Lecture Notes in Computer Science 4224

Commenced Publication in 1973
Founding and Former Series Editors:
Gerhard Goos, Juris Hartmanis, and Jan van Leeuwen

Editorial Board

David Hutchison
  Lancaster University, UK
Takeo Kanade
  Carnegie Mellon University, Pittsburgh, PA, USA
Josef Kittler
  University of Surrey, Guildford, UK
Jon M. Kleinberg
  Cornell University, Ithaca, NY, USA
Friedemann Mattern
  ETH Zurich, Switzerland
John C. Mitchell
  Stanford University, CA, USA
Moni Naor
  Weizmann Institute of Science, Rehovot, Israel
Oscar Nierstrasz
  University of Bern, Switzerland
C. Pandu Rangan
  Indian Institute of Technology, Madras, India
Bernhard Steffen
  University of Dortmund, Germany
Madhu Sudan
  Massachusetts Institute of Technology, MA, USA
Demetri Terzopoulos
  University of California, Los Angeles, CA, USA
Doug Tygar
  University of California, Berkeley, CA, USA
Moshe Y. Vardi
  Rice University, Houston, TX, USA
Gerhard Weikum
  Max-Planck Institute of Computer Science, Saarbruecken, Germany

Emilio Corchado   Hujun Yin
Vicente Botti   Colin Fyfe (Eds.)

Intelligent Data Engineering and Automated Learning – IDEAL 2006

7th International Conference
Burgos, Spain, September 20-23, 2006
Proceedings

 Springer

Volume Editors

Emilio Corchado
Universidad de Burgos
09001 Burgos, Spain
E-mail: escorchado@ubu.es

Hujun Yin*
The University of Manchester
Manchester, M60 1QD, UK
E-mail: hujun.yin@manchester.ac.uk

Vicente Botti
Universidad Politécnica de Valencia, Camino de Vera s/n
46022 Valencia, Spain
E-mail: vbotti@dsic.upv.es

Colin Fyfe
University of Paisley, PA1 2BE
Scotland
E-mail: FYFE-CI0@wpmail.paisley.ac.uk

* Corresponding editor

Library of Congress Control Number: 2006932576

CR Subject Classification (1998): H.2.8, F.2.2, I.2, F.4, K.4.4, H.3, H.4

LNCS Sublibrary: SL 3 – Information Systems and Application, incl. Internet/Web and HCI

ISSN   0302-9743
ISBN-10   3-540-45485-3 Springer Berlin Heidelberg New York
ISBN-13   978-3-540-45485-4 Springer Berlin Heidelberg New York

This work is subject to copyright. All rights are reserved, whether the whole or part of the material is concerned, specifically the rights of translation, reprinting, re-use of illustrations, recitation, broadcasting, reproduction on microfilms or in any other way, and storage in data banks. Duplication of this publication or parts thereof is permitted only under the provisions of the German Copyright Law of September 9, 1965, in its current version, and permission for use must always be obtained from Springer. Violations are liable to prosecution under the German Copyright Law.

Springer is a part of Springer Science+Business Media

springer.com

© Springer-Verlag Berlin Heidelberg 2006
Printed in Germany

Typesetting: Camera-ready by author, data conversion by Scientific Publishing Services, Chennai, India
Printed on acid-free paper   SPIN: 11875581   06/3142   5 4 3 2 1 0

Preface

Since its establishment in Hong Kong in 1998, the international Intelligent Data Engineering and Automated Learning (IDEAL) conference has become a reference for researchers in both theoretical and practical aspects of learning and information processing, data mining, retrieval and management, bioinformatics and bio-inspired models, agents and hybrid systems and financial engineering. The purpose of IDEAL conferences has been to provide a broad and interdisciplinary forum for scientists, researchers, and practitioners in these areas from around the world. A special feature of IDEAL conferences is cross-disciplinary exchange of ideas in emerging topics and application in these areas. Data analysis and engineering and associated learning paradigms are playing increasingly important roles in an increasing number of applications and fields. The multidisciplinary nature of contemporary research is pushing the boundaries and one of the principal aims of the IDEAL conferences is to promote interactions and collaborations across disciplines.

This volume of *Lecture Notes in Computer Science* contains accepted papers presented at IDEAL 2006 held at the University of Burgos, Spain, during, September 20–23, 2006. The conference received 557 submissions from over 40 countries around the world, which were subsequently refereed by the Programme Committee and many additional reviewers. After rigorous review, 170 top-quality papers were accepted and included in the proceedings. The acceptance rate was only 30%, which ensured an extremely high-quality standard of the conference. The buoyant number of submitted papers is a clear proof of the vitality and increased importance of the fields related to IDEAL, and is also an indication of the rising popularity of the IDEAL conferences.

IDEAL 2006 enjoyed outstanding keynote speeches by distinguished guest speakers: José Mira of the Universidad Nacional de Educación a Distancia, Spain, Xin Yao of the University of Birmingham, UK, Hojjat Adeli of Ohio State University, USA and Nigel Allinson of the University of Sheffield, UK. Delegates also enjoyed a special session on "Nature -Inspired Data Technologies" sponsored by NISIS.

This year IDEAL also teamed up with three international journals, namely, the *International Journal of Neural Systems*, *Integrated Computer-Aided Engineering* and the *Journal of Mathematical Modelling and Algorithms*. Three special issues on *Bioinformatics and Bio-inspired Models*, *Soft Computing and Hybrid Systems* and *Algorithms for Mining Large Data Sets*, respectively, have been scheduled from selected papers from IDEAL 2006. The extended papers, together with contributed articles received in response to subsequent open calls, will go through further rounds of peer refereeing in the remits of these three journals.

We would like to thank the International Advisory Committee and the Steering Committee for the guidance and influential and useful advice. We would particularly like to acknowledge the diligent work of our Programme Committee Members who performed admirably under tight deadlines.

Particular thanks go to the Applied Research Group of the University of the Burgos, in particular Álvaro Herrero, Bruno Baruque and David Martín, and also Juan Manuel Corchado of the University of Salamanca for his suggestions on organization and promotion of IDEAL 2006. And we must also mention and thank our technical staff at Viajes Ojeda. We were fortunate to have the support from Junta de Castilla y León, University of Burgos, NISIS, GCI, FEC-Burgos, Caja de Burgos and Caja Círculo.

We also wish to thank the publisher Springer, especially Alfred Hofmann, Anna Kramer and Ursula Barth for their continued support and collaboration in this demanding publication project.

Last but not the least, we thank all the authors and participants for their great contributions that made this conference a successful and enjoyable event.

July 2006

Emilio Corchado
Hujun Yin
Vicente Botti
Colin Fyfe

Organization

General Chairs

José M. Leal Rector of the University of Burgos, Spain
Hujun Yin University of Manchester, UK
Hojjat Adeli (Honorary) Ohio State University, USA

International Advisory Committee

Lei Xu (Chair) Chinese University of Hong Kong, China
Yaser Abu-Mostafa CALTECH, USA
Shun-ichi Amari RIKEN, Japan
Michael Dempster University of Cambridge, UK
Nick Jennings University of Southampton, UK
Sun-Yuan Kung Princeton University, USA
Erkki Oja Helsinki University of Technology, Finland
Latit M. Patnaik Indian Institute of Science, India
Burkhard Rost Columbia University, USA

Steering Committee

Hujun Yin (Co-chair) University of Manchester, UK
Lai-Wan Chan (Co-chair) Chinese University of Hong Kong, China
Nigel Allinson University of Sheffield, UK
Yiu-ming Cheung Hong Kong Baptist University, Hong Kong, China
Marcus Gallagher University of Queensland, Australia
Marc van Hulle K. U. Leuven, Belgium
John Keane University of Manchester, UK
Jimmy Lee Chinese University of Hong Kong, Hong Kong, China
Malik Magdon-Ismail Rensselaer Polytechnic Institute, USA
Zheng Rong Yang University of Exeter, UK
Ron Sun Rensselaer Polytechnic Institute, USA
Ning Zhong Maebashi Institute of Technology, Japan

Organizing Committee

Emilio Corchado (Chair) University of Burgos, Spain
Juan Manuel Corchado University of Salamanca, Spain
Álvaro Herrero University of Burgos, Spain

Organizing Committee (continued)

Bruno Baruque	University of Burgos, Spain
Raúl Marticorena	University of Burgos, Spain
David Martín	University of Burgos, Spain
Jose Manuel Sáiz	University of Burgos, Spain
Leticia Curiel	University of Burgos, Spain
Juan Carlos Pérez	University of Burgos, Spain
Lourdes Sáiz	University of Burgos, Spain
Pedro Burgos	University of Burgos, Spain
Miguel Ángel Manzanedo	University of Burgos, Spain
Carlos López	University of Burgos, Spain
Carlos Pardo	University of Burgos, Spain
Belén Vaquerizo	University of Burgos, Spain
Eduardo Renedo	University of Burgos, Spain
Óscar J. González	University of Burgos, Spain
Jacinto Canales	CPIICyL, Spain

Programme Committee

Vicente Botti (Co-chair)	Polytechnic University of Valencia, Spain
Colin Fyfe (Co-chair)	University of Paisley, UK
Ajith Abraham	Chung-Ang University, Republic of Korea
Khurshid Ahmad	Trinity College Dublin, Ireland
Nigel Allinson	University of Sheffield, UK
Ángel Alonso	University of León, Spain
Luis Alonso	University of Salamanca, Spain
Martyn Amos	University of Exeter, UK
Jiyuan An	Deakin University, Australia
Davide Anguita	University of Genoa, Italy
Bruno Apolloni	University of Milano, Italy
Bernard De Baets	Ghent University, Belgium
Federico Barber	Polytechnic University of Valencia, Spain
Alan Blair	University of New South Wales, Australia
Mikael Boden	University of Queensland, Australia
Juan Botía	University of Murcia, Spain
Teodoro Calonge	University of Valladolid, Spain
Carlos Carrascosa	Polytechnic University of Valencia, Spain
André de Carvalho	University of São Paulo, Brazil
Matthew Casey	Surrey University, UK
Sheng Chen	University of Southampton, UK
Songcan Chen	Nanjing Univ. of Aeronautics and Astronautics, China
Sung-Bae Cho	Yonsei University, Korea
Sungzoon Cho	Seoul National University, Korea

Programme Committee (continued)

Emilio Corchado	University of Burgos, Spain
Juan Manuel Corchado	University of Salamanca, Spain
Rafael Corchuelo	University of Seville, Spain
David Corne	Heriot-Watt University, UK
Ernesto Costa	University of Coimbra, Portugal
Miguel Delgado	University of Granada, Spain
José Dorronsoro	Autonomous University of Madrid, Spain
Zhao Yang Dong	University of Queensland, Australia
Tom Downs	University of Queensland, Australia
Richard Everson	University of Exeter, UK
Fernando Fernández	Carlos III University of Madrid, Spain
Marcus Frean	Victoria University of Wellington, New Zealand
Richard Freeman	Capgemini, UK
Toshio Fukuda	Nagoya University, Japan
Bogdan Gabrys	Bournemouth University, UK
Marcus Gallagher	University of Queensland, Australia
Francisco Garijo	Telefónica I+D, Spain
John Qiang Gan	University of Essex, UK
Mark Girolami	University of Glasgow, UK
Antonio F. Gómez	University of Murcia, Spain
Ana González	Autonomous University of Madrid, Spain
Jennifer Hallinan	University of Queensland, Australia
Francisco Herrera	University of Granada, Spain
James Hogan	Queensland University of Technology, Australia
Tony Holden	University of Cambridge, UK
Jaakko Hollmen	Helsinki University of Technology, Finland
Robert J. Howlett	University of Brighton, UK
David Hoyle	University of Exeter, UK
Hisao Ishibuchi	Osaka Prefecture University, Japan
Paul Jackway	CSIRO, Australia
Gareth Jones	Dublin City University, Ireland
Vicente Julián	Polytechnic University of Valencia, Spain
Ata Kaban	Birmingham University, UK
Hoon Kang	Chung Ang University, Korea
Juha Karhunen	Helsinki University of Technology, Finland
Samuel Kaski	Helsinki University of Technology, Finland
Dong Hwa Kim	Hanbat National University, Korea
Irwin King	Chinese University of Hong Kong, Hong Kong
Aldebaro Klautau	Federal University of Para (UFPA), Brazil
Mario Köppen	Fraunhofer IPK, Germany
Kostadin Korutchev	Autonomous University of Madrid, Spain
Rudolf Kruse	University of Magdeburg, Germany

Programme Committee (continued)

Jimmy Lee	Chinese University of Hong Kong, Hong Kong, China
Kwong S. Leung	Chinese University of Hong Kong, Hong Kong, China
Carlos Linares	Carlos III University of Madrid, Spain
Paulo Lisboa	Liverpool John Moores University, UK
Malik Magdon-Ismail	Rensselaer Polytechnic Institute, USA
Frederic Maire	Queensland University of Technology, Australia
Roque Marín	University of Murcia, Spain
José F. Martínez	INAOE, Mexico
Simon Miles	University of Southampton, UK
José Mira	Universidad Nacional de Educación a Distancia, Spain
José Manuel Molina	Carlos III University of Madrid, Spain
Carla Moller-Levet	University of Manchester, UK
Ajit Narayanan	University of Exeter, UK
Ricardo del Olmo	University of Burgos, Spain
Ramón Otero	University of A Coruña, Spain
Joaquín Pacheco	University of Burgos, Spain
Juan Pavón	University Complutense of Madrid, Spain
Witold Pedrycz	University of Alberta, Canada
David Pelta	University of Granada, Spain
David Powers	Flinders University, Australia
José Principe	University of Florida, USA
Mª José Ramirez	Polytechnic University of Valencia, Spain
Omer Rana	University of Wales, Cardiff, UK
Vic Rayward-Smith	University of East Anglia, UK
Perfecto Reguera	University of León, Spain
Bernardete Ribeiro	University of Coimbra, Portugal
José Riquelme	University of Seville, Spain
Ramón Rizo	University of Alicante, Spain
Shazia Sadiq	University of Queensland, Australia
José Santos	University of A Coruña, Spain
Michael Small	Hong Kong Polytechnic University, Hong Kong, China
P. N. Suganthan	Nanyang Technological University, Singapore
David Taniar	Monash University, Australia
Peter Tino	Birmingham University, UK
Miguel Toro	University of Seville, Spain
Marc Van Hulle	K. U. Leuven, Belgium
Alfredo Vellido	Technical University of Catalonia, Spain
José Ramón Villar	University of Oviedo, Spain
Lipo Wang	Nanyan Technological University, Singapore
Dong-Qing Wei	Shanghai Jiaotong University, China

Programme Committee (continued)

Ian Wood	Queensland University of Technology, Australia
Gordon Wyeth	University of Queensland, Australia
Zheng Rong Yang	University of Exeter, UK
Yong Xu	University of Birmingham, UK
Nobuyoshi Yabuki	Muroran Institute of Technology, Japan
Ronald R. Yager	Iona College, USA
Hujun Yin	University of Manchester, UK
Du Zhang	California State University, USA
Yanqing Zhang	Georgia State University, USA
Ning Zhong	Maebashi Institute of Technology, Japan
Rodolfo Zunino	University of Genoa, Italy

Additional Reviewers

Aitor Mata	Universidad de Salamanca, Spain
Angélica González	Universidad de Salamanca, Spain
Daniel González	Universidad de Vigo, Spain
Dante Israel Tapia	Universidad de Salamanca, Spain
Dymitr Ruta	British Telecom, UK
Eva Lorenzo	Universidad de Vigo, Spain
Fernando Díaz	Universidad de Valladolid, Spain
Florentino Fernández	Universidad de Vigo, Spain
Javier Bajo	Universidad Pontificia de Salamanca, Spain
José Adserias	Universidad de Salamanca, Spain
José Ramón Méndez	Universidad de Vigo, Spain
Lourdes Borrajo	Universidad de Vigo, Spain
Manuel González	Universidad Carlos III de Madrid, Spain
Marcos Valiño	Universidad de Vigo, Spain
Rosalía Laza	Universidad de Vigo, Spain
Yanira de Paz	Universidad de Salamanca, Spain
Álvaro Herrero	University of Burgos, Spain
Bruno Baruque	University of Burgos, Spain

Table of Contents

Learning and Information Processing

On Some of the Neural Mechanisms Underlying Adaptive Behavior 1
   José Mira Mira

On Correlation Measures of Intuitionistic Fuzzy Sets 16
   Zeshui Xu

A More Effective Constructive Algorithm for Permutation Flowshop Problem 25
   Xingye Dong, Houkuan Huang, Ping Chen

A Fast Algorithm for Relevance Vector Machine 33
   Zheng Rong Yang

Time Series Relevance Determination Through a Topology-Constrained Hidden Markov Model 40
   Iván Olier, Alfredo Vellido

A Fast Data Preprocessing Procedure for Support Vector Regression 48
   Zhifeng Hao, Wen Wen, Xiaowei Yang, Jie Lu, Guangquan Zhang

Classification by Weighting, Similarity and kNN 57
   Naohiro Ishii, Tsuyoshi Murai, Takahiro Yamada, Yongguang Bao

An Improved EM Algorithm for Statistical Segmentation of Brain MRI 65
   Yong Yang

Process State and Progress Visualization Using Self-Organizing Map 73
   Risto Hakala, Timo Similä, Miki Sirola, Jukka Parviainen

Exploiting Spatio–temporal Data for the Multiobjective Optimization of Cellular Automata Models 81
   Giuseppe A. Trunfio

Comparing Support Vector Machines and Feed-forward Neural Networks with Similar Parameters 90
   Enrique Romero, Daniel Toppo

A New Model Selection Method for SVM 99
  G. Lebrun, O. Lezoray, C. Charrier, H. Cardot

Speed-Up LOO-CV with SVM Classifier 108
  G. Lebrun, O. Lezoray, C. Charrier, H. Cardot

Integration of Strategies Based on Relevance Feedback into a Tool
for the Retrieval of Mammographic Images 116
  A. Fornells, E. Golobardes, X. Vilasís, J. Martí

Generalization Performance of Exchange Monte Carlo Method
for Normal Mixture Models 125
  Kenji Nagata, Sumio Watanabe

Evolutionary Design of gdSOFPNN for Modeling and Prediction
of NOx Emission Process 133
  Tae-Chon Ahn, Ho-Sung Park

Upper Bounds for Variational Stochastic Complexities of Bayesian
Networks 139
  Kazuho Watanabe, Motoki Shiga, Sumio Watanabe

A Neural Stochastic Optimization Framework for Oil Parameter
Estimation 147
  Rafael E. Banchs, Hector Klie, Adolfo Rodriguez, Sunil G. Thomas,
  Mary F. Wheeler

Bootstrap Prediction Intervals for Nonlinear Time-Series 155
  Daisuke Haraki, Tomoya Suzuki, Tohru Ikeguchi

Effectiveness of Considering State Similarity for Reinforcement
Learning 163
  Sertan Girgin, Faruk Polat, Reda Alhajj

On the Structural Robustness of Evolutionary Models of Cooperation 172
  Segismundo S. Izquierdo, Luis R. Izquierdo

Prediction of Chaotic Time Series Based on Multi-scale Gaussian
Processes 183
  Yatong Zhou, Taiyi Zhang, Xiaohe Li

Visual Sensitivity Analysis for Artificial Neural Networks 191
  Roberto Therón, Juan Francisco De Paz

Performance of BSDT Decoding Algorithms Based on Locally Damaged
Neural Networks 199
  Petro Gopych

K Nearest Sequence Method and Its Application to Churn Prediction.... 207
  Dymitr Ruta, Detlef Nauck, Ben Azvine

Evolutionary Computation Technique Applied to HSPF Model
Calibration of a Spanish Watershed 216
  F. Castanedo, M.A. Patricio, J.M. Molina

Genetic Algorithms and Sensitivity Analysis Applied to Select Inputs
of a Multi-Layer Perceptron for the Prediction of Air Pollutant
Time-Series 224
  Harri Niska, Mikko Heikkinen, Mikko Kolehmainen

Genetic Algorithms for Estimating Longest Path from Inherently Fuzzy
Data Acquired with GPS 232
  José Villar, Adolfo Otero, José Otero, Luciano Sánchez

The Topographic Neural Gas 241
  Marian Peña, Colin Fyfe

A Fast Classification Algorithm Based on Local Models 249
  Sabela Platero-Santos, Oscar Fontenla-Romero,
  Amparo Alonso-Betanzos

Human Activity Recognition in Videos: A Systematic Approach 257
  Sameer Singh, Jessica Wang

Application of Artificial Neural Network to Building Compartment
Design for Fire Safety 265
  Eric Wai Ming Lee, Po Chi Lau, Kitty Kit Yan Yuen

A Method of Motion Segmentation Based on Region Shrinking 275
  Zhihui Li, Fenggang Huang, Yongmei Liu

A Family of Novel Clustering Algorithms 283
  Wesam Barbakh, Malcolm Crowe, Colin Fyfe

Vector Quantization Segmentation for Head Pose Estimation 291
  José Lopes, Sameer Singh

Neural Network Detectors for Composite Hypothesis Tests 298
  D. de la Mata-Moya, P. Jarabo-Amores, R. Vicen-Bueno,
  M. Rosa-Zurera, F. López-Ferreras

Automatic Sound Classification for Improving Speech Intelligibility
in Hearing Aids Using a Layered Structure 306
  Enrique Alexandre, Lucas Cuadra, Lorena Álvarez,
  Manuel Rosa-Zurera, Francisco López-Ferreras

Directed Laplacian Kernels for Link Analysis 314
  Pawel Majewski

Pruning Adaptive Boosting Ensembles by Means of a Genetic
Algorithm... 322
  Daniel Hernández-Lobato, José Miguel Hernández-Lobato,
  Rubén Ruiz-Torrubiano, Ángel Valle

On the Fusion of Polynomial Kernels for Support Vector Classifiers...... 330
  Isaac Martín de Diego, Javier M. Moguerza, Alberto Muñoz

Speech and Gesture Recognition-Based Robust Language Processing
Interface in Noise Environment 338
  Jung-Hyun Kim, Kwang-Seok Hong

Heterogeneous Answer Acquisition Methods in Encyclopedia QA 346
  Hyo-Jung Oh, Chung-Hee Lee, Changki Lee, Ji-Hyun Wang,
  Yi-Gyu Hwang, Hyeon-Jin Kim, Myung-Gil Jang

Face Recognition Using DCT and Hierarchical RBF Model 355
  Yuehui Chen, Yaou Zhao

Chaotic Dynamics for Avoiding Congestion in the Computer Network ... 363
  Takayuki Kimura, Tohru Ikeguchi

Combined Effects of Class Imbalance and Class Overlap
on Instance-Based Classification 371
  V. García, R. Alejo, J.S. Sánchez, J.M. Sotoca, R.A. Mollineda

Melt Index Predict by Radial Basis Function Network Based
on Principal Component Analysis 379
  Xinggao Liu, Zhengbing Yan

Thinking Capability of Saplings Growing Up Algorithm................ 386
  Ali Karci, Bilal Alatas

Functional Networks and the Lagrange Polynomial Interpolation 394
  Cristina Solares, Eduardo W. Vieira, Roberto Mínguez

The Evolution of OSI Network Management by Integrated the Expert
Knowledge 402
  Antonio Martín, Carlos León, Iñigo Monedero

Learning the Complete-Basis-Functions Parameterization
for the Optimization of Dynamic Molecular Alignment by ES 410
  Ofer M. Shir, Joost N. Kok, Thomas Bäck, Marc J.J. Vrakking

Multi Criteria Wrapper Improvements to Naive Bayes Learning 419
  José Carlos Cortizo, Ignacio Giraldez

BP Neural Networks Combined with PLS Applied to Pattern
Recognition of Vis/NIRs 428
  Di Wu, Yong He, Yongni Shao, Shuijuan Feng

Speeding Up Shape Classification by Means of a Cyclic Dynamic Time
Warping Lower Bound 436
  Vicente Palazón, Andrés Marzal

Using Genetic Algorithm for Network Status Learning and Worm Virus
Detection Scheme 444
  Donghyun Lim, Jinwook Chung, Seongjin Ahn

Clustering by Integrating Multi-objective Optimization with Weighted
K-Means and Validity Analysis 454
  Tansel Özyer, Reda Alhajj, Ken Barker

Improving the Classification Accuracy of RBF and MLP Neural
Networks Trained with Imbalanced Samples 464
  R. Alejo, V. Garcia, J.M. Sotoca, R.A. Mollineda, J.S. Sánchez

Learning Discrete Probability Distributions with a Multi-resolution
Binary Tree 472
  F.A. Sanchís, F. Aznar, M. Sempere, M. Pujol, R. Rizo

Combining Unsupervised and Supervised Approaches to Feature
Selection for Multivariate Signal Compression 480
  Victor Eruhimov, Vladimir Martyanov, Peter Raulefs, Eugene Tuv

Cohesion Factors: Improving the Clustering Capabilities
of Consensus 488
  Guiomar Corral, Albert Fornells, Elisabet Golobardes, Jaume Abella

Using Neural Networks to Detect Microfossil Teeth in Somosaguas Sur
Paleontological Site 496
  R. Gil-Pita, N. Sala-Burgos

A Fast Grid Search Method in Support Vector Regression Forecasting
Time Series 504
   Yukun Bao, Zhitao Liu

Fast Global k-Means with Similarity Functions Algorithm 512
   Saúl Lóez-Escobar, J.A. Carrasco-Ochoa, J. Fco Martínez-Trinidad

NN-Based Detector for Known Targets in Coherent Weibull Clutter 522
   R. Vicen-Bueno, M. Rosa-Zurera, M.P. Jarabo-Amores, R. Gil-Pita

ICA with Sparse Connections 530
   Kun Zhang, Lai-Wan Chan

Two-Stage User Mobility Modeling for Intention Prediction
for Location-Based Services 538
   Moon-Hee Park, Jin-Hyuk Hong, Sung-Bae Cho

Partition-Based Similarity Joins Using Diagonal Dimensions in High
Dimensional Data Spaces 546
   Hyoseop Shin

Evolving Feed-forward Neural Networks Through Evolutionary
Mutation Parameters 554
   M. Annunziato, I. Bertini, R. Iannone, S. Pizzuti

Computer Interface Using Eye Tracking for Handicapped People 562
   Eun Yi Kim, Se Hyun Park

Local Negative Correlation with Resampling 570
   Ricardo Ñanculef, Carlos Valle, Héctor Allende, Claudio Moraga

Convex Perceptrons 578
   Daniel García, Ana González, José R. Dorronsoro

Hybridizing Cultural Algorithms and Local Search 586
   Trung Thanh Nguyen, Xin Yao

ICA and Genetic Algorithms for Blind Signal and Image Deconvolution
and Deblurring 595
   Hujun Yin, Israr Hussain

Data Mining, Retrieval and Management

Electroencephalogram Signals from Imagined Activities: A Novel
Biometric Identifier for a Small Population 604
   Ramaswamy Palaniappan

Resolving Ambiguities in the Semantic Interpretation of Natural
Language Questions 612
    Serge Linckels, Christoph Meinel

Mining the K-Most Interesting Frequent Patterns Sequentially 620
    Quang Tran Minh, Shigeru Oyanagi, Katsuhiro Yamazaki

Discovering Non-taxonomic Relations from the Web 629
    David Sánchez, Antonio Moreno

A New Algorithm of Similarity Measuring for Multi-experts' Qualitative
Knowledge Based on Outranking Relations in Case-Based Reasoning
Methodology 637
    Hui Li, Xiang-Yang Li, Jie Gu

Comparing and Combining Spatial Dimension Reduction Methods
in Face Verification 645
    Licesio J. Rodríguez-Aragón, Cristina Conde, Ángel Serrano,
    Enrique Cabello

A New Semi-supervised Dimension Reduction Technique for Textual
Data Analysis 654
    Manuel Martín-Merino, Jesus Román

CBR Model for the Intelligent Management of Customer Support
Centers 663
    Stella Heras Barberá, Juan Ángel García-Pardo,
    Rafael Ramos-Garijo, Alberto Palomares, Vicente Julián,
    Miguel Rebollo, Vicent Botti

Non Parametric Local Density-Based Clustering for Multimodal
Overlapping Distributions 671
    Damaris Pascual, Filiberto Pla, J. Salvador Sánchez

Application of Bidirectional Probabilistic Character Language Model
in Handwritten Words Recognition 679
    Jerzy Sas

Efficient Classification Method for Complex Biological Literature
Using Text and Data Mining Combination 688
    Yun Jeong Choi, Seung Soo Park

Classifying Polyphony Music Based on Markov Model 697
    Yukiteru Yoshihara, Takao Miura

Two Phase Semi-supervised Clustering Using Background Knowledge 707
  Kwangcheol Shin, Ajith Abraham

Using Rough Set to Find the Factors That Negate the Typical
Dependency of a Decision Attribute on Some Condition Attributes 713
  *Honghai Feng, Hao Xu, Baoyan Liu, Bingru Yang, Zhuye Gao,
  Yueli Li*

Automatic Extraction and Classification of Footwear Patterns 721
  Maria Pavlou, Nigel M. Allinson

Description of Combined Spatial Relations Between Broad Boundary
Regions Based on Rough Set 729
  Shihong Du, Qimin Qin, Qiao Wang, Haijian Ma

Active Sketch for Finding Primary Structures in Images 738
  Shulin Yang, Cunlu Xu, Qin Lei

Shape Matching Using Chord-Length Function 746
  Bin Wang, Chaojian Shi

Spectral High Resolution Feature Selection for Retrieval of Combustion
Temperature Profiles 754
  Esteban García-Cuesta, Inés M. Galván, Antonio J. de Castro

Sentence Ordering in Extractive MDS 763
  Zengchang Zhang, Dexi Liu

Query Expansion with an Automatically Generated Thesaurus 771
  José R. Pérez-Agüera, Lourdes Araujo

An Interactive Hybrid System for Identifying and Filtering Unsolicited
E-mail 779
  M. Dolores del Castillo, J. Ignacio Serrano

Topological Tree Clustering of Web Search Results 789
  Richard T. Freeman

Reduced Attribute Oriented Inconsistency Handling in Decision
Generation 798
  Yucai Feng, Wenhai Li, Zehua Lv, Xiaoming Ma

A Non-parametric Method for Data Clustering with Optimal Variable
Weighting 807
  Ji-Won Chung, In-Chan Choi

A Closed Model for Measuring Intangible Assets: A New Dimension
of Profitability Applying Neural Networks 815
   Ana Maria Lara Palma, Lourdes Sáiz Bárcena, Joaquín Pacheco

Audio and Video Feature Fusion for Activity Recognition
in Unconstrained Videos 823
   José Lopes, Sameer Singh

Multi-stage Classification for Audio Based Activity Recognition 832
   José Lopes, Charles Lin, Sameer Singh

A Simple Approximation for Dynamic Time Warping Search in Large
Time Series Database 841
   Jie Gu, Xiaomin Jin

Regression Analisys of Segmented Parametric Software Cost Estimation
Models Using Recursive Clustering Tool 849
   M. Garre, M.A. Sicilia, J.J. Cuadrado, M. Charro

An Efficient Attribute Reduction Algorithm 859
   Yuguo He

Conceptual Classification to Improve a Web Site Content 869
   *Sebastián A. Ríos, Juan D. Velásquez, Hiroshi Yasuda,
   Terumasa Aoki*

Automated Learning of RVM for Large Scale Text Sets: Divide
to Conquer 878
   Catarina Silva, Bernardete Ribeiro

Using Rules Discovery for the Continuous Improvement of e-Learning
Courses 887
   *Enrique García, Cristóbal Romero, Sebastián Ventura,
   Carlos de Castro*

Generating Adaptive Presentations of Hydrologic Behavior 896
   Martin Molina, Victor Flores

A New Measure for Query Disambiguation Using Term
Co-occurrences 904
   Hiromi Wakaki, Tomonari Masada, Atsuhiro Takasu, Jun Adachi

Unsupervised Word Categorization Using Self-Organizing Maps
and Automatically Extracted Morphs 912
   Mikaela Klami, Krista Lagus

Effective Classification by Integrating Support Vector Machine
and Association Rule Mining 920
  Keivan Kianmehr, Reda Alhajj

A Design of Dynamic Network Management System 928
  Myung Jin Lee, Eun Hee Kim, Keun Ho Ryu

QoS Multicast Routing Based on Particle Swarm Optimization 936
  Jing Liu, Jun Sun, Wenbo Xu

Evolutionary Search of Optimal Features............................... 944
  Manuel del Valle, Luis F. Lago-Fernández, Fernando J. Corbacho

Biased Minimax Probability Machine Active Learning for Relevance
Feedback in Content-Based Image Retrieval 953
  Xiang Peng, Irwin King

Evidential Integration of Semantically Heterogeneous Aggregates
in Distributed Databases with Imprecision 961
  Xin Hong, Sally McClean, Bryan Scotney, Philip Morrow

Describing Customer Loyalty to Spanish Petrol Stations Through Rule
Extraction 970
  Alfredo Vellido, Terence A. Etchells, David L. García, Ángela Nebot

Strangeness Minimisation Feature Selection with Confidence Machines ... 978
  Tony Bellotti, Zhiyuan Luo, Alex Gammerman

Indexing and Mining of Graph Database Based on Interconnected
Subgraph 986
  Haichuan Shang, Xiaoming Jin

Evaluation of Decision Tree Pruning with Subadditive Penalties......... 995
  Sergio García-Moratilla, Gonzalo Martínez-Muñoz, Alberto Suárez

Categorization of Large Text Collections: Feature Selection for Training
Neural Networks 1003
  Pensiri Manomaisupat, Bogdan Vrusias, Khurshid Ahmad

Towards Healthy Association Rule Mining (HARM): A Fuzzy
Quantitative Approach 1014
  Maybin Muyeba, M. Sulaiman Khan, Zarrar Malik, Christos Tjortjis

State Aggregation in Higher Order Markov Chains for Finding Online
Communities 1023
  Xin Wang, Ata Kabán

Functional Networks and Analysis of Variance for Feature Selection 1031
    Noelia Sánchez-Maroño, María Caamaño-Fernández,
    Enrique Castillo, Amparo Alonso-Betanzos

Automatic Categorization of Patent Applications Using Classifier
Combinations 1039
    Henrik Mathiassen, Daniel Ortiz-Arroyo

Best Subset Feature Selection for Massive Mixed-Type Problems 1048
    Eugene Tuv, Alexander Borisov, Kari Torkkola

Planning Under Uncertainty with Abstraction Hierarchies 1057
    Letícia Maria Friske, Carlos Henrique Costa Ribeiro

Fusion of Domain Knowledge for Dynamic Learning in Transcriptional
Networks 1067
    Oscar Harari, R. Romero-Zaliz, C. Rubio-Escudero, I. Zwir

An Improved Discrete Immune Network for Multimodal Optimization ... 1079
    Jing-Xin Xie, Chun-Tian Cheng, Zhen-Hui Ren

Bioinformatics and Bio-inspired Models

Using Fuzzy Patterns for Gene Selection and Data Reduction
on Microarray Data 1087
    Fernando Díaz, Florentino Fdez-Riverola, Daniel Glez-Peña,
    Juan M. Corchado

Applying GCS Networks to Fuzzy Discretized Microarray Data
for Tumour Diagnosis 1095
    Fernando Díaz, Florentino Fdez-Riverola, Daniel Glez-Peña,
    Juan M. Corchado

Refractory Effects of Chaotic Neurodynamics for Finding Motifs
from DNA Sequences 1103
    Takafumi Matsuura, Tohru Ikeguchi

Neighborhood-Based Clustering of Gene-Gene Interactions 1111
    Norberto Díaz-Díaz, Domingo S. Rodríguez-Baena,
    Isabel Nepomuceno, Jesús S. Aguilar-Ruiz

Gene Expression Profiling Using Flexible Neural Trees 1121
    Yuehui Chen, Lizhi Peng, Ajith Abraham

Multivariate Crosstalk Models 1129
    Natasha Young, Zheng Rong Yang

Decision Making Association Rules for Recognition of Differential Gene
Expression Profiles 1137
    C. Rubio-Escudero, Coral del Val, O. Cordón, I. Zwir

Application of Chemoinformatics to the Structural Elucidation
of Natural Compounds 1150
    José Luis López-Pérez, Roberto Theron, Esther del Olmo,
    David Díez, Miguel Vaquero, José Francisco Adserias

Agents and Hybrid Systems

Intelligent Coordinated Control of Multiple Teleoperated Robots 1158
    Wusheng Chou, Tianmiao Wang

SMas: A Shopping Mall Multiagent Systems 1166
    Javier Bajo, Yanira de Paz, Juan Francisco de Paz, Quintín Martin,
    Juan M. Corchado

Protecting Agent from Attack in Grid Computing[II] 1174
    Byungryong Kim

A Graph Transformation System Model of Dynamic Reorganization
in Multi-agent Systems 1182
    Zheng-guang Wang, Xiao-hui Liang, Qin-ping Zhao

Efficient Search of Winning Strategies in Multi-agent Systems
on Random Network: Importance of Local Solidarity 1191
    Tin Yau Pang, K.Y. Szeto

Heterogeneous Domain Ontology for Location Based Information
System in a Multi-agent Framework 1199
    Virginia Fuentes, Javier Carbó, José Manuel Molina

Intelligent Data Analysis for the Verification of Multi-Agent Systems
Interactions 1207
    Juan A. Botía, Jorge J. Gómez-Sanz, Juan Pavón

Multi-agent Based Hybrid System for Dynamic Web-Content
Adaptation 1215
    Jaewoo Cho, Seunghwa Lee, Eunseok Lee

Strategic Software Agents in Continuous Double Auction Under
Dynamic Environments 1223
   Marta Posada

Student Modeling for Adaptive Teachable Agent to Enhance Interest
and Comprehension 1234
   *Sung-il Kim, Myung-Jin Lee, Woogul Lee, Yeonhee So,
Cheon-woo Han, Karam Lim, Su-Young Hwang, Sung-Hyun Yun,
Dong-Seong Choi, Misun Yoon*

An Agent-Based Model of Personal Web Communities 1242
   José I. Santos, José M. Galán, Ricardo del Olmo

A Conceptual Framework for Automated Negotiation Systems 1250
   Manuel Resinas, Pablo Fernandez, Rafael Corchuelo

Development of New IFC-BRIDGE Data Model and a Concrete Bridge
Design System Using Multi-agents 1259
   Nobuyoshi Yabuki, Zhantao Li

Multi-Agent Systems over RT-Java for a Mobile Robot Control 1267
   *Marti Navarroa, Vicente Julian, Stella Heras, Jose Soler,
Vicent Botti*

Financial Engineering

Financial Risk Modeling with Markov Chains......................... 1275
   *Arturo Leccadito, Sergio Ortobelli Lozza, Emilio Russo,
Gaetano Iaquinta*

CNY Realignment and USD Expectation: Empirical Study Based
on RND Function of Currency Option 1283
   Zhongzhong Ning

Investment Selection and Risk Management for Insurance Corporation... 1289
   Yan-Ling Wang, De-Li Yang

Knowledge-Based Risk Assessment Under Uncertainty in Engineering
Projects 1296
   Rashid Hafeez Khokhar, David A. Bell, Jiwen Guan, QingXiang Wu

Fuzzy Regression with Quadratic Programming: An Application
to Financial Data 1304
   Sergio Donoso, Nicolás Marín, M. Amparo Vila

Special Session on Nature-Inspired Date Technologies

Improving Search in Unstructured P2P Systems: Intelligent Walks
(I-Walks) 1312
  Francis Otto, Song Ouyang

Evolutionary Product-Unit Neural Networks for Classification 1320
  *F.J. Martínez-Estudillo, C. Hervás-Martínez, P.A. Gutiérrez Peña,
  A.C. Martínez-Estudillo, S. Ventura-Soto*

Uncentered (Absolute) Correlation Clustering Method Fit
for Establishing Theoretical SAPK/JNK Signaling Pathway in Human
Soft Tissue Sarcoma Samples 1329
  *Jinling Zhang, Yinghua Lu, Lin Wang, Hongxin Zhang, Bo Zhang,
  Yeqiu Wang, Kai Wu, Stefan Wolfl*

Guiding Genetic Program Based Data Mining Using Fuzzy Rules 1337
  James F. Smith III, ThanhVu H. Nguyen

Neural Network Models for Language Acquisition: A Brief Survey 1346
  Jordi Poveda, Alfredo Vellido

Incorporating Knowledge in Evolutionary Prototype Selection 1358
  Salvador García, José Ramón Cano, Francisco Herrera

Evidence Relationship Matrix and Its Application to D-S Evidence
Theory for Information Fusion 1367
  Xianfeng Fan, Hong-Zhong Huang, Qiang Miao

Soft Computing in Context-Sensitive Multidimensional Ranking 1374
  *Weber Martins, Lauro Eugênio Guimarães Nalini,
  Marco Antonio Assfalk de Oliveira,
  Leonardo Guerra de Rezende Guedes*

Ontology-Based Classifier for Audio Scenes in Telemedicine 1382
  Cong Phuong Nguyen, Ngoc Yen Pham, Eric Castelli

PSO and ACO in Optimization Problems 1390
  Lenka Lhotská, Martin Macaš, Miroslav Burša

Constraints in Particle Swarm Optimization of Hidden Markov
Models 1399
  Martin Macaš, Daniel Novák, Lenka Lhotská

Nature-Inspired Approaches to Mining Trend Patterns in Spatial
Databases... 1407
    Ashkan Zarnani, Masoud Rahgozar, Caro Lucas

A Proposal of Evolutionary Prototype Selection for Class Imbalance
Problems 1415
    Salvador García, José Ramón Cano, Alberto Fernández,
    Francisco Herrera

MOVICAB-IDS: Visual Analysis of Network Traffic Data Streams
for Intrusion Detection 1424
    Álvaro Herrero, Emilio Corchado, José Manuel Sáiz

Maximum Likelihood Topology Preserving Ensembles 1434
    Emilio Corchado, Bruno Baruque, Bogdan Gabrys

Author Index... 1443

On Some of the Neural Mechanisms Underlying Adaptive Behavior

José Mira Mira

Dpto. de Inteligencia Artificial. ETS Ing. Informática. UNED. Madrid. Spain
jmira@dia.uned.es

Abstract. After a summary of AI development, from its neurocybernetic origins to present paradigms, we establish the distinction between the description-based "top-down" approach and the mechanism-based "bottom-up" approach. Then we analyze the different types of neural circuits that repeatedly appear in the sensory, motor and association regions of the nervous system. Finally, we propose an abstraction process that allows us to interpret the functions of these circuits at knowledge level.

1 Introduction

In "Finality and Form in Nervous Activity" W.S. McCulloch wrote: "Problems in the theory of knowledge and of value must be stated and resolved as questions concerning the anatomy and the physiology of the nervous system (NS). In those terms we are inquiring into the *a priori* forms and limitations of knowing and willing determined by the structure of the NS and by the mode of action of its elements" [1].

This mechanist and functional view of intelligence was dominant during the Neurocybernetic era, before the official birth of Artificial Intelligence (AI) in the summer of 1956. Fifty years of scientific and technical work have elapsed which have been dominated mainly by the symbolic view (representational) of AI [2] in which the initial objectives of "synthesizing general intelligence in machines" have not been achieved and some of the scientific community is again considering the AI issue from a bottom-up view. Works on situated robotics [3,4] and recognition of the excessively abstract and pre-scientific nature of the term intelligence makes us look to the classical cybernetic proposals and consider intelligence as a gradual concept, as an emerging property of the cooperation-competition of a large number of *adaptation mechanisms* of an organism that interacts dynamically with its environment [5,6]. At different levels, this idea of intelligence as an emerging property of the interaction of a network of non-intelligent agents is present in Minsky's "*Society of Mind*" [7], in Varela's "self made of self-less components", and in all the current movement on "multi-agent systems" (MAS) [8].

Some of the criticisms of the bottom-up view (functional and mechanism-based) of AI are based on its apparent reductionist nature that prevents it from handling high-level linguistic and cognitive concepts such as intention, purpose, representation, diagnosis, reasoning, classification, learning, perception, memory or planning [9]. In this work we argue that the apparent justification of this criticism disappears at the moment when we consider the different adaptation mechanisms in the methodological context of the theory of levels (physical, symbolic and knowledge) and domains (own and the external observer's) of a calculus description performed by a neural mechanism, where the figure of the observer is essential who *interprets* in his natural language what this calculus "means", using cognitive terms that have no causal effect on the mechanism's own operation domain. From this perspective it is easy to see that what we call "purposes" are closed loop feedback mechanisms, for example.

The rest of the work is organized as follows. In the second section we briefly review AI development from its neurocybernetic origins and its baptism in 1956 to present paradigms. In the third section we introduce the mechanism idea and its relation with the agent concept. In the fourth section we view the functional paradigm proposed by Newell and Simon to describe "intelligent agent" behavior. This diagram includes perception, action, association and learning tasks in terms of which neurophysiology and psychology describe the interaction of a living creature with its environment. Section fourth also includes a set of basic mechanisms that appear in one or more of these tasks. Section five is devoted to adaptation and learning. The sixth section has two examples to interpret the meaning of the calculus performed by these mechanisms (lateral inhibition and reflex arches) at knowledge level. Finally, the tenth section is the conclusion.

2 From Neurocybernetics to Present AI Paradigms

The interest in simulating nervous system functions and animal behavior electronically and computationally stems from neurocybernetics, which aims to understand the cerebral function in terms of the network of neural mechanisms from which it emerges. "Minds are simply what brains do", Minsky says [7]. The foundation works by McCulloch-Pitts [1] and Rosemblueth, Wiener and Bigelow [10] gave rise to formal neuron models and modular finite state automata, pattern recognition, associative memory, learning by reinforcement, information theory and self-organization and self- reproduction, among others [11,12].

From 1956 the connectionist view was overshadowed by the symbolic approach (top-down), which tackles the AI problem in terms of declarative and modular descriptions in natural language of entities (concepts) and relations between these entities (inferential rules). It thus forgets that all calculus emerges from a mechanism that calculates (all knowing depends on the structure that knows, Maturana says) and nervous system functions are interpreted in terms of manipulations of symbolic descriptions, confusing the map with the territory. Clancey, Searle, Edelman, Dreyfus and Gibson, among others criticise this view of AI [5]. In the late 1980s the interest in connectionism and the cybernetic view of intelligence now called situated paradigm [3] and before embodiments of mind [1] and epistemological physiology reappeared.

We thus reach the present state in which the three paradigms coexist: (1) the *symbolic*, obviously useful in knowledge engineering where it begins with a description in natural language of the task and the method used to develop a knowledge-based system (KBS), irrespective of its validity to explain cognitive processes, (2) the *connectionist* with its two aspects (adaptive numeric classifiers with fixed architecture and special-purpose neural mechanisms) and (3) the *situated*, also with two aspects (the ethological and the mechanism based). The approach that we defend in this work coincides with the mechanism-based aspects of the connectionist and situated paradigms, as illustrated in figure 1.

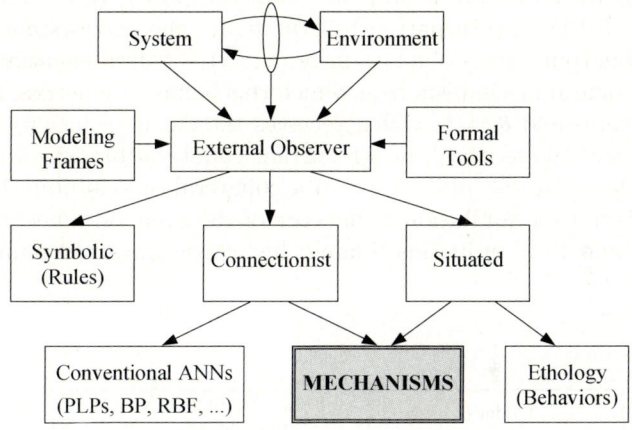

Fig. 1. AI paradigms

In fact there are only two paradigms with different paths: (1) the paradigm based on *program* descriptions that run on a general-purpose machine and (2) the paradigm based on *mechanisms* of a special-purpose machine. The first type stresses the external observer domain (EOD) and takes for granted that there is a set of organizations interposed between the description of a calculus and its final hardware implementation. This approach includes the symbolic one, the conventional ANNs and the descriptions of behaviors in situated robotic. The second type stresses own domain (OD), in the direct causality of the mechanisms, and only uses the EOD as a framework of interpretation. This approach includes bioinspired connectionism and the branch of situated robotics which is concerned with the mechanisms from which the observed behaviors emerge. In terms of the agent theory, in the first approach the agent implementation is software, in the second it is special-purpose hardware.

We conclude this summary of the historical development of AI remembering the concept of "knowledge level" introduced by Newell [13] and Marr [14] and the external observer figure proposed by Maturana [15] and Varela [16] in biology and Mira and Delgado in computation [17]. The superposition of both contributions has given rise to the three-level methodological framework (signals, symbols and knowledge) and two description domains for each level, own domain (OD) and that of the external observer's (EOD), which we will use to interpret the meaning of the calculus performed by a specific neural mechanism.

3 Mechanisms Versus Agents

Every mechanism (OD entity) is the structural support (internal implementation) of an agent (EOD entity) and, seen from outside, every agent is the functional description (external) of the behavior that emerges from a mechanism or an organized set of mechanisms (an organism) structurally coupled to its environment. In figure 2 we show a simple example proposed by W.S. McCulloch to establish this distinction. In part (a) of the figure the correspondence between the input and output values of an oddness detection neural agent is shown. Part (b) shows the neural mechanism from which this behavior emerges. It is a formal neuron with threshold $\theta = 1$, which receives the state of activity of an external signal, x, and the feedback of a recurrent collateral branch of its own axon as inputs. This collateral inhibits x and a collateral of x inhibits the recurrent feedback. This mutual inhibition is the core of the even/odd mechanism. In the words of McCulloch "... in its functioning this neuron says, the number that has been is odd."

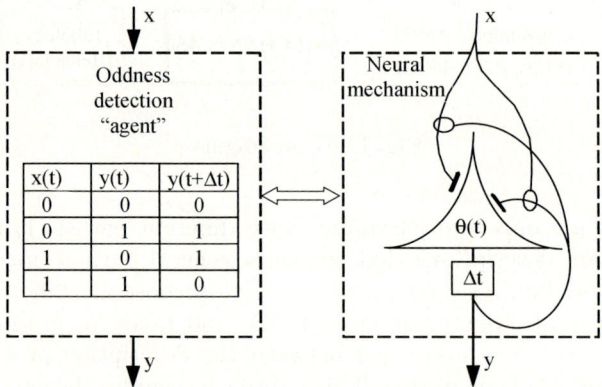

Fig. 2. External description versus internal mechanism in McCullochs formal neuron for oddness detection example

Both the mechanisms and their associated agents can be considered simple or *composed*. A mechanism is considered simple when it decides not to continue delving deeper into its analysis and it accepts for itself a single external description (functional). Conversely, a mechanism is considered *composed* when we accept the need to know its internal structure to obtain a satisfactory explanation of its function. This internal structure is described in terms of a network of interconnections between other mechanisms that we have accepted as simple. Obviously, the process is recursive.

4 Functional Systems Underlying Reflex and Voluntary Motor Acts

Luria distinguishes between *function* of a specific tissue (a photoreceptor that detects light), which can have a highly specific location, and *functional system* (FS) that requires the coordinated action of different neural structures and distinguishes four basic types: (1) sensor functional system (SFS), (2) motor (MFS), (3) association and decision (ADFS) and (4) adaptation and learning (ALFS), on which another system is superimposed responsible for regulating the state of tone and supervises all the rest (figure 3). If we call these functional systems proposed by Luria agents, the scheme in figure 3 coincides with the "intelligent-agent" proposal made by Newell and Simon in 1974 and currently reactivated by situated robotics and the multi-agent system theory [8,18].

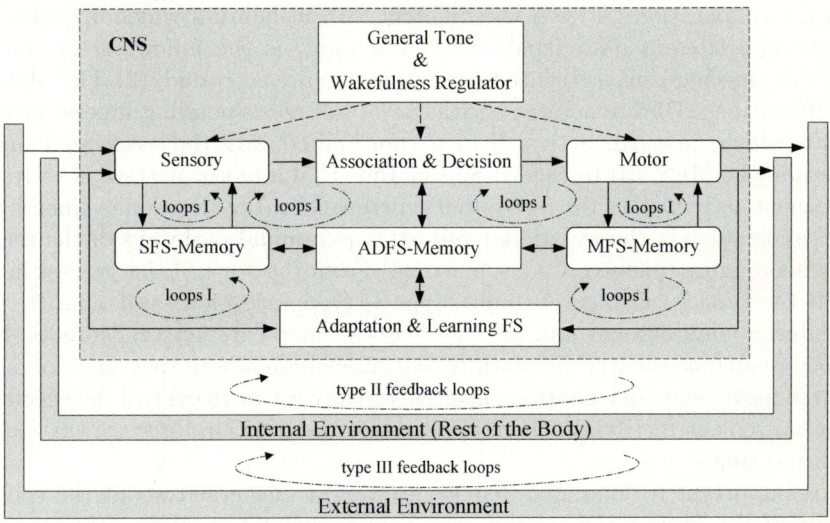

Fig. 3. Functional systems and feedback loops involved in reflex and voluntary motor acts

The system interacts with the rest of the body (internal environment) and with the external environment via a set of sensors and effectors that close many feedback loops. W.S. McCulloch [1] distinguished three types of loops. Type (I) loops are those that close inside an FS or among different FS, within the nervous system. Type (II) loops close via the rest of the body (internal environment) and type (III) close via the external environment, using the specific set of sensors and effectors developed in every living creature to structurally connect its body with its environment. Type (I) loops have to do with the timing, control-memory, sequential -association and decision-making, motor-planning and output-pattern-generation mechanisms. Type (II) loops are associated with homeostasis and reflex actions. Finally, type (III) loops have to do with the integration of perception-action and the control of voluntary acts, based on values, purposes and intentions. The large number of type I, II and III feedback loops is the first family of neural mechanisms on which adaptive behavior is based [19,20,21].

Now let us view a description of the function that we associate with each of these functional systems in relation to their anatomical support and the new types of mechanism that are appearing, in addition to the feedback loops already mentioned. We will stress the SFS and the ADFS habituation, sensitization and conditioning mechanisms more, because they are the most well known and include the lateral inhibition circuits and reflex arches that we will later use to illustrate the abstraction process that allows us to interpret the neural function at knowledge level. The construction of a more complete library of neural mechanisms is a long-term objective.

An ingenuous view of how we believe the voluntary motor act is organized from the cooperation between the different SFS in figure 3 which organize the afferent and efferent data (spatial and temporal) is the following: (1) in the ADFS the mechanisms associated with an action are activated. (2) This state of activity in the ADFS generates activation of the corresponding kinetic melody in SFS which, in turn, activates in a coordinated way the associated motor pattern in the MFS. (3) In the MFS, each time that a motor pattern is activated subsequent activation of the associated synergisms and "vedette" movements and the connections via the pyramidal and extra-pyramidal pathways of the sets of corresponding motoneurons takes place. (4) From the start of the process in the ADFS the type I (with cerebellum), type II (propioception) and type III (via the external environment and the SFS) control loops are active. Moreover, the sensory reafferences carry the data to the cerebellum where they are compared with the movement coordination patterns, already learnt to control the execution of the movement rectifying where appropriate the position-force correlations in space and time.

It is important to highlight that we are not so concerned about the specific aspects of this description of the voluntary motor act as pinpointing the difficulty inherent in every "bottom-up" approach. It is not easy to pass from an anastomotic network of local mechanisms to a coherent explanation of the global organization of the motor act, which, moreover, is experimentally verifiable.

The function of the *sensor functional system* (SFS) is to construct a representation of the external and internal environment dynamically in three stages: (1) sensation (2) perception and (3) conceptualization by plurisensorial association (integration of the different sensory modalities).

The first stage is repeated for each sensory modality and includes receptor, corresponding thalamic nucleus and primary cortical area. Here the stimulus is detected but not identified. For example, for the visual pathway it would be:

1. Receptor (retina, optic nerve and chiasma)
2. Thalamic nucleus (external geniculate body)
3. Primary cortical area

The second stage (perception) constitutes the first gnostic level. Here there is already semantics. It is where the stimulus is coded and identified. It is the process that the sensory information undergoes from the thalamic nucleus of the previous level to the secondary cortical areas, passing through the corresponding associative thalamic nucleus.

The third stage (plurisensorial association and stimulus conceptualization) includes the confluence and interaction of secondary areas corresponding to the different sensory modalities. Here the supramodal (symbolic) scheme take place, the base for the complex forms of activity.

Observe that advancing from the receptor to the cortex in each sensory pathway, modal specificity is combined with the capacity to integrate, associate and generalise. Moving up towards the cortex, integration increases (stimulus semantics) and modal specificity decreases.

When the SFS is analysed from the peripheric receptors to cortex, we find, at least, the following types of mechanisms (figure 4):

1. Monotonic (linear and non linear) and non-monotonic transducers, tuned to different types and intervals of stimuli quality and intensity.
2. *Divergent* and *convergent* processes.
3. *Modulated*, *delayed* and *thresholded* transmission lines.
4. *Lateral inhibition* (contrast enhancement) and other spatio-temporal feature extraction circuits.
5. *Intersensorial transformations* that increase the discriminant power in those situations that are indistinguishable using a single sensory modality. The mechanisms underlying intersensorial transformation are the same as (2), (3) and (4), but now in the cortex, at the third level of semantics.

Of all the mechanisms mentioned in this section, except the non-linear ones, the one that has the greatest capacity for integration is lateral inhibition (LI) because since the shape of its nuclei changes it allows us to formulate practically all the relevant processes, first in the feature extraction and after in the discrimination and classification tasks. In the visual pathway of higher mammals we find LI circuits in the retina (photoreceptor feet, amacrines in the external and internal plexiform layers, horizontal, bipolar and ganglion cells). There is also LI in the lateral geniculate body (LGB) and in the connections that the LGB projects in the cortex, where LI is responsible for the formation of ocular dominance columns and the preference for certain orientations in the stimuli.

There are two basic connectivity schemes: (1) *non-recurrent LI*, and (2) *recurrent LI* with feedback. In both instances the shape and size of the receptive fields (RFs) specifies the network connectivity (cooperation-competition area) and calculation details (tuning, orientations, shapes, speeds, etc.). The most usual shape these RFs is an approximation of a Laplace Gaussian obtained from subtracting two Gaussians.

The *motor functional system* (MFS) structure is similar to the SFS specular image. There it started from the external data and its semantics increased until it reached the cortex where it constituted the input of the association and decision system. Here, it starts from the action decision and is broken down first

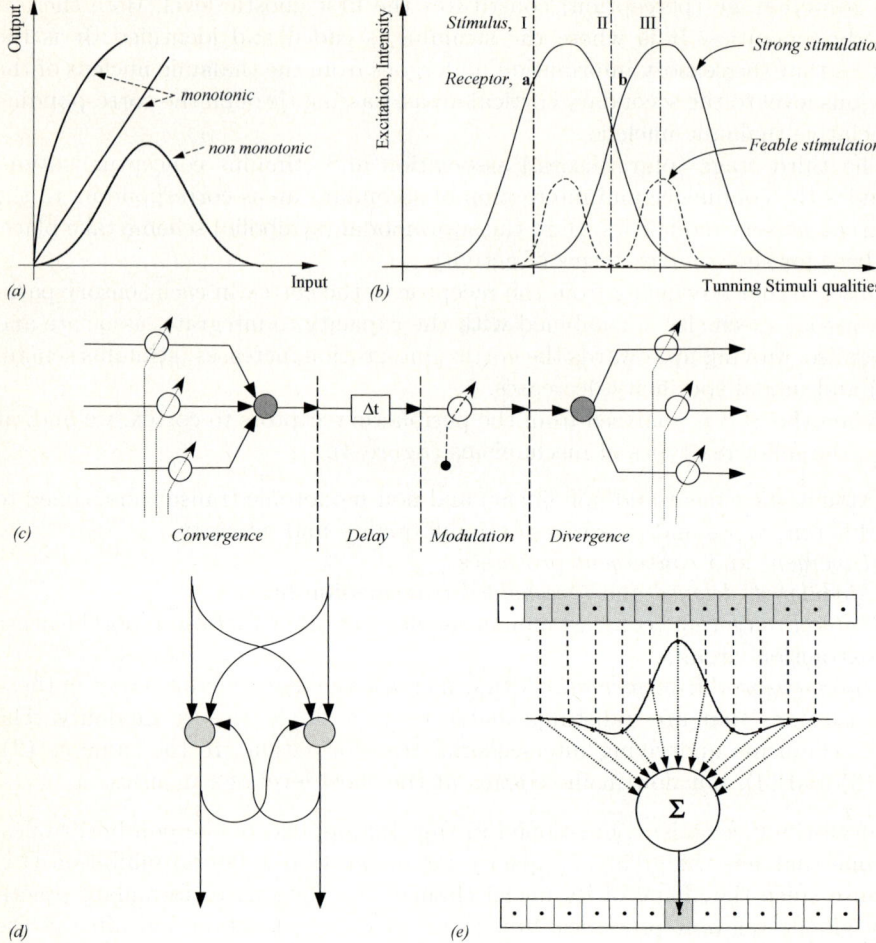

Fig. 4. Sensorial mechanism. (a) Monotonic and non-monotonic transference functions. (b) Excitation levels of two hypothetical receptors responding to stimuli of equal energy but different quality (i.e. sound frequency). The overlapping area is a function of the intensity level. (c) Hypothetical transmission line including convergence, delay, modulation, and divergence. (d) Recurrent and non-recurrent LI circuits. (e) Continuous case formulation.

in terms of a plan, and after in terms of a set of elementary actions until it reaches the effector level (medula) that links again with the external environment, thus closing the perception-action loop. This FS embraces the following areas: primary motor area, sensor module (postcentral cortex), premotor areas, nuclei (subcortical system) and cerebellum.

All the mechanisms that intervene in the most central part of the MFS are still not known. Those in the peripheral part, nearest to the motoneurons, are: (1) convergent and divergent connections integrated in reflex pathways, (2) groups of interneurons coordinating timing processes and opposite muscle innervation, (3) rhythmic locomotion pattern generators, (4) oscillatory loops, (5) cerebellar PROM-like mechanisms, and (6) spinal reflexes.

The *association and decision functional system* (ASFS), also called psycho-emotive, basically corresponds to Lurias third functional unit, from which we have separated its executive level (the MSF). It is usually associated with the task of programming, *regulating* and *verifying* the action. Based on experiments on the functional deficit and the residual function after local traumatic or surgical injuries, it is accepted that this FS houses the mechanisms underlying our purposes and intentions, the activation of plans and decision processes on the motor actions relevant to each stimulus configuration and each internal state. Their circuits are activated by sensory and motor memories and their efferent pathways act on the MFS to control the analysis and execution of the motor planes.

It also includes the levels of psychic activity, intellectual content and emotive coloring of feeling and response. It is decision system for voluntary activities. The cerebral organization of this functional unit is located in the front regions of the hemispheres (prefrontal cortex). Its output channel is the MFS and its most distinctive characteristics are:

1. Its wealth of bi-directional connections with the rest of the cortical and subcortical structures (MSF and SFC), and with the reticular formation.
2. Its superstructure on the rest of the cortex suggests a much more general function to regulate planned, purpose-directed rational behavior.

The destruction of the prefrontal cortex alters the behavior programs and causes lack of inhibition of immediate responses to irrelevant stimuli, slows down the decision processes and deteriorates motor coordination. It is easy to understand, faced with this pathology, that the mission of the prefrontal cortex is very extensive. It collaborates in the regulation of the cortical tone, in the decision of the behavior mode and in all action based on *language* and higher forms of voluntary activity.

Identification and description of the specific neural mechanisms of the ASFS do not fall within the scope of this work. It is however obvious that the ASFS includes all the mechanisms mentioned earlier when describing the SFS and MFS.

5 Adaptation and Learning Functional System (ALFS)

The learning mechanisms, the same as memory, are distributed on all the structures of the brain and appear in the different levels of integration, from the cellular to global behavior, passing through the different functional systems described above.

Starting with the cellular level, and in accordance with Kandel [20], the most elementary forms of learning are the processes of: (1) Habituation, (2) sensitization, and (3) conditioning. Habituation is a mechanism whereby the response of a neural unit is diminished when the eliciting stimulus is repeatedly presented. Its mission is to distinguish between what is known and what is new in a stimulus and in the second instance, activate the orientation reflexes. It is the basis of selective attention mechanisms. In a complementary way, sensitization is a mechanism that increases the response of a neural unit as a result of the presentation of a strong or noxious stimulus. It mission, once more, is to modulate attention but now focusing it on potentially dangerous or painful stimuli. Figure 5(a) shows the composition of both mechanisms from Kandel and his collaborators' proposals for the aplixia. Part b of the figure shows their interpretation of classical conditioning as an "associative enhancement of presynaptic facilitation".

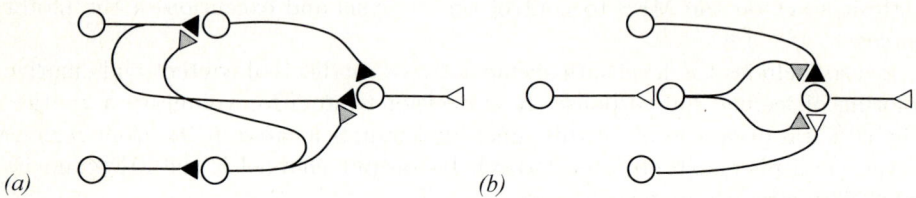

Fig. 5. (a) Elementary learning mechanisms in Aplixia. Habituation and Sensitisation. (b) Classical conditioning (adapted from Kandel [20]).

In both instances, habituation and sensitization, the same as in Hebbs conjecture, the physiological support of the elementary learning processes at cellular level is the temporal modification of synaptic effectiveness which modifies in turn the function and/or the structure of the neural network into which this synapsis is integrated. The mechanism whereby the value of the magnitude and sign of change is controlled in this synaptic parameter is the one that gives the name to the process. Thus, in habituation it is the temporal persistence of a stimulus, in sensitization it is the presence of strong or noxious stimuli and in self-organizational or Hebbian learning it is the persistence in the temporal coincidence between the states of pre- and postsynaptic activity. The same occurs with *classical conditioning*, only that here the event controlling the change has to do with the relational structure of the environment since what is associated is not so much the spatio-temporal coincidence of the unconditioned stimuli (US) with the conditioned stimuli (CS), as the relation between the two. This relation is used by animals to predict the occurrence of US from the presence of CS because both, CS and US, seem to form "a unitary and significant whole" in this animals environment. It is because of this that *extinction* is so important, because it makes the response stop to "cues that are no longer significant".

This idea of modifying the value of a set of parameters that determines the calculus of a neural network has given rise to virtually all the field of "Artificial Neural Nets", which are adaptive numerical classifiers where the value of their parameters, the weights matrix is modified in accordance with "supervised" procedures (BP and reinforcement) or non-supervised (hebbian mechanisms). For the higher forms of learning (induction, abduction, and learning for insight) their neurophysiological support is still not precisely known.

Paulov extended the idea of an organization based on the creation and modification of a wide network of sensory-motor connections via the creation of new pathways between the cortical areas that are simultaneously active to the cortex. Thus, the US become previous reflex signals and trigger their response. As a result of these associations, any agent active on the receptors can become a stimulus integrated into the animals experience and evoke the appropriate activity of the organism to match this stimulus. This makes it possible to multiply the number of "congruent interactions" between an organism and its environment.

From our point of view, the important thing is to find a series of mechanisms that enable the association, the creation of *connecting pathways* between main lines related to animal survival, and secondary lines. This necessarily implies the existence of a mechanism to *compare* the states of activity of both lines, of another mechanism to *integrate* the result of this comparison and a third mechanism to *forget* the associations that are no longer significant. It is not important at this level if these processes for creating/destroying lines of association are biologically supported by changes in synaptic effectiveness or by irradiation of cortex excitement and subsequent raising of tone (excitement facility) in the areas near to the excited point, making possible the firing of these areas via temporal connections. Nor is it relevant now if we implement these processes analogically (controlled charge and discharge of a condenser), digitally (reversible counter) or with a program (algorithm). The relevant thing is the proposal underlying all connectionism which tells us that the general learning mechanism consists of dynamically creating and modifying a network of associations that provide an increasingly wealthier relational structure of our representation of the environment and the connections of this representation with our repertory of actions in this environment. Learning is constructing and updating a hierarchy of significant associations in a specific environment.

6 Neural Mechanisms Interpreted at the Knowledge Level: Two Case Studies

When a neural circuit is analyzed outside the organism it can give the impression that its function is not particularly important. For example, to say that lateral inhibition (LI) circuits are detectors of contrasts or that reflex arches (RA) are elementary learning mechanisms, does not highlight their capacity to adapt. Braitenberg says that behaviors always seem more complex than the mechanisms from which they emerge.

The purpose of this section is to illustrate a way of interpreting neural mechanisms as inferential schemes at knowledge level. For this we have taken the usual route in reverse neurophysiology for two basic mechanisms, LI and RA. We start with their anatomical description in own domain (OD) of the physical level. After we propose an *abstraction* process consisting of substituting the circuit elements with verbs that best describe their function (comparing, selecting, evaluating,

...) and the physical signals with dynamic roles. Thus the mechanism becomes a multi-agent system (MAS) and the local processes simple agents (inferences). Finally, the initial circuits are now instantiations of an inferential scheme. In other words, a specific implementation of MAS. In fact, if we now do direct engineering starting from these models we obtain a set of different programs and circuits, which include the initial ones.

This abstraction process, regarding recurrent LI, generates the inferential scheme in figure 6 where data in the center (C) and the periphery (P) of the receptive field are evaluated, the results of these evaluations are compared (match inference) and dialogue is entered into with the proposals of the neighboring agents in a cooperation process that generates a consensued result.

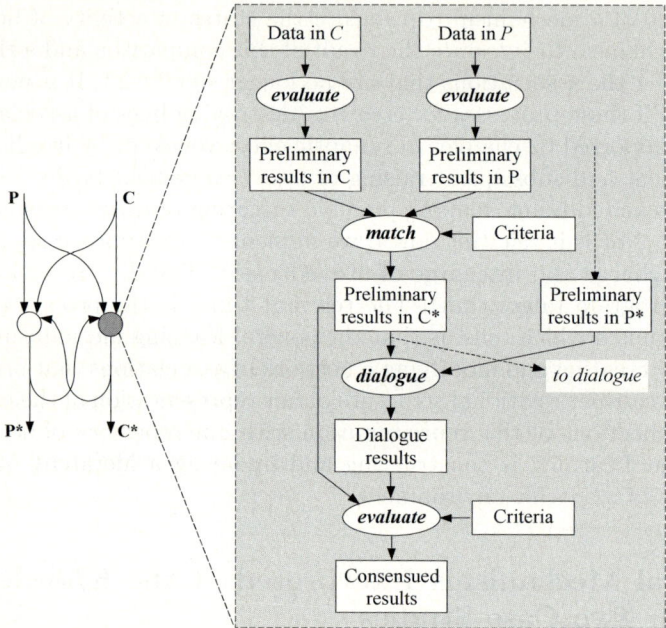

Fig. 6. A knowledge level interpretation of the recurrent LI circuit function

If we now repeat the process for an RA circuit, (figure 7) we see that the inferential scheme corresponding to this neural mechanism consists of: (1) *detecting* several relevant *perceptual schemes*, (2) *calculating* the temporal *persistence* of the associations between these schemes, (3) *activating* (creating) new functional pathways of sensorimotor association and (4) *deactivating* (destroying) these pathways when the association ceases or decreases. The process is also recurrent. Once an association has been created it acts as a base for creating other new ones.

In this work we are not so interested in stressing the details of the abstraction process followed in two types of specific neural mechanisms as the underlying

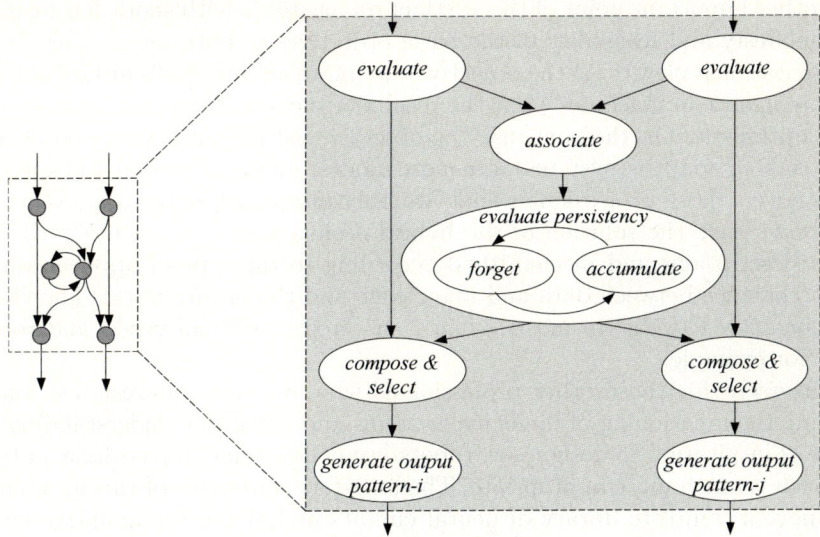

Fig. 7. Inferential scheme of the RA at knowledge level

idea that provides us with a way of looking at neural circuits as a support of a calculus whose meaning is only complete when complementary descriptions of an external observer are added to the obvious description of the physical level. The external observer with his own semantics injects the symbol level and knowledge level knowledge. Just pausing one moment to reflect makes us realize that this is what occurs in all computation. In a specific program, it will be difficult for us to understand the meaning of what a digital mechanism does (register, ALU, FIFO memory, ...) unless we add computer architecture and programming language knowledge. These examples for interpreting mechanisms at knowledge level can also be used to reason in the other direction. In other words, behind many behaviors that we label cognitive or intelligent, there are relatively simple neural mechanisms. What complicates them is the semantics used by the external observer to interpret their function.

7 Conclusions

A key point to understand the distinction between the symbolic paradigm of AI and the mechanism-based approach that we have presented in this work is to remember the difference between the calculus performed by a special-purpose circuit, where the correlation between structure and function or the meaning of the different signals and their transformations are never lost, and the calculus programmed, starting from a description in natural language, in a general-purpose machine where conventional users only know the syntax and the semantics of the programming language that they use.

Another important point of this distinction has to do with short and medium-term modesty and feasibility of the basic objectives in both approaches. In the representational view of AI the objectives are more ambitious ("synthesizing general intelligence in machines") but the results of the last fifty years are not excessively optimistic. On the contrary, the objectives of the mechanism-based view (constructing adaptive systems), are more modest and feasible and still splendid.

Moreover, those professionals that are only interested in the applied part of AI, always have the solution of the hybrid architectures, which integrate both views (descriptions and mechanisms) according to the type of application, the specific balance between data and knowledge and the nature of this knowledge. It is currently like this in most applications in the artificial vision and robotic fields, for example.

Conversely, for those other professionals who are more interested in understanding the functioning of biological systems and using this understanding as a source of inspiration to design new robots, we believe that the mechanism-based approach is much more appropriate. The long-term objective of this approach is to achieve a complete library of neural circuits underlying the adaptive behavior of a living creature in its environment. The reduction of high-level cognitive processes to mechanisms is still a much longer long-term objective.

Acknowledgments. I acknowledge the support of the CICYT project TIN2004-07661-C02-01.

References

1. W.S. McCulloch. *Embodiments of Mind.* The MIT Press, Cambridge, Mass., 1965.
2. S.C. Shapiro, editor. *Encyclopedia of artificial intelligence.*, volume Vol. I and II. John Wiley & Sons, New York, 2nd edition, 1990.
3. R.A. Brooks. Intelligence without reason. A.i. memo, MIT, N°. 1293 1991.
4. W.J. Clancey. *Situated cognition. On human knowledge and computer representation.* Univ. Press, Cambridge, 1997.
5. N. Wiener. *Cybernetics.* The Technology Press. J. Wiley & Sons, New York, 1948.
6. R.D. Beer. *Intelligence as adaptive behavior.* Academic Press, 1990.
7. M. Minsky. *The society of mind.* Simon and Schuster, New York, 1985.
8. S. Russell and P. Norvig. *Artificial Intelligence. A Modern Approach.* Prentice Hall, Upper Saddle River, New Jersey, 1995.
9. J. Mira. On the use of the computational paradigm in neurophysiology and cognitive science. In José Mira and José R. Álvarez, editors, *Mechanisms, Symbols, and Models Underlying Cognition.* IWINAC 2005, volume LNCS 3561, pages 1–15. Springer, 2005.
10. A. Rosenblueth, N. Wiener, and J. Bigelow. Behavior, purpose and teleology. *Philosophy of Science,* 10, 1943.
11. C.E. Shannon and J. McCarthy, editors. *Automata Studies.* Princeton University Press, Princeton, 1956.
12. J. A. Anderson and Rosenfeld, editors. *Neurocomputing: Foundations of Research.* The MIT Press, Cambridge, 1989.
13. A. Newell. The knowledge level. *AI Magazine,* 120, 1981.

14. D. Marr. *Vision*. Freeman, New York, 1982.
15. H.R. Maturana. Ontology of observing. the biological foundations of self consciousness and the physical domain existence. http://www.inteco.cl/biology/ontology/, 2002.
16. F.J. Varela. *Principles of Biological Autonomy*. The North Holland Series in General Systems Research, New York, 1979.
17. J. Mira and A.E. Delgado. Some comments on the antropocentric viewpoint in the neurocybernetic methodology. In *Proc of the Seventh International Congress of Cybernetics and Systems*, pages 891–95, 1987.
18. R.R. Murphy. *Introduction to AI robotics*. MIT Press., Cambridge, MA, 2002.
19. F.O. Schmitt and F.G. Worden. *The Neuroscience Fourth Study Program*. The MIT Press, Cambridge, Mass, 1979.
20. E.R. Kandel, J.H. Schwartz, and T.M. Jessell. *Principles of Neural Science*. Prentice Hall, 1991.
21. M. Arbib, editor. *The Handbook of Brain Theory and Neural Networks*. The MIT Press, Cambridge, MA., 1995.

On Correlation Measures of Intuitionistic Fuzzy Sets

Zeshui Xu

Department of Management Science and Engineering
School of Economics and Management
Tsinghua University, Beijing 100084, China
Xu_zeshui@263.net

Abstract. The intuitionistic fuzzy set, developed by Atanassov [1], is a useful tool to deal with vagueness and uncertainty. Correlation analysis of intuitionistic fuzzy sets is an important research topic in the intuitionistic fuzzy set theory and has great practical potential in a variety of areas, such as engineering, decision making, medical diagnosis, pattern recognition, etc. In this paper, we propose a new method for deriving the correlation coefficients of intuitionistic fuzzy sets, which has some advantages over the existing methods. Furthermore, we extend the developed method to the interval-valued intuitionistic fuzzy set theory, and show its application in medical diagnosis.

1 Introduction

In the conventional fuzzy set theory of Zadeh [2], there is only a membership degree of an element in a fuzzy set, and the non-membership degree equals one minus the membership degree. In real life, however, a person may assume that an object belongs to a set to a certain degree, but it is possible that he/she is not so sure about it [3]. The fuzzy set theory is somewhat unsuitable for dealing with this situation. In [1], Atanassov extended this theory, and defined the notion of intuitionistic fuzzy set (IFS), which assigns to each element a membership degree and a non-membership degree with a hesitation degree. Thus, the IFSs are very interesting and useful and give us the possibility to model hesitation and uncertainty by using an additional degree [4]. Later, Atanassov and Gargov [5] further introduced the interval-valued intuitionistic fuzzy set (IVIFS), which is a generalization of the IFS. The fundamental characteristic of the IVIFS is that the values of its membership function and non-membership function are intervals rather than exact numbers. Over the last two decades, the IFS theory has been widely studied and applied in a variety of fields, such as decision making [6,7], logic programming [8], medical diagnosis [9,10], machine learning and market prediction [11], etc. Correlation analysis of IFSs is an important research topic in the IFS theory, which has received much attention from researchers [12-18]. Gerstenkorn and Manko [12] defined a function measuring the correlation of IFSs, and introduced a coefficient of such a correlation and examined its properties. Hong and Hwang [13] studied the concepts of correlation and correlation coefficient of IFSs in probability spaces. Hung [14] and Mitchell [15] derived the correlation coefficient of IFSs from a statistical viewpoint by interpreting an IFS as an ensemble of ordinary fuzzy sets. Hung and Wu [16] proposed a method to calculate the correlation coefficient of IFSs by means of "centroid". Furthermore, they extended the "centroid" method to the IVIFS theory. Bustince and Burillo [17] introduced the concepts of correlation and correlation coefficient of IVIFSs and gave two decomposition theorems of the correlation of IVIFSs in terms of the correlation of interval-valued fuzzy sets and the entropy of IFSs. Hong [18] generalized the concepts of correlation and correlation coefficient of IVIFSs in a general probability space. However, all the existing methods can't guarantee that the correlation coefficient of any two IFSs (or IVIFSs) equals one if and only if these two IFSs (or IVIFSs) are the same. To overcome this drawback, in this paper, we propose a new method for deriving the correlation coefficient of IFSs, and then extend the developed method to the IVIFS theory. Finally, we show its application in medical diagnosis.

2 Basic Concepts

In the following, we review some basic concepts related to IFSs and IVIFSs:

Definition 2.1 [2]. *Let X be a universe of discourse, then a fuzzy set is defined as:*

$$A = \{<x, \mu_A(x)> | x \in X\} \qquad (1)$$

which is characterized by a membership function $\mu_A : X \to [0,1]$, where $\mu_A(x)$ denotes the degree of membership of the element x to the set A.

Atanassov [1] extended the fuzzy set to the IFS, shown as follows:

Definition 2.2 [1]. *An IFS A in X is given by*

$$A = \{<x, \mu_A(x), v_A(x)> | x \in X\} \qquad (2)$$

where $\mu_A : X \to [0,1]$ and $v_A : X \to [0,1]$, with the condition

$$0 \leq \mu_A(x) + v_A(x) \leq 1, \forall x \in X \qquad (3)$$

The numbers $\mu_A(x)$ and $v_A(x)$ represent, respectively, the membership degree and non-membership degree of the element x to the set A.

Definition 2.3 [1]. *For each IFS A in X, if*

$$\pi_A(x) = 1 - \mu_A(x) - v_A(x), \text{ for all } x \in X \qquad (4)$$

then $\pi_A(x)$ is called the degree of indeterminacy of x to A.

However, sometime it is not approximate to assume that the membership degrees for certain elements of A are exactly defined, but a value range can be given. In such cases, Atanassov and Gargov [5] introduced the notion of IVIFS as follows:

Definition 2.4 [5]. *Let X be a universe of discourse. An IVIFS $\tilde{A}$ over X is an object having the form:*

$$\tilde{A} = \{<x, \tilde{\mu}_{\tilde{A}}(x), \tilde{v}_{\tilde{A}}(x)> | x \in X\} \qquad (5)$$

where $\tilde{\mu}_{\tilde{A}}(x) \subset [0,1]$ and $\tilde{v}_{\tilde{A}}(x) \subset [0,1]$ are intervals, and

$$\sup \tilde{\mu}_{\tilde{A}}(x) + \sup \tilde{v}_{\tilde{A}}(x) \leq 1, \text{ for each } x \in X \tag{6}$$

Especially, if $\mu_{\tilde{A}}(x) = \inf \tilde{\mu}_{\tilde{A}}(x) = \sup \tilde{\mu}_{\tilde{A}}(x)$ and $v_{\tilde{A}}(x) = \inf \tilde{v}_{\tilde{A}}(x) = \sup \tilde{v}_{\tilde{A}}(x)$, then the IVIFS $\tilde{A}$ is reduced to an ordinary IFS.

3 Correlation Measures

Let $A = \{<x_i, \mu_A(x_i), v_A(x_i)> | x_i \in X\}$ and $B = \{<x_i, \mu_B(x_i), v_B(x_i)> | x_i \in X\}$ be two IFSs, and let $X = \{x_1, x_2, ..., x_n\}$ be a finite universe of discourse. In [12], Gerstenkorn and Manko introduced the concept of correlation coefficient of the IFSs A and B as below:

$$\rho_1(A, B) = \frac{c_1(A, B)}{(c_1(A, A) \cdot c_1(B, B))^{1/2}} \tag{7}$$

where $c_1(A, B) = \sum_{i=1}^{n}(\mu_A(x_i) \cdot \mu_B(x_i) + v_A(x_i) \cdot v_B(x_i))$ is the correlation of the IFSs A and B. Furthermore, they proved that:

Theorem 3.1 [12]. *The correlation coefficient $\rho_1(A, B)$ satisfies the following properties:* 1) $0 \leq \rho_1(A, B) \leq 1$; 2) $A = B \Rightarrow \rho_1(A, B) = 1$; and 3) $\rho_1(A, B) = \rho_1(B, A)$.

Hong and Hwang [13] further considered the situations in which X is an infinite universe of discourse, and defined

$$\rho_2(A, B) = \frac{c_2(A, B)}{(c_2(A, A) \cdot c_2(B, B))^{1/2}} \tag{8}$$

as a correlation coefficient of the IFSs A and B, where

$$c_2(A, B) = \int_X (\mu_A(x)\mu_B(x) + v_A(x)v_B(x))dx \tag{9}$$

is the correlation of the IFSs A and B.

Clearly, $\rho_2(A, B)$ has also all the properties in Theorem 3.1.

Hung [14] gave another correlation coefficient of the IFSs A and B as: $\rho_3(A, B) = (\rho_{1,1} + \rho_{2,2})/2$, where $\rho_{1,1}$ and $\rho_{2,2}$ are, respectively, the correlation coefficients of $\mu_A(x)$ and $\mu_B(x)$ and of $v_A(x)$ and $v_B(x)$:

$$\rho_{1,1} = \frac{\int_X (\mu_A(x) - \bar{\mu}_A) \times (\mu_B(x) - \bar{\mu}_B)dx}{\left(\int_X (\mu_A(x) - \bar{\mu}_A)^2 dx \int_X (\mu_B(x) - \bar{\mu}_B)^2 dx\right)^{1/2}}, \quad \rho_{2,2} = \frac{\int_X (v_A(x) - \bar{v}_A) \times (v_B(x) - \bar{v}_B)dx}{\left(\int_X (v_A(x) - \bar{v}_A)^2 dx \int_X (v_B(x) - \bar{v}_B)^2 dx\right)^{1/2}} \tag{10}$$

where $\bar{\mu}_A$ and $\bar{\mu}_B$ are, respectively, the sample means of the membership functions $\mu_A(x)$ and $\mu_B(x)$; $\bar{v}_A$ and $\bar{v}_B$ are the sample means of the non-membership functions $v_A(x)$ and $v_B(x)$.

Mitchell [15] gave an improved version of Hung' results. He interpreted the IFSs A and B as the ensembles of the ordinary membership functions $\phi_A^{(h)}(x)$ and $\phi_B^{(k)}(x)$, $h, k = 1, 2, ..., n$:

$$\phi_A^{(h)}(x) = \mu_A(x) + \pi_A(x) \times p_h(x), \quad \phi_B^{(h)}(x) = \mu_B(x) + \pi_B(x) \times p_k(x) \tag{11}$$

where for each x, $p_h(x)$ and $p_k(x)$ are two uniform random numbers chosen from the interval $[0,1]$, and then calculated the correlation coefficient $\rho_{h,k}$ of each pair of membership functions $\phi_A^{(h)}$ and $\phi_B^{(h)}$ as:

$$\rho_{h,k} = \frac{\int_X (\phi_A^{(h)}(x) - \bar{\phi}_A^{(h)}) \times (\phi_B^{(h)}(x) - \bar{\phi}_B^{(h)}) dx}{\left(\int_X (\phi_A^{(h)}(x) - \bar{\phi}_A^{(h)})^2 dx \int_X (\phi_B^{(k)}(x) - \bar{\phi}_B^{(k)})^2 dx \right)^{1/2}} \tag{12}$$

where $\rho_{h,k} \in [-1,1]$, $\bar{\phi}_A^{(h)}$ and $\bar{\phi}_B^{(h)}$ are, respectively, the sample means of the ordinary membership functions $\phi_A^{(h)}(x)$ and $\phi_B^{(k)}(x)$, $h, k = 1, 2, ..., n$, then he defined the correlation coefficient of the IFSs A and B as: $\rho_3(A, B) = F(\rho_{h,k} \mid h, k = 1, 2, ..., n)$, where F is a mean aggregation function.

In [16], Huang and Wu proposed a method to calculate the correlation coefficient of the IFSs A and B by means of "centroid", shown as:

$$\rho_4(A, B) = \frac{c_4(A, B)}{\left(c_4(A, A) \cdot c_4(B, B) \right)^{1/2}} \tag{13}$$

where $c_4(A, B) = m(\mu_A) m(\mu_B) + m(v_A) m(v_B)$ is the correlation of A and B, and

$$m(\mu_A) = \frac{\int_X x \mu_A(x) dx}{\int_X \mu_A(x) dx}, \quad m(v_A) = \frac{\int_X x v_A(x) dx}{\int_X v_A(x) dx} \tag{14}$$

$$m(\mu_B) = \frac{\int_X x \mu_B(x) dx}{\int_X \mu_B(x) dx}, \quad m(v_B) = \frac{\int_X x v_B(x) dx}{\int_X v_B(x) dx} \tag{15}$$

are, respectively, the centroids of μ_A, v_A, μ_B and v_B.

Huang and Wu [16] further extended the "centroid" method to the IVIFS theory: Let $\tilde{A} = \{<x, \tilde{\mu}_{\tilde{A}}(x), \tilde{v}_{\tilde{A}}(x)> \mid x \in X\}$ and $\tilde{B} = \{<x, \tilde{\mu}_{\tilde{B}}(x), \tilde{v}_{\tilde{B}}(x)> \mid x \in X\}$ be two IVIFSs, where $\tilde{\mu}_{\tilde{A}}(x) = [\tilde{\mu}_{\tilde{A}}^L(x), \tilde{\mu}_{\tilde{A}}^U(x)]$, $\tilde{\mu}_{\tilde{B}}(x) = [\tilde{\mu}_{\tilde{B}}^L(x), \tilde{\mu}_{\tilde{B}}^U(x)]$, $\tilde{v}_{\tilde{A}}(x) = [\tilde{v}_{\tilde{A}}^L(x), \tilde{v}_{\tilde{A}}^U(x)]$,

$\tilde{v}_{\tilde{B}}(x) = [\tilde{v}_{\tilde{B}}^L(x), \tilde{v}_{\tilde{B}}^U(x)]$, $\tilde{\mu}_{\tilde{A}}^L(x) = \inf \tilde{\mu}_{\tilde{A}}(x)$, $\tilde{\mu}_{\tilde{A}}^U(x) = \sup \tilde{\mu}_{\tilde{A}}(x)$, $\tilde{v}_{\tilde{A}}^L(x) = \inf \tilde{v}_{\tilde{A}}(x)$, $\tilde{v}_{\tilde{A}}^U(x) = \sup \tilde{v}_{\tilde{A}}(x)$, $\tilde{\mu}_{\tilde{B}}^L(x) = \inf \tilde{\mu}_{\tilde{B}}(x_i)$, $\tilde{\mu}_{\tilde{B}}^U(x) = \sup \tilde{\mu}_{\tilde{B}}(x)$, $\tilde{v}_{\tilde{B}}^L(x) = \inf \tilde{v}_{\tilde{B}}(x)$, $\tilde{v}_{\tilde{B}}^U(x) = \sup \tilde{v}_{\tilde{B}}(x)$, and let the centroids of $\tilde{\mu}_{\tilde{A}}^L, \tilde{\mu}_{\tilde{A}}^U, \tilde{v}_{\tilde{A}}^L, \tilde{v}_{\tilde{A}}^U, \tilde{\mu}_{\tilde{B}}^L, \tilde{\mu}_{\tilde{B}}^U, \tilde{v}_{\tilde{B}}^L$ and $\tilde{v}_{\tilde{B}}^U$ be $m(\tilde{\mu}_{\tilde{A}}^L), m(\tilde{\mu}_{\tilde{A}}^U), m(\tilde{v}_{\tilde{A}}^L), m(\tilde{v}_{\tilde{A}}^U), m(\tilde{\mu}_{\tilde{B}}^L), m(\tilde{\mu}_{\tilde{B}}^U), m(\tilde{v}_{\tilde{B}}^L)$ and $m(\tilde{v}_{\tilde{B}}^U)$, respectively, then they defined the correlation coefficient of the IVIFSs $\tilde{A}$ and $\tilde{B}$ as:

$$\rho_5(\tilde{A}, \tilde{B}) = \frac{c_5(\tilde{A}, \tilde{B}))}{\left(c_5(\tilde{A}, \tilde{A}) \cdot c_5(\tilde{B}, \tilde{B})\right)^{1/2}} \tag{16}$$

where $c_5(A, B) = m(\tilde{\mu}_{\tilde{A}}^L)m(\tilde{\mu}_{\tilde{B}}^L) + m(\tilde{\mu}_{\tilde{A}}^U)m(\tilde{\mu}_{\tilde{B}}^U) + m(\tilde{v}_{\tilde{A}}^L)m(\tilde{v}_{\tilde{B}}^L) + m(\tilde{v}_{\tilde{A}}^U)m(\tilde{v}_{\tilde{B}}^U)$ is the correlation of the IVIFSs $\tilde{A}$ and $\tilde{B}$.

Bustince and Burillo [17] also investigated the correlation coefficient of the IVIFSs $\tilde{A}$ and $\tilde{B}$, and defined it as:

$$\rho_6(\tilde{A}, \tilde{B}) = \frac{c_6(\tilde{A}, \tilde{B}))}{\left(c_6(\tilde{A}, \tilde{A}) \cdot c_6(\tilde{B}, \tilde{B})\right)^{1/2}} \tag{17}$$

where $c_6(A, B) = \frac{1}{2} \sum_{i=1}^{n} \left(\tilde{\mu}_{\tilde{A}}^L(x_i) \tilde{\mu}_{\tilde{B}}^L(x_i) + \tilde{\mu}_{\tilde{A}}^U(x_i) \tilde{\mu}_{\tilde{B}}^U(x_i) + \tilde{v}_{\tilde{A}}^L(x_i) \tilde{v}_{\tilde{B}}^L(x_i) + \tilde{v}_{\tilde{A}}^U(x_i) \tilde{v}_{\tilde{B}}^U(x_i) \right)$, $x_i \in X$ is the correlation of the IVIFSs $\tilde{A}$ and $\tilde{B}$, and $X = \{x_1, x_2, ..., x_n\}$ is a finite universe of discourse. Later, Hong [18] introduced the concept of correlation coefficient of the IVIFSs $\tilde{A}$ and $\tilde{B}$ in a general probability space, shown as:

$$\rho_7(\tilde{A}, \tilde{B}) = \frac{c_7(\tilde{A}, \tilde{B}))}{\left(c_7(\tilde{A}, \tilde{A}) \cdot c_7(\tilde{B}, \tilde{B})\right)^{1/2}} \tag{18}$$

where $c_5(\tilde{A}, \tilde{B}) = \frac{1}{2} \int_X \left(\tilde{\mu}_{\tilde{A}}^L(x) \tilde{\mu}_{\tilde{B}}^L(x) + \tilde{\mu}_{\tilde{A}}^U(x) \tilde{\mu}_{\tilde{B}}^U(x) + \tilde{v}_{\tilde{A}}^L(x) \tilde{v}_{\tilde{B}}^L(x) + \tilde{v}_{\tilde{A}}^U(x) \tilde{v}_{\tilde{B}}^U(x) \right) dx$ is the correlation of the IVIFSs $\tilde{A}$ and $\tilde{B}$, and X is an infinite universe of discourse.

All the correlation coefficients $\rho_i(A, B)$ ($i = 3, 4$) and $\rho_i(\tilde{A}, \tilde{B})$ ($i = 5, 6, 7$) have the properties 2) and 3) in Theorem 3.1, and satisfy the following: 1) $|\rho_i(A, B)| \leq 1$, $i = 3, 4$; 2) $|\rho_5(\tilde{A}, \tilde{B})| \leq 1$; and 3) $0 \leq \rho_i(\tilde{A}, \tilde{B}) \leq 1$, $i = 6, 7$.

However, from Theorem 3.1 we notice that all the above correlation coefficients can't guarantee that the correlation coefficient of any two IFSs (or IVIFSs) equals one if and only if these two IFSs (or IVIFSs) are the same. Thus, how to derive the correlation coefficients of the IFSs (or IVIFSs) satisfying this desirable property is an interesting research topic. To solve this issue, in what follows, we develop a new method to calculate the correlation coefficient of the IFSs A and B.

Definition 3.1. Let A and B be two IFSs, and let $X = \{x_1, x_2, ..., x_n\}$ be a finite universe of discourse, then we define

$$\rho(A,B) = \frac{1}{2n} \sum_{i=1}^{n} \left(\frac{\Delta\mu_{\min} + \Delta\mu_{\max}}{\Delta\mu_i + \Delta\mu_{\max}} + \frac{\Delta v_{\min} + \Delta v_{\max}}{\Delta v_i + \Delta v_{\max}} \right) \quad (19)$$

as a correlation coefficient of the IFSs A and B, where

$$\Delta\mu_i = |\mu_A(x_i) - \mu_B(x_i)|, \ \Delta v_i = |v_A(x_i) - v_B(x_i)|$$
$$\Delta\mu_{\min} = \min_i\{|\mu_A(x_i) - \mu_B(x_i)|\}, \ \Delta v_{\min} = \min_i\{|v_A(x_i) - v_B(x_i)|\}$$
$$\Delta\mu_{\max} = \max_i\{|\mu_A(x_i) - \mu_B(x_i)|\}, \ \Delta v_{\max} = \max_i\{|v_A(x_i) - v_B(x_i)|\}$$

Obviously, the greater the value of $\rho(A,B)$, the closer A to B. By Definition 3.1, we have

Theorem 3.2. The correlation coefficient $\rho(A,B)$ satisfies the following properties:
1) $0 \leq \rho(A,B) \leq 1$; 2) $A = B \Leftrightarrow \rho(A,B) = 1$; and 3) $\rho(A,B) = \rho(B,A)$.

In the following, we generalize Definition 3.1 to the IVIFS theory:

Definition 3.2. Let $\tilde{A}$ and $\tilde{B}$ be two IVIFSs, then we define

$$\rho(\tilde{A},\tilde{B}) = \frac{1}{4n} \sum_{i=1}^{n} \left(\frac{\Delta\mu_{\min}^L + \Delta\mu_{\max}^L}{\Delta\mu_i^L + \Delta\mu_{\max}^L} + \frac{\Delta\mu_{\min}^U + \Delta\mu_{\max}^U}{\Delta\mu_i^U + \Delta\mu_{\max}^U} + \frac{\Delta v_{\min}^L + \Delta v_{\max}^L}{\Delta v_i^L + \Delta v_{\max}^L} + \frac{\Delta v_{\min}^U + \Delta v_{\max}^U}{\Delta v_i^U + \Delta v_{\max}^U} \right) \quad (20)$$

as a correlation coefficient of the IVIFSs $\tilde{A}$ and $\tilde{B}$, where

$$\Delta\mu_i^L = |\mu_{\tilde{A}}^L(x_i) - \mu_{\tilde{B}}^L(x_i)|, \ \Delta\mu_i^U = |\mu_{\tilde{A}}^U(x_i) - \mu_{\tilde{B}}^U(x_i)|$$
$$\Delta v_i^L = |v_{\tilde{A}}^L(x_i) - v_{\tilde{B}}^L(x_i)|, \ \Delta v_i^U = |v_{\tilde{A}}^U(x_i) - v_{\tilde{B}}^U(x_i)|$$
$$\Delta\mu_{\min}^L = \min_i\{|\mu_{\tilde{A}}^L(x_i) - \mu_{\tilde{B}}^L(x_i)|\}, \ \Delta\mu_{\min}^U = \min_i\{|\mu_{\tilde{A}}^U(x_i) - \mu_{\tilde{B}}^U(x_i)|\}$$
$$\Delta v_{\min}^L = \min_i\{|v_{\tilde{A}}^L(x_i) - v_{\tilde{B}}^L(x_i)|\}, \ \Delta v_{\min}^U = \min_i\{|v_{\tilde{A}}^U(x_i) - v_{\tilde{B}}^U(x_i)|\}$$
$$\Delta\mu_{\max}^L = \max_i\{|\mu_{\tilde{A}}^L(x_i) - \mu_{\tilde{B}}^L(x_i)|\}, \ \Delta\mu_{\max}^U = \max_i\{|\mu_{\tilde{A}}^U(x_i) - \mu_{\tilde{B}}^U(x_i)|\}$$
$$\Delta v_{\max}^L = \max_i\{|v_{\tilde{A}}^L(x_i) - v_{\tilde{B}}^L(x_i)|\}, \ \Delta v_{\max}^U = \max_i\{|v_{\tilde{A}}^U(x_i) - v_{\tilde{B}}^U(x_i)|\}$$

Similar to Theorem 3.2, we have

Theorem 3.3. The correlation coefficient $\rho(\tilde{A},\tilde{B})$ satisfies the following properties:
1) $0 \leq \rho(\tilde{A},\tilde{B}) \leq 1$; 2) $\tilde{A} = \tilde{B} \Leftrightarrow \rho(\tilde{A},\tilde{B}) = 1$; and 3) $\rho(\tilde{A},\tilde{B}) = \rho(\tilde{B},\tilde{A})$.

4 Application of the Method in Medical Diagnosis

In this section, we apply the developed method to medical diagnosis (adapted from [10]). To make a proper diagnosis $D = \{Viral\ fever, Malaria, Typhoid,$

Stomach problem , Chest problem} for a patient with the given values of the symptoms $S = \{temperature, \ headache, stomach \ pain, cough, chest \ pain\}$ a medical knowledge base is necessary that involves elements described in terms of IFSs. The data are given in Table 1—each symptom is described by two parameters (μ, v), i.e., the membership μ and non-membership v. The set of patients is $P = \{Al, Bob, Joe, Ted\}$. The symptoms are given in Table 2. We need to seek a diagnosis for each patient p_i, $i = 1,2,3,4$.

Table 1. Symptoms characteristic for the considered diagnoses

	Viral fever	Malaria	Typhoid	Stomach problem	Chest Problem
Temperature	(0.4, 0.0)	(0.7, 0.0)	(0.3, 0.3)	(0.1, 0.7)	(0.1, 0.8)
Headache	(0.3, 0.5)	(0.2, 0.6)	(0.6, 0.1)	(0.2, 0.4)	(0.0, 0.8)
Stomach pain	(0.1, 0.7)	(0.0, 0.9)	(0.2, 0.7)	(0.8, 0.0)	(0.2, 0.8)
Cough	(0.4, 0.3)	(0.7, 0.0)	(0.2, 0.6)	(0.2, 0.7)	(0.2, 0.8)
Chest pain	(0.1, 0.7)	(0.1, 0.8)	(0.1, 0.9)	(0.2, 0.7)	(0.8, 0.1)

Table 2. Symptoms characteristic for the considered patients

	Temperature	Headache	Stomach pain	Cough	Chest pain
Al	(0.8, 0.1))	(0.6, 0.1)	(0.2, 0.8)	(0.6, 0.1)	(0.1, 0.6)
Bob	(0.0, 0.8)	(0.4, 0.4)	(0.6, 0.1)	(0.1, 0.7)	(0.1, 0.8)
Joe	(0.8, 0.1)	(0.8, 0.1)	(0.0, 0.6)	(0.2, 0.7)	(0.0, 0.5)
Ted	(0.6, 0.1)	(0.5, 0.4)	(0.3, 0.4)	(0.7, 0.2)	(0.3, 0.4)

We utilize the correlation measure (19) to derive a diagnosis for each patient p_i, $i = 1,2,3,4$. All the results for the considered patients are listed in Table 3.

Table 3. Correlation coefficients of symptoms for each patient to the considered set of possible diagnoses

	Viral fever	Malaria	Typhoid	Stomach problem	Chest Problem
Al	0.8000	**0.8224**	0.7728	0.7308	0.6258
Bob	0.7332	0.6688	0.7536	**0.8000**	0.7381
Joe	**0.8207**	0.7459	0.7529	0.7121	0.7092
Ted	**0.9167**	0.6977	0.8435	0.6862	0.7702

From the arguments in Table 3, we derive a proper diagnosis as follows:
Al suffers from malaria, Bob from a stomach problem, and both Joe and Ted from viral fever.
If we utilize the correlation formulas (7) to derive a diagnosis, then we get the following results (Table 4):

Table 4. Correlation coefficients of symptoms for each patient to the considered set of possible diagnoses

	Viral fever	Malaria	Typhoid	Stomach problem	Chest Problem
Al	0.8856	**0.9003**	0.8316	0.4546	0.4194
Bob	0.6096	0.4258	0.7872	**0.9714**	0.6642
Joe	0.8082	0.7066	**0.8822**	0.5083	0.4828
Ted	**0.8709**	0.8645	0.7548	0.5997	0.5810

The results in Table 4 show that Al suffers from malaria, Bob from a stomach problem, Joe from typhoid, and Ted from viral fever. The difference between the results derived by the above two methods is only the diagnosis for Joe.

From the data in Table 3, we know that for Joe the correlation coefficient of his symptoms and the symptoms characteristic for viral fever is the largest one, while the correlation coefficient of his symptoms and the symptoms characteristic for typhoid ranks second. But in Table 4, the ranking is just reverse. The difference is because the results derived by using (7) are prone to the influence of unfair arguments with too high or too low values, while the method developed in this paper can relieve the influence of these unfair arguments by emphasizing the role of the considered arguments as a whole.

5 Conclusions

In this work, we have developed a method for deriving the correlation coefficients of IFSs, and extended it to the IVIFS theory. The prominent characteristic of the method is that it can guarantee that the correlation coefficient of any two IFSs (or IVIFSs) equals one if and only if these two IFSs (or IVIFSs) are the same, and can relieve the influence of the unfair arguments on the final results.

Acknowledgement

The work was supported by the National Natural Science Foundation of China under Grant (70571087).

References

1. Atanassov, K.: Intuitionistic fuzzy sets. Fuzzy Sets and Systems 20(1986) 87-96.
2. Zadeh, L. A.: Fuzzy Sets. Information and Control. 8(1965) 338-353.
3. Deschrijver, G., Kerre, E.E.: On the composition of intuitionistic fuzzy relations. Fuzzy Sets and Systems 136(2003) 333-361.
4. Deschrijver, G., Kerre, E.E.: On the representation of intuitionistic fuzzy t-norms and t-conorms. IEEE Transactions on Fuzzy Systems 12(2004) 45-61.
5. Atanassov, K., Gargov, G.: Interval-valued intuitionistic fuzzy sets. Fuzzy Sets and Systems 31(1989) 343-349.
6. Chen, S.M., Tan, J.M.: Handling multicriteria fuzzy decision-making problems based on vague set theory. Fuzzy Sets and Systems 67(1994) 163-172.

7. Hong, D.H., Choi, C.H.: Multicriteria fuzzy decision-making problems based on vague set theory. Fuzzy Sets and Systems 114(2000) 103-113.
8. Atanassov, K., Georgiev, C.: Intuitionistic fuzzy prolog. Fuzzy Sets and Systems 53(1993) 121-128.
9. De, S.K., Biswas, R., Roy, A.R.: An application of intuitionistic fuzzy sets in medical diagnosis. Fuzzy Sets and Systems 117(2001) 209-213.
10. Szmidt, E., Kacprzyk, J.: A similarity measure for intuitionistic fuzzy sets and its application in supporting medical diagnostic reasoning. Lecture Notes in Artificial Intelligence 3070(2004) 388-393.
11. Liang, Z.Z., Shi, P.F.: Similarity measures on intuitionistic fuzzy sets. Pattern Recognition letters 24(2003) 2687-2693.
12. Gerstenkorn, T., Manko, J.: Correlation of intuitionistic fuzzy sets. Fuzzy Sets and Systems 44(1991) 39-43.
13. Hong, D.H., Hwang, S.Y.: Correlation of intuitionistic fuzzy sets in probability spaces. Fuzzy Sets and Systems 75(1995) 77-81.
14. Hung, W.L.: Using statistical viewpoint in developing correlation of intuitionistic fuzzy sets. International Journal of Uncertainty Fuzziness Knowledge-Based Systems 9(2001) 509-516.
15. Mitchell, H.B.: A correlation coefficient for intuitionistic fuzzy sets. International Journal of Intelligent Systems 19(2004) 483-490.
16. Hung, W.L., Wu, J.W.: Correlation of intuitionistic fuzzy sets by centroid method. Information Sciences 144(2002) 219-225.
17. Bustince, H., Burillo, P.: Correlation of interval-valued intuitionistic fuzzy sets. Fuzzy Sets and Systems 74(1995) 237-244.
18. Hong, D.H.: A note on correlation of interval-valued intuitionistic fuzzy sets. Fuzzy Sets and Systems 95(1998) 113-117.
19. Szmidt, E., Kacprzyk, J.: Distances between intuitionistic fuzzy sets. Fuzzy Sets and Systems 114(2000) 505-518.

A More Effective Constructive Algorithm for Permutation Flowshop Problem

Xingye Dong, Houkuan Huang, and Ping Chen

School of Computer and IT, Beijing Jiaotong University, 100044 Beijing, China
dong.xingye@163.com, hkhuang@center.njtu.edu.cn, chenpingbjtu@gmail.com

Abstract. NEH (Nawaz et al., 1983) is an effective heuristic for solving the permutation flowshop problem with the objective of makespan. It includes two phases. PE-VM (Li et al., 2004), which is based on NEH, is analyzed and we conclude that its good performance is partially due to the priority rule it used in phase I. Then, we propose a new measure to solve job insertion ties which may arise in phase II. The measure is based on the idea of balancing the utilization among all machines. Finally, we propose a heuristic NEH-D (NEH based on Deviation), which combines the priority rule of PE-VM and the new measure. Computational results show that the measure is effective and NEH-D is better than PE-VM. There is one parameter in NEH-D, and we design an experiment to try to find a near optimized value of it for tuning the performance of NEH-D.

1 Introduction

Permutation flowshop sequencing problem (PFSP) is one of the best known production scheduling problems, which has a strong engineering background and has been proved to be strongly NP-complete. Among desired objectives, makespan minimization has attracted a lot of attention. Many approximate algorithms have been developed to find good solutions in a short time. These algorithms can be classified into two categories: improvement methods and constructive methods. Improvement methods are mainly metaheuristics, such as genetic algorithm (GA), simulated annealing (SA) and tabu search (TS) algorithm. As for constructive methods, several heuristics had been developed in relatively early decades, e.g., heuristics by Palmer [1], Campbell et al. [2], Gupta [3], Dannenbring [4] and Nawaz et al. (denoted by NEH) [5], and more recently, by Koulamas [6] and Li et al. (denoted by PE-VM, which means Partial Enumeration method based on Variance-Mean) [7]. All the above heuristics are designed for minimizing makespan. Recently heuristics about minimizing flowtime or flowtime and makespan have been developed, e.g., heuristics by Woo [8] and Framinan et al. [9, 10]. All these three heuristics use the search strategy of NEH heuristic. Early comparisons among constructive heuristics aimed to minimize makespan conclude that NEH heuristic is the most effective one [11]. Moreover, Koulamas claimed that his heuristic performs as well as NEH, and Li et al. claimed that their heuristic performs better than NEH. The search strategy of NEH is applied in both heuristics.

Generally speaking, improvement methods are quite time-consuming, so they are not fit to solve large scale problems. On the other hand, constructive methods are mainly simple heuristics. They can construct a solution very quickly, but the solution is usually not so good as expected. Improvements of constructive methods usually include the use of certain strategies or priority rules. Intuitively, improvement can also be expected when such strategies or rules are used in metaheuristics. Therefore, such strategies and priority rules are worthy to be deep studied.

As mentioned above, NEH is the best among earlier heuristics, and PE-VM is claimed better than NEH. NEH includes two phases: firstly, generate an initial job sequence by decreasing sums of processing times of each job; secondly, insert these jobs in sequence into a partial schedule to construct a complete schedule. It's easy to see that there exist a lot of priority rules which can be used in phase I, and a lot of ties for job insertion in phase II. Then an issue arises naturally: can we improve this search strategy by using a more effective priority rule in phase I and a more reasonable measure to deal with these ties in phase II?

The remainder of this paper is organized as follows. In Section 2, we describe the formulation of PFSP briefly. In Section 3, we analyze PE-VM algorithm, and point out that the reason for its good performance is partially due to the priority rule it uses in phase I. We illustrate our effective measure in Section 4 and propose an improved heuristic NEH-D in Section 5. Then we present some computational results in Section 6 and conclude the paper in Section 7.

2 Problem Formulation

The PFSP can be formulated as follows. Each of n jobs from the job set $J = \{1, 2, \ldots, n\}$ has to be processed on m machines. Job $j \in J$ consists of a sequence of m operations; each of them needs a slot of uninterrupted processing time $p_{ij} \geq 0$ on machine i. Machine i, $i = 1, 2, \ldots, m$, can execute at most one job at a time, and it is assumed that each machine processes the jobs in the same order. All the jobs are available at time zero. We use π to denote a permutation, which represents a job processing order, on the set J. In this paper, we only focus on the objective of makespan (C_{max}). Using the widely accepted triple notation [12], it can be denoted by $F_m|prmu|C_{max}$. Given $\pi = (j_1, j_2, \ldots, j_n)$, then the completion time of every job $j_1, \ldots, j_n$ on each machine i can be computed easily through a set of recursive equations:

$$C_{i,j_1} = \sum_{l=1}^{i} p_{l,j_1} \quad i = 1, \ldots, m \qquad (1)$$

$$C_{1,j_k} = \sum_{l=1}^{k} p_{1,j_l} \quad k = 1, \ldots, n \qquad (2)$$

$$C_{i,j_k} = max\{C_{i-1,j_k}, C_{i,j_{k-1}}\} + p_{i,j_k} \quad i = 2, \ldots, m; k = 2, \ldots, n \qquad (3)$$

Then, $C_{max} = C_{m,j_n}$.

Although the two-machine problem $F_2|prmu|C_{max}$ is polynomially solvable by using Johnson's rule [12, 13], the general problem with more than two machines is strongly NP-complete.

3 Analysis of PE-VM

Firstly, we present the NEH algorithm as follows:

1. Order the n jobs by decreasing sums of processing times on the machines;
2. Take the first two jobs and schedule them in order to minimize the partial makespan as if there were only two jobs;
3. For the kth job, $k = 3, \ldots, n$, insert it at the place, among k possible ones, which minimizes the partial makespan.

It is easy to see that NEH heuristic consists of two phases: firstly, the jobs are sorted by descending sums of their processing times; secondly, a job sequence is constructed by evaluating the partial schedules originating from the initial order of phase I. In our implementation, we choose heap sort algorithm in phase I. For the job insertion in phase II, we always insert a job at the first feasible position.

Li et al. [7] improve NEH by using a priority rule in phase I. The priority rule is based on the following hypothesis: the larger deviation of processing time of a job on every machine, the higher priority it should have. Then they use a priority rule $\alpha AVG_j + (1-\alpha)D_j$ in phase I to sort the jobs in a descending way, where $\alpha \in [0,1]$, $AVG_j = \frac{1}{m}\sum_{i=1}^{m} p_{ij}$ means the average processing time of job j, $D_j = [\sum_{i=1}^{m}(p_{ij}-AVG_j)^2]^{1/2}$ reflects the deviation of processing time of job j. For different α, different initial job sequence may be generated. In their algorithm, they choose $L+1$ different α ($\alpha = 0, \frac{1}{L}, \ldots, 1$), then construct one solution for each α and choose the best solution as the final output.

From the above description, we can guess the good performance of PE-VM is partially due to the initial job sequence generated in phase I. In order to verify this, we design an experiment to compare the effect of three priority rules used in phase I on benchmarks of Taillard [14], while the phase II is identical with that of NEH. Firstly, we define AVG_j as above, $Dev_j = [\frac{1}{m-1}\sum_{i=1}^{m}(p_{ij}-AVG_j)^2]^{1/2}$ the standard deviation of processing time of job j. The three rules are Avg, Dev and AvgDev, where Avg means ordering jobs according to AVG_j (the same as NEH), Dev means ordering jobs according to Dev_j, and AvgDev means ordering jobs according to $AVG_j + Dev_j$. The results are shown in Table 1 in terms of average relative deviation (in percent). The relative deviation can be calculated by $100\% * (C_{max}^H - UB)/UB$, where $H \in \{$Avg, Dev, AvgDev$\}$, UB are the upper bounds provided by Taillard [14]. From the table, we can see that the NEH modified by using AvgDev performs the best, and the NEH modified by using Dev performs the worst. So we can conclude that considering the deviation in phase I is a reason for good performance of PE-VM.

4 New Measure

For the job insertion of NEH in phase II, there may be ties, i.e., there may exist several partial sequences which have the same partial makespan. For example, as shown in Fig. 1, the makespans of three partial sequences generated by inserting job 3 at three different possible places are equal. But the original NEH algorithm

Table 1. Effect of Priority Rules in Phase I on Taillard's Benchmarks

	Avg	Dev	AvgDev
20|5	3.091	3.107	2.662
20|10	5.025	4.576	4.084
20|20	3.668	4.571	3.816
50|5	0.776	1.514	1.107
50|10	4.226	4.656	3.971
50|20	5.219	5.691	5.154
100|5	0.379	0.592	0.378
100|10	2.281	2.437	1.887
100|20	3.675	3.841	3.889
200|10	1.078	1.372	1.052
200|20	2.514	2.660	2.649
500|20	1.257	1.439	1.279
all	2.766	3.038	2.661

does not provide a strategy to solve these ties. Considering the complexity of the problem, we can conclude that there does not exist a single strategy which can always solve these ties optimally, but we can hypothesize intuitively that there may exist certain strategies which can solve these ties near optimally with great probability. With this consideration, we propose the following new measure.

Firstly, we define several notes as follows. For a permutation π, let $\pi(x)$ denote the job in the xth position, $C_{i,\pi(x)}$ denote the earliest possible completion time of job $\pi(x)$ on machine i, $S_{i,\pi(x)}$ denote the latest possible start time of job $\pi(x)$ on machine i, then the following two measures can be computed for job $\pi(x)$ as follows:

$$E_{\pi(x)} = \frac{1}{m} \sum_{i=1}^{m} \frac{p_{i,\pi(x)}}{S_{i,\pi(x+1)} - C_{i,\pi(x-1)}} \qquad (4)$$

$$D_{\pi(x)} = \sum_{i=1}^{m} (\frac{p_{i,\pi(x)}}{S_{i,\pi(x+1)} - C_{i,\pi(x-1)}} - E_{\pi(x)})^2 \qquad (5)$$

Note that there exist exceptions: let $S_{i,\pi(x+1)}$ equal to the latest possible completion time of job $\pi(x)$ if $\pi(x)$ is the last job in the partial sequence; let $C_{i,\pi(x-1)}$ equal to the earliest possible starting time of job $\pi(x)$ when job $\pi(x)$ is the first in the partial sequence; if $S_{i,\pi(x+1)} = C_{i,\pi(x-1)}$, then $p_{i,\pi(x)}$ must be zero, and we let $p_{i,\pi(x)}/(S_{i,\pi(x+1)} - C_{i,\pi(x-1)})$ equal to zero in this case. Then, when inserting a job into the partial sequence, we firstly choose the place which minimize the makespan, and if there exist ties, we choose the place x which minimize $D_{\pi(x)}$. The idea behind this is that choosing the place in this way is more likely to balance the utilization of each machine.

For the example in Fig. 1, in order to compute the above two measures, we illustrate these three cases in Fig. 2 in another way. In Fig. 2, the jobs prior to the insertion place (include the inserted job itself if it is not the last job in the partial sequence) are scheduled as early as possible and the jobs succeeding

(a) Insert job 3 at the 1st position

(b) Insert job 3 at the 2nd position

(c) Insert job 3 at the 3rd position

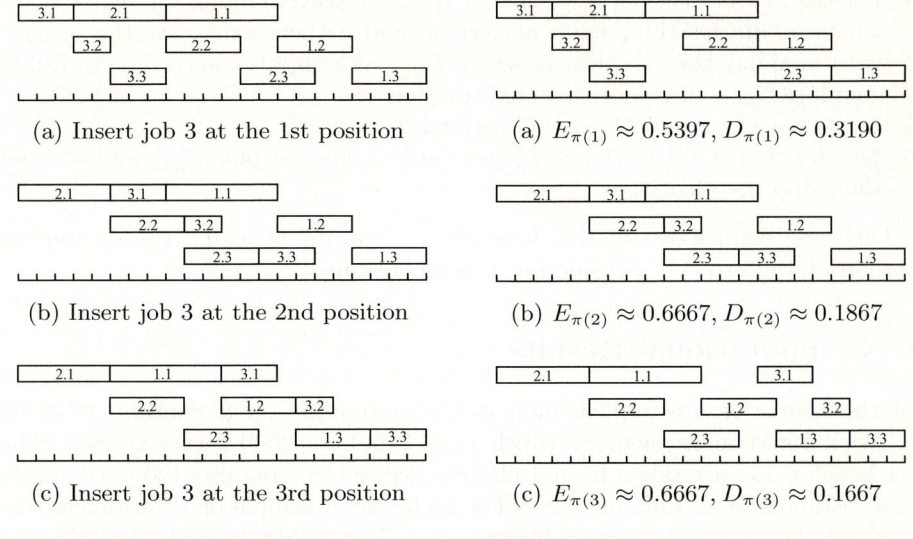

Fig. 1. Ties for job insertion

(a) $E_{\pi(1)} \approx 0.5397, D_{\pi(1)} \approx 0.3190$

(b) $E_{\pi(2)} \approx 0.6667, D_{\pi(2)} \approx 0.1867$

(c) $E_{\pi(3)} \approx 0.6667, D_{\pi(3)} \approx 0.1667$

Fig. 2. Illustration of $E_{\pi(x)}$ and $D_{\pi(x)}$

to the insertion place are scheduled as late as possible. From Fig. 2(a), we can see that $E_{\pi(1)} = \frac{1}{3}(\frac{3}{3-0} + \frac{2}{10-3} + \frac{3}{14-5}) \approx 0.5397$ and $D_{\pi(1)} = (\frac{3}{3-0} - E_{\pi(1)})^2 + (\frac{2}{10-3} - E_{\pi(1)})^2 + (\frac{3}{14-5} - E_{\pi(1)})^2 \approx 0.3190$. The measures for Fig. 2(b) and Fig. 2(c) can be computed similarly. For D_3 in Fig. 2(c) is the smallest, inserting job 3 to position 3 is preferred.

5 Improved Heuristic

From the above discussions, if we modify NEH by combining the initial job sequence described in Section 3 into phase I and the new measure described in Section 4 into phase II, then better performance can be expected. The improved algorithm is presented completely as follows. In the algorithm, the variable with an asterisk superscript refers to the best values found in the constructing process. The algorithm is named NEH-D, which means NEH algorithm improved by using deviation.

Algorithm NEH-D:

1. Compute the average processing time AVG_j and the standard deviation of processing time Dev_j for every job j, where AVG_j and Dev_j are defined in Section 3; set $iter = 0$; set $L \geq 1$; set C^*_{max} be a very large number;
2. Sort jobs in descending order according to $\alpha * Dev_j + (1 - \alpha) * AVG_j$, where $\alpha = iter/L$;
3. Take the first two jobs and schedule them in order to minimize the partial makespan as if there were only two jobs;

4. For the kth job, $k = 3, \ldots, n$, insert it at the place, among k possible ones, which minimizes the partial makespan; and if there exist ties, the place x with minimal $D_{\pi(x)}$ is chosen, where $D_{\pi(x)}$ is computed according to Eq. 5; compute C_{max} of the constructed solution π;
5. If $C^*_{max} > C_{max}$, set $C^*_{max} = C_{max}$ and $\pi^* = \pi$;
6. Set $iter = iter + 1$; if $iter \leq L$, go to step 2, else output C^*_{max} and π^*, and then stop the algorithm.

The time complexity of this heuristic is $O(mn^2)$ by using the computing method of Taillard [11], considering L is a constant.

6 Computational Results

All the heuristics are implemented in C++, running on a Pentium IV 2.4G PC with 256M main memory which runs Windows 2000 server version. The test benchmarks are taken from Taillard's [14], which contains 120 particularly hard instances of 12 different sizes. For each size, a sample of 10 instances was provided. The scale of these problems is varied from 20 jobs and 5 machines to 500 jobs and 20 machines. Firstly, we use the benchmarks of Taillard to validate the effectiveness of the measure described in Section 4, and then we compare the performance of NEH-D with NEH and PE-VM on the given benchmarks.

In order to check the influence of the new measure on the results with different initial job sequences, we design the following experiment. In the experiment, we collect the results of six different cases, i.e., three different initial job sequences combined with two search strategies. The different initial job sequences are denoted by Avg, Dev and AvgDev, respectively, whose meanings are the same as those in Section 3. The two search strategies are denoted by C_{max} and NewM, which means the original search strategy of NEH and the search strategy described in Section 4, respectively. The results are shown in Table 2 in terms of average deviation from the upper bounds provided by Taillard [14]. From the table, we can see that for a specific initial job sequence, better solutions can be constructed by using the new search strategy on the whole. Just as what we anticipate, the new strategy does not perform well on all instances. It performs a little worse on small instances, e.g., 20 jobs and 5 machines instances. For relatively large instances, the new search strategy performs quite well. On the whole, the new measure does work well.

We compare the performance of NEH-D with NEH and PE-VM in total average relative deviation from the upper bounds in Taillard [14]. Since the performance of NEH is already shown in the first column of Table 1 and Table 2, and NEH is a single-pass constructive heuristic, we will only show the performance of NEH-D and PE-VM here. On the other hand, there is one parameter L to tune the heuristic of NEH-D and PE-VM, and there would not exist an optimal value for all instances. In order to find a near optimal value for all instances and compare their performances, we run both heuristics with $L = 1, 2, \ldots, 300$, respectively, and collect the average relative deviation for all the instances. The results are shown in Fig. 3. From this figure, we can see that NEH-D performs

Table 2. Influence of New Measure on Taillard's Benchmarks

$n\|m$	Avg		Dev		AvgDev	
	C_{max}	NewM	C_{max}	NewM	C_{max}	NewM
20|5	3.091	**2.442**	**3.107**	3.314	**2.662**	2.772
20|10	5.025	**4.519**	4.576	**4.152**	4.084	**3.752**
20|20	**3.668**	3.703	**4.571**	4.588	3.816	**3.644**
50|5	**0.776**	0.881	**1.514**	1.767	1.107	**0.894**
50|10	4.226	**3.636**	4.656	**3.899**	3.971	**3.732**
50|20	5.219	**4.752**	5.691	**5.214**	5.154	**4.848**
100|5	**0.379**	0.421	0.592	**0.520**	0.378	**0.369**
100|10	2.281	**1.660**	2.437	**1.993**	1.887	**1.431**
100|20	3.675	**2.997**	3.841	**3.687**	3.889	**3.228**
200|10	1.078	**0.843**	1.372	**0.982**	1.052	**0.738**
200|20	2.514	**1.824**	2.660	**2.120**	2.649	**1.848**
500|20	1.257	**0.938**	1.439	**1.015**	1.279	**0.806**
all	2.766	**2.385**	3.038	**2.771**	2.661	**2.339**

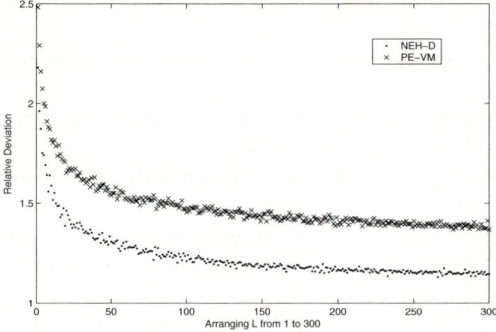

Fig. 3. The relative deviation trend with growing L

Table 3. CPU Time Comparison

$n\|m$	NEH	PE-VM	NEH-D
20|5	0.186	0.445	0.586
20|10	0.328	0.680	0.820
20|20	0.597	1.095	1.303
50|5	0.457	1.299	2.342
50|10	0.855	2.247	2.998
50|20	1.553	3.872	4.666
100|5	0.989	3.356	7.614
100|10	1.761	6.005	9.791
100|20	3.233	11.136	14.609
200|10	3.733	17.444	36.442
200|20	6.997	35.122	46.613
500|20	20.775	164.977	250.491

better than PE-VM. With the increase of L, both algorithms are improved obviously and quickly when L is less than about 23, and then the improvements of both are slowing down. Both of them perform better than NEH.

For the L is set to 23 in the experiment of Li. et al. [7], we set $L = 23$ to compare NEH-D with PE-VM. The total average relative deviation of NEH-D is 1.3946, while that of PE-VM is 1.6624. From our experiments, we find that $L = 23$ is quite good for all instances, and this is the same as that of [7].

In order to compare running times, we run NEH, PE-VM and NEH-D 100 times with $L = 23$ for PE-VM and NEH-D, then collect total CPU time in seconds and average them according to problem size. The results are reported in Table 3. From this table, we can see that NEH-D is quite efficient. It can solve 500 jobs and 20 machines instance within about 2.5 seconds.

7 Conclusions

In this paper, we analyze the reason for good performance of PE-VM, and propose a new measure trying to solve job insertion ties in the original NEH. The idea is based on trying to balance the utilization of each machine. We also propose an improved heuristic NEH-D. Experiments show that our new measure does work and NEH-D is more effective. Because there also exist job insertion ties in some metaheuristics (tabu search for instance), their performance may be improved by applying the new measure into their searching processes. We will exploit it in our future work.

References

1. Palmer, D.S.: Sequencing jobs through a multistage process in the minimum total time: a quick method of obtaining a near-optimum. Operational Research Quarterly, 16, pp. 101-107, 1965.
2. Campbell, H.G., Dudek, R.A., Smith, M.L.: A heuristic algorithm for the n job, m machine sequencing problem. Management Science, 16, pp. B630-B637, 1970.
3. Gupta, J.N.D.: Heuristic algorithms for multistage flowshop scheduling problem. AIIE, Transactions, 4, pp. 11-18, 1972.
4. Dannenbring, D.G.: An evaluation of flowshop sequence heuristics. Management Science, 23, pp. 1174-1182, 1977.
5. Nawaz, M., Enscore, E.E., Ham, I.: A heuristic algorithm for the m-machine, n-job flowshop sequencing problem. OMEGA, 11, pp. 91-95, 1983.
6. Koulamas, C.: A new constructive heuristic for the flowshop scheduling problem. European Journal of Operational Research, 105, pp. 66-71, 1998.
7. Li, X.P., Wang, Y.X., Wu, C.: Heuristic algorithms for large flowshop scheduling problems. Proceedings of the 5th world congress on intelligent control and automation, Hangzhou, China, pp. 2999-3003, 2004.
8. Woo, H.S., Yim, D.S.: A heuristic algorithm for mean flowtime objective in flowshop scheduling. Computers & Operations Research, 25(3), pp. 175-182, 1998.
9. Framinan, J.M., Leisten, R., Ruiz-Usano, R.: Efficient heuristics for flowshop sequencing with the objectives of makespan and flowtime minimisation. European Journal of Operational Research, 141, pp. 559-569, 2002.
10. Framinan, J.M., Leisten, R.: An efficient constructive heuristic for flowtime minimisation in permutation flow shops. OMEGA, 31, pp. 311-317, 2003.
11. Taillard, E.: Some efficient heuristic methods for the flow shop sequencing problem. European Journal of Operational Research, 47, pp. 65-74, 1990.
12. Michael Pinedo: Scheduling: theory, algorithms, and systems. Prentice Hall, 2nd edition, 2001.
13. Johnson, S.M.: Optimal two and three-stage production schedule with setup times included. Naval Research Logistics Quarterly, 1(1), pp. 61-68, 1954.
14. Taillard, E.: Benchmarks for basic scheduling problems. European Journal of Operational Research, 64, pp. 278-285, 1993.

A Fast Algorithm for Relevance Vector Machine

Zheng Rong Yang

School of Engineering, Computer Science and Mathematics
University of Exrter, UK

Abstract. This paper presents a fast algorithm for training relevance vector machine classifiers for dealing with large data set. The core principle is to remove dependent data points before training a relevance vector machine classifier. The removal of dependent data points is implemented by the Gram-Schmidt algorithm. The verification using one group of toy data sets and three benchmark data sets shows that the proposed fast relevance vector machine is able to speed up the training time significantly while maintaining the model performance including testing accuracy, model robustness and model sparseness.

Keywords: relevance vector machine, classification, Gram-Schmidt algorithm.

1 Introduction

The relevance vector machine (RVM) [9] uses the Bayesian learning framework, in which an *a priori* parameter structure is placed based on the automatic relevance determination theory (ARD) [6] for removing irrelevant data points, hence producing sparse models. The removal of irrelevant data points in a RVM model is implemented through zeroing the weighting parameters of the irrelevant data points through the use of ARD theory. RVM has been applied to some real tasks, for instance, the classification of submerged elastic targets [3], optical diagnosis of cancer [7], laser data analysis [2], and the identification of non-coding regions in genomes [4].

However, the computational cost associated with RVM is still challenge because of matrix inverse and the inner loop of weight update. The complexity of the former is known to be $\mathcal{O}(\ell^3)$, where ℓ is the number of data points [1]. The time complexity of the latter normally depends on how long the a weight update process can converge. Because of the high computational cost, RVM cannot compete with the support vector machine [10] in terms of training time although it can deliver much sparse models. This is why RVM since developed has not yet been widely applied to many real tasks with thousands or hundred of thousands of data points. Bear in mind, training a RVM classifier for a thousand data points with about 20 independent variables may take a couple of days using a PC with 500Hz.

This paper therefore presents a novel algorithm which can speed up training RVM classifiers for large data sets. It is known that the relevance vectors selected from the available data points are those which are prototypic, hence most informative. In terms of this, each relevance vector is a data point which *must* be independent on the other data points. From this, we develop an idea of removing dependent data points as they certainly cannot be candidate relevance vectors. The basic principle of this algorithm is therefore to detect the linear dependence between data points. If a data point is linear dependent on the others, the data point may not play an important role in modeling, i.e. the data point is less likely to be a candidate relevance vector. Rather than using all the available data points, we can remove dependent data points and employ a much parsimonious input matrix for RVM to use. This means that the time complexity of training of a RVM classifier can be much more reduced. Technically, the size of an input matrix for training a RVM classifier can be reduced significantly.

The Gram-Schmidt algorithm is commonly used for matrix orthogonalization during which it needs to detect if a new orthogonal vector has a zero norm. If this happens, it means that the corresponding data point is linear dependent on the recruited orthogonal vectors or the used data points. In other words, the data point could be non-informative. This paper therefore presents an algorithm termed as fRVM which can speed up the training time of RVM classifiers.

2 Algorithm and Methods

We denote by $\mathbf{x}_n \in \mathbb{R}^d$ (d is the dimension) and $t_n \in \{0,1\}$ an input vector and a target value, respectively. Note that $\mathbb{R}$ is a set of real numbers. Correspondingly, we denote by $\{\mathbf{x}_n\}_{n=1}^{\ell}$ and $\{t_n\}_{n=1}^{\ell}$ an input set and a target set, respectively. A sigmoid function based on the kernel principle [9] can be used as a classifier

$$y_n = \frac{1}{1+\exp(-\boldsymbol{\varphi}_n \cdot \mathbf{w})} \tag{1}$$

where $\boldsymbol{\varphi}_n = (\phi(\mathbf{x}_n,\mathbf{x}_1),\phi(\mathbf{x}_n,\mathbf{x}_2),\cdots,\phi(\mathbf{x}_n,\mathbf{x}_\ell))^T$. In the above equation, $\phi(\mathbf{x}_n,\mathbf{x}_m)$ is commonly implemented using a radial basis function in many vector machines where the inputs are numerical. The likelihood function of the classification model using the cross-entropy function is as follows

$$p(\mathbf{t} \mid \mathbf{w}) = \prod_{n=1}^{\ell} y_n^{t_n}(1-y_n)^{1-t_n} \tag{2}$$

An automatic relevance determination (ARD) prior [6] is used to prevent over-fitting over the coefficients [9]

$$p(\mathbf{w} \mid \boldsymbol{\alpha}) = \prod_{n=1}^{\ell} \mathcal{G}(0,\alpha_n^{-1}) \tag{3}$$

where $\boldsymbol{\alpha} = (\alpha_1,\alpha_2,\cdots,\alpha_\ell)^T$. The posterior of the coefficients is as follows

$$p(\mathbf{w} \mid \mathbf{t},\boldsymbol{\alpha}) \propto |\boldsymbol{\Sigma}|^{-1/2} \exp\left\{-\frac{1}{2}(\mathbf{w}-\mathbf{u})^T \boldsymbol{\Sigma}^{-1}(\mathbf{w}-\mathbf{u})\right\} \tag{4}$$

The mean vector and the covariance matrix are

$$\mathbf{u} = \boldsymbol{\Sigma}\boldsymbol{\Phi}^T \mathbf{B} \mathbf{t} \tag{5}$$

and

$$\boldsymbol{\Sigma} = (\boldsymbol{\Phi}^T \mathbf{B} \boldsymbol{\Phi} + \mathbf{A})^{-1} = \mathbf{H}^{-1} \tag{6}$$

where $\mathbf{t}=(t_1,t_2,\cdots,t_\ell)^T$, $\mathbf{B}=\text{diag}\{y_n(1-y_n)\}$, $\mathbf{A}=\text{diag}\{\alpha_1,\alpha_2,\cdots,\alpha_\ell\}$ and $\mathbf{\Phi}$ is a squared input matrix $\mathbf{\Phi}=\{\phi(\mathbf{x}_i,\mathbf{x}_j)\}_{1\le i,j\le\ell}$. The marginal likelihood can be obtained through integrating out the coefficients [9]

$$p(\mathbf{t}\mid\mathbf{\alpha})\propto|\mathbf{B}^{-1}+\mathbf{\Phi}\mathbf{A}^{-1}\mathbf{\Phi}^T|^{-1/2}\exp\left\{-\frac{1}{2}\mathbf{t}^T(\mathbf{B}^{-1}+\mathbf{\Phi}\mathbf{A}^{-1}\mathbf{\Phi}^T)^{-1}\mathbf{t}\right\} \quad (7)$$

In learning, $\mathbf{\alpha}$ can be estimated

$$\alpha_n(\tau+1)=(1-\alpha_n(\tau)\Sigma_{nn})/u_n^2(\tau) \quad (8)$$

where τ is the iterative time. The weight update can follow

$$\Delta\mathbf{w}=-\mathbf{H}^{-1}\nabla\mathcal{L} \quad (9)$$

where

$$\mathcal{L}=-\log\left\{|\mathbf{\Sigma}|^{-1/2}\exp\left[-\frac{1}{2}(\mathbf{w}-\mathbf{u})^T\mathbf{\Sigma}^{-1}(\mathbf{w}-\mathbf{u})\right]\right\} \quad (10)$$

Note that $\mathbf{H}$ is the Hessian matrix. Equation (9) is a close form where we have to use an iterative algorithm to update weights.

As seen above, RVM deals with intensive matrix operations which are very computationally costing. It is known that matrix inverse has the time complexity of $O(\ell^3)$ [1]. Meanwhile, an inner loop must be used to update weights as indicated by equation (9) which is also time consuming.

In order to reduce the training cost of RVM, it is clear that the size of the input matrix $\mathbf{\Phi}$ must be reduced. As we know that a matrix can be converted into two parts, one orthogonal and one upper triangular, $\mathbf{\Phi}=\mathbf{OV}$ [5]. The orthogonal matrix $\mathbf{O}$ is $\mathbf{O}=(\mathbf{o}_1,\mathbf{o}_2,...,\mathbf{o}_\ell)$ satisfying

$$\mathbf{O}^T\mathbf{O}=\mathbf{\Lambda} \quad (11)$$

where $\mathbf{\Lambda}$ is diagonal.

The Gram-Schmidt algorithm is commonly used for the conversion of an input matrix into an orthogonal matrix and an upper triangular matrix. With the algorithm the first orthogonal vector is $\mathbf{o}_1=\mathbf{\varphi}_1$. The nth orthogonal vector is estimated as follows

$$\mathbf{o}_n=\mathbf{\varphi}_n-\sum_{i=1}^{n-1}z_{in}\mathbf{o}_i \quad (12)$$

where $n=2,3,...,\ell$. The coefficients are

$$z_{in}=\mathbf{o}_i^T\mathbf{\varphi}_n/\mathbf{o}_i^T\mathbf{o}_i \quad (13)$$

where $1\le i<n$, $n=2,3,...,\ell$.

It should be noted that during the use of the Gram-Schmidt algorithm, some times we will have $\mathbf{o}_n\to 0$. It implies

$$\varphi_n \approx \sum_{i=1}^{n-1} z_{in} \mathbf{o}_i \qquad (14)$$

In other words, φ_n is linearly dependent on $\{\mathbf{o}_i\}_{i=1}^{n-1}$ with respect to $\{z_{in}\}_{i=1}^{n-1}$. Because of this, φ_n can be regarded as a redundant data point and can be ignored for the selection as a potential relevance vector. The larger the data size, the more data points could be dependent for a same data distribution. It can be seen that the pre-process of removing these dependent data points could significantly improve the time needed for training RVM classifiers.

Having understood that the Gram-Schmidt algorithm can be used to remove linearly dependent data points which are probably non-informative for building a RVM classifier, we then develop a novel algorithm termed as fRVM. We will remove all the columns corresponding to the non-informative data points from the input matrix $\mathbf{\Phi}$. This means we will use a reduced matrix $\mathbf{\Phi}_\kappa$ with ℓ rows and $\kappa \ll \ell$ (informative data points) columns, $\mathbf{\Phi}_\kappa = \{\phi(\mathbf{x}_i, \mathbf{x}_j)\}_{1 \le i, j \le \kappa}$ rather than a full matrix $\mathbf{\Phi}$. The mean vector and the covariance matrix then become

$$\mathbf{u}_\kappa = \mathbf{\Sigma}_\kappa \mathbf{\Phi}_\kappa^T \mathbf{B} \mathbf{t} \qquad (15)$$

and

$$\mathbf{\Sigma}_\kappa = (\mathbf{\Phi}_\kappa^T \mathbf{B} \mathbf{\Phi}_\kappa + \mathbf{A}_\kappa)^{-1} \qquad (16)$$

where $\mathbf{A}_\kappa = \mathrm{diag}\{\alpha_1, \alpha_2, \cdots, \alpha_\kappa\}$. It can be seen that both the size of the covariance matrix is decreased from ℓ to κ and the number of weights to be updated in the inner loop using equation (9) is decreased from ℓ to κ as well.

3 Results

This fast RVM algorithm is applied to one group of toy data sets and three benchmark data sets for the verification of the algorithm in this section. The toy data with four point swarms from two classes is generated. They follow $\mathcal{G}(\mathbf{u}, \Sigma)$, where $\mathbf{u}_1 = (0.25, 0.25)^T$, $\mathbf{u}_2 = (0.75, 0.75)^T$, $\mathbf{u}_3 = (0.25, 0.75)^T$, $\mathbf{u}_4 = (0.75, 0.25)^T$ and $\Sigma = \sigma^2 \mathbf{I}$. $\sigma = 0.02$. Note that $\mathbf{u}_1$ and $\mathbf{u}_2$ are assigned to one class while $\mathbf{u}_3$ and $\mathbf{u}_4$ are assigned to the other class. Each swarm contains m (100, 150, 200, 250 and 300) data points. In total, we have five data sets with 400, 600, 800, 1000 and 1200 data points. The use of five data sets with different sizes for the same data distribution is to demonstrate that the time complexity between RVM and fRVM will become large when the number of dependent data points becomes large.

Five-fold cross-validation is used for the verification. Four indicators were used for the evaluation of the proposed fast RVM algorithm. They are the true negative fraction (specificity), the true positive fraction (sensitivity), the total accuracy and the receiver operating characteristic (ROC) curve [8]. Let TN, TP, FN, FP denote the true negative, the true positive, the false negative and the false positive, respectively. The sensitivity is

$$TPf = TP/(TP+FN) \qquad (17)$$

the specificity is

$$TNf = TN/(TN+FP) \qquad (18)$$

the total accuracy is

$$Total = (TN+TP)/(TN+FP+TP+FN) \qquad (19)$$

In this study, the area under a ROC curve (AUR) is used as it is a quantitative measurement of robustness of a built machine. It is also regarded as the Wilcoxon statistic with a score of 50% representing random and 100% perfect classification [11]. Table 1 shows the simulation results on the data using RVM and fRVM. It can be seen that fRVM gives much faster running time compared with RVM while maintaining similar performance including testing accuracy (TNF, TPf and Total) and AUR. Besides, fRVM models employ similar number of relevance vectors. Note that all CPU times are in seconds.

Table 1. The results on the toy data using RVM and fRVM

	RVM					
	TNf	TPf	Total	AUR	RV	CPU
400	93.7(3.2)	93.7(2.4)	93.6(1.2)	0.97(0.02)	5(1)	6148
600	93.6(4.3)	91.3(2.8)	92.5(1.9)	0.98(0.01)	6(1)	22147
800	92.6(1.6)	91.9(2.4)	92.3(0.7)	0.98(0.01)	5(1)	73110
1000	92.8(1.1)	92.9(3.1)	92.9(2.0)	0.98(0.01)	6(1)	161173
1200	93.8(3.5)	92.2(1.5)	93.0(2.0)	0.98(0.01)	6(1)	399131
	fRVM					
	TNf	TPf	Total	AUR	RV	CPU
400	93.2(2.7)	93.2(2.6)	93.1(1.1)	0.97(0.01)	7(1)	40
600	94.3(3.5)	90.0(1.8)	92.2(1.3)	0.97(0.01	7(1)	71
800	92.9(1.7)	92.3(2.4)	92.6(0.6)	0.98(0.01)	8(1)	107
1000	92.4(1.1)	93.2(2.7)	92.8(1.8)	0.98(0.01)	8(1)	168
1200	93.5(4.0)	92.3(2.0)	92.9(2.4)	0.98(0.01)	7(1)	209

We then consider three benchmark data sets collected from the UCI Machine Learning Repository. The Liver data has 345 instances with six variables. The Pima data has 768 instances with eight variables. The Wisconsin data has 569 instances with 30 variables.

Table 2 shows the simulation results for these three data sets. It can be seen again that fRVM outperforms RVM in using CPU times. Meanwhile fRVM can maintain similar performance as RVM in testing accuracy, model robustness and model structure. In fact, fRVM models even employ smaller model structures in the Liver and Pima data sets. It can be seen how significantly fRVM improves the time complexity compared with RVM. Note that all CPU times are in seconds.

Table 2. The results on the benchmark data using RVM and fRVM

	\multicolumn{6}{c}{RVM}					
	TNf	TPf	Total	AUR	RV	CPU
Liver	68.2(4.5)	66.2(14.2)	66.7(8.9)	0.64(0.08)	12(1)	1166
Pima	85.3(4.5)	62.5(5.4)	77.3(1.8)	0.84(0.01)	7(1)	33446
Wisconsin	97.5(1.1)	95.7(3.9)	96.7(1.7)	0.99(0.01)	7(1)	15080
	\multicolumn{6}{c}{fRVM}					
	TNf	TPf	Total	AUR	RV	CPU
Liver	66.5(4.2)	66.2(8.8)	65.7(0.2)	0.63(0.08)	11(1)	163
Pima	85.7(4.2)	58.8(6.2)	76.2(1.3)	0.84(0.01)	6(0)	338
Wisconsin	98.1(1.0)	96.0(2.5)	97.2(0.7)	0.99(0.01)	7(0)	549

4 Summary

This paper has presented a fast algorithm for training a relevance vector machine classifier. The basic idea is to use the Gram-Schmidt algorithm to remove dependent data points to make the input matrix smaller containing only informative data points as candidate relevance vectors. The relevance vector machine is then applied to the reduced input matrix. From this, the training time of the relevance vector machine can be significantly reduced. The more the dependent data points, the larger the reduction in training time complexity is when using fRVM. One group of toy data sets and three benchmark data sets have been used for the verification of this fast relevance vector machine algorithm. The results show that this algorithm does reduce the training speed significantly while maintaining the model performance including testing accuracy, model robustness and model sparseness. It is therefore concluded that data pre-process is very important to most machine learning algorithms. Another algorithm which can speed up RVM training for regression has also been developed. In terms of page limit, the algorithm has been drafted for other publication.

References

1. Atkinson, K.E.: An Introduction to Numberical Analysis, John Wiley & Sons (1978)
2. Bowd, A., Medeiros, F.A., Zhang, Z., Zangwill, L.M., Hao, J., Lee, T.W., Sejnowski, T.J., Weinreb, R.N., Goldbaum, M.H.: Relevance vector machine and support vector machine classifier analysis of scanning laser polarimetry retinal nerve fiber layer measurements. Invest Ophthalmol Vis Sci. 46 (2005) 1322-1329
3. Dasgupta, N., Carin, L.: Time-reversal imaging for classification of submerged elastic targets via Gibbs sampling and the Relevance Vector Machine. Acoust Soc Am. 117 (2005) 1999-2011
4. Down, T.A., Hubbard, T.J.: What can we learn from noncoding regions of similarity between genomes? BMC Bioinformatics. Sept 15 (2004) 131
5. Golub, G.H., van Loan, C.F.: Matrix Computations, 2nd edn., The John Hopkins University Press (1989)
6. MaCkay, D.J. A practical Bayesian framework for backpropagation networks. Neural Computation, 4 (1992) 448-472

7. Majumder, S.K., Ghosh, N., Gupta, P.K.: Relevance vector machine for optical diagnosis of cancer. Lasers Surg Med. 36 (2005) 323-333
8. Metz, C.E.: Basic principles of ROC analysis. Seminars in Nuclear Medicine 8(1978) 283-298
9. Tipping, M.E.: The relevance vector machine. Advances in Neural Information Processing Systems, 12 (2000) 652-658
10. Vapnik, V.: The Nature of Statistical Learning Theory. Springer-Verlag, New York (1995)
11. Ward, J.J, Sodhi, J.S., McGuffin, L.J., Buxton, B.F., Jones, D.T.: Prediction and functional analysis of native disorder in proteins from the three kingdoms of life. Journal of Molecular Biology 337 (2004) 635-645

Time Series Relevance Determination Through a Topology-Constrained Hidden Markov Model

Iván Olier and Alfredo Vellido

Department of Computing Languages and Systems (LSI)
Polytechnic University of Catalonia (UPC)
C/. Jordi Girona, 1-3. 08034, Barcelona, Spain
{iaolier, avellido}@lsi.upc.edu

Abstract. Most of the existing research on multivariate time series concerns supervised forecasting problems. In comparison, little research has been devoted to unsupervised methods for the visual exploration of this type of data. The interpretability of time series clustering results may be difficult, even in exploratory visualization, for high dimensional datasets. In this paper, we define and test an unsupervised time series relevance determination method for Generative Topographic Mapping Through Time, a topology-constrained Hidden Markov Model that performs simultaneous time series data clustering and visualization. This relevance determination method can be used as a basis for time series selection, and should ease the interpretation of the time series clustering results.

1 Introduction

The data mining of multivariate time series has long ago become an established research area. Methods to deal with this problem have stemmed from traditional statistics and also from the machine learning field, where neural networks have provided some of the most fruitful approaches [1]. These methods usually consider the problem as supervised, being prediction the main goal of the analysis. In comparison, little attention has been paid to methods of unsupervised clustering for the exploration of the dynamics of time series.

Some of the most interesting time series clustering results have been obtained with different variants of Kohonen's SOM ([2], [3], and [4]) although, in general, without accounting for the violation of the independent identically distributed (i.i.d.) condition. Despite attempts to fit SOM into a probabilistic framework, it has mostly retained its heuristic definition, which is at the origin of some of its limitations. The Generative Topographic Mapping (GTM: [5]) is a latent model of the manifold learning family that was originally devised as a probabilistic alternative to SOM, aiming to overcome its limitations. The GTM, which can also be understood as a constrained mixture model, is suited for data clustering but also, as a latent variable model, is embodied with visualization capabilities that are akin to those of the SOM. The GTM Through Time (henceforth referred to as GTM-TT: [6]) is one of the many possible extensions of the standard GTM allowed by its probabilistic definition. It was defined as a topology-constrained

Hidden Markov Model (HMM) for the analysis of multivariate time series, and its capabilities for exploratory visualization have only recently been assessed in certain detail [7].

Feature selection plays an important role in pattern recognition and data analysis. In the context of multivariate time series analysis, one approach to data reduction would be the selection of a subset of time series on the basis of a relevance ranking. Some strides have already been made in feature selection for time series prediction but little has been accomplished in unsupervised time series clustering settings (one exception is the recent work by Yoon et al., [8]). The interpretation of the GTM-TT clustering results through exploratory visualization might be difficult for data sets consisting of a large number of time series and, therefore, the data analyst would benefit from a method that allowed ranking the features according to their unsupervised relative relevance and, ultimately, from a feature selection method based on it. Recently, an unsupervised feature relevance determination method for the standard GTM was defined in [9]. In this paper, we extend this approach and define a method for time series relevance determination (TSRD) for GTM-TT that should ease the interpretation of the time series clustering results. The rest of the paper is structured as follows: In section 2, an introduction to the GTM as a constrained mixture of Gaussians is provided, followed by a description of GTM-TT and the TSRD method. In section 3, several experiments for the assessment of the performance of the proposed TSRD method are carried out and the corresponding experimental results discussed. The paper wraps up with a conclusion section.

2 Generative Topographic Mapping

The GTM was originally conceived as a model that could provide most of the functionality of SOM, while overcoming some of its limitations through a probability theory-based definition. GTM can be thought of as a nonlinear latent variable model of the manifold learning family. It performs simultaneous clustering and visualization of the observed multivariate data through a nonlinear and topology-preserving mapping from a visualization latent space in $\mathcal{R}^L$ (with L being usually 1 or 2 for visualization purposes) onto the space $\mathcal{R}^D$ in which the observed data reside. The mapping that generates the embedded manifold takes the functional form:

$$\mathbf{y} = \mathbf{W}\mathbf{\Phi}(\mathbf{u}) \tag{1}$$

where $\mathbf{u}$ is an L-dimensional point in latent space, $\mathbf{W}$ is the matrix that generates the mapping, and $\mathbf{\Phi}$ consists of S basis functions ϕ_S (radially symmetric Gaussians in the standard model for continuous static data). To achieve computational tractability, the prior distribution of $\mathbf{u}$ in latent space is constrained to form a uniform discrete grid of M centres, analogous to the layout of the SOM units, in the form $p(\mathbf{u}) = M^{-1}\sum_{i=1}^{M}\delta(\mathbf{u}-\mathbf{u}_i)$. This way defined, the GTM can also be understood as a constrained mixture of Gaussians model. A density model in data space is generated for each component i of the mixture, which, assuming that the observed data points $\mathbf{x}_n$ are i.i.d., leads to the definition of a log-likelihood in the form:

$$L(\mathbf{W}, \beta | \mathbf{X}) = \sum_{n=1}^{N} \ln p(\mathbf{x}_n | \mathbf{W}, \beta) = \sum_{n=1}^{N} \ln \left\{ \frac{1}{M} \sum_{i=1}^{M} p(\mathbf{x}_n | \mathbf{u}_i, \mathbf{W}, \beta) \right\}, \quad (2)$$

where,

$$p(\mathbf{x}_n | \mathbf{u}_i, \mathbf{W}, \beta) = \left(\frac{\beta}{2\pi} \right)^{D/2} \exp \left\{ -\frac{\beta}{2} \|\mathbf{y}_i - \mathbf{x}_n\|^2 \right\} \quad (3)$$

In Eq. 3, $\mathbf{y}_i = \mathbf{W}\mathbf{\Phi}(\mathbf{u}_i)$ is a D-dimensional prototype point in data space: the centre of the ith constrained mixture component, and β is the estimated common inverse variance of the isotropic Gaussian distributions in data space whose centres are $\mathbf{y}_i$. The adaptive parameters of the model $(\mathbf{W}, \beta)$ can be optimized using the EM algorithm. Details can be found in [5].

2.1 Generative Topographic Mapping Through Time: The GTM-TT

Multivariate time series are not i.i.d. data and, therefore, the standard definition of the GTM summarized in the previous paragraphs can only provide a rough approximation to their proper modelling. A variation on the standard model, namely the GTM Through Time or GTM-TT, was defined as a topology-constrained HMM in [6] to deal with this limitation. In GTM-TT, the points in latent space are considered as hidden states and temporal dependencies are captured through their coupling. Furthermore, the emission probabilities are controlled by the GTM mixture distribution. The joint probability distribution of the multivariate time data $\mathbf{X}$ and the hidden states $U = \{\mathbf{u}_{i_1}, \mathbf{u}_{i_2}, \ldots, \mathbf{u}_{i_n}, \ldots, \mathbf{u}_{i_N}\}$ is based on HMM and takes the form:

$$p(U, \mathbf{X}) = \pi_{i_1} \prod_{n=2}^{N} p_{i_{n-1} i_n} \prod_{n=1}^{N} p(\mathbf{x}_n | \mathbf{u}_{i_n}), \quad (4)$$

where π_{i_1} defines the initial state probability of U; $p_{i_{n-1} i_n} = p(\mathbf{u}_{i_n} | \mathbf{u}_{i_{n-1}})$ is the probability of transition from one hidden state to another (capturing the temporal dependencies); and $p(\mathbf{x}_n | \mathbf{u}_{i_n})$, is the probability found in Eq.3. This leads to the definition of the following likelihood for the GTM-TT model:

$$L = p(\mathbf{X}) = \sum_{\text{all } U} p(U, \mathbf{X}), \quad (5)$$

which can be efficiently calculated using the *forward-backward procedure* [10].

In addition to parameters $(\mathbf{W}, \beta)$, which can be obtained in the M-step of the EM algorithm as for the standard GTM, GTM-TT modelling entails the estimation of the initial state probabilities $\{\pi_i\}$ and the state transition probabilities $\{p_{ij}\}$. Details of their estimation can be found in [6].

As mentioned in the introduction, the GTM is embodied with visualization capabilities that are akin to those of the SOM. Multivariate time series can be summarily visualised in the low-dimensional latent space (in 1 or 2 dimensions) of GTM-TT by means of the posterior-mode projection [5], defined as $i_n^{max} = \arg\max_{\{i_n\}} R_{in}$, where R_{in} is known as *responsability* and defines the probability of being in the state i at time n, given the data and the model. This projection is used later on in Fig. 2. The distribution of the responsibility over the latent space of states can also be directly visualized [7].

2.2 Time Series Relevance Determination Using GTM-TT

For a time series clustering solution to be considered useful in practical applications, it has to be interpretable, and this interpretability would improve if clusters could be described using only the time series that are most relevant for the definition of the cluster structure. Therefore, the development of an unsupervised method for TSRD should sensibly increase the GTM-TT model interpretability and, as a result, its usefulness. Recently, a method for feature selection in unsupervised model-based clustering with mixture models was presented in [11] and extended to the GTM for static data in [9]. This method calculates an unsupervised feature saliency as part of the EM algorithm. Such saliency measures the relevance of a feature on the definition of the cluster structure defined by the model. Here, this method is extended to TSRD for the GTM-TT.

Formally, the saliency of a time series d is defined as $\rho_d = P(\eta_d = 1)$, where $\eta = \{\eta_1, \ldots, \eta_D\}$ is a set of binary indicators that can be integrated in the GTM-TT optimization algorithm as missing (latent) labels. A value of $\eta_d = 1$ would indicate the full relevance of time series d. According to this definition, the distribution of $\mathbf{x}_n$ can be written as

$$p(\mathbf{x}_n|\mathbf{u}_{i_n}, \mathbf{W}, \beta, \mathbf{w}_o, \beta_o, \rho) = \prod_{d=1}^{D} \{\rho_d p(x_d|\mathbf{u}_{i_n}, \mathbf{w}_d, \beta) + (1-\rho_d) q(x_d|w_{o,d}, \beta_{o,d})\} \quad (6)$$

where $\mathbf{w}_d$ is the vector of $\mathbf{W}$ corresponding to time series d and $\rho = \{\rho_1, \ldots, \rho_D\}$. The distribution p is a time series-specific version of Eq. 3, and the relevance of a given time series d is defined by ρ_d; correspondingly, a time series d is irrelevant if it follows a density $q(x_d|w_{o,d}, \beta_{o,d})$, common to all the states-components of the mixture. This common component requires the definition of two extra adaptive parameters $\mathbf{w}_o = \{w_{o,1}, \ldots, w_{o,D}\}$ and $\beta_o = \{\beta_{o,1}, \ldots, \beta_{o,D}\}$. The joint probability distribution $p(U, \mathbf{X})$ is redefined as:

$$p(U, \mathbf{X}) = \pi_{i_1} \prod_{n=2}^{N} p_{i_{n-1} i_n} \prod_{n=1}^{N} (a_{i_n,d} + b_{n,d}) \quad (7)$$

where

$$a_{i_n,d} = \rho_d \left(\frac{\beta}{2\pi}\right)^{1/2} \exp\left[-\frac{\beta}{2}\left(x_{n,d} - \sum_m \phi_m(\mathbf{u}_{i_n}) w_{m,d}\right)^2\right] \quad (8)$$

and
$$b_{n,d} = (1 - \rho_d)\left(\frac{\beta_{o,d}}{2\pi}\right)^{1/2} \exp\left[-\frac{\beta_{o,d}}{2}(x_{n,d} - \phi_o(\mathbf{u}_o)\mathbf{w}_o)^2\right] \quad (9)$$

The likelihood can be defined as in Eq. 5. The parameters π_i and p_{ij} can also be calculated as for the standard GTM-TT. The maximization of the expected likelihood yields the following update formulae for the model parameters:

$$\rho_d^{new} = \frac{1}{N} \sum_{i,n} R_{in} u_{i_n,d} \quad (10)$$

where $u_{i_n,d} = \frac{a_{i_n,d}}{a_{i_n,d} + b_{n,d}}$;

$$\beta^{new} = \frac{\sum_{i,n} R_{in} \sum_d u_{i_n,d}}{\sum_{i,n} R_{in} u_{i_n,d} \left(\sum_m \phi_m(\mathbf{u}_{i_n}) w_{md} - x_{nd}\right)^2} \quad (11)$$

$$\beta_{o,d}^{new} = \frac{\sum_{i,n} R_{in} \nu_{i_n,d}}{\sum_{i,n} R_{in} \nu_{i_n,d} (\phi_o(\mathbf{u}_o) w_{o,d} - x_{nd})^2}, \quad (12)$$

where $\nu_{i_n,d} = \frac{b_{n,d}}{a_{i_n,d} + b_{n,d}}$. The elements of matrix $\mathbf{W}^{new}$, for each time series d, are obtained as the solution of the system of equations $\mathbf{\Phi}^T \mathbf{G}^* \mathbf{\Phi} \mathbf{W}_d^{new} - \mathbf{\Phi}^T \mathbf{R}^* \mathbf{X}_d = 0$, where the elements of $\mathbf{\Phi}$ are $\Phi_{is} = \Phi_s(\mathbf{u}_i)$, $\mathbf{R}^*$ has elements $R_{in}^* = u_{i_n,d} R_{in}$ for a given time series d^*, and $\mathbf{G}^*$ has elements $g_{ii'}^* = \begin{cases} \sum_{n=1}^N R_{in}^* & i = i' \\ 0 & i \neq i' \end{cases}$. Similarly, we obtain $\mathbf{w}_o^{new}$, for each time series, as the solution of $\phi_o^T \mathbf{g}^* \phi_o \mathbf{w}_{o,d}^{new} - \phi_o^T \mathbf{r}^* \mathbf{X}_d = 0$, where $\mathbf{r}^*$ has elements $r_n^* = \sum_i R_{in}^* = \sum_i \nu_{i_n,d} R_{in}$ for a given time series d^*, and $\mathbf{g}^* = \sum_{i,n} R_{in}^*$.

3 Experiments

A set of experiments was designed to evaluate the proposed multivariate TSRD method for GTM-TT. The first goal was the generation of time series relevance rankings that, in practical applications, might be used as a basis for time series selection. Depending on the application requirements, different saliency thresholds might be set, so that time series with a saliency below the given threshold would be considered of not enough interest for cluster interpretation through exploratory visualization.

3.1 Experimental Data Sets

Two data sets were used for the TSRD method evaluation experiments:

(1) *Artificial_data*: This artificial data set consists of three series with two brisk transitions between relatively stable periods, plotted in (Fig. 1, Left), to which four randomly generated series are added. The latter are less likely to have cluster structure (and, therefore, are less likely to be relevant) than the former.

(2) *Shuttle_data*: These 6-variate time series consist of 1000 data points obtained from various inertial sensors from Space Shuttle mission STS-57[1]. They contain subsequences of little variability followed by sudden transition periods and are likely to yield a clear cluster structure.

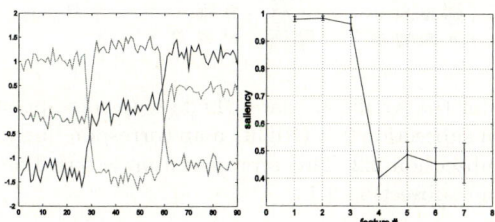

Fig. 1. (Left) the three series from *Artificial_data* with highest expected relevance. (Right) estimated values (represented by their means, over 20 runs of the algorithm, plus and minus one standard deviation) of the saliencies ρ for all features from *Artificial_data*, using random varying initialization.

3.2 Experimental Results and Discussion

In a first experiment, we aimed to test whether the TSRD method for GTM-TT was capable of gauging this relevance in *Artificial_data*. The model was run 20 times with different random parameter initializations. The resulting saliencies from Eq. 10 are plotted in Fig. 1(Right). As expected, the three time series including brisk transitions between relatively stable periods yield the highest saliencies ($\bar{\rho}_d > 0.95$) and they are, therefore, the most relevant or, in other words, those which the model considers to be generating most of the data cluster structure. On the contrary, the extra four variables without clear clustering pattern yield saliencies in the area of 0.5, corresponding to some relative relevance but not much when compared with the other three. It is also worth noting that the smaller bars for the three time series including brisk transitions suggest that the model is more certain of the relevance of these series.

These results are reinforced by the GTM-TT maps in Fig. 2. The map on the left, corresponding to the standard GTM-TT, suggests the presence of three well-differentiated clusters of states, which are of course generated by the three time series with the two brisk transitions. We would expect that the application of the TSRD method generated a sharper separation between the three clusters of states. This is the case, as evidenced by the map on the right hand side plot of Fig. 2, which shows not only wider gaps between the three main groups of states than the map on the left hand side, but also a higher concentration of time points in only a few individual states. Exploring such effect was the second goal of these experiments, and the results can be easily explained: The TSRD method is not only providing a ranking of time series, but it is also actively limiting the effect of the less relevant series during the data fitting process, while enhancing

---
[1] Available from: www.cs.ucr.edu/~eamonn

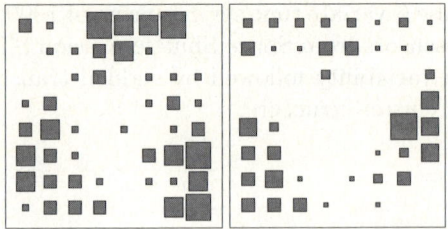

Fig. 2. Cluster maps for the Artificial_data. (Left) map corresponding to the standard GTM-TT described in subsection 2.1. (Right) map corresponding to the GTM-TT with TSRD described in subsection 2.2. This representation is based on the posterior mean proyection described in subsection 2.1.

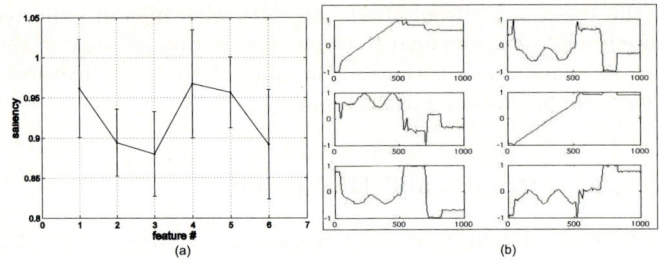

Fig. 3. (a) Estimated values of the saliencies ρ for all features from *Shuttle_ data* (displayed as in Fig. 1). (b) Individual time series of *Shuttle_ data* (1st to 6th from top to bottom and left to right), including their mean saliencies.

the effect of the most relevant ones. As a result, the final cluster structure mainly reflects what enhances it most.

These relevance determination experiments are now repeated with the real *Shuttle_ data*. The time series saliency results are reported in Fig. 3. In this case, the differences in saliency between the six available series are much smaller, and all series are attributed high relevance ($\bar{\rho}_d > 0.85$) in defining the cluster structure of the data. Interestingly though, the series with highest saliency, all with $\bar{\rho}_d > 0.95$, namely 1, 4 and 5, correspond to those with the neatest and simplest combinations of quasi-stationary periods and broad magnitude shifts.

4 Conclusions

Little research has been devoted to unsupervised methods for the clustering and visual exploration of multivariate time series. The GTM-TT [6], a stochastic latent model of the manifold learning family, is one such method. For real applications of time series analysis, we would like the clustering results and their visualization to be both interpretable and actionable. Unfortunately, the interpretation of the GTM-TT clustering results through exploratory visualization might be difficult for data sets consisting of a large number of time series: a problem that might be eased by a time series relevance ranking method and a selection method based on it. In this paper, we have defined one such TSRD method that is an integral part of the GTM-TT model data fitting process. It has been tested and the results show not only that it can properly gauge the relative relevance of individual time series, but also that it can produce neater clustering results by effectively minimizing the negative impact of the least relevant series on the clustering process itself.

Acknowledgements

Alfredo Vellido is a research fellow within the Ramón y Cajal program of the Spanish Ministry of Education and Science.

References

1. Zhang, G., Patuwo, B., Hu, M.: Forecasting with artificial neural networks: The state of the art. Int. J. of Forecasting **14** (1998) 35–62
2. Chappel, G., Taylor, J.: The temporal Kohonen map. Neural Networks **6** (1993) 441–445
3. Strickert, M., Hammer, B.: Merge SOM for temporal data. Neurocomputing **64** (2005) 39–71
4. Voegtlin, T.: Recursive self-organizing maps. Neural Networks **15** (2002) 979–991
5. Bishop, C., Svensen, M., Williams, C.: GTM: The Generative Topographic Mapping. Neural Comput. **10** (1998) 215–234
6. Bishop, C., Hinton, G., Strachan, I.: GTM through time. In: IEE Fifth Int. Conf. on Artif. Neural Net., Cambridge, U.K. (1997) 111–116
7. Olier, I., Vellido, A.: Capturing the dynamics of multivariate time series through visualization using Generative Topographic Mapping Through Time. In: IEEE ICEIS06, Islamabad, Pakistan. (2006)
8. Yoon, H., Yang, K., Shahabi, C.: Feature subset selection and feature ranking for multivariate time series. IEEE Trans. on Knowledge and Data Eng. **17** (2005) 1186–1198
9. Vellido, A., Lisboa, P.J.G., Vicente, D.: Robust analysis of MRS brain tumour data using t-GTM. Neurocomputing (in press) Accepted for publication.
10. Baum, L., Egon, J.: An inequality with applications to statistical estimation for probabilistic functions for a Markov process and to a model for ecology. B. Am. Meteorol. Soc. **73** (1967) 360–363
11. Law, M.H.C., Figueredo, M.A.T., Jain, A.K.: Simultaneous feature selection and clustering using mixture models. IEEE Trans. Pattern Anal. **26** (2004) 1154–1166

A Fast Data Preprocessing Procedure for Support Vector Regression

Zhifeng Hao[1], Wen Wen[2], Xiaowei Yang[1,3], Jie Lu[3], and Guangquan Zhang[3]

[1] School of Mathematical Science, South China University of Technology, Guangzhou, 510641, China
mazfhao@scut.edu.cn
[2] College of Computer Science and Engineering, South China University of Technology, Guangzhou, 510641, China
mathww@126.com
[3] Faculty of Information Technology University of technology Sydney, PO Box 123, Broadway, NSW 2007, Australia

Abstract. A fast data preprocessing procedure (FDPP) for support vector regression (SVR) is proposed in this paper. In the presented method, the dataset is firstly divided into several subsets and then K-means clustering is implemented in each subset. The clusters are classified by their group size. The centroids with small group size are eliminated and the rest centroids are used for SVR training. The relationships between the group sizes and the noisy clusters are discussed and simulations are also given. Results show that FDPP cleans most of the noises, preserves the useful statistical information and reduces the training samples. Most importantly, FDPP runs very fast and maintains the good regression performance of SVR.

1 Introduction

Support Vector Machine (SVM), introduced by Vapnik [1] is a useful tool for data mining, especially in the fields of pattern recognition and regression. During the past few years, its solid theoretical foundation and good behaviors have a number of researchers, and it has been demonstrated to be an effective method for solving real-life problems [2-3].

According to Vapnik's *"the nature of statistical learning theory"* [1], using tactics such as introducing a kernel function, both nonlinear pattern recognition problems and regression problems can be converted into linear ones, and finally deduced to mathematical problems of Quadratics Programming (QP). As a result, the time-consuming procedure of solving QP problems, especially when the data set is huge, became a bottleneck of SVM. Since then, researchers have proposed many methods based on iteration or decomposition strategies for solving QP problems. The Kernel Adatron algorithm [4] and Successive Over Relaxation (SOR) [7] are good examples of iterative methods. The Chunking method [5], Sequential Minimal Optimization [11] and SVM light [6] are typical examples of decomposition methods.

For the time consumed on solving QP problems is proportional to the number of variables, which is the number of samples in SVM, another category of methods based on effective sample-selection was proposed. These methods aim at reducing training samples while keeping the error caused by sample-reduction as low as possible. Yu, *et al.* [8] provides a strategy based on clustering for sample-selection, which has been demonstrated to be quite effective when dealing with classification data. Their basic idea comes from a clustering feature tree, which provides an effective recursive rule for sample-selection. However, since the characteristics of classification data and regression data are different, the sample-selection method for regression data should be somewhat different. Wang and Xu propose a heuristic training method for support vector regression, which they called Heuristic SVM (HSVM) [9]. This method has been demonstrated to be applicable when the dataset is small; however, since it firstly calculates the similarity between two samples and then calculates the similarity between a sample and a centroid, the process takes a lot of time, especially when data set is large. And in addition, HSVM just works for data that are ordered.

In this paper, focusing on the sample-selection problem of regression data and using the basic idea of subset clustering, we introduce a fast clustering-based sample-selection procedure for support vector regression. The rest of this paper is organized as follows: a basic data-preprocessing procedure is proposed and then extended to a fast version in Section 2. The simulation results and discussions are given in section 3, and conclusions are presented in Section 4.

2 The Proposed Data Preprocessing Method

2.1 Data Preprocessing Procedure Based on K-Means Clustering

One purpose of data preprocessing is to reduce the samples without losing much information. Since in K-means clustering [12], the centroid contains the statistical information of the group and the number of centroids is usually much smaller than the original data volume, therefore an intuitive idea is to use centroids to surrogate the original data set.

Another purpose of data preprocessing is to eliminate the noises in the data set. In most cases, there are two categories of noises: one category is dependent on the regression curve (denoted by "Dependent Noises"); the other is independent of the regression curve (denoted by "Independent Noises"). The following discussions are based on two *assumptions*: (1) Dependent noises are distributed along the regression curve and have a small symmetric deviation from it. (2) Independent noises are much sparser than the dependent ones, and they are randomly but approximately uniformly distributed in the input space.

For the dependent noises, using cluster centroid may reduce their negative effect, because the centroid's coordinate is actually the average coordinate of the data within a group. When the noises are symmetric on the output, the average value may reduce their deviations from the regression curve. For the independent noises, we may also find them by using clustering, because the "independently noisy groups" (groups composed of independent noises) usually contain fewer samples than the others. Thus we may eliminate them according to their *group size (defined as the number of samples contained in a cluster)*.

The whole data preprocessing process is summarized as follows (Fig. 1.):

Step1: Use K-means clustering to find K centroids.
Step2: Order the centroids by their group size;
Step3: Eliminate the last p_d percent (discarding proportion) centroids;
Step4: Use the rest $K(1-p_d)$ centroids to train SVR.

Fig. 1. SVR with data preprocessing procedure

In the proposed method, K-means clustering is implemented on the input variables, that is, distance is defined as $r(x_i, x_j) = \sum_{d=1}^{x\_dim}(x_{id} - x_{jd})^2$ without considering the output variable. However, the output variable is considered after clustering, that is, centroid involved in the afterward procedures is the average position of the cluster samples on both input features and output feature. This guarantees each input intervals have representative samples and meanwhile negative influence caused by noises can be reduced by calculating average values on output feature.

Generally, after K-means clustering, the original data set is divided into three categories of groups: (a) Groups composed of dependent noises. Since the dependent noises are much more concentrated than the independent ones, these groups usually have large group sizes. (b) Groups composed of independent noises. These groups have small sizes. (c) Groups containing both independent noises and dependent noises. These groups have the group size between group type (a) and group type (b) and are hard to be distinguished; however, in most cases these groups are quite near to the regression curve, so whether they are eliminated hardly influences the SVR-training. Furthermore, empirical study shows that if we can choose an appropriate number of *K*, the size of group type (a) would be widely different from group type (b). Thus, to eliminate the centroids that have small group size will reduce the independent noises. In the following sections, we refer to it as CDPP (A clustering-based data preprocessing procedure).

2.2 Fast Data Preprocessing Version

In the K-means clustering, k distances are calculated for each sample in each iteration, which leads to $n \bullet k \bullet I$ calculations in the whole process (n is the total samples in the dataset, k is the clustering constant and I is the total iterations needed for clustering). Therefore K-means clustering tends to suffer long computational time when the dataset grows. To deal with this problem, we propose an improved version, in which one firstly partitions the original data into several subsets according to their output values (Y-value), and then implements K-means clustering in each subset. The pseudo codes are shown in Fig. 2.

Notice that in the improved version, K-means clustering is implemented in l subsets. Each subset contains n_i $(i=1,\cdots,l)$ samples and is clustered into k_i groups. During the data preprocessing procedure, $\sum_{i=1}^{l}(n_i \bullet k_i)$ calculations are made in each iteration. In respect that

$$n = \sum_{i=1}^{l} n_i , k = \sum_{i=1}^{l} k_i , n \bullet k = \sum_{i=1}^{l}\sum_{i=1}^{l}(n_i \bullet k_i) >> \sum_{i=1}^{l}(n_i \bullet k_i), (l >= 2) \quad (1)$$

much less calculations are involved in each iteration in the improved version than does in the original one. Additionally, for the samples in each subset are much less than the ones in the whole dataset, the novel method takes much fewer iterations to reach the stop condition than the original one does, that is $I_i < I$, therefore

$$\sum_{i=1}^{l}(n_i \bullet k_i \bullet I_i) << n \bullet k \bullet I \quad (2)$$

Due to the above reasons, the improved version can reduce the computational time. We name it fast data preprocessing procedure (FDPP). In the case of *Num_of_layer=1*, FDPP is identical to CDPP.

In FDPP, the dataset is divided into several layers according to their output value. This guarantees that in each output interval there are some representative centroids. Empirical study shows that compared with CDPP, FDPP is also much easier to distinguish the independent noisy centroids from the dependent ones.

```
/* Initialize */
  For(l=0; l<Num_of_layer;l++)
    {Subset[i]= ∅ ;}
/* Subset Division */
  for(i=0; i<Num_of_Samples; i++)
    { Find Y_max and Y_min; }
  step=(Y_max-Y_min)/Num_of_Layer;
  for(l=0;l<Num_of_Layer;l++)
    { For(i=0; i<Num_of_Samples; i++)
      if(Y_i<Y_min+step*(l+1) and Y_i>=Y_min+step*l)
        { Subset[i]= Subset[i] +{(X_i,Y_i)};}
    }
/* Cluster in each Subset */
  for(l=0; l<Num_of_Layer;l++)
    { K_i=int (Clustering_proportion*Samplenum_in_layer[l]);
      Implement K_i-Means clustering in Subset[i];
      Record the centroids and the corresponding group sizes
    }
  Descendantly order the centroids according to their group size
  Eliminate the last Discarding_proportion* ∑ k_i centroids
```

Fig. 2. Pseudo codes of FDPP

3 Simulations and Results

To verify the validities of the proposed data preprocessing method, a program including the data preprocessing module and the SORSVR module is written in VC++6.0 and run on a personal computer with 3.0GB memory and Windows XP OS. Each instance consists of dependent noisy samples and independent noises. Dependent noisy samples are generated from three sampling functions:

$$f_1(x) = \frac{\sin(2x)}{2x} + \xi_1, \quad f_2(x) = x^3 + \xi_2, \quad f_3(x) = \frac{\sin\left(\sqrt{x_1^2 + x_2^2}\right)}{\sqrt{x_1^2 + x_2^2}} + \xi_3;$$

Independent noises are randomly generated in the space. The proportion of dependent noisy samples to independent noises is 10:1. Table 1 shows the running parameters in the simulations. Table 2 shows the comparisons between the CDDP and FDDP. The visual results from one of the twenty tests are illustrated in Figs. 3(a)~5(b): Figs. 3(a), 4(a) and 5(a) show the distributions of original datasets and Figs. 3(b), 4(b) and 5(b) show the distributions of selected samples after FDPP.

From Figs. 3(b), 4(b) and 5(b), we can see that most of the independent noisy centroids are eliminated and the useful ones are preserved. However, as shown in Fig. 5(b), there still exist a few independent noisy centroids that are not eliminated,

Table 1. Running parameters of each instance

Eg.	ξ_i	Sampling Interval	Para. of FDPP			Para of SVR	
			N	p_c	p_d	σ	ε
1	U[-0.05,0.05]	$x \in [-1.5,1.5]$	1650	0.1	0.3	1	0.1
2	U[-0.2,0.2]	$x \in [-3,3]$	1650	0.1	0.3	1	0.3
3	U[-0.05,0.05]	$x_1 \in [-1,5]$ $x_2 \in [-5,5]$	3422	0.1	0.3	1	0.3

n: total samples p_c: clustering proportion p_d: discarding proportion

Table 2. Comparisons between FDPP and CDPP

Eg.	Method	L	K	Time(s)
Dataset1	FDPP	15	111	0.20
		10	112	0.40
		5	115	0.55
	CDPP	-	116	1.60
Dataset2	FDPP	15	111	0.35
		10	113	0.55
		5	115	1.1
	CDPP	-	116	2.5
Dataset3	FDPP	15	235	3.20
		10	237	4.60
		5	238	7.80
	CDPP	-	240	18.85

K: Count of selected centroids L: Setting of Num_of_layer Time: Average time of 20 tests

which is caused by the incompletely uniformly-distributed independent noises. Fortunately, in most cases these points are so few that they rarely affect the SVR training.

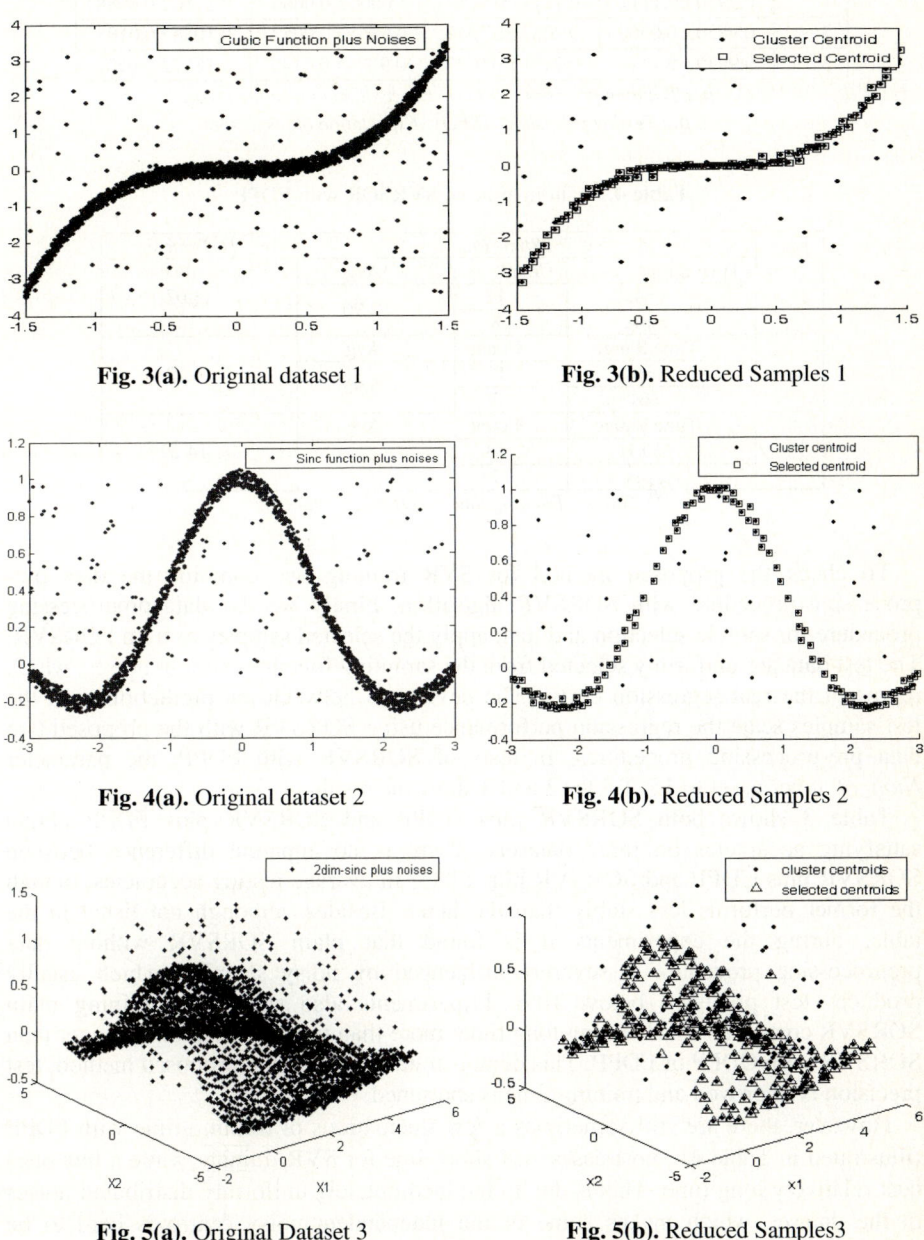

Fig. 3(a). Original dataset 1   **Fig. 3(b).** Reduced Samples 1

Fig. 4(a). Original dataset 2   **Fig. 4(b).** Reduced Samples 2

Fig. 5(a). Original Dataset 3   **Fig. 5(b).** Reduced Samples3

Table 3. Testing accuracy comparison

Eg.	CDPP+SORSVR		FDPP+SORSVR	
	p_{ts}	TSEerr	p_{ts}	TSEerr
1	0.9930±0.1111	0.1211±0.0219	1.0000±0.0000	0.1150±0.0088
2	0.9850±0.0560	0.2063±0.0319	0.9865±0.0052	0.1058±0.0105
3	0.9930±0.1111	0.1437±0.0311	0.9704±0.0140	0.1817±0.0201

p_{tr}: Training precision TREerr: Expectation of training errors
p_{ts}: Testing precision TSEerr: Expectation of test errors

Table 4. Training time of SVRSOR with FDPP

Eg.	TRtime (s)			Avg_TOTtime (s)
1	Time Range	Count	Avg.	3.07
	<=4s	12	2.90	
	>=4s	8		
2	Time Range	Count	Avg.	6.12
	<=6s	17	5.95	
	>6s	3		
3	Time Range	Count	Avg.	14.29
	<=14s	13	12.45	
	>14s	7		

TRtime: Training time TOTtime: Total time

To check the proposed method for SVR training, we combine the data pre-processing procedure with SORSVR algorithm: Firstly we use data preprocessing procedure for sample selection and then apply the selected samples to train SORSVR. The test data are uniformly selected from the sampling function without noises, which represent the real regression curve. The deviations between the predictions and the test samples scale the regression performance using SORSVR with the proposed two data pre-processing procedures. In tests of SORSVR with FDPP, the parameter *Num_of_layer* is set to 15. Tables 3 and 4 show the results.

Table 3 shows both SORSVR plus CDPP and SORSVR plus FDPP obtain satisfying accuracies on three datasets. There is no apparent difference between SORSVR plus CDPP and SORSVR plus FDPP in average testing accuracies, though the former performs less stably than the latter. Besides, although not listed in the table, during the experiments it is found that plain SORSVR without data preprocessing procedure is severely influenced by noisy samples, which usually produces test precision below 10%. Experiments also show that training plain SORSVR costs an overwhelming long time: more than two hundred times longer than SORSVR with CDPP or FDPP. This demonstrates that with the proposed method, test precision is improved and training time is shortened.

However, there are still sometimes a few fluctuations of training time with FDPP (illustrated in Table 4): most cases cost short time for SVR training while a few ones cost relatively long time. This is due to the incompletely uniformly-distributed noises in the dataset, which makes some of the independent noisy centroids hard to be eliminated and furthermore affects the training time of SORSVR. But in the whole, the fluctuations of training time are acceptable and the proposed method is effective.

4 Conclusions

In this paper we firstly introduced CDPP, a clustering-based data preprocessing procedure for support vector regression. As for itself drawbacks: computationally expensive, we have furthermore proposed FDPP, a fast version based on CDPP. FDPP eliminates most of the independent noises and meanwhile preserves the useful centroids that contain the useful statistical information. What is most important is FDPP runs fast, which hardly needs any extra computational time. The experimental results show that the proposed method is valid and effective for support vector regression.

However, FDPP does not work for datasets that contain bad independent noises, which are excessively concentrated in some area of the input space. Our future work is to find new methods based on FDPP, and extend the noise-cleaning ability of FDPP to these "worse" cases.

Acknowledgements

The authors would like to thank the anonymous reviewers for their valuable comments and advices. This work has been supported by the National Natural Science Foundation of China (10471045, 60433020), the program for New Century Excellent Talents in University(NCET), Natural Science Foundation of Guangdong Province (031360, 04020079), Excellent Young Teachers Program of Ministry of Education of China, Fok Ying Tong Education Foundation (91005), Social Science Research Foundation of MOE (2005-241), Key Technology Research and Development Program of Guangdong Province (2005B10101010, 2005B70101118), Key Technology Research and Development Program of Tianhe District (051G041) and Natural Science Foundation of South China University of Technology (B13-E5050190).

References

[1] Vapnik, V.: The Nature of Statistical Learning Theory, John Wiley, New York, USA, 1995.
[2] Wu, C. H.: Travel-Time Prediction with Support Vector Regression, IEEE Transactions on Intelligent Transportation Systems, 5 (2004) 276-281.
[3] Yang, H. Q., Chan, L. W., King, I.: Support Vector Machine Regression for Volatile Stock Market Prediction, Proceedings of the Third Intelligent Data Engineering and Automated Learning, (2002) 391-396.
[4] Frie, T. T., Chistianini, V. N., Campbell, C.: The Kernel Adatron Algorithm: A Fast and Simple Learning Procedure for Support Vector Machines, Proceedings of the 15th International Conference of Machine Learning, Morgan Kaufmann, San Fransisco, CA, 1998.
[5] Vapnik, V.: Estimation of Dependence Based on Empirical Data, Springer, New York, 1982.
[6] Joachims, T.: Making large-scale support vector machine learning practical, Advances in Kernel Methods: Support Vector Learning, MIT Press, Cambridge, MA, (1998) 169-184.

[7] Mangasarian, O. L., Musicant, D. R.: Successive Overrelaxation for Support Vector Machines, IEEE Transactions on Neural Networks, 10 (1999) 1032-1037.
[8] Yu, H. J., Yang, J., Han, J. W., Li, X. L.: Making SVMs Scalable to Large Data Sets using Hierarchical Cluster Indexing, Data Mining and Knowledge Discovery, 2005 (published online)
[9] Wang, W. J., Xu, Z. B.: A Heuristic Training for Support Vector Regression, Neurocomputing, 61 (2004) 259-275.
[10] Quan, Y., Yang, J., Yao, L. X., Ye, C. Z.: Successive Overrelaxation for Support Vector Regression, Journal of Software on 15 (2004) 200-206.
[11] Platt, J.: Fast Training of Support Vector Machines Using Sequential Minimal Optimizationg, Advances in Kernel Methods: Support Vector Learning, MIT Press, Cambridge, MA, (1998) 185-208.
[12] Webb, A. R.: K-means clustering, Statistical Pattern Recognition, John Wiley & Sons, Inc. (2002) 296-299.

Classification by Weighting, Similarity and kNN

Naohiro Ishii, Tsuyoshi Murai, Takahiro Yamada, and Yongguang Bao

Aichi Institute of Technology, Yakusacho, Toyota , Japan 470-0392
ishii@aitech.ac.jp

Abstract. In this paper, the grouping method of the similar words, is proposed for the classification of documents. It is shown that the grouping of words has equivalent ability to the LSA in the classification accuracy. Further, a new combining method is proposed for the documents classification, which consists of Grouping, Latent Semantic Analysis(LSA) followed by the k-Nearest Neighbor classification (k-NN). The combining method proposed here, shows the higher accuracy in the classification than the conventional methods of the kNN, and the LSA followed by the kNN. Thus, the grouping method is effective as a preprocessing before the conventional method.

Keywords: text classification, LSA, kNN, words similarity.

1 Introduction

There are classification methods based on the distances in which the distance between vectors is used as the difference between documents[1,2]. The length of the document might have thousands of dimensions with words. Therefore, the classification technique for treating the words vector needs a considerable computational complexity. In the statistical text classification, the reduction of attributes in their dimension, becomes a problem.

The reduction of dimension was paid to attention by analyzing the statistical appearance patterns by using the technique of the Latent Semantic Analysis (LSA)[3,4]. Moreover, it will be classified by taking out a potential structure of the document while removing the noise and reducing the dimension. Though the LSA is theoretically clear and established method, we checked whether the LSA is best in the practical applications by proposing a simple grouping method, which is used in nearest neighbor classification. In this paper, the grouping method of the similar words, is almost equivalent to the LSA for the classification ability of documents, which is shown in the Reuters international news. Further, a new combining method including the grouping of words, is proposed for the documents classification, which consists of Grouping, LSA followed by the k-Nearest Neighbor classification (k-NN). The combining method shows the higher accuracy than the conventional method of the LSA followed by the k-NN. This shows that grouping of words is useful as a preprocessing before the conventional method of the LSA followed by k-NN.

2 Vector Space Model

The most commonly used document representation is so called vector space model. In the vector space model, a document is represented by a vector of words. Usually, one has a collection of documents which is represented by a word-by-document matrix A, where each entry represents the occurrences of a word in a document, i.e., $A = (a_{ik})$, where a_{ik} is the weight of the word i in the document k.

The number M of rows in matrix A, corresponds to the number of words in the dictionary. The $k-th$ document is represented by the characteristic vector

$$x_k = (a_{1k}, a_{2k}, ..., a_{Mk}),$$

where the suffix, $1k$ of a_{1k} is the 1-st vector component and M shows the number of the words in the dictionary, $dic = \{word_i | 1 \le i \le M\}$. To determine a_{ik}, the following approach is taken:

(1) Term Frequency, which means by the occurrence of terms(words) in the document.
(2) Document Frequency, which means by the occurrence of words in all the collected documents.

Let f_{ik} be the number of occurrence of the word i in the document k, N be the number of all the collected documents, M be the number of words after the removal of the unnecessarily words and n_i be the number of the occurrence of the word i in the all the collected documents. Then, the weight a_{ik} is determined by the following methods[1,2,7].

Word frequency weighting: The number of occurrence of the targeted word in the document, becomes the weight, i.e,

$$a_{ik} = f_{ik}$$

tf×idf – weighting: tf means by the term frequency, f_{ik}, while df means by the document frequency, n_i. The smaller n_i, will mean the high ability for characterizing the word i. Thus, the inverse value of n_i, is computed. Then, $idf_i = \log(N/n_i)$ is defined. The weight of the word i in the document k, becomes

$$a_{ik} = f_{ik} \times \log(N/n_i)$$

tfc – weighting: tfc-weighting is the normalized tf×idf-weighting

Itc – weighting: By the log transformation of tf×idf – weighting and its normalization.

3 k – Nearest Neighbor Classification

The training of documents is shown by the 2-tuple $d = (x, y)$, where x shows the characteristic vector of the document and y shows the given category of the document. From the trained documents set $D = \{d_i | 1 \leq i \leq n\}$, the unclassified document d_q is classified by k-nearest neighbor as follows,

1) Let the trained documents be $d_{n1}, d_{n2} \ldots d_{nk} \in D$, which are nearest neighbors of the unclassified document d_q. Then, the similarity of documents d_i and d_j, is computed as follows,

$$sim(d_i, d_j) = \cos(vec\, x_i, vec\, x_j) = \frac{vec\, x_i \cdot vec\, x_j}{|vec\, x_i||vec\, x_j|},$$

where $vec\, x_i \cdot vec\, x_j$ shows a inner product of vectors, $vec\, x_i$ and $vec\, x_j$.

2) For the unclassified document d_q, the class category is determined from the following rank computation denoted by $rank_{c_j}(d_q)$, which is defined as

$$rank_{c_j}(d_q) = \frac{\sum_{i=n1}^{nk}(sim(d_q, d_i) \times \delta(c_j, y_i))}{\sum_{i=n1}^{nk} sim(d_q, d_i)},$$

where the suffix c_j is the j-th category among all classes, $c_j (j = 1 \ldots l)$ and $\delta(c_j, y_i) = 1$ if $c_j = y_i$ and $\delta(c_j, y_i) = 0$ if $c_j \neq y_i$.

3) The unclassified document is assigned to the class c_j, which satisfies the relation $rank_{c_j}(d_q) \geq \theta$, where θ is the threshold value, which is given in advance.

4 Latent Semantic Indexing and Grouping of Words

Assuming that we have a $m \times n$ word-by-document matrix A, where m is the number of words, and n is the number of documents. The singular value decomposition of A is given by :

$$A = U \sum V^T,$$

where $U(m \times r)$ and $V(r \times n)$ have orthogonal columns and $(r \times r)$ is the diagonal matrix of singular values. $r \leq \min(m, n)$ is rank of A. If the singular values of A are ordered by size, the k largest may be kept and the remaining smaller ones set to zero. The matrix A_k that is an approximation to A with rank k as shown in the following.

$$A_k = U_k \sum_k V^T_k ,$$

where $\sum_k (k \times k)$ is obtained by deleting the zero rows and columns of $\sum$ and $U_k (m \times n)$ and $V_k (n \times k)$, are obtained from U and V, respectively.

The similarity between words, is carried out by the cosine of two rows in the approximated matrix A_k or $U_k \sum_k$ The set of similar words, will be useful for the classification of documents. The set is made from the aggregation of similar words by the following procedure. Let the word in the document, be $k_i (i=0,1,...,n)$ and each set be $K_j (j=0,1,...,m(<n))$, where K_j is represented as follows,

$$K_j = \bigcup_{s \leq r(k_i, k_l)} k_l$$

The relation $s \leq r(k_i, k_l)$ shows the similarity relation $r(k_i, k_l)$ between words, k_i and k_l, which is computed from cosine of words described above. The s is the threshold of the similarity relation. By the similarity relation of the given threshold, the words are grouped into the same class, which is assumed as a new word K_j. Thus the grouped set of the new words, is made as $\{K_j\}$. The schematic diagram of grouping process of words, is shown in Fig. 1. The d_1 shows a document consisting of words. By the grouping of words, which is carried out by the similarity relation in the above Section 3, the dimension of words is reduced and the grouping words will make the uncorrelated points in the vector space.

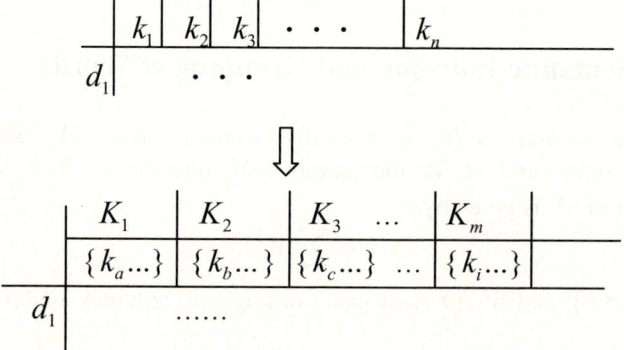

Fig. 1. Schematic diagram of grouping words

5 Experimental Method and Results

The computer experiments were carried out by the well known news data called Reuters21578[9], which consists of international politics and economical news documents. The documents are classified to 10 categories (cocoa, copper, cpi, gnp, rubber, fuel, gold, jobs, alum, coffee) [9]. Classification of Reuters news data, was carried out by the conventional kNN method and the proposed combining method of Grouping, LSA and kNN.

To measure the classification accuracy in the class c_i, three indexes, $Recall_{ci}$, $Precision_{ci}$, and $Accuracy_{ci}$ are defined as follws[1,5,7], the ratio of documents classified to the class c_i within the total documents in the class c_i, the ratio of documents classified correctly in the class c_i within the documents assigned to the class c_i, and the ratio of documents classified correctly to the class c_i and other c_i among all the documents, respectively. Data weighting is an important pre-processing for vector space model of the classification of documents. To compute the best results in those weighting, the classification in kNN with tf×idf weighting, showed the highest values in the data weighting, which is applied here.

The parameter k in the kNN, was chosen to be k=14, in numerical experiments. The bold numerals in Table 1 , shows the almost or same higher values than those in case of combining Grouping, LSA and kNN method in Table 5 . Table 1 and 2 show the result by the traditional method by the LSA followed by kNN.

Table 1. Classification indexes (LSA + kNN)

Class	kNN (LSA + kNN)		
	Recall	Precision	Accuracy
alum	**0.6842**	0.9286	0.9583
cocoa	**0.8461**	**1.0000**	**0.9881**
coffee	**1.0000**	0.8276	0.9702
copper	**0.8125**	0.9286	0.9762
cpi	0.7500	0.9231	0.9702
fuel	0.4000	**1.0000**	0.9643
gnp	**1.0000**	0.5676	**0.9048**
gold	0.9260	0.9259	0.9762
jobs	**0.7273**	**1.0000**	0.9702
rubber	0.7273	0.8889	0.9762

Table 2. Classification indexes (LSA + kNN)

micro-average	0.8274	0.8274	0.9655
macro-average	0.7873	0.8790	0.9655

Results of the Grouping followed by kNN, are shown in Table 3 and 4. The Grouping is better than the conventional LSA followed by kNN in classification indexes.

Table 3. Classification indexes (Grouping + kNN)

Class	kNN (Grouping + kNN)		
	Recall	Precision	Accuracy
alum	0.6316	**1.0000**	0.9583
cocoa	**0.8461**	**1.0000**	**0.9881**
coffee	**1.0000**	0.8276	0.9702
copper	**0.8125**	**1.0000**	**0.9821**
cpi	0.7500	0.9231	0.9702
fuel	**0.5000**	**1.0000**	0.9702
gnp	**1.0000**	0.5385	0.8929
gold	**0.9630**	0.8966	**0.9762**
jobs	**0.7273**	**1.0000**	**0.9821**
rubber	0.7273	0.8889	0.9762

Table 4. Classification indexes (Grouping + kNN)

micro-average	0.8333	0.8333	0.9667
macro-average	0.7958	0.9075	0.9667

Table 5 and 6 show the results of the Grouping followed by LSA and kNN.

Table 5. Classification indexes in combining Grouping, LSA and kN

Class	kNN (Grouping + LSA + kNN)		
	Recall	Precision	Accuracy
alum	**0.6842**	**1.0000**	**0.9643**
cocoa	**0.8461**	**1.0000**	**0.9881**
coffee	**1.0000**	**0.8571**	**0.9762**
copper	**0.8125**	**1.0000**	**0.9821**
cpi	**0.8125**	**0.9286**	**0.9762**
fuel	**0.5000**	**1.0000**	**0.9702**
gnp	**1.0000**	**0.5676**	**0.9048**
gold	**0.9630**	**0.8966**	**0.9762**
jobs	**0.7273**	**1.0000**	**0.9821**
rubber	**0.8182**	**0.9000**	**0.9821**

Table 6. Classification indexes in combining grouping, LSA and kNN

micro-average	0.8512	0.8512	0.9702
macro-average	0.8164	0.9150	0.9702

The bold numerals in Table 5 and 6, show the higher values of classification indexes in the proposed method than those indexes in the LSA+kNN or Grouping + kNN. The accuracy of the unknown documents in each class of Reuters news, are improved in the classification indexed as shown in Table 5 and 6.

6 Classification by Multiple Weightings

To improve the accuracy of classification, a new integrated weighting method is discussed here, which combine the several weights in the section 3. The algorithm proposed, is as follows, (1) Multiple weights are computed from the methods described in the section 3 for the training data. (2) Ranking computations a re carried out by (2) in Section 3. (3) The final rank for class C_j in the unknown data d_q is computed as the average value of the ranking computations at the above (2), which satisfies inequality $rank_{C_j, knn_i}(d_q) \geq \theta$.

The average is defined here as follows,

$$rank_{C_j}(d_q) = \frac{\sum_{i=1}^{m} \{rank_{C_j, knn_i}(d_q)\}}{m}$$

The final class C_j is determined from the maximum value of the above average.

To evaluate this ranking algorithm, the 11-point aveage precision method for the ranking category was developed (Yang 1999) as the accuracy of classification. The experimental results are shown in Table 7, in which bold face is the maximum value. This shows the combining weighting factors improves the classification accuracy.

Table 7. Average precision by combining weighting factors

weighting classs	word frequency	tf×idf	tfc, tf×idf,entropy	tf×idf, Itc,entropy	tf×idf, Itc, tfc,entropy
4 class	0.813	0.845	**0.867**	0.861	0.861
5 class	0.795	0.822	**0.847**	0.842	0.861
6 class	0.782	0.844	0.857	**0.866**	0.862

7 Conclusion

Text and document classification still have received a lot of attention by the unsupervised manner. In the classification, the accuracy is an important measure to assign the correct class for the unknown objects. This paper proposes a simple preprocessing method of grouping of words before the conventional method of the LSA followed by kNN. Thus, the combining classification method, which consists of data grouping ,reduction of data dimension(LSA), followed by the kNN method. Text classification experiments are carried out to compare the accuracy of the classification by the conventional method of the LSA followed by kNN with the proposed method of Grouping, followed by the LSA and kNN. The combining proposed method shows the higher accuracy in the classification.

References

1. Grossma, D. A. and Frieder, O., Information Retrieval - Algorithms and Heuristics- , Springer-Verlag, pp.332, 2004
2. Sebastiani, F., " A tutorial on automated text categorization ", Proc. of ASAI-99, 1st Argentinian Symposium on Artificial Intelligence, pp.7-35, Buenos Aires, 1999
3. Derrwester, S., Dumais, S.T. ,Furnas,G.W., Landauer, T.K. and Harshman, R., " Indexing by latent semantic analysis ", Journal of the American Society for Information Science, No.41, pp.391-407, 1990
4. Landauer, P.W., Folz, T.K. and Laham, D., " Introduction to latent semantic analysis", Discourse Processes, No.25, pp.259-284, 1998
5. Sebastiani, F., " Machine learning in automated text categorization", ACM Computing Surveys, Vol.34, No.1, pp.1-47, 2002
6. Bao, Y. and Ishii, N., " Combining multiple k-nearest neighbor classifiers for text classification by reducts", Proc. 5th Int. Conference on Discovery Science, Lecture Notes in Artificial Intelligence, Vol.2534, Springer-Verlag, pp.361-368, 2002
7. Sirmakessis, S., Text Mining and its Application, Springer-Verlag, pp.204, 2003
8. Baldi, P., Frasconi, P. and Smyth, P., Modeling the Internet and the Web, Wiley, pp.285, 2003
9. http://kdd.ics.uci.edu//databases/reuters21578/reuters21578.html
10. Bao, Y., Tsuchiya ,E., Ishii, N. and Du, X., "Classification by Instance-Based Learning Algorithm", 6th Int. Conference on Intelligent Data Engineering and Automated Learning- IDEAL 2005, Lecture Notes in Computer Science, LNCS 3578, Springer-Verlag,pp.133-140, 2005

An Improved EM Algorithm for Statistical Segmentation of Brain MRI

Yong Yang

School of Information Management, Jiangxi University of Finance and Economics,
Nanchang 330013, P.R. China
greatyyy765@sohu.com

Abstract. To overcome the limitations of standard expectation maximization (EM) algorithm, an improved EM algorithm is proposed. Based on this algorithm, a novel statistical approach for segmentation of brain magnetic resonance (MR) image data is presented in this paper, which involves three steps. Firstly, after pre-processing the image with the curvature anisotropic diffusion filter, the background (BG) and brain masks of the image are obtained by applying a combination approach of thresholding with morphology. Secondly, the connected threshold region growing technique is employed to get the preliminary results of white matter (WM), gray matter (GM) and cerebrospinal fluid (CSF) on a brain MRI. Finally, the previous results are served as the priori knowledge for the improved EM algorithm to segment the brain MRI. The performance of the proposed method is compared with those of standard EM algorithm and the popular used fuzzy-C means (FCM) segmentation. Experimental results show our approach is effective, robust and significantly faster than the conventional EM based method.

1 Introduction

Magnetic resonance imaging (MRI) is an important diagnostic imaging technique to obtain high quality brain images in both clinical and research areas because it is virtually noninvasive and it possesses a high spatial resolution and an excellent contrast of soft tissues [1], [2]. MR images are widely used not only for detecting tissue deformities such as cancers and injuries, but also for studying brain pathology [3]. In order to offer useful and accurate clinical information, the segmentation and recognition algorithms of MR images are becoming important subject of the study on medical image processing. Various approaches for MR image segmentation have been developed and applied in the last decades. Clarke *et al.* [4] gave an early survey about MRI segmentation, they divided the techniques into the following groups: threshold-based segmentation, statistical methods and region growing methods. Rajapakse *et al.* [5] proposed a more exact summarization: the available methods for MR image segmentation can be categorized into classical, statistical, fuzzy, and neural network techniques. In this paper, we take the recently most used statistical approach as has been done by many others for MR image segmentation [1], [2], [3], [5], [6], [7].

Most previous reported statistical approaches used the expectation maximization (EM) [8] algorithm to compute the maximum likelihood (ML) estimation of the segmentation parameters. However, since the EM is an iterative algorithm, it always meets the problem of slow convergence or painfully slow computing [6], which influences its practical clinical applications. To overcome the above problem, an improved EM algorithm named statistical histogram based expectation maximization (SHEM) algorithm is presented in this paper. Based on this SHEM algorithm, a novel statistical method is then proposed for segmentation of the brain MR image data instead of the conventional EM based method. The core idea of this approach is to combine the SHEM algorithm and the connected threshold region-growing algorithm that is used to provide the priori knowledge for the segmentation. Experimental results demonstrate the proposed method is efficient and robust.

2 Methods for Preliminary Results

A. Curvature Anisotropic Diffusion Filtering

Acquired medical images are often degraded by various types of artifacts resulting in a lowering of signal-to-noise ratio (SNR) or contrast-to-noise ratio (CNR) [9]. The conventional filtering techniques such as mean and median filtering, along with reducing the noise, they often blur important structures such as boundaries and detailed structures. The modified curvature diffusion equation (MCDE) is employed in this sub-section. This method has been proved more aggressive than ordinary anisotropic diffusion at enhancing and preserving edges and detailed structures. The MCDE equation is given as:

$$f_t = |\nabla f| \nabla \cdot c(|\nabla f|) \frac{\nabla f}{|\nabla f|} \quad (1)$$

where $f = f(x, y, t)$ and $f(x, y, 0) = I(x, y)$, the input image. $c(\ )$ is called conductance function and is a monotonically decreasing function containing a free parameter k, which determines the contrast of edges that will have significant affects on the smoothing. Fig.1 illustrates the effect of this filter on a MRI proton density (PD) weighted image of the brain from the digital brain phantom [10]. In this example the filter was run with a time step of $t = 0.125$, a conductance value of $k = 1.0$ and 5 iterations. Fig.1 (b) shows how homogeneous regions are smoothed and edges are preserved compared with Fig.1 (c), which is the result of conventional mean filtering.

B. Generate BG and Brain Masks

After the image has been filtered, an initial segmentation into foreground/background is achieved using simple intensity thresholding, thus a BG mask binary image is produced. Then we segment the inside of the brain from non-brain tissues and remove small connections between the brain and surrounding tissues. The segmentation methods used here is thresholding with morphology. We use an automated method as described in [3] to find the binary threshold; the result of BG mask is shown in Fig.2

(a). A morphological erosion operation is then applied with a 5×5 rectangular structural element. After erosion, a labeling algorithm is used to find the largest single region. Finally, binary dilation with the same 5×5 kernel as for erosion is performed on the remaining region to make it close to the original size. The final brain mask is shown in Fig.2 (b) and the corresponding result of brain MRI is presented in Fig.2 (c).

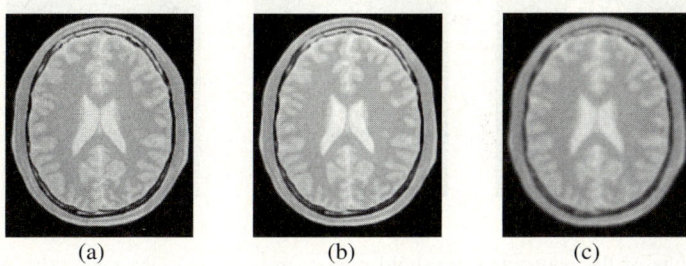

Fig. 1. Results of filtering. (a) Original PD-weighted image. (b) Image after MCDE filtering. (c) Image after mean filtering.

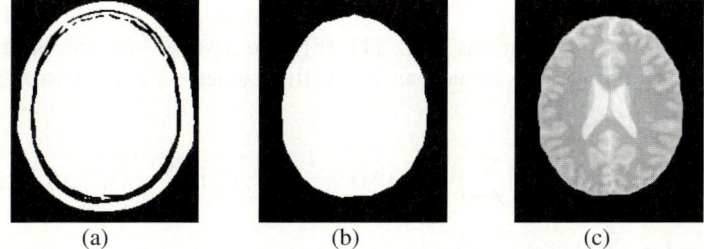

Fig. 2. Results of cerebral region masks and brain MRI. (a) BG mask. (b) Brain mask. (c) Brain MRI.

C. Connected Threshold Region Growing

Region growing (often called flood-fill) algorithms have been proven to be an effective approach for image segmentation. A simple region growing method is introduced here, namely connected threshold. The criterion used by the connected threshold is based on an interval of intensity values. Values of lower and upper threshold should be provided. The region-growing algorithm includes those pixels whose intensities are inside the interval.

$$I(x, y) \in [Lower, Upper] \qquad (2)$$

The problem is the definition of these two intervals. We do this by statistical evaluation about the gray value distribution, which can be done by fitting a Gaussian curve to the histogram of the image. Thus the two intervals are determined automatically. Then, we can easily segment the major anatomical structures by providing seeds in the appropriate locations. These seeds are manually selected in the different distinct areas of the image. After binary thresholding with these two steps, we can get the three clusters' masks. The experiment results are shown in Fig.3. From Fig.3 (a) and (c), we notice that the GM and CSF are not being completely segmented. This illustrates the vulnerability of the region growing methods. However, these incomplete segmentation masks can be used as *a priori* for the following SHEM algorithm.

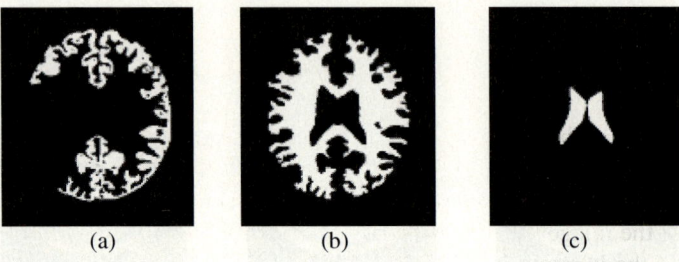

Fig. 3. Results of the connected threshold region growing. (a) GM mask. (b) WM mask. (c) CSF mask.

3 Statistical Histogram Based EM Algorithm

As proposed in the publications (e.g., [1], [5]), we assume here the brain image intensity corresponding to a tissue can be well modeled as a multivariate Gaussian distribution.

$$p(x_t|\theta_k) = (2\pi)^{-M/2} |\Sigma_k|^{-1/2} \cdot \exp\left(-\frac{1}{2}(x_t - \mu_k)^T \Sigma_k^{-1}(x_t - \mu_k)\right) \qquad (3)$$

where $\theta_k = (\mu_k, \Sigma_k)$ is the vector of parameter associate with each type of tissue (or class) k, μ_k is the mean vector, and Σ_k is the covariance (positive definite symmetric) matrix associate with class k, $1 \leq k \leq K$ where K is the number of classes, M is the number of channels or spectra in the image, and T denotes matrix transpose. In this paper, we consider only a single MR image of the object such an image is referred as single-channel image (i.e., $M = 1$). The model of (3) can then take the form as follows:

$$p(x_t|\theta_k) = \frac{1}{\sqrt{2\pi}\sigma_k} \exp\left[-\frac{1}{2\sigma_k^2}(x_t - \mu_k)^2\right] \qquad (4)$$

where σ_k is the standard deviation of class k. As the brain is the mixture of different tissues, and the tissues are assumed tissue-independent. With these assumptions, the likelihood of the image data can be written as:

$$L(\phi) = \prod_{t=1}^{n} \sum_{k=1}^{K} w_k p(x_t|\theta_k) \qquad (5)$$

where $\phi = \{\mu_k, \sigma_k^2, w_k\}$ for $k = 1, 2, \cdots, K$, n is the total number of the image pixels and w_k is the proportion of each tissue component, where $\sum_{k=1}^{K} w_k = 1$ and $w_k \geq 0$. The log-likelihood can then be expressed by:

$$\log L(\phi) = \sum_{t=1}^{n} \log \sum_{k=1}^{K} w_k p(x_t | \theta_k) \tag{6}$$

Many numerical techniques have been proposed to perform the ML estimation of the above class parameters, among which EM algorithm is the most used method as many authors have reported [5], [6], [7]. The above used EM algorithm is based on the intensity of the image, which counts the parameters pixel-by-pixel, as a result, the convergence of the iteration is slow, more computational time is needed. In this section, we use the statistical histogram of the image to overcome the problems.

Define the non-negative integrate set $G = \{L_{\min}, L_{\min+1}, \cdots, L_{\max}\}$ as gray level, where $L_{\min}$ is the minimum gray level, $L_{\max}$ is the maximum gray level, so the grayscale is $L_{\max} - L_{\min}$. For image size $U \times V$, at point (u,v), $f(u,v)$ is the gray level with $0 \leq u \leq U-1$, $0 \leq v \leq V-1$. Use $His(g)$ to denote the number of pixels having gray level g, $g \in G$. The statistical histogram function is as follows:

$$His(g) = \sum_{u=0}^{U-1} \sum_{v=0}^{V-1} \delta(f(u,v) - g) \tag{7}$$

where $g = \{L_{\min}, L_{\min+1}, \cdots, L_{\max}\}$, $\delta(0) = 1$ and $\delta(g \neq 0) = 0$.

Let i be the intensity of the pixel with $L_{\min} \leq i \leq L_{\max}$, and all pixels of the k th tissue cluster have a mean intensity μ_k, variance σ_k^2, and proportional ratio w_k. The K mixed Gaussian distribution can be written as:

$$p(i|\phi) = \sum_{k=1}^{K} w_k p(i|\theta_k) \tag{8}$$

where $\sum_{k=1}^{K} w_k = 1$ and

$$p(i|\theta_k) = \frac{1}{\sqrt{2\pi}\sigma_k} \exp\left[-\frac{1}{2\sigma_k^2}(i - \mu_k)^2\right] \tag{9}$$

The above parameters can be obtained by equating the first partial derivatives of (6) with respect to unknown parameters to zero. With the statistical histogram, the SHEM algorithm can then be expressed by:

A. The E-step

$$\psi_{ik}^{(b+1)} = \frac{p(i|\theta_k^{(b)}) \cdot w_k^{(b)}}{\sum_{k=1}^{K} p(i|\theta_k^{(b)}) \cdot w_k^{(b)}} \quad (10)$$

ψ_{ik} is the posterior probability that intensity i belongs to class k.

B. The M-step

The second step updates the unknown parameters with the statistical histogram $His(i)$.

$$T_k^{(b+1)} = \sum_{i=L\min}^{L\max} \psi_{ik}^{(b+1)} \cdot His(i) \quad (11) \qquad w_k^{(b+1)} = \frac{T_k^{(b+1)}}{U \cdot V} \quad (12)$$

$$\mu_k^{(b+1)} = \frac{\sum_{i=L\min}^{L\max} \psi_{ik}^{(b+1)} \cdot i \cdot His(i)}{T_k^{(b+1)}} \quad (13) \qquad \left(\sigma_k^{(b+1)}\right)^2 = \frac{\sum_{i=L\min}^{L\max} \psi_{ik}^{(b+1)} \cdot \left(i - \mu_k^{(b+1)}\right)^2 \cdot His(i)}{T_k^{(b+1)}} \quad (14)$$

where b is the iteration number.

4 Experimental Results

In this section, both standard EM and SHEM algorithms are used for the segmentation of the filtered PD-weighted MRI. The segmentation was implemented in VC++6.0 language on a PC. We attempt to segment the MRI into four clusters (GM, WM, CSF, and BG), and apply the previous corresponding segmentation mask results to compute the initial value of $\phi^{(0)}$. The algorithm was terminated after the convergence is stable. The final results are gained by extracting the brain region from the results of SHEM algorithm. The segmentation results are shown in Fig.4. Compared with the connected threshold region growing results in Fig.3 (a) and (c), GM and CSF are extracted completely and accurately as shown in Fig.4 (a) and (c).

(a)
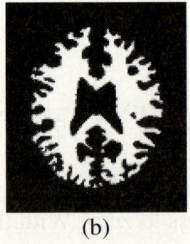
(b)
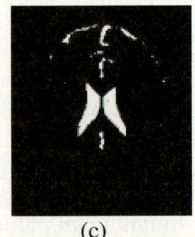
(c)

Fig. 4. Results of SHEM algorithm. (a) GM. (b) WM. (c) CSF.

In the experiment, we see both EM and SHEM spend the same iterations to accomplish the segmentation process and get the same results, however the proposed SHEM algorithm consumes less time than the standard EM algorithm. In this example, the standard EM algorithm spends 0.64 seconds in each iteration, while the corresponding time for SHEM algorithm is nearly 0.004 seconds. In this case, the SHEM algorithm converged approximately 160 times faster than the EM algorithm. Because most brain MR scans consist of more than 100 2D slices, the proposed SHEM algorithm can save significantly large computational time. Therefore, the clinical information can be provided more quickly than that of standard EM algorithm.

To test the performance of the proposed approach, we compared the method with the popular used fuzzy C-means (FCM) [11] algorithm to segment the MRI. The algorithm is implemented with the total number classes $C = 4$ and the weighting exponent $m = 2$. After convergence, the *maximum membership segmentation* is applied to each pixel of the image. The GM, WM and CSF results of FCM segmentation are shown in Fig.5 (a)-(c). Compared to the corresponding results in Fig.4 (a)-(c), it can be seen by FCM algorithm the results of CSF is over-segmented, WM is under-segmented, and GM on the top and bottom is somewhat under-segmented while in some other place over-segmented.

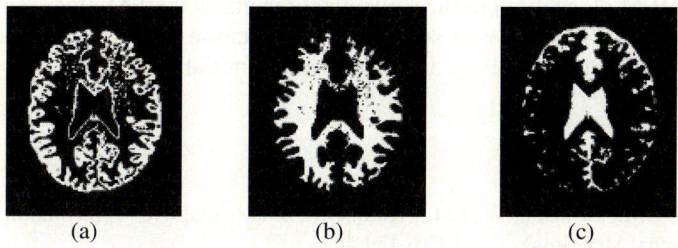

(a) (b) (c)

Fig. 5. Results of FCM segmentation. (a) GM. (b) WM. (c) CSF.

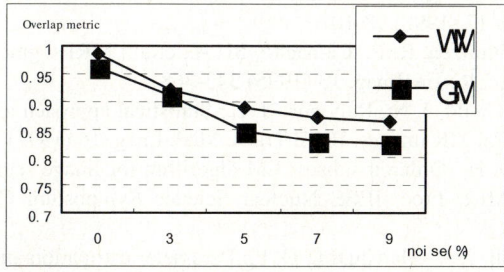

Fig. 6. Overlap metrics with different noise level for SHEM based segmentation on T1-weighted MR phantoms

Finally, to further quantitatively testify the performance the algorithm, our method is realized to segment the digital MR phantoms [10] with different noise level. Here in our experiments, we use the high-resolution T1-weighted MR phantoms with slice thickness of 1mm, no intensity inhomogeneites and 0-9% noises. To measure the segmentation accuracy, the overlap metric is utilized as the criteria. Larger metric means more similar for results. Fig. 6 gives the overlap metrics of WM and GW. It is satisfied that as the level of noise increases, the overlap metric of our algorithm gradually degrades that is because no spatial information is incorporated into the algorithm. However, it is important to note that at 0% noise level, the overlap metrics of both WM and GM are higher than 0.95, even if at 3% noise level, the corresponding over metrics are still higher than 0.90. The results presented here can prove that our method is effective and can obtain correct segmentation results at low noise level. Future work will focus on combining the spatial context into the algorithm to improve its robustness to noise while segmentation.

5 Conclusions

In this paper, a novel statistical approach based on an improved EM algorithm called SHEM algorithm for segmentation of the brain MRI is proposed and tested. After a preliminary processing, the four clusters' (GM, WM, CSF, BG) masks are extracted, which are served as *a priori* for the SHEM algorithm. The tissue regions of the image are satisfactorily segmented in this way, which demonstrates the method is effective. We compared our results with those of standard EM algorithm and FCM segmentation. The SHEM algorithm produces identical results as the EM algorithm with faster convergence. The SHEM based statistical segmentation outperformed the FCM segmentation on both the effectivity and robustness to initialization.

References

1. Wells, W. M., Grimson, W. E. L., Kikins, R., et al.: Adaptive segmentation of MRI data. IEEE Trans. Med. Imag. 15 (1996) 429-442
2. Held, K., Kops, E. R., Krause, B. J., et al.: Markov random field segmentation of brain MR images. IEEE Trans. Med. Imag. 16 (1997) 878-886
3. Atkins, M. S., Mackiewich, B. T.: Fully automatic segmentation of the brain in MRI. IEEE Trans. Med. Imag. 17 (1998) 98-107
4. Clarke, L. P., Velthuizen, R. P., Camacho, M. A., et al.: MRI segmentation: Methods and applications. Magn. Reson. Imag. 13 (1995) 343-368
5. Rajapakse, J. C., Giedd, J. N., Rapoport, J. L.: Statistical approach to segmentation of single-channel cerebral MR images. IEEE Trans. Med. Imag. 16 (1997) 176-186
6. Hashimoto, Kudo, H.: Ordered-subsets EM algorithm for image segmentation with application to brain MRI. Proc. IEEE Nuclear Science Symposium Conference Record. 3 (2000) 118- 121
7. Liang, Z., MacFall, J. R., Harrington, D. P.: Parameter estimation and tissue segmentation from multispectral MR images. IEEE Trans. Med. Imag. 13 (1994) 441-449
8. Dempster, P., Laird, N. M., Rubin, D. B.: Maximum-likelihood from incomplete data via the EM algorithm. J. Roy. Statist. Soc. 39 (1977) 1-38
9. Gerig, G., Kübler, O., Kikinis, R., et al.: Nonlinear anisotropic filtering of MRI data. IEEE Trans. Med. Imag. 11 (1992) 221-232
10. Collins, D. L., Zijdenbos, A. P., Kollokian, V., et al.: Design and construction of a realistic digital brain phantom. IEEE Trans. Med. Imag. 17 (1998) 463-468
11. Bezdek, J.: Pattern Recognition with Fuzzy Objective Functions Algorithms. New York: Plenum Press, (1981)

Process State and Progress Visualization Using Self-Organizing Map

Risto Hakala, Timo Similä, Miki Sirola, and Jukka Parviainen

Helsinki University of Technology,
Laboratory of Computer and Information Science,
P.O. Box 5400, FI-02015 HUT, Finland

Abstract. The self-organizing map (SOM) [1] is used in data analysis for resolving and visualizing nonlinear relationships in complex data. This paper presents an application of the SOM for depicting state and progress of a real-time process. A self-organizing map is used as a visual regression model for estimating the state configuration and progress of an observation in process data. The proposed technique is used for examining full-scope nuclear power plant simulator data. One aim is to depict only the most relevant information of the process so that interpretating process behaviour would become easier for plant operators. In our experiments, the method was able to detect a leakage situation in an early stage and it was possible to observe how the system changed its state as time went on.

1 Introduction

Understanding complex nonlinear systems is a problematic research area in information science. For instance, industrial processes are mostly too complex to be analyzed completely by analytical system models. Artificial neural networks (ANN) are able to acquire knowledge directly from data without an explicit physical model by resolving nonlinear input-output relationships in complex systems. The self-organizing map (SOM) [1] is an important ANN method that is based on competetitive, unsupervised learning. The SOM has been used in many engineering applications [2], e.g., in state identification and monitoring in process analysis [3]. The usability of the SOM method in decision support has also been discussed in our other study [4].

In control rooms, operators should be able to observe changes in the system and interpret these changes [5]. Therefore, it is worth considering how information is presented to the operator. A good presentation method should make the interpretation task easier by hiding unnecessary information of the system. Traditionally, display systems in power plants have been based on trend curves and mimic diagrams, with the measured values displayed as digits. These display methods are problematic, since it is hard to tell which information is more important than other. The SOM provides a technique for depicting system behaviour by hiding unnecessary information. In fact, the SOM may be used for hiding measurement values completely and visualizing how the process moves between predefined states. This is beneficial for providing an overall view of the system, as humans tend to describe system behaviour without exact measurement values. Hence, a part of the interpretation task can be performed automatically.

This paper presents a method for visualizing process state and progress using the SOM. We examine how a boiling water reactor nuclear power plant simulator run can be observed without actual measurement values. One aim is to be able to detect failures in the process in an early stage. The focus of this paper is in the methodology, and the experiment with simulator data is carried out to demonstrate the usability of the method.

2 Methods

Consider a process, which has p possible states where it can belong to with different degrees of membership, and the current state configuration depends on m process variables. Denote the ith observation of the variables by $x_i \in \mathbb{R}^m$ and states by $s_i \in \{s : \mathbf{1}^T s = 1, s \geq \mathbf{0}\} \subset \mathbb{R}^p$, both observed at time t_i. A high value of s_{ij} means that the process can mainly be determined by the jth state at time t_i. Suppose that we have a training data set consisting of process variables and states observed at some time instances $t_1, t_2, \ldots$

The goal is to explore what the process variables can tell us about the states and progress of the process based on the data. More formally, we fit a predictive model $(\hat{s}, \hat{t}) = F(x)$ and then analyse the shape of the function F. When a novel time series of variables $x(t)$ appears, the predictions of states $\hat{s}(t)$ and progress $\hat{t}(t)$ can be computed. We avoid using the term time since $\hat{t}$ is related to the time scale of the training data. Instead, by plotting $\hat{t}$ against the actual time t it is possible to follow the progress of a time series compared to the training data. Figure 1 depicts a situation, where a process starts near the first state and traverses toward the second one. Since the progress curve is pointing upward, the studied process moves in the same direction as the process used in training. A downward pointing curve would indicate progress in the opposite direction between the two processes.

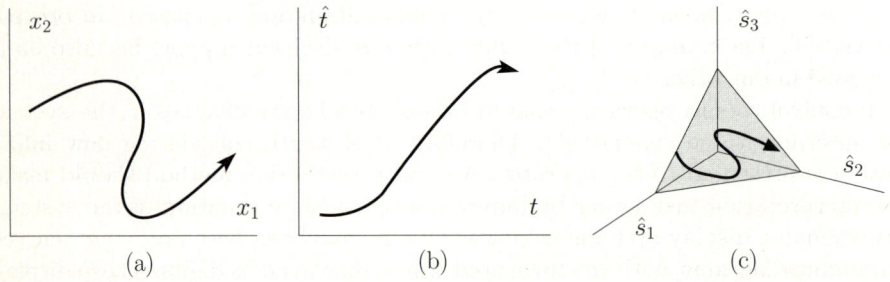

Fig. 1. Illustration of a process with $p = 3$ states and $m = 2$ process variables. (a) corresponds a time series of measurements $x(t)$, (b) estimated progress of the time series with respect to the training data $\hat{t}(t)$, and (c) estimated states $\hat{s}(t)$ in the time series.

Since the goal is rather explorative than predictive, we use a variant of the SOM to build the model F. The SOM has been successfully used as a visual regression model earlier [6,7]. Let $(\hat{s}_k, \hat{x}_k, \hat{t}_k)$ denote the prototype vector of the kth node and $\hat{r}_k$ its position in a low-dimensional lattice. The prototype vectors represent nodes of a grid in a multidimensional data space and the grid can be unfolded to form a visual lattice display. The algorithm iterates the following two steps. Firstly, pick a training data point (s_i, t_i, x_i) randomly and find the nearest node in the subspace of the process variables

$$c = \underset{k}{\operatorname{argmin}} \|x_i - \hat{x}_k\|. \tag{1}$$

Secondly, update the prototype vectors of all nodes

$$\begin{bmatrix} \hat{s}_k \\ \hat{t}_k \\ \hat{x}_k \end{bmatrix} \leftarrow \begin{bmatrix} \hat{s}_k \\ \hat{t}_k \\ \hat{x}_k \end{bmatrix} + h_{ck} \begin{bmatrix} s_i - \hat{s}_k \\ t_i - \hat{t}_k \\ x_i - \hat{x}_k \end{bmatrix}, \tag{2}$$

where the neighborhood function h_{ck} is a decreasing function of the distance $\|\hat{r}_c - \hat{r}_k\|$ in the lattice. We use a hexagonal 2D lattice and a Gaussian neighborhood function. For other possible choices, see [1].

Suppose that the state prototype vectors are initialized to the same plane, where the training data lie, i.e. $\hat{s}_k \in \{s : \mathbf{1}^T s = 1, s \geq \mathbf{0}\}$. Then they are there after the training process as well since the update (2) is always made along this plane. The main principal components of the data go through the plane and can, thus, be used in initialization. The prototype vectors $\hat{x}_k$ in the subspace of the process variables adapt in the same way as in the standard SOM [1], i.e. according to the joint distribution of the data. However, $\hat{s}_k$ and $\hat{t}_k$ are updated conditional on the nearest node found in the process variable space, which evokes regression. After the training process, the state configuration and progress of a novel observation x are estimated $F(x) = (\hat{s}_c, \hat{t}_c)$, where c refers to the node nearest to x according to (1). The training data should be able to be divided into continuous time periods so that each period represents one unique state. If the training data contains multiple separate time periods with similar process variable values, the progress variable $\hat{t}_k$ may get values that do not depict the corresponding state very well, which is unwanted. In other words, regression gives inaccurate results in such case.

The SOM can be applied in the visualization of multidimensional data in many ways. In this paper, we focus on the component plane representation [1], see Fig. 3. Each variable of the data space has its own plane, where the lattice is shown with a color-coding. The colors on a single plane fix the positions of the nodes in terms of the corresponding variable. By observing all the planes, we can analyze the grid in the multidimensional data space. Due to the topological ordering property of the SOM, nearby nodes in the lattice are nearby in the data space as well. The grid itself is static, and dynamical processes can be visualized by mapping the observations on the lattice sequentially, while also holding some of the past values, to form a trajectory similar to the one in Fig. 1.

3 Experiments

Data from a full-scope nuclear power plant (NPP) training simulator of Teollisuuden Voima Oy is used in the experiments. The two power plants and their simulator are located in Olkiluoto, Finland. In general, NPPs are classified into groups according to their reactor types. The Olkiluoto NPP is of the boiling water reactor (BWR) type. A BWR has a primary circuit, which contains a reactor vessel, a turbine, and a condenser. Water vaporizes into steam in the reactor vessel. The steam runs through the turbine and a part of the energy is converted into mechanical work, which drives the generator. The steam is then condensed back into water and pumped to the reactor core.

Abnormal events in NPPs are grouped into three categories [8]: (1) events caused by a pipe break or leakage in the primary system, (2) transients leading to imbalance between the rate of heat release and heat removal in the reactor, and (3) external events. In this paper, we concentrate on leakages, which were found out most interesting, as the possibilities to notice this type of events in an early stage are rather good.

To present how our visualization method works in practice, we utilized two data sets, which are denoted as Data set I and Data set II. Both data sets were collected from simulator runs at the Olkiluoto NPP. Data set I is used as a training data for the SOM. Equations (1) and (2) are used for training the SOM. After the training, we examine Data set II with the SOM-based model. The data sets were collected from fairly similar runs. Both runs begin in a normal operation state. After a while, a leakage happens in the high-pressure preheater and the process drifts into an abnormal state. The leakage leads to a bypass of the preheater, which is followed by a partial reactor shutdown and the reactor pressure drops dramatically. As a result of the bypass, feed water temperature starts to decrease. Finally, after a few minutes, happens a turbine and a reactor shutdown, which ends the runs. The run in Data set I progresses slightly slower than the run in Data set II. The leakage lasts approximately two minutes in Data set I and approximately one minute in Data set II.

Both data sets consist of $m = 9$ process variables, each observed once per second. In addition, $p = 4$ state variables have been assigned to each observation in the training data, so the data points can be described as $(\boldsymbol{s}_i, t_i, \boldsymbol{x}_i)$. The values for the process variables were collected from indicators located around the primary circuit. The indicators measured water level and pressure in the reactor, coolant temperature, feedwater flow and temperature. Also, power range in the reactor was monitored at four different spots. The state variables represent normal operation, leakage, partial reactor shutdown and (full) reactor shutdown. Figure 2 represents the time series of the state variables $\boldsymbol{s}_i$ in the training data. The values of $\boldsymbol{s}_i$ for each i have been normalized so that $\mathbf{1}^T \boldsymbol{s}_i = 1$, $\boldsymbol{s}_i \geq \mathbf{0}$ applies. Since it is not completely clear to which state the process belongs in the beginning of the leakage, a partial membership to the normal state and to the leakage state is used to depict this imprecision.

A component plane representation of the SOM is presented in Fig. 3. Component planes are completely static – trajectories [9] are used for depicting

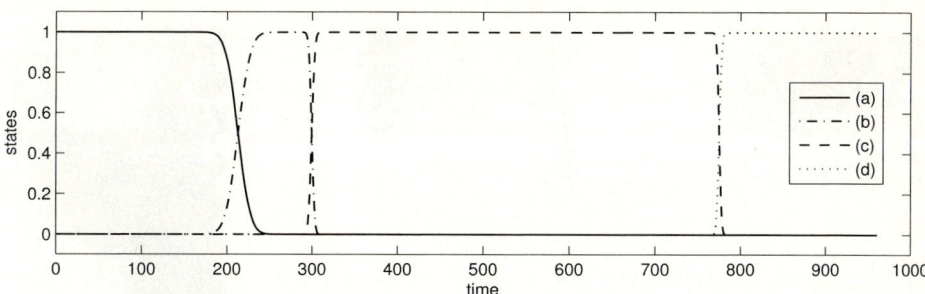

Fig. 2. The states s_i in Data set I as a function of time t. (a) corresponds normal state, (b) leakage state, (c) partial reactor shutdown state, and (d) reactor shutdown state.

behaviour of a dynamic system. Traditionally, trajectories are drawn on component planes that correspond process variables. This may appear complicated as there are usually many process variables in the data. The approach in this paper is different: only the component planes that represent a certain state in the process are used. Figure 3 shows how different parts of the SOM lattice represent different states. For example, a trajectory moving on the upper part of the SOM lattice depicts a process in a normal operation state. This type of representation hides values of the process variables $x(t)$ and can be thought as an abstraction level. Instead of observing how the process behaves based on values of $x(t)$, the operator can simply observe the predictions of states $\hat{s}(t)$. The sum of state values equals one like it does in the training data. This should help observing the process, as it is not possible for an observation to belong to multiple states with a high degree of membership. The progress plane can be used for observing how the process progresses compared to the training data. A trajectory moving toward darker areas on the progress plane indicates that the corresponding process progresses to the same direction as the training data.

As an example, Data set II is examined with the trained SOM. The trajectory in Fig. 3 depicts a sequence of observations in Data set II estimated with the SOM-based model. Clearly, the process starts in the normal state and progresses to the leakage state and then to the partial reactor shutdown state. Just by observing the normal state plane it is possible to follow when the process drifts away from normal operation state. The advantage of this method is in real-time observation: history and current development of the process can be quickly seen on the state planes. Hence, the proposed method provides an overall view of the system. The progress and state values can also be plotted. Figure 4 depicts predicted values of the whole run and shows also that the run ends in the reactor shutdown state. The progress speed compared to the training data can be determined by plotting values of $\hat{t}(t)$. If the curve grows faster than t in the training data, then the process also progresses relatively faster. The leakage in Data set II starts at 121 seconds from the beginning. This is also when the leakage starts according to Fig. 4.

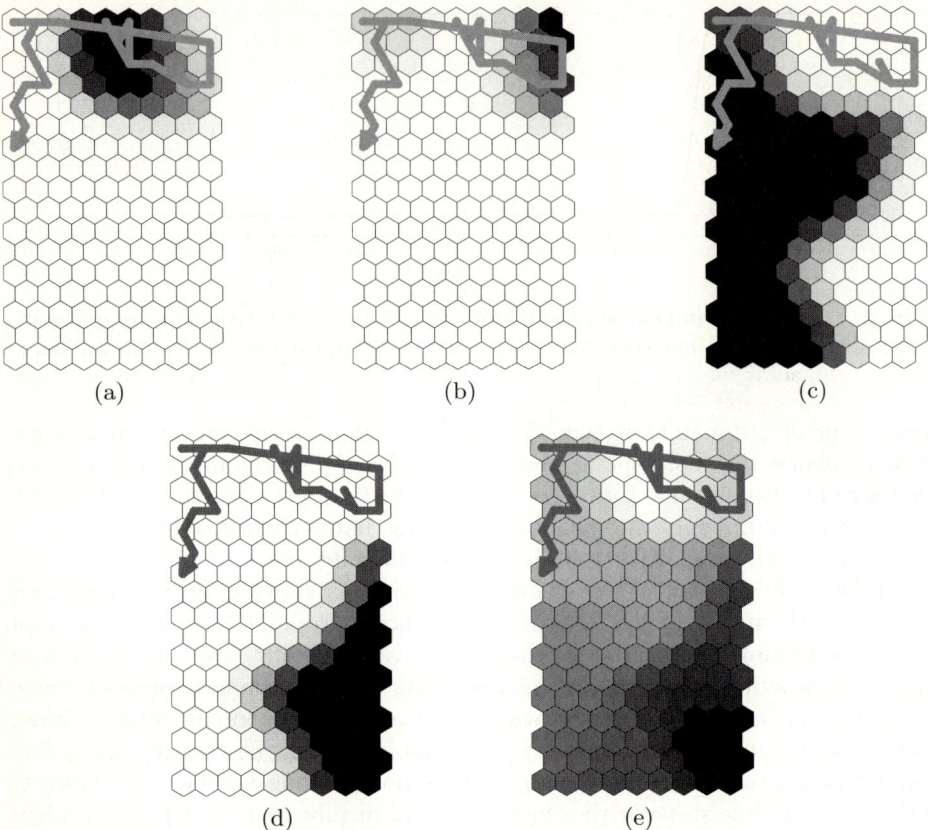

Fig. 3. A component plane representation of the trained SOM. Only component planes corresponding (a) normal state, (b) leakage state, (c) partial reactor shutdown state, (d) reactor shutdown state, and (e) progress are displayed. Dark color on a cell indicates high component value. The trajectory depicts a sequence of observations $x(100)$–$x(250)$ from Data set II mapped on the SOM. The process starts in the normal state and progresses to the partial reactor shutdown state.

4 Conclusions

In this study, we examined application of the SOM to process state monitoring. The SOM is used as a visual regression model to predict the state and progress of a process based on actual process data. The purpose is to depict a complex process so that it would be easily observable for plant operator. Rather than visualizing a set of process variables, the prediction of state and progress are visualized. We used the proposed method to analyze boiling water reactor nuclear power plant simulator data.

To present how the method can be used in practice, we utilized two data sets that had been obtained from the simulator. Both data sets represent fairly similar runs. The first data set was used as a training data for the SOM, which

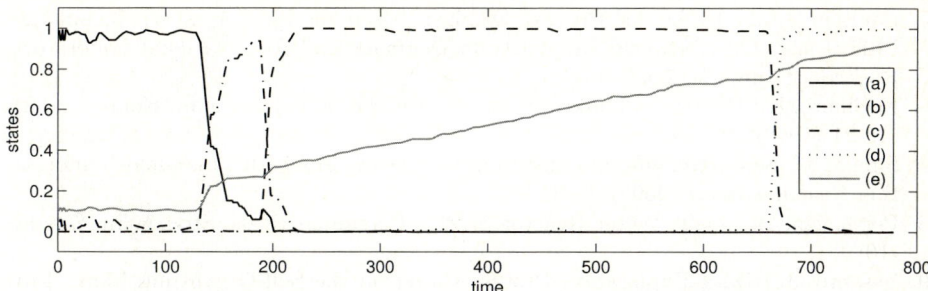

Fig. 4. A 10-second running average of the predictions of state and progress for Data set II. (a) corresponds normal state, (b) leakage state, (c) partial reactor shutdown state, (d) reactor shutdown state, and (e) progress. The values of $\hat{t}(t)$ have been scaled so that they are plotted relatively on the same scale as values of t in the training data but between $[0, 1]$. Also, the sum of state values for each t equals one as in the training data.

was then used as a predictive model. We examined the dynamic behaviour of the run in the second data set by mapping a sequence of measurements on the trained SOM. The mapped values were displayed as a trajectory on component planes. This makes it possible for a plant operator to observe process state and progress in real-time. We were able to detect a leakage situation in an early stage and observe how the system changed its state as time went on.

The strength of the proposed method is in hiding unnecessary information from the operator. This is an important requirement for display systems as the operator should not be exposed to confusing amount of information. With the proposed method, measurement values are hidden completely and the process is depicted in more intelligible terms. Therefore, the operator may observe an overall view of the system easily. A similar idea has been used before, when displays for control rooms have been designed. For example, a polar plot of selected variables shows deviations in process behaviour clearly, since the polar graph becomes asymmetric in such case [5]. A polar graph does not, however, preserve history of the process behaviour. Neither does it show the state of the process in simple terms. With the proposed method, it is possible not only to determine the state, but also to see how the process reached the state.

References

1. Kohonen, T.: Self-Organizing Maps. 3rd edn. Volume 30 of Springer Series in Information Sciences. Springer, Berlin, Heidelberg, New York (2001)
2. Simula, O., Vesanto, J., Vasara, P., Helminen, R.R.: Self-organizing map in industry analysis. In: Industrial Applications of Neural Networks. CRC Press (1999) 87–112
3. Alhoniemi, E., Hollmén, J., Simula, O., Vesanto, J.: Process monitoring and modeling using the self-organizing map. Integrated Computer-Aided Engineering **6** (1999) 3–14
4. Sirola, M., Lampi, G., Parviainen, J.: SOM based decision support in failure management. International Scientific Journal of Computing **3** (2005) 124–130

5. Paulsen, J.L.: Design of Process Displays based on Risk Analysis Techniques. PhD thesis, The Technical University of Denmark and Risø National Laboratory, Roskilde, Denmark (2004)
6. Kiviluoto, K.: Predicting bankruptcies with the self-organizing map. Neurocomputing **21** (1998) 191–201
7. Similä, T.: Self-organizing map learning nonlinearly embedded manifolds. Information Visualization **4** (2005) 22–31
8. Pershagen, B.: Light Water Reactor Safety. Pergamon Press, Stockholm, Sweden (1989)
9. Vesanto, J.: Data Exploration Process Based on the Self-Organizing Map. PhD thesis, Helsinki University of Technology, Espoo, Finland (2002)

Exploiting Spatio–temporal Data for the Multiobjective Optimization of Cellular Automata Models

Giuseppe A. Trunfio

DAP – University of Sassari
Palazzo del Pou Salit, Piazza Duomo, 6, I07041 Alghero (SS), Italy
trunfio@uniss.it

Abstract. The increased availability of remotely sensed spatio-temporal data offers the chance to improve the reliability of an important class of Cellular Automata (CA) models used for the simulation of real complex systems. To this end, this paper proposes a multiobjective approach, based on a genetic algorithm, which can present some significant advantages if compared with standard single-objective optimizations. The method exploits the available temporal sequences of spatial data in order to produce CAs which are non-dominated with respect to multiple objectives. The latter represent, in different metrics, the level of agreement between the simulated and real spatio-temporal processes. The set of non-dominated CAs proves to be a valuable source of information about potentialities and limits of a specific CA model structure.

1 Introduction

Modern Cellular Automata (CA) models allow for the simulation of the dynamic evolution of a large class of complex systems, incorporating knowledge from various sources. For this reason, they are considered a valuable tool in many scientific fields, including ecology, biology, geology, medicine, urban studies and many others. CAs are discrete dynamical systems, which can be thought as an n-dimensional lattice of cells, each one embedding an identical finite automaton. The cell state changes according to the finite automaton transition function, the input of which is constituted by the states of some neighbouring cells and of the cell itself. The CA initial configuration is defined by the finite automata states at time $t = 0$. The global behaviour of the system emerges, step by step, as a consequence of the simultaneous application of the transition function to each cell of the cellular space.

A CA model can be built to simulate the dynamic evolution over time and space of a real system, the evolution of which emerges from the local interactions of its constituent parts. Often, the final aim is to perform predictive tasks, that is, given an initial configuration, to predict the final one at a certain future instant of time. In most models of this kind [1,2,3,4]: (*i*) each cell corresponds to a portion of a real space (e.g. a location on the Earths surface); (*ii*) the states of the cell correspond to spatial characteristics which are important to the model (e.g. slope, temperature); (*iii*) the transition function models some local interactions among the system components; and (*iv*) each CA step corresponds to an interval of time.

The reliability of CA-based predictive models is maximized by some standard procedures, such as *model optimization*. Broadly speaking, model optimization is the process by which the transition function is defined in all its aspects (e.g. numerical values are assigned to the model parameters), in such a way that the model accurately reproduces some real spatio-temporal patterns. Since the availability of spatio-temporal data has increased dramatically in recent years, mainly due to the growth of satellite remote sensing and other technologies, the CA optimization phase has been correspondingly the object of deep investigations. Essentially, most research efforts have been addressed at achieving better CA models, in terms of reliability, accuracy and efficiency, adopting some kind of information extraction from the temporal sequences of spatial data concerning the real system. In particular, after an earlier phase of manually-optimized models, it was recognized that a formal, well-structured and automated optimization procedure was particularly necessary for models used in real forecasting applications. At present, many techniques have been used to automatically exploit spatio-temporal sequences for CA optimizations. Among these can be found techniques based on exhaustive search [2], as well as intelligent machine-learning approaches based on Artificial Neural Networks [3,5,6], Decision Tree learning [4] and Genetic Algorithms (GAs) [1,7]. The specific approach used is strictly related to the particular form assumed for the transition function. For example, there are parameter-dependent transition functions, for which GAs are frequently used to find the optimal set of parameters.

In this paper a multiobjective approach, based on a GA, is suggested to exploit the available spatio-temporal sequences with the purpose of optimizing CA models. The difference from existing applications [1,7], where single-objective GAs have been used, lies in the simultaneous consideration of different fitness measures. This is accomplished on the basis of the concept of dominance [8], which resolves in the production of a set of candidate non-dominated solutions. It will be shown that the multiobjective approach can lead to a better exploitation of the data, providing significant advantages to the whole modelling process.

2   A Parameterized CA Modelling Approach

One of the most common CA-based modelling approaches is based on a generalization of the classical CA formulation, where the states of the cell are represented by the values of numeric variables. Moreover, in many applications of the method the transition function is parameter-dependent.

In particular, in such CA models a d-dimensional domain $\mathcal{D} \in \mathbb{R}^d$ is discretized in n cells. The set $D = \{\mathbf{c}_1, \mathbf{c}_2, ..., \mathbf{c}_n\}$ collects the n cells in terms of d-dimensional index vectors $\mathbf{c}_i \in \mathbb{Z}^d$ representing space sites. Every relevant characteristic, relative to the space portion corresponding to a given cell, is described as a scalar variable s_i belonging to a nonempty set $\mathcal{R}(s_i)$ [9]. Thus, each cell $\mathbf{c}$ corresponds to a vector *state* $\mathbf{s} = \mathbf{s}(\mathbf{c}) = [s_1, \ldots, s_m]^T$ belonging to the set $\mathcal{R}(s_1) \times \cdots \times \mathcal{R}(s_m)$.

Given a generic set of cells $Y \subseteq D$, with $|Y| = k$, the $m \times k$ matrix $\boldsymbol{\Omega}_Y$ is defined, the columns of which are the vectors $\mathbf{u}(\mathbf{c}_j), \forall \mathbf{c}_j \in Y$. The matrix $\boldsymbol{\Omega}_Y$ is called the *configuration* of Y. In the following, the configuration of the whole automaton, that is $\boldsymbol{\Omega}_Y$ with $Y \equiv D$, will be simply indicated by $\boldsymbol{\Omega}$.

The states of the cells in the set $D_A \subset D$ of *active cells* simultaneously evolve in discrete steps. To each $\mathbf{c} \in D_A$ a set $N \subset D$ called *neighbourhood* is associated; the states of the cells belonging to N can influence the evolution of $\mathbf{s}(\mathbf{c})$. At each time-step the state of a cell is updated using the *transition function* φ, which encapsulates the mechanism upon which the discrete dynamic model evolves. The function φ depends on the current neighbourhood configuration $\boldsymbol{\Omega}_N$ and, in most CA models, on a vector of parameters $\mathbf{p} = [p_1, \ldots, p_r]^T$. Each parameter p_i, which is constant in time and space, belongs to a set of definition $\mathcal{P}(p_i)$. Thus, the updated cell's state is given by:

$$\mathbf{s}^{(t+1)} = \varphi(\boldsymbol{\Omega}_N^{(t)}; \mathbf{p}) \tag{1}$$

where the superscripts refer to the time step. All of the local transition functions (1), acting simultaneously on each cell, can be thought as an overall transition function Φ which acts on the entire automaton and gives the global configuration at the step $t + 1$ as:

$$\boldsymbol{\Omega}^{(t+1)} = \Phi(\boldsymbol{\Omega}^{(t)}, \mathbf{p}) \tag{2}$$

Thus, the iterative application of the function Φ to the successive configurations, starting from an initial one $\boldsymbol{\Omega}^{(0)}$, leads to the dynamic process

$$\boldsymbol{\Omega}^{(0)} \xrightarrow{\Phi} \boldsymbol{\Omega}^{(1)} \xrightarrow{\Phi} \cdots \xrightarrow{\Phi} \boldsymbol{\Omega}^{(t)} \tag{3}$$

representing the automaton evolution. For a given set $Y \subseteq D$ we can write

$$\boldsymbol{\Omega}^{(t)} = \Phi^t(\boldsymbol{\Omega}^{(0)}, \mathbf{p}) \tag{4}$$

expressing the automaton configuration at the time step t as a function of both the initial configuration and the parameters, with the other automaton characteristics (i.e. the model structure) being fixed.

3 Multiobjective Model Optimization

Eq. (3) shows that the dynamic process depends on both the initial configuration and the vector of parameters. With respect to the latter, the model can be optimized to maximise the correspondence, expressed by proper measures of accuracy, between the simulated patterns and the real ones.

To formalize the problem, let us suppose the existence of spatio-temporal datasets collecting some automaton configurations, which come from experiments of the real system behaviour. Let each dataset $\tilde{\mathcal{V}}$ be composed by a series of q automaton configurations:

$$\bar{\mathcal{V}} = \{<\bar{\boldsymbol{\Omega}}^{(0)}, \tau_0>, <\bar{\boldsymbol{\Omega}}^{(1)}, \tau_1>, \ldots, <\bar{\boldsymbol{\Omega}}^{(q)}, \tau_q>\} \tag{5}$$

where the attribute τ_i indicates the instant of time in which the configuration $\bar{\boldsymbol{\Omega}}^{(i)}$ is known. Starting from the configuration $\bar{\boldsymbol{\Omega}}^{(0)}$, and given a vector $\mathbf{p}$ of parameters, the process (3) can be executed for the computation of the $q-1$ automaton configurations:

$$\mathcal{V} = \{\boldsymbol{\Omega}^{(1)}, \ldots, \boldsymbol{\Omega}^{(q)}\} \tag{6}$$

where $\boldsymbol{\Omega}^{(j)} = \Phi^j(\bar{\boldsymbol{\Omega}}^{(0)}, \mathbf{p})$. Thus, the optimization process consists of the determination of a proper value of the vector $\mathbf{p}$, which leads to the best agreement between the real spatio-temporal sequence (5) and the simulated one (6). In many applications it is desirable that the model reproduces different aspects of the real system evolution in space and time. Thus, in general, r measures of fitness are defined:

$$\theta_i = \Theta_i\left(\bar{\mathcal{V}}, \mathcal{V}\right) = \Theta_i\left(\bar{\mathcal{V}}, \mathbf{p}\right) \qquad i = 1, \ldots, r \tag{7}$$

Each function Θ_i corresponds to an optimization objective and accounts for a specific aspect of the agreement between simulated and real patterns. Clearly, optimization of the model to one of the multiple objectives does not guarantee accurate simulations with respect to the other objectives. Optimization to multiple targets is typically done by combining the multiple objectives into a single one. To this end, often, multiplicative (e.g. [2,7]) or additive weighted aggregations are used. However, the selection of the aggregation method is largely subjective and can significantly affect the optimal parameter values.

The alternative proposed in this paper is to conduct a full multiobjective optimization that identifies a set of non-dominated or Pareto solutions [8] within a single optimization run. In particular, the optimization is done using a multiobjective Genetic Algorithm (GA). The GA is used to evolve a randomly initialized population, whose generic *chromosome* is a vector encoding an r-dimensional vector of parameters $\mathbf{p}$. The i-th element of the chromosome is obtained as the binary encoding of the parameter p_i, using a suitable number of bits and its set of definition $\mathcal{P}(p_i)$. Each chromosome can be decoded in a vector of parameters $\mathbf{p}$ and, through performing a CA simulation, the objective functions can be computed.

In the multiobjective GA, to avoid the aggregation of multiple objectives, the comparison of two candidate solutions, with respect to different objectives, is achieved through the concepts of Pareto optimality and dominance. In particular, we say that a solution $\mathbf{p}^*$ (strongly) *dominates* the solution $\mathbf{p}$ if:

$$\forall i : \Theta_i\left(\bar{\mathcal{V}}, \mathbf{p}^*\right) \geq \Theta_i\left(\bar{\mathcal{V}}, \mathbf{p}\right) \quad \wedge \quad \exists j : \Theta_j\left(\bar{\mathcal{V}}, \mathbf{p}^*\right) > \Theta_j\left(\bar{\mathcal{V}}, \mathbf{p}\right) \tag{8}$$

In other words, $\mathbf{p}^*$ dominates $\mathbf{p}$ if $\mathbf{p}^*$ is better or equivalent to $\mathbf{p}$ with respect to all objectives, and better in at least one objective. A non-dominated solution is optimal in the Pareto sense (i.e. no criterion can be improved without worsening at least one other criterion). Rather than a single solution, a search based on such a definition of optimum produces a set of non-dominated solutions.

The adopted multiobjective GA is the well known NSGA-II [10], which has been extensively investigated and successfully tested. The NSGA-II algorithm is based on the idea of transforming the objectives to a single fitness measure by the creation of a number of fronts, sorted according to non-domination. The fronts are created using a 'non-dominated sorting' procedure, which works as follows: (*i*) all non-dominated individuals in the current population are inserted in the first front, which corresponds to the highest fitness; (*ii*) these individuals are virtually removed from the population and the next set of non-dominated individuals are inserted in a second front, corresponding to the second-highest fitness; (*iii*) the phases *i-ii* are reiterated until all of the individuals have been assigned a fitness. When each front has been created, its members are assigned so-called *crowding distances* (i.e., normalized distance to closest neighbors in the front in objective space), to be used in the next phase with the objective of promoting an uniform sampling of the Pareto set.

In the NSGA-II algorithm, selection is performed by binary tournaments [10], where the individual with the lowest front number wins. If the solutions come from the same front, the one with the highest crowding distance wins, since a high distance to the closest neighbors indicates that the solution is located in a sparsely populated part of the front. If N is the size of the population, in each generation N new individuals are generated trough a standard crossover with a predefined probability p_c. Then, a mutation with a probability p_m is applied to each offspring at each position in the chromosome. The algorithm is elitist, in the sense that out of the $2N$ individuals, the best N individuals are kept for the next generation.

4 An Application Example

The multiobjective optimization approach has been applied in conjunction with SLEUTH, which is one of the most popular CA models for the simulation, as a diffusion process, of urban growth and related land use changes over time [2,11]. The program name comes from the GIS data layers that are required as input to the model: Slope, Landuse, Exclusion layer, Urban, Transportation, and Hillshade. SLEUTH has been widely applied [11], showing good capacity of forecasting landscape changes. The adopted CA uses square cells, with a neighborhood of eight cells. The cell states account for some static characteristics, corresponding to the GIS data layers above cited, as well as dynamic characteristics, that is, urbanization condition and land-use class. The transition function depends on five integer parameters, which belong in the interval $[1, \ldots, 100]$. Namely, they are: *Diffusion*, which determines the overall dispersiveness of the urbanization; *Breed*, which expresses the likelihood that a new isolated urban cell will start its own growth cycle; *Spread*, which controls the diffusion by contagion from existing urbanized cells; *Slope Resistance*, which influences the likelihood of new urbanization on steep slopes; and *Road Gravity*, which regulates the generation of new urbanization towards and along roads.

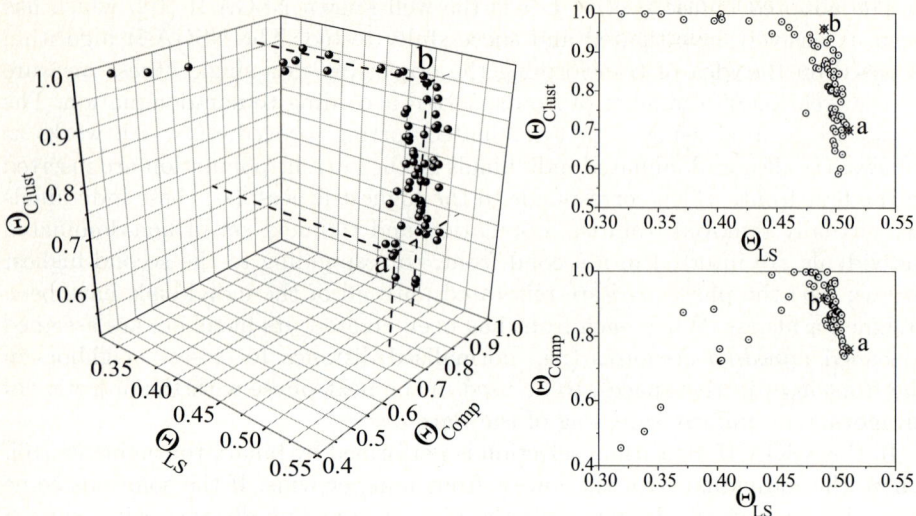

Fig. 1. The set of computed non-dominated solutions in the space of the objective functions. The selected solutions are labelled.

In order to perform predictive tasks, the parameters of SLEUTH must be optimized for a specific scenario, given the required GIS layers for some control years in the past. The goal of optimization is to determine which of the 100^5 possible combinations of parameters gives a specific urban region the best agreement between the historical citys real extent and shape and the simulated ones. To measure the "goodness-of-fit", SLEUTH makes available 12 spatial metrics. Each metric gives a different measure of the optimizations fit relative to the historical spatio-temporal data provided. For the model optimization, the authors recommend using a kind of "brute force" method, which consists of a methodical, but computationally expensive, exploration of the the parameter space. As an alternative, a single-objective Genetic Algorithm was successfully experimented [7]. In both cases, existing applications use either a single fitness measure or the product of some selected measures.

Instead, in the present application SLEUTH has been coupled with the NSGA-II algorithm, and three fitness measures (i.e. objectives) have been selected for conducting a multiobjective optimization. The spatio-temporal data set used in this preliminary test is that which is distributed with the program source code [11], and it concerns a hypothetical city. It is composed of the GIS data layers required by the model in four control years, namely in 1930, 1950, 1970 and 1990. During the genetic optimization, the three objectives have to be computed for each individual (i.e. vector of parameters) in the population. To this end, a run of SLEUTH is performed, starting from the older scenario (i.e. 1930) and assuming that each CA time step corresponds to one year. At the end of the simulation, the three objectives are computed using the CA outcomes and the GIS layers corresponding to the remaining three control years (i.e. 1950, 1970, 1990), according to Eq. 7. In particular, the three spatial metrics were:

- $\Theta_{LS} = (U_m \cap U_a)/(U_m \cup U_a)$, where U_m is the modelled and U_a the actual urbanized area. This shape index [12] measures the spatial fit between the model's growth and the known urban extent for the control years;
- $\Theta_{Comp} = [$ if $u_m < u_a$ then (u_m/u_a) else $(1 - u_m/u_a)]$, where u_m is the modelled number of urbanized cells for the last control year, while u_a is the correspondent quantity for the actual scenario;
- Θ_{Clust}, defined as the least squares regression score (r^2) for the number of modeled urban clusters compared to known urban clusters;

For all objectives the value of one, indicates an exact match of model outcomes to the real spatio-temporal sequence, while a value below one indicates no match.

The NSGA-II algorithm was executed using the settings experimented in [10] for a wide range of tests, that is, a population of $N = 100$ individuals, crossover probability $p_c = 0.9$, and mutation probability $p_m = 1/\ell$, where ℓ is the number of bits in the chromosome.

The non-dominated set obtained after 150 generation is represented in Fig. 1. It shows that Θ_{LS} ranges in the interval $[0.32, 0.51]$, Θ_{Comp} in the interval $[0.46, 0.99]$ and Θ_{Clust} in the interval $[0.59, 0.99]$. Two solutions were selected from the non-dominated set (see also Table 1). The first one, labelled with the letter a, leads to the best value of the metric Θ_{LS}, which is important for measuring the spatial matching. On the other hand, such a value of Θ_{LS} can be achieved, at the price of having relatively low values of the other metrics considered, that is, $\Theta_{Comp} = 0.76$ and $\Theta_{Clust} = 0.70$. The second solution, labelled with the letter b, leads to a lower value of Θ_{LS} but better values of Θ_{Comp} and Θ_{Clust}. Fig. 2 shows the final (i.e. 1990) urbanization patterns obtained through the two non-dominated CAs, compared with the actual one. In the case examined, there are solutions offering a good compromise among all objectives (e.g. the solution b). This means that the model can reproduce the actual phenomenon with good performances, even considering all three of the metrics. This might not always be the case. Indeed, significant trade-offs in fitting two or more objectives may indicate an error in the model structure (e.g. a relevant physical process may not be accounted for in the transition function). In this sense the multiobjective approach can provide useful information about the model, exploiting the available historical data about the real system.

Table 1. The characteristics of the selected solutions

Solution	Θ_{LS}	Θ_{Comp}	Θ_{Clust}	Dispersion	Breed	Spread	Slope	Road Gravity
a	0.51	0.76	0.70	1	2	14	4	12
b	0.49	0.92	0.96	1	4	17	15	32

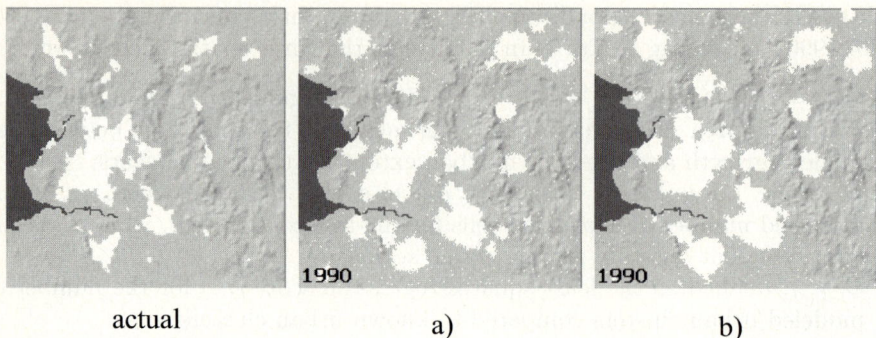

Fig. 2. The actual final urbanization pattern compared with those produced by the selected non-dominated CAs

5 Conclusions and Future Work

In existing GA-based optimizations of CA, modellers use either a single fitness measure [1,13] or the combination of some selected measures [2,14]. For example in the SLEUTH optimization exercise presented in [7], which was based on a single-objective GA, the metric of fit was comprised of the product of three spatial metrics: Θ_{LS}, Θ_{Clust} and Θ_{Urb}, the latter being a measure of agreement on the number of urban cells. The population was comprised of 18 chromosomes and the optimization took 200 generations. As result of the computation, a combination of values of parameters which leads to a good value of the composite fitness measure was found. Even if the multiobjective example presented in this paper refers to a different urban region, a comparison and some general considerations can be made. In particular, the computational requirements are roughly of the same order of magnitude. Nevertheless, in the single-objective approach the result of the optimization consists of a single value of the vector of parameters, whereas the multiobjective optimization provides a set of non-dominated solutions (i.e. non-dominated CAs). The latter explicitly represent trade-offs among the various objectives. Thus, the solution eventually chosen can be attained by examining and exploring the full range of possibilities offered by the CA model. For example, non-dominated solutions show explicitly to what extent a single metric can contribute to a composite fitness, allowing the modeller to choose with awareness and to learn something more, with respect to the single-objective case, about the CA model. In other words, the set of non-dominated solutions offers a representation rich in valuable information about the CA model, thereby potentially leading to better optimizations and improved understanding of the model potentialities and limits. Besides, no arbitrary combination of the different metrics is required by the multiobjective optimization, since they are treated independently.

On the other hand, the proposed approach is suitable only when the agreement between actual and simulated spatio-temporal patterns is expressed in terms of multiple metrics (i.e. objectives), each accounting for a different aspect of the simulated phenomenon. In addition, in the multiobjective approach the final choice of the preferred solution could be difficult, especially when dealing with many objectives and high number of non-dominated solutions.

Further work could be addressed in experimenting with different search heuristics, in order to provide non-dominated sets of better quality. Moreover, in the future, the approach should be tested on different CAs and datasets.

References

1. Spataro, W., D'Ambrosio, D., Rongo, R., Trunfio, G.A.: An evolutionary approach for modelling lava flows through cellular automata. In: ACRI 2004. Volume 3305 of LNCS. (2004) 725–734
2. Clarke, K., Hoppen, S., Gaydos, L.: A self-modifying cellular automaton model of historical urbanization in the San Francisco bay area. Environment and Planning B-Planning and Design **24** (1997) 247–261
3. Yeh, A.G.O., Li, X.: Neural-network-based cellular automata for simulating multiple land use changes using GIS. Int. Journal of Geogr. Inf. Science **16** (2002) 323–343
4. Li, X., Yeh, A.G.O.: Data mining of cellular automata's transition rules. International Journal of Geographical Information Science **18** (2004) 723–744
5. Yeh, A.G.O., Li, X.: Simulation of development alternatives using neural networks, cellular automata, and GIS for urban planning. Photog. Eng. & Remote Sensing **69** (2003) 1043–1052
6. Trunfio, G.A.: Enhancing cellular automata by an embedded generalized multi-layer perceptron. In: Artificial Neural Networks: Biological Inspirations. Volume 3696 of Lecture Notes in Computer Science. (2005) 343–348
7. Goldstein, N.C.: Brains vs. brawn comparative strategies for the calibration of a cellular automata based urban growth model. In: Proceedings of the 7th International Conference on GeoComputation. (2003)
8. Pareto, V.: Cours d'Economie Politique. Volume I, II. F. Rouge, Lausanne (1896)
9. Di Gregorio, S., Serra, R.: An empirical method for modelling and simulating some complex macroscopic phenomena by cellular automata. Future Generation Computer Systems **16** (1999) 259–271
10. Deb, K., Agrawal, S., Pratap, A., Meyarivan, T.: A fast and elitist multiobjective genetic algorithm: NSGA-II. IEEE Trans. Evol. Comp. **6** (2002) 182–197
11. Project Gigalopolis, NCGIA: http://www.ncgia.ucsb.edu/projects/gig/. (2003)
12. Lee, D., Sallee, G.: A method of measuring shape. Geographical Review **60** (1970) 555–563
13. Yang, X., Lo, C.: Modelling urban growth and landscape change in the Atlanta metropolitan area. International Journal of Geographical Information Science **17** (2003) 463–488
14. Silva, E., Clarke, K.: Calibration of the sleuth urban growth model for Lisbon and Porto, Portugal. Computers, Environment and Urban Systems **26** (2002) 525–552

Comparing Support Vector Machines and Feed-forward Neural Networks with Similar Parameters

Enrique Romero[1] and Daniel Toppo[2]

[1] Departament de Llenguatges i Sistemes Informàtics
Universitat Politècnica de Catalunya, Barcelona, Spain
`eromero@lsi.upc.edu`
[2] I&C School of Computer and Communication Sciences
Swiss Federal Institute of Technology, Onex, Switzerland
`daniel.toppo@epfl.ch`

Abstract. From a computational point of view, the main differences between SVMs and FNNs are (1) how the number of elements of their respective solutions (SVM-support vectors/FNN-hidden units) is selected and (2) how the (both hidden-layer and output-layer) weights are found. Sequential FNNs, however, do not show all of these differences with respect to SVMs, since the number of hidden units is obtained as a consequence of the learning process (as for SVMs) rather than fixed *a priori*. In addition, there exist sequential FNNs where the hidden-layer weights are always a subset of the data, as usual for SVMs. An experimental study on several benchmark data sets, comparing several aspects of SVMs and the aforementioned sequential FNNs, is presented. The experiments were performed in the (as much as possible) same conditions for both models. Accuracies were found to be very similar. Regarding the number of support vectors, sequential FNNs constructed models with less hidden units than SVMs. In addition, all the hidden-layer weights in the FNN models were also considered as support vectors by SVMs. The computational times were lower for SVMs, with absence of numerical problems.

1 Introduction

Support Vector Machines (SVMs) and Feed-forward Neural Networks (FNNs) are two alternative Machine Learning frameworks for classification and regression problems with different inductive bias and very interesting properties [1,2].

However, although both schemes have been developed from very different starting points of view, they share a number of elements that allow to make a direct correspondence between their respective obtained solutions. In fact, they are structurally identical, since both SVMs and FNNs induce a function which is expressed as a linear combination of simpler functions: $f(x) = b + \sum_{k=1}^{N} \lambda_k h(\omega_k, x)$. For SVMs, N is the number of support vectors, h is the kernel function, $\{\omega_k\}_{k=1}^{N}$ are the support vectors and $\{\lambda_k\}_{k=1}^{N}$ are the coefficients found by the constrained optimization problem posed. For FNNs (fully connected with one hidden layer of units and output linear units), N is the number of units in the hidden layer, h is the activation function, $\{\omega_k\}_{k=1}^N$ are the hidden-layer weights and $\{\lambda_k\}_{k=1}^N$ are the output-layer weights.

The differences between the solutions obtained by both models lie in the way the elements of that linear combination are found. This is a consequence of their respective inductive bias. The first important difference is related to the number of elements in the combination (number of support vectors for SVMs and number of hidden units for FNNs). Whereas for SVMs the number of support vectors is also a consequence of the optimization problem posed, for FNNs the number of hidden units is usually fixed *a priori*. A second difference lies in the hidden-layer weights $\{\omega_k\}_{k=1}^N$. For SVMs, they are always a subset of the data (the support vectors), as a consequence of the optimization problem posed. For FNNs, in contrast, that property does not usually hold. Finally, the values of the output-layer weights $\{\lambda_k\}_{k=1}^N$ may be very different, since both schemes solve different optimization problems (the maximization of the margin for SVMs and the minimization of the sum-of-squares error for FNNs).

There exist, however, FNN models [3,4,5] that do not show all of these differences with respect to SVMs. On the one hand, the architecture is sequentially constructed, so that the number of hidden units is a consequence of the learning process rather than fixed *a priori*. On the other hand, the hidden-layer weights are always a subset of the data, as usual for SVMs. Indeed, the may use kernels as activation functions. For a review of sequential FNNs see, for example, [6].

This work focuses on the aforementioned sequential FNNs schemes and their comparison with SVMs. An experimental study on several benchmark data sets, comparing several aspects of these learning models, namely the accuracy of the obtained solutions, the quantity and quality of the support vectors and the computational cost, is presented. The experiments were performed in the (as much as possible) same conditions for both models. To this end, the same activation functions were tested with the same training and test data sets, so that the set of simple functions $\{h(\omega_k, x)\}$ available to construct the solution was the same for both models.

These experiments can be seen as a comparison of the respective inductive bias of SVMs and FNNs when both models are restricted to use similar kernels and hidden-layer weights. Accuracies were found to be very similar. Regarding the number of support vectors, sequential FNNs construct models with less hidden units than SVMs. In addition, all the hidden-layer weights in the FNN models were also considered as support vectors by SVMs. In contrast, the computational times were lower for SVMs, with absence of numerical problems.

2 Background

In order to fix the notation, consider the classification task given by a data set $X = \{(x_1, y_1), \ldots, (x_L, y_L)\}$, where each instance x_i belongs $\mathbb{R}^N$, $y_i \in \{-1, +1\}^T$, and T is the number of classes. For 2-class problems, usually $y_i \in \{-1, +1\}$.

2.1 Support Vector Machines

Using Lagrangian and Kuhn-Tucker theory, the maximal margin hyperplane for a binary classification problem given by a data set X is a linear combination of simple functions depending on the data: $f_{SVM}(x) = b + \sum_{i=1}^{L} y_i \alpha_i K(x_i, x)$, where $K(u,v)$ is a kernel function and the vector $(\alpha_i)_{i=1}^{L}$ is the (1-norm soft margin) solution of the following constrained optimization problem in the dual space [2]:

$$\begin{array}{l} \text{Maximize}_\alpha -\frac{1}{2} \sum_{i,j=1}^{L} y_i \alpha_i y_j \alpha_j K(x_i, x_j) + \sum_{i=1}^{L} \alpha_i \\ \text{subject to } \sum_{i=1}^{L} y_i \alpha_i = 0 \quad \text{(bias constraint)} \\ \quad 0 \leqslant \alpha_i \leqslant C \quad i = 1, \ldots, L. \end{array} \quad (1)$$

for a certain constant C. The points x_i with $\alpha_i > 0$ (active constraints) are named *support vectors*. An example is well classified if and only if its functional margin $y_i f_{SVM}(x_i)$ with respect to f_{SVM} is positive.

The parameter C allows to control the trade-off between the margin and the training errors. By setting $C = \infty$, one obtains the hard margin hyperplane. The most usual kernel functions $K(u,v)$ are polynomial, Gaussian-like or sigmoidal functions. It is worth noting that the kernel function depends on a certain parameter γ (that is, $K(u,v) := K_\gamma(u,v)$), usually fixed in advance. In many implementations b is treated apart (fixed *a priori*, for example) in order to avoid the bias constraint.

2.2 Sequential FNNs Where the Hidden-Layer Weights Are a Subset of the Data

Different from SVMs, the most usual cost function for fully connected FNNs with one hidden layer of N units and output linear units is the sum-of-squares error:

$$\sum_{i=1}^{L} \frac{1}{2} (f_{FNN}(x_i) - y_i)^2, \quad (2)$$

where $f_{FNN}(x) = b_0 + \sum_{k=1}^{N} \lambda_k \varphi(\omega_k, x)$. As usual, $\{\omega_k\}_{k=1}^{N}$ are the hidden-layer weights and $\{\lambda_k\}_{k=1}^{N}$ are the output-layer weights. The most common activation functions $\varphi(b, \omega, x)$ for the hidden units are sigmoidal for Multi-layer Perceptrons (MLPs) and radially symmetric for Radial Basis Function Networks (RBFNs), although other functions may be used [1]. Similar to kernel functions, the activation functions φ usually depends on a certain parameter γ, which is usually named "gain factor" for sigmoidal functions or "width" for radial basis functions.

The architecture of the network (i.e., connections, number of hidden units and activation functions) is usually fixed in advance, whereas the weights are learned during the training process.

There exist, however, FNN models that sequentially construct the architecture, so that the number of hidden units is a consequence of the learning process rather than fixed *a priori* (for a review of constructive FNNs see, for example, [6]). Among them, some models select the hidden-layer weights to be always a subset of the data, such as the Orthogonal Least Squares Learning algorithm [3], Kernel Matching Pursuit with *pre-fitting* [4] and the Sequential Approximation with Optimal Coefficients and Interacting Frequencies algorithm [5]. At every step, in order to select the hidden-layer weights of the new hidden unit, every input example in the data set is temporarily installed in the network as a hidden-layer candidate weights vector. Then, the optimal (in a least squares sense) output-layer weights of the whole network are computed (by solving a linear equations system). The input example that allows a greater reduction of the whole error is selected. We will refer to these schemes as Support Vector Sequential FNNs (SVSFNNs).

3 Comparing SVMs and SVSFNNs

3.1 Motivation

Apart from the structurally identical form of their respective output functions (see section 2), a parallelism can be done between SVMs and SVSFNNs. On the one hand, the number of terms of the approximation (support vectors or hidden units, respectively) is a consequence of the learning process itself. On the other hand, they share the property that the hidden-layer weights are always a subset of the data, leading to sparse solutions. Only those input examples that, according to their respective inductive bias, have some influence on their respective approximations are present in the obtained solutions.

One of the disadvantages of SVSFNNs with respect to SVMs is that, due to their greedy approach, SVSFNNs does not usually find a global minimum of the problem. Nevertheless, finding a good local minimum is many times enough to achieve good performance. In contrast, an advantage with respect to SVMs is that the sparsity of the model is explicitly controlled.

The aim of this work is to compare SVMs and SVSFNNs with respect to the accuracy of the obtained solutions, the quantity and quality of the support vectors and the computational cost.

3.2 Methodologies

The following methodologies were followed in our experiments:

1. Preprocess the data.
2. SVMs: Choose a kernel.
   SVSFNNs: Choose an activation function.
3. Select suitable parameters for the model.
4. SVSFNNs: Choose a stopping criterion.
5. Train and test the model.

Note that the only difference when comparing the respective methodologies for SVMs and SVSFNNs is that a stopping criterion is provided to SVSFNNs. This stopping criterion is used to stop the addition of new hidden units.

Software. For SVMs, we used the LIBSVM software [7] For SVSFNNs, we used our own implementation.

Preprocessing. Categorical attributes were converted to *dummy* variables. The rest of the data were linearly scaled in $[0,1]$.

Kernel and activation function. SVM models were obtained using the following kernels: Gaussian $e^{-\gamma\|\boldsymbol{u}-\boldsymbol{v}\|^2}$, 2-degree polynomial $(\gamma\,\boldsymbol{u}'\boldsymbol{v}+1)^2$ and sigmoidal $tanh(\gamma\boldsymbol{u}'\boldsymbol{v})$. For SVSFNNs, equivalent activation functions (Gaussian RBF, polynomial MLP and sigmoidal MLP) were used to obtain the networks.

Parameters. In order to perform the experiments in the (as much as possible) same conditions both for SVMs and SVSFNNs, the following correspondence between the parameters of the respective models can be made:

1. The γ parameter of the kernel can be considered equivalent to the MLP-gain factor or RBF-width of the activation function (see section 2).
2. Similar to the restriction related to the C parameter for SVMs (see (1)), a hidden-layer candidate weights vector was not considered valid for SVSFNNs if the 2-norm of the solution (the output-layer weights) of its associated linear equations system was greater than a certain value C, regardless of the error reduction obtained with that vector.

In order to get adequate γ and C parameters for SVMs, a cross-validation (CV) process was performed (using a *grid search* provided by the LIBSVM software). The parameters with the best CV accuracy were kept to build the model. For SVSFNNs, the γ found for SVMs was set as the starting point of the search of the MLP-gain factor or RBF-width. The C parameter was set to the value found for SVMs. This process was repeated for every kernel function.

Stopping criterion. For SVSFNNs, an early stopping procedure with a validation set was used. No more hidden units were added when the error on the validation set (see below) did not improve for 5 consecutive hidden units.

Train and test the model. For the early stopping procedure performed by SVSFNNs, a validation data set must be provided. Depending on the number of available data, different resampling techniques were used.

When the number of examples in the data set was considered small, a *double* CV (2CV) procedure was performed as follows. A simple ν-fold CV splits the data set into ν folds of equal size (one fold is used to test the model, and the remaining $\nu-1$ folds to obtain the model). The 2CV procedure performs an internal $(\nu-1)$-fold CV with the $\nu-1$ folds of the simple (external) ν-fold CV. It considers $\nu-2$ folds to train the network, and the last one to validate it. Finally, the obtained model is tested with the test fold of the external ν-fold CV. This procedure is repeated for every test fold of the external ν-fold CV.

When the number of examples in the data set was considered sufficient, no 2CV was applied. A fixed subset was used to test the models and a simple CV procedure was applied to the rest of the data in order to obtain the models.

Table 1. Description of the benchmark data sets used. The column '#Var' shows the number of variables, the column '#Cla' the number of classes and the column '#Examples' the number of examples.

Data Set	#Var	#Cla	#Examples	Missing
Abalone	8	6	4,177	No
Australian Credit	15	2	690	Yes
German Credit	20	2	1,000	No
Pima Indians Diabetes	8	2	768	Yes
Hepatitis	19	2	155	Yes
Ionosphere	33	2	351	No
Sonar	60	2	208	No

To be as fair as possible for the comparison, the validation sets used by SVSFNNs, needed by the early stopping procedure, were not used for SVMs. Therefore, the training and test data sets and the number of training and test processes were exactly the same for SVMs and SVSFNNs.

4 Experiments

4.1 Data Sets

Several data sets from the UCI repository were used for the comparison, namely *Abalone, Australian Credit, German Credit, Pima Indians Diabetes, Hepatitis, Ionosphere* and *Sonar*. Table 1 shows a brief description of these data sets. A 10-9-fold 2CV (an external 10-fold CV and an internal 9-fold one) was performed for all the data sets except for the *Abalone* one, that was split into 3,132 examples to obtain the model (with a 9-fold CV) and 1,045 examples to test it.

4.2 Results

Table 2 shows the results obtained with SVMs and SVSFNNs, using the methodology previously described, for the following activation functions: Gaussian, polynomial and sigmoidal. The average results of the cross-validation processes (test accuracies) are shown. Columns #SV and #HU indicate the average number of support vectors and hidden units for SVMs and SVSFNNs, respectively.

Accuracies found with SVSFNNs are similar to those for SVMs. Actually, results found with SVSFNNs are a little better than the results for SVMs. However, these differences are not considered as qualitatively important. They can be explained by the respective search procedures of the γ parameter (more exhaustive for SVSFNNs than for SVMs) and by the stopping criterion for SVSFNNs.

The number of support vectors (hidden units) are in the same range for every data set, regardless of the kernel/activation function used. It is noteworthy that the number of hidden units/support vectors was much lower for SVSFNNs than for SVMs. This can be explained because the objective of SVSFNNs is that of

Table 2. SVM and SVSFNN results with the Gaussian $e^{-\gamma\|\boldsymbol{u}-\boldsymbol{v}\|^2}$ (top), polynomial $(\gamma \boldsymbol{u}'\boldsymbol{v}+1)^2$ (middle) and sigmoidal $tanh(\gamma \boldsymbol{u}'\boldsymbol{v})$ (bottom) kernel/activation functions.

Data Set	SVM γ	Test %	#SV	SVSFNN γ	Test %	#HU
Abalone	0.5	72.25	2,187.0	0.25	73.34	5.89
Australian credit	0.33	67.54	488.4	0.2	70.04	3.42
German credit	0.009	76.00	506.8	0.075	76.09	6.64
Pima Indians Diabetes	0.009	75.85	393.0	0.1	78.87	5.42
Hepatitis	0.008	100.00	46.4	0.075	100.00	12.69
Ionosphere	0.072	94.29	90.9	0.1	95.49	2.78
Sonar	0.09	85.71	129.8	0.25	86.12	9.14
Abalone	0.5	73.21	2,211.0	0.4	72.72	12.56
Australian credit	0.008	67.82	455.7	0.025	70.08	2.76
German credit	0.008	75.75	503.7	0.01	76.06	7.13
Pima Indians Diabetes	0.007	77.53	383.6	0.025	78.77	7.54
Hepatitis	0.008	100.00	43.5	0.008	100.00	16.52
Ionosphere	0.44	89.43	77.5	0.075	90.46	3.88
Sonar	0.44	82.24	86.2	0.005	85.96	6.21
Abalone	0.002	72.57	2,272.0	0.002	73.58	7.33
Australian credit	0.008	67.23	399.6	0.025	68.43	6.59
German credit	0.001	76.00	492.0	0.25	75.68	8.00
Pima Indians Diabetes	0.01	76.75	376.9	0.005	76.30	5.63
Hepatitis	0.008	100.00	54.5	0.008	99.93	14.37
Ionosphere	0.0007	80.57	91.2	0.072	82.55	3.09
Sonar	0.0004	75.71	126.4	0.001	75.01	5.79

minimizing the empirical error (the approximation to the data), and the only (or at least the most important) way to control the complexity of the model is by means of the number of hidden units. According to the Structural Risk Minimization principle [2], in contrast, SVMs minimize a combination of the empirical error and the complexity of the model, so that the number of terms is not so important.

In addition, for every data set and activation function, all the hidden-layer weights selected by an SVSFNN were also found among the support vectors of the corresponding SVM model. This can be intuitively explained if we note that both the SVSFNN and SVM solutions are expressed as a sum of hyperplanes, each one defined by the inner product with an input example in the data set (the support vectors in the SVM model). Support vectors are near the decision boundary. Therefore, these examples are also likely to be selected as the most discriminating ones for SVSFNNs (recall that only the input examples in the data set are considered as the hidden-layer candidate weights vectors).

For SVSFNNs, numerical problems were encountered in some cases, motivated by the bad conditioning of the matrix of the associated linear equations systems. The computational times were lower for SVMs than for SVSFNNs. We cannot directly compare the execution times, because the respective methods were implemented with different programming languages and implementation optimizations. The publicly available LIBSVM software was implemented in C, and we used C++ to implement SVSFNNs. With these implementations, the relative execution times for SVSFNNs ranged between 1.6 and 6.2 times the mean execution time for SVMs.

5 Conclusions and Future Work

The experiments in this work can be seen as a comparison of the respective inductive bias of SVMs and FNNs. When both models are restricted to use similar kernels/activation functions and hidden-layer weights, their accuracies are very similar, with a high correlation between their performance with the same kernels/activation functions.

One might wonder if the performance of SVMs and FNNs may be more influenced by the fact that hidden-layer weights are a subset of the data rather than by their respective inductive bias It would be worthy to perfrom a comparison with other models that also select their hidden-layer weights within the data, such as the Relevance Vector Machine [8], for example.

Note that sequential FNNs tested in this work can be directly extended in several ways that SVMs cannot (or at least not so easily). First, any activation function can be used, without the restriction to be a kernel function. Second, they can be easily extended to be able to deal with heterogeneous data [9], without the necessity to construct specific kernels for every type of heterogeneity (any similarity could indeed be used).

Acknowledgments. This work was supported by the Consejo Interministerial de Ciencia y Tecnología (CICYT), under project CGL2004-04702-C02-02.

References

1. Bishop, C.M.: Neural Networks for Pattern Recognition. Oxford University Press Inc., New York (1995)
2. Vapnik, V.N.: The Nature of Statistical Learning Theory. Springer-Verlag, NY (1995)
3. Chen, S., Cowan, C.F.N., Grant, P.M.: Orthogonal Least Squares Learning Algorithm for Radial Basis Function Networks. IEEE Transactions on Neural Networks **2**(2) (1991) 302–309
4. Vincent, P., Bengio, Y.: Kernel Matching Pursuit. Machine Learning **48**(1-3) (2002) 165–187 Special Issue on New Methods for Model Combination and Model Selection.
5. Romero, E., Alquézar, R.: A Sequential Algorithm for Feed-forward Neural Networks with Optimal Coefficients and Interacting Frequencies. Neurocomputing **69**(13-15) (2006) 1540–1552
6. Kwok, T.Y., Yeung, D.Y.: Constructive Algorithms for Structure Learning in Feedforward Neural Networks for Regression Problems. IEEE Transactions on Neural Networks **8**(3) (1997) 630–645

7. Chang, C.C., Lin, C.J.: LIBSVM: A Library for Support Vector Machines (2002) http://www.csie.ntu.edu.tw/~cjlin/libsvm.
8. Tipping, M.: Sparse Bayesian Learning and the Relevance Vector Machine. Journal of Machine Learning Research **1** (2001) 211–244
9. Valdés, J., García, R.: A Model for Heterogeneous Neurons and Its Use in Configuring Neural Networks for Classification Problems. In: International Work-conference on Artificial Neural Networks (Lecture Notes in Computer Science 1240). (1997) 237–246

A New Model Selection Method for SVM

G. Lebrun[1], O. Lezoray[1], C. Charrier[1], and H. Cardot[2]

[1] LUSAC EA 2607, groupe Vision et Analyse d'Image, IUT Dépt. SRC,
120 Rue de l'exode, Saint-Lô, F-50000, France
{gilles.lebrun, c.charrier, o.lezoray}@chbg.unicaen.fr
[2] Laboratoire Informatique (EA 2101), Université François-Rabelais de Tours,
64 Avenue Jean Portalis, Tours, F-37200, France
hubert.cardot@univ-tours.fr

Abstract. In this paper, a new learning method is proposed to build Support Vector Machines (SVMs) Binary Decision Functions (BDF) of reduced complexity and efficient generalization. The aim is to build a fast and efficient SVM classifier. A criterion is defined to evaluate the Decision Function Quality (DFQ) which blends recognition rate and complexity of a BDF. Vector Quantization (VQ) is used to simplify the training set. A model selection based on the selection of the simplification level, of a feature subset and of SVM hyperparameters is performed to optimize the DFQ. Search space for selecting the best model being huge, Tabu Search (TS) is used to find a good sub-optimal model on tractable times. Experimental results show the efficiency of the method.

1 Introduction

Data mining is considered as one of the challenging research fields of the 21th century. Extracting knowledge from raw data is a difficult problem which covers several disciplines: Artificial Intelligence, Machine Learning, Statistics, Data Bases. Machine learning methods aim at providing classification methods which induce efficient decision functions. Among all possible inducers, SVMs have particular high generalization abilities and became very popular these last years. However decision functions provided by SVMs have a complexity which increases with the training set size [1,2,3]. Therefore, time processing with SVMs on huge datasets is not directly tractable. In recent years, there has been a lot of interest to improve learning methods using SVMs. One way is to optimize the SVM algorithm [1,4] to solve the associated quadratic problem. Other approaches use a simplification step to reduce the training set size [2,3,5,6,7]. For learning methods using SVM, model selection is critical. Many studies have shown that SVM generalization efficiency depends on the choices of SVMs parameters [8,9,10]. Other studies [11] have shown that multiclass SVMs are efficient if an efficient model selection is performed for each involved binary SVM. Therefore, as regards these considerations, new approaches aim at merging simplification step and model selection [5,3]. Although the SVM algorithms are lesser sensitive to curse of dimensionality [12], dimension reduction techniques can improve the efficiency of SVMs [8,10,12]. Our approach aims at unifying feature selection, simplification of training set and hyperparameters tuning as a complete model selection in order to produce efficient and low complexities BDFs with SVMs. For this new model selection method, a criterion named DFQ has been defined which takes into account the recognition rate of the BDF but also the number of support vectors (SV) and the number of features selected. For the simplification of the training set, the LBG algorithm used in vector quantization field [13] has been retained because it can produce good prototypes representing the initial dataset. Moreover the simplification level is controled by a single integer parameter whose values are few and can range from extreme simplification with only one prototype by class to no simplification. However, the proposed learning method is sufficiently general to be extended to other simplification methods. To have a proper tuning of hyperparameters and an accurate selection of relevant features, an adapted TS method is proposed for SVM model selection since usual SVM model selection have local minima [14]. Moreover TS has proved its suitability for such model selection problems [15,16]. The section 2 gives overviews and definitions used by our model selection method. The section 3 describe this new method and section 4 gives experimental results with it.

2 Overviews and Definitions

Support Vector Machines (SVM): SVMs were developed by Vapnik according to structural risk minimization principle from statistical learning theory [17]. Given training data (x_i, y_i), $i = \{1, \ldots, m\}$, $x_i \in \mathbb{R}^n$, $y_i \in \{-1, +1\}$, SVM maps an input vector x into a high-dimensional feature space $\mathbf{H}$ through some mapping function $\phi : \mathbb{R}^n \to \mathbf{H}$, and constructs an optimal separating hyperplane in this space. The mapping $\phi(\cdot)$ is performed by a kernel function $K(\cdot, \cdot)$ which defines an inner product in $\mathbf{H}$. The optimal solution α^* of corresponding convex quadratic programming problem [17] specifies the coefficients for the optimal hyperplane $w^* = \sum_{i=1}^{m} \alpha_i^* y_i \phi(x_i)$. The SV subset (i.e., $\alpha_i^* > 0$) gives the BDF $h(x) = \text{sign}(f(x))$ with $f(x) = \sum_{i \in \text{SV}} \alpha_i^* y_i K(x_i, x) + b^*$ where the threshold b^* is computed via the SVs [17]. SVMs being binary classifiers, several binary SVMs classifiers are combined to define a multi-class SVM scheme [11].

Vector Quantization (VQ): VQ is a classification technique used in the compression field [13]. VQ maps a vector x to another vector x' that belongs to m' *prototypes* vectors which is named *codebook*. The *codebook* S' is built from a training set S_t of size m ($m >> m'$). The algorithm must produce a set S' of prototypes which minimizes the distorsion $d' = \frac{1}{m} \sum_{i=1}^{m} \min_{1 \leq j \leq m'} d(x_i, x_j)$ ($d(.,.)$ is a $\mathcal{L}_2$ norm). LBG is an iterative algorithm [13] which produces 2^k prototypes after k iterates.

Decision Function Quality (DFQ): We consider that the DFQ of a given model θ depends on the recognition rate R_R but also on the complexity C_P of the DF h_θ when processing time is critical. Let $q(h_\theta) = R_R(h_\theta) - C_P(h_\theta)$ be the DFQ. For SVMs the complexity of the DF depends on the number of both SVs and selected features. The empirical model we propose to model the complexity of a SVM BDF is: $C_P(h_\theta) = c_{p_1} \log_2(n_{SV}) + c_{p_2} \log_2(\text{cost}(\beta))$. β is a boolean vector of size n representing selected features. Constants c_{p_1} and c_{p_2} fix the trade-off between classification rate improvement and complexity reduction. Let κ_i denote the cost for the extraction of the ith feature, the value of $cost(\beta)$ linked to the subset of selected features is defined by: $cost(\beta) = \sum \beta_i \kappa_i$. When these costs are unknown, $\kappa_i = 1$ is used for all features. Strictly speaking, a doubly of the number of SVs (extraction cost) is accepted in our learning method if it is related to a recognition rate increase of at least c_{p_1} (repectively c_{p_2}).

Tabu Search (TS): TS is a metaheuristic for difficult optimization problems [15]. TS belongs to iterative neighbourhood search methods. The general step, at the it iteration, consists in searching from a current solution θ^{it} a next best solution θ^{it+1} in a neighborhood. This new solution may be less efficient than the previous one, however it avoids local minimum trapping problems. That is why, TS uses short memory to avoid moves which might led to recently visited solutions (*tabu* solutions). TS methods generally use intensification and diversification strategies (alternately). In a promising region of space, the intensification allows extensive search to optimize a solution. The diversification strategy enables large changes of the solution to find quickly another promising region. Although the basic idea of TS is straightforward, the choice of solution coding, objective function, neighborhood, *tabu* solutions definition, intensification and diversification strategies, all depend on the application problem.

3 New Model Selection Method

The idea of our method is to produce fast and efficient SVM BDF using few features and SVs. A SVM is therefore trained from a small dataset S'_t representative of the initial training set S_t in order to reduce the complexity of the BDF and consequently training time. The LBG algorithm has been used to perform the simplification (reduction) of the initial dataset. Algorithm in Table 1 gives the details of this simplification[1]. As the level of simplification k cannot be easily fixed in an arbitrary way, a significant concept in our method is to regard k as variable. The optimization of SVM DFQ thus requires for a given kernel function K the choice of: the simplification level k, the feature subset β, the regularization constant C and kernel parameter σ. The search of the values of those variables is called model selection. Let θ be a model and k_θ, β_θ, C_θ, σ_θ be respectively the values of all the variables to tune. The search for the exact θ^* which optimizes the DFQ not being tractable, we decided to use tabu search as metaheuristic. Let the model θ be a vector of n' integer values[2] with $(\theta_1, \ldots, \theta_{n'}) = (\beta_1, \ldots, \beta_n, k, C', \sigma')$. A move for TS method is

---
[1] To speed up model selection, at each new value of k, the simplification result is stored for future steps which might use the same simplification level.
[2] $C_\theta = 2^{C'/2}$ with $C' \in [-10, \ldots, 20]$ (inspired by the *grid search* method [4]).

Table 1. Algorithm synopsis

Simplification(S,k)	SVM-DFQ(θ,S_l)
$S' \Leftarrow \emptyset$ **FOR** $c \in \{-1,+1\}$ | $T = \{x \mid (x,c) \in S\}$ | **IF** $2^k < \|T\|$ **THEN** $T' \Leftarrow \text{LBG}(T,k)$ | **ELSE** $T' \Leftarrow T$ | $S' \Leftarrow S' \cup \{(x,c) \mid x \in T'\}$ **RETURN** S'	$(S_t, S_v) \Leftarrow \text{Split}(S_l)$ $S'_t \Leftarrow \text{Simplification}(S_t, k_\theta)$ $h_\theta \Leftarrow \text{TrainingSVM}(S'_t, K_{\beta_\theta}, C_\theta, \sigma_\theta)$ $R_R \Leftarrow \frac{m^{\text{correct}}_{-1}}{2m_{-1}} + \frac{m^{\text{correct}}_{+1}}{2m_{+1}}$ $C_P \Leftarrow \text{Complexity}(h_\theta)$ $q(\theta) \Leftarrow R_R - C_P$
Intensification(θ^{it})	Diversification(θ^{it})

IF $q(\theta^{it}) > \eta_{\text{promising}} \cdot q(\theta_{\text{best-known}})$
   THEN $\Theta_{\text{next}} \Leftarrow \text{ExtensiveSearch}(\theta^{it})$
   ELSE $\Theta_{\text{next}} \Leftarrow \text{FastExtensiveSearch}(\theta^{it})$
 $\theta^{it+1} \Leftarrow \text{BestNotTabu}(\Theta_{\text{next}})$
 IF $q(\theta^{it+1}) > q(\theta_{\text{intensification}})$
 THEN
   $\theta_{\text{intensification}} \Leftarrow \theta^{it+1}$
   $n_{\text{WithoutImprove}} \Leftarrow 0$
 ELSE
   $n_{\text{WithoutImprove}} \Leftarrow n_{\text{WithoutImprove}} + 1$
   IF $n_{\text{WithoutImprove}} > n_{\text{max}}$
   THEN
     $n_{\text{failure}} \Leftarrow n_{\text{failure}} + 1$
     stategy $\Leftarrow$ Diversification
     IF $n_{\text{failure}} > n^{\text{max}}_{\text{failure}}$ **THEN** STOP
	$\delta \Leftarrow n_{\text{failure}+1}$
	 $i \Leftarrow$ SelectEligibleVariable
	 $\Theta_{\text{next}} \Leftarrow \text{TwoMove}(\theta^{it}, i, \delta)$
	 $\theta^{it+1} \Leftarrow \text{BestNotTabu}(\Theta_{\text{next}})$
	 IF $q(\theta^{it+1}) > q(\theta_{\text{diversification}})$
	 THEN
	   $\theta_{\text{diversification}} \Leftarrow \theta^{it+1}$
	   $n_{\text{diversification}} \Leftarrow n_{\text{diversification}} + 1$
	   IF $n_{\text{diversification}} > n_{\text{max}} \cdot n_{\text{failure}}$
	   THEN
	     $\theta^{it+1} \Leftarrow \theta_{\text{diversification}}$
	     stategy $\Leftarrow$ Intensification

to add or substract δ ($\delta = 1$ for a basic move in intensification strategy) to one of those integer variables (i.e., $\theta^{it+1}_i = \theta^{it}_i \pm \delta$). The synopsis in Table 1 gives the details of the estimation of DFQ $q(\theta)$ from a model θ and a learning set S_l with $q(\theta) \equiv \text{SVM-DFQ}(\theta, S_l)$ the objective function to optimize. S_t, S_v sets produced by Split function ($|S_t| = \frac{2}{3}|S_l|$, $|S_v| = \frac{1}{3}|S_l|$) respectively indicate the bases used for SVM simplification step (training dataset) and for recognition rate estimation (validation dataset). This dissociation is essential to avoid the risk of overfitting when empirical estimation is used. For a given class $y \in \{+1, -1\}$, m_y represents the number of examples and m^{correct}_y the correctly identified ones. This evaluation is more adapted when unbalanced class data are used. The kernel functions used is : $K_\beta(x_i, x_j) = \exp\left(-\sum_{l=1}^{n} \beta_l (x_{i,l} - x_{j,l})^2 / \sigma^2\right)$ with $x_{i,l}$ the lth feature of example i. Feature selection is embedded in kernel functions by using β binary vectors ($\sigma = 2^{\sigma'/2}$ and σ' have the same range that C' in θ representation). The model selection TS algorithm has to deal with two kinds of problems. Firstly, testing all moves between two iterations with a great number of features can be time expensive. In particular, it is a waste of time to explore moves which are linked to features when the actual solution is not sufficiently promising. Therefore, intensification strategy focusing on moves which are only linked to SVM hyperparameters or simplification level is more efficient to discover fastly new promising regions. Secondly, it is difficult for TS method to quickly escape from deep valleys of poor solutions when only using the short memory and resulting not taboo solutions. Using more diversified solutions can overcome this problem. This is dealt by increasing step size ($\delta > 1$) of moves and by forcing to use all types of moves (except feature selection moves for previous reason) in diversification strategy. Table 1 gives details of these two strategies. In intensification sysnopsis, `ExtensiveSearch` explores all eligible basic moves, whereas `FastExtensiveSearch` explores only eligible basic moves which are not related to feature selection (i.e. changing the value of β). $\eta_{promising}$ controls when the actual solution is considered as sufficiently promising. The set of all solutions θ which are tabu at the it iteration step of TS is: $\Theta_{tabu}^{it} = \{\theta \in \Omega \mid \exists\, i, t' : t' \in [1,\ldots,t],\ \theta_i \neq \theta_i^{it-1} \wedge \theta_i = \theta_i^{it-t'}\}$ with Ω the set of all solutions and t an adjustable parameter for the short memory used by TS (for experimental results $t = \sum_{i=1}^{n'} \max(\theta_i) - \min(\theta_i)$). `BestNotTabu` corresponds to the best solution on all possible moves from θ^{it} which are not tabu at this iteration. n_{max} is the maximum number of intensification iterations for which no improve of the last best intensification solution ($\theta_{intensification}$) are considered as failure of the intensification strategy. In diversification sysnopsis, an eligible variable (those which do not have a relationship with features) is selected (`SelectEligibleVariable`) and a jump of $\pm \delta$ is performed by modifying the random selected variable in the actual solution. There are the two only explored moves (`TwoMove`) and this forces diversification. The jump size increases with the number of successive failures ($n_{failure}$) of the intensification strategy in order to explore more and more far regions. During the diversification iterations, the best visited solution is stored ($\theta_{diversification}$) and selected as the start solution for the next intensification step. At any time of TS exploration, if aspiration is involved, strategy automatically switch to intensification and the number of failures is reseted ($n_{failure} = 0$). The TS is stopped when the number of failures is higher than a fixed value and the best known solution is returned.

4 Experimental Results

We used the following datasets described in Table 2 (m, n_c and n are respectively the number of: examples, classes and features). *Adults* and *Shuttle* come from UCI repository [18], *Web* from [1] and *ClassPixels* from [7]. Learning and test sets contain respectively 2/3 and 1/3 of initial datasets. Test sets are used to estimate recognition rate (R_R) after model selection. For multiclass classification problem, the one-versus-all decomposition scheme is used. It produces n_c (number of class) binary classification problems [11]. For each one a model selection is realized. Figures 1(a) to 1(c) illustrate model selection experiments with Gaussian kernel for different

Table 2. Datasets description

bases	m	n_c	n
Shuttle	58000	6	9
Adults	45222	2	103
Web	49749	2	300
ClassPixels	224636	3	27

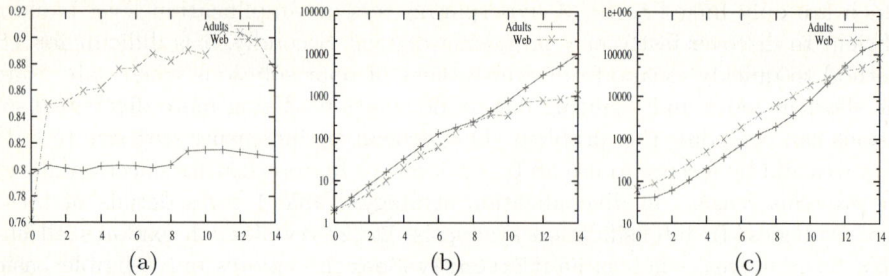

Fig. 1. Best recognition rate (a) and number of SVs (b) of BDF for a given simplification level k. *Grid search* method are used to select best model (C,σ). (c) gives total training time in seconds for grid search at each simplification level k.

simplification levels. Figure 1(a) shows that the level for which increasing training set size does not significantly improves recognition rate depends on dataset (*i.e.* importance of redundancy in dataset). Figure 1(c) shows that direct training with the whole dataset is time expensive for model selection. Moreover, complexity of decision function (fig. 1(b)) is directly linked to training set size of this one.

The objective of our learning method is to automatically select different parameters for producing SVM BDF which optimize the DFQ. However new parameters have been introduced and this can be problematic. Next experiments show how to deal with them. Our learning method is applied[3] on *Adults* dataset and table 3 (top) shows that an increase of $\eta_{\text{promising}}$ reduces the learning time without reducing quality of solution. Experiments with other datasets gave the same results and $\eta_{\text{promising}}$ can be fixed at 99%. Similar experiments have shown that a good compromise between learning time and quality of produced solution is $n_{\max} = 5$ and maximum of accepted failure $n_{\text{failure}}^{\max} = 5$.

Tables 3 (middle and bottom) illustrates the complexity evolution obtained with our learning method by using different penalties (c_{p_1} and c_{p_2}). Results show that higher penalties significantly reduce the number of SVs, the number of selected features and learning time while the recognition rate decrease is low if penalty is not too high. Of course good compromise depends on the considered application. Another interesting observation for a multiclass SVM scheme is that selected simplification levels could be different for each binary SVMs (*Shuttle* set in tab. 3). If training time are compared to the classical *grid search* methods without simplification of training set (fig. 1(c)), training time is greatly reduced (except for very low penality and feature selection) whereas our method preforms in addition feature and simplification level selection. Let n_k be the number of solutions θ examined by TS for which simplification level is equal to k. Global SVM training time of our method is $O(\sum n_k (2^k)^\gamma)$ with $\gamma \approx 2$. The examination of our method shows that n_k decreases while k increases. This effect increases when c_p values increases and explains the efficient training time of our method. In

---

[3] Starting solution is: $k = \lfloor log_2(m/n_c)/3 \rfloor$, $C' = 0$, $\sigma' = 0$ and $n_{\text{feature}} = n$.

Table 3. Top: Influence of $\eta_{\text{promising}}$ for model selection (*Adults* dataset, $c_{p_1} = c_{p_2} = 10^{-3}$). Middle: Trade off between recognition rate and complexity (*Adult*(A) or *Web*(W) dataset, $\eta_{\text{promising}} = 99\%$). Bottom: Models selection for one-versus-all scheme (*Shuttle* dataset, $\eta_{\text{promising}} = 99\%$). For all tables T_{learning} is the learning time for model selection in seconds, n_{feature} is the number of selected features, DFQ is computed on the validation dataset (value of R_R in DFQ criterion) and selected model R_R is evaluated on a test dataset.

$\eta_{\text{promising}}$	T_{learning}	k	$\log_{\sqrt{2}}(C)$	$\log_{\sqrt{2}}(\sigma)$	n_{VS}	n_{feature}	R_R	DFQ
99.5 %	6654	6	0	0	50	9	79.3%	0.789
99.0 %	9508	1	-3	6	4	22	81.7%	0.803
98.0 %	160179	4	0	8	18	20	81.1%	0.804
95.0 %	195043	0	10	5	2	41	81.9%	0.803
0.0 %	310047	12	1	5	3286	44	81.8%	0.805

		with feature selection					without				
S	$c_{p_1} = c_{p_2}$	T_{learning}	k	n_{VS}	n_{feature}	R_R	DFQ	T_{learning}	k	n_{VS}	R_R	DFQ
A	0.0100	5634	0	2	44	81.5%	0.762	1400	0	2	79.4%	0.789
A	0.0020	16095	4	12	44	81.9%	0.793	2685	3	6	79.9%	0.800
A	0.0001	127096	10	764	55	81.8%	0.817	7079	13	5274	81.7%	0.811
W	0.1000	4762	1	3	44	82.2%	0.598	1736	1	3	84.1%	0.695
W	0.0100	25693	2	5	149	87.3%	0.846	4378	5	39	87.5%	0.835
W	0.0010	197229	9	506	227	89.7%	0.881	18127	11	730	90.4%	0.898

	$c_{p_1} = c_{p_2} = 0.01$					$c_{p_1} = c_{p_2} = 0$				
BDF	T_{learning}	k	n_{VS}	n_{feature}	R_R	T_{learning}	k	n_{VS}	n_{feature}	R_R
1-vs-all	207	4	7	2	99.85%	38106	15	127	3	99.83%
2-vs-all	67	0	2	1	99.93%	14062	10	20	3	99.95%
3-vs-all	45	0	2	1	99.94%	7948	11	38	3	99.95%
4-vs-all	152	5	9	2	99.91%	31027	14	63	4	99.94%
5-vs-all	44	3	2	1	99.98%	36637	7	13	2	99.96%
6-vs-all	113	2	5	1	99.97%	394	6	24	6	99.97%

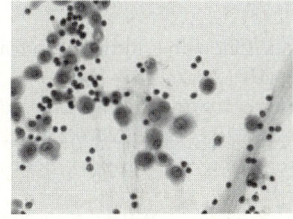
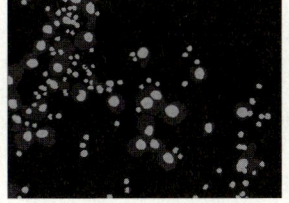
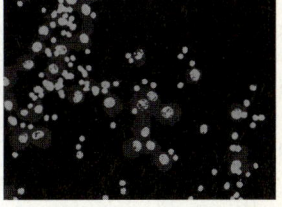

(a) Microscopic image. (b) Expert segmentation. (c) Pixel classification.

Fig. 2. Pixel classification ($R_R = 90.1\%$) using feature extraction cost

our last experiments, pixel classification is performed for microscopical images. On such masses of data, the processing time is critical and we can assign a weight to each color feature of pixel: let $\kappa_i = n \cdot T_i / T$ be the weight with T_i the time to extract the ith color feature ($T = \sum_{i \in [1,...,n]} T_i$). With our model selection method, pixel classification (fig. 2) can be performed with only 7 SVs and 4 color features (see [7] for further details).

5 Conclusions and Discussions

A new learning method is proposed to perform efficient model selection for SVMs. This learning method produces BDFs whose advantages are threefold: high generalization abilities, low complexities and selection of efficient features subsets. Moreover, feature selection can take into account feature extraction cost and many kinds of kernel functions with less or more hyperparameters can easily be used. Future works will deal with the influence of other simplification methods [2,6,5]. In particular, because QV methods can be time expensive with huge datasets.

References

1. Platt, J.: Fast training of SVMs using sequential minimal optimization, advances in kernel methods-support vector learning. MIT Press (1999) 185–208
2. Yu, H., Yang, J., Han, J.: Classifying large data sets using SVM with hierarchical clusters. In: SIGKDD. (2003) 306–315
3. Lebrun, G., Charrier, C., Cardot, H.: SVM training time reduction using vector quantization. In: ICPR. Volume 1. (2004) 160–163
4. Chang, C.C., Lin, C.J.: Libsvm: a library for support vector machines. Sofware Available at http://www.csie.ntu.edu.tw/~cjlin/libsvm (2001)
5. Ou, Y.Y., Chen, C.Y., Hwang, S.C., Oyang, Y.J.: Expediting model selection for SVMs based on data reduction. In: IEEE Proc. SMC. (2003) 786–791
6. Tsang, I.W., Kwok, J.T., Cheung, P.M.: Core vector machines: Fast SVM training on very large data sets. JMLR **6** (2005) 363–392
7. Lebrun, G., Charrier, C., Lezoray, O., Meurie, C., Cardot, H.: Fast pixel classification by SVM using vector quantization, tabu search and hybrid color space. In: CAIP. (2005) 685–692
8. Chapelle, O., Vapnik, V., Bousquet, O., Mukherjee, S.: Choosing multiple parameters for support vector machines. Machine Learning **46** (2002) 131–159
9. Chapelle, O., Vapnik, V.: Model selection for support vector machines. In: Advances in Neural Information Processing Systems. Volume 12. (1999) 230–236
10. Fröhlich, H., Chapelle, O., Schölkopf, B.: Feature selection for support vector machines using genetic algorithms. IJAIT **13** (2004) 791–800
11. Rifkin, R., Klautau, A.: In defense of one-vs-all classification. JMLR **5** (2004) 101–141
12. Christianini, N.: Dimension reduction in text classification with support vector machines. JMLR **6** (2005) 37–53
13. Gersho, A., Gray, R.M.: Vector Quantization and Signal Compression. Kluwer Academic (1991)
14. Staelin, C.: Parameter selection for support vector machines. http://www.hpl.hp.com/techreports/2002/HPL-2002-354R1.html (2002)
15. Glover, F., Laguna, M.: Tabu search. Kluwer Academic Publishers (1997)

16. Korycinski, D., Crawford, M.M., Barnes, J.W.: Adaptive feature selection for hyperspectral data analysis. SPIE **5238** (2004) 213–225
17. Vapnik, V.N.: Statistical Learning Theory. Wiley edn. New York (1998)
18. Blake, C., Merz, C.: Uci repository of machine learning databases. advances in kernel methods, support vector learning. (1998)

Speed-Up LOO-CV with SVM Classifier

G. Lebrun[1], O. Lezoray[1], C. Charrier[1], and H. Cardot[2]

[1] LUSAC EA 2607, groupe Vision et Analyse d'Image, IUT Dépt. SRC,
120 Rue de l'exode, Saint-Lô, F-50000, France
{gilles.lebrun, c.charrier, o.lezoray}@chbg.unicaen.fr
[2] Laboratoire Informatique (EA 2101), Université François-Rabelais de Tours,
64 Avenue Jean Portalis, Tours, F-37200, France
hubert.cardot@univ-tours.fr

Abstract. Leave-one-out Cross Validation (LOO-CV) gives an almost unbiased estimate of the expected generalization error. But the LOO-CV classical procedure with Support Vector Machines (SVM) is very expensive and cannot be applied when training set has more that few hundred examples. We propose a new LOO-CV method which uses modified initialization of Sequential Minimal Optimization (SMO) algorithm for SVM to speed-up LOO-CV. Moreover, when SMO's stopping criterion is changed with our adaptive method, experimental results show that speed-up of LOO-CV is greatly increased while LOO error estimation is very close to exact LOO error estimation.

1 Introduction

LOO-CV is an useful measure to estimate the generalization of an inducer [1]. Model selection is the main aim of LOO measure [2], especially when dataset size is considered as too small to split it into training and test sets. SVM is an efficient inducer, but training time increases quickly with training set size [3] and it would be a bad candidate for model selection with direct LOO-CV. But others properties of SVM made it a good candidate for smart LOO-CV [4,5]. Decoste et al [4] and others [2,5] have proposed new methods to speed-up exact (or very close) evaluation of LOO error with SVM. All these methods are based either on changing initialization, stopping criterion, or both of SMO algorithm. Next sections present an overview of speed-up LOO-CV methods and explain in what way our method improves them. Many experimental results are also described to highlight the efficiency of our method and to compare it with previous ones.

2 SVM and SMO Overview

Consider a data set S ($S = \{z_1, ..., z_m\} = \{(x_1, y_1), ..., (x_m, y_m)\}$) with m instances (or examples) where each data information z_i is a couple (x_i, y_i) with $y_i \in \{+1, -1\}$ and $x_i \in \mathbb{R}^n$. The main task for training SVM is to solve the following dual quadratic optimization problem [6]:

$$\min_{\alpha} W(\alpha) = \tfrac{1}{2} \sum \alpha_i \alpha_j Q_{ij} - \sum \alpha_i \quad (1a)$$
$$\text{subject to } 0 \leq \alpha_i \leq C \text{ and } \sum \alpha_i y_i = 0 \quad (1b)$$

with $Q_{ij} = y_i y_j K(x_i, x_j)$ and $K(x_i, x_j)$ is a kernel function. Let us define (see [7] for more details on those formulations):

$$G_i = \sum \alpha_j Q_{ij} - 1 \quad (2a)$$
$$I_{up}(\alpha) \equiv \{t | \alpha_t < C, y_t = +1 \text{ or } \alpha_t > 0, y_t = -1\} \quad (2b)$$
$$I_{low}(\alpha) \equiv \{t | \alpha_t < C, y_t = -1 \text{ or } \alpha_t > 0, y_t = +1\} \quad (2c)$$
$$m(\alpha) = -y_{i_1} G_{i_1} | i_1 = \operatorname*{argmax}_{i \in I_{up}} -y_i G_i, \; M(\alpha) = -y_{i_2} G_{i_2} | i_2 = \operatorname*{argmin}_{i \in I_{low}} -y_i G_i \quad (2d)$$

A solution α is optimal for problem (1) if and only if [7]

$$m(\alpha) < M(\alpha) \quad (3)$$

Let α^* be an optimal solution and $\{I_0, I_m, I_{bound}\}$ a partition of examples indexes $I = \{1, \ldots, m\}$ in function of α values with $I_0(\alpha) \equiv \{t | \alpha_t = 0\}$, $I_m(\alpha) \equiv \{t | 0 < \alpha_t < C\}$, $I_{bound}(\alpha) \equiv \{t | \alpha_t = C\}$. A decision function h produced by SVM has the following expression:

$$h(x) = \operatorname{sign}(f(x)), f(x) = \sum \alpha_i^* y_i K(x_i, x) + b^* \quad (4)$$

with $b^* = -y_i G_i^*$, $\forall i \in I_m(\alpha^*)$ and f the output of SVM [6].

An efficient iterative algorithm named SMO was proposed by Platt [3] to find optimal solution of (1) by using test condition (3). The main idea of this algorithm is that at each iteration only two variables α_{i_1} and α_{i_2} are modified to decrease (1a) value. The synopsis of SMO is given by algorithm 1. $\epsilon = 10^{-3}$ and $\forall i : \alpha_i = 0, G_i = -1$ are classical default initialization values for SMO. As SMO is only asymptotically convergent, the previous ϵ value is an efficient admissible choice for checking optimality [7]. Without any kind of information on optimal solution localization, $\alpha = 0$ ($W(\alpha) = 0$) is a efficient starting solution [3]. Mainly, because for other α values, G_i values must be computed using (2a), which is time expensive. But also because objective initial value could be worst (i.e. $W(\alpha) > 0$) and increase the number of iterations for convergence. In order to have the lowest number of iterations for SMO, the procedure BESTCOUPLE must select i_1 and i_2 which produce the maximum decrease of (1a) [3]. Variation of (1a) when only two variables are modified is equal to:

$$\Delta W(i_1, i_2) = \Delta \alpha_{i_1} G_{i_1} + \Delta \alpha_{i_2} G_{i_2} + \Delta \alpha_{i_1} \Delta \alpha_{i_2} Q_{i_1, i_2} \\ + \tfrac{1}{2} \left(\Delta \alpha_{i_1}^2 Q_{i_1, i_1} + \Delta \alpha_{i_2}^2 Q_{i_2, i_2} \right) \quad (5)$$

Algorithm 1. SMO(α, G, ϵ)

---
  while $m(\alpha) - M(\alpha) > \epsilon$ do
    (i_1, i_2)=BESTCOUPLE()
    ($\Delta \alpha_{i_1}, \Delta \alpha_{i_2}$)=OPTIMALVARIATION($i_1, i_2$)
    (α, G)=UPDATE($\alpha, G, (i_1, \Delta \alpha_{i_1}), (i_2, \Delta \alpha_{i_2})$)
  end while

Search of optimal couple with equation (5) is time expensive ($O(m^2)$), and heuristics were proposed (see [7] and references in). The most common one is to select the couple which maximum violates the stopping criterion of SMO (*i.e.* respectively i_1 and i_2 in equations (2d)). A recent alternative is to select the first α_i using previous heuristic (i_1 for example) and to use equation (5) to select the second [7]. After selecting good candidates, the OPTIMALVARIATION procedure computes $\Delta\alpha_{i_1}$ and $\Delta\alpha_{i_2}$ values in order to have the maximal decrease of W (see [3,7] for more details). The UPDATE procedure uses (6) to compute variations of G values in function of $\Delta\alpha_{i_1}$ and $\Delta\alpha_{i_2}$.

$$\forall j : \Delta G_j = \Delta\alpha_{i_1} Q_{j,i_1} + \Delta\alpha_{i_2} Q_{j,i_2} \tag{6}$$

3 Speed-Up LOO-CV

LOO-CV definition: Let h_θ^S be the decision function produced by a learning algorithm with training set S. θ is the set of parameters (also named model) used by the training algorithm. The error e_{LOO} measured by LOO-CV procedure is defined by:

$$e_{\text{LOO}}(\theta) = \frac{1}{m} \sum_{i=1}^{m} l\left(h_\theta^{S_i}(x_i), y_i\right) \tag{7}$$

with $S_i = S\backslash\{z_i\}$ training sets and $l(x,y) = \begin{cases} 0 & \text{if } x = y \\ 1 & \text{else} \end{cases}$ the loss function.

LOO error and SVM relation: For many training algorithms, the estimation of e_{LOO} is realized by m trainings on S_i datasets. A better way to do this with SVMs is to first realize a training with all the m examples. This first optimal solution α^* provides several useful informations [5]. Those informations allow to determine values of $l(h_\theta^{S_i}(x_i), y_i)$ without any training with several datasets S_i. For example: $h_\theta^{S_i}(x_i) = y_i$, if $\alpha_i = 0$ in α^* (see [5] for more details). Let I_{LOO} denote set of examples for which SVM trainings with datasets S_i are necessary. Experimental results in [5] illustrate how the size of those set changes in function of θ. Those results show that the rate $|I_{\text{LOO}}|/m$ is not negligible for many models θ. Then, model selection using LOO-CV is always time expensive when m increases, even if only $|I_{\text{LOO}}|$ SVM trainings must be realized. To speed-up those SVM trainings, two possibilities exist: (1) the solution of first training with S could help to determine a better $\tilde{\alpha}$ starting solution for SMO (and associated $\tilde{G}$ values), (2) ϵ stopping value of SMO could be increased. For the next sections, let α_S, G_S denote the final results of SMO training with S.

Alpha Seeding methods: DeCoste and Wagstaff named Alpha Seeding (AS-SMO) a method which determines $\tilde{\alpha}$ next SVM initial solution in function of previous SVM trainings [4]. For LOO-CV with SVM, a starting solution $\tilde{\alpha}$ with $\tilde{\alpha}_i = 0$ is deduced from α_S to realize SVM training with S_i datasets. $\tilde{\alpha}_i=0$ reflects the fact that example z_i is removed from training set S. Moreover, the modification of α_S must respect constraints (1b) to produce a $\tilde{\alpha}$ feasible solution. To have speed-up effect, starting solution $\tilde{\alpha}$ must be near optimal solution $\tilde{\alpha}^*$.

Initially proposed method [4] consists in uniformly adding an equal portion of α_i to each in-bound α_j within the same class (i.e. $j \in I_m$, $y_j = y_i$ and $j \neq i$). α_i is then decreased in the same proportion. Due to constraint (1b), $\tilde{\alpha}_i = 0$ could fail, then this action is repeated with remaining in-bound $\tilde{\alpha}_j$ until $\tilde{\alpha}_i = 0$. The main problem with this method is that many α_i variables are modified. The computation cost for updating $\tilde{G}$ values from G_S is then too high. Lee et al noticed this problem and proposed a method which changes only few variables [5]. The main idea is to redistribute an amount δ from α_i to α_k (i.e. $\Delta\alpha_i = -\delta$ and $\Delta\alpha_k = y_i y_k \delta$) and to select $k \in I_m(\alpha_S)$ in order to reduce magnitude variation of G. This corresponds to solve: $k = \operatorname*{argmin}_{k \in I_m, k \neq i} (\max_j |\Delta G_j|)$ with $k \equiv i_1$ and $i \equiv i_2$ in (6). This problem has however a too high complexity. Lee proposes as a heuristic to look only at variations of G_k (see [5] for more details). This corresponds to solve the simplified problem : $k = \operatorname*{argmin}_{k \in I_m, k \neq i} (|\Delta G_k|)$ and to make the hypothesis that all other ΔG_i have same or less magnitude variations than $|\Delta G_k|$ when α_k is modified. This procedure is repeated until $\tilde{\alpha}_i = 0$.

New AS-SMO method: Previous studies highlight that an efficient AS-SVM method must modify the lesser possible variables in α_S for a reduce of G update cost. It must also produce a starting solution $\tilde{\alpha}$ for which SMO algorithm has a minimum of iterations to reach the stopping condition. DeCoste et al method [4] focuses only on second key point by making the hypothesis that building a close and valid solution $\tilde{\alpha}$ from α_S produces a solution near the optimal, but neglecks completely the first point. Lee et al method [5] advantages the first point and manages the second point by taking into account heuristic informations. Our proposed method tries to deal with those two key points at the same time. The main idea is to search which α_k variable allows by its modification, to decrease α_i to zero in respect to contraints (1b) and has the lowest $W(\tilde{\alpha})$ (i.e., nearest to optimal solution $\tilde{\alpha}^*$). The synopsis of this new method is resumed in algorithm 2 with $I_1(\alpha, i) = \{k | 0 \leq \alpha_k + y_k y_i \alpha_i \leq C, k \neq i\}$ the set of α_k variables which allow to have $\alpha_i = 0$ under contraint (1b) by modifying only one of them, $I_\delta(\alpha, i) = \{k | \exists \delta > 0 : 0 \leq \alpha_k + y_k y_i \delta \leq C, k \neq i\}$ the set of α_k variables which allow to decrease α_i and $\delta_{max}(k, i)$ the maximal decrease of α_i when only α_k is modified. $(\tilde{\alpha}, \tilde{G}) = \text{AS-SMO}(\alpha_S, G_S, i)$ are initialization values of

---

Algorithm 2. AS-SMO(α,G,i)

while $\alpha_i > 0$ do
  if $I_1(\alpha, i) \neq \emptyset$ then
    $\Delta\alpha_i = -\alpha_i$, $\Delta\alpha_k = y_k y_i \alpha_i$ with $k = \operatorname*{argmax}_{k \in I_1(\alpha,i)} -\Delta W(k, i)$
  else
    $k = \operatorname*{argmax}_{k \in I_\delta(\alpha,i)} [\Delta W_{\max} - \Delta W(k, i)] \cdot \delta_{\max}(k, i)$ with $\Delta W_{\max} = \operatorname*{argmax}_{k \in I_\delta(\alpha,i)} \Delta W(k, i)$
    $\Delta\alpha_k = y_k y_i \delta_{\max}(k, i)$, $\Delta\alpha_i = -\delta_{\max}(k, i)$
  end if
  $(\tilde{\alpha}, \tilde{G}) = \text{Update}(\alpha, G, (i, \Delta\alpha_i), (k, \Delta\alpha_k))$
end while

SMO when training set S_i is used. In general case, when I_1 is not empty, it is possible to have $\alpha_i = 0$ by modifying only another α_k variable. As regards the first key point, this action has the lowest cost. When I_1 has more than one element, which is generally true, the modified α_k variable must be the one which produces an $\tilde{\alpha}$ starting SMO solution which has the lower $W(\tilde{\alpha})$ value to deal with the second key point. $\Delta\alpha_i = -\alpha_i$ and $\Delta\alpha_k = y_k y_i \alpha_i$ by using contraint (1b). $\Delta W(i,k)$ is determined directly by using (5) and the optimal choice of k has a time complexity of $O(m)$. Paying attention to this method highlights a strong similarity with one step of SMO algorithm, especially by comparing it with *second order* SMO step in [7]. Computing cost for determination of $\tilde{\alpha}$ from α_S is close to one SMO iteration for general case. In the rare case for which $|I_1| = \emptyset$, more than one α variable must be modified. The approach is a greedy one and is guided by a criterion which makes a trade-off between bringing $\tilde{\alpha}$ close to optimal and decreasing greatly α_i in order to have few α modified variables.

Stopping ϵ value change: SMO implementations [8] use low values of ϵ to ensure efficient solution as regards theoretical convergence criterion. This has for effect that the reponse of decision function does not change for many iterations [9]. It is then natural to want to increase ϵ value in order to stop earlier SMO algorithm. But the problem is to select an efficient ϵ. Too high ϵ leads too early stopping and the solution does not correspond to the SVM problem. Too low ϵ does not sufficiently decrease the number of iterations of SMO. Lee [2] compares e_{LOO} variations between $\epsilon = 10^{-1}$ and classical $\epsilon = 10^{-3}$ with several datasets and hyperparameters values. Conclusion is that e_{LOO} estimations are very similar for both ϵ values, but training time is greatly reduced using $\epsilon = 10^{-1}$. In [5] an adaptive ϵ method is proposed. The main idea is to stop SMO algorithm, step by step, for $\epsilon \in [10^{-1}, 10^{-2}, 10^{-3}]$ and to use a heuristic criterion to test if SMO must continue (see [5] for more details). The advantage is that e_{LOO} estimation is more accurate than with the previous method. The disadvantage is that speed-up is reduced mainly because more than one evaluation of the SVM output (4) must be realized [5].

New adaptive method: Taking into account that an efficient stopping ϵ value for SMO training with dataset S must be also efficient for training with datasets S_i, due to the closeness of S and S_i datasets, our new proposed method uses the first training not only to produce an α_S helpful guidline for SMO, but also to deduce an efficient ϵ_{LOO} for LOO-CV with AS-SVM. Let $W_t \equiv W(\alpha_t)$, $Q_t = |(W_t - W_\infty)/W_\infty|$ and $\Delta M_t \equiv m(\alpha_t) - M(\alpha_t)$ respectively denote values of the objective function, a proximity measure of optimal solution and maximum violation of KKT criterion at SMO iteration t. As W_∞ could not be evaluated, SMO classic ending is used: $W_\infty = W_{t_{\max}}$ with $t_{\max}$ the number of SMO iterations when training set is S and $\epsilon = 10^{-3}$. Let t_ϵ be the first SMO iteration for which $\forall t \geq t_\epsilon : \Delta M_t < \epsilon$. An ϵ choice is efficient if Q_{t_ϵ} is close to zero. Let $Q_{t_\epsilon} \leq 10^{-3}$ be a transcription of "Q_{t_ϵ} is close to zero" and $t_S = \max\limits_{1 \leq t \leq t_{\max}} \{t | Q_t > 10^{-3}\}$ be the last SMO iteration with training set S for which this condition is not true. The ϵ_{LOO} corresponding choice is determined by using W_t and ΔM_t recorded values with this one SMO's training:

$$\epsilon_{\text{LOO}} = \min_{1 \leq t \leq t_S} \Delta M_t \tag{8}$$

4 Experimental Results

For experiments, four datasets are used. Three are from Statlog collection: **Australian (Au)**, **Heart (He)** and **German (Ge)**. Fourth one is from UCI collection: **Adult (Ad)**. General information about used datasets are provided in table 1 where n and $|S|$ are respectively the number of features of examples and the training set sizes.

Table 1. Datasets information

Data sets (S)	n	$|S|$
Australian (Au)	14	390
Heart (He)	13	180
German (Ge)	24	400
Adult (Ad)	123	1605

Let T_M^{LOO} and n_M^{niter} be respectively total training time and total number of iterations to evaluate LOO error by using a SMO initialization method M. For all this section, gain $G_{\text{LOO}}^T = T_{M_2}^{\text{LOO}}/T_{M_1}^{\text{LOO}}$ ($G_{\text{LOO}}^{\text{iter}} = n_{M_2}^{\text{niter}}/n_{M_1}^{\text{niter}}$) corresponds to the gain in time (resp. total number of iterations) realized by using a given SMO initialization method M_1 in comparison of classical SMO initialization method M_2 (i.e $\alpha = 0, \epsilon = 10^{-3}$) for e_{LOO} computation. To illustrate the robustness of our method, experiments are conducted for a great number of θ hyperparameters values. Used procedure corresponds to the well known *grid search* method [8]. Tested values for C SVM hyperparameter are in: $\{2^x | x \in [-2, ..., 12]\}$. For Gaussian kernel: $k(x_i, x_j) = \exp(-\gamma ||x_i - x_j||^2)$, tested values for γ are in: $\{2^x | x \in [-10, ..., 2]\}$. For Polynomial kernel: $k(x_i, x_j) = (1+ < x_i, x_j >)^\gamma$, tested values for γ are in: $[2, ..., 6]$. Statistical measures within minimal, maximal, average and standard deviation for all tested models (C, γ) are respectively denoted by min, max, STD and AVG acronyms in tables 2. Experimental results with use of Gaussian or Polynomial kernel are mentioned in tables 2 and 3 by using respectively G or P letters between parenthesis after dataset's abreviation name.

Proposed method: First experimentation highlights the speed-up effect of using SMO $\tilde{\alpha}$ initialization produced by our method ($\epsilon_{\text{LOO}} = 10^{-3}$ for M_1 also). Table 2 (up-left) gives statistical measures of gain G_{LOO}^T with different data sets. Results here, show that $\tilde{\alpha}$ deduced from α_S is an efficient starting solution for SMO in average and in the worst case it is not as bad as $\alpha = 0$. However, the global speed-up for model selection is not sufficient for LOO error evaluation when training size grows (too expensive with **Adult** dataset for exemple). Second experimentation focuses on the effect of combining $\tilde{\alpha}$ and ϵ_{LOO} SMO initialization of our method. Table 2 (up-right) gives statistical measures of ϵ_{LOO} variation. In a similar way to first experimentation, table 2 (bottom-left) gives statistical information of gain variations in function of θ model. To estimate gain with **Adult** dataset, we made the hypothesis that training time (number of iterations) with $m-1$ and m examples are identical with SMO classical

Table 2. Statistical measures of: G_{LOO}^T with only our alpha seeding method (up-left) and with our complete method (bottom-left), ϵ_{LOO} with our adaptive ϵ_{LOO} method (up-right) and Δe_{LOO} between an adaptive ϵ_{LOO} and a fixed $\epsilon_{LOO} = 10^{-3}$ for stopping SMO (bottom-right)

G_{LOO}^T	min	max	AVG	STD
Au(G)	0.95	119.1	**9.67**	18.97
He(G)	1.25	81.38	**8.24**	14.90
Ge(G)	1.34	78.85	**7.13**	8.32

ϵ_{LOO}	min	max	AVG	STD
Au(G)	0.057	1.665	**0.164**	0.186
He(G)	0.062	1.785	**0.178**	0.216
Ge(G)	0.056	1.986	**0.149**	0.218
Ad(G)	0.058	1.854	**0.287**	0.300

G_{LOO}^T	min	max	AVG	STD
Au(G)	12.72	364.44	**99.01**	60.79
He(G)	25.08	379.59	**52.10**	63.75
Ge(G)	17.96	224.43	**102.43**	50.70
Ad(G)	82.30	26580	**1587**	4159

Δe_{LOO}	min	max	AVG	STD
Au(G)	-2.0%	+3.67%	**+0.16%**	±0.86%
He(G)	-1.67%	+5.0%	**+0.59%**	±1.05%
Ge(G)	-0.5%	+7.5%	**+1.23%**	±1.85%

initialization[1]. The variation of e_{LOO} with SMO's classical initialization have also been measured. Table 2 (bottom-right) gives statistical information for Statlog collection datasets. Results show that combining efficient alpha seeding and adaptive increase of ϵ stopping criterion permits to speed-up greatly LOO procedure. Speed-up could be spectacular for some θ models, in particular when training set size increases. Even with worse θ cases, the speed-up are not negligible and are in favour of greater training sets again. Moreover, e_{LOO} evaluations have small perturbations when stopping criterion is increased with our method. When results of Δe_{LOO} are examined in more detail, variations close to min or max values in bottom-right table 2 are almost always located in regions with high e_{LOO}. Consequently, model selection is very few impacted by those variations and e_{LOO} value for selected model is very close to values found with $\epsilon = 10^{-3}$. Average values in up-right table 2 highlight the global efficiency of Lee's $\epsilon = 0.1$ heuristic choice, but also the limit of a fixed value.

Comparaison with previous methods: First experimental comparisons have for objective to highlight difference between our adaptive ϵ_{LOO} stopping criterion and fixed $\epsilon_{LOO} = 10^{-1}$. Table 3 resumes results from this comparison. Our alpha seeding method is used for those experiments. Looking at table 3, it is obvious that SMO algorithm stopped earlier in average with our method without important increase of e_{LOO} deviation. Second experimental comparison has for objective to highlight difference between the three alpha seeding methods (ϵ_{LOO} adaptive is used for all of them). In table 3, n_{α_S} corresponds to the number of variables α modified to produce $\tilde{\alpha}$. It is a good indicator of G update cost. G_{LOO}^{iter} (G_{LOO}^T) is gain between an alpha seeding method and classical ($\alpha = 0$, $\epsilon = 10^{-3}$) SMO initialization. Results in table 3 show that DeCoste et al method can produce very efficient starting solution (**He(G)** and **Ge(G)**), but update cost of (6) is too high and penalizes G_{LOO}^T. It is particularly obvious with **Adult**

---

[1] Inspect of experimental results with the three Stalog datasets corroborate this hypothesis (*i.e.* variation of training times are negligible).

Table 3. Comparison between: (a) our adaptive or fixed ϵ value for SMO stopping criterion and (b) the three alpha seeding methods: AS_1, AS_2 and AS_3 which are respectively our method, Lee et al [5] and DeCoste et al [4] method

	(a) SMO's ϵ stopping criterion				(b) AS-SMO methods								
	adaptive		fixed		n_{α_S}			G_{LOO}^{iter}			G_{LOO}^{T}		
$S(K)$	G_{LOO}^{iter}	Δe_{LOO}	G_{LOO}^{iter}	Δe_{LOO}	AS_1	AS_2	AS_3	AS_1	AS_2	AS_3	AS_1	AS_2	AS_3
Au(G)	100	1.6 ± 0.9	76	1.8 ± 0.6	1.0	2.9	110	100	89	110	99	82	41
Au(P)	166	1.1 ± 1.6	31	0.5 ± 1.3	1.0	4.9	58	166	152	118	96	86	63
He(G)	49	0.6 ± 1.0	39	0.5 ± 0.9	1.1	2.4	82	49	51	112	52	51	28
He(P)	34	0.9 ± 0.9	31	0.9 ± 0.9	1.0	1.6	50	34	36	28	36	38	26
Ge(G)	109	1.2 ± 1.8	102	0.8 ± 1.3	1.1	2.7	223	109	109	341	102	104	38
Ge(P)	64	1.4 ± 1.3	62	1.1 ± 1.2	1.1	5.2	69	64	65	53	62	59	49
Ad(G)	1787	-	467	-	1.0	5.1	789	1787	529	699	1587	460	115
Ad(P)	1561	-	348	-	1.0	7.2	912	1561	421	731	1419	389	167

dataset. Lee method has a lower update cost, although our method has the lowest, especially when training set size increases.

5 Conclusion and Discussion

We developed an efficient method to speed-up e_{LOO} estimation. Experimental results show that our method outperforms in average previous proposed methods [4,5]. Moreover, speed-up of e_{LOO} evaluation increases with training set size. Our experiments have also highlighted that e_{LOO} deviations, when ϵ stopping criterion is increased efficiently, are mainly due to numerical instabilities when SVM ouptut is not confident. Future works have to extend this method to speed-up bootstrap and k fold cross-validation (with high k value but lower that m).

References

1. Duan, K., Keerthi, S.S., Poo, A.N.: Evaluation of simple performance measures for tuning svm hyperparameters. Neurocomputing **51** (2003) 41–59
2. Lee, J., Lin, C.: Automatic model selection for support vector machines. technical report. http://www.csie.ntu.edu.tw /~cjlin/papers/modelselect.ps.gz (2000)
3. Platt, J.: Fast training of SVMs using sequential minimal optimization, advances in kernel methods-support vector learning. MIT Press (1999) 185–208
4. DeCoste, D., Wagstaff, K.: Alpha seeding for support vector machines. In: Int. Conf. Knowledge Discovery Data Mining. (2000) 345–349
5. Lee, M.M.S., Keerthi, S.S., Ong, C.J., DeCoste, D.: An efficient method for computing leave-one-out error in SVM with gaussian kernels. JAIR **15** (2004) 750–757
6. Vapnik, V.N.: Statistical Learning Theory. Wiley edition (1998)
7. Fan, R.E., Chen, P.H., Lin, C.J.: Working set selection using the second order information for training SVM. JMLR **6** (2005) 1889–1918
8. Chang, C.C., Lin, C.J.: Libsvm: a library for Support Vector Machines. Software Available at http://www.csie.ntu.edu.tw/~cjlin/libsvm (2001)
9. Burbidge, R.: Stopping criteria for SVMs. Available at http://stats.ma.ic.ac.uk/rdb/public/~html/pubs/hermes.pdf (2002)

Integration of Strategies Based on Relevance Feedback into a Tool for the Retrieval of Mammographic Images

A. Fornells[1], E. Golobardes,[1] X. Vilasís[2], and J. Martí[3]

[1] Research Group in Intelligent Systems, Ramon Llull University
[2] Automatic and Control Section, Ramon Llull University
Enginyeria i Arquitectura La Salle, Quatre Camins 2-4, 08022 Barcelona (Spain)
{afornells, elisabet, xvilasis}@salle.url.edu
http://www.salle.url.edu/GRSI
[3] Computer Vision and Robotics Group, University of Girona,
Avda Lluís Santaló s/n, 17071 Girona (Spain)
joanm@eia.udg.es

Abstract. The incidence of breast cancer varies greatly among countries, but statistics show that every year 720,000 new cases will be diagnosed world-wide. However, a high percentage of these cases can be 100% healed if they are detected in early stages. Because symptoms are not visible as far as advanced stages, it makes the treatments more aggressive and also less efficient. Therefore, it is necessary to develop new strategies to detect the formation in early stages.

We have developed a tool based on a Case-Based Reasoning kernel for retrieving mammographic images by content analysis. One of the main difficulties is the introduction of knowledge and abstract concepts from domain into the retrieval process. For this reason, the article proposes integrate the human experts perceptions into it by means of an interaction between human and system using a Relevance Feedback strategy. Furthermore, the strategy uses a Self-Organization Map to cluster the memory and improve the time interaction.

Keywords: Breast Cancer, Bioinformatics Tools, Relevance Feedback, Knowledge Discovery & Retrieval Data, Case-Based Reasoning, Self-Organization Map.

1 Introduction

Breast cancer is the most common cancer among western women and is the leading cause of cancer-related death in women aged 15-54. Screening programs have proved to be good practical tools for prematurely detecting and removing breast cancer, and increasing the survival percentage in women [19]. In an attempt to improve early detection, a number of Computer Aided Diagnosis (CAD) techniques have been developed in order to help experts in the diagnosis.

We focus on a CAD tool for retrieving mammographic images by content analysis [12,5] called HRIMAC[1]. A mammographic image is like a breast

---
[1] HRIMAC is a project financed by Spanish government - TIC 2002-04160-C02-02.

radiography, which allows the extraction information on the tissue composition. The main purpose is to allow human experts to access a certain type of digital mammographic images typology stored in several public databases. This way, the results returned by the system allow experts to enhance their interpretations, and consequently, to improve the reliability of their diagnosis.

The retrieval process is based on Case-Based Reasoning (CBR) [1] because it justifies results by means of similarity criterion. It is based on solving new problems using its experience, as humans do. The 'experience' is a case memory containing previously solved cases. The CBR cycle can be summarized in the next steps: (1) It retrieves the most similar cases, (2) It adapts them to propose a new solution to the new environment, (3) It revises whether the solution is valid, and finally, (4) It stores it following a learning policy. One of the main difficulties is the definition of the similarity criterion through a similarity function, which is the responsibility of comparing the cases and defining a value of similarity.

Nowadays, HRIMAC only uses the physical features extracted from *mammographic* images previously diagnosed, called microcalcifications (μCa). A sample can contain several μCa in a large variety of sizes and locations making it almost impossible to introduce these abstract concepts into the similarity function. We may improve the precision if we could model the problem domain. That is why we have previously studied a wide set of general purpose of similarity functions and strategies to define similarity functions [5]. However, the experts - using their experiences and their human abstraction abilities - can form concepts which cannot be detected by the system using only the physical information. For this reason, we want to make them participate in the retrieval process by means of a Relevance Feedback strategy [13]. Thus, they can lead the search depending on their points of view through an interactive iterative process. Also, with the aim of reducing the execution time of each interaction, we organize the CBR case memory using a Self-Organization Map.

The article is organized as follows. Section 2 surveys some related work about Relevance Feedback. Section 3 sets the background techniques needed to implement the strategy. Section 4 describes the experimentation. Finally, section 5 summarizes the conclusions and the further work.

2 Relevance Feedback

Relevance Feedback are strategies used to introduce human subjectivity in the retrieval process. This is done by an iterative process in which the expert and the system interact. First, the system shows a set of results parting from an initial question/query from the expert. Next, the expert marks the positives (relevant) and negatives (non-relevant) examples - according to his own perception - from the results. Finally, the system rebuilds the query and shows them again. The process ends when the expert finds what he is looking for. This way, the system auto-adjusts itself according to the perception of expert, in order to obtain more accurate results. Therefore, its application reduces the differences in the similarity concepts of the human expert and the system.

These techniques can be classified according to the next properties: (1) Low level features (using physical properties) versus High level concepts (using concepts or contexts, as humans do) [2,17]; (2) Learning from the feedback of the users or not. This is dangerous if feedback is not fully objective [3]; (3) Positives Feedback, negative Feedback, or both [13]; (4) Category (the user looks for concepts), Objective (the user searches for a specific set of examples), or Exploring (the user does not know what he is exactly looking for) search [3]; (5) Query by example (the query are images) or Query by word (the query are keywords) [2]. Some properties are more recommended than others depending on the domain and the experts. Even they were originally oriented to document retrieval, their usage has been extended to image retrieval (Content Base Image Retrieval).

3 Integration of Relevance Feedback into HRIMAC

3.1 Definition of the Strategy

The requirements needed in our Relevance Feedback strategy are the next: (1) Management of low level features because HRIMAC only uses physical data extracted from mammographic images. Thus, system uses low level features; (2) Positives and negatives Feedbacks; (3) Queries by example or by keyword; (4) Category search; (5) System does not learn from the interaction due to the complexity of the domain and the difference in perception and experiences of each expert when analysing mammographic images.

The time between interactions need to be short because they are done in real time. Retrieve phase is the main neck bottle because CBR compares with all cases from the case memory, which can be useful or not. For this reason, we need to minimize the number of comparison by means of a selective retrieval in which the system only compares with potentially useful cases. The best way is indexing or clustering the case memory depending on the properties of the cases. For this purpose we use a framework called SOMCBR [4] developed by us, which clusters the case memory using a Kohonen or Self-Organizing Map (SOM) [10].

3.2 Integration of SOMCBR into the Relevance Feedback Strategy

SOM [10] is one of the major unsupervised learning paradigms in the family of artificial neural networks. It has many important properties which make it useful for clustering [7]: (1) It preserves the original topology; (2) It works well even though the original space has a high number of dimensions; (3) It incorporates the selection feature approach; (4) Although one class has few examples they are not lost; (5) It provides an easy way to show data; (6) It is organized in an autonomous way to be adjusted better to data. Moreover, Kohonen Maps are a Soft Computing technique that allows the management of uncertain, approximate, partial truth and complex knowledge. These capabilities are useful in order to manage real domains, which are often complex and uncertain. On the other hand, the drawbacks are that it is influenced by the order of the training samples, and it is not trivial to define how many clusters are needed.

```
input     : Let R be the set of retrieved elements from SOMCBR; let $D^+$ be the set of
            relevant elements; let $D^-$ be the set of non-relevant elements; let I be the actual
            element that is being evaluated;
1 Function Full Strategy is
2     $D^-=\emptyset$, $D^+=\{initial\ mammography\ image\}$
3     forall I de $D^+$ do
4         //Retrieve the most similar cases from the X most similar model
5         $R=R+(SOMCBR(I)-D^-)$
6     //Show the results to the user
7     if human expert finds what he is looking for then
8         End the execution
9     else
10        //The user marks the positive and negative images/cases
11        $D^+=$<Relevant elements>
12        $D^-=D^- \cup$ <Non-relevant element>
```

Fig. 1. Relevance Feedback strategy using the SOMCBR framework

They have successfully been used in a variety of clustering applications for CBIR. Zhang was the first in used them to filter images according to the colour and texture [20]. Next, Han and Myaeng [6] used them to define the outline of objects. Also, they have been used to develop search engines as in PicSOM [11] or WEBSOM [9].

SOM allows the projection of the original n-input data space into a new shorter m-output space in order to highlight the more important data features. This property allows the defining of clusters represented by a vector, which models certain patterns. These clustering capabilities are used in SOMCBR [4] to do a selective retrieval. This way, CBR only compares with cases belonging to the X most similar clusters instead of comparing with all cases from the case memory. The definition of the X value depends on the relation between time execution and error rate desired, because it determines the number of cases used in the comparison. Finally, figure 1 describes the SOMCBR integration in the Relevance Feedback strategy.

4 Experiments and Results

It is difficult to measure the improvement of Relevance Feedback into HRIMAC. There is not a standard benchmarking because evaluation is completely related to domain, its complexity, and the points of view of the expert. However, the introduction of an expert into the retrieval process allows system to obtain more accurate results under the perception of the expert, and consequently, its integration can be considered as positive. However, we can evaluate how SOMCBR works instead of the CBR without clustering (CBRWC) into the Relevance Feedback strategy. It means, the impact of using less cases in the retrieve phase on the error rate. Because we only study the measure capabilities, both systems are studied using a 1-NN in the retrieve phase.

Our main goal is to reduce the case retrieval mean time, which is related with the cases used in the retrieve phase. The number of models used determines this value as we can see in the figure 1. Let I be the number of interactions; let D be the results marked by expert as positives from CBR in each interaction; let K be the map size; let S be the size of case memory; and considering the mean number of elements by cluster as S/K^2, the number of comparisons in retrieve phase can be modeled in equation 1 and 2. They show how the number of operations in SOMCBR is smaller than in CBRWC for short X values, and how the operations are incremented for bigger values of X. Also, SOMCBR and CBRWC work similar when X is equal to the number of cases.

$$number\ of\ operations\ in\ CBRWC = (1 + D \cdot (I-1)) \cdot S \qquad (1)$$
$$number\ of\ operations\ in\ SOMCBR = (1 + D \cdot (I-1)) \cdot (K^2 + X \cdot S/K^2) \qquad (2)$$

Next, we study these equations over several datasets (see table 1) from HRI-MAC with the aim studying this in a more quantifiable way. The µCa dataset [12] contains samples from Trueta Hospital (in Girona), while DDSM [8] and MIAS [18] are public mammographic images datasets, which have been studied and preprocessed in [15,14] respectively. The µCa dataset contains samples of mammographies previously diagnosed by surgical biopsy, which can be benign or malign. DDSM and MIAS-Bi classify mammography densities, which was found relevant for the automatic diagnosis of breast cancer. Experts classify them either in four classes (according to BIRADS [16] classifications) or three classes (classification used in Trueta Hospital). Therefore, all this information is used with to aims: (1) Detecting abnormalities or espicular lesions in shape of µCa, and analysing whether they are benign or malign; (2) Defining the density of tissue to improve the mammographic interpretation.

The charts in figure 2 show the evolution of the number of operations. They have been build using the equation 2, and supposing common values for I (5) and D (3 and 5) variables. Also, we have test situations with few (K=2) and many clusters (K=8). It is obvious that SOMCBR strategy drastically reduces the number of comparisons required, and consequently, SOMCBR is better than CBRWC in terms of execution time.

The next step is to evaluate the influence of the reduction in the number of comparisons on the precision of results. We have three parameters to tune: the similarity function, the X value, and the map size. The similarity function in CBR used is Minkowski with r=1 because it provides the best error rate. Also, we focus on the worst situation for SOMCBR, that is, when X value is 1. Finally, we do not know the optimal number of clusters. For this reason, we study several map sizes in order to represent situations defined by many clusters

Table 1. Description of datasets from HRIMAC

Dataset	Attributes	Class distribution
µCa	22	benign (121), malign (95)
DDSM	143	b1(61), b2(185), b3(157), b4(98)
Mias-Bi	153	b1(128), b2(78), b3(70), b4(44)
Mias-3C	153	fatty(106), dense(112), glandular(104)

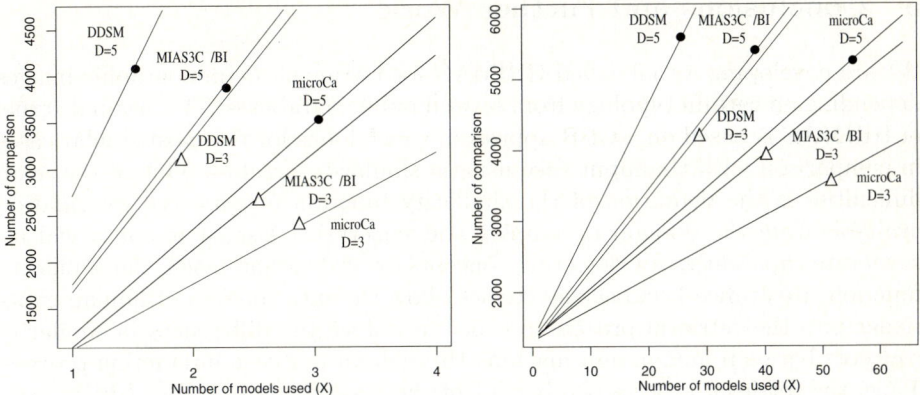

Fig. 2. Evolution for the number of operations in Relevance Feedback strategy using SOMCBR configured with 2×2 and 8×8 respectively, applying the equation 2. The 'Δ' and '$\bullet$' symbols represent the configurations for $D=3$ and 5 respectively.

with few cases, and defined by few clusters with many cases. The configurations tested are: 2×2 (4 clusters), 4×4 (16 clusters), and 8×8 (64 clusters).

Table 2 summarizes the error rates, their standard deviation, and the case retrieval mean time in milliseconds for the CBRWC and for several SOMCBR configurations. All computes have been done applying a 10-fold stratified Cross Validation. Comparing the error rates, we can observe that strategy based on clustering the case memory maintains the error rate for the datasets, and it provides equivalent results if we apply a t-student at 95% of confidence level. This is produced because the Soft Computing capabilities of SOM allows the management of uncertain, approximate, partial truth and complex knowledge. Thus, the SOMCBR strategy is able to manage these complex data, and it does not affect negatively the error rate. Also, the results show the improvement of time, which is significantly better when the CBR case memory is clustered, that is, in SOMCBR strategy.

Therefore, we can conclude that the application of SOMCBR as kernel of our Relevance Feedback strategy is positive, because we drastically reduce the number of comparisons in retrieve phase, and consequently the execution time, without negatively affecting the error rate.

Table 2. Summary of error rates, their standard deviation, and the case retrieval mean time in milliseconds for CBR and SOMCBR using several map sizes $(K \times K)$, $X=1$, and Minkowski (r=1) as similarity function

Code	CBRWC		SOMCBR - 2×2		SOMCBR - 4×4		SOMCBR - 8×8	
	%AR(std.)	Time	%AR(std.)	Time	%AR(std.)	Time	%AR(std.)	Time
μCa	31.02(10.5)	0.1	34.26(9.5)	0.04	33.80(7.7)	0.02	34.26(8.1)	0.01
DD	55.49(5.8)	1.9	53.49(5.6)	1.30	53.89(5.2)	1.18	54.29(4.3)	1.10
MB	30.94(11.4)	1.5	29.69(5.5)	0.69	31.25(7.4)	0.61	32.19(5.8)	0.59
M3	29.81(6.4)	1.5	29.19(6.2)	0.69	29.81(6.2)	0.61	31.06(8.5)	0.59

5 Conclusions and Further Work

We are developing a tool called HRIMAC for retrieving mammographic images depending on certain typology from several public databases. The original kernel of HRIMAC is based on a CBR approach, which looks for the most similar cases in comparison with the input case using a similarity function. One of the main difficulties is the definition of the similarity function because the information available from the domain is complex and uncertain. Also, it is not trivial incorporate capabilities for detecting concepts or abstraction inside the similarity function. Relevance Feedback strategies allow the introduction of human experience into the retrieval process in order to reduce the differences in similarity concepts between human and machine through an iterative interaction process. Thus, the retrieval process can benefit of the experts abilities for creating concepts and relationships that systems usually can not detect. For this reason, we want to integrate this strategy into HRIMAC in order to make the task of retrieving mammographic images easier.

On the other hand, the interaction needs to be fast because it is done in real time. The CBR retrieve phase is the bottle neck because it has to compare with all the cases from the case memory. One way of improving it is by means of a selective retrieval, in which CBR only compares with potentially useful cases. For this reason, we have proposed the use of SOMCBR as kernel of our Relevance Feedback strategy because it is a CBR with a case memory clustered by SOM. SOM is a clustering algorithm that projects the original space into other more reduced with the aim of highlighting the more important features. This property is used to build clusters that model the information. Thus, CBR can organize the case memory to improve the retrieval time. Also, SOM has Soft Computing capabilities that allow the management of uncertain, approximate, partial truth and complex knowledge and, consequently, improve the management capacity. The experiments done show that error rate has not been negatively influenced by the reduction of the information used. Therefore, SOMCBR strategy is better than CBR in these datasets because it improves the execution time without negatively affecting the error rate.

The further work is focused on improving the Relevance Feedback strategy allowing semantic content by means of the introduction of keywords, which represent concepts of experts, in order to improve the capacity of retrieving results more accurately. This goal requires two previous steps: (1) Experts have to mark all the mammographic image in order to set high level relations, (2) We need to define a similarity function capable of managing and measuring distances between concepts.

Acknowledgements

We would like to thank the Spanish Government for the support under grants TIC 2002-04160-C02-02 and TIN 2005-08386-C05-04, and the *Generalitat de*

Catalunya (DURSI) for the support under grants 2005SGR-302 and 2006FIC-0043. Also, we would like to thank *Enginyeria i Arquitectura La Salle* of Ramon Llull University for the support to our research group.

References

1. A. Aamodt and E. Plaza. Case-based reasoning: Foundations issues, methodological variations, and system approaches. *IA Communications*, 7:39–59, 1994.
2. Z. Chen, L. Wenyin, C. Hu, M. Li, and H. Zhang. ifind: a web image search engine. In *Proceedings of the 24th annual international ACM SIGIR conference on Research and development in information retrieval*, page 450. ACM Press, 2001.
3. I.J. Cox, T.P. Minka, and T.V. Papathomas. The bayesian image retrieval system, pichunter: Theory, implementation, and psychophysical experiments. *IEEE Transaction on Image Processing – special issue on digital libraries*, 9:20–37, 2000.
4. A. Fornells, E. Golobardes, D. Vernet, and G. Corral. Unsupervised case memory organization: Analysing computational time and soft computing capabilities. In *8th European Conference on Case-Based Reasoning*, 2006. In press.
5. E. Golobardes, X. Llorà, M. Salamó, and J. Martí. Computer aided diagnosis with case-based reasoning and genetic algorithms. *Journal of Knowledge Based Systems*, 15:45–52, 2002.
6. K. Han and S. Myaeng. Image organization and retrieval with automatically constructed feature vectors. *SIGIR Forum*, special issue:157–165, 1996.
7. S. Haykin. *Neural Networks: A Comprehensive Foundation*. Prentice Hall, 2nd edition, 1999.
8. M. Heath, K. Bowyer, D. Kopans, R. Moore, and P.J. Kegelmeyer. The digital database for screening mammography. *Int. Workshop on Dig. Mammography*, 2000.
9. S. Kaski, T. Honkela, K. Lagus, and T. Kohonen. Websom: Self-organizing maps of document collections. *Neurocomputing*, 21(1):101–117, 1998.
10. T. Kohonen. *Self-Organization and Associative Memory*, volume 8 of *Springer Series in Information Sciences*. Springer, Berlin, Heidelberg, 1984. 3rd ed. 1989.
11. J. Laaksonen, M. Koskela, and E. Oja. Picsom: Self-organization maps for content-based image retrieval. In *Proceedings of Int. Joint Conference on NN*, 1999.
12. J. Martí, J. Español, E. Golobardes, J. Freixenet, R. García, and M. Salamó. Classification of microcalcifications in digital mammograms using case-based reasonig. *International Workshop on Digital Mammography*, 2000.
13. H. Müller, Wolfgang Müller, Stéphane Marchand-Maillet, and Thierry Pun. Strategies for positive and negative relevance feedback in image retrieval. *International Conference on Pattern Recognition*, 1:1043–1046, 2000.
14. A. Oliver, J. Freixenet, A. Bosch, D. Raba, and R. Zwiggelaar. Automatic classification of breast tissue. In *Iberian Conference on Pattern Recognition and Image Analysis*, pages 431–438, 2005.
15. A. Oliver, J. Freixenet, and R. Zwiggelaar. Automatic classification of breast density. *IEEE International Conference on Image Processing*, 2:1258–1261, 2005.
16. T. H. Samuels. *Illustrated Breast Imaging Reporting and Data System BIRADS*. American College of Radiology Publications, 3rd edition, 1998.
17. Stan Sclaroff, Leonid Taycher, and Marco LaCascia. Imagerover: A content-based image browser for the world wide web. Technical Report 5, 1997.

18. J. Suckling, J. Parker, and D.R. Dance. The mammographic image analysis society digital mammogram database. In A.G. Gale et al., editor, *Proceedings of 2nd International Workshop on Digital Mammography*, pages 211–221, 1994.
19. D. Winfields, M. Silbiger, and G. Brown. Technology transfer in digital mamography. *Report of the Joint National Cancer Institute, Workshop of May 19-20, Invest Radiololgy*, pages 507–515, 1994.
20. H. Zhang and D. Zhong. A scheme for visual feature based image indexing. In *Storage and Retrieval for Image and Video Databases III*, volume 2420, 1995.

Generalization Performance of Exchange Monte Carlo Method for Normal Mixture Models

Kenji Nagata[1] and Sumio Watanabe[2]

[1] Department of Computational Intelligence and Systems Science, Tokyo Institute of Technology, MailBox R2-5,4259, Nagatsuta, Midori-ku, Yokohama, 226-8503 Japan
kenji.nagata@cs.pi.titech.ac.jp
[2] P&I Lab.,Tokyo Institute of Technology
swatanab@pi.titech.ac.jp

Abstract. A normal mixture model, which belongs to singular learning machines, is widely used in statistical pattern recognition. In singular learning machines, the Bayesian learning provides the better generalization performance than the maximum likelihood estimation. However, it needs huge computational cost to realize the Bayesian posterior distribution by the conventional Monte Carlo method. In this paper, we propose that the exchange Monte Carlo method is appropriate for the Bayesian learning in singular learning machines, and experimentally show that it provides better generalization performance in the Bayesian learning of a normal mixture model than the conventional Monte Carlo method.

1 Introduction

A normal mixture model is a learning machine which estimates the target probability density by sum of normal distributions. This learning machine is widely used in statistical pattern recognition and data clustering. Normal mixture models belong to singular learning machines because they have singular points where the Fisher information matrices are degenerate. In singular learning machines, it is well known that the Bayesian learning provides better generalization performance than the maximum likelihood estimation that tends to produce a learning machine overfitting the data[1].

In the Bayesian learning, it is necessary to realize the Bayesian posterior distribution accurately around the singular points. A Markov Chain Monte Carlo (MCMC) method is often used to generate a sequence of Markov chain that converges to the target distribution. Recently, it has been shown that the Metropolis algorithm, one of the MCMC methods, needs huge computational cost to approximate the Bayesian posterior distributions of singular learning machines [3]. This is because the Bayesian posteriors of the singular learning machines are widely and complexly distributed in the parameter space.

On the other hand, an improved MCMC method has recently been developed based on the idea of an extended ensemble method, which is surveyed in [4]. This method gives us a general strategy for overcoming the problem of huge computational cost. An exchange Monte Carlo (MC) method is well known as one of the extended ensemble method [5], and its effectiveness has been shown in a spin glass [5], a strongly correlated system, an optimization problem and many other applications.

In this paper, we propose that the exchange MC method is appropriate to compute the Bayesian learning in singular learning machines, and experimentally show that the exchange MC method provides better generalization performance in the Bayesian learning of a normal mixture model than the Metropolis algorithm.

This paper consists of five sections. In Section 2, we introduce the normal mixture models and the frameworks of the Bayesian learning and the MCMC method respectively. In Section 3, the exchange MC method and its application to the Bayesian learning are described. In Section 4, we state the experimental result. Finally, discussion and conclusion are followed in Section 5.

2 Background

2.1 Normal Mixture Models

Suppose that $g(x|b, \Sigma)$ is a density function of an M-dimensional normal distribution whose mean is $b \in R^M$ and variance-covariance matrix is $\Sigma \in R^{M \times M}$. A normal mixture model $p(x|w)$ of an M-dimensional input $x \in R^M$ with a parameter vector w is defined by $p(x|w) = \sum_{k=1}^{K} a_k g(x|b_k, \Sigma_k)$, where the integer K is the number of components and $\{a_k | a_k \geq 0, \sum_{k=1}^{K} a_k = 1\}$ is the set of coefficients. The parameter w of this learning machine is $w = \{a_k, b_k, \Sigma_k\}_{k=1}^{K}$.

In some applications, the parameter is confined to the mean of each component and it is supposed that there are no correlation between each input dimension. In this case, the learning machine is rewritten by

$$p(x|w) = \sum_{k=1}^{K} \frac{a_k}{\sqrt{2\pi\sigma_k^2}^M} \exp\left(-\frac{||x - b_k||^2}{2\sigma_k^2}\right),$$

where $\sigma_k > 0$ is a constant. This means $w = \{a_k, b_k\}_{k=1}^{K}$. Hereafter, we consider learning in this type of normal mixture models.

Normal mixture models belong to singular learning machines because they have singular points in their parameter space. Let us illustrate the singularities by the simplest example. Assume that the true distribution $q(x)$ of a one-dimensional input x is defined by $q(x) = \frac{1}{\sqrt{2\pi}} \exp\left(-\frac{(x-b^*)^2}{2}\right)$. This distribution has one component. Also assume that a learning machine is defined by $p(x|w) = \frac{a}{\sqrt{2\pi}} \exp\left(-\frac{(x-b_1)^2}{2}\right) + \frac{1-a}{\sqrt{2\pi}} \exp\left(-\frac{(x-b_2)^2}{2}\right)$, which has two components. The set of true parameter is $\{a = 1, b_1 = b^*\} \cup \{a = 0, b_2 = b^*\} \cup \{b_1 = b_2 = b^*\}$. This set has singular points where two sets of true parameters are crossing (Figure 1). At a singular point, Fisher information matrix is degenerate. Therefore, it is generally difficult to clarify the property of learning for singular learning machines theoretically.

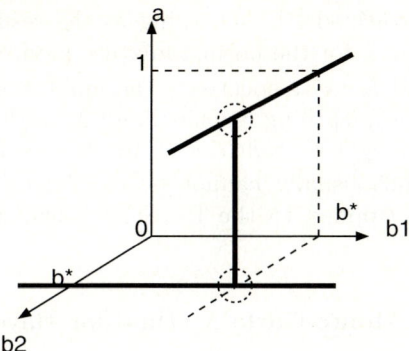

Fig. 1. Singularity of normal mixture models. Thick lines are set of true parameters. Circle center indicates a singular point.

2.2 Frameworks of Bayesian Learning

Let $X^n = (X_1, X_2, ..., X_n)$ be n training samples independently and identically taken from the true distribution $q(x)$. In the Bayesian learning of a learning machine $p(x|w)$ whose parameter is w, the prior distribution $\varphi(w)$ of the parameter w needs to be set. Then the posterior distribution $p(w|X^n)$ is defined by the given dataset X^n and the prior distribution $\varphi(w)$ as follows,

$$p(w|X^n) = \frac{1}{Z(X^n)} \varphi(w) \prod_{i=1}^{n} p(X_i|w),$$

where $Z(X^n)$ is the normalization constant, which is also known as the marginal likelihood or as the evidence. In the Bayesian learning, the predictive distribution $p(x|X^n)$ is given by averaging the learning machine over the posterior distribution,

$$p(x|X^n) = \int p(x|w) p(w|X^n) dw,$$

which estimates the true density function of x given dataset X^n.

The generalization error is defined by

$$G(X^n) = \int q(x) \log \frac{q(x)}{p(x|X^n)} dx,$$

which indicates the Kullback-Leibler divergence from the true distribution to the predictive distribution. The averaged generalization error has the following asymptotic form,

$$E_{X^n}[G(X^n)] = \frac{\lambda}{n} - \frac{m-1}{n \log n} + O\left(\frac{1}{n \log n}\right),$$

where the notation $E_{X^n}[\,]$ shows the value of expectation over all sets of training samples. The values of rational number λ and natural number m depend on the learning machine and the prior distribution. Recently, an algebraic geometrical method for singular learning machines has been established, and their learning coefficients have been clarified [1]. According to the results, in the redundant case, the upper bound of λ for the normal mixture models is $\lambda \leq \frac{MK_0+K_0-1}{2} + \frac{K-K_0}{2}$ [2], where K_0 and K are respectively the number of components for the true distribution and for a learning machine, and M is the dimension for data.

In the Bayesian learning, we need to compute the expectation over the posterior distribution, which usually cannot be carried out analytically. Hence, the MCMC method is applied to the Bayesian learning in singular learning machines.

2.3 Markov Chain Monte Carlo Method for Bayesian Learning

The MCMC method is the algorithm to obtain the sample sequence which converges in law to the random variable subject to a target probability distribution. The Metropolis algorithm is well known as one of MCMC methods[9]. Given the target density function, the Metropolis algorithm can be applied even if the normalization constant is not clarified. Therefore, the sample sequence from the Bayesian posterior distribution can be obtained by the Metropolis algorithm.

However, when the Metropolis algorithm is employed in the computation of expectation over the Bayesian posterior distribution of a singular learning machine, it requires vast computational resources [3]. The characteristic time to generate a sample sequence which converges to the Bayesian posterior distribution increases rapidly as the number n of the training samples increases. This is caused by the fact that the target distribution is complexly distributed in the parameter space.

The Bayesian posterior distribution has most of its density around the true parameters. The variance of this distribution becomes small as the number n of training samples increases. As we mentioned in Section 2.1, in singular learning machines, the set of true parameter(s) is not a point but an analytic set like Figure 1. Therefore, the Bayesian posterior distribution for a singular learning machine is complexly distributed in the parameter space. On the contrary, Metropolis algorithm is based on local updating. Moreover, the smaller the variance of target distribution is, the more local the updating of Metropolis algorithm has to become. Consequently, it requires huge cost to generate a sample sequences to converge to the Bayesian posterior distribution for a singular learning machine by the Metropolis algorithm.

3 Proposal

In this paper, we propose that the exchange MC method is appropriate for Bayesian learning in singular learning machines.

3.1 Exchange Monte Carlo Method

The exchange MC method treats a compound system which consists of noninteracting L sample sequences of the system concerned. The elements of the l-th sample sequence $\{w_l\}$ converge in law to the random variable which is subject to the following probability distribution

$$P_l(w) \propto \exp(-t_l \hat{H}(w)) \quad (1 \leq l \leq L),$$

where $t_1 < t_2 < \cdots < t_L$. Given a set of the temperatures $\{t\}$, the simultaneous distribution for finding $\{w\} = \{w_1, w_2, \cdots, w_L\}$ is expressed as a simple product formula by $P(\{w\}; \{t\}) = \prod_{l=1}^{L} P_l(w)$. The exchange MC method is based on two types of updating in constructing a Markov chain. One is conventional updates based on the Metropolis algorithm for each target distribution $P_l(w)$. In addition to the Metropolis algorithm, we carry out the position exchange between two sequences, that is, $\{w_l, w_{l+1}\} \to \{w_{l+1}, w_l\}$. The transition probability $P(w_l, w_{l+1}; t_l, t_{l+1})$ is defined by

$$P(w_l, w_{l+1}; t_l, t_{l+1}) = \min(1, \exp(-\Delta))$$
$$\Delta(w_l, w_{l+1}; t_l, t_{l+1}) = (t_{l+1} - t_l)(\hat{H}(w_l) - \hat{H}(w_{l+1})).$$

Under these updates, the simultaneous distribution is invariant because these updates satisfy the detailed balance condition for the simultaneous distribution.

Consequently, the following two steps are carried out in alternate shifts:

1. Each sequence is simulated simultaneously and independently for a few iteration by Metropolis algorithm.
2. Two positions are exchanged with the probability $P(w_l, w_{l+1}; t_l, t_{l+1})$.

3.2 Application to the Bayesian Learning

The exchange MC method can be applied to Bayesian learning by defining the probability distribution $p_l(w|X^n)$ as

$$p_l(w|X^n) = \frac{1}{Z_l(X^n)} \varphi(w) \left(\prod_{i=1}^{n} p(X_i|w) \right)^{t_l}.$$

As mentioned in Section 2.3, the Bayesian posterior distribution, which is equal to $p_l(w|X^n)$ for $t_l = 1$, is complexly distributed. In the case that $0 < t_l < 1$, the distribution $p_l(w|X^n)$ is distributed less complexly than the Bayesian posterior distribution. Moreover, the distribution $p_l(w|X^n)$ for $t_l = 0$ has no complexity because it is equal to the prior distribution. Therefore, by using the distribution $p_l(w|X^n)$ for $0 \leq t \leq 1$ as the target distribution for the exchange MC method, we expect to obtain a sample sequence to converge to the posterior distribution in less samples than the Metropolis algorithm. In this paper, we propose that the exchange MC method is appropriate for computing the Bayesian learning in the singular learning machines, and show its effectiveness by experimental results.

4 Experiment

In this section, we present the experimental results where the Bayesian learning is simulated for the mixture model with the 3-dimensional gaussian component

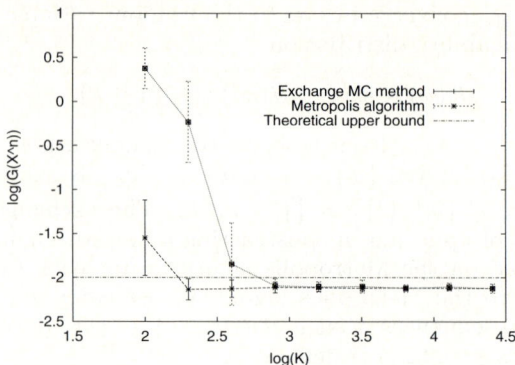

Fig. 2. The results of generalization error using the exchange MC method and the Metropolis algorithm

$c(x|b) = \frac{1}{(2\pi)^{3/2}} \exp(-\frac{||x-b||^2}{2})$. This means $M = 3$. We compare the exchange MC method with the Metropolis algorithm by applying each method to sample producing from the Bayesian posterior distribution.

In these experiments, the number K_0 of components in the true distribution is set as 2, and the number K in the learning machine 5. The true distribution is set to $q(x) = 0.52 * c(x|(-1.19, 1.43, 3.50)^T) + 0.48 * c(x|(3.54, 2.01, 2.35)^T)$. We prepare a sample set with the sample size $n = 500$ from this true distribution. The prior distributions for the parameter a_k and b_k are respectively defined as a uniform distribution with the range $[0,1]$ and a 3-dimensional standard gaussian distribution.

The number L of the set of the temperatures $\{t_1, \cdots, t_L\}$ is configured as 42, and the temperature t_l is defined as

$$t_l = \begin{cases} 0 & \text{(if } l = 1) \\ (1.25)^{-L+l} & \text{(otherwise)}. \end{cases}$$

Note that $t_L = 1$. The initial value of the parameter w is randomly selected from the prior distribution $\varphi(w)$. For calculating the expectation, we use the last fifty percents of the sample sequence in order to reduce the influence of the initial value. An iteration for Step 1 of the exchange MC method is set as 1. In the exchange MC method, the rule for selecting the exchange pairs is $\{(w_1, w_2), (w_3, w_4), \cdots, (w_{41}, w_{42})\}$ if the number k of MC iteration is odd, and $\{(w_2, w_3), (w_4, w_5), \cdots, (w_{40}, w_{41})\}$ otherwise.

Firstly, for the evaluation of the algorithm, we calculate the generalization error, which is approximated by $\frac{1}{n'} \sum_{i=1}^{n'} \log \frac{q(x_i')}{p(x_i'|X^n)}$ with test data $\{x_i'\}_{i=1}^{n'=2500}$ generated from the true distribution. Figure 2 shows the average of the generalization errors. The horizontal axis shows the base-10 logarithm of MC iteration, and the vertical one the base-10 logarithm of the generalization error. The value of MC iteration is changed from 100 to 25600. The horizontal line shows the theoretical upper bound of the generalization error. Comparing two results of each algorithm, convergence of generalization error for the exchange

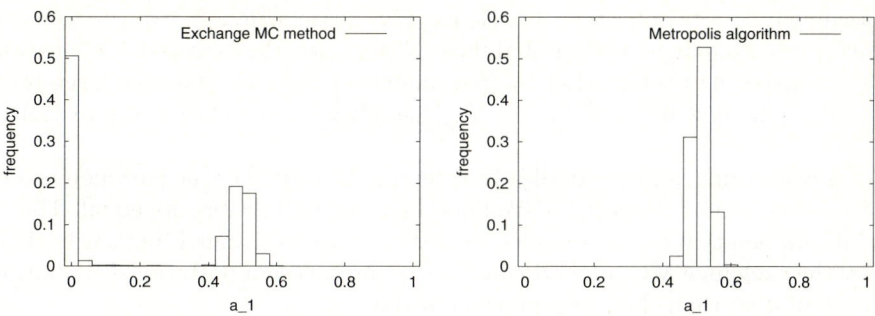

Fig. 3. The histograms of the parameter a_1. The left is obtained by the exchange MC method and the right by the Metropolis algorithm.

MC method is faster than that for Metropolis algorithm. However, after each algorithm is converged, there is little difference between two algorithms. Note that the computational cost of the exchange MC method is higher than that of the Metropolis algorithm. However, by the parallel processing, we can make the computational time of the exchange MC method equal to that of the Metropolis algorithm.

Secondly, we compare the distribution of the sample sequences obtained by the exchange MC method with that by the Metropolis algorithm. Figure 3 shows the histograms of the parameter a_1, the coefficient of one of 5 components. The left part of Figure 3 is obtained by the exchange MC method and the right part the Metropolis algorithm. Considering the true parameters, the marginal distribution for the parameter a_1 has peaks near $a_1 = 0$ and near $a_1 = 0.5$. Consequently, the exchange MC method generates the correct histogram while the Metropolis algorithm generates the localized histogram.

5 Discussion and Conclusion

In this paper, we proposed that the exchange MC method is appropriate for the Bayesian learning of the singular learning machines and clarified its effectiveness experimentally by simulating learning of the normal mixture model. As a result, we found that the experimental value of the generalization error using the exchange MC method converges in the smaller number of MC iterations than using the Metropolis algorithm. Moreover, after converging, the exchange MC method can approximate the Bayesian posterior distribution more accurately than the Metropolis algorithm.

In this section, we discuss experimental results. In the setting of Section 3.2, the transition probability for the exchange MC method depends on minus of the logarithm likelihood, that is,

$$\Delta(w_l, w_{l+1}; t_l, t_{l+1}) = (t_{l+1} - t_l)(L(w_l) - L(w_{l+1})),$$

$$L(w) = -\sum_{i=1}^{n} \log p(X_i|w)$$

We assume $t_{l+1} > t_l$ in Section 3.1. Hence, if $L(w_l) < L(w_{l+1})$, two positions,w_l and w_{l+1}, are exchanged with probability 1. Therefore, the exchange MC method works to make the likelihood of the parameter w_L for $t = 1$ become large preferentially. This is why the value of the generalization error using the exchange MC method converges fast.

After converging, all the samples $\{w_l\}$ tend to be near the true parameters. On the true parameters, the value of likelihood for any parameters are equal. Therefore, all combination of two samples w_l and w_{l+1} are exchanged frequently. This is why the exchange MC method can realize the Bayesian posterior distribution more accurately than the Metropolis algorithm.

However, in spite of the fact that the Metropolis algorithm produce the localized sample sequence, the generalization error has less difference between the exchange MC method and the Metropolis algorithm. One of our future works is to clarify the relationship between the convergence accuracy of a sample sequence and the generalization error or other expectation values.

Acknowledgement. This research was partially supported by the Ministry of Education, Science, Sports and Culture, Grant-in-Aid for JSPS Fellows 18-5809 and for Scientific Research 15500130, 2006.

References

1. S.Watanabe, "Algebraic analysis for nonidentifiable learning machines," Neural Computation, Vol.13, No.4, pp.899-933, 2001.
2. K.Yamazaki, S,Watanabe, "Singularities in mixture models and upper bounds of stochastic complexity," Neural Networks, Vol.16, No.7, pp.1029-1038, 2003.
3. N.Nakano, K.Takahashi, S.Watanabe, "On the Evaluation Criterion of the MCMC Method in Singular Learning Machines" , Trans. of IEICE, Vol.J88-D-2, No.10, pp.2011-2020, 2005.
4. Y.Iba, "Extended Ensemble Monte Carlo", International Journal of Modern Physics, C12, pp.623-656, 2001.
5. K.Hukushima, K.Nemoto, "Exchange Monte Carlo Method and Application to Spin Glass Simulation", Journal of the Physical Society of Japan, Vol.65, No.6, pp.1604-1608, 1996.
6. P.Sengupta, A.W.Sandvik, D.K.Campbell, "Bond-order-wave phase and quantum phase transitions in the one dimensional extended Hubbard model", Physical Review B, vol.65, 155113, 2002.
7. K.Pinn, C.Wieczerkowski, "Number of magic squares from parallel tempering Monte Carlo", Int. J. Mod. Phys. C9, 541, 1998.
8. K.Hukushima, "Extended ensemble Monte Carlo approach to hardly relaxing problems", Computer Physics Communications, 147, pp.77-82, 2002.
9. K.Nagata, S.Watanabe, "Exchange Monte Carlo Method for Bayesian Learning in Singular Learning Machines", Proc of International Joint Conference on Neural Networks 2006 (IJCNN2006), to appear.

Evolutionary Design of gdSOFPNN for Modeling and Prediction of NOx Emission Process

Tae-Chon Ahn and Ho-Sung Park

Department of Electrical Electronic and Information Engineering, Wonkwang University,
344-2, Shinyong-Dong, Iksan, Chon-Buk, 570-749, South Korea
tcahn@wonkwang.ac.kr

Abstract. In this study, we proposed **g**enetically **d**ynamic optimized **S**elf-**O**rganizing **F**uzzy **P**olynomial **N**eural **N**etworks (SOFPNN) with information granulation based Fuzzy Polynomial Neuron(FPN) (**gdSOFPNN**), develop a comprehensive design methodology involving mechanisms of genetic optimization. The proposed gdSOFPNN gives rise to a structurally and parametrically optimized network through an optimal parameters design available within the FPN (viz. the number of input variables, the order of the polynomial, input variables, the number of membership functions, and the apexes of membership function). Here, with the aid of the information granulation, we determine the initial location (apexes) of membership functions and initial values of polynomial function being used in the premised and consequence part of the fuzzy rules respectively. The performance of the proposed gdSOFPNN is quantified through experimentation that exploits standard data already used in fuzzy modeling.

1 Introduction

When the dimensionality of the model goes up (the number of system's variables increases), so do the difficulties. In the sequel, to build models with good predictive abilities as well as approximation capabilities, there is a need for advanced tools [1].
To help alleviate the problems, one among the first approaches along systematic design of nonlinear relationships between system's inputs and outputs comes under the name of a Group Method of Data Handling (GMDH) [2], [3]. The GMDH-type algorithms have been extensively used since the mid-1970's for prediction and modeling complex nonlinear processes. While providing with a systematic design procedure, the GMDH comes with some drawbacks. To alleviate the problems associated with the GMDH, Self-Organizing Neural Networks were introduced by Oh et al. [3], [4], [5], [6] as a new category of neural networks or neuro-fuzzy networks. Although the SOFPNN has a flexible architecture whose potential can be fully utilized through a systematic design, it is difficult to obtain the structurally and parametrically optimized network because of the limited design of the nodes located in each layer of the SOFPNN.

In this study, in considering the above problems coming with the conventional SOFPNN, we introduce a new structure and organization of fuzzy rules as well as a new genetic design approach. The determination of the optimal values of the parameters available within an individual FPN (viz. the number of input variables, the order of the polynomial, a collection of preferred nodes, the number of MF, and the apexes of membership function) leads to a structurally and parametrically optimized network through the genetic approach.

2 SOFPNN with FPN and Its Topology

The FPN consists of two basic functional modules. The first one, labeled by **F**, is a collection of fuzzy sets that form an interface between the input numeric variables and the processing part realized by the neuron. The second module (denoted here by **P**) is about the function – based nonlinear (polynomial) processing. The detailed FPN involving a certain regression polynomial is shown in Table 1.

Table 1. Different forms of regression polynomial building a FPN

Order of the polynomial		No. of inputs		
Order	FPN	1	2	3
0	Type 1	Constant	Constant	Constant
1	Type 2	Linear	Bilinear	Trilinear
2	Type 3	Quadratic	Biquadratic-1	Triquadratic-1
	Type 4		Biquadratic-2	Triquadratic-2

1: Basic type, 2: Modified type

3 The Structural Optimization of the gdSOFPNN

3.1 Information Granulation by Means of HCM Clustering Method

Information granulation is defined informally as linked collections of objects (data points, in particular) drawn together by the criteria of indistinguishability, similarity or functionality [7]. We extract information for the real system with the aid of Hard C-Means (HCM) clustering method [4], [5], which deals with the conventional crisp sets. Through HCM, we determine the initial location (apexes) of membership functions and initial values of polynomial function being used in the premise and consequence part of the fuzzy rules respectively. The fuzzy rules of the gdSOFPNN is as followings.

$$R^j : If\ x_1\ is\ A_{ji}\ and\ \cdots x_k\ is\ A_{jk}\ then\ y_j - M_j = f_j\{(x_1 - v_{j1}), (x_2 - v_{j2}), \cdots, (x_k - v_{jk})\}$$

Where, A_{jk} means the fuzzy set, the apex of which is defined as the center point of information granule (cluster). M_j and v_{jk} are the center points of new created input-output variables by information granule.

3.2 Genetic Optimization of the gdSOFPNN

Let us briefly recall that GAs is a stochastic search technique based on the principles of evolution, natural selection, and genetic recombination by simulating a process of "survival of the fittest" in a population of potential solutions to the given problem. The main features of genetic algorithms concern individuals viewed as strings, population-based optimization and stochastic search mechanism (selection and crossover). In order to enhance the learning of the gdSOFPNN and augment its performance, we use genetic algorithms to obtain the structural optimization of the network by optimally selecting such parameters as the number of input variables (nodes), the order of polynomial, input variables, and the number of MF within a gdSOFPNN. Here, GAs uses serial method of binary type, roulette-wheel as the selection operator, one-point crossover, and an invert operation in the mutation operator [8].

4 The Algorithm and Design Procedure of the gdSOFPNN

[Step 1] *Determine system's input variables.*
[Step 2] *Form training and testing data.*
[Step 3] *Decide initial information for constructing the gdSOFPNN structure.*
[Step 4] *Decide FPN structure using genetic design.*
The 1st sub-chromosome contains the number of input variables, the 2nd sub-chromosome involves the order of the polynomial of the node, the 3rd sub-chromosome contains input variables, and the 4th sub-chromosome (remaining bits) involves the number of MF coming to the corresponding node (FPN).
[Step 5] *Design of structurally optimized gdSOFPNN.*
In this step, we design the structurally optimized gdSOFPNN by means of the FPNs that obtained in [Step 4].
[Step 6] *Identify the membership value using dynamic searching method of GAs.*
Fig. 1 shows the identification of membership value using dynamic searching method of GAs.

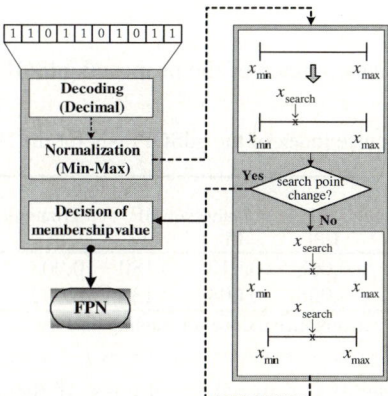

Fig. 1. Identification of membership value using dynamic searching method

[Step 7] *Design of parametrically optimized gdSOFPNN.*
The fitness function reads as

$$F(\textit{fitness function}) = 1/E \tag{1}$$

Where, E means the objective function with weighting factor ($E=\theta\times PI+(1-\theta)\times EPI$).

5 Experimental Studies

We illustrate the performance of the network and elaborate on its development by experimenting with data coming from the NOx emission process of gas turbine power plant [9]. To come up with a quantitative evaluation of network, we use the standard MSE performance index.

Table 2. Computational aspects of the genetic optimization of the gdSOFPNN

	Parameters	1st layer	2nd layer	3rd layer
GA	Maximum generation	100		
	Total population size	300×No. of 1st layer node		
	Crossover rate	0.65		
	Mutation rate	0.1		
	String length	90		
gdSO FPNN	Maximal no.(Max) of inputs to be selected	1≤l≤Max(2~3)	1≤l≤Max(2~3)	1≤l≤Max(2~3)
	Polynomial type (Type T) of the consequent part of fuzzy rules	1≤T*≤4	1≤T≤4	1≤T≤4
	Membership Function (MF) type	Triangular Gaussian	Triangular Gaussian	Triangular Gaussian
	No. of MFs per input	2 or 3	2 or 3	2 or 3

l, T, Max: integers, T* means that entire system inputs are used for the polynomial in the conclusion part of the rules.

Table 3 shows the performance index of the proposed gdSOFPNN.

Table 3. Performance index of the gdSOFPNN for the NOx process data

Model	Layer M.F Max	3rd layer						
		Triangular MF		Gaussian MF		Triangular MF*		Gaussian MF*	
		PI	EPI	PI	EPI	PI	EPI	PI	EPI
gdSOFPNN	2	0.016	0.068	0.012	0.180	0.003	0.017	0.002	0.024
	3	0.014	0.036	0.004	0.134	0.002	0.008	0.001	0.023

PI and EPI are standard MSE performance indexes of training data and testing data, respectively.

Fig. 2 illustrates the detailed optimal topologies of the gdSOFPNN for 3 layers (PI=0.002, EPI=0.008). In nodes (FPNs) of Fig. 2, 'FPNn' denotes the nth FPN (node) of the corresponding layer, the number of the left side denotes the number of nodes (inputs or FPNs) coming to the corresponding node, and the number of the right side denotes the polynomial order of conclusion part of fuzzy rules used in the corresponding node. And rectangle means no. of MFs.

Fig. 3 illustrates the different optimization process between the IG_gSOFPNN [13] and the proposed gdSOFPNN by visualizing the values of the performance index obtained in successive generations of GA when using Type T*.

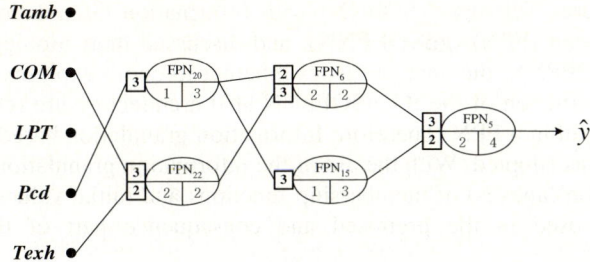

Fig. 2. The gdSOFPNN architecture

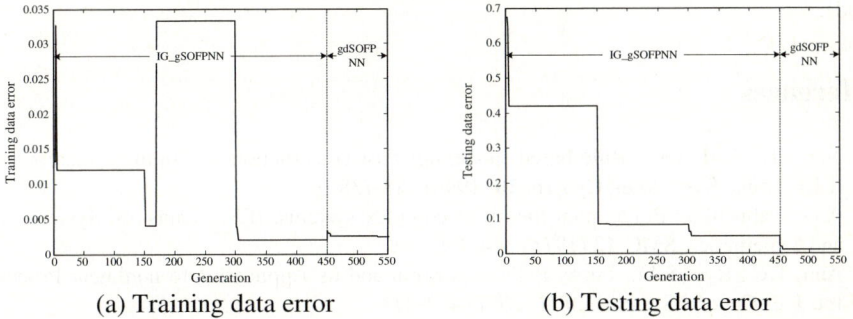

(a) Training data error (b) Testing data error

Fig. 3. The optimization process quantified by the values of the performance index

Table 4. Comparative analysis of the performance of the network; considered are models reported in the literature

Model				PI	EPI
Regression model				17.68	19.23
FNN model[10]	GA	Simplified		7.045	11.264
		Linear		4.038	6.028
	Hybrid	Simplified		6.205	8.868
	(GA+Complex)	Linear		3.830	5.397
Multi-FNNs[11]		Simplified		2.806	5.164
gHFPNN[12]	Max=2 (Type T*)	Triangular	3rd layer	0.008	0.082
			5th layer	0.008	0.081
		Gaussian-like	3rd layer	0.016	0.132
			5th layer	0.016	0.116
IG_gSOFPNN[13]	Max=2 (Type T*)	Triangular	3rd layer	0.002	0.045
		Gaussian-like		0.001	0.027
Proposed gdSOFPNN	Max=2 (Type T*)	Triangular	3rd layer	0.003	0.017
		Gaussian-like		0.002	0.024
	Max=3 (Type T*)	Triangular		0.002	0.008
		Gaussian-like		0.001	0.023

6 Concluding Remarks

In this study, we introduced and investigated a new architecture and comprehensive design methodology of **g**enetically **d**ynamic optimized **S**elf-**O**rganizing **F**uzzy

Polynomial Neural Networks (SOPNN) with Information Granulation based Fuzzy Polynomial Neuron (FPN) (**gdSOFPNN**), and discussed their topologies. In the design of the gdSOFPNN, the characteristics inherent to entire experimental data being used in the construction of the IG_gSOFPNN [13] architecture are reflected to fuzzy rules available within a FPN. Therefore Information granulation based on HCM clustering method was adopted. With the aid of the information granulation, we determine the initial location (apexes) of membership functions and initial values of polynomial function being used in the premised and consequence part of the fuzzy rules respectively.

Acknowledgement. This work was supported by the Korea Research Foundation Grant funded by the Korean Government (MOEHRD, Basic Research Promotion Fund).

References

1. Nie, J.H., Lee, T.H.: Rule-based modeling: Fast construction and optimal manipulation. IEEE Trans. Syst., Man, Cybern. **26** (1996) 728-738
2. A.G. Ivahnenko.: Polynomial theory of complex systems. IEEE Trans. on Systems, Man and Cybernetics. SMC-**12** (1971) 364-378
3. Ahn, T.C., Ryu, S.M.: Fuzzy PNN Algorithm and its Application to nonlinear Processes. Int. J. of General Systems. **30-4** (2001) 463-478
4. Oh, S.K., Pedrycz, W.: The design of self-organizing Polynomial Neural Networks. Information Science. **141** (2002) 237-258
5. Oh, S.K., Pedrycz, W., Park, B.J.: Polynomial Neural Networks Architecture: Analysis and Design. Computers and Electrical Engineering. **29** (2003) 703-725
6. Oh, S.K., Pedrycz, W.: Fuzzy Polynomial Neuron-Based Self-Organizing Neural Networks. Int. J. of General Systems. **32** (2003) 237-250
7. Zadeh, L.A.: Toward a theory of fuzzy information granulation and its centrality in human reasoning and fuzzy logic. Fuzzy sets and Systems. **90** (1997) 111-117
8. Jong, D.K.A.: Are Genetic Algorithms Function Optimizers? Parallel Problem Solving from Nature 2, Manner, R. and Manderick, B. eds., North-Holland, Amsterdam (1992)
9. Vachtsevanos, G., Ramani, V., Hwang, T.W.: Prediction of gas turbine NOx emissions using polynomial neural network. Technical Report. Georgia Institute of Technology. Atlanta. (1995)
10. Oh, S.K., Pedrycz, W., Park, H.S.: Hybrid identification in fuzzy-neural networks. Fuzzy Sets and Systems. **138** (2003) 399-426
11. Oh, S.K., Pedrycz, W., Park, H.S.: Multi-FNN identification based on HCM clustering and evolutionary fuzzy granulation. Simulation Modeling Practice and Theory. **11** (2003) 627-642
12. Oh, S.K., Pedrycz, W., Park, H.S.: Multi-layer Hybrid Fuzzy Polynomial Neural Networks: A Design in the Framework of Computational Intelligence. Neurocomputing. **64** (2005) 397-431
13. Park, H.S., Oh, S.K. Ahn, T.C.: A Novel Self-Organizing Fuzzy Polynomial Neural Networks with Evolutionary FPNs: Design and Analysis. Advances in Neural Networks. Lecture Notes in Computer Science, **3971**(2006) 780-785

Upper Bounds for Variational Stochastic Complexities of Bayesian Networks

Kazuho Watanabe[1], Motoki Shiga[2], and Sumio Watanabe[3]

[1] Department of Computational Intelligence and Systems Science, Tokyo Institute of Technology, Mail Box:R2-5, 4259 Nagatsuta, Midori-ku, Yokohama, 226–8503 Japan
kazuho23@pi.titech.ac.jp
[2] Bioinformatics Center, Institute for Chemical Research, Kyoto University Gokasho, Uji, Kyoto 611-0011, Japan
shiga@kuicr.kyoto-u.ac.jp
[3] P&I Lab, Tokyo Institute of Technology, Mail Box:R2-5, 4259 Nagatsuta, Midori-ku, Yokohama, 226–8503 Japan
swatanab@pi.titech.ac.jp

Abstract. In recent years, variational Bayesian learning has been used as an approximation of Bayesian learning. In spite of the computational tractability and good generalization performance in many applications, its statistical properties have yet to be clarified. In this paper, we analyze the statistical property in variational Bayesian learning of Bayesian networks which are widely used in information processing and uncertain artificial intelligence. We derive upper bounds for asymptotic variational stochastic complexities of Bayesian networks. Our result theoretically supports the effectiveness of variational Bayesian learning as an approximation of Bayesian learning.

1 Introduction

Recently, Bayesian networks have been widely used in information processing and uncertain artificial intelligence[6,5]. For example, they are applied to bioinformatics, image analysis and so on. In spite of the wide range of their applications, the statistical properties such as the generalization error have yet to be clarified.

The main reasons are due to their non-identifiability. In general, a learning model is described by the probability function $p(x|w)$, where w is the parameter. If the mapping from the parameter to the probability density function is one-to-one, then the model is called identifiable, otherwise, non-identifiable.

One of the difficulties in the analysis of the non-identifiable model is that we cannot apply the asymptotic theory of regular statistical models to a non-identifiable one. If the learning model attains the true distribution from which sample data are taken, the true parameter is not one point but an analytic set with singularities in the parameter space. This is why the mathematical properties of the non-identifiable models have been unknown.

In recent years, however, a method to analyze non-identifiable models has been developed on the basis of algebraic geometry[10,12]. The method revealed the relation between model's singularities and its statistical properties. For Bayesian

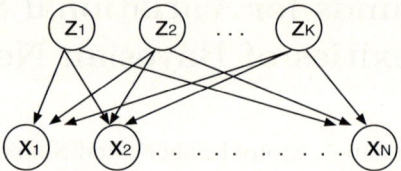

Fig. 1. Graphical structure of the Bayesian network

networks, the Bayesian stochastic complexity was derived[12]. The result shows that the stochastic complexity of Bayesian networks is much smaller than regular models. However, for non-identifiable models, performing Bayesian learning is computationally intractable.

The variational Bayesian framework was proposed as an approximation method of Bayesian learning[3] and extended for statistical models with hidden variables[1,2]. This framework provides computationally tractable posterior distributions over the hidden variables and parameters with an iterative algorithm. Variational Bayesian learning has been applied to various learning machines and it has performed good generalization with only modest computational costs compared to Markov Chain Monte Caro (MCMC) methods that are the major schemes of Bayesian learning. Recently, the variational stochastic complexities of mixture models and hidden Markov models were derived[9,4].

In this paper, we analyze the statistical property in variational Bayesian learning of Bayesian networks. We derive an upper bound of the variational stochastic complexity. And we show that the variational stochastic complexity becomes smaller than those of regular models, which implies the advantage of Bayesian learning still remains in variational Bayesian learning.

2 Bayesian Networks

A graphical model can express the relations among random variables by a graph. Bayesian networks are included in graphical models. The Bayesian network is defined by a directed graph and conditional probabilities[5].

In this paper, we focus on the Bayesian network whose states of all hidden nodes influence those of all observation nodes and assume that it has N observation nodes and K hidden nodes. Fig. 1 shows the graphical structure of the Bayesian networks. The observation nodes are denoted by a vector $x = (x_1, x_2, \ldots, x_N)$, and the set of states of the observation node x_j is $x_j \in \{1, 2, \ldots, Y_j\}$. The hidden nodes are denoted by a vector $z = (z_1, z_2, \ldots, z_K)$, and the set of states of the hidden node z_k is $z_k \in \{1, 2, \ldots, T_k\}$.

The probability that the state of the hidden node z_k is i, $(1 \leq i \leq T_k)$, is expressed as

$$a_{(k,i)} := P(z_k = i). \qquad (1)$$

Because $\{a_{(k,i)}, i = 1, 2, \ldots, T_k\}$ is a probability distribution, $\sum_{i=1}^{T_k} a_{(k,i)} = 1$, holds for $k = 1, 2, \ldots, K$.

And the conditional probability that the jth observation node x_j is l, ($1 \leq l \leq Y_j$), given the condition that the states of hidden nodes are $z = (z_1, z_2, \ldots, z_K)$, is

$$b_{(j,l|z)} := P(x_j = l|z). \tag{2}$$

Define $a := \{a_{(k,i)}\}$, $b := \{b_{(j,l|z)}\}$ and let $\omega = \{a, b\}$ be the set of all parameters. Then the joint probability that the states of observation nodes are $x = (x_1, x_2, \ldots, x_N)$ and the states of hidden nodes are $z = (z_1, z_2, \ldots, z_K)$ is

$$P(x, z|\omega) = \prod_{k=1}^{K} a_{(k,z_k)} \prod_{j=1}^{N} b_{(j,x_j|z)}. \tag{3}$$

Therefore the marginal probability that the states of observation nodes are x is

$$P(x|\omega) = \sum_z P(x, z|\omega) = \left\{ \prod_{k=1}^{K} \sum_{z_k=1}^{T_k} \right\} \prod_{k=1}^{K} a_{(k,z_k)} \prod_{j=1}^{N} b_{(j,x_j|z)}, \tag{4}$$

where we use the notation $\sum_z = \left\{ \prod_{k=1}^{K} \sum_{z_k=1}^{T_k} \right\} := \sum_{z_1=1}^{T_1} \sum_{z_2=1}^{T_2} \cdots \sum_{z_K=1}^{T_K}$ for the summation over all states of hidden nodes.

3 Bayesian Learning

Suppose n training samples $X^n = \{X_1, X_2, \ldots, X_n\}$ are independently and identically taken from the true distribution $p_0(x)$. In Bayesian learning, the prior distribution $\varphi(\omega)$ on the parameter ω is set. Then the posterior distribution $p(\omega|X^n)$ is computed from the given dataset and the prior by

$$p(\omega|X^n) = \frac{1}{Z(X^n)} \exp(-nH_n(\omega))\varphi(\omega), \tag{5}$$

where $H_n(\omega) = \frac{1}{n} \sum_{i=1}^{n} \log \frac{p_0(X_i)}{p(X_i|\omega)}$, and $Z(X^n)$ is the normalization constant called the marginal likelihood or the evidence of the dataset X^n [7]. The Bayesian predictive distribution $p(x|X^n)$ is given by averaging the model over the posterior distribution as follows,

$$p(x|X^n) = \int p(x|\omega)p(\omega|X^n)d\omega. \tag{6}$$

The Bayesian stochastic complexity $F(X^n)$ is defined by

$$F(X^n) = -\log Z(X^n), \tag{7}$$

which is also called the free energy and is important in most data modeling problems. Practically, it is used as a criterion by which the model is selected and the hyperparameters in the prior are optimized[8].

Let $E_{X^n}[\cdot]$ be the expectation over all sets of training data. It was proved that the Bayesian stochastic complexity has the following asymptotic form [10],

$$E_{X^n}[F(X^n)] \approx \lambda \log n - (m-1) \log \log n + O(1), \tag{8}$$

where λ and m are the rational number and the natural number respectively which are determined by the singularities of the true parameter. In regular models, 2λ is equal to the number of parameters and $m = 1$, while in non-identifiable models, 2λ is not larger than the number of parameters and $m \geq 1$[12]. This means non-identifiable models have an advantage in Bayesian learning.

However, Bayesian learning requires integration over the posterior distribution, which typically cannot be performed analytically. As an approximation, the variational Bayesian framework was introduced in neural networks[3] and was extended to deal with statistical models containing hidden variables[1].

4 Variational Bayesian Learning for Bayesian Networks

4.1 Variational Bayesian Learning

Let $\{X^n, Z^n\}$ be the complete data added the corresponding hidden variables $Z^n = \{Z_1, Z_2, \ldots, Z_n\}$. Variational Bayesian framework approximates the Bayesian posterior $p(Z^n, \omega | X^n)$ of the hidden variables and the parameters by the variational posterior $q(Z^n, \omega | X^n)$, which factorizes as

$$q(Z^n, \omega | X^n) = Q(Z^n | X^n) r(\omega | X^n), \tag{9}$$

where $Q(Z^n | X^n)$ and $r(\omega | X^n)$ are posteriors on the hidden variables and the parameters respectively. And the variational posterior $q(Z^n, \omega | X^n)$ is chosen to minimize the functional $\overline{F}[q]$ defined by

$$\overline{F}[q] = \sum_{Z^n} \int q(Z^n, \omega | X^n) \log \frac{q(Z^n, \omega | X^n) p_0(X^n)}{p(X^n, Z^n, \omega)} d\omega, \tag{10}$$

$$= F(X^n) + K(q(Z^n, \omega | X^n) \| p(Z^n, \omega | X^n)), \tag{11}$$

where $K(q(Z^n, \omega | X^n) \| p(Z^n, \omega | X^n))$ is the Kulback information between the true Bayesian posterior $p(Z^n, \omega | X^n)$ and the variational posterior $q(Z^n, \omega | X^n)$. This leads to the following theorem. The proof is well known[2].

Theorem 1. *If the functional $\overline{F}[q]$ is minimized under the constraint eq.(9) then the variational posteriors, $r(\omega | X^n)$ and $Q(Y^n | X^n)$, satisfy*

$$r(\omega | X^n) = \frac{1}{C_r} \varphi(\omega) \exp < \log p(X^n, Z^n | \omega) >_Q, \tag{12}$$

$$Q(Z^n | X^n) = \frac{1}{C_Q} \exp < \log p(X^n, Z^n | \omega) >_r, \tag{13}$$

where C_r and C_Q are the normalization constants [1].

---
[1] Hereafter we use the notations $< \cdot >_r$ and $< \cdot >_Q$ for the expectation over $r(\omega | X^n)$ and $Q(Z^n | X^n)$ respectively.

Note that eq.(12) and eq.(13) give only necessary conditions for the functional $\overline{F}[q]$ to be minimized. The variational posteriors that satisfy eq.(12) and eq.(13) are computed by an iterative algorithm whose convergence is guaranteed.

We define the variational stochastic complexity $\overline{F}(X^n)$ by the minimum value of the functional $\overline{F}[q]$, that is,

$$\overline{F}(X^n) = \min_{r,Q} \overline{F}[q]. \tag{14}$$

From eq.(11), the difference between $\overline{F}(X^n)$ and the Bayesian stochastic complexity $F(X^n)$ shows the accuracy of the variational Bayesian approach as an approximation of Bayesian learning.

4.2 Variational Posterior for Bayesian Networks

We assume that the prior distribution $\varphi(\omega)$ of parameters $\omega = \{a, b\}$ is the conjugate prior distribution. Then $\varphi(\omega)$ is given by $\left\{\prod_{k=1}^{K} \varphi(a_k)\right\}\left\{\prod_z \prod_{j=1}^{N} \varphi(b_{(j,\cdot|z)})\right\}$ where

$$\varphi(a_k) = \frac{\Gamma(T_k \phi_0)}{\Gamma(\phi_0)^{T_k}} \prod_{z_k=1}^{T_k} a_{(k,z_k)}^{\phi_0 - 1} \quad, k = 1, 2, \ldots, K, \tag{15}$$

$$\varphi(b_{(j,\cdot|z)}) = \frac{\Gamma(Y_j \xi_0)}{\Gamma(\xi_0)^{Y_j}} \prod_{x_j=1}^{Y_j} b_{(j,x_j|z)}^{\xi_0 - 1} \quad, j = 1, 2, \ldots, N, \tag{16}$$

are Dirichlet distributions with hyperparameters $\phi_0 > 0$ and $\xi_0 > 0$. Let $\delta(n)$ be 1 when $n = 0$ and 0 otherwise, and define

$$\bar{n}^z_{(k,z_k)} := \sum_{i=1}^{n} \left\langle \delta(Z_i^{(k)} - z_k) \right\rangle_Q, \text{ and } \bar{n}^x_{(j,x_j|z)} := \sum_{i=1}^{n} \delta(X_i^{(j)} - x_j) \left\langle \prod_{k=1}^{K} \delta(Z_i^{(k)} - z_k) \right\rangle_Q.$$

Here $X_i^{(j)}$ is the state of the jth observation node and $Z_i^{(k)}$ is the state of the kth hidden node when the ith training datum is observed. From eq.(12), the variational posterior distribution of parameters $\omega = \{a, b\}$ is given by $r(\omega|X^n) = \left\{\prod_{k=1}^{K} r(a_k|X^n)\right\} \left\{\prod_z \prod_{j=1}^{N} r(b_{(j,\cdot|z)}|X^n)\right\}$,

$$r(a_k|X^n) = \frac{\Gamma(n + T_k \phi_0)}{\prod_{z_k=1}^{T_k} \Gamma(\bar{n}^z_{(k,z_k)} + \phi_0)} \prod_{z_k=1}^{T_k} a_{(k,z_k)}^{\bar{n}^z_{(k,z_k)} + \phi_0 - 1}, \tag{17}$$

$$r(b_{(j,\cdot|z)}|X^n) = \frac{\Gamma(\bar{n}^x_z + Y_j \xi_0)}{\prod_{x_j=1}^{Y_j} \Gamma(\bar{n}^x_{(j,x_j|z)} + \xi_0)} \prod_{x_j=1}^{Y_j} b_{(j,x_j|z)}^{\bar{n}^x_{(j,x_j|z)} + \xi_0 - 1}, \tag{18}$$

where $\bar{n}^x_z := \sum_{i=1}^{n} \left\langle \prod_{k=1}^{K} \delta(Z_i^{(k)} - z_k) \right\rangle_Q$. Then it follows that

$$\bar{n}^x_z = \sum_{x_j=1}^{Y_j} \bar{n}^x_{(j,x_j|z)}, \text{ for } j = 1, \cdots, N, \text{ and } \bar{n}^z_{(k,z_k)} = \sum_{z_{-k}} \bar{n}^x_z, \tag{19}$$

where $\sum_{z_{-k}}$ denotes the sum over z_i ($i \neq k$).

5 Main Result

We assume the following conditions.

(A1). The true distribution is defined by a Bayesian network with H hidden nodes and each hidden node has S_k states, where $H \leq K$ and $S_k \leq T_k$ holds for $k = 1, 2, \ldots, H$. Then the true distribution $p_0(x)$ is

$$p(x|\omega^*) = \left\{\prod_{k=1}^{H} \sum_{z_k=1}^{S_k}\right\} a^*_{(k,z_k)} \prod_{j=1}^{N} b^*_{(j,x_j|z)}, \quad (20)$$

where $\omega^* = \{\{a^*_{(k,z_k)}\}, \{b^*_{(j,x_j|z)}\}\}$ is the true parameter.

(A2). The prior distribution of parameters $\omega = (a,b)$ is the conjugate prior distribution, $\varphi(\omega) = \left\{\prod_{k=1}^{K} \varphi(a_k)\right\} \left\{\prod_z \prod_{j=1}^{N} \varphi(b_{(j,\cdot|z)})\right\}$, where $\varphi(a_k)$ and $\varphi(b_{(j,\cdot|z)})$ are given by eqs.(15),(16).

Under these conditions, we prove the following theorem.

Theorem 2. *Assume the conditions (A1) and (A2). If the learning machine is given by eq.(4) and the true distribution is given by eq.(20), then for an arbitrary natural number n, the variational stochastic complexity satisfies,*

$$\overline{F}(X^n) \leq \nu \log n + C, \quad (21)$$

where C is a constant independent of n and

$$\nu = \phi_0 \sum_{k=1}^{K} T_k - \phi_0 K + \left(\phi_0 - \frac{1}{2}\right) H + \left(\frac{1}{2} - \phi_0\right) \sum_{k=1}^{H} S_k + \frac{1}{2} \prod_{k=1}^{H} S_k \sum_{j=1}^{N} (Y_j - 1). \quad (22)$$

6 Outline of the Proof

From eq.(13), we can rewrite the variational stochastic complexity as follows,

$$\overline{F}(X^n) = \min_r \left[-\left(S(X^n) + \log C_Q\right) + K\left(r(\omega|X^n)\|\varphi(\omega)\right) \right], \quad (23)$$

where $S(X^n) = -\sum_{i=1}^{n} \log p_0(X_i)$ and

$$\log C_Q = \log \sum_{Z^n} \exp \left\langle \log p(X^n, Z^n|\omega) \right\rangle_r. \quad (24)$$

We can approximate the term in the bracket in eq.(24) and the second term $K\left(r(\omega|X^n)\|\varphi(\omega)\right)$ in eq.(23) as follows:

$$\left\langle \log p(X^n, Z^n|\omega) \right\rangle_r = \sum_{k=1}^{K} \sum_{z_k=1}^{T_k} \left\{ \log \frac{\bar{n}^z_{(k,z_k)} + \phi_0}{n + T_k \phi_0} - \frac{1}{2(\bar{n}^z_{(k,z_k)} + \phi_0)} + \frac{1}{2(n + T_k \phi_0)} \right.$$
$$\left. + \sum_{j=1}^{N} \sum_{x_j=1}^{Y_j} \left\{ \log \frac{\bar{n}^x_{(j,x_j|z)} + \xi_0}{\bar{n}^x_z + Y_j \xi_0} - \frac{1}{2(\bar{n}^x_{(j,x_j|z)} + \xi_0)} + \frac{1}{2(\bar{n}^x_z + Y_j \xi_0)} + O\left(\frac{1}{(\bar{n}^x_{(j,x_j|z)})^2}\right) \right\}, \quad (25)$$

$$K\left(r(\omega|X^n)||\varphi(\omega)\right) = \sum_{k=1}^{K}\left\{\left(T_k\phi_0 - \frac{1}{2}\right)\log(n + T_k\phi_0)\right\}$$

$$-\sum_{k=1}^{K}\sum_{z_k=1}^{T_k}\left\{\left(\phi_0 - \frac{1}{2}\right)\log\left(\bar{n}^z_{(k,z_k)} + \phi_0\right)\right\} + \sum_{z}\sum_{j=1}^{N}\left\{\left(Y_j\xi_0 - \frac{1}{2}\right)\log(\bar{n}^x_z + Y_j\xi_0)\right\}$$

$$-\sum_{z}\sum_{j=1}^{N}\sum_{x_j=1}^{Y_j}\left\{\left(\xi_0 - \frac{1}{2}\right)\log\left(\bar{n}^x_{(j,x_j|z)} + \xi_0\right)\right\} + O(1). \tag{26}$$

Here we use the asymptotic expansions of the psi function, $\Psi(x) = \log x - \frac{1}{2x} + O\left(\frac{1}{x^2}\right)$ and the log gamma function, $\log \Gamma(x) = (x - \frac{1}{2})\log x - x + O(1)$.

From eq.(23), since $\overline{F}(X^n)$ is given as the minimum value of the function of $\{\bar{n}^x_{(j,x_j|z)}\}$, we can obtain an upper bound of $\overline{F}(X^n)$ by substituting each $\bar{n}^x_{(j,x_j|z)}$ by any specific value. Therefore substitute for each j and x_j,

$$\bar{n}^x_{(j,x_j|z)} = \begin{cases} (\prod_{k=1}^{H} a^*_{(k,z_k)})b^*_{(j,x_j|z)}n & (1 \leq z_1 \leq S_1, \cdots, 1 \leq z_H \leq S_H, \\ & z_{H+1} = \cdots = z_K = 1), \\ 0 & \text{(otherwise)}. \end{cases} \tag{27}$$

From eqs.(24), (25), (27), and (19), we obtain

$$\log C_Q = -S(X^n) + \text{Const.} . \tag{28}$$

And from eqs.(26), (27), and (19), we obtain

$$K\left(r(\omega|X^n)||\varphi(\omega)\right) = \nu \log n + \text{Const.} . \tag{29}$$

From eqs.(23), (28), (29), we complete the proof. □

7 Discussion and Conclusions

In this paper, we showed the asymptotic upper bounds of the variational stochastic complexities of Bayesian networks. Let us compare the variational stochastic complexities to the Bayesian stochastic complexities of Bayesian networks and those of regular statistical models. The Bayesian stochastic complexities of regular models are also called the Bayesian information criterion(BIC)[8].

For an arbitrary natural number n, the following inequality holds for the Bayesian stochastic complexity[12],

$$E_{X^n}[F(X^n)] \leq \mu \log n + \text{Const.} ,$$

$$\mu = \frac{1}{2}\sum_{j=1}^{N}(Y_j - 1)\prod_{k=1}^{H}S_k - \frac{1}{2}\sum_{k=1}^{H}S_k + \frac{1}{2}H + \sum_{k=1}^{K}T_k - K. \tag{30}$$

These upper bounds are obtained under the conditions (A1), (A2), and $\phi_0 = 1$ in eq.(15). Also the penalty term in the BIC is given by $\frac{d}{2}\log n$ where

$$d = \sum_{k=1}^{K}(T_k - 1) + \sum_{j=1}^{N}(Y_j - 1)\prod_{k=1}^{K}T_k, \tag{31}$$

is the number of parameters. By putting $\phi_0 = 1$ in eq.(22), from eqs.(30) and (31), we obtain
$$\nu = \mu < d/2.$$

This means the variational stochastic complexity is much smaller than the BIC and close to the Bayesian stochastic complexity. In other words, this implies the effectiveness of the variational Bayesian approach in terms of approximating the Bayesian posterior distributions and estimating the Bayesian stochastic complexities. It would be important to assess the variational approximation in terms of the generalization error or approximating the Bayesian predictive distributions in the future study. It is also important to show the lower bound of the variational stochastic complexity as well as the upper bound. To obtain lower bounds, the identifiability of Bayesian networks should be taken into account[11].

Acknowledgement. This research was partially supported by the Ministry of Education, Science, Sports and Culture, Grant-in-Aid for JSPS Fellows 16-4637 and for Scientific Research 15500130, 2006.

References

1. H. Attias (1999). Inferring parameters and structure of latent variable models by variational Bayes, *Proc. of UAI-99*, Stockholm, Sweden, pp. 21–30.
2. M. J. Beal (2003). *Variational algorithms for approximate Bayesian inference* , Ph.D. Thesis, University College London.
3. G. Hinton, D. van Camp (1993). Keeping neural networks simple by minimizing the description length of weights, *Proc. of COLT'93*, Santa Cruz, USA, pp. 5–13.
4. T. Hosino, S. Watanabe (2005). Stochastic complexity of variational Bayesian hidden Markov models, *Proc. of IJCNN 2005*, Vol.2, pp.1114–1119.
5. F. V. Jensen (2001). *Bayesian Networks and Decision Graphs*, New York, Springer.
6. M. I. Jordan (1999). *Learning in graphical models*, Cambridge, MIT Press.
7. D. J. Mackay (1992). Bayesian interpolation, *Neural Computation*, Vol.4, N0.2, pp.415–447.
8. G. Schwarz (1978). Estimating the dimension of a model, *Annals of Statistics*, Vol.6, No.2, pp.461–464.
9. K.Watanabe, S.Watanabe (2006). Variational Bayesian stochastic complexity of mixture models, *Advances in NIPS*, Vol.18, MIT Press, pp.1465–1472.
10. S. Watanabe (2001). Algebraic analysis for non-identifiable learning machines, *Neural Computation*, Vol.13, No.4, pp.899–933.
11. M. Whiley, D.M.Titterington (2002). Model identifiability in naive Bayesian networks, Technical Report 02-1, Department of Statistics, University of Glasgow.
12. K. Yamazaki, S. Watanabe (2003). Stochastic complexity of Bayesian networks, *Proc. of UAI-03*, Acapulco, Mexico, pp. 592–599.

A Neural Stochastic Optimization Framework for Oil Parameter Estimation[*]

Rafael E. Banchs[1], Hector Klie[2], Adolfo Rodriguez[2],
Sunil G. Thomas[2], and Mary F. Wheeler[2]

[1] GPS, TSC, Polytechnic University of Catalonia, Barcelona, Spain
rbanchs@gps.tsc.upc.edu
[2] CSM, ICES, The University of Texas at Austin, Texas, USA
{klie, adolfo, sgthomas, mfw}@ices.utexas.edu

Abstract. The main objective of the present work is to propose and evaluate a neural stochastic optimization framework for reservoir parameter estimation, for which a history matching procedure is implemented by combining three independent sources of spatial and temporal information: production data, time-lapse seismic and sensor information. In order to efficiently perform large-scale parameter estimation, a coupled multilevel, stochastic and learning search methodology is proposed. At a given resolution level, the parameter space is globally explored and sampled by the simultaneous perturbation stochastic approximation (SPSA) algorithm. The estimation and sampling performed by SPSA is further enhanced by a neural learning engine that evaluates the objective function sensitiveness with respect to parameter estimates in the vicinity of the most promising optimal solutions.

1 Introduction

The continuous growth of computing power and communication technology is bridging gaps in many scientific applications by allowing traditional information processing and modeling techniques to be performed in a more complete multi-dimensional and multivariate framework. In the particular case of geosciences, specialized sensors are capable of measuring at a high local resolution, fluid and rock properties (see e.g., [1,2] and references therein). These advances, in conjunction with time-lapse seismic studies, are revealing enormous potentials to reduce the uncertainty in both reservoir characterization and production scenarios. Meanwhile, new stochastic optimization and statistical learning methods are arising as promising tools to find nontrivial correlations between data measurements and responses and to develop optimal reservoir exploitation plans ([3,4,5,6,7,8]).

The main objective of the present work is to propose and evaluate a neural stochastic optimization framework for reservoir parameter estimation. The proposed optimization framework is demonstrated and evaluated by means of a

---

[*] The research presented in this paper is supported in part by the National Science Foundation ITR Grant EIA-0121523/EIA-0120934 and the Spanish Ministry of Education and Science.

history matching procedure that combines information conveyed by production data, time-lapse seismic and specialized sensor measurements as independent sources of spatial and temporal information. All sensor information of pressures, concentrations and fluid velocities is incorporated, along with seismic and production data, into a multi-dimensional objective function that quantifies the mismatch between observed and predicted data. This set of objective functions evaluates the impact that each information component has in the quality of the permeability estimation, which allows for relating detailed changes in fluid flow and seismic traveltimes to permeability field distribution.

The proposed optimization framework consists of the use of a hybrid multilevel approach to gradually perform parameter estimation from low to high resolution levels. In this way, the parameter space is globally explored and sampled by the simultaneous perturbation stochastic approximation (SPSA) algorithm at a given resolution level. Then, the estimation and sampling performed by SPSA is further enhanced by a neural learning engine which is trained to provide a smooth representation of the multi-dimensional objective function within the region explored by SPSA. This combination of global stochastic searches with local estimations via artificial neural networks (ANNs) also provides means to study the objective function sensitivity with respect to parameter estimates in the vicinity of the most promising optimal solutions, which consequently allows for further resolution refinements to the parameter estimation process.

2 The Neural Stochastic Optimization Framework

As already mentioned, the proposed methodology consists of the use of a hybrid multilevel approach to gradually perform parameter estimation from low- to high-resolution levels. We restrict our attention to permeability although the proposed framework could also be employed for other reservoir parameters of interest, such as porosity, PVT data, stress and fracture distribution.

Starting from a coarse grid, the parameter estimation is first carried out with the simultaneous perturbation stochastic approximation (SPSA) algorithm [7] with different initial guesses. This not only augments the chances for finding a global optimal solution, it also allows for a rich sampling of the parameter space. Moreover, the search performed by the SPSA algorithm guides the sampling toward promising regions containing a global solution ("hot spots"). We provide more details on the SPSA algorithm below. Due to the size of the coarse grid, thousands of computations are affordable in a few hours.

Based on the mapping between parameters and the objective function provided by SPSA samples, we train an artificial neural network (ANN) that provide us with an approximate smooth representation of the objective function within the region of the most promising optimal solutions explored by SPSA. The trained ANN also provides means to study the objective function sensitivity with respect to parameter estimates in the vicinity of explored regions. This sensitivity analysis allows to further refine the solution of the optimization. Therefore, points evaluated by the ANN are validated against the simulator. If these evaluations lead to a better optimizer, then the final estimation is used as an initial guess for the next finer resolution permeability grid. In this way, the ANN acts as a surrogate model or metamodel for the simulation model.

The simulation model consists of the integrated functionality of independent multiphase flow, petrophysics and seismic models. The flow component is provided by the Integrated Parallel Accurate Reservoir Simulation (IPARS) framework ([9,10]). The petrophysics model follows the Biot-Gassman theory [11], which describes seismic velocity changes resulting from changes in pore-fluid saturations and pressures. Given the resulting seismic velocities, it is possible to perform wave propagation modeling through the porous media. In the first stage of the present effort, we are momentarily disregarding amplitude effects and, instead, reporting on traveltime measurements generated by the FERMAT raytracer algorithm [12]. Therefore, the simulation model allows us to evaluate a collection of objective functions of the form:

$$\Phi(\theta) = \Phi(\mathbf{p}, \mathbf{c}, \mathbf{u}, \mathbf{q}, \tau) = \\ \sum_{i=1}^{T} \left[\left\| \mathbf{w}_{p,i} \left(\mathbf{p}_i^d - \mathbf{p}_i \right) \right\|_2 + \left\| \mathbf{w}_{c,i} \left(\mathbf{c}_i^d - \mathbf{c}_i \right) \right\| + \left\| \mathbf{w}_{u,i} \left(\mathbf{u}_i^d - \mathbf{u}_i \right) \right\|_2 \right] + \\ \sum_{i=1}^{T} \left[\left\| \mathbf{w}_{q,i} \left(\mathbf{q}_i^d - \mathbf{q}_i \right) \right\|_2 + \left\| \mathbf{w}_{\tau,i} \left(\tau_i^d - \tau_i \right) \right\|_2 \right], \quad (1)$$

where p, c and u denote pressure, concentration and velocity vectors at discrete times, respectively. Here, q represents data at production wells, i.e. bottom hole pressure, gas/oil ratio and cumulative production. The variable τ stands for the traveltime vector. Superscript d indicates measured data. The weight operators, w_x, include scaling factors and allow for the flexible selection of sensor, production and seismic measurements. Note that the above formulation may include measurements at selected locations and at discrete times throughout the simulation interval $[0, T]$.

3 Global Stochastic Optimization Via SPSA

The simultaneous perturbation stochastic approximation (SPSA) for equation (1) is defined by the following recursion for the parameter vector θ:

$$\theta_{k+1} = \theta_k - a_k \hat{g}_k(\theta_k), \quad (2)$$

where a_k is a positive scalar that monotonically decreases with respect to k, and $\hat{g}_k(\theta_k)$ is a stochastic approximation to the gradient given by a simultaneous perturbation of all elements of θ_k, that is,

$$\hat{g}_k(\theta_k) = \frac{1}{2c_k} \left[\Phi(\theta_k + c_k \Delta_k) - \Phi(\theta_k - c_k \Delta_k) \right] \Delta_k^{-1}, \quad (3)$$

where c_k is also a positive scalar that monotonically decreases with respect to k, Δ_k is a vector consisting of $\{-1, 1\}$ values randomly generated with a Bernoulli distribution and Δ_k^{-1} stands for the componentwise reciprocal of each of the entries of Δ_k. The parameters a_k and c_k are chosen to ensure asymptotic convergence of the algorithm; for more details and pointers on SPSA see [7].

The SPSA algorithm has received considerable attention for global optimization problems where it is difficult or impossible to compute first order derivative information associated with the problem. As indicated by (3), this algorithm only requires two function evaluations per iteration independently of the parameter space size to generate a stochastic descent direction for (2).

4 The Neural Learning Engine

The ANN implementation used in the present work considers a multilayer perceptron architecture under the supervised learning framework [13]. Supervised learning implies the existence of an "adviser" entity able to quantify the network performance, which in many practical applications, reduces to the availability of a set of input data for which the expected output data is known. In the case of the proposed methodology, this data is numerically generated by the SPSA algorithm which certainly explores a specific region of the objective function when converging to a promising optimal solution. Special attention should be paid to this sampling process in order to guarantee collected samples to provide a good representation of the parameter space. Hence, several runs of SPSA within the same neighborhood might be necessary to ensure a good parameter space representation.

These parameter space samples, along with their corresponding objective function values, constitute the training data set for the ANN model. This data set is used to calibrate the multilayer perceptron parameters, as well as for the final training of the ANN model. The training of the multilayer perceptron considered here is implemented by using the classical back-propagation algorithm [13]. In the proposed optimization framework, the ANN engine is used with a twofold objective in mind. First, it should provide an efficient and smooth estimator of the mismatch objective function, which will allow for further enhancing the global solution provided by the SPSA algorithm. Special care must be taken when performing a local search over the smooth estimator provided by the ANN since the ANN representation is only valid inside the core region explored by the SPSA. In order to avoid going out the valid region of search, some constraining conditions should be artificially imposed to this local search. Second, it should allow for capturing the intrinsic complexities of the mismatch objective function with respect to variations of individual permeability field values. This will enable performance of a fast sensitivity analysis of the overall model response with respect to each individual model parameter, which will provide useful information about the specific gridblocks for which further scale refinements are required.

5 Numerical Experiments

Computational experiments were performed on a coarse grid representation of model 1 of the SPE 10th Comparative Solution Project [14]. This reference coarse permeability field, consisting of $10 \times 2 = 20$ gridblocks, was obtained by successively upscaling the original 100 × 20 model with a wavelet transformation using the Haar basis [15]. A fixed production strategy was adopted with one gas injecting well located at the leftmost side of the model and a production well at the opposite side. Sensor measurements of pressures, concentrations and flow velocities were assumed to be active midway between the two wells and along the wellbore. An *a priori* permeability model was obtained by an upscaled low-resolution model of the original permeability field. Each iteration of the SPSA algorithm involved two function evaluations by using the simulation model described at the end of section 2. The SPSA converged in about 2000 iterations for a total computation time of about half an hour.

Two ANN models were calibrated and trained by using the sample points generated by the SPSA algorithm. The ANN-1 model corresponds to an ANN architecture of only one hidden layer with ten units, and the ANN-2 model corresponds to an architecture of two hidden layers with eight and five units, respectively. The number of units was empirically selected by using a cross-validation procedure to compare different networks of similar complexities (in terms of their total amount of weights). A local search was performed over each ANN model space in order to further improve the SPSA solution. Each of these searches converged in about 1000 iterations for a total computation time of about 13 seconds. Table 1 presents both actual and estimated objective function values for four specific permeability fields of interest: the *a priori* permeability model, the SPSA solution model and both ANN model improved solutions.

Table 1. Actual and estimated objective function values for *a priori* permeability model, SPSA solution, and ANN-1 and ANN-2 improved solutions

Objective Function	*A priori* Model	SPSA Solution	ANN-1 Solution	ANN-2 Solution
IPARS Value	0.0761578849	0.0042390311	0.0041412518	0.0039853471
ANN-1 Estimation	0.0761588044	0.0042386536	0.0041278380	
ANN-2 Estimation	0.0758141299	0.0042406859		0.0038237641

Two important observations can be drawn from table 1. First, these figures reveal that although both ANN models were able to capture the behavior of the 20-dimensional objective function under consideration, no significant improvement with respect to the SPSA solution was achieved. This might suggest that the SPSA algorithm probably reached, or got very close, to the basin minimum. Nevertheless, it is seen that a little improvement of the permeability field was achieved in both cases. The second observation refers to the mismatch between the actual objective function values and the estimations provided by the ANN models. It is interesting to notice that although ANN-1 estimations are better than ANN-2 estimations, this latter model is the one which allows for a better improvement of the SPSA solution model. Figure 1 presents the individual permeability estimations for the global SPSA-based optimization and both local ANN-based refinements along with the true permeability values.

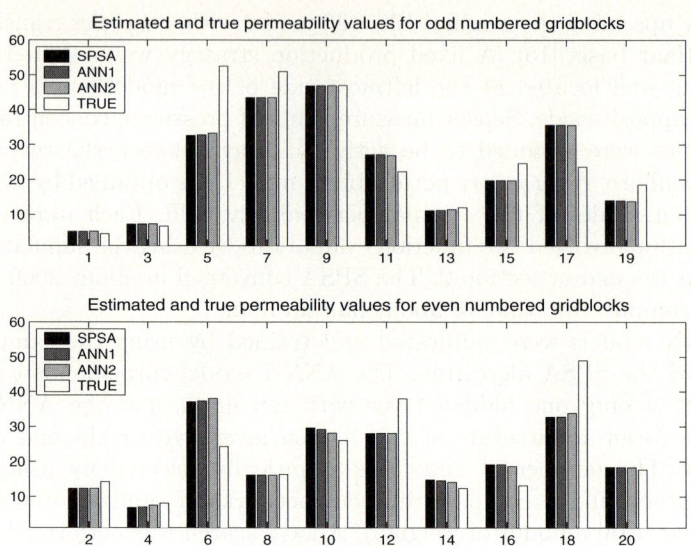

Fig. 1. True permeability values and permeability estimations for the global SPSA-based optimization and both local ANN-based refinements

The following step in the proposed methodology is to proceed to generate a higher resolution estimate of the initial coarse permeability field. In order to achieve this in an efficient manner, only those gridblocks with a significant impact on the objective function cost are subdivided into smaller gridblocks, while all others are maintained at their original level of resolution. The selection of significant gridblocks is supported by a sensitivity analysis which is performed with the smooth estimator provided by the ANN. Table 2 presents the percentage variations of the objective function value around the ANN-2 solution when each individual permeability value is varied from -1% to $+1\%$ of its value.

Table 2. Percentage variations of the objective function for individual permeability value variations of 2%

Block1	Block3	Block5	Block7	Block9	Block11	Block13	Block15	Block17	Block19
0.158%	0.751%	0.720%	2.940%	2.141%	1.113%	0.481%	0.466%	0.440%	0.339%
Block2	Block4	Block6	Block8	Block10	Block12	Block14	Block16	Block18	Block20
0.110%	0.186%	0.262%	2.941%	0.980%	0.561%	0.685%	0.641%	0.464%	1.698%

As seen from table 2, gridblocks 7, 8, 9, 11 and 20 are the most sensitive ones. This shows the important incidence of sensor information on the overall estimation process, since those gridblocks are precisely the closest ones to both the midway and wellbore located sensors. The detailed objective function behavior for each individual permeability value variation is depicted in figure 2, were each panel (numbered in a row-wise fashion) corresponds to the varying permeability gridblock.

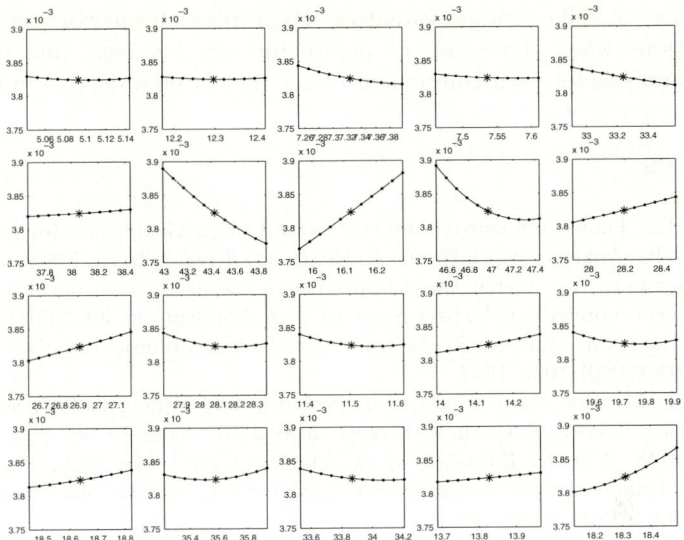

Fig. 2. Objective function variations corresponding to each individual gridblock permeability variation (gridblocks are presented in a row-wise fashion)

Finally, according to the sensitivity analysis results, further resolution refinements should be performed at those particular gridblocks which have a stronger incidence on the objective function behavior. Once this new multi-resolution grid representation of the permeability field model is implemented, a global search should be performed again by using SPSA in order to readjust all permeability values of the new model. This global search result might be enhanced again by a new ANN-based local search and sensitivity analysis.

6 Conclusions

According to the preliminary results presented in this work, the proposed methodology promises to provide a very attractive framework for parameter estimation, especially when the problem complexity makes derivative computation unfeasible and when computational times strongly limit the search performance. As already discussed, for the example presented here, although model enhancements achieved by the ANN-based search were actually small compared to the global search performed by SPSA, the ANN model not only helped for better understanding the search space, but also provided a good estimator of the objective function allowing for much faster computations.

Moreover, this type of hybrid approach may be convenient when models and data are subject to dynamic changes as the understanding of the reservoir increases. Ongoing efforts are currently focused on a deeper analysis of the value that sensor information has in time-lapse seismic history matching. To that end, the research team will continue evaluating the proposed framework for enhancing the estimations when thousands of parameters are involved, and performing sensitivity analysis for each component of the mismatch objective function.

References

1. Lumley, D.: Time-lapse seismic reservoir monitoring. Geophysics **66** (2001) 50–53
2. Versteeg, R., Ankeny, M., Harbour, J., Heath, G., Kostelnik, K., Matson, E., Moor, K., Richardson, A.: A structured approach to the use of near-surface geophysics in long-term monitoring. Expert Systems with Applications **23** (2004) 700–703
3. van der Baan, M., Jutten, C.: Neural networks in geophysical applications. Geophysics **65** (2000) 1032–1047
4. Nikravesh, M.: Soft computing-based computational intelligent for reservoir characterization. Expert Systems with Applications **26** (2004) 19–38
5. Bangerth, W., Klie, H., Parashar, M., Mantosian, V., Wheeler, M.F.: An autonomic reservoir framework for the stochastic optimization of well placement. Cluster Computing **8** (2005) 255–269
6. Parashar, M., Klie, H., Catalyurek, U., Kurc, T., Bangerth, W., Matossian, V., Saltz, J., Wheeler, M.F.: Application of grid-enabled technologies for solving optimization problems in data-driven reservoir studies. Future Generation of Computer Systems **21** (2005) 19–26
7. Spall, J.C.: Introduction to stochastic search and optimization: Estimation, simulation and control. John Wiley & Sons, Inc., New Jersey (2003)
8. Keane, A., Nair, P.: Computational Approaches for Aerospace Design: The Pursuit of Excellence. Wiley, England (2005)
9. Parashar, M., Wheeler, J.A., Pope, G., Wang, K., Wang, P.: A new generation EOS compositional reservoir simulator. Part II: Framework and multiprocessing. In: Fourteenth SPE Symposium on Reservoir Simulation, Dalas, Texas. (1997) 31–38
10. Wang, P., Yotov, I., Wheeler, M.F., Arbogast, T., Dawson, C.N., Parashar, M., Sepehrnoori, K.: A new generation EOS compositional reservoir simulator. Part I: Formulation and Discretization. In: Fourteenth SPE Symposium on Reservoir Simulation, Dalas, Texas, Society of Petroleum Engineers (1997) 55–64
11. Bourbie, T., Coussy, O., Zinszner, B.: Acoustics of Porous Media. Institut français du pétrole publications, Editions TECHNIP (1987)
12. Nishi, K.: A three dimensional robust seismic ray tracer for volcanic regions. Earth Planets Space **53** (2001) 101–109
13. Haykin, S.: Neural Networks: A Comprehensive Foundation. Macmillan College Publishing Company, New York (1994)
14. Christie, M., Blunt, M.: Tenth SPE Comparative Solution Project: A Comparison of Upscaling Techniques. SPE Reservoir Engineering **12** (2001) 308–317
15. Daubechies, I.: Ten Lectures on Wavelets. SIAM, Philadelphia (1992)

Bootstrap Prediction Intervals for Nonlinear Time-Series

Daisuke Haraki[1], Tomoya Suzuki[2], and Tohru Ikeguchi[1]

[1] Graduate School of Science and Engineering, Saitama University,
225 Shimo-Ohkubo, Sakura-ku, Saitama-city 338-8570, Japan
daisuke@nls.ics.saitama-u.ac.jp
[2] Department of Information Systems Design, Doshisya University,
1-3 Tatara Miyakodani, Kyotanabe-city 610-0394, Japan

Abstract. To evaluate predictability of complex behavior produced from nonlinear dynamical systems, we often use normalized root mean square error, which is suitable to evaluate errors between true points and predicted points. However, it is also important to estimate prediction intervals, where the future point will be included. Although estimation of prediction intervals is conventionally realized by an ensemble prediction, we applied the bootstrap resampling scheme to evaluate prediction intervals of nonlinear time-series. By several numerical simulations, we show that the bootstrap method is effective to estimate prediction intervals for nonlinear time-series.

1 Introduction

Several prediction methods have been proposed for analyzing complex, possibly chaotic, time-series, for example, the Lorenz' method of analogues[1], the Jacobian matrix estimation[2], the Bootstrap nonlinear prediction[3], and the kNN technique[4]. In the field of nonlinear time-series analysis, these prediction methods are important not only to predict future values of the time-series, but also to analyze long-term unpredictability and short-term predictability, or one of the essential characteristics of deterministic chaos[5].

To evaluate the prediction accuracy, we usually use a normalized root mean square error between true points and predicted points. In such a case, prediction must be described as a point even if its predictability is unreliable due to small size data or noise in the data. In this paper, we evaluate prediction accuracy from another viewpoint: we estimate prediction intervals in which the future point would fall.

In statistical literatures, several attempts have been made on evaluation of prediction intervals. For example, in Ref.[6], the bootstrap method is used to evaluate prediction intervals for autoregressive models. In Ref.[7], a parametric bootstrap method is applied to financial time-series. In Ref.[8], the endogenous lag order method of Kilian[9] applied to sieve bootstrap prediction intervals. However, an application of the bootstrap method is usually evaluated through a linear model such as ARMA.

Although a nonlinear model for a stochastic volatility is used in Ref.[7], however, there is no application of the bootstrap method to more general class of nonlinear dynamical systems, possibly producing chaotic response. In this paper, we apply the concept to the prediction problem of nonlinear, possibly chaotic, time-series.

The concept of the prediction intervals does not directly evaluate the prediction accuracy but statistically estimates a spatial distribution of the future point which might be included in a bounded interval. One of the conventional methods for evaluating such a prediction interval is the ensemble prediction[10]. However, because the ensemble prediction needs large size data to evaluate ensemble properties, estimated prediction intervals[6,7] might be unreliable in the case that we cannot use large size data. In Ref.[3], we have already reported effectiveness of the bootstrap resampling scheme[11] for nonlinear prediction even if the data size is small. This paper [3] showed that the bootstrap resampling method improves prediction accuracy for nonlinear chaotic dynamical systems.

Thus, it is expected that the concept of the bootstrap method would also work well for the present issue. In this paper, we compared the performances of the ensemble prediction and the bootstrap method on the basis of accuracy or efficiency of estimated prediction intervals. By several numerical simulations, we reveal that the bootstrap method has advantages on the evaluation of prediction intervals for nonlinear time-series.

2 Local Linear Prediction Methods

Although there are several local linear prediction methods[1,2,4,5], we introduced two basic methods[1,2] which are used for estimating prediction intervals in the following sections. At first, let us consider a nonlinear dynamical system:

$$\boldsymbol{x}(t+1) = \boldsymbol{f}(\boldsymbol{x}(t)), \tag{1}$$

where $\boldsymbol{f}$ is a k-dimensional nonlinear map, $\boldsymbol{x}(t)$ is a k-dimensional state at time t. To estimate the Jacobian matrix of $\boldsymbol{f}$, we linearize Eq.(1) as follows:

$$\delta\boldsymbol{x}(t+1) = \boldsymbol{Df}(\boldsymbol{x}(t))\delta\boldsymbol{x}(t), \tag{2}$$

where $\boldsymbol{Df}(\boldsymbol{x}(t))$ is the Jacobian matrix at $\boldsymbol{x}(t)$, and $\delta\boldsymbol{x}(t)$ is an infinitesimal deviation at $\boldsymbol{x}(t)$. To evaluate $\boldsymbol{Df}(\boldsymbol{x}(t))$ only with local information at $\boldsymbol{x}(t)$, we first extract a near-neighbor set of $\boldsymbol{x}(t)$. Let us denote the i-th near neighbor of $\boldsymbol{x}(t)$ by $\boldsymbol{x}(t_{k_i})$, $(i = 1, 2, \ldots, M)$. Here, M is the total number of near neighbors. After temporal evolution, displacement vectors can be denoted as $\boldsymbol{y}_i = \boldsymbol{x}(t_{k_i}) - \boldsymbol{x}(t)$ and $\boldsymbol{z}_i = \boldsymbol{x}(t_{k_i}+1) - \boldsymbol{x}(t+1)$. Here, $\boldsymbol{y}_i$ corresponds to $\delta\boldsymbol{x}(t)$, and $\boldsymbol{z}_i$ corresponds to $\delta\boldsymbol{x}(t+1)$ in Eq.(2). If the norms of $\boldsymbol{y}_i$ and $\boldsymbol{z}_i$ and the corresponding temporal evolution is small enough, we can approximate the relation between $\boldsymbol{z}_i$ and $\boldsymbol{y}_i$ by the linear equation: $\boldsymbol{z}_i = \boldsymbol{G}(t)\boldsymbol{y}_i$, where the matrix $\boldsymbol{G}(t)$ is an estimated Jacobian matrix $\boldsymbol{Df}(\boldsymbol{x}(t))$ in Eq.(2). Then, we estimate

$G(t)$ by the least-square-error fitting which minimizes the average square error $S = \frac{1}{M}\sum_{i=1}^{M}|z_i - G(t)y_i|$. In other words, we can estimate $G(t)$ by the following equations: $G(t)W = C$, where W is the variance matrix of y_i, and C is the covariance matrix between y_i and z_i. If W has its inverse matrix, we can obtain $G(t)$ from $G(t) = CW^{-1}$[2,12].

Because we do not know a future value of $x(t)$, we cannot use dynamical information of z_i, and then cannot have direct information of $G(t)$. To solve the problem, we use the information of the nearest neighbor $x(t_{k_0})$ of $x(t)$. Then, we calculate a displacement vector $y' = x(t) - x(t_{k_0})$. Next, we can estimate the Jacobian matrix $G(t_{k_0})$ at $x(t_{k_0})$ by the above procedure. If we define $\hat{x}(t+1)$ as the predicted future value of $x(t)$, we can denote the predicted displacement vector $\hat{z}' = \hat{x}(t+1) - x(t_{k_0}+1)$ by $\hat{z}' = G(t_{k_0})y'$. Then, we can predict $\hat{x}(t+1)$ as follows: $\hat{x}(t+1) = G(t_{k_0})(x(t) - x(t_{k_0})) + x(t_{k_0}+1)$. Repeating the scheme for p time iteratively, we can predict the p step future of $x(t)$[13].

We introduced another prediction method to estimate a dynamical system f[1,5]. First, in this method, we search for the near neighbors $x(t_{k_i})(i=0,1,\ldots,K)$ of $x(t)$ on the reconstructed attractor. Then, we calculate a future value of $x(t)$ as

$$\hat{x}(t+1) = \sum_{i=0}^{K} \exp(-d_i) x(t_{k_i}+1) \Big/ \sum_{i=0}^{K} \exp(-d_i),$$

where $d_i = |x(t_{k_i}) - x(t)|$. This method is called a weighted average prediction.

3 Estimating Prediction Intervals

As a conventional measure to evaluate the prediction accuracy, we can use a normalized root mean square error:

$$E = \sqrt{\sum_{t=1}^{N}\sum_{d=1}^{k}(x_d(t+1) - \hat{x}_d(t+1))^2} \Big/ \sqrt{\sum_{t=1}^{N}\sum_{d=1}^{k}(x_d(t+1) - \bar{x}_d)^2},$$

where N is the data length, $\bar{x}_d(t+1)$ is the d-th variable of a predicted point, and $\bar{x}_d = \frac{1}{N}\sum_{t=1}^{N} x_d(t)$. For evaluating the prediction accuracy, E is basic and essential. However, any prediction methods cannot predict future points perfectly. Instead, it is important to offer a prediction interval in which the true future point might be included.

3.1 Ensemble Prediction

Generally, the prediction intervals can be generated by the ensemble prediction[10] whose technical procedure is described as follows: first, we select several ensemble samples $x^{(m)}(t)(m = 0, 1, 2, \ldots, M)$ from near neighbors $x(t_{k_i})$. In this paper, we set $M = K$, where K is the number of near neighbor data. We predict a future state of $\boldsymbol{x}^{(m)}(t)$ as $\hat{\boldsymbol{x}}^{(m)}(t+1)$ with estimating $\boldsymbol{f}$ by some prediction method, and we calculate the future of $\boldsymbol{x}(t)$ as

$$\hat{\boldsymbol{x}}(t+1) = \frac{1}{M} \sum_{m=1}^{M} \hat{\boldsymbol{x}}^{(m)}(t+1).$$

Next, to perform multi-steps prediction, we predict the futures of $\hat{\boldsymbol{x}}^{(m)}(t+1)$, respectively. Then, repeating this scheme for p times, we can predict the p step future as $\hat{\boldsymbol{x}}^{(m)}(t+p)$.

The prediction intervals can be calculated from the spatial distribution of $\hat{\boldsymbol{x}}^{(m)}(t+p)$. In this paper, the prediction intervals $\boldsymbol{E}(t+p)$ is defined by an ellipse, the center of which is $\bar{\boldsymbol{x}}(t+1)$. Then, the equation of the ellipse is defined by

$$\boldsymbol{E}(t+p) = \sum_{i=1}^{d} \frac{\hat{z}_i^2(t+p)}{\sigma_i^2} - 1$$

where $\hat{z}_i(t+p)$ is the i-th principle component, obtained by the application of PCA to the data set $\hat{\boldsymbol{x}}^{(m)}(t+p), (m = 1, 2, \ldots, M)$, and σ_i corresponds to the variance.

3.2 Prediction Intervals by Using the Bootstrap Method

Because the ensemble prediction needs large data sets to evaluate ensemble properties, estimated prediction intervals might be unreliable in the case that we cannot use large size data. In Ref.[3], we have already reported effectivity of the bootstrap method[11] for nonlinear prediction problem even if data size is small. Thus, to evaluate more accurate prediction intervals and to perform stable prediction, it is expected that the bootstrap method may work as well.

The bootstrap resampling scheme[11] is described as follows. First, we selected near-neighbor points of $\boldsymbol{x}(t)$ to predict $\boldsymbol{x}(t)$. The data set is denoted by $\boldsymbol{D} = \{\boldsymbol{x}(t_{k_0}), \boldsymbol{x}(t_{k_1}), \cdots, \boldsymbol{x}(t_{k_L})\}$, where L is the number of near-neighbor points to make a predictor. In this paper, we set $L = M$. Next, we performed a sampling with replacement of $\boldsymbol{D}$ to obtain a new near-neighbor data set $\boldsymbol{D}^{(1)} = \{\boldsymbol{D}^{(1,1)}, \boldsymbol{D}^{(1,2)}, \cdots, \boldsymbol{D}^{(1,l)}, \cdots, \boldsymbol{D}^{(1,L)}\}$. Here, $\boldsymbol{D}^{(1,l)}$ means the l-th sampling with replacement at the first bootstrap trial. Then, we estimate a predictor $\tilde{\boldsymbol{f}}^{(1,l)}$ on each $\boldsymbol{D}^{(1,l)}$, and we predict a future point of $\boldsymbol{x}(t)$ by $\tilde{\boldsymbol{x}}^{(1,l)}(t+1) = \tilde{\boldsymbol{f}}^{(1,l)}(\boldsymbol{D}^{(1,l)})$.

We repeated such bootstrap estimates for B times. Namely, the b-th bootstrap predicted point is described by $\tilde{\boldsymbol{x}}^{(b,l)}(t+1) = \tilde{\boldsymbol{f}}^{(b,l)}(\boldsymbol{D}^{(b,l)})$, where $b = 1, 2, \ldots, B$. Next, we predict the future of each bootstrap predicted point $\{\tilde{\boldsymbol{x}}^{(b,1)}(t+1), \cdots, \tilde{\boldsymbol{x}}^{(b,L)}(t+1)\}$. Therefore, predicted two-steps futures of bootstrap estimates was described as $\tilde{\boldsymbol{x}}^{(b,l)}(t+2)$ whose size is $(B \cdot L)^2$. That is, this dimension is $(B \cdot L)^p$. If we perform a p-steps prediction with the bootstrap method, the computational load would grow exponentially. Thus, in this paper, at the second prediction step, we randomly select B elements from $\{\tilde{\boldsymbol{x}}^{(b,l)}(t+2)\}$ to prevent the number of bootstrap samples from exploding exponentially. Repeating this scheme for p times, we can predict the p-step future of bootstrap estimates $\{\tilde{\boldsymbol{x}}^{(b,l)}(t+p)\}$, whose size is B^2. Finally, we decided the prediction interval $\boldsymbol{R}(t+p)$ in the same way as the ensemble prediction as described in 3.1.

4 Numerical Simulations

To confirm the validity of estimating prediction intervals by the proposed method, we applied the proposed method to an example test: the Ikeda map[14], which is described as follows:

$$\begin{cases} x(t+1) = a + b\bigl(x(t)\cos(\theta(t)) - y(t)\sin(\theta(t))\bigr) \\ y(t+1) = b\bigl(x(t)\sin(\theta(t)) + y(t)\cos(\theta(t))\bigr), \end{cases}$$

$$\theta(t) = \kappa - \alpha/(1 + x^2(t) + y^2(t)),$$

where a, b, κ, and α are parameters. The Ikeda map is suitable to check the validity of the proposed method because it has higher order nonlinearity. In simulations, the parameters were set as $a = 1.0$, $b = 0.9$, $\kappa = 0.4$ and $\alpha = 6.0$, the data length of $x(t)$ and $y(t)$ is 1,000, respectively. Then, we disturbed the system both by observational and dynamical noise. In this paper, the noise level is quantified by the signal-to-noise ratio, which is calculated by SNR[dB] = $10\log_{10}\sigma_o^2/\sigma_\eta^2$, where σ_o^2 is the variance of the original data and σ_η^2 is the variance of Gaussian observational/dynamical noise.

For estimating prediction accuracy, we introduced a measure to evaluate the prediction interval: we counted how many times the true point were included in the prescribed prediction interval. The number is denoted by V, which is averaged on several trials. We also introduced the size of prediction interval S_r, defined by $S_r(p) = \sqrt{\sum_{d=1}^{k}\hat{\sigma}_d^2(t+p)}$ in the case of the ensemble prediction, or $S_r(p) = \sqrt{\sum_{d=1}^{k}\tilde{\sigma}_d^2(t+p)}$ in the case of the bootstrap method, and p is the prediction step.

We compared two prediction methods: the Jacobian matrix estimation, and the weighted average prediction. Figs.1–3 show the results of the comparisons among four cases to estimate prediction intervals: the bootstrap method with the Jacobian prediction or the Lorenz' method of analogues, or the ensemble prediction with the same local prediction methods. Figure 1 shows the result of the noiseless data, Fig.2 shows the case that the data are disturbed by observational noise and Fig.3 shows the case that the data are disturbed by dynamical noise.

To evaluate applicability of the proposed method to real data, the data might be produced from a nonlinear chaotic dynamical system. we applied our method

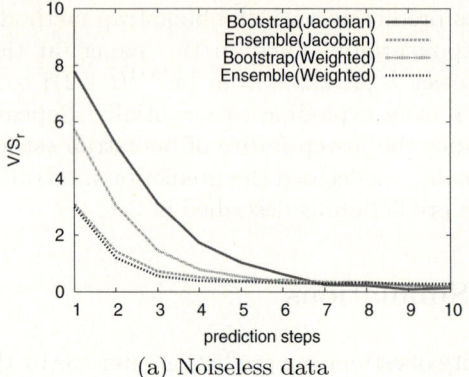

(a) Noiseless data

Fig. 1. Comparisons of four methods to estimate prediction intervals for noiseless data. The horizontal axis shows the prediction steps p, and the vertical axis shows the estimation accuracy $V(p)/S_r(p)$.

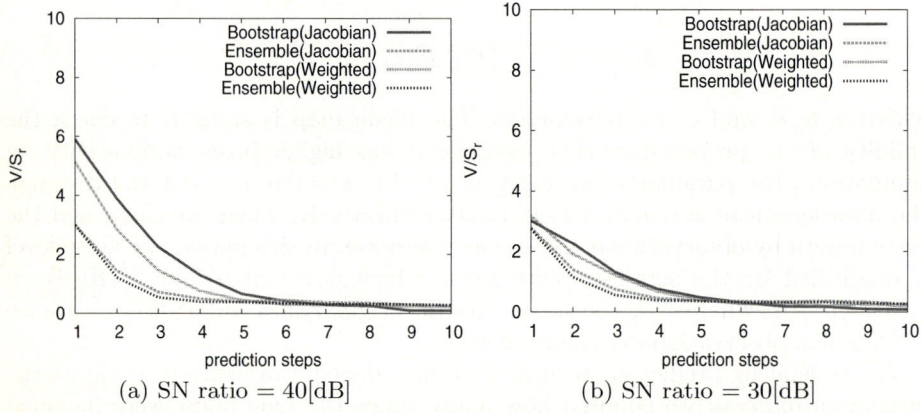

Fig. 2. The same as Fig.1, but to the observational noise data

to the Japanese vowels /a/ which is example of a real time-series. This data is suitable for benchmark tests because this data has been analyzed and discussed in several studies[14-16].

5 Discussion

These results show that the bootstrap method is more reasonable to make efficient prediction intervals if p is less than six. Namely, the bootstrap prediction method adjusts intervals size more accurately and efficiently than the ensemble prediction method. The performance of V/S_r of the bootstrap method and the ensemble method is almost the same as the observational/dynamical noise level

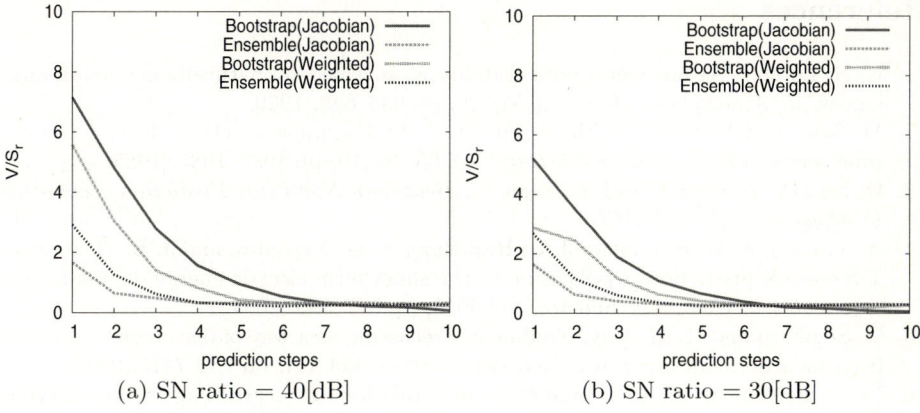

Fig. 3. The same as Fig.2, but to the dynamical noise data

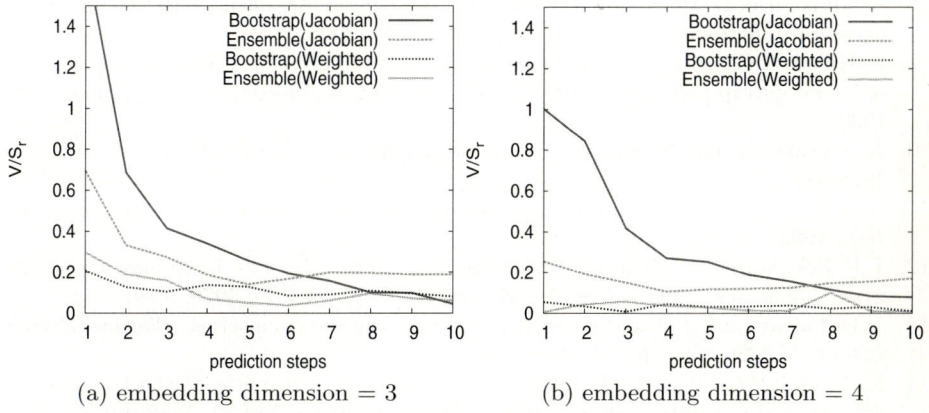

Fig. 4. Results of the Japanese vowels /a/. The axis is same as Fig.1.

becomes larger. In the case of noiseless data, the bootstrap method with the Jacobian prediction showed the best performance.

6 Conclusion

In this paper, we proposed a new framework for estimating the prediction intervals by using the bootstrap method with local-linear prediction methods. In particular, the proposed framework improves short-term predictability comparing to the conventional ensemble prediction. Moreover, the bootstrap method adjusts the size of the prediction intervals effectively according to the difficulty of prediction. The authors would like to thank Dr. Hiroki Hashiguchi for his valuable comments and discussions. The research of TI was partially supported by Grant-in-Aids for Scientific Research (C) (No.17500136) from JSPS.

References

1. E. N. Lorenz. Atmospheric predictability as revealed by naturally occurring analogues. *J. Atmospheric Sciences*, Vol.26, pp.636–646, 1969.
2. M. Sano and Y. Sawada. Measurement of the lyapunov spectrum from a chaotic time series. *Physical Review Letters*, Vol.55, No.10, pp.1082–1085, 1985.
3. D. Haraki, T. Suzuki, and T. Ikeguchi. Bootstrap Nonlinear Prediction. submitted to *Physical Review E*, 2005.
4. A. T. Lora, J. M. R. Santos, J. C. Riquelme, A. G. Expósito, and J. L. M. Ramos. Time-series prediction: Application to the short-term electric energy demand. *Lecture Notes in Computer Science*, Vol.3040, pp.577–586, 2004.
5. G. Sugihara and R. M. May. Nonlinear forecasting as a way of distinguishing chaos from measurement error in time series. *Nature*, Vol.344, pp.734–741, 1990.
6. M. Grigoletto. Bootstrap prediction intervals for autoregressions: Some alternatives. *International Journal of Forecasting*, Vol.14, pp.447–456, 1998.
7. Yun-Huan Lee and Tsai-Hung Fan. Bootstrapping prediction intervals on stochastic volatility models. *Applied Economic Letters*, Vol.13, pp.41–45, 2006.
8. A. M. Alonso, D. Pēna, and J. Romo. Introducing model uncertainty in time series bootstrap. *Statistica Sinica*, Vol.14, pp.155–174, 2004.
9. L. Kilian. Accounting for lag uncertainty in autoregressions: The endogenous lag order bootstrap algorithm. *Journal of Time Series Analysis*, Vol.19, pp.531–548, 1998.
10. T. Hurukawa and S. Sakai. Ensemble prediction. *Tokyo-doh Press*, 2004, in Japanese.
11. B. Efron and R. J. Tibshirani. *An Introduction to the Bootstrap*. Chapman and Hall, 1993.
12. J. P. Eckmann, S. O. Kamphorst, D. Ruelle, and S. Ciliberto. Lyapunov exponents from time series. *Physical Review A*, Vol.34, No.6, pp.4971–4979, 1986.
13. J. D. Farmer and J. J. Sidorowich. Predicting chaotic time series. *Physical Review Letters*, Vol.59, No.8, pp.845–848, 1987.
14. K. Ikeda. Multiple-valued stationary state and its instability of the transmitted light by a ring cavity system. *Optics Communications*, Vol.30, No.2, pp.257–261, 1979.

Effectiveness of Considering State Similarity for Reinforcement Learning[*]

Sertan Girgin[1,2], Faruk Polat[1], and Reda Alhajj[2,3]

[1] Department of Computer Eng., Middle East Technical University, Ankara, Turkey
[2] Department of Computer Science, University of Calgary, Calgary, AB, Canada
[3] Dept. of Computer Science, Global University, Beirut, Lebanon

Abstract. This paper presents a novel approach that locates states with similar sub-policies, and incorporates them into the reinforcement learning framework for better learning performance. This is achieved by identifying common action sequences of states, which are derived from possible optimal policies and reflected into a tree structure. Based on the number of such sequences, we define a similarity function between two states, which helps to reflect updates on the action-value function of a state to all similar states. This way, experience acquired during learning can be applied to a broader context. The effectiveness of the method is demonstrated empirically.

1 Introduction

Reinforcement learning (RL) is the problem faced by an agent that must learn behavior through trial-and-error interactions with a dynamic environment by gaining percepts and rewards from the world and taking actions to affect it [1,2]. In most of the realistic and complex domains, the task that the agent is trying to solve is composed of various subtasks and has a hierarchical structure formed by the relations between them [3]. Each of these subtasks repeats many times at different regions of the state space. Although, all instances of the same subtask, or similar subtasks, have almost identical solutions (sub-behaviors), without any (self) guidance an agent has to learn these solutions independently by going through similar learning stages again and again. This situation affects the learning process in a negative way, making it difficult to converge to optimal behavior in a reasonable time.

The main reason of the problem is the lack of connections, that would allow to share solutions, between similar subtasks scattered throughout the state space. One possible way to build the connections, based on *temporally abstract actions* formalism [4], is to identify subgoals of the problem, store the sub-policies solving these subgoals, and then reuse them when necessary. Methods based on this approach identify subgoals by using various statistics (such as visit frequencies of states) [5,6] or graph theoretical notions (such as bottleneck states connecting

---

[*] This work was supported NSERC-Canada, and by the Scientific and Technological Research Council of Turkey under Grant No. 105E181(HD-7).

the strongly connected components of the state space) [7,8]. They explicitly generate subpolicies solving them using reinforcement learning processes such as action replay [9] executed on restricted sub-problems with artificial rewards.

An alternative approach is to identify similar subtasks and corresponding region of the state space during the learning process. Then, instead of explicitly generating solutions, transfer and apply experience acquired on solving one instance to all other instances, reducing the repetitions in learning and therefore improving the performance. In this paper, we propose a method to identify states with similar sub-policies, and show how they can be integrated into reinforcement learning framework to improve the learning performance. Using the collected history of states, actions and rewards, traces of possible optimal policies are generated and then translated into a tree form to efficiently identify states with similar sub-policy behavior based on the number of common action sequences. Updates on the action-value function of a state are then reflected to all similar states, expanding the influence of new experiences. We demonstrate the effectiveness of the proposed approach empirically on the taxi domain.

The paper is organized as follows. Section 2 describes the standard reinforcement learning framework. Our approach to reinforcement learning with similar state update is presented in Section 3 on an illustrative example. A method to find similar states during the learning process is described in Section 4. We present experimental results in Section 5. Section 6 is conclusions.

2 Background

A *Markov decision process*, MDP, is a tuple $\langle S, A, T, R \rangle$, where S is a finite set of states, A is a finite set of actions, $T : S \times A \times S \rightarrow [0, 1]$ is a state transition function such that $\forall s \in S, \forall a \in A, \sum_{s' \in S} T(s, a, s') = 1$, and $R : S \times A \rightarrow \Re$ is a reward function. $T(s, a, s')$ denotes the probability of making a transition from state s to state s' using action a. $R(s, a)$ is the *immediate* expected reward received when action a is executed in state s. A (stationary) *policy*, $\pi : S \times A \rightarrow [0, 1]$, is a mapping that defines the probability of selecting an action from a particular state. If $\forall s \in S, \pi(s, a_s) = 1$ and $\forall a \in A, a \neq a_s, \pi(s, a) = 0$ then π is called a *deterministic policy*. The *value* of a policy π at state s, $V^\pi(s)$, is the expected infinite discounted sum of reward that the agent will gain if it starts in state s and follows π [1]. Let $Q^\pi(s, a) = R(s, a) + \gamma \sum_{s' \in S} T(s, a, s') V^\pi(s')$, where $0 \leq \gamma < 1$ is the discount factor, denote the expected infinite discounted sum of reward that the agent will gain if it selects action a at s, and follows π afterward. Then, we have $V^\pi(s) = \sum_{a \in A_s} \pi(s, a) Q^\pi(s, a)$; $V^\pi(s)$ and $Q^\pi(s, a)$ are called policy's state value function and action value function, respectively. In a Markov decision process, the objective of an agent is to find an *optimal policy*, π^*, which maximizes the state value function for all states (i.e., $\forall \pi, \forall s \in S, V^{\pi^*}(s) \geq V^\pi(s)$). Every MDP has a deterministic stationary optimal policy; and the following Bellman equations hold $\forall s \in S$: $V^*(s) = \max_{a \in A_s} \left(R(s, a) + \gamma \sum_{s' \in S} T(s, a, s') V^*(s') \right) = \max_{a \in A_s} Q^*(s, a)$ Here, V^* and Q^* are called the optimal value functions. Accordingly, $\pi^*(s)$ can be defined based on the value of Q^* at state s.

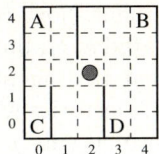

Fig. 1. Dietterich's taxi domain of size 5×5

When the reward function, R, and the state transition function, T, are known, π^* can be found by using *dynamic programming* techniques [1,2]. When such information is not readily available, it is possible to use Monte Carlo or temporal-difference (TD) learning methods, which rely on experience in the form of sample sequences of states, actions, and rewards collected from on-line or simulated trial-and-error interactions with the environment. In TD learning methods, estimate of the optimal state-(action) value function is kept and updated in part on the basis of other estimates. Various algorithms basically differ from each other on how they update the estimation of the optimal value function. In simple TD learning algorithms, the update of estimation is based on just the one next reward, using the value of the state one step later as a proxy for the remaining rewards. In n-step TD and TD(λ) algorithms, such as Sarsa(λ), a sequence of observed rewards and discounted average of all such sequences are used respectively. Hierarchical RL algorithms [3] further extend traditional methods to include temporally abstract actions that may last for a period of time once executed and involve sub-abstractions.

3 RL with Similar State Update

Dietterich's Taxi domain [10] is an episodic task, in which a taxi agent moves around on a $n \times n$ grid world, containing obstacles that limit the movement (Fig. 1). The agent tries to transport a passenger from one predefined location to another. At each time step, the agent can execute one of six actions: move one square in one of four main directions, attempt to *pickup* a passenger, or attempt to *drop-off* the passenger being carried. Should a move action cause the agent to hit a wall/obstacle, the position of the agent will not change. The movement actions are non-deterministic and agent may move perpendicular to the desired direction with 0.2 probability. An episode ends when the passenger is successfully transported to its destination and the agent receives a reward of +20. There is an immediate negative reward of −10 if pickup or drop-off actions are executed incorrectly, and −1 for any other action. In order to maximize the overall cumulative reward, the agent must transport the passenger as quickly as possible, i.e. using minimum number of actions. Let $L = \{l_1, \ldots, l_k\}$ be the set of possible locations on $n \times n$ version of the taxi problem. Then, each possible state can be represented by a tuple of the form $\langle r, c, l, d \rangle$, where $r, c \in \{0, \ldots, n-1\}$ denote the taxi's position, $l \in L \cup \{T\}$ denotes the location of the passenger (either one of predefined locations or in case of $l = T$ picked-up by the taxi), and $d \in L$

denotes the destination of the passenger. Now, consider two different instances of the problem where passenger is located at l_1, but wants to go to l_2 in one of them and to l_3 in the other. Suppose that taxi agent starts at the same position on the grid. Although different state trajectories will be visited, in both cases, until the passenger is picked-up, the optimal sub-policy (i.e. go to l_1 and then pick up the passenger) that can be executed by the agent has the same pattern. One can easily observe that, any two states of the form $\langle r, c, l, d_i \rangle$ and $\langle r, c, l, d_j \rangle$ such that $d_i, d_j \in L, d_i \neq d_j$ have similar sub-policies. In general, such similar states exist in most of the reinforcement problems that have a hierarchical structure, and contain subtasks that need to be solved by the agent. By taking advantage of this similarity relation, it is possible to improve the performance of learning.

Let $\Omega(s)$ be the set of states similar to s. Suppose that while learning the optimal policy, the agent selects action a at state s which takes it to state s' with an immediate reward r, and consequently the estimate of the state-action value funtion, $Q(s, a)$, is updated based on this experience. Let $\Delta Q(s, a)$ be the difference between Q-values before and after the update. An increase in the value of $Q(s, a)$ roughly indicates that selecting action a at state s could be a good choice leading to a better solution, whereas a decrease indicates the opposite. Since states in $\Omega(s)$ are similar in terms of optimal sub-policies, it is very likely that selecting action a at those states also has a similar effect, i.e., for $t \in \Omega(s)$, increases $Q(t, a)$ if $\Delta Q(s, a) > 0$, and decreases $Q(t, a)$ if $\Delta Q(s, a) < 0$. Then, based on $Q(s, a)$ and $\Delta Q(s, a)$, we can update the Q-value of each state t similar to s according to the following learning rule in order to speed up the learning process: $Q(t, a) = Q(t, a) + \rho \varsigma(s, t) f(Q(t, a), Q(s, a), \Delta Q(s, a))$ where $\rho \in [0, 1)$ is the learning rate, $\varsigma(s, t)$ is the degree of similarity between s and t, and f is the *reflection* function such that $sign(f(\cdot, \cdot, \Delta Q(s, a))) = sign(\Delta Q(s, a))$, i.e., its value is positive for $\Delta Q(s, a) > 0$ and negative for $\Delta Q(s, a) < 0$. Since it is possible that states similar to s would have different optimal state-action values depending on the reward formulation, it may not be feasible to use $\Delta Q(s, a)$ directly to update $Q(t, a)$. Function f maps the change in $Q(s, a)$, i.e., $\Delta Q(s, a)$, to $Q(t, a)$ in a problem specific way. It can be a static function, such as $f(\cdot, \cdot, \Delta Q(s, a)) = c \cdot sign(\Delta Q(s, a))$, where c is a constant that decreases with time, or reflects the change proportionally, such as $f(Q(t, a), Q(s, a), \Delta Q(s, a)) = Q(t, a) \frac{\Delta Q(s, a)}{Q(s, a)}$.

The method described above assumes that similar states, and consequently ς function, is already known. However, in general it is not easy to specify similar states prior to learning, since optimal policies and relations between states are not known in advance. In the next section, we describe a method to approximate ς and identify similar states on-line using the collected history of events.

4 Finding Similar States

Let $h = s_t, a_t, r_{t+1}, s_{t+1}, a_{t+1}, \ldots, r_\tau, s_\tau$ be the sequence of states, actions and rewards observed by the agent starting from time t until τ. Following [4], we will call this sequence the *history* from t to τ. $A_h = a_t a_{t+1} \ldots a_\tau$ and $S_h = \bigcup_{i=t..\tau} \{s_i\}$ are the action sequence and state set of h, respectively. A history that starts with state s and obtained by following a policy π until the end of an episode is called a π-history of s. For non-episodic tasks, a variety of methods can be used to determine a termination condition for π-history such as when a reward peak is reached.

Now consider the set of π^*-histories of two states u and v for an optimal policy π^*. If u and v are parts of two similar subtasks or repeated instances of the same subtask, then they are expected to have similar sub-policies. This means that their π^*-histories will exhibit similar patterns of state transition and action selection up to a number of steps t. The number of common action sequences in such histories will be high for states that are similar to each other, and on the contrary will be low for states with different sub-policies. Therefore, given any two states, the number of common action sequences in their π^*-histories approximately reflect the degree of similarity between them. During learning, since optimal policy is not known, π^*-histories of a given state s are not available to the agent, and the number of common action sequences can not be directly counted. However, in RL methods where the behavior of the agent converges to optimal policy as the learning progresses, it is possible to utilize observed histories instead of optimal histories. Let π' denote the agent's current policy and $h' = s_1 a_1 r_2 \ldots r_t s_t$ be a π'-history of length t for state s_1. Total cumulative reward of h' is defined as $r(h') = r_2 + \gamma r_3 + \ldots + \gamma^{t-1} r_t$. Now suppose that in h' a state appears at two positions i and j, i.e., $s_i = s_j, i \neq j$; and consider the sequence $h'' = s_1 a_1 r_2 \ldots r_i s_i a_{j+1} r_{j+1} \ldots r_t s_t$ where s_i and s_j are united and the sequence in between is removed; h'' is also a π'-history for state s_1 and could be a better candidate for being a π^*-history if $r(h'') > r(h')$. Also, every suffix of h' of the form $h'_i = s_i a_i r_{i+1} \ldots r_t s_t$ for $i = 2..t-1$ is also a π'-history. Combining these two observations, we can generate a set of π^*-history candidates by processing h' from back to front. Let bh'_s denote the π'-history for state s with maximum total cumulative reward; initially $bh'(s_{t-1}) = s_{t-1} a_{t-1} r_t s_t$. For each $s_i, i = t-2..1$, if s_i is not encountered before (i.e., for $j > i, s_j \neq s_i$) or $r_i + \gamma r(bh'_{s_{i+1}})$ is higher than the total cumulative reward of the current bh'_{s_i}, $r(bh'_{s_i})$, then bh'_{s_i} is replaced by $s_i a_i r_{i+1} bh'_{s_{i+1}}$. Finally, for each unique s_i in $(s_1, \ldots, s_t)$, resulting $bh's_i$ is used as a probable π^*-history for state s_i. This process of creating probable π^*-histories from the observed history also helps to reduce the effects of bogus transitions due to non-determinism of the environment.

In order to calculate the similarity between states, we need to store probable π^*-histories for each state, and enumerate common action sequences generated by them. This process must be repeated at certain intervals during learning, since sets of probable π^*-histories are not static but rather change with time. Also, as the agent experiences new probable π^*-histories for a state s, previous ones that are no longer eligible must be eliminated. These issues can be handled efficiently by using an auxiliary structure called *path tree*. A path tree stores the prefixes of action sequences of π-histories for a given set of states. There is one node for every unique action sequence and two nodes representing action sequences u and v are connected by an edge with label a if $v = ua$. The root node represents the empty action sequence. Let σ_u denote the action sequence

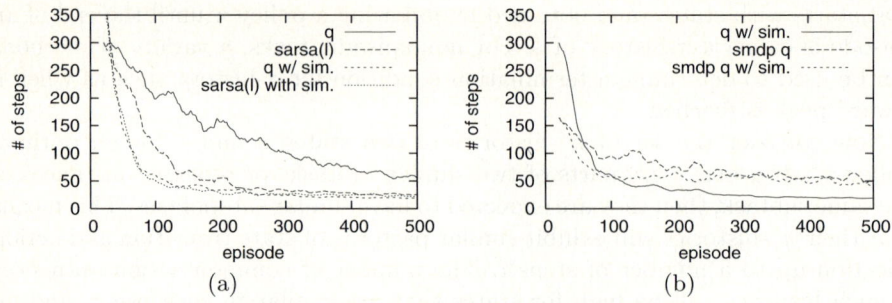

Fig. 2. Taxi problem with one passenger

associated with node u. Each node u holds a list of $\langle s, \xi \rangle \in S \times \mathcal{R}$ tuples, stating that state s has one or more π-histories starting with action sequence σ_u. ξ is the *eligibility value* of σ_u for state s, which denotes the visit frequency. It is incremented every time a new π-history for state s starting with action sequence σ_u is added to the path tree, and gradually decremented otherwise. A π-history $h = s_1 a_1 r_2 \ldots r_t s_t$ can be added to a path tree T by starting from the root node and following edges according to their label. Let $\hat{n}$ denote the active node of T, which is initially the root node. For $i = 1..(t-1)$, if there is a node n such that $\hat{n}$ is connected to n by an edge with label a_i, then either ξ of the tuple $\langle s_1, \xi \rangle$ in n is incremented or a new tuple $\langle s_1, 1 \rangle$ is added to n if it doesn't exist, and $\hat{n}$ is set to n. Otherwise, a new node containing tuple $\langle s_1, 1 \rangle$ is created, and $\hat{n}$ is connected to this node by an edge with label a_i. The new node becomes the active node.

After each episode, based on the sequence of states, actions and rewards observed during the episode (or between two termination conditions in case of non-episodic tasks), a set of probable π^*-histories are generated and added to the path tree. The eligibility values of tuples in the nodes of the tree are decremented by a factor of $0 < \xi_{decay} < 1$, called *eligibility decay rate*. For a given state s, tuples in nodes representing action sequences that are frequently used starting from s would have high eligibility values, whereas for sequences that are used less would decay to 0 and those with eligibility value less than a small threshold value, ξ_{thres}, can be removed. If two states u and v have π-histories with same action sequence prefixes, then tuple lists of nodes corresponding to those prefixes in T would contain entries for both u and v. Let $\nu_k(u)$ be the number of nodes representing action sequences of length at most k that contain a tuple for state u, and $\kappa_k(u,v)$ be the number of such nodes that contain a tuple for state v also. Then, $\varsigma_k(u,v) = \frac{\kappa_k(u,v)}{\nu_k(v)}$ is an approximate measure of the similarity between u and v when sub-policies of length k are considered. Note that, action sequences will eventually deviate and follow different courses as the subtask that they are part of ends. As a result, for k larger than some threshold value, ς_k would inevitably decrease and no longer be a permissible measure of the state similarity. On the contrary, for very small values of k, it may over estimate the amount of similarity since number of common action sequences can be high for short sequences. Also, since optimal value of k depends on the subtasks of the problem, to increase robustness it is necessary to take into account action sequences of various lengths. In this work, we used the maximum value of $\varsigma_i(s, s')$ over a range of i values, k_{min} to k_{max}, to combine the results of evaluations and calculate $\varsigma(u, v)$. This can be efficiently realized by traversing the path tree in breadth-first order and incrementally updating $\varsigma(u, v)$ values when necessary by comparing with $\frac{\kappa_i(u,v)}{\nu_i(v)}$ at level i. Once ς values are calculated, state pairs with ς greater than a threshold value τ_{sim}, can be regarded as similar and incorporated into learning. Note that, for the purpose of $\varsigma(u, v)$ calculations, only nodes up to level k_{max} are considered, and therefore, it is not necessary to store nodes at higher levels, reducing the size of the path tree.

5 Experiments

We applied the similar state update method described in Section 4 to various RL algorithms on single and multiple passenger versions of the 5×5 taxi problem and compared their performance. In the multiple passenger version, the taxi agent must transport passengers successively to their destinations. Rewards and action characteristics are the same as defined in Section 3. State representation is extended to include multiple passenger locations and destinations. Passengers can not be co-located at the same position, but their destinations can be the same. In all cases, the initial Q-values are set to 0. After systematic initial testing, the learning rate and discount factor are set as $\alpha = 0.125$ and $\gamma = 0.9$, respectively. ϵ-greedy action selection mechanism is used with $\epsilon = 0.1$. For $Sarsa(\lambda)$ algorithm, we used $\lambda = 0.9$. Initial position of the taxi agent, locations and destinations of the passengers are selected randomly with uniform probability.

Fig. 2 shows sliding window (20 episodes) average number of steps for successful transportation of the standard version averaged over 30 runs. State similarities are computed every 5 episodes starting from the 20th episode in order to let the agent gain experience for the initial path tree. While updating the path tree, $\xi_{decay} = 0.95$ and $\xi_{thres} = 0.1$ are used as eligibility decay rate and threshold values. In similarity calculations, the following parameters are used: $k_{min} = 3$, $k_{max} = 7$, and $\tau_{sim} = 0.2$. Reflection function is defined as $f(\cdot, \cdot, \Delta Q(s, a)) = \Delta Q(s, a)$. In Sarsa($\lambda$) with similar state update, Q-value updates based on eligibility traces are also reflected to similar states. As presented in Fig. 2(a), both Q-learning with state update and Sarsa(λ) with state update outperform their regular counterparts and learn in less number of steps. In SMDP Q-learning [3], in addition to primitive actions, the agent can select and execute hand-coded options, extended actions, which move the agent from any position to one of predefined locations in minimum number of steps. Although SMDP Q-learning has a very steep learning curve in the initial stages, by utilizing similarities more effectively Q-learning with similar state update perform better in the long run (Fig. 2(b)). When state similarity update is applied to SMDP Q-learning, we ignored the execution time of extended actions. In domains where not only the state that the extended action leads to but the transition time is

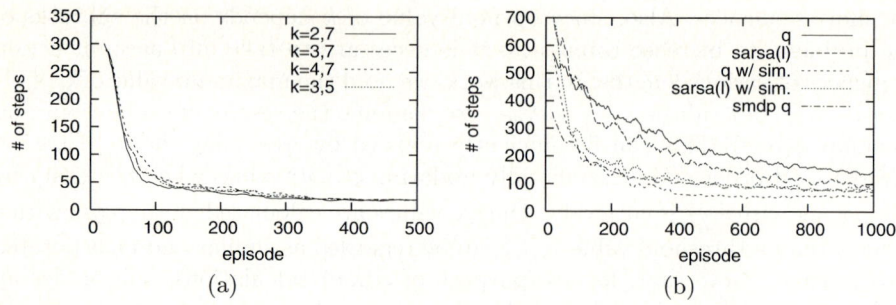

Fig. 3. (a) Effect of k_{min} and k_{max}, and (b) Taxi problem with two passengers

also important, π-histories and path tree need to be extended to include temporal information. The results are found to be consistent for a range of k_{min} and k_{max} values, Fig. 3(a). Results for the taxi problem with two passengers, which has a larger state space and contains more similar sub-policies, is presented in Fig. 3(b). Although the convergence rate of regular algorithms decreases in this case, those with similar state update still perform well.

6 Conclusions

We have shown that states that are similar to each other with respect to sub-policies can be identified on-line in a reinforcement learning system. Our experimental results suggest that experience transfer performed by the algorithm is an attractive approach to make learning systems more effective and allows to improve the learning performance using less information, i.e. interaction with the environment. Future work will examine convergence guarantees of the method and its adaptation to larger domains, possibly involving continuous variables.

References

1. Kaelbling, L., Littman, M., Moore, A.: Reinforcement learning: A survey. Journal of Artificial Intelligence Research **4** (1996) 237–285
2. Sutton, R.S., Barto, A.G.: Reinforcement Learning: An Introduction. MIT Press, Cambridge, MA (1998)
3. Barto, A.G., Mahadevan, S.: Recent advances in hierarchical reinforcement learning. Discrete Event Dynamic Systems **13** (2003) 341–379
4. Sutton, R.S., Precup, D., Singh, S.: Between MDPs and semi-MDPs: a framework for temporal abstraction in reinforcement learning. Artificial Intelligence **112** (1999) 181–211
5. Stolle, M., Precup, D.: Learning options in reinforcement learning. In: Proc. of the 5th Int. Symp. on Abstraction, Reformulation and Approximation. (2002) 212–223
6. McGovern, A., Barto, A.G.: Automatic discovery of subgoals in reinforcement learning using diverse density. In: Proc. of the 18th ICML. (2001) 361–368
7. Menache, I., Mannor, S., Shimkin, N.: Q-cut - dynamic discovery of sub-goals in reinforcement learning. In: Proc. of the 13th ECML. (2002) 295–306

8. Simsek, O., Wolfe, A.P., Barto, A.G.: Identifying useful subgoals in reinforcement learning by local graph partitioning. In: Proc. of the 22nd ICML. (2005)
9. Lin, L.J.: Self-improving reactive agents based on reinforcement learning, planning and teaching. Machine Learning **8** (1992) 293–321
10. Dietterich, T.G.: Hierarchical reinforcement learning with the MAXQ value function decomposition. Journal of Artificial Intelligence Research **13** (2000) 227–303

On the Structural Robustness of Evolutionary Models of Cooperation

Segismundo S. Izquierdo[1] and Luis R. Izquierdo[2]

[1] Social Systems Engineering Centre (INSISOC), University of Valladolid, 47011, Spain
[2] The Macaulay Institute, Craigiebuckler, AB15 8QH, Aberdeen, UK
segis@eis.uva.es, l.izquierdo@macaulay.ac.uk

Abstract. This paper studies the structural robustness of evolutionary models of cooperation, i.e. their sensitivity to small structural changes. To do this, we focus on the Prisoner's Dilemma game and on the set of stochastic strategies that are conditioned on the last action of the player's opponent. Strategies such as Tit-For-Tat (TFT) and Always-Defect (ALLD) are particular and classical cases within this framework; here we study their potential appearance and their evolutionary robustness, as well as the impact of small changes in the model parameters on their evolutionary dynamics. Our results show that the type of strategies that are likely to emerge and be sustained in evolutionary contexts is strongly dependent on assumptions that traditionally have been thought to be unimportant or secondary (number of players, mutation-rate, population structure...). We find that ALLD-like strategies tend to be the most successful in most environments, and we also discuss the conditions that favor the appearance of TFT-like strategies and cooperation.

Keywords: Evolution of Cooperation; Evolutionary Game Theory; Iterated Prisoner's Dilemma; Tit for Tat; Agent-based Modeling.

1 Introduction

The evolutionary emergence and stability of cooperation is a problem of fundamental importance that has been studied for decades in a wide range of disciplines. The value of understanding such a question is clear: in the social and biological sciences, the emergence of cooperation is at the heart of subjects as diverse as the first appearance of life, the ecological functioning of countless environmental interactions, the efficient use of natural resources, the development of modern societies, and the sustainable stewardship of our planet. From an engineering point of view, the problem of understanding how cooperation can emerge and be promoted is crucial for the design of efficient decentralized systems where collective action can lead to a common benefit but individual units may (purposely or not) undermine the collective good for their own advantage.

At the most elementary level, the problem of cooperation can be formalized using the symmetric Prisoner's Dilemma (PD), a two-person game where each player can either cooperate or defect. The payoff that players gain when they both cooperate (R)

is greater than the payoff obtained when they both defect (P); a single cooperator obtains S, whereas a single defector receives T. The essence of the problem of cooperation is captured by the fact that both players prefer any outcome in which the opponent cooperates to any outcome in which the opponent defects ($T > R > P > S$), but they both have clear incentives to defect. Specifically, both the temptation to cheat ($T > R$) and the fear of being cheated ($S < P$) put cooperation at risk.

Thus, the fundamental challenge of understanding the evolutionary emergence and stability of cooperation can be enlightened, at the most elementary level, by identifying the conditions under which a finite number of units that interact by playing the PD may cooperate. These units might be able to adapt their individual behavior (i.e. learn), or the population of units as a whole may adapt through an evolutionary process (or both). While formalizing the problem of cooperation in this way significantly decreases its complexity (and generality), the question still remains largely unspecified: how many units form the population? How do they interact? What strategies can they use? What is the value of each of the payoffs in the game? and, crucially, what are the processes governing the dynamics of the system?

It is well known since the early years of the study of the evolution of cooperation that, in general, the question of how – if at all – cooperation emerges in a particular system significantly depends on all of the above defining characteristics of the system (see e.g. [1], [2], [3] and [4]). Having recognized this, the method that scientists have naturally followed to advance our formal understanding of the emergence of cooperation has been to study those systems that are tractable with the tools of analysis available at the time. Until not long ago, such tools have derived almost exclusively from the realm of mathematics, and they have given rise to mainstream evolutionary game theory [5]. Mainstream (analytical) Evolutionary Game Theory (EGT) has proven to be tremendously useful, but its use has had important implications in terms of the *classes of systems* that have been investigated, and in terms of the *kind of conclusions* that have been drawn on such systems.

In terms of *classes of systems*, in order to achieve mathematical tractability, EGT has traditionally analyzed *idealized systems*, i.e. systems that *cannot* exist in the real world (e.g. a system where the population is assumed to be infinite). Typically, mainstream EGT has also imposed various other assumptions that simplify the analysis, but which do not necessarily make the system ideal in our terminology (i.e. impossible to exist in the real world). Some examples of such assumptions are: *random* encounters, *infinitely repeated* interactions, *finite* sets of *deterministic* strategies, *proportional fitness rule*, and *arbitrarily small homogenous* invasions. Applying mainstream EGT to non-idealized systems can be very problematic because the validity on non-idealized systems of conclusions drawn from extremely similar idealized systems is not as straightforward as one may think. As an example, Beggs [6] demonstrates that when analyzing some types of evolutionary idealized systems, results can be widely different depending on the order in which certain limits are taken: if one takes the limit as population size becomes (infinitely) large and then considers the limit as the force of selection becomes strong, then one obtains different results from those attained if the order of the limits is inverted. Thus, Beggs [6] warns that "care is therefore needed in the application of these approximations".

The need to achieve mathematical tractability has also influenced the *kind of conclusions* obtained in mainstream EGT. Thus, mainstream EGT has focused on analyzing the stability of incumbent strategies to arbitrarily small mutant invasions, but has not paid much attention to the overall dynamics of the system in terms of e.g. the size of the basins of attraction of different evolutionary stable strategies, or the average fraction of time that the system spends in each of them.

Nowadays it has just become possible to start addressing the limitations of mainstream EGT outlined above. The current availability of vast amounts of computing power through the use of computer grids is enabling us to conduct formal and rigorous analyses of the dynamics of non-idealized systems through an adequate exploration of their sensitivity both to basic parameters and to their structural assumptions. These analyses can complement previous studies by characterizing dynamic aspects of (idealized and non-idealized) systems beyond the limits of mathematical tractability. It is this approach that we follow in this paper.

The specific aim of this paper is to study the structural robustness of evolutionary models of cooperation. To do this, we analyze simple non-idealized models of cooperation and we study their sensitivity to small structural changes (e.g. slight modifications in the way players are paired to play the PD, or in how a generation is created from the preceding one). The impact of the assumptions that we study here has not been, to our knowledge, investigated in a formal and consistent way before arguably because a) it is only recently that we can thoroughly analyze non-idealized models, and/or because b) the effect of such assumptions has been considered unimportant. Thus, in broader terms, our results also shed light on the robustness of the conclusions obtained from EGT as we know it nowadays – i.e. can these conclusions be readily applied to non-idealized systems?

Following this introduction, in section 2 we review some previous work on the robustness of evolutionary models of cooperation. Section 3 describes our modeling framework: EVO-2x2. In section 4 we provide and discuss the main results obtained, and finally, in section 5, we present our conclusions.

2 Previous Work

In this section we report previous work that has shed light on the robustness of evolutionary models of cooperation. We find it useful to place these models in a fuzzy spectrum that goes from mathematically tractable models with strict assumptions that limit their applicability (e.g. work on idealized systems), to models with the opposite characteristics. The rationale behind the construction and use of such a spectrum is that when creating a formal model to investigate a certain question (e.g. the evolution of cooperation), there is often a trade-off between the applicability of the model (determined by how constraining the assumptions embedded in the model are) and the mathematical tractability of its analysis (i.e. how deeply the functioning of the model can be understood given a certain set of available tools of analysis).

The former end is mostly populated by models *designed to* ensure its mathematical tractability. Near this end we find papers that study the impact of some structural assumptions, whilst still keeping others which ensure the model remains tractable and which, unfortunately, also tend to make the model retain its idealized nature. Gotts et al. [4] review many of such papers in sections 2 and 4. Some of these investigations have considered finite vs. infinite populations [7, 8, 9], different pairing settings or population structures (see section 6 in [4]), deterministic vs. stochastic strategies [10, 11], and finite vs. infinitely repeated games [12]. While illuminating, the applicability of most of these studies is somewhat limited since, as mentioned before, the models investigated there tend to retain their idealized nature.

Near the opposite end, we find models that tend to be slightly more applicable (e.g. they consider non-idealized systems), but they are often mathematically intractable. It is from this end that we depart in this paper. To our knowledge, the first relevant study with these characteristics was conducted by Axelrod [13]. Axelrod had previously organized two open tournaments in which the participant strategies played an iterated PD in a round robin fashion [1]. Tit for Tat (TFT) was the winner in both tournaments, and also in an *ecological analysis* that Axelrod [1] conducted after the tournaments. Encouraged by these results, Axelrod [13] investigated the generality of TFT's success by studying the evolution of a randomly generated population of strategies (as opposed to the arguably arbitrary set of strategies submitted to the tournament) using a particular genetic algorithm. The set of possible strategies in this study consisted of all deterministic strategies able to consider the 3 preceding actions by both players. From this study, Axelrod [13] concluded that in the long-term, "reciprocators [...] spread in the population, resulting in more and more cooperation and greater and greater effectiveness". However, the generality of Axelrod's study [13] is doubtful for two reasons: (1) he used a very specific set of assumptions, the impact of which was not tested, and (2) even if we constrain the scope of his conclusions to his particular model, the results should not be trusted since Axelrod only conducted 10 runs of 50 generations each. As a matter of fact, Binmore [14, 15] cites unpublished work by Probst [16] that contradicts Axelrod's results.

In a more comprehensive fashion, Linster [17] studied the evolution of strategies that can be implemented by two-state Moore machines in the infinitely repeated PD. He found a strategy called GRIM remarkably successful. In particular, GRIM was significantly more successful than TFT. GRIM always cooperates until the opponent defects, in which case it switches to defection forever. Linster [17] attributed the success of GRIM over TFT to the fact that GRIM is able to exploit poor strategies while TFT is not. Linster's investigation was truly remarkable at its time, but technology has advanced considerably since then, and we are now in a position to expand his work significantly by conducting parameter explorations beyond what was possible before. As an example, note that Linster [17] could only consider deterministic strategies and one specific value for the mutation rate; furthermore, in the cases he studied where the dynamics were not deterministic, there is no guarantee that his simulations had reached their asymptotic behavior.

In the following section we describe the relevant aspects of our modeling framework, which is aimed at facilitating a more consistent and systematic exploration of the impact of competing assumptions in non-idealized evolutionary models of cooperation.

3 Our Modeling Framework: EVO-2x2

EVO-2x2 was developed using NetLogo [18]. In EVO-2x2 there is a population of **num-players** players. Events occur in discrete time-steps, which can be interpreted as successive generations. At the beginning of every generation every player's payoff (which denotes the player's fitness) is set to zero. Then, every player is paired with another player to play a 2-player match, according to one of two possible pairing algorithms (***pairing-settings***):

- *random pairings*: Pairs are made at random, without any bias.
- *children together*: Players are paired preferentially with their siblings (and at random among siblings). Once all the possible pairs between siblings have been made, the rest of the players are paired at random. This procedure was implemented because it seems plausible in many biological contexts that individuals belonging to the same family tend to interact more often among them than with individuals from other families.

Every player plays one single match per generation. Each match consists of a number of sequential rounds (***rounds-per-match***). In each round, the two members of the pair play a symmetric PD once. The action selected by each of the players determines the magnitude of the payoff that each of them receives in that round (***CC-payoff***, ***CD-payoff***, ***DC-payoff***, ***DD-payoff***). The total payoff that a player obtains in a match is the sum of the payoffs obtained in each of the rounds. Players differ in the way they play the match, i.e. they generally have different strategies. The strategy of a player is determined by three numbers between 0 and 1:

- *PC*: Probability to cooperate in the first round.
- *PC/C*: Probability to cooperate in round n ($n > 1$) given that the other player has cooperated in round $(n-1)$.
- *PC/D*: Probability to cooperate in round n ($n > 1$) given that the other player has defected in round $(n-1)$.

The set of possible values that *PC*, *PC/C* or *PC/D* can take depends on the value of the binary variable ***infinite-strategies?***, which is either on or off. If on (default option), the set of possible values is any (floating-point) number between 0 and 1. If off, only ***num-strategies*** (≥ 2) values are allowed for each of the variables *PC*, *PC/C*, and *PC/D*; the permitted values are evenly distributed between 0 and 1 (both included). Once every player has played one – and only one – match, two evolutionary processes come into play to replace the old generation with a brand new one: natural selection (***selection-mechanism***) and mutation (***mutation-rate***). Successful players (those with higher payoffs) tend to have more offspring than unsuccessful ones. This marks the end of a generation and the beginning of a new one, and thus the cycle is completed. In this paper we only consider a ***selection-mechanism*** called *roulette wheel*, which involves conducting ***num-players*** replications that form the new generation. In each replication, players from the old generation are given a probability of being chosen to be replicated that is proportional to their total payoff. A mutant is a player whose strategy (the 3-tuple formed by *PC*, *PC/C*, and *PC/D*) has been determined at random. The probability that any newly created player is a mutant is ***mutation-rate***.

4 Results and Discussion

We use EVO-2x2 to conduct a systematic exploration of the parameter space for the PD, in order to assess the impact of various competing assumptions. All the simulations reported in this paper have been run on computer grids.

Defining a state of the system as a certain particularization of every player's strategy, it can be shown that all simulations in EVO-2x2 with positive mutation rates can be formulated as irreducible positive recurrent and aperiodic (sometimes called ergodic) discrete-time Markov chains. Thus, there is a unique long-run distribution over the possible states of the system, *i.e.* initial conditions are immaterial in the long-run [19, Theorem 3.15]. Although calculating such (dynamic) distributions analytically is unfeasible, we can estimate them using the computer simulations. The problem is to make sure that a certain simulation has run for long enough, so the limiting distribution has been satisfactorily approximated. To make sure that this is the case, for each possible combination of parameters considered, we ran 8 different simulations starting from widely different initial conditions. These are the 8 possible initial populations where every individual has the same pure strategy (the 8 corners of the strategy space). Then, every simulation run is conducted for 1,000,000 generations. Thus, in those cases where the 8 distributions are similar, we have great confidence that they are showing a distribution close to the limiting distribution.

A useful summary of the results produced in a simulation run is the accumulated frequency of different types of strategies throughout the course of a simulation run. This is something that can be plotted in a 3D contour plot, and in complementary 2D density plots, as shown in figure 1.

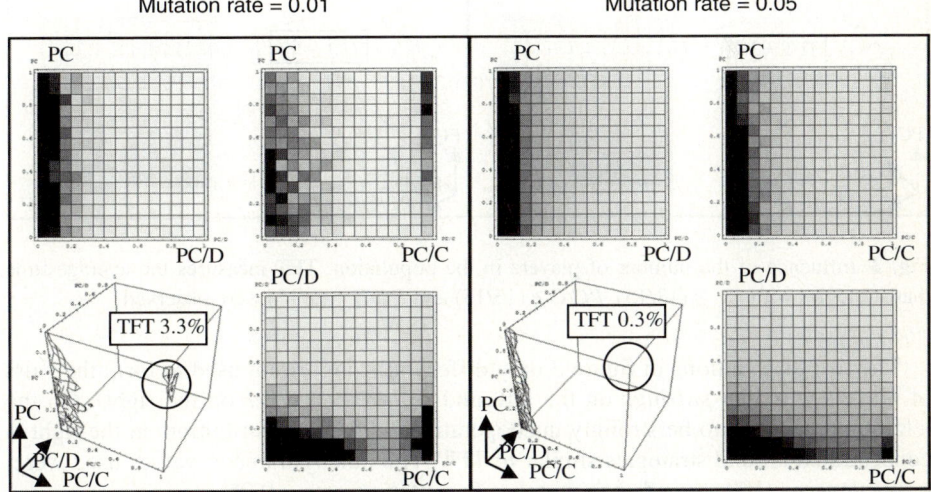

Fig. 1. Influence of the mutation rate on the dynamics of the system. TFT measures the average time that strategies with $PC \geq (13/15)$, $PC/C \geq (13/15)$ and $PC/D \leq (2/15)$ were observed.

Here we report several cases where it can be clearly seen that some of the assumptions that are sometimes thought to have little significance (e.g. mutation-rate, number of players, or population structure) can have a major impact on the type of strategies that emerge and are sustained throughout generations. The payoffs used in all simulations are: ***CC-payoff*** = 3; ***CD-payoff*** = 0; ***DC-payoff*** = 5; ***DD-payoff*** = 1.

The two distributions in figure 1 only differ in the value of the mutation rate used (0.01 on the left, and 0.05 on the right). The distribution on the left shows the evolutionary emergence and (dynamic) permanence of strategies similar to TFT ($PC \approx 1$, $PC/C \approx 1$, and $PC/D \approx 0$). Such strategies do not appear for slightly higher mutation rates (distribution on the right). The other parameter values used were ***num-players*** = 100; ***pairing-settings*** = *random pairings*; ***rounds-per-match*** = 50.

The two distributions in figure 2 only differ in the number of players in the population (100 on the left, and 10 on the right). The distribution on the left shows the evolutionary emergence and (dynamic) permanence of strategies similar to TFT, whereas such strategies do not appear in smaller populations. The other parameter values are: ***pairing-settings*** = *random pairings*; ***rounds-per-match*** = 50; ***mutation-rate*** = 0.01.

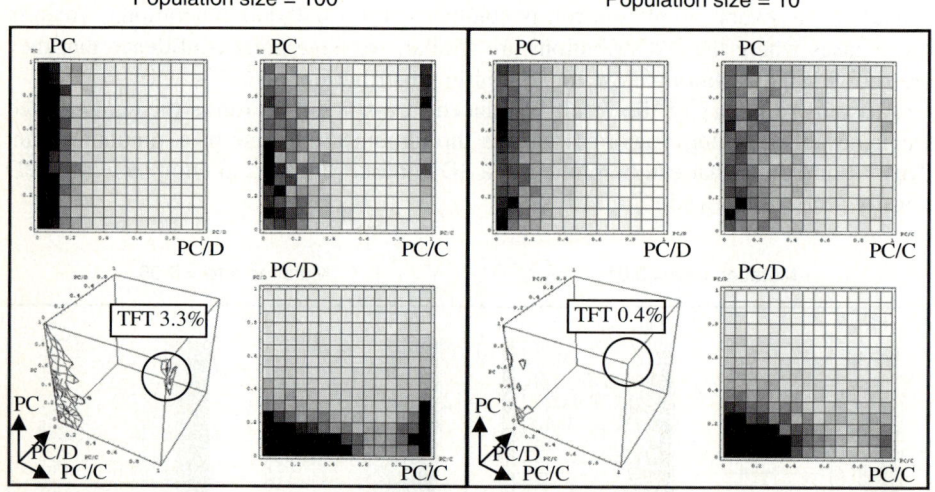

Fig. 2. Influence of the number of players in the population. TFT measures the average time that strategies with $PC \geq (13/15)$, $PC/C \geq (13/15)$ and $PC/D \leq (2/15)$ were observed.

The two distributions in figure 3 only differ in the algorithm used to form the pairs of players (*random pairings* on the left, and *children together* on the right). On the left, strategies tend to be strongly uncooperative, while the distribution on the right is concentrated around strategies similar to TFT. The other parameter values used were: ***num-players*** = 100; ***rounds-per-match*** = 5; ***mutation-rate*** = 0.05.

The two distributions in figure 4 only differ in the set of possible values that PC, PC/C or PC/D can take. For the distribution on the left the set of possible values is any (floating-point) number between 0 and 1, and the strategies are mainly uncooperative, similar to ALLD ($PC \approx 0$, $PC/C \approx 0$, and $PC/D \approx 0$). For the distribution on the right, the set of possible values is only {0, 1}, and the distribution is concentrated in TFT. The other parameter values used were: **num-players** = 100; **mutation-rate** = 0.05; **rounds-per-match** = 10; **pairing-settings** = *random pairings*.

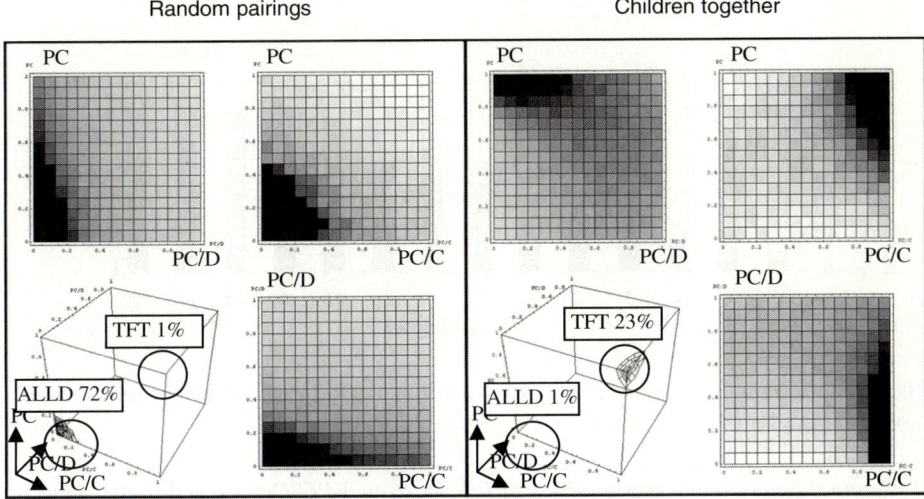

Fig. 3. Influence of different pairing mechanisms. TFT measures the average time that strategies with $PC \geq (10/15)$, $PC/C \geq (10/15)$ and $PC/D \leq (5/15)$ were observed; ALLD measures the average time that strategies with $PC \leq (5/15)$, $PC/C \leq (5/15)$ and $PC/D \leq (5/15)$ were observed.

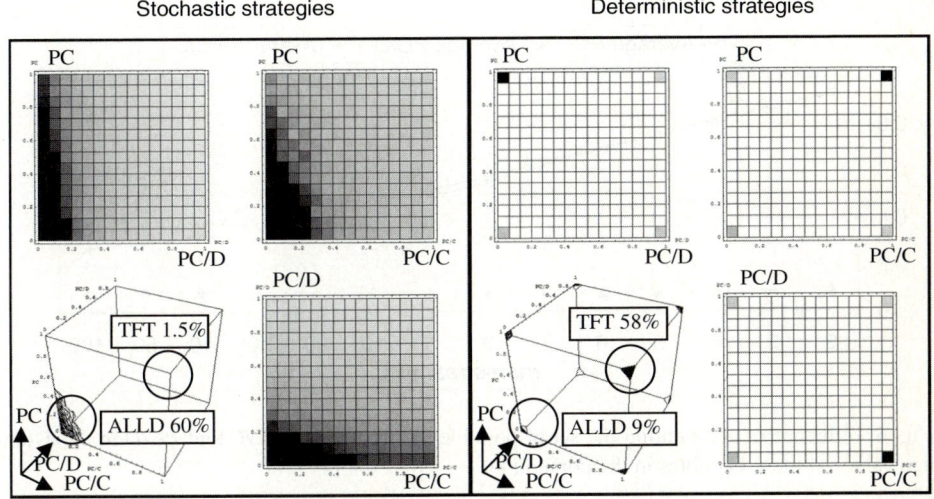

Fig. 4. Stochastic (mixed) strategies vs. deterministic (pure) strategies: influence in the system dynamics. TFT measures the average time that strategies with $PC \geq (10/15)$, $PC/C \geq (10/15)$ and $PC/D \leq (5/15)$ were observed; ALLD measures the average time that strategies with $PC \leq (5/15)$, $PC/C \leq (5/15)$ and $PC/D \leq (5/15)$ were observed.

In figures 5 and 6 we show the effect of gradually increasing the set of possible values for *PC*, *PC/C* and *PC/D* (i.e. **num-strategies**). Figure 5 shows the (average) number of each possible outcome of the game (CC, CD/DC or DD) in observed series of 10^6 matches (this number of matches is selected so the effect of changing the initial state is negligible, i.e. results are close to the stationary limiting distribution).

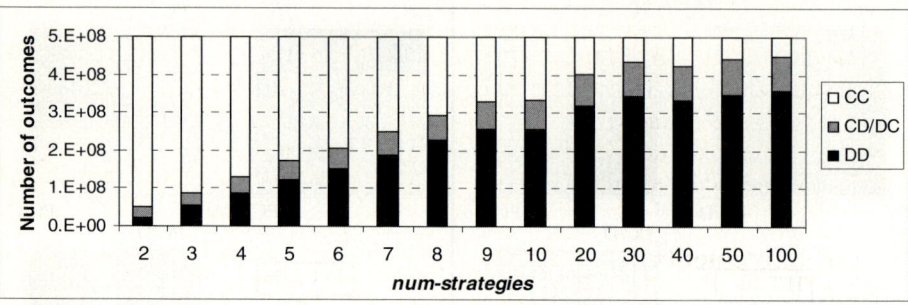

Fig. 5. Influence in the distribution of outcomes (CC, CD/DC or DD) of augmenting the set of possible values for *PC*, *PC/C* and *PC/D*

Figure 6 shows the average values of *PC*, *PC/C* and *PC/D* observed in the same series. Augmenting the set of possible values for *PC*, *PC/C* and *PC/D* undermines cooperation and favors the emergence of ALLD-like strategies. The other parameter values used were: **num-players** = 100; **mutation-rate** = 0.01; **rounds-per-match** = 10; **pairing-settings** = *random pairings*.

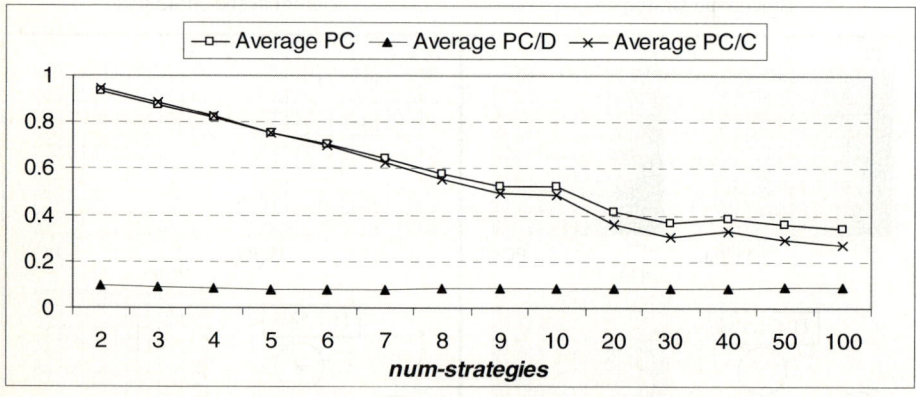

Fig. 6. Influence of augmenting the set of possible values for *PC*, *PC/C* and *PC/D* in the average values of these variables in the population

5 Conclusions

In this paper we have presented, for the Prisoner's Dilemma, several results on the evolutionary dynamics of stochastic strategies that are conditioned on the last action of the player's opponent. Popular strategies such as TFT and ALLD are particular (extreme) cases within this framework, and we have studied the possible appearance and evolutionary robustness of such strategies. Our results show that:

- The type of strategies that are likely to emerge and be sustained in evolutionary contexts is strongly dependent on assumptions that traditionally have been thought to be unimportant or secondary (value of mutation-rate, number of players, population structure...)
- Strategies similar to ALLD tend to be the most successful in most environments.
- Strategies similar to TFT tend to spread best with the following factors: in large populations, where individuals with similar strategies tend to interact more frequently, when only deterministic strategies are allowed, with low mutation rates, and when interactions consist of many rounds.

Acknowledgements

We would like to gratefully acknowledge financial support from the Spanish Ministerio de Educación y Ciencia research project DPI2005-05676 "SIGAME" and from the Scottish Executive Environment and Rural Affairs Department.

References

1. Axelrod, R.: The Evolution of Cooperation. Basic Books USA (1984)
2. Bendor, J., Swistak, P.: 1995. Types of evolutionary stability and the problem of cooperation. Proceedings of the National Academy of Sciences USA **92** (1995) 3596-3600
3. Bendor, J., Swistak, P.: Evolutionary Equilibria: Characterization Theorems and Their Implications. Theory and Decision **45** (1998) 99-159.
4. Gotts, N.M., Polhill, J.G., Law, A.N.R.: Agent-based simulation in the study of social dilemmas. Artificial Intelligence Review, **19**(1) (2003) 3-92.
5. Weibull, J. W.: Evolutionary Game Theory. MIT Press (1995)
6. Beggs, A.: Stochastic evolution with slow learning. Economic Theory **19** (2002) 379-405
7. Imhof, L.A., Fudenberg, D., Nowak M.A.: Evolutionary cycles of cooperation and defection. Proceedings of the National Academy of Sciences USA, **102**(31) (2005) 10797-10800
8. Nowak, M.A., Sasaki, A., Taylor, C., Fudenberg, D.: Emergence of cooperation and evolutionary stability in finite populations. Nature **428** (2004) 646-650
9. Taylor, C., Fudenberg, D., Sasaki, A., Nowak, M.A.: Evolutionary Game Dynamics in Finite Populations. Bulletin of Mathematical Biology **66** (2004) 1621–1644
10. Nowak, M.A., Sigmund K.: The evolution of stochastic strategies in the Prisoners' Dilemma. Acta Applicandae Mathematicae **20** (1990) 247-265
11. Nowak, M.A., Sigmund K.: Tit for tat in heterogeneous populations. Nature **355** (1992) 250-253
12. Nowak, M.A., Sigmund K.: Invasion Dynamics of the Finitely Repeated Prisoner's Dilemma. Games and Economic Behavior **11**(2) (1995) 364-390
13. Axelrod, R.: The Evolution of Strategies in the Iterated Prisoner's Dilemma. In: Davis, L. (Ed.): Genetic Algorithms and Simulated Annealing. London Pitman, Los Altos CA, Morgan Kaufman (1987) 32-41. Reprinted in Axelrod, R.: The complexity of cooperation. Agent-based models of competition and collaboration. Princeton NJ, Princeton University Press (1997)

14. Binmore, K.: Playing Fair: Game Theory and the Social Contract I. MIT Press, Cambridge MA (1994)
15. Binmore, K.: Review of the book: The Complexity of Cooperation: Agent-Based Models of Competition and Collaboration, by Axelrod, R., Princeton NJ, Princeton University Press, (1997). Journal of Artificial Societies and Social Simulation **1**(1) (1998) http://jasss.soc.surrey.ac.uk/1/1/review1.html
16. Probst, D.: On Evolution and Learning in Games. PhD thesis, University of Bonn (1996)
17. Linster, B.: Evolutionary stability in the repeated Prisoners' Dilemma played by two-state Moore machines. Southern Economic Journal **58** (1992) 880-903
18. Wilensky, U.: NetLogo. http://ccl.northwestern.edu/netlogo/. Center for Connected Learning and Computer-Based Modeling, Northwestern University, Evanston, IL (1999)
19. Kulkarni, V.G.: Modelling and Analysis of Stochastic Systems. Chapman & Hall/CRC (1995)

Prediction of Chaotic Time Series Based on Multi-scale Gaussian Processes

Yatong Zhou, Taiyi Zhang, and Xiaohe Li

Dept. Information and Communication Engineering,
Xi'an Jiaotong University,
710049 Xi'an, P.R. China
{zytong, tyzhang, lixh}@mailst.xjtu.edu.cn

Abstract. This paper considers the prediction of chaotic time series by proposed multi-scale Gaussian processes (MGP) models, an extension of classical Gaussian processes (GP) model. Unlike the GP spending much time to find the optimal hyperparameters, MGP employs a covariance function that is constructed by a scaling function with its different dilations and translations, ensuring that the optimal hyperparameter is easy to determine. Moreover, the scaling function with its different dilations and translations can form a set of complete bases, resulting in that the MGP can acquire better prediction performance than GP. The effectiveness of MGP is evaluated using simulated Mackey-Glass series as well as real-world electric load series. Results show the proposed model outperforms GP on prediction performance, and takes much less time to determine hyperparameter. Results also show that the performance of MGP is competitive with support vector machine (SVM). They give better performance compared to the radial basis function (RBF) networks.

1 Introduction

Chaotic time series prediction has attracted considerable interest in the past few years. Not only is it an efficient method to reconstruct a dynamical system from an observed time series, but it also has many applications in engineering problems. Traditional machine learning methods, such as multi-layer perceptron (MLP) [1], RBF networks [2], and SVM [3] have been developed for chaotic series prediction.

Recently, there has been a good deal of excitement about the use of Gaussian processes (GP) model for function regression and prediction within the machine learning community [4]. The GP model has the merit of simplicity and flexibility. In contrast to the traditional methods mentioned above, it obtains not only a point prediction but also a predictive distribution. Moreover, there are strong similarities between the GP model and these traditional methods. For instance, the SVM uses a covariance kernel, but differs from GP by using a different data fit term [5].

The GP model has been successfully applied to the prediction of nonstationary time series [6]. However, little attention has been paid to apply GP to the prediction of chaotic time series, although the problem is essentially important for real applications. In this paper, we focus on prediction tasks of chaotic time series by proposed MGP models, an extension of classical GP model. Unlike the GP spending much time to find the optimal hyperparameters, MGP employs a covariance function that is constructed by a scaling function with its different dilations and translations, ensuring that the optimal hyperparameter is easy to determine. Furthermore, whether in GP or in MGP, the function to be estimated can be represented by a set of bases. For instance, if squared exponential (SE) function——most frequently used covariance functions is employed by the GP model, it is proved that the set of bases is composed of radial basis functions centered at different points [5]. However this set of bases is incomplete, so the representation is only an approximation. On the contrary for the MGP model, the scaling function with its different dilations and translations can form a set of complete bases, ensuring that the representation is accurate. From this perspective, it is anticipated that the MGP has better prediction performance than GP.

2 Chaotic Time Series Prediction

Assume that a chaotic time series $s(n)$ is defined as a function s of an independent variable n, generated from an unknown dynamical system. Our goal is to predict the future behavior of the series. Takens' theorem [7] ensures that, for almost all τ and for some d there is a smooth function f such that

$$s(n) = f\left[s(n-\tau), s(n-2\tau), \cdots, s(n-d\tau)\right] , \tag{1}$$

where d is embedding dimension and τ is time delay respectively. If f were known, the value $s(n)$ is uniquely determined by its d values in the past. Therefore, the problem of prediction becomes equivalent to the problem of estimating f.

To estimate f one needs to construct a training set D_N with the capability N. For simplicity of notation, we define the scalar $t_n \equiv s(n)$ and the d-dimensional vector $\mathbf{x}_n \equiv (s(n-\tau), s(n-2\tau), \cdots, s(n-d\tau))^T$ in a phase space. Thus the training set D_N can be constructed as follows: $D_N = \{(\mathbf{x}_n, t_n) \mid n = 1, \cdots, N\}$. Correspondingly, Eq. (1) can be written simply as

$$t_n = f(\mathbf{x}_n) . \tag{2}$$

3 Overview on GP Model for Prediction

Given the training set D_N, the GP would like to estimate $f(\mathbf{x})$. Now assume $f(\mathbf{x})$ be represented by a fixed basis functions with a weight vector $\mathbf{w} = (w_1, w_2, \cdots w_H)^T$

$$f(\mathbf{x}) = \sum_{h=1}^{H} w_h \phi_h(\mathbf{x}) . \tag{3}$$

If the prior distribution of $\mathbf{w}$ is Gaussian with zero mean, it follows that $f(\mathbf{x})$ is a Gaussian process. Let $\mathbf{t}_N = (t_1, t_2, \cdots t_N)^T$ be the collection of target values, in terms of Eq. (2) and (3) we can infer that

$$\mathbf{t}_N \sim N(0, \mathbf{C}_N) \quad, \tag{4}$$

where the matrix $\mathbf{C}_N$ is given by a covariance function $C(\mathbf{x}_n, \mathbf{x}_{n'})$. For example, the covariance function most frequently used is the SE function

$$C(\mathbf{x}_n, \mathbf{x}_{n'}) = \sqrt{\pi \sigma_c^2} \exp\left(-\sum_{l=1}^{d} \xi_l (x_{nl} - x_{n'l})^2 / 4\sigma_c^2\right) \quad, \tag{5}$$

where σ_c is so called lengthscale and x_{nl} is the l-th component of $\mathbf{x}_n$.

If the GP employs Eq. (5) as its covariance function, the set of bases $\{\phi_h(\mathbf{x})\}_{h=1}^{H}$ given in Eq. (3) would be composed of radial basis functions centered at different points $\mathbf{x}_h$, that is $\phi_h(\mathbf{x}) \propto \exp\left(-\|\mathbf{x}-\mathbf{x}_h\|_2^2 / 2\sigma_c^2\right)$, $h = 1, 2, \cdots H$ [5]. However this set of bases is incomplete in the square integrable space, so the function $f(\mathbf{x})$ can only be represented approximately.

Let us assume that the covariance function (5) has been chosen, but it depends on undetermined hyperparameters $\boldsymbol{\theta} = (v_0, v_1, \varsigma_0, \varsigma_1, \cdots, \varsigma_d)^T$. To use conjugate gradient method to find the maximum likelihood $\boldsymbol{\theta}_{MP}$ one needs to calculate the log likelihood Γ and its derivatives. The partial derivatives of Γ with respect to $\boldsymbol{\theta}$ is expressed by

$$\partial \Gamma / \partial \boldsymbol{\theta} = -0.5 Trace\left[\mathbf{C}_N^{-1} \cdot (\partial \mathbf{C}_N / \partial \boldsymbol{\theta})\right] + 0.5 \mathbf{t}_N^T \mathbf{C}_N^{-1} (\partial \mathbf{C}_N / \partial \boldsymbol{\theta}) \mathbf{C}_N^{-1} \mathbf{t}_N \quad. \tag{6}$$

where $Tr(\cdot)$ stands for the trace of a matrix.

4 Proposed MGP Model for Chaotic Time Series Prediction

4.1 Proposed MGP Model

One of the areas of investigation in multi-scale analysis has been the emerging theory of multi-scale representations of function and wavelet transforms [8]. Unlike the GP model representing $f(\mathbf{x})$ as in Eq. (3), MGP seeks a multi-scale representation as

$$f_j(\mathbf{x}) = \sum_k w_k^{(j)} \phi_{jk}(\mathbf{x}) \quad, \tag{7}$$

where $w_k^{(j)}$ is the k-th weight coefficients and the set of bases $\phi_{jk}(\mathbf{x}) = 2^{-j/2} \phi(2^{-j}\mathbf{x} - k)$, $(j, k \in Z)$ is composed of the dilations and translations of a scaling function ϕ. If suitable ϕ has been chosen, it follows Ref. [8] that this set of bases is complete in the square integrable space, ensuring the representation of $f_j(\mathbf{x})$ is accurate.

To set up the MGP model, the set of N variables $\mathbf{f}_N^{(j)} = \left(f_j(\mathbf{x}_1), f_j(\mathbf{x}_2), \cdots f_j(\mathbf{x}_N)\right)^T$, modeling the function values at $\mathbf{x}_1, \mathbf{x}_2, \cdots \mathbf{x}_N$ respectively, is introduced. Following that, a Gaussian prior distribution is specified over the vector $\mathbf{f}_N^{(j)}$:

$$\mathbf{f}_N^{(j)} \sim N\left(0, \mathbf{Q}_N^{(j)}\right) \quad.$$

This is equivalent to specify a Gaussian process prior over $f_j(\mathbf{x})$ since that a Gaussian process is fully defined by giving a Gaussian distribution for every finite subset of variables. The (n, n') entry of covariance matrix $\mathbf{Q}_N^{(j)}$ is given by

$$Q_j(\mathbf{x}_n, \mathbf{x}_{n'}) = \sum_k 2^{-j} \phi(2^{-j}\mathbf{x}_n - k) \phi(2^{-j}\mathbf{x}_{n'} - k) \;.$$

If t_n is assumed to differ by additive Gaussian noise with variance σ_v^2 from the corresponding function value $f_j(\mathbf{x}_n)$ then $\mathbf{t}_N$ also has a Gaussian distribution

$$\mathbf{t}_N \sim N(0, \mathbf{C}_N^{(j)}) \;. \tag{8}$$

It is inferred that the (n, n') entry of $\mathbf{C}_N^{(j)}$ is given by the covariance function

$$C_j(\mathbf{x}_n, \mathbf{x}_{n'}) = Q_j(\mathbf{x}_n, \mathbf{x}_{n'}) + \sigma_v^2 \delta_{nn'} \;, \tag{9}$$

where $\delta_{nn'} = 1$ if $n = n'$ and 0 otherwise.

Having formed the covariance function defined in Eq. (9) our task is to infer $t^{(j)}(\mathbf{x})$, the target of $\mathbf{x}$ at the scale j. Assume $\mathbf{C}_{N+1}^{(j)}$ is the $(N+1) \times (N+1)$ covariance matrix for the combination of $\mathbf{t}_N$ and $t^{(j)}(\mathbf{x})$. Given such assumption, the analytic form of predictive distribution over $t^{(j)}(\mathbf{x})$ can be derived. It is a Gaussian

$$P(t^{(j)}(\mathbf{x}) \mid \mathbf{t}_N) \propto \exp\left\{ \left[t^{(j)}(\mathbf{x}) - \hat{t}^{(j)}(\mathbf{x})\right]^2 / 2 \left[\sigma_N^{(j)}(\mathbf{x})\right]^2 \right\} \;, \tag{10}$$

where the mean and variance are given by

$$\hat{t}^{(j)}(\mathbf{x}) = \left[\mathbf{k}_j(\mathbf{x})\right]^T \left(\mathbf{C}_N^{(j)}\right)^{-1} \mathbf{t}_N \;, \tag{11}$$

$$\sigma_N^{(j)}(\mathbf{x}) = \sqrt{\kappa_j(\mathbf{x}) - \left[\mathbf{k}_j(\mathbf{x})\right]^T \left(\mathbf{C}_N^{(j)}\right)^{-1} \left[\mathbf{k}_j(\mathbf{x})\right]^T} \;. \tag{12}$$

where $\mathbf{k}_j(\mathbf{x})$ and $\kappa_j(\mathbf{x})$ are sub-blocks of the matrix $\mathbf{C}_{N+1}^{(j)}$.

The mean $\hat{t}^{(j)}(\mathbf{x})$ is regarded as the prediction of MGP on the test sample $\mathbf{x}$ at the scale j, that is, $f_j(\mathbf{x}) = \hat{t}^{(j)}(\mathbf{x})$. The interval $\left[\hat{t}^{(j)}(\mathbf{x}) - 2\sigma_N^{(j)}(\mathbf{x}), \hat{t}^{(j)}(\mathbf{x}) + 2\sigma_N^{(j)}(\mathbf{x})\right]$ is called the error bar. It is a confidence interval of $\hat{t}^{(j)}(\mathbf{x})$ that represents how uncertain we are about the prediction at the point $\mathbf{x}$ assuming the model is correct.

4.2 Determining the Optimal Scale j

The MGP takes Eq. (9) as its covariance function. As seen from the equation, the sole hyperparameter needs to determined is the scale j. We would like to obtain the optimal j by maximum likelihood estimation. The posterior of j comprises three parts

$$P(j \mid \mathbf{t}_N) = P(\mathbf{t}_N \mid j) P(j) / P(\mathbf{t}_N) \;. \tag{13}$$

The evidence term $P(\mathbf{t}_N)$ is independent of j and will be ignored for the time being. The two remaining terms, the likelihood $P(\mathbf{t}_N \mid j)$ and the prior $P(j)$, will be considered in terms of their logs. The log of the likelihood Γ is

$$\Gamma = \log P(\mathbf{t}_N \mid j) = -0.5\log\left|\mathbf{C}_N^{(j)}\right| - 0.5\mathbf{t}_N^T \mathbf{C}_N^{(j)-1}\mathbf{t}_N - 0.5N\log 2\pi \quad . \tag{14}$$

It is common practice to ignore the log prior and maximize the log likelihood Γ. For the MGP model, unlike GP model where the partial derivatives of Γ with respect to $\boldsymbol{\theta}$ should be implemented, each of the discrete values for j can be substituted into Eq. (14), the one that maximizes Γ is selected for the optimal value.

5 Experiments

Experiments 1: Benchmarking the Mackey-Glass time series
Our first experiment is with the Mackey-Glass (MG) chaotic time series. This series may be generated by numerical integration of a time-delay differential equation

$$ds/d\varsigma = \left[0.2s(\varsigma-\Delta)\right]/\left[1+s(\varsigma-\Delta)^{10}\right] - 0.1s(\varsigma) \quad .$$

In this experiment we consider two series with parameters $\Delta = 17, 30$, $s(0)=1.2$, and $s(\varsigma)=0$ for $\varsigma<0$. We denote these two series by MG$_{17}$ and MG$_{30}$. To test the performance of the MGP model and compare it with classical GP model, 1000 samples are generated by sampling two series with $d=4$ and $\tau=6$. We use the samples 1-300 for training, while the samples 600-800 for testing. The GP employs Eq. (5) as covariance function. The function ϕ we chosen is the scaling function of the Daubechies (DB) wavelet with order 10. It is a compact supported scaling function. Being in a noiseless environment, σ_ν is set to 0. Mean square error (MSE) and prediction error (PE) are used to measure the prediction performance.

Fig.1 shows the prediction results on the MG$_{17}$ series using the MGP and GP respectively. It is can be seen that both the MGP and GP show excellent performance. The difference between the original series and the predicted values is very small. This is why we can only see one curve in the first and second plot. The prediction error is shown in the third plot with a much finer scale. However, it can be easily seen that the MGP can provide smaller prediction error than the GP model. The whole prediction results in MSE are given in Table 1. As can be seen from the table, the MGP outperforms GP both on MG$_{17}$ and MG$_{30}$ series. We also note that whether for MGP or for GP, the MG$_{30}$ series has a significantly higher MSE value than MG$_{17}$. This is probably because the MG$_{30}$ is more difficult to predict than MG$_{17}$.

Now we compare the CPU time in seconds consumed for determining hyperparameters. Simulations were conducted in the MATLAB environment running on an ordinary PC with single 2.8GHZ CPU (Celeron) and 256MB size of memory. The results are illustrated in Table 1. It is found that the CPU time consumed by MGP is much less than that by the standard GP.

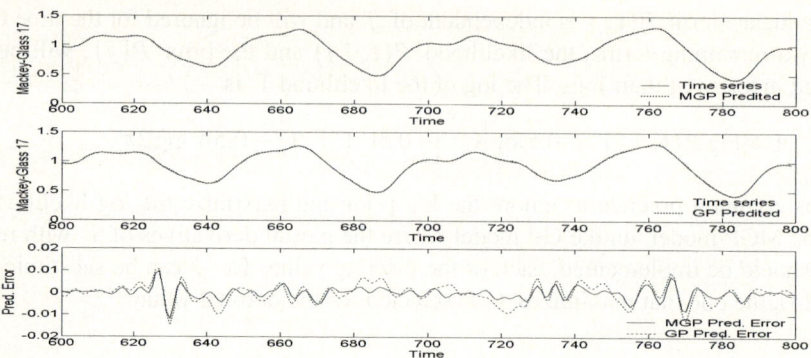

Fig. 1. Comparison of prediction results on the MG_{17} series between the MGP and GP model

Table 1. Comparison of the MGP and GP model for predicting MG_{17} and MG_{30} series. TH denotes the time in seconds consumed for determining hyperparameters.

Models	MG_{17} MSE ($\times 10^{-5}$)	TH (s)	MG_{30} MSE ($\times 10^{-5}$)	TH (s)
MGP	0.683	0.195	1.781	0.196
GP	1.111	5.207	2.495	5.412

For the MGP model, to see how to determine the optimal scale j in the prediction of MG_{17} and MG_{30} series, we substitute each integer value in the interval [-6,12] to Eq. (14). The minus logarithm Γ plotted as a function of j is illustrated in Fig. 2. As seen in the figure, the optimal scales determined are $j = -1$ and $j = -4$ respectively.

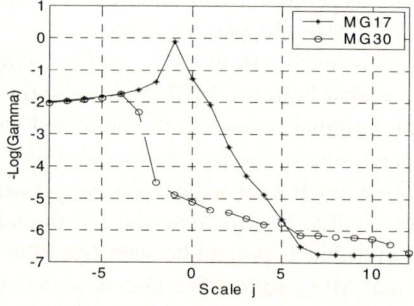

Fig. 2. Graphs of the minus logarithm Γ with respect to different scale j for the MGP model

Experiments 2: Electric load prediction
This experiment provides an in-depth comparison of MGP with SVM and RBF networks based on the electric load prediction. The electric load acquired from Northwest China Grid Company (NCGC) has been normalized to lie in the range [0,1]. It appears periodical approximately due to the nature of load. After $d = 2$ and $\tau = 1$ are chosen, we generate 700 samples by sampling the load. Samples of point 1-500 are used for training and consequent 168 samples are used for testing.

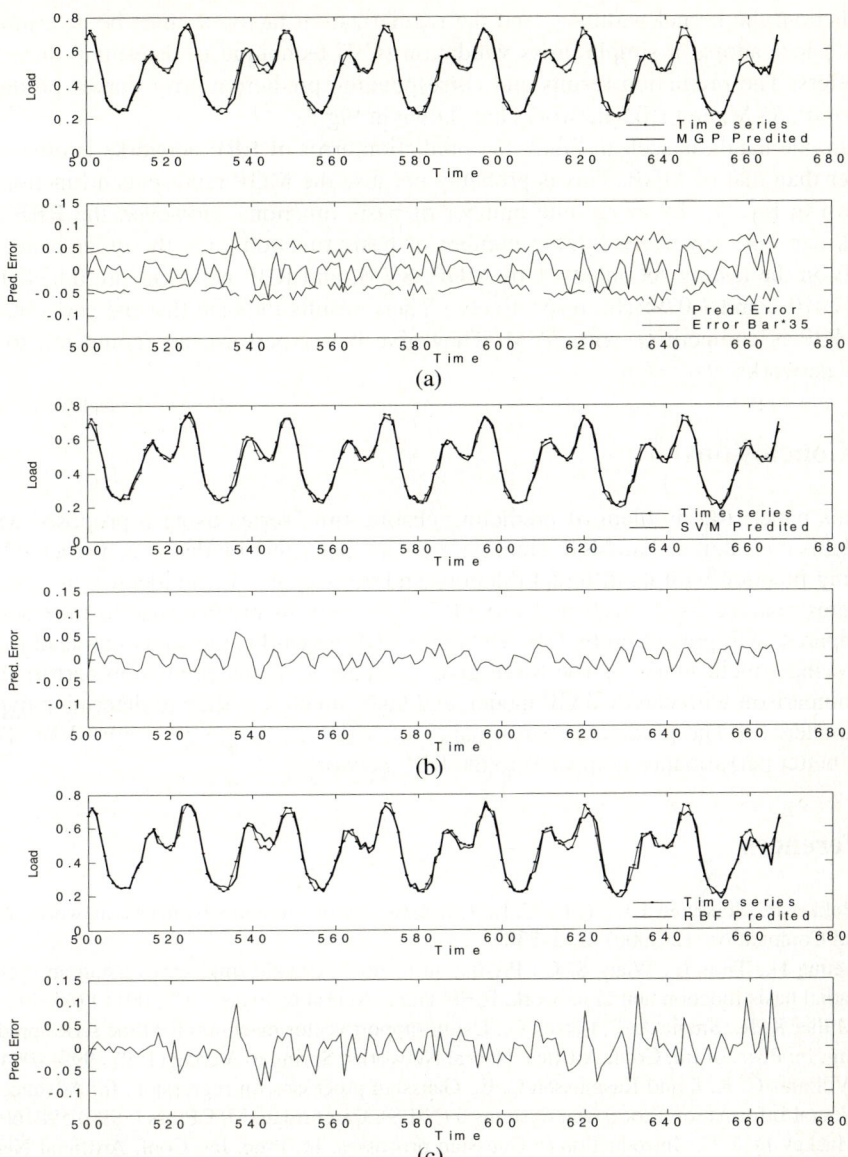

Fig. 3. Comparison of prediction results and prediction error between the (a) MGP model, (b) SVM, and (c) the RBF networks. For convenience to plot, the error bar shown in (a) is multiplied by a factor of 35.

For the MGP model, the function ϕ and the parameter σ_v are set as same as those in experiment 1. The RBF networks are trained based on the methods of Moody [9]. However, the output weights, the RBF centers and variances are adaptively adjusted during the training procedure. When SVM employed a Gaussian kernel is used for prediction, the kernel width w_σ and the regularization factor λ must be determined. This paper adopts a simple cross validation (CV) technique to determine these parameters. The prediction results and corresponding prediction error curves produced by MGP, SVM, and RBF networks are shown in Fig.3.

On one hand, as seen in Fig.3, the prediction error of RBF networks is obviously larger than that of MGP. This is probably because the MGP represents a function, as shown in Eq. (7), by an infinite number of basis functions. However, the RBF network can only involve a limited number of basis functions. On the other hand, the MSE on the testing set achieved by MGP, SVM, and RBF networks are 0.634×10^{-3}, 0.547×10^{-3}, and 1.079×10^{-3} respectively. These results indicate that the performance of MGP is competitive with SVM. They give better performance compared to the RBF networks.

6 Conclusions

In this paper, the problem of predicting chaotic time series using a proposed MGP model is considered. The MGP employs a covariance function that is constructed by a scaling function with its different dilations and translations. It can identify the chaotic systems characteristics well and provide a new way to predict chaotic time series. Compared with prediction by GP, SVM and RBF networks, the study can lead to the following conclusions. (1) The MGP gives a relatively better prediction performance in comparison with classical GP model, and takes much less time to determine hyperparameter. (2) The prediction performance of MGP is competitive with SVM. They give better performance compared to the RBF networks.

References

1. Bakker R., Schouten J. C., Giles C. L.: Learning chaotic attractors by neural networks. Neural Compuation. 12(2000) 2355–2383
2. Leung H., Titus L., Wang S. C.: Prediction of noisy chaotic time series using an optimal radial basis function neural network. IEEE Trans. Neural Networks. 12(2001) 1163–1172
3. Müller K. R., Smola A. J., Rätsch G.: Using support vector machines for time series predicting, In: Proc. of Int. Conf. Artifical Neural Networks, Springer -Verlag (1997) 999–1004
4. Williams C. K. I. and Rasmussen C. E.: Gaussian processes for regression. In: Advances in Neural Information Processing Systems 8 (NIPS), Cambridge, MIT Press (1996) 598–604
5. Mackay D. J. C.: Introduction to Gaussian processes. In: Proc. Int. Conf. Artificial Neural Networks (ICANN'97), (1997) 1-28
6. Bellhouari S. B., Bermak A.: Gaussian process for nonstationary time series prediction. Computational Statistics and Data Analysis. 47 (2004) 705–712
7. Takens, F.: Detecting strange attractors in fluid turbulence. In: Rand D., Young L. S. (eds.): Dynamical systems and turbulence, Springer-Verlag, Berlin (1981) 366–381
8. Mallat, S.: A theory for multiresolution signal decomposition: The wavelet representation. IEEE Trans. PAMI. 11 (1989) 674-693
9. Moody J., Darken C.: Fast learning in networks of locally-tuned processing units. Neural Computation. 1 (1989) 281-294

Visual Sensitivity Analysis
for Artificial Neural Networks*

Roberto Therón and Juan Francisco De Paz

Departamento de Informática y Automática
Facultad de Ciencias - Universidad de Salamanca
Plaza de la Merced s/n. 37008. Salamanca, Spain
theron@usal.es, fcofds@usal.es

Abstract. A challenge in ANN research is how to reduce the number of inputs to the model in high dimensional problems, so it can be efficiently applied. The ANNs black-box operation makes not possible to explain the relationships between features and inputs. Some numerical methods, such as sensitivity analysis, try to fight this problem. In this paper, we combine a sensitivity analysis with a linked multi-dimensional visualization that takes advantage of user interaction, providing and efficient way to analyze and asses both the dimension reduction results and the ANN behavior.

1 Introduction

Many disciplines (such as bioinformatics, economics, climatology, etc.) face a classification or prediction problem involving large number of features. However, the high dimensionality of the data can lead to inaccurate results or even disqualify the use of machine learning methods. The *curse of dimensionality* stipulates that it is hard to apply a statistical technique to high-dimensional data.

Feature selection and dimension reduction techniques are both used to remove features that do not provide significant incremental information. Numerous studies have revealed that in high-dimensional data, feature selection and dimension reduction methods are essential to improve the performance of a classifier report on dimension reduction techniques such as principal component analysis (PCA) or factor analysis [1].

Despite the great success in many fields, ANNs are still regarded as black-box methods [2] where it is difficult for the user to understand the nature of the internal representations generated by the network in order to respond to a certain problem. In order to overcome this problem, different rule extraction and numerical methods are applied to study the contribution of variables in a neural network; sensitivity analysis is one of the most broadly used [3].

In recent years the field of information visualization has played an important role providing insight through visual representations combined with interaction techniques that take advantage of the human eye's broad bandwidth pathway

---
* This work was supported by the MCyT of Spain under Integrated Action (Spain-France) HF2004-0277 and by the Junta de Castilla y León under project SA042/02.

to the mind, allowing experts to see, explore, and understand large amounts of information at once. In this work we combine a sensitivity analysis with a linked multi-dimensional visualization, mainly based on interactive parallel coordinates[4], that can help to understand the behavior of the neural network, analyze its sensitivity, and provide a way to interpret the relationship between features and outputs.

1.1 Related Work

Tzeng and Ma [5] provide a survey of several visualization techniques for understanding the learning and decision-making processes of neural networks. These techniques include Hinton diagrams, bond diagrams, response-function plots, hyperplane diagrams, and trajectory diagrams [6], that are used to illustrate the idea of neural networks but are not practical due to the difficulty of showing a large network clearly. The visualization method in [5] allows the user to probe into the data domain and visualize the corresponding network, errors, and uncertainty visualization, by means of Parallel coordinates [4], to help both the designer and the user of a neural network. In [7] an interactive visualization tool for feed-forward neural networks, based on tree/graph visualization, is described. Although the visualization tool is useful both as an educational device (to aid in the understanding of neural networks, search spaces, and genetic drift), and as a practical tool for solving complex problems with neural networks, the authors recognize that its main limitation is that the graphical feedforward network depiction does not scale well to networks with large numbers of nodes.

A projection on a lattice of hypercube nodes to visualize the hidden and output node activities in a high dimensional space is used in [8]. Scatterograms of the images of training set vectors in the hidden space help to evaluate the quality of neural network mappings and understand internal representations created by the hidden layers. Visualization of these representations leads to interesting conclusions about optimal architectures and training of such networks.

In [9], Cook and Yin discuss visualization methods for discriminant analysis adapted from results in dimension reduction for regression (sliced inverse regression and sliced average variance estimation). The method are good identifying outliers. The graphical representations used for regression visualization are Summary plots, where the structural dimension of the data is used, so such plots have the minimal complexity needed to explain the structure of the model and to make predictions.

2 Visual Sensitivity Analysis

In order to add power to ANNs in their explanatory capacity and understand the complex relationships that occur between the variables, sensitivity analysis [10][11][3] have been used. Having trained a neural network, an input sensitivity analysis is conducted on the trained network, using the training data.

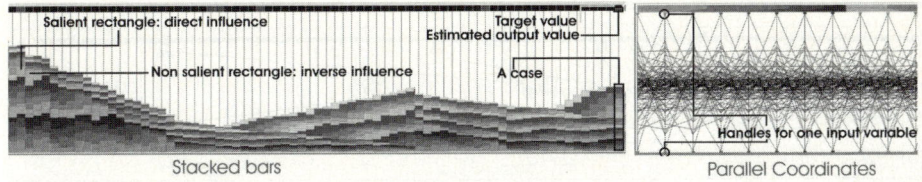

Fig. 1. Visual techniques used in visual sensitivity analysis

In the Jacobian matrix S, each line represents an output to the network and each column represents an input to the network, so that the element S_{ki} represents the sensitivity of the output y_k with respect to the input x_i, calculated as a partial derivative of the output with respect to the input, $S_{ki} = \frac{\partial y_k}{\partial x_i}$. This way, the higher the value of S_{ki}, the more important it is x_i with respect to y_k. The sign indicates the kind of influence (direct or inverse).

From a practical point of view it is more interesting to understand how different inputs affect to a given output for the training pairs (cases). Thus, the purpose of the visual sensitivity analysis is to provide a representation of the relationships between the output y_k with each of the inputs x_i for each of the cases. Furthermore, the inputs and their output values will also be represented to be able to compare the input data and the sensitivity analysis.

2.1 Visualization Techniques

In this section we will explain the information visualization techniques used in the visual sensitivity analysis. The interface consists of two clearly differentiated areas: one for stacked bars and another one for parallel coordinates. Both areas are linked so the interaction on one implies changes in the other one.

Each case in a problem is represented as a stacked bar (see figure 1), divided into as many fragments (rectangles) as input variables. On top of each bar, both the output value estimated by the ANN and the target are represented.

Each stacked bar is color coded in order to distinguish each of the variables of the case. The height of the rectangle is used to represent the value of the variable. On the other hand, bars are represented in 3D, so that the rectangles with salient appearance represent positive values (direct influence), while negative values (inverse influence), are represented without relief (see figure 1).

Target and estimated output values are also color coded, from blue (lowest value, 0) to red (highest value, 1). This way, we can determine in a visual and quick way erroneous network estimates (note the last case on the right in figure 1) or **see** the group to which each case belongs.

Parallel Coordinates Plot (PCP) [4] is one of the most successful techniques in multi-dimensional visualization. Each case is drawn as a polyline passing through parallel axis, which represent the input variables (see figure 2).

Each axis represents an input variable; thus, the handles (see figure 1) are colored using the corresponding color of the rectangles in the stacked bars. A case (bar) is also a polyline in the PCP (see two cases highlighted in figure 2).

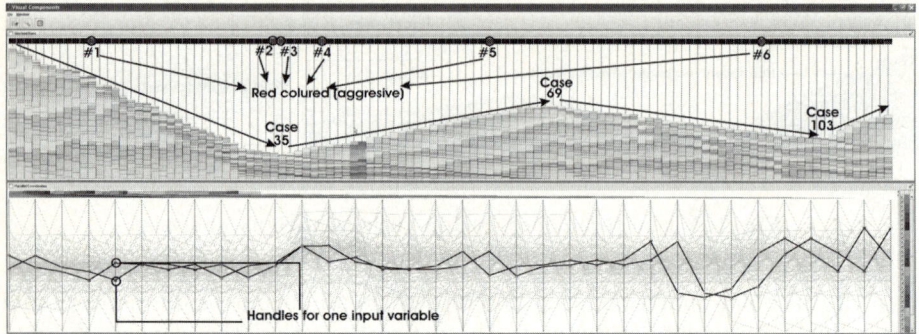

Fig. 2. Selecting cases: bars and polylines

Our aim was to design a highly interactive visual interface that would allow to compare relationships between the variables and their values, through the cases and to determine the ranges of variable values that separate the individual cases into groups. Several interaction techniques [12] have been integrated to allow brushing [13], linking, focus + context, etc., for exploratory analysis and knowledge discovery purposes. Thus, it is possible to select one or several bars and the corresponding polylines are highlighted, and vice versa (see figure 2); the order of bars and axis can be altered; tooltips are used to give details on demand; handles in axis can be used to filter cases based upon interesting variables ranges (see how the handles were used to filter cases in figure 2), etc.

3 Case Study: Aggressive Behavior in High School Students

Following, the visual sensitivity analysis for the aggressive behavior in high school students is explained. 111 students of 7 schools with ages ranging from 14 to 17 years answered to 114 questions. The dimension of the problem was reasonably high for building a neural network classifier, so a factor analyis with a PCA extraction method was performed to reduce the number of variables. As a result, 34 factors were extracted, i.e., the actual number of variables used to train a Multilayer Perceptron (MLP). Having the input/output and sensitivity data, this visualization technique can be used with other types of ANNs.

Once the MLP was trained, an analysis of sensitivity was carried out. The results of this process are then used in the visual sensitivity analysis, in order to study the relationship of the input variables with the aggressive behavior of students (i.e., the target used for the network training).

3.1 Sensitivity Analysis

The visual sensitivity analysis for the MLP trained after dimension reduction can be seen in figure 2. Red colors on outputs (on top of stacked bars) represent an

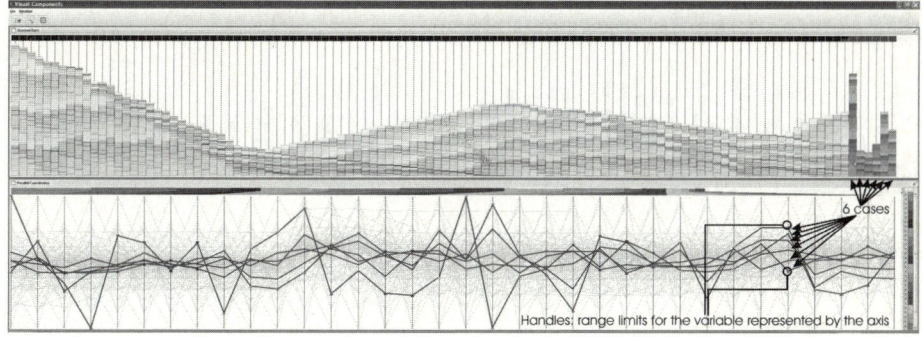

Fig. 3. Visualization of sensitivity ranges for aggressive behavior

aggressive behavior. Note an estimate error on the last case: the target (above) is blue (non aggressive), while the estimated value (below) is red (aggressive).

Focusing in the stacked bars, different areas can be observed, depending on how different cases (students) were affected by the components. Concretely, in a first group, a falling trend in the influence of the inputs to the output is found; this can be observed up to the third aggressive student (red colored target, case 35). Then a growing trend begins arriving to a local maximum, a non aggressive student (case 69). Finally, there is another falling phase arriving to student 103 and a small growing one up to the 111.

This result is quite curious; we had 34 neurons in the input layer and the changes take place every 34+1 cases. In order to explain this, two neighbor bars were selected and the polylines examined: they are almost identical but displaced (see figure 2). All couples of neighbor bars (cases) offer the same result, except for trend change places. That is, during the training, the influence of the input neurons in the output goes moving toward the end of the input neurons, then a small variation takes place. The training order does not change this situation.

An interesting question is if there exists a value for the coordinates that separate the aggressive students. The cases were ordered according to an increasing value of target. Then, the aggressive cases were selected so the ranges were automatically delimited by the axis handles (see figure 3). The only polylines that were active and highlighted were those corresponding to the selected bars (aggressive students). The remaining cases are drawn with soft colors in the background so the context of the problem is not lost.

3.2 Target Data

This analysis is similar to the previous one and complements it. Now, instead of the influences, the the MLP input values are represented. The result is shown in figure 4. It can be observed that the height of the bar does not follow any certain pattern: no relationship similar to that observed for the analysis of sensitivity can be found. In this case, few conclusions can be reached starting from the stacked bars. There are many cases in which the values of the answers are low

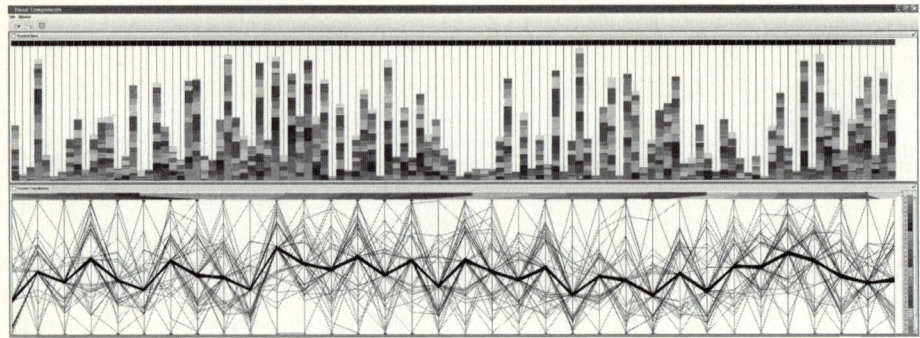

Fig. 4. Visual inputs analysis

(very small bars), but this does not separate the aggressive students. In this case, the color code of the bars, as opposed to what happened in the sensitivity analysis, does not contribute much information.

In this case, it is more useful the parallel coordinates plot. It can be easily seen that a mass of polylines exists in the central part of the plot. They correspond to the bars with the smaller heights. This permits to understand that, possibly, there was a group of students that were not interested in the survey and they answered similarly to all the questions. Another explanation is that they may form a differentiated class; this should be kept in mind when choosing cases for the sample. Repeating the previous process, ordering the bars according to height, and selecting only the smaller bars, it can be seen that these students actually form a separated group (see the polyline pattern in figure 5).

Now, the main question is if it is possible to determine if a student is aggressive according to his/her answers. By selecting the aggressive students (as context, the rest are maintained in the background). The handles in the parallel axis are automatically placed so they indicate that if the answers are inside those ranges, the student is aggressive (see figure 6). This a quick and easy way to determine if the variables are actually good to classify the students. In this particular

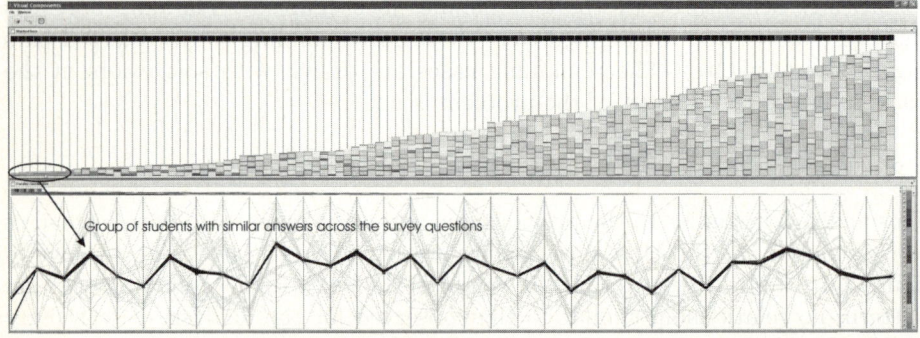

Fig. 5. Discovering a group of students

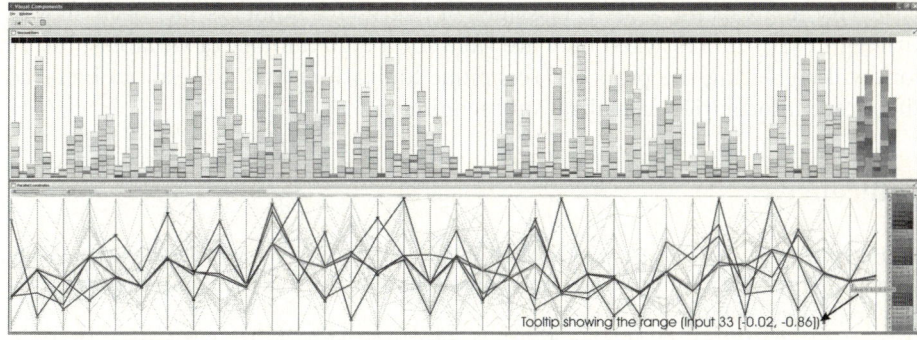

Fig. 6. Visualization of sensitivity ranges for aggressive behavior

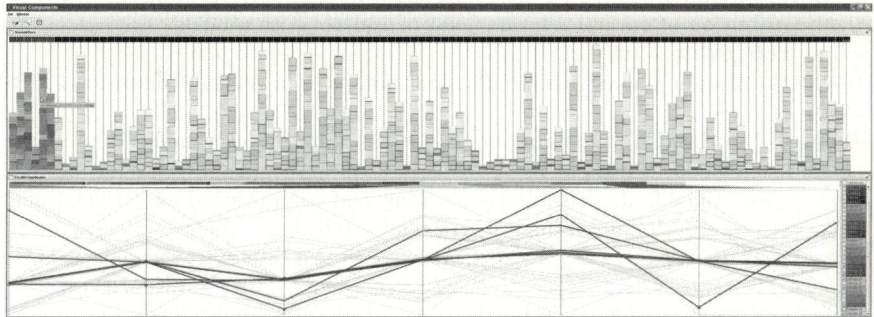

Fig. 7. Discovering the relevant factors in input analysis

situation the result has been affirmative. Note how aggressive students form an independent group: there are not blue polylines selected anymore.

Finding the smaller range in the axis will provide the more important inputs to classify the students behavior. Note the tooltip of input 33 (figure 6) showing the range in which the answer of an aggressive student should be. Remember that inputs are the result of dimensionality reduction, so a conversion to the actual answers of the student should be performed. Furthermore, we can go on removing axis (inputs) and seeing that there are not aggressive cases inside the range. After this process the most important variables that allow the isolation of the students are inputs 1, 23, 25, 26, 28, 32 and 34 (see checked boxes on the right of the PCP, figure 7). Same behavoir is observed in the sensitivity analysis.

4 Conclusions

A novel method for the visualization and exploration of the relationship between features and outputs in ANNs was presented. The combination of sensitivity analysis with information visualization techniques for multi-dimensional data provides a solution to face the curse of dimensionality. As case study, a visual sensitivity analysis for a MLP classifier of aggressive students has been shown. Although PCPs and Stacked bars are valid for a high number of variables, future work will be testing the proposed technique limitations and if these can be faced with other information visualization techniques.

References

1. Berrar, D.P., Downes, C.S., Dubitzky, W.: Multiclass cancer classification using gene expression profiling and probabilistic neural. In: Pacific Symposium on Biocomputing. Volume 8. (2003) 5–16
2. Sjoberg, J., Zhang, Q., Ljung, L., Benveniste, A., Delyon, B., Glorennec, P., Hjalmarsson, H., Juditsky, A.: Nonlinear black-box modeling in system identification: a unified overview. Automatica **31** (1995) 1691–1724
3. Gevrey, M., Dimopoulos, I., Lek, S.: Review and comparison of methods to study the contribution of variables in artificial neural network models. Ecological Modelling, **160** (2003) 249–264
4. Inselberg, A.: The plane with parallel coordinates. The Visual Computer **1** (1985) 69–91
5. Tzeng, F.Y., Ma, K.L.: Opening the black box - data driven visualization of neural networks. In: Proceedings of IEEE Visualization '05 Conference. (2005) 383–390
6. Craven, M., Shavlik, J.: Visualizing learning and computation an artificial neural networks. International Journal on Artificial Intelligence Tools **1** (1992) 399–425
7. Streeter, M.J., Ward, M.O., Alvarez, S.A.: Nvis: An interactive visualization tool for neural networks. In: Proceedings of SPIE Symposium on Visual Data Exploration and Analysis. (2001) 234–241
8. Duch, W.: Visualization of hidden node activity in neural networks: I and ii. In: Proceedings of the International Conference on Artificial Intelligence and Soft Computing. (2004) 38–49
9. Cook, R.D., Yin, X.: Special invited paper: Dimension reduction and visualization in discriminant analysis (with discussion). Australian & New Zealand Journal of Statistics **43** (2001) 147–199
10. Hwang, J.N., Choi, J.J., Oh, S., II, R.J.M.: Query-based learning applied to partially trained multilayer perceptrons. IEEE Transactions on Neural Networks **2** (1991) 131–136
11. Fu, L., Chen, T.: Sensitivity analysis for input vector in multilayer feedforward networks. In: Proceedingd of IEEE International Conference on Neural Networks. Volume 1. (1993) 215–218
12. Keim, D.A.: Information visualization and visual data mining. IEEE Transactions on Visualization and Computer Graphics **8** (2002) 1–8
13. Becker, R.A., Cleveland, W.S.: Brushing scatterplots. Technometrics **29** (1987) 127–142

Performance of BSDT Decoding Algorithms Based on Locally Damaged Neural Networks

Petro Gopych

V.N. Karazin Kharkiv National University, 4 Svoboda sq., Kharkiv 61077, Ukraine
pmg@kharkov.com

Abstract. Traditional signal detection theory (SDT) and recent binary signal detection theory (BSDT) provide the same basic performance functions: receiver operating characteristic (ROC) and basic decoding performance (BDP) curves. Because the BSDT may simultaneously be presented in neural network (NN), convolutional, and Hamming distance forms, it contains more parameters and its predictions are richer. Here we discuss a formal definition of one of specific BSDT parameters, the confidence level of decisions, and demonstrate that the BSDT's ROCs and BDPs, as functions of the number of NN disrupted links, have specific features, though rather strange at first glance but consistent with psychophysics experiments (for example, judgment errors in cluttered environments).

1 Introduction

Traditional signal detection theory [1] (SDT) operates mainly with a kind of continuous signals (sinusoids as a rule) distorted by an additive noise distributed according to a continuous probability distribution function (Gaussian as a rule), a natural assumption in 1940s-1960s—the era of analogous (vacuum-tube and transistor) communication technologies. Recent binary signal detection theory [2-5] (BSDT) operates with digital (binary) signals (messages) distorted by binary noise and distributed according to a discrete finite-range (binomial) probability distribution function, a natural assumption in 2000s—the era of digital (VLSI and computer) communication technologies.

The BSDT's decoding algorithm exists simultaneously in functionally equivalent NN, convolutional, and Hamming distance forms each of which is optimal in the sense of pattern recognition quality [2,4]. For BSDT decoding algorithms based on intact NNs, their performance functions, receiver operating characteristic (ROC) curves and basic decoding performance (BDP) curves (universal psychometric functions [3]), may easily be found even analytically [2]. For each locally damaged NN with specific arrangement of its disrupted links, formulae for computing its decoding probabilities have separately to be derived, but that is a rather complicate problem, taking into account the large amount of possible damage arrangements even for small NNs with rather small damage degrees (see the legend to Fig. 1). The solution required may routinely be found by the method of multiple computations [4,5], using the BSDT NN decoding algorithm with decision rules specified in ref. 4.

2 Confidence Levels of Decisions

The decision confidence is usually understood through the value of corresponding false-alarm probability, F: the smaller the F the larger the confidence is. As the BSDT's parameters may be calculated one through the other [3], to quantify confidence levels, we ascribe to each discrete F its unique number j and interpret it as the confidence level of decisions. For intact NNs, relations between confidence levels, j, false alarms, F_j, and their underlying triggering threshold intervals, $\Delta\theta_j$, are shown, for example, in Fig. 1b of ref. 3 ($j = N - i$ where i is an auxiliary index from Table 1 [3]; if $j = 0$ then $F_j = 1$); for damaged NNs, similar relations Fig. 1 illustrates.

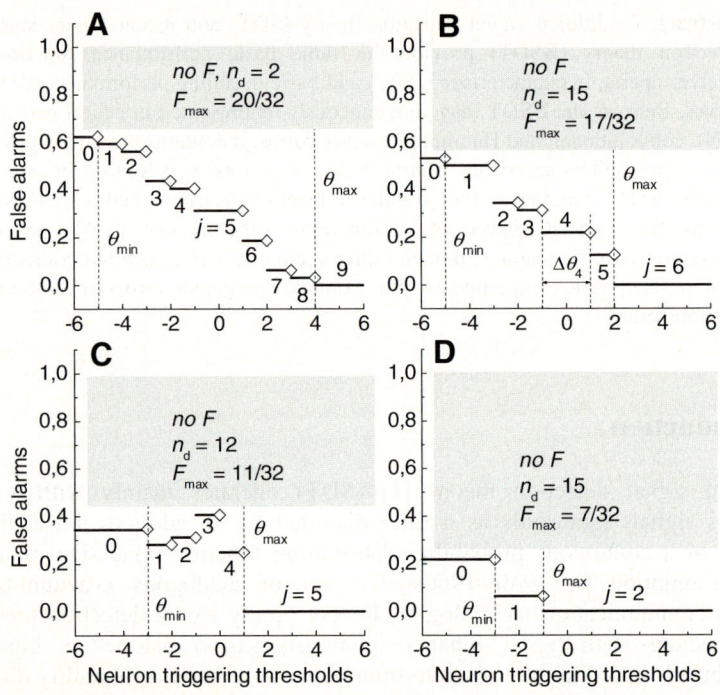

Fig. 1. False alarms, F, vs. neuron triggering thresholds, θ, for the BSDT's decoding algorithms based on NNs of the size N [4] with n_d local damages (disrupted links). Confidence levels of decisions, j (digits), their corresponding false alarms, F_j (horizontal line segments), and their underlying neuron threshold intervals, $\Delta\theta_j$ (lengths of horizontal line segments; in particular, $\Delta\theta_4$ in **B**), are indicated; θ_{min} and θ_{max} are bounds for $\Delta\theta_{left} = (-\infty, \theta_{min})$ and $\Delta\theta_{right} = [\theta_{max}, +\infty)$; N = 5. Arrangements of NN disrupted links (entrance-layer-neuron, exit-layer-neuron) and their total number, $n_a(N, n_d) = N^2!/(N^2 - n_d)!/n_d!$, are as follows. **A**, $n_d = 2$: (1,2) and (4,5); $n_a(5,2) = $ 300. **B**, $n_d = 4$: (1,1), (1,4), (3,4), and (5,4); $n_a(5,4) = 12\ 650$. **C**, $n_d = 12$: (5,1), (1,2), (3,2), (5,2), (1,3), (2,3), (1,4), (2,4), (3,4), (4,4), (2,5), and (4,5); $n_a(5,12) = 520\ 030$. **D**, $n_d = 15$: (3,1), (4,1), (1,2), (2,2), (3,2), (5,2), (1,3), (2,3), (3,3), (4,3), (5,3), (1,4), (2,4), (1,5), and (3,5); $n_a(5,15) = 3\ 268\ 760$. In shaded areas, $F_{max} < F \leq 1$, values of F do not exist; points, where the function $F(\theta)$ is not defined [3], are plotted as diamonds. Calculations were performed by multiple computations [4,5] (at $\theta \geq 0$ and $\theta < 0$ Equations A and a from Table 1 of ref. 4 were used, respectively); in **A** and ref. 4, the same NN example is considered.

3 ROCs and BDPs for Locally Damaged NNs

The BSDT operates with binary vectors x; their properties are defined by binomial probability distribution functions [2,3] which are discrete-valued and finite-ranged ones. For this reason, in contrast to traditional SDT [1], the BSDT's performance functions, ROCs and BDPs, are discrete-valued and finite-ranged [2,3]. Their discreteness and the discreteness and finiteness of their arguments are the BSDT's inherent property and, consequently, its discrete-valued predictions imply the existence of fundamentally discrete-valued empirical data whose discreteness is also their inherent property, not a result of an imperfection in measurement tools or of the specificity of measurement protocols.

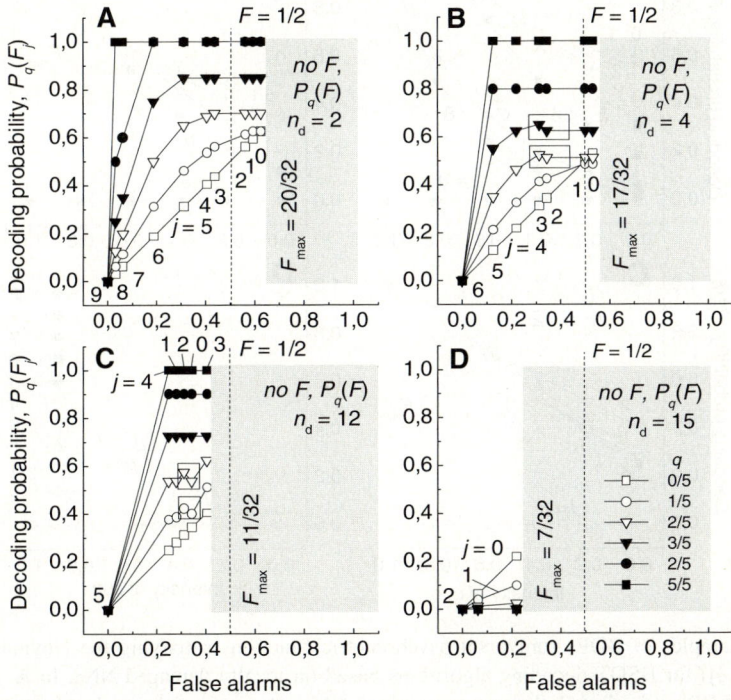

Fig. 2. Examples of ROCs for BSDT algorithms based on locally damaged NNs. In **A**, **B**, **C**, and **D**, those ROCs are plotted that correspond to NNs whose confidence levels of decisions, damage degrees, and damage arrangements are specified in Fig. 1**A**, **B**, **C**, and **D**, respectively (for different values of q, intensity of cue, they are shown in different signs). Other arrangements of disrupted links could produce other ROCs that are not shown. Digits enumerate confidence levels; shaded rectangles indicate the areas where probabilities F_j and $P_q(F_j)$ are not defined ($F_{max} < F_j \leq 1$, $0 \leq P_q(F_j) \leq 1$; F_{max} is the largest F_j provided by a given locally damaged NN); in **B** and **C**, cases, where the next $P_q(F_j)$ is smaller than the previous one, are boxed; vertical dashed lines ($F = 1/2$) indicate the axis of symmetry in distributions of F_j for intact NNs [2,3]; **A** displays ROCs for the NN discussed in ref. 4. For further details see the legend to Fig. 1.

Even the continuousness and the infiniteness of the neuron triggering threshold parameter, θ, is actually consistent with above assertions because the whole range of θ, $-\infty < \theta < \infty$, is naturally divided into a finite number of neuron threshold intervals, $\Delta\theta_j$ (see Fig. 1), and each θ related to a particular interval ($\theta \in \Delta\theta_j$) exerts an equal influence on final BSDT predictions (decoding probabilities). Infinite bounds of the left-most threshold interval, $\Delta\theta_{\text{left}} = (-\infty, \theta_{\min})$, and the right-most threshold interval, $\Delta\theta_{\text{right}} = [\theta_{\max}, +\infty)$, mean only that any $\theta \in \Delta\theta_{\text{left}}$ is smaller than $\theta_{\min}$ ($\theta < \theta_{\min}$) and any $\theta \in \Delta\theta_{\text{right}}$ is equal to or larger than $\theta_{\max}$ ($\theta \geq \theta_{\max}$); the infiniteness of these intervals does not imply the infiniteness of thresholds in real neurons.

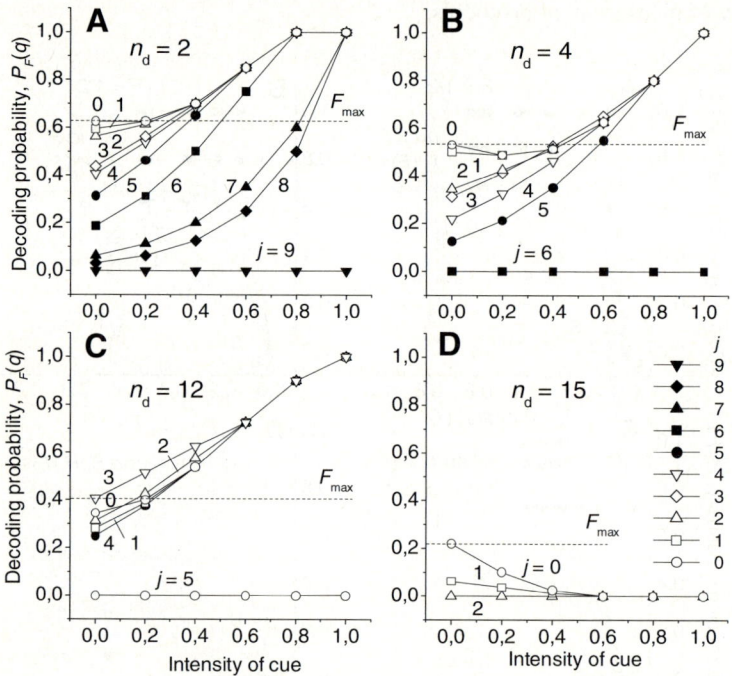

Fig. 3. Examples of BDPs (universal psychometric functions satisfying the Neyman-Pearson objective [3]) for BSDT decoding algorithms based on locally damaged NNs. In **A**, **B**, **C**, and **D**, those BDPs are plotted that correspond to NNs whose confidence level specifications, damage degrees, damage arrangements, and ROCs are presented in Figs. 1 and 2 (panels **A**, **B**, **C**, and **D**, respectively). BDPs, corresponding to different confidence levels, j, or false alarms, F_j ($F_j = P_F(q)$ at $q = 0$ [2,3]), are shown in different signs; $F_{\max}$ is as in Figs. 1 and 2.

There are many similarities and distinctions between the SDT and the BSDT. For the case of BSDT algorithms based on intact NNs, in part they have already been discussed [3]. Below, we focus on specific distinctions between the performance of BSDT algorithms based on intact NNs and based on locally damaged NNs (they were perfectly learned [2-5] but afterward some of their connections were disrupted).

For a locally damaged BSDT NN of the size N with a given arrangement of n_d disrupted links, from the inspection of Figs. 1-3, one can infer that:

1. The more the n_d the smaller the F_{max} is (Figs. 1-3).
2. An ROC's arguments, values of F_j, are asymmetrically distributed relative to $F = 1/2$, $0 \leq F_j \leq F_{max} < 1$, and, consequently, such an ROC cannot contain the point (1,1) (Figs. 1 and 2); for intact NNs, $F_{max} = 1$, $0 \leq F_j \leq 1$, F_j are symmetrically distributed relative to $F = 1/2$, and the ROC point (1,1) is always present.
3. The number of theoretical confidence levels of a decision (the number of neuron threshold intervals, $\Delta\theta_j$, values of F_j, or points along an ROC) depends not only on N but also on n_d and the damage arrangement; for intact NNs, the number of ROC points is always $N + 2$, including the points (0,0) and (1,1).
4. At different q, the right-most ROC points, $P_q(F_{max})$, are different in general; for rather large cues (e.g., $q > 1/2$) and not too large damage degrees, n_d, right-most parts of ROCs are flat (Fig. 2A and B). If $q = 0$ (by-chance decoding) then all the ROCs are linear, $P_q(F_j) = F_j$, but they are shorter than the main diagonal (Fig. 2).
5. For some q, non-monotonous ROCs are possible (signs boxed in Fig. 1B and C); for intact NNs, ROCs are never-decreasing functions.
6. A 'false' correspondence between j and F_j is possible when larger values of j (confidence levels) may correspond to smaller values of F_j (Figs. 1C-4C).
7. Severely (catastrophically) damaged NNs do not recognize the own standard pattern (memory trace) x_0; in such a case, BDPs and ROCs are zero-valued: if $q = 1$ then $P_F(q) = 0$ (Fig. 3D) and $P_q(F_j) = 0$ (Fig. 2D).
8. The genuine 'two-point' ROCs (with two theoretical confidence levels) are possible for catastrophically damaged NNs only (Fig. 2D), but two-point empirical ROCs may result from theoretically many-point ROCs (Fig. 4A and C).
9. Positions of bounds θ_{min} and θ_{max} of intervals $\Delta\theta_{left}$ and $\Delta\theta_{right}$ depend on N, n_d, and a particular damage arrangement (Figs. 1-3); in general, the more the n_d the smaller the distance $\theta_{max} - \theta_{min}$ is (Fig. 1); for intact NNs, $\theta_{min} = -N$ and $\theta_{max} = N$.
10. Some of $n_a(N,n_d)$ different damage arrangements (see the legend to Fig. 1) may generate different ROCs and BDPs, but some of them may also produce equal performance functions. Moreover, the arrangements are possible that generate such ROCs and BDPs as intact NNs do (e.g., Table 1 in ref. 5).

BSDT theoretical predictions discussed above and illustrated by Figs. 1-3 are rich, diverse, rather strange (with respect to both the SDT and the BSDT based on intact NNs), and have to be verified by comparing with an experiment. Recent findings, for example in the field of perceptual (visual) decisions in cluttered environments [6], provide one of such possibilities.

4 Judgment Errors in Cluttered Environments

In psychophysics, traditional SDT [1] is extremely popular for empirical data analysis, because usually SDT-based theories of memory and/or perception describe corresponding data quite well, e.g. [6-8]. But scrutinizing of large sets of available data and methods for their SDT-based analysis reveal discrepancies between the theory and experiment and lead to new versions of the SDT [7] (and theories [6] based on it) which contain additional, sometimes disputable, assumptions. The SDT can also not describe any cognitive phenomena, as it does not contain any cognitive parameters. To demonstrate the BSDT's advantages, we consider, for example, a rather surprised finding according to which in cluttered environments, when a target may be confounded with competing stimuli, subjects demonstrate high confidence of their (erroneous) perceptual decisions [6]. This inference has many potential practical consequences but cannot be explained by SDT-based theories of (visual) perception.

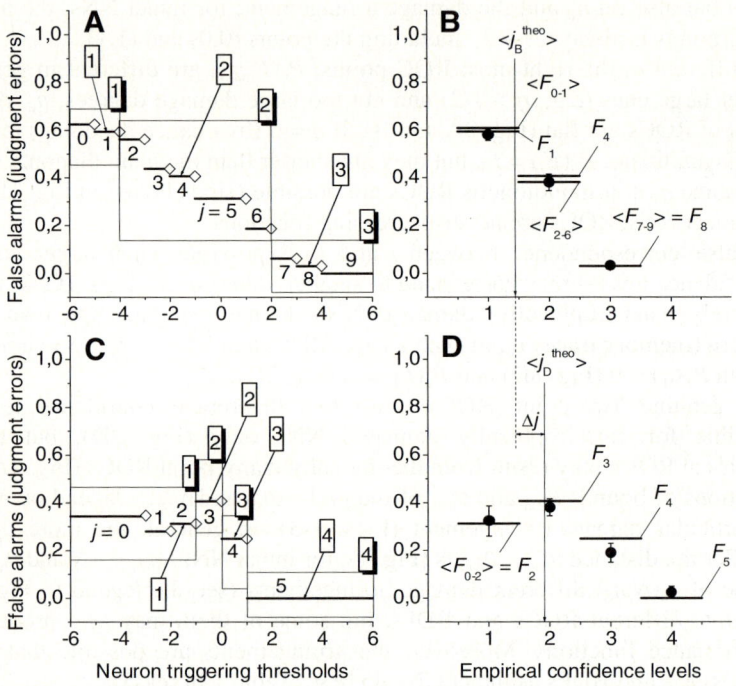

Fig. 4. Theoretical and empirical probabilities of judgement errors. **A**, Possible relations between 10 theoretical (Fig. 1A) and 3 empirical [6] confidence levels; digits, boxed digits, and shadowed digits enumerate respectively theoretical confidence levels, those of them that may individually represent empirical confidence levels, and groups of them that may jointly represent empirical confidence levels (corresponding F_j are boxed). **B**, Judgement errors vs. empirical confidence levels of decisions; circles (they correspond to red patterned bars in Fig. 7A [6]), the proportion of erroneous responses in trials when targets were presented in isolation; horizontal line segments, separate theoretical false alarms (F_j) or false-alarm values ($<F>$) averaged across a set of F_j boxed in **A**. **C**, Possible relations between 6 theoretical (Fig. 1C) and 4 empirical [6] confidence levels; designations are as in **A**. **D**, The same as in **B**; circles (they correspond to green bars in Fig. 7A [6]), the proportion of erroneous responses in trials when targets were presented in a cluttered environment; horizontal line segments, theoretical false alarms and their averaged value designated as in **C**. In **B** and **D**, arrows indicate the averaged theoretical decision confidences, $<j_B^{theo}> = 31173/21582 \approx 1.44$ and $<j_D^{theo}> = 60/31 \approx 1.93$; $\Delta j = <j_D^{theo}> - <j_B^{theo}>$; the fact that $<j_D^{theo}>$ is grater than $<j_B^{theo}>$ explains the subject's preferences for high-confidence (erroneous) decisions in cluttered environments [6].

For decision data measured in rating experiments, the BSDT's cognitive metric (confidence levels, j) allows to compare directly the theoretical predictions about human cognitive abilities (Fig. 1) with corresponding empirical data (Fig. 7 in ref. 6). As the number of theoretical and empirical confidence levels may not coincide, in Fig. 4A and C two possible ways of how to compare them are considered.

Fig. 4B and D demonstrate that BSDT false alarms, presented in any of forms shown in Fig. 4A and C, consist equally well with judgement errors found in experiment [6]. Averaged theoretical decision confidences, $<j_B^{theo}> \approx 1.44$ and $<j_D^{theo}> \approx 1.93$ (Fig. 4B and D), coincide with corresponding empirical data, $<j_B^{exper}> = 1.44 \pm 0.02$ and $<j_D^{exper}> = 1.93 \pm 0.08$ (Fig. 7A in ref. 6), also quite well. Consequently, it may be thought of that on isolated targets (Fig. 4B) decisions are generated by a slightly damaged NN (for its properties see Figs. 1A-4A), while decisions concerning the target embedded in distractors (Fig. 4D) are produced by an NN with a rather large damage degree (for its properties see Figs. 1C-4C). The BSDT not only describes successfully decision confidences measured in simple (Fig. 4B) and complex (cluttered, Fig. 4D) environments but provides also a clear 'idea of the neural representations on which observers base their response' [6]. For explaining the bimodality of response distributions observed in cluttered environments [6], the BSDT-based theory for vision [5] may be used.

5 Conclusion

For a simple example by a method of multiple computations, performance functions for BSDT decoding algorithms based on locally damaged NNs (ROC and BDP curves) have exactly been calculated and classified using a specific BSDT cognitive parameter, the confidence level of decisions. It has been demonstrated that the version of the BSDT considered provides rich, diverse, and strange at first glance predictions. Some of them were applied to the first explanation of recent experimental findings concerning a cognitive experiment (judgment errors in cluttered environments). As a result, empirical data have been reproduced both qualitatively and quantitatively.

Acknowledgments. I am grateful to the HINARI (Health InterNetwork Access to Research Initiative) for free on-line access to some full-text journals, to anonymous reviewers for their comments, to M. Gopych and other my family members and friends for their help and support.

References

1. Green, D. Swets, J.: Signal Detection Theory and Psychophysics. Wiley, New York (1966)
2. Gopych, P.M.: ROC Curves within the Framework of Neural Network Assembly Memory Model: Some Analytic Results. Int. J. Inf. Theo. Appl. **10** (2003) 189-197
3. Gopych, P.M.: Sensitivity and Bias within the Binary Signal Detection Theory, BSDT. Int. J. Inf. Theo. Appl. **11** (2004) 318-328
4. Gopych, P.M.: Neural Network Computations with Negative Triggering Thresholds. In: Duch, W. et al. (eds.): Artificial Neural Networks: Biological Inspirations. Lecture Notes in Computer Sciences Vol. 3696. Springer-Verlag, Berlin-Heidelberg (2005) 223-228

5. Gopych, P.M.: Generalization by Computation through Memory. Int. J. Inf. Theo. Appl. **13** (2006) 145-157
6. Baldassi, S., Megna, N., Burr, D.: Visual Clutter Causes High-Magnitude Errors. PloS Biol. **4** (2006) e56
7. Rotello, C.M., Macmillan, N.A., Reeder, J.A.: Sum-Difference Theory of Remembering and Knowing: A Two-Dimensional Signal Detection Model. Psychol. Rev. **111** (2004) 588-616

K Nearest Sequence Method and Its Application to Churn Prediction

Dymitr Ruta, Detlef Nauck, and Ben Azvine

British Telecom (BT) Group, Chief Technology Office
Adastral Park, Orion MLB 1, PP12, Ipswich IP53RE, UK
dymitr.ruta@bt.com

Abstract. In telecom industry high installation and marketing costs make it between six to ten times more expensive to acquire a new customer than it is to retain the existing one. Prediction and prevention of customer churn is therefore a key priority for industrial research. While all the motives of customer decision to churn are highly uncertain there is lots of related temporal data sequences generated as a result of customer interaction with the service provider. Existing churn prediction methods like decision tree typically just classify customers into churners or non-churners while completely ignoring the timing of churn event. Given histories of other customers and the current customer's data, the presented model proposes a new k nearest sequence (kNS) algorithm along with temporal sequence fusion technique to predict the whole remaining customer data sequence path up to the churn event. It is experimentally demonstrated that the new model better exploits time-ordered customer data sequences and surpasses the existing churn prediction methods in terms of performance and offered capabilities.

1 Introduction

Most of telecom companies are in fact customer-centric service providers and offer to its customers variety of subscription services. One of the major issues in such environment is customer churn known as a process by which a company loses a customer to its competitor. Recent estimates suggest that churn rates in the telecom industry could be anything between 25% to 50% [1]. Moreover average acquisition costs standing at around $400 take years to recoup [1] and are estimated to be between 5 to 8 times higher than average retention costs [2]. In such circumstances, it makes every economic sense to have a strategy to retain customers which is only possible if the customer intention to churn is detected early enough. In the presence of large data warehouses packed with terabytes of data, data mining techniques are being adopted to business applications [3] in an attempt to understand, explain and predict customer interaction with the company that leads to churn. Many churn prediction models are available in the market, however churn is only being modelled statically by analysing customer data and running regression or predictive classification models at a particular time instance [4]. On the research arena the focus is shifted towards more complex classification and nonlinear regression techniques like neural networks [5] or support vector machines [6] yet still applied in the same static context to customer data.

In this work the weaknesses of static churn prediction are addressed resulting in a proposition of a new temporal churn prediction system. It uses novel k nearest sequence algorithm that learns from the whole available customer data path and is capable to generate future data sequences along with precisely timed predicted churn events.

The remainder of the paper is organised as follows. Section 2 formulates the problem of churn prediction and explains the sequential data model used for predictions. Next section shows Gamma distribution-based modelling of customer lifetime as a prerequisite tool for kNS algorithm described in Section 4. Section 5 provides comparative churn prediction results from experiments carried out upon real customer data. Finally the concluding remarks are drawn Section 6.

2 Problem Formulation and Data Model

Assuming a constant stream of N customers from whom n_{churn} customers churn while n_{new} customers join the company in a considered time window let $n_{churn} = n_{new}$ and let $p_{prior} = n_{churn}/N$ stand for a prior churn probability. As only churn predictions are actionable and incur some cost, the performance measures evaluating the model should focus on measuring efficiency of churn predictions. Considering predictability limits in the optimal scenario all churn predictions made are correct, whereas in the worst case i.e. by predicting k churners at random, on average kp_{churn} churners will be correctly recognised at the cost of $(1 - kp_{churn})$ wrong churn predictions. The churn prediction results can be presented in a form of confusion matrix as shown in Table 1. The churn recognition rate evaluating efficiency of churn predictions can be expressed

Table 1. Confusion matrix representation: $c_{0|0}$ - true negatives, $c_{1|0}$ - false negatives, $c_{0|1}$ - false positives, $c_{1|1}$ - true positives, where churn is denoted by 1 and non-churn by 0

Actual\Predicted	NonChurn	Churn
NonChurn	$c_{0|0}$	$c_{1|0}$
Churn	$c_{0|1}$	$c_{1|1}$

by: $p_{churn} = c_{1|1}/(c_{1|1} + c_{1|0})$. In order to truly reflect the quality of model predictions compared to the random predictions it is sensible to use a gain measure which expresses how many times the predictor's churn rate is better than the prior churn rate p_{prior}:

$$G = \frac{p_{churn}}{p_{prior}} = \frac{c_{1|1}(c_{1|1} + c_{1|0} + c_{0|1} + c_{0|0})}{(c_{1|1} + c_{1|0})(c_{0|1} + c_{1|1})} \quad (1)$$

Or in order to scale the gain within the achievable limits of $(1, 1/p_{prior})$ a simple normalisation can be used to finally give the relative gain measure defined as follows:

$$G_r = \frac{p_{churn} - p_{prior}}{1 - p_{prior}} = \frac{c_{1|1}c_{0|0} - c_{1|0}c_{0|1}}{(c_{1|1} + c_{1|0})(c_{0|0} + c_{1|0})} \quad (2)$$

Using the above performance measures it is demonstrated that the successful churn prediction strategy depends on comprehensive exploitation of temporal data. These data are generated on the course of customer interaction with the service provider and can be interpreted as a time-directed trajectories in the multidimensional data space generated from customer events. This way not only information coming in the sheer data is used for prediction but also additional information about data sequentiality patterns. The model assumes periodically collected customer data. The duration of each time interval will form the time resolution for customer behaviour analysis and should be selected inline with company routines, data availability and the required time-resolution of generated predictions. Once this is decided, the elementary data unit x_{cti} represents a value of the ith column (feature), collected at time interval t for the customer identified by c. For each customer c the complete life cycle would be defined by the time ordered sequence of customer data that can be stored in a matrix profile as follows:

$$X_c = \begin{bmatrix} x_{c,1,1} & x_{c,1,2} & \cdots & x_{c,1,M} \\ \cdots & \cdots & \cdots & \cdots \\ x_{c,T,1} & \cdots & \cdots & x_{c,T,M} \end{bmatrix} \quad (3)$$

where T is the total number of time intervals of a sequence and M stands for the number of features. To increase storage efficiency customer data matrices were piled together into a single table D with the customer identifier and time interval index moved into the two first identifying columns. This tabular data model is more suitable for SQL processing in databases and allows for instant and effortless update of table D. Due to data availability issues, in our models the time resolution has been set to 1 month such that the annual customer data form an ordered sequence of 12 points.

3 Customer Lifetime

Customer lifetime in itself provides unconditional estimation of the churn timing blind to any additional data describing customer interaction with the service provider. Historical lifetime data from different customers gives information about the lifetime distribution which then allows to link the churn event to a random process with certain probability distribution and hence describe churn in probabilistic terms. Denoting by x_i a random series of customer lifetimes extracted from the available data the first goal is to find its distribution. Customer lifetime can be modelled as a random process modelling random event occurrence where the waiting time (i.e. lifetime) before the event (i.e. churn) is relatively long. The three distributions that match this process have been identified: exponential, Gamma and Weibull distributions. All of these distributions have reported applications to lifetime modelling [7]. Yet further analysis in which distributions were fitted to certain ranges of lifetimes e.g. for lifetimes greater than 5 years showed that only Gamma distribution consistently fits well the data despite its changing characteristics. Settling on the Gamma distribution, the probability density function (PDF) of the lifetime x is defined by:

$$y = f(x|a,b) = \frac{x^{a-1}e^{-x/b}}{b^a \Gamma(a)} \qquad \Gamma(a) = \int_0^\infty e^{-t}t^{a-1}dt \quad (4)$$

where a and b are the distribution parameters and $\Gamma(a)$ is a gamma function. Given the density (4) the cumulative distribution function (CDF) can be obtained by:

$$p = F(x|a,b) = \int_0^x f(x)dx = \frac{1}{b^a \Gamma(a)} \int_0^x t^{a-1} e^{-t/b} dt \tag{5}$$

The CDF function $F(x)$ returns the probability that an event drawn from gamma distribution will occur no later than at x. In case of customer lifetime modelling the only event expected is customer churn, hence the CDF becomes immediately the churn risk expressed as a function of the customer life with the service provider. Complementing the event of churn occurrence to a certain event, i.e. $S(x) = 1 - F(x)$ gives the customer survival function showing the probability $S(x)$ of a customer surviving up to the period x. Figures 1(a)-1(b) show examples of the fitted gamma distribution along with corresponding cumulative probability distribution and the survival function.

Exploiting further the properties of the gamma distribution one can immediately obtain the average customer lifetime expectancy and its variability which correspond to the gamma mean $\mu = ab$ and variance $\nu = ab^2$.

The lifetime analysis carried out so far applies to a customer who just joined the service. In reality at any snapshot of a time one might need to ask about the remaining lifetime of a customer who already stayed with the service provider for some time. The problem of a remaining lifetime from the mathematical point of view is quite simple.

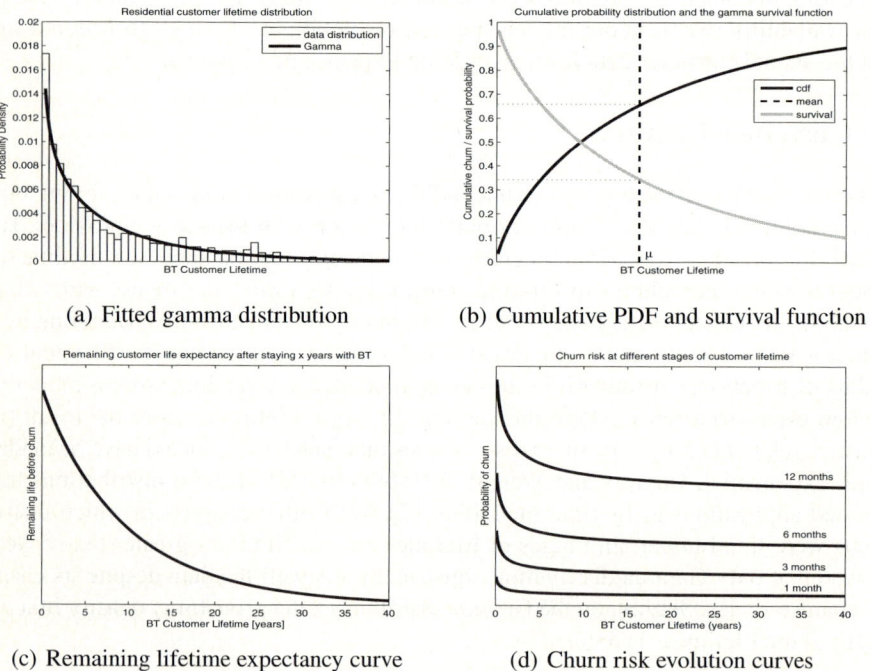

(a) Fitted gamma distribution (b) Cumulative PDF and survival function

(c) Remaining lifetime expectancy curve (d) Churn risk evolution curves

Fig. 1. Gamma PDF distribution fitted to the customer lifetime data. 1(a) Gamma PDF fitted to customer lifetime data 1(b) Cumulative probability distribution of the fitted gamma distribution. 1(c) Remaining lifetime expectancy curve. 1(d) Churn riskl evolution curves.

The remaining lifetime of a customer at age t can be found by an integration of the survival function from t to ∞ and renormalisation which can be expressed by:

$$L(t) = \frac{1}{S(t)} \int_t^\infty S(x) dx \tag{6}$$

Note that if the customer has just joined the company i.e. when $t = 0$, the remaining lifetime simplifies to the Gamma mean parameter: $L(0) = \int_0^\infty S(x)dx = \mu$.

Figure 1(c) shows the plot of the remaining lifetime for incremental periods that the customer already stays with the company obtained by numerical integration shown in (6). Finally the most interesting characteristics from the churn prediction point of view is the churn risk evolution over time. Assuming that the churn probability relates to fixed time ahead τ, its evolution over time $H(t)$ can be calculated by the integration of gamma PDF function from t to $t + \tau$ and renormalisation i.e.:

$$H_\tau(t) = \frac{\int_t^{t+\tau} f(x)dx}{\int_t^\infty f(x)dx} = \frac{F(t+\tau) - F(t)}{1 - F(t)} = \frac{S(t) - S(t+\tau)}{S(t)} \tag{7}$$

Using formula (7) examples of churn risk evolution curves were obtained for 1, 3, 6 and 12 months as shown in Figure 1(d)

The presented analysis indicates that entrants have much higher churn rate than the customers who stayed long with the service provider. For churn prediction purposes this information means that the random churn prediction strategy from previous section would give much higher performance if applied only to entrants or in general to customers with the service age at which the churn risk is the highest.

4 K Nearest Sequence Algorithm

As mentioned in Section 1 temporal classification approach to churn prediction struggles from its underlying static form in which a classifier can only give the answer on whether the churn will occur or not in the particular time slot. Such models either loose information through the necessity of temporal data aggregation or ignore it by not being able to exploit the dynamics of data evolution over time. The timed predictions of churn and its circumstances is beyond the capabilities of temporal classification models.

In an answer to these challenges an original, simple and efficient non-parametric model called k Nearest Sequence (kNS) has been developed. This model uses all available sequences of customer data on input and generates the whole remaining future data sequences up to the churn event as an output. An interesting part is that this model does not require learning prior to the prediction process. Instead it uses customer sequence as a template and automatically finds the k best matching data subsequences of customers who already churned and based on their remaining subsequences kNS predicts the most likely future data sequence up to the time-stamped churn even. The model is further supported by the remaining lifetime estimate presented in Section 3 which is used to add the estimated lifetime feature to the training data.

Let for notation simplicity $S(c, t, \tau)$ stand for a data sequence for a customer identified by c, starting from the time period t and having the length τ i.e.:

$$S(c, t, \tau) = \{\mathbf{x}_{c,t}, \ldots, \mathbf{x}_{c,t+\tau}\} \quad \tau = 1, 2, .. \tag{8}$$

Formally the objective of kNS is to predict the future sequences of customer data $S(c, t_{cur}+1, R)$, where R is the remaining customer lifetime and t_{cur} is the current time, given the existing customer data sequence to date $S(c, t_{cur}-\tau, \tau)$, where τ is the data availability timeframe, and the historical and live data of former and current customers $S(c_i, 0, L_i)$, where L_i is a lifetime of the customer identified by c_i.

In the first step kNS finds the k nearest sequences, i.e. the customers whose data sequences match the considered sequence the most. This task is split into 2 subtasks. First, all customer sequences are scanned to find the best matching subsequences i.e. the subsequences $S(c_i, t_i-\tau, \tau)$ that have the closest corresponding points to the considered sequence pattern $S(c, t_{cur}-\tau, \tau)$ in the Euclidean distance sense, that is:

$$t_i = \arg\min_{t=\tau}^{L_i} \|S(c, t_{cur}-\tau, \tau) - S(c_i, t-\tau, \tau)\| = \arg\min_{t=\tau}^{L_i} \sum_{j=0}^{\tau} \|\mathbf{x}_{c,t_{cur}-j} - \mathbf{x}_{c_i,t-j}\| \quad (9)$$

Then all best subsequences $S(c_i, t_i-\tau, \tau)$ are sorted according to their distance from the sequence in question in order to determine first k best matching patterns. The remaining subsequences of these best matches i.e. $S(c_i, t_i, L_i - t_i)$, $i = 1,..,k$, are referred to as k nearest remainders, and are used directly for predicting the future sequence in question $S(c, t_{cur}, L)$. The prediction is done by a specific aggregation of the k nearest remainders, which due to different lengths of the remaining subsequences has been supported by the time stretch of the sequences such that they all terminate in the same average churn point. First, the remaining lifetime is calculated by taking average from the last points of k nearest remainders:

$$R = \frac{1}{k} \sum_{i=1}^{k} L_i - t_i \quad (10)$$

Then denoting by $s_i = (L_i - t_i)/R$, $i = 1,..,k$ the transition step for each of k nearest remainders, each jth point $\mathbf{x}_{c,t_{cur}+j}$, $j = 1,..,R$ of the predicted sequence can be calculated using the following formula:

$$\mathbf{x}_{c,t_{cur}+j} = \frac{1}{k} \sum_{i=1}^{k} [(\lceil js_i \rceil - js_i) x_{c_i,t_i+\lfloor js_i \rfloor} + (js_i - \lfloor js_i \rfloor) x_{c_i,t_i+\lceil js_i \rceil}] \quad (11)$$

which uses interpolation of in-between sequence points spaces to obtain higher precision when dealing with unequally lengthened sequence reminders. This way kNS algorithm would predict the churn taking place in $L = t_{cur} + R$ time period along with the data path $S(c, t_{cur}, R)$ leading to this event.

In realistic scenario the data availability timeframe is very narrow compared to customer lifetime, which means that instead of having complete data sequences of customers from their acquisition up to churn there is only a tiny time slice of data available. In this time slice the turnover of customers and hence the number of churners that can be observed is on average $\tau N/L$ and . Most of the data in such It is therefore expected that vast majority of data relate to the existing customers who did not churn yet. In this case it is very likely that among k nearest sequences most would relate to existing customers with unknown churn time. In this case the kNS algorithm is aided by the unconditional remaining lifetime estimate covered in Section 3. The data sequence predictions are provided only up to the data availability limit and then overall customer average sequence is filled in up to the predicted churn event. The complete kNS algorithm is visualised in Figure 2.

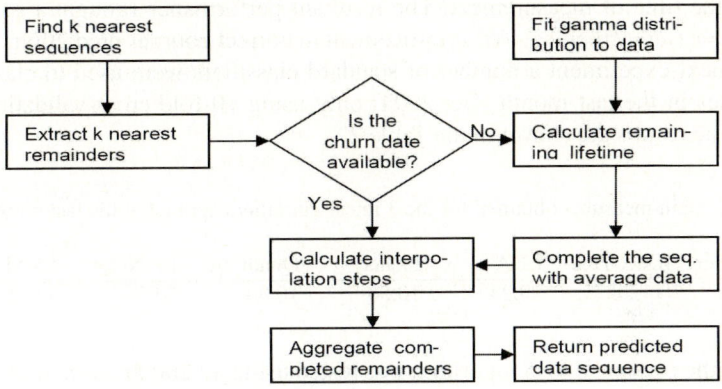

Fig. 2. Flowchart of the k nearest sequence algorithm

5 Experiments

In order to demonstrate the capabilities of the presented kNS algorithm a set of comparative experiments have been carried out on the real BT customer data sample. Due to data security issues only selected features describing customer provisions, fault repairs and complaints events were used excluding possibly crucial but sensitive customer billing data. They were prepared compliant to data model presented in Section **??** with first column of customer identifier, second keeping monthly time period, third holding customer lifetime up to the current month, and fourth keeping the churn label i.e. a binary flag indicating whether the customer churned in this month or not. This follows with 24 columns of customer data features extracted from customer events database and including events counters, durations and many other mostly quantitative measures describing these events. The data were sampled at random from the database but due to very narrow data availability timeframe of just 10 months churners have been selected for only last month in order to keep customer sequences the longest possible and of consistent length. All the customers data selected for the experiment had at least one event of each type. As a result about 20000 10-months customer sequences have been extracted with many missing data. These missing data have been treated using exponential continuous decay function of the form $y(t) = e^{-ln(2)t/T}$, where T stands for the half-decay period, which intends to simulate fading intensity of human emotions caused by certain event over time. The 2-weeks half-decay period was used following some quick manual optimisation. The prior churn probability i.e. the average likelihood that random customer will churn in particular month turned out to be very low and is denoted by p_{prior} as summarised in Section 2. Due to security reasons the real value of p_{prior} can not be shown here and for the same reasons in all experiments the model performance is expressed by a gain measure as described in Section 2.

The first experiment concerned predicting customer lifetime based on lifetime analysis presented in Section 3. Based on gamma distribution fitted to customer lifetimes, the period with the highest churn density was identified to be the first year of contract and accordingly random churn prediction was applied to the customers who stay less than a year at the time of measurement. The resultant performance brought a gain of just $G_{lifetime} = 1.46$ achieving 46% improvement in correct churner prediction.

In the next experiment a number of standard classifiers were used to classify customer states in the last month (Oct-2004) only using 10-fold cross-validation testing method. The results are shown in the Table 2.

Table 2. Gain measures obtained for the 3 linear classifiers applied to the last month data

Classifier	Dec. Tree	LDA	Fisher	Quadratic	FF NNet	SVM
Gain	11.28	10.24	10.58	10.86	9.97	11.06

Finally the presented kNS algorithm was tested using all 20000 10-months customer sequences with approximated missing data when necessary. Due to the fact that kNS returns precise churn timing it has been assumed that correct churn recognition occurs when the predicted timing deviates no more than 2 months from the actual churn date. The experiment was run for 5 different nearest sequence parameters $k = 1, .., 5$ and for 5 different lengths of the matching template i.e. for $\tau = 1, .., 5$ months. For each setup the performances have been converted to the gain measures which are shown in Figure 3 along with the diagram depicting differences between these measures. The results show very clearly that above $k \geq 3$ performance gain obtained for kNS becomes higher than for any other tested classifier, shown in Table 2. When $\tau = 1$ the algorithm converges to a standard kNN algorithm for which the performance is comparable to other classifiers from Table 2. The sequential strength starts to take effects from $\tau > 1$ and the results shown in Figure 3 confirm that the highest performance gains are observed for τ ranging between 2 and 4 months with the highest gain of 13.29 obtained for 3-months sequences matched to 4 nearest sequences. These results outperform static non-sequential classification by around 20% and thereby confirm the contribution of the sequential modelling to the churn prediction performance. Due to the lack of space the whole issue of data sequences prediction, coming as a by-product of kNS-based churn prediction, was ignored and left for further investigations within a wider framework of of customer behaviour modelling.

6 Conclusions

Summarising, this work uncovered a new perspective on customer churn prediction and highlighted the importance of the sequential analysis for events prediction. The traditional methods of churn prediction based static classification have been shown conceptually unable to handle the sequential nature of customer relationship path up to churn and therefore unable to time the predictions. The presented kNS algorithm was

k \ τ	1	2	3	4	5
1	6.53	6.53	8.05	7.37	7.58
2	8.80	11.20	10.71	7.61	9.06
3	9.00	11.25	10.75	12.87	9.09
4	10.62	12.82	**13.29**	13.18	12.87
5	11.05	13.02	12.35	12.33	12.42

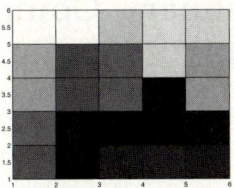

Fig. 3. Gain performance measures obtained for kNS predictor for 5 different nearest sequence parameters k and template sequence lengths τ, shown in a tabular form (left) and graphical diagram (right). Darker shades correspond to higher gain measures.

designed specifically to learn from customer data sequences and is capable to handle the whole customer life cycle rather than individual customer state caught in a snapshot of time. The kNS algorithm is prepared for limited data availability timeframe and can effectively handle missing data. Moreover kNS is capable of exploiting both former customers with completed lifetime data paths and the existing customer sequences by using Gamma distribution applied to model expected customer lifetime. Due to the lack of space and the churn focussed theme of this work the whole aspect of data sequences prediction, coming as a by-product of kNS-based churn prediction, was ignored and left for further investigations within a wider framework of customer behaviour modelling.

References

1. G. Furnas. Framing the wireless market. The Future of Wireless, WSA News:Bytes 17(11):4-6, 2003.
2. L. Yan, D.J. Miller, M.C. Mozer, R. Wolniewicz. Improving prediction of customer behaviour in non-stationary environments. In Proc. of Int. Joint Conf. on Neural Networks, 2001, pp. 2258-2263.
3. M. Morgan. Unearthing the customer: data mining is no longer the preserve of mathematical statisticians. Marketeers can also make a real, practical use of it (Revenue-Generating Networks). Telecommunications International, May, 2003.
4. R.O. Duda, P.E. Hart, D.G. Stork. Pattern classification. John Wiley & Sons, 2001.
5. M. Mozer, R.H. Wolniewicz, D.B. Grimes, E. Johnson, H. Kaushansky: Churn Reduction in the Wireless Industry. Neural Information Processing Systems Conf. 1999, pp 935-941.
6. K. Morik, H. Kopcke: Analysing customer churn in insurance data. Eur. Conf. on Principles and Practice of Knowledge Discovery in Databases, Pisa, Italy, 2004, pp 325-336.
7. M.S. Finkelstein. On the shape of the mean residual lifetime function. Applied Stochastic Models in Business and Industry 18(2):135 - 146, 2002.

Evolutionary Computation Technique Applied to HSPF Model Calibration of a Spanish Watershed*

F. Castanedo, M.A. Patricio, and J.M. Molina

Computer Science Department.
Universidad Carlos III de Madrid, Spain.
Avda. Universidad Carlos III 22, 28270-Colmenarejo (Madrid)
{fcastane, mpatrici}@inf.uc3m.es, molina@ia.uc3m.es

Abstract. Hydrological Simulation Program Fortan (HSPF) is a mathematical modelling program developed by the United States Environmental Protection Agency (EPA). HSPF is used for simulating of watershed hidrology and water quality. In this paper, an evolutionary algorithm is applied to automated watershed model calibration. The calibration stage of the model is very important in order to reduce the errors in hydrological predictions. Results show the capacity of the proposed method to simulate watershed streamflows.

1 Introduction

The movement and storage of water at watershed scales is a complex process primarily affected by climatic, topographic, soil, vegetative, geologic and land use factors. The complex nature of the processes inherent in surface and subsurface hydrology is best investigated by computer models that simulate these processes over short and long intervals. In recent years a number of conceptual watershed models have been developed to assess the impacts of changes in land use, land cover, management practices, or climatic conditions on water resources and water quality at watershed scales [1]. They range in capability, complexity, scale and resolution and may have different data requirements. Moreover the accuracies of the resulting simulation may vary [2].

One of this models is Hydrological Simulation Program in Fortran (HSPF) [3] developed by the United States Environmental Protection Agency (EPA) [4] for simulating many processes related to water quantity and quality in watersheds of almost any size and complexity. An extensive description of HSPF is given in [5].

HSPF allows modelers to emphasize the hydrologic process that are dominant in a watershed by adjusting parameter values during calibration (see Table 1). All of them depend on the physical conditions of the river basin and reflect specific

---

* Funded by projects CICYT TSI2005-07344, CICYT TEC2005-07186 and CAM MADRINET S-0505/TIC/0255.

watershed physical values that need to be adjusted to adapt the HSPF model to a particular river basin. But, the estimation of actual parameter values from physical measurements is either difficult or impossible [6]. Therefore, parameter values are generally obtained through the calibration process. In some hydrological models where the number of parameters is small enough - up to three according to [7] - they can be adjusted using trial and error methods. But the bigger the number of parameters is, the more efficient optimization algorithms should be applied.

There are a few works concerned the HSPF model calibration. In [17], the authors use HSPexp [16] for the calibration stage. They adjusted only eleven out of the twenty parameters of HSPF model (see Table 1), since they did not used the snow module. They applied this calibrated HSPF model to evaluate water quality in Virginia (USA). Computer programs like PEST [18] can be used to estimating the parameters. If we are modelling an US watershed, the calibration could be done using HSPF Parameter Database (HSPFParm) [19]. In [20] the authors propose the optimization of WATCLASS hydrology model calibration using fuzzy Tagaki Sugeno Kang method (TSK).

Evolutionary computation (EC) comprises several robust search mechanisms based on underlying biological metaphor. EC techniques have been established as a valid approach to problems requiring efficient and effective search, furthermore, EC are increasingly finding widespread application in business, scientific and engineering circles. There are very few works that use evolution search strategies in model calibration, the first attempt was undertaken by [15] who applied Genetic Algorithms (GA) [14] in a model with only 7 parameters.

The purpose of this contribution is to show the improvement of the calibration stage in the HSPF model by means of evolutionary computation techniques. In order to assess our proposal, we had calibrated a Spanish watershed using the calibration process presented in this paper.

This paper is organized as follows, first section 2 presents how HSPF model works. Then an evolutionary algorithm for the calibration stage is presented in section 3. The experimental results are presented in section 4. Finally section 5 shows the conclusions of this work.

2 HSPF

HSPF is a very robust, high resolution, flexible, reliable, and comprehensive hydrologic model for simulation of watershed hydrology and water quality. As a physical-process-based model, HSPF uses minimal input data to describe hydrological conditions in a watershed. As a time series management system, it can simulate continuously the hydrologic and associated water quality processes on pervious and impervious land surfaces as well as in streams. Derived from the Stanford Watershed Model (SWM) developed by [8], HSPF considers all streamflow components (runoff, interflow and baseflow) and thier pollutant contributions, snow accumulation is also included in the HSPF model.

HSPF model has been used to simulate: (1) a wide variety of hydrologic conditions [9] [10], (2) transport of various non-point source pollutants, including

Table 1. Adjusted parameters during the calibration stage

Parameter	Definition	Unit
RDCSN	Relative density of new snow at -18 °C	none
COVIND	Empirical parameter used to give the areal coverage of snow in a land segment	none
SNOEVP	Parameter used to adjust the calculation to field conditions	none
CCFACT	Parameter used to correct melt values to field conditions	none
MELEV	Lower mean elevation	meters
SHADE	Parameter indicating the fraction of the land segment which is shaded	none
MWATER	Parameter specifying the maximum liquid water content of the snowpack	(mm/mm)
CEPSC	Interception storage capacity of vegetation	mm
INFILT	Index to mean soil infiltration rate. High values of INFILT divert more water to the subsurface flow paths	(mm/interval)
INFILD	Parameter giving the ratio of maximum and mean soil infiltration capacity over the land segment	none
INFEXP	Infiltration equation exponent >1	none
INTFW	Interflow coefficient that governs the amount of water that enters the ground from surface detention storage	none
UZSN	Parameter for upper zone nominal storage. Defines the storage capacity of the upper-unsaturated zone	(mm)
LZSN	Lower zone nominal storage parameter. Defines the storage capacity of the lower-unsaturated zone	(mm)
LZETP	Lower zone evapotranspiration parameter. 0<=LZETP<1	(mm)
DEEPFR	Fraction of infiltrating water that is lost to deep aquifiers. Represents the fraction of ground water that becomes inactive ground water and does not discharge to the model stream channel	none
AGWRC	Active ground water recession rate	(1/interval)
KVARY	Ground water recession flow parameter. Describes nonlinear ground water recession rate	(1/mm)
AGWETP	Active ground water evapotransporation. Represents the fraction of stored ground water that is subject to direct evaporation and transpiration by plans whose roots extend below the active ground water table	none
IRC	Interflow retention coefficient. Rate at which interflow is discharged from the upper-zone storage	1 per day

contaminated sediment [11] and pesticides [12], and (3) land use management and flood control scenarios [13].

HSPF is usually classified as a Lumped model[1] and it can reproduce spatial variability by dividing the basin in hydrologically homogeneous land segments and simulating runoff for each land segment independently, using different meteorologic input data and watershed parameters.

In HSPF, the various hydrologic processes are represented mathematically as flows and storages. In general, each flow is an outflow from a storage, usually expressed as a function of the current storage amount and the physical characteristics of the subsystem. Thus the overall model is physically based. Although

---

[1] A model in which the physical characteristics of the catchment are assumed to be homogeneous.

this requires the use of calibrated parameters, it has the advantage of avoiding the need of giving the physical dimensions and characteristics of the flow system.

The key steps in modelling a watershed with HSPF are the mathematical representation of the watershed, the preparation of input meteorological and hydrological time series and the estimation of parameters in calibration. For HSPF model calibration proposes, we must have a set of historical data inputs and their respective output values. Once the model is calibrated, we are able to use it with predicted meteorological values as inputs in order to generate hydrological predictions.

HSPF requires eight meteorological time series to simulate the hydrological cycle in a watershed. These are air temperature, dew-point temperature, cloudiness, wind velocity, atmospheric pressure, solar radiation and precipitation, and this is considered as the model inputs. The parameters that governs the streamflow simulation in HSPF are categorized as fixed and adjusted parameters. Fixed parameters can be measured or are well documented in the literature, such as the length, slope, width, depth and roughness of a watershed. Fixed parameters are held constant in HSPF during model calibration. On the other hand, adjusted parameters are highly variable in the environment or are immeasurable [6], such as the infiltration rate ($INFILT$). A model calibration process lies in searching these adjusted parameters in order to estimate the measured flow of a watershed from the meteorological values and the present state of the watershed. Table 1 shows the 20 adjusted parameters used in the calibration stage.

3 Model Calibration Using Evolutionary Computation

In this section, we show the evolutionary technique used for HSPF model calibration of a specific Spanish watershed. The aim of the calibration stage is to find the best parameters values for the physical area. The model was calibrated using meteorological inputs and their respective measured flow over 33 years period. The data set was divided in two subsets. First, we used 21 years (from 01/02/1968 to 12/31/1989) as calibration set, and the remainder (from 02/01/1990 to 12/31/2000) as validation set. The simulated flow results for the 21 year period were compared with the observed daily discharge records during the simulation period.

Since we have used a huge data set for calibrating (a daily data set of 21 years), the computational cost of evaluating an individual is very high. Therefore, we have implemented a steady-state evolutionary algorithm. The steady-state evolutionary algorithm uses overlapping populations. In each generation, a portion of the population is replaced by the newly generated individuals. We only replace one individual in each generation (close to 100% overlap). Since the algorithm only replaces one individual in each generation, the best individuals are more likely to be selected and the population quickly converges. As a result, the steady-state algorithm often converges prematurely to a sub-optimal solution. The crossover and mutation operators are the key to the algorithm performance. A crossover operator that generates children unlike their parents

Table 2. Parameters Values

Parameter	Manual value	Optimized Value	Value Range
RDCSN	0.15	0.166751	(0.1 , 0.2)
COVIND	47.0	45.05150	(20.0 , 55.0)
SNOEVP	0.20	0.230342	(0.1 , 0.3)
CCFACT	4.0	3.797310	(3.0 , 5.0)
MELEV	800	1127.930	(500 , 1300)
SHADE	0.05	0.064753	(0.01 , 0.1)
MWATER	0.015	0.066278	(0.001 , 0.1)
CEPSC	2.6	2.847270	(2.0 , 3.2)
INFITL	23.0	23.17990	(18.0 , 28.0)
INFILD	2.3	2.583510	(1.8 , 2.8)
INFEXP	2.5	3.135000	(1.5 , 3.5)
INTFW	3.9	3.380480	(2.0 , 4.0)
UZSN	19.0	19.32750	(15.0 , 23.0)
LZSN	70.0	65.14050	(60.0 , 80.0)
LZETP	0.25	0.390257	(0.01 , 0.5)
DEEPFR	0.01	0.005994	(0.0001 , 0.02)
AGWRC	0.975	0.989731	(0.96 , 0.99)
KVARY	1.5	0.019585	(0.01 , 2.99)
AGWETP	0.1	0.066748	(0.0001 , 0.2)
IRC	0.80	0.8711780	(0.60 , 0.90)

and/or a high mutation rate can delay the convergence. Each individual are encoded as an array of 20 elements of double data type. Each element represents the parameter value of Table 1 and all of them represents one possible solution to the calibration problem. The range values for these parameters are shown in the fourth column of the Table 2. The crossover operator is implemented by use of one point sexual (two parents) crossover operator. The new individual has the first 10 values of the father and the last 10 values of the mother. The mutation was performed based on the mutation rate. For each parameter if a random number between 0 and 1 is greater than the mutation rate the parameter change and its obtained a new parameter. The selection operator chosen was a fitness proportionate selection, also known as roulette wheel selection. Candidate solutions with higher fitness has more probability of selection.

The fitness function is the result of calling the HSPF simulator over 21 years (calibration period) and evaluate

$$F(x) = \frac{K - \sum_{i=1}^{n}(Q_{obs,i} - Q_{sim,i})^2}{K} \quad (1)$$

where $Q_{obs,i}$ is the observed streamflow at day i and $Q_{sim,i}$ is the model simulated streamflow at day i with the specific parameters and the meteorological input values for that day, and K is a constant for scaling propose. In our case, we have used the value of $K = \sum_{i=1}^{n}(2Q_{obs,i})^2$.

4 Experimentation and Results

As we have mentioned above, we use two data sets: calibration set and validation set. First, it is used for model calibration purpose and comprises 7665 samples (21 years). In order to validate the calibrated model, we use the second data set, which 4015 samples (11 years) are not involved in the calibration process.

Table 3. Evolutionary Algorithm Experiments (2000 generations)

Population Size	Mutation Rate	Best Fitness	Worst Fitness	Average Fitness
10	10%	0.985348	0.909932	0.965289
10	20%	0.992765	0.895047	0.969007
10	30%	0.994031	0.900430	0.967297
20	10%	0.986759	0.369053	0.928430
20	20%	0.987637	0.767560	0.955034
20	30%	0.986759	0.369053	0.928430
30	10%	0.986865	0.909145	0.948826
30	20%	0.991004	0.846900	0.960567
30	30%	0.986865	0.909145	0.948826

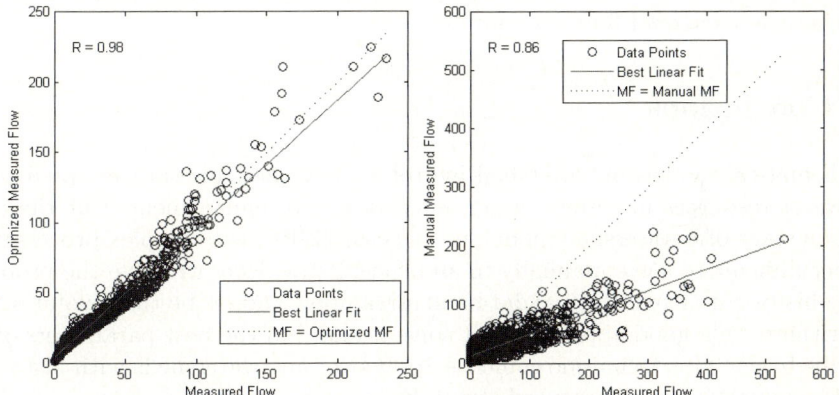

Fig. 1. Correlation coefficient for the estimation of the Watershed Measured Flow using (a) the evolutionary algorithm and (b) the manual process

We have run several experiments using different parameters of the evolutionary algorithm. In Table 3, we present the results obtained with different values for the *Population Size* and *Mutation Rate* parameters. The Table 3 also exhibits, for each experiment, the *Best*, *Worst* and *Average* fitness of the population. We can see as the individual with best fitness is obtained using *Population Size* of 10 individuals and *Mutation Rate* of 30%. The optimized values of this individual for the HSPF model parameters are shown in the third column of the Table 2.

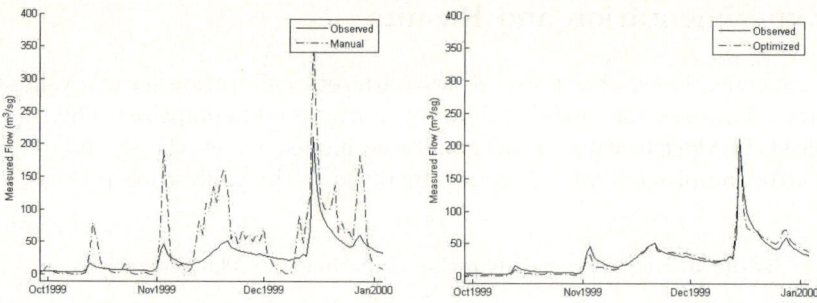

Fig. 2. Observed, optimized and manual measured flow

In order to show the improvement of this evolutionary technique, we have compared the calibrated HSPF model using these optimized parameters with another calibrated manually using the validation data set. The *try and error* is the most usual technique for searching manually these parameters. The HSPF calibrated model using the evolutionary algorithm provided a good fit ($r^2 = 0.98$) (Figure 1a) concerning the HSPF model manually calibrated ($r^2 = 0.86$) (Figure 1b). In Figure 2 we display the *Observed*, *Optimized* and *Manual Measured Flow* for the first two months of the year 1996. Notice how the optimized model fits the true measured flow successfully.

5 Conclusions

Mathematical models of watershed hydrology have now become accepted tools for water resources planning, design operation and management. But the calibration stage of a watershed model, in this case HSPF, is a complex process that is very difficult to solve manually in an efficient way. Here we solve the problem using historical meteorological data and streamflow and probe that evolutionary algorithms are a good approach that solve it and find the best parameters of an specific basin. This technique could be apply over any watersheds with historical meteorologic data and measured streamflows information.

Acknowledgements. We would like to thank Meteologica S.A. for providing us the rainfall and streamflow measured data.

References

1. Singh VP, Woolhiser D A. Mathematical modeling of watershed hydrology. Journal of Hydrologic Engineering,2002,7(4):270-292.
2. Singh VP. Environmental Hydrology. Borton, MA. Kluwer Academic. 1995.
3. http://water.usgs.gov/software/hspf.html
4. http://www.epa.gov/

5. Bricknell, B.R., Imhoff, J.C., Kittle, J.L. Jr., Donigian, A.S., Johanson, R.C., 1997. Hydrological Simulation Program - Fortran. User's Manual for Realese 11. EPA-600/R-97-080, USEPA, Athens, GA, 755 p.
6. Jacomino, V.M.F., Fields, D.E., 1997. A critical approach to the calibration of a watershed model. J. Am. Water Resour. Assoc. 33, 143-154.
7. Liong, S.Y., Van Nguyen, V.T., Gautam, T.R. and Wee, L. Alternative well calibrated rainfall-runoff model: genetic programming scheme. Paper presented at World Water and Environmental Resources Congress 2001 (papers on CD-ROM), 20-24 May 2001, Orlando, Florida, USA, 2001.
8. Crawford, H.H., Linsley, R.K., 1966. Digital Simulation in Hydrology: Stanford Watershed Model IV. Technical Report No. 39, Dept. of Civil Eng., Stanford University, Stanford, CA.
9. Srinivasan, M.S., Hamlett, J.M., Day, R.L., Sams, J.I., Peterson, G.W., 1998. Hydrologic modeling of two glaciated watersheds in northeast Pennsylvania. J. Am. Water Resour. Assoc. 34, 963-978.
10. Zarriello, P.J., Ries, K.G., III, 2000. A Precipitation-Runoff Model for Analysis of the Effects of Water Withdrawals on Streamflow, Ipswich River Basin, Massachusetts. USGS Water Resources Investigations Report 00-4029, 99 p.
11. Fontaine, T.A., Jacomino, V.M.F., 1997. Sensitivity analysis of simulated contaminated sediment transport. J. Am. Water Resour. Assoc. 33, 313-326.
12. Laroche, A.M., Gallichand, J., Lagace, R., Pesant, A., 1996. Simulating atrazine transport with HSPF in a agricultural watershed. ASCE J. Environ. Wngng. 122, 622-630.
13. Donigian, A.S.Jr., Chinnaswamy, R.V., Jobes, T.H., 1997. Conceptual Design of Multipurpose Detention Facilities for flood protection and Nonpoint Source Pollution Control, Aqua Terra Consultants, Mountain View, CA, 151 p.
14. Goldberg, D.E. Genetic algorithm in search, optimization, and machine learning. Addison-Wesley, Reading, Masss.,1989.
15. Wang, Q. J., 1991. The Genetic Algorithm and its Application to Calibrating Conceptual Rainfall-Runoff Models, Water Resour. Res., 27(9), 2467-2471.
16. http://water.usgs.gov/software/hspexp.html
17. Douglas, L. Moyer and Kenneth E. Hyer. Use of Hydrological Simulation Program - Fortran and Bacterial Source Tracking for Development of the Fecal Coliform Total Maximum Daily Load (TMDL) for Blacks Run, Rockingham Country, Virginia. U.S. Geological Survey. Water Resources Investigations Report 03-4161. 2003.
18. http://www.sspa.com/pest/pesthspf.html
19. Donigian, A.S.Jr., Imhoff, J.C., Kittle, J.L., Jr., 1999. HSPFParm - An interactive database of HSPF model parameters, Version 1.0. EPA-823-R-99-004, USEPA, Washington, DC, 40 p.
20. Kamali, M., Ponnambalam, K., Soulis, E.D. 2005. Hydrologic model Calibration using Fuzzy TSK surrogate model. NAFIPS 2005. Annual Meeting of the North American Fuzzy Inf. Proc. Soc.

Genetic Algorithms and Sensitivity Analysis Applied to Select Inputs of a Multi-Layer Perceptron for the Prediction of Air Pollutant Time-Series

Harri Niska, Mikko Heikkinen, and Mikko Kolehmainen

Department of Environmental Sciences, University of Kuopio, PO Box 1627, FIN-70211
Kuopio, Finland
{Harri.Niska, Mikko.Heikkinen, Mikko Kolehmainen}@uku.fi

Abstract. The aim of this paper was to evaluate genetic algorithms (GA) and sensitivity analysis (SA) for selecting inputs of a multi-layer perceptron model (MLP) applied to forecast time-series of urban air pollutant. The main objective was to compare usability and efficiency of the methods. The results in general showed that the methods based on the SA and GA can be used efficiently to select relevant variables and thus, to enhance the performance of MLP.

Keywords: Genetic algorithms, Multi-layer perceptron, Sensitivity analysis, Input selection, Time-series forecasting.

1 Introduction

The modeling of real-world processes such as urban air pollution using a multi-layer perceptron (MLP) model is challenging due to the limitations of MLP [1], [2]. The selection of an optimal model inputs (features) is one of the main topics because irrelevant or noisy variables disturb the training process leading to complex model structure and poor generalization power. In real-word problems a high number of measurements are usually available and thus, the selection of an optimal input subset should be considered.

A wide variety of different input selection algorithms have been developed. The selection schemes are based either on the filter or the wrapper approach [3]. In the filter approach, the selection is based on data only as in the wrapper approach the selection is made using the model itself. Both the schemes have their own pros and cons. However, in most cases, the wrapper approach seems to lead better performance but heavy computation efforts are required because the model is involved into calculations.

The MLP models have been successfully applied in the field of air quality forecasting [2], [4]. For a more detailed description of MLP in air quality modelling, the reader is referred to the article written by Gardner and Dorling [2]. However, the selection of optimal inputs has been challenging task due to the excessively large number of potential meteorological input variables and complex interactions between them. Part of these variables may have negligible effect or be totally irrelevant, and should be removed from the modelling.

The aim of this study was to evaluate input selection techniques based on genetic algorithms and sensitivity analysis to enhance a MLP model for the forecasting of urban air pollution time-series. The paper is organised as follows. First technical outlines of input selection methods are presented, that is followed by the presentation of experiments made to evaluate methods. Finally, the numerical results of experiments are presented and discussed.

2 Methods for Selecting Inputs

2.1 Sensitivity of Inputs

Irrelevant, noisy or correlated input variables may disturb the training of MLP leading to poor generalisation on "unseen" data. Correlation analysis could be used to eliminate the features having strong dependency. For large number of inputs there are $O(N^2)$ pairs of features to correlate and thus, the use of methods based on the correlation is difficult. Another way is to retrain MLP with various subsets of inputs to determine the best input subset. However, due to exhaustive enumeration such approach is not practical for large number of inputs [5].

Therefore, the examination of sensitivity of inputs is potential way to go about the input selection problem. A method due to Belue and Bauer [6] uses the MLP itself in the selection of relevant features. In this scheme, the MLP with one hidden layer is first trained over the full set of inputs and the training is used to determine the relevance of the inputs. Final inputs are determined by eliminating the input features having low relevancy. A simple relevancy metric is based on the squared sum of weights between input node and hidden neurons [5].

The approach utilised, denoted here as SA, was based on the study proposed by Moody and Utans [7] where the selection of inputs is based on the sensitivity of MLP model trained with all the input variables. The sensitivity of an input is estimated by replacing input variable in test set by its average computed on the training set (should be variance scaled) and calculating the effect of elimination on the output of the MLP. To measure the accuracy of MLP we have used the index of agreement [8] calculated as follows:

$$d = 1 - \left[\frac{\sum_{i=1}^{N}(P_i - O_i)^2}{\sum_{i=1}^{N}\left(|P_i - \overline{O}| + |O_i - \overline{O}|\right)^2} \right] \quad (1)$$

where N is the number of observations, O_i is the observed data point, P_i is the predicted data point and $\overline{O}$.

The sensitivity of inputs was then defined here according to the absolute change of performance as follows:

$$S = |d(\overline{x}) - d| \quad (2)$$

where $d(\overline{x})$ is the index of agreement achieved when replacing unselected input variable by its means and d is the index of agreement achieved using all input variables.

2.2 Genetic Algorithms

Genetic algorithms [9] are stochastic search strategies developed as the inspiration of biologic evolution. They have been successfully used to solve different optimization problems in wide range of application areas. The advantage of GAs is that they are capable of searching complex search spaces with multiple local minima that cannot be yielded using the conventional optimization algorithms. However, a major drawback of GAs is related to computational burden which is due to the stochastic search strategy. Therefore, a particular attention should be laid on an objective function to minimise computational burden.

GAs are especially well suited to the selection of input features as the problem can be represented directly as a bit string where 1-bit corresponds to presence and 0-bit corresponds to absence. In this study, the implementation of GA was based on the toolbox of genetic and evolutionary algorithms (GEATbx). The selection of structure and control parameters of GA was made experimentally. One population having 30 individuals was evolved for 150 generations with the elitist selection scheme (20% of the best individuals were maintained).

2.3 Multi-Objective GAs

Relatively new approach is to pose input selection as the multi-objective optimisation problem where two optimisation criteria are minimised, namely, (1) the number of inputs and (2) the modelling error. Such approach has many appealing features compared to the pure GA, such as the guidance of the search towards interesting areas of search space and small number of potential inputs.

In recent years, multi-objective GAs (MOGAs) has been applied in this domain. The combination of MOGA and SA has showed to be successful in the field of pattern recognition [10]. In this study, the implementation of MOGA was based on the functions of GEATbx which follows mainly Fonsecas and Flemmings work [12] and utilises the well-known Pareto-ranking technique. The selection of appropriate recombination operator has been found necessary to ensure efficient search and maintain diversity over Pareto-front. We have utilised subset size-oriented common features (SSOCF) recombination [11] which has been found to be appropriate in this domain. The rest of search parameters were similar to ones used in the GA.

3 Experimental Study

3.1 Air Quality Forecasting Using MLP

The forecasting of urban air pollutant concentrations is largely based on the modelling of complex relationships between meteorological and air pollutant variables. Moreover, timing data has an important role because the major source of air pollution is usually traffic and the activity of traffic varies over time. In operational situation, the use of numerical weather prediction (NWP) data enhances the performance of forecasting [13] because it describes the meteorological condition of time which forecast applies.

In our experiments, we have focused on the forecasting of hourly concentration of NO_2 which is one of the most significant urban airborne pollutants. In the calculations, we have utilised both the meteorological and the NWPs of the HIRLAM [4] as the input of the MLP model [13], 14]. The NWPs are applied from time which forecast applies. The use of the NWP data increases the number of potential number of inputs drastically because the variables are utilised from several model surfaces. In addition to the NWP, air pollutant data is utilised to describe the air pollution situation of the previous day. Overall picture of the input variables and their time-lags is presented in Table 1.

Table 1. The list of input variables (N=92) used in the MLP model for the forecasting (T+24) of NO_2 cocentrations. The input time T+24 is the time (next +24 hours), for which the forecast applies; N is the number of variables.

Input variable(s)	Unit(s)	Time Lags	N
Temporal variables			
Sine and cosine of year, week day and hour	–	T + 24	2x3
Weekend	–	T + 24	1
Concentration variables			
NO_x, NO_2, O_3, PM_{10} and $PM_{2.5}$	µg/m^3	T	5
Meteorological variables			
Pressure, temperature and humidity	Pa, K, %	T	3
State of ground and albedo	–	T	2
Cloudiness	(0-8)/8	T	1
Dewpoint, wetbulb and temp. scale	K	T	3
Rain	mm	T	1
Height of low clouds	m	T	1
Sine and cosine of direction of flow	–	T	2
Wind speed	m/s	T	1
Sunshine duration and solar elevation	h, rad	T	2
Solar and net radiations	W/m2	T	2
Moisture parameter	–	T	1
Monin-Obukhov length	m	T	1
Friction and convective velocities	m/s	T	2
Turb. and latent heat flux	W/m2	T	2
Mixing height	m	T	1
Gradient of potential temperature	K/m	T	1
HIRLAM forecasts for the model surface levels from 26 to 31			
U- and V-components of wind	m/s	T + 24	6x2
Kinetic energy of turbulence	J/kg	T + 24	6x1
Temperature	K	T + 24	6x1
Specific humidity and cloud condensate	kg/kg	T + 24	6x2
Total cloud cover	%	T + 24	6x1
Pressure and temperature at 2m	Pa, K	T + 24	6x2

The implementation of the MLP was based on the functions of Matlab Neural Network Toolbox. The MLP model was back-propagation (BP) trained using early-stopping criteria. One fully connected hidden layer was utilised with the number of neurons determined as follows sqrt(p)*2 where p is the the number of inputs and sqrt is the square root. Non-linear tangent sigmoid functions were used for hidden units and linear transfer function was used for output.

3.2 Evaluation Scheme

The selection of inputs was performed using the methods based on the sensitivity analysis of inputs and the genetic algorithms, namely the SA, the SA+GA, SA+MOGA, the GA and the MOGA. The correlation based selection scheme, denoted as CORR, was utilised for benchmarking the methods. In the CORR, the inputs having averagely greater linear correlation with output were selected. Moreover, the random selection of variables (N=20) was employed to reflect the importance of input selection.

The GA and MOGA were based on the actual training of MLP where the fitness of input set was estimated as the average index of agreement of three 10% random samples of training data sets. In the case of the SA, the selection of relevant was performed according to the average sensitivity S_x. All the inputs having sensitivity greater than S_x were selected to the final set of inputs (Fig. 1). In the case of the SA+GA and the SA+MOGA the input sets having minimum sensitivities were selected.

The data used for evaluating the MLP models contained overall 24215 measurement rows gathered during the period 1 May 2000 to 30 April 2003 in Helsinki; for more detailed information of data, the reader is referred to Niska et al. [13]. The training and testing of the MLP (during the input selection) was performed using the data from the period 1 May 2000 to 30 April 2002; 30% random sample was used to test MLP for input sets. The rest of data (the last year cycle) was used to perform final evaluation of the models.

The final evaluation of input selection methods was based on the statistical analysis of the prediction accuracies of the MLP obtained with selected input subsets. The runs were repeated several times (10 times) to achieve error marginals of statistical measures. Three statistical indices were calculated, namely, the index of agreement (Eq. 1), the root mean square error (RMSE) and the coefficient of determination (R^2).

4 Numerical Results and Discussion

The numerical performance indices of the evaluation are presented in Table 2. The results showed that sensitivity analysis of inputs is efficient and appropriate for the selection of MLP input variables. The performances obtained with SA, SA+GA and SA+MOGA varied within the same range. Slightly better average performances were obtained with MOGA, in terms of index of agreement, which applies the actual training of MLP instead of the sensitivity analysis. However, the approaches based on the actual training of MLP are computationally very demanding and thus, the use of them is not usually practical. The results obtained with the CORR showed that moderately good results can be achieved simply by applying correlation analysis to decide input variables.

Table 2. Statistical evaluation of MLP models trained with selected input sets where N is the number of inputs

Method	Model performance for selected inputs			N
	d	RMSE	R2	
No selection	0.77 ± 0.02	15.19 ± 0.53	0.41 ± 0.03	92
SA	0.81 ± 0.01	13.25 ± 0.33*	0.49 ± 0.02*	19 ± 3
SA+GA	0.82 ± 0.01	13.27 ± 0.27	0.49 ± 0.01*	48 ± 3
SA+MOGA	0.81 ± 0.01	13.29 ± 0.26	0.48 ± 0.02	18 ± 5
GA	0.82 ± 0.01	13.43 ± 0.35	0.48 ± 0.02	43 ± 2
MOGA	0.83 ± 0.02*	13.40 ± 0.67	0.48 ± 0.04	36 ± 10
CORR	0.80 ± 0.00	13.67 ± 0.21	0.46 ± 0.01	28
RAND	0.73 ± 0.03	14.76 ± 0.51	0.36 ± 0.03	20

*The best value

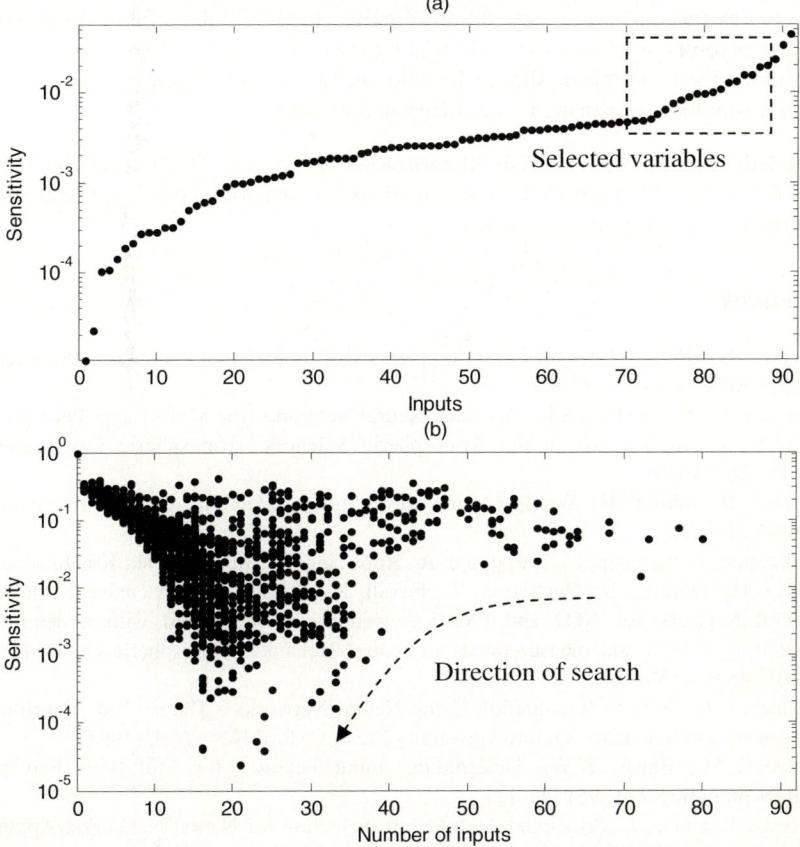

Fig. 1. The basic outlines of (a) the sensitivity analysis and (b) the multi-objective genetic algorithm (MOGA)

When comparing the GA and the MOGA it can be seen that the major advantage of MOGA is that it is capable of investigating more potential (less inputs) regions of search space. Moreover, the MOGA produces several optimal input sets, i.e., Pareto optimal sets to be selected by user. On the whole, it seems that there are multiple "optimal" input sets having different number of inputs which are capable of yielding the good model accuracy. The optimal number of input variables varies between ~20 and 50. If larger number of variables (>~50) are utilised the prediction accuracy of MLP model seems to be decreased. It could be concluded that the selection of inputs enhances the generalisation ability of the MLP (d: 0.77<0.83) by eliminating irrelevant variables and decreasing the model complexity.

5 Summary

In this study, the GAs and the SA were evaluated for selecting inputs of MLP model applied in the air pollution modelling. The numerical results in general showed that the SA is sufficient technique to identify significant input variables of MLP. Moreover, it was seen that the combination of SA and GA or MOGA did not improved the performances any more. Finally, it should be emphasised that the evaluation of input selection methods was based here on the one-year validation set. In the future more attention should be laid on the model validation itself, and the evaluation should be performed with different data sets

Acknowledgements. The Finnish Meteorological Institute (FMI) and the Helsinki Metropolitan Area Council (YTV) are thanked for providing the numerical weather prediction and the air quality data sets.

References

1. Haykin, S.: Neural Networks: A Comprehensive Foundation. 2nd edn. Prentice Hall, Upper Saddle River NJ (1999)
2. Gardner, M.W., Dorling, S.R.: Artificial Neural Networks (the Multi-Layer Perceptron) - a Review of Applications in the Atmospheric Sciences. Atmospheric Environment 32 (1999) 2627-2636
3. Kohavi, R., John, G.H.: Wrappers for Feature Subset Selection. Artificial Intelligence 97 (1997) 273-324
4. Kukkonen, J., Partanen, L., Karppinen, A., Ruuskanen, J., Junninen, H., Kolehmainen, M., Niska, H., Dorling, S., Chatterton, T., Foxall, R., Cawley, G.: Extensive Evaluation of Neural Networks of NO2 and PM10 concentrations, compared with a deterministic modelling system and measurements in central Helsinki. Atmospheric Environment 37 (2003) 4539-4550
5. Looney, C.G.: Pattern Recognition Using Neural Networks - Theory and Algorithms for Engineers and Scientists. Oxford University Press, Oxford New York (1997)
6. Belue, L.M., Bauer, K.W.: Determining Input Features for Multilayer Perceptrons. Neurocomputing 7 (1995) 111-121
7. Moody, J., Utans, J.: Principled Architecture Selection for Neural Networks: Application to Corporate Bond Rating Predictions. In: Moody, J., Hanson, S.J., Lippmann, R.P. (eds.): Proceedings of Advances in Neural Information Processing Systems. Morgan Kaufmann, San Mateo CA (1991) 683-690

8. Wilmott, C.J.: On the Validation of Models. Physical Geography 2 (1981) 184-194
9. Goldberg, D.E.: Genetic Algorithms in Search, Optimization and Machine Learning. Addison-Wesley, Reading Massachusetts (1989).
10. Oliveira L.S., Sabourin R., Bortolozzi F., and Suen C.Y.: A Methodology for Feature Selection Using Multi-Objective Genetic Algorithms for Handwritten Digit String Recognition. International Journal of Pattern Recognition and Artificial Intelligence 17 (2003) 903-930
11. Emmanouilidis, C., Hunter, A., MacIntyre, J.: A Multiobjective Evolutionary Setting for Feature Selection and a Commonality-Based Crossover Operator. In: Congress on Evolutionary Computation. IEEE, New Jersey (2000) 309-316
12. Fonseca, C. M., Fleming, P. J.: Genetic Algorithms for Multi-Objective Optimization: Formulation, Discussion and Generalization. In: Forrest, S. (eds.): 5th International Conference on Genetic Algorithms. Morgan Kauffman, California (1993) 416-423
13. Niska, H., Rantamäki, M., Hiltunen, T., Karppinen, A., Kukkonen, J., Ruuskanen, J., Kolehmainen, M.: Evaluation of the Integrated Modelling System Containing a Multi-Layer Perceptron Model and the Numerical Weahter Prediction Model HIRLAM for the Forecasting of Urban Airborne Pollutant Concentrations. Atmospheric Environment 39 (2005) 6524-6536
14. Eerola, K.: The Operational HIRLAM at the Finnish Meteorological Institute. HIRLAM Newsletter 41 (2002) 19-24

Genetic Algorithms for Estimating Longest Path from Inherently Fuzzy Data Acquired with GPS

José Villar, Adolfo Otero, José Otero, and Luciano Sánchez*

Computer Science Department, Universidad de Oviedo, Edificio Departamental 1,
Campus de Viesques s/n Gijon (Spain)
otero@uniovi.es, jotero@uniovi.es, luciano@uniovi.es,
villarjose@uniovi.es

Abstract. Measuring the length of a path that a taxi must fare is an obvious task: when driving lower than certain speed threshold the fare is time dependent, but at higher speeds the length of the path is measured, and the fare depends on such measure. When passing an indoor MOT test, the taximeter is calibrated simulating a cab run, while the taxi is placed on a device equipped with four rotating steel cylinders in touch with the drive wheels. This indoor measure might be inaccurate, as the information given by the cylinders is affected by tires inflating pressure, and only straight trajectories are tested. Moreover, modern vehicles with driving aids such as ABS, ESP or TCS might have their electronics damaged in the test, since two wheels are spinning while the others are not. To surpass these problems, we have designed a small, portable GPS sensor that periodically logs the coordinates of the vehicle and computes the length of a discretionary circuit. We will show that all the legal issues with the tolerance of such a procedure (GPS data are inherently imprecise) can be overcome if genetic and fuzzy techniques are used to process and analyze the raw data.

1 Introduction

One of the tasks to be performed in the Spanish VTSS is the test and control of the taximeters in the taxicabs. This supervision must be performed every year because the taxicabs' fares are revised and published by the authorities every year. The process a taxicab owner must follow includes driving the taxicab to a specialized garage to change the fares in the taximeter. When the fares are changed, a MOT test must be done. In this MOT test, the tester engineer verifies if both the distance traveled and the waiting time fares lie between the limits imposed.

The verification of the fares can be done in two ways. The simplest way consists in doing a cab run in a previously measured circuit, manually computing the fare. More over, one person from the MOT agency must do it. One second approach is to use a machine capable of the recovering of the speed of the cab to select

---

* This work was funded by Spanish M. of Education, under the grant TIN2005-08386-C05.

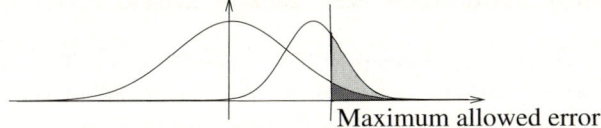

Fig. 1. If the owners of the taxis calibrated their taximeters in good faith, the density of the errors in the measures of taximeters should be centered in 0. Field measures show that the density is centered near 9% (the legal cut point is 10%). A small deviation in the tolerance of our measure, which would be unnoticed under theoretical circumstances (dark gray area,) will cause a high percentage of rejections (light gray area).

the waiting fare or the traveled fare and to compute the time elapsed and the distance. Currently, such device is used, but fails when active safety systems nowadays present in cars trigger, moreover these systems may be damaged.

In this situation, a new method of testing taximeters must be developed. This system should be designed taking into account that it is not desirable to block one MOT test engineer when testing a taximeter. We have decided to use GPS technology to track the position of a vehicle in an actual road, and process this information on-line [13]. Moreover, the taxi driver can be sent alone to cover a distance, and no personal of MOT agency is needed, making the process cheaper.

There are some drawbacks, though. GPS generates imprecise data, and the degree of imprecision of every sample is different. The differences in tolerances must be taken into account in the algorithm that analyzes the data. The significance of this step is crucial for our system to compute the upper bound of the length of the trajectory, which must be provided in the case that a taximeter is rejected. The legal margin of error of a taximeter in Spain is 10%. We can not reject a taxi with a deviation of 7% if we can not warrant a tolerance lower than 3%, say. This could seem a minor problem, and it would be, if the density of the errors in the taxis resembled the left Gaussian in Fig. 1. Unfortunately, our study revealed that the calibration of taximeters is far from unbiased. Small changes in the tolerance produce important changes in the number of rejections. Therefore, it is needed a procedure to determine the bounds of the measure with high accuracy and it is also needed that all the tolerance errors benefit the owner of the taxi. In other words, we need to compute the lowest upper bound (LUB) of the trajectories compatible with the (imprecise) GPS measures.

In this paper we will explain a new method for estimating the LUB of the trajectory from imprecise data. Through multiobjective genetic algorithms, the measures are filtered to obtain the smallest set of samples that define a multi polygonal covering the input data. The LUB of the path is found by means of a deterministic algorithm that processes this multi polygonal.

The structure of this work follows: In next section, how GPS measures are obtained is detailed. Then, a description of the proposal is done in Sect. 3. The genetic algorithms are detailed in Sect. 3.1, while the deterministic algorithm for estimating the maximum length is detailed in Sect. 3.2. In Sect. 4 experiment and results are shown. Finally, conclusions and future work are presented.

2 GPS-Based Measures Are Fuzzy Data

The term Global Positioning System (GPS) refers to a set of devices (satellites and receiver) working together to get a fix (the position) of the receiver. The receiver can get some signals from the satellites and compute a set of measures: longitude, latitude, altitude, number of satellites in use, time, etc. Each signal received from a satellite contains information about the time that the signal lasts from the satellite to the receiver.

The higher the number of satellites, the better the accuracy. But even with a high number of satellites in use (12 to 16) the geometry or constellation of the satellites must be taken into account to estimate the fix accuracy. This is done using DOP (Dilution of Precision), a measure of the probability of the effects of the constellation on the fix accuracy; a higher value of DOP indicates a weaker geometry of satellites. In the case of GPS longitude and latitude accuracy, the HDOP (latitude and longitude DOP) value must be taken into account. Related with HDOP is the CEP (Circular Error Probable), a given value of CEP at probability P means that the receiver is inside a circle of radius CEP, centered at the measured fix with that probability. When using consumer-grade receivers, it is very common to obtain accuracies like 3 meter CEP (50%) and 7 meters (90%). Given the number of satellites n used for the measure and an accuracy probability P, the CEP is computed by means of equation Eq. 1. Constants A, B, C and D are device dependant [16] .

$$CEP = \left(-((A \cdot (\frac{C}{n^2} + D))^2 + B^2) \cdot \ln(1 - P(Err \leq CEP|HDOP)\right)^{0.5} \quad (1)$$

2.1 Fuzzy Interpretation of GPS-Values

Under the imprecise probabilities framework, it makes sense to understand a fuzzy set as a set of tolerances, each one of them is assigned a confidence degree, being the lower degree the narrower tolerance [9]. In particular, it has stated that, given an incomplete set of confidence intervals for a random variable, we can build a fuzzy random variable, whose α-cuts are confidence intervals with degree $1 - \alpha$, that contains all the information we know about the unknown random variable [4]. In our case, the GPS sensor provides two confidence intervals at 50% and 90% (the mentioned circle of radius CEP,) and therefore the fuzzy representation of GPS coordinates is immediate.

3 Determining the Length of Trajectories Using Fuzzy Data

GPS data is recorded at regular time intervals. Each sample is a fuzzy set, as mentioned, whose α-cuts are circles. In turn, every circle is a confidence interval for the coordinates of the taxicab at that moment. It is remarked that taking the centers of these circles is not a valid estimation. We need to compute the

LUB of the paths whose extremes are contained in the circles, and this length will always be higher than the value obtained from the centers.

The answer to the problem is not easy, though. If we try to compute the maximum length of all compatible piecewise linear paths that are contained in the circles it is obvious that, the shorter the sampling period, the longer the estimation. This is not correct, and we wish the estimation of the length not to be too influenced by the sampling period [12]. We have decided to process the fuzzy data and remove all redundant information with the help of a genetic algorithm, as we will show in the section that follows.

When using crisp data, the geometric problem of simplifying polygonal lines has been studied in [7]. The most similar approach to ours, up to our best knowledge, uses fuzzy data from a geographical database for reconstruction of 3D images by means of B-splines[1], where a fuzzy point is said to be covered by the fuzzy B-spline if the fuzzy set induced by the latter completely contains the former, we use this concept next.

3.1 Multiobjective Fuzzy Fitness Genetic Algorithm for Filtering the Fuzzy Input Data

The fuzzy GPS measures are filtered using a multiobjective genetic algorithm. The output is the minimum set of fuzzy input data that defines a fuzzy trajectory covering as many points as possible. Using those fuzzy points, and for each α-cut, a distance value is computed by means of a deterministic algorithm, which will be detailed later.

Every candidate solution is evaluated as follows: we first build a polygonal chain for each α-cut of the selected data, using the tangent surfaces to the selected fuzzy data set [1]. We wish that this chain contain as many data as possible, while having the minimum area.

Both objectives are fuzzy numbers and define a multicriteria problem [3], and two different approaches had been used for solving the problem. The first one is using the NSGA-II algorithm [5,6]. The second approach is using the multi-objective genetic operators simulated annealing (MOSA) [14]. Further details of those algorithms follow.

Coding of Individuals. Each individual is a boolean vector, marking the corresponding fuzzy input data to be or not part of the hypothesis: those marked with true are used to define the polygonal chain. To generate an individual, a probability value p is given, and for each fuzzy point in the vector of input fuzzy data, it is included in the hypothesis with probability less of equal than p. The origin and the end of the ride must be always included.

Genetic Operators. The definitions of crossover and mutation must reduce the number of vertexes in the population, and therefore they are unbiased.

---

[1] This chain might include some extra points not covered by the input data, but this fact always would benefit the taxi, thus it is legally correct.

Given two parents A and B, the offspring are two new chains C and D such that a $A \cap B \subseteq C$ and $A \cap B \subset D$; a vertex $v \in A - B$ has a probability p^+ of being in C, and a vertex in $B - A$ has a probability p^- of being in C, where p^- is much lower that p^+. The chain D is built the same way. Mutation is defined as the random removing of a point of the chain, different from the first or last one. The operation named *toggle* is very similar to mutation, but it can alter the state of inclusion in the hypothesis of a randomly selected fuzzy data. Toggle is used as genetic operation for MOSA. When generating a neighborhood of current individual a random number of toggle operations are done. The number of operations is temperature dependent, and so the neighborhood of new individual, as well.

Multiobjective Fuzzy Fitness. As stated before, two criteria are to be reached: the minimization of polygonal chain area and the maximization of the percentage of data covered. Both of them are fuzzy numbers. This means that it is needed an operator *less than* and an operator *less or equal than*, both defined for fuzzy numbers, so dominance could be evaluated. Some work has been done in evaluating Pareto dominance with fuzzy fitness. In [17] the Pareto dominance concept is extended to fuzzy dominance, and different levels of α-cut are used for each decision making process, using the concept known as α-dominance. In [11] it is proposed a fuzzy rule to determine the *degree of dominance of x over y*, and another fuzzy rule to determine the *degree of been dominated of x by y*. Then, aggregating those rules by means of the max t-conorm, a crisp rank of dominance is obtained for each individual x. In [10] a totally different approach is used. It defines a comparison between fuzzy numbers, so Pareto dominance could be used as stated in its definition. In [8] a generalization of the Pareto dominance concept is proposed. In that work, instead of using especial operators *less than* and *less or equal than*, fuzzy Pareto dominance is defined so the result of such redefinition is that decision surface is obtained. For the purposes of this work, α-dominance approach is used.

3.2 Deterministic Longest Path Estimation

Once the data is preprocessed by means of genetic algorithms, LUB is computed. For each α-cut of the fuzzy b-splines that contains the taxi trajectory, we get a polygonal set constructed with trapezoids, as it can be seen in right side of Fig. 2. The motion direction is indicated by the thin dashed arrow. Each trapezoid vertex is denoted with a pair of integers, those at the left of the arrow have zero at first and those at the right have one at first. The other number is the step in motion sequence. The longest path at each step i goes through $(0, i)$ vertex or $(1, i)$. The set of vertexes that defines the longest path, can be computed by exhaustive exploration of all possible combinations, but this is very expensive in terms of computational cost and proved impracticable in a realistic trajectory with 700 points, for instance. This problem has been studied in the area of Computational Geometry and is related with Longest Path with Forbidden Pairs [2], that is NPO PB-complete. Because of this and given that

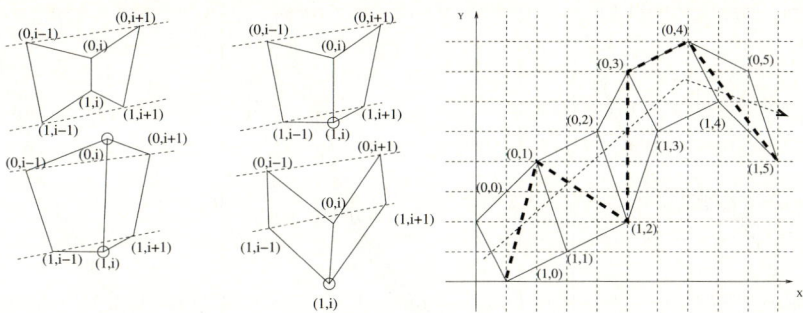

Fig. 2. Left: Possible relative positions of vertex and lines between prior and next vertex. Right: Example of longest path estimation.

in a realistic trajectory the changes of direction and the changes in distance between left and right vertex are limited due to the dynamics of the taxi, the geometry of the road and GPS behavior, we use a heuristic that is lineal in time with the number of vertex. The heuristic is based in the selection of convex vertexes: when a vehicle turns, the longest path goes through the exterior of the trajectory curvature. The convexity of a vertex is analyzed using the straight lines that rely on previous and next vertexes, the possible relative positions of the central vertex can be seen in right side of Fig. 2, where convex vertex are marked with a small circle and the lines that pass through vertex $(0, i-1)$, $(0, i+1)$ and $(1, i-1)$, $(1, i+1)$ are drawn. From left to right and up to bottom, if both vertexes lie between the lines, both are concave. If only one is outside of the lines, it must be convex. If both are out of the lines, either both are convex (left) or one is concave and the other one convex. In both cases, if the farthest one from the nearest line is chosen , then it is convex.

The heuristic is as follows: the first segment of the longest path goes from a convex vertex in step 1 to the vertex at step 0 that gives the maximum segment length. From vertex 1 to the one before the last, the path goes through this vertex if there is only a convex vertex, throught the farthest one if there are two convex vertexes or there is not any convex vertex. Last segment ends in the farthest vertex from the previous one. In right side of Fig. 2 the path computed with this heuristic is marked with a thick dashed line. The first segment goes from $(1,0)$ to $(0,1)$ because $(0,1)$ is convex and the distance to $(0,0)$ is shorter. Then the longest path continues to $(1,2)$ because is the only convex. The same situation happens with $(0,3)$ and $(0,4)$. Finally, the path ends in $(1,5)$ because it is farther from $(0,4)$ than $(0,5)$).

4 Experiments and Results

In the experiments presented here, the parameters of the NSGA-II algorithm are: 4000 generations, 15 individuals in the population, 0.1 and 0.7 of mutation and crossover probabilities, $p^+ = 0.7$ and $p^- = 0.01$. Each individual must cover

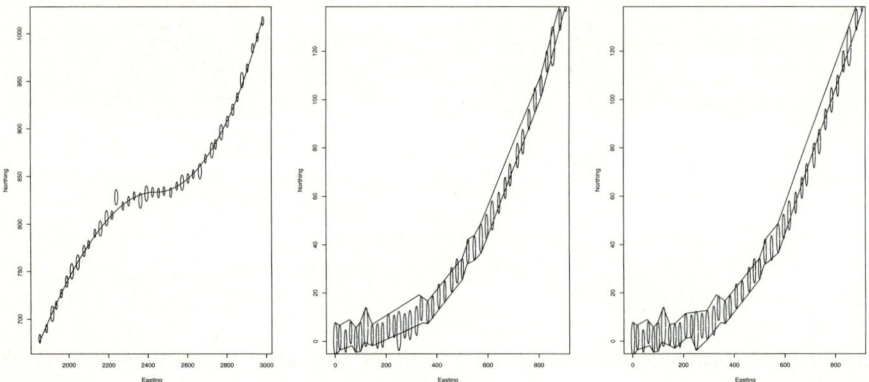

Fig. 3. Left: Example of GPS generated data along with the real trajectory. Center: Part of the first trajectory simplified by NSGA-II algorithm. Rigth: Same data simplified by MOSA.

a minimum of 85 percent of input data to be included in the Pareto front. When using MOSA, delta is 1/4000, T0 is 1.0 and T1 is 0.0, while the rest of parameters are the same to those of NSGA-II. We have decided to evaluate our algorithm in a realistic path that covers the situations usually found when the MOT test of a taxi is done, and computing HDOP, CEP, and projecting earth measures adequately [16,15].

The trajectory is sampled each second, obtaining 1000 points, the total length of the trajectory is 21273.21 meters. At each location, we take a random number from 4 to 9 as the number of available satellites, that we found representative for real data. From this data, we build a dataset of GPS measures, sampled at each second. Each measurement is simulated using the following procedure, with a probability of 0.95, a point is selected that is closer in distance to the real one less than the CEP at that probability. With 0.05 probability the point is selected further than the corresponding CEP from the original data. This resembles the uncertainty that occurs using GPS, and the obtained data can be used to test how tight the bounds obtained with our algorithm are. The reader must remember that the goal is to obtain a multi polygonal chain that covers most of the GPS fixes with minimum number of vertexes and with the minimum area. In left side of Fig. 3 is shown part of the generated data. GPS measures are represented with circles (actually ellipsoids due to scaling issues) with radius equal to 95% CEP and the original trajectory with a continuous line. As it can be seen, most of the circles intersect the trajectory, that is, most of the points of the real trajectory (in fact 95%) are inside the circles with CEP radius, centered in GPS fixes.

We perform two experiments with two subset of the complete dataset with 120 points each. The true length of the first trajectory is 3228.574 meters. The estimated length of the longest path compatible with the 85 % of the points of the first processed trajectory polygonal chain using NSGA-II is 3471.75, and 3555.34 using MOSA. If the taximeter reports a distance longer more than 10% than this upper bound, it should be rejected because even in the worst case the taximeter is out of tolerance. The distance through the GPS fixes is 3238.521, that is much closer to the real data, but the taxi owner can argue about the uncertainty of the procedure saying that it is inaccurate, if we compute an upper bound of the length compatible with GPS data there is no chance for this.

The length of the second trajectory is 2741.306 meters. The estimated length of the longest path compatible with the 85 % of the points of the corresponding processed trajectory polygonal chain using NSGA-II is 3059.1, while using MOSA is 3130.48. In this case the bound is less tight since the trajectory has stronger turns and this leads to longest path compatible with the data. In center and right of Fig. 3 can be see how the simplification of the trajectory works with NSGA-II and MOSA algorithms showing part of the data from the first trajectory. The data correspond to the individuals with less total length. Both algorithms cover most of the data, but differ in which data must be preserved.

5 Conclusions and Future Work

During the development of this application we found that if we report directly the data obtained with GPS equipment, there were legality issues about the uncertainty of the measures. Taxi owners could easily gain in courts any reclamation where the uncertainty of the GPS measures were revealed. As result, the upper bound of the trajectory length compatible with GPS data is computed. In this way there is no doubt to reject a taximeter with reported length above of this measure. Additionally, this alternative is less restrictive with the real data given the biased error detected in the taximeters. In the experiments, MOSA has shown to be almost as accurate as NSGA-II but much more faster. We have found that our algorithm performs worst when the trajectory includes more and stronger turns, this issue must be solved in future modifications with an additional heuristic that includes the dynamic behavior of a real driver using the time information in GPS measures.

Future work includes also using different fuzzy dominance approaches that should be tested to better fit the longest path better.

References

1. A.M. Anile, B. Falcidieno, G. Gallo, M. Spagnuolo and S. Spinello, *Modeling uncertain data with fuzzy B-splines*, Fuzzy Sets and Systems 113, 397–410, 2000.
2. Berman, P., and Schnitger, G. (1992), "On the complexity of approximating the independent set problem", Inform. and Comput. 96, 77-94.
3. C. A. Coello, *An Updated Survey of Evolutionary Multiobjective Optimization Techniques : State of the Art and Future Trends*, 1999 Congress on Evolutionary Computation, IEEE Service Center, 1999.
4. I. Couso, S. Montes, P. Gil The necessity of the strong alpha-cuts of a fuzzy set International Journal of Uncertainty, Fuzziness and Knowledge-Based Systems 9-2, 249-262, 2001

5. K. Deb, S. Agrawal, A. Pratab, and T. Meyarivan, *A Fast Elitist Non-Dominated Sorting Genetic Algorithm for Multi-Objective Optimization: NSGA-II*, In Marc Schoenauer, Kalyanmoy Deb, Günter Rudolph, Xin Yao, Evelyne Lutton, Juan Julian Merelo, and Hans-Paul Schwefel, editors, Proceedings of the Parallel Problem Solving from Nature VI Conference, 849-858, Springer. Lecture Notes in Computer Science, 2000.
6. K. Deb and T. Goel, *Controlled Elitist Non-dominated Sorting Genetic Algorithms for Better Convergence*, In Eckart Zitzler, Kalyanmoy Deb, Lothar Thiele, Carlos A. Coello Coello, and David Corne, editors, First International Conference on Evolutionary Multi-Criterion Optimization, 67-81. Springer-Verlag. Lecture Notes in Computer Science No. 1993, 2001.
7. R. Estkowski and J. S. B. Mitchell, *Simplifying a polygonal subdivision while keeping it simple*, SCG '01: Proceedings of the seventeenth annual symposium on Computational geometry, ISBN 1-58113-357-X, 40–49, ACM Press, New York, NY, USA, 2002.
8. M. Farina and P. Amato, *Fuzzy Optimality and Evolutionary Multiobjective Optimization*, in Carlos M. Fonseca, Peter J. Fleming, Eckart Zitzler, Kalyanmoy Deb and Lothar Thiele (editors), Evolutionary Multi-Criterion Optimization. Second International Conference, EMO 2003, pp. 58–72, Springer. Lecture Notes in Computer Science. Volume 2632, Faro, Portugal, April 2003.
9. Goodman, Nguyen. *Uncertainty Models for Knowledge-based Systems.* North-Holland. 1985
10. M. Hapke, A. Jaszkiewicz and R. Slowinski, *Pareto Simulated Annealing for Fuzzy Multi-Objective Combinatorial Optimization*, Journal of Heuristics, 6(3), 329-345, August 2000.
11. M. Köppen, K. Franke and B. Nickolay, *Fuzzy-Pareto Dominance Driven Multiobjective Genetic Algorithm*, In Proceedings of the 10th IFSAWorld Congress (IFSA 2003), pages 450-453, Istanbul, Turkey, June, 2003.
12. N. Meratnia and R. A. de By, *Trajectory representation in location-based services : problems and solutions*, in Proceedings of the 3rd IEEE Workshop on Web and Wireless Geographical Systems (W2GIS 2003) in conjunction with the Fourth International Conference on Web Information Systems Engineering (WISE), Rome, Italy, 2003.
13. A. Otero and J. Otero and L. Sánchez and J. R. Villar, , *Longest path estimation from inherently fuzzy data acquired with GPS using genetic algorithms*, 2nd International Symposium on Evolving Fuzzy Systems, University of Lancaster, UK, 2006
14. L. Sánchez, J. Otero and J. R. Villar, *Boosting of fuzzy models for high-dimensional imprecise datasets*, in Proceedings of the Information Processing and Management of Uncertainty in Knowledge-Based Systems IPMU06, Paris, 2006.
15. Snyder, J. P., "Map Projections Used by the U. S. Geological Survey", 2nd edition, Geol. Survey Bulletin 1532, 313 p., U. S. Government Printing Office, Washington, D. C., 1982.
16. Wilson, D., "David L. Wilson's GPS Accuracy Web Page", http://users.erols.com/dlwilson/gps.html.
17. J. Zhang, B. Pham, and P. Chen,*Fuzzy Genetic Algorithms Based on Level Interval Algorithm*, In Kazmierczak, E, Eds. Proceedings The 10th IEEE International Conference on Fuzzy Systems, pages pp. 1424-1427, Melbourne, Australia, 2001.

The Topographic Neural Gas

Marian Peña and Colin Fyfe

University of Paisley, Paisley PA1 2BE, Scotland
marian.pena@paisley.ac.uk,
colin.fyfe@paisley.ac.uk

Abstract. We have recently investigated a family of algorithms which use the underlying latent space model developed for the Generative Topographic mapping(GTM) but which train the parameters in a different manner. Our first model was the Topographic Product of Experts (ToPoE) which is fast but not so data-driven as our second model, the Harmonic Topographic Mapping (HaToM). However the HaToM is much slower to train than the ToPoE. In this paper we introduce ideas from the Neural Gas algorithm to this underlying model and show that the resulting algorithm has faster convergence while retaining the good quantization properties of the HaToM.

1 Introduction

Clustering is one of the fundamental problems in data mining. There are different techniques, the most popular being K-means and its harmonic variant K-Harmonic Means [11]. These are sometimes combined with topology-preserving algorithms such as Neural Gas (NG)[6], the Self-organizing Map (SOM)[5] and the Generative Topographic Mapping (GTM)[1] which tend to be used for visualisation of datasets. The neighborhood cooperation in these algorithms also reduces the influence of initialisation [2]. The topology preservation however may limit the efficiency of clustering due to the fixed topology in the algorithm.

One drawback of K-Means is its sensitivity to initialisation of the centres, that can lead to convergence to a local minima. The SOM algorithm can be considered as a topology preserving mapping generalisation of K-Means. We[4][9][10] have recently investigated a family of algorithms which use the underlying latent space model developed for the Generative Topographic Mapping (GTM) but which train the parameters in a different manner. Our first model was the Topographic Product of Experts (ToPoE).

K-Harmonic Means overcomes the initialisation problem by using harmonic means instead of arithmetic means. Recently we have used this clustering technique in a topology preserving map called The Harmonic Topographic Mapping (HaToM) that shares a common structure with the GTM map, but the centres are organised by K-Harmonic Means.

We have shown that HaToM is more responsive to the data than ToPoE but this comes at a cost of an increase in computation time. In this paper, we introduce ideas from the Neural Gas algorithm and show that the resulting method retains the good quantization properties of HaToM but is much faster.

2 GTM, ToPoE and HaToM

The GTM[1] was introduced as a principled alternative to Kohonen's SOM[5]. It begins with a fixed set of points, $t_k, k = 1, ..., K$, in latent space which have some regular topology, such as lying on a grid. These latent points are then mapped through a set of nonlinear basis functions, typically Gaussians, to an intermediate feature space which is then mapped to a set of centres, m_k, in data space. This last mapping is a linear mapping with a set of parameters, W, which are updated by treating the complete mapping as a mixture of experts. [1] uses the Expectation Maximization (EM) algorithm to train the parameters such that the m_k lie on the data manifold and so, by investigating the responsibilities that each latent point has for each data point, the resulting mapping can be used to visualize the data.

ToPoE[4] uses the same underlying mapping, $t_k \to m_K$, but treats the structure as a product of experts. Training is done by gradient descent on the resulting mapping. HaToM[9,10] again uses this underlying mapping but uses K-Harmonic Means[11] to train the parameters. We have previously shown that this algorithm is more data driven than ToPoE but this comes at increased computational expense.

3 Neural Gas

Vector quantization methods encode a set of data points in n-dimensional space with a smaller set of reference vectors m_k, $k = 1, ..., N$. The m_k are determined such that the expected Euclidean distance between all data vectors and their corresponding reference vectors becomes minimal. Neural Gas [6] is a vector quantization technique with soft competition between the units. In each training step, the squared Euclidean distances

$$d_{ik} = \|\mathbf{x}_i - \mathbf{m}_k\| = (\mathbf{x}_i - \mathbf{m}_k)^T * (\mathbf{x}_i - \mathbf{m}_k) \quad (1)$$

between a randomly selected input vector x_i from the training set and all reference vectors m_k are computed; the vector of these distances is d. Each centre k is assigned a rank $r_k(d) = 0, ..., N - 1$, where a rank of 0 indicates the closest and a rank of N-1 the most distant centre to x. The learning rule is then

$$m_k = m_k + \varepsilon * h_\rho[r_k(d)] * (x - m_k) \quad (2)$$

The function

$$h_\rho(r) = e^{(-r/\rho)} \quad (3)$$

is a monotonically decreasing function of the ranking that adapts all the centres, with a factor exponentially decreasing with their rank. The width of this influence is determined by the neighborhood range ρ. The learning rule is also affected by a global learning rate ε. The values of ρ and ε decrease exponentially from an initial positive value ($\rho(0)$, $\varepsilon(0)$) to a smaller final positive value ($\rho(T)$, $\varepsilon(T)$) according to

$$\rho(t) = \rho(0) * [\rho(T)/\rho(0)]^{(t/T)} \quad (4)$$

and
$$\varepsilon(t) = \varepsilon(0) * [\varepsilon(T)/\varepsilon(0)]^{(t/T)} \tag{5}$$
where t is the time step and T the total number of training steps, forcing more local changes with time.

There is also a Growing version of Neural Gas[3] that learns the topology of the data by combining NG with Competitive Hebbian Learning (CHL), which is then closer to the SOM algorithm. In our algorithm Neural Gas is embeded in a GTM-like structure.

4 Topographic Neural Gas

Topographic Neural Gas (ToNeGas) unifies the underlying structure in GTM for topology preservation, with the technique of Neural Gas. We thus have a number of latent points (organised in a two dimensional grid as in the SOM algorithm), that are mapped to a feature space by M Gaussian functions, and then into the data space by a matrix W. Each latent point, indexed by k is mapped, through a set of M basis functions, $\Phi_1(), \Phi_2(), \cdots, \Phi_M()$ to a centre in data space, $\mathbf{m}_k = \Phi(t_k) * W$. The centres in data space are then clustered using the NG algorithm. The algorithm has been implemented based on the Neural Gas algorithm code included in the SOM Toolbox for Matlab [8].

The steps of the algorithm are as follows:

1. Initialise K to 2. Initialise the W weights randomly and spread the centres of the M basis functions uniformly in latent space.
2. Initialise the K latent points uniformly in latent space. Set count=0.
3. Calculate the projection of the latent points to data space. This gives the K centres, $\mathbf{m}_k = \Phi(t_k)^T * W$.
4. Select randomly a datapoint
5. Calculate the distances between the datapoint selected and all the centres
6. Calculate the rank of each centre depending of the previous distance, and the neighborhood function $h_\rho(r) = e^{(-r/\rho)}$
7. Recalculate centres using the learning rule $\mathbf{m}_k = \mathbf{m}_k + \varepsilon * h_\rho[r_k(d)] * (\mathbf{x} - \mathbf{m}_k)$
8. If count<MAXCOUNT, count= count +1 and return to 4
9. Recalculate W using

$$W = \begin{cases} (\Phi^T\Phi + \delta I)^{-1}\Phi^T\Xi & \text{if } K < M \\ (\Phi^T\Phi)^{-1}\Phi^T\Xi & \text{if } K \geq M \end{cases}$$

10. If $K < K_{max}$, $K = K + increment$ and return to 2.
11. For every data point, $\mathbf{x}_i$, calculate the Euclidean distance between the ith data point and the kth centre as $d_{ik} = ||\mathbf{x}_i - \mathbf{m}_k||$.
12. Calculate responsibilities that the kth latent point has for the ith data point and the projections of each datapoint in latent space

$$r_{nk} = \frac{C_\lambda(n,k)}{\sum_{j=1}^{K} C_\lambda(n,j)} \text{ and } y_n = \sum_{k=1}^{K} r_{nk} t_k \tag{6}$$

where t_k is the position of the kth latent point in latent space, and $C_\lambda(n,k)$ the tri-cube Kernel

$$C_\lambda(n,k) = D\left(\frac{|\mathbf{x}_n - \mathbf{m}_k|}{\lambda}\right) \text{ where } D(t) = \begin{cases} \frac{3}{4}(1-t^2) & \text{if } |t| < 1 \\ 0 & \text{otherwise} \end{cases} \quad (7)$$

We have used this growing method with HaToM but have found with the addition of the NG learning, we can increment the number of latent points by e.g. 10 each time we augment the map. With HaToM, the increase can only be one at a time to get a valid mapping. The visualisation is provided by the projection of each datapoint to latent space y_n, using the responsibilities of all the centres for each data point r_{nk}, and the fixed centres in latent space t_k. The responsibilities include the tri-cube Kernel that proved to be better also for HaToM[10]. One of the advantages of this algorithm is that the Neural Gas part is independent of the non-linear projection, thus the clustering efficiency is not limited by the topology preservation restriction.

5 Simulations

We apply this new algorithm to a real dataset of 18 dimensions, and two artificial datasets from the Fundamental Clustering Problems Suite that are complicated to cluster for different reasons.

5.1 The Algae Data Set

This is a set of 118 samples from a scientific study of various forms of algae some of which have been manually identified. Each sample is recorded as an 18 dimensional vector representing the magnitudes of various pigments. 72 samples have been identified as belonging to specific classes of algae which are labeled from 1 to 9. 46 samples have yet to be classified and these are labeled 0. ToNeGas is able to cluster this data correctly (Figure 1). In this case we used wider responsibilities to spread the clusters, but as with HaToM, the projection depicts tighter clusters with narrower responsibilities.

5.2 The Hepta and Target Dataset

We use two of the datasets that appear in The Fundamental Clustering Problems Suite (FCPS)[1]. We use specifically the Hepta and the Target algorithm; the first one has clusters with different densities while the second one includes several outliers.

For both datasets (Figure 2 and Figure 3) the Topographic Neural Gas separates well the clusters, projecting the right topology into the latent space. The centres (bottom left of the Figures) are mainly located within the clusters.

---

[1] http://www.mathematik.uni-marburg.de/ databionics/

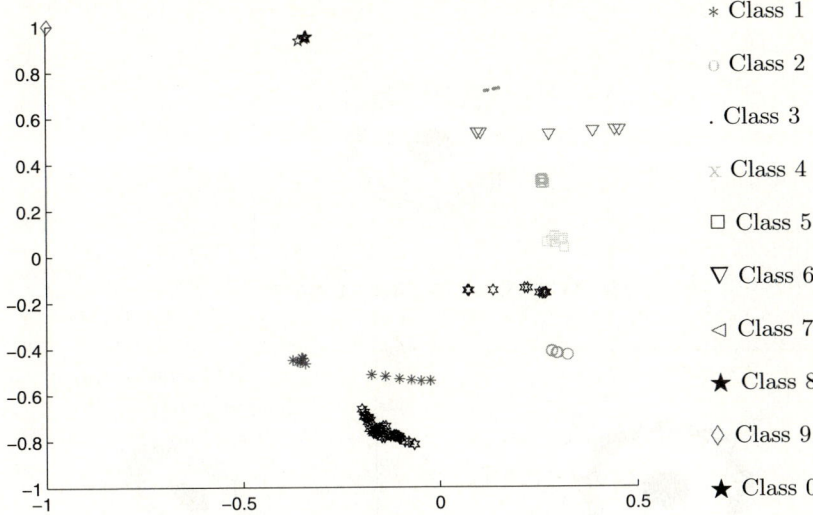

Fig. 1. ToNeGas projection of the 9 labelled algae classes and 1 unlabelled class (0)

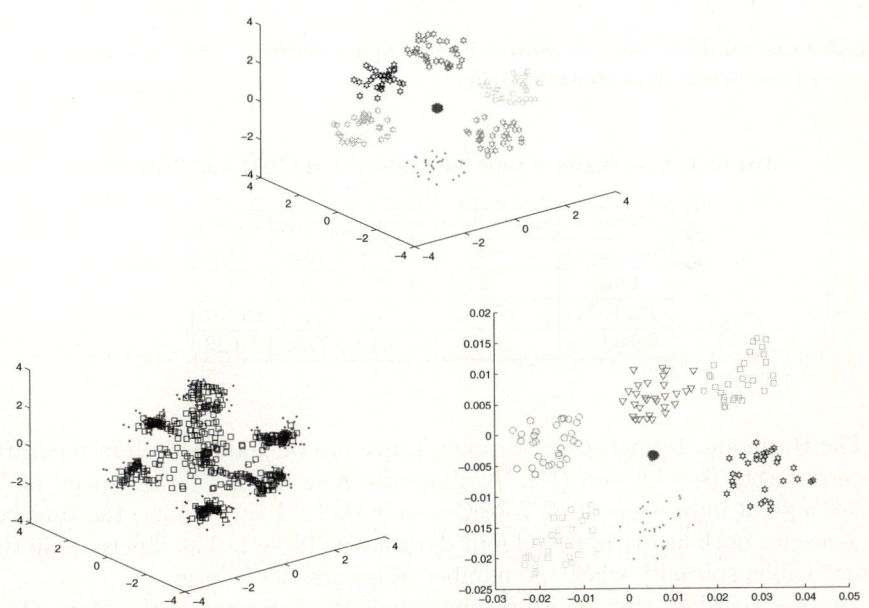

Fig. 2. Original data (top), □ centres in data space (bottom left) and ToNeGas projection of the hepta data (bottom right)

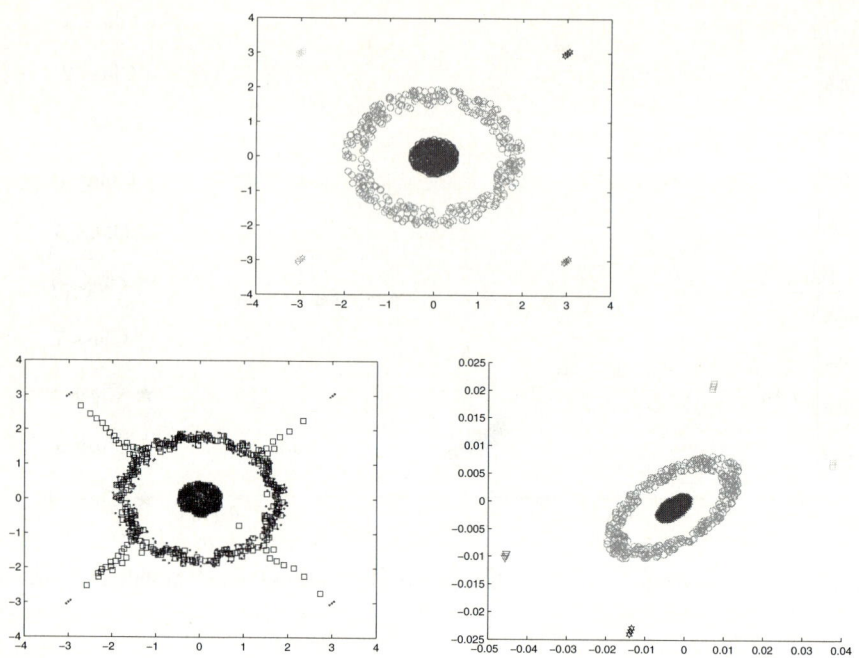

Fig. 3. Original data (top), □ centres in data space (bottom left), and ToNeGas projection of the target data (bottom right)

Table 1. Convergence time (seconds) for HaToM and ToNeGas

Dataset	Four clusters	Algae	Hepta	Target
No points	800	118	212	770
Dim	2	19	3	2
HaToM	174.47	7.07	17.19	155.19
ToNeGas	20.21	6.10	7.24	19.23

The Harmonic Topographic Mapping proved to be good as well in separating these datasets (see [9] and [10]). To illustrate how the clustering speed of NG makes a great improvement of ToNeGas over HaToM we evaluate the time convergence for both algorithms and four datasets in Table 1. The difference in time is noticeable, specially when the number of datapoints is large.

Another possible criterion for comparison is the reduction in the Mean Quantisation error (MQE) while growing the map. In this experiment we calculate the MQE every time we add new latent points to the map, that is after finishing each run of the clustering technique (K-Harmonic Means for HaToM and Neural Gas for ToNeGas). We can see in Figure 4 that both techniques reduce the MQE, but the change is much more remarkable for ToNeGas.

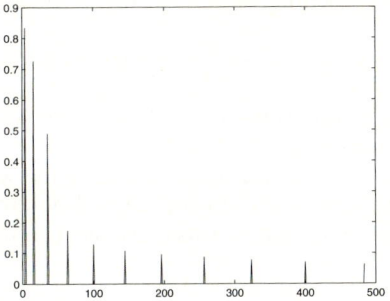 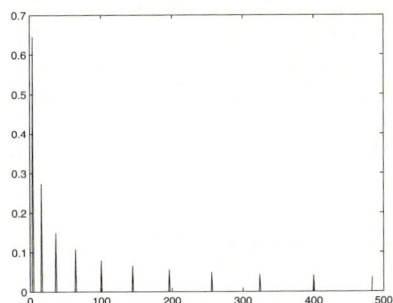

Fig. 4. Mean quantisation error over time for the Harmonic Topographic Mapping (left) and the Topographic Neural Gas (right)

6 Conclusions

We have presented a new algorithm for vector quantization and visualisation that integrates the Neural Gas and the underlying structure of the GTM algorithm. The clustering speed of Neural Gas gives an important improvement over the previously developed algorithm, the Harmonic Topographic Mapping, and has also proved to reduce the mean quantisation error much more than the latter.

The Topographic Neural Gas gains advantages from the Neural gas clustering as well as from the GTM like structure. Three main advantages of NG model are [6]: (1) faster convergence to low distortion errors, (2) lower distortion error than that resulting from K-means clustering, maximum-entropy clustering and Kohonens self-organizing map algorithm [5], obeying a stochastic gradient descent on an explicit energy surface. From the non-linear projection from latent space to data space, the algorithm obtains topology preservation as well as a visualisation application in a low dimensional grid.

References

1. Bishop, C. M. and Svensen, M. and Williams, C. K. I.: GTM: The Generative Topographic Mapping. Neural Computation (1997)
2. Cottrell,M and Hammer,B and Hasenfu, A and Villmann, T. Batch neural gas. WSOM 2005.
3. Fritzke, F.A Growing Neural Gas Network Learns Topologies. Advances in Neural Information Processing Systems 7 (NIPS'94), pages 625–632, Cambridge, 1995. MIT Press.
4. Fyfe, C. Two topographic maps for data visualization, Data Mining and Knowledge Discovery, 2006.
5. Kohonen, T. Self-Organization and Associative Memory. Springer-Verlag (1984)
6. Martinetz,T.M. and Berkovich, S.G. and Schulten, K.J. 'Neural-gas' network for vector quantization and its application to time-series prediction. IEEE Transactions on Neural Networks. **4** Volume 4 (1993) 558–569

7. Martinetz, Th. and Schulten, K. Topology representing networks. Neural Networks, 7 (1994) 507522
8. Neural Networks Research Centre, Helsinki University of Technology, SOM Toolbox, http://www.cis.hut.fi/projects/somtoolbox/
9. Peña,M. and Fyfe, C.: Model- and Data-driven Harmonic Topographic Maps. WSEAS Transactions on Computers **4** Volume 9 (2005) 1033-1044
10. Peña, M. and Fyfe, C.: Outlier Identification with the Harmonic Topographic Mapping. 14 th European Symposium on Artificial Neural Networks , ESANN (2006)
11. Zhang, B.:Generalized K-Harmonic Means – Boosting in Unsupervised Learning. Tech. report. HP Laboratories, Palo Alto. (2000)

A Fast Classification Algorithm Based on Local Models*

Sabela Platero-Santos, Oscar Fontenla-Romero, and Amparo Alonso-Betanzos

Department of Computer Science, University of A Coruña,
Facultad de Informática, Campus del Elviña s/n, 15071,
A Coruña, Spain
sabelaplatero@wanadoo.es, {ofontenla, ciamparo}@udc.es
http://www.dc.fi.udc.es/lidia

Abstract. This work presents a new classification method based on the iterative combination of two steps: a clustering technique and a set of one-layer neural networks. First, the clustering algorithm divides the input space in several regions (local models). Subsequently, a one-layer neural network, for each local region, is used to fit the model (classifier) for a specific group of data points. Experimental results on three different data sets are showed to verify the validity of the proposed method. Besides, a comparative study with a feedforward neural network is included. This study exhibits that the presented algorithm is a fast procedure that obtains, in many cases, better results than the other technique.

1 Introduction

Most of the proposed algorithms in the Machine Learning field for pattern classification are based on a global model of the data points. This kind of approaches tries to obtain a single complex model that explains the global behavior of the system that generate the data. An alternative approach to global modeling is local modeling. This last approach is supported on the old "divide and conquer" strategy. It tries to solve a complex problem using simpler solutions for local regions of the input space. Specifically, it divides the input space into local areas and learn simple (constant/linear) models in each region. Figure 1 shows an example of the behavior of these two kind of techniques in their application for a classification problem. In the global modeling approach, figure 1(a), a single non-linear decision curve is obtained for all the data set, whereas in the local modeling approach, figure 1(b), the examples are split in several groups (delimited by the dashed lines in the figure) and a simpler classifier (in this case, a linear model) is employed for each one of the clusters.

Algorithms such as Associative Neural Networks [1], classification and regression trees (CART) [2] and the hierarchical mixtures of experts (HME) algorithms [3], are local approximation models where the input space is split, at training

---

* This work has been funded by the project TIC2003-00600 of the Ministerio de Ciencia y Tecnología, Spain (partially supported by FEDER funds).

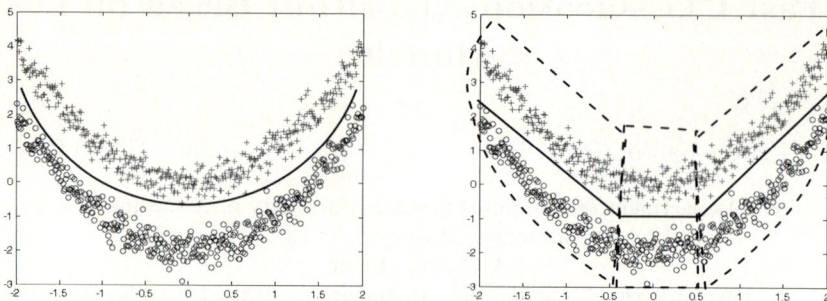

(a) An example of a global model of the data

(b) An example of local models of the data

Fig. 1. Example of local and global modeling

time, into a set of regions where simple surfaces are fit to the local data. Lawrence et al. [4] did an empirical comparison of several global and local methods for estimating a function mapping. In that work, they observed, in the considered data sets, that the local approximations perform better that global ones when the density of the function to be approximated varies more as we move around the input space. In addition, they note that local approximators can exhibit slow convergence and difficulties to determine the optimal number of regions. One of the usual solutions to this last problem is to employ a fixed number of clusters, but of course this is neither optimal nor efficient. In this paper, a new and fast local modeling approach is presented which dynamically estimates the number of local models to fit.

2 Algorithm

The proposed method is based on a two stage procedure that is iteratively repeated until it converges. In the first stage, a clustering method (k-means) is used to divide the input space into two regions (local models). The second stage is employed to fit a classifier for each one of the regions obtained by the previous phase. This is accomplished using a set of one-layer neural networks trained using a fast algorithm based on a set of linear equations. The following subsections show this phases in a more detailed way.

2.1 Clustering Stage

This phase consist on the successive division of a data set into two clusters. For this task the k-means algorithm was used due to its simplicity and operation speed. The data belonging to each of the two generated clusters will be the input patterns for a one-layer neural network (second stage of the process). Let m be the number of attributes (variables) for each pattern in the data set, then the method can be summarized by the following algorithm:

1. Insert in a stack (S) the initial training set (single initial cluster)
2. Do while the stack is not empty
   (a) Pop the cluster (C) on the top of S (this cluster contains n instances)
   (b) For C train the associate one-layer neural network to obtain the optimal weights.
   (c) If ($n > 2m + 1$) and *classification error* > 0 then divide C in C_1 (with j instances) and C_2 (with k instances) using the clustering technique (k-means)
   Option 1 :
   If ($j > m + 1$) and ($k > m + 1$) then push C_1 and C_2 in S
   else, store the weights and the centroid of the cluster C. This will be one of the final local models.
   Option 2 :
   If ($k > m + 1$) push C_2 in S
   If ($j > m + 1$) push C_1 in S
   If ($j \leq m + 1$) or ($k \leq m + 1$) store the weights and the centroid of the cluster C. This will be one of the final local models.
   (d) Else, store the weights and the centroid of the cluster C. This will be one of the final local models.

In the presented algorithm, the general conditions that should be fulfilled by a cluster to be split are (step 2(c)):

1. The classification error of the associated model for this cluster must be greater that zero. In this topic two approaches were tried: the classification error obtained in the training set or the error in a validation set. This last approach is similar to the early stopping criteria.
2. The number of elements in the cluster must be greater than twice the number of inputs of the classifier ($n > 2m+1$). This condition was added to guarantee that the new clusters generated could have a classifier with at least more data points than inputs.

Using the iterative procedure presented in the algorithm a binary tree is obtained where each node represents one of the clusters. The tree is obtained in a deep-first way. Figure 2 shows an example. In this figure, several iterations of the method (iterations of the loop in step 2) are represented. As can be observed, in each iteration one of the nodes is split in two clusters and a one-layer artificial neural network (ANN) is used to fit the model for each particular cluster. Finally, only the leaf nodes and the corresponding ANNs are considered as final local models. As can be observed, the number of clusters is not prefixed but it is dynamically determined during the learning process. Besides, it is important to remark that in step 2(c) two alternative options are proposed. These two options produce two different implementations of the method and different behaviors in its operation:

1. In option 1, the children nodes (clusters), generated by the division of a cluster in the tree, are considered as valid if the number of data points in

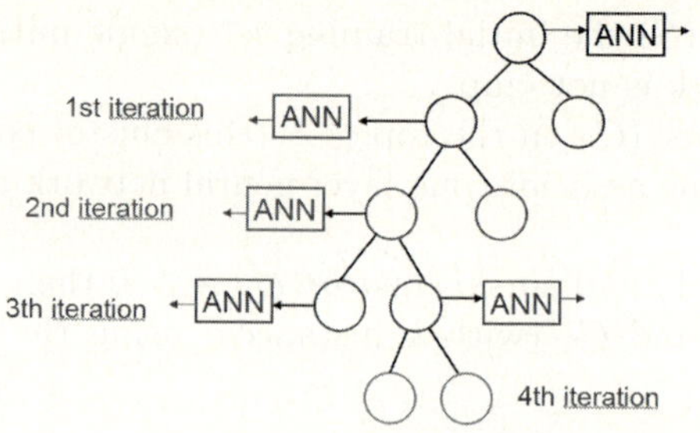

Fig. 2. Example of binary tree obtained by the proposed method

both clusters are equal o greater than the number of inputs in the classifier. In this case, both clusters are stored in the stack and the cluster father is discarded because it is divided.

2. In option 2, it is not necessary that both clusters must have more data points than inputs in the classifier. If only one of them fulfil this requirement then the other is discarded and the father is also kept.

2.2 Model Fitting Stage

In the step 2(b) of the algorithm presented in the previous section, a model is fitted using only the data of the associated cluster. The model employed was a one-layer neural network trained with a fast procedure proposed in [5]. The advantages of this learning method is that it always obtain the global optimum and is a very fast procedure because it obtains the solution using a linear system of equations. Due to space restrictions the details of this method are not included, but interested readers can access to complete information in reference above.

3 Experimental Results

In this section, the results obtained using three different data sets are showed. The first data set is an artificial problem used to show visually the behavior of the proposed method. The other two data sets are real problems from the UCI Machine Learning Repository [6]. In addition, a comparative study was accomplished with a feedforward neural network (multilayer perceptron) with logistic activation functions. The learning method used in this case was the scaled conjugate gradient [7] as it is one of the fastest supervised methods for this kind of networks. Several topologies were trained using one hidden layer and different number of hidden neurons. In this section, only the results for the more relevant topologies are showed (5, 9 and 14 hidden neurons). For all the experiments, a 10-fold cross validation was used to estimate the real error of all the classifiers. Besides, 50 different simulations, using different initial parameters, were accomplished to check the variability of the methods.

3.1 Artificial Data Set

This first example is a two input dimensional data set that contains 800 data catalogued in two classes. Figure 3(a) depicts the 2-dimensional data points and the class of each one using different markers. The dots represent the data of the first class and the crosses the data of the second class. As it can be observed, this is a non-linear classification problem. Figure 3(b) shows an example of the clusters obtained by the proposed method for one of the simulations. In this case, 6 final clusters (local models) were choosen, each one represented by a different color and marker. Figure 4 shows the results for this data set. It contains the mean accuracy, over the 50 simulations, of the train and test set using the 10-fold cross-validation. As can be seen, the option 2 of the proposed method achieves better results than the other one. Besides, the results for the test set are better than the ones obtained for the feedforward neural network. Anyway, although the differences between the methods are not very significant, it can be observed

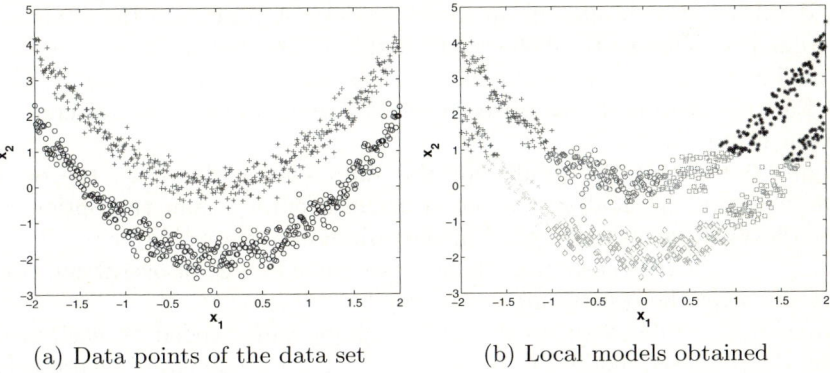

(a) Data points of the data set   (b) Local models obtained

Fig. 3. Example of the clusters achieved by the proposed method for the Artificial data set

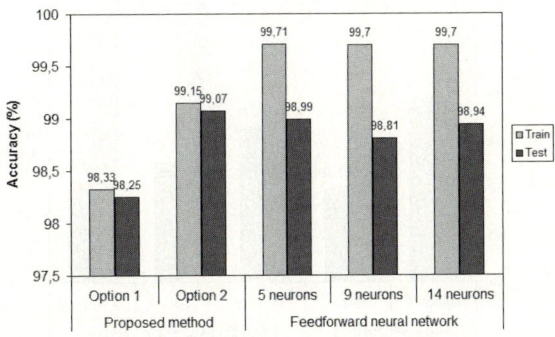

Fig. 4. Results of the Artificial data set

Table 1. Mean training time (in seconds) for each method using the the Artificial data set

Method	Mean time ± std
Proposed method (option 1) without early stopping	0.06 ± 0.01
Proposed method (option 1) with early stopping	0.10 ± 0.03
Proposed method (option 2) without early stopping	0.07 ± 0.02
Proposed method (option 2) with early stopping	0.12 ± 0.03
Feedforward Neural Network (5 hidden neurons)	13.73 ± 6.06
Feedforward Neural Network (9 hidden neurons)	24.44 ± 5.35
Feedforward Neural Network (14 hidden neurons)	31.14 ± 2.91

in table 1 that the proposed method is a very fast algorithm, much faster than the feedforward neural network.

3.2 Wisconsin Breast Cancer Database

This database was obtained from the University of Wisconsin Hospitals, Madison from Dr. William H. Wolberg. It contains 699 instances, 458 benign and 241 malignant cases, but 16 were not used as they contain incomplete information. Each example is characterized by 9 attributes measured in a discrete range between 1 and 10.

Figure 5 contains the results for this data set. In this case, the option 1 of the proposed method gets a better mean accuracy than the option 2 and the feedforward neural network. This last method achieves better results in the training set, but it is clear that there exists some degree of overfitting because the results over the test set are not so good.

Furthermore, table 2 shows the mean training time needed for each method. Again, the proposed method is much faster than the feedforward neural network using the scaled conjugate gradient algorithm. Besides, it can be observed than the option 1 of the presented method is faster than the option 2. This is due to in the first case the number of clusters generated is lesser than in the other case.

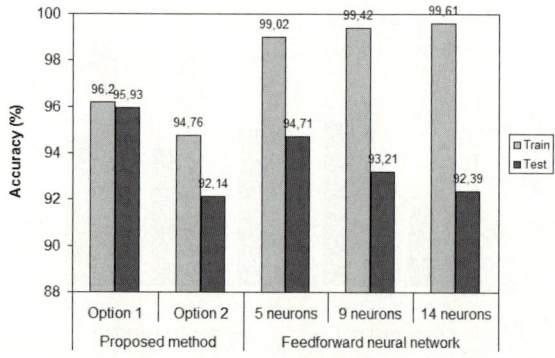

Fig. 5. Results of the Wisconsin Breast Cancer database

Table 2. Mean training time (in seconds) for each method using the Wisconsin Breast Cancer Database

Method	Mean time ± std
Proposed method (option 1) without early stopping	0.06 ± 0.03
Proposed method (option 1) with early stopping	0.02 ± 0.02
Proposed method (option 2) without early stopping	0.16 ± 0.01
Proposed method (option 2) with early stopping	0.15 ± 0.08
Feedforward Neural Network (5 hidden neurons)	17.80 ± 2.73
Feedforward Neural Network (9 hidden neurons)	22.26 ± 1.53
Feedforward Neural Network (14 hidden neurons)	29.42 ± 2.63

3.3 Pima Indians Diabetes Database

Figure 6 illustrates the accuracies obtained for this data set. As in the previous example, the option 1 of the presented method performs better than the option 2. In this case the results are similar to those obtained for the feedforward neural network. In any case, the training time needed for the proposed method is much lesser than the neural network, as can be seen in table 3. In the worst case, the proposed algorithm is up to 56 times faster than the other method.

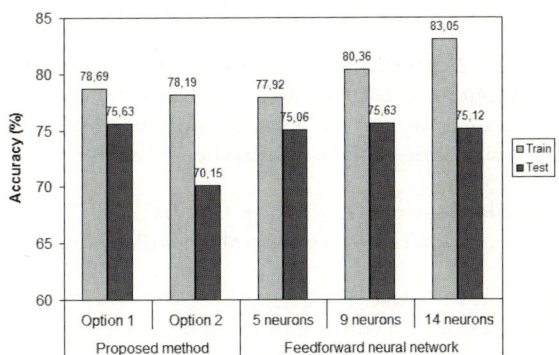

Fig. 6. Results of the Pima Indians Diabetes database

Table 3. Mean training time (in seconds) for each method using the Pima Indians Diabetes Database

Method	Mean time ± std
Proposed method (option 1) without early stopping	0.29 ± 0.03
Proposed method (option 1) with early stopping	0.11 ± 0.12
Proposed method (option 2) without early stopping	0.34 ± 0.03
Proposed method (option 2) with early stopping	0.32 ± 0.18
Feedforward Neural Network (5 hidden neurons)	19.31 ± 3.30
Feedforward Neural Network (9 hidden neurons)	25.49 ± 1.34
Feedforward Neural Network (14 hidden neurons)	29.40 ± 0.54

4   Discussion and Conclusions

In this paper a new method for pattern classification has been presented. The performance obtained over several benchmark classification problems has demonstrated its soundness. The main advantages of the proposed algorithm are: (a) it does not assume a prefixed number of local models (clusters) but they are dynamically estimated during the learning process, and (b) it is a fast learning method which could be very relevant in real time applications.

Two different options of the algorithm were presented and, although in the artificial data set the first one obtains the best performance, the second one presents the best results over the real problems thus it is the most recommended. In the all the performed experiments, the proposed method obtains similar results, in the test set, than a multilayer perceptron but employing a lesser computational time. Besides, the proposed method seems to exhibit a better generalization behavior due to the relative small differences between the training and test errors.

References

1. Tetko, I.: Associative neural network. Neural Processing Letters **16** (2002) 187–199
2. Duda, R., Hart, P., Stork, D.: Pattern Classification. Wiley-Interscience, New York, NY (2001)
3. Titsias, M., Likas, A.: Mixture of experts classification using a hierarchical mixture model. Neural Computation **14**(9) (2002) 2221–2244
4. Lawrence, S., Tsoi, A.C., Back, A.D.: Function approximation with neural networks and local variance and smoothness. Australian Conference on Neural Networks (ACNN96) (1996) 16–21
5. Castillo, E., Fontenla-Romero, O., Guijarro-Berdias, B., Alonso-Betanzos, A.: A global optimum approach for one-layer neural networks. Neural Computation **14**(6) (2002) 1429–1449
6. Newman, D., Hettich, S., Blake, C., Merz, C.: UCI repository of machine learning databases [http://www.ics.uci.edu/~mlearn/mlrepository.html], University of California, Irvine, Dept. of Information and Computer Sciences (1998)
7. Moller, A.: A scaled conjugate gradient algorithm for fast supervised learning. Neural Networks **6** (1993) 525–533

Human Activity Recognition in Videos: A Systematic Approach

Sameer Singh and Jessica Wang

Research School of Informatics, Loughborough University, Loughborough LE 11 3TU, UK
S.Singh@lboro.ac.uk

Abstract. The identification of human activity in video, for example whether a person is walking, clapping, waving, etc. is extremely important for video interpretation. In this paper we present a systematic approach to extracting visual features from image sequences that are used for classifying different activities. Furthermore, since different people perform the same action across different number of frames, matching training and test sequences is not a trivial task. We discuss a new technique for video shot matching where the shots matched are of different sizes. The proposed technique is based on frequency domain analysis of feature data and it is shown to achieve very high accuracy of 94.5% on recognizing a number of different human actions.

1 Introduction

Human activity recognition from video streams has a wide range of applications such as human-machine interaction, security surveillance, choreography, content-based retrieval, sport, biometric applications, etc. Human activity recognition in video streams is used in a wide range of applications such as human-machine interaction, surveillance, choreography, content-based image/video retrieval, biometric applications, gesture recognition, etc. [9,21,24]. A number of different approaches have been applied in the literature to solve the problem of human activity recognition using video data for the purposes of understanding gestures, gait and full body activities. These include the matching of spatio-temporal surfaces and curves (Tsai et al. [22], Rangarajan *et al.* [15], Rao *et al.* [16]), spatial distribution of optic flow (Little and Boyd [10]), Hidden Markov Models [20] (Bobick and Ivanov [2], Masoud and Papanikolopoulos [11], Ramamoorthy *et al.* [14], Ou et al.' [12], Starner and Pentland [19], Zobl *et al.* [24]), Finite State Machines (Ayers and Shah[1], Stark *et al.* [18]), Template matching using key frames only (Kim and Park [8]) and on feature based templates derived from video data (Bobick and Davis [3], Huang and Nixon [7]), string matching using edit distances [4], and popular classifiers that can be trained to recognize differences between spatio-temporal patterns of different activities (e.g. the use of Support Vector Machines by Schüldt et al. [17], Bayesian analysis of trajectory features by Hongeng et al. [6] and a rule based system using spatial features of body part coordinates Ozki et al. [13]).

In our work, we focus on: *passive action* e.g. sit and do nothing, or thinking, or turning the head to follow someone across the room (watch the world go by); and *active action* e.g. waving, clapping (repetitive actions), or lifting, reading (non-repetitive actions). These actions can be performed with the person sitting or standing. Our aim is to develop a machine learning system that uses training data on different actions (performed by a number of subjects) to automatically classify (identify) actions in test videos. A systematic approach to extracting important features for classification includes:

a) *Video capture*: In our analysis we use co-registered optical and thermal videos of the same human activity. The videos are captured in an unconstrained environment with the person sitting or standing.
b) *Skin detection*: A Gaussian Mixture Model approach is used for skin detection in optical video, whereas simple image thresholding is used in the thermal video. A pixel is considered to be skin if and only if it is deemed to be a skin pixel in both videos.
c) *Hand and Face Identification*: This process is based on skin region analysis: shape and size constraints are used on skin region along with semantic information (e.g. face region is in between hand regions) to label.
d) *Landmark feature identification*: The centroid of the face region (A) and the tip of the longest fingers of left and right hand (B, C) are used as landmarks.
e) *Features for Classification*: A number of geometric features based on the triangle ΔABC are extracted and used in classification. These are described in section 2.
f) *Feature Post-processing*: The raw features are further preprocessed to ensure that the information used as input to a classifier from a video of any frame size is of the same length.
g) *Classification*: Any classifier can be used for analysis. In our broad research work both neural networks and nearest neighbour classifiers have been used.

2 Some Important Issues

There are three key issues when recognizing human activity through video. These include: (a) Robustness of the image processing algorithms in automatically detecting skin, and accurate landmark location detection; (b) Large variability in how the same action can be performed by different people; and (c) Algorithms for extracting features such that different sized image sequences can be matched because the same action can be of any length depending on the sampling rate and the speed with which the action is performed. We explain these issues now.

a) *Robustness of the image processing algorithms*: This is directly dependent on the quality of skin detection, ellipse fitting and landmark location determination algorithms. A detailed treatment on these is available in Wang [23]. In this paper we experimentally evaluate the robustness of these algorithms in our experimental section.

b) *Large variability in how the same action can be performed by different people*: People perform the same action differently. No two image sequences showing a human activity are exactly the same. For example Figure 1 shows a sample trajectory; the shape and length of the trajectory varies with the person performing the action.

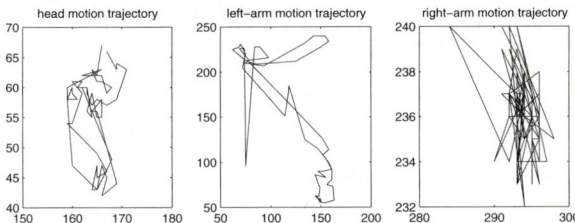

Fig. 1. A sample head motion, left-arm and right-arm trajectory for the action "drinking"

(c) *Algorithms for extracting features such that different sized image sequences can be matched*: The main problem with matching training and test video shots (a shot is a sequence of video frames) is that each shot is of a different length and exact matching is impossible. For example, consider two people waving in two different videos. This action in the first video v_1, say, takes L_1 frames and this action in the second video v_2 takes L_2 frames. In addition, these actions would most likely start at different times in their corresponding shots since there might be some random action in some frames. Hence it is not trivial to solve the problem: "*Given*: videos v_1 and v_2 that have been preprocessed to have shots: $v_1 = (a_1, a_2, ..., a_n)$ and $v_2 = (b_1, b_2, ..., b_n)$. The video v_1 is training video, with shot a_i ground truthed as "waving" and v_2 is test video. *Problem*: Match all shots of v_2 with a_i to confirm if any of them are "waving". This will be based on a measure of similarity. The problem of speed variation is however more difficult. The solution to such a problem requires a complex search for the optimum match with various sequence lengths and phase shifts.

3 Feature Extraction and Matching

In this section we discuss: (a) The process for extracting relevant features once the landmark features have been identified; and (b) Feature post-processing such that effective matching is possible (matching a test sample to find the nearest training sample is the same as predicting the class of an unknown test pattern). The processes of video capture, co-registration, skin detection, hand and face identification and landmark feature identification are described in detail in Wang [23] and not the focus of this paper.

The classification accuracy depends on the quality of features used. We generate features at two levels. Firstly, a set of p features $(f_1, ..., f_p)$ is computed directly from the hand and face location information. For a video sequence V consisting of N frames, we get a set of p features per frame. Secondly, these features are processed in the frequency domain to generate a new set of features $(g_1, ..., g_q)$ that define the overall video sequence V. It is expected that two video sequences of different lengths will each finally yield a total of q features. In the following description we first define the features $(f_1,...,f_{41})$ that can be computed from the output of hand/face localization step.

Features (f_1, f_2, f_3, f_4): Type of triangles—Given the centroid of the head region (C_x, C_y), the (x, y) position of the tip of the left arm (L_x, L_y) (i.e. the end of major axis of the left arm ellipse) and the (x, y) position of the tip of the right arm (R_x, R_y) (i.e. the end of major axis of the right arm ellipse). If $L_y > C_y$ and $R_y > C_y$, then it is triangle type 1 (see Fig. 2(a))- $f_1 = 1$, else $f_1 = 0$; if $L_y > C_y$ and $R_y \leq C_y$, then it's triangle type 2 (see Fig. 2(b))- $f_2 = 1$, else $f_2 = 0$; if $L_y \leq C_y$ and $R_y > C_y$, then it's triangle type 3 (see Fig. 2(c))- $f_3 = 1$, else $f_3 = 0$; and if $L_y \leq C_y$ and $R_y \leq C_y$, then it's triangle type 4 (see Fig. 2(d))- $f_4 = 1$, else $f_4 = 0$.

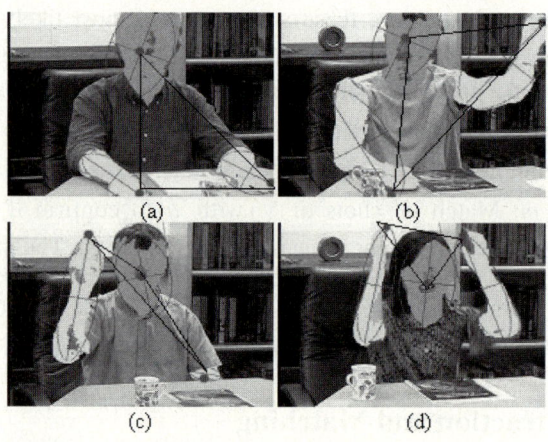

Fig. 2. a) Triangle type1; b) type2; c) type3; d) type 4

Features (f_5, f_6, f_7): The first feature f_5 is used to determine whether the triangle area changes significantly or not, and features (f_6, f_7) denote the direction of change, i.e. area increases or decreases.

Features $(f_8,...,f_{34})$: These 27 features are calculated to find the spatial relationships between head, left arm and right arm regions.

Features (f_{35}, f_{36}, f_{37}): These features determine the movement and direction of left arm oscillation when moving in horizontal directions (left and right).

Feature (f_{38}, f_{39}, f_{40}): These features determine the amount and direction of right arm oscillation when moving in horizontal plane (left and right), and these are computed in the same way as (f_{35}, f_{36}, f_{37}).

Feature (f_{41}) : This feature calculates whether the area of the head region changes significantly across two frames which indicates head movement.

For each video sequence we extract the above described 41 features. Each feature contains a binary vector of size N, $(b_1,...,b_N)$, for a total of N frames. From the above set of features, we generate the following set of post-processed features that separate the high and low frequency components in our data.

Algorithm Fourier Feature Selection
Given: A video containing N frames, from which 41 features ($f_1,..., f_{41}$) have been extracted. Each feature can be represented as a vector of binary numbers, i.e. $f_i = (b_{i1},...,b_{iN})$.

Step 1: Discrete Fourier transform is applied on a given feature which generates a Fourier representation $\Im(f_i) = (u_{i1},...,u_{iN})$, where u_i is a complex number, and its magnitude can be used for further analysis.
Step 2: Compute the mean μ_i and standard deviation σ_i of the Fourier magnitudes of u_i.
Step 3: The final 82 Fourier features used for classification are now given as $(\mu_1,\sigma_1,...\mu_{41},\sigma_{41})$. This can now be represented as the new feature set $(g_1,...g_{82})$. Perform feature selection to find the most discriminatory features. In this manner, irrespective of the length of the video sequence, each video is now represented by only 82 features.

4 Experimental Methodology

On the basis of the above features, we investigate the recognition of the following human activities: class c_1) sit and do nothing; class c_2) turning the head; class c_3) thinking1 (with one of the hand under the chin); class c_4) clapping; class c_5) waving; class c_6) drinking; class c_7) reading; and class c_8) thinking2 (with both the hands under the chin). We evaluate how well our systematic approach to human activity recognition performs on real data. Our experiments will be conducted using k nearest neighbour classifier with leave-one-out cross-validation..

A total of 22 subjects were asked to perform the 8 actions. Each action could be performed either using the left or the right hand or both hands, and the activity duration ranged between the shortest of 10 seconds (sitting) to the longest of 2 minutes (reading). In order to get an adequate number of frames per action which vary in terms of their duration, the frame rate was variable for each action, e.g. for slow actions such as "sitting and not doing anything", the frame rate was set at 1 frame per second, whereas for clapping and waving it was set to 8 frames per second. The image frames are extracted and individually analysed for detecting landmark features (temporal information is used from previous frames). Each video sequence is manually ground-truthed for activity class. There is considerable variability in the length of the sequences for each action performed by different subjects (Figure 3).

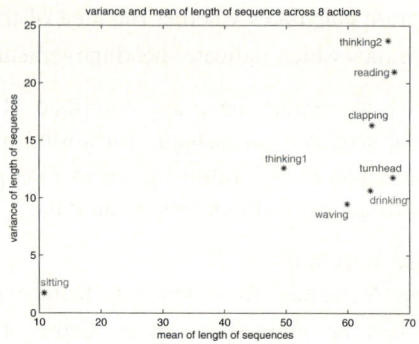

Fig. 3. Variability in the duration of sequences across different activities (mean plotted against variance)

The above plot confirms that robust classification of data is not a trivial task. On feature selection (based on the correlation between features and class labels), the best 42 features are selected for classification.

5 Results

We achieve 95.4% average classification success with a nearest neighbour classifier with leave-one-out cross validation on all eight activities. The confusion matrix output shows that the following mistakes are made: 4.2% of class c_5 (waving) is mistaken as class c_4 (clapping); 20% of samples of class c_6 (drinking) are mistaken as class c_7 (reading), and 3.8% of samples of class c_7 (reading) are mistaken as class c_4 (clapping). These mistakes are understandable since in actions "drinking" and "reading", a subject often raises their hand close to their face to either bring the cup to the mouth for drinking or for turning the pages of a newspaper. The problem can be solved if the video is captured from more than one viewpoint where such differences can be highlighted.

We next compare our approach on the same data with the following studies: Ben-Arie et al. [4], Rao and Shah [26] and Wang and Singh [37]. We implemented the algorithms detailed in the above publications and performed the leave-one-out classification in exactly the same manner as before. The results showed 19.1% with Ben Arie [4], 33.5% classification accuracy with Rao and Shah [26], and 55% classification accuracy with Wang and Singh [37]. This shows that our proposed model is highly successful. A careful analysis of the confusion matrices generated by the other models shows that the mistakes generated by our model are repeated by all other models too. Some of the confusion in classes exists because of similar body movements to a large degree for two actions even though some phases may be discriminatory.

We finally evaluate the robustness of our model. The location of the landmark features is noise contaminated such that we randomly introduce an error between 1 and 15 pixels. A total of five experimental trials are conducted with varying levels of error and at each trial the leave-one-out cross-validation accuracy exceeded 90% on eight class classification. This shows that our model is relatively robust to image analysis errors. This is obvious since the geometric features described earlier are not varied much by small changes in landmark features and continue to give good results with small errors.

6 Conclusions

In this paper we present an approach to understanding human activity in unconstrained videos. Such analysis has two elements: image processing, and machine learning. The first aspect deals with the identification of relevant features from video that can be used for classification. In these areas we make the following contributions: i) Our approach to skin detection is quite novel as we fuse the decisions made on a co-registered set of optical and thermal images; (ii) The detection of landmark features was achieved with high accuracy. Our results show that the novel geometric features are highly robust to minor errors in image processing stage. (iii) The use of Fourier analysis to post-process geometric features and achieve a final set of features for classification that are invariant to video size (number of frames) is a major contribution; and (iv) We have shown that our approach is superior to three other baseline approaches. In contrast to other approaches, our methodology is simpler and cheaper to compute (Wang, 2005). On the whole, our study has shown a general workplan of how to recognize human activities. In the future using similar approach we can extend the system to include the recognition of other activities such as full body gestures.

References

1. D. Ayers and M. Shah, "Monitoring Human Behavior from Video Taken in an Office Environment", Image and Vision Computing, Vol. 19, pp. 833-846, 2001.
2. A. F. Bobick and Y. A. Ivanov, "Action Recognition using Probabilistic Parsing", Proceedings of IEEE Conference on Computer Vision and Pattern Recognition, pp. 196-202, 1998.
3. A. F. Bobick and J. W. Davis, "The Recognition of Human Movement using Temporal Templates", IEEE Transactions on PAMI, Vol.23, No.3, pp. 257-267, March 2001.
4. R. Duda, P. E. Hart and D. Stork, "Pattern Classification", 2nd ed., New York: John Wiley and Sons, 2001.
5. C. Faloutsos, M. Ranganathan and Y. Manolopoulos, "Fast Subsequence Matching in Time-Series Databases", Proceedings ACM SIGMOD Conference, Mineapolis, MN, pp. 419-429, 1994.
6. S. Hongeng, R. Nevatia and F. Bremond, "Video-based Event Recognition: Activity Representation and Probabilistic Recognition Methods", Computer Vision and Image Understanding, vol. 96, pp. 129-162, 2004.
7. P. S. Huang, C. J. Haris, M. S. Nixon, "Human Gait Recognition in Canonical Space using Temporal Templates", IEEE Proceedings—Vision, Image and Signal processing, Vol. 146, pp. 93–100, 1999.

8. S. H. Kim and R-H. Park, "An Efficient Algorithm For Video Sequence Matching Using The Modified Hausdorff Distance and the Directed Divergence", IEEE Transactions on Circuits and Systems for Video Technology, Vol. 12, pp. 592-296, 2002.
9. R-H. Liang and M. Ouhyoung, "A Real-Time Continuous Gesture Recognition System for Sign Language", Proc. Int. Conference on Automatic Face and Gesture Recognition, Nara, Japan, pp. 558-565, 1998.
10. J. Little and J. Boyd, "Recognizing People by Their Gait: the Shape of Motion", VIDERE, Vol. 1, Number 2, 1998.
11. O. Masoud and N. Papanikolopoulos, "A Method for Human Action Recognition", Image and Vision Computing, Vol. 21, pp. 729-743, 2003.
12. J. Ou, X. Chen and J. Yang, "Gesture Recognition for Remote Collaborative Physical Tasks using Tablet PCs", ICCV Workshop on Multimedia Tech. in E-Learning and Collaboration, 2003.
13. M. Ozki, Y. Nakamura and Y. Ohta, "Human Behavior Recognition for an Intelligent Video Production System", IEEE Pacific Rim Conference on Multimedia, pp. 1153-1160, 2002.
14. A. Ramamoorthy, N. Vaswani, S. Chaudhury and S. Banerjee, "Recognition of Dynamic Hand Gestures", Pattern Recognition, Vol. 36, pp. 2069-2081, 2003.
15. K. Rangarajan, B. Allen and M. Shah, "Matching Motion Trajectories", Pattern Recognition, Vol.26, pp. 595-610, 1993.
16. C. Rao, A. Yilmaze and M. Shah, "View-Invariant Representation and Recognition of Actions", International Journal of Computer vision, Vol. 50, Issue 2, pp. 203-226, 2002.
17. C. Schüldt, I. Laptev and B. Caputo, "Recognizing Human Actions: A Local SVM Approach", ICPR, Vol.3, pp. 32-36, 2004.
18. M. Stark, M. Kohler and P. G. Zyklop, "Video Based Gesture Recognition for Human Computer Interaction", Informationstechnik und Technische Informatik, 38(3), pp. 15-20, 1996.
19. T. Starner and A. Pentland, "Visual Recognition of American Sign Language using Hidden Markov Models", Proc. Int. Workshop on Automatic Face and Gesture Recognition, 1995.
20. A. Stolcke, "Bayesian Learning of Probabilistic Language Models", Phd., University of California at Berkeley, 1994.
21. A. Tolba, "Arabic Glove: A Communication Aid for the Vocally Impaired", Pattern Analysis and Applications, Vol. 1, Issue 4, pp. 218-230, 1998.
22. P-S. Tsai, M. Shah, K. Keiter and T. Kasparis, "Cyclic Motion Detection", Computer Science Technical Report, University of Central Florida, Orlando, 1993.
23. J. Wang and S. Singh, "Video Based Human Dynamics: A Review", Real Time Imaging, Vol. 9, No.5, pp. 321-346, 2003.
24. J. Wang, "Video Based Understanding of Human Dynamics: A Machine Learning Approach, PhD Thesis, Exeter Univ, 2005.
25. M. Zobl, F. Wallhoff anf G. Rigoll, "Action Recognition in Meeting Scenarios using Global Motion Features", Proceedings Fourth IEEE International Workshop on Performance Evaluation of Tracking and Surveillance, J Ferryman, Ed., Graz, Osterreich, University of Reading, pp. 32-36, March 2003.

Application of Artificial Neural Network to Building Compartment Design for Fire Safety

Eric Wai Ming Lee[1], Po Chi Lau[2], and Kitty Kit Yan Yuen[1]

[1] Fire Safety and Disaster Prevention Research Group, Department of Building and Construction, City University of Hong Kong, Kowloon Tong, Hong Kong (SAR), People of Republic of China
ericlee,@cityu.edu.hk, yuen.ky@student.cityu.edu.hk
[2] Asian Institute of Intelligent Buildings, c/o Department of Building and Construction, City University of Hong Kong, Kowloon Tong, Hong Kong (SAR), People of Republic of China
Lau_po_chi007@yahoo.com.hk
http://www.aiib.net

Abstract. Computational fluid dynamics (CFD) techniques are currently widely adopted to simulate the behaviour of fire but it requires extensive computer storage and lengthy computational time. Using CFD in the course of building design optimization is theoretically feasible but requires lengthy computational time. This paper proposes the application of an artificial neural network (ANN) approach as a quick alternative to CFD models. A novel ANN model that is denoted as GRNNFA has been developed specifically for fire studies. As the available training samples may not be sufficient to describe system behaviour, especially for fire data, additional knowledge of the system is acquired from a human expert. The expert intervention network training is developed to remedy the established system response surface. A genetic algorithm is applied to evaluate the close optimum set of the design parameters.

1 Introduction

Currently, Computational Fluid Dynamics (CFD) is the most widely adopted approach to simulate the behaviour of fire systems. It divides the domain of a system into finite numbers of small volumes. The nonlinear system behaviour of the fire system is determined by solving a large set of differential equations that describe the interactions between the small volumes. The major drawback of CFD is the requirement of extensive computer storage and lengthy computational time. Hence, it may be impractical to rely solely on the CFD model in the fire system design optimisation. However, various approaches have been adopted for thermal-fluid system optimisation. Hou [1] proposed the optimisation of the thermal system by applying the response surface method. This approach applies different orders of polynomials to fit the data that was obtained from the simulation software – DOE-2.1D [2]. However, the order choice of the polynomial is critical to the success of the model. Pioneer works in the application of the Artificial Neural Network (ANN) to study the behaviour of heat exchangers were carried out in [3-4]. A comprehensive study on the application of the ANN and a GA in thermal engineering was also conducted by [5] which founded the basis of applying soft computing techniques in thermal-fluid systems. Currently, ANN techniques are only applied to fire detection systems [6,7]. However, the application of ANN techniques to determine the consequences of fire is very limited. Lee et al. [8] successfully applied ANN techniques to determine sprinkler actuation and the occurrence of flashover [9]. Lee et al. have also developed a probabilistic inference engine (PEMap) [10] addressing the uncertainties that are embedded in fire data. An ANN model denoted as GRNNFA [11] has been developed specifically for predicting the height of the thermal interface in a single compartment [12]. These pioneer works have confirmed the applicability of ANN techniques in the determination of fire consequences. The high speed computation of the GRNNFA facilitates the formulation of a soft computation based optimisation model.

2 GRNNFA-GA Design Optimization Approach

2.1 The GRNNFA Model

The GRNNFA [11] model is a hybrid model employing Fuzzy ART (FA) [13] model as the preprocessor of the General Regression Neural Network (GRNN) [14]. The architecture of the GRNNFA model is shown in Fig. 1.

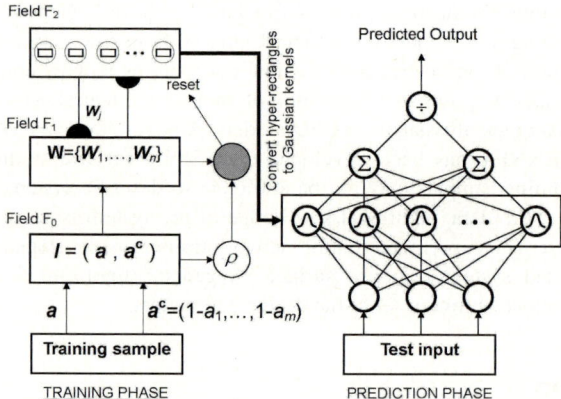

Fig. 1. The architecture of the GRNNFA model comprises of two portions. The Fuzzy ART module (left) clusters the training samples to fewer numbers of prototypes in the training phase. The information of the prototype is used to establish the Gaussian kernels of the GRNN module (right). When an input vector presents to the GRNN module, the corresponding responses of the kernels to the input vectors are fed into the summation and division operators to produce the predicted output.

The proposed compression scheme of the GRNNFA model converting the prototypes of the FA modules to the Gaussian kernels of the GRNN module also facilitates the removal of the noise embedded in the training samples. This feature is particularly important for processing fire data. Readers may refer to [11] for the detail formulation of the GRNNFA model.

2.2 Human Expert Intervention Network Training

Most of the intelligent systems [15,16] are designed to minimize human intervention in the network training phase for the purpose of automation. However, limited training samples (e.g. fire data) may not be sufficient to describe the system behaviour.

Expert experience can provide the information that is missing from the limited training samples. The approach of the human expert intervention network training algorithm is summarized Fig.2.

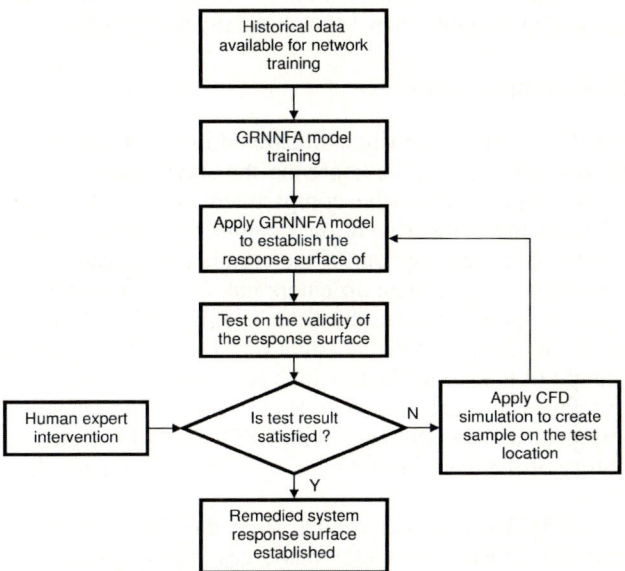

Fig. 2. The GRNNFA model establishes the response surface of system behaviour described by the training samples. The response surface is tested and examined by human expert to determine the validity. If the expert does not satisfy the test result, CFD simulation will be carried out to create an extra training sample to supplement the knowledge of the original samples.

2.3 GRNNFA-GA Design Optimization Approach

A Genetic Algorithm (GA) [17, 18] can be applied on the remedied system surface to arrive at a close optimum solution. The scheme employing GRNNFA and GA for optimization is denoted as GRNNFA-GA hereunder. The overall design optimization approach is shown in Fig. 3.

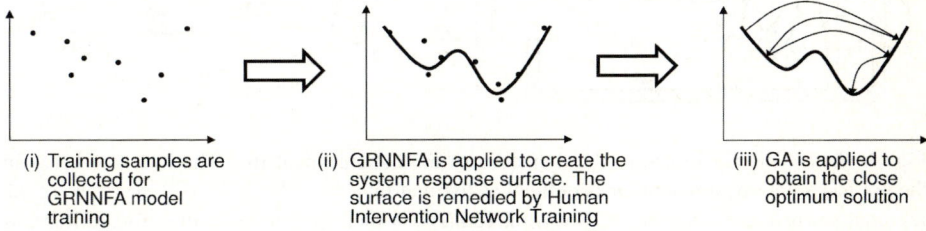

(i) Training samples are collected for GRNNFA model training

(ii) GRNNFA is applied to create the system response surface. The surface is remedied by Human Intervention Network Training

(iii) GA is applied to obtain the close optimum solution

Fig. 3. This figure shows the concept of the GRNNFA-GA design parameter optimization. The GRNNFA model creates the response surface according to the knowledge of the noise corrupted training samples. Human expert knowledge is introduced to supplement the training samples to remedy the system response surface. Then, GA can be applied to obtain a close optimum set of design parameters.

3 Application to Building Compartment Design Optimization

This section presents the application of the GRNNFA-GA optimization approach to determine the minimum door width of a compartment with which the height of the thermal interface (HTI) is higher than 1.0m above the floor level.

3.1 Dynamics of Compartment Fire

The dynamics of the compartment fire is illustrated in Fig. 4. During the development of compartment fire, the hot gases comprising the sooty smoke created from the fire source rises to the upper part of the compartment due to the buoyancy. When it reaches the ceiling of the compartment, it accumulates and descends down. The hot gases and the sooty smoke emerge out of the compartment when they reach the door soffit. At the same time, the ambient air enters into the fire compartment and entrains into the fire plume to support the combustion. The dynamics of the compartment fire is shown in Fig. 4. The Height of the Thermal Interface (HTI) indicated as Z_i in Fig. 4 represents the height of the smoke layer which is mathematically defined as the height with maximum temperature gradient. The HTI is one of the crucial factors to determine the tenability of a compartment. If the HTI is too low, the sooty smoke will reduce the visibility of the evacuees which may induce the untenable condition of the fire room.

The value of the HTI can be determined from the CFD simulation result but the simulation requires extensive computer resources and lengthy computational time especially for design parameter optimization which requires a series of trials. Instead, the following sections demonstrate the application of the GRNNFA-GA design optimization approach to determine the minimum door width of a fire compartment.

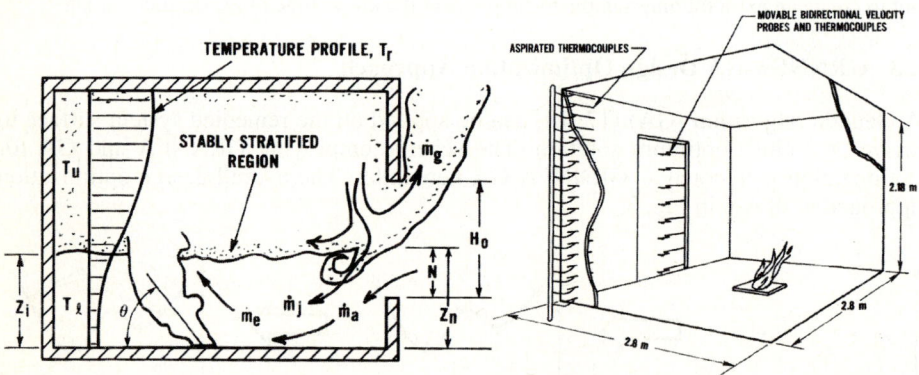

Fig. 4. (*Left*) This figure shows the dynamics of the compartment fire. The interface between the hot gases and the ambient air is defined as thermal interface. (*Right*) The dimensions of the fire compartment are 2.8m(W) ×2.8m(L)×2.18m(H). A methane burner with porous diffuser is placed at the floor of the compartment. Thermocouples and velocity probes were provided at the doorway to measure properties of the ambient air and hot gases flowing across the door opening. The figures are adopted from [19].

3.2 Training of the GRNNFA Model

The fire experimental data for the GRNNFA model training was extracted from [19]. The experimental setup is shown in Fig. 4 (*Right*). It is a set of full-scale steady state experiments of flow that was induced in a single compartment fire. A total of 55 experiments were performed that included different fire locations, fire intensities and window and door sizes. Owing to the diffusion and mixing effects of the fluid flow, the thermal interface height could not be determined precisely. It was ascertained that the interface height could only be achieved within a range of ±8% to ±50% accuracy [19]. The values of the interface height that were recorded in the format of mean ± error were used to compare the GRNNFA predictions. Different controlled parameters were varied to produce different measurements. Table 1 summarizes the parameters and measurements in [19]. The HTI was chosen to be the target output of the GRNNFA model. All of the controlled parameters were taken to be the model inputs.

Table 1. Controlled parameters and the measured results of Steckler's Experiment

Controlled parameters (*Model Inputs*)	Measurements
- Width of opening - Height of the sill of the opening - Fire Strength - Distance of fire bed from the front wall - Distance of fire bed from the centerline - Ambient temperature	- Air mass flow rate - Neutral plane location - Height of the thermal interface (*Model Output*) - Average temperature of the upper hot gases layer - Average temperature of the lower ambient air layer - Maximum mixing rate - Air velocity profile at opening - Temperature profile at opening

3.3 Human Expect Intervention for Remedying System Response Surface

The above procedures established the system response surface of GRNNFA and the training samples that were adopted from [19]. In this step, the expert intervention is involved in the network training. Five different cases which were unseen from the training samples were examined by an expert. The five cases and the original sample distribution are shown in Fig. 6.

The findings in [12], which are considered as expert knowledge, reveal two behaviours of the thermal interface that the HTI can be raised by (i) increasing the door width; or (ii) shifting the fire bed away from the door opening. According to these findings, the ranking of the HTIs of the five cases is expected to be $HTI_{II} > HTI_{I} > HTI_{III} > HTI_{IV} > HTI_{V}$. The trained GRNNFA model was applied to the five cases to evaluate the HTIs of the five cases and the result is: HTI_{II} (1.207m) > HTI_{I} (1.225m) > HTI_{III} (0.95m) > **HTI_{V} (0.91m)** > HTI_{IV} **(0.90m)**. It is noted that the ranking of HTI_{V} and HTI_{IV} are different from the human expert expectation. The system response surface of GRNNFA may be required to be remedied. Referring to [10], the accuracy of the prediction is significantly affected by the data distribution density. This applies particularly to the knowledge distribution of [19]. As the data distribution density at case IV is less than that at case V as shown in Fig. 6 (right), it may be concluded that

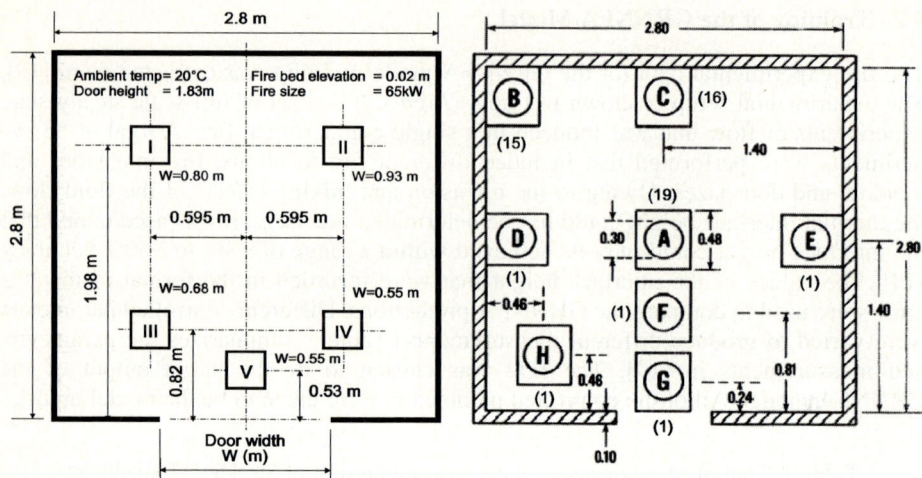

Fig. 6. (*Left*) This figure shows the fire bed locations of the five test cases which do not appear in the training sample. (*Right*) The figure shows the locations of the fire beds of the training samples. Bracketed figures are the number of samples in the experiment [19].

the available samples are not sufficient to describe the system behaviour at case IV. CFD simulation by Fire Dynamic Simulator (FDS) [20] was carried out for case IV and the HTI was determined. The GRNNFA was re-trained by the original 55 samples together with the extra sample that was created by the FDS. The re-trained model is denoted as GRNNFA*. Fig. 7 shows the ranking of the HTIs of the five test cases predicted by the models before (i.e. GRNNFA) and after (i.e. GRNNFA*) the network re-training.

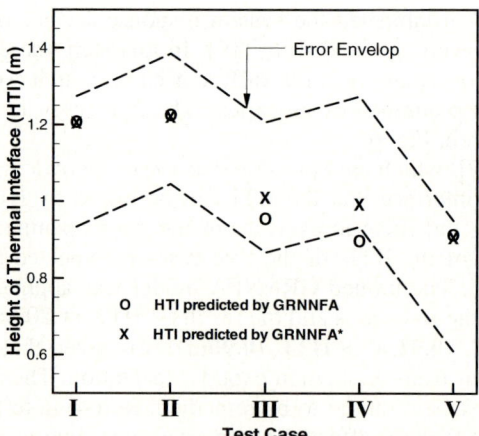

Fig. 7. This figure shows that the extra sample remedy the system response surface that the ranking of the HTIs is rectified and agrees with the human expert's expectation

The ranking predicted by GRNNFA* is HTI_{II} (1.20m) > HTI_I (1.22m) > HTI_{III} (1.01m) > **HTI_{IV} (0.99m)** > **HTI_V (0.91m)** which is in line with the human expert expectation. The error envelope that is indicated in Fig. 7 was estimated by the CFD simulations in the five test cases with the minimum error range of the HTI as indicated in [19] that was incorporated. It shows that the network re-training with the extra sample drags case IV back so that it falls within the error envelope. Other cases have also benefited from the re-training as they have also been moved closer to the centre of the error range. The above example demonstrates the remedy of the system response surface by the human expert intervention network training. The human expert knowledge was not meant to be quantified but employed for identifying the defective location of the system response surface.

3.4 Optimization of Door Width for Fire Safety

The remedied system response surface was ready to be used after the network training. The objective of this design parameter optimization was to determine the minimum door width with which the HTI would not be lower than 1.0m above the floor level, regardless of the location of the fire. The optimization is, in fact, to determine the width of door opening such that the HTI will be 1.0m. The objective function is defined in Equation (1) where H is the HTI that results from the door width w, the distance of the fire bed from the room centre D_x and from the front wall D_y. The value of H is to be determined by the trained GRNNFA model. The physical domain of the fire bed location is defined as Ω.

$$W(D_x, D_y) = \underset{w}{Min}\left\{\left[H(D_x, D_y, w) - 1.0\right]^2\right\} \; ; \; \{D_x, D_y\} \in \Omega \qquad (1)$$

The objective is to evaluate the value of W given a particular location of the fire bed inside the compartment such that the HTI will be 1.0m. It should be noted that W is the minimum door width above which the HTI will be higher than 1.0m according to the findings in [12]. Since different set of {w, Dx, Dy} may result from the same value of HTI, the minimum door width regardless of the location of the fire bed is determined by Monte-Carlo approach. The total 10,000 fire bed locations were randomly chosen within the physical domain Ω to arrive at 10,000 corresponding door widths with which the HTIs were higher than 1.0m. The typical progress of the GA optimisation is shown in Fig. 8 (Left). It can be observed that the close optimum solution was reached by only 10 generations. The distribution of the 10,000 door widths is presented by the histogram that is shown in Fig. 8 (Right). By counting 99.9% of the 10,000 samples (i.e. 9990 samples) from the leftmost, the door width of the 9990th sample falls into the range of 0.85–0.9m. The following conclusion can be drawn: there is at least a 99.9% confidence level that the average height of the thermal interface that is induced by the fire (62.9kW) will not be lower than 1.0m above the floor level when the door width is 0.9m, regardless of the location of the fire inside the compartment that is identical to the experimental setup of [19].

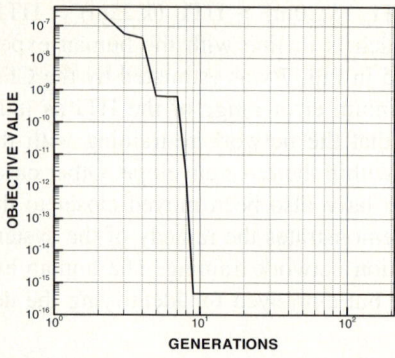 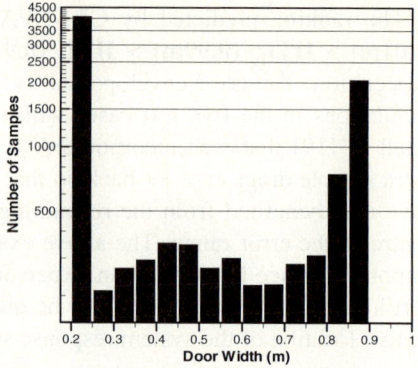

Fig. 8. (Left) The progress of the GA optimization shows that the close optimum set of parameters is achieved after 10 generations. (Right) The distribution of the 10,000 samples shows that the corresponding door widths of the 10,000 samples are less than 0.9m.

4 Conclusions

This paper presented the development of a set of generic optimisation procedures with applications of the GRNNFA model, the expert intervention network training and a GA. The GRNNFA model established the preliminary system response surface according to the information of the available training samples. As the available samples may not be sufficient to describe the general behaviour of the system, human expert intervention network training was developed to remedy the system response surface through the implementation of the human expert's knowledge. Subsequently, the GA was applied to the remedied system response surface to arrive at a close optimum solution.

This optimisation approach was demonstrated by application to determine the door width of a single compartment with which the HTI would not be lower than 1.0m above the floor level regardless of the location of the fire bed. Steckler's experimental results [19] were adopted as the training samples. The trained GRNNFA model revealed the two conjectures of the HTI's behaviour (i.e. the HTI will be raised by placing the fire bed away from the door opening or increasing the width of the door opening). The conjectures were also validated theoretically and numerically. The established system response surface was examined by the expert. The defective location of the surface was then determined by the expert's knowledge. A CFD simulation was carried out at the location to create an additional sample for the network retraining. The re-trained GRNNFA produced the remedied system response surface. It was shown that the human knowledge together with the CFD simulation significantly improved the system response. After the completion of the GA optimisation was applied to the response surface, the close optimum door width was found to be 0.9m.

Comparing the GRNNFA model and the FDS model in terms of computational time, the GRNNFA and FDS require, respectively, 1 second and 8.3 hours to determine the value of HTI of the same fire scenario. The comparative high speed of the GRNNFA model realize the proposed building compartment design optimization while FDS is considered impractical to be implemented in the GA for the optimization due to its lengthy computational time. Regarding the model complexity, the network structure of the GRNNFA as shown in Fig.1 is much simpler than the CFD model which is also considered as a complex model by Muller and Messac [21]. This study demonstrates the superiority of the GRNNFA model and its application to the building compartment design optimization for fire safety.

Acknowledgments. The work described in this paper was fully supported by a grant from the Research Grant Council of the Hong Kong Special Administrative Region, Chain [Project No. CityU 115205].

References

1. Hou, D.: Thermal Design and Optimization by Integration of Simulation and Response Surface Method – Methodologies and Applications. PhD Thesis, The University of Texas at Austin (1998)
2. Lawrence Berkeley Laboratory, DOE-2 supplement version 2.1D, Report LBL-8706, Rev 5 Supplement. Berkeley, CA, Lawrence Berkeley Laboratory (1989)
3. Jambunathan, K., Hartle, S.L., Ashforth-Frost, S. and Fontana, V.N.: Evaluating convective heat transfer coefficients using neural networks. International Journal of Heat and Mass Transfer, Vol. 39, No. 11 (1996) 2329-2332
4. Pacheco-Vega, Sen, M. and Yang, K.T.: Simultaneous determination of in- and out-tube heat transfer correlations in heat exchangers by global regression. International Journal of Heat and Mass Transfer, Vol. 46 (2003) 1029-1040
5. Sen, M. and Yang, K.T.: Applications of artificial neural networks and genetic algorithms in thermal engineering. in F. Kreith (Ed.), CRC Handbook of Thermal Engineering, Section 4.24 (2000) 620-661
6. Milke, J.A. and Mcavoy, T.J.: Analysis of signature patterns for discriminating fire detection with multiple sensors. Fire Technology, Vol. 31, No. 2 (1995) 120-136
7. Pfister, G.: Multisensor / multicriteria fire detection: A new trend rapidly becomes state of art, Fire Technology. Vol. 33, No. 2 (1997) 115-139
8. Lee, W.M., Yuen, K.K., Lo, S.M. and Lam, K,C.: Prediction of sprinkler actuation time using the artificial neural networks. Journal of Building Surveying, Vol. 2, No. 1 (2000) 10-13.
9. Lee, E.W.M, Yuen, R.K.K., Lo, S.M. and Lam, K.C.: Application of Fuzzy ARTMAP for prediction of flashover in compartmental fire. Proceedings of International conference on Construction Hong Kong, 19-21 June 2001 (2001) 301-311
10. Lee, E.W.M, Yuen, R.K.K., Lo, S.M. and Lam, K.C.: Probabilistic Inference with Maximum Entropy for Prediction of Flashover in Single Compartment Fire. Advanced Engineering Informatics, Vol. 16 (2002) 179-191
11. Lee, E.W.M., Lim, C.P., Yuen, R.K.K. and Lo, S.M.: A hybrid neural network for noisy data regression. IEEE Transactions on Systems, Man and Cybernetics – Part B, Vol. 34, No. 2 (2004) pp. 951-960
12. Lee, E.W.M., Yuen, R.K.K., Lo, S.M. and Lam, K.C.: A novel artificial neural network fire model for prediction of thermal interface location in single compartment fire. Fire Safety Journal, Vol. 39 (2004) 67-87
13. Carpenter, G.A., Grossberg, S., David, B.R.: Fuzzy ART: Fast Stable Learning and Categorization of Analog Patterns by an Adaptive Resonance System. Neural Networks, Vol. 4 (1991) 759-771

14. Specht, D.F.: A general regression neural network. IEEE Transaction on Neural Networks, Vol. 2, No. 6 (1991) 568-576
15. Penny, W.D. and Roberts, S.J.: Bayesian neural networks for classification: how useful is the evidence framework?, Neural Networks, Vol. 12 (1999) 877-892
16. Fogel, D.B. and Chellapilla, K.: Verifying Anaconda's expert rating by competing against Chinook: experiments in co-evolving a neural checkers. Neurocomputing, Vol. 42 (2002) 69-86
17. Holland, J.H.: Adaptation in Natural and Artificial System. MIT Press (1975)
18. Holland, J.H.: Genetic Algorithm. Scientific American, Vol. 267, No. 1 (1992) 66-72
19. Steckler, K.D., Quintiere, J.D. and Rinkinen, W.J.: Flow induced by fire in a compartment. NBSIR 82-2520, National Bureau of Standards, Washington D.C. (1982)
20. McGranttan, K.B., Baum, H.R., Rehm, R.G., Hamins: A. and Forney, G.P., Fire Dynamics Simulator. Technical Reference Guide, NISTIR 6467 2000, National Institute of Standards and Technology, Gaithersburg, MD (2000)
21. Mullur, A.A. and Messac A.: Metamodeling using extended radial basis functions: a comparative approach. Engineering with Computers, Vol. 21, No. 3 (2006) 203-327.

A Method of Motion Segmentation Based on Region Shrinking

Zhihui Li, Fenggang Huang, and Yongmei Liu

School of Computer Science and Technology, Harbin Engineering University, Harbin 150001, China
lizhh@126.com

Abstract. Motion segmentation needs to estimate the parameters of motion and its supporting region. The usual problem in determining the supporting region is how to obtain a complete spatial consistence. On the basis of maximum posterior marginal probability (MPM-MAP) algorithm this paper presents a new algorithm based on region shrinking to locate the supporting area. First the motion parameters are estimated by MPM-MAP algorithm. In this algorithm pixels of maximum probabilities belonging to a motion are considered to be preselected pixels for supporting area. Then the region shrinking algorithm is used to determine the region of maximum density of the preselected pixels to be the range of supporting area. Finally the active contour based on gradient vector flow (GVF) is adopted to obtain the accurate shape of supporting region. This method obtains a solid region to be supporting area of a motion and extracts the accurate shape of moving objects, so it offers a better way in motion segmentation to solve the problem of spatial continuity.

Keywords: region shrinking; motion segmentation; MPM-MAP; active contour; gradient vector flow.

1 Introduction

Motion-based segmentation of image sequences is an important problem in computer vision. In the image sequences there are several moving objects on the background of complex scene. The difficulty in solution of such problem is to estimate not only the parameters of motion model but also the corresponding region of every motion (supporting region). Wang and Adelson[1] presents that the regions of moving objects are represented by "layer". A motion image consists of several layers and every layer is a supporting region of the motion. The motion to estimate is usually described by affine model. The effective kind of methods to estimate motion is based on probabilistic frame. EM algorithm[2-3] is used to estimate the motion parameters without considering consistent constraint. The consistent constraint based on Markov random field(MRF) is adopted to eliminate the noise in motion fields[4]. The estimating process is divided into two steps which are motion estimation and supporting region estimation and the EM algorithm are replaced by maximum posterior marginal probability(MPM-MAP) algorithm[5]. Ref.[6] offers a fast algorithm on MPM-MAP. The consistent methods in Ref.[5] are still based on MRF.

The most often used consistent methods are mainly MRF-based methods or local smoothing methods usually used in computation of optical flow. These methods can remove isolate pixels or small holes to some degree but will fail when the holes or isolated regions enlarge a little. The comparatively big holes appear easily in motion field estimation when the color in central area of object is consistent. So the MRF-based methods can't solve fundamentally the problems in spatial consistence. This paper presents a new method in motion segmentation to get supporting areas by region shrinking. First the MPM-MAP algorithm is responsible to estimate the motion parameters. Then the region shrinking algorithm is used to locate the supporting regions accurately. Finally active contour based on gradient vector flow (GVF) is adopted to extract the exact supporting region. Because the accurate motion parameters and area location bring forward the accurate initial position of active contour the exact region of motion field can be obtained in fewer iterations than before.

2 Bayesian Frame in Motion Estimation

Some effective motion segmentation methods are model fitting based on probabilistic frame. Several motion models with unknown parameters are defined then the parameters are derived by maximum posterior probability (MAP) or maximum likelihood(ML) criterion. Assume F is image sequence function .$r=(x,y)^T$ is a pixel in an image and a 2-d positional vector . $F(r)=\{f_1(r), f_2(r),…, f_N(r)\}$ are motion image sequences. $\Phi(r;\theta_k)(k=1,2,…K)$ is a set of motion model. θ_k is the parameter set and character of each model. A model k is supported effectively in the region R_k. The motion field v at each pixel is as follow equation.

$$v(r) = \sum_{k=1}^{K}\Phi(r;\theta_k)b_k(r) \quad (1)$$

Where b(r) is the instructive function of R_k.

$$b_k(r) = \begin{cases} 1 & r \in R_k \\ 0 & elsewise \end{cases}$$

All pixels that $b_k(r)=1$ form the supporting region of R_k. If the motion model and supporting region are given the probability of data $p(f|b,\theta)$, probability model for every pixel $l_k(r)$ can be calculated according to the definitions in Ref.[5]. The definition of motion model $\Phi(r;\theta_k)$ can be seen in Ref.[5] too.

The probability of spatial consistence proposed in this paper is as follows.

$$p(b|\theta) = \frac{1}{S_{R_k}}\sum_{r \in R_k}\eta_k \quad (2)$$

$$\eta_k = \begin{cases} 1 & p_k(r) > p_{k'}(r), k' \neq k \\ 0 & elsewise \end{cases}$$

The more pixels belonging to the motion field k the region R_k includes the larger the $p(b|\theta)$ is . The determination of supporting area is in section 4.

$$p(f,b|\theta) = p(f|b,\theta)p(b|\theta) \qquad (3)$$

The likelihood function is defined in equation (4)

$$Q(b,\theta) = \log(p(g,b|\theta)) = Q_1 + Q_2 \qquad (4)$$

$$Q_1 = \sum_{k=1}^{K}\sum_{r \in R_k} b_k(r)\log(l_k(r))$$

$$Q_2 = \sum_{k=1}^{K}\sum_{r \in R_k} \frac{\eta_k}{S_{R_k}}$$

The posterior probability can be calculated by follow equation according to Bayesian Theorem.

$$p(b,\theta|f) = \frac{p(f,b|\theta)p(\theta)}{p(f)} \qquad (5)$$

P(b,θ|f) can be calculated by equation (3)-(5). p(f) is a normalized constant. If prior knowledge about parameter vector θ is unknown it can be assumed to be a constant. So P(b,θ|f) is in direct proportion to P(f,b |θ). By MAP criterion

$$(\hat{b},\hat{\theta}) = \arg\max_{b,\theta} p(b,\theta|f) = \arg\max_{b,\theta}(p(f,b|\theta) = \arg\min_{b,\theta}(Q(b,\theta))) \qquad (6)$$

3 Motion Estimation by MPM-MAP Method

Under ideal condition b andθin equation (6) can be derived from iteration of EM algorithm according to MAP criterion. But such method is computationally complex so the MPM-MAP algorithm is used here. The advantages of MPM-MAP are showed in Ref.[5]. First assume that b is known andθmaking equation (4) maximum is computed. Thenθis assumed to be given ,so the supporting region making equation (4) maximum is calculated ,which is to compute b making function Q(b, θ) maximum . The above approaches are the two steps in each iteration . In each step the maximum marginal probability of b or θ is computed. The algorithm is as follows.

1) Set the initial value ofθand t=1.
2) Determine the supporting region byθ.That's to say ,b is computed assuming that θis set with the method in section 4.
3) After the supporting region is defined assuming b is known compute optimal θ asθ$^{(t+1)}$according to equation (4)and (6).
4) Repeat step (2) and (3) till the iteration is convergent.
5) Determine the accurate region of moving object by method of active contour introduced in section 5.

There are many ways to deriveθmaking function Q maximum. The over-slacking algorithm in Ref.[7] is adopted here. It belongs to a kind of method of descent gradient and has the advantage of assurance of convergence.

4 Determining of Supporting Region

4.1 Method of Supporting Region's Determination

After model parameter θ is obtained its corresponding region needs to be determined, which is to calculate b at each pixel. First the preselected pixels of R_k are chosen, which is to define R_k' (the initial value of R_k) ,and η_k of each pixel is calculated according to equation (7).

$$R_k' = \{r \mid p_k(r) > p_{k'}(r), k' \neq k\} \tag{7}$$

R_k' consists of pixels having maximum probability belonging to motion θ_k. If R_k' is the target supporting region function Q is maximum for definite θ. This Q is denoted as Q'. Because of errors these preselected pixels usually can't gather in one region. There are always some isolated pixels ,small regions and holes, which were removed by local smoothing methods such as MRF before. But such methods are computationally complex and can't ensure the overall elimination of all small isolated regions and holes. This paper proposes a method to determine supporting area by region shrinking ,which can guarantee the integrity of the region.

This method dosen't use R_k' as supporting area. The target area R_k should make Q maximum, that is to say the target Q should approximate Q' as possible as it can. Assume that when $r \in R_k'$, $l_k(r)$ is approximate to a constant and it is 0 elsewise. The difference between pixels in R_k' can be disregarded and so as to pixels out R_k'. Q changes its expression into the following equation.

$$Q = Q_1 + Q_2 \tag{8}$$

$$Q_1 = \sum_{k=1}^{K} \sum_{r \in f} \eta_k (-\log(l_k(r))) \qquad Q_2 = \sum_{k=1}^{K} \sum_{r \in f} \frac{\eta_k}{S_{R_k}}$$

Here $\sum \eta_k$ is equal to the number of pixels in R_k and belonging to R_k'. In equation (10) the maximum of Q_1 is S_{R_k} which is the area of R_k'. S_{R_k} is equal to the number of pixels in R_k'. That means all pixels in R_k' belong to R_k, which is almost impossible in practice obviously. η_k and S_{R_k} are impossible to derive from Q_1 so they can only get by Q_2. That is

$$(\eta_k, S_{R_k}) = \arg\max Q_2 \tag{9}$$

(η_k, S_{R_k}) by Equation (9) is to make R_k the region with maximum density of preselected pixels. Theoretically this method isn't as near to Q' as MRF-based method in Ref.[5]. But when the moving object is solid and has comparatively simple shape the value by equation(9) is a hypo-optimal value suited to practice better. In figure 1 R_k' is the set of all white pixels while R_k is a rectangular region.

The region with maximum density of preselected pixels is in the area whose center is at mean and range around the center no matter what its distribution is like. According to Chebyshev equation in 3σ (σ is variance) range there is more than 89% probability while in 2σ there is more than 75%. In practice there is always a region with higher density of preselected pixels. So the range with higher density of preselected pixels can be derived from their mean and variance and the supporting area can be obtained from region shrinking.

The method is to compute the mean and variance for all preselected pixels. Every time pixels in the area whose center is at mean μ and range in 2σ are kept and the pixels out of it are deleted. The area in 2σ last time are the all pixels now. μ and σ are recomputed. The region of preselected pixels shrinks and the density increases every time till the increment of the density is smaller than threshold T then the supporting area of motion field is found.

Keeping range of 2σ in region shrinking is suitable for any distribution of probability. In this paper if the difference in probability between preselected pixels is ignored σ can be regarded as average distance of all pixels to the center. The number of pixels in range σ must be larger than that out σ. It means that there is more than 50% probability in range σ. So σ can be used as keeping range instead of 2σ considering that there is always a region in which preselected pixels cluster in.

4.2 Algorithm of Supporting Region's Determination

Rectangle is used to be the shape of preserving region ,which can keep preselected pixels in preserving range. The parameters can be calculated according to rectangular even distribution. The algorithm is as follow.

(1) Assume that the probability of each pixel is same. Calculate the mean μ and covariance matrix C.
(2) According to C derive the eigenvalue λ_1, λ_2 and eigenvector v_1, v_2. μ is center and $2x_r, 2y_r$ is the side length of rectangular region. v_1, v_2 instruct its two main axises. x_r, y_r can be calculated according to equation (10).

$$x_r = \frac{1}{2}\sqrt{12 \cdot \lambda_1} \quad y_r = \frac{1}{2}\sqrt{12 \cdot \lambda_2} \tag{10}$$

(3) Preserve all inner preselected pixels and remove those out of the rectangular region. Then turn to step (1) recompute μ and C till the increment in density of preselected pixels in the region is smaller than threshold T(In this paper T is 0.02). The region with maximum density of preselected pixels can be obtained. In figure 1(b) and 2(b) the rectangular regions from large to small are the computed supporting regions every time. It shows that the accurate position of supporting region can be got by this method.

5 Extraction of Exact Shape of Moving Region

Region shrinking algorithm determines the region with maximum density of preselected pixels but this region is only in a rough shape and needs to be refined to make it exact. It can be achieved in many ways and the GVF-based active contour[9] is chosen here. An initial ellipse contour is defined by supporting region got by the algorithm above-mentioned. μ is its center , x_r, y_r are its two radiuses and v_1, v_2 instruct its two main axises. x(s) represents the active contour whose energy function is defined as equation(11)

$$E = \int_0^1 \frac{1}{2}(\alpha \mid x'(s) \mid^2 + \beta \mid x'(s) \mid^2) + E_{ext}(x(s))ds \tag{11}$$

α and β are used to control the tension and rigidity of the curve. $x'(s)$ and $x''(s)$ denote the first and second derivatives of the curve. Here the external energy function E_{ext} changes as follow:

$$E_{ext}(s) = -(\mid \nabla M_k(r) \mid)^2 \tag{12}$$

$M_k(r)$ is the set of preselected pixels in the supporting region. The details of GVF-based active contour algorithm are described in Ref.[9]. A comparatively accurate region of motion field can be achieved both for the accurate initial contour provided by region shrinking algorithm and the effectiveness of the GVF algorithm.

6 Experiments

Some experiments were performed to validate the algorithm. The results in figure 1 and 2 show the effectiveness of the method used in this paper.

The algorithm in this paper is effective to the objects with simple shape. It has remarkable advantage when the color in the central area of the objects is consistent, such as the images in figure 2.Under above situations this algorithm is better than MRF-based methods. Because the comparatively big holes in objects can't be filled by MRF methods. In results of MRF the outer contours are often larger than the true ones while the holes are filled just as figure 1(e) shows .

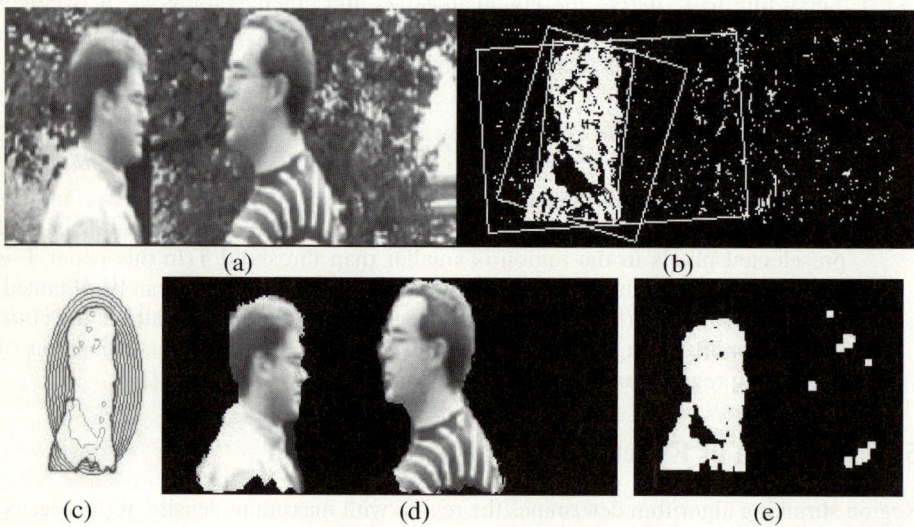

Fig. 1. Segmentation of image 1 (a) Original image (b)Process of region shrinking (c)Process and result of iteration of active contour (d)Extracted moving objects (e)Result of MRF based algorithm

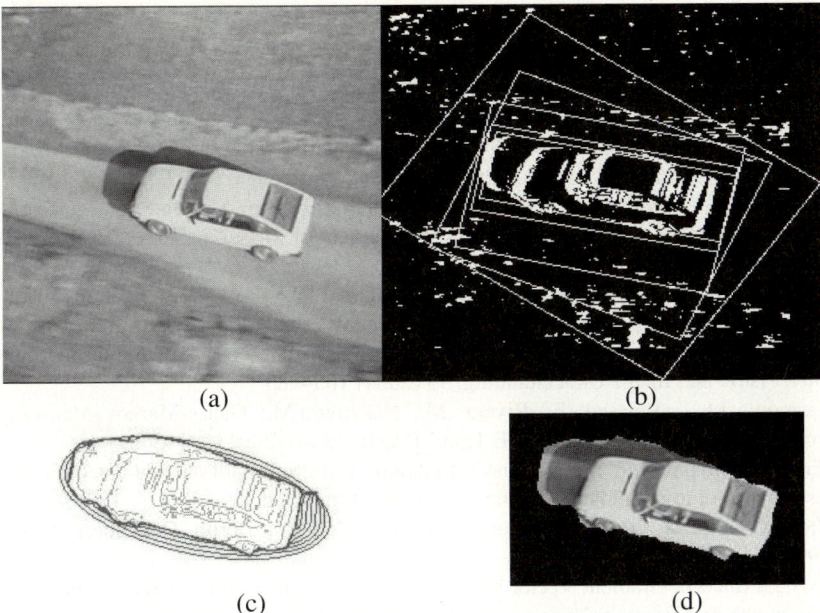

Fig. 2. Segmentation of image 2 (a) Original image (b)Process of region shrinking (c)Process and result of iteration of active contour (d)Extracted moving object

But when the shapes of the objects in images are complex or camera moves the MRF-based methods are better than the method in this paper.

7 Conclusion

On the basis of MPM-MAP algorithm this paper presented a new method of motion segmentation based on region shrinking. First the motion parameters are estimated by MPM-MAP algorithm. The pixels with maximum probabilities belonging to a motion are considered to be preselected pixels for supporting area. Then a method of region shrinking is used to determine the supporting region with maximum density of the preselected pixels. Finally the active contours based on gradient vector flow (GVF) are adopted to derive the precise supporting regions. The advantages of this method are the accurate estimation in both the motion fields and positions of moving objects and the robusticity in the extraction of objects.

However, there are some problems in this method. One is that it is effective to the objects with comparatively simple outer contours, such as human ,car etc.. But it fails for the objects with complex shape such as tree. Another problem is that it can't distinguish the original hole in object. Although some problems exist in this method it offers a new idea to segment objective region and is valuable to be improved in future.

References

1. Wang ,J.Y.A., Adelson, E.H.: Representing Moving Images with Layers. IEEE Trans. Image Process. 3(1994) 625–638.
2. Weiss,Y. :Smoothness in Layers: Motion Segmentation Using Nonparametric Mixture Estimation. In: Proc.IEEE Conf. Comput. Vision Pattern Recogn. (1997)520–527.
3. Weiss ,Y., Adelson,E.H.: A Unified Mixture Framework for Motion Segmentation: Incorporing Spatial Coherence and Estimating the Number of Model. In: Proc. IEEE Conf. Comput. Vision Pattern Recogn.(1996) 321–326.
4. Celeux ,G., Forbes ,F. :EM Procedures Using Mean Field-Like Approximations for Markov Model-Based Image Segmentation. Pattern Recognition 36 (2003) 131 – 144.
5. Calderon, F., Marroquin, J. L.: The MPM–MAP Algorithm for Motion Segmentation. Computer Vision and Image Understanding. 95 (2004) 165–183
6. Marroquin,J.L. , Velasco ,F., Rivera ,M., Nakamura,M.: Gauss-Markov Measure Field Model for Low-Level Vision. IEEE Trans. PAMI 23 (4) (2001) 337–348.
7. Black ,M., Anandan ,P. :The Robust Estimation of Multiple Motions: Parametric and Piecewise-Smooth Flow Fields. Computer Vision and Imag Understanding 63(1)(1996) 75–104
8. Blake,A.,Asard,M. :Active Contours. Springer-Verlag , Berlin Heidelberg New York (1998)
9. Xu ,C., Prince,J.: Gradient Vector Flow -- A New External Force for Snakes. In:IEEE Proc. Conference on Computer Vision and Pattern. Recognition (CVPR'97).

A Family of Novel Clustering Algorithms

Wesam Barbakh, Malcolm Crowe, and Colin Fyfe

Applied Computational Intelligence Research Unit,
The University of Paisley,
Scotland
{wesam.barbakh, malcolm.crowe, colin.fyfe}@paisley.ac.uk

Abstract. We review the performance function associated with the familiar K-Means algorithm and that of the recently developed K-Harmonic Means. The inadequacies in these algorithms leads us to investigate a family of performance functions which exhibit superior clustering on a variety of data sets over a number of different initial conditions. In each case, we derive a fixed point algorithm for convergence by finding the fixed point of the first derivative of the performance function. We give illustrative results on a variety of data sets. We show how one of the algorithms may be extended to create a new topology-preserving mapping.

1 Introduction

The K-Means algorithm is one of the most frequently used investigatory algorithms in data analysis. The algorithm attempts to locate K prototypes or means throughout a data set in such a way that the K prototypes in some way best represents the data. The algorithm is one of the first which a data analyst will use to investigate a new data set because it is algorithmically simple, relatively robust and gives 'good enough' answers over a wide variety of data sets: it will often not be the single best algorithm on any individual data set but be close to the optimal over a wide range of data sets. However the algorithm is known to suffer from the defect that the means or prototypes found depend on the initial values given to them at the start of the simulation: a typical program will converge to a local optimum. There are a number of heuristics in the literature which attempt to address this issue but, at heart, the fault lies in the performance function on which K-Means is based. In this paper, we investigate alternative performance functions and show the effect the different functions have on the effectiveness of the resulting algorithms. We are specifically interested in developing algorithms which are effective in a worst case scenario: when the prototypes are initialised at the same position which is very far from the data points. If an algorithm can cope with this scenario, it should be able to cope with a more benevolent initialisation.

2 Performance Functions for Clustering

The performance function or distortion measure for K-Means may be written as

$$J_K = \sum_{i=1}^{N} \min_{j=1}^{K} \| \mathbf{x}_i - \mathbf{m}_j \|^2 \tag{1}$$

which we wish to minimise by moving the prototypes to the appropriate positions. Note that (1) detects only the centres closest to data points and then distributes them to give the minimum performance which determines the clustering. Any prototype which is still far from data is not utilised and does not enter any calculation that give minimum performance, which may result in dead prototypes, prototypes which are never appropriate for any cluster. Thus initializing centres appropriately can play a big effect in K-Means.

Recently, [7] there have been several investigations of alternative performance functions for clustering algorithms. One of the most effective updates of K-Means has been K-Harmonic Means which minimises

$$J_{HA} = \sum_{i=1}^{N} \frac{K}{\sum_{k=1}^{K} \frac{1}{d(\mathbf{x}_i, \mathbf{m}_k)^2}} \tag{2}$$

for data samples $\{\mathbf{x}_1, , \mathbf{x}_N\}$ and prototypes $\{\mathbf{m}_1, , \mathbf{m}_K\}$. Then we wish to move the centres using gradient descent on this performance function

$$\frac{\partial J_{HA}}{\partial \mathbf{m}_k} = -K \sum_{i=1}^{N} \frac{4(\mathbf{x}_i - \mathbf{m}_k)}{d(\mathbf{x}_i, \mathbf{m}_k)^3 \{\sum_{l=1}^{K} \frac{1}{d(\mathbf{x}_i, \mathbf{m}_l)^2}\}^2} \tag{3}$$

Setting this equal to 0 and "solving" for the $\mathbf{m}_k$'s, we get a recursive formula

$$\mathbf{m}_k = \frac{\sum_{i=1}^{N} \frac{1}{d_{i,k}^3 (\sum_{l=1}^{K} \frac{1}{d_{i,l}^2})^2} \mathbf{x}_i}{\sum_{i=1}^{N} \frac{1}{d_{i,k}^3 (\sum_{l=1}^{K} \frac{1}{d_{i,l}^2})^2}} \tag{4}$$

where we have used $d_{i,k}$ for $d(\mathbf{x}_i, \mathbf{m}_k)$ to simplify the notation. There are some practical issues to deal with in the implementation details of which are given in [7,6].

[7] have extensive simulations showing that this algorithm converges to a better solution (less prone to finding a local minimum because of poor initialisation) than both standard K-means or a mixture of experts trained using the EM algorithm. However we have investigated this algorithm using a number of extreme cases such as when the prototypes are initialised in identical positions and/or are far from the data (see below), and found the algorithm wanting. We thus investigate new algorithms.

3 A Family of Algorithms

We have previously investigated this initialization effect in detail in [1]. We might consider the following performance function:

$$J_A = \sum_{i=1}^{N} \sum_{j=1}^{K} \parallel \mathbf{x}_i - \mathbf{m}_j \parallel^2 \tag{5}$$

which provides a relationship between all the data points and prototypes, but it doesn't provide useful clustering at minimum performance since

$$\frac{\partial J_A}{\partial \mathbf{m}_k} = 0 \implies \mathbf{m}_k = \frac{1}{N}\sum_{i=1}^{N} \mathbf{x}_i, \forall k \qquad (6)$$

Minimizing the performance function groups all the prototypes to the centre of data set regardless of the intitial position of the prototypes which is useless for identification of clusters.

We wish to form a performance function with following properties:

- Minimum performance gives an intuitively 'good' clustering.
- It creates a relationship between all data points and all prototypes.

(5) provides an attempt to reduce the sensitivity to prototypes' initialization by making a relationship between all data points and all prototypes while (1) provides an attempt to cluster data points at the minimum of the performance function. Therefore it may seem that what we want is to combine features of (1) and (5) to make a performance function such as:

$$J_1 = \sum_{i=1}^{N}\left[\sum_{j=1}^{K} \| \mathbf{x}_i - \mathbf{m}_j \| \right] \min_{k=1}^{K} \| \mathbf{x}_i - \mathbf{m}_k \|^2 \qquad (7)$$

We derive the clustering algorithm associated with this performance function by calculating the partial derivatives of (7) with respect to the prototypes. We call the resulting algorithm Weighted K-Means (though recognising that other weighted versions of K-Means have been developed in the literature). The partial derivatives are calculated as

$$\frac{\partial J_{1,i}}{\partial \mathbf{m}_r} = -(\mathbf{x}_i - \mathbf{m}_r)\{\| \mathbf{x}_i - \mathbf{m}_r \| + 2\sum_{j=1}^{K} \| \mathbf{x}_i - \mathbf{m}_j \|\} = -(\mathbf{x}_i - \mathbf{m}_r)a_{ir} \qquad (8)$$

when $\mathbf{m}_r$ is the closest prototype to $\mathbf{x}_i$ and

$$\frac{\partial J_{1,i}}{\partial \mathbf{m}_k} = -(\mathbf{x}_i - \mathbf{m}_k)\frac{\| \mathbf{x}_i - \mathbf{m}_r \|^2}{\| \mathbf{x}_i - \mathbf{m}_k \|} = -(\mathbf{x}_i - \mathbf{m}_r)b_{ik} \qquad (9)$$

otherwise.

We then solve this by summing over the whole data set and finding the fixed point solution of

$$\frac{\partial J_1}{\partial \mathbf{m}_r} = \sum_{i=1}^{N} \frac{\partial J_{1,i}}{\partial \mathbf{m}_r} = 0 \qquad (10)$$

which gives a solution of

$$\mathbf{m}_r = \frac{\sum_{i\in V_r} \mathbf{x}_i a_{ir} + \sum_{i\in V_j, j\neq r} \mathbf{x}_i b_{ir}}{\sum_{i\in V_r} a_{ir} + \sum_{i\in V_j, j\neq r} b_{ir}} \qquad (11)$$

We have given extensive analysis and simulations in [1] showing that this algorithm will cluster the data with the prototypes which are closest to the data points being positioned in such a way that the clusters can be identified. However there are some potential prototypes which are not sufficiently responsive to the data and so never move to identify a cluster. In fact, these points move to (a weighted) centre of the data set. This may be an advantage in some cases in that we can easily identify redundancy in the prototypes however it does waste computational resources unnecessarily.

3.1 A New Algorithm

Consider the performance algorithm

$$J_2 = \sum_{i=1}^{N} \left[\sum_{j=1}^{K} \frac{1}{\| \mathbf{x}_i - \mathbf{m}_j \|^p} \right] \min_{k=1}^{K} \| \mathbf{x}_i - \mathbf{m}_k \|^n \tag{12}$$

Let $\mathbf{m}_r$ be the closest centre to $\mathbf{x}_i$. Then

$$J_2(\mathbf{x}_i) = \left[\sum_{j=1}^{K} \frac{1}{\| \mathbf{x}_i - \mathbf{m}_j \|^p} \right] \| \mathbf{x}_i - \mathbf{m}_r \|^n$$

$$= \| \mathbf{x}_i - \mathbf{m}_r \|^{n-p} + \sum_{j \neq r} \frac{\| \mathbf{x}_i - \mathbf{m}_r \|^n}{\| \mathbf{x}_i - \mathbf{m}_j \|^p} \tag{13}$$

Therefore

$$\frac{\partial J_2(\mathbf{x}_i)}{\partial \mathbf{m}_r} = -(n-p)(\mathbf{x}_i - \mathbf{m}_r) \| \mathbf{x}_i - \mathbf{m}_r \|^{n-p-2}$$

$$- n(\mathbf{x}_i - \mathbf{m}_r) \| \mathbf{x}_i - \mathbf{m}_r \|^{n-2} \sum_{j \neq r} \frac{1}{\| \mathbf{x}_i - \mathbf{m}_j \|^p}$$

$$= (\mathbf{x}_i - \mathbf{m}_r) a_{i,r} \tag{14}$$

$$\frac{\partial J_2(\mathbf{x}_i)}{\partial \mathbf{m}_j} = p(\mathbf{x}_i - \mathbf{m}_j) \frac{\| \mathbf{x}_i - \mathbf{m}_r \|^n}{\| \mathbf{x}_i - \mathbf{m}_j \|^{p+2}} = (\mathbf{x}_i - \mathbf{m}_j) b_{i,j} \tag{15}$$

At convergence, $E(\frac{\partial J_2}{\partial \mathbf{m}_r}) = 0$ where the expectation is taken over the data set. If we denote by V_j the set of points, $\mathbf{x}$ for which $\mathbf{m}_j$ is the closest, we have

$$\frac{\partial J}{\partial \mathbf{m}_r} = 0 \iff \int_{\mathbf{x} \in V_r} \{(n-p)(\mathbf{x}_i - \mathbf{m}_r) \| \mathbf{x}_i - \mathbf{m}_r \|^{n-p-2}$$

$$+ n(\mathbf{x} - \mathbf{m}_r) \| \mathbf{x} - \mathbf{m}_r \|^{n-2} \sum_{j \neq r} \frac{1}{\| \mathbf{x} - \mathbf{m}_j \|^p} P(\mathbf{x})\} d\mathbf{x}$$

$$+ \sum_{j \neq r} \int_{\mathbf{x} \in V_j} p(\mathbf{x} - \mathbf{m}_j) \frac{\| \mathbf{x} - \mathbf{m}_r \|^n}{\| \mathbf{x} - \mathbf{m}_j \|^{p+2}} P(\mathbf{x}) d\mathbf{x} = 0 \tag{16}$$

where $P(\mathbf{x})$ is the probability measure associated with the data set. This is, in general, a very difficult set of equations to solve. However it is readily seen that, for example, in the special case that there are the same number of prototypes as there are data points, that one solution is to locate each prototype at each data point (at which time $\frac{\partial J}{\partial \mathbf{m}_r} = 0$). Again solving this over all the data set results in

$$\mathbf{m}_r = \frac{\sum_{i \in V_r} \mathbf{x}_i a_{ir} + \sum_{i \in V_j, j \neq r} \mathbf{x}_i b_{ir}}{\sum_{i \in V_r} a_{ir} + \sum_{i \in V_j, j \neq r} b_{ir}} \quad (17)$$

From (16), we see that $n \geq p$ if the direction of the first term is to be correct and $n \leq p + 2$ to ensure stability in all parts of that equation. We compare results with $n = p + 1$ and $n = p + 2$ below.

In practice, we have found that a viable algorithm may be found by using (15) for all prototypes (and thus never using (14) for the closest prototype). We will call this the Inverse Weighted K-Means Algorithm.

4 Comparative Study

In order to compare the convergence of these algorithms, we have created a number of data sets with varying degrees of difficulty (see Table 1). The data sets are all two dimensional to make visual identification of the convergence easy. Each data set consists of 4 clusters each of 10 data points drawn from uniform distributions in the four disjoint squares, $\{(x,y) : 0 \leq x < 1, 0 \leq y < 1\}, \{(x,y) : 3 \leq x < 4, 0 \leq y < 1\}, \{(x,y) : 0 \leq x < 1, 3 \leq y < 4\}$, and $\{(x,y) : 3 \leq x < 4, 3 \leq y < 4\}$.

Example 1. We begin with 4 prototypes, initialised in the first square cluster and success is having each of the 4 prototypes identify one of the clusters.
Example 2. Again 4 prototypes but now each prototype is initialised to the same position very distant from the data, the point (100,100).
Example 3, 4. We have 40 prototypes all initialised in the first cluster. Now successful convergence requires each prototype to identify a single data point. This measures the responsiveness of the algorithm to the data.
Example 5. 40 prototypes all initialised to the same position (100,100) far from the data and success is as for Example 3.
Example 6, 7. 40 prototypes randomly initialised throughout $\{(x,y) : 0 \leq x < 4, 0 \leq y < 4\}$ and success is as for Example 3.

We see the results in Table 1. K-Means fails to converge to successful solutions on all these simple data sets. K-Harmonic Means fails in two cases, both of which correspond to the situation in which all prototypes are initialised to the same position far from the data. Weighted K-Means always converges to successful solutions but some simulations take many iterations to converge. Inverse Weighted K-Means also always converges to successful solutions and does so very much faster than Weighted K-Means. In general, it appears that convergence with $n = p + 1$ is faster than when $n = p + 2$, though not in the case of data in Example 5.

Table 1. Number of iterations to convergence on 7 data sets (see text) using the various algorithms. Top: K-Means fails on all 7 data sets, Second Row: K Harmonic Means fails on 2 data sets. Third Row: Weighted K-Means algorithm. Next 5 rows; the Inverse Weighted K-Means with $n = p + 1$. Last 5 rows show results with the the Inverse Weighted K-Means with $n = p + 2$.

	Ex. 1	Ex. 2	Ex. 3	Ex. 4	Ex. 5	Ex. 6	Ex. 7
K-Means	-	-	-	-	-	-	-
KHM	6	-	23	19	-	22	25
WKM	3	7	81	106	142	45	67
IWKM, p=1,n=2	5	7	25	29	100	27	21
IWKM, p=2,n=3	7	6	34	17	88	17	21
IWKM, p=3,n=4	5	8	27	15	83	22	17
IWKM, p=4,n=5	8	8	25	18	92	24	19
IWKM, p=5,n=6	5	6	26	14	86	23	17
IWKM, p=1,n=3	4	6	44	23	93	29	24
IWKM, p=2,n=4	5	9	33	37	88	29	22
IWKM, p=3,n=5	5	7	44	42	81	42	18
IWKM, p=4,n=6	6	7	50	77	85	49	20
IWKM, p=5,n=7	6	13	50	38	88	35	47

Note that the reason which the current algorithm succeeds in these extreme cases when other algorithms fail is because we have available two sets of updates rather than a single update for all prototypes. This is a symmetry-breaking factor which enables local minima to be avoided.

5 A Topology Preserving Mapping

A topographic mapping (or topology preserving mapping) is a transformation which captures some structure in the data so that points which are mapped close to one another share some common feature while points which are mapped far from one another do not share this feature. The Self-organizing Map (SOM) was introduced as a data quantisation method but has found at least as much use as a visualisation tool.

Topology-preserving mappings such as the Self-organizing Map (SOM) [4] and the Generative Topographic Mapping(GTM) [2] have been very popular for data visualization: we project the data onto the map which is usually two dimensional and look for structure in the projected map by eye. We have recently investigated a family of topology preserving mappings [3] which are based on the same underlying structure as the GTM.

The basis of our model is K latent points, $t_1, t_2, \cdots, t_K$, which are going to generate the K prototypes, $\mathbf{m}_k$. To allow local and non-linear modeling, we map those latent points through a set of M basis functions, $f_1(), f_2(), \cdots, f_M()$. This gives us a matrix Φ where $\phi_{kj} = f_j(t_k)$. Thus each row of Φ is the response of the basis functions to one latent point, or alternatively we may state that each column of Φ is the response of one of the basis functions to the set of latent points. One of the functions, $f_j()$, acts as a bias term and is set to one for every input. Typically the others are gaussians centered in the latent space. The output of these functions are then mapped by a set of weights, W, into data space. W is $M \times D$, where D is the dimensionality of the data space, and is the sole parameter which we change during training. We will use $\mathbf{w}_i$ to represent the ith column of W and Φ_j to represent the row vector of the mapping of the jth latent point. Thus each basis point is mapped to a point in data space, $\mathbf{m}_j = (\Phi_j W)^T$.

We may update W either in batch mode or with online learning: with the Topographic Product of Experts [3], we used a weighted mean squared error; with the Harmonic Topographic Mapping [5], we used Harmonic K-Means. We now apply the Inverse Weighted K-Means algorithm to the same underlying structure to create a new topology preserving algorithm.

We create a simulation with 20 latent points deemed to be equally spaced in a one dimensional latent space, passed through 5 Gaussian basis functions and then mapped to the data space by the linear mapping W which is the only parameter we adjust. We generated 60 two dimensional data points, (x_1, x_2), from the function $x_2 = x_1 + 1.25\sin(x_1) + \mu$ where μ is noise from a uniform distribution in [0,1]. Final results from the algorithm are shown in Figure 1. The left diagram shows results with $n = p+1, p = 1$, the right with $n = p+2, p = 1$. We see that, in each case, a topology-preserving mapping has been found.

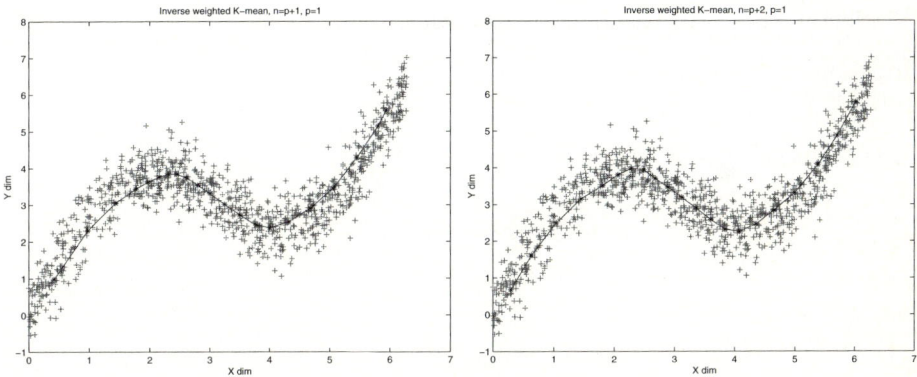

Fig. 1. In both diagrams, the data are shown as red '+'s and the prototypes as blue '*'s. The prototypes have been joined in their natural order. Left: The Inverse Weighted Topolographic Mapping, $n = p+1, p = 1$. Right: Same, $n = p+2, p = 1$.

6 Conclusion

We have reviewed K-Means and K-Harmonic Means and their associated performance functions. We have developed new performance functions and derived fixed point algorithms based on their derivatives. We have shown that the Inverse Weighted K-Means is a better algorithm in terms of convergence to the most informative solutions over a variety of artificial data sets. We emphasise again that the reason which the current algorithm succeeds in extreme cases when other algorithms fail is because we have available two sets of updates rather than a single update for all prototypes. This is a symmetry-breaking factor which enables local minima to be avoided. We have also shown how one of these algorithms can be used as a base for effective topology preserving algorithms as was done with K-Harmonic Means in [3]. Future work will investigate these mappings on real data sets.

References

1. W. Barbakh and C. Fyfe. Performance functions and clustering algorithms. *Computing and Information Systems*, 10(2):2–8, 2006. ISSN 1352-9404.
2. C. M. Bishop, M. Svensen, and C. K. I. Williams. Gtm: The generative topographic mapping. *Neural Computation*, 1997.
3. C. Fyfe. Two topographic maps for data visualization. *Data Mining and Knowledge Discovery*, 2006.
4. Tuevo Kohonen. *Self-Organising Maps*. Springer, 1995.
5. M. Peña and C. Fyfe. Model- and data-driven harmonic topographic maps. *WSEAS Transactions on Computers*, 4(9):1033–1044, 2005.
6. B. Zhang. Generalized k-harmonic means – boosting in unsupervised learning. Technical report, HP Laboratories, Palo Alto, October 2000.
7. B. Zhang, M. Hsu, and U. Dayal. K-harmonic means - a data clustering algorithm. Technical report, HP Laboratories, Palo Alto, October 1999.

Vector Quantization Segmentation for Head Pose Estimation

José Lopes and Sameer Singh

Research School of Informatics, Loughborough University, Loughborough, LE11 3TU, UK
J.E.F.C.Lopes@lboro.ac.uk, S.Singh@lboro.ac.uk

Abstract. Head pose estimation is an important area of investigation for understanding human dynamics. Appearance-based methods are one of the popular solutions to this problem. In this paper we present a novel approach using vector quantization that adds spatial information to the feature set. We compare this with raw, Gabor filtered and Wavelet features using the Carnegie Mellon PIE database. Our approach shows increased performance over the other methods.

1 Introduction

There has been a great amount of interest in finding human faces in images and videos and understanding human behavior [21][17][19]. Examples of practical applications include intelligent surveillance systems, smart rooms technology, teleconferencing, and human-computer interaction (HCI) [3]. The understanding of head pose is extremely important for understanding human behavior and human-object interaction. It is directly related to estimating the direction of eye gaze and understanding the attention that the human observer is paying to a particular object. In addition, head pose estimation is also important for performing tasks such as face recognition where template matching or feature based classification are based on information taken from a specific pose image.

The task of head pose estimation is not trivial and several solutions have been proposed in the literature. There is considerable variability in the approaches involved, e.g. some methods classify discrete subsets of the rotation space while others estimate the pose angle to a certain degree of precision; some studies use monocular or stereo images, while others track pose over a video sequence.

The motivation for this work is to investigate the validity of using vector quantization image segmentation to process the face appearance. We hypothesize that by using intensity and spatial information of the clusters, we can improve on standard appearance-based techniques.

This paper is laid out as follows. Section 2 provides the background to the research field. In section 3, we provide the theory and implementation details of our method. We present experimental results in section 4 and conclude in section 5.

2 Background

The problem of estimating head pose can be defined by the process of obtaining the six components that describe the head in 3D space (x, y, z, θ, ϕ, γ), i.e. the position and orientation angles (yaw, pitch and roll) of the head in 3D space. In our study, these values are to be estimated from a monocular grayscale image. Also, while the more generic situation concerns estimating the actual angles to a given degree of precision in the classification case, poses are aggregated into discrete sets containing similar orientation angles. There are several methods proposed to address the problem of head pose estimation. We organize these into three main categories: Feature, Model and Appearance based approaches. These are described in brief below.

2.1 Feature Based Approach

Feature-based procedures derive from a very intuitive concept: "that after identifying facial landmarks, it is possible to estimate head pose from their spatial relationships" (e.g. if we know the positions of eyes, mouth, nose or ears and their relationship, it is possible to make an educated guess about orientation of the head). Hence, this process involves detecting facial features and computing orthographic or affine projection to extrapolate the original 3D pose [4].

A number of studies have used feature-based approaches to pose estimation [8][10][2]. The main issue when using feature based pose estimation is that we need to have good image resolution so that the features are detected with a high degree of success and localized with high precision. Secondly, for systems that require identification of large ranges of rotation, it is necessary to deal with feature occlusion, which requires that different methods handle different feature occurrences (e.g. if someone turns sideways, we can only locate one eye). Finally, this approach introduces errors in both stages, consequently propagating the error from the feature detection stage to the final transformation result.

2.2 Model Based Approach

Model based approaches map an artificially generated 3D model to the image acquired. This involves the creation of a 3D structure, representing a generic face, which is manipulated to fit the image input. Once the transformed model fits the input, we can claim that both share the same pose. Examples that use this type of method include [11] and [9]. The main problem when using model-based methods is that we need a robust and generic design of the model to match different faces. Unfortunately, high computational complexity of most algorithms often prevents such models to be used in real-time.

2.3 Appearance Based Approach

This approach uses the face image as a whole after some form of pre-processing and generates a model from an image database using statistical or pattern recognition techniques. The input image can then be applied to a classifier or other type of decision algorithm to be labeled as of a certain pose. The main challenge in developing a robust technique is to reduce the influence of unwanted information such as illumination variance and background clutter.

Appearance based approaches have been very popular. They usually involve pre-processing the images, e.g. filtering [20], texture analysis [14]. The appearance vector is then used as classification data. Different types of classification schemes have also been explored [13][17][5][6][1][15].

Appearance-based algorithms present some benefits over the other approaches since: (a) feature-based techniques require high-resolution images and are prone to occlusion problems; (b) model-based need 3D structure definition that can be computationally complex. Nevertheless, by concentrating on the facial appearance as a whole, they fail to explore explicitly the spatial relation between pertinent features.

3 Head Pose Estimation Using Vector Quantization

Vector Quantization (VQ) has been used extensively in a variety of applications such as signal processing and compression. In particular, it can be used for image segmentation and object tracking [6].

VQ is the process of mapping k-dimensional vectors in the space R^k into a finite set of vectors V = {v_i: i = 1,2,...,N} called codewords or prototypes [11].

For image segmentation and clustering, similar to [6] each pixel in a grayscale images is defined as feature vector $f_{ij} = (I_{ij}, i, j)$. The image is the set of all pixels: $X = \{f_{ij}, \forall i \forall j\}$.

The process of clustering if finding the set of prototypes that minimize the sum of quantization errors $\sum_{ij} f_{ij} - p_{\min}$ where $p_{\min}$ is the prototype closest to f_{ij}.

There are several techniques to arrive at a suboptimal solution. We start with one cluster that encompasses all points in X.

In each iteration, we select the cluster with higher variance. This cluster is divided in two by a hyperplane perpendicular to the direction of higher variance (the covariance matrix first eigenvector).

A prototype is attributed to each set as the mean value of the set.

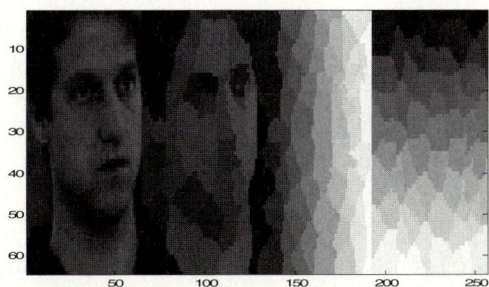

Fig. 1. Example of Vector Quantization Segmentation. From left to right: Original picture; Prototype intensity, Prototype centers x and y.

Stopping conditions can be the number of clusters or a threshold to the quantization error. In the case of this work, we decided empirically on 64 clusters as a good representation of the images used.

Finally, for recognition purpose, we replace each pixel with its prototype, thus conveying information in a visual appearance manner about the grayscale and position of each cluster.

An example of the segmentation end result is shown in figure 1.

4 Experimental Evaluation

Our experimental setup uses Carnegie Mellon University's Pose, Illumination and Expression (PIE) database [16], which includes pictures of 68 subjects taken with 13 different camera angles and under different illumination conditions (for a detailed description of the exact angles and conditions see [16]). We use images with neutral expression and normal illumination for a total of images. Each face is cropped from the image (we selected the smallest rectangular area that includes all facial skin colored pixels), resized to 64x64 pixels and converted to a grayscale image (figure 2).

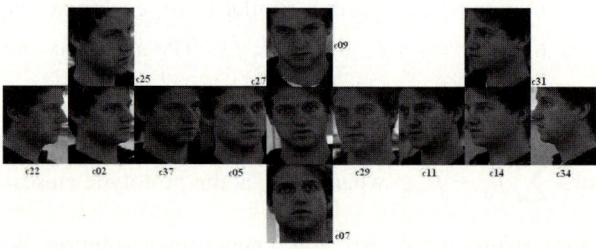

Fig. 2. Pre-processed images of one subject from CMU PIE Database

To compare the performance of the vector quantized data, we use the following alternatives:

- Raw data: X ;
- Gabor filtered data as described in [1] use a 2D feature vector instead of the more complex 3D model to represent information. In their method, face images are convoluted with four different templates: a 3x3 Gaussian mask and three 11x11 rotation-invariant Gabor templates, with (σ, ω) = (1,0.5), (2,0.25) and (4,0.0125). These are defined as:

$G(\sigma, \omega) = g(\sigma, \omega, 0) + g(\sigma, \omega, 45) + g(\sigma, \omega, 90) + g(\sigma, \omega, 135)$,

where $g(\sigma, \omega, \theta) = C \times e^{\frac{-(x^2+y^2)}{2\sigma^2}} \times \cos[(x\cos(\theta) + y\sin(\theta)) \times \omega]$, C is a standardization constant and x and y the coordinates of the template.
- We perform a two-level discrete wavelet transform (DWT) using the biorthogonal wavelet family as described in [14].

Although the literature mentions different classification procedures, we decided to use support vector machines according to [6]. Future work will compare the performance and complexity of using alternative classifiers.

The experiments evaluate the average success rate of an n-fold cross-validation of the classification procedure. Given N number of samples (68 in our case), we divide the overall dataset into n groups (folds). In our experiments we chose n as 2, 3, 5 and 10 and show results as an average of results on these numbers of folds. If n=10 then we divide the set into 10 groups each consisting of 7 subjects except 2 groups that have 6 subjects. Then we use n-1 groups for training and 1 group for testing. We repeat this process n times using a different training and testing set each time and average the success rate. Hence, as the value of n increases in our experiments, we have more training data and less test data per fold (e.g. the training and test samples per fold are as follows, respectively: 2 folds (442:442); 3 folds (590:294); 5 folds (708:176) and 10 folds (796:88). The test results are shown on the same number of test samples that aggregated across all folds, equal the total number of samples we have for analysis.

Figure 3 shows the success rates of the four processing techniques. Results are shown as classification accuracy averaged on 2-fold, 3-fold, 5-fold and 10-fold cross-validation (the results get better for 10 fold cross-validation since we have a larger training data set). It is clear that the vector quantized data outperforms the other three achieving an average success rate of 86% for the 10 fold case.

We can also confirm that performance improves in general as the number of folds increases. This supports the argument that the amount of training data is crucial for good classification.

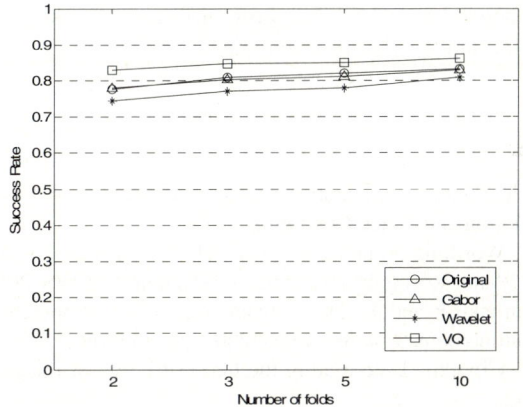

Fig. 3. Classification Mean Success Rates

Finally, a t-test was performed to compare the mean results across the different 10-fold cross-validation results. The statistical significance results are displayed in table 1. This shows that the classification performance of the VQ algorithm to be statistically significantly different to the other models. Furthermore, both Gabor and Wavelet samples produce results that are not statistically different from using the original data.

This result is quite important. More extensive experiments with other classification setups are required to determine exactly the benefits of using such preprocessing techniques.

Table 1. Mean comparison; significance (p-value associated with t-statistic) at 5% significance level

	Gabor	Wavelet	VQ
Original	0.7661	0.0782	0.0002
Gabor		0.0732	0.0086
Wavelet			0.0015

5 Conclusion

Head pose estimation is an important field of research in image processing. Some of its most popular approaches involve classification methodologies applied to the face appearance itself.

We argued that by segmenting the appearance we can provide spatial information about the location of clusters, which can be beneficial to the classification process.

Comparing this method with established techniques offers evidence that in fact such system is better.

Further work is needed to investigate how different processing techniques behave when used with different classification schemes.

References

[1] L. Brown and Y. Tian, "Comparative Study of Coarse Head Pose Estimation", IEEE Workshop on Motion and Video Computing, 2002.
[2] K.N. Choi, P.L. Worthington and E.R. Hancock, "Estimating Facial Pose Using Shape-From-Shading", Patter Recognition Letters, v.23 n.5, pp.533-548, 2002.
[3] T. Fong, I. Nourbakhsh and K. Dautenhahn, "A survey of socially interactive robots", Robotics and Autonomous Systems, 42(3), 2003, pp. 143-166.
[4] A.H.Gee and R. Cipolla, "Determining the Gaze of Faces in Images", Image and Video Computing, 1994.
[5] S. Gong, E. Ong, S. McKenna, "Learning to Associate Faces across Views in Vector Space of Similarities to Prototypes", Biological Motivated Computer Vision, 1998.
[6] B. Heisele, U. Kressel, and W. Ritter, "Tracking nonrigid, moving objects based on color cluster flow," Proc. IEEE Conf. Computer Vision and Pattern Recognition, pp. 257–260, June 1997.
[7] J. Huang, X. Shao, H. Wechsler, "Face Pose Discrimination Using Support Vector Machines (SVM)", Proc. of ICPR, 1998.
[8] Q. Ji, "3D Face Pose Estimation and Tracking from a Monocular Camera", Image and Vision Computing, v.20, issue 7, pp.499-511, 2002.
[9] V. Krueger and G. Sommer, "Gabor Wavelet Networks for Efficient Head Pose Estimation", Image and Vision Computing, 20, pp.665-672, 2002.

[10] C. Lin, K. Fan, "Pose Classification of Human Faces by Weighting Mask Function Approach", Pattern Recognition Letters 24(12), pp.1857-1869, 2003.
[11] Y. Linde, A. Buzo and R. M. Gray, "An algorithm for vector quantizer design", IEEE Trans. On Communications, vol.28, pp. 84-95, Jan. 1980.
[12] M. Malciu and F. Pretuex, "A Robust Model-Based Approach for 3D Head Tracking in Video Sequences", Fourth IEEE International Conference on Automatic Face and Gesture Recognition, 2000.
[13] S. McKenna and S. Gong, "Real-time Face Pose Estimation", International Journal on Real Time Imaging, Vol. 4, pp. 333-347, 1998.
[14] M.C. Motwani and Q. Ji, "3D Face Pose Discrimination Using Wavelets", Proc. of ICIP, 2001.
[15] R. Rae and H.J. Ritter, "Recognition of Human Head Orientation Based on Artificial Neural Networks", IEEE Trans. Neural Networks, No. 2, March 1998.
[16] T. Sim, S. Baker, and M. Bsat, "The CMU Pose, Illumination, and Expression Database", IEEE Trans. on Patter Analysis and Machine Intelligence, Vol. 25, No. 12, December, 2003, pp. 1615 – 1618.
[17] S. Srinivasan and K.L. Boyer, "Head Pose Estimation Using View Based Eigenspaces", Proc. of ICPR, 2002.
[18] R. Stiefelhagen, J. Yang and A. Waibel, "Tracking Eyes and monitoring Eye Gaze", Proceedings of Workshop on Perceptive User Interfaces, pp. 98-100, 1997.
[19] J. Wang and S. Singh, "Video Based Human Dinamics: A Survey", Real Time Imaging, vol. 9, issue 5, pp. 321-346, 2003.
[20] Y.C. Wei, L. Fradet, T.N. Tan, "Head Pose Estimation using Gabor Eigenspace Modeling", Proc. of ICIP, 2002.
[21] M.-H. Yang, D. Kriegman, and N. Ahuja. "Detecting faces in images: A survey", IEEE Transactions on Pattern Analysis and Machine Intelligence, 24(1), 2002, pp. 34-58.

Neural Network Detectors for Composite Hypothesis Tests

D. de la Mata-Moya, P. Jarabo-Amores, R. Vicen-Bueno,
M. Rosa-Zurera, and F. López-Ferreras

Departamento de Teoría de la Señal y Comunicaciones,
Escuela Politécnica Superior, Universidad de Alcalá
Ctra. Madrid-Barcelona, km. 33.600, 28805, Alcalá de Henares - Madrid, Spain
{david.mata, mpilar.jarabo, raul.vicen, manuel.rosa,
francisco.lopez}@uah.es
http://www2.uah.es/teose/

Abstract. Neural networks (NNs) are proposed for approximating the Average Likelihood Ratio (ALR). The detection of gaussian targets with gaussian autocorrelation function and unknown one-lag correlation coefficient, ρ_s, in Additive White Gaussian Noise (AWGN) is considered. After proving the low robustness of the likelihood ratio (LR) detector with respect to ρ_s, the ALR detector assuming a uniform distribution of this parameter in [0, 1] has been studied. Due to the complexity of the involved integral, two NN based solutions are proposed. Firstly, single Multi-Layer Perceptrons (MLPs) are trained with target patterns with ρ_s varying in [0, 1]. This scheme outperforms the LR detector designed for a fixed value of ρ_s. MLP with 17 hidden neurons is proposed as a solution. Then, two MLPs trained with target patterns with ρ_s varying in [0, 0.5] and [0.5, 1], respectively, are combined. This scheme outperforms the single MLP and allows to determine a solution of compromise between complexity and approximation error. A detector composed of MLPs with 17 and 8 hidden units each one is proposed.

1 Introduction

Neural networks (NNs) are proposed as a solution for approximating the Average Likelihood Ratio (ALR) detector in composite hypothesis-tests. While in simple hypothesis tests, the likelihood functions, $f(\mathbf{z}|H_0)$ and $f(\mathbf{z}|H_1)$, are known, in composite hypothesis ones, one of them or both depends on some parameters. When the probability density function (pdf) of the parameters governing the hypothesis are known, the decision rule resulting of comparing the output of the ALR with a detection threshold fixed attending to probability of false alarm (P_{FA}) requirements, is an implementation of the optimum detector in the Neyman-Pearson (NP) sense [1]. The NP detector maximizes the probability of detection (P_D), while maintaining the P_{FA} lower than or equal to a given value. This decision criterion is commonly used in radar detection, where it is difficult to assing realistic costs or a priori probabilities.

In a radar detection problem, the interference parameters can be estimated from measurements in the operating environment, but target parameters can not. Because of that, the radar detection problem can be formulated as a composite hypothesis test, where the likelihood function under hypothesis H_1 depends on a set of parameters θ. If the pdf of θ is known, the ALR can be calculated with (1), where χ is the parameter space [1]:

$$\Lambda(\mathbf{z}) = \frac{f(\mathbf{z}|H_1)}{f(\mathbf{z}|H_0)} = \frac{\int_\chi f(\mathbf{z}|\theta, H_1) f(\theta) d\theta}{f(\mathbf{z}|H_0)} \quad (1)$$

$f(\theta)$ is usually unknown, and the optimum test is the ALR assuming that it is uniform in the variation interval [2]. In many situations, this approach leads to intractable integrals without a closed-form solution.

NNs are known to be able to approximate the optimum Bayessian classifier [3,4,5], and they have been widely applied to classification tasks. But there are less examples of their application to detection problems attending to the NP criterion. The possibility of approximating this detector using adaptive systems trained in a supervised manner for minimizing an error function, has been proven in [6]. Multi-Layer Perceptrons (MLPs), have been applied to approximate the NP detector in simple hypothesis tests [7,8,9,10]. In this paper, NNs are proposed as tools to approximate the ALR detector in composite hypothesis tests, not only to overcome the difficulty of solving the integral in the numerator of (1), but to obtain an approximation with lower computational cost than other numerical ones.

2 Case of Study

The problem of detecting gaussian targets with gaussian autocorrelation function (ACF) and zero doppler shift, in additive white gaussian noise (AWGN) is considered. The target echo is modelled as a zero mean complex vector, $\mathbf{z} \in \mathcal{C}^n$, with covariance matrix $(\mathbf{M}_s)_{h,k} = p_s \cdot \rho_s^{|h-k|^2}$, where ($h, k = 1, 2, ..., n$), and p_s and ρ_s are, respectively, the target power and the one-lag correlation coefficient. The covariance matrix of the interference is given by $(\mathbf{M}_n)_{h,k} = p_n \delta_{hk}$, where p_n is the noise power and δ_{hk} is the Kronecker delta. p_n is assumed equal to 2, and the signal-to-noise ratio is calculated as $SNR = 10 log_{10}(p_s/p_n) = 10 log_{10}(p_s/2)$.

As a first step, the simple hypothesis test for detecting targets with known ρ_s and SNR values is considered. In this case, the likelihood ratio (LR) is the optimum one [1], and a study of its robustness with respect to ρ_s and SNR is carried out. After proving the low robustness with respect to ρ_s, the calculus of the ALR is proposed assuming that ρ_s is uniformly distributed in [0, 1].

2.1 Robustness of the LR Detector with Respect to SNR and ρ_s

When p_s and ρ_s have known specific values, the log-likelihood ratio (LLR) can be easily calculated and, after eliminating immaterial constants, the NP decision rule can be expressed as in (2), where $\mathbf{z}^T$ denotes the transposed vector, while $\mathbf{z}^*$ denotes the complex conjugate one.

$$\mathbf{z}^T[\mathbf{M}_n^{-1} - (\mathbf{M}_n + \mathbf{M}_s) - \mathbf{I}]\mathbf{z}^* \underset{H_0}{\overset{H_1}{\gtrless}} \eta_1(P_{FA}) \qquad (2)$$

The statistic of rule (2) depends on the SNR and ρ_s values, because matrix $\mathbf{M}_s$ does. These are the design SNR and ρ_s values that will be denoted as $DSNR$ and ρ_s^d, respectively. On the other hand, the observation vector is generated with SNR and ρ_s values known as *simulation* ones, that will be denoted as $SSNR$ and ρ_s^s, respectively. Clearly, the detector is only optimum for input vectors with $SSNR = DSNR$ and $\rho_s^s = \rho_s^d$.

In order to study the robustness of rule (2) with respect to the $DSNR$, given a $SSNR$ value, ROC curves have been plotted for different $DSNRs$. As in Air Traffic Control radar, the usual number of collected pulses in a scan is $n = 8$, this is the dimension of the complex input vector $\mathbf{z}$. In all cases, $\rho_s^s = \rho_s^d$, and both are denoted as ρ_s. For saving space, only the results obtained for $SSNR = 7dB$, $DSNR = 0, 3, 7, 10dB$ and different ρ_s values are presented (left side of figure 1). In general, the dependence on $DSNR$ reduces as $SSNR$ increases. The value of $SSNR = 7dB$ has been selected because in this case P_D values are suitable for all ρ_s ones, in the range of P_{FAs} that are of interest in practical situations. Results show a low dependence on $DSNR$ for SNR values that fulfill these conditions.

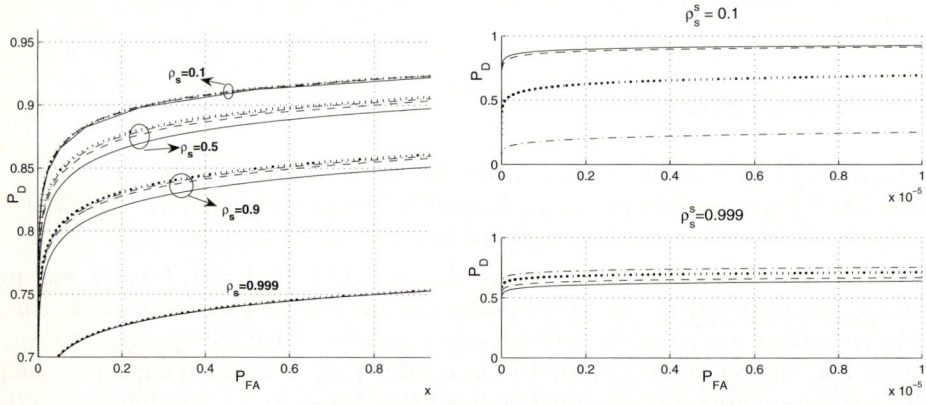

Fig. 1. Left: ROC curves for $SSNR = 7dB$ and different ρ_s and $DSNR$ values. Right: ROC curves for $DSSN = SSNR = 7dB$, two ρ_s^s values, and $\rho_s^d = 0.1$ (solid), $\rho_s^d = 0.5$ (dashed), $\rho_s^d = 0.9$ (dotted) and $\rho_s^d = 0.999$ (dashdot).

To evaluate the robustness with respect to ρ_s, given a ρ_s^s, ROC curves have been plotted for $DSNR = SSNR = 7dB$, and different ρ_s^d values. Results are shown on the right side of figure 1. For low values of ρ_s^s, the dependence on ρ_s^d is very important, and P_D decreases dramatically when ρ_s^d tends to unity. On the other hand, the ρ_s^d dependence is lower for high values of ρ_s^s, but it is still important (a 10% decrease is observed in P_D for $\rho_s^d = 0.1$ and $\rho_s^s = 0.999$).

2.2 The ALR Detector for Targets of Unknown ρ_s

Assuming that ρ_s can be modelled as a random variable with uniform pdf in the interval $[0,1]$, and according to (1), the optimum decision rule in the NP sense involves the calculus of the following integral:

$$\int_0^1 \frac{1}{\pi^n \cdot \det\left[\mathbf{M_s}(\rho_s) + \mathbf{M}_n\right]} \exp\left\{-\mathbf{z}^T[\mathbf{M_s}(\rho_s) + \mathbf{M}_n]^{-1}\mathbf{z}^*\right\} d\rho_s \qquad (3)$$

As $[\mathbf{M_s}(\rho_s) + \mathbf{M}_n)]$ is a function of ρ_s, its determinant and the argument of the exponential in (3) are complex functions of ρ_s. Because of that, the calculus of this integral is very complex. NN based detectors are proposed to approximate an expression equivalent to the ALR.

3 NN Based Detectors

Two NN based approaches are studied for approximating the ALR for gaussian targets with gaussian ACF, and unknown ρ_s in AWGN:

- In a first approach, detectors based on one MLP are trained to approximate the ALR, using training and validation sets where target patterns have ρ_s values that vary uniformly in $[0,1]$.
- In a second approach, the detectors compare the outputs of two MLPs trained using training and validation sets where target patterns have ρ_s values that vary uniformly in $[0, 0.5]$ and $[0.5, 1]$, respectively.

Taking into consideration the results presented in [6], in both cases, the MLPs are able to converge to the ALR for the corresponding pair of hypothesis. In the first case, the NN converges to the desired function, so its output must be compared to a detection threshold fixed attending to P_{FA} requirements in order to decide if target is present or not. In the second strategy, the approximation capabilities of the NNs are exploited to approximate the ALR for smaller intervals of variations of ρ_s. This strategy can be explained taking into consideration the results presented in [10,11], which prove that the minimum number of hidden units that are necessary to enclose the decision boundary is expected to be between 3 and 17 (for $\rho_s = 1$ and $\rho_s = 0$, respectively). So, there is a strong relation between the structure of the MLP and the range of variation of ρ_s. Reducing this range, a given structure is expected to converge with lower approximation error. Also, this structure can be minimized in order to reduce the computational charge associated to the combination of MLPs.

3.1 Design of the Experiments

As the considered MLPs use real arithmetic, the n-dimension complex vectors are transformed in $2n$-dimension real ones, composed of the real and imaginary parts of the complex samples. MLPs with $2n = 16$ inputs, a hidden layer and an output neuron have been trained. In this context, the design parameters previously defined are known as 'training parameters'. The Training Signal-to-Noise ratio ($TSNR$) is the value selected for generating the training and validation sets, while the $SSNR$ is the value selected for generating the simulation sets for evaluating the performance of the trained NNs. According to the results presented in section 2.1, all ROC curves are presented for $TSNR = SSNR = 7dB$.

MLPs have been trained for minimizing the cross-entropy error, using the strategy proposed in [12]. A cross-validation technique has been used to avoid over-fitting and all NNs have been initialized using the Nguyen-Widrow method [13]. For each case, the training process has been repeated ten times. Only the cases where the performances of the ten trained networks were similar in average, have been considered to extract conclusions.

P_{FA} values have been estimated using Importance Sampling techniques (relative error lower than 10% in the presented results) [14]. P_D values have been estimated using conventional Montecarlo simulation.

4 Results

4.1 Detectors Based on a MLP

Results are presented for detectors that use a single MLP trained with ρ_s varying uniformly in $[0, 1]$. According to results presented in [10,11], the minimum number of hidden units could have been set to 17, although MLPs with lower number of hidden units have also been trained. ROC curves for $TSNR = SSNR = 7dB$ and 14, 17, 20 and 23 hidden units are presented on the left side of figure 2. This results prove that for less than 17 hidden units, a loss in detection capabilities is observed, while for bigger NNs, there is no significative improvement in detection capabilities. On the right side of the figure, the MLP with 17 hidden units is compared to the LR detectors designed for $\rho_s^d = 0.1$ and $\rho_s^d = 0.999$, respectively, for the same sets of simulation patterns. Clearly, the MLP based detector outperform the LR ones designed for fixed values of ρ_s^d.

4.2 Detectors Based on Two MLPs

In this section, neural detectors composed of two MLPs trained with targets whose ρ_s varies uniformly in $[0, 0.5]$ and $[0.5, 1]$, respectively, are analyzed. The former will be denoted as MLP_1 while the latest will be denoted as MLP_2. Again, as a starting point, MLPs with 17 hidden units have been trained. On the left side of figure 3, the ROC curve for $TSNR = SSNR = 7dB$ is compared to that obtained for a single MLP with 17 hidden units and the same set of simulation patterns, showing that the new detector outperforms the previous one significatively. To study the cause of this performance improvement, ROC curves have been simulated for targets with $\rho_s^s = 0.1$ and $\rho_s^s = 0.999$ (right side of figure 3). Results show that for $\rho_s^s = 0.999$ the performance of the detector composed of two MLPs is slightly worse than that of the single MLP. For $\rho_s^s = 0.1$ the detector

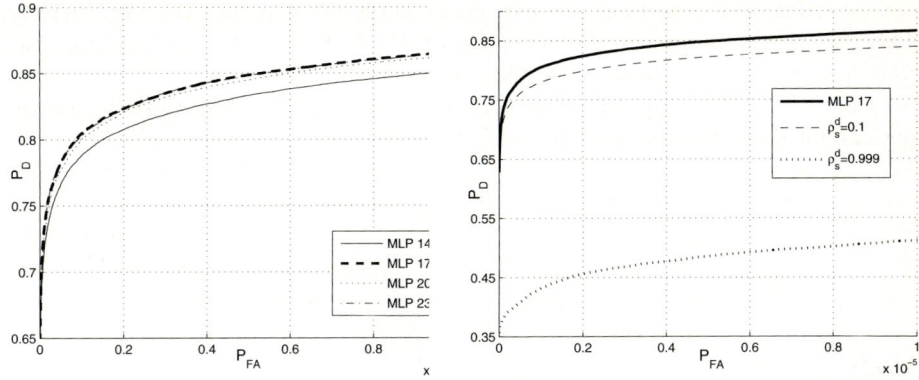

Fig. 2. Left: MLPs with 14, 17, 20 and 23 hidden neurons. Right: MLP with 17 hidden units and LR detectors with $\rho_s^d = 0.1$ and $\rho_s^d = 0.999$. In all cases $TSNR = SSNR = 7dB$ and ρ_s^s varies uniformly in $[0, 1]$.

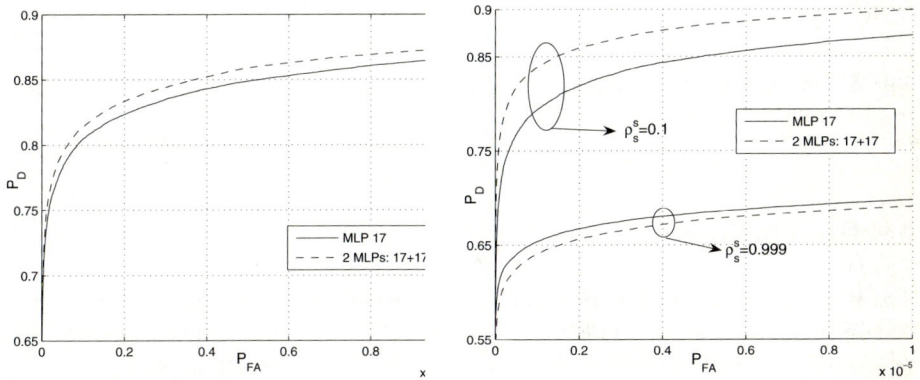

Fig. 3. Left: Single MLP with 17 hidden neurons and two MLPs with 17 hidden neurons when ρ_s^s varies uniformly in $[0, 1]$ and $TSNR = SSNR = 7dB$. Right: The same detectors when $\rho_s^s = 0.1$ and $\rho_s^s = 0.999$

composed of two MLPs outperforms the single MLP. These results prove why, in average, the detector composed by two MLPs outperforms the single one for ρ_s varying in $[0, 1]$. Note that in 2.1 we proved that the dependence on ρ_s^d is bigger for low values of ρ_s^s. Considering [10,11], these results suggest that to improve the approximation implemented by MLP_1, its number of hidden units should be increased, while, in the case of MLP_2, a reduction in complexity could simplify the training process and give rise to a better approximation. A study of the influence of the number of hidden neurons of each MLP has been carried out, and the obtained results are presented in figure 4.

In a first step, the number of hidden neurons of MLP_2 has been reduced, while the number of hidden neurons of MLP_1 has been fixed to 17. Results presented on the left side of figure 4 show that the number of hidden neurons of MLP_2

can be reduced to 8 without decreasing the detection capabilities significatively. Then, fixing the number of hidden units of MLP_2 to 8, a study of the influence MLP_1 size has been carried out. On the right side of figure 4, ROC curves are presented for different number of hidden units in MLP_1. Results show that no performance improvement is obtained when MLP_1 size is increased.

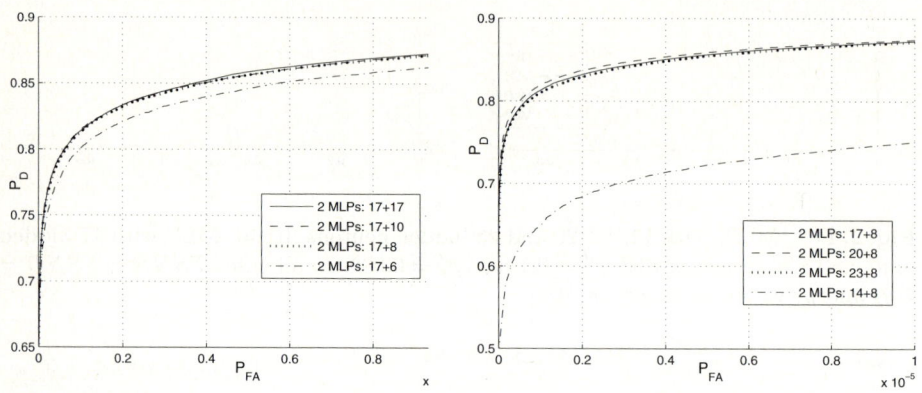

Fig. 4. Left: the number of hidden units of MLP_1 is fixed to 17, while for MLP_2 varies from 17 to 6. Right: the number of hidden units of MLP_2 is fixed to 8, while for MLP_1 varies from 14 to 23. ρ_s varies uniformly in $[0, 1]$ and $TSNR = SSNR = 7dB$

5 Conclusions

Taking into consideration previous results where NNs are proved to be able to approximate the NP detector, two different NN based approaches are proposed and analyzed for approximating the ALR in composite hypothesis-testing problems. In many practical cases the ALR involves the calculus of intractable integrals that can have no closed solution, but its suitability is proved in that cases where the robustness of the LR detector for a simple hypothesis test with respect to the statistical models assumed for the hypothesis is very low. In this paper, the case of detecting gaussian targets with gaussian ACF and unknown one-lag correlation coefficient, ρ_s, in AWGN is considered. After proving the low robustness of the LR detector with respect to ρ_s, the ALR detector assuming a uniform distribution of this parameter in $[0, 1]$ has been studied. Due to the complexity of the involved integral, NN based solutions are proposed. MLPs are trained with target patterns with ρ_s varying in $[0, 1]$, and results prove that this scheme outperforms the LR detector designed for a fixed value of the parameter. MLPs with 17 hidden neurons are proposed as a solution after observing no significative performance improvement when the number of hidden units is increased. Attending to the influence of ρ_s on the decision boundary, and how a MLP build it, a detector based on two MLPs trained for ρ_s ranging in $[0, 0.5]$ and $[0.5, 1]$ has been designed and analyzed. Results show that this scheme outperforms the single MLP and allows to understand network size influence in order to determine a solution of compromise between complexity and approximation error. Two MLPs with 17 and 8 hidden units are proposed as the best solution.

References

1. Van Trees, H.L.:Detection, estimation, and modulation theory, Vol. 1. Wiley (1968).
2. Aref, M.R., Nayebi, M.M.: Likelihood-ratio detection. IEEE Int. Symp. on Information Theory. Trondheim, Norway (1994) 260.
3. Ruck, D.W., Rogers, S.K., Kabrisky, M., Oxley M.E., Suter, B.W.: The multilayer perceptron as an aproximation to a Bayes optimal discriminant function. IEEE Transactions on Neural Networks, Vol. 1, No. 4 (1990) 296-298.
4. Wan, E.A.: Neural network classification: a bayesian interpretation. IEEE Transactions on Neural Networks, Vol. 1, No. 4 (1990) 303-305.
5. Richard, M.D., Lippmann, R.P.: Neural network classifiers estimate Bayessian a posteriori probabilities. Neural Computation, Vol. 3, (1991) 461-483.
6. Jarabo-Amores, P., Rosa-Zurera, M., Gil-Pita, R., López-Ferreras, F.: Suficient Condition for an Adaptive System to Approximate the Neyman-Pearson Detector. Proc. IEEE Workshop on Statistical Signal Processing. Bordeaux, France (2005).
7. Gandhi, P.P., Ramamurti, V.: Neural networks for signal detection in non-gaussian noise. IEEE Transactions on Signal Processing, Vol. 45, No. 11 (1997) 2846-2851.
8. Andina, D., Sanz-Gonzlez, J.L.: Comparison of a neural network detector vs. Neyman-Pearson optimal detector. Proc. ICASSP 1996, Atlanta, GA (1996) 3573-3576.
9. Munro, D.J., Ersoy, O.K., Bell, M.R., Sadowsky, J.S.: Neural network learning of low-probability events. IEEE Transactions on Aerospace and Electronic Systems, Vol. 32, No. 3 (1996) 898-910.
10. Mata-Moya, D., Jarabo-Amores, P., Rosa-Zurera, M., López-Ferreras, F., Vicen-Bueno, R.: Approximating the Neyman-Pearson detector for Swerling I Targets with Low Complexity Neural Networks. Lecture Notes in Computer Science, No. 3697. Springer-Verlag, Berlin Heidelberg New York (2005) 917-922.
11. Jarabo-Amores, P., Gil-Pita, R., Rosa-Zurera, M., López-Ferreras, F.: MLP and RBFN for detecting white gaussian signals in white gaussian interference. Lecture Notes in Computer Science, No. 2687 Springer-Verlag, Berlin Heidelberg New York (2003) 790-797.
12. El-Jaroudi, AA., Makhoul, J.: A new error criterion for posterior probability estimation with neural nets. Proc. of the Int. Conf. on Neural Networks IJCNN, U.S.A., June (1990) 185-192.
13. Nguyen, D., Widrow, B.: Improving the learning speed of 2-layer neural networks by choosing initial values of the adaptive weights. Proc. f the Int. Joint Conf. on Neural Networks (1990) 21-26.
14. Sanz-Gonzalez, J.L., Andina, D.: Performance analysis of neural network detectors by importance sampling techniques. Neural Proc. Letters, No. 9 (1999) 257-269.

Automatic Sound Classification for Improving Speech Intelligibility in Hearing Aids Using a Layered Structure*

Enrique Alexandre, Lucas Cuadra, Lorena Álvarez,
Manuel Rosa-Zurera, and Francisco López-Ferreras

Dept. de Teoría de la Señal y Comunicaciones. Escuela Politécnica Superior.
Universidad de Alcalá. 28805 Alcalá de Henares, Spain
enrique.alexandre@uah.es

Abstract. This paper presents some of our first results in the development of an automatic sound classification algorithm for hearing aids. The goal is to classify the input audio signal into four different categories: speech in quiet, speech in noise, stationary noise and non-stationary noise. In order to make the system more robust, a divide and conquer strategy is proposed, resulting thus in a layered structure. The considered classification algorithms will be based on the Fisher linear discriminant and neural networks. Some results will be given demonstrating the good behavior of the system compared with a classical approach with a four-classes classifier based on neural networks.

1 Introduction

Hearing aids are usually designed and programmed for only one listening environment. However it has been shown that their users usually prefer to have different amplification schemes in different listening conditions [1][2]. Thus, modern digital hearing aids usually allow the user to manually select between different programs (different frequency responses or other processing options such as compression methods, directional microphone, feedback canceller, etc.) depending on the listening conditions. The user has therefore to recognize the acoustic environment and choose the program that best fits this situation by using a switch on the hearing instrument or some kind of remote control.

This indicates the need for hearing aids that can be automatically fitted according to user preferences for various listening conditions. In a study with hearing-impaired subjects, it was observed that the automatic switching mode of the instrument was deemed useful by a majority of test subjects, even if its performance was not perfect [3].

The two most important listening environments for a hearing aid user are speech in quiet and speech in noise [4]. While the first situation is usually easy

---
* This work has been partially financed by the Universidad de Alcalá (UAH PI2005/081) and Comunidad de Madrid/Universidad de Alcalá (CAM-UAH2005/036).

to handle, nevertheless speech in noise is a much more difficult environment for the hearing aid user as a consequence of its low signal-to-noise ratio. Therefore, automatic detection of noise in the listening environment can be helpful to the user, since it would allow switching on or off different features of the hearing aid, such as directional microphone or a noise suppression algorithm.

This paper shows our first results in the problem of classifying between speech in quiet, speech in noise, stationary noise and non-stationary noise. Noise will be referred to as any other signal different from speech, and therefore would include not only environmental noise but also music, both instrumental and vocal. The complete implementation and functionality of the hearing aid will not be covered in this paper.

The paper is structured as follows: first the implemented method will be described, including the feature extraction process, the sound database used for the experiments and the structure of the classifier. After that, some results will be shown, to illustrate the behavior of the proposed system. The paper will conclude with a brief discussion on the results obtained.

2 Method

2.1 Features Extraction

The input audio signal is divided into frames with a length of 512 samples (23.22 ms for the considered sampling frequency), and with no overlap between adjacent frames. Then, a Discrete Cosine Transform (DCT) is computed [5], and all the considered features are calculated. Finally, the mean and standard deviation values are computed every 2 seconds in order to soften the values.

The features that will be considered in this work will be now briefly described. More detailed descriptions of these features can be found, for instance, in [6], [7] and [8].

Spectral Centroid. The spectral centroid can be associated with the measure of brightness of a sound, and is obtained by evaluating the center of gravity of the spectrum:

$$Centroid_t = \frac{\sum_{k=1}^{N} |X_t[k]| \cdot k}{\sum_{k=1}^{N} |X_t[k]|} \quad (1)$$

where $X_t[k]$ represents the k-th frequency bin of the spectrum at frame t, and N is the number of samples.

Spectral Roll-off. The spectral roll-off ($RollOff_t$) is usually defined as the frequency bin below which a PR% of the magnitude distribution is concentrated:

$$\sum_{k=1}^{RollOff_t} |X_t[k]| = PR \cdot \sum_{k=1}^{N} |X_t[k]| \ . \quad (2)$$

A typical value for PR is PR=85%. The spectral roll-off can give an idea of the shape of the spectrum.

Spectral Flux. It is associated with the amount of spectral local changes, and is defined as follows:

$$Flux_t = \sum_{k=1}^{N} (|X_t[k]| - |X_{t-1}[k]|)^2 \quad . \tag{3}$$

Zero Crossing Rate (ZCR). The ZCR is computed from the temporal signal $x[n]$ using the expression:

$$ZCR_t = \frac{1}{2} \sum_{n=1}^{N} |sign(x[n]) - sign(x[n-1])| \tag{4}$$

where $sign(\cdot)$ represents the sign function, which returns 1 for positive arguments and -1 for negative ones. This parameter takes higher values for noise and unvoiced speech than for voiced speech.

High Zero Crossing Rate Ratio (HZCRR). This feature, proposed in [7], is computed from the ZCR, and is defined as the number of frames whose ZCR is 1.5 times above the mean ZCR on a window containing M frames.

It can be demonstrated [7] that the HZCRR takes higher values for speech than for music since speech is usually composed by alternating voiced and unvoiced fragments, while music does not follow this structure.

Short Time Energy (STE). It is defined as the mean energy of the signal within each analysis frame.

Low Short-Time Energy Ratio (LSTER). Similarly to the HZCRR, the LSTER is obtained from the STE, and defined as the ratio of frames whose STE is 0.5 times below the mean STE on a window that contains M frames.

Mel-Frequency Cepstral Coefficients (MFCCs). These are a set of perceptual parameters calculated from the STFT [9] that have been widely used in speech recognition. They provide a compact representation of the spectral envelope, such that most of the signal energy is concentrated in the first coefficients. The application of these parameters for music modeling was discussed by Logan in [10]. To represent speech, 13 coefficients are commonly used, although it has been demonstrated that for classification tasks, it is enough to take into account only the first five coefficients [11].

Voice2White (V2W). This parameter, proposed in [6], is a measure of the energy inside the typical speech band (300-4000 Hz) respect to the whole energy of the signal.

Percentage of Low Energy Frames (LEF). It is defined as the proportion of frames with RMS power less than 50% of the mean RMS power within a one-second window [12].

Activity Level. The activity level of the audio signal is calculated according to the method for the objective measurement of active speech published by the ITU-T in its recommendation P.56 [13].

Loudness. Defined as an exponential function of the energy of the audio signal: $Loudness_t = Energy_t^{0.23}$.

Spectral Flatness Measure (SFM). This feature gives an idea of the flatness of the spectrum, and according to [14], is defined as the relation between the geometric and arithmetic means of the power spectral density for each critical band.

2.2 Classification System

As it was commented before, the objective of this work is to classify the input audio signal as speech in quiet, speech in noise, stationary noise or non-stationary noise. While it would be possible to use a single classifier to distinguish among the four considered classes, this approach has some disadvantages for this particular application. To explain this, let us consider that the input signal is speech in quiet. If the classification algorithm confuses it with noise, the hearing aid will reduce the gain and the user will probably loose all the information. On the contrary, if the speech in quiet is confused with speech in noise, the hearing aid will switch on some mechanisms, in this case unnecessary, to reduce the noise, without affecting too much to the received speech information. From this it can be observed that the distinction between speech (with and without noise) and noise is much more critical in terms of maximum allowed probability of error than the distinction between speech in noise and speech in quiet.

To solve this problem a divide and conquer strategy was applied, that is, rather than using one single classifier, the use of three more specialized binary classifiers is proposed, as shown in Fig. 1. Each one of these classifiers may be based on a different algorithm, and will be separately trained.

Two particular classification algorithms will be considered in this work: the Fisher linear discriminant and a neural network. A k-nearest neighbors classifier was also studied at first, but the results obtained were clearly below those achieved by the two considered algorithms and therefore it was not included in this work.

Fisher Linear Discriminant. The basic idea behind this algorithm is that the data are projected onto a line, and the classification is performed in this one-dimensional space. The projection maximizes the distance between the means of the two classes while minimizing the variance within each class [15].

Neural Networks. Neural networks can be viewed as massively parallel computing systems consisting of a large number of simple processors with many interconnections [16][17]. A three-layer feedforward backpropagation neural network (also called multilayer perceptron or MLP) was implemented.

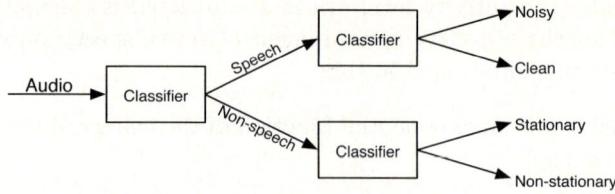

Fig. 1. Scheme of the proposed system, consisting of three specialized classifiers arranged in a two-layer structure

The nodes in the hidden layer used a hyperbolic tangent as the activation function, while a linear transfer function was used for the nodes in the output layer. The weights of each node were adjusted using a gradient descent algorithm to minimize the mean squared error (MSE) between the output of the network for a certain training data set and the desired output. The network was trained using the Levenberg-Marquardt backpropagation algorithm.

2.3 Database Used

The sound database used for the experiments consisted of a total of 2936 files, with a length of 2.5 seconds each. The sampling frequency was 22050 Hz with 16 bits per sample. The files corresponded to the following categories: speech in quiet (509 files), speech in stationary noise (727 files), speech in non-stationary noise (728 files), stationary noise (486 files) and non-stationary noise (486 files). Noise sources were varied, including those corresponding to the following environments: aircraft, bus, cafe, car, kindergarden, living room, nature, school, shop, sports, traffic, train, train station. Music files, both vocal and instrumental, were also considered as noise sources. The files with speech in noise presented different Signal to Noise Ratios (SNRs) ranging from 0 to 10 dB.

The database was then divided into three different sets for training, validation and test, including 1074 (35%), 405 (15%) and 1457 (50%) files respectively. The division was made randomly and ensuring that the relative proportion of files of each category was preserved for each set.

3 Results

This section presents the results obtained with the proposed system. For the sake of clarity, the results for each one of the classification tasks will be shown separately. Four different sets of features were considered for our experiments, since they proved to provide the best results:

- **Set 1**: Five first Mel Frequency Cepstral Coefficients.
- **Set 2**: Centroid, Voice2White and Zero Crossing Rate.
- **Set 3**: All the features except the spectral flux and Low Energy Frames.
- **Set 4**: All the features.

Table 1. Probabilities of correct classification obtained for the speech/non-speech and clean/noisy speech tasks

	Speech/Non-speech		Clean/Noisy speech	
	Fisher	MLP	Fisher	MLP
Set 1	92.9%	95.2%	95.9%	95.1%
Set 2	84.3%	90.7%	77.8%	81.3%
Set 3	91.6%	94.9%	96.0%	95.5%
Set 4	93.4%	94.9%	95.8%	94.5%

3.1 Speech/Non-speech Classification

The objective of this first task is to classify the input file as either speech or non-speech. Speech files include those with speech in quiet as well as those with speech in noise. Non-speech files are those with either music or background noise.

Table 1 shows the results obtained for the different algorithms and sets of features used. The MLP has 3 layers, with seven nodes in the hidden layer. This configuration obtained the best results in terms of MSE for the validation set. The result shows the probability of correct classification achieved for the test set using the network with lower MSE for the validation set.

As it can be observed, the best result is obtained with the MLP, with a probability of correct classification close to 95%. Slightly lower results are obtained with the Fisher linear discriminant. The matrixes of confusion corresponding to these cases are shown in Table 2.

3.2 Clean/Noisy Speech Classification

The goal of this second task is to distinguish between speech in quiet and speech in noise. Table 1 shows the results obtained. As occurred in the Speech/non-speech classification task in Sect. 3.1, the MLP resulted in having three layers with seven nodes in the hidden layer, and the shown probability corresponds to the network which presented the lower MSE for the validation set.

Table 2. Matrixes of confusion for the speech/non-speech and clean/noisy speech classification tasks

	Speech/Non-speech classification			
	Fisher (Feature set 4)		MLP (Feature set 1)	
	Speech	Non-speech	Speech	Non-speech
Speech	897	63	919	41
Non-speech	33	464	28	469
	Clean/Noisy speech classification			
	Fisher (Feature set 3)		MLP (Feature set 3)	
	Clean	Noisy	Clean	Noisy
Clean	228	16	223	21
Noisy	15	523	14	524

This time the results achieved by the Fisher linear discriminant and the MLP are almost equal, being close to 96%, the results achieved by the Fisher linear discriminant being slightly better. Taking this into account, and in order to reduce the overall computational complexity of the system, a Fisher linear discriminant is proposed for this task. Table 2 shows the matrixes of confusion obtained for the considered configurations.

3.3 Stationary/Non-stationary Noise Classification

Finally, noise files were classified into two classes attending to the characteristics of the noise. All the noises were manually divided into two different classes corresponding to stationary and non-stationary files.

With this taxonomy, the results achieved by the Fisher linear discriminant and the MLP were very similar, as for the previous task, and, like before. A Fisher linear discriminant was used given its lower computational complexity. The final achieved probability of correct classification for this task was 98.4%.

4 Discussion

This paper has presented our first results in the development of a sound classification algorithm for hearing aids. For the considered application, the relative importance of each particular probability of classification is different (e.g., the speech/non-speech discrimination is more critical than the clean/noisy speech classification). For this reason, the proposed approach is based on a divide and conquer strategy, in order to obtain a more robust system.

The overall mean probability of correct classification of the proposed system is 92.5%, considering a MLP for the speech/non-speech classification and two Fisher linear discriminants for the remaining two tasks. If a Fisher linear discriminant is used instead of a MLP for the speech/non-speech classification, this probability of correct classification drops to a 90.5%. For comparison purposes, a three-layer neural network was trained to classify between the four considered classes (speech in quiet, speech in noise, stationary noise and non-stationary noise), and the best result obtained was a probability of correct classification equal to 89%.

From this we can conclude that the proposed system provides very good results compared with a single four-classes classifier in terms of overall probability of correct classification. Moreover, the proposed system provides a significantly higher probability of correct classification for the most critical task (speech/non-speech classification), being thus more appropriate for our objective.

References

1. Keidser, G.: The relationships between listening conditions and alterative amplification schemes for multiple memory hearing aids. Ear Hear **16** (1995) 575–586
2. Keidser, G.: Selecting different amplification for different listening conditions. J. of the American Academy of Audiology **7** (1996) 92–104

3. Büchler, M.: Algorithms for sound classification in hearing instruments. PhD thesis, Swiss Federal Institute of Technology, Zurich (2002)
4. Nordqvist, P., Leijon A.: An efficient robust sound classification algorithm for hearing aids. J. Acoustic Soc. Am. **115**(6) (2004) 3033–3041
5. Alexandre, E., Rosa, M., Cuadra, L., Gil-Pita, R.: Application of Fisher linear discriminant analysis to speech/music classification. In: AES 120th Convention. (2006)
6. Guaus, E., Batlle, E.: A non-linear rhythm-based style classification for broadcast speech-music discrimination. In: AES 116th Convention. (2004)
7. Lu, L., Zhang, H.J., Jiang, H.: Content analysis for audio classification and segmentation. IEEE Transactions on speech and audio processing **10**(7) (2002) 504–516
8. Scheirer, E., Slaney, M.: Construction and evaluation of a robust multifeature speech/music discriminator. In: ICASSP. (1997)
9. Davis, S., Mermelstein, P.: Experiments in syllable-based recognition of continuous speech. IEEE Transactions on Acoustics, Speech and Signal Processing **28** (1980) 357–366
10. Logan, B.: Mel frequency cepstral coefficients for music modeling. In: Int. Symp. Music Information Retrieval (ISMIR). (2000)
11. Tzanetakis, G., Cook, P.: Musical genre classification of audio signals. IEEE Transactions on speech and audio processing **10**(5) (2002) 293–302
12. Saunders, J.: Real time discrimination of broadcast speech/music. In: ICASSSP. (1996) 993–996
13. ITU-T: Objective measurement of active speech level. Recommendation P.56 (1993)
14. Batlle, E., Neuschmied, H., Uray, P., Ackerman, G.: Recognition and analysis of audio for copyright protection: the RAA project. Journal of the American Society for Information Science and Technology **55**(12) (2004) 1084–1091
15. Fisher, R.: The use of multiple measurements in taxonomic problems. Annals of Eugenics (7) (1936) 179–188
16. Haykin, S.: Neural Networks: A comprehensive foundation. Prentice Hall (1999)
17. Jain, A.K., Duin, R.P., Mao, J.: Statistical pattern recognition: a review. IEEE Transactions on pattern analysis and machine intelligence **22**(1) (2000) 4–37

Directed Laplacian Kernels for Link Analysis

Pawel Majewski

Gdańsk University of Technology,
Narutowicza 11/12, 80-952 Gdańsk, Poland
Pawel.Majewski@eti.pg.gda.pl

Abstract. Application of kernel methods to link analysis is presented. Novel kernels based on directed graph Laplacians are proposed and their application as measures of relatedness between nodes in a directed graph is presented. The kernels express relatedness and take into account the global importance of the nodes in a citation graph. Limitations of existing kernels are given with a discussion how they are addressed by directed Laplacian kernels. Links between the kernels and PageRank ranking algorithm are also presented. The proposed kernels are evaluated on a dataset of scientific bibliographic citations.

1 Introduction

Web and bibliographic data can be described in terms of graphs where each node represents a web page or a paper, and edges represent relationships between documents, e.g. citing or linking. Now, link analysis can be formulated in terms of graph problems. Some of the emerging ones are to assess relatedness and importance of nodes in such a graph. Co-citation and bibliographic coupling are popular measures of *relatedness* of scientific papers. HITS [1] or PageRank [2] are among the best known algorithms evaluating the *global importance* of nodes. Existing measures of importance and relatedness face some serious limitations, though. Co-citation captures relationships between two papers only if they are cited together by some papers. Web ranking calculate only global importance of nodes in a graph while one might be interested in importance relative to some node, etc. To address some of the issues Ito *et al.* [3] have recently proposed application of kernels on graphs to link analysis. They showed that diffusion kernels might serve as a measure of *relative importance* [4], defined as an importance relative to some root nodes.

In this paper we propose Laplacian kernels on directed graphs that are an extension to their undirected counterparts. Later, we show that these kernels could be used as measures of relatedness between nodes in a directed graph. They likely outperform Ito's measures based on undirected kernels in problems that are directed in their nature, e.g. link analysis. We also show how these kernels address some of the limitations of undirected Laplacians. Links between directed Laplacians and PageRank ranking algorithm are also presented.

The paper is organized as follows. In the second section we formulate the problem and give some preliminary definitions used throughout the paper. The third section brings a short review of existing kernels on graphs. In the following section we formulate Laplacian kernels on directed graphs and discuss their properties with respect to application as a relatedness measure. In the fifth section we present the results of the experimental evaluation of the proposed kernels. Finally, we conclude in the last section.

2 Preliminaries

2.1 Problem Formulation

We want to define a measure of relatedness between nodes of directed graph G, relative to one node and based on directed edges in the graph. The proposed measure must take into account the importance of the nodes visited on the walks between considered nodes. Important nodes that presumably are members of many walks should be treated as less discriminative.

We will use two toy graphs (see Fig. 1) to illustrate intuitive rationale behind assessing relatedness of nodes. This will allow us to explicitly show the problem, limitations of existing measures and propose possible solutions later in the paper.

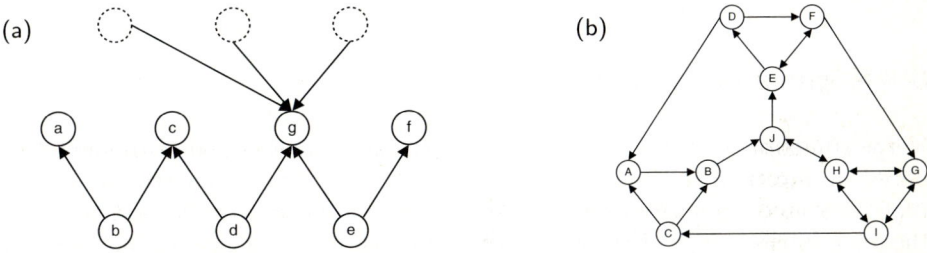

Fig. 1. Toy graphs: (a) with a frequently cited node g [3]; (b) directed graph with each node of degree three [4]

Let's take a look at the left graph first (Fig. 1a). Consider the node d as the root node. This node links to two other nodes c and g. While c is referenced by one more node, node g represents some highly cited paper or a popular web site, like Yahoo, Google, etc. We may intuitively consider g important but since g is so popular it might be referenced by many documents that are not so closely related to each other. Therefore, the relationship between d and c should be ranked higher then d and g. Consequently, longer (indirect) relationships should also follow similar rule. Neither a or f are explicitly linked by d but they seem somehow related to d due to being referenced by nodes that point to the same nodes as d. However, a should be considered more closely related to d than f to d since it is linked through less popular (or less globally important) nodes.

To address the problem of walks going through popular nodes Ito *et al.* [3] proposed application of undirected Laplacian kernels. These kernels penalize connections through a node relative to its degree. Therefore, nodes with many neighbors are assigned a high discounting factor. There are some limitations of that heuristics, though. Let's take a look at the graph on the right (Fig. 1b). If we neglect the direction of the edges, as in Ito's setting, all nodes have the same degree, and will be treated as equally important. On the other hand if we apply a ranking algorithm on that graph, it will show that the central and mutually connected nodes H, G and J, are much more important than the rest (see Table 2). Measure of relatedness proposed later in the paper captures that phenomena and overcomes the limitation of undirected Laplacians.

2.2 Definitions

A *directed graph* (sometimes called *digraph*) G is defined as a set of vertexes $V(G)$ and set of edges $E(G)$, where edges are ordered pairs of vertexes (u, v). Sometimes notation $u \to v$ is used to indicate that there is a directed edge going from u to v. Undirected graphs have bidirectional edges. Graph G can also be represented by its *adjacency matrix* A. It is a $n \times n$ matrix, with $A_{uv} = 1$ if there is an edge (u, v) from u to v, and 0 otherwise. A *random walk* is defined by a transition probability matrix P, where $P(u, v)$ denotes the probability of transition from vertex u to v. The probability is non-zero only if there is an edge connecting two vertexes, and is usually equal for every out-edges.

3 Kernels on Graphs

Kernel function $\kappa(x, x')$, $\kappa : \Omega \times \Omega \mapsto \mathbb{R}$, expresses some kind of similarity between objects in the data domain Ω. There are no special constraints on the type of desired similarity except for symmetry and positive semi-definiteness of the relation [5]. In case of graphs and other finite domains the kernel function can be represented by a $|\Omega| \times |\Omega|$ matrix K, where element $K_{ij} = K_{ji}$ corresponds to $\kappa(x_i, x_j)$. The positive semi-definiteness constraint is met if all eigenvalues of K are non-negative. In this paper we also exploit the matrix representation of kernel functions. The data domains will be limited to adjacency matrices or their modifications, i.e. graph Laplacians and transition probability matrices.

We used two diffusion kernels on graphs to calculate similarity between nodes in a graph, namely von Neumann [6] and exponential [7] kernels. The former is defined by

$$K^{(N)} = H \sum_{k=0}^{\infty} \lambda^k H^k = H(I - \lambda H)^{-1} \qquad (1)$$

and the latter by

$$K^{(exp)} = \sum_{k=0}^{\infty} \frac{\beta^k H^k}{k!} = \exp(\beta H). \qquad (2)$$

In both kernels H is any symmetric matrix, usually referred as *generator matrix*. The parameters λ and β are decaying factors that control the diffusion process. The additional restriction $0 < \lambda < \|H\|_2^{-1}$, where $\|H\|_2^{-1}$ is a spectral radius of

H, assures that the von Neumann kernel is positively defined [8]. Both kernels are very similar to each other. The difference is a stronger decaying factor in exponential kernel that highly penalizes longer walks.

The adjacency matrix A of any undirected graph is symmetric, therefore can be used as H in the definitions above to obtain the kernel values on that graph. Since every entry a_{uv}^k of the A^k matrix contains the number of walks between nodes u and v requiring exactly k steps then the kernel value $\kappa(u,v) = K_{uv}$ expresses the weighted sum of walks of all lengths between nodes v and u. Ito et al. [3] also showed that when co-citation matrix $A^T A$ is used as H and $\lambda \to \|H\|_2^{-1}$, then von Neumann kernel function, $\kappa^{(N)}$, tends to HITS authority ranking, while for $\lambda = 0$ the kernel subsumes co-citation matrix.

3.1 Laplacian Kernels

There is a family of kernels introduced to machine learning community by Kondor and Lafferty [7] that have attractive properties with respect to relatedness measures. In general, they are diffusion kernels, either von Neumann or exponential, but instead of adjacency or co-citation matrices, negated Laplacians are applied as generator matrices H in (1) or (2).

Laplacian of undirected graph is usually defined by $L = D - A$ where A is an adjacency matrix and D is a diagonal matrix with entries $D_{uu} = \sum_v A_{uv} = d_u$. The normalized version of L, called *Regularized Laplacian*, is defined as $\mathcal{L} = D^{-\frac{1}{2}} L D^{-\frac{1}{2}} = I - D^{-\frac{1}{2}} A D^{-\frac{1}{2}}$. Both Laplacians can be used to formulate kernels on undirected graphs. Substituting H in (1) or (2) with negatives of Laplacian or Regularized Laplacian yields four different diffusion kernels (Table 1).

Table 1. Laplacian diffusion kernels

Exponential Laplacian kernel	$K^{(exp\ L)} = \sum_{k=0}^{\infty} \frac{\beta^k(-L)^k}{k!} = \exp(-\beta L)$
Exponential regularized Laplacian kernel	$K^{(exp\ \mathcal{L})} = \sum_{k=0}^{\infty} \frac{\beta^k(-\mathcal{L})^k}{k!} = \exp(-\beta \mathcal{L})$
von Neumann Laplacian kernel	$K^{(N\ L)} = \sum_{k=0}^{\infty} \lambda^k(-L)^k = (I + \lambda L)^{-1}$
von Neumann regularized Laplacian kernel	$K^{(N\ \mathcal{L})} = \sum_{k=0}^{\infty} \lambda^k(-\mathcal{L})^k = (I + \lambda \mathcal{L})^{-1}$

Laplacian kernels are also known as heat kernels since they originate from differential equations describing heat diffusing in material [9]. They can also model relatedness between nodes in citations graphs. The difference between adjacency matrices and negated Laplacians are the diagonal entries expressing negated number of nodes incident to the node. When computation of the diffusion kernels takes place the negative self-loops are also taken into account and penalize walks going through nodes. The higher degree of the node the higher penalty (discounting). Recall, the toy graph in Fig. 1a. Node g is connected to five other nodes, therefore every walk that visits g will be penalized relatively high. This matches our intuitive assessment that d is more related to c then to

g. Discounting also affects indirect relationships between d and node b or e. Nevertheless, the undirected Laplacian kernels unify the importance with degree of the nodes. Therefore, they can not cope with graphs that have balanced degrees of nodes (e.g. the one in Fig. 1b).

4 Laplacian Kernels on Directed Graphs

The definitions of kernels on undirected graphs given above make use of the symmetry of their adjacency matrices. Such assumption does not hold for directed graphs, though. In general, adjacency matrices of directed graphs are not symmetric. Therefore, they can not be plugged in the definitions of kernels given above to obtain their directed counterparts.

In contrast to large literature on Laplacians on undirected graphs the directed graphs have not gained that much attention. There are some simple propositions of Laplacians on directed graphs that have an analogy to Kirchhoff's law but for construction of Laplacian kernels on directed graphs we use the definition proposed just recently in [10].

Definition 1 (Chung). *Given a directed graph G with transition probability matrix P and the Perron vector φ of P, its* directed Laplacian *is defined by*

$$\mathcal{L}_{dir} = I - \frac{\Phi^{\frac{1}{2}} P \Phi^{-\frac{1}{2}} + \Phi^{-\frac{1}{2}} P^* \Phi^{\frac{1}{2}}}{2} \qquad (3)$$

where Φ is a diagonalization of Perron vector φ with entries $\Phi(v,v) = \varphi(v)$ and H^* denotes the conjugated transpose of H. The combinatorial Laplacian *is defined as*

$$L_{dir} = \Phi - \frac{\Phi P + P^* \Phi}{2}. \qquad (4)$$

Since the definitions of Laplacians on directed graphs yield symmetric matrices, this allows us to formulate Laplacian kernels on directed graphs. When we plug negations of the directed graph Laplacians into (1) and (2), we obtain two *directed Laplacian kernels* and two *directed combinatorial Laplacian kernels*, respectively.

The definitions of Laplacian (3) and combinatorial Laplacian (4) given above utilize Perron vector φ of transition probability matrix P. The Perron vector is a stationary probability vector of Markov chain and can be found by solving either the eigenvector problem [11], $\varphi P = \varphi$, or by solving homogeneous linear system

$$\varphi(I - P) = \mathbf{0}, \qquad (5)$$

where both formulations are subject to normalization constrain $\sum_v \varphi(v) = 1$. For a general directed graph there is no closed form solution for φ [10]. Note, however, that (5) resembles linear formulation of PageRank problem [11];

$$\boldsymbol{\pi}(I - \alpha P) = (1 - \alpha + \alpha\gamma)\boldsymbol{v}, \qquad (6)$$

where $\boldsymbol{\pi}$ is the PageRank vector, α is a PageRank's "personalization parameter", $\boldsymbol{v} = \frac{1}{n}\mathbf{1}$ and γ is a normalization parameter corresponding to dangling nodes[1]. Hence, the Perron vector φ is nothing else but famous Google's PageRank importance ranking vector for its "personalization parameter" $\alpha \to 1$.

Directed Laplacian matrix can be seen as a transition probability matrix weighted by a PageRank vector. Every entry l_{ij} of directed Laplacian contains a mean value of probabilities of transitions from i to j and from j to i, weighted by importance factors of nodes i and j. Diagonal entries express global importance of the nodes. Therefore, during kernel evaluation the diagonal entries are a discounting factor. In directed setting, however, the penalty assigned to a walk when crossing a node corresponds only to its importance. Therefore, really important nodes will be penalized relatively highly, while less important nodes will avoid discounting despite larger number of out-links. This is in contrast to the undirected Laplacians and allows to overcome their limitations pointed out during problem formulation.

In case of web pages or scientific literature it is natural that papers considered important are usually cited more frequently than less known publications. Nevertheless, significant ones usually become very popular and referenced even by papers that are not so closely related to the subject of the cited paper. This effect decreases their applicability as an indicator of a specific topic. Some niche papers might be a better choice for discriminators. On the other hand a reference from a significant publication boosts the importance of a paper and is also a hint that these documents are related to each other. This is exactly how directed Laplacian kernels model the relatedness. In this setting the connections between important nodes are reinforced by a product of importance of the papers but at the same time walks through important and highly cited papers are penalized.

5 Evaluation

We have evaluated all eight kernels, both undirected and directed, on a toy graph (Fig. 1b). Table 2 presents rankings of the nodes relative to the central node J. Since the degree of all nodes is the same all rankings based on undirected Laplacians score the relatedness of nodes only depending on the distance between them. In all cases the direct neighbors are rated highest, then the nodes that are one step apart from the root node and so forth. The kernels based on directed Laplacians exploit additional information on the direction of the edge to produce the rankings. All the directed rankings also place the neighbors on the top but the scores are not equal this time. Due to a mutual connection, H is considered the most related node to J in all rankings. Node B, as another neighbor comes next, followed by more distant nodes. As an illustration we enclosed a PageRank ranking as a measure of global importance of nodes in the graph.

We used part of Cora dataset [12] for experiments on real data. The data set consists of abstracts of scientific papers with citations. We dropped the texts and used the bibliographic information only. After filtering out the papers that had

---
[1] Dangling nodes are the ones without out-neighbors, $d_v^{out} = 0$.

Table 2. Rankings on toy graph (b) with J as a root node; for exponential kernels $\beta = 1$, PageRank computed for $\alpha = 0.9999$, for Neumann kernels $\lambda = 0.999\|H\|_2^{-1}$

Rank	PR		$K^{(exp\mathcal{L})}$		$K^{(exp\mathcal{L}_d)}$		$K^{(N\mathcal{L})}$		$K^{(N\mathcal{L}_d)}$		$K^{(expL)}$		$K^{(expL_d)}$		$K^{(NL)}$		$K^{(NL_d)}$	
1	H	15.4	J	43.2	J	42.2	J	40.7	J	38.4	J	17.0	J	88.6	J	23.6	J	80.2
2	G	12.6	B	13.5	H	16.1	B	11.0	H	16.6	B	12.1	H	5.2	B	10.9	H	7.7
3	J	12.5	E	13.5	B	14.3	E	11.0	B	11.3	E	12.1	B	3.0	E	10.9	B	5.1
4	I	11.2	H	13.5	E	11.2	H	11.0	E	9.8	H	12.1	E	2.8	H	10.9	E	4.5
5	E	10.4	A	2.7	G	3.7	A	4.4	G	5.9	A	7.8	G	0.2	A	7.3	G	0.9
6	F	8.5	C	2.7	A	3.6	C	4.4	I	5.2	C	7.8	I	0.1	C	7.3	I	0.7
7	C	8.1	D	2.7	I	3.1	D	4.4	D	4.9	D	7.8	F	0.1	D	7.3	F	0.4
8	B	7.9	F	2.7	F	3.0	F	4.4	F	4.7	F	7.8	A	0.1	F	7.3	A	0.3
9	A	7.5	G	2.7	D	2.3	G	4.4	D	3.7	G	7.8	D	0.04	G	7.3	D	0.2
10	D	5.9	I	2.7	C	0.6	I	4.4	C	2.5	I	7.8	C	0.0	I	7.3	C	0.04

no citations at all or referred to papers outside the dataset, the experimental data counted 2708 papers. Following [4], we used K-Min (minimizing Kendall distance) metric [13] to measure distances between the top-10 lists produced by different kernels. We normalized the results so that K-Min equals 0 when the rankings are perfectly matching each other and 1000 when they are in a reverse order. To evaluate the stability of proposed kernels over their parameters ranges we compared rankings generated by the same kernel function with varying parameters values. Every node in a graph was taken as a root node and the results were averaged on all nodes. Table 3a shows results of pairwise correlations between rankings obtained from directed regularized Laplacian kernel with varying parameter β. The kernels exhibit almost perfect stability since the variations of K-Min do not exceed 2. We have also examined the correlation between rankings obtained with directed and undirected kernels with different parameters settings. Table 3b shows the results of the comparison for exponential regularized Laplacians. The rankings are highly correlated in whole parameters range. This might be partially explained by the properties of the data. Since the average degree of

Table 3. (a) Correlations (K-Min) between top-10 lists obtained with directed exp. reg. Laplacian kernel for different β, PageRank computed for $\alpha = 0.9999$, ($\alpha \to 1$, see eq. (5) and (6)); (b) Correlations (K-Min) between top-10 lists obtained with directed and undirected exp. reg. Laplacian kernels, PageRank computed for $\alpha = 0.9999$.

(a) β	0.01	0.1	0.5	1.0	10	100	1000
0.01	0.00	1.34	1.13	0.95	1.00	1.32	1.31
0.1		0.00	1.07	0.65	0.91	0.72	1.03
0.5			0.00	1.10	1.34	1.03	1.47
1.0				0.00	0.38	0.38	0.54
10					0.00	0.47	0.47
100						0.00	0.43
1000							0.00

(b) β	0.01	0.1	0.5	1.0	10	100	1000
0.01	1.24	1.31	1.61	1.26	1.28	1.10	1.17
0.1		1.24	0.78	1.24	0.73	0.84	1.08
0.5			0.89	0.78	0.54	0.82	0.89
1				0.65	0.84	0.55	0.74
10					0.77	0.74	0.93
100						0.54	1.06
1000							0.47

node is about 6 and direct neighbors are considered the most related for every kernel, then the variations in the top-10 are relatively small. There might be bigger differences on further positions of the rankings. The results of von Neumann kernels were omitted due to lack of space but are very similar.

6   Conclusions

In this paper we proposed application of directed graph kernels to link analysis. We gave definitions of graph kernels based on directed graph Laplacians that could be used as measures of relatedness between nodes in a directed graph. We also showed how these kernels address some of the limitations of undirected Laplacians. Links between directed Laplacians and PageRank ranking algorithm were also explored. Evaluation has confirmed that proposed method expresses relatedness in a more intuitive way than previous works.

Acknowledgments. This work was supported by KBN grant 3 T11C 047 29.

References

1. Kleinberg, J.M.: Authoritative sources in a hyperlinked environment. Journal of the ACM **46** (1999) 604–632
2. Brin, S., Page, L., Motwani, R., Winograd, T.: The PageRank citation ranking: bringing order to the Web. Technical Report 1999-0120, Computer Science Department, Stanford University (1999)
3. Ito, T., Shimbo, M., Kudo, T., Matsumoto, Y.: Application of kernels to link analysis. In: Proceedings of KDD. (2005) 586–592
4. White, S., Smyth, P.: Algorithms for estimating relative importance in networks. In: Proceedings of SIGKDD. (2003) 266–275
5. Schölkopf, B., Smola, A.: Learning with Kernels. MIT Press (2001)
6. Kandola, J., Shawe-Taylor, J., Cristianini, N.: Learning semantic similarity. In: NIPS 15, Cambridge, MA, MIT Press (2003) 657–664
7. Kondor, R.I., Lafferty, J.: Diffusion kernels on graphs and other discrete structures. In: Proceedings of MGTS at ECML/PKDD. (2002) 315–322
8. Shawe-Taylor, J., Cristianini, N.: Kernel Methods for Pattern Analysis. Cambridge University Press (2004)
9. Smola, A.J., Kondor, R.: Kernels and Regularization on Graphs. In: Proceedings of Conference on Learning Theory, COLT/KW. (2003)
10. Chung, F.R.K.: Laplacians and the Cheeger inequality for directed graphs. Annals of Combinatorics **9** (2005) 1–19
11. Langville, A.N., Meyer, C.D.: Deeper inside PageRank. Internet Mathematics **1** (2005) 335–380
12. McCallum, A.K., Nigam, K., Rennie, J., Seymore, K.: Automating the construction of internet portals with machine learning. Information Retrieval **3** (2000) 127–163
13. Fagin, R., Kumar, R., Sivakumar, D.: Comparing top k lists. SIAM Journal of Discrete Mathematics **17** (2003) 134–160

Pruning Adaptive Boosting Ensembles by Means of a Genetic Algorithm

Daniel Hernández-Lobato[1], José Miguel Hernández-Lobato[1], Rubén Ruiz-Torrubiano[1], and Ángel Valle[2]

[1] Escuela Politécnica Superior,
Universidad Autónoma de Madrid,
C/ Francisco Tomás y Valiente, 11, Madrid 28049 Spain,
{daniel.hernandez, josemiguel.hernandez, ruben.ruiz}@uam.es
[2] Cognodata,
C/ Caracas 23, 4ªplanta, Madrid 28010 Spain,
angel.valle@cognodata.com

Abstract. This work analyzes the problem of whether, given a classification ensemble built by Adaboost, it is possible to find a subensemble with lower generalization error. In order to solve this task a genetic algorithm is proposed and compared with other heuristics like *Kappa* pruning and *Reduce-error* pruning with backfitting. Experiments carried out over a wide variety of classification problems show that the genetic algorithm behaves better than, or at least, as well as the best of those heuristics and that subensembles with similar and sometimes better prediction accuracy can be obtained.

1 Introduction

The algorithm Adaboost, proposed by Freund and Schapire [1], is one of the most successful ensemble algorithms in the field of machine learning. Following the idea of boosting algorithms, Adaboost produces a very accurate prediction rule using many simple and slightly better than random-guessing weak-hypothesis. Weak-hypotheses are generated iteratively forcing each one to focus on the examples misclassified by the previous hypothesis itself. This way Adaboost obtains a set of diverse weak hypotheses with little correlation that, when combined by a voting procedure, they often outperform the result of a single hypothesis. Adaboost ensembles built by using decision trees like C4.5 [2] or CART [3] as weak hypotheses have reported excellent results on several benchmarks [4,5,6,7].

Some recent investigations [8,9] have shown that it is possible to reduce the generalization error of an ensemble method like bagging [10] by ruling out some of the classifiers generated. This process is called pruning the ensemble and most of the times it is an NP-complete task, so only approximate solutions are feasible. There have been some attempts to prune boosting ensembles like [11,12] where approximate solutions like *Kappa* pruning and *Reduce-error* pruning with backfitting are proposed. However, experiments in these works considered rather small ensembles or no statistical test were carried out. In this document we analyze whether it is possible to prune boosting ensembles and compare the performance of a genetic algorithm devised to carry out this task with *Kappa* and *Reduce-error* heuristics.

2 Adaboost Algorithm

Adaboost pseudocode is shown in Algorithm 1. The algorithm is fed with a training set of examples S and a constant T that indicates how many weak hypotheses will be generated. The algorithm maintains a set of weights $\mathbf{w}_t$ over the training examples that are normalized to obtain a probability distribution p_t. A weak learner is trained with the examples and the distribution p_t to obtain a hypothesis h_t whose training error is $\epsilon_t < 0.5$. Next, a new weight vector $\mathbf{w}_{t+1}$ is generated by using β_t, a variable that depends on ϵ_t and takes values between 0 (when h_t has error 0) and 1 (when h_t has error 0.5). The weight of each example that is correctly classified by h_t is multiplied by β_t, and therefore it is reduced since $0 \leq \beta_t \leq 1$. The new weight vector $\mathbf{w}_{t+1}$ will be used during the next iteration to generate hypothesis h_{t+1} forcing it to focus on the examples misclassified by h_t. The process is repeated until T weak hypotheses are generated. Finally, a hypothesis h_f is produced by combining the outputs of the T weak hypotheses in a weighted majority vote scheme. In this voting system the weight of each hypothesis h_t depends on its error on the training examples according to distribution p_t: the lower the error the higher the weight.

Algorithm 1. Adaboost.

Input: Set S of m labeled examples: $S = \{(\mathbf{x}_i, y_i) : i = 1, 2, ..., m\}$. Constant T. Labels $Y = \{1, ..., k\}$. Weak learner like C4.5 or CART

1. initialize $\mathbf{w}_t(i) = 1/m, \forall i = 1, ..., m$
2. for $t = 1$ to T do:
    (a) $p_t(i) = \mathbf{w}_t(i)/(\sum_i \mathbf{w}_t(i)), \forall i = 1, ..., m$
    (b) $h_t = weakLearner(p_t, S)$
    (c) $\epsilon_t = \sum_i p_t(i) I\{h_t(\mathbf{x}_i) \neq y_i\}$
    (d) $\beta_t = \epsilon_t/(1 - \epsilon_t)$
    (e) $\mathbf{w}_{t+1}(i) = \mathbf{w}_t(i) \beta^{1-I\{h_t(\mathbf{x}_i) \neq y_i\}}, \forall i = 1, ..., m$

Output: $h_f(\mathbf{x}) = argmax_{y \in Y} \{\sum_{t=1}^{T} (\log 1/\beta_t) I\{h_t(\mathbf{x}) = y\}$

---

3 The Boosting Pruning Problem

Suppose we have an ensemble of classifiers (alongside with their weights) generated by Adaboost. Could it be possible to find a subensemble (the weights are not changed) with lower generalization error than the original ensemble and than any other subensemble? This question summarizes the boosting pruning problem. We can make the assumption that minimizing the ensemble error over a validation set has as consequence the minimization of the generalization error. Then, the problem is to find a subensemble whose error on a validation set is the lowest possible. Using a validation set to prune the original ensemble has as its major drawback the reduction of the the training set size and hence, the accuracy of the resulting ensemble, but as we are focused on finding an answer to the question stated before, our main objective is far from achieving the lowest possible error rate.

The boosting pruning problem can be formalized as follows. We build a $T \times m$ matrix M, where T is the number of classifiers generated by Adaboost and m is the number of examples in a validation set $V = \{\mathbf{x}_1, ..., \mathbf{x}_m\}$. The element M_{ij} of the matrix M is defined as $M_{ij} = w_i I\{h_i(\mathbf{x}_j) = y_j\} - w_i I\{h_i(\mathbf{x}_j) \neq y_j\}$, where y_j is the class of example $\mathbf{x}_j$ and w_i is the weight of classifier i. The boosting pruning problem is to find a vector $\mathbf{v} \in \{0,1\}^T$ so that $\mathbf{v}^t M = \mathbf{z}^t$ and $\mathbf{z}$ is a vector that has the fewest possible negative components. Due to the optimization nature of the problem it is very likely to be NP-complete [13], so only approximate solutions would be feasible.

4 Previous Pruning Methods

In this section we describe some already existing heuristics designed to prune boosting ensembles [11]. The most successful algorithms so far are *Reduce-error* pruning with backfitting and *Kappa* pruning. We also include another pruning technique called *Early Stopping*.

4.1 Reduce-error Pruning with Backfitting

Reduce-error [11] uses a validation set to prune an ensemble of classifiers. It follows a greedy strategy beginning with an empty subensemble of classifiers. It progressively adds to the subensemble the classifier that, when added, makes the new subensemble have the lowest error on a validation set. It adds classifiers until the subensemble contains exactly M classifiers.

The add-on of backfitting implements the chance of reviewing previously added classifiers. Each time a classifier is added to the subensemble, all the previous classifiers (included the one just added) are checked. When checked, a classifier is progressively replaced by each one of all the remaining classifiers to see if the error of the set is reduced. If that is the case, then the original classifier is replaced and it becomes available, otherwise it stays in the subensemble. In the case that one classifier is replaced then the process of reviewing previously added classifiers repeats until a maximum of 100 times.

4.2 Kappa Pruning

Kappa pruning [11] focuses on obtaining a subensemble of diverse classifiers. In order to determine how much two classifiers h_a and h_b differ from each other the *Kappa* measure is used. Consider a dataset S with m examples and L possible classes, an $L \times L$ matrix C is calculated as

$$C_{ij} = \#\{\mathbf{x} \in S | h_a(\mathbf{x}) = i \text{ and } h_b(\mathbf{x}) = j\}. \quad (1)$$

If h_a and h_b are identical only the diagonal will contain non-zero values, otherwise the more different they are the more non-zero values that there will be outside the diagonal. The probability Θ_1 that both classifiers are identical is

$$\Theta_1 = \frac{\sum_{i=1}^{L} C_{ii}}{m}. \quad (2)$$

Nonetheless, Θ_1 is not a formal measure of agreement. If one class is much more common than the others it is natural to think that all classifiers will agree on most of the examples of that class, otherwise their error would be too high. In this situation Θ_1 will have a high value for all classifiers and it will not take into account how the classifiers differ in the examples from the less numerous classes. For this reason we calculate the probability that two classifiers h_a and h_b agree by chance as

$$\Theta_2 = \sum_{i=1}^{L} \left(\frac{\sum_{j=1}^{L} C_{ij}}{m} \cdot \frac{\sum_{j=1}^{L} C_{ji}}{m} \right) \quad (3)$$

then we define the κ measure as

$$\kappa = \frac{\Theta_1 - \Theta_2}{1 - \Theta_2} \quad (4)$$

which takes value 0 when the agreement of the two classifiers h_a and h_b equals the expected level of agreement by chance, and it takes value 1 when both classifiers agree on every example.

Kappa pruning algorithm proceeds as follows. Given an ensemble of classifiers, the κ measure for each pair of classifiers in the ensemble is calculated. Then, the pairs are sorted in an ascending order regarding the κ value and the pair with the lowest κ value is taken until M classifiers are selected. If one classifier has already been taken and a pair with that classifier appears again then the pair is ignored. Although *Kappa* pruning does not need a validation set, we use one to calculate the κ value for each pair of classifiers. This way, we avoid training bias and make the heuristic more competitive against the other methods.

4.3 Early Stopping

Early-stopping [11] is the simplest of the pruning techniques. It consists in taking only the first M classifiers of the $T \geq M$ classifiers returned by Adaboost.

5 Evolutionary Approach

We propose a Genetic Algorithm (GA) [14] as a heuristic to solve the boosting pruning problem. The evolutionary approach is well suited for this problem because of the combinatorial nature of the optimization problem, which involves finding the best subset of a given set of classifiers.

Let S be the set of size T which contains the classifiers returned by Adaboost. Our algorithm searches in the space $\Omega = \wp(S)$, where $\wp(S)$ represents the set of all possible subsets of S. To represent the population that will undergo evolution we use binary fixed-length strings in the space $\{0,1\}^T$. As a result, the cardinality of the search space is $|\Omega| = 2^{|S|}$. We define the crossover operator as one-point crossover where each point is chosen uniformly in the interval $[1,T]$. The probability of carrying out crossover was set to $p_c = 0.6$. Mutation is defined as the bitwise flip, and it is applied with probability $p_m = 5 \cdot 10^{-3}$ on every allele.

The fitness function takes into account the error $\epsilon(s, V)$ of the classifier ensemble $s \in \Omega$ over a validation set of examples V

$$\epsilon(s, V) = \frac{1}{|V|} \sum_{\mathbf{x} \in V} I\{h_s(\mathbf{x}) \neq y\} \quad (5)$$

where h_s is the voted combination of the classifiers in s. The fitness function of an individual s over a set of examples V is defined thus as

$$\Phi(s) = 1 - \epsilon(s, V). \quad (6)$$

The fitness is scaled linearly in order to avoid outstanding individuals from generating too many offspring, something which would reduce variability. The probability of selecting an individual for reproduction at epoch n is proportional to its fitness:

$$P_{rep}(s) = \frac{\Phi(s)}{\sum_{t \in \mathcal{P}_n} \Phi(t)} \quad (7)$$

where $\mathcal{P}_n$ is the population set at epoch n. The rest of the parameters of the GA were set empirically. The initial population was set to 60 individuals and the algorithm was run over 1000 generations. Individuals $s \in \Omega$ are generated randomly in the first generation by setting $P(s_i = 1) = P(s_i = 0) = 0.5$ for every bit $s_i, 1 \leq i \leq T$.

6 Experiments and Results

In order to compare the performance of the previously exposed pruning methods, we carried out experiments over a set of classification problems from the UCI Repository [15]. Table 1 displays the number of instances, attributes and classes of each problem, as well as the size of the training, validation and test sets used in the experiments. We used CART trees [3] as base learners for the Adaboost algorithm (p_t distribution is obtained by resampling). All computations were carried out using the R statistics software and the CART decision trees package *rpart*. For each of the real world classification problems we built 100 random independent training, validation and test partitions of size $\frac{4}{9}$, $\frac{2}{9}$ and $\frac{1}{3}$ of the original problem size respectively. For the synthetic classification problems *Waveform*, *Twonorm* and *Ringnorm* we generated 100 independent train, validation and test sets of sizes showed in Table 1. Error estimates for

Table 1. Characteristics of the data sets used in the experiments

Problem	Cases	Attr.	Train	Val.	Test	Classes
Glass	214	9	95	48	71	7
Chess	928	36	413	206	309	2
Ionosphere	351	34	156	78	117	2
Waveform	-	21	300	100	5000	3
Twonorm	-	20	300	100	5000	2
Ringnorm	-	20	300	100	5000	2
Pima	768	8	341	171	256	2
Tic-tac-toe	958	9	426	213	319	2
Vowel	990	10	440	220	330	11
Segment	210	19	93	47	70	7
Sonar	208	60	93	46	69	2
Vehicle	846	18	376	188	282	4

each problem were obtained as the average of each pruning method over the 100 random independent partitions.

The computation of the error estimates involved repeating 100 times the following steps. (i) Generate random partitions of the original data as described above. (ii) Call *Adaboost* to build a boosting ensemble of 100 classifiers using the training set. (iii) Prune the ensemble returned by *Adaboost* by means of our genetic algorithm using the validation set. (iv) Perform *Kappa* and *Reduce-error* pruning over the original ensemble so that the resulting subensemble has the same size as the one returned by the genetic algorithm. The validation set is also used for this task. (v) Prune the original ensemble using the *Early Stopping* method. (vi) Estimate the generalization error of all the obtained subensembles and the original ensemble over the test set.

Table 2 shows the averaged test error of each pruning method for each problem. On most of the problems the genetic approach obtained lower or similar error results than the other methods, and in some problems it even outperforms the generalization error of the full ensemble. A paired *t-test* performed over the differences between the errors of each pruning method and the genetic approach states that there is statistical evidence for a difference in their generalization error in some of the problems investigated (see Table 3). Table 2 also shows the average size of the subensemble returned by the genetic algorithm on each problem. It is interesting to notice that the average size is usually a bit less that half the size of the original ensemble. This has no relation with the probabilities $P(s_i = 1) = P(s_i = 0) = 0.5$ used to generate the initial population in the genetic algorithm because similar results were obtained with $P(s_i = 1) = 0.9$, $P(s_i = 0) = 0.1$.

In the *Tic-tac-toe* and *Vowel* problems the GA approach outperforms all the other pruning techniques while in all the other problems (except *Waveform*) its performance is as good as the best of them. In the problems *Waveform* and *Pima*, both *Reduce-error* and the genetic algorithm overfit the validation set and have a worse result on the test set, both with similar error values. This overfitting is more clear in the synthetic problem where *Early stopping*, which does not use

Table 2. Test error values for the original ensemble and each pruning algorithm alongside with the size of the resulting pruned ensemble. Error values in bold indicate the best pruning approach.

Problem	Original	GA	RE	Kappa	ES	#Trees
Chess	2.25±1	**2.13±0.9**	2.15±0.91	3.59±1.39	2.33±1.04	45.75±5.82
Glass	26.99±5.42	**26.56±5.66**	27.27±5.06	29.13±5.69	28.25±5.38	42.47±5.96
Ionosphere	7.2±2.49	**7.42±2.66**	7.45±2.46	9.44±2.93	7.67±2.42	44.66±5.47
Pima	26.5±2.58	27.12±2.47	26.93±2.43	28.61±2.47	**26.88±2.58**	38.54±5.19
Ringnorm	5.35±0.61	**6.36±0.79**	6.39±0.77	8.01±0.97	6.44±0.73	48.7±5.48
Segment	11.19±4.01	10.76±3.66	**10.67±3.77**	12.26±4.06	11.33±4.16	45.47±6.99
Sonar	19.86±4.82	**20.29±4.57**	20.3±4.63	22.25±4.49	20.8±4.87	44.23±6.11
Tic-tac-toe	2.17±0.99	**2.24±0.87**	2.47±0.96	4.35±1.5	2.59±1.12	49.81±5.33
Twonorm	4.12±0.35	4.82±0.5	**4.8±0.48**	5.09±0.57	4.85±0.46	47.67±5.94
Vehicle	24.63±2.11	25.18±2.28	**24.91±2.14**	25.46±2.08	25.2±2.42	38.24±5.03
Vowel	11.94±2.27	**11.58±2.21**	12.04±2.25	12.84±2.26	13.04±2.39	42.48±4.52
Waveform	17.21±0.78	18.1±0.82	18.01±0.72	18.63±0.83	**17.96±0.75**	41.27±6.06

Table 3. Results of a paried t-test performed over the differences in test error values between the GA and the other methods. It is highlighted where there is statistical evidence in favor of the GA (bold) and against it (underline).

Problem	Original	RE	Kappa	ES
Chess	$4.5 \cdot 10^{-2}$	$7.2 \cdot 10^{-1}$	$4 \cdot 10^{-23}$	$5.7 \cdot 10^{-3}$
Glass	$2.5 \cdot 10^{-1}$	$5.9 \cdot 10^{-2}$	$\mathbf{4.1 \cdot 10^{-7}}$	$\mathbf{1.2 \cdot 10^{-4}}$
Ionosphere	$1.8 \cdot 10^{-1}$	$8.4 \cdot 10^{-1}$	$\mathbf{3.6 \cdot 10^{-14}}$	$1.6 \cdot 10^{-1}$
Pima	$\underline{1.9 \cdot 10^{-3}}$	$3.7 \cdot 10^{-1}$	$\mathbf{2.1 \cdot 10^{-9}}$	$2.4 \cdot 10^{-1}$
Ringnorm	$\underline{1.7 \cdot 10^{-34}}$	$6.3 \cdot 10^{-1}$	$\mathbf{4.6 \cdot 10^{-40}}$	$1.7 \cdot 10^{-1}$
Segment	$\mathbf{3.9 \cdot 10^{-2}}$	$6.7 \cdot 10^{-1}$	$\mathbf{2 \cdot 10^{-6}}$	$\mathbf{8 \cdot 10^{-3}}$
Sonar	$3.4 \cdot 10^{-1}$	$9.7 \cdot 10^{-1}$	$\mathbf{2.9 \cdot 10^{-4}}$	$2.8 \cdot 10^{-1}$
Tic-tac-toe	$3.4 \cdot 10^{-1}$	$\mathbf{6.4 \cdot 10^{-3}}$	$\mathbf{1.6 \cdot 10^{-28}}$	$\mathbf{3.9 \cdot 10^{-4}}$
Twonorm	$\underline{4 \cdot 10^{-37}}$	$6.9 \cdot 10^{-1}$	$\mathbf{2.2 \cdot 10^{-8}}$	$3.7 \cdot 10^{-1}$
Vehicle	$\underline{2.2 \cdot 10^{-3}}$	$1.3 \cdot 10^{-1}$	$1.5 \cdot 10^{-1}$	$9.2 \cdot 10^{-1}$
Vowel	$\mathbf{9 \cdot 10^{-3}}$	$\mathbf{4.2 \cdot 10^{-3}}$	$\mathbf{7.4 \cdot 10^{-14}}$	$\mathbf{4.8 \cdot 10^{-17}}$
Waveform	$\underline{9.6 \cdot 10^{-28}}$	$1.3 \cdot 10^{-1}$	$\mathbf{7.9 \cdot 10^{-13}}$	$\underline{2.7 \cdot 10^{-2}}$

a validation set, obtains the best result. We point out the bad results of *Kappa* pruning similar to those obtained in [12]. Finally, we notice that pruning only improves performance in the problems *Chess*, *Segment* and *Vowel* while in the others it has a detrimental effect. This means that the question of whether to apply the known pruning thecniques or not is problem dependent.

7 Conclusion

In this work we have proposed a genetic algorithm to find an approximate solution to the boosting pruning problem. Experimental results over a wide variety of classification problems show that this evolutionary approach most of the times obtains similar and sometimes better error values than other existing heuristics like *Kappa* and *Reduce-error*. Moreover, the observed error rates of pruned ensembles indicate that it is possible to extract subensembles with better prediction accuracy than the full Adaboost ensemble. However, a validation set must be used for this task. Finally, we have also shown that the question of whether to apply the available pruning thecniques or not is problem dependent.

Acknowledgment

This work has been supported by *Consejería de Educación de la Comunidad Autónoma de Madrid, European Social Fund, Universidad Autónoma de Madrid* and *Dirección General de Investigación* under project TIN2004-07676-C02-02. All authors would like to thank A. Sierra, M. Alfonseca and A. Ortega.

References

1. Freund, Y., Schapire, R.E.: A decision-theoretic generalization of on-line learning and an application to boosting. In: Proc. 2nd European Conference on Computational Learning Theory. (1995) 23–37
2. Quinlan, J.R.: C4.5 programs for machine learning. Morgan Kaufmann (1993)
3. Breiman, L., Friedman, J.H., Olshen, R.A., Stone, C.J.: Classification and Regression Trees. Chapman & Hall, New York (1984)
4. Quinlan, J.R.: Bagging, boosting, and C4.5. In: Proc. 13th National Conference on Artificial Intelligence, Cambridge, MA (1996) 725–730
5. Freund, Y., Schapire, R.E.: Experiments with a new boosting algorithm. In: International Conference on Machine Learning. (1996) 148–156
6. Dietterich, T.G.: An experimental comparison of three methods for constructing ensembles of decision trees: Bagging, boosting, and randomization. Machine Learning **40**(2) (2000) 139–157
7. Breiman, L.: Arcing classifiers. The Annals of Statistics **26**(3) (1998) 801–849
8. Zhou, Z.H., Wu, J., Tang, W.: Ensembling neural networks: Many could be better than all. Artificial Intelligence **137**(1-2) (2002) 239–263
9. Martínez-Muñoz, G., Suárez, A.: Pruning in ordered bagging ensembles. In: International Conference on Machine Learning. (2006) 609–616
10. Breiman, L.: Bagging predictors. Machine Learning **24**(2) (1996) 123–140
11. Margineantu, D.D., Dietterich, T.G.: Pruning adaptive boosting. In: Proc. 14th International Conference on Machine Learning, Morgan Kaufmann (1997) 211–218
12. Tamon, C., Xiang, J.: On the boosting pruning problem. In: Proc. 11th European Conference on Machine Learning. Volume 1810., Springer, Berlin (2000) 404–412
13. Garey, M.R., Johnson, D.S.: Computers and Intractability; A Guide to the Theory of NP-Completeness. W. H. Freeman & Co., New York, NY, USA (1990)
14. Goldberg, D.E.: Genetic Algorithms in Search, Optimization and Machine Learning. Addison-Wesley Longman Publishing Co., Inc., Boston, MA, USA (1989)
15. Blake, C.L., Merz, C.J.: UCI repository of machine learning databases (1998)

On the Fusion of Polynomial Kernels for Support Vector Classifiers

Isaac Martín de Diego[1], Javier M. Moguerza[1], and Alberto Muñoz[2]

[1] University Rey Juan Carlos, c/ Tulipán s/n, 28933 Móstoles, Spain
{isaac.martin, javier.moguerza}@urjc.es
[2] University Carlos III de Madrid, c/ Madrid 126, 28903 Getafe, Spain
alberto.munoz@uc3m.es

Abstract. In this paper we propose some methods to build a kernel matrix for classification purposes using Support Vector Machines (SVMs) by fusing polynomial kernels. The proposed techniques have been successfully evaluated on artificial and real data sets. The new methods outperform the best individual kernel under consideration and they can be used as an alternative to the parameter selection problem in polynomial kernel methods.

1 Introduction

It is well known that the choice of kernel parameters is often critical for the good performance of Support Vector Machines (SVMs). Nevertheless, to find optimal values in terms of generalization performance for the kernel parameters is an open and hard to solve question. An a priori kernel selection for SVM is a difficult task [2]. The polynomial kernel function is one of the most popular classical SVM kernels. Several practical proposals to automatically select the polynomial kernel function and its optimum degree for SVM have been made [9,1]. However, there is not a simple and unique technique to select the best set of parameters to build a kernel matrix. Our proposal is based on the fusion of the different polynomial kernel matrices that arise with the use of a range of values for the unkown parameters. Fusing kernels provides a solution that minimizes the effect of a bad parameter choice. An intuitive and usual approach to build this fusion is to consider linear combinations of the matrices. This is the proposal in [6], which is based on the solution of a semi-definite programming problem to calculate the coefficients of the linear combination. Nevertheless, the solution of this kind of optimization problem is computationally very expensive [14].

In this paper we propose several methods to build a kernel matrix from a collection of polynomial kernels generated from different values of the unkown parameters in the polynomial kernel function. The functions involved in the proposed methods take advantage of class conditional probabilities and nearest neighbour techniques.

The paper is organized as follows. The general framework for the methods is presented in Section 2. The proposed methods are described in Section 3. The experimental setup and results on artificial and real data sets are described in Section 4. Section 5 concludes.

2   General Framework

Consider the general expression of the polynomial kernel function:

$$K(x_i, x_j) = (a + bx_i^T x_j)^d, \qquad (1)$$

where a, b and d are the function parameters, and x_i and x_j are data points in the sample. If $a = 0$ and $b = d = 1$, then the classical linear kernel is obtained. As already mentioned, our proposal is based on the generation of a collection of kernel matrices using a wide range of values for the unkown polynomial kernel parameters. Once the collection has been built, we will fuse the matrices in order to build a unique kernel.

There is an explicit relation between a kernel matrix and a distance-based similarity matrix. If K is a polynomial kernel matrix, then $D^2 = ke^T + ek^T - 2K$ is a matrix of square Euclidean distances [5], where k is a vector made up of the diagonal elements of K. It is well known that every distance is a dissimilarity measure, and several methods to transform dissimilarities into similarities have been proposed in the literature (see [10] for a complete review). For instance, we can use:

$$S = -\frac{1}{2} H D^2 H, \qquad (2)$$

where $H = I_n - \frac{1}{n} 1_n 1_n^T$, I_n is the identity matrix of order n, 1_n is a column vector of ones and n is the sample size. Therefore, in the following we will work with similarities. This is not a constraint since, given a kernel matrix and using the previous arguments, it is immediate to build a similarity matrix.

In order to fuse the similarity matrices we make use of the concept of functional fusion of matrices. This concept is based on the one introduced originally in [8].

Let $S_1, S_2, ...S_M$ be a set of M normalized input polynomial similarity matrices defined from (1) on a data set X, and denote by S^* the desired output combination. Let y denote the label vector, where for simplicity $y_i \in \{-1, +1\}$ (the extension to the multiclass case is straightforward).

Consider the following (functional) weighted sum:

$$S^* = \sum_{m=1}^{M} W_m \otimes S_m, \qquad (3)$$

where $W_m = [w_m(x_i, x_j)]$ is a matrix whose elements are nonlinear functions $w_m(x_i, x_j)$, and '$\otimes$' denotes the element by element product between matrices (Hadamard product). Notice that if $w_m(x_i, x_j) = \mu_m$, where $\mu_m, m = 1, \ldots M$ are constants, then the method reduces to calculate a simple linear combination of matrices:

$$S^* = \sum_{m=1}^{M} \mu_m S_m. \qquad (4)$$

Several methods have been suggested to learn the coefficients μ_m of the linear combination [4,6]. Thus, the formulation used in these papers is a particular case of the formula we propose. For instance, if we take $\mu_m = \frac{1}{M}$, the average of the input matrices is obtained.

Regarding our proposals, consider the (i, j) element of the matrix S^* in (3):

$$S^*(x_i, x_j) = \sum_{m=1}^{M} w_m(x_i, x_j) S_m(x_i, x_j). \tag{5}$$

This is the general formula of our approximation. In this way, we will generate a particular weight for each pair of elements under consideration.

An aspect that has to be treated before describing the methods is the fact that the matrix arising from the combination has to be a positive semi-definite matrix. Since this can not be guaranteed in advance, we make use of some of the several solutions that have been proposed to solve this difficulty [12]. For instance, consider the spectral decomposition $S^* = Q \Lambda Q^T$, where Λ is a diagonal matrix containing (in decreasing order) the eigenvalues of S^*, and Q is the matrix of the corresponding eigenvectors. Assume that Λ has at least p positive eigenvalues. We can consider a p-dimensional representation by taking the first p columns of Q: $Q_p \Lambda_p Q_p^T$. We will refer to this technique as 'Positive Eigenvalue Transformation'. A computationally cheaper solution is to consider the definition of a new kernel matrix as S^{*2}. Notice that, in this case, the new matrix is: $Q \Lambda^2 Q^T$. We call this method 'Square Eigenvalue Transformation'. In practice, there seems not to be a universally best method to solve this problem [11].

3 Some Specific Proposals

The next section describes a common feature to the methods we propose: The use of conditional class probabilities in order to build the weights $w_m(x_i, x_j)$ introduced in the previous section.

3.1 Conditional Class Probabilities

Consider the pair (x_i, y_i) and an unlabelled observation x_j. Given the observed value x_j, define $P(y_i|x_j)$ as the probability of x_j being in class y_i. If x_i and x_j belong to the same class this probability should be high. Unfortunately, this probability is unknown and has to be estimated. In our proposals, we will estimate it by:

$$P(y_i|x_j) = \frac{n_{ij}}{n}, \tag{6}$$

where n_{ij} is the number of the n-nearest neighbours of x_j belonging to class y_i.

Notice that each similarity matrix induces a different type of neighborhood. Hence, it is advisable to estimate this probability for each representation, that is, for the matrix S_m we will estimate the conditional probabilities $P_m(y_i|x_j)$ using the induced distances matrix D_m^2. We will need the average of this conditional probabilities over the similarity matrices:

$$\bar{p}(x_i, x_j) = \frac{\bar{P}(y_i|x_j) + \bar{P}(y_j|x_i)}{2}, \tag{7}$$

where $\bar{P}(y_i|x_j) = \frac{1}{M}\sum_{m=1}^{M} P_m(y_i|x_j)$.

To estimate the conditional class probabilities, the appropriate size of the neighbourhood has to be determined. We propose a dynamic and automatic method: given two points x_i and x_j, we look for the first common neighbour. For each data point (x_i and x_j), the size k of the neighbourhood will be determined by the number of neighbours nearer than the common neighbour. To be more specific, let $R(x_i, n) = \{n\text{-nearest neighbours of } x_i\}$, then $k = \operatorname{argmin}_n\{R(x_i, n) \cap R(x_j, n) \neq \emptyset\}$. Obviously, the size k of the neighbourhood depends on the particular pair of points under consideration.

At this point, we have the tools to implement some particular proposals of combination methods.

3.2 The 'MaxMin' Method

The 'MaxMin' method (first used in [8]) produces a functional fusion of two similarity matrices, namely, the maximum and the minimum of the ordered sequence of similarities, being zero the weight assigned to the rest of the similarities. Consider the ordered sequence:

$$\min_{1\leq m\leq M} S_m(x_i, x_j) = S_{[1]}(x_i, x_j) \leq \ldots \leq S_{[M]}(x_i, x_j) = \max_{1\leq m\leq M} S_m(x_i, x_j),$$

where the subscript $[\cdot]$ denotes the position induced by the order. This method builds each element of S^* using the formula:

$$S^*(x_i, x_j) = \bar{\rho}(x_i, x_j)S_{[M]}(x_i, x_j) + (1 - \bar{\rho}(x_i, x_j))S_{[1]}(x_i, x_j). \quad (8)$$

If x_i and x_j belong to the same class then the conditional class probabilities $\bar{\rho}(x_i, x_j)$ will be high and the method guarantees that $S^*(x_i, x_j)$ will be large. On the other hand, if x_i and x_j belong to different classes the conditional class probabilities $\bar{\rho}(x_i, x_j)$ will be low and the method will produce a value close to the minimum of the similarities. In the following, this method will be refered as **MaxMin**.

3.3 The Percentile-in Method

Next we propose a method whose assignment of positive weights $w_m(x_i, x_j)$ is based on the order induced by the similarities. The method builds each element of S^* using the following formulae:

$$S^*(x_i, x_j) = S_{\lceil \bar{\rho}(x_i, x_j)M \rceil}, \quad (9)$$

where the subscript $\lceil \cdot \rceil$ denotes the upper rounding of the argument.

We denote this method by **'Percentile-in'** method [8]. If the class probability $\bar{\rho}(x_i, x_j)$ is high, we can expect a high similarity between x_i and x_j and the method will guarantee a high $S^*(x_i, x_j)$. If the class probability $\bar{\rho}(x_i, x_j)$ is low, $S^*(x_i, x_j)$ will be also low.

3.4 The Percentile-out Method

As in the previous method, the last proposed technique is based on the order induced by the similarities. However, in this case two similarities are considered. Each element of the S^* matrix is built as follows:

$$S^*(x_i, x_j) = \frac{1}{2}\left(S_{\lceil \bar{P}(y_i|x_j)M \rceil} + S_{\lceil \bar{P}(y_j|x_i)M \rceil}\right), \qquad (10)$$

where the subscript $\lceil \cdot \rceil$ denotes the upper rounding of the argument. We denote this method by **'Percentile-out'** method [8].

If the conditional class probabilities $\bar{P}(y_i|x_j)$ and $\bar{P}(y_j|x_i)$ are high, we can expect a high similarity between x_i and x_j and both methods will guarantee a high $S^*(x_i, x_j)$. If the conditional class probabilities $\bar{P}(y_i|x_j)$ and $\bar{P}(y_j|x_i)$ are both low, $S^*(x_i, x_j)$ will be also low.

4 Experiments

To test the performance of the proposed methods, a SVM (with the upper bound on the dual variables fixed to 1) has been trained on several real data sets using the output matrix S^* constructed.

In order to classify a non-labelled data point x, $S^*(x, i)$ has to be evaluated. We calculate two different values for $S^*(x, i)$, the first one assuming x belongs to class $+1$ and the second assuming x belongs to class -1. For each assumption, we compute the distance between x and the SVM hyperplane and assign x to the class corresponding to the largest distance from the hyperplane.

Since our technique is based on the calculation of the nearest neighbours, we have compared the proposed methods with the k-Nearest Neighbour classification (k-NN, using the optimal value $k = l^{\frac{4}{p+4}}$, where l is the sample size and p is the data dimension [13]). In order to evaluate the improvement provided by our proposals, we have carried out a Wilcoxon signed-rank test (see for instance [7]). This nonparametric test is used to compare the median of the results for different runs of each method. So, the null hypothesis of the test is that our methods do not improve the individual kernels.

4.1 The Three Spheres Example

The data set contains 300 data points in $\mathbb{R}^4$. We generate three different groups of observations (100 observations per group) corresponding to three spheres in $\mathbb{R}^3$. The center is the same for the three spheres $(0, 0, 0)$ and the radii are different (0.1, 0.3, and 1 respectively). The 100 points on the sphere with radio equals to 0.3 belong to class $+1$, and the other 200 points belong to class -1. Finally a fourth random additional dimension is added to the data set, following a Normal distribution (centered in 0 and with 10^{-2} as standard deviation). We use 50% of the data for training and 50% for testing.

Let $\{K_1, \ldots, K_5\}$ be a set of polynomial kernels with parameters $d = 1, 2, 3, 4, 5$ respectively, and $a = b = 1$. We use the Square Eigenvalue Transformation method to solve the problem of building a positive semi-definite matrix. Table 1 shows the performance of the proposed methods when fusing these kernel matrices. The results have been averaged over 10 runs.

The MaxMin and Percentile methods show the best overall performance. All our fusion methods provide better results than the best polynomial kernel, often using a significant lower number of support vectors. Regarding the Wilcoxon signed-rank test for the comparison of our methods with the best individual polynomial kernel, the p-values are smaller than 0.001 for all our methods. So the improvement obtained by the use of our proposals is statistically significant. Notice that the results using any of the single kernels are very poor, while the results obtained using any of our combination methods are significatively better.

Table 1. Percentage of missclassified data, sensitivity (Sens.), specificity (Spec.) and percentage of support vectors for the three spheres data set. Standard deviations in brackets.

Method	Train Error Sens. Spec.	Test Error Sens. Spec.	Support Vectors
Polynomial$_{d=1}$	31.8 (2.5) 0.000 1.000	34.9 (2.5) 0.000 1.000	69.5 (5.0)
Polynomial$_{d=2}$	31.8 (2.5) 0.000 1.000	34.9 (2.5) 0.000 1.000	75.7 (7.9)
Polynomial$_{d=3}$	30.6 (1.8) 0.200 0.909	36.1 (1.8) 0.200 0.891	71.7 (5.6)
Polynomial$_{d=4}$	23.7 (7.3) 0.377 0.893	31.7 (7.0) 0.293 0.816	69.5 (4.6)
Polynomial$_{d=5}$	14.7 (2.5) 0.541 0.958	24.1 (7.0) 0.436 0.798	69.5 (4.6)
MaxMin	4.0 (0.8) 0.964 0.958	5.5 (2.5) 0.921 0.958	8.4 (1.2)
Percentile-in	5.5 (1.4) 0.907 0.963	6.9 (3.2) 0.864 0.967	7.6 (1.4)
Percentile-out	4.5 (1.1) 0.941 0.959	6.9 (2.9) 0.886 0.957	8.5 (1.5)
k-NN	10.9 (2.4) 0.795 0.934	15.7 (4.2) 0.725 0.904	— (—)

4.2 Ionosphere Data Set

In this section we have worked with a database from the UCI Machine Learning Repository: the Johns Hopkins University Ionosphere database [3]. In this case, the data set consists of 351 observations with 34 continous predictor attributes variables each. We have used 60% of the data for training and 40% for testing.

For this data set we have considered the fusion of three polynomial kernels with $d = 1$, $d = 2$ and $d = 3$ respectively. We use the Positive Eigenvalue Transformation to solve the problem of building a positive semi-definite matrix.

The classification results are shown in Table 2. The MaxMin method, the Percentile-in method, and the Percentile-out method clearly improve the individual polynomial kernels under consideration. The improvement obtained by the use of our proposals is statistically significant: the p-values for the comparison of our methods with the best individual polynomial, using the Wilcoxon signed-rank test, are smaller than 0.01 for all our methods.

Table 2. Percentage of missclassified data and percentage of support vectors for the ionosphere data set. Standard deviations in brackets.

Method	Train Error	Test Error	Support Vectors
Polynomial$_{d=1}$	4.6 (0.3)	11.9 (2.0)	25.2 (1.6)
Polynomial$_{d=2}$	0.0 (0.0)	15.9 (3.9)	27.9 (2.1)
Polynomial$_{d=3}$	0.0 (0.0)	16.7 (2.8)	31.0 (1.4)
MaxMin	2.5 (0.6)	5.5 (1.4)	23.0 (1.5)
Percentile-in	3.1 (0.4)	5.7 (1.0)	23.6 (1.9)
Percentile-out	3.9 (0.6)	7.0 (2.2)	23.0 (1.9)
k-**NN**	19.7 (2.1)	21.8 (4.0)	— (—)

5 Conclusions

In this paper, we have proposed some methods for the fusion of polynomial kernels in order to improve their classification ability. The proposed techniques are specially usefull when does not exist an overall and unique best polynomial kernel. The suggested kernel fusion methods compare favorably to the single use of one of the polynomial kernels involved in the combination. Further research will focus on the theoretical properties of the methods. In particular, the methods shown in this paper do not take full advantage of the concept of the functional weighted sum described in (3): we think that there is room for improvement and more sophisticated ways for the calculus of the weights for the particular case of polynomial kernel matrices may be designed.

A natural extension of this work would be its generalization for the fusion of different types of kernels but, in this case, the normalization of the kernels has to be carefully studied.

Acknowledgments. This research has been partially supported by Spanish grants TIC2003-05982-C05-05, MTM2006-14961-C05-05, and SEJ 2004-03303.

References

1. S. Ali and K.A. Smith. Automatic parameter selection for polynomial kernel. pages 243–249. Proceedings of the 2003 IEEE International Conference on Information Reuse and Integration, IRI-2003, 2003.
2. S. Amari and S. Wu. Improving support vector machine classifiers by modifying kernel functions. *Neural Networks*, 12:783–789, 1999.
3. C. L. Blake and C. J. Merz. Uci repository of machine learning databases. university of carolina, Irvine, Department of Information and Computer Sciences, http://www.ics.uci.edu/~mlearn/MLRepository.html, 1998.

4. O. Bousquet and D.J.L. Herrmann. On the complexity of learning the kernel matrix. In S. Becker, S. Thurn, and K. Obermayer, editors, *Advances in Neural Information Processing Systems, 15*, pages 415–422. Cambridge, MA: The MIT Press, 2003.
5. J. C. Gower and P. Legendre. Metric and euclidean properties of dissimilarity coefficients. *Journal of Classification*, 3:5–48, 1986.
6. G. R. G. Lanckriet, N. Cristianini, P. Barlett, L. El Ghaoui, and M. I. Jordan. Learning the kernel matrix with semi-definite programming. *Journal of Machine Learning Research*, 5(Jan):27–72, 2004.
7. E. L. Lehmann. *Nonparametrics: Statistical Methods Based on Ranks*. McGraw-Hill, 1975.
8. J. M. Moguerza, I. Martín de Diego, and A. Muñoz. Improving support vector classificacion via the combination of multiple sources of information. In *Proc. of the IAPR International Workshops SSPR 2004 and SPR 2004, Vol. 3138 of LNCS*, pages 592–600. Berlin: Springer, 2004.
9. Y-Y. Ou, C-Y. Chen, S-C. Hwang, and Y-J. Oyang. Expediting model selection for support vector machines based on data reduction. page 786. IEEE International Conference on Systems, Man and Cybernetics, 2003.
10. E. Pękalska and R. P. W. Duin. *The Dissimilarity Representation for Pattern Recognition. Foundations and Applications*. World Scientific, Singapore., 2005.
11. E. Pękalska, R. P. W. Duin, S. Günter, and H. Bunke. On not making dissimilarities euclidean. In *Proc. of the IAPR International Workshops SSPR 2004 and SPR 2004, Vol. 3138 of LNCS*, pages 1145–1154. Berlin: Springer, 2004.
12. E. Pękalska, P. Paclík, and R. P. W. Duin. A generalized kernel approach to dissimilarity-based classification. *Journal of Machine Learning Research, Special Issue on Kernel Methods*, 2(12):175–211, 2001.
13. B. Silverman. *Density Estimation for Statistics and Data Analysis*. Chapman and Hall, London, 1986.
14. L. Vandenberghe and S. Boyd. Semidefinite programming. *SIAM Review*, 38(1):49–95, 1996.

Speech and Gesture Recognition-Based Robust Language Processing Interface in Noise Environment

Jung-Hyun Kim and Kwang-Seok Hong

School of Information and Communication Engineering, Sungkyunkwan University, 300,
Chunchun-dong, Jangan-gu, Suwon, KyungKi-do, 440-746, Korea
kjh0328@skku.edu, kshong@skku.ac.kr
http://hci.skku.ac.kr

Abstract. We suggest and implement WPS (Wearable Personal Station) and Web-based robust Language Processing Interface (LPI) integrating speech and sign language (the Korean Standard Sign Language; KSSL). In other word, the LPI is integration language recognition and processing system that can select suitable language recognition system according to noise degree in given noise environment, and it is extended into embedded and ubiquitous-oriented the next generation language processing system that can take the place of a traditional uni-modal language recognition system using only 1 sensory channel based on desk-top PC and wire communication net. In experiment results, while an average recognition rate of uni-modal recognizer using KSSL only is 92.58% and speech only is 93.28%, advanced LPI deduced an average recognition rate of 95.09% for 52 sentential recognition models. Also, average recognition time is 0.3 seconds in LPI.

1 Introduction

The Multi-Modal Interface (MMI) for man-machine interaction aims to make considerable advances in interface technology by offering users a wide range of interaction facilities within the same interface system. In other word, the multi-modal interfaces integrating various sensory channels such as speech, vision and haptic can increase the bandwidth and application of human-computer interaction and it may improve the interactive properties and functions of the system [1]. Nowadays, multi-modal systems are at the center of many research areas like computer science, philosophy, mathematics, linguistics, social science, and economics [2], [3]. However, desktop PC and wire communications net-based traditional studies on pattern recognition and multimodal interaction generally have some restrictions and problems according to using of the vision technologies for recognition and acquisition of the haptic-gesture information. That is, according as most of traditional studies like this keep the accent on an implementation of uni-modal recognition and translation system that recognizes and represents one of various natural components based on wire communications net and a vision technology, they have not only several restrictions such as limitation of representation, conditionality on the space and limitation of the motion, but also some problems such as uncertainty of measurement and a necessity of complex computational algorithms according to using of vision technologies. Consequently, we suggest and implement advanced LPI integrating speech and KSSL gestures based on the VXML for web-based speech recognition and ubiquitous computing-oriented WPS with a built-in KSSL recognizer.

2 Wearable Personal Station-Based Embedded KSSL Recognizer

2.1 Regulation and Components of the KSSL

Not only a absolute natural learning and interpretation of the KSSL very difficult and takes a long time to represent and translate it fluently in hearing person, but also understanding and learning of spoken language in the hearing-impaired is impossible and uncertain. In other words, because the KSSL is very complicated and is consisted of considerable numerous gestures, motions and so on, it are impossible that recognize all dialog components which are represented by the hearing-impaired. Therefore, we prescribe that this paper is a fundamental study for perfect dialog and communication between the hearing-impaired and hearing person, and selected 25 basic KSSL gestures connected with a travel information scenario according to the "Korean Standard Sign Language Tutor (hereinafter, "KSSLT")[4]". And necessary 23 hand gestures for travel information - KSSL gestures are classified as hand's shapes, pitch and roll degree. Consequently, we constructed 52 sentential KSSL recognition models according to associability and presentation of hand gestures and basic KSSL gestures.

2.2 Improved KSSL Input Module Using Wireless Haptic Devices

For the KSSL input module, we adopted blue-tooth module for wireless sensor network, 5DT company's wireless data (sensor) gloves and fastrak® which are one of popular input devices in the haptic application field. Wireless data gloves are basic gesture recognition equipment that can acquires and capture various haptic information (e.g. hand or finger's stooping degree, direction) using fiber-optic flex sensor.. Each flexure value has a decimal range of 0 to 255, with a low value indicating an inflexed finger, and a high value indicating a flexed finger. Also, the fastrak® is electromagnetic motion tracking system, a 3D digitizer and a quad receiver motion tracker. And it provides dynamic, real-time measurements of six degrees of freedom; position (X, Y, and Z Cartesian coordinates) and orientation (azimuth, elevation, and roll) [5]. The architecture and composition of KSSL input module is shown in Fig. 1.

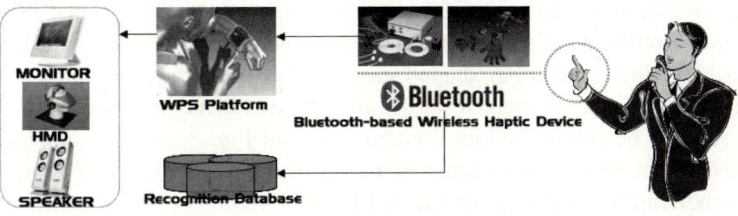

Fig. 1. The architecture and composition of the KSSL input module

2.3 Feature Extraction and Recognition Models Using RDBMS

A statistical classification algorithms such as K-means clustering, QT (Quality Threshold) clustering, fuzzy c-means clustering algorithm and Self-Organizing Map (SOM) had been applied universally in a traditional pattern recognition systems with unsupervised training, including machine training, data mining, pattern recognition, image analysis and bioinformatics [6], [7], [8]. However, such classification algorithms have some restrictions and problems such as the necessity of complicated mathematical computation according to multidimensional features, the difficulty of application in a distributed processing system, relativity of computation costs by patterns (data) size, minimization of memory swapping and assignment. Accordingly, for a clustering method for efficient feature extraction and a construction of training/recognition models based on a distributed computing, we suggest and introduce improved RDBMS (Relational Data-Base Management System) clustering module to resolve such a restrictions and problems. The RDBMS has the capability to recombine the data items from different files, providing powerful tools for data usage [9], [10]. A clustering rule to segment valid gesture record set and invalid record set in the RDBMS classification module is shown in Fig. 2.

SerialNO	F1THUMB	F1INDEX	F1MIDDLE	F1RING	F1LITTLE	F1X-POSI.	F1Y-POSI.	F1Z-POSI.	F1_Px	F1_Py	GESTURE DATA...	VALIDITY
22	73	86	255	255	255	50.90	-14.53	-4.74	55.42	-5.71		X
23	51	48	255	255	255	52.05	-11.97	-2.13	53.29	-4.95		X
24	32	15	255	255	255	53.99	-9.50	0.01	50.02	-4.75		X
25	17	0	255	255	255	51.03	-10.50	-1.05	51.11	-4.83	Omission...	X
26	7	0	255	255	255	52.01	-9.85	-1.02	49.85	-5.23		
27	0	0	255	254	255	52.78	-8.77	-1.75	51.85	-6.02		
28	0	0	253	254	255	49.87	-10.18	-2.12	48.97	-5.27		
29	0	0	255	255	254	48.71	-9.43	-1.92	52.85	-4.89		
30	0	0	255	255	255	51.09	-8.75	-1.75	47.93	-4.94		

1. Difference Between Preceding Average(preceding 3 and 1) and Current Row Value
2. Decide validity : Preceding Average - Current Value = 52-17 = 35

Average Between 3 Preceding and 1 Preceding from Current Row : 52

1. Difference between Preceding Average and Current Row Value > 5
2. 'X'(Invalidity Record) check

Fig. 2. The clustering rules to segment in the RDBMS classification module

2.4 Fuzzy Max-Min Composition-Based the KSSL Recognition

Fuzzification and Membership Function. We applied trapezoidal shaped membership functions for representation of fuzzy numbers-sets, and this shape is originated from the fact that there are several points whose membership degree is maximum. To define and describe trapezoidal shaped membership functions, we define trapezoidal fuzzy numbers-set A as $A = (a, b, c, d)$, and the membership function of this fuzzy numbers-set will be interpreted as Equation (1) and Fig. 3. Also, a suppositions and basic rules for its design and representation are as following and the proposed the fuzzy membership functions are shown in Fig. 4.

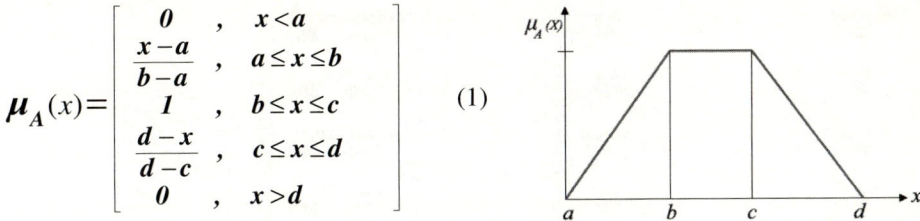

$$\mu_A(x) = \begin{bmatrix} 0 & , & x<a \\ \dfrac{x-a}{b-a} & , & a\leq x\leq b \\ 1 & , & b\leq x\leq c \\ \dfrac{d-x}{d-c} & , & c\leq x\leq d \\ 0 & , & x>d \end{bmatrix} \quad (1)$$

Fig. 3. Trapezoidal fuzzy numbers-set A as $A = (a, b, c, d)$

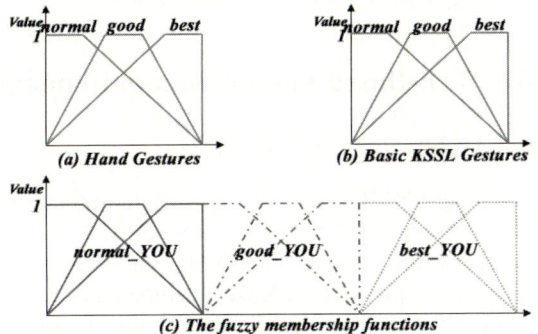

Fig. 4. The fuzzy membership functions for KSSL recognition. Because fuzzy numbers-sets according to KSSL recognition models are very various and so many, we represent membership functions partially: "YOU" in KSSL).

Max-Min Composition of Fuzzy Relation. In this paper, we utilized the fuzzy max-min composition to extend a crisp relation concept to relation concept with fuzzy proposition and to reason approximate conclusion by composition arithmetic of fuzzy relation. Two fuzzy relations R and S are defined on sets A, B and C (we prescribed the accuracy of hand gestures and basic KSSL gestures, object KSSL recognition models as the sets of events that are happened in KSSL recognition with the sets A, B and C). The composition $S \bullet R = SR$ of two relations R and S is expressed by the relation from A to C, and this composition is defined in Equation (1) [11].

$$\text{For } (x, y) \in A \times B,\ (y, z) \in B \times C,$$
$$\mu_{S\bullet R}(x, z) = \underset{y}{Max}\ [Min(\mu_R(x,y), \mu_S(y,z))] \quad (1)$$

$S \bullet R$ from this elaboration is a subset of $A \times C$. That is, $S \bullet R \subseteq A \times C$. If the relations R and S are represented by matrices M_R and M_S, the matrix $M_{S\bullet R}$ corresponding to $S \bullet R$ is obtained from the product of M_R and M_S; $M_{S\bullet R} = M_R \bullet M_S$. Also, the matrix $M_{S\bullet R}$ represents max-min composition that reason and analyze the possibility of C when A is occurred and it is also given in Fig. 5.

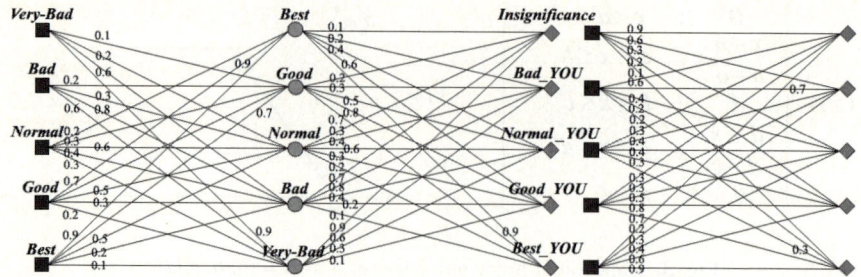

Fig. 5. Composition of fuzzy relation

3 Voice-XML for Web-Based Speech Recognition and Synthesis

3.1 Components and Architecture of Voice-XML

VXML is the W3C's standard XML format for specifying interactive voice dialogues between a human and a computer [12]. A document server (e.g. a Web server) processes requests from a client application, the VXML Interpreter, through the VXML interpreter context. The server produces VXML documents in reply, which are processed by the VXML interpreter. The VXML interpreter context may monitor user inputs in parallel with the VXML interpreter. The implementation platform is controlled by the VXML interpreter context and by the VXML interpreter. The components and architecture of VXML 2.0 by W3C are shown in Fig. 6.

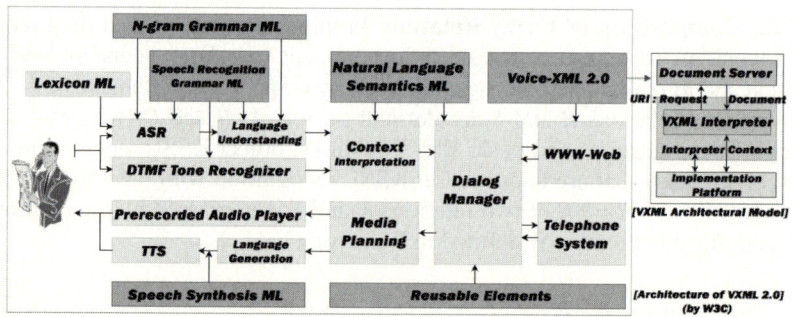

Fig. 6. The components of architectural model and architecture of W3C's VXML 2.0

3.2 Integration Scheme of Speech and KSSL for the LPI

The user connects to VXML server through web and telephone network using WPS based on wireless networks and telephone terminal, and input prescribed speech and KSSL. The user's sentential speech data which is inputted into telephone terminal transmits to ASR-engine and saves sentential ASR results to MMI database. Also, the KSSL data which is inputted into embedded WPS is recognized by sentential KSSL recognizer, transmits and saves sentential recognition results to VXML server using TCP/IP protocol based on middleware and wireless sensor networks. Sentential ASR and KSSL recognition results execute comparison arithmetic by internal SQL logic, and transmit arithmetic results to the LPI. Arithmetic results are definite intention that user presents. Finally, user's intention is provided to user through speech (TTS) and visualization. The KSSL recognition processes of the LPI synchronize with the speech recognition and synthesis using VXML and MMI database.

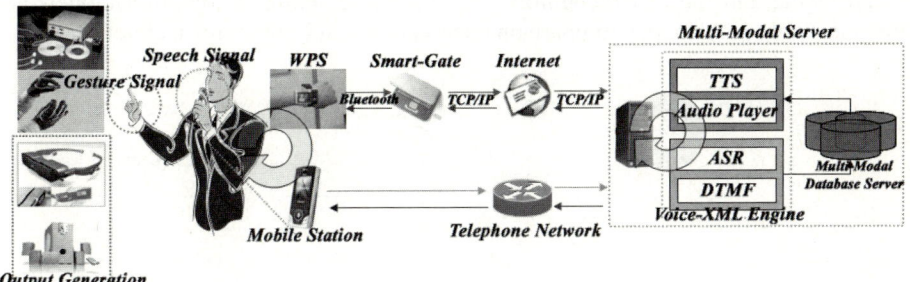

Fig. 7. The components and architecture of the LPI using speech and sign language

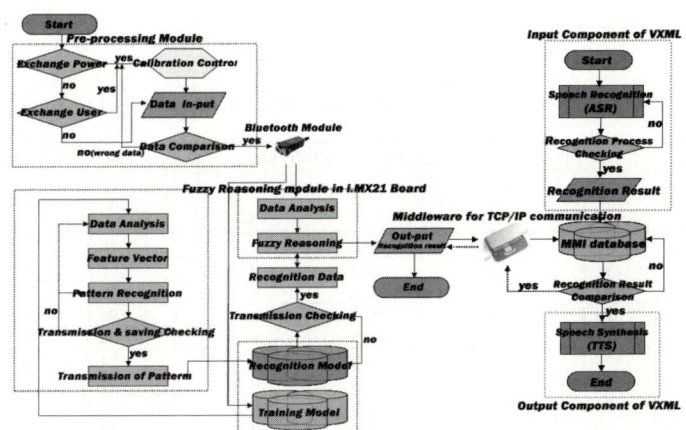

Fig. 8. The flowchart of the LPI integrating VXML and KSSL Recognizer

Also, even if speech recognition system of laboratory environment that have the high recognition rate, because its recognition performance is fallen greatly in noise environment, could deduce the higher recognition rate according as give suitable weight by noise degree to each language recognition system. The suggested a scenario and architecture of the LPI using speech and KSSL are shown in Fig. 7. And a flowchart of the LPI integrating VXML for web-based speech recognition and synthesis and ubiquitous-oriented sentential KSSL recognizer is shown in Fig. 8.

4 Experiments and Results

Experimental set-up is as follows. The distance between the KSSL input module and embedded WPS for processing of the KSSL recognition composed in about radius 10M's ellipse form. When user inputs the KSSL and speech, we move data gloves and receivers of motion tracker to prescribed position. For every 15 reagents, we repeat this action 10 times. While user inputs the KSSL using data gloves and motion tracker, speak using blue-tooth headset of telephone terminal. Experimental results, the uni-modal and the LPI recognition rate for 52 sentential recognition models are shown in Table 1. Also, the comparison charts are given in Fig.9 respectively.

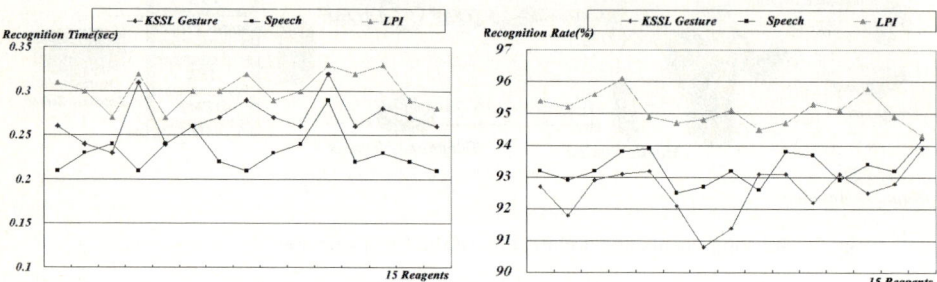

Fig. 9. Average recognition rate of the uni-modal and the LPI

Table 1. Uni-modal and the the LPI recognition rate for 52 sentential recognition models

Evaluation (R: Recognition) Reagent	Uni-modal Language Processing Interface				LPI 52 Sentence models	
	The KSSL (%)		Speech (%)			
	R-Rate (%)	R-Time(sec)	R-Rate (%)	R-Time(sec)	R-Rate (%)	R-Time(sec)
Reagent 1	92.7	0.26	93.2	0.21	95.4	0.31
Reagent 2	91.8	0.24	92.9	0.23	95.2	0.30
Reagent 3	92.9	0.23	93.2	0.24	95.6	0.27
Reagent 4	93.1	0.31	93.8	0.21	96.1	0.32
Reagent 5	93.2	0.24	93.9	0.24	94.9	0.27
Reagent 6	92.1	0.26	92.5	0.26	94.7	0.30
Reagent 7	90.8	0.27	92.7	0.22	94.8	0.30
Reagent 8	91.4	0.29	93.2	0.21	95.1	0.32
Reagent 9	93.1	0.27	92.6	0.23	94.5	0.29
Reagent10	93.1	0.26	93.8	0.24	94.7	0.30
Reagent11	92.2	0.32	93.7	0.29	95.3	0.33
Reagent12	93.1	0.26	92.9	0.22	95.1	0.32
Reagent13	92.5	0.28	93.4	0.23	95.8	0.33
Reagent14	92.8	0.27	93.2	0.22	94.9	0.29
Reagent15	93.9	0.26	94.2	0.21	94.3	0.28
Average	92.58	0.27	93.28	0.23	95.09	0.30

5 Summary and Conclusions

Multimodal interaction provides the user with multiple modes of interfacing with a system beyond the traditional keyboard and mouse input/output. The most common such interface combines a visual modality with a voice modality. Suggested LPI for multi-modal interaction support the two major types of multi-modality for language recognition based on embedded and ubiquitous computing: 1) sequential multi-modality allows users to move seamlessly between speech and the KSSL recognition modes. Sequential multi-modality offers real value when different steps of a single application are more effective in one mode than the other. Particularly, in a language recognition application, it is more effective to speak the user's intentions (speech recognition mode) than to represent the KSSL in noiseless environment, yet it may be preferable to recognize the KSSL (sign language recognition mode) than to listen in noise environment. The swap between speech and the KSSL recognition modes may be initiated by the application or by the user, 2) simultaneous multi-modality, where the device has both modes active, empowers the user to use speech and sign language communication simultaneously according to the noise degree. In experiment results, the LPI is more efficient and powerful than uni-modal recognition system that uses one in the KSSL or speech. Especially, while the average recognition rate of uni-modal recognition system that use KSSL (gesture) only is 92.58%, the LPI deduced an average recognition rate of 95.09% and showed difference of an average recognition rate as much as about 2.51%.

Acknowledgement

This research was supported by MIC, Korea under ITRC IITA-2005-(C1090-0501-0019).

References

1. M. Fuchs, P. et al.: Architecture of Multi-modal Dialogue System. TSD2000. Lecture Notes in Artificial Intelligence, Vol. 1902. Springer-Verlag, Berlin Heidelberg New York (2000) 433–438
2. M. J. Wooldridge and N.R. Jennings. Intelligent agents: Theory and practice. Know. Eng. Review, 10(2):115-152, 1995.
3. R. Fagin, J.Y. Halpern, Y. Moses, and M.Y. Vardi. Reasoning about Knowledge. MIT Press, 1995.
4. S.-G.Kim.: Korean Standard Sign Language Tutor, 1st, Osung Publishing Company, Seoul (2000)
5. J.-H.Kim. et al.: Hand Gesture Recognition System using Fuzzy Algorithm and RDBMS for Post PC. FSKD2005. Lecture Notes in Artificial Intelligence, Vol. 3614. Springer-Verlag, Berlin Heidelberg New York (2005) 170-175
6. Richard O. Duda, Peter E. Hart, David G. Stork.: Pattern Classification, 2nd, Wiley, New York (2001)
7. Dietrich Paulus and Joachim Hornegger.: Applied Pattern Recognition, 2nd, Vieweg (1998)
8. J. Schuermann.: Pattern Classification: A Unified View of Statistical and Neural Approaches, Wiley&Sons (1996)
9. Relational DataBase Management System.: http://www.auditmypc.com/acronym/RDBMS.asp
10. Oracle 10g DW Guide.: http://www.oracle.com
11. W. B. Vasantha kandasamy.: Smaranda Fuzzy Algebra. American Research Press, Seattle (2003)
12. Scott McGlashan et al.: Voice Extensible Markup Language (VoiceXML) Version 2.0. W3C Recommendation, http://www.w3.org (1992)

Heterogeneous Answer Acquisition Methods in Encyclopedia QA

Hyo-Jung Oh, Chung-Hee Lee, Changki Lee, Ji-Hyun Wang, Yi-Gyu Hwang, Hyeon-Jin Kim, and Myung-Gil Jang

ETRI, 161 Gajeong-dong, Yuseong-gu, Daejeon, 305-700, Korea
{ohj, forever, leeck, jhwang, yghwang, jini, mgjang}@etri.re.kr

Abstract. We propose an enhanced QA model with combination of heterogeneous answer acquisition methods. Our QA system is based on web encyclopedia in Korean. We investigated characteristic features of the encyclopedia and incorporate them in our answer acquisition methods. We defined three different types of answer extraction methods: learning-based, pattern-based, and traditional statistical methods. By empirical experiments, we obtained 59% improvement on MRR as well as 2.3 times speedy response.

Keywords: Question Answering, Knowledge acquisition, Machine learning.

1 Introduction

Most of early studies on Question Answering (QA) have performed a single strategy for acquiring answer. Typical QA consists roughly of question analysis, answer retrieval, and candidate answer indexing [1]. Although a typical QA system classifies questions based on expected answer types, it adopts the same strategy for candidate answer indexing.

For revealing various question and answer types, we collected real users' questions from the commercial web site logs[1]. We gathered 2,569 questions during three months. Over 80% questions could find the answer in encyclopedia except questions from gossips or scandals about entertainers. Contrary to some web documents which contain indefinite information in terms of uncertainty of web, encyclopedia contains the facts which were already approved or occurred in the past. Moreover, the Web, while nearly infinite in content, is not a complete repository of useful information, thus we need to prepared answers in advance.

On the other hand, there are many typical sentences which can be patternized or be learnable in encyclopedia. That means we might prepare candidate answers based on knowledge acquisition approach in advance. For example, a sentence, 'Capital: Paris', in the document which explains about 'France', contains the answer for *"where is the capital of France?"*. Based on these observations, we investigate three different answer extraction methods based on Korean encyclopedia. We utilize machine-learning and pattern-matching techniques. Our system combines pre-acquired answers

---
[1] Nate Encyclopedia Service(http://100.nate.com), Naver manual QA Service(http://kin.naver.com), Yahoo Korea Encyclopedia Service(http://kr.dic.yahoo.com).

for finding answer, thus attempts to improve the QA performance in terms of response accuracy. It is against the fact that typical QA retrieves answers in real-time when a user question entered.

2 Heterogeneous Answers in Encyclopedia

Figure 1 shows our QA system using four different answer bases and a document containing various answers. A question about a diseases or syndrome might ask for 'alias', 'discovery date', or 'discovery person'. The second highlighted sentence in Figure 1 has information about alias of a Down syndrome. It might be an answer for a question, *"what is alias of Down syndrome?"*. We notice that the Information Extraction (IE) system is successful in the closed domain such as encyclopedia [2].

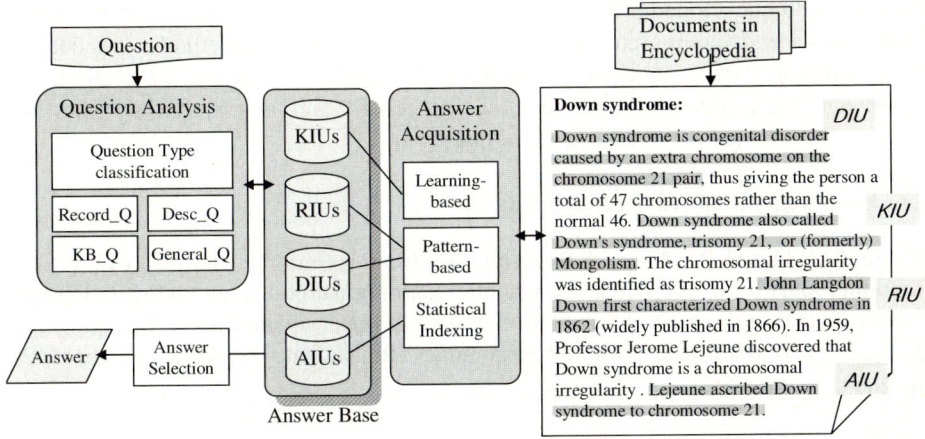

Fig. 1. System Architecture

As second type, we focused on stereotyped sentences. The third sentence contains record answer for *"who did disclose Down syndrome for the first time?."* Sentences including record information generally have specific words which indicate that the sentence is record sentence [3]. Another typical sentence type is descriptive sentence, such as the first sentence in Figure 1. Because encyclopedia contains facts about many different subjects or one particular subject explained for reference, there are many sentences which present definition such as *"X is Y."* On the other hand, some sentences describe the process of some special event (i.e. the 1st World War), so that they consist of particular syntactic structures (5W1H) like news article. Record and descriptive answer sentences in corpus form particular syntactic patterns.

When user question arrives at QA engine, we firstly perform linguistic process contained Part-of-Speech (POS) tagging, Answer Type (AT) tagging (similar to the extended named entity recognizer) and parsing. To find appropriate answers in our pre-built answer bases, we perform query processing to determine user question types, especially looking for record and descriptive answers. If a user question can be generated by a LSP (Lexico-Syntactic Pattern), then the answer for that question might be found in knowledge-base (KB). We differentiate user questions into four types: record, descriptive, KB, and general type. According to question type, our system extracts the answer in one of four different answer bases: one is traditional index database (AIUs: Answer Index Units) for ordinarily question and the others are KB (KIUs), record (RIUs), and descriptive answers (DIUs), which are focused on this paper.

3 Answer Acquisition Methods

The ultimate purpose of our various answer acquisition methods is to help a QA system by providing correct answer as well as fast response time. Our QA system is based on web encyclopedia in Korean. We investigated characteristic features of the encyclopedia and incorporate them in our answer acquisition methods. We defined three different types of answer extraction method: *learning-based* method for knowledge base, *pattern-based* method for record and descriptive answer, and traditional *statistical* method for general question.

3.1 Learning-Based Answer Acquisition

We built a knowledge-base (KB) using machine learning technique, Conditional Random Fields (CRF) [4]. CRF is a machine learning method using undirected graphs trained to maximize a conditional probability. A linear-chain CRF with parameters $\Lambda = \{\lambda_1,...\}$ defines a conditional probability for a state (such as a label "BP (birthplace)" in Fig. 2) sequence $s = <s_1,...,s_T>$ given an input sequence $o = <o_1,...,o_T>$ to be

$$p_\Lambda(s|o) = \frac{1}{Z_o} \exp\left(\sum_{t=1}^{T} \sum_i \lambda_i f_i(s_{t-1}, s_t, o, t)\right) \qquad (1)$$

Where z_0 is the normalization constant that makes the probability of all state sequences sum to one, $f_i(s_{t-1}, s_t, o, t)$ is a feature function that is often binary-valued, but can be real-valued, and λ_i is a learned weight associated with feature f_i.

To construct the KB, a specific schema for encyclopedia domains is required [2]. KB schema consists of an entity and its properties: The entity is a target object on a user's question, and the property which explains the characteristics of the object is an answer candidate on a user's question. Properties might be grouped into topics. Those reflect most frequently asked themes in user questions. For example, the questions about a person can be grouped by theme, such as 'alias', 'birth', 'death', and so on. We defined 110 topics and 268 specific properties for 14 domains. Table 1 shows topics and its properties for the 'PERSON' domain.

Table 1. Examples of Properties for 'PERSON' domain

Domain	Topic	Properties
PERSON	Birth	birth data, birth place
	Death	death date, death place, death reason
	Name	Family origin, pseudonym
	Career	joining date, position
	Discovery	a discovery, discovery date, discovery place.
	Assertion	asserted theory
	Education	graduate school, graduate data,
	Record	championship title, championship date
	Work	Debut journal, debut date, debut work
	...	
14 Domains	110	268

Title: Marie Curie
Sentence1: She was born in Warsaw, Poland on November 7, 1867.

- Generating feature for a given sentence:

  Sentent1: She was born in Warsaw, Poland on November 7, 1867
  -Feature: {word-2=born word-1=in word=Warsaw word+1=, ord+2=Poland
  tag-2=VBD tag-1=IN tag=NN tag+1=,..., verb=born}

- Labeling sentence using CRF:

  Sentent1: She was born in Warsaw, Poland on November 7, 1867
  - Label: O O O O BP BP BP O BD   BDBD BD

- Storing in Knowledge Base:
  - **Entity: Marie Curie**

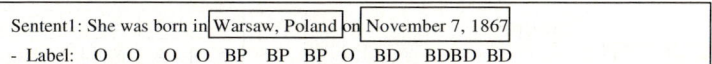

	Properties	Value	Score
KIU	Birth – place (BP)	Warsaw, Poland	0.72
	Birth – date (BD)	Nov.7, 1867	0.72

Fig. 2. KB extraction flow

Figure 2 depicts the processes of KB extraction. First, we generate features from the words in a sentence of the encyclopedia. The words are then tagged with their corresponding labels (ex, BP-'Birth Place', BD-'Birth Date', O, etc) using CRF. In this example, 'Warsaw, Poland' and 'November 7, 1869' are labeled as BP and BD tags, respectively. Then we save them as KIU (Knowledge Indexing Unit), one of answer bases. Finally, we extracted 408,628 KIUs from encyclopedia and constructed about 1.2 giga-bytes of knowledge base.

3.2 Pattern-Based Answer Acquisition

3.2.1 Record Answer Acquisition

We utilized pattern-based approach for extracting record answer. We defined specific words as '*RI(Record Indicating)-term*' to identify record information and determined Record Type (RT) by it. Example 1 is a sentence including '*the first*' as RI-term.

Example 1: 영국의 피시하우스는 세계 최초의 수족관이다.
Fish House of the Britain is the first aquarium in the world

Not all sentences which contain RI-term are useful. For example, a sentence, *"This song was made on the most sensitive season."* has '*the most*' as RI-term. However, the sentence does not contain record information. We extract valid record information only when the sentence satisfies context restrictions on structure and term. We defined '*record sentence*' for sentences which contain RI-term and satisfy constrains. Context restriction on structure can be formalized as a template, such as 'A is the first C in B' for *"ENIAC is the first computer in the world."* In this example, A, B, and C represent answer, location and kind of answer, respectively. We defined 220 templates as context restrictions on structure for record sentences.

We define Record Answer Indexing Template (RAIT) that can represent contextual information of the record sentence. RAIT reflects context restriction which consists of six units: RI-term, Answer Type, location where the record occurs, and parsing result formed predicate-argument <verb, subject, object>. Figure 3 describes automatic acquired RIU (Record Index Unit) from a record sentence that matches with the context. By this method, 8,810 RIUs are extracted.

Record Sentence: The whale shark is the largest fish in the world.

RAIT

Indexing info.	Verb	Loc.	AT	Subj.	Obj.	Answer
	be	C	B	NULL	NULL	A
Sent. Context	A is the largest B in C.					

RIU

Verb	Loc.	AT	Subject	Object	Answer
is	world	fish	NULL	NULL	Whale shark

Fig. 3. Example of RIU extraction

3.2.2 Descriptive Answer Acquisition

Our QA system is a domain specific system for encyclopedia. Among 2,569 questions, 901 questions (35%) find long descriptive statement. For example, *"Who is Jacques Chirac?"* and *"Why is sky blue?"* are 'descriptive' question. By analyzing 200 sample documents, we found that the fact that encyclopedia has many descriptive sentences, about 20%. Descriptive answer sentences in corpus show particular syntactic patterns such as appositive clauses, parallel clauses, and adverb clauses of cause and effect. We defined 10 DATs (Descriptive Answer Types) to reflect these features of sentences in encyclopedia. Table 2 shows example sentences and patterns for each DAT.

As shown in Table 2, descriptive answer sentences generally have particular syntactic structures. To extract these descriptive patterns, we first build initial patterns. We constructed pre-tagged corpus with 10 DAT tags, then performed sentence alignment by the surface tag boundary. The tagged sentences are processed through POS tagging in the first step. In this stage, we can get descriptive clue terms and structures, such as "X is caused by Y" for 'Reason', 'X was made for Y" for 'Function', and so on.

In the second step, we used linguistic analysis including chunking and parsing to extend initial patterns automatically. Initial patterns are too rigid because we look up only surface of sentences in the first step. If some clue terms appear with long distance in a sentence, it can fail to be recognized as a pattern. To solve this problem, we added sentence structure patterns on each DAT patterns, such as appositive clause patterns for 'Definition', parallel clause patterns for 'Kind', and so on.

Finally, we generalized patterns to conduct flexible pattern matching. We need to group patterns to adapt to variations of terms which appear in un-seen sentences. Several similar patterns under the same DAT tag were integrated into regular-expression union which is to be formulated automata. For example, 'Definition' patterns are represented by [X<NP> be called/named/known as Y<NP>].

We built a pattern matching system based on Finite State Automata (FSA) [3] which consists 3,254 patterns. We extracted 300,252 DIUs from the whole encyclopedia using descriptive pattern matching method.

Table 2. Examples of Descriptive Answer Type

DAT	Example/Pattern
DEFINITION	쓰나미란 급격한 지진으로 인해 발생한 긴 파장의 해일이다. *A tsunami* is a large wave, often caused by an earthquake. [X is Y]
FUCTION	부레는 물고기가 물의 깊이에 따라 상하로 이동할 때 내부의 가스량을 조절하는 역할을 한다. *Air bladder* is an air-filled structure in many fishes that functions to maintain buoyancy or to aid in respiration. [X that function to Y]
KIND	미국 동전에는 1 센트, 5 센트, 25 센트, 100 센트 짜리가 있다. *The coins* in States are 1 cent, 5 cents, 25 cents, and 100cents. [X are Y_1, Y_2,... and Y_n]
METHOD	감기를 예방하는 방법은 손을 자주 씻는 것이다. *The method that prevents a cold* is washing your hand often. [The method that/of X is Y]
CHARACTER	해마는 수직인 자세로 헤엄치며 갈고리 모양의 꼬리는 갖는 특징이 있다. *Sea horse*, characteristically swimming in an upright position and having a prehensile tail. [X is characteristically Y]
OBJECTIVE	자동차는 이동을 위해 사용되는 수단이다. *An automobile* used for land transports. [X used for Y]
REASON	쓰나미란 급격한 지진으로 인해 발생한 긴 파장의 해일이다. *A tsunami* is a large wave, often caused by an earthquake. [X is caused by Y]
COMPONENT	자동차는 보통 4 개의 바퀴와 엔진, 휠 등으로 구성된다. *An automobile* usually is composed of 4 wheels, an engine, and a steering wheel. [X is composed of Y_1, Y_2,... and Y_n]
PRINCIPLE	삼투압의 원리는 투과되지 않는 막에 양쪽에 용액과 순용매를 따로 넣으면, 용매의 일정량이 용액 속으로 침투하여 평형에 이르는 과정이다. *Osmosis* is the principle, transfer of a liquid solvent through a semipermeable membrane that does not allow dissolved solids to pass. [X is the principle, Y]
ORIGIN	아킬레스힘줄이란 이름은 그리스 신화에 나오는 영웅인 아켈레우스의 이름에서 유래한 것이다. *The Achilles tendon* is the name from the mythical Greek hero Achilles. [X is the name from Y]

3.3 Statistical Answer Retrieval

We take statistical retrieval approach for general questions, which do not correspond to question types explained in previous sections. For this approach, we rely on natural language processing techniques including morphological process, word sense disambiguation, AT tagging and syntactic analysis. The indexer generates AIU (Answer Index Unit) structures using the answer candidates (the AT annotated words) and the content words which can be founded within the same context boundary. It seems to be indexing stage in context of Information Retrieval (IR).

The answer processing module searches the relative answer candidates from index DB using question analysis and calculates the similarities and then extracts answers. This module is composed of question term-weighting part and answer-ranking part as same with typical QA [5]. We calculate the weight of a keyword using the BM25 weighting scheme [6]:

$$f_K = \frac{tf_k}{K\left[(1-b)+b\frac{document\ length}{avg.\ document\ length}\right]+tf_k} \times \log \frac{N-df+0.5}{df+0.5} \quad (2)$$

4 Experiments

The encyclopedia used in our system, Pascal[2], currently consists of 100,373 entries and 14 domains in Korean. For our experimental evaluations we constructed an operational system in the Web, named "AnyQuestion 3.0[3]." To show improvement of our model, we built test collection, named KorQAEval judged by 4 assessors from different groups. KorQAEval 3.0 consists of 873 <question, answer> pairs including general factoid, record, and descriptive questions for all categories in encyclopedia. Table 3 details distribution of our test set. For performance comparisons, we used MRRs (Mean Reciprocal Ranks, [1]) and Top 5 measure: precision, recall and F-score (F1[4]). Top 5 is a measure to consider whether there is a correct answer in top 5 ranking or not. MRR is a measure to reflect the answer order, such as 1/rank weight.

Table 3. Distribution of KorQAEval 3.0

Test Set	KB (KIU)	Record (RIU)	Descriptive (DIU)	General (AIU)	Total
Tuning	60	15	45	191	311
Evaluation 1	44	24	39	161	268
Evaluation 2	22	29	55	158	294
Total	126	68	139	540	873

The goal of combining heterogeneous answer acquisition methods is to help a QA system by providing correct answer as well as fast response time. We compared traditional QA method with combined QA, proposed in this paper, using Evaluation 1 and 2. While traditional QA performs statistical retrieval in AIU answer base, combined QA uses four different answer base, including RIU, KIU, DIU and AIU, according to question types. Table 4 shows the result.

---

[2] Pascal[tm] Encyclopedia. http://www.epascal.co.kr
[3] AnyQuestion (http://anyq.etri.re.kr): Korean Encyclopedia QA system.
[4] F1=2*Precision*Recall/(Precision+Recall). It mean that recall and precision are evenly weighted.

Table 4. Comparison with Traditional QA and Combined QA

Model	Test Set	Retrieved	Correct	Precision	Recall	F-score	MRRs
Traditional QA	Evaluation 1	157	136	0.87	0.51	0.64	0.46
	Evaluation 2	191	120	0.62	0.41	0.50	0.33
	Overall	348	256	0.74	0.46	0.56	0.39
Combined QA	Evaluation 1	206	175	0.85	0.65	0.74	0.60
	Evaluation 2	239	206	0.86	0.71	0.77	0.63
	Overall	441	380	0.86	0.68	0.76	0.62

As expected, we obtained 59% improvement in MRR (0.39 to 0.62). While traditional QA provide 256 correct answers, combined QA find 380 correct answers among 562 (268 in Evaluation 1 + 294 in Evaluation 2) questions. Besides, the response time of combined QA (avg. 0.35 sec.) is 2.3 times as fast as traditional QA (avg. 0.82 sec.) since statistical retrieval computes similarity between question and a mass of AIUs in real-time. On the other hand, combined QA finds candidate in pre-acquired answers. To reveal effects of individual answer acquisition methods, we made a close investigation of the result of Evaluation 1. Table 5 shows the details.

Table 5. Performance of Individual Answer Base with Evaluation 1

Test Set	KB (KIU)	Record (RIU)	Descriptive (DIU)	General (AIU)	Total
# of Question	44	24	39	161	268
# of Retrieved	35	24	33	114	206
# of correct	30	23	30	94	175
Precision	0.86	0.96	0.91	0.82	0.85
Recall	0.68	0.96	0.77	0.57	0.65
F-score	0.76	0.96	0.83	0.67	0.74

As a result, 40% (107) questions should be covered by combined approach QA. Record QA shows the highest performance, whereas general QA (traditional QA) shows the lowest. KB QA has low recall since pre-defined properties for KIU are not sufficient to represent various themes in user questions.

5 Conclusion

We have proposed an enhanced QA model with combination of heterogeneous answer acquisition methods. We also presented the evaluation result of a system in which we had built four different answer bases: knowledge base (KIU), record information (RIU), descriptive answers (DIU), and traditional index DB (AIU). We developed learning-based method using CRF for knowledge base. For record and descriptive QA, we utilized pattern-based approaches. To handle general questions, we developed statistical indexing method as same as traditional QA. We had shown that our combined models outperformed the traditional QA system with some experiments.

The result showed that MRR of proposal QA model is higher than traditional model by about 59%; moreover, the response time of combined QA is 2.3 times as faster as typical QA. From the overall comparison, we prove that our model which combined pre-acquired answers has enhanced with correct answer as well as fast response time. As the future work, we plan to expand restriction information and use sophisticated linguistic processing for improving recall. In pattern-based approach, our further works will concentrate on reducing human efforts for building patterns or templates. Finally, we will compare with other systems which participated in TREC by translating questions of TREC in Korean.

References

1. E. M. Voorhees. Overview of TREC 2003 QA Track. In Proceedings of TREC-12, 2003
2. Lee, C.-K. Wang, J.-H. et al., Extracting template for knowledge-based question-answering using conditional random fields, The proceedings of 28th ACM SIGIR Workshop on Mathematical/Formal Methods in IR , 2005.
3. Oh, H.-J., Lee, C.-H. et al., Enhanced Question Answering with combination of pre-acquired answers, Lecture Notes in Computer Science, Vol. 3689, Oct. 2005
4. J. Lafferty, A. McCallum, and F. Pereia, Conditional random fields: probabilistic models for segmenting and labeling sequence data, The proceedings of ICML, 2001
5. Kim, H. J. Lee, C. H., et al., A LF based Answer Indexing Method for Encyclopedia Question-Answering System, Lecture Notes in Computer Science, Vol. 3689, Oct. 2005
6. S. E. Roberson, S. Walker, Some simple effective approximations to the 2-poisson model for probabilistic weighted retrieval, The proceedings of 17th ACM SIGIR, 1994. 345-354

Face Recognition Using DCT and Hierarchical RBF Model

Yuehui Chen and Yaou Zhao

School of Information Science and Engineering
Jinan University, Jinan 250022, P.R. China
yhchen@ujn.edu.cn

Abstract. This paper proposes a new face recognition approach by using the Discrete Cosine Transform (DCT) and Hierarchical Radial Basis Function Network (HRBF) classification model. The DCT is employed to extract the input features to build a face recognition system, and the HRBF is used to identify the faces. Based on the pre-defined instruction/operator sets, a HRBF model can be created and evolved. This framework allows input features selection. The HRBF structure is developed using Extended Compact Genetic Programming (ECGP) and the parameters are optimized by Differential Evolution (DE). Empirical results indicate that the proposed framework is efficient for face recognition.

1 Introduction

Face recognition has become a very active research area in recent years mainly due to increasing security demands and its potential commercial and law enforcement applications. Face recognition approaches on still images can be broadly grouped into geometric and template matching techniques. In the first case, geometric characteristics of faces to be matched, such as distances between different facial features, are compared. This technique provides limited results although it has been used extensively in the past. In the second case, face images represented as a two dimensional array of pixel intensity values are compared with a single or several templates representing the whole face. More successful template matching approaches use Principal Components Analysis (PCA) or Linear Discriminant Analysis (LDA) to perform dimensionality reduction achieving good performance at a reasonable computational complexity/time. Other template matching methods use neural network classification and deformable templates, such as Elastic Graph Matching (EGM). Recently, a set of approaches that use different techniques to correct perspective distortion are being proposed. These techniques are sometimes referred to as view-tolerant. For a complete review on the topic of face recognition the reader is referred to [1] and [2].

Neural networks have been widely applied in pattern recognition for the reason that neural-networks-based classifiers can incorporate both statistical and structural information and achieve better performance than the simple minimum distance classifiers [2]. Multilayered networks(MLNs), usually employing the backpropagation (BP) algorithm, are widely used in face recognition [3]. Recently, RBF neural networks have been applied in many engineering and scientific applications including face recognition [7]. HRBF networks consist of multiple RBF networks assembled in different level or cascade architecture in which a problem was divided and solved in more than one step. Mat Isa et al. used Hierarchical Radial Basis Function (HiRBF) to increase RBF performance in diagnosing cervical cancer [4]. Hierarchical RBF network has been proved effective in the reconstruction of smooth surfaces from sparse noisy data points [5]. In order to improve the model generalization performance, a selective combination of multiple neural networks by using Bayesian method was proposed in [6].

In this paper, an automatic method for constructing HRBF networks is proposed. Based on a pre-defined instruction/operator set, the HRBF network can be created and evolved. The HRBF network allows input variables selection. In our previous studies, in order to optimize the Flexible Neural Tree (FNT) and the hierarchical TS fuzzy model (H-TS-FS), the hierarchical structure of FNT and H-TS-FS was evolved using Probabilistic Incremental Program Evolution algorithm (PIPE) [11][12] and Ant Programming with specific instructions. In this research, the hierarchical structure is evolved using the Extended Compact Genetic Programming (ECGP). The fine tuning of the parameters encoded in the structure is accomplished using the DE algorithm. The novelty of this paper is in the usage of HRBF model for selecting the important features and for face recognition.

2 Discrete Cosine Transform

Like other transforms, the Discrete Cosine Transform (DCT) attempts to decorrelate the image data [8]. After decorrelation each transform coefficient can be encoded independently without losing compression efficiency. This section describes the DCT and some of its important properties.

The 2-D DCT is a direct extension of the 1-D case and is given by

$$C(u,v) = \alpha(u)\alpha(v) \sum_{x=0}^{N-1} \sum_{y=0}^{N-1} f(x,y) \cos\frac{\pi(2x+1)u}{2N} \cos\frac{\pi(2y+1)}{2N} \quad (1)$$

for $u, v = 0, 1, 2, \ldots, N-1$ and $\alpha(u)$ and $\alpha(v)$ are defined as follows, $\alpha(u) = \sqrt{1/N}$ for $u = 0$, and $\alpha(u) = \sqrt{2/N}$ for $u \neq 0$. The inverse transform is defined as

$$f(x,y) = \sum_{u=0}^{N-1} \sum_{v=0}^{N-1} \alpha(u)\alpha(v) C(u,v) \cos\frac{\pi(2x+1)u}{2N} \cos\frac{\pi(2y+1)}{2N} \quad (2)$$

for $x, y = 0, 1, 2, \ldots, N-1$.

The DCT possess some fine properties, i.e., de-correlation, energy compaction, separability, symmetry and orthogonality. These attributes of the DCT have led to its widespread deployment in virtually every image/video processing standard of the last decade [8].

For an $N \times N$ image, an DCT coefficient matrix covering all the spatial frequency components of the image. The DCT coefficients with large magnitude are mainly located in the upper-left corner of the DCT matrix. Accordingly, we scan the DCT coefficient matrix in a zig-zag manner starting from the upper-left corner and subsequently convert it to a one-dimensional (1-D) vector. As a holistic feature extraction method, the DCT converts high-dimensional face images into low-dimensional spaces in which more significant facial features such as outline of hair and face, position of eyes, nose and mouth are maintained. These facial features are more stable than the variable high-frequency facial features. As a matter of fact, the human visual system is more sensitive to variations in the low-frequency band.

In this paper, we investigate the illumination invariant property of the DCT by discarding its several low-frequency coefficients. It is well-known that the first DCT coefficient represents the dc component of an image which is solely related to the brightness of the image. Therefore, it becomes DC free (i.e., zero mean) and invariant against uniform brightness change by simply removing the first DCT coefficient.

3 The RBF Network

An RBF network is a feed-forward neural network with one hidden layer of RBF units and a linear output layer. By an RBF unit we mean a neuron with multiple real inputs $\boldsymbol{x} = (x_1, \ldots, x_n)$ and one output y computed as:

$$y = \varphi(\xi); \quad \xi = \frac{\|\boldsymbol{x} - \boldsymbol{c}\|_C}{b} \tag{3}$$

where $\varphi : R \to R$ is a suitable activation function, let us consider Gaussian radial basis function $\varphi(z) = e^{-z^2}$. The center $\boldsymbol{c} \in R^n$, the width $b \in R$ and an $n \times n$ real matrix $\boldsymbol{C}$ are a unit's parameters, $\|\cdot\|_C$ denotes a weighted norm defined as $\|\boldsymbol{x}\|_C^2 = (\boldsymbol{C}\boldsymbol{x})^T(\boldsymbol{C}\boldsymbol{x}) = \boldsymbol{x}^T \boldsymbol{C}^T \boldsymbol{C} \boldsymbol{x}$.

Thus, the network represents the following real function $\boldsymbol{f} : R^n \to R^m$:

$$f_s(\boldsymbol{x}) = \sum_{j=1}^{h} w_{js} e^{-\left(\frac{\|\boldsymbol{x} - \boldsymbol{c}\|_C}{b}\right)^2}, \quad s = 1, \ldots, m, \tag{4}$$

where $w_{js} \in R$ are weights of s-th output unit and f_s is the s-th network output.

The goal of an RBF network learning is to find suitable values of RBF units' parameters and the output layer's weights, so that the RBF network function approximates a function given by a set of examples of inputs and desired outputs $T = \{\boldsymbol{x}(t), \boldsymbol{d}(t); t = 1, \ldots, k\}$, called a *training set*. The quality of the learned RBF network is measured by the *error function*:

$$E = \frac{1}{2} \sum_{t=1}^{k} \sum_{j=1}^{m} e_j^2(t), \quad e_j(t) = d_j(t) - f_j(t). \tag{5}$$

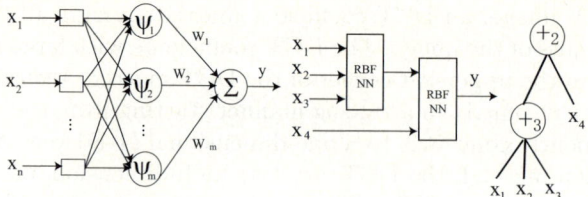

Fig. 1. A RBF neural network (left), an example of hierarchical RBF network (middle), and a tree-structural representation of the HRBF network (right)

4 The Hierarchical RBF Network

4.1 Encode and Calculation

A function set F and terminal instruction set T used for generating a HRBF network model are described as $S = F \bigcup T = \{+_2, +_3, \ldots, +_N\} \bigcup \{x_1, \ldots, x_n\}$, where $+_i (i = 2, 3, \ldots, N)$ denote non-leaf nodes' instructions and taking i arguments. $x_1, x_2, \ldots, x_n$ are leaf nodes' instructions and taking no arguments. The output of a non-leaf node is calculated as a HRBF network model (see Fig.1). In this research, Gaussian radial basis function is used and the number of radial basis functions used in hidden layer of the network is same with the number of inputs, that is, $m = n$.

In the creation process of HRBF network tree, if a nonterminal instruction, i.e., $+_i (i = 2, 3, 4, \ldots, N)$ is selected, i real values are randomly generated and used for representing the connection strength between the node $+_i$ and its children. In addition, $2 \times n^2$ adjustable parameters a_i and b_i are randomly created as radial basis function parameters. The output of the node $+_i$ can be calculated by using Eqn.(1) and Eqn.(2). The overall output of HRBF network tree can be computed from left to right by depth-first method, recursively.

4.2 Tree Structure Optimization by ECGP

Finding an optimal or near-optimal HRBF is formulated as a product of evolution. In this paper, the ECGP [13] is employed to find an optimal or near-optimal HRBF structure. ECGP is a direct extension of ECGA to the tree representation which is based on the PIPE prototype tree. In ECGA, Marginal Product Models (MPMs) are used to model the interaction among genes, represented as random variables, given a population of Genetic Algorithm individuals. MPMs are represented as measures of marginal distributions on partitions of random variables. ECGP is based on the PIPE prototype tree, and thus each node in the prototype tree is a random variable. ECGP decomposes or partitions the prototype tree into sub-trees, and the MPM factorises the joint probability of all nodes of the prototype tree, to a product of marginal distributions on a partition of its sub-trees. A greedy search heuristic is used to find an optimal MPM mode under the framework of minimum encoding inference. ECGP can represent the probability distribution for more than one node at a time. Thus, it extends PIPE in that the interactions among multiple nodes are considered.

4.3 Parameter Optimization with DE Algorithm

The DE algorithm was first introduced by Storn and Price in 1995 [9]. It resembles the structure of an evolutionary algorithm (EA), but differs from traditional EAs in its generation of new candidate solutions and by its use of a 'greedy' selection scheme. DE works as follows: First, all individuals are randomly initialized and evaluated using the fitness function provided. Afterwards, the following process will be executed as long as the termination condition is not fulfilled: For each individual in the population, an offspring is created using the weighted difference of parent solutions. The offspring replaces the parent if it is fitter. Otherwise, the parent survives and is passed on to the next iteration of the algorithm. In generation k, we denote the population members by $x_1^k, x_2^k, \ldots, x_N^k$. The DE algorithm is given as follows [10]:

S1 Set $k = 0$, and randomly generate N points $x_1^0, x_2^0, \ldots, x_N^0$ from search space to form an initial population;
S2 For each point $x_i^k (1 \leq i \leq N)$, execute the DE offspring generation scheme to generate an offspring $x_i^{(k+1)}$;
S3 If the given stop criteria is not met, set $k = k + 1$, goto step S2.

The DE Offspring Generation approach used is given as follows,

S1 Choose one point x_d randomly such that $f(x_d)$ $f(x_i^k)$, another two points x_b, x_c randomly from the current population and a subset $S = \{j_1, \ldots, j_m\}$ of the index set $\{1, \ldots, n\}$, while $m < n$ and all j_i mutually different;
S2 Generate a trial point $u = (u_1, u_2, \ldots, u_n)$ as follows:
DE Mutation. Generate a temporary point z as follows,

$$z = (F + 0.5)x_d + (F - 0.5)x_i + F(x_b - x_c); \quad (6)$$

Where F is a give control parameter;
DE Crossover. for $j \in S$, u_j is chosen to be z_j; otherwise u_j is chosen a to be $(x_i^k)_j$;
S3 If $f(u) \leq f(x_i^k)$, set $x_i^{k+1} = u$; otherwise, set $x_i^{k+1} = x_i^k$.

4.4 Procedure of the General Learning Algorithm

The general learning procedure for constructing the HRBF network can be described as follows.

S1 Create an initial population randomly (HRBF network trees and its corresponding parameters);
S2 Structure optimization is achieved by using ECGP algorithm;
S3 If a better structure is found, then go to step S4, otherwise go to step S2;
S4 Parameter optimization is achieved by DE algorithm. In this stage, the architecture of HRBF network model is fixed, and it is the best tree developed during the end of run of the structure search;

S5 If the maximum number of local search is reached, or no better parameter vector is found for a significantly long time then go to step S6; otherwise go to step S4;

S6 If satisfactory solution is found, then the algorithm is stopped; otherwise go to step S2.

5 Face Recognition Using HRBF Paradigm

We performed extensive experiments on two benchmark face datasets, namely the ORL and the Yale face database. In all the experiments, the background is cut out, and the images are resized to 92 × 112. No other preprocessing is done. Besides our method, the PCA based method, LDA-based method, neural networks etc. were also tested for comparisons.

5.1 The Face Database

For ORL face dateset, 40 persons with variations in facial expression and . All images were taken under a dark background, and the subjects were in an upright frontal position, with tilting and rotation tolerance up to 20 degree, and tolerance of up to about 10%. Fig. 2(left) shows 12 images of one subject from the selected dataset. The Yale face database contains 165 images of 15 subjects. There are 11 images per subject with different facial expressions or lightings. Fig. 2(right) shows the 11 images of one subject. For each experiment, 5 images are generated randomly to form the training data set and the remaining were chosen as test data set. This process was repeated to 20 times for each experiment.

5.2 Experiments on ORL and Yale Face Database

For this simulation, the DCT is employed to training and testing data sets, respectively. The extracted 60 input features are used for constructing a HRBF model. A HRBF classifier was constructed using the training data and then the classifier was used on the test data set to classify the data as an face ID or not. The instruction sets used to create an optimal HRBF classifier is

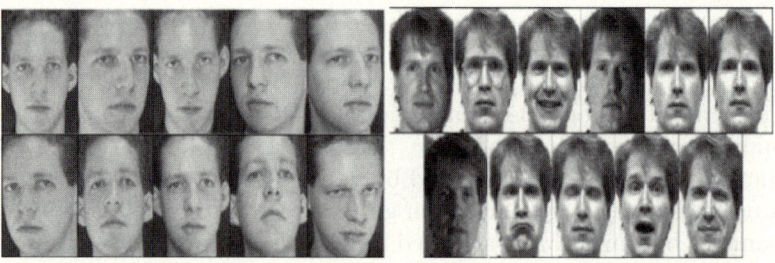

Fig. 2. Example in ORL face dataset (left), and example in YALE data set (right)

Table 1. Comparison of different approaches for ORL face recognition (test)

Method	Recognition rate
PCA+RBF [14]	94.5%
LDA+RBF [14]	94.0%
FS+RBF [14]	92.0%
NN [15]	94.64%
PCA [15]	88.31%
LDA [15]	88.87%
DCT+HRBF (this paper)	97.68%

Table 2. Comparison of different approaches for Yale face recognition (test)

Method	Recognition rate
NN [14]	83.51%
PCA [14]	81.13%
LDA [14]	98.69%
DCT+HRBF (this paper)	98.95%

$S = \{+_2, +_3, \ldots, +_6, x_0, x_1, \ldots, x_{59}\}$. Where $x_i (i = 0, 1, \ldots, 59)$ denotes the 60 features extracted by DCT.

A comparison of different feature extraction methods and different face classification methods for ORL face dataset (average recognition rate for 20 independent runs) is shown in Table 1. Table 2 depicts the face recognition performance of the HRBF by using the 60 features for Yale data set. The HRBF method helps to reduce the features from 60 to 6-15. For each experiment, the true positive rate (fp), false positive rate (fp) were also computed. For save space, they're not shown here.

6 Conclusions

In this paper DCT based feature extraction method and HRBF classification model are proposed for face recognition. The ORL and Yale database images are used for conducting all the experiments. Facial features are first extracted by the DCT which greatly reduces dimensionality of the original face image as well as maintains the main facial features. Compared with the well-known PCA approach, the DCT has the advantages of data independency and fast computational speed. The presented HRBF model for face recognition with a focus on improving the face recognition performance by reducing the input features. Simulation results on ORL and Yale face database also show that the proposed method achieves high training and recognition speed, as well as high recognition rate. More importantly, it is insensitive to illumination variations.

Acknowledgment

This research was partially supported the Natural Science Foundation of China under contract number 60573065, and The Provincial Science and Technology Development Program of Shandong under contract number SDSP2004-0720-03.

References

1. Zhao, W., Chellappa R., Rosenfeld A. and Phillips P.J.: Face Recognition: A literature survey. Technical Report CART-TR-948. University of Maryland, Aug. 2002.
2. Chellappa R., Wilson, C.L., and Sirohey, S.: Human and machine recognition of faces: A survey, Proc. IEEE, 83(5): 705C740, 1995.
3. Valentin D., Abdi H., Toole, A. J. O., and Cottrell, G. W.: Connectionist models of face processing: A survey, Pattern Recognit., 27: 1209C1230, 1994.
4. N. A. Mat Isa, Mashor, M. Y., and Othman, N. H., "Diagnosis of Cervical Cancer using Hierarchical Radial Basis Function (HiRBF) Network," In Sazali Yaacob, R. Nagarajan, Ali Chekima (Eds.), Proceedings of the International Conference on Artificial Intelligence in Engineering and Technology, pp. 458-463, 2002.
5. S. Ferrari, I. Frosio, V. Piuri, and N. Alberto Borghese, "Automatic Multiscale Meshing Through HRBF Networks," IEEE Trans. on Instrumentation and Measurment, vol.54, no.4, pp. 1463-1470, 2005.
6. Z. Ahmad, J. Zhang, "Bayesian selective combination of multiple neural networks for improving long-range predictions in nonlinear process modelling," Neural Comput & Applic. Vol. 14. pp. 78C87, 2005.
7. Yang F. and Paindavoine M.: Implementation of an RBF neural network on embedded systems: Real-time face tracking and identity verification, IEEE Trans. Neural Netw., 14(5): 1162C1175, 2003.
8. Sorwar G., Abraham A. and Dooley L., Texture Classification Based on DCT and Soft Computing, The 10th IEEE International Conference on Fuzzy Systems, FUZZ-IEEE'01, IEEE Press, Volume 2, pp. 545 -548, 2001.
9. R. Storn, and K. Price, "Differential evolution - a simple and efficient adaptive scheme for global optimization over continuous spaces," Technical report, International Computer Science Institute, Berkley, 1995.
10. K. Price, "Differential Evolution vs. the Functions of the 2nd ICEO," In proceedings of 1997 IEEE International Conference on Evolutionary Computation (ICEC'97), Indianapolis, USA, pp. 153-157, 1997.
11. Chen, Y., Yang, B. and Dong, J.: Nonlinear System Modeling via Optimal Design of Neural Trees. International Journal of Neural Systems. 14 (2004) 125-137
12. Chen, Y., Yang, B., Dong, J. and Abraham, A.: Time-series Forecasting using Flexible Neural Tree Model. Information Science. 174 (2005) 219-235
13. Sastry, K. and Goldberg, D. E.: Probabilistic model building and competent genetic programming. In: R. L. Riolo and B. Worzel, editors, Genetic Programming Theory and Practise. (2003) 205-220
14. Su, H., Feng D., Zhao R.-C.: Face Recognition Using Multi-feature and Radial Basis Function Network, Proc. of the Pan-Sydney Area Workshop on Visual Information Processing (VIP2002), Sydney, Australia, 183-189, 2002.
15. Huang, R. and Pavlovic, V. and Metaxas, D.N: A hybrid face recognition method using markov random fields, ICPR04, pp. 157-160, 2004.

Chaotic Dynamics for Avoiding Congestion in the Computer Network

Takayuki Kimura and Tohru Ikeguchi

Graduate school of Science and Engineering, Saitama University,
255 Shimo-Ohkubo Saitama 338–8570, Japan
kimura@nls.ics.saitama-u.ac.jp

Abstract. We proposed a new algorithm for packet routing problems using chaotic neurodynamics and analyze its statistical behavior. First, we construct a basic neural network which works in the same way as the Dijkstra algorithm that uses information of shortest path lengths from a node to another node in a computer network. When the computer network has a regular topology, the basic routing method works well. However, when the computer network has an irregular topology, it fails to work, because most of packets cannot be transmitted to their destinations due to packet congestion in the computer network. To avoid such an undesirable problem, we extended the basic neural network to employ chaotic neurodynamics. We confirm that our proposed method exhibits good performance for complex networks, such as scale-free networks.

1 Introduction

In the social system, the Internet is a great tool to obtain a wide variety of information instantaneously. In a computer network such as the Internet, huge amounts of packets of various types are exchanged. Even if the frequency band width becomes wider, we cannot avoid nuisance situation: some of packets are often delayed or lost. To avoid such undesirable situation, it is very important to consider packet routing problem, or optimize packet routing in the computer network.

A computer network comprises nodes and links. A packet is transmitted from one node to another through the links. A packet can be transmitted from the nodes and multiple packets can be received simultaneously. Every node stores some amounts of packets in a buffer and all packets are transmitted according to First-In-First-Out basis. Then, when a buffer of the node is full, the packet transmitted to the node will be removed. In addition, the packet flow is regulated by an upper limit. Thus, every packet is also removed if it exceeds this limit. When a packet is removed, the packet is retransmitted from its source until it will be transmitted to the destination of the packet.

Packet routing strategies are generally classified into two types controls–centralized control and decentralized control. Centralized control is a technique with which a centralized unit controls all packet routing in the network. This control exhibits good performance in relatively small-scale networks. However, once the network size increases, the centralized control fails to work because the computational load on the central unit also increases. Then, the centralized control does not work well in large-scale network. Therefore, under practical situation, it is almost impossible to control the transmission of all packets to their destinations using centralized control.

On the other hand, decentralized control is more applicable for large-scale networks because packets are transmitted to their destinations autonomously and adaptively. However, if we adopt the decentralized control, we have to design our algorithm for transmitting packets at each node. In an ideal computer network, every node has an infinite buffer size and throughputs. In such a network, the Dijkstra algorithm[1], one of the basic strategies to find a shortest path between two node in the network, may work well[1]. However, under a real situation, the buffer sizes are finite and the throughputs at each node are different, which eventually leads to congest the route to transmit packets. Then it is inevitable to consider how to avoid such congested routes. It means that an ideal packet routing problem is easy to be solved, but real packet routing problems probably become very difficult and possibly may be a hard problem such as $\mathcal{NP}$ hard problems.

As for solving $\mathcal{NP}$ hard class combinatorial optimization problems, for example, the traveling salesman problems (TSP) or the quadratic assignment problems(QAP), it is well-known that a method which combines a heuristic algorithm and chaotic neurodynamics is very effective[2,3,4,5]. The main idea in these methods[2,3,4,5] is an extension of tabu search strategy[6,7], which avoids to search a solution that has already been searched for a while. Because the tabu search strategy is modified to involve chaotic neurodynamics[2,3,4,5], the method exhibits better performance not only for bench mark problems of TSP[8] or QAP[9], but also for real life problems such as bipartitioning problems[10], motif extraction problems from DNA sequences[11], time tabling problems[12], and vehicle routing problems with soft time windows[13].

In this paper, we proposed a new packet routing method to introduce such techniques[2,3,4,5,10,11,12,13]. To simulate real computer networks, we applied the proposed algorithm to two different packet generating properties. In the first one, packet generation is stationary, which means that the packet generation probability in the network is fixed to a constant value. In the second one, the packet generation is nonstationary, which means that the packet generating probability depends on the time.

Using the two packet generating properties, we conducted computer simulation. As a result, our proposed method is very effective for two packet generation properties in comparison with the Dijkstra algorithm and a packet routing method using a tabu search[6,7].

2 A Packet Routing Method Using Chaotic Neurodynamics

To realize chaotic neurodynamics, we used a chaotic neural network[14] as a basic part. In this paper, a computer network model has N nodes. In the computer network, the i-th node has N_i adjacent nodes ($i = 1, \ldots, N$). In this framework, each node has its own neural network, and N_i adjacent neurons are assigned to each node. The ij-th neuron corresponds to the connection between the i-th node and its j-th adjacent node. We first compose a basic neural network that operates to minimize a distance of transmitting packets from the i-th node to the destinations. To realize this method, we consider the following internal state of the ij-th neuron:

$$\xi_{ij}(t+1) = \beta \left(1 - \frac{d_{ij} + d_{jo}}{d_c}\right), \qquad (1)$$

where d_{ij} is the distance between the i-th node to the j-th adjacent node; d_{jo} is the distance from the j-th adjacent node to the destination of the i-th node; d_c is a control parameter which expresses the size of the computer network; β is a normalization parameter. If $\xi_{ij}(t+1)$ is the largest value in the neurons of the i-th node, the ij-th neuron fires, which means that the j-th adjacent node is selected to transmit a packet from the i-th node. The decent down-hill dynamics of Eq.(1) corresponds to the basic Dijkstra algorithm[1] and works well for the ideal case.

However, under real situation we have to consider both network topologies and packet congestion at each node. If the network topology is not regular, the number of links of each node is biased. In addition, the number of routes through which the packets are transmitted to the destinations also increases. When we conduct a packet routing for an irregular network, if we only consider to minimize the shortest distance, many packets might be transmitted to the nodes which are connecting many adjacent nodes. This behavior leads to delay or lost packets. To avoid such an undesirable situation, we use a refractory effect of a chaotic neuron model[14] described as follows:

$$\begin{aligned}\zeta_{ij}(t+1) &= -\alpha \sum_{d=0}^{t} k_r^d x_{ij}(t-d) + \theta, \\ &= k_r \zeta_{ij} - \alpha x_{ij}(t) + \theta(1 - k_r),\end{aligned} \qquad (2)$$

where α is a control parameter of the refractory effect; k_r is a decay parameter of the refractory effect; $x_{ij}(t)$ is the output of the ij-th neuron at time t; θ is a threshold.

The refractory effect plays an essential role for decentralizing the packets in the adjacent nodes. Because the refractory effect is related to the information of a past routing history, we expect that the packets are transmitted to their destination by avoiding the nodes to which packets have just been transmitted to and in which many packets possibly have already been stored.

In addition, we control firing rates of neurons by mutual connection, because too frequent firing often leads to a fatal situation of the packet routing. The mutual connection is defined as follows:

$$\eta_{ij}(t+1) = W - W \sum_{j=1}^{N_i} x_{ij}(t), \qquad (3)$$

where W is a positive parameter and N_i is the number of adjacent nodes at i-th node.

Then, the output of the ij-th neuron is defined as follows:

$$x_{ij}(t+1) = f\{\xi_{ij}(t+1) + \zeta_{ij}(t+1) + \eta_{ij}(t+1)\}, \tag{4}$$

where $f(y) = 1/(1+e^{-y/\epsilon})$. In this algorithm, if $x_{ij}(t+1) > 0.5$, the ij-th neuron fires; the packet at the i-th node is transmitted to the j-th node. If the outputs of multiple neurons exceed 0.5, we defined that the neuron which has the largest output only fires.

3 Evaluation of the Proposed Method in Complex Networks

We compared the proposed method with two packet routing methods. The first one is a neural network which decides to transmit packets only by Eq.(1). The neural network routes packets only with the gain effect of Eq.(1); it has a descent down hill dynamics of Eq.(1)(the DD method). In other words, the DD method has the same dynamics as the Dijkstra algorithm which only considers shortest distances.

The second one routes packets using a tabu search strategy(The TS method). To realize the TS method, Eq.(2) in the proposed method is replaced by the following equation:

$$\gamma_{ij}(t+1) = -\alpha \sum_{d=0}^{s_i-1} x_{ij}(t-d), \tag{5}$$

where $\alpha \to \infty$, s_i is a tabu tenure of the i-th node, and $x_{ij}(t)$ is an output of the ij-th neuron that takes 0(resting) or 1(firing). In the TS method, each neuron has the gain effect(Eq.(1)) and the tabu effect(Eq.(5)). The ij-th neuron fires if the value of $\xi_{ij}(t+1) + \gamma_{ij}(t+1)$ is the largest.

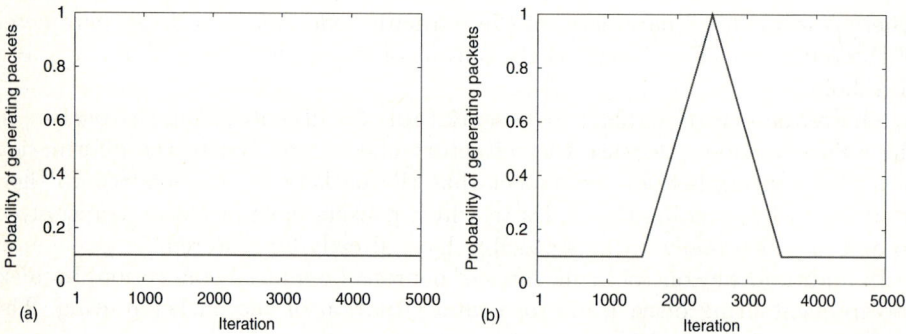

Fig. 1. Temporal changes of packet generation probabilities p_g. (a) p_g is fixed to 0.1 and (b) p_g has a peak.

We conducted computer simulations of the packet routing by the following procedures. First, we assigned random values from one to five, which correspond to throughputs at all nodes. In addition, each node calculates the shortest distance from the node to other nodes. In other words, each node has a routing table which contains information of shortest distances. Then, packets are generated at each node using packet generating probability p_g at each iteration. In this paper, we introduced two different packet generating properties. The first one is a stationary type: the amounts of packets flowing in the network are stationary for all iteration. The second one is a nonstationary: the amounts of packets flowing in the network drastically change. Thus, we realized these two different properties by using two different packet generating probability p_g. They are shown in Fig.1 Moreover, each packet has a destination and the destinations are assigned randomly using uniformly distributed random numbers. Then, the selection of an adjacent node and the transmission of the packet are simultaneously conducted at every node. The packets transmitted from a node is stored at the tail of the buffer of the adjacent node. We set the buffer size of the i-th node to $1,000$ times of the number of adjacent nodes of the i-th node. We also set the upper limit of the packet movement to 64. A packet is removed when the buffer is full and the packet exceeds the limit. The packet is retransmitted from a source to its destination until it will be certainly delivered to the destination.

We repeated the packet transmission for $5,000$ iterations. We set the parameters of Eqs.(1)–(3) as follows: $\beta = 1.5$, $\alpha = 0.045$, $k_r = 0.98$, $\epsilon = 0.05$ $W = 0.05$ and $\theta = 0.5$. We also set d_c as the longest path length in the network. We set $\alpha = 500$ in Eq.(5) and s_i in Eq.(5) to one third of the number of adjacent nodes of the i-th node.

To evaluate performance of the proposed method, we introduced the following measures:

N_a : the number of packets arriving at their destinations,
N_{dp}: the number of lost packets without arriving at their destinations.

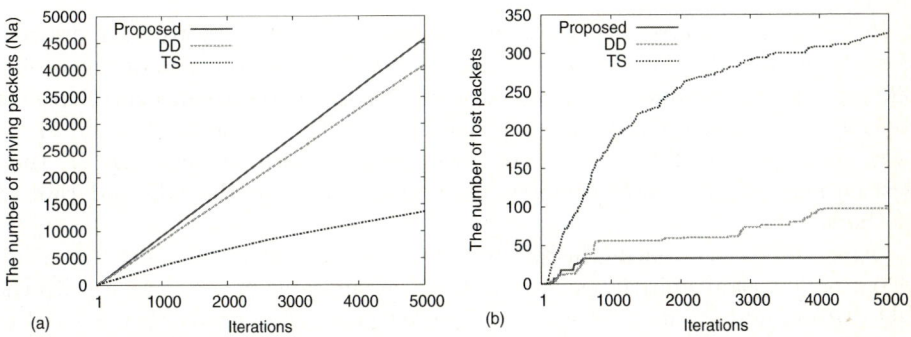

Fig. 2. Relationships between the iterations and (a) the number of packets arriving at their destinations (N_a), and (b) the number of lost packets without arriving at their destinations (N_{lp}) when the packet generating probability p_g is fixed to 0.1(Fig.1(a))

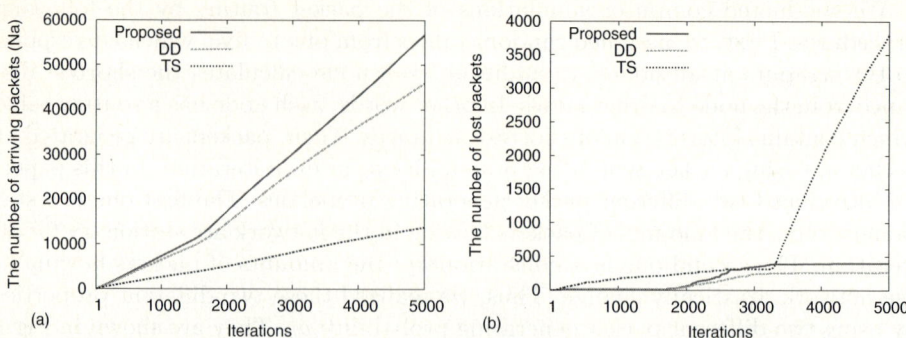

Fig. 3. Relationships between the iterations and (a) the number of packets arriving at their destinations (N_a), and (b) the number of lost packets without arriving at their destinations (N_{lp}) when the packet generation probability p_g has a peak(Fig.1(b))

We conducted computer simulations on the scale-free networks. It is widely acknowledged that the structure of the Internet has scale-free property. The scale-free networks are generated in the same way as Barábasi and Albert[15]. This network is constructed by the following procedure: First, we made a complete graph of four nodes, then we put a new node with three links to the graph at every time step with the probability $\Pi(k_i) = \dfrac{k_i}{\sum_{j=1}^{n} k_j}$, where k_i is the degree of the i-th node ($i = 1, \ldots, n$); n is the number of nodes at a current iteration. In this simulation, the scale-free networks comprise 100 nodes.

Results for the scale-free networks are shown in Figs.2 and 3. In Fig.2(a), the proposed method transmits many packets to their destinations in comparison with the DD and the TS methods when the packet generating probability is fixed to 0.1. In addition, in Fig.2(b), the proposed method reduces the number of lost packets without arriving at their destinations (N_{lp}) in comparison with the DD and the TS methods.

In Fig.3(a), the proposed method transmits more packets to their destinations than the DD and the TS methods even if the packet generating probability p_g is nonstationary(Fig.3). As a result, our method can control packet routing even under the situation that packet generation is nonstationary. Moreover, in Fig.3(b), the number of lost packets without arriving at their destinations (N_{lp}) in the proposed method is less than the DD and the TS methods.

Using the packet routing history, our proposed method can select better adjacent node to transmit the packets to their destinations in comparison with the DD method and TS method when the packet generation probability is fixed to a small value. Furthermore, when the packet generation probability has a peak, the amount of the packets flowing in the computer network changes drastically during a simulation, our method can transmit more packets to their destinations than the DD method and TS method.

4 Conclusion

In this paper, we proposed a new algorithm for routing packets using chaotic neurodynamics. By introducing a refractory effect, which is an essential characteristic of real neurons, the proposed method shows the highest performance for the scale-free networks in comparison with the descent down hill dynamics and the tabu search method when the amounts of packets flowing in the computer network are stationary or nonstationary. As a result, our method can control packet routing even under the situation that packet generation is nonstationary.

It has been shown that a meta-heuristic algorithm by the chaotic neural network[14] is effective for solving traveling salesman problems (TSP) and quadratic assignment problems (QAP)[4,5]. Although we used almost the same strategy to employ chaotic neurodynamics as in Refs.[2,3,4,5], the results obtained in this paper indicate important point, because the packet routing problem has a different property from TSP and QAP. Usually, TSP and QAP are static because the state of the problem (the number of cities in TSP, the dimension of matrices in QAP) is fixed. However, the computer network always changes its state because of the flowing of the packets. Namely, the packet routing problem is a dynamical optimization problem. In particular, we showed that our method can adapt the packet routing for nonstationary situation. Therefore, the results shown in this paper is good evidence that the chaotic neurodynamics could also be effective for solving the nonstationary optimization problems whose constraints are always changed.

Many methods of packet routing which decentralize packets in the computer network have also been proposed. In this paper, we do not compare the performance of the proposed method with such routing methods. Thus, it is an important future task to compare the performance of the proposed routing method with such routing methods.

We are grateful to H. Nakajima, Y. Horio, M. Adachi, M. Hasegawa, and H. Sekiya for their valuable comments and discussions. The research of TI is partially supported by Grant-in-Aid for Scientific Research (B) from JSPS (No.16300072).

References

1. D.Bertsekas and R.Gallager. *Data Networks*. Prenticehall, 1987.
2. M.Hasegawa, T.Ikeguchi, and K.Aihara. Exponential and chaotic neurodynamics tabu searches for quadratic assignment problems. *Control and Cybernetics*, 29:773–788, Sep. 2000.
3. M.Hasegawa, T.Ikeguchi, and K.Aihara. Combination of chaotic neurodynamics with the 2-opt algorithm to solve traveling salesman problems. *Physical Reveiw Letters*, 79:2344–2347, Sep. 1997.
4. M.Hasegawa, T.Ikeguchi, and K.Aihara. Solving large scale traveling salesman problems by chaotic neurodynamics. *Neural Networks*, 15:271–283, Mar. 2002.
5. M.Hasegawa, T.Ikeguchi, K.Aihara, and K.Itoh. A novel chaotic search for quadratic assignment problems. *European J. Oper. Res.*, 139:543–556, Jun. 2002.

6. F.Glover. Tabu search I. *ORSA Journal on Computing*, 1:190–206, 1989.
7. F.Glover. Tabu search II. *ORSA Journal on Computing*, 2:4–32, 1990.
8. TSPLIB. http://www.iwr.uni-heidelberg.de/groups/comopt/software/TSPLIB95/.
9. QAPLIB. http://www.seas.upenn.edu/qaplib/.
10. E.Mardhana and T.Ikeguchi. Neurosearch: A program library for neural network driven search meta-heuristics. *Proceedings of 2003 IEEE International Symposium on Circuits and Systems*, V:697–700, May 2003.
11. T.Matsuura, T.Ikeguchi, and Y.Horio. Tabu search and chaotic search for extracting motifs from DNA sequences. *Proceedings of the 6th Metaheuristics International Conference*, pages 677–682, Aug. 2005.
12. T.Ikeguchi. Combinatorial optimization with chaotic dynamics. *Proceedings of 2005 RISP International Workshop on Nonlinear Circuits and Signal Processing*, pages 263–266, Mar. 2005.
13. T.Hoshino, T.Kimura, and T.Ikeguchi. Solving vehicle routing problems with soft time window. *Tech. Rep of IEICE*, 105:17–22, 2006. in Japanese.
14. K.Aihara, T.Tanabe, and M.Toyoda. Chaotic neural network. *Physics Letters A*, 144:333–340, Mar. 1990.
15. A.-L.Barábsi and R.Albert. Emergence of scaling in random networks. *Science*, 286:509–512, Oct. 1999.

Combined Effects of Class Imbalance and Class Overlap on Instance-Based Classification

V. García[1,2], R. Alejo[1,2], J.S. Sánchez[1], J.M. Sotoca[1], and R.A. Mollineda[1]

[1] Dept. Llenguatges i Sistemes Informàtics, Universitat Jaume I
Av. Sos Baynat s/n, 12071 Castelló de la Plana, Spain
[2] Lab. Reconocimiento de Patrones, Instituto Tecnológico de Toluca
Av. Tecnologico s/n, 52140 Metepec, México

Abstract. In real-world applications, it has been often observed that class imbalance (significant differences in class prior probabilities) may produce an important deterioration of the classifier performance, in particular with patterns belonging to the less represented classes. This effect becomes especially significant on instance-based learning due to the use of some dissimilarity measure. We analyze the effects of class imbalance on the classifier performance and how the overlap has influence on such an effect, as well as on several techniques proposed in the literature to tackle the class imbalance. Besides, we study how these methods affect to the performance on both classes, not only on the minority class as usual.

1 Introduction

The common assumption that the naturally occurring class distribution (i.e., the relative frequency of examples of each class in the data set) is best for learning is now being questioned. This is because of the increasingly common need to limit the size of large data sets and because classifiers built from data sets with high class imbalance perform poorly on minority-class instances.

There is a considerable amount of research on how to build "good" learning algorithms when the class distribution of data in the training set is imbalanced. For simplicity, and consistently with the common practice [1,3,5,10], only two-class problems are here considered. A data set is said to be imbalanced when one of the classes (the minority one) is heavily under-represented in comparison to the other (the majority) class. This issue is particularly important in those applications where it is costly to misclassify minority-class examples. High imbalance occurs in real world domains where the decision system is aimed to detect a rare but important case, such as fraudulent telephone calls [6], diagnosis of an infrequent disease [18], or text categorization [15].

Most of the research addressing this problem can be classified into three categories. One consists of assigning distinct costs to the classification errors for positive and negative examples [4,7,13]. The second is to resample the original training set, either by over-sampling the minority class [3,11] and/or under-sampling the majority class [10] until the classes are approximately equally represented. The third focuses on internally biasing the discrimination-based process so as to compensate for the class imbalance [1,6,13]. Other techniques consist of combining several of these general methods [2,1,10].

Although it is often assumed that class imbalance is responsible for significant loss of classifier performance, recent investigations have directed their efforts to question whether class imbalance is directly correlated to the loss of performance or whether the class imbalance is not a problem by itself. For example, some authors have focused on the small disjuncts problem [8,9,16], whereas others on the problem of class overlap [12,14]. These works suggest that there exists a connection between such problems, stating that the loss of performance when learning from unbalanced data is potentiated by other factors.

The aim of the present paper is to analyze the relation between class imbalance and class overlap, and their effects on the classification performance. We are also interested in investigating how these factors affect to both classes, since most of the proposals deal with the patterns of the minority class only, thus overlooking the consequences over the majority class. This study is performed in the framework of the Nearest Neighbor (NN) algorithm, as one of the most significant representatives of the instance-based learning.

2 Algorithms to Handle the Class Imbalance

In the present section, the algorithms used for dealing with the class imbalance are briefly described. Specifically, we focus on three different strategies: downsizing the majority class, over-sampling the minority class and, internally biasing the discrimination-based process.

Within the category of handling the imbalance by means of under-sampling the majority class, the simplest technique randomly selects a number of negative patterns to be further removed from the training set. Nevertheless, since downsizing the majority class can result in throwing away some useful information, this must be done carefully. Accordingly, other schemes employ some filtering and/or condensing algorithms to pick out and eliminate a number of negative examples [1,10]. The method we adopt in this work consists of iteratively removing noisy and atypical patterns belonging to the majority class [1] by using the well-known Wilson's editing algorithm (WE) [17].

In the case of over-sampling the minority class, one of the most popular techniques refers to the SMOTE algorithm [3]. This consists of taking each positive pattern and introducing synthetic examples along the line segments joining any/all of the k minority class nearest neighbors. Depending upon the amount of over-sampling required, the neighbors from the k nearest neighbors are randomly chosen. Synthetic samples are generated by taking the difference between the sample under consideration and its nearest neighbor. This difference is multiplied by a random number between 0 and 1, and added to the corresponding feature vector.

On the other hand, for internally biasing the discrimination procedure, we make use of a weighted distance function to be applied in the classification of new patterns [1]. Let $d_E(\cdot)$ be the Euclidean metric, and let Y be a new sample to classify. Let x_i be a training example belonging to class i, let n_i be the number of examples from class i, let n be the training set size, and let d be the dimensionality of the feature space. Then, the weighted distance measure is defined as:

$$d_W(Y, x_i) = (n_i/n)^{1/d} d_E(Y, x_i) \qquad (1)$$

The idea is to compensate for the imbalance in the training set without actually altering the class distribution. Weights are assigned, unlike in the usual weighted k-NN rule, to the respective classes and not to the individual examples. In that way, since the weighting factor is greater for the majority class than for the minority one, the distance to positive examples is reduced much more than the distance to negative examples. This produces a tendency for the new patterns to find their neighbor among the positive examples.

2.1 Classifier Performance for Imbalanced Data Sets

The average predictive accuracy is the standard performance measure in Pattern Recognition and Machine Learning research. However, using this form evaluation metric assumes that the error costs (the cost of a false positive and false negative) are equal, which can be criticized as being unrealistic [6,10]. It has to be noted that highly unbalanced problems generally have highly non-uniform error costs that favor the minority class (often the class of primary interest). Therefore, classifiers that optimize average accuracy are of questionable value in these cases since they rarely will predict the minority class.

Table 1. Confusion matrix for a two-class problem

	Positive prediction	Negative prediction
Positive class	True Positive (TP)	False Negative (FN)
Negative class	False Positive (FP)	True Negative (TN)

Alternative methods for evaluating the classifier performance are ROC analysis and the geometric mean. For a two-class problem, these can be described using the confusion matrix as plotted in Table 1. In the present work, we are primarily interested in analyzing the classification performance on positive and negative classes independently. From the confusion matrix, these measures can be defined as $a^+ = TP/(TP + FN)$ and $a^- = TN/(TN + FP)$, respectively.

3 Experimental Results on Synthetic Data Sets

In this section, we run a number of experiments on several artificial data sets whose characteristics can be fully controlled, allowing to better interpret the results. Pseudo-random bivariate patterns have been generated following a uniform distribution in a square of length 100, centered at $(50, 50)$. There are 400 patterns from the majority class and 100 in the minority class. Six different situations of increasing overlap have been considered, always keeping the majority/minority ratio equal to 4. In all cases, positive examples are generated in the range [50..100], while those belonging to the majority class are as follows: in [0..50] for 0% of class overlapping, in [10..60] for 20%, in [20..70] for 40%, in [30..80] for 60%, in [40..90] for 80%, and in [50..100] for 100% of overlap. Fig. 1 illustrates two examples of these data sets.

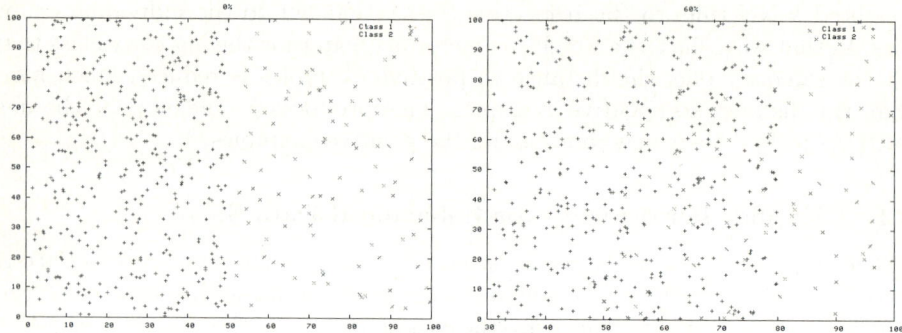

Fig. 1. Two different levels of class overlapping: 0% and 60%

For each data set (degree of overlap), we have studied the techniques described in Sect. 2. In the case of downsizing the majority class, the Wilson's editing algorithm has been applied with both the Euclidean metric (WE) and the weighted distance (WEW). Moreover, WE and WEW have been also applied to both classes (not only to the majority class). Wilson's editing has been always run with $k = 3$. On the other hand, the SMOTE algorithm (with $k = 5$) has been used to over-sampling the minority class. After preprocessing the training set, we have employed the NN rule with the Euclidean (NNe) and the weighted (NNw) distances to classify patterns from an independent test set.

Fig. 2 shows the classification performance on positive (a^+) and negative (a^-) patterns when using the NNe and NNw rules directly, that is, without preprocessing the training set. From this, it is worth remarking several issues. First, when there exists no overlapping (0%), we obtain the same performance on both classes. Second, although the majority/minority ratio keeps constant along the distinct situations, the accuracies degrade as overlap increases. Both of these results suggest that the class imbalance by itself does not strongly affect to the classifier performance. Finally, the use of the weighted distance in the NN rule allows to increase the performance on the minority class but at the same time, the accuracy on the majority class suffers from an important degradation. In fact, from 40% of overlap, it can be noted that the performance on the minority class becomes even better than that on the majority class.

Table 2 reports the performances on each class when preprocessing the training set by means of the techniques previously described and then using the NNe or the NNw classifiers. The values corresponding to the original training set

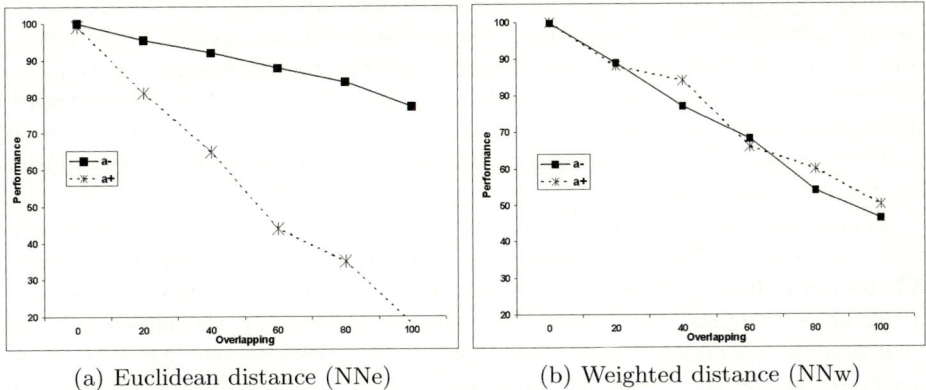

(a) Euclidean distance (NNe)   (b) Weighted distance (NNw)

Fig. 2. Performance evaluation on each class when using the NN rule – synthetic data

Table 2. Performance on each class with NNe and NNw (synthetic data sets)

	0%		20%		40%		60%		80%		100%	
	a^-	a^+	a^-	a^+	a^-	a^+	a^-	a^+	a^-	a^+	a^-	a^+
	NNe											
Original	100	99.0	95.5	81.0	92.0	65.0	87.8	44.0	84.0	35.0	77.3	18.0
WE	-	-	93.8	82.0	89.5	67.0	85.5	52.0	79.0	37.0	68.3	23.0
WE both classes	100	96.0	98.5	80.0	99.5	54.0	97.3	40.0	98.8	17.0	97.8	1.0
WEW	100	100	90.3	85.0	82.8	74.0	71.8	61.0	63.0	58.0	53.0	48.0
WEW both classes	100	99.0	93.0	83.0	91.3	69.0	83.0	53.0	74.3	42.0	69.3	34.0
SMOTE	100	99.0	94.3	86.0	84.8	75.0	78.8	58.0	69.8	47.0	62.3	34.0
	NNw											
Original	99.8	100	89.0	88.0	77.0	84.0	68.3	66.0	54.0	60.0	46.3	50.0
WE	-	-	88.6	87.0	76.8	85.0	68.5	65.0	53.8	60.0	46.5	54.0
WE both classes	100	99.0	94.3	82.0	96.0	63.0	89.5	49.0	83.0	29.0	61.5	32.0
WEW	99.3	100	85.3	92.0	70.3	88.0	60.5	78.0	48.3	72.0	37.8	59.0
WEW both classes	99.5	100	89.0	91.0	79.8	79.0	67.0	69.0	56.0	60.0	50.0	51.0

(without any preprocessing) are also included as a baseline. The first comment refers to the results over the data set with no overlap (0%), in which all methods obtain similar performance on both classes. As already pointed out, it seems that the class imbalance does not constitute an important difficulty for the learning system under such a "simple" situation. In contrast, as class overlap increases, the effect of the imbalance on the performance becomes clear enough.

When comparing the preprocessing methods, one can observe a different behavior depending on the use of the Euclidean distance (NNe) or the weighted distance (NNw) for the classification of new patterns. In the case of NNe, except the application of Wilson's editing (WE) to both classes, all algorithms improve the performance on the minority class (a^+), but at the cost of reducing the performance on the majority class (a^-). It has to be noted that WEW (editing only the majority class) and SMOTE allow the highest increase in performance on the minority class, independently of the degree of class overlap. Nevertheless, both of these techniques produce an important loss of performance on negative examples. On the other hand, editing both classes does not seem to be an appropriate alternative: it is able to "clean" the class overlap but, at the same time, it clearly increases the imbalance due to the removal of patterns from the majority and the minority classes.

Focusing on the results with NNw, the effect just described is still more evident. In this case, when there exists a very high overlapping, all schemes (except WE on both classes) invert the classifier behavior: the performance on the minority class becomes even better than the performance on the majority class. As a preliminary conclusion of these experiments, one can see that most techniques to handle the class imbalance are able to improve the performance on the positive examples, although producing some decrease in performance on the negative patterns.

4 Experimental Results on Real Data Sets

We here experimented with four real data sets taken from the UCI Machine Learning Database Repository (http://www.ics.uci.edu/~mlearn), to validate the results obtained over the synthetic databases. All data sets were transformed into two-class problems to facilitate comparison with other published results [1]. Five-fold cross validation was employed.

Table 3 reports, for each real data set, the performance on both classes when preprocessing the original training sets by means of different techniques and classifying with NNe and NNw. Analyzing the results with NNe over the original training sets (without preprocessing), one can observe that in the Phoneme

Table 3. Performance on each class with NNe and NNw (real data sets)

	Phoneme		Satimage		Glass		Vehicle	
	a^-	a^+	a^-	a^+	a^-	a^+	a^-	a^+
	NNe							
Original	79.1	68.8	91.7	54.8	98.9	76.0	82.8	37.6
WE	74.5	75.3	90.4	58.3	97.7	76.0	78.2	50.5
WE both classes	79.5	68.6	91.7	48.1	99.4	72.0	89.7	25.2
WEW	73.1	77.0	89.2	60.6	97.7	76.0	76.8	54.8
WEW both classes	77.0	73.1	90.1	54.6	99.4	72.0	87.0	31.4
SMOTE	76.0	71.2	86.2	69.1	98.3	80.0	80.5	44.3
	NNw							
Original	71.1	82.3	88.4	65.1	97.1	80.0	78.5	45.2
WE	68.1	84.2	87.5	66.2	96.6	80.0	75.0	56.2
WE both classes	74.1	79.3	89.4	54.1	98.3	76.0	85.7	31.0
WEW	66.9	84.8	86.7	67.5	95.6	80.0	73.8	60.0
WEW both classes	71.8	81.2	88.0	59.2	98.3	80.0	81.7	38.6

database both classes show similar and quite low performances, thus suggesting that there probably exists high overlap and low class imbalance (the majority/minority ratio is 2.41). Conversely, in the case of the Satimage database, the performance on the majority class is high enough and clearly better than the performance on the minority class, which indicates a very considerable class imbalance (the majority/minority ratio is 9.28).

It has to be remarked that in all data sets, the use of the weighted distance for classification (NNw) produces an important improvement in the performance on the minority class, and it does not lead to a significant loss of performance on the majority class. On the other hand, when the training set has been preprocessed, it seems that the best results are achieved with the editing schemes applied only to the negative examples, that is, WE and WEW. In fact, as already observed in the artificial data sets, the schemes based on downsizing both classes are not able to appropriately balance the data sets.

5 Conclusions and Future Work

The class imbalance by itself does not seem to constitute a crucial problem for instance-based classification. In fact, in the presence of imbalance with 0% of overlap, the NN classifier provides high performance on both classes. In contrast, the combination of class imbalance and class overlapping suppose an important deterioration of the performance. These results suggest that the imbalance in the overlap region has a strong influence on the classification performance.

The experiments carried out suggest that the application of some undersampling technique to both classes leads to poor performance on the minority class. Conversely, the use of editing combined with NNw classification makes the performance on the majority class to become worse than that on the minority class. This is mainly due to the fact that in the overlap region, after editing the negative examples, the minority class is more represented than the majority class. On the other hand, although SMOTE has been recognized as one of the best techniques to handle the imbalance problem, the experiments demonstrate that in the presence of high overlap it is not better than editing, since the generation of synthetic patterns involves an increase of noise in the data set.

Future work is primarily addressed to characterize the data sets by means of data complexity (or problem difficulty) measures, thus obtaining a better description of data and allowing a more accurate application of specific techniques to tackle the class imbalance and the class overlap situations.

Acknowledgments

This work has been partially supported by grants TIC2003-08496 from the Spanish CICYT and SEP-2003-C02-44225 from the Mexican CONACyT.

References

1. Barandela, R., Sánchez, J.S., García, V., Rangel, E.: Strategies for learning in class imbalance problems. *Pattern Recognition*, 36:849–851, 2003.
2. Batista, G.E., Pratti, R.C., Monard, M.C.: A study of the behavior of several methods for balancing machine learning training data. *SIGKDD Explorations*, 6:20–29, 2004.
3. Chawla, N.V., Bowyer, K.W., Hall, L.O., Kegelmeyer, W.P.: SMOTE: synthetic minority over-sampling technique. *Journal of Artificial Intelligence Research*, 16:321–357, 2002.
4. Domingos, P.: Metacost: a general method for making classifiers cost-sensitive. In: *Proc. 5th Intl. Conf. on Knowledge Discovery and Data Mining*, 155–164, 1999.
5. Eavis, T., Japkowicz, N.: A recognition-based alternative to discrimination-based multi-layer perceptrons, In: *Proc. Workshop on Learning from Imbalanced Data Sets*, Technical Report WS-00-05, 2000.
6. Fawcett, T., Provost, F.: Adaptive fraud detection. *Data Mining and Knowledge Discovery*, 1:291–316, 1996.
7. Gordon, D.F., Perlis, D.: Explicitly biased generalization. *Computational Intelligence*, 5:67–81, 1989.
8. Japkowicz, N.: Class imbalance: are we focusing on the right issue?. In: *Proc. Intl. Workshop on Learning from Imbalanced Data Sets II*, 2003.
9. Jo, T. Japkowicz, N.: Class imbalances versus small disjuncts. *SIGKDD Explorations*, 6:40–49, 2004.
10. Kubat, M., Matwin, S.: Adressing the curse of imbalanced training sets: one-sided selection. In: *Proc. 14th Intl. Conf. on Machine Learning*, 179–186, 1997.
11. Ling, C.X., Li, C.: Data mining for direct marketing: problems and solutions. In: *Proc. 4th Intl. Conf. on Knowledge Discovery and Data Mining*, 73–79, 1998.
12. Orriols, A., Bernardó, E.: The class imbalance problem in learning classifier systems: a preliminary study. In: *Proc. Conf. on Genetic and Evolutionary Computation*, 74–78, 2005.
13. Pazzani, M., Merz, C., Murphy, P., Ali, K., Hume, T., Brunk, C.: Reducing misclassification costs. In: *Proc. 11th Intl. Conf. on Machine Learning*, 217–225, 1994.
14. Prati, R.C., Batista, G.E., Monard, M.C.: Class imbalance versus class overlapping: an analysis of a learning system behavior. In: *Proc. 3rd Mexican Intl. Conference on Artificial Intelligence*, 312–321, 2004.
15. Tan, S.: Neighbor-weighted K-nearest neighbor for unbalanced text corpus. *Expert Systems with Applications*, 28:667–671, 2005.
16. Weiss, G.M.: *The Effect of Small Disjuncts and Class Distribution on Decision Tree Learning*. PhD thesis, Rutgers University (2003)
17. Wilson, D.L.: Asymptotic properties of nearest neighbour rules using edited data. *IEEE Trans.on Systems, Man and Cybernetics*, 2:408–421, 1972.
18. Woods, K., Doss, C., Bowyer, K.W., Solka, J., Priebe, C., Kegelmeyer, W.P.: Comparative evaluation of pattern recognition techniques for detection of microcalcifications in mammography. *International Journal of Pattern Recognition and Artificial Intelligence*, 7:1417–1436, 1993.

Melt Index Predict by Radial Basis Function Network Based on Principal Component Analysis

Xinggao Liu and Zhengbing Yan

National Laboratory of Industrial Control Technology,
Department of Control Science and Engineering,
Zhejiang University,
Hangzhou 310027, P.R. China
`liuxg@iipc.zju.edu.cn`

Abstract. Melt index is considered important quality variable determining product specifications. Reliable prediction of melt index (MI) is crucial in quality control of practical propylene polymerization processes. In this paper, a radial basis function network (RBF) model based on principal component analysis (PCA) and genetic algorithm (GA) is developed to infer the MI of polypropylene from other process variables. Considering that the genetic algorithm need long time to converge, chaotic series are explored to get more effective computation rate. The PCA-RBF model is also developed as a basis of comparison research. Brief outlines of the modeling procedure are presented, followed by the procedures for training and validating the model. The research results confirm the effectiveness of the presented methods.

1 Introduction

The melt index is defined as the mass rate of extrusion flow through a specified capillary under prescribed conditions of temperature and pressure [1]. Because the index determines the flow properties as well as other mechanical properties of polymer products, it is considered one of the important quality variables in the manufacturing process.

However, the direct measurement of the melt index in the laboratory is not only costly but also time consuming which make the real-time control of the product quality difficult or even impossible and therefore, yield off-spec products, resulting in enormous economic losses. Hence, many researchers have strived to infer the melt index indirectly with mathematical models that relate the melt index to other readily measurable process variables and let modeling and analyzing polymerization processes more cheaply and quickly with the huge amount of measurement data stored in the RTDBs.

Neural networks have been widely adopted to model and control dynamic processed because of their extremely powerful adaptive capabilities in response to nonlinear behaviors. Wai-Man Chan et al.[2] presents the approach of back propagation neural networks for modeling of free radical polymerization in high pressure tubular reactors and compare it with the mechanistic model. Results showed the promising capability of a neural network as an alternative approach to model polymeric systems.

Kong and Yang [3] presented RBF network models combing PCA and PLS for the melt index prediction problem for the propylene polymerization process. Shi Jian and Liu Xinggao [4] propose a novel soft-sensor model with principal component analysis, radial basis function networks and multi-scale analysis which provides promising prediction reliability and accuracy. Unfortunately, the selections of the model parameters were not considered.

In this article, the radial basis function network based on principal component analysis [5-6] is explored to predict the melt index in the polypropylene processes. Two model selection methods, genetic algorithm [7] and chaos genetic algorithm [8] are then employed to obtain the optimal set of parameters. Detailed comparisons among PCA-GA-RBF and PCA-CGA-RBF models are then carried out. The PCA-RBF model of PP process presented by Kong [3] is also developed as a basis of comparison research.

2 Melt Index Modeling

2.1 Radial Basis Function Network

The radial basis function network, proposed by Moody and Darken [5-6], employs local receptive fields to perform function mapping. Fig. 1 shows the schematic diagram of an RBFN with three receptive field units; the output of ith receptive field unit (or hidden unit) is

$$w_i = R_i(\vec{x}) = R_i(\|\vec{x} - \vec{c}_i\| / \sigma_i), i = 1, 2, ..., M \tag{1}$$

where $\vec{x}$ is an N dimensional input vector, $\vec{c}_i$ is a vector with the same dimension as $\vec{x}$, M is the number of receptive field units, and $R_i(\bullet)$ is the ith receptive field response with a single maximum at the origin. Typically, $R_i(\bullet)$ is chosen as a Gaussian function

$$R_i(\vec{x}) = \exp\left[-\frac{\|\vec{x} - \vec{c}_i\|^2}{\sigma_i^2}\right] \tag{2}$$

Thus the radial basis function w_i computed by the ith hidden units is maximum, when the input vector $\vec{x}$ is near the center $\vec{c}_i$ of that unit.

The output of an RBFN can be computed in two ways. For the simpler one, as shown in Fig. 1, the output is the weighted sum of the function value associated with each receptive field:

$$f(\vec{x}) = \sum_{i=1}^{M} f_i w_i = \sum_{i=1}^{M} f_i R_i(\vec{x}) \tag{3}$$

where f_i, is the function value, or strength, of ith receptive field. With the addition of lateral connections (not shown in Fig. 1) between the receptive field units, the network can produce the normalized response function as the weighted average of the strengths:

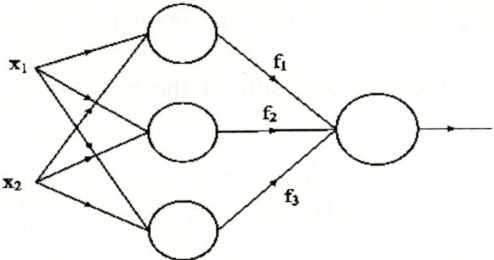

Fig. 1. An RBFN

$$f(\vec{x}) = \frac{\sum_{i=1}^{M} f_i w_i}{\sum_{i=1}^{M} w_i} = \frac{\sum_{i=1}^{M} f_i R_i(\vec{x})}{\sum_{i=1}^{M} R_i(\vec{x})} \quad (4)$$

To minimize the square errors between desired output and model output, several learning algorithms have been proposed to identify the parameters ($\vec{c}_i$, σ_i and f_i) of an RBFN. Moody et al. use a self-organizing technique to find the centers ($\vec{c}_i$) and widths (σ_i) of the receptive fields, and then employ the supervised Adeline or LMS learning rule to identify f_i. On the other hand, Chen et al. [9] apply orthogonal least squares learning algorithm to determine those parameters.

2.2 Genetic Algorithm

In the RBFN, the parameter $\vec{c}_i$, σ_i have to be selected carefully. These parameters play a key role in the RBF performance. Parameters inappropriately chosen result in over-fitting or under-fitting. These parameters are sometimes guessed by users. In this paper, genetic algorithm (GA) is employed to select optimal set of parameters because of its characteristic of global optimization.

In this paper, the real coded scheme of variables is selected, because it performs better than binary encoded scheme in constrained optimization problems. The initial values of the designed parameters are distributed in the solution space as even as possible. The reciprocal of the mean RMSE of L-folder cross validate is proposed as the fitness function:

$$fit = 1 \Big/ (\frac{1}{L} \sum_{i=1}^{L} rmse_i) \quad (5)$$

Here, the method of survival of the fittest was used to select the next generation individual. The probability of a_i selected as the next generation one is as follow:

$$P(a_i) = \frac{fit(a_i)}{\sum_{j=1}^{m} fit(a_j)} \quad (6)$$

where, $fit(a_i)$ is the fitness function of the individual a_i, m is the size of the population.

Due to the real-encoding scheme is utilized; the crossover operator in this paper is defined as:

$$c_1 = aP_1 + (1-a)P_2$$
$$c_2 = (1-a)P_1 + aP_2 \qquad (7)$$

where P_1 and P_2 are the two parents to be implemented the crossover operation, c_1 and c_2 are the children.

The mutation operator varies a point represented by an individual to another point in the solution space randomly. When the average fitness has not changed significantly for five generations, the program terminates and exports the optimal set of parameters.

2.3 Chaos Genetic Algorithm

As a result of mis-selection of many parameters such as crossover and mutation probabilities, pure random can not ensure the extension so that Gas fall into a situation of key gene deficiency and destruction of efficient form work, which leads to algorithm premature convergence. Genetic operators are fabricated by means of chaos to make the different generation seen random on a short-term basis while, in the long-term, there does exist a variety of 'exquisite' interior relationship, from which a set of Gas based on the chaotic set are acquired [8].

Let $I \subseteq [0,1]$ and I's measure is more than measure zero or it is a denumerable set including many elements. Let x_k is Logistic sequence:

$$x_{k+1} = vx_k(1-x_k), k = 0,1,... \qquad (8)$$

Suppose a certain code altogether has N+1, divides interval [0,1] into (N+1) subinterval I0,I1,...IN; among which

$$I_i \cap I_j = \phi (i \neq j) \qquad (9)$$

$$\bigcup_{i=1}^{N} I_i = [0,1] \qquad (10)$$

When $x \in I$ and $i \neq 0$, crossover operation can be conducted, and crossover site is ith locus. However when $x \in I_0$, no crossover operation happens.

3 Results and Discussion

A PP polymerization process currently operated for commercial purposes. To prepare a set of modeling data, the measurements of the process and quality variables from the RTDB and LIMS for the PP polymerization process are retrieved. Data from the records of the process variables and MI are separated into training, test and generalization sets that are constructed from the time series of recorded plant data. And the test set is obtained from the same batch as the training set, while the generalization set is derived from another batch.

To infer the MI of manufactured products from real process variables, RBF networks are used to characterize the nonlinearity of the process, and PCA is carried out to select the most relevant process features and to eliminate the correlations of the input variables, which will simplify the neural architecture and reduce the time needed for training without the loss of significant information. Genetic algorithm (GA) is employed to select optimal set of parameters of the PCA and RBF. Chaos is then introduced into GA to surmount the defects caused by pure random in the standard GAs.

The PCA-RBF model is developed as the basis of comparison research. The PCA-GA-RBF model is developed to get the optimal set of parameters. The PCA-CGA-RBF model is further developed to get more effective computation rate.

3.1 Predictive Effective

The prediction performances of the PCA-GA-RBF and PCA-CGA-RBF models can be assessed from table 1 and 2, which list the mean relative error (MRE), root mean squared error (RMSE), Theil's Inequality Coefficient (TIC), standard deviation (STD) defined as follows:

$$MRE = \frac{1}{N}\sum_{i=1}^{N}\left|\frac{y_i - \hat{y}_i}{y_i}\right| \tag{11}$$

$$RMSE = \sqrt{\sum_{i=1}^{n}(\hat{y}_i - y_i)/n} \tag{12}$$

$$TIC = \frac{\sqrt{\sum_{i=1}^{N}(y_i - \hat{y}_i)^2}}{\sqrt{\sum_{i=1}^{N}y_i^2} + \sqrt{\sum_{i=1}^{N}\hat{y}_i^2}} \tag{13}$$

$$STD = \sqrt{\frac{1}{N-1}\sum_{i=1}^{N}(e_i - \bar{e})^2} \tag{14}$$

where, $e_i = y_i - \hat{y}_i$, $\bar{e} = \frac{1}{N}\sum_{i=1}^{N}e_i$ and y_i, $\hat{y}_i$ denote the measured value and predicted result respectively.

The data listed in Table 1 clearly show that the PCA-GA-RBF model gives the best prediction performance for the test set, with MRE of 4.49%, better than the PCA-RBF and PCA-CGA-RBF models with those of 5.02%, 4.6049%, respectively. The RMSE listed also in Table I have confirmed the prediction accuracy of the proposed methods. The RMSEs of the PCA-GA-RBF and PCA-CGA-RBF models are 0.0294, 0.0300 respectively, compared with that of 0.0373 of the PCA-RBF model. The PCA-GA-RBF and PCA-CGA-RBF models give the similar predictive stability for the testing data set, with STD of 0.1304, 0.1300 respectively, better than the PCA-RBF model with that of 0.1622. TICs of the PCA-GA-RBF and PCA-CGA-RBF models are smaller than that of the PCA-RBF model, which indicates a good level of agreement between the proposed model and the studied process.

A detailed comparison of the generalization data set is presented in Table 2. It clearly shows that the all four criterions of the PCA-GA-RBF and PCA-CGA-RBF models are better than that of the PCA-RBF model.

Table 1. Performance for the testing data sets

Methods	MRE (%)	RMSE	TIC	STD
PCA-RBF	5.02	0.0373	0.0337	0.1622
PCA-GA-RBF	4.49	0.0294	0.0270	0.1304
PCA-CGA-RBF	4.60	0.0300	0.0276	0.1300

Table 2. Performance for the generating data sets

Methods	MRE (%)	RMSE	TIC	STD
PCA-RBF	5.16	0.0620	0.0279	0.0479
PCA-GA-RBF	2.31	0.0282	0.0124	0.0389
PCA-CGA-RBF	2.36	0.0301	0.0132	0.0378

3.2 Computation Time

The comparison between PCA-GA-RBF and PCA-CGA-RBF on computational rate is listed in Table 3. It has been shown that the CPU running time of PCA-CGA-RBF model is significantly smaller than PCA-GA-RBF model, decreasing from 922s to 327s, while the similar predict performance is guaranteed simultaneously.

Table 3. Computation time (Pentium IV 1.4G/512M)

Methods	Computation time(s)
PCA-GA-RBF	922
PCA-CGA-RBF	327

4 Conclusions

In this paper, the PCA-GA-RBF and PCA-CGA-RBF models are presented to infer MI of polypropylene from other process variables. The PCA-RBF model is also developed as the basis of comparison research. The PCA-GA-RBF and PCA-CGA-RBF models predict MI with MRE of 4.49% and 4.60% respectively, compared with that of 5.02% obtained from the PCA-RBF model.

The comparison between the PCA-GA-RBF and PCA-CGA-RBF models on computation time also indicate that the PCA-CGA-RBF model is more computationally efficient than PCA-GA-RBF with the same predictive performance guaranteed, which is more convenient for use in more interesting engineering studies like the simulation of different types of polypropylene reactors, optimization, control etc and supposed to have promising potential for practical use.

Acknowledgements

This work is supported by Zhejiang provincial Natural Science Foundation of China (Grant Y105370), National Natural Science Foundation of China (Grant 20106008), National HI-TECH Industrialization Program of China (Grant Fagai-Gaoji-2004-2080) and Science Fund for Distinguished Young Scholars of Zhejiang University (Grant 111000-581645), and their supports are thereby acknowledged.

References

1. Bafna, S. S., Beall, A.M.: A design of experiments study on the factors affecting variability in the melt index measurement. J. Appl. Polym. Sci. 65(2) (1997) 277-288
2. Chan, Wai-Man, Nascimento, C. A. O.: Use of neural networks for modeling of olefin polymerization in high pressure tubular reactors. J. Appl. Polym. Sci. 53(10) (2003) 1277-1289
3. Kong, W., Yang, J.: Prediction of polypropylene melt index based on RBF networks. J. Chem. Ind. Eng. (Chinese) 54(8) (2003) 1160-1163
4. Shi, Jian, Liu, Xinggao: Melt index prediction by neural soft-sensor based on multi-scale analysis and principal component analysis. Chinese J. Chem. Eng. 13(6) (2005) 849-852
5. Moody, J., Darken, C.: Learning with localized receptive fields. In Proc. 1988 Connectionist Models Summer School, Touretzky, D., Hinton, G. and Sejnowski, T. Eds,. Carnegie Mellon University, Morgan Kaufmann Publishers (1988)
6. Moody, J., Darken, C.: Fast learning in networks of locally-tuned processing units. Neural Comp. 1 (1989) 281-294
7. Zheng, Chunhong, Jiao, Licheng: Automatic parameters selection for SVM based on GA. Proceedings of the 5th world congress on intelligent control and automation, Hangzhou, P.R. China (2004)
8. Lin, C.T., Jou, C.P.: Controlling chaos by GA-based reinforcement learning neural network. IEEE T. Neural Networ. 10(4) (1999) 846-859
9. Chen, S., Cowan, C.F.N., Grant, P.M.: Orthogonal least squares learning algorithm for radial basis function networks. IEEE T. Neural Networ. 2(2) (1991) 302-309

Thinking Capability of Saplings Growing Up Algorithm

Ali Karci and Bilal Alatas

Firat University, Department of Computer Engineering, 23119, Elazig / Turkey
{akarci, balatas}@firat.edu.tr

Abstract. Saplings Growing up Algorithm (SGA) is a novel computational intelligence method inspired by sowing and growing up of saplings. This method contains two phases: Sowing Phase and Growing up Phase. Uniformed sowing sampling is aim to scatter evenly in the feasible solution space. Growing up phase contains three operators: *mating, branching, and vaccinating* operator. In this study thinking capability of SGA has been defined and it has been demonstrated that sapling population generated initially has diversity. The similarity of population concludes the interaction of saplings and at consequent, they will be similar. Furthermore, the operators used in the algorithm uses similarity and hence the population has the convergence property.

1 Introduction

The thinking is a social activity, and human culture and cognition are aspects of a single process [1, 2]. People learn from one another not only facts but methods for processing those facts. If knowledge and skills spread from person to person, the population converges on optimal processes. The social activities in a population can be categorized in three levels.

- Individuals learn locally from their neighbors. People are aware of interacting with their neighbors, gleaning insights from them, and sharing their own insights in turn, and local social learning is an easily measured and well-documented phenomenon.
- The spread of knowledge through social learning results in emergent group-level processes. This sociological, economic, or political level of phenomenon is seen as regularities in beliefs, attitudes, behaviors, and other attributes across individuals within a population. A society is self-organized system with global properties that cannot be predicted from the properties of the individuals who make up.
- Culture optimizes cognition. Though all interactions are local, insights and innovations are transported by culture from the originator to distant individuals; further, combination of various innovations results in even more improved methods. This global effect is largely transparent to actors in the system who benefit from it.

The probability of human interaction is a function of the similarity of two individuals: The basic idea is that agents who are similar to each other are likely to interact and then become even more similar.

E. Corchado et al. (Eds.): IDEAL 2006, LNCS 4224, pp. 386–393, 2006.
© Springer-Verlag Berlin Heidelberg 2006

Similarity is a precondition for social interaction and subsequent exchange of cultural features. The probability of interaction depends on similarity and culture is seen to spread and finally stabilize through links between similar individuals. Individuals become more similar as they interact; populations do not converge on unanimity.

The effect of similarity as a casual influence in Axelrod's model is to introduce polarization. Dissimilarity generates boundaries between cultural regions. Inter-individual similarities do not facilitate convergence, but rather, when individuals contain no matching features, the probability of interaction is defined as 0.0, and cultural differences become insurmountable.

In this study, we defined the thinking capability of saplings growing up algorithm (SGA) [3-4]. In order to introduce the thinking skill of algorithm, we used a simple encoding (binary encoding) for sake of understandability and simplicity without lose of generality.

The second part of this paper introduces the Saplings Growing up Algorithm (SGA). Third section describes the thinking skill of algorithm and finally, the last section concludes the paper.

2 Saplings Growing Up Algorithm (SGA)

Solution space can be considered as a garden of saplings, and hence all saplings must be scattered in the garden uniformly (Fig. 1). Each sapling is a potential solution, unless there is multi-criteria problem. In the multi-criteria case, all saplings are solutions. If a farmer wants to sow saplings, he will trivially sow them in equi-length distance for the sake of growing up of saplings more quickly (Fig. 1). In order to solve a problem by simulating the growing up of saplings, arbitrary solutions to be generated initially must be scattered evenly in the feasible searching space. In order to scatter saplings in the garden, the uniform population method in genetic algorithms for generating initial population uniformly can be used [5-10]. Each sapling consists of branches, and initially each sapling contains no branch and it is a body. The algorithm for generation of initial population is seen in Algorithm 1.

Fig. 1. Scattering saplings in garden uniformly

After being sowed, saplings must grow up (mating, branching and vaccinating). The aim of mating operator (denoted as ⊗) is to generate a new sapling from currently exist saplings by inter-changing genetic information. There will be a mating factor for each pair of saplings, since the distance between a pair is the most important factor which causes the mating of pair or not.

```
Algorithm 1. SowingSaplings
    // P is population, I is indices set and I_e is the enlarged indices set.
1.  Create two saplings such as one of them P[1] contains all upper bounds for
    variables as branches and the other P[2] contains all lower bounds for
    variables as branches.
2.  Index←3
3.  k←2
4.  While P is not saturated do
       Let i_e be an element of I_e and each i_e are enlarged with bit value and this
    bit value corresponds to part.
       i←1
       While P is not saturated and all saplings are not generated for a specific
    value of k (and i≤2^k-2) do
          i is a k-bit number and i_e corresponds to the enlarged value of i. Each bit
    of i is enlarged upto length of corresponding part of P[0] and P[1].
             For j←1 to n do
             If j^th bit of i_e is 1 then j^th branch of P[Index] is equal to P[1]*r
             else   j^th branch of P[Index] is equal to P[2]*r
                r is a random number in interval [0,1] and it is a real number.
             Index←Index+1
          i←i+1
       k←k+1
```

Let $G=g_1g_2...g_i...g_n$ and $H=h_1h_2...h_i...h_n$ be two saplings. The distance between G and H affects the mating process' taking place or not, and it depends on the distance between current pair. Let $P(G,H)$ be probability of not mating of saplings G and H, and $P_m(G,H)$ is mating probability of saplings G and H.

$$P(G,H)= \frac{\left(\sum_{i=1}^{n}(g_i - h_i)^2\right)^{1/2}}{R} \quad (1)$$

$$R=\left(\sum_{i=1}^{n}(u_i - l_i)^2\right)^{1/2} \quad (2)$$

u_i is the upper bound for the corresponding distance between the pair of currently selected saplings, and l_i is the lower bound for the corresponding distance between the pair of currently selected saplings. The probability of mating of two saplings depends on the distance between both saplings. G and H are saplings and the probability of their mating is

$$P_m(G,H)=1- \frac{\left(\sum_{i=1}^{n}(g_i - h_i)^2\right)^{1/2}}{R} \quad (3)$$

Wind and other effects in the nature affect the mating probability. With the mating operator, a sapling gets a branch from the mating partner or sends its branch to mating partner and thus, G⊗H may yield 2n new saplings.

The mating process takes place for each pair of branches (g_i and h_i), if $P_m(G,H)$ satisfies the mating condition. The mating condition is $P_m(G,H)$ and this is the mating rate for G and H. A random number is generated and if this random number is smaller than or equal to this mating rate, then these saplings are mated.

```
Algorithm 2. Mating(G,H)
1.  j←1, ..., n
2.  compute P_m(G,H)=1- (Σ_{j=1}^{n}(g_j - h_j)^2)^{1/2} / R
3.  i←1,...,n
4.      if P_m(G,H)≥random[0,1) then
5.          G←G-g_i, and H←H-h_i
6.          G←G+h_i, and H←H+g_i  // G←G+h_i, and h_i is added to position of g_i, and
            H←H+g_i and g_i is added to position of h_i,
```

In order to grow up a branch on any point on the body of sapling, there should be no near branch previously occurred there. Assume that a first branch was occurred at point **1** as seen in Fig. 2, the probability of branch occurring on the point **2** is less than the probability of branch occurring on the points **3**. This logic can be used as a method for searching solution locally. This is a local change on the current solution(s).

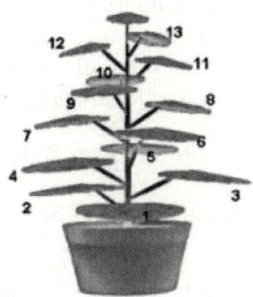

Fig. 2. Effects of the point where a branch trying to grow up

There is a branch growing up at point **1**. The probability of a branch growing up at point different from **1** is proportional to $1-\frac{1}{d^2}$ where d is the distance between that point and point **1**. The probability of a branch growing up at point **2** is $1-\frac{1}{d_1^2}$, where d_1 is the distance between and point **1** and **2**. The probability of a branch growing up at point **3** is $1-\frac{1}{(d_1+d_2)^2}$ if d_2 is the distance between point **2** and **3**.

Let $G=g_1g_2...g_i...g_n$ be a sapling. If a branch occurs in point g_i (the value of g_i is changed), then the probability of a branch occurring in point g_j could be calculated in two ways: linear and non-linear.

The distance between g_i and g_j can be considered as $|j-i|$ or $|i-j|$. If g_i is a branch, then the probability of g_j being a branch is $P(g_j | g_i) = 1 - \frac{1}{(|j-i|)^2}$, $i \neq j$ in linear case, and $P(g_j|g_i)$ is similar to conditional probability, however, it is not pure conditional probability. In the non-linear case, the probability can be considered as $P(g_j | g_i) = 1 - \frac{1}{e^{(|j-i|)^2}}$. If $i=j$, then $P(g_j|g_i)=0$.

```
Algorithm 3. Branching(G)
1.   i←1,..., n
2.       j←i+1,...,n
3.           if there is no branch then
4.               P(g_j|g_i)=1 and branching process is applied
5.           else
6.               P(g_j|g_i) = 1 - 1/(|j-i|)^2 ,  i≠j  or  P(g_j|g_i) = 1 - 1/e^(|j-i|)^2
7.           if P(g_j|g_i)≥random[0,1] then
8.               g_j will be a branch
```

The vaccinating process takes place between two different saplings in case of similarity of saplings. Since the similarity of saplings affects the success of vaccinating process, and also vaccinating success is proportional to the similarity of both saplings. In this study, the similarity of saplings is computed in two ways. $G = g_1 g_2 \ldots g_i \ldots g_n$ and $H = h_1 h_2 \ldots h_i \ldots h_n$ for $1 \leq i \leq n$, $g_i, h_i \in \{0,1\}$.

$$Sim(G,H) = \sum_{i=1}^{n} g_i \oplus h_i$$

The vaccinating process takes place as follow, if $Sim(G,H) \geq$ threshold.

$$G' = \begin{cases} g_i & \text{if } g_i = h_i \\ random(1) & \text{if } g_i \neq h_i \end{cases} \text{ and } H' = \begin{cases} h_i & \text{if } h_i = g_i \\ random(1) & \text{if } h_i \neq g_i \end{cases}$$

where G' and H' are obtained as consequence of applying vaccinating process to G and H. Saplings are not vaccinated arbitrarily. The saplings to be vaccinated must satisfy the inequality defined by the similarity ($Sim(G,H) \geq$ threshold). The initial value of threshold depends on the problem solvers. The smaller value of threshold results in more accurate solution, and the bigger value of threshold results in more non-accurate solution.

```
Algorithm 4. Vaccinating(G,H)
1.   i←1 ,..., n
2.       Sim(G,H) = Σ_{i=1}^{n} g_i ⊕ h_i
3.       if Sim(G,H)≥r then
4.           G' = {g_i    if g_i = h_i    and  H' = {h_i    if h_i = g_i
                 {random(1)  if g_i ≠ h_i         {random(1)  if h_i ≠ g_i
         where r is a threshold value defined by problem solver. random(1)
         generates a random number which is 0 or 1.
```

In order to determine the quality of saplings, in contrast to genetic algorithm objective function is used. The objective function measures the goodness of the saplings in the population space and there is no necessity to take objective function scores and processes them to produce a number for each sapling.

3 Thinking Capability

Assume that the length of a sapling is n (a sapling has n branches), and the initial population contains m saplings. In order to demonstrate the thinking capability of SGA, we must firstly see the structure of initial population. The amount of knowledge in the initial population and its type must be known.

Algorithm 1 generates the initial population and this population has the following knowledge. Let S_1 and S_2 be two saplings.

$S_1 = \boxed{s_1 s_2 \ldots\ldots\ldots\ldots\ldots\ldots s_n}$ $\qquad S_2 = \boxed{\bar{s}_1 \bar{s}_2 \ldots\ldots\ldots\ldots \bar{s}_n}$

These two saplings are deterministically generated initially. Then the remaining saplings are generated with respect to the rules in Algorithm 1 up to population is completed.

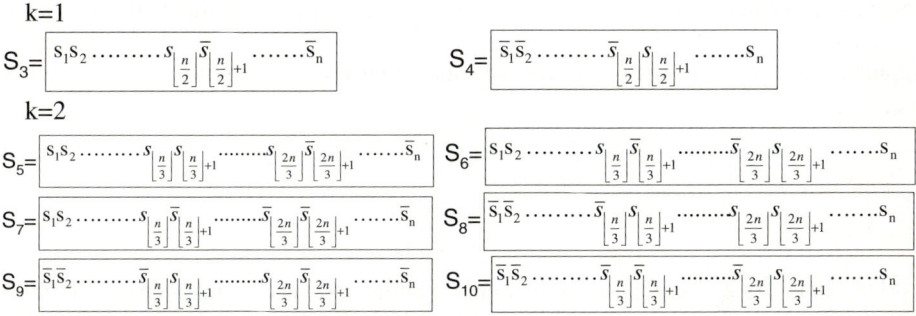

For any branch s_i, $1 \leq i \leq n$, the number of 1s and number of 0s are equal to each other. This case is valid for all branches.

Theorem: The probability of similarity of population is greater than or equal to 0.5.

Proof: The similarity of population means that $\forall S_i$, S_j, $1 \leq i, j \leq m$, $i \neq j$, $Sim(S_i, S_j) > 0$. In order to prove this theorem, the knowledge contained by the initial population must be determined. $Sim(S_i, S_j) = n$ means that S_i and S_j saplings are not similar and their similarity is zero, since they do not have branches that have same values.

Initially generated saplings

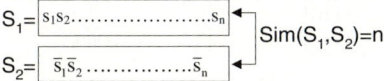 $Sim(S_1, S_2) = n$

Generated saplings for k=1

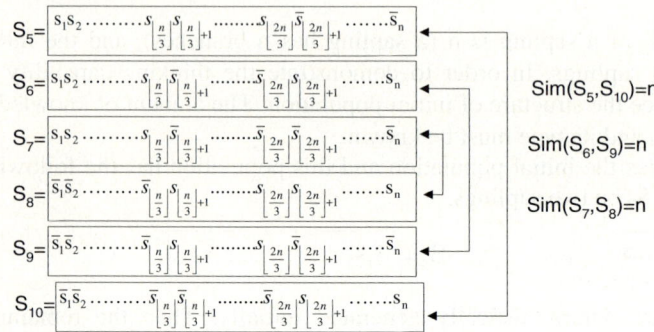

Generated saplings for k=2

This situation is conserved for all values of *k*. The number of disjoint saplings in the initial population is $m/2$ and there are $\binom{m}{2}$ pairs. So, there are $\binom{m}{2} - m/2$ saplings have branches whose values are equal to each others. Hence

$$\frac{\binom{m}{2} - \frac{m}{2}}{\binom{m}{2}} = \frac{m-2}{m-1}. \text{ For } m \geq 3, \frac{m-2}{m-1} \geq 0.5 \qquad \blacklozenge$$

The similarity in the population is used in mating and vaccinating steps of the SGA. Mating operator is a global search operator and uses similarity between saplings. Let S_0, S_1, S_2, and S_3 be the saplings and let them be encoded with binary strings as shown in Table 1. In growing up step, mating points are determined. If the mating points are 2, 3, 2, 1, 4, and 3; then new saplings 12 new sapling are created as shown in Table 2.

Table 1. Generated saplings

	Saplings
S_0	00000
S_1	11111
S_2	00011
S_3	11100

Table 2. Mating

	New candidate saplings	New candidate saplings
$S_0 \otimes S_1$	11000	00111
$S_0 \otimes S_2$	00000	00011
$S_0 \otimes S_3$	11000	00100
$S_1 \otimes S_2$	01111	10011
$S_1 \otimes S_3$	11101	11110
$S_2 \otimes S_3$	11111	00000

Vaccinating operator is a search operator and aims to generate new saplings from currently existing saplings which are similar. In vaccinating step, $\text{Sim}(S_0, S_1) = 0$;

$Sim(S_0,S_2)=3$; $Sim(S_0,S_3)=2$; $Sim(S_1,S_2)=2$; $Sim(S_1,S_3)=3$; $Sim(S_2,S_3)=0$. If threshold value is greater than 3, vaccinating process will not be performed. If it is less than 3, then S0 and S3; S1 and S2 are vaccinated. $S_0 \oplus S_3 = \{01100, 01100\}$, $S_1 \oplus S_2 = \{00011, 00111\}$.

Briefly, similarity is used in the SGA operators. When the algorithm continues, mating operator uses similarity measures and makes a global search. Vaccinating is also uses similarity and similar saplings are vaccinated. Competition and cooperation are observed among saplings.

4 Conclusions

The generated population with respect to SGA has disjoint saplings. However, the probability of similarity of population is greater than or equal to 0.5. This means that a similar population has diversity, and this is a desired case for obtaining better result. The similarity of population concludes the interaction of saplings and at consequent, they will be similar. Furthermore, the operators used in the algorithm uses similarity and hence, the population has the convergence property.

Acknowledgement

This study is supported by Turkish Scientific and Technical Research Council grant 105E144.

References

1. Axelrod, R.: The Evolution of Cooperation. New York: Basic Book (1984).
2. Axelrod, R.: The Dissemination of Culture: A Model with Local Convergence and Global Polarization. Journal of Conflict Resolution, 41 (1997) 203-226.
3. Karci, A., Alatas, B., Akin, E.: Sapling Growing up Algorithm (in Turkish). INISTA, Turkey (2006).
4. Karci, A., Alatas, B., Akin, E.: Evolutionary Algorithms and Imitating the Saplings (in Turkish). IKECCO 2006, Kyrgyzstan (2006).
5. Gundogan K. K., Alatas, B. Karci, A., Tatar, Y.: Comprehensible Classification Rule Mining with Two-Level Genetic Algorithm. 2nd FAE International Symposium, TRNC (2002) 373-377.
6. Alatas, B., Karci, A.: Genetik Sürecin Düzenlilik Operatoruyle Global Cozume Dogru Harekete Zorlanmasi. ELECO'2002, 364-368, Turkey (2002) 18-22.
7. Karci, A., Arslan, A.: Uniform population in genetic algorithms. I.U. Journal of Electrical & Electronics, 2 (2) (2002) 495-504.
8. Karci, A., Cinar, A.: Comparison of Uniform Distributed Initial Population Method and Random Initial Population Method in Genetic Search. The 15th International Symposium on Computer and Information Sciences, Istanbul / Turkey (2000) 159-166.
9. Karci, A.: Novelty in the Generation of Initial Population for Genetic Algorithms. Lecture Notes in Artificial Intelligence, 3214 (2004) 268-275.
10. Karci, A., Arslan, A.: Bidirectional evolutionary heuristic for the minimum vertex-cover problem. Journal of Computers and Electrical Engineering, vol. 29 (2003) 111-120.

Functional Networks and the Lagrange Polynomial Interpolation

Cristina Solares*, Eduardo W. Vieira, and Roberto Mínguez

University of Castilla-La Mancha, Spain
Cristina.Solares@uclm.es,
Eduardo.Vieira@uclm.es,
Roberto.Minguez@uclm.es

Abstract. A new approach is presented for the approximation of a scalar function defined on a discrete set of points. The method is based on the application of functional networks and the Lagrange interpolation formula. The interpolation mechanism of the separable functional networks when the neuron functions are approximated by Lagrange polynomials, is explored. The coefficients of the Lagrange interpolation formula are estimated during the learning of the functional network by simply solving a linear system of equations. Finally, several examples show the effectiveness of the proposed interpolation method.

1 Introduction

The approximation of functions defined on a finite set of argument values plays an essential role in the problem of experimental data processing. Diverse methods have been developed and are widely applied in constructing approximating functions in the form of polynomial or trigonometric functions [4]. Among them, the Lagrange interpolation polynomials occupy an important place in the finite element function approximation method [5,6,7]. In the finite element method, in order to approximate an unknown function, the domain is divided into subdomains (finite elements) and the approximation is carried out over these subdomains and then, based on these results, the approximation is established for the entire domain. It has been shown that the use of polynomials is especially advantageous and convenient for establishing the above approximation of the unknown scalar function (see [6] for further details).

Functional networks have been introduced by Castillo [1] and Castillo, Cobo, Gutiérrez and Pruneda [2] as an efficient generalization of neural networks, which allow combining both domain and data knowledge. Unlike neural networks, in these models the internal neuron functions are not fixed but learnable from data and there are no weights associated with the links connecting neurons (their effect is subsumed by the neuron functions). During the functional network

---

* The author is indebted to the Spanish Ministry of Science and Technology (Project BFM2003-05695) and to the Junta de Comunidades de Castilla-La Mancha (Project PAI-05-044) for partial support.

learning process, a method based on minimizing a least squares error function is used. One advantage of working with this kind of models is that the learning procedure is based on solving a linear system of equations.

In this paper, a nontraditional approach for the approximation of one, two and three-variable scalar functions, defined on the above finite elements, is presented. The proposed method is based on the application of a separable functional network which calculates the Lagrange interpolation polynomials (element shape or element interpolation functions) and the interpolation coefficients during the functional network learning process without knowing the values of the function at the nodal points.

2 Construction of the Interpolation Function

Consider a function $F(\mathbf{x})$ defined on a finite set of argument values $\{\mathbf{x}_1, \mathbf{x}_2, \ldots, \mathbf{x}_n\}$. If the values of $F(\mathbf{x})$ at intermediate $\mathbf{x}$ values are required for the solution of the problem, then it is convenient to construct a function $\hat{F}(\mathbf{x})$, which assumes the values of $\{z_1 = F(\mathbf{x}_1), z_2 = F(\mathbf{x}_2), \ldots, z_n = F(\mathbf{x}_n)\}$ and which approximates $F(\mathbf{x})$ with some degree of accuracy in the rest of its domain. The function $\hat{F}(\mathbf{x})$ is called interpolating function.

2.1 One-Variable Function Approximation

Given a set of nodal points $\{\theta_1, \theta_2, \ldots, \theta_n\}$ the interpolating function $\hat{F}(x)$ can be built as

$$\hat{F}(x) = \sum_{i=1}^{n} w_i \phi_i(x) \qquad (1)$$

where $w_i = F(\theta_i)$ and the functions $\phi_i(x)$ are the Lagrange polynomials. The Lagrange polynomials are defined as

$$\phi_i(x) = \prod_{k=1, k \neq i}^{n} \frac{x - \theta_k}{\theta_i - \theta_k}, 1 \leq i \leq n. \qquad (2)$$

The functions $N_i(x) = \phi_i(x)$ in (1) are the shape functions at the nodal points θ_i in the finite element function approximation method.

The nodal points θ_i can be taken as equally spaced points in the interval $[-1, 1]$, i.e., $\theta_i = i/n$ or as the clustered Chebyshev points, obtained by projecting equally spaced points on the unit circle down to the unit interval $[-1, 1]$. The Chebyshev points of the first kind are given by

$$x_j = \cos\left(\frac{(2j+1)\pi}{2n+2}\right), j = 0, \ldots, n.$$

When the function domain (finite element domain) is an arbitrary interval $[a, b]$, a linear change of variables

$$x = \frac{1}{2}[(b-a)z + (b+a)] \qquad (3)$$

can be applied to transform it into $[-1, 1]$.

For determining the coefficients w_i in (1) is necessary to have the values of the function $F(x)$ at the nodal points $\theta_i, i = 1\ldots, n$, but in the practice, this is not always possible.

2.2 Two-Variables Function Approximation

Given the set of nodal points $\{(\theta_1, \delta_1), (\theta_2, \delta_2), \ldots, (\theta_n, \delta_n)\}$ the interpolating function $\hat{F}(x, y)$ can be built as

$$\hat{F}(x, y) = \sum_{i=1}^{n} \sum_{j=1}^{n} w_{ij} \phi_i(x) \psi_j(y) \tag{4}$$

where $w_{ij} = F(\theta_i, \delta_j)$ and the functions $\phi_i(x)$ and $\psi_j(y)$ are the Lagrange polynomials in x and y directions.

For determining the coefficients w_{ij} in (4) it is necessary to have the values of the function $F(x, y)$ at the nodal points $(\theta_i, \delta_j), i = 1\ldots, n, j = 1\ldots, n$.

2.3 Three-Variables Function Approximation

As in the previous sections, we can construct the interpolating function $\hat{F}(x, y, z)$

$$\hat{F}(x, y, z) = \sum_{i=1}^{n} \sum_{j=1}^{n} \sum_{l=1}^{n} w_{ijl} \phi_i(x) \psi_j(y) \nu_l(z) \tag{5}$$

where the functions $\phi_i(x)$, $\psi_j(y)$ and $\nu_l(z)$ are the Lagrange polynomials in x, y and z directions.

For determining the coefficients w_{ijl} in (5) it is necessary to have the values of the function $F(x, y, z)$ at the nodal points $(\theta_i, \delta_j, \lambda_l), i = 1\ldots, n, j = 1\ldots, n, l = 1\ldots, n$.

3 Description of the Functional Network

In this section, we consider a separable functional network model for function approximation, which permits the calculation of the coefficients w_i in (1), w_{ij} in (4) and w_{ijl} in (5) without knowing the values of the function F at the nodal points. The above coefficients are calculated from arbitrary initial points during the network learning process.

The separable model of functional network

$$\begin{aligned} z = \hat{F}(x, y) = \\ f_1(x)g_1(y) + f_2(x)g_2(y) + f_3(x)g_3(y) + \ldots + f_n(x)g_n(y) \end{aligned} \tag{6}$$

is proposed to approximate $z = F(x, y)$ (see Castillo et al. [2] for further details). This is an interesting functional network architecture with many applications and which combines the separate effects of the input variables. The one-dimensional case is a particular case of (6), taking $g_i(y) = 1, i = 1, \ldots, n$ we approximate the function $y = F(x)$ as

$$y = \hat{F}(x) = f_1(x) + f_2(x) + f_3(x) + \ldots + f_n(x). \tag{7}$$

The problem of learning the functional network (6) reduces to estimating the neuron functions $f_1, f_2, \ldots, f_n$ and $g_1, g_2, \ldots, g_n$ from the available training data $\{(x_1, y_1, z_1), (x_2, y_2, z_2), \ldots, (x_m, y_m, z_m)\}$ where $z_i = F(x_i, y_i), i = 1, \ldots, m$. To this aim, each neuron function f_j in (6) is supposed to be a linear combination of the Lagrange polynomials $\{\phi_1(x), \phi_2(x), \ldots, \phi_n(x)\}$ and each neuron function g_j in (6) is supposed to be a linear combination of Lagrange polynomials $\{\psi_1(y), \psi_2(y), \ldots, \psi_n(y)\}$

$$\hat{f}_j(x) = \sum_{i=1}^{n} a_{ji} \phi_i(x), j = 1, \ldots, n, \tag{8}$$

$$\hat{g}_j(y) = \sum_{i=1}^{n} b_{ji} \psi_i(y), j = 1, \ldots, n, \tag{9}$$

where the coefficients a_{ji} and b_{ji} are the parameters of the functional network which are estimated using the least squares criterion. The above Lagrange polynomials are the polynomials defined in Section 2.2 at the nodal points $\{(\theta_1, \delta_1), (\theta_2, \delta_2), \ldots, (\theta_n, \delta_n)\}$.

Replacing (8) and (9) in (6) we obtain the interpolating function for the two-dimensional case

$$\hat{F}(x, y) = \sum_{i=1}^{n} \sum_{j=1}^{n} c_{ij} \phi_i(x) \psi_j(y) \tag{10}$$

where $N_{ij}(x, y) = \phi_i(x) \psi_j(y), i = 1, \ldots, n; j = 1, \ldots, n$ are the shape functions at the nodal points (θ_i, δ_j) and $\hat{F}(x, y)$ is proposed to approximate $F(x, y)$. The architecture of this functional network is represented in Figure 1. The problem of learning the above functional network reduces to estimating the parameters c_{ij} in (10) from the training data $(x_i, y_i, z_i), i = 1, \ldots, m$. Then, the proposed functional network model (10) allows the calculation of the coefficients $w_{ij}, i = 1, \ldots, n; j = 1, \ldots, n$ in (4) from the available training data.

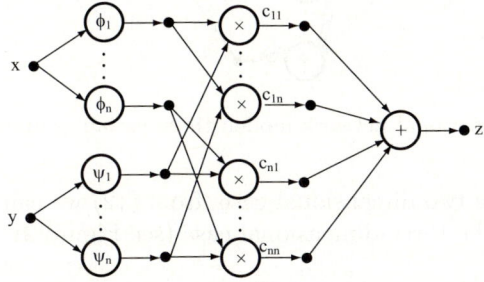

Fig. 1. Separable functional network model: two-variable function approximation

To find the optimum coefficients in (10) we minimize the sum of square errors

$$E = \sum_{k=1}^{m} e_k^2; \text{ where } e_k = z_k - \sum_{i=1}^{n}\sum_{j=1}^{n} c_{ij}\, \phi_i(x_k)\, \psi_j(y_k) \qquad (11)$$

and m is the number of training data. Using the Lagrange multipliers the minimum can be obtained by solving a linear system of equations where the unknowns are the coefficients c_{ij} in (10) (see Castillo et al. [2] for further details). The main advantage of working with this kind of models is that the learning procedure is based on solving a linear system of equations. We apply the Orthogonalization Algorithm [3] to obtain the solution of the above system of linear equations. The Orthogonalization Algorithm is a robust pivoting algorithm of complexity equivalent to Gauss Elimination Algorithm.

Analogously, the separable model of functional network

$$\begin{aligned} u = \hat{F}(x,y,z) = \\ f_1(x)g_1(y)h_1(z) + \ldots + f_n(x)g_n(y)h_n(z) \end{aligned} \qquad (12)$$

is proposed to approximate a three-variables scalar function $u = F(x,y,z)$ (see Castillo et al. [2] for further details).

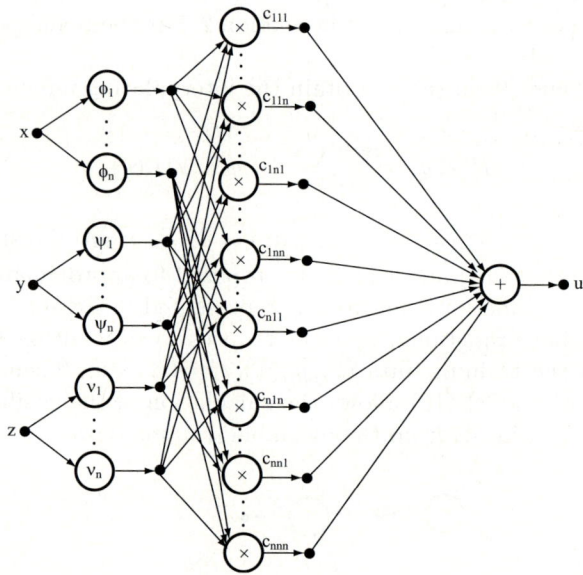

Fig. 2. Separable functional network model: three-variables function approximation

Working as in the two dimensional case, from (12) we can build the interpolating function for the three-dimensional case (see Figure 2)

$$\hat{F}(x,y,z) = \sum_{i=1}^{n}\sum_{j=1}^{n}\sum_{l=1}^{n} c_{ijl}\, \phi_i(x)\, \psi_j(y)\, \nu_l(z) \qquad (13)$$

where $N_{ijl}(x,y,z) = \phi_i(x)\psi_j(x)\nu_l(z), i = 1,\ldots,n; j = 1,\ldots,n; l = 1,\ldots,n$ are the shape functions at the nodal points $(\theta_i, \delta_j, \lambda_l)$. The proposed functional network model (13) allows the calculation of the coefficients $w_{ijl}, i = 1,\ldots,n; j = 1,\ldots,n; l = 1,\ldots,n$ in (5), from the available training data $(x_i, y_i, z_i, w_i), i = 1,\ldots,m$.

4 Examples of Application

In the finite element method, in order to approximate an unknown function, the domain is divided into subdomains (finite elements) and the approximation is carried out over these subdomains.

In this section we show some examples of function approximation working with the above functional network models. The approximation is carried out over a finite element $(x,y) \in [-1,1] \times [-1,1]$ in the two-dimensional case and $(x,y,z) \in [-1,1] \times [-1,1] \times [-1,1]$ in the three-dimensional case.

Example 1. In the first example we aproximate the function $z = f(x,y) = xy + xy^3$ over the finite element $(x,y) \in [-1,1] \times [-1,1]$. For that, we use the functional network (10) with $m = 10$ random training points. The points $\{\theta_1 = -1, \theta_2 = 1\}$ and $\{\delta_1 = -1, \delta_2 = -1/3, \delta_3 = 1/3, \delta_4 = 1\}$ are considered to construct the Lagrange polynomials and to approximate the neuron functions. This element, which has two nodes in the x-direction and four nodes in the y-direction, is useful when the function variation is more pronounced in the y-direction than in the x-direction.

The approximation function obtained is

$$\begin{aligned}
z = &\, 0.562(1-x)(1-y)\left(y-\tfrac{1}{3}\right)\left(y+\tfrac{1}{3}\right) - 0.562 \\
&(x+1)(1-y)\left(y-\tfrac{1}{3}\right)\left(y+\tfrac{1}{3}\right) + 0.312(1-x)(y-1) \\
&(y+1)\left(y+\tfrac{1}{3}\right) - 0.312(x+1)(y-1)(y+1)\left(y+\tfrac{1}{3}\right) - \\
&0.562(1-x)\left(y-\tfrac{1}{3}\right)(y+1)\left(y+\tfrac{1}{3}\right) + 0.563(x+1) \\
&\left(y-\tfrac{1}{3}\right)(y+1)\left(y+\tfrac{1}{3}\right) + 0.312(1-x)(y-1)\left(y-\tfrac{1}{3}\right) \\
&(y+1) - 0.312(x+1)(y-1)\left(y-\tfrac{1}{3}\right)(y+1)
\end{aligned} \quad (14)$$

and the RMSE error obtained is 0.0.

Example 2. In the second example we approximate the function $z = F(x,y) = x\cos(\pi y) + y\sin(\pi x)$ where $(x,y) \in [-1,1] \times [-1,1]$, using the functional network (10). Firstly, we consider $m = 50$ training points to estimate the coefficients of the functional network. The x_i and y_i coordinates of the above data are random values generated in accordance with an uniform distribution in the interval $[-1,1]$. The neuron functions are approximated using the Lagrange polynomials with the Chebyshev nodes $\{\theta_1 = \delta_1 = -0.965926, \theta_2 = \delta_2 = -0.707107, \theta_3 = \delta_3 = -0.258819, \theta_4 = \delta_4 = 0.258819, \theta_5 = \delta_5 = 0.707107, \theta_6 = \delta_6 = 0.965926\}$. The Root Mean Square Error (RMSE) obtained is 0.0103836. Secondly, we consider $m = 100$ training points to estimate the coefficients of the functional network. The neuron functions are approximated using the

Lagrange polynomials with the Chebyshev nodes $\{\theta_1 = \delta_1 = -0.980785, \theta_2 = \delta_2 = -0.831469, \theta_3 = \delta_3 = -0.555570, \theta_4 = \delta_4 = -0.195090, \theta_5 = \delta_5 = 0.195090, \theta_6 = \delta_6 = 0.555570, \theta_7 = \delta_7 = 0.831469, \theta_8 = \delta_8 = 0.980785\}$. The Root Mean Square Error (RMSE) obtained is 0.000270944 (see Figure 3).

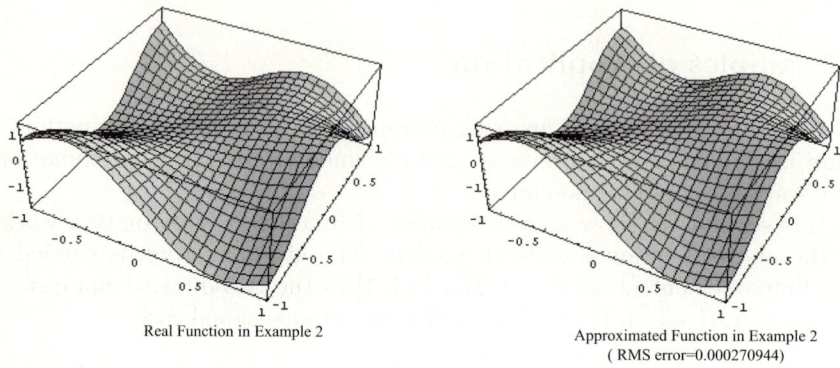

Real Function in Example 2

Approximated Function in Example 2
(RMS error=0.000270944)

Fig. 3. Approximated functions in Example 2

Example 3. In the third example we approximate the function $z = F(x, y) = 0.5\sin(x) + \sin(z)y$ where $(x, y, z) \in [-1, 1] \times [-1, 1] \times [-1, 1]$, using the functional network (13). We consider $m = 70$ training points to estimate the coefficients of the functional network. The x_i, y_i and z_i coordinates of the above data are random values generated in accordance with an uniform distribution in the interval $[-1, 1]$. The neuron functions are approximated using the Lagrange polynomials at the Chebyshev nodal points $\{\theta_1 = \delta_1 = -0.92388, \theta_2 = \delta_2 = -0.382683, \theta_3 = \delta_3 = 0.382683, \theta_4 = \delta_4 = 0.92388\}$. The Root Mean Square Error (RMSE) obtained is 0.000333034.

5 Conclusions

In this paper we show the interpolation mechanism of functional networks, when the neuron functions are approximated as linear combinations of the Lagrange polynomials. We study its application to the approximation of a scalar function defined on a discrete set of points. Applying the least squares criterion we obtain the coefficients of the Lagrange interpolation formula and the element shape functions at the nodal points. One advantage of working with this kind of models is that the learning procedure is based on solving a linear system of equations. Finally, several examples show the effectiveness of the proposed interpolation method.

References

1. Castillo, E.: Functional networks. Neural Processing Letters **7** (1998) 151–159
2. Castillo, E., Cobo, A., Gutiérrez, J.M., Pruneda, R.E.: An introduction to functional networks with applications. Kluwer Academic Publishers (1999)

3. Castillo, E., Cobo, A., Jubete, F., Pruneda, R.E.: Orthogonal sets and polar methods in linear algebra. Applications to matrix calculations, systems of equations and inequalities, and linear programming. John Wiley, New York (1999)
4. Davis, P.J.: Interpolation & approximation. Dover Publications, Inc. (1975)
5. Hughes, T.J.R.: The Finite Element Method: Linear static and dynamic finite element analysis. John Wiley & Sons (1987)
6. Ottosen, N., Petersson H.: Introduction to the finite element method. Prentice Hall (1992)
7. Thompson, E.G.: Introduction to the finite element method. John Wiley & Sons (2005)

The Evolution of OSI Network Management by Integrated the Expert Knowledge

Antonio Martín, Carlos León, and Iñigo Monedero

Escuela Superior de Ingeniería Informática, Universidad de Sevilla,
Avda. Reina Mercedes, 41012 Sevilla, Spain
{toni, cleon, imonedero}@us.es
http://www.dte.us.es

Abstract. The management of modern telecommunications networks must satisfy ever-increasing operational demands. Operation and quality service requirements imposed by the users are also an important aspect to consider. In this paper we have carried out a study for the improvement of intelligent administration techniques in telecommunications networks. This task is achieved by integrating knowledge base of expert system within the management information used to manage a network. For this purpose, an extension of OSI management framework specifications language has been added and investigated in this study. A new property named RULE has also been added, which gathers important aspects of the facts and the knowledge base of the embedded expert system. Networks can be managed easily by using this proposed integration.

1 Introduction

Current communications networks support a large demand of services for which the traditional model of network management is inadequate. It is thus necessary to develop new models, which offer more possibilities. These models are called *Integrated Management Expert Systems*.

We propose a new technique which integrates the Expert System completely within the Management Information Base (MIB) [1]. The expert rules that make up the Knowledge Base are joined to the management objects definitions that belong to the network. These definitions integrate the specifications of management objects representing the network resource and the management expert rules which allow for the intelligent control and administration of the resources represented. In this document we explain the main aspects of this proposal. To achieve this we have used the OSI network management model and the Guidelines for the Definition of Managed Objects, GDMO (ISO/IEC 10165-4 (ITU X.722)) [2].

We present an extension of the standard GDMO, to accommodate the intelligent management requirements. We describe how to achieve this goal using a new extension called GDMO+. This extension presents a new element RULE, which defines the knowledge base of the management expert system.

2 GDMO and Expert Management

Information architecture is based on an object-oriented approach and the agent/manager concepts that are of paramount importance in the open system interconnection (OSI) systems management [3]. The denominated Managed Objects have an important role in the normalization. A managed object is the OSI abstract view of a logical or physical system resource to be managed. These special elements provide the necessary operations for the administration, monitoring and control of the telecommunications network. The managed objects are defined according to the International Standardization Organization (ISO) Guidelines for the Definition of Managed Objects (GDMO), which defines how network objects and their behavior are to be specified, including the syntax and semantics [4].

Within the OSI (Open Systems Interconnection) management framework [5], the specification language GDMO (Guidelines for the Definition of Managed Objects) has been established as a means to describe logical or physical resources from a management point of view. GDMO has been standardized by ITU (International Telecommunication Union) in ITU-T X.722 and is now widely used to specify interfaces between different components of the TMN (Telecommunication Management Network) architecture [6].

GDMO is organized into templates, which are standard formats used in the definition of a particular aspect of the object. A complete object definition is a combination of interrelated templates. There are nine of these templates: class of managed objects, package, attribute, group of attributes, action, notification, parameter, connection of name and behavior.

3 Extension of the GDMO Standard

The elements that at the moment form the GDMO standard do not make a reference to the knowledge base of an expert system. To answer these questions, it will be necessary to make changes on the template of the GDMO standard.

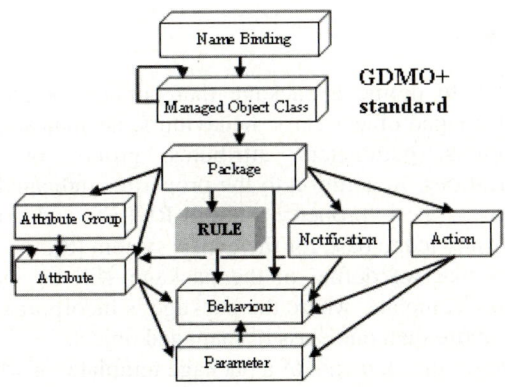

Fig. 1. Relations between proposed standard Templates

Specifically, by means of a new item named RULE. This template groups the knowledge base supplied by an expert in a specific management dominion. It allows the storage of the management knowledge in the definition of the resources that form the system to be managed [7], Fig.1.

The standard we propose contains the singular template RULE and its relations to other templates. Two relationships are essential for the inclusion of knowledge in the component definition of the network: Managed Object Class and Package Template. In the standard we propose, both templates have the new property RULES. Let us study both relationships.

3.1 Template for Management of Object Classes

This template is used to define the different kinds of objects that exist in the system. The definition of a managed Object Class is made uniformly in the standard template, eliminating the confusion that may result when different persons define objects of different forms. This way we ensure that the classes and the management expert rules defined in system A can be easily interpreted in system B.

```
<class-label> MANAGED OBJECT CLASS
    [DERIVED FROM  <class-label>  [,<class-label>]*;]
    [CHARACTERIZED BY <package-label> [,<package-label]*;]              (1)
    [CONDITIONAL PACKAGES
         <package-label>  PRESENT IF condition;
         ,<package-label>] PRESENT IF condition]*;]
    REGISTERED AS object-identifier;
```

DERIVED FROM plays a very important role, when determining the relations of inheritance which makes it possible to reutilize specific characteristics in other classes of managed objects. In addition, a great advantage is the reusability of the object classes and therefore of the expert rules which are defined.

This also template can contain packages and conditional packages, including the clauses CHARACTERIZED BY and CONDITIONAL PACKAGES.

3.2 Package Template

This template is used to define a package that contains a combination of many characteristics of a managed object class: behaviours, attributes, groups of attributes, operations, notifications, parameters, attributes, groups of attributes, actions, behaviour and notifications. In addition to the properties indicated above, we suggest the incorporation of a new property called RULES, which contains all the specifications of the knowledge base for the expert system [8].

All the properties that we define in the package will be included later in the Managed Object Class Template, where the package is incorporated. A same package can be referenced by more than one class of managed objects.

Next definition shows the elements of a package template, in which it is possible to observe the new property RULES.

```
<package-label> PACKAGE
    [BEHAVIOUR <behaviour-label> [,<behaviour-label>]*;]
    [ATTRIBUTES <attribute-label> propertylist [,<parameter-label>]*
        [,<attribute-label> propertylist [,<parameter-label>]*]*;]
    [ATTRIBUTE GROUPS   <group-label> [<attribute-label>]*
            [<group-label> [<attribute-label>]*]* ;]
    [ACTIONS <action-label> [<parameter-label>]*
            [<action-label> [<parameter-label>]*]* ;
    [NOTIFICATIONS <notification-label> [<parameter-label>]*
        [<notification-label> [<parameter-label>]*]* ;]
    [RULES    <rule-label>   [,<rule-label>]*;]
REGISTERED AS object-identifier;
```
(2)

The property RULES allows a treatment similar to the other properties, including the possibility of inheritance of rules between classes. Like the rest of the other properties defined in a package, the property RULES need a corresponding associated template.

4 Expert Rule Template

This template permits the normalised definition of the specifications of the expert rule to which it is related. This template allows a particular managed object class to have properties that provide a normalised knowledge of a management dominion. The structure of the RULE template is shown here:

```
<rule-label> RULE
    [PRIORITY    <priority> ;]
    [BEHAVIOUR   <behaviour-label> [,<behaviour-label>]*;]
    [IF     occurred-event-pattern [,occurred-event-pattern]*]
    [THEN   sentence [, sentence]* ;]
  REGISTERED AS object-identifier;
```
(3)

The first element in a template definition is headed. It consists of two sections:

- <rule-label>: This is the name of the management expert rule. Rule definitions must have a unique characterizing name.
- RULE: A key word indicates the type of template, in our case a definition template and the specifications for the management expert rule.

After the head, the following elements compose a normalised definition of an expert rule.

- BEHAVIOUR: This construct is used to extend the semantics of previously defined templates. It describes the behaviour of the rule. This element is common to the others templates of the GDMO standard.
- PRIORITY: This represents the priority of the rule, that is, the order in which competing rules will be executed.

- IF: It contains all the events that must be true to activate a rule. Those events must be defined in the Notification template. The occurrence of these events is necessary for the activation of the rule and the execution of their associated actions. We can add a logical condition that will be applied on the events occurred or their parameters.
- THEN: This gives details of the operations performed when the rule is executed. Those operations must be previously defined in the Action template. These are actions and diagnoses that the management platform makes as an answer to network events occurred.
- REGISTERED AS is an object-identifier: A clause identifies the location of the expert rule on the ISO Registration Tree. The identifier is compulsory.

5 Application of the GDMO+ Standard System Network Management

This section present a tool based on the proposed GDMO+ standard, which helps administrators in expert network management. Our tool understands transceivers and multiplex equipment. We will describe the basic structure and concepts of our software, especially of the knowledge base. Related work is briefly discussed in the next section.

5.1 Related Work

In this section we present a rule-based expert system applied to error diagnosis in the communications system of SEVILLANA-ENDESA (a major Spanish power utility). Part of SEVILLANA-ENDESA's long-distance traffic is controlled by a wireless system distributed throughout the Endesa network. Expert systems are part of the system dedicated to the management of a power utility's communications system, which we call NOMOS [9]. NOMOS is implemented in Brightware's

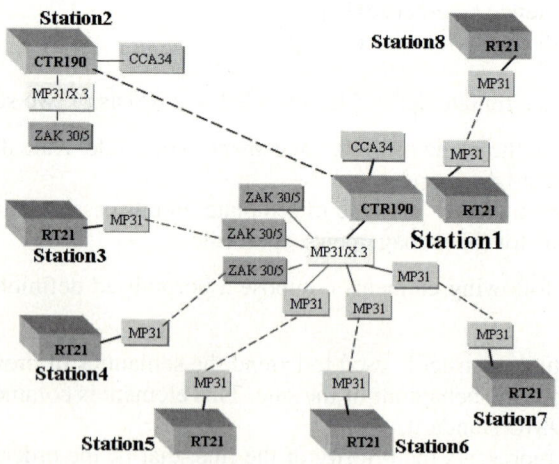

Fig. 2. Power Company Network

ART*Enterprise. ART*Enterprise is a set of programming paradigms and tools that are focused on the development of efficient, flexible, and commercially deployable knowledge-based systems. NOMOS+ is an extension for intelligent decision-making and diagnostic reasoning controlled by its own integrated expert system. NOMOS+ is the first production software written and integrated in GDMO+.

The knowledge base is included within the specifications of the managed resources, following the proposed prescriptions in standard GDMO+. These new specifications contain management information of managed resources and include also the set of expert rules that provides the knowledge base of the expert system, Fig.2.

5.2 Implementation

Our tool has three major components: a knowledge base, an inference engine and a user interface [10]. This structure is typical for expert systems. Those elements are briefly discussed in the following:

The knowledge base: The core of the system, this is a collection of facts and if-then production rules that represent stored knowledge about the problem domain. The knowledge base of our system is a collection of expert rules and facts expressed in the ARTScript programming language ART*Enterprise.

The knowledge base contains both static and dynamic information and knowledge about different network resources and common failures. The knowledge base of our system can be extended by adding new higher level rules and facts. To this purpose we can employ user interface.

The inference engine: This is the processing unit that solves any given problems by making logical inferences on the given facts and rules stored in the knowledge base. In our tool we used the ART*Enterprise. By using an existing general purpose tool we were able to build a standard and extensible platform with proven performance and quality.

The user interface: This controls the inference engine and manages system input and output. The user interface of our tool contains a preprocessor for parsing GDMO+ specification files, a set of input and output handling routines, and a simple command prompt interface for managing the system. Also, the user interface components allow administrators to inspect the definitions of management object classes interactively, this allows to modify or include new experts management rules in the managed objects definition.

The prototype has a preprocessor module. A previous phase to the inference is realized by a unit processor-translator, which processes the file that contains the GDMO+ specifications and extracts the normalized knowledge from the expert system. Two exits are obtained: a file with management expert rules and another file with GDMO definitions of the managed object classes. The preprocessor also translates the expert rules into a valid syntax for the programming language of inference engine. Procedures are coded in ART*Enterprise's ARTScript language, a dynamic interpreted language similar in syntax to LISP, Fig. 3.

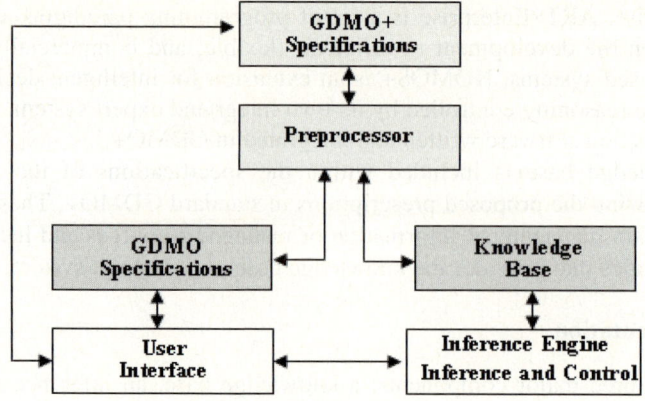

Fig. 3. Elements of the prototype NOMOS+

5.3 Final Prototype Verification

The purpose is to achieve a functionally correct prototype. To verify the system we feed it with an alarms arbitrary amount. The result of this proof are including in Table 1.

Table1. Prototype Testing Results

Alarms Initial Number	Number After Filtration	Filtered Alarms	Fired Rules	Preceding time	Rules/Sec.	Indications to the Operator
100	1	99	51	0,118 Sec.	432,2034	1
200	10	95	102	0,412 Sec.	247,5728	6
300	31	89,6	155	1,250 Sec.	124,0000	20
400	31	92,25	201	1,438 Sec.	139,7775	16
500	32	93,6	254	2,975 Sec.	85,3782	19
600	38	93,66	293	5,249 Sec.	55,8202	16
700	44	93,71	346	17,982 Sec.	19,2415	18
800	55	93,125	394	26,938 Sec.	14,6262	23

From these result we can establish the following conclusions:

- Filtration process effectiveness is very high: almost 90% of the whole. This has the advantage of a decreasing percentage in the amount of indications presented to the operator.
- The speed of the system improves diminishing the number of alarms on which the rest of rules act.

6 Conclusions

Current networks are very complex and demand ever-increasing levels of quality, making their management a very important aspect to take into account. The traditional model of network administration has certain deficiencies that we have tried to overcome by using a model of intelligent integrated management. To improve the techniques of expert management in a communications network, we propose the possibility of integrating and normalising the expert rules of management within the actual definition of the managed objects. Through the integration of the knowledge within the new extension of the GDMO standard, we can simultaneously define the management information and knowledge.

Thus, the management platform is more easily integrated and allows a better adaptation for the network management. We conclude pointing out an important aspect of the obtained integration: by using only and exclusively the extended GDMO specification, the administration platform will be able to obtain the management necessary information with respect to the managed objects as well as the expert rules of management that make up the knowledge base of the expert system.

References

1. Morris, Stephen B.: Network Management, MIBs and MPLS: Principles, Design and Implementation By Publisher: Addison Wesley (2003).
2. 2. CCITT X. 722 / ISO 10165-4 ISO, Structure of management information. Part 1: Guidelines for the definition of managed objects.
3. Black, U.D.: Network Management Standards. McGraw Hill (1995).
4. Hebrawi, B.: GDMO, Object modeling and definition for network management. Technology appraisals (1995)
5. ITU-T Recommendation X.700, Management Framework for Open Systems Interconnection (OSI). CCITT Applications (1992).
6. ITU-T Rec. M.3010, Principles for a Telecommunications Management Network (TMN). Study Group IV (1996).
7. Stallings, William.: SNMP, SNMPv2, and CMIP: the practical guide to network. Publication Reading, Mass. [etc.] Addison-Wesley, (2000).
8. Garcia, R.C.; Cannady, J.: Boundary expansion of expert systems: incorporating evolutionary computation with intrusion detection solutions. SoutheastCon 2001. Proceedings. IEEE, (2001) 96-99.
9. Leon, Carlos. Mejias, Manuel. Luque, Joaquin. Gonzalo, Fernando: Expert System for the Integrated Management of a Power Utility's Communication System. IEEE Trans on Power Delivery, Vol. 14, No. 4, Octubre, (1999), pp 1208-1212
10. Joseph C. Giarratano, Gary D. Riley.: Expert Systems: Principles and Programming. Book, Brooks/Cole Publishing Co. (2005).

Learning the Complete-Basis-Functions Parameterization for the Optimization of Dynamic Molecular Alignment by ES

Ofer M. Shir[1], Joost N. Kok[1], Thomas Bäck[1,*], and Marc J.J. Vrakking[2]

[1] Natural Computing Group
Leiden University
Niels Bohrweg 1, 2333 CA Leiden
The Netherlands
[2] Amolf-FOM, Institute for Atomic and Molecular Physics
Kruislaan 407, 1098 SJ Amsterdam
The Netherlands

Abstract. This study further investigates the *complete-basis-functions parameterization method* (CBFP) for Evolution Strategies (ES), and its application to a challenging real-life high-dimensional *physics* optimization problem, namely *Femtosecond Laser Pulse Shaping*.

The CBFP method, which was introduced recently for tackling efficiently the learning task of n-variables functions, is combined here, for the first time, with *niching techniques*, and shown to boost the learning process of the given laser problem, and to yield satisfying multiple optima.

Moreover, a technique for learning the basis-functions and improving this method is outlined.

1 Introduction

Traditionally, the advancement of physical understanding through experimental research involves the definition of controlled experiments where a problem of interest is studied as a function of one or more relevant experimental parameters, and where the outcome of the experiment then provides insight into the specific role of these parameters. This approach dates back all the way to the days of Galileo, who, in a famous series of experiments, measured how far a ball rolls down a gradient as a function of the parameter time, and concluded that the distance traveled by the ball is proportional to the square of the time. This approach has led to an enormous wealth of accumulated knowledge. However, it fails when the number of parameters relevant to the problem of interest becomes very large. These days more and more of these situations are encountered. In problems in physics that depend on a large number of parameters, great advances can be made using a new approach based on evolutionary algorithms. The large number of parameters limits the usefulness of experiments where only some of

---

* NuTech Solutions, Martin-Schmeisser-Weg 15, 44227 Dortmund, Germany.

these parameters are varied in a prescribed manner. An evolutionary approach is a viable alternative in many of these situations. In this approach the system of interest is studied within a closed loop strategy, where in each iteration the set of system parameters is modified to some extent by means of specialized mutation and recombination operators. After doing an actual experiment on the system with these parameters, the best performing values for achieving a given objective are selected for the next round. The key advantage of this iterative evolutionary optimization approach is that one does not need to know a priori the details of the working mechanism of the complex system. Instead, the goal is to learn about the underlying physics by interpreting the sets of parameters produced by the evolutionary algorithm. This is in contrast to performing experiments with controlled variations (i.e., knowledge-based or trial-and-error-based variations by human experts) of these parameters.

The advent of modern **laser pulse shaping** techniques in the *femtosecond* regime has made it possible to control the motion of nuclei and even electrons by a judicious choice of the pulses shapes. The application to *dynamic molecular alignment* (see, e.g., [1]) is of considerable interest in this context because of its many practical consequences: a multitude of chemical and physical processes ranging from bimolecular reactions [2] to high harmonic generation [3] are influenced by the angular distribution of the molecular sample. Furthermore, in many fundamental molecular dissociation or ionization experiments the interpretation of the collected data becomes much easier when the molecules are known to be aligned with respect to a certain axis. Hence, techniques to generate molecular alignment are much needed.

This study further investigates the *complete-basis-functions parameterization* (CBFP) method [4] for Evolution Strategies (ES) [5] and its application to this real-world challenging problem of *laser pulse shaping*. The CBFP method, which was introduced recently for learning efficiently n-variables functions, with emphasis on the speeding-up of convergence, is combined here, for the first time, with *niching techniques* [6], and shown to boost the learning process of the given laser problem. The speeding-up effect is important for an evolutionary loop with an **experimental laser in the laboratory** [7], where the fast computation is needed. Thus the main motivation for the combination of techniques is boosting the convergence velocity in the numerical domain as a preparation for the optimization in the experimental domain. Furthermore, a technique for learning the basis-functions and improving this method is outlined.

The remainder of the paper is organized as follows. Section 2 presents briefly the physics problem, namely *femtosecond laser pulse shaping*. Section 3 introduces the algorithms used. In section 4 we briefly present our modus operandi for applying niching combined with the parameterization method. This is followed by the description of the experimental setup and the numerical results. In section 5 we draw conclusions and outline how to proceed further with this research.

2 The Problem: Laser Pulse Shaping

The goal of this study is to optimize the *alignment* of an ensemble of molecules after the interaction with a shaped laser pulse. By applying a self-learning loop using an evolutionary mechanism, the interaction between the system under study and the laser field can be steered, and optimal pulse shapes for a given optimization target can be found. In our work, the role of the experimental feedback in the self-learning loop is played by a **numerical simulation** [8].

To calculate the time-dependent alignment, the Schrödinger's equation for the angular degrees of freedom of a model diatomic molecule under the influence of the shaped laser field is solved. Explicitly, the time-dependent profile of the pulse, which completely determines the dynamics after the transition to the rotating frame has been performed, is described by:

$$E(t) = \int_{-\infty}^{\infty} A(\omega) \exp(i\phi(\omega)) \exp(i\omega t) \, d\omega, \tag{1}$$

where $A(\omega)$ is a Gaussian window function describing the contribution of different frequencies to the pulse and $\phi(\omega)$, the *phase function*, equips these frequencies, which are equally distributed across the spectrum of the pulse, with different complex phases. Hence, by changing $\phi(\omega)$, the temporal structure of $E(t)$ can be altered. In a real life pulse shaping experiment, $A(\omega)$ is fixed and $\phi(\omega)$ is used to control the shape of the pulses. We have used the same approach in our numerical simulations, i.e. **the search space is in the frequency domain while the fitness evaluation is performed in the time domain**.

The alignment's quantity, i.e. the success-rate or fitness, is defined as the expectation value of the *cosine-squared* of the angle of the molecular axis with respect to the laser polarization axis. Moreover, since a high degree of alignment with a peak intensity as low as possible was the desired result, an additional constraint was introduced as a *punishment term* for pulses that are too intense. Explicitly, we have used

$$I_p = \int_0^T E^2(t) \cdot \Theta\left(E^2(t) - I_{thr}\right) \, dt \tag{2}$$

where $\Theta(x)$ is the *Heaviside step function*. Hence, the fitness function, i.e. the objective value, assigned to a pulse shape is given by

$$F = \max_{E(t)=0} \left\langle \cos^2(\theta) \right\rangle - \lambda I_p. \tag{3}$$

By choosing λ large enough, I_{thr} can be used to effectively operate the evolutionary algorithms only on a subset of pulses whose maximum peak intensity approaches the threshold intensity from below.

A typical phase function and a typical laser pulse, obtained by an evolutionary optimization, are given for illustration as Fig. 1 and Fig. 2, respectively.

It should be noted that this *laser pulse shaping problem*, based on numerical simulations, has been already tackled at several levels [4] [9] [10].

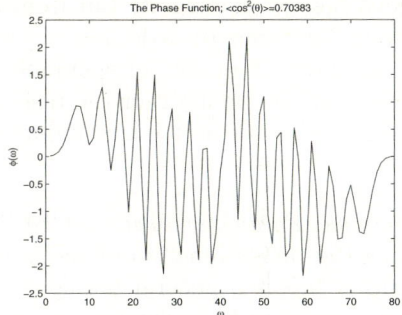

Fig. 1. A phase function obtained by an evolutionary search (frequency domain)

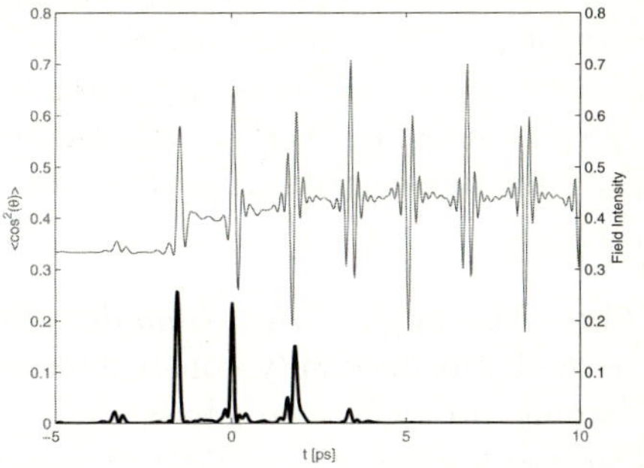

Fig. 2. Given the phase function - thin red line: alignment; thick black line: intensity of the laser pulse (time domain)

3 Algorithms

We provide here a short review of the algorithms used.

3.1 The Covariance Matrix Adaptation Evolution Strategies

The *covariance matrix adaptation evolution strategy* [11], is a variant of ES that has been successful for treating correlations among object variables. This method tackles the critical element of Evolution Strategies, the adaptation of the mutation parameters. We provide here a short description of the principal elements of the $(1, \lambda)$-CMA-ES.

The fundamental property of this method is the exploitation of information obtained from previous successful mutation operations. Given an initial search point x^0, λ offspring are sampled from it by applying the mutation operator. The best search point out of those λ offspring is chosen to become the parent of the next generation. The action of the *mutation operator* for generating the λ samples of search points in generation $g + 1$ is defined as follows:

$$x^{g+1} \sim \mathcal{N}\left(x_k^{(g)}, \sigma^{(g)^2} \mathbf{C}^{(g)}\right), \qquad k = 1, ..., \lambda \qquad (4)$$

where $\mathcal{N}(m, \mathbf{C})$ denotes a normally distributed random vector with mean m and covariance matrix $\mathbf{C}$. The matrix $\mathbf{C}$, the crucial element of this process, is initialized as the *unity matrix* and is learned during the course of evolution, based on cumulative information of successful mutations (the so-called *evolution path*). The global step size, $\sigma^{(g)}$, is based on information from the *principal component analysis* of $\mathbf{C}^{(g)}$ (the so-called *"conjugate" evolution path*). We omit most of the details and refer the reader to Hansen and Ostermeier [11].

3.2 The Complete-Basis-Functions Parameterization Method

Motivation. An infinite series of *complete basis functions* converges to any "reasonably well behaving" function. It is straightforward to approximate a given function with a finite series of those functions, i.e. by cutting its tail from a certain point. In principle, the sum can always be found to a desired degree of accuracy by adding up enough terms of the series. The idea of spanning a function using a set of complete basis-functions can also be used for the task of learning an n-variables function, and in particular when its profile is unknown a priori.

The Method. The *Complete-Basis-Functions Parameterization* (CBFP) method was originally constructed for learning the target function of the laser shaping problem (the phase $\phi(\omega)$), but is nevertheless a general method for learning a generic n-variables function [4]. The idea is to learn the target function by means of the coefficients of a complete set of functions which will span it, rather than learning function values to be interpolated. Assuming that the desired discretization of the target function is up to a resolution of N points in the interval, the number of elements in the expansion series is then limited to n, where preferably $n \ll N$. By that the method obtains a dramatic dimensionality reduction of the search space, aiming to achieve a speeding-up of the convergence. An evolutionary search is eventually applied to the n coefficients of the building functions, where a simple transformation is done for every fitness evaluation.

3.3 Dynamic Niching with Covariance Matrix Adaptation ES

The *dynamic niching with CMA-ES* algorithm [12] is a niching method which uses the Covariance Matrix Adaptation ES as its core evolutionary mechanism. The aim of this approach is to find multiple local optima simultaneously, within one run of the ES. Given q, the estimated/expected number of peaks, $q + p$ "CMA-sets" are initialized, where a CMA-set is defined as the collection of all the dynamic variables of the CMA algorithm which uniquely define the search at a given point of time. Such dynamic variables are the current search point, the covariance matrix, the step size, as well as other auxiliary parameters. At every point in time the algorithm stores exactly $q + p$ CMA-sets, which are associated with $q + p$ search points: q for the peaks and p for the "non-peaks domain". The $(q+1)^{th}...(q+p)^{th}$ CMA-sets are individuals which are randomly re-generated in every generation as potential candidates for niche formation. Until stopping criteria are met, the following procedure takes place. Each search point samples λ offspring, based on its evolving CMA-set. After the fitness evaluation of the new $\lambda \cdot (q+p)$ individuals, the classification into niches of the entire population is done using the DPI algorithm, and the peaks become the new search points. Their CMA-sets are inherited from their parents and updated according to the CMA method.

4 Applying Niching with CBFP to Laser Pulse Shaping

Background. As introduced earlier, the phase function $\phi(\omega)$ is the target function to be calibrated. To this end, we interpolated $\phi(\omega)$ at N frequencies $\{\omega_i\}_{i=1}^N$;

the N values $\{\phi(\omega_i)\}_{i=1}^{N}$ are our decision parameters to be optimized. In order to achieve a good trade-off between high resolution and optimization efficiency, the value of $N = 80$ turned to be a good compromise.

We define this calibration of $\phi(\omega)$, i.e. learning $N = 80$ function values and interpolating, as the so-called *'plain-parameterization'* optimization.

The *CBFP* method as well as the *dynamic niching with CMA-ES* were both successfully applied to this *molecular alignment problem*, however separately:

1. The *CBFP* was applied to the problem using $n = 40$ components of various sets of complete-basis-functions. The best parameterization for the problem was the *Hermite polynomials*. Overall, the method achieved a significant speeding-up of the convergence process of the given problem; the obtained solutions were at least as good as any other solutions known to us, but were achieved faster. For more details see [4].
2. Dynamic niching with CMA-ES was applied successfully to this molecular alignment problem. The distance metric had to be chosen carefully, due to some invariance properties of the Fourier transformation, but in total the obtained pulses in the *time domain* had indeed different characteristics, and in particular their shapes differed in a satisfying manner. Moreover, the obtained alignment values **for all niches** were as good as the other good solutions known to us. For more details we refer the reader to [9].

Modus Operandi. In this study we combine the two methods, and compare niching with plain parameterization versus niching with Hermite parameterization on a variant of the molecular alignment problem. This variant is a simplified version of the original problem, which considers only the ground rotational level ($J = 0$) at temperature $T = 0$ in the initial distribution, rather than the range of initial rotational levels at a finite temperature. This version reduces the duration of a single function evaluation from $35sec$ to $7sec$ (on an HT Pentium-4 2.6GHz), and thus allows us to run more experiments. This is the first time that we perform experiments on this variant, and hence we lack a reference for numerical comparison.

The regime of good solutions begins with alignment values of 0.93.

Preliminary Runs. In order to test this variant of the alignment problem, we constructed a series of runs to compare the plain parameterization versus the Hermite parameterization, based on the CMA-ES mechanism as before, with a $(1,10)$ strategy. Each run was limited to 5000 function evaluations. The numerical results are consistent with those obtained for the original problem at [4],

Table 1. Parameterizations: Performance Results

Parameterization	Averaged Best-Fitness	Evaluations for 0.93
Plain-Param	0.9303 ± 0.07	2346.0 ± 175.3
Hermite	0.9375 ± 0.02	1692.8 ± 180.3

i.e. the Hermite parameterization has faster convergence, and yields on average higher alignment values.

The results, averaged over 20 runs, are given in table 1, where the number of function evaluations required to cross the threshold of the 0.93 regime is specified.

Applying Niching: Numerical Results. The chosen niching strategy is similar to [9] - the aim is for $q = 3$ niches, with a $(1,10)$-CMA mechanism for each niche. The distance metric for the plain parameterization is the Euclidean distance at the second derivative space of the phase function, whereas it is the Euclidean distance at the decision space (coefficients space) for the Hermite parameterization. Each run was limited to 15000 function evaluations (5000 evaluations per niche). The numerical results, averaged over 10 runs, are summarized in table 2.

The results of our experiments will be discussed at several levels:

1. We can conclude from the numerical results that the Hermite parameterization speeds up the convergence also when applied under niching. It seems to get punishment values at first (Eq. 2), but afterwords it speed-up and crosses the 0.93 threshold faster. A comparison between 2 typical runs of the 2 parameterizations is given as Fig. 3.

    Moreover, the Hermite parameterization also obtains on average higher alignment (fitness) values.

2. The CMA niching method achieved the highest alignment value known to us, i.e. the value of 0.9486 (The revival structure of this best solution is given as Fig. 4). For both parameterizations, the 2nd and 3rd niches also obtained good results, usually very close to the result of the 1st niche. A plot of the best run with respect to alignment values for the Hermite parameterization is given as Fig. 5.

3. Our definition of the distance metric for this problem has been shown to be successful also for the Hermite parameterization (it was already shown to work for the plain parameterization at [9], but was not at all guaranteed to work for a different parameterization). The obtained pulses in the time domain had indeed different characteristics for both parameterizations, and in particular their shapes differed in a satisfying manner. An illustrative example of the diversity of the optima for the Hermite parameterization is given as Fig. 6.

Table 2. Niching with Parameterizations: Performance Results for Best Niche

Parameterization	Averaged Best-Fitness	Evaluations for 0.93
Plain-Param	0.9318 ± 0.11	2120.0 ± 226.1
Hermite	0.9391 ± 0.09	1777.5 ± 122.0

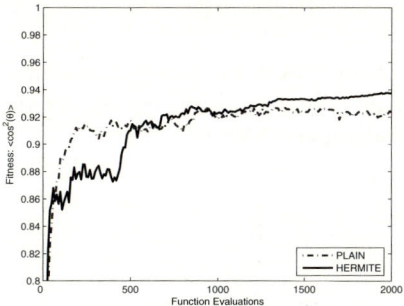
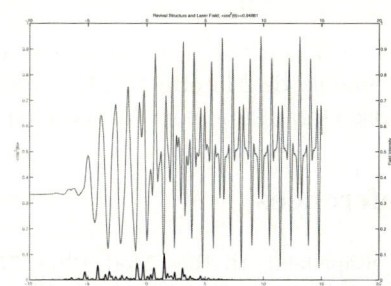

Fig. 3. Typical convergence process: Hermite-param gets punished at first, but then overtakes and reaches 0.93 faster

Fig. 4. Revival structure of the best solution obtained by the Hermite parameterization

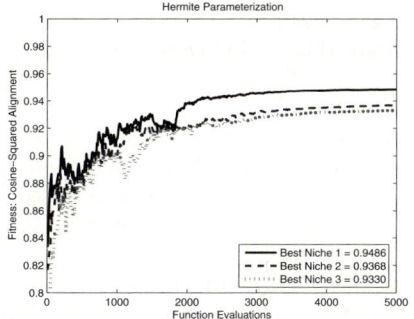
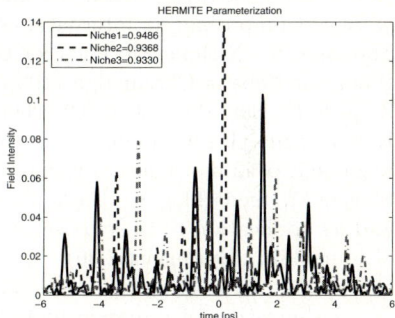

Fig. 5. Typical evolution process of the Hermite parameterization of the 3 niches

Fig. 6. Hermite-Param: Best run with pulses in the time domain of the 3 niches: clear diversity

5 Conclusions and Outlook

We have introduced a simplified variant of the laser pulse shaping problem, and presented a combination of modern evolutionary approaches to this problem of molecular alignment. Given two parameterizations of the problem, we have applied a *niching* technique, which obtained highly-fit optima with high diversity among them. The Hermite parameterization managed to boost the convergence process within the niches, in consistency with previous results.

We would like to propose a future direction for this study - learning the basis functions. The idea is to consider adaptive building blocks, rather than fixed, as in the CBFP method. By applying evolutionary optimization to the internal parameters of the functions, their profile can be tuned to parameterize better the original search space of the problem. The decision parameters are the coefficients of those functions, as well as their characteristic parameters.

Acknowledgments

This work is part of the research programme of the 'Stichting voor Fundamenteel Onderzoek de Materie (FOM)', which is financially supported by the 'Nederlandse Organisatie voor Wetenschappelijk Onderzoek (NWO)'.

References

1. Stapelfeldt, H. Rev. Mod. Phys. **75** (2003)
2. Friedrich, B., Herschbach, D. Phys. Chem. Chem. Phys. **2** (2000)
3. Hay, N. Phys. Rev. **A 65** (2000)
4. Shir, O.M., Siedschlag, C., Bäck, T., Vrakking, M.J.: The complete-basis-functions parameterization in es and its application to laser pulse shaping. In: Proceedings of the Genetic and Evolutionary Computation Conference. (2006)
5. Beyer, H.G., Schwefel, H.P.: Evolution strategies a comprehensive introduction. Natural Computing: an international journal **1** (2002)
6. Mahfoud, S.: Niching Methods for Genetic Algorithms. PhD thesis, University of Illinois at Urbana Champaign (1995)
7. Zamith, S. Eur. Phys. J. D **12** (2000)
8. Rosca-Pruna, F., Vrakking, M.: Revival structures in picosecond laser-induced alignment of i2 molecules. Journal of Chemical Physics **116** (2002) 6579–6588
9. Shir, O.M., Siedschlag, C., Bäck, T., Vrakking, M.J.: Niching in evolution strategies and its application to laser pulse shaping. In: Lecture Notes in Computer Science. Volume 3871., Springer (2006)
10. Shir, O.M., Siedschlag, C., Bäck, T., Vrakking, M.J.: Evolutionary algorithms in the optimization of dynamic molecular alignment. In: Proceedings of the 2006 Congress on Evolutionary Computation. (2006)
11. Hansen, N., Ostermeier, A.: Completely derandomized self-adaptation in evolution strategies. Evolutionary Computation **9** (2001)
12. Shir, O.M., Bäck, T.: Dynamic niching in evolution strategies with covariance matrix adaptation. In: Proceedings of the 2005 Congress on Evolutionary Computation CEC-2005, Piscataway, NJ, USA, IEEE Press (2005)

Multi Criteria Wrapper Improvements to Naive Bayes Learning

José Carlos Cortizo[1,2] and Ignacio Giraldez[2]

[1] Artificial Intelligence and Network Solutions S.L.
jccp@ainetsolutions.com
http://www.ainetsolutions.com/jccp
[2] Universidad Europea de Madrid
Villaviciosa de Odón, 28670 Madrid, Spain
{josecarlos.cortizo, ignacio.giraldez}@uem.es

Abstract. Feature subset selection using a wrapper means to perform a search for an optimal set of attributes using the Machine Learning Algorithm as a black box. The Naive Bayes Classifier is based on the assumption of independence among the values of the attributes given the class value. Consequently, its effectiveness may decrease when the attributes are interdependent. We present FBL, a wrapper that uses information about dependencies to guide the search for the optimal subset of features and we use the Naive Bayes Classifier as the black-box Machine Learning algorithm. Experimental results show that FBL allows the Naive Bayes Classifier to achieve greater accuracies, and that FBL performs better than other classical filters and wrappers.

Keywords: Naive Bayes, (In)Dependent Attributes, Wrapper, Feature Subset Selection, Machine Learning, Data Analysis, Data Mining.

1 Introduction and Motivation

Machine Learning algorithms try to learn from experience, usually coded as a set of training instances defined as a set of attribute-value pairs. As a general rule, the algorithms' classification accuracy depends on the attributes and values given to those attributes, and it degrades in performance when faced with many features that are not neccesary for predicting the desired output ([11]).

Work in feature subset selection can be summarized in two main trends: the *filter model* and the *wrapper model*. In the *filter model* (e.g. [9], [1], [7]) the features are filtered according to a certain metric but independent of the Machine Learning algorithm. In the *wrapper model* ([8]), the feature subset selection algorithm uses the classification algorithm as a part of the evaluation function.

The Naive Bayes Classifier provides the most probable target value $v_m \in V$ for a new instance according to the concrete values of the attributes on the instance $(a_1, a_2 \ldots a_n)$. The most probable target value is

$$v_m = argmax_{v_j \in V} P(v_j | a_1, a_2 \ldots a_n) \tag{1}$$

This expression is rewritten using the Bayes Theorem and ignoring the common denominator:

$$v_m = argmax_{v_j \in V} P(a_1, a_2 \ldots a_n | v_j) P(v_j) \quad (2)$$

In Equation 2 is easy to estimate $P(v_j)$ because it represents the a priori probability of the value v_j of the class and can be obtained dividing the number of instances belonging to that category by the total number of instances. Estimating $P(a_1, a_2 \ldots a_n | v_j)$ is not so simple, but assuming independence among the attribute values given the class value (v_j), the the probability $P(a_1, a_2 \ldots a_n | v_j)$ can be factorized as the product $P(a_1|v_j) \ldots P(a_n|v_j)$. Replacing this into Equation 2, we obtain the Naive Bayes Classifier [10]

$$v_m = argmax_{v_j \in V} P(v_j) \prod P(a_i | v_j) \quad (3)$$

To obtain the Naive Bayes Classifier, we must assume independence among the attributes values. Our goal, as in [3], is to *modify the Naive Bayes Classifier to obtain an extended-Naive Bayes algorithm robust to attribute dependencies*. As [13] or [16], we propose a wrapper (FBL) to improve Naive Bayes, where the evaluation function is the accuracy obtained by the Naive Bayes. But where [13] and [16] performed a greedy search, we propose a search guided by the information about the dependencies among attributes. As starting point, we have used linear regression [5] (as a first kind of dependency for guiding the search), which is a classical statistical solution to the problem of determining the relationship between two random variables X and Y (or even more than two random variables). We can extend the behaviour of the system adding other kind of dependencies.

In section 2 we present FBL, a strength-of-dependency based wrapper for attribute selection. Section 3 explains the experiments made for testing the FBL algorithm and the comparisons to other attribute selection methods. In section 4 we discuss the results and present our conclusions.

2 FBL Algorithm

We propose a method to improve the Naive Bayes Classifier based on a previous filtering of the attributes used for representing the data (the additional flow required by FBL to classify instances is represented in Figure 1). It filters out the dependent attributes of a given dataset, as a result, the set of attributes used to represent the data is modified. Then it transforms the original data set so it complies with the new representation.

The Naive Bayes Classifier works under the assumption of independent attributes, and that is why we perform a first stage where we detect all the dependencies between attributes for a later processing, trying to achieve a representation free of dependent attributes. This is performed at the first stage called "Dependency Analysis". The complete dependency search and clean algorithm can be decomposed into four main steps detailed next.

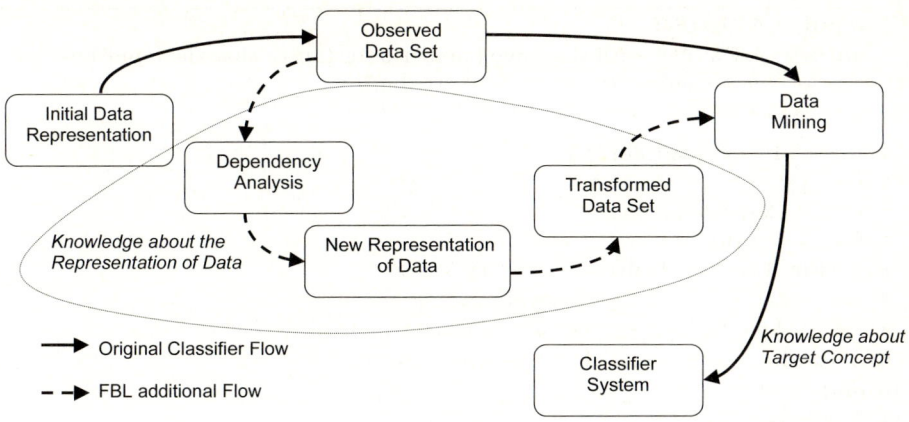

Fig. 1. Naive Bayes original data flow and FBL extended flow for performing a complete classification

First step: Definitions and initialization. First we define and initialize some variables and lists. Being $S = \{A_1, A_2 \ldots A_n\}$ the original set of attributes and $V = \{v_1, v_2 \ldots v_m\}$ the possible class values, $e_j = \{\overrightarrow{x}, v\}$ is a trainning ex ample where $\overrightarrow{x} = (a_1, a_2 \ldots a_n)$ is a point that belongs to the input space (X) and $v \in V$ is a point belonging to the output space (V). We also initialize an empty list, L_{IG}, a list of attributes ordered by the inverse of their Information Gain ([12]).

Second step: Dependencies analysis. We search for dependencies of the form $a_i = \alpha + \beta \cdot a_v$ where $a_i \neq a_v \wedge a_i, a_v \in S$ and $\alpha, \beta \in \aleph$. For each a_i we calculate the squared correlation (R_i^2) beetween its attribute values (this value measures how well the regression curve fits the points), then $d_i = (a_i, R_i^2)$. We define $L = \{d_i\}$ for $i = 1 \ldots n$, which contains all the possible dependencies between pairs of attributes ($\sum_{i=1}^{N-1} i$ possible dependencies) and is in a strength-of-dependency (R^2) decremental order.

Third step: Dependency based filtering. At this step we use L to obtain the final attribute set by deleting (or not) the most dependent attributes until no accuracy improvement is achieved. At each step, the algorithm considers two dependencies, one is the next dependency not previously seen in L, and the other is the next to this one[1]. As each dependency is represented by two attributes: the dependent one (a_i) and the independent one (a_v), at each step we are dealing with four attributes, two from the first dependency and two from the next dependency. For each of the four attributes we delete it from the previous dataset and calculate the accuracy of the Naive Bayes over the resultant dataset and then we select the attribute that when removed from the dataset produces the greater accuracy improvement. When an attribute(a_j) is deleted from the dataset, L is updated deleting all the dependencies where a_j appears as one of

---
[1] We use two dependencies at each stage because some dependent attributes are also very informative when dealing with the target class and should not be removed.

```
input  : A DataSet
output : A DataSet with the same number of instances that the input but
         only a subset of the original attributes
 1  F ← S;
 2  L_{IC} ← IGInverseOrder(S);
 3  L ← {};
 4  P_{init} ← NaiveBayes(S);
 5  for A_i ∈ S do
 6      for A_j ∈ S − A_i do
 7          L_S ← {A_i, A_j, g(A_i, A_j)};
 8          L ← L ⋃ L_S;
 9      end
10  end
11  L ← Order(L);
12  pos ← 0;
13  fin ← false;
14  while (fin = false)&&(pos < L.length) do
15      L_1 ← L[pos];
16      Attributes ← {L_1.A_i, L_1.A_j};
17      if pos < (L.length − 1) then
18          L_2 ← L[pos + 1];
19          Attributes ← Attributes ⋃ {L_2.A_i, L_2.A_j};
20      else
21          Atr ← GetBest(Attributes);
22      end
23      if Atr = null then
24          fin ← true;
25      else
26          L_{IC} ← L_{IC} − Atr;
27          L ← DeleteDependencies(L, Atr);
28          F ← DeleteAttribute(F, Atr);
29          T ← Transform(F);
30          P_i ← NaiveBayes(T);
31      end
32  end
33  pos ← 0;
34  while pos < L_{IG}.length do
35      Atr ← L_{IG}[pos];
36      F_{aux} ← DeleteAttribute(F, Atr);
37      P_p ← NaiveBayes(F_{aux});
38      if P_p > P_i then
39          P_i ← P_p;
40          F ← F_{aux};
41      end
42  end
43  return P_i
```

Algorithm 1. FBL Algorithm

the two dependent attributes, and also L_{IG} is updated deleting a_j. The third step concludes when in one iteration no performance of the classifier could be achieved deleting any of the four related attributes.

Fourth step: IG based filtering. A further attribute filtering is performed by considering the Information Gain values of the attributes. For every attribute in the resulting L_{IG} we consider if we should delete it by comparing the accuracy of the classifier over the dataset versus the accuracy of the classifier over the dataset when removing the attribute. Once finished the whole process, we obtain $F = \{A_i, A_j \ldots A_z | A_k \in S\}$ that is a subset of S that contains the best possible attributes.

Table 1. Description of the methods referenced from the Algorithm

Method	Description
IGInverseOrder	Method that orders a list of attributes by its IG value.
NaiveBayes	Deletes the atributes given as parameter from the dataset and returns the accuracy obtained by the NB on the resultant data.
Order	Receives a list containing dependencies and returns the list in strength-of-dependecy decremental order.
GetBest	Returns the attribute (from Attributes) that when deleted from the previous set of attributes (F), makes the Naive Bayes achieve a greater accuracy. If the greater accuracy is achieved when no attribute is deleted, then returns Null.
DeleteDependencies	Deletes all the dependencies from L where Atr is one of the independent or dependent attributes.
DeleteAttribute	Deletes the given attribute from a list of attributes.
Transform	Deletes from the original dataset all the attributes that are not in F.

Having F, we modify each element in T deleting all the information that does not correspond with the final attributes (F). Being g the regression method used and t a function that transforms each trainning instance deleting the values of the attributes that belonging to S are not in F, the FBL algorithm is implemented as shown in Algorithm 1.

3 Experiments

In this section some experiments are present to evaluate our hypothesis and the Wrapper proposed in this paper. To study the behaviour of FBL, 13 synthetic data sets were generated from 5 original data sets taken from [2]: Contraceptive Method, Balance Scale, Glass Identification, Wine Recognition and TAE. Linear dependencies were introduced by generating synthetic attributes in the way $SyntheticAttribute = a \cdot OriginalAttribute_1 + b$, being a and b two random integers. For each original dataset, different synthetic attributes (from different original attributes and parameters) were used, resulting in some final datasets (for example, for the ContraceptiveMethod dataset CM1, CM2 and CM3 were generated). As can be seen in Table 2, in the 13 synthetic domains the Naive Bayes Classifier works worst than in the original ones where the synthetic dependencies are not present.

Table 2. Comparison of the performance of 6 Machine Learning Algorithms working with data containing dependencies. The values represent the variation in the percentage of accuracy from the original dataset to the resultant dataset where synthetic attributes have been added. The datasets are: Contraceptive Method (CM), Breast Cancer (BC), Balance Scale (BS), Glass Identification (GI), Wine Recognition (WR) and TAE. For each dataset we have generated one or some synthetic ones (which can be differentiated by the final number). All the accuracies are calculated using ten-fold cross validation.

Algorithm	CM1	CM2	CM3	BC1	BC2	BC3	BC4	BS1	BS2	BS3	GI1	WR1	TAE
Naive Bayes	-1.15	-2.45	-1.02	-0.14	-0.14	-0.14	-0.14	-9.11	-5.23	-0.68	-0.08	-0.07	-0.04
C4.5	-0.61	1.77	0.68	1.72	3.72	2.72	0.14	0.00	0.45	0.68	0.13	0.01	0.89
C4.5 rules	0.34	0.81	1.08	0.72	1.58	0.29	0.86	-2.74	-1.60	-0.91	0.72	1.58	-0.29
KNN(N=1)	-1.29	-0.61	-1.29	0.04	0.28	0.28	-0.15	-0.23	0.91	1.14	-0.13	-0.28	0.23
KNN(N=4)	-0.81	-0.88	-0.88	0.15	0.72	0.72	-0.43	-1.14	-0.91	-2.50	-1.16	-0.72	0.01
SMO	0.06	0.06	0.00	-0.14	-0.14	-0.14	0.00	0.22	-0.23	-0.46	0.00	-0.04	0.54

In contrast to other Machine Learning algorithms used, Table 2 shows that Naive Bayes is the only algorithm that invariably worsens its accuracy when interdependent attributes are used. Once proven this, the next step is to study if non-synthetic datasets reveal the same behaviour. To check this, 15 datasets have been selected from [2], and have been studied without adding any synthetic feature.

The effectiveness of FBL can be evaluated by comparing the FBL attributes selection to the best possible subset selection. To calculate the best subset we have performed an exhaustive search over the space of attributes of each one of the 15 datasets selected. Table 3 shows the result of this exhaustive search, showing the accuracy of the Naive Bayes Classifier over the best possible subset of attributes, the number of attributes of the best subset and also the number of attributes of the original dataset for establishing a comparison. In 13 from 15 datasets we are able to find a subset of attributes that allows the Naive Bayes Classifier to perform better than using the original ones. In addition, we can see the best subsets are composed, generally, by a few number of attributes, which means a drastic reduction of the complexity of the classifier's model.

Once obtained the superior level for the attributes selection, we compare these results with the behaviour of the FBL algorithm. We have performed some experiments using the FBL algorithm over the same 15 UCI domains, and also we have studied the behaviour of two classical ways of attribute selection as are the filtering using the Information Gain value and also the filtering using the Chi^2 value and the Principal Components Analysis (PCA, [17]) method to extract a subset of more or less independent attributes. For the filtering using Chi^2 and IG, we have generated a ranking of the attributes according to those metrics and

Table 3. Comparison between the accuracy obtained by the Naive Bayes (NB), the Naive Bayes over the best possible attribute selection (Best), the FBL algorithm and using filters based on Information Gain (IG) or Chi^2, PCA or the Langley algorithm in a forward (LF) or a backward mode (LB). O/B means the number of original attributes (O) and the number of attributes in the best subset selection (B). As the best subset selection is an exhaustive search, we couldn't obtain the results for some highly dimensional data sets and we set them as NA. All the results are obtained by 10-fold cross validation.

DataSet	NB	Best	O/B	FBL	IG	Chi^2	PCA	LF	LB
Abalone	0.240	0.266	9/2	0.266	0.266	0.266	0.245	0.265	0.265
Adult	0.827	0.835	15/13	0.835	0.752	0.752	ND	0.791	0.835
Cmc	0.508	0.554	10/4	0.554	0.508	0.508	0.453	0.553	0.537
Glass	0.495	0.603	10/3	0.579	0.556	0.556	0.542	0.598	0.598
Ionosphere	0.826	≥0.984	36/NA	0.915	0.863	0.872	0.920	0.984	0.900
Iris	0.960	0.967	5/2	0.967	0.967	0.967	0.933	0.960	0.953
Nursery	0.903	0.903	9/9	0.903	0.876	0.903	0.883	0.903	0.903
OpDigits	0.913	≥0.939	64/NA	0.913	0.865	0.881	0.939	0.925	0.918
PenDigits	0.857	0.865	16/13	0.865	0.615	0.836	0.886	0.864	0.864
Spam	0.793	≥0.908	57/NA	0.908	0.793	0.793	0.737	0.837	0.902
TAE	0.503	0.510	6/5	0.510	0.470	0.510	0.470	0.503	0.509
TicTacToe	0.696	0.724	9/5	0.718	0.699	0.699	0.742	0.718	0.728
WdbCancer	0.929	≥0.959	31/NA	0.956	0.924	0.923	0.937	0.959	0.945
Wine	0.966	0.989	13/10	0.977	0.792	0.977	0.983	0.989	0.977
Yeast	0.577	0.577	7/7	0.577	0.577	0.577	0.558	0.577	0.577

then, from an empty set of features, we have added one attribute from the ordered list to the set of features until no improvement of the classifier is achieved. For PCA we have studied the behaviour of the Naive Bayes Classifier over the studied domains covering 4 different levels of variance (0.65, 0.75, 0.85 and 0.95) and then we select the best value for each dataset. The results are shown in Table 3.

Table 4. Sumary table where, for each algorithm proven, it is shown the average accuracy over the 15 datasets proven, the times the algorithm obtains the best accuracy and the percentage of accuracy reduced

Algorithm	N.B.	FBL	PCA	LF	LB	IG	Chi^2
Avg. Accuracy	0.7331	0.7629	0.7327	0.7619	0.7610	0.7016	0.7346
Trim	0.00%	11.17%	-0.15%	10.78%	10.45%	-11.79%	0.57%
Times Best	ND	8	3	6	4	3	3

Finally, Table 4 is a sumary table. Having the average accuracy obtained for the 15 datasets proven, the times that each algorithm obtains the best accuracy, and the percentage of improved accuracy, we are able to compare more carefully all the algorithms used in this paper. FBL obtains the best possible value 8 times from 15 possible, being the algorithm that more times obtains the best value. Also obtains the best accuracy value, and we can assure it is the best option from all the proposed in this paper. The forward greedy search proposed by Langley is near FBL in accuracy values, but is not as good as FBL and also performs a greedy search, wasting too much time. It seems interesting the results obtained by PCA and the Information Gain based selection as, in average, obtain worse results than using the Naive Bayes without any previous transformation or filtering.

4 Discussion and Future Work

We have presented a simple alternative to the Naive Bayes which works well even in domains where strong linear dependencies [2] are present. The proposed algorithm performs a non greedy search based on the previous estimation of the dependencies strength between attributes, and the filtering according to these values and also according to the Information Gain values for each attribute.

We have run several experiments over 15 UCI domains, comparing the accuracy of the FBL algorithm presented in this paper to the accuracy obtained by the Naive Bayes and the accuracies obtained by performing some attribute filters: PCA, the forward and backward attribute selection algorithms proposed by Langley and a Information Gain and a Squared Chi based filterings.

Experimental results show that using the FBL Wrapper allows us to obtain better accuracy results when applying the Naive Bayes Classifier. It should be remarked that on 13 from 15 real datasets we can perform a better classification when those dependencies are not present, which shows we are not working on a synthetic problem, this is a reality. We have demonstrated that a classical attributes extraction technique such as PCA does not make the Naive Bayes to perform better. We have also proved that filters based on Information Gain and Squared Chi metrics are not a good way to make the Naive Bayes perform better and that FBL is as good (or better) than the greedy algorithms proposed by Langley but performing a more guided search that implies to try less attribute sets, resulting in a lower running time.

As FBL modifies the data to meet the simplifying assumptions of the Naive Bayes classifier, it achieves better accuracies. Another way to deal with the simplifying assumption would be modelling the dependences (Bayesian Networks) but we have selected the first way because we obtain a simpler model which be think is an advantage but in future work we would compare these two approximations and study the behaviour of each one over each possible application domain.

Applications as Spam are excelent scenarios to apply FBL as their domains are composed by words extracted from texts, and those words are not independent attributes as some words should appear, commonly, in pairs, or the appearance of some of them should be much related to the appearance of other words. Any other applications on the Information Retrieval area should be also susceptible to be improved with the use of FBL, as could be [6]. As traffic flows shows dependencies

---

[2] FBL can be extended to use other kind of dependencies.

(two roads ending in another road is a clear example of dependency), a domain like [4] could be improved with FBL.

Summarizing, the FBL algorithm performs better than Naive Bayes, PCA and other attribute filters under 13 from 15 UCI domains as it is able to deal with the dependencies presented on those domains.

References

1. Almuallim, H., Dietterich, T. G.: Learning with Many Irrelevant Features. 9th National Conference on Artificial Intelligence (1991) Mit Press. 547–552.
2. Blake, C. L. and Merz, C. J.: UCI Repository of Machine Learning Databases. [http://www.ics.uci.edu/ mlearn/MLRepository.html]. Irvine, University of California. Department of Information and Computer Science.
3. Cortizo, J. C. and Giraldez J. I.: Discovering Data Dependencies in Web Content Mining. IADIS International Conference WWW/Internet. (2004) 881–884.
4. Exposito, D. and Giraldez J. I.: Control MultiAgente del trfico rodado mediante Redes WIFI Conferencia Iberoamericana IADIS WWW/Internet. (2004) 473–476.
5. Fisher, R.: Statistical Methods for Research Workers. Macmillan Pub Co (1925)
6. Gomez, J. M., Buenaga, M., Cortizo, J. C.: The Role of Word Sense Disambiguation in Automated Text Categorization NLDB 2005 Springer Verlag, LNCS **3513**. (2005) 298–309.
7. Jakulin, A. and Bratko, I.: Analyzing Attribute Dependencies. Proceedings of Knowledge Discovery in Data (PKDD) Springer Verlag, LNAI. (2003) 229–240.
8. John, G. H., Kohavi, R., Pfleger, K.: Irrelevant Features and the Subset Selection Problem. Proceedings of the International Conference on Machine Learning (1994), 121–129.
9. Kira, K., Rendell, L. A.: A Practical Approach to Feature Subset Selection. 9th International Conference on Machine Learning (1992) Morgan Kauffman.
10. Kononenko, I.: Comparison of inductive and naive Bayesian learning approaches to automatic knowledge adquisition. B. Wielinga Editors, Current trends in Knowledge Adquisition. Amsterdam: IOS Press (1990) 190–197.
11. Kohavi, R., Sommerfield, D.: Feature Subset Selection Using the Wrapper Method: Overfitting and Dynamic Search Space Topology. 1st International Conference on Knowledge Discovery and Data Mining (1995) 192–197.
12. Kullback, S., Leibler, R. A.: On Information and Sufficiency. Annals of Mathematical Statistics **22**, (1951) 79–86.
13. Langley, P: Induction of recursive Bayesian Classifiers. Proceedings of the 1993 European Conference on Machine Learning (1993) 153–164.
14. Montes, C.: Metodo de Induccion Total. PhD Thesis. Universidad Politcnica de Madrid, Boadilla del Monte, Spain.
15. Neter, J., Kutner, M. H., Wasserman, W., Nachtsheim C. J.: Applied Linear Statistical Models. Irwin Editors, (1996).
16. Pazzani, M.: Searching for dependencies in Bayesian Classifiers. Artificial Intelligence and Statistics IV. Springer Verlag, New York, USA. (1997)
17. Shlens, J.: A tutorial on Principal Component Analysis. Systems Neurobiology Laboratory, Salk Institute for Biological Studies (2005).

BP Neural Networks Combined with PLS Applied to Pattern Recognition of Vis/NIRs

Di Wu, Yong He, Yongni Shao, and Shuijuan Feng

College of Biosystems Engineering and Food Science, Zhejiang University, 310029,
Hangzhou, China
yhe@zju.edu.cn

Abstract. Vis/NIRs technique can be used in non-destructive measurement of the material internal quality in many fields. In this study, a mixed algorithm combined with back-propagation neural networks (BPNNs) and partial least squares (PLS) method was applied in the predicting the acidity of yogurt. The reflectance of optimal wavebands selected by PLS process were set as input neurons of BPNNs to establish the prediction model. By training the 130 yogurt samples in the BPNNs of topological structure 19:11:1, the acidity of the remaining 25 samples were predicted. The correlation between the measured and predicted values shows an excellent prediction performance with the value of 0.97, higher than the result (0.916) obtained only by PLS. Thus, it is concluded that the algorithm construct by BPNNs combined with partial least square applied to pattern recognition is an available alternative for pattern recognition based on Vis/NIRs.

1 Introduction

In the resent years, pattern recognition which has the function of data prediction has attracted many eyes and has excellent performances in many fields. Based on the Vis/NIRs technique, the whole spectral bands data can be made quantitative analysis and qualitative analysis. Because of its advantage of low cost, high efficiency, fast analytical speed, ease of operation, non-destruction and limited preparation, this technique has been widely used in many fields such as the food industry, petroleum chemical, engineering, military, biometrics and the medicine etc [1] [2] [3]. The information of Vis/NIRs data which is used to predict the composition and quantities of the samples is contained in the spectral curve. It is difficult to extract the relevant information from many overlapping peaks, so pivotal step for spectroscopy technique is how to extract quantitative data from them. Several multivariate calibration techniques are usually applied to data treatment like principal component analysis (PCA), soft independent modeling of class analogy (SIMCA), herachical cluster analysis (HCA), canonical analysis (CA), discriminant analysis (DA), principal component regression (PCR). However, most of those methods have some limitation such as accuracy is not very high and the training speed is a little slow. Thus, we hope to find a method that can offset these deficiencies.

Artificial neural networks (ANNs) is a non-linear dynamical data processing system consisted of lots of simple processing units for prediction, classification, data association, data conceptualization, and data filter. ANNs use mass but simple unites to connect a neural network in order to execute its function. With the characteristic of high-speed parallelism, calculation, abundant association, great robustness, strong capacity of self-adaptive, self-organization and self-learning [4], As its prominent ability to mining the obscure relationship between diverse variables, this methodology has been demonstrated and considered to be an excellent system in the field of scientific prediction by scientific scholar [5]. Due to the changing of prediction environment which may make the collected data imprecise and incorrect, the conventional methods are deficient in solving those problems. So only when the parameters in ANN models changed with the environment will gain the correct and precise results. Instead, the BPNNs is widely applied in most of the fields as a result of its high-nonlinear mapping ability of computing model possessing at present.

In order to design a simple optical sensor that can discriminate between healthy and diseased canopies, it is important to reduce the number of selected wavebands to a minimum. PLS is usually considered for a large number of applications in spectrum analysis. It performs the decomposition on both the spectral and concentration data simultaneously, as it takes the advantage of the correlation relationship that already exists between the spectral data and the constituent concentrations. The latent variables (LVs) calculated by PLS are several major variables which are related to the data. While in this paper, the aim of PLS is to obtain the optimal wavebands for acidity prediction thought the loading values of each LV.

This paper proposed a new method which is constructed with PLS analysis and BPNNs. The aim of this study is to evaluate the use of Vis/NIRs in measuring the acidity of yogurt. The PLS analysis combined with BP neural network was applied to find out a better mathematic model in pattern recognition.

2 Theory

2.1 PLS Methodology

PLS is a bilinear modeling method where the original independent information (X-data) is projected onto a small number of LVs to simplify the relationship between X and Y for predicting with the smallest number of LVs [6]. Through full cross validation, PLS was executed on the spectra from 400 to 1000nm to reduce the variable dimensions of the original independent information (X-data) and extract few but primary LVs which can present the characteristics (Y) of spectra belong to each sample. The extracting process is performed including both X and Y data through exchanging the score of X and Y before every new principle component is calculated and this is the different and better against PCR. So the LVs are related to dependent variables, not only to the independent variables. The loading values are the unit vector values of each LV and can present the importance of each original vector which is the wavebands in this study. The whole process was achieved in the Unscrambler V9.2 (CAMO Process AS.), a statistical software for multivariate calibration.

2.2 BP Neural Network Model

The most popular type of neural network for use in analytical applications is ANN with the back-propagation learning algorithm [7]. It is a one-way multilayer feed-forward network [8] and can be used for the data compression tasks as well as property prediction tasks. The BPNNs learning algorithm is optimizing network weights to minimize the global error of the system by error-back-propagation. The network is trained by initially selecting the weights random at the beginning of the training then presenting all training data repeatedly. The weight of every node is adjusted along gradients when the outputs run back through the hidden neuron connection and reduce the global error which obtained by external information specifying the correct result until all the errors are within the required tolerance. The delta rule was used as the learning rule, which specifies how connection weights are changed during the learning process. The sigmoid transfer function was chosen for the non–linear function that transfers the internally generated sum for each node to a potential output node. Three-layered back propagation fundamental topological structure of networks is composed of input layers, hidden layers and output layers. A schematic diagram of multilayer neural network architecture is shown in Fig. 1.

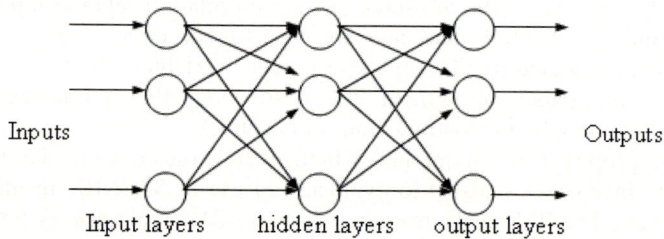

Fig. 1. Schematic diagram of the topological structure of BPNNs

The transfer function of net-node takes the form:

$$f(x) = \frac{1}{1 + e^{-x/Q}} \qquad (1)$$

Where, Q is the parameter of function *Sigmoid*.

3 Application to a Case

Because of high value of nutrition, a good taste and many salutary functions, yogurt is widely preferred. But the favorite is not uniform due to different consumer groups, so it is necessary to use a method which can identify the value of acidity of yogurt. At present, the domestic and international measurements of acidity of yogurt always use chemical methods which are carried out at destructive state, involve a considerable amount of manual work, and cost plenty of time. Therefore, the aim of this study is to measure the acidity of yogurt basing on Vis/NIRs technique.

3.1 Experimental Materials and Reflectance Measurement

Five different brands of yogurt include Mengniu (Neimenggu), Junyao (Shanghai), Guangming (Shanghai), Yili (Neimenggu), Shuangfeng (Hang Zhou), which are produced at the one day, were purchased in a supermarket. 32 samples (total 155 samples) selected from each brand equally were used in the measurement of Vis/NIR-spectroscopy. All the samples were stored in a refrigerator to keep at cold temperature (4±1°C). All the samples were first equilibrated to room temperature before Vis/NIRS analysis and the whole experiment was carried through at 23°C.

In order to reducing the error of operation during the whole experiment, samples were extended upperly throughout the bottom surface of glass containers of 65 mm diameter and 14mm height. The height of yogurt surface is 7mm. For each sample, reflection spectra with total 30 scan times were taken with a field spectroradiometer (FieldSpec Pro FR (325–1075 nm)/ A110070) placed at a height of approximately 150 mm above the sample cup, Trademarks of Analytical Spectral Devices, Inc. (ASD), the interval of sampling is 1.5cm, using RS2 software for Windows. Considering its 20° field-of-view (FOV). The light source of Lowell pro-lam 14.5V Bulb/128690 tungsten halogen that could be used in Vis/NIRs region was placed about 300 mm from the center of the container to make the angle between the incident light and the detector optimally about 45°. The acidity of each sample was determined at 23°C with a pH meter (LIDA-PHS-3C), after measured immediately,

3.2 Preprocessing of the Optical Data

The reflectance spectra needed to be transformed to absorbency and also for each data which was imported into Unscramble for further process must be ASCII datum, the ASD software was used to achieve these two purposes. Due to the own system might be a little imprecise, there were some scattering which could be observed in the beginning and end of the spectral data. As those data would affect the accuracy of measurements, the first 75 and the last 75 wavelength values were taken out of total values. Starting from here all the considerations were based on this range of wavelengths (400-1000nm) until the optimal wavebands were chosen [9].

In order to reduce the influence of the noise, after compared with the final prediction results by using different preprocessing methods, there were two preprocessing methods were selected in this study. First type of processing was Moving Average Smoothing which was used to average the spectral data in order. It had been proved that many high frequency noises could be eliminated by this smooth. By using the different numbers (3 to 21), the results presented that number 9 was best in this study. The second type of processing was the use of the multiplicative scatter correction (MSC). This technique was used to correct for additive and multiplicative effects in the spectra [10]. Due to the fresh light scattering, the light does not always travel the same distance in the sample before it is detected. A longer light traveling path corresponds to a lower relative reflectance value, since more light is absorbed. This causes a parallel translation of the spectra. This kind of variation was not of use for the calibration models and was eliminated by MSC.

The sample data (155 yogurt samples) was separated randomly into two groups: a calibration set used to develop the calibration set (130 samples with 5 brands equally) and the remaining samples of the population were used to validation set (25 samples with 5 brands equally).

4 Result and Discussion

The average absorbance spectral curves from 325 to 1075 nm for certain randomly selected every one sample are showed in Fig. 2. Excluding the little overlapping of the wavebands at the 'violet edge' (i.e., 400-520nm), the spectral curves indicate the potential of discriminating one yogurt from another via NIRs especially at the visible wavelength (i.e., 520-920nm).

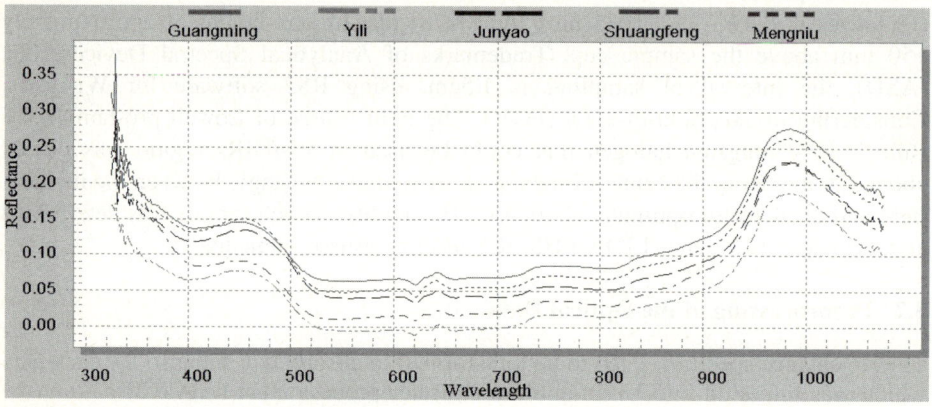

Fig. 2. NIR reflectance spectra of three different varieties peaches

4.1 Partial Least Square (PLS) Used Only

Calibration model was developed using PLS with cross-validation and the number of LVs was determined by the PRESS (predicted error sum of squares) function in order to avoid overfit of the models [11]. As a result, yogurt samples for modeling were split into a calibration set and a validation set. The quality of the calibration model was quantified by the standard error of calibration (SEC), and r (coefficient of correlation) and the one of validation set was quantified by the standard error of validation (SEV) and r. The prediction accuracy of the calibration model was tested using the predicting set, and evaluated by the standard error of prediction (SEP) and the r between the predicted and the measured parameters [11]. An excellent model should have lower SEC, SEV and SEP, higher r but smaller differences between SEC and SEV, because large ones indicate that too many latent variables are introduced in the model and the noises are also modeled. In addition, the minimum plot of the root mean square error of validation (RMSEV) was used to determine the optimal model without overfittedness or underfittedness [11]. PLS prediction result for acidity is presented in scatter plots (Fig.3). The ordinate and abscissa axes represent the predicted and measured fitted values of the acidity. The performance of each model established by PLS in the study was shown in Table 1.

Table 1. The performance of each model established by PLS

Calibration	Validation	Prediction	SEC	SEV	SEP	RMSEP
0.932535	0.907743	0.916	0.02244	0.038973	0.037	0.042

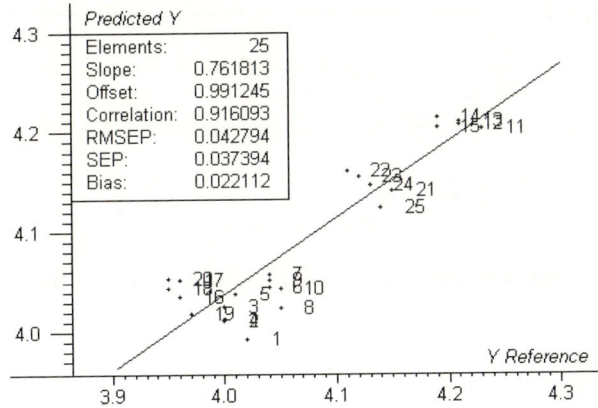

Fig. 3. Vis/NIR prediction results from the PLS models for acidity

4.2 BPNNs Combined with PLS

Determination of Optimal Wavebands. After the preprocessing of spectral data and PLS process carried out with all the 155 samples were finished, the number of LVs was determined as 8 by cross-validation. By choosing spectral wavebands with the first three highest loading values in each of those 8 LVs across the entire spectral region, those wavelengths were chose as the optimal ones: 61nm, 62nm, 63nm (in LV1), 519nm, 520nm, 521nm (in LV2), 236nm, 237nm, 238nm (in LV3), 62nm, 413nm, 414nm (inLV4), 105nm, 106nm, 107nm (in LV5), 222nm, 223nm, 224nm (in LV6), 237nm, 238nm, 239nm (in LV7) and 223nm, 224nm, 225nm (in LV8). After wiped off the same wavebands, there were 19 left. The reflectance values of those 19 wavebands were set as input neurons of BPNNs to establish the prediction model.

BPNNs Model Based on Optimal Wavebands. The whole wave-band of spectra is from 400 to 1000nm. If it is used as the input of BPNNs directly, it not only affects the training rate, but also decreases the discrimination accuracy. Based on the first three highest loading values in each of those 8LVs, the reflectance values of those 19 wavebands were set as input neurons of BPNNs to establish the prediction model. The node of input layer, hidden layer, and output layer was 19, 11 (chose by comparing the prediction results with different integral value from 9 to 19), and 1 (the value of acidity). 130 samples were used as training set and reminder samples formed the prediction set. The speed of learning was set as 0.1. Prediction result for acidity is presented in scatter plot (Fig. 4). The ordinate and abscissa axes represent the predicted and measured fitted values of the acidity. The correlation between the measured and predicted values shows an excellent prediction performance with the value of 0.97, higher than the result (0.916) obtained by the use of PLS only.

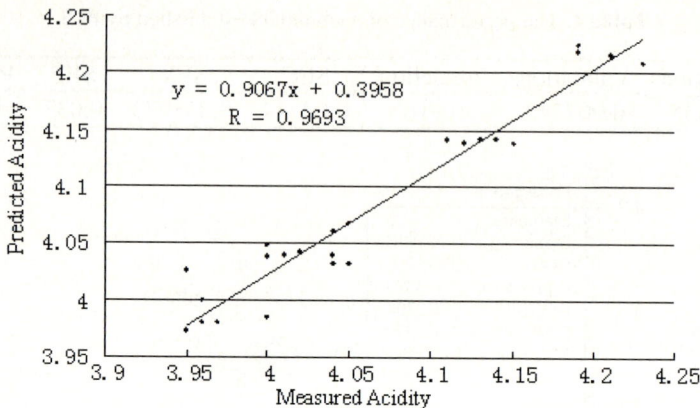

Fig. 4. Prediction performance by using PLS- BPNNs

5 Conclusions

Vis/NIR Spectrum technique with the advantage of low cost, high efficiency, fast analytical speed, ease of operation, non-destruction and limited preparation, has been widely used in many fields. The pivotal step for spectroscopy technique is how to extract quantitative data from mass spectral curves. This paper proposed a mixed algorithm constructed with PLS analysis and BPNNs and shows an excellent prediction performance. After the PLS process carried out with all the 155 samples, the number of LVs was determined as 8 by cross-validation. Each reflectance of 19 optimal wavebands was set as input neurons of BPNNs to establish the prediction model. The node of input layer, hidden layer, and output layer was 19, 11, and 1. 130 samples were used as training set and reminder samples formed prediction set. After the training, the result shows that the correlation between the measured and predicted values shows an excellent prediction performance with the value of 0.97, higher than the result (0.916) obtained only by used the algorithm of PLS. Thus, it is concluded that the algorithm construct by BPNN combined with PLS applied to pattern recognition is an available alternative for pattern recognition based on Vis/NIRS.

This model could be applied in other non-destructive measurement of the material internal quality, as artificial neural network was highly effective to complete the nonlinear-system predication in response to its great capability of self-learning and nonlinear computation. Further work is required to optimize, standardize and implement this technique. Also more fundamental research is required to provide a physical-chemical background of spectra.

Acknowledgements

This study was supported by the Teaching and Research Award Program for Outstanding Young Teachers in Higher Education Institutions of MOE, P. R. C., Natural Science Foundation of China (Project No: 30270773), Specialized Research

Fund for the Doctoral Program of Higher Education (Project No: 20040335034), Natural Science Foundation of Zhejiang (Project No: RC02067) and Science and Technology Department of Zhejiang Province (Project No. 2005C21094).

References

1. Slaughter, D. C.: Non-destructive Determination of Internal Quality in Peaches and Nectarines, Transactions of the ASAE, Vol. 38. (1995) 617–623
2. Antihus, H. G., Yong, H., Annia, G. P.: Non-Destructive Measurement of Acidity, Soluble Solids and Firmness of Satsuma Mandarin Using Vis/NIR-Spectroscopy Techniques, Journal of Food Engineering, Vol.77(2006)313-319
3. Yong, H., Xiaoli, L., Yongni, S.: Discrimination of Varieties of Apple Using Near Infrared Spectra Based on Principal Component Analysis and Artificial Neural Network Model, Spectroscopy and Spectral Analysis, Vol.26(2006)850-853
4. Jiangang, Y.: Tutorial of Artificial Neural Networks. Zhejiang University Press, Hangzhou (2001) 13–36
5. Yong, H.: Study on the Theory and Methods of Analysis and Optimization of Grain Post-production System and Their Applications. PhD Dissertation of Zhejiang University, Hangzhou (1998) 21–42
6. The Unscrambler 7.8 for Windows.User Manual, Camo, Norway (1998)
7. Dou,Y., Sun, Y., Ren,Y. Q., Ren,Y. L.: Artificial Neural Network for Simultaneous Determination of Two Components of Compound Paracetamol and Diphenhydramine Hydrochloride Powder on NIR Spectroscopy, Analytica Chimica Acta, 528 (2005) 55–61.
8. Widyanto, M. R., Novuhara, H., Kawamoto, K., Hirota, K., Kusumoputro, B.: Improving Recognition and Generalization Capablility of Back-Propagation NN Using a Self-organized Network Inspired by Immune Algorithm (SONIA), Applied Soft Computing, (2005) 72–84
9. Qi, X. M., Zhang, L. D., Du, Z. L.: Quantitative Analysis Using NIR by Building PLS-BP Model, Spectroscopy and Spectral Analysis, Vol. 23 (2003) 870–872
10. Yong, H., Xiaoli, L.: Discrimination of Varieties of Waxberry Using Near Infrared Spectra, J. Infrared Millim. Waves, Vol.25(2006)192-194,212
11. Naes, T., Isaksson, T., Fearn,T., & Davies, A.M.: A User-friendly Guide to Multivariate Calibration and Classification, NIR Publications, UK, (2002)

Speeding Up Shape Classification by Means of a Cyclic Dynamic Time Warping Lower Bound

Vicente Palazón and Andrés Marzal*

Dept. Llenguatges i Sistemes Informàtics. Universitat Jaume I de Castelló. Spain
{palazon, amarzal}@lsi.uji.es

Abstract. Cyclic Dynamic Time Warping (CDTW) is a good measure of contour shapes dissimilarity, but it is computationally expensive. We introduce a lower bound for CDTW inspired in the Bunke and Bühler that leads to a significant speed up of contours classification in real tasks, as the experiments show.

1 Introduction

Content-based image retrieval is being increasingly demanded in many applications: digital libraries, broadcast media selection, multimedia editing, etc [11]. The shape of 2D/3D objects usually provides a more powerful semantical clue for similarity matching than colour or texture: humans can recognize characteristic objects from their contour. Contours can be considered *cyclic sequences*: sequences with no beginning or end. The sequences can be Freeman chaincodes, series of 2D points, curvature values, distances to the shape's centroid, etc.

Given two cyclic sequences of lengths m and n, respectively, their dissimilarity can be measured by means of the *cyclic edit distance* (CED), which is defined as the weight of the best sequence of edit operations needed to transform any cyclic shift of one string into any cyclic shift of the other. Maes proposed in [7] an $O(mn \lg m)$ time procedure to compute the CED and applied it in [6] to the recognition of shapes described with polygons. As Maes pointed out, the CED has some drawbacks when comparing contours: it is sensitive to segmentation inconsistencies in the polygons and to the number of edges representing similar regions. A Dynamic Time Warping based dissimilarity measure seems more natural for optimally aligning contours. In [8], the authors defined a Cyclic Dynamic Time Warping (CDTW) measure and presented an $O(mn \lg m)$ algorithm to compute it. The CDTW was shown to outperform other contour comparison methods in shape retrieval and classification tasks.

In nearest neighbour (NN) classification systems, where the running time of the comparison algorithm is a major concern, it is possible to take advantage of fast lower bounding functions to avoid the computation of expensive comparisons between cyclic sequences: when comparing two cyclic sequences, the exact

---

* This work has been supported by the *Conselleria d'Empresa, Universitat i Ciència* under grant GV06/302.

comparison can be avoided if the lower bounding function is greater or equal than the best dissimilarity measure computed so-far. A well-known approximate method to compute the CED is the so-called Bunke and Bühler (BB) algorithm, which runs in $\mathcal{O}(mn)$ time [3]. When comparing two cyclic sequences, the BB method yields a value which is a lower bound of the CED [3]. In [4], an efficient lower bounding function for Dynamic Time Warping (DTW) was presented; however, there is a lack in CDTW at this respect. As we show in this paper, the BB method can be used to lower bound the CDTW. We use this lower bound to speed up NN pattern classification.

The paper is organized as follows: In section 2, the CDTW is reviewed. In section 3, the BB algorithm is also reviewed and we show that it can be used as a lower bound function for CDTW. The lower bounding method for CDTW is presented in section 4. Finally, in sections 5 and 6, some experimental results and conclusions are presented.

2 Cyclic Dynamic Time Warping

Let $X = x_0 x_1 \ldots x_{m-1}$ and $Y = y_0 y_1 \ldots y_{n-1}$ be two sequences from an alphabet Σ and let Σ^* be its closure under concatenation of Σ. An *alignment* between X and Y is a sequence of pairs $(i_0, j_0), (i_1, j_1), \ldots, (i_{k-1}, j_{k-1})$ such that (a) $0 \leq i_\ell < m$ and $0 \leq j_\ell < n$; (b) $0 \leq i_{\ell+1} - i_\ell \leq 1$ and $0 \leq j_{\ell+1} - j_\ell \leq 1$; and (c) $(i_\ell, j_\ell) \neq (i_{\ell+1}, j_{\ell+1})$. The pair (i_ℓ, j_ℓ) is said to *align* x_{i_ℓ} with y_{j_ℓ}. Each pair is weighted by means of a local dissimilarity function $\gamma : \Sigma \times \Sigma \to \mathbb{R}^{\geq 0}$ and the weight of an alignment is $\sum_{0 \leq \ell < k} \gamma(x_{i_\ell}, y_{j_\ell})$.

An alignment between X and Y is optimal if its weight is minimum among that of all possible alignments. The DTW dissimilarity measure between X and Y will be denoted with $DTW(X, Y)$ and is defined as the weight of the optimal alignment between both sequences. The DTW dissimilarity can be computed as $DTW(X, Y) = d(m - 1, n - 1)$, where d is this recurrence:

$$d(i,j) = \begin{cases} \gamma(x_0, y_0), & \text{if } i = j = 0; \\ d(i-1, j) + \gamma(x_i, y_0), & \text{if } i > 0 \text{ and } j = 0; \\ d(i, j-1) + \gamma(x_0, y_j), & \text{if } i = 0 \text{ and } j > 0; \\ \min \begin{Bmatrix} d(i-1, j-1), \\ d(i-1, j), \\ d(i, j-1) \end{Bmatrix} + \gamma(x_i, y_j), & \text{if } i > 0 \text{ and } j > 0. \end{cases} \quad (1)$$

This equation formulates the $DTW(X, Y)$ computation problem as a shortest path problem in the so-called *warping graph*, an array of nodes (i, j) for $0 \leq i < m$ and $0 \leq j < n$. Each node (i, j) is connected to nodes $(i-1, j), (i, j-1)$, and $(i-1, j-1)$ by an arc of weight $\gamma(x_i, y_j)$. There is a one-to-one correspondence between alignments and path departing from $(0, 0)$ and arriving to $(m-1, n-1)$: the alignment between X and Y contains a pair (i, j) for each traversed node (i, j). The weight of a path (and of its corresponding alignment) is the sum of the weights of its arcs. Since the warping graph is acyclic, the optimal path can be computed by Dynamic Programming in $\mathcal{O}(mn)$ time.

A cyclic sequence can be viewed as the set of sequences obtained by cyclically shifting a representative sequence, i.e., by choosing different starting points. A cyclic shift σ of X is a mapping $\sigma : \Sigma^* \to \Sigma^*$ defined as $\sigma(x_0 x_1 \ldots x_{m-1}) = x_1 x_2 \ldots x_{m-1} x_0$. Let σ^k denote the composition of k cyclic shifts and let σ^0 denote the identity. Two sequences X and X' are cyclically equivalent if $X = \sigma^k(X')$ for some k. A cyclic sequence is an equivalence class $[X] = \{\sigma^k(X) : 0 \leq k < m\}$. Let $[X] = [x_0 x_1 \ldots x_{m-1}]$ and $[Y] = [y_0 y_1 \ldots y_{n-1}]$ be two cyclic sequences. A *cyclic alignment* between $[X]$ and $[Y]$ is a sequence of pairs (i_0, j_0), (i_1, j_1), ..., (i_{k-1}, j_{k-1}) such that, for $0 \leq \ell < k$, (a) $0 \leq i_\ell < m$ and $0 \leq j_\ell < n$; (b) $0 \leq i_{(\ell+1) \bmod m} - i_\ell \leq 1$ and $0 \leq j_{(\ell+1) \bmod n} - j_\ell \leq 1$; and (c) $(i_\ell, j_\ell) \neq (i_{(\ell+1) \bmod m}, j_{(\ell+1) \bmod n})$. The *weight of a cyclic alignment* (i_0, j_0), (i_1, j_1), ..., (i_{k-1}, j_{k-1}) is defined as $\sum_{0 \leq \ell < k} \gamma(x_{i_\ell}, y_{j_\ell})$, where γ is the local dissimilarity measure. An optimal cyclic alignment is a cyclic alignment of minimum weight.

The Cyclic Dynamic Time Warping (CDTW) measure $CDTW([X], [Y])$ is defined as the weight of the optimal cyclic alignment between X and Y. First, we are going to show that the optimal cyclic alignment can be defined in terms of alignments between non-cyclic sequences, i.e., in terms of $DTW(\cdot, \cdot)$; then, we will present an efficient procedure to compute it[1].

Lemma 1. *If $m, n > 1$ and (i_0, j_0), (i_1, j_1), ..., (i_{k-1}, j_{k-1}) is an optimal alignment between two sequences $x_0 x_1 \ldots x_{m-1}$ and $y_0 y_1 \ldots y_{n-1}$, there is at least one ℓ such that $i_\ell \neq i_{(\ell+1) \bmod m}$ and $j_\ell \neq j_{(\ell+1) \bmod n}$.*

Lemma 2. *The CDTW dissimilarity between $[X] = [x_0 x_1 \ldots x_{m-1}]$ and $[Y] = [y_0 y_1 \ldots y_{n-1}]$, can be computed as*

$$CDTW([X], [Y]) = \min_{0 \leq k < m} \min_{0 \leq \ell < n} DTW(\sigma^k(X), \sigma^\ell(Y)).$$

According to Lemma 2, the value of $CDTW([X], [Y])$ can be trivially computed in $O(m^2 n^2)$ time by solving mn recurrences. Maes showed in [7] that the Cyclic Edit Distance (CED), a related dissimilarity measure, can be computed in $O(m^2 n)$ time by performing cyclic shifts only on one of the sequences. This observation finally led to a $O(mn \lg m)$ time algorithm.

Is it possible to perform cyclic shifts on only one of the sequences when computing the CDTW? The answer is no: in general, $CDTW([X], [Y])$ is neither $\min_{0 \leq k < m} DTW(\sigma^k(X), Y)$ nor $\min_{0 \leq k < n} DTW(X, \sigma^k(Y))$, as the following counter-example shows: let z and w be two elements from Σ such that $\gamma(z, w) = 1$; the value of $CDTW([zwz], [wzw])$ is 0, since $DTW(zzw, zww) = 0$, but $DTW(zwz, wzw) = 2$ and $DTW(wzz, wzw) = DTW(zzw, wzw) = DTW(zwz, zww) = DTW(zwz, wwz) = 1$. Therefore, an equivalent of Maes' algorithm for the CED computation cannot be directly applied to CDTW dissimilarity computation.

Theorem 1. *The CDTW dissimilarity between two cyclic sequences, $[X]$ and $[Y]$, can be computed as*

$$CDTW([X], [Y]) = \min_{0 \leq k < m} \left(\min(DTW(\sigma^k(X), Y), DTW(\sigma^k(X) x_k, Y))\right).$$

---
[1] The reader is addressed to [8] to obtain proofs for the following lemmas and theorem.

The value of $DTW(\sigma^k(X), Y)$ and $DTW(\sigma^k(X)x_k, Y)$, for each k, can be obtained by computing shortest paths in an *extended warping graph* similar to the extended edit graph defined by Maes [7] (see Fig. 1 (a)). Since the non-crossing property of edit paths also holds for alignment paths (see Fig. 1 (b)), the Divide-and-Conquer approach proposed by Maes can be applied to CDTW. It should be taken into account that, unlike in Maes' algorithm, the optimal path starting at $(k, 0)$ can finish either at node $(k + m - 1, n - 1)$ or $(k + m, n - 1)$.

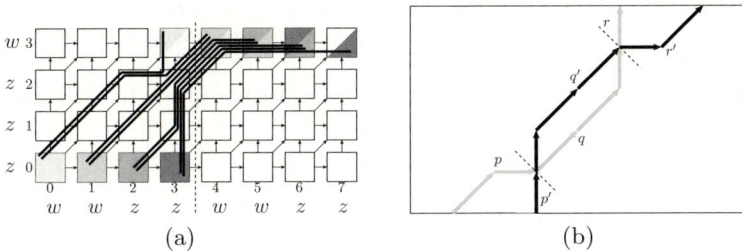

Fig. 1. (a) Extended warping graph for $X = wwzz$ and $Y = zzzw$. $\gamma(z, w) = 1$. Arcs ending at node (i, j) are weighted $\gamma(x_i, y_j)$. The optimal alignment for $[X]$ and $[Y]$ is the minimum weight path starting from any colored node in the lower row and ending at a node containing the same color in the upper row (all path candidates are shown with thick lines). (b) Optimal crossing paths can be avoided: if the weight of the subpath q is greater than the weight of the subpath q', the black path can be improved by traversing q' instead of q.

3 A Lower Bounding Function for the Cyclic DTW

Bunke and Bühler presented in [3] a method to approximate the Cyclic Edit Distance. These authors proposed to search for an optimal path in the edit graph underlying the computation of the Edit Distance between Y and $X \cdot X$, i.e., the concatenation of one of the sequences with itself. The optimal path can start and end at several nodes in the graph and it corresponds to the substring in $X \cdot X$ that most resembles Y.

We can adapt Bunke and Bühler's algorithm in order to efficiently approximate $CDTW([X], [Y])$. First, we define the "extended warping graph" (see Fig. 1a) as the warping graph underlying the computation of $DTW(X \cdot X, Y)$. The optimal path departing from any node $(k, 0)$ for $0 \leq k < m$, and arriving to any node $(k', n - 1)$, for $m - 1 \leq k' < 2m$, corresponds to the optimal alignment between a subsequence of $X \cdot X$ and Y. The BB estimation of $CDTW([X], [Y])$, that will be denoted as $BB(X, Y)$, is performed by initializing all starting nodes with 0 and computing the minimum value of any optimal path arriving at a final node. Thus, the BB algorithm can be computed in $\mathcal{O}(mn)$ time complexity.

It should be noted that every possible cyclic shift of X is a subsequence of $X \cdot X$ and, therefore, the optimal path in the extended warping graph corresponds to an optimal alignment between a subsequence of $X \cdot X$ and Y. All the optimal paths considered by the CDTW algorithm are paths in the extended warping

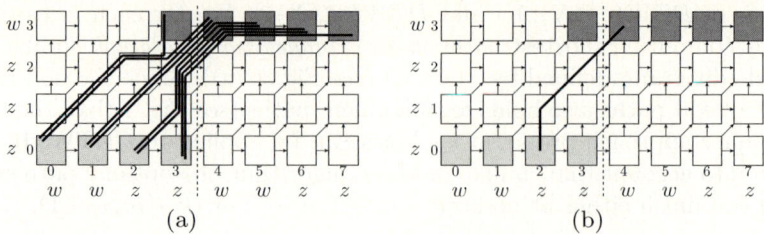

Fig. 2. (a) We can find all the paths corresponding to $DTW(\sigma^k(X), Y)$ and $DTW(\sigma^k(X)x_k, Y)$ for $0 \leq k < m$, departing from any node $(k, 0)$ for $0 \leq k < m$ (light grey nodes), and arriving to any node $(k', n-1)$, for $m-1 \leq k' < 2m$ (dark grey nodes). (b) The BB algorithm path that approximates the CDTW dissimilarity in the extended warping graph for X and Y. $\gamma(z, w) = 1$. The path must start from any light grey node in the lower row and end at a dark grey node in the upper row.

graph (see Fig. 1a and Fig. 2a); but, since there is no control over the length of the subsequence aligned by the optimal path in the extended edit graph, the optimal path underlying $BB(X, Y)$ may not correspond the optimal path found by the CDTW algorithm. The suboptimality of this method is due to the fact that the optimal path that it finds could start going from $(k, 0)$ and finish to $(k', n-1)$, with $k' \neq k+m-1$ and $k' \neq k+m$, while the path corresponding to $CDTW([X], [Y])$ should verify $k' = k+m-1$ or $k' = k+m$. The corresponding alignment path can be considered as a *pseudo-alignment* between $[X]$ and Y (see Fig. 2b). The following theorem is straightforward from the above discussion:

Theorem 2. *The BB estimation is a lower bound of the CDTW:*

$$BB(X, Y) \leq CDTW([X], [Y]).$$

4 NN Classification with the BB Lower Bound

The CDTW is a relatively expensive algorithm: it runs in $O(mn \lg n)$ and it requires to explicitly compute and store alignment paths. The BB algorithm is asymptotically faster (it runs in $O(mn)$ time) and leads to an efficient computation where only the weight of the optimal path is computed. When the CDTW is used to compute the nearest neighbour of a cyclic sequence in a set of cyclic sequences (for instance, for the purpose of classification), we use the lower bounding function BB to avoid the execution of the more computationally expensive, exact CDTW algorithm in many cases. The BB value obtained for a pair of cyclic sequences is compared with the lowest, exact CDTW value computed so far. The CDTW between this pair of cyclic sequences is compared only in case that their BB value is lower.

It is still possible to further speed up computation if we abort BB evaluation whenever we can guarantee that the final result will not improve the best CDTW known so far: we can stop the computation at the first row where all the values are greater than this external bound. The modified version of the BB algorithm is depicted in Fig. 3.

Algorithm BB
input: X, Y, $best\_so\_far$, output: $distance$
for i in 0 .. $|X| - 1$ do
  $M[i][0] = \gamma(X[i], Y[0])$
for i in $|X|$ .. $2|X| - 1$ do
  $M[i][0] = M[i-1][0] + \gamma(X[i], Y[0])$
for j in 1 .. $|Y| - 1$ do
  $M[0][j] = M[0][j-1] + \gamma(X[0], Y[j])$
for i in 1 .. $2|X| - 1$ do
  for j in 1 .. $|Y| - 1$ do
    $M[i][j] = \min(M[i-1][j-1], M[i-1][j], M[i][j-1]) + \gamma(X[i], Y[j])$
  if every element at row i is $\geq best\_so\_far$ then
    $distance = \infty$
    return
$distance = \min(M[i][|Y|-1]$ for i in $|X| - 1$ .. $2|X| - 1)$

Fig. 3. BB algorithm with anticipated end of computation using an external bound

5 Evaluation and Results

In order to assess the behaviour of the lower bounding function in a nearest neighbour computation problem, we have performed experiments on shape recognition tasks using three publicly available databases:

- MPEG-7 Core Experiments CE-Shape-1 (partB) [5]. It contains 1440 shapes divided in 70 categories, each categoriy with 20 images (see Fig. 4a).
- SQUID Demo database [9]. It consists of 1100 contours of marine species. Its developers do not provide information about categories (see Fig. 4b).
- Silhouette database [10]. It contains 1070 silhouettes. The shapes belong to 41 categories representing different objects: animals, tools, bones, hands, etc.

For each database we have performed nearest neighbour classification using leaving-one-out. Every shape was compared to the rest ones in the database in a randomized order to avoid time improvements related to a sequential order of the categories.

To describe the contours, two descriptors were used:

- a derivative of 2D landmark points of the contour obtained by Fourier Descriptors [1].
- a sequence of shape contexts [2]. Given a sequence of landmark points of the contour, for each point, an histogram of the relative coordinates of the remaining points is computed, where bins are uniform divisions of the log-polar space centred at that point.

In both cases, we have performed experiments with cyclic sequences of lengths 32 and 64.

The classification error results for the MPEG-7 and Silhouette databases with BB and CDTW are shown in Fig. 5. It can be seen that the classification results

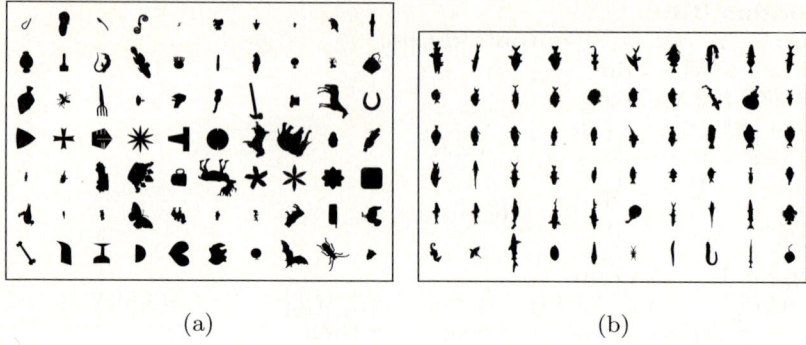

Fig. 4. Some images in (a) the MPEG-7 CE-Shape-1 and (b) the SQUID databases

		Derivative		Shape Contexts	
		32 points	64 points	32 points	64 points
BB	MPEG-7	56.64%	75.28%	16.00%	11.93%
	Silhouette	56.96%	70.90%	8.14%	3.85%
CDTW	MPEG-7	5.57%	5.35%	5.15%	2.35%
	Silhouette	5.98%	4.78%	3.84%	2.15%

Fig. 5. BB and CDTW classification error rates

	Derivative		Shape Contexts	
	32 points	64 points	32 points	64 points
MPEG-7	32.32%	38.79%	42.75%	48.34%
SQUID	32.15%	21.73%	35.53%	41.02%
Silhouette	31.77%	30.97%	39.10%	47.46%

Fig. 6. Percentage of time to compute the nearest neighbour with CDTW and the BB lower bound with respect to a pure CDTW-based procedure

	Derivative		Shape Contexts	
	32 points	64 points	32 points	64 points
MPEG-7	18.12%	21.18%	2.62%	2.56%
SQUID	18.23%	26.31%	1.48%	2.12%
Silhouette	16.79%	20.01%	2.12%	2.13%

Fig. 7. Pruning power. Percentage of times CDTW algorithm is computed.

of the BB algorithm are much worse than those obtained with CDTW. On the other hand, shape contexts offer a better classification since this descriptor contains much more information than the contour derivative, but it also supposes an increase of the time needed to compute each local dissimilarity between components of the sequence.

In Fig. 6, it is shown the time saved in each experiment using the BB algorithm as a lower bounding function and the external bound explained in section 4. In Fig. 7, it is the pruning power that is the fraction of total comparisons that does not require the computation of CDTW while still allowing use to guarantee that we have found the nearest match to a nearest-neighbour query.

6 Discussion

The BB function can approximate the CDTW and it is also a lower bound that can be used to speed up classification tasks. The BB algorithm has been modified to accept an external bound that speeds up computation, stopping whenever it can be guaranteed that $BB(X, Y)$ is greater than the best result obtained so far. The experiments show that the proposed method saves a considerable amount of time while preserving the error rate in classification problems.

References

1. I. Bartolini, P. Ciaccia, and M. Patella. WARP: Accurate Retrieval of Shapes Using Phase of Fourier Descriptors and Time Warping Distance. *IEEE Transactions on Pattern Analysis and Machine Intelligence*, 27(1):142–147, 2005.
2. Serge Belongie, Jitendra Malik, and Jan Puzicha. Shape matching and object recognition using shape contexts. *IEEE Trans. Pattern Anal. Mach. Intell*, 24(4):509–522, 2002.
3. H. Bunke and H. Bühler. Applications of approximate string matching to 2D shape recognition. *Pattern Recognition*, 26(12):1797–1812, 1993.
4. Eamonn J. Keogh. Exact indexing of dynamic time warping. In *VLDB*, pages 406–417, 2002.
5. J. Latecki, R. Lakämper, and U. Eckhardt. Shape descriptors for non-rigid shapes with a single closed contour. In *Proc. of the IEEE Conf. on Computer Vision and Pattern Recognition*, pages 424–429, 2000.
6. M. Maes. Polygonal Shape Recognition using String Matching Techniques. *Pattern Recognition*, 24(5):433–440, 1991.
7. M. Maes. On a Cyclic String-to-String Correction Problem. *Information Processing Letters*, 35:73–78, 1990.
8. Andrés Marzal and Vicente Palazón. Dynamic time warping of cyclic strings for shape matching. In *ICAPR (2)*, volume 3687 of *Lecture Notes in Computer Science*, pages 644–652. Springer, 2005.
9. F. Mokhtarian, J. Kittler, and S. Abbasi. Shape queries using image databases. http://www.ee.surrey.ac.uk/Research/VSSP/imagedb/demo.html.
10. D. Sharvit, J. Chan, H. Tek, and B.B. Kimia. Symmetry-based Indexing of Image Databases. In *CBAIVL98*, pages 56–62, 1998.
11. T. Sikora. The mpeg-7 visual standard for content description – an overview. *IEEE Transactions on Circuits and Systems for Video Technology*, 11(6):696–702, 2001.

Using Genetic Algorithm for Network Status Learning and Worm Virus Detection Scheme*

Donghyun Lim[1], Jinwook Chung[1], and Seongjin Ahn[2],**

[1] Dept. of Computer Engineering, Sungkyunkwan Univ.,
300 ChunChun-Dong JangAn-Gu, Suwon, South Korea, 440-746
{dhlim, jwchung}@songgang.skku.ac.kr
[2] Dept. of Computer Education, Sungkyunkwan Univ.,
53 MyungRyun-Dong JongRo-Gu, Seoul, South Korea, 110-745
sjahn@comedu.skku.ac.kr

Abstract. This paper tries to propose the worm virus detection system that focuses on many connection attempts, more frequently occurring in the process of scanning than their common transmission processes. And this paper tries to determine the critical value of connection attempt by using the ordinary time network traffic learning technique which applies the genetic algorithm in order to ensure accurate detection of virus, depending on the status of network. This system can reduce the damage from worm virus more quickly than the pattern-founded worm virus detection system because it applies the common characteristics of worm viruses to detect them, and the criteria for judgment can be altered in its application though the network may change.

1 Introduction

Recently, many efforts are being made to detect and isolate worm virus which threaten the reliability and stability of network resources. Some of the most noticeable examples include the network resource and security management architecture which uses the network interception algorithm [6], the network access control system that applies the architect address counterfeiting and VLAN filtering [7], and network security management which uses ARP counterfeiting [8], and so on.

Worm virus is defined as a malicious code which is characterized by its active dissemination through the network with some help or without any assistance of human being [1]. For the worm virus to be spread there should be a scanning process to search for and select the object to be attacked. The host infected with the worm virus in that scanning process tends to have dramatically increased number of IP address which is communicating with the unit of time. Though several methods have been proposed to detect the worm virus, most of those methods which analyze and compare the patterns of specific worm virus have

---

* This work was supported by grant No. R01-2004-000-10618-0 from the Basic Research Program of the Korea Science and Engineering Foundation.
** Corresponding author.

the drawbacks of not being able to detect the virus if the pattern of attack changes or a new set of attack happens. In respond to that, this paper tries to detect the worm virus by applying the specific characteristics [4] of scanning that attempts to make many connections within a short time mentioned in the above.

And it is necessary to study the network traffic to ensure accurate detection of virus as the number of scanning by worm virus can change depending on the status of network. For that, this researcher tries to propose the system that adapts itself to the network status by using genetic algorithm (GA).

The Section 2 of this paper examines the characteristics, detection techniques, Intrusion Detection System and genetic algorithm of worm virus as part of related study, and the Section 3 explains worm virus detection technique that uses the characteristics of scanning process. The Section 4 explains the learning technique which uses the genetic algorithm. Finally, the Section 5 draws the conclusion.

2 Related Study

2.1 Analysis on the Characteristics of Worm Virus

Worm virus is a program that takes advantage of the weakness of unspecific system from remote places to replicate itself and disseminate to other system. Generally, it referred to the program that replicates itself within the memory, but recently it refers to the program that replicates itself through the network on computer. The worm virus that replicates itself has the optimal environment condition to operate in the Internet, and that poses a great problem. Some of the most noticeable worm viruses include the Code Red, Nimda worm and so forth.

---

1. Scanning : Search for and select the next object to be attacked

2. Taking the control : Taking advantage of the weakness of host to be attacked to take the control

3. Spreading the virus : Replicating the malicious virus code to the host subject to its attack

4. Installation and execution: Installing the virus in the host to be attacked and then executing it.

Fig. 1. Propagation Processes of Worm Virus

The operation of worm virus is classified into direct worm and indirect worm at large, depending on the method of operation [2]. Direct worm virus takes the control on its own to spread the virus, whereas indirect worm relies on other means of transmission, such as email, to spread the virus indirectly. The direct worm usually takes advantage of the weakness of system such as buffer overflow, has a relatively broader scope of dissemination than the indirect worm, and is very fast in spreading the virus. Meanwhile the indirect worm usually spreads the virus via the following process.

2.2 Intrusion Detection System

The Intrusion Detection System [5] is a type of information protection system that detects the abnormal use, abuse and misuse which compromises the confidentiality, integrity and availability of system resources, and automatically takes countermeasures or transmits the alarm message to the manager to cope with the intrusion. It is a security system that monitors the use of network or system and detects the intrusion in real time by applying the intrusion pattern database and expert system, etc, a function beyond the ordinary access control. In other words, the Intrusion Detection System is a software that detects and cope with those illegal trespassing quickly, and various software exist, ranging from simple log file analysis to complicated real time Intrusion Detection System.

The intrusion detection technique is classified into the misuse detection and anomaly detection at large. Generally, the misuse detection defines the known behavior from the attack or abnormal behavior and determines the intrusion if the collected data matches the defined behavior. Anomaly detection is also called statistical detection technique, and is a system that informs of the detected intrusion if an event which causes dramatic change or rare event happens by defining the normal and usual status as the criteria for the comparison.

In detecting the intrusion, there are problems of false positive and false negative. False positive means that what is not the intrusion is determined as the intrusion and false negative means that the actual intrusion fails to be detected. The former causes users to complain due to unnecessary policy and may undermine the productivity, while the latter fails to achieve the original goal. Therefore, Intrusion Detection System should remove the false negative and false positive as much as possible.

2.3 Genetic Algorithm

Genetic algorithm is the optimization technique that uses the mechanism of genetics and evolution in the nature to solve the problem. The genetic algorithm was introduced for the first time in the "Adaptation on Natural and Artificial Systems" written by John Holland in 1975.

If the information is transmitted to the living thing through genes from parents, the genetic information of individual which possesses greater adaptive power to cope with the environment than other individuals is primarily transmitted to the following generation. That is because the individual with inferior adaptive power is short-lived and cannot multiply. At the same time, species with weak adaptive power is wed out naturally. Based on that principle, individuals highly capable of adapting themselves to the environment multiply generation after generation. This is the basic principle of heredity and evolution.

Genetic algorithm expresses the possible solutions to problems as the data structure of defined pattern, and then creates better solutions by changing them gradually. In other words, it expresses possible solutions to problems as chromosomes and then changes them gradually to create better solutions. Each possible solution is deemed to be the organism or individual, and their collection is called 'population'.

One individual is composed of one or various chromosomes and the operators that change the chromosomes are called genetic operators. Basic operator includes the selection which selects the individual subject to the crossover, the crossover which replaces the genes between two chromosomes to generate new individual, and mutation which changes specific area of gene based on probability.

3 Worm Virus Detection Technique

There are very wide ranging types or worm viruses and their pattern of operation is very far ranging. Detection plan should be established on the basis of their operating patterns to detect various worm viruses. The character of scanning process which is among the method of worm viruses' operation is used in this paper to detect the worm virus. The process of looking for the next target is required because worm viruses can spread themselves. This process creates the IP address on a random basis to search for the IP address to be attacked next time.

At this time, the connection to IP address which is not actually used can be attempted because the IP address is created randomly. Moreover, a lot of IP addresses are searched within a short time for the fast dissemination speed of worm virus. Using this character, worm virus can be detected on the basis of the number of IP address that the host is communicating with within the unit of time. At this time, though a method to install the agent system in all hosts can be considered, I propose the method that installs the agent system at the location where all traffics of network pass in order to analyze all traffics. Agent system collects and analyzes the packet and compares the source IP address and destination IP address to investigate the number of the communicating IP address for each managing IP address.

In this paper, the packing monitoring is performed for three items as shown in Fig. 2 to ensure the maximum detection with the minimum analysis. First, analyze the address resolution protocol (ARP)[3] packet and investigate the case where the host tries to approach other host. Here, it is not the number of ARP-requesting packet but the source address and destination address of ARP-requesting packet that should be investigated. This host can judge that the scanning is being performed inside the network if same source address requests MAC value for countless destination addresses. Specifically, if the own IP address is the virus that fixes the a.b.c and creates d randomly to search for the following destination address in the event that the own IP address is a.b.c.d, this method assures an easy detection. This is an improved ARP detection method, and it was considered that the ARP requesting pack is not to be transmitted if

MAC address is already possessed. It is the method that is used to investigate the number of host that is in process of linking in case of the network with same source address and destination address. In this method, only the source of IP address and the address of destination are compared and other fields are not to be investigated in order to improve the detection function at the maximum. This final method is used in scanning through the external network, and includes both methods in the above, and considered that most of worm viruses take advantage of similar weakness. Considering a vast majority of worm viruses tend to attack the known port of Window Operating System such as 80, 135, 445 port, I used the method that analyzes only the packet for specific port among the collected packets. Compare the source and destination IP address and record the number of the connecting host for the IP address subject to the management if the packet is collected, the port is investigated and included in the port subject to the investigation.

```
1. packet ← New Captured Packet

2. if (packet = ARP)

3.    then Database .arp_mark[packet.source_ip][packet.target_ip] = checked

4. else if (packet = IP)

5.    then if (packet.source ip ∈ Managed IP List and packet .target_ip ∈ Managed IP List )

6.        then Database .ip[packet.source_ip][packet.target_ip] = checked

7.    if (packet = TCP) or (packet = UDP)

8.        then if (packet.target_port = WeakPort List )

9.            then if (packet.target_ip ∉ Database .port[packet.source_ip] List)
10.                add packet.target_ip in Database .port[packet.source_ip] List
```

Fig. 2. Algorithm of Worm Virus Detection (Packet Monitoring)

After it collect information through packet monitoring as Fig. 2, it set up critical value numer about ARP, IP and a connection host of port and compare with collection data about each IP address in a managed object IP address list as Fig. 3. Perceive to a host infected with a Worm virus than the value which set up if large.

4 Learning Technique That Applies the Genetic Algorithm (GA)

The detection of worm virus relies on the APP, IP, number of the connection host of port, and critical value. If the critical value of those numbers are too low, false positive occurs which mixes up even the normal connection with the worm,

```
1. α ← ARP threshold value, β ← IP threshold value, γ ← Port threshold value
2. for ip in Managed IP addresses List
3.   arp_count ← count checked database.ARP[ip]
4.     if (arp_count > α)
5.       then notify ip is infected.
6.     else
7.       initalize database.ARP[ip]
8.   ip_count ← count checked database.IP[ip]
9.     if (ip_count > β)
10.      then notify ip is infected.
11.    else
12.      initalize database.IP[ip]
13.  port_count ← count checked database.PORT[ip]
14.    if (port_count > γ)
15.      then notify ip is infected.
16.    else
17.      initalize database.PORT[ip]
```

Fig. 3. Algorithm of Worm Virus Detection (Counting Connections)

whereas false negative occurs which fails to detect the worm if the critical value is too high. GA is used to determine the optimal value of those critical values. In the proposed system, GA learns the input value of fuzzy controller. Learning data is required for the learning. The learning data is composed by the pair of [the number of connection host of ARP/IP/Port] [Whether there is any worm virus infection] The learning program learns the fuzzy value by using learning data shown in Table 1. In order to learn the fuzzy input value, the fuzzy section should be converted to a genetic type than can be used by GA as Fig. 4.

Table 1. Structure of Learning Data

IP Count	Infection or Not	ARP Count	Infection or Not	Port Count	Infection or Not
84	True	12	False	37	False
12	False	77	True	61	True
1	False	50	True	48	False
8	False	23	False	72	True
..	..	..	..	..	..

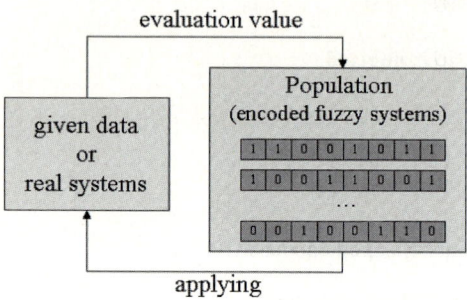

Fig. 4. Diagram Showing the Structure of Fuzzy System That Uses GA

The proposed system had the fuzzy section in the form of trapezoid, and used each point as the genetic value. Each section in Fig. 5 can be expressed by the following equation.

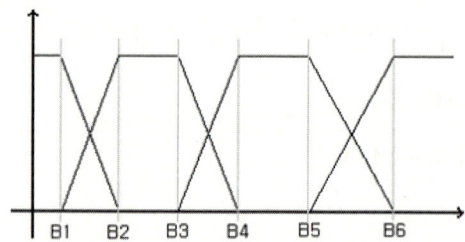

Fig. 5. Section of Genetic Type

Section 1: (0, 0) (0, 1) (B1, 1) (B2, 2)

Section 2: (B1, 0) (B2, 1) (B3, 1) (B4, 0)

Section 3: (B3, 0) (B4, 1) (B5, 1) (B6, 0)

Fig. 6. Indication of Genetic Type of Trapezoid Section

The section is divided into 9 sections all told, and a total of 16 points from B1 to B16 are created which define the section in this case. Therefore, the gene

```
RULE 0: IF IP_Count is B1 THEN Low;
RULE 1: IF IP_Count is B2 THEN Low;
RULE 2: IF IP_Count is B3 THEN Low;
RULE 3: IF IP_Count is B4 THEN Slightly_High;
RULE 4: IF IP_Count is B5 THEN Slightly_High;
RULE 5: IF IP_Count is B6 THEN High;
RULE 6: IF IP_Count is B7 THEN High;
RULE 7: IF IP_Count is B8 THEN Very_High;
RULE 8: IF IP_Count is B9 THEN Very_High;
```

Fig. 7. Proposed Fuzzy Rule

```
If the result from the input learning data is False:
  - If the result value of fuzzy controller is Low, the fitness is +5 scores.
  - If the result value of fuzzy controller is Slightly_High, the fitness is +2 scores.
  - If the result value of fuzzy controller is High, the fitness is +1 score.
  - If the result value of fuzzy controller is Very_High, the fitness is 0 score.
If the result from the input learning data is True:
  - If the result value of fuzzy controller is Low, the fitness is 0 score.
  - If the result value of fuzzy controller is Slightly_High, the fitness is +1 score.
  - If the result value of fuzzy controller is High, the fitness is +3 score.
  - If the result value of fuzzy controller is Very_High, the fitness is +5 scores.
```

Fig. 8. Fitness evaluation of Fuzzy input

can be defined in the form of [B1 B2 B3 ... B15 B16]. In creating the initial individual, 16 integers are created randomly, and then they become the genetic types if they are arranged in ascending order. Rule is not separately learned but fixed because the input variable is only one. The proposed fuzzy rule is like this;

The result value is divided into 4 values which indicate the possibility of worm infection: Low, Slightly_High, High, Very_High. As for the learning, the fitness is determined depending on the result obtained by fuzzy controller after the genetic type is converted to input value, and crossover for the superior individual is performed. The fitness of fuzzy input value is evaluated by the following method.

The evaluation algorithm of GA derives the fitness in the wake of the learning of all learning data. If the fitness is obtained, the crossover of superior individual is performed. The individual is based on the RouletteWheel which has the possibility of selection proportional to the fitness, and the selection value is defined as 4. The crossover method is 2 point crossover, and the mutation rate was defined to be 0.15

If the aforesaid fitness method was applied, definitive evaluation (if false, low, or if true, very high) would be made to get the top score in case that GA is sure that the input value is certainly the worm virus. If GA is unsure, it will make ambiguous evaluation (slightly_ High) to avoid the cut in scores as much as possible. As a result, Slightly_High will be learned at the boundary line where the infection of worm virus is determined, and if that value is exceeded, High or Very_High will be determined as to the fuzzy section.

5 Conclusion

This paper made it possible to detect fast detection of worm virus by using the function that detects the host infected with worm virus. In addition, this paper proposed the method that enables the optimized system itself to determine the worm virus status by using the fuzzy value for critical value, instead of the absolute value that users enter, and learning through genetic algorithm.

This researcher tries to experiment to find how much efficiency the system that learns the critical value on its own through the precise simulation on the network identical to real situation, which applies this system, can achieve in the future, compared to the existing structure which requires users to input. Moreover, it seems that it will identify and complement the problem arising from the simulation, and through that process, more improved system may be developed.

References

1. Darrell M. Kienzle and Matthew C. Elder, "Recent worms: a survey and trends," Proceedings of the 2003 ACM workshop on Rapid Malcode, 2003
2. Jason C. Hung, Kuan-Cheng Lin, Anthony Y. Chang, Nigel H. Lin and Louis H. Lin, "A bahavior-based anti-worm system," In Proceedings on AINA'03, China, 2003
3. David C. Plummer, "An ethernet address resolution protocol," RFC 826, 1982
4. Vincent Berk and George Bakos, "Designing a framework for active worm detection on global networks," in Proceedings of the First IEEE International Workshop on Information Assurance, 2003
5. Wagner D. and Dean R., "Intrusion detection via static analysis," in Proceedings of 2001 IEEE Symposium on Security and Privacy, 2001

6. Jahwan Koo, Seongjin Ahn, Jinwook Chung, "Network blocking algorithm and architecture for network resource and security management," in Proceedings of International Scientific-Practical Conference "Problems of Operation of Information Networks", 2004
7. Wonwoo Choi, Hyuncheol Kim, Seongjin Ahn and Jinwook Chung, "A network access control system using on address spoofing and VLAN filtering," The 4th Asia Pacific International Symposium on Information Technology, 2005
8. Kyohyeok Kwon, Seongjin Ahn and Jinwook Chung, "Network security management using ARP spoofing," in Proceedings of ICCSA 2004, 2004
9. D. E. Goldberg, Genegic Algorithm in Search, Optimization, and Machine Learnig, Addison-Wesley publishing company, Inc. 1989
10. D. Dasgupta and F. A. Gonzalez, "An intelligent decision support system for intrusion detection and response," In Proceedings of International Workshop on Mathematical Methods, Models and Architecture for Computer Networks Security, pp 1-14, May 2001
11. M. Crosbie and G. Spafford, "Applying genetic programmings of to intrusion detection," In Proceedings of AAAI Symposium on Genetic Programming, pp. 1-8 November 1995.

Clustering by Integrating Multi-objective Optimization with Weighted K-Means and Validity Analysis

Tansel Özyer[1,3], Reda Alhajj[1,2], and Ken Barker[1]

[1] Dept. of Computer Science, University of Calgary, Calgary, Alberta, Canada
[2] Dept. of Computer Science, Global University, Beirut, Lebanon
[3] Dept. of Comp. Eng., TOBB Economics & Technology University, Ankara, Turkey

Abstract. This paper presents a clustering approach that integrates multi-objective optimization, weighted k-means and validity analysis in an iterative process to automatically estimate the number of clusters, and then partition the whole given data to produce the most natural clustering. The proposed approach has been tested on real-life dataset; results of both weighted and unweighed k-means are reported to demonstrate applicability and effectiveness of the proposed approach.

1 Introduction

Clustering is unsupervised classification; the number of classes is not given a priori. K-means [1] is a well known clustering technique. A recent study related to k-means involves feature weighting for mixed type data. For instance, Desarbo et al [2] proposed the first method for variable weighting for k-means in the SYNCLUS algorithm. Modha and Spangler [3] developed a method for variable weighting in k-means. Another study [4] presents W-k-means, which can automatically weight variables based on their importance in clustering. Friedman and Meulman [5] published a method to cluster objects on subsets of attributes; instead of assigning a weight to each variable for the entire dataset, they compute a weight for each variable in each cluster.

Realizing the importance of simultaneously considering multiple criteria in clustering, we started a challenging project MOKGA (Multi-Objective K-Means Genetic Algorithm), which integrates multi-objective optimization, k-means and validity analysis. The target is to derive alternative solutions with identified characteristics, rather than forcing the clustering towards a single solution. Another advantage of this approach is automatically deciding on possible number of clusters by validating the alternative solutions to favor a particular solution. The two objectives utilized in the previous approach are minimizing the number of clusters and minimizing the total within cluster variation. The developed initial approach has been reported successful in clustering datasets from different domains [6,7]. However, we identified three main weaknesses of the initial approach, which are actually directions to enrich it into the more sophisticated approach described in this paper: it skips some main objectives; it does not scale well for large datasets; and it does not utilize external validity indexes in analyzing alternative clustering.

We realized that each alternative solution reported by our previous approach does not necessarily reflect the most natural clustering because it only emphasizes within cluster homogeneity and neglects separateness between clusters. Further, the first approach does not scale well for large datasets because it considers the whole dataset for encoding the chromosomes. To overcome these weaknesses, we developed alternative solutions, including a divide and conquer based approach [8], and the approach presented in this paper, which integrates weighted k-means to enrich the process. This approach solves the scalability problem by breaking the whole clustering process into two stages. It depends on sampling techniques in the first stage to estimate the most appropriate number of clusters; and then the whole dataset is clustered in the second stage. To sum up, the first stage utilizes sampling techniques and involves an iterative process that integrates weighted k-means with a multi-objective genetic algorithm. Each iteration runs for a particular number of clusters k (from prespecified range) to estimate corresponding alternative clustering; and validity analysis is then applied to select the most natural single clustering for the considered value of k. To speedup the process, an iteration starts with the result produced by the predecessor iteration, if any. This leads to additional computational advantage by efficiently using the pre-computed results. The outcome from this first stage is the most natural single clustering for each value of k in the prespecified range. In the second stage, validity analysis is applied on these alternative clustering results to estimate the most natural number of clusters, which is then used to cluster the whole data. These are actually the main contributions of the work described in this paper. At the end, some key features of this approach may be enumerated as follows: using weighted k-means integrated with k-means clustering for suggesting several partitions with varying feature weights; improves external cluster validity indexes by exploiting the multi-objective results to find the reference partition to use against the clusters; using multi-objective genetic algorithm in clustering of mixed-type data sets; at the end of each generation, we used k-means to achieve quick convergence, and the features are weighted after that; individuals obtained at the last generation are analyzed to end up with the pairwise correlation analysis of the weights among features in order to determine the kind of relationship that exists between them.

The rest of the paper is organized as follows. Section 2 introduces the proposed approach. Section 3 reports test results of both weighted and unweighed k-means on real-life dataset from UCI Machine Learning Repository. Section 4 is summary and conclusions.

2   The Proposed Clustering Method

In this section, we describe the proposed approach which integrates multi-objective optimization, weighted k-means and validity analysis to produce optimal clustering. We try to estimate the most natural clustering by employing sampling techniques and two objectives, namely maximizing inter-cluster similarity and minimizing intra-cluster similarity. This iteratively reports the most natural clustering alternatives for all numbers of clusters in prespecified range. We start with the range [2, 10], as most datasets reported optimal number of clusters in this range. However, because some datasets may have optimal number of clusters larger than 10, we adapted into the process a step that enlarges the checked range such that, as long as the process selects the optimal number of clusters to be the upper bound of the checked range, the range size is enlarged by 5 and the the iterative process is resumed to consider the new possible candidates. At the end of each iteration, cluster validity analysis is applied to favor the optimal clustering within each reported alternative set. After the optimal clustering is obtained for each tested number of clusters, validity analysis is utilized once again to report the most appropriate number of clusters for the tested dataset. Finally, the actual clustering is performed on the whole dataset based on the estimated number of clusters parameter.

For cluster validation, we use the Clest algorithm adapted to multi-objective optimization [9]; it uses a re-sampling technique. The original dataset is split into two non-overlapping subsets, which are clustered as classifier and test. The classifier is checked with the rest of the data not used in the classification, and the similarity between the classification and the test subset is measured. The same is done for uniform data, which may be obtained in two ways: either random feature values are selected, or the shape may be preserved by using principle component values to compile the uniformly distributed instances. Finally, we measure the similarity between two partitions, say P_1 and P_2, using [10]: $F\&M(P_1, P_2) = \frac{C_{11}}{\sqrt{m_1 m_2}}$, where C_{11} is the number of pairs of data points that are in the same cluster in P_1 and P_2; m_1 and m_2 are the number of pairs co-occurring in the same cluster within P_1 and P_2, respectively.

A reference data set is generate and partitioned. The aim of the clustering is to get the predictor as the true labeled a priori known class label. These are obtained by using the mean values of the static estimator of the samples, based on the assumption that there is small statistical bias and clustering results are validated with the reference data.

The proposed process for iterative multi-objective weighted k-means with validity analysis is depicted in Algorithm 1.

Algorithm 1. *Iterative Multi-Objective Weighted K-Means with Cluster Validity*
Input: *k_{min} and k_{max}: number of clusters parameter range; D: original dataset; trial number of samples; subtrial number of splits over samples.*
Output: *number of cluster values that have difference d_k greater than d_{min} and p_k less than p_{max}.*

for $k_{min} = 1$ to k_{max} {
  for $l = 1$ to trial {
    scores[k][l] = 0.00
    for $m = 0$ to subtrial   randomscores[k][l][m] = 0.00 } }
for $k_{min} = 1$ to k_{max} {
  for $l = 1$ to trial {
    $(D', D'') = Split(D)$

$Pop'_{k,l,0} = Cluster(D')$
$BestIndividual'_{k,l,0} = FindClosest(Pop'_{k,l,0})$
$\overline{Individual}_{k,l,0} = Classify(Pop'_{k,l,0}, D')$
$Pop''_{k,l,0} = Cluster(D'')$
$BestIndividual''_{k,l,0} = FindClosest(Pop''_{k,l,0})$
$scores[k][l] = Compare(\overline{Individual}_{k,l,0}, BestIndividual''_{k,l,0})$
$S^l = SampleData(D)$
for $m = 1$ to subtrial {
  $(D', D'') = Split(S^l)$
  $Pop'_{k,l,m} = Cluster(D')$
  $BestIndividual'_{k,l,m} = FindClosest(Pop'_{k,l,m})$
  $\overline{Individual}_{k,l,m} = Classify(Pop'_{k,l,m}, D')$ } }
  $Pop''_{k,l,m} = Cluster(D'')$
  $BestIndividual''_{k,l,m} = FindClosest(Pop''_{k,l,m})$
  $randomscores[k][l][m] = Compare(\overline{Individual}_{k,l,m}, BestIndividual''_{k,l,m})$ } }
if $(l == 0)$ $AvgScore[k][l] = median(scores[k][l][0])$
else $AvgScore[k][l] = median(randomscores[k][l][1..m])$
$K = \{k_{\min} \leq k \leq k_{\max} : p_k \leq p_{\max}, d_k \geq d_{\min}\}$

endAlgorithm

Algorithm 1 finds the largest significant difference. For every k, d_k denotes the difference between $scores[k][l][0]$ and avg_{score} (the average of $AvgScore[k][l], l > 0$). For every value of d_k, the significance of the difference should be greater than the threshold value d_{min}; and p_{max} is the percentage of the number of cases where $AvgScore[k][l] > scores[k][l][0]$. If K is null, then $\hat{k} = 1$; otherwise $\hat{k} = arg\ max\ d_k$. Finally, the main functions/terms used in Algorithm 1 are described next. $SampleData(D)$: Data sampling under the assumption that there is uniformity in the distribution. $(D', D'') = Split(S^l)$: Splitting the data into two non-overlapping sets. $BestIndividual'_{k,l,0} = FindClosest(Pop'_{k,l,0})$: The partition is obtained based on the closeness to all the other derived solutions; all results use clustering objectives according to non-dominated solutions.

Definition 1 (Best Individual). *Given a reference dataset D', the partitions after executing $Cluster(D', k)$ are represented by $Pop'_{k,l,0}$. $BestIndividual'_{k,l,0}$ is the individual chosen from the most agreed upon pairwise partitioning among all solutions, such that $\forall j, j = 1..popsize, Pop'_{k,l,0}[j] \in Pop'_{k,l,0}$ and $Average(F\&M(BestIndividual'_{k,l,0}) \leq Average(F\&M(Pop'_{k,l,0}[j], Pop'_{k,l,0}[m])$*

$\overline{Individual}_{k,l,0} = Classify(Pop'_{k,l,0}, D')$: This is done based on the comparison of two partitioning. Here, we utilize F&M external validity index to compare the two partitions. Multivariate Gaussian conditional density is used for the maximum likelihood discriminant rule, DLDA (Diagonal Linear Discriminant Analysis), as in the original Clest algorithm. $C(x) = \arg\min_{1 \leq j \leq k} \sum_{d=1..D} \frac{x_d - \mu_{jd}}{\sigma_j}$

Sub-goals can be defined as fitness functions; and instead of scalarizing them to find the goal as the overall fitness function with the user defined weight values, we expect the system to find the set of best solutions, i.e., the pareto-optimal front. By using the specified formulas, in each generation, each chromosome in the population is evaluated and assigned a value for each fitness function.

Concerning the objectives, we used the the following inter-cluster separability formulas for the separateness, where C and D denote clusters.

Average Linkage: $d(C,D) = \frac{1}{|C|\cdot|D|} \sum_{(x \in C,\ y \in D)} d(x,y)$; note that the cardinalities of C and D may be omitted to reduce the scaling factor.

Complete Linkage: $d(C,D) = \max_{(x \in C,\ y \in D)} d(x,y)$

Centroid Linkage: $d(C,D) = d(v_C, v_D)$, where v_C and v_D are the centroids of the two clusters.

Average to Centroid: $d(C,D) = \frac{1}{|C|+|D|} \left(\sum_{x \in C} d(x, v_D) + \sum_{y \in D} d(y, v_C) \right)$

For homogeneity, we used the intra-cluster distance formula, namely

Total Within Cluster Variation: $TWCV = \sum_{n=1}^{N} \sum_{d=1}^{D} X_{nd}^2 - \sum_{k=1}^{K} \frac{1}{Z_k} \sum_{d=1}^{D} SF_{kd}^2$,

where $X_1, X_2, \ldots, X_N$ are N objects, X_{nd} denotes feature d of pattern X_n ($n= 1$ to N); SF_{kd} is the sum of the dth features of all the patterns in cluster $k(G_k)$; Z_k denotes the number of patterns in cluster $k(G_k)$. Actually, SF_{kd} is computed as: $SF_{kd} = \sum_{\vec{x}_n \in G_k} X_{nd}$, $(d = 1, 2, \ldots D)$.

We modified the two objectives into minimization; the separateness value is multiplied by -1 for the minimization. After that, both objectives are normalized by dividing their values by the corresponding maximum values.

Initially, the *current generation* is set to zero. Each individual in the population is represented by a chromosome of length n, where n is the number of instances in the sample dataset. Every gene is represented by an allele, where allele i is the cluster number of instance i in the dataset. Every chromosome in the population suggests a partition. If the chromosome represents k clusters, then each gene a_n ($n=1$ to N) takes a value from the interval $[1, k]$. The program starts by initializing the population. Then for the next generation, parent chromosomes are selected by using pareto domination tournament. The recombination operation occurs between parent individuals (crossover and mutation). This is followed by one time k-means iteration to reorganize the assigned cluster numbers for quick convergence. Features are re-weighted according to their contribution to the clustering.

The selection using pareto domination tournament step picks two candidate items from (*population size*- t_{dom}) to participate in the pareto domination tournament against the t_{dom} individuals for their survival in the population. In the selection part, t_{dom} individuals are randomly picked from the population. With two randomly selected chromosome candidates from (*population size*- t_{dom}) individuals, each candidate is compared against each individual in the comparison set, t_{dom}. If a candidate is dominated by the comparison set, then it is deleted from the population permanently; otherwise, it resides in the population.

After running some initial tests using alternative cross-over operators from the literature, it was realized that one-point cross-over satisfies the target and has lower cost. So, it is applied on randomly chosen two chromosomes. It is carried out on the population with probability p_c. After the crossover, mutation is applied on the current population to guarantee convergence. After every generation, a data point is assigned to the closest cluster with respect to the inter-intra cluster distance average value. The process terminates when either when the difference between two generation satisfies a predefined threshold, or after running up to the maximum number of generations.

As feature weighting is concerned, we refer to the work described in [4]. Assume data $X = X_1, X_2, .., X_N$ is composed of N objects with m features, i.e., $X_i = x_{i1}, x_{i2}, .., x_{im}$. The objective function is to minimize:

$$P(U, Z, W) = \sum_{l=1}^{k} \sum_{i=1}^{N} \sum_{j=1}^{m} u_{il} w_j^\beta d(x_{ij}, z_{lj}) \qquad (1)$$

subject to $\sum_{l=1}^{k} u_{il} = 1, \ 1 \leq i \leq N$

$u_{il} \in \{0, 1\} \ 1 \leq i \leq N, 1 \leq l \leq k$

$\sum_{l=1}^{k} w_j = 1, \ 1 \leq j \leq m$

Here, U is an $N \times k$ indicator function, where N is the number of objects and k is the number of clusters; $Z = Z_1, Z_2, ..Z_k$ is the partition of k clusters, and function $d(x_{ij}, z_{lj})$ is the distance between the jth attribute of object i and partition z_{lj}; W is $1 \times m$ row vector representing the weight per attribute of the partition. Weight values are computed by using Lagrange multiplier:

$$\hat{w} = \frac{1}{\sum_{t=1}^{h} \left[\frac{D_j}{D_t}\right]^{\frac{1}{\beta-1}}} \qquad (2)$$

where D_j is the total distance $d(x_{ij}, z_{lj})$ with hard membership value for attribute j, and D_t is the total distance value [4]; $\hat{w} = 0$ if $D_j = 0$. Since we have two objectives in the iterative process, we use two different weight values, one per objective, by employing the same formula for homogeneity and separateness. We take the average of the two weights as the final weight for each attribute.

3 Experiments and Results

The tests have been conducted using Wine from UCI Machine Learning Repository. **Wine** from an Italian region are classified into 3 classes; 13 constituents are detected inside as continuous features, 178 examples and 3 classes (59, 71, and 48). The tests were run on PC with Intel 4, 2GHz CPU, 512MB RAM, running Windows XP. The proposed algorithm was implemented with GAlib (C++ Library with GA Components (2.4.6) [11], and NSGA-II source code (Compiled with g++). Necessary parts were (re)implemented for the multi-objective case, and NSGA-II ranking mechanism was incorporated after it was transformed into C++. The cluster validity section was done using Matlab 7.0.

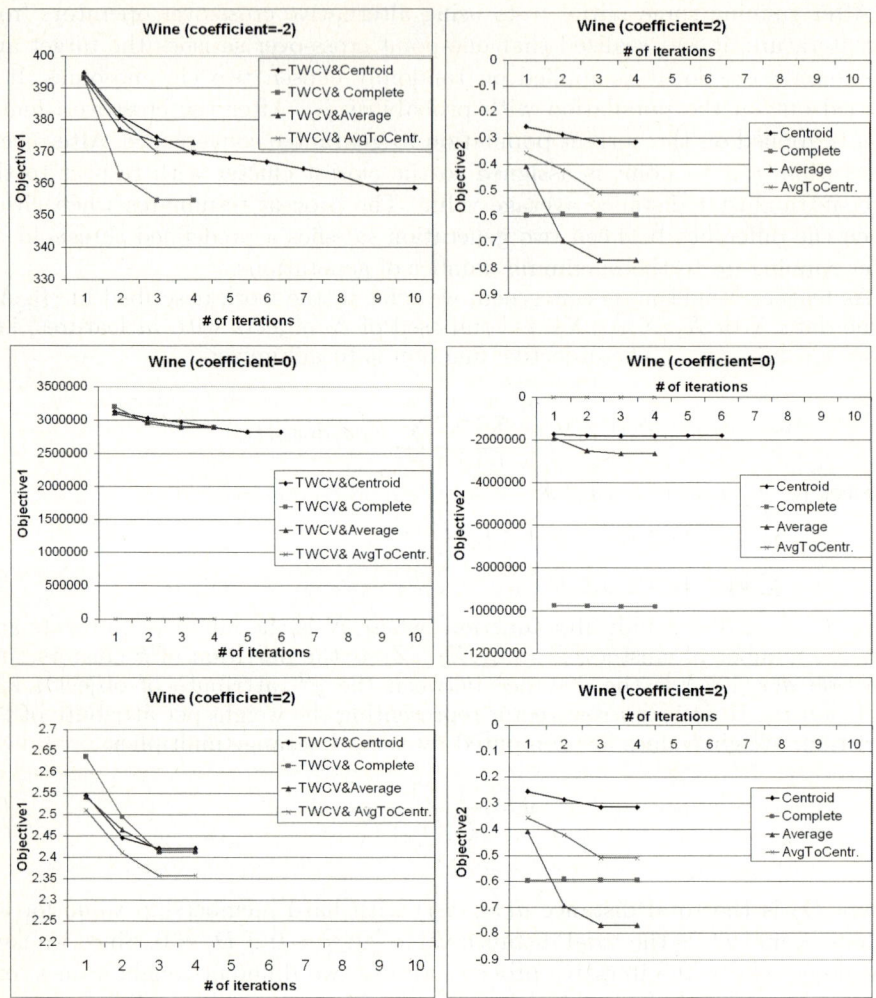

Fig. 1. Convergence of Intra-cluster and Inter-Cluster Distance for $\beta \in \{-2, 0, 2\}$

We run our implementation 20 times for each data set with the following parameters, which have been selected by running some initial experiments; in each initial experiment all the parameters were fixed except the one for which the appropriate value is to be estimated. *population size*=100; t_{dom} *for the selection* is 10; *tournament size* is approximately $\frac{no\ of\ items}{5}$, (20% of the entire data set); *p(crossover)* for the selection is 0.9; and *p(mutation)*= 0.05.

For the cluster validity part of the iterative process, the number of cluster parameter is estimated for the described objectives within the given range. For the estimation, we used re-sampling techniques with the external cluster validity index, *F&M*. We tested four cases: (1) TWCV and Centroid; (2) TWCV and Complete; (3) TWCV and Average; (4) TWCV and Average To Centroid. Also,

Table 1. External Index Values w.r.t. Real Partition

	β	Proposed Method				Best Values for Final Population			
		Rand	Mirkin	F&M	Jacc	Rand	Mirkin	F&M	Jacc
(1)	-2	0.71	0.29	0.57	0.401	0.73	0.267	0.614	0.440
	0	0.72	0.28	0.58	0.406	0.73	0.272	0.625	0.448
	2	0.84	0.16	0.77	0.619	0.93	0.0745	0.888	0.801
(2)	-2	0.71	0.29	0.57	0.39	0.74	0.259	0.655	0.471
	0	0.71	0.29	0.58	0.403	0.73	0.273	0.660	0.471
	2	0.81	0.19	0.73	0.570	0.9	0.09	0.850	0.740
(3)	-2	0.71	0.29	0.57	0.401	0.74	0.263	0.620	0.438
	0	0.72	0.28	0.59	0.417	0.73	0.266	0.618	0.44
	2	0.89	0.11	0.84	0.723	0.94	0.059	0.911	0.837
(4)	-2	0.72	0.28	0.58	0.412	0.74	0.258	0.625	0.444
	0	0.72	0.28	0.59	0.414	0.73	0.271	0.612	0.433
	2	0.92	0.08	0.88	0.784	0.94	0.0594	0.911	0.837

we used three different values for coefficient β, namely -2, 0 and 2. At the end, for the final cluster validity analysis, we used Clest based algorithm. We did the sampling 10 times by using .75 of the original data set and split each sample into two different parts.

In order to show the convergence of the proposed algorithm while clustering the tested dataset, the two objectives, inter-cluster distance and intra-cluster distance, are displayed in Figure 1 as objective 1 and objective 2 versus the number of iterations. Here, the number of iterations is small because of using the k-means operator.

At the end of the clustering process, we accept every clustering solution and try to find the most similar to the rest. In other words, the most agreed upon solution is proposed as the natural clustering solution. For this purpose, we utilize F&M validity index, which considers only the co-occurring partitions in a cluster. Here, it would also be possible to show the best clustering solution among the population by using the reference partition, which holds predefined true class labels of the dataset. Both solutions are presented for different scenarios to demonstrate the effectiveness of the proposed multi-objective genetic algorithm based approach.

We used four external cluster validity indexes: Rand, Mirkin, F&M and Jaccard to check the similarity between the partition we found and the partition with the real class labels. Rand index takes into account the number of pairs that exist in different and same clusters; it is scaled to the number of object pairs in the dataset. Jaccard coefficient is the ratio of the number of objects in the same cluster for both partitions to the possible number of object pairs except object pairs in different clusters for both partitions. Mirkin index considers only object pairs in different clusters for both partitions and finds the dissimilarity. So, Mirkin's formula is based on the disagreement (dissimilarity) of partitions, while the other three indexes measure the agreement (similarity). These measurements vary based on whether pairs of objects are in the same cluster or not. By considering these four indexes, the results reported in Tables 1 reflect the validity analysis for Wine.

As a result, effectiveness of weighted k-means clustering has been reported. According to the obtained index values, Wine clustering performance increase by fixing the weight at 2. Weighting helps in finding the most and the least effective features in clustering, so features that are more noisy will be less contributive than others. We tried different β values and validate the results using external validity indexes. The data set used in this study has continuous numeric features, and several experiments are performed with unweighted clustering methods. Here, we took the approach of analyzing different values for weighted (-2,0,2) and unweighted coefficients. By using weighting, the features are fuzzified from another perspective.

4 Summary and Conclusions

Multi-objective optimization is more suitable to handle real life problems because most problems intuitively involve more than one objective. We identified clustering as a multi-objective problem and developed a multi-objective based clustering approach, which automates the process of finding the number of clusters as part of the overall clustering process to minimize user input and to produce more natural clustering. The developed approach produces the clustering in two stages by using sampling and multi-objective genetic algorithm with three objectives integrated with weighted and un-weighted k-means. The first stage iteratively benefits for the next iteration from every good result produced in a previous iteration. This considerably decreased the run-time of the algorithm. We tested different alternatives for computing some of the objectives. We realized that integrating k-means in the process highly improved the performance of the developed approach. We validated the results using external validity indexes, which validate the results independent of any particular parameters like size and shape. The reported results for the tested dataset are encouraging; they demonstrate the applicability and effectiveness of the proposed approach.

References

1. Hartigan, J.: Clustering algorithms. John Wiley and Sons, New York, NY (1975)
2. Desarbo, W., Carroll, J., Clark, L., Green, P.: Synthesized clustering: A method for amalgamating clustering bases with differential weighting variables. Psychometrika **49** (1984) 57–78
3. Modha, D., Spangler, W.: Feature weighting in k-means clustering. Machine Learning **52**(3) (2003)
4. Huang, J., Ng, M., Rong, H., Li, Z.: Automated variable weighting in k-means type clustering. IEEE PAMI **27**(5) (2005) 657–668
5. Friedman, J., Meulman, J.: Clustering objects on subsets of attributes. J. Royal Stat. Soc. B. (2002)
6. Liu, Y., Özyer, T., Alhajj, R., Barker, K.: Integrating multi-objective genetic algorithm and validity analysis for locating and ranking alternative clustering. European Journal of Informatica **29**(1) (2005) 33–40
7. Liu, Y., Özyer, T., Alhajj, R., Barker, K.: Cluster validity analysis of alternative solutions from multi-objective optimization. Proc. of SIAM DM (2005)

8. Özyer, T., Alhajj, R.: Achieving natural clustering by validating results of iterative evolutionary clustering approach. In: Proceedings of IEEE International Conference on Intelligent Systems. (2006)
9. Fridyland, J., Dudoit, S.: A prediction-based resampling method for estimating the number of clusters in a dataset. Genome Biology **3**(7) (2002)
10. Fowlkes, E., Mallows, C.: A method for comparing two hierarchical clusterings. Journal of American Statistical Association (78) (1983) 553–569
11. Wall, M.: GAlib Documentation. Massachusetts Institute of Technology. (2005)

Improving the Classification Accuracy of RBF and MLP Neural Networks Trained with Imbalanced Samples

R. Alejo[1,2], V. Garcia[1,2], J.M. Sotoca[1], R.A. Mollineda[1], and J.S. Sánchez[1]

[1] Dept. Llenguatges i Sistemes Informàtics, Universitat Jaume I
Av. Sos Baynat s/n, 12071 Castelló de la Plana (Spain)
[2] Lab. de Reconocimiento de Patrones, Instituto Tecnológico de Toluca
Av. Tecnológico S/N, 52140, Metepec, (México)

Abstract. In practice, numerous applications exist where the data are imbalanced. It supposes a damage in the performance of the classifier. In this paper, an appropriate metric for imbalanced data is applied as a filtering technique in the context of Nearest Neighbor rule, to improve the classification accuracy in RBF and MLP neural networks. We diminish atypical or noisy patterns of the majority-class keeping all samples of the minority-class. Several experiments with these preprocessing techniques are performed in the context of RBF and MLP neural networks.

1 Introduction

An imbalanced training sample (TS), can be defined as a sample in which the number of patterns of a (minority) class is much smaller than those in the other classes. This scenario strongly affects many types of classifiers, in particular, the artificial neural networks trained with procedures of iterative adjustment [7]. Following a common practice [10], we consider a simplified version with only two classes (majority-class and minority-class). Several proposals reduce the influence of class imbalance in training. In general, three categories [4] can be identified: *over-sampling* replicates examples in the minority-class, *under-sampling* eliminates examples from the majority-class and *biasing* the discrimination process to compensate the class imbalance.

A very established strategy to reduce the majority-class and compensate the imbalance has been exhaustively studied in the Nearest Neighbor (NN) rule [3]. The process removes redundant, atypical, and noisy patterns producing less confusing in the TS and improving the NN classification accuracy. These techniques do not produce a considerable reduction of the majority-class size and in general, do not solve the imbalanced distribution between classes. In this sense, a further preprocessing of the TS addressed to remove redundant patterns has been proposed [2], conducting to a significant reduction of the majority-class size. In the context of NN classifiers, these majority-class reduction techniques have led to better classifier performances than the plain use over all classes.

A number of papers have studied the imbalance problem in neural network frameworks. Three main general approaches have been proposed. One of them is aimed to reduce the imbalance effects [11]. So, a first method multiplies the number of samples of the minority class, while a second one makes a two-step dynamic training of the neural networks considering first samples of the minority class and then, gradually adds samples of the majority class. A second approach focuses in adapting the backpropagation algorithm for imbalance situations [1], speeding up the convergence of the learning process for two-class problems. Finally, a third approach is directed to find appropriate parameters of the neural network models to improve their performance [5,7].

This work analyzes the behavior of two neural network models at classifying imbalance problems: Radial Basis Function (RBF) and Multilayer Perceptron (MLP). Through a resampling strategy, we remove examples of the majority-class from the overlap region, producing a local balance of the two classes. For this, the only requirement is that all samples of the minority class must be kept in the TS. As downsizing of the majority class can throw away significant information, an editing scheme is applied. Note that a global balance in the class sizes is not achieved.

The rest of the paper is organized as follow. In Sect. 2, the main characteristics of RBF and MLP neural networks are briefly described. The methodology of resampling used in the TS is presented in Sect. 3. Section 4 discusses the classification performance with a synthetic data set in different situations. as well as when applied to real databases. Finally, the main conclusions and possible future research are outlined in Sect. 5.

2 RBF and MLP Neural Networks

In the last years, the MLP (Backpropagation) has become popular in many tasks of machine learning, pattern recognition and data mining. In particular, it has been applied in image interpretation of remote sensing, whereas RBF neuronal networks have been used widely in applications with function approximation, interpolation with noise and tasks of classification. However, the knowledge about these models seems insufficient, what is translated into poor capacity of generalization in different applications.

By the simplicity of their architecture and training method, RBF networks are an attractive alternative respect to MLP. At the moment, RBF and MLP are two models of neural networks with great popularity in pattern recognition tasks. They are a clear example of feedforward neural networks with nonlinear layers. These techniques can be used as universal approximation [9], and are trained in a similar way with descendent gradient method [6]. In this kind of problems there always exists a RBF capable to make equal the MLP accuracy or viceversa. However, both networks have important differences [8].

1. The RBF has a single hidden layer, and the MLP can have one or more.
2. Generally, in the MLP all hidden and output nodes have the same neural model. On the other hand, in the RBF the hidden and output nodes have different neural models.

3. The parameters of the activation function for each hidden node in RBF are calculated with the Euclidean distance between the input vector and the prototype vector. Moreover, the parameters of the activation function of each hidden unit in a MLP is calculated from the sum of the product between the input vector and the synaptic weights of each unit.
4. The MLP generates a global approximation for the nonlinear association of input-output. Furthermore, the RBF networks generate a local approximation for the nonlinear association of input-output.

3 Methodology

The aim is increasing the classification accuracy of RBF and MLP neural networks in class imbalance problems, by improving the quality of the TS. The MLP neural network here used is a simplified version of the one proposed in [12], with a hidden layer and three hidden neurons. In our experiments, the learning rate and momentum are set to 0.9 and 0.7, respectively. The shutdown criterion settled down with an error smaller than 0.01 or maximum of 5000 training epochs. The RBF neural network was trained with the Backpropagation algorithm [13], four hidden neurons, and a learning rate equal to 0.9. The shutdown criterion settled down with an error smaller than 0.01 or maximum of 5000 training iterations.

For internally biasing the balance between classes in the overlap region, we have used the weighted distance used in [3] in resampling tasks. This weighted distance is defined as

$$d_w(y, x_0) = (n_i/n)^{1/m} d_E(y, x_0) \tag{1}$$

where $d_E(.)$ is the Euclidean metric between the new sample to classify y, x_0 is a sample of the TS that belongs to the class i, n_i is the number of patterns of the class i, n is the total number of patterns in the TS, and m represents the dimensionality of the feature space.

In the preprocessing of the TS, we have utilized an editing technique based upon distances. These methods are an easy and simple strategy to eliminate noisy or atypical patterns from the TS. In this work, the classical Wilson's proposal (WE) is utilized for this purpose, finding the k nearest neighbors (with $k = 3$) of each instance from the TS. Three practical scenarios are proposed in the use of WE: editing with Euclidean distance in both classes, editing of the majority-class with Euclidean distance, and editing of the majority-class with the weighted distance shown above (Eq. 1).

With respect to the performance of the classifier, the average geometric mean is here used as the evaluation criterion. This measure is more appropriate in environments with imbalanced class distributions. The geometric mean is defined as follows:

$$g = \sqrt{a^+ \cdot a^-} \tag{2}$$

where (a^+) is the accuracy on the minority-class and (a^-) denotes the accuracy on the majority-class. This measure tries to maximize the accuracy on each of the two classes while keeping these accuracies balanced. For instance, higher (a^+) with lower (a^-) results in a poor value of g.

4 Experiments and Discussion

To evaluate the effect of class overlapping on neural network classifiers with imbalanced classes, we have generated six synthetic databases with different levels of overlapping. Each domain is described by two classes with two dimension and uniform distributions: A0 = 0% (that is, non-overlapped), A20 = 20%, A40 = 40%, A60 = 60%, A80 = 80%, and A100 = 100%(that is, absolutely overlapped). Each artificial database consists of 500 patterns for training and 500 patterns for test (400 patterns for the majority-class and 100 patterns for the minority-class. The nature of the data is illustrated in Fig. 1.

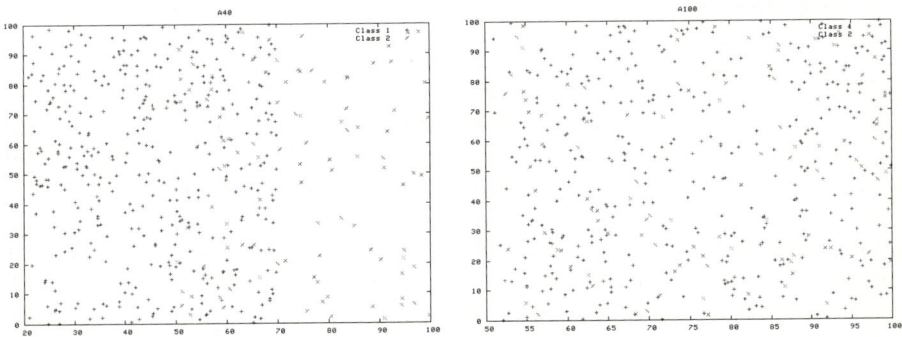

Fig. 1. Several degrees of imbalance: 40% and 100%

Furthermore, we also include three real databases (see Table 1) from the UCI Machine Learning Database Repository (http://www.ics.uci.edu/~mlearn). All data sets were transformed into two-class problems to provide a comparison with other published results [3]. A five-fold cross-validation error estimate method is employed in the classification tasks.

Table 1. A brief summary of the real databases

Data set	Features	Minority class	Majority class
Glass	9	29	185
Phoneme	5	1586	3818
Vehicle	18	212	634

In Table 2 and Table 3, the results with RBF and MLP neural networks are shown. Rows represent the results with the different preprocessing techniques applied to the TS respect to the original set. Moreover, the accuracy of neural networks using the average geometric mean are represented for WE on the majority-class (Euclidean distance and weighted distance), and WE in both classes. This strategy is applied three times until the number of atypical or noise patterns is sufficiently small.

Table 2. RBF neural networks: average values of the geometric mean

		A0	A20	A40	A60	A80	A100
Original TS		98.99	89.32	74.83	61.64	37.42	0
WE	1st application	98.99	90.61	78.47	61.42	35.60	0
(majority class)	2nd application	98.99	89.15	77.22	61.82	35.60	0
	3 rd application	98.99	89.15	**78.04**	**61.88**	**38.10**	0
weighted WE	1st application	99.49	89.86	78.13	64.8	51.99	0
(majority class)	2nd application	**100**	89.62	77.81	72.57	57.97	30.78
	3 rd application	**100**	**89.62**	**79.42**	**72.74**	**54.89**	**32.11**
WE(both class)		98.49	89.44	72.11	58.3	37.42	0

The application of WE in the majority-class (see Table 2) equalizes or outperforms the classification accuracy for RBF classifier in all data sets. This improvement is remarkable in the case of A40, A60 and A80 databases for WE with Euclidean distance, and for all data sets when WE with the weighted distance is applied.

In general, the use of the weighted distance obtains better results than the Euclidean distance with WE in the majority class for the RBF neural networks. On the other hand, WE applied in both classes presents worse results, and in some cases does not improve the accuracy of the original TS.

Table 3. MLP neural networks: average values of the geometric mean

		A0	A20	A40	A60	A80	A100
Original TS		99.50	**90.19**	76.81	62.45	44.55	**34.21**
WE	1st application	99.50	90.61	76.81	62.45	0	0
(majority class)	2nd application	99.50	90.50	76.81	62.45	0	0
	3rd application	99.50	90.50	76.81	62.45	**59.03**	9.91
weighted WE	1st application	100	87.98	**79.61**	64.23	**60.77**	0
(majority class)	2nd application	100	87.62	74.65	65.91	54.67	0
	3rd application	**100**	87.62	76.68	**70.25**	55.10	0
WE(both class)		100	89.22	74.83	61.51	43.53	9.87

In the MLP neural network, we can observe that a data reduction in the majority-class does not enhance the classification accuracy meaningfully for this classifier (see Table 3). So, it is not clear the advantages of the weighted distance in WE for MLP neural network as editing technique to clean the TS.

In Table 4, a study of the classification accuracy for each individual class is presented in A60 database. Whenever the accuracy of the minority-class (a^+) increases, the accuracy of the majority-class (a^-) diminishes. The same characteristics was found for NN rule in problems with imbalanced classes [4].

Table 4. Partial accuracy for the A60 database. (a^-) the minority-class and (a^+) the majority-class.

		RBF		MLP	
		a^-	a^+	a^-	a^+
	Original TS	100.0	38.00	100.0	39.00
WE	1st application	96.75	39.00	100.0	39.00
(majority class)	2nd application	98.00	39.00	100.0	39.00
	3rd application	95.75	40.00	100.0	39.00
Weighted WE	1st application	87.50	48.00	93.75	44.00
(majority class)	2nd application	75.25	70.00	90.50	48.00
	3rd application	73.50	72.00	69.50	71.00
WE(both class)		100.00	34.00	97.00	39.00

Table 5. Size in the original TS and applying editing techniques

	A0	A20	A40	A60	A80	A100
Original TS	400	400	400	400	400	400
WE (majority class)	400	381	372	353	351	336
Weighted WE (majority class)	392	351	303	239	215	203
WE(both class)	400/94	385/82	379/53	369/41	364/21	355/5

When the weighted distance is used in WE, this reduction can be up to 50% of the size of the majority-class (a^-) (see Table 5). However, this does not mean a balance in the size of both classes. For example, WE with weighted distance in A100 database significantly reduces the size of the majority-class (a^-), but it does not reach a good balance in the size of both classes. Also, it is observed that the WE applied to both classes drastically reduces the size of the minority-class (a^+) to 5 patterns in A100 database.

Table 6 shows the classification accuracy before and after WE is applied in real data sets. In this case, we do not know the level of overlap between classes, and there is not information of atypical or noisy patterns. In RBF neural networks, the performance of the classifier improves when the majority-class of the TS is edited. Furthermore, the weighted distance is better than the Euclidean distance for the *Vehicle* and *Phoneme* data sets and worse for the *Glass* database.

In the case of MLP neural networks, one can see different behaviors and it only improves the results for the *Vehicle* database. In this classifier, it is not clear the benefits obtained when a WE in the majority-class is applied. The WE in both classes (see Table 6) obtains worse results than the original TS, except

Table 6. Average values of the geometric mean with real data sets

		Glass		Vehicle		Phoneme	
		RBF	MLP	RBF	MLP	RBF	MLP
Original TS		85.97	82.05	46.63	70.62	69.84	**56.77**
WE	1st application	87.26	78.38	60.77	71.56	69.80	44.43
(majority class)	2nd application	87.26	78.38	63.59	76.06	70.01	49.13
	3rd application	**87.26**	78.38	64.81	**76.06**	70.01	50.57
Weighted WE	1st application	86.97	76.20	62.80	70.52	70.53	50.50
(majority class)	2nd application	86.97	76.20	66.63	68.63	70.26	50.44
	3rd application	86.97	76.20	**66.45**	73.93	**71.32**	46.83
WE(both class)		81.52	**86.43**	39.86	67.23	67.89	47.80

with *Glass* database. It can be due to a smooth of the decision boundaries in the editing process. So, other issues such as the data complexity or the nature of the classifier must be analyzed in the editing process for imbalanced classes.

5 Conclusions

A preprocessing technique to filter the TS by removal of noise or atypical patters is applied to clean the data, and enhance the classification accuracy in neural networks. In the case of RBF neural networks, the application of editing techniques with an adequate metric to imbalanced classes increases the classification accuracy. Despite the successful results in RBF neural networks, a common problem to all these downsizing techniques is that they do not allow a control on the number of patterns to be removed.

Nevertheless, this strategy to clean the decision boundaries has a worse behavior in the case of MLP neural networks. It can be due to a smoothing of the decision boundaries in the editing process. A study of the data complexity and the nature of the classifier is required to deepen the influence of the editing process with imbalanced classes.

Acknowledgments

This work has been supported in part by grants TIC2003–08496 from the Spanish CICYT, P1–1B2004–08 from Fundació Caixa Castelló–Bancaixa, and SEP-2003-C02-44225 from the Mexican CONACyT.

References

1. R. Anand, K. G. Mehrotra, C. K. Mohan, and S. Ranka. An Improved Algorithm for Neural Network Classification of Imbalanced Training Sets. IEEE Transactions on Neural Networks, vol. 4, no. 6, (1993) 962–969.
2. R. Barandela, N. Cortés, A. Palacios. The nearest neighbour rule and the reduction of the training sample size. 9th. Spanish Symposium on Pattern Recognition and Image Analysis, vol. 1, Benicassim, Spain, 2001, 103–108.

3. R. Barandela, J.S. Sánchez, V. García, E. Rangel. Strategies for learning in class imbalance problems. Pattern Recognition, vol. 36, no. 3 (2003) 849–851
4. R. Barandela, R.M. Valdovinos, J.S. Sánchez, F.J. Ferri. The imbalanced training sample problem: under or over sampling?. Joint IAPR International Workshops on Structural, Syntactic, and Statistical Pattern Recognition (SSPR/SPR'04). Lecture Notes in Computer Science 3138, Springer-Verlag 2004, Lisbon (Portugal), 2004, 806–814.
5. V. L. Berardi, G. P. Zhang. The Effect of Misclassification Costs on Neural Network Classifiers. Decision Sciences, vol. 30, no. 3, 1999, 659–682
6. S.Q. Ding, C. Xiang. From multilayer perceptrons to radial basis function networks: a comparative study. IEEE. Conference on Cybernetics and Intelligent Systems, vol. 1, Singapore, 1-3 December, 2004, 69–74
7. X. Fu, L. Wang, K.S. Chua, F. Chu. Training RBF neural networks on unbalanced data. IX International Conference on Neural Information Processing (ICONIP'02), Singapore, 2002, 1016–1020.
8. S. Haykin. Neuronal Networks - a comprehensive foundation. Ed. Prentice Hall, second edition, New Jersey, 1999, 278–282
9. J.M. Hutchinson, A. Lo, T. Poggio. A Nonparametric Approach to Pricing and Hedging Derivates Securities Via Learning Networks. Technical Report, Artificial Intelligence Laboratory and Center for Biological and Computational Learning, MIT, memo 1471, no. 92, 1994.
10. M. Kubat, S. Matwin. Addressing the curse of imbalanced training set: one-sided selection. 14th International Conference on Machine Learning, Nashville, USA, 1997, 179–186
11. Y. Lu, H. Guo, and L. Feldkamp. Robust neural learning from unbalanced data examples. IEEE International Joint Conference on Neural Networks, 1998, 1816–1821
12. Y. H. Pao, Adaptive Patter Recognition and Neuronal Networks. Addison-Wesley, Reading. MA., 1989
13. F. Schwenker, H. A. Kestler, and G. Palm. Three learning phases for radial-basis-function networks. Neural Networks, vol.14 no. 4-5, May 2001, 439–458

Learning Discrete Probability Distributions with a Multi-resolution Binary Tree

F.A. Sanchís, F. Aznar, M. Sempere, M. Pujol, and R. Rizo

Department of Computer Science and Artificial Intelligence
University of Alicante
fasp@alu.ua.es,
{fidel, mireia, mar, rizo}@dccia.ua.es

Abstract. In this paper a method for learning and representing joint probabilistic distributions, using binary trees, is shown. This method could be used with the Bayesian Programming formalism, being a very useful tool when working with real world data. It has the advantage of learning unknown probabilistic distributions directly from raw data, and to remain more balanced than other previous methods. Finally, an application to learn a fuzzy control system, using this approach, will be presented.

1 Introduction

When an agent develops any task in real world, it must understand the environment. In this way an agent must have a set of sensors of different types. One of the most important problems on robotic agents is related to the transformation of input information collected from sensors into a description of the world. This problem is mainly associated to uncertainty and incompleteness of information.

Bayesian programming is a formalism where a probability distribution (called description) is linked to a logical value. This formalism can deal with incomplete information transforming it into uncertainty. As can be seen in [1], [2], [3], [4], Bayesian programming is also a useful tool for designing robotic systems. However, it is not easy to specify a Bayesian program.

A common problem for this specification is how to learn and represent probabilistic distributions. When we learn a distribution from experimental data, we try to approximate it with a parametrical function. This method requires the programmer to previously know the distribution form. Moreover, there are probability distributions hard to approximate with any decomposition based on parametrical functions.

In this paper, a method for representing and learning probabilistic distributions, in an efficient way, is presented. This method approximates large probabilistic joint distributions, being very useful for the Bayesian Programming formalism.

We will start at section 2 by introducing probabilistic learning. Next, some existing techniques for explicit representation of probability distributions will be seen. Our model is presented at section 3, including a small graphical example and an algorithm for constructing a tree, in order to learn unknown distributions. Section 4 shows a real application using the approach presented here. Finally, conclusions and future lines will be described.

2 Probabilistic Learning

A simple method for learning a probabilistic joint distribution is to build an explicit representation for it. The simplest representation we could use is a probabilistic table. A probabilistic table is an array of probabilistic values with size equal to the variables product. A drawback of this representation is table size because it grows exponentially with the number of variables. A review of some important methods for learning probabilistic distributions can be found in [5].

More specifically, [6] presents an efficient algorithm for representing probabilistic distributions, using a Multi-resolution Binary Tree. From now on we will call this algorithm MRBT. The key idea beside the MRBT is to store more information from the most probable space regions, and less information about the less probable ones. A leaf in a MRBT represents both, the probability of a single point and the probability of a region.

In order to use a MRBT, a method that generates space points relating to its probability is needed. Thus, more points will be generated from high mass probability regions. Also, a method to obtain the probability of a given point (to be inserted to the MRBT) is needed. However, obtaining the probability of a given point may be a difficult task in some problems.

In this paper we present an improvement of the basic MRBT algorithm. This allows learning probabilistic distributions without the need for calculating the probability of the point to be inserted.

3 Proposed Method

As commented above, the MRBT algorithm presented in [6] inserts pairs $(x, P(X = x))$ into the tree. Then the leaf node, that contains the point x, is searched using dichotomy. In this way the region represented by this node is divided (dimension after dimension, each level of the tree) until the two points (the one we are inserting, and the other already contained in the node) are splitted into different nodes.

In our method we cannot insert points linked with their own probabilities (because we don't know the probability of a point to be drawn). Instead we simply insert points to the tree. Every time a point is inserted its relative frequency is incremented. After enough points are inserted, the tree will contain reliable statistical information.

To achieve a good resolution using this method is very difficult (except for small problems). However, this is not a problem at all, since we only need to have high resolution for high mass probability regions.

The generated tree will contain in its leafs the region probability they represents (or the probability of a single point if the surrounding region has enough mass probability) by inserting real data points.

When a new point is inserted into the tree, the region, that contains it, is splitted into two smaller subregions. Next, the relative frequency of this region is divided equally for both subregions. Finally, the relative frequency of the subregion that contains the new point is increased in one unit.

Note that, contrary to the MRBT approach, the point information is never stored into the tree. In fact, there is no advantage in doing so when we don't know the probability for a given point at insertion time. In our approach we learn the probability of regions and points without comparing the point to be inserted with the existing ones.

3.1 A Small Example

We will use a system composed by two discrete variables, A and B, with four possible states. The combination space for this variables is $A \otimes B = [\{a_1, a_2, a_3, a_4\} \otimes \{b_1, b_2, b_3, b_4\}]$. For this example we will assume that the probability for a given point $\{a_i, b_j\}$ is bigger when $i = j$.

A set of points from $A \otimes B$ will be generated following the previous representation (the one that we want to learn). Figure 1 shows the points generated and the insertion order. It also represents the relative frequency for each region (leaf node) and the mass probability for each region (gray level). Figure 2 shows the tree generated by our approach, where each node is labelled with its weight. Moreover, the region that represents each node is shown (in order to understand the tree representation, since we don't need to store these ranges in the nodes).

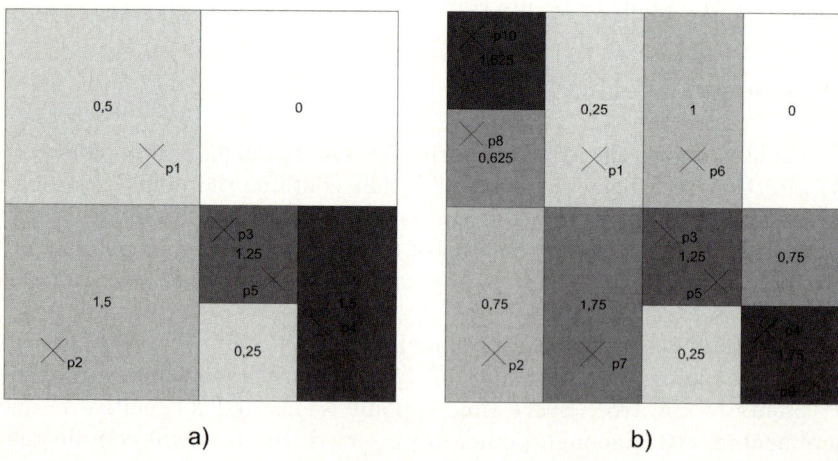

Fig. 1. Points generated. Gray level represents the probability of each region (white is 0). a) After 5 insertions, b) After 10 insertions.

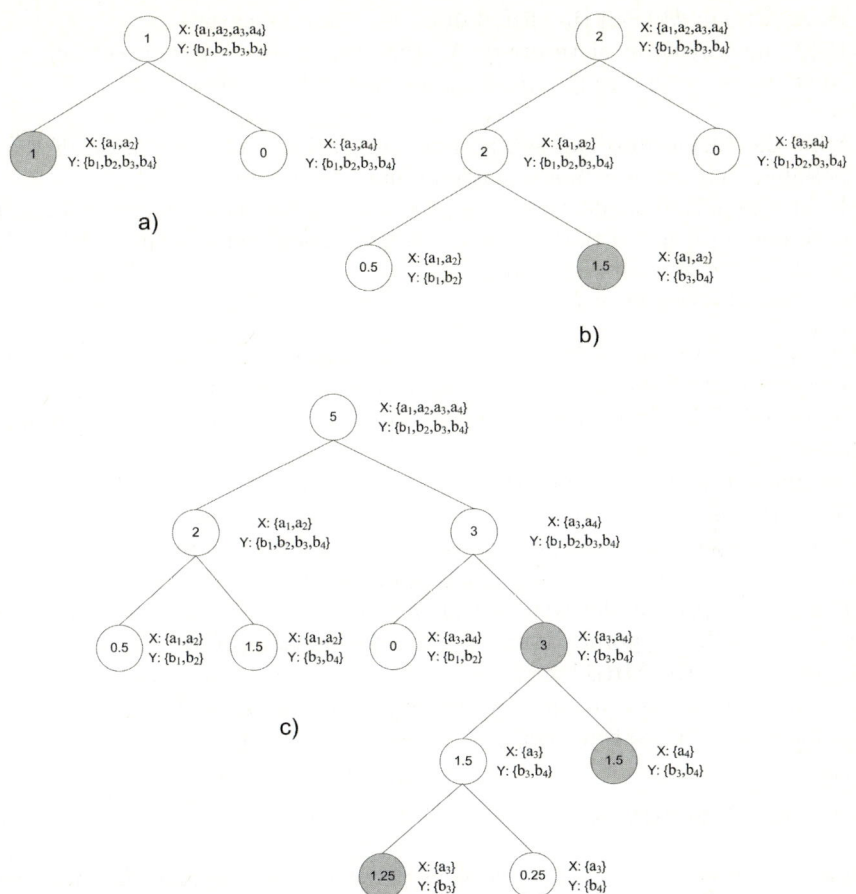

Fig. 2. a) Tree generated after one insertion. We see how starting from the root node, that represents all the space, the point $p1(a2, b2)$ is inserted. In this way two child nodes are created from the root node, splitting the values of X in two halfs. As $p1$ is contained by the left child, both nodes, their parent and it, increment in a unit their weight. b) Tree generated after two insertions. A second point has been inserted $p2(a1, b4)$. At this position two new subnodes has been added, splitting Y values. For each subnode the half weight of its father has been assigned (0.5). Right subnode (an all its ancestors) increases its weight a unit. In this way 1.5 is assigned to right subnode weight, 2 for their parent and 2 for the root node. c) Tree generated after five insertions following the same procedure.

3.2 Learning a Distribution

To insert a new point into the tree is the key of this learning process. It is an incremental process where a distribution is better approximated when each new point is inserted into the tree. This learning process is defined by the following steps:

1. Draw a point P from the distribution we want to learn.
2. Find the leaf node of the tree, N, that represents a region containing P. Next, increase the weight of all nodes visited from the root in 1 (excluding N).
3. Split the region into two sub-regions, dimension after dimension, if that is possible (the region is not a single point)
4. If the region is divisible, the previous node becomes into two new child nodes, each one with half a part of the N weight. Then increase the weight of the child node that contains P in 1.
5. Increase the weight of N in 1.

This approach requires less space for representing a probability distribution than a probability table. Moreover, it can be trained in real time by simply inserting more points into the tree (learning more accurately unknown probabilistic distributions).

It is important to highlight that this method has some advantages respect to the MRBT algorithm. If two very nearly points are drawn from a low-mass probability region, the tree generated with the MRBT approach will become very unbalanced, since this two points require the tree to grow until a very deep level. In our approach the tree will grow only one level deeper for the region containing the drawn point. However, when trying to represent known probability distributions, the MRBT method needs less points to learn small probability regions than our approach. Anyway our method is still better balanced, and only needs more training to learn correctly these small regions.

4 Case of Study

In this section an application example is presented. We assume that we have a fuzzy logic system for the navigation of a robot. There are seven input variables that represent the measures from seven sensors arranged at different angles. The fuzzy logic system takes that seven input variables ($S1, ..., S7$) and returns two output variables (lineal Vl and rotational Vr velocity).

The problem is that our fuzzy logic system is too slow, and we want to reproduce the same behaviour with a faster technique due to temporal restrictions. We can learn the probability distribution generated by the fuzzy logic system with our method and then ask to the tree a value for the unknown variables.

4.1 Learning Process

First, we need to discretize system variables. Each variable is discretized using four possible states (S: close, middle-close, middle-far, far; Vl, Vr : slow, normal, fast, very fast). We need to generate points of the joint distribution, in this way we simply make the fuzzy logic system to control the robot for a time. During this time we record the data from the sensors obtaining the values for Vl and Vr returned by the fuzzy system.

We read this data during 5 minutes, obtaining ten values (for each of the nine variables) per second. Around three thousand points will be inserted for the space $Vl \times Vr \times S1 \times ... \times S7$. In this way we want to learn the distribution:

$$P(Vl \otimes Vr|S1 \otimes ... \otimes S7) \times P(S1 \otimes ... \otimes S7) = \\ P(Vl \otimes Vr \otimes S1 \otimes ... \otimes S7) \tag{1}$$

4.2 Questions to the Tree

Different questions can be asked to the tree, many of them in an efficient way. Some of the questions described in [6] are also valid for our approach (i.e. compute the probability of a given point; draw a point from the distribution...)

More complex questions can be asked to the tree too. In this section two of them will be described. Both are related with drawing a point knowing some input variables. Before explaining these questions a definition for node dimension is required. We call dimension of a node the dimension (or variable name) that split a child from its node (i.e.: a node has the dimension $S3$ if its region is divided between its child by splitting the state values of the variable $S3$)

We will control the robot reading the values from the sensors, discretizing those values, and asking the tree the values for Vl and Vr given the known values $S1, ..., S7$.

First Question: Finding the Best Probability. This question asks the values of the most probable unknown variables given the known variables (in this case the sensor readings):

$$\forall_{Vr',Vl'} (Vl', Vr') \neq (Vl, Vr), \\ P(Vl \otimes Vr|S1 \otimes ... \otimes S7) \geq P(Vl' \otimes Vr'|S1 \otimes ... \otimes S7) \tag{2}$$

We can answer the previous question using the following recursive algorithm:

1. Start at root node.
2. If current node is a leaf, return a pair consisting of a random point in the region defined by the node, and the node weight.
3. Current node has a known dimension,
   (a) If true then advance to the child node, that contains the state of the known variable, and go to step 2.
   (b) If false then obtain a pair of the left child and another pair of the right child applying the same process. The pair returned by this node is the one with the higher weight.

Second Question: Drawing a point. This question draws a point from the probability distribution, with the restriction of the known variables:

$$P(Vl \otimes Vr|S1 \otimes ... \otimes S7) \tag{3}$$

We can answer it following the same strategy described in the previous section. Even thought there is a problem when a node of an unknown dimension has to return a value for its parent. In this case it does not return the most weighted result of his children, it selects one of them randomly. A point will be selected more probably as more high is his weight. The weight assigned to that point is the sum of the two weights of its children.

4.3 Experimental Results

To test the proposed system we use a model of the Pioneer 3-DX robot provided by activMedia[1] with the saphira simulator[7]. The obtained results are presented in figure 3. First the joint distribution $P(Vl \otimes Vr \otimes S1 \otimes ... \otimes S7)$ is learned using the fuzzy system. We could see how the fuzzy system controls the robot (dotted line). Next, using the learned tree, the question $P(Vl \otimes Vr|S1 \otimes ... \otimes S7)$ is answered. Using this question we read sensor variables obtaining the Vr and Vl velocity. We send Vr, Vl to the robot controller developing the following robot path (continuous line).

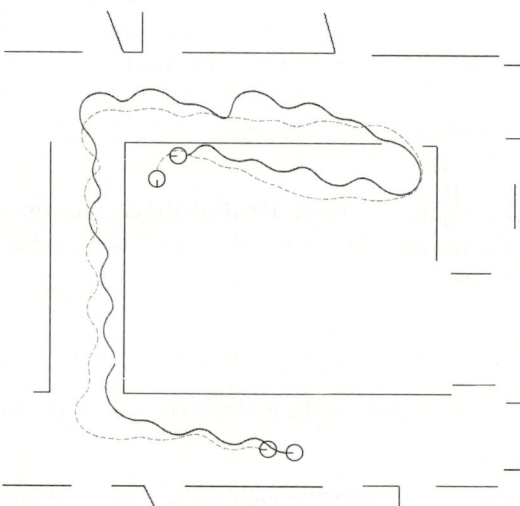

Fig. 3. Path developed by the fuzzy system (dotted line) and learned by our method (continuous line)

5 Conclusions and Future Lines

In this paper an approach to learn and represent joint probabilistic distributions was presented. Based on the MRBT method, our approach has the advantage of being able to learn unknown probabilistic distributions, and to remain more balanced than the MRBT does.

When trying to represent known probability distributions, the MRBT method needs less points to correctly learn little high-probability regions than our

---

[1] http://www.mobilerobots.com/

approach. Anyway, our method is still better balanced, and only needs some further training to correctly learn that small regions.

An application example, that learns a fuzzy control system using our method, has been presented too. This method can be very useful in robotic, for example in order to learn complex system behaviours. Moreover, we want to use this method for learning and representing experimental data working with Bayesian programs.

Future studies will try to state speed optimizations for some specific tree questions and to represent some experimental data, of our Bayesian programs, previously presented using this method.

References

1. Bellot, D., Siegwart, R., Bessière, P., Coué, C., Tapus, A., Diard, J.: Bayesian reasoning for real world robotics: Basics, scaling and examples. Book Chapter in LNCS/LNAI (2004)
2. Coué, C., Fraichard, T., Bessière, P., E., M.: Using bayesian programming for multi-sensor data fusion in automotive applications. IEEE Intelligent Vehicle Symposium (2002)
3. Lebeltel, O., Bessière, P., Diard, J., Mazer, E.: Bayesian robots programming. Autonomous Robots **16** (2004) 49–79
4. Aznar, F., Pujol, M., Rizo, R.: Robot security and failure detection using bayesian fusion. AI*IA 2005 - 9th Congress of the Italian Association for Artificial Intelligence. LNAI 3673-518. ISSN 0302-9743 (2005) 518–521
5. Bessière, P., Group, I.R.: Survei:probabilistic methodology and tecniques for artefact conception and development. INRIA (2003)
6. Bellot, D., Bessiere, P.: Approximate discrete probability distribution representation using a multi-resolution binary tree. 15th IEEE International Conference on Tools with Artificial Intelligence (ICTAI'03) (2003) 498
7. Konolige, K., Myers, K.L., Ruspini, E.H., Saffiotti, A.: The saphira architecture: A design for autonomy. Journal of experimental & theoretical artificial intelligence (JETAI) (1997)

Combining Unsupervised and Supervised Approaches to Feature Selection for Multivariate Signal Compression

Victor Eruhimov, Vladimir Martyanov, Peter Raulefs, and Eugene Tuv

Intel, Analysis & Control Technology
victor.eruhimov@intel.com, vladimir.martyanov@intel.com,
peter.raulefs@intel.com, eugene.tuv@intel.com

Abstract. A problem of learning from a database where each sample consists of several time series and a single response is considered. We are interested in maximum data reduction that preserves predictive power of the original time series, and at the same time allows reasonable reconstruction quality of the original signals. Each signal is decomposed into a set of wavelet features that are coded according to their importance consisting of two terms. The first depends on the influence of the feature on the expected signal reconstruction error, and the second is determined by feature importance for the response prediction. The latter is calculated by building series of boosted decision tree ensembles. We demonstrate that such combination maintains small signal distortion rates, and ensures no increase in the prediction error in contrast to the unsupervised compression with the same reduction ratio.

1 Introduction

The paper considers a problem of multivariate time series compression. We start with a dataset where each sample consists of several time series and a single response value. Individual series from the same sample correspond to the different variables with different physical characteristics generated by a process. Our goal is to reduce the representation size of time series, and at the same time preserve the important information about the underlying process.

This work is motivated by the manufacturing applications where a set of sensors log down various physical properties of a wafer processing over time. The number of time series varies from several dozens up to hundreds (an example is a set of Fourier coefficients of 2MHz signal averaged over a window of 1 second). After a manufacturing step a wafer undergoes a so-called metrology, where the process quality is verified by taking additional measurements from the wafer. One of our key objectives is predicting the performance (metrology) of the tool given sensors data.

A very important property of the manufacturing data is low variability of time series – signal profiles from the same sensors are generally very similar to each other.

The amount of raw data is much larger than what we can store, but potentially could be very useful in predicting the process performance. In this context we are interested in reducing the representation size of time series data. A desirable compression algorithm, therefore, would benefit from the low variability among the signal profiles, and would be aware of the response variable.

The problem of lossy signal compression is well studied – its basics are described in [13],[8]. Data denoising by filtering in wavelet space is covered by [5], [4]. A wavelet decomposition of signals for the manufacturing process fault detection is used in [11]. [10] use a thresholding technique to shrink data by filtering out small coefficients, and then use the decision tree-based fault classification engine to estimate the impact of the compression.

Our approach combines methods of signal processing and learning theory. We intend to show that manufacturing time series data with low variability can be efficiently compressed using simple quantization-based techniques without a significant loss in prediction power.

Here is a brief summary of the proposed approach. We start with a dataset where each sample consists of several time series and a single response value. First, we extract a set of features from each time series that is sufficient or superfluous for the original series reconstruction. Next, we perform the standard SureShrink wavelet denoising [4]. A generic multivariate feature selection mechanism then assigns relevance scores for the derived features with respect to the response variable. We compress the signals by quantizing each wavelet coefficient in a number of bins. The number of bins per wavelet feature depends on its importance for both reconstruction of the signal profile distribution, and the prediction of the response. The resulting quantized signal represented with a set of categorized feature coefficients can be efficiently stored using Huffman code [12]. The novelty of this approach is in using the feature importance rank wrt response prediction for bit allocation, i.e. for the number of bits we spend to store an individual feature.

The outline of the paper is as follows. Section 2 provides the background on the supervised learning techniques and variable selection methods that was used, Section 3 focuses on the feature quantization scheme, Section 4 describes datasets we tested the compression on, and Section 5 contains experimental results.

2 Tree Ensembles

This section gives background on supervised learning techniques that we employ both for feature selection and for the response prediction. We try to address a problem of feature filtering, or removal of irrelevant inputs in very general supervised settings: the target variable could be numeric or categorical, the input space could have variables of mixed type with non-randomly missing values, the underlying relationship of response Y and predictors X could be very complex and multivariate, and the data could be massive in both dimensions (tens of thousands of variables, and millions of observations). Ensembles of unstable but very fast and flexible base learners such as trees (with embedded feature weighting) can address the most of the listed challenges. They have proved to be very effective for variable ranking in problems with up to a hundred thousand predictors [1,14]. A more comprehensive overview of feature selection with ensembles is given in [15].

Gradient Tree Boosting (GBT) [6], [7] has been proven to be among the most accurate and versatile state-of-the-art learning machines. GBT is an iteratively learned serial ensemble where every new tree is fitted to the generalized residuals of the current ensemble. GBT builds shallow trees using all variables (on a subsample of the training data), and hence, it can handle large datasets with a moderate number of inputs. Very high dimensional data (thousands or even several hundreds of features) is extremely challenging for GBT. A modification of GBT [1] suggests a different ensemble learning strategy so that processing of very high dimensional datasets is feasible with almost no loss in prediction accuracy.

Random Forest [2] is a distinguished representative of tree ensembles that extends the "random subspace" method [9]. It grows a forest of random trees on bagged samples showing excellent results comparable with the best known classifiers.

Both ensembles inherit all nice properties of a single tree and also provide (as a byproduct) a more reliable estimate of the variable importance by averaging it over all trees in the ensemble.

We use GBT ensemble for response prediction since our response is a numeric variable and GBT is natively better adjusted for the regression task. At the same time Random Forest is used in the process of feature selection for performance reasons. It is important to note that we could use any of these methods for both tasks.

Relative feature ranking provided by the ensembles mentioned above, does not separate relevant features from irrelevant. Only a list of importance values is produced without a clear indication which variables to include, which to discard. Also, trees tend to split on variables with more distinct values. This effect is more pronounced for categorical predictors with many levels. It often makes a less relevant (or completely irrelevant) input variable more "attractive" to split on only because it has high cardinality. [16] provides a feature selection method that reduces a problem of selecting relevant features to a formal statistical test. The output of this method is a subset of features that are ranked according to their influence on response variable.

3 Feature Quantization

We decompose each time series $\{f_i\}_{i=1..I}$ into Daubechies wavelets D8 [13], [3]. The decomposition coefficients $\{w_i\}_{i=1..I}$ satisfy the Plancherel equation:

$$\sum_i f_i^2 = \sum_i w_i^2, \qquad (1)$$

The focus of this paper is in learning a predictive model that helps compressing time series data by selecting the right features. We argue that lossy compression with high rate can remove or distort features important for prediction. In order to account for this we consider a quantization scheme where compression-induced losses in each feature depend on its contribution to the original signal reconstruction as well as its relevance to the response variable.

There are two measures of how good a quantization is: the approximation error and the entropy. The approximation error estimates how different is the quantized signal from the original:

$$\varepsilon_a = \sum_i \sum_j \min_k \left| v_i^{(k)} - w_i^{(j)} \right|^2. \qquad (2)$$

Here j enumerates samples, $v_i^{(k)}$ is a set of bin centers, k takes values from 1 to N_i. The entropy measures the average number of bits per symbol coded by Huffman algorithm that follows the quantization. Since we are interested in a high-quality compression, we use equal bin length quantization that is proved to be optimal for a high resolution quantization (see, for example, [13]). Under the same assumption the optimal value for $v_i^{(k)}$ is the bin mass center. The bin length is different from one feature to another since we take into account the supervised feature importance.

Each feature i is quantized independently with bin length L_i that is determined by

$$N_i = \max(\alpha f_i^{(e)}, \beta f_i^{(p)}). \qquad (3)$$

Here $f_i^{(e)}$ is equal to the standard deviation of the corresponding energy term in (1) across samples:

$$f_i^{(e)} = \left(\langle w_i^4 \rangle - \langle w_i^2 \rangle^2 \right)^{1/2}. \qquad (4)$$

$f_i^{(p)}$ is equal to the variable importance obtained from feature selection algorithm [16]. α and β are coefficients that are used to control the influence of the corresponding term on the total number of bins per feature, and hence, on the compression rate. We will call $f_i^{(e)}$ and $f_i^{(p)}$ energy and prediction importances correspondingly.

The algorithm that selects the number of bins according to (3) we will call "*supervised* compression". We also compare it with the algorithm that ignores the second term so that $N_i = \alpha f_i^{(e)}$, and we will refer to this problem as "*unsupervised* compression".

4 Data Generation

Due to confidentiality of the manufacturing process information we used a data generator designed specifically to mimic most of the challenges we face in the real environment. Each sample in the dataset consists of several time series and the response value is generated using the following algorithm. First, we sample a vector V of N parameters from a given distribution. Then, we generate time series as parameterized functions of time and V. The response is generated by computing a sum of linear and quadratic forms of V:

$$y = AV + V^T BV + \varepsilon. \tag{5}$$

Here A is a vector $1 \times N$, B is a matrix $N \times N$ and ε is Gaussian noise. It is a challenge for any predictive engine to recover this functional relationship due to the complex dependence of time series on V and the problem dimensionality. All parameters are normalized so that the standard deviation of y across the dataset is equal to 1. The prediction error of a GBT model can be varied from 0.001 up to 0.5 by changing the values of A and B.

5 Experimental Results

We ran our experiments on several datasets created by a data generator described in the previous section. All of them consist of 3000 samples. The main one that we will address to as G10P, has 20 time series per sample. Each time series contained 128 values and all of them were defined on the same time values. We extracted a set of 128 wavelet coefficients from each signal followed by SureShrink [4] denoising. For each wavelet feature variations of energy terms (1) were calculated. For a supervised problem setting we built a GBT model and a feature selection model that estimates the importance of each wavelet feature from each time series for the response. The dataset was split into 70% of samples for learning and 30% for estimating the model generalization error. We used (3) to calculate the number of bins for individual features (in an unsupervised problem the second term in (3) is disregarded). The feature selection model ignored the most of the features, therefore β did not influence much the total number of levels. At the same time, the value of β was crucial for the prediction qulaity. Obviously, we could always make sure that the prediction error does not suffer from the compression by keeping β value sufficiently high – this ensures features important for response prediction get enough quantization bins. Since the number of these features was small compared to the overall feature set, β did not influence the compression rate significantly. In all our experiments β was kept at a constant value, and we tuned α to balance between the compression rate and the signal reconstruction error. Each feature was quantized with a given number of bins. The resulting dataset was encoded with Huffman code.

Figure 1, (a) shows energy $f^{(e)}$ and prediction $f^{(p)}$ importances for all wavelet features. Missing values for $f^{(p)}$ indicate that the corresponding features have zero importance. Figure 1, (b) shows the average number of bits per feature (BPF) that we use to encode quantized variables for supervised (i.e. (3) is used to calculate the number of bins) and unsupervised (the second term from (3) is ignored) problems. It is calculated as a number of bits needed to represent the whole sample with the Huffman code divided by the number of features in the sample. BPF here does not include the size of the coding vocabulary, but the latter is negligible since the number of samples is large. The parameter α plotted along the horizontal axis is a coefficient from (3). Since a regular representation of single precision floating points values is 32 bits, the compression rate can be calculated as $32/BPF$. Figure 1, (c) shows L_2 distance between the original and the reconstructed signals averaged over the dataset. It is normalized by the average distance between original signals from different samples. Note that even for compression rate equal to 80 ($BPF \sim 0.4$ corresponding to $\alpha = 0.01$) the reconstruction error is still about 20% from the average distance between original signals.

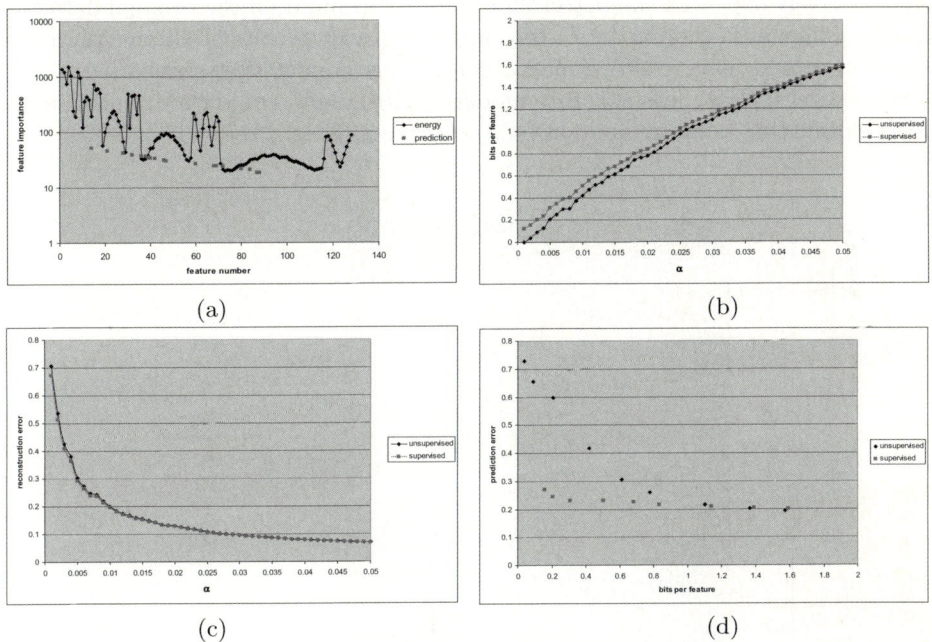

Fig. 1. Compression of time series from G10P dataset: (a) feature importance $f_i^{(u)}$ and $f_i^{(s)}$; (b) average bits per feature (BPF) versus α; (c) signal reconstruction error (normalized by the average distance between signals over the sample) versus α; (d) prediction error versus BPF

Figure 1, (b) shows that supervised and unsupervised BPF are close to each other. This indicates that BPF is not influenced much by the second term in (3). The same conclusion can be made about the reconstruction error from Figure 1, (c). However the prediction term has a dramatic effect on the prediction error plotted on Figure 1, (d) against BPF. One can see that for the small BPF values (high compression rates) such as $BPF \sim 0.4$ the prediction error for the supervised compression is 30-50% lower than for unsupervised case as more resolution is given to the features relevant to the response. The number of such features is small, and therefore the average compression rate is hardly influenced by this change. It also important to note that a GBT model trained on the compressed signals with $BPF = 0.4$ had a predictive power at least as good as a model built using the original uncompressed signals.

The next set of experiments studied improvement due to the supervised compression for different levels of predictability. As it was described in the Section 4 we could vary the generalization error the GBT model could potentially achieve using the original signals from 0.001 up to 0.5 by changing the values of A and B in the underlying dependence (5). Figure 2 demonstrates the relative improvement due to the supervised compression for different levels of max predictability. As intuitively expected the better model we could build on the original data the more significant is the impact of the supervised term on the predictive power of the compressed features. The magnitude of this impact is less sensitive to the compression rate for less accurate models (G10U), and could be dramatic even for small feature compression for very accurate models (G10S).

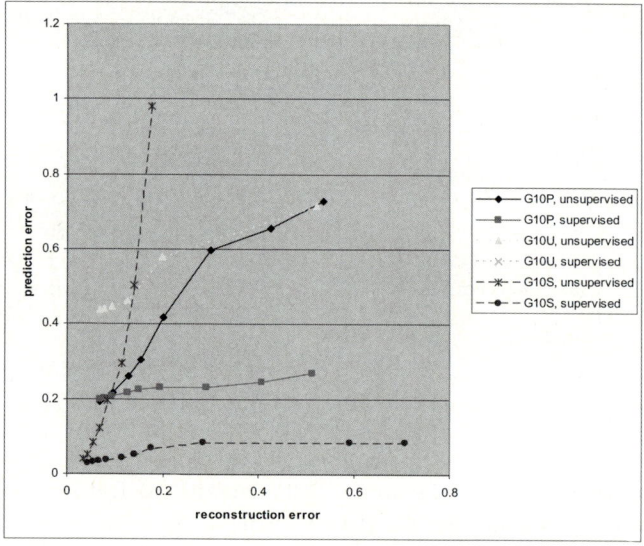

Fig. 2. Impact of the supervised compression for different levels of predictability

6 Summary

We considered a supervised feature selection method to reduce the representation size of time series that are used as predictors. The experimental setup corresponded to the challenges high precision semiconductor manufacturing faces routinely. The proposed approach enhancing an unsupervised data reduction method demonstrated high compression ratios (more than 30) while preserving predictive capacity of the original time series. This is in contrast with significant loss in accuracy (30-50%) when just unsupervised compression is done with the same data reduction ratio.

References

1. A. Borisov, V. Eruhimov, and E. Tuv. Dynamic soft feature selection for tree-based ensembles. In I. Guyon, S. Gunn, M. Nikravesh, and L. Zadeh, editors, *Feature Extraction, Foundations and Applications*. Springer, New York, 2005.
2. L. Breiman. Random forests. *Machine Learning*, 45(1):5–32, 2001.
3. I. Daubechies. *Ten lectures on wavelets*. SIAM, Philadelphia, PA, 1992.
4. David L. Donoho and Iain M. Johnstone. Adapting to unknown smoothness via wavelet shrinkage. *Journal of the American Statistical Association*, 90(432):1200–1224, 1995.
5. D.L. Donoho. Denoising via soft-thresholding. *IEEE Trans. Infrom. Theory*, 41(3):613–627, 1995.
6. J.H. Friedman. Greedy function approximation: a gradient boosting machine. Technical report, Dept. of Statistics, Stanford University, 1999.
7. J.H. Friedman. Stochastic gradient boosting. Technical report, Dept. of Statistics, Stanford University, 1999.
8. Allen Gersho and Robert M. Gray. *Vector Quantization and Signal Compression*. Springer, 1991.
9. T. K. Ho. The random subspace method for constructing decision forests. *IEEE Transactions on Pattern Analysis and Machine Intelligence*, 20(8):832–844, 1998.
10. Myong K. Jeong, Jye-Chyi Lu, and Xiaoming Huo et al. Wavelet-based data reduction techniques for process fault detection. *Technometrics*, 48(1):26–40, 2006.
11. Jionchua Jin and Jianjun Shi. Automatic feature extraction of waveform signals for in-process diagnostic performance improvement. *Journal of Intellifent Manufacturing*, 12:257–268, 2001.
12. David J. C. MacKay. *Information Theory, Inference, and Learning Algorithms*. Cambridge University Press, 2003. available from http://www.inference.phy.cam.ac.uk/mackay/itila/.
13. Stephane Mallat. *A Wavelet Tour on Signal Processing*. Academic Press, 1999.
14. Kari Torkkola and Eugene Tuv. Ensembles of regularized least squares classifiers for high-dimensional problems. In Isabelle Guyon, Steve Gunn, Masoud Nikravesh, and Lofti Zadeh, editors, *Feature Extraction, Foundations and Applications*. Springer, 2005.
15. E. Tuv. Feature selection and ensemble learning. In I. Guyon, S. Gunn, M. Nikravesh, and L. Zadeh, editors, *Feature Extraction, Foundations and Applications*. Springer, New York, 2005.
16. E. Tuv and K. Torkkola. Feature filtering with ensembles using artificial contrasts. *accepted for publication in IEEE Intelligent Systems Journal*, 2005.

Cohesion Factors: Improving the Clustering Capabilities of Consensus

Guiomar Corral, Albert Fornells, Elisabet Golobardes, and Jaume Abella

Research Group in Intelligent Systems
Ramon Llull University, Enginyeria i Arquitectura La Salle
Quatre Camins 2-4, 08022 Barcelona (Spain)
{guiomar, afornells, elisabet, jaumea}@salle.url.edu

Abstract. Security has become a main concern in corporate networks. Security tests are essential to identify vulnerabilities, but experts must analyze very large data and complex information. Unsupervised learning can help by clustering groups of devices with similar vulnerabilities. However an index to evaluate every solution should be calculated to demonstrate results validity. Also the value of the number of clusters should be tuned for every data set in order to find the best solution. This paper introduces SOM as a clustering method to evaluate complex and uncertain knowledge in Consensus, a distributed security system for vulnerability testing; it proposes new metrics to evaluate the cohesion of every cluster, and also the cohesion between clusters; it applies unsupervised algorithms and validity metrics to a security data set; and it presents a method to obtain the best number of clusters regarding these new cohesion metrics: Intracohesion and Intercohesion factors.

Keywords: AI applications, Unsupervised Learning, Self-Organization Map, K-means, Network security.

1 Introduction

Computer attacks and network vulnerabilities have increased dramatically over the last years. Nowadays the best approach to keep a network protected consists of understanding how services are running and their vulnerabilities [6]. Thus security experts need solutions for an optimal treatment of the data obtained from network security tests. Moreover, security applications require of some intelligence to recognize malicious data, unauthorized traffic, identify intrusion data patterns and learn from previous decisions [3,15]. Security experts have noticed that collecting logs, capturing network traffic and identifying potential threats is becoming difficult to handle with large data sets. So there is a need for methods that help identifying abnormal data from everyday network activity.

Clustering techniques permit dividing the space into K regions based on some similarity metric where the value of K may or may not be known a priori. The real challenge is to be able to evolve a proper value of the number of clusters and provide the appropriate clustering solution. Thus a validity method must be applied to verify clusters quality.

We have already successfully applied Artificial Intelligence (AI) techniques to find similarities and dissimilarities within information resulting from security tests in Consensus [3], an integrated computer-aided system to automate network security tests [2,4]. The nature of our domain has forced us to start working with unsupervised techniques, as the domain and the different classes have not been defined yet. This study was achieved using clustering algorithms based on K-means [10], which allows discovering hidden patterns, abnormal system configurations, or other valuable information for network security analysts [3]. Even this data categorization improves the time needed to analyze the security testing results, it is difficult to measure cluster quality due to the amount of factors that influence the results, and also because of data complexity.

For these reasons, in this paper we propose new indices of cluster validity called Intracohesion and Intercohesion factors. These metrics will help security experts in the task of analyzing clusters in order to validate their results. Another contribution concerns the computation of the proper value of the number of clusters in network security domain using the proposed indices. We also study the application of Self-Organization Maps (SOM) [13] in Consensus [3]. As the amount of data and complexity is high in our domain, their Soft Computing capabilities can improve the discovery of implicit and previously unknown knowledge using a better feature extraction in a high dimensional space[9] to cluster data.

This paper is organized as follows. Section 2 surveys related work about the application of AI in network security and validity metrics. Section 3 explains how clustering and cohesion factors are applied. Section 4 describes the experimentation and results. Finally, Section 5 presents conclusions and further work.

2 Related Work

Network security testing is currently demanding for new ways of finding patterns in large data sets. Some research projects have used K-means as a clustering method to find natural grouping of similar alarm records [1], SOM as a clustering method to study computer attacks [7], or unsupervised anomaly detection for network intrusion detection [14]. Also Case-Based Reasoning has been applied in dynamic, imprecise and adversarial domains, like network security [15].

Consensus is a vulnerability testing system that automates mechanisms to perform a network security test [4]. Consensus simplifies network security experts' work, as all collected information is stored in the system database for its future analysis. A corporate network can handle many devices, thus a thorough test can result in a great amount of data that must be processed by security analysts. Unsupervised learning helps analysts to find groups of devices with similar patterns. Clustering partition methods have been introduced in Consensus, like K-means [10] and X-melan [3] and their results were successfully evaluated by network security experts [3]. On the other hand, other partition methods as SOM [13] are effective when dealing with problems that present a huge amount of information and complex data [9]. Thus SOM will be also included in Consensus to compare its clustering results with the other methods.

Validation of unsupervised clustering results is a main task in order to demonstrate its correctness. Cluster validation refers to procedures that evaluate the clustering results in a quantitative and objective function. Several proposals have been analyzed. One possibility is based on evaluating the same function that clustering algorithms optimize. The main problem is that it is not normalized with respect to the number of clusters. Other indices of cluster validity are Davies-Boudin (DB) [5], Dunn's separation [8], or Silhouette [17]. All indices calculate clustering validity by using the same features included in the data set. However, in our case we want to validate clustering results using not only the features used for classifying, but also other features that were not in the input data set. As stated before, Consensus database contains complex information that is hard to introduce as classification features but can be helpful to analyze the quality of the obtained clusters. Also determining the correct number of clusters in a data set is one of the most common applications of cluster validity, as it cannot always be known a priory in unsupervised environments.

3 Improving the Clustering Capabilities of Consensus

3.1 Clustering Methods: From K-Means to SOM

K-means [10] is a representative example of partition methods [11]. It divides data-points into K clusters, where each one is represented by a pattern or a model called centroid. First centroids are randomly initialized. Next, they are iteratively adjusted by assigning the samples into the nearest centroid using an average squared distance between points and centroids. Training ends when there is no change in two iterations. K-means is sensitive to the choice of initial centroids, so a bad choice can greatly impact on both performance and distortion.

K-means was included in Consensus to automate the process of classifying devices related to their vulnerabilities [3,9]. Obtained results showed a valid clustering that grouped devices with similar open ports and operating systems (OSs) without using features related to vulnerabilities, regarding to the opinion of the human expert on network security. However K-means does not have good capabilities when managing complex data. In this sense, we use SOM in order to introduce Soft Computing capabilities in Consensus, that allows the management of uncertain, approximate, partial truth and complex knowledge.

SOM [13] is one of the major unsupervised learning paradigms in artificial neural networks. It projects the n-input data space into a new shorter m-output space to highlight the most important data features. SOM defines clusters which represent certain patterns of the original data. Its properties make it useful for clustering [12]: it preserves the original topology; it works well even though the original space has many dimensions; it has feature selection; classes with few examples are not lost; it provides an easy way to show data; it is organized in an autonomous way to be adjusted better to data. However, the order of training samples affects results, and the definition of the number of clusters is not trivial.

SOM properties are very useful for Consensus data. Different tools are used during a security test and their results can be approximate or inconsistent. When scanning the same device, Nessus [18] may resemble Nmap [16] results. Also the huge amount of information obtained produces a data set with many dimensions. In addition, a class can contain few examples, because it represents a group of devices with similar vulnerabilities, and maybe only few devices have these specific vulnerabilities. Thus, SOM features conform to Consensus data characteristics. A drawback is related to the election of the number of clusters. However, our proposal introduces new metrics ad hoc to Consensus domain to decide how many clusters are needed depending on every data set.

3.2 Cohesion Factors: Intracohesion and Intercohesion

A very important point after implementing a clustering method is to evaluate the quality of each resulting configuration according to a given validity index. However cluster validation cannot rely on given patterns to conclude whether a cluster is right or wrong, as given patterns do not exist in unsupervised domains. Thus, cluster validity may depend on the human expert related to that domain.

One of the main goals of this paper is a new proposal to computer-aided validate the clusters from Consensus data sets. Our criterion to assess the quality of a solution is related to the coherence and cohesion of clusters. Different evaluation measures have been proposed. DB [5] evaluates a cluster structure, but does not show the worthiness of every cluster and the dependences between them. Silhouette [17] estimates only the best cluster. Dunn [8] compares inter and intracluster distances and cluster diameters. All apply the same clustering features, so new features can not be used to evaluate clustering results.

The proposed validity measures focus not only on the clustering features, but also on more information already stored in Consensus. Results obtained after a port scanning, OS fingerprinting, vulnerability testing and denial of service attacks are stored for every tested device. Only port scanning and OS fingerprinting were selected as clustering features due to data complexity [3] and these are the results we want to evaluate with these measures. In fact, data from these two processes is what a security expert would analyze first to find patterns in tested devices. So Consensus obtains clusters that group devices with similar open ports and OSs [3]. Consequently, clusters should group devices with similar vulnerabilities since devices with similar OSs and open ports usually hold the same vulnerabilities. As complex information about detected vulnerabilities is also stored this data will be used to assess cluster validation. Other measures like DB or Dunn would also validate the clusters, but would not test the dependence between OSs, ports and network vulnerabilities.

The *Intracohesion factor* evaluates the cohesion between the elements of a cluster. This factor is a distance measure on the set of data points in a cluster C_k. Then, the *Similarity* (S) between two elements of a cluster $x_i, x_k \in C_k$ is calculated by adding the vulnerabilities common in both elements. This value is divided by the number of vulnerabilities of one of the compared devices. S is calculated for every different pair of elements in a cluster and it is divided by the number of different pair of elements. Finally, the *mean Intracohesion factor* is the average of the Intracohesion obtained from every cluster in the system. The higher the *Intracohesion factor*, the better the result.

$$S(x_i, x_j) = \frac{Common\,Vulnerabilities(x_i, x_j)}{Total\,Vulnerabilities(x_i)} \quad (1)$$

$$Mean\,Intracohesion = \frac{1}{K}\sum_{k=1}^{K} \frac{\sum_{x_i \in C_k} \sum_{\substack{x_j \in C_k \\ x_j \neq x_i}} S(x_i, x_j)}{|C_k|^2 - |C_k|} \quad (2)$$

The *Intercohesion factor* evaluates the cohesion between clusters. It is the distance measure on the set of clusters. Therefore, the lower the value, the better the result. Firstly, the *Distance* (D) between the different clusters must be calculated. D checks the coincidence of vulnerabilities between two clusters and divides this value by the number of vulnerabilities that all the elements of one cluster have in common. Finally, the *mean Intercohesion factor* calculates D for every pair of different clusters and normalizes this value.

$$D(C_i, C_j) = \frac{Common\,Vulnerabilities(C_i, C_j)}{Common\,Vulnerabilities(C_i)} \quad (3)$$

$$Mean\,Intercohesion = \frac{\sum_{i=1}^{K} \sum_{\substack{j=1 \\ j \neq i}}^{K} D(C_i, C_j)}{K^2 - K} \quad (4)$$

4 Experiments and Results

In this section we describe the implemented testbed with Consensus data and we present the clustering evaluation applying the *Cohesion metrics*. Finally, results have also been validated with the help of network security testing experts.

4.1 Testbed Description

Data used for clustering came from Consensus, which runs several open-source tools in order to obtain information regarding port scanning, OS fingerprinting, vulnerability testing and denial of service attacks and stores all the results in a PostgreSQL database. Input data sets only include features related to port scanning and OS fingerprinting, as they are very related to the types of vulnerabilities a device can handle. The features consist of a list of all available ports and the reliability percentage of having certain OSs installed in every device[3].

After testing 44 real devices from the university network to obtain real data using Consensus, an input file with more than 160 features has been created. This is because a wide variety of devices have been tested to get as much representation as possible. Therefore these devices have different open ports and implement very diverse OSs. This input file has been applied to K-means with K=3..8, and SOM with size maps of $2 \times 2, 3 \times 3, 4 \times 4, 5 \times 5$ and 6×6, in order to find different clusters configurations. Also, 15 different random seeds have been tested to check the initialization influence. Results are shown in the next section.

Table 1. Summary of the mean of Intracohesion and Intercohesion values for K-means and SOM algorithms using different number of clusters (C). It also includes the difference between both factors. The best results are marked in **Bold**.

Clusters (C)	K-means			SOM		
	Intrach. (std.)	Interch. (std.)	Diff.	Intrach. (std.)	Interch. (std.)	Diff.
3	0.661 (0.09)	0.183 (0.08)	0.477	0.680 (0.07)	0.095 (0.13)	0.584
4	0.687 (0.06)	**0.161 (0.03)**	0.52	**0.875 (0.01)**	0.088 (0.01)	**0.786**
5	0.693 (0.04)	0.216 (0.02)	0.477	0.678 (0.07)	0.231 (0.12)	0.447
6	**0.706 (0.01)**	0.217 (0.01)	0.488	0.748 (0.08)	0.288 (0.08)	0.459
7	—	—	—	0.762 (0.04)	0.318 (0.04)	0.443
8	—	—	—	0.817 (0.03)	0.355 (0.09)	0.461

4.2 Evaluation of Clustering Techniques Using Consensus Data

Here we present the results obtained from analyzing vulnerability testing data using clustering techniques. The main goal of Consensus is to define a set of clusters, which group devices depending on their similarities based on their vulnerabilities, considering that no directly related information about vulnerabilities has been used. Mean Intracohesion and mean Intercohesion factors have been calculated for different number of clusters (C) using the same data set. The similarity function in both algorithms is the Manhattan distance. Table 1 represents the mean of the mean of the Intracohesion factor, and the mean of the mean Intercohesion factor for every execution with their standard deviation respectively, and also the difference between their values. Although K-means has been configured with $K=8$, it has not been able to build more than 6 clusters. Still, SOM has been able to create more than 6 clusters in several map configurations.

Best results should include a high Intracohesion and a low Intercohesion. If Intracohesion is high, every element is very similar to the elements of the same cluster. If Intercohesion is low, clusters are different. Considering only the mean Intracohesion value, it increases when C increases. When having more clusters, cluster size decreases as there are more groups to insert the devices; therefore, it is easier that elements in a cluster look like more similar. However, when C increases also the mean Intercohesion increases. The more clusters, the higher possibility that two clusters become more similar because maybe devices' differences are not so significant to create so many clusters. Thus a compromise between both cohesion metrics should be achieved and this compromise will fix the best C for this data set. Another useful value is the difference between the mean Intracohesion and the mean Intercohesion. A higher value is desired.

Figure 1 shows the evolution of Intracohesion and Intercohesion comparing both clustering approaches. The best solution for SOM Intracohesion consists of four clusters, whereas K-means considers six clusters, although other solutions have similar Intracohesion rate. Regarding to Intercohesion, both algorithms agree in the best $C=4$. Although K-means obtained a better Intracohesion for $C=6$, its Intercohesion was lower. In conclusion, the best number of clusters for this data set is 4. Also, SOM has the best configuration.

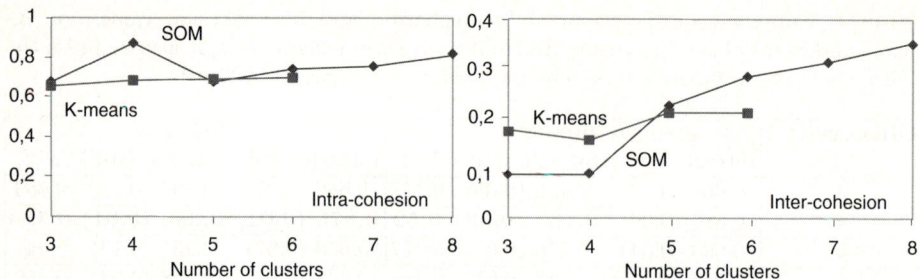

Fig. 1. Intracohesion and Intercohesion evolution for K-means (■) and SOM (♦)

Network security experts have also analyzed results obtained after clustering the data set. Regarding to $C=4$, human experts have observed that K-means grouped devices prioritizing OSs. Still, SOM grouped devices with similar vulnerabilities although they had different OSs. Both clustering proposals were accepted, as they can help analysts handling information obtained from security tests in order to detect devices with similar vulnerabilities, abnormal groups of devices or atypical system behaviors.

5 Conclusions and Further Work

This paper has presented new indices for cluster validation in a network security domain. Intracohesion factor shows the coherence between elements of a same cluster, whereas Intercohesion factor registers the difference between clusters. These indices have been introduced in Consensus, an integrated computer-aided sytem to help network security analysts in order to discover groups of similar devices or hidden patterns in network devices, after performing a security test.

The high amount of data obtained after a security test, its complexity and uncertainty justify the incorporation of SOM, as Soft Computing techniques improve managing complex data. Afterwards the initial clustering algorithm used in Consensus, K-means, and the SOM approach have been evaluated using Intracohesion and Intercohesion factors. Furthermore, Consensus has become an hybrid system that implements unsupervised learning based on inductive learning and also artificial neural networks learning. This hybrid system can also evaluate the obtained memory case using the proposed metrics. Results show that in most cases SOM perform better than K-means cohesion factors.

One of the main concerns with unsupervised learning is the ability to find a proper value of the number of clusters. Cohesion factors help on selecting C. The higher the Intracohesion and the lower the Intercohesion, the better the result. Thus a compromise between both values must be achieved, which reveals the best C, as security analyst experts have confirmed in a later study. Furthermore, the limitations of K-means and SOM regarding to the election of the best C is overcome applying a clustering evaluation ad hoc to the domain. Further work includes the analysis of other metrics. Also the introduction of the knowledge of security experts to guide the process will be further researched.

Acknowledgements

We would like to thank the Spanish Government for their support under grants TIN 2005-08386-C05-04, FIT-360000-2004-81 and CIT-390000-2005-27, and *Generalitat de Catalunya* (DURSI) for its support under grants 2005SGR-302 and 2006FIC-0043. We also thank Pete Herzog and ISECOM for their support to this project. Finally, we thank *Enginyeria i Arquitectura La Salle* of Ramon Llull University for their support to our research group.

References

1. E. Bloedorn, A.D. Christiansen, W. Hill, and C. Skorupka. Data mining for network intrusion detection: How to get started. In *The MITRE Corporation*, 2001.
2. G. Corral, X. Cadenas, A. Zaballos, and M. Cadenas. A distributed security system for wlans. In *1st. IEEE International Conference on Wireless Internet*, 2005.
3. G. Corral, E. Golobardes, O. Andreu, I. Serra, E. Maluquer, and A. Martínez. Application of clustering techniques in a network security testing system. *Artificial Intelligence Research and Devolopment*, 131:157–164, 2005.
4. G. Corral, A. Zaballos, X. Cadenas, and A. Grané. A distributed security system for an intranet. In *39th IEEE Int. Carnahan Conf. on Security Technology*, 2005.
5. D. Davies and D. Bouldin. A cluster separation measure. *IEEE Transactions on Pattern Analysis and Machine Intelligence*, 1(4):224–227, 1979.
6. J. Dawkins and J. Hale. A systematic approach to multi-stage network attack analysis. *Second IEEE Int. Inf. Assurance Workshop*, 2004.
7. L. DeLooze. Classification of Computer Attacks using a Self-Organizing Map. *Proc. of the 2004 IEEE, Workshop on Information Assurance*, pages 365–369, 2004.
8. J.C. Dunn. Well separated clusters and optimal fuzzy partitions. *J. Cybernetics*, 4:224–227, 1974.
9. A. Fornells, E. Golobardes, D. Vernet, and G. Corral. Unsupervised case memory organization: Analysing computational time and soft computing capabilities. In *8th European Conference on Case-Based Reasoning*, 2006. In press.
10. J. Hartigan and M. Wong. A k-means clustering algorithm. In *Applied Statistics*, pages 28:100–108, 1979.
11. J.A. Hartigan. *Clustering Algorithms*. John Wiley and Sons, New York, 1975.
12. S. Haykin. *Neural Networks: A Comprehensive Foundation*. Prentice Hall, 1999.
13. T. Kohonen. *Self-Organization and Associative Memory*, volume 8 of *Springer Series in Information Sciences*. Springer, Berlin, Heidelberg, 1984. 3rd ed. 1989.
14. K. Leung and C. Leckie. Unsupervised anomaly detection in network intrusion detection using clusters. In *Conf. in Research and Practice in Inf. Tech.*, 2005.
15. F. Martin. *Case-Based Sequence Analysis in Dynamic, Imprecise, and Adversarial Domains*. PhD thesis, Universitat Politècnica de Catalunya, 2004.
16. Nmap. Insecure. http://www.insecure.org/nmap.
17. P.J.Rousseew. Silhouttes: a graphical aid to the interpretation and validation of cluster analysis. *J. of Computational Applications in Math*, 20:53–65, 1987.
18. Internet Scanner. http://www.nessus.org.

Using Neural Networks to Detect Microfossil Teeth in Somosaguas Sur Paleontological Site

R. Gil-Pita and N. Sala-Burgos*

Departamento de Teoría de la Señal y Comunicaciones, Universidad de Alcalá, Spain
Departamento de Paleontología, Universidad Complutense de Madrid, Spain
roberto.gil@uah.es, nohemisala@hotmail.com

Abstract. Automatic microfossil detection system allows to extract the position of the microfossils in a concentrate of mineral grains, speeding up the time required to analyze each sample. In this paper we study the use of Multilayer Perceptrons and Radial Basis Function Networks applied to the automatic microfossil teeth detection problem, focusing on the dependence of the performance with the size of the network, and with the size of the training set. The data used in the experiments are three images of concentrates with micromammal teeth from Somosaguas paleontological site, in Madrid (Spain). The obtained results demonstrate RBFNs perform better than MLPs in most of the considered cases, detecting most of the microfossil teeth in the images.

1 Introduction

Microfossils are very important in order to determinate the age of a geological layer with a high grade of accuracy. They are also the fund of any micropaleontological studies. Actual techniques used to extract microfossils are manual, and require of a high amount of time and human resources. This fact makes interesting the study of other more complex techniques, that speed up the extraction of the microfossils. So, the volume of analyzed terrain can be increased, and, consequently, the accuracy of the microfossil studies is improved.

Automatic microfossil detection consists in a real-time video system, that allows to detect the position of the microfossils in a concentrate of stone grains, speeding up the time required to analyze each sample. A high resolution camera is disposed over the concentrate, so that video data can be processed and monitored. The output of the detection system is a binary image, where the pixels considered as fossil are marked, like in a radar image. This systems must be operating in real time, and, therefore, the computational cost of the algorithms is a very important issue.

There are not many articles dedicated to the study of this application in the literature. In [1] the authors describe three systems designed to automatically

---

* We thank Somosaguas Project manager N. López Martínez, and photographer C. Alonso. Somosaguas Project is jointly supported by the "Universidad Complutense de Madrid" and the "Museo nacional de Ciencias Naturales" under their agreement with the Spanish "Consejería de Cultura de la Comunidad de Madrid".

recognize calcareous microfossils. They deal with the classification of different types of coccoliths using convolutional neural networks, but it does not consider the detection, since it is not a difficult task in the study of the coccoliths.

Other article related with the work presented is the paper [2], that studies the use of a Multilayer Perceptron with 20 hidden neurons for detecting micromammal teeth. Experimental studies were carried out using a single image, just for generating the training, validating and testing sets. The parameters used in the detection task were the red, green and blue components of each pixel, and the red, green and blue components of the eight d-distanced neighbors of each pixel. Using not only the information of the pixel, but its neighbors, the detection task was improved, due to the use of texture information. The paper studied the variation of the performance of the MLP in function of the parameter d, obtaining the best results with a value of $d = 12$.

The work presented in this paper compares the use of Multilayer Perceptrons (MLPs) and Radial Basis Function Networks (RBFNs) applied to the automatic microfossil detection problem, and it focuses on the dependence of the performance with experimental parameters like the architecture and size of the network, and the size of the training set. The analyzed material are three different images, that have been obtained from Somosaguas Sur paleontological site, in Madrid (Spain).

2 Material and Methods

The Universidad Complutense de Madrid's Somosaguas Campus is placed in Pozuelo de Alarcón (Spain), and includes two vertebrate fossil sites: Somosaguas Sur and Somosaguas Norte. They have yielded about 600 identifiable rests in different preservation states, belonging to 22 species.

Somosaguas Sur paleontological site is located at the top of a clay layer that contains quartz and feldspar grains, floating next to small and very small fossils of micromammals [3]. It is one of the richest sites in microvertebrates in Madrid, and it has provided hamster rodents (*Megacricetodon collongensis*, *Democricetodon darocensis* and *Democricetodon cf. D. Lacombai*), squirrels (*Heteroxerus grivensis* and *Heteroxerus rubricati*), dormices (*Armantomys tricristatus*, *Microdyromys koenigswaldi* and *Microdyromys monspeliensis*) lagomorph pikas (*lagopsis penai* and *Prolagus cf. Oeningensis*), insectivores (*Galerix exilis* and *Miosorex cf. grivensis*) and reptiles (lacertids, anguids and quelonids) [4]. The presence of these species determines the biochronology of the Somosaguas site, placing it in the Middle Miocene E biozone (Middle Aragonian), about 14 million of years ago. In addition, they allow the reconstruction of an arid climate epoch in the Madrid basin during middle Miocene times, occupied by subtropical woodlands and savannahs with strong floods and without permanent rivers [5].

The microvertebrate paleontologic studies consist in recovering small fossils of vertebrates. Based on them, evolutionary, paleoecological and paleoclimatic models can be obtained, and their application in Bioestratigraphy has made them indispensable for geological dating of deposits [6]. The most common microvertebrate fossils are teeth and bones, and their sizes are usually of the order of 0.5 mm. Due to their small size, their extraction techniques are special and quite different to macrofossil extraction ones. In first place, several kilograms of sediment are extracted. The quantity of sediment varies in function of the site. Once extracted the sediment, it is sun dried during several hours. Then, it is introduced in a recipient with water so the clay is completely dissolved. When the sample is disintegrated, the wash sieve process is carried out. This process consists on making the sample go through a series of sieves of different sizes using pressure water. So, several concentrates of mineral grains, bones and teeth are separated from the sediment, and classified in different sizes. In Somosaguas Sur site the proportion of concentrates is about 3.5 Kg over 50 Kg of sediment [3], and the number of microfossils founded in the concentrates is about 1500, giving a ratio lower than 0.8 % (less than 28 g).

The most common technique to separate microfossils from the concentrates is denominated picking. It consists on dividing the concentrate in small fractions for a visual examination and manual separation of the fossils. When grain size is lower than 1 mm, it is necessary the use of binocular magnifying glasses. The picking technique is relatively easy for an expert in microfossil recognition, but however it is quite tedious and requires a high amount of time. In this paper we study the viability of the use of machine learning methods, in order to speed up the picking process. So, we study the use of different neural network-based detection techniques applied to high resolution images of the concentrates.

The data used in the experiments of this paper are three high definition photographies of three different samples of concentrate extracted form Somosaguas Sur site. These three images have been used to generate three sets of data, respectively: the training set, the validation set and the test set. The training set has been used to train the network. The validation set has been used to early stop the training process, and to calculate the values of the free parameters of the experiments. The test set has been used to evaluate the detector performance, and it has not been used during the training and validating process.

The average size of the grains is over 2 mm, and each image represents about 4.65x5.70 cm of sample (1550x1900 pixels, giving 0.3 mm per pixel). All microfossils have been identified, with special interest over micromammal teeth. Teeth are more useful than bones in order to obtain paleontological information, because they can determine the specie more accurately than bones, and they provide information about the feeding habits, and therefore about habitat and climatic conditions. So for this study we will focus on the detection of teeth, ignoring the bone fragments. The training image contains 12 teeth (4 incisives of continuous growth, and 8 molars and premolars), the validation image contains 6 teeth (1 incisive of continuous growth, and 5 molars and premolars), and the test image contains 10 teeth (1 incisive of continuous growth, and 9 molars and premolars). Figure 2 shows the third photograph of the sample, the test image, and the position of the teeth in this sample.

The input data has been collected using the red, green and blue components of the pixels of the image. For each pixel, a vector **z** has been created using the

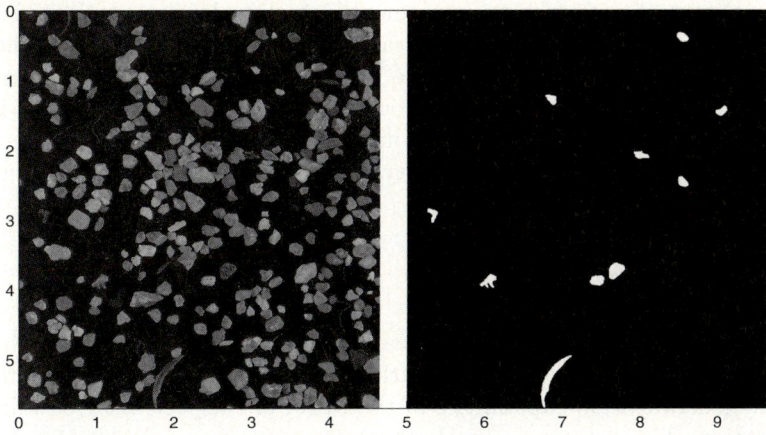

Fig. 1. Photograph of the first sample, the test image, used to generate the test set (left), and desired output of the system for the same image (right)

values of the components of the pixel, and the values of the components of eight neighbors placed at a distance $d = 12$. This value has been selected, according to the results previously obtained in [2]. The output data has been one for the points belonging to a fossil tooth, and zero for the rest.

3 Problem Formulation

Automatic microfossil detection can be formulated as a binary hypothesis test, in which the Neyman-Pearson criterion can be applied. The detection system has to decide if the observation is originated either from a mineral grain (the null hypothesis H_0) or from a fossil tooth (the alternative hypothesis H_1). Considering $P(\mathbf{z}|H_i)$ is the probability density function of the observation vector $\mathbf{z}$ under hypothesis H_i, and $P(H_i)$ is the prior probability of the hypothesis H_i, then equation (1) is an implementation of the Neyman-Pearson detector.

$$g_{np}(\mathbf{z}) = \frac{P(H_1)P(\mathbf{z}|H_1)}{P(H_0)P(\mathbf{z}|H_0)} \gtrless \eta_{np} \qquad (1)$$

If $g_{np}(\mathbf{z})$ is higher than a given threshold η_{np}, then the Neyman-Pearson criterion decides in favor of hypothesis H_1, and if it is lower, then the it decides in favor of hypothesis H_0. This detector maximizes the probability of detection (P_D), while maintaining the probability of false alarm (P_{FA}) lower than or equal to a specified value. The characteristics of each detector are reflected in the curve that relates P_D to P_{FA} [7]. This criterion needs the likelihood functions under both, the null and the alternative hypotheses, to be implemented. Unfortunately, the designers hardly ever know the likelihood functions.

Neural networks are proposed as a solution because they can be trained in order to implement detectors without prior knowledge of the likelihood functions.

The use of neural networks to implement detectors is also motivated by the demonstration that a feed-forward neural network trained to minimize the mean square error criterion, approximates the Bayes optimal discriminant function [8]. If the neural network is trained to produce 1 when the feature vector is from class H_1 and 0 when the vector is from class H_0, then the network is trying to approximate the posterior probability posterior probability $P(H_1|\mathbf{z})$, given in expression (2):

$$g_0(\mathbf{z}) = P(H_1|\mathbf{z}) = \frac{1}{1 + \frac{P(H_0)P(\mathbf{z}|H_0)}{P(H_1)P(\mathbf{z}|H_1)}} \gtrless \eta \qquad (2)$$

where $\mathbf{z}$ is the feature vector. $g_0(\mathbf{z})$ can be used to implement the Neyman-Pearson detector when is compared with a detection threshold, η. When evaluating the generalization capabilities of the MLP, one aspect must be taken into consideration: The detection threshold, η, is necessary to decide if a target is present or not. The P_{FA} is a function of η, and the pairs (P_{FA}, η) must be estimated in each detector. This values can be estimated by presenting a set of H_0 patterns, and applying the Monte-Carlo simulation.

An interesting conclusion related to the prior probabilities is extracted from equation (2). Let's consider a neural network trained with data with the same probability density functions, but with different prior probabilities $P'(H_0)$ and $P'(H_1)$. Then the relationship between $g_0(\mathbf{z})$ and function approximated by this network, $g'_0(\mathbf{z})$, is obtained using equation (3).

$$g'_0(\mathbf{z}) = f(g_0(\mathbf{z})) = \frac{1}{1 + \frac{P'(H_0)P'(H_1)}{P(H_0)P(H_1)} (g_0(\mathbf{z})^{-1} - 1)} \qquad (3)$$

So, taking into account that the function $f(\cdot)$ defined in equation (3) is a continuous and strictly increasing function in the interval $(0,1)$, which is the range of the function $g_0(\mathbf{z})$, then function $g'_0(\mathbf{z})$ is valid for implementing the Neyman-Pearson detector under the original data. This implies that, considering a sufficiently high number of patterns over each hypothesis, then the network can be trained with a proportion of the data that differs from the prior probabilities.

Due to the high amount of available data under hypothesis H_0, the proportion of the training and validation data $p = P'(H_0)/P'(H_1)$ has been a parameter of the experiments. In order to generate the training and validation sets, all the N_1 patterns belonging to hypothesis H_1 has been selected, and $N_0 = pN_1$ patterns belonging to the null hypothesis has been randomly selected. The values of the parameter p considered are 1, 2, 4, 8 and 16. So, taking into account that the training image contains $N_1 = 23819$ pixels belonging to class H_1, the highest number of training patterns used belonging to class H_0 asociated with $p = 16$ is $N_0 = 16 \cdot N_1 = 381104$.

4 Description of the Experiments

The MLPs trained in this paper have one hidden layer, and use the sigmoidal function as the activation function for all the neurons. They have been trained

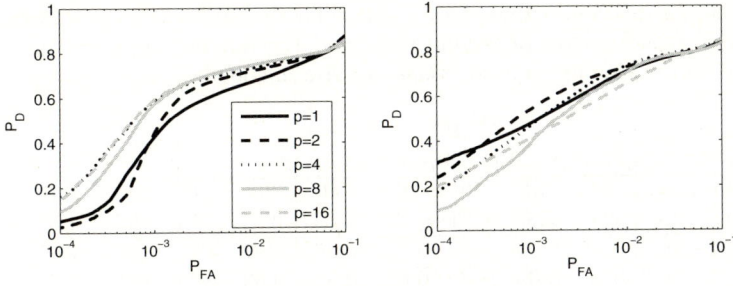

Fig. 2. P_D versus P_{FA} for the MLPs (left) and the RBFNs (right) which obtained lowest validation error, trained with $p = 1$, $p = 2$, $p = 4$, $p = 8$, and $p = 16$

using the Levenberg-Marquardt algorithm [9], and have been regularized using Bayesian regularization [10]. The number of inputs of the network is 27, corresponding to the red, green and blue components of the nine points considered for each pattern.

In the case of RBFNs, the hidden units are radial basis functions, defined by equation (4).

$$G_i(\mathbf{z}) = exp\left(-\frac{1}{2\sigma^2}|\mathbf{z} - \mathbf{t}_i|^2\right) \quad (4)$$

where $\mathbf{z}$ is the sample vector, $\mathbf{t}_i$ is the center of the radial basis function, and σ is a smoothing parameter. All the hidden radial basis neurons on the hidden layer are connected to the output neuron, which is a linear neuron. So, the function implemented by the network is a linear combination of the radial basis functions. To train the RBFNs, we applied a three-phased learning strategy: first, the centers of the radial basis functions $\mathbf{t}_i$ are determined by the k-means algorithm; then, the smoothing parameter σ is set to the value that minimizes the mean square error over the validation set; and finally, the output weights that allow the least squares solution are determined using LMS algorithm.

In order to implement a detector, both MLPs and RBFNs have one output, which has been thresholded with a value η, calculated for each P_{FA} using Monte-Carlo experiment. The number of hidden units of both MLPs and RBFNs has been a parameter of the experiments, varying it from 10 to 60 in steps of 10. Each experiment has been repeated 5 times, and the mean square error over the validation set has been used to select the best network.

5 Results

Figure 2 shows the results obtained by the MLPs (left) and the RBFNs (right), selected by the validation set. Each curve represents the relationship between the P_{FA} and the P_D, for a given proportion p. For the MLPs, the best results are obtained by the lower values of p. The RBFNs show their best with high values of p, being quite similar the results obtained with $p = 4$, $p = 8$, and $p = 16$.

Table 1. P_D for different values of P_{FA} and p, for the MLPs and the RBFNs selected by validation. The number of hidden units and the number of simple operations in millions needed to classify the test image are also included.

	MLP					RBFN				
	$p=1$	$p=2$	$p=4$	$p=8$	$p=16$	$p=1$	$p=2$	$p=4$	$p=8$	$p=16$
Hidden units	50	40	50	30	30	20	20	20	20	30
Op. (millions)	8331	6682	8331	5033	5033	4971	4971	4971	4971	7415
$P_{FA} = 1 \cdot 10^{-2}$	0.71	0.73	0.74	0.70	0.66	0.67	0.72	0.73	0.75	0.74
$P_{FA} = 5 \cdot 10^{-3}$	0.64	0.69	0.67	0.63	0.58	0.63	0.69	0.70	0.72	0.71
$P_{FA} = 1 \cdot 10^{-3}$	0.48	0.54	0.47	0.39	0.42	0.43	0.44	0.59	0.57	0.59
$P_{FA} = 5 \cdot 10^{-4}$	0.42	0.45	0.38	0.28	0.35	0.26	0.17	0.46	0.40	0.47
$P_{FA} = 1 \cdot 10^{-4}$	0.30	0.24	0.17	0.09	0.20	0.05	0.03	0.16	0.10	0.15

Table 1 shows a comparison of the results obtained by the MLPs and the RBFNs. It shows the P_D for different values of P_{FA}, for the networks that obtained the lowest mean square error over the validation set. Results show the best performance of RBFNs for intermediate P_{FA} values. The MLPs are only an interesting option when the lowest P_{FA} value is selected.

In addition, the table shows the number of neurons of the selected networks, and the number of operations (in millions of simple operations) needed to process the whole test image. The number of neurons of the MLPs selected by validation is in general higher than the number of neurons of the RBFNs. On the other hand, the computational complexity of both solutions is quite similar.

At last, figure 3 shows the obtained output for the RBFN with $p = 16$, and $P_{FA} = 5 \cdot 10^{-3}$ (left) and $P_{FA} = 5 \cdot 10^{-4}$ (right). Taking into account the real position of the teeth in the sample (see figure 2), the second one clearly detects eight of the teeth, and it wrongly detects one or two mineral grains. The two

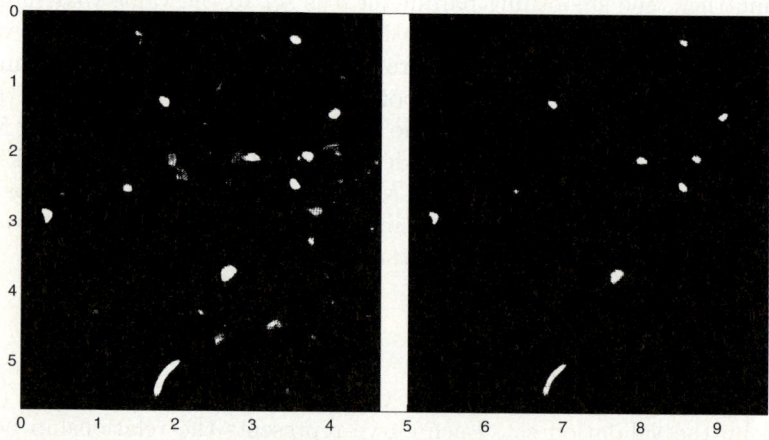

Fig. 3. Output for the test image of the RBFN trained with $p = 16$, for a $P_{FA} = 5 \cdot 10^{-3}$ (left), and for a $P_{FA} = 5 \cdot 10^{-4}$ (right)

missed teeth are not represented in the images, because they are completely different from those in the training image.

6 Conclusion

Automatic systems designed in order to aid in the picking process in micropaleontology can be very beneficial for actual geological and paleontological research. In this paper we study the use of MLPs and RBFNs applied to the automatic microfossil detection problem, considering the number of neurons and the size of the training set as parameters of the experiments.

The obtained results demonstrate RBFNs performs better than MLPs in most of the P_{FA} values considered, and they can detect most of the microfossil teeth of the sample. This fact makes RBFNs a quite interesting option in order to implement microfossil real-time detection systems, that can reduce the time required to analyze concentrates in most of the micropaleontological researches.

References

1. J. Bollmann, P. Quinn, M. Vela, B. Brabec, S. Brechner, M.Y. Corts, H. Hilbrecht, D.N. Schmidt, R. Schiebel, H.R. Thierstein, Automated particle analysis: calcareous microfossils, "Image Analysis, Sediments and Paleoenvironments", Kluwer Academic Publishers, Dordrecht, The Netherlands, 2003.
2. N. Sala-Burgos, R. Gil-Pita "Automatic Microfossil Detection in Somosaguas Sur paleontologic site (Pozuelo de Alarcón, Madrid, Spain) using Multilayer Perceptrons", *WSEAS Trans. on Signal Processing* Issue 2, Vol. 2, 2006, pp. 218-223.
3. A. Luis, J.M. Hernando, "The microvertebrates of the Middle Miocene of Somosaguas Sur (Pozuelo de Alarcón, Madrid, Spain)", *Coloquios de Paleontología*, Vol. 51, 2000, pp. 87-136.
4. D. Mínguez Gandú "Marco estratigráfico y sedimentológico de los yacimientos Miocenos de Somosaguas (Madrid, Spain)", *Coloquios de Paleontología*, Vol. 51, 2000, pp. 183-196.
5. N. López Martinez, J. Élez Villar, J. M. Hernando Hernando, A. Luis Cavia, A. Mazo, D. Minguez Gandú, J. Morales, I. Polonio Martín, M. J. Salesa, and I.M. Snchez, "The fossil vertebrates from Somosaguas (Pozuelo, Madrid, Spain)", *Coloquios de Paleontología*, Vol. 51, 2000, pp. 69-85.
6. N. López Martínez, Técnicas de Estudio de Microvertebrados. Los micromamíferos y su interés bioestratigráfico, "Paleontología de Vertebrados. Faunas y filogenia, aplicación y sociedad", Ed. Univ. País Vasco, 1992, pp. 345-365.
7. H.L. Van Trees, *Detection, estimation, and modulation theory* Vol. 1. Wiley, 1968.
8. D.W. Ruck, S.K. Rogers, M. Kabrisky, M.E. Oxley, B.W. Suter, "The multilayer Perceptron as an approximation to a Bayes optimal discriminant function", *IEEE Transactions on Neural Networks*, Vol. 1, No. 1, 1990, pp. 296-298.
9. M.T. Hagan, M.B. Menhaj, "Training Feedforward Networks with the Marquardt Algorithm", *IEEE Trans. on Neural Networks*, Vol. 5, No. 6, 1994, pp. 989-993.
10. D.J.C. MacKay, "Bayesian interpolation", *Neu. Comp.*, Vol. 4, 1992, pp. 415-447.

A Fast Grid Search Method in Support Vector Regression Forecasting Time Series

Yukun Bao and Zhitao Liu

Department of Management Science & Information System, School of Management,
Huazhong University of Science and Technology, Wuhan 430074, China
yukunbao@mail.hust.edu.cn

Abstract. Selection of kernel function parameters is one of the key problems in support vector regression(SVR) for forecasting because these free parameters have significant impact on the performances of forecasting accuracy. The commonly used grid search method is intractable and computational expensive. In this paper, a fast grid search method is proposed for tuning multiple parameters for SVR with RBF kernel for time series forecasting. Empirical results confirm the feasibility and validation of the proposed method.

Keywords: Grid Search; Support Vector Regression; Parameters Tuning.

1 Introduction

The performance of Support Vector Regression forecasting time series is significantly affected by kernel parameters [1, 2]. One commonly used parameters selection method of SVM, Grid search method, is very time consuming [3].

Hsu et al. suggested exponentially growing sequences of C and *gamma* is a practical method to identify optimal parameters. and Kim and Bao used this method in forecasting financial time series and got acceptable results [2, 4].

Recently, a gradient descent approach has been introduced in [5] which reduces drastically the search steps of the optimal parameters. Some improvement based on it have been done in ref. [6, 7].

Gradient descent approach has a general purpose in improving the learning process and the measures used are still computational expensive compared with some specific application scenario. Our method is under a situation of forecasting time series. Here we put more attention on the prediction accuracy during training and testing. So we take such kind of measures such as NMSE which are less time consuming than gradient descent approach proposed in [5].

This paper consists of five sections. Section 2 reviews SVMs regression. Section 3 presents our proposed fast grid search method. Section 4 shows the experiment design and results concerned with the detailed procedures. Conclusions and discussion for further research hints are included in the last section.

2 Support Vector Regression

Given a set of data points $G = \{(x_i, d_i)\}_i^n$ (x_i is the input vector, d_i is the desired value and n is the total number of data patterns), SVMs approximate the function using the following:

$$y = f(x) = \omega\phi(x) + b \qquad (1)$$

where $\phi(x)$ is the high dimensional feature space which is non-linearly mapped from the input space x. The coefficients ω and b are estimated by minimizing

$$R_{SVMs}(C) = C\frac{1}{n}\sum_{i=1}^{n} L_s(d_i, y_i) + \frac{1}{2}\|\omega\|^2 \qquad (2)$$

$$L_s(d, y) = \begin{cases} |d - y| - \varepsilon, & |d - y| \geq \varepsilon \\ 0 & \text{otherwise} \end{cases} \qquad (3)$$

In the regularized risk function given by Eq.(2), the first term $C(\frac{1}{n})\sum_{i=1}^{n} L_s(d_i, y_i)$ is the empirical error (risk). They are measured by the ε-insensitive loss function given by Eq.(3). This loss function provides the advantage of enabling one to use sparse data points to represent the decision function given by Eq.(1). The second term $\frac{1}{2}\|\omega\|^2$, on the other hand, is the regularization term. C is referred to as the regularized constant and it determines the trade-off between the empirical risk and the regularization term. Increasing the value of C will result in the relative importance of the empirical risk with respect to the regularization term to grow. ε is called the tube size and it is equivalent to the approximation accuracy placed on the training data points. Both C and ε are user-prescribed parameters.

To obtain the estimations of ω and b, Eq.(2) is transformed to the primal function given by Eq.(4) by introducing the positive slack variables ξ_i and ξ_i^* as follows:

$$\text{Minimize} \quad R_{SVMs}(\omega, \xi^{(*)}) = C\sum_{i=1}^{n}(\xi_i + \xi_i^*) + \frac{1}{2}\|\omega\|^2$$
$$\text{Subject to} \quad \begin{array}{l} d_i - \omega\phi(x_i) - b_i \leq \varepsilon + \xi_i, \\ \omega\phi(x_i) + b_i - d_i \leq \varepsilon + \xi_i^*, \xi^* \geq 0 \end{array} \qquad (4)$$

Finally, by introducing Lagrange multipliers and exploiting the optimality constraints, the decision function given by Eq.(1) has the following explicit form:

$$f(x, a_i, a_i^*) = \sum_{i=1}^{n}(a_i - a_i^*)K(x, x_i) + b \qquad (5)$$

In Eq.(5), a_i and a_i^* are the so-called Lagrange multipliers. They satisfy the equalities $a_i * a_i^* = 0$, $a_i \geq 0$ and $a_i^* \geq 0$ where $i = 1,2,\ldots,n$ and are obtained by maximizing the dual function of Eq.(4) which has the following form:

$$R(a_i, a_i^*) = \sum_{i=1}^{n} d_i(a_i - a_i^*) - \varepsilon\sum_{i=1}^{n}(a_i + a_i^*)$$
$$-\frac{1}{2}\sum_{i=1}^{n}\sum_{j=1}^{n}(a_i - a_i^*)(a_j - a_j^*)K(x_i, x_j) \qquad (6)$$

with the constraints

$$\sum_{i=1}^{n}(a_i - a_i^*),$$
$$0 \leq a_i \leq \mathcal{C}, \quad i=1,2,\ldots,n$$
$$0 \leq a_i^* \leq \mathcal{C}, \quad i=1,2,\ldots,n$$

Based on the Karush-Kuhn-Tucker (KKT) conditions of quadratic programming, only a certain number of coefficients $(a_i - a_i^*)$ in Eq.(5) will assume non-zero values. The data points associated with them have approximation errors equal to or larger than ε and are referred to as support vectors. These are the data points lying on or outside the ε-bound of the decision function. According to Eq.5 it is evident that support vectors are the only elements of the data points that are used in determining the decision function as the coefficients $(a_i - a_i^*)$ of other data points are all equal to zero. Generally, the larger the ε, the fewer the number of support vectors and thus the sparser the representation of the solution. However, a larger ε can also depreciate the approximation accuracy placed on the training points. In this sense, ε is a trade-off between the sparseness of the representation and closeness to the data.

$K(x_i, x_j)$ is defined as the kernel function. The value of the kernel is equal to the inner product of two vectors X_i and X_j in the feature space $\phi(x_i)$ and $\phi(x_j)$, that is, $K(x_i, x_j) = \phi(x_i) * \phi(x_j)$. The elegance of using the kernel function is that one can deal with feature spaces of arbitrary dimensionality without having to compute the map $\phi(x)$ explicitly. Any function satisfying Mercer's condition can be used as the kernel function. The typical examples of kernel function are as follows:

Linear: $\quad K(x_i, x_j) = x_i^T x_j$
Polynomial: $\quad K(x_i, x_j) = \left(\gamma x_i^T x_j + r\right)^d, \gamma > 0.$
Radial basis function(RBF): $K(x_i, x_j) = \exp\left(-\gamma \|x_i - x_j\|^2\right), \gamma > 0.$
Sigmoid: $\quad K(x_i, x_j) = \tanh\left(\gamma x_i^T x_j + r\right).$

Here, γ, r and d are kernel parameters. The kernel parameter should be carefully chosen as it implicitly defines the structure of the high dimensional feature space $\phi(x)$ and thus controls the complexity of the final solution.

3 Proposed Fast Grid Search Method

Our research effort aims at finding the largest error decreasing path during training. Figure1 illustrates the error surface with NMSE, C and γ on data set EXJU. Figure1a is NMSE on the training data. And Figure1b is NMSE on the test data. We can observe that the error surface varies smoothly and looks like a concave. The main idea of our proposed method is to walk along the direction with relatively largest error decrease (by computing the prediction measures)in the parameter grid map until we get out of the boundary or walk back to one tested point. The pseud code of the algorithm is as follows:

```
input C[], gamma[]
variable walk[], error[]

main fastGridSearch {
  start with a small pair of (C,1/gamma) in the grid map;
  while(true) {
    next = findNextStep(current);
    if(next == null)
      break;
    walk[next] = true
  }
  select suitable C and gamma from the exploited path
  via computing the prediction measures;
}

proc findNextStep(current) {
  for(p in the eight adjacent points of current)
    getErrorFromCache(p);
  next = the point with relatively largest error decrease;
  if(walk[next] == true)
    return null;
  return next;
}

proc getErrorFromCache(p) {
  if(p is out range of the grid map)
    return NaN;
  if(error[p] was caculated)
    return error[p];
  training SVM with the corresponding C and gamma,
  store and return the result error;
}
```

4 Experiment

4.1 Data Sets

We collects four data sets from different backgrounds to prove the performance of the proposed fast grid search method. The four data sets are:

1. Data Set D (SanD) from the Santa Fe Competition;
2. Japan/U.S foreign exchange rate (EXJU) from the Financial Forecast Center;
3. ShangZhen Stock Composite Index (SZSI) from www.stockstar.com;
4. rainfall-runoff data (RAIN) from the ISF'06 ANNEX Neural Network Forecasting Competition (www.isf2006.org).

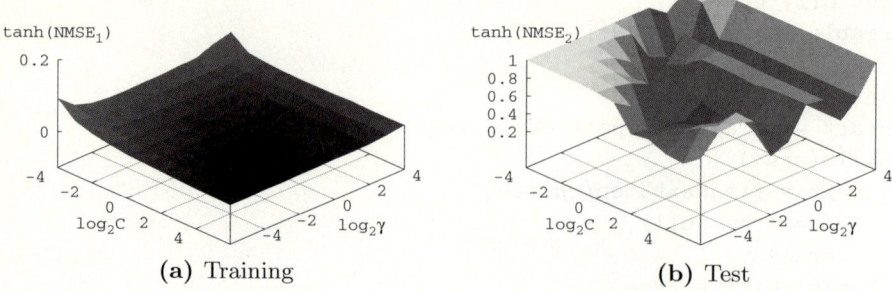

Fig. 1. Error surface on EXJU using RBF kernel

Data set SanD is generated by a high-dimensional operation with weak non stationarity. The original source provided by the Santa Fe time series competition contains 100,000 points. The first 505 points are used here.

Data set EXJU are Japan to U.S. foreign exchange rates covers the period January 1 1971 to January 1 2006. Data are sampled in monthly interval.

Data set SZSI are daily stock indices from January 2 2004 to February 9 2006. Each example contains the open, high, low and close price of one day. We aimed at predicting the closing price from previous examples.

Data set RAIN contains 729 examples covers the period 1 October 1993 to 31 March 1994. It contains flow data (stage, m) at three upstream sites (US1, US2, US3), rainfall data at five catchment rain gauges (mm) (RG1, RG2, RG3, RG4, RG5) and flow (stage, m) at the target site (Q). It covers three different domain of attributes and is a relatively high dimension data set.

More details of the data sets are listed in Table 1. The first column is the abbreviation of the data set, the second column is the number of attributes, the next four column are the average, unit variation, minimum and maximum of the target attribute, the last two columns are the number of training and testing examples respectively.

Table 1. Details of Data Set

DataSet	Attrs	Avg	Var	Min	Max	Train	Test
SanD	1	0.397	0.207	0.053	0.807	439	60
EXJU	1	179.345	71.974	83.690	357.400	395	20
SZSI	4	1313.717	200.280	1011.500	1777.520	435	60
RAIN	8	1.852	0.992	0.631	4.997	663	60

4.2 Data Scaling

Normalization performs a linear transformation on the original data. Suppose that min_A and max_A are the minimum and maximum values of an attribute A. A Min-Max normalization maps a value v of A to v' in the range min'_A and max'_A by computing

$$vI = \frac{v - min_A}{max_A - min_A}(max'_A - min'_A) + min'_A \qquad (7)$$

Here we let $min'_A = -1$ and $max'_A = 1$, thus, all data are scaled to the range $[-1, +1]$.

4.3 Performance Evaluation

We use normalized mean squared error (NMSE) as the performance criteria.

$$\text{NMSE} = \frac{1}{\delta^2 n} \sum_{i=1}^{n}(y_i - p_i)^2 \qquad (8)$$

$$\delta^2 = \frac{1}{n-1} \sum_{i=1}^{n}(y_i - \bar{y})^2$$

Where y_i represents the actual value, p_i represents the predicted value, $\bar{y}$ represents the mean of the actual value. NMSE is the most commonly used measure of success of numeric prediction. It stands for the deviation between the actual and predicted values. The smaller the values of NMSE, the closer the predicted time series values to the actual values.

To evaluate the generalization performance of Support Vector Machines, the stratified k-fold cross-validation technique is used, which is a well-known sampling approach to determining the machine parameters. In this study, 5-fold is adopted, thus, the training data set are randomly partitioned into five folds, of which four folds are used as the training set for building up the forecast model, and the remaining fold as the valid set for justifying the performance of the model. Idea parameters of SVR are chosen based on the machines' average performance on the cross-validation set. In addition, we reserves some samples from the end of the source data set as an independent test set to see can the trained model works well in the future. Parameter optimization are only based on the cross-validation set, not on the test set! Each experiment is repeated 10 times.

We use subscript 1 and 2 to distinguish error on the 5-fold cross-validation set and independent test set, e.g. NMSE_1 and NMSE_2. If no subscript is given, we refer to the former.

4.4 Results

Figure 2 shows the exploited path on error surface by fast Grid-Search algorithm. Figure 2a uses EXJU data set and Figure 2b uses RAIN data set. C is set from 2^{-2} to 2^{12}, $1/\gamma$ is set from 2^{-2} to 2^{10}. Color area in the figure is the fast Grid-Search path contrasting to traditional Grid-Search. We can see, by adopting the fast Grid-Search strategy, the training process avoids wasting time on parameters combination with poor performance, and quickly locate the idea parameter set.

Table 2 shows the NMSE1(for training data), NMSE2 (for test data), training time (in seconds) of traditional Grid Search and Fast Grid Search on all the four data sets.

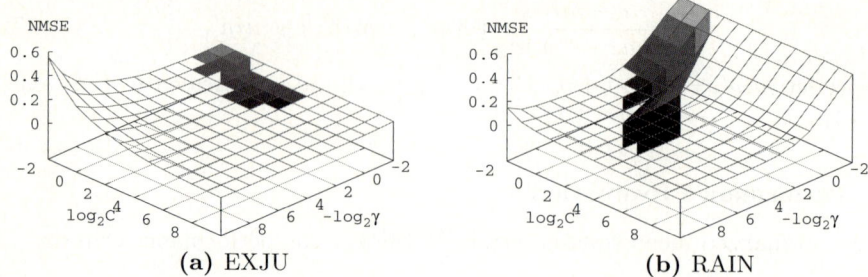

Fig. 2. Fast Grid-Search Path on EXJU and RAIN

Table 2. Compare Grid-Search and fast Grid-Search

	Grid-Search				Fast Grid-Search			
	Grid	NMSE$_1$	NMSE$_2$	Time	Grid	NMSE$_1$	NMSE$_2$	Time
SanD	5,2	0.014	0.099	122	4,1	0.015	0.103	41
EXJU	3,2	0.008	0.678	16	1,2	0.011	0.595	1
SZSI	1,4	0.035	0.125	8	-1,2	0.033	0.121	1
RAIN	3,6	0.020	0.423	160	3,6	0.020	0.423	46

5 Conclusions and Acknowledgements

In this paper we proposed fast grid search method for forecasting time series by support vector regression. The experiment shows a better result and indicates one possible research direction on specific application of support vector regression forecasting time series.

This research is granted by National Science Foundation of China(70401015) and Hubei Provincial Key Social Science Research Center of Information Management.

References

1. E. H. T. Francis and L. Cao. Application of support vector machines in financial time series forecasting. Omega: International Journal of Management Science, vol. 29, pp. 309-317, 2001.
2. K.J. Kim. Financial time series forecasting using support vector machines. Neurocomputing, vol. 55, pp. 307-319, 2003.
3. Hsu, C.-W., Chang, C.-C., Lin, C.-J. A practical guide to support vector classification. Technical Report, Department of Computer Science and Information Engineering, National Taiwan University. Available at http://www.csie.ntu.edu.tw/cjlin/papers/guide/guide.pdf, 2004.
4. Bao YK, Lu YS and Zhang JL. Forecasting stock price by SVMs regression. Lecture Notes in Artifical Intelligence, Vol.3192,2004:295-303.

5. Chapelle O, Vapnik V, Bousquet O, Mukherjee S . Choosing multiple parameters for support vector machines. Machine Learning, 46 (2002) : 131-159.
6. S. Boughorbel, J. P. Tarel, and N. Boujemaa. The LCCP for optimizing kernel parameters for SVM. Lecture Notes in Artificial Intelligence, vol. 3697, pp. 589-594, 2005.
7. Bo, L. F., L. Wang, et al. Multiple parameter selection for LS-SVM using smooth leave-one-out error.Lecture Notes in Computer Science, 2005, Vol.3496: 851-856.

Fast Global *k*-Means with Similarity Functions Algorithm

López-Escobar Saúl, Carrasco-Ochoa J.A., and Martínez-Trinidad J. Fco

National Institute for Astrophysics, Optics and Electronics
Luis Enrique Erro No.1 Sta. Ma. Tonantzintla, Puebla, México C. P. 72840
{slopez, ariel, fmartine}@inaoep.mx

Abstract. The global *k*-means with similarity functions algorithm is an algorithm that allows working with qualitative and quantitative features (mixed data), but it involves a heavy computational cost. Therefore, in this paper, an algorithm that accelerates the global *k*-means with similarity functions algorithm without significantly affecting the quality of the solution is proposed. Our algorithm called fast global *k*-means with similarity functions algorithm is tested and compared against the *k*-means with similarity functions algorithm and the global *k*-means with similarity functions algorithm.

1 Introduction

Clustering has been applied in many fields including pattern recognition, machine learning, data mining, image processing, etc., and it can be defined as the process of partitioning a set of patterns into disjoint and homogeneous meaningful groups, called clusters [5]. Clustering has been studied in a variety of applications domains, such as bioinformatics, data classification and compression, data mining and knowledge discovery, medical image processing, and statistical data analysis.

A popular algorithm used to solve the clustering problem is the *k*-means algorithm, in this algorithm it is necessary to know the number of clusters in which the data set will be divided. The *k*-means algorithm minimizes an objective function and it is a local search procedure which heavily depends on the initial conditions.

The global *k*-means algorithm was proposed to solve the dependency on the initial conditions of the *k*-means algorithm [1]. This algorithm finds a global solution and does not depend on the initial conditions or any other external parameter. This finding involves a heavy computational cost, which represents its main disadvantage. For that reason in [1] the fast global *k*-means algorithm was proposed, this algorithm constitutes a straightforward method to accelerate the global *k*-means algorithm without significantly affecting the quality of the results.

The algorithms described above are based on a distance in a *n*-dimensional space, so, the objects must be described in terms of features such that the distance among them can be evaluated. Nevertheless, in soft sciences such as Geology, Medicine, Sociology, etc. commonly the objects are described in terms of qualitative and quantitative features (mixed data). In this kind of descriptions could be not possible to use a distance, only the degree of similarity between objects can be determined, through a similarity function. Therefore the k-means with similarity functions algorithm was proposed [2], but it depends on the initial conditions. For that reason, following the idea of the global k-means algorithm, the global k-means with similarity functions algorithm was proposed [4]. But this algorithm involves a heavy computational cost. So, in this paper we propose an algorithm that accelerates the global k-means with similarity functions algorithm without significantly affecting the quality of the solution. The proposed algorithm maximizes the similarity among objects belonging to the same cluster and minimizes the similarity among different clusters.

This paper is organized as follows: section 2 describes related work. In section 3, the fast global k-means with similarity functions algorithm is introduced. Experimental results are shown in section 4 and finally, section 5 provides conclusions and future work.

2 Related Work

One of the main problems of the k-means algorithm is its dependency on the initial conditions, a good solution depends on good initial conditions; for that, usually the algorithm is executed multiple times in order to find a better clustering.

Several attempts have been reported to solve the cluster initialization problem [6,7,8]. These attempts make the k-means algorithm more independent on initial conditions. However, they do not guarantee to get a global solution. Likas et al [1] proposed the global k-means algorithm which constitutes a deterministic effective global clustering algorithm which does not depend on the initial conditions or any other parameter. The global k-means algorithm uses the k-means algorithm as a local search procedure. The basic idea underlying this algorithm is that an optimal solution for a clustering problem with k clusters can be obtained through a series of local searches using the k-means algorithm. At each local search k-1 clusters centers are placed at their optimal position corresponding to the solution of the clustering problem with k-1 clusters and the remaining center is searched verifying each object in the data set.

The attractiveness of the global k-means algorithm lies in finding a global solution, this finding involves a heavy computational cost, which represents its main disadvantage. For that reason the fast global k-means algorithm was proposed [1], this algorithm constitutes a straightforward method to accelerate the global k-means algorithm without significantly affecting the quality of the results. The difference lies in the way a solution for the problem with k-cluster is obtained. Given a solution for the problem with k-1 clusters, to solve the problem with k-clusters the algorithm does not verify each object of the data set, instead of this, it only uses a small subset of suitable candidates.

The algorithms described above only allow working with numerical features, therefore, in [2] the k-means with similarity functions algorithm was proposed. This algorithm allows working with quantitative and qualitative features (mixed data), but it heavily depends on the initial conditions, so, following the idea of the global k-means algorithm, the global k-means with similarity algorithm was proposed [4], this algorithm finds a global solution for the clustering problem with *k*-clusters, and it uses the *k*-means with similarity functions algorithm instead of the *k*-means algorithm.

3 Fast Global *k*-Means with Similarity Functions Algorithm

Since the global *k*-means with similarity functions algorithm involves a heavy computational cost, in this paper an algorithm that accelerates it without significantly affecting the quality of the solution is proposed. The proposed algorithm and finds a global solution and uses the *k*-means with similarity functions algorithm as a local search procedure, which allows working with mixed data.

Suppose that a data set $X=\{x_1,\ldots,x_m\}$ is given, where each object is described by a set $R=\{y_1,\ldots,y_n\}$ of features and it is required partitioning the data set in k clusters $M_1,\ldots,M_k$. Each feature takes values in a set of admissible values D_i, $y_i(x_j) \in D_i$ $i=1,\ldots,n$. Thus, the features can be of any nature (qualitative: Boolean, multi-valued, etc. or quantitative: integer, real). A similarity function $\Gamma:(D_1 \times D_2 \times \ldots \times D_n)^2 \to [0,1]$, which allows comparing objects is defined. In this work, the similarity function used was:

$$\Gamma(x_i, x_j) = \frac{1}{n} \sum_{p=1}^{n} C_p(y_p(x_i), y_p(x_j)) \qquad (1)$$

where C_p is the comparison function between features values of y_p.

The comparison function for qualitative features used in this work was:

$$C_p(y_p(x_i), y_p(x_j)) = \begin{cases} 1 & \text{if } y_p(x_i) = y_p(x_j) \\ 0 & \text{otherwise} \end{cases} \qquad (2)$$

and for quantitative features was:

$$C_p(y_p(x_i), y_p(x_j)) = 1 - \left| \frac{|y_p(x_i)|}{|\max(y_p(x_s))|} - \frac{|y_p(x_j)|}{|\max(y_p(x_s))|} \right| \qquad (3)$$

where $s = 1,\ldots,m$.

In this kind of problems, it could be impossible to calculate means; so objects from the sample, called representative objects x_j^r are used instead of means. These objects are in average the most similar with objects in the same cluster and, at the same time are the least similar with the rest of the representative objects (see [2] for details). The representative objects x_j^r are used as centers of the clusters M_j, $j=1,\ldots,k$.

In this context, the clustering problem consists in maximizing the following objective function:

$$J(x_1^r,\ldots,x_k^r) = \sum_{j=1}^{k} \sum_{i=1}^{m} I_j(x_i) \Gamma(x_j^r, x_i) \qquad (4)$$

where

$$I_j(x_i) = \begin{cases} 1 & \text{if} \quad \Gamma(x_j^r, x_i) = \max_{1 \le q \le k}\{\Gamma(x_q^r, x_i)\} \\ 0 & \text{otherwise} \end{cases} \qquad (5)$$

That is, an object x_i will be assigned to the cluster such that its representative object is the most similar with x_i.

The global k-means with similarity functions algorithm finds an optimal solution for a clustering problem with k clusters, this is made through a series of local searches using the k-means with similarity functions algorithm. At each problem with k clusters, k-1 representative objects corresponding to the solution of the clustering problem with k-1 clusters are placed at their optimal position and the remaining representative object is searched for verifying each object in the data set. In this algorithm, the solution for the problem with one cluster is the object which is the most similar to all the objects of the data set.

The global k-means with similarity functions algorithm involves a heavy computational cost; this is because the k-means with similarity functions algorithm is executed too many times. Therefore it is necessary to reduce the number of times that the k-means with similarity functions algorithm is executed without significantly affecting the quality of the results. This can be made by computing a bound $J_i \ge J + b_i^*$ on the value that the objective function J_i could reach for each possible position x_i searching for a solution of the k clusters problem from the k-1 clusters, where J is the value of the objective function (4) in the solution for the problem with k-1 clusters and b_i^* is defined as follows:

$$b_i^* = \sum_{j=1}^{m} \max(\Gamma(x_i, x_j) - \Gamma_{k-1}^j, 0) \qquad (6)$$

where Γ_{k-1}^j is the similarity between x_j and the representative object of the cluster where x_j belongs to in the solution of the problem with k-1 clusters.

The position of the new representative object is initialized at the objects that maximize J_i, or equivalently that maximize b_i^*, and the k-means with similarity functions algorithm is executed to obtain the solution for the problem with k clusters.

The quantity b_i^* measures the *guaranteed* increment in the objective function (4) by inserting a new cluster at object x_i.

Suppose the solution for the problem with k-1 clusters is $(x_1^{r*}(k-1), x_2^{r*}(k-1), \ldots, x_{k-1}^{r*}(k-1))$, when a new representative object is added as the object x_i the new cluster will allocate all objects x_j whose similarity with x_i is greater than the similarity Γ_{k-1}^j from their previously most similar center. For example, if an object has a similarity of 0.7 with the representative object of its cluster, and the similarity with the object x_i is 0.9, then this object will be allocated in the new cluster where x_i is the representative object. So, the objective function will has an increment of at least 0.2. Therefore, the sum $\sum_{j=1}^{m} \max(\Gamma(x_i, x_j) - \Gamma_{k-1}^j, 0)$ measures the increment in the objective function when a new cluster is added at object x_i. Due we use an implementation of the k-means with similarity functions algorithm that keeps the best value of the objective function with its representative objects in all steps, the value of the objective will have an increment of at least b^*_i. In this way, the objects which maximizes the function b^*_i could produce a bigger increment in the objective function.

If the k-means with similarity functions algorithm is executed with $(x_1^{r*}(k-1),$ $x_2^{r*}(k-1),\ldots,x_{k-1}^{r*}(k-1), x_t)$ as the initial set of representative objects, where $x_1^{r*}(k-1), x_2^{r*}(k-1),\ldots,x_{k-1}^{r*}(k-1)$ is the solution for the k-1 clusters and x_t are the objects which maximizes b^*_i. Since it is guaranteed that the objective function will be increased in at least b^*_i, the increment in the objective function that will be obtained by executing the k-means with similarity functions algorithm after inserting a new representative object at object x_i can be bounded by $J + b^*_i$.

The pseudo code of the fast global algorithm is depicted as follows:

```
Input: k = number of clusters
       n = number of objects of the data set
Output: RO [1,...,k] /* Representative Objects */
        OF /* Value of the objective function */
Count = 0
Seeds [1,...,k] = 0
// For the problem with one cluster, the object which is the most
// similar to the data set.
Seeds[1] = most similar object to the data set
for k'=2 to k
   Bi = 0 // Variable that saves the maximum value of the Bi's
   for i=1 to m
      // Obtain B_i* using formula (6)
      Baux = ObtainBi (i)
      if Baux > Bi
         Bi = Baux
   // Get the objects which maximizes Bi and save it in a vector
   Vector[] = GetObjectsMaxBi ()
   m' = length (Vector)
   for i=1 to m'
      xi = Vector[i]
      if xi ≠ Seeds[1,...,k'-1]
         [SRO,J] = KMeansWithSimilarityFunctions(Seeds[1,...,k'-1],xi)
         /* SRO is the set of representative objects */
         /* J is the objective function */
         if J>count then
            count = J
            Seeds = SRO
RO = Seeds
OF = count
```

4 Experimental Results

The proposed algorithm was tested on several data sets; two kinds of data sets were used: data sets with mixed data, and data sets containing only numerical features. The data sets were taken from the repository of machine learning databases of the University of California, Irvine [3]. In all data sets, experiments considering only information of the features and ignoring class labels were done. The quality of the obtained solutions was evaluated in terms of the objective function (4).

The data sets containing only numerical features were: Ecoli, Glass, Iris and Wine; the data sets with mixed data were: Bands, Credit, Flags and Machine.

For all data sets, the following experiments were done:

- One run of the global k-means with similarity functions algorithm for the problem with $k=2,\ldots,15$.
- One run of the fast global k-means with similarity functions algorithm for the problem with $k=2,\ldots,15$.
- m runs (where m is the number of objects of the data set) of the k-means with similarity functions algorithm for each problem with $k=2,\ldots,15$ starting with random initial representative objects. For each data set, the average, the maximum and the minimum of the objective function were calculated.

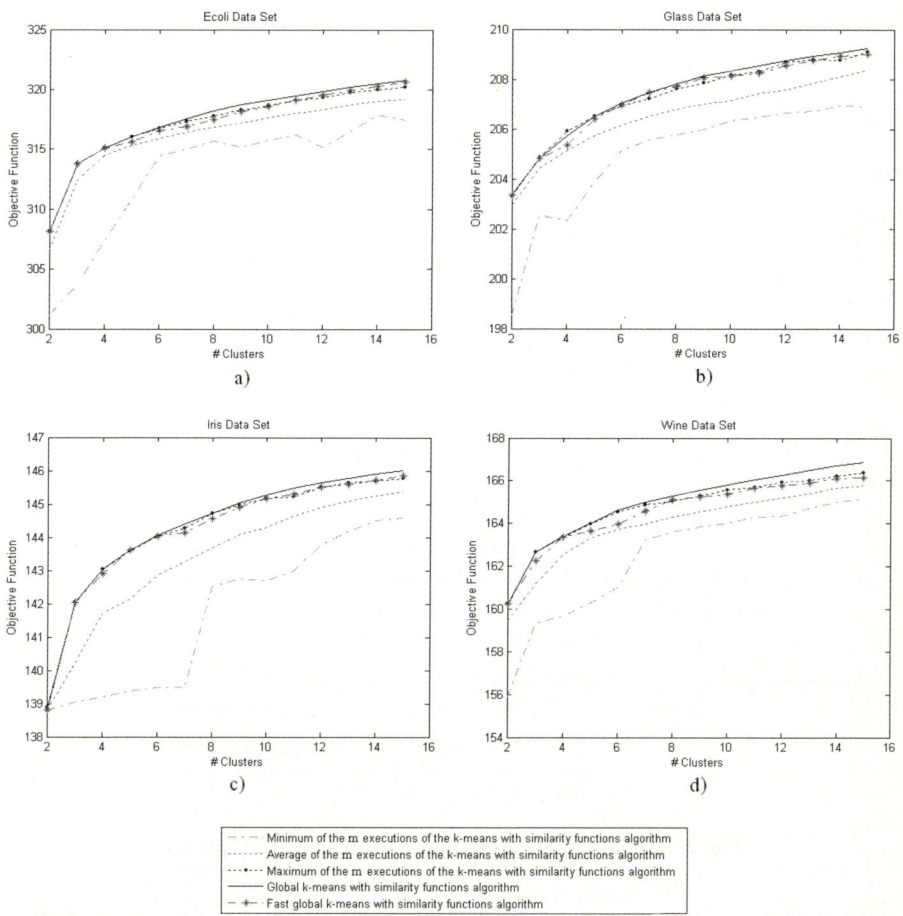

Fig. 1. Experimental results obtained with numerical data sets

Figure 1 shows the results obtained by applying the fast global k-means with similarity functions, the global k-means with similarity functions and the m executions of the k-means with similarity functions algorithm on four data sets containing only numerical features (Ecoli, Glass, Iris and Wine).

In all the experiments, the results obtained by the fast global k-means with similarity functions algorithm were better than the average of the m executions of the k-means with similarity functions algorithm and in a few cases the results were equal to the maximum. Compared against the global k-means with similarity functions algorithm, the fast global k-means with similarity functions obtains almost the same results but in less time.

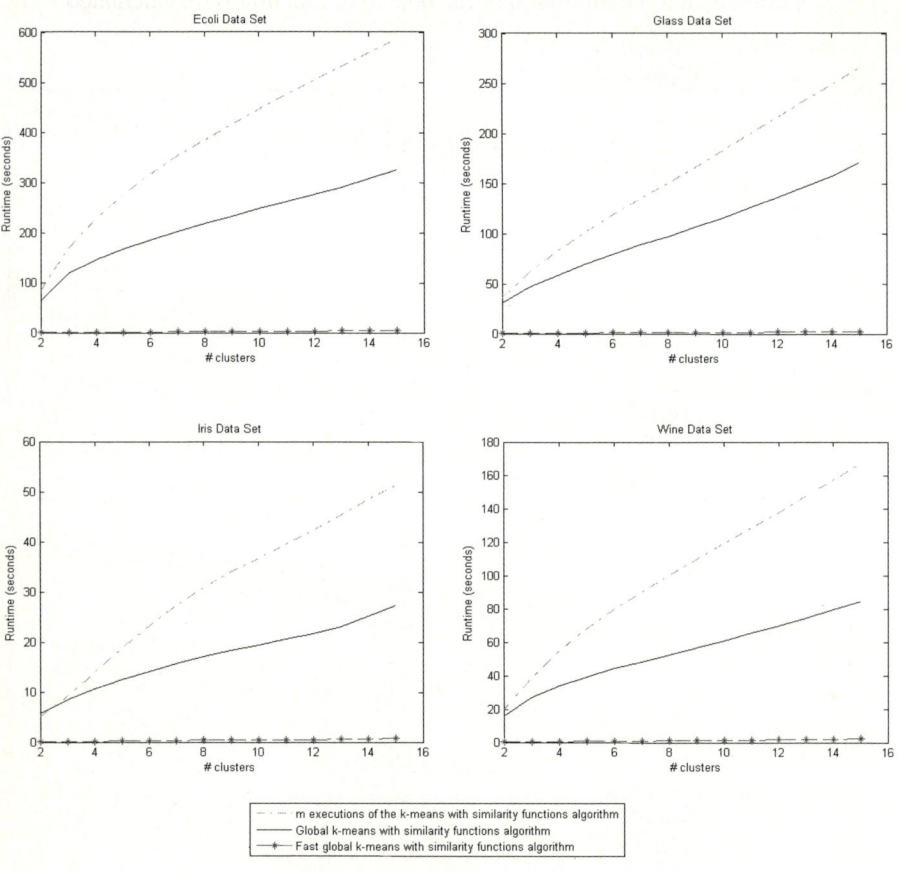

Fig. 2. Runtimes of the experiments with numerical data sets

The runtimes of the experiments with numerical data sets are depicted in figure 2. In terms of the runtime, the fast global k-means with similarity functions algorithm was better than the others because its runtimes were significantly smaller as it is shown in figure 2, this is because our algorithm at each step with k-clusters does not execute m-$(k$-$1)$ times the k-means with similarity functions algorithm as the global k-means with similarity functions algorithm does and each execution converges faster due it starts with better initial representative objects. In our experiments with numerical data sets, in average at each step only executes 5 times the k-means with similarity functions algorithm. The runtimes of the m executions of the k-means with similarity functions algorithm were greater the than the runtime of the global k-means with similarity functions algorithm and the fast global k-means with similarity functions algorithm. The runtimes obtained by applying the fast global k-means with similarity functions were the smallest, they are close to the X axis in the graphs of figure 2.

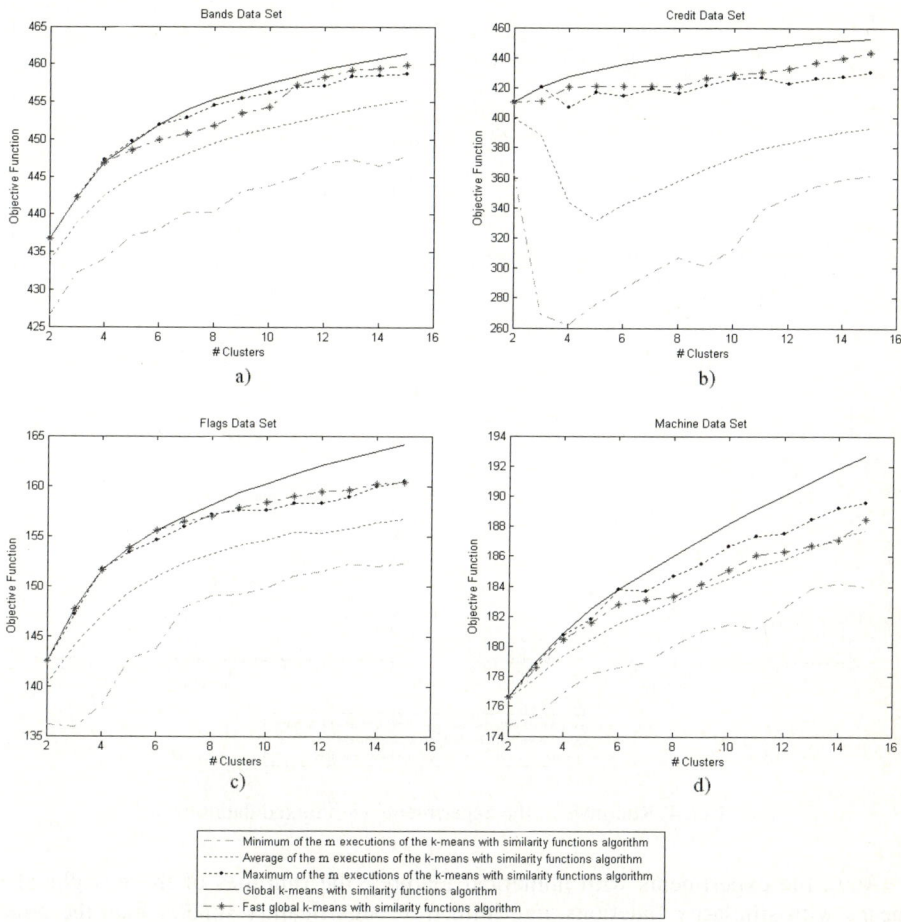

Fig. 3. Experimental results obtained with mixed data sets

Figure 3 shows the results obtained by applying the fast global k-means with similarity functions, the global k-means with similarity functions and the m

executions of the *k*-means with similarity functions algorithm on four data sets containing mixed features (Bands, Credits, Flags and Machine).

In these experiments, in almost all the data sets, the results of the fast global *k*-means with similarity functions algorithm were equal or better than the average of the *m* executions of the *k*-means with similarity functions, excepting in one case where the result was slightly less than the average (Machine data set with 14-clusters). The fast global *k*-means with similarity functions algorithm obtains good results compared against the global *k*-means with similarity functions algorithm, but in less time.

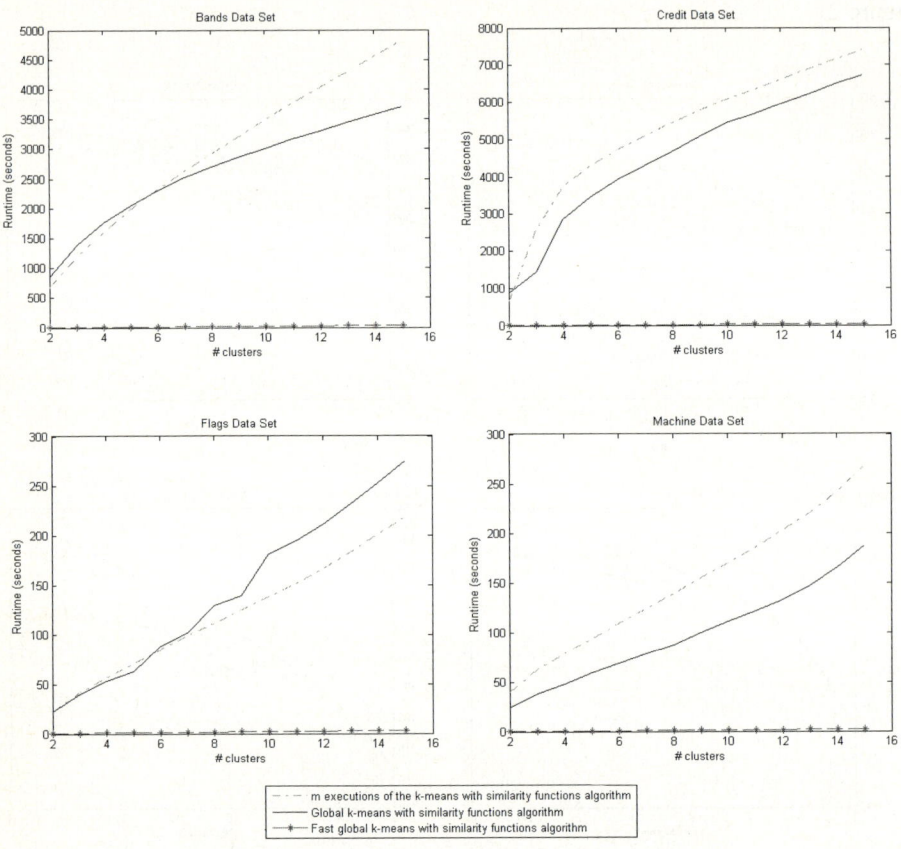

Fig. 4. Runtimes of the experiments with mixed data sets

As in the experiments with numerical features, the runtimes of the fast global *k*-means with similarity functions algorithm were significantly smaller than the others as it is shown in figure 4. This is because the fast global *k*-means with similarity functions algorithm does not execute m-$(k-1)$ times the *k*-means with similarity functions algorithm at each step and each execution converges faster due the best initial representative objects. In our experiments with mixed data, the fast global *k*-means with similarity functions in average only executes 8 times the *k*-means with similarity functions at each step.

5 Conclusions

In this paper, the fast global k-means with similarity functions algorithm was introduced. This algorithm is independent of the initial conditions and allows working with mixed data. It was tested with data sets containing mixed features and data sets containing only numerical features, and was compared against the k-means with similarity functions algorithm and the global k-means with similarity functions.

In all the experiments excepting in one case, the quality of the results with the proposed algorithm were equal or better than the average of m executions of the k-means with similarity functions algorithm. In the experiments with numerical features, the results were better that the average of m executions of the k-means with similarity functions algorithm.

Compared against the global k-means with similarity functions, the fast global k-means with similarity functions algorithm is significantly faster because at each step for k clusters it does not execute m-$(k$-$1)$ times the k-means with similarity functions algorithm (it is executed in average, only 5 times with numerical data sets and 8 times with mixed data sets); the proposed algorithm gives solutions of equal or better quality than the average of m executions of the k-means with similarity functions algorithm in a significantly less runtime.

Even though the fast global k-means with similarity functions algorithm is much faster than the global k-means with similarity functions algorithm and obtains good results, it is not feasible to apply it to large data sets. Therefore, as future work, we are going to find a strategy to apply it to large data sets.

References

1. Aristidis Likas, Nikos Vlassis, and Jakob J. Verbeek: The Global k-Means Clustering Algorithm. Pattern Recognition 36 (2003) 451-461
2. Javier R. García Serrano and J. F. Martínez-Trinidad: Extension to c-Means Algorithm for the Use of Similarity Functions. 3rd European Conference on Principles and Practice of Knowledge Discovery in Databases Proceedings. Prague, Czech Rep. (1999) 354-359
3. C.L. Blake, C. J. Merz: UCI Repository of Machine Learning Databases, University of California, Irvine, Departament of Information and Computer Sciences (1998)
4. Saúl López Escobar, J. A. Carrasco Ochoa, J. Fco. Martínez Trinidad: Global k-Means with Similarity Functions. Progress in Pattern Recognition, Image Analysis and Applications, LNCS 3773 (2005) 392-399
5. D. K. Tasoulis, M. N., Vrahatis: Unsupervised Clustering on Dynamic Databases. Pattern Recognition Letters 26 (2005) 2116-2127
6. Paul S.Bradley, Usama M. Fayyad: Refining Initial Points for k-Means Clustering. Proceedings of the 15th International Conference on Machine Learning. San Francisco, CA (1998) 91-98
7. Shehroz S. Khan, Amir Ahmad: Cluster Center Initialization for k-Means Clustering. Pattern Recognition Letters 25 (2004) 1293-1302
8. Peña, J. M., Lozano, J. A., Larrañaga, P.: An Empirical Comparison of Four Initialization Methods for the k-Means Algorithm. Pattern Recognition Letters 20 (1999) 1027-1040

NN-Based Detector for Known Targets in Coherent Weibull Clutter

R. Vicen-Bueno, M. Rosa-Zurera, M.P. Jarabo-Amores, and R. Gil-Pita

Signal Theory and Communications Department
Escuela Politécnica Superior, Universidad de Alcalá
Ctra. Madrid-Barcelona, km. 33.600, 28805, Alcalá de Henares - Madrid, Spain
{raul.vicen, manuel.rosa, mpilar.jarabo, roberto.gil}@uah.es

Abstract. Radar detection of targets in clutter and noise is an usual problem presented in radar systems. Several schemes based on statistical signal processing are proposed as detectors. In some cases, the Neural Networks (NNs) are applied to this problem. In this article, a radar detector based in a class of NN, the MultiLayer Perceptron (MLP), is proposed. This MLP can be trained in a supervised way to minimize the Mean Square Error (MSE) criterion. Moreover, it is demonstrated that the MLP trained in that way approximates the Neyman-Pearson detector. The NN-based detector proposed is compared with a Target Sequence Known A Priori (TSKAP) detector. The last detector is only took as reference because it is not realizable due to it is necessary to know when the target exists and its magnitude and shape. The results show how the proposed detector improves the performance of the TSKAP one for different conditions of the target measured with the Signal-to-Noise Ratio (SNR) and the skewness or shape parameter (a) of the Weibull-distributed clutter. Finally, several figures show which is the improvement of the NN-based detector.

1 Introduction

Neural Networks (NNs) are proposed for approximating the Neyman-Pearson (NP) detector for detecting known targets in coherent Weibull clutter. The NP detector is usually used in radar systems design. This detector maximizes the probability of detection (Pd) maintaining the probability of false alarm (Pfa) lower than or equal to a given value [1]. The detection of targets in presence of clutter is the main problem in radar detection. Many clutter models have been proposed in the literature [2]. One of the most used models is the Weibull one [3][4][5].

The optimum detector for target and clutter with arbitrary Probability Density Functions (PDFs) has been set in [4]. Only suboptimal solutions were proposed, like the Target Sequence Known A Priori (TSKAP) detector taken as reference for the experiments. Also, these solutions convey implementation problems, some of which make them non-realizable.

NNs, paying special attention to the MultiLayer Perceptrons (MLPs), have been probed to be able to approximate the NP detector when they are trained in a supervised way to minimize the Mean Square Error (MSE) [6]. MLPs have been applied to the detection of known targets in different environments [7][8].

In [2], NNs are applied for detecting radar targets in K-distributed clutter. In this work, MLPs are trained to approximate the NP detector for known targets in coherent Weibull clutter. The NN approach is probed to be able to outperform the suboptimum solution proposed in [4] overcoming all the implementation problems.

2 Target and Interference Models

The radar is assumed to collect N pulses in a scan, so input vectors (z) are composed of N complex samples, which are presented to the detector. Under hypothesis H0 (target absent), z is composed of N samples of clutter and noise. Under hypothesis H1 (target present), a known target characterized by a fixed amplitude (A) and phase (θ) for each of the N pulses is summed up to the clutter and noise samples. Also, a doppler frequency in the target model of $\frac{1}{2}PRF$ is assumed, where PRF is the Pulse Repetition Frequency of the system or the sampling rate of the discrete process.

The noise is modeled as a white Gaussian complex process of variance equal to 1, i.e., a power of $\frac{1}{2}$ for the quadrature and phase components. The clutter is modeled as a coherent correlated sequence with Gaussian AutoCorrelation Function (ACF), whose complex samples have a modulus with a Weibull PDF. The autocorrelation matrix of the clutter is given by

$$(\mathbf{M_c})_{h,k} = P_c \rho_c^{|h-k|^2} e^{j(2\pi(h-k)\frac{f_c}{PRF})}, 1 \leq h \leq N, 1 \leq k \leq N \qquad (1)$$

where P_c is the power, ρ_c is the one-lag correlation coefficient and f_c is the doppler frequency of the clutter.

The Weibull PDF depends of two parameters: the skewness or shape (a) and the scale (b). The relationship between these parameters and the P_c is expressed in (2).

$$P_c = \frac{2b^2}{a} \Gamma\left(\frac{2}{a}\right) \qquad (2)$$

where $\Gamma()$ is the *Gamma function* [9].

Taking in consideration that the complex noise samples are of unity variance (power), the following power relationships are considered for the study:

$$Signal-to-NoiseRatio: SNR = 10log_{10}\left(A^2\right) \qquad (3)$$

$$Signal-to-InterferenceRatio: SIR = 10log_{10}\left(\frac{A^2}{(1+P_c)}\right) \qquad (4)$$

$$Clutter-to-NoiseRatio: CNR = 10log_{10}\left(P_c\right) \qquad (5)$$

In [3] and [4] a model for generating coherent Weibull sequences is presented. Fig. 1 shows the proposed scheme composed of two blocks. The first one is the

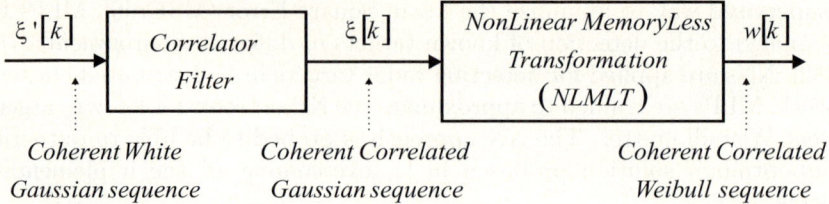

Fig. 1. Generator of coherent correlated Weibull sequences

Correlator Filter, which is used to obtain a coherent correlated Gaussian sequence (CCGS) from a coherent white Gaussian sequence (CWGS). The second block performs a PDF transformation to obtain the coherent correlated Weibull sequence (CCWS) from the CCGS.

To transform the CWGS ($\xi'[k] = \mathbf{x}'[k] + j\mathbf{y}'[k], k = 1, ..., N$), in the desired CCGS, the following linear function is implemented [3]:

$$\xi = \mathbf{U}^* \mathbf{L}^{\frac{1}{2}} \xi' \qquad (6)$$

where $\mathbf{U}$ and $\mathbf{L}$ are the matrixes with the eigenvectors and the eigenvalues (diagonal matrix) of the autocorrelation matrix of the clutter sequence, respectively. The size of both matrixes is NxN, where N is the length of the ξ and ξ' sequences, where both are taken as column vectors.

The NonLinear MemoryLess Transformation (NLMLT) transforms the CCGS into a CCWS one [3] with the relationship:

$$\mathbf{w}[k] = \xi[k]|\xi[k]|^{\frac{2}{a}-1} \qquad (7)$$

Several relationships exist between the powers and the correlation coefficients of the sequences involved in the generation.

The CCWS power (P_c) is obtained with (2) and the CCGS power (P_{cG}) is related with a and b in that way:

$$P_{cG} = b^a \qquad (8)$$

The relationship between the ρ_c and the correlation coefficient of the CCGS (ρ_{cG}) is given by

$$\rho_c = \frac{a\rho_{cG}}{2\Gamma(\frac{2}{a})} \left(1 - \rho_{cG}^2\right)^{\frac{2}{a}+1} \Gamma^2\left(\frac{1}{a} + \frac{3}{2}\right) F\left(\frac{1}{a} + \frac{3}{2}; \frac{1}{a} + \frac{3}{2}; 2; \rho_{cG}^2\right) \qquad (9)$$

where $F(A; B; C; D)$ is the *Gauss Hypergeometric function* [9].

3 Optimum and Suboptimum NP Detectors

In [3] the problem of optimum radar detection of targets in clutter is explored when both are time correlated and have arbitrary PDFs. The optimum detector

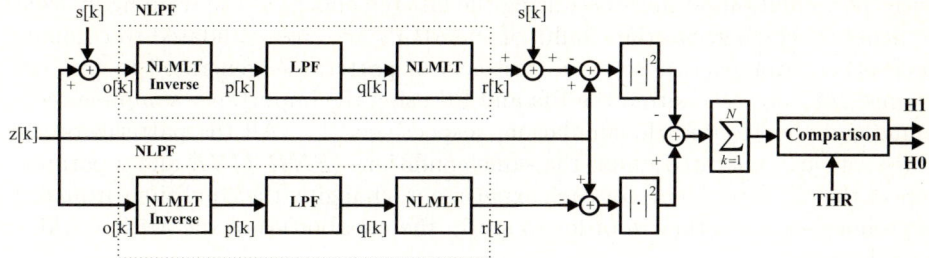

Fig. 2. TSKAP Detector

scheme is built around two non-linear estimators of the disturbances in both hypothesis, which minimize the mean square error. The study of the detection of Gaussian correlated targets in Gaussian correlated clutter plus noise is carried out, but for the cases where the hypothesis are non-gaussian distributed, only suboptimal solutions are studied.

The proposed detectors basically consist of two channels. The upper channel is matched to the conditions that the sequence to be detected is the sum of the target (hypothesis H1) plus clutter in presence of noise . While the lower one is matched to the detection of clutter (hypothesis H0) in presence of noise.

For the detection problem considered in this paper, the suboptimum detection scheme (TSKAP) shown in the figure 2 is taken.

Considering that the CNR is very high (CNR>>1), the inverse of the NLMLT is assumed to transform the Weibull clutter in a Gaussian one, so the Linear Prediction Filter (LPF) is a N-1 order linear one. Then, the NLMLT transforms the filter output in a Weibull sequence. Besides being suboptimum, this scheme presents two important drawbacks: 1) The prediction filters have N-1 memory cells that must contain the suitable information to predict correct values for the N samples of each input pattern. So N+(N-1) pulses are necessary to decide if target is present or not; 2) The target sample must be subtracted from the input of the H1 channel. There is no sense in subtracting the target component before deciding if this component is present or not. It makes this scheme non-realizable in a practice case.

4 NN-Based Detector

A detector based on a MultiLayer Perceptron (MLP) is proposed, in order to overcome the drawbacks of the scheme proposed in the Section 3. Also, as MLPs have been probed to approximate the NP detector when minimizing the MSE [6], it can be expected that they outperform the suboptimum scheme proposed in [3].

The standard *Back-Propagation Algorithm* [10] with momentum and varying learning rate is used in combination with cross-validation to train each MLP. In order to minimize the MSE criterion, training and validation sets were synthetically generated for the training. The training is stopped if the MSE estimated with the validation set increase during the last ten epochs of the training in order to avoid overfitting. So, the results of the MLPs are cross-validated to compare each other. Moreover, a new set (test set) of patterns is generated to test the trained MLP for estimating the Pfa and Pd using the importance sampling technique and the Montecarlo simulation, respectively [11]. All the patterns of the three sets are generated under the same conditions (SNR, CNR and a parameters of the radar problem) for each experiment, changing the conditions from one experiment to the other in order to study the capabilities of the MLP working as a detector.

MLPs have been initialized using the Nguyen-Widrow method [12] and in all cases the training process has been repeated ten times to guarantee that the performance of the ten MLPs were similar in average. Once the ten MLP trainings are made, the best MLP in terms of the MSE estimated with the validation set is selected, in order to avoid the problem of keeping in local minima at the end of the training.

The architecture of the MLP considered for the experiments is $I/H/O$, where I is the number of MLP inputs, H is the number of hidden neurons in its hidden layer and O is the number of MLP outputs. As the MLPs work with real arithmetic, if the input vector (z) is composed of N complex samples, the MLP will have 2N inputs (the N in phase and the N in quadrature components of the N complex samples). Taking into consideration the memory of the prediction filters of the suboptimum (TSKAP) detector proposed in [3], MLPs of 2N and 2(N+(N-1)) inputs have been trained. Note that the MLP with 2(N+(N-1)) inputs requires the same input vector size than the suboptimum detector proposed, while the MLP with 2N inputs requires less number of samples to take the decision.

5 Results

The performance of the detectors exposed in the previous sections is shown in terms of the Receiver Operating Characteristics (ROC) curves, which gives the Pd estimated for a desired Pfa. The experiments were made for $N = 2$. So, in order to test correctly the TSKAP detector, patterns of length 3 ($N + N - 1$) complex samples were generated, due to memory requirements of the detector. The architecture of the MLP used to generate the NN-based detector is 6/10/1. The number of MLP inputs (6) is establish by the patterns length. The number of hidden neurons in its hidden layer is established to 10. Although it is not shown an exhaustive study of the architecture size and its influence in the detector performance, this number of hidden neurons gives enough intelligence to the system. Finally, the number of MLP outputs (1) is established by the problem (binary detection). Moreover, another MLP architecture has been tested, which architecture size is 4/10/1. The number of hidden neurons and the number of MLP outputs is the same as above, but the number of MLP inputs is the same as two times the number of pulses that integrates the TSKAP for $N = 2$. The first MLP architecture (6/10/1) is took in order to compare the NN-based

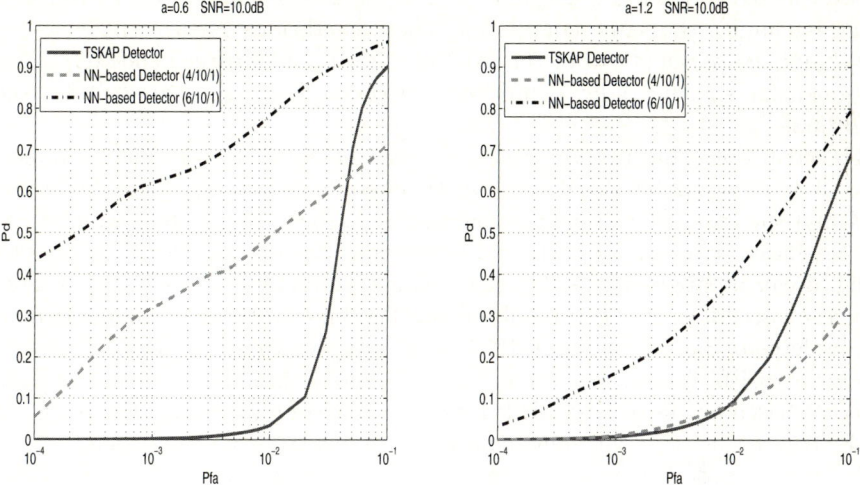

Fig. 3. TSKAP and NN-based detector performances for SNR=10dB, CNR=30dB and a=[0.6,1.2]

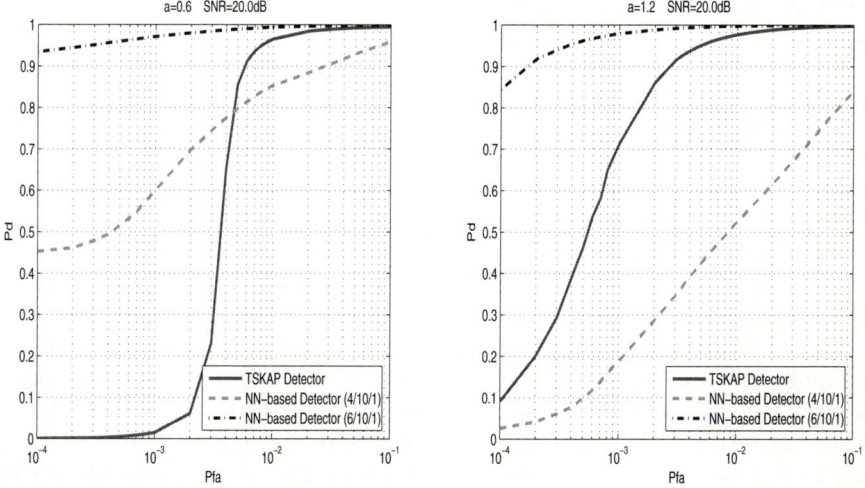

Fig. 4. TSKAP and NN-based detector performances for SNR=20dB, CNR=30dB and a=[0.6,1.2]

detector to the TSKAP detector when they have the same information. While the second MLP architecture (4/10/1) is took to compare them in the case they take the decision under the same quantity of information, because TSKAP take the decision over $N = 2$ pulses.

Three sets of patterns were generated for each experiment: train, validation and test sets. Each of them have 5000 patterns, where the a priori probabilities of hypothesis $H0$ and $H1$ are the same. The patterns of all the sets are synthetically generated under the same conditions. These conditions involve the SNR, the CNR and the parameter a of the Weibull-distributed clutter. The ROC curves are given for specific radar conditions, so the sets are generated under these conditions.

The conditions that usually models several real data clutter involves values of $a = 0.6$ and $a = 1.2$ for the Weibull-distributed clutter. In fig. 3 can be appreciated that the lower is the skewness parameter a, the better is the performance of the NN-based detector for SNR and CNR values of 10 and 30 dB, respectively. In fig. 4 can be appreciated almost the same characteristics as in fig. 3, but in this case two differences can be observed. The first one is that the performance of the detector based on the 4/10/1 MLP is lower than the TSKAP detector one for high Pfa values. The second one is related with the performance loss of detector based on the 4/10/1 MLP for high values of a ($a = 1.2$). For the 6/10/1 MLP (comparing it in the same conditions of availability of information as the TSKAP detector) it does not occur.

The differences appreciated between the TSKAP and NN-based detectors appear because the first one is a suboptimum detector. So, the NN-based detector is better than the TSKAP detector under certain circumstances as shown above, but it will be always under the optimum detector. An analytical expression for the optimum detector cans not be obtained in the case of detecting targets in presence of Weibull-distributed clutter.

6 Conclusions

This article shows the comparison of two radar detectors that work in a Weibull-distributed clutter plus white Gaussian noise environment: one based in a suboptimal solution (TSKAP detector) and other based in NNs trained in a supervised way to minimize the MSE (NN-based detector). The detector proposed (NN-based detector) is able to solve the problems of the TSKAP detector: the necessity of N-1 extra complex samples to fill the LPF internal registers and the most important, its non-realizability because it is necessary know a priori the target. So, the NN-based detector eliminate both drawbacks. Moreover, the NN approximates the NP detector and improves the performance of the TSKAP detector in the case it is taken 3 pulses (integrating 2 of them) to decide whether a target is present (hypothesis $H1$) or not (hypothesis $H0$). Although, it is not made an exhaustive investigation of the MLP size that composes the NN-based detector, it is demonstrated that the size took for the experiments is good enough.

The results show that the lower is the skewness parameter a of the Weibull-distributed clutter, the better is the performance of the NN-based detector. On the other hand, it is appreciated that the lower is the SNR, the better is its performance. So, this detector can be considered for detect known targets in presence of noise and Weibull-distributed clutter.

References

1. Van Trees, H.L.: Detection, Estimation and Modulation Theory. Part I. John Wiley and Sons, New York (1997).
2. Cheikh, K.,Faozi S.: Application of Neural Networks to Radar Signal Detection in K-distributed Clutter. First Int. Symp. on Control, Communications and Signal Processing Workshop Proc. (2004) 633-637.
3. Farina, A.,Russo, A., Scannapieco, F., Barbarossa, S.: Theory of Radar Detection in Coherent Weibull Clutter. In: Farina, A. (eds.): Optimised Radar Processors. IEE Radar, Sonar, Navigation and Avionics, Series 1. Peter Peregrinus Ltd., London (1987) 100-116.
4. Farina, A., Russo, A., Scannapieco, F.: Radar Detection in Coherent Weibull Clutter, IEEE Trans. on Acoustics, Speech and Signal Processing, Vol. ASSP-35, No. 6 (1987) 893-895.
5. DiFranco, J.V., Rubin, W.L.: Radar Detection. Artech House. U.S.A. (1980).
6. Jarabo-Amores, P., Rosa-Zurera, M., Gil-Pita, R., Lopez-Ferreras, F.: Sufficient Condition for an Adaptive System to Aproximate the Neyman-Pearson Detector. Proc. IEEE Workshop on Statistical Signal Processing (2005) 295-300.
7. Gandhi, P.P., Ramamurti, V.: Neural Networks for Signal Detection in Non-Gaussian Noise. IEEE Trans. on Signal Processing, Vol. 45, No. 11 (1997) 2846-2851.
8. Andina, D., Sanz-Gonzalez, J.L., Comparison of a Neural Network Detector Vs Neyman-Pearson Optimal Detector. Proc. of ICASSP-96 (1996) 3573-3576.
9. Gradshteyn, I.S., Ryzhik, I.M.: Table of Integrals, Series ans Products. Academic Press. USA (1965).
10. Haykin, S.: Neural Networks. A Comprehensive Foundation (Second Edition). Prentice-Hall. London (1999).
11. Sanz-Gonzalez, J.L., Andina, D.: Performance Analysis of Neural Network Detectors by Importance Sampling Techniques. Neural Processing Letters, No. 9 (1999) 257-269.
12. Nguyen, D., Widrow, B.: Improving the Learning Speed of 2-layer Neural Networks by Choosing Initial Values of the Adaptive Weights. Proc. of the Int. Joint Conf. on Neural Networks (1999) 21-26.

ICA with Sparse Connections

Kun Zhang and Lai-Wan Chan[*]

Department of Computer Science and Engineering
The Chinese University of Hong Kong
Shatin, Hong Kong
{kzhang, lwchan}@cse.cuhk.edu.hk

Abstract. When applying independent component analysis (ICA), sometimes that the connections between the observed mixtures and the recovered independent components (or the original sources) to be sparse, to make the interpretation easier or to reduce the model complexity. In this paper we propose natural gradient algorithms for ICA with a sparse separation matrix, as well as ICA with a sparse mixing matrix. The sparsity of the matrix is achieved by applying certain penalty functions to its entries. The properties of the penalty functions are investigated. Experimental results on both artificial data and causality discovery in financial stocks show the usefulness of the proposed methods.

1 Introduction

Independent component analysis (ICA) aims at recovering latent independent sources from their observable linear mixtures [4]. Denote by $\mathbf{x} = (x_1, ..., x_n)^T$ the vector of observable signals. $\mathbf{x}$ is assumed to be generated by $\mathbf{x} = \mathbf{As}$, where $\mathbf{s} = (s_1, ..., s_n)^T$ with mutually independent components and $\mathbf{A}$ is the mixing matrix. Here for simplicity we assume the number of observed signals is equal to that of the independent sources. Under certain conditions on $\mathbf{A}$ and the distribution of s_i, ICA applies the following linear transformation on $\mathbf{x}$:

$$\mathbf{y} = \mathbf{Wx} \qquad (1)$$

The separation matrix $\mathbf{W}$ is tuned such that the components of $\mathbf{y} = (y_1, ..., y_n)^T$ are mutually as independent as possible, and finally y_i provide an estimate of the original sources s_i.

When performing ICA, sometimes it is desirable not only to achieve the independence between outputs, but also to make the transformation matrix (the separation matrix $\mathbf{W}$ or the mixing matrix $\mathbf{A}$) as sparse as possible, i.e. to make its zero entries of the transformation matrix as many as possible, for the following reasons. First, consider the case where the data dimension is high and the true values of some entries of the transformation matrix are 0. If the zero entries can be automatically detected and are set to 0 during the learning process,

---

[*] This work was partially supported by a grant from the Research grants Council of the Hong Kong Special Administration Region, China.

the model complexity will be reduced and the parameters will be estimated more reliably. Second, a sparse mixing matrix means that the observations x_i are affected by only a smaller subset of the independent sources s_i, and this makes the interpretation easier. The third reason is application-oriented. Recently, ICA was proposed for identifying the linear, non-Gaussian, acyclic causal model (LiNGAM) [8]. If the data are generated according to the LiNGAM model, theoretically, the ICA separation matrix $\mathbf{W}$ can be permuted to lower triangularity. However, in practice this may not be true, due to the finite sample effect, noise effect, or slight violation of the model. So in order to estimate LiNGAM, $\mathbf{W}$ with as many as possible zero entries is preferred.

In this paper we propose methods to perform ICA with a sparse transformation matrix. The sparsity of the transformation matrix is achieved by maximizing the likelihood function of the ICA model together with suitable penalties on the ICA transformation matrix. We first discuss the properties of various penalty functions which can produce sparse coefficients in the linear regression problem, and also propose a new one. Under certain regularity conditions, likelihood-based models can also incorporate the above penalties to produce sparse parameters. In this way we develop the natural gradient-based ICA algorithm producing a sparse separation matrix, as well as that producing a sparse mixing matrix.

2 Penalties Producing Sparse Coefficients in Linear Regression

In the statistics literature, the behavior of different penalties in the linear regression problem has been intensively studied. By incorporating the L_γ penalty on the regression coefficients β_i, the penalized least square error (LSE) estimate for the coefficients $\boldsymbol{\beta} = (\beta_0, ..., \beta_n)^T$ is obtained by minimizing the mean square error plus the penalty term $\lambda \sum_{j=1}^{n} |\beta_j|^\gamma$, where $\lambda \geq 0$ is a parameter controlling the extent to which the penalty influences the solution. $\gamma = 2$ results in ridge regression, which tends to make coefficients smaller, but cannot set any coefficient to 0. The L_2 penalty also results in the weight decay regularizer in neural networks learning. The least absolute shrinkage and selection operator (Lasso) emerges when $\gamma = 1$, i.e. the L_1 penalty is adopted [9]. The L_1 penalty corresponds to a Laplacian prior on β_i. It automatically sets insignificant coefficients to 0 with a suitable λ; however, it has the disadvantage that it also influences the estimate of significant coefficients.

In [3] it was claimed that a good penalty function producing sparse parameters should result in an estimator with three properties. They are: 1. unbiasedness for the resulting estimator of significant parameters, 2. sparsity, which means that insignificant coefficients are automatically set to 0, to reduce the model complexity, and 3. continuity of the resulting estimator with respect to changes in data to avoid unnecessary variation in model prediction. Furthermore, the smoothly clipped absolute deviation (SCAD) penalty, which possesses the above properties, was proposed. The derivative of the SCAD penalty (including the coefficient λ) is given by (for $\beta > 0$)

$$P'_\lambda(\beta) = \lambda \left\{ I(\beta \leq \lambda) + \frac{(a\lambda - \beta)_+}{(a-1)\lambda} I(\beta > \lambda) \right\}, \text{ for some } a > 2 \quad (2)$$

where $I(\cdot)$ is the indicator function. The typical value for a is 3.7, which is obtained from the Bayesian viewpoint [3]. The SCAD penalty corresponds to an improper prior on β. It was also shown that with a proper choice of regularization parameter, the SCAD penalty exhibits the so-called oracle property. This property is very appealing, meaning that the coefficients whose true values are zero are automatically estimated as zero, and that the remaining coefficients are estimated as well as if the correct submodel were known in advance. For details of the SCAD penalty, see [3].

Now we propose a generalized version of the SCAD penalty and consider some computational problems. In fact, in the SCAD penalty (Eq. 2), the parameter controlling the strength of the penalty and that controlling the range the penalty applies to are not necessarily equal; we then propose the following generalized SCAD (GSCAD) (for $\beta \geq 0$):

$$P'_{\boldsymbol{\lambda}}(\beta) = \lambda \left\{ I(\beta \leq \lambda_1) + \frac{(a\lambda_1 - \beta)_+}{(a-1)\lambda_1} I(\beta > \lambda_1) \right\} \quad (3)$$

GSCAD plays a trade-off between SCAD and the L_1 penalty. When λ_1 is very large, it tends to be the L_1 penalty. When the data are very noisy, we can choose the parameter $\lambda_1 > \lambda$ so that the penalty operates on a wider range in the parameter space than SCAD. The penalty for weight elimination in neural networks learning [10] can be considered as a heuristic approximate to GSCAD. But it just shrink small parameters and can not set any parameter to 0.

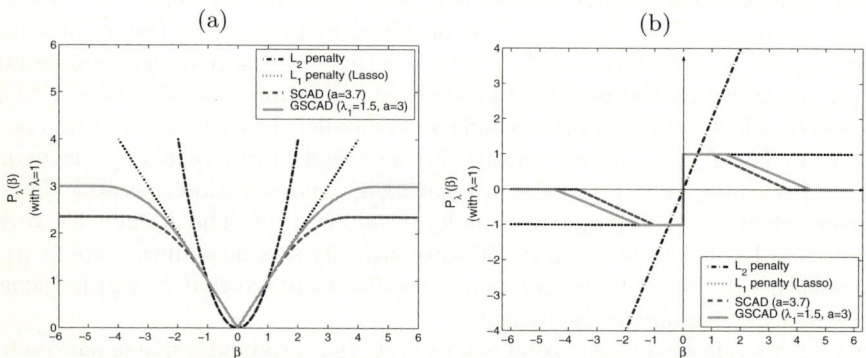

Fig. 1. (a) Curves of the four penalty functions with $\lambda = 1$. (b) Their derivatives.

Any penalty which can set small parameters to 0 and result in a continuous estimator, including the L_1 penalty and (G)SCAD, must be singular (not differentiable) at the origin [3]. Consequently, we can not use the gradient-based learning rule to optimize the objective function when β is very close to 0. Here we use some approximation to tackle this computational problem. We can use the function tanh($m\beta$) (m is a large number, say 200) to approximate the derivative of $|\beta|$. The GSCAD (Eq. 3) is then approximated by

$$P'_\lambda(\beta) = \lambda\left\{\tanh(m\beta) \cdot I(\beta \leq \lambda_1) + \tanh(m\lambda_1) \cdot \frac{(a\lambda_1 - \beta)_+}{(a-1)\lambda_1} I(\beta > \lambda_1)\right\} \quad (4)$$

As the price of the approximation, β will not exactly shrink to 0 even if its true value is 0; it will converge to a very small number (about 10^{-2}) instead. In practice, after the convergence of the algorithm, we need to set the parameters whose values are small enough, say, smaller than 0.02, to 0. For the illustrative purpose, Fig. 1 depicts the penalty functions discussed above, as well as their derivatives.

3 ICA with Sparse Transformation Matrix

Under weak regularity conditions, the ordinary maximum likelihood estimates are asymptotically normal [5], and the above penalties can be applied to likelihood-based models [3]. As ICA algorithms can be derived from a maximum likelihood point of view [7], ICA with a sparse transformation matrix can be derived with the data (log-)likelihood together with the above penalties as the objective function.

3.1 ICA with Sparse Separation Matrix

Denote by $p_i(s_i)$ the probability density function of the source s_i, and let $\mathbf{w}_i$ be the i-th column of $\mathbf{W}^T$. According to the ICA model (Eq. 1), the log-likelihood of the data $\mathbf{x}$ is

$$\ell(\mathbf{x}; \mathbf{W}) = \sum_{t=1}^{T}\sum_{i=1}^{n} \log p_i(\mathbf{w}_i^T \mathbf{x}_t) + T \log|\det \mathbf{W}| \quad (5)$$

where T denotes the number of samples. The penalized log-likelihood (divided by T) is

$$\ell_P = \frac{1}{T}\ell(\mathbf{x}; \mathbf{W}) - \sum_{i,j=1}^{n} P_\lambda(w_{ij}) \quad (6)$$

Its gradient w.r.t $\mathbf{W}$ is

$$\frac{d\ell_P}{d\mathbf{W}} = -E\{\boldsymbol{\psi}(\mathbf{y})\mathbf{x}^T\} + [\mathbf{W}^T]^{-1} - [P'_\lambda(w_{ij})] \quad (7)$$

where $\boldsymbol{\psi}(\mathbf{y}) = (\psi_1(y_1), ..., \psi_n(y_n))^T$ denotes the score function of $\mathbf{y}$, with $\psi_i(y_i) = -\frac{p'_i(y_i)}{p_i(y_i)}$, and $[P'_\lambda(w_{ij})]$ denotes the matrix whose (i,j)-th entry is $P'_\lambda(w_{ij})$. Multiplying the above equation from the right-hand side with $\mathbf{W}^T\mathbf{W}$, the corresponding natural gradient learning rule [1] for $\mathbf{W}$ can be obtained:

$$\triangle \mathbf{W} \propto \left(\mathbf{I} - E\{\boldsymbol{\psi}(\mathbf{y})\mathbf{y}^T\} - [P'_\lambda(w_{ij})]\mathbf{W}^T\right)\mathbf{W} \quad (8)$$

$\mathbf{W}$ and y_i estimated by ICA have the scaling indeterminacy. However, in the penalized log-likelihood (Eq. 6), the value of the penalty $P_\lambda(w_{ij})$ depends on the scale of w_{ij}, and the scaling indeterminacy should be avoided. A convenient way is to replace the diagonal entries of the right-hand side of Eq. 8 with $1 - E\{y_i^2\}$ to ensure that y_i are of unit variance at convergence.

3.2 ICA with Sparse Mixing Matrix

Now we give the learning rule for ICA with a sparse mixing matrix. The gradient of the penalized log-likelihood (Eq. 6) w.r.t $\mathbf{A}$ is

$$\frac{d\ell_P}{d\mathbf{A}} = [A^T]^{-1}(\boldsymbol{\psi}(\mathbf{y})\mathbf{y}^T - \mathbf{I}) - [P'_\lambda(a_{ij})] \qquad (9)$$

where $[P'_\lambda(a_{ij})]$ denotes the matrix whose (i,j)-th entry is $P'_\lambda(a_{ij})$. The corresponding natural gradient learning rule for $\mathbf{A}$ [1,6] is

$$\triangle \mathbf{A} \propto \mathbf{A}\left(\boldsymbol{\psi}(\mathbf{y})\mathbf{y}^T - \mathbf{I} - \mathbf{A}^T[P'_\lambda(a_{ij})]\right) \qquad (10)$$

In our implementation the diagonal entries of the right-hand side of the above equation are replaced by $1 - E\{y_i^2\}$ to avoid the scaling indeterminacy.

3.3 To Determine Parameters in Penalty Functions

The performance of the penalies is affected by the choice of the parameters in them. For example, in order to possess the oracle property (see Section 2) for the SCAD penalty, λ should satisfy the condition $\lambda_T \to 0$ and $\sqrt{T}\lambda_T \to \infty$ as $T \to \infty$. Note that here we use the subscript T to indicate that the choice of λ depends on the sample size T. The popular ways to select the parameters in the penalties are cross-validation and generalized cross-validation [3]. The choice of these parameters can also be application-oriented. For instance, in Section 4.2 we will discuss how to select the parameter λ when applying ICA with a sparse separation matrix (Eq. 8) to estimate the LiNGAM model, in the situation that the LiNGAM assumption is slightly violated.

4 Experiments

We now present two experiments to show the usefulness and the behavior of the proposed methods.[1] In the first experiment, we use artificial data to illustrate and compare properties of various penalty functions discussed in Section 2. In the second experiment, ICA with a sparse separation matrix is used to discover the LiNGAM causal relations among a set of stocks selected from the Hong Kong stock market.

---

[1] We also have exploited ICA with a sparse separation matrix to analyze high-dimensional gene expression data (with 77 conditions and 6180 genes). The regularization parameter λ is selected by five-fold cross-validation, and ICA with a sparse separation matrix gives much more stable separation results than traditional ICA. This result is not reported in detail due to space limitation.

4.1 With Artificial Data

In this experiment four independent sources are a sine wave (s_1), a uniformly distributed white signal (s_2), a sign signal (s_3) with a different frequency as s_1, and a normally distributed white signal (s_4). The entries of the mixing matrix **A** are randomly generated between -0.5 and 0.5, and some of them are set to 0 to make **A** sparse:

$$\mathbf{A} = \begin{pmatrix} 0.1518 & -0.2793 & 0 & 0 \\ -0.4472 & -0.1934 & 0 & 0 \\ -0.2707 & 0.2207 & -0.3748 & 0 \\ 0.0874 & 0.4544 & -0.3338 & -0.2310 \end{pmatrix}$$

The observations are generated by $\mathbf{x} = \mathbf{As} + \mathbf{n}$, where $\mathbf{n} = (n_1, ..., n_4)^T$ denotes isotropic Gaussian noise. Here we use the ratio of the standard deviation of n_i to the average standard deviation of $x_i - n_i$ to measure the noise level.

We compare the performance of four ICA methods for estimating **A** at different noise levels. These methods all exploit the natural gradient-based algorithm (Eq. 10), but different penalty functions are applied to entries of the estimate of **A**. The first one does not use any penalty, i.e. it is the traditional natural gradient ICA algorithm. The penalties in the other methods are the L_1 penalty, SCAD (Eq. 2), and GSCAD (Eq. 3), respectively. The parameters in the penalty functions are chosen empirically. $\lambda = 0.05$ for all the above penalties. In SCAD, $a = 3.7$. In GSCAD, $\lambda_1 = 1.5\lambda$ and $a = 3.3$.

At each noise level, we repeat the above methods for 30 runs. In each run, the sources s_2 and s_4 and the noise **n** are randomly generated. Fig. 2(a) shows the estimate of the entry a_{14} at different noise levels (with columns of the estimate of **A** correctly permuted). Note that here the estimate of a_{14} will not be exactly 0 since we use $\tanh(ma_{ij})$ to approximate the gradient of $|a_{ij}|$. Fig 2(b) compares the Amari performance index [2] obtained by the above methods. The smaller the Amari performance index, the better separation performance. From these figures we can see that when the noise level is not very high, the last three methods always performs better than traditional ICA. From the error bar in Fig. 2(a) we can see that they all provide a more stable estimate. Among the three penalties, the L_1 penalty is not as good as the others. The reason is probably that it penalizes all entries of the estimate of **A**, including the significant and reliable ones. SCAD and GSCAD give very similar performance. However, when the noise level is comparatively high (greater than 0.3), GSCAD behaves slightly better than SCAD.

4.2 For Estimation of LiNGAM Among Stock Returns

If the ICA separation matrix **W** of observed variables can be permuted to lower triangularity, these variables follow the LiNGAM model and **W** implies the causal relations among them [8]. In practice, **W** produced by traditional ICA is unlikely to have many zero entries, especially when the LiNGAM assumption is slightly violated. In [8], statistical tests were proposed to prune entries of **W** such

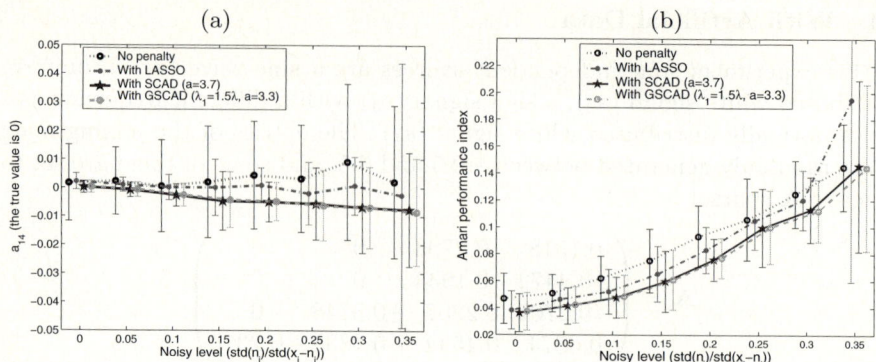

Fig. 2. (a) The estimate of the entry a_{14} (the true value is 0) at different noise levels. The error bar denotes the standard deviation of the results of 30 runs. The curves are shifted a little for clarity. (b) The Amari performance index.

that it is permuted to lower triangularity. However, it does not adjust $\mathbf{W}$ continuously, and consequently, small changes in data may result in sudden changes in the result. In addition, the interaction among entries of $\mathbf{W}$ is neglected when do pruning, and after an entry is pruned, the value and significance of others are changed. ICA with a sparse separation matrix provides a more reliable way to estimate the LiNGAM model.

When using ICA with a sparse separation matrix for estimation of the LiNGAM model, we need to choose a suitable λ such that the resulting $\mathbf{W}$ can be permuted to lower triangularity. A greedy scheme can be adopted for determining λ. (When using the GSCAD penalty, we set $\lambda_1 = 1.5\lambda$ and $a = 3.3$ empirically.) Starting from a small value, each time λ is increased by a fixed increment. After the algorithm converges for the new value of λ, we check whether the LiNGAM assumption holds by examining $\mathbf{W}$. The check can be easily done with Algorithm B in [8]. Once the LiNGAM assumption holds, we stop the above procedure and the LiNGAM model is estimated by analyzing $\mathbf{W}$; if λ reaches the upper bound set in advance or the correlations of y_i become significant, we terminate the above procedure and conclude that the data do not follow the LiNGAM model.

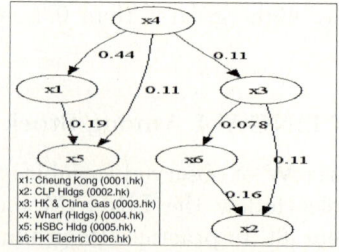

Fig. 3. LiNGAM causal relations among the six stocks

The computation involved in this method is not high, since the convergence of the algorithm for the new value of λ usually requires just several iterations.

The data to be analyzed are returns of six stocks selected from the Hong Kong stock market. The stocks (0001.HK~0006.HK) are given in the legend of Fig. 3. Starting from $\lambda = 0.04$ and increased by 0.04 each time, finally when $\lambda = 0.16$ the LiNGAM assumption holds for $\mathbf{W}$ estimated by ICA with a sparse separation matrix (Eq. 8). Fig. 3 gives the LiNGAM causal relations. x_2, x_3, and x_6 are components of the Hang Seng Utilities Index, and they are interconnected. x_1, x_4, and x_5 are closely related. This figure also tells us how their returns are influenced by others.

5 Conclusion

ICA with sparse connections is more suitable than traditional ICA for some real-world problems. In this paper We have proposed natural gradient algorithms for ICA with a sparse separation matrix and ICA with a sparse mixing matrix. The algorithms are derived by maximizing the ICA likelihood penalized by certain functions. Various penalty functions which can produce sparse parameters have been discussed and compared. A direct application of the proposed methods is to estimate the LiNGAM model. The proposed methods have been applied to both artificial data and real-world data, and the experimental results support the theoretical claims.

References

1. S. Amari. Natural gradient works efficiently in learning. *Neural Computation*, 10:251–276, 1998.
2. S. Amari, A. Cichocki, and H. H. Yang. A new learning algorithm for blind signal separation. In *Advances in Neural Information Processing Systems*, 1996.
3. J. Fan and R. Li. Variable selection via nonconcave penalized likelihood and its oracle properties. *Journal of the American Statist. Assoc.*, 96:1348–1360, 2001.
4. A. Hyvärinen, J. Karhunen, and E. Oja. *Independent Component Analysis*. John Wiley & Sons, Inc, 2001.
5. E.L. Lehmann. *Theory of Point Estimation*. John Wiley & Sons, Inc., 1983.
6. M. Lewicki and T.J. Sejnowski. Learning nonlinear overcomplete represenations for efficient coding. In *Advances in Neural Information Processing Systems 10*, pages 815–821, 1998.
7. D.T. Pham and P. Garat. Blind separation of mixture of independent sources through a quasi-maximum likelihood approach. *IEEE Trans. on Signal Processing*, 45(7):1712–1725, 1997.
8. S. Shimizu, P.O. Hoyer, A. Hyvärinen, and A.J. Kerminen. A linear non-Gaussian acyclic model for causal discovery. Submitted to Journal of Machine Learning Research, 2006.
9. R. Tibshirani. Regression shrinkage and selection via the lasso. *Journal of the Royal Statistical Society*, 58(1):267–288, 1996.
10. A.S. Weigend, D.E. Rumelhart, and B.A. Huberman. Generalization by weight elimination with application to forecasting. In *Advances in Neural Information Processing Systems 3*, 1991.

Two-Stage User Mobility Modeling for Intention Prediction for Location-Based Services

Moon-Hee Park, Jin-Hyuk Hong, and Sung-Bae Cho

Dept. of Computer Science, Yonsei University
Shinchon-dong, Seodaemun-ku,
Seoul 120-749, Korea
{moonypark, hjinh}@sclab.yonsei.ac.kr, sbcho@cs.yonsei.ac.kr

Abstract. Although various location-sensing techniques and services have been developed, most of the conventional location-based services provide only static service. They do not consider user's preference but only a current location. Considering the trajectory might help to understand the user's intention and to provide a proper service. We propose a novel method that predicts user's mobility to provide service corresponding to the intention. The user's movement trajectory is analyzed by two stage modeling of recurrent self-organizing maps (RSOM) and Markov models. Using a GPS data set collected on the campus of Yonsei University, we have verified the usefulness of the proposed method.

1 Introduction

Location-based services (LBS) are a hot topic in the field of wireless networks and mobile communication services. If it might be delivered to predict the user intention, a proper service can be provided at appropriate time.

At the network level, there are several management tasks that are deeply influenced by the user's mobility, such as handoff management, flow control, resource allocation [1], congestion control, call admission control, and quality of service (QoS) provisioning [2]. At the service level, the importance of mobility prediction techniques stems from the LBS [3,4], which provides the users with improved wireless services based on a combination of their profile and current or predicted location. Such services include pushed online advertising, map adaptation, user-solicited information, such as local traffic information, weather forecasts, instant messaging for communication with people within the same or nearby localities, mapping/route guidance, and directing people to reach their destination.

It is an essential element to incorporate location information into a real map in order to implement location-based services. We can easily obtain the location information using location sensing device such as GPS, but it is difficult to incorporate a complicated real map with them. In [5], the environment context describes information regarding the landscape and environment of the user represented using a Spatial Conceptual Map (SCM). As defined in [5], an SCM is "an abstraction of a real map representing a portion of the urban environment."

To increase the accuracy of location prediction, recent research trends predict user's movement through modeling the user's moving behavior by storing all the possible movement paths and related mobility patterns that are derived from the long-term history of moving events of the mobile user [6]. A closely related work has been carried out by Ashbrook and Starner [3], where a GPS system is used to collect location information over time. The system then automatically clusters GPS data taken into meaningful locations at multiple scales. These locations are then incorporated into a similar Markov model to predict the user's future movement based on the highest probability transition from the current location. However, this model is dependent only the current location or place of the user. In [7], Liu and Maguire further pursued this method by modeling the user's movement behavior as repetitions of some elementary movement patterns. Tabbane [8] proposed that a mobile terminal's location can be derived from its quasi-deterministic mobility behavior and can be represented as a set of movements in a user profile.

This paper proposes a method that analyzes a user's movement in order to predict the user's future movement. In first stage, the location information in the real world are abstracted into a map using RSOM, and Markov models for each cell of the map is trained to classify into the type of mobility at the second stage.

2 Domain Analysis

The user's trajectories were collected at Yonsei university (about 800×900 m^2) for 20 days by using the GPS sensor, which includes the error range of 10 meters.

Table 1. User's movement path

Class	Path		Goal
	Start Location	End Location	
1	Main Gate	Engineering Hall I	Lecture
2	Engineering Hall I	College of Liberal Arts II	Part-time job
3	College of Liberal Arts II	Auditorium	Lecture
4	Auditorium	College of Social Science	Lecture
5	College of Social Science	Engineering Hall III	Lecture
6	Engineering Hall III	Student Union	Have Lunch
7	Student Union	Engineering Hall III	Lecture
8	Engineering Hall III	Central Library	Study
9	Central Library	College of Liberal Arts I	Club activity
10	College of Liberal Arts I	Main Gate	Go home
11	Engineering Center	Student Union	Have Lunch
12	Engineering Center	Student Union	Personal work
13	Engineering Center	College of Business	Lecture
14	Engineering Center	College of Business	Lecture

Analyzing the data, we recognized 11 representative places for attending a lecture, having lunch, studying, personal work and participating club activity as shown in Table 1. We define 14 classes of movement patterns while each class has 9 instances. The data shows that the movement path is changed according to the user's intention class; each data is the same start location and end location such as class 11 and 12, class 13 and 14. In Table 1, class 11 and 12 mean movement patterns in case of a different movement goal. Going to the Student union in order to have lunch with friends, the student usually leaves the Engineering center and passed by the Engineering hall 3 (class 11); going to the Student union in order to conduct personal activities, the student directly goes toward the Student union (class 12). Class 13 and 14 present movement patterns of user's different states. Moving from the Engineering center to the College of business to deliver a lecture, if the student is late, she selects a shortcut which is a hill passing by the Science hall (class 13). Otherwise, she chooses a long flat path which is passed by the Student union (class 14).

3 Mobility Modeling Based a Two-Stage Model

The proposed framework is comprised of three phases as shown in Fig. 1: Information gathering, user modeling, and prediction module. In the information gathering phase, the GPS sensor collects user's location information and then it is stored on the knowledge base. User modeling contains two stages such as the feature abstraction and the trajectory classification. The feature abstraction summarizes a real map onto a 2D map and discovers meaningful patterns using RSOM. In the trajectory classification, Markov model is used to model the mobility for each cluster of the map. Finally, the prediction module predicts the future movement using the user's model built at the previous phase.

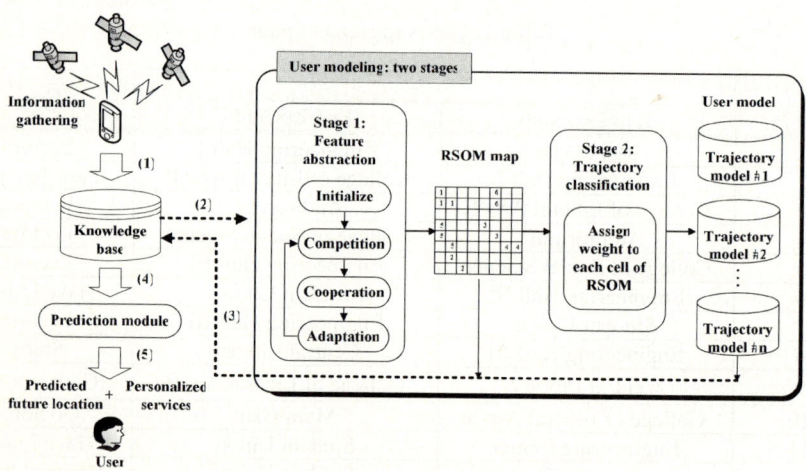

Fig. 1. Overview of the proposed framework

3.1 Stage 1: Feature Abstraction Using RSOM

RSOM, one type of SOM, copes with temporal sequence processing and inherits original properties of SOM [9]. It can organize nodes topographically to provide users with an abstract representation of the real map. It allows storing temporal context from consecutive input vectors. In this problem, the input vector, $x(n)$, is GPS data observed at time n, which is two dimensional vector composed of user's longitude and latitude. The RSOM simplifies a real map which has the complicated location information, corresponding to the SOM map. It is possible for similar movements to map onto neighborhood locations in RSOM output space. User's movement data set was clustered by RSOM and then each cluster was learned. The algorithm for training RSOM is as follows:

1. ***Initialize***: The codebook vector $w_i(0)$ is initialized by assigning random numbers.
2. ***Competition***: An input pattern $x(n)$ from input space is drew between current input pattern and each unit in output map is computed using Euclidean distance measure as follows:
$$y_i(n) = (1-\alpha)y_i(n-1) + \alpha(x(n) - w_i(n))$$
where α is the leaking coefficient, $y_i(n)$ is the leaked difference vector at step n and $x(n)$ is the input vector at step n. The best matching unit at time step n selected as the unit of minimum difference.
$$b(n) = \arg\min_i \| y_i(n) \|$$
By this process, a continuous input pattern is mapped onto discrete output space.
3. ***Cooperation***: The topological neighborhood is defined with respect to the lattice structure, not according to difference between the current input pattern and map units. The following Gaussian function h is typically used as a neighborhood function.
$$h_{b(x),i}(n) = \exp(-\frac{d^2_{b,i}}{2\sigma^2(n)})$$
4. ***Adaptation***: The weights of units inside the neighborhood are updated in relation to input vector using the following equation.
$$w_i(n+1) = w_i(n) + \eta(n)h_{b(n),i}(n)y_i(n)$$

The learning rate parameter $\eta(n)$ also varies during learning. By the neighborhood function, the units in neighborhood are updated in a distance-weighted manner instead of being uniformly updated. The algorithm is continued with competition steps until no noticeable changes in output map are observed. The difference vectors are reset to zero after learning each input sequence.

3.2 Stage 2: Trajectory Classification Using Markov Model

A Markov model is a stochastic process based on the Markov assumption, under which the probability of a certain observation only depends on the observation that directly precedes it [10]. A Markov model has a finite number of states, $1,2,\cdots,n$ which are defined by a transition probability matrix and an initial probability distribution.

$$p = \begin{pmatrix} p_{11} & p_{12} & \cdots & p_{1n} \\ p_{11} & p_{22} & \cdots & p_{1n} \\ \vdots & \vdots & \cdots & \vdots \\ p_{n1} & p_{n2} & \cdots & p_{nn} \end{pmatrix}$$

$$Q = \{q_1, q_2, \cdots, q_n\}$$

where p_{ij} is the probability of state transition from i to j, q_i is the probability of which the state i is observed at time 0.

$$\sum_{j=1}^{n} p_{ij} = 1$$

We can learn a Markov model by computing the transition probability and the initial probability distribution from the training data as follows:

$$p_{ij} = \frac{N_{ij}}{N_i}$$

where N_{ij} is the number of state transitions from state i to state j and N_i is the number of observation of state i.

$$q_i = \frac{N_i}{N}$$

N is the total number of observations. The trajectory models are built using the first-order Markov models. A Markov model learns the sequences of the best matching units instead of the raw GPS data. Changes to the best matching units during the processing sequence can be considered as changes of state because the SOM approximates the input space.

3.3 Intention Prediction

Evaluating current movement: The state i in Markov model corresponds to the i th output unit in RSOM because the sequences of the best matching units are used as inputs. In order to avoid the effect from the length of an input sequence, the probability for each class is normalized constantly for each movement of the sequence. The probability is computed as follows:

$$P(b(0), b(1), \cdots, b(N) \mid LM_i) = q_{b(0)} \prod_{t=2}^{T} P_{b(t-1)b(t)}$$

Selecting the closest movement pattern: The prediction of user's future movement is made by using the probabilities of local models, which are built by training each output space of RSOM using Markov model. The simplest solution to select the most likely movement pattern is maybe applying the predefined threshold to the probability of the local model. However, this method lacks the flexibility because the level of probability varies according to the length of the movement. The significance of a local model is used instead of the direct use of the local model probability. The significance of a local model is computed as follows:

$$significance(LM_j) = p(M_k^b | LM_j) - \sum_{i=1st.k \neq I}^{I} \frac{p(M_k^b | LM_i)}{I-1}$$

M_k^b means the sequence of best matching unit $\{b(0), b(1), …, b(T)\}$ and LM_i represents a local model associated to the ith output node. Using this method, we can predict user's movement as soon as the probable pattern is found.

4 Experimental Results

We have verified the proposed method with the dataset described in Section 2. In the experiment, a 16×16 map was used for RSOM. The initial learning rate and the initial neighborhood radius were set as 0.03 and 4, respectively. It repeated 5,000 times.

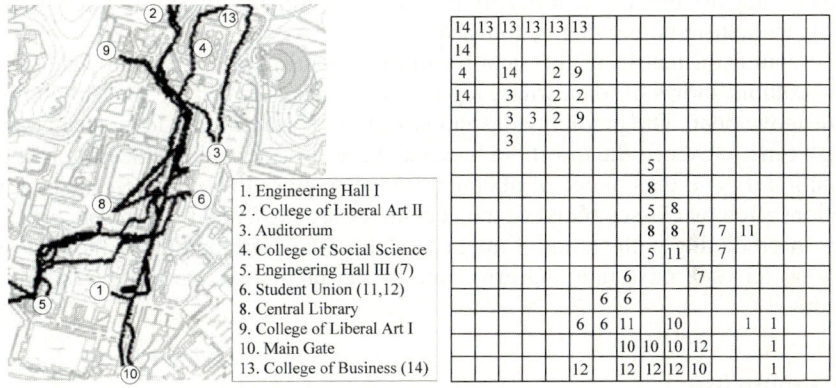

Fig. 2. Data superimposed on real campus map and labeled output units of RSOM

Fig. 2 presents the collected GPS data superimposed on real campus map and the labeled output units of RSOM. The real map is labeled in accordance with class number of the end location in Table 1. After training RSOM, each output unit is labeled by one of 14 classes. We evaluate the training data using the RSOM and each movement pattern is associated with its last best matching unit. Each cell shows an output unit and the empty cell presents the output unit which does not participate in the clustering. As shown in Fig. 2, the same moving patterns are located at near locations. In addition, we can find out two large groups: Top-left side and bottom-right side. In top-left side of map, there are 2, 3, 4, 9, 13 and 14. 1, 5, 6, 7, 8, 10, 11 and 12 are at bottom-right side. The top-left side group ends in the northern part of campus. On the other hand, the bottom-right group ends in the southern part of

Table 2. Confusion matrix

		Predicted (M: Miss, A: Accuracy)														
		1	2	3	4	5	6	7	8	9	10	11	12	13	14	M	A
Actual	1	5											1			3	0.56
	2		6							2			1				0.67
	3			8										1			0.89
	4				8										1		0.89
	5					8									1		0.89
	6						6		3								0.67
	7							8			1						0.89
	8						6		2					1			0.22
	9									4				1		3	0.44
	10									8			1				0.89
	11										3	1	3	1			0.33
	12											7					0.78
	13										1		8				0.89
	14		1			1						4	2	**1**			0.11

campus. They are due to the topology preservation property of SOM which helps the user browse clustered moving patterns easily.

The confusion matrix of the samples in this experiment is given in Table 2. The 'miss' column shows the data whose significance do not exceed the threshold until the end of movement. The prediction accuracies of class 1 and 9 are low. There was not enough time to exceed the threshold because the main gate and engineering hall I, the central library and the college of liberal arts I are so close to each other. In ambiguous situations such as classes 6 and 8, the accuracies are 0.67 and 0.22, respectively. All errors in predicting paths 6 and 8 might be due to the confounding of the two paths. The total hit rate, miss rate and error rate of the prediction are 0.65, 0.05 and 0.3, respectively.

5 Conclusion

In this paper, we presented a method to predict user's future movement and to provide a service by reasoning user's states and movement goals. The complexity of data is reduced by RSOM for the raw GPS data, where multiple Markov models are learned for each cell of RSOM. When a new sequence input, the user is immediately provided with an assigned service if it is similar to pattern of local model and over the predefined threshold.

It is too difficult to accomplish intelligent services by accurately predicting user's moving intension using only current location information. As the future work, we will gather information such as not only location but also schedules, moving time, pictures of the space, *etc.* to infer user's movement intensions. In addition, we will compare the proposed method with other techniques using evidential reasoning of Dempster-Shafer's theory [11] or REKF.

References

1. J. Chan and A. Seneviratne, "A practical user mobility prediction algorithm for supporting adaptive QOS in wireless networks," *Proc. IEEE Int'l Conf. Networks (ICON '99)*, pp. 104-111, 1999.
2. W. Soh and H. Kim, "QOS provisioning in cellular networks based on mobility prediction techniques," *IEEE Comm. Magazine*, vol. 41, no. 1, pp. 86-92, Jan. 2003.
3. D. Ashbrook and T. Starner, "Learning significant locations and predicting user movement with GPS," *Proc. Sixth Int'l Symp. Wearable Computers (ISWC 2002)*, pp. 101-108, Oct. 2002.
4. N. Marmasse and C. Schmandt, "A user-centered location model," *Personal and ubiquitous computing*, vol. 6, no. 5-6, pp. 318-321, Dec. 2002.
5. D. Kettani and B. Moulin, "A spatial model based on the notions of spatial conceptual map and of object's influence areas," *Proc. Conf. Spatial Information Theory (COSIT 1999)*, pp. 401-416, Aug. 1999.
6. S. Nancy and K. Ahmed, "A mobility prediction architecture based on contextual knowledge and spatial conceptual maps," *IEEE Transactions on Mobile Computing*, vol. 4, no. 6, pp. 537-551, 2005.
7. G. Liu and G. Maguire, "A class of mobile motion prediction algorithms for wireless mobile computing and communication," *ACM Int'l J. Wireless Networks*, vol. 1, no. 2, pp. 113-121, 1996.
8. S. Tabbane, "An alternative strategy for location tracking," *IEEE J. select. Areas Commus*, vol. 13, pp. 880-892, Jun. 1995.
9. T. Koskela, M. Varsta, J. Heikkonen and K. Kaski, "Temporal sequence processing using recurrent SOM," *Proc. of 2nd Int. Conf. on Knowledge-based Intelligent Engineering System*, vol. 1, pp.290-297, Adelaide, Australia. Apr. 1998.
10. W. Winston, *Operations Research: Applications and Algorithm*, Belmont, CA: Duxbury, 1994.
11. S. Nancy and K. Ahmed, "A mobility prediction architecture based on contextual knowledge and spatial conceptual maps," *IEEE Transactions on Mobile Computing*, vol. 4, no. 6, Nov. 2005.

Partition-Based Similarity Joins Using Diagonal Dimensions in High Dimensional Data Spaces*

Hyoseop Shin

Department of Internet and Multimedia Engineering
Konkuk University, Seoul, Korea
hsshin@konkuk.ac.kr

Abstract. Distributions of very high dimensional data are, in most cases, not even, but skewed. For this reason, there can be more effective dimensions than others in partitioning a high dimensional data set. Effective dimensions can be used to partition the data set in more balanced way so that data are located in more evenly distributed. In this paper, we present schemes to select dimensions by which high dimensional data sets are partitioned for efficient similarity joins. Especially, in order to efficiently reduce the number of partition dimensions, we propose a novel scheme using diagonal dimensions compared with perpendicular dimensions. The experimental results show that the proposed schemes substantially improve the performance of the partition-based similarity joins in high dimensional data spaces.

1 Introduction

Data derived from image and multimedia applications, time-series databases, and data mining are usually very high dimensional that even well-known multi-dimensional index structures [5,6,7] are not adequate for use. Distributions of very high dimensional data are, in most cases, not even, but skewed. For this reason, if we partition the data set along dimension axes, there can be more effective dimensions than others. Effective dimensions can be used to partition the data set in more balanced way so that data are located in more evenly distributed. In this respect, finding effective dimensions are crucial in searching objects in high dimensional data sets.

Similarity joins in a high dimensional space is considered as an important primitive operator in the applications listed above. For two data sets, R and S, of d-dimensional data points, a similarity join query is formulated as:

$$R \bowtie S = \{(r,s) \mid (\sum_{i=1}^{d} \mid r_i - s_i \mid^p)^{1/p} \leq \varepsilon, r \in R, s \in S\} \quad (1)$$

where r and s are represented as $[r_1, r_2, ..., r_d]$ and $[s_1, s_2, ..., s_d]$, respectively.

---

* This paper was supported by Konkuk University in 2006.

Similarity join queries are similar to spatial join queries [1,2] or distance join queries [3,4] in the spatial databases. The difference mainly lies in the dimensionality. In a low dimensional space, many index structures including R-tree [5] and its variants[6,7] are available and these indexes can be useful in processing spatial joins efficiently. Even without indexes available, some partition-based spatial join algorithms[8,9] are known to be competitive to the algorithms using indexes. Basically, most of these spatial join methods are based on the assumption that a data space can be partitioned in an efficient way. Unfortunately, this assumption is not applicable to similarity join queries in high dimensional spaces.

With increasing dimensions, the domain cardinality of a data space grows exponentially ($O(c^d)$ for a dimension d), and accordingly data points in a high dimensional data space are likely to be distributed sparsely and skewedly in most regions of the data space. This data skewness can also happen when data points are projected into each dimension axis. So, it is desirable to select dimension axes that show more uniform data distributions for efficient partitioning of a data space. As the similarity join processing associate two input data sets, a dimension which yields rather uniform data distribution on one input data set may yield non-uniform data distribution on the other input data set. Furthermore, the degree of the uniformity even for one data set can change according to the cut-off similarity value. For these reasons, the partitioning dimensions for the similarity joins should be selected under the consideration of the associated two input data sets as well as the cut-off similarity value.

To address this problem, this paper proposes the schemes of selection of dimensions by which the high dimensional data space is partitioned and the given data sets are split into partitions for efficient partition-based similarity joins. Furthermore, in order to further reduce the cost of the similarity join, we propose a novel method of using diagonal dimensions instead of perpendicular dimensions only as the partitioning dimension. The advantage of the diagonal dimension over the perpendicular dimensions is that the diagonal dimension can have the larger data space and thus the data sets can be distributed more evenly.

This paper is organized as follows. Section 2 explains the overview of the partition-based similarity join. Section 3 summarizes the perpendicular dimension selection algorithm for partition-based similarity join processing. Section 4 presents the diagonal dimension selection algorithm. Experimental results for the proposed methods are reported in Section 5. In Section 6 related work is described. In Section 7, the conclusion of this paper is presented.

2 Background

In this section, the general approach of the partition-based similarity join is described and the difficulties in applying the approach for high dimensional data are explained. The partition-based similarity join consists of two steps, partition step and join step. In the partition step, the entire data space is partitioned into cube-shaped cells by dividing each dimension. We assume without loss of generality that all the data points are within an unit hypercube. As each dimension value ranges between [0,1], each dimension is partitioned into $\lceil 1/\varepsilon \rceil$ intervals of the width, ε. And then, each point in the data sets, R and S, which participate in the similarity join, is assigned to the cell to which it belongs. Note that two separate sets of cells exist for the two data sets. The Fig. 1 illustrates the partitioned data space after the partition step. The small rectangles in the figure represent the resulted cells.

In the join step of the partition-based similarity join, actual join computations are performed between cells from the two input data sets. Each cell from R does not need to be paired with every cell from S, but is paired only with the cells which it overlaps or neighbors in the data space. For example, in the Fig.1, a cell, P shall be paired with one cell overlapping with it and eight cells surrounding it. Generally, in d dimensional data space, a cell in a data set that is not located at a border of the unit hypercube should be paired with 3^d cells in the other set.

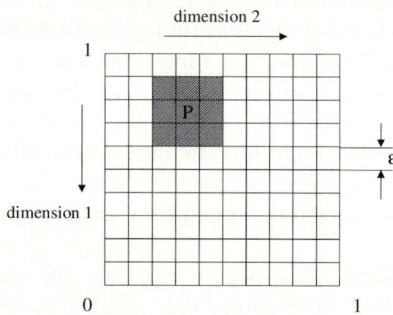

Fig. 1. Partition-Based Similarity Join: The Partition Step

3 Using Perpendicular Dimensions Only

To determine partitioning dimensions, the expected join cost for each dimension is pre-computed when data points of the input data sets are projected onto each dimension axis. After the join cost for each dimension compared, the d_p dimensions for which the join costs are smallest are selected as the partitioning dimensions.

The join cost for a dimension is computed as follows. First, as the space of a dimension axis is divided by a similarity cut-off value, ε, the space is divided into $\lceil 1/\varepsilon \rceil$ cells of length, ε. Second, the number of data points to be included in each cell from the input data sets is counted. Third, each cell in one input data set is paired with three cells in the other input data set, a cell at the left side of it, one at the right side of it, and one overlapping with it.

The cost of a join between two cells is computed by counting the number of distance computations between data points from the two cells. The number of distance computations between cells is computed by multiplying the number of data points of the cells. The total join cost for a dimension is obtained by the summation of the join costs between cells. The detail of the algorithm, *PerDimSelect*, is represented in the preivous paper[14].

4 Using Diagonal Dimensions

In case of high dimensions, if a data space is divided by employing all the dimensions during the partition step, the number of cells resulted from the partitioning may explode so that the data skew problem can be serious. This consequently causes to lessen the effect of search space reduction by space partitioning, while increasing additional costs during the join step.

Theoretically, under an assumption that data points are uniformly distributed in the data space, given the two input data sets, R and S, and the number of partitioning dimensions, d_p, the CPU cost of the partition-based similarity join, which is computed by counting the number of distance computations between data points, is formulated as follows:

$$Cost(CPU) = |R| \times |S| \times (\frac{3}{\lceil 1/\varepsilon \rceil})^{d_p} \qquad (2)$$

Meanwhile, the disk I/O cost, which is computed by counting the number of disk blocks visited, is formulated as follows:

$$Cost(IO) = |R|_{block} + 3^{d_p} \times |S|_{block} \qquad (3)$$

for the total number of disk blocks, $|R|_{block}$ for R and $|S|_{block}$ for S.

According to the Equation 2 and 3, as the partitioning dimension, d_p, increases, the CPU cost of the partition-based similarity join decreases(if we assume that $\lceil 1/\varepsilon \rceil > 3$), while the I/O cost increases. This implies that there is a trade-off between the CPU cost and the I/O cost in regard to the performance of the partition-based similarity joins and it is desirable to determine the converging dimensionality. In this respect, it would be more desirable to lessen the CPU cost without enlarging the IO cost.

To address this problem, we propose a method of using diagonal dimensions instead of perpendicular dimensions only as the partitioning dimension for the partition-based similarity joins. The data space of a diagonal dimension combined from k perpendicular dimensions is $\sqrt{k}$ times as large as that of a perpendicular dimension. Note that the number of partitioned cells is proportional to the size of the data space of the partitioning dimension and accordingly the CPU cost of the partition-based similarity join decreases. From the equation (2), given the two input data sets, R and S, and the number of diagonal partitioning dimension across k perpendicular dimensions, d_k, the CPU cost is reduced as follows:

$$Cost(CPU) = |R| \times |S| \times (\frac{3}{\lceil \sqrt{k}/\varepsilon \rceil})^{d_p} \qquad (4)$$

while the IO cost remains same as the equation (3).

Given a vector point $P = (p_1, p_2, ..., p_k)$ in k dimensional space, the projected coordinate value of the point on the diagonal dimension axis combined from the k perpendicular dimensions is easily computed as $\frac{1}{\sqrt{k}} \times \sum_{i=1}^{k} p_i$.

Fig 2 represents a projected point on the diagonal dimension for the two perpendicular dimensions.

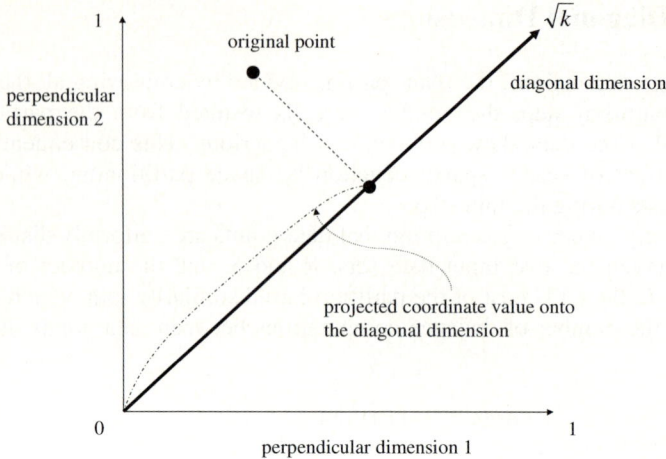

Fig. 2. Projected coordinate value onto diagonal dimension for 2 perpendicular dimensions

Although a diagonal dimension combining more perpendicular dimensions will have a larger data space than one with less perpendicular dimensions, larger data space does not guarantee less CPU cost because the CPU cost also depends upon data skewness in addition to the size of a data space. To obtain the near-optimal diagonal dimension, we utilize the sorted list of the dimensions that were selected to be efficient in partitioning dimensions. We iterate to combine the first i efficient dimensions in order to obtain a diagonal dimension by increasing i. In each step within the iteration, we compute the expected number of distance computations for the diagonal dimension. The iteration stop condition is when the $(i+1)$-th diagonal dimension is expected to have more CPU cost than the i-th one. Algorithm 1 represents the algorithm, *DiaDimSelect*, of selecting diagonal dimensions.

5 Experimental Results

In this section, we evaluate the proposed methods for the partition-based similarity join in high dimensional data spaces. We implemented *PerDimSelect*[14], *DiaDimSelect* and the partition-based similarity join algorithm based on them. In the experiments, we used two sets of 5,000 256-dimensional points, each of which is a color histogram value of an image.

we compare between *PerDimSelect* and *DiaDimselect*. While *PerDimSelect* uses k efficient perpendicular dimensions to partition the data space, *DiaDimSelect* use only single diagonal dimension that is made by combining the exacly same k perpendicular dimensions above. As far as *PerDimSelect* algorithm is concerned, , the performance was the smallest around at three, and at more than that, the performance monotonously got reduced.(Fig 3). This is due to the increase in the IO cost and in the cost of locating data points in higher dimensions. Meanwhile, the single diagonal dimension consistently shows better performance than multiple perpendicular dimensions.

set number of partitions, $np \leftarrow \lceil \sqrt{k}/\varepsilon \rceil$;
initialize sampled data sets R_s, S_s;
initialize partition arrays, $P_R[1...d][1...np]$, $P_S[1...d][1...np] \leftarrow 0$;
initialize number of distance computations, $JoinCost[1...d] \leftarrow 0$;
initialize sorted list of efficient dimensions resulting from *PerDimSelect*, $PerDim[1...d]$;

// compute the number of entities for each partition
for each entity $<e_1,e_2,...,e_d>$ in R_s **do**
  for each dimension k in $[1...d]$ **do**
$$P_R[k][\lceil np \times \frac{1}{\sqrt{k}} \times \sum_{i=1}^{k} p_i \rceil]\text{++};$$
  end
end
for each entity $<e_1,e_2,...,e_d>$ in S_s **do**
  for each dimension k in $[1...d]$ **do**
$$P_S[k][\lceil np \times \frac{1}{\sqrt{k}} \times \sum_{i=1}^{k} p_i \rceil]\text{++};$$
  end
end

for each dimension i in$[1...d]$ **do**
  for each partition number p in $[1...np]$ **do**
    if ($i>1$) $JoinCost[i] \leftarrow JoinCost[i] + P_R[i][p] \times P_S[i][p-1]$;
    $JoinCost[i] \leftarrow JoinCost[i] + P_R[i][p] * P_S[i][p]$;
    if ($i<np$) $JoinCost[i] \leftarrow JoinCost[i] + P_R[i][p] \times P_S[i][p+1]$;
  end
  if ($JoinCost[i+1] > JoinCost[i]$) **break;**
end

return the i-th diagonal dimension;

Algorithm 1. *DiaDimSelect* : Diagonal Dimension Selection Algorithm

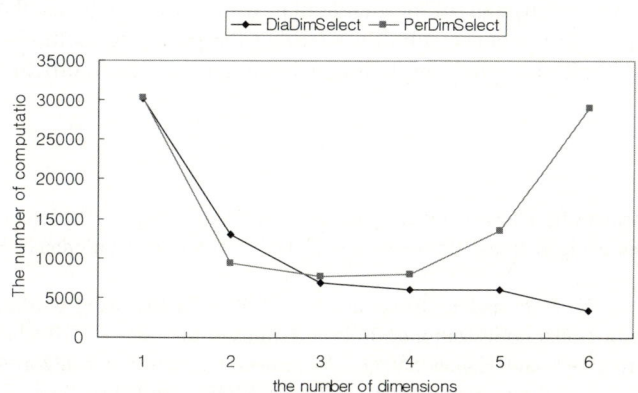

Fig 3. Diagonal Dimension vs Perpendicular Dimensions

6 Related Work

Several methods for similarity join processing in high dimensional data spaces have been reported in the literature. Shim et al.[10] proposed an indexing structure, ε-kdB-tree, to process similarity join queries. The data space is subdivided into a series of stripes of the width, ε, along one selected dimension axis. And then, each stripe is constructed as a main memory data structure, ε-kdB-tree in which dimension axes are chosen in order to partition the space recursively so that the search space is reduced while processing joins between nodes of the ε-kdB-trees. Koudas and Sevick [11] proposed to use space filling curves to partition the high dimensional spaces. Bohm et al.[12] proposed the epsilon grid order algorithm for the similarity join problem. A regular grid of the side-length, ε, is laid over the data space, anchored in the origin. Then, the lexicographical order is defined on the grid cells. With this ordering of data points, it can be shown that all join mates of a point p lie within an interval of the file. The lower and upper limit of the interval is determined by subtracting and adding the vector $[\varepsilon, \varepsilon, ..., \varepsilon]^T$ to p, respectively. The number of grid cells in an interval, however, tends to get larger as the dimension increases.

The TV-tree[13] has been proposed as a structure to index the high dimensional data using only part of the entire dimensions. The TV-tree is mainly for efficient search on single data set, while the dimension selection method in this paper dynamically selects the dimensions for efficient similarity joins on two associated data sets.

7 Conclusion

Partition-based approaches are not directly applicable to the similarity join processing in high dimensional data spaces. This is mainly because the number of cells resulted from partitioning is too large and thus unreasonable CPU and IO costs are spent. This paper proposed a dimension selection method which dynamically selects the most efficient dimensions to be partitioned for the similarity join. Furthermore, in order to further reduce the cost of the similarity join, we proposed a novel method of using diagonal dimensions instead of perpendicular dimensions only as the partitioning dimension. The experimental results showed that the proposed methods enhanced the partition-based similarity join in high dimensional data spaces significantly.

References

1. Thomas Brinkhoff, Hans-Peter Kriegel, and Bernhard Seeger, "Efficient processing of spatial joins using R-trees," Proceedings of the 1996 VLDB Conference, Bombay, India, Sep. 1996.
2. Y.W. Huang, N. Jing, and E. Rundensteiner, "Spatial joins using R-trees: Breadth-first traversal with global optimizations," In Proceedings of the 1997 VLDB Conference, 1997.
3. Gisli R. Hjaltason and Hanan Samet, "Incremental distance join algorithms for spatial databases," Proceedings of the 1998 ACM-SIGMOD Conference, pp. 237-248, Seattle, WA, June 1998.

4. Hyoseop Shin, Bongki Moon, and Sukho Lee, "Adaptive multi-stage distance join processing," In Proceedings of the 2000 ACM-SIGMOD Conference, pp. 343-354, Dallas, TX, May 2000.
5. Antonin Guttman, "R-trees: A dynamic index structure for spatial searching," In Proceedings of the 1984 ACM-SIGMOD Conference, pp. 47-57, Boston, MA, June 1984.
6. N. Beckmann, H.-P. Kriegel, R. Schneider, and B. Seeger, "The R*-tree: An efficient and robust access method for points and rectangles," Proceedings of the 1990 ACM-SIGMOD Conference, pp. 322-331, Atlantic City, NJ, May 1990.
7. S. Berchtold, D. A. Keim, and H.-P. Kriegel, "The X-tree: An index structure for high-dimensional data," In Proceedings of the 1996 Conference, Bombay, India, September 1996.
8. Jignesh M. Patel and David J. Dewitt, "Partition based spatial-merge join," In Proceedings of the 1996 ACM-SIGMOD Conference, pp. 259-270, Montreal, Canada, June 1996.
9. Ming-Ling Lo and Chinya V. Ravishankar, "Spatial hash join," In Proceedings of the 1996 ACM-SIGMOD Conference, pp. 247-258, Montreal, Canada, June 1996.
10. K. Shim, R. Srikant, and R. Agrawal, "High-dimensional similarity joins," In Proceedings of the 1997 IEEE International Conference on Data Engineering, 1997.
11. N. Koudas and C. Sevcik, "High dimensional similarity joins: Algorithms and performance evaluation," In Proceedings of the 1998 IEEE International Conference on Data Engineering, 1998.
12. C. Bohm, B. Braunmuller, F. Krebs, and H.-P. Kriegel, "Epsilon grid order" An algorithm for the similarity join on massive high-dimensional data," In Proceedings of the 2001 ACM-SIGMOD Conference, 2001.
13. King-Ip Lin, H. V. Jagadish, and Christos Faloutsos, "The TV-Tree: An Index Structure for High-Dimensional Data," VLDB Journal 3(4), pp. 517-542, 1994.
14. Hyoseop Shin, Bongki Moon and Sukho Lee, "Partition-Based Similarity Join in High Dimensional Data Spaces," Proceedings of the 13th DEXA conference, pages 741-750, Aix-en-Provence, France, September, 2002

Evolving Feed-forward Neural Networks Through Evolutionary Mutation Parameters

Annunziato M.[1], Bertini I.[1], Iannone R.[2], and Pizzuti S.[1]

[1] Energy New technologies and Environment Agency, 'Casaccia' R.C.
Via Anguillarese 301, 00060 Rome, Italy
{mauro.annunziato, ilaria.bertini,
stefano.pizzuti}@casaccia.enea.it
[2] University of Rome 'La Sapienza', Dept. of Computer Science
Via Salaria 113, Rome, Italy
rob.iannone@gmail.com

Abstract. In this paper we show a preliminary work on evolutionary mutation parameters in order to understand whether it is possible or not to skip mutation parameters tuning. In particular, rather than considering mutation parameters as global environmental features, we regard them as endogenous features of the individuals by putting them directly in the genotype. In this way we let the optimal values emerge from the evolutionary process itself. As case study, we apply the proposed methodology to the training of feed-forward neural netwoks on nine classification benchmarks and compare it to other five well established techniques. Results show the effectiveness of the proposed appraoch to get very promising results passing over the boring task of off-line optimal parameters tuning.

1 Introduction

Artificial Neural Networks (ANN) and Evolutionary Algorithms (EA) are both abstractions of natural processes. They are formulated into a computational model so that the learning power of neural networks and adaptive capabilities of evolutionary processes can be harnessed in an artificial life environment. 'Adaptive learning', as it is called, produces results that demonstrate how complex and purposeful behavior can be induced in a system by randomly varying the topology and the rules governing the system. Evolutionary algorithms can help determine optimized neural network architectures giving rise to a new branch of ANN known as Evolutionary Neural Networks [30] (ENN). It has been found [1] that, in most cases, the combinations of evolutionary algorithms and neural nets perform equally well (in terms of accuracy) and were as accurate as hand-designed neural networks trained with backpropagation [9]. However, some combinations of EAs and ANNs performed much better for some data than the hand-designed networks or other EA/ANN combinations. This suggests that in applications where accuracy is a premium, it might pay off to experiment with EA and ANN combinations.

In this context methodological efforts ranged from the simple weights optimization to the simultaneous evolution of weights and topological neural structures [16][19]

[22][28]. ENN applications are wide as well and ranged from modelling (es. [3],[25]) to classification tasks (es. [10]).

However, all the proposed methodologies and applications consider the algorithm's parameters as static (at most adaptive) global environmental features and do not take into account the possibility of considering them as endogenous features of the individuals, although it is known that the evolutionary adaptation of mutation rates playes an important role in the molecular evolution of life [24].

In order to face this new challenge, evolutionary programming has started to study evolving mutation rates in an effort to automate control of evolutionary search for function optimisations. Preliminary efforts proved that automated control is feasible [5] [15], and continuing research is fine-tuning this process [12]. In particular, in [5] it is presented an approach in which a basic idea from Evolution Strategies (ESs) is transferred to EAs. Mutation rates, instead of being handled as a global constant external parameters, are changed into endogenous items which are adapting during the research process. In this work experimental results indicate that environment-dependent self-adaption of appropriate settings for the mutation rate is possible.

Later, it has been demonstrated [17] that energy dependent mutation rate adaptation can play a pivotal role in the evolution of complexity. In [7], through a model consisting of a two-dimensional world with a fluctuating population of evolving agents, it is provided evidence that evolving mutation rates adapt to values around a transition among qualitatively different kinds of complex adaptive systems (meta-stable, quasi-clonal systems, and randomly fluctuating systems). Results provide an especially simple illustration of how the evolution of evolvability creates and tunes the capacity of complex adaptive systems to generate order through adaptive evolution.

In this context, the goal of the proposed work is to study the effectiveness of using evolutionary mutation rates, applied to the evolution of weights in feed forward neural networks, in order to achieve good results without the off-line optimal parameter tuning process.

2 The Evolutionary Environment

2.1 The Alife Algorithm

The implemented artificial environment is inspired by the 'Artificial Life (*ALIFE*)' methodology [20][21]. This approach has been tested for the optimisation of static well known benchmark problems, like the Travelling Salesman Problem, as well as real life problems [4]. The *ALIFE* context is a two-dimensional lattice (*life space*) representing a flat physical space where the artificial *individuals* can move around. At each iteration (or *life cycle*), individuals move in the life space and, in case of meeting with other individuals, interaction occurs. Each individual has a particular set of rules that determines its interactions with other agents basically based on a competition for energy in relation to the performance value. Individuals can self-reproduce via haploid mutation and can occur only if the individual has an *energy* greater than a specific *birth energy*. In fact, during reproduction, an amount of energy equal to the birth energy is transferred from the parent to the child. In the haploid reproduction a probabilistic test for self reproduction is performed at every life cycle and a probabilistic-random mutation occurs on the genes according to the mutation rate and the mutation amplitude (see next paragraph). When two individuals meet, fighting occurs. The winner is the individual characterized by a greater value of performance and the loser transfers an amount of energy *(fighting energy)* to the winner. At every life cycle each individual *age* is increased and the age reaches a value close to the *average lifetime*, the probability of natural death increases. This ageing mechanism is very important to warrant the possibility to lose memory of very old solutions and follow the process evolution. Another mechanism of death occurs when the individual reaches the null energy due to reproduction or fighting with other individuals. In this way, when there is a reproduction event the population size increases of one unit while in a death event the population size decreases of one unit. Therefore, the population size is dynamic and it is limited by the dimension of the physical space. The reader interested in further details can refer to [2].

2.2 Implementation

In the genotype of the individuals it is stored the information concerning the problem to be solved and the individuals' fitness is calculated as function of the genotype itself. In the case we are facing here, each individual represents a feed forward neural network in competition with the others by means of the proper fitness, which depends on the capability of reconstructing the training database. The fitness of the individuals is measured referring to the global error in modelling the training database with the following formula:

$$\text{Fitness} = 1 - \text{RMSE} \qquad (1)$$

Where *RMSE* is the classical Root Mean Squared Error (2) normalised in the lattice [0,1] used by the back-propagation (BP) algorithm. This cost function has been chosen in order to directly compare the results with the ones obtained with BP methodology.

$$\text{RMSE} = \sqrt{\frac{1}{n}\sum_{1}^{n}(0.5*\sum_{1}^{m}(y-y_t)^2)} \qquad (2)$$

Where n is the dimension of the training data set, m is the number of output neurons, y is the estimated output and y_t is the corresponding target. All the inputs and outputs of the networks are normalized between 0 and 1 (as well as the targets) and there are no differences among the activation functions for hidden and output nodes. As measure of the level reached in the training stage, we take the fitness of the best individual corresponding to the best performing neural network.

The genotype is therefore composed (see table 1) by the network features (weights and biases) to be optimised, by the mutation rate (*Rate*), representing the number of genes to be mutated during the reproduction stage, for weights, biases and, associated to each gene, by the highest mutation amplitude (*Delta*). Therefore, during evolution both topological features (solutions) and parameters are simultaneously evolved.

Table 1. Individuals' genotype

Solutions	GENOTYPE
	Parameters
Weight 1	Rate Delta(1)
...	...
...	...
Weight k	Delta(k)
Bias 1	Delta($k+1$)
...	...
...	...
Bias h	Delta($k+h$)

3 Experimentation

Experimentation concerned the optimal training of feed forward neural networks in order to solve nine classification benchmarks taken from the UCI repository [8].

The neural optimisation task has been accomplished using the proposed evolutionary approach and compared to the following five well established methodologies: Multilayer Perceptron (*MLP*) [26] trained with the Back-Propagation algorithm, Kstar[11], MultiBoost (*MB*)[27], Voting Feature Interval (*VFI*) [14] and Particle Swarm Optimisation (*PSO*) [18]. For the first four the WEKA tool [29] has been used and for PSO we took the results presented in [13]. Each data set (see table 2) has been split in two parts: training (75% of the whole data set) and testing set (25% of the whole data set).

Table 2. Data sets features

Problem	Data set size	Training set Size	Testing set Size	Classes	Input size
Card	690	517	173	2	51
Diabetes	768	576	192	2	8
Glass	214	160	54	6	9
Heart	303	227	76	2	35
Horse	364	273	91	3	58
Iris	150	112	38	3	4
Wdbc	569	426	143	2	30
WdbcInt	699	524	175	2	9
Wine	178	133	45	3	13

In our experimentation we compared the mentioned techniques to the evolutionary neural networks trained with (*EvoNN*) and without (*ENN*) the evolutionary mutation parameters. For these two experimentations we used a physical space of 25X25 cells corresponding to a maximum population size of 625 individuals. The neural topologies used in the *EvoNN*, *ENN* and *MLP* tests are reported in table 3 and results are in table 4 where we show the average of the classification error (percentage) on the testing set. For each of the mentioned techniques, we performed ten runs on each problem. Moreover, to avoid over-fitting in the MLP and ENN tests, we used the early stopping criterion trying different number of generations and then choosing the number of iterations which gave the best testing results. The same number of generations were therefore used in the *EvoNN* test. On average, the best ENN and EvoNN experimentations needed about 300000 performance evaluations.

All the other parameters of the other techniques were not optimised because the goal of this work is to get results without the off-line tuning of parameters which, in this case, are optimised during the evolutionary process (figure 1).

Table 3. Neural topologies

Problem	Neural Topology (input-hidden-output)
Card	51-4-2
Diabetes	8-3-2
Glass	9-2-6
Heart	35-4-2
Horse	58-4-3
Iris	4-4-3
Wdbc	30-4-2
WdbcIn	9-3-2
Wine	13-3-3

Table 4. Experimental testing results (classification error)

	EvoNN	MLP	KSTAR	ENN	PSO	MB	VFI
Card	17.98%	16.7%	24.28%	24.1%	22.84%	**13.8%**	25.43%
Diabete	**21.82%**	21.9%	32.29%	22.1%	22.5 %	26.5%	54.69%
Glass	35.00%	37%	**25.93%**	40.3%	41.69%	61.1%	46.30%
Heart	14.87%	17.1%	25.00%	16.4%	17.46%	**10.5%**	18.42%
Horse	38.24%	38.4%	**34.07%**	36.1%	40.98%	36.2%	42.86%
Iris	**2.63%**	**2.63%**	5.26%	7.11%	**2.63%**	7.90%	7.90%
Wdbc	**1.75%**	2.10%	5.59%	3.15%	5.73%	2.80%	5.59%
WdbcIn	**1.09%**	1.71%	1.14%	3.54%	2.87%	4.00%	1.71%
Wine	3.33%	**2.22%**	**2.22%**	4.22%	4.44%	22.2%	11.11%
Average	**15.19%**	15.5%	17.31%	17.4%	17.91%	20.5%	23.78%

These results show the effectiveness of the proposed methodology based on evolutionary mutation parameters. In fact, this method provides the best global performance obtaining the best results on four problems. In particular, it is interesting the comparison with the MLP ANNs, trained with the Back-Propagation Algorithm, and the original ENN with constant mutation parameters. This comparison directly shows the performance improvement when using the suggested technique.

As regards cpu time, KSTAR, MB and VFI are very fast (1-2 seconds) because they are statistical clustering techniques which do not require a training stage. For PSO we got the results from [13] which does not report such an information and for the other methods the cpu training time ranges from 25 to 190 seconds.

After all, in figure 1 we can see how the mutation parameters evolve compared to the performance behaviour. From this graph it is interesting to point out that after several generations the optimal parameter values emerge and tend to stabilize as well as the performance. This is remarkable because it is the evidence that the evolutionary environment is able to optimise the problem itself and to find the best parameters for that problem avoiding the off-line tuning of the parameters.

Fig. 1. Evolution of mutation parameters

4 Conclusion

In this paper we showed a preliminary work on how evolutionary mutation parameters affect the performance of the optimization in an evolutionary environment. In particular, rather than considering the mutation parameters as global environmental features, we regarded them as endogenous features of the individuals by putting them directly in the genotype.

The final goal of this work is that we can achieve very good results without the need of parameters tuning because, making them evolutionary, their optimal values emerge from the evolutionary optimization itself.

As case study, we applied the proposed methodology to the training of feed-forward neural netwoks. We tested it on nine classification benchmarks and compared it to other five well established techniques. Results on testing data showed that the proposed methodology performs globally better than the others achieving the best results on four problems.

In the end, we studied the evolution of the mutation parameters and we found out they tend to emerge and stabilize around some optimal values as well as the achieved performance. These preliminary results are extremely encouraging and future work will focus on finding out a formal justification of the solution, on testing the proposed approach on real problems and on comparing the evolutionary environment to other similar techniques (like genetic algorithms).

References

1. Alander, J. T.: An indexed bibliography of genetic algorithms and neural networks. Technical Report 94-1-NN, University of Vaasa, Department of Information Technology and Production Economics (1998).
2. Annunziato, M., Bertini, I., Lucchetti, M., Pannicelli, A. and Pizzuti, S. : Adaptivity of Artificial Life Environment for On-Line Optimization of Evolving Dynamical Systems, in Proc. EUNITE01, Tenerife (Spain) (2001).
3. Annunziato, M., Bertini, I., Pannicelli, A., Pizzuti, S. : Evolutionary feed-forward neural networks for traffic prediction , proceedings of EUROGEN2003, Barcelona, Spain (2003)
4. Annunziato M. , Lucchetti M., Orsini G., Pizzuti S. : ARTIFICIAL LIFE AND ONLINE FLOWS OPTIMISATION IN ENERGY NETWORKS, IEEE Swarm Intelligence Symposium, Pasadena (CA), USA, 2005
5. Bäch, T. : Self-adaptation in genetic algorithms", in *Towards a Practice of Autonomous Systems*, F. J. Varela & P. Bourgine (Eds.), Cambridge, MA: Bradford/MIT Press, (1992) 263-271.
6. Balakrishnan, K. and Honavar, V : Evolutionary Design of Neural Architectures - A Preliminary Taxonomy and Guide to Literature, Technical Report CS TR95-01, Dept. of Computer Science, Iowa State University (1995)
7. Bedau, M. A. and Seymour R.: Adaptation of Mutation Rates in a Simple Model of Evolution, Complexity International, vol.2, (1995)
8. Blake, C. L and Merz, C. J. : UCI repository of machine learning databases, University of California, Irvine, http://www.ics.uci.edu/~mlearn/MLRepository.html (1998)
9. Cant-Paz, E. and Kamath, C. : An empirical comparison of combinations of evolutionary algorithms and neural networks for classification problems. IEEE Transactions on Systems, Man, and Cybernetics-Part B: Cybernetics (2005) 915-927.
10. Cantú-Paz, E. and Kamath, C. : Evolving neural networks for the classification of galaxies," Proceedings of the Genetic and Evolutionary Computation Conference, GECCO 2002, Morgan Kaufmann Publishers, San Francisco (CA), (2002) 1019-1026
11. Cleary, J. G. and Trigg, L. E. : K*: An Instance- based Learner Using an Entropic Distance Measure, Proceedings of the 12th International Conference on Machine learning (1995) 108-114
12. Davis, M. W.: The natural formation of gaussian mutation strategies in evolutionary programming, Proceedings of the 3rd Annual Conference on Evolutionary Programming, A. V. Sebald & L. J. Fogel (Eds.), River Edge, NJ: World Scientific (1994).

13. De Falco, I. , Della Coppa, A. and Tarantino, E. : Impiego della particle swarm optimization per la classificazione in database, II Italian Artificial Life Workshop, Rome, Italy, ISTC-CNR (2005)
14. Demiroz, G. and Guvenir, A. : Classification by voting feature intervals, ECML-97 (1997)
15. Fogel, D. B., Fogel, L. J. & Atmar J. W.: Meta-evolutionary programming, Proceedings of the 25th Asilomar Conference on Signals, Systems and Computers, R. R. Chen (Ed.), San Jose: Maple Press, (1991) 540-545.
16. Hwang, M. W., Choi, J. Y., and Park, J.: Evolutionary projection neural networks, in Proceedings of the 1997 IEEE International Conference on Evolutionary Computation, ICEC'97, (Piscataway, NJ, USA), IEEE Press, (1997) 667-671.
17. Jan, T. and Kim : Energy Dependent Adaptation of Mutation Rates in Computer Models of Evolution, Proceedings of ALIFE VI, Los Angeles, CA, (1998)
18. Kennedy, J. and Eberhart R.C. : Particle swarm optimization. Proc. IEEE International Conference on Neural Networks, IV. Piscataway, NJ: IEEE Service Center, (1995) 1942–1948
19. Kenneth, O. Stanley and Miikkulainen, R. : Evolving Neural Networks Through Augmenting Topologies (2002)
20. Langton, C. G. : Artificial life in Artificial life, C. Langton (Ed.). Addison-Wesley. (1989)
21. Langton, C. G. : The Garden in the Machine, The Emerging Science of Artificial Life, Princeton University Press (1989)
22. Liu, Y. and Yao, X., : Evolutionary design of artificial neural networks with different nodes, in Proc. of the 1996 IEEE Int'l Conf. on Evolutionary Computation (ICEC'96), Nagoya, Japan, IEEE Press, New York, NY 10017-2394, (1996) 670-675
23. Matteucci, M. : ELeaRNT: Evolutionary Learning of Rich Neural Network Topologies, Technical Report N CMU-CALD-02-103, Department of Computer Science - Carnegie Mellon University, Pittsburgh PA (2002)
24. Metzgar, D. and Wills, C. : Evidence for the Adaptive Evolution of Mutation Rates, Cell, Vol. 101, (2000) 581-584
25. Prudencio, R.B.C. and Ludermir, T.B. : Evolutionary Design Of Neural Networks: Application To River Flow Prediction, Proceedings of the IASTED International Conference on Artificial Intelligence and Applications, AIA 2001, Marbella, Spain (2001)
26. Rumelhart, D. E., Hinton, G. E., and Williams, R. J. : Learning representations by backpropagating errors. Nature, 323 (1986) 533–536
27. Webb, G. I. : MultiBoosting: a technique for combining boosting and wagging, Machine Learning, vol. 40 (2), (2000) 159-196
28. White, D. and Ligomenides, P.: GANNet: a genetic algorithm for optimizing topology and weights in neural network design, in Proc. of Int'l Workshop on Artificial Neural Networks (IWANN'93), Springer-Verlag, Lecture Notes in Computer Science, Vol. 686 (1993) 322-327
29. Witten, I. H. and Frank, E.: Data mining: practical machine learning tool and technique with Java implementation, San Francisco: Morgan Kaufmann (2000)
30. Yao, X., "Evolving Artificial Neural Networks", Proceedings of the IEEE, 87(9): (1999)1423-1447

Computer Interface Using Eye Tracking for Handicapped People

Eun Yi Kim[1] and Se Hyun Park[2,*]

[1] Department of Internet and Multimedia Engineering, Konkuk Univ., Korea
eykim@konkuk.ac.kr
[2] School of Computer and Communication, Daegu Univ., Korea
Tel.: +82-53-850-6637; Fax: +82-2-850-6637
sehyun@daegu.ac.kr

Abstract. In this paper, a computer interface for handicapped people is proposed, where input signals are given by eye movement of the handicapped people. Eye movement is detected by neural network (NN)-based texture classifier, which enables our system to be not obliged to constrained environment. To be robust the natural motion of a user, we first detect a user's face using skin-color information, and then detect her or his eyes using neural network (NN)-based texture classifier. After detection of eye movements, the tracking is performed using mean-shift algorithms. We use this eye-tracking system as an interface to control the surrounding system such as audio, TV, light, phone, and so on. The experimental results verify the feasibility and validity of the proposed eye-tracking system to be applicable as an interface for the handicapped people.

1 Introduction

The eye-tracking device has become one of the most important human machine interfaces in which eye movements are related to the information processing demands of a task [1-6]. The interface using the eye movement is can be used as an interface to control a computer, a robot, game, and so on. These interfaces using the eye movement can support the people who can not use the keyboard or mouse due to severe disabilities. Due to these, such an interface using eye movements has gained many attractions, so far many systems have been developed [1]-[6]. Then they can be classified into two techniques: intrusive method using some devices such as glasses, head band, etc., and non-intrusive method using image processing techniques. Between them, the handicapped people actually prefer the non-intrusive method to the intrusive method because non-intrusive method is more comfortable.

To be practically used, automatic detection and tracking of faces and eyes in real-life situation should be first supported. However, in most of the current commercial systems, the initial eye or face position are manually given or some conditions are used. In [5], the interface to use head and eye movement for handicapped people was developed, where the user at the beginning of the system was requested to blink his or

---

* Corresponding author.

her eyes during a couple of times so as to localize the eye region through the subtraction of two successive frames. In [4], the user initially clicks on the features to be tracked via a mouse. Moreover, most of the current systems have used strong assumptions to make the problems more tractable. Some common assumptions are the images contain frontal facial view, the illumination is constant, the light source is fixed, and the face has no facial hair or glasses. However, in most of the real-life situation, it can not be assured that the observed subject will remain immovable, as assumed by some methods.

To solve these difficulties, this paper proposes the eye tracking method that can automatically locate the accurate eye regions under the cluttered background with no constraints. In our system, the facial region is first obtained using skin color model. And then, the eye regions are localized by a NN-based texture classifier that discriminates each pixel in the extracted facial regions into the eye-class and non-class using the texture property. This enables us to accurately detect user's eye region even if they put on the glasses. Once the eye regions are detected in the first frame, they are continuously tracked by a mean-shift procedure. After the system transfers the coordinates of eyes' center in the images to the display coordinate, it will determine the point at which the user gazed on the display, and then execute the menu to locate that point. We use this eye-tracking system as an interface to control the surrounding system such as audio, TV, light, phone, and so on. The experimental results verify the feasibility and validity of the proposed eye-tracking system to be applicable as an interface for the handicapped people.

2 Outline of Welfare Interface

Our system consists of a PC camera and a computer. The system receives and displays a live video of the user sitting in front of the computer. The video is taken by a camera that is mounted above the monitor of the computer. Watching this video, the user can move the computer's mouse and select the menu which is displayed on the computer monitor. One example of the menu is shown in Fig. 1, where five menu items are shown. A user faces the display monitor and selects one item among five menu items by gazing at it.

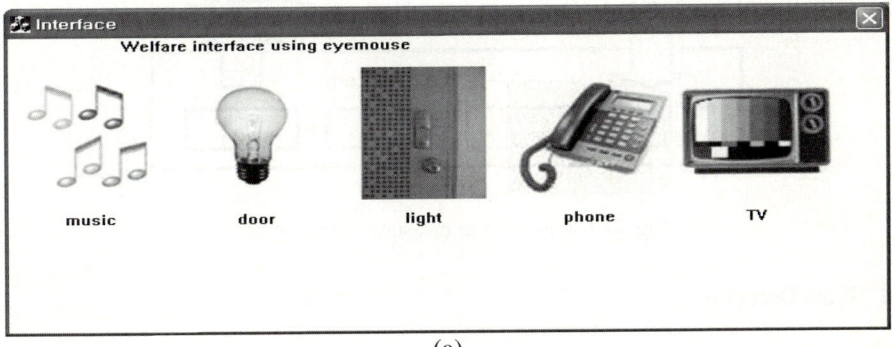

(a)

Fig. 1. Examples of menu selection. (a) main menu, (b) sub-menu of 'music'.

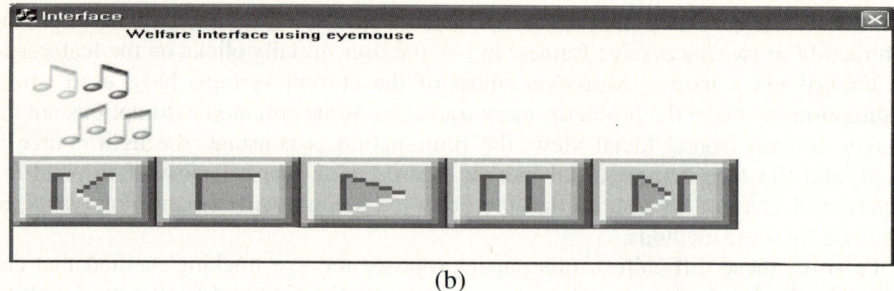

(b)

Fig. 1. (*Continued*)

Suppose the user select the 'music' menu in Fig. 1(a), then the next sub-menu of 'music' is displayed on the computer monitor is shown in Fig. 1(b). Here, suppose the user select the first menu item, then the interface starts to connect the audio automatically. Similarly every item on the menu has sub-menu if necessary.

3 Eye Movement Measurement

In our system, the user moves the mouse pointer or clicks menus by moving his or her eyes. For processing the user's movement, our system consists of four modules (as shown in Fig.2): face extractor, eye detector, eye tracker. We extract a user's face using skin color model. Then the user's eyes are detected using neural network (NN)-based texture classifier. Then, the eyes are continuously tracked using mean-shift algorithm. Based on the tracking results, mouse operations such as movement or click are implemented and then the control signal is sent to the surroundings systems such as 'telephone', 'audio', 'video and so on.

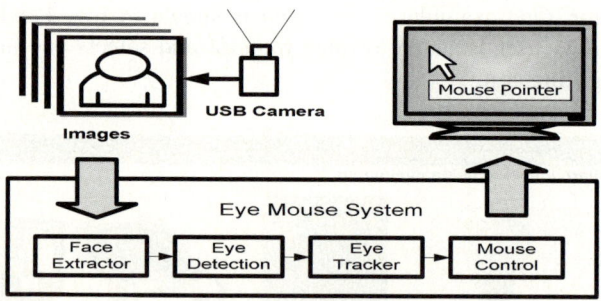

Fig. 2. The process to measure eye movement

3.1 Face Detector

A face region is easily detected thanks to the distinct color distributions of the faces from other objects. An input frame is divided into skin-color regions and non-skin-color regions using skin-color model that is represented as a 2D Gaussian model in the chromatic color space. Then, the results are filtered using connected-component analysis. The biggest CC to be located at the center in an image is considered as the facial region.

Fig. 3 shows the examples of face detection results on a video sequence. Fig. 3(a) shows the original frames and Fig. 3(b) shows the extracted facial regions after connected-component analysis.

(a)   (b)

Fig. 3. Face detection results. (a) original images, (b) extracted facial regions.

3.2 Eye Detector Using Neural Network

Our goal is to detect the eye in the facial region and track it through the whole sequence. Generally, the eye region has the following properties: 1) it has the high brightness contrast between white eye sclera and dark iris and pupil, along the texture of the eyelid; 2) it has place in the upper of the facial region. These properties help reduce the complexity of the problem, and facilitate the discrimination between the eye regions from the whole face. Here, we use a neural network as a texture classifier to automatically discriminate the pixels of the facial regions into eye regions and non-eye ones in various environments. The network scans all the pixels in the upper facial region so as to classify them as eye or non-eye. A diagram of our eye detection scheme is shown in Fig. 4.

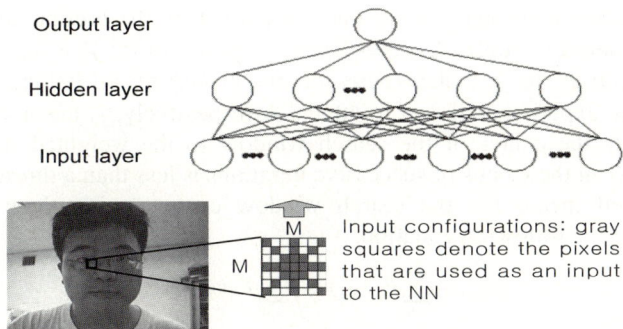

Fig. 4. A diagram of eye detection scheme

An input image is scanned by the MLP, which receive the gray values of a given pixel and its neighbors within a small window. Then, instead of using all pixels in the input window, a configuration for autoregressive features (gray squares in Fig. 4) is used. The MLP's output is in the range [0, 1], and represents the probability that the corresponding input pixel is a part of eye regions. If a pixel has a larger value than 0.5, it is considered as an eye pixel.

Although we use the bootstrap method to make the eye detection, the detection result from the MLP includes many false alarms. As such we still encounter difficulties in filtering out high-frequency and high-contrast non-eye regions. In this paper, we use the connected-component analysis result posterior to the texture classification. The generated components are filtered by their attributes, such as size, area, and location.

Fig. 5 shows the classification result using the neural network. Fig. 5(a) is an input frame and Fig. 5(b) is the extracted facial regions, and then the result of detected eye pixels is shown in Fig. 5(c). In Fig. 6(c), the pixels to be classified as eyes are marked as black. We can see that all of the eyes are labeled correctly, but there are some misclassified regions as eye. These misclassified regions are filtered by the heuristics, then the resulting image is shown in Fig. 5(c), where the extracted eye region is filled blue for the better viewing.

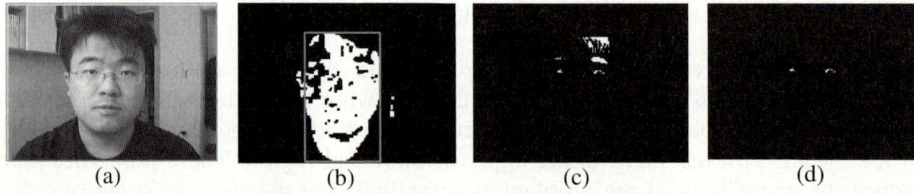

Fig. 5. An example of eye detection. (a) a original image, (b) the extracted facial regions (c) the classified image by the neural network, (d) the detected eye region after post-processing.

3.3 Mean-Shift Based Eye Tracker

To track the detected eyes, a mean shift algorithm is used, which finds the object by seeking the mode of the object score distribution [7]. In the present work, the color distribution of detected pupil, $P_m(g_s) = -(2\pi\sigma)^{-1/2}\exp\{(g_s-\mu)^2\sigma^{-1}\}$ is used as the object score distribution at site s, which represents the probability of belonging to an eye. The μ and σ are experimentally set to 40 and 4, respectively. A mean shift algorithm iteratively shifts the center of the search window to the weighted mean until the difference between the means of successive iterations is less than a threshold.

The weighted mean, i.e. the search window center at iteration $n+1$, m_{n+1} is computed using the following equation,

$$m_{n+1} = \sum_{s \in W} P_m(g_s) \cdot s \bigg/ \sum_{s \in W} P_m(g_s) \qquad (1)$$

The search window size for a mean shift algorithm is generally determined according to the object size, which is efficient when tracking an object with only a small motion. However, in many cases, objects have a large motion and low frame rate, which means the objects end up outside the search window. Therefore, a search window that is smaller than the object motion will fail to track the object. Accordingly, in this paper, the size of the search window of the mean shift algorithm is adaptively determined in direct proportion to the motion of the object as follows:

$$W_{width}^{(t)} = \max\left(\alpha\left|m_x^{(t-1)} - m_x^{(t-2)}\right| - B_{width}, 0\right) + \beta B_{width}$$
$$W_{height}^{(t)} = \max\left(\alpha\left|m_x^{(t-1)} - m_x^{(t-2)}\right| - B_{height}, 0\right) + \beta B_{height} \quad (t>2) \tag{2}$$

where α and β are constant and t is the frame index. This adaptation of the window size allows for accurate tracking of highly active objects.

Fig. 6 shows the results of the eye tracking, where the eyes are filled out white for the better viewing. As can be seen in Fig. 7, the eye regions are accurately tracking. Moreover, the proposed method can determine the gaze direction.

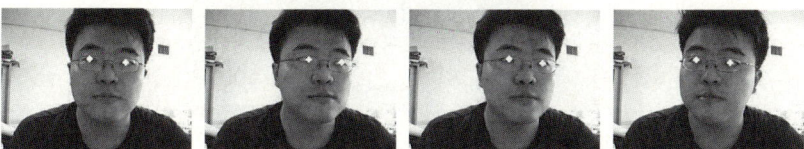

Fig. 6. An eye tracking result

3.4 Mouse Controller

The system determines the center of eyes in the first frame as the initial coordinates of mouse, and then computes it automatically in subsequent frames. If there is not a difference in the coordinates for one more second, our system will determine the point at which the user gazed on the display, and then execute the menu to locate that point. The control signal is sent to the surrounding system using the socket programming, then the user can control it with only eye movement.

In our system, to cover the eye movement at window resolution of 1024×768, the x and y coordinates of real eye movement are multiplied by 5 and 11, respectively.

4 Experimental Results

In this paper, we use this eye-tracking system as an interface to control the surrounding system such as audio, TV, light, phone, and so on. To assess the effectiveness of the proposed method, it was tested with twenty-peoples under the various environments.

Fig. 7 is the experimental setup. The PC camera, which is connected to the computer through the USB port, supplies 15 color images of size 320 x 240 per second. The computer is a 600-MHz with the Window XP operating system, and then it translates the user's gestures into the mouse movements by processing the images received from the PC camera.

The user accesses a computer by moving her or his eyes. The tracking results are shown in Fig. 8. The extracted eyes have been filled white for better viewing. The features are tracked throughout the 100 frames and not lost once.

Twenty people tested the interface using our eye tracking method. Table 1 presents the average time to be taken to control the menu, when using the standard mouse and our interface. The average time with the standard mouse was the more fast than one of our method. In the experiments, the difference is highly significant. The major reason in these comparisons is the waiting time to be required for our interface. In our system, we consider a menu to be clicked when the difference of the coordinates in between successive frames is not occurred one more second.

Fig. 7. Experimental setup

Fig. 8. Tracking Results in the uncluttered environments

Table 1. Timing comparison between standard mouse and our system

Method	Measure	Time/sec
Standard Mouse	Mean	0.44s
	Deviation	0.07s
Eye Mouse	Mean	1.67s
	Deviation	0.21s

Even if it is slower than the standard mouse, can process more than 30 frames/sec on a notebook without any additional hardware, for the 320×240 size input image, which is enough to apply to the real-time application. Moreover, the implemented system is not needed any additional hardware except a general PC and an inexpensive PC camera, the system is very efficient to realize many applications using real-time interactive information between users and computer systems.

Consequently, the experiment showed that it has a potential to be used as interface for handicapped people and generalized user interface in many applications.

5 Conclusions

In this paper, a computer interface was developed for the handicapped people, where input signals are given by eye movement of the handicapped people. Eye movement is detected by neural network (NN)-based texture classifier, which enables our system to be not obliged to constrained environment. To be robust the natural motion of a user, we first detect a user's face using skin-color information, and then detect her or his eyes using neural network (NN)-based texture classifier. After detection of eye movements, the tracking is performed using mean-shift algorithms.

We used this eye-tracking system as an interface to control the surrounding system such as audio, TV, light, phone, and so on. The experimental results showed that our method has the following advantages: 1) it is robust to the time-varying illumination and less sensitive to the specula reflection, 2) it works well on the input image of the low resolutions. However, it has some problems. Although it is fast enough to apply for user interface and other application, the proposed method is slower than the standard mouse. Thus, we are currently investing the speed-up of our method.

Acknowledgments. This research was supported by the Daegu University Research Grant, 2004.

References

1. Kaufman, A. E., Bandopadhay, A., S., Bernard, D. An Eye Tracking Computer User Interface. 1993. Proceedings., IEEE Symposium on Research Frontiers in Virtual Reality 25-26.
2. Liu, T., Zhu, S., 2005. Eyes Detection and Tracking based on Entropy in Particle Filter. International Conf. on Control and Automation 1002-1007.
3. Yoo, D., Chung, M. J., 2004. Eye-mouse under Large Head Movement for Human-Computer Interface. IEEE International Conf. on Robotics and Automation 237-242.
4. Betke, M., Gips, J., Fleming, P., 2002. The Camera Mouse: Visual Tracking of Body Features to Provide Computer Access for People with Severe Disabilities. IEEE Transactions on Neural Systems and Rehabilitation Engineering 10 (1) 1 – 10.
5. Takami, O., Morimoto, K., Ochiai, T., Ishimatsu, T. 1995. Computer Interface to Use Head and Eyeball Movement for Handicapped People. IEEE International Conference on Systems, Man and Cybernetics 1119-1123.
6. Lin, C., Huan, C., Chan, C., Yeh, M., Chiu, C. 2004. Design of a Computer Game using an Eye-tracking Device for Eye's Activity Rehabilitation. Optics and Lasers in Engineering 42 91-108.
7. Kim, K. I., Jung, K. 2003. Texture-based Approach for Text Detection in Images using Support Vector Machines and Continuously Adaptive Mean Shift Algorithm. IEEE Transactions on Pattern Analysis and Machine Intelligence 25 (12) 1631-1639.

Local Negative Correlation with Resampling*

Ricardo Ñanculef[1], Carlos Valle[1], Héctor Allende[1], and Claudio Moraga[2,3]

[1] Universidad Técnica Federico Santa María,
Departamento de Informática, CP 110-V Valparaíso, Chile
{jnancu, cvalle, hallende}@inf.utfsm.cl
[2] European Centre for Soft Computing 33600 Mieres, Asturias, Spain
[3] Dortmund University, 44221 Dortmund, Germany
claudio.moraga@udo.edu

Abstract. This paper deals with a learning algorithm which combines two well known methods to generate ensemble diversity - error negative correlation and resampling. In this algorithm, a set of learners iteratively and synchronously improve their state considering information about the performance of a fixed number of other learners in the ensemble, to generate a sort of local negative correlation. Resampling allows the base algorithm to control the impact of highly influential data points which in turns can improve its generalization error. The resulting algorithm can be viewed as a generalization of *bagging*, where each learner no longer is independent but can be locally coupled with other learners. We will demonstrate our technique on two real data sets using neural networks ensembles.

1 Introduction

Ensemble methods have emerged as an effective paradigm to approach the problem of learning from examples. The basic idea behind these methods is to train a set of simple predictors $S = \{f_0, f_1, \ldots, f_{n-1}\}$ obtained from some base space H and then build a final decision function F using an operator that combines the individual decisions.

It seems obvious that to get advantages from using a single learner it is necessary that the group exhibits a sort of heterogeneity or *diversity* that allows this to compensate individual errors and reach a better expected performance. Several diversity creation methods have been explored in the literature [4], including manipulation of the architecture of the learners, modification of the objective function each learner optimizes and sampling methods both on the training patterns and the training features. Recently, new advances have been made for explaining the advantages of using resampling. Using concepts of algorithmic stability [7], Rifkin et.al. [10] show that an α-stable regressor can become strongly α-stable by the use of bagging with appropriate sampling schemes. This

---

* This work was supported in part by Research Grant Fondecyt (Chile) 1040365 and 7050205, and in part by Research Grant DGIP-UTFSM (Chile). Partial support was also received from Research Grant BMBF (Germany) CHL 03-Z13.

means that averaging different regressors can improve significatively the generalization bounds of the base regressor. In [6] experimental evidence is presented to support the hypothesis that bagging stabilizes prediction by equalizing the influence of training examples. In many situations, highly influential points are outliers, and their down-weighting could help to get more robust predictions.

In this paper we deal with a learning algorithm which combines the two learning strategies indicated above: diversity and stability by means of resampling. We start by presenting an algorithm where a set of learners is trained iteratively to improve their state considering information about the performance of a fixed number of other learners in the ensemble. This algorithm encourages a sort of local negative correlation between the individual errors, to get a set of diverse predictors. Resampling allows this base algorithm to control the impact of highly influential data points which in turns can improve its generalization error. The resulting algorithm can be also explained as generalization of *bagging*, where each learner no longer is independent but locally coupled with other learners.

The remainder of this paper is organized as follows. In the next section we present an algorithm to locally generate diversity in a ensemble by means of error negative correlation. In section number 3, we explain the benefits of resampling and propose to modify the base algorithm introduced previously to control the influence of the training patterns. In section 4 we provide a set of experimental results on two real data sets to assess the introduced algorithm and compare this with two other algorithms. Conclusions and future work close this article.

2   Local Negative Correlation Learning (LNC)

One of the principles that allows to explain the success of various well-performed ensembles methods is diversity of its component learners. For regression estimation a theoretically motivated way to measure diversity is the so called *Ambiguity Decomposition* [3] of the quadratic loss of an ensemble F which is obtained as combination of a set of n predictors $f_0, f_2, \ldots, f_{n-1}$. Defining F as

$$F(x) = \sum_{i=0}^{n-1} w_i f_i(x) \qquad (1)$$

with $\sum_i w_i = 1$, it can be proved that

$$\bar{e} = (F - y)^2 = \sum_{i=0}^{n-1} w_i (y - f_i)^2 - \sum_{i=0}^{n-1} w_i (f_i - F)^2 \qquad (2)$$

This decomposition states that the error of the ensemble can be decomposed into two terms, where the first is the aggregation of the individual errors ($y - f_i$) and the second (called ambiguity) measures deviations of these individual predictions around the ensemble prediction. If the ambiguity is positive, the ensemble loss is guaranteed to be less than the averaged individual errors. Similar measures of diversity can be defined for pattern recognition problems using the conditional densities of each class [12].

Ambiguity decomposition suggests that individual learners should be trained considering information about their deviations around the ensemble. For example, in the *Negative Correlation Learning* algorithm (NC) described in [14] [9] and [3], the i-th learner is trained using the following objective function

$$e_i = (y - f_i)^2 - \lambda (f_i - F)^2 \qquad (3)$$

where the parameter λ weights the importance of the ambiguity component versus the individual performance. If the parameter $\lambda = 0$ each learner is trained independently. In [3] a theoretical argument is presented to choose λ according to

$$\lambda = 2 \cdot \gamma \cdot (1 - \frac{1}{n}) \qquad (4)$$

where n is the size of the ensemble and the value of $\gamma \in [0,1]$ is problem dependent.

Recently [8] we have proposed an algorithm to generate ensemble diversity using a set of locally coupled learners. Each learner f_i is related with a reduced and fixed subset of other learners V_i through the definition of a linear neighborhood function of order ν

$$\psi(i,j) = 1 \Leftrightarrow (i-j) \bmod n \leq \nu \text{ or } (j-i) \bmod n \leq \nu \qquad (5)$$

such that, the learner f_j belongs to the neighborhood V_i of f_i if and only if $\psi(i,j) = 1$. Geometrically, we dispose the learners on a ring, where two learners are neighbors if they are contiguous up to ν steps. The objective function for each learner is obtained noting that decomposition (2) can be alternatively stated as

$$(F - y)^2 = \sum_{i=0}^{n-1} w_i^2 (y - f_i)^2 + \sum_{i=0}^{n-1} \sum_{j \neq i} w_i w_j (f_i - y)(f_j - y) \qquad (6)$$

As in the ambiguity decomposition, the first term measures the individual performance of the estimators while the second measures the error correlation between the different predictors. From this decomposition it seems reasonable to train each learner $i = 0, \ldots, n-1$ with the training function

$$\tilde{e}_i = (y - f_i)^2 + \alpha \sum_{j \neq i} (f_i - y)(f_j - y) \qquad (7)$$

where as in NC, $\alpha > 0$ controls the importance of the group performance versus the individual performance. We can make this objective function local by restricting this to the neighborhood of the i-th learner

$$e_i^{local} = (y - f_i)^2 + \alpha \sum_{j \in V_i} (f_i - y)(f_j - y) \qquad (8)$$

It seems reasonable to choose α as

$$\alpha = \frac{\kappa}{2 \cdot \nu} \qquad (9)$$

because this allows to recover the global training (7) by linearly aggregating the local training functions (8). The interesting result is that we can demonstrate that synchronously training the set of learners with these local objective functions is independent of the neighborhood order ν. This means that a minimal degree of overlapping ($\nu = 2$) between the learners is enough to propagate the information about the performance of each learner by all the group. On the other hand it should be clear that this algorithm is much faster than a global algorithm like NC.

3 Introducing Resampling to LNC

Probably the most investigated method to generate diversity is the manipulation of the training data each member of the ensemble uses to learn. Different learners are provided with different training examples or different training features to learn different "aspects" about the same task. In this family of ensemble algorithms resampling methods have proved to be highly effective. One example is bagging [2] where each learner is provided with a set of patterns obtained randomly resampling the original set of examples and then trained independently of the other learners. Although very simple, this algorithm exhibit results in many cases superior to more elaborated algorithms.

Recent works are very clarifying about the benefits of resampling. In [10] it is shown that for well behaved loss functions[1], certain sampling schemes can provide generalization bounds with a rate of convergence of the same order as Tikhonov regularization [11]. The key observation is that an β-stable algorithm can become strongly β-stable with appropriate sampling schemes. Let S be a training sample and $S^{i,u}$ the same sample but with the i-th example replaced with an arbitrary new point u. An algorithm is said to be β-stable if

$$\forall S, \forall S^{i,u} \forall x \left| f_S(x) - f_{S^{i,u}(x)} \right| \leq \beta \tag{10}$$

where f_D is the function obtained training the algorithm with the sample D. An algorithm is said strongly β-stable if $\beta = O(1/l)$ where l is the size of the sample S.

Let us suppose that the original sample is divided in n disjoint subsets of size p to generate each one of the n members of the ensemble at equation 1. Then, it is easy to show that if the base learning algorithm is β-stable, the ensemble is strongly β-stable with $\beta_{bagg} = p\beta/l$. Similar results can be obtained for random resampling schemes if we can bound the probability that a point belongs to a given sample. In fact, using resampling with replacement as in standard bagging, the probability that a pattern appears in the resulting sample is exactly $(1-1/l)^l$ which converges to ~ 0.632 with $l \to \infty$.

The key fact in the previous analysis is that certain sampling schemes allow some points affect only a subset of learners in the ensemble. The importance of this property of well-performed sampling schemes is also remarked in [6] [5].

---
[1] The result is proved for σ-admissible loss functions [7].

In these works, empirical evidence is presented to show that bagging equalizes the influence of training points in the estimation procedure in way such that points highly influential (the so called leverage points) are down-weighted. Since in most situations leverage points are badly influential, bagging can improve generalization by making robust an unstable base learner. From this point of view, resampling has an effect similar to *robust M-estimators* where the influence of sample points is (globally) bounded using appropriate loss functions, for example Huber's robust loss or Tukey's bisquare loss.

Since in uniform resampling all the points in the sample have the same probability of being selected, it seems counterintuitive that bagging has the ability to selectively reduce the influence of leverage points. The explanation is in the nature of leverage points itself. Leverage points are usually isolated in the feature space while non-leverage points act in groups - which is consistent with the concepts of stability previously introduced. To remove the influence of a leverage point it is enough to eliminate this point from the sample but to remove the influence of a non-leverage point we must in general remove a group of observations. Now, the probability that a group of size k be completely ignored by bagging is $(1 - k/l)^l$ which decays exponentially with k. For $k = 2$ for example $(1 - k/l)^l \sim 0.14$ while $(1 - 1/l)^l \sim 0.37$.

In the previous section we have introduced an algorithm to locally generate diversity between a set of learners. However this algorithm not only does not prevent the potentially bad effect of a leverage point but propagates this effect through the whole ensemble. Since the algorithm encourages mutual cooperation, when a point induces a significant error in a single machine other machines will try to compensate this error. In other words, the algorithm has two potential sources of instability: the individual measure of performance - first term in equation (8) - and the group measure of performance - second term in (8).

We propose to modify the previously introduced algorithm in a way such that each learner works with a different set of training patterns obtained randomly resampling the original set of examples. Resampling allows to restrict the influence of leverage points to only a subset of learners in the ensemble while the training criterion (8) still encourages cooperation between learners. As depicted in figure 1, at each iteration each learner takes into account the performance of the group but respect to its own set of training patterns. Then, the influence of each training pattern is restricted to the learners whose training set contains the point.

As we have said, parameter λ controls the importance of the group performance relative to the individual performance. It should be noted that if $\lambda = 0$ we obtain bagging, an algorithm where the learners are trained independently without any information about the group performance. If $\lambda > 0$ this information is incorporated in the estimation process and we obtain an ensemble explicitly cooperative.

1: Let $S = \{(x_i, y_i); i = 1, \ldots, m\}$ be a set of training patterns.
2: Let f_i $i = 0, \ldots, n-1$ be a set of n learners and f_i^t the function implemented by the learner f_i at time $t = 0, \ldots, T$.
3: Let V_i be the neighborhood of f_i.
4: Generate n new samples S^i, $i = 1, \ldots, n$ sampling randomly with replacement the original set of examples S.
5: **for** $t = 1$ to T
6:     Make one epoch on the learner f_i with the learning function
$$e_i^t = (y - f_i)^2 + \lambda \sum_{j \in V_i} (f_i - y)\left(f_j^{t-1} - y\right)$$
and the set of examples S^i.
7: **end for**
8: Set the ensemble at time t to be $F(x) = 1/n \sum_{i=0}^{n-1} f_i(x)$

Fig. 1. LNC with Resampling (RLNC)

4 Experimental Results

In this section we present empirical results to evaluate the proposed approach in two well-known data sets namely *Boston Housing* and NO_2, available in [1] and [13] respectively. For comparison purposes, three algorithms will we evaluated: *Bagging*, *Negative Correlation* (NC) and the proposed one (RLNC).

The NC algorithm depends on the parameter γ of equation (equation 4). Similarly, RLNC depends on the parameter κ at equation (equation 9) which measures the importance of the overlapping between learners. In the following experiments we will empirically determine the best values of λ and κ for each data set. Since we have previously shown [8] that local learning rules (8) are practically insensitive to the value ν we will use the minimal value this parameter, i.e. $\nu = 2$ which gives a more efficient algorithm.

Additionally neural networks with five sigmoidal hidden units and trained with standard backpropagation were employed as base learners. For each experiment t-student confidence intervals will be reported with a significance of 0.02 obtained after 50 simulations. The estimation process is carried out with a 75% of the available observations and testing with the rest 25%.

Figure (2) shows confidence intervals for the *mean squared error* of the algorithms versus the number of learners in the ensemble; the error was computed in the training set and the testing set respectively. The circle-solid curve corresponds to bagging, square-dotted to NC and cross-dashed to the proposed algorithm (RLNC). For this data set, the best values of γ and κ were found at 0.5 and 0.95 respectively. It is interesting to note that for this task the performance is almost monotonically improved increasing κ between 0.0 and 1.0. Near 1.0 instabilities and divergence is observed.

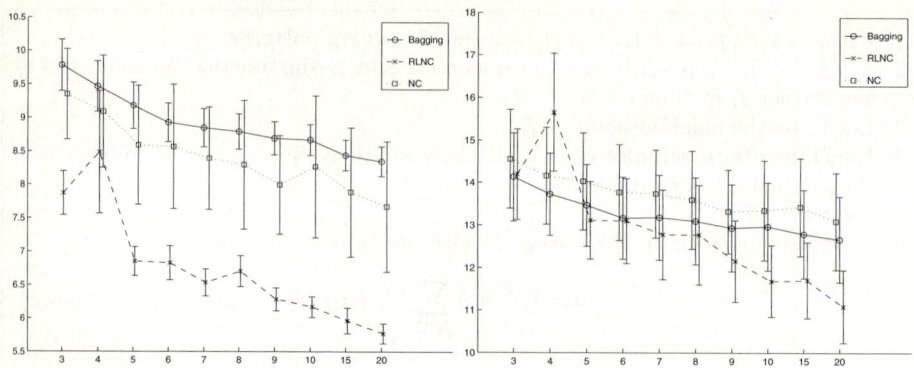

Fig. 2. MSE versus number of learners, corresponding to the (Boston) training set (at left) and testing (at right)

Figure (3) shows confidence intervals for the *mse* of the algorithms versus the number of learners in the ensemble. The circle-solid curve corresponds to bagging, square-dotted to NC and cross-dashed to RLNC.

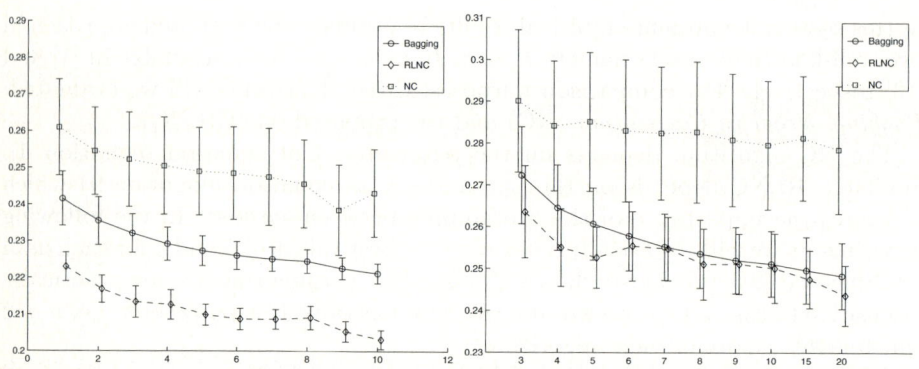

Fig. 3. MSE versus number of learners, corresponding to the (NO_2) training set (at left) and testing set (at right)

For this data set, the best values of γ and κ were found at 0.4 and 0.5 respectively.

5   Conclusions and Final Remarks

In this paper we have combined two main ideas in *ensemble learning*: diversity and stability generated using resampling. The resulting algorithm (RLNC) can be viewed as a generalization of bagging where the learners are locally coupled using a neighborhood function and trained to be explicitly cooperative.

Experiments with neural network ensembles, in two real data sets have demonstrated that this algorithm obtain a better performance than bagging, which only uses resampling and a better performance than negative correlation learning (NC) which only encourages diversity between the learners. Advantages of the proposed algorithm tend to be more significant when we increase the number of learners.

Experiments can also lead to conclude that, at least in the two considered problems, the effect of resampling is more relevant than the effect of the error negative correlation principle studied in several works [14] [9] and [3].

Future research has to study the benefits of local coupling using other resampling schemes such as adaptive boosting-like approaches and partitional (maybe competitive) ones.

References

1. C.L. Blake and C.J. Merz, *UCI repository of machine learning databases*, 1998.
2. L. Breiman, *Bagging predictors*, Machine Learning **24** (1996), no. 2, 123–140.
3. G. Brown, *Diversity in neural network ensembles*, Ph.D. thesis, School of Computer Science, University of Birmingham, 2003.
4. R. Harris G. Brown, J. Wyatt and X. Yao, *Diversity creation methods: A survey and categorisation*, Information Fusion Journal (Special issue on Diversity in Multiple Classifier Systems) **6** (2004), no. 1, 5–20.
5. Y. Grandvalet, *Bagging down-weights leverage points*, IJCNN, vol. IV, 2000, pp. 505–510.
6. _____, *Bagging equalizes influence*, Machine Learning **55** (2004), no. 3, 251–270.
7. O.Bousquet and A. Elisseeff, *Stability and generalization.*, Journal of Machine Learning Research **2** (2002), 499–526.
8. H. Allende R. Ñanculef, C. Valle and C. Moraga, *Ensemble learning with local diversity*, ICANN'06, To Appear 2006.
9. B. Rosen, *Ensemble learning using decorrelated neural networks*, Connection Science (Special Issue on Combining Artificial Neural Networks: Ensemble Approaches) **8** (1999), no. 3-4, 373–384.
10. R. Rifkin T. Poggio and S. Mukherjee, *Bagging regularizes*, Tech. Report 214/AI Memo 2002-003, MIT CBCL, 2002.
11. A. Tikhonov and V. Arsenin, *Solutions of ill-posed problems*, Winston, 1977.
12. K. Tumer and J. Ghosh, *Error correlation and error reduction in ensemble classifiers*, Connection Science **8** (1996), no. 3-4, 385–403.
13. P. Vlachos, *StatLib datasets archive*, 2005.
14. X. Yao Y. Lui, *Ensemble learning via negative correlation*, Neural Networks **12** (1999), no. 10, 1399–1404.

Convex Perceptrons

Daniel García, Ana González, and José R. Dorronsoro*

Dpto. de Ingeniería Informática and Instituto de Ingeniería del Conocimiento
Universidad Autónoma de Madrid,
28049 Madrid, Spain

Abstract. Statistical learning theory make large margins an important property of linear classifiers and Support Vector Machines were designed with this target in mind. However, it has been shown that large margins can also be obtained when much simpler kernel perceptrons are used together with ad–hoc updating rules, different in principle from Rosenblatt's rule. In this work we will numerically demonstrate that, rewritten in a convex update setting and using an appropriate updating vector selection procedure, Rosenblatt's rule does indeed provide maximum margins for kernel perceptrons, although with a convergence slower than that achieved by other more sophisticated methods, such as the Schlesinger–Kozinec (SK) algorithm.

1 Introduction

While Rosenblatt's perceptrons (pcps) were the first successful attempt at neural network learning and subsymbolic artificial intelligence, their linear nature resulted in a limited usefulness as a tool for classifier construction and they were superseded by the more flexible and powerful sigmoid multilayer percpetrons (MLP). Recently, however, linear classifiers have regained a wide interest when used jointly with kernel methods, as they may provide simple but powerful classfiers in very large dimension spaces, the best known example being Support Vector Machines (SVMs) [8,10]. Since statistical learning theory [10] places a great importance on achieving large margins for linear classifiers, SVM training explicitly seeks to maximize them. More precisely, assume we have a training sample $\mathcal{S} = \{(X_i, y_i) : i = 1, \ldots, N\}$, where $y_i = \pm 1$, and want to construct classifiers of the form $c(X) = W \cdot X + b$. The margin of such a linear classifier (W, b) is then

$$m(W, b) = \min \left\{ \frac{y_i(W \cdot X_i + b)}{\|W\|} : i = 1, \ldots, N \right\},$$

and we want an optimum (W^*, b^*) such that $m(W^*, b^*) \geq m(W, b)$ for any other classifier (W, b). It can be argued that, equivalently, one may seek [8] to solve the problem

$$(W^*, b^*) = \operatorname{argmin}_{(W,b)} \|W\|^2 \tag{1}$$

where the (W, b) must satisfy the constraints $y_i(W \cdot X_i + b) \geq 1$ for all sample points.

---

* With partial support of Spain's TIN 2004–07676.

SVMs have a well established theory and are the tool of choice in many classification problems. However, and although several simplified methods have been proposed [2,5], SVM training is relatively complex, as a quadratic programming has to be solved. On the other hand, pcps can be easily used in a kernel setting and their training is very fast. This has led many researchers to propose simpler, pcp–based methods for large margin linear classifier construction that somehow modify Rosenblatt's weight update rule in ways better suited to the large margin goal. Examples of this are the Relaxed Online Maximal Margin algorithm [4] and, particularly, the Schlesinger–Kozinec algorithm [1], which we briefly describe next in its 1–vector form.

We slightly change our notation by considering extended patterns $\tilde{X} = (X, 1)$ and weight vectors $\tilde{W} = (W, b)$. The constraints then become $y_i \tilde{W} \cdot \tilde{X}_i \geq 1$. We shall drop in what follows the $\tilde{\ }$ and write simply W and X for the extended weight and pattern vectors. Now, let us write $\tilde{\mathcal{S}}$ for the set $\tilde{\mathcal{S}} = \{y_i X_i : i = 1, \ldots, N\}$. We then have [1] the following characterization of the maximum margin vector W^*:

$$W^* = \arg\min\{\|W\| : W \in C(\tilde{\mathcal{S}})\} \qquad (2)$$

where $C(A)$ denotes the convex hull of a set A. This suggests to keep the successive weight updates W_t inside the $C(\tilde{\mathcal{S}})$ set. Moreover, it can be proved that $m^* = m(W^*) = \|W^*\|$, where $m(W)$ denotes the margin of W. As a consequence, for any other $W \in C(\mathcal{S})$ we have $m(W) \leq m(W^*) = \|W^*\| \leq \|W\|$. In particular, setting $g(W) = \|W\| - m(W)$, we have $0 = g(W^*) \leq g(W)$.

The Schlesinger–Kozinec (SK) algorithm uses g as a criterion function to stop pcp training when it becomes smaller than a specified value. It also performs pcp weight updates as

$$W_{t+1} = (1 - \lambda^*)W_t + \lambda^* y_{l(t)} X_{l(t)} \qquad (3)$$

where $l(t)$ is the index of the pattern $X_{l(t)}$ chosen at step t and

$$\lambda^* = \arg\min\nolimits_\lambda \{\|(1 - \lambda)W_t + \lambda X_{l(t)}\|\}.$$

If we start at a random $W_0 = X_{l_0}$, these updates guarantee that $W_{t+1} \in C(\tilde{\mathcal{S}})$ and also that $\|W_{t+1}\| \leq \|W_t\|$. There are several options to choose the pattern $X_{l(t)}$. In standard pcp training one would randomly choose an $l(t) = l$ such that $y_l W_t \cdot X_l < 0$ and stop the algorithm when no such X_l can be found. However, such a possibly too early stopping has to be avoided in margin maximization, and in the SK algorithm we choose at each iteration an index l such that

$$l = \arg\min\nolimits_i \{y_i W_t \cdot X_i\}, \qquad (4)$$

even if all patterns are correctly classified. As we shall argue in section 2, this choice makes the new margin at X_l larger that the previous one. In summary, the SK algorithm causes the $\|W_t\|$ to decrease while making the margin $m(W_t)$ likely to increase. This explains the speed at which it causes the difference $g(W) = \|W\| - m(W)$ tend to zero, that makes it competitive with more sophisticated state–of–the–art SVM methods [1].

At first sight, Rosenblatt's rule for standard pcp training seems quite far from the above considerations. However, it can be observed that if pattern selection is performed according to (4), the margins $m(W_t)$ of the succesive weights tend to increase. In this work we shall analyze this behavior, showing in section 2 that if we write Rosenblatt's standard weight updates as $W'_{t+1} = W'_t + y_{l(t)} X_{l(t)}$, the vectors $W_t = W'_t/t$ verify

$$W_{t+1} = \left(1 - \frac{1}{t}\right) W_t + \frac{1}{t} y_{l(t)} X_{l(t)} \qquad (5)$$

and therefore $W_t \in C(\tilde{S})$; we will call (5) the convex Rosenblatt rule and convex pcps the resulting linear classifiers. To select the updating vector, we can choose between update (4) to improve on the margin, or an alternative such as

$$l = l(t) = \arg \min_i \left\| \left(1 - \frac{1}{t}\right) W_t + \frac{1}{t} y_i X_i \right\| \qquad (6)$$

that we shall see that would imply $\|W_{t+1}\| \leq \|W_t\|$. In section 3 we shall numerically demonstrate that the weight norms $\|W_t\|$ will then decrease and, as consequence, large margins can be achieved with Rosenblatt's rule, although with a decrease rate of the $g(W)$ criterion slower than that achieved by the SK algorithm. Since linear separation usually cannot be achieved in original pattern space, we shall also show in section 2 how to set up the resulting procedures in a kernel setting, paying attention to complexity issues. In section 3 we shall experimentally compare the performance of the convex Rosenblatt's rule with respect to that of the SK algorithm, in terms not only of the margin achieved, but also of test set errors. The paper will end with a short discusion and pointers to futher work.

2 Convex Perceptron Training

Recall that we write Rosenblatt's standard weight update rule as $W'_t = W'_{t-1} + y_{l(t)} X_{l(t)}$, with $l = l(t)$ is the index of the pattern (X_l, y_l) that is used in the t-th update. Starting at an initial $W'_0 = X_{l_0}$, it follows that $W'_t = \sum_0^t y_{l(j)} X_{l(j)}$ and, therefore,

$$W_t = \frac{1}{t} W'_t = \frac{1}{t} \sum_0^t y_{l(j)} X_{l(j)} = \frac{1}{t} \left(\sum_0^{t-1} y_{l(j)} X_{l(j)} + y_{l(t)} X_{l(t)} \right)$$
$$= \frac{1}{t} \left(W'_{t-1} + y_{l(t)} X_{l(t)} \right) = \left(1 - \frac{1}{t}\right) W_{t-1} + \frac{1}{t} y_{l(t)} X_{l(t)}. \qquad (7)$$

As a consequence, $W_t \in C(\tilde{S})$ for all t. We turn next our attention to the updating pattern selection. To simplify the notation, we shall consider general updates

$$W_t = (1 - \lambda) W_{t-1} + \lambda y_l X_l = \mu W_{t-1} + \lambda y_l X_l. \qquad (8)$$

If we use (4) to choose the updating vector X_l, we have $y_l W_{t-1} \cdot X_l = m(W_{t-1}) \|W_{t-1}\|$ and the new margin of X_l after update (8) verifies

$$y_l W_t \cdot X_l = y_l ((1 - \lambda) W_{t-1} + y_l \lambda X_l) \cdot X_l = (1 - \lambda) y_l W_{t-1} \cdot X_l + \lambda \|X_l\|^2$$
$$= W_{t-1} \cdot X_l + \lambda \left(\|X_l\|^2 - W_{t-1} \cdot X_l \right),$$

Table 1. Evolution of weight norm and margin values for the SK and convex pcp algorithms over the Ripley data set

	SK		convex pcp	
Iter.	norm	margin	norm	margin
100	0.4474 ± 0.0000	-0.0104 ± 0.0018	0.4495± 0.0000	-0.0141 ± 0.0021
500	0.2302 ± 0.0013	0.1082 ± 0.0035	0.2330 ± 0.0013	0.1036 ± 0.0028
1000	0.2150 ± 0.0017	0.1745 ± 0.0026	0.2171 ± 0.0016	0.1563 ± 0.0023
5000	0.2122 ± 0.0017	0.2092 ± 0.0017	0.2120 ± 0.0017	0.2017 ± 0.0017
10000	0.2121 ± 0.0017	0.2103 ± 0.0017	0.2119 ± 0.0017	0.2069 ± 0.0018
50000	0.2119 ± 0.0017	0.2114 ± 0.0017	0.2118 ± 0.0017	0.2109 ± 0.0017

which will be larger that the previous margin $W_{t-1} \cdot X_l$ at X_l if $y_l W_{t-1} \cdot X_l < \|X_l\|^2$. This will certainly be the case in the first iterations, as linear separability may not have been achieved yet and the left side will be negative. Moreover, since $|y_l W_{t-1} \cdot X_l| \leq \|W_{t-1}\| \cdot \|X_l\|$ and the norms $\|W_t\|$ will decrease, the margin should also increase in later iterations, as then we should likely have $\|W_{t-1}\| \leq \|X_l\|$.

Alternatively, we can try to ensure that $\|W_t\| \leq \|W_{t-1}\|$. Observe that if $W' = \mu W + \lambda y_i X_i$

$$\delta = \|W\|^2 - \|W'\|^2 = (1-\mu^2)\|W\|^2 - \lambda^2\|X_i\|^2 - 2\lambda\mu y_i W \cdot X_i,$$

and to maximize δ and, hence, to obtain a largest norm decrease, we should select an X_l such that

$$l = \arg\min_i \{\lambda\|X_i\|^2 + 2\mu y_i W \cdot X_i\}. \tag{9}$$

Notice that if all X_i have the same norm, procedures (4) and (9) give the same updating vector.

As mentioned in the introduction, we have to consider kernel versions of pcps in order to achieve linear separability, for which we have to rewrite (7) in dual form [7]. More precisely, we shall assume $X = (\phi(x), 1) = \Phi(x)$ with x a low dimension pattern and ϕ a nonlinear transformation into a high dimensional space such that there is a kernel $k(x, z)$ that verifies $X \cdot Z = 1 + \phi(x) \cdot \phi(z) = 1 + k(x, z) = K(x, z)$. To write (7) in kernel form, we assume that

$$W_t = \sum_j \alpha_j^t y_j X_j = \sum_l \alpha_j^t y_j \Phi(x_j).$$

Then (7) becomes

$$W_t = \sum_j \alpha_j^t y_j X_j = \left(1 - \frac{1}{t}\right) W_{t-1} + \frac{1}{t} y_l X_l$$

$$= \left(1 - \frac{1}{t}\right) \sum_j \alpha_j^{t-1} y_j X_j + \frac{1}{t} y_l X_l. \tag{10}$$

which gives

$$\alpha_j^t = \left(1 - \frac{1}{t}\right) \alpha_j^{t-1} + \frac{1}{t} \delta_{j\,l}. \tag{11}$$

Table 2. Evolution of weight norm and margin values for the SK and convex pcp algorithms over the Pima data set

Iter.	SK		convex pcp	
	norm	margin	norm	margin
100	0.4474 ± 0.0012	-0.0116 ± 0.0007	0.4496 ± 0.0014	-0.0124 ± 0.0014
500	0.2479 ± 0.0013	0.1792 ± 0.0027	0.2512 ± 0.0013	0.1562 ± 0.0027
1000	0.2446 ± 0.0013	0.2311 ± 0.0016	0.2453 ± 0.0013	0.1970 ± 0.0022
5000	0.2438 ± 0.0014	0.2414 ± 0.0014	0.2437 ± 0.0014	0.2349 ± 0.0014
10000	0.2437 ± 0.0014	0.2425 ± 0.0014	0.2436 ± 0.0014	0.2394 ± 0.0014
50000	0.2436 ± 0.0014	0.2433 ± 0.0014	0.2436 ± 0.0014	0.2427 ± 0.0014

To speed up the vector selection procedure, we shall use vectors D^t such that $D_j^t = y_j W_t \cdot X_j$. Since $W_t \cdot X_j = (\mu W_{t-1} + \lambda y_l X_l) \cdot X_j$, it follows that

$$D_j^t = \mu D_j^{t-1} + \lambda y_l y_j K(x_l, x_j).$$

Then (4) becomes

$$l = l(t) = \arg\min_i \left\{ D_i^{t-1} \right\}.$$

while (9) becomes

$$l = l(t) = \arg\min_i \left\{ \lambda K(x_i, x_i) + 2\mu D_i^{t-1} \right\}.$$

It is clear that the choice of the vector X_l to be used at step t has a cost $O(N)$ (it does not require kernel evaluations), and the D_j^t updates have a cost of $O(N)$ kernel computations. Thus, the cost of a T iteration SK or convex pcp training becomes $O(T \times N)$ kernel computations, while memory requirements are just $O(N)$.

3 Numerical Experiments

In this section we shall contrast the performance of convex perceptrons with that of the SK algorithm over two datasets taken from the UCI problem database [9], the Pima Indians diabetes and the Wisconsin breast cancer, and also over a synthetic problem, the Ripley dataset [6]. We shall normalize the original patterns to componentwise 0 mean and 1 variance and use the gaussian kernel

$$k(x, y) = \exp\left(-\frac{\|x-y\|^2}{\sigma^2}\right);$$

with $\sigma = 0.5$ for the Ripley dataset and $\sigma = 50$ for the other two datasets. Notice that for this kernel $\|X_i\|$ is constant for all X_i, and the updating vector selection procedures (4) and (9) give the same updating pattern sequence. In order to guarantee linear separability for the training set, we shall use the standard trick of extending the projected patterns $X = \Phi(x)$ as

$$X_i' = \left(X_i, 0, \ldots, \frac{y_i}{2C}, \ldots, 0\right)$$

Table 3. Evolution of weight norm and margin values for the SK and convex pcp algorithms over the breast cancer data set

Iter.	SK		convex pcp	
	norm	margin	norm	margin
100	0.4569 ± 0.0012	0.0250 ± 0.0036	0.4588 ± 0.0011	0.0363 ± 0.0041
500	0.3125 ± 0.0047	0.2445 ± 0.0067	0.3150 ± 0.0047	0.2290 ± 0.0056
1000	0.3064 ± 0.0049	0.2934 ± 0.0051	0.3060 ± 0.0049	0.2686 ± 0.0056
5000	0.3059 ± 0.0049	0.3051 ± 0.0049	0.3059 ± 0.0003	0.2991 ± 0.0051
10000	0.3059 ± 0.0049	0.3056 ± 0.0050	0.3059 ± 0.0049	0.3025 ± 0.0050
50000	0.3059 ± 0.0049	0.3058 ± 0.0049	0.3059 ± 0.0049	0.3053 ± 0.0049

Table 4. Final test set errors for the three datasets: both methods achieve the same values

Dataset	SK accuracy	conv. pcp acc.
Ripley	0.9049 ± 0.0195	0.9049 ± 0.0195
Pima	0.7769 ± 0.0482	0.7769 ± 0.0482
Breast	0.9500 ± 0.0181	0.9500 ± 0.0181

which requires us to work with extended kernel

$$K'(x,z) = K(x,z) + \frac{1}{2C}\delta_{xz};$$

we shall use a common C value of 10.

The comparison criteria we shall discuss are final test set accuracy and final separating weight norm and margin values. Tables 1, 2 and 3 show evolution values for up to

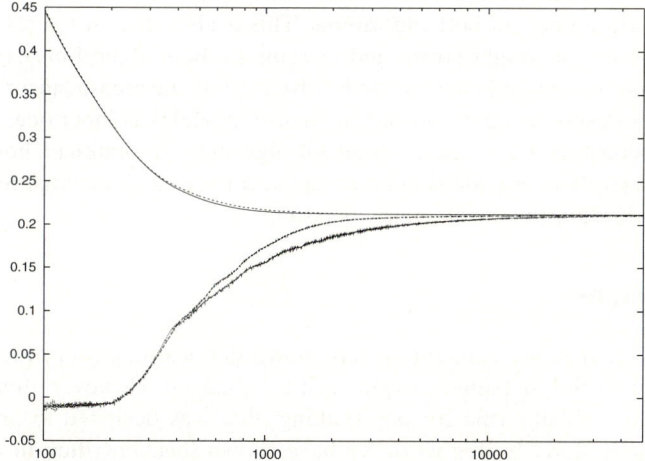

Fig. 1. Norm and margin evolution for convex pcp (outer curves) and the SL algorithm (inner curves) for the Ripley dataset

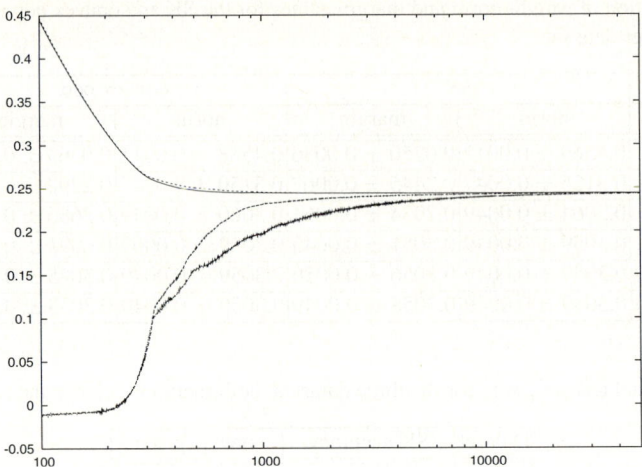

Fig. 2. Norm and margin evolution for convex pcp (outer curves) and the SL algorithm (inner curves) for the Pima dataset

50.000 iterarions of the weight norm and margin values for the Ripley, Pima and breast cancer datasets. They have been computed by 10–times cross validation, where the full data sets have been randomly split in 10 train–test pairs, with the training set taking 90% of all patterns. Values shown are the averages over the 10 runs. We point out that a standard way in machine learning to obtain larger average samples is to use a number of random starting vectors for each train–test set pair. However, this procedure tends to give nearly identical evolutions for both methods, and we have not followed it. Notice that while the weight norm decreases at about the same speed in both methods, margins go upward faster in the SK algorithm. Table 4 shows final test set accuracies; as it can be seen, they are similar for both algorithms. This is also clear in figures 1 and 2, that show the evolution of weight norms and margins for both algorithms over the Ripley and Pima dataset (a similar behavior can be observed on the breast cancer dataset). The outer curves correspond to the convex pcp algorithm while the inner ones, that demonstrate a faster convergence, to the 1-vector SK algorithm. In summary, both the convex pcp and SK algorithms provide similar test set accuracies and maximal margin values, although the SK algorithm convergence is faster.

4 Conclusions

Modern study of standard perceptrons has shown that learning procedures can be defined for them so that maximal margins can be obtained. However, this was not the objective of Rosenblatt's rule for pcp training, that was designed to provide a simple learning procedure. In this work we have shown that, rewritten in a convex update setting and using an appropriate updating vector selection procedure, Rosenblatt's rule does indeed provide maximal margins in a way much simpler than that offered by SVMs. In any case, the margin convergence speed is slower than that of specific methods such as the Schlesinger–Kozinec (SK) algorithm, that also works in a convex setting and uses the same updating vector selection procedure. The reason probably lies on the different update rule used by the SK algorithm, that seems to ensure a faster margin increase, something that may not happen for convex pcps (weight norms seem to decrease at about the same speed for both methods). How to achieve faster increasing margins for convex pcps and, more generally, how to increase convergence speed are questions currently under research.

References

1. V. Franc, V. Hlavac, An iterative algorithm learning the maximal margin classier, Pattern Recognition 36 (2003) 1985-1996.
2. T. Joachims, Making Large-Scale Support Vector Machine Learning Practical, in **Advances in Kernel methods**, B. Schölkopf, C. Burges, A. Smola (Eds.), MIT Press, 1999, 169-184.
3. S.S. Keerthi, S.K. Shevade, C. Bhattacharyya, K.R.K. Murthy, A fast iterative nearest point algorithm for support vector machine classier design, IEEE Trans. Neural Networks 11 (2000) 124-136.
4. Yi Li, P.M. Long, The relaxed online maximum margin algorithm, in **Advances in Neural Information Processing Systems**, Vol. 12, S.A. Solla, T.K. Leen, K.R. Muller (Eds.), MIT Press, 2000, 498–504.
5. J.C. Platt, Fast training of support vector machines using sequential minimal optimization, in **Advances in Kernel methods**, B. Schölkopf, C. Burges, A. Smola (Eds.), MIT Press, 1999, 185–208.
6. B.D. Ripley, Neural networks and related methods for classication, J. R. Statist. Soc. Ser. B 56 (1994) 409-456.
7. J. Shawe-Taylor, N. Cristianini, **Kernel Methods for Pattern Analysis**, Cambridge Univ. Press, 2004.
8. B. Schölkopf, A. J. Smola, **Learning with Kernels**, MIT Press, 2001.
9. UCI-benchmark repository of machine learning data sets, University of California Irvine, http://www.ics.uci.edu.
10. V.N. Vapnik, **The Nature of Statistical Learning Theory**, Springer, Berlin, 1995.

Hybridizing Cultural Algorithms and Local Search

Trung Thanh Nguyen and Xin Yao

The Centre of Excellence for Research in Computational Intelligence and Applications
(CERCIA), School of Computer Science,
University of Birmingham, B15 2TT, United Kingdom
{T.T.Nguyen, X.Yao}@cs.bham.ac.uk

Abstract. In this paper, we propose a new population-based framework for combining local search with global explorations to solve single-objective unconstrained numerical optimization problems. The idea is to use knowledge about local optima found during the search to a) locate promising regions in the search space and b) identify suitable step sizes to move from one optimum to others in each region. The search knowledge was maintained using a Cultural Algorithm-based structure, which is updated by behaviors of individuals and is used to actively guide the search. Some experiments have been carried out to evaluate the performance of the algorithm on well-known continuous problems. The test results show that the algorithm can get comparable or superior results to that of some current well-known unconstrained numerical optimization algorithms in certain classes of problems.

Keywords: Unconstrained Numerical Optimization, Cultural Algorithm, Iterated Local Search, Evolutionary Algorithm, Brent Direct Search.

1 Introduction

In this paper, we propose a new population-based framework for combining local search (Brent Direct Search [1, 2]) with global exploration to solve single-objective unconstrained numerical optimization problems. The idea is to use knowledge about local optima found during the search to a) locate promising regions in the search space and b) identify the suitable step size to move from one optimum to others in each region. The general properties of the framework could be described as follow:

- A population of individuals is maintained. Each individual is a mobile agent equipped with two heuristics: one internal local search to find local optima and one adaptive move length to get out of the current basin of attraction.
- To successfully get out of the current basin as well as to approach promising areas, individuals need to share their knowledge about the search space with others. They do that by contributing their knowledge to a shared source called *belief space*. It contains the following information: (1) positions of best optima; (2) successful move lengths that was used to find these optima; and (3) promising area to search.
- All individuals can contribute their knowledge to the belief space, but only the most successful one is used as exemplars for others to follow. Here are the details:
  - At the beginning of a generation, a *promising region* was created from positions of all best optima. Individuals are attracted to this region.

- Each individual then uses rank selection to adopt with modification a successful move length from the belief space.
  - During its lifetime, an individual can change its move length by selecting with modification a new one from the belief space.
- At each move, an individual can proceed along either a random direction or a direction heading to a selected optimum depending on a certain probability. To guarantee search diversity, the more the trials, the larger the probability is.

Some details described in the framework above have already been mentioned in existing literature. The idea of iteratively taking the local search and using mutation to escape from current basin of attraction has been mentioned by Martin et al. [3], and then was named Iterated Local Search (ILS) by Lourenco et al. [4]. The idea of maintaining exemplars from current solutions and using them to influence the next-generation population was also described by Reynolds [5] in his Cultural Algorithms (CA). Our new algorithm is a hybrid version of CA and ILS. We named it "CA-ILS".

Several new issues are proposed in CA-ILS. Firstly, different from current CA versions for continuous unconstrained optimization [6, 7], which concentrate on evolving solutions, we tried to evolve behaviors that individuals can use to find better solutions. These include lengths, directions and regions for the move. Because there are evidences that in reality phenotypic information may evolve much faster than genetic evolution [8], or even dominate it [9, 10], it might be interesting to evolve only this information to investigate the impact of cultural evolution on optimization.

Secondly, while existing versions of CA perform the search in all feasible solutions S [5-7, 11-13, 16-17], CA-ILS takes the search in a sub-set of optima S^* only. When optima are not randomly distributed, but form a specific pattern, it may make senses to detect that pattern using information from found local optima. Several researches points out that such patterns exist in real-world continuous problems [14, 15].

We have carried out some empirical experiments on well-known multi-modal test problems to evaluate the strength and weakness of CA-ILS. The test results show that CA-ILS could get comparable performances to that of some current state-of-the-art algorithms in at least some classes of multimodal functions. We expect that the performance could be improved further when CA-ILS's parameters are tuned.

The rest of this paper is organized as follows: Section 2 provides a detail implementation of CA-ILS, section 3 describes experiments on test functions and section 4 concludes with some discussions and future research directions.

2   CA-ILS – Implementation

Definition 1 (Population and individuals)
We define a population P of μ individuals, in which each individual $X \in P$, $X = <x, x', \Delta, \hat{u}, l(x)>$, is an entity moving around the space during its lifetime, where:

x – current position - a real vector represent individual X's current position
x' – previous position - a real vector represents X's previous position
Δ – move length – the step size that the individual takes to jump from one basin to others. This may change during individual's lifetime

$\hat{u}$ – direction – unit vector representing X's moving direction
$l(x)$ - the internal local search method that X uses to find local optima

Definition 2 (Belief space)
Reynolds and Sverdlik [16] proposed the concept of *belief* space as a kind of "problem-solving" knowledge derived from "behaviours" of individuals and is used to actively constrain the traits acquired in future populations. In CA-ILS, we use the belief space to maintain behaviors (move lengths, directions) leading to best solutions.

A belief space in CA-ILS can be described by the tuple <S, N, T> as follows:

Definition 2.1 (Situational knowledge)
S denotes the *situational knowledge* [17] – a set of exemplary behaviours for others to follow. In CA-ILS, S corresponds to a set of k triples <x_j, f_j, δ_j>, $j=1,...,k$, where x_j, f_j are the *co-ordinations* and *fitness score* of the jth optimum in S, respectively, and δ_j is the *move length* used by an individual to find that optimum.

Definition 2.2 (Normative knowledge)
N denotes the *normative knowledge* - acceptable ranges limiting individuals' behaviors. In CA-ILS, N is represented as the pair <N^{bnd}, N^{ml}>, where:

- N^{bnd} is a *promising region boundary* containing positions of all optima in S:
  $N^{bnd} = <l, u>$, where l, u are two n-component real vectors; $l_i = \min[x_i(j)]$, $u_i = \max[x_i(j)]$, $j =1, ..k$, $i = 1, ..n$, where $x_i(j)$ is the i-th coordination of the j-th optima in S, and n is the *number of variables* in the objective function.
- N^{ml} is the *move length range* bounded by the smallest (l) and largest (u) acceptable move lengths from the situational knowledge S.
  $N^{ml} = <l, u>$, where $l = \min(\delta_j)$, $u = \max(\delta_j)$, $\forall$ move length $\delta_j \in S$, $j=1, ..., k$.

Definition 2.3 (Global temperature)
T denotes a *temperature* parameter, inspired from Simulated Annealing [18]. The higher T is, the more the probability p that individuals should not take oriented moves to known good optima but random ones, where $p = \exp(-1/T)$. T is gradually reduced after each move. Its reduction is controlled by the *rate* β ($0 < \beta < 1$): $T_t = T_{t-1} \cdot \beta$.

CA-ILS - main procedures
1. *Initialize*: Initialize the population and all necessary parameters.
2. *SearchForOptima*: Each individual invokes the following routines η times:
   2.1. *Local search*: Take a local search from individual's current position to find the optimum
   2.2. *Choose direction*: Modify its current strategy and direction basing on the *belief space*.
   2.3. *Global Search*: Take a global move to jump out of the current basin
3. *Adjust*: Search results and strategies found in step 2 are used to adjust the *belief space*:
   3.1. *Select exemplar*: Retain top ρ percent of best optima as exemplars for others to follow
   3.2. *Select move length*: Move lengths leading to these best optima are also selected
   3.3. *SetPromisingRegion*: Use these optima to form a promising region to attract individuals
4. *Influence*: The adjusted belief space is used to influence a new generation
   4.1. *InfluencePosition*: Move new individuals to the promising region.
   4.2. *InfluenceMoveLength*: Individuals use rank selection to adopt with modification a move length from the belief space
5. If the search criteria are not satisfied, go to step 2.

Initialize
1. *Initialize the population*: At initial, each individual $X \in P$ is initiated as follow:
   (a) The current position x of X was distributed randomly in the space.
   (b) X's move length $\Delta = (\sqrt{n}/\tau) \cdot \min[\text{size}(I_i)]$, where τ is set by users; size(I_i) is the *size* of the interval I for the ith variable, $i = 1, ..., n$
   (c) X is provided with a random initial direction.
2. *Initialize the belief space*
   (a) $S = \{\emptyset\}$,
   (b) $N^{\text{bnd}} = <\boldsymbol{0}, \boldsymbol{u}>$, where $\boldsymbol{u}$ are a n-component real vector, $u_i = \text{size}(I_i)$, $i = 1, ..., n$; $N^{\text{ml}} = <0, \min[\text{size}(I_i)]/2>$, $i = 1, ..., n$.
   (c) Initialize the global temperature T
   (d) Initialize η - the *maximum moves* for each individual per generation

SearchForOptima
1. Set the *iteration counter* $m = 1$
2. For each individual X of the population P, perform the following steps:
2.1. Local search
   a. Invoke the local search algorithm to get to the nearest optimum x^*,
   b. If X did not escape from the current basin, randomly select from S a larger move length δ as exemplar for its move length Δ :

   Let $\Delta_0 = \Delta$; then set $\Delta = \delta + N(0,1) \bullet \max(|\delta - l|, |u - \delta|)$, (1)

   where $\delta \in S$ such that $\delta < \Delta_0$, l and u are bounds of N^{ml}, and $N(0,1)$ denotes a normally distributed random variable.
   c. Update information to the belief space: If X has found a new optimum x^* which has better fitness score than at least one optimum in S then
   - set the distance from the previous optimum x' found by X to x^* as X's move length Δ: $\Delta = \sqrt{\sum_{1}^{n}(x'_j - x^*_j)^2}$, n - number of variables
   - record x^*, its fitness score $f(x^*)$ and X's move length Δ to the situational knowledge S. $S \leftarrow (x^*, f(x^*), \Delta)$
2.2. Choose a moving direction for the global move of X:
   a. Check $p = \exp(-1/T)$ to determine X's direction: If $U(0,1) > p$, where $U(0,1)$ is a uniform distribution variable, then the direction is random.
   b. If X should move along a random direction, randomize its unit vector $\hat{\boldsymbol{u}}$:
   c. If X should take a directed move toward an already-known optimum:
   - Select an optimum with position x^d from S using rank selection,
   - Set the direction vector from x^* to x^d as the unit vector $\hat{\boldsymbol{u}}$ for X
2.3. Global search: Take a global jump to move out of the current basin using the acquired move length Δ and direction $\hat{\boldsymbol{u}}$: $x_i = x_i + \Delta \cdot \hat{u}_i$, $i = 1, ..., n$.
2.4. Decrease T: $T = T \cdot \beta$, where β is the reduction rate.
3. $m = m + 1$. If stopping criteria is satisfied, stop. If $m < \eta$, go to step 2.

Adjust
After each generation, results found are used to adjust the *belief space* as follows:
   1. *Adjust S:* Retain only a top ρ percent of optima based on their fitness scores.

2. *Adjust N^{bnd}* : $N^{bnd} = <l, u>$, with $l_i = \min[x_i(j)]$, $u_i = \max[x_i(j)]$, $j =1, ...,k$; $i=1, .., n$ where $x_i(j)$ is the i-th coordination of the j-th optima in S.
3. *Adjust N^{ml}* : $N^{ml} = <l, u>$, with $l = \min(\delta_i)$, $u = \max(\delta_i)$, $\forall\ \delta_i \in S$, i=1, ..., n.

Influence

The new belief space is used to influence behaviors of the new generation:
1. *Influence Position*:
   1.1 Individuals outside the *promising region* move to random places within this.
   1.2 Individuals inside the promising region have their places unchanged.
2. *Influence Move length*: Move length Δ of X is influenced from an exemplar $\delta \in S$ as follow: $\Delta = |\delta + N(0,1) \bullet \max(|\delta - l|, |u - \delta|)|$, where l, u are bounds of N^{ml}.

   In addition, in some situations we may want Δ to not be larger than $1/s$ minimum size of the promising region. Otherwise, s should be set as zero.

3 Experiments

We took three different types of experiments. First, we compared the performance of CA-ILS with that of two well-known CA algorithms specialized for unconstrained optimization - CAEP [6] and FCAEP [7] - in six multi-modal functions (Fig. 1 - 3) described in [6, 7]. Among many versions of these two algorithms, only the best for each problem are used to compare with CA-ILS. Our purpose is to evaluate the efficiency of applying the new issues mentioned in *section 1* to CA.

Second, we evaluated the performance of CA-ILS in nine multi-modal functions described by Yao and Liu [19] and compared it with the classics FEP algorithm to find out in which condition CA-ILS work well. Among these functions, six (F8 – F13) are hard functions with many local minima in 30 dimensions and the three left (F21 – F23) are special functions that are usually hard to solve for algorithm combined of local and global search [19].

Finally, we took a comparison between CA-ILS and some of the latest developed algorithms - 11 algorithms selected for publishing in CEC'05 special session on Real-Parameter Optimization [20]. The purpose of this experiment is to compare CA-ILS's performance with that of most recent advances in the field. At the time of writing this paper we have made comparisons on only first three multi-modal hard problems (F6 – F8) provided in [20]. Other comparisons will be published in the near future.

For a fair comparison, we use the same configurations for all test cases in each type of experiments (**Table 1**). The main measures for the first experiment are *success rate* and *numbers of function evaluations* needed to reach minimum values , as described in [6] and [7]. The main measures for the second experiment are the *mean best* (MB), as described in [19], and the main measures for the last experiment are the average of *ranks* that each algorithm got in all three considered functions and also their *averaged success rate*. Detail performance of each algorithm in the top eleven algorithms of CEC05's special session can be found in [21], and detail performance of CA-ILS for F6 – F8 can be found in [22].

Because the nature of CA-ILS is to search in the space of optima, we interested in testing only functions that have more than 10 optima in all experiments.

In experiment 1, **Fig. 2** and **Fig. 3** show that CA-ILS required fewer averaged function-evaluations than that required by CAEP and FCAEP to find global optima in most of the given problems, except the Ackley. In experiment 2, as can be seen in **Table 2** CA-ILS performed better than FEP in six out of 9 test functions. In the last experiment with three given problems tested in 10 and 30 dimensions, CA-ILS was ranked third and fourth, respectively, in comparing with 11 top algorithms (**Table 3**).

However, CA-ILS did not perform so well in some problems and in some others it did not become superior to the compared algorithms. In experiment 1, CA-ILS did not 100% succeed in the Foxholes and Griewank problems. It stuck early at some local optima and consequently did not find the global optima. The reason for this phenomenon is the low value of the exemplary percentage ρ (default is 30%). When we increased ρ to a certain value (35% for Foxholes and 98% for Griewank), CA-ILS succeeded 100% and outperformed CAEP/FCAEP. The same thing happened in experiment 2 while we tested CA-ILS on function F8. F8 was reported as having a fake global optimum and that might cause CA-ILS to improperly converge.

Another problem that CA-ILS encountered during the test is that sometimes the Brent Direct local search needed to perform a large number of function evaluations. This prolonged operation reduced the number of global explorations, hence reduced algorithm's performance. As a result, when CA-ILS was used to solve such problems as with many optima as Rastrigin, Ackley and their variations in high dimensions, it may need a large number of evaluations and become less effective than some other algorithms. These shortcomings suggest that further investigations on how to effectively use the internal local searches should be taken in future research.

4 Conclusions

CA-ILS proved to have comparable or superior performance to that of some current well-known algorithms in at least some classes of multimodal functions.

Further studies may be needed to investigate why CA-ILS work well in some of the given problems, but one reason might be that it can detect problems' structural patterns. Some of the tested problems have a big valley structure, in which good optima clustered around the global optimum. As expected the algorithm can quickly find the valley and heading to the good regions. These findings also support the mentioned issue of searching in the space of optima S^* instead of the whole space S.

Another reason for the success of CA-ILS may be that it can adaptively change the global move lengths and move directions to quickly find the next better optima. This success shows that the evolvement of individuals' behaviors actually have positive effects on improving search performance in certain situations.

There are many related research topics may be pursued in the future to improve and further evaluate the algorithm. One of these is to investigate the impact of decomposing the search space to better identify promising regions. Another interesting issue is about how to maintain diversity for the search process. Another one is about when to apply local searches and how to avoid optima recycling.

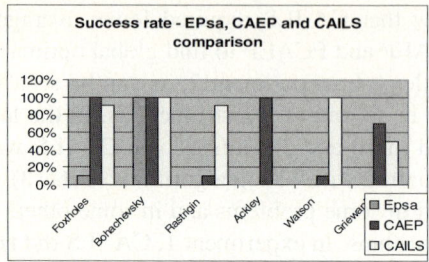

Fig. 1. Success ratio (experiment 1)

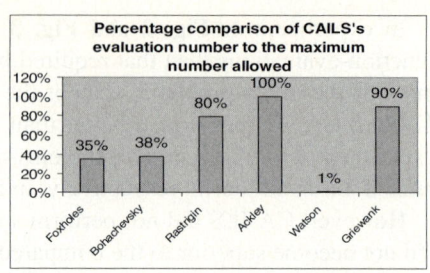

Fig. 2. Percent of evaluations that CAILS needed, compared to that of CAEP (exp. 1)

Table 1. Parameter settings of CA-ILS

Prm	References	Value
β	Definition 2.3	0.838
μ	Definition 1	3
η	proc. Initialize	10^*; $5^{**,***}$
ρ	proc. Adjust	30%
τ	proc. Initialize	0.5/0.1/0.02
T	Definition 2.3	100
t	formula (6.10) in [4]	1.0e-2
s	proc. Influence	$2^{*,**}$; 0^{***}

* experiment 1: compare with CAEP & FCAEP
** experiment 2: compare with FEP
*** exp. 3: compare with top algorithms from CEC05

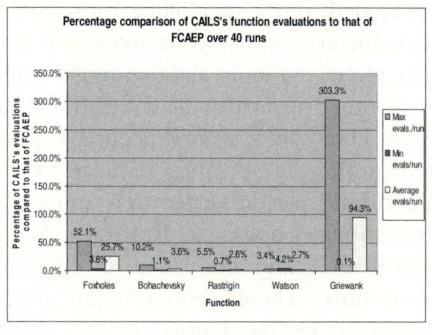

Fig. 3. Percent of evaluations that CAILS needed, compared to that of FCAEP (exp. 1)

Table 2. CA-ILS vs FEP (exp. 2)

	CA-ILS		FEP	
f	MB	SD	MB	SD
8	-10129.2	538.0	**-12554.5**	52.6
9	7.8E+00	2.4E+00	**4.6E-02**	1.2E-02
10	**2.4E-03**	6.5E-04	1.8E-02	2.1E-03
11	**1.8E-09**	1.7E-09	1.6E-02	2.2E-02
12	3.0E-05	6.4E-05	**9.2E-06**	3.6E-06
13	**3.2E-07**	3.5E-07	1.6E-04	7.3E-05
21	**-9.9E+00**	1.3E+00	-5.5E+00	1.6E+00
22	**-9.6E+00**	1.9E+00	-5.5E+00	2.1E+00
23	**-1.0E+01**	1.3E+00	-6.6E+00	3.1E+00

Table 3. CA-ILS vs CEC'05 algos (exp. 3)

10 dimensions			30 dimensions		
Algorithms	Rank	%	Algorithms	Rank	%
G-CMA-ES	1.7	67	L-CMA-ES	1.7	67
L-CMA-ES	1.7	67	G-CMA-ES	2.0	67
CA-ILS	1.7	48	BLX-GL50	4.0	67
L-SaDE	3.3	41	**CA-ILS**	4.3	47
DMS-L-PSO	4.3	39	K-PCX	5.7	32
BLX-GL50	5.7	45	DMS-L-PSO	6.7	64
K-PCX	6.7	29	EDA	7.0	33
DE	8.3	35	DE	7.0	29
EDA	8.7	31	SPC-PNX	8.7	23
BLX-MA	9.7	0	BLX-MA	9.0	0
CoEVO	10.0	0	L-SaDE	9.3	27
SPC-PNX	10.3	1	CoEVO	9.3	15

We also interest in applying different strategies, both globally and locally, in the algorithm. Although the current framework has only single available type of local search, its flexibility allows us to mix and adaptively choose different search algorithms in both local and global levels.

Acknowledgements

This research was supported by Vietnamese Overseas Scholarship Program, coded 322, and partly by School of Computer Science, University of Birmingham. The authors are grateful to colleagues from CERCIA and other institutions for their fruitful discussions and to the anonymous reviewers for their useful comments. The first author is grateful to Truyen T. Tran for his introduction to ILS, and to Hang T. Nguyen for her proof reading.

References

1. Brent, R., P. Algorithms for Minimization without Derivatives, Prentice-Hall, NJ (1973).
2. Gegenfurtner, K. R. PRAXIS: Brent's algorithm for function minimization. Behavior Research Methods, Instrument, & Computers. 24(4) (1992) 560 – 564.
3. Martin, O., Otto, S. W. and Felten, E. W. Large-step Markov chains for the traveling salesman problem. Complex Systems. 5(3) (1991) 299--326.
4. Lourenco, H. R. Martin, O. and Stuetzle. T. A beginner's introduction to Iterated Local Search. In Proceedings of the 4th Metaheuristics International Conference , v1 (2001) 1-6.
5. Reynolds, R. G. An introduction to cultural algorithms. In Sebald, A.V., Fogel, L.J. (eds.): Proceedings of the 3rd Annual Conf. Evolutionary Programming, (1994) 131-139.
6. Reynolds, R.G. and Chung, C.J. Knowledge-based self-adaptation in evolutionary programming using cultural algorithm. In Proc. of the International Conference on Evolutionary Computation (1997) 71-76.
7. Reynolds, R. G. and Zhu, S. Knowledge-based function optimization using fuzzy cultural algorithms with evolutionary programming. IEEE Transactions on Systems, Man, and Cybernetics, Part B, *31*(1) (2001) 1-18.
8. Lumsden, C. J. and Wilson, E. O. *Genes, Mind and Culture*. Harvard University Press, Cambridge, MA (1981).
9. Stebbins, G. L. Darwin to DNA: molecules to humanity. W. H. Freeman & Co. (1982).
10. Ayala, F., Biology precedes, culture transcends: an evolutionist's view of human nature. Zygon, 33, (1998) 507-523.
11. Ostrowski, D., Tassier, T., Everson, M., and Reynolds, R. Using Cultural Algorithms to Evolve Strategies in Agent-Based Models. In Proceedings of World Congress on Computational Intelligence, (2002) 741 - 746.
12. Becerra, R., L., and Coello Coello, C., A. Optimization with constraints using a cultured differential evolution approach. In Proceedings of the GECCO Conference, (2005) 27– 34.
13. Reynolds, R. G., and Peng, B. Knowledge Learning and Social Swarms in Cultural Algorithms. Journal of Mathematical Sociology, London, Routledge, Vol. 29 (2005) 1-18.
14. Wales, D. J., and Scheraga, H. A. Global optimization of clusters, crystals and biomolecules. *Science*, 285 (1999) 1368–1372.
15. Doye, J. P. K. Physical perspectives on the global optimization of atomic clusters. In Pinter, J. D. (ed.) Global Optimization: Scientific and Engineering Case Studies, Springer, (2006).
16. Reynolds, R. G., and Sverdlik, W. Problem Solving Using Cultural Algorithms. In Proceedings of IEEE World Congress on Computational Intelligence, 2 (1994) 645 - 650.
17. Saleem, S., and Reynolds, R. G. Cultural Algorithms in Dynamic Environments. In Proceedings of the Congress on Evolutionary Computation, Vol. 2 (2000) 1513-1520.

18. Kirkpatrick, S., Gelatt, C. D., and Vecchi, M. P. . Optimization by Simulated Annealing. Science, 220, (1983) 671-680.
19. Yao, X. and Liu, X. Fast evolutionary programming. In *Proceedings of the Fifth Annual Conference on Evolutionary Programming (EP'96)*, MIT Press, CA. (1996). 451-460.
20. Suganthan, P. N.; Hansen, N.; Liang, J. J.; Deb, K.; Chen, Y.-P.; Auger, A. and Tiwari, S. Problem definitions and evaluation criteria for the CEC 2005 special session on real-parameter optimization, TR, Nanyang Technology University, Singapore(2005). [Online]. http://www.ntu.edu.sg/home/epnsugan/index_files/CEC-05/Tech-Report-May-30-05.pdf
21. Hansen, N. Compilation of Results on the 2005 CEC Benchmark Function Set. (2006) [Online]. http://www.ntu.edu.sg/home/epnsugan/index_files/CEC-05/compareresults.pdf
22. Nguyen, T. T., Compare CA-ILS with 11 top algorithms (in CEC'05, special session on Real-Parameter Optimization) in functions F6, F7, and F8 in CEC'05 test suites. (2006). [Online]. Available at http://www.cs.bham.ac.uk/~txn/Papers/CA-ILSvsCEC05_F6-F8.pdf.

ICA and Genetic Algorithms for Blind Signal and Image Deconvolution and Deblurring

Hujun Yin and Israr Hussain

School of Electrical and Electronic Engineering
The University of Manchester
Manchester, M60 1QD, UK
`h.yin@manchester.ac.uk, i.hussain@postgrad.manchester.ac.uk`

Abstract. Signals and images often suffer from blurring or point spreading with unknown filter or point spread function. Most existing blind deconvolution and deblurring methods require good knowledge about both the signal and the filter and the performance depends on the amount of prior information regarding the blurring function and signal. Often an iterative procedure is required for estimating the blurring function such as the Richardson-Lucy method and is computational complex and expensive and sometime unstable. In this paper a blind signal deconvolution and deblurring method is proposed based on an ICA measure as well as a simple genetic algorithm. The method is simple and does not require any priori knowledge regarding the signal and the blurring function. Experimental results are presented and compared with some existing methods.

1 Introduction

A long-standing problem in image restoration is to reconstruct from a blurred and/or noisy image with as little as possible *a priori* knowledge of the original image, blurring function and the nature of added noise. The blurring degradation may be due to misfocus, motion or atmospheric turbulence. The resultant image should be as close to the original image as possible. Some related past efforts can be found in [1,6,7]. Here the motivation is to come up an effective and efficient method to perform blind deblurring.

The degraded system can be represented by a general block diagram shown in Fig.1. Most blurring models rely on a standard model of a shift invariant kernel and additive noise, which mathematically can be represented as,

$$x(n_1,n_2) = f(n_1,n_2) \otimes b(n_1,n_2) + \eta(n_1,n_2) \qquad (1)$$

where $\otimes$ is the convolution operator. The degraded image $x(n_1,n_2)$ is the result of convoluting the original image $f(n_1,n_2)$ with a point spread function (PSF) $b(n_1,n_2)$ and then adding noise $\eta(n_1,n_2)$.

Various techniques have been applied to recover the actual image. Traditional approaches like median-based approaches are inadequate and limited. The ideal approach to deblurring is to directly inverse the PSF that degrades the image (same is true with the presence of noise). For the case when there is no or little noise, the direct

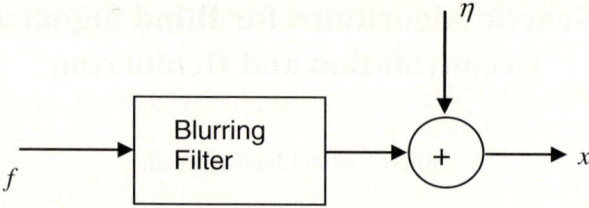

Fig. 1. Blurring model. x is the corrupted or observed image, f is the original image and η is added noise.

inverse filter can be done easily in spectral (frequency) domain, where the convolution process becomes multiplication,

$$F(\omega_1,\omega_2) = \frac{X(\omega_1,\omega_2)}{B(\omega_1,\omega_2)} \tag{2}$$

In most cases the PSF is not available. However, there are certain situations in which one may make certain valid assumption on the PSF or at least some properties. For example, if the blurring in the image is due to linear movement of the scene or camera during exposure, the PSF is like a sinc function, as shown in Fig. 2 (a). So the most straightforward approach is to recover the image through deconvolution with the inverse filtering. Another instance in which one may estimate the PSF to some degree is when there is a lens or other circular aperture causing the blur due to misfocus. In this case, the frequency response of the PSF takes on the form as shown in Fig. 2 (b) Although inverse filtering method is very simple in principle, but finding the correct values of the corresponding PSF is never an easy task in practical cases.

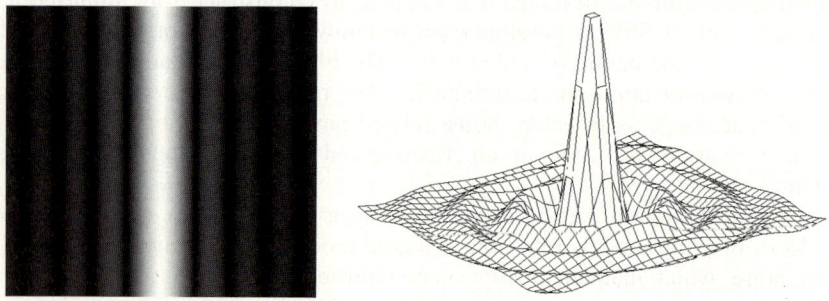

Fig. 2. PSF frequency response for (a) linear motion, (b) lens misfocus

In blind deconvolution, a convoluted version of x is obtained without knowing the signal f and deconvolution kernel h [7-9]. The problem is to find a separating filter h so that $f = h \otimes x$. The equalizer h can be assumed to be a FIR filter of sufficient length, so that the truncation effects can be ignored. A special case of blind deconvolution that is especially interesting in our context is the case where it is assumed that the values of the signal f at two different points of time are statistically independent. Under certain assumptions, this problem can be solved by simply whitening the signal x. However, to solve the problem in full generality, one must assume that the signal f is non-Gaussian, and use higher-order information [5,10]. Thus the techniques used for solving this special case of the problem are very similar to the techniques used in other higher-order methods.

2 Richardson–Lucy Method

The main disadvantage of the majority of the blind deconvolution algorithms is that the performance is directly proportional to the amount of a priori knowledge of either f or b. In an effort to address this weakness, Ayers and Dainty [2] proposed an iterative deconvolution algorithm developed independently in the 1970's by Richardson [3] and Lucy [4], which has become a widely used method for blind deblurring. The algorithm for iteratively solving for f is written as,

$$f_{k+1}(n_1,n_2) = f_k(n_1,n_2)(b(n_1,n_2) \otimes \frac{x(n_1,n_2)}{r_k(n_1,n_2)}) \qquad (3)$$

where $r_k(n_1,n_2)$ represents a reblurred image given by,

$$r_k(n_1,n_2) = f_k(n_1,n_2) \otimes b(n_1,n_2) \qquad (4)$$

This method has an added benefit of robustness to noise if it may be modelled as Poisson noise. If the noise is Gaussian in nature, an alternative algorithm is given by,

$$f_{k+1}(n_1,n_2) = f_k(n_1,n_2)(b(n_1,n_2) \otimes x(n_1,n_2) - r_k(n_1,n_2)) \qquad (5)$$

Ayers and Dainty [2] first proposed to extend this deconvolution to unknown PSF as well, by alternately iterating on each of the unknowns in

$$b_{k+1}(n_1,n_2) = b_k(n_1,n_2)(f_k(n_1,n_2) \otimes \frac{x(n_1,n_2)}{r_k(n_1,n_2)}) \qquad (6)$$

$$f_{k+1}(n_1,n_2) = f_k(n_1,n_2)(b_k(n_1,n_2) \otimes \frac{x(n_1,n_2)}{r_k(n_1,n_2)}) \qquad (7)$$

where both f and b are unknown quantities. Initial values of each of these functions are necessary for the algorithm. The recommended starting values are constant images with a DC value equal to the DC value of the blurred image and unity for the deblurred image and PSF, respectively. It should be noted that there is no clear consensus on the best iteration scheme for this algorithm.

None of the techniques studied worked particularly well for every type of the images, as they require a prior knowledge about the point spread function or the image in many circumstances. Therefore these schemes fall short in performance in any real test cases. Richardson-Lucy iterative blind deconvolution method is computationally expensive and requires good initial estimates; it also exhibits some instabilities that one often does not expect.

3 ICA and Nongaussianity

Independent Component Analysis (ICA) is a technique that recovers a set of independent source signals from a set of observed, mixed signals without a priori knowledge of the sources, thus is also termed as blind source separation (BSS). It is assumed that each measured signal is a linear combination of the independent original signals, and that there are an equal number of measured signals and independent signals. Furthermore it is assumed that the sources are nongaussian.

ICA starts with a vector of observations, x_i, $i=1, 2, \ldots n$. Then each of these observations is a liner combination of a set of n independent components:

$$x_i = a_{i1}s_1 + a_{i2}s_2 + \ldots + a_{in}s_n, \quad i=1, 2, \ldots, n \tag{8}$$

Or, using a matrix notation, $X=AS$. Here $S= (s_1, \ldots, s_n)$ is a random vector, the latent variables or independent sources, and A is the mixing matrix. The task is to find both S and A. It is worthwhile to mention here that the underlying sources are to be linearly independent and nongaussian, in fact at most only one source can be Gaussian. Basic working methodology behind such a scheme is to look for nongaussianity in recovered signals.

The output of a linear system usually has a close to gaussian output, because of the Central Limit Theorem. ICA tries to find a solution that maximises the nongaussianity of the recovered signal. Because of that, the techniques usually do not work with gaussian signals, since they have higher cumulants equal to zero. The Central Limit Theorem states that, 'the sum of several independent random variables, such as those in X, tends towards a Gaussian distribution'. So $x_i=a_{i1}s_1+ a_{i2}s_2$ is more gaussian than either s_1 or s_2. The Central Limit Theorem implies that if we can find a re-combination of the measured signals X with minimal gaussian properties, then that signal will be one of the independent signals. Once demixing matrix is determined it is a simple matter to invert it to find A. In order to do this, some way to measure the nongaussianity is required.

Kurtosis is the classical method of measuring nongaussianity. When data is pre-processed to have unit variance, kurtosis is equal to the fourth moment of the data. In an intuitive sense, kurtosis measured how "spikiness" of a distribution or the size of the tails. Kurtosis is extremely simple to calculate, however, it is very sensitive to outliers in the data set. Its values may be based on only a few values in the tails which means that its statistical significance is poor. Kurtosis may not be robust enough.

Mathematically kurtosis, is defined as,

$$Kurt(y) = E\{y^4\} - 3(E\{y^2\})^2 \tag{9}$$

or, in cases where y has unit variance, $Kurt(y) = E\{y^4\} - 3$. In other words, kurtosis is a normalised version of the fourth moment. Kurtosis is relatively easy to use, in part because of its linearity: If x_1 and x_2 are random variables, $Kurt(x_1 + x_2) = Kurt(x_1) + Kurt(x_2)$ and $Kurt(\alpha x) = \alpha^4 Kurt(x)$.

The other measure used for measuring nongaussanity is negentropy. Negentropy is based on the information theoretic quantity of differential entropy. The entropy of a discrete signal Y is equal to the sum of the products of probability of each event and the log of those probabilities,

$$H(Y) = \sum P(Y = \alpha) \log P(Y = \alpha) \qquad (10)$$

In all random variables with equal variance, normal distribution is the one, which has the maximum entropy, indicating that it is the least structured. The entropy of a random variable thus can be used for as a measure of non-normality, in practice that term is negentropy. Negentropy is simply the differential entropy of a signal, minus the differential entropy of a gaussian signal with the same covariance.

$$J(Y) = H(Y_{gaussian}) - H(Y) \qquad (11)$$

Negentropy is always positive and is zero only if the signal is a pure Gaussian. It is stable but difficult to calculate. Therefore some estimation techniques for measuring negentropy are applied.

4 Proposed Deconvolution Method and Experimental Results

Here we present a blind image deconvolution approach using independent component analysis and genetic algorithms. The method makes use of the difference between blurred thus correlated and unblurred original images, using the very fact by 'Central Limit Theorem', that is the system output after blurring would be more Gaussian than the actual image. Therefore actual image can be solved using any nongaussianity measure, i.e. kurtosis or negentropy like ICA uses to find the independent components. Here nongaussianity measure (e.g. kurtosis) is used to differentiate between the correlated (blurred) and uncorrelated (deblurred) images. Deblurring is to make the resulting more independent than the blurred, observed image. The mentioned cost function is used to optimize the estimated PSF $b(n_1, n_2)$ by a simple genetic algorithm in an iterative manner. The operation is conducted in the frequency domain. The approach is computationally simple and efficient. The entire process can be described in the following steps:

- Initialize the genetic algorithm parameters, population size, initial filter parameters, cross-over rate, mutation rate, etc.
- Calculate the kurtosis or negentropy of the blurred image and Fourier coefficients of the blurred image.
- Perform first iteration and for different values of the spreading parameter (i.e. sigma in this case); find the restored image through inverse filtering in the spectral domain. Convert the image to spatial domain and calculate its kurtosis or negentropy (i.e. fitness function) for different population samples.
- Generate the child population for next iteration by evolving from the parents on the basis of the fittest function, and optimize the fitness function in subsequent iterations (generations).

The proposed algorithm has been tested on both 1D and 2D blind deconvolution problems. For a 1D demonstration a square wave was blurred using a Gaussian blurring function. Then proposed algorithm was used to estimate the required blurring function and the estimated signal. The results are shown in Fig. 3.

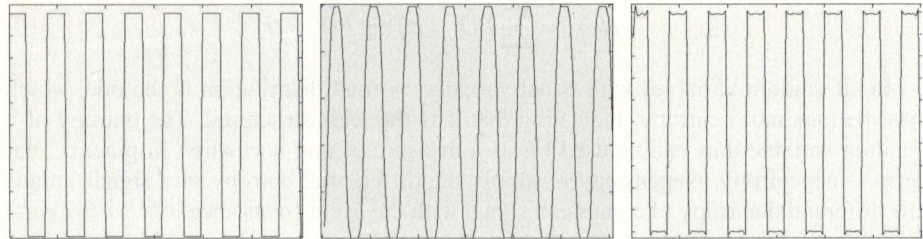

Fig. 3. Original (left), blurred (centre) and restored (right) signals using proposed method

2D case study was conducted on three test images (check board, cameraman and Lena)– shown in Fig. 4. Original images were blurred using a Gaussian PSF of spreading (sigma) of 3-5. The proposed method is able to display advantageous results both qualitatively, as shown in Fig. 5, and quantitatively -the PSNR performance results for checkboard and Lena images are given in Table 1.

Fig. 4. Original test images (check board, cameraman and Lena)

Table 1. PSNR performance for test Images

Image	Gaussian Blurring Parameter	PSNR of Blurred Image	PSNR of Restored Image
Checkboard	Sigma = 3	57 db	81 db
	Sigma = 5	55 db	104 db
Lena	Sigma = 3	22.76 db	32.49 db

A qualitative (visual) and PSNR comparison of the proposed method with some existing techniques (such as Wiener filter, regularised filter, Richardson Lucy method and blind Richardson Lucy method) was carried out; with Lena image, the performance results are shown in Fig. 6 and Table 2. The proposed method is not only able to display the superior results in terms of improved perception but also in quantitative (PSNR) terms. It is further noted worthy that the comparison of the exiting techniques was done with the actual point spread function (PSF) such as

Wiener and Regularization filter techniques where the deconvolution techniques are not blind, where as Richardson Lucy is both blind and non blind, hence required a prior knowledge of the PSF for the its subsequent processing.

Fig. 5. Blurred images (left) and restored images (right) using the proposed method

Table 2. PSNR comparison of proposed method with other techniques for Lena image

Blurred Image	Wie-ner Filter	Regularised Filter	Richardson Lucy Method	Blind Richardson-Lucy Method	Proposed Method
22.76 db	23.96 db	23.96 db	25.36 db	25.43 db	**32.49** db

Fig. 6. Blurred images (top left), restored using the proposed method (top right), Richardson Lucy (middle left), regularised filter (middle right), Wiener Filter (bottom left) and blind Rishardson Lucy method (bottom right).

5 Discussion and Conclusions

A new method based on nongaussianity measure of Independent Component Analysis along with the Genetic algorithm for optimization in frequency domain for blind deconvolution and deblurring of images has been proposed. The proposed method is simple and easy to implement. Although the method is only applied for estimation of one parameter (e.g. sigma) of Gaussian blurring filter in the experiment, it can be extended to estimate other unknown blurring parameters. Hence the algorithm can be extended to estimate any blurring function without prior knowledge of the image and the function. The method has few limitations, firstly as it is based on the Genetic algorithm therefore it is iterative process for optimizing the cost function; further as the processing is done in frequency domain therefore it can be a bit computationally expensive. The fitness function, if based on kurtosis, can be prone to outliers, therefore can have convergence issue in some cases. To alleviate the convergence issues, negentropy instead of kurtosis can be a suitable alternative as a fitness function in the Genetic algorithm.

The experimental results show that the proposed method is able to blind deblur signals and images effectively without much adverse distortion. A comparison with existing deconvolution methods also indicates improved performance of the proposed. Future endeavor is to tackle noise and outliners during function optimization.

References

1. William H. Richardson, W., H.: Bayesian-based iterative method of image restoration. J. Opt. Soc. of America A, 62 (1972) 55–59.
2. Ayers, G.,R., and Dainty, J., C.: Iterative blind deconvolution method and its applications. Opt. Letts., 13 (1988) 547–549.
3. Lucy, L., B.: An iterative technique for the rectification of observed images. The Astronomical Journal, 79 (1974) 745–754.
4. Richard, L., W.: Image restoration using the damped Richardson-Lucy method. In R. J. Hanisch and R. L. White, editors, The Restoration of HST Images and Spectra II, Baltimore, MD, Space Telescope Science Institute (1994).
5. Hyvärinen, A. and Oja, E.: Independent component analysis: algorithms and applications. Neural Networks, 13 (2000) 411-430.
6. Moayeri, N. and Konstantinides, K.: An algorithm for blind restoration of blurred and noisy images, Hewlett-Packard Lab Report (http://www.hpl.hp.com/techreports).
7. Rabie, T., F., Rangayyan, R., M., and Paranjape, R., B.: Adaptive-neighborhood image deblurring, J. Electronic Imaging, 3 (1994) 368-378.
8. Tan, S. and Savoie, T.: Blind Deconvolution Techniques for Image Deblurring (6.344 Project, Spring 2000) at http://www.mit.edu/people/savoie/portfolio
9. Vural C. and Sethares, W., A.: Blind deconvolution of noisy blurred images via dispersion minimization, 14th IEEE Int. Conf. on DSP, Santorini, Greece, July (2002).
10. Hyvärinen, A.: Survey on independent component analysis. Neural Computing Surveys, 2 (1999) 94-128.

Electroencephalogram Signals from Imagined Activities: A Novel Biometric Identifier for a Small Population

Ramaswamy Palaniappan

Dept. of Computer Science, University of Essex, Colchester, United Kingdom
rpalan@essex.ac.uk

Abstract. Electroencephalogram (EEG) signals extracted during imagined activities have been studied for use in Brain Computer Interface (BCI) applications. The major hurdle in the EEG based BCI is that the EEG signals are unique to each individual. This complicates a universal BCI design. On the contrary, this disadvantage is the advantage when it comes to using EEG signals from imagined activities for biometric applications. Therefore, in this paper, EEG signals from imagined activities are proposed as a biometric to identify the individuality of persons. The approach is based on the classification of EEG signals recorded when a user performs either one or several mental activities (up to five). As different individuals have different thought processes, this idea would be appropriate for individual identification. To increase the inter-subject differences, EEG data from six electrodes are used instead of one. A total of 108 features (autoregressive coefficients, channel spectral powers, inter-hemispheric channel spectral power differences and inter-hemispheric channel linear complexity values) are computed from each EEG segment for each mental activity and classified by a linear discriminant classifier using a modified 10 fold cross validation procedure, which gave perfect classification when tested on 500 EEG patterns from five subjects. This initial study has shown the huge potential of the method over existing biometric identification systems as it is impossible to be faked.

Keywords: Biometrics, Brain Computer Interface, Electroencephalogram, Imagined activities.

1 Introduction

Person identification, which is different from authentication, is the process in which a person's identity is recognized. Nowadays, automatic identification through the use of computers has become an everyday issue. The biometric approach to this is commonly through fingerprint recognition [1, 2]. It is becoming more important to find alternative biometric methods to replace or augment the fingerprint technology. In this regard, there are other biometrics like voice [1], palmprint [3], hand geometry [4], iris [5], face [6], ear force fields [7], heart signals [8], odor [9], and brain signals [10-12] that have been proposed.

However, using EEG during imagined activities has yet to be studied as a biometric as far as the knowledge of the author is concerned. There have been other types of EEG signals that have been studied for biometrics [10-12]. In [10], alpha rhythm EEG signals were used to classify 4 subjects, while in another study [11], AR modeling of EEG obtained when the subjects had their eyes open or closed were used as a biometric. Visual evoked potentials recorded while subjects perceived a picture were used in [12] to identify the subjects. However, this method required 61 channels, which is cumbersome and also required the individuals to perceive a visual stimulus, which is drawback for the visually impaired.

In previous study [13], it has been shown that classification of EEG signals during imagined activities is a suitable technique for use in the design of Brain Computer Interfaces (BCIs) to aid the disabled to communicate or control devices. BCIs are also useful for hands-off menu activation, which could be used by anyone. In this paper, the same approach but using different feature extraction and classification methodologies is proposed for a different application: to identify the individuality of the subjects.

2 Data

The EEG data used in this study were collected by Keirn and Aunon [14]. Data from five subjects were used in this study. The description of the data and recording procedures are as follows. The subjects were seated in noise controlled room. An electrode cap was used to record EEG signals from positions C3, C4, P3, P4, O1 and O2 defined by the 10-20 system of electrode placement. The impedances of all electrodes were kept below 5 KΩ and measurements were made with reference to electrically linked mastoids, A1 and A2. The electrodes were connected through a bank of amplifiers with analog band-pass filters set from 0.1 to 100 Hz. The data were sampled at 250 Hz with 12-bit precision. The system was calibrated before each recording. Signals were recorded for 10 seconds during each of the five imagined activities and each activity was repeated for 10 different day sessions.

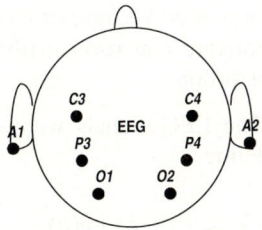

Fig. 1. Electrode placement

These imagined activities were:

Baseline activity. The subjects were asked to relax and think of nothing in particular.

Math activity. The subjects were given nontrivial multiplication problems, such as 79 times 56 and were asked to solve them without vocalizing or making any other physical movements. The activities were non-repeating and designed so that an immediate answer was not apparent. The subjects verified at the end of the activities whether or not he/she arrived at the solution and no subject completed the activity before the end of the 10 s recording session.

Geometric figure rotation activity. The subjects were given 30 s to study a particular three-dimensional block object, after which the drawing was removed and the subjects were asked to visualize the object being rotated about an axis. The EEG signals were recorded during the mental rotation period.

Mental letter composing activity. The subjects were asked to mentally compose a letter to a friend without vocalizing. Since the activity was repeated for several times the subjects were told to continue with the letter from where they left off.

Visual counting activity. The subjects were asked to imagine a blackboard and to visualize numbers being written on the board sequentially, with the previous number being erased before the next number was written. The subjects were instructed not to verbalize the numbers but to visualize them. They were also told to resume counting from the previous activity rather than starting over each time.

Keirn and Aunon [11] specifically chose these activities since they involve hemispheric brainwave asymmetry (except for the baseline activity).

3 Feature Extraction

In this study, each of the EEG signal was segmented into 20 segments with length 0.5 s, so each EEG segment was 125 data points (samples) in length. The EEG signals were referenced to the common reference (i.e. centered to zero mean across all the channels) and also were centered to zero mean in each of the channel. The preliminary results indicated that both these operations decreased the classification error and hence were adopted. Elliptic Finite Impulse Response (FIR) was used to high-pass filter the EEG signals above 0.5 Hz (to reduce baseline noise). The filter specifications were: 30 dB minimum attenuation in the stop-band with 0.5 dB ripple in the pass-band. Elliptic filter was used because of its low order as compared to other FIR filters like Butterworth. Forward and reverse filtering was performed to ensure that there would be no phase distortion.

Autoregressive coefficients. The EEG signals were subjected to feature extraction using autoregressive (AR) modeling:

$$x(n) = -\sum_{k=1}^{p} a_k x(n-k) + e(n) , \qquad (1)$$

where p is the model order, $x(n)$ is the signal at the sampled point n, a_k are the real valued AR coefficients and $e(n)$ represents the error term independent of past samples. In this paper, Burg's method [15] was used to estimate the AR coefficients. In computing AR coefficients, order six was used because other researchers [13, 14, 16] have suggested the use of order six for AR process for mental activity classifications. Therefore, six AR coefficients were obtained for each channel, giving 36 features for each EEG segment for a mental activity. When two mental activities were used, the size of the features was 72 and so forth.

Channel spectral powers and inter-hemispheric channel spectral power differences. Next, Elliptic filters with similar specifications as used earlier were utilized to extract EEG in three spectral bands: alpha, beta and gamma. Delta and theta bands were ignored since there is seldom any EEG in these low frequencies during a mental activity. The frequency ranges of each bands were alpha (8-13 Hz), beta (14-20 Hz) and gamma (21-50 Hz). Channel spectral power in each band was computed using the variance of the filtered output. Next, inter-hemispheric channel spectral power differences in each spectral band was computed using

$$Power_{difference} = \left[\frac{P_1 - P_2}{P_1 + P_2}\right], \quad (2)$$

where P_1 and P_2 are the powers in different channels in the same spectral band but in the opposite hemispheres. Overall, this gave 18 channel spectral powers and 27 inter-hemispheric channel spectral power differences (nine spectral power differences for six channels in opposite hemispheres x three bands) for each mental activity. These numbers increase in multiplicative order for more mental activities.

Inter-hemispheric Channel Linear Complexity. For C-channel signals, linear complexity is defined as [17]:

$$\Omega = \exp(-\sum_{i=1}^{C} \xi_i \log \xi_i), \quad (3)$$

where the eigenvalues, λ are computed from the covariance of the C-channel EEG signal matrix and normalized using

$$\xi_i = \lambda_i \Big/ \sum_{i=1}^{C} \lambda_i . \quad (4)$$

Roughly, the linear complexity, Ω measures the amount of spatial synchronization. Large values of Ω indicates low correlation between the signals in the channels and vice versa. Here, Ω is computed to measure the inter-hemispheric channel linear complexity for each spectral band where the two channels used were one each from the opposite hemispheres. There were nine inter-hemispheric channel linear complexity values times three bands, totaling 27 for each mental activity. These numbers increase in multiplicative order for more mental activities.

4 Feature Reduction and Classifier

Principal Component Analysis (PCA). The standard PCA was used to reduce the feature size. In this work, the principal components that contributed to 99.99% of the total variance were retained. This variance value to be retained was obtained after some preliminary simulations. The reduced feature sizes were 78, 125, 150, 169 and 182, in increasing number of mental activity combinations. These features were normalized to the range [-1,1], using maximum and minimum values of each feature.

Linear Discriminant Classifier. Linear Discriminant Classifier (LDC) [18] is a linear classification method that is computationally attractive as compared to other classifiers like artificial neural network. It could be used to classify two or more groups of data. Here, LDC was used to classify the EEG feature vectors into one of the five categories representing the subject. The EEG feature vector size would depend on the number of used mental activities (as mentioned earlier). A total of 1000 EEG feature vectors (20 segments for EEG each signal x 10 sessions x 5 subjects) were used in the experimental study. Half of the patterns were used in training and the remaining half in testing. The selection of the patterns for training and testing were chosen randomly. A modified 10 fold cross validation procedure was used to increase the reliability of the results. In this procedure, the entire data for an experiment (i.e. 1000 EEG feature vectors) were split into 10 parts, with equal number of feature vectors from each subject. Training and testing were repeated for five times where for each time, five different parts were used for training and the remaining five parts for testing. This was done to increase the reliability of the classification results.

5 Results and Discussion

Table 1 shows the classification results (in terms of percentage error) using one mental activity, while Tables 2, 3, 4 and 5 shows the classification results using combinations of two, three, four and five mental activities, respectively. The results were obtained using the modified 10 fold cross validation procedure mentioned earlier. The maximum, minimum and average of the five repeated experiments using the modified 10 fold cross validation procedure are reported in the Tables.

Table 1. Results with modified 10 fold cross-validation using one mental activity

	Classification error (%)		
Mental activity	Min	Max	Average
Baseline	2.00	2.80	2.32
Count	0.80	3.40	1.60
Letter	0.80	2.40	1.36
Maths	2.20	4.20	3.12
Rotation	1.40	3.40	2.16
Overall average	1.44	3.24	2.11
Minimum	0.80	2.40	1.36
Best mental activity (using average value): Letter			

From Table 1, the best mental activity that discriminated the subjects was Letter activity, while from Table 2, it could be seen that the best combination of mental activity pair was Maths-Letter (using the values in the average column). There was a reduction in classification error by using the mental activity pairs instead of a single mental activity. Similarly, there were reductions in classification error with increasing mental activity combinations, which was as anticipated. When all five mental activities were used, there was no classification error.

The increase in recognition accuracy that followed the higher number of mental activities resulted in additional complexity and computational time. However, the increase in computational time is insignificant especially with the easy availability of fast computing power. The computational times required were approximately 40 μs, 77.5 μs, 155 μs, 235 μs and 390 μs for one, two, three, four and five mental activities, respectively. The increase in complexity is a cause for concern but the method is simple as the subjects have to think of the different mental activities only, which could be easily mastered with some training. With the use of active electrode caps, the placement of electrodes will not be cumbersome and a simple hat that fits most heads could be designed. If necessary, the EEG signals could be transmitted wirelessly to the computer for processing. Combined with the 0.5 s required for a single mental activity, operation of the system requires about 2.89 s for five mental activities, which is feasible to be implemented.

Table 2. Results with modified 10 fold cross-validation using two mental activities

Mental activity combinations	Classification error (%)		
	Min	Max	Average
Baseline, Count	0	1.80	0.40
Baseline, Letter	0.20	0.60	0.40
Baseline, Maths	0.20	0.60	0.40
Baseline, Rotation	0	1.40	0.48
Letter, Count	0	1.40	0.40
Letter, Rotation	0.20	1.00	0.44
Maths, Count	0.20	2.20	0.68
Maths, Letter	0	0.40	0.24
Maths, Rotation	0.40	1.00	0.76
Rotation, Count	0	2.00	0.60
Overall average	0.5	0.99	0.46
Minimum	0	0.40	0.24
Best mental activity combination (using average value): Maths, Letter			

Table 3. Results modified 10 fold cross-validation using three mental activities

Mental activity combinations	Classification error (%)		
	Min	Max	Average
Baseline, Letter, Count	0	1.40	0.28
Letter, Count, Maths	0	1.40	0.32
Maths, Baseline, Count	0	1.40	0.32
Maths, Baseline, Letter	0	0.40	0.12
Rotation, Baseline, Count	0	1.60	0.40
Rotation, Baseline, Letter	0	0.40	0.16
Rotation, Letter, Count	0	1.60	0.40
Rotation, Maths, Baseline	0	0.60	0.16
Rotation, Maths, Count	0	1.60	0.36
Rotation, Maths, Letter	0	0.20	0.12
Overall average	0	1.06	0.26
Minimum	0	0.20	0.12
Best mental activity combination (using average value): Maths, Baseline, Letter or Rotations, Maths, Letter			

Table 4. Results with modified cross-validation using four mental activities

Mental activity combinations	Classification error (%)		
	Min	Max	Average
Maths, Letter, Count, Baseline	0	1.00	0.2
Rotation, Baseline, Letter, Count	0	0.60	0.12
Rotation, Maths, Count, Baseline	0	1.00	0.2
Rotation, Maths, Count, Letter	0	1.40	0.32
Rotation, Maths, Letter, Baseline	0	0	0
Overall average	0	0.80	0.17
Minimum	0	0	0
Best mental activity combination (using average value): Rotation, Maths, Letter, Baseline			

Table 5. Results with modified cross-validation using five mental activities

Mental activity combination	Classification error (%)		
	Min	Max	Average
Rotation, Maths, Count, Letter, Baseline	0	0	0

6 Conclusion

In this paper, a novel method of identifying individuals using classification of feature vectors from six EEG signals recorded during mental activities has been proposed. The features consisted of sixth order AR coefficients, channel spectral powers, inter-hemispheric channel spectral power differences and inter-hemispheric channel linear complexity values. LDC was used to classify the EEG feature vectors, where a modified 10 fold cross validation procedure was used to improve the reliability of the results. The perfect classification over 500 test EEG feature vectors from five subjects show promise for the method to be studied further as a biometric tool for individual identification. The method could be used as a uni-modal (stand alone) or in part of a multi-modal individual identification system and is mainly advantageous because of the difficulty in establishing another persons exact EEG output. Nevertheless, further extensive research with more subjects would be necessary in order to determine the stability of the EEG features over time. Another future work could be on authentication of users using similar approach.

Acknowledgment. The author would like to acknowledge the assistance of Dr. C. Anderson of Colorado State University, USA for giving permission to use the EEG data.

References

1. Wayman, J., Jain, A., Maltoni, D., Maio, D. (eds.): Biometric Systems: Technology, Design and Performance Evaluation. Springer-Verlag (2004)
2. Pankanti, S., Prabhakar, S., Jain, A.K.: On the individuality of fingerprints. IEEE Transactions on Pattern Analysis and Machine Intelligence, Vol. 24, No. 8 (2002) 1010-1025

3. Duta, N., Jain, A.K., Mardia, K.V.: Matching of palmprints. Pattern Recognition Letters, Vol 23, No. 4 (2002) 477-485
4. Jain, A.K., Ross, A., Pankanti, S.: A prototype hand geometry-based verification system. Proceedings of 2nd International Conference on Audio and Video-Based Biometric Person Identification, Vol. 1 (1999) 166-171
5. Daugman, J.: Recognizing persons by their iris patterns. In Jain, A.K., Bolle, R., Pankanti, S. (eds.): Biometrics: Personal Identification in Networked Society. Kluwer Academic (1999)
6. Samal, A., Iyengar, P.: Automatic recognition and analysis of human faces and facial expressions: a survey. Pattern Recognition, Vol. 25, No. 1 (1992) 65-77
7. Hurley, D. Nixon, M., Carter, J.: Force field feature extraction for ear biometrics. Computer Vision and Image Understanding, Vol. 98, No. 3 (2005) 491-512
8. Biel, L., Pettersson, O., Philipson, L., Wide, P.: ECG analysis: a new approach in human identification. IEEE Transactions on Instrumentation and Measurement, Vol. 50, No. 3 2001 808-812
9. Korotkaya, Z.: Biometric Person Authentication: Odor. Available: http://www.it.lut.fi/kurssit/03-04/010970000/seminars/Korotkaya.pdf (2003)
10. Poulos, M., Rangoussi, M., Chrissikopoulos, V., Evangelou, A.: Person identification based on parametric processing of the EEG. Proceedings of the 6th IEEE International Conference on Electronics, Circuits, and Systems, Vol. 1, (1999) 283-286
11. Paranjape, R.B., Mahovsky, J., Benedicenti, L., Koles, Z.: The electroencephalogram as a biometric. Proceedings of Canadian Conference on Electrical and Computer Engineering, Vol.2 (2001) 1363-1366
12. Palaniappan, R.: A new method to identify individuals using VEP signals and neural network. IEE Proceedings - Science, Measurement and Technology Journal, Vol. 151, No. 1 (2004) 16-20
13. Palaniappan, R., Paramesran, R., Nishida, S., Saiwaki, N.: A new brain-computer interface design using fuzzy ARTMAP. IEEE Transactions on Neural System and Rehabilitation Engineering, Vol. 10 (2002) 140-148
14. Keirn, Z.A., Aunon, J.I.: A new mode of communication between man and his surroundings. IEEE Transactions on Biomedical Engineering, Vol. 37, No.12 (1990) 1209-1214
15. Shiavi, R.: Introduction to Applied Statistical Signal Analysis, 2nd edition. Academic Press (1999)
16. Anderson, C.W., Stolz, E. A., Shamsunder, S.: Multivariate autoregressive models for classification of spontaneous electroencephalogram during mental activities. IEEE Transactions on Biomedical Engineering, Vol. 45, No. 3 (1998) 277-286
17. Wackermann, J.: Towards a quantitative characterization of functional states of the brain: from the non-linear methodology to the global linear description. International Journal of Psychphysiology, Vol. 34 (1999) 65-80
18. Fukunaga, K.: Introduction to Statistical Pattern Recognition, 2nd edition. Academic Press (1990)

Resolving Ambiguities in the Semantic Interpretation of Natural Language Questions

Serge Linckels[1,2] and Christoph Meinel[1]

[1] Hasso-Plattner-Institut (HPI), Potsdam University, P.O. Box 900460, D-14440 Potsdam, Gremany
[2] Luxembourg International Advanced Studies in Information Technologies (LIASIT), L-1511 Luxembourg, Luxembourg

Abstract. Our project is about an e-librarian service which is able to retrieve multimedia resources from a knowledge base in a more efficient way than by browsing through an index or by using a simple keyword search. The user can formulate a complete question in natural language and submit it to the semantic search engine.

However, natural language is not a formal language and thus can cause ambiguities in the interpretation of the sentence. Normally, the correct interpretation can only be retrieved accurately by putting each word in the context of a complete question.

In this paper we present an algorithm which is able to resolve ambiguities in the semantic interpretation of NL questions. As the required input, it takes a linguistic pre-processed question and translates it into a logical and unambiguous form, i.e. $\mathcal{ALC}$ terminology. The *focus function* resolves ambiguities in the question; it returns the best possible interpretation for a given word in the context of the complete user question. Finally, pertinent documents can be retrieved from the knowledge base.

We report on a benchmark test with a prototype that confirms the reliability of our algorithm. From 229 different user questions, the system returned the right answer for 97% of the questions, and only one answer, i.e. the best one, for nearly half of the questions.

1 Introduction

Our vision is to create an *e-librarian service* which is able to retrieve multimedia resources from a knowledge base in a more efficient way than by browsing through an index or by using a simple keyword search. The user formulates a complete question in natural langauge (NL), then the e-librarian service retrieves the most pertinent document(s) in which the user finds the answer to her/his question. The user's NL question is processed in three steps. Firstly, the linguistic pre-processing (section 3), secondly the translation of the linguistic pre-processed user question into a computer readable and unambiguous form w.r.t. a given ontology (section 4), and thirdly the retrieval of pertinent documents (section 5).

The main contribution of this paper is an algorithm, which is able to resolve ambiguities in the user question. The *focus function* returns the best interpretation for a given word in the context of the complete user question. A benchmark test confirms the reliability of this algorithm (section 6).

2 Related Work

In this section, we present some related work from the fields of "Natural Language Interfaces to Databases" and "Question-Answering Systems". In general, the main difference is that our system's corpus is about a specific and well defined domain (computer history or fractions in mathematics), whereas other related projects deal with larger corpora and/or other domains. Also, some projects focus more on the NLP of the user question; we only use linguistic tools to overcome this step. Furthermore, other projects do not have an "ontological approach" like in our case in order to map a sentence into an logical and unambiguous form, i.e. $\mathcal{ALC}$ terminology.

START [2] is the first question-answering system available on the Web. Several improvements have been made since it came online in 1993. However, the NLP is not always sound, e.g. the question "What did Jodie Foster before she became an actress?" returns "I don't know what Jodie fostered before the actress became an actress". Also, the question "Who invented the transistor?" yields two answers: the inventors of the transistor, but also a description about the transistor (the answer to the question: "What is a transistor").

AquaLog [4] is a portable question-answering system which takes queries expressed in NL and an ontology as input, and returns answers drawn from one or more knowledge bases. User questions are expressed as triples: <subject, predicate, object>. If the several translation mechanisms fail, then the user is asked for disambiguation. The system also uses an interesting learning component to adapt to the user's "jargon". AquaLog has currently a very limited knowledge space. In a benchmark test over 76 different questions, 37 (48.68%) where handled correctly.

The prototype PRECISE [5] uses ontology technologies to map semantically tractable NL questions to the corresponding SQL query. It was tested on several hundred questions drawn from user studies over three benchmark databases. Over 80% of the questions are semantically tractable questions, which PRECISE answered correctly, and recognized the 20% it could not handle, and requests a paraphrase. The problem of finding a mapping from the tokenization to the database requires that all tokens must be distinct; questions with unknown words are not semantically tractable and cannot be handled.

FALCON is an answer engine that handles questions in NL. When the question concept indicating the answer type is identified, it is mapped into an answer taxonomy. The top categories are connected to several word classes from WordNet. Also, FALCON gives a cached answer if the similar question has already been asked before; a similarity measure is calculated to see if the given question is a reformulation of a previous one. In TREC-9, FALCON generated a score of 58% for short answers and 76% for long answers, which was actually the best score.

LASSO relies on a combination of syntactic and semantic techniques, and lightweight abductive inference to find answers. The search for the answer is based on a form of indexing called paragraph indexing. The advantage of processing paragraphs instead of full documents determines a faster syntactic parsing. The extraction and evaluation of the answer correctness is based on empirical abduction. A score of 55.5% for short answers and 64.5% for long answers was achieved in TREC-8.

3 Linguistic Pre-processing

In our e-librarian service, the linguistic pre-processing is performed with a part-of-speech (POS) tagger; we use *TreeTagger*. The linguistic pre-processing step contributes in three points. Firstly, the word category of each word is made explicit, e.g. article, verb. Secondly, the tagger returns the canonical form (*lemma*) for each word (*token*). Thirdly, the sentence is split into linguistic clauses. A linguistic clause is a triple of the form <subject;verb;object>. Each triple is then processed individually, e.g. the question $q =$ "Who invented the transistor and who founded IBM?" is split into the two clauses: $q'_1 =$ [Who invented the transistor?], conj = [and], $q'_2 =$ [Who founded IBM?].

4 Ontology Mapping

4.1 Ontology Preliminaries

The e-librarian service masters a domain language L_H over an alphabet Σ^*, which may or may not contain all the possible words L used by the user to formulate his question, so that $L_H \subseteq L \subseteq \Sigma^*$. The semantics are attached to each word by classification in the knowledge source, which is structured in a hierarchical way like *hyperonyms*, *hyponyms*, *synonyms*, and *homonyms*, e.g. *WordNet*.

Definition 1 (Concept taxonomy). *A concept taxonomy $H = (V, E, v_0)$ is a directed acyclic graph where each node, except the root-node (v_0), has one or more parents. E is the set of all edges and V is the set of all nodes (vertices) with $V = \{(s, T) \mid s \in S\}$ where s is a unique label, S the set of all labels in the ontology, and T is a set of words from L_H that are associated to a node so that $T \subseteq L_H$.*

A node v_i represents a concept. The words that refer to this concept are regrouped in T_i. We assume that each set of words T_i is semantically related to the concept that the node v_i represents. Of course, a certain word can refer to different concepts, e.g. "Ada" is the name of a programming language but also the name of a person. Not all words in L_H must be associated with a concept. Only words that are semantically relevant are classified. In general, nouns and verbs are best indicators of the sense of a question.

4.2 Semantic Interpretation

The representation of context-independent meaning is called the *logical form*, and the process of mapping a sentence to its logical form is called *semantic interpretation* [1]. The logical form is expressed in a certain knowledge representation language; we use the *Description Logics* (DL) $\mathcal{ALC}$ language, which is sufficiently expressive for our purposes. Firstly, DL have the advantage that they come with well defined semantics and correct algorithms. Furthermore, the link between DL and NL has already been established [6]. Finally, translating the user question into DL allows direct reasoning over the OWL-DL encoded knowledge base (section 5). A DL terminology is composed, firstly, of *concepts* (unary predicates), which are generally nouns, question words (*w-words*) and proper names, and secondly, of *roles* (binary predicates), which are generally verbs, adjectives and adverbs. The core part of the semantic interpretation is a mapping algorithm—commonly called *non-standard inference* [3]—which maps each word from the user question to one or more ontology concepts, and resolves the arguments of each role by analyzing the syntactic structure of the sentence.

Definition 2 (Mapping). *The meaning of each word $w_k \in L$ is made explicit with the mapping function $\varphi : L \to V$ over an ontology dictionary $L_H \subseteq L \subseteq \Sigma^*$ and an $\mathcal{ALC}$ concept taxonomy $H = (V, E, v_0)$ so that $\varphi(w_k)$ returns a set of interpretations Φ defined as follows,*

$$\Phi = \varphi(w_k) = \{v_i \mid \exists x \in ft(v_i) : w_k \equiv x\}.$$

The function $ft(v_i)$ returns the set of words T_i associated to the node v_i (definition 1), and $w_k \equiv x$ are two equivalent words respecting a given tolerance. This solution gives good results even if the user makes spelling errors. Furthermore, only the best matching is considered for the mapping, e.g. the word "comXmon" will be considered as "common", and not as "uncommon". Both words, "common" and "uncommon", will be considered for the mapping of "comXXmon". The ambiguity will be resolved in a further step (focus function).

It is possible that a word can be mapped to different concepts at once, so that $|\Phi| > 1$. We introduce the notion of *focus* to resolve this ambiguity. The focus is a function (f), which returns the best interpretation for a given word in the context of the complete user question.

Definition 3 (Focus). *The focus of a set of interpretations Φ is made explicit by the function f which returns the best interpretation for a given word in the context of the complete question q. The focus is written $f_q(\varphi(w_k \in q)) = v'$.*

Let us consider as illustration the word "Ada", which is called a multiple-sense word. In fact, in the context of computer history, "Ada" can refer to the programming language named "Ada", but it can also be the name of the person "Augusta Ada Lovelace". The correct interpretation can only be retrieved accurately by putting the ambiguous word in the context of a complete question. For example, the context of the sentences "Who invented Ada?" and "Did the firms Bull and Honeywell create Ada?" reveals that here Ada is the programming language, and not the person Ada.

The focus function uses the role's signature. A role r has the signature $r(s_1, s_2)$, where s_1 and s_2 are labels. The signature of each role defines the kind of arguments that are possible. For example $wasInventedBy(Thing, Creator)$ is the role $r = wasInventedBy$ that has the arguments $s_1 = Thing$ and

$s_2 = Creator$. In the question $q =$ "Who invented Ada?" the following mappings are computed:

$$\varphi("\text{Who}") = \{Creator\}$$
$$\varphi("\text{invented}") = \{wasInventedBy(Thing, Creator)\}$$
$$\varphi("\text{Ada}") = \{Person, Language\}$$

The system detects an ambiguity for the word "Ada", which is mapped to an instance of the concept $Person$, but also to an instance of the concept $Language$. The focus function computes the following combinations to resolve the ambiguity:

1. Was Ada invented by who?* $wasInventedBy("Ada","Who")$
2. Was Ada invented by Ada? $wasInventedBy("Ada","Ada")$
3. Was who invented by Ada?* $wasInventedBy("Who","Ada")$
4. Was who invented by who?* $wasInventedBy("Who","Who")$

Cyclic combinations like (2) and (4) are not allowed. As for (3), it does not match the role's signature because $s_1 = Creator$ ("Who"), but $Thing$ is required. As for (1), s_1 can be $Person$ or $Language$ ("Ada"). The role's signature requires $Thing$, therefore $Person$ is excluded as valid interpretation because $Person \not\sqsubseteq Thing$. As $Language \sqsubseteq Thing$, a valid interpretation is found, and in the context of this question the word "Ada" refers to the programming language Ada. Finally, the result of the focus function is:

$$f_q(\varphi("\text{Ada}")) = Language.$$

In deed, (1) represents the question "Who invented Ada?". It is still possible that the focus function cannot resolve an ambiguity, e.g. a given word has more interpretations but the focus function returns no result. In a such case, the system will generate a semantic query for each possible interpretation. Based on our practical experience we know that users generally enter simple questions where the disambiguation is normally successful.

Definition 4 (Semantic interpretation). *Let q be the user question, which is composed of linguistic clauses, written $q = \{q'_1, ..., q'_m\}$, with $m \geq 1$. The sematic interpretation of a user question q is the translation of each linguistic clause into an $\mathcal{ALC}$ terminology w.r.t. a given ontology H written,*

$$q_i^H = \prod_{k=1}^{n} f_{q'_i}(\varphi(w_k \in q'_i))$$

with q'_i a linguistic clause $q'_i \in q$, and n the number of words in the linguistic clause q'_i.

If a user question is composed of several linguistic clauses, then each one is translated separately. The logical concatenation of the different interpreted clauses q_i^H depends on the conjunction word(s) used in the user question, e.g. "Who invented the transistor *and* who founded IBM?". If no such conjunction word is found, then the "or" operator is preferred over the "and" operator.

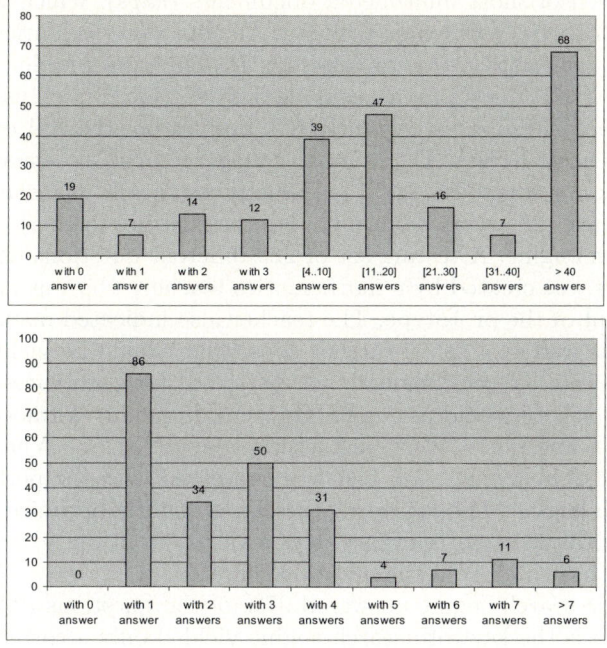

Fig. 1. Number of results yielded by a (1) keyword and by a (2) semantic search engine with a set of 229 questions

5 Retrieval

Logical inference over the non-empty ABox from the knowledge base $\mathcal{K}$ is possible by using a classical DL reasoner; we use *Pellet* [7]. The returned results are logical consequences of the inference rather than of keyword matchings. The nature of the question (*open* or *close*) reveals the missing part. An *open question* contains a question word, e.g. "Who invented the transistor?", whereas a *close question* (logical- or yes/no question) does not have a question word, e.g. "Did Shockley contribute to the invention of the transistor?". As for the first kind of questions, the missing part—normally not an individual but a concept—is the subject of the question and therefore the requested result. The result of the query is the set of all models $\mathcal{I}$ in the knowledge base $\mathcal{K}$. As for the second kind of questions, there is no missing part. Therefore, the answer will be "yes" if $\mathcal{K} \models q^H$, otherwise it is "no".

6 Benchmark Tests

Our background theory was implemented prototypically in an educational tool about fractions mathematics. We used an educational knowledge base about fractions in mathematics from the university of Luxembourg. The knowledge base is composed of short multimedia documents (*clips*), which were recorded with tele-TASK (http://www.tele-task.de). All clips were semantically described with OWL-DL metadata, w.r.t. an ontology H. The same ontology H was used to translate the NL questions as explained in section 4. Let us remark that although our algorithm does currently not profit from the full expressivity of OWL-DL, which is $\mathcal{SHOIN}(\mathbf{D})$, it allows to have compatible semantics between the OWL-DL knowledge base, and the less expressive $\mathcal{ALC}$ translated questions.

In a benchmark test we used our prototype to measure the performance of our semantic search engine. A testing set of 229 different questions about fractions in mathematics was created by a mathematics teacher, who was not involved in the development of the prototype. The teacher also indicated manually the best possible clip, as well as a list of further clips, that should be yielded as correct answer. The questions were linguistic correct, and short sentences like students in a secondary school would ask, e.g. "How can I simplify a fraction?", "What is the sum of $\frac{2}{3}$ and $\frac{7}{4}$?", "What are fractions good for?", "Who invented the fractions?", etc. This benchmark test was compared with the performance of a keyword search engine. The keyword search was slightly optimized to filter out stop words (words with no relevance, e.g. articles) from the textual content of the knowledge base and from the questions entered.

The semantic search engine answered 97% of the questions (223 out of 229) correctly, whereas the keyword search engine yielded only a correct answer (i.e. a pertinent clip) in 70% of the questions (161 out of 229). For 86 questions, the semantic search engine yielded just one—the semantically best matching—answer (figure 1). For 75% of the questions (170 out of 229) the semantic search engine yielded just a few results (one, two or three answers), whereas the keyword search yielded for only 14% of the questions less than 4 answers; mostly (138 questions out of 229) more than 10 answers. For example, the semantic interpretation of the question "What is the sum of $\frac{2}{3}$ and $\frac{7}{4}$?" is the following valid $\mathcal{ALC}$ terminology and its corresponding ABox query:

$$Fraction \sqcap \exists hasOperation.(Operation \sqcap \exists hasType.Operator)$$

$$Fraction(x1) \wedge hasOperation(x1, x2) \wedge Operation(x2) \wedge hasType(x2, sum)$$

The keyword search engine yields all clips, in which keywords like "sum" are found, e.g. a clip that explains how to represent a complex function in terms of additions, and a clip that explain how to describe situations with simple fractions.

The experiment revealed also two major weaknesses of our e-librarian service that should be improved in future. Firstly, the system is not able to make the difference between a question, where there is no answer in the knowledge base, and a question that is out of the topic, e.g. "Who invented penicillin?". Secondly, in its current state, the e-librarian service does not handle number restrictions, e.g. "How many machines did Konrad Zuse invent?". The response will be the list of Zuse's machines, but not a number. Furthermore, the question "What is the designation of the third model of Apple computers?" will yield a list of all models of Apple computers.

7 Conclusion

In this paper we presented an algorithm which is able to resolve ambiguities in the semantic interpretation of NL questions. It takes as input a linguistic pre-processed question and translates it into a logical and unambiguous form, i.e. $\mathcal{ALC}$ terminology. The *focus function* resolves ambiguities in the question; it returns the best interpretation for a given word in the context of the complete user question. Finally, pertinent documents can be retrieved from the knowledge base.

In our further work, we will try to improve the translation from the NL question into an $\mathcal{ALC}$ terminology, e.g. use number restrictions. We also want to investigate if a more precise grammatical analyze of the user question can help in the interpretation step, or if this would reduce the users liking of the interface (because of the smaller tolerance of the system). Another important topic is the maintenance facilities; how can unknown words from the user query (i.e. the user's "jargon") be included in the dictionary, and how can external "thrusted" knowledge sources been accessed by the e-librarian service?

References

1. J. Allen. *Natural Language Understanding*. Addison Wesley, 1994.
2. B. Katz. Annotating the world wide web using natural language. In *5th RIAO conference on computer assisted information searching on the internet, Montreal, Canada*, 1997.
3. R. Küsters. *Non-Standard Inferences in Description Logics*, volume 2100 of *Lecture Notes in Artificial Intelligence*. Springer-Verlag, 2001. Ph.D. thesis.
4. V. Lopez, M. Pasin, and E. Motta. Aqualog: An ontology-portable question answering system for the semantic web. In *The Semantic Web: Research and Applications, Second European Semantic Web Conference, ESWC 2005, Heraklion, Crete, Greece*, pages 546–562, 2005.
5. A.-M. Popescu, O. Etzioni, and H. A. Kautz. Towards a theory of natural language interfaces to databases. In *8th International Conference on Intelligent User Interfaces, January 12-15, Miami, FL, USA*, pages 149–157, 2003.
6. R. A. Schmidt. Terminological representation, natural language & relation algebra. In *16th German AI Conference (GWAI)*, volume 671 of *Lecture Notes in Artificial Intelligence*, pages 357–371, 1993.
7. E. Sirin and B. Parsia. Pellet: An owl dl reasoner. In *International Workshop on Description Logics (DL2004), Whistler, British Columbia, Canada, June 6-8*, volume 104 of *CEUR Workshop Proceedings*. CEUR-WS.org, 2004.

Mining the K-Most Interesting Frequent Patterns Sequentially

Quang Tran Minh, Shigeru Oyanagi, and Katsuhiro Yamazaki

Graduate school of Science and Engineering Ritsuimeikan University, Kusatsu city Japan
quang@cpsy.cs.ritsumei.ac.jp, quang_tranbk@yahoo.com

Abstract. Conventional frequent pattern mining algorithms require users to specify some minimum support threshold, which is not easy to identify without knowledge about the datasets in advance. This difficulty leads users to dilemma that either they may lose useful information or may not be able to screen for the interesting knowledge from huge presented frequent patterns sets. Mining *top-k* frequent patterns allows users to control the number of patterns to be discovered for analyzing. In this paper, we propose an optimized version of the *ExMiner*, called *OExMiner*, to mine the *top-k* frequent patterns from a large scale dataset efficiently and effectively. In order to improve the user-friendliness and also the performance of the system we proposed other 2 methods, extended from *OExMiner*, called *Seq-Miner* and *Seq-BOMA* to mine *top-k* frequent patterns sequentially. Experiments on both synthetic and real data show that our proposed methods are much more efficient and effective compared to the existing ones.

1 Introduction

Recently frequent pattern mining has become a fundamental problem in data mining and knowledge discovery. There are several methods to improve the performance of the mining task which extended and based upon the two seminal approaches: *Apriori* method [1] and *FP-growth* methods [2] have been proposed.

However, the conventional frequent patterns mining algorithms require users to provide a support threshold which is very difficult to identify without knowledge about the dataset in advance. A large minimum support threshold results in a small set of frequent patterns which users may loss useful information. On the other hand, if the support threshold is small, users may not be able to screen for the actual useful knowledge from a huge resulted frequent pattern set. In recent years, various researches have been dedicated to mine frequent patterns based upon user-friendly concepts such as maximal pattern mining [3][4], closed pattern mining [5][6], and mining the most interesting frequent patterns *(top-k mining)* [7][8][9][10][11][12]. With regard to the usability and user-friendliness, *top-k* mining permits users to mine the *k-most* interesting frequent patterns without providing a support threshold. In real applications, it is more convenient for users to control the number of *k* highest frequency patterns for extracting the interesting knowledge. If they fail to discover useful knowledge, they can continue with the next *top-k* frequent patterns and so on.

An essential problem in mining *top-k* frequent patterns is that the minimum support threshold, which is useful for algorithms to prune the search space, is not given in advance (initially set to *0*). This value has to be found gradually, according to a given number *k*, by the *top-k* mining algorithms. A good algorithm is the one that can raise the support value (i.e. from *0*) to the actual value effectively and efficiently.

As our best knowledge, *Top-k FP-growth* [11] is a sound method for *top-k* mining which extended the *FP-growth* method [2] and adopted a reduction array to trace the potential patterns for the final *top-k* frequent patterns. However, *Top-k FP-growth* is an exhaustive approach causes to slow down the performance. *ExMiner* [12] was an effective and efficient method for *top-k* mining which resolved the weakness of *Top-k FP-growth* method. In turn, this method still requires a large number of items to be examined to mine *top-k* frequent patterns thus restricted the improvement of the algorithm. This paper proposes an optimized version of *ExMiner*, called *OExMiner* to mine *top-k* frequent pattern more efficiently. Beside that, to improve the user-friendliness as well as the performance of the mining system, we also introduced other 2 methods, extended from *OExMiner*, called *Seq-Miner* and *Seq-BOMA*, to mine *top-k* frequent patterns sequentially. These methods are very valuable in real applications.

The rest of the paper is organized as follows. Section 2 is the preliminary definitions and *OExMiner* algorithm is described in section 3. The idea of mining *top-k* frequent patterns sequentially is explained in section 4. Section 5 is the experimental evaluation and we conclude the paper in section 6.

2 Preliminary Definitions

Let $I = \{i_1, i_2, ..., i_n\}$ be a set of items. An itemset or a pattern, X, is a non-empty subset of I where set of k items is called a *k-itemset*. A transaction T is a duple $<T_{id}, X>$, where T_{id} is the identifier. A transaction database D is a set of transactions.

Definition 1. The support of an itemset X, denoted as $Sup(X)$ is the number [1] of transactions in D that contain X.

Definition 2. Let θ be the minimum support threshold. An itemset X is called a frequent itemset (frequent pattern) if $Sup(X)$ satisfies θ (is not smaller than θ).

Definition 3. Let α be the support of the kth pattern in a set of frequent patterns which are sorted by the descending order of their support. The *k-most* interesting frequent patterns is a set of patterns whose support value satisfies α.

3 ExMiner vs. OExMiner Algorithms

ExMiner (explorative miner) algorithm [12] proceeds from the observation of mineral mining activities in the real world in which some explorative mining activities should be performed before the actual mining. The actual mining phase examines the dataset in an effective way to pick up the *final internal support threshold*, θ which is given to the actual mining phase later. The actual mining phase mines the *top-k* frequent patterns efficiently by using the *final internal support threshold* θ. However, *ExMiner*

---

[1] The *support* can be defined as a relative value, that is the fraction of the occurrence frequency per the total number of transactions in the considered dataset.

requires *k* singletons (items) to be examined before concluding the *final internal support threshold θ*. In fact, a set *k* singletons can generate $2^k - 1$ patterns, thus one may think that not all *k* items are used to mine *top-k* frequent patterns but a smaller number of items will be actually used. In order to improve the performance by reducing the number of singletons to be examined hence reducing the search space, an optimized version of *ExMiner* called *OExMiner* is introduced. *OExMiner* initially sets the *boundary_sup* (represents for the *"final internal support threshold"*) to the support of an item in some position, say *l*, in the middle of the *F-list* instead to that of the kth item as in *ExMiner*. For example, the support of the $k/2^{th}$ or $k/4^{th}$ item in the list of sorted items *F-list* should be chosen. If the chosen item is near to the top of the *F-list* the *boundary_sup* has higher possibility to get a large value. After that the algorithm examines the *FP-tree* and traces the supports of potential frequent patterns. The greater initial *boundary_sup* is, the narrower the search space is, thus avoiding the unnecessary additional computation time for examining unripe potential patterns.

However, if the initial *boundary_sup* is set to a very large value (*l* is near to the top of *F-list*), the number of examined potential patterns may be smaller than *k*. If this situation occurs, it is required to reselect another farther item in *F-list* and continue to examine. The position of the new item is at some place distance with an offset, say *Δl*, from the former position *l*. When a new position is chosen, the *boundary_sup* is then reset to the support of the newly selected item. The explorative mining routine, called the *VirtualGrowth* routine, is repeated according to the new *boundary_sup*. This process is repeated until all *top-k* potential patterns are examined. The pseudo code of the *OExMiner* is depicted in Figure 1 and described as follows.

Steps *1-3* are to construct the *FP-tree* based on the given dataset, *D*, and a number, *k*. The initial position, *l*, and the offset, *Δl*, are set to the round of *k/2* and *k/5*, respectively, by default (they can be customized by users). Every element in *supQueue* (contains *k* lements) is initially set to *0* and an upper boundary for the minimum support *upper_sup*, is set (step 5). Since the *VirtualGrowth* might not be able to finish in an iteration, the variable *upper_sub* is necessary for checking the duplication (ref. step 2 of the *VirtualGrowth* procedure). The *VirtualGrowth* is called in step 6 returning a converged *supQueue* whose last element is extracted as the *final minimum support threshold θ*, (step 7). *FP-growth* algorithm is then involved, given *θ* as the support threshold, to extract *top-k* frequent patterns. The *VirtualGrowth* routine is also depicted in Figure 1 and described as follows.

The temporary *boundary_sup* called *lower_sup*, is set to the support of the element at position *l* in *F-list* (step 1). The supports of elements in *F_list* which are greater than *lower_sup* but smaller than *upper_sup*, are used to replace *0's* elements in *supQueue* (steps 2, 3). Since some elements in the *F-list* may have the same supports, the position *l* is updated to position of the last element in *F-list* whose support is equal to *lower_sup* (step 4). The *supQueue* is checked whether it converged (step 5). If *supQueue* has already converged, the routine returns and terminates (step 6), else it calls the *success_Mining* routine to traverse the tree and virtually mine the tree for potential frequent patterns (step 8). We can see in Figure 2 that the *success_Mining* returns TRUE when the *supQueue* converged (the support of the considered item in the header table dose not pass the minimum element of *supQueue* – ref. step 24 in Figure 2). Turning back to the *VirtualGrowth* routine in Figure 1, it will terminate when receives the TRUE value returned by *success_Mining* routine (step 9). On the other hand (the *supQueue* is not converged), a new iteration for *VirtualGrowth* is needed. A new position for *l* is set (step 11), the upper boundary for the minimum support is reset to the *lower_sup* (step 12) to avoid duplicating the consideration of the already considered potential frequent patterns. After that, the *VirtualGrowth* is recalled recursively in which *upper_sup* is served as the new support's upper boundary, (step 13). Noted that the new lower boundary for the minimum support, *lower_sup* is recalculated inner the routine based on the *F_list* and new value of *l*.

```
    Procedure ExMiner(dataset D, int k)
    Input: Dataset D, number of patterns k
    Output: top-k frequent patterns
    Method:
1.  Scan D to count support of all 1-itemsets
2.  According to k, set border_sup and generate F-list
3.  Construct an FP-tree according to F-list
4.  l=⌈k/2⌉; Δ₁=⌈k/5⌉;//default setting, user can customize these
    values
5.  upper_sub = sub(F_list[1])+1; supQueue[i] = 0 for all i;
6.  call VirtualGrowth(supQueue, Tree, l, F_list, upper_sb).
7.  θ = suqQueue[last]; // the final internal support threshold
8.  FP-growth algorithm is involved given θ as the support threshold
    to mine top-k frequent patterns.

    Procedure VirtualGrowth(supQueue, Tree, l, F_list, upper_sb)
    Input: an integer array, subQueue, the FP-tee, Tree; position, l;
           F_list, the upper-bound support value upper_sub
    Output: converged subQueue
    Method:
1.  lower_sup = sup(F-list[1]); i = 1;
2.  While (lower_sup ≤ sup(F-list[i++]) ≤ upper_sup)
3.          replace supQueue[j] by sup(F-list[i]) where supQueue[j] =
    0;
4.  l = i; // update l to the new position
5.  p = supQueue.find(0); // look for 0 element in supQueue
6.  If (p ≠ supQueue.end()) Return;
7.  Else
8.      If success_Mining(supQueue, Tree, Root, lower_sup, upper_sup)
9.          Return
10.     Else{
11.         l+= Δ₁;
12.         upper_sub = lower_sup;
13.         VirtualGrowth(supQueue, Tree, l, F_list, upper_sb)
14.     }
```

Fig. 1. Pseudo code of the *OExMiner* algorithm

Figure 2 is the pseudo code for the *success_Mining* procedure. This procedure examines the *FP-tree* to identify and trace the supports of potential frequent patterns which are used to make the *supQueue* converge. In this routine, to be satisfied for replacing an element in *supQueue* the support of a potential frequent pattern (represented by $sup(a_i)$) has to pass two conditions: greater than min_q and smaller than *upper_sub* (steps 6, 14 and 15). Finally, when the support of the considering item in the header table does not pass the min_q (step 24), the *supQueue* is converged and the routine returns TRUE.

```
Procedure success_Mining(supQueue, Tree, α, lower_sup, upper_sup){
(1) If Tree contains a single path P {
            i = 1; δ = sup(n_i); min_q = max(lower_sup, supQueue[last]);
            // n_1 represents for the 1st "real" node under Root
(2)     While (δ > min_q) {
(3)         If (α ≠ null) c = 2^(i-1);
(4)         Else c = 2^(i-1) - 1;
(5)         For each of c value of δ
(6)             If (min_q ≤ δ ≤ upper_sup) {
(7)                 replace supQueue[j] by sup(F-list[i]) where supQueue[j] = 0;
(8)                 min_q = max(min_q, supQueue[last]);
                    //supQueue is sorted automatically
(9)             }
                i++;
(10)        If (n_i ≠ null) δ = sup(n_i) Else δ = 0;
(11)    }// end While
(12) } // end If
(13) Else {
(14)    While (sup(a_i) > min_q){ // a_i in the header table, H
(15)        If ((α ≠ null)&& (sup(a_i)<upper_sup)){
(16)            replace supQueue[j] by sup(F-list[i]) where supQueue[j] = 0;
(17)            min_q = max(min_q, supQueue[last]);
(18)        }
(19)        β = a_i U α; a_i <- next item in header the table;
(20)        Construct β's conditional FP-tree, Tree_β;
                // based on its conditional pattern base
(21)        If (Tree_β ≠ empty)
(22)            call success_Mining(supQueue, Tree_β, β, min_q, upper_sup);
(23)    }// end While
(24)    If (a_i ≠ null) Return TRUE;
(25)    Else Return FALSE;
(26) }
```

Fig. 2. Pseudo code of the *success-Mining* procedure

4 Seq-Minner: Mining Top-k Frequent Patterns Sequentially

OExMiner has reduced the number of required singletons significantly compared to the *ExMiner*, but it still required a large number of singletons. In practice, especially in dense datasets which contain long patterns, just a very small number of items (compared to *k*) are examined to generate *top-k* frequent patterns. For example, in a real dataset, named *Connect-4* [2], only the first *15* (not 1000) items can generate *top-1000* frequent patterns and even only *19* (not 10,000) items can generate *top-10,000*

---

[2] Available at UCI Machine Learning Repository (http://www.ics.uci.edu/~mlearn/MLRepository.html).

frequent patterns. The smaller number of items an algorithm considers, the more efficient the algorithm is. However, the problem is *"how to ensure such a small number of items is adequate to mining for top-k frequent patterns correctly?"* The idea of mining *top-k* frequent patterns sequentially, or *Seq-Miner* for short, can solve this problem soundly.

The idea of mining *top-k* frequent patterns sequentially consists of two major advantages. *1)* It provides users the flexibility by proposing users n_c^3 highest frequency patterns first to examine interesting information. If they are not satisfied with the result, next *top-n_c* frequent patterns (i.e. *top-n_c+1* to *2n_c*) are proposed and so on. Users can stop the program when the interesting information is found or whenever they want. *2)* After finding *top-n_c* frequent patterns, algorithm can identify the number of items that is adequate for mining the next *top-n_c* ones correctly and efficiently. For example, if the algorithm recognized that only *15* items, for example, were actually examined for mining *top-1000*, then it will consider only *1015* items *(15+1000)* to mine *top-1001* to *2000* frequent patterns in the next mining iteration. In contrast, conventional algorithms have to consider at least *2000* items in this case. The fewer items are examined the better the algorithm is. Figure 3 is the block diagram of the *Seq-Miner* method.

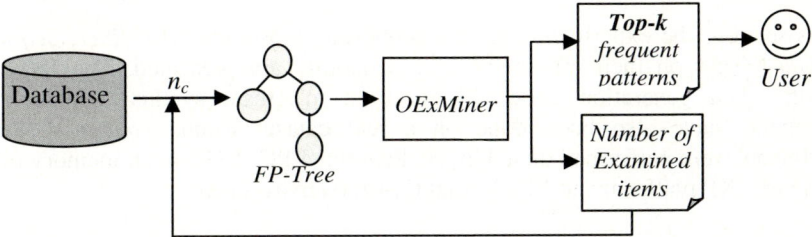

Fig. 4. The block diagram of the *Seq-Miner* method

In both *OExMiner* and *Seq-Miner* algorithm, a new *FP-tree* has to be rebuilt from the scratch whenever a given *top-k* is changed. If a "large" *FP-tree* which can be re-used to mine *top-k* frequent patterns with any different value of *top-k* is built in advance, the algorithm can significantly save the computation time. The idea of "<u>b</u>uild <u>o</u>nce <u>m</u>ine <u>a</u>nytime" *(BOMA)* allows us to do that. Moreover, the synthesis of *Seq-Miner* and the *BOMA* idea, called *Seq-BOMA* approach, can improve the performance surprisingly. This idea is illustrated in Figure 4 and described as follows.

A "large" *FP-tree* is built and saved into the hard disk. This information will be read to reconstruct the original "large" *FP-tree* (in the memory) when a *top-k* mining is required. After handling the original *FP-tree*, the *Seq-Miner* algorithm can be applied to mine for any *top-k* frequent patterns sequentially. The major computation time *of seq-BOMA* approach is the time to build the "large" *FP-tree*. However, since the tree is built only once and can be built in the computer-free time this approach becomes more practical in real applications. Another advantage of this approach is

---

[3] n_c is a chunk size which can be set by users or set to 1000 automatically by the algorithm.

that with an initial medium *FP-tree* many *top-k* frequent patterns, where the value of *k* is much greater than the number of items contained in the tree, can be mined sequentially. This feature improves the scalability of the algorithm and could not be found in any traditional *top-k* frequent patterns mining approach.

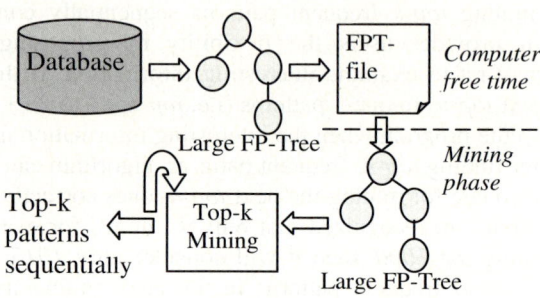

Fig. 4. The work flow of the *Seq-BOMA* approach

5 Experimental Evaluations

In this section, the experiments for the proposed algorithms *OExMiner*, *Seq-Miner*, and *Seq-BOMA* on their efficiency, and scalability are presented. The IBM quest synthetic data generation code [13] is used to create synthetic datasets. The experiments have also been done on a real dataset named *connect-4*. All the experiments were performed on a 3.2GHz Pentium 4 PC, 1 GB main memory running on Window XP platform and MS. Visual C++ 6.0 environment.

a. Efficiency Evaluation
In order to evaluate the efficiency of *OExMiner*, *Seq-Miner* and *seq-BOMA*, their computation time is compared to that of the *"optimal FP-growth"*, *"optimal Apriori"* and *Top-k FP-growth* [11] algorithms (*Top-k FP-growth* has been re-implemented in our machine). The *"optimal FP-growth"* is the *FP-growth* algorithm with the *best tuned* minimum support threshold to obtain an exactly desired number of *top-k* patterns (*"optimal Apriori"* is defined as the same way). The *best tuned* support threshold for a desired *top-k* pattern can be obtained by using *OExMiner* algorithm.

Figure 5 is the comparison between algorithms running on dataset D_1: *T10I4D1000kN1000k*. In this experiment, *top-k* frequent patterns where *k* varied from *1000* to *7000* with an interval of *1000* are mined. The figure shows that *OExMiner* is superior to the *TopK-FPGrow* and even faster than *optimal Apriori* with a factor of *2*. Other interesting things are that *Seq-Minner* is comparable to, and the *Seq-BOMA* is even better than the *optimal FP-growth*, the theoretically ideal method. To execute the *Seq-BOMA* algorithm in this experiment, a "large" *FP-tree* containing *7000* items (to mine *top-7000* patterns safely) is built in advance only once at the computer-free time.

The experiment on *connect-4* (*67,557* transactions with *43* items in each one) is shown in Figure 6. Since it is a dense dataset containing very long patterns, *Apriori* becomes extremely costly and incomparable to the remaining algorithms. Figure 6 excludes the *optimal Apriori* duce to the above reason. The figure shows that

OExMiner is about *3* times faster than *TopK-FPGrow* whereas *Seq-BOMA* is about *7* times faster than *TopK-FPGrow* and almost the same as the *optimal FP-growth*.

b. Scalability Evaluation

To evaluate the scalability of the proposed methods we use another synthetic dataset, named D_2: *T10I4D1000kN2000k*, which contains 2 million items (twice of that in D_1). As shown in Figure 7, *OExMiner* is still better than *TopK-FPGrow*; *Seq-Miner* is still comparable to, while *Seq-BOMA* is clearly better than *optimal FP-growth*. This result reveals that our proposed methods scale well in the large datasets.

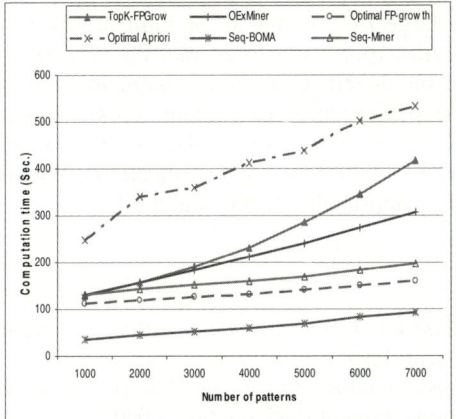 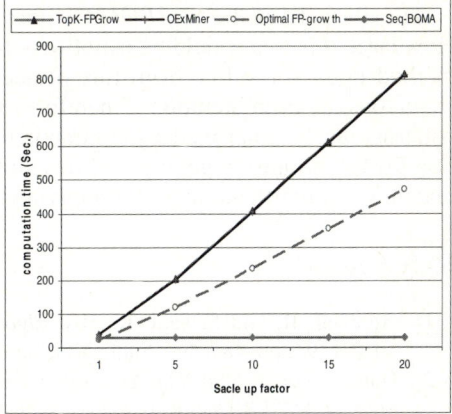

Fig. 7. Time comparison on D_1 *T10I4D1000kN2000k*

Fig. 8. Time comparison on scaled up *Connect 4*

In real applications, many datasets such as customer transactional datasets of super markets, or electronic shops contain many duplicated transactions. To experiment how well the proposed methods execute on those kinds of dataset we duplicate dataset *connect-4* with some scale up factors and test on those scaled up datasets.

Figure 8 shows the experimental results where number of desired *top-k* patterns is fixed to *10,000*. The computation time of *Seq-BOMA* is constant at the value of *29* or *30* second while the computation time of three remaining algorithms increases very fast. When the scale up factor is *20*, *Seq-BOMA* is faster than *optimal FP-growth* about *17* times. The reason for *Seq-BOMA* keeping a constant computation time is that when the dataset is duplicated, the structure and the size of the original "large" *FP-tree* do not change. Therefore the time of reading, reconstructing and mining the tree for *top-k* frequent patterns in *Seq-BOMA* does not change as well. The result of this experiment reveals that *Seq-BOMA* can be worthily applied to mine *top-k* frequent patterns in such datasets that contain many duplicating transactions. Note that Figure 8 excludes the computation time for *Seq-Miner* since it is the same as the *OExMiner*. The reason is that the number of items to be examined increases much more slowly than the number of *top-k* patterns does, *15* items for *top-1000* patterns while only *19* items for *top-10,000* patterns, for example. Therefore the *Seq-Miner* is not robust in this case (for a very and very dense dataset).

6 Conclusions and Future Work

This research proposed an optimized version of the *ExMiner* method, called *OExMiner,* to mine *top-k* frequent patterns more efficiently and effectively. *Seq-Miner* is then proposed based on the extension of the *OExMiner* to mine *top-k* frequent pattern *sequentially* by which improves not only the performance but also the user-friendliness of the algorithm. *Seq-BOMA* approach, the combination between *Seq-Miner* algorithm and the idea of "build once mine anytime", proposed many beneficial features for the real applications. The experiments on both synthetic and real datasets revealed that our proposed methods are scaled well on large datasets and superior to the existing algorithms.

The obstacle of the *Seq-BOMA* is that a large *FP-tree* has to be built in advance. How large this tree should be is not easy for un-expert users to decide. The *Seq-Miner* method does not suffer from this obstacle but it still examines a large number of singletons in each iteration. Therefore, the performance of mining *top-k* frequent patterns can be improved by optimizing these methods. Obviously, *Seq-Miner* and *Seq-BOMA* promise a great possibility of being applied into real applications. We are planning to investigate more for applying these approaches to the real works.

References

[1] Agrawal, R, and Srikant, R. *Fast algorithm for mining association rules*. In proc. of VLDB '94. pp. 487-499, Santiago, Chille, Sept. 1994.
[2] Han, J., Pei, J., and Yin, Y. *Mining frequent patterns without candidate generation*. In proc. of ACM SIGMOD Conference on Management of Data, pp. 1-12, 2000.
[3] Bayard, R.J. *Efficiently mining long patterns from databases*. In proc. of ACM SIGMOD Conference on Management of Data, pp. 85-93, 1998.
[4] Grahne, G., and Zhu, J. *High performance mining of maxima frequent itemsets*. In proc. of SIAM'03 workshop on High Performance Data Mining, 2003.
[5] Grahne, G., and Zhu, J. *Efficiently using prefix-tree in mining frequent itemsets*. In proc. of IEEE ICDM workshop on Frequent Itemsets Mining Implementations, 2003.
[6] Pei, J., Han, J., and Mao, R. *CLOSET: An efficient algorithm from mining frequent closed itemsets*. In proc. of DMKD'00, 2000.
[7] Fu, A.W., Kwong, R.W., Tang, J. *Mining N most interesting itemsets*. In proc. of ISMIS'00, 2000.
[8] Han, J., Wang, J., Lu, Y. and Tzvetkov, P. *Mining top-k frequent closed patterns without minimum support*. In proc. of IEEE ICDM Conference on Data Mining, 2002.
[9] Ly, S., Hong, S., Paul, P., and Rodney, T. *Finding the N largest itemsets*. In Proc. Int. Conf. on Data Mining, Rio de Janeiro, Brazil, pp. 211-222., 1998.
[10] Wang, J., Han, J., Lu, Y. and Tzvetkov, P. *TFP: An efficient algorithm for mining top-k frequent closed itemsets*. In proc. of IEEE Knowledge and Data Engineering, vol 17, no.5 pp. 652-663, 2005.
[11] Hirate, Y., Iwahashi, E., and Yamana, H. *TF^2P-growth: An efficient algorithm for mining frequent patterns without any thresholds*. In proc. of ICDM., 2004.
[12] Quang, T.M., Oyanagi, S., and Yamazaki, K. *ExMiner: An efficient algorithm for mining top-K frequent patterns*. In LNAI 4093, Springer-verlag Berlin Heidelberg , 2006, pp. 436 – 447.
[13] IBM Quest Data Mining Project. Quest synthetic data generation http://almaden.ibm.com/software/quest/Resources/index.shtml

Discovering Non-taxonomic Relations from the Web

David Sánchez and Antonio Moreno

Universitat Rovira i Virgili (URV)
Computer Science and Mathematics Department
43007 Tarragona, Catalonia, Spain
{david.sanchez, antonio.moreno}@urv.net

Abstract. The discovery of non-taxonomical relationships is one of the less studied knowledge acquisition tasks, even though it is a crucial point in ontology learning. We present an automatic and unsupervised methodology for extracting non-taxonomically related concepts and labelling relationships, using the whole Web as learning corpus. We also discuss how the obtained relationships may be automatically evaluated, using relatedness measures based on WordNet.

1 Introduction

The Web is an invaluable repository of knowledge. It has been considered that the number of resources available in the Web is so vast and the amount of people generating web pages is so enormous, that the Web information distribution approximates the actual real distribution as used in society [1]. Moreover, the redundancy of information in such a wide environment can represent a measure of relevance and trustiness of information for a certain domain. For those reasons, many authors [2][3][4] have been using the Web as the corpus for different knowledge acquisition tasks.

One of the most researched tasks is *ontology learning* from the Web. However, most of the approaches [4][5] are focused on the acquisition of taxonomical relationships and often neglect the importance of interlinkage between concepts. In fact, the discovery of non-taxonomic relations is understood as the least tackled aspect within ontology learning [6]. In general, two tasks have to be performed: first, detect which concepts are related and, second, assign a label for the relation (typically using verb phrases).

So, in this paper, we present an *automatic method for discovering non-taxonomic relationships from the Web*. This task involves the *i)* discovery of semantic patterns used for expressing non-taxonomic relationships in a specific domain (verb phrases) *ii)* retrieval of a corpus according to the acquired knowledge from where to extract candidates and *iii)* selection of the most appropriate concepts and relationships incorporating them to the ontology. This method has been designed as an extension of another one [7] that covers the taxonomical aspect of ontology learning.

The main features of our contribution are:

1. Unsupervised operation during the Web analysis and the learning process. This is important due to the amount of resources, avoiding the need of a human expert.
2. Automatic operation, allowing to perform easily executions to maintain the results updated. This characteristic fits very well with the dynamic nature of the Web.

3. Domain independent solution, because no domain assumptions are formulated and no predefined knowledge is needed. This is interesting when dealing with technological domains where specific and non widely-used concepts may appear. The only restriction here is that it can be only applied with English written resources.
4. Incremental learning with dynamic adaptation of the evaluated corpus as new knowledge is acquired. This results in an optimization of the computational cost of the analysis, retrieving only the most concrete and appropriate web resources.

The rest of the paper is organized as follows. Section 2 introduces the premises and techniques that configure the base of our proposal. Section 3 describes the proposed methodology to extract and label non-taxonomical relationships. Section 4 discusses the evaluation of results using WordNet based relatedness measures. Section 5 introduces related works and the final section presents the conclusions and lines of future work.

2 Knowledge Acquisition Framework

In this section, we comment some aspects of the knowledge acquisition techniques used to discover, extract and select non-taxonomical relationships from the Web:

– Lightweight analysis techniques are needed to achieve good scalability in such an enormous environment like the Web [8]. So, in order to perform an efficient analysis, the amount of processed information for each resource should be reduced to the minimum. Concretely, only those pieces of text that present knowledge in a simple, direct and unambiguous way (typically called *text nuggets* [8]) can be analysed.
– Statistical analysis applied over knowledge acquisition tasks is a good deal if enough information is available to obtain relevant measures. As introduced before, the Web environment is especially suitable for this task due to its size and heterogeneity. Moreover, web search engines can provide confident measures (*web-scale statistics*) in an immediate way if the appropriate search queries are formulated [9]. In our case, this is a crucial point because it allows us to obtain robust statistics about information distribution in a very scalable and efficient way.
– The use of linguistic patterns can be an effective technique to extract knowledge without expert's supervision and without predefined knowledge. For the taxonomical case, domain independent linguistic patterns [10] are a very common manner of discovering relationships. However, for the non-taxonomical case, aside from a reduced set of predefined relationships (e.g. meronymy, antonymy, synonymy, etc), there do not exist domain independent patterns, as those relationships are typically expressed by a verb that relates a pair of concepts [6]. If we want to use this pattern-based approach to extract non-taxonomical knowledge, a previous step for learning suitable patterns (verb phrases) for the analysed domain is required.
– As learning in a completely unsupervised and automatic way is difficult, an incremental approach in which several learning steps are defined and each one is enriched (bootstrapped) with the most relevant knowledge already acquired can be suitable. In our case, bootstrapping is used to constrain the search process contextualizing the queries formulated to the search engine in order to obtain appropriate corpus of documents and web-scale statistics for the specific domain. Bootstrapped information involves already acquired concepts and linguistic patterns.

3 Non-taxonomical Learning

The first step in our non-taxonomical learning is the discovery of linguistic patterns that express non-taxonomical relationships. In this case, those relationships are typically expressed by a verb relating a pair of concepts. Due to the potential amount of verbs available in the English language, we should find which of them are truly relevant for the particular domain (in our case, a domain is expressed by an initial keyword, such us *hypertension*). In order to do this, we query a web search engine with the initial keyword to obtain a set of web resources covering the specific domain. For each one, a lightweight syntactical analysis is performed, considering the neighbourhood terms that surround the initial keyword in order to find verb phrases (conjugated verb and, optionally, prepositions), composing a list of candidates. Those candidates are classified in function of their position within the sentence: *predecessors* (e.g. "*is associated with* hypertension") or *successors* (e.g. "hypertension *is treated with*") of the initial keyword.

Each candidate is evaluated in order to decide if it is really closely related to the search domain. As we base our unsupervised analysis in statistical measures, we consider measures of co-occurrence between the verb phrase and the domain's keyword as a measure of relatedness between them. In order to obtain a robust measure, we use the mentioned web-scale statistics that represent the distribution of a queried concept in the whole Web. Concretely, for each verb phrase candidate that has been extracted as a *predecessor* of the initial keyword, we compute the following relatedness score (1) by asking the number of hits returned by a web search engine for the following queries:

$$Score(\frac{verbPhrase}{initKey}) = \frac{hits("verbPhrase\ initKey")}{hits("verbPhrase")} \quad (1)$$

Alternatively, if the candidate has been extracted as a *successor* of the initial keyword, we compute the same relatedness but specifying the inverse order in the corresponding query (*hits("initKey verbPhrase")*). Those formulas are derived from the score measures presented in [9] that are typically used to compute the degree of relationship between two words. Note also that double quotes are used to force the search of the exact string to ensure that the verb phrase is truly linked with the initial keyword.

The returned values are used to rank the list of domain dependent linguistic pattern candidates (verb phrases) and select those that are more closely related to the analysed domain (see examples in Table 1, for the *hypertension* example).

Once those domain dependent linguistic patterns have been obtained, the next step is to use them to discover concepts that are non-taxonomically (verb-labelled) related with the initial keyword. So, we query a web search engine with the pair "verb-phrase initial-keyword" or "initial-keyword verb-phrase" depending on whether the verb phrase precedes or succeeds the initial keyword. The result will be a set of web resources that contain the specified query. Our objective in this case is to evaluate their content to obtain concepts that immediately precede (e.g. "*salt intake* is associated with hypertension") or succeed (e.g. "hypertension is treated with *diuretics*") the specified query. Those new concepts become candidates for being non-taxonomically related with the initial keyword, labelling this relation with the verb phrase.

Next, we have to decide again which of the extracted concepts (e.g. "salt intake") are closely related to the searched domain (e.g. "hypertension"). In order to perform this

Table 1. Firsts elements of the ranked list of verb phrases (173 total candidates) for the *Hypertension* domain, according to their position (PREdecessors or SUCcessors of the initial keyword)

Verb phrase	Position	Relatedness	Verb phrase	Position	Relatedness
is diagnosed in	SUC	0.12	is indicated for	PRE	0.11
are diagnosed as	PRE	0.10	is diagnosed as	PRE	0.08
is associated with	PRE	0.06	are associated with	PRE	0.06
is aggravated by	SUC	0.05	is cured by	SUC	0.03
is caused by	SUC	0.03	occurs during	SUC	0.03
is influenced by	SUC	0.03	suffer from	PRE	0.02
is treated with	SUC	0.02	accelerates	SUC	0.02

selection process we use again web scale statistics about the co-occurrence of those two terms. In this case, the relatedness score is computed in the following manner (2):

$$Score(\frac{Concept}{initKey}) = \frac{hits("initKey" \ AND \ "Concept")}{hits("Concept")} \quad (2)$$

In this case, the AND operator ensures that those two terms co-occur within the text but not necessarily in the same sentence. If we use double quotes or add the verb phrase to the query, it will become too restrictive to obtain robust measures.

Those concepts whose relatedness is higher than a threshold (see some examples for *hypertension* in Table 2) are selected and incorporated into the ontology, with a relation that is labelled according to the verb phrase used to discover them (e.g. "salt intake" "is associated with" "hypertension"). Note that the direction of the relation corresponds to the role that each concept plays in the sentences (subject or object).

Finally, results are integrated with those from a methodology for learning taxonomies [7] using a standard ontology representation language (OWL), providing a tool that covers the main aspects of ontology learning.

Table 2. Examples of verb-labelled non-taxonomical relations for the *Hypertension* domain. Those in *italic* represent rejected candidates (relatedness below 0.1).

Subject (NP)	Verb (VP)	Object (NP)	Relat.
diuretic therapy	is indicated for	hypertension	0.61
salt intake	is associated with	hypertension	0.45
latter factors	*are associated with*	*hypertension*	*0.08*
hypertension	*is diagnosed in*	*individuals*	*0.006*
hypertension	is aggravated by	obesity	0.12
hypertension	*is aggravated by*	*the increase*	*0.01*
hypertension	is influenced by	sodium retention	0.65
hypertension	*is influenced by*	*some factors*	*0.02*
hypertension	is treated with	antihypertensives	0.55
hypertension	accelerates	renal disease	0.49
hypertension	*accelerates*	*the development*	*0.003*

4 Evaluation

Evaluating results of an automatic learning methodology is a difficult task. In general, either an expert opinion is needed to check the results manually or a repository is required to perform any automatic evaluation. Due to the nature of the learning environment (the huge and changing Web) and the learning method (domain independent, automatic and unsupervised) we focus on the automatic side.

The biggest and most widely used general purpose English electronic repository is WordNet [11]. It offers a lexicon, a thesaurus and semantic linkage between English terms. Using all this information it is possible to compute the similarity and relatedness between concepts. In this sense, the software *WordNet::Similarity* [12] offers an implementation of some standard measures that have been widely used for different knowledge related tasks [13]. Concretely, similarity measures use information found in an *is-a* hierarchy of concepts and quantify how much a concept A is like another B. WordNet is particularly well suited for similarity measures, since it organizes nouns and verbs into *is-a* hierarchies and, therefore, it can be very adequate for evaluating taxonomical relations. However, concepts can be related in many ways beyond being similar to each other. As such, WordNet provides relations beyond *is-a*, including *has-part*, *is-made-of* and *is-an-attribute-of*. In addition, each concept is defined by a short gloss that may include an example of use. All this information can be brought to bear in creating measures of relatedness. As a result, these measures tend to be more general and, in our case, more appropriate for evaluating non-taxonomically related terms.

Among the different relatedness measures implemented by *WordNet::Similarity*, we have chosen *vector-pairs* [13] because it does not depend on the interlinkage between words that, in many situations, has a poor coverage in the WordNet semantic network. This measure incorporates information from WordNet glosses as a unique representation for the underlying concept, creating a cooccurrence matrix from a corpus made up of the WordNet glosses. Each content word used in a WordNet gloss has an associated context vector. Each gloss is represented by a gloss vector that is the average of all the context vectors of the words found in the gloss. Relatedness between concepts is measured by finding the cosine between a pair of gloss vectors. For a pair of terms, the bigger the measure is, the more related the terms are (in a range between 0 and 0.5).

However, in general, all relatedness measures have serious limitations because they assume that all the semantic content of a particular term is modelled by semantic links and/or glosses in WordNet and, in consequence, in many situations, truly related terms obtain a low score due to WordNet's poor coverage. However, these measures are some of the very few fully automatic general purpose ways of evaluating results.

Applied to our approach, we check our Web based relatedness measure between two non-taxonomically related concepts by comparing it against *vector-pairs*, using *WordNet::Similarity* whenever both terms are in WordNet. The result can be represented in a plane in which each axis corresponds to one of those measures. Adding the limit that represents the selection threshold over both axis, it is also possible to evaluate the correctness of our candidate selection procedure visualizing correctly classified concepts (selected or discarded) and incorrectly classified ones (selected or discarded). An example of the type of results that we are able to obtain (whenever the particular domain is contained in WordNet) is represented in Figure 1 for the *Hypertension* domain.

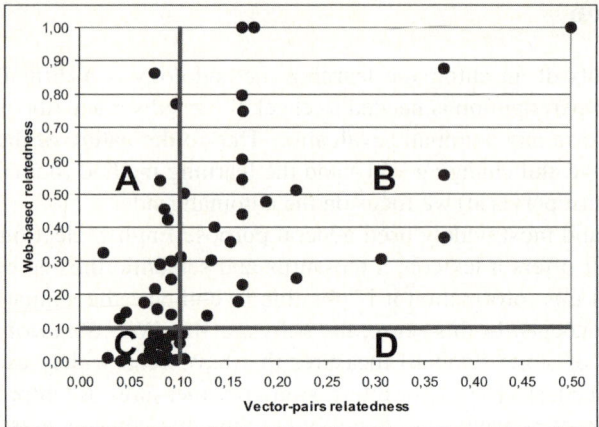

Fig. 1. Comparison of our Web-based relatedness measure against *vector-pairs* for the *Hypertension* domain. A: false positives; B: true positives; C: true negatives; D: false negatives.

Analysing this example (that shows a common tendency observed in several domains), we can extract the following conclusions:

- *True positives* (section B) cover a big area, with relatedness (using both measures) values above 0.1. *False negatives* (section D) are almost nonexistent apart from a pair of examples observed over the boundaries of the selection threshold. These facts indicate that when a pair of concepts are closely related according to the *vector-pairs* measure, our measure also indicates the same.
- *True negatives* (section C) tend to conform a compact set that have a value of relatedness (using both measures) below 0.1. However *false positives* (section A) are quite common, showing a discordance between both measures. Analysing them, we have observed that the poor performance is caused in many situations by the way in which *vector-pairs* (and in general all WordNet based relatedness measures) works. As has been introduced previously, those measures completely depend on WordNet's coverage for each concept (semantically expressed by interlinks or glosses); in consequence, when concepts are slightly considered in WordNet, those measures return a value that does not fully represent the reality. For example *vector-pairs* returns a very low value of 0.007 between *diuretics* and *hypertension* even though the first is a common treatment for the second; this is because, in Wordnet, this fact is not mentioned in the *diuretics*' gloss. In contrast, our measure depends on the Web's coverage for a particular term and, taking into consideration its size compared to WordNet, it can be seen why we are able to provide more consistent results over a wider set of concepts (returning a value of 0.6 for the mentioned example).

Finally, one may realize that the evaluation does not consider the verb used to label the relations. This is because relatedness measures are intended for nouns (concrete things with specific meaning). However, as final concepts are obtained through verb phrases, their quality (evaluated here) also depends on the quality of extracted verbs.

5 Related Work

Faure and Nedellec [14] presented an interactive machine learning system, ASIUM, which hierarchically clusters nouns based on the verbs that they co-occur with and vice versa. The proposal by Byrd and Ravin [15] extracts named relations when they find particular syntactic patterns, such as an appositive phrase. They derive unnamed relations from concepts that co-occur by calculating the measure for mutual information between terms. Finkelstein and Morin [16] combine supervised and unsupervised extraction of relationships between terms, assigning them default labels. Maedche and Staab [17] use shallow text processing methods to identify linguistically related pairs of words. Thereby, they use the background knowledge from a taxonomy to propose relations at the appropriate level of abstraction but without considering the problem about labelling. Kavalec *et al.* [6] apply co-occurrence analyses to extract related terms. Then, they hypothesised that the 'predicate' of a non-taxonomic relation can be characterised by verbs frequently occurring in the neighbourhood of pairs of lexical entries. Other approaches based on clustering of documents using self-organizing maps (SOM) [18] or topological trees are able to express relationships between clusters unsupervisedly.

Studying those systems, the conclusion is that most of these approaches apply co-occurrences analysis in order to find out which concepts are related. In some cases, those unnamed relations are labelled using the verbs. Those aspects also conform the base of our approach, but the way in which we obtain resources to evaluate, the linguistic analysis and the computing of statistical measures are especially adapted to achieve good performance and efficiency in the Web environment.

6 Conclusions and Future Work

The presented methodology does not start from any predefined knowledge and, in consequence, it can be applied over domains that are not typically considered in semantic repositories. The automatic operation eases the updating of the results in highly changing domains without depending on a human expert. Those aspects conform an unsupervised and domain independent methodology for extracting non-taxonomical relationships from the Web.

As future lines of research, firstly, we can consider problems about semantic ambiguity presented in natural language resources. In this sense, complementary methods have been developed for dealing with polysemy [7] and synonymy [19] specially adapted to our working environment (web resources, search engines and lack of predefined knowledge) that we plan to integrate into our learning methodology.

Secondly, regarding the discovered verb labelled relationships, in order to obtain a computer understandable knowledge base that allows inference, verb labels should be interpreted (e.g. the verb phrase *"is included into"* expresses a *"part of"* type relationship). Standard classifications of verbs [20] could be used for this purpose, adding additional information about the semantic content of verb labelled relationships.

Finally, the proposed evaluation methodology should be improved in order to tackle the limitations described in Section 4. Maintaining the automatic operation (WordNet based), we plan to combine *vector-pairs* [13] with other additional relatedness measures [12] in order to improve the performance.

Acknowledgements. The work has been supported by *Departament d'Universitats, Recerca i Societat de la Informació de la Generalitat de Catalunya i del Fons Social Europeu* of Catalonia.

References

1. Cilibrasi, R., Vitanyi, P.: Automatic meaning discovery using Google (2004) Available at: http://xxx.lanl.gov/abs/cs.CL/0412098.
2. Brill, E., Lin, J., Banko, M., Dumais, S.: Data-intensive Question Answering. In: 10th Text Retrieval Conference. (2001)
3. Agirre, E., Ansa, O., Hovy, E., Martinez, D.: Enriching very large ontologies using the WWW. In: Workshop on Ontology Construction (ECAI-00), Berlin, Germany (2000)
4. Etzioni, O., Cafarella, M., Downey, D., Popescu, A., Shaked, T., Soderland, S., Weld, D., Yates, A.: Unsupervised named-entity extraction form the Web: An experimental study. Artificial Intelligence **165** (2005) 91–134
5. Cimiano, P., Staab, S.: Learning by Googling. SIGKDD **6** (2004) 24–33
6. Kavalec, M., Maedche, A., Skátek, V.: Discovery of Lexical Entries for Non-taxonomic Relations in Ontology Learning. In: SOFSEM'04. Volume 2932 of LNCS. (2004) 249–256
7. Sánchez, D., Moreno, A.: Automatic Generation of Taxonomies from the WWW. In: 5th International Conference on Practical Aspects of Knowledge Management. Volume 3336 of LNAI., Vienna, Austria (2004) 208–219
8. Pasca, M.: Finding Instance Names and Alternative Glosses on the Web: WordNet Reloaded. In: CICLing 2005. Volume 3406 of LNCS., Springer (2005) 280–292
9. Turney, P.: Mining the Web for synonyms: PMI-IR versus LSA on TOEFL. In: 12th European Conference on Machine Learning, Germany (2001)
10. Hearst, M.: Automatic acquisition of hyponyms from large text corpora. In: 14th International Conference on Computational Linguistics, France (1992) 539–545
11. Miller, G.: Wordnet: A lexical database. Communication of the ACM **38** (1995) 39–41
12. Pedersen, T., Patwardhan, S., Michelizzi, J.: WordNet::Similarity - Measuring the Relatedness of Concepts. In: 5th Annual Meeting of the North American Chapter of the Association for Computational Linguistics, Boston, USA (2004)
13. Patwardhan, S.: Incorporating Dictionary and Corpus Information into a Context Vector Measure of Semantic Relatedness (2003) Master of Science Thesis.
14. Faure, D., Nedellec, C.: Corpus-based conceptual clustering method for verb frames and ontology acquisition. In: LREC-98 Workshop on Adapting Lexical and Corpus Resources to Sublanguages and Applications, Granada, Spain (1998)
15. Byrd, R., Ravin, Y.: Identifying and extracting relations from text. In: 4th International Conference on Applications of Natural Language to Information Systems. (1999)
16. Finkelstein-Landau, M., Morin, E.: Extracting Semantic Relationships between Terms: Supervised vs. Unsupervised Methods. In: Workshop on Ontological Engineering on the Global Information Infrastructure. (1999)
17. Maedche, A., Staab, S.: Discovering Conceptual Relations from Text. In: 14th European Conference on Artificial Intelligence, Amsterdam, Netherlands (2000)
18. Kohonen, T., Kaski, S., Lagus, K., Salojarvi, J., Honkela, J., Paatero, V., Saarela, A.: Self organization of a massive document collection. IEEE Transactions on Neural Networks **11** (2000) 574–585
19. Sánchez, D., Moreno, A.: Automatic Discovery of Synonyms and Lexicalizations from the Web. In: Artificial Intelligence Research and Development. Volume 131. (2005) 205–212
20. Levin, B.: English Verb Classes and Alternations. Chicago University, Chicago, USA (1993)

A New Algorithm of Similarity Measuring for Multi-experts' Qualitative Knowledge Based on Outranking Relations in Case-Based Reasoning Methodology*

Hui Li[1], Xiang-Yang Li[1], and Jie Gu[2]

[1] School of Management, Harbin Institute of Technology, Harbin 150001
Heilongjiang Province, China
{lihuihit, lixiangyanghit}@sohu.com
[2] School of Software, Tsinghua University, Beijing 100084, China
guj05@mails.tsinghua.edu.cn

Abstract. Qualitative knowledge reasoning is a key content in knowledge science. Case-based reasoning is one of the main reasoning methodologies in artificial intelligence. Outranking relation methods, called ELECTRE and others, have been developed. In this research, a new algorithm of similarity measuring for qualitative problems in the presence of multiple experts based on outranking relations in case-based reasoning was proposed. Strict preference, weak preference, and indifference relations were introduced to formulate imprecision, uncertainty, incompleteness knowledge from multi-experts. Case similarities were integrated through aggregating house on the foundation of outranking relations. Experiments indicated that the new algorithm got accordant outcome with traditional quantitative similarity mode but extended its application range.

1 Introduction

Expert Systems (ES) focus on applying experts' task-specific knowledge that transferred from a human to a computer, whose trend is to develop ES towards expertise orientation [1]. The mode to deal with experts' knowledge of traditional ES is storing them in computer to provide specific advices when called on [2]. Hence, knowledge representation is a key step, which is becoming a bottle-neck. The stress of expertise orientation includes implementing knowledge reasoning in the presence of experts, if the knowledge is qualitative or difficult to be represented and entered into computer. Qualitative knowledge reasoning methodology is important because experts' knowledge is always qualitative and quantification value of experts' knowledge is subject to imprecision and inconsistency. The idea of case-based reasoning (CBR), which was firstly discussed by Schank [3], is to adapt solutions of previous problems to solve new problems on the assumption that similar problems have similar solutions [4]. The common accepted model of CBR is the R^4 model, which constitutes four processes:

---

* This work is supported by the National Natural Science Foundation of China (# 70571019), the National Defense Basic Science and Research Project of China (# A2320060097), and National Center of Technology, Policy and Management, Harbin Institute of Technology.

retrieve, reuse, revise, and retain [5]. However, there are some other models [6], [7]. Their common drawback is that they are all on the assumption that the case base is ready for the first process. Finnie and Sun (2003) integrated case representation and proposed a R^5 model [8]. It is common that quantification value of experts' knowledge is subject to imprecision. Thus, there are many conditions the R^5 model is hard to get satisfaction. So, similarity algorithms dealing with qualitative problems in the presence of experts had better to be counted on.

This research attempts to build a new algorithm of similarity measuring for qualitative problems based on outranking relations in the presence of multiple experts. The rest of the paper is divided into four sections. Section 2 is a brief description on traditional case similarity algorithm. Section 3 builds up the new similarity algorithm, and experiment is discussed and analyzed in section 4. Section 5 makes conclusions.

2 Common Case Similarity Algorithm in Case Retrieval

The most common type of distance measure in nearest-neighbor retrieval is based on the location of objects in Euclidean space. Let CB=$\{c_1, c_2, ..., c_N\}$ denotes a case library. Each case can be identified by a set of corresponding features, which can be expressed as $\{F_j\}$ ($j = 1, 2, ..., n$). The ith case c_i in case base can be represented as an n-dimensional vector, $c_i = (x_{i1}, x_{i2}, ..., x_{in})$, where x_{ij} corresponds to the value of feature F_j ($1 \leq j \leq n$). Let the weight of each feature F_j be expressed as w_j ($w_j \in [0,1]$). For a pair of cases c_p and c_q in case base, a weighted distance metric can be defined as

$$SIM_{p,q}^{(w)} = SIM^{(w)}(c_p,c_q) = \frac{1}{1+d_{p,q}^{(w)}} = 1 \Big/ (1+\alpha(\sum_{j=1}^{n} w_j^2 (x_{p,j} - x_{q,j})^2)^{0.5}). \quad (1)$$

The distance measure for the jth feature denotes as d_j which has the following properties: $d_j(a, b) = 0$ if and only if a = b, $d_j(a, b) = d_j(b, a)$, $d_j(a, c) \leq d_j(a, b) + d_j(b, c)$. And,

$$d_j(a, b) = |a - b| \text{ if a and b are real numbers}. \quad (2)$$

$$d_j(a, b) = \begin{cases} 0 & \text{if a = b} \\ 1 & \text{if a} \neq \text{b} \end{cases} \text{ if a and b are qualitative or symbols}. \quad (3)$$

In these circumstances, the similarity between c_p and c_q can be computed by

$$SIM_{p,q}^{(w)} = SIM^{(w)}(c_p,c_q) = \frac{1}{1+d_{p,q}^{(w)}} = 1 \Big/ (1+\alpha(\sum_{j=1}^{n} w_j^2 (d_j(a,b))^2)^{0.5}). \quad (4)$$

Formula (3) is the method used in dealing with qualitative problems. Though it is simple and straightforward, it lacks a firm methodological basis, and doesn't take expertise into consideration.

3 The New Similarity Algorithm for Qualitative Problems

What is thus required is a method that is relatively simple and with a methodological basis, which insures that the quantification of qualitative description reflects the experts' actual preference. In order to deal with conflicting multi-criteria in complex systems, Roy developed pseudo-criterion, indifference and preference thresholds [9], [10]. Thus, outranking relations can be drawn out on experts' actual preferences in terms of what he believes, and it is more reasonable than *Formula (3)*. Indifference threshold, q_k, and preference threshold, p_k, are hidden values in experts' experience. Even if experts can not point out the real number of the two types of thresholds, they can express their knowledge through outranking relations on the basis of them. Thus, qualitative problems can be quantificated by outranking relations based on expertise.

Let stored cases be denoted as $Ent = \{ent(1), ent(2), ..., ent(i), ..., ent(n)\}$, experts be denoted as $Dag = \{dag(1), dag(2), ..., dag(j), ..., dag(m)\}$, corresponding features be denoted as $Ind = \{ind(k)\}$, and feature weights be denoted as $Wei_j = \{wei_j(k)\}$. Thus, actual preference information of expert $dag(j)$ can be denoted as.

$$dag(j)_d = \begin{pmatrix} ind(1)_{ent(1)} & \cdots & ind(k)_{ent(1)} \\ \vdots & \ddots & \vdots \\ ind(1)_{ent(i)} & \cdots & ind(k)_{ent(i)} \end{pmatrix} = (ind(k)_{ent(i)})_{n \times Num(Ind)} \quad (5)$$

In which, $ind(k)_{ent(i)}$ expresses actual preference of expert $dag(j)$ on the kth feature of the ith case, which is qualitative or quantification value that is subject to imprecision, and uncertainty. The new similarity algorithm for qualitative problems in case retrieval is based on confirmation approaches of outranking relations. Entered data are experts' knowledge, and output data, outranking relation indexes among stored cases.

3.1 Confirming Outranking Relations

Definitions below are operated on *Formula (5)*. How expertise is dealt with can be denoted by these *definitions*. Firstly, single expert involved condition is considered. Generally, it can be assumed that larger value is preferred to smaller one.

Definition 1: $P_{k,j}(ind(k)_{ent(i1)}, ind(k)_{ent(i2)})$. $\forall\ ent(i1) \in Ent, \forall\ ent(i2) \in Ent, \forall\ ind(k) \in Ind, \forall\ dag(j) \in Dag, \exists\ p_k \in R^+$. If the condition, $ind(k)_{ent(i1)} - ind(k)_{ent(i2)} > p_k$, is met based on knowledge of expert $dag(j)$. Then, what the expert believes is that $ind(k)_{ent(i1)}$ is strict preferred to $ind(k)_{ent(i2)}$ if feature $ind(k)$ is taken into consideration. That can be denoted as $P_{k,j}(ind(k)_{ent(i1)}, ind(k)_{ent(i2)})$, and in this *definition*, p_k is a preference threshold and a qualitative description that expresses what the expert believes.

Definition 2: $I_{k,j}(ind(k)_{ent(i1)}, ind(k)_{ent(i2)})$. $\forall\ ent(i1) \in Ent, \forall\ ent(i2) \in Ent, \forall\ ind(k) \in Ind, \forall\ dag(j) \in Dag, \exists\ p_k \in R^+$. If the condition, $|ind(k)_{ent(i1)} - ind(k)_{ent(i2)}| \leq q_k$, is met based on knowledge of expert $dag(j)$. Then, what the expert believes is that $ind(k)_{ent(i1)}$ is indifference to $ind(k)_{ent(i2)}$ if feature $ind(k)$ is taken into consideration. That can be denoted as $I_{k,j}(ind(k)_{ent(i1)}, ind(k)_{ent(i2)})$. In this *definition*, q_k is an indifference threshold and a qualitative description that expresses what the expert believes.

Definition 3: $W_{k,j}(ind(k)_{ent(i1)}, ind(k)_{ent(i2)})$. $\forall\ ent(i1) \in Ent, \forall\ ent(i2) \in Ent, \forall\ ind(k) \in Ind, \forall\ dag(j) \in Dag, \exists\ p_k \in R^+, \exists\ q_k \in R^+, q_k < p_k$. If the condition, $q_k < ind(k)_{ent(i1)} - ind(k)_{ent(i2)} \leq p_k$, is met based on knowledge of expert $dag(j)$. Then, what the expert believes is that $ind(k)_{ent(i1)}$ is weak preferred to $ind(k)_{ent(i2)}$ if feature $ind(k)$ is taken into consideration. That can be denoted as $W_{k,j}(ind(k)_{ent(i1)}, ind(k)_{ent(i2)})$, and in this definition, q_k is an indifference threshold, p_k is a preference threshold, and they are both qualitative descriptions that express what the expert believes.

3.2 Concordance Index and Discordance Index

Definition 4: $c_{k,j}(ent(i1), ent(i2))$. $\forall\ ent(i1) \in Ent$, $\forall\ ent(i2) \in Ent$, $\forall\ ind(k) \in Ind$, $\forall\ dag(j) \in Dag$, $\exists\ p_k \in R^+$, $\exists\ q_k \in R^+$, $q_k < p_k$. Let the concordance index of $ent(i1)$ to $ent(i2)$ on the feature of $ind(k)$ based on what the expert $dag(j)$ believes denote as: $c_{k,j}(ent(i1), ent(i2))$. If $P_{k,j}(ind(k)_{ent(i1)}, ind(k)_{ent(i2)})$ then $c_{k,j}(ent(i1), ent(i2))=1$ and $c_{k,j}(ent(i2), ent(i1))=0$, else if $I_{k,j}(ind(k)_{ent(i1)}, ind(k)_{ent(i2)})$ then $c_{k,j}(ent(i1), ent(i2))=1$ and $c_{k,j}(ent(i2), ent(i1))=1$, else if $W_{k,j}(ind(k)_{ent(i1)}, ind(k)_{ent(i2)})$ then $c_{k,j}(ent(i1), ent(i2))=1$ and $0 < c_{k,j}(ent(i2), ent(i1)) < 1$:

$$c_{k,j}(ent(i1),ent(i2))=((ind(k)_{ent(i1)}-ind(k)_{ent(i2)})-q_k)/(p_k-q_k). \quad (6)$$

Outranking relation and concordance index on feature $ind(k)$ can be denoted as Fig. 1.

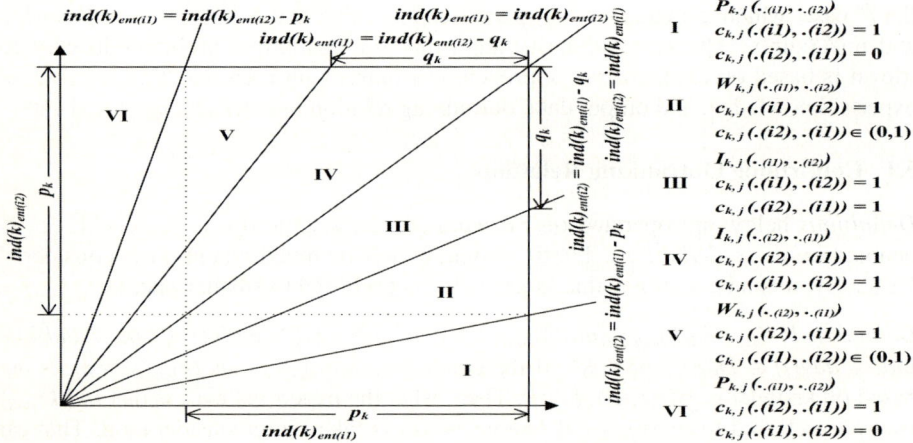

Fig. 1. Outranking relation and concordance index of $ent(i1)$ to $ent(i2)$ on feature $ind(k)$

Definition 5: $C_j(ent(i1), ent(i2))$. $\forall\ ent(i1) \in Ent$, $\forall\ ent(i2) \in Ent$, $\forall\ ind(k) \in Ind$, $\forall\ wei_j(k) \in Wei_j$, $\forall\ dag(j) \in Dag$. Let the concordance index of $ent(i1)$ to $ent(i2)$ based on what the expert $dag(j)$ believes denote as: $C_j(ent(i1), ent(i2))$.

$$C_j(ent(i1),ent(i2))=(\sum_{k=1}^{Num(Ind)}(w_j(k) \times c_{k,j}(ent(i1),ent(i2))))/\sum_{k=1}^{Num(Ind)}w_j(k). \quad (7)$$

Definition 6: $d_{k,j}(ent(i1), ent(i2))$. $\forall\ ent(i1) \in Ent$, $\forall\ ent(i2) \in Ent$, $\forall\ ind(k) \in Ind$, $\forall\ dag(j) \in Dag$, $\exists\ v_k \in R^+$, $\exists\ p_k \in R^+$, $p_k < v_k$. Let the discordance index of $ent(i1)$ to $ent(i2)$ on the feature of $ind(k)$ based on what the expert $dag(j)$ believes denote as: $d_{k,j}(ent(i1), ent(i2))$. If $ind(k)_{ent(i2)} - ind(k)_{ent(i1)} \leq p_k$ then $d_{k,j}(ent(i1), ent(i2)) = 0$, else if $ind(k)_{ent(i2)} - ind(k)_{ent(i1)} > v_k$ then $d_{k,j}(ent(i1), ent(i2)) = 1$, else if $p_k < ind(k)_{ent(i2)} - ind(k)_{ent(i1)} \leq v_k$ then $0 < d_{k,j}(ent(i1), ent(i2)) < 1$:

$$d_{k,j}(ent(i1), ent(i2)) = ((ind(k)_{ent(i2)} - ind(k)_{ent(i1)}) - q_k)/(v_k - q_k). \quad (8)$$

In which, v_k is a veto threshold that the outranking of $ent(i2)$ by $ent(i1)$ is refused. Discordance index of $ent(i1)$ to $ent(i2)$ on feature $ind(k)$ can be expressed as Fig. 2.

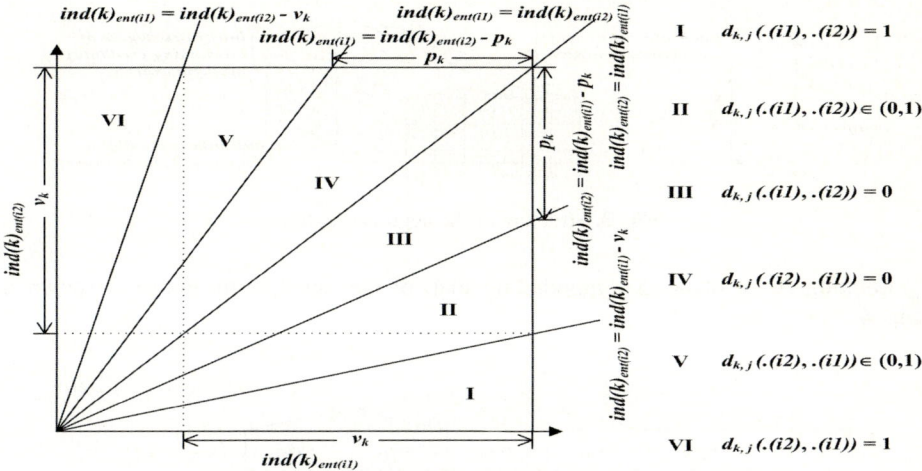

Fig. 2. Discordance index of $ent(i1)$ to $ent(i2)$ on feature $ind(k)$

3.3 Outranking Credibility Degree of a Single Expert

The degree of credibility of outranking of $ent(i2)$ by $ent(i1)$ is defined as follows.

Definition 7: $S_j(ent(i1), ent(i2))$. $\forall\ ent(i1) \in Ent$, $\forall\ ent(i2) \in Ent$, $\forall\ ind(k) \in Ind$. On the basis of concordance index of $ent(i1)$ to $ent(i2)$ and discordance index of $ent(i1)$ to $ent(i2)$ on feature $ind(k)$, Let the degree of credibility of outranking of $ent(i2)$ by $ent(i1)$ based on what expert $dag(j)$ believes denote as: $S_j(ent(i1), ent(i2))$.

$$S_j(ent(i1), ent(i2)) = \begin{cases} C_j(ent(i1), ent(i2)) \prod_{k \in J_j(ent(i1), ent(i2))} \dfrac{1 - d_{k,j}(ent(i1), ent(i2))}{1 - C_j(ent(i1), ent(i2))} \\ \qquad \text{if } d_{k,j}(.(i1),.(i2)) > C_j(.(i1),.(i2))\ \exists k \\ (\text{where } J_j(.(i1),.(i2)) = \{k : d_{k,j}(.(i1),.(i2)) > C_j(.(i1),.(i2))\}) \\ C_j(ent(i1), ent(i2)) \quad \text{if } d_{k,j}(.(i1),.(i2)) \leq C_j(.(i1),.(i2))\ \forall k \end{cases} \quad (9)$$

The degree of credibility of outranking is thus equal to the concordance index where no criterion is discordant. Where, discordances do exist, the concordance index is lowered in direct relation to the importance of those discordances. Integration based on distance between concordance index and discordance index of $ent(i1)$ to $ent(i2)$ can get consistent outcome with *Formula (9)* [11]. Thus,

$$S_j(ent(i1), ent(i2)) = C_j(ent(i1), ent(i2)) - \left(\sum_{k=1}^{Num(Ind)} (w_j(k) \times d_{k,j}(ent(i1), ent(i2)))\right) \bigg/ \sum_{k=1}^{Num(Ind)} w_j(k). \quad (10)$$

3.4 Collaborative Degree of Outranking Credibility of Multiple Experts

Secondly, when multiple experts are taken into consideration, experts' opinions can be placed into an $n \times n \times m$ cube, and integration process can be expressed by housetop of the cube. Thus, an aggregating house is formed, which is shown in Fig. 3.

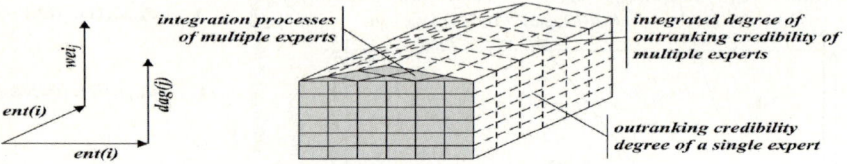

Fig. 3. Structure of the aggregating house

Looking-down plane decompounding map of the aggregating house is shown in Fig. 4.

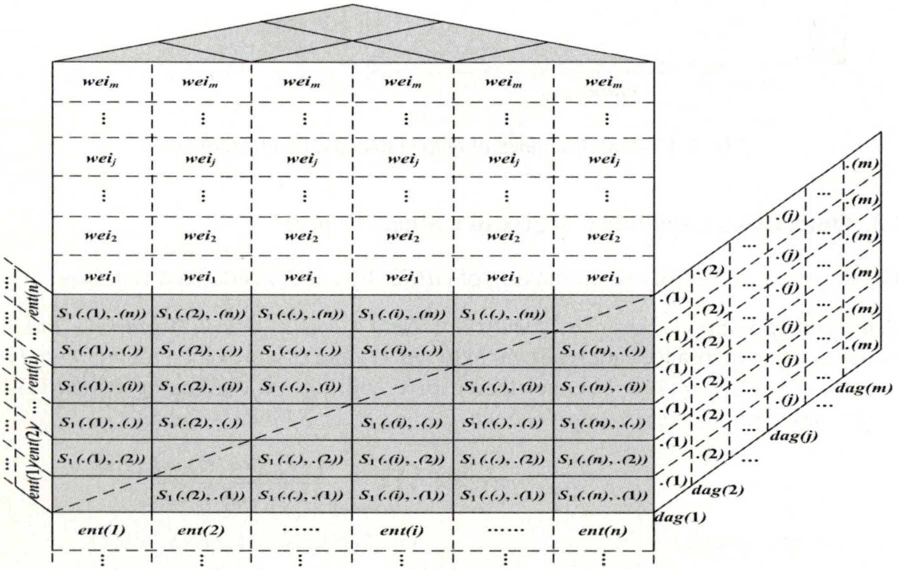

Fig. 4. Looking-down plane decompounding map of the aggregating house

Firstly, the comparability among $S_j(ent(i1), ent(i2))$ should be assured. Thus, the concept of standard degree of outranking credibility, $S'_j(ent(i1), ent(i2))$, is introduced, which can be expressed as follows.

$$S'_j(ent(i1), ent(i2)) = \frac{S_j(ent(i1), ent(i2)) - \min_j(S_j(ent(i1), ent(i2)))}{\max_j(S_j(ent(i1), ent(i2))) - \min_j(S_j(ent(i1), ent(i2)))} \quad (11)$$

Standard degrees of outranking credibility will be collected to form the integrated degree of outranking credibility, $S_j(ent(i1), ent(i2))$.

$$S(ent(i1),ent(i2))=(\sum_{j=1}^{m}(wei_j\times S_j^{'}(ent(i1),ent(i2))))/\sum_{j=1}^{m}wei_j.\qquad(12)$$

And the looking-down plane map of aggregating housetop after the process of integration is shown as Fig. 5.

ent(n)	S(.(1),.(n))	S(.(2),.(n))	S(.(.),.(n))	S(.(i),.(n))	S(.(.),.(n))		
⋮	S(.(1),.(.))	S(.(2),.(.))	S(.(.),.(.))	S(.(i),.(.))			S(.(n),.(.))
ent(i)	S(.(1),.(i))	S(.(2),.(i))	S(.(.),.(i))		S(.(.),.(i))	S(.(n),.(i))
⋮	S(.(1),.(.))	S(.(2),.(.))			S(.(i),.(.))	S(.(.),.(.))	S(.(n),.(.))
ent(2)	S(.(1),.(2))			S(.(.),.(2))	S(.(i),.(2))	S(.(.),.(2))	S(.(n),.(2))
ent(1)		S(.(2),.(1))	S(.(.),.(1))	S(.(i),.(1))	S(.(.),.(1))	S(.(n),.(1))
	ent(1)	ent(2)	……	ent(i)	……	ent(n)

Fig. 5. Looking-down plane map of aggregating housetop

If *Formula (9)* is adopted, two distillation procedures, the downward and upward systems, are employed. While, if *Formula (10)* is adopted, collaborative degree of outranking credibility (*CDOR*) can be computed as follows.

$$CDOR(ent(i1))=(\sum_{i2=1}^{n}S(ent(i1),ent(i2)))/n.\qquad(13)$$

4 Experiment

The new similarity algorithm based on outranking relation expands the quantification method of traditional one. Hereby, the consistent outcome between traditional quantitative similarity algorithm that is based on Euclidean distance and the new one should be firstly assured. Secondly, a comparison should be made to observe if the new algorithm really can get better outcome than traditional quantification method. MATLAB 6.5 was employed to develop and compare the two similarity algorithms

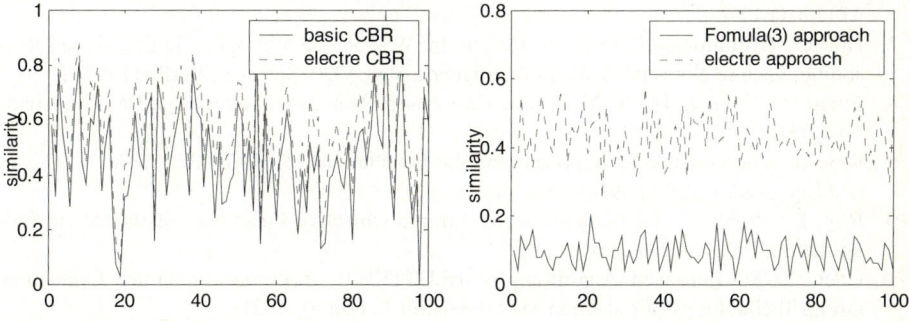

Fig. 6. Comparison between the new similarity algorithm and Euclidean based one

on the conditions of $n = 50$, $a = 1$, same weights, and 100 cases. Comparison between the new similarity algorithm and Euclidean distance based quantitative one is shown in Fig. 6 (a), and Comparison between the new similarity algorithm and Euclidean based *Formula (3)* is shown in Fig. 6 (b).

Conclusion can be drawn from Fig. 6 (a) that there are similar curves of the two algorithms. Ascending/descending trends of the two algorithms are also similar. We discover from Fig. 6 (b) that the new similarity algorithm based on outranking relation fluctuate more heavily than Euclidean distance based qualitative one on the adoption of the traditional quantification method.

5 Conclusion

In order to support qualitative knowledge reasoning in the presence of multiple experts, outranking relation was introduced into CBR to improve traditional method in dealing with qualitative data. Collaborative degree of outranking credibility of multiple experts was integrated through aggregating house. This approach is relatively simple and with a methodological basis which insures that quantification of qualitative description reflects experts' actual preference. Experiments indicated that the new similarity algorithm for qualitative problems based on outranking relation had consistent outcome with traditional quantitative similarity algorithm based on Euclidean distance, and was more sensitive than the traditional one.

References

1. Liao, S.-H.: Expert System Methodologies and Applications – A Decade Review from 1995 to 2004. Expert Systems with Applications 28 (2005) 93-103
2. Turban, E., Aronson, J.E.: Decision Support Systems and Intelligent Systems. 6th edn. Prentice International Hall, Hong Kong (2001)
3. Schank, R.C.: Dynamic Memory: A Theory of Learning in Computers and People. Cambridge University Press, New York (1982)
4. Schank R.C., Leake, D.: Creativity and Learning in a Case-Based Explainer. Artificial Intelligence 40 (1989) 353-385
5. Aamodt, A., Plaza, E.: Case-based Reasoning: Foundational Issues, Methodological Variations, and System Approaches. Artificial Intelligence Communications 7 (1994) 39-59.
6. Allen B.P.: Case-based Reasoning: Business Applications. Communications of the ACM 37 (1994) 40-42
7. Hunt, J.: Evolutionary Case Based Design. In: Waston (eds.): Progress in Case-based Reasoning, Lecture Notes in Artificial Intelligence, Vol. 1020. Springer, Berlin (1995) 17-31
8. Finnie, G., Sun, Z.-H.: R^5 Model for Case-based Reasoning. Knowledge-Based Systems 16 (2003) 59-65
9. Roy, B.: The Outranking Approach and the Foundations of ELECTRE Methods. Theory and Decision 31 (1991) 49-73
10. Roy, B.: Problems and Methods with Multiple Objective Functions. Mathematical Programming 1 (1971) 239-266.
11. Chen, Z.-X.: Improved Algorithms of ELECTRE-I for Production Order Evaluation. Group Technology & Production Modernization 22 (2005) 19-21

Comparing and Combining Spatial Dimension Reduction Methods in Face Verification

Licesio J. Rodríguez-Aragón, Cristina Conde,
Ángel Serrano, and Enrique Cabello

Universidad Rey Juan Carlos, c\ Tulipán, s/n,
E-28933, Móstoles, Madrid, Spain
{licesio.rodriguez.aragon, cristina.conde,
angel.serrano, enrique.cabello}@urjc.es
http://frav.escet.urjc.es

Abstract. The problem of high dimensionality in face verification tasks has recently been simplified by the use of underlying spatial structures as proposed in the 2DPCA, 2DLDA and CSA methods. Fusion techniques at both levels, feature extraction and matching score, have been developed to join the information obtained and achieve better results in verification process. The application of these advances to facial verification techniques using different SVM schemes as classification algorithm is here shown. The experiments have been performed over a wide facial database (FRAV2D including 109 subjects), in which only one interest variable was changed in each experiment. For training the SVMs, only two images per subject have been provided to fit in the small sample size problem.

1 Introduction

Many face recognition techniques have been developed over the past few decades. Some of them are based on dimension reduction methods such as Eigen Face method [1], using principal component analysis to obtain a most expressive subspace for face representation. Others are based on Fisher Face method [2], that uses linear discriminant analysis to obtain the most discriminant subspace. These methods as other improved variations treat input images as vectors [3]. Some recent works have begun to treat images as two dimensional matrices.

These new Spatial Dimension Reduction Methods give way to a set of vectors (2DPCA, 2DLDA) or even smaller matrices (CSA), instead of producing a single feature vector over a new lower dimensional space. To obtain the highest verification rate, different approaches have been proposed combining features either in a fusion at extraction level or at matching score level for each method, and then combining the best obtained results from the different methods [4]. SVM has been used as the classifier throughout all the experiments.

Another problem present in face recognition tasks is learning in the small sample size problem [5], what is of great practical interest. In face recognition it is not easy to collect a database with a large number of images of each individual.

Furthermore, it is often difficult to collect training or testing data to cover all possible variations as illumination, pose, expression, occlusion, or even age. A set of different experiments with only two training images per subject to fit the small sample size problem has been carried out.

2 Feature Extraction

Traditional feature extraction techniques require that 2D face images are vectorized into a 1D row vector to then perform the dimension reduction [6]. Recently, Two-Dimensional PCA (2DPCA), Two-Dimensional LDA (2DLDA) and Coupled Subspace Analysis (CSA) have been developed for bidimensional data feature extraction. These methods are based on 2D matrices rather than 1D vectors, preserving spatial information. As base line method Principal Component Analysis [1] has been used.

2.1 Two-Dimensional Principal Component Analysis

Given a set of images $I_1, I_2, \ldots, I_N$ of height h and width w, the consideration of images $I_{h \times w}$ as 1D vectors instead as 2D structures is not the right approach to retain spatial information. Pixels are correlated to their neighbours and the transformation of images into vectors produces a loss of information preserving the dimensionality.

The idea recently presented as a variation of traditional PCA, is to project an image $I_{h \times w}$ onto X^{2DPCA} by the following transformation [7,8],

$$Y_{h \times 1} = I_{h \times w} \cdot X^{2DPCA}_{w \times 1}. \tag{1}$$

As result, a h dimensional projected vector Y, known as projected feature vector of image I, is obtained. The total covariance matrix S_X over the set of projected feature vectors of training images $I_1, I_2, \ldots, I_N$ is considered. The mean image $\bar{I}$ of the training set, is taken into account.

$$S_X = \frac{1}{N} \sum_{i=1}^{N} [(I_i - \bar{I})X][(I_i - \bar{I})X]^T \tag{2}$$

The maximization of the total scatter of projections is chosen as the criterion to select the vector X^{2DPCA}. The total scatter of the projected samples is characterized by the trace of the covariance matrix of the projected feature vectors. It has been considered the optimal projection axis X^{2DPCA} as the is the unitary vector that maximizes $tr(S_X)$, which corresponds to the eigenvector of largest associated eigenvalue of the image covariance matrix S, defined as a $w \times w$ nonnegative matrix that can be directly evaluated using the training samples,

$$S = \frac{1}{N} \sum_{i=1}^{N} [(I_i - \bar{I})^T (I_i - \bar{I})]. \tag{3}$$

2.2 Two-Dimensional Linear Discriminant Analysis

The idea presented as 2DPCA, has been upgraded to consider the class information [9,10]. Suppose there are L known pattern clases having M samples for each class, $N = L \cdot M$. The idea is to project each image as in (1), but to obtain X^{2DLDA} with the information provided by the classes. The covariance over the set of images can be decomposed into between-class and within-class. The mean image as in 2DPCA, as well as the mean image of the class $\overline{I^j}$, $j = 1, \ldots, L$, are taken into account.

$$S_{XB} = \sum_{j=1}^{L} M[(\overline{I^j} - \overline{I})X][(\overline{I^j} - \overline{I})X]^T; \quad S_{XW} = \sum_{j=1}^{L}\sum_{i=1}^{M}[(I_i^j - \overline{I^j})X][(I_i^j - \overline{I^j})X]^T \quad (4)$$

The objective function maximized in this case to select X^{2DLDA} is considered a class specific linear projection criterion, and can be expressed as a quotient of the traces: $tr(S_{XB})/tr(S_{XW})$. The total between and within covariances are defined as $w \times w$ nonnegative matrices and can be directly evaluated.

$$S_B = \sum_{j=1}^{L} M[(\overline{I^j} - \overline{I})][(\overline{I^j} - \overline{I})]^T; \quad S_W = \sum_{j=1}^{L}\sum_{i=1}^{M}[(I_i^j - \overline{I^j})][(I_i^j - \overline{I^j})]^T \quad (5)$$

Both matrices are formally identical to the corresponding traditional LDA, and by maximizing the traces quotient, the within-class scatter is minimized, whereas the between-class scatter is maximized, giving as result the maximization of discriminating information. The optimal projection axis X^{2DLDA} corresponds to the eigenvector of $S_B \cdot S_W^{-1}$, of largest associated eigenvalue.

2.3 Coupled Subspace Analysis

Recently a new approach has been presented to reconstruct the original image matrices with two low dimensional coupled subspaces, in the sense of least square error [11]. These two subspaces encode the row and column information of the image matrices.

Let us denote Y_i, of height h' and width w', as the lower dimensional matrix representation of sample I_i, $i = 1, \ldots, N$, derived from two projection matrices $B_{h \times h'}$ and $C_{w \times w'}$,

$$Y_{h' \times w'} = B_{h' \times h}^T \cdot I_{h \times w} \cdot C_{w \times w'}. \quad (6)$$

The matrices B and C are chosen as those that best reconstruct the original images from the projections, in the sense of least square error satisfying the following optimal matrix reconstruction criterion,

$$(B^*, C^*) = \underset{B,C}{\operatorname{argmin}} \sum_i \|B \cdot Y_i \cdot C^T - I_i\|_F^2. \quad (7)$$

Being $\|\cdot\|_F$ the Frobenius norm of a matrix.

The objective function has no closed form and to obtain a local optimal solution, an iterative procedure has been presented. The whole procedure is called Coupled Subspace Analysis or Generalized Low Rank Approximation [11,12]. As it has been shown, this procedure is connected with traditional PCA and 2DPCA. Principal Component Analysis is a special case of CSA algorithm with $w = 1$ and 2DPCA is a special case of CSA algorithm with fixed $B = Id$.

3 Projection and Reconstruction

In 2DPCA and 2DLDA, as in traditional PCA, a proportion of retained variance can be fixed, $\sum_1^d \lambda_i / \sum_1^w \lambda_i$, where $\lambda_1 > \lambda_2 > \cdots > \lambda_w$ are the eigenvalues and $X_1, X_2, \ldots, X_d$ are the eigenvectors corresponding to the d largest eigenvalues.

Once d is fixed, $X_1, X_2, \ldots, X_d$ are the ortonormal axes used to perform the feature extraction. Let $V = [Y_1, Y_2, \ldots, Y_d]$ and $U = [X_1, X_2, \ldots, X_d]$, then

$$V_{h \times d} = I_{h \times w} \cdot U_{w \times d}. \tag{8}$$

A set of projected vectors, $Y_1, Y_2, \ldots, Y_d$, are obtained for both methods. Each projection over an optimal projection vector is a vector, instead of a scalar as in traditional PCA. A feature matrix $V_{h \times d}$ for each considered dimension reduction method is produced, containing either the most amount of variance, or the most discriminating features of image I.

In CSA the projection is performed through the optimal projection matrices $B^*_{h \times h'}$ and $C^*_{w \times w'}$ as in (6). As result, the extracted features form a lower dimensional matrix of height h' and width w'. In these dimension reduction methods, a reconstruction of the images from the features is possible (Fig. 1). It is possible to obtain an approximation of the original image with the retained information determined by d for PCA, 2DPCA and 2DLDA, $\widetilde{I}_{h \times w} = V_{h \times d} \cdot U^T_{d \times w}$, or by (h', w') for CSA, $\widetilde{I}_{h \times w} = B_{h \times h'} \cdot Y_{h' \times w'} \cdot C^T_{w' \times w}$.

4 Facial Verification Using SVM

SVM is a method of learning and separating binary classes [13]; it is superior in classification performance and is a widely used technique in pattern recognition and especially in face verification tasks [3,6].

Given a set of features $y_1, y_2, \ldots, y_N$ where $y_i \in \mathbb{R}^n$, and each feature vector associated to a corresponding label $l_1, l_2, \ldots, l_N$ where $l_i \in \{-1, +1\}$, the aim of a SVM is to separate the class label of each feature vector by forming a hyperplane. The optimal separating hyperplane is determined by giving the largest margin of separation between different classes. This hyperplane is obtained through a minimization process subjected to certain constrains. Theoretical work has solved the existing difficulties of using SVM in practical application [14].

As SVM is a binary classifier, a *one vs. all* scheme is used. For each class, each subject, a binary classifier is generated with positive label associated to feature vectors that correspond to the class, and with negative label associated to all the other classes.

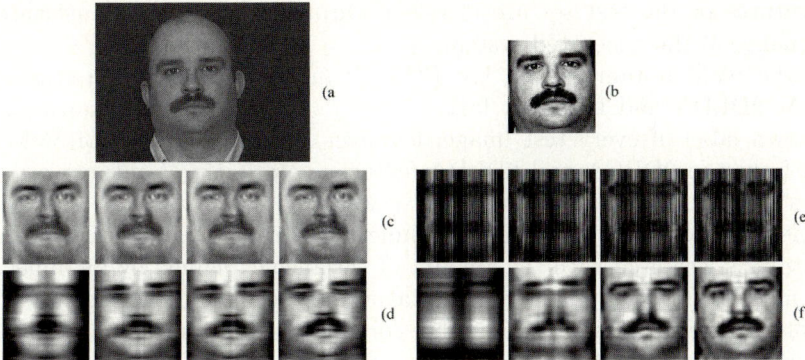

Fig. 1. a) One of the original frontal images in our database. b) Automatically selected window containing the facial expression of the subject in equalized gray scale. From left to right: c) reconstructed images, for $d = 30, 90, 150, 210$, from PCA projection. d) and e) reconstructed images, for $d = 2, 4, 6, 8$, from 2DPCA and 2DLDA projections respectively. f) reconstructed images, for $h' = w' = 3, 9, 15, 21$, from CSA projection.

In our experiments and in order to fit in the small sample size problem [5], the same two frontal and neutral images of every subject are selected as the training set for every experiment. A disjoint group of images, all of them affected by the same perturbation, is selected as the test set. The training set is used in the feature extraction process through PCA, 2DPCA, 2DLDA and CSA. Then, the training images are projected onto the new ortonormal axes and the feature vector (PCA), vectors (2DPCA,2DLDA), or low dimensional matrix (CSA) are obtained. The required SVMs are trained for each subject.

Several strategies have been used to train and combine the SVMs. When training and classifying PCA features, each image generates one feature vector $Y_{d \times 1}$ and one SVM is trained for each subject, with its feature vectors labelled as $+1$ and all the other feature vectors as -1.

For feature vectors obtained from 2DPCA and 2DLDA, each image generates a set of projected vectors, $V_{h \times d} = [Y_1, Y_2, \ldots, Y_d]$, which are considered under three different strategies. The first strategy, considered as a fusion at extraction level, generates a unique feature vector through a concatenation of d projected vectors, and then one SVM is trained for each subject as in PCA. The second and third approaches, fusion at matching score level, consider d projected vectors and, consequently, d SVMs are trained for each subject. These d outputs are then combined to produce a final classification output, first through an arithmetic mean, and secondly through a weighted mean.

On the other hand, applying CSA produces a low dimensional matrix $Y_{h' \times w'}$ for every image. This feature matrix is then transformed into a vector, $Y_{h' \cdot w' \times 1}$, and as in PCA one SVM is trained for each subject.

Once the SVMs are trained, each image from the test set is projected obtaining the corresponding features for each dimension reduction method (1,6).

The features of the test set are classified through the SVMs to measure the performance of the generated system.

For the SVM obtained from the PCA, from the concatenation strategy of 2DPCA, 2DLDA and the CSA feature vectors, the output is compared with the known label of every test image. However, for the ensemble of SVMs obtained from the 2DPCA and 2DLDA feature vectors, the d outputs are combined whether through an arithmetic or a weighted mean. Arithmetic approach combines the d outputs through an arithmetic mean. At weighted approach, every output is weighted with the amount of variance explained by its dimension, which means that each output will be taken into account proportionally to the value of the eigenvalue associated to the corresponding eigenvector: $\lambda_i / \sum_{j=1}^{d} \lambda_j$ is the weight for the i−SVM, $i = 1, 2, \ldots, d$.

To measure the system performance, a cross validation procedure is carried out. The Equal Error Rate, EER, that is the value for which false positive rate (FP) is equal to false negative rate (FN) is a valuable reference of the performance of the system.

4.1 Combining Results

To combine the results obtained by the three novel methods, 2DPCA, 2DLDA and CSA, a fusion at matching score level has been performed for the best approaches of each method. The scores obtained by the SVMs of the three methods have been linearly combined.

$$\text{Final Score} = \alpha \cdot \text{2DPCA} + \beta \cdot \text{2DLDA} + \gamma \cdot \text{CSA} \qquad (9)$$

Being α, β and $\gamma \in [0, 1]$, and verifying $\alpha + \beta + \gamma = 1$. To reach this combination two sources have been considered: firstly the scores obtained have been directly combined and secondly, a previous standardization of the scores has been performed, before combining the individual scores. The aim of this process is not only to achieve better results by combining the different Spatial Dimension Reduction Methods, but to weight the contribution of each of them towards the best performance in the verification process.

5 Design of Experiment

Although a large number of very complete facial databases acquired under very good conditions are available for the scientific community, our research group has found valuable to collected FRAV2D, a quite complete set of facial images including 109 subjects. This particular database has been created under extremely detailed procedures with a deep control of each of the acquiring conditions. All the images have been taken under 8 different conditions varying pose, expression and illumination and only varying one interest variable for each of them. 32 images of each subject were taken, being 12 frontal, 4 preforming a 15° rotation, 4 performing a 30° rotation, 4 with zenithal instead of diffuse illumination, 4 with expression changes and 4 occluding parts of the face. This database as well as other facial databases are freely available upon request at the research group home page[1].

Each experiment has been performed for the 109 subjects from our database. In all the experiments, the train set for the extraction of features and for the classifiers training is formed by the same 2 frontal and neutral images of each subject, in order to fit in the small sample size problem. Then, the classifiers have been tested over 5 different groups of images. Firstly, the 10 remaining frontal and neutral images for each subject have been used to perform the cross validation process. In a second experiment, the 4 images obtained with zenithal illumination have formed the test set. The 4 15° turn images have been selected to measure the performance of the system to pose variations. In the fourth experiment 4 images with expressions changes have been used. And finally, 4 occluded images for each subject have formed the test set.

6 Results

Tests, varying the dimensions of the different feature spaces, have been carried out for the four dimension reduction methods. For PCA, experiments have been performed for values $d = 30, 60, 90, 120, 150, 180, 210$. For 2DLDA and 2DPCA, values $d = 1, 2, 3, \ldots, 10$ are used under the three different classification strategies (Concatenation, Arithmetic and Weighted). And for CSA, low dimensional square matrices of sizes $h' = w' = 3, 6, 9, 12, 15, 18$ have been considered.

The lowest EER values in percentage, corresponding to each experiment and to each dimension reduction method under the different strategies, are presented in Table 1, as well as the values of d or $(h' \times w')$ for which they were achieved.

The optimum strategies for each method have been combined as proposed (9), and the results for the standardized option are shown to be the best performance (Table 1).

7 Conclusions

Better results for spatial dimension reduction methods (2DPCA, 2DLDA and CSA) than for traditional PCA are evidently achieved as shown in the EER values presented in Table 1.

The fusion at the matching score level used (Arithmetic and Weighted) never improves the fusion at the feature extraction level (Concatenation strategy).

Better results are achieved in all the experiments by means of the combination of the three scores, even thought in some of them the improvements are not significant. The coefficients of the optimal linear combination weighs the contribution of each method to the best solution.

2DLDA is theoretically the best approach as it distinguishes between within-class and between-class scatter and the criterion minimizes the first, while the second is maximized. As can be observed in the results of the 5 experiments

---

[1] http://frav.escet.urjc.es

Table 1. First, best EER (in percentage), values obtained for each dimension reduction method in each experiment: 1) Frontal, 2) Illumination, 3) 15° Rotated, 4) Expression, 5) Occluded. In brackets: the dimension for which they are achieved. Second, EER for the best combination (9) of the standardized scores of every method and the coefficients α for 2DPCA, β for 2DLDA and γ for CSA in which it occur.

Exp.	PCA	2DPCA			2DLDA		
		Conc.	Arith.	Weigh.	Conc.	Artith.	Weigh.
1)	3.0 (210)	1.3 (9)	1.9 (6)	1.9 (10)	**1.2 (6)**	1.9 (6)	1.9 (9)
2)	6.5 (210)	2.9 (7)	3.6 (6)	3.7 (9)	**2.0 (9)**	3.0 (7)	3.2 (10)
3)	21.5 (120)	**13.9 (1)**	13.9 (1)	13.9 (1)	16.9 (2)	17.5 (2)	20.6 (2)
4)	12.7 (210)	9.4 (10)	11.0 (5)	11.5 (9)	**7.2 (6)**	9.0 (5)	8.5 (9)
5)	30.7 (120)	25.2 (10)	24.8 (10)	24.7 (10)	24.6 (9)	26.5 (6)	27.3 (6)

Exp.	CSA	Fusion:	EER	α	β	γ
1)	1.3 (12 × 12)		1.2	0	0.4	0.6
2)	2.7 (18 × 18)		2.0	0	1	0
3)	20.6 (24 × 24)		13.6	0.3	0.3	0.4
4)	8.5 (12 × 12)		7.0	0	0.8	0.2
5)	**22.6 (24 × 24)**		22.0	0	0.4	0.6

carried out (Table 1), 2DLDA achieves the best results for 3 of them (frontal, illumination and expression). On the other hand 2DPCA (for 15° rotated) and CSA (for occluded) achieve the best results for 2 experiments with images suffering from very strong difficulties.

The results of these experiments show how difficult is to provide guidelines and information for practitioners to select not only the best performing method, but also an adequate choice in the dimension d or $(h' \times w')$. What we can clearly state as a main conclusion is that in none of the 5 experiments that have been exhaustively carried out the result of the fusion at the matching score level following (9) worsen the best result achieved individually by the best performing method for each experiment. On the contrary, results are equal or slightly improved, though no significantly, by the fusion strategy.

Therefore, the main guideline proposed in our work is the use of fusion at the matching score level schemes with different dimension reduction methods as the ones used in this work. We can consider that there is not a specific best approach to face the variations to appear in a face verification problem. Our present work shows, under the small sample size problem assumptions, that the fusion approach can obtain as good results as the obtained by the best individual approach.

Deeper work has to be done to combine and use in an optimum way all the information provided by the dimension reduction methods. The inclusion of recently presented variations and extensions, as Non-iterative Generalized Low Rank Approximations [15], face new challenges on the way of combining the different scores.

References

1. Turk, M., Pentland, A.: Eigenfaces for recognition. Journal of Cognitive Neurosicience **3** (1999) 71–86
2. Belhumeur, P., Hespanha, J., Kriegman, D.: Eigenfaces vs. fisherfaces: recognition using class specific linear projection. IEEE Transactions on Pattern Analysis and Machine Intelligence **19** (1997) 711–720
3. Fortuna, J., Capson, D.: Improved support vector classification using PCA and ICA feature space modiffication. Pattern Recognition **37** (2004) 1117–1129
4. Ross, A., Jain, A.: Information fusion in biometrics. Pattern Recognition Letters **24** (2003) 2115–2125
5. Guo, G., Dyer, C.: Learning from examples in the small sample case: face expression recognition. IEEE Transactions on Systems, Man, and Cybernetics-Part B **35** (2005) 477–488
6. Pang, S., Kim, D., Bang, S.Y.: Memebership authentication in the dynamic group by face classification using SVM ensemble. Pattern Recognition Letters **24** (2003) 215–225
7. Yang, J., Yang, J.: From image vector to matrix: a straightforward image projection technique–IMPCA vs. PCA. Pattern Recognition **35** (2002) 1997–1999
8. Yang, J., Zhang, D., Frangi, F., Yang, J.: Two-dimmensional PCA: A new approach to apperance-based face representation and recognition. IEEE Transacctions on Pattern Analysis and Machine Intelligence **26** (2004) 131–137
9. Chen, S., Zhu, Y., Zhang, D., Yang, J.: Feature extraction approaches based on matrix pattern: MatPCA and MatFLDA. Pattern Recognition Letters **26** (2005) 1157–1167
10. Li, M., Yuan, B.: A novel statistical linear discriminant analysis for image matrix: two-dimensional fisherfaces. In: Proceedings of the International Conference on Signal Processing. (2004) 1419–1422
11. Xu, D., Yan, S., Zhang, L., Liu, Z., Zhang, H.: Coupled subspace analysis. Technical Report MSR-TR-2004-106, Microsof Research (2004)
12. Ye, J.: Generalized low rank approximations of matrices. Machine Learning **61** (2005) 167–191
13. Cortes, C., Vapnik, V.: Support vector network. Machine Learning **20** (1995) 273–297
14. Joachims, T.: Making large scale support vector machine learning practical. In: Advances in Kernel Methods: Support Vector Machines. MIT Press, Cambridge, MA (1998)
15. Liu, J., Chen, S.: Non-iterative generalized low rank approximation of matrices. Pattern Recognition Letters **27** (2006) 1002–1008

A New Semi-supervised Dimension Reduction Technique for Textual Data Analysis

Manuel Martín-Merino and Jesus Román

Universidad Pontificia de Salamanca
C/Compañía 5, 37002, Salamanca, Spain
mmartinmac@upsa.es, jaromanga.eui@upsa.es

Abstract. Dimension reduction techniques are important preprocessing algorithms for high dimensional applications that reduce the noise keeping the main structure of the dataset. They have been successfully applied to a large variety of problems and particularly in text mining applications.

However, the algorithms proposed in the literature often suffer from a low discriminant power due to its unsupervised nature and to the 'curse of dimensionality'. Fortunately several search engines such as Yahoo provide a manually created classification of a subset of documents that may be exploited to overcome this problem.

In this paper we propose a semi-supervised version of a PCA like algorithm for textual data analysis. The new method reduces the term space dimensionality taking advantage of this document classification. The proposed algorithm has been evaluated using a text mining problem and it outperforms well known unsupervised techniques.

1 Introduction

The analysis of high dimensional datasets remains a challenging task for common machine learning techniques due to the well known 'curse of dimensionality' [1,6]. It has been suggested in the literature [6,12] that the dimension reduction techniques can help to overcome this problem because they reduce the noise keeping the main structure of the dataset. Several algorithms have been proposed to this aim such as Principal Component Analysis (PCA), Correspondence Analysis or neural based techniques (see for instance [4,11,12]). In this paper we focus on the Torgerson Multidimensional Scaling algorithm (MDS) [8] which is analogous to linear PCA and works directly from a dissimilarity matrix. This algorithm is robust and efficient and has been applied to a wide range of problems.

An interesting application of linear PCA is the analysis of the semantic relations among terms or documents in textual databases. However, the algorithms proposed in the literature often have a low discriminant power due mainly to their unsupervised nature. Therefore, the resulting projection is often useless to identify the different semantic groups in a given textual collection [14].

Fortunately in several search engines such as for instance Yahoo a classification of a subset of documents is usually available [15]. Notice that certain techniques such as the linear discriminant analysis (LDA) profit from this classification looking for a projection that maximizes the class separability [6]. However they do not preserve the structure of the dataset. Moreover in the problem we are dealing with terms are not usually classified because this is a complex task. Therefore new techniques should be developed that are able to reduce the term dimensionality considering a classification in the space of documents.

In this paper we present a new semi-supervised version of the Torgerson MDS algorithm that profits from the document categorization carried out by human experts to reduce the term dimensionality. To this aim, a semi-supervised similarity is defined that takes into account the document class labels. Next, the Torgerson MDS algorithm is applied to represent this dataset in a low dimensional space considering this similarity matrix. Finally the new algorithm has been tested using a real textual collection and has been exhaustively evaluated through several objective functions.

This paper is organized as follows. In section 2 the Torgerson MDS algorithm is introduced. Section 3 presents the new semi-supervised dimension reduction algorithm. In section 4 the algorithm is applied to the analysis of the semantic relations among terms in textual databases. Finally section 5 gets conclusions and outlines future research trends.

2 The Torgerson MDS Algorithm

In this section we introduce briefly the Torgerson MDS algorithm, which can be considered a dimension reduction technique analogous to the well known Principal Component Analysis (PCA). Next, the main properties of this technique in the context of text mining applications are summarized.

Let $\boldsymbol{X}(n \times d)$ be a matrix of n objects represented in $\mathbb{R}^d$ and $\boldsymbol{D} = (\delta_{ij})$ the dissimilarity matrix made up of the object proximities. The Torgerson MDS algorithm looks for a projection $W : \mathbb{R}^p \to \mathbb{R}^k$ to a lower dimensional space such that the Euclidean distances in $\mathbb{R}^k$ preserve as much as possible the original dissimilarities.

The object coordinates that verify this condition are obtained as follows. Define the matrix $\boldsymbol{A}$ as $[\boldsymbol{A}]_{ij} = a_{ij} = -\frac{1}{2}\delta_{ij}^2$, and hence the inner product matrix as:

$$\boldsymbol{B} = \boldsymbol{HAH} \qquad (1)$$

where $\boldsymbol{H}$ is a centering matrix defined as:

$$\boldsymbol{H} = \boldsymbol{I} - \frac{1}{n}\boldsymbol{1}\boldsymbol{1}^T \qquad (2)$$

with $\boldsymbol{1} = (1, 1, \ldots, 1)^T$.

It can be shown that the object coordinates for the projection that maximizes the preservation of the original dissimilarities are given by [8]:

$$\hat{\boldsymbol{X}} = \boldsymbol{V}_k \boldsymbol{\Lambda}_k^{\frac{1}{2}}, \qquad (3)$$

where V_k is the $n \times k$ orthonormal matrix whose columns are the kth first eigenvectors of B and $\Lambda_k = diag(\lambda_1, \ldots, \lambda_k)$ is a diagonal matrix with elements the first eigenvalues of B. The object coordinates are usually obtained through an SVD. This operation is particularly efficient when only the first eigenvectors are need [9] as it happens in our practical problem.

Besides it can be easily shown [8] that the object coordinates (3) obtained by the Torgerson MDS algorithm with the Euclidean distance are the same that those one obtained by linear PCA. However, notice that the Torgerson MDS algorithm is able to work directly from a dissimilarity matrix while PCA needs to know the object coordinates.

The Torgerson MDS originally proposed considers that the dissimilarity δ_{ij} is a Euclidean distance. However, we can work with any dissimilarity which gives rise to a semi-definite positive matrix B. Additionally the algorithm can be extended to the non-linear case or to more general dissimilarities using the kernel trick [16,13].

The Torgerson MDS algorithm exhibits several interesting properties for text mining problems that are worth to mention. First, the algorithm is equivalent to a linear PCA and hence can be solved efficiently through a linear algebraic operation such as the SVD. Second, the optimization problem doesn't have local minima which is an important requirement for text mining applications. Finally, the Torgerson MDS algorithm can be considered with certain similarities equivalent to the Latent Semantic Indexing (LSI) [3]. This technique has been successfully applied by the Information Retrieval community as a dimension reduction technique [4].

3 A Semi-supervised Dimension Reduction Technique

The Torgerson MDS algorithm often suffers from a low discriminant power. That is, due to the unsupervised nature of the algorithm the different topics of the textual collection overlap significantly in the projection. Moreover, due to the "curse of dimensionality" the original Euclidean distances become often meaningless and the resulting projection increases particularly the overlapping of the more specific terms (see [14,5] for more details). Therefore any clustering or classification algorithm that is applied in the projected space will not perform well.

In this section we explain how the document categorization carried out by human experts can be exploited to improve the discriminant power of the resulting projection. The novelty of this problem relies in that we are trying to improve an unsupervised technique that works in the space of terms considering a classification in the space of documents. To this aim two supervised measures are first defined considering the document class labels. Next they are properly combined with an unsupervised similarity which gives rise to a semi-supervised measure. This similarity will reflect the semantic classes of the textual collection and the term relationships inside each class. Finally the Torgerson MDS algorithm will be applied to reduce the term dimensionality considering this similarity.

Let t_i, t_j be the vector space representation [2] of two terms and $\{C_k\}_{k=1}^{c}$ the set of categories created by human experts. The association between terms and categories are usually evaluated in the Information Retrieval literature by the Mutual Information [18] defined as:

$$I(t_i; C_k) = \log \frac{p(t_i, C_k)}{p(t_i)p(C_k)}, \tag{4}$$

where $p(t_i, C_k)$ denotes the joint coocurrence probability of term t_i and class C_k. $p(t_i)$, $p(C_k)$ are the a priori probability of occurrence of term t_i and class C_k respectively. The Mutual Information is able to capture non-linear relationships between terms and categories.

However, it has been pointed out in the literature [18] that the index (4) gives higher score to rare terms. To overcome this problem we have considered a weighted version of the previous index defined as

$$I'(t_i; C_k) = p(t_i, C_k) \log \frac{p(t_i, C_k)}{p(t_i)p(C_k)}. \tag{5}$$

This index reduces obviously the weight of the less frequent terms.

Now, we can define a similarity measure between terms considering the class labels. This measure will be referred as supervised similarity from now on. Obviously, this similarity should become large for terms that are related/unrelated with the same categories. This suggests the following definition for the term similarity:

$$s_1(t_i, t_j) = \frac{\sum_k I'(t_i; C_k) I'(t_j; C_k)}{\sqrt{\sum_k (I'(t_i; C_k))^2} \sqrt{\sum_k (I'(t_j; C_k))^2}}. \tag{6}$$

The numerator of this similarity will become large for terms that are correlated with similar categories. Notice that the index (6) can be considered a cosine similarity between the vectors $I'(t_i; \cdot) = [I'(t_i; C_1), \ldots, I'(t_i; C_c)]$ and $I'(t_j; \cdot) = [I'(t_j; C_1), \ldots, I'(t_j; C_c)]$. This allow us to interpret the new similarity as a non-linear transformation to a feature space [16] where a cosine similarity is computed. Finally the similarity (6) is translated and scaled so that it takes values in the interval $[0, 1]$.

The similarity defined above can be considered an average over all the categories. Next, we provide an alternative definition for the supervised similarity that considers only the class with higher score. It can be written as

$$s_2(t_i, t_j) = \max_k \{\bar{I}(t_i; C_k) * \bar{I}(t_j; C_k)\}, \tag{7}$$

where $\bar{I}$ is a normalized Mutual Information defined as

$$\bar{I}(t_i; C_k) = \frac{I(t_i; C_k)}{\max_l \{I(t_i; C_l)\}}. \tag{8}$$

This normalization factor guarantees that $s_2(t_i, t_i) = 1$ which is usually required by common Multidimensional Scaling algorithms [8]. The similarity (7) will get large when both terms are strongly correlated with one of the classes.

The supervised measures proposed earlier will score high terms that are related with the same categories. However, it is also interesting to reflect the semantic relations among the terms inside each class or among the main topics. This information is provided by unsupervised measures such as for instance the cosine [7]. This justify the definition of a semi-supervised similarity as a convex combination of a supervised and an unsupervised measure. This similarity will reflect both, the semantic groups of the textual collection and the term relationships inside each topic. It is defined as follows:

$$s(t_i, t_j) = \lambda s_{sup}(t_i, t_j) + (1 - \lambda) s_{unsup}(t_i, t_j), \qquad (9)$$

where s_{sup} and s_{unsup} denote the supervised and unsupervised measures respectively. The parameter λ verifies $0 \leq \lambda \leq 1$. This parameter will determine if the resulting projection reflects better the semantic classes of the textual collection (λ large) or the semantic relations among the terms (λ small).

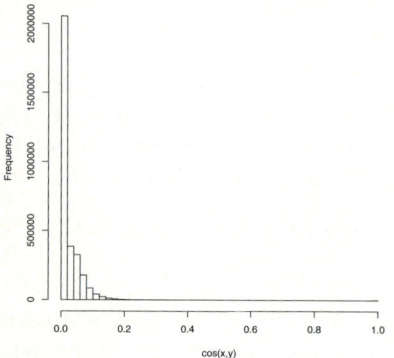

Fig. 1. Cosine similarity histogram

Fig. 2. Histogram of the average semi-supervised similarity measure

The semi-supervised similarity (9) has an interesting property that is worth to mention. Figure (1) shows the similarity histogram for an unsupervised measure such as the cosine while figure (2) shows the histogram for a semi-supervised one. It can be seen that the standard deviation for the semi-supervised similarity is larger than for the cosine similarity and that the histogram is smoother. This suggests that the semi-supervised similarity is more robust to the 'curse of dimensionality' and consequently any algorithm based on distances will perform better [5].

Besides figure 4 suggests that for textual data, the semi-supervised measures defined give rise to an inner product matrix B semi-definite positive. Therefore the Torgerson MDS algorithm can be used to get an approximate representation of the data in a space of dimension $< n - 1$ where n is the sample size.

Finally, notice that the semi-supervised algorithm proposed here differs from Partial Least Squares (PLS) [10] in several aspects. First, our algorithm works directly from a dissimilarity matrix. This feature allow us to consider a wide variety of unsupervised dissimilarities such as the χ^2 [7] that perform better than the Euclidean distance in textual data analysis. However, PLS relies on the Euclidean distance. Second, in the algorithm proposed, the equation (9) allow us to control the weight of the supervised component on the derivation of the projection. However, it has been pointed out in [10] that in PLS the weight of the unsupervised component (the variance) can not be controlled and tends to dominate the process. Finally, our algorithm is based on the Mutual Information and therefore is able to capture the non-linear correlation between the input and output variables. However, PLS maximizes a linear correlation.

4 Experimental Results

In this section we apply the proposed algorithms to the analysis of the semantic relations among terms in textual databases. The textual collection considered, is made up of 2000 *scientific abstracts* retrieved from three commercial databases 'LISA', 'INSPEC' and 'Sociological Abstracts'. For each database a thesaurus created by human experts is available. The thesaurus induces a classification of terms into seven groups according to their semantic meaning. This will allow us to exhaustively check the term associations suggested by the projection.

The algorithms proposed in this paper have been evaluated from different viewpoints through several objective functions. This guaranty the objectivity and validity of the experimental results.

The objective measures considered quantify the agreement between the semantic word classes induced in the projected space and the thesaurus. Therefore, once the objects have been projected to a low dimensional space, they are grouped into seven topics with a clustering algorithm (for instance k-means). Next we check if words that have been assigned to the same cluster belong to same semantic class according to the thesaurus. To this aim, three objective functions are considered that evaluate the partition from several viewpoints.

The F measure [2] has been widely used by the Information Retrieval community and evaluates if words from the same class according to the thesaurus are clustered together. The entropy measure [17] that will be denoted in this section as E, evaluates the uncertainty for the classification of words from the same cluster. Small values suggest little overlapping among different topics in the projection and are preferred. Finally the Mutual Information [18] that will be denoted in this section as I, is a nonlinear correlation measure between the word classification induced by the thesaurus and the word classification given by the clustering algorithm. This measure gives more weight to specific words and therefore provides valuable information about the position of the more specific terms in the projection.

Table 1 compares the semi-supervised Torgerson MDS algorithm with PCA, a dimension reduction technique widely used in the Information Retrieval literature [4]. The terms have been previously normalized by the L_2 norm so that the Euclidean distance becomes equivalent to the cosine similarity which is more appropriate for textual data analysis [4]. Notice that after the normalization,

Table 1. Evaluation of the semi-supervised dimension reduction techniques over a collection of scientific abstracts

	F	E	I
PCA	0.62	0.41	0.22
Torgerson MDS (Average)	0.83	0.18	0.38
Torgerson MDS (Maximum)	0.87	0.20	0.38

the PCA algorithm gives a projection similar to the one obtained by the Torgerson MDS algorithm with the cosine dissimilarity [8]. Thus PCA can be considered a particular case of the semi-supervised MDS algorithm presented in this paper just considering $\lambda = 0$ in equation 9 and the cosine similarity as unsupervised measure. Therefore, the PCA algorithm allow us to evaluate objectively if the supervised component of the algorithm ($\lambda \neq 0$) helps to improve a projection technique that relies solely on unsupervised measures. Obviously, the semi-supervised algorithm presented can incorporate other dissimilarities such as the χ^2 [11,7] that have been recommended to text mining problems.

Concerning the λ parameter in the semi-supervised measure (9) it has been set up to 0.5 in all the experiments. This value achieves a good balance between the preservation of the word relationships and the preservation of the semantic classes of the textual collection. However, for classification purposes this parameter can be tuned by cross-validation.

In all the experiments the terms have been projected to a space of dimension 12. Next a standard clustering algorithm such as k-means has been run with k the number of classes in the textual collection. Finally, the objective measures evaluate the agreement between the semantic classes induced by the clustering algorithm and by the thesaurus.

Table 1 suggests that the semi-supervised measures (rows 2-3) help to reduce significantly the overlapping among the different topics in the projection. This is supported by a drastic improvement of the measures E and I. Finally the F measure usually considered by the Information Retrieval community is improved up to 40%.

The maximum semi-supervised similarity (row 3) gives better results than the average. This can be explained because the maximum supervised similarity is defined considering only the class that is more correlated with the terms. This feature may improve the separation of the topics in the projection.

Finally, figures 3 and 4 show the eigenvalues for the cosine similarity and for the average semi-supervised measure respectively. Notice that the semi-supervised MDS algorithm (fig. 4) is able to reduce the dimension more aggressively than PCA. Thus, for dimensions greater than 12 the eigenvalues for the semi-supervised MDS become close to 0. However, the eigenvalues for PCA (fig. 3) decrease slowly and it is very difficult to determine the optimal value to represent the data. This behavior is originated by the sparsity and dimensionality of the text mining data [1,14]. This suggests that as we have mentioned in section 3 the semi-supervised measures proposed in this paper help to overcome the 'curse of dimensionality'.

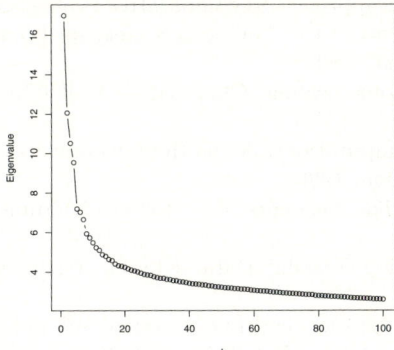 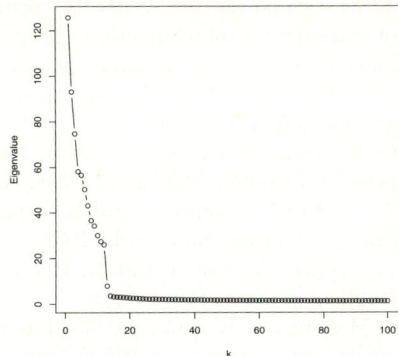

Fig. 3. Eigenvalues considering the cosine similarity

Fig. 4. Eigenvalues considering a semi-supervised measure

5 Conclusions and Future Research Trends

In this paper we have proposed a semi-supervised version of a well known dimension reduction technique for textual data analysis. The new model takes advantage of a categorization of a subset of documents to improve the discriminant power of the projection. The algorithm proposed has been tested using a real textual collection and evaluated through several objective functions.

The experimental results suggest that the proposed algorithm improves significantly well known alternatives that rely solely on unsupervised measures. In particular the overlapping among different topics in the projected space is significantly reduced improving the discriminant power of the algorithm.

Future research will focus on the development of new semi-supervised clustering algorithms.

References

1. C. C. Aggarwal. Re-designing distance functions and distance-based applications for high dimensional applications. In Proc. of SIGMOD-PODS, 1:13-18, 2001.
2. R. Baeza-Yates and B. Ribeiro-Neto. Modern information retrieval. Addison Wesley, Wokingham, UK, 1999.
3. B. T. Bartell, G. W. Cottrell, R. K. Belew. Latent Semantic Indexing is an Optimal Special Case of Multidimensional Scaling. Proceedings of the Fifteenth Annual International ACM SIGIR Conference, 161-167, Copenhagen, Denmark, 1992.
4. M. W. Berry, Z. Drmac, and E. R. Jessup. Matrices, vector spaces and information retrieval. SIAM review, 41(2):335-362, 1999.
5. A. Buja, B. Logan, F. Reeds and R. Shepp. Inequalities and positive default functions arising from a problem in multidimensional scaling, Annals of Statistics, 22, 406-438, 1994.
6. V. Cherkassky and F. Mulier. Learning from Data. John Wiley & Sons, New York, 1998.

7. Y. M. Chung and J. Y. Lee. A corpus-based approach to comparative evaluation of statistical term association measures, Journal of the American Society for Information Science and Technology, 52, 4, 283-296, 2001.
8. T. F. Cox and M. A. A. Cox. Multidimensional scaling. Chapman & Hall/CRC, 2nd edition, USA, 2001.
9. G. H. Golub and C. F. Van Loan. Matrix Computations. Johns Hopkins university press, Baltimore, Maryland, USA, third edition, 1996.
10. T. Hastie, J. Friedman, and R. Tibshirani. The Elements of Statistical Learning. Springer Verlag, New York, 2002.
11. L. Lebart, A. Salem and L. Berry. Exploring Textual Data. Kluwer Academic Publishers, Netherlands, 1998.
12. J. Mao and A. K. Jain. Artificial neural networks for feature extraction and multivariate data projection. IEEE Transactions on Neural Networks, 6(2), March 1995.
13. M. Martin-Merino and A. Muñoz. Extending the SOM algorithm to non-euclidean distances via the kernel trick. Lecture Notes on Computer Science (LNCS-2130), 150-157, Springer Verlag, Belin, 2004.
14. M. Martín-Merino and A. Muñoz. A New Sammon Algorithm for Sparse Data Visualization. International Conference on Pattern Recognition, 1:477-481, Cambridge, August, 2004.
15. D. Mladenié. Turning Yahoo into an Automatic Web-Page Classifier. Proceedings of the 13th European Conference on Aritficial Intelligence. 473-474, Brighton, UK, 1998.
16. Schölkopf, B. and A. J. Smola. Learning with Kernels, MIT Press, Cambridge, 2002.
17. A. Strehl, J. Ghosh, and R. Mooney. Impact of similarity measures on web-page clustering. Proceedings of the 17th National Conference on Artificial Intelligence: Workshop of Artificial Intelligence for Web Search , Austin, USA, 58-64, July 2000.
18. Y. Yang and J. O. Pedersen. A comparative study on feature selection in text categorization, Proc. of the 14th International Conference on Machine Learning, Nashville, Tennessee, USA, July, 412-420, 1997.

CBR Model for the Intelligent Management of Customer Support Centers

Stella Heras Barberá[1,*], Juan Ángel García-Pardo[1], Rafael Ramos-Garijo[1], Alberto Palomares[2], Vicente Julián[1], Miguel Rebollo[1], and Vicent Botti[1]

[1] Information Systems and Computing Department,
Universidad Politécnica de Valencia, 46022 Valencia, Spain
{sheras, jgarciapardo, rramosgarijo}@dsic.upv.es
[2] TISSAT S.A., Parque Tecnológico,
Av. Leonardo Da Vinci, 5, 46980 Paterna - Valencia, Spain
apalomares@tissat.es

Abstract. In this paper, a new CBR system for Technology Management Centers is presented. The system helps the staff of the centers to solve customer problems by finding solutions successfully applied to similar problems experienced in the past. This improves the satisfaction of customers and ensures a good reputation for the company who manages the center and thus, it may increase its profits. The CBR system is portable, flexible and multi-domain. It is implemented as a module of a help-desk application to make the CBR system as independent as possible of any change in the help-desk. Each phase of the reasoning cycle is implemented as a series of configurable plugins, making the CBR module easy to update and maintain. This system has been introduced and tested in a real Technology Management center ran by the Spanish company TISSAT S.A.

1 Introduction

Technology Managemet Centers (TMCs) are control centers in charge of managing all processes implicated in the provision of technological and customer support services in private companies and public administration organisms. Usually, the company managing the TMC also has a call center, where a group of operators attend to requests of customers with the help of a help-desk software. The call center is also an effective way to communicate government organisms and citizens. Therefore, the operators of the call center must deal with queries coming from very diverse domains.

Nowadays, differentiating a company from its competitors in the market just by its products, prices and quality is becoming very difficult. Thus, companies try to take advantage by a high-quality customer support. A big amount of commercial activity is performed via phone, being necessary to avoid situations as

---

[*] Financial support from Spanish government under grant PROFIT FIT-340001-2004-11 is gratefully acknowledged.

busy lines, to ask the customer to repeat the query several times or to give incoherent answers. Moreover, a good customer support depends on the experience and skills of the company operators. There is an obvious need for saving their experience and for giving a suitable answer to each query as quick as possible.

From the 90s, Case-Based Reasoning (CBR) systems have been used to cope with this need in help-desks applied to call centers [1][2][3][4][5][6][7]. More recently, the internal CAD/CAM help-desk system *Homer* [8][9] has been developed in the course of the *INRECA-II* project [10]. There are also many companies that sell software tools for applying CBR to help-desks (e.g. *eGain* [11], *Kaidara* [12] and *Empolis* [13]). Therefore, most of the systems reported have either been specifically adapted to cover the needs of a private company by using some CBR tool [14][15][16] or developed for research purposes.

We were asked to implement a CBR system with specific features and observing some constraints. On one hand, the CBR system had to be flexible and modular, in order to be easily integrated in an existing help-desk application as an intelligent module for advising solutions to customer requests. On the other hand, we were not allowed to use any CBR tool that is only available for research purposes or copyrighted by any vendor. Therefore, we considered to implement a new CBR system able to fulfil these requirements.

The rest of the paper is structured as follows. In section 2 we briefly introduce the environment where our CBR system has been introduced. In section 3 we explain the CBR module proposed. In section 4 we show the results of the tests performed over the system. Finally, we summarise the conclusions of this paper.

2 I2TM – Intelligent and Integrated Ticketing Manager

The Spanish company TISSAT S.A. [17] runs a Technology Management Center (TMC) that offers customer support, communication and Internet services for public administration organisms and private companies. TISSAT works either with problems related to computer errors or with other domains, such as the international emergency phone 112 of Valencia (Spain), which covers the emergencies of over four and a half million of citizens.

TISSAT attends to customer requests via a call center. This call center can receive queries via phone, e-mail, Internet or fax. There is a maximum time to provide a correct solution for each query. This time is agreed between TISSAT and its customers in the Service Level Agreements (SLA's). When the maximun time to solve a problem is exceeded, the company is economically penalized.

In order to efficiently manage its call center, TISSAT has developed a helpdesk toolkit called I2TM (**I**ntelligent and **I**ntegrated **T**icketing **M**anagement). I2TM manages customer requests, integrates the available channels to make a request and manages the inventory. The system also helps operators to solve new problems by searching for solutions successfully applied to similar problems in the past. This will ease their work and thus, they will be able to provide quicker and more accurate answers to customer problems. In order to cope with this functionality, we have developed a tool called CBR-TM (**C**ase-**B**ased **R**easoning for **T**icketing **M**anagement). This tool works as a separate module of the I2TM system, which allows to make changes in the I2TM implementation without affecting the CBR-TM module and vice versa. Figure 1 shows the overview of the entire system. I2TM and CBR-TM communicates and synchronises their data via webservice calls. The CBR-TM module will be explained in detail in section 3.

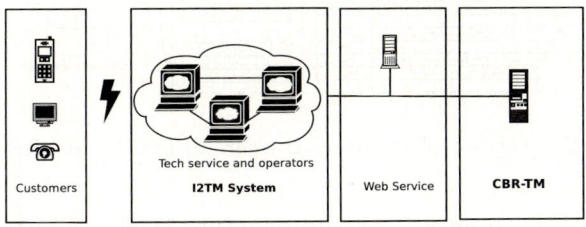

Fig. 1. System architecture

3 CBR-TM – CBR for Ticketing Management

Before the implementation of the CBR-TM module and the new I2TM system itself, some weaknesses to improve in the call center operation were identified. On one hand, it was necessary to save the knowledge and experience of the operators in an appropriate format (previously it was simply written in hand-written notes or in reference manuals that were usually out of date). This would avoid losing valuable information whenever the operators leave the company and it may also be used to train new operators. Moreover, the information about problems that had been already solved by other operator was not available on-line and the operators lost time solving them again. On the other hand, the information to manage comes from a wide range of domains and data types.

In order to facilitate the update of the CBR-TM module, each phase of the reasoning cycle [18][19] (*Retrieve, Reuse, Revise* and *Retain* [20]) is implemented as a *plugin algorithm*. Thus, CBR-TM is a flexible system and any change in the algorithms that implement the phases, or even the introduction of new algorithms, does not affect the entire CBR-TM system. The specific algorithm that has to be used in each phase is specified in a *XML configuration file*. The following sections describe with more detail the reasoning phases of the CBR-TM module.

3.1 Data Acquisition

An important task in this project has been to obtain a test database to validate our CBR system during its development. In order to extract this information, we analysed the old call center database. The registers of the database (*tickets*) contain information about previously solved problems. Therefore, a *ticket* in our

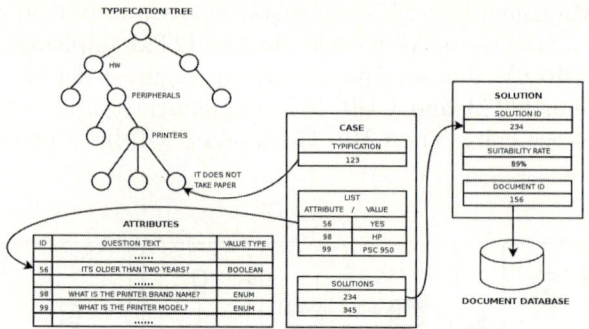

Fig. 2. Overview of the data structure in I2TM and CBR-TM

system is a new case to solve. The data structure in CBR-TM and the relations with the structure of the new databases of I2TM is shown in Figure 2.

TISSAT maintains a non-disjoint tree (*Typification Tree*) that contains the taxonomy of the problem types (categories) in a hierarchical order (from less to more specific categories). These categories are set by TISSAT depending on the application domain of each project managed by the company. The first level nodes of the tree represent projects and the nodes below them are the categories of those projects. The CBR-TM module is able to reread the tree whenever a new project is added or any category is modified. In this sense, CBR-TM is a multi-domain system able to work with different types of problems. TISSAT also maintains a database of answers to questions that the operators ask to the customer when a query is made. These answers are saved as *attributes* in a database and they provide more specific information about the problem represented by the categories. In addition, TISSAT registers successfully applied solutions in a *document database*. In CBR-TM, a case is the prototyped representation of a set of tickets sharing the same categories and attributes. Each case has one or more associated solutions. One solution of the document database can also be associated with more than one case. CBR-TM stores the cases in a *case-base*.

3.2 Retrieve

The first step when CBR-TM is asked to solve a new ticket is to retrieve a set of cases from the case-base that are related to the same problem as the ticket. I2TM uses a webservice call named *GetSolutions* to start this process in the CBR-TM module. The call needs as parameters the values of the ticket attributes and its categorisation. The retrieval process comprises three steps: *Indexation*, *Mapping* and *Similarity* calculation. At the end of the retrieval phase, a list of cases sorted by similarity with the ticket is obtained. This phase is implemented through three different types of plugin algorithms: the *Indexer*, the *Mapper* and the *Similarity* algorithms. The *Indexer* algorithm hierarchically organises the cases of the case-base in order to facilitate their retrieval. Currently, the operators perform the indexation by categorising manually the ticket. The *Mapper* algorithm explores the

Typification Tree to retrieve the category nodes of the ticket and its predecessors (since upper categorisations represent more generic problems, but they are also related with the current problem and their solutions might also be suitable). Then, the algorithm searches in the case-base and retrieves all the cases with either the same categorisation as the ticket or a more generic one.

Once the set of similar cases has been selected, it is sorted by similarity with the ticket. The *Similarity* algorithm performs this arrangement. Here arises the problem of finding the similarity between cases that share some attributes and have different ones. Note that the cases associated with different categories of the *Typification Tree* can have different attributes. Moreover, there are many possible attribute types. The attributes can also have missing values, which makes more complicated the calculation of the similarity between cases. In order to test the CBR-TM module, we have adapted and implemented some similarity measures: two similarity measures based on the Euclidean distance (classic *Euclidean* and *NormalizedEuclidean*) and a similarity measure based on the ratio model proposed by *Tversky* [21]. In addition, we have implemented a set of distance metrics that allow us to work with different attribute types (numeric, nominal and enumerated). The *Similarity* algorithms use the distance metrics to compute local distances between the attributes of the cases, and the similarity measures to compute global distances between the cases (the similarity between the cases). Finally, the set of retrieved cases is sorted by means of a *k-nearest neighbour* algorithm.

3.3 Reuse

The reuse phase is implemented by means of the *SolutionSelection* plugin algorithm. At the end of the reuse phase, we obtain a sorted list of solutions to apply to the ticket. First, the *SolutionSelection* algorithm proposes the solutions of the most similar case to the ticket, sorted from higher to lower degree of suitability. Next, it proposes the solutions of the second most similar case, and so on. Note that the solutions themselves are not adapted, but proposed directly in a specific order to use them to solve the current ticket. When this process is finished, CBR-TM answers the *GetSolutions* webservice call and returns it with the list of proposed solutions and their associated suitability for the ticket.

3.4 Revise

In the revision phase, the I2TM system uses the *CloseQuestion* webservice call to report to the CBR-TM module the customer degree of satisfaction with the proposed solution. The tickets that were not requested to CBR-TM, but solved directly by the operator, are also reported. This phase, implemented by means of the *Rewarder* plugin algorithm, helps CBR-TM to improve its performance. When CBR-TM is reported a solved ticket, it performs the retrieval phase in order to discover whether this ticket has already a prototype case in the case-base. If such case exists and the solution applied to the reported ticket is already associated with this case, the degree of suitability of this solution is increased. Otherwise, the new solution is associated with the case. If there is not a similar enough case in the case-base, a new case with its solution is created. The similarity threshold has been found experimentally and it can be changed to any desired value.

Note that the retrieval phase would be avoided here if we were able to know which case was used to propose its solution to solve the ticket. Moreover, this solution could be penalized if it does not fit the ticket. However, we consider that in the current implementation of our system this is not appropriate. On one hand, the CBR-TM module may be reported a ticket that was not requested previously to the module. In this situation we have to perform the retrieval phase in order to check if there is a similar case in the case-base or, otherwise, to create a new one. On the other hand, it is possible that CBR-TM had proposed an invalid solution but it had not made any mistake, since this is not a completely automated system and, for instance, the operators can fail in their categorisations. Moreover, do not use a proposed solution does not necessary mean that this solution is erroneous, but the operator may have chosen other solution for any reason.

3.5 Retain

As it is explained above, each time that a ticket is solved, the I2TM system reports back to the CBR-TM module. The retention phase is also done by means of the *Rewarder* algorithm, which checks if it is necessary to create a new prototype case for the ticket. Therefore, the retention phase can be viewed as a consequence of the revision phase. If the ticket that has been reported to CBR-TM is not similar enough to any case of the case-base (it exceeds the similarity threshold that has been specified), a new case will be added to the case-base.

4 Evaluation

Using the *Ticket Database*, we have run several tests to validate the CBR-TM module. The tests have been performed using a cross-partition technique, separating the ticket database into two databases for training (loading the case-base) and testing the system. We wanted to check on the computer error domain the behaviour of the similarity measures implemented. Therefore, the tests have been repeated setting the system to work with a different similarity measure each time.

First of all, we have checked the system performance. This performance may be influenced by the size of the database or by the number of customers performing simultaneous requests. Figure 3a shows that as the number of tickets in the database used to create the case-base of CBR-TM increases the mean error in the answers to the requests decreases. Note that, as we are performing a supervised learning, it is considered an error when CBR-TM does not propose the same solution as the one we have recorded in the *Ticket Database* for the ticket that has been requested. It demonstrates that, the more problems CBR-TM solves, the more it increases its knowledge to solve new ones.

Figure 3b shows the response time of the CBR-TM module when the number of customers performing simultaneous requests increases. Although in this test it is considered that the customers are making the requests almost at the

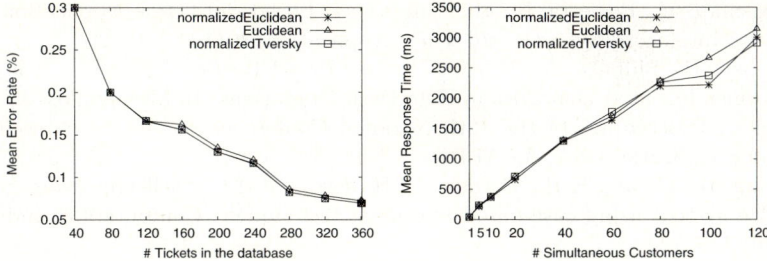

Fig. 3. a: Influence of the database size on the CBR-TM system performance; b: Influence of the number of simultaneous customers on the CBR-TM system performance

same time, CBR-TM is able to answer all of them quickly. With regard to the behaviour of the different similarity measures, we can appreciate that their performance in this domain is almost the same.

5 Conclusions

We have developed a CBR system for ticketing management called CBR-TM, which acts as an intelligent module for the I2TM help-desk application in the Spanish company TISSAT S.A. The CBR-TM module searches for solutions successfully applied in the past and thus, helps the operators to rapidly solve new problems. This saves time and prevents I2TM from losing the knowledge acquired when a problem is solved. The results of the CBR-TM evaluation show that the system has a good performance when it attends to the requests of simultaneous customers. As it is expected, the CBR-TM accuracy improves as the case-base increases and the system learns properly the new solutions created by the I2TM operators.

The system has been tested in a help-desk whose purpose is to solve computer errors, but TISSAT is planning to apply it to other domains. The system is recently implanted and an intensive research to improve the techniques applied will be done. One of the main objectives in a near future is to develop an automatic categorisation method, in order to prevent the CBR-TM module from human mistakes. Current research is done in studying automatic methods to set appropriate weights to the attributes of the cases and improve the similarity calculation.

References

1. Acorn, T., Walden, S.: SMART: Support Management Automated Reasoning Technology for Compaq Customer Service. In Scott, A., Klahr, P., eds.: Proceedings of the 2 International Conference on Intelligent Tutoring Systems, ITS-92 Berlin. Volume 4., AAAI Press (1992) 3–18
2. Simoudis, E.: Using Case-Based Retrieval for Customer Technical Support. IEEE Intelligent Systems **7** (1992) 7,10–12

3. Kriegsman, M., Barletta, R.: Building a Case-Based Help Desk Application. IEEE Expert: Intelligent Systems and Their Applications **8** (1993) 18–26
4. Shimazu, H., Shibata, A., Nihei, K.: Case-Based Retrieval Interface Adapted to Customer-Initiated Dialogues in Help Desk Operations. In Mylopoulos, J., Reiter, R., eds.: Proceedings of the 12th National Conference on Artificial Intelligence. Volume 1., Seatle, USA, AAAI Press (1994) 513–518
5. Raman, R., Chang, K.H., Carlisle, W.H., Cross, J.H.: A self-improving helpdesk service system using case-based reasoning techniques. Computers in Industry **2** (1996) 113–125
6. Kang, B.H., Yoshida, K., Motoda, H., Compton, P.: Help Desk System with Intelligent Interface. Applied Artificial Intelligence **11** (1997) 611–631
7. Roth-Berghofer, T., Iglezakis, I.: Developing an Integrated Multilevel Help-Desk Support System. In: Proceegings of the 8th German Workshop on Case-Based Reasoning. (2000) 145–155
8. Goker, M., Roth-Berghofer, T.: The development and utilization of the case-based help-desk support system HOMER. Engineering Applications of Artificial Intelligence **12** (1999) 665–680
9. Roth-Berghofer, T.R.: Learning from HOMER, a case-based help-desk support system. In Melnik, G., Holz, H., eds.: Advances in Learning Software Organizations, Springer-Verlag (2004) 88–97
10. Bergmann, R., Althoff, K.D., Breen, S., Göker, M., Manago, M., Traphöner, R., Wess, S.: Developing Industrial Case-Based Reasoning Applications . The INRECA Methodology. 2nd edn. Volume 1612 of Lecture Notes in Artificial Intelligence. Springer-Verlag (2003)
11. eGain: www.egain.com (2006)
12. Kaidara Software Corporation: http://www.kaidara.com/ (2006)
13. Empolis Knowledge Management GmbH - Arvato AG: http://www.empolis.com/ (2006)
14. Althoff, K.D., Auriol, E., Barletta, R., Manago, M.: A Review of Industrial Case-Based Reasoning Tools. AI Perspectives Report. Goodall, A., Oxford (1995)
15. Watson, I.: Applying Case-Based Reasoning. Techniques for Enterprise Systems. Morgan Kaufmann Publishers, Inc., California (1997)
16. empolis: empolis Orenge Technology Whitepaper. Technical report, empolis GmbH (2002)
17. Tissat S.A: www.tissat.es (2006)
18. Giraud-Carrier, C., Martinez, T.R.: An integrated framework for learning and reasoning. Journal of Artificial Intelligence Research **3** (1995) 147–185
19. Corchado, J.M., Borrajo, M.L., Pellicer, M.A., Yanez, J.C.: Neuro-symbolic system for Business Internal Control. Advances in Data Mining, LNIA Springer-Verlag **3275** (2004) 1–10
20. Aamodt, A., Plaza, E.: Case-based reasoning: foundational issues, methodological variations and system approaches. AI Communications **7, no. 1** (1994) 39–59
21. Tversky, A.: Features of similarity. Psychological Review **84, no.4** (1997) 327–352

Non Parametric Local Density-Based Clustering for Multimodal Overlapping Distributions*

Damaris Pascual[1], Filiberto Pla[2], and J. Salvador Sánchez[2]

[1] Dept de Ciencia de la Computación, Universidad de Oriente,
Av. Patricio Lumumba s/n, Santiago de Cuba, CP 90100, Cuba
dpascual@csd.uo.edu.cu
[2] Dept. Llenguatges i Sistemes Informàtics, Universitat Jaume I,
12071 Castelló, Spain
{pla, sanchez}@lsi.uji.es

Abstract. In this work, we present a clustering algorithm to find clusters of different sizes, shapes and densities, to deal with overlapping cluster distributions and background noise. The algorithm is divided in two stages. In a first step, local density is estimated at each data point. In a second stage, a hierarchical approach is used by merging clusters according to the introduced cluster distance, based on heuristic measures about how modes overlap in a distribution. Experimental results on synthetic and real databases show the validity of the method.

1 Introduction

Many application problems require tools aimed at discover relevant information and relationships in databases. These techniques are mainly based on unsupervised pattern recognition methods like clustering. The problem of clustering can be defined as: Given n points belonging to a d-dimensional space, and provided some measure of similarity or dissimilarity, the aim is to divide these points into a set of clusters so that the similarity between patterns belonging to the same cluster is maximized whereas the similarity between patterns of different clusters is minimized.

There are two main approaches in clustering techniques: the partitioning approach and the hierarchical approach [8]. The partitioning methods build a partition splitting a set of n objects into k clusters. These algorithms usually assume a priori knowledge about the number of classes in which the database must be divided. The K-means is one of the best known partitioning algorithms.

Other clustering algorithms are based on parametric mixture models [3]. However, this work focuses on non parametric approaches, since they can be applied in a more general way to metric and non metric feature spaces, just defining a dissimilarity measure in the feature space.

Hierarchical methods consist of a sequence of nested data partitions in a hierarchical structure, which can be represented as a dendogram. There exist two hierarchical

---

* This work has been partially supported by projects ESP2005-07724-C05-05 and TIC2003-08496 from the Spanish CICYT.

approaches: agglomerative and divisive. The first one can be described in the following way: initially, each point of the database form a single cluster, and in each level, the two most similar clusters are joined, until either a single cluster is reached containing all the data points, or some stopping condition is defined, for instance, when the distance between the clusters is smaller than certain threshold. In the divisive approach, the process is the other way around.

The Single Link (SL) and the Complete Link (CL) methods are the most well known hierarchical strategies [4]. Some hierarchical algorithms are based on prototypes selection, as CURE [5]. On the other hand, in density–based algorithms, the clusters are defined as dense regions, where clusters are separated by low density areas [6]. Some of the most representative works of the density-based approach are DBSCAN [1], KNNCLUST [8] and SSN [2] algorithms.

The main problems of these algorithms are the fact that clusters are not completely separable, due to the overlapping of cluster distributions, and the presence of noisy samples. The main contribution of the work presented here is the use of a hybrid strategy between the hierarchical and density-based approaches, and the cluster dissimilarity measure introduced, both aimed at dealing with overlapped clusters and noisy samples, in order to discover the most significant density based distributions in databases with high degree of cluster overlapping and clusters with multiple modes.

2 Clustering Process

The objective of the algorithm here presented is to detect clusters of different shapes, sizes and densities even in the presence of noise and overlapping cluster distributions. The algorithm here presented is a mixture of a density-based and a hierarchical-based approach, and it is divided in two stages. In the first stage, the initial clusters are constructed using a density-based approach. In a second stage, a hierarchical approach is used, based on a cluster similarity function defined in terms of cluster density measures and distances, joining clusters until either arriving to a pre-defined number or reaching a given stopping criterion.

2.1 Point Density Estimation

Let X be a set of patterns provided with a similarity measure between patterns d. Let x be an arbitrary element in the dataset X, and $R>0$. The neighbourhood V_R of radius R of x is defined as the set $V_R(x)=\{y/d(x,y) \leq R\}$, and the local density $p(x)$ of the non-normalized probability distribution at point x as:

$$p(x) = \sum_{x_i \in V_R(x)} \exp\left(-\frac{de^2(x,x_i)}{R^2}\right) \qquad (1)$$

where x_i are the points that belong to the neighbourhood of radius R of x, V_R, and de, the Euclidean distance.

In the algorithm presented here, we will differentiate between two concepts: *core cluster* and *cluster*. We will refer to *core clusters* to the sets that are obtained after applying the first stage of the algorithm, and we will refer to *clusters* to the groups of core clusters that will be grouped into clusters in a further stage.

2.2 Di-similarities Between Clusters

As part of the hierarchical approach, we need to define a di-similarity measure that takes into account two possible facts, when clusters are overlapped or completely separated. Let us define the following di-similarty function d between two clusters K_i and K_j,

$$d(K_i, K_j) = do(K_i, K_j) \ (1 + ds(K_i, K_j)) \tag{2}$$

where $do(K_i, K_j)$ is a measure of overlapping between clusters K_i and K_j, and $ds(K_i, K_j)$ is a measure of separability between those clusters.

The separability measure can be defined as

$$ds(K_i, K_j) = \min \{dsc(C_m, C_n)\}, \ \forall \ C_m, C_n / C_m \in K_i \text{ and } C_n \in K_j$$

where C_m, C_n are two core clusters, one from each cluster, and let us define the distance between two core clusters as:

$$dsc(C_m, C_n) = \min \{de(x_m, x_n)\}; \ \forall \ x_m, x_n / x_m \in C_m \text{ and } x_n \in C_n$$

That is, the distance or di-similarity measure of separability between two clusters is the shortest distance between any pair of points, one point from each cluster. Therefore, for overlapped clusters, $ds=0$.

On the other hand, about the cluster overlapping measure in equation (2), $do(K_i, K_j)$, let us suppose that each cluster corresponds to one mode in Figure 1. A non parametric measure of the degree of overlapping of such modes can be defined referring to the density value of the border point x_b between both modes.

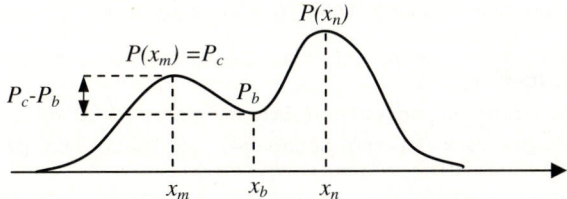

Fig. 1. Overlapping measures between two distribution modes

Therefore, let us define the overlapping degree of the two modes in Figure 1, $doc(C_m, C_n)$, as the relative difference between the density of the modes centres, x_m and x_n, with respect to the density at the border x_b between both modes. We can express this relative measures as

$$d(C_m, C_n) = \frac{P_c - P_b}{P_c} \tag{3}$$

Given a core cluster C_m, the centre of the core cluster x_m is defined as the point whose density is maximal within the core cluster. Let x_m and x_n be the centres of C_m and C_n respectively. Therefore, P_c in equation (3) is defined as the minimum density of the core cluster centres x_m and x_n, that is, $Pc=\min(p(x_m),p(x_n))$. Note that the di-similarity measure of overlapping in equation (3) is normalized in the range [0,1].

In equation (3), P_b is the density at the midpoint of the border between both core clusters, which is defined as the midpoint between the nearest points xb_m and xb_n, one from each core cluster, C_m and C_n. Finally, the measure of the degree of overlapping between two clusters $do(K_i, K_j)$, is be defined as

$$do(K_i, K_j) = \min \{doc(C_m, C_n)\}; \ \forall \ C_m, C_n \ / \ C_m \in K_i \text{ and } C_n \in K_j$$

In a few words, the di-similarity measure defined in (2) is aimed at considering that clusters are more similar when their probability distributions are either nearer in the feature space, measured by means of the separability measure $ds()$, or when their probability distributions are more overlapped. When the probability distributions are overlapped ($ds=0$), the measure of similarity becomes the overlapping degree of the probability density term $do()$, which is a heuristic local estimate of the mixed probability distributions at the border between clusters (Figure 1).

2.3 Clustering Algorithm

The clustering algorithm here presented consists of a hierarchical agglomerative strategy based on a Single Link approach, using the di-similarity measures defined in the previous Section. The use of such di-similarity measures defines the behaviour of the clustering process and the response to the overlapping of the local distributions of patterns in the data set.

Therefore, the proposed algorithm can be summarized in two stages as follows:

First stage:
```
Input:  radius R, data points and density noise threshold
Output: data points grouped into N core clusters
```

1. Initially, each point of the database is assigned to a single core cluster.
2. For each point x, calculate its neighbourhood of radius R, $V_R(x)$
3. For each point x in the database, estimate its probability density p(x) according to expression (1).
4. Assign each point x to the same core cluster of the point xc in its neighbourhood, being xc the point with maximal density in the neighbourhood of x.
5. Mark all core clusters with density less than the density noise threshold as noise core clusters. The rest of the core clusters are the resulting N core clusters.

Second stage
```
Input:  N core clusters
Output: K clusters
```

```
1.    Initially, assign each one the N core clusters from the first
      stage to a single cluster. Therefore, there are initially N
      clusters with one core cluster.
2.    Repeat until obtaining K clusters,
           2.1 Calculate the distance between each pair of clusters
               using expression (2)
           2.2 Join the two clusters in step 2.1 that their distance
               is minimum
3     Eventually, assign the noise core clusters to a nearest.
```

3 Experimental Results

In this section, some experimental results are presented aimed at evaluating the proposed algorithm, hereafter named *H-density*, and to compare it with some other similar algorithms referred in the introduction, DBSCAN, CURE and K-means. In order to test the algorithm, three groups of experiments are performed. The first one uses synthetic databases based on overlapped Gaussian distributions, in order to see the response of the proposed algorithm in these controlled conditions. The second experiment uses two synthetic databases from [7], for comparison purposes, and to test the problem of the presence of noise, overlapping, and clusters of different sizes and shapes. Finally, some experiments are performed on three real databases.

3.1 Gaussian Databases

Several databases using Gaussian distributions were generated with different number Gaussians, sizes and overlapping degrees. The results obtained in one of these databases are shown in Figure 2, where we can notice how the algorithm has been able to correctly detect each one of the existing Gaussian distributions, even in the presence of significant overlapping.

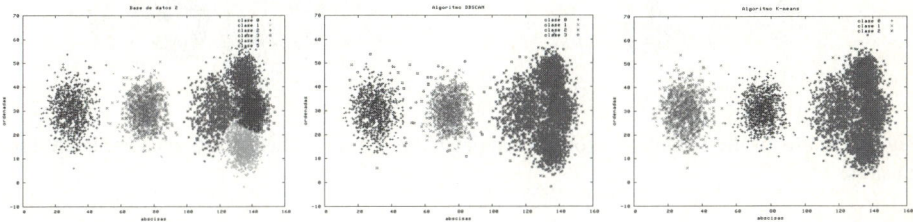

Fig. 2. Results on a Gaussian database of (left to right) H-density, DBSCAN and k-means

The DBSCAN algorithm did not correctly detect all the Gaussians in different data-bases because it is not able to separate the overlapped distributions. The CURE and K-means algorithms correctly detected the three main clusters. However, in the case of trying to find six clusters, they could not detect the 4 Gaussians highly overlapped.

3.2 Synthetic Databases

In [7], some experiments were presented for the DBSCAN and CURE algorithms using the databases of Figure 3 (see [7] for comparison results with those algorithms and note the satisfactory results of the proposed H-density algorithm). Notice the presence of clusters of different shapes, sizes, noise and overlapping. Figure 4 shows the result of applying the proposed H-density algorithm on these databases. Note how the algorithm has correctly grouped the main clusters present in the data set. Figure 4 shows the result of the K-means algorithm for 6 clusters (left) and 9 clusters (right) of the corresponding databases. The errors in the grouping are noticeable.

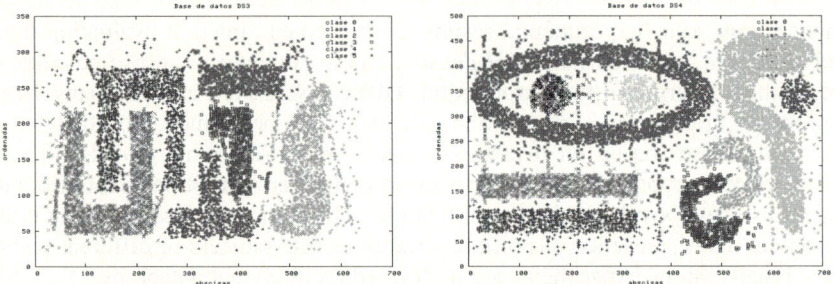

Fig. 3. Results of the H-density algorithm on databases from [7]

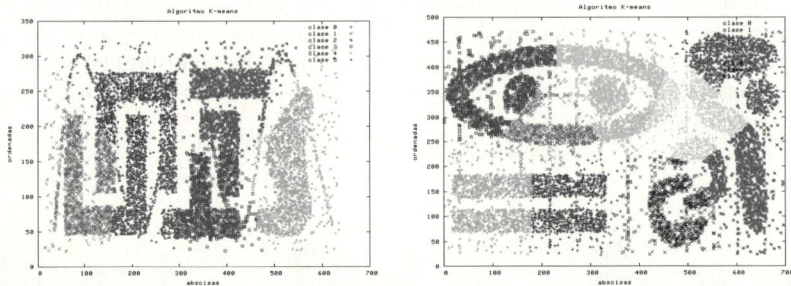

Fig. 4. Results of the K-means algorithm on databases from [7]. Left: for 6 clusters. Right for 9 clusters.

3.3 Real Databases

Two real databases were used in this experiment, Iris and Cancer. These databases were used for comparison purposes with the results presented in [4]. The first one is a database of Iris plants containing 3 known class labels, with a total of 150 elements, 50 each of the three classes: Iris Setosa, Iris Versicolour, Iris Virginica. The number of attributes is 4, all numeric. The first class, Iris Setosa, is linearly separable from the other two classes.

In order to compare the clustering results with the ones presented in [4], there was provided an error classification measure using the NN classifier, taking as training set the resulting clusters of the clustering algorithms, and as a test set the original labelled data set. The class assigned to each cluster was the class of the majority of patterns with the same class from the original dataset.

In the first experiment, all the algorithms were run to obtain two classes, and all of them obtained 100% of correct grouping or classification, that is, all the tested algorithms were able to correctly separate the Setosa class from the other ones.

In a second experiment, the algorithms were run to find three clusters. The results are shown in Table 1. Notice how, due to the overlapping between Versicolour and Virginica classes, the proposed H-density algorithm outperforms the other ones reaching a 94% correct classification. In the case of the Cancer database, it has 2 classes. The proposed H-density algorithm obtained a 95.461% of correct classification, the same as CURE (Table 2).

Table 1. Classfification rate of the clustering algorithm on Iris database

Algorithm	% in two classes	% in three classes
DBSCAN	100	71.33
CURE	100	83.33
K-means	100	88.33
H-Density	100	94.00

Table 2. Classification rate of the clustering algorithms in Cancer database (two classes)

Database	DBSCAN	CURE	K-means	H-Density
Cancer	94.28	95.461	95.04	95.461

Finally, the H-Density algorithm was run on a dataset consisting of the chroma values of the *Lab* representation of the "house" image (Figure 5 left). This image has 256x256 pixels, and the clustering was performed in the *ab* space to find 5 different colour classes. Note how the algorithm has been able to correctly identify 5 different clusters with a high degree of overlapping and different shapes and sizes (Figure 5 right). To see the goodness of the clusters found Figure 3 (middle) shows the labelled pixels with the corresponding assigned clusters.

5 Conclusions and Further Work

A hierarchical algorithm based on local probability density information has been presented. The way the density of the probability distribution is estimated, and the use of this information in the introduced dissimilarity measure between clusters, provides to the algorithm a mechanism to deal with overlapping distributions and the presence of noise in the data set. The experiments carried out show satisfactory and promising results to tackle these problems usually present in real databases. The experiments also show the proposed algorithm outperforms some existing algorithms. Future work is directed to unify the treatment of noise and overlapping in the process, and to introduce a measure to assess the "natural" number of clusters in the hierarchy.

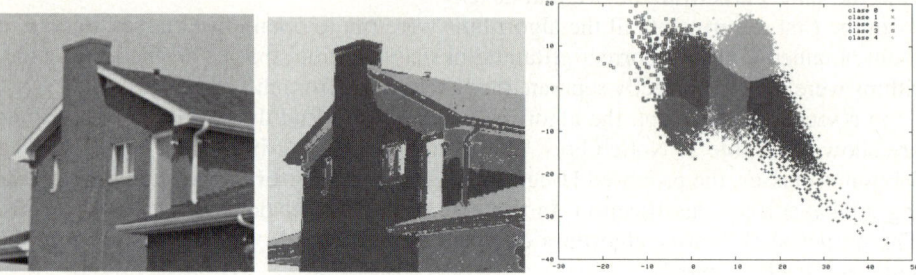

Fig. 5. Result of the H-density algorithm on the "house" image. Left: original image. Middle: labelled image. Right: 5 colour clusters found of pixels in the *ab* space.

References

1. Ester, M.; Kriegel, H. P.; Sander, J. and Xu, X.; A density-based algorithm for discovering clusters in large spatial databases with noise. In Proc. of the second International Conference on Knowledge Discovery and Data Mining, Portland, (1996) 226-231.
2. Ertöz, L.; Steinbach, M. and Kumar V.: Finding Clusters of Different Sizes, Shapes, and Densities in Noisy, High Dimensional Data. In Proceedings of Third SIAM International Conference on Data Mining, (2003).
3. Figueiredo, M. and Jain, A.K.; Unsupervised Learning of Mixture Models, IEEE Trans. on PAMI, Vol 24, No 3 (2002) 381-396.
4. Fred A. L. and Leitao J.: A New Cluster Isolation Criterion Based on Dissimilarity Increments. IEEE Transactions on Pattern Analysis and Machine Intelligence. Vol 25, No 8, (2003) 944-958.
5. Guha, S.; Rastogi, R. and Shim, K.; CURE: An Efficient Clustering Algorithm for Large Databases. In Proceedings of ACM SIGMOD International Conference on Management of Data, . ACM, New York, (1998) 73-84.
6. Hinneburg A. and Keim D.A.: An efficient Approach to Clustering in Large Multimedia Databases with Noise. In Proc. of the ACM SIGKDD, (1998).
7. Karypis, G.; Han, E.H. and Kumar, V.; Chameleon: A Hierarchical Clustering Algorithm Using Dynamic Modeling. In the IEEE Computer Society. Vol 32, No 8 (1999) 68-75.
8. Tran T. N., Wehrens R. and Buydens L.M.C.: Knn Density-Based Clustering for High Dimensional Multispectral Images. Analytica Chimica Acta 490 (2003) 303–312.

Application of Bidirectional Probabilistic Character Language Model in Handwritten Words Recognition

Jerzy Sas

Wroclaw University of Technology, Institute of Applied Informatics, Wyb.
Wyspianskiego 27, 50-370 Wroclaw, Poland
jerzy.sas@pwr.wroc.pl

Abstract. This paper presents a concept of bidirectional probabilistic character language model and its application to handwriting recognition. Character language model describes probability distribution of adjacent character combinations in words. Bidirectional model applies word analysis from left to right and in reversed order, i.e. it uses conditional probabilities of character succession and character precedence. Character model is used for HMM creation, which is applied as a soft word classifier. Two HMMs are created for left-to-right and right-to-left analysis. Final word classification is obtained as a combination of unidirectional recognitions. Experiments carried out with medical texts recognition revealed the superiority of combined classifier over its components.

1 Introduction

Despite of four decades of intensive researcher efforts, the handwriting recognition techniques, based merely on feature extraction from text images, are still not sufficiently accurate for practical applications. It was proved that the text recognition accuracy may be greatly increased by limiting the recognizable items to the set of words contained in a domain specific lexicon, especially if the relative word frequencies are also included in it.

Unfortunately, it is very common that domain lexicons are not available for domains the analyzed texts come from or available lexicons are highly incomplete. For this reason, to improve the recognition accuracy, other information sources about the recognized words must be used. One of them may be the information about the probabilistic properties of character succession and precedence. The set of probability distributions describing these properties will be called Probabilistic Character Language Model (PCLM). PCLM contains conditional probabilities of character succession and precedence as well as the probability distribution of the leading and trailing characters in a word. Data contained in PCLM seem to be specific for overall language of texts being recognized and are domain invariant. Therefore the general corpus of texts in the language can be used to estimate probabilities in PCLM.

The concept of word recognizer based on isolated character recognition results and on PCLM is discussed in this paper. Character bi-gram and tri-gram models are proposed and experimentally compared. Hidden Markov Model (HMM) is used as word recognizer. Soft classification concept ([2]) is applied on the level of words recognition. It makes possible to easily reuse results of isolated words recognition on higher levels of text recognition system, where complete sentences are recognized using methods of natural language processing.

Character n-grams and HMMs were used also by other researchers in constrained handwriting recognition ([1], [5]). The novelty of our proposal consists in application of bidirectional analysis. At the first stage of the word recognition two independent HMMs are used. One of them uses the character succession probabilities and analyses the word in left-to-right direction. The second one utilizes character precedence probabilities and analyses the word in reversed order. At the second stage, the results of both classifiers are combined, yielding the final word soft recognition.

The classifier described in this article either can be used as a stand-alone tool for word recognition or it can be combined with a lexicon based classifier in similar way as it is usually done on the word level ([3], [6]). Experiments described in Section 4 showed that the combined classifier outperforms its components.

2 Problem Statement

Let us consider the problem of correctly segmented word recognition. The word consists of M characters, each of them belongs to alphabet $\mathcal{A} = \{c_1, c_2, ..., c_L\}$. On the character level, isolated characters $c_{i_j}, j = 1..M$ are recognized independently by crisp character classifier $\Phi(x_j)$, where x_j is an image of isolated character. All further references to recognized characters mean characters recognized by crisp classifier.

On the word level we have three kinds of information, which can be used by word classifier:

– results of crisp character classification $(\Phi(x_1), \Phi(x_2), ..., \Phi(x_M))$ for isolated characters constituting the word,
– confusion matrix $E_{L \times L}$ of character recognizer; $e_{i,j} = p(\Phi(x) = c_i \mid c_j)$ is a probability that character classifier recognizes c_i while the actual character on the image x is c_j,
– PCLM consisting of:
  • probability distribution of leading and trailing characters (i.e. characters standing at the beginning and at the end of words) $P^I = (p_1^I, p_2^I, ..., p_L^I)$ and $P^E = (p_1^E, p_2^E, ..., p_L^E)$,
  • matrix $A_{L \times L}^S$ of character succession conditional probabilities, where $a_{i,j}^S = p(c_i \mid c_j)$ is the probability that the next character in a word is c_i provided that the preceding character is c_j,
  • matrix $A_{L \times L}^P$ of character precedence conditional probabilities, where $a_{i,j}^P = p(c_i \mid c_j)$ is the probability that the preceding character in a word is c_i provided that the next character is c_j.

Precedence and succession matrices can be obtained by simple analysis of text corpus. Character succession (and precedence) probability distribution seems to be general property of the language in which recognized texts are written, so it is domain invariant. Hence the texts in the corpus does not have to be from the particular area of interest. Large corpora of general texts in the language can be used to estimate A^S and A^P matrices.

On the word level soft classification paradigm is applied ([2]). Soft classification consists in finding the set of N most likely words and evaluating support values for selected words. Word classifier produces the set of pairs $\{(w_1, d_1^W), ..., (w_I, d_N^W)\}$, where w_i is the word and d_i^W is its support value. Our aim is to utilize all available sources of information in order to obtain the word classifier having possibly high accuracy.

3 Bidirectional Word Classifier Based on PCLM

Let us consider the probability $p_f(c_i \mid c_j)$ of character c_i appearance, given that preceding character is c_j. Probabilities $p(c_1 \mid c_i), ..., p(c_L \mid c_i)$ are distributed nonuniformly for most characters c_i from the alphabet. Classification of preceding character c_j and probabilities $p(c_i \mid c_j)$ can be utilized to support recognition of the next character. Improvement of the whole word recognition accuracy can be expected by applying this technique to classification of successive characters in the word. Described procedure is based on character succession probabilities and proceeds from the beginning to the end of word, so can be called *forward chaining*. Similar technique can be applied in reversed order, i.e. by proceeding from last to the first character and using character precedence probabilities $p(c_i \mid c_j)$ which are conditional probabilities of preceding character c_i provided that the next character is c_j *(backward chaining)*. Classifiers using backward and forward chaining can be combined. Although succession and precedence probabilities seem to be redundant (precedence probabilities can be calculated having succession and prior character probabilities), recognizers built using forward and backward chaining give different results and their combination results in further improvement of recognition quality. This observation can be explained by the fact, that Markov assumption (that conditional probabilities of a long sequence of events can be reasonably approximated as a product of low order conditional probabilities) introduces error for different prefixes/suffixes in the two models.

Both forward and backward classifiers have been constructed as Hidden Markov Models. HMM for words recognition can be entirely constructed using available PCLM described in Section 2. Here the construction of forward recognizer is explained. Backward classifier can be constructed in analogous way. HMM is defined by the following data:

- $\mathcal{Q} = \{q_1, ..., q_L\}$ - set of states,
- $\mathcal{O} = \{o_1, ..., o_L\}$ - set of visible states,
- $\mathcal{P}^B = (p_1^B, ..., p_L^B)$ - probability distribution of initial states,
- $\mathcal{A}_{L \times L}$ - matrix of transition probabilities,

- $\mathcal{B}_{L \times L}$ - matrix of observed states emission probabilities ($b_{i,j}$ - is the probability that visible state j is emitted when actual state is i).

Here HMM is used to model sequences of characters constituting word being recognized. Sets $\mathcal{Q}$ and $\mathcal{O}$ are both equivalent to the alphabet $\mathcal{A}$. States reached by HMM in successive steps are actual characters of the word being recognized. Here we apply the convention that observations are emitted by states. States represent characters recognized by character classifiers. Having the vector of observations $(o_1,..,o_M)$ (i.e. characters recognized by character classifiers on successive character positions in the word) we are searching the most probable trajectory of HMM $(q_1^*,...,q_M^*)$ on condition that the sequence $(o_1,...,o_M)$ was observed. To be more precise, for further application of word recognition results in whole sequence recognition, we need N most probable trajectories. HMM for lexicon independent word recognition is created in the following way:

- each of L hidden states represents actual character in the word being recognized, the set of observable states is equal to the set of hidden states,
- state transition probability matrix $\mathcal{A}$ determines conditional probabilities of adjacent characters succession in the word, hence the character succession probability matrix A^S from PCLM can be directly applied as $\mathcal{A}$,
- initial state probabilities $\mathcal{P}^B$ are the probabilities of characters on the beginning of words determined in PCLM as P_I,
- visible state emission matrix $\mathcal{B}$ is equivalent to confusion matrix E, where hidden states correspond to actual characters and observed states correspond to characters recognized by the character recognizer.

The procedure of word recognition with HMM consists in finding the most probable sequences of actual states, provided that given sequence of visible states was observed. The observed sequence of states is the word recognized by character recognizer. For further processing we need N most probable characters sequences. In our experiments we used $N = 100$ most probable words recognized by HMM. Finding N-best words is achieved by extended Viterbi procedure. The HMM based classifier yields the set of N most probable characters sequences with their conditional probabilities interpreted as support factors

$$R^F = \{(w_1, d_1^F), ..., (w_N, d_N^F)\}. \tag{1}$$

Support factors d_i^F are approximations of the conditional word probabilities $p(w_i \mid (o_1,...,o_M))$ calculated as a by-product of Viterbi procedure and normalized so as to sum up to 1.0.

Another similar HMM can be used for backward chaining. The only differences in building backward chaining HMM are that the probability distribution of trailing characters P^E (i.e characters standing at the end of word) is used instead of P^I and A^P is used instead of A^S as transition probability matrix. Let R^B denotes the soft recognition set created by backward chaining HMM, analogous to the one defined in (1). Results produced by forward and backward HMMs are combined giving ultimate word soft classification. Because both HMMs seem to be equally robust, the following combination procedure can be proposed:

- let the set Z^{FB} of words recognized by combined HMM will be the sum of word sets Z^F and Z^B appearing in R^F and R^B,
- for words w_j belonging to Z^{FB} but not belonging to Z^F let $d_j^F = 0$, for words belonging to Z^F use support factors d_j^F provided by forward HMM,
- for words w_j belonging to Z^{FB} but not belonging to Z^B let $d_j^B = 0$, for words belonging to Z^B use support factors d_j^B provided by backward HMM,
- calculate support factors d_j^{FB} for all words in Z^{FB} as geometric mean $\sqrt{d_j^F * d_j^B}$,
- normalize factors obtained in this way so as to sum up to 1.0 over whole set Z^{FB}.

Finally we obtain the soft recognition of combined bidirectional HMM.

$$R^{FB} = \{(w_1, d_1^{FB}), ..., (w_{N_{FB}}, d_{N_{FB}}^{FB})\}, \qquad (2)$$

where N_{FB} is the count of elements in the set Z^{FB} ($N_{FB} \geq N$). Experiments showed that classification accuracies obtained by forward and backward HMMs are similar, although the sets of words produced by both classifiers are usually different. Four methods of support factor calculation were tested: arithmetic mean $d_j^F + d_j^B$, geometric mean $\sqrt{d_j^F * d_j^B}$, maximum of d_j^F and d_j^B and minimum of d_j^F and d_j^B. Best results of combined HMM classifier were obtained when geometric mean was used as fusing rule, so this method is finally recommended. Some remarks about results of remaining rules application are presented in Section 4.

3.1 Implementation of Tri-gram Model Using HMM

The prediction of the next character may be more accurate if the sequence of $(n-1)$ preceding characters is taken into account. It leads to n-gram model frequently used in natural language processing for analyzing word sequences. Similar concept can be applied to character sequences. Because of the limitations of text corpus size, we restricted our considerations to tri-gram models, where the character occurrence depends on the sequence of two preceding characters. In first order Markov model, the probability distribution of the next state depends only on the previous state, so dependence on two preceding states cannot be directly modeled. For this reason in tri-gram HMM model we represent sequences of two characters as a single states. It leads to the following definition of HMM-based tri-gram model:

- set of visible states $\mathcal{O} = \{c_1, ..., c_L, c_{bl}\}$ consists all characters from alphabet $\mathcal{A}$ extended with blank character c_{bl},
- set of states $\mathcal{Q}$ consists of $(L+1)^2$ states q_{c_i, c_j}, each of them represents pair of characters c_i, c_j from $\mathcal{A} \cup \{c_{bl}\}$,
- probability distribution of initial states is determined as follows:

$$p(q_{c_i,c_j}) = \begin{cases} p_j^I & \text{for } c_i = c_{bl} \text{ and } c_j \in \mathcal{A} \\ 0 & \text{otherwise} \end{cases} \qquad (3)$$

- $\mathcal{A}_{(L+1)^2 \times (L+1)^2}$ - matrix of transition probabilities, which elements a determine conditional probabilities $p(c_k \mid (c_i, c_j))$ in character sequences $c_i c_j c_k$:

$$a(q_{c_i c_j}, q_{c_l c_k}) = \begin{cases} p(c_k \mid (c_i, c_j)) & \text{if } c_j = c_l \text{ and } c_l, c_k \neq c_{bl} \\ 0 & \text{otherwise} \end{cases} \quad (4)$$

- visible states emission probability matrix $\mathcal{B}$ is defined taking into account that each state $q_{c_i c_j}$ actually represents single character c_j in the word being recognized, preceded by the character c_i; so the probability of c_k emission is equal in all states q_{c_i, c_j} with the same c_j, i.e:

$$b(q_{c_i c_j}, c_k) = p(\Phi(x_j) = c_k \mid x_j \text{ is an image of } c_j) = e(k, j), \quad (5)$$

where $e(k, j)$ is an element of character classifier confusion matrix.

The tri-gram HMM created as described above is based on forward chaining. In the way analogous to the one described for b-gram HMM, similar tri-gram backward HMM can be constructed, and results of forward and backward word soft recognitions can be combined.

4 Experiments

The aim of experiments carried out was to asses the improvements in word recognition accuracy achieved due to PCLM application. Because the work being described here is a part of wider project that consists in automatic recognition of handwritten medical texts, excerpts from authentic patient records stored in a hospital information system have been used in experiments. The acquired corpus consisted of 15961 texts stored as ASCII strings. Text set was divided into training part consisting of 12691 texts and testing part containing remaining 3600 passages. The training part was used to estimate probabilities in PCLM.

Unfortunately, we were not able to collect sufficiently numerous set of handwritten texts from the same field as texts in corpus. Therefore, simulated experiment was carried out, where text images were artificially created using the a set of 5080 images of correctly recognized isolated handwritten characters. For the sake of automatic recognition accuracy assessment, actual characters on these images were recognized by a human and this classification was assumed to be correct. The image creation procedure consisted of the following steps. First, the text passage to be recognized was randomly drawn from the testing subset of corpus. Next, for each character in selected text, one image of this character was randomly chosen from the set of character samples. Finally, the drawn character images were arranged side by side, constituting artificial text image.

The alphabet consisted of 35 Polish letters including 9 diacritic characters. Five character classifiers were used in experiments:

- **MLP** - neural network classifier using directional features extracted according to the method described in [4] - accuracy: 91.7%,
- **KNN** - k-NN classifier (k=9) using directional features - accuracy: 88.9%,

- **EM_88** - NN classifier based on dissimilarity measure and unconstrained elastic matching as described in [7] - accuracy: 88.4%,
- **EM_79** - the classifier analogous to EM_88 but trained with reduced learning set - accuracy: 79.3%,
- **EM_45** - the classifier analogous to EM_88 but trained with strongly reduced learning set - accuracy: 44.8%.

In the experiment all HMM classifiers described in Section 3 were tested and compared:

- **BI_FWD** - bi-gram HMM classifier with forward chaining,
- **BI_BWD** - bi-gram HMM classifier with backward chaining,
- **BI_2DIR_AM**, **BI_2DIR_GM** - combination of bi-gram forward and backward chaining classifiers based on arithmetic mean and geometric mean fusing rules correspondingly,
- **TRI_FWD**- tri-gram HMM classifier with forward chaining,
- **TRI_BWD** - tri-gram HMM classifier with backward chaining,
- **TRI_2DIR_AM**, **TRI_2DIR_GM** - combination of tri-gram forward and backward chaining classifiers based on arithmetic mean and geometric mean fusing rules.

The results of words recognition can be used as an input to higher level of handwritten text recognition system, where complete sentences are recognized. Natural language processing methods used there expect that word classifier applied to successive words delivers the rank of most likely words for each word position in the sentence. In such cases, it is not the most essential that the actual word has the highest support factor in support vector (2). Rather it is expected that the actual word is in the small subset of words with highest support factors. Therefore, in evaluating the word soft classifiers accuracy, we consider as erroneous such soft recognition result, where the actual word is not among k words with highest support factors. Error rates of word classification for all tested word classifiers for $k = 1$ and $k = 5$ are given in Tab. 1. $k = 1$ is equivalent to word crisp recognition.

It can be noticed that in all the cases accuracies of forward and backward chaining HMM recognizers are similar. Combination of backward and forward chaining results in noticeable boost of accuracy in relation to unidirectional HMM for both combination rules based on geometric and arithmetic means. Geometric mean gives best results of all tested fusing rules. Combination rules based on maximum and minimum of component classifier support factors were also tested. Calculating final support factors with "rule of maximum" gives results close to the ones obtained using arithmetic mean. "Rule of minimum" gives worst results, close to the results of worse of component classifiers. In the case of best character classifier (MLP) the error rate reduction resulting from application of bidirectional model instead of unidirectional one in case of tri-gram HMM and for $k = 1$ (crisp classification) is 1.29(error rate reduced from 10.2% to 7.9%).

Word recognition accuracy achieved with the tri-gram model is significantly better than that achieved with bi-gram one. Relative error reduction resulting

Table 1. Word recognition error rates of HMM classifiers

Formula	MLP	KNN	EN_88	EN_79	EN_45
k=1:					
BI_FWD	17.2%	26.3%	28.1%	50.3%	76.3%
BI_BWD	16.4%	26.1%	28.8%	50.2%	79.2%
BI_2DIR_AM	15.5%	24.4%	27.1%	47.5%	73.7%
BI_2DIR_GM	13.2%	20.8%	23.4%	42.6%	69.1%
TRI_FWD	11.2%	14.5%	14.4%	28.3%	52.9%
TRI_BWD	10.2%	13.6%	15.1%	27.7%	55.8%
TRI_2DIR_AM	8.8%	11.3%	13.5%	25.5%	48.5%
TRI_2DIR_GM	7.9%	10.5%	11.7%	21.0%	43.2%
k=5:					
BI_FWD	2.6%	6.5%	6.8%	24.0%	58.1%
BI_BWD	2.7%	5.9%	7.0%	24.0%	58.2%
BI_2DIR_AM	2.4%	5.9%	6.3%	21.7%	56.8%
BI_2DIR_GM	2.0%	5.1%	5.9%	18.7%	49.9%
TRI_FWD	1.7%	2.7%	2.4%	7.2%	28.7%
TRI_BWD	2.0%	3.0%	2.4%	7.0%	29.4%
TRI_2DIR_AM	0.4%	1.1%	1.3%	5.8%	25.2%
TRI_2DIR_GM	0.4%	0.9%	1.1%	5.4%	23.0%

from bidirectional tri-gram HMM application in relation to bidirectional bi-gram model for $k = 1$ and for MLP character classifier is 1.67 (error rate reduced from 13.2% to 7.9%).

5 Conclusions

In the paper the problem of handwritten words recognition with the use of unlimited lexicon is addressed. The proposed algorithm applies probabilistic language character model that describes properties of character succession, which are specific for the language being recognized. Neither the lexicon of admissible words nor the text corpus specific for the domain being considered is necessary to create the language character model. It can be created using easily available corpus of arbitrary texts in the given language. Bidirectional word analysis is applied which boosts the word recognition quality.

Experiments carried out on the medical texts corpus have proved that the word recognition accuracy necessary for practical application is possible with the use of proposed method, even if character classifiers are of a relatively low quality. It is especially important for the case of "analytic" paradigm of cursive script recognition, where the segmentation of words into characters constitutes a serious problem and the segmented character recognition accuracy is low.

The final word recognition accuracy could be probably further improved by using more advanced methods of forward and backward classifier combination.

One of possibilities is to use classifier combination based on component classifier confidence assessment, e.g. as described in [7].

Acknowledgement. This work was financed from the State Committee for Scientific Research (KBN) resources in 2005 - 2007 years as a research project No 3 T11E 005 28.

References

1. Brakensiek A., Rottland J., Kosmala A., Rigoll G.: Off-Line Handwriting Recognition Using Various Hybrid Modeling Techniques and Character N-Grams, Proc. of the Seventh Int. Workshop on Frontiers in Handwriting Recognition, (2000) 343-352
2. Kuncheva L.: Combining Classifiers: Soft Computing Solutions, [in.] Pattern Recognition: from Classical to Modern Approaches, Pal S., Pal A. [eds.], World Scientific (2001) 427-451
3. Marti U.V., Bunke H.: Using a Statistical Language Model to Improve the Performance of an HMM-Based Cursive Handwritting Recognition System, Int. Journ. of Pattern Recognition and Artificial Intelligence, Vol. 15 (2001) 65-90
4. Liu C., Nakashima K., Sako H.: Handwritten Digit Recognition: Benchmarking of State-of-the-Art Techniques. Pattern Recognition, Vol. 36. (2003) 2271-2285
5. l-Nasan A., Nagy G., Veeramachaneni S.: Handwriting recognition using position sensitive n-gram matching, Proc. 7th Int. Conf. on Document Analysis and Recognition (2003) 577-582
6. Vinciarelli A., Bengio S., Bunke H.: Offline Recognition of Unconstrained Handwritten Text Using HMMs and Statistical Language Models, IEEE Trans. on PAMI, Vol. 26 (2004) 709-720
7. Sas J., Luzyna M.: Combining Character Classifier Using Member Classifiers Assessment, Proc. of 5th Int. Conf. on Intelligent Systems Design and Applications, ISDA 2005, IEEE Press (2005) 400-405

Efficient Classification Method for Complex Biological Literature Using Text and Data Mining Combination

Yun Jeong Choi and Seung Soo Park

Department of Computer Science & Engineering,
Ewha Womans University, Seoul 127-150, Korea
cris@ewhain.net, sspark@ewha.ac.kr

Abstract. Recently, as the size of genetic knowledge grows faster, the automated analysis and systemization into high-throughput database has become a hot issue. In bioinformatics area, one of the essential tasks is to recognize and identify genomic entities and discover their relations from various sources. Generally, biological literatures containing ambiguous entities, are laid by decision boundaries. The purpose of this paper is to design and implement a classification system for improving performance in identifying entity problems. The system is based on reinforcement training and post-processing method and supplemented by data mining algorithms to enhance its performance. For experiments, we add some intentional noises to training data for testing the robustness and stability. The result shows significantly improved stability on training errors.

1 Introduction

As the advanced computational technology and systems have been developed, the amount of new biomedical knowledge and their scientific literature has been increased exponentially. Consequently, the automated analysis and systemization in high- throughput system has become a hot issue. Most of biological and medical literatures have been published online, such as journal articles, research reports, and clinical reports. These literatures are invaluable knowledge source for researchers. When we perform knowledge discovery from large amount of biological data, one essential task is to recognize and identify genomic entities and discover their relations. Recently, many effective techniques have been proposed to analyze text and documents. Yet, accuracy seems to be high only when the data fits the proposed model well. We explain the motivation and issues to be solved in this section.

1.1 Automated Analysis of Biological Literature and Identification Problem

Biological literature contains many ambiguous entities including biological terms, medical terms and general terms, and so on. Genes and their transcripts often share the same name, and there are plenty of other examples of the multiplicity of meanings. The task of annotation can be regarded as identifying and classifying the terms that appear in the texts according to a pre-defined classification. However, disambiguated annotation is hard to achieve because of multiplicity of meanings and types. Generally, documents containing ambiguous entities are laid by decision boundaries and it is not easy for a machine to perform a reasonable classification(Fig.1). These problems reduce the accuracy of document retrieval engines and of information extraction system. Most of classifiers ignore the semantic aspects of the linguistic contents.

1.2 Classification Algorithms and Evaluation of the Performance

Automated text classification is to classify free text documents into predefined categories automatically, and whose main goal is to reduce the considerable manual process required for the task. Generally, when you evaluate the performance of automated text classification, you simply consider what kind of classifier and how many documents have been used. Traditionally, classification approaches are either statistical methods or those using NLP(Natural Language Processing) methods. Simple statistical approaches are efficient, and fast but usually lack deep understanding, and hence prone to ambiguity errors. Knowledge based NLP techniques, however, are very slow even though the quality of the result is usually better than that of statistical approaches[1,2]. Also, there are tons of classifiers based on rule base model, inductive learning model, information retrieval model, etc. Some classifiers such as Naïve Bayesian and Support Vector Machines(SVMs) is based on inductive learning based model. These classifiers have pros and cons.

1.3 Classification Problem in Complex Data

As the data size and its complexity grow fast, finding optimal line to classify is more difficult. Fig.1 shows the example of documents represented in vector. It displays the difficulty in automated classification of complex documents. A set of documents which has simple contents with lower complexity, are represented as (a). Complex documents which have multiple concepts are represented as (b). Usually, the documents located around decision boundary have multiple subjects and features. This is the area where our research is focused on.

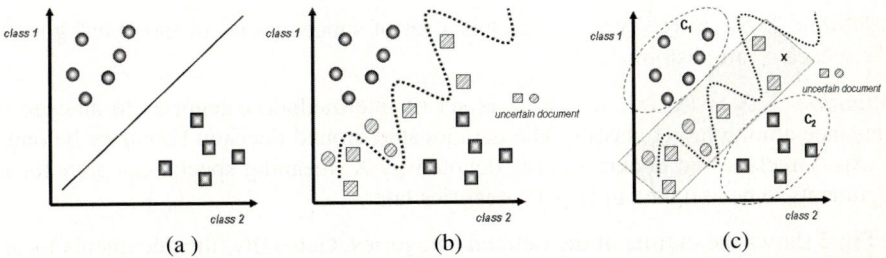

Fig. 1. Finding decision rule or line for classification : A set of documents which has simple contents and lower complexity, are represented as(a). Complex documents which have multiple concepts are represented as(b). Usually, documents located around decision boundaries have multiple subjects.

In this paper, we propose a new approach based on a reinforcement training method and text and data mining combination. We have designed and implemented a text classification system, *RTPost*, for identifying entity based on reinforcement training and post-processing method. We show that we do not need to change the classification techniques itself to improve accuracy and flexibility. This paper is organized as follows. We describe our proposed method in section 2. Section 3 presents the experimental results on the newsgroup domain. Finally, section 4 concludes the paper.

2 Method

Our goal is to maximize the classification accuracy while minimizing training costs using a refined training method and post-processing analysis. Specifically, we focus our attention to complex documents. Most of them can be misclassified, which is one of the main factors to reduce the accuracy. In this section, we present a RTPost system, which is designed in a different style from traditional methods, in the sense that it takes a fault tolerant system approach as well as a data mining strategy. We use text classification system based on text mining as a front-end system, which performs clustering and feature extraction basically. The output of the text mining, then, is fed into a data mining system, where we perform automated training using a neural net based procedure. This feedback loop can be repeated until the outcome is satisfactory to the user. In this section we describe our propose method focusing on refinement training and post-processing.

2.1 Training : Category Design and Definition

Most of the training algorithms deal with the selection problem under a fixed condition of target category. We expand the problem into designing and definition of more categories. We add a new category, X, in addition to the target category, C, to generate the initial classification results, L ,based on probabilistic scores. We define some types of class for classification purpose.

Definition 1. $C = \{c_1, c_2, \ldots, c_n\}$ is a set of final target categories, where c_i and c_j are disjoint each other.($i \neq j$)

Definition 2. $SC_n = \{c_{n1}, c_{n2}, \ldots, c_{nk}\}$ is a set of subcategories of target category c_i, where each c_{nj} are disjoint.

Definition 3. $X = \{x_1, x_2, \ldots, x_{n-1}\}$ is set of intermediate categories to analyze the relevance among target classes. The data located around decision boundary belong to X. Also, unclassified documents are denoted by X, meaning special category for the documents to be assigned to target categories later.

Fig.2 shows the outline of the defined categories. Generally, the documents located along the decision boundary, lead to poor performance as they contain multiple topics and multiple features in similar frequencies. These are the typical cases which induce false positive errors and lower accuracies. We simply select and construct training samples in each class by collecting obviously positive cases. If we define a set of target categories as $C = \{c_1, c_2\}$, and number of subcategory = 2, the actual training is performed on, $T = \{c_{11}, c_{12}, x_1, x_2, c_{21}, c_{22}\}$, where x_1's are intermediate categories. The decision of the final target categories of complex documents, class x_1, and x_2, is done by the computation of distance function in the post-processing step[11].

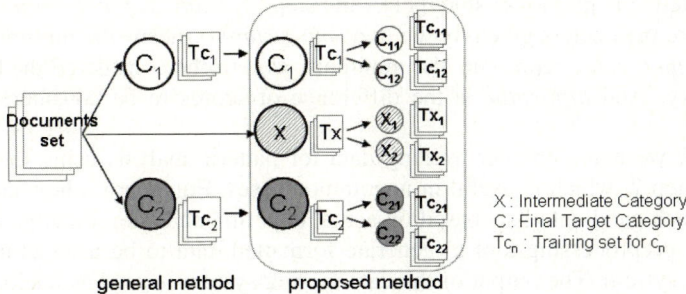

Fig. 3. Organizing method of training data : In complex documents decision boundary is not a line but a region. The data in this region is predicted as false positive. We separate the training set into target and intermediate category.

2.2 Reinforcement Post-processing Method in *RTPost* System

The main goal is to overcome these problems and limitations of traditional methods using the data mining approach. The main feature of our system is the way that we assign complex documents to the corresponding classes. We combine data mining and text mining so that they can complement each other. It is based on the structural risk minimization principle for error-bound analyses. This post–processing method consists of two stages. The front part is to assign a category to a document using the initial score calculated from the text classification result. Then, the second part is to make feedback rules to give guidelines to the previous step.

D_i\L	1 (w_m=0.02)		2 (w_m=0.15)		3 (w_m=0.25)		4 (w_m=0.31)		5 (w_m=0.35)		D_i^{size}	Step1	Step2	Assign	Actual Class
1	C_{21}	.98	C_{11}	.01	X_1	.01	X_2	.01	C_{12}	.00	726.33	$C_{21} \rightarrow C_2$	-	C_2	C_2
2	C_{21}	.39	C_{12}	.20	X_2	.17	C_{11}	.13	X_1	.10	31.6	X	C_2	C_2	C_2
3	X_2	.29	C_{11}	.28	C_{12}	.17	C_{21}	.15	X_1	.01	514.42	X	C_1	C_1	C_1
4	X_1	.28	C_{21}	.23	X_2	.17	C_{11}	.16	C_{12}	.15	287.12	X	C_2	C_2	C_2

Fig. 4. Assignment examples by computation of distance between pivot category and candidate categories defined categories and experimental condition. It shows how computation is done in each candidate lists based on actual experimental data.

As a limitation of pages we simply explain about step 1 and step 2, which performs comparisons using rank scores given by the text classification result. This work is well-presented in previous study[11]. In step 1, *min_support*, *min_value* and *diff_value* are parameters given by the user, *min_support* means the minimum support values, and *min_value* represents the minimum score to be considered the best candidate category. And *diff_value* is the difference of scores to be considered they are different.

In step 3, we make another training data for pattern analysis using the results of step 1 and step 2, which is useful in uncommon cases. Fig.3 shows how computation is done in each candidate lists based on actual experimental data. Finally, we use text mining as a preprocessing tool to generate formatted data to be used as input to the data mining system. The output of the data mining system is used as feedback data to the text mining to guide further categorization

In step 4, we analyze a whole process until classifying of document D_i is done. As input values, integrated results of previous steps are used. The goal is to minimize classification error in *RTPost* system and maintain stability in a fault tolerant manner. Fault tolerant system is designed to automatically detect faults and correct a fault effect concurrently at the cost of either performance degradation or considerable hardware or software overhead.

Table 1. Evaluation matrix for effectiveness by variance of results

Location / Input Data	Result from each step (feedback time =1)						
	C_n^1.step1	C_n^1.step2	C_n^2	C_{n+1}^1.step1	C_{n+1}^1.step2	C_{n+1}^2	
d_1	X	1	1	1	-	-	Good
d_2	X	0	1	1	-	-	Good
d_3	X	0	0	1	-	-	Poor
d_4	1	1	1	1	-	-	Fair
d_5	1	0	1	1	-	-	Fair
d_6	1	1	0	1	-	-	Poor
d_7	1	0	0	1	-	-	Poor
d_8	0	1	1	1	-	-	Good
d_9	0	0	1	1	-	-	Good
d_{10}	0	1	0	1	-	-	Poor
	✓	✓	✓	✓	-	-	

where C_n^e.*process*, $n = 0,1,2 ...$: *feedback time*, e : *a type of input data*, 1= *documents* 2=*candidate lists of documents* *process*= *step1, step2*

In our system, the types of faults are classified to design error, parameter error and training error. We integrated results from each steps and make evaluation matrix like table 1. Table 1 is evaluation table to observe classification progress and to catch out the errors Where C_n^e.*process*, *n* refers to feedback time, and *e* is a type of input date; '1'=documents, '2' = candidate lists of documents, *process* refers to step1 and step2. We denote 1 when each predicted value is true, and we denote X when the document was unclassified. We can expect the location that the error is occurred as analysis of these variances in the matrix. In step 1, it is caused by parameters and category scheme, and in step2, computation of distance between pivot category and target categories is a important factor. Based on this table, we define effectiveness function to assess how the process works well. We divide result into 3 states: *good, fair, poor* and simply make an effectiveness function, like (1).

$$E(RTPost) = \frac{1}{N}\left[\sum Good(d_i) \times benefit + \frac{1}{N}\sum Fair(d_i) - \frac{1}{N}\sum Poor(d_i) \times penalty\right] \quad (1)$$

$$benefit = log\ (n) + 1.0 \quad (2)$$

$$penalty = log\ (n) + 1.5 \quad (3)$$

If documents d_i is located around decision boundary and the result value in step1 is true, then we regard it as '*good*' case, it means *RTPost* system works very well. If d_i is not located around decision boundary and the result values in step1 and step2 are both false, then we regard it as 'poor' case, it means that there were problem in entire process. So we give penalty. Also, if d_i is not located around decision boundary and the result value in step1 is true, then we regard it as 'fair' case, it mean there is no critical problem in the process. (2) and (3) are weight values for '*good*' state and '*poor*' state. For example, the range of *E(RTPost) is* -4.5 < *E* < 4, when 1000 of test documents were used. At this time, there are above 30% of 'poor' cases without any '*good*' cases, then, *E(RTPost)* has the score below 0. If *E(RTPost)* score is lower that defined reasonable value, we need to assess that there are critical problems over the entire process.

3 Experiments

To measure the performance of our system, We experiment our system in a field where ambiguous words can cause errors in grouping and affect the result. In particular, we focused on the Rb(retinoblastoma)-related documents from the PubMed abstracts. The main difficulty of automatic classification of the documents is the ambiguity of the intended meaning of Rb, which can only be interpreted correctly when full context is considered. Possible interpretations include cancer(C), cell line(L), protein(P), gene(G), and ion(I). We perform the same experiments using Naïve Bayesian and SVM, with and without the post-processing steps, for two situations(with and without noise). We present the test conditions in Table 2 and report. Since the proposed system is developed by using a component based style using BOW toolkit[10] and C, it can be easily adapted to deal with other data or other data mining algorithms.

3.1 Classification for Disambiguation of 'RB'

Our goal is to identify the words 'Rb' or 'retinoblastoma' through the classification task. The examples of the successful tagging is as follows :

(1) P130I mediates TGF-beta-induced cell-cycle arrest inn **Rb** mutant HT-3 cells. *(gene)*

(2) The INK4alpha/ARF locus encodes p14(ARF) and p16(INK4alpha) , that function to arrest the cell cycle through the p53 and **RB** pathways, respectively. *(protein)*

(3) Many tumor types are associated with genetic changes in the **retinoblastoma** pathway, leading to hyperactivation of cyclin-dependent kinases and incorrect progression through the cell cycle. *(cancer)*

(4) The Y79 and WERI-Rb1 **retinoblastoma** cells, as well as MCF7 breast cancer epithelial cells, all of which express T-channel current and mRNA for T-channel subunits, is inhibited by pimozide and mibefradil with IC(50)= 8 and 5 microM for pimozide and mibefradil, respectively). *(cell line)*

3.2 Experimental Setting

In RB-related documents, most documents is connected with protein(P), gene(G) and cancer(C). Hence, there are a few documents connected with ion(I) and which size are very small. In this paper, we experimented with 3 classes by defined categories as shown in table 2. We equally divided each target category into two parts, and added two intermediate categories. Finally, we performed classification on the set of candidate categories, SC={P1, P2, X1, G1, G2, X2, D1, D2}. For experiments, we collected about 20,000 abstracts, and we verified our result using 200 abstracts. Especially, we put some intentional noises by adding incorrectly classified documents to target categories, which is about 10% of the total. Actually, these documents get high classification errors because these have many ambiguous features, and their contents are very intricate.

Table 2. Defined categories and Experimental Condition

Definition of category			Number of training documents (correct + incorrect)		
Target category (C)	Candidate category (SC)	Intermediate category(X)	Correct Documents	Incorrect documents (10%)	Total (300, 318)
Protein	P1		30	5	60(36)
	P2		30	1	
		X1	60	0	60
Gene	G1		30	3	60(36)
	G2		30	3	
		X2	60	0	60
Disease, Cancer	D1		30	6	60(36)
	D2		30	0	

We defined parameter values to assign documents in text classification, as shown in figure 3: min_support=100(bytes), min_value=0.6, diff_value=0.2. We performed analysis based on effectiveness factor, 0.5 and one-time feedback.

3.3 Experimental Result and Discussion

Table 3, 4 show the experimental results on the correct training data. According to the results, our method works very well when applied to the Naïve Bayesian or SVM classifiers. Especially, SVM and NB perform badly on the *protein* class, which is the fraction of protein-related documents that are with high complexity and multiplicity, which share multiple topics and features in the similar frequency.

Table 3. Experimental Result: Exising method and RTPost method with correct document

method / performance	Accuracy	Protein Predict Power	Gene Predict Power	Disease Predict Power	Misclassification rate
Naïve Baysian(NB)	0.69	51%	82%	74%	31%.
SVM	0.74	64%	83%	76%	29%
RTPost Algorithm(with NB)	0.89	81%	94%	92%	11%
RTPost Algorithm(with SVM)	0.91	88%	91%	94%	8%

Table 4. Experimental Result: Exising method and RTPost method with incorrect document

method / performance	Accuracy	Protein Predict Power	Gene Predict Power	Disease Predict Power	Misclassification rate
Naïve Baysian(NB)	0.45	52%	65%	17%	55%.
SVM	0.47	54%	61%	26%	64%
RTPost Algorithm(with NB)	0.85	84%	92%	75%	15%
RTPost Algorithm(with SVM)	0.87	87%	91%	81%	11%

Our system enhances both classifiers by relatively high rates. On the average, the refined classifiers are on average about 25% better the original. Especially, our method have high predict power about *gene* class consisting of '*Gene*', '*DNA*', '*mRNA*' as main features, and *cancer* class consisting of '*cancer*', '*disease*' and so on.

Table 4 shows the experimental result on the data containing incorrect training samples. According to the result, the accuracy of original method decreased 0.45 and 0.47. Generally, it is well known that Naïve Bayesian is less influenced by the training errors. However, it's predict power drops down to 17% in '*disease*' class. It clearly shows that the important features among the classes were generalized because of incorrect documents. Also, it reveals the assignment problem and the limitation of improving performance by reforming computation method based on probability models or vector models. Hence, our method significantly improved stability on training errors.

4 Conclusion

In this paper, we proposed a refinement method to enhance the performance of identifying entity using text and data mining combination. It provides a comparatively cheap alternative to the traditional statistical methods. We applied this method to analyze Rb-related documents in PubMed and got very positive results. We also have shown that our system has high accuracy and stability in actual conditions. It does not depend on some of the factors that have important influences to the classification power. Those factors include the number of training documents, selection of sample data, and the performance of classification algorithms. In the future research, we plan to simplify the effectiveness function without raising the running costs of the entire process.

References

1. Agrawal R., R. Bayardo, and R. Srikant. :Athena: Mining-based Interactive Management of Text Databases, *In Proc. of the International Conference on Extending Database Technology* (2000) 365-379
2. Koller D. and S. Tong.:Active learning for parameter estimation in Bayesian networks. *In Neural Information Processing Systems(* 2001)
3. Bing Liu, Haoran Wu and Tong Heng Phang :a Refinement Approach to Handling Model Misfit in Text Categorization, SIGKDD(2002)
4. Castillo M. D.,, J.L.Serrano:A Multistrategy Approach for Digital Text Categorization form Imbalanced Documents, SIGKDD, vol 6(2004) 70-79
5. Sheng Gao, Wen Wu, et al,:A MFoM Learning Approach to Robust Multiclass Multi-Label Text Categorization, *In Proceedings of the 21th* Intenational Conference on Machine Learning(2004)
6. Joachims T.,, :Text categorization with support vector machines: learning with many relevant features. *In Proceedings of ECML-98, 10th European Conference on Machine Learning(1998)* 137-142
7. Hasenager M.,.: Active Data Selection in Supervised and Unsupervised Learning. PhD thesis, Technische Fakultat der Universitat Bielefeld(2000)
8. Hatzivassiloglou, V., P.A. Duboue, and A.Rzhetsky. : Disambiguating Proteins, Genes and RNA in Text: a Machine Learning Approach. *Bioinformatics*(2001) Vol.17, S97-106
9. Lifeng Chen, Hongfang Liu and Caroal Friedman, : Gene Name Ambiguity of Eukaryotic Nomenclatures, Bioinformatics, Vol21, No.2, pages 248-256,. Jan 15, 2005 .
10. BOW toolkit : http://www.cs.cmu.edu/~mccallum/bow/
11. Choi, Y.J., Park, S.S. : Refinement Method of Post-processing and Training for Improvement of Automated Text Classification", *In Proc. Of the International Conference, ICCSA(2006)*

Classifying Polyphony Music Based on Markov Model

Yukiteru Yoshihara and Takao Miura

Dept.of Elect.& Elect. Engr., HOSEI University
3-7-2 KajinoCho, Koganei, Tokyo, 184–8584 Japan

Abstract. In this investigation we propose a novel approach for classifying polyphonic melodies. Our main idea comes from *Probability Stochastic Processes* using Markov models where the characteristic features of polyphonic melodies are extracted from each bar. The similarity among harmonies can be considered by means of the features. We show the effectiveness and the usefulness of the approach by experimental results.

Keywords: Melody Classification, Melody Features, Markov process, Markov Modeling.

1 Background

In this investigation we propose a novel approach for automatic classification of polyphonic melodies by means of *Probability Stochastic Processes* based on Markov models where the characteristic features of the melodies are extracted from each bar. Here we concern *content information* but don't assume any *secondary* or *meta* information such as music names nor identifiers. Basic motivation comes similarly from recognizing hand-written characters or pictures.

Generally *melodies* play important roles of most part of impression, and we could apply this property to the problem of *melody classification*. Melody classification is really useful for many applications. For instance, it help us to assist copyright aspects as well as naive composition and arrangement. Also we might manage and classify anonymous and unknown music consistently since we can access archive library thru internet.

Since early 60's music information retrieval (MIR) has been investigated and nowadays we see several sophisticated techniques for multimedia information in a context of information retrieval such as N-gram, vector space model and search engines. In MIR, most parts of the techniques take *monophonic property* into consideration although we see a wide range of interesting music in *polyphony* where *monophony* is a melody where at most *one* tone arises at each time while *polyphony* consists of several melodies. It is hard to see what parts play *important* roles in polyphony music, because usually changes of keys or rhythm arise many times dependent upon parts and the many sequences go at the same time thus we should examine the relationship among all the parts.

In this investigation we propose a novel approach for classifying polyphonic melodies. Our main idea comes from *Probability Stochastic Processes* using

Markov models where the characteristic features, called *pitch spectrum*, to polyphonic melodies are extracted from each bar. Also we introduce the similarity among polyphonies in terms of the features. We generate Markov models from the features and calculate the probabilities of the state transitions with the similarity.

Here readers are assumed to be familiar with basic notions of music[4] and basic IR techniques[3]D Section 2 contains several definition of features for melody description that have been proposed so far. In section 3 we review probability stochastic processes and Markov models. We show some experiments and some relevant works in section 4. We conclude our investigation in section 5.

2 Features for Melodies

To specify and classify melodies, we should examine what kinds of semantics they carry and we should describe them appropriately. Since we need score based features for classification purpose, we should examine notes over score or in bars. We discuss several kinds of features, and, in this investigation, we put these characteristic values into vector spaces using Vector Space Model (VSM)[3].

First of all, let us examine several features for melody description. *Melody Contour* is one of the major technique proposed so far[2,6,11]. *Pitch Contour* is the one where we put stress on incremental transition of pitch information in monophonic melody. This contour expression is relative to keys and keeps identical against any transposition but varies according to noises and falls down one after another. Querying melody corresponds to perform *inexact match* to text strings.

Given a melody on score, we introduce *Pitch Spectrum* per bar in the melody for similarity measure[7]. *Pitch Spectrum* is a histogram in which each column represents total duration of a note within a bar. The spectrum constitutes a vector of $12 \times n$ dimensions for n octaves range. We calculate pitch spectrum to every bar and construct characteristic vectors prepared for querying to each music. By pitch spectrum we can fix several problems against incomplete melody. In fact, the approach improves problems in swinging and grace. Note that score approach improves issues in rhythm, keys, timbre, expression, speed, rendition and strength aspects of music. Some of the deficiencies are how to solve transposition (relative keys) issues and how to distinguish majors from minors[7]. Especially the latter issue is hard to examine because we should recognize the contents.

In polyphonic music, there is no restriction about the occurrence of tones and we could have unlimited numbers of the combination. That's why several features suitable for monophony is *not* suitable for polyphonic music in a straightforward manner. There have been some ideas proposed so far based on IR such as N-gram[1] or Dimensionality reduction[10], and based on probability (such as Markov Model (MM) [9] or Hidden MM. Here we assume that polyphonic scores are given in advance to obtain the feature values [9].

In this investigation we propose a new kind of feature based on pitch spectrum to polyphonic music. We extract all the tones in each bar from polyphonic music and put them into a spectrum in a form of vector. Clearly the new spectrum reflects not only all the tones in the bar but also all the noises for classification like grace/trill notes. For this issue, we take modulo 12 to all the notes (i.e., we ignore octave). Then we define *(polyphonic) pitch spectrum* as the pitch spectrum as mentioned that consists of only n biggest durations considered as a chord. If there exist more than n candidates, we select the n tones of the highest n pitch. Note that we select n tones as a chord but ignore their explicit duration. And finally we define the *feature description* of the length m as a sequence $w_1, ..., w_m$ where each feature w_j is extracted from i-th bar of music of interests. Since we define our chords syntactically but different from music theory, we don't need to reduce our spectrums to any combination of harmonies[9] according to the law of harmony.

Example 1. Let us describe our running example "A Song of Frogs" in a figure 1. Here are all the bars where each collection contains notes with the total duration counted the length of a quarter note as 1. The sequence of the pitch spectrums constitute the new features for all the bars by top 3 tones. In this case we get the feature description <DEF, CDE, EGA, EFG> for the first 4 bars.

```
Bar1 : {C:1, D:1, E:1, F:1} = {DEF}
Bar2 : {C:2, D:2, E:2, F:1} = {CDE}
Bar3 : {C:1, D:1, E:2, F:1, G:1, A:1} =
       {EGA}
Bar4 : {E:2, F:2, G:2, A:1} = {EFG}
```

Fig. 1. Score of "A Song of Frogs"

3   Markov Process and Music Classification

In this section we discuss how to classify polyphonic music d by using Markov Model (MM) approach. We assume that the music d is represented as a *list* $< w_1, ..., w_m >$ of feature vectors w_j described in the previous section.

3.1   Markov Process

First of all let us review some basic notion of probability stochastic processes in the context of music. Given $d =< w_1, ..., w_m >$ and a collection of classes (or labels) $\mathcal{C} = \{c_1, ..., c_w\}$, we say d is *classified* as $c \in \mathcal{C}$ if we assign c to d. We also say it is *correctly* classified if the class of d is known in some way and is c.

By $P(d)$, we define the probability of the event d which can be described as the product of conditional probabilities $P(w_j|w_1,..,w_{j-1}), j = 1,..,m$. However it is hard to estimate them and very often we take an assumption that the probability depends on last N events. This approximation of the transition process is called *N-Markov process*. This means that the probability of N-gram for melody d_j at j-th event can be expressed by the following simple rule: $P(d_j|d_{j-1}) = P(w_j|w_{j-N})$. This is interesting because we could classify music if we see some chord transition. In our case let d_j be the first j features, then we can obtain $P(d)$ if all the conditional probabilities $P(d_j|d_{j-1})$ or $P(w_j|w_{j-N})$ are known in advance.

However, it is not practical to obtain all the $P(w_j|w_{j-N})$ in advance since there can be huge number of the chord combination. Here we take $N = 1$, the most simple Markov process, then it is enough to examine all the possible chord combination of our case.

Example 2. Let us illustrate the Markov Model of our running examples with chords of top 3 tones. We have *A Song of Frog* (d_1) and two more music, "Ah, Vous dirai-Je, Maman" in C Major, KV.265, by Mozart (d_2). and Symphony Number 9 (Opus 125) by Beethoven (d_3), that is classified to d_1 or d_2 later on.

Fig. 2. Mozart KV.265   **Fig. 3.** Beethoven Symphony No.9,Op.125

Putting each first 8 or 9 bars of d_1, d_2 and d_3 into abc format, we get the following expressions:

(d_1) {CDEF}, {EDC,CDEF}, {EFGA,EDC}, {GFE,EFGA}, {CC, GFE}, {CC, CC}, {C/2C/2D/2D/2E/2E/2F/2F/2, CC}, {EDC, C/2C/2D/2D/2E/2E/2F/2F/2}, {CDE}
(d_2) {CCGG, CCEC}, {AAGG,FCEC}, {FFEE, DBCA}, {DD3/4E/4C2, FGC}, {CCGG, CCEC}, {AAGG, FCEC}, {FFEE, DBCA}, {DD3/4E/4C2, FGC}
(d_3) {FFGA},{AGFE},{DDEF},{F3/2E/2E2},{FFGA},{AGFE},{DDEF},{E3/2D/2D2}

Then by summarizing all the tones in each bar, we choose the features by the chords. By counting all the appearance of chord transition, we get all the probabilities of transitions between chords, i.e., two Markov Models for d_1 and d_2 as below:

Table 1. Chords and Features

Bar	1	2	3	4	5	6	7	8	9
d_1	DEF	CDE	EGA	EFG	CFG	C	CEF	CDE	CDE
d_2	CEG	CGA	EFB	CDG	CEG	CGA	EFB	CDG	
d_3	FGA	FGA	DEF	EF	FGA	FGA	DEF	EF	

Table 2. Markov Model

	CDE	CEF	CFG	DEF	EFG	EGA	C
CDE	0.5	0	0	0	0	0.5	0
CEF	1	0	0	0	0	0	0
CFG	0	0	0	0	0	0	1
DEF	1	0	0	0	0	0	0
EFG	0	0	1	0	0	0	0
EGA	0	0	0	0	1	0	0
C	0	1	0	0	0	0	0

(a)A Song of Frogs

	CDG	CEG	CGA	EFB
CDG	0	1	0	0
CEG	0	0	1	0
CGA	0	0	0	1
EFB	1	0	0	0

(b)KV.265

3.2 Classification by Markov Process

In N-Markov process, it is possible to say that a probability of any event depends on an initial state and the transitions from the state. Formally, given event sequence $w_1, ..., w_m$, the probability of the transition from 1 to m, $P(w_1^m)$, can be desribed as the product of intermediate probabilities of the transition: $P(w_1^m) = \prod_{j=1}^{m} P(w_j|w_1^{j-1})$. In our case, we assume simple Markov process ($N = 1$), and we can simplify our situation since the transition depends on the just prior state: $P(d) = P(w_1^m) = \prod_{j=1}^{m} P(w_j|w_{j-1})$.

All the transition probabilities are called *Markov Model* which can be illustrated by means of *transition diagram*. To classify music d to a class c by means of simple Markov process, we should obtain a conditional probability $P_c(d)$ which can be calculated by the transition probabilities as above. Here let us summarize the procedure.

1. Input: a training collection of music (a set of labeled music) and a set of music to be classified. They are represented as feature descriptions by examining score description (such as abc format[12]).
2. We generate Markov Model by examining labeled music.
3. Given unknown music d, using the Markov Model, we obtain the class membership probabilities $P_{c_i}(d)$ for all the $i = 1, .., w$
4. We estimate the class c_k by Maximum Likelihood Estimation (MLE): $c_k = ArgMax_{c \in \mathcal{C}} P_c(d)$

Let us note that the probability 0.0 means that event can't happen. Once we see the probability 0.0, the transition never arises afterward. We will revisit this issue.

Here we describe how to classify polyphonic music based on Markov Model. Let D be a set of polyphonic music without any label. Given $d \in D$, let $w_i(d)$ be the i-th feature of d and $P_c(d)$ be the membership probability of d in a class $c \in \mathcal{C}$. As described previously, by definition, we have :

$$P_c(d) = \prod_{i=1}^{m} P_c(w_i|w_{i-1}) \qquad (1)$$

During comparison of feature descriptions of two music d_1, d_2, it is likely to have some feature (a chord) w in d_1 but not in d_2 at all. In this case, the probability must be 0.0 in d_2 and the membership probability should be zero. Then the two music can't belong to a same class even if the most parts look much alike. Such situation may arise in the case of noises or trills.

To solve this problem, usually some sort of revisions are introduced but we don't expect excellent classification because the probability tends to be smaller by multiplication, thus we can't decide the amount of revision easily. Alternatively we introduce a notion of similarity between each pair of chords and we adjust the probabilities with them.

Given two features w, w', we define the similarity $sim(w, w')$ as the cosine value: $sim(w, w') = \frac{w \cdot w'}{|w||w'|}$. Then we adjust the transition probability $P(w_i|w_{i-1})$

from w_{i-1} to w_i into $P'(w_i|w_{i-1})$ by summarizing the probability multiplied with similarity over all the possible chords with w_{i-1} defined below: $P'(w_i|w_{i-1}) = \sum_g P(w_i|g) \times sim(g, w_{i-1})$. Note we concern only chords g that transit to w_i and that have non-zero similarity, which we can pick up easily in the Markov Model. Thus our new criteria for MLE should be adjusted as below:

$$P'(c|d) = \prod_{i=1}^{|m|} P'_c(w_i|w_{i-1}) \qquad (2)$$

Note $P'(c|d)$, called *weighted probability*, is not the probability any more but is useful because we apply MLE for classification. We process all the music in advance for classification and examine the weighted probabilities by MLE.

Example 3. Let us classify Symphony Number 9 (Opus 125) by Beethoven (d_3), i.e., which is more similar for d_3 to d_1 or d_2 ? According to the probability values of each Markov Model examining similarities, we obtain the following (extended) probabilities:

$P(Frogs|d_3) = 0.0181 \times 0.0181 \times 0.0375 = 1.23 \times 10^{-5}$
$P(KV.265|d_3) = 0.0417 \times 0.0347 \times 0.0170 = 2.46 \times 10^{-5}$

Thus we out the label KV.265 to d_3, that is, we have estimated d_3 belogs to Mozart KV.265.

4 Experiments

To see how well our proposed scheme works, let us show several experimental results. Here we discuss 3 famous variations by Mozart, Schubert and Beethoven. We consider each title as a class and its theme as the corresponded (representative) labeled melody. All other variations are considered unlabeled and we classify them. Let us note that, in theory of music, no formal rule exists in "variations" but the main concern is how elaborately the theme varies.

4.1 Preliminaries

Here we adopt 3 variations, "Ah, Vous dirai-Je, Maman" in C Major (KV. 265) by Mozart, "Impromptus" in B flat Major (Op.142-3) by Schubert and "6 Variations on theme of Turkish March" in D Major (Op.76) by Beethoven. They contain 12, 5 and 6 variations respectively and 23 variations in total. Note there is no test collection reported so far.

All 3 themes and the variations are processed in advance into a set of feature descriptions. Here we calculate the feature descriptions of all the bars of the 3 themes to obtain Markov Models. Then we calculate the two collections of the feature descriptions, one for the first 4 bar, another for the first 8 bars to all the variations. In this experiment, we examine 3 kinds of chords consisting of the 3, 4 and 5 longest tone. Thus we have $23 \times 2 \times 3 = 138$ features.

We have 3 classes (labels), *Mozart, Schubert* and *Beethoven* according to the composers. By our procedure, we classify all the 23 unlabeled melodies into one of three labels. We say a variation is *correctly* classified if the music is composed by the label. Formally the correctness ratio is defined as

$$\frac{\text{Number of Correctly Classified Melodies}}{23}$$

4.2 Results

We show all the extended probabilities of all the variations to each class to the first 4 and 8 bars in table 3, figures 4 and 5.

Table 3. Extended Probabilities: 3 Chord

	4 Bars			8 Bars		
	Mozart	Schubert	Beethoven	Mozart	Schubert	Beethoven
Mozart v1	$7.497\ 10^{-5}$	$1.292\ 10^{-6}$	$6.384\ 10^{-7}$	$2.516\ 10^{-10}$	$3.959\ 10^{-14}$	$4.648\ 10^{-15}$
v2	$4.895\ 10^{-5}$	$3.066\ 10^{-6}$	$2.140\ 10^{-6}$	$9.985\ 10^{-11}$	$2.385\ 10^{-13}$	$5.345\ 10^{-14}$
v3	$5.604\ 10^{-5}$	$2.910\ 10^{-6}$	$3.034\ 10^{-6}$	$2.036\ 10^{-10}$	$1.764\ 10^{-13}$	$9.124\ 10^{-14}$
v4	$2.257\ 10^{-4}$	$1.923\ 10^{-6}$	$9.237\ 10^{-7}$	$4.047\ 10^{-9}$	$3.852\ 10^{-14}$	$4.682\ 10^{-15}$
v5	$8.335\ 10^{-5}$	$1.898\ 10^{-6}$	$1.530\ 10^{-6}$	$2.788\ 10^{-10}$	$6.669\ 10^{-14}$	$3.353\ 10^{-14}$
v6	$1.827\ 10^{-4}$	$2.331\ 10^{-6}$	$7.621\ 10^{-7}$	$2.163\ 10^{-9}$	$1.132\ 10^{-13}$	$5.755\ 10^{-15}$
v7	$6.125\ 10^{-5}$	$2.970\ 10^{-6}$	$9.249\ 10^{-7}$	$1.560\ 10^{-10}$	$4.688\ 10^{-14}$	$8.624\ 10^{-15}$
v8	$6.417\ 10^{-5}$	$1.782\ 10^{-5}$	$1.057\ 10^{-6}$	$7.913\ 10^{-11}$	$9.745\ 10^{-12}$	$1.189\ 10^{-14}$
v9	$4.434\ 10^{-5}$	$1.229\ 10^{-5}$	$9.714\ 10^{-7}$	$1.153\ 10^{-10}$	$3.767\ 10^{-12}$	$1.054\ 10^{-14}$
v10	$3.936\ 10^{-5}$	$8.525\ 10^{-6}$	$1.003\ 10^{-6}$	$1.231\ 10^{-10}$	$7.571\ 10^{-13}$	$5.520\ 10^{-15}$
v11	$6.801\ 10^{-5}$	$9.203\ 10^{-6}$	$1.814\ 10^{-6}$	$2.391\ 10^{-10}$	$2.059\ 10^{-12}$	$5.617\ 10^{-14}$
v12	$2.415\ 10^{-5}$	$8.412\ 10^{-6}$	$1.069\ 10^{-6}$	$2.121\ 10^{-11}$	$2.293\ 10^{-12}$	$7.002\ 10^{-14}$
Schubert v1	$1.961\ 10^{-6}$	$1.608\ 10^{-5}$	$1.155\ 10^{-5}$	$2.394\ 10^{-12}$	$1.285\ 10^{-11}$	$5.642\ 10^{-13}$
v2	$6.319\ 10^{-6}$	$3.563\ 10^{-5}$	$8.079\ 10^{-6}$	$3.857\ 10^{-13}$	$4.468\ 10^{-11}$	$2.513\ 10^{-12}$
v3	$1.548\ 10^{-5}$	$2.418\ 10^{-5}$	$2.429\ 10^{-6}$	$8.988\ 10^{-12}$	$1.010\ 10^{-11}$	$5.125\ 10^{-14}$
v4	$6.221\ 10^{-5}$	$1.854\ 10^{-5}$	$4.496\ 10^{-7}$	$1.977\ 10^{-11}$	$2.134\ 10^{-11}$	$2.417\ 10^{-14}$
v5	$3.212\ 10^{-5}$	$2.091\ 10^{-5}$	$2.068\ 10^{-6}$	$6.763\ 10^{-12}$	$1.354\ 10^{-11}$	$7.304\ 10^{-14}$
Beethoven v1	$5.943\ 10^{-6}$	$9.357\ 10^{-6}$	$6.138\ 10^{-5}$	$5.455\ 10^{-13}$	$1.606\ 10^{-12}$	$3.163\ 10^{-11}$
v2	$7.563\ 10^{-6}$	$1.380\ 10^{-5}$	$6.987\ 10^{-6}$	$7.135\ 10^{-13}$	$4.240\ 10^{-12}$	$1.785\ 10^{-12}$
v3	$4.065\ 10^{-6}$	$1.003\ 10^{-5}$	$2.370\ 10^{-5}$	$5.780\ 10^{-11}$	$2.013\ 10^{-12}$	$2.207\ 10^{-12}$
v4	$5.372\ 10^{-6}$	$2.674\ 10^{-5}$	$7.352\ 10^{-6}$	$3.143\ 10^{-12}$	$2.966\ 10^{-13}$	$5.968\ 10^{-12}$
v5	$6.174\ 10^{-6}$	$6.447\ 10^{-6}$	$2.851\ 10^{-5}$	$8.236\ 10^{-13}$	$1.124\ 10^{-12}$	$2.356\ 10^{-11}$
v6	$2.026\ 10^{-6}$	$1.878\ 10^{-5}$	$5.476\ 10^{-5}$	$2.051\ 10^{-13}$	$1.486\ 10^{-11}$	$1.082\ 10^{-10}$

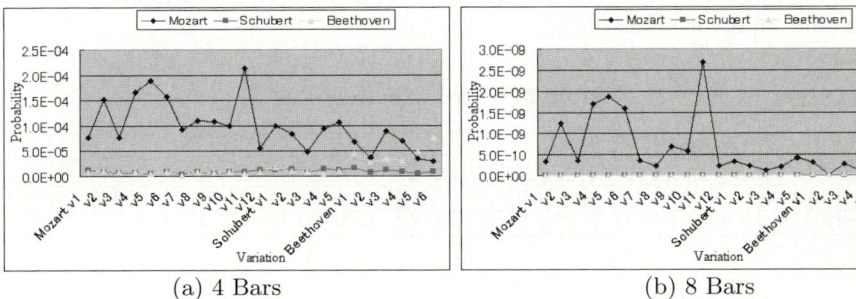

(a) 4 Bars (b) 8 Bars

Fig. 4. Extended Probabilities : 4 Chord

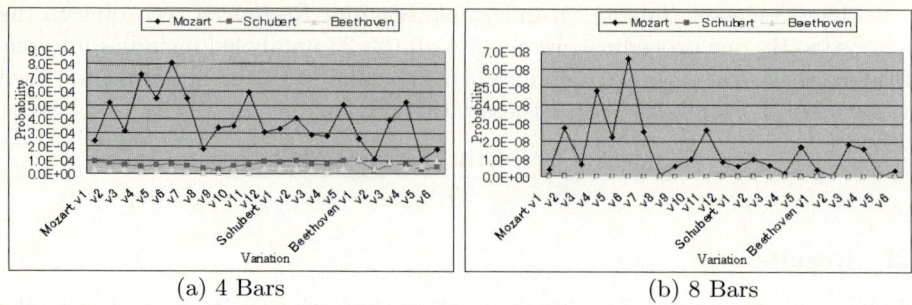

(a) 4 Bars   (b) 8 Bars

Fig. 5. Extended Probabilities : 5 Chord

A table 4 shows the summary of our all the experiments In all the cases, we get the better results in 8 bars compared to 4 bars. Especially the correctness ratio in "Schubert" shows better results in 3 bars, and the one in "Mozart" is perfect in every case.

Table 4. Correctness Ratio

Chord/Bars	Correct Answers				Ratio
	Mozart	Schubert	Beethoven	Total(%)	
3/4	12/12	2/5	3/6	17/23	73.9
3/8	12/12	5/5	4/6	21/23	91.3
4/4	12/12	0/5	2/6	14/23	60.9
4/8	12/12	0/5	2/6	14/23	60.9
5/4	12/12	0/5	0/6	12/23	52.2
5/8	12/12	0/5	0/6	12/23	52.2

4.3 Discussion

As shown in the results, it is clear that we get better results with more bars. In fact, we got 91.3% (8 bars) compared to the average 73.9% (4 bars). This is because there happens the first parts are similar with each other. For example, the 3rd variation of Schubert has the feature description {CFB} {CEF} {CFB} {CFB} {CFB} {CEF} {CEB} {CFB}. Looking at the first 4 bars, this is similar to Mozart since there appear many C, E, F, B tones in both music as shown in a table 5. On the other hand, there exist few common chords in the latter part of 8 bars, and no error arises.

Table 5. Chord Occurrences

	4 Bars	8 Bars
Schubert v3	{CFB} {CEF}	+{CEB}
Mozart theme	{DFB} {CFA} {DEB} {DGB} {CEF} {CEB} {CFB}	+{DFB}{DAB}
Schubert theme	{CEG} {CGA} {CEF} {DEF} {EFA} {EFB} {CDF} {CDG}	-

Let us examine why some variations are incorrectly classified. One possibility comes from *the number of beats*. The 12 th variation of Mozart takes $\frac{12}{8}$ beats while the theme has $\frac{4}{4}$ beats. Since we summarize all the feature values per bar, we can hardly describe music across bars. We wonder whether it is enough to have only 4 bars for characteristic features, but still we see 73.9% correctness ratio.

Another important aspect is that we get the worse results with bigger chords except Mozart. We see the more tones we have the less characteristics we have. In fact, two chords {`C:2,D:2,E:2,F:1,G:1` }, {`C:1,D:1,E:2,F:2,G:2`} have {`CDE`} and {`EFG`} as dominant 3 chords, but share {`CDEFG`} as 5 chords. In our case, many variations have been declared as Mozart because of 5 chord.

To our experiment, we can't say many tones are needed for classification of polyphony music.

There is no investigation of polyphony classification to compare directly with our results. In [8,9], given about 3000 music of polyphony, classification as been considered as query and the results have been evaluated based precision. They got 59.0% at best.

We have ever examined melody classification of monophony music by means of EM algorithm[13]. Here we have classified several variations given themes. Let us show the two best results in 6 where we extract pitch spectrum of the first 4 bars based on Bayesian classifier with EM algorithm. Note, for example, EM10 means the result by of 10 loops EM step.

Table 6. Correctness Ratio (Monophony) by EM algorithm

	EM loops					
	EM0	EM5	EM10	EM15	EM20	EM25
Similarity 0.30	87	91.3	91.3	91.3	91.3	91.3
Similarity 0.50	78.3	91.3	91.3	87.0	87.0	87.0

EM0 means naive Bayesian that provides us with 87.0 % correctness ratio, and we got 91.3 % correctness ration at best by EM algorithm. Compared to this case where all the melodies are monophony that are much simpler, we got the similar correctness ratio with 3-chords over 8 bars to polyphony melodies.

5 Conclusion

In this investigation, we have proposed a new method to classify polyphony music based on Markov Model approach. Given training music, we have extracted sequence of chords syntactically in terms of pitch spectrum, and obtained transition probabilities. Based on Maximum likelihood Estimation using the Markov Model, we have shown highly precise classification to variation music.

References

1. Dowaisamy, S. and Ruger, S.M. : A comparative and fault-tolerance study of the use of n-gram with polyphonic music, ISMIR 2002, pp.101-116
2. Dowling, W.J. : Scale and Contour – two components of a theory of memory for melodies, *Psychological Reviews* 85-4, 1978, pp.341-354

3. Grossman, D. and Frieder, O.: Information Retrieval – Algorithms and Heuristics, Kluwer Academic Press, 1998
4. Ishigeta, M. et al: Theory of Music, Ongaku-No-Tomo-Sha, 2001 (in Japanese)
5. Iwasaki, M.: Foundation of Incmplete Data Analysis, Economicst Sha, 2002 (in Japanese)
6. Kim, Y. et al.: Analysis of A Contour-based Representation for Melody, *Intn'l Symp. on Music Information Retrieval* (ISMIR), 2000
7. Miura, T. and Shioya, I: Similarities among Melodies for Music Information Retrieval, ACM *Conf. on Information and Knowledge Management*(CIKM), 2003
8. J.Pickens: A Comparison of Language Modelling and Probabilistic Text Information Retrieval Approaches to Monophonic Music Retrieval, *Intn'l Symp. on Music Information Retrieval* (ISMIR), 2000
9. Pickens, J. and Crawford, T.: Harmonic Models for Polyphonic Music Retrieval, ACM *Conf. on Information and Knowledge Management*(CIKM), 2002
10. Uitdenbogerd, A.L. et al.: Manipulation of Music For Melody Matching, ACM *MultiMedia* Conf., 1998
11. Uitdenbogerd, A.L. et al.: Matching Techniques for Large Music Databases, ACM *Multimedia Conf.*, 1999
12. Walshaw, C.: abc Ver.1.6, `http://www.gre.ac.uk/~c.walshaw/abc2mtex/abc.txt`
13. Yoshihara,Y. and Miura, T.: Melody Classification Using EM Algorithm. *COMPSAC*, pp. 204-210, 2005

Two Phase Semi-supervised Clustering Using Background Knowledge

Kwangcheol Shin and Ajith Abraham

School of Computer Science and Engineering, Chung-Ang University
221, Heukseok-dong, Dongjak-gu, Seoul 156-756, Korea
kcshin@archi.cse.cau.ac.kr, ajith.abraham@ieee.org

Abstract. Using background knowledge in clustering, called semi-clustering, is one of the actively researched areas in data mining. In this paper, we illustrate how to use background knowledge related to a domain more efficiently. For a given data, the number of classes is investigated by using the must-link constraints before clustering and these must-link data are assigned to the corresponding classes. When the clustering algorithm is applied, we make use of the cannot-link constraints for assignment. The proposed clustering approach improves the result of COP k-means by about 10%.

1 Introduction

In data mining, clustering is an unsupervised method to classify unlabeled data. Unsupervised means that it does not have any prior knowledge of the problem domain to formulate the number of clusters (classes). However, in some real situations, background knowledge that might help the clustering problem is available. One of representative back ground knowledge is the *must-link* and *cannot-link* constraints. Wagstaff and et al. [1] illustrated that their modified *k*-means algorithm (COP k-means), gives better results than the original k-means by using the *must-link* and *cannot-link* constraints.

Adami et al. [2] proposed a baseline approach that classifies documents according to the class terms, and two clustering approaches, whose training is constrained by the a priori knowledge encoded in the taxonomy structure, which consists of both terminological and relational aspects.

Shen et al. [3] proposed a novel approach, the so-called "supervised fuzzy clustering approach" that is featured by utilizing the class label information during the training process. Based on such an approach, a set of "*if-then*" fuzzy rules for predicting the protein structural classes are extracted from a training dataset. It has been demonstrated through two different working datasets that the overall success prediction rates obtained by the supervised fuzzy clustering approach are all higher than those by the unsupervised fuzzy c-means.

Zio and Baraldi [4] studied the Mahalanobis metric for each cluster for analyzing the complexity and variety of cluster shapes and dimensions. The a priori known information regarding the true classes to which the patterns belong is exploited to select, by means of a supervised evolutionary algorithm, the different optimal Mahalanobis metrics. Further, the authors illustrated that the diagonal elements of the matrices defining the metrics can be taken as measures of the relevance of the features employed for the classification of the different patterns.

Eick et al. [6] introduced a novel approach to learn distance functions that maximizes the clustering of objects belonging to the same class. Objects belonging to a dataset are clustered with respect to a given distance function and the local class density information of each cluster is then used by a weight adjustment heuristic to modify the distance function so that the class density is increased in the attribute space. This process of interleaving clustering with distance function modification is repeated until a "good" distance function has been found. We implemented our approach using the k-means clustering algorithm.

Some recent research [6] sought to address a variant of the conventional clustering problem called semi-supervised clustering, which performs clustering in the presence of some background knowledge or supervisory information expressed as pairwise similarity or dissimilarity constraints. However, existing metric learning methods for semi-supervised clustering mostly perform global metric learning through a linear transformation. Chang and Yeung [6] proposed a new metric learning method that performs nonlinear transformation globally but linear transformation locally.

In this paper, we present a novel algorithm which uses background knowledge more efficiently. At first, before the clustering process, graphs are constructed by using must-link constraints to find out how many classes do the dataset has and we make use of cannot-link constraints when the k-means clustering algorithm is applied. The proposed method could adaptively determine the k value empirical results illustrate about 10% of improvement over the COP k-means algorithm on some popular datasets.

2 Proposed Algorithm

We make use of basic background knowledge, must-link and cannot-link constraints. The algorithm is divided into two parts. The first part is for finding number of classes by using must-link constraints and assigns must-link data to the corresponding class and the other part is for applying the k-means algorithm effectively using cannot-link constraints.

2.1 The Constraints

Must-link and cannot link constraints are defined as follows [1]:

- Must-link constraints specify that two instances have to be in the same cluster
- Cannot-link constraints specify that two instances must not be placed in the same cluster

Two instances within the constraints are randomly selected. The number of constraints is important to apply our algorithm.

2.2 Phase I : Find Number of Class by Using Must-link Constraints

In the first part of our algorithm, namely phase I, we make use of the must-link constraints to find the number of classes of the given dataset based on the following assumption. If we have enough must-link constraints to get at least one of must-link constraints in each class, then we can find out the number of class.

Two instances (a, b) are in must-link if they should be assigned to a same class. This is illustrated as an undirected graph in Figure 1.

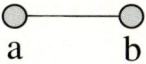

Fig. 1. Must-link graph

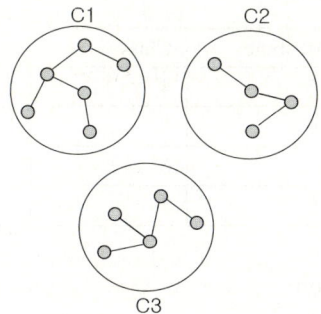

Fig. 2. Must-link graphs

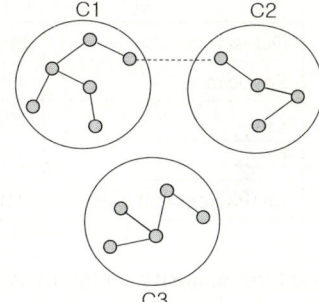

Fig. 3. Merging graphs according to class label

If there are lots of must-link constraint data, more graphs could be constructed as depicted in Figure 2.

Each graph has a class label because must-link data gives that information. We can merge graphs which has the same label as illustrated in Figure 3 (if C1 and C2 has the same label). By merging graphs, we can figure out the number of classes if we pick up sufficient number of must-link data. We also assign the must-link data to corresponding class before phase II.

2.3 Phase II : Applying Clustering Algorithm Effectively by Using Cannot-Link Constraints

In phase II, rest of the data is assigned to the preset-up classes by applying modified k-means clustering algorithm. 'Modified' means that we use cannot-link constraints to assign data. If two instances have a cannot-link relation, it cannot be in a same class. So, our algorithm does not assign data to the class which has the data that has cannot-link relationship with the assigning data. Suggested algorithm is depicted below.

1. Construct must-link graphs using must-link constraints
2. Merge graphs which has the same category ID (classes)
3. Construct clusters using graphs of step 2 (this determines proper number of clusters automatically).
4. For each point d_i in D, except must-link data already assigned at step 3, assign it to the closest cluster C_j such that C_j does not have cannot-link data with d_i. If no such

cluster exists, print "fail" and exit program.
5. For each cluster C_i, update its center by averaging all of the points that have been assigned to it.
6. Repeat step 4 and 5 until the whole data is covered.

3 Experimental Results

We used 4 datasets to verify our method as shown in Table 1.

Table 1. Test dataset used

Dataset	Instance	Attribute	Class
Soybean	47	35	4
Zoo	101	16	7
Glass	214	9	6
Image Segmentation	2100	19	7

We used the majority voting to evaluate the results.

$$MajorityVote(C_i) = \frac{Number\ of\ MajorityData(C_i)}{Number\ of\ Data(C_i)} \quad (1)$$

The majority voting formula gives high value when there are lots of same labeled data in the class.

We tested 5 times for COP k-means with user-providing the values for k and the proposed method could automatically determine the k value in phase I. We obtained an average value from 5 trials for each of the tested number of constraints. The proposed method gives better results about 13%, 4%, 12% and 8% over COP k-means as illustrated in Figures 4-7. An important observation here is COP k-means does not give better results than original k-means except for the Soybean dataset. The proposed method gives better results when compared to the original k-means and COP k-means.

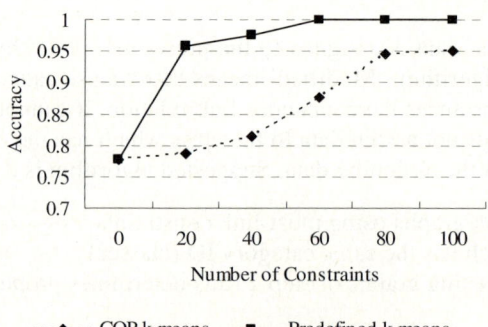

Fig. 4. Test result for soy bean dataset

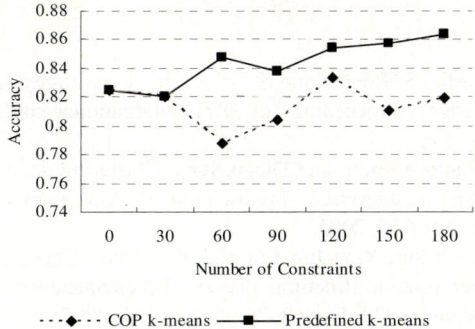

Fig. 5. Test result for zoo dataset

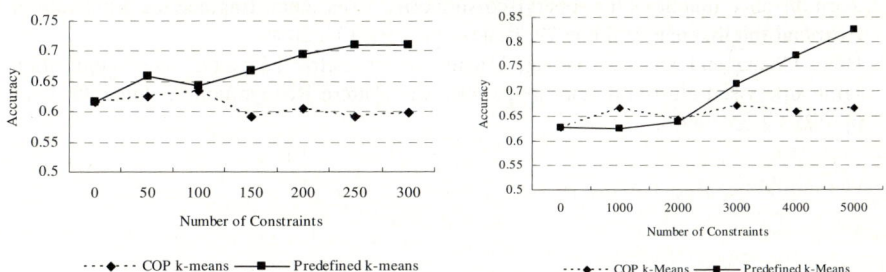

Fig. 6. Test result for glass   **Fig. 7.** Test result for image segmentation

4 Conclusions

Recent research has shown the importance of the conventional clustering problem called semi-supervised clustering, which performs clustering in the presence of some background knowledge or supervisory information. This paper proposed a new method to use background knowledge related to a domain more efficiently. For a given data, the number of classes is investigated by using the must-link constraints before clustering and these must-link data are assigned to the corresponding classes. The proposed clustering approach improves the result obtained by the direct COP k-means by about 10% on average.

Acknowledgments

Work supported by the MIC (Ministry of Information and Communication), Korea, under the Chung-Ang University HNRC-ITRC (Home Network Research Center) support program supervised by the IITA (Institute of Information Technology Assessment).

References

[1] K. Wagstaff, C. Cardie, S. Rogers and S. Schroedl, "Constrained k-means clustering with background knowledge", Proceedings of 18'th international conf. on machine learning, 2001, p. 577-584.
[2] Giordano Adami, Paolo Avesani and Diego Sona, Clustering documents into a web directory for bootstrapping a supervised classification, Data & Knowledge Engineering, Volume 54, Issue 3, pp. 301-325, 2005.
[3] Hong-Bin Shen, Jie Yang, Xiao-Jun Liu and Kuo-Chen Chou, Using supervised fuzzy clustering to predict protein structural classes, Biochemical and Biophysical Research Communications, Volume 334, Issue 2, 26 pp. 577-581, 2005.
[4] E. Zio and P. Baraldi, Identification of nuclear transients via optimized fuzzy clustering, Annals of Nuclear Energy, Volume 32, Issue 10, pp. 1068-1080, 2005.
[5] Christoph F. Eick, Alain Rouhana, A. Bagherjeiran and R. Vilalta, Using clustering to learn distance functions for supervised similarity assessment, Engineering Applications of Artificial Intelligence, Volume 19, Issue 4, pp. 395-401, 2006.
[6] Hong Chang and Dit-Yan Yeung, Locally linear metric adaptation with application to semi-supervised clustering and image retrieval, Pattern Recognition, Volume 39, Issue 7, pp. 1253-1264, 2006.

Using Rough Set to Find the Factors That Negate the Typical Dependency of a Decision Attribute on Some Condition Attributes

Feng Honghai[1,2], Xu Hao[3], Liu Baoyan[4], Yang Bingru[2], Gao Zhuye[3], and Li Yueli[1]

[1] Hebei Agricultural University, 071001 Baoding, Hebei, China
[2] University of Science and Technology Beijing, 100083 Beijing, China
[3] Beijing Sino-Japen Friendship Hospital, 100029 Beijing, China
[4] China Academy of Traditional Chinese Medicine, 100700 Beijing, China
liuby@tcmcec.com

Abstract. In real world, there are a lot of knowledge such as the following: most human beings that are infected by a kind of virus suffer from a corresponding disease, but a small number human beings do not. Which are the factors that negate the effects of the virus? Standard rough set method can induce simplified rules for classification, but cannot generate this kind of knowledge directly. In this paper, we propose two algorithms to find th**e** factors. In the first algorithm, the typical rough set method is used to generate all the variable precision rules firstly; secondly reduce attributes and generate all the non-variable precision rules; lastly compare the variable precision rules and non-variable precision rules to generate the factors that negate the variable precision rules. In the second algorithm, firstly, induce all the variable precision rules; secondly, select the examples corresponding to the variable precision rules to build decernibility matrixes; thirdly, generate the factors that negate the variable precision rules. Three experimental results show that using the two algorithms can get the same results and the computational complexity of the second algorithm is largely less than the firs one.

1 Introduction

In real world, there are a lot of knowledge such as the following: most people suffer from hyperpyrexia when they take a heavy cold, whereas some people do not; most earthquakes in the sea cannot cause a ground sea, but in 2005 the earthquake in Indian Ocean cause a ground sea and cause thousands upon thousands people death. Which are the factors that negate the effects of virus, or a heavy cold? And which factors make an earthquake cause the Indian Ocean ground sea? Standard rough set method [1] can induce simplified rules for classification, but cannot generate this kind of knowledge directly. Other machine learning theories such as SVM [2], ANN [3] and Bayesian networks have not been found that they can be used to induce this kind of knowledge.

All the disasters such as floods, dam collapses, terror events, epidemics etc are exceptional cases. The factors that cause these disasters are significant to us. Additionally, the exceptional students education, exceptional customers service, exceptional patients therapy and nurse etc need the factors that cause exceptional rules.

The decernibility matrix in rough set theory is a valid method for attribute reduction and rule generation whose main idea is to compare the examples that are not in the same class. However, generally, the decernibility matrix is used to the whole data set [4], can it be used to partial data to induce the knowledge with which we can find the factors that negate the typical dependency of a decision attribute on some condition attributes? The answer is affirmative.

2 Basic Concepts of Rough Set Theory

A decision table is composed of a 4-tuple DT=$\langle U, A, V, f \rangle$, where $U = \{x_1, x_2, \cdots, x_n\}$, is a nonempty, finite set called the universe; A is a nonempty, finite set of attributes; $A = C \cup D$, in which C is a finite set of condition attributes and D is a finite set of decision attributes; $V = \bigcup_{a \in A} V_a$, where V_a is a domain (value) of the attribute a, and $f: U \times A \rightarrow V$ is called the information function such that $f(x,a) \in V_a$ for every $a \in A, x_i \in U$.

For every set of attributes $B \subset A$, an indiscernibility relation $IND(B)$ is defined in the following way: two objects, x_i and x_j, are indiscernible by the set of attributes B in A, if $f(b, x_i) = f(b, x_j)$ for every $b \subset B$. The equivalence class of $IND(B)$ is called elementary set in B because it presents the smallest discernible groups of objects. For any element x_i of U, the equivalence class of x_i in relation $IND(B)$ is represented as $[x_i]_{IND(B)}$. The construction of elementary sets is the first step in classification with rough sets.

By a discernibility matrix of $B \subseteq A$ denoted $M(B)$ a $n \times n$ matrix is defined as

$$(c_{ij}) = \{a \in B : f(a, x_i) \neq f(a, x_j)\} \text{ for } i, j = 1, 2, \ldots, n.$$

Thus entry c_{ij} is the set of all attributes that discern objects x_i and x_j.

It is easily seen that the core is the set of all single element entries of the discernibility matrix $M(B)$, i.e.,

$$CORE(B) = \{a \in B : c_{ij} = \{a\}, \text{ for some } i, j\}$$

Every discernibility matrix $M(B)$ defines uniquely a discernibility (boolean) function $f(B)$ defined as follows.

Let us assign to each attribute $a \in B$ a binary Boolean variable $\bar{a}$, and let $\Sigma\delta(x, y)$ denote Boolean sum of all Boolean variables assigned to the set of attributes $\delta(x, y)$. Then the discernibility function can be defined by the formula

$$f(B) = \prod_{(x,y) \in U^2} \{\Sigma\delta(x, y) : (x, y) \in U^2 \text{ and } \delta(x, y) \neq \varnothing\}.$$

Where $\prod$ denotes the Boolean multiplication.

The following property establishes the relationship between disjunctive normal form of the function $f(B)$ and the set of all reducts of B.

All constituents in the minimal disjunctive normal form of the function $f(B)$ are all reducts of B.

In order to compute the value core and value reducts for x we can also use the discernibility matrix as defined before and the discernibility function, which must be slightly modified:

$$f^x(B) = \prod_{y \in U}\{\Sigma\delta(x, y): y \in U \text{ and } \delta(x, y) \neq \emptyset\}.$$

3 Algorithms

(1) Algorithm 1

   (a) Generate all the variable precision rules.
   (b) Attribute reduction.
   (c) Select the reduced attribute set with the attributes that are in the variable precision rules.
   (d) Generate the non-variable precision rules.
   (e) Select the non-variable precision rules whose preconditions are the same as the variable precision rules whereas the postcondition is not the same as the variable precision rules.
   (f) Compare the variable precision rules and their corresponding to generate the factors that negate the variable precision rules.

(2) Algorithm 2

   (a) For every condition attribute A, (or select anyone among all the condition attributes) calculate its equivalence classes or partition
      $IND(A)=\{A_1, A_2, \ldots, A_n,\}$. And for the decision attribute D, calculate $IND(D)=\{D_1, D_2, \ldots, D_m,\}$.
   (b) For (i=0; i<n; i ++)// n: amount of equivalence classes of condition attribute //A
   (c) For (j=0; j<m; j++)// m: amount of equivalence classes of decision attribute D.

$$\text{If } \alpha = \frac{|A_i \cap D_j|}{|A_i|} > s \quad // \ 0.5 < s \neq 1 \text{ and chosen by user.}$$

   (d) Select the examples with A_i, and build a decernibility matrix
   (e) For the examples whose decision attribute values are not included in D_j to use Boolean multiplication and Boolean sum to induce the factors that negate the rule $A_i \rightarrow D_j$ with α. That is, use $f^x(B) = \prod_{y \in U}\{\Sigma\delta(x, y): y \in U$ and $\delta(x, y) \neq \emptyset\}$ to get the factors.

4 Hand-Written Chinese Characters Recognition

We have generated the feature vectors of 4 hand-written Chinese characters, where the values 1, 2, 3 and 4 of Y denote the 4 different hand written Chinese characters (Figure 1), examples 1 and 2, 3 and 4, 5 and 6, 7 and 8 are the same hand-written Chinese characters respectively, after discretization we get Table 1.

Fig. 1. 4 hand-written Chinese characters

Table 1. The information table of 4 hand-written Chinese characters

U	A	B	C	D	E	F	Y
1	17	8	5	4	2	1	1
2	18	8	5	3	2	1	1
3	17	9	5	5	2	2	2
4	17	9	5	3	2	1	2
5	18	7	6	4	2	1	3
6	18	8	6	4	3	2	3
7	15	8	5	4	3	2	4
8	16	8	5	5	3	2	4

(1) Using algorithm 1 to induce the factors
  (a) The variable precision rules are:
    1) $A=17 \rightarrow Y=2$ with $\alpha =2/3$; 2) $A=18 \rightarrow Y=3$ with $\alpha =2/3$; 3) $E=3 \rightarrow Y=4$ with $\alpha =2/3$.
  (b) After attribute reduction we get the following new condition attributes combinations: $\{A, B, C\}, \{A, B, E\}, \{A, B, F\}, \{A, D\}, \{B, C, E\}, \{B, C, F\}$.
  (c) Select $\{A, B, C\}, \{A, B, E\}, \{A, B, F\}, \{A, D\}, \{B, C, E\}, \{A, C, E, F\}$, since the attribute sets $\{B, C, F\}$ and $\{B, C, D, F\}$ do not contain attribute A and E that are in the variable precision rules.
  (d) For the selected attribute sets, the following rules are generated:
    4) $A=17 \wedge B=8 \rightarrow Y=1$; 5) $A=18 \wedge D=3 \rightarrow Y=1$; 6) $B=9 \rightarrow Y=2$; 7) $B=7 \rightarrow Y=3$; 8) $A=18 \wedge D=4 \rightarrow Y=3$; 9) $A=15 \rightarrow Y=4$; 10) $A=16 \rightarrow Y=4$; 11) $B=8 \wedge E=2 \rightarrow Y=1$; 12) $A=18 \wedge E=3 \rightarrow Y=3$; 13) $B=8 \wedge F=1 \rightarrow Y=1$; 14) $A=18 \wedge F=2 \rightarrow Y=3$; 15) $A=17 \wedge D=4 \rightarrow Y=1$; 16) $A=17 \wedge D=5 \rightarrow Y=2$; 17) $A=17 \wedge D=3 \rightarrow Y=2$; 18) $C=6 \rightarrow Y=3$; 19) $C=5 \wedge E=3 \rightarrow Y=4$; 20) $A=18 \wedge C=5 \rightarrow Y=1$; 21) $B=8 \wedge C=5 \wedge F=2 \rightarrow Y=4$.
  (e) For variable precision rule 1) $A=17 \rightarrow Y=2$ with $\alpha =2/3$, rule 4) $A=17 \wedge B=8 \rightarrow Y=1$ and rule 15) $A=17 \wedge D=4 \rightarrow Y=1$ should be selected, and after comparing rule 1) with rule 4) and rule 15) respectively, we can get that: $B=8$ and

$D=4$ are the factors that negate rule 1) $A=17\rightarrow Y=2$ with $\alpha =2/3$. For rule 2) $A=18\rightarrow Y=3$ with $\alpha =2/3$, rule 5) $A=18 \wedge D=3\rightarrow Y=1$ and rule 20) $A=18 \wedge C=5\rightarrow Y=1$ should be selected, and after comparing it with rule 5) rule 20) respectively, we can get that: $D=3$ and $C=5$ are the factors that negate the rule $A=18\rightarrow Y=3$ with $\alpha =2/3$. For rule 3) $E=3 \rightarrow Y=4$ with $\alpha =2/3$, rule 12) $A=18 \wedge E=3\rightarrow Y=3$ should be selected, and after comparing rule 3) with rule12), we can get that: $A=18$ is the factor that negate $E=3 \rightarrow Y=4$ with $\alpha =2/3$.

(2) Using algorithm 2 to induce the factors

(a) The partitions of all the attributes can be gotten as follows:

$IND(A)=\{A_1,A_2,A_3,A_4\}=\{\{1,3,4\},\{2,5,6\},\{7\},\{8\}\}$,
$IND(B)=\{B_1,B_2,B_3\}=\{\{1,2,6,7,8\},\{3,4\},\{5\}\}$,
$IND(C)=\{C_1,C_2\}=\{\{1,2,3,4,7,8\},\{5,6\}\}$,
$IND(D)=\{D_1,D_2,D_3\}=\{\{1,2,6,7,8\},\{3,4\},\{5\}\}$,
$IND(E)=\{E_1,E_2\}=\{\{1,2,3,4,5\},\{6,7,8\}\}$,
$IND(F)=\{F_1,F_2\}=\{\{1,2,4,5\},\{3,6,7,8\}\}$,
$IND(Y)=\{Y_1, Y_2, Y_3, Y_4\}=\{\{1,2\},\{3,4\},\{5,6\},\{7,8\}\}$.

Obviously, only $\frac{|A_1 \cap Y_2|}{|A_1|}=\frac{2}{3}>0.5$, $\frac{|A_2 \cap Y_3|}{|A_2|}=\frac{2}{3}>0.5$ and $\frac{|E_2 \cap Y_4|}{|E_2|}=\frac{2}{3}>0.5$ can be held.

So for $A_1=\{1,3,4\}$, we select examples 1, 3, and 4 to build the decernibility matrix, since the example 1 belongs to class 1, and examples 3, 4 belong to class 2; they should in different places in decernibility matrix, and for example 1 we using Boolean multiplication and Boolean sum to induce the factors that negate the variable rule.

From Table 2, since $(B \vee D \vee F) \wedge (B \vee D) = B \vee D$, we can conclude that $B=8$ and $D=4$ are the factors that negate rule 1) $A=17\rightarrow Y=2$ with $\alpha =2/3$, or make $A=17 \wedge B=8\rightarrow Y=1$ and $A=17 \wedge D=4\rightarrow Y=1$. Namely we get the following knowledge:

$A=17\rightarrow Y=2$ with $\alpha =2/3$
$A=17 \wedge B=8\rightarrow Y=1$ with $\alpha =1$
$A=17 \wedge D=4\rightarrow Y=1$ with $\alpha =1$
$B=8$ and $D=4$ are the factors that negate the rule $A=17\rightarrow Y=2$ with $\alpha =2/3$

Table 2. Decernibility matrix for the examples in A_1

	3	4
1	BDF	BD

For $A_2=\{2,5,6\}$, we select examples 2, 5, and 6 to build the decernibility matrix.

Table 3. Decernibility matrix for the examples in A_2

	5	6
2	BC D	CDEF

Since $(B \vee C \vee D) \wedge (C \vee D \vee E \vee F) = C \vee D$, we get that $D=3$ and $C=5$ are the factors that negate the rule $A=18 \rightarrow Y=3$ with $\alpha = 2/3$, or make $A=18 \wedge C=5 \rightarrow Y=1$ and $A=18 \wedge D=3 \rightarrow Y=1$.

5 Micronutrient Data Set Experiments

(1) SARS Data Set and Discretization

The SARS data are the experimental results of micronutrients that are essential in minute amounts for the proper growth and metabolism of human beings. Among them, examples 31~60 are the results of SARS patients and 61~90 are the results of healthy human beings. Attributes "1", "2", "3", "4", "5", "6", "7" denote micronutrient Zn, Cu, Fe, Ca, Mg, K and Na respectively, and decision attribute "C" denotes the class "SARS" and "healthy". $V_C = \{0,1\}$, where "0" denotes "SARS", "1" denotes "healthy".

After discretization, some examples become a repeat. The amount of the total examples is reduced from 60 to 39. Table 4 describes the left 39 examples after discretization.

Table 4. Left examples after discretization

U	1	2	3	4	5	6	7	C	U	1	2	3	4	5	6	7	C	U	1	2	3	4	5	6	7	C
31	1	1	1	0	1	1	1	0	54	0	0	1	0	0	1	1	0	69	1	1	1	2	2	1	2	1
32	2	1	1	0	1	1	1	0	55	1	0	1	0	1	1	1	0	70	1	2	2	2	2	2	1	1
34	1	1	1	0	1	2	1	0	56	0	1	1	0	0	1	1	0	71	1	1	2	1	1	1	1	1
39	1	1	0	0	0	1	1	0	59	0	0	0	0	0	2	1	0	72	2	1	1	2	2	1	1	1
41	0	1	1	0	0	2	2	0	60	1	2	1	0	1	1	1	0	73	1	1	2	1	2	1	1	1
42	2	1	1	0	1	2	1	0	61	2	1	1	2	2	0	1	1	74	2	1	2	2	2	1	1	1
43	2	1	1	0	2	1	1	0	62	1	1	1	1	1	1	1	1	76	2	1	1	2	1	1	1	1
47	0	1	0	0	0	1	1	0	63	1	1	1	2	1	0	1	1	78	1	1	2	2	2	1	1	1
48	2	1	0	2	1	1	1	0	64	2	1	2	2	1	1	1	1	79	2	2	1	2	2	1	1	1
49	1	1	1	1	1	1	2	0	65	1	1	1	2	1	1	1	1	85	2	1	1	2	1	0	0	1
50	0	1	1	0	0	2	1	0	66	1	1	1	2	1	0	0	1	86	2	1	1	2	2	1	0	1
52	1	1	2	0	1	1	1	0	67	1	1	1	2	2	1	1	1	87	2	1	1	2	2	1	1	1
53	1	1	1	1	1	0	1	0	68	1	1	1	1	1	1	0	1	88	2	1	2	2	2	1	1	1

(2) Induce the Negating Attribute Values

1) For examples 64, 70, 71, 73, 74, 78 and 88, we can conclude that "Fe=2 $\rightarrow$ C=1", whereas for example 52, we hold "Fe=2 $\rightarrow$ C=0". Namely "Fe=2 $\rightarrow$ C=1" with $\alpha = 7/8$, and "Fe=2 $\rightarrow$ C=0" with $\alpha = 1/8$ can be held. Which are the attribute value that negate the rule of "Fe=2 $\rightarrow$ C=1"? With the partial decernibility matrix we can find the factors.

Firstly, the examples with Fe=2 are selected. Secondly, generate the decernibility matrix with these examples. Thirdly, use the decernibility matrix to induce the rules that include the factors negating the rule "Fe=2 $\rightarrow$ C=1". Table 5 gives the results of the decernibility matrix.

Table 5. Decernibility matrix for the examples with Fe=2

	64	70	71	73	74	78	88
52	1,4	2,4,5,6	4	4,5	1,4,5	4,5	1,4,5

The attribute value that negates the rule "Fe=2 → C=1" can be induced as follows:

$(1 \vee 4) \wedge (2 \vee 4 \vee 5 \vee 6) \wedge 4 \wedge (4 \vee 5) \wedge (1 \vee 4 \vee 5) \wedge (4 \vee 5) \wedge (1 \vee 4 \vee 5) = 4$ (Ca)

So for example 52, the following knowledge can be gotten:

"Fe=2 → C=1"   with $\alpha = 7/8$;
"Fe=2 → C=0"   with $\alpha = 1/8$;
"Fe=2 ∧ Ca=0 → C=0" with $\alpha = 1$;

"Ca=0" is the factor that negate the rule "Fe=2 → C=1" with $\alpha = 7/8$ (see Table 1).

2) For the examples 61, 63, 64, 65, 66, 67, 69, 70, 72, 74, 76, 78, 79, 85, 86, 87 and 88, we can conclude that "Ca=2 → C=1", while for example 48, we hold "Ca=2 → C=0". Similarly we get the following knowledge:

"Ca=2 → C=1"   with $\alpha = 17/18$;
"Ca=2 → C=0"   with $\alpha = 1/18$;
"Ca=2 ∧ Fe=0 → C=0" with $\alpha = 1/18$;

"Fe=0" is the factor that negate the rule "Ca=2 → C=1" with $\alpha = 17/18$.

3) For examples 49 and 53, we can induce that "Ca=1 → C=0", whereas for examples 62, 68, 71 and 73 we can get that "Ca=1 → C=1". Table 6 gives the results of the decernibility matrix.

Table 6. Decernibility matrix for the examples with Ca=1

	62	68	71	73
49	7	7	3,7	3,5,7
53	6	6,7	3,6	3,5,6

With $7 \wedge 7 \wedge (3 \vee 7) \wedge (3 \vee 5 \vee 7) = 7$ (Na) for example 49 and with $6 \wedge (6 \vee 7) \wedge (3 \vee 6) \wedge (3 \vee 5 \vee 6) = 6$ (K) for example 53, we can get the following knowledge:

"Ca=1 → C=1"   with $\alpha = 4/6$;
"Ca=1 → C=0"   with $\alpha = 2/6$;
"Ca=1 ∧ Na=2 → C=0"   with $\alpha = 1$;
"Ca=1 ∧ K=0 → C=0"   with $\alpha = 1$;

"Na=2" (see example 49) and "K=0" (example 53) are the factors that negate the rule "Ca=1 → C=1" with $\alpha = 4/6$.

6 Coronary Heart Disease Data Experiments

We have gotten 441 coronary heart disease cases from Beijing, and among all the 441 cases there are 161 ones who suffer from heart failure with 638 records in the course of being in hospital. Among all the 638 records we get the following rules:

(1) Heart failure=true → Breath sounds in lungs = gruff (not sharp) with 192/638 and souffles in hearts =true with only 4/192;
(2) Heart failure=true → Breath sounds in lungs = decrease in soundness with 205/638 and souffles in hearts =true with 111/192;

7 Conclusions and Discussions

1) Three experimental results show that using the two algorithms can get the same results.

2) Since algorithm 1 contains the step of attribute reduction and the computational complexity of attribute reduction is NP hard, the computational complexity of algorithm 1 is NP hard too, whereas algorithm 2 does not need the step of attribute reduction, especially the amount of selected examples for building a decernibility matrix will be very small even there are only several ones. So the computational complexity of algorithm 2 is largely less than the one of algorithm 1.

3) The factors that negate a typical dependency embody the correlation between two rules, i.e., the factors negate a rule (dependency) whereas support another rule (dependency). This kind of knowledge differs from the exceptional rules, since the factors can give us the information of two rules, which is a kind of comparative knowledge, whereas the exceptional rule can only give us the information of one rule.

4) ANN, SVM, etc models can be viewed as "population based" as a single model is formed for the entire population (test data set), while the rough set approach follows an "individual (data object) based" paradigm. The "population based" tools determine features that are common to a population (training data set). The models (rules) created by rough set are explicit and easily understood. So for inducing easily understood knowledge, the rough set theory has an advantage over the black-box based machine learning methods such as ANN, SVM etc.

5) This kind of knowledge give us the knowledge that how a typical pattern change to the exceptional pattern.

6) The idea of decernibility matrix can be used to not only the whole data set but also the partial data. The current use of the decernibility matrix need whole data set, i.e., whether a part of data of the whole data set can be selected to be applied to the decernibility matrix for inducing particular knowledge has not been offered up to now.

References

1. Pawlak Z.: Rough sets. Int. J. of Computer and Information Science. 11 (1982): 341-356
2. V.N. Vapnik: Statistical Learning Theory. John Wiley & Sons, (1998).
3. S.B.Cho."Pattern recognition with neural networks combined by genetic algorithm", Fuzzy sets and systems 103 (1999) 339-347,
4. Wong S K, Ziarko W.: On optimal decision rules in decision tables. Bulletin of Polish Academy of Sciences. 33(1985) 357-362

Automatic Extraction and Classification of Footwear Patterns

Maria Pavlou and Nigel M. Allinson

University of Sheffield, Sheffield, S1 3JD, UK
{m.pavlou, n.allinson}@sheffield.ac.uk

Abstract. Identification of the footwear traces from crime scenes is an important yet largely forgotten aspect of forensic intelligence and evidence. We present initial results from a developing automatic footwear classification system. The underlying methodology is based on large numbers of localized features located using MSER feature detectors. These features are transformed into robust SIFT or GLOH descriptors with the ranked correspondence between footwear patterns obtained through the use of constrained spectral correspondence methods. For a reference dataset of 368 different footwear patterns, we obtain a first rank performance of 85% for full impressions and 84% for partial impressions.

1 Introduction

Recent changes of UK police powers allows for collected footwear marks and evidence to be treated in the same way as fingerprint and DNA evidence. This generally untapped forensic source can be used to identify linked crime scenes, can link suspects in custody to other crime scenes and can sometimes provide strong courtroom evidence. Footwear evidence is quite common at crime scenes, frequently more so than finger prints [1], and of which approximately 30% is usable for forensic purposes [2]. In the UK the recovery rate of footwear evidence from crime scenes is expected to increase greatly from the current average of 15%. Changes in police procedures are expected to expand the current work load and there is need for practical systems to allow effective matching of footwear patterns to national databases. The provision of the underpinning technology is the focus of this study.

Automatic matching of footwear patterns has been little explored in the literature. Early works [4,5,2,7,6] have employed semi-automatic methods of manually annotated footwear print descriptions using a codebook of shape and pattern primitives, for example, wavy patterns, geometric shapes and logos. Searching for an example print then requires its encoding in a similar manner as that used for the reference database. This process is laborious and can be the source of poor performance as similar patterns may be inconsistently encoded by different users. One automated approach proposed in [3] employs shapes automatically generated from footwear prints using various image morphology operators. The spatial positioning and frequencies of these shapes are used for classification with a neural network. The authors did not report any performance statistics for their system. Work in [8, 9] makes use of fractals to represent the footwear prints and a mean square noise error method is used for classification. They report a 88% success in classifying 145 full-print images with no spatial or rotational variations. More recently in [10], Fourier Transforms (**FT**) are used for the classification of full and partial prints of varying quality. The **FT** provides invariance to translation and rotation effects and encodes spatial frequency information. They report first rank classification results of 65% and 87% for rank 5 on full-prints. For partial prints, a best performance of 55% and 78% is achieved for first and fifth ranks respectively. Their approach is promising and shows the importance of encoding local information. Although the footwear prints are processed globally they are encoded in terms of the local information evident in the print. Finally in [11] pattern edge information is employed for classification. After image de-noising and smoothing operations, extracted edge directions are grouped into a quantized set of 72 bins at 5 degree intervals. This generates an edge direction histogram for each pattern which after applying a Discrete **FT** provides a description with scale, translational and rotational invariance. On a dataset of 512 full-print patterns which were randomly noised (20%), randomly rotated and scaled they achieve rank 20 classification of 85%, 87.5%, and 99.6% for each variation group. Their approach deals well with these variations and a larger dataset, however their query examples originate from the learning set and no performance statistics are provided for partial prints.

2 Approach

From discussion with police forces, two main aspects of footwear processing have been identified. The first regards the automatic acquisition, categorization/encoding and storage of footwear patterns at police custody suites. The second is the identification and verification of scene evidence with stored reference samples or with other scene evidence.

Our work has initially approached the task of footwear categorization and encoding. In this case footwear patterns of good quality can easily be obtained and digitized either from scanning prints from specialist paper or by directly scanning or imaging. The former is a good representation and is similar to ones obtained from a scene. The direct scan or image can however contain more information but is slow and suitable equipment is not always easily available.

2.1 Local Feature Detection and Description

Research on covariant region detectors and their descriptors is now well advanced and have been used extensively as building blocks in general recognition systems. Based on recent research [12,13] it is possible to select a number of affine invariant feature extractors suitable for footwear patterns. From these studies the Harris-Affine (**HA**) corner detector and Maximally Stable Extremal Region (**MSER**) detector are identified as being robust and having a high repeatability under varied conditions such as affine transformations and image degradations (lighting, blurring, etc.).

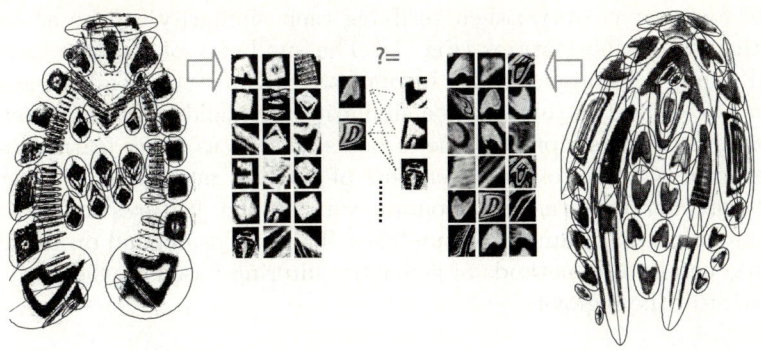

Fig. 1. Pair of footwear prints and some of their detected MSER features

The **MSER** detector (a watershed-based segmentation algorithm) performs well on images containing homogeneous regions with distinctive boundaries. Near-binary images of footwear patterns exhibit this set of characteristics. The **HA** detector provides a higher number of affine stable regions centered on corner features. These features sets are complementary as they have different properties and their overlap is usually small if not empty. Additionally their abundance is useful in matching images with occlusion and clutter. The **HA** detector can be used for footwear verification as its properties are well suited to corner-like features such as small cuts and grooves which are abundantly found in footwear patterns and can be the 'unique' features need to provide courtroom evidence. As a first step however, for footwear pattern matching and classification the **MSER** detector is employed as it is better suited for discriminating general patterns or shapes of footwear marks into classes.

Once a number of features have been found a suitable feature descriptor is needed to code the appearance or properties of the local features. In [14] the performance of a number of feature descriptors was evaluated using the above feature detectors and others. In most of the tests performed, the Gradient Location and Orientation Histogram (**GLOH**) descriptor provided the best results, closely followed by the Scale Invariant Feature Transform (**SIFT**) descriptor. The **SIFT** descriptor, computed for a normalized image patch, is a 3D gradient location and orientation histogram constructed using 8 quantized orientations and a 4×4 patch location grid. The resulting descriptor is of dimension 128. The **GLOH** is an extension of the **SIFT** descriptor designed to increase robustness and distinctiveness using a log-polar location grid with 3 bins in radial direction and 8 in angular direction. The gradient orientations are quantized into 16 bins. This gives a 272 bin histogram which is reduced in size using PCA to 128 dimensions.

2.2 Feature Matching

A combination of the above studies suggests that good matching performance is possible using **MSER** features encoded with **SIFT** or **GLOH** descriptors. Given images of footwear patterns, then verifying their similarity can be achieved by finding their matching features (Fig. 1). The similarity of features can be determined using a suitable metric. In our case a Gaussian weighted similarity metric has been used as this allows a similarity threshold to be easily set. However, matching on descriptors alone is not sufficient as some features may be mismatched or a many-to-many mapping of features may occur. Furthermore, different footwear patterns may contain very similar features and so further steps are required to disambiguate matches. These steps depend on the application, but generally use methods of geometric filtering based on the local spatial arrangement of the regions.

2.3 Spectral Correspondence Matching with Constraint Kernels

The problem of finding feature correspondence between two or more images is well known and is of crucial importance for many image analysis tasks. A number of techniques can be used to tackle this problem and can be broadly categorized into three groups based on their application and approach. These are Point Pattern Matching, Graphical Models and Spectral Methods.

Point Pattern Matching attempts to decide whether a pattern or spatial arrangement of points appears in an image. This involves the matching of isometries where a mapping is sought which transforms the query pattern onto a gallery pattern. Graphical Models also find mappings of graph structures and are based in representations of factored joint probability distributions. Both approaches and early Spectral Methods have been successful in graph matching problems. However they lack the ability to incorporate additional properties of the points being matched.

A simple and direct approach of associating features of two arbitrary patterns was proposed by Scott and Longuet-Higgins [16]. Applying singular value decomposition (SVD) to a suitable proximity matrix of feature locations it is possible to find good correspondences. This result stems from the properties of the SVD to satisfy *exclusion* (one-to-one mappings) and *proximity* principles [17]. One of the limitations of such spectral methods is their particular susceptibility to the effect of size differences between point samples and structural errors. To improve performance Pilu [15] included a feature similarity constraint based on the local gray patches around any feature point.

Similarly a number of feature similarity constraints are used in this work. As a first step a basic feature similarity constraint is enforced. Assume that two pattern images $\mathcal{I}_A$, $\mathcal{I}_B$ are given along with their set of feature descriptors $\mathcal{F}_A$ and $\mathcal{F}_B$. By employing a Gaussian function,

$$K(i,j) = e^{\frac{-\|\mathcal{F}_i - \mathcal{F}_j\|^2}{2\sigma^2}} \quad (1)$$

between every pairing of the features in each image a Gaussian feature similarity matrix $G_{ij}^{\mathcal{F}}$ can be formed. Multiplying $G^{\mathcal{F}}$ with the Gaussian proximity matrix $G^{\mathcal{D}}$ (based on the coordinate positions of features) results in a similar formulation to that used in [15]. Applying the SVD based algorithm of [16] at this point gives

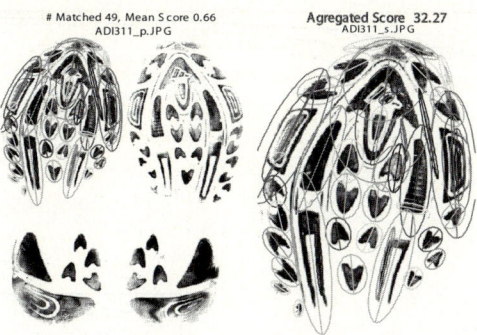

Fig. 2. An example of a matched partial to its reference image. Corresponding coloured ellipses indicate matched features with corresponding neighbourhoods.

a high proportion matching of features. However, as the number of features can be high, strong correspondences cannot be found.

To enhance the performance of the algorithm, locality and neighbourhood constraint kernels are also applied. This allows the SVD algorithm to consider features which are strongly matched in terms of their neighbours. The neighbourhood constraint kernel $G^\mathcal{N}$ enforces features matches whose neighbouring features are also similar. Constructing $G^\mathcal{N}$ is straight forward since $G^\mathcal{F}$ has already been obtained. All that is required is to construct an index list h^i of suitable neighbours for every feature i. Using feature coordinates the nearest N surrounding features are selected as neighbours. $G^\mathcal{N}$ can now be constructed as follows:

$$G^\mathcal{N}_{ij} = \frac{1}{N} \sum_{p,q=1}^{N} G^\mathcal{F}_{h^i_p, h^j_q}. \qquad (2)$$

The locality constraint kernel enforces feature pairings whose neighbouring features are similarly positioned around the central feature. This positioning is defined in terms of the angle between neighbours relative to the nearest neighbour. For each feature i the angle to its first nearest neighbour is found and the remaining neighbours angles, θ, are recorded relative to the first. The locality constraint kernel is then constructed as follows:

$$G^\mathcal{L}_{ij} = \frac{1}{N-2} \sum_{p=1}^{N-2} e^{\frac{\|\theta^i_p - \theta^j_p\|^2}{2\sigma^2}}. \qquad (3)$$

With a suitable selection of σ's for $G^\mathcal{D}$, $G^\mathcal{F}$ and $G^\mathcal{L}$ based on the maximum feature distance, similarity and neighbour angle deviations a final constrain matrix is obtained as follows:

$$G_{ij} = \sqrt[4]{G^\mathcal{D}_{ij} \times G^\mathcal{F}_{ij} \times G^\mathcal{N}_{ij} \times G^\mathcal{L}_{ij}}, \qquad (4)$$

for $i, j = 1 \ldots |\mathcal{F}_B|, |\mathcal{F}_B|$. After using G in the algorithm proposed in [16] and obtain pairings $\{i, j\}$ the matched pairs are further thresholded by keeping only

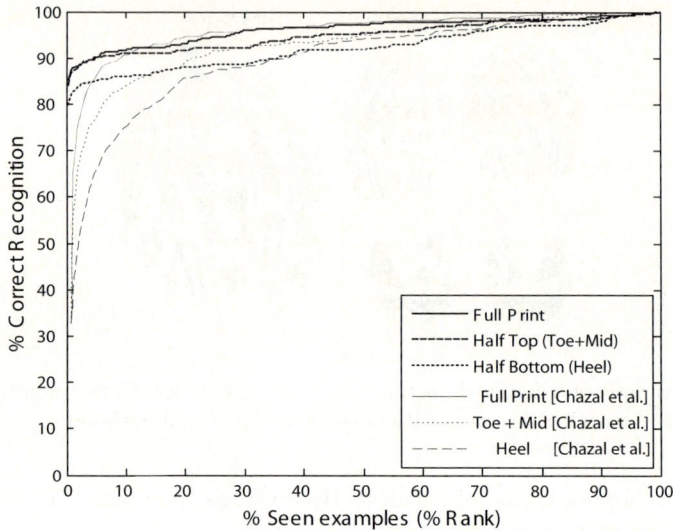

Fig. 3. Rank Recognition Performance of matching with full and partial prints

those who's $G_{i,j} > e^{-1}$. This is a convenient threshold provided reasonable values of σ have been set for the constraint kernels. An example of a partial match using the above approach is shown in Fig. 2.

3 Experiments

A subset of 368 different footwear patterns from the Forensic Science Service database is used [18]. Each pattern class consists of two images, a reference set image containing a whole left and right print and a test set image of either a complete left or right print. The test set print is a different print of varying quality of the same class as that in its corresponding reference image. In order to test on partial prints two additional test sets were produced from the approximate division of the test images into sole and heel sections.

Testing proceeds by applying the above approach for every pairing of reference and test image. The output of each matching attempt returns a list of paired features along with their individual match score G_{ij}, where i and j are feature indexes of the test and reference images. A total match score is taken as the sum of the feature match scores. A best match is that having the highest aggregate score. The value of $2\sigma^2$ is set at 0.3 for the feature similarity constraint and 5 for the locality constraint and the number of neighbours N is set to 5.

4 Results

Performance was measured on the observed reference images, in terms of the highest aggregate score, before the correct match was found. Figure 3 shows the

Table 1. Comparison of proposed algorithm with proposed approach of Chazal et al. [10]

Approach	Number of unique patterns	% Seen images (Rank)	Full-print	Partial-prints Toe-Mid	Heel
Chazal et al. [10]	140	0.7 **(1)**	65	55	41
	140	5 **(7)**	87	78	66
	140	20 **(28)**	95	89	86
Proposed Method	368	0.3 **(1)**	85	**84**	**80**
Sec. 2	368	1.6 **(6)**	**88**	**87**	**83**
	368	5.4 **(20)**	**90**	**90**	**85**

correct recognition rate (CRR) for full and partial prints. It can be seen that a good matching performance is achieved, starting at 85% for first rank on full-prints and rising to 91% for the best 6 matches. The performance of our approach is strong even for partial prints. For example, when matching 'Half Top' partial prints our system returns a rank '1' CRR of 84% rising to 90% at rank '6'.

5 Discussion and Conclusions

Our programme of work to develop robust footwear recognition systems will be expanded to much larger reference databases: the current national database contains over 13,000 footwear patterns. Nevertheless, we are greatly encouraged by these initial results, as good performance is possible using only a direct pattern matching approach with no explicit model of outsole appearance. It is difficult to compare different published approaches as different datasets and testing procedures are used. However, we attempt a comparison with the recent work reported in [10]. Table 1 shows this comparison based on similar rank numbers, while the best results of [10] are plotted in Fig. 3. Bearing in mind that the number of different patterns used in our study is over twice that used in [10], a marked increase in performance was achieved. This is especially true in the early ranking figures where we report a 90% CRR from viewing only 5% of the database.

The foundations of our proposed automated footwear classification system are based on local shape and pattern structure. The selected feature and pattern descriptors are affine invariant and so can cope with relative translations and rotations. The abundance and localized nature of these features permit good recognition performance for partial impressions. Our on-going work will also explore the ability to match footwear marks retrieved from crime scenes to specified shoes recovered from suspects.

Acknowledgments

The work is financially supported by the UK EPSRC (Grant reference EP/D03633X) in collaboration with the UK Home Office Police Standard Unit and ACPO.

References

1. W. J. Bodziak, Footwear impression evidence detection, recovery and examination, Second ed. CRC Press, 2000
2. A. Girod, Computer classification of the shoeprint of burglars' shoes, Forensic Science Int., 82, 1996, p59-65.
3. Z. Geradts and J. Keijzer, The image-database REBEZO for shoeprints with developments on automatic classification of shoe outsole designs, Forensic Science Int., 82, 1996, p21-31.
4. N. Sawyer, SHOE-FIT A computerised shoe print database, Proc. European Convention on Security and Detection, 1995, p86-89.
5. W. Ashley, What shoe was that? The use of computerised image database to assist in identification, Forensic Science Int., 82(1), 1996, p7-20.
6. S. Mikkonen, V. Suominen and P. Heinonen, Use of footwear impressions in crime scene investigations assisted by computerised footwear collection system, Forensic Science Int., 82, 1996, p67-79.
7. S. Mikkonen and T. Astikainen, Databased classification system for shoe sole patterns - identification of partial footwear impression found at a scene of crime. Journal of Forensic Science, 39(5), 1994, p1227-1236.
8. A. Bouridane, A. Alexander, M. Nibouche and D. Crookes, Application of fractals to the detection and classification of shoeprints, Proc. 2000 Int. Conf. Image Processing, 1, 2000, p474-477.
9. A. Alexander, A. Bouridane and D. Crookes, Automatic classification and recognition of shoeprints, Proc. Seventh Int. Conf. Image Processing and Its Applications, 2, 1999, p638-641.
10. P. de Chazal, J. Flynn and R. B. Reilly, Automated processing of shoeprint images based on the Fourier Transform for use in forensic science, IEEE Trans. Pattern Analysis & Machine Intelligence, 27(3), 2005, p341-350.
11. L. Zhang and N. Allinson, Automatic shoeprint retrieval system for use in forensic investigations, UK Workshop On Computational Intelligence (UKCI05), 2005.
12. K. Mikolajczyk, T. Tuytelaars, C. Schmid, A. Zisserman, J. Matas, F. Schaffalitzky, T. Kadir and L. Van Gool, A comparison of affine region detectors, Int. Journal of Computer Vision, 65(1/2), 2005, p43-72.
13. K. Mikolajczyk and C. Schmid, Scale and affine invariant interest point detectors, Int. Journal of Computer Vision 60(1), 2004, p6386.
14. K. Mikolajczyk and C. Schmid, A performance evaluation of local descriptors, IEEE Trans. Pattern Analysis & Machine Intelligence, 27(10), 2004, p1615-1630.
15. M. Pilu, A direct method for stereo correspondence based on singular value decomposition, IEEE Conf. Computer Vision & Pattern Recognition (CVPR'97), 1997, p261.
16. G. Scott and H. Longuet-Higgins. An algorithm for associating the features of two patterns. Proc. Royal Society London, B244, 1991, p21-26.
17. S. Ullman. The interpretation of Visual Motion. MIT Press, Cambridge, MA, 1979.
18. Data taken from the UK National Shoewear Database, Forensic Science Service, Birmingham, B37 7YN, UK.

Description of Combined Spatial Relations Between Broad Boundary Regions Based on Rough Set

Shihong Du[1], Qimin Qin[1], Qiao Wang[2], and Haijian Ma[1]

[1] Institute of Remote Sensing and GIS, Peking University, Beijing, 100871, China
dshgis@hotmail.com, qmqin@pku.edu.cn
[2] College of Geographical Science, Nanjing Normal University, Nanjing, 210097, China
wangqiao@zhb.gov.cn

Abstract. The uncertain regions are modeled by broad boundary regions, while the description and reasoning of combined spatial relations between them are still unresolved problems. So far, the research about describing spatial relations mainly focuses on single-kind of spatial relation between simple and certain objects, rather than the combination of multi-kinds of spatial relations between uncertain regions. In addition, the uncertainty of formalizing combined spatial relations between uncertain regions is still a puzzle problem. Based on this point, the rough set theory is introduced into describing combined spatial relations between broad boundary regions. First, topological relations, exterior direction relations and detailed direction relations are approximated by a lower and an upper rough set, respectively, and then the difference set between the two sets indicates the uncertainty of spatial relations. Finally, the combination of the topological and direction relations between broad boundary regions is used to describe combined spatial relations.

Keywords: Broad boundary region, direction relation, topological relation.

1 Introduction

The description of spatial relations between uncertain regions attracts much attention of many researchers in the field of spatial relations. Uncertain regions are derived from the position uncertainty of crisp regions and vague of fuzzy objects, and usually approximated by broad boundary regions. For an area object defined clearly, the position uncertainty or attribute uncertainty makes the boundary of a region be not a geometry line any more, but a broad boundary, i.e., broad boundary region. The important aspects for describing, combining and deriving spatial relations between broad boundary regions are the partition of topology and direction. Therefore, these partitions must handle with the uncertainty led by the broad boundary. Clementini et al. used the extended 9-intersection to deal with topological relations between broad boundary regions in [1], [2]. However, this extended model does not describe the uncertainty of topological relations in a straightforward way. Du et al. [3] introduced the rough set theory [4] into the formalization of direction relations between broad boundary regions. The rough set approximated the uncertain region, direction relations and their reasoning by an upper and a lower set, and the difference between the two sets represents the uncertainty of regions, direction relations and the reasoning results, respectively, but the combined spatial relations are still not involved. Although the qualitative model for combining topological and direction relations improves the power to discern spatial relations, and is helpful to describe and derive spatial relations, the combined methods still only handle with spatial relations between simple and certain regions, not between broad boundary regions. Especially, they cannot process the uncertainty of spatial relations. Accordingly, the methods for describing combined spatial relations between broad boundary regions and their uncertainties need to be investigated further.

Aiming at the shortcomings abovementioned, the rough set is introduced to describe combined spatial relations between broad boundary regions and relations between broad boundary regions and certain regions. Firstly, the exterior and detailed direction relations between broad boundary regions are approximated by two rough sets: the upper and lower. Meanwhile, the topological relations are also approximated by the two rough sets. The notable difference between our method and the extended 9-intersection is that our model handles directly with the uncertainty of topological relations between broad boundary regions by combining the eight basic topological relations between simple and certain regions, while the extended model describes the uncertainty indirectly by increasing the number of basic topological relations [1]. This is an important advancement because the more the number of the topological relations is, the harder the understanding of them is, the more complex the combination of topological and direction relations is. Finally, rough sets of direction and topological relations between broad boundary regions, and relations between broad boundary regions and certain regions are combined to improve ability of distinguishing spatial relations. The uncertainty of direction relations, topological relations, combined spatial relations and their reasoning results are represented by the differences between the corresponding upper and lower rough set, respectively.

2 The Existing Qualitative Model for Spatial Relations

2.1 Topological Relations

Topological relations between simple and certain regions are modeled by the 9-intersection [4]. A certain region can be divided into three subsets: interior ($A°$), boundary (∂A) and exterior (A^-). Accordingly, the topological relations between two certain regions, A and B, can be determined by a 3×3 matrix constructed by the nine intersections of the three subsets of A and those of B. Because the intersection has two states: empty (0) and non-empty (1), the 9-intersection can determine 512 relations at most in theory. Nevertheless, there are only eight meaningful topological relations between two certain regions since other relations are meaningless.

Because the 9-intersection can not discern the topological relations between broad boundary regions, Clementini *et al.* extended the 9-intersection by replacing the boundary with the broad boundary, while kept the interior and exterior unchanged. The extended 9-intersection can discern 44 topological relations between simple broad boundary regions [1], and 12 ones between complex uncertain regions [2]. The extended model uses the qualitative method to represent the uncertainty of topological relations between broad boundary regions. In addition, this uncertainty is represented by increasing the number of topological relations, but which relations are uncertain and which are certain are not pointed out.

2.2 Direction Relations

At present, there are many models for direction relations, such as direction relation matrix [6], the cone-based [7], the projection-based [8] and 2D-String [9], etc. All of these models compute the direction relations by approximate shapes of the target and the reference object, not by their real shapes. For example, the cone-based method uses points to approximate the reference and target object, so it can not consider the size and shape of objects; 2D-String model does not represent direction relations directly, the derivation is needed to obtain direction information from the symbol stings; direction-relation matrix computes the direction relations by replacing the reference objects with its Minimum Bounding Rectangle (MBR) and the real shape of the target object. Comparing with other models, direction relation matrix is more accurate to describe direction relations between certain regions.

Although direction-relation matrix is more powerful than other models, as it still uses the MBR of a reference object to compute direction relations, provided that the MBRs of any two reference objects are identical, no matter how different their shapes, the directions partitioned around the two reference objects are same. On the other hand, direction-relation matrix only handles with the direction information outside the MBR, while not describes some direction concepts people often used, such as "east part of a region", "west part of a region" and "east boundary of a region", etc. The common characteristics of these concepts are that all of them are inside the MBR. Accordingly, the space extents of those directions are inside the MBR of a reference object, but the direction-relation matrix only regards them as "same direction", not considers their differences.

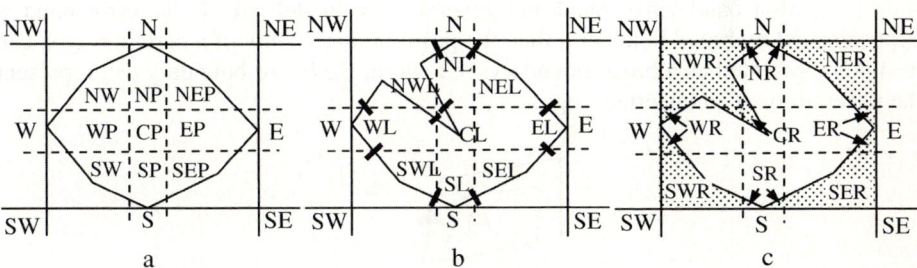

Fig. 1. Detailed direction relations model: (a) interior direction relations; (b) boundary direction relations; (c) ring direction relations

In order to overcome the shortcomings of direction relation matrix abovementioned, Du *et al.* suggested a detailed direction relations model to describe the direction information inside the MBR of a reference object [10]. Detailed direction relations model is composed of interior, boundary and ring direction relations. The interior of a reference region is partitioned into nine directions at most, such as *EP, WP, SP, NP, NEP, NWP, SEP, SWP* and *CP*. The interior direction *EP* means east part of a region. Other interior directions have similar meanings. The boundary of a reference region is divided into nine components at most, such as *EL, WL, SL, NL, NEL, NWL, SEL, SWL* and *CL*. The boundary direction *EL* means east boundary of a region, so do other boundary directions. The ring, the difference between the MBR and the reference region, is also divided into nine parts at most, such as *ER, WR, SR, NR, NER, NWR, SER, SWR* and *CR*. The ring directions have not real meanings, but they have important effects on discerning the shape of a reference region. The detailed information about interior, boundary and exterior directions is explained in [10], [11].

It is worth while to point out that the detailed direction relations and the existing direction relations are different. Therefore, the existing direction relations described by direction relations matrix are called exterior direction relations. Although both the exterior and detailed atomic directions are concepts people often used, they have different meanings and spatial extent, so they are different atomic directions. These atomic directions complement each other, and their combinations can simulate natural languages about spatial relations more powerfully than only exterior or direction relations can do.

3 Rough Description of Combined Spatial Relations Between Broad Boundary Regions

3.1 Broad Boundary Regions

The broad boundary not only describes the vague of fuzzy objects, but also the position uncertainty of certain objects. The vague of fuzzy objects is indicated by the membership degree of each element. Therefore, if a fuzzy object is regarded as a fuzzy set, the broad boundary region can be constructed by the α-cut set of the fuzzy set. The position uncertainty of certain regions refers to the position difference between the stored objects in GIS and their real positions, which is modeled by error band models, such as epsilon band, error band and general error model, etc. If the error band is approximated by broad boundary, then the position uncertainty of a certain region can also be represented as a broad boundary. In a word, the broad boundary can represent the uncertainty of an uncertain region.

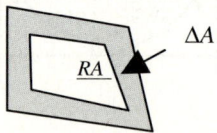

Fig. 2. Broad boundary region

The rough set approximates a set by two rough sets: an upper and a lower. Accordingly, the broad boundary region can also approximated by two rough sets. As illustrated in Fig. 2, the interior of a broad boundary region A is represented as a lower set $\underline{RA}$, the union of the broad boundary and the lower is denoted by a upper set $\overline{RA}$, so the difference between the upper and lower is the broad boundary $\Delta A = \overline{RA} - \underline{RA}$, which indicates the uncertainty.

3.2 The Uncertainty of Combined Spatial Relations Between Broad Boundary Regions

The extended 9-intersection in [1] can determine 56 topological relations between two broad boundary regions, but it can not tell which relations are uncertain and which ones are certain. Making the difference between uncertain and certain relations is important for recognizing uncertainty of relations. Because broad boundary regions can be approximated by two approximate rough sets, the spatial relations related to broad boundary regions can also be represented as an upper and a lower rough set ($\overline{R_\alpha}$ and $\underline{R_\alpha}$). The lower set of spatial relations is computed by the lower sets of broad boundary regions, while the upper set is computed by the upper sets of broad boundary regions. The possibilities of relations in lower set are larger than the ones of elements that is in the upper set and not in the lower set, so the difference between the upper and the lower set indicates the uncertainty of spatial relations. The accuracy of rough spatial relations is measured by $\alpha_R(R) = |\underline{R_\alpha}|/|\overline{R_\alpha}|$, where $|\overline{R_\alpha}|$ means computing the number of elements in $\overline{R_\alpha}$. The roughness is defined as $\rho_R(R) = 1 - \alpha_R(R)$. It is clearly that the larger the accuracy is, the smaller the roughness is. When the two sets $\overline{R_\alpha}$ and $\underline{R_\alpha}$ are equal, the accuracy is 1, while the roughness is 0, which indicates the uncertainty of spatial relations is low.

Rough method represents the combined spatial relations as two rough sets composed of simple and basic spatial relations determined by existing models; therefore the process of combined spatial relations will be simpler than other methods. The combined spatial relations related to broad boundary regions can fall into three categories: relations between certain regions and broad boundary regions, relations between broad boundary regions and certain regions and relations between broad boundary regions.

3.3 The Rough Description of Combined Spatial Relations Between Certain Regions and Broad Boundary Regions

The rough description of combined spatial relations between certain regions and broad boundary regions is the combination of topological and direction relations between them. The certain region is regarded as the reference object, while the broad boundary region as the target object (Fig. 3). Since the broad boundary region is the target object, it can not influence the partition of direction relations. That is, the spatial extent of direction is certain, while the directions which the broad boundary region falls inside are uncertain because the broad boundary does not belong to a region completely.

Let the reference object be the certain region A, the target object be the broad boundary region $\tilde{B}$ approximated by the lower and the upper set $\underline{RB}$ and $\overline{RB}$, then the lower set of topological relations between A and $\tilde{B}$ can be defined as $\underline{T}_{AB} = \{T_{A\underline{B}}\}$, and the upper set $\overline{T}_{AB} = \{T_{A\underline{B}}, T_{A\overline{B}}\}$, where $T_{A\underline{B}}$ represents the topological relation between two certain region A and $\underline{RB}$ determined by the 9-intersection; $T_{A\overline{B}}$ means the relation between A and $\overline{RB}$. The upper and lower set of exterior direction relations can be defined as $\underline{O}_{AB} = \{O_{A\underline{B}}\}$ and $\overline{O}_{AB} = \{O_{A\underline{B}}, O_{A\overline{B}}\}$, respectively, where $O_{A\underline{B}}$ represents the exterior direction relations between A and $\underline{RB}$ computed by direction relation matrix. In the same way, we can obtain the rough sets of the interior, boundary and exterior direction relations. Accordingly, the combination of exterior and detailed direction relations is approximated by two corresponding rough sets: the lower $\underline{D}_{AB} = (\underline{O}_{AB}, \underline{R}_{AB}, \underline{L}_{AB}, \underline{P}_{AB})$ and the upper $\overline{D}_{AB} = (\overline{O}_{AB}, \overline{R}_{AB}, \overline{L}_{AB}, \overline{P}_{AB})$, where $\underline{R}_{AB}$, $\underline{L}_{AB}$ and $\underline{P}_{AB}$ are the lower set composed of interior, boundary and ring directions, respectively, decided by the detailed direction relations model discussed in section 2.2. Based on the upper and lower rough set of spatial relations, the uncertainty of combined spatial relations is indicated by the difference between the upper and lower rough set. Like the broad boundary representing the uncertainty of uncertain regions, the difference of two rough set of combined spatial relations also represents the uncertainty of spatial relations, denoted as ΔD_{AB} and ΔT_{AB} for combined direction relations and topological relations, respectively.

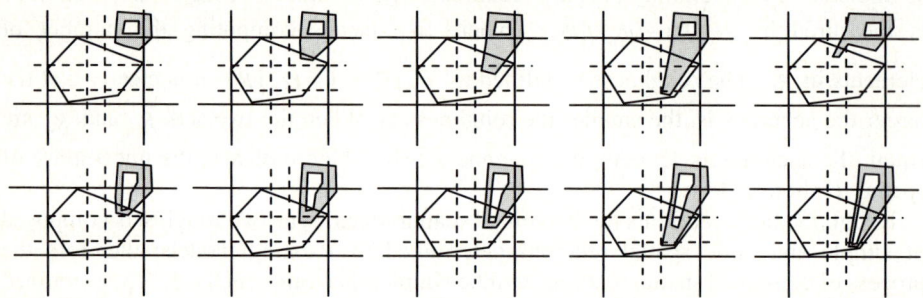

Fig. 3. Rough description of combined spatial relations between certain regions and broad boundary regions

For example, for the geometry graphics of column 4 and row 1 in Fig. 3, $\underline{D}_{AB} = \{\{N\}, \emptyset, \emptyset, \emptyset\}$, $\overline{D}_{AB} = \{\{N, NE, C, E\}, \{NER\}, \{NEL\}, \{NEP, EP, SEP\}\}$, the difference, the boundary ΔD_{AB} of combined direction relations, is $\{\{NE, C, E\}, \{NER\}, \{NEL\}, \{NEP, EP, SEP\}\}$; $\underline{T}_{AB} = \{disjoint\}$, $\overline{T}_{AB} = \{disjoint, overlap\}$, the boundary ΔT_{AB} of topological relations is $\{overlap\}$. This means that the possibility of the topological relation *disjoint* between the geometry graphics is larger than that of the relation *overlap*. In the same way, for the geometry graphics in column 4 and row 2 in Fig. 3, $\underline{D}_{AB} = \{\{N, O\}, \{NER\}, \{NEL\}, \{NEP, EP\}\}$, $\overline{D}_{AB} = \{\{N, NE, C, E\}, \{NER\}, \{NEL\}, \{NEP, EP, SEP\}\}$, $\Delta D_{AB} = \{\emptyset, \emptyset, \{SEP\}\}$; $\underline{T}_{AB} = \{disjoint\}$, $\overline{T}_{AB} = \{disjoint\}$, $\Delta T_{AB} = \emptyset$. For the former example, the roughness, i.e., uncertain degree of topological relations is 0.5, while for the latter, the uncertain degree is 0.

3.4 The Rough Description of Combined Spatial Relations Between Broad Boundary Regions and Certain Objects

Because the broad boundary region is reference object, the broad boundary can influence spatial extent of detailed and exterior directions, thus results in the uncertainty of spatial extent of directions.

Let the reference object be broad boundary region $\tilde{A}$ approximated by two sets: the lower $\underline{RA}$ and the upper $\overline{RA}$, while the target object be certain object B, then the lower set $\underline{T}_{AB}$ of topological relations between $\tilde{A}$ and B is defined as $\underline{T}_{AB} = \{T_{\underline{AB}}\}$, the upper one $\overline{T}_{AB} = \{T_{\underline{AB}}, T_{\overline{AB}}\}$, where $T_{\underline{AB}}$ and $T_{\overline{AB}}$ mean the topological relations between $\underline{RA}$ and B, and that between $\overline{RA}$ and B, respectively; the lower set $\underline{O}_{AB}$ of exterior direction relations is defined as $\underline{O}_{AB} = \{O_{\underline{AB}}\}$, and the upper $\overline{O}_{AB} = \{O_{\underline{AB}}, O_{\overline{AB}}\}$, where $O_{\underline{AB}}$ and $O_{\overline{AB}}$ represent the exterior direction relation between $\underline{RA}$ and B and that between $\overline{RA}$ and B computed by direction relation matrix, respectively. In the same way, we can obtain the rough set of the interior, boundary and exterior direction relations. Accordingly, the combination of exterior and detailed direction relations is also approximated by corresponding two rough sets: the lower $\underline{D}_{AB} = (\underline{O}_{AB}, \underline{R}_{AB}, \underline{L}_{AB}, \underline{P}_{AB})$ and the upper $\overline{D}_{AB} = (\overline{O}_{AB}, \overline{R}_{AB}, \overline{L}_{AB}, \overline{P}_{AB})$.

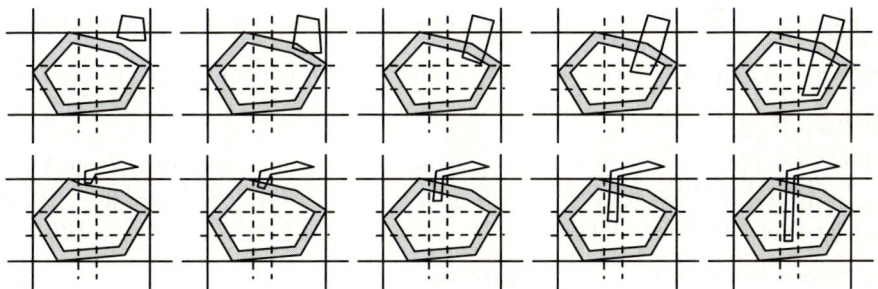

Fig. 4. Rough description of combined spatial relations between broad boundary regions and certain regions

For example, for the geometry graphics of column 1 and row 2 in Fig. 4, $\underline{D}_{AB} = \{\{N,C\},\{NER\},\{\emptyset,\emptyset\}\}$, $\overline{D}_{AB} = \{\{N,C\},\{NER\},\{NEL\},\{NEP\}\}$, so $\Delta D_{AB} = \{\emptyset,\emptyset,\{NEL\},\{NEP\}\}$; $\underline{T}_{AB} = \{disjoint\}$, $\overline{T}_{AB} = \{disjoint, overlap\}$, $\Delta T_{AB} = \{overlap\}$. Like the combined spatial relations between certain regions and broad boundary regions, the boundary of topological and direction relations manifests the uncertainty of topology and direction led by broad boundary regions.

3.5 The Rough Description of Combined Spatial Relations Between Broad Boundary Regions

In the combined spatial relations between broad boundary regions, both the reference and the target object are broad boundary regions, so both the spatial extent of directions and the directions that the target object fall insides are uncertain.

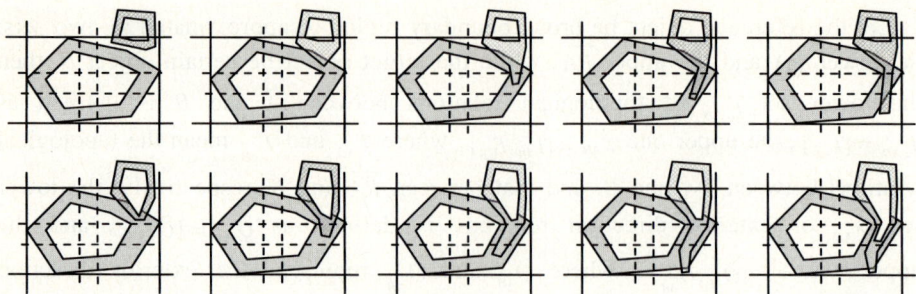

Fig. 5. Rough description of combined spatial relations between broad boundary regions

Let the reference and the target object be broad boundary region $\tilde{A}$ and $\tilde{B}$, respectively, and $\underline{RA}$, $\overline{RA}$, $\underline{RB}$ and $\overline{RB}$ are their corresponding lower and upper rough set, then for topological relations, the lower rough set $\underline{T}_{AB} = \{T_{\underline{AB}}\}$, and the upper $\overline{T}_{AB} = \{T_{\underline{AB}}, T_{\overline{AB}}, T_{\underline{AB}}, T_{\overline{AB}}\}$; for exterior direction relations, the lower $\underline{O}_{AB} = \{O_{\underline{AB}}\}$, the upper $\overline{O}_{AB} = \{O_{\underline{AB}}, O_{\underline{AB}}, O_{\overline{AB}}\}$; for ring, boundary and interior direction relations, the lower $\underline{R}_{AB} = \{R_{\underline{AB}}\}$, $\underline{L}_{AB} = \{L_{\underline{AB}}\}$ and $\underline{P}_{AB} = \{P_{\underline{AB}}\}$, the upper $\overline{R}_{AB} = \{R_{\overline{AB}}\}$, $\overline{L}_{AB} = \{L_{\partial A\overline{B}}\}$ and $\overline{P}_{AB} = \{P_{\overline{AB}}\}$.

For example, for the geometry graphics of column2 and row 2 in Fig. 5, $\underline{D}_{AB} = \{\{N,C\}, \{NER\}, \{\varnothing, \varnothing\}\}$, and $\overline{D}_{AB} = \{\{N,C\}, \{NER\}, \{NEL\}, \{NEP\}\}$, so the boundary of direction relations $\Delta D_{AB} = \{\varnothing, \varnothing, \{NEL\}, \{NEP\}\}$; $\underline{T}_{AB} = \{disjoint\}$, $\overline{T}_{AB} = \{disjoint, overlap\}$, $\Delta T_{AB} = \{overlap\}$.

4 Conclusions

The rough description of combined spatial relations can deal with the uncertainty led by broad boundary regions, especially this method transforms the complex combination of topological and direction relations between broad boundary regions into the combination of simple topological and direction relations between simple and certain objects, so does the reasoning of complex combined spatial relations. The method uses the basic spatial relations accepted comprehensively by people to represent the spatial relations between broad boundary regions, and directly measures the uncertainty of the topological and direction relations by the differences between the upper and lower rough set, not by increasing the number of basic topological relations used in the extended 9-intersection. The rough description and reasoning of combined spatial relations between broad boundary regions can be applied in querying, analyzing and matching uncertain spatial data.

Acknowledgements. The work described in this paper was substantially supported by grants from the National Natural Science Foundation of China (No. 40271090).

References

1. Clementini E and Felice P D. Approximate Topological Relations. International Journal of Approximate Reasoning, 16(1997) 173 – 204.
2. Clementini, E., and Felice, P. D.: A Spatial Model for Complex Objects with a Broad Boundary Supporting Queries on Uncertain Data. Data & Knowledge Engineering, 3(2001) 285–305
3. Du, S. H., Wang, Q., and Wei, B., etc.: Spatial Direction Relations Rough Reasoning. Acta Geodaetica et Cartographica Sinica, 2(2004) 334–338 (in Chinese)
4. Pawlak, Z.: Rough Sets — Theoretical Aspects of Reasoning about Data. Kluwer Academic Publishers, Dordrecht, The Netherlands, (1991)
5. Egenhofer, M. J., and Herring, J.: Categorizing Binary Topological Relations between Regions, Lines and Points in Geographic Databases. Technical Report, Department of Surveying Engineering, University of Maine, Orono, USA, (1991)
6. Goyal, R.: Similarity Assessment for Cardinal Directions between Extended Spatial Objects. Ph.D. Thesis, the University of Maine, Orono, USA, (2000)
7. Peuquet, D., and Zhang. C. X.: An Algorithm to Determine the Directional Relationship between Arbitrailly Shaped Polygons in the Plane. Pattern Recognition, 1(1987) 65–74
8. Frank, A. U.: Qualitative Spatial Reasoning: Cardinal Directions as an Example. In: Mark, D., and White, D. (Eds.): Auto-Carto 10, Baltimore, USA, (1995) 148–167
9. Chang, S. K., Shi, Q. Y., and Yan, C. W.: Iconic Indexing by 2D Strings. IEEE Transactions on Patter Analysis and Machine Intelligence, 3(1987) 413–428
10. Du, S. H., Wang, Q., and Yang, Y. P.: A Qualitative Description Model of Detailed Direction Relations. Journal of Image and Graphics, 12(2004) 1496–1503 (in Chinese)
11. Du, S. H.: Theories and Methods for Fuzzy Description and Combined Reasoning of Spatial Relations. PH.D Thesis, Institute of Remote Sensing Applications, Chinese Academy of Sciences, Beijing, China, (2004) (in Chinese)

Active Sketch for Finding Primary Structures in Images

Shulin Yang[1], Cunlu Xu[2,*], and Qin Lei[3]

[1] Dept. of Computer Science and Engineering, Fudan Univ., PRC, 200433
[2] School of Information Science and Engineering, Lanzhou Univ., PRC, 730000
[3] School of Mathematics, Physics and Software Engineering, Lanzhou Jiaotong Univ., PRC, 730070

Abstract. The vision system of human beings is very sensitive to lines. Sketches composed of line drawings provide a useful representation for image structures, which can be used for recognition and which is capable of serving as intermediate data structures of images for further analysis. However, traditional schemes tackling the line detection problem for sketch generation are stuck to one of the two problems: lack of global supervision for line detection over an image or confinement of hard global constraints on the configuration of detected lines. In this paper, we propose an active sketch model for finding primary structures in the form of line drawings, overcoming shortcomings of the traditional schemes by combining local line finding techniques with supervision of a global saliency measure while imposing no global constraint on the configuration of the line drawings. Test results show that our model is able to sketch out lines in an image representing the most salient image discontinuity without imposing any shape or topology constraint on the sketch.

1 Introduction

Studies in cognitive psychological have indicated that human beings can identify objects represented by line drawings almost as well as in full gray-level pictures [1]. Line drawings provide a good way for presenting edge information in images, which carries an important part of the structural information. Therefore, a sketch composed of line drawings provides a natural way to represent the content of an image. In fact, this representation has a wide use in many high level vision tasks: Saund uses sketches and drawings to find perceptually closed paths [2]; Gao and Leung used a line edge map composed of line segments for face recognition [3]; moreover, methods for generating such a sketch can be used to detect roads and ridges in remotely sensed images [4] and to extract image structures for recognition, retrieval, etc [5].

Generating a sketch made up of line drawings is to find the lines in an image. There are generally two groups of approaches related to finding lines in images. One group is based on edge detection and edge linking, following a bottom-up way to construct lines by linking edges detected by local features [6]. These approaches are free from improper constraints imposed on the configuration of the lines, however, they lack a global supervision for line detection over a whole image. Extraction of lines in one part of an image has nothing to do with extraction of lines in another part of the image.

---

* Corresponding author.

Even if preprocessing steps are added to calculate some global thresholds, effective estimations for the thresholds are hard to be achieved before all lines are extracted.

The other group of schemes are highly global supervised and are based on certain constraints imposed on the configuration of all potential lines, and they follow a top-down way to locate them. These constraints vary from specific features of the lines, like the templates used in Hough transformation [7], to the widely used boundary finding targets, like segmentation [8], contour finding [9], etc. Some of these approaches have achieved very good results with incorporation of their global constraints, but because of their strong reliance on such prior knowledge, they are not widely applicable in the task of sketch generation in which no shape or topology constraints should be imposed on the global configuration of lines. Improper use of prior knowledge and global supervision will hurt the performance of an algorithm badly. Fig.1 are several images that are hard to impose the inclusive constraints used in these schemes like segmentation, contour extraction or template fitting.

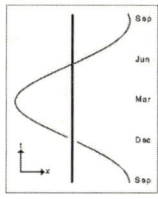

Fig. 1. Images that conventional top-down schemes have difficulty in generating sketches for

In this paper, an active sketch model is proposed to find primary structures in images. This model differs from the approaches mentioned above in that it combines the merits of both top-down schemes and bottom-up schemes by combining global supervision of a saliency measure with local line finding techniques. An active sketch is a system of straight line segments that can adjust their number and positions, seeking for a configuration to best represent the primary structure in the image. Local adjustments of the positions and the number of the line segments are implemented under the supervision of a global criterion, which evaluates how well a sketch satisfies our intuitive expectation for it. Primary structures in images emerge as outputs of the model.

The approach of using a global criterion, while performing a supervision over the whole sketch generation process for a desirable sketch structure, is consistent with the general local line fitting targets- to connect together line segments and to drag the lines to places where large image discontinuity occurs. Meanwhile, no shape or topology constraint is imposed on the global configuration of lines in an active sketch. As a result, the problem of over supervision that occurs to traditional global supervised schemes as mentioned above will not occur to the active sketch model.

In the following parts of this paper, we first give a description of the active sketch model in Section 2. Then, a genetic algorithm is involved as optimization techniques of the active sketch model in Section 3. Section 4 provides tests to verify the effectiveness of the model. And finally, conclusions and future work are given in Section 5.

2 Active Sketch Model

2.1 Representation with Line Segments

A natural idea of representing line drawings on an image is to use a point set, recording the sites the line drawings go through, like the way that is used in most line detection approaches. However, line drawings are more than just a set of points. An expression carrying direction information is more consistent with the spatial feature discontinuity in images that lines represent.

In the proposed model, a sketch τ is composed of N straight line segments of a given length l,

$$\tau = \{L_i\} \qquad (i = 1, 2, ..., N), \tag{1}$$

Each line segment L_i is determined by a coordinate and an orientation ranging from 0 to π, denoting the central location and the obliquity of L_i,

$$L_i = \{x_{L_i}, y_{L_i}, \theta_{L_i}\} \qquad (\theta_{L_i} \in [0, \pi)). \tag{2}$$

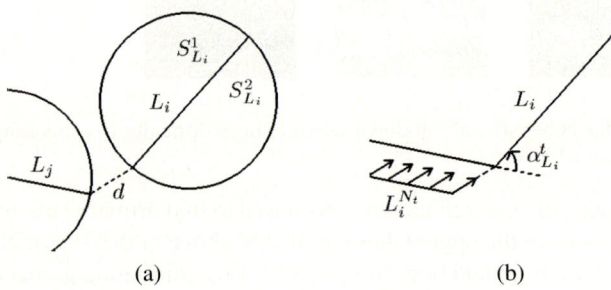

(a)   (b)

Fig. 2. (a)The neighborhood of L_i and its neighbors L_j; (b)The orientation difference between L_i and its nearest neighbor $L_i^{N_t}$

$e_I(L_i)$ denotes the amount of edge strength represented by L_i in image I, and it is measured by the spatial feature disparity (including local information like intensity, color, texture, etc) between image patches by the two sides of L_i. Areas on image I that have an effect on the value of $e_I(L_i)$ is called the *Neighborhood* of L_i.

In this model, the *Neighborhood* of L_i is a round area on image I (Fig.2(a)), and L_i is positioned at the center of its *Neighborhood*. $S_{L_i}^1$ and $S_{L_i}^2$ are respectively half of the Neighborhood of L_i, each by one of its two sides. $e_I(L_i)$ is the normalized difference of weighted sums of the gray scale of pixels in $S_{L_i}^1$ and $S_{L_i}^2$,

$$e_I(L_i) = \frac{4}{\pi l^2} |\gamma_{S_{L_i}^1}(L_i) - \gamma_{S_{L_i}^2}(L_i)|, \tag{3}$$

where $\gamma_{S_i^t}(L_i)$ is a weighted sum of the gray scale of all pixels in area S_i^t ($t = 1, 2$), estimating the gray scale of the area represented by L_i. $g(p)$ is the gray scale of pixel

p, and $d(p, L_i)$ is its distance to L_i. Obviously, the more close p is to L_i, the better p is represented by line segment L_i,

$$\gamma_{S_i^t}(L_i) = \int_{p \epsilon S_i^t} g(p)(1 - \frac{4d^2(p, L_i)}{l^2})dp. \quad (4)$$

$c(L_i)$ is evaluation of continuity and smoothness of L_i. Calculating $c(L_i)$ involves the concepts of *Neighbor* and the *Nearest Neighbor* of L_i: considering any line segment L_j other than L_i ($i \neq j$), if L_j has an endpoint within a threshold distance d_0 ($d_0 \leq \frac{l}{2}$) to one end of L_i ($d < d_0$ as in Fig.2(a)), L_j is a *Neighbor* of L_i; and of all *Neighbors* of L_i, it has two *Nearest Neighbors* $L_i^{N_1}$ and $L_i^{N_2}$, each of which has an endpoint with the shortest distance to one end of L_i. If L_i has no *Neighbor* at one end (no endpoint has a distance smaller than d_0 to one end of L_i), $L_i^{N_t} = Nil$ ($t \in \{1, 2\}$).

In this model, $c(L_i)$ is the average value of $\alpha_{L_i}^t$ ($t = 1, 2$), which reflects the relationship between L_i and its *Nearest Neighbor* $L_i^{N_t}$.

$$c(L_i) = \frac{\alpha_{L_i}^1 + \alpha_{L_i}^2}{2\pi}, \quad (5)$$

when L_i has no neighbor at one end ($L_i^{N_t} = Nil$ ($t = 1, 2$)), $\alpha_{L_i}^t$ has a maximal value π, showing that this end of L_i is a breakpoint of the sketch. Otherwise, $\alpha_{L_i}^t$ estimates the orientation difference of L_i and $L_i^{N_t}$, and is obtained from Fig.2(b), resulting from a translation of $L_i^{N_t}$. In the translation, $L_i^{N_t}$ is moved to a place where an endpoint of L_i is connected to the endpoint of $L_i^{N_t}$ that has the nearest distance to the end of L_i. $\alpha_{L_i}^t$ is a supplementary angle of the angle between L_i and the new position of $L_i^{N_t}$ ($\alpha_{L_i}^t \in [0, \pi)$). Here, the larger $\alpha_{L_i}^t$ is, the less smooth τ is considered at around L_i.

2.2 Saliency Measure of an Active Sketch

An active sketch is aimed at adjusting the number and positions of the line segments in it to best represent the primary structure in an image. To achieve this goal, a global criterion is used to evaluate how well an image is represented by a sketch. Then, the task of finding a representative sketch is equivalent to maximizing the value of the criterion.

Usually, two things are concerned in evaluating a representation: relationship between the representation and the original data, and the attributes of the representation. Specifically, a sketch for an image is expected to fully represent information of the image data and to be meaningful in itself - the features and the configuration of line drawings in the sketch are supposed to be consistent with people's prior knowledge for them. We call the former external requirements on a sketch and the latter internal requirements. Both should be considered when an evaluation criterion is proposed.

Concerning external requirements in this model, an active sketch is expected to represent a sufficient amount edge information in an image, meanwhile, the edge information it represents is supposed to be the most salient part over the image. This requires a tradeoff between the total amount of edge strength represented by the sketch and average edge strength over the sketch, which means to increase the value $\sum_{L_i \in \tau} e_I(L_i)$

and $\sum_{L_i \in \tau} e_I(L_i)/(Nl)$ at the same time. On the other hand, with internal requirements concerned, a meaningful sketch calls for continuous and smooth line drawings in it, which means to minimize total $c(L_i)$ of all the line segments: $\sum_{L_i \in \tau} c(L_i)$.

Evaluation of a sketch should be consistent with the items listed above $\sum_{L_i \in \tau} e_I(L_i)$, $\sum_{L_i \in \tau} e_I(L_i)/(Nl)$ and $\sum_{L_i \in \tau} c(L_i)$. Increases of the first two items and reduction of the last item will result in a better representation. In this model, a global evaluation criterion is proposed by simply summing up logarithms of these items.

$$E_I[\tau] = ln \sum_{L_i \in \tau} e_I(L_i) - k_1 ln(Nl) - k_2 ln \sum_{L_i \in \tau} c(L_i) \qquad (0 < k_1 < 1, k_2 > 0) \quad (6)$$

An active sketch that makes the best representation have a maximal value for $E_I[\tau]$.

3 Saliency Measure Optimization

In this section, a sketch with the maximal value for its saliency measure is to be found on an image. Genetic algorithms (GAs) is one of the most widely used artificial intelligent techniques for optimization. A GA is a stochastic searching algorithm based on the mechanisms of natural selection and genetics, and it has been proved to be very efficient and stable in searching for global optimal solutions. Usually, a GA creates a population of solutions in the form of chromosomes and applies genetic operators to evolve the solutions in order to find the best one(s).

In this model, a genetic algorithm is employed to optimize the saliency measure $E_I[\tau]$ in (6), searching for the best subset of line segments in composing a sketch. Details of the genetic algorithm are described as follows:

(1) Chromosome encoding: Each chromosome represents a configuration of all the line segments on an image. In a chromosome, the parameters ($\{x_{L_i}, y_{L_i}, \theta_{L_i}\}$) of no more than 100 line segments are encoded into its gene bits, each parameter encoded with five bits $'0'/'1'$. In this way, the structure and position of a sketch can be recorded very precisely with a chromosome.

(2) Fitness function: $E_I[\tau]$ in (6) is used as the fitness function of the GA.

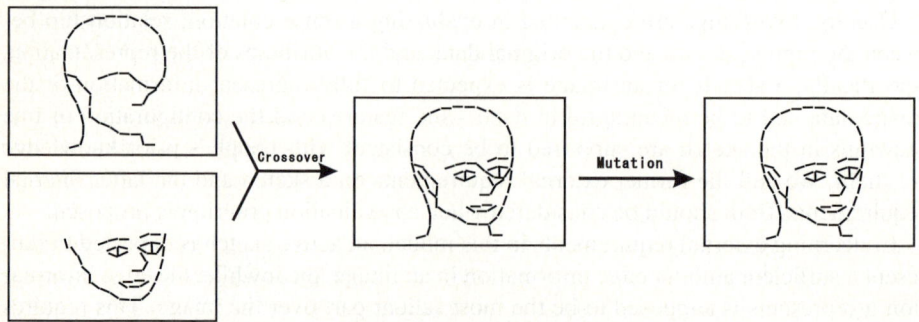

Fig. 3. Crossover and mutation of the chromosomes

(3) Genetic operations: As is shown in Fig.3, the crossover operation finds out a possible combination of two parent sketches, and generates a new sketch which is composed of parts from both of the parent sketches. The mutation operation makes random modifications to a parent sketch, adding, removing or replacing several line segments in it, or modifying positions of some line segments of the parent sketch. The gene pool is initialized with N_g chromosomes, each of which consists 100 line segments randomly scattered at the places with $e_I(L_i) > e_0$. Then, the evolution process is performed iteratively with parameters p_c and p_m. Roulette wheel selection is used as the selection rule in this algorithm. Parameters used here are provided in the next section.

4 Experimental Results and Discussions

In this part, experiments are designed to test the attributes and the effectiveness of active sketch of finding lines. In our tests, the length l of all line segments is 20, and the distance threshold d_0 which is used in the definition of *Neighbor* is 10. The parameters in the saliency measure $k_1 = 0.7$ and $k_2 = 0.2$. According to our former tests, the values always produce the best sketch results for natural images. The parameters used in the genetic algorithm for optimization goes as $p_c = 0.9$, $p_m = 0.1$, the population size $N_g = 50$, and e_0 is the standard deviation of the gray level of all pixels of an image. The optimization process is stopped after 100 generations of population where a satisfying solution can be achieved.

In our experiments, first, we test our approach on some real images by finding their primary structure which has a maximal value for the saliency measure $E_I[\tau]$. Results of our approach are compared with the results of a line fitting method [6].

These test images are all gray scale images, and they are normalized to be within the size of 160×160. Fig.4 shows our test results on them. Column 1 are the original gray scale image; column 2 are the results of the canny detector [10]; column 3 are results of the line fitting algorithm proposed by Nevatia and Babu [6], using Kovesi's software ("http://www.csse.uwa.edu.au/ pk/research/matlabfns/"). Column 4 are the results of our active sketch model. As can be seen from the resultant images, active sketch is good at generating continuous lines, but it does not require all lines to be connected in its results. Different from the line fitting methods of Nevatia and Babu, the output of active sketch consists only of the most salient lines of an image, rather than including all the edges that can be found. As a result, the model is capable of generating "clean" sketches for the test images, properly leaving out most of the noisy lines. Although a few meaningful lines are missed in the outputs, active sketch is successful in presenting most of the useful edge information with continuous and smooth lines.

Then, active sketch is applied to images (a), (b) and (c) in Fig.5 to illustrate its ability to extract the most salient edge information - the ability of sketching out lines covering a mild decrease of edge strength rather than a sharp decrease. Test images (a) and (b) have a great part with the same edge strength (the worm), however, this part is sketched out with lines in only one resultant image (d) (for (a)) but not in (e) (for (b)). These lines in image (d) are drawn out because they cover the strongest edge strength of image (a). But image (e) has no such lines found out as in (d) because other lines that can represent much stronger edge strength of image (b) have already been found.

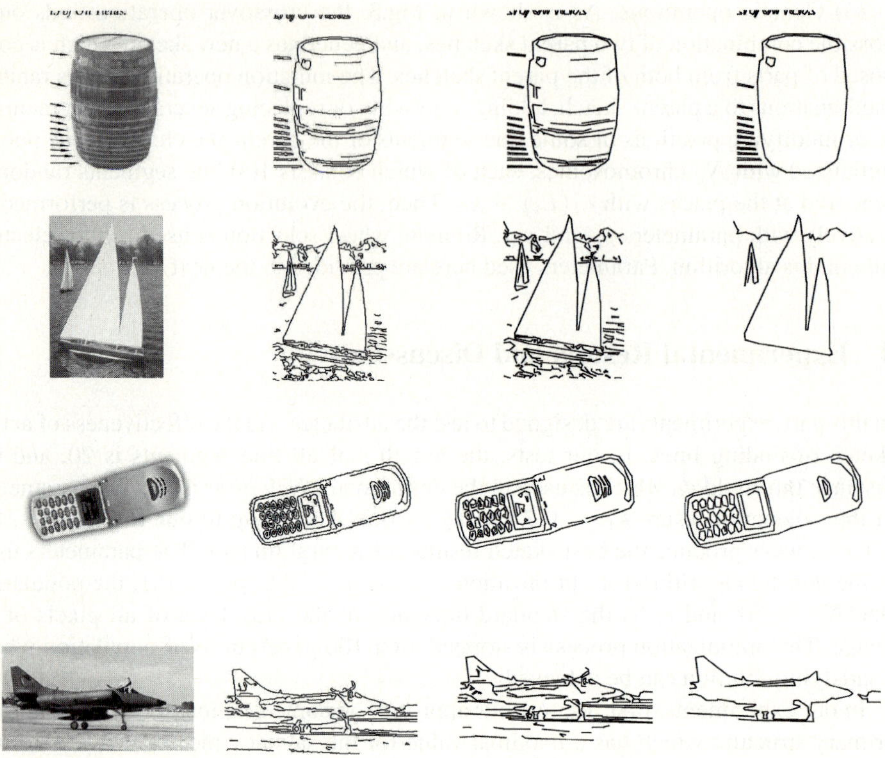

Fig. 4. Test results on several gray scale images

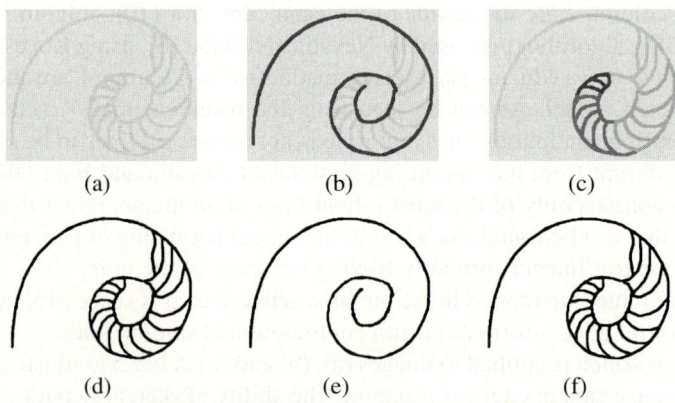

Fig. 5. Extraction of the most salient edges

Another comparison can be made on test images (b) and (c), which have the same strongest edge strength and the same faintest edge strength. But in their sketch generation results, lines that can represent the faintest edge strength in (c) are drawn out in its sketch (f), while the same edge strength in (b) fails to be sketched out in its sketch (e). The results are caused by the fact that edge strength over image (c) decreases mildly from strong to faint, while edge strength over image (b) decreases sharply, making a cascade of edge strength. Active sketch allows for a mild edge strength decrease rather than a sharp one under the supervision of the global criterion. This feature of active sketch is quite reasonable, because a severe reduction in edge strength usually denotes a transition from useful edge information to noises in an image. In test image (c) where there is no obvious division between useful edge information and noises, all lines that can be detected are drawn out.

5   Conclusions and Future Work

This paper has presented a novel active sketch model for finding primary structures in images with line drawings. The model achieves a balance between two traditional line detection approaches: the top-down schemes and the bottom-up schemes, locally finding lines under supervision of a global saliency measure, which take into consideration several intuitive expectations for a sketch, including the total amount of edge strength represented by the sketch, the average edge strength over it and continuity and smoothness features of the lines in it. Future work can be done on application of active sketch for higher level vision tasks such as object recognition and segmentation. Meanwhile, the saliency measure used in this model can be modified to incorporate prior knowledge of a sketch for sketch generation with specific objectives.

References

1. Bruce, V., Hanna, E., Dench, N., Healy, P., Burton, A.: The importance of 'mass' in line drawing of faces. Applied Cognitive Psychology **6** (1992) 619–628
2. Saund, E.: Finding perceptually closed paths in sketches and drawings. IEEE Trans. Pattern Anal. Machine Intell. **25** (2003) 475–491
3. Gao, Y., Leung, M.: Face recognition using line edge map. IEEE Trans. Pattern Anal. Machine Intell. **22** (1998) 764–779
4. Prinet, V., SongDe, M., Monga, O.: Scale selection for curvilinear structures detection from remote sensing images. (2000)
5. Iqbal, Q., Aggarwal, J.: Image retrieval via isotropic and anisotropic mappings. Pattern Recognition Journal **35** (2002) 2673–2686
6. Nevatia, R., Babu, K.: Linear feature extraction and description. Comput. Vis., Graph., Image Processing **33** (1980) 257–269
7. Duda, R., Hart, P.: Use of hough transform to detect lines and curves in pictures. Commun. ACM **15** (1972) 11–15
8. Mumford, D., Shah, J.: Boundary detection by minimizing functionals. In Proc. IEEE Conference on Computer Vision and Pattern Recognition (1985) 22–26
9. Kass, M., Witkin, A., Terzopoulos, D.: Snake: active contour models. INT J Computer Vision (1988) 321–331
10. Canny, J.: A computational approach to edge detection. IEEE Trans. Pattern Anal. Machine Intell. **8** (1986) 679–698

Shape Matching Using Chord-Length Function

Bin Wang[1,*] and Chaojian Shi[1,2]

[1] Department of Computer Science and Engineering, Fudan University,
Shanghai, 200433, P.R. China
[2] Merchant Marine College, Shanghai Maritime University,
Shanghai, 200135, P.R. China
wangbin.cs@fudan.edu.cn, cjshi@shmtu.edu.cn

Abstract. A novel shape descriptor, chord length function (CLF) which can be obtained by equal arc length partitions of a contour, is proposed. The difference of two shapes is measured by the distance between their corresponding CLF. The proposed CLF is invariant to rotation, scaling and translation. It is robust to noise and simple to compute. Experimental results indicate that CLF is an effective shape descriptor.

1 Introduction

Shape matching is one of the most important tasks in computer vision and pattern recognition. Shape description is key to shape matching. A good shape description scheme is expected to possess the following properties: (1) Invariance to rotation, scaling and translation. (2) Robustness to noise. (3) Simplicity in computation. (4) Reflecting both global and local shape characteristics.

A widely used shape description scheme is contour function [1]. The basic idea is to reduce a 2-D shape to a 1-D function, which is easier to handle than the original shape [2]. The primary consideration for the contour functions include the choice of the variable and the choice of the geometric quantity as the value for the function to take. Two candidate variables are in frequent use: one is the angle from a given direction (Fig. 1a), the other is the arc length from a given starting point (Fig. 1b). Most of the existing contour functions can be classified as function of angle or function of arc length.

Distance-versus-angle function (DAF)[1] and curvature function (CF) [3] are two widely used contour functions. On the choice of the variable, DAF chooses the angle from given direction as its variable. The potential drawback is that some contours cannot be described as 1-D functions through DAF because some angle may correspond to several different distance values (Fig. 2). Different from DAF, CF chooses the arc length from the starting point as variable, the main advantage is that CF always exists for any contour.

On the choice of the characterizing geometric quantity, DAF adopts the distance between the contour points and the contour's centroid as the function value. As the centroid is collectively determined by the whole contour, the distance from the contour points to the centroid reflects the contour shape in a

---

* Corresponding author.

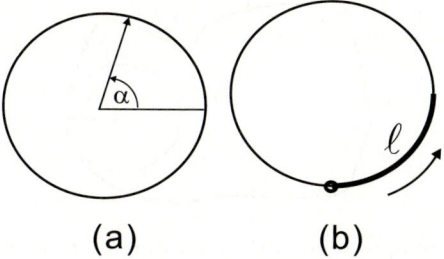

Fig. 1. Two candidate variables that can be chosen. (a) Angle from a given direction. (b) Arc length from a given starting point.

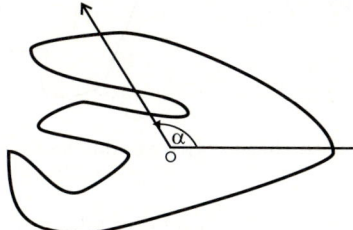

Fig. 2. Multiple intersections and distances

global manner. CF, on the other hand, uses the curvature on the contour points as the function value. Curvature describes the extent to which the contour bends. The curvature at a point on the contour can be obtained by computing the reciprocal of the radius of the osculating circle [4] (Fig. 3). As such, CF reflects the local property of the contour and its global characterizing ability is limited. Here, we give an example for illustrating this fact. Fig. 4 shows two shapes, their local features (wavy lines) are very similar, if we use curvature to characterize the contour, it will be very difficult to distinguish them. In contrast, if we use the distance to the contour to characterize the contour, we can distinguish them easily.

In this paper, we propose a novel contour function, chord length function (CLF), which is obtained through partitioning a contour into arcs of the same length. It combines the advantages of DAF and CF and overcomes their drawbacks. That is: (1) CLF exists for arbitrary contour. (2) CLF globally reflects the shape while the local features are also considered. (3) CLF is robust to noise and simple to compute. The experimental results show its promising performance.

2 Chord Length Function

A contour can be denoted as a sequence of N points $C = \{x_0, x_1, \ldots, x_{N-1}\}$, where the next point to x_{N-1} is x_0. Let $L = \sum_{i=0}^{N-1} d(x_i, x_{i+1})$ be its perimeter

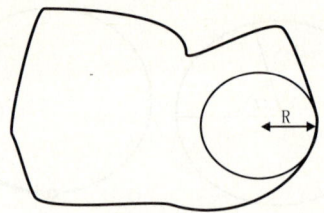

Fig. 3. The computation of the curvature on a point of a contour

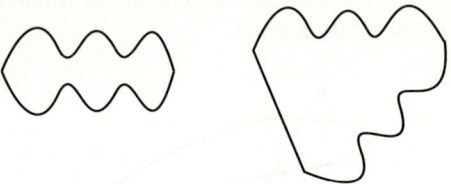

Fig. 4. Two shapes with similar local features

and $D = \max_{0 \leq i,j \leq N-1} d(x_i, x_j)$ be its diameter, where $d(.)$ denotes the Euclidean distance metric. Let us start from a point $x_i \in C$ and follow the contour anti-clockwise to divide it into k sections, $\widehat{x_i s_1}, \widehat{s_1 s_2}, \ldots, \widehat{s_{k-1} x_i}$, of equal arc length and obtain $k-1$ chords $\overline{x_i s_1}, \overline{x_i s_2}, \ldots, \overline{x_i s_{k-1}}$, where s_j is the jth division point and $k > 1$ is a pre-specified parameter. We now have $k-1$ chord lengths $L_1^{(i)}, L_2^{(i)}, \ldots, L_{k-1}^{(i)}$, where $L_j^{(i)}$ is the length of the chord $\overline{x_i s_j}$. Fig. 5 shows an equal arc length partition of a contour at point x_i into eight segments. As the point x_i moves along the contour, the chord length $L_j^{(i)}$ vary accordingly, where $j = 1, \ldots, k-1$. In other words, $L_j^{(i)}$ are function of x_i. Without loss of generality, we specify x_0 as the reference point. Then each point x_i can be uniquely identified with the length $l_i \in [0, L]$ of arc $\widehat{x_0 x_i}$. Therefore each chord length $L_j^{(i)}$ can be considered as a function of arc length l_i. Then we obtain a set of chord length functions $\Phi = \{L_1, L_2, \ldots, L_{k-1}\}$.

It can be seen that each function in Φ is invariant to rotation and translation. To make it invariant to scaling, we use the perimeter L and the diameter D to normalize respectively the arc length and chord length. Then each function in Φ will be linearly rescaled to a function from $[0, 1]$ to $[0, 1]$. Chord length function is also robust to noise. Fig. 6 gives an example to illustrate it. In Fig. 6, there are two shapes, one is a rectangle and the other is a noised rectangle. Their chord length functions with parameter $k = 2$ are compared. The result is shown in (c) of Fig. 6. From the comparison, we can see that there is little difference between them. So the chord length function is not sensitive to noise. Note that changing the location of the reference point x_0 by an amount $t \in [0, 1]$ along the perimeter of contour C corresponds to a horizontal shift of the function L_i and it is simple to compute the new function $L_i(l + t)$. From the definition of CLF, we can see that k is the only parameter of the proposed method. CLF with small parameter

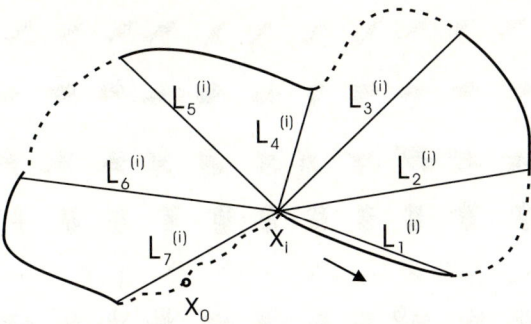

Fig. 5. An example of emanating seven chords from a contour point to partition the contour into eight equal-length arcs

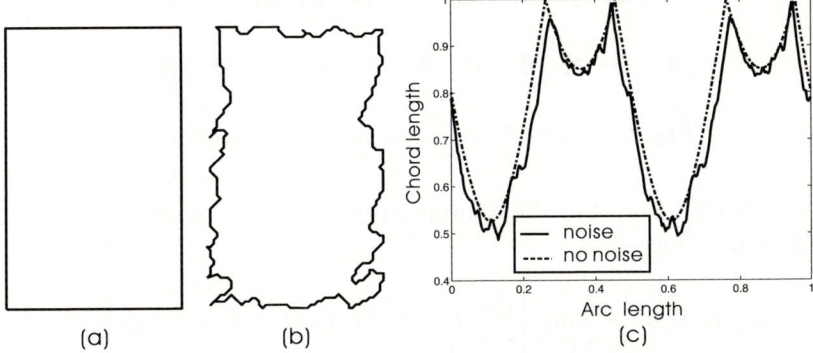

Fig. 6. An example for illustrating the chord length functions' robustness to noise. (a) rectangle. (b) noised rectangle. (c) Comparison of their chord length functions with parameter k=2.

k will be prone to characterize the shape's global feature, while CLF with large parameter k will reflect both global and local shape characteristics. Therefor, if we expect higher accuracy in shape distinction, k will be set lager.

3 Difference Measure

We have presented a CLF description $\Phi = \{L_1, L_2, \ldots, L_{k-1}\}$ for a contour. The comparison of two shapes can be performed using their associated CLFs, namely, the degree to which shape A and shape B are different can be measured by the distance between $\Phi_A = \{L_1^{(A)}, L_2^{(A)}, \ldots, L_{k-1}^{(A)}\}$ and $\Phi_B = \{L_1^{(B)}, L_2^{(B)}, \ldots, L_{k-1}^{(B)}\}$ using a metric for function spaces such as the L^P metrics. To remove the dependence of the description on the reference point, we shift the reference point along the contour of B by an appropriate amount $t \in [0, 1]$, then each function $L_i^{(B)}(s)$ in Φ_B will be changed into $L_i^{(B)}(s+t)$. We need to find the minimum

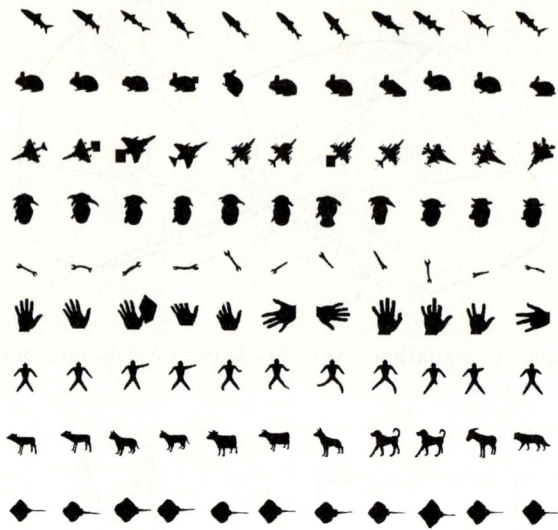

Fig. 7. Images of test shapes used in literature [5]

over all such shift t to find the appropriate one. So we define the L_1 distance between A and B as

$$diff(A,B) = \min_{t \in [0,1]} \left[\sum_{i=1}^{k} \int_0^1 | L_i^{(A)}(s) - L_i^{(B)}(s+t) | \, ds \right]. \tag{1}$$

4 Experimental Results and Discussions

The performance of the proposed CLF is tested on the benchmark shapes used in literature [5] as shown in Fig. 7. The benchmark shapes includes nine categories and eleven instances are included in each categories to allow for variations in form, as well as for occlusion, articulation, missing parts, etc., resulting in a total of 99 shape instances. The size of each image in Fig. 7 ranges from 120×91 pixels to 148×148 pixels.

We select two widely used contour functions, distance-versus-angle function (DAF) and curvature function (CF), for comparison. A task of shape retrieval is conducted using DAF, CF and the proposed CLF respectively, on the benchmark shapes. Common performance measures, precision and recall of the retrieval [6,7], are used as the evaluation of the query result. In this evaluation scheme, each shape in the benchmark is taken as a query to match all the other shapes. Top n matched shapes are returned and the number of similar shapes of the same class was counted in these returned shapes, where n equals 11 in our experiments. The precision p and recall r are calculated as

$$p = c/m, \quad r = c/n \tag{2}$$

where c is the number of the returned shapes which are in the same class as that of the query shape, m is the number of returned shapes and n is the number of the shapes which are in the same class (n=11 in this case). When 11 top matched shapes are returned, the precision is the same as the recall. Since there are 11 shapes in the same class, there is no need to report the precision for the number of the returned shapes being greater than 11. For $m = 1, 2, \ldots, 11$, the average precision and recall of all the queries are calculated and a precision-recall plot for each method are presented as shown in Fig. 8, where the parameter for the proposed method CLF is set to $k = 2, 4$ and 8 respectively. The horizontal axis in such a plot corresponds to the measured recall, while the vertical axis corresponds to precision. Since precision and recall values are computed from $m = 1$ to 11, where m is the number of the returned shapes, each curve contains exactly 11 points. The top-left point of a precision/recall curve corresponds to the precision/recall values for the best match, i.e, $m = 1$, while the bottom-right point corresponds to the precision/recall values on the case of $m = 11$.

A method is better than another if it achieves better precision and recall. From the Fig. 8, the proposed method CLF with parameter $k = 4$ and 8 achieves higher precision and recall than the methods DAF and CF. Therefore we can see that the proposed CLF with parameter $k = 4$ and 8 is better than DAF and CF. It is noted that the two precision/recall curves, which correspond to the method DAF and the proposed CLF with $k = 2$ respectively, intersect. This means that DAF perform better when the the number of returned shapes m is small ($m <= 9$), while the proposed CLF with $k = 2$ perform better when m is larger ($m > 9$). Since the method achieving higher precision and recall for the lager number of returned shapes is considered to be the better method [8], the proposed method CLF with parameter $k = 2$ is also better than the method DAF.

From the above experimental results, we can also see that, for the proposed CLF, the larger the parameter k is, the better the retrieval performance is. This is because with the parameter k increased, the more local information of the shape can be obtained, in other words, the more details of the shape can be characterized. So the shape will be described more accurately.

Invariance to rotation, scaling and translation is a basic requirement for a good shape descriptor. For examining the invariance of CLF, the following experiments are conducted.

For all the 99 shapes as shown in Fig. 7, we increase them in scale by 400%, scale them down by 50% and simultaneously scale them down by 50% and rotate them by 90^0. Through these geometric transformations, we obtain three new shape sets. Then each original shape in Fig. 7 is used as a query to match all the three new shape sets respectively. The resulting precision-recall plot are shown in Fig. 9. From it, we can see that, using the proposed CLF, the results of retrieving are nearly identical regardless of their scale and rotation. Therefore, the proposed CLF is an invariant shape description method.

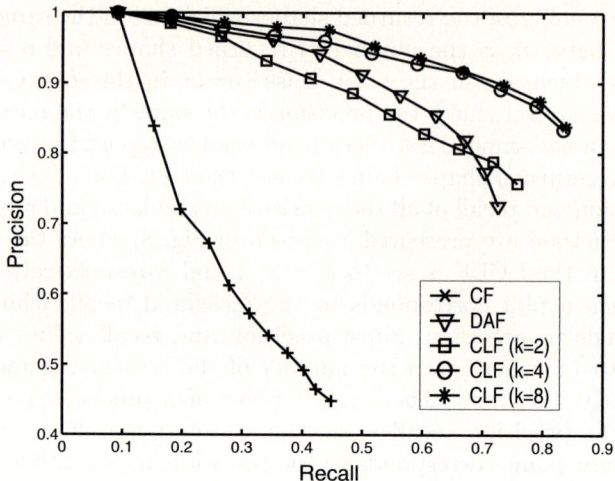

Fig. 8. The resulting precision-recall plot for distance-versus-angle function (DAF), curvature function (CF) and the proposed CLF with parameter $k = 2, 4$ and 8 respectively

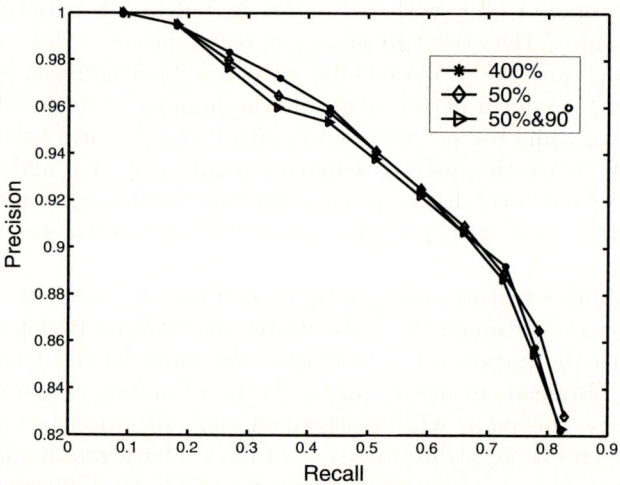

Fig. 9. The precision-recall plot for the three shape sets obtained by different geometric transformations of the images in Fig. 7

5   Conclusion

The proposed chord length function (CLF) is a simple and effective shape description method. It is obtained using the equal arc length partitions of a contour. The proposed CLF is invariant to rotation, scale and translation and robust to noise. It can capture both global feature and local feature of the contour and it is simple to compute. The experiment results show that it performs better than two widely used descriptors.

Acknowledgement

The research work in this paper is partially sponsored by Shanghai Leading Academic Discipline Project, T0603.

References

1. Voldymyr V. Kindratenko, "On Using Functions to Describe the Shape," *Journal of Mathematical Imaging and Vision*", 18, 225-245, (2003).
2. Rafael C. Gonzalez, Richard E. Woods, "Digital Image Processing," , 2, 648-649.
3. C.-L. Huang and D.-H Huang, "A Content-Based Image Retrieval System" *Image and Vision Computing*, 16, 149-163, (1998).
4. Francisco J. Sanchez-Marin, "The Curvature Function Evolved in Scale-Space as a Representation of Biological Shapes" *Comput. Biol. Med*, 27, 77-85, (1997).
5. Thomas Bernier, Jacques-Andre Landry, "A New Method for Representing and Matching Shapes of Natural Objects," *Pattern Recognition*, 36, 1711-1723, (2003).
6. A.D. Bimbo, "Visual Information Retrieval," *Morgan Kaufmann Publishers*, Inc., San Fancisco, USA, 56-57, (1999).
7. G.Salton, "The State of Retrieval System Evaluation," *Inform. Process. Manage*, 28 (4), 441-450, (1992).
8. G.Salton, "Matching and Retrieval of Distorted and Occluded Shapes Using Dynamic Programming," *IEEE Transactions on Pattern Analysis and Machinge Intelligence*, 24 (11), 1501-1516 (2002).

Spectral High Resolution Feature Selection for Retrieval of Combustion Temperature Profiles

Esteban García-Cuesta[1], Inés M. Galván[2], and Antonio J. de Castro[1]

[1] Physics Department
[2] Computer Science Department
Carlos III University -Avenida de la Universidad, 30 - 28911 Leganés (Madrid), Spain
egc@fis.uc3m.es, igalvan@inf.uc3m.es, decastro@fis.uc3m.es

Abstract. The use of high spectral resolution measurements to obtain a retrieval of certain physical properties related with the radiative transfer of energy leads a priori to a better accuracy. But this improvement in accuracy is not easy to achieve due to the great amount of data which makes difficult any treatment over it and it's redundancies. To solve this problem, a pick selection based on principal component analysis has been adopted in order to make the mandatory feature selection over the different channels. In this paper, the capability to retrieve the temperature profile in a combustion environment using neural networks jointly with this spectral high resolution feature selection method is studied.

1 Introduction

Progress in optoelectronic technologies during last decade has led to the fabrication of new sensors to measure the radiated energy focused on new measurement concept based on high spectral resolution measurements. High resolution measurements leads a priori to better accuracy in retrieval of physical properties in radiative transfer of energy (RTE) problems. However, as the number of data increases, it makes more difficult the use of conventional data regression techniques to retrieve the physical information involved in the problem. One problem is related with the amount of samples needed to cover this high dimensionality space, which is so-called the curse of dimensionality. Also, the high dimensionality increase the complexity of regression models used to retrieve the information and consequently the number of operations to solve it. This make impractical the use of these kind of techniques when the dimensionality is large and encourage the use of new techniques for this kind of inverse problems.

The industrial fuel fired furnace is a context where optoelectronic technologies have some advantages over conventional temperature monitoring devices such thermocouples. These advantages are mainly three: it is not intrusive, it does not disturb the measurement, and it can undergo the harsh furnace environment. In this context it is very important to have devices that monitor and control the combustion process in order to minimise pollutant emissions as well as to optimise energy losses. Flame temperature appears, among others, as a very important parameter to be monitored[1][2][3][4].

The retrieval of temperature profiles from high resolution measurements of radiative transfer of energy is related to ill-posed problems or under-constrained since we are trying to retrieve a continuous function from a finite measurements[5].

The use of artificial neural networks as inverse model for the RTE seem to be an alternative to retrieve the temperature profiles. One important advantage of neural networks is their speed. Once the neural network has been trained, the results of the inversion method are almost instantaneous compared to regression models. Some other advantages over classical physical-statistical techniques are the not need of good initial conditions for the inversion model and the independence of a rapid direct model for iterative inversion algorithms[6].

The purpose of this study is to show an approximation to retrieve the temperature profile of combustions processes composed by CO_2 and water vapor from optical spectroradiometric measurements. The use of artificial neural networks and the improvement obtained with an specific selection of spectra channels in this kind of problems will be tested based on the accuracy of the results obtained for the retrieval.

Two approaches are presented in this paper to validate the use of neural networks and the improvement obtained using statistical techniques to introduce a priori knowledge in the reducing dimensionality process. In a initial approach a multilayer perceptron neural network has been trained using all the data belonging to a spectrum which implies a huge number of input nodes including redundancies and possible noisy information. A priori, as more data is included better results would be expected, but in the other hand this high dimensionality could prevent an appropriate performance of MLP.

To prevent this disadvantages using high spectral resolution measurements a refined approach to reduce the dimensionality is proposed. There are different ways to make a reduction of the dimensionality: feature extraction(linear or not linear), transformation of data (principal components analysis projections) and feature selection[7]. Because of the importance of semantic interpretation, a feature selection is adopted instead of methods which find a mapping between the original feature space to lower dimensional feature space. Principal Components Analysis (PCA)[8][9], and typical methods as B2 and B4 to select a subset of original variables[10] has been tested without successful results. Here, a feature selection with a pick peak selector is proposed which tries to spread the selection according to a priori physical knowledge. Then a MLP is trained with the selected channels reducing the complexity of the network and improving it's performance.

The the paper is organised as follows: In Sect. 2 a context description of retrieval of temperature profiles in flames is made, describing the simulations carried out and the obtained results. This section includes also the use of PCA and peak selection to reduce the dimensionality of the input space for the MLP. Discussion and conclusions are presented in Sect. 3.

2 Temperature Retrieval Using Neural Networks

Neural networks techniques can be used as an approach to solving problems of fitting experimental data. In the context of approximation of nonlinear maps, the architecture most widely used is the MLP. It is relatively quite straightforward to use and it has been proven by different authors that they are universal approximators ([11], [12]), in the sense that any continuous function may be represented by a MLP with one hidden layer. Here the MLP is used as inverse model for the RTE.

In previous works, neural networks have been used to invert the RTE in atmospheric problems[13]. However, important differences can be pointed out in relation to the combustion problem involved in this work. Values and variation ranges for temperature and gas concentrations are different. Moreover, the optic path length is unknown from the point of view of transmitter-receptor.

In this context of industrial fuel fired furnace, given a high spectral spectrum energy measurement from a sensor (spectroradiometer) which are related to the Eq. (1), the goal is to recover the temperature profile inside a hot gas cloud. The dependence of the energy measured by the sensor and temperature and optical-path length of the hot gas is expressed by the RTE

$$R_\nu = (I_0)_\nu \tau_\nu(z_o) + \int_{z_0}^{\infty} B_\nu\{T_{(z)}\}\frac{d\tau_\nu(z)}{dz}dz \qquad (1)$$

where ν_i are the different channels of energy, $B_\nu\{T_{(z)}\}$ is the Planck function which indicates the radiance emitted by a blackbody at temperature T and τ_ν is the hot gas transmission at channel ν between the sensor and the depth z. The value of τ depends in a non-linear way of T and z; $\tau = -exp^{[KTz]}$, where K is a constant provided by HITRAN/HITEMP database[14].

The problem to obtain the temperature profile from such a spectrum is not straightforward. Energy emission at each channel depends in a non-linear way on parameters like the spatial distribution of temperature and the gas cloud width. Moreover each channel emission depends in a different way on these parameters.

In the next, the procedure to obtain the data sets to train MLPs is explained. After, the results of different experimental simulations are shown. In an initial approach, the whole spectrum variables are used as input to MLPs. The refined approach try to reduce the input dimensionality of the network using the pick peak selector to make a feature selection.

The performance of different approaches is measured, in one hand, in terms of mean square error over the training and test data sets and, in other hand, in terms of average temperature error per profile and for the hottest cell. The hottest cell is used as criterion because its retrieval is the most difficult due to the fact that energy emitted by this cell is absorbed by the others which behave as a mask.

2.1 Experimental Data Sets

The data set is composed of large number of synthetic emission spectra generated with a computer code developed at University Carlos III (CASIMIR)[15] based on the well known HITRAN/HITEMP[14] spectral database. The total number of cases simulated are 1040 covering many possible sceneries of a typical flame combustion. Data set generation has been performed under the following assumptions:

- Synthetic spectra will correspond to energy emission of hot gas cloud of width L. Temperature and gas concentrations present gradients inside the cloud.
- The spectral range selected for this data set is $2110 cm^{-1}$-$2410 cm^{-1}$. In this spectral range, the CO_2 emission band is by far the most important emission feature, being the water emission nearly negligible. Due to this fact, only the emission associated to the CO_2 will be considered.

- For retrieval scheme, we have used an spatial discretization with five cells of equal width (L/5). Each cell has an average value of temperature and gas concentration.
- The concentration profiles for carbon dioxide and water vapour will keep unchanged for the whole data set. Numerical values for these concentrations have been selected from typical combustion experiments.
- Four basic temperature profiles have been chosen to simulate different temperature gradient. The step between the temperature of two consecutive synthetics flames is $\Delta T = 50$ K, with a variation in the hottest cell between 540 K and 1140 K. And for each of these variations of temperature, a variation of cell's length is done. These variation have an step of $\Delta w = 0.02$ meters for each cell which means a total step variation $\Delta W = 0.1$ meters, covering a range between 0.1 and 2 meters. These profiles have been adjusted to a spatial discretization of five cells. All the value ranges for temperature and length have been chosen to be representative for hot gases clouds associated to fossil fuel combustion.
- Experimental noise of spectra has not been simulated in order to extract pure features associated with physical characteristics.

2.2   Initial Approach: Using the Whole Frequency Spectrum

In a first phase, the MLP has been designed with a number of inputs equal to the spectrum of energy dimensionality. Such that, each input neuron is associated with an energy channel value. In this case the experiments have been done with 4000 dimensions (high spectral resolution) which implies 4000 input neurons. As it has been explained in Sect. 2.1 the temperature profile to retrieve is discretized in five cells, so the output layer will have six neurons, one for each temperature cell and another one for the total length[1]. We must include the length because of both parameters, temperature and optical depth or total length, have influence in the composition of the spectrum in agreement to the Beer's law.

Different architectures of MLP varying the number of hidden neurons have been trained until to reach the minimum value in validation error, not allowing overfitting. In Table 1, the mean square error over the trained and test data for different architectures are shown. The table also included the mean error per profile, the mean error on the hottest cell and standard deviation.

In any of the architectures tested the results obtained have not been good. The MLP converges in any case without good results and there is not almost difference although the best results are with 30 hidden neurons. Also could be seen how the train error and the test error are quite different possibly due to the input dimension and the bad generalization due to the ratio number of samples and high dimensionality.

2.3   Refined Approach: Feature Selection for Dimension Reduction Based on PCA

In order to introduce a priori knowledge of the problem in the MLP learning process and improve the results, a reduction using feature selection approach has been assumed.

---

[1] We are assuming in the discretization that all the cells have the same length so we do not include one per each cell.

Table 1. Errors for the hot gas temperature retrieval using a MLP with 4000 inputs and different architectures

Hidden neurons	MSE Train	MSE Test	Mean error per profile (K)	Mean error hottest cell (K)	Standard Deviation
10	0.00418	0.02817	21.65	19.20	16.40
20	0.00178	0.03224	21.08	19.13	14.78
30	0.00099	0.02871	18.80	17.08	13.22
60	0.00989	0.03208	25.88	21.89	17.20

This reduction try to conserve all the information of any possible scenery in a few original variables stressing the importance of that wavelengths whose influence in the temperature and length profile are important. To make this selection PCA analysis has been applied. The central idea of PCA is to reduce the dimensionality of data set where there are a large number of interrelated variables, while retaining as much as possible of the variation present in the data set. This reduction is achieved by transforming to a new set of variables, the principal components, which are uncorrelated, and which are ordered so that the first few retain most of the variation present in all of the original variables[10]. The new base is composed of a set of axes which will be orthogonal between them and are calculated as a lineal combination of the old base.

Also a dimension reduction could be done using the projections of the original data over this new base, but during the experiments realized the results obtained have been always worst than with a feature selection method and consequently has been rejected. Let $C=\{e_1^M,\ldots,e_n^M\}$ be a data set of n spectrum of dimension M variables. Let Σ be the covariance matrix of the data set C with dimension M x M. Let V the M x M matrix with columns equal to eigenvectors of Σ and let L be the diagonal M x M matrix with the M associated eigenvalues (by definition $\Sigma \cdot V = V \cdot L$).

Table 2. Cumulated percentage of variance for spectrum data set generated

Number of PCA components	Cumulated variance
1	95.15
2	98.20
3	99.04
4	99.42
5	99.58
...	...
14	99.90

The selection of m specific channels from M variables where m ≪ M, allows to work with lower dimensionality. This m subset of variables contains virtually all the information available in M variables. The problem then is to find the value of m, and to decide the subset or subsets of m variables are the best. Here we want to find those variables which best represent the internal variation of C to find out which channels are significant (feature selection). In other cases the linear correlation between PCs and channels are used to interpret the physical meaning[16], or to get a first retrieval approximation[17]. To resolve the question about how many m variables we have to consider, we must check the number of PCs that account for most of the variation in a spectrum e_x of the data set C. This can also be interpreted as finding the effective dimensionality of e_x. If e_x can be successfully described by only m PCs, then it will often be true that M can be replaced by a subset m (or perhaps slightly more) variables, with a relative small loss of information[10].

The results of this analysis as cumulative percentage of variance are shown in Table 2. Between thirdteen and sixteen principal component, around the 99.9% of the total variation it is covered and the spectrum could be reconstruct almost without error. Furthermore we have visualized the projections of the data set for this first principal components trying to find clusters and we have found that with five PCs we can do a first approximation clustering (k-means) by temperature and total length. It means that the projections in these first five PCs have information about temperature and length scales.

The results obtained for the temperature retrieval with typical selection methods as B2(backward selection) and B4(forward selection) were not successful. Thus, to select a subset of variables from this first five PCs, a pick peak selector has been proposed trying to search for the most important groups coefficients of each eigenspectrum[2] in absolute value. This pick peak selector firstly look for all the possible peaks in each eigenspectrum. Then a threshold is established, and every peak greater than this threshold will be chosen. This will allow to catch not only the most relevant information of each eigenspectrum but the mainly second, third,... and carry on most important variables either.To limit the number of variables to select the threshold could be adapted to adjust it.

From a physical point of view each of these eigenspectrums does not contain only information about the temperature of one area of the gas, but also have information about the temperature and the spatial distribution over the different channels. Thus, the pick peak selector tries to get not only variables from one channel area but spread this selection over all the eigenspectrum guiding the selection.

The first 6 eigenspectrums can be seen in Fig. 1. Each one gives specific information about different channels. Because we are not trying to get the best reduction, a permissive threshold has been assumed to avoid taking out any relevant channel. Finally the number of channels selected have been 86 which are the inputs for the MLP. As in the previous approach, different number of hidden neurons has been tested with these input channels, and the results are shown in Table 3.

This refined approach improve quantitatively the results obtained using all the spectra channels. The mean temperature error retrieval is 3.36 K and 2.81 K in the hottest area for the best case. In the initial approach (see Table 1) the train error tends to decrease to 0 however the test error tends to level off which implies a bad performance in the MLP learning process. In this refined approach both errors tends to decrease together which means that the learning and generalization processes are working well and also the results obtained are better.

---

[2] Eigenspectrum is the eigenvector matrix which corresponds to the Σ matrix of the spectrum data set.

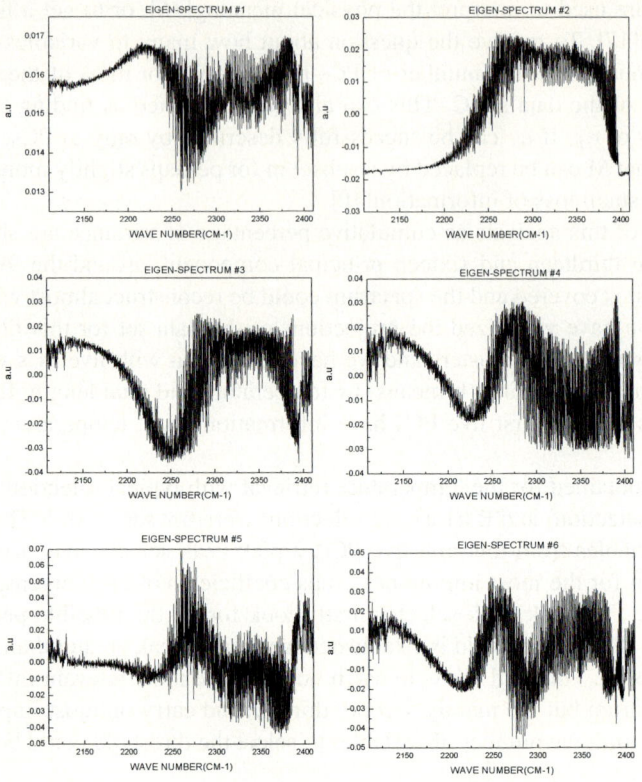

Fig. 1. First 6 eigenspectrums, infrared region ($2110 cm^{-1}$ - $2410 cm^{-1}$)

Table 3. Errors for the hot gas temperature retrieval using a MLP with 86 inputs and different architectures

Hidden neurons	MSE Train	MSE Test	Mean error per profile (K)	Mean error hottest cell (K)	Standard Deviation
10	0.00058	0.00067	6.82	5.10	4.60
20	0.00021	0.00033	3.94	2.95	3.56
30	0.00024	0.00029	3.36	2.81	2.90
40	0.00022	0.00040	3.72	3.14	3.18

3 Discussion and Conclusions

We have presented here an efficient approach to prevent the problems related with the use of high spectral resolution measurements jointly with neural networks for inversion of radiative transfer equation in combustion processes.

All the samples data set of typical combustions emission gases used in this paper has been generated with CASIMIR[15] at high spectral resolution ($0.05 cm^{-1}$). For this temperature sounding the range selected has been $2110 - 2410 cm^{-1}$ and the number of inputs with the resolution mentioned is 4000. This high number of inputs is a serious drawback to the use of neural networks in this framework.

The spectral feature selection has been supported by the statistical technique principal component analysis which has allowed a reduction of dimensionality of factor 46, choosing those channels specially important for temperature sounding profiles.

The results presented in Sect. 2.2 with 4000 input variables without any previous treatment over data are not acceptable. The same results are reproduced for different architectures of MLP without any sensible improvement. The best results obtained in this approach have been 18.80 K mean error over the whole profile and 17.08 K on the hottest cell with a standard deviation of 13.22 K. Reference values in literature show that a temperature measurement with an error of 0.5–1% is considered an accurate measurement in the range of 1200–2000 K. The DT025 sensor is a commercial "intrusive" thermocouple with a maximum error of 0.5%. This sensor is considered to be "extremely accurate".

The digital image system[3] also has relative errors no greater than 1% in the range 1280–1690 °C. If the results for this initial approach are compared with the intrusive methods we can conclude that they are not acceptable since the relative medium error of 2.2% is sensitive bigger than 1.0%. In this case the use of neural networks as inverse model with 4000 inputs is not useful.

With the refined approach the input dimensionality space is much smaller and the results obtained have improved significantly the previous ones. The best results have a relative error on the hottest cell of 0.34% which are in the same magnitude that the ones obtained with the intrusive methods mentioned above but with the advantages explained in the introduction, as it is not intrusive and can be applied in harsh environments.

From this physical point of view these results are acceptable, and we can conclude that neural networks techniques can be applied successfully as inverse model for this problems with a priori treatment of the data. This previous treatment reduce the dimensionality of the inputs conserving the important data and limits the grades of flexibility. As consequence the MLP convergence is faster and better as has been showed in this paper.

The use of high spectral feature selection jointly with neural networks can contribute in an efficient way to retrieve the temperature profiles with some advantages over classical physical-statistical techniques as speed and generalization.

Acknowledgments

This article has been financed by the Spanish founded research MEC project OPLINK:: UC3M, Ref: TIN2005-08818-C04-02.

References

1. Romero, C., Li, X., K.S., Rossow, R.: Spectrometer-based combustion monitoring for flame stoichiometry and temperature control. Appl. Therm. Eng. **25** (2005) 659–676
2. Thakur, M., Vyas, A., Shakher, C.: Measurement of temperature and temperature profile of an axisymmetric gaseous flames using lau phase interferometer with linear gratings. Opt. Laser Eng. **36** (2001) 373–380

3. Lu, G., Yan, Y., Colechin, M.: A digital imaging based multifuncional flame monitoring system. IEEE T. Instrum. Meas. **53** (2004) 1152–1158
4. Liu, L.H., Jiang, J.: Inverse radiation problem for reconstruction of temperature profile in axisymmetric free flames. J. Quant. Spectrosc. Radit. Transfer **70** (2001) 207–215
5. McCornick, N.J.: Inverse radiative transfer problems: a review. Nuclear Science and Engineering **112** (1992) 185–198
6. Eyre, J.R.: Inversion methods for satellite sounding data. Lecture Notes NWP Course. European Centre for Medium-Range Weather Forecasts (ECMWF) (2004)
7. Bishop, C.M.: Neural Networks for Pattern Recognition. Oxford University Press (1999)
8. Pearson, K.: On lines and planes of closet fit to systems of points in space. Phil. Mag. **2** (1901) 559–572
9. Hotelling, H.: Analysis of a complex of statistical variables into principal components. Educ. Physhol. **24** (1933) 417–441. 498–520
10. Jollife, I.T.: Principal Component Analysis (2nd Ed.). Springer Series in Statistics Springer-Verlag, New York (2002)
11. Cybenko, G.: Approximation by superposition of a sigmoidal function. Mathematics of Control, Signals, and Systems **2** (1989) 303–314
12. Hornik, K., Stinchcombe, M., White, H.: Multilayer feedforward networks are universal approximators. Neural Networks **2** (1989) 359–366
13. Aires, F., Chédin, A., Scott, N.A., Rossow, W.B.: A regularized neural net approach for retrieval of atmospheric and surface temperatures with the iasi instrument. Journal of Applied Meteorology **41** (2001) 144–159
14. Rothman, L.S.: The hitran molecular spectroscopic database: edition of 2000 including updates through 2001. J. Quant. Spectrosc. Radiat. Transfer (2003)
15. García-Cuesta, E.: CASIMIR: Cálculos Atmosféricos y Simulación de la Transmitancia en el Infrarrojo. University Carlos III L/PFC 01781, Madrid (in Spanish) (2003)
16. Huang, H.L., Antonelli, P.: Application of principal component analysis to high-resolution infrared measurement compression an retrieval. J. Clim. Appl. Meteorol. **40** (2001) 365–388
17. Aires, F.: Remote sensing from the infrared atmospheric sounding interferometer instrument. J. Geophys. Res. **107** (2002) ACH6–1–15

Sentence Ordering in Extractive MDS

Zengchang Zhang[1] and Dexi Liu[1,2]

[1] School of Physics, Xiangfan University, Xiangfan 441053, P.R. China
[2] School of Computer, Wuhan University, Wuhan 430079, P.R. China
dexiliu@gmail.com

Abstract. Ordering information is a critical task for multi-document summarization(MDS) because it heavily influent the coherence of the generated summary. In this paper, we propose a hybrid model for sentence ordering in extractive multi-document summarization that combines four relations between sentences - chronological relation, positional relation, topical relation and dependent relation. This model regards sentence as vertex and combined relation as edge of a directed graph on which the approximately optimal ordering can be generated with PageRank analysis. Evaluation of our hybrid model shows a significant improvement of the ordering over strategies losing some relations and the results also indicate that this hybrid model is robust for articles with different genre.

1 Introduction

Automatic text summarization [1] that provides users with a condensed version of the original text, tries to release our reading burden, and most summarization today still relies on extraction of sentences from the original document [2]. In extractive summarization, a proper arrangement of these extracted sentences must be found if we want to generate a logical, coherent and readable summary. This issue is special in multi-document summarization. Sentence position in the original document, which yields a good clue to sentence arrangement for single-document summarization, is not enough for multi-document summarization because we must consider inter-document ordering at the same time [3].

Barzilay et al. [4] showed the impact of sentence ordering on readability of a summary and explored some strategies for sentence ordering in the context of multi-document summarization. Lapata [5] proposed another method to sentence ordering based on an unsupervised probabilistic model for text structuring that learns ordering constraints from a large corpus. However, the limitation of above-mentioned strategies is still obvious. Barzilay's strategy paid attention to chronological and topical relation whereas ignored sentence original ordering in the articles where summary comes from. Hence, if the articles are not event-based, the quality of summary will decrease because the temporal cue is invalid. As for Lapata's strategy, the probabilistic model of text structure is trained on a large corpus, so it performs badly when genre of the corpus and the article collection are mismatched.

To overcome the limitation mentioned above, we propose a hybrid model for sentence ordering in extractive multi-document summarization that combines four relations between sentences - chronological relation, positional relation, topical relation and dependent relation. Our model regards sentence as vertex and combined relation as edge of a directed graph on which the approximately optimal ordering can be generated with PageRank analysis. Evaluation of our hybrid model shows a significant improvement of the ordering over strategies losing some relations and the results also indicate that this hybrid model is robust for articles with different genre.

2 Four Relations

Positional Relation. Most of the sentence ordering strategies in extractive single-document summarization arrange sentences according to their original positions in the article. So we employ positional relation to match the original ordering arranged by author. Suppose si and sj are two sentences in article collection, quantitatively positional relations between si and sj are defined as follow:

$$P_{i,j} = \begin{cases} 1, \text{ if } s_i, s_j \text{ are extrated from the same article and } s_i \text{ precedes } s_j \\ 0, \text{ else} \end{cases}. \quad (1)$$

Topical Relation. Investigations into the interpretation of narrative discourse have shown that specific lexical information (e.g., verbs) plays an important role in determining the discourse relations between propositions [6]. Centering Theory (CT)[7] is an entity-based theory of local coherence, which claims that certain entities mentioned in an utterance are more central than others and that this property constrains a speaker's use of certain referring expressions (in our model, noun is considered as entity). Accordingly, stemmed verbs and nouns are selected while calculating the sentence topical relation and other words are ignored. Topical relation can be operationalized in terms of word overlap:

$$T_{i,j} = \frac{2|words(s_i) \cap words(s_j)|}{|words(s_i)| + |words(s_j)|}. \quad (2)$$

Where $words(s_i)$ is the set of nouns and stemmed verbs in sentence s_i, $|words(s_i)|$ is the number of words in $words(s_i)$.

Dependent Relation. Following the same methodology used by Lapata [5], we use $P(s_i|s_{i-1})$ to describe the dependent relation of sentence s_i on its antecedent s_{i-1}. Of course estimating would be impossible if s_i and s_{i-1} are actual sentences because it is unlikely to find the exact same sentence repeated several times in a corpus. What we can find and count is the number of occurrences a given word appears in the corpus. We will therefore estimate - from features that express its content.

$$P(s_i|s_{i-1}) = P(\langle a_{i,1}, a_{i,2}, ..., a_{i,n}\rangle | \langle a_{i-1,1}, a_{i-1,2}, ..., a_{i-1,m}\rangle). \quad (3)$$

Where $\langle a_{i,1}, a_{i,2}, ..., a_{i,n}\rangle$ are features of sentence s_i and $\langle a_{i-1,1}, a_{i-1,2}, ..., a_{i-1,m}\rangle$ are of sentence s_{i-1}.

In our model, noun and stemmed verb are employed as the features of a sentence. We assume that these features are independent and that $P(s_i|s_{i-1})$ can be estimated from the pairs in the Cartesian product defined over the features expressing sentences s_i and s_{i-1}: $\langle a_{i,r}, a_{i-1,k} \rangle \in s_i \times s_{i-1}$. Under these assumptions $P(s_i|s_{i-1})$ can be written as :

$$P(s_i|s_{i-1}) = P(a_{i,1}|a_{i-1,1})P(a_{i,1}|a_{i-1,2})...P(a_{i,r}|a_{i-1,k})...P(a_{i,n}|a_{i-1,m})$$
$$= \prod_{(a_{i,r}, a_{i-1,k}) \in s_i \times s_{i-1}} P(a_{i,r}|a_{i-1,k}) \tag{4}$$

The probability $P(a_{i,r}|a_{i-1,k})$ is estimated as:

$$P(a_{i,r}|a_{i-1,k}) = \frac{f(a_{i,r}, a_{i-1,k})}{\sum_{a_{i,r}} f(a_{i,r}, a_{i-1,k})}. \tag{5}$$

where $f(a_{i,r}, a_{i-1,k})$ is the number of occurrences feature $a_{i,r}$ is preceded by feature $a_{i-1,k}$ in the corpus. The denominator expresses the number of occurrences $a_{i-1,k}$ is attested in the corpus (preceded by any feature).

Instead of a large corpus, the article collection is used as training data because we try to make full use of text structure of the original articles. Furthermore, mismatch between the article collection and training corpus is resolved. In additional, we do not smooth the probability because all sentences in summary are extracted from the corpus (the article collection), and consequently, it is impossible that the occurrence of $a_{i-1,k}$ is equal to zero.

Then, we define the dependent relation between two sentences. For two sentence s_i and s_j, suppose s_i is immediately preceded by s_j, the dependent relation of s_i on s_j is defined according to formula (6).

$$D_{i,j} = P(s_i|s_j) = \prod_{(a_{i,r}, a_{j,k}) \in s_i \times s_j} P(a_{i,r}|a_{j,k}). \tag{6}$$

Chronological Relation. Multi-document summarization of news typically deals with articles published on different dates, and articles themselves cover events occurring over a wide range of time. Using chronological relation in the summary to describe the main events helps the user understand what has happened. In our model, we approximate the sentence time by its first publication date. It is an acceptable approximation for news events because the first publication date of an event usually corresponds to its occurrence in real life [4].

Suppose sentence s_i and s_j come from the xth and the yth article individually. The chronological relation between sentence s_i and s_j is defined as:

$$C_{i,j} = \begin{cases} 1 & \text{, if the } x^{th} \text{ article has earlier publication date than the } y^{th} \\ 0 & \text{, else} \end{cases}. \tag{7}$$

3 Hybrid Model

For the group of sentences extracted from the article collection, we construct a directed graph (we call it Precedence Graph). Let $G = (V, E)$ be a directed graph with the set of vertices V and set of directed edges E, where E is a subset of $V \times V$. For a given vertex V_i, let $In(V_i)$ be the set of vertices that point to it (predecessors), and let $Out(V_i)$ be the set of vertices that vertex V_i points. In our hybrid model, the Precedence Graph is constructed by adding a vertex for each sentence in the summary, and edges between vertices are established using sentence relations. Three of the predefined quantitative relations are integrated to precedent relation using linear model as follows.

$$R_{i,j} = \lambda_P P_{i,j} + \lambda_D D_{i,j} + \lambda_C C_{i,j}. \tag{8}$$

where λ_P, λ_D, λ_C are the weight of positional relation, dependent relation and chronological relation individually. If $R_{i,j}>0$, there exist a directed edge with value $R_{i,j}$ from V_i to V_j (see figure 1). In our case, we set λ_P=0.3, λ_D=0.4, λ_C=0.3 manually. By the way, figure 1 does not contain topical relation because it will be used only after the first vertex has been selected.

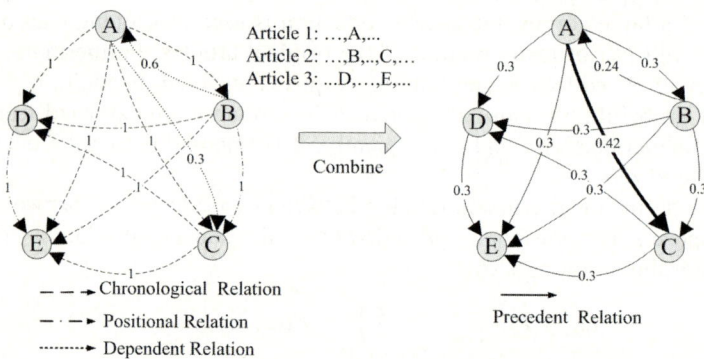

Fig. 1. An example for the hybrid model

Unfortunately, the next critical task of finding an optimal road according to the Precedence Graph is a NP-complete problem. However, using a modified version of topological sort provides us with an approximate solution. For each node, Barzilay et al. [4] assign a weight equal to the sum of the weights of its outgoing edges minus the sum of the weights of its incoming edges. In his method, the node with maximum weight first picked up and arranged as the first sentence in summary. Then the node just selected and its outgoing edges are deleted from the Precedence Graph, and the weights of the remaining nodes in the graph are updated properly. This operator iterates through all nodes until the graph is empty. However, the method only considering the local relationship between two sentences is not precise enough. For example in figure 2, vertex "A" precedes vertex "B" and should be arranged before "B", but we get an ordering "B, A" according to Barzilay's method.

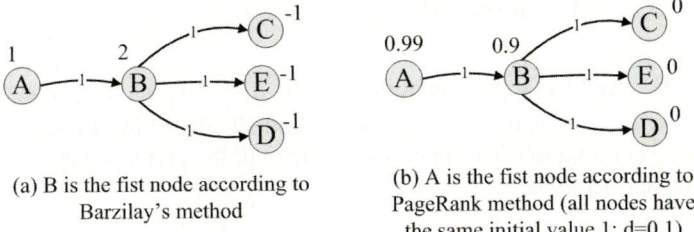

(a) B is the fist node according to Barzilay's method

(b) A is the fist node according to PageRank method (all nodes have the same initial value 1; d=0.1)

Fig. 2. An example for PageRank method and Barzilay's method

Our model employs PageRank method [8], which is perhaps one of the most popular ranking algorithms, and was designed as a method for Web link analysis. PageRank method is a graph-based ranking algorithm to decide the importance of a vertex within a graph, by taking into account global information recursively computed from the entire graph, rather than relying only on local vertex-specific information. The basic idea implemented by the ranking model is that of "voting" or "recommendation". When one vertex links to another one, it is basically casting a vote for that other vertex. The higher the number of votes that are cast for a vertex, the higher the importance of the vertex. Score of vertex V_i is defined as:

$$S(V_i) = (1-d) + d * \sum_{V_j \in In(V_i)} \frac{S(V_j)}{|Out(V_j)|} . \quad (9)$$

where d is a parameter set between 0 and 1 (we let d=0.1 in our experiments).

In the context of Web link analysis, it is unusual for a vertex to include partial links to another vertex, and hence the original definition for graph-based ranking algorithms is assuming unweighted graphs. However, the Precedence Graph in our model includes partial links between the vertices. For example in figure 1, the precedent relation (or link) between two vertices has "weight" in [0, 1]. In formula (9), where vertex with higher "in degree" has higher score, but it is contrary in our model that vertex with higher "out degree" should has higher score. The ranking model therefore is amended as:

$$S(V_i) = (1-d) + d * \sum_{V_j \in Out(V_i)} R_{i,j} \frac{S(V_j)}{\sum_{V_k \in In(V_j)} R_{k,j}} . \quad (10)$$

While the final vertex scores (and therefore rankings) for weighted graphs differ significantly with their unweighted alternatives, the number of iterations to convergence and the shape of the convergence curves is almost identical for weighted and unweighted graphs.

The next step following PageRank algorithm is the selection of vertex. We first select the vertex with highest score as the first sentence in summary. For the following vertices, not only the score itself but also the topical relation with immediately previous vertex should be taken into consideration. So the succeed vertex of V_k should satisfy:

$$V_i = \arg\max_{V_{\hat{i}}}((1-\lambda_T)S(V_{\hat{i}}) + \lambda_T T_{k,\hat{i}}). \tag{11}$$

where λ_T is the weight of topical relation (we let λ_T =0.4 in our experiments). When the succeed vertex of V_k is picked up, vertex V_k and all edges linked with it are deleted from the Precedence Graph. This operator iterate until the graph is empty, and then an ordered summary is produced.

4 Experiments

We collected three groups of summaries generated by three different participants of task 2 in DUC2004 [9]. Three selected groups have high (id=65), fair (id=138), and low (id=111) ROUGE score [10] individually so that we can observe the degree of influence that our model affects on summarizer with different performance. For each group, we randomly selected 10 from 50 summaries produced by one participant. Five postgraduates were employed and everyone built one ordering manually for each summary. To test the adaptive performance of our hybrid model, we also randomly selected the fourth group of testing data from DUC2005, which has different genre with DUC2004.

We use Kendall's strategy [11], which based on the number of inversions in the rankings, to measure the distance between two ranking.

$$\tau = 1 - \frac{2\times \mathrm{Inv}(O_i, O_j)}{N(N-1)/2} \tag{4}$$

where N is the number of sentences being ranked and $\mathrm{Inv}(O_i, O_j)$ is the number of interchanges of consecutive elements necessary to arrange them in their natural ordering (manual ordering in this case). If we think in terms of permutations, then τ can be interpreted as the minimum number of adjacent transpositions needed to bring one ordering to the other. We use the minimal one from 5 distance values corresponding to the 5 "ideal" orderings produced manually. Figure 2 shows the evaluation results.

As Figure 3 indicates, our hybrid ordering (HO) model yields more satisfactory result (as a whole) than any other model taking part in the comparison, including the strategy employed by the summarizer that produces the original ordering (OO). Although partially hybrid strategies such as HO-C (hybrid ordering model without chronological relation), HO-P (hybrid ordering model without positional relation), HO-T (hybrid ordering model without topical relation, and HO-D (hybrid ordering model without dependent relation) are all worse than HO, we found that different relation has significantly different influence on the ordering strategy performance. In context of DUC2004 dataset (group 1, 2, 3), HO-C performs worst and HO-T is slightly better than HO-C, whereas there aren't significant difference between HO-P, HO-D, and HO. In other word, the ordering strategy depend more on chronology and topical relation than on positional and dependent relation for DUC2004 dataset. After investigating the failure ordering of HO-C, we found that most of the articles have been used for task 2 in DUC2004 are event-based, so chronological cue is very important for ordering. Moreover, for the limitation of summary length, number of

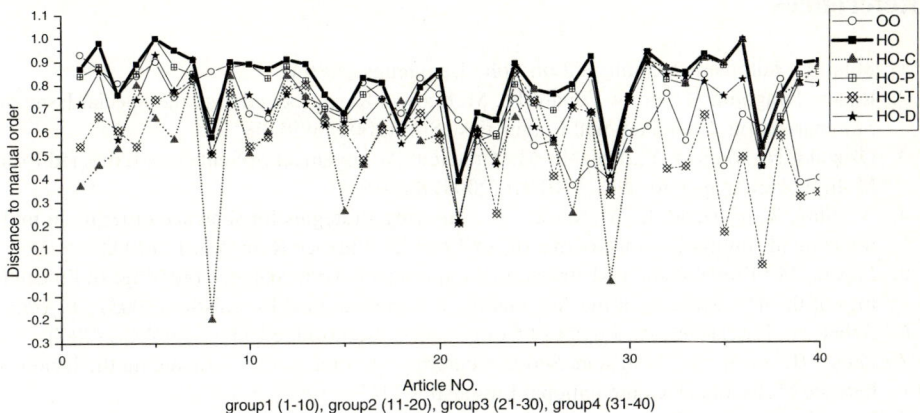

Fig. 3. Results and comparison of different models

sentences in most summaries is less than 10 – the number of articles from which summary extracted, so the probability of two sentences coming from the same article is very low. Hence the importance of positional relation is not distinct.

On the contrary, HO-T and HO-P perform much worse than HO on DUC2005 dataset (group 4) while HO-D and HO-C perform closely to HO. Reason for this change is that most articles for DUC2005 are biography, where chronological cue is not so important for ordering. Although different relation plays different role in ordering summary with different genre, our hybrid model combining these relations together has robust performance. Figure 3 indicates clearly that the results of HO have no distinct change when article genre change from event-based to biography-based. Furthermore, after reordering, the improvement for "poor" summaries (group 3) is better than for "good" summaries (group 1) because the summaries generated by a good summarizer are more readable than by bad one.

5 Conclusions

In this paper, we propose a hybrid model for sentence ordering in extractive multi-document summarization. We combine the four relations between sentences using a linear model and we call it precedent relation. To find a proper ordering for the group of sentences extracted from an article collection, our hybrid model regards sentence as vertex and precedent relation as edge of a directed graph, and employs PageRank analysis method to generate an approximately optimal ordering. We evaluate the automatically generated orderings against manual orderings on the testing dataset extended from DUC2004 and DUC2005. Experiment results show that the hybrid model has a significant improvement compared with other partially hybrid model. Moreover, experiment results on DUC2004 dataset and DUC2005 dataset indicates that our hybrid model is robust for articles with different genre.

References

1. Mani, I.: Automatic Summarization. John Benjamins (2001)
2. Radev, Dragomir R., Hovy, Eduard H., McKeown, K.: Introduction to the Special Issue on Summarization. Computational Linguistics 28(4) (2002) 399-408
3. Okazaki, N., Matsuo, Y., Ishizuka M.: Coherent Arrangement of Sentences Extracted from Multiple Newspaper Articles. PRICAI (2004) 882-891
4. Barzilay, R., Elhadad, E., McKeown, K.: Inferring strategies for sentence ordering in multidocument summarization. Journal of Artificial Intelligence Research, 17 (2002) 35–55
5. Lapata, M.: Probabilistic text structuring: experiments with sentence ordering. In Proceedings of the 41st Meeting of the Association of Computational Linguistics (2003) 545–552
6. Asher, N., Lascarides, A.: Logics of Conversation. Cambridge University Press (2003)
7. Grosz, B., Joshi, A., Weinstein, Scott.: Centering: A framework for modeling the local coherence of discourse. Computational Linguistics 21(2) (1995) 203–225
8. Brin, S., Page, L.: The anatomy of a large-scale hypertextual Web search engine. Computer Networks and ISDN Systems, 30 (1998) 1–7
9. Paul, O., James, Y.: An Introduction to DUC-2004. In Proceedings of the 4th Document Understanding Conference (DUC 2004). (2004)
10. Lin, C.Y., Hovy, E.: Automatic Evaluation of Summaries Using N-gram Co-Occurrence Statistics. In Proceedings of the Human Technology Conference (HLTNAACL-2003), Edmonton, Canada (2003)
11. Lebanon, G., Lafferty, J.: Combining rankings using conditional probability models on permutations. In Proceedings of the 19th International Conference on Machine Learning. Morgan Kaufmann Publishers, San Francisco, CA. (2002) 363-370

Query Expansion with an Automatically Generated Thesaurus*

José R. Pérez-Agüera and Lourdes Araujo

Departamento de Sistemas Informáticos y Programación.
Universidad Complutense de Madrid. Spain
jose.aguera@fdi.ucm.es, lurdes@sip.ucm.es

Abstract. This paper describes a new method to automatically obtain a new thesaurus which exploits previously collected information. Our method relies on different resources, such as a text collection, a set of source thesauri and other linguistic resources. We have applied different techniques in the different phases of the process. By applying indexing techniques, the text collection provides the set of *initial terms* of interest for the new thesaurus. Then, these terms are searched in the source thesauri, providing the initial structure of the new thesaurus. Finally, the new thesaurus is enriched by searching for new relationships among its terms. These relationships are first detected using similarity measures and then are characterized with a type (equivalence, hierarchy or associativity) by using different linguistic resources. We have based the system evaluation on the results obtained with and without the thesaurus in an information retrieval task proposed by the Cross-Language Evaluation Forum (CLEF). The results of these experiments have revealed a clear improvement of the performance.

1 Introduction

A thesaurus is a structured list of terms, usually related to a particular domain of knowledge. Thesauri are used to standardize terminology and to provide alternative and preferred terms for any application. They are specially useful in indexing and retrieving information processes, by providing the different forms which a concept can adopt.

The three basic relationships between thesaurus terms are equivalence, hierarchy and associativity. Terms related by the equivalence relationship have an equivalent meaning, in different senses (they are synonyms, one is the translation to the other, its archaic form, etc). In a set of equivalent terms, one of them, distinguished as the *preferred* one, is the one used in the hierarchies and for indexing. Preferred terms are arranged into hierarchies with different numbers of levels. These levels go from the broadest type of term to the narrowest and most specific one. Finally, there can be associative relationships between terms which are not connected by a hierarchy, for example because they are narrower terms of different broad terms, but they still present some kind of relationship.

---

* Supported by project TIC2003-09481-C04.

In spite of the great interest thesaurus have reached nowadays for web applications, most of them are manually generated, what is very expensive and limits its availability to some particular topics. Furthermore, a thesaurus usually requires to be periodically updated to include new terminology, in particular in modern terms, such as those related to computer science. These reasons make the automatic generation of thesauri an interesting area of research which is attracting a lot of interest. Research on automatic thesaurus generation for information retrieval began with Sparck Jones's works on automatic term classification [5], G. Salton's work on automatic thesaurus construction and query expansion [9], and Van Rijsbergen's work on term co-occurrence [10]. In the nineties Qui and Frei [7] [6] [8] worked on a term-vs-term similarity matrix based on how the terms of the collection are indexed. Recently, Zazo, Berrocal, Figuerola and Rodríguez [1] have developed a work using similarity thesauri for Spanish documents. Jing and Croft [4] have carried out an approach to automatically construct collection-dependent association thesauri using large full-text documents collections. Those approaches obtain promising results when applied to improve information retrieval processes.

This paper proposes to apply a combination of techniques to automatically obtain a new thesaurus for a particular knowledge domain. The method relies on different resources from which we extract selected information, thus taking advantage of the information previously gathered and processed, what improve both the accuracy and the efficiency. The domain of knowledge to which the new thesaurus is devoted, is characterized by a set of terms extracted from a document collection about the intended topic. This is done by applying indexing techniques. Then we use the information previously collected in other thesauri about these terms to construct the initial structure of the new one. Finally, the new thesaurus is enriched by searching for new relationships among its terms. These relationships are first detected using co-occurrence measures and then its type (equivalence, hierarchy or associativity) is characterized by using different linguistic resources, such as a dictionary and a POS tagger. Apart from the specific methods that we have applied, our proposal differs from previous works in that the relationship type (equivalence, hierarchy or associativity) of the generated thesaurus is identified. The system has been evaluated by comparing the results obtained in an information retrieval task, for which the expected results are perfectly defined, when a set of query terms are directly consulted, and when they are previously expanded with the generated thesaurus.

The rest of the paper proceeds as follows: section 2 describes the general scheme of the system, presenting their different phases and tools; sections 3 describes the enrichment of the relationships between the thesaurus terms and the identification of its type; section 4 presents and discusses the experimental results, and section 5 summarizes the main conclusions of this work.

2 System Overview

We combine different techniques to obtain a new thesaurus for a particular domain of knowledge. Figure 1 shows a scheme of the process. First of all, we

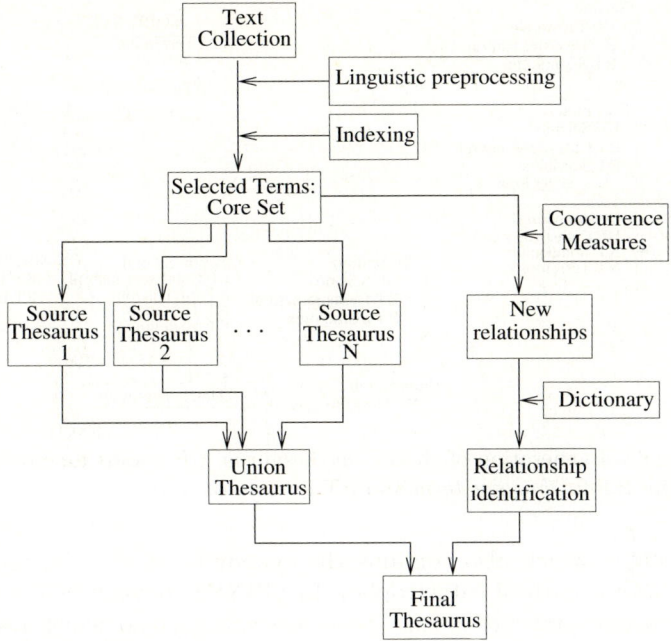

Fig. 1. Process to generate a new thesaurus

perform a selection of terms, called the *core set*, from a text collection concerning the intended thesaurus domain. In this phase we apply linguistic pre-processing which consists of a POS tagging which allows selecting only those words of noun category, stemming, and elimination of stopwords. We apply TF-IDF to the candidate words in order to obtain the initial list of thesaurus terms.

The next step of the process is the generation of the *union thesaurus* from a set of source thesauri. The source thesauri that we have used are the following ones:

- EUROVOC, which contains concepts on the activity of the European Union.
- SPINES, a controlled and structured vocabulary for information processing in the field of science and technology for development.
- ISOC, thesaurus aimed at the treatment of information on economy.

Terms which appear in both, the core set and any source thesauri, are the term list of the *union* thesaurus. Furthermore, the relationships among the terms included in the new thesaurus are provided by the source thesauri. Figure 2 shows an example of generation of the *union* thesaurus. When the term *terremoto* (earthquake), which belongs to the core set, is searched in the source thesauri two entries are found, one in SPINES and the other one in EUROVOC. In EUROVOC *terremoto* (earthquake) belongs to an entry whose preferred term is *seísmo* (seism) and which also contains *desastre natural* (natural disaster) (BT), and *sismología* (seismology) (RT). In SPINES *terremoto* is the preferred

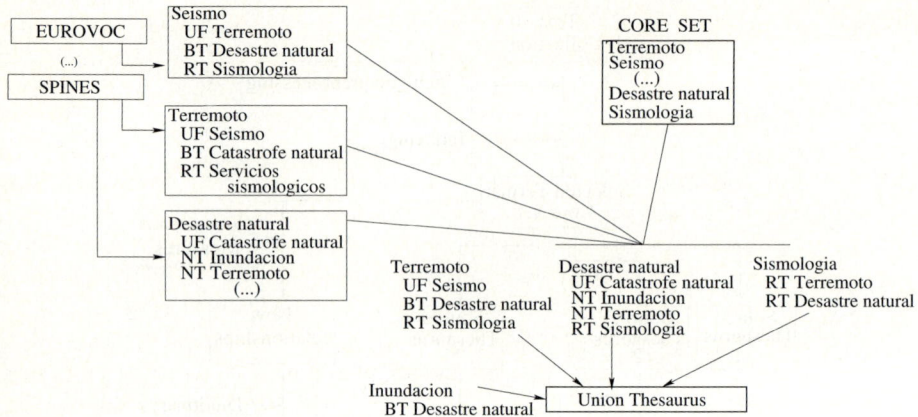

Fig. 2. Example of generation of the *union* thesaurus. UF stands for *used for*, NT for *narrower term*, BT for *broader term* and RT for *related term*.

term of an entry which also contains the synonym *seísmo*, the broader term *catástrofe natural* (natural catastrophe). In SPINES, *terremoto* also appears in other entry whose preferred term is *desastre natural*, and which also contains the synonym *catástrofe natural*, and the narrower terms *inundación* (flood) and *terremoto*. Accordingly, the *union* thesaurus presents entries whose preferred terms are *terremoto*, *desastre natural*, *sismología* and *inundación*, the terms of the core set.

The *union* thesaurus just described is now extended by detecting new semantic relationships among the terms of the set compose of the core set plus the terms taken from the source thesauri.

3 Enriching the Hierarchies

If a couple of terms to be related, appears in some of the source thesauri, this indicates the kind of its relationships. If they do not appear in the source thesauri, its possible relationship has to be investigated. The first step is to detect any kind of relationship, and then, in a second step the type of the detected relationship is identify.

For the extraction of semantic relations between terms we have chosen the statistical method of the Vector Space Model [3]. To apply the vectorial model we defined a vector of features for each term from the documents in which it appears. The values of this vector are estimated by counting the co-occurrences of the terms in the documents. After testing different classic measures, such as Dice, Jaccard and Cosine, we have chosen Cosine, which provides the best results for our work.

Once we have determined the pairs of terms for which the semantic similarity is significant enough (the similarity is above a threshold value of 0.3), we have to determine the type of the relationship between these pairs of terms: equivalence, hierarchy or associativity. We assume that the degree of semantic similarity between a term and a preferred one depends on the type of the relationship between them: equivalent terms have the highest values, followed by terms which belong to the same hierarchy, and related terms have the lowest values. Accordingly, we concentrate in detecting the hierarchical relationships, and the higher and lower values of semantic similarity of these pairs are considered respectively as the top and the bottom threshold values of this type of relationship. Then term pairs with sematic similarity over the top threshold are assigned the equivalence relationship, while terms with a value of semantic similarity below the bottom threshold are considered related terms.

Let us now to consider the technique used to detect hierarchical relationships. It relies on the assumption that in a dictionary the entries for a term which is an instance of a more general concept contain a reference to the term for this general concept. Furthermore, we assume that the references to more general terms usually adopt some predefined structures. We have considered the following set of structures for the detection of hierarchical relationships:

> noun
> noun adjective
> noun noun
> noun preposition noun
> noun preposition article noun

We have developed our experiments in Spanish, using the RAE (Real Academia Española) dictionary, applying a part-of-speech (POS) tagging of the dictionary entries in order to detect the selected structures. For query expansion we use the method proposed by Qiu y Frei [7], which selects expansion terms according to their similarity with all query terms.

4 Experiments and Results

The prototype developed for our experiments has been implemented using the programming language Java. This prototype has been run on a computer Intel Pentium IV Hyper-Threading 3.40 GHz, with 2GB of RAM memory.

In order to provide a quantitative measure for the quality of the generated thesaurus, we have decided to evaluate its usefulness when it is applied to an information retrieval task. Specifically, we used the thesaurus to perform a term-to-term query expansion, i.e. for identifying terms related with the query terms in order to improve the retrieval capability.

With the aim at being as fair as possible, in the selection of tests we have taken a set of tests used in the CLEF (Cross-Language Evaluation Forum) for the Spanish language. The collection and tests used come from EFE94.

For the evaluation of the system we have used *trec_eval* package, with the measures of precision and recall [2]. Recall is the fraction of the relevant documents which have been retrieved and precision is the fraction of the retrieved documents which are relevant. Besides, we use R-precision, which is the precision

Table 1. Comparison of results obtained applying query expansion with different thesauri

Query	Precision	Recall	Improve. Precision	Improve. Recall
Baseline	0.4460	0.7584	–	–
Spines	0.3624	0.6416	- 18.74%	- 15.40%
Eurovoc	0.3730	0.6550	- 16.37%	- 13.63%
ISOC-Economy	0.3728	0.6415	- 16.41%	- 15.41%
Union Thesaurus	0.3727	0.6556	-16.43%	- 13.55%
Final Thesaurus	0.4927	0.8426	+ 9,47%	+ 9.99%

after retrieving R documents, where R is the total number of relevant documents for the query. As test set we have used a total of 50 queries extracted from the batteries provided by CLEF in 2001.

Table 1 shows the results obtained performing query expansion with different thesauri. We can observe that the results for the automatically generated thesaurus (last row) are significantly better than those obtained with the source and *union* thesauri, since we obtain a general improvement of 9,47% in the precision and of 9.99% in the recall, while the source and *union* thesauri obtain negative results. On the one hand, the query expansion achieved by using the thesaurus enlarges the set of search terms and thus recall improves. On the other hand, precision also improves because the percentage of relevant documents retrieved with the query expansion is larger than the percentage for the original query. Because the Qui & Frei expansion method that we apply for the query expansion requires similarity measures to work appropriately, the source and *union* thesauri, which do not provide such measures, do not achieve any improvement in the retrieval. We have also tested a direct expansion method, which does not use similarity measures, and it also provides much worse results for the source and *union* thesauri.

We have performed a number of experiments in order to determine the influence of the different steps of the linguistic preprocessing on the results. Table 2 shows the results with and without POS tagging. The first row shows the results without query expansion. The other two rows present the results expanding with the thesaurus generated without (second row) and with POS tagging (third row). We can observe that the POS tagging not only improve the different measures (precision, R-precision and recall) but also reduces the index size, what leads to a significative decrease of the execution time.

Table 2. Comparison of results obtained applying POS tagging in the thesaurus generation. Th. w. POS stands for Thesaurus with POS tagging. Time is given in minutes.

Query	Precision	R-Precision	Recall	Index size	Time
Baseline	0.4460	0.4482	0.7584	352.534	-
Thesaurus	0.4789 (+ 6.86%)	0.4745 (+ 5.54%)	0.8460 (+ 10.35%)	352.534	242
Th. w. POS	0.4906 (+ 9.09%)	0.4886 (+ 8.71%)	0.8454 (+ 10.29%)	321.612	220

Table 3. Comparison of results obtained applying stemming in the thesaurus generation. Th. w. Stem. stands for Thesaurus with stemming. Time is given in minutes.

Query	Precision	R-Precision	Recall	Index size	Time
Baseline	0.4460	0.4482	0.7584	352.534	-
Thesaurus	0.4789 (+ 6.86%)	0.4745 (+ 5.54%)	0.8460 (+ 10.35%)	352.534	242
Th. w. Stem.	0.4832 (+ 7.69%)	0.4815 (+ 6.91%)	0.8428 (+ 10.01%)	315.457	216

Table 4. Comparison of results obtained by eliminating specific stopwords in the thesaurus generation. Th. wo. SSW stands for Thesaurus without specific stopwords. Time is given in minutes.

Query	Precision	R-Precision	Recall	Index size	Time
Baseline	0.4460	0.4482	0.7584	352.534	-
Thesaurus	0.4906 (+ 9.09%)	0.4906 (+ 9.09%)	0.4906 (+ 9.09%)	321.612	220
Th. wo. SSW	0.4927 (+ 9.47%)	0.4916 (+ 9.27%)	0.8426 (+ 9.99%)	321.503	220

Table 3 shows the results with and without stemming. As in the case of POS tagging, stemming not only improves the different measures but also reduces the index size, and thus the execution time.

Table 4 compares the results when *specific stopwords* are eliminated of the core set. Specific stopwords are not typical stopwords, but they are words too frequent in the collection to be good discriminators for thesaurus construction. Examples of specific stopwords are months, name of the days, etc. The default thesaurus has been generated with POS tagging and stemming. In this case the improvement of the measures is smaller than in the other cases. We think that it is because the frequency must not be the only factor to take into account to determine the specific stopwords, but the degree of relationship with other words of the intended domain must also be considered.

5 Conclusions and Future Works

This paper shows how to use handmade thesauri for the automatic generation of new thesauri. There exists a large amount of handmade thesauri, which are very useful as knowledge bases for the automatic generation of thesauri[1]. Furthermore, we have defined a methodology to combine linguistic methods and statistical methods for the automatic generation of thesauri. This is one of the ways in which natural language processing can improve the performance of information retrieval processes. Results have shown the usefulness of the generated thesaurus, improving both, recall and precision measures in an information retrieval task. Recall improves because the list of search terms is enlarged with the query expansion. And precision also improves since most of the new documents added to the retrieved list are relevant, and thus the rate of relevance improves.

---

[1] Web Thesaurus Compendium: http://www.ipsi.fraunhofer.de/ lutes/thesoecd.html

We have also shown the advantages of some preprocessing steps, such as POS-tagging and stemming, used in the process of selection of the term list which characterizes the intended domain.

Given the promising results obtained, we plan to investigate how to improve the different phases of this process. In particular, we plan to apply a more exhaustive linguistic analysis for the identification of semantic relationships, as well as using Wordnet as another source of information for the thesaurus generation.

References

1. Angel F. Zazo and Carlos G. Figuerola and Jose L. Alonso Berrocal and Emilio Rodríguez. Reformulation of queries using similarity thesauri. *Information Processing and Management*, 41(5):1163–1173, 2005.
2. Ricardo A. Baeza-Yates and Berthier A. Ribeiro-Neto. *Modern Information Retrieval*. ACM Press / Addison-Wesley, 1999.
3. G. Salton. *Automatic Information Organization and Retrieval*. McGraw Hill Book Co, 1968.
4. Y. Jing and W. Bruce Croft. An association thesaurus for information retrieval. In *Proceedings of RIAO-94, 4th International Conference "Recherche d'Information Assistee par Ordinateur"*, pages 146–160, New York, US, 1994.
5. K. Sparck Jones and R.M. Needham. Automatic Term Classification and Retrieval. *Information Processing and Management*, 4(1):91–100, 1968.
6. Yonggang Qiu and Hans-Peter Frei. Applying a similarity thesaurus to a large collection for information retrieval, 1993.
7. Yonggang Qiu and Hans-Peter Frei. Concept-based query expansion. In *Proceedings of SIGIR-93, 16th ACM International Conference on Research and Development in Information Retrieval*, pages 160–169, Pittsburgh, US, 1993.
8. Yonggang Qiu and Hans-Peter Frei. Improving the retrieval effectiveness by a similarity thesaurus. Technical Report 225, Dept of Computer Science, Swiss Federal Institute of Technology (ETH), Zürich, Switzerland, 1995.
9. G. Salton, C. Buckley, and C. T. Yu. An evaluation of term dependence models in information retrieval. In *SIGIR '82: Proceedings of the 5th annual ACM conference on Research and development in information retrieval*, pages 151–173, New York, NY, USA, 1982. Springer-Verlag New York, Inc.
10. C.J van. Rijsbergen, D.J. Harper, and M.F. Porter. The selection of good search terms. *Information Processing and Management*, 17(2):77–91, 1981.

An Interactive Hybrid System for Identifying and Filtering Unsolicited E-mail

M. Dolores del Castillo and J. Ignacio Serrano

Instituto de Automática Industrial, CSIC, Ctra. Campo Real km 0.200 – La Poveda,
28500 Arganda del Rey, Madrid. Spain
{lola, nachosm}@iai.csic.es

Abstract. This paper presents a system for automatically detecting and filtering unsolicited electronic messages. The underlying hybrid filtering method is based on e-mail origin and content. The system classifies each of the three parts of e-mails separately by using a sinole Bayesian filter together with a heuristic knowledge base. The system extracts heuristic knowledge from a set of labelled words as the basis on which to begin filtering instead of conducting a training stage using a historic body of pre-classified e-mails. The classification resulting from each part is then integrated to achieve optimum effectiveness. The heuristic knowledge base allows the system to carry out intelligent management of the increase in filter vocabularies and thus ensures efficient classification. The system is dynamic and interactive and the role of the user is essential to keep the evolution of the system up to date by incremental machine learning with the evolution of spam. The user can interact with the system over a customized, friendly interface, in real time or at intervals of the user's choosing.

Keywords: e-mail classification, machine learning, heuristic knowledge.

1 Introduction

Unsolicited commercial e-mail, known as "spam", is widely recognized as one of the most significant problems facing the Internet today. According to a report [5] from the Commission of European Communities, more than 25% of all e-mail currently received is spam. More recent reliable data indicate that this percentage has increased by over 50%.

There are techniques for preventing addresses from being discovered and used by spammers, such as encoding or hiding the kinds of data that spammers target. Unfortunately, these techniques are not in widespread use [21]. Since spam growth is exponential and prevention is both extremely difficult and rare, the problem must be tackled on a technical front, by developing methods to analyse e-mail traffic in order to identify and reject spam communications. This introduction provides a review of the properties of the different filter types that are currently available.

Filtering can be classified into two categories, origin-based filtering or content-based filtering, depending on the part of the message chosen by the filter as the focus for deciding whether e-mail messages are valid or illegitimate [6]. Origin-based filtering focuses on the source of the e-mail, which is recorded in the domain name and address of the sender device. Two types of origin-based filters are available [12]:

White-list filtering. This kind of filtering only lets e-mail from explicitly confidential or reliable lists of e-mail addresses (white lists) through. TDMA [20] and ChoiceMail [16] are paradigms of white-list filtering.

Black-list filtering. These filters use lists of e-mail addresses that are widely known to be spam sources (black lists). Razor [23] and Pyzor [15] are tools that use black-list filtering.

Content-based filters conduct an analysis whose goal is to review the text content of e-mail messages. Depending on the analysis technique used, these filters may be differentiated as follows [12]:

Rule-based filters. This type of filter extracts text patterns or rules [4] and assigns a score to each rule based on the occurrence frequency of the rule in spam and non-spam e-mail in a historic body of e-mail. SpamAssassin is the most popular application using rule-based filtering [18].

Bayesian filters. These filters analyse every word of a message and assign a spam probability and a non-spam probability to each word based on statistical measurements. Next, the Bayes theorem is used to compute the message total probability [1], and the message is categorized according to the higher probability value. There are a great many filters that use these properties [10], [11].

Memory-based filters. These filters use e-mail comparison as their basis for analysis. E-mail messages are represented as feature or word vectors that are stored and matched with every new incoming message. Some examples of this kind of filter are included in [2], [7]. In [6], case-based reasoning techniques are used.

Other filters. Some of the content-based approaches adopted do not fall under the previous categories. Of these, the most noteworthy are the ones based on support vector machines [9] or neural networks [22].

Other features exist that can be used to classify filters in other ways as well. These features include filter location (in a client or dedicated server), ease of use, configuration ability, and filtering options. One of the basic properties of filters is their dynamism or ability to evolve over time. Only some filters have this ability to learn from past mistakes. Bayesian filters evolve by updating word probabilities and including new words in their vocabularies, while memory-based filters evolve by increasing the number of stored e-mail messages. Filters that rely on lists updated by users are also dynamic. Other filtering systems, such as some rule-based filters, are static and once such filters have been installed, their behaviour and performance never change.

Most current filters achieve an acceptable level of performance, detecting 80%-98% of spam. The main difficulty is to detect false positives, i.e., the messages that are misidentified as spam. Some filters obtain false positives in nearly 2% of the tests run on them. These filters are used commercially, but they show two key issues for which there is no solution at present: 1) Filters are tested on standard sets of examples that are specifically designed for evaluating filters. Since the features of real-life spam are always changing, these sets do not reflect the real world where filters have to operate with any degree of certainty, and 2) In response to the acceptable performance of some filters, spammers have hit upon methods of circumvention. They study the techniques filters use, and then create masses of "suicide" e-mail (messages intended to be filtered out), so that the filters will learn from them. Next, the spammers generate new messages that are completely different in terms of content and format. This is the major spam battlefield.

This paper describes a client-side system called JUNKER, which was designed and built to detect and filter unsolicited e-mail automatically, using several sources of knowledge that are handled by a single processing method. The system obtains optimum results and is highly effective at classifying e-mail, and highly efficient at managing resources. It is a dynamic interactive system that learns from and evolves with the evolution of spam. The user owns the control over the e-mails that he/she receives by making the decision about which e-mails he/she wants to receive. The system can learn directly from data in a user's mail inbox and this system can be customized to the user's particular preferences.

2 The JUNKER System

JUNKER is based on a hybrid filtering method that employs a novel way of filtering based on content and origin. JUNKER architecture is composed of a heuristic knowledge base and a Bayesian filter. JUNKER classifies the three parts of e-mails in the same way and then integrates the classifications resulting from each part before making a final decision about the class of e-mails.

Usually, when a Bayesian filter is trained using a historic body of valid and invalid e-mail messages, a vocabulary of valid and invalid words is created. JUNKER does not require a training stage designed to create an exhaustive vocabulary that is obsolete within a short period of time. JUNKER learns the vocabulary incrementally starting from a previously extracted knowledge base, which is formed by a set of rules and set of heuristic words without associated semantics. This word set includes words that are invalid because their morphology does not meet the morphological rules of all the languages belonging to the Indo-European family. The e-mails containing these types of invalid words are primarily conceived to fool spam filters.

2.1 Heuristic Knowledge Base

Different algorithms exist for automatically acquiring grammars. Dupont [8] proposes a general scheme for selecting the most appropriate algorithm that infers a grammar with a certain representation under different conditions. According to these ideas, the Error Correcting Grammatical Inference (ECGI) algorithm was selected for inferring a grammar that JUNKER uses to recognize well-formed words. ECGI [17] focuses on a heuristic construction of a regular grammar so that the resulting automata representing the grammar allows general and flexible recognition.

The finite state automata is used to automatically identify the words or tokens that are formed correctly and to differentiate them from invalid words. A well-formed word is composed of a term sequence. A term can be a consonant ("c"), a vowel ("v"), a number ("n"), or a symbol ("s").

The automata is created from a set of examples of well-formed words collected randomly from a set of dictionaries of several Indo-European languages. For example, the valid word "scientific-technical", represented as the string of terms "c c v v c c v c v c s c v c c c v c v c", should be recognized by the automata. If the automata recognizes a word, then it is a well-formed word. Words taken from e-mails labelled as spam, like "v1@gra" represented by the string "c n s c c v", are not recognized by the automata as valid words, and are thus identified as misleading words.

The strings of terms that are not recognized as valid words are represented according to different parameters or criteria, including length, the type of terms contained, or the adjacency of the terms, among others. An unsupervised learning algorithm is used [13] to build a set of clusters and their descriptions. Every cluster and its description is represented by a rule relating one or more morphological criteria with a label or heuristic word. Thus, the content of the heuristic knowledge base is a set of heuristic rules whose left-hand sides evaluate some morphological criteria in words and whose right-hand sides are heuristic words:

$Rule_i$: *((Morphological Criterion)$_i$, (Heuristic Word)$_i$)*

An example of two possible rules of this base may be written as:

Rule 1: ((number of consonants running together in a word is higher than 4), (Non-sense word 1))
Rule 2: ((number of accents in a word is higher than 3), (Non-sense word 2))

The heuristic words, i.e., Non-sense words, constitute the initial vocabulary of the Bayesian filter and it is the same for all the system end-users.

2.2 Bayesian Filtering

The filter was developed to identify and filter e-mail based on the Naïve Bayes statistical classification model [14]. This method can adapt to and learn from errors, and performs well when dealing with high-dimension data.

In general, a Bayesian classifier learns to predict the category of a text from a set of training texts that are labelled with actual categories. In the training stage, the probabilities for each word conditioned to each thematic category are estimated, and a vocabulary of words with their associated probabilities is created. The filter classifies a new text into a category by estimating the probability of the text for each possible category C_j, defined as $P(C_j \mid text) = P(C_j) \cdot \Pi_i P(word_i \mid C_j)$, where $word_i$ represents each word contained in the text to be classified. Once these computations have been carried out, the Bayesian classifier assigns the text to the category that has the highest probability value. The effectiveness of the classifier, measured by *precision* (percentage of predicted documents for a category that are correctly classified) and *recall* (percentage of documents for a category that are correctly classified), is calculated on a test set of documents with known thematic categories.

The vocabulary required by JUNKER to begin to classify e-mails is formed by the heuristic words. Initially, every heuristic word has spam and non-spam probabilities fixed beforehand. The initial value for the spam probability (*Psp*) of heuristic words is greater than the initial value for their non-spam probability (*Pnsp*). When JUNKER analyses the words of a text to be classified, it checks whether a word matches the left-hand side of any rule. If this is the case, the system substitutes the word for a heuristic word. When a word fulfils more than one rule, the system assigns the heuristic word with the lowest spam probability value to the invalid word. This bias aims to generate the minimum number of false positives. Next, the Bayesian filter uses the probabilities of the heuristic word in the same way as the valid words present in both the text and vocabulary in order to classify the text. For example, when JUNKER receives the following text to classify: {*youuuuu, play, game*} and its vocabulary content is {(*Non-sense w1*, (Psp-w1, Pnsp-w1)), (*Non-sense w2*, (Psp-w2, Pnsp-w2)), (*play*, (Psp-play, Pnsp-play)), (*piano*, (Psp-piano, Pnsp-piano))}, it finds that "*youuuuu*" matches the heuristic word Non-sense w1 and "*play*" belongs to both the text and the vocabulary. Next, JUNKER computes the spam and non-spam probabilities of the text as P (SP | text) = P (SP) . Psp-w1 . Psp-play and P(NSP | text) = P (NSP) . Pnsp-w1 . Pnsp-play.

In order for the filter to adapt to e-mail evolution and thus maintain its performance level, the filter must evolve. The user interacts with the system by prompting false positives and negatives so that the system learns incrementally from them, either after classification has just been done or periodically. The heuristic vocabulary is just the initial state of the system vocabulary when the Bayesian filter begins to operate. As the classifier system learns, the vocabulary is updated, in terms of the number of words and word-probability values for both types of words, heuristic and learned words, and the system learns based on user prompts after classifying with an interactive interface.

2.3 Integrated Content Classification

An e-mail message can be seen as a text document composed of three separate parts: the sender, the subject, and the body of the message. Most content-based e-mail classifier systems analyse all of the parts as a single vector of words.

The design and development of the JUNKER classifier system is based on the assumption that in most cases a user can detect unsolicited e-mail just by looking at the sender and subject parts of the message. Accordingly, the system has been conceived to analyse and classify each part of the message separately. The final category of the message is the weighted integration of the resulting classifications for each part.

Since Bayesian filters are known to yield successful results, the classifier system applies a Bayesian filter to each part of the message. Each part of the message has its own vocabulary, which is initially the same as the heuristic vocabulary for the subject and body parts and is empty for the sender part. As the system learns and evolves, the various vocabularies are updated in terms of the number of words and word probabilities associated with the spam and non-spam categories.

When a new message is received, the system composes a word vector associated with each part of the message. Next, the filter computes the *Psp* and *Pnsp* probabilities for every vector by consulting the corresponding vocabulary. Any words in the message that are included in a vocabulary take on the probabilities assigned within the vocabulary. The remaining words are not considered, because they do not provide any useful information about the e-mail category.

In order to generate the minimum number of false positives, once the *Psp* and *Pnsp* probabilities have been computed for each part of the message, the system evaluates the distance between these two probability values and labels a message part as spam whenever this distance is greater than an empirically determined threshold, as follows in equation:

$$\text{Distance}_i \ (\text{Psp} \ (\text{part}_i) \ | \ \text{Pnsp} \ (\text{part}_i)) > u_1 \Rightarrow \text{Category} \ (\text{part}_i) = \text{spam} \qquad (1)$$

Thus, the system creates a bias in order to avoid generating false positives. After the system has analysed and computed the distance between the spam and non-spam categories for all three parts of the message, it computes the final category of the message by weighting the distances of all of the parts, defined as:

$$\text{Distance (Psp (email) | Pnsp (email))} = (\sum_i w_i * \text{Distance}_i) / 3 \qquad (2)$$

The sender and the subject of a message may provide the user with the most obvious clues as to the intention behind the message. This factor is taken into account in the final overall distance, because w_1 and w_2 take higher values than w_3 by default.

Since the bias against generating false positives is included at all of the system decision points, the system only classifies a message as spam when the overall distance is above a global threshold termed "filter confidence". The user can interactively modify the filter confidence.

3 Intelligent Management of Vocabularies and Resources

Once the system has classified incoming messages and the user has been informed of the resulting classification, the user can note the system errors, in real time or periodically, using a friendly interface. The interface also allows the user to remove correctly classified e-mail from the filter domain.

The properties of the system allow carrying out an intelligent vocabulary management to prevent an exhaustive increase in vocabulary. On the one hand, vocabulary upgrades do not include the new words contained in correctly classified and removed e-mail from the filter domain. The reason why such e-mail is correctly classified is that the words that are present in messages and vocabularies alike are enough to categorize the e-mail into its target class. Although increasing the vocabulary size may provide a filter with a greater capacity to discriminate, very large vocabularies require more classification time and are accordingly less efficient.

On the other hand, when the system has to learn from misclassified e-mails, the invalid words in these e-mails, which match some rule of the knowledge base and are identified as heuristic words, are not added to the vocabulary. Instead, the system updates the spam and non-spam probabilities of the heuristic words in the vocabulary that has been found in the e-mail.

The system hybrid behaviour based on filtering origin and content lies in applying the Bayesian filter to the sender part of the message first of all. If the filter finds the sender in its vocabulary, the message is directly classified as non-spam, and the system stops filtering the remaining two parts of the message. If the sender is not found, the system goes on to analyse the content of the subject and body parts of the message. The method used to integrate the classifications of all three parts by giving priority to the sender classification prevents the system from wasting processing resources on classifying e-mail and thereby increases its efficiency.

3.1 Updating the Sender, Subject, and Body Vocabularies

The Bayesian filter begins with an empty vocabulary in the sender part. The system initially classifies this part of the incoming messages into the non-spam category. The integrated classification of the three message parts is what finally categorizes e-mail as spam or non-spam. When the user accepts the classification made by the system, the system stores only the address of the senders of non-spam e-mail whose non-spam probability is greater than its spam probability in the sender vocabulary.

When the filter has to learn from the misclassifications pointed out to it by the user, the system stores only the senders of false positives, i.e., the senders of e-mails classified as spam that are actually non-spam. The senders of false negatives, i.e., the senders of spam that is erroneously assigned to the non-spam category, are ignored, because the majority of unsolicited e-mail hardly ever comes from the same senders twice. Thus, as the system operates over time, the system builds the vocabulary of the sender part using the list of the trusted senders, or white list, which is processed by the Bayesian filter the same as the other two message parts. The initial subject and body vocabularies are formed by the heuristic words, and the system begins to classify these parts of the messages by searching for the words in the vocabularies. When the system has to learn from misclassifications highlighted by the user, these vocabularies are upgraded with the words from the misclassified messages, including false positives and negatives. These new words receive the values of the spam and non-spam probabilities that the system sets for them by default.

Both the correctly classified messages and the new words from misclassified messages prompt the filter to update the probabilities for the entire vocabularies of both parts, so that the vocabularies contain the system's current knowledge.

4 Empirical Evaluation

JUNKER was evaluated on two different set of messages. The first one, LingSpam [1], is composed of 2,412 legitimate messages and 481 spam messages received by LingSpam authors during a given period of time. The messages in LingSpam collection were pre-processed by removing the "from" part, applying a stop list, stemming the words, and removing all the invalid words from a morphological viewpoint. The corpus was split by LingSpam authors into 10 folds in order to apply a 10-fold cross validation. The second corpus, SpamAssassin Corpus [19], is composed of 4,149 legitimate messages and 1,896 spam messages that were collected from individual e-mail boxes.

The SpamAssassin corpus was not pre-processed like LingSpam although all the e-mails came from different senders. In spite of the fact that both corpora were collected from real users, they do not represent the current, actual situation of the users' mail inboxes, since these e-mails were somehow pre-processed and nearly all the noise had been removed. Thus, JUNKER is not able to test some of its most novel properties on these e-mail collections. Anyway, the system presented in this paper obtained good results on both corpora, as shown in Fig. 1 a), b), c) and d).

In [3] several techniques, ranging from Naïve Bayes to Support Vector Machines and Genetic Programming, were evaluated on the LingSpam corpus and the results obtained were nearly 99.5% recall and nearly 81% precision when classifying e-mails in the spam class. The same paper showed that if the corpus is not stemmed and stop listed, the precision in the spam class improves. The classification performance of a modified and fine-tuned Naïve Bayes algorithm evaluated on the SpamAssassin corpus was nearly 99.9% recall and 95% precision in the spam class [24].

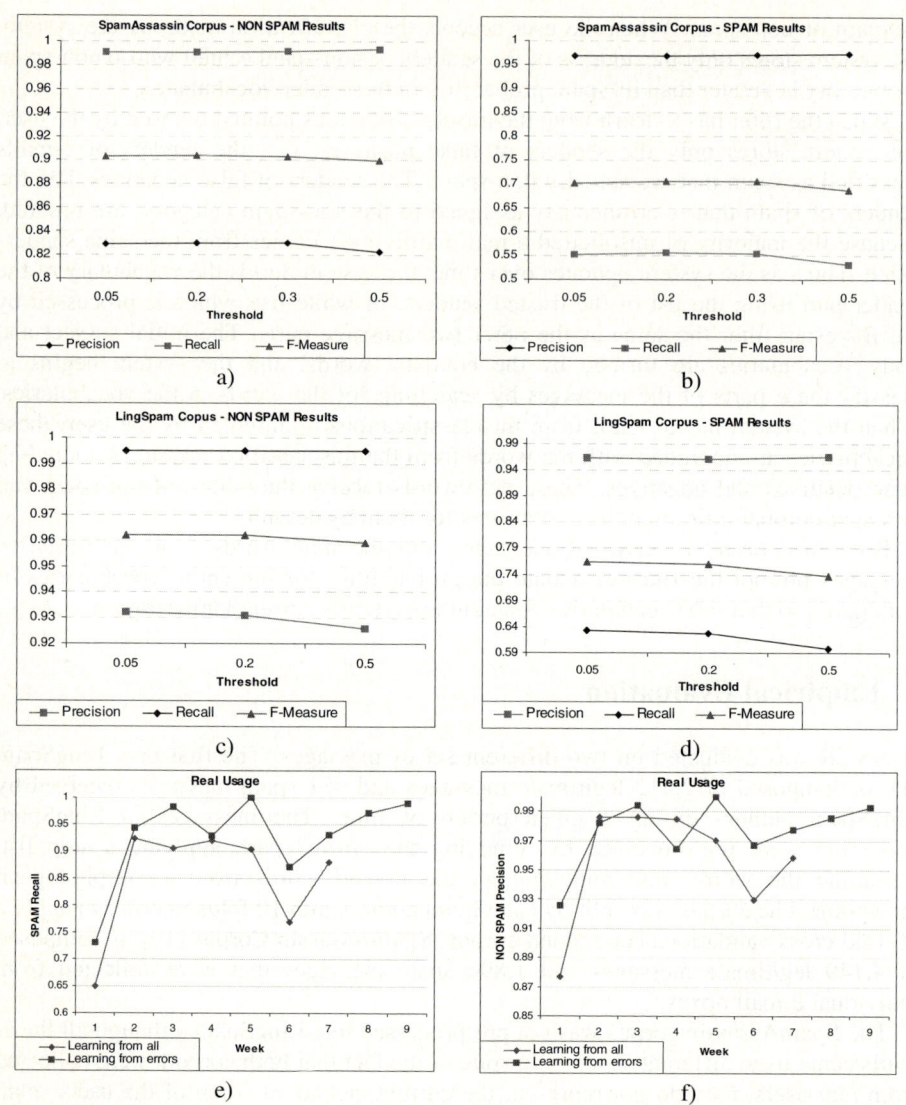

Fig. 1. JUNKER results: a) Non-Spam category on SpamAssassin Corpus, b) Spam category on SpamAssassin Corpus, c) Non-Spam category on LingSpam Corpus, d) Spam category on LingSpam Corpus, for different threshold values, and e) Spam recall and f) Non-Spam precision on real usage during a period of time

JUNKER has been also checked on real usage, by dealing with the e-mails received by the authors of this paper at real-time during a period of time. The initial heuristic vocabulary of the system consisted of 5 heuristic words. The evolution of JUNKER using a distance threshold of 0.3 has been evaluated in two ways: 1) the system only learned from misclassifications for 9 weeks, and 2) the system learned from both correctly and misclassified e-mails for the next 7 weeks (see results in Fig. 1 e) and f)). The relation between the increase of the number of received e-mails and the size of the vocabularies is logarithmic-like. The increase of the vocabulary is smoother when the system only learns from misclassifications.

5 Conclusion

JUNKER works as a customized filter by analysing the e-mail messages of every user individually. It is an effective system, not only for avoiding the creation of false positives, but also for filtering. Its main advantage is that it slows down spammer attempts to fool the filter. Its good performance is reached without a training stage that uses e-mail that has first been received by the user. This classification performance is easier to achieve because of integrating the classifications of the three parts of each message and because of the homogeneous processing of these parts by a single Bayesian filter. The system procedure for evaluating the sender part first allows the system to give high performance in terms of resource management and in terms of response time for classifying and learning from errors.

The system features an easy, friendly interface that provides the user with a way of highlighting misclassifications and guiding the system evolution, based on the e-mail the user receives. JUNKER has been designed for client-side operation. However, thanks to its underlying inner nature, it does allow for straightforward expansion to multiple-user support.

References

1. Androutsopoulos, I., Paliouras, G., Karkaletsis, G., Sakkis, G., Spyropoulos, C., Stamatopoulos, P.: Learning to filter spam e-mail: A comparison of a naive bayesian and a memory-based approach. Workshop on Machine Learning and Textual Information Access, 4th European Conference on Principles and Practice of Knowledge Discovery in Databases (2000)
2. Androutsopoulos, I., Koutsias, J., Chandrinos, K. V., Paliouras, G., Spyropoulos, C. D.: An Evaluation of Naive Bayesian Anti-Spam Filtering. Proc. of the workshop on Machine Learning in the New Information Age, 11th European Conference on Machine Learning (ECML) (2000) 9-17
3. Carreras X., Márquez L.: Boosting Trees for Anti-Spam Email Filtering. In: Mitkov, R., Angelova, G., Bontcheva, K., Nicolov, N., Nikolov, N. (eds.). Proceedings of RANLP-01, 4th International Conference on Recent Advances in Natural Language Processing. Tzigov Chark, BG (2001) 58-64
4. Cohen, W.: Learning rules that classify e-mail. AAAI Spring Symposium on Machine Learning in Information Access (1996)
5. Commission of the European Communities: Communication from the Commission to the European Parliament, the Council, the European Economic and Social Committee of the Regions on unsolicited commercial communications or 'spam', Brussels (2004)
6. Cunningham, P., Nowlan, N., Delany, S.J., Haahr M.: A Case-Based Approach to Spam Filtering that Can Track Concept Drift. Technical Report at Trinity College, TCD-CS-2003-16, Dublin (2003)

7. Daelemans, W., Zavrel, J., van der Sloot, K., van den Bosch, A.: TiMBL: Tilburg Memory-Based Learner - version 4.0 Reference Guide (2001)
8. Dupont, P.: Inductive and Statistical Learning of Formal Grammars. Technical Report, research talk, Department of Ingenerie Informatique, Universite Catholique de Louvain (2002)
9. Drucker, H., Wu, D., Vapnik, V. N.: Support Vector Machines for Spam Categorization, IEEE Transactions on Neural Networks, 10(5) (1999)
10. Graham, P.: A plan for spam. (2002), http://www.paulgraham.com/spam.html
11. Graham, P.: Better Bayesian Filtering. Proc. of Spam Conference 2003, MIT Media Lab., Cambridge (2003)
12. Mertz, D.: Spam Filtering Techniques. Six approaches to eliminating unwanted e-mail. Gnosis Software Inc. (2002)
13. Michalsky R.S.: A theory and methodology of inductive learning. In: Michalsky R.S., Carbonell J.G., and Mitchell T.M. (eds.): Machine Learning: An Artificial Intelligence Approach. Springer-Verlag (1983) 83-134
14. Mitchell, T.M.: Machine Learning. McGraw-Hill (1997)
15. Pyzor, http://pyzor.sourceforge.net
16. Randazzese, V. A.: ChoiceMail Eases Antispam Software Use While Effectively Figthing Off Unwanted E-mail Traffic. CRN (2004)
17. Rulot, H.: ECGI. Un algoritmo de Inferencia Gramatical mediante Corrección de Errores. Phd Thesis, Facultad de Ciencias Físicas, Universidad de Valencia (1992)
18. Sergeant, M.: Internet-Level Spam Detection and SpamAssassin 2.50. Proceedings of Spam Conference 2003, MIT Media Lab. Cambridge (2003) http://spamassassin.org
19. http://www.spamassassin.apache.org
20. Tagged Message Delivery Agent Homepage, http://tmda.net
21. Teredesai, A., Dawara, S.: Junk Mail, a Bane to Messaging. Technical Report of STARE Project, Rochester Institute of Technology, http://www.cs.rit.edu/~sgd9494/STARE.htm, (2003)
22. Vinther, M.: Junk Detection using neural networks. MeeSoft Technical Report (2002) http://logicnet.dk/reports/JunkDetection/JunkDetection.htm
23. Vipul's Razor, http://razor.sourceforge.net
24. Yerazunis, W. S.: The Spam-Filtering Accuracy Plateau at 99,9% Accuracy and How to Get Past It. Proceedings of MIT Spam Conference (2004)

Topological Tree Clustering of Web Search Results

Richard T. Freeman

Capgemini, Business Information Management
No. 1 Forge End, Woking, Surrey, GU21 6DB
United Kingdom
richard.freeman@capgemini.com
http://www.rfreeman.net

Abstract. In the knowledge economy taxonomy generation, information retrieval and portals in intelligent enterprises need to be dynamically adaptive to changes in their enterprise content. To remain competitive and efficient, this has to be done without exclusively relying on knowledge workers to update taxonomies or manually label documents. This paper briefly reviews existing visualisation methods used in presenting search results retrieved from a web search engine. A method, termed topological tree, that could be use to automatically organise large sets of documents retrieved from any type of search, is presented. The retrieved results, organised using an online version of the topological tree method, are compared to the visual representation of a web search engine that uses a document clustering algorithm. A discussion is made on the criterions of representing hierarchical relationships, having visual scalability, presenting underlying topics extracted from the document set, and providing a clear view of the connections between topics. The topological tree has been found to be a superior representation in all cases and well suited for organising web content.

Keywords: Information retrieval, document clustering, search engine, self organizing maps, topological tree, information access, faceted classification, guided navigation, taxonomy generation, neural networks, post retrieval clustering, taxonomy generation, enterprise portals, enterprise content management, enterprise search, information management.

1 Introduction

The rapidly growing volume of electronic content is leading to an information overload. On the Internet, the use of web search engines is critical to finding and retrieving relevant content. Despite the numerous advances in information visualisation [1], the most popular way of presenting search results still remain ranked lists. In this format, the user generally never looks beyond the first three pages, after which they will rather lengthen their search query by adding more terms or refine the initial query [2]. Although ranking mechanisms help order the web pages in terms of their relevance to the users query (e.g. Google[1]), they do not provide any guide as to the overall themes described in the web pages or their relationships. Some efforts

---

[1] http://www.google.com/

have been made to provide different visual representation of the search results, such as suggesting keywords to refine the search (e.g. Webcrawler[2]), representing a graph view of the relations between pages (e.g. Kartoo[3]) or clustering the results (Vivisimo[4]). A major review of the methods and algorithms can be found in [3] [4].

This paper deals with methods that *organise documents* (retrieved by a web search engine) into *automatically extracted* topics. A method which clusters web pages dynamically, whilst creating a topology between them in a tree view, is presented in this paper. The *topological tree* method, first introduced by the author [3], is enhanced through weighting terms depending on their relation to the query term and making the algorithm function efficiently with dynamic datasets. Results and discussions confirm that the topological tree representation can be used to provide a user with a more intuitive and natural representation for browsing documents and discovering their underlying topics.

2 Visual Representation of Retrieved Content

2.1 The Importance of Clustering and Topology

In information access systems, the major visual representations are Self-Organising Maps (SOMs), binary or n-way trees, graphs, and ranked lists. In some cases a combination of these representations can be used. This section describes the limitations of these methods, and illustrates the benefits of using the topological tree structure.

Clustering algorithms can be used to sort content into categories which are discovered automatically based on a similarity criterion. Its typical output representation is a binary tree or generic n-way tree. n being the number of nodes at each level, value which can be fixed or dynamic at each level in the tree. Binary trees quickly become too deep as each level only has two nodes; this representation has been used for retrieval rather than browsing. n-way trees are typically generated using partitioning algorithms (e.g. k-means), or can be manually constructed such as with social bookmarks (e.g. Del.icio.us[5]) and web directories (e.g. Dmoz[6]). Web directories are particularly beneficial to users who are not familiar with the topics and their relations. However, even if some show cross links with related topics, they do not show the relations between topics at the same level, rather the topics are sorted alphabetically or by popularity. Other search engines such as Vivisimo do cluster results, however at each level in the tree there is always a category "other topics" where many document are clustered to. In addition, as with the other n-way trees, there is no relationship between the topics at each level.

Another important trend in industry is the taxonomy generator packages, e.g. Autonomy / Verity Thematic Mapping [5]. These allow the construction of topic hierarchies that can be used for browsing or classification (matching a new document

---

[2] http://www.webcrawler.com/
[3] http://www.kartoo.com/
[4] http://www.vivisimo.com/
[5] http://del.icio.us/
[6] http://www.dmoz.org/

to existing topics). However they are out of the scope of this document, as they are generally constructed offline and / or manually by subject matter experts. As with other tree representations, these taxonomies rarely represent the relationships between the topics at any one level, i.e. only the hierarchical relations and limited cross links are shown.

Graph representations or SOMs can be used to compensate for this lack of topology in these tree representations or taxonomies. Graphs can represent hyperlinks, relationships or links between topics. A web example of a graph generated representation is Kartoo. Other knowledge representations such as Topic Maps (e.g. Omnigator[7]), can also be represented as graph structures. Although they do capture the inter topic / document relations, the major drawback is that they cannot scale easily, i.e. the more nodes / links are added the less legible it becomes. SOMs typically have a 2-dimensional grid structure which adapts to the content space and the number of nodes need not change to represent the underlying number of topics. The SOM-based methods have two distinct properties over other methods, namely non-linear dimensionality reduction and topology preservation. The non-linear projection property ensures that the input space is mapped onto a lower dimensional space with minimum information distortion. The topology preserving clustering enables documents that are similar to be located closely on the map. However one the major weakness of 2-dimensional SOMs, is it is difficult to navigate between different levels of detail. Hierarchical variants of the SOM, such as the Growing Hierarchical SOM [6] have been developed for this purpose; however only one map can be shown at any time and their size is sensitive to fixed parameters. In addition, tables or complex graphics are required to represent the 2-dimensional maps efficiently.

The topological tree method, first proposed by the author [3], compensates for all these factors by exploiting a simple tree view structure to represent both *hierarchical* and *topological relationships* between topics. Previous work undertaken by the author focused on clustering a fixed set of documents. This paper deals with the clustering of search results of multi author / non-uniform documents with different formatting and content. The topological tree can be used to combine the tree structure with that of the topology inherent in SOMs. The tree structure allows a user to visualise different levels of detail and hierarchical relationships. The topology, a novel feature specific to the topological trees and SOMs, additionally allows the viewing of the relationships between the topics. Fig. 1 clearly shows the difference between having a topology and not having one. On the left, the topics appear to be randomly placed, but on the right they naturally flow downward as economics, microeconomics, finance, biology, and anatomy making it more intuitive and natural to the user.

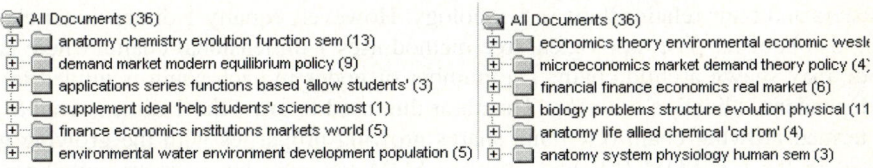

Fig. 1. – k-mean with no topology (left) and root level in the topological tree (right)

---

[7] http://www.ontopia.net/omnigator/models/index.jsp

3 The Topological Tree Method

3.1 Overview of the Method

There are a number of essential steps in the method:

1. The user enters a query term into the local web application, and selects the search options and search engine.
2. The application submits the query term to the search engine and crawls the returned results.
3. Each page is indexed and transformed into a document vector.
4. Feature selection and term weighting is performed on the vector.
5. The documents are organised in a growing chain (see section 0).
6. Each chain is labelled and added to the topological tree, if further child chains are required (see section 0) return to 4.
7. The user is presented with the resulting generated topological tree.

3.2 Text Pre-processing

Text pre-processing is essential to any search or retrieval system, since the quality of the terms will have an impact on the results. There are generally three steps, the indexing, feature selection and term weighting. In the first step of indexing, the HTML is parsed and extracted terms are transformed into vector forms to allow fast mathematical comparisons. The second step involves selecting the most relevant terms. This feature selection is required to reduce the number of terms and select the most discriminative terms. The terms that are not frequent or too frequent can be discarded, as they do not help find common patterns in the document set.

In the third step, the remaining terms are weighted to give more mathematical importance to potentially more significant terms. The keyword query term, as well as their context, can be considered more relevant to the search; hence these are weighted more heavily in the document vectors. In essence the terms in the web metadata, title, search engine snippet (distinct excerpt from retrieval results), and context of the query are all weighted more heavily since these are likely to be most significant. In the growing chain, these weighted document vectors are used to compute similarities to a node's weight vector via a dot product.

3.3 Growing Chains and Topological Tree Method

SOMs are generally associated with 2-dimensional structures that help visualise clusters and their relationships in a topology. However, equally 1-dimensional chains can also be used. The topological tree method uses 1-dimensional chains where each node may spawn a child chain. The number of nodes in each chain is guided by an independent validation criterion. The algorithm used to grow the 1-dimensional SOM is termed growing chain (GC) and shares growing properties with the growing grid (used in the GH-SOM [6]) and growing SOM variants, but is more suited for 1-dimension.

As with the SOM, there are two major steps in the GC algorithm: the search for the best matching unit and the update of the winner and its neighbouring nodes. At time t, an input document vector **x** is mapped to a chain consisting of n nodes with a weight vector **w**. The best matching unit $c(\mathbf{x})$ is the node with the maximum dot product amongst nodes j and document vector $\mathbf{x}(t)$,

$$c(\mathbf{x}) = \arg\max_{j}\{S_{dot}(\mathbf{x}(t), \mathbf{w}_j)\}, \quad j = 1, 2, \ldots n \qquad (1)$$

where n is the current number of nodes. Once the winner node $c(\mathbf{x})$ is found the neighbouring weights are updated using,

$$\mathbf{w}_j(t+1) = \frac{\mathbf{w}_j(t) + \alpha(t)h_{j,c(x)}(t)\mathbf{x}(t)}{\|\mathbf{w}_j(t) + \alpha(t)h_{j,c(x)}(t)\mathbf{x}(t)\|} \qquad (2)$$

where $\alpha(t)$ is the monotonically decreasing learning rate and $h_{j,c(x)}(t)$ the neighbourhood function, typically a Gaussian kernel. When the learning has stabilised for the current number of nodes n, the entropy of the chain is recorded and a new node is inserted next to the node with the highest number of wins. The weights of the new node are initialised by interpolating or extrapolating existing nodes weight values. New nodes are added until n_{max} nodes are reached which corresponds to the maximum allowable chain size. Finally the validation criterion, the entropy-based Bayesian Information Criterion that penalises complexity, gives the optimum number of nodes per chain as:

$$\tau = \arg\min_{n}\left\{\frac{1}{m}\sum_{j=1}^{n}m_j \cdot H(C_j) + \frac{1}{2}n\log m\right\}, n = 2, \ldots, n_{max} \qquad (3)$$

where m is the number of documents, n the current number of nodes in the chain, $H(C_j)$ is the total normalised and weighted sum of entropies for cluster C_j.

Then in the hierarchical expansion process, each node in the chain is tested to determine if it will spawn a child chain. This is performed using several tests. The first test counts the number of document clustered to that node to see if it is less than a fixed threshold. The next test analyses the vocabulary present in those documents to determine if there is a sufficient number of terms. The final test uses cluster tendency method. It aims to test if a set of documents contains random documents with no or few relations or if there are strong underlying clusters[7]. If any of these tests fail for a particular node, then it does not spawn a child chain and becomes a leaf node in the final topological tree representation.

Finally each node in the chain is labelled using the most representative terms of the node's weight and its frequency. Once the chain is labelled, then it is added to the current topological tree structure. If further hierarchical expansions in its child chains are required, then the process is repeated for each of the child chains, otherwise the process is terminated and the results presented to the user. The full pre-processing and topological tree method is shown in Fig. 2.

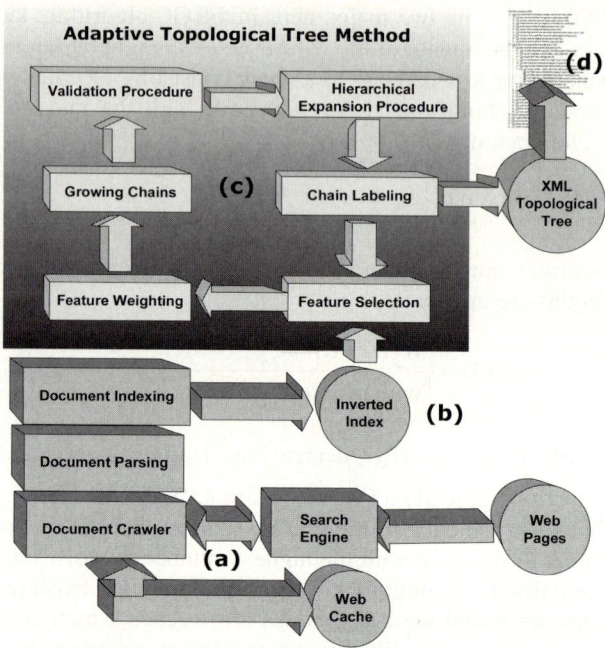

Fig. 2. The Topological Tree Method. (a) The search engine is queried, the pages are returned and crawled by the Web Application. (b) An inverted index is generated from the retrieved documents. (c) The closed loop represents the necessary processing for each growing chain in the topological tree. It is grown using an independent validation procedure that estimates the optimum number of nodes that maximise the information value. (d) Once the topological tree is complete it is exported to XML.

4 Results and Discussions

The dataset was dynamically generated from a search query. The query was "cookie"; other queries were also tested but omitted for space considerations. The Vivisimo tree, shown in Fig. 3, was generated by directly submitting the same query to the search engine and taking a sample snapshot of the tree. Fig. 4 shows the topological tree that was generated from running a Google query and crawling the returned ranked listing.

4.1 Comparison

Although Vivisimo uses meaningful pre-crafted labels compared to the topological tree, it suffers from the fact that the number of categories tends to grow large at root level and this number seems arbitrary. In addition the relations between topics at each level are ambiguous (only the hierarchical relations are represented) and many documents remain unclassified as "other topics". In comparison, the topological tree representation appears more intuitive and natural to the user, as closely related topics are located close to one another in each chain. Each chain does not grow to a large number of nodes, as this number is guided by an independent validation criterion that penalises complexity. In addition hierarchical relations between a parent node and child chain help abstract different levels of detail.

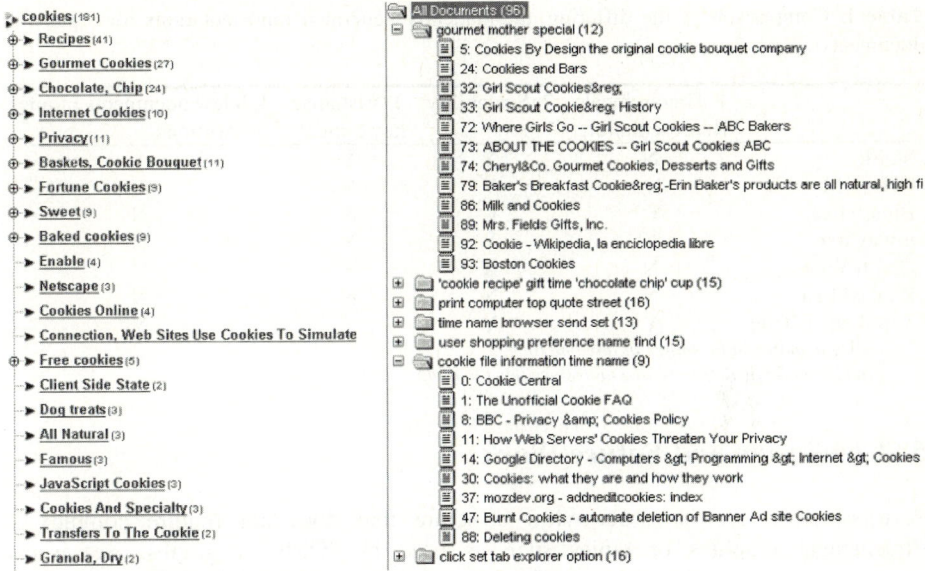

Fig. 3. – A partial snapshot of a tree generated using Vivisimo on the query "cookies". Clearly the tree becomes confusing as the web and edible cookies ordering is intermingled at the same level in the tree, making it less understandable

Fig. 4. – A topological tree generated from the pages retrieved using the query "cookies". Clearly the topology ensures that the web cookies and edible cookies are separated. From top to bottom the main theme of edible cookies, cookie recipes, cookies sales, web cookies in browsers, and data stored in cookies can be observed making it visually intuitive.

4.2 Discussion

There are four important criteria for creating an effective browsing experience of documents and topics:

1. Hierarchical Representation: the topics need to show different levels of detail simultaneously. This is especially true when the number of topics is large, e.g. the Dewey decimal classification or web directories.
2. Scalability: the ability to view a large number of topics and documents in the same window.
3. Visualise key topics and their related documents: key topics should be easily be discernable using a label and documents should be shown to belong to one of more of them.
4. Visualise key relationships: the ability to visualise the relationships between different topics as well as the connections between documents.

Table 1 compares the differences between visualisation methods based on these four criteria. It shows that only the topological tree meets all hierarchical, scalability, major topics and topology visual criterions required for efficient browsing.

Table 1. Comparison of the differing automatically generated representations for organising documents

	1. Hierarchical Representation	2. Scalability	3. Visualise key topics	4. View documents / topics connections
SOM	N	Y	Y	Y
GH-SOM	N^1	Y	Y	Y
Binary tree	Y^2	Y^2	N	N
n-way tree	Y	Y	Y	N
Graph View	N	N	Y	Y
Ranked List	N	N	N	N
Topological Tree	Y	Y	Y	Y

[1] only one map can be shown at any one time.
[2] not efficiently as there are two nodes per level leading to a deep structure.

5 Conclusion and Future Work

A topological tree is a tree view structure that does not require complex 2-dimensional graphics or tables such as used in SOMs or graphs. Yet it can complement current faceted classification solutions (e.g. guided navigation used in Endeca), by showing the key relationships between extracted topics thus helping reveal previously unknown associations automatically. It also helps make a tree structure appear more intuitive, i.e. related topics are located close to one another in the tree. This topology can be thought of as a graph representation that has been optimised into a tree view, where only the strongest relationships between topics are preserved. Through building on top of existing search engines, the topological tree method benefits from pre-filtered content where it only needs to organise a relevant subset of the content. This paper has shown that the topological tree can be built on top of a typical web search engine and produce an insightful overview of the underlying topics contained in the top ranking web pages. Future work could look at extracting and combining knowledge from web directories and social networks, with results returned from a web search engine, into a topological tree.

References

[1] Herman, I., Melancon, G., and Marshall, M., Graph visualization and navigation in information visualization: A survey. IEEE Transactions on Visualization and Computer Graphics. **6**(1). 24-43, 2000.
[2] Search Engine User Behavior Study, White Paper, iProspect, April 2006.
[3] Freeman, R.T. and Yin, H., Adaptive Topological Tree Structure for Document Organisation and Visualisation. Neural Networks. **17**(8-9). 1255-1271, 2004.

[4] Freeman, R.T., Web Document Search, Organisation and Exploration Using Self-Organising Neural Networks, PhD Thesis, Faculty of Engineering and Physical Sciences, School of Electrical & Electronic Engineering, University of Manchester: Manchester, 2004.
[5] Chung, C.Y., et al. Thematic Mapping – From Unstructured Documents to Taxonomies. in Proceedings of the 11th International Conference on Information and Knowledge Management VA, 2002.
[6] Rauber, A., Merkl, D., and Dittenbach, M., The Growing Hierarchical Self-Organizing Map: Exploratory Analysis of High-Dimensional Data. IEEE Transactions on Neural Networks. **13**(6). 1331-1341, 2002.
[7] Freeman, R.T. and Yin, H., Web Content Management by Self-Organization. IEEE Transactions on Neural Networks. **16**(5). 1256-1268, 2005.

Reduced Attribute Oriented Inconsistency Handling in Decision Generation

Yucai Feng, Wenhai Li, Zehua Lv, and Xiaoming Ma

Department of Computer Science, Huazhong University of
Science and Technology, Wuhan 430074, Hubei, China
lwhaymail@21cn.com

Abstract. Due to the discarded attributes, the effectual condition classes of the decision rules are highly different. To provide a unified evaluative measure, the derivation of each rule is depicted by the reduced attributes with a layered manner. Therefore, the inconsistency is divided into two primary categories in terms of the reduced attributes. We introduce the notion of joint membership function wrt. the effectual joint attributes, and a classification method extended from the default decision generation framework is proposed to handle the inconsistency.

1 Introduction

Classification in rough set theory [1] is mainly composed of two components: *feature extraction* and *decision synthesis*. Many researches focus on the construction of classification algorithm, such as probabilistic method [2], decision trees[3] and parameterized rule inducing method [4]. The purpose of these methods is to generate rules with high precision and simple expression. In view of the comprehensiveness and conciseness of the training rules, many discernibility matrices based rule extracting methods [5] concerning both approximate inducing and accurate decision are proposed to classify the objects previously unseen. We would like to point out the dynamic reduct [6], variable thresholds based hierarchical classifier [7]. The synthesis methods place emphasis on how to efficiently resolve the conflicts of training rules for the test objects, such as the stable coverings based synthesis [6], hierarchical classifier [7] and lower frequency first synthesis [8].

This paper, based on the default rule extracting framework [5], analyzes the conflicts [9] with two categories of inconsistent rules, and a synthesis stratagem with the notion of joint membership function is proposed to resolve the inconsistency [10]. In the sequel, a report from our experiments with the medical data sets is given to indicate the availability of our classification method.

2 Rough Set Preliminaries

The starting point of rough set based data analysis is an *information system* denoted by IS, which is a pair $\mathcal{A}(U, A)$ [1]. An IS is a *decision system* when the attributes $\mathcal{A}$ can be further classified into disjoint sets of condition attributes C and decision attributes D. With every subset of attributes $B \subseteq \mathcal{A}$ in $\mathcal{A}$, the *indiscernibility relation* denoted by $IND(B)$ is defined as follows:

$$IND(B) = \{(x,y) \in U \times U | \forall_{a \in B}, (a(x) = a(y))\}. \quad (1)$$

By $U/IND(B)$ we indicate the set of all equivalence classes in $IND(B)$. Two objects $x, y \in U$ with equation (1) held are indistinguishable from each other. In other words, each object in the universe can be expressed by its own equivalence class $E_i \in U/IND(B)$. For a set of objects $X \subseteq U$, based on $U/IND(B)$, the lower and upper approximations denoted by $\underline{B}X$ and $\overline{B}X$ are $\cup\{E \in U/IND(B) | E \subseteq X\}$ and $\{E \subseteq U/IND(B) | E \cap X \neq \emptyset\}$ respectively. For an information system $\mathcal{A}(U, A)$, the *discernibility matrix* denoted by $M_D(\mathcal{A})$ is expressed as an $n \times n$ matrix $\{m_D(i,j)\}$, where $n = |U/IND(A)|$ and

$$m_D(i,j) = \{a \in A | \forall_{i,j=1,2...n}, (a(E_i) \neq a(E_j))\}, \quad (2)$$

which implies the set of attributes of A which can distinguish between the two classes $E_i, E_j \in U/IND(A)$. For a decision system $\mathcal{A}(U, C \cup \{d\})$, the *relative discernibility matrix* $M'_D(\mathcal{A})$ is composed of $m'_D(i,j) = \emptyset$ if $d(E_i) = d(E_j)$ and $m'_D(i,j) = m_D(i,j) \setminus \{d\}$, otherwise.

Following this, a unique boolean variable $\overline{a}$ is associated with each attribute a, and $\overline{m}_D(i,j)$ is transformed from $m_D(i,j)$ in terms of $\overline{a}$. Therefore, the *discernibility function* of the attribute set A in an information system $\mathcal{A}(U, A)$ is defined by:

$$f(A) = \bigwedge_{i,j \in \{1...n\}} \vee \overline{m}_D(E_i, E_j), \quad (3)$$

where $n = |U/IND(A)|$, and the *relative discernibility function* $f'(C)$ in $\mathcal{A}(U, C \cup \{d\})$ is constructed from $\overline{M}'_D(\mathcal{A})$ like equation (3). Similarly, for $n = |U/IND(C)|$, the *local discernibility function* of any $E_i \in U/IND(C)$ is given as:

$$f'(E_i, C) = \bigwedge_{j \in \{1...n\}} \vee \overline{m}'_D(E_i, E_j). \quad (4)$$

For $\mathcal{A}(U, A)$, a *dispensable* attribute a of A implies $IND(A) = IND(A \setminus \{a\})$, and its counterpart called the *indispensable* has an opposite implication. A *reduct* of A denoted by $RED(A)$ is *a minimal set* of attributes $A' \subseteq A$ so that all attributes $a \in A \setminus A'$ are dispensable, namely $IND(A') = IND(A)$. For $\mathcal{A}(U, C \cup \{d\})$, the *relative reducts* $RED(C,d)$ of C to d are judged by $f'(C)$ similarly with the determination of $f(A)$ on $RED(A)$ [6]. Accordingly, we entitle an attribute (set) $C_{Cut} \subseteq C$ relatively indispensable to d iff $\forall_{c \in C_{Cut}} \vee c$ can construct a conjunct of $f'(C)$, and the *prime implicants* of $f'(E_i, C)$ is utilized to determine the *local reduct* of a condition class E_i in $\mathcal{A}$. For $X \subseteq U$ and $B \subseteq A$, the *rough membership* function of X with respect to any class $E_i \in U/IND(B)$ is

$$\mu_B(E_i, X) = \frac{|E_i \cap X|}{|E_i|}, \quad 0 \leq \mu_B(E_i, X) \leq 1. \quad (5)$$

3 Rule Extracting from Training Tables

Though not entirely correct wrt. the classical rule extracting methods [1, 4, 7], the *default rule extracting* framework in [5] provides at lest two advantages, namely *simplicity and generalization*. Therefore, we will use this framework as a basis to validate our research under a restriction of vast rules generation.

For a given *training* table $\mathcal{A}(U, C \cup \{d\})$, taking the prime implicants of $f'(E_i, C)$ of each class $E_i \in U/IND(C)$ for the *predecessor* while regarding the prime implicants of d of each $\{X_j \in U/IND(\{d\}) \mid E_i \cap X_j \neq \emptyset\}$ as the *successor*, all the simpler rules can be expressed as $R : Des(E_i, C) \to Des(X_j, \{d\})$ with $\mu_C(E_i, X_j)$ no less than a filtering threshold μ_{tr}. By introducing an iterative reduct stratagem, thereby, new training rules by deserting the relatively indispensable attributes are generated as much as possible to handle *test* objects. Accepting $\mathcal{A}$ and a given threshold μ_{tr} as the input, the primary extracting framework can be described as the following four steps:

Step 1. $INIT(\Psi)$. Calculate $U/IND(C)$, $U/IND(\{d\})$ and $M'_D(\mathcal{A})$. For $\forall E_i \in U/IND(C)$, calculate $f'(E_i, C)$ and make a rule $R : Des(E_i, C) \to Des(X_j, \{d\}) | \mu_C(E_i, X_j)$ for $\forall X_j \in U/IND(d)$ if $\mu_C(E_i, X_j) \geq \mu_{tr}$. Let $C_{Pr} = C$ and goto Step 4.

Step 2. Exit if $ISEND(\Psi)$; let $\mathcal{A}'(U, C' \bigcup \{d\})$ equal to $NEXT(\Psi)$ and let $C_{Pr} = C'$. Calculate $U/IND(C_{Pr})$ and $M'_D(\mathcal{A}')$.

Step 3. For any $E_{(k, C_{Pr})} \in U/IND(C_{Pr})$, calculate $f'(E_i, C_{Pr})$ and generate a rule $\Delta : Des(E_{(k, C_{Pr})}, C_{Pr}) \to Des(X_j, \{d\}) | \mu_{C_{Pr}}(E_{(k, C_{Pr})}, X_j))$ for each $X_j \in U/IND(d)$ if $\mu_C(E_{(k, C_{Pr})}, X_j) \geq \mu_{tr}$, while the blocks to this rule $\mathcal{F} : Des(E_i, C_{Pr}) \to \neg Des(X_j, \{d\})$ are made if $\forall_{E_i \in U/IND(C)}, E_i \subseteq E_{(k, C_{Pr})} \wedge E_i \cap X_j = \emptyset$.

Step 4. Calculate $f'(C_{Pr})$. For each attribute set C_{Cut} emerging in the conjuncts of $f'(C_{Pr})$, select the projections $C'_{Pr} = C_{Pr} \backslash C_{Cut}$, then $INSERT(\Psi)$ with $\mathcal{A}'(U, C'_{Pr} \cup \{d\})$. Goto step2.

Where the *cursor queue* Ψ composed of all the *subtable* $\mathcal{A}'$ has four main operations $\{INIT; INSERT; ISEND; NEXT\}$. Different from the *classical queue*, $ISEND$ judges if the *cursor* is pointing to a $NULL$ subtable, and $NEXT$ is utilized to get the subtable pointed by cursor and move the cursor to the next

Table 1. An illustrative example

V	a	b	c	d
E_1	1	2	3	1 (50×)
E_2	1	2	1	2 (5×)
E_3	2	2	3	2 (30×)
E_4	2	3	3	2 (10×)
$E_{5,1}$	3	5	1	3 (4×)
$E_{5,2}$	3	3	1	4 (1×)

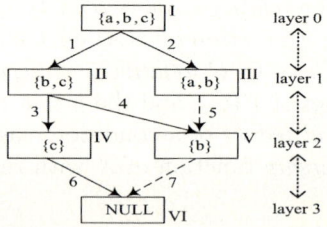

Fig. 1. Flow graph of reduct

subtable. To elucidate the generation of the *rule set*(denoted by $RUL(\mathcal{A})$), an illustrative sample displayed in table 1 results from having observed a total of one hundred objects that were classified according to the condition attributes $C = \{a, b, c\}$ and decision attributes $\{d\}$. Furthermore, the decision classification followed with the cardinality of each $U/IND(C \cup \{d\})$ is represented as $D = \{d\}$.

The real line with the executing sequence number in figure 1 illustrates the projection order of the default algorithm on Table 1, and the dashed denotes the duplicate projection prevented by the cursor queue. The node represents condition attribute set derived from the corresponding projection. Furthermore, the partial relation exists in the nodes which are in different layers and connected by the bidirectional line.

4 Inconsistency Classifying Based on Reduced Layer

The *default decision generation* method [5] extracts the rules measure up to a membership threshold as much as possible, also, it employs the membership as the interface to resolve the synthesis of the training rules for the test objects. Unfortunately, the conflict of the decision generation can not be resolved completely under this framework. To parse the causation of the conflict, a notion of *reduced layer* is defined recursively as follows:

Definition 1. *For a given training decision table* $\mathcal{A}(U, C \cup \{d\})$, *the reduced layer* L *of each subtable* $\mathcal{A}'(U, C' \cup \{d\}) \in \Psi$ *denoted by* $L(\mathcal{A}')$ *is*

- 0 *iff* $IND(C) = IND(C')$;
- $k+1$ *iff* $\exists_{\mathcal{A}''(U,C''\cup\{d\})\in\Psi}, L(\mathcal{A}'') = k \wedge C''\backslash C' \in CON(f'(C''))$.

Where $CON(f'(C''))$ accepts the attribute sets emerging in all the conjuncts of $f'(C'')$ as its elements, and each element corresponding to a *conjunct* in $f'(C'')$ includes all the attributes emerging in this conjunct. We call $\mathcal{A}''$ the *parent* of $\mathcal{A}'$ (i.e $\mathcal{A}''\mathcal{P}\mathcal{A}'$) iff $C''\backslash C' \in CON(f'(C''))$. Simultaneously, P is used to depict the partial relation between C'' and C'. If $\mathcal{A}_1\mathcal{P}\mathcal{A}_2$ and $\mathcal{A}_2\mathcal{P}\mathcal{A}_3$, due to the transitivity of $\subseteq$, subtable $\mathcal{A}_1$ is called the *forefathers* of $\mathcal{A}_3$ (i.e. $\mathcal{A}_1\mathcal{F}\mathcal{A}_3$ or C_1FC_3). From the above, obviously, the original table $\mathcal{A}(U, C \cup \{d\})$ is with the reduced layer 0. Any subtable $\mathcal{A}'(U, C'\cup\{d\})$ in Ψ with reduced layer larger than 0 is homogenous with $\mathcal{A}$ except for $C' \subseteq C$, where C' is called *reduced attributes*. Let us now assume that the considered original table had no condition attributes with the same equivalence classes, i.e. $\forall_{c_1,c_2 \in C}, IND/\{c_1\} \neq IND/\{c_2\}$, and it is commonly satisfied in the large-scale environments.

Proposition 1. *For two reduced attributes* C'' *and* C' *which belong to* $\mathcal{A}''$ *and* $\mathcal{A}'$ *respectively,* $U/IND(C') \subseteq U/IND(C'')$ *exists iff* $C''FC'$, *namely* $\mathcal{A}''\mathcal{F}\mathcal{A}'$.

When considering the necessity, due to the transitivity of relation $\mathcal{P}$ among all the middle subtables between $\mathcal{A}'$ and $\mathcal{A}''$, $U/IND(C') \subseteq U/IND(C'')$ can be easily proven. When considering the sufficiency, we suppose there exists another subtable $\mathcal{B}(U, B \cup \{d\})$ with $L(\mathcal{B}) = L(\mathcal{A}'') \wedge \mathcal{B}\mathcal{F}\mathcal{A}'$ held, and due to the greedy manner of the default rule extracting framework discussed in [5], we assert $U/IND(\mathcal{B}) = U/IND(\mathcal{C}'')$; also because both $\mathcal{B}$ and $\mathcal{A}''$ root in the original table $\mathcal{A}$ with several indispensable attributes deserted, $\mathcal{B} = \mathcal{C}'''$ can be obtained. And thus $\mathcal{C}''\mathcal{F}\mathcal{C}'$ and $\mathcal{A}''\mathcal{F}\mathcal{A}'$ are proven.

As discussed in section 3, a set of rules with the form of $r_k : Pred(r_k) \to Succ(r_k)|\mu(r_k)$ can be generated by applying the four steps to a given training table $\mathcal{A}(U, C \cap \{d\})$. For the universe W, each object $u \in W$ can be classified to a decision class $CLS(Succ(r_k))$ iff any attribute $a \in A$ emerging in $Pred(r_k)$ is supported by u, and it's denoted by $Mat(r_k, u) : \forall_{a \in A}, a(Pred(r_k)) \neq \emptyset \to a(u) = a(Pred(r_k))$. Therefore, the inconsistency consists in $RUL(\mathcal{A})$ iff

$$\exists_{r_i, r_j \in RUL(\mathcal{A})}, Mat(r_i, u) \wedge Mat(r_j, u) \wedge CLS(Succ(r_i)) \neq CLS(Succ(r_j)), \quad (6)$$

where $Mat(r_i, u)$ denotes $Pred(r_i)$ is supported by u, and $CLS(Succ(r_i))$ denotes the decision class determined by $Succ(r_i)$. Therefore, $RUL(\mathcal{A})$ is inconsistent due to the existence of any $r_i, r_j \in RUL(\mathcal{A})$ with both $\forall_{a \in A}, a(Pred(r_i)) \neq \emptyset \wedge a(Pred(r_j)) \neq \emptyset \to a(Pred(r_i)) = a(Pred(r_j)))$ and $CLS(Succ(r_i)) \neq CLS(Succ(r_j))$ held. To distinguish the rules derived from different subtables, each $r \in RUL(\mathcal{A})$ is expressed by $Des(E_i^r, C^r) \to Des(X_j, \{d\})$, where $Des(E_i^r, C^r)$ implies $Pred(r)$ comprising the local reduct of E_i^r in subtable $\mathcal{A}^r(U, C^r \cup \{d\})$. Based on the correlative notions of reduced layer, the inconsistency among the rules can be divided into two cases according to their condition class.

Corollary 1. *For two inconsistent rule r_1 and r_2 derived respectively from $\mathcal{A}^{r_1}$ and $\mathcal{A}^{r_2}$, suppose $L(\mathcal{A}^{r_2}) \geq L(\mathcal{A}^{r_1})$, we shall say that this inconsistency is:*

$$\begin{cases} inherited & \text{iff } C^{r_2} \subseteq C^{r_1}, \\ varietal & \text{iff } C^{r_2} \not\subseteq C^{r_1}. \end{cases} \quad (7a), (7b)$$

The *inherited* inconsistency can be ulteriorly divided into two cases, i.e. $L(\mathcal{A}^{r_2}) = L(\mathcal{A}^{r_1}) \to C^{r_2} = C^{r_1}$ and $L(\mathcal{A}^{r_2}) > L(\mathcal{A}^{r_1}) \to C^{r_2} \subset C^{r_1}$, and the *varietal* inconsistency has two similar cases. In figure 1, the consistency between the rules from node II and the rules from node IV belongs to the inherited, and the consistency arising from node III and node IV is varietal. With little consideration of the difference among the subtables, the rule certainty is converted into the original table oriented evaluation measures which are based on the cardinality to achieve high-frequency rule.

5 Methods of Inconsistency Handling

In this paper, to complement the default decision generation method, we mainly discuss the inconsistency from different layers and suppose $L(\mathcal{A}^{r_2}) > L(\mathcal{A}^{r_1})$. For two inconsistent rules $r_1 : Des(E_{i_1}^{r_1}, C^{r_1}) \to Des(X_{j_1}, \{d\})$ and $r_2 : Des(E_{i_2}^{r_2}, C^{r_2}) \to Des(X_{j_2}, \{d\})$, if $C^{r_2} \subset C^{r_1}$ exists, it's obvious that the condition classes could hold either $E_{i_1}^{r_1} \subset E_{i_2}^{r_2}$ or $E_{i_1}^{r_1} \cap E_{i_2}^{r_2} = \emptyset$. Being comparable with the condition class determined by r_1, the *effectual set* covered by r_2 is only composed of the classes which leads to $Succ(r_2)$ while belonging to $U/IND(C^{r_1})$, namely:

$$ES(E_{i_2}^{r_2}, C_{r_1}) = \{E_i^{r_1} \in IND/C^{r_1} | E_i^{r_1} \cap X_{j_2} \neq \emptyset \wedge E_i^{r_1} \subseteq E_{i_2}^{r_2}\}. \tag{8}$$

When measuring the rules r_1 and r_2 with the relation $C^{r_2} \subset C^{r_1}$ held, due to the desertion of the relatively indispensable attributes $C^{r_1} \backslash C^{r_2}$, the condition classes in $U/IND(C^{r_1})$ which could not lead to the decision $Succ(r_2)$ are taken into account, and it may depress the rule r_2. Hence, for disposing the inherited inconsistency, the notion of *joint membership function* can be determined by the cardinality-based evaluation measure of the effectual set.

Definition 2. *For two inconsistent rules r_1, r_2 with $C^{r_2} \subset C^{r_1}$ held, the joint membership function of r_2 with respect to C^{r_1} is defined as:*

$$\mu_{C^{r_1}}(E_{i_2}^{r_2}, X_{j_2}) = \frac{\sum_{E_k \in ES(E_{i_2}^{r_2}, C_{r_1})} |E_k \cap X_{j_2}|}{\sum_{E_k \in ES(E_{i_2}^{r_2}, C_{r_1})} |E_k|}, \quad 0 \leq \mu_{C^{r_1}}(E_{r_2}, X_{j_2}) \leq 1. \tag{9}$$

Where the denominator denotes the cardinality of the effectual set for r_2 under the condition attributes C^{r_1}, and the numerator denotes the cardinality of the objects which support r_2. Clearly, one can perceive that the rough membership function is a special case of the joint membership function, i.e. $\mu_{C^{r_1}}(E_{i_2}^{r_2}, X_{j_2}) = \mu_{C^{r_2}}(E_{i_2}^{r_2}, X_{j_2}))$ iff $C^{r_1} = C^{r_2}$.

When considering the varietal inconsistency, for the above two rules r_1 and r_2, $C^{r_2} \not\subseteq C^{r_1}$ comes into existence as discussed in corollary 1. Similarly with the analysis of the inherited case, it can be divided into two subcases, i.e. $L(\mathcal{A}^{r_2}) = L(\mathcal{A}^{r_1}) \rightarrow C^{r_2} \neq C^{r_1}$ and $L(\mathcal{A}^{r_2}) > L(\mathcal{A}^{r_1}) \rightarrow C^{r_2} \not\subset C^{r_1}$. In figure 1, one may conclude the inconsistent rules from node II and node III to be the former and the ones from III and IV the latter. Due to the necessity of proposition 1, the condition attribute set $C^{r_1} \cup C^{r_2}$ is the forefather of the both subset, denoted by $(C^{r_1} \cup C^{r_2})FC^{r_1}$ and $(C^{r_1} \cup C^{r_2})FC^{r_2}$. Therefore, $C^{r_1} \cup C^{r_2}$ can be utilized to evaluate the rule certainty, and called by the *effectual joint attributes*.

Proposition 2. *For two inconsistent rules r_1, r_2 with $L(\mathcal{A}^{r_2}) = L(\mathcal{A}^{r_1}) \rightarrow C^{r_2} \neq C^{r_1}$ held, we shall say that the rule certainty can be evaluated by the joint membership function $\mu_{C^{r_1} \cup C^{r_2}}(E_{i_1}^{r_1}, X_{j_1})$ and $\mu_{C^{r_1} \cup C^{r_2}}(E_{i_2}^{r_2}, X_{j_2})$.*

It's obvious that $C^{r_1} = C^{r_1} \cup C^{r_2}$ iff $C^{r_2} \subseteq C^{r_1}$, thus proposition 2 provides a unified evaluative condition attributes for the both rules, and the both categories of inconsistency can be disposed by choosing the rules with higher joint membership function. All the above accounts for the inconsistency between two rules, but when two rules r_1, r_2 are consistent with both the predecessor and the successor (denoted by $r_1 Cst\ r_2$), i.e. $\forall_{a \in A}, a(Pred(r_1)) \neq \emptyset \wedge a(Pred(r_2)) \neq \emptyset \rightarrow a(Pred(r_1)) = a(Pred(r_2)) \wedge CLS(Succ(r_1)) = CLS(Succ(r_2))$, to compete with any $r_3 \in RUL(\mathcal{A})$ which is inconsistent with (by $r_3 Inc\ r_1$) the both rules, all the consistent pairs of each rule must be treated like the inconsistent pairs for obtaining the most credible rule. To achieve the forementioned, the rule is constructed by a header followed with an array of consistent rule descriptions and an array of inconsistent rule descriptions, and the header include six members:

$$Idt : Rule : Block : Strength : Layer : Pds : CstArray : IncArray. \qquad (10)$$

For any $r_a \in RUL(\mathcal{A})$, the symbol Idt denotes the identifier of r_a and $Strength(r_a) = |E_{i_a}^{r_a} \cap X_{j_a}|$ denotes the cardinality of the r_a supported objects. $Layer$ denotes the reduced layer of $\mathcal{A}_a^r$. Pts points to the r_a related decision sub-table in the cursor queue Ψ, and r_a is also pointed by its related subtable. Each element in the last two arrays is composed of an identifier $Idt(r_b)$ and a pair of joint membership function value $(\mu_{C^{r_a} \cup C^{r_b}}(E_{i_a}^{r_a}, X_{j_a}), \mu_{C^{r_a} \cup C^{r_b}}(E_{i_b}^{r_b}, X_{j_b}))$, in which $CstArray$ records all the consistent rules to r_a and $IncArray$ includes all the inconsistent ones. To achieve the four members and the two arrays, two main modifications are made on the rule extracting phase:

+ **Step 2.** Add a layer marker in $\mathcal{A}'$, and the four members are obtained from Step 2.
+ **Step 3.** Following Step 3, according to the established subtables in Ψ, each *generated rule* is fetched to be compared with r_a. Following this, as discussed in definition 2:
  join $Idt(r_b) : (\mu_{C^{r_a} \cup C^{r_b}}(E_{i_a}^{r_a}, X_{j_a}), \mu_{C^{r_a} \cup C^{r_b}}(E_{i_b}^{r_b}, X_{j_b}))$ into $CstArray$ if $r_a Cst\ r_b$;
  join $Idt(r_b) : (\mu_{C^{r_a} \cup C^{r_b}}(E_{i_a}^{r_a}, X_{j_a}), \mu_{C^{r_a} \cup C^{r_b}}(E_{i_b}^{r_b}, X_{j_b}))$ into $IncArray$ if $r_a Inc\ r_b$.

From the above, + Step 3 implies that the both arrays only record the corresponding rules which are generated from the subtable with the reduced layer smaller than $\mathcal{A}^{r_a}$. Due to the reflexivity of both Cst and Inc, this can reduce the complexity of extracting and synthesis. From all above, we assert the time and space complexity of reduced attributes oriented rule extracting algorithm are of order $O(n^4 \cdot m^2)$ and $O(n \cdot m + m^2)$, respectively. According to the above structures, suppose several rules $M = (r_1...r_k)$ are supported by a test object u, then the most credible rule can be obtained by:

1. Classify $\forall r_a \in M$ into several (suppose it's K) consistent subsets according to X_{j_a}.
2. For each consistent subset, with a dimidiate manner, chose the rule with the maximal joint membership value by $CstArray$; if the result is not unique, chose the rule with the largest $Strength$, and $M' = (r^1...r^K)$ is obtained.
3. For $\forall r^a, r^b \in M'$, with a dimidiate manner, chose the one with the maximal joint membership value by $IncArray$; if the result is not unique, chose the rule with the largest $Strength$, and the most credible rule for u is found.

In 2 and 3, for comparing rules pairs, fetch the $CstArray$ or $IncArray$ of the rule with the larger $Layer$. The random selection is applied if both the joint membership value and $Strength$ of any pair are the same.

6 Computational Experiments

To indicate the validity of our method, three medical data from the UCI Machine Learning Repository are used in our experiments. Let us notice that the data sets used in our experiments are assumed to be complete. To achieve this, except the Lymphography dataset, the medical data were slightly modified by:

1. Remove the attribute of which more than 1/3 values are missing, which is the fifth attribute in the Primary tumor with 155 missing values out of 339 ones.
2. The other 79 missing values in the total 234 missing ones are selected in the corresponding value domain with a statistic manner: in each decision class, choose the most arisen value of the attribute. 9 missing values in the above 79 ones are from the Breast cancer, and the rest 70 ones originate from the Primary tumor.

To insure the comparability, 10 fold cross-validation reclassification technique was performed. And in order to indicate the availability of our Reduced Attributed oriented Rule Generation method, three synthesis methods based on vast rules generation algorithm [5] are given for comparison. In which, Std is the standard discernibility applying a random rule selection to the rules with equal membership, HFF uses the high frequency first strategy of inconsistent rule-choosing and LFF is it's opposite. Moreover, we consult two popular rough sets based rule induction systems, i.e. new version of LERS (New LERS) and the classification coefficient oriented synthesis system based on the object-oriented programming library (RSES-lib). For the purpose of comparison, the membership value threshold for Std, HFF, LFF and RARG are all 0.55 and the coefficient threshold for RSES-lib is 0.75, which are quoted by the corresponding authors.

Table 2. Computational result with the medical datasets

Algorithm	Lymphography			Breast cancer			Primary tumor		
	Rule number	Error rate Train	Test	Rule number	Error rate Train	Test	Rule number	Error rate Train	Test
New LERS	984	0.000	0.233	1163	0.063	0.342	8576	0.245	0.671
RSES-lib	427	0.000	0.195	756	0.152	0.277	6352	0.136	0.687
Std	1321	0.000	0.320	2357	0.060	0.361	7045	0.175	0.764
HFF	1321	0.000	0.267	2357	0.042	0.338	7045	0.147	0.742
LFF	1321	0.000	0.341	2357	0.245	0.470	7045	0.360	0.720
RARG	1321	0.000	0.207	2357	0.051	0.292	7045	0.125	0.598

As shown in table 2, since HFF refined the default decision generation framework, its performance exceeds the later in all the three datasets. Due to the different granularity distribution of both classes, LFF works well in the first and the third datasets while falling across a sharply decrease in the breast cancer dataset. Because RARG provides a unified evaluation criterion for conflicts, with the irrelevant condition classes filtered, it guarantees the decision with the largest ratio of the sustaining decision objects to the effectual condition objects. For the tested objects, it refers to the most accordant rule with respect to other conflict ones. Therefore, RARG is particularly outstanding in the applications with voluminous inconsistency, such as the third dataset displayed in the result.

In conclusion, RARG takes on a comparatively high performance in the above four methods. The results also show that RARG is comparable with the other two systems, and especially, it exceeds them in the Primary tumor dataset.

References

1. Pawlak, Z., Skowron, A.: A rough set approach to decision rules generation, *Research Report 23/93, Warsaw University of Technology* (1993) 1-19
2. Michie, D., Spiegelhalter, D.J., Taylor, C.C.: *Machine learning, neural and statistical classification.* Ellis Horwood, New York. (1994)
3. Quinlan J.R.: Induction of decision trees. *Machine Learning* 1 (1986) 81-106
4. Grzymala-Busse, J.W.: A new version of the rule induction system LERS. *Fundamenta Informaticae* 31 (1887) 27-39
5. Mollesta, T., Skowron, A.: A rough set framework for data mining of propositional default rules, In *9th Int. Sym. Proc. On Found. of Intelligent Systems* (1996) 448-457
6. Bazan, J., Nguyen, H.S., Synak P., Wrblewski J.: Rough set algorithms in classification problems. *Rough set methods and applications. New Developments in Knowledge Discovery in Information Systems, Fuzziness and Soft Computing* (2000) 49-88
7. Skowron, A., Wang, H., Wojna, A., Bazan, J.G.: A hierarchical approach to multimodal classification. In *RSFDGrC05* 2 (2005) 119-127
8. Wang, G.Y., Wu, Y., Liu, F.: Generating rules and reasoning under inconsistencies. *IEEE Int. Conf. on Ind. Electronics, Control and Instrumentation* (2000) 2536-2541
9. Grzymalao-Busse, J.W., Hu, M.: A comparison of several approaches to missing attribute values in data mining. In *Ziarko and Yao (ed.), RSCTC00* (2000) 378-385
10. Dzeroski, S.: Normalized decision functions and measures for inconsistent decision tables analysis. In *Fundamenta Informaticae* 44(3) (2000) 291-319

A Non-parametric Method for Data Clustering with Optimal Variable Weighting*

Ji-Won Chung[1] and In-Chan Choi[2,**]

[1] Department of Industrial Systems and Information Engineering, Korea University,
Anamdong, Seongbookku, Seoul 136, Republic of Korea
`jiwon@idi.re.kr`

[2] Department of Industrial Systems and Information Engineering, Korea University,
Anamdong, Seongbookku, Seoul 136, Republic of Korea
Tel.: +82-2-3290-3388; Fax: +82-2-929-5888
`ichoi@korea.ac.kr`

Abstract. Since cluster analysis in data mining often deals with large-scale high-dimensional data with masking variables, it is important to remove non-contributing variables for accurate cluster recovery and also for proper interpretation of clustering results. Although the weights obtained by variable weighting methods can be used for the purpose of variable selection (or, elimination), they alone hardly provide a clear guide on selecting variables for subsequent analysis. In addition, variable selection and variable weighting are highly interrelated with the choice on the number of clusters. In this paper, we propose a non-parametric data clustering method, based on the W-k-means type clustering, for an automated and joint decision on selecting variables, determining variable weights, and deciding the number of clusters. Conclusions are drawn from computational experiments with random data and real-life data.

1 Introduction

In [24], variable weighting is described as a generalization of variable selection. Although it is possible to use the weighting results for the variable selection with human interface, the variable weighting itself does not provide any specific guide on which variables should remain in a subsequent analysis. Moreover, many variable selection methods, when used in the first stage of cluster analysis, may lose vital information [12], [13]. A different approach of discriminant analysis, which requires prior knowledge of the classes, is widely accepted in the context of cluster recovery [21], [23]. In this approach, however, both the variable selection and the variable weighting are heavily dependant on the choice of an important parameter, the number of clusters. The results on the variable selection and variable weighting may vary erratically, depending on the choice of the number of clusters.

The purpose of this paper is to propose a non-parametric clustering method for simultaneously deciding the number of clusters, determining variable weights, and

---

* This work was supported by the Korea Research Foundation Grant (KRF-2003-041-D00629).
** Corresponding author.

selecting contributory variables to include in the analysis, based on the weighted K-means algorithm. While many studies have introduced clustering indices to compute the number of clusters [20], little attention has been given to the combined problem of selecting variables with respect to the computed variable weights and determining the number of clusters.

A handful number of variable weighting methods deal with weighting and clustering problems jointly, rather than clearly separating the two tasks. The concept underlying these algorithms is to assign larger weights to contributory variables. Under this strategy for variable weights, the true cluster structure need not be assumed beforehand. Using this concept, [5] proposed SYNCLUS as a new clustering procedure, which combined K-means clustering [16] with a weighting method that used stress-type measures relevant to the amount of data in each clusters. The performance of SYNCLUS, however, was not encouraging [7].

An optimal variable weighting algorithm for hierarchical clustering, based on ultrametricity, was proposed in [6]. The method was later extended to additive tree structures [4] and it was further extended to the K-means clustering [17]. The optimal variable weighting (OVW) model of [17] used the subjective maximum limit for variable weights to avoid trivial solutions, which occurred due to the linearity of the objective function of variable weights. In [10], the W-k-means clustering method was proposed, in which the subjective maximum limit on variable weights was no longer needed. However, the combined problem of selecting variables and also determining the number of clusters simultaneously has not been explicitly addressed in the previous studies, despite variable selection and variable weights are determined as a consequence of the choice on the number of clusters.

In this paper, we present a non-parametric clustering method, in which the number of clusters, variable selection, and variable weights are not known *a priori*. The method incorporates the existing W-k-means clustering and cluster validity index, which selects the best number of clusters and variables in compliance with the computed variable weights. Finally, the results of computational experiments with randomly-generated and real-life data are provided with some conclusions.

2   The Existing Methods

The W-k-means clustering model deals with classifying n objects into distinct m clusters and simultaneously computing weights $\mathbf{w}=\{w_1,w_2,\ldots,w_p\}$ for p variables. The $n \times p$ object-by-variable data matrix $\mathbf{O}$ is used to represent n measurements on p variables. The binary decision variable x_{ik} indicates that object i belongs to group k and the continuous decision variable w_l represents the attribute weight for variable l. Indices i and j denote objects, and k and l denote group and variable indices, respectively. The following notation is used throughout this paper.

o_{il} : observed value of object i in variable l,

d_{ijl} : distance between object i and j in variable l,

n_k : the number of objects in the kth group,

S : the within-group sum-of-squares, WGSS, $S = \sum_{l=1}^{p} S_l$

S_l : WGSS computed by using attribute l only,
T : the total sum-of-squares, TSS,
T_l : TSS obtained by using attribute l only.

2.1 The W-k-Means Clustering Method

In the W-k-means model of [10], variable weights were automatically computed when the number of clusters is given as a parameter. The model can be reformulated as

$$\min \quad S(w,x) = \sum_{k=1}^{m}\sum_{i=1}^{n-1}\sum_{j=i+1}^{n}\sum_{l=1}^{p}(w_l d_{ijl})^2 x_{ik} \cdot x_{jk} / n_k \qquad (1)$$

$$s.t. \quad \sum_{k=1}^{m} x_{ik} = 1, \quad \text{for } i = 1,\ldots,n \qquad (2)$$

$$\sum_{l=1}^{p} w_l = 1, \qquad (3)$$

$$x_{ik} = 0,1, \quad w_l \geq 0, \quad \text{for } i = 1,\ldots,n,\ l=1,\ldots,p,\ k = 1,\ldots,m \qquad (4)$$

where $d_{ijl} = (o_{il} - o_{jl})$ and $n_k = \sum_{i=1}^{n} x_{ik}$.

The objective function (1) represents the weighted WGSS of all pairs of objects. Constraint (2) forces an object to belong to exactly one group. Constraint (3) excludes the trivial solution of zero weights for all p dimensions. The above formulation corresponds to the case when β of w_l^β in the original formulation of [10] is set to 2. Thus, the optimal weight for given partition $\mathbf{x}$ is obtained as $w_l^* = (S_l \sum_{i=1}^{p} S_i^{-1})^{-1}$.

2.2 The Pseudo F-Statistic

When the number of clusters, k, is not known *a priori*, the W-k-means algorithm could be used to find the correct number of clusters by an exhaustive search on different values of k for $k_{min} \leq k \leq k_{max}$, where k_{min} and k_{max} are the lower and upper bounds, respectively. The search would try to maximize or minimize a specific validity index.

The Calinski-Harabasz [2] pseudo F-statistic (CH) is a cluster validity index for determining the number of clusters in homogeneous clustering. In the simulation studies of [20], it is reported that CH performed the best for hierarchical clustering algorithms with multivariate normal data sets. Besides its superior computational performance, CH is intuitively appealing for characterizing the quality of the true cluster structure because internal cohesion and external isolation are both well represented.

Despite the advantages, CH may not identify the correct number of clusters for data with noisy dimensions (see the simulation results in section 4.2), because it does not explicitly consider variable weights to remove noisy variables. It is possible to incorporate weights directly in computing distances T and S of CH as in Eq. (5). However, such an approach would produce poor results because, without a user-supplied upper bound on the variable weight, it would result in one-dimensional solutions.

$$WCH(k) = (T(w)/S(k,w) - 1) \cdot (n-k)/(k-1) \qquad (5)$$

In [3], an improved index of CH, *MCH*, was proposed to incorporate variable selection and also to handle data with noisy variables. CH is replaced with *MCH* in the clustering procedure, where indicator variables u_l's represent variable selection. When the number of clusters is given as k, $MCH(k, u)$ is defined as

$$MCH(k,u) = \left(\sum_{l=1}^{P} T_l u_l \Big/ \sum_{l=1}^{P} S_l u_l - 1\right) \cdot (n-k)/(k-1) \tag{6}$$

In Eq. (6), the indicator variable u_l represents whether variable l is selected or not, and it is determined by Eq. (7) below.

$$u_l = \begin{cases} 0, & \text{if } CH_l^- > \alpha \\ 1, & \text{otherwise} \end{cases} \tag{7}$$

where CH_l^- is the CH value for the within-group sum-of-squares S for all but dimension l, i.e.

$$CH_l^- = \left(\left(T - \sum_{i=1,i \neq l}^{P} S_i(k)\right) \Big/ \sum_{i=1,i \neq l}^{P} S_i(k)\right) \cdot ((n-k)/(k-1))$$

and

$$\alpha = a(CH^-) + s(CH^-).$$

where $a(CH^-)$ and $s(CH^-)$ denote the average and the standard deviation of CH_l^-, $l=1$, ..., p, respectively. Thus, $a(CH^-)$ represents the average loss (gain) of information when each dimension is removed.

3 The Non-parametric Algorithm

The W-k-means method unified with *MCH* as a cluster validity index solves automatically and simultaneously four problems with reciprocal relationship, variable weighting, variable selection, determining the number of clusters, and clustering.

The algorithm for the non-parametric clustering method implements the W-k-means algorithm iteratively within a specified range of the number of clusters, and calculates *MCH* values for the partition with the minimum S at each number of clusters. Finally, the algorithm selects the partition with the maximum *MCH* value as the best solution. Thus, *MCH* determines the number of clusters with relevant variables for computing the number of clusters from the output of the W-k-means algorithm.

In the algorithm, twenty initial centers, which are randomly generated among data objects, are used for each run of W-k-means. Moreover, equal weight of $1/p$ is used as initial variable weights rather than a multiple number of random initial weights as used in [10]. The proposed algorithm employs the general sequential strategy in [8], [22] and uses the maximum number of clusters, m. We note that a small number for m, compared to the number of data points, is preferred in data mining [1], [9]. The complete algorithm is given in Fig. 1 below:

```
For k=2,3,…,m do {
  Generate 20 sets of random initial cluster centers.
  For i=1,2,…,20 do {
    Initialize variable weights to 1/p.
    While (any improvements in S(w)) {
        Run K-means with given weights and i^th initial center.
        Compute variable weights from the resulting partition of W-
        k-means, using the closed form solution.
    } EndWhile
  } EndFor i
    Select the best solution P_i with the minimum S(w) i = 1,2,…,20.
    Determine u_i by using Eq (7).
    Compute MCH for the W-k-means solution P_i using u_i.
} EndFor k
Select the best solution P_{ki} with the maximum MCH among k=2,3,…,m.
Output the selected partition and the variable weights.
```

Fig. 1. The algorithm of the W-k-means with *MCH*

4 Computational Experiments

4.1 Description of Data

To test the performance of the proposed method, we conducted computational experiments with two different artificial data sets and two real-life data sets. The first artificial data set is the synthetic data set considered by [4]. The second artificial data set was randomly generated by using the algorithm for generating artificial test clusters for a simulation study of [19] as in [20]. The real-life data sets were obtained from the UCI Repository of Machine Learning Databases at [http://www.ics.uci.edu/~mlearn/MLRepository].

In the experiment with the second artificial data set, four factors, corresponding to the number of clusters, the number of dimensions, the density levels, and the number of objects, formed a four-way factorial design. With choices of two to five clusters and of four-, six-, and eight-dimensional Euclidean spaces in the problem generation, the factorial design considered 144 cells. Moreover, three replicates were generated for each cell. Therefore, 432 datasets were produced for each error condition, resulting in 2,160 datasets over five different error conditions.

The first error type considered was error-free data; the second included 20% additional data points, which were outliers; the third involved perturbation of the error-free coordinate values with a mean of zero and a standard deviation corresponding to the cluster and dimension of each point; and the fourth and fifth error types involved the addition of one and three random noise dimensions, respectively, to the basic set of variables. Moreover, the data generated by the Milligan's algorithm were standardized using a sample range in preparing the simulation datasets.

The performance of the Non-parametric Clustering method (NC) was compared with OVW and equal weighted K-means with CH (K-CH). In the comparison, the original OVW code of [17] was used without modification and with the parameters given in their paper, *i.e.*, the variable weight limit was set to 0.7 and the number of runs was set to 10. To replicate the OVW simulation results, we used the K-means code of [14] without modification and with the same twenty random starts. Moreover, the maximum number of clusters, *m*, for W-k-means was set to twenty.

4.2 Computational Results

De Soete's data in [4] has a predefined structure: first two dimensions separate objects into three clusters and the other two dimensions are random noise with uniform distribution. The three clusters are {1,2,3,4},{5,6,7,8}, and {9,10,11,12}. NC identified exactly the three clusters, but OVW and K-CH partitioned the data into two subgroups, {1,2,3,4,9,10,11,12} and {5,6,7,8}.

In the experiment with the second artificial data set, the effectiveness of the non-parametric method NC was measured against those of OVW and K-CH, based on the corrected Rand Index (CRI), which measures similarity between two partitions of an object set [11]. Maximum value 1.0 of CRI indicates perfect match of the two partitions and value 0.0 indicates matches at the chance level.

Table 1. Mean values of the corrected Rand Index for OVW, K-CH, and NC

No of obj.	No of var.	Error-free OVW	K-CH	NC	Outliers OVW	K-CH	NC	Error-perturbed OVW	K-CH	NC	1 noise dim. OVW	K-CH	NC	3 noise dim. OVW	K-CH	NC	Average OVW	K-CH	NC	Average CPU Time OVW	K-CH	NC
50	4	0.723	0.904	0.966	0.624	0.770	0.837	0.679	0.888	0.894	0.738	0.642	0.968	0.735	0.703	0.880	0.700	0.782	0.909	1.3	0.5	1.4
50	6	0.831	0.963	0.979	0.635	0.819	0.818	0.750	0.931	0.966	0.872	0.777	0.958	0.890	0.801	0.971	0.795	0.858	0.939	1.5	0.6	1.7
50	8	0.837	0.973	0.974	0.652	0.751	0.856	0.811	0.964	0.958	0.872	0.891	0.952	0.873	0.885	0.948	0.809	0.893	0.938	1.8	0.7	2
100	4	0.757	0.900	0.984	0.655	0.772	0.794	0.733	0.898	0.899	0.758	0.594	0.965	0.805	0.585	0.865	0.742	0.750	0.901	2.3	1.0	3.8
100	6	0.857	0.969	0.991	0.765	0.878	0.892	0.761	0.973	0.958	0.872	0.826	0.995	0.929	0.801	0.983	0.837	0.889	0.964	3.1	1.3	4.8
100	8	0.871	0.986	0.987	0.748	0.865	0.886	0.841	0.984	0.964	0.912	0.946	0.986	0.895	0.898	0.983	0.853	0.936	0.961	4	1.6	6.0
150	4	0.817	0.880	0.921	0.714	0.836	0.851	0.796	0.910	0.920	0.794	0.659	0.929	0.823	0.695	0.863	0.789	0.796	0.897	3.4	1.9	7.0
150	6	0.810	0.955	0.948	0.760	0.832	0.879	0.805	0.926	0.939	0.907	0.739	0.968	0.937	0.746	0.978	0.844	0.840	0.943	4.9	2.4	9.4
150	8	0.922	0.961	0.991	0.760	0.840	0.878	0.871	0.953	0.955	0.891	0.856	0.990	0.849	0.827	0.965	0.859	0.887	0.956	5.9	3.1	11.6
200	4	0.785	0.921	0.897	0.704	0.806	0.830	0.809	0.893	0.878	0.835	0.642	0.948	0.801	0.665	0.853	0.787	0.786	0.881	5.0	2.7	11.3
200	6	0.792	0.988	0.988	0.755	0.884	0.893	0.754	0.975	0.963	0.847	0.819	0.962	0.936	0.890	0.972	0.817	0.911	0.956	7.3	3.8	14.9
200	8	0.879	0.992	0.992	0.789	0.890	0.905	0.849	0.991	0.989	0.883	0.874	0.981	0.882	0.917	0.972	0.856	0.933	0.968	8.9	5.0	18.8
Average		0.823	0.949	0.968	0.713	0.829	0.860	0.788	0.940	0.940	0.848	0.772	0.967	0.863	0.785	0.936	0.807	0.855	0.934	4.1	2.0	7.7

Table 1 summarizes the simulation results for OVW, NC, and K-CH for the non-parametric case in terms of the mean values of CRI; NC outperforms OVW and K-CH in every case for every error condition. The average computation time for each method is also included in the last three columns of the table. Fig. 2 shows the gross mean value of the three algorithms for different numbers of objects and dimensions. The figure shows the consistency in the performance of NC over OVW and K-CH. In all computation, a Pentium IV PC with a 3.0-GHz CPU and 256 MB RAM is used in the time estimation.

Table 2 summarizes the results of the experiments with Iris and Breast cancer data [18]. In it, the number of computed clusters and CRI value are given for different number of initial random centers in each method. The overall performance of NC is better than or comparable to that of K-CH and OVW for 200 initial random centers. Although the performance of NC and OVW seems to be more sensitive to the choice of initial centers than that of K-CH for Iris data set, Table 2 shows that their results could potentially be further improved with a larger number of initial random centers.

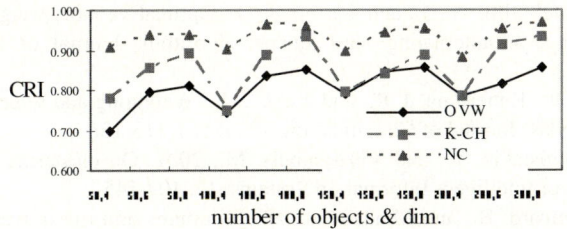
number of objects & dim.

Fig. 2. Mean values of CRI for the non-parametric method

Table 2. Experiment results with real life datasets

Data	IRIS DATA									BREAST CANCER DATA								
	OVW			K-CH			NC			OVW			K-CH			NC		
no. of init. centers	20	100	200	20	100	200	20	100	200	20	100	200	20	100	200	20	100	200
no. of cl.	3	3	3	3	3	3	4	4	3	3	3	3	2	2	2	2	2	2
CRI	0.716	0.886	0.886	0.716	0.716	0.716	0.663	0.663	0.886	0.627	0.627	0.627	0.847	0.847	0.847	0.830	0.830	0.830

5 Summary and Future Works

In this paper, we presented a non-parametric method to solve simultaneously four problems with reciprocal relationship, variable weighting, variable selection, determining the number of clusters, and clustering. The method selects variables complying with the computed variable weights in proportion to their contribution to the resultant clustering.

The results of the Monte Carlo studies of the algorithm showed that the proposed method outperformed both OVW and K-CH, but results with the real-life data tested introduced a need for further study on determining the proper number of initial centers. Furthermore, the efficiency of the proposed algorithm for large-scale datasets using vector-parallel computing remains to be investigated.

References

1. Bezdek, J. C. and Pal, N. R.: Some new indexes of cluster validity, IEEE Transaction on Systems, Man, and Cybernetics, 28(3) (1998), 301-315
2. Calinski, T. and Harabasz, J.: A dendrite method for cluster analysis, Communications in statistics, 3(1) (1974), 1-27
3. Chung, J-W. and Choi, I-C.: A new clustering index for datasets with noise dimensions, Under review, Department of ISIE, Korea University, Republic of Korea, (2006)
4. De Soete, G.: Optimal variable weighting for ultrametric and additive tree clustering, Quality and Quantity, 20 (1986), 169-180
5. DeSarbo, W. S., Carroll, J. D., Clark, L., and Green, P. E.: Synthesized clustering: a method for amalgamating alternative clustering bases with differential weighting of variables, Psychometrika, 49 (1984), 59-78

6. De Soete, G., DeSarbo, W. S., and Carroll, J. D.: Optimal variable weighting for hierarchical clustering: an alternating least-squares algorithm, Journal of Classification, 2 (1985), 173-192
7. Gnanadesikan, R., Ketterning, J. R., and Tsao, S. L.: Weighting and selection of variables for cluster analysis, Journal of Classification, 12 (1995), 113-136
8. Halkidi, M., Batistakis, Y., and Vazirgiannis, M., 2001. On clustering validation techniques, Journal of Intelligent Information Systems, 17, 107-145
9. Hansen, P., Jaumard, B., and Mladenovic, N.: Minimum sum of squares clustering in a low dimensional space, Journal of Classification, 15 (1998), 37-55
10. Huang, J. Z., Ng, M. K., Rong, H., and Li, Z.: Automated variable weighting in k-means type clustering, IEEE Transactions on Pattern Analysis and Machine Intelligence, 27(5) (2005), 657-668
11. Hubert, L. and Arabie, P.: Comparing partitions, Journal of Classification, 2 (1985), 193-218
12. Kim, M., Yoo, H., and Ramakrishna, R. S.: Cluster validation for high-dimensional datasets, AIMSA 2004, LNAI, 3192 (2004), 178-187
13. Last, M., Kandel, A., and Maimon, O.: Information-theoretic algorithm for feature selection, Pattern Recognition Letters, 22 (2001), 799-811
14. Legendre, P.: *Program K-means*, <http://www.fas.umontreal.ca/biol/legendre/> (2000)
15. Likas, A., Vlassis, N., and Verbeek, J. J.: The global k-means clustering algorithm, Pattern Recognition, 36 (2003), 451-461
16. MacQueen, J.: Some methods for classification and analysis of multivariate observations, Proceedings of the Fifth Berkeley symposium in Mathematical Statistics and Probability, 1 (1967), 231-297
17. Makarenkov, V. and Legendre, P.: Optimal variable weighting for ultrametric and additive trees and k-means partitioning: methods and software, Journal of Classification, 18 (2001), 247-271, <http://www.fas.umontreal.ca/biol/legendre/>
18. Mangasarian, O. L., Setiono, R., and Wolberg, W.H.: Pattern recognition via linear programming: Theory and application to medical diagnosis, in Large-scale numerical optimization, Coleman, T. F. and Li, Y. editors, SIAM Publications, Philadelphia, (1990), 22-30.
19. Milligan, G. W.: An algorithm for generating artificial test clusters, Psychometrika, 50(1) (1985), 123-127, <http://www.pitt.edu/~csna/Milligan/readme.html>
20. Milligan, G. W. and Cooper, M. C.: An examination of procedures for determining the number of clusters in a data set, Psychometrika, 50(2) (1985), 159-179
21. Kumar, N. and Andreou, A. G. : A generalization of linear discriminant analysis in maximum likelyhood framework, Proceedings of the Joint Statistical Meeting, Statistical Computing section, (1996)
22. Ray, S. and Turi, R. H.: Determination of number of clusters in k-means clustering and application in colour image segmentation, Proceedings of the 4th International Conference on Advances in Pattern Recognition and Digital Techniques, (1999), 137-143
23. Swets, D. L., and Weng, J. J.: Using discriminant eigenfeatures for image retrieval, IEEE Transaction on Pattern Analysis and Machine Intelligence, 18(8) (1996), 831-836
24. Wettschereck, D., Aha, D., and Mohri, T.: A review and empirical evaluation of feature weighting methods for a class of lazy learning algorithms, Artificial Intelligence Review, 11 (1997), 273-314

A Closed Model for Measuring Intangible Assets: A New Dimension of Profitability Applying Neural Networks

Ana Maria Lara Palma[1], Lourdes Sáiz Bárcena[1], and Joaquín Pacheco[2]

[1] Department of Civil Engineering, [2] Department of Applied Economy
University of Burgos, Spain
{amlara, lsaiz, jpacheco}@ubu.es

Abstract. The definition of a model should contain something more than purely conceptual development. Its discriminatory characteristics should harbour, in practice, the intention to uncover unknown opportunities in times of globalization. Quantification of the intangible value of the service sector must become another management strategy; thereby consolidating the wealth of each company and gearing up -just like in a mechanism- the variables that can predict the value of these environments which are abound in opportunities, something that has been hardly considered until lately. The rest of this paper deals with the development of M6PROK (Model of the Six Profitability Stages of Knowledge) using an artificial neural architecture. M6PROK is a mirror in which companies can look at themselves and whose reflection should provide a basis for the solution of issues concerning the profitability that knowledge brings about and the awareness of this, as well as supporting decision-making processes to consolidate business strategies.

Keywords: Knowledge management, intangibility, profitability, neuronal networks.

1 Knowledge Management: Repercussion in the Managerial World

Knowledge has meant an enormous contest for companies. It represents an extraordinary challenge for human beings, and its acquisition is sought out with a view to improving and developing our thought structures. The most innovative approach has been the suggestion to manage as well as to assign a value to it by the organizations.

We can thus appreciate the mutations that companies have undergone over the last few hundred of years, moving from being solely concerned with their survival to valuing a series of other factors, such as the development of their workers' potential and abilities, the sustained growth of new economies, the co-existence of professional and personal values, the centralization of needs, and the renewal of training or the valuation of the learning processes and knowledge management. It is therefore the precise and detailed review carried out by [1] what becomes the most accurate justification to the assertion: "Why is it that it has taken so long for knowledge to be considered as a key strategic factor!"

The sector which is the object of this research, the "service sector" provides it with flavour. Here, knowledge management has no boundaries, as its use is not only limited to large firms where the volume of work, invoicing and its payroll are overwhelming, but also to small environments and on occasions, traditional family businesses. The following section unveils how learning influences knowledge and what connotations it has for the service sector regarding knowledge.

2 Modeling Knowledge Using M6PROK

The objective that we have set out with this maxim is to prove, in accordance with the aforementioned parameters, the value of acquiring -or not acquiring- knowledge in PYMES and therefore, the transformation that these can experience in relation to the measurement of the intangible value generated, applying a model of our own creation called "Model of the Six Profitability Stages of Knowledge" (M6PROK).

All too often, the introduction of a model consists simply of presenting a graphical logic of the same without mentioning anything but its most outstanding qualities. However in this presentation, we consider modelling knowledge by examining each stage of its creation, the justification for which is based in the effect that each level has in the companies. Thus, the architecture of this model is structured in a matrix setting using four intangibility measurement ratios [2] that share two relevant characteristics; one is that their selection has a direct relationship with the cost factor, and, two, that they are caused by the lack of knowledge. These four ratios define the four axes on which the model is based on and on which results are determined.

The M6PROK is structured in a matrix setting and the way it works follows a route that is referred to as outside-in, which puts together not only the environment and structure of the company, but also its economic characteristics. In relation to the first, the relevance of the thematic index -which is the relationship between the number of times that knowledge that belongs to a specific category is used and its economical repercussion on the company- and of the state of knowledge -the definition of which takes into account the situation that the sector is facing in relation to the learning capacity and the generation of new knowledge- which give rise to the so-called external matrix.

On the other hand, the cost of knowledge has been considered -the suggestion of a cost that derives from activities focused on the acquisition of the same- performance costs calculated on the basis of knowledge acquisition -and the cost of non-knowledge- conceptualized as the cost deriving from insufficient awareness of concepts that pertain to the sector- which configure the internal matrix.

It should be added that its design and structure were drawn from a second stage in which the matrix of the model was divided into four areas to reflect the situation of each company in relation to its knowledge, according to the different thematic indexes, and the relevance of each of these. The naming of each area in the matrix corresponds to a combination of factors and circumstances, and they are: control area (outlined in green), critical situation area (outlined in red), inflection area (outlined in blue) and growth area (outlined in orange). The restructuring of the profitability levels of knowledge takes place under these. Fig. 1 shows the combination of the two stages in the chosen grouping and the exchange of values between the variables in order to create the basic operational and intangibility measurement structure.

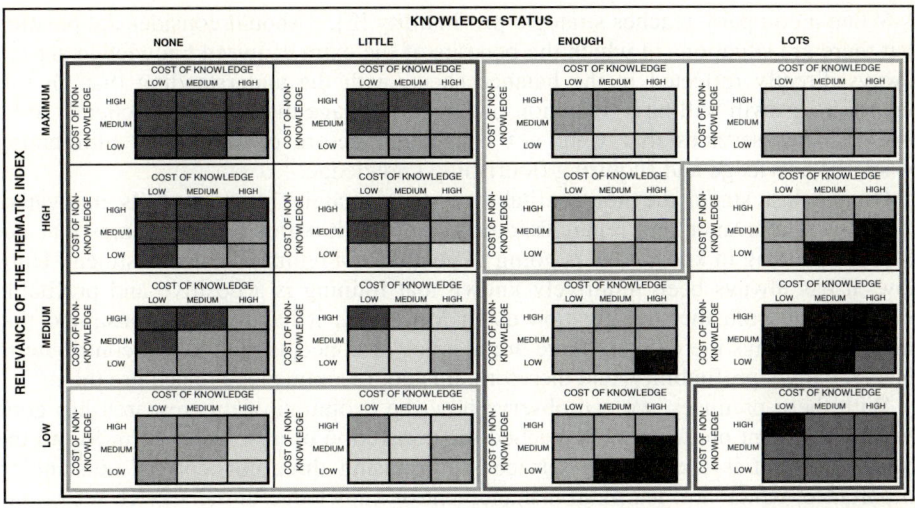

Fig. 1. Flow Diagram of the Sequence for the Handling of Information in the M6PROK Model

3 Handling of Information and Display of the Profitability Stages

Having presented the sequence of matrix restructuring, the operational handling of the model takes place. All the knowledge of each activity (that is already located in one of the parcels of the model due to the fact that the information provides both the relevance of the knowledge and its status) is displayed, rating each one of them according to its knowledge and non-knowledge evaluation.

At this point, it is now possible to use a tool called the Matrix of Grouped Data, the structure of which allows the regrouping of all the activities and knowledge in order of equality between two of its parameters which are the cost of knowledge and of non-knowledge. Fig. 2 depicts schematically and in synthesis the handling of information and the sequential procedures that must be followed.

The results obtained from the use of the model lead to a series of conclusions that underline the causes and their corresponding effects and the need for the necessary steps for knowledge to be a source of growth and continuous improvement. In this regard, the output of the model is profitability at very short-term that leads into an immediate profit gain once the company acquires specific knowledge.

In second place is the short-term profitability, noting that in this case the acquisition of knowledge continues to be profitable, but that the return on the investment is not as immediate as in the previous case. A sure bet is the medium-term profitability, in the sense that knowledge is being gained without urgency, allowing for it to be profitable in a relatively short period of time.

A very advantageous situation occurs if the company involves itself in long-term profitability, as this places the company in a better situation when it comes to its knowledge status, so that, regardless of the frequency of the demand for its services, it will always be prepared to undertake the projects that are presented to it. Therefore, in principle, the acquisition of knowledge continues to be a profitable exercise, although the results will only be seen in a longer period of time.

When a company reaches strategic profitability [3], it should consider the position that there are situations in which the benefits of the extra acquired knowledge are not always directly reflected in the balance sheet, with the understanding that, in this regard, its growth will be a reflection of the good image that it offer its clients, to be able to offer services that were not considered before or simply by eliminating obsolete knowledge and acquiring flourishing knowledge.

On the last stage, the non-profitability stage, mainly because of its innovative concept, its relevance and repercussions, given that it warns the companies that not always investing in knowledge is going to guarantee a return on the investment. Until now, it has always been intuitively known that training is a positive and profitable practice, but from the investigation using M6PROK, it has been demonstrated that this is not always the case, as there are a series of concepts that do not contribute to the company's profitability, and therefore, it is not recommended to acquire them.

With these premises, we can observe how the evolution of this research has gone through different phases until it reached the concretion of a stratified form for all the knowledge that is used in the service sector, using three concepts of outstanding importance, which are: learning, management of knowledge in the service sector and the viable quantification of the intangible value that lies in these environments.

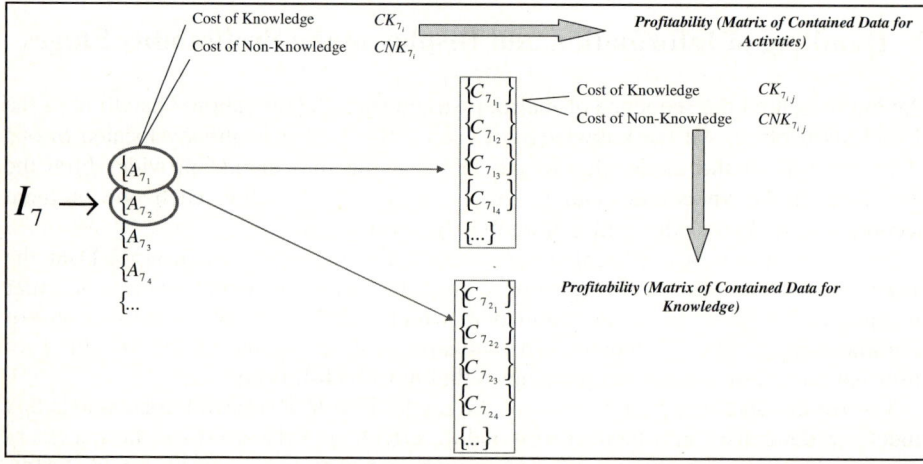

Fig. 2. Sequence of the Treatment of the Information in the M6PROK

4 Neural Network Methodology for the M6PROK Model

A multiple-layer model is going to be considered for predicting the State of the Knowledge about a specific subject inside one company (SK), studying three parameters: the Cost of acquiring that knowledge (CK-Cost of Knowledge), how many looses the company will have due to not having full domain of the knowledge (CNK-Cost of Non Knowledge) and the relevance of that concrete knowledge (RTI-Relevance of the Thematic Index).

For this study, it will be used a multiple-layer perceptron with one hidden layer, where n will be the number of input variables (CK, CNK and RTI, so n=3), and m the number of neurons in the hidden layer (according to the different stages of Profitability of the Knowledge, PROK (see Fig. 1), so m=9). On the output layer, only one neuron is considered. The selected program language was PASCAL, and the compiler was Delphi (version 5) from Borland. A schematic representation is shown in Fig. 3 [4].

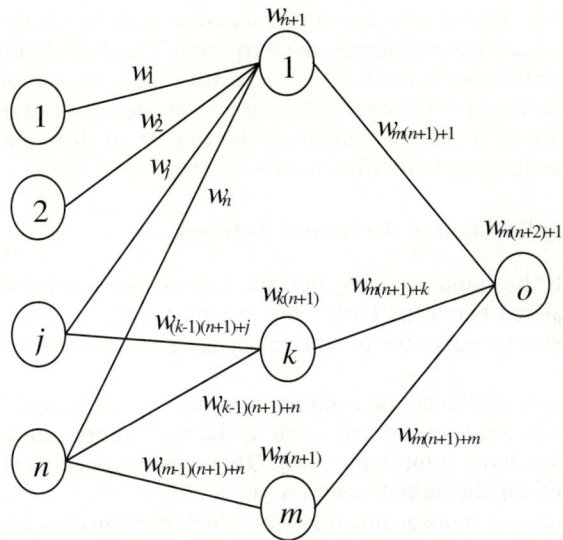

Fig. 3. Neural network architecture

The network reads input values (CK, CNK and RTI) and propagates from one layer to another until the output is produced (SK). Then, weights are sequentially numbered such that the weights that link the input layer with the first neuron of the hidden layer range from w_1 to w_n where their bias term is w_{n+1}.

The network reads an input vector $e = (e_j)$ and the information propagates from one layer to another until output s is produced. Thus, the input information of each neuron, $k = 1, ..., m$, of the hidden layer is given by:

$$z_k = w_{k(n+1)} + \sum_{j=1}^{n} w_{(k-1)(n+1)+j}\, e_j , \qquad (1)$$

and the output neuron receives the following data:

$$w_{m(n+2)+1} + \sum_{k=1}^{m} w_{m(n+1)+k} a_k \qquad (2)$$

where a_k are the outputs from the hidden neurons. In our example, a sigmoid function (a_k) is used as a transfer function for the hidden layer and an identity function (s) is used for the output neuron. Thus,

$$a_k = \frac{1}{1+e^{-z_k}}, \qquad (3)$$

$$s = w_{m(n+2)+1} + \sum_{k=1}^{m} w_{m(n+1)+k}\, a_k\ . \qquad (4)$$

As the M6PROK Model was developed together with the help of many experts working for several service companies, the purpose of this NN algorithm is to use this work to extrapolate the results to all different sectors. This is a sample of using NN in order to support the Human Resources Department inside a firm to develop a sensible Training Policy. Even, it allows comparing the impact of different Training Policy between companies that work in different environments or sectors.

4.1 The Training Problem of the Neural Network

Prior to start with the training of the net, the values of each variables of the input vectors are normalized between -1 (the lowest value in the training set) and +1 (the highest) for the training stage; the output values are also normalized between 0.8 and +0.8 [5].

There are several methods for training this neural net model in the literature. Algorithms based on gradient descent, such as the back-propagation method [6], [7], [8] and [9], but they have some limitations. They convergence to poor local optimal and are dependent on the initial solution. In addition, they are not applicable to network models that use transfer functions for which derivatives cannot be calculated. On the other hand, Genetic Algorithms have been highlighted in works such as [10], [11], [12], [13], [14] and [15].

In this work a Memetic Algorithm [16] for the training of this neural network model is selected. One aspect to take into account is that due to the type of transfer functions used, these methods only seek weight values in the hidden layer. Those in the output layer are obtained by the least squares method, ensuring good results [5].

Usually a subset of values are used for training the net and some subsets (test subsets) are used for checking that "trained" net performs well. In the original M6PROK Model there were used 2.779 values (all the different Knowledge inside the electric companies working in the service sector). From the NN study, a subset of 1.379 of them were selected as the training set, and 10 subsets of 140 values each were taken as test sets. The next table summarizes the results (success ratio = percentage of "good predictions") obtained by the net.

Table 1. Summary of Results

	SUCCESS RAT.
TRAINING SET	75,1
TEST SETS	
Minimum	70,4
Mean	71,2
Maximum	72,1

Therefore it can be diagnosed where the service sector companies should invest their training budgets, in order to get the most out from their money.

5 Conclusions

This paper started explaining how learning is configured as the root that feeds creative minds. Without learning, creativity does not exist; neither does critical formulations, deviations in the generation of explicit ideas or originality. Learning is, therefore, [17] a measurement of the organizational value, although, considering that it is people who develop it and make it productive.

Nowadays, the service sector environment is prone to achieve good management of its intellectual assets. M6PROK provides a response to this need. This management strategy tool places the service sector in an advantage position against non-structured companies, by allowing these to set in operation the model's own capabilities and the body of knowledge developed for all the structures that make it up, be it the clients, workers, technicians, the competition and the lack of quality. In turn, and as a consequence of the use of the model, six levels of profitability become apparent (very short-term profitability, short-term profitability, medium-term profitability, long-term profitability, strategic profitability and non-profitability) providing enough information for a company to take corrective measures depending on the results of the four variables that make up the model.

According to the results, knowledge management is not merely a theoretical concept: it establishes a practical framework that can quantify the market value that lies on small and medium companies, allowing them to analyze and direct their efforts towards operational excellence.

Acknowledgments. Authors are grateful to Spanish Ministry of Education for Financial Support (National Plan R&D, Project SEJ-2005 08923/ECON).

References

1. Nadal, J., Benaul, J. M., Sudría, C.: Atlas de la Industrialización de España, 1750-2000. Fundación BBVA. Editorial Crítica, S. L. Barcelona (2003)
2. Cameli, A., Tishler, A.: The Relationships Between Intangible Organizational Elements and Organizational Performance. Strategic Management Journal, Vol. 25. Chichester (2004) 1257-1279
3. Camillus, J. C.: Turning Strategy into Action. Tools and Techniques for Implementing Strategic Plans, an APQC Best Practise Research Report. APQC Research Report. Harvard Business Review, New York (2004)
4. Laguna, M., Martí, R.: Neural Network Prediction in a System for Optimizing Simulations. IEE Transactions (2002)
5. Sexton, R. S., Alidaee, B., Dorsey, R. E., Johnson, J. D.: Global Optimization for Artificial Neural Networks: A Tabu Search Application, European Journal of Operational Research (1998)
6. Werbos, P.: Beyond Regression: New Tools for Prediction and Analysis in the Behavioral Sciences. PhD thesis. Harvard, Cambridge (1974)

7. Parker, D.: Learning Logic, Technical Report TR-87. Center for Computational Research in Economics and Management Science, MIT, Cambridge (1985)
8. Lecun, Y.: Learning Process in an Asymmetric Threshold Network. In: Disordered Systems and Biological Organization. Springer, Berlin (1986) 233-240
9. Rumelhart, D., Hinton, G., Williams, R.: Learning Internal Representations by Error Propagation. In: Rumelhart, D., McCleeland, J. (eds.): Parallel Distributed Processing, Explorations in the Microstructure of Cognition. Vol.1. MIT Press, Cambridge (1986)
10. Montana, D. J., Davis, L.: Training Feedforward Neural Networks Using Genetic Algorithms. In: Kaufmann, M.: Proceedings of the Third International Conference on Genetic Algorithms, San Mateo, CA. (1989) 379-384
11. Schaffer, J. D.: Combinations of Genetic Algorithms with Neural Networks or Fuzzy Systems. In: Zurada, J. M., Marks, R. J., Robinson, C. J. (eds.): Computational Intelligence: Imitating Life. IEEE Press (1994) 371-382.
12. Schaffer, J. D., Whitley, D., Eshelman, L. J.: Combinations of Genetic Algorithms and Neural Networks: A survey of the State of the Art. In: COGANN-92 Combinations of Genetic Algorithms and Neural Networks, IEEE Computer Society Press, Los Alamitos, CA. (1992) 1-37
13. Dorsey, R. E., Johnson, J. D., Mayer, W. J.: A Genetic Algorithm for the Training of Feedforward Neural Networks. In: Johnson, J. D., Whinston, A. B. (eds.): Advances in Artificial Intelligence in Economics, Finance and Management, Vol. 1. JAI Press, Greenwich, CT, (1994) 93-111
14. Topchy, A. P., Lebedko, O. A., Miagkikh, V. V.: Fast Learning in Multilayered Networks by Means of Hybrid Evolutionary and Gradient Algorithms. In: Proceedings of International Conference on Evolutionary Computation and its Applications (1996)
15. Sexton, R. S., Dorsey, R. E., Johnson, J. D.: Optimization of Neural Networks: A Comparative Analysis of the Genetic Algorithm and Simulated Annealing, Vol. 114. European Journal of Operational Research (1999) 589-601
16. Aragon, A., Krasnogor, N., Pacheco, J.: Memetic Algorithms. Book Chapter in Metaheuristics in Neural Networks Learning. Eds. Rafael Marti and Enrique Alba, Kluver (2006)
17. De Treville, S.: Disruption, Learning and System Improvement in JIT Manufacturing. Thesis GSB, Harvard University, Ann Arbor (Michigan) (1987)

Audio and Video Feature Fusion for Activity Recognition in Unconstrained Videos

José Lopes and Sameer Singh

Research School of Informatics, Loughborough University, Loughborough, LE11 3TU, UK
J.E.F.C.Lopes@lboro.ac.uk, S.Singh@lboro.ac.uk

Abstract. Combining audio and image processing for understanding video content has several benefits when compared to using each modality on their own. For the task of context and activity recognition in video sequences, it is important to explore both data streams to gather relevant information. In this paper we describe a video context and activity recognition model. Our work extracts a range of audio and visual features, followed by feature reduction and information fusion. We show that combining audio with video based decision making improves the quality of context and activity recognition in videos by 4% over audio data and 18% over image data.

1 Introduction

The objective of this paper is to develop an automated feature extraction and classification scheme that discriminates between different activities in audiovisual sequences. These activities captured in unconstrained videos include the recognition of a vehicle driving past, a person clapping his/hers hands, a person opening, going through and closing a door, a person walking, a person talking, a train going past, a person typing at a keyboard [9]. These activities can be recognized both using audio [9] and visual classifiers but we show that their recognition is greatly enhanced by information fusion across these two modalities. This problem is unique in the literature; most work using both modalities has limited itself to human computer interaction or person recognition and verification [13]. We analyze the combination methods for fusing audio-visual decisions and evaluate a number of audio and video features to determine which are best suited for the task. Integration of different modalities for video information classification can enhance system performance through the cooperation and interaction between dissimilar data sources. This integration can take many forms as proposed by Martin et al. [11], e.g. transfer, equivalence, specialization, redundancy and complementarity. Several approaches to audio and video fusion have been suggested in the literature. These can be classified into three main groups: data fusion, feature fusion and decision fusion [15] (Figure 1). Data fusion is rarely found in multi-modal systems because raw data is usually incompatible. Audio is represented by one-dimensional high frequency data whereas video is organized in two-dimensional frames over time at a much lower rate. There are issues when synchronizing both sources, as well as the fact that video only represents the space covered by the camera frustum. As a result, in this paper, we concentrate on decision fusion and feature fusion.

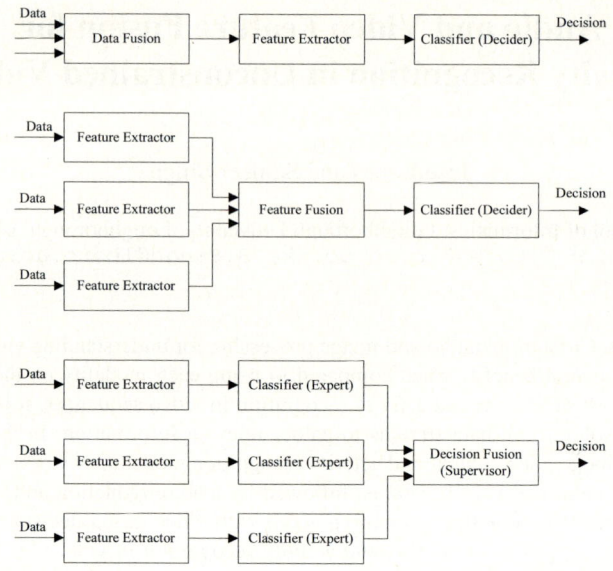

Fig. 1. Fusion levels: Data fusion; Feature fusion; Decision fusion

This paper is organized as follows: Section 2 describes the problem and data collection in detail. Section 3 provides an overview of features extracted and used in the classification stage (discussed in Section 4) and finally, in Section 5, the results are interpreted and further work is proposed.

2 Problem Domain

Our work tackles the problem of identifying activities or events that are commonly present in natural and highly unconstrained videos of day-to-day situations. Since the problem domain is very broad, a limited number of classes has been selected to represent situations where both audio and video cues are present. The following activities form distinct classes for recognition:

- Class c_1 : Car - a vehicle driving past;
- Class c_2 : Clap – a person clapping his/hers hands;
- Class c_3 : Door – a person opening, going through and closing a door;
- Class c_4 : Step – a person walking;
- Class c_5 : Talk – a person talking;
- Class c_6 : Train – a train going past;
- Class c_7 : Type – a person typing at a keyboard.

The samples of the above seven different activities were collected using a digital video camera. The only constraint is the fact that only one (at most two in some cases, e.g. two hands clapping or person+door) objects have spatial movement in the scene.

Each of these sample video clips was later reduced to 8 seconds in length. The audio signal was extracted and saved in a mono, uncompressed PCM .wav file, sampled at 44.1 kHz at 16 bits. One of the major problems with audio analysis is the presence of background noise. We decided not to perform any preprocessing to remove such noise because of the risks involved with affecting the signal of interest and the difficulty in modeling the differences between the signal of interest and other signals. The database used contained 30 samples (videos) per class - a total of 210 samples (videos).

A preliminary visual inspection of the audio files shows that the signals across these seven classes are not totally distinguishable. The 'clap', 'step' and 'type' class signals are periodic and regular, whereas 'train' and 'car' are loud and noisier. The class 'talk' is more erratic, and because speaking can be done both indoors and outdoors, some of the samples are noisier than others. However, some classes have similar characteristics. For example, the 'step' and 'door' classes are similar because both 'door' clips have stepping sounds. 'Car' and 'train' videos are similar because they contain vehicles that are present in an outdoor environment and contain higher ambient sounds.

In video, visual features can be extracted on object motion, texture, colour and shape to recognize them and understand their behaviour. A preliminary inspection of the videos show that visual features are not very robust given the changes in illumination, variability in object viewpoint and different instances of the same object, unpredictable object motion, changes in skin tone, and so on. As a result, the identification of objects and their activities based on visual information alone is highly challenging. In the next section we describe the audio and visual features extracted from videos and discuss their correlation.

3 Feature Extraction

3.1 Audio Features

Signal and audio processing are mature fields with several well-established, reliable techniques. We computed several popular audio features to be included in our machine learning system. These included:

Bandwidth Features BW (a_1 - a_{90}) [7] – This includes the width between two frequency bands f_1 and f_2 over the whole signal. For the purpose of this work, it represents the width of the smallest frequency band within which a signal can fit. This uses the frequency centroid value of each time component to deduce its value.

FCVC4 (a_{91}) [7] – Frequency Component of the Volume Contour around 4Hz.

FQC (a_{92}-a_{181}) [7] – Frequency Centroid. This feature represents the clarity of the signal by evaluating the centre of each frequency domain obtained by the Fourier transform and the magnitude information.

Gabor (a_{182}-a_{545}) [3] – The Gabor function is widely used as a filter and as a basis function for de-correlation. For this study, the signals were Gabor filtered and then the corresponding main LPC coefficients were used as features for classification.

HPS (a_{546}-a_{674}) [5] – Harmonic Product Spectrum is a methodology employed to approximate fundamental frequency f_0.

LPC (a_{675}-a_{1029}) [3] – Linear Predictive Coefficients exploit the auto-correlated characteristics of the input waveform by estimating the value of the current sample using a linear combination of the previous samples.

MFCC (a_{1030}-a_{2049}) [1] – The Mel Frequency Cepstral Coefficients emphasize the lower frequencies which are perceptually more meaningful in speech.

Power (a_{2050}-a_{2089}) [8] – The power spectrum is the energy present in the signal's Fourier transform.

Silence and VDR (a_{2090}, a_{2091}) [8] – based on the Volume Contour (VC – divide the signal into overlapping frames and take the Root Mean Square of the signal magnitude within each frame). Silence reports the ratio between the period of time with low VC and the time with high VC. VDR corresponds to VC range.

HER features – the High Energy Region uses the spectrogram of the audio signal. It is defined by the highest energy peak, together with the left and right thresholds defined as a fraction of that peak. Several features are computed within this region as defined below:

- Area (a_{2092}) – The energy area within the HER: ($\forall f \in spec : energy_f = \sum_{\omega \in f} |A_\omega|$,

  where f is a frame, ω is frequency and A_ω the corresponding Fourier coefficient);
- Average Distance (a_{2093}) between peaks. This is achieved by finding other high energy peaks and computing their average temporal distance.
- Duration (a_{2094}) – The duration of the HER.
- Spectogram Moment (a_{2095}) –

$$\sum_{f,\omega \in HER} |A_\omega| \times d((f,\omega),\mu), \; \mu = \begin{pmatrix} mean(f), mean(\omega) \\ f \in HER \quad f \in HER \end{pmatrix}$$

and $d(.)$ is the Euclidean distance.

- Peak value itself (a_{2096});
- In addition, we also compute the previous features within this region (sBW, sFCVC4, sFQC, sGabor, sHPS, sLPC, sMFCC and sPower) (a_{2097}-a_{2234}).

3.2 Visual Features

For recognizing activities we can obtain cues from both the object itself and its motion behavior. Image object segmentation is a research area on its own and not the focus of this work. In our study the objects were segmented by motion based region clustering. A number of well-established image processing features were computed to reflect the object's colour, texture and shape characteristics as described below:

Colour Spaces (v_1-v_{108}) – statistics (mean, standard deviation, skewness, kurtosis, entropy and energy) of each channel of the RGB, rgb, YIQ, HSI, TSL and LCH colour spaces.

Laws Masks (v_{109}-v_{558}) [6] – the RGB channels were convoluted with 5x5 Laws masks to enhance texture structure and the same statistics were produced.

Colour Moments (v_{559}-v_{563}) [12] – invariant to illumination and viewpoint, these features are commonly used in characterizing object colour and to some extent shape (we used feature set G from [12]).

Wavelet (v_{564}-v_{707}) [16] – we computed statistics on the coefficients resulting from discrete wavelet decomposition to 3 levels using Daubechies basis functions.

Ellipse fitting (v_{708}-v_{717}) [2] – Least Squares Ellipse fitting of the mask allow the extraction of some shape features (ratio between major and minor axis, angle, ellipse coefficients and the ratio between number of pixels inside and outside the ellipse).

To describe object movement, we performed Fourier phase motion compensation [17] to stabilize the background and then processed the sequence with a KLT tracker [10] (v_{718}-v_{740}). The 10 tracked points displaying most movement through the sequence are selected for feature extraction. We compute the global magnitude of displacement, average displacement and the first DFT components in the x and y directions.

4 Experimental Setup

All experiments were performed by randomly dividing the data set into separate training and data sets with 15 samples for each class in the training set and the same amount in test set. Hence, there are 105 samples in training and 105 samples in test set. We perform feature selection to reduce the number of discriminatory features. This is important for several reasons. We need to avoid the curse of dimensionality and select a number of features that are relevant and reduce redundancy. It can also provide evidence that selecting features from both modalities is beneficial (as discussed later). For this purpose, we use the Sequential Forward Floating Selection (SFFS) algorithm [14]. The measure of separability used for SFFS was the success rate of a leave-one-out kNN classifier using the training data.

Once the appropriate features are selected, in order to study the benefit of combining both modalities, we compare the performance of different systems using the same classification setup. The kNN classifier was chosen for all experiments. All experiments were performed on a selection of 35 features using SFFS and used $k = 7$ for the kNN classifier.

Figure 2 shows the correlation matrix in a graphical form for the entire 2974 feature set (740 video + 2234 audio). Each pixel represents a correlation value and rows and columns of pixels (left to right, top to bottom) index the features in ascending order. Brighter areas denote high correlation. The matrix presents a block diagonal structure, suggesting some dependency between features of each set and, more

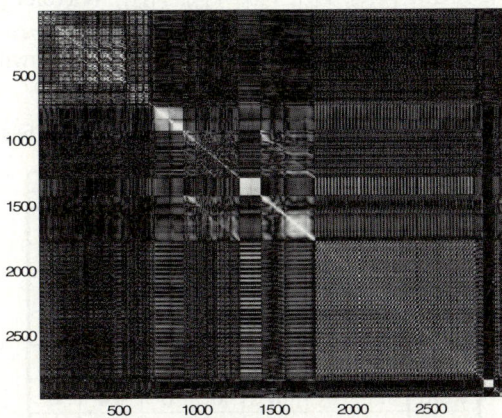

Fig. 2. Correlation matrix of video and audio features

importantly, low correlation between features of different modalities. This is the property we intend to explore – that by selecting features from different sets, the recognition rate will improve. This figure shows that there are several regions of high image intensity confirming that there is high correlation amongst features and sufficient scope for removing redundant features.

4.1 Classification Results Based on Audio Only

The application of SFFS feature selection methodology on audio features alone yielded the following features: Gabor [a_{251}]; LPC [a_{750}, a_{763}, a_{759}, a_{731}]; MFCC [a_{1105}, a_{1492}, a_{1390}, a_{1063}, a_{1528}]; Power [a_{2075}, a_{2073}, a_{2071}, a_{2054}]; Silence [a_{2099}]; sFCVC4 [a_{2098}]; sMFCC [a_{2195}, a_{2187}]; sPower [a_{2234}, a_{2232}, a_{2231}, a_{2230}, a_{2229}, a_{2229}, a_{2218}, a_{2233}, a_{2228}, a_{2223}, a_{2222}, a_{2221}, a_{2220}, a_{2219}, a_{2213}, a_{2208}, a_{2204}, a_{2200}]. Using these features for testing, we obtain the following confusion matrix and a success rate of 65% (Table 1).

Table 1. Confusion matrix for 7NN test using audio features

Audio	car	clap	door	step	talk	train	type
car	**12**	0	0	2	0	0	1
clap	0	**12**	0	1	0	0	2
door	0	1	**9**	1	1	0	3
step	0	0	6	**4**	1	0	4
talk	3	0	0	0	**11**	0	1
train	2	0	0	0	0	**13**	0
type	0	2	2	2	1	0	**8**

4.2 Classification Results Based on Video Only

The application of SFFS feature selection methodology on visual features alone yielded the following features: rgb [v_{26}, v_{27}]; YIQ [v_{48}]; HIS [v_{66}]; TSL [v_{73}, v_{77}, v_{85}, v_{78}]; LCH [$v1_{08}$, v_{91}]; LMM [v_{359}, v_{481}, v_{196}, v_{329}, v_{114}]; Wavelet [v_{590}, v_{681}, v_{689}, v_{669}, v_{664}, v_{663}, v_{641}, v_{699}]; Shape [v_{712}, v_{709}]; KLT [v_{718}, v_{738}, v_{732}, v_{740}, v_{739}, v_{733}, v_{729}, v_{736}, v_{735}, v_{737}]. These features produced a success rate of 78% as shown in Table 2.

Table 2. Confusion matrix for 7NN test using video features

Video	car	clap	door	step	talk	train	type
car	**12**	1	0	0	0	2	0
clap	1	**11**	0	0	3	0	0
door	0	2	**12**	1	0	0	0
step	0	1	6	**5**	2	0	1
talk	0	1	0	0	**14**	0	0
train	1	0	0	0	0	**14**	0
type	0	0	0	0	1	0	**14**

4.3 Classification Results Based on Audio and Video Decision Level Fusion

There are several approaches to combining classifier decisions. Kittler et al. [4] explored a variety of rules based on the *a posteriori* probabilities modeled by each classifier. Based on their work, we take the outputs of the classifiers used in section 5.1 and 5.2 and use the sum rule (which exhibited good efficiency and is robust to errors). The success rate achieved was 83%, an increase of 5% and 18% over video and audio alone, respectively.

Table 3. Confusion matrix for 7NN test using decision fusion

Audio	car	clap	door	step	talk	train	type
car	**14**	0	0	0	0	1	0
clap	0	**14**	0	1	0	0	0
door	0	2	**11**	1	0	0	1
step	0	0	5	**6**	1	0	3
talk	1	0	0	0	**14**	0	0
train	1	0	0	0	0	**14**	0
type	0	0	0	1	0	0	**14**

4.4 Feature Level Fusion of Audio and Video

The application of SFFS feature selection methodology on audio and video features together yielded the following features: RGB [v_4]; LMM [v_{193}]; Wavelet [v_{671}, v_{593}, v_{567}, v_{575}]; KLT [v_{718}]; Gabor [a_{182}]; LPC [a_{675}]; MFCC [a_{1177}, a_{1921}]; Power [a_{2087}, a_{2078}, a_{2086}, a_{2080}, a_{2063}, a_{2055}, a_{2054}]; sPower [a_{2231}, a_{2219}, a_{2204}, a_{2199}, a_{2234}, a_{2233}, a_{2232}, a_{2220}, a_{2201}, a_{2200}, a_{2229}, a_{2202}, a_{2198}, a_{2221}, a_{2213}, a_{2212}, a_{2207}]. As expected, features from both modalities were selected, indicating that there are advantages in exploring their interaction. Furthermore, the classification success rate on the test set improved to 82% (table 4), which is a similar performance increase to the decision fusion model. It is noteworthy to mention that while in the decision fusion model we select 35 features for each modality, the feature fusion model also uses only 35 features. Therefore, we obtain similar results with half the information with feature fusion model.

Table 4. Confusion matrix for 7NN test using feature fusion

Video+Audio	car	clap	door	step	talk	train	type
car	**14**	1	0	0	0	0	0
clap	0	**15**	0	0	0	0	0
door	1	0	**13**	1	0	0	0
step	0	2	6	**4**	1	0	0
talk	0	0	1	1	**13**	0	0
train	0	0	0	0	0	**15**	0
type	0	0	0	3	0	0	**12**

Finally, we need to mention the fact that all models exhibit some confusion between the classes 'door' and 'step'. This is due to the presence of people walking with the objective of opening the door. There is no simple solution to this problem unless further semantic information is used in our model.

5 Conclusion

In this paper we have performed exhaustive experimentation to demonstrate that audio-visual information can be effectively combined for robust classification of activities in unconstrained video sequences. We have performed detailed analysis on a large number of videos by extracting a large number of features. Our results show that substantial classification gains are possible both using feature and decision level fusion. This process is very important to the future of autonomous systems (e.g. robots) that will need to understand scene context and object activity recognition by combing audio and visual cues. Our future work needs to explore the proposed context on a very large video benchmark and improve upon object detection. We also need to address the problems of object occlusion, viewpoint, illumination changes and improved data pre-processing.

References

1. P. Boersma, "Accurate Short-Term Analysis of the Fundamental Frequency and the Harmonics-to-Noise Ratio of a Sampled Sound", Institute of Phonetic Sciences, University of Amsterdam, Proceedings 17, 1993.
2. R. Halif and J. Flusser, "Numerically Stable Direct Least Squares Fitting of Ellipses," Department of Software Engineering, Charles University, Czech Republic, 2000.
3. Y. H. Hu and J.-N. Hwant, "Handbook of Neural Network Signal Processing", CRC Press.
4. J. Kittler, M. Hatef, R.P.W. Duin and J. Matas, "On Combining Classifiers", IEEE Transactions on Pattern Analysis and Machine Intelligence, vol. 20(3), pp. 226-239, 1998.
5. R. Kobes and G. Kunstatter, "Physics 1501 – Modern Technology", Physics Department, University of Winnipeg.
6. K. I. Laws, "Textured image segmentation", Ph.D. thesis, University of Southern California, 1980.
7. Z. Liu and Y. Wang, "Audio Feature Extraction and Analysis for Scene Segmentation and Classification", Journal of VLSI Signal Processing, pp. 61-79, 1998.
8. Z. Liu, J. Huang and Y. Wang, "Classification of TV Programs Based on Audio Information Using Hidden Markov Model", IEEE Workshop on Multimedia Signal Processing, 1998.
9. J. Lopes, C. Lin and S.Singh, "Multi-stage Classification for Audio based Activity Recognition", Submited to International Conference on Intelligent Data Engineering and Automated Learning, 2006.
10. B. D. Lucas and T. Kanade, "An Iterative Image Registration Technique with an Application to Stereo Vision", International Joint Conference on Artificial Intelligence, pages 674-679, 1981.
11. J.C. Martin, R. Veldman and D. Beroule, "Developing multimodal interfaces: a theoretical framework and guided propagation networks", In Multimodal Human-Computer Communication. H. Bunt, R.J. Beun, & T. Borghuis, (Eds.), 1998.

12. F. Mindru, T. Moons, L. Van Gool, "Recognizing color patterns irrespective of viewpoint and illumination", Proc. IEEE Conf. on Computer Vision and Pattern Recognition (CVPR'99), 1999, pp. 368-373.
13. M. R. Naphade and T. Huang, "Extracting semantics from audiovisual content: the final frontier in multimedia retrieval", IEEE Transactions on Neural Networks, 13, pp. 793-810, 2002.
14. P.Pudil, J. Navovicova, and J.Kittler, "Floating search methods in feature selection", Pattern Recognition Letters, 15(1994), 1119-1125.
15. R. Sharma, V. I. Pavlovic and T. S. Huang, "Toward multimodal human-computer interface", In Proceedings of the IEEE, vol. 86(5), pp. 853-869, 1998.
16. M. Sonka, V. Hlavac, R. Boyle. Image Processing, Analysis and Machine Vision. Brooks/Cole, 1999.
17. J. Watkinson, "The Engineer's Guide to Motion Compensation", Petersfield, Snell & Wilcox, 1994.

Multi-stage Classification for Audio Based Activity Recognition

José Lopes, Charles Lin, and Sameer Singh

Research School of Informatics, Loughborough University, Loughborough LE11 3TU, UK
J.E.F.C.Lopes@lboro.ac.uk, S.Singh@lboro.ac.uk

Abstract. Context recognition in indoor and outdoor surroundings is an important area of research for the development of autonomous systems. This work describes an approach to the classification of audio signals found in both indoor and outdoor environments. Several audio features are extracted from raw signals. We analyze the relevance and importance of these features and use that information to design a multi-stage classifier architecture. Our results show that the multi-stage classification scheme is superior than a single stage classifier and it generates an 80% success rate on a 7 class problem.

1 Introduction

The human auditory system is very good at differentiating in what we hear, as well as filtering background noise. However, the classification of audio signals is not a trivial problem. Auditory scene analysis has been widely studied [4]. This is a challenging area of research, because sounds can be highly variable, mixed, distorted and noisy. Audio analysis has been used in a number of applications including automatic speaker recognition [3], musical genre classification [17][20], speech recognition [14], blind source separation (BSS) and independent component analysis (ICA) [2]. Features used include time-domain and frequency-domain features [9]. Time-domain features include techniques such as zero-crossing rate [20] and LPC [5] and frequency domain methods include MFCC. Some of these features are described in more detail in section 2. A number of classifiers have been experimented with for audio classification. These include kNN and rule based systems [12] Neural Networks [16], Support Vector Machines [20] and Gaussian Mixture Models [21].

The objective of our project is to develop an automated feature extraction and classification scheme that recognizes different audio signals. We propose the use of a multi-stage classifier architecture. We aim to evaluate a number of audio features and determine which features are best suited for the task. The paper is organized as follows: Section 2 describes the problem and data collection aspects in detail. Section 3 provides an overview of features extracted and used in the classification stage, which is presented in section 4. Finally, in section 5, the results are commented and further work is proposed.

2 Problem Domain

The audio signals come from the following activities and form distinct classes for recognition.

Class c_1 : Car - a vehicle driving past;

Class c_2 : Clap – a person clapping his/hers hands;

Class c_3 : Door – a person opening, going through and closing a door;

Class c_4 : Step – a person walking;

Class c_5 : Talk – a person talking;

Class c_6 : Train – a train going past;

Class c_7 : Type – a person typing at a keyboard.

The samples of the above seven different activities were collected using a digital video camera, taking care that only one activity is present in each sequence (in a practical application, different audio sources would initially be separated using techniques such as BSS). Each of these sample video clips was later reduced to 8 seconds in length. As the clips have both video and audio signal, the audio signal was extracted and saved in a mono, uncompressed PCM .wav file, sampled at 44.1 kHz at 16 bits. One of the major problems with audio analysis is the presence of background noise. We decided not to perform any preprocessing to remove such noise because of the risks involved with affecting the signal(s) of interest and the difficulty in modeling the differences between the signal of interest and other signals. The database used contained 30 samples per class and a total of 210 samples. We try to maximize the validity of this work by using leave-one-out techniques to estimate success rates on different disjoint training and test sets.

A preliminary glance at the wave files (Figure 1) shows that the signals across these seven classes are not easily distinguishable. The 'clap', 'step' and 'type' class signals are periodic and regular, whereas 'train' and 'car' are loud and noisier. The class 'talk' is more erratic, and because speaking can be done both indoors and outdoors, some of the samples are noisier than others. Also, some classes have similar characteristics. For example, the 'step' and 'door' classes are similar because 'door' clips have stepping sounds. 'Car' and 'train' are similar because they are both vehicles and exist in an outdoor environment producing higher ambient sounds.

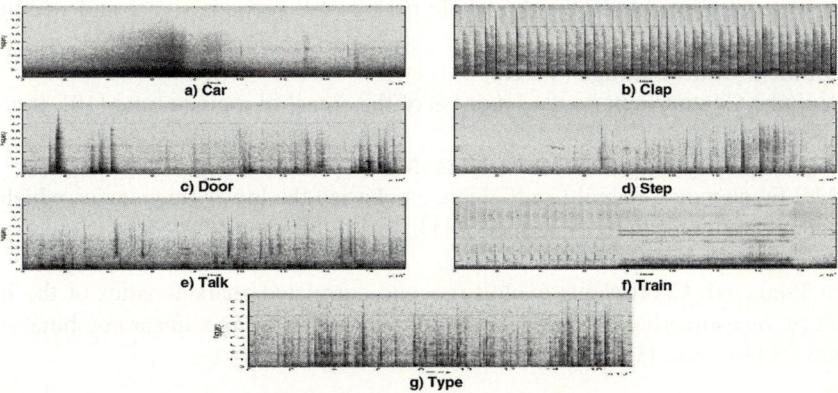

Fig. 1. Spectrograms of one sample of each class

3 Audio Analysis

Signal and audio processing are mature fields with many well-established, reliable techniques. We explored several popular audio features to determine whether they can be included in our machine learning system. These included:

- **High Energy Region (HER)**

In the real world, the loudest sound attracts the most attention. A simple way to identify a loud sound is to use the spectrogram of the audio signal (spec), and first compute the sum of the magnitude of each frame ($\forall f \in spec : energy_f = \sum_{\omega \in f} |A_\omega|$, where f is a frame, ω is frequency and A_ω the corresponding Fourier coefficient) is a measure of its corresponding energy.

The HER is defined by the highest energy peak, together with the left and right thresholds defined as a fraction of that peak (Figure 1).

From the HER, several features can be computed:
- The peak value itself (Peak);
- The duration of the HER (Duration): $t_r - t_l$, where t_r is the time associated with the region's right threshold and t_l the left threshold;
- The energy area (Area): $\sum_{f \in HER} energy_f$
- HER spectrogram moment: $\sum_{f, \omega \in HER} |A_\omega| \times d((f, \omega), \mu)$, where $d(.)$ is the Euclidean distance and $\mu = \left(\underset{f \in HER}{mean(f)}, \underset{f \in HER}{mean(\omega)} \right)$;
- Average distance between peaks: this is achieved by finding other high energy peaks and computing their average temporal distance.

The HER information was also used sub-sequentially to the remaining features, which were computed both for the whole period of 8 seconds signal and within the HER duration period.

- **Volume Dynamic Range (VDR)**

The Volume Contour reports the loudness of the signal in a given time [10]. It corresponds to the Volume Contour range.

- **Mel Frequency Cepstral Coefficients (MFCC)**

The Mel Frequency Cepstral Coefficients emphasize the lower frequencies which are perceptually more meaningful in speech [1].

- **Linear Predictive Coefficients (LPC)**

Linear Predictive Coefficients exploit the auto-correlated characteristics of the input waveform by estimating the value of the current sample using a linear combination of the previous samples [5].

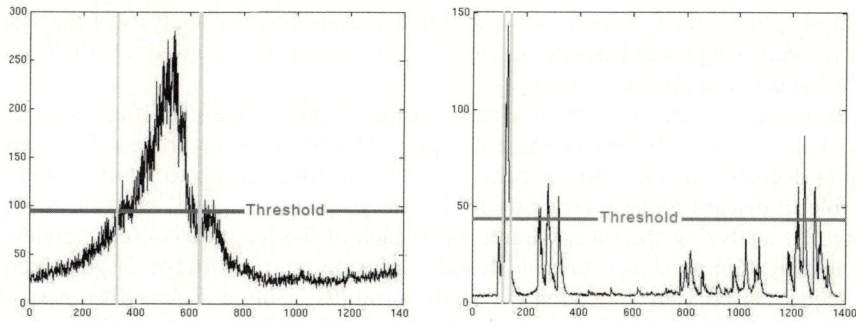

Fig. 2. Example of High Energy Region determination for samples of 'car' and 'talk' respectively

- **Gabor Mask**

The Gabor function is widely used as a filter and as a basis function for decorrelation. For this study, the signals were Gabor filtered and then the corresponding main LPC coefficients were used as features for classification [5].

- **Wavelets**

Wavelets, like Fourier transform, convert the time domain information into the frequency domain, splitting signals into component frequencies but varying the time-frequency resolution [8].

- **Frequency Centroid (FQC)**

This feature represents the clarity of the signal by evaluating the centre of each frequency domain obtained by the Fourier transform and the magnitude information [9].

- **Bandwidth (BW)**

This includes the width between two frequency bands f_1 and f_2 over the whole signal. For the purpose of this work, it represents the width of the smallest frequency band within which a signal can fit. This uses the frequency centroid value of each time component to deduce its value [9].

- **Harmonic Product Spectrum (HPS)**

Harmonic Product Spectrum is a methodology employed to approximate fundamental frequency f_0 [8].

- **Frequency Component of the Volume Contour around 4Hz (FCVC4)**

Frequency Component of the Volume Contour around 4Hz [9].

4 Classification Scheme

With regards to the classification process, several issues need to be addressed with regards to the amount of data and the features extracted. First, some feature vectors, such as MFCC and LPC have a large size nearly equal to the magnitude of the original raw audio data. In such cases, to reduce the corresponding dimensionality, only components associated with the most significant information (i.e. lower frequencies) were used. Second, feature selection is important to reduce the ratio of features to samples, and also use only discriminatory features. This is important because several features might be correlated, i.e. there is irrelevant data, and because a lower dimensional input vector simplifies the classification setup. Finally, a preliminary analysis of the system performance using a *k*nn classifier using all features extracted, showed a high degree of confusion between all seven classes.

The last two issues can be tackled by using a multi-stage classifier architecture [15]. This approach breaks down a complex decision-making process into several simpler decision stages, with the benefit that the result is easier to interpret and it is possible to discard unnecessary data in the design phase. Feature selection was performed by analyzing the success rates when each of the features is used individually for classification as shown in table 1 and confusion matrices (table 2) generated by the Sequential Forward Selection (SFS) algorithm [6] using a 7 class *k*NN classifier. The results of table 2 are clearly not good enough for a reliable system, although most of them are better than random class prediction (14.3%). The best results are obtained using LPC, MFCC and Gabor features.

Table 1. Success Rates for different features with a KNN classifier

Feature	SR	Feature	SR	Feature	SR
Peak	36%	VDR (whole clip)	29%	Peak + Area	36%
Area	36%	LPC (whole clip)	57%	Peak + Average Distance	54%
Average Distance	27%	MFCC (whole clip)	57%	Peak + Duration	57%
Duration	53%	Wavelet	21%	Peak + Moment	38%
Moment	50%	LPC + Gabor (whole clip)	57%	Average Distance + Duration	46%
HPS (HER)	53%	HPS (whole clip)	14%	Area + Average Distance	54%
Frequency Centroid (HER)	38%	Frequency Centroid (whole clip)	39%	Average Distance + Moment	32%
Bandwidth (HER)	35%	Bandwidth (whole clip)	14%	Area + Moment	39%
FCVC4 (HER)	40%	FCVC4 (whole clip)	39%	Duration + Moment	59%
LPC (HER)	60%	HPS + BW	44%	Area + Duration	56%
MFCC (HER)	60%	LPC + MFCC	58%	Duration + Peak + Area	54%
Gabor (HER)	65%	LPC + MFCC + HPS	60%	HPS + FQC + BW	58%

From the confusion matrices in table 2 certain observations can be made. Although the area feature only produces 36% global accuracy, it does not confuse the 'clap' class and the 'type' class like the others do. With the Duration and Moment features, a relatively high (59% rate) can be achieved, as a result of good classification of 'car' and 'train', even though, some samples of the two classes are confused with each other. This feature also shows confusion between 'clap' and 'type' which the area feature does not.

Table 2. Confusion matrices for Area and Duration+Moment features after SFFS. Average result of area classifier is 36% and duration+ moment classifier 59%.

Area						36%		Duration + Moment						59%
	car	clap	door	step	talk	train	type		car	clap	door	step	talk	train	type
car	**0.33**	0	0.16	0.10	0.20	0.13	0.06	Car	**0.76**	0	0	0	0	0.23	0
clap	0.13	**0.43**	0	0.03	0	0.40	0	Clap	0	**0.80**	0.03	0	0.03	0	0.13
door	0.16	0	**0.36**	0.13	0.16	0.03	0.13	Door	0	0	**0.46**	0.26	0.13	0.06	0.06
step	0.06	0.03	0.20	**0.33**	0.20	0.03	0.13	Step	0	0.03	0.10	**0.33**	10	0.10	0.10
talk	0.16	0	0.23	0.03	**0.23**	0.03	0.30	Talk	0	0	0.16	0.23	**0.50**	0	0.10
train	0.13	0.26	0	0	0.03	**0.56**	0	Train	0.10	0.03	0.03	0.06	0.10	**0.66**	0
Type	0.03	0	0.20	10	0.16	0	**0.26**	Type	0.03	0.13	0.10	0.03	0.10	0.03	**0.56**

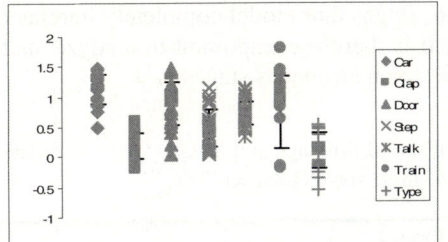 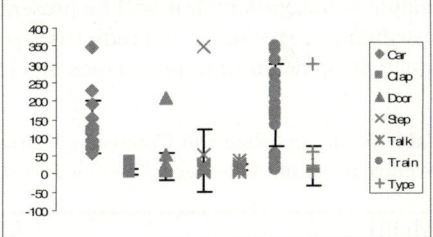

Fig. 3. Measure of variability for a) Duration and b) first Gabor+LPC component

Examining feature variability is an additional method of determining which features are good candidates to separate certain classes or groups of classes. Figure 3 shows an example of data variability for 2 features. These graphs display corresponding feature data points together with error bars representing 1-standard deviation variation. In the case of HER Duration, it is possible to conclude that generally, 'car' and 'train' exhibit longer HER regions. This suggests that this feature might be a good discriminator between these and other activities. A similar situation is observed for classes 'clap' and 'type' when examining the first Gabor+LPC component. After analyzing such results using other features as well, we gather the necessary information required to explore a multi-level binary kNN classifier. The architecture of our classifier uses a series of singular classification blocks, each using a set of features that proved efficient when dealing with different groupings of the original data. e.g. in the final design, the first step is to discriminate the 'car' class from all other classes using a set of 3 types of features.

The structure of the classifier was built following the methodology defined below:

1. For each class, find a combination of feature vectors (with a limit of 3 vectors) that separates it from the rest.
2. For the remaining classes, group the classes in pairs and repeat step 1 for each group.

3. For each discriminated group, find a combination of feature vectors that separates those two classes between each other.
4. Join them into a complete system.

The final system is shown in Figure 4. At each level a binary decision is made, e.g. at the first level a "car vs. not car" decision is made. The "not car" data consists of all six other classes. At the second level, a decision of "train vs. not train" is made, where the "not train" class consists of the remaining five more classes. For each binary classification a different set of features are used as shown. The results are compared with a simple kNN classifier using the same reduced set of features (table 3). The benefits of using such architecture are clear. Most classes achieve a better success rate than the one obtained with the single-stage classifier. However, an interesting observation can be made for the results of the 'step' class. In the multi-stage architecture its detection rate is lower. Furthermore, it is no longer confused with the class 'door' (as we pointed in section 2) but instead confused with 'talk' and 'clap'. This odd disparity is due to errors in earlier stages of classification (in this case, stages 3 and 4). Once a sample is misclassified, it will be presented to stages that model completely unrelated distributions, producing unpredicted results. It is therefore important to analyze such situations in detail in future studies and handle such erroneous stages.

Table 3. Success Rate and Confusion Matrices of the Multi-stage and Single-stage classifiers. Average result of multi-stage classifier is 80% and single stage classifier 70%.

Multi-stage	car	clap	door	step	talk	train	type	80% One-Stage	car	clap	door	step	talk	train	type	70%
car	**0.90**	0	0.03	0	0.06	0	0	Car	**0.93**	0	0	0	0	0	0.06	
clap	0	**0.86**	0	0.06	0	0	0.06	Clap	0	**0.66**	0.03	0	0	0	0.30	
door	0.06	0	**0.73**	0.03	0.10	0	0.06	Door	0	0	**0.53**	0.30	0	0	0.16	
step	0	0.10	0.06	**0.50**	0.20	0	0.13	Step	0	0	0.16	**0.63**	0.03	0	0.16	
talk	0	0	0.16	0	**0.83**	0	0	Talk	0.03	0	0	0.06	**0.70**	0	0.20	
train	0.10	0	0	0	0.03	**0.86**	0	Train	0.33	0	0	0	0.03	**0.63**	0	
type	0	0.03	0.03	0	0.03	0	**0.90**	Type	0	0.03	0	0.06	0	0	**0.90**	

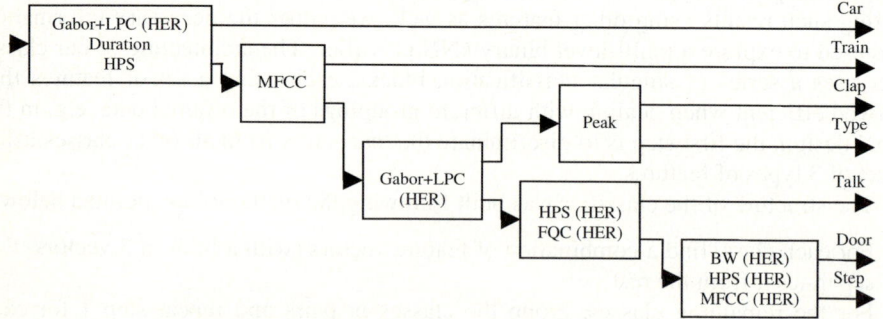

Fig. 4. The multi-stage classifier for audio classification

5 Conclusion

Our work is intended to recognize every day activities based on audio signals alone. In this paper a number of different audio techniques were investigated and applied as feature extractors and a multi-stage classification method was used and compared with a single stage system. After employing a wide range of audio feature extraction schemes, a simple empirical feature selection process was used to determine the most discriminatory features. The benefits of using a multi-stage architecture are quite apparent. By performing a series of binary decisions improves the subsequent stages of classification and the overall recognition rate. Each classification step also becomes simpler as it processes a limited number of features and classes. Although our multi-stage architecture paradigm is useful, it can be very sensitive to errors, especially in early stages of classification. When designing these systems, it is very important to detect situations that might affect subsequent performance. In future, our audio-based classification scheme can be used with the development of autonomous systems that use both audio and video cues to recognize their environment. The multi-stage classification scheme will present in such scenarios advantage not only for improved recognition accuracy but will also be quicker when only binary decisions are needed to recognize specific classes.

References

1. P. Boersma, "Accurate Short-Term Analysis of the Fundamental Frequency and the Harmonics-to-Noise Ratio of a Sampled Sound", Institute of Phonetic Sciences, University of Amsterdam, Proceedings 17, 1993.
2. S. Choi, A. Cichocki, H.-M. Park and S.-Y. Lee, "Blind Source Separation and Independent Component Analysis: A Review", Neural Information Processing – Letters and Review, vol. 6, no. 1, pp. 1-57, 2005.
3. M. N. Do, "An Automatic Speaker Recognition System", Audio Visual Communications Laboratory, Swiss Federal Institute of Technology, Lausanne, Switzerland.
4. D. Gerhard, "Audio Signal Classification: History and Current Techniques", Technical report TR-CS 2003-07, 2003.
5. Y. H. Hu and J.-N. Hwant, "Handbook of Neural Network Signal Processing", CRC Press.
6. A. Jain and A. Zongker, "Feature selection: evaluation, application, and small sample performance", IEEE Transactions PAMI, vol. 19, no. 2, pp. 153-158, 1997.
7. M. Kleinschmidt, "Methods for capturing spectro-temporal modulations in automatic speech recognition", Acustica united with acta acustica, vol.88, no. 3, pp. 416-422, 2002.
8. R. Kobes and G. Kunstatter, "Physics 1501 – Modern Technology", Physics Department, University of Winnipeg.
9. Z. Liu and Y. Wang, "Audio Feature Extraction and Analysis for Scene Segmentation and Classification", Journal of VLSI Signal Processing, pp. 61-79, 1998.
10. Z. Liu, J. Huang and Y. Wang, "Classification of TV Programs Based on Audio Information Using Hidden Markov Model", IEEE Workshop on Multimedia Signal Processing, 1998.
11. B. Logan, "Mel Frequency Cepstral Coefficients for Music Modelling", Cambridge Research Laboratory.

12. L. Lu, H-J. Zhang and H. Jiang, "Content Analysis for Audio Classification and Segmentation", IEEE Transactions on Speech and Audio Processing, v.10, pp. 504-516, 2002.
13. S. Mallat, "A wavelet tour of signal processing", Academic Publishers.
14. L. R. Rabiner and R. W. Schafer, "Digital Processing of Speech Signals", Prentice-Hall (Signal Processing Series), 1978.
15. S.R. Safavian, D.A. Landgrebe," A Survey of decision tree classifier methodology", IEEE Trans SMC, pp. 660-674, 1990.
16. E. Scheirer and M. Slaney, "Construction and Evaluation of a Robust Multifeature Music/Speech Discriminator", Proceedings of IEEE ICASSP, vol. 2, pp. 1331-1334, 1997.
17. G. Tzanetakis and P. Cook, "Audio Information Retrieval (AIR) Tools", Department of Computer Science and Department of Music, Princeton University.
18. G. Tzanetakis and P. Cook, "Multifeature Audio Segmentation for Browsing and Annotation", Proc. IEEE Workshop on Applications of Signal Processing to Audio and Acoustics, pp. 103-106, 1999.
19. O. Viikki and K. Laurila, "Cepstral domain segmental feature vector normalization for noise robust speech recognition", Speech Communication, vol.25, pp. 133-147, 1998.
20. C. Xu, N. Maddage, X. Shao, F. Cao and O. Tian, "Musical Genre Classification using Support Vector Machines", IEEE ICASSP, 2003.
21. R.E. Yantorno, A.N. Iyer, J.K. Shah and B.Y. Smolenski, "Usable Speech Detection Using a Context Dependent Gaussian Mixture Model Classifier", IEEE International Symposium on Circuits and Systems, 2004.

A Simple Approximation for Dynamic Time Warping Search in Large Time Series Database

Jie Gu[1] and Xiaomin Jin[2]

[1] Software School of Tsinghua University
guj05@mails.tsinghua.edu.cn
[2] Software School of Tsinghua University
xmjin@tsinghua.edu.cn

Abstract. The problem of similarity search in time series database has attracted a lot of interest in the data mining field. DTW(Dynamic Time Warping) is a robust distance measure function for time series, which can handle time shifting and scaling. The main defect of DTW lies in its relatively high computational complexity of similarity search. In this paper, we develop a simple but efficient approximation technique for DTW to speed up the search process. Our method is based on a variation of the traditional histograms of the time series. This method can work with a time linear with the size of the database. In our experiment, we proved that the proposed technique is efficient and produces few false dismissals in most applications.

1 Introduction

Time series data has composed of a large portion of the current data being used, naturally similarity search in time series data set becomes an important issue. The size of the time series data set is extremely large in many applications, thus how to speed up the search process on time series has attracted a lot of research interest. In the past many searching methods have been developed to tackle the problem and most of them are focused on the Euclidean distance function. Given two time series X and Y, the Euclidean distance function requires the two time series be of the same length, e.g., n . The Euclidean distance is defined as follows:

$$D(X,Y) = \sqrt{\sum_{i=1}^{n}(X[i]-Y[i])^2}$$

Euclidean distance function is widely used in many applications and also is very efficient in the measurement of equal-length time series. But it can not handle the condition when there is a time shifting and scaling in time series, i.e., Euclidean distance can not measure the distance between time series of different length. Another shortcoming of Euclidean distance is that it is sensitive to noise.

Dynamic Time Warping distance (DTW) is introduced to time series field to solve the problem of time shift and scaling. DTW allows time series to be stretched or compressed along the axis thus it is efficient to measure time series of different length or sampled at different rates. Time warping is a generalization of classical algorithms for comparing discrete sequences to sequences of continuous values[3]. Instead of treating the elements of time series independently as the Euclidean distance does, DTW searches for a minimal value from the global point of view. This feature of DTW provides a more accurate result. More details about DTW will be introduced in Section 2.

The defect of DTW is that it has a relatively high computational complexity $O(mn)$, where m and n are the length of the two time series being compared. Then sequential scanning in the search process is not feasible given a large time series data set. Most of the existing query techniques have a poor performance in the DTW field or can not be used at all for they are designed for Euclidean distance. In this paper, we introduce a simple but efficient approximation method which can be applied in the query search based on DTW distance. The method is based on a variation of the traditional histograms of the time series. It considers both the value distribution and position of the elements in the time series, which are relative to the DTW distance. The variation of histograms is defined as Binary Histograms. With Binary Histograms we can prune most false candidates at a low cost. The proposed method can be constructed and revised easily, and it also provides a high efficiency in the search process.

The rest of the paper is organized as follows: In Section 2 we will have a review of the DTW distance function and the query methods for DTW. The Binary Histograms is introduced in Section 3. Section 4 gives an overall description of the proposed method and the search process. Several experiments to evaluate the performance of the novel approximation technique is conducted in Section 5, which show the advantage of our proposed method. Section 6 provides the conclusions and suggestions for further work.

2 Related Work

2.1 Dynamic Time Warping Distance

Dynamic Time Warping first appeared in the language recognition field. It is introduced to handle with time shifting and scaling in time series. In order to find the minimal difference of two time series being compared, DTW maps each element of a time series to one or more elements of another time series.

Definition 1. ***Dynamic Time Warping Distance:*** *Given two time series X and Y of length m and n, respectively. $X = \{X_1, X_2, ..., X_m\}$ and $Y = \{Y_1, Y_2, ..., Y_n\}$. The DTW distance is defined as follows:*

$$D_{tw}(X,Y) = \sqrt{D_{base}(X,Y)^2 + minD(X,Y)^2}$$

$$D_{base}(X,Y) = |X[1] - Y[1]|$$

$$minD(X,Y) = min \begin{cases} D_{tw}(X[1..m], Y[2...n]) \\ D_{tw}(X[2..m], Y[1...n]) \\ D_{tw}(X[2..m], Y[2...n]) \end{cases}$$

In the above definition, $X[1]$ means the first element of time series X. $X[i...n]$ denotes a subsequence of X containing the elements from i to n. Given two time series X and Y, $D_{tw}(X,Y)$ can easily be calculated with a dynamic programming technique. DTW is used to find the best possible alignment between two time series. This feature of DTW makes it more reasonable and efficient in real-world applications.

2.2 Current Methods

Since DTW employs a dynamic programming algorithm, it works with a time complexity of $O(MN)$, where M and N is the two time series being compared. This heavy computation cost makes it impossible to do sequential scanning in the similarity search based on DTW distance. Several technique has been developed to speed the query process for DTW distance.

Discrete Fourier Transform (DFT)[1] is used to reduce the dimensionality of time series. In [2,4], time series are transformed into frequency domain and mapped into multi-dimensional points which are indexed by an R-tree. The two methods are both based on Euclidean distance and thus can not be applied to DTW directly. Yi et al.developed a lower bounding approach for DTW[6]. They use the lower bounding distance to get a small candidate set and then evaluate the real DTW distance. Kim et al. proposed another index technique for DTW[7]. Hsul employed a suffix tree to index the DTW[8]. The index structure is efficient but the space cost of the index is too high.

3 The Approximation Method

We propose a simple but efficient approximation technique to speed up the similarity search based on DTW. We develop a new histograms, defined as **Binary Histograms**, to represent time series.

3.1 Traditional Histograms

A time series is defined as a sequence of real values, each sample at a specific time. $X = \{X_1, X_2, ..., X_n\}$ is a time series with n elements. The traditional histograms of time series is defined as follows: Select the maximum and minimum element from the given time series X, denoted as X_{max} and X_{min}, respectively. The range $[X_{min}, X_{max}]$ can be divided into m equal size sub-regions, called *histogram bins*. The histograms H can be constructed by counting the number of data points h_i that are located in each histogram bins: $H = [H_1, H_2, ..., H_m]$. Traditional histograms has been used a lot in the similarity search based on Euclidean distance. If the Euclidean distance between two time series is as small as 0, the two time series must has the same histograms. Generally, if the Euclidean distance of two time series is under a specified threshold(usually a small value), the two time series must has similar histograms. This feature of histograms makes it possible to conduct approximation in Euclidean space.

3.2 Binary Histograms

In our method, the traditional histograms described above is not employed. Though the traditional histograms can approximate the Euclidean distance well at a certain degree, it has a poor performance when used to approximate the DTW distance. Considering the DTW calculating process, one element of a time series may be mapped to several elements of another time series. Thus the traditional histograms cannot approximate the DTW distance. Even when the DTW distance between two time series is 0, they may have quite different histograms. Take two time series $X = \{3,3,3,5,5,8,8,8,8\}$ and $Y = \{3,5,8\}$ for example. Dividing the range [3,8] into 3 equal-size subregions [3,4], [5,6] and [7,8], their histograms are $h_X=\{3,2,4\}$ and $h_Y=\{1,1,1\}$. Though $D_{tw}(X,Y)=0$, h_X and h_Y are totally different. Then the challenge is how to improve the approximation ability of histograms in DTW space. Since the computation complexity of DTW is relatively high, if the histograms can be used as in the Euclidean space, the overall performance of DTW similarity search will be enhanced greatly.

We develop a new form of histograms from the traditional histograms. The new histograms has considered the special calculation process of the DTW and is suitable to be used as an approximation tool.

As mentioned above, in the DTW calculating process, one element of a time series may be mapped to several elements of another time series. Thus the number of elements in a specified sub-region $[X_{j-1}, X_j]$ is no longer important, since a great number of elements and a single element may have the same impact on the value of the DTW distance. We neglect the exact number of elements in a specified sub-region $[X_{j-1}, X_j]$, but focus on whether there exists such element. This modification of traditional histograms makes it more reasonable and accurate in the approximation of DTW distance.

Given a time series $X = \{X_1, X_2, ..., X_n\}$, the first step is to divide the range $[X_{min}, X_{max}]$ into m equal size sub-regions, which is the same as in the traditional histograms. For every sub-region $[X_{j-1}, X_j]$, its corresponding value is H_j in the histogram $H = [H_1, H_2, ..., H_m]$. In our definition, $H_j = 1$ if and only if there exists at least one X_i in the sub-region $[X_{j-1}, X_j]$, where X_i is the element of the given time series X. If there is no X_i in the sub-range $[X_{j-1}, X_j]$, then $H_j = 0$. The construction algorithm of binary histograms is shown in Figure.3.

The new histograms we developed is defined as *Binary Histograms* since it only contains the binary value 0 and 1. In the rest of this paper, it is denoted as B_h for short. Compared with the traditional histograms, B_h has a more powerful approximation ability in DTW space. Still considering the above two time series $X = \{3,3,3,5,5,8,8,8,8\}$ and $Y = \{3,5,8\}$, while $D_{tw}(X,Y) = 0$, their binary histograms are $B_{hX} = \{1,1,1\}$ and $B_{hY} = \{1,1,1\}$. The binary histograms of two time series will be similar if their DTW distance is small enough. This nice feature of binary histograms makes it possible to be used in the similarity search based on DTW.

```
BinaryHistogramsConstruction(X, int n, BinH) {
 /*X=the time series from which binary histograms is constructed;
    n=the number of sub-regions in the binaryhistograms;
    BinH=the binary histograms with n elements;*/
    for all elements BinH[i] in Binh
            BinH[i]=0;
    /*initialization of the binary histograms*/
    min=X[1]; max=X[1];
    for all elements X[i] in time series X
      {if(X[i]>max) max=X[i];
        if(X[i]<min) min=X[i];
      } /*find the minimal and maximal element of X*/
    size=(max-min)/n;
    /* the length of each sub-regions*/
    for all elements X[i] in time series X
        / int index=(X[i]-min)/size;
           if(BinH[index]==0)  BinH[index]=1;
        /
           return Binh;
}
```

Fig. 1. The Binary Histograms Construction Process

4 The Search Process Based on Binary Histograms

4.1 Binary Histograms Construction for Time Series Data Set

For all the time series in the data set, they share the same sub-region partition to construct their histograms. The problem is that several outliers will influence the sub-region partition greatly. Thus we have to first analyze the value distribution of all the elements in the time series data set and eliminate several outliers when choose the minimal and maximal value in the data set. After this process, we construct a binary histogram for each of the time series in the data set using the construction algorithm proposed above. The only difference is that we no longer extract the min and max elements from each time series. Instead, every time series have the same min and max elements which are extract from the whole data set.

After all the binary histograms have been constructed, we define the number of 1 in each binary histograms as the **Size of Binary Histograms**. Then sort all the time series by the size of their corresponding binary time series. This structure will be of great help in the search process.

4.2 Similarity Search Process

The similarity search process using binary time series is a tradeoff between the time cost and recall of the query. With the help of binary histograms, the efficiency of the similarity search is improved greatly with little loss of recall. When one query time series is coming, the search process can be described as follow:

- Step.1 Construct the binary histograms of the query time series.
- Step.2 Calculate the size of the binary histograms constructed in Step.1, denoted as S_{query}.
- Step.3 For all the time series with a binary histograms whose size is within a specified threshold from S_{query}, add them to the candidate set.
- Step.4 For all the time series in the candidate set, validate them by calculating the true DTW distance between them and the query time series.

5 Experiment Evaluation

In this section, we conducted several experiments to evaluate the accuracy and efficiency of our proposed technique. The data sets we use is SP500 stock data. This data contains information about 500 companies for about 250 days.

5.1 Approximation Ability of Binary Histograms

The reason we can employ binary histograms in the DTW similarity search is based on such fact: when the two time series have a small DTW distance, they must have similar or even the same binary histograms. In this experiment , we show the approximation ability of binary histograms.

Table 1. Approximation Ability of Binary Histograms

DTW \ EOBH	0	1	2	3	4	5	6	7	total
100	1477	1642	253	8	1	0	0	0	3381
150	2853	3849	1060	158	16	0	0	0	7936
200	4146	6059	2240	529	91	6	0	0	13701

In the above table, we show the relationship between the DTW distance and binary histograms. We find 3381 pairs of time series in the data set whose DTW distance is less than 100. For each pair of time series, we divide them into 50 subregions and construct the binary histograms. We calculate the distance between the two corresponding histograms with the Euclidean distance function. From the first of the table, we can see that 1477 pairs of similar time series have the same binary histograms. For most similar time series, the Euclidean distance between their binary histograms is no less than 2. If the threshold is specified to be 200, there are 13701 pairs of time series in the data set and he binary histograms also approximate the DTW distance well.

5.2 Precision and Recall

Precision and recall are the two most important factor we should consider in the similarity process. In our binary histograms based approach, we conduct the validation in the last step, so we have 100% precision. In this experiment, we select 500 time series from the data set as the query time series. For each query time series, we conduct range queries on the data set and average the results.

Table 2. Precision and Recall

Threshold	Recall
50	100%
100	99.7%
150	97.8%
200	90.8%

Above show the recall of the query results. When the specified threshold is not so large, we can get a considerably high recall. The recall declines as the threshold grows. As discussed in previous section, our approach is a tradeoff between efficiency and the recall of the results. From this experiment, we can see the loss of recall is absolutely acceptable in most cases.

5.3 Time Cost

In this experiment, we evaluate the time cost of our proposed technique. Time cost of the search process is influenced by the structure of the histograms. In Fig.4, we show the relationship between the time cost and the number of subregions of each binary histograms. Our technique is compared with the naive method which conduct sequential scanning on the data set. From the figure

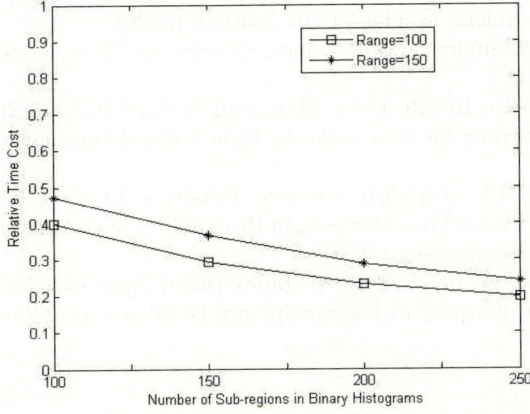

Fig. 2. The alignment of measurements by DTW

we can see our technique outperforms the naive method greatly. The time cost declines as the sub-regions in each binary histograms grows. This is because the approximation ability of binary histograms will improve if the number of sub-regions grows. Thus the candidate set in each query process will be smaller and the overall time cost benefits.

6 Conclusion

In this paper, we develop a novel approximation technique for DTW distance in time series data set. The method is easy to implement and have a nice performance in the search process on time series database. The proposed binary histograms have a nice approximate performance on the DTW distance. The similarity search process in DTW data set can be greatly improved with our method, as have shown in our experiment.

Acknowledgment

The work was supported by the NSFC 60403021 and the National Basic Research Program of China 2004CB719400.

References

1. R.Agrawal, C.Faloutsos, and A.N.Swami.: Efficient similarity serach in sequence database. Proc. Conf.of Foundations of Data Organization and Algorithms. (1993)
2. R.Agrawal, K.I.Lin, H.S.Sawhney, and K.Shim.: Fast Similarity in the presence of noise, scaling, and translation in time-series databases.In the VLDB Journal. (1995)
3. Sanghyun Park, Wesley W. Chu, Jeehee Yoon, and Jungim Won.: Similarity search of time-warped subsequences via a suffix tree. Information Systems, Volume 28, Issue 7 (2003)
4. K.Chakrabarti, M.N.Garofalakis, R.Rastogi, and K.Shim.: Approximate Query Processing Using Wavelets. In The VLDB Journal. (2000)
5. T.Kahveei and A.Singh.:Variable Length Queries for Time Series Data. In Proc. of The ICDE. (2001)
6. Selina Chu, Eamonn Keogh, David Hart.,and Michael Pazzani.:Iterative deepening dynamic time warping for time series.In Proc 2 SIAM International Conference on Data Mining.
7. Byoung-Kee Yi, H.V. Jagadish, Christos Faloutsos.:Efficient Retrieval of Similar Time Sequences Under Time Warping.In Proceedings of the 14th International Conference on Data Engineering (1998)
8. Sang-Wook Kim, Sanghyun Park.An Index-Based Approach for Similarity Search Supporting Time Warping in Large Sequence Databases.In ICDE (2001)

Regression Analisys of Segmented Parametric Software Cost Estimation Models Using Recursive Clustering Tool

M. Garre[1], M.A. Sicilia[1], J.J. Cuadrado[1], and M. Charro[2]

[1] University of Alcalá, Ctra. Barcelona km 33.6 - 28871,
Alcalá de Henares, Madrid, Spain
{miguel.garre, jjcg, msicilia}@uah.es
[2] Dept. Applied Sciences, Torrejón Air Base - Technical School, 28850 - Torrejón de Ardoz, Madrid, Spain

Abstract. Parametric software effort estimation models rely on the availability of historical project databases from which estimation models are derived. In the case of large project databases with data coming from heterogeneous sources, a single mathematical model cannot properly capture the diverse nature of the projects under consideration. Clustering algorithms can be used to segment the project database, obtaining several segmented models. In this paper, a new tool is presented, Recursive Clustering Tool, which implements the EM algorithm to cluster the projects, and allows use different regression curves to fit the different segmented models. This different approaches will be compared to each other and with respect to the parametric model that is not segmented. The results allows conclude that depending on the arrangement and characteristics of the given clusters, one regression approach or another must be used, and in general, the segmented model improve the unsegmented one.

Keywords: Software Engineering, Effort estimation, Segmented parametric model, Recursive Clustering Tool (RCT), Clustering, EM algorithm.

1 Introduction

Segmented parametric software estimation models has been used against not segmented, in a variety of works. Concretely J.J. Cuadrado [1] show the influence of cost drivers, CASET (Use of Case Tools) and METHO (Use of a Methodology), on estimation effort using segmented parametric models. In the work of M. Garre [2], a recursive process is described to obtain a set of segments that shows more homogeneous characteristics than previously. Finally the same author, compares the two models (segmented and not segmented) in [3]. These works are based in the use of the EM algorithm [7,5,4], which has been integrated into a software tool: "Recursive Clustering Tool" (RCT).

Segmented parametric estimation models have arisen in contrast to not segmented, due to the use of heterogeneous historical projects databases on the estimation process. For example the projects database ISBSG (International

Software Benchmarking Standards Group[1]) contains information about 2028 projects, which have been collected from a variety of organizations during the last decade. One important aspect of the process of deriving models from databases is the heterogeneity of data. Heteroscedasticity (i.e. non–uniform variance) is known to be a problem affecting data sets that combine data from heterogeneous sources [8]. When using such databases, traditional application of curve regression algorithms to derive a single mathematical model results in poor adjustment to data and subsequent potential high deviations. This is due to the fact that a single model can not capture the diversity of distributions of different segments of the database points.

Serge Oligny et. al [9] use the ISBSG version 4 to obtain a empirical time-prediction model, based on effort. The relation between time and effort are established by means of regression analysis. The most important aspect of this work is that it uses three estimation models. One to the 208 *mainframe* projects, the other to the 65 *mid-range* projects, and the last one to the 39 *pc* projects. The authors distinguish between the different development platforms used to get the model, obtaining a relation for each one of the groups. This study can be considered as supporting evidence for the segmentation approach described in this paper, even though the partitioning of the data is carried out without using a clustering algorithm.

Clustering is a suitable technique that has been used to segment the project database in different clusters. The projects clusters obtained this way show more homogeneous characteristics than others not clusterized. After that, a set of parametrics models are gotten, one for each cluster. This models are calibrated using curve regression analysis.

Parametric estimation techniques are nowadays widely used to measure and/or estimate the cost associated to software development [6]. The *Parametric Estimating Handbook* (PEH) [10] defines parametric estimation as "a technique employing one or more cost estimating relationships (CERs) and associated mathematical relationships and logic". Parametric techniques are based on identifying significant CERs that obtain numerical estimates from main *cost drivers* that are known to affect the effort or time spent in development. Parametrics uses the few important parameters that have the most significant cost impact on the software being estimated.

This paper presents several curve regression approaches, and it shows the results gotten using this curves into the segmented parametric model.

In order to support the development and posterior evaluation of the parametric segmented model, a new tool have been created. This tool, RCT, will be described in Section 3.

The rest of this paper is structured as follows. In Section 2, the different curve regression approaches are provided. Section 3 briefly describes the Recursive Clustering Tool. Section 4 provides the discussion and the empirical evaluation of the approaches carried out. Finally, conclusions and future research directions are described in Section 5.

---

[1] http://www.isbsg.org/

2 Curve Regression Approaches

Regression analysis research the relation between two o more variables. In this paper, work effort and function points are related, using a power function:

$$e = A_0 \cdot fp^{A_1} \tag{1}$$

or a linear function:

$$e = A_0 + A_1 \cdot fp \tag{2}$$

where e is the dependent variable work effort, A_0 and A_1 are founded parameters, and fp is the independent variable function points.

The model can be linealized to do power function regression analysis more simple. For example, this function could be linealized like this:

$$e' = log(e), \; fp' = log(fp) \tag{3}$$

getting the lineal form:

$$e' = log(A_0) + A_1 \cdot fp' \tag{4}$$

using it to make all the operations. A double logarithmic transformation of the effort and function points are made. It is named in RCT, *Linear log-log Plot* regression.

Some times the formula 1 is directly solved, using complex numeric algorithms, specifically the Levenberg-Marquardt [11] is used. This approach is named in RCT *Non-Linear Power*.

To make a linear regression like formula 2, the traditional methods are used. In RCT the word *Linear* represents this.

The regression curve of the model is obtained using a set of pairs (e_1, fp_1), $\ldots (e_n, fp_n)$. The more close are the points to the curve the more accurate it will be. According to least squares principle, the curve accuracy depends on the vertical distances (deviation) between the points and the curve. The fit quality measure is the sum squares of this deviations. The best curve regression has the minimum sum squares.

The least squares method is widely used, although when outliers appears, it is necessary to treat them. There are two possibility:

1. One possibility would be to leave out this points. This would be correct if this dates come from registry or experimental errors.
2. Other possibility would be to assign less weight to the extreme points than least squares, like *least absolute deviation* does. This method is developed through an iterative process.

In this paper, the second approach is used.

3 Recursive Clustering Tool

In this section a brief description of the RCT will be carried out. The only objective is to show the characteristics directly related to the present work.

First, the clustering process of the training data will be shown, resulting in a set of segments. Second, the different approaches of regression analysis will be described. Last, the full report for the test data is provided.

In figure 1 the main window of RCT can be seen.

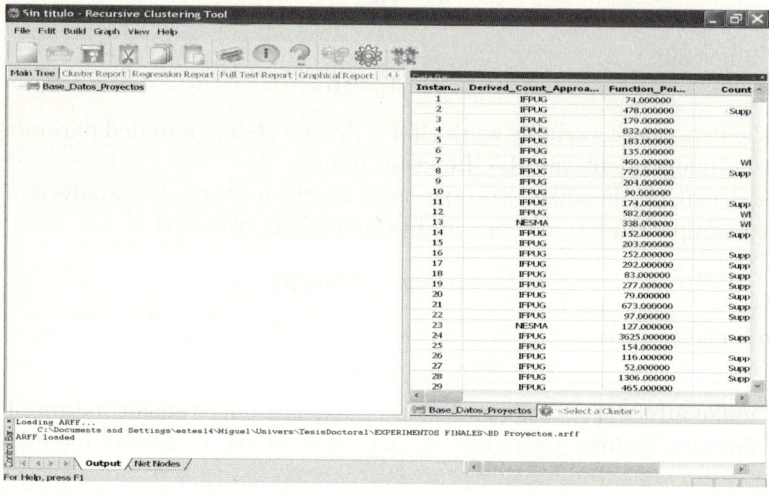

Fig. 1. Principal window of RCT

3.1 Creation of Clusters

The first step consist on separate the training and test data. It can be done by means of the option *Build → Separate Test Instances*. Now the training data are clusterized, clicking on *Build → Create Clusters*.

There are several options and parameters to the clustering process using the EM algorithm, for example:

1. Select the desired attributes
2. Build the *mixture model* [12] selecting the probability density function that best represents the points. For example normal, log-normal or t-student distribution
3. It is possible to select the number of splits for cross validation in opposite to the *Minimum Description Length* [13] criterion, to get the optimum number of clusters
4. Besides is possible to establish the maximum number of clusters or the maximum number of iterations in EM algorithm, etc.

When this has been done, the clustering process begins, and the obtained segments must be modeled.

3.2 Regression Analysis

For each one of the segments it is necessary make regression analysis.

RCT provides five different approaches to get the segments curve regression:

Linear (least-absolute-deviation). Uses the formula 2 to fit the points to the curve, and the least absolute deviation to minimize the estimated error. It is appropriate when there is a strong lineal dependency between the two variables e and fp, and the points are scattered.

Linear (least-squares). The points fitting are made using the formula 2, and the least squares method is used to minimize the estimated error. It is appropriate when there is a strong lineal dependency between the two variables e and fp, and the points are not too much scattered.

Linear log-log Plot (least-absolute-deviation). Uses the formula 1 to fit the software projects. It is linealized by means of double logarithmic transformation, formulas 3 and 4. Besides, uses least absolute deviation to minimize points deviation. It is appropriate when there is not a lineal dependency between the two variables e and fp, and the points are scattered.

Linear log-log Plot (least-squares). It is the same as the one before, but uses least squares to minimize the error.

Non-Linear Power (least-squares). It fits the points using formula 1 without any transformation. This approach would make similar results to previous one.

All of these possibilities will allow to make a lot of different combinations, with the target of getting the best fit of the given projects.

After select one of this approximations, we have one curve for each one of the given clusters.

3.3 Curve and Full Test Report

There are two possibilities to test the segmented parametric model:

1. Get the MMRE and PRED values for the given curves of each one of the clusters. An average value of all this values can be calculated. Option *Build → Data Analysis* of RCT.
2. Get the MMRE and PRED values for a set of test data instances. Option *Build → Full Test* of RCT.

The first measure give us an idea of the predictive capacity of each one of the curves, and the average values of MMRE and PRED give the predictive capacity of all the curves. The second one give us the predictive capacity of the whole model. Both measures will be used to evaluate the segmented parametric model.

4 Clustering and Evaluation of Process with RCT

This section can be divided into three subsections, the first one describes the filtering process of the ISBSG-8 database, the second one provides the results of the clustering process using different regression curves. The last one shows the analysis of results.

4.1 Data Preparation

The entire ISBSG-8 database containing information about 2028 projects was used as the project database. The database contained attributes about size, effort and many other project characteristics. However, before applying clustering techniques to the dataset, there are a number of issues to be taken into consideration dealing with cleaning and data preparation.

An important attribute is the *data quality rating* that can take values from A (where the submission satisfies all criteria for seemingly sound data) to D (where the data has some fundamental shortcomings). According to ISBSG only projects classified as A or B should be used for statistical analysis.

The first cleaning step was that of removing the projects with null or invalid numerical values for the fields effort ("Summary Work Effort" in ISBSG-8) and size ("Function Points"). Then, the projects with "Recording method" for total effort other than "Staff hours" were removed. The reason for this is that the other methods for recording were considered to be subject to subjectivity. For example, "productive time" is a rather difficult magnitude to assess in a organizational context. Since size measurements were considered the main driver of project effort, the database was further cleaned for homogeneity in this respect. Concretely, the projects that used other size estimating method ("Derived count approach") than IFPUG, NESMA, Albretch or Dreger were removed, since they represent smaller portions of the database. The differences between IFPUG and NESMA methods are considered to have a negligible impact on the results of function point counts [14]. Counts based on Albretch techniques were not removed since in fact IFPUG is a revision of these techniques, similarly, the Dreger method refers to the book [15], which is simply a guide to IFPUG counts.

Another question is the consistency of the attribute values. For example some times the fields appear empty while some times appear with the value "don't know". There are another cases in which the used language is COBOL 2 or COBOL II, it is necessary give them the same value, because it is the same language.

After this, 1546 projects remains in the database, which will be used in the next section.

4.2 Results of the Clustering Process

The clustering process is performed over 1246 projects, leaving 300 for test purposes. All of then are randomly selected. The considered attributes are effort and function points. The mixture model is made with a normal n-dimensional distribution.

The objective is to compare the given results using the different regression curves, getting which of them offers the best behaviour to the software projects used.

After the first segmentation step using the effort and function points attributes, the clusters of table 1 are given, describing the clusters properties, as average, standard deviation, correlation coefficient, etc. The figure 2 shows the graphical representation of this clusters, besides the test data that will be used in the full test report.

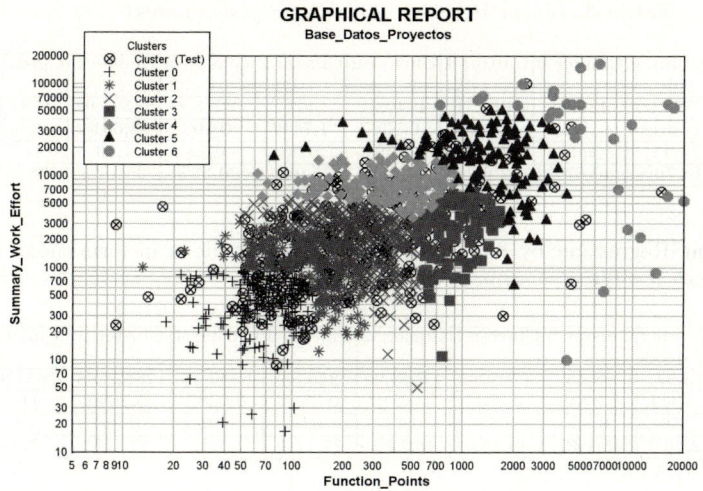

Fig. 2. Clusters given with RCT

Table 1. Properties of the clusters given with RCT

	Cluster 0	Cluster 1	Cluster 2	Cluster 3	Cluster 4	Cluster 5	Cluster 6
N Projects	177	306	321	114	169	128	31
Probability	0,133	0,235	0,245	0,095	0,157	0,105	0,027
Average e	474,532	1257,227	2533,056	2892,66	7334,681	17849,586	46689,829
Average fp	75,4	135,429	269,177	846,109	406,073	1495,645	6159,518
Stand Dev e	252,233	614,618	1329,888	1646,118	3337,86	11052,253	38191,984
Stand Dev fp	29,352	57,965	119,354	368,016	198,57	801,413	5062,282
Correl coeff e-fp	0,1029	-0,2965	-0,4704	0,31	0,036	-0,1946	-0,3377

Next, tables 2, 3, 4, 5 and 6, provide the A_0 and A_1 constants for each one of the different regression curve approach that implements RCT, besides the MMRE and PRED(0,3) respective values. At the first column of each one of the tables appear the values associated to all training projects, without clustering.

Finally, table 7 describes a comparative analysis among all regression approximations. At the first column appear the MMRE and PRED(0,3) average predictive values, and at the second one appear the MMRE and PRED(0,3) model predictive values. In each one of the rows appear a different type of regression of the segmented and not segmented model.

Table 2. Linear Regression: *Linear (least-absolute-deviation)*

	Training Projects	Cluster 0	Cluster 1	Cluster 2	Cluster 3	Cluster 4	Cluster 5	Cluster 6
A_0	1041,36	211,88	1813,016	4168,13	1734,26	7495,35	22657,5	66951,63
A_1	3,606	2,9411	-4,2756	-5,7552	1,0772	0,7585	-4,0293	-3,7789
MMRE	1,68	1	0,53	0,7	0,9	0,26	0,93	21,5
PRED(0,3)	23,86%	44,06%	49,01%	50,46%	35,96%	61,53%	43,75%	41,93%

Table 3. Linear Regression: *Linear (least-squares)*

	Training Projects	Cluster 0	Cluster 1	Cluster 2	Cluster 3	Cluster 4	Cluster 5	Cluster 6
A_0	3578,98	421,44	1934,76	4440,94	1362,7	8215,8	24527,98	68741,06
A_1	3,4611	0,5451	-4,6393	-6,5387	1,7117	0,193	-3,6314	-3,056
MMRE	4,11	1,07	0,56	0,69	0,93	0,28	1,13	24,29
PRED(0,3)	14,76%	40,67%	47,05%	51,09%	35,96%	60,35%	35,15%	38,7%

Table 4. Linear Regression by means of double logarithmic transformation: *Linear log-log Plot (least-absolute-deviation)*

	Training Projects	Cluster 0	Cluster 1	Cluster 2	Cluster 3	Cluster 4	Cluster 5	Cluster 6
A_0	38,94	88,23	7783,84	43563,99	245,83	6649,36	128378,68	5763486,49
A_1	0,7343	0,3738	-0,3845	-0,5212	0,3554	0,0287	-0,2899	-0,6075
MMRE	1,58	0,96	0,55	0,74	0,9	0,26	0,95	15,1
PRED(0,3)	22,44%	45,19%	48,36%	46,72%	37,71%	61,53%	37,5%	32,25%

Table 5. Linear Regression by means of double logarithmic transformation: *Linear log-log Plot (least-squares)*

	Training Projects	Cluster 0	Cluster 1	Cluster 2	Cluster 3	Cluster 4	Cluster 5	Cluster 6
A_0	41	163,88	13797,4	111094,49	19,61	9062,12	248456,92	38312472,85
A_1	0,7174	0,2012	-0,5187	-0,7112	0,7099	-0,0238	-0,3924	-0,8736
MMRE	1,52	0,9	0,51	0,64	0,78	0,26	0,86	12,62
PRED(0,3)	22,97%	38,41%	44,44%	40,8%	30,7%	59,17%	37,5%	25,8%

To get the average MMRE and PRED(0,3) values, the cluster 6 has not been considered, because it holds not much projects and they are scattered.

4.3 Analysis of Results

In figure 2, the cluster 6 projects are very scattered, the function points range of values is 1.000-20.000, that point out a difficult regression curve fitting. There are other clusters that presents this characteristic, but less scattered.

Following with cluster 6, and watching tables 2, 3, 4, 5 and 6, we realize that the MMRE values are very high, and the logarithmic transformation models yield best values. The least absolute deviation method, supplies the best fit to clusters with high level of dispersion, which give less weight to remote points. For example in table 4, with least absolute deviation, PRED(0,3)=32,25% against PRED(0,3)=25,8% for least squares in table 5.

Regarding to the average prediction values in table 7, any of the regression approaches provide similar values of MMRE and PRED(0,3). With respect to the model prediction values, there is not much difference between the segmented and not segmented parametric model, but there are differences between the regression approaches, the logarithmic transformation, with least absolute deviation, supplies the best prediction behaviour. This can be due to this method work very well for remote points, which are very abundant in the ISBSG database.

Table 6. Exponential regression: *Non-Linear Power (least-squares)*

	Training Projects	Cluster 0	Cluster 1	Cluster 2	Cluster 3	Cluster 4	Cluster 5	Cluster 6
A_0	207,15	316,53	5554,27	29443,88	74,36	8876,21	62584,75	683358,03
A_1	0,5653	0,0892	-0,303	-0,4423	0,5405	-0,0115	-0,1678	-0,3147
MMRE	3,43	1,06	0,59	0,78	0,93	1,07	1,15	22,12
PRED(0,3)	18,05%	40,67%	48,69%	50,77%	35,08%	40,82%	38,28%	38,7%

Table 7. Comparative of the different regressions

	Curves Average Prediction		Model Prediction	
	MMRE	PRED(0,3)	MMRE	PRED(0,3)
RCT. Linear (l.a.d.)	0,72	47,46%	3,94	21%
M. Not Segmented. Linear (l.a.d.)	1,68	23,86%	1,36	22%
RCT. Linear (l.s.)	0,77	45,04%	7,39	13%
M. Not Segmented. Linear (l.s.)	4,11	14,76%	3,48	13,34%
RCT. Linear log-log Plot (l.a.d.)	0,72	46,16%	32,89	23,33%
M. Not Segmented. Linear log-log Plot (l.a.d.)	1,58	22,44%	1,41	22,34%
RCT. Linear log-log Plot (l.s.)	0,65	41,8%	112,72	22%
M. Not Segmented. Linear log-log Plot (l.s.)	1,52	22,97%	1,33	23%
RCT. Non-Linear Power (l.s.)	0,93	42,38%	11,77	15,66%
M. Not Segmented. Non-Linear Power (l.s.)	3,43	18,05%	3,09	16%

The curves average prediction values are higher than model prediction values. This can not be due to a bad selection of the data test because they are very well distributed, figure 2.

Besides it can be seen that the segmented parametric model curves average prediction values, improve the respective values for the not segmented models.

5 Conclusions and Future Research Directions

With the inception of several organizations such as ISBSG, there are a number of repositories of project management data. The problem faced by project managers is the large disparity of the their instances so that estimates using classical techniques are not accurate. The use of clustering techniques using data mining can be used to group instances from software engineering databases. In our case, this was used to provide segmented models such that each cluster had an associated estimation mathematical model, with five different posible regression approaches. This has proven to be more accurate.

The comparison of using segmented parametric models with different regression approaches for each cluster, and the unsegmented model has resulted in evidence that the parametric approach improve the curves average prediction values of MMRE and PRED(0,3). In general, it is better to use the set of segmented model curves provides by the cluster process, than use a unique curve for all the database projects.

When we deal with a new problem, the best choice will be to use different regression curves, depending on the form and characteristics of the given clusters. It is a good idea to use different regression approaches, because all the clusters have not the same characteristics.

Further work will consist on using recursive clustering to improve, for example, the cluster 6 behaviour, which have several scattered points. Recursive clustering can be applied to improve the clusters obtained at one step of the clustering process, getting other set of clusters of a lower level.

References

1. Cuadrado, J.J., Sicilia, M.A., Garre, M., Rodrguez, D.: An empirical study of process-related attributes in segmented software cost-estimation relationships. Journal of Systems and Software **79** 3 2006 351–361
2. Garre, M., Cuadrado, J.J., Sicilia, M.A.: Recursive segmentation of software projects for the estimation of development effort. Proceedings of the ADIS 2004 Workshop on Decision Support in Software Engineering, CEUR Workshop proceedings, **120** 2004
3. Garre, M., Cuadrado, J.J., Sicilia, M.A., Charro, M., Rodrguez, D.: Segmented Parametric Software Estimation Models: Using the EM algorithm with the ISBSG 8 database. Information Technology Interfaces 2005
4. G. McLachlan, T. Krishnan: The EM Algorithm and Extensions. Wiley series in probability and statistics, John Wiley & Sons, 1997
5. G. McLachlan, D. Peel.: Finite Mixture Model. Wiley, New York, 2000
6. Boehm, B., Abts, C., Sunita Chulani.: Software Development Cost Estimation approaches – a survey. USC Center for Software Engineering Technical Report # USC-CSE-2000-505
7. A. Dempster, N. Laird, D. Rubin.: Maximum Likelihood from Incomplete Data via the EM Algorithm. Journal of the Royal Statistical Society, Series B **39** 1 1977 1–38
8. Stensrud, E., Foss, T., Kitchenham, B., Myrtveit, I.: An Empirical Validation of the Relationship Between the Magnitude of Relative Error and Project Size. In Proceedings of the Eighth IEEE Symposium on Software Metrics 2002
9. Oligny, S., Bourque, P., Abran, A.,Fournier, B.: Exploring the relation between effort and duration in software engineering projects. Proceedings of the World Computer Congress 2000 175-178
10. Parametric Estimating Initiative. Parametric Estimating Handbook 1999 2nd edition.
11. Marquardt, D.W.: An algorithm for least squares estimation of nonlinear parameters. Journal of the Society for Industrial and Applied Mathematics, **11** 1963 431–441
12. McLachlan, G., Basford, K.: Mixture Models: Inference and Applications to Clustering, Marcel Dekker, New York 1988
13. Rissanen, J.: A Universal Prior for Integers and Estimation by Minimum Description Length, Annals of Statistics, **2** 11 1983 417–431
14. NESMA (1996). NESMA FPA Counting Practices Manual (CPM 2.0)
15. Dreger, J. Brian. Function Point Analysis. Englewood Cliffs, NJ: Prentice Hall, 1989

An Efficient Attribute Reduction Algorithm

Yuguo He

Department of Computer Science and Engineering, Beijing Institute of Technology, 100081
Beijing, China
yuguo@bit.edu.cn

Abstract. Attribute reduction is an important issue of data mining. It is generally regarded as a preprocessing phase that alleviates the curse of dimensionality, though it also leads to classificatory analysis of decision tables. In this paper, we propose an efficient algorithm TWI-SQUEEZE that can find a minimal (or irreducible) attribute subset, which preserves classificatory consistency after two scans of a decision table. Its worst-case computational complexity is analyzed. The outputs of the algorithm are two different kinds of classifiers. One is an IF-THEN rule system. The other is a decision tree.

1 Introduction

Concept learning and symbolic rule learning are defined as non-trivial extraction of potentially useful structural patterns from given symbolic data. As is well known, the traditional machine learning methods, such as version space, ID3, AQ11, CN2 etc., can handle such problems. The main part of these methods can be regarded as a process of data reduction. That is, a process leading to a shorter attribute-value description of original data, which in the same time preserves initial classificatory consistency. Here consistency means: if two objects are different in their categorical labels, they should also be different in some of their features. Otherwise, these two objects cannot be determinately classified. Therefore, if object x determinately belongs to class y before reduction, x should still determinately belong to class y after reduction. Rough set theory [1-3], which is strict and elegant, aims to find the "maximum" reduction of the raw data. That is, finding a model as small as possible to fit the training samples best. Relative reduct (in the sequel we will use "reduct" instead), as defined by Pawlak, is a minimal (or irreducible) attribute subset that preserves initial classificatory consistency, and hence the ability to perform classifications as the whole attribute set does (this is a definition of reduct identical to the original one [4]). Finding a reduct is a basic and classical mathematical problem in rough set theory that serves as a jumping-off point to reach other goals, such as finding good quality (approximate) reducts that can be used to classify unseen objects well. In this paper we present an algorithm, which can find a reduct efficiently. Rather than exploring the way of finding good quality (approximate) reducts, we concentrate ourselves on the core well-defined mathematical problem which was proposed by Pawlak. It means we look the problem as a problem of summarizing raw data, not as a generalization problem. Thus, we can focus on the soundness and computational complexity analyses of our algorithm, as other related works do.

Tabular knowledge systems are extensively studied and used for data mining. A data set is represented as a table, where each row represents an object, or an event. Every column represents an attribute that can be measured for each object. Decision table is a kind of tabular knowledge system. In decision table, there is a distinct attribute, the value of which decides the category an object belongs to. We call this attribute as decision attribute, which is denoted by "d". And we call other attributes as conditional attributes, the set of which is denoted by C. Assume there are t_C attributes in C. We use the ith column in a table to represent C_i ($C_i \in C$, $1 \le i \le t_C$) and use the (t_C+1)th column to represent decision attribute d. C_{t_C} is called the rightmost conditional attribute in decision table. If $i<j$, we say C_i is on the left side of C_j in the table. Formally, a decision table can be represented as $KS=(U, C \cup \{d\})$. Here U is a non-empty finite set of objects called the universe. C is non-empty finite set of conditional attributes. $C \cap \{d\} = \phi$. For any $a \in C \cup \{d\}$, $a: U \to Va$, where Va is called the value set of a [4]. After sorting the rightmost column that is denoted by "d", decision table is divided into r_D groups according to the values of d. We call these groups as "D-Region". r_D is the number of equivalence classes induced by decision attribute d.

If two objects are regarded as different according to conditional attribute or decision attribute in a decision table, we say there is a *demarcation* between these two objects. If they are different according to both conditional attribute and decision attribute, we say there is a *relative demarcation* between them. Furthermore, if one of these two objects is consistent with all the other objects, we say the relative demarcation is valid. We've proved that reduction, including both attribute reduction and value reduction, is a process that preserves *valid relative demarcations* of the original decision table.

Note that, in rough set literature, researchers used the word "discern" instead of "demarcate". Whereas, the word "discern" has no proper corresponding noun. Therefore, we use the word "demarcate" (*vt.*) and the word "demarcation" (*n.*) throughout this paper.

We can see that the set of all valid relative demarcations is sufficient and necessary for preserving the consistency. The proof is simple. Our task is to find a reduct, which preserves all the *valid relative demarcations* of the original system, and any of its subset cannot do so.

The rest of this paper is organized as follows. Section 2 introduces the ideas of an algorithm called TWI-SQUEEZE. The algorithm can find a reduct after two scans of a decision table, just like squeezing water from a sponge by pressing on two sides of it. Section 3 reports on the experimental results. Section 4 concludes.

2 Attribute Reduction

2.1 Squeezing a Reduct from Decision Table: An Example

Imagine that conditional attributes are many distinctive robots working on a product line. Their tasks are to demarcate some objects. Our attribute reduction program assigns some of these robots, as few as possible, to finish their tasks. For any robot working on the product line, its *task*, together with what it can demarcate, decides the task of next robot on the line. We should not represent (relative) demarcations made by a robot directly because space complexity will be a problem in large applications. Therefore, we represent task it has to face instead. And fortunately, there is a simple way that saves both space and time complexity.

Assume every object has a serial number. Let $\{[a, b]_i, [c, d]_i, [e, f]_k\}^{CR}$ be the compact representation of set $\{(x, y)| x \in [a, b]$ or $[c, d], y \in [e, f]\}$. The subscript "i" in "$[a, b]_i$" means $[a, b]$ falls into D-Region i. That is, for any $x \in [a, b]$, $d(x)=i$. Since it won't cause confusion, we omit the superscript "CR" from now on. In this paper, $[a, b]$, $[c, d]$ and $[e, f]$ are called segments.

Here is a small example. Table 1 is a small decision table $KS=(U, C \cup \{d\})$, where $C=\{C_1, C_2, C_3, C_4, C_5\}$. There are 11 objects in the universe. We first sort them by the decision attribute d. And the set of demarcations induced by attribute d can be represented as $\{[1,5]_0, [6,11]_1\}$. We call it T_D. Clearly, the set of all the (valid) relative demarcations is a subset of it. Any subset of T_D is called a *task*. Note that a task can be represented in the compact form of a set of segments.

Now we look at C_5 and see which relative demarcations it can induce and which it cannot. To know it, we sort (or split) the segments in T_D (that is [1,5] and [6,11]) by the values of attribute C_5. The result can be seen on the right side of Table 1. It is clear that object x and y can be demarcated both by attribute C_5 and d, for any $x \in [1,2]$ and $y \in [9,11]$. In other words, $\{[1,2]_0, [9,11]_1\}$ is a set of relative demarcations. So is $\{[3,5]_0, [6,8]_1\}$.

Assume we have an attribute list *s_reduct*. We want to make *s_reduct* be the super reduct which contains at least one reduct. Hence, we can put C_5 into *s_reduct* because C_5 can induce some relative demarcations. But the objects belonging to [1,2] cannot be demarcated from the objects belonging to [6,8] by C_5. And the same is applicable to [3,5] and [9,11]. These pairs of objects need to be demarcated by other attributes. Hence, new task is formed: The first subtask is $\{[1,2]_0, [6,8]_1\}$ and the second subtask is $\{[3,5]_0, [9,11]_1\}$. We use CT_5 to denote this new task, a union of these two subtasks. In this paper, we also call CT_i a *cascade task* since it decides CT_{i-1}, together with attribute C_{i-1}. CT_i is just the task faced by "robot" C_{i-1} in our previous metaphor.

Now we have to consider attribute C_4 since $CT_5 \neq \phi$. The segments in CT_5 are split according to the values of C_4, which implies that $CT_4 \neq CT_5$. In other words, C_4 can induce some relative demarcations that cannot be induced by C_5. Hence, we put C_4 into *s_reduct*. Clearly, $\{[1,2]_0, [6,6]_1\}$ and $\{[3,3]_0, [9,11]_1\}$ form a new cascade task, which can be represented as CT_4. Note that $CT_3 = CT_4$. Thus, C_3 is dispensable to $\{C_4, C_5\}$ and can be skipped. Since $CT_2=\{[1,2]_0, [6,6]_1\} \neq CT_3$, we put C_2 into the attribute list *s_reduct*.

Because $CT_1=CT_2$, C_1 is dispensable to $\{C_2, C_4, C_5\}$. And in the same time we find that $\{[1,2]_0, [6,6]_1\}$ are the demarcations that cannot be induced by the conditional attributes but can be induced by the decision attribute. It means that the objects 1, 2, 6 cannot be assigned to one class determinately. We simply mark them by a special token "?". For a segment $[x, y]$, if any object $z \in [x, y]$ is marked by "?", we say the *segment is marked*.

s_reduct, which contains at least one *reduct*, has three attributes: C_2, C_4, C_5 (we can represent it simply by $\{2, 4, 5\}$). C_2 can induce some *valid relative demarcations* that

Table 1. The table sorted in the firt scan (from right side of the table to its left side)

C_1	C_2	C_3	C_4	C_5	d		Ad	C_1	C_2	C_3	C_4	C_5	d
0	1	0	0	0	0		?1	0	1	0	0	0	0
0	1	0	0	0	0		?2	0	1	0	0	0	0
1	0	1	0	1	0	Sort	3	1	0	1	0	1	0
0	1	1	0	1	1	→	4	1	0	0	1	1	0
1	1	1	0	1	1		5	0	0	0	1	1	0
1	1	0	0	1	1		?6	0	1	0	0	0	1
1	0	1	1	0	1		7	1	0	1	1	0	1
0	0	0	1	0	1		8	0	0	0	1	0	1
0	1	0	0	0	1		9	0	1	1	0	1	1
1	0	0	1	1	0		10	1	1	1	0	1	1
0	0	0	1	1	0		11	1	1	1	0	1	1

cannot be induced by all the other conditional attributes because CT_4 is not empty and it is not completely composed of marked segments. Therefore, C_2 is indispensable to $\{C_4, C_5\}$. Include C_2 into a *reduct*, which is empty initially.

In the algorithm, we should resort to an auxiliary array called "Ad", as shown in Table 2. The indices of the items of Ad are used in the first scan to form CT_i. The items of Ad have two sorts of values: the values of one kind are the serial numbers used in the second scan to form CT'; those of the other kind are the "pointers", i.e. the indices of objects of the original table, which are used to avoid movement of the objects in sorting (they haven't been shown in table 1). Note that the serial numbers have no use in the first scan. They are set to be equal to the indices of the items of Ad at the beginning of the second scan. Ad can also be substituted by two ordinary one-dimensional integer arrays, which is actually adopted in our implementation.

Now, in the second scan, we scan the table from left to right, as shown in Table 2. A cascade task, which includes two subtasks $T_{20}'=\{[3,5]_0, [7,8]_1\}$ and $T_{21}'= \{[1,2]_0^?, [6,6]_1^?, [9,11]_1\}$, are the set of relative demarcations that cannot be induced by attribute C_2. (Here "2" in the subscript of T_{20}' comes from C_2. "0" in T_{20}' means: For any object belonging to those segments of T_{20}', "0" is its value measured on C_2.) We use CT' to denote this task.

To decide whether C_4 is indispensable to other attributes in *s_reduct* or not, we need check $CT' \cap CT_5$. If it is empty or completely composed of *marked* segments, C_4 is dispensable to other attributes because all the valid relative demarcations that can be induced by C_4 can also be induced by C_2 and C_5. Otherwise, C_4 is indispensable to other attributes and CT' will be split by C_4 to form new CT'. In this case, $CT' \cap CT_5$ is composed of marked segments $[1,2]_0^?$ and $[6,6]_1^?$. Therefore, C_4 is dispensable to other attributes and should not be included in the *reduct*. CT' remains unchanged.

Since CT' is neither empty nor completely composed of marked segments, and there is no attribute that can induce the valid relative demarcations denoted compactly by CT' except C_5, include C_5 directly into the *reduct*.

At last, we can obtain a *reduct*, $\{C_2, C_5\}$, in this way. This example has disclosed the basic ideas of algorithm TWI-SQUEEZE, which will be introduced in section 2.2.

Table 2. The table sorted in the second scan (from left to right)

Ad	C_2	C_4	C_5	d
3	0	0	1	0
4	0	1	1	0
5	0	1	1	0
?1	1	0	0	0
?2	1	0	0	0
7	0	1	0	1
8	0	1	0	1
?6	1	0	0	1
9	1	0	1	1
10	1	0	1	1
11	1	0	1	1

Decision tree:
- T_D splits on $C_2=0$ to T_{20}' and $C_2=1$ to T_{21}'
- T_{20}' splits on $C_5=0$ (→ $d=1$) and $C_5=1$ (→ $d=0$)
- T_{21}' splits on $C_5=0$ (→ $d=0$) and $C_5=1$ (→ $d=1$)

Indices: 1, 2, 3, 4, 5, 6, 7, 8, 9, 10, 11
Ad: 3, 4, 5, ?1, ?2, 7, 8, ?6, 9, 10, 11

(The serial numbers in the items of Ad; The indices of the items of Ad; The pointers in the items of Ad)

Once a reduct is found, IF-THEN rules can be easily constructed by overlaying the *reduct* over the original decision table and reading off the values. Conditional attribute-value pairs of an object form a conjunction in the rule antecedent ("IF" part). And decision attribute-value pair forms the rule consequent ("THEN" part) [4]. For example, we can draw rule "If $C_2=1$ and $C_5=0$ Then $d=0$" from table 2. Here, the value of d is decided by majority voting.

Note that, when CT' is splitting, the algorithm is also creating a decision tree by adding links from a task to its children tasks and those segments that cannot form children tasks, as shown in table 2. This tree is in fact the decision tree shown in Fig. 1 (*a*). In this case it is shorter than the tree created by ID3, which is shown in Fig. 1 (*b*). It is not surprising because the algorithm uses the second scan to prune all dispensable attributes, which may be useful due to the principle of Occam's razor, although "short" does not always mean "good".

From the tree shown in Table 2, we can draw conclusions at any depth of the tree, because we have elements of both condition values and decision values at every node. For inconsistent rules, we can draw rules like "If $C_2=1$ and $C_5=0$ Then $d=0$ (2) or $d=1$ (1)" instead of simply assigning most common values to their decision attribute values. The numbers in parentheses are the numbers of objects that match the rule. Various frequency-related numerical quantities may be computed from these numbers. Concepts in disjunction form are useful in life. If they have a corresponding superordinate level concept [8], we can also draw a more general rule by attribute-oriented induction [9].

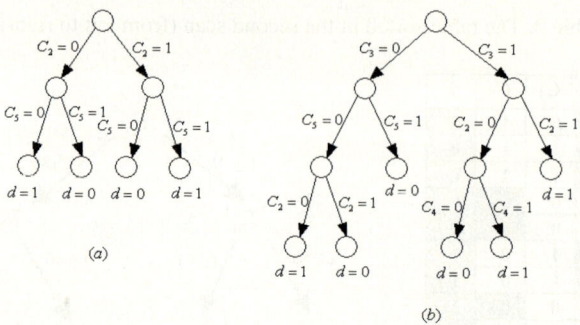

Fig. 1. Decision trees: (a) is produced by TWI-SQUEEZE; (b) is created by ID3

Therefore, after attribute reduction, we obtain two different classifiers: one is a rule system and the other is a decision tree. As far as efficiency of classification is concerned, decision tree is favorable, whereas rules are more understandable to people.

We've briefly discussed the outputs of algorithm TWI-SQUEEZE and regard them as classifiers. However, it is not the main topic of this paper. What we are presenting is an efficient algorithm for attribute reduction, which is introduced more formally in the following section.

2.2 Algorithm TWI-SQUEEZE

Now we can understand why we need a data structure like the one in Fig. 2. In the algorithm to be proposed, cascade task CT_i stores the relative demarcations needed to be induced by $\{C_1, C_2, \cdots, C_{i-1}\}$, since these demarcations cannot be induced by $\{C_i, C_{i+1}, \cdots, C_p\}$ ($p=|C|=t_C$). $|C|$ is the cardinality of set C. As have been shown in Fig. 2, CT_i is composed of some sets, which are its subtasks. The elements of a subtask are segments. A segment is composed of first position of segment (addr_first), last position of segment (addr_last), and a label denoting the D-Region it falls into, and a label denoting which subtask it belongs to. We can use segment to represent a task.

In Fig. 2, the subtasks in CT_i are linked as a list, which is clear and easy to be understood. The "5" appeared in subtask 1 is the number of segments in this subtask. This number must be larger than one. For any object belonging to these segments, "a" is its value measured on C_i. In fact, cascade tasks can be realized using two-dimension dynamic arrays, based on the STL.

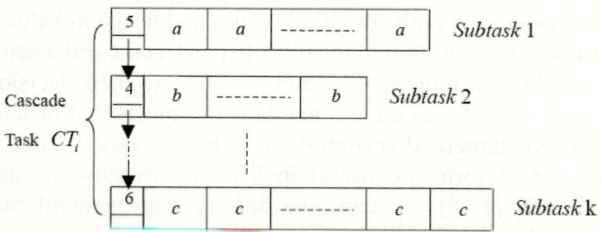

Fig. 2. Data structure of cascade task

At the beginning of the algorithm, objects will be sorted by decision attribute d. Assume the result is: $\{Seg_1, Seg_2, \cdots, Seg_{r_D}\}$. Thus, T_D is formed. These r_D segments correspond to r_D D-Regions. r_D is assumed to be larger than 1. These segments will be sorted according to the rightmost conditional attribute C_p. In other words, they are split and form some subsegments. Objects in a subsegment have the same value of C_p. All the subsegments that have a same value will be put together to form a new task (a set of segments). A cascade task split by some attribute will generate many new tasks, which are its children tasks. These children tasks form a new cascade task. We call these children tasks as the subtasks of this new cascade task.

Below is a formal ADL description of the algorithm TWI-SQUEEZE (The parameter after period is the output variable. The Knuth style notations are omitted).

Algorithm R2L-SQUEEZE (KS, C. s_reduct)
/* This subroutine finds a s_reduct. **Assume** $|C| = t_c$.*/
(1) $k \leftarrow t_c + 1$.
(2) $CT_k \leftarrow T_D$. $s\_reduct \leftarrow \{\}$.
(3) WHILE $CT_k \neq \phi$ DO
   (IF $k=1$ THEN mark inconsistent objects and RETURN.
    Split CT_k by C_{k-1}, forming CT_{k-1}.
    IF $CT_{k-1} \neq CT_k$ THEN $s\_reduct \leftarrow s\_reduct \cup \{k-1\}$.
    $k \leftarrow k-1$.) ■

Algorithm L2R-SQUEEZE (KS, s_reduct. $reduct$)
/* This subroutine squeezes a $reduct$ from s_reduct. */
(1) $k \leftarrow 1$.
(2) $CT' \leftarrow T_D$. $reduct \leftarrow \{\}$.
(3) WHILE $CT' \neq \phi$ AND it is not completely composed of marked segments DO
   ($s \leftarrow s\_reduct[k]$. /*Assume attribute $s\_reduct[i]$ is on the left side of $s\_reduct[j]$ in the
               table where $i < j$. */
   IF $k = length(s\_reduct)$ THEN ($reduct \leftarrow reduct \cup \{s\}$. RETURN.)
   $t \leftarrow s\_reduct[k+1]$.
   IF $CT' \cap CT_t \neq \phi$ AND the intersection is not completely composed of marked segments
      THEN ($reduct \leftarrow reduct \cup \{s\}$. Split CT' by Cs, forming new CT'.
        Add links. /*This step is used to form a tree*/)
$k \leftarrow k+1$.) ■

Algorithm TWI-SQUEEZE (KS. $reduct$)
/* The Main Part: find a $reduct$ in decision table KS.*/
(1) Give the conditional attributes an order. /*The most important and/or costliest attributes should be set on the right side of the table. The importance can be measured by many kinds of metrics. And the order can also be arbitrary */
(2) Sort the objects by decision attribute d, forming D-Regions. Assume the result is: $\{Seg_1, Seg_2, \cdots, Seg_{r_D}\}$. T_D is formed. It is a global variable that will be used in (3-4)
(3) $s\_reduct \leftarrow$ R2L-SQUEEZE (KS, C).
(4) $reduct \leftarrow$ L2R-SQUEEZE(KS, s_reduct). ■

All the algorithms that find one reduct depend (e.g. [10]) or implicitly depend on the order of attributes (e.g. [6]) they choose to deal with. A good order means a good reduct. By controlling the order of conditional attributes in table with some heuristic information such as entropy or Johnson's strategy [6] or just a-priori, the algorithm can find a suboptimal reduct. Generally, good a-priori can lead to good quality approximate reduct [7]. Algorithm TWI-SQUEEZE can ensure that the approximate one is a real reduct. Moreover, the algorithm can find more reducts with some additional time.

The main part of time needed in the algorithm is sorting. Assume the number of attributes actually scanned by R2L-SQUEEZE is r and the number of objects in table is N, the sorting needs $O(rN\ln N)$ steps, where $1 \le r \le t_C$. Note that, we can use secondary sorting to subdue unsteadiness of sorting in L2R-SQUEEZE.

The other part of time needed in the algorithm is counting the intersection of two cascade tasks, it needs only $O(N\ln N)$ steps.

Hence, the worst-case time complexity of TWI-SQUEEZE is: $O(rN\ln N)$.

In R2L-SQUEEZE, we keep all cascade tasks CT_i ($C_i \in s\_reduct$) in memory, taking a memory-resident view. In L2R-SQUEEZE, only one new cascade task CT' is needed. All these cascade tasks occupy $O(rN)$ units. These are additional or auxiliary space. In the same time, we need only put a small fraction of the total table, the projection of one or more attributes of the table, into the memory. Thus only $O(N)$ units are needed. Therefore the total space needed is $O(rN)$. However, we can also do not maintain all cascade tasks CT_i in the memory, but write these tasks to disk. From this disk-resident view, the algorithm needs only $O(N)$ memory space, with some read-in and write-out disk operations.

Let $length(CT_i)$ be the sum of sizes of segments in CT_i and assume $length(CT_{i-1})/length(CT_i) \le \mu$ ($0 \le \mu \le 1$) for any $i \in [2, t_C+1]$ in R2L-SQUEEZE, the worst-case time complexity of the algorithm is: $O\left(Min\left(t_C, \log_\mu \frac{2}{N}\right) \times N \ln N\right)$ since at most $Min\left(t_C, \log_\mu \frac{2}{N}\right)$ attributes need to be scanned. Generally, the algorithm works much better than it works in worst case. The previous fastest algorithm, let us called it NERS (the efficient rough set algorithm of Nguyen Sinh Hoa and Nguyen Hung Son), which finds a reduct, needs to scan table t_C times [6]. Its worst-case time complexity is $O(t_C^2 N \ln N)$.

3 Experiments

Experiments are performed on three data sets listed in Table 3. The results reflect the performance time (measured in seconds) of algorithms compared. These data sets come from the UCI Machine Learning Repository [11] where detailed descriptions of them can be found. The data set "Promoter Gene Sequences" includes 57 conditional attributes, one decision attribute and 106 objects; "Primate splice-junction gene sequences (DNA) with associated imperfect domain theory" has 60 plus one attributes and 3190 objects; and "Optical Recognition of Handwritten Digits" has 64 plus one attributes, which has 3823 objects. Note that we did not take the object names of the two molecular biology databases into account.

We haven't compare the classifier accuracy because the reducts found by these algorithms happen to be the same. It is also worth mention that the reduct of the data set "Optical Recognition of Handwritten Digits" cannot be used directly to classify unseen objects. In this case, attribute reduction, as a data preprocessing method, should combine with other classification algorithms, such as kNN.

Table 3. Comparison of the efficiency of NERS, NERSA, TWI-SQUEEZE on classification tasks

	NERS	NERSA	TWI-SQUEEZE
Promoter Gene Sequences	0.35	0.21	0.02
Primate splice-junction gene sequences (DNA)	202.181	94.816	1.232
Optical Recognition of Handwritten Digits	333.56	165.749	1.172

A factor that influences the efficiency of NERS significantly is movement of the objects in the sorting. To be fair, we added an ancillary array to NERS to avoid such movement. We call this improvement as NERSA. For the same sake, we avoid heuristic search in these algorithms. These algorithms are implemented using C++. The experiment is taken on a computer with windows XP, Intel Pentium III 651 MHz processor and 384M memory. From the experiments, we can see that TWI-SQUEEZE is a faster attribute reduction algorithm, compared with NERS and NERSA. Generally speaking, TWI-SQUEEZE can show its advantages in the face of a large number of attributes. But in our viewpoint, the more stringent limitation on data mining is memory. Maybe it is the reason for the infeasibility of the discernibility matrix based algorithms in face of large data sets [6] (they are still usable when the number of different elements of the matrix is moderate). And it is said that some algorithms from the embedded RSES library of ROSETTA are not applicable to decision tables larger than some predetermined size, currently 500 objects and 20 attributes. Although NERS and NERSA have relieved this curse, they need put the whole table into the memory, which also imposes a demand on memory. As have been explained, TWI-SQUEEZE can avoid this problem by putting a column or several into the memory step by step, which makes it more suitable for the requirements of data mining.

4 Conclusions

We propose a simple and efficient algorithm TWI-SQUEEZE that finds one reduct. This algorithm finds one reduct instead of all for two reasons. On the one hand, finding all reducts in huge database is proved to be NP-hard [5]. On the other hand, excessive reducts are unmanageable even for an expert.

The outputs of the algorithm are two different style classifiers. One is a set of IF-THEN rules. The other is a decision tree. It is an advantage of algorithm TWI-SQUEEZE since other attribute reduction algorithms cannot do it. The other merit deserving some words is that the algorithm can relieve the curse of memory limitation by reading part of a data set into memory in every phase because it deals with a column of the table every time.

References

1. Marek, W., and Pawlak, Z.: Rough Set and Information Systems. Fundamenta Informaticae, 17, 1984, pp. 105-115
2. Pawlak, Z.: Rough Sets. International Journal of Computer and Information Sciences, 11, 1982, pp. 341-356
3. Pawlak, Z. Rough Sets: Theoretical Aspects of Reasoning about Data. Kluwer Academic Publishers (1991)
4. Komorowski, J., Pawlak, Z., Polkowski, L., and Skowron, A.: Rough Sets: A Tutorial. In: Rough Fuzzy Hybridization --A New Trend in Decision Making, Springer, 1998, pp. 3-98
5. Skowron, A., and Rauszer, C.: The Discernibility Matrices and Functions in Information System, Intelligent Decision Support-Handbook of Applications and Adbvances of the Rough Set Theory, Kluwer Academic Publishers, 1992
6. Hoa, N.S., and Son, N.H.: Some efficient algorithms for rough set methods. In Proceedings of the Conference of Information Processing and Management of Uncertainty in Knowledge-Based Systems, 1996
7. Hu, Q., Pao, W., and Yu, D.: Improved reduction algorithm based on A-Priori. Computer Science, 29, 2002, pp. 115-117
8. Best, J.B.: Cognitive Psychology. Heinle and Heinle Publishers, Boston, MA (1998)
9. Han, J., and Kamber, M.: Data Mining: Concepts and Techniques. Morgan Kaufmann, San Francisco, CA (2000)
10. Wang, J., Wang, Ju.: Reduction algorithms based on discernibility matrix: The ordered attributes method. Journal of Computer Science and Technology, 16, 2001, pp. 489-504
11. Newman, D.J. & Hettich, S. & Blake, C.L.& Merz, C.J.: UCI Repository of machine learning databases [http://www.ics.uci.edu/~mlearn/MLRepository.html],1998

Conceptual Classification to Improve a Web Site Content

Sebastián A. Ríos[1], Juan D. Velásquez[2], Hiroshi Yasuda[1], and Terumasa Aoki[1]

[1] Applied Information Engineering Laboratory, University of Tokyo, Japan
{srios, yasuda, aoki}@mpeg.rcast.u-tokyo.ac.jp
[2] Department of Industrial Engineering,
University of Chile, Chile
jvelasqu@dii.uchile.cl

Abstract. This paper presents a conceptual based approach for improving a Web site content. Usually Web Usage Mining (WUM) techniques study the visitors' browsing behavior to obtain interesting knowledge. However, most of the work in the area leave behind the semantic information of web pages. We propose to combine the Concept-Based Knowledge Discovery in Text with the visitors sessions to perform the personalization task. This way, it is possible to obtain information about which are the users' goals when browsing a web site. Moreover, it is possible to give better browsing recomendations and help managers improving the content of their Web site. We test this idea on a real Web site to show its effectiveness.

1 Introduction

The World Wide Web has became an important way to reach information on almost any topic rapidly and effortlessly. Also, the Web has opened a new way of doing businesses, i.e. amazon.com that is one of the most used examples.

One important issue is how to deal with an overwhelming amount of documents. Most of the better search engines like google, yahoo, altavista, among others use algorithms based on keywords. However, when the web users perform a searching task have some questions, ideas or goals in mind [4]. Similarly, when a user finally reach a web site, she/he need to read the content in order to find if this information is suitable to her/his needs or goals. These problems get worse with the fast growing of the Web and forces to a new way of designing and developing web sites [3] to give a better browsing experience to the visitors.

Improving the web site usability, structure and content to keep the visitors interested on it is a challenging task [7]. Many techniques like Web Text Mining (WTM), Web Structure Mining (WSM), Web Usage Mining (WUM), Web Personalization (WP), etc. are used to help managers and web masters improve a web site [1] or automatically giving an on-line recommendation directly to the visitors. Many times when applying such techniques combined with keyword based algorithms the semantics of the web pages is lost. We define concepts trying to give a simple solution which consider this semantic factor. We show that the resulting process better fit users' needs and goals.

The paper is organized as follows. Section 2, we show a short review about related research work. Section 3 explains how to identify and define concepts and how to apply the conceptual approach for web pages classification. Afterwards, in Section 4, we show how to improve the WUM using the conceptual information. Section 5, an experiment in a real-world case is presented. Finally, Section 6 presents the main conclusions and future work.

2 Related Work

There are more than one approach for improving the visitors' browsing experience in a web site. Many researchers focus on text content improvements [9,10], to do so they use a text preprocessing stage, sometimes a stemming process is applied to reduce the number of features and obtain better results in the generalization process which will applied later. Finally, the expert's collaboration to validate the results is always desirable.

Other researchers argue that in order to improve a Web Site we need to focus on how the users browse on it. This is called Web Usage Mining (WUM) and several works have been developed in this area, one example is Mobasher et al [5,12]. However, other researchers realize that better web sites' improvements recomendations can be obtained using a combination of visitors browsing behavior plus the textual content of the pages visited, some examples are [8,11,13].

All these techniques probe their effectiveness to help improve sites' usability. However, non of them take into consideration the semantic information of the web pages. Some authors realize this issue, and developed approaches aiming to consider the semantics of documents when performing the mining technique. A very good example is the Semantic Web Personalization System (SEWeP) [3], this system use concepts defined on a domain taxonomy to obtain the semantics of documents, afterwards, enhance the Web personalization process.

Other interesting work related with semantics but not with personalization is the one developed by Chau et al. in [2]. She is focused in the semantics from multilingual documents written in Chinese and English. She uses fuzzy logic to define concepts and afterwards she run a Fuzzy K-Means algorithm to filter the multilingual documents in topics regardless of the language. Afterwards, a Self Organizing Map (SOM) is used to obtain a topic-oriented multilingual text classification.

In our case, we intended to use the concept-based knowledge discovery in text proposed by Loh et al. in [4] to improve the WUM process. In his proposal Fuzzy Logic is used in order to define concepts which express the semantics of documents. Then he applied a fuzzy reasoning model to classify the documents into its concepts. Finally the application of statistical techniques allow to discover interesting patterns in concept distribution.

3 Conceptual Approach for Web Pages Classification

To begin with the conceptual approach we need to understand the meaning of the word "concept". From a Spanish dictionary a "concept" is an "idea, opinion or thought", from WordNet 2.0 is "an abstract or general idea inferred or derived from specific instances". Both definitions show the ambiguity and subjectivity of the word. Also, they show the inference capacity which humans have for performing different tasks.

3.1 Identification and Definition of Concepts

We worked with the web site of the Faculty of Sciences Physics and Mathematics of the University of Chile. Identification of concepts was performed with sites' expert help. This way was possible to establish a set of concepts which can be important for the visitors of the site as shown in Table 1.

Table 1. Small sample of concepts identified for the site in Spanish

CONCEPTOS	CONCEPTS
ACTIVIDADES EVALUATIVAS	EVALUATIVE ACTIVITIES
SERVICIOS GENERALES	GENERAL SERVICES
SERVICIOS PERSONALES	PERSONAL SERVICES
ACTIVIDADES EXTRAPROGRAMATICAS	EXTRACURRICULAR ACTIVITIES
CALENDARIO DE PRUEBAS	TEST SCHEDULE

Note that we don't use all possible concepts, just the most important to the visitors based on the expert criteria. Afterwards, we need to define these concepts by a coherent combination of words [3,4]. To do so, we used a synonyms dictionary to extract words to characterize each concept also we use quasi-synonyms. A quasi-synonym from the dictionary is "a term in a controlled vocabulary, such as a thesaurus, that is treated as if it means the same thing as another term". For example. In the case of "Personal services" we consider words like "agenda" or "u-agenda" which is the name of the agenda system for the students and professors of the Faculty. Other example is the incorporation of the word "U-Cursos" that is the name of the portal for all courses in the Faculty. This contains all the classes documents (.ppt, .doc, etc), bibliography and many other useful information.

3.2 Fuzzy Logic for Pages Classification

We decided to apply the Fuzzy Reasoning model proposed by Loh et al. [4]. To characterize the documents of the web site. This solution is based in the idea that we need to gather the relation between the concepts and the documents which can be represented as a fuzzy composition, shown in Eq.(1). In that expression the terms $[Concepts \times Terms]$ and $[Terms \times Words]$ are fuzzy relations, therefore matrices. The operator ○ represent the compositional rule of inference according to Nakanishi et al. [6]. From this point we call "terms" to the special words that represent a concept and "words" to any word in a document like a web page.

$$[Concepts \times Words] = [Concepts \times Terms] \circ [Terms \times Words] \qquad (1)$$

In order to apply the expression in Eq.(1) we defined a list of concepts and terms that represent these concepts in the previous section. However, we still

Table 2. A column extracted from the compositional matrix [$Concepts \times Words$]

URL: http://escuela.ing.uchile.cl/servicios.htm	
ACTIVIDADES EVALUATIVAS	=> 0
SERVICIOS GENERALES	=> 0.707106781187
SERVICIOS PERSONALES	=> 0.424264068712
REGLAMENTACION	=> 0
INFORMACION GENERAL ESCUELA INGENERIA	=> 0.707106781187
CLASES	=> 0
CALENDARIO DE PRUEBAS	=> 0
....	

need to set up the membership values for this relation. Once again we use the experts' knowledge to define this values (direct method with one expert).

We used a simple model that use relative words frequency on each document to deffine the second fuzzy relation [$Terms \times Words$]. The documents were preprocessed to eliminate the HTML and JavaScript code and using a stop word list we also erased words that are not important. We intended to keep nouns, adjectives and verbs. At this point we decided to not use stemming process to maintain the words intact and compare it with its synonyms and quasi-synonyms without problems of having one stem and more than one possible word.

After applying the compositional rule of inference we obtain the [$Concepts \times Words$] matrix were each row is a concept and each column is a web page and each value in the matrix represent the degree of possibility of a concept to be represented in a web page (i.e. the membership value of the composition shown in Eq.(1)). Therefore, we achieved a Conceptual based classification for each web page on the site. An example is shown in Table 2, where we have the column that represent "http://escuela.ing.uchile.cl/servicios.htm" (services.htm in English) and then we have the concepts and its membership values. In this case this page contains information of services for students, professors and links to them. We can see that the concept "SERVICIOS GENERALES" (General Services) has a membership value of 0.707106781187 and "SERVICIOS PERSONALES" (Personal Services) has a membership value of 0.424264068712. As we mention before this can be interpreted as "the degree of the concept X to be represented in the page servicios.htm". In this particular example we can observe for example that the page is more semantically related to the concept "SERVICIOS GENERALES" than "SERVICIOS PERSONALES" this is because most of the services are not only for students or professors but also for the whole comunity. Similarly others concepts in Table 2 have a membership value of 0 which means that the page doesn't talk about these concepts.

4 Mining User Sessions

Several techniques to perform WUM over a site exists. We chose to perform a WUM that combine the text of the documents and the visitors' sessions according to [11,13] and then compare its results with the concept-based approach.

To begin with WUM process we need to transform the web pages in a more useful way. We use the Vector Space Model to represent each document as a vector of words combined with the $TF*IDF$ to establish the wight of every word (frequency) on each document. On the other hand, we need to pre-process the web servers' logs to figure out which are the visitors' sessions. We perform a time heuristic sessionization over the web logs. After this step, we have the pages and time spend on each document visited for the visitors.

4.1 Visitors' Session Classification

After the pre-processing stage we have to apply the generalization process. We selected to use a Self Organizing Feature Map (SOFM) because it is an unsupervised algorithm which means we don't need to know before hand how many clusters are. We used a process similar to the one published in a previous works [13,11].

We based our work in a similarity measure proposed by Velasquez et al in [13] that combines the visitors sessions and the content of the web pages. However, we intended to generate more semantically related results rather than textual contents related. This is why we modified this similarity in order to apply the conceptual classification obtained before. The similarity measure used is shown in Eq.(2) were $CS(S^i, S^j)$ is the similarity between the session S^i from visitors i and session S^j from visitor j. The sessions S should be of the same length so we sort the pages per time spent on each. Then we use the first ι pages where the visitor spend most of his time. The formula uses the $S^j_\tau(k)$ as the time in seconds spent by visitor j in page k and similarly for visitor i. The term $S^j_\rho(k)$ is a vector which contains the concepts and the degree of membership for page k of visitor j session (Section 3.2) . This way, the equation is unaltered from its original form but we are using concepts instead of terms frequency to compare the sessions.

$$CS(S^i, S^j) = \frac{1}{\iota} \sum_{k=1}^{\iota} min(\frac{S^i_\tau(k)}{S^j_\tau(k)}, \frac{S^j_\tau(k)}{S^i_\tau(k)}) * PD(S^i_\rho(k), S^j_\rho(k)) \qquad (2)$$

Finally, we obtain clusters that are related by its conceptual meaning. Therefore, we obtain a conceptual classification of the documents on each visitors' session.

5 Experiments in a Real Web Site

We applied this process to the web site of the School of Engineering and Sciences of the University of Chile [1]. This web site has 182 web pages and it is almost static throw the year (only the news page change continuously), thus we used the version of March 2006 of the web site. Besides, we took approximately 2 months of web logs 2006.

---

[1] http://escuela.ing.uchile.cl

We detect 12 important concepts, we defined them using a dictionary, a thesaurus and the experts' help. Afterwards, each document was classified into its concepts as explained before (see Table 2).

We decided to use a SOFM of 7×7 neurons. Then we kept the 3 pages per session were the visitors spend most of its time. Afterwards, we compute the similarity measure in Eq.(2) for the SOFM through 50 epochs. In order to compare the results obtained with the conceptual approach. We also compute the traditional approach that uses $TF * IDF$ words vector instead of a vector of concepts in Eq.(2). Using the same network size, epochs, and session length.

Our results using the traditional approach are shown in the Table 3. We can observe that we obtain three clusters for the users sessions $\{0, 1, 2\}$. Each cluster found, is represented for several visitors' sessions, e.g for cluster $ID = 0$ we have a list of nine sessions $\{1, 2, 50, 58, 64, 66, 78, 127, 262\}$. Each number in this list is the ID of a visitor session. For example, the session ID=1, has 3 pages which are $\{mail2.htm, barraizquierda.htm, maincalendarios.htm\}$ where the visitor spent most of his/her time (See Section 4.1). The problem in this case is we have the pages that the visitors browsed and we now that he/she was interested in the text inside that pages. Usually the recommendation is to link those pages. However, with the conceptual approach we can discover what topic he/she is interested in and we can give a family of pages that satisfy his/her needs, even if the pages are not present in the cluster sessions.

Table 3. Results of traditional approach

CLUSTER ID	SESSIONS [IDs.]
0	$\{1, 2, 50, 58, 64, 66, 78, 127, 262\}$
1	$\{54, 57, 66, 67, 69, 74, 90, 112, 146\}$
2	$\{0, 66, 93, 123, 184, 224, 256, 267\}$

The results of the conceptual approach proposed are shown in Table 4. This time we discovered five clusters (two more clusters than using the traditional approach). Afterwards, we extracted the concepts on the real sessions representative of each cluster. To do so, we computed the common concepts to all documents on the cluster. The result of this is shown on Table 5. If there is no concept common to all of the documents on the cluster sessions, then the value "N/A" is given to that cluster.

Observing this results on Table 5 we can notice that Cluster $ID = 1$ is about people who is looking for contact information, telephone numbers, the name and e-mail of people in charge of the administrative office or certificate office or other area. Other interesting information is obtained from cluster $ID = 0$ where the concepts are { *Vacations Schedule, News/Advertisements, Seminars/Extention, Extracurricular Activities, Organizations* }. This means that the students look for activities to do on vacations. Other interpretation is that when a visitor to the site (most of them students) search for vacations schedule, also is looking for activities to do on his/her free time. This is way he/she also browse for

Table 4. Results of conceptual approach

CLUSTER ID	SESSIONS [IDs.]
0	{57, 66, 93, 102, 224, 230, 268}
1	{56, 66, 90, 93, 269}
2	{66, 78, 224, 256, 268}
3	{4, 57, 66, 78, 239, 267}
4	{2, 66, 78, 223, 265}

Table 5. Concepts obtained from clusters

CLUSTER ID	CONCEPTS
0	{ Vacations Schedule, News/Advertisements, Seminars/Extention, Extracurricular Activities, Organizations }
1	{ Location Information / Physical Addresses, Contact Information }
2	{ Classes Material, Tests Schedule, Classes Inforation. }
3	N/A
4	{ Reglaments, Classes Information, Tests schedule }

extracurricular activities information, Organizations Information (Photography Club, Role Gamimg Club, etc).

If we study the structure of the pages on the cluster sessions, we notice that many of the page in the session, are not close one to the other. In the case of Cluster $ID = 1$, the schedules are in a section different from the section of the Organizations and this both in a section different from the section of extracurricular activities. The visitors must browse all the sections doing several clicks to reach the calendars then exit this section and browse down in the next section to find the information about Role Gaming Club. Then, the recommendation in this case is to link the relevant pages on this cluster. Many alternative exist, from creating one single page with all this information, to link the existing pages among them. Moreover, since we have all web pages classified by its conceptual meaning we do not need to limit the recommendation to those pages in the cluster. We can also generate a single page where all the pages with information about extra curricular activities or organizations we have. When we talk about a concept we talk about a family of web pages that express the concept in a certain degree.

5.1 Discussion

After extracting the concepts form each real page on the session, we discover that cluster $ID = 3$ it is not valid from concepts perspective. If we use other manner to extract concepts from the cluster we can obtain results. However, we need more work to do in this area, because it is not simple and the results can change greatly depending on the technique used to extract the concepts form the sessions.

We need more work about the concepts base used. Our experiment only take into consideration a small amount of concepts (12) however, it is possible to define a wider concepts base to obtain more information about our visitors.

6 Conclusions

Many different techniques and methodologies exists to help managers or web masters improve web sites' usability. However, most of them do not consider the semantic information from the web documents. We propose a simple process to achieve a conceptual classification of documents using a fuzzy reasoning model. Then a Self Organizing Feature Map for the Generalization stage.

We use this process to improve the Web Usage Mining process results, to obtain patterns that have more relation with the visitors goals and then recommend managers changes in the web sites' content.

We perform two experiments using a traditional WUM approach and then we used our proposal in a real Web site.

We are working in more experimental results as well as in the evaluation of the whole concept-based usage minig process proposed in this work.

References

1. S. Chakrabarti. Data Mining for Hypertext: A Tutorial Survey. *SIGKDD Explorations*, 1, 2000.
2. R. Chau and C.-H. Yeh. Filtering multilingual web content using fuzzy logic and self-organizing maps. *Neural Comput. Appl.*, 13(2):140–148, 2004.
3. M. Eirinaki, C. Lampos, S. Paulakis, and M. Vazirgiannis. Web personalization integrating content semantics and navigational patterns. In *WIDM '04: Proceedings of the 6th annual ACM international workshop on Web information and data management*, pages 72–79, New York, NY, USA, 2004. ACM Press.
4. S. Loh, J. P. M. D. Oliveira, and M. A. Gameiro. Knowledge discovery in texts for constructing decision support systems. *Applied Intelligence*, 18(3):357–366, 2003.
5. B. Mobasher, R. Cooley, and J. Srivastava. Automatic personalization based on web usage mining. *Commun. ACM*, 43(8):142–151, 2000.
6. H. Nakanishi, I. B. Turksen, and M. Sugeno. A review and comparison of six reasoning methods. *Fuzzy Sets and Systems*, 57(3):257–294, Aug. 1993.
7. J. Nielsen. User Interface directions for the web. *Communications of ACM*, 42(1):65–72, 1999.
8. M. Perkowitz and O. Etzioni. Adaptive web sites. *Commun. ACM*, 43(8):152–158, 2000.
9. S. A. Ríos, J. D. Velásquez, E. S. Vera, H. Yasuda, and T. Aoki. Establishing guidelines on how to improve the web site content based on the identification of representative pages. In *IEEE/WIC/ACM Int. Conf. on Web Intelligence and Intelligent Agent Technology*, pages 284–288, Compiegne, France, September 2005. IEEE Computer Scociety.
10. S. A. Ríos, J. D. Velásquez, E. S. Vera, H. Yasuda, and T. Aoki. Using SOFM to Improve Web Site Text Content. In *Advances in Natural Computation: 1st Int.l Conf., ICNC 2005*, volume 3611 of *Lecture Notes in Computer Science*, pages 622–626, Changsha, China, August 2005. Springer-Verlag GmbH.

11. S. A. Ríos, J. D. Velásquez, H. Yasuda, and T. Aoki. Web Site Improvements Based on Representative Pages Identification. In *AI 2005: Advances in Artificial Intelligence: 18th Australian Joint Conference on Artificial Intelligence*, volume 3809 of *Lecture Notes in Computer Science*, pages 1162–1166, Sydney, Australia, November 2005.
12. M. Spiliopoulou, B. Mobasher, B. Berendt, and M. Nakagawa. A Framework for the Evaluation of Session Reconstruction Heuristics in Web-Usage Analysis. *INFORMS J. on Computing*, 15(2):171–190, 2003.
13. J. D. Velásquez, S. A. Ríos, A. Bassi, H. Yasuda, and T. Aoki. Towards the identification of keywords in the web site text content: A methodological approach. *International Journal of Web Information Systems*, 1(1):11–15, March 2005.

Automated Learning of RVM for Large Scale Text Sets: Divide to Conquer

Catarina Silva[1,2] and Bernardete Ribeiro[2]

[1] School of Technology and Management of the Polytechnic Institute of Leiria, Morro do Lena - Alto do Vieiro, Portugal, P-2411-901 Leiria, Portugal
[2] Department of Informatics Engineering, Center for Informatics and Systems (CISUC), University of Coimbra, Polo II, P-3030-290 Coimbra, Portugal
catarina@dei.uc.pt, bribeiro@dei.uc.pt

Abstract. Three methods are investigated and presented for automated learning of Relevance Vector Machines (RVM) in large scale text sets. RVM probabilistic Bayesian nature allows both predictive distributions on test instances and model-based selection yielding a parsimonious solution. However, scaling up the algorithm is not workable in most digital information processing applications. We look at the properties of the baseline RVM algorithm and propose new scaling approaches based on choosing appropriate working sets which retain the most informative data. Incremental, ensemble and boosting algorithms are deployed to improve classification performance by taking advantage of the large training set available. Results on Reuters-21578 are presented, showing performance gains and maintaining sparse solutions that can be deployed in distributed environments.

1 Introduction

With the explosion of electronically stored text, automatic Text Classification (TC) plays a decisive role in document processing and visualization, Web mining, digital information search, patent analysis, etc. The task in TC is often defined as assigning previously defined classes to documents (natural language texts), by analyzing their content. Different methods to choose a classifier are selected according to experiments on a particular problem instance. No single classifier is always best [1], so for practical purposes we need to develop an effective methodology for combining them. In addition, several challenges are the cutting-edge of TC research, namely scaling up the classifiers to large data sets, since independently of the application at hand this issue usually causes problems for many standard learning algorithms.

While many techniques have successfully been used in tackling the problem of TC, current research is focused on kernel-based algorithms mainly due to their performance of accuracy and sparsity of the final solution. Examples are Vapnik's Support Vector Machines (SVM) [2] which implement the principle of structural minimization and Tipping's Relevance Vector Machines (RVM) [3] which are a Bayesian approach leading to a probabilistic non-linear model with a prior on the weights that promotes sparse solutions. RVM's advantage over non-Bayesian kernel methods, comes from explicit probabilistic formulation that yields predictive distributions for test instances and allows Bayesian model selection. However, the computational cost is $O(n^3)$ where n is the number of training instances which results in huge computational cost for large data sets. Furthermore, computing a test case requires $O(n)$ cost for calculating the mean and $O(n^2)$ cost for computing the variance. These heavy scaling properties obstruct the use of RVM in large scale problems.

There are clear benefits of combining multiple classifiers based on different classification methods and these have been discussed in [4]. Our own approach is to use a combination method for text classifiers based on randomly selecting small working chunks from the large data and using an efficient scheme of combination such as voting or boosting.

In section 2 we present related work that establishes background for baseline results. In section 3 we describe the large scale TC instance problem, performance measures and the benchmark used. In section 4 kernel-based learning methods such as, SVM and RVM, are introduced and baseline results are presented. Section 5 focuses on the proposed approaches of combining and scaling-up classifiers, analyzes the results and compares them on Reuters-21578 benchmark. In section 6 conclusions and future work are addressed.

2 Related Work

Yang [5] presents a scalability analysis of classifiers in TC that although do not including RVM, compares KNN and Support Vector Machines (SVM). Sebastiani in [1] provides an overview of standard classification methods for TC such as, Naive Bayes, logistic regression, and decision trees. Joachims in [6] describes an approach with SVM, which yields results considered state-of-the-art, by making SVM computationally more efficient and therefore applicable to a large set of applications. Despite these results, SVM suffer from some limitations that can become important on TC. Namely SVM hard classification decision function does not allow to estimate the conditional probability distribution in order to capture the uncertainty in the prediction and the error/margin trade-off parameter has to be estimated.

Relevant Vector Machines (RVM)[3] appear as a powerful alternative to SVM in this problem, by introducing a probability distribution over possible parameter values of the learned classifier. This not only provides one solution to overfitting problems, but also provides a mathematical way to allow domain knowledge to influence the parameter values that result from learning. However, a known problem with Bayesian approaches is their relative inability to scale with large problems, like TC.

3 Text Classification

In the last two decades the production of textual documents in digital form has increased exponentially, due to the increased availability of hardware and software [7]. As a consequence, there is an ever-increasing need for automated solutions for organizing the huge amount of digital texts produced.

A recurrent issue in TC is the scale of the data sets that usually causes difficulties for many standard learning algorithms. Documents are represented by vectors of numeric values, with one value for each word that appears in any training document, making it a large scale problem. High dimensionality increases both processing time and the risk of overfitting, i.e., the learning algorithm inducing a classifier that reflects accidental properties of the particular training examples rather than the systematic relationships between the words and the categories [8].

For the experiments, Reuters-21578 dataset (http://kdd.ics.uci.edu/databases/reuters21578/reuters21578.html) was used. It is a financial corpus with news articles averaging 200 words each. Reuters-21578 has 12000 classified stories into 118 possible categories. We use 10 categories generally accepted as a benchmark: earn, acq, money-fx, grain, crude, trade, interest, ship, wheat and corn. The ModApte split was used, using 75% of the articles (9603 items) for training and 25% (3299 items) for testing.

TC tasks have specific characteristics that demand particular performance measures. Most TC applications have highly unbalanced classes. For instance, corn category in Reuters-21578 has only 164 positive training examples. Therefore common error or accuracy measures are not suitable, since they value equally both false positives (negative testing examples classified as positive) and false negatives (positive testing examples classified as negatives). To define customised measures a contingency table (table 1) is built and F_β (1), an weighted harmonic average of Precision ($a/(a+b)$) and Recall ($a/(a+c)$), is used with $\beta = 1$ to evaluate binary classifiers in natural language applications like TC.

$$F_\beta(h) = \frac{(\beta^2 + 1)\,a}{(\beta^2 + 1)\,a + b + \beta^2\,c} \qquad (1)$$

Table 1. Contingency table. Possible target (y)/hypothesis (h) combinations

	y=1	y=-1
h(x)=1	a	b
h(x)=-1	c	d

4 Kernel-Based Learning Algorithms for TC

This section presents results achieved with linear versions of SVM and RVM on Reuters-21578 benchmark data set, that serve as baseline of comparison.

4.1 SVM

SVM are a learning method introduced by Vapnik [2] based on his Statistical Learning Theory and Structural Minimization Principle. When using SVM for classification, the basic idea is to find the optimal separating hyperplane between the positive and negative examples. The optimal hyperplane is defined as the one giving the maximum margin between the training examples that are closest to it. Support vectors are the examples that lie closest to the separating hyperplane. Once this hyperplane is found, new examples can be classified simply by determining on which side of the hyperplane they are. The best SVM F1 average result obtained was 79.88% with an average of 618 support vectors when all documents were used, with SVM^{light} package (http://svmlight.joachims.org/) default parameters.

4.2 RVM

The RVM was proposed by Tipping [3], as a Bayesian treatment of the sparse learning problem. The RVM preserves the generalization and sparsity of the SVM, yet it also yields a probabilistic output, as well as circumvents other limitations of SVM, such as the need of Mercer kernels and the definition of the error/margin trade-off parameter C. The output of an RVM model is very similar to the Vapnik proposed SVM model [2], and can be represented as:

$$g(\mathbf{x}) = \sum_{i=1}^{N} w_i k(\mathbf{x}, \mathbf{z}_i) + w_0, \mathbb{R} \qquad (2)$$

where $\mathbf{x}$ is an input vector and $g : \mathbb{R}^M \to \mathbb{R}$ is the scalar-valued output function, modelled as a weighted sum of kernel evaluations between the test vector and the training examples. The kernel function, $k : \mathbb{R}^M \times \mathbb{R}^M \to \mathbb{R}$ can be considered either as a similarity function between vectors, or as a basis function centered at $\mathbf{z}_i$. Training determines the weights, $\mathbf{w} = [w_0, ..., w_N]$ while the sparsity property will rise if some of the w_i are set to zero. As can be seen in table 2, average

Table 2. F1, RV and CPU training time (in seconds) for Baseline RVM

	1000 docs			2000 docs		
	F1	RV	CPU	F1	RV	CPU
earn	95.70%	23	95	97.52%	35	1218
acq	86.69%	26	100	91.57%	49	1257
money-fx	45.32%	19	96	57.14%	35	1193
grain	72.86%	22	96	76.52%	28	1110
crude	64.11%	16	90	69.51%	28	1125
trade	42.46%	19	103	50.27%	37	1076
interest	45.40%	16	84	58.29%	35	1133
ship	37.84%	15	78	66.21%	26	1130
wheat	71.01%	19	90	75.18%	19	1133
corn	62.63%	15	82	67.37%	27	952
average	62.40%	19.0	91.4	70.96%	31.9	1132.7

F1 classification performance is of 62.40% for the RVM trained with 1000 documents and of 70.96% for the one trained with 2000 documents. CPU times increase supra-linearly, preventing the full training set to be used. As referred, this RVM scaling inability constitutes one of the main motivations for the work presented in this paper. Since the average number of relevant vectors (RV) and the training times remain fairly constant for the same number of training examples, hereafter results will be reported concerning only classification performance (F1 measure).

5 Proposed RVM Scaling Techniques

In this section we develop and compare three techniques on RVM, namely incremental, boosting and ensemble methods. The underlying idea is to preserve the RVM probabilistic Bayesian nature, together with the sparse solutions achieved, while improving classification performance, by using all training documents available.

5.1 Incremental RVM

Incremental RVM, represented in figure 1a), starts by dividing the available training set in smaller chunks of 1000 and 2000 documents, resulting in two sets of RVM models. Larger chunks were not considered since their computational burden would risk the algorithm scalability. For each set, the Relevant Vectors (RV) of each RVM model are gathered and a new RVM model is trained. Table 3 presents the results achieved.

Table 3. F1 values for incremental RVM

Category	1000 docs	2000 docs
earn	93.42%	91.17%
acq	87.79%	96.76%
money-fx	63.33%	69.97%
grain	76.09%	76.26%
crude	59.65%	73.97%
trade	62.01%	65.90%
interest	58.96%	56.50%
ship	50.79%	68.93%
wheat	66.67%	77.37%
corn	59.26%	62.86%
average	67.80%	73.97%

5.2 Boosting RVM

Boosting generates many weak classifiers and combines them into a single highly accurate classification rule, assigning different importance weights to different training examples, increasing significance of examples which are hard to classify.

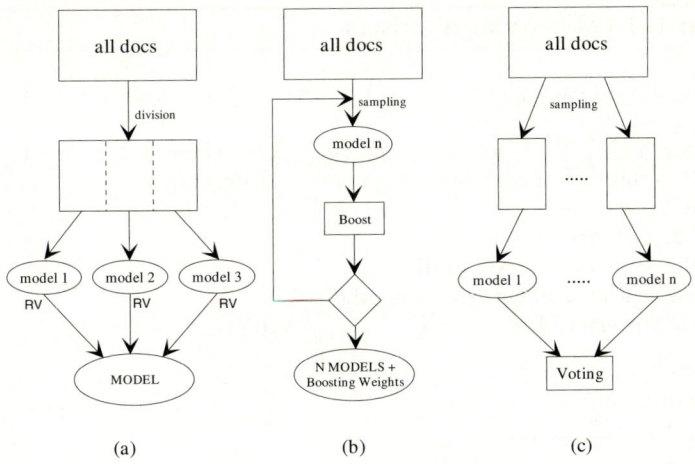

Fig. 1. (a) Incremental RVM; (b) Boosting RVM; (c) Ensemble RVM

Table 4. F1 results for boosting 20 classifiers of 2000 documents

Iterations	20	40	60
earn	97.40%	97.26%	97.35%
acq	92.05%	91.95%	91.87%
money-fx	62.84%	64.39%	64.39%
grain	83.27%	83.27%	83.27%
crude	73.87%	75.00%	75.00%
trade	66.03%	66.99%	66.99%
interest	65.14%	65.91%	65.91%
ship	70.75%	70.75%	70.75%
wheat	85.08%	84.81%	84.21%
corn	71.26%	71.26%	71.26%
average	76.77%	76.99%	77.39%

Boosting RVM uses all the training examples, sampling them into small working sets. If enough models are generated all distinctive aspects of the class are captured and represented in the final classifier. Two major innovations were performed to adapt the AdaBoost [9] algorithm to RVM boosting, as represented in figure 1b). First, instead of using the training set for training and for boosting, a separate boosting set was defined, to avoid overfitting problems that may occur by boosting the classifier with the same set. Second, as the RVM classifiers are in fact *not so weak classifiers*, as the AdaBoost assumes, the same set of classifiers was presented repeatedly to the boosting algorithm. Algorithm 1 shows the RVM boosting algorithm. The 20 base RVM classifiers were trained randomly sampling 2000 documents from the training set. For each classifier, the rest of the training set was used for boosting. Table 4 presents the results achieved.

Algorithm 1. RVM boosting algorithm

Input:
N training labeled examples: $<(\mathbf{x}_1, y_1), ..., (\mathbf{x}_N, y_N)>$, where $y_i \in \{-1, +1\}$
N_{boost} boosting labeled examples:
$<(\mathbf{x}_{N+1}, y_{N+1}), ..., (\mathbf{x}_{N+N_{boost}}, y_{N+N_{boost}})>$, where $y_i \in \{-1, +1\}$
integer NC - number of classifiers, T - number of iterations
Initialize $X_1(i) = \frac{1}{N_{boost}}$
for $s = 1, 2, ..., T$ **do**
  $c = s$; **if** $c = 0$ **then** c=NC **endif**
  Call weak learner and get weak hypothesis h_c;
  Calculate the error of h_s: $\epsilon_s = \sum_{i:h_c(x_i) \neq y_i} X_s(i)$
  Set $\alpha_s = \frac{1}{2} ln\left(\frac{1-\epsilon_s}{\epsilon_s}\right)$
  Update distribution:
  $X_{s+1} = \frac{X_s(i) \, e^{-\alpha_s y_i h_s(x_i)}}{Z_s}$
  $\quad\quad = \frac{X_s(i)}{Z_s} \times e^{-\alpha_s}$, if $h_c(x_i) = y_i$
  $\quad\quad = \frac{X_s(i)}{Z_s} \times e^{\alpha_s}$, if $h_c(x_i) \neq y_i$
  where Z_s is a normalization factor.
end for
Output: the final hypothesis:
$h_{fin}(x) = sign\left(\sum_{s=1}^{T} \alpha_s h_c(x)\right)$.

5.3 Ensemble RVM

To use all training examples available in TC, ensemble RVM shown in figure 1c), consists in the construction of several smaller training sets of 2000 documents: 40 classifiers were trained by randomly choosing the 2000 examples from the training set and a majority voting scheme was implemented. Table 5 presents the maximum, average and voting F1 results for each category.

5.4 Discussion of Results

Table 6 presents the summary of the proposed approaches results, presenting an improvement regarding the baseline RVM classifier. Figure 1 depicts the resulting models which are basically distinguished in the way chosen training chunks are combined. The incremental approach, using RV gathered from models trained with sub sets of the training set, shows the first evidence that using the entire training information can be useful, improving circa 3% the average performance. The boosting approach that ranks the classifiers according to their performance on harder-to-classify examples allows a 7% surplus and the ensemble approach presents a greater performance improvement of 9%, by using majority voting.

6 Conclusions and Future Work

We proposed incremental, boosting and ensemble methods to adapt RVM to large scale text sets, maintaining RVM probabilistic Bayesian nature and providing sparse solutions. The resulting models allow for the use of information from the entire training set, yielding significant improvement (9%) over baseline RVM performance. The outlined methods rely on a selection of small working chunks from the training set and then explore different combining strategies. From the comparison of the algorithms, majority voting approaches were found to provide the best results for Reuters-21578, suggesting further research to determine more elaborate combination schemes.

By dividing the huge data set into smaller tractable chunks, the computational load usually associated with training RVM is mitigated. Moreover, due to the independence of the RVM classifiers, it is possible to distribute the computational burden in a cluster or other distributed environment.

CISUC and Portuguese Foundation for Science and Technology through Project POSI/SRI/41234/2001 are gratefully acknowledged for financing support.

Table 5. F1 values for ensemble of 40 chunks of 2000 documents with Ensemble Voting

Category	Maximum	Average	Ensemble
earn	96.77%	96.12%	97.69%
acq	90.36%	88.84%	94.97%
money-fx	68.29%	60.54%	71.81%
grain	84.83%	79.16%	81.62%
crude	75.08%	70.13%	78.34%
trade	66.67%	62.46%	70.25%
interest	67.02%	62.10%	70.47%
ship	66.67%	60.43%	77.99%
wheat	85.71%	80.83%	81.48%
corn	70.83%	64.06%	66.67%
average	77.22%	72.46%	79.13%

Table 6. Results summary

Baseline	Incremental	Boosting	Ensemble
70.96%	73.93%	77.30%	79.13%

References

1. F. Sebastiani, "Machine Learning in Automated Text Categorization", *ACM Computing Surveys*, 34, 2002, pp 1-47.
2. V. Vapnik, "The Nature of Statistical Learning Theory", Springer, 1995.
3. M. Tipping, "Sparse Bayesian Learning and the Relevance Vector Machine", *Journal of Machine Learning Research I*, 2001, pp 211-214.
4. L. Kuncheva, "Combining Patt. Classifiers: Methods and Algorithms", Wiley, 2004.
5. Y. Yang, J. Zhang, B. Kisiel, "A Scalability Analysis of Classifiers in Text Categorization", *SIGIR '03*, ACM Press, 2003, pp 96-103.
6. T. Joachims, "Learning to Classify Text Using SVM", Kluwer, 2002.

7. F. Sebastiani, "Classification of Text, Automatic", *The Encyclopedia of Language and Linguistics*, In Keith Brown (ed.), Volume 14, 2nd Edition, Elsevier, 2006.
8. S. Eyheramendy, A. Genkin, W. Ju, D. Lewis, D. Madigan, "Sparse Bayesian Classifiers for Text Classification", *Journal of Intelligence Community R&D*, 2003.
9. R. Schapire, Y. Singer, "Boostexter: A Boosting-based System for Text Categorization", *Machine Learning*, 39(2/3), pp. 135-168, 2000.

Using Rules Discovery for the Continuous Improvement of e-Learning Courses

Enrique García, Cristóbal Romero, Sebastián Ventura, and Carlos de Castro

Escuela Politécnica Superior. Universidad de Córdoba
14071 Córdoba, Spain
{egsalcines, cromero, sventura, cdecastro}@uco.es

Abstract. This paper presents a cyclical methodology for the continuous improvement of e-learning courses using data mining techniques applied to education. For this purpose, a specific data mining tool has been developed, which discovers relevant relationships between data about how students use a course. Unlike others data mining approaches applied to education, which focus on the student, this method is aimed professors and how to help them improve the structure and contents of an e-learning course by making recommendations. We also use a rule discovery algorithm without parameters in order to be easily used by non-expert users in data mining. The results of experimental tests performed on an online course are also presented, demonstrating the usefulness of the proposed methodology and algorithm.

Keywords: association rule, e-learning, authoring tool.

1 Introduction

The huge increase in Internet access means that online education or e-learning is now a reality. Increasingly more private and public teaching institutions provide their students with web-based learning management systems (LMS). WebCT, Virtual-U and TopClass are examples of commercial LMS, although freely distributed learning management systems, such as Moodle, ATutor, ILIAS [1], and educational adaptive hypermedia courses as Interbook, ELM-ART and AHA [2] are also gaining importance. These systems accumulate a vast amount of information which is very valuable in analyzing students' behavior and to assist authors in detecting possible errors, shortcomings and improvements. However, due to the vast quantities of data these systems can generate daily, it is very difficult to manage manually, and authors demand tools which assist them in this task, preferably on a continuous basis. In order to solve this problem, some specific educational data mining tools have been developed to help educators in analyzing different aspect of the learning process: personalization of learning systems [3]; recommendation systems [4] that classify students and contents in order to recommend optimum resources and routes; and systems that detect irregularities [5], discovering irregular browsing patterns. These systems can be classified according to the field of application or focus [6]: 1) aimed at students [7], to suggest good learning experiences depending on the students' preferences, needs and level of knowledge; and 2) aimed at professors [8], so they can know more about the students that learn on the net, assess students according to their browsing patterns, classify students into groups or restructure website contents in order to customize the course. This paper looks at the use of data mining techniques applied to e-learning but from the point of view of the course professor or creator. The main aim of the proposed system is to detect possible problems in the course structure or contents, based on information about how students use the course. This is an increasingly important area of research, which enables the enormous amount of information generated when students interact with the system to be put to efficient use. It also introduces a feedback stage so that the course designed can be continuously improved.

2 Methodology for the Improvement of e-Learning Courses

We propose to use a continuous improvement of e-learning courses methodology to detect possible problems in the design and contents of e-learning courses [9]. This cyclical methodology includes a feedback or maintenance stage based on how the students use the course, and consists of the following stages:

- **Course creation.** This is the first stage, when the course is created. The professor usually creates the adaptive course, providing all the contents and structural information required. A generic or specific authoring tool [10] is normally used to make this task easier. At the end of this stage, the course should be uploaded onto a web server so that students can use it remotely.
- **Course completion.** In order to complete the course, students must use a web browser to connect to the Web Server where the course is stored. As the students are completing the course, usage data are collected and stored on the server, depending on the data model used, as well as the different log files.
- **Course improvement.** The data generated as students complete the course is used as input. The methodology applies a data mining algorithm to this data to detect any possible problems. The results of this process are displayed to the professor in the form of recommendations about how to improve the course structure or contents. Our aim, therefore, is to discover relevant information from a teaching point of view and about the effectiveness of the course in the form of rules based on the data stored about all the students who complete the course. The sub-sections below describe each of the modules that make up the Course Improvement stage, which is the nucleus of the proposed methodology (see Figure 1).

The data mining modules used in the course improvement are:

- **Data mining module without parameters.** This module aims to find association rules about a specific data set once the data have been pre-processed and converted into a single summary table that guarantees the quickest possible management of this information. The output of this module is then analyzed by the subjective analysis module. A comparative study between the main algorithms that are currently used to discover association rules can be found in [11]: APriori [12], FP-Growth [13], MagnumOpus [14], Closet [15]. The most widely used algorithm is Apriori, to which many improvements have been made. The Apriori algorithm uses two parameters, the minimum support and the minimum confidence, to find all the rules that exceed the thresholds specified by the user. However, the user must possess a certain amount of expertise in order to find the right balance between support and confidence that gives the best N rules. Weka [16] package implements an Apriori-type algorithm that solves this problem partially. This algorithm, reduces iteratively the minimum support, by the factor delta support (Δs) introduced by user, until minimum support is reached or required number of rules (NR) has been generated. Another improved version of the Apriori algorithm is the Predictive Apriori algorithm [17], which automatically resolves the problem of balance between these two parameters, maximizing the probability of making an accurate prediction for the data set. In order to achieve this, a parameter called the *exact* expected predictive accuracy (acc) is defined and calculated using the Bayesian method, which provides information about the accuracy of the rule found.

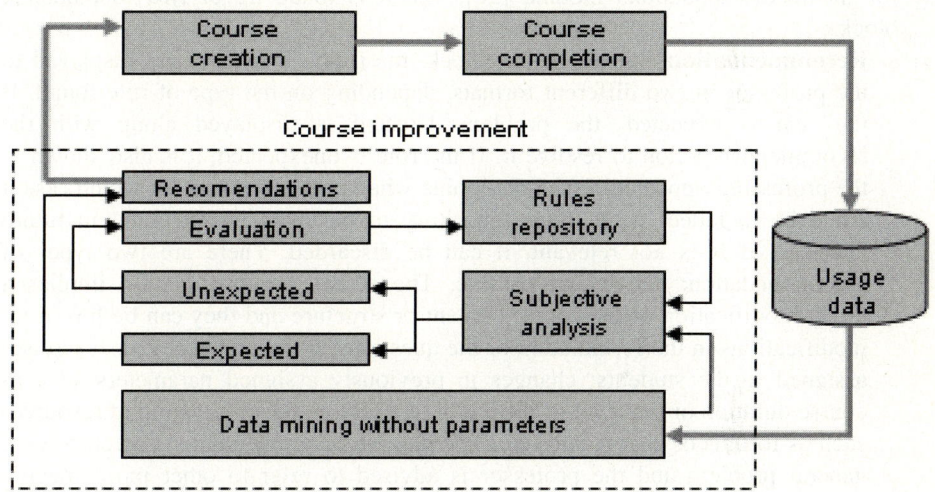

Fig. 1. Methodology for the continuous improvement of e-learning courses

- **Subjective analysis module.** The Predictive Apriori algorithm finds the best N rules without the intervention of the user. However, this method does not guarantee that the rules obtained will be relevant or useful to the professor to detect problems in the e-learning course. Therefore, they need to be assessed in order to find the most relevant ones. For this purpose, objective relevance measurements can be used such as the support and confidence parameters, as well as purely statistical measurements [18] such as Chi-Squared, correlation coefficients, profit or entropy functions, to measure the dependency inference between data variables. However, the use of subjective measurements is becoming increasingly important, measurements based on subjective factors guided by the users. In most approaches to finding relevant rules subjectively, the user has to express, in accordance with his/her previous knowledge, which rules he/she finds relevant. In [19] it is

describes a system that compares the rules discovered with the user's knowledge about the field in question. Using their own specification language, the users indicate their knowledge base about a certain subject, through relationships between fields or items in the database. Our analysis module applies this algorithm, adapting it to our data format and types of rules in order to classify them as expected rules, if they coincide with the knowledge base we have about the domain, or unexpected rules if they do not. The knowledge base is a rules repository of contents that is made up of rules discovered by other LMS users in previous experiences or courses, as well as rules proposed by experts in this area. Expected rules are used as a basis for recommendations to improve the course and unexpected rules should be analyzed by the professor to determine if they are relevant, in which case they could be included in the repository.

- **Recommendations module.** The output of the previous module becomes the input for the recommendations module [20], which is made up of two fundamental blocks:
  - **Recommendations block.** In this block, the rules discovered are displayed to the professor in two different formats, depending on the type of rule found. If the rule is expected, the problem detected is displayed along with the recommended action to resolve it. If the rule is unexpected, it is also shown to the professor, who should then determine whether it is relevant, in which case it could be included in the rules repository to be taken into account in future analyses; if it is not relevant, it can be discarded. There are two types of recommendation: active and passive. The active recommendation implies a direct modification of the course content or structure and they can be linked to: modifications in the formulation of the questions or the practical tasks/exercises assigned to the students; changes in previously assigned parameters such as course duration or the level of difficulty of a lesson; the elimination of resources such as forums or chat rooms, etc. The passive recommendation detects a more general problem and the professor is advised to refer to other more specific recommendations. An example is: IF U_FINAL_SCORE(N) = LOW THEN C_SCORE = HIGH, which detects a problem in unit n and advises the professor to check with other problems related to this unit.
  - **Rules repository block.** This is the knowledge base from which the recommendations are made. The success of the modifications made to the course depends on the content and structure of this module. The repository can initially be empty, if the professor has not yet discovered any rules, or it can contain an initial set of rules, which the user considers to be reasonably precise knowledge [19] about the domain. In addition to the rule itself, two fundamental fields are included: the problem detected by the proposed rule and a possible recommendation for its solution. Each time a rule is included in the repository, additional identification data are also included, such as author, date and the type of course where said rule was discovered. Based on teaching and our experience of e-learning courses, we have proposed an initial set of rules and their respective recommendations to be included in the repository.

3 Implementation

In order to implement the proposed architecture and to make it easier for the course professor or author to perform the data mining process, a tool called CIECoF (*Continuous improvement of e-learning courses framework*) has been developed in the Java programming language (see Figure 2). The main feature is its specialization in education, using specific attributes, filters and restrictions for course usage data; hence it is better suited for use in educational contexts than general purpose tools. To make the rules discovered more comprehensible and to reduce significantly the run time of the search algorithm, these attributes must be discretized. The transformation to discreet variables can be seen as a categorization of the attributes that takes a small set of values. The basic idea involves partitioning the values of the continuous attributes within a small list of intervals. Our discretization process used three possible nominal values: LOW, MEDIUM and HIGH and three discreet transformation methods were implemented: equal width method, equal frequency method, manual method [21], where the user sets the limits of the categories manually. In the case of discretization of times, an additional option is included to eliminate noisy values that exceed a specific threshold in order to avoid erroneous data, for example if a concept or exercise remains on the screen for a long time owing to the fact that the student left without finishing that section.

Once the application's parameters have been configured or using the default values, the professor must select specific data and attributes in order to restrict the search domain. Another panel displays the results obtained in a table with the

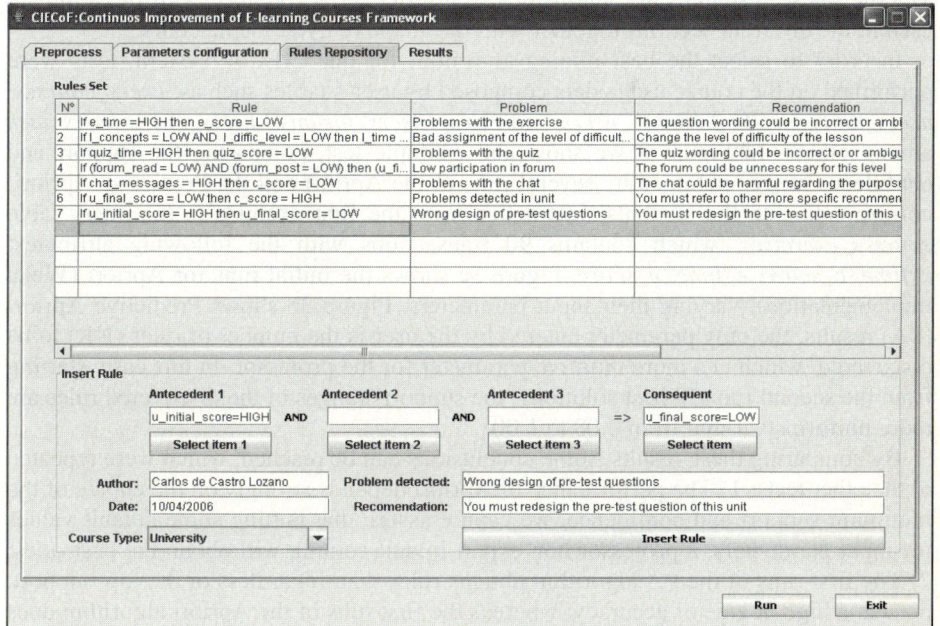

Fig. 2. CIECoF interface

following fields: rule, problem detected, recommendation and an APPLY button if the recommendation is active. By clicking on the APPLY button, the user will see the area of the course the recommendation or modification is referring to.

4 Results Obtained and Discussion

In order to test our architecture, we needed data to which the mining process could be applied. During the academic year 2004-2005, the first pilot experiment aimed at improving the technological literacy of women living in rural Spanish areas was carried out in Cordoba, called "Cordobesas Enredadas". This experiment was performed on 90 students from three villages in the province of Cordoba. For this project, 7 courses were developed based on the subjects studied for the ECDL (European Computer Driving Licence) and which were based on the Linux Operating System (distributed by Guadalinex) and the freeware office software package Open Office. The courses were developed using the authoring tool INDESAHC [22], which creates adaptive hypermedia courses that they can be executed on Moodle. The definition of the course syllabus is based on a hierarchical model of the domain, which is made up of learning units divided into lessons. Each lesson contains a series of concepts to explain or assess the contents through scenarios or web pages. An adaptation model was also included to adapt the contents to the knowledge of the student. For this purpose, the unit contents were classified in accordance with the different levels of difficulty and links can be hidden [23] accordingly. Other teaching resources such as forums, chat rooms, quiz and tasks are also introduced from the INDESAHC interface. Once the course has been generated and uploaded using Moodle, these resources are automatically inserted in accordance with the template used in the different sections together with the adaptive hypermedia course.

In order to select the best mining algorithm for our CIECoF system, tests were performed on the course usage data composed by user's tables such as: *users_courses*, *users_units*, *users_lessons*, *users_exercises*, *users_forums*, *users_quiz*, *users_task* among others. In Figure 3 we show and example test, comparing the support and confidence ranges obtained by several runs of the Apriori and the Predictive Apriori, corresponding to the students' interaction with the first exercise in the query table *courses_exercises*, which contains 90 transactions with the following attributes: *c_time, c_score, e_time, e_score*. Figure 3a shows the initial runs for Apriori (Weka implementation), varying their input parameters. Figure 3b shows Predictive Apriori (PA) results, the only parameter entered by the user is the number of rules (NR) to be discovered, which is a more intuitive parameter for the professor. In this case, starting from the second run (20 best solutions) the supports ranges of the discovered rules are more uniforms varying from 0.08 to 1.00.

By comparing these results, some conclusions can be reached, which were repeated in the other tests: 1) The performance of Apriori depends strongly on the choice of the minimum support and confidence, we cannot assure that putting some default values for input parameters, a professor non expert in data mining will obtain the best rules; 2) The first runs of the PA algorithm obtains rules that, regardless of the low support, present a high degree of accuracy; whereas the first runs of the Apriori algorithm does not obtain these rules, therefore the Apriori had to be run several times, varying its inputs parameters to obtain similar results to the PA; 3) the PA also discovers rules with low support and high confidence; these rules are interesting in education because they enable small groups that differ from the average to be detected. In fact, when professor find these type of rules, they can ask the programme to identify those students in order to give them more personalised attention. Hence, for all the abovementioned reasons, the PA was chosen as the basic algorithm of the CIECoF system data mining model.

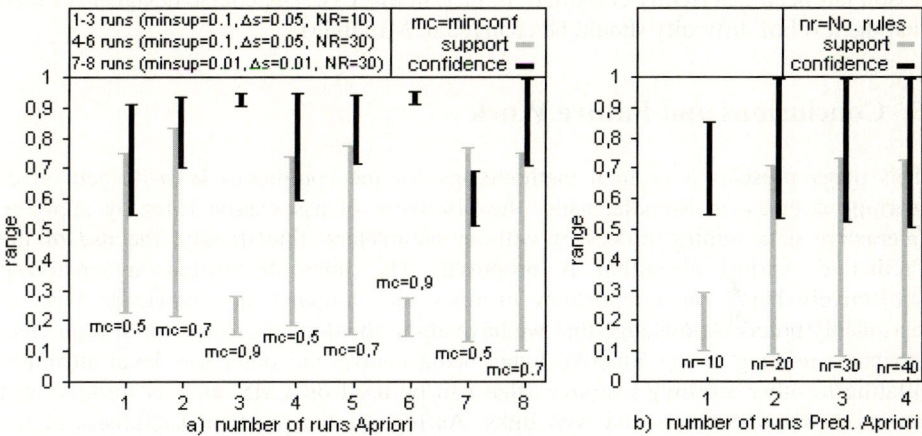

Fig. 3. Results of running the Apriori and Predictive Apriori algorithms on the query table *courses_exercises*

The results discussed below correspond to the tests carried out on course three, entitled "Word Processing". Below, two examples of discovered rules are described: one expected rule, which coincides with the knowledge base and one unexpected rule, which was classified as relevant.

The first rule is:

```
IF    (E_TIME[25]    =    HIGH)    THEN    (E_SCORE[25]    =    LOW),
ACCURACY=0.92.
```

In this case, the system showed the professor the following recommendation: You must analyze the wording of exercise 25, which corresponds to the subject "Use of the application", lesson "First steps using the word processor" and the concept "Saving and renaming documents", (an INDESAHC interactive video scenario where the student used the mouse to simulate an activity). When the professor clicked in the APPLY button the system showed this question wording. In this particular case, the question wording was found to be ambiguous and could be interpreted in several ways and so was corrected. Other rules with a similar format were also found but they were related to test type questions.

The other rule is:

```
IF   (L_CONCEPTS[13]    =    LOW   AND   L_DIFFIC_LEVEL[13]   =   LOW
THEN  (L_TIME  [13]   =   HIGH),
ACCURACY=0.85.
```

This rule was unexpected and the message showed to the professor was: if the number of concepts included in the lesson is LOW and the level of difficulty assigned to that lesson is LOW, then the time taken to complete the lesson is HIGH. By analyzing this rule, the following interpretation could be reached: since no score-related attributes have been used in relation to the level of the lesson, the fact that students have spent a long time completing a lesson that supposedly is not very difficult and contains few concepts could indicate that the level of difficulty of the lesson has been incorrectly classified. In fact, in this case, the course designer decided that the level of difficulty should be changed to MEDIUM.

5 Conclusions and Future Work

This paper presents a cyclical methodology for the continuous improvement of e-learning courses on Moodle, using the discovery of association rules by applying interactive data mining processes without parameters. Specifically, the use of the Predictive Apriori algorithm is proposed. The rules discovered are analyzed subjectively based on a repository of rules that contains the knowledge base or reasonably precise knowledge that we have about the domain from a set of high level attributes relating to the adaptive hypermedia course and other low level attributes relating to other teaching resources that can be used on LMS such as forums, chat rooms, tasks, documents and web links. As regards the practical usefulness of the rules discovered for making decisions, experimental tests were performed on a Moodle course created using the authoring tool INDESAHC and specific examples of the rules discovered were described along with the problem that they have helped to resolve. In order to facilitate this knowledge discovery process, the CIECoF tool has been developed. This tool pre-processes data about the use of web courses, enables a set of restrictions to be defined about the type of information to be discovered, and also applies data mining algorithms to the extraction of rules and how they are displayed. Owing to the usefulness of this tool to detect and correct problems in e-learning courses, and in order to ensure that this tool can be applied to all kinds of fields, we are currently working on the definition of an ontology based on standard SCORM [24] metadata with the aim of providing a better understanding of the knowledge to be discovered and so that this knowledge can be exchanged and improved on, using a common language.

Acknowledgments. This "Cordobesas Enredadas" project was financed by the Provincial Government, reference ECDL/DIPUCO/MEM/04-0001bis.

References

1. Itmazi, J.A.S. Sistema Flexible de gestión del elearning para soportar el aprendizaje en las universidades tradicionales y abiertas. PhD Thesis. University of Granada, Spain. (2005)
2. Brusilovsky, P., Adaptative Educational Systems on the World-Wide-Web: A Review. Int. Conf. on Intelligent Tutoring Systems. San Antonio. (1998)
3. Srivastava, J.; Mobasher, B.; Cooley, R. Automatic Personalization Based on Web Usage Mining. Communications of the Association of Computing Machinery. (2000) 142-151

4. Li, J.; Zaiane, O.R. Combining Usage, Content and Structure Data to Improve Web Site Recommendation. Int. Conf. on Electronic Commerce and Web Technologies. Spain. (2004)
5. Barnett, V.; Lewis, T.; Outliers in Statistical Data. John Wiley & Sons. (1994)
6. Romero, C, Ventura, S., Hervás, C. Estado actual de la aplicación de la minería de datos a los sistemas de enseñanza basada en web. III Taller de Minería de Datos y Aprendizaje, TAMID. Granada. (2005) 49-56.
7. Zaïane, O.Z. Web Usage Mining for a Better Web-Based Learning Environment. Conference on Advanced Technology for Education. pp 60-64. Alberta. (2001)
8. Romero, C.; Ventura, S.; de Bra, P. Knowledge Discovery with Genetic Programming for Providing Feedback to Courseware Author. User Modeling and User-Adapted Interaction. Vol. 14. No. 5. (2005) 425-464
9. Romero, C., Ventura, S., Castro, C., Hall W. and Hong M.. Using Genetic Algorithms for Data Mining in Web-based Educational Hypermedia Systems. Adaptive Hypermedia. Workshop on Adaptive Systems for Web-based Education. Málaga. (2002) 137-142
10. Developing adaptive educational systems: From Design Models to Authoring tools. Authoring Tools for Advanced Technology learning environments. Netherlands: Kluwer Academic Publishers. (2003) 377-409.
11. Zheng Z., Kohavi R., Mason L. Real world performance of association rules. In Proceedings of the Sixth ACM-SIGKDD. (2001)
12. Agrawal, R., Srikant, R. Fast algorithms for mining association rules. Proceedings of 20th VLDB CVonf. Santiago de Chile. (1996)
13. Han, J., Pei, J., and Yin, Y. Mining frequent patterns without candidate generation. In Proceedings of ACM-SIGMOD International Conference on Management of Data. 1999.
14. Webb, G.I. OPUS: An efficient admissible algorithm for unordered search. Journal of Artificial Intelligence Research. (1995) 431-465
15. Pei, J., Han, J., and Mao, R. CLOSET: An efficient algorithm for mining frequent closed itemsets. In Proceedings of ACM_SIGMOD International DMKD'00, Dallas, TX. (2000)
16. The University of Waikato. Weka:Waikato Environment for Knowledge Analysis. Available at: http://www.cs.waikato.ac.nz/ml/weka/ in May of the 2006.
17. Tobias S. Finding Association Rules That Trade Support Optimally against Confidence. Lecture Notes in Computer Science, Vol. 2168. (2001) 424+
18. P. Tan, V. Kumar. Interesting Measures for Association Patterns: A Perspectiva. Technical Report TR00-036. Department of Computer Science. University of Minnnesota. (2000)
19. Liu B., Wynne H., Shu C. Yiming M. Analyzing the Subjective Interestingness of Association Rules. IEEE Inteligent System. (2000)
20. T. Tang, G. McCalla,. Smart Recommendation for an Evolving E-Learning System: Architecture and Experiment. International Journal on E-Learning 4(1). (2005) 105-129
21. H. Liu, F. Hussain, C.L. Tan, and M. Dash. Discretization: An enabling technique. Journal of Data Mining and Knowledge Discovery. (2002) 393-423
22. De Castro, C., García, E., Romero, C., Ventura, S. Herramienta autor INDESAHC para la creación de cursos hipermedia adaptativos. Revista latinoamericana de tecnología educativa. Vol. 3, 1. (2004)
23. De Bra, P., Calvi, L.. AHA! An Open Adaptive Hypermedia Architecture. The New Review of Hypermedia and Multimedia, 4. Taylor Graham Publishers. (1998) 115-139
24. Advanced Distributed Learning. Shareable content object reference model (SCORM): The SCORM overview. Available: http://www.adlnet.org in May of the 2006.

Generating Adaptive Presentations of Hydrologic Behavior

Martin Molina and Victor Flores

Department of Artificial Intelligence, Universidad Politécnica de Madrid,
Campus de Montegancedo S/N 28660 Boadilla del Monte, Madrid, Spain
{mmolina, vflores}@fi.upm.es

Abstract. This paper describes a knowledge-based approach for summarizing and presenting the behavior of hydrologic networks. This approach has been designed for visualizing data from sensors and simulations in the context of emergencies caused by floods. It follows a solution for event summarization that exploits physical properties of the dynamic system to automatically generate summaries of relevant data. The summarized information is presented using different modes such as text, 2D graphics and 3D animations on virtual terrains. The presentation is automatically generated using a hierarchical planner with abstract presentation fragments corresponding to discourse patterns, taking into account the characteristics of the user who receives the information and constraints imposed by the communication devices (mobile phone, computer, fax, etc.). An application following this approach has been developed for a national hydrologic information infrastructure of Spain.

1 Introduction

One of the main tasks of water control centers is to help to react in the presence emergency situations as a consequence of floods. In this context, the state of the hydrological basin is measured with the help of sensors that send periodically to the control center quantitative values about rainfall, water levels and flows. When the dimension and complexity of the information is high, a large number of values need to be summarized and adequately presented. Automatic tools can help in this task in order to minimize the time response of human operators in the presence of emergencies. In general, this is a complex task that normally requires specific knowledge about the dynamic system. In fact, summarization and presentation modeling have received important attention in the research community of Artificial Intelligence where certain general solutions have been proposed [1][2].

In this paper we describe an innovative knowledge-based approach to perform automatically this task in the context of the surveillance of hydrologic networks. The main contribution of our approach is that we take the advantage of the system representation to support specific strategies for summarizing and presentation. As a result, we propose an efficient solution to generate automatically adaptive multimodal reports according to prefixed management goals. In the following, the paper describes a general view of the method as a knowledge-based architecture. It is illustrated with the application in the field of hydrology. At the end of the paper we make a comparative discussion with similar approaches.

2 A General View of the Method

The goal of the method is to present relevant information about the behavior of the dynamic system at an adequate level of abstraction close to the decision processes. This information is presented as concise as possible and it is accompanied with additional information to facilitate a complete understanding. The information is presented in different modes (text, graphics, animations, etc.) using different devices for reception (computer, mobile phone, fax, etc.).

The method has been designed following a knowledge-based approach (according to recent knowledge engineering methodologies [3]) with a set of general inference steps that use domain specific knowledge. The method performs two main tasks: (1) *summarize* the most important information (i.e., *what* to inform) and (2) generate a *presentation plan* according to the type of end-user and the communication media (*how* to present the information).

2.1 Summarization

Our method for summarization is based on an explicit representation of the dynamic system (see [4] for more details). The method was designed to simulate professional human operators in control centers with partial and approximated knowledge about the dynamic system. This is formulated following an approach based on representations and ontologies of qualitative physics [5] [6] [7].

The structure of the dynamic system is represented with hierarchies of components with quantities for physical magnitudes and qualitative states. The model includes a simplified view of the system behavior represented with causal relations between quantities with labels such as temporal references about approximated delay and type of influence. Historical values also help to represent information about behavior (e.g., average values, maximum historical values, etc.). This representation includes a *qualitative interpretation model* to determine the qualitative state of every single component from physical quantities and an *aggregation model* to determine the state of complex components based on the state of simpler components (both models are represented using rules).

The representation also includes what we call the *salience model* to determine when certain event is relevant and should be reported to the operator. In general, we consider a relevant event as an event that (1) changes with respect to the immediate past and (2) produces a change in the *distance* between the state of the dynamic system and the desired state established by the management goals. This distance is a way to quantify the degree of relevance of events. Based on our assumption for system modeling (with approximated knowledge for system behavior) the representation of relevance establishes preferences between states based on relations that summarize sets of behaviors [4].

The strategy of inference receives as input sensor data and uses this representation to produce what we call a *summarization tree*. This tree is a particular representation that summarizes the most relevant information to be reported to the user. To construct this tree, the inference procedure performs the following steps. For every single component, its qualitative state is computed using as input the interpretation model and the quantitative measures of sensors. Then, these states are ranked according to the heuristics of the salience model. Causes and effects are removed following the order in this set. Finally, the states of similar components are condensed by *aggregation* (states of components with the same type are aggregated by the state of a more global component) and *abstraction* (two states of components of different type are abstracted by the most relevant state). This produces the *summarization tree* (see figure 2) where the root is the most representative event and the branches include aggregated and abstracted states. The salience model plays the role of control knowledge in the inference procedure because it directs the search for qualitative states of complex components using first the most relevant states of simpler components. This strategy provides an adequate condensation of information by aggregation based on relevance.

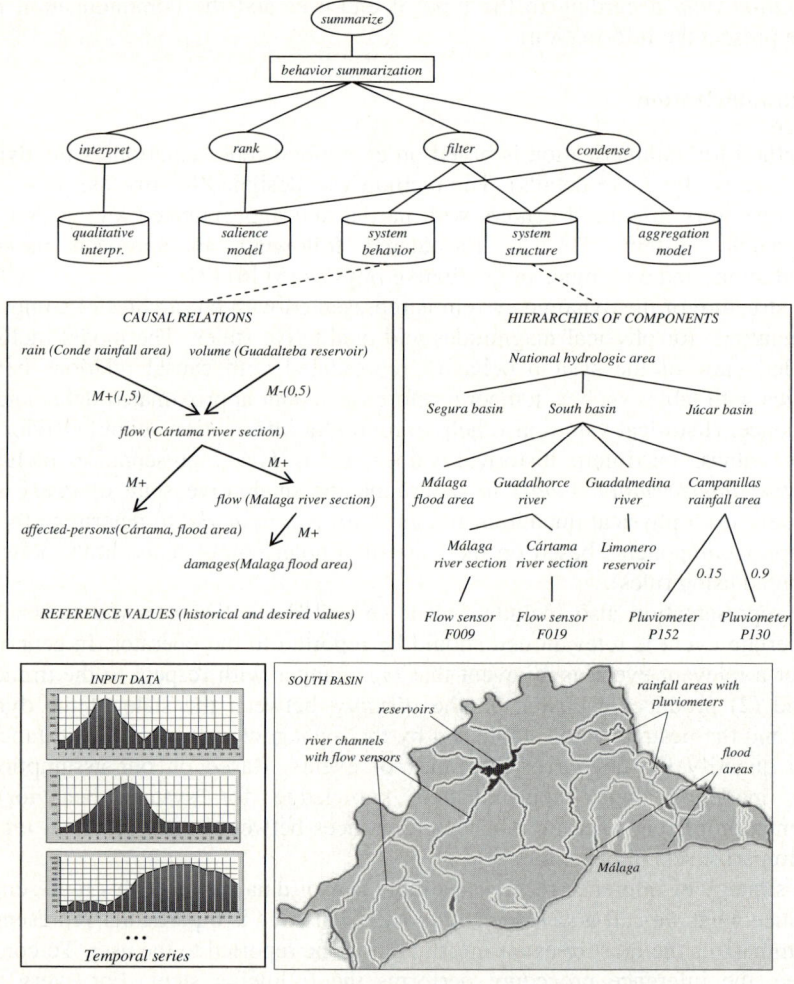

Fig. 1. A global view of the method for summarization in the hydrologic domain

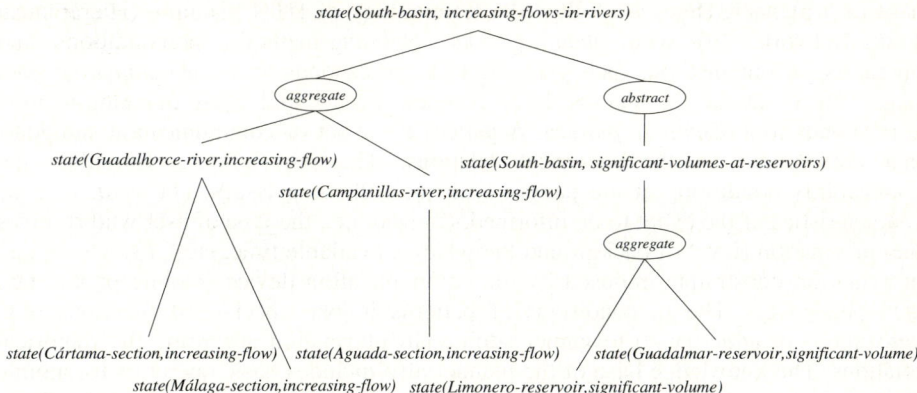

Fig. 2. Example of summarization tree

2.2 Presentation Planning

Once the relevant information to be reported to the operator is determined (*what* to inform) it is necessary to generate an adequate presentation plan (*how* to present the information). For this purpose, the method gathers related information that helps to understand relevant events and determines the type and detail of the presentation taking into account the end-user and the communication devices (mobile telephone, fax, computer screen with 3D animations, etc.).

In order to bring together the information related to relevant events, the method develops discourse strategies that connect information modules with rhetorical relations (as used in Rhetorical Structure Theory [8]). For this purpose, we have formulated a set of model-based gathering strategies for rhetorical relations applicable in our context of dynamic system surveillance (see table 1) following the system representation and our notion of relevance.

To articulate rhetorical relations for a particular discourse the method uses *discourse patterns*. Each pattern is a template that expresses how to develop a part of the discourse. The total set of discourse patterns is implemented as the knowledge

Table 1. Examples of gathering strategies for rhetorical relations

Rhetorical relation	Gathering strategy
causes	The method gathers related causes. A cause is related if its state has changed in the last Δt, where Δt is the delay between each cause and the event.
effects	The method gathers related effects. An effect is related if its state is not assumed by default. Default values are either goal values or values already reported to the user.
contrast	The method gathers the goal value of an event according to the management strategy. This goal value is informed in contrasts to the current value of the event.
evidence	The method gives evidence of a fact with the measured values of the corresponding sensor.
details	Details of the state of an aggregated component correspond to the state of the simpler component with greater distance to the goal value and a list of the rest of components with the same state.

base of a planner. Here, we follow the terminology of HTN planning (Hierarchical Task Network) [9] with planning-tasks, planning-methods, preconditions and operators. In our method, each planning-task corresponds to a *communication goal* (e.g., inform about the details of a relevant event) and each planning-method corresponds to a *discourse pattern*. A pattern has a set of communication sub-goals that corresponds to the rhetorical relations. The preconditions formulate the applicability conditions of the pattern with the following issues: (1) *what*, i.e., the characteristics of the event to be informed, (2) *who*, i.e., the type of user who receives the information (level of background knowledge, available time, etc.), (3) *where*, i.e., presentation constraints imposed by the communication device (mobile phone, fax, web page, etc.). The preconditions of patterns invoke specialized functions (e.g, *causes(x,y)* or *effects(x,y)*) to gather additional information according the rhetorical relations. The knowledge base of the planner also includes basic operators for atomic communication goals, i.e., for goals that are not divided into other sub-goals. These operators are implemented as specialized presentation primitives in the form of textual descriptions and parameterized functions that compose text, illustrate with 2D graphics and construct 3D animations.

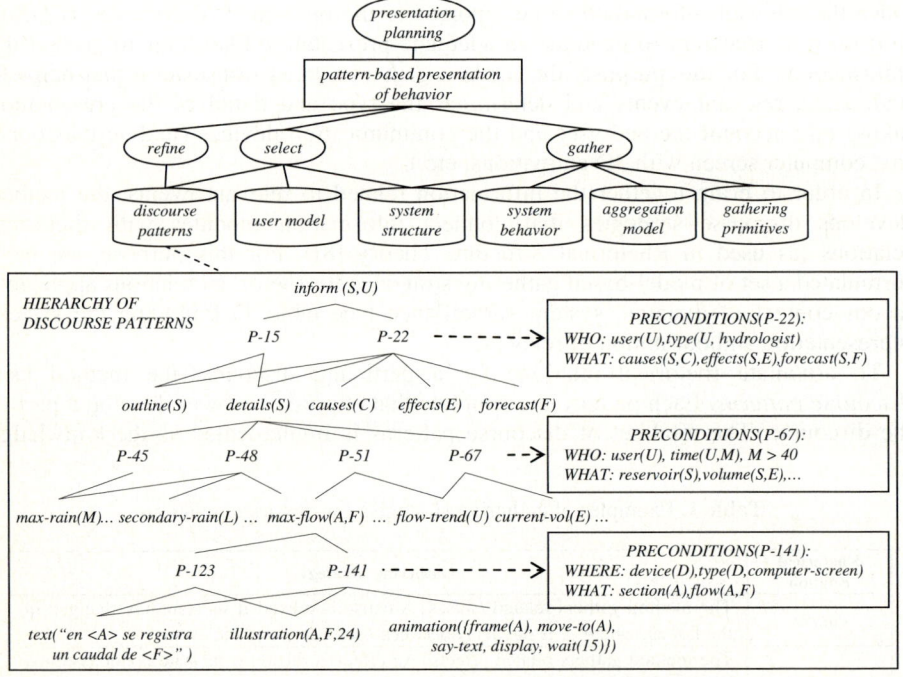

Fig. 3. Summary of the method for presentation planning

Figure 3 shows a summary of the method for presentation planning. To construct the complete plan the method follows a recursive planning procedure that, in every step performs the following subtasks: (1) *select* a discourse pattern that satisfies the preconditions, (2) *gather* additional information according to the preconditions, and

(3) *refine* the communication goal with the sub-goals. The second subtask uses the system model (structure and behavior) together with the aggregation model to construct additional summarization trees for the presentation.

3 Discussion

The previous method has been developed to work with real time data of SAIH systems (SAIH: Spanish acronym for Automatic Information System in Hydrology) developed by a National Programme of Spain. It was conceived to help to react in the presence emergency situations as a consequence of river floods, as a component of a more complex intelligent system for emergency management [10]. In this context, information is received periodically in a control center about rainfall at certain locations, water levels and flow discharge of reservoirs and flows in certain river channels. Figure 4 shows an example of the presentation that can be generated with the help of the method presented in this paper.

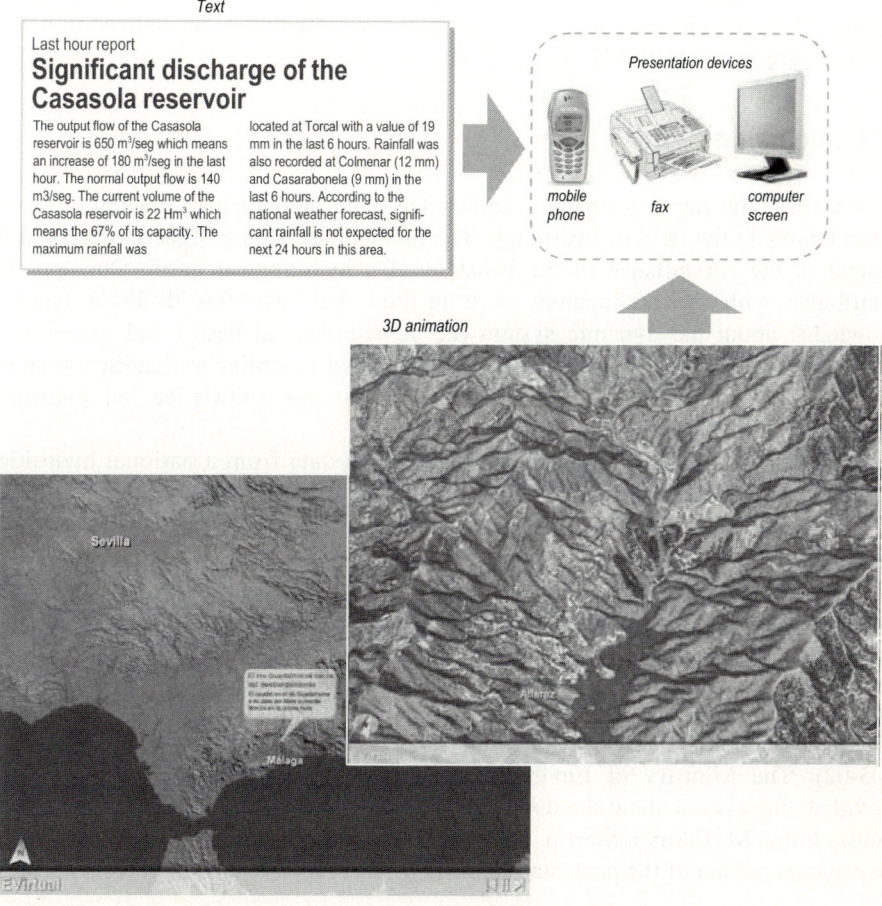

Fig. 4. Examples of information reported in the field of hydrology

Our method for presentation can be compared to techniques of artificial intelligence such as explanation generators and presentation modeling. For example, our method generates explanations that help to understand the relevant events. Compared to methods for diagnosis [11] our approach does not look for hidden causes for a set of given symptoms. Instead, it complements the relevant information by selecting data in the measured information using causal knowledge.

Compared to the field of presentation models we integrate and extend some general ideas about multimodal presentation planning of the WIP project [2] [12] for the case of dynamic systems (for example, our method defines gathering primitives specialized in the system model). For the particular case of text composition we follow a template-based approach [13]. Concerning text composition, our solution also presents certain similarities for the case of ILEX [14] although with different model representation, notion of relevance and abstraction method.

Related to our method, other solutions for presentation generation in the field of meteorology have been proposed. For example, the system of Kerpedjiev [15] follows a multimodal approach based on WIP [12] but it is restricted to documents and 2D graphics. In this field there are other examples for presentation specialized in natural language generation [16][17].

4 Conclusions

In summary, the paper presents a knowledge-based approach to generate adaptive presentations in the field of hydrology. The method has been designed to work in the context of the surveillance of the behavior of a hydrological basin. Our approach contributes with the architecture of a method that identifies different types of knowledge about the dynamic system (i.e. a hydrological basin) and model-based strategies for presentation planning that are organized according to rhetorical relations for discourse generation. The approach is, up to our knowledge, an innovative application in the hydrologic domain.

The method has been designed to operate with data from a national hydrologic information infrastructure (the SAIH systems in Spain). A preliminary validation of the method in this context with partial models has been carried out with satisfactory results. Currently, we are working on a more extensive evaluation with complete models. The presentation method was developed for the domain of hydrology, but we are also working on a general approach to be used in other domains.

Acknowledgements. This research work has been supported partially by the Ministry of Education and Science of Spain within the E-VIRTUAL project (REN2003-09021-C03-02). The Ministry of Environment of Spain (*Dirección General del Agua*) provided information about the domain in hydrology. The authors would like to thank Sandra Lima, M. Carmen Martín, Nuria Andrés and Enrique Parodi for their work on the implementation of the presentation method.

References

1. Wahlster W.: "User and discourse models for multimodal communication". In Sullivan, J. W., Tyler, S. W. & Sherman, W. editors, Intelligent User Interfaces. New York: ACM Press, S. 45-67. 1991.
2. Maybury M. T.: "Generating Summaries from Event Data". Information Processing and Management: an International Journal. Volume 31, Issue 5 (special issue: Summarizing Text) Pages: 735 – 751.September 1995.
3. Schreiber G., Akkermans H., Anjewierden A., De Hoog R., Shadbolt N., Van de Velde W., Wielinga B.: "Knowledge engineering and management. The CommonKADS methodology" MIT Press, 2000.
4. Molina M., Flores V.: "A knowledge-based approach for automatic generation of summaries of behavior". Proc. 12th International Conference on Artificial Intelligence: Methodology, Systems, Applications. AIMSA 06. Lecture Notes of Artificial Intelligence. Springer. Varna, Bulgaria, 2006.
5. Iwasaki Y. and Low C.: "Model Generation and Simulation of Device Behavior with Continuous and Discrete Changes". Intelligent Systems Engineering, Vol. 1 No.2. 1993.
6. Gruber T. R. and Olsen G. R.: "An Ontology for Engineering Mathematics". In Jon Doyle, Piero Torasso, & Erik Sandewall, Eds., Fourth International Conference on Principles of Knowledge Representation and Reasoning, Gustav Stresemann Institut, Bonn, Germany, Morgan Kaufmann, 1994.
7. Borst P., Akkermans J. M., Pos A., and Top. J. L.: "The PhysSys ontology for physical systems". In R. Bredeweg, editor, Working Papers Ninth International Workshop on Qualitative Reaso ning QR'95. Amsterdam, NL, May 16-19. 1995.
8. Mann W.C., Thompson S.A.: "Rhetorical Structure Theory: Toward a Functional Theory of Text Organization". Text journal, Vol. 8, N. 3, 243-281. 1988.
9. Ghallab M., Nau D., Traverso P.: "Automated Planning: Theory and Practice". Morgan Kaufmann, 2004.
10. Molina, M.: "Building a Decision Support System with a Knowledge Modeling Tool". Journal of Decision Systems. Special issue "Design, Building and Evaluation of Intelligent Decision-making Support Systems". Lavoisier, France, 2006.
11. Benjamins R.: "Problem-solving methods for diagnosis". PhD thesis, University of Amsterdam, Amsterdam, The Netherlands. 1993.
12. Wahlster W., André E., Graf W., Rist, T.: "Designing illustrated texts: how language production is influenced by graphics generation", Proceedings of the fifth conference on European chapter of the Association for Computational Linguistics, p.8-14, April 09-11, 1991, Berlin, Germany.
13. Reiter E.: "NLG vs. Templates". In Fifth European Workshop on Natural Language Generation". Leiden, 1995.
14. O'Donnell M.: "Intermixing Multiple Discourse Strategies for Automatic Text Composition". Revista Canaria de Estudios Ingleses (RCEI), No. 40 (April): Special Issue on Intercultural and Textual Approaches to Systemic-Functional Linguistics, 2000.
15. Kerpedjiev S. M.: "Automatic generation of multimodal weather reports from datasets". Proceedings of the third Conference on Applied Natural Language Processing. Trento, Italy. 48 – 55.1992.
16. Kittredge R., Polguere A., Goldberg E.: "Synthesizing weather forecasts from formatted data". COLING-86, Proceedings, Bonn, August 1986.
17. Bourbeau L., Carcagno D., Goldberg E., Kittredge R., Polguere A.: "Synthesizing Weather Forecasts in an Operational Environment". In Proc. 13th International Conference COLING, vol. 3, 318-320, Helsinki, August 1990.

A New Measure for Query Disambiguation Using Term Co-occurrences

Hiromi Wakaki[1], Tomonari Masada[2], Atsuhiro Takasu[2], and Jun Adachi[2]

[1] The University of Tokyo, Graduate School of Information Science and Technology,
Hongo 7-3-1, Bunkyo-ku, Tokyo, Japan 113-0033
hiromi@nii.ac.jp
[2] The National Institute of Informatics,
Hitotsubashi 2-1-2, Chiyoda-ku, Tokyo, Japan 101-8430
{masada, takasu, adachi}@nii.ac.jp

Abstract. This paper explores techniques that discover terms to replace given query terms from a selected subset of documents. The Internet allows access to large numbers of documents archived in digital format. However, no user can be an expert in every field, and they trouble finding the documents that suit their purposes experts when they cannot formulate queries that narrow the search to the context they have in mind. Accordingly, we propose a method for extracting terms from searched documents to replace user-provided query terms. Our results show that our method is successful in discovering terms that can be used to narrow the search.

1 Introduction

The Internet allows us to access large numbers of documents archived in digital format. However, when a search presents many documents, we usually look at only a few top-ranked documents. Further, the search results often contain a large number of unrelated documents. Therefore, we need results to be more compact and relevant to our intentions. This is why we should use query terms that indicate our needs exactly when we search in the Internet. However, queries consisting of two or three terms are often not reliable enough to gather appropriate Web pages, because such queries are intrinsically ambiguous. Moreover, we cannot be experts in every field, so we often cannot formulate queries that narrow the search to the context we have in mind. In many cases, we hit upon only a few terms to refine the initial query, and end up with unsatisfactory search results even after refining the query. Therefore, the research challenge of query processing has been to find more appropriate query terms and to provide search results that can meet the needs of various users[1]. To meet this challenge, we propose a method for extracting terms from a given set of documents to replace or add to the original query terms. Our results show that our method is successful in discovering terms that can be used to narrow the search.

Our method analyzes the co-occurrence of terms in the top-ranked documents of the initial search result and extracts terms having a special feature called

Tangibility. When a term refers to a specific concept or denotes a particular thing, we say the term has Tangibility. A proper noun is a typical example of a term that has Tangibility. Our method is based on the following observation: we can easily disambiguate a short query by adding just one term that has Tangibility. Our method works regardless of the retrieval method we used. Moreover, the method can extract terms to expand queries without using additional data such as word networks or structural directories of concepts. Our approach is unique because we propose a new term-weighting formula that can extract terms that imply a distinct topic. Our experiments have shown that the terms extracted by our method are qualitatively different from those extracted by other existing measures.

The rest of the paper is organized as follows: Section 2 introduces our new concept, Tangibility; Section 3 reports the details and results of our experiments; Section 4 discusses prior work; and Section 5 concludes with a summary of the paper and an indication of future work.

2 Tangibility

2.1 Hypothesis of Tangibility

To cope with ambiguities in queries, we propose a new method for selecting terms. The aim of our method is to find more specific terms than the query terms the user has given; these specific terms can match more easily with distinct topics and resolve query ambiguity. Here we are introducing a new concept called *Tangibility*. We say that a term has Tangibility when it keeps a fairly close relationship with the given query and, at the same time, is strongly related to a distinct topic, regardless of whether or not the topic is principal in the retrieved document set. We measure the Tangibility of a term t by focusing on the variety of terms frequently co-occurring with t. To obtain numerical estimates of Tangibility, we formulate our hypothesis as follows:

> *A term co-occurring frequently with a limited number of terms in a retrieved document set can establish a distinct topic in the document set.*

We call this the *hypothesis of Tangibility*. We say two terms *co-occur* when they appear in the same document. Each term is counted only once, even if it appears many times within the document. In the following subsection, we propose two numerical estimates for term Tangibility: TNG1 and TNG2.

2.2 TNG1: First Formulation of Tangibility

Suppose we have a document corpus U. Let $S \subset U$ be the set of the top l ranked documents retrieved with a query. $U(t_i)$ (resp. $S(t_i)$) denotes the set of documents from U (resp. S), in which the term t_i appears. $V(d)$ denotes the number of terms in document d. Our first numerical estimate of Tangibility, denoted by TNG1, is based on the hypothesis described in Section 2.1. To obtain

TNG1, we introduce the average number of terms that appear in documents that include term t_i, and denote it by $F(t_i)$. More formally, $F(t_i)$ is defined as follows:

$$F(t_i) = \frac{\sum_{d \in S(t_i)}(V(d)-1)}{|S(t_i)|}. \tag{1}$$

$F(t_i)$ shows how many terms appear with t_i in S. Therefore, we can regard a term with small $F(t_i)$ as a term representing a distinct topic. However, a term having small $|S(t_i)|$ intrinsically has small $F(t_i)$. We therefore introduce an additional component into our formula so that terms of small $|S(t_i)|$ should not always be regarded as having Tangibility. Consequently, we obtain the following formula as TNG1, which expresses the Tangibility of a term t_i:

$$TNG1(t_i) = \frac{|S(t_i)|^2}{|U(t_i)|} \cdot \frac{1}{F(t_i)}, \tag{2}$$

where the first half is obtained by multiplying $|S(t_i)|$ by $|S(t_i)|/|U(t_i)|$. $|S(t_i)|$ is simply the document frequency of t_i in S and indicates how strongly t_i is *unconditionally* related to S. In contrast, $|S(t_i)|/|U(t_i)|$ indicates how strongly t_i is related to S *in comparison with U*.

2.3 TNG2: Second Formulation of Tangibility

To provide the second formulation TNG2, we rewrite Equation (1) as follows:

$$F(t_i) = \sum_{t_j \neq t_i} \frac{|S(t_i \wedge t_j)|}{|S(t_i)|}, \tag{3}$$

where $|S(t_i \wedge t_j)|$ is defined to $|S(t_i) \cap S(t_j)|$. Since we can interpret $|S(t_i \wedge t_j)|/|S(t_i)|$ as the probability of the occurrence of t_j among the documents including t_i, we denote it by $P(t_j|t_i)$. According to TNG1, t_i has Tangibility when $\sum_{t_j \neq t_i} P(t_j|t_i)$ is small. In contrast, we devise the second formulation, TNG2, by requiring $P(t_j|t_i)$ to be *smaller than* $P(t_j)$ for a large number of t_js ($j \neq i$). TNG1 and TNG2 share the same intuition. However, we introduce an elaboration into TNG2, i.e., the comparison of $P(t_j|t_i)$ with $P(t_j)$. For the discrepancy evaluation of the two probability distributions, Kullback–Leibler Divergence (KLD) is often used. In our case, $P(t_j|t_i)$ and $P(t_j)$ are to be compared. Moreover, the event complementary to the occurrence of t_j is the non-occurrence of t_j, denoted by $\neg t_j$. Therefore, the KLD for our evaluation can be written as:

$$KL(t_j; t_i) = P(t_j|t_i) \log \frac{P(t_j|t_i)}{P(t_j)} + P(\neg t_j|t_i) \log \frac{P(\neg t_j|t_i)}{P(\neg t_j)}.$$

However, $\sum_{t_j \neq t_i} KL(t_j; t_i)$ cannot evaluate the Tangibility of t_i, because this sum is large when any of the following two conditions holds for many t_js:

(a) $P(t_j|t_i) \log \dfrac{P(t_j|t_i)}{P(t_j)} < 0 \ \left(\text{and thus } P(\neg t_j|t_i) \log \dfrac{P(\neg t_j|t_i)}{P(\neg t_j)} > 0 \text{ also holds}\right)$

(b) $P(t_j|t_i) \log \dfrac{P(t_j|t_i)}{P(t_j)} > 0$ $\left(\text{and thus } P(\neg t_j|t_i) \log \dfrac{P(\neg t_j|t_i)}{P(\neg t_j)} < 0 \text{ also holds}\right)$

Only (a) is important for the Tangibility of t_i. Therefore, we propose a new measure, called Signed Kullback–Leibler (SKL), as follows:

$$SKL(t_j; t_i) = -P(t_j|t_i) \log \frac{P(t_j|t_i)}{P(t_j)} + P(\neg t_j|t_i) \log \frac{P(\neg t_j|t_i)}{P(\neg t_j)}. \quad (4)$$

SKL is derived from the KLD by changing the sign of the first term. Consequently, we propose the following as the second formula for Tangibility:

$$TNG2(t_i) = \frac{|S(t_i)|^2}{|U(t_i)|} \cdot \sum_{t_j \neq t_i} SKL(t_j; t_i).$$

3 Experiment

3.1 Metrics for Term Selection

Before describing our experiment in detail, we present the various term-weighting schemes that we tested. Term weight $W(t_i)$ for term t_i is computed by multiplying two weights: $|S(t_i)|^2/|U(t_i)|$ and $CW(t_i)^\sigma$. The former weight was introduced in Section 2.2. As for $CW(t_i)^\sigma$, we obtain $CW(t_i)$ by summing $cw(t_i, t_j)$ for all t_js ($j \neq i$), i.e., $CW(t_i) = \sum_{t_j \neq t_i} cw(t_i, t_j)$, where each summand $cw(t_i, t_j)$ is computed based on the co-occurrence of t_i and t_j; σ takes a value of 1 or -1. When we want an increase (resp. decrease) in $CW(t_i)$ to contribute to an increase of $W(t_i)$, σ is set to 1 (resp. -1).

Many recent studies have proposed various term-weighting methods for term extraction. Some of them use term co-occurrence frequencies as in our formulations of Tangibility. We compared eight term-weighting methods[13] (see Table 1). *UnitWeight* is so called because $CW(t_i) = 1$ for any t_i. This method ignores the effect of term co-occurrence. That is, *UnitWeight* is intended to reveal how the difference of $CW(t_i)$ works in each of the other term-weighting methods. Co-occurrence Frequency (CF) is prepared for ranking terms based on the intuition contrary to that of TNG1. Mutual Information (MI) [14], KLD, and χ^2 measure the discrepancy between $P(t_j|t_i)$ and $P(t_j)$. Thus, they are all based on nearly the same intuition about term importance. With these measures, however, we cannot distinguish the two cases (a) and (b) shown in Section 2.3. Since these methods and our two methods use term co-occurrence frequencies, we next discuss the computational cost to obtain co-occurrence frequencies for all pairs of terms. Let m be the number of terms that appear in S. In the worst case, the computational cost is proportional to m^2. However, for most t_i, $|\{t_j : |S(t_i \wedge t_j)| > 0\}| \ll m$ holds. Therefore, the actual computational cost can be reduced by choosing an appropriate data structure. Robertson's selection value (RSV) [10] is a term weight used for query expansion in information retrieval[11]; it does not use co-occurrence information. The exact formulation is as follows:

$$RSV = (\frac{|S(t_i)|}{|S|} - \frac{|U(t_i)|}{|U|})$$

$$\cdot \left\{ \alpha \cdot \log \frac{|U|}{|U(t_i)|} + (1-\alpha) \cdot \log \frac{\frac{|S(t_i)|+0.5}{|S|-|S(t_i)|+0.5}}{\frac{|U(t_i)|-|S(t_i)|+0.5}{|U|-|U(t_i)|-|S|+|S(t_i)|+0.5}} \right\},$$

where α is a parameter. We set $\alpha = 1/2$ in our experiment.

Table 1. Formulations used in our experiments. We replace $P(t_j|t_i)$, $P(t_j|\neg t_i)$, $P(\neg t_j|t_i)$, $P(\neg t_j|\neg t_i)$, and $|S(t_i)|^2/|U(t_i)|$ with A, B, C, D, and U, respectively.

method	$cw(t_i, t_j)$	$W(t_i) = U \cdot \left\{ \sum_{t_j \neq t_i} cw(t_i, t_j) \right\}^\sigma$
TNG1	$|S(t_i \wedge t_j)|/|S(t_i)|$	$U \cdot \left\{ \sum_{t_j \neq t_i} cw(t_i, t_j) \right\}^{-1}$
TNG2	$-A \log \frac{A}{P(t_j)} + C \log \frac{C}{P(\neg t_j)}$	$U \cdot \sum_{t_j \neq t_i} cw(t_i, t_j)$
UnitWeight	—	$U \cdot 1$
CF	$|S(t_i \wedge t_j)|/|S(t_i)|$	$U \cdot \sum_{t_j \neq t_i} cw(t_i, t_j)$
MI	$P(t_i) \left\{ A \log \frac{A}{P(t_j)} + C \log \frac{C}{P(\neg t_j)} \right\}$ $+ P(\neg t_i) \left\{ B \log \frac{B}{P(t_j)} + D \log \frac{D}{P(\neg t_j)} \right\}$	$U \cdot \sum_{t_j \neq t_i} cw(t_i, t_j)$
KLD	$A \log \frac{A}{P(t_j)} + C \log \frac{C}{P(\neg t_j)}$	$U \cdot \sum_{t_j \neq t_i} cw(t_i, t_j)$
χ^2	$\frac{\{A-P(t_j)\}^2}{P(t_j)} + \frac{\{C-P(\neg t_j)\}^2}{P(\neg t_j)}$ $+ \frac{\{B-P(t_j)\}^2}{P(t_j)} + \frac{\{D-P(\neg t_j)\}^2}{P(\neg t_j)}$	$U \cdot \sum_{t_j \neq t_i} cw(t_i, t_j)$

3.2 Experimental Procedure and Results

We used a document set prepared for the NTCIR3 Web Retrieval Task[3]. This set includes about ten million Web pages written in Japanese. We denote this Web page set by U. The Web pages in U are decomposed into terms by using a morphological analyzer MeCab[8] equipped with a Japanese dictionary ipadic-2.5.1[6]. There are 47 queries prepared for the NTCIR3 Web task, and each query includes two or three query terms. First, we issued the queries and obtained the top 1000 Web pages for each query. Although our experiment adopted an Okapi-type term-weighting scheme for Web page retrieval[4], our method can be applied to the search results obtained with other term-weighting schemes. From the top 1000 pages of each of the 47 retrieval results, we gathered terms appearing in five or more pages. We obtained about 10,000 terms for each query. We did not delete stop words. Next, we computed the eight term weights described in Section 3.1. As a result, we obtained eight term rankings by sorting the terms with respect to their eight kinds of weights. For every term ranking, we added each of the top five terms (a, b, c, d, and e) separately to the original query term set $\{A, B, C\}$ and made five expanded sets of query terms $\{A, B, C, a\}$, $\{A, B, C, b\}$, ..., $\{A, B, C, e\}$. Finally, we retrieved the Web pages with these expanded query term sets. Consequently, we obtained five search results for each query. We computed the average precisions of these five results by using `trec_eval`[12]. Of these five

Table 2. Overall precisions and their improvements compared to the baseline. The baseline overall precision is 0.1606.

method	overall precision	improvement(%)
UnitWeight	0.1765	9.9
TNG1	**0.1847**	15.0
TNG2	**0.1899**	18.2
CF	0.1801	12.1
MI	0.1829	13.9
KLD	0.1733	7.9
χ^2	0.1751	9.0
RSV	**0.1867**	16.3

average precisions, we kept only the best one, because this average precision can be taken as the performance measure of the information retrieval most desirable for users who are supposed to issue the corresponding query. Finally, we regarded the mean of the best average precisions of the 47 queries as the overall precision for each term-weighting method.

For the original 47 queries, we obtained 0.1606 as the overall precision and regarded it as the baseline. Among the eight term-weighting formulae, TNG1, TNG2, and RSV significantly increased overall precision (Table 2). TNG2 achieved the best overall average precision with an 18.2% improvement. The most important point is that TNG1 and TNG2 showed qualitative differences from RSV. While RSV tends to extract terms having general meanings, TNG1 and TNG2 can extract many technical terms used in specific domains relative to the query. For a query including "loudspeaker", "comparison", and "evaluation", our method extracted such technical terms as "woofer" and "bass reflex" (Table 3). For a query involving "the World Tree", "Norse mythology", and "name", our method extracted "Yggdrasill", which is the name of a mythological tree in Norse mythology and is a synonym of "the World Tree" (Table 4).

4 Related Work and Discussion

Numerous studies have been done on keyword extraction. Most of them report methods for extracting topic-centric terms, such as technical terms and proper nouns[2][9]. Rennie and Jaakkola [9] introduced a new informativeness measure, the Mixture score, which focuses on the difference in log-likelihood between a mixture model and a simple unigram model, to identify informative words. They compare it against a number of other informativeness criteria, including the Inverse Document Frequency (IDF) and Residual IDF (RIDF)[2]. While the results show their measure works well when compared with existing methods, the documents they used are all posts to a restaurant discussion bulletin board, so these results cannot be seen as conclusive.

The method proposed by Hisamitsu et al. [5] compares the term frequency distributions in an entire document set with those in the set of documents

Table 3. Terms extracted for the query consisting of "loudspeaker", "comparison", and "evaluation". (The baseline average precision is 0.0596.)

Query terms are "スピーカー (loudspeaker)", "比較 (comparison)", and "評価 (evaluation)"

method	rank	top five terms	average precision
RSV	1	"アンプ (amplifier)"	0.0067
	2	"可能 (possible)"	0.0279
	3	"結果 (result)"	0.0341
	4	"システム (system)"	0.0246
	5	"音 (sound)"	**0.0593**
TNG1	1	"アンプ (amplifier)"	0.0067
	2	"ウーファー (woofer)"	0.0660
	3	"ソフトドームツィーター(soft dome tweeter)"	0.0154
	4	"スーパーウーファー (super-woofer)"	0.0177
	5	"バスレフ (bass reflex)"	**0.0661**
TNG2	1	"アンプ (amplifier)"	0.0067
	2	"ウーファー (woofer)"	0.0660
	3	"バスレフ (bass reflex)"	**0.0661**
	4	"サブウーファー (sub-woofer)"	0.0640
	5	"低音 (bass sound)"	0.0434

Table 4. Terms extracted for the query consisting of "the World Tree", "Norse mythology", and "name". (The baseline average precision is 0.0675.)

Query terms are "世界樹 (the World Tree)", "北欧神話 (Norse mythology)", and " 名前 (name)"

method	rank	top five terms	average precision
RSV	1	"神 (God)"	0.0253
	2	"たち (they)" *1	0.0280
	3	"それ (it)" *2	**0.0377**
	4	"歴史 (history)"	0.0266
	5	"物語 (tale)"	0.0198
TNG1	1	"Pandaemonium"	0.0586
	2	"イグドラシル (Yggdrasill)"	**0.3767**
	3	"ソグネフィヨルド(Sognefjorden)"	0.0523
	4	"エッダ (Edda)"	0.0525
	5	"シルマリル (Silmaril)"	0.0533
TNG2	1	"イグドラシル (Yggdrasill)"	**0.3767**
	2	"古事記 (Kojiki)" *3	0.0227
	3	"ギリシア (Greece)"	0.0160
	4	"ノルウェー (Norway)"	0.0203
	5	"フィヨルド (fjord)"	0.0287

*1 A suffix used to make Japanese nouns plural.
*2 A kind of Japanese pronoun.
*3 The oldest known historical book about the ancient history of Japan.

containing a specific term t. When a large discrepancy exists between them, t is said to have *representativeness*. This method estimates a discrepancy similar to ours. However, our concern lies in the *direction* of the discrepancy. We ask whether the frequency of terms other than t in an entire set is higher or lower than that in a set of documents including t. When the latter is less than the former with respect to a large number of terms, we say that t has Tangibility. Therefore, we believe Tangibility is novel. Matsuo et al. [7] also proposed a term extraction method based on term co-occurrences. Their method combines term ranking by the χ^2 measure with term clustering. However, this method is designed for application to a single document. In contrast, our aim is to disambiguate a query by finding the terms corresponding to distinct topics latent in a set of hundreds of retrieved documents. Therefore, we have proposed a new measure for term extraction.

5 Conclusion and Future Work

We proposed a co-occurrence-based measure, called Tangibility, for term extraction to disambiguate queries. Our experiments obtained very interesting results worthy of further investigation. Both of our numerical estimates for term tangibility, TNG1 and TNG2, realized good average precisions. In addition, many of the extracted terms were related to more specific topics than that implied by the original ambiguous query terms. Our method may be used as a key component of a system that helps users to discover specific topics from a given corpus simply by using fairly general terms as search keywords. As future work, we plan to propose a method of clustering the terms that have Tangibility; we will test to determine whether the term clusters correspond to distinct topics implied by the initial query terms.

References

1. R. Baeza-Yates and B. Ribeiro-Neto. *Modern Information Retrieval*. Addison Wesley, 1999.
2. K. Church and W. Gale. Inverse document frequency (IDF): A measure of deviations from poisson. In *Proc. of 3rd Workshop on Very Large Corpora*, pages 121–130, 1995.
3. K. Eguchi, K. Oyama, E. Ishida, N. Kando, and K. Kuriyama. Overview of the Web retrieval task at the third NTCIR workshop. In *Proc. of NTCIR-3*, pages 1–24, 2003.
4. H. Fang, T. Tao, and C. Zhai. A formal study of information retrieval heuristics. In *Proc. of SIGIR 2004*, pages 49–56, 2004.
5. T. Hisamitsu, Y. Niwa, S. Nishioka, H. Sakurai, O. Imaichi, M. Iwayama, and A. Takano. Extracting terms by a combination of term frequency and a measure of term representativeness. *Terminology*, 6(2):211–232, 2001.
6. ipadic-2.5.1. http://chasen.naist.jp/stable/ipadic/.
7. Y. Matsuo and M. Ishizuka. Keyword extraction from a single document using word co-ocurrence statistical information. *International Journal on Artificial Intelligence Tools*, 13:157–169, 2004.
8. MeCab. http://mecab.sourceforge.jp/.
9. J. Rennie and T. Jaakkola. Using term informativeness for named entity detection. In *Proc. of SIGIR'05*, pages 353–360, 2005.
10. S. E. Robertson. On term selection for query expansion. *Journal of Documentation*, 46(4):359–364, 1990.
11. M. Toyoda, M. Kitsuregawa, H. Mano, H. Itoh, and Y. Ogawa. University of Tokyo/RICOH at NTCIR-3 Web retrieval task. In *Proc. of NTCIR-3*, pages 31–38, 2003.
12. TREC. trec_eval, http://trec.nist.gov/trec_eval/.
13. Y. Yang and J. Pedersen. A comparative study on feature selection in text categorization. In *Proc. of ICML-97*, pages 412–420, 1997.
14. M. Yoshioka and M. Haraguchi. Study on the combination of probabilistic and boolean ir models for www documents retrieval. In *Working Notes of NTCIR-4 (Supplement Volume)*, pages 9–16, 2004.

Unsupervised Word Categorization Using Self-Organizing Maps and Automatically Extracted Morphs

Mikaela Klami and Krista Lagus

Adaptive Informatics Research Centre, Helsinki University of Technology
P.O. Box 5400, FI-02015 TKK, Finland
mikaela.klami@hut.fi

Abstract. Automatic creation of syntactic and semantic word categorizations is a challenging problem for highly inflecting languages due to excessive data sparsity. Moreover, the study of colloquial language resources requires the utilization of fully corpus-based tools. We present a completely automated approach for producing word categorizations for morphologically rich languages. Self-Organizing Map (SOM) is utilized for clustering words based on the morphological properties of the context words. These properties are extracted using an automated morphological segmentation algorithm called Morfessor. Our experiments on a colloquial Finnish corpus of stories told by young children show that utilizing unsupervised morphs as features leads to clearly improved clusterings when compared to the use of whole context words as features.

1 Introduction

Gathering lexical information based on authentic word usage has become a reasonable avenue due to the availability of vast language resources. Detailed syntactic and semantic information on words is valuable for a wide variety of fundamental natural language processing tasks, including information retrieval, question answering, and machine translation.

One way of capturing information regarding the syntactic or semantic relatedness of words is through obtaining a classification or a cluster structure of them. Over the years, many researchers have examined the use of statistical, corpus-based methods for clustering words [1,2,3,4,5].

In the task of word clustering, first a set of informative features representing the words is determined, and for each word, the values for the features are recorded. Then, a clustering method is used for grouping the words based on their feature vector values. Typically, the features used are individual words occurring in the immediate context of the words being clustered [1,2,5] or having some other grammatical relationship with the words [6,7]. This is a feasible approach for languages like English with manageable amounts of word inflection. But even there, data sparsity is a problem: many samples of a word form are needed in order to obtain a reliable feature representation for it.

For a language like e.g. Finnish which relies heavily on inflection and other morphological processes, the data sparsity problem is yet intensified due to the much larger number of possible context word forms. Finnish word forms typically contain masses of potentially valuable semantic information inside them. As counting the occurrences of individual words is generally an infeasible strategy for such morphologically rich languages, one solution is to use features that utilize the inflectional or derivational properties within words [5,8]. However, suitable morphological analyzers do not exist for all languages, and the manually designed analyzers also typically fail to cope with e.g. language change or the colloquial language found in everyday conversations. Fortunately, in the recent years, tools that discover a rudimentary morphological segmentation automatically from text corpora have emerged, e.g. Linguistica [9] and Morfessor [10].

The purpose of this study was to find out whether the use of completely automatically discovered morphological segmentations can improve the quality of word categorizations for highly inflecting languages. We also selected an unusual and challenging corpus for our task, a collection of stories told by young Finnish children. The data set was chosen in the purpose of studying the language use and language acquisition process of children of different ages, but only the technical results of our work will be presented here due to space limitations.

In our experiments, we employ an unsupervised morphological segmentation algorithm called Morfessor [10] for extracting morphological features for the words that are to be categorized. We then use the morph features in training word category maps using the Self-Organizing Map (SOM) algorithm [11]. We evaluate and compare the utilization of different feature sets, with both whole context word features and sets of Morfessor-extracted morphs. Our experiments show that the use of automatically extracted morph features instead of whole words leads to improved quality of the resulting word category maps. We expect the presented results also to be of interest for solving many other lexical acquisition tasks than word categorization, and there is reason to believe that similar benefits will be obtained for also other languages with rich morphology.

2 Segmenting Words into Morphs Using Morfessor

Morfessor [10,12] is an automated learning algorithm for extracting the morphology of a language from text corpora. Morfessor is able to segment the words of an unlabeled text corpus into morpheme[1]-like units (morphs), and it is especially applicable to highly inflecting, morphologically rich languages like Finnish, Spanish or Turkish. The Morfessor algorithm not only seeks to find the most accurate segmentation possible, but it also learns a representation of the language from the data it was applied to, namely an inventory of the morphs of the language. In this work, we chose to apply the Categories-ML variant of Morfessor, which uses a Hidden Markov Model (HMM) to model morph sequences and estimates the model parameters by maximizing the likelihood of the data. The

---

[1] Morphemes can be defined as parts of words that constitute the smallest meaningful units in the grammar of a language.

algorithm is based on the Expectation Maximization (EM) principle, and the Viterbi algorithm is used for optimizing the model.

The output of the Morfessor algorithm is a lexicon of the words from the corpus, segmented at the proposed morpheme boundaries into morphs. The more recent versions of Morfessor also label the resulting morphs as either 'STM' (word root), 'PRE' (prefix) or 'SUF' (suffix). For example, the verb form "aivastivat" ('they sneezed') is correctly segmented as "aivast/STM + i/SUF + vat/SUF".

Morfessor has been tested on Finnish and English text corpora with good results [12], making it an able tool for producing the morphological segmentation used in this work. Previously it has been shown that the use of Morfessor-extracted morphs was able to improve Finnish large vocabulary speech recognition accuracy considerably [13].

3 Self-Organizing Maps

The Self-Organizing Map (SOM) [11,14] is an unsupervised neural network algorithm that is able to organize multidimensional data sets into a two-dimensional, ordered map grid. The data samples are then projected on the map so that their relative distances reflect their similarity according to the chosen feature set, i.e. similar input samples will generally be found close to each other on the map.

The map grid of a SOM consists of nodes, each of which corresponds to a prototype vector. Together, the prototype vectors form an approximation of the data set. During the training process of the SOM, sample vectors (or feature vectors) are compared to the prototype vectors, and the samples are mapped according to their Best Matching Unit (BMU) on the map grid. The algorithm thus simultaneously obtains a clustering of the data based on the prototype vectors, and a nonlinear projection of the input data from the multidimensional input space onto the two-dimensional ordered map.

3.1 SOMs in Word Categorization

Word category SOMs are word maps trained on sample word forms from an input text corpus [1,2]. The general idea is to have implicit word categorizations emerge automatically from the input data itself. The similarity or dissimilarity of word forms is usually based on their textual contexts in the corpus, i.e. word forms that have similar elements in their contexts should appear close to each other on the resulting word category SOM.

A set of training words for training a word SOM is usually chosen based on a word form frequency list of the corpus, and a feature vector for each training word is then calculated from the corpus. Traditionally, the feature sets of word SOMs have consisted of the occurrences of whole corpus words in the contexts of the training word samples. The size of the context window of the sample words may vary; in the experiments of this paper, the context window size was fixed at 1, meaning that only the two words that were immediately before and after the training word were considered as its context.

In this work, a novel approach to word SOM feature sets is adopted. Instead of using the context word forms for features as such, they are segmented into morphs by using the Morfessor algorithm, and the context of a training word is now checked for the presence of feature morphs rather than for whole, unsegmented words. Also Lagus et al. [5] utilized morphological features in a study on categorizing Finnish verbs using SOM, but instead of automatically extracted word segments, they used as features only 21 different morphemes obtained with a linguistic morphological analyzer. However, such an approach would be inapplicable here due to the particular colloquial nature of our corpus.

4 Data Set and Feature Extraction

The data set for our experiments consisted of 2642 stories or fairytales in Finnish, told by children aged from 1 to 14. In total, the stories form a Finnish text corpus of 198 036 word forms (after preprocessing).

The stories were collected using a method called *Storycrafting* [15]: they were told orally and transcribed by an adult exactly as they were heard, without correcting any potential mistakes or colloquialisms by the child. This gives the corpus a particular nature as the conversational and authentic use of language of young Finnish children. Because of this challenging, often non-orthographical nature of the data, statistical, completely automated learning methods were assumed to prove especially useful in analyzing it.

The stories were preprocessed, which included stripping metadata, removal of punctuation, changing numbers to the special symbol NUM, and changing uppercase letters to lower-case. Finally, a morphological segmentation of the corpus was obtained using the Categories-ML variant of the Morfessor algorithm.

5 Experiments on SOM Feature Sets

The objective of these experiments was to find out the best way of producing word categorizations with the Self-Organizing Map. The experiments on comparing word SOMs with different types of features are described in the following.

5.1 Evaluation Measure

For evaluating the quality of word SOMs, an automatical evaluation measure was needed. The evaluation measure developed for this work is based on using the part-of-speech (POS) information of the 200 most frequent word forms in the corpus. Each word form was manually assigned a list of all its possible POS tags, according to a recent descriptive book of Finnish grammar [16].

The idea of the evaluation measure is to find out how tightly word forms are clustered on a particular word SOM according to their POS classifications. For each word form on a SOM, a percentage is calculated which tells the portion of the words in the same or the immediately neighboring map node having at least one POS in common with the word form under examination. An average percentage for the whole word SOM is then calculated over these results of individual word forms. More precisely, the evaluation measure for a single word SOM can be written as $1/N \sum_{i=1}^{N} A_i/B_i$, where N is the number of word forms projected on the SOM, B_i denotes the number of words having their Best Matching Unit (BMU) in the neighborhood of the BMU of the ith word, and A_i is the number of words in the neighborhood sharing at least one POS with the ith word.

Finally, in order to rule out the possibility of chance, the final results for each type of word SOM were calculated over the individual results of 100 randomly initialized word SOMs of that type, yielding the final quality score for the word SOM type. This quality score can be seen as a kind of a POS cluster density score for the emergent word clusters of the particular SOM variant.

5.2 Feature Sets for Different Experiments

We evaluated and compared word SOM variants with different numbers and types of features. The feature sets used will be described below in more detail.

Morph vs. whole context word features. In order to see whether using morph features can improve the quality of a word SOM, two maps were trained: one with the 200 most frequent corpus word forms as features, and one with the 200 most frequent Morfessor-extracted morphs as features (with all types of morphs).

Different types of morph features. In addition to the SOM experiments with morph features in general, a few variants with different types of morph features were trained. Here, two morph type experiments are presented, namely one word SOM with the 200 most frequent root morphs as features, and one with the 80 suffix morphs that Morfessor extracted from the story corpus.

Other experiments. Some experiments on combining together different types of feature morphs as well as on the effect of the number of features in the feature set were also studied, but they will not be further considered in this paper as the results fell between the reported figures.

Baseline. For comparison, also a baseline similarity measure was included. It counts for every word form in the training word set the percentage of other training words sharing at least one POS with it. Again, the result is an average over all the words in the training set. This corresponds roughly to the idea of a SOM organized in a completely random fashion.

6 Results

The evaluation results of the experiments can be found in Fig. 1. As can be seen, all word SOMs clearly outperform the (rather crude) baseline similarity, whether they had morphs or whole context words as features. This indicates that all the word SOM variants that were evaluated succeeded in creating word categorizations which surpass in quality a random organization of the data.

All but one of the word SOMs that utilized morphological information in their feature sets seemed to fare better in the evaluation than the traditional

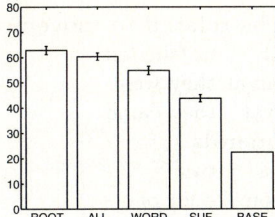

Feature sets:

ROOT : root morphs (200 most frequent)
ALL : all morphs (200 most frequent)
WORD : whole words (200 most frequent)
SUF : suffix morphs only (80 most frequent)
BASE : baseline similarity measure

Fig. 1. The accuracies of the experiments (error bars mark one standard deviation)

word SOMs with whole context words as features. The best results were yielded by word SOMs with only root morphs as features, but when also suffixes were added to feature sets, the evaluation results seemed to slightly decline. Further, the only morph-featured word SOM variant that actually fared worse than the traditional SOMs with whole context words as features was the one with only suffix morphs in its feature set.

These results imply that, firstly, utilizing automatically discovered morphological units in the feature set of a word SOM does indeed improve the quality of the resulting word category SOM. Due to the highly inflecting nature of Finnish, the better performance of morph features as compared to whole feature words is hardly a surprise. With context words segmented into roots and into a variety of derivational or inflectional affixes, it is clear that some of the data sparsity problems caused by the diversity of Finnish inflected word forms are solved.

Secondly, it seems that not all morphs make equally good features: the best-quality word SOMs were constructed by using only root morphs as features. The fact that the POS-based quality evaluation measure we developed seemed to penalize the inclusion of other types of morphs (prefixes, suffixes) into the feature set appears to imply that most of the semantic and POS information of Finnish word forms is carried in their roots, not so much in the affixes attached to these roots. However, affix morphs should not be too hastily rejected as bad features on the basis of these evaluation results, as it may e.g. be the case that they encode some entirely different characteristic of words than their POS class.

6.1 Example of a Word SOM Analysis

Another objective of our research was to analyze the unique Finnish children's stories corpus (see Sect. 4) using SOMs. With the optimal features discovered in the experiments, we trained word category SOMs on the whole data set and also on story data from different age categories of children. As including also suffix morphs into the feature set appeared to bring some additional benefits from the point of view of analyzing and interpreting the story data, the final analysis maps were trained using a feature set of the 200 most frequent root morphs combined with the 20 most frequent suffixes.

An example word category SOM, constructed using the whole story corpus and the feature set described above, can be found in Fig. 2. Some emergent

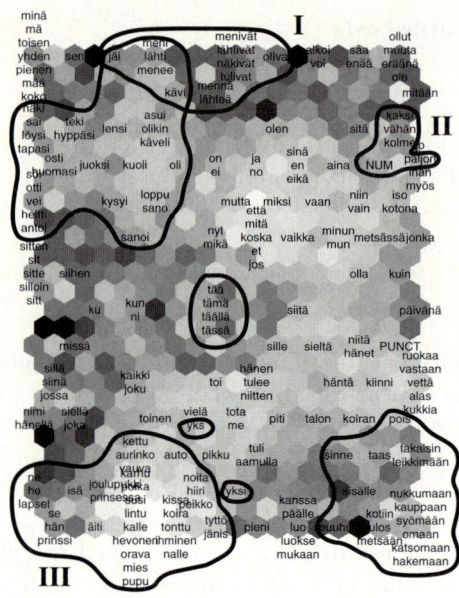

Fig. 2. The U-matrix representation of a word category SOM trained on the whole children's stories corpus. Some interesting clusters of semantically similar words have been manually highlighted, and some words from three of them are presented in more detail on the side of the map (with English translations). Notice for example how the nouns in group III are typical agents in the children's stories.

groups of intuitively similar words have been manually highlighted to the resulting word map. However, we will not go here into a further analysis of the language use of young Finnish children due to space limitations.

7 Conclusions

We trained word category SOMs on Finnish text data using morphologically informed features that were extracted from the corpus itself with an unsupervised morphological segmentation algorithm called Morfessor. Experiments were performed on different kinds of SOM feature sets with morphs and whole context words. The resulting word SOMs were evaluated with an evaluation measure developed for this task, based on a list of part-of-speech -classified word forms.

Our experiments showed that the use of Morfessor-extracted morphs as word SOM features clearly improves the POS density -based quality of the resulting word SOMs, as opposed to using unsegmented context words for features. However, some types of morphs seem to make better features than others. The best resulting word SOMs were trained by using a feature set with only root morphs, chosen from the top of a morph frequency list calculated from the data.

The work described in this paper is the first completely automated categorization of Finnish word forms with morphology-utilizing word SOMs. It is also a study on the problem of lexical acquisition in a highly inflecting language in general. Particularly, the method we described aims at – and succeeds in – tackling the critical problem of data sparsity, typical to morphologically rich languages (as opposed to e.g. languages like English).

In future, the current work could be extended in many ways. First, the experiments should be re-run on data in other languages, and maybe also on another, larger corpus in Finnish. Further, the morphological features of also the training word itself could be utilized, examining e.g. only some very high-frequency morphs like common suffixes. Finally, the Morfessor-extracted morphological features could be used in many other lexical acquisition tasks, like e.g. finding verb subcategorization patterns or selectional preferences of words.

References

1. Ritter, H., Kohonen, T.: Self-Organizing Maps. Biological Cybernetics **61** (1989) 241–254
2. Honkela, T., Pulkki, V., Kohonen, T.: Contextual relations of words in Grimm tales analyzed by self-organizing map. In: Proceedings of ICANN-95. Volume 2., Paris, EC2 et Cie (1995) 3–7
3. Redington, M., Chater, N., Finch, S.: Distributional information: A powerful cue for acquiring syntactic categories. Cognitive Science **22**(4) (1998) 425–469
4. Schütze, H.: Automatic word sense discrimination. Computational Linguistics **24**(1) (1998) 97–123
5. Lagus, K., Airola, A., Creutz, M.: Data analysis of conceptual similarities of Finnish verbs. In: Proceedings of the CogSci 2002, Fairfax, Virginia (2002) 566–571
6. Pereira, F., Tishby, N., Lee, L.: Distributional clustering of English words. In: ACL 30. (1993) 183–190
7. Schulte im Walde, S.: Clustering verbs semantically according to their alternation behaviour. In: COLING-00. (2000) 747–753
8. Light, M.: Morphological cues for lexical semantics. In: ACL 34. (1996) 25–31
9. Goldsmith, J.: Unsupervised learning of the morphology of a natural language. Computational Linguistics **27**(2) (2001) 153–198
10. Creutz, M., Lagus, K.: Unsupervised discovery of morphemes. In: Proceedings of the Workshop on Morphological and Phonological Learning of ACL-02, Philadelphia, Pennsylvania (2002) 21–30
11. Kohonen, T.: Self-organized formation of topologically correct feature maps. Biological Cybernetics **43** (1982) 59–69
12. Creutz, M., Lagus, K.: Inducing the morphological lexicon of a natural language from unannotated text. In: Proceedings of AKRR'05, Espoo (2005) 106–113
13. Hirsimäki, T., Creutz, M., Siivola, V., Kurimo, M., Virpioja, S., Pylkkönen, J.: Unlimited vocabulary speech recognition with morph language models applied to Finnish. Computer Speech and Language **20**(4) (2006) 515–541
14. Kohonen, T.: Self-Organizing Maps. 3rd edn. Springer, Berlin (2001)
15. Riihelä, M.: The Storycrafting Method. Stakes, Helsinki, Finland (2001)
16. Hakulinen, A., Vilkuna, M., Korhonen, R., Koivisto, V., Heinonen, T., Alho, I.: Iso suomen kielioppi. Suomalaisen Kirjallisuuden Seura, Helsinki (2004)

Effective Classification by Integrating Support Vector Machine and Association Rule Mining

Keivan Kianmehr[1] and Reda Alhajj[1,2]

[1] Dept. of Computer Science, University of Calgary, Calgary, Alberta, Canada
[2] Dept. of Computer Science, Global University, Beirut, Lebanon

Abstract. In this study, we propose a new classification framework, CARSVM model, which integrates association rule mining and support vector machine. The aim is to take advantages of both knowledge represented by class association rules and the power of SVM algorithm to construct an efficient and accurate classifier model. Instead of using the original training set, a set of rule-based feature vectors, which are generated based on the discriminative ability of class association rules over the training samples, are presented to the learning process of the SVM algorithm. The reported test results demonstrate the applicability, efficiency and effectiveness of the proposed model.

Keywords: classification, association rule mining, associative classifiers, class association rules, support vector machine, machine learning.

1 Introduction

Data objects stored in a database are identified by their attributes; and the main idea of classification [1] is to explore through data objects (training set) to find a set of rules, which determine the class of each object according to its attributes. A wide variety of research has considered the use of popular machine learning techniques in classification problems. Despite their good performance in real world applications, machine learning techniques have some shortcomings. They work based on mathematical and statistical algorithms, and use domain independent biases to extract the rules. Therefore, they are not able to discover all the interesting and understandable rules in the analyzed data set.

To overcome the understandability problem of the classification task [2,3], association rule-based classification techniques, known as associative classification, have been recently proposed and have received a great consideration. In associative classification, a classifier is built by using a subset of association rules, namely CARs [4], where the consequent of each rule is single class attribute. The related literature indicates that associative classifiers have better results than machine learning classification algorithms. However, they suffer from efficiency issues. First, the rule generator algorithm generates a large number of rules, and it is difficult to store the rules, retrieve the related rules, prune and sort the rules [5]. Second, it is challenging to find the best subset of rules to build the most robust and accurate classifier.

In this paper, we propose a new classification framework, called CARSVM. The CARSVM model attempts to overcome the drawbacks of machine learning and associative classification algorithms by integrating support vector machine and class association rules. SVM is a new and modern method based on statistical learning theory [6]. Compared to other machine learning algorithms, SVM has been successfully applied to many real world classification problems such as gene expression analysis [7] and hot-spot crime prediction [8]. We take advantages of both SVM as a machine learning algorithm and associative classification techniques to integrate the two trends into a novel, efficient and accurate classification technique by directly dealing with the following problems. The first problem is to provide more discriminative knowledge to the learning process of the SVM algorithm, by incorporating class association rules in the form of rule-based feature vectors. In our previous study [9], we developed a set of binary rule-based feature vectors to be used as inputs to the SVM algorithm, and the result are outstanding. However, in this study we propose the use of weighted rule-based feature vectors in the classifier model. The use of rule-based feature vectors helps to improve the interpretability and understandability of the classification task for experts in the area under research. The second problem is to develop an effective ranking method to filter out the best subset of rules to be incorporated into the final classifier. We hope to improve the accuracy of the classifier by eliminating the deterioration effect of the rule ranking and selection approach in associative classification algorithms.

The rest of this paper is organized as follows. Section 2 describes the associative classification problem. Section 3 presents a review of associative classifier techniques and highlights our contribution to this problem. Section 4 explains in detail our approach to build an associative classifier. Section 5 provides explanation on the selected evaluation model, the conducted experiments and the achieved results. Section 6 is summary and conclusions.

2 Associative Classification

Associative classification algorithms produce classification models that are easy to understand by end-users because models are constructed based on interesting and interpretable rules. Their understandability and high accuracy have made associative classifiers very popular in real world applications such as medical diagnoses.

A more formal definition of associative classification can be described as follows. **Given** a transactional database D consisting of n transactions $T = \{T_1, \ldots, T_n\}$; a set of items $I = \{I_1, \ldots, I_k\}$ consisting of all items in D, which is also the domain of possible values for transactions; a set of class labels $L = \{L_1, \ldots, L_m\}$; and $minsupp$ and $minconf$ thresholds; **the objective** is generating the set of strong class association rules in the form: $Class_i : X_i \Rightarrow L_i, i = 1, 2, \ldots, m$, where $L_i \in L$ and X_i is an instance of the cross product of a subset of I that denotes a tuple as belonging to L_i; and ranking and selecting the best CARs to build a classifier that can predict the class of a previously unseen object. The **constraints** are: transactional database D is a normalized dataset to positive integer values; each transaction in D belongs to one and only one of m classes; class association rules are in the form ($attributes \Rightarrow class$).

3 Related Work and Our Contribution

As described in the literature, associative classification includes two major techniques: classification based on single class association rule and classification based on multiple class association rules. Alternative approaches have been also proposed to combine different techniques to improve the classification efficiency. In the rest of this section, we briefly describe several well-known associative classification algorithms; and finally highlight the main contributions of this paper.

for classification based on single class association rules, a subset of strong rules, called candidate set, is sorted in descending order of rules' accuracy (a rule is accurate if both its confidence and support are above the pre-determined thresholds). When classifying a new unseen data object, the first rule in the sorted candidate set that matches the object makes the prediction. The candidate set also contains a default class at the end. The class label of uncovered training data objects by the last rule in the candidate set, which has the majority, is identified as the default class. When there is no rule to cover the new coming data object, it is classified to the default class. CBA [4] and C4.5 [10] are two techniques that work based on single class association rules.

For classification based on multiple class association rules, the candidate set of strong rules is not sorted and most matching rules may participate in the classification process. Simply, if the new data object is covered by all candidate rules, it will be assigned to the class label of candidate rules; otherwise the majority vote of candidate rules will specify the class label of the new object. CPAR [11] employs this technique to classify new data objects. Another method is to divide candidate rules into groups according to class labels, and then to compute the actual effect obtained from the multiple rules for all groups. The group with the highest efficiency will identify the class of the new object; CMAR [5] employs this method.

The main contribution of this study is CARSVM system, which is a new classification framework that extracts class association rules from a dataset and incorporate them in the process of building a classifier model using SVM algorithm. The use of class association rules improves the interpretability and understandability of the classification task for experts in the area under research. The SVM algorithm in turn helps to improve the effectiveness and efficiency of the associative classifiers.

4 The CARSVM Model

CARSVM is a general classification framework that attempts to make the classification task more understandable and efficient by integrating association rule mining and SVM technique. CARSVM consists of two major phases: generating class association rules and building a classifier model based on the rules. In the first phase, the task is to extract all association rules whose consequents are class labels, i.e, class association rules (CARs), from a normalized dataset. In the second phase, extracted CARs are first ranked and sorted based on a scoring metric strategy. The score calculated by the scoring method is also used as the weight of the rule. Then, a subset of high score rules, called discriminator CARs set, is selected to be used in the process of generating rule-based feature vectors. The validity of the rules from discriminator CARs set for every row in the dataset is used to generate a set of feature vectors. Each row in the dataset is represented by a feature vector. Every feature of the vector corresponds to an individual rule in the discriminator CARs set. The value of every individual feature for any row in the dataset is set to the weight of the corresponding rule if the rule is covered by the selected row; otherwise the value is set to 0. Generated feature vectors represent the coverage distribution of the discriminator CARs over the original dataset. Eventually rule-based feature vectors are given to the SVM algorithm to build a classifier model. The accuracy of the classifier is then evaluated by using the cross validation technique. In the rest of this section, the components of CARSVM will be described in more details.

Data Preprocessing: The problem in class association rule mining arises mainly when the dataset used for classification contains continuous values for some attributes or categorical (discrete) attributes. Indeed, mining association rules in such datasets is still a major research problem. The general approach used to address this issue is data discretization and data normalization. Normalization is the process of mapping values associated with categorical attributes to unique integer labels. Discretization is the process of mapping the range of possible values associated with a continuous attribute into a number of intervals each denoted by a unique integer label; and converting all the values associated with this attribute to the corresponding integer labels. In our study, discretization and normalization are done using a method developed by LUCS-KDD group [12].

Class Association Rule Mining: The method used for class association rule mining follows the CBA rule generator approach, called CBA-RG [4]. In CBA-RG, the Apriori algorithm [13] is adapted to find all class association rules that have support and confidence values greater than the given thresholds. Please refer to [4] for further information about the CBA-RG algorithm.

Rules Ranking and Sorting: Ranking and sorting class association rules play an important role in most associative classification algorithms because the main goal of these techniques is to select a set of rules that can represent the strong discrimination ability of the class association rules over the training set. We follow the same basic idea in our classification algorithm. After extracting CARs, CARSVM ranks and sorts them based on a scoring metric strategy. Our goal is to select a subset of the most discriminative class association rules such that it would be able to represent the discrimination ability of the rules over the training set when used in the SVM classification algorithm. However, most of the existing approaches rank the class association rules based on the confidence value of every individual rule. A better idea for ranking the rules should take into consideration the statistical importance of a rule as well, i.e., the support value of the rules. As a result, a good scoring metric for ranking the rules involve both support and confidence values of the rules. In our model, we use the scoring method introduced in [14]; however, our classification approach is different than their technique. We also use *weighting* instead of *scoring* as the former has better interpretation in our model. The weight of a class association rule is computed according Equation 1.

$$W\left(r^{C_i}\right) = r^{C_i}.conf \times r^{C_i}.sup/d_{C_i} \qquad (1)$$

where r^{C_i} denotes a class association rule $r \in CARs$ whose antecedent is class C_i; and d_{C_i} denotes the distribution of class C_i over the training set, i.e., the number of training data instances whose class labels are C_i.

Constructing Rule-Based Feature Vectors: In order to make the learning process more understandable to domain experts, we construct a new rule-based feature vector for each sample from the original training set by utilizing class association rules. Feature vectors constructed using our method describe the distribution validity of high discriminative rules over the training set. That is, we first select a predefined portion of class association rules starting from the beginning of the ranked-order CARs set. Then, we check the validity of rules within this set against the original training set. A feature in the rule-based feature vector is defined as a predicator indicating whether every individual rule from the selected CARs set is covered by a data item from the training set. As a result, the number of features in the rule-based feature vector is equal to the number of selected rules. If a rule is valid for a sample (i.e., the rule is covered by the sample), the weight corresponding to the rule is set to the value of the feature representing that rule in the feature vector; otherwise, the value is set to 0. A <feature, value> pair in a rule-based feature vector takes the following form.

$$f^{r_i} = \begin{cases} w_i & \text{if } r_i \text{ is covered by the data item } d \\ 0 & \text{otherwise} \end{cases} \qquad (2)$$

where f^{r_i} is a feature that represents a rule from the selected CARs set, w_i is its corresponding weight, and d is a data item from the training set D.

Building SVM Classifier Model: The task of building a classifier model in CARSVM is to apply the SVM algorithm to build a classifier model. The input to the SVM algorithm is a set of rule-based feature vectors. The SVM learning algorithm uses these feature vectors to train a classifier model. For building the classifier model, we apply both linear and non-linear SVM algorithms to analyze how it would influence the effectiveness of CARSVM classifier model. To evaluate the accuracy of our classifier model, we use the cross validation technique. The input to the cross validation procedure are the parameters of the classifier model built by the SVM algorithm and the rule-based feature vectors (training set). The output of the cross validation process is the accuracy of the classifier model.

5 Experimental Results

In this section, we report the test results of the experiments conducted using two well-known datasets, namely Breast and Glass, downloaded from UCI ML Repository [16]. They consist of 2 and 7 class labels, respectively. Thus, the binary and multi-class classification are applicable. We conducted an extensive performance study to evaluate the accuracy of the proposed technique. We also compare the proposed method with other existing approaches. For the experiments, we used Personal Computer with Intel P4 2.4GHZ CPU and 1GB memory. Our main performance metric is classification accuracy. An increase in the classification accuracy is an indicator of how accurate the proposed model is. A 10-fold cross validation is used to estimate the accuracy of the proposed classification technique. First, the datasets are discretized and normalized using a method developed by LUCS-KDD group [12]. The SVM technique used in our classification method is implemented using a Matlab interface of LIBSVM [15] in Matlab 7.

In the first set of experiments, we evaluated the impact of the number of selected CARs integrated in the CARSVM model. This threshold can be defined by system users, preferably domain experts. Because of the absence of domain

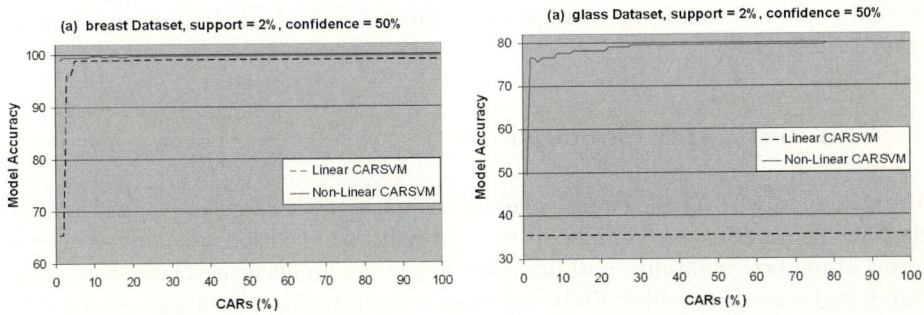

Fig. 1. Model accuracy as a function of selected CARs percentage

Table 1. Comparison of C4.5, CBA, CMAR, CPAR, SVM and *CARSVM* on model classification accuracy

Dataset	C4.5	CBA	CMAR	CPAR	SVM		CARSVM
					Linear	Non-Linear	
breast	95.0	96.3	96.4	96.0	45.8	46.2	**99.7**
glass	68.7	73.9	70.1	74.4	69.2	65.9	**79.9**

knowledge in our study, we decided to define the best possible threshold associated with the best accurate CARSVM model. The process works as follows: after building the ranked-order set of CARs, we increased the number of selected rules starting from 1% to 100% by steps of 1. In each step, the discriminative ability of the selected rules is identified by training the SVM on corresponding rule-based feature vectors and building the CARSVM model. The less the prediction error rate of CARSVM, the higher is the discriminative ability of the selected rules. The percentage of the selected rules associated with the rule-based feature vectors used in the learning process of the best CARSVM model was considered to define the possible best threshold. The results of these experiments are displayed in Figure 1; and demonstrate that it is possible to improve the performance of the model by increasing the number of the selected CARs threshold. However, after a certain percentage of the selected CARs, increasing the threshold does not improve model accuracy. Moreover, we observed in some experiments that involving more rules in the CARSVM classifier may lead to a degradation in model accuracy. This is based on the fact that if the CARs set integrated into the learning process of CARSVM is too large, the training feature vectors may be overfit.

In terms of classification accuracy, we compared the performance of CARSVM model with C4.5, CBA, CPAR and CMAR from the family of associative classifiers, and with SVM as a machine learning technique. To keep the comparison fair, we set the minimum support value to 2%, and minimum confidence value to 50% for CARSVM model as the associative classifiers mentioned above used the same values. Besides, we report the best result obtained from the previous set of experiments reported in Figure 1. Table 1 lists the classification accuracy on the two tested datasets. Accuracy rates on each dataset are obtained from 10-fold cross-validation. As can be seen, the CARSVM model outperforms all other techniques.

6 Summary and Conclusions

In this paper, we proposed a new classification framework, which integrates association rule mining and SVM in order to provide users with more convenience in terms of understandability and interpretability via an accurate class association rule-based classifier model. First, we used a discretization technique to convert a given dataset to a normalized form appropriate for association rule mining algorithm. Then, we adapted an existing association rule mining algorithm to extract, from the normalized dataset, all association rules whose consequents are class labels and have a support and confidence greater than given thresholds. After extracting CARs, we ranked and sorted them based on a scoring metric strategy to select a subset of the top-ranked CARs, such that it would be able to monotonously represent the discrimination ability of the rules over the training set. The validity of CARs from this subset on the tuples of the training set was used to generate a set of rule-based feature vectors. Rule-based feature vectors were then given to the SVM algorithm to build a classifier model. Finally, the cross-validation technique was used to evaluate the performance of the classifier in terms of accuracy. The performance of the proposed system was compared with five well-known existing methods; and it was concluded from the results that a considerable increase in classification accuracy was obtained when the rule-based feature vectors were integrated in the learning process of the SVM algorithm. This confirms the significance of rule-based feature vectors in the process of building a classifier model, and consequently shows that rule-based feature vectors present a high-quality knowledge extracted from the training set.

References

1. J. Han and M. Kamber: *Data Mining Concepts and Techniques*, Morgan Kanufmann, 2000.
2. P. Clark and S. Matwin: "Using qualitative models to guide induction learning," *Proc. of ICML*, pp.49–56, 1993.
3. M. Pazzani, S. Mani and W. R. Shankle: "Beyond concise and colorful: learning intelligible rules," *Proc. of ACM KDD*, 1997.
4. B. Liu, W. Hsu and Y. Ma: "Integrating Classification and Association Rule Mining," *Proc. of ACM KDD*, 1998.
5. W. Li, J. Han and J. Pei: "CMAR: Accurate and Efficient Classification Based on Multiple Class-Association Rules," *Proc. of IEEE ICDM*, 2001.
6. V.N. Vapnik: *Statistical Learning Theory*, John Wiley, NY, p.732, 1998.
7. M. P. Brown, W. N. Grundy, D. Lin, N. Cristianini, C. W. Sugnet, T. S. Furey, M. Ares Jr. and D. Haussler: "Knowledge-based analysis of microarray gene expression data by using support vector machines," *Nat. Acad. Sci.*, vol.97, pp.262267, 2000.
8. K. Kianmehr and R. Alhajj: "Crime Hot-Spots Prediction Using Support Vector Machine," *Proc. of ACS/IEEE International Conference on Computer Systems and Applications*, Dubai, March 2006.
9. K. Kianmehr and R. Alhajj: "Support Vector Machine Approach for Fast Classification," *Proc. of DAWAK*, Springer-Verlag LNCS, Poland, Sep. 2006.
10. J.R. Quinlan: "C4.5: Programs for Machine Learning," San Mateo, CA:Morgan Kaufmann, 1993.
11. X. Yin and J. Han: "CPAR: Classification based on predictive association rules", *Proc. of SIAM International Conference on Data Mining*, 2003.
12. F. Coenen: "LUCS-KDD DN Software (Version 2)," Department of Computer Science, The University of Liverpool, UK, 2003.
13. R. Agrawal and R. Srikant:"Fast algorithms for mining association rules", *Proc. of VLDB*, 1994.
14. G. Cong, K.-L. Tan, A. K. H. Tung and X. Xu: "Mining Top-k Covering Rule Groups for Gene Expression Data", *Proc. of ACM SIGMOD*, pp.670–681, 2005.
15. C.C. Chang and C.J. Lin: "LIBSVM: A Library for Support Vector Machines", 2001. URL: http://www.csie.ntu.edu.tw/ cjlin/libsvm.
16. C.J, Merz and P. Murphy: UCI repository of machine learning database, [http://www.cs.uci.edu/ mlearn/MLRepository.html], 1996.

A Design of Dynamic Network Management System*

Myung Jin Lee**, Eun Hee Kim***, and Keun Ho Ryu

Research and Development Center, GALIM Information Technology, Korea**
Database and Bioinformatics Laboratory, Chungbuk National University, Korea
mjlee@galimit.com**
{ehkim, khryu}@dblab.chungbuk.ac.kr

Abstract. With the increasing expansion of network scale, users consume much cost for network that is composed of various network environments. In this paper, we propose a dynamic network management system employing the management program actively generating facilities in order to reduce the cost and time of system development. The proposed system consists of basic components for real time network management and Automatic Generation Technique of Network Components (AG-NC) in order to actively support information generation for network management objects through these basic components. The basic components includes configuration management, performance management, and fault management. AG-NC includes NE Basic Info Handler, MIB Handler, Template Handler, and Operation Handler. This system is able to generate a network management program with SNMP manager using the information of network objects. Our system actively generates network objects in an automatic manner instead of the manual manner of the existing systems. Finally, we can make the network structure expansion because the development time and cost of the network management program can be reduced dramatically through our system.

1 Introduction

Due to internet development with spread of the Web, most information systems are constructed based on the network environment connected with various network devices. The Network management has become important because the network structure is complex and growing fast. The beginning of network management is how to catch the connection status of end-to-end network using ICMP (Internet Control Message Protocol). However, it requires the information of network objects such as node, interface, and service rather than the simple status of the network. In addition, we need a standard network management scheme to manage network in a common way for the different network devices. IETF (Internet Engineering Task Force) made SNMP (Simple Network Management Protocol) [1] as standardization for easy internet management. It has been broadly used for most internet managements until now. Its advantages were easiness of implementation and interoperability. Therefore,

---

* This research was supported by ETRI and the MIC (Ministry of Information and Communication), Korea, under the ITRC (Information Technology Research Center) support program supervised by the IITA (Institute of Information Technology Assessment).
*** Corresponding author.

it exposed many limitations in network management and operation in the SNMP-based network management as high-speed telecommunication network appeared.

In this paper, we propose a dynamic network management system that automates the generation of information for management of network objects. The proposed system can generate a network management program automatically using information that has been provided along with the network equipments and SNMP library. Thus, we can make the network structure expansion while reducing the development time and cost of the network management program dramatically through proposed system.

This paper is organized as the following. In Section 2, we briefly review related work and describe their weaknesses. We introduce the proposed system architecture in Section 3. We describe the result of analysis of experiment through our system in Section 4, followed by the conclusion which summarizes our contributions and discusses future work in Section 5.

2 Related Work

SNMP has many advantages like easy implementation and a simple structure. However, the high-speed telecommunication network enlarges volume of network and makes structure of network complex. Therefore it becomes more difficult that we manage various network devices and hosting systems. Especially, network management application development is more difficult. The network management application should orchestrate network management objects automatically.

In order to complement the disadvantages of the SNMP-based network management system, many researchers have applied XML as a scheme to transfer and process large amount of data generated from a broad network [2], [3] effectively. These researches are to express managed information using XML and transfer these XML documents by HTTP [3], [4]. Moreover, when data is stored in database or processed by user application, it uses XML standardization [5].

Web based structure accelerates lots of new application programs by providing various kinds of data which was distributed in the internet and platform-independent easily. Therefore, there is a number of researches integrating existing different managed protocols and tools by applying web techniques into the network management or system management [6], [7], [8], [9]. However, the researches do not concentrate on management as they are SNMP agent, and depend on manual work in order to develop a network management program. Therefore, it requires expensive cost and time for developing a network management program. Also, a network manager spends a lot of time on modifying errors. Moreover, commercial network management systems such as OpenView [10], and MRTG [11] generates network management program manually.

This paper focuses on how to solve the problems that increase the cost and time in development of network management applications. Whenever changes happen in the network, the network manager must modify or create a new management application to manage network management objects. Therefore this works increases the cost and time for developing network management application and distributing the network management application to the newly added network devices. We need a tool to generate management program automatically for the newly added network management objects.

In this paper, we present a system which can develop network management object management program automatically. When we try to develop the management program for the newly added network management objects, the proposed system is able to reduce network development cost and time because it uses and stores common and frequent information.

3 Architecture of Dynamic Network Management System

The proposed system consists of Configuration Management, Fault Management, Performance Management, AG-NC ([12], [13]), SNMP API, and Database interface for managing complex network widely as Fig. 1.

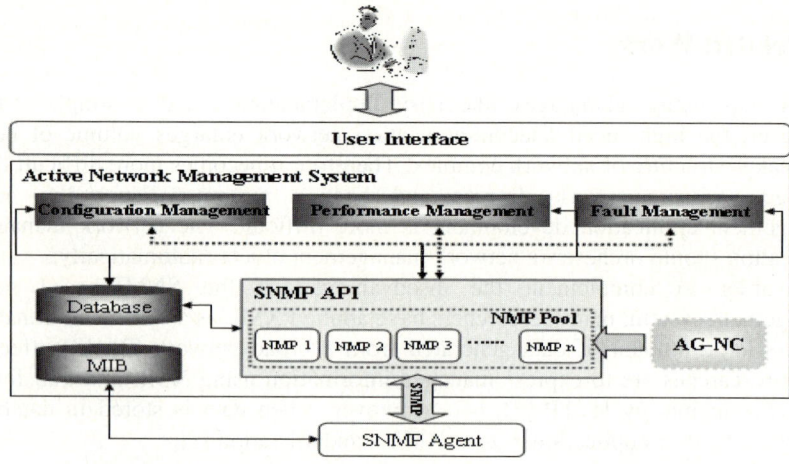

Fig. 1. Overall architecture of dynamic network management system

3.1 Configuration Management

Configuration Management takes charge of managing network equipments and all contents configure of network equipments in network. The network manager manages group unit classifying departments or regions of department configuring network. We need to manage node configuration information such as *sysDescr, sysObjectID, sysName, sysContact, sysLocation, and sysServices* and interface information such as *ifDescr, ifType, ifMTU, ifSpeed, ifPhyAddress, ifAdminStatus, and ifOperStatus*.

3.2 Performance Management

Performance Management can optimize traffic performance of network through adjustment design of network by monitoring status occurring in the network. In here, Network manager can accomplish node, interface, and service management. First, node performance management is managed by CPU and Memory usages, and if collected performance value over set up threshold, then node performance management can generate a TCA (Threshold Crossing Alert). The TCA is control attribute for performance management that information can identify occurring status from network management object. Second, we use data such as interface input usage, input throughput, input error rate, and input discard rate for interface performance management. Finally, service performance management manages by using status, node, and interface information of current network service.

3.3 Fault Management

Fault Management takes charge of supporting information in real time that automatically monitor fault about node, interface, and service in network. The proposed system divides into four levels as follows. First, critical level is a serious fault which causes serious problem in the system. Second, major level is important fault which causes important problem in the system and occur problem in operation of network. Third, minor level is general fault, which causes problem in the system, but the operation of network is normal. Lastly, warning level is just notice, which need a system check for operation of network.

3.4 AG-NC

Fig. 2 shows inner components relationship of AG-NC. In order to generate network management program automatically, AG-NC consists of NE Basic Info Handler, MIB Handler, Template Handler, and Operation Handler.

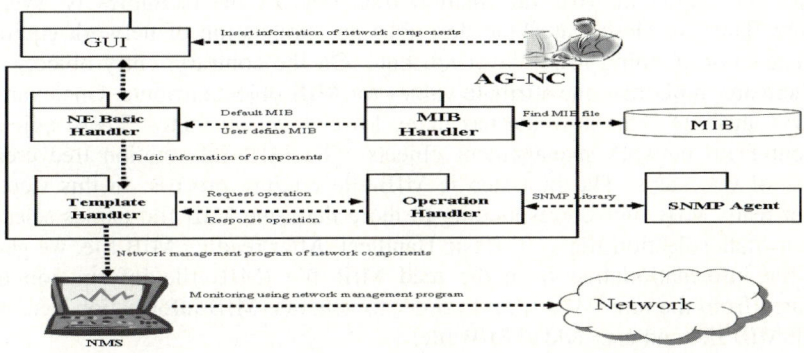

Fig. 2. Inner components relationship of AG-NC

The functions of these components in AG-NC are described in detail in the next section.

A. NE Basic Info Handler

This component takes charge of storing and creating basic information of network management objects. In order to create basic information, we need some information. First, a class name of new network management program and program name of network management objects. Second, a file name of MIB that network manager uses to specify network management objects. Third, object name for the specific network management object. Fourth, acceptance or rejection of method for set operation of SNMP. Finally, acceptance or rejection of method switching over from a specific numeric data contained in MIB to character data. We will generate a network management program based on this information.

B. Operation Handler
Operation handler manages operations for SNMP execution. SNMP protocol has four kinds of operation such as Get, Get Next, Set, and Trap. Get operation reads management information such as status and run-time of network management object. When the operation handler reads information of a specific component, a manager as a sender of message enquires of an agent small application which marks the network management objects. Get Next operation takes lower layer information from the hierarchical tree structure. Set operation has the control of handling MIB of the network management object. The manager can initiate or reconfigure network management object by requesting to agent according to application. Trap operation is threshold or event which is reported to the manager.

C. MIB Handler
MIB handler takes charge of building MIB information tree to generate network management application. MIB information tree makes a hierarchy of MIB objects. MIB handler extracts identification values of MIB objects which is a target for the network management application from MIB information tree, and builds a tree after parsing the content of MIB file. The MIB objects are managed and classified by single and entry objects single object means that MIB object attribute corresponds to one attribute value in MIB information tree. One of the examples is 'sysDescr' attribute. This 'sysDescr' attribute describes an explanation of network equipment, also it has not anything lower layer attribute. On the contrary, entry objects means that there are more than one attribute values for MIB object attribute. One example is 'ifEntry' attribute. This attribute has many lower layer attributes. These objects are different from network management objects. The MIB information tree creates a process of two steps. The first step is MIB file reading process. In this step, MIB handler reads MIB files corresponding to more than one MIB file names selected in the basic data selection step (NE Basic Handler). After reading MIB file, we generate MIB file information tree from the read MIB file (MIB file information tree is generated from the read MIB file). In order to generate MIB information tree, we use default MIB file and user-added MIB file.

D. Template Handler
Template Handler supports formal information such as template header and template tail, which are commonly used in generated network management application. In the template header, name of network management application and necessary application variables are defined. In the template tail, source code that configures method for debugging is defined.

The proposed framework generates an automatic application with not only single objects, but also entry objects, and also the generation process of network management application for them is the same.

4 Experimental Analysis

In this section, we evaluate the efficiency of the generated application through our system. Efficiency of application is how exactly the information is obtained from various kinds of network objects.

4.1 Analysis Result

We assume that it is impossible to collect the information of the network objects in network with manually generated network management program and automatically generated network management in AG-NC because network management system manages status of network in real time. It is because the volume of traffic which is input every time is different by characteristics of network. Therefore we would compare the network management program which is created manually with which is generated automatically in the same network environment and for the same network object. We would also evaluate the efficiency, development time and error rate. Also, we would analyze the reliability of proposed system through the test about how exactly to manage network status of network object. In order to verify the generated network management program between our system and the existing method (manual manner), we get information from one network objects as shown in Table 1.

Table 1. Example of Network object

Object Name	Network Object Description
CISCO Router	Cisco Internetwork Operating System Software IOS (tm) C3550 Software (C3550-I5Q3L2-M), Version 12.1(13)EA1, RELEASE SOFTWARE (fc1) Copyright (c) 1986-2003 by cisco Systems, Inc. Compiled Tue 04-Mar-03 03:10 by yenanh

For CICSO Router object, we must analyze MIB of 1416 lines and total 5705 lines. Total 5705 lines mean that 4868 lines are common module and 839 lines are only CISCO module. In here, we are considering CISCO module. In order to verify the result of CISCO module, we repeat test step followed by error modification until no error existing. Next, we employ this module in the network management system. The verifying processing terminates when this module monitor CISCO Router normally. Otherwise, we do again the same process.

Fig. 3 shows the test results of two methods. That is, the existing method consumes much time about one week for analyzing total lines and 3 days for developing only CISCO module. There we can reduce 36% totally generating time of network management program through our system.

We obtain the result that the collected information from CISCO Router object using the generated network management program through our system has no errors. Also, we can reduce consuming cost for maintenance and management of network management system. These results verified confidence of our system. Fig. 4 shows the monitoring results of input/output traffics of CISCO Router connecting to the network using generated network program through our system. Where upper line is output traffic and lower line is input traffic.

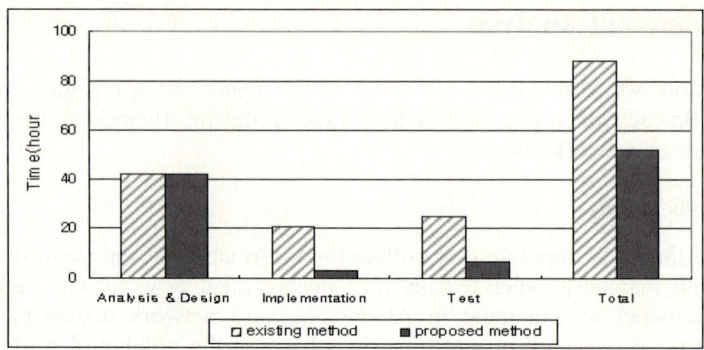

Fig. 3. Development Time compare between the manual manner and the proposed method

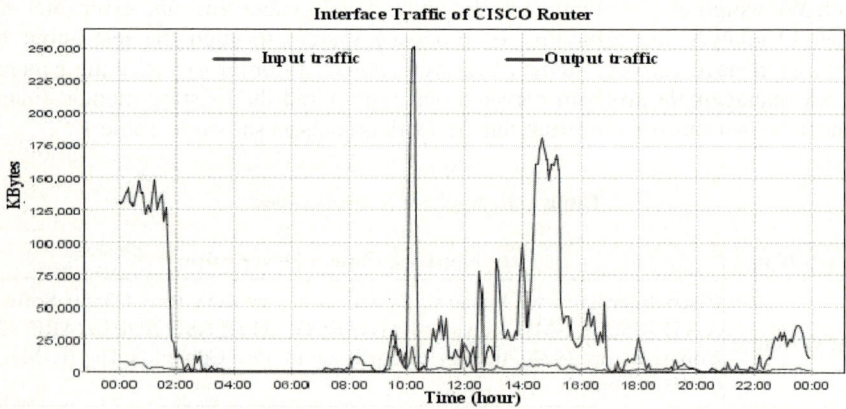

Fig. 4. Result of Input/Output traffics of CISCO Router using generated network program through our system

5 Conclusion

The existing SNMP based network management systems create the network management program manually for network objects, when adding new network device or network components to the network. Moreover, it can cause large amount of overhead in developing network management program because of developing new network management object (e.g. network device) continuance.

Therefore, we proposed a dynamic network management system that considers automatically network management program in the paper. The proposed system consists of basic components for real time network management and AG-NC in order to actively support information generation for network management objects through these basic components. The basic components includes configuration management, performance management, and fault management. AG-NC includes NE Basic Info Handler, MIB Handler, Template Handler, and Operation Handler. It can create an automatic network management program that accomplishes network management with SNMP manager using information of network objects. As a result, we show capability to reduce time and cost for maintaining network with evaluation of time consumed and error rate in the generation of network management program by applying in an actual network environment.

Our dynamic network management system contributes not only an objects automatically generating network program, but also improves accuracy of network program.

References

1. Stallings, W.: SNMP, SNMPv2, SNMPv3, and RMON 1 and 2. 3rd edn, Addison-Wesley, Reading, MA, USA (1999)
2. Ju, H.T., Han, S.H., Oh, Y.J., Yoon, J.H., Lee, H.J., Hong, J.W.: An Embedded Web Server Architecture for XML-Based Network Management. the IEEE/IFIP Network Operations and Management Symposium, Florence, Italy (2002) 5-18
3. Kim, Y.D., Cho, K.Y., Heo, J.H., Cheon, J.K., Cho, S.H.: Network management system by using transfer SNMP. Proc. of KNOM Conference, Taejeonn, May (2001) 102-106
4. Barillaud, F., Deri, L., Fedirum, M.: Network Management Using Internet Technologies. Proc. IEEE/IFIP International Symp. On Integrated Network Management, San Diego CA (1997)
5. Deri, L.: HTTP-Based SNMP and CMIP Network Management. Internet Draft, IBM Zurich Research Laboratory (1996)
6. Pell, H.A., Mellquist, P. E.: Web-Based System and Network Management. Internet Draft, Hewlett-Packard (1996)
7. WBEM : http://wbem.freerange.com
8. Perkins, D., McGinnis, E.: Understanding SNMP MIBs, Prentice-Hall (1997)
9. Case, J.(et al): Management Information Base for Version 2 of the Simple Network Management Protocol. IETF, RFC-1907 (1996)
10. OpenView : http://www.openview.com
11. MRTG : http://people.ee.ethz.ch/~oetiker/webtools/mrtg
12. Lee. M. J.: A Network Management System Based on Active Program Generation. Ph.D. Thesis, Chungbuk National University, Korea (2005)
13. Kim, E. H., Lee, M. J., Ryu, K. H.: An Automatic Generation Technique of Network Components for Dynamic Network Management: International Conference on Intelligent Computing, China, (2006)

QoS Multicast Routing Based on Particle Swarm Optimization

Jing Liu, Jun Sun, and Wenbo Xu

Center of Intelligent and High Performance Computing,
School of Information Technology, Southern Yangtze University
No. 1800, Lihudadao Road, Wuxi,
214122 Jiangsu, China
{liujing_novem, sunjun_wx, xwb_sytu}@hotmail.com

Abstract. The purpose of this paper is to solve Quality-of-Service (QoS) multicast routing problem by Particle Swarm Optimization (PSO). The QoS multicast routing optimization problem was transformed into a quasi-continuous problem by constructing a new integer coding and the constrained conditions in the problem were solved by the method of penalty function. The experimental results indicated that the proposed algorithm could converge to the optimal on near-optimal solution with less computational cost. It also appeared that PSO outperformed Genetic Algorithm on QoS the tested multicast routing problem.

Keywords: Quality-of Service, Multicast Routing, Particle swarm optimization.

1 Introduction

Multicast services have been used by various continuous media applications. The provision of Quality-of-Service (QoS) guarantees is of utmost importance for the development of the multicast services. Multicast routing has continued to be a very important research issue in the areas of networks and distributed systems. QoS multicast routing relies on state parameters specifying resource availability at network nodes or links, and uses them to find paths with enough free resources. An efficient allocation of network resources to satisfy the different QoS requirements is the primary goal of QoS-based multicast routing. However the inter-dependency and conflication among multiple QoS parameters makes the problem difficult. It has been demonstrated that it is NP-Complete to find a feasible multicast tree with two independent additive path constraints.

With introduction of QoS to network service, the multicast problem becomes more challenging. The QoS requirements can be classified into link constraints (e.g., bandwidth), path constraints (e.g., end to end delay) and tree constraints (e.g., delay-jitter). Generally, heuristics are employed to solve this NP-complete problem. Some GAs has been used to solve the problem from different aspects [8]. GA reassures a higher chance of reaching a global optimum by starting with multiple random search points and considering several candidate solutions simultaneously.

A recent development in optimization theory sees the emergence of Swarm Intelligence, a category of stochastic search methods for solving Global Optimization

(GO) problems. Particle Swarm Optimization (PSO) method is one of its member. It was originally proposed by J. Kennedy as a simulation of social behavior of bird flock, and it was initially introduced as an optimization method in 1995 ([9]). PSO is related with Artificial life, and specifically to swarm theories, and also with Evolutionary Computation, especially Evolutionary Strategy and GA. It can be easily implemented and it is computationally inexpensive, since its memory and CPU speed requirements are low. PSO has been proved to be an efficient method for many GO problems and in some cases it does not suffer the difficulties encountered by GA [1].

PSO was originally proposed to solve the continuous functions optimization. So far, it has rarely been used to discrete Combinatory Optimization Problems (COP). The purpose of this paper is to solve QoS multicast routing problem via PSO, which is an attempt to explore the applicability of PSO to COPs. The rest of the paper is organized as follows. In Section 2, the network model of QoS multicast routing problem is introduced. The origin and the development of PSO is described in Section 3. Section 4 is our proposed PSO-based QoS multicast routing algorithm. The experiment results are given in Section 5 and the paper is concluded in Section 6.

2 Network Model

A network is usually represented as a weighted digraph G = (V, E), where V denotes the set of nodes and E denotes the set of communication links connecting the nodes. |V| and |E| denote the number of nodes and links in the network, respectively, Without loss of generality, only digraphs are considered in which there exists at most one link between a pair of ordered nodes [7].

Let $s \in V$ be source node of a multicast tree, and $M \subseteq \{V - \{s\}\}$ be a set of end nodes of the multicast tree. Let R be the positive weight and R+ be the nonnegative weight. For any link $e \in |E|$, we can define the some QoS metrics: delay function delay (e): $E \to R$, cost function cost (e): $E \to R$, bandwidth function bandwidth (e): $E \to R$; and delay jitter function delay-jitter (e): $E \to R^+$. Similarly, for any node $n \in V$, one can also define some metrics: delay function delay (n): $V \to R$, cost function cost (n): $V \to R$, delay jitter function delay-jitter (n): $V \to R^+$ and packet loss function packet-loss (n): $V \to R^+$. We also use $T(s,M)$ to denote a multicast tree, which has the following relations:

$$delay(p(s,T)) = \sum_{e \in p(s,T)} delay(e) + \sum_{n \in p(s,T)} delay(n) \qquad (1)$$

$$cost(T(s,M)) = \sum_{e \in p(s,M)} cost(e) + \sum_{n \in p(s,M)} cost(n) \qquad (2)$$

$$bandwidth(p(s,T)) = \min(bandwidth(e)), e \in p(s,T) \qquad (3)$$

$$delay - jitter(p(s,T)) = \sum_{e \in p(s,T)} delay - jitter(e) + \sum_{n \in p(s,T)} delay - jitter(n) \qquad (4)$$

$$packet - loss(p(s,T)) = 1 - \prod_{n \in p(s,T)} (1 - packet - loss(n)) \qquad (5)$$

where $p(s,T)$ denotes the path from source s to end node t to T(s, M). With QoS requirements, the problem can be represented as finding a multicast tree T(s, M) satisfying the following constraints:

1. Delay Constraint: delay(p(s,T))≤D;
2. Bandwidth Constraint: bandwidth(p(s,T))≥B ;
3. Delay-jitter Constraint: delay-jitter(p(s,T))≤J ;
4. Packet-loss Constraint: packet-loss(p(s,T))≤L;

QoS multicast routing problem is a NP-complete hard problem, which is also a challenging problem for high-performance networks.

3 Particle Swarm Optimization

Particle Swarm Optimization (PSO), originally proposed by J. Kennedy and R. Eberhart [5], has become a most fascinating branch of evolutionary computation. The underlying motivation for the development of PSO algorithm was social behavior of animals such as bird flocking, fish schooling, and swarm theory. Like genetic algorithm (GA), PSO is a population-based random search technique but that outperforms GA in many practical applications, particularly in nonlinear optimization problems [1]. In the standard PSO model, each individual is treated as a volume-less particle in the D-dimensional space, with the position and velocity of ith particle represented as $X_i = (X_{i1}, X_{i2}, \cdots, X_{iD})$ and $V_i = (V_{i1}, V_{i2}, \cdots, V_{iD})$ [10]. The particles move according to the following equation:

$$V_{id} = w*V_{id} + c_1*rand(\cdot)*(P_{id} - X_{id}) + c_2*Rand(\cdot)*(P_g - X_{id}) \tag{6}$$

$$X_{id} = X_{id} + V_{id} \tag{7}$$

where c_1 and c_2 are positive constant and rand() and Rand() are two random functions in the range of [0,1]. Parameter w is the inertia weight introduced to accelerate the convergence speed of the PSO. Vector $P_i = (P_{i1}, P_{i2}, \cdots, P_{iD})$ is the best previous position (the position giving the best fitness value) of particle i called **pbest**, and vector $P_g = (P_{g1}, P_{g2}, \cdots, P_{gD})$ is the position of the best particle among all the particles in the population and called **gbest**.

Since the origin of PSO, many researchers have been devoted to improving its performance, and therefore, many revised versions of PSO have been proposed, among which the most important are those proposed in ([2][3][4][5][6]). These various improved versions, generally speaking, can enhance the convergence performance and the search ability of PSO considerably.

4 The Proposed Algorithm

In this section, we proposed our PSO-based QoS Multicast Routing Algorithm.

4.1 Coding

The coding is one of important problems to solve the QoS multicast routing problem using Particle Swarm Optimization (PSO) algorithm. It involves encoding a path serial into a feasible solution (or a position) in the search space of the particle. In this paper, we design a new integral coding scheme for PSO so that it can be employed to solve the discrete combinatory optimization problem. In our scheme, the number of paths (no loop) reaching each end node $t \in M$ worked out. With the number of end nodes denoted by $|M|$, the number of paths to end node i is represented as $n_i (1 \leq i \leq |M|)$. The paths to end node i can be numbered by an integer variable $t_i (1 \leq i \leq |M|)$, where $t_i \in [1, n_i](1 \leq i \leq |M|)$. Therefore we can obtain a $|M|$-dimensional integral vector $(t_1, t_2, \cdots, t_{|M|})$ denoting a possible path serial with each component t_i varying in the interval $[1, n_i]$. In the PSO for Qos Multicasting routing problem, such an integral vector represents the position of the particle and the combinatory optimization problem is reduced to a $|M|$-dimensional integral programming.

The initial population is a matrix with row vectors representing particles' positions. The dimension of a row vector is the number of end nodes. The value of the ith component of a row vector denotes the number of a path from the source node to end node i, which is initialized by randomly select an integer number in the interval, $[1, n_i]$.

4.2 Fitness Function

In our proposed method, the fitness unction is defined as :

$$f(x) = \frac{\omega_1}{cost(T(s,M))}(\omega_2 * f(d) + \omega_3 * f(j) + \omega_4 * f(p)) \tag{8}$$

where ω_1, ω_2, ω_3 and ω_4 is the weight of cost, delay, delay-jitter and packet loss, respectively; f(d), f(j) and f(p) are defined as:

$$f(d) = \prod_{t \in M} F_d(delay(p(s,t)) - D), \tag{9}$$

$$F_d(delay(p(s,t)) - D) = \begin{cases} 1, delay\ (p(s,t)) < D \\ \alpha, delay\ (p(s,t)) \geq D \end{cases} \tag{10}$$

$$f(j) = \prod_{t \in M} F_j(delay\_jitter(p(s,t)) - J), \tag{11}$$

$$F_j(delay\_jitter\ (p(s,t)) - J) = \begin{cases} 1, delay\_jitter\ (p(s,t)) < J \\ \beta, delay\_jitter\ (p(s,t)) \geq J \end{cases} \tag{12}$$

$$f(p) = \prod_{t \in M} F_p(packet\_loss(p(s,t)) - L), \tag{13}$$

$$F_p(packet\_loss(p(s,t)) - L) = \begin{cases} 1, packet\_loss(p(s,t)) < L \\ \sigma, packet\_loss(p(s,t)) \geq L \end{cases} \tag{14}$$

where $F_d(x)$, $F_j(x)$ and $F_p(x)$ are penalty functions for delay, delay-jitter and packet loss, respectively, and α, β and σ are positive numbers smaller than 1.

4.3 Implementation of PSO on the Problem

PSO-based QoS Multicast Routing Algorithm
Input: The dimension of the particles' positions (equal to the number of end nodes); Population size; Parameters of the network model.
Output: The best fitness value after PSO executes for MAXITER iterations; optimal multicast tree.
The proposed algorithm is described as follows:
1. Initialize the population;
2. **for** t=1 to MAXITER
3. Compute the fitness value of each particle according to (17);
4. Update the personal best position P_i;
5. Update the global best position P_g;
6. **for** each particle in the population
7. Update each component of the particle's velocity and position by (9) and (10) and adjust the component t_i as an integer in $[1, n_i]$;
8. **endfor**
9. **endfor**

4.4 Loop-Deletion Operation

Implementation of PSO on the problem yields an optimal multicast tree denoted by a path serial. The path serial is a $|M|$-dimensional integral vector with each component being the path number of a path from the source code to corresponding end node. To make the multicast tree a feasible solution of the problem, we must delete loops existing in it. The operation of loop deletion is as follows.

Loop-deletion Operation:
1. **for** i=1 to $|M|$
2. **for** j=1 to I+1
3. **if** there exists loop between ith and jth path of the path serial;
4. Compare the costs of the routs that constitute the loop and delete the more expensive rout;
5. **endif**
6. **endfor**
7. **endfor**

By the above operation, we can obtain a non-loop optimal multicast tree with lowest cost.

5 Experiment

To test the performance of the PSO-based Multicast Routing Algorithm, we use the network model in Figure 1 as our tested problem. In the experiments, it is assumed that all the end nodes of multicast satisfy the same set of QoS constraints without regard to the characteristics of the nodes. The characteristics of the edges described by a quaternion (d, j, b, c) with the components representing delay, delay-jitter, bandwidth and cost, respectively. For performance comparison, Genetic Algorithm (GA) was applied to test the problem. The experiments were realized with Visual C++6.0 on Windows XP and executed on a PC with 2.10GHz-CPU and 256MB-RAM.

The experiment configuration is as follows. The population size for PSO is 50 and maximum number of iterations is for all three algorithms and the number of the end nodes is 5. The fitness function is formula (8) with $\omega_1=1$, $\omega_2=0.5$, $\omega_3=0.5$, $\omega_4=0.3$, $\alpha=0.5$, $\beta=0.5$, $\sigma=0.5$. There are 23 nodes in the network model (Figure 1), and we assume node 0 to be the source node; the set of end nodes to be M={4,9,14,19,22}. The inertia weight w in PSO decreases linearly from 0.9 to 0.4 over a running and acceleration coefficients c1 and c2 are fixed at 2.0. For GA, the population size is 100 and binary tournament selection is used. The probability of crossover operation is 0.2 and that of mutation operation is 0.002.

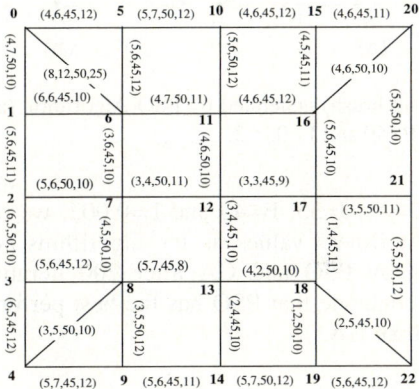

Fig. 1. A network model as the testing paradigm in our experiments

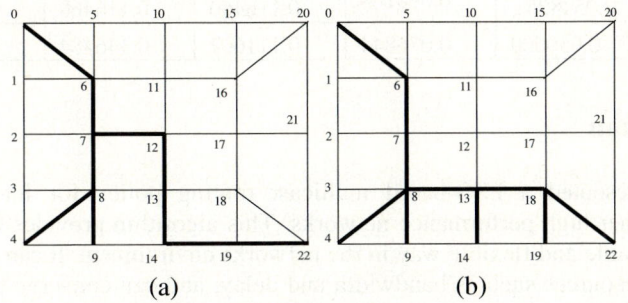

Fig. 2. Multicast trees (broad-brush) generated by Genetic Algorithm. (a). D=20, J=30, B=40 and L=0.002; (b). D=25, J=35, B=40 and L=0.002.

We adopt two sets of constraints in the experiments:

1. When delay constraint D=20, delay-jitter constraint J=30, bandwidth constraint B=40 and packet loss constraint L=0.002, the multicast trees generated by the three algorithms are shown in Figure 2(a), Figure 3(a) and Figure 4(a), respectively.
2. When delay constraint D=25, delay-jitter constraint J=35 and bandwidth constraint B=40 and packet loss constraint L=0.002, the multicast trees generated by the three algorithms are shown in Figure 2(b), Figure 3(b) and Figure 4(b), respectively.

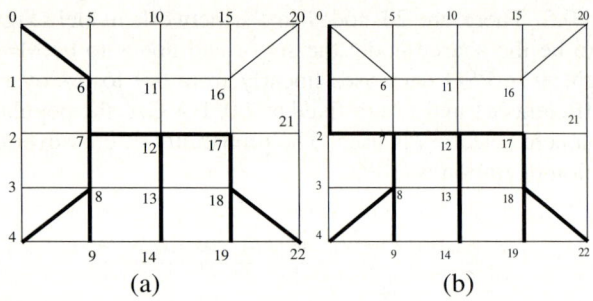

Fig. 3. Multicast trees (broad-brush) generated by PSO Algorithm. (a). D=20, J=30, B=40 and L=0.002; (b). D=25, J=35, B=40 and L=0.002.

For constraints that D=25, J=35, B=40 and L=0.002, we recorded in Table 1 the dynamic changes of best fitness values as the algorithms are executing. The best fitness values generated by PSO and GA after 200 iterations are 0.223214 and 0.116460. Thus we can conclude that PSO has the best performance and could yield the better multicast tree than GA.

Table 1. Dyanmic changes of best fitness values of GA, PSO and QPSO

Iter	20	50	100	150	200
GA	0.054825	0.098168	0.116460	0.116460	0.116460
PS	0.050000	0.076844	0.111607	0.146484	0.223214

6 Conclusion

The paper presented a PSO-based multicast routing policy for Internet, mobile network or other high-performance networks. This algorithm provides QoS-sensitive paths in a scalable and flexible way in the networks environment. It can also optimize the network resources such as bandwidth and delay, and can converge to the optimal on near-optimal solution within fewer iterations. The incremental rate of computational cost can close to polynomial and is less than exponential rate. The availability and efficiency of PSO on the problem have been verified by experiments. We also test for performance comparison, and the experiment results show that PSO outperforms GA on QoS the tested multicast routing problem. Our future work will focus on using PSO to solve QoS multicast routing in network environment with uncertain parameter.

References

1. P. J. Angeline.: Evolutionary Optimization Versus Particle Swarm Optimization: Philosophy and Performance Differences. Evolutionary Programming VII, , Springer, *Lecture Notes in Computer Science* 1447 (1998) 601-610
2. F. Van den Bergh, A. P. Engelbrecht.: A New Locally Convergent Particle Swarm Optimizer. IEEE International Conference on systems, Man and Cybernetics (2002)
3. J. Kennedy.: Sereotyping: Improving Particle Swarm Performance with Cluster Analysis. Proc. Congress on Evolutionary Computation (2000) 1507-1512
4. P. N. Suganthan.: Particle Swarm Optimizer with Neighborhood Operator. Congress on Evolutionary Computation (1999) 1958-1962
5. M. Clerc.: The Swarm and Queen: Towards a Deterministic and Adaptive Particle Swarm Optimization. Congress on Evolutionary Computation (1999) 1951-1957.
6. M. Clerc and J. Kennedy.: The Particle Swarm: Explosion, Stability, and Convergence in a Multi-dimensional Complex Space. IEEE Transaction on Evolutionary Computation (2002) no. 6, 58-73
7. Roch A. Guerin and Ariel Orda.: QoS Routing in Networks with Inaccurate Information: Theory and Algorithms. IEEE/ACM. Trans. On Networking (1999) no.3, vol.7 350-363.
8. Abhishek Roy, Sajal K. Das.: QM^2RP: a QoS-based Mobile Multicast Routing Protocol Using Multi-objective Genetic Algorithm. Kluwer Academic Publishers Hingham (2004), MA, USA, vol. 10, 271-286
9. J. Kennedy, R. C. Eberhart.: Particle Swarm Optimization. IEEE Conference on Neural Networks, IV (1995) Piscataway, NJ 1942-1948
10. Y. Shi and R. Eberhart.: Empirical Study of Particle Swarm Optimization. Congress on Evolutionary Computation (1999) 1945-1950

Evolutionary Search of Optimal Features

Manuel del Valle[1], Luis F. Lago-Fernández[1,2], and Fernando J. Corbacho[1,2]

[1] Escuela Politécnica Superior, Universidad Autónoma de Madrid,
28049 Madrid, Spain
[2] Cognodata Consulting, C/ Caracas 23, 28010 Madrid, Spain

Abstract. In data mining problems, the selection of appropriate input transformations is often crucial to obtain good solutions. The purpose of such transformations is to project the original attribute space onto a new one that, being closer to the problem structure, allows for more compact and interpretable solutions. We address the problem of automatic construction of input transformations in classification problems. We use an evolutionary approach to search the space of input transformations and a linear method to perform classification on the new feature space. Our assumption is that once a proper data representation, which captures the problem structure, is found, even a linear classifier may find a good solution. Linear methods are free from local minima, while the use of a representation space closer to the problem structure will in general provide more compact and interpretable solutions. We test our method using an artificial problem and a real classification problem from the UCI database. In both cases we obtain low error solutions that in addition are compact and interpretable.

1 Introduction

In a data mining problem, one tries to fit a model to known data in order to extract useful patterns [1]. Common modeling methods include induction of decision trees, artificial neural networks, support vector machines, etc. Any of them may perform better than the others for a subset of particular problems. However, independently of the method used, a previous data preprocessing step is essential in any data mining problem, and to a great extent it is determinant of the quality of the final result. Data preprocessing is usually driven by a human analyst, who constructs a new data representation, derived from the initial problem data, based on a priori knowledge of the problem structure. Starting from the set of original input attributes, new features are constructed by selecting different subsets of attributes (input selection) and transformations to be applied on them (transformation selection). These two processes can be automated to some degree by heuristic search, which is related to the fields of *feature selection* [2,3,4] and *feature construction* [5,6,7,8,9,10,11].

In this paper we focus on *pattern classification* problems [12], where each of the examples in a set of data items must be assigned to one of several classes. We emphasize the preprocessing phase, aiming at the automatic construction of a data representation space that is close to the problem structure and simplifies as much as possible the subsequent learning stages. The underlying hypothesis is that, once a proper representation has been found for the problem data, classification can be performed by a linear method. So we concentrate on the automatic construction of a new set of *optimal features*, defined as those that allow for a linear solution of the problem.

We explore this approach using evolutionary computation to search the representation space for the optimal features. A given set of newly constructed attributes is evaluated by computing the classification error rate of a linear classifier that uses the attributes as input. The error rate is then used by the search algorithm to find the best set of attributes. In particular, we use *genetic programming* (GP) [13] in combination with linear discriminant analysis (LDA) [12]. We apply this method to two different classification problems. The first one is a synthetic problem in two dimensions, which in the original input space presents a complex overlap between the two classes [14]. The proposed methodology is able to find different representations, based on the trigonometric functions, that allow linear classification, while other classification algorithms fail to find a solution. The second problem is the well known BUPA Liver Disorder from the UCI database [15]. Our algorithm finds error competitive solutions, that in addition are more compact and easier to interpret than other solutions in the literature [8].

Evolutionary approaches have been widely used in the field of feature construction [7,8,9,16,17]. Our approach differs from previous ones in the use of a linear method to perform classification. This presents some advantages. First, linear methods do not suffer from local minima, and the optimal solution can often be found analytically. Second, a linear projection will be in general easier to interpret than a non-linear mapping. Finally, using a data representation that is closer to the problem structure usually produces more compact solutions, avoiding overfitting and in turn allowing for better generalization. The use of a linear classifier in combination with evolutionary search of the input transformation space was first explored by [18]. They used genetic algorithms to find new features that consisted of polynomial combinations of the original problem attributes. In a previous research we extended their work by allowing different bases to be searched by the genetic algorithm [14]. We showed that the use of trigonometric functions can be useful when the problem has certain hidden periodicity. In the present work, we replace the genetic algorithms by genetic programming, which is a more powerful language to construct symbolic functions. In addition, in order to control the explosive combinatorial power intrinsic to the GP search, we introduce a new complexity control mechanism.

2 Implementation Details

We use GP to evolve a population of individuals, each one consisting of a set of transformations that, applied to the original input data, define a new set of features. For any of such individuals, classification of the whole training set is performed by a linear classifier that uses the new features as input. The classification error rate, combined with a complexity term that favors simple transformations, determines the fitness of the individual in the evolutionary process.

2.1 Evolutionary Search of Optimal Transformations

Automatic feature selection and construction are computationally expensive processes. When the number of input variables is too large, an exhaustive search of the transformation space is not feasible. In such a situation, alternatives based on evolutionary computation are a good choice. They provide a global search mechanism that avoids exhaustive search. In this context, genetic programming (GP) appears particularly useful, as it provides a powerful language to construct and evolve symbolic expressions using a very intuitive tree representation [13].

In our genetic program, each individual defines a new set of features, and is given by a tree-shaped expression constructed from the following set of node operators: $\{F, +, -, *, /, sin, cos, log\}$. The node F is reserved for the tree root. It has an arbitrary number of descendants, n, which determines the number of new features. The set $\{+, -, *, /\}$ consists of binary operators that perform arithmetic operations, and the set $\{sin, cos, log\}$ consists of unitary operators that perform the sine, the cosine and the logarithm respectively. As terminal nodes, we allow any of the original variables, as well as some symbolic constants such as π. Figure 1 shows an example of the tree representation of a GP individual for a 2D problem.

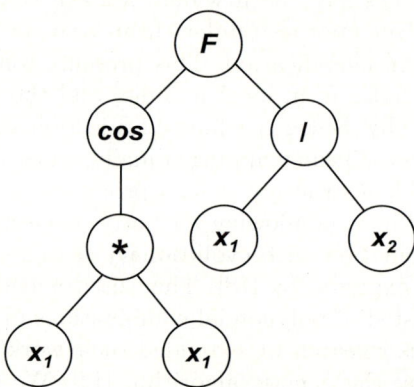

Fig. 1. Tree representation of a GP individual for a 2D problem for the variables x_1 and x_2. The number of new attributes is set to $n = 2$. The set of new features generated by this tree is $\{cosx_1^2, x_1/x_2\}$.

To perform the experiments, we use the BEAGLE Puppy library [19], configuring the genetic program parameters in a standard way. The evaluation of a GP individual, T, is performed by computing the following fitness function:

$$f(T) = (1 - \alpha)A(T) + \alpha(1 - C(T)) \qquad (1)$$

where $A(T)$ measures the accuracy of the linear classifier that uses the features in T; $C(T)$ measures the tree complexity; and the parameter α, which varies between 0 and 1, weights the balance between accuracy and complexity. The accuracy and complexity contributions to the fitness function are described below.

2.2 Accuracy

In order to compute the accuracy of a given GP individual T, we must classify the whole training set using the features defined in T. We use Linear Discriminant Analysis (LDA) to perform the classification. The classification error, $E(T)$, is calculated as the percentage of misclassified patterns, and it is used to calculate the accuracy contribution to the fitness function as follows:

$$A(T) = \frac{1 - E(T)}{1 + E(T)} \qquad (2)$$

This definition of $A(T)$ uses standardized error [13], which emphasizes the differences for higher accuracy values. The accuracy equals 1 when there is no classification error, and it is 0 when all the patterns are misclassified.

2.3 Complexity Control

When using GP for feature construction, some mechanism to control tree complexity must be considered. Otherwise the evolved trees become extremely complex, and provide features that overfit the training data given the classification method. This obviously reduces the generalization capabilities and must be avoided. Typical complexity control policies limit the maximum tree depth and the maximum number of nodes. The latter option is generally preferred [9], since the former tends to produce balanced trees of the maximum allowed depth.

We use both policies. First, we limit the maximum tree depth d. Second, we introduce a complexity term in the fitness function which penalizes trees with a high number of nodes. The complexity term $C(T)$ takes into account the ratio between the actual number of tree nodes and its maximum possible value. It is given by:

$$C(T) = \frac{N(T)}{n 2^{d-1}} \qquad (3)$$

where $N(T)$ is the number of nodes in the individual T which are at depth larger than 2; and n is the number of features in T. This complexity measure takes its minimum value of 0 for a minimal tree with $n + 1$ nodes and depth 1. Such a minimal tree represents a subset of n of the original input attributes. The maximum complexity value of 1 is given for a complete tree of depth d.

3 Test Problems

To illustrate our methodology, we show the results on two classification problems. The first one is a 2 class synthetic problem in a bidimensional input space. The original data representation makes the problem very difficult to solve for traditional learning methods. The second problem is the well known BUPA Liver Disorder from the UCI database [15].

Table 1. Three different sets of optimal features for the 2D synthetic problem. Each set is composed of 3 attributes that are used to classify the problem examples with LDA. The resulting projection coefficients are also shown.

	Att. 1	Att. 2	Att. 3
Set 1	$\sin\pi x \sin\pi y$	0	0
Coefs. 1	−8.66	0	0
Set 2	$\cos\pi(x+y)$-$\cos\pi(x-y)$	$\cos\pi(x+y)$-$\cos\pi(x-y)$	$\cos\pi(x-y)$-$\cos\pi(x-y)$
Coefs. 2	2.33	2.33	0
Set 3	$\cos\pi$	3.01	$\cos\pi(x+y)$-$\cos\pi(x-y)$
Coefs. 3	0	0	4.33

3.1 Synthetic Problem in Two Dimensions

The first problem consists of two classes, A and B, in a two-dimensional input space, given by the attributes x and y. It is constructed in such a way that (i) there exists an appropriate non-linear transformation that is able to separate the classes with no error; and (ii) in the original input space the classes present a very high overlap and, given the number of examples, seem to follow the same distribution (see figure 2, left). This last fact makes the problem difficult to solve for traditional learning algorithms, such as neural networks or decision trees, which provide errors close to 50% [14]. Class A patterns are defined in the following way:

$$(x,y) \in A \longleftrightarrow mod(int(x),2) = mod(int(y),2) \qquad (4)$$

where $int(x)$ is the integer part of x and $mod(x,2)$ is the remainder of $x/2$. Class B patterns are those that do not satisfy the equality in eq. 4. The two classes can be separated with no error using the transformation $z = \sin\pi x \sin\pi y$ (figure 2, right). However, as far as the number of patterns is small, it becomes quite complicated to discover the hidden structure.

We have applied the previous methodology to the problem, using the operators $\{+, -, *, /, sin, cos\}$. As terminal nodes we allow the two input variables x and y, the symbolic constant π, and randomly generated constants. We use populations of 1000 individuals, and perform evolution during 30 epochs. The number of new features associated to an individual is $n = 3$, and the complexity control parameter is set to $\alpha = 0.5$. In table 1 we present three different sets of optimal features obtained in three different runs, together with their associated projection coefficients. Note that LDA sets to 0 the coefficients for those features that do not contribute to the problem solution. Any of the three sets represents a transformation that allows for a linear separation of the problem. GP does not find a unique solution for this problem. Surprisingly, trigonometric equivalences are found by the algorithm. In fact, the attributes in sets 2 and 3 of the table are showing the equivalence $sinAsinB = (cos(A-B) - cos(A+B))/2$.

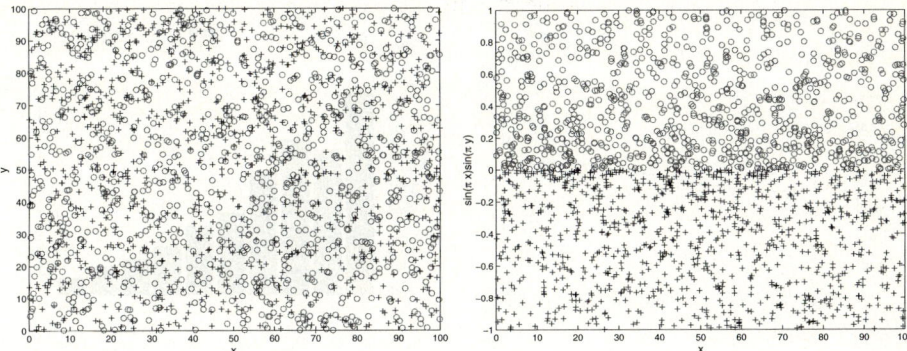

Fig. 2. Left. Input patterns for a problem with two classes and two attributes x and y. There are 1000 patterns of class A (circles) and 1000 patterns of class B (crosses). Apparently the two classes follow the same (uniform) distribution in the considered interval. Right. Class distributions in the new feature space $\{x, sin\pi x sin\pi y\}$.

Table 2. Three different sets of constructed attributes for the BUPA problem. Each set is composed of 4 attributes that are used to classify the problem examples with LDA. The resulting projection coefficients are also shown. The last column indicates the test error obtained for the attribute set.

	Att. 1	Att. 2	Att. 3	Att. 4	Error
Set 1	$log(n_2 + n_3)$	n_3	n_5	n_4	
Coefs. 1	-0.33	0.86	-0.28	-0.78	0.29
Set 1	n_4	$log(n_6) + n_6 + n_2 + n_5/n_6$	n_5	n_3	
Coefs. 1	-1.08	0.21	-0.37	0.91	0.26
Set 1	$log(n_6)$	n_3	n_4	$n_4 n_6$	
Coefs. 1	0.47	0.75	-1.04	0.21	0.29

3.2 BUPA Liver Disorder

This problem consists of predicting whether or not a male patient has a liver disorder, based on blood test and alcohol consumption. There are 345 records consisting of six continuous input attributes and a class variable. Of these, 145 examples belong to class 0 (absence) and 200 belong to class 1 (presence of disease). We have tackled the problem using 1000 individuals with $n = 4$ associated features, evolved during 100 epochs. Node operators include arithmetic functions, and the *cos* and *log* functions. Terminal nodes allow the 6 original input variables and random constants. We have performed simulations for different values of the control parameter α, ranging from 0 to 1. For each value of α, the classification error rate is calculated as an average over 10 CV sets.

The results of our experiments are summarized in figure 3 and table 2. Figure 3A shows the error rate versus α. For increasing α, the classification error rate slightly increases for the training set, as more complex trees can better adapt

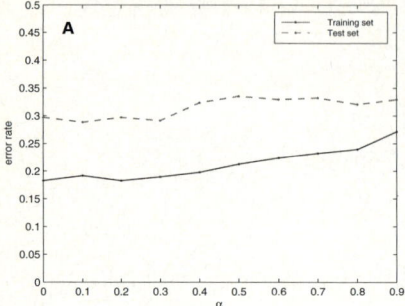 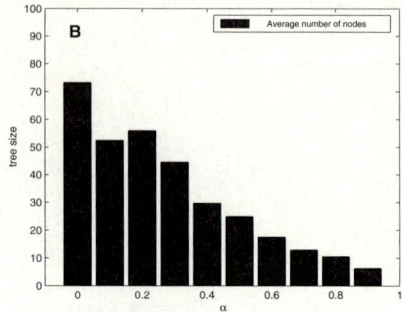

Fig. 3. A. Average error rate versus control parameter α for the BUPA problem. Solid line is for the training set, dashed line is for the test set. The error values are averages over 10 CV sets. B. Average tree size (number of nodes) versus α.

to the regularities of the training data. For the test set, however, the error remains almost constant for the full range of α values. Figure 3B displays the average tree size for different αs. Simpler trees are obtained for the higher values of the control parameter. Comparing the two graphs we see that, for high α, much simpler models can be obtained at almost no expense on the error rate. In table 2 we show some of the attribute sets obtained for $\alpha = 0.8$, together with their projection coefficients and error rate on the test set. The computed errors are similar to those reported in the literature [8,20], yet they are achieved with much simpler models. For instance, [8] obtain too complex models, such as $((n_2 - (n_2/n_3))/(n_5 + (n_2 + n_6)/n_3))/(n_4/n_3)$. The much simpler models that we obtain allow for easier interpretation of the problem structure.

4 Discussion

The traditional approach in pattern classification is biased towards the learning algorithm. Data manipulation techniques, such as feature construction and selection, are viewed as preprocessing steps that aid the learning method. In this paper we propose a change of view that considers the search for the optimal problem representation as the main goal. This search is guided by the error rate of the classification method, which acts as a tool but not as the final objective. In this context, we define an optimal problem representation as the one that allows classification by means of a linear method.

As a counter-argument to the use of linear classifiers, it could be argued that a more complex learning algorithm, such as a multilayer perceptron, can compute linear functions, and introduce non-linear terms if needed. Nevertheless, this option presents some problems that must be considered. First, the combination of complex attribute construction and complex learning algorithm leads to an overall complex process which has a larger tendency to overfitting and loss of generalization. Second, non-linear learning methods have multiple locally optimal solutions, and so the fitness of a given set of attributes is not well defined, but depends on the particular run of the learning process. Using a linear classifier this problem is avoided, and the fitness measure for any set of input attributes is uniquely defined. In addition, the computation of the optimal solution can be performed avoiding training during a long number of epochs.

We use genetic programming to construct non-linear features using a rich set of basis functions. In order to avoid the construction of too complex features that may induce to overfitting, a new complexity measure is introduced. The obtained new problem representation is evaluated using a linear discriminant. The methodology here presented gives rise to much simpler models than the ones previously developed in the literature [8,20]. These simpler models allow for an easier interpretation of the problem structure.

References

1. Fayyad, U.M., Piatetsky-Shapiro, G., Smyth, P.: From data mining to knowledge discovery: an overview. In: Advances in Knowledge Discovery and Data Mining, U.M. Fayyad, G. Piatetsky-Shapiro, P. Smyth, and R. Uthurusamy (eds.). Menlo Park, CA, AAAI Press (1996) 1–34
2. Forman, G.: An extensive empirical study of feature selection metrics for text classification. J. Mach. Learn. Res. 3 (2003) 1289–1306
3. Guyon, I., Elisseeff, A.: An Introduction to Variable and Feature Selection. J. Mach. Learn. Res. 3 (2003) 1157–1182
4. Stoppiglia, H., Dreyfus, G., Dubois, R., Oussar, Y.: Ranking a random feature for variable and feature selection. J. Mach. Learn. Res. 3 (2003) 1157–1182
5. Flach, P.A., Lavrac, N.: The role of Feature Construction in Inductive Rule Learning. ICML (2000) 1–11
6. Kramer, S.: Demand-Driven Construction of Structural Features in ILP. ILP 2157 (2001) 132–141
7. Kuscu, I.: A Genetic constructive induction model. Proc. Congress on Evolutionary Computation, P.J Angeline et al., eds., vol. 1. IEEE Press (1999) 212–217
8. Muharram, M., Smith G.D.: Evolutionary Constructive Induction. IEEE Trans. Knowl. Data Eng. 17, 11 (2005) 1518–1528
9. Otero, F.E.B., Silva, M.M.S., Freitas, A.A., Nievola, J.C.: Genetic Programming for Attribute Construction in Data Mining. LNCS 2610 (2003) 383–393
10. Rennie, J.D.M., Jaakkola, T.: Automatic Feature Induction for Text Classification. MIT Artificial Intelligence Laboratory Abstract Book (2002)
11. Utgoff, P.E., Precup, D.: Constructive Function Approximation. In: Feature Extraction, Construction and Selection: a Data Mining Perspective, H. Liu and H. Motoda (eds.). Boston, Kluwer Academic (1998) 219–235
12. Duda, R.O., Hart, P.E., Stork, D.G.: Pattern classification. John Wiley and Sons (2001)
13. Koza, J.: Genetic Programming: On the Programming of Computers by Means of Natural Selection. MIT Press (1992)
14. del Valle, M., Sánchez, B., Lago-Fernández, L.F., Corbacho, F.J.: Feature discovery in classification problems. LNCS 3646 (2005) 486–496
15. Blake, C.L., Merz, C.J.: UCI Repository of Machine Learning Database (1998) http://www.ics.uci.edu/~mlearn/MLRepository.html
16. Haring, S., Kok J.N., van Wezel M.C.: Feature selection for neural networks through functional links found by evolutionary computation. LNCS 1280 (1997) 199–210

17. Hu, Y.: Constructive Induction: Covering Attribute Spectrum. In: Feature Extraction, Construction and Selection: a Data Mining Perspective, H. Liu and H. Motoda (eds.). Boston, Kluwer Academic (1998) 257–272
18. Sierra, A., Macías, J.A., Corbacho, F.: Evolution of Functional Link Networks. IEEE Trans. Evol. Comp. 5, 1 (2001) 54–65
19. Gagne, C., Parizeau, M.: BEAGLE Puppy Genetic Programming Library. http://beagle.gel.ulaval.ca/puppy
20. Lim, T., Loh, W., Shih, Y.: A Comparison of Prediction Accuracy, Complexity, and Training Time of Thirty-three Old and New Classification Algorithms. Mach. Learn. 40 (2000) 203–229

Biased Minimax Probability Machine Active Learning for Relevance Feedback in Content-Based Image Retrieval

Xiang Peng and Irwin King

Department of Computer Science and Engineering
The Chinese University of Hong Kong
Shatin, N.T., Hong Kong
{xpeng, king}@cse.cuhk.edu.hk

Abstract. In this paper we apply Biased Minimax Probability Machine (BMPM) to address the problem of relevance feedback in Content-based Image Retrieval (CBIR). In our proposed methodology we treat relevance feedback task in CBIR as an imbalanced learning task which is more reasonable than traditional methods since the negative instances largely outnumber the positive instances. Furthermore we incorporate active learning in order to improve the framework performance, i.e., try to reduce the number of iterations used to achieve the optimal boundary between relevant and irrelevant images. Different from previous works, this model builds up a biased classifier and achieves the optimal boundary using fewer iterations. Experiments are performed to evaluate the efficiency of our method, and promising experimental results are obtained.

1 Introduction

Content-based Image Retrieval (CBIR) has attracted a lot of research interests in the past decade [9]. For Content-based Image Retrieval, i.e., searching in image database based on their content, the focus was on Query By Example (QBE). A representative CBIR system contains four major parts: image representation, high-dimensional image indexing, similarity measurement between images and system design [12]. At the early stage of CBIR research, scientists focused on the feature extraction for the best representation of the content of images. However these features are often low-level features. Therefore two semantically similar objects may locate far from each other in the feature space, while two absolutely different images may lie close to each other [12]. This is known as the problem of semantic gap between low-level features and high-level concepts and the subjectivity of human perception [2]. Although many features have been investigated for some CBIR systems, and some of them demonstrated good performance, the problem has been the major encumbrance to more successful CBIR systems.

Relevance feedback has been shown to be a powerful tool to address the problem of the semantic gap and the subjectivity of human perception problems in CBIR [2]. Widely used in text retrieval, relevance feedback was first introduced by Rui et al. [8] as an iterative tool in CBIR. Since then it becomes a major research topic in this area. Recently, researchers proposed a number of classification techniques to attack relevance feedback tasks, in which SVM-based techniques are considered as the most promising and effective techniques [2]. The major SVM technique treats the relevance feedback problem as a strict binary classification problem. However, these methods do not consider the imbalanced dataset problem, which means the number of irrelevant images are significantly larger than the relevant images. This imbalanced dataset problem would lead the positive data (relevant images) be overwhelmed by the negative data (irrelevant images). Furthermore, how to reduce the number of iterations in order to achieve the optimal boundary in this learning task is also a critical problem for image retrieval from large datasets.

In this paper, we propose a relevance feedback technique to incorporate both Biased Minimax Probability Machine and Active Learning to attack these two problems, which can better model the relevance feedback problem and reduce the number of iterations in the learning interaction.

The rest of the paper is organized as follows. In Section II, we review some previous work on relevance feedback. In Section III we first provide an introduction for Active Learning and Biased Minimax Probability Machine (BMPM), then we formulate the relevance feedback technique employing BMPM and Active Learning. Furthermore we show the advantages compared with conventional techniques. Experiments, performance evaluations are given in Section IV. Finally, Section V concludes our work and shows some directions for future work.

2 Related Work

In text retrieval, relevance feedback was used early on and had proven to improve results significantly. The adoption of relevance feedback in CBIR is more recent, and it has evolved to incorporate various machine learning techniques into applications recently. In [7], Decision Tree was employed to model the relevance feedback task. In [1], Bayesian learning was conducted to attack the problem of relevance feedback. Apart from these, many other conventional machine learning methods were also proposed, e.g., Self-organizing Map [5], Artificial Neural Network [9], etc. Furthermore, many state-of-the-art classification algorithms were suggested to model and solve the relevance feedback problem, e.g., Nearest Neighborhood classifier [9] and Support Vector Machine (SVM) [11], etc. Among these techniques, SVM-based techniques are the most effective techniques to address the relevance feedback task in CBIR.

However, conventional relevance feedback techniques by SVMs or other learning models are based on strict binary classification tasks. In other words, they do not consider the imbalanced dataset problem in relevance feedback. Moreover, these techniques always consume a number of iterations to obtain an optimal boundary which is not suitable for image retrieval from large datasets. In order to address this imbalance classification task and make relevance feedback more efficient, we propose the Biased Minimax Probability Machine Active Learning to construct the relevance feedback technique in CBIR.

3 Relevance Feedback by Active Learning Using BMPM

In this section, we introduce the concepts of Active Learning and Biased Minimax Probability Machine. We then present and formulate our proposed Biased MPM methodology with Active Learning, applying to relevance feedback.

3.1 Active Learning

In supervised learning, often the most time-consuming and costly process in designing classifiers is object labelling when we face large scale learning tasks. Instead of randomly picking instances to be manually labelled for training dataset, active learning is a novel mechanism for selecting unlabelled objects based on the result of past labelled objects. Under this framework, the learner could construct a classifier as quickly as possible while active learning method just provides fewer optimal data.

Based on the different criterion for optimal data, there are three main types of active learning method: "Most Information", "Minimizing the Expected Error" and "Farthest First" active learning methodologies. In each iteration of learning, the examples with highest classification uncertainty is chosen for manual labelling [12]. Then the classification model is retrained with additional labelled example. The key issue in active learning for relevance feedback is how to measure the information associated with an unlabelled images. In [6], various of distinct classifier models were first generated. Then, the classification uncertainty of a test image is measured by the amount of disagreement among the test images. Another batch of methodologies measure the information associated with a test example by how far the example is away from the classification boundary. One of the most promising approaches within this group is the SVM active learning developed by Tong and Chang [11].

Let O_i, $i = 1, 2, ..., N$ be the objects in the database, and $\mathbf{x}, \mathbf{y}$ be the two classes we want to perform classification. For each object O_i, we define probability P_{ic} to be the probability that this object belongs to a particular class $\mathbf{x}$ or $\mathbf{y}$. Furthermore we define $P_{ix}=1$ if the object O_i has been labelled to class $\mathbf{x}$, and $P_{ix}=0$ if it has been classified to class $\mathbf{y}$. P_{iy} is defined likewise. If the object has not been labelled, P_i is estimated by its nearest neighborhood. In order to derive the expected information gain when we label a certain object, we define an uncertainty measurement as follows:

$$G_i = \Phi(P_{ix}, P_{iy}), \qquad i = 1, 2, ..., N \qquad (1)$$

where G_i is the information measurement and $\Phi(\cdot)$ is a function on the class probabilities of object O_i. Moreover, we use the entropy formulation to define the information measurement as

$$G_i = \Phi(P_{ix}, P_{iy}) = -P_{ix}\log P_{ix} - P_{iy}\log P_{iy} \qquad (2)$$

3.2 Biased Minimax Probability Machine

We assume two random vectors **x** and **y** represent two classes of data with mean and covariance matrices as $\{\overline{x}, \Sigma x\}$ and $\{\overline{y}, \Sigma y\}$, respectively in a two-category classification task, where $\mathbf{x}, \mathbf{y}, \overline{x}, \overline{y} \in R^n$, and $\Sigma x, \Sigma y \in R^{n \times n}$. We also use **x** and **y** to represent the corresponding class of the **x** data and the **y** data respectively.[1]

With given reliable $\{\overline{x}, \Sigma x\}$, $\{\overline{y}, \Sigma y\}$ for two classes of data, we try to find a hyperplane $\mathbf{a}^T \mathbf{z} = b$ ($\mathbf{a} \neq 0, \mathbf{z} \in R^n, b \in R$, here the superscript T denotes the transpose) with $\mathbf{a}^T \mathbf{z} > b$ being considered as class **x** and $\mathbf{a}^T \mathbf{z} < b$ being judged as class **y** to separate the important class of data **x** with a maximal probability while keeping the accuracy of less important class of data **y** acceptable. We formulate this objective as follows:

$$\begin{aligned}
& \max_{\alpha, \beta, b, \mathbf{a} \neq \mathbf{0}} \quad \alpha \\
& \text{s.t.} \quad \inf_{\mathbf{x} \sim (\overline{\mathbf{x}}, \Sigma_{\mathbf{x}})} \mathbf{Pr}\{\mathbf{a}^T \mathbf{x} \geq b\} \geq \alpha, \\
& \qquad \inf_{\mathbf{y} \sim (\overline{\mathbf{y}}, \Sigma_{\mathbf{y}})} \mathbf{Pr}\{\mathbf{a}^T \mathbf{y} \leq b\} \geq \beta, \\
& \qquad \beta \geq \beta_0,
\end{aligned} \qquad (3)$$

where α represents the lower bound of the accuracy for the classification, or the worst-case accuracy of future data points **x**; likewise β. The parameter β_0 is a pre-specified positive constant, which represents an acceptable accuracy level for the less important class **y**.

The above formulation is derived from MPM, which requires the probabilities of correct classification for both classes to be an equal value α. Through this formulation, the BMPM model can handle the biased classification in a direct way. This model provides a different treatment on different classes, i.e., the hyperplane $\mathbf{a}_*^T \mathbf{z} = b_*$ given by the solution of this optimization problem will favor the classification of the important class **x** over the less important class **y**.

Given the reliable mean and covariance matrices, the derived decision hyperplane is directly associated with two real accuracy indicators of classification of the future data, i.e., α and β, for each class. Furthermore with no assumption on the data distribution, the derived hyperplane seems to be more general and valid than generative classifiers.

3.3 Proposed Framework

Here we describe how to formulate the relevance feedback algorithm by employing the BMPM technique and Active Learning. Applying BMPM-based techniques in relevance feedback is similar to the classification task. However, the relevance feedback needs to construct an iterative function to produce the retrieval results. The following is our proposed methodology for image retrieval tasks in CBIR:

---

[1] The reader may refer to [3] for a more detailed and complete description.

Strategy 1. $BMPM_{active}$ loop summary

1: Randomly pick n_0 images from the pool and check their labels
2: Learn a BMPM on the current images whose labels are known
3: Select m images from the dataset based on the criterion of Eq. 2 with the highest value
4: Loop till local optimal boundary achieved or get to maximum number of iterations

After the iterations of relevance feedback have been performed, $BMPM_{active}$ returns the $Top - k$ most relevant images and learn a final BMPM based on the label known images.

Strategy 2. $BMPM_{active}$ final output

1: Learn a final BMPM from the labeled images
2: This decision line maybe the a local optimal one for the whole image dataset.
3: The final BMPM boundary separates relevant images from irrelevant ones.

When we train and engage BMPM in the classification task, the choice of parameters is very direct, for example a typical settings could be $n_0=10$, $m=10$, and $k=50$. Users can also set them empirically by experience.

4 Performance Evaluation

In this section, we will show some experimental results and we compare the performance of two different algorithms for relevance feedback: SVMs and our proposed $BMPM_{active}$. Both of them are based on Radial Basis Function Kernel. The experiments are evaluated on two real world image datasets: a two-category and a ten-category image dataset. These image datasets were collected from COREL Image CDs. All our works are done on a 3.2GHz machine with Intel Pentium 4 processor and having 1Gb RAM.

4.1 Experiment Setup

COREL Image Datasets. The real-world images are chosen from the COREL image CDs. We organize the datasets which contain various images with different semantic meanings, such as *bird, pyramid, model, autumn, dog* and *glacier*, etc.

(A) *Two-Bird set*. The 180 images in this dataset belong to two groups - *bird* which contains 80 images, and *pyramid* which consists of 100 images. And we assume the category of *bird* is relevant class.

(B) *Ten-Dog set*. The 480 images in this dataset fall into ten categories - *dog, autumn, bird, pyramid, Berlin, model, church, wave, tiger, Kenya*. In this set we assign the class of *dog* to be the user wanted group and it contains 80 images while the other categories have 100 images each belonging to the irrelevant classes.

Fig. 1. Example Images from COREL Image Database

Image Representation. For the real-world image retrieval, the image representation is an important step for evaluating the relevance feedback algorithms. We extract three different features to represent the images: color, shape and texture.

The color feature employed is the color histograms since it is closer to human natural perception and widely used in image retrieval. We quantized the number of pixels into 10 bins for each color channel (H, S, and V) respectively. Thus we could get a 30-dimensional color histogram.

We use edge direction histogram as shape feature to represent an image [4]. We first calculate the edge images by Canny edge detector and obtain the edge direction histogram by quantize it into 15 bins of 20 degrees. Therefore a 15-dimensional edge direction histogram is generated as the edge feature.

Texture is an important cue for image feature extraction. We apply the wavelet-based texture in our experiments [?]. Gabor Wavelet Decomposition is first performed and we compute the features for each Gabor filter output afterwards. Following this approach we use a 16-dimensional vector to describe the texture information for each image.

4.2 Experimental Results

In the following, we present the experimental results by this algorithm on real-world images. The metric of evaluation is Recall vs. Precision for each query, and the Average Precision which is defined as the average ratio of the number of relevant images of the returned images over the total number of the returned images.

The System performances are defined as precision **Pre** and recall **Rec** during the retrieval progress as,

$$\begin{aligned} \mathbf{Pre} &= \frac{r}{\mathbf{A}}, \\ \mathbf{Rec} &= \frac{r}{\mathbf{R}}. \end{aligned} \quad (4)$$

where **A** is the number of images returned, r is the number of relevant images retrieved, and **R** is the total number of relevant images in the pool. In general, recall increases as more images are retrieved while precision decreases.

Since we define $n_0 = 10$, $m = 10$, and $k = 50$ in the experiments, two positive examples and eight negative examples are randomly picked from the dataset for the first iteration, then SVMs and $BMPM_{active}$ are applied with the same start point. For the iterations afterward, both methods select 10 image based on their

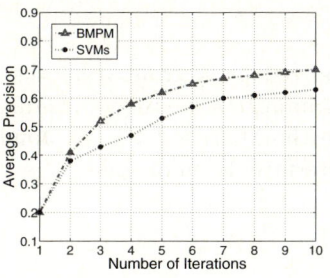 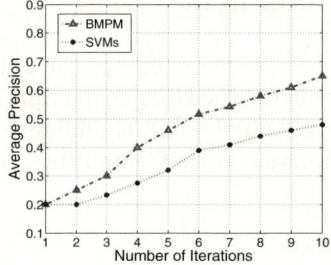

(a) Evaluation on Two-Bird Set   (b) Evaluation on Ten-Dog Set

Fig. 2. Experimental results over COREL Images Dataset

own strategies. For SVM-based method in our evaluation we select images closest to the boundary from the dataset. In the iterative procedure, the precision and recall are recorded, and the maximum loop used to obtain the average precision is set to be 10 iterations for both methods.

Fig. 2 shows the evaluation results on the Two-Bird dataset and Ten-Dog dataset. From the results on the image sets, we can see that our proposed framework outperforms the other approach.

The following table shows the retrieval results after certain number of iterations by these two methods. We could get a more detailed comparison between these two methods. Here k could be 10, 20, 50, and 100 respectively since we define 10 returns for every iteration. In the right sub-table we notice that when BMPM return most of the relevant images from the pool within 7 iterations while for SVMs it takes more than 10 iterations. From this point we could say BMPM achieves the optimal decision line much earlier than SVMs.

Table 1. Number of relevant images in Top-k Returns

Two-Bird Dataset	No. of Iterations					Ten-Dog Dataset	No. of Iterations				
	1	2	5	7	10		1	2	5	7	10
BMPM	2	8	31	47	70	BMPM	2	5	23	38	65
SVM	2	7	26	42	63	SVM	2	4	16	28	48

5 Conclusion

In this paper, we address the problem of biased classification needed by the relevance feedback in CBIR and present a novel learning tool, Biased Minimax Probability Machine Active Learning, to treat this problem more precisely. In contrast to the traditional methods, the BMPM provides a more elegant way to handle biased classification tasks. We evaluate the performance of the BMPM based on the COREL image dataset and obtain promising retrieval results.

Acknowledgment

The work described in this paper is supported by a grant from the Research Grants Council of the Hong Kong Special Administrative Region, China (Project No. CUHK4235/04E) and is affiliated with the Microsoft-CUHK Joint Laboratory for Human-centric Computing and Interface Technologies.

References

1. I. Cox, M. Miller, T. Minka, and P. Yianilos. An optimized interaction strategy for bayesian relevance feedback. In *Proceedings of 1998 IEEE Conference on Computer Vision and Pattern Recognition*, pages 553–558, Santa Barbara, USA, 1998.
2. C. H. Hoi, C. H. Chan, K. Huang, M. R Lyu, and I. King. Biased support vector machine for relevance feedback in image retrieval. In *Proceedings of International Joint Conference on Neural Networks*, pages 3189–3194, Budapest, Hungary, 2004.
3. K. Huang, H. Yang, I. King, and M. R Lyu. Learning classifiers from imbalanced data based on biased minimax probability machine. In *Proceedings of IEEE Conference on Computer Vision and Pattern Recognition*, pages 558–563, 2004.
4. A. Jain and A. Vailaya. Shape-based retrieval: a case study with trademark image database. *Pattern Recognition*, 9:1369–1390, 1998.
5. J. Laaksonen, M. Koskela, and E. Oja. PicSOM: Self-organizing maps for content-based image retrieval. In *Proceedings of International Joint Conference on Neural Networks, Washington, D.C., USA, July 10–16*, 1999.
6. D. Lewis and W. Gale. A sequential algorithm for training text classifiers. In *Proceedings of ACM International Conference on Research and Development in Information Retrieval*, pages 3–12, Dublin, IE, 1994.
7. S. MacArthur, C. Brodley, and C. Shyu. Relevance feedback decision trees in content-based image retrieval. In *IEEE Workshop on Content-based Access of Image and Video Libraries*, pages 68–72, 2000.
8. Y. Rui, T. Huang, M. Ortega, and S. Mehrotra. Relevance feedback: A power tool for interactive content–based image retrieval. *IEEE Transactions on Circuits and Systems for Video Technology*, 8(5):644–655, 1998.
9. A. Smeulders, M. Worring, S. Santini, A. Gupta, and R. Jain. Content-based image retrieval at the end of the early years. *IEEE Transactions on Pattern Analysis and Machine Intelligence*, 22(12):1349–1380, 2000.
10. J. Smith and S. F. Chang. Automated image retrieval using color and texture. *IEEE Transactions on Pattern Analysis and Machine Intelligence*, November 1996.
11. S. Tong and E. Chang. Support vector machine active learning for image retrieval. In *Proceedings of ACM International Conference on Multimedia*, pages 107–118, 2001.
12. C. Zhang and T. Chen. An active learning framework for content-based information retrieval. *IEEE Transactions on Multimedia*, 4(2):260–268, June 2002.

Evidential Integration of Semantically Heterogeneous Aggregates in Distributed Databases with Imprecision

Xin Hong, Sally McClean, Bryan Scotney, and Philip Morrow

School of Computing and Information Engineering
University of Ulster, Coleraine, Northern Ireland, UK
{x.hong, si.mcclean, bw.scotney, pj.morrow}@ulster.ac.uk

Abstract. The mass function of evidential theory provides a means of representing ignorance in lack of information. In this paper we propose mass function models of aggregate views held as summary tables in a distributed database. This model particularly suits statistical databases in which the data usually presents imprecision, including missing values and overlapped categories of aggregate classification. A new aggregation combination operator is developed to accomplish the integration of semantically heterogeneous aggregate views in such distributed databases.

1 Introduction

In a distributed database system local databases may comprise physically distributed datasets from a common population. Examples of such distributed data exist in the different State Statistical Institutes where data must be merged for the purpose of central government and large-scale epidemiological studies. To merge the distributed data, the straight way is moving distributed data to the operational site. This however is impractical considering the massive volume of a modern database, security threats of directly accessing data sources and unavailability of data at the time. Aggregate views held as summary tables are commonly used for summarizing data in very large databases [4]. Such aggregates may be combined at a high level without having to revert to the original data. Aggregate integration may be used to provide information on properties and patterns of the data over the population. Variations of classification of summary data in a distributed database may arise due to the use of different attribute domains in different local databases [3]. In this paper we are concerned with integrating semantically heterogeneous aggregate views of distributed datasets.

The mass function of the Dempster-Shafer theory of evidence (evidential theory, DS theory) has the capability of representing imprecision due to lack of information. In this paper we propose a mass function model to represent aggregate views on local classification schemes, and extend it to represent aggregates on the common classification scheme derived from the local schemes. This representation is particularly suited to statistical databases which usually include imprecise data due to missing values or different classification schemes used by different local databases.

The paper extends our previous work [5] on aggregation of imprecise and uncertain datasets from different experts, to integration of aggregates in a distributed database. We propose a new aggregation combination operator *DAggCom* for integrating semantically heterogeneous aggregate views to which the mass distributions of individual datasets have already been assigned. Our aggregation combination also takes into account weights of different datasets. Essentially we weight each dataset according to the "credibility" of its beliefs where "credibility" is represented by the number of tuples (cardinality) underlying the mass distributions. Distributed data sites only pass on aggregate views and weights to the operational site, which means that the aggregation combination needs minimal communication between local and the operational sites, aggregation combination is therefore computationally efficient.

The remainder of the paper is organised as follows. The next section defines terminologies for representing semantically heterogeneous aggregates. Section 3 proposes our mass function model of aggregates. Section 4 presents a novel mechanism for integrating semantically heterogeneous aggregate views from different data sources in a distributed database. The last section concludes our work and highlights directions for further research.

2 Representation of Semantically Heterogeneous Aggregate Views of Distributed Databases

Notation 1. A set of all possible values of attribute A forms the *domain* of A, $D = \{v_1, ..., v_k\}$. The elements of D are grouped to make up categories (classes) of *classification* C, $C = \{c_1, ..., c_l\}$. For *aggregate data view* V^r, $r = 1, ..., m$, the domain D is partitioned into classes $C^r = \{c_1^r, ..., c_{T_r}^r\}$, T_r is the number of classes in classification C^r. Class c_t^r, for $t = 1, ..., T_r$, is associated with the *cardinality*, i.e. the number of tuples that hold a value from c_t^r on A, denoted by n_t^r. The cardinality of a database, denoted by N^r, is the total number of the tuples in the database. In the format of the classification scheme C^r partitioning the domain,

$$N^r = \sum_{t=1}^{T_r} n_t^r.$$

Definition 1. An *ontology* is defined as the Cartesian-product of a number of attributes, along with their corresponding classifications. An ontology, in the form of classification schemes, is a set of classes, $C = \{c_1, ..., c_m\}$.

In a distributed database environment, there usually exists a global ontology to which all constituent databases are committed, denoted by G, $G = \{g_1, ..., g_n\}$. The different ontologies used by local databases are semantically equivalent in the sense that there are mappings between local ontologies and the global ontology.

Definition 2. In a distributed database, L is a local classification scheme, $L = \{l_1, ..., l_m\}$; G is the global ontology, $G = \{g_1, ..., g_n\}$. A *correspondence mapping* Γ is a mapping, assigning to each category of L a set of categories $\Gamma(l_i)$ of G, $i = 1, ..., m$.

$$\Gamma: L \to 2^G$$

To illustrate the above concepts we employ a running example based on the EU Labour Force Survey, which is carried out in each of the EU countries. Such data, which may be published according to different ontologies, are then used to compare and contrast the member states. The global ontology for the *job status* attribute is given in Table 1.

Table 1. The global ontology for the *job status* attribute

Category code	Value label	Category code	Value label
g_1	Full-time self-employed	g_5	Unemployed (receiving benefits)
g_2	Full-time employees	g_6	In full-time education
g_3	Part-time employment	g_7	Economically inactive but not in full-time education
g_4	On government training scheme		

Two local classification schemes are as follows.

Scheme 1: $\{<l_1^1$: in employment$>$, $<l_2^1$: non-self employed including government training schemes$>$, $<l_3^1$: unemployed$>$, $<l_4^1$: economically inactive$>\}$

Scheme 2: $\{<l_1^2$: in employment$>$, $<l_2^2$: part-time employment including government training scheme$>$, $<l_3^2$: unemployed$>$, $<l_4^2$: in full-time education$>$, $<l_5^2$: economically inactive but not in full-time education$>\}$

Associated respectively with the two local schemes, the correspondence mappings in tabular format are drawn in Table 2 (the numbers in the brackets are cardinalities produced as a result of extracting views of data from the local databases.)

Table 2. Correspondence mappings of local scheme 1, 2 to the global ontology respectively

Local scheme 1	l_1^1 (257)	l_2^1 (260)	l_3^1 (14)	l_4^1 (196)	
Global ontology	g_1, g_2, g_3	g_2, g_3, g_4	g_5	g_6, g_7	
Local scheme 2	l_1^2 (540)	l_2^2 (138)	l_3^2 (33)	l_4^2 (370)	l_5^2 (30)
Global ontology	g_1, g_2, g_3	g_3, g_4	g_5	g_6	g_7

3 Evidential Model of Imprecise Aggregate Views

We first discuss some imprecision that aggregate views may present and then briefly introduce mass functions of evidential theory. To represent aggregates with imprecision, we propose *mass function models* of aggregate views.

3.1 Aggregate Views with Imprecision

Imprecision means that an attribute value is not uniquely specified from within the set of domain values, but is taking a subset of the domain [5]. In a distributed database, two causes mainly contribute to imprecision of aggregates. One is that aggregates from different sources may use different classification schemes. It is quite usual that the granularity of a local scheme is coarser than the global ontology. For example, in the EU Labour Force Survey example, each category of local scheme 1 is the subset of the *Job status* attribute domain (the global ontology). Category l_2^1 is represented by the set of g_3 and g_4 of the global ontology; the aggregate view on l_2^1 provides the summary over the set of g_3 and g_4, neither g_3 nor g_4 individually. Moreover, aggregates on l_1^1 and l_2^1 both contain the summary of g_3, but cannot separate it from that of the set of g_1, g_2 and g_3, and of g_3 and g_4 respectively. Such aggregates are imprecise from the view of the global ontology.

The second cause of imprecision is that tuples in a local database may have empty values for an attribute and cannot be specified from within the attribute domain set. For instance, we now have a slightly changed version of the aggregate on local scheme 1 in the EU Labour Survey (changes are highlighted):

Scheme 1: {<l_1^1 : in employment, **252**>, <l_2^1 : non-self employed including government training schemes, 260>, <l_3^1 : unemployed, **11**>, <l_4^1 : economically inactive, **192**>, <l_5^1 : **unknown, 12**>}

The new category l_5^1 indicates that 12 tuples in the database have empty values for the *Job status* attribute. To accommodate this type of imprecision, we expand the **global ontology** to include an extra category g_8: **unknown**, to which tuples with the empty *Job status* value in a local database can be classified. The category l_5^1 has the one-to-one reflection of category g_8 in the global ontology.

3.2 Mass Distribution of Evidential Theory

Evidential theory [1, 7] is considered a generalization of traditional probability theory. One of the prominent features of evidential theory lies in its capability of representing ignorance in lack of information [2]. Let Θ denote the domain of an attribute, which is a set of mutually exclusive and exhaustive possible values that can be assigned,

Mass distribution: A mass distribution m is a mapping: $2^\Theta \rightarrow [0, 1]$, satisfying the following properties:

(a) $m(\phi) = 0$, where ϕ is an empty set (b) $\sum_{A \subseteq \Theta} m(A) = 1$

A mass distribution is also called a *mass function* or *basic probability assignment*. The subset A is called a focal element if $m(A) > 0$. It is possible that two focal elements may overlap. If all focal elements are the singletons of the domain Θ, the mass distribution is exactly a probability distribution on Θ. In this sense, mass distributions are generalized probability distributions. If the domain set becomes the only focal element, it describes the total ignorance.

3.3 Mass Function Model of Aggregates

In a distributed database consisting of Q local databases, the qth local database uses the classification scheme L^q, $L^q = \{l_1^q, ..., l_{I_q}^q\}$. The **aggregate view** of the qth database with associated mass distribution m_i^q for l_i^q, $i = 1, ..., I_q$, can be represented by the set S_q:

$$S_q = \{<l_i^q, m_i^q>, i = 1, ..., I_q\}$$

The mass distribution may be calculated from cardinalities if provided in the aggregate view,

$$m_i^q = \frac{n_i^q}{\tilde{N}^q}, \quad \tilde{N}^q = \sum_{i=1}^{I_q} n_i^q, \quad i = 1, ..., I_q$$

where n_i^q is the associated cardinality with category l_i^q of L^q. However, when local schemes contain overlapping categories, the calculation may favour the overlapped categories more than others by double counting cardinalities of overlapped categories.

Below we present a method of calculating mass distributions without over calculating overlapping values. The method was initially used in [6] in a different context: that of combining data from different heterogeneous, but non-overlapping, classifications. Let N^q be the cardinality of the local database. G represents the global ontology (including the category *Unknown*), $G = \{g_1, ..., g_m\}$. We have the following equation,

$$A^q G = n^q$$

where A^q is the $(I_q+1) \times m$ matrix, $A_{ij}^q = 1$ if $g_j \in l_i^q$; $A_{ij}^q = 0$ otherwise, for $i = 1, ..., I_q$, $j = 1, ..., m$; $A_{(I_q+1)j}^q = 1$, for $j = 1, ..., m$ if the aggregate includes missing values; $A_{(I_q+1)j}^q = 1$, for $j = 1, ..., m-1$, $A_{(I_q+1)j}^q = 0$, for $j = m$, otherwise. The I_q-vector n^q contains the cardinalities n_i^q for $i = 1, ..., I_q$ (n_i^q is the cardinality of l_i^q in L^q) and N^q. The m-vector G contains cardinalities n_{g_i} of g_i in G, $i = 1, ..., m$. By use of the Gauss-Jordan elimination algorithm, we obtain $A^{q'} G = n^{q'}$, where $\sum_{i=1}^{I_q+1} n_i^{q'} = N^q$. $A^{q'}$ is the row reduced echelon form of A^q. The refined aggregate view can then be derived based on $A^{q'}$. For each class $l_i^{q'}$ associated with the cardinality $n_i^{q'}$ in the refined classification scheme, the mass function m_i^q can then be calculated by:

$$m_i^q = \frac{n_i^{q'}}{N^q}, \quad i = 1, ..., (I_q+1).$$

The procedure has the effect of discriminating the overlapping values and provides an efficient allocation of mass functions to the local datasets.

For example, the matrix representations of local scheme 1 (revised one given in section 3.1) and 2 in the EU Labour Force Survey example are shown in equations (1a) and (2a). Equations (1b) and (2b) are their row reduced echelon forms respectively.

$$\begin{bmatrix} 1 & 1 & 1 & 0 & 0 & 0 & 0 & 0 \\ 0 & 1 & 1 & 1 & 0 & 0 & 0 & 0 \\ 0 & 0 & 0 & 0 & 1 & 0 & 0 & 0 \\ 0 & 0 & 0 & 0 & 0 & 1 & 1 & 0 \\ 0 & 0 & 0 & 0 & 0 & 0 & 0 & 1 \\ 1 & 1 & 1 & 1 & 1 & 1 & 1 & 1 \end{bmatrix} \begin{bmatrix} g1 \\ g2 \\ g3 \\ g4 \\ g5 \\ g6 \\ g7 \\ g8 \end{bmatrix} = \begin{bmatrix} 252 \\ 260 \\ 11 \\ 192 \\ 12 \\ 500 \end{bmatrix} \text{(1a)} \quad \begin{bmatrix} 1 & 0 & 0 & 0 & 0 & 0 & 0 & 0 \\ 0 & 1 & 1 & 0 & 0 & 0 & 0 & 0 \\ 0 & 0 & 0 & 1 & 0 & 0 & 0 & 0 \\ 0 & 0 & 0 & 0 & 1 & 0 & 0 & 0 \\ 0 & 0 & 0 & 0 & 0 & 1 & 1 & 0 \\ 0 & 0 & 0 & 0 & 0 & 0 & 0 & 1 \end{bmatrix} \begin{bmatrix} g1 \\ g2 \\ g3 \\ g4 \\ g5 \\ g6 \\ g7 \\ g8 \end{bmatrix} = \begin{bmatrix} 25 \\ 227 \\ 33 \\ 11 \\ 192 \\ 12 \end{bmatrix} \text{(1b)}$$

$$\begin{bmatrix} 1 & 1 & 1 & 0 & 0 & 0 & 0 & 0 \\ 0 & 0 & 1 & 1 & 0 & 0 & 0 & 0 \\ 0 & 0 & 0 & 0 & 1 & 0 & 0 & 0 \\ 0 & 0 & 0 & 0 & 0 & 1 & 0 & 0 \\ 0 & 0 & 0 & 0 & 0 & 0 & 1 & 0 \\ 1 & 1 & 1 & 1 & 1 & 1 & 1 & 0 \end{bmatrix} \begin{bmatrix} g1 \\ g2 \\ g3 \\ g4 \\ g5 \\ g6 \\ g7 \\ g8 \end{bmatrix} = \begin{bmatrix} 540 \\ 138 \\ 33 \\ 370 \\ 30 \\ 1000 \end{bmatrix} \text{(2a)} \quad \begin{bmatrix} 1 & 1 & 0 & 0 & 0 & 0 & 0 & 0 \\ 0 & 0 & 1 & 0 & 0 & 0 & 0 & 0 \\ 0 & 0 & 0 & 1 & 0 & 0 & 0 & 0 \\ 0 & 0 & 0 & 0 & 1 & 0 & 0 & 0 \\ 0 & 0 & 0 & 0 & 0 & 1 & 0 & 0 \\ 0 & 0 & 0 & 0 & 0 & 0 & 1 & 0 \end{bmatrix} \begin{bmatrix} g1 \\ g2 \\ g3 \\ g4 \\ g5 \\ g6 \\ g7 \\ g8 \end{bmatrix} = \begin{bmatrix} 429 \\ 111 \\ 27 \\ 33 \\ 370 \\ 30 \end{bmatrix} \text{(2b)}$$

Table 3 displays in tabular format the refined schemes 1' and 2' with mapping to the global ontology, accompanied with the mass distributions calculated from cardinalities provided originally.

Table 3. The mass distributions of the two aggregate views based on local scheme 1' and 2'

Local scheme 1' category	$l_1^{1'}$	$l_2^{1'}$	$l_3^{1'}$	$l_4^{1'}$	$l_5^{1'}$	$l_6^{1'}$
Global ontology categories	g_1	g_2, g_3	g_4	g_5	g_6, g_7	g_8
m^1	0.050	0.454	0.066	0.022	0.384	0.024
Local scheme 2' category	$l_1^{2'}$	$l_2^{2'}$	$l_3^{2'}$	$l_4^{2'}$	$l_5^{2'}$	$l_6^{2'}$
Global ontology categories	g_1, g_2	g_3	g_4	g_5	g_6	g_7
m^2	0.429	0.111	0.027	0.033	0.370	0.030

4 Integration of Semantically Heterogeneous Aggregates

In what follows, we define our use of the term *common ontology* for integration of semantically heterogeneous distributed databases. The mass function model of aggregate views is then extended from local schemes to the common ontology. We develop a new combination operator *DAggCom* for distributed databases, for integrating semantically heterogeneous aggregate views to which the mass distributions have already been assigned. *DAggCom* also takes into account weights of different datasets.

4.1 The Common Ontology

Definition 3. For Q local ontologies of a distributed database, $L^q = \{l_1^q,...,l_{I_q}^q\}$ ($q = 1$, ..., Q), the *common ontology* denoted by C, is defined as the union of L^q,

$$C = \bigcup_{q=1}^{Q} L^q .$$

The common ontology C in the form of classification schemes is the set of classes,
$$C = \{c_j, j = 1, ..., J\}$$
where (a) if $i \neq j$, then $c_i \neq c_j$, $i, j = 1, ..., J$; (b) $L^q \subseteq C$, $q = 1, ..., Q$; (c) $1 \leq J \leq \sum_{q=1}^{Q} I_q$.

The common ontology is the ontology of discourse at which to carry out the integration of aggregate views.

From local schemes 1' and 2' on the *job status* attribute in the EU Labour Force Survey example, the common ontology can be derived as shown in Table 4.

Table 4. The common ontology of the *job status* attribute

Common ontology	c_1	c_2	c_3	c_4	c_5	c_6	c_7	c_8	c_9	c_{10}
Global ontology	g_1	g_2, g_3	g_4	g_5	g_6, g_7	g_8	g_1, g_2	g_3	g_6	g_7

4.2 Extended Mass Function Model

Suppose that the common ontology C, $C = \{c_1, ..., c_J\}$, is derived from Q local ontologies in a distributed database. For the aggregate view on local ontology L^q, $L^q = \{l_1^q,...,l_{I_q}^q\}$, we introduce the trivial extension of the set S_q defined in section 3.3.

$$\tilde{S}_q = \{<c_j, \tilde{m}_j^q>, j = 1,...,J\} ,$$

where

$$\tilde{m}_j^q = \begin{cases} m_i^q & \text{if } \exists i \in \{1, ..., I_q\} \text{ for which } c_j = l_i^q. \\ 0 & \text{otherwise.} \end{cases}$$

It can obviously be seen that $\tilde{m}^q$ is also a mass function.

4.3 Aggregation Combination Operator

Consider that a distributed database contains Q local databases, each of which uses a different ontology $L^q = \{l_1^q,...,l_{I_q}^q\}$ for $q = 1,..., Q$. The aggregate view of a local database is represented by $S_q = \{<l_i^q, m_i^q>, i = 1,..., I_q\}$ with associated weight W_q. The common ontology derived from the Q local databases is denoted by $C = \{c_j, j = 1,$

..., J}. The set $\tilde{S}_q = \{<c_j, \tilde{m}_j^q>, j=1,...,J\}$ is the extension of S_q on the common ontology. The Q aggregate views in the extension form may then be combined using the aggregation combination operator *DAggCom* defined as follows:

$$DAggCom(\tilde{S}_q, q=1,...,Q) = \{<c_j, m_j>, j=1,...,J\}$$

where $m_j = \sum_{q=1}^{Q} (\frac{W_q}{\sum_{q=1}^{Q} W_q} \times \tilde{m}_j^q)$.

Theorem 1. The operator *DAggCom* yields a mass function.

The output of the *DAggCom* operator is a set of the common ontology categories along with the associated mass distribution.

For illustration purposes, consider again the EU Labour Force Survey example. With the common ontology in table 4, the extended mass function distributions of the two aggregates $\tilde{m}^1$ and $\tilde{m}^2$ can be calculated from m^1 and m^2. We now use the aggregation combination operator *DAggCom* to calculate m by combining $\tilde{m}^1$ and $\tilde{m}^2$. Here weights are cardinalities, so $W_1 = 500$, $W_2 = 1000$, $\frac{W_1}{W_1+W_2} = \frac{500}{500+1000}$ =0.333, $\frac{W_2}{W_1+W_2} = \frac{1000}{500+1000} = 0.667$. The results are displayed in Table 5.

Table 5. The common classification scheme for the *job status* attribute

Common ontology categories	$\tilde{m}^1$	$\tilde{m}^2$	m	Common ontology categories	$\tilde{m}^1$	$\tilde{m}^2$	m
c1	0.050	0.000	0.017	c6	0.024	0.000	0.008
c2	0.454	0.000	0.152	c7	0.000	0.429	0.286
c3	0.066	0.027	0.040	c8	0.000	0.111	0.074
c4	0.022	0.033	0.029	c9	0.000	0.370	0.247
c5	0.384	0.000	0.128	c10	0.000	0.030	0.020

5 Conclusions and Future Work

In this paper, we have presented an evidential approach to representing and combining semantically heterogeneous aggregate views of different datasets from the same population. The mass function of evidential theory is used to model aggregate views on classification schemes in which categories may overlap, not be restricted to attribute domain partitions only. A new aggregation combination operator (*DAggCom*) is developed to perform the integration of semantically heterogeneous aggregates from distributed data sources. The operational site only needs classification schemes with mass distributions (or cardinalities) from distributed data sites, no direct consultation with the raw data in distributed sources takes place. The future work includes investigating whether and how integration may provide finer aggregate results.

References

1. Dempster, A. P.: A Generalisation of Bayesian Inference. J. Royal Statistical Soc., B 30 (1968) 205 – 247.
2. Guan, J. W., Bell, D. A.: Evidence Theory and Its Applications: Vol 1. Studies in Computer Science and Artificial Intelligence (1991), Elsevier, North-Holland.
3. McClean, S., Scotney, B.: Using Evidence Theory for the Integration of Distributed Databases. Int'l J. Intelligent Systems, Vol.12 (1997) 763 – 776.
4. McClean, S., Scotney, B., Greer, K.: A Scalable Approach to Integrating Heterogeneous Aggregate Views of Distributed Databases. IEEE Trans. Knowledge and Data Eng., Vol. 15 No. 1 (2003) 232 – 236.
5. Scotney, B., McClean, S.: Database Aggregation of Imprecise and Uncertain Evidence. Int'l J. Information Sciences, Vol. 155 (2003) 245 – 263.
6. Scotney, B., McClean, S., Rodgers, M.: Optimal and Efficient Integration of Heterogeneous Summary Tables in a Distributed Database. Data and Knowledge Engineering, Vol. 29 (1999) 337 – 350.
7. Shafer, G.: The Mathematical Theory of Evidence. Princeton Uni. Press 1976.

Describing Customer Loyalty to Spanish Petrol Stations Through Rule Extraction

Alfredo Vellido[1], Terence A. Etchells[2], David L. García[1], and Ángela Nebot[1]

[1] Department of Computing Languages and Systems. Technical University of Catalonia.
C. Jordi Girona, Barcelona, 08034 Spain
{avellido, dgarcia, angela}@lsi.upc.edu
[2] School of Computing and Mathematical Sciences, Liverpool John Moores University,
Byrom Street, L3 3AF, Liverpool, UK
t.a.etchells@ljmu.ac.uk

Abstract. Globalization and deregulation are modifying the competitive framework in the majority of economic sectors and, as a result, many companies are changing their commercial model to focus on the preservation of existing customers. Understanding customer loyalty therefore represents an element of competitive advantage. In this brief paper, we investigate loyalty in the Spanish petrol station market, according to the *customer satisfaction* and *switching barriers* constructs. Satisfaction and behavioural intentions are analysed within a classification framework using Bayesian neural networks. The necessary interpretability and actionability of the results is achieved through the use of a feature selection process embedded in the network training and a novel rule extraction method.

1 Introduction

The ongoing processes of globalization and deregulation are modifying the competitive framework in the majority of economic sectors. The appearance of new competitors and technologies has produced a sharp increase in competition and a growing preoccupation among companies with creating stronger bonds with customers. Faced with this new scenario, many companies are shifting resources from the goal of capturing new customers to the preservation of existing ones. According to this model, an understanding of how customer loyalty construction mechanisms work represents a clear element of competitive advantage. Two key factors of customer loyalty are *customer satisfaction* and *switching barriers*; these concepts have been qualitatively and quantitatively studied in some detail [1, 2, 3]. Customers who experience high levels of satisfaction with the service received seem to form loyalty bonds with their current service providers. However, in some cases, customer satisfaction is not enough to avoid provider switching and the existence of switching barriers has to be considered.

In this brief paper, we analyze the specific case of satisfaction and loyalty in customers of Spanish petrol stations. A survey of several thousand customers is used to classify them according to satisfaction levels and behavioural intention to recommend the service, using an artificial neural network (ANN) defined within a

Bayesian framework [4] that allows for the automatic determination of the relevance of individual data features.

One of the potential drawbacks affecting the application of ANN models to classification problems is that of the limited interpretability of the results they yield. One way to overcome this limitation is by pairing the ANN model with a rule extraction method. The interpretability of the classification results could be greatly improved by their description in terms of reasonably simple and actionable rules. For this, we used Orthogonal Search-based Rule Extraction (OSRE), a novel overlapping rule extraction method [5].

The paper is structured as follows. First, the concepts of customer loyalty, satisfaction, and switching barriers are described in more detail. This is followed by a summary description of the analysed survey data. In section 4, the Bayesian ANN model used for classification and the OSRE method for rule extraction are, in turn, introduced. The satisfaction survey data are then summarily described. This is followed by the presentation of the experimental results and their discussion. Some conclusions are finally summarised.

2 Customer Satisfaction, Loyalty and Switching Barriers

Data mining, applied to market surveyed information, can provide assistance to churn (customer attrition) management processes. Efficient churn management requires a model of both preventive and treatment actions: preventing dissatisfaction before it occurs and treating it when it has already set in. We propose one such model in Fig. 1.

This paper focuses on the prevention side of customer loyalty management and, especially, on customer satisfaction. Satisfaction with the received service is likely to act as an antecedent to loyalty, consolidating customer permanence and avoiding substitution by a competitor. It might be a necessary condition for loyalty, but perhaps not sufficient. Therefore, the development of active barriers by the company in order to make the switch to another provider difficult (such as, for instance, the "cost incurred in the change") should also be explored as an antecedent to customer loyalty.

Several models that attempt to clarify the structure of the relationships between customer satisfaction, service value and behavioural intentions have been described in the recent marketing literature. The service value construct contains many of the factors here defined as switching barriers. Most existing models consider perception of satisfaction and value to be antecedents of behavioural intentions [1, 2].

3 Petrol Station Customer Satisfaction Survey Data

The data analysed in this study correspond to a survey carried out among customers of Spanish petrol station main brands. A total of 350 service stations on the Spanish market, sampled by location (urban vs. road) and type of service (with attendant vs. self-service), were selected for the exercise. The survey questionnaire was answered by over 3,500 clients during the last quarter of 2005.

The classification and rule extraction analyses described in the next section considered two binary dependent variables: *overall satisfaction* and *intention to recommend*, with possible answers: *satisfied / dissatisfied* and *definitely recommend / definitely not recommend*. *Overall satisfaction* would measure the customer satisfaction construct, whereas *intention to recommend* would measure a type of behavioural intention. The questionnaire included 20 variables, listed in table 1, measured in a Likert scale. They fit into two qualitative categories: attributes of satisfaction with service and switching barriers.

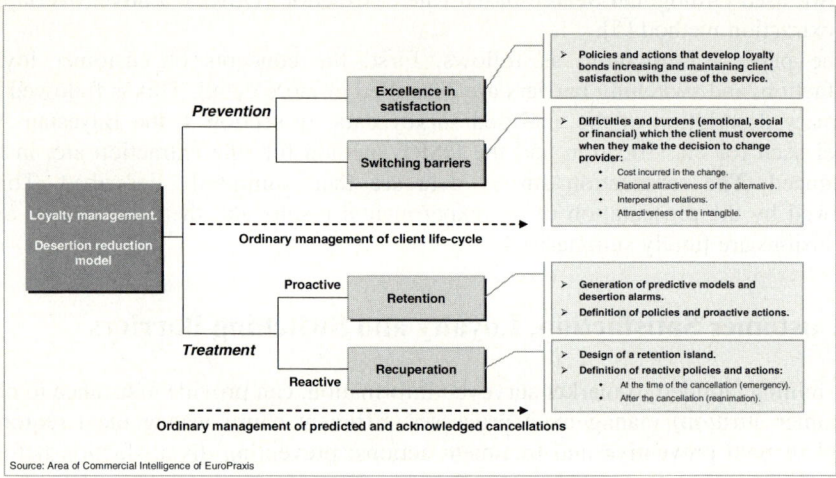

Fig. 1. Conceptual model of customer loyalty management

4 Experiments

In this study, we aim to describe, through reasonably simple and actionable rules, the drivers towards customer satisfaction and intention to recommend the service on the basis of a survey conducted amongst the customers of several Spanish petrol station brands. The method underlying the experiments can be summarily described as follows:

- The survey data described in section 3 were used to predict customer satisfaction and intention to recommend the service. A Bayesian ANN [4] with embedded Automatic Relevance Determination (ARD: [6]) was used to classify the data.
- The ARD technique allowed ranking the variables according to their relevance in the classification task. This naturally leads to a process of selection on the basis of this ranking.
- The variables selected in the previous step of the method were used to describe the classification performed by the ANN through rules, using a novel technique known as Orthogonal-Search Rule Extraction (OSRE: [5]).

The different elements of this method are described next.

Table 1. Description of the 20 variables used in this study and their adscription to the marketing constructs of *satisfaction, switching barriers* and *loyalty*

Independent variables		Conceptually linked to:		
		Satisfaction	Switching barriers	Loyalty
1.	Personal attention from staff	+		+
2.	Speed and efficiency of staff	+		+
3.	Additional services	+		+
4.	Ease of access to installations, well-indicated	+		+
5.	Signs inside installations	+		+
6.	Modern and attractive installations	+		+
7.	Hygiene and maintenance of the installations	+		+
8.	Basic services well-maintained and always in working order	+		+
9.	Extended opening hours	+		+
10.	Cleanliness of toilets	+		+
11.	Exact and reliable pumps	+		+
12.	Feeling of security and absence of risk	+		+
13.	Top quality fuel	+		+
14.	Attractive and stocked shop	+		+
15.	Price		+	+
16.	Payment cards with discounts		+	+
17.	Cards to collect points for gifts		+	+
18.	Brand which inspires trust		+	+
19.	Brand with an extensive network of service stations		+	+
20.	Environmental awareness		+	+

4.1 Bayesian ANN and Automatic Relevance Determination

The Bayesian approach to the training of a multi-layer perceptron ANN differs from the standard Maximum Likelihood approach in that it does not simply attempt to find a single optimal set of weights; instead, it considers a probability distribution over the weights, which reflects better the uncertainty resulting from the use of finite data sets. In that way, the outputs of the ANN in a classification problem can be interpreted as posterior probabilities of class membership given the data and the weights,

$$P(C_i|\mathbf{x},\mathbf{w}) = y(\mathbf{x};\mathbf{w}) \qquad (1)$$

where y is the network function, $\mathbf{x}$ is an input vector, $\mathbf{w}$ is the vector of weights and biases, and C_i is class i. The probability of class membership for a test vector can be obtained by integrating Eq.1 over the weights:

$$P(C_i|\mathbf{x},D) = \int y(\mathbf{x};\mathbf{w})p(\mathbf{w}|D)d\mathbf{w} \qquad (2)$$

where D are the target data for the training set. This conditional probability can be adequately approximated [4].

ANNs are frequently considered as *black boxes* due to, amongst other things, their supposed incapacity to identify the relevance of independent variables in nonlinear terms. Automatic Relevance Determination (ARD: [6]), for supervised Bayesian ANNs, is a technique that tackles that shortcoming: In ARD, the weight decay or regularization term can be interpreted as a Gaussian prior over the network parameters of the form $p(\mathbf{w}) = A\exp\left(-\alpha_c \sum_c^C n_{w(c)} \sum_i^{N_w} w_i^2 / 2\right)$, where $\mathbf{w} = \{w_i\}$ is the vector of network weights and biases, so that individual regularization terms with coefficients α_c are associated with each group c of fan-out weights from each input to the hidden layer (i.e. with each input variable). Therefore C = (number of ANN inputs + 2), $n_{w(c)}$ is the number of parameters in group c, so that $\sum_c^C n_{w(c)} = N_w$, where N_w is the total number of network parameters. The adaptive hyperparameters α_c associated with irrelevant variables will be inferred to be large, and the corresponding weights will become small. Therefore, ARD performs soft feature selection, and a direct inspection of the final { α_c } values indicates the relative relevance of each variable. ARD has shown to be a useful feature selection method for classification problems [7].

4.2 Orthogonal Search-Based Rule Extraction

Orthogonal Search-based Rule Extraction (OSRE: [5]) is an algorithm that efficiently extracts comprehensible rules from smooth models, such as those created by the Bayesian ANN in this study. OSRE is a principled approach and is underpinned by a theoretical framework of continuous valued logic.

In essence, the algorithm extracts rules by taking each data item, which the model predicts to be in a particular class, and searching in the direction of each variable to find the limits of the space regions for which the model prediction is in that class. These regions form hyper-boxes that capture in-class data and they are converted to conjunctive rules in terms of the variables and their values. The obtained set of rules is subjected to a number of refinement steps: removing repetitions; filtering rules of poor specificity and sensitivity; and removing rules that are subsets of other rules. Specificity is defined as one minus the ratio of the number of out-of-class data records that the rule identifies to the total number of out-of-class data. Sensitivity is the ratio of the number of in-class data that the rule identifies to the total number of in-class data. The rules are then ranked in terms of their sensitivity values to form a hierarchy describing the in-class data. Testing against benchmark datasets [8, 9] has showed OSRE to be an accurate and efficient rule extraction algorithm. Details of the algorithm can be found in [5].

4.3 Results and Discussion

4.3.1 Automatic Relevance Determination and Feature Selection

The application of the ARD described in section 4.1 for the classification of *overall satisfaction* and *intention to recommend* using the 20 variables of Table 1, yielded sensible and interesting results: As shown in Fig.2 (left), two variables turn out to be the most relevant for the classification of *overall satisfaction*, namely numbers 1 (*Personal attention from staff*) and 7 (*Hygiene and maintenance of the installations*), followed by a subset of variables with similar relevance, namely numbers 3, 5, 6, 14 and 16 (see Table 1). The relevance of the rest of variables falls clearly behind. Most, if not all, of these variables are easily actionable (easy to act upon) in terms of service management, which comes to validate the usefulness of the ARD process. It is worth noting that all but one (number 16) of the most relevant variables were *a priori* considered as elements of the satisfaction construct (see Table 1).

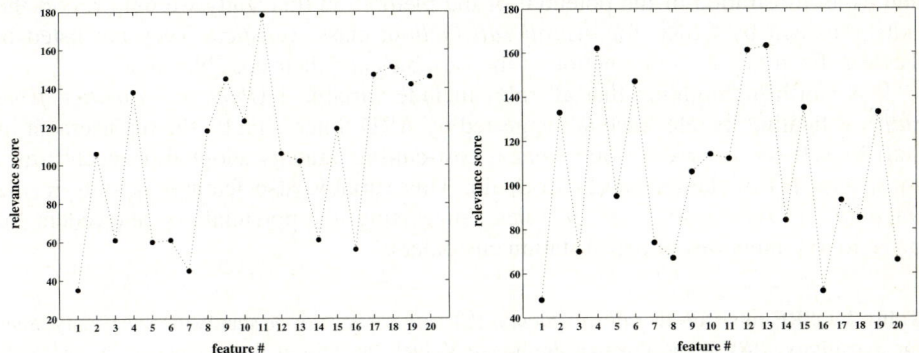

Fig. 2. Cumulative ranking of relevance calculated according to the ranking of variables on each of the 10 ANN runs. The lower the score, the more relevant the variable (A value of 10 would indicate that the variable was ranked 1st in all ANN runs, whereas a value of 200 would mean that the variable has been ranked as the least relevant in all runs).

Fig.2 (right) displays the ARD ranking of relevance for the classification of *intention to recommend*. Again, two variables turn out to be the most relevant, namely numbers 1 (*Personal attention from staff*) and 16 (*Payment cards with discounts*), followed by a subset of variables with similar relevance, namely numbers 3, 7, 8, and 20. This time, overall, the variables considered as elements of the switching barriers construct play a more relevant role in the classification. Given that *intention to recommend* is a behavioural intention, this result indirectly validates the satisfaction and loyalty models presented in [1, 2, 3], where both customer satisfaction and switching barriers are shown to be antecedents of behavioural intentions.

4.3.2 Rule Extraction Using OSRE

The available survey data described in section 3 are strongly unbalanced in terms of class prevalence, both for *overall satisfaction* and *intention to recommend*, with only small percentages of customers declaring themselves unsatisfied or lacking the intention to recommend. This makes rule extraction a challenging task. The Bayesian ANN training was adapted to compensate for this unbalance, using a strategy described in [10] (see eqs. 6 and 8) that entailed modifying the log-likelihood and the network output.

Firstly, OSRE was tested using all 20 variables (full results not reported here). As an example, for *customer satisfaction*, whilst the overall specificity was poor, the specificity of each individual extracted rule was quite good; this means that each rule identified different groups of customers who are satisfied for different reasons. The overall coverage of the extracted rules was in the area of 75% and concerned 15 out the 20 variables, a far too complex description for marketing purposes.

Secondly, the selections of variables obtained by ARD were used to extract the rules: for *overall satisfaction*: 1, 3, 5, 6, 7, 14 and 16 (see Table 1); for *intention to recommend*: 1, 3, 7, 8, 16 and 20. In both cases, rules were extracted for two classes (*satisfied / dissatisfied*) and (*recommend / not recommend*). Due to space limitations and as an illustration of the potential of the method, in this study we only report the rules obtained by OSRE for *overall satisfaction*; class: *satisfied*. They are listed in Table 2. Each rule is a conjunction of the variables and their possible values.

It is worth highlighting that all rules include variable 1 (*Personal attention from staff*), validating its relevance as suggested by ARD. Interestingly, the replacement of staff by self-service was a controversial cost-cutting strategy adopted in recent times by several petrol station brands in Spain. This variable also features heavily in the *intention to recommend* set of rules, suggesting its potential as antecedent of behavioural intentions of petrol station customers.

Table 2. OSRE rules for *overall satisfaction* (Class: *satisfied*). *Spec* stands for Specificity; *Sens* for Sensitivity; *PPV* is the Positive Predictive Value: the ratio of the number of in-class data that the rule predicts to the total number of data the rule predicts. The expression vn stands for variable n, following the numbering in Table 1. The possible variable values, in a Likert scale, range from 1: very good, to 5: very bad. Value 6: NA.

	CLASS: *satisfied*	For this rule only			For ALL rules up to row n		
n	RULE	Spec	Sens	PPV	Spec	Sens	PPV
1	v1=1 ∧ v7={1,4,6}	0.95	0.18	0.85	0.95	0.18	0.85
2	v1=1 ∧ v6={2,3,4,5,6} ∧ v7={1,2,4,6} ∧ v14={1,2,3,4}	0.94	0.14	0.79	0.89	0.29	0.81
3	v1=1 ∧ v6={2,3,5,6} ∧ v14={2,4}	0.95	0.14	0.81	0.85	0.37	0.80
4	v1={1,2,6} ∧ v7={1,2,4,6} ∧ v14={1,2,4}	0.95	0.11	0.75	0.75	0.53	0.77
5	v1=1 ∧ v3={1,4,5,6} ∧ v7={1,2,4,5,6} ∧ v14={1,2,3,4}	0.94	0.18	0.82	0.73	0.56	0.77
6	v1=1 ∧ v14={1,2,4}	0.95	0.16	0.83	0.71	0.58	0.76
8	v1=1 ∧ v7={1,2,4,6} ∧ v14={1,2,3,4}	0.95	0.15	0.82	0.69	0.61	0.76
9	v1={1,2} ∧ v3={1,3,4,5} ∧ v7={1,2,4} ∧ v14={1,2,3,4}	0.95	0.16	0.83	0.68	0.62	0.76
10	v1={1,2} ∧ v6={2,3,5} ∧ v14={1,2,4}	0.96	0.11	0.80	0.67	0.63	0.75

5 Conclusions

Strongly competitive globalised markets drive towards strategies for the preservation of existing customers. In this scenario, understanding how customer loyalty construction mechanisms work, especially from the point of view of customer satisfaction, becomes a relevant task for service providers.

Data from a survey of customers of Spanish petrol stations has been used in this study to predict customer satisfaction and intention to recommend the service, using a Bayesian ANN model. The ARD technique embedded in this model has been used for feature selection. The subset of selected features has, in turn, been used to describe the classification performed by the ANN through rules, through the novel OSRE method. OSRE has been able to describe the factors driving customer satisfaction and intention to recommend in a reasonably simple and interpretable way that could be swiftly integrated in service management processes.

References

1. Cronin Jr., J.J., Brady, M.K., Hult, G.T.M.: Assessing the effects of quality, value, and customer satisfaction on consumer behavioral intentions in service environments. J. Retailing **76**(2) (2000) 193-218.
2. Dabholkar, P.A., Shepherd, C.D., Thorpe, D.I.: A comprehensive framework for service quality: An investigation of critical conceptual and measurement issues through a longitudinal study. J. Retailing **76**(2) (2000) 139-173
3. Bell, S.J., Auh, S., Smalley, K.: Customer relationship dynamics: Service quality and customer loyalty in the context of varying levels of customer expertise and switching costs. J. Acad. Market. Sci. **33**(2) (2005) 169-183.
4. Mackay, D.J.C.: The evidence framework applied to classification networks. Neural Comput. **4**(5) (1992) 720-736.
5. Etchells, T.A., Lisboa, P.J.G.: Orthogonal search-based rule extraction (OSRE) method for trained neural networks: A practical and efficient approach, IEEE T. Neural Networ. **17**(2) (2006) 374-384.
6. MacKay, D.J.C.: Bayesian Methods for Back-Propagation Networks. In: Domany, E., van Hemmen, J.L., Schulten, K. (eds.): Models of Neural Networks III, Springer, New York (1994) 211-254.
7. Penny, W.D, Roberts, S.J.: Bayesian neural networks for classification: How useful is the evidence framework?. Neural Networks **12**(6) (1999) 877-892.
8. Etchells, T.A., Jarman, I.H., Lisboa, P.J.G.: Empirically derived rules for adjuvant chemotherapy in breast cancer treatment. In: IEE Proc. of the MEDSIP Int. Conf., Malta, (2004) 345- 351.
9. Etchells, T.A., Nebot, A., Vellido, A., Lisboa, P.J.G., Mugica, F.: Learning what is important: feature selection and rule extraction in a virtual course. In: Proc. of the 14th ESANN, Bruges, Belgium, (2006) 401-406.
10. Lisboa, P.J.G., Vellido, A., Wong, H.: Bias reduction in skewed binary classification with Bayesian neural networks. Neural Networks **13**(4-5) (2000) 407-410.

Strangeness Minimisation Feature Selection with Confidence Machines

Tony Bellotti, Zhiyuan Luo, and Alex Gammerman

Computer Learning Research Centre, Royal Holloway, University of London, Egham,
Surrey TW20 0EX, UK
zhiyuan@cs.rhul.ac.uk

Abstract. In this paper, we focus on the problem of feature selection with confidence machines (CM). CM allows us to make predictions within predefined confidence levels, thus providing a controlled and calibrated classification environment. We present a new feature selection method, namely Strangeness Minimisation Feature Selection, designed for CM. We apply this feature selection method to the problem of microarray classification and demonstrate its effectiveness.

1 Introduction

Confidence machine (CM) is a framework for constructing learning algorithms that predict with confidence. In particular, we use CM to produce hedged predictions with accuracy controlled by predefined confidence level. Predictions using CM are not only accurate but also, unlike many conventional algorithms, well-calibrated [2,5]. This method is ideally suited to the problem of providing measured and controlled risk of error for microarray analysis. In this paper, we focus on the problem of feature selection with CM and describe a new feature selection method, namely Strangeness Minimisation Feature Selection, designed for CM. We apply this feature selection method to the problem of microarray classification and demonstrate its effectiveness.

2 Confidence Machines

CM is a general learning framework for making well-calibrated predictions, in the sense that test accuracy is controlled. Intuitively, we predict that a new example (eg microarray data for a new patient with unknown diagnosis) will have a label (eg disease diagnosis) that makes it similar to previous examples in some specific way, and we use the degree to which the specified type of similarity holds within the previous examples to estimate confidence in the prediction. Formally, CMs work by deriving a p-value based on a *strangeness measure*. A strangeness measure is a function that provides an indication of how strange or typical a new example is in relation to a given sequence of examples.

Once a strangeness measure A is defined, we can compute the p-value for a new example. Given a sequence of labelled examples for training $(z_1, ..., z_{n-1})$

where each example z_i consists of an object $\mathbf{x}_i$ and its label y_i, and a new example $\mathbf{x}_n$ with label withheld, we calculate p-values for each $y \in Y$, where Y is the set of all possible class labels, as

$$p_y = \frac{|\{i : i \in \{1, ..., n\}, \alpha_i \geq \alpha_n\}|}{n} \quad (1)$$

where $\alpha_i = A(z_i, (z_1, ..., z_n))$ and $z_n = (\mathbf{x}_n, y)$ for $i \in \{1, ..., n\}$. So, p_y is computed from the sequence $(z_1, ..., z_{n-1}, (\mathbf{x}_n, y))$. Clearly $\frac{1}{n} \leq p_y \leq 1$. The p-value p_y gives a measure of typicalness for classifying $\mathbf{x}_n$ with label y. The use of p-values in this context is related to the Martin-Löf test for randomness [3]. Indeed, the p-values generated by CM form a valid randomness test under the iid assumption.

A region prediction for $\mathbf{x}_n$ is then computed as $R = \{\{y : p_y > \delta\} \cup \arg\max_y(p_y)\}$ where $1 - \delta$ is a confidence level supplied prior to using CM (and arg max here returns the *set* of arguments giving the maximum value). This region prediction will always predict the label with the highest p-value, but may also hedge this prediction by including any other label with a p-value greater than δ. If $|R| = 1$, i.e. only one label is predicted, it is called a *certain prediction*. Otherwise, if $|R| > 1$, it is an *uncertain prediction*. Clearly, certain predictions are more efficient than uncertain ones, so an objective of learning with region predictions is to make as many certain predictions as possible. A region prediction is correct if the true label for the example is a member of the predicted region. Otherwise it is an error. Region predictions are well-calibrated, in the sense that we expect the number of errors for k predictions to be approximately less than or equal to $k\delta$ [11].

CM can operate as an on-line or off-line learner. In the on-line learning setting the examples are presented one by one. Each time, the classifier takes an object to predict its label. Then the classifier receives the true label from an ideal teacher and goes on to the next example. The classifier starts by observing $\mathbf{x}_1$ and predicting its label $\hat{y}_1$. Then the classifier receives feedback of the true label y_1 and observes the second object $\mathbf{x}_2$, to predict its label $\hat{y}_2$. The new example $(\mathbf{x}_2, y_2)$ is then included in the training set for the next trial. And so on. At the nth trial, the classifier has observed the previous examples $(\mathbf{x}_1, y_1), ..., (\mathbf{x}_{n-1}, y_{n-1})$ and the new object $\mathbf{x}_n$ and will predict $\hat{y}_n$. We expect the quality of the predictions made by the classifier to improve as more and more examples are accumulated. In the off-line learning setting, the classifier is given a training set $(\mathbf{x}_1, y_1), (\mathbf{x}_2, y_2), ..., (\mathbf{x}_n, y_n)$ which is then used to make predictions on new unlabelled examples $\mathbf{x}_{n+1}, \mathbf{x}_{n+2}, ..., \mathbf{x}_{n+k}$. For on-line learning, it is possible to prove that CM is well-calibrated, in the sense that the test errors form a Bernoulli sequence with parameter δ if we assume identically and independently distributed (iid) data. Calibration to confidence level is a useful property of CM allowing direct control of risk of error. For example, CM has been applied successfully to the problem of reliable diagnosis from microarray data and proteomics patterns [2,5]. In order to achieve calibration, the strangeness measure needs to be *exchangeable* in the sense that the strangeness value α_i is not dependent on the order of the sequence of labelled examples given to Equation (1) [11].

3 Feature Selection

Most microarray gene expression data sets suffer from the dual problem of low sample size and high-dimensional feature space [8]. It is well known that dimension reduction is necessary when high dimensional data is analysed. This is because,

1. large number of features may cause over-fitting, if they are not relevant features, and if the underlying distributions are not estimated accurately,
2. large number of features makes it difficult to design a classifier due to time and space complexity issues.

Previous work with gene expression data has shown that the use of feature selection during classification can lead to improvements in performance, in light of these problems; eg Yeoh et al [12].

Feature selection is the process of selecting a subset of features from a given space of features with the intention of meeting one or more of the following goals:

- choose the feature subset that maximises the performance of the learning algorithm;
- minimise the size of the feature subset without reducing the performance of a learning algorithm on a learning problem significantly;
- reduce the requirement for storage and computational time to classify data.

There are three general methods for feature selection: filters, wrappers and embedded feature selection. The filter method employs a feature ranking function to choose the best features. For example, the signal to noise ratio (SNR) is a ranking function that scores a feature by how well it is a signal for the classification label. Wrapper methods are general purpose algorithms that search the space of feature subsets, testing performance of each subset using a learning algorithm. Some learning algorithms include an embedded feature selection method. Selecting features is then an implicit part of the learning process. This is the case, for example, with decision learners like ID3.

It is possible to derive feature selection from within the CM framework. In this paper, we propose a new method called Strangeness Minimisation Feature Selection (SMFS) that selects the subset of features that minimise the overall strangeness values of a sequence of examples. The intuition for this approach is that reducing overall strangeness implies an increase in conformity amongst the examples in the sequence. Therefore, the set of features that minimise overall strangeness are most relevant to maximising conformity between training examples.

3.1 Strangeness Minimisation Feature Selection

The SMFS goal is defined in relation to any strangeness measure. Let $\tilde{A}$ be an exchangeable measure. The optimal strangeness minimisation feature subset S_0 of size t for a sequence $(z_1, ..., z_n) \in Z^n$ with feature space F is the SMFS goal,

$$S_0 = \arg\min_{S \in G} \sum_{i=1}^{n} \tilde{A}(z_i, (z_1, ..., z_n), S) \qquad (2)$$

where $G = \{R : R \subseteq F, |R| = t\}$. We establish that this is an exchangeable feature selection function and can be implemented in CM. In common with wrapper feature selection methods, it requires a search over the space of all subsets of F, although restricted to subsets of size t. For m features, in the typical case when $t < m$, this search has computational complexity of $O(m^t)$. The number of selected features t does not need to be very large for this to become intractable. Fortunately, practical implementations of SMFS are possible if we restrict our attention to a subclass of linear strangeness measures. The problem becomes tractable without the need for ad-hoc heuristics that are often required with wrapper methods. Within CM framework, we can still implement useful versions of CM based on learning algorithms such as nearest centroid and SVM. We find that SMFS is a principled, broad and practical feature selection framework, for which distinct feature selection methods are determined by strangeness measures.

The function $\tilde{A} : \mathbf{Z} \times \mathbf{Z}^n \times 2^F \to \mathbf{R}$ is a linear measure based on the transformation function $\phi : \mathbf{Z} \times F \times \mathbf{Z}^n \to \mathbf{R}$ if

$$\tilde{A}(z_i, (z_1, ..., z_n), S) = \sum_{j \in S} \phi(z_i, j, (z_1, ..., z_n)) \qquad (3)$$

for all $z_i \in Z$, and $S \subseteq F$.

In CM, strangeness examples are computed as α-strangeness values for each example, see Eq (1). By using linear strangeness measures, we can compute strangeness values for each feature. We call them β-strangeness measures. The β-strangeness value for feature j is defined as

$$\beta_j = \sum_{i=1}^{n} \phi(z_i, j, (z_1, ..., z_n)). \qquad (4)$$

We reformulate the SMFS goal to minimise the sum of β-strangness measure values across subsets of features of size t,

$$S_0 = \arg\min_{S \in G} \sum_{j \in S} \beta_j \qquad (5)$$

where $G = \{R : R \subseteq F, |R| = t\}$. It is easy to see that this minimum is computed from the set of features giving the smallest β-strangeness values. Hence, the SMFS goal can be solved by

1. computing β-strangeness values for each feature,
2. sorting the β-strangeness values in ascending order and choosing the top t.

Clearly, this solution is tractable and is a great improvement on the computational complexity for SMFS in general.

We now consider implementing SMFS using two examples of linear strangeness measures and construct strangeness measures based on the Nearest Centroid (NC) classifier [8] and linear classifier. In both cases, we derive an exchangeable transformation function and the corresponding β-strangeness measure.

For the NC classifier, a linear strangeness measure can be given using specifically one of family of Minkowski distance metrics,

$$\tilde{A}_{NC}((x_0, y_0), (z_1, ..., z_n), S) = \sum_{j \in S} \left(\frac{|x_{0j} - \underline{\mu}_{(y_0)j}|}{\sigma_j}\right)^k \quad (6)$$

where $\underline{\mu}_{(y_0)j}$ is the within class mean for label y_0 and σ_j variance for feature j based on the sequence $(z_1, ..., z_n)$. If we consider NC with the usual Euclidean distance measure ($k = 2$), the β-strangeness measure corresponding to the NC linear strangeness measure $\tilde{A}_{NC}$ is

$$\beta_j = \frac{\sum_{y \in Y} (|C_y| \sigma^2_{(y)j})}{\sigma_j^2} \quad (7)$$

where $|C_y|$ is the number of examples with label y.

We have described a strangeness measure for SVM based on the Lagrange multipliers defined in the dual form optimisation problem for SVM [5]. Although these work for SVM, they cannot be applied to other linear classifiers in general. Also, the range of strangeness values that are output is small since all nonsupport vector examples will have a strangeness value of zero. This means strangeness cannot be measured between these examples. We define a new strangeness measure which resolves both these difficulties, by measuring the distance between an example and the separating hyperplane. The linear classifier strangeness measure is the function $\tilde{A}_{LC}$ defined for all (x_0, y_0) and $(z_1, ..., z_n)$ as

$$\tilde{A}_{LC}((x_0, y_0), (z_1, ..., z_n), S) = -y_0 \left(\sum_{j \in S} w_j x_{0j} + b\right) \quad (8)$$

where the hyperplane (w, b) has been computed using a linear inductive learner based on the sequence $(z_1, ..., z_n)$. We can take the threshold b as an extra weight on a new constant-valued feature without loss of generality. The β-strangeness measure corresponding to the above linear classifier strangeness measure $\tilde{A}_{LC}$ is

$$\beta_j = -w_j \sum_{i=1}^{n} y_i x_{ij}. \quad (9)$$

4 Experiments

Our experiments are based on two public databases of Affymetrix HG-U133A oligonucleotide microarrays for children with acute leukaemia. These microarrays provide gene expression measurements on over 22,000 gene probes for human

substructure-based method sharply increases with the size of graph. On the other hand, if we increase the size of the index to maintain the number of candidate answers, the size of index structure will exponentially increases. This is because when we enumerate subgraphs as the index, the number of subgraphs increases with the size of subgraph at an exponential rate. This yields a requirement for introducing more informative index items into the index to increase its pruning power in order to reduce the candidate answer set size.

In this paper, we demonstrate that degree information can help solve this problem. We also propose a new index structure (D-index) based on the subgraph and the degree information. D-index preserves the information of relationships between the subgraph and the other parts outside this subgraph. Furthermore, D-index maintains a compact feature set whose size is much smaller than the subgraph-based approaches when they achieve the same performance. Experimental results show that D-index reduces the size of candidate answer set by 20%-50%, and thus reduce the execution time by 20%-50%. Moreover, this improvement over existing methods increases with the graph size.

2 The D-subgraph and D-indexing

We focus on the retrieval of graphs in which the query is a subgraph. Briefly, if G' is a subgraph of G, we say G contains G'. Given a query graph Q and a graph database D, the subgraph query is to extract all the graphs G in D which contain Q.

To help process the graph query, we build an index which consists of the features extracted from the graph database. Given a graph query, the first stage is searching the index to find which graphs contain all the features of the graph query. Then, the second stage is verifying whether the graph query is a subgraph of the graphs found in first stage. To build this index, we study which information should be contained in the index items (Section 2.1) and how the index organizes these index items (Section 2.2). The index item should be both small enough to be stored in the index and strong enough to represent the features of the graph. Therefore, we propose a new index structure (D-index) which uses the subgraph and the degree information as the index item.

2.1 The Index Item

In this section, we will discuss the structure of the index item, and we also introduce an approach to sequentialize the index item in order to remove the isomorphic index items.

Our approach is based on the index item, called D-subgraph. D-subgraph is defined as a structure which consists of a subgraph divided from an original graph and the vertex degree information of the original graph. For example, considering the graphs shown in fig.1, some D-subgraphs of these graphs are shown the fig.2. It is meaningful to introduce the degree information, because the substructure with degree information is more discriminative than the subgraph. This is because the degree information can help represent the relationship between the subgraph and the other parts of the graph. Considering the graphs shown in fig.1, although subgraph C-C-C is frequent (appearing

4 times in the database), subgraph C-C-C cannot distinguish the four graphs in the database because all graphs contain C-C-C. The D-subgraphs with the subgraph C-C-C in the above database are shown in fig 2, where degree information is indicated in the brackets. In D-subgraph, we can distinguish the four graphs by the subgraph C-C-C and its degree information.

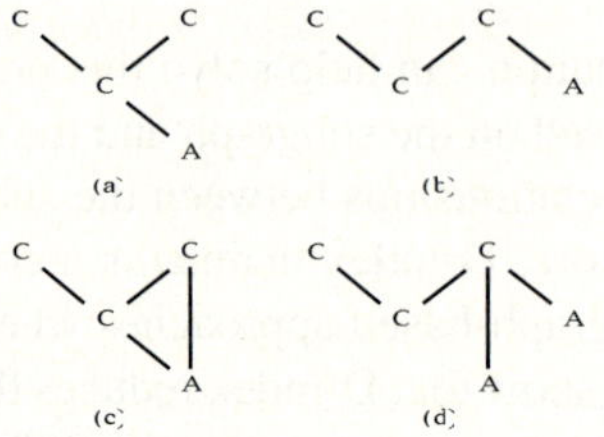

Fig. 1. Graph database

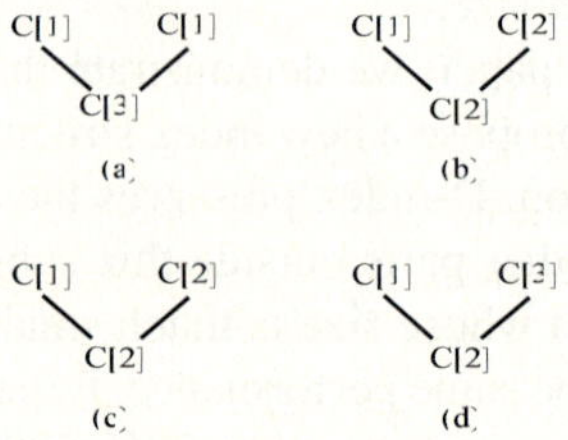

Fig. 2. D-subgraphs

Based on the notion above, our index structure, D-subgraph, is an index item that introduces degree information into an existing subgraph-based index item. It can be viewed as two parts. The first part is for indexing the subgraph. All the existing approaches designed for subgraph indexing can be applied to this part, such as FSG [6], DFS-tree [2] and GraphGrep [5]. In this paper, we use DFS-tree [2] as a case study and use it in our experiments. The second part is for maintaining the degree information. It is organized in a degree-structure, which is an index item used to build the degree tree. (This will be discussed in Section 2.2). For example, the graph (a) in fig.3 could be stored in 8 different ways by the DFS-tree. (We do not consider edge labels in this paper for simplicity.) Graph (b), (c) and (d) in fig.3 are three isomorphic index items.

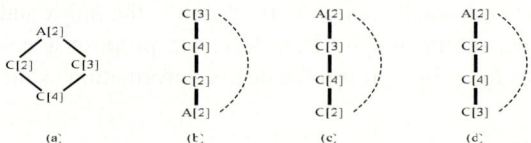

Fig. 3. Three D-index structures generated from a same D-subgraph

The index item (D-subgraph) can be derived as follows: (1) derive the DFS-trees of the sub-graph; (2) count the degree information in the original graph; and (3) sequentialize the D-subgraph by ruling out the isomorphic D-subgraphs. The first stage is similar to the existing method. The second stage can be easily achieved by counting the graph stored in the adjacency matrix or the adjacency list. In the third stage, we restrict the linear order to choose the **Minimum D-subgraph** in the isomorphic D-subgraphs. This **Minimum D-subgraph** will be an index item in the index structure, D-index.

In the first stage and the second stage, we use DFS-tree as a case study. The DFS-tree of a D-index is created by a DFS algorithm. (The detail of this approach is represented in [3].) After that, when we transform the DFS-tree into an edge table, we affix the degree information into the end of the table. Table1 is the information of graph (b), (c) and (d) in figure 3. Specifically, which is different from subgraph based method, when there exist many D-index with a same DFS-tree, we should consider all these DFS-tree and distinguish them by their degree information. As fig.3 (c), (d) and table.1 (C), (D), they have same edge-structures and different degree-structures.

Table 1. The index item information of fig.3(b)(c)(d). The top four rows are the edge-structures describing the edges of the D-subgraph. The bottom row is a degree-structure describing the degree information of the D-subgraph.

D-index(B)	D-index (C)	D-index (D)
(0,1,C,C)	(0,1,A,C)	(0,1,A,C)
(1,2,C,C)	(1,2,C,C)	(1,2,C,C)
(2.3.C,A)	(2,3,C,C)	(2,3,C,C)
(3.0,A,C)	(3,0,C,A)	(3,0,C,A)
(3,4,2,2)	(2,3,4,2)	(2,2,4,3)

In the third stage, we restrict the order of D-subgraphs to rule out the isomorphic D-subgraphs.

For two edge-structures $a = (v_1, v_2, l_1, l_2)$, $b = (v_1', v_2', l_1', l_2')$: (i)if $l_1 < l_1'$, then $a < b$; (ii)else if $l_1 = l_1'$ $l_2 < l_2'$, then $a < b$ (iii) $l_1 = l_1'$ $l_2 = l_2'$ $v_1 < v_1'$, then $a < b$; (iv)else if $l_1 = l_1'$ $l_2 = l_2'$ $v_1 = v_1'$ $v_2 < v_2'$, then $a < b$; (v)else if $l_1 = l_1'$ $l_2 = l_2'$ $v_1 = v_1'$, $v_2 = v_2'$ then $a = b$

For two degree-structures a=$(d_1, d_2...d_n)$, b=$(d_1', d_2'...d_n')$ if $\exists t, 0 \leq t \leq n$, $d_k = d_k'$ for $k < t$, $d_t < d_t'$, then $a < b$.

The D-subgraph lexicographic linear order is defined as follow. If the D-subgraph $a = (a_0, a_1...a_n)$ and the D-subgraph b=$(b_0, b_1...b_m)$, $a < b$ if one of the following is true.

(1) $\exists t, 0 \leq t \leq \min(m, n), a_k = b_k$, for k<t a_t and b_t are edge-structure, $a_t < b_t$.

(2) $\exists t, 0 \leq t \leq \min(m, n), a_k = b_k$, for k<t; a_t is a degree-structure and b_t is a edge-structure.

(3) $\exists t, 0 \leq t \leq \min(m, n), a_k = b_k$, for k<t; a_t and b_t are degree-structure, $a_t < b_t$.

For the D-index in Table.1 ,(D)<(C)<(B)

Definition 1 (Minimum D-index). Given a D-subgraph G, the minimum D-index of all D-indices generated from G is called Minimum D-index.

2.2 The Index Construction

In this section, we will consider the construction of D-index. Briefly, we add **Minimum D-subgraphs** into the index structure. The root part of the D-index is

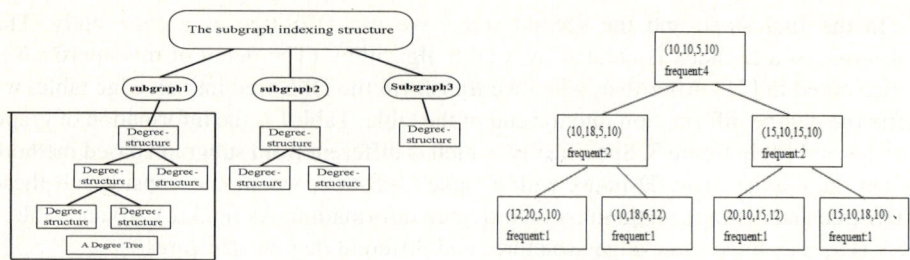

Fig. 4. The overview of the D-index **Fig. 5.** Mergence of the degree structures

subgraph index. For each subgraph indexed in the root part, the D-subgraphs are organized as a degree tree shown in Fig.4. There are three sub-problems should be considered: (1) which subgraphs should be included as the root part of the D-index; (2) which **Minimum D-subgraphs** should be included in the degree tree of D-index; and (3) how the D-subgraphs in the degree tree are organized. All the existing approaches designed for subgraph indexing can be applied to the first sub-problem. In this paper, we adopt the gIndex [2, 3], because the discriminative selection existed in the subgraph-based approach can be easily extended to D-subgraph. For the second problem and the third problem, we present the mergence tree to solve these problems.

Frequent Selection and Discriminative Selection. The frequent number is the least appearance times of the indexing D-subgraph. The discriminative selection based on subgraph can be found in [2]. The D_X is the set of graphs which contain D-subgraph x in the database. Fragment x is discriminative with respect to graph sets F, if $|D_X| \ll |\cap f \in F \wedge f \subset x) D_f|$.

The subgraph of D-subgraph. Both selection need to define the subgraph of D-subgraph. If D-subgraph X is a subgraph of D-subgraph Y, X can be created by the combination of the operations as follow:

(1) Reduce the degree of Y's vertex.
(2) Remove edges of Y, when Y is still a connected graph
(3) Remove edges of Y, and remove the isolated vertexes created by this remove.

The mergence tree of degree-structures. The subgraph-based index can be generated by enumerating all the graphs in a certain bound of graph size. However, we cannot enumerate all D-subgraphs. Our approach is that we search the D-subgraphs by their edge-structure. Then, we use a tree to merge the nearest two D-indices whose edge-structures are same. The distance of two D-indices is the addition of all the absolute dispersions between each vertex pair. The parent of these two D-indices consist of the minimum degree of each vertex pair. For example, as shown in fig.5, the distance between (12,20,5,10) and (10,18,6,12) is 7, and their parent is (10,18,5,10). At last, we check whether the D-index is discriminative in the tree to judge the indexing ability. Because this approach does not need additional subgraph isomorphism operations, the runtime of index construction is close to that of subgraph-based approaches.

2.3 Applications of a D-index

Given a query graph G, the searching method is straightforward. The query is processed as follows:
Set candidate answer set $C=D$.

(1) Search the index to find out D-index x whose edge-structure is a subgraph of the query graph G.
(2) For each D-index x found in step (1), if all vertex degrees in the D-index x are smaller than the vertex degrees in the query graph G, then $C = C \cap D_x$.

This approach can be used in mining frequent subgraph in graph database. Especially, when implemented on large graph databases or the database whose size of the index is restricted, our approach achieves considerable performance improvements over subgraph-based approaches as shown in the experiments.

3 Experiments

We compare our approach with the state-of-the-art subgraph-based approach, gIndex. The purpose of our experiments is to compare the performance on various database sizes and the graph sizes.

Because the time of the search on index is much less than the time spent in candidate answer verification, the query response time (T_{query}) can be presented as follows: $T_{query} = T_{index\_search} + |C| \times T_{subgraph\_iso\_testy} \approx |C| \times T_{subgraph\_iso\_test}$, where T_{index_search} is the time spent in searching on index, $T_{subgraph\_iso\_test}$ is the average time of subgraph isomorphism test and C is the candidate answer set. Thus, the performance of an index can be defined as follows:

$$Performance = \frac{1}{|T_{query}|} \approx \frac{1}{|C| \times T_{subgraph\_iso\_test}}$$

As a result, it achieves an average 30% to 80% improvement in terms of the query response time compared to the state-of-the-art subgraph-based method, gIndex.

The experiments are performed on a computer with 2.4GHZ CPU and 512M memory. We generate the databases by a graph generator. We use these databases instead of the real database because the size of graphs and the number of graphs can be successfully controlled which is necessary for our experiment. The databases contain 1000-5000 graphs and the number of vertexes in the databases is from 10 to 14. The performance is average over 200 runs on different query graphs. We measure the results by the number of candidate answers. Because the time spent in searching of index is much less than that cost on the verification of subgraph. Therefore, the number of candidate answers exactly represents the execution time.

The results of the relationship between the size of candidate answer set and the size of graphs are shown in fig.6. When the size of the graph increases, the difference between the candidate answer set size of D-index and that of gIndex also increases.

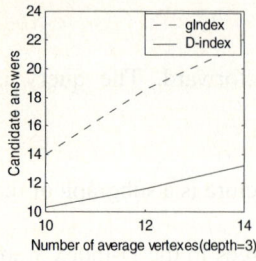 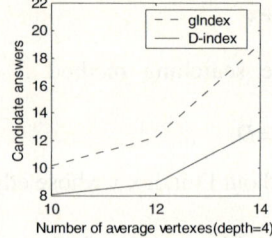 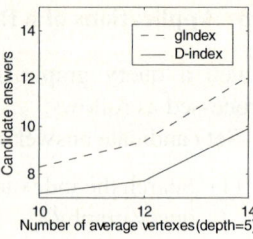

Fig. 6. Performance vs. size of graphs

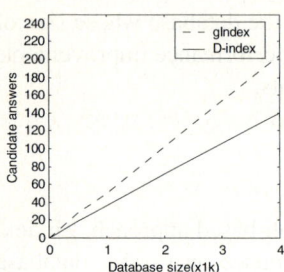 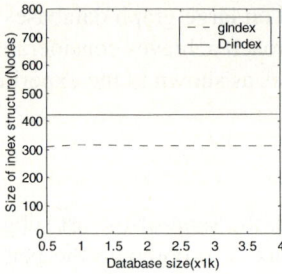 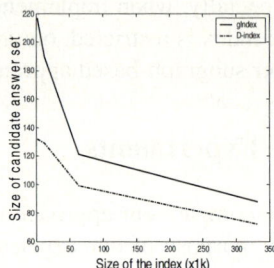

Fig. 7. Performance on various sizes of database   **Fig. 8.** Index size on various sizes of database   **Fig. 9.** Performance on various sizes of index

This is because the number of subgraphs divided from a graph increases with the size of graphs. This increase, however, decreases the pruning power of the subgraph-based approach, because this approach cannot represent the information between the subgraph and the original graph. This also indicates that degree information can successfully maintain the relationship between the subgraph and the original graph, and therefore, decrease the size of candidate answer set. This made our approach superior to the existing approaches.

Fig.7 shows that the performance of both D-index and gIndex scaled linearly with the database size. Furthermore, this difference is more remarkable especially when the database was extremely large.

Fig.8 indicates that the database size have no impact on the size of index structure. This is due to the construction method of the index. Note that, recall from the results shown in Fig. 6, the improvement of our approach increases with the size of graphs. Although our approach is less storage efficient, the size of the index structure is stabile. Therefore, this disadvantage can be ignored when the size of database is large. Actually, D-index reduces the size of candidate answer set by 20%-50%. According to the definition of performance in the end of Section 3, it achieves a 30% to 80% improvement in terms of execution time over the gIndex when restricted in same size of storage.

Although the improvement decreases when the size of the index increases, Fig. 9 depicts that the D-index at least reduces the size of candidate answer set by 20%. The experimental results suggest that D-index works well in any condition especially when implemented on large graph databases or the database whose size of the index is restricted. It at least achieves a 30% improvement due to reducing the size of candidate answer set by 20%.

4 Conclusion

Subgraph query is a very important problem for many information retrieval and data mining tasks on graph database. The graph indexing has attracted increasing attentions due to its wide usefulness.

In this paper, we have explored a different approach to graph indexing. Our approach suggests that the introducing of degree information can help increase the pruning power of the index. Especially, when implemented on large graph databases or the database whose size of the index is restricted, D-index can help represent the whole features of graph by several small index items.

Experimental results also show that D-index reduces the size of candidate answer set by 20%-50%. According to the definition of performance in the end of Section 3, it achieves a 30% to 80% improvement in terms of execution time over the state-of-the-art approach, gIndex. When implemented on large graph databases, D-index achieves more considerable performance improvements over subgraph-based approaches than it does on small database.

Acknowledgments. This work is supported by the National Science Foundation of China (60403021) and the 973 Program (2004CB719400).

References

1. D. Shasha, J TL. Wang, and R. Giugno. Algorithmics and applications of tree and graph searching. Proceedings of the twenty-first ACM SIGMOD-SIGACT-SIGART symposium on Principles of database systems 2002, Madison, Wisconsin June 03-05, 2002.
2. X. Yan, PS. Yu and J. Han. Graph indexing: A frequent structure based approach. Proceedings of the 2004 ACM SIGMOD international conference on Management of data 2004, Paris, France June 13 - 18, 2004.
3. X.Yan and J.Han. gspan: Graph-based substructure pattern mining. Second IEEE International Conference on Data Mining (ICDM'02), 2002.
4. B. Goethals, E. Hoekx and J. Van den Bussche. Mining tree queries in a graph. Proceeding of the eleventh ACM SIGKDD international conference on Knowledge discovery in data mining 2005, Chicago, Illinois, USA August 21 - 24, 2005.
5. R. Giugno and D.Shasha. Graphgrep: A fast and universal method for querying graphs. 16th International Conference on Pattern Recognition (ICPR'02) Volume 2, 2002.
6. M.Kuramochi and G.Karypis. Frequent subgraph discovery. First IEEE International Conference on Data Mining (ICDM'01), 2001.
7. J. Wang, Z. Zeng and L. Zhou. CLAN: An Algorithm for Mining Closed Cliques from Large Dense Graph Databases. Proceedings of the 22nd International Conference on Data Engineering (ICDE'06) April 03 - 07, 2006.

8. J. Huan, W. Wang, J. Prins and J. Yang. SPIN: Mining Maximal Frequent Subgraphs from Graph Databases. Proceedings of the tenth ACM SIGKDD international conference on Knowledge discovery and data mining 2004, Seattle, WA, USA August 22 - 25, 2004.
9. X. Yan, F. Zhu, J. Han and PS. Yu. Searching Substructures with Superimposed Distance. 22nd International Conference on Data Engineering (ICDE'06), 2006.
10. X. Yan, PS. Yu and J. Han. Substructure Similarity Search in Graph Databases. Proceedings of the 2005 ACM SIGMOD international conference on Management of data 2005, Baltimore, Maryland June 14 - 16, 2005.

Evaluation of Decision Tree Pruning with Subadditive Penalties

Sergio García-Moratilla, Gonzalo Martínez-Muñoz, and Alberto Suárez

Universidad Autónoma de Madrid,
Avenida Francisco Tomás y Valiente, 11,
Madrid 28049, Spain
sergio.garcia@uam.es, gonzalo.martinez@uam.es, alberto.suarez@uam.es

Abstract. Recent work on decision tree pruning [1] has brought to the attention of the machine learning community the fact that, in classification problems, the use of subadditive penalties in cost-complexity pruning has a stronger theoretical basis than the usual additive penalty terms. We implement cost-complexity pruning algorithms with general size-dependent penalties to confirm the results of [1]. Namely, that the family of pruned subtrees selected by pruning with a subadditive penalty of increasing strength is a subset of the family selected using additive penalties. Consequently, this family of pruned trees is unique, it is nested and it can be computed efficiently. However, in spite of the better theoretical grounding of cost-complexity pruning with subadditive penalties, we found no systematic improvements in the generalization performance of the final classification tree selected by cross-validation using subadditive penalties instead of the commonly used additive ones.

1 Introduction

Decision trees are one of the most extended types of classifiers. The reasons for their wide use are the availability of efficient algorithms for the automatic induction of decision trees from labeled data (CART [2], C4.5 [3]), the high processing speed and accuracy that can be obtained in many classification problems of practical interest, and the interpretability of the classification models generated.

A decision tree is a hierarchical questionnaire that partitions the data into disjoint subsets according to the result of tests associated to each of the non-terminal nodes of the tree. By applying the sequence of tests at the internal nodes, an example is associated to a single leaf node on the fringe of the decision tree. The classification given by the tree is the class label of the leaf node to which the example is assigned. Assuming that only Boolean tests are used, as in CART, the decision tree is a rooted binary tree. The root node has all the examples associated to it and yields as a classification the majority class of the examples in the whole training set. The binary decision tree is grown from the root node by performing a test that splits the data into two disjoint subsets. Each of these subsets is associated to one of the two child nodes of the root node, which becomes an internal node of the tree. Each of the newly generated child nodes becomes labeled with the majority class of the training examples associated to it. The split is chosen to maximize a quantity that is correlated with the classification accuracy of the tree (for instance impurity reduction [2], information gain, information gain ratio [3], etc.) This divide-and-conquer process is repeated for each of the newly generated nodes until either all examples are correctly classified or a termination criterion is satisfied.

Trees grown with this greedy algorithm need not be globally optimal. Furthermore, if they are grown until they reach the minimum classification error on the training data, they typically exhibit poor generalization performance and yield overly optimistic estimates of the true classification error. To avoid overfitting to the training data, the tree growing process could be stopped when a properly designed termination criterion is fulfilled. However, it has proved difficult to design appropriate stopping rules [2]. Instead, the strategy that is commonly used is to overgrow the decision tree until all training examples are correctly classified, and then to prune the fully-grown tree upward, in an appropriate order, until the optimal tree is found. Biases can be avoided if the pruning process is guided by using classification error rates estimated on a validation set, an independent collection of labeled examples, which have not used in the construction of the tree [4]. While this may be an appropriate strategy for problems in which labeled training data is either abundant or easy to obtain, in data-poor problems, or when the labeling process is costly, one should avoid using separate portions of the training set for the growing and for the pruning process [5]. An alternative to this procedure is the cost-complexity pruning proposed in CART, where the goal is to minimize a function that considers both misclassification costs and a measure of the tree complexity [2].

The complexity penalty used in most cost-complexity pruning methods for decision trees, and in particular in CART, is additive. Additive penalties increase linearly with the size of the decision tree. Recent results in statistical learning theory suggest that subadditive penalties, and in particular a penalty term that varies as the square root of the size of the tree, may be more appropriate for classification problems [1,6,7,8,9]. A subadditive penalty is monotonic but its increase with the size of the tree is slower than linear. The theoretical support for subadditive penalty terms comes from complexity regularization theory [7] and from structural risk minimization formulas that provide bounds for the generalization error of a decision tree [6]. Generally, additive penalties are used because one can design pruning algorithms that are fast, efficient in memory use, and easy to implement [1]. Little o no theoretical justification is given for the choice of a linear penalty term.

The goal of the present work is to investigate whether cost-complexity pruning with subadditive penalties, which seems to be theoretically well grounded, improves the results of other pruning strategies in a collection of benchmark problems. Previous research devoted to performing extensive comparisons between different pruning strategies [5,10] did not consider the possibility of subadditive penalties. To carry out this comparison we implement the efficient pruning algorithms designed in [1] and confirm the main results of this work. In particular we corroborate that in all cases the family of trees selected by pruning with a subadditive penalty is a subset of the nested family of trees obtained by pruning with additive penalties. Following CART, we select a single tree from the family of pruned trees using cross-validation error estimates. The performance of the selected tree is then compared with the corresponding standard CART tree, which is induced using an additive penalty.

2 Cost-Complexity Pruning Using Subadditive Penalties

Consider T, a binary decision tree. Any subtree S of T containing the root node is a pruned subtree of T. This relation is denoted by $S \preccurlyeq T$. The set of terminal nodes of T is $\tilde{T}$ and the number of terminal nodes is $|T|$.

The idea behind cost-complexity pruning is to avoid overfitting by balancing the performance on the training data and the complexity of the generated model. The performance is quantified by a cost function $\rho(S)$. In classification trees the cost function typically used is the training classification error. The complexity of the model is measured by a penalty function $\Phi(S)$, which, for decision trees, is a function of the size of the tree or, equivalently, of the number of terminal nodes. The following assumptions can be made about these functions: (i) $\rho(S)$ is a monotonically non-increasing function. That is, if $S_1 \preccurlyeq S_2$ then $\rho(S_1) \geq \rho(S_2)$, (ii) $\rho(S)$ is additive; i.e. it can be calculated by $\rho = \sum_{t \in \tilde{T}} \rho(t)$ and (iii) the penalty function $\Phi(|S|)$ is a monotonically increasing function of the tree size. That is, if $S_1 \prec S_2$ then $\Phi(|S_1|) < \Phi(|S_2|)$, where $S_1 \prec S_2$ indicates that $S_1 \preccurlyeq S_2$ and that $S_1 \neq S_2$.

To balance the importance of $\rho(S)$ with respect to $\Phi(|S|)$ a tuning parameter α is introduced. For a given value of α the optimal tree according to the cost-complexity function is

$$T^*(\alpha) = \underset{S \preccurlyeq T}{argmin} \left[\rho(S) + \alpha \Phi(|S|) \right]. \qquad (1)$$

The final classification tree is selected by estimating the value of α using cross-validation. Given that $|T| < \infty$, the solutions of Eq. (1) are a finite set of pruned subtrees $R_l \preccurlyeq T$, $l = 1, \ldots, m$ such that $|R_1| > |R_2| > \cdots > |R_m| = 1$. Each of these trees is optimal for a range of values of α

$$\alpha \in [\alpha_{l-1}, \alpha_l) \Rightarrow T(\alpha) = R_l, \qquad 0 = \alpha_0 < \alpha_1 < \cdots < \alpha_m = \infty \qquad (2)$$

The goal is to select the optimally pruned tree from R_l, $l = 1, \ldots, m$ by determining the correct value of α. For both additive and subadditive penalties the family of pruned subtrees is unique and nested [1,2]

$$root = R_m \prec \cdots \prec R_2 \prec R_1 \preccurlyeq T. \qquad (3)$$

Another important result demonstrated in [1] is that the family of subtrees obtained using subadditive penalties is a subset of the family generated using additive penalties. This implies that there are less trees available for selection

Input: Fully developed tree T
Output: Minimum cost trees $T^k = T_1^k$, $k = 1, 2, \ldots, |T|$

```
1. for t = 2|T| - 1 to 1 {
2.     set T_t^1 = t
3.     if (t is not a terminal node) {
4.         for k = 2 to |T_t| {
5.             set mincost = ∞
6.             for i = max(1, k - |T_{r(t)}|) to min(|T_{l(t)}|, k - 1) {
7.                 set j = k - i
8.                 set cost = ρ(T_{l(t)}^i) + ρ(T_{r(t)}^j)
9.                 if cost < mincost {
10.                    set mincost = cost
11.                    set T_t^k = merge(t, T_{l(t)}^i, T_{r(t)}^j)
12.                }
13.            }
14.        }
15.    }
16. }
```

Fig. 1. Pseudocode for computing minimum cost trees

Input: Minimum cost trees T_1^k, $k = 1, 2, \ldots, |T|$
Output: Family of prunings R_l and thresholds α_l

```
1. set k_1 = argmin (ρ(T^k) = ρ(T))
               k
2. set R_1 = T^{k_1}
3. set l = 1
4. while k_l > 1 {
5.     set α_l = ∞
6.     for k = k_l - 1 to 1 {
7.         set γ = (ρ(T^k) - ρ(T^{k_l}))/(Φ(k_l) - Φ(k))
8.         if γ < α_l {
9.             set α_l = γ
10.            set k_{l+1} = k
11.        }
12.    }
13.    set l = l + 1
14.    set R_l = T^{k_l}
15. }
```

Fig. 2. Pseudocode for computing the family of pruned subtrees

using cross-validation. Despite having a smaller range of trees to choose from, the extra trees that appear when additive penalties are used may actually have poorer generalization performance, in which case it would be better not to consider them for selection [1].

The algorithms presented in Figs. 1 and 2 generate the family of subtrees pruned with a general size-based penalty term of increasing strength [1]. The algorithm detailed in Fig. 1 constructs the minimum cost pruned subtrees of sizes 1 to $|T|$ from the fully grown tree T. Tree nodes are indexed by numbers 1 to $2|T|-1$ in such a way that children nodes always have a larger index than their parents. The root node has index 1. The expression T_t denotes the full tree rooted at node t (hence $T = T_1$) and T_t^k denotes the lowest cost pruned subtree of T_t of size k (i.e. $|T_t^k| = k$). The expressions $l(t)$ and $r(t)$ refer to the left child and right child of t, respectively. The algorithm given in Fig. 2 generates the family of pruned subtrees R_l and thresholds α_l of Eq. (2) from the minimum cost tree set ($T^k = T_1^k$, $k = 1, 2, \ldots, |T|$) returned from the algorithm in Fig. 1.

3 Experiments

In order to compare the performance of pruning strategies using either linear (additive) or square-root (subadditive) penalties we carry out experiments in eight datasets from the UCI repository [11] and in two synthetic datasets proposed by Breiman *et al.* [2]. The datasets are selected to sample a variety of problems from different fields of application. The characteristics of the selected datasets and the testing method are shown in Table 1.

The experiments consist in 100 executions for each dataset. For real-world datasets we perform a 10×10-fold cross-validation. For the synthetic datasets (*Led24* and *Waveform*) random sampling was applied to generate each of the 100 training and testing sets. Each experiment involves the following steps: (i) Obtain the training and testing sets (by 10-fold-cv or by random sampling) and build a fully grown tree T with the training dataset using the CART tree growing algorithm [2]. (ii) Compute the family of pruned subtrees R_l of T and thresholds α_l, using a square-root penalty (i.e. $\Phi(|S|) = \sqrt{|S|}$) in the algorithms of Figs. 1 and 2. (iii) Obtain by V-fold-cv on the training dataset V trees ($T^{(1)}, \ldots, T^{(V)}$) and their respective families of pruned subtrees $R_m^{(v)}$ for $v = 1, \ldots, V$. The value $V = 10$ is used. Select one subtree from each of the V families for each of the

Table 1. Characteristics of the datasets and testing method

Dataset	Instances	Test	Attrib.	Classes
Australian	690	10-fold-cv	14	2
Breast W.	699	10-fold-cv	9	2
Diabetes	768	10-fold-cv	8	2
German	1000	10-fold-cv	20	2
Heart	270	10-fold-cv	13	2
Ionosphere	351	10-fold-cv	34	2
Led24	200	5000 cases	24	10
New-thyroid	215	10-fold-cv	5	3
Tic-tac-toe	958	10-fold-cv	9	2
Waveform	300	5000 cases	21	3

following α values: $\alpha_{geom}^l = \sqrt{\alpha_{l-1}\alpha_l}$, $l = 1, \ldots, m$. For each value of α_{geom}^l calculate the error of the selected subtrees using the independent set and obtain the average cv-error (e_{cv}^l) and standard deviation (se_{cv}^l). (iv) Select the pruned subtree from (R_l, $l = 1, \ldots, m$) corresponding to the α_{geom}^l value producing the smallest cv-error e_{cv}^{l*}. Denote this tree by CV-0SE. We also select the smallest tree corresponding to cv-error such that $e_{cv}^l < e_{cv}^{l*} + se_{cv}^{l*}$ and denote it by CV-1SE. Breiman *et al.* advocate the selection of CV-1SE (the 1 SE rule in [2]) because it is the simplest tree whose accuracy is comparable to CV-0SE (the optimal tree according to the cross-validation procedure) when the uncertainty in the cross-validation error estimates is taken into account. (v) Repeat steps 2-4 using additive penalties $\Phi(|S|) = |S|$. This configuration results in standard CART trees.

The results of the experiments performed are in agreement with the theoretical results demonstrated in [1]. In particular, the family of pruned subtrees obtained when applying a square-root subadditive penalty term is a subset of the family of trees obtained when considering additive penalties.

Table 2 displays the average test error and average size of the selected trees for the different pruning configurations and datasets. The best average test error for each classification task is highlighted in boldface. The test errors are very similar in trees selected with either subadditive or additive penalties. The differences between CV-0SE and CV-1SE (and between these and unpruned trees) are actually larger. Another important observation is that there does not seem to be a systematic trend in the variations in performance. In some datasets the more complex trees perform better (*New-thyroid, Tic-tac-toe*). In other problems the minimum is obtained for medium-sized trees (*Breast W., Heart, Led24, Waveform*). Finally, there are some datasets where the smaller trees are slightly better (*Australian, Diabetes, German*). The lack of a clear tendency in the results is apparent in the *Ionosphere* dataset, where the highest error corresponds to a tree of intermediate size.

Table 2. Test errors and sizes of the decision trees selected

| | Unpruned | | CV-0SE | | | | CV-1SE | | | |
| | | | Subadd. | | CART | | Subadd. | | CART | |
Dataset	error	size	error	size	error	size	error	size	error	size
Australian	18.7	151.2	15.1	9.8	15.2	9.9	**14.7**	3.6	**14.7**	3.8
BreastW.	5.6	67.4	**5.3**	31.3	5.5	29.7	6.0	12.3	6.2	12.5
Diabetes	29.9	247.1	26.0	19.1	**25.8**	22.5	25.9	8.1	**25.8**	6.8
German	30.8	329.2	26.0	26.9	26.0	23.6	26.1	10.8	**25.8**	11.1
Heart	26.8	83.9	**22.7**	15.7	**22.7**	16.4	23.4	9.0	23.3	8.5
Ionosphere	**10.4**	44.3	11.3	16.0	11.4	15.5	10.8	5.9	10.7	5.7
Led24	43.6	146.3	**32.7**	21.7	32.9	24.7	33.7	18.6	33.6	18.6
New-thyroid	**6.6**	22.9	7.6	17.6	7.6	17.5	9.2	10.6	9.1	10.7
Tic-tac-toe	**5.5**	143.1	5.9	105.4	5.9	106.1	6.7	69.1	6.7	71.0
Waveform	29.6	78.9	**28.9**	31.7	29.0	28.3	30.2	16.0	30.3	15.7

Table 3. Family size and number of coincidences in the tree selected

Dataset	Average m		# same tree is selected	
	Subadd.	CART	CV-0SE	CV-1SE
Australian	10.74	13.32	79	96
Breast W.	10.01	10.54	59	70
Diabetes	11.24	16.02	64	82
German	13.52	19.52	44	65
Heart	9.47	10.19	64	71
Ionosphere	7.59	8.25	92	97
Led24	11.19	15.76	76	94
New-thyroid	5.85	6.60	99	95
Tic-tac-toe	13.40	17.22	78	75
Waveform	11.23	12.20	67	70

The average sizes of the trees selected using subadditive and additive penalties are very similar. This can be seen in the second and third columns of Table 3, which display the average size of the families of subtrees for subadditive and additive penalties, respectively. The differences are small for most datasets. In fact, they are less that one on average for half of the studied datasets (*Breast, Heart, Ionosphere, New-thyroid, Waveform*). This indicates that the size of the final tree selected with both types of penalties is very similar. The fourth and fifth columns of Table 3 show the number of times (out of the 100 executions) in which both penalties actually selected the same final pruned subtree for CV-0SE and CV-1SE, respectively. The fact that in most instances the same tree is selected, irrespective of the type of complexity penalty used, accounts for the similarity of the values of test errors.

4 Conclusions

Despite the large body of work on decision trees, there has been little research into the problem of how to prune fully grown trees to their optimal size using complexity penalty terms. This paucity of theoretical investigations may be ascribed to the fact that pruning with additive penalties, which are commonly used in cost-complexity pruning, can be readily and efficiently implemented. Furthermore, classification trees that are selected using cross-validation from a family of trees pruned with additive penalties seem to perform well in many problems of practical interest. Recent work on statistical learning theory for classification problems indicates that subadditive penalties may have a sounder theoretical basis than the additive penalty terms commonly used in cost-complexity pruning. In this research we implement the efficient algorithms designed in [1] to generate families of decision trees pruned with nonadditive penalty terms. The family of pruned trees is generated using a subadditive complexity penalty that increases with the square root of the size of the tree. From this family a tree is selected as the final classifier using cross-validation error estimates.

Experiments on benchmark problems from the UCI repository show that, in the datasets investigated, there is no systematic improvement of the classification performance of decision trees selected by cross-validation from a family of pruned trees induced with a square-root penalty. Since the family of trees pruned using subadditive penalties is necessarily smaller than or equal to the family pruned using additive ones, there is little room for improvement and, in fact, the decision trees selected using either a square-root penalty or linear penalty are often equal. This conclusion should also obtain for other subadditive penalties. In summary, despite the implications of recent theoretical work, we have found no evidence in the classification problems analyzed of systematic improvements in generalization performance by using subadditive penalties instead of the usual additive ones.

Acknowledgments

The authors acknowledge financial support from the Spanish *Dirección General de Investigación*, project TIN2004-07676-C02-02.

References

1. Scott, C.: Tree pruning with subadditive penalties. IEEE Transactions on Signal Processing **53**(12) (2005) 4518–4525
2. Breiman, L., Friedman, J.H., Olshen, R.A., Stone, C.J.: Classification and Regression Trees. Chapman & Hall, New York (1984)
3. Quinlan, J.R.: C4.5 programs for machine learning. Morgan Kaufmann (1993)
4. Quinlan, J.R.: Simplifying decision trees. Int. J. Man-Mach. Stud. **27**(3) (1987) 221–234
5. Esposito, F., Malerba, D., Semeraro, G., Kay, J.: A comparative analysis of methods for pruning decision trees. IEEE Transactions on Pattern Analysis and Machine Intelligence **19**(5) (1997) 476–491
6. Mansour, Y., McAllester, D.A.: Generalization bounds for decision trees. In: COLT '00: Proceedings of the Thirteenth Annual Conference on Computational Learning Theory, San Francisco, CA, USA, Morgan Kaufmann Publishers Inc. (2000) 69–74
7. Nobel, A.: Analysis of a complexity-based pruning scheme for classification trees. IEEE Transactions on Information Theory **48**(8) (2002) 2362–2368
8. C., S., R., N.: Dyadic classification trees via structural risk minimization. Advances in Neural Information Processing Systems 15 (2003)
9. Scott, C., Nowak, R.: Minimax-optimal classification with dyadic decision trees. IEEE Transactions on Information Theory **52**(4) (2006) 1335–1353
10. Mingers, J.: An empirical comparison of pruning methods for decision tree induction. Machine Learning **4**(2) (1989) 227–243
11. Blake, C.L., Merz, C.J.: UCI repository of machine learning databases (1998)

Categorization of Large Text Collections: Feature Selection for Training Neural Networks

Pensiri Manomaisupat[1], Bogdan Vrusias[1], and Khurshid Ahmad[2]

[1] Department of Computing, University of Surrey
Guildford, Surrey, UK
{P.Manomaisupat, B.Vrusias}@surrey.ac.uk
[2] Department of Computer Science, O'reilly Institute, Trinity College
Dublin 2, Ireland
Khurshid.Ahmad@cs.tcd.ie

Abstract. Automatic text categorization requires the construction of appropriate surrogates for documents within a text collection. The surrogates, often called *document vectors*, are used to train learning systems for categorising unseen documents. A comparison of different measures (*tfidf* and *weirdness*) for creating document vectors is presented together with two different state-of-the-art classifiers: supervised Kohonen's SOFM and unsupervised Vapniak's SVM. The methods are tested using two 'gold standard' document collections and one data set from a 'real-world' news stream. There appears to be an optimal size both for the of document vectors and for the dimensionality of each vector that gives the best compromise between categorization accuracy and training time. The performance of each of the classifiers was computed for five different surrogate vector models: the first two surrogates were created with *tfidf* and weirdness measures accordingly, the third surrogate was created purely on the basis of high-frequency words in the training corpus, and the fourth vector model was created from a standardised terminology database. Finally, the fifth surrogate (used for evaluation purposes) was based on a random selection of words from the training corpus.

Keywords: Feature selection, Text categorisation, Information extraction, Self-organizing feature map (SOFM), Support vector machine (SVM).

1 Introduction

News text streams, like Reuters and Bloomberg, supply documents in a range of topic areas and the topic 'code(s)' are marked on the news texts. The assignment of topic codes requires the definition of topics. For the automatic topic assignment, a semantic concept space of relevant terms has to be created. There is a degree of arbitrariness in the assignment of topic codes by the news agency (subeditors) [1]. The problems relating to the choice of terms can be obviated to an extent by using information retrieval measures like *tfidf* where statistical criteria are used to select terms that are specific enough to be characteristic of a domain and characteristic of a the majority of documents within the domain. More problems are encountered when topics are closely related (for example in one of our experiments we found that the terminology of *currency markets* and *bond markets* has substantial overlaps). Due to the large volumes of new, covering different topics, that are becoming available, it is important to have a system that not only can categorise but can also learn to categorise. Once trained to a certain performance measure, the system is then tested with an arbitrary selection of unseen texts from the domain.

Typically, a text categorization system is presented with a representative sample of texts comprising one or more topic areas: each text is then represented by a surrogate vector – usually containing keywords that characterize a specific document or sets of keywords that may represent a domain [2]. The choice of the keywords – based on information-theoretic measures – is not without controversy or problems. Once the keywords are chosen the training of a text categorization begins: essentially, given the training texts and a lexicon of keywords to construct the vectors, a (supervised) learning system learns to categorize texts according to the categories that are prescribed by a teacher; or in the case of an unsupervised learning system, the vectors are clustered according to a similarity measure and the resulting clusters are expected to have some relation to the given categories of news texts in the training data set. The supervised learning systems require the pre-knowledge of the categories and the keywords that may be used to construct the surrogate vectors. In the case of unsupervised systems, only the knowledge of keywords is required; however, the categories generated by an unsupervised method may be at considerable variance with real world categories. The discussions in the information retrieval/extraction literature focus largely on supervised or semi-supervised classification [3, 5] and a keen interest in recent developments in machine learning, especially support vector machines (SVM) [5]. The success of the unsupervised text categorization systems, precipitated by the development of WEBSOM [7, 8], where they looked at a number of different methods for describing the 'textual contents of documents statistically', and have made comments about traditional information retrieval measures: *tfidf* and *latent semantic indexing (LSI)*. An important finding here is that LSI particularly is computationally more complex than 'random projection techniques', that compress the feature vector space by around 1%, and that the use of LSI is not as straightforward as it appears. It has been noted that the use of LSI does not offer significant advantage over term space reduction methods in the context of neural classifiers [9].

The measures used for selecting the keywords for surrogate vectors have been debated in the text categorization literature extensively. Consider how such vectors were created for the 'largest WEBSOM map [...][that interfaces] a data base of 6,840,568 patent abstracts' written in English with average length of 132 words [6, pp. 581]. A total of 733,179 base forms exist in this patent-abstract corpus: WEBSOM designers decided intuitively to remove all words 'occurring less than 50 times in the whole [patent] corpus, as well as a set of common words in a stop-word list of 1335 words': the 'remaining vocabulary consisted of 43,222 words'; 122,524 abstracts in which less than five words of the vocabulary were 'omitted'. The self-organising system thus trained had an excellent classification accuracy of around 60% and took 'about six weeks on a six-processor SGI O2000 computer' (ibid, pp 582). The choice of keywords appears inspired and what is needed is to look at ways in which the choice itself is automated as the training is. This is the burden of argument in this paper.

In our work we have looked at news wire either organised according to specific topics (the TREC 96 collection) or provided by a news agency covering a range of topics. The latter comprise two text collections: the topic diversified RCV1 corpus and daily financial news wire supplied by Reuters Financial over a month. A part of the three news collections – also referred to as news wire corpora – was used for training two text categorisation systems and another smaller part used for testing. We have contrasted the performance of the two systems trained on two very different training algorithms for potentially eliminating the bias due to the algorithms used. The keywords used in the construction of vectors, for training the two systems, were extracted automatically from the text collections using two different methods: the first method uses the well-known *tfidf* measure [3, 4] and the second uses information about the use of English in everyday context and then selects keywords on the basis of the contrast in the distribution of the same word in a specialist and a general language context (*weirdness* [11]). In order to evaluate the effectiveness of the two methods we have compared the performance of systems trained using words selected (i) randomly; (ii) purely on the basis of being above an arbitrary frequency threshold, and (iii) using keywords already available from an on-line thesaurus; techniques (i)-(iii) will be referred to as 'baseline' vectors.

The performance measurements for the supervised learning system included the use of a contingency table for contrasting the correctly/incorrectly recalled documents from the same category with that of the category of a test document; we have used 'break-even point' statistic to evaluate the performance of the SVM-based text categorization system.

The results presented here had involved us in training an SOFM and an SVM with very large vectors (starting from a 27 component vector through to 6561 component vector) and large number of documents (600 to 22,418). The computation for 27 component vector takes about 1 minute for 1000 input vectors and 6561 component vector takes about 30 hours for 10,000 input vectors. These computations were carried out over many thousands of iterations. In this paper we report the results of one single run for the two methods over 4 different lengths of vector together with 5 different methods of choosing keywords. Altogether we carried out 64 experiments each for SOFM and SVM (24 for TREC-AP, 20 each for RCV1 and Reuters Financial) over a period of about 10 weeks. Ideally we should have repeated these experiments especially for the SOFM and reported an aggregated result together with the values of standard deviations. This work is in progress.

2 Method

In the following section we describe measures for creating document vectors (2.1). The goal of a text classification algorithm is to assign a label to a document based upon its contents. We wish to explore the effect of how the choice of keywords to build a surrogate vector affects the ability of a system that is learning to classify documents. It may be argued that for supervised systems a complicating factor may be the choice of a 'teacher' and for the unsupervised system the factor may be the manner in which clusters are created and subsequently labelled [14]. In order to avoid such complications we use two popular and very different techniques: an exemplar unsupervised algorithm – Kohonen's SOFM [7]) (2.2); and an exemplar supervised algorithm – Vapniak's SVM [11] (2.3).

2.1 Measures for Creating Document Vectors from Text Collections

The first measure Term Frequency Inverse Document Frequency, *tfidf*, facilitates the creation of a set of vectors for a document collection by looking at the importance of a term within a document collection, document by document. Subsequently, a weight is assigned to individual terms based on the observation as to whether a given term can help in identifying a class of documents within the collection: the more frequent a term is in a specific collection of documents, and the less it appears in other collections, the higher its *tfidf* value.

The second measure is based on contrasting the frequency distribution of a word within a document collection, or a sub-collection, with the distribution of the same word within a non-specialist, but representative general language collection, for example, the 100 million words British National Corpus for English language. The ratio of the relative frequency in specialist and general language collections indicates whether or not a token is a candidate term. The ratio varies between zero (token not in the specialist collection) to infinity (token not used in the general language collection); the ratio of unity is generally found for the closed class words. Tokens with higher ratio are selected as feature terms [11].

For creating baseline vectors we have used three 'measures': first 'measure' relates to the random selection of words from the text collection excluding the closed class words; the second measure relates to the selection of most frequent words, excluding closed-class words, from a given text collection; the third 'measure' relates to the selection of using only those words that occur in a publicly available terminology database for the specialist domain where the texts in the collection originate. For the standardised term selection, we have used a web-based *glossary of financial terms* comprising 6,000 terms divided over 25 financial sub-categories [13] (see Table 1). In order to asses the optimum length of a surrogate vector, we have repeated our experiments with 3^n tokens (where $n=1-6$).

Table 1. The computation of term weighting used in the creation of vectors in the different models: the weighting is the product of term frequency (a) and text frequency (b) [14])

Methods	Text type	Term Frequency (a)	Text Frequency (b)
Term frequency/Inverse	Individual Documents d in a collection C	$tf_{t,d}$	df_t
Contrastive Linguistic	Documents in a specialist collection 'C' and in a general language collection 'G'	$tf_{t,c}$	$\dfrac{N_G}{N_C} * \dfrac{1}{tf_{t,G}}$
Baseline			
Random	Collection C	$tf_{t,d}$	NA
Pure Frequency	Collection C	$tf_{t,d}$ >threshold	NA
Standardised term	Collection C and Terminology database T_{DB}	$tf_{t,c}$	=1 if $t \in T_{DB}$ =0 otherwise

2.2 Self Organised Feature Map

The self-organising feature map is based on a grid of artificial neurons whose weights are adapted to match the input vectors presented during the training process. Unlike supervised neural networks, the SOFM does not produce an error based on an expected output; rather the SOFM learns to cluster similar data. An SOFM produces visualisations of the original high-dimensional data onto a two-dimensional surface/map. The two dimensional map produces clusters of input vectors based on 'detailed topical similarities' as the document categories are not known, *a priori* for the unsupervised system [6, 14]: The lack of *a priori* category information is a given for rapidly updated text collections. Financial news collections are a case in point: the categorisation at a sub-domain is quite critical (e.g. *financial news → currency news → US$ news*); where a sub-domain may disappear (for instance financial news → currencies of national states now in the Euro zone); and, new domains may appear (e.g. *financial news → derivative trading of currencies*). We have used following algorithm for training a SOFM:

STEP 1. Randomize the map's nodes' weight vectors
STEP 2. Take an input vector
STEP 3. Traverse each node in the map
   a. Use Euclidean distance to measure the distance between the input and all map's nodes
   b. Track the node that produces the smallest distance (the Best Matching Unit - *BMU*)
STEP 4. Update the BMU and all nodes in the neighbourhood by pulling them closer to the input vector according to Kohonen's formulae.
STEP 5. Repeat step 3-4 with a new input vector until all the input has been taken.
STEP 6. Update training parameters accordingly
STEP 7. Repeat step 5 and 6 for the desired number of cycles.

The weights $w_{ij}(t+1)$ of the winning neuron and its neighbourhood are adjusted as the incremental-learning occurs following the formulae:

$$w_{ij}(t+1) = w_{ij}(t) + \alpha(t) \times \gamma(t) \times (x_j - w_{ij}(t)) \tag{1}$$

w_{ij} is the current weight vector, x_j is the target input, t is the current iteration and $\alpha(t)$ is the learning restraint due to time. $\alpha(t)$ is given by:

$$\alpha(t) = (\alpha_{max} - \alpha_{min}) \times e^{\frac{t \times \ln\left(\frac{1}{t_{max}}\right)}{t_{max}}} + \alpha_{max} \tag{2}$$

where α_{max} is the starting learning rate and α_{min} is the final learning rate. The t value is the current cycle and the t_{max} is the total number of cycles. γ decays exponentially with increasing training cycles and neighbourhood distances [8].

In this experiment, the number of exemplar input vectors has a fixed size similar to the output grid which is determined during the unsupervised training process. Training commences with an output layer, consisting of 15x15 nodes. This training process is repeated for a fixed number λ of training iterations, we set $\lambda = 1,000$ cycles. The key parameters for successfully SOFM training include the learning rate (α) and the neighbourhood size (γ). We have used a typical initial setting for the training parameters, $\alpha=0.9$, $\gamma=8$, that eventually both decreased to zero towards the end of the training process. The testing regimen involves the computation of the Euclidian distance of a text input vector from the most 'excited' (winner takes all) node on the output map of the 15x15 trained SOFM, which will eventually determine the classification of the test input.

2.3 Support Vector Machine

A Support Vector Machine is a relatively new learning approach for solving two-class pattern recognition problems [16, 17]. An SVM attempts to find a hyperplane that maximises the margin between positive and negative training examples, while simultaneously minimizing training set misclassifications. Given a training set of instance-level pairs (x_i, y_i), $i=1,\ldots,l$ where $x_i \in R^n$ and $y \in \{1, -1\}^l$, when perfect separation is not possible along two class lines a slack variable (ξ) is introduced, and w defined as the weight vector. The support vector machines require the solution of the following optimisation problem:

$$\min_{w,b,\xi} \tfrac{1}{2} w^T w + C \sum_{i=1}^{l} \xi_i \qquad (3)$$

subject to $\qquad y_i (w^T \phi(x_i) + b) \geq 1 - \xi_i; \qquad$ where $\xi_i \geq 0 \qquad (4)$

In a binary classification task m labelled examples $(x_1, y_1),\ldots, (x_m, y_m)$ are used, where $x_i \in X$ are training data points and $y_i \in \{-1, +1\}$ are the corresponding class labels for the elements in X and b is a parameter. In order to make the data linearly separable, data points are mapped from the input space X to a feature space F with a mapping $\Phi: X \rightarrow F$ before they are used for training or for classification. The training vector x_i is mapped into a higher dimensional space by the function Φ. The support vector machine is expected to find a linear separating hyperplane with the maximal margin in this higher dimensional space. ($C > 0$ is the penalty parameter of the error term).

Following Yang and Liu [18]; Dumais *et al* [19] or Hearst [11], we have used the SVM with the RBF kernel function. The RBF kennel function is defined by as:

$$K(x_i, x_j) = \exp(-\gamma \|x_i - x_j\|^2), \gamma > 0 \qquad (5)$$

For computing C and γ the open-source implementation due to Hsu *et al* [20] was used.

3 Performance Measures

Two key metrics for determining the performance of SOFM's were used – the so-called *classification accuracy* and the *average quantization error* (AQE). For SVM performance we chose the *Break-even points* measure for measuring the effectiveness of the classification task.

Classification accuracy: Our evaluation method is similar to Kohonen et al [7] and Hung et al [19, 21]. Kohonen defines the categorisation error in terms of 'all documents that represented a minority newsgroup at any grid point were counted as classification errors.' We have used a majority voting scheme: given that a node in the SOFM has "won" many news reports from the same topic category, then our system can check the category information (which not used during the training process). If a majority of the news reports belonging to one category have been won over, then that node is assigned the majority's category. The classification accuracy is computed during testing by simply checking whether the category of the test news report matched that assigned to the BMU by the majority voting scheme.

Average quantization error (AQE): The best SOFM is expected to yield the smallest average quantization error qE. The mean of quantization error (AQE) as:

$$AQE = \frac{1}{N} \sum_{i=1}^{N} \|\vec{x}_i - \vec{w}_i\|, \qquad (6)$$

where N is the total number of input patterns, $\vec{x}_i$ is the sequences of the training vectors, and $\vec{w}_i$ is the initial values of the input pattern i [7].

Break-even points (BEP): For supervised networks, that have access to correct category information, information retrieval measures of precision and recall are used. Break-Even Points measure is an equally weighted combination of recall and precision.

4 Experiments and Results

We report on experiments carried out for selecting an 'appropriate' vector representation model for training and testing an unsupervised and supervised neural networks for text classification. The data sets used in creating representative vectors are publicly available. The systems used for training and testing can be downloaded by request to the authors.

We have used two data sets that have been used extensively in testing and evaluating text categorisation systems over the last 10 years: the TREC-AP-News wire (http://www-nlpir.nist.gov/projects/duc/pubs.html and ttp://trec.nist.gov/faq.html), the Reuters-22173 text collection (RCV1). These data sets were chosen by text retrieval experts from the 'noisy' real world news wire: we have used a third data set, only available through subscription – Reuters Financial News Stream (Table 2).

Table 2. The text collections used in our study. The texts were selected from a large dataset: TREC-AP news corpus comprises 242,918 documents; RCV1 has 806,791. For Reuters Financial we chose a month's news supply which was 22,418 news stories for that month.

Collection	Training Set		Testing Set	
	# of Document	# of Words	# of Document	# of Words
TREC- AP news	1,744	962,322	543	321,758
RCV1	600	114,430	180	64,217
Reuters Financial	13,670	6,710,000	8,748	4,074,174

4.1 SOFM Classifier Results

We begin by describing the results obtained on the TREC-AP collection. Recall that experts carefully chose this collection and their focus was on 10 well-defined topics. We created five vector sets of sizes 27, 81, 243, 2187 and 6561 – multiples of powers of 3.

The classification accuracy improves when increasing the vector size, therefore increasingly larger number of features, for both the key feature selection measures – *weirdness* and *tfidf*. However, the accuracy quickly reached 99% mark when the vector size was increased from 27 to 81 dimensions and the accuracy remained about the same despite the increase in the vector size to 6561 (See Table 1).

The comparison with our first benchmark –*randomly-selected keyword* vectors indicates that for small vector sizes the SOFM trained with randomly selected keywords has a classification accuracy of 60% for a 27 component vector and 72% for a 243 component vector: compare these with 96% and 99% for a SOFM trained using words of high weirdness and *tfidf*. As the number of components increase the randomly selected vector comes to within 10% of the classification accuracy for 6561 component vector. The second benchmark – *high-frequency* vector – has better or equal accuracy for all the six component vectors (between 27 and 6561 components).

Table 3. Classification Accuracy results using different size of vectors in TREC-AP collection

Feature Selection Measure			Benchmarking Measures			
Vector Size	Weirdness	tfidf	Random	High-frequency	Term-base
27	96.2%	96.3%	60.2%	99.1%	97.0%
81	99.3%	92.5%	66.8%	98.8%	97.1%
243	99.1%	93.7%	72.9%	99.0%	97.8%
2187	99.3%	98.8%	88.9%	99.0%	99.3%
6561	99.1%	98.8%	88.1%	98.1%	-

As expected, the average quantization error increases when the vector sizes are increased for both the key feature selection measures and for the three benchmark measures (See Table 4). The quantization error determines the extent to which the categories are isolated from each other. Recall that we are using a fixed size output surface (15X15) but we are increasing the components of the input vector 2-3 orders of magnitude. Perhaps, the increased resolution of the input vector, thereby allowing

Table 4. AQE of five feature selection methods for TREC-AP

Feature Selection Measure			Benchmarking Measures			
Vector Size	Weirdness	tfidf	Random	High-frequency	Term-base
27	0.002	0.001	0.02	0.01	0.02
81	0.01	0.02	0.004	0.03	0.02
243	0.05	0.04	0.01	0.07	0.04
6561	0.12	0.12	0.13	0.19	-

for more potential categories, should have been matched by an increment in the output map. As the output map was fixed, then that nodes that had 'won' different categories could not have been isolated enough. Higher AQE does not necessarily indicate that the classification will be bad. It simply indicates that there are no clear cluster boundaries. We are investigating the use of AQE in this respect.

The classification errors for the Reuters RCV1 corpus are substantially higher than that of TREC-AP as this corpus is more diffuse. The increment in the size of the vectors does decrease the error and again there is a plateau when the vector length increases beyond 243 (3^5). The keyword selection method shows a mild impact: vectors constructed using *tfidf* show a marginally poor performance than those constructed using weirdness analysis, especially for vectors of longer lengths (>243). As expected, the more diffuse Reuters Financial News Stream Corpus was categorized with much poorer classification accuracy partly because the number of terms used in the corpus is far higher than the maximum vector length of 6561: the weirdness measure appears to be performing better than the *tfidf* measure of constructing the vectors.

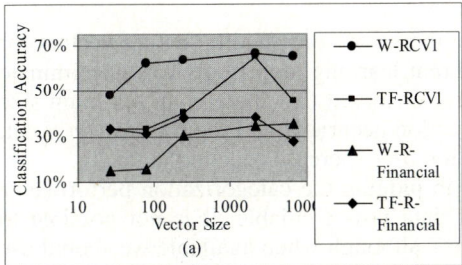 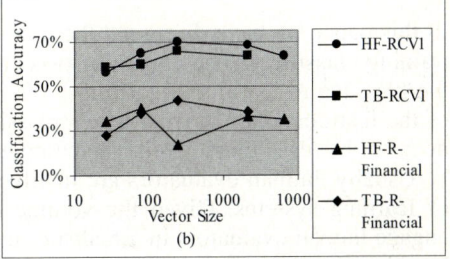

Fig. 1. shows the results for the benchmark vectors and a simple choice of very high frequency words as the basis of feature selection. This simple choice of keywords pays handsome dividends in terms of roughly the same or better classification accuracy obtained when compared with results of weirdness or *tfidf* measures. The other empirical choice of keywords – constructing vectors based on the entries in a terminology database appears to give similar results.

4.2 SVM Classifier

The performance of the support vector machines was quantified using the *break-even point* (BEP) computation – a combination of precision and recall measures. The results are, as expected, better than those obtained with the SOFM classifiers. The increase in the size of the vector eventually beyond 243 keywords both for weirdness-based and *tfidf* constructions and the former measure gives better BEP than the later (Figure 2a).

The high frequency vector outperforms all other methods of construction followed closely by vectors constructed exclusively from term bases (Figure 2b).

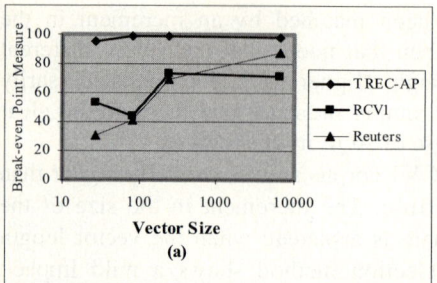 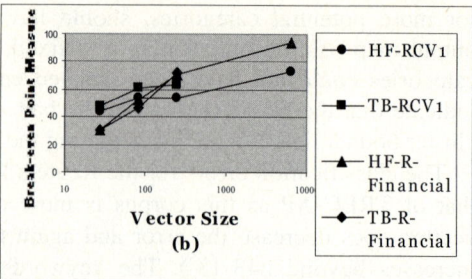

Fig. 2. Classification accuracy (CA) for SVM for different methods of constructing training vectors for learning categories in the two diffuse corpora (Reuters - *RCV1* and Reuters - *Financial News Stream*). Figure 2(a) shows the comparison of CA between weirdness-based measures (*W*) and the *tfidf* measure. Figure 2(b) shows the comparison between the 'benchmark' vectors using high-frequency terms in the RCV1 and R-Financial corpora and using terms in a terminology database only.

5 Conclusions and Future Work

In this paper we have discussed the relative merits of constructing feature vectors for training classifiers. The choice of two different learning algorithms was to eliminate the bias due to learning algorithms. We have observed that there is an optimum size of the feature vector beyond which classification accuracy, and the break-even point, does not increase much whilst the computation time increases due to the length.

Usually, human evaluators are involved in judging the categorization performance of learning systems. Given the volume of data now available, it is not possible to engage human evaluators in a realistic sense – although when available we should use human volunteers. One way to circumvent this problem is to use feature vectors with randomly selected terms from the training, or to select terms whose frequency is above a certain threshold within the corpus, or to construct a vector from a terminology data base without reference to the training corpus. Terms selected on the basis of simple frequency (or other frequency based measures like *tfidf* and *weirdness*) appear to lead to training vectors that, in turn, lead to higher classification accuracy (or BEP).

Work on large corpora needs further research due largely to the sheer volume of data and the computation time involved. All our results on CA and BEP are averages over thousands of trials, but in the case of Reuters Financial Corpus we need to carry more computations to deal with this topic-diverse corpus.

Acknowledgments. Two of the authors (P. Manomaisupat and B. Vrusias) gratefully acknowledge the support of the UK EPSRC sponsored REVEAL project (EPSRC GR/S98450/01). K. Ahmad acknowledges the support of Trinity College, Dublin.

References

1. Manomaisupat, P.: Term Extraction for Text Categorisation, (2006) (Unpublished PhD Dissertation, Department of Computing, University of Surrey)
2. Liao, D., Alpha, S. and Dixon, P.: Feature Preparation in Text Categorisation. Technical Report, Oracle Corporation Available at: http://www.oracle.com/technology/products/text/index.html Accessed: May 25, 2005

3. Croft, W.B. and Lewis, D.D.: Term Clustering of Syntactic Phrases. Proc. of the 13th Annual Int. ACM SIGIR Conf. on R&D in Information Retrieval, Brussels, Belgium (1990) 385-404
4. Manning, C. D., and Schütze, H.: Foundations of Statistical Natural Language Processing, Cambridge (Mass.) & London: The MIT Press (1999/2003)
5. Beitzel, S.M., Eric C. Jensen, E.C., Frieder, O., Lewis, D.D., Chowdhury, A., and Kołcz, A.: Improving Automatic Query Classification via Semi-Supervised Learning. IEEE Int. Conf. on Data Mining (ICDM'05) (2005) 42-49
6. Lewis, D. D.: Applying Support Vector Machines to the TREC-2001 Batch Filtering and Routing Tasks (2001)
7. Kohonen, T., Kaski, S., Lagus, K., Salojärvi, J., Honkela, J., Paatero, V. and Saarela A.: Self Organization of a Massive Document Collection. IEEE Trans. NN, vol.11, no.3 (2000) 574-585
8. Kohonen, T.: Self-Organizing Maps, Springer Verlag (2001)
9. Sebastiani, F.: Machine Learning in Automated Text Categorization. ACM Computing Surveys, vol. 34, no.1 (2002) 1–47
10. Xu R. and Wunsch D.: Survey of Clustering Algorithms. IEEE Transactions on Neural Networks, vol. 16, no. 3 (2005) 645-678
11. Hearst, M. A.: Support Vector Machines. IEEE Intelligent Systems, vol. 13, no. 4 (1998) 18-28
12. Ahmad, K., and Rogers, M. A.: Corpus Linguistics and Terminology Extraction. In (Eds.) S-E Wright and G. Budin. *Handbook of Terminology Management* (Volume 2). Amsterdam & Philadelphia: John Benjamins Publishing Company (2001) 725-760
13. Investorwords.com (www.Investorwords.com) [Accessed on 5 September, 2005]
14. Manomaisupat, P. and Ahmad, K.: Feature Selection for Text Categorisation Using Self-Organising Map. Proc. ICNN&B Int. Conf. on Neural Networks and Brain, vol. 3 (Oct 2005) 1875-1880
15. Arnulfo P. Azcarraga, Teddy N. Yap Jr., Tat Seng Chua and Jonathan Tan.: Evaluating Keyword Selection Methods for WEBSOM Text Archives. IEEE Trans. on DKE, vol 16, no.3 (2004) 380-383
16. Keerthi, S.S. and Line, C.J.: Asymptotic Behaviours of Support Vector Machines with Gaussian Kernel. Neural Computation, vol.15 (2003) 1667-1669
17. Hsu, W., Chang, C.C. and Line, C.J.: A Practical Guild to Support Vector Classification. Technical Report, Dept of CS and Info. Engineering, National Taiwan University, Taipei (2003)
18. Yang, Y. and Liu, X.: A Re-examination of Text Categorization methods. Proc. of the 22nd Int. ACM SIGIR Conf. of Research and Development in Information Retrieval (SIGIR), (1999) 42-49
19. Dumais, S. T., Platt, J., Heckerman, D. and Sahami, M.: Induction Learning Algorithms and Representations for Text Categorization. Proc. of the 7th ACM Int. Conf. on Information and Knowledge Management CIKM-98, Washington, US (1998) 148-155
20. Hung, C. and Wermter, S.: A Dynamic Adaptive Self-Organizing Hybrid Model for Text Clustering. Proc. of the 3rd IEEE Int. Conf. Data Mining (ICDM 03), IEEE Press (2003) 75-82
21. Hung, C., Wermter, S. and Smith, P.: Hybrid Neural Document Clustering Using Guided Self-Organization and WordNet. IEEE Intelligent Systems, vol.19, no.2 (2004) 68-77

Towards Healthy Association Rule Mining (HARM): A Fuzzy Quantitative Approach

Maybin Muyeba[1], M. Sulaiman Khan[1], Zarrar Malik[2], and Christos Tjortjis[2]

[1] Liverpool Hope University, School of Computing, Liverpool, UK
[2] University of Manchester, School of Informatics, UK
`muyebam@hope.ac.uk, m_sulaiman78@yahoo.com,`
`Zarrar.Malik@postgrad.manchester.ac.uk,`
`Christos.Tjortjis@manchester.ac.uk`

Abstract. Association Rule Mining (ARM) is a popular data mining technique that has been used to determine customer buying patterns. Although improving performance and efficiency of various ARM algorithms is important, determining Healthy Buying Patterns (HBP) from customer transactions and association rules is also important. This paper proposes a framework for mining fuzzy attributes to generate HBP and a method for analysing healthy buying patterns using ARM. Edible attributes are filtered from transactional input data by projections and are then converted to Required Daily Allowance (RDA) numeric values. Depending on a user query, primitive or hierarchical analysis of nutritional information is performed either from normal generated association rules or from a converted transactional database. Query and attribute representation can assume hierarchical or fuzzy values respectively. Our approach uses a general architecture for Healthy Association Rule Mining (HARM) and prototype support tool that implements the architecture. The paper concludes with experimental results and discussion on evaluating the proposed framework.

Keywords: Association rules, healthy patterns, fuzzy rules, primitive and hierarchical queries, nutrients.

1 Introduction

Association rules (ARs) [1] have been widely used to determine customer buying patterns from market basket data. Most algorithms in the literature have concentrated on improving performance through efficient implementations of the modified *Apriori* algorithm [2], [3]. Although this is an important aspect in large databases, extracting health related information from association rules or databases has mostly been overlooked. People have recently become "healthy eating" conscious, but largely they are unaware of qualities, limitations and above all, constituents of food. For example, how often do people who buy baked beans bother with nutritional information other than looking at expiry dates, price and brand name? Unless the customer is diet conscious, there is no explicit way to determine nutritional requirements and consumption patterns. As modern society is concerned with health issues, association rules can be used to determine healthy buying patterns by analysing product nutritional information, here termed Healthy Association Rule Mining (HARM), using market basket data. The term Healthy Buying Patterns (HBP) is introduced and signifies the level of nutritional content in an association rule per item.

The paper is organised as follows: section 2 presents background and related work; section 3 gives a problem definition; section 4 discusses the proposed methodology; section 5 details the proposed architecture; section 6 reviews experimental results, and section 7 concludes the paper with directions for future work.

2 Background and Related Work

In almost all AR algorithms, thresholds (both confidence and support) are crisp values. This support specification may not suffice for our approach and we need to handle linguistic terms such as "low protein" etc. in queries and rule representations.

Fuzzy approaches [4], [5] deal with quantitative attributes [6] by mapping numeric values to boolean values. A more recent overview is given in [7]. Little attention has been given to investigating healthy buying patterns (HBP) by analysing nutrition consumption patterns. However [8] presents fuzzy associations by decreasing the complexity of mining such rules using a reduced table. The authors also introduce the notion of mining for nutrients in the antecedent part of the rule but it is not clear how the fuzzy nutrient values are dealt with and consequently how membership functions are used. Nutrient analysis is therefore more complex a process than mere search for element presence. Our approach determines whether customers are buying healthy food, which can easily be evaluated using recommended daily allowance (RDA) standard tables. Other related work dealing with building a classifier using fuzzy ARs in biomedical applications is reported in [9].

3 Problem Definition

The problem of mining fuzzy association rules is given following a similar formulation in [10]. One disadvantage discussed, is that discretising quantitative attributes using interval partitions brings sharp boundary problems where support thresholds leave out transactions on the boundaries of these intervals. Thus the approach to resolve this, using fuzzy sets, is adopted in this paper.

Given a database D of transactions and items $I = \{i_1, i_2, ..., i_m\}$, we also define edible set of items $E \subseteq I$ where any $i_j \in E$ consists of quantitative nutritional information $\bigcup_{k=1}^{p} i_j^k$, where each i_j^k is given as standard RDA numerical ranges. Each quantitative item i_j is divided into various fuzzy sets $f(i_j)$ and $m_{i_j}(l, v)$ denotes the membership degree of v in the fuzzy set l, $0 \leq m_{i_j}(l, v) \leq 1$. For each transaction $t \in E$, a normalization process to find significance of an items contribution to the degree of support of a transaction is given by equation (1):

$$m'_{i_j} = \frac{m_{i_j}(l, t.i_j)}{\sum_{l=1}^{f(i_j)} m_{i_j}(l, t.i_j)} \qquad (1)$$

The normalisation process ensures fuzzy membership values for each nutrient are consistent and are not affected by boundary values. To generate fuzzy support (FS) value of an item set X with fuzzy set A, we use equation (2):

$$FS(X, A) = \frac{\sum_{t_i \in T} \pi_{x_j \in X} m_{x_j}(a_j \in A t_i . x_j)}{|E|} \qquad (2)$$

A quantitative rule represents each item as <item, value> pair. For a rule $< X, A > \rightarrow < Y, B >$, the fuzzy confidence value (FC) where $X \cup Y = Z, A \cup B = C$ is given by equation (3):

$$FC(< X, A > \rightarrow < Y, B >) = \frac{\sum_{t_i \in T} \pi_{z_z \in X} m_{z_j}(c_j \in C t_i . z_j)}{\sum_{t_i \in T} m_{x_j}(a_j \in A t_i . x_j)} \qquad (3)$$

where each $z \in \{X \cup Y\}$. For our approach, $X, Y \subset E$, where E is a projection of edible items from D. Depending on the query, each item i_j specified in the query and belonging to a particular transaction, is split or converted into p nutrient parts $\bigcup_{k=1}^{p} i_j^k, 1 \leq j \leq m$. For each transaction t, the bought items contribute to an overall nutrient k by averaging the total values of contributing items i.e. if items i_3, i_4 and i_7 are in a transaction t_1 and all contain nutrient k=5 in any proportions, their contribution to nutrient 5 is $\sum \frac{|i_j^5|}{3}$, j∈ {3,4,7}. These values are then aggregated into an RDA table with a schema of nutrients (see table 2, in 4.1) and corresponding transactions. We use the same notation for an item i_j with nutrient k, i_j^k, as item or nutrient i_k in the RDA table. Given that items i_k are quantitative (fuzzy) and we need to find fuzzy support and fuzzy confidence as defined, we introduce membership functions for each nutrient or item since for a normal diet intake, ideal intakes for each nutrient vary. However, five (5) fuzzy sets for each item are defined as {very low, low, ideal, high, very high}.

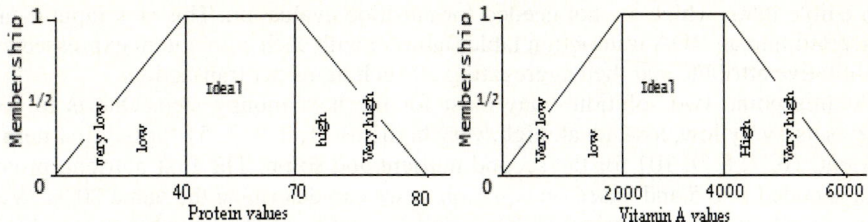

Fig. 1. Fuzzy membership functions

$$\mu(x,\alpha,\beta,\gamma,\delta,\theta) = \begin{cases} 0, \delta < x < \alpha \\ \dfrac{(\alpha - x)\theta}{(\alpha - \beta)}, \alpha \leq x \leq \beta \\ \theta, \theta = 1 \\ \dfrac{(\delta - x)\theta}{(\delta - \gamma)}, \gamma \leq x \leq \delta \end{cases} \quad (4)$$

Examples of fuzzy membership functions for some nutrients are shown in figue 1 (Protein and Vitamin A). The functions assume a trapezoidal shape since nutrient values in excess or in deficiency mean less than ideal intake according to expert knowledge. Ideal nutrients can assume value 1 naturally, but this value could be evaluated computationally to 0.8, 0.9 in practical terms. Equation 4 [11] represents all nutrient membership functions with input range of ideal values and the initial and final range of all values.

Note that equation 4 gives values equal to $m_{i_k}(l,v)$ in equations 1, 2 and 3. We can then handle any query after a series of data transformations and fuzzy function evaluations of associations between nutritional values.

4 Proposed Methodology

The proposed methodology consists of various HARM queries, each of which is evaluated using fuzzy sets for quantitative attributes as mentioned earlier. We can use any Apriori-type algorithm to generate rules but in this case Apriori TFP (Total From Partial) ARM algorithm is used as it is efficient and readily available to us. Apriori TFP stores large items in a tree and pre-processes input data to a partial P tree thus making it more efficient than Apriori and can also handle data of duplicate records. We have discovered three techniques to obtain HBPs as described in the next sections.

4.1 Normal ARM Mining

To mine from the transactional file (table 1), input data is projected into edible database on-the-fly thereby reducing the number of items in the transactions and possibly transactions too. The latter occurs because some transactions may contain non-edible items which are not needed for nutrition evaluation. This new input data is converted into an RDA transaction table (table 2) with each edible item expressed as a quantitative attribute and then aggregating all such items per transaction.

At this point, two solutions may exist for the next mining step. One is to code fuzzy sets {very low, low, ideal, high, very high} as {1, 2, 3, 4, 5} for the first item or nutrient, {6, 7, 8, 9, 10} for the second nutrient and so on. The first nutrient, protein (Pr), is coded 1 to 5 and based on equation 4, we can determine the value 20 as "Very Low" or VL etc. Thus nutrient Pr has value 1 in table 3. The encoded data (table 3) can be mined by any non-binary type association rule algorithm to find frequent item sets and hence association rules. This approach only gives us, for instance, the total support of various fuzzy sets per nutrient and not the degree of support as expressed in equations 1 and 2.

Table 1. Transaction file

TID	Items
1	X, Z
2	Z
3	X, Y, Z
4	..

Table 2. RDA transactions

TID	Pr	Fe	Ca	Cu
1	20	10	30	60
2	57	70	0	2
3	99	2	67	80
4	..	..	..	..

Table 3. Fuzzy transactions

TID	Pr	Fe	Ca	Cu
1	1	7	15	24
2	3	10	11	20
3	5	6	15	25
4				

Table 4. Linguistic transaction file

TID	VL	L	Ideal	H	VH	VL	L	Ideal	H	VH	..
1	0.03	0.05	0.9	0.01	0.01	0.2	0.1	0.8	0	0.7	..
2	0.2	0.1	0.0	0.7	0.1	0.23	0.2	0	0.5	0.1	..
3	0.7	0.2	0.03	0.15	0.12	0	0.5	0.3	0.3	0.11	..
4	..	..	..	..	..	..	..	..	..	..	

The other approach is to convert RDA transactions (table 2) to linguistic values for each nutrient and corresponding degrees of membership for the fuzzy sets they represent above or equal to a fuzzy support threshold. Each transaction then (table 4), will have repeated fuzzy values {very low, low, ideal, high, very high} for each nutrient present in every item of that transaction. Table 4 actually shows only two nutrients. A data structure is then used to store these values (linguistic value and degree of membership) and large itemsets are found based on the fuzzy support threshold. To obtain the degree of fuzzy support, we use equations 1 and 2 on each fuzzy set for each nutrient and then obtain ARs in the normal way with HBP values.

4.2 Rule Query on Nutrient Associations

To mine a specific rule, X→Y, for nutritional content, the rule base (table 5) is scanned first for this rule and if found, converted into an RDA table (table 6) otherwise, the transactional database is mined for this specific rule. The latter involves projecting the database with attributes in the query, thus reducing the number of attributes in the transactions, and mining as described in 4.1.

In the former case, HBP is calculated and the rule stored in the new rule base with appropriate support, for example [proteins, ideal] → [carbohydrates, low], 35%. A rule of the form "Diet Coke → Horlicks, 24%" could be evaluated to many rules including for example, [Proteins, ideal] → [Carbohydrates, low], 45%; where, according to rule representations shown in section 3, X is "Proteins", A is "ideal" and Y is "Carbohydrates", B is "low" etc. The same transformation to an RDA table occurs and the average value per nutrient is calculated before conversion to membership degrees or linguistic values. Using equations 1, 2, 3 and 4, we evaluate final rules with HBP values expressed as linguistic values. The following example shows a typical query as described in 4.1 where TID is transaction ID, X,Y, Z are items and Pr (protein), Fe (Iron), Ca (calcium), Cu (Copper) are nutritional elements and support of N% is given:

Table 5. Rule base

Rules	Support
X→Y	24%
Y→Z	47%
X,Y→Z	33%
..	..

Table 6. RDA table and HBP rule

	Pr	Fe	Ca	Cu	..
X→Y	20	10	30	60	..

X→Y [Proteins, Very Low] → [Carbohydrates, Low], s=45%, c=20%;

4.3 Hierarchical Rule Query

To make the system usable by a variety of users, hierarchical queries may be needed and a tree parsing algorithm can be used to obtain leaf nodes or concepts of the hierarchical query terms can be retrieved. After obtaining leaf terms, the mining algorithm proceeds as in section 4.2. For example, a hierarchical rule query such as:

Vegetable (V) → Meat (P)

where Vegetable is parsed to lettuce, cabbage etc. and meat to beef, liver etc. can be a typical query for other types of users.

5 Architecture

The proposed framework has a number of components in the architecture (see figure 2). Firstly, a user query is given for a specific task and the HARM Manager through the Query Detector determines the query type. If it is a query type described in section 4.1, the edible filter is activated and an RDA table generated for the given transactions for edible items. The Data Mining (DM) module then invokes an appropriate association rule algorithm. If the query is as in 4.2, then the RDA Converter is activated to generate RDA transactions for that rule and then an algorithm in the DM module is used. In our approach, we have thought it useful, for future use, to keep generated RDA transactions so that we can test other AR algorithms.

The fuzzy module involves tree parsing of hierarchical query terms (items) and determining fuzzy sets for these items' leaf concepts which become predefined rules. After filtration and RDA conversion is done, the query is then passed to the DM module where an appropriate algorithm is run for a particular query. Rules are generated and stored in the rule base.

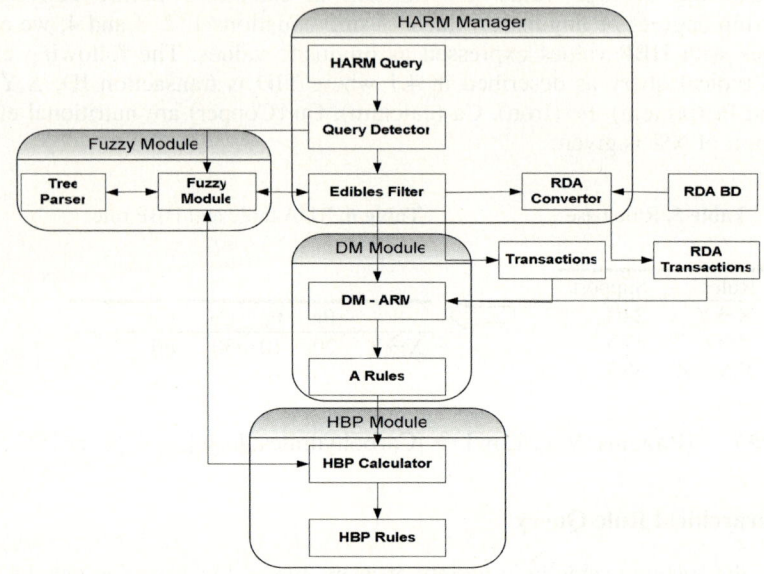

Fig. 2. HARM Architecture

After generating the rule base or finding the support and confidence for predefined rules, the rules are passed to the HBP Module where the HBP calculator is activated which uses fuzzy functions to evaluate the HBP strength of given rules as outlined in section 4.2.

6 Experimenta Results

In order to show the defined frameworks effectiveness, we performed experiments using the prototype system with synthetic data (1 million transactions with 30 edible items out of 50 items) and used a real nutritional standard RDA table to derive fuzzy values. Our choice of association rule algorithm [12] was based on efficiency and availability. We also implemented the algorithms for analysing rule queries and calculating fuzzy support and fuzzy confidence. For missing nutrient values or so called "trace" elements, the fuzzy function evaluated zero degree membership. We run AprioriTFP on the data to produce a rule base. Some of the rule queries are as follows:

Rule 1: Milk → Honey, Support=29%

The rule is evaluated accordingly (see 4.2) as

HBP is
- 44% - Very Low in [Calcium Cholesterol Fats Iodine Magnesium Manganese Phosphorus Sodium VitaminA VitaminC VitaminD VitaminK]
- 3% - Low in [VitaminB12]
- 14% - Ideal in [Fiber Protein VitaminB6 Zinc]
- 7% - High in [Niacin VitaminE]
- 29% - Very High in [Biotin Carbohydrate Copper Folacin Iron Riboflavin Selenium Thiamin]

Rule 2: Cheese, Eggs → Honey, Support=19%

HBP is
- 37% - Very Low in [Calcium Fats Iodine Magnesium Phosphorus VitaminA VitaminB12 VitaminC VitaminD VitaminK]
- 3% - Low in [Carbohydrate]
- 22% - Ideal in [Manganese Protein Sodium VitaminB6 VitaminE Zinc]
- 3% - High in [Cholesterol]
- 33% - Very High in [Biotin Copper Fiber Folacin Iron Niacin Riboflavin Selenium Thiamin]

Rule 3: Jam → Milk, Support=31%

HBP is
- 48% - Very Low in [Calcium Cholesterol Fats Iodine Iron Magnesium Phosphorus] etc.

It is surprising to see that for most rules (at least these shown here), calcium purchases from calcium rich products like milk and cheese are very low. Contrary, Biotin (Vitamin H, rules 1 and 2) deficiency that causes cholesterol, loss of appetite, hair loss etc is very high possibly because it is found in egg yolks and milk (dry skimmed). These inferences could be useful in real data applications.

7 Conclusion and Future Work

In this paper, we presented a novel framework for extracting healthy buying patterns (HBP) from customer transactions by projecting the original database into edible attributes and then using fuzzy association rule techniques to find fuzzy rules. In this new approach, a user can formulate different types of queries to mine ARs either from the transactions, or from a given rule from the rule base or using a hierarchical query. Standard health information for each nutrient is provided as fuzzy data to guide the generation and evaluation of the rules.

In future, we intend to evaluate our approach on real and larger customer data. The determination of comparative complexity between typical Apriori-like or similar algorithms [13] and our presented approach for nutrient analysis is also important and viable future work. Overall, the approach presented here could be very useful for both the customer and health organizations.

References

1. Agrawal, R., Imielinski, T. and Swami, A. N.: Mining Association Rules Between Sets of Items in Large Databases. In Proceedings of the 1993 ACM SIGMOD Conference on Management of Data, (1993), 207-216.
2. Bodon, F.: A Fast Apriori Implementation. Proceedings of the IEEE ICDM Workshop on Frequent Itemset Mining Implementations, Vol. 90, (2003).
3. Lee, C.-H., Chen, M.-S., Lin, C.-R. : Progressive Partition Miner: An Efficient Algorithm for Mining General Temporal Association Rules. IEEE Transactions on Knowledge and Data Engineering, Vol. 15, No. 4, (2003), 1004 - 1017.
4. Chen, G. and Wei, Q.: Fuzzy Association Rules and the Extended Mining Algorithms, Information Sciences-Informatics and Computer Science: An International Journal archive, Vol. 147, No. (1-4), (2002), 201 - 228.
5. Au, W-H. and Chan, K. : Farm: A Data Mining System for Discovering Fuzzy Association Rules. In Proceedings of the 18th IEEE Conference on Fuzzy Systems, (1999), 1217-1222.
6. Srikant, R. and Agrawal, R.: Mining Quantitative Association Rules in Large Relational Tables. In Proceedings of ACM SIGMOD Conference on Management of Data. ACM Press, (1996), 1-12.
7. Dubois, D., Hüllermeier, E. and Prade, H.: A Systematic Approach to the Assessment of Fuzzy Association Rules. To appear in Data Mining and Knowledge Discovery Journal, (2006).
8. Xie, D. W.: Fuzzy Association Rules discovered on Effective Reduced Database Algorithm, In Proceedings of IEEE Conference on Fuzzy Systems, 2005.
9. 9. He, Y., Tang, Y., Zhang, Y-Q. and Synderraman, R.: Adaptive Fuzzy Association Rule Mining for Effective Decision Support in Biomedical Applications, International Journal Data Mining and Bioinformatics, Vol. 1, No. 1, (2006), 3-18.
10. Gyenesei, A.: A Fuzzy Approach for Mining Quantitative Association Rules, Acta Cybernetical, Vol. 15, No. 2, (2001), 305-320.
11. Klir, G. J. and Yuan, B.: Fuzzy Sets and Fuzzy Logic, Theory and Applications, Prentice-hall, (1995).
12. F. Coenen, Leng, P. , Goulbourne, G. : Tree Structures for Mining Association Rules. Journal of Data Mining and Knowledge Discovery, Vol. 15, No. 7, (2004), 391-398.
13. Wang, C. and Tjortjis, C.: PRICES: An Efficient Algorithm for Mining Association Rules. In Proceedings of the 5th Conference on Intelligent Data Engineering Automated Learning, Lecture Notes in Computer Science Series, Vol. 3177, Springer-Verlag, (2004), 352-358.

State Aggregation in Higher Order Markov Chains for Finding Online Communities

Xin Wang and Ata Kabán

School of Computer Science, The University of Birmingham,
Birmingham, B15 2TT, UK
{X.C.Wang, A.Kaban}@cs.bham.ac.uk

Abstract. We develop and investigate probabilistic approaches of state clustering in higher-order Markov chains. A direct extension of the Aggregate Markov model to higher orders turns out to be problematic due to the large number of parameters required. However, in many cases, the events in the finite memory are not equally salient in terms of their predictive value. We exploit this to reduce the number of parameters. We use a hidden variable to infer which of the past events is the most predictive and develop two different mixed-order approximations of the higher-order aggregate Markov model. We apply these models to the problem of community identification from event sequences produced through online computer-mediated interactions. Our approach bypasses the limitations of static approaches and offers a flexible modelling tool, able to reveal novel and insightful structural aspects of online interaction dynamics.

1 Introduction

With the growing spread of web-based online communication applications, there is a growing demand for developing tools that allow us to learn from the wealth of data being generated. Community identification [8] is one of the most important learning tasks, because discovering communities and their evolution may be useful in bringing individuals with common interests together, tracking trends and facilitating the transmission of information and targeted marketing.

In social sciences, relationships are typically represented by edge-weighted, directed graphs. Communities are then identified by finding densely connected subgraphs [3]. This an NP-complete problem. Approximate polynomial-time algorithms include the maximum flow algorithms [3] and spectral-methods [4] (based on eigen-computations), such as the Hypertext Induced Topic Search (HITS) [7] and PageRank [1] algorithms, which identify authoritative or influential web pages from the graph formed by the interconnected pages. Probabilistic counterparts of some of these ideas with a desirable clear generative semantics have also been devised and shown to have certain advantages. These include the Aggregate Markov (AM) model [11], developed in language modelling, which introduces a hidden 'bottleneck' variable to infer the state groupings. Essentially the same model has later been employed for bibliometric analysis, for finding related publications [2] and it can be seen as a probabilistic version of the HITS model, and therefore has also been termed as the probabilistic HITS (PHITS).

However the AM model makes the first-order assumption of Markovianity. In this paper we extend it to higher-order Markov chains in various ways.

2 Model Formulation

Let $X = \{x_1, x_2, \cdots, x_N\}$ denote a discrete state sequence with each symbol $x_n \in \{1, 2, \cdots, S\}$ coming from a S-symbol state space.

2.1 A Higher-order Aggregate Markov Model (HAM)

Retaining the idea of a 'bottleneck' latent variable, we may directly attempt to extend the Aggregate Markov (AM) model to higher orders. The resulting generative model is then the following.

- Conditional on the finite memory of past events, generate a class $k \sim$ Multinomial $P(k|x_{n-1}, ..., x_{n-L})$.
- Generate the next symbol $x_n \sim$ Multinomial $P(x_n|k)$, conditional on class k.

Thus, the probability of observing state x_n under the above generative process is the following.

$$P(x_n|x_{n-1}, \cdots, x_{n-L}) = \sum_{k=1}^{K} P(x_n|k) P(k|x_{n-l}, ..., x_{n-L}) \quad (1)$$

Although conceptually very simple, there is an obvious problem with this approach in that the number of parameters in the term $P(k|x_{n-l}, ..., x_{n-L})$ grows exponentially with L. This makes the approach impractical and it is most probably the reason why it was never pursued in the literature. We need to make further assumptions in order to make progress. A natural assumption that we exploit in the sequel is that the past events $x_{n-l}, ..., x_{n-L}$ are not equally salient and at each time n there is a single most salient event. Somewhat differently from model-based saliency estimation in static generative models [12], in the dynamic context this leads us to mixed-memory formulations.

The idea of mixed transition Markov models was first introduced in the statistical literature by Raftery [9], as an approximation to higher order Markov models with a reduced parameter complexity. Later [10] have proposed a version of this model which employs a separate parameter transition for each time-lag and the resulting model was termed as the mixed-memory Markov model.

2.2 Mixed-memory Aggregate Markov Chains (MAMC)

Let $P^l(k|x_{n-l})$ denote the probability of cluster k conditional on the event x_{n-l}. Further, let $P(x_n|k)$ be the probability of choosing state x_n from cluster k.

Our model assumption proposes a generative process according to which the generation of each symbol x_n of the sequence $X = \{x_1, \cdots, x_N\}$ is the following:

- Generate the salient lag $l \sim$ Multinomial $P(l)$
- Conditional on the salient lag, generate a class $k \sim$ Multinomial $P^l(k|x_{n-l})$, conditional on the symbol observed at lag l
- Generate the next symbol $x_n \sim$ Multinomial $P(x_n|k)$, conditional on class k.

The probability of observing state x_n under the above generative process is the following:

$$P(x_n|x_{n-1},\cdots,x_{n-L}) = \sum_{l=1}^{L} P(l) \sum_{k=1}^{K} P(x_n|k) P^l(k|x_{n-l}) \qquad (2)$$

Analogously to the two different versions of Mixed-memory Markov models, namely that of [9], where a single transition parameter matrix is employed, i.e $P^l(x_n|x_{n-l}) = P(x_n|x_{n-l})$ versus that of [10], where a separate transition parameter matrix is kept for all lags $l = 1 : L$, we shall also consider two versions of our model. For consistency, by m_MAMC we will refer to our model as described above, while s_MAMC will stand for the version in which $P^l(k|s_l) = P(k|s_l)$ is the same for all lags. Further, it is easy to see that both versions of our model recover AM as a special case, at $L = 1$, and s_MAMC is identical to the model we have recently introduced in [5], and termed deconvolutive state clustering. In the later sections of this paper, we will assess these two versions comparatively. However, the formalism is sufficient to be given for the more general version, which is the m_MAMC.

2.3 Estimation of MAMC Models

In this section we derive an efficient iterative estimation algorithm for MAMC, based on maximum likelihood (ML). Simple manipulation of (2) yields the log likelihood of a sequence $X = \{x_1, \cdots, x_N\}$ under the MAMC model as follows:

$$\mathcal{L}(\Theta|X) \equiv \log P(X|\Theta) = \sum_{s_0,s_1,\cdots,s_L=1}^{T} N_{s_0,s_1,\cdots,s_L} \log \sum_{l=1}^{L} P(l) \sum_{k=1}^{K} P^l(k|s_l) P(s_0|k)$$

where $(s_0, s_1, \cdots, s_l, \cdots, s_L)$ is used to denote a $(L+1)$-gram $(x_n = s_0, x_{n-1} = s_1, \cdots, x_{n-L} = s_L)$, $s_0, s_1, \cdots, s_l, \cdots, s_L$ are symbols $\in \{1, 2, \cdots, T\}$. $N_{s_0,s_1,\cdots,s_L}$ is the frequency of $(L+1)$-gram $s_L \to s_{L-1} \to \cdots \to s_0$ being observed. $x_{n-L} = s_L, \cdots, x_{n-l} = s_l, \cdots, x_n = s_0$, and $s_l \in \{1, 2, \cdots, T\}$ and $l \in \{1, \cdots, L\}$.

We employ the standard procedure for ML estimation in latent variable models, the Expectation-Maximisation methodology, and obtain the following algorithm:

- E-step

$$P(l|s_0, s_1, \cdots, s_L) \propto P(l) \sum_{k=1}^{K} P^l(k|s_l) P(s_0|k)$$

$$P(k, l|s_0, s_1, \cdots, s_L) \propto \frac{P^l(k|s_l) P(s_0|k)}{\sum_{k'=1}^{K} P^l(k'|s_l) P(s_0|k')} P(l|s_0, s_1, \cdots, s_L)$$

– M-step

$$P(l) \propto \sum_{s_0,s_1,\cdots,s_L=1}^{T} N_{s_0,s_1,\cdots,s_L} P(l|s_0, s_1, \cdots, s_L)$$

$$P^l(k|s_l) \propto \sum_{s_0,\cdots,s_{l-1},s_{l+1},\cdots,s_L=1}^{T} N_{s_0,s_1,\cdots,s_L} P(k,l|s_0, s_1, \cdots, s_L)$$

$$P(s_0|k) \propto P(s_0|k) \sum_{s_1,\cdots,s_L=1}^{T} \sum_{l=1}^{L} N_{s_0,s_1,\cdots,s_L} P(k,l|s_0, s_1, \cdots, s_L)$$

This is guaranteed to converge to a local optimum of the likelihood and is applicable to both versions (m_MAMC and s_MAMC) of our model. In the case of s_MAMC, the substitution $P^l(k|s_l) = P(k|s_l)$ needs to be made throughout.

Implementation issues It is advantageous to perform a complete E-step before each of the three M-step updates. By doing this, we can effectively replace the E-step expressions into the M-step expressions and avoid storing the burdensome posteriors. In the case of s_MAMC, the algorithm in [5] is recovered.

2.4 Model Complexity

Time complexity Theoretically, the time complexity of the algorithms is $O(T^{L+2} \times L \times K)$. However usually the real data are quite sparse. Let S denote non-zero elements (grams) in the observed data. Both algorithms scale as $O(S \times L \times K)$. Usually $L \times K \ll S$, so we can say that both of the two algorithms scale linearly with the number of observed non-zero $(L+1)$-grams.

Space complexity. The space complexity consists of two parts, the space for model parameters and space for the data, counts of $(L+1)$-grams $N_{s_0,s_1,\cdots,s_L}$. For models with large T, the number T^{L+1} of potential patterns can be extremely large, thus it is not practical to store the $(L+1)$-dimensional count matrix. This problem can be solved by a hashing algorithm. We proceeded by labelling a pattern $(s_0, s_1, \cdots, s_L)$ by all the $L+1$ indices followed by the frequency of the pattern occurred in the observed data, so the $(L+1)$-dimensional count matrix is substituted by a $S \times (L+2)$ matrix, S is the observed non-zero $(L+1)$-grams in the data. So the space for storing data is $O(S \times L)$. *The number of free parameters* to be stored is $P = (L-1) + (T-1) \times K + (K-1) \times T$ for s_MAMC and $P = (L-1) + (T-1) \times K + L \times (K-1) \times T$ for m_MAMC respectively. Note, the number of free parameters are an important characteristic that may be used in model selection criteria (AIC will be used in some of our experiments). Therefore by summing the above two parts, the total space complexity of the algorithm is $O(K \times T \times L + S \times L)$ for m_MAMC, or in the simpler s_MAMC case it is $O(K \times T + S \times L)$ instead. Further, when the data is very sparse, $L \times K \ll S$ and $L \times K \ll T$, the space complexity can be simplified to $O(S+T)$.

3 Experiments

3.1 Model Identification from Synthetic Data

As a first experiment, we generate data sequences from both s_MAMC and m_MAMC, of 1,000 symbols each, over a 15-symbol state space. The model order of $K = 3$ and $L = 2$ and a memory depth distribution $P(l = 2) = 1, P(l \neq 2) = 0$ have been defined. The AIC-penalised log likelihood is then calculated over a range of L and K in order to assess the correctness of model identification. This is shown on Fig. 1. In both cases, the model order as well as the generating parameters are correctly recovered. We also conducted model order identification using the out-of-sample likelihood on a separate test sequence and the results were qualitatively similar for both MAMC models. In addition, we observe that due to its extremely compact parameterisation, the AIC score for s_MAMC does not decrease so quickly with increasing L. This suggests that in the case of large state-space problems the compactness of s_MAMC may be expected be more advantageous. As shown on the rightmost plot of Fig. 1, at larger values of L, the distribution of memory depths, $P(l)$, is still recovered. By contrary, experiments with high-order AM (HAM) have indicated serious overfitting problems. A lot longer sequences would be required for a full HAM to be reliably estimated.

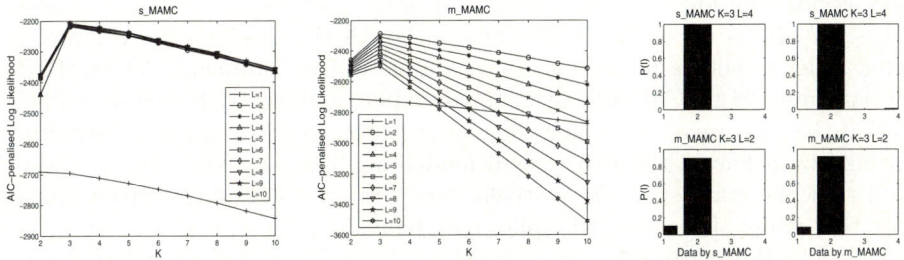

Fig. 1. Model estimation from generated data. From left to right: AIC-penalised log likelihood for s_MAMC, AIC-penalised log likelihood for m_MAMC and the recovered distributions, $P(l)$, for both data and model pairs.

3.2 Results on Real Data

Finding Communities from Internet Chat Participation. In this experiment, a sequence of userID-s from real-world IRC chat participation is analysed. This encompasses $N = 25,355$ contributions from $S = 844$ chat participants and the observed transition counts are very sparse. For a range of model orders K and L, the models were trained 20 times to avoid local optima. Fig. 2 shows the AIC curves obtained with the MAMC models. As expected, simple higher-order AM model experienced overfitting from the start and is therefore not included on the plots. Also, as we can see from the figure, for m_MAMC, the model with $L = 1, K = 7$ has the highest value. This is essentially just a

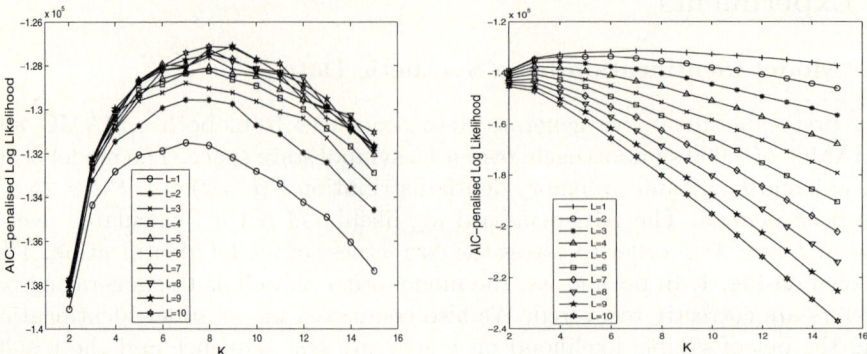

Fig. 2. The left hand plot shows the AIC curves for s_MAMC, peaking at $L = 9, K = 9$, which means the optimum number of clusters in this data is 9, with a maximum allowed lag of 9. The right hand plot corresponds to m_MAMC and this peaks at $L = 1$ and $K = 7$, which is essentially an Aggregate Markov model with 7 clusters. As the two MAMC versions at $L = 1$ are both identical to the AM model, it is clear that s_MAMC outperforms both AM and m_MAMC on this data.

first-order AM model. However, inspecting the left-hand plot, we see the AM curve is now the lowest of all s_MAMC results, and the optimal model order with s_MAMC is $L = 9, K = 9$. Thus, although there is clearly evidence for higher-order structure in the dynamics, the more free parameters of the HAM or even the m_MAMC do not seem to contribute sufficiently to the data likelihood at the expense of increasing the model complexity. Revealing the structure can only be achieved through careful modelling. This shouldn't be surprising, given that the state space is relatively large. In addition, it intuitively makes sense that many of the delayed replies may be mainly due to concurrency rather than due to the existence of a genuinely different dynamics at different lags. This explains the advantage of s_MAMC over m_MAMC for this kind of data and therefore in the reminder of experiments, only the s_MAMC model will be employed.

With the optimal model order selected above, the development of the communities identified is presented on Fig. 3.

This is the actual event aggregation as obtained with the optimal model, visualised as event components versus discrete time. Each row corresponds to the context-conditional state cluster probabilities for one cluster k, marginalised over the time lag variable, i.e. $P(k|s_0, s_1, \cdots, s_L) = \sum_{l=1}^{L} P(k, l|s_0, s_1, \cdots, s_L)$ and time goes on the horisontal axis $t = 1, ..., T$. We see the evolution of nearly all communities are characterised by bursts of activity over time, indicating our model manages to capture the bursty nature [6] of the stream in a natural manner. This has not been the case with a Hidden Markov Model (HMM), which instead tends to produce sharp boundaries between time segments. As previously shown [6], additional constraints on the transition probability structure would be required for a HMM to model bursty activity.

Fig. 3. The time evolution of chatting communities

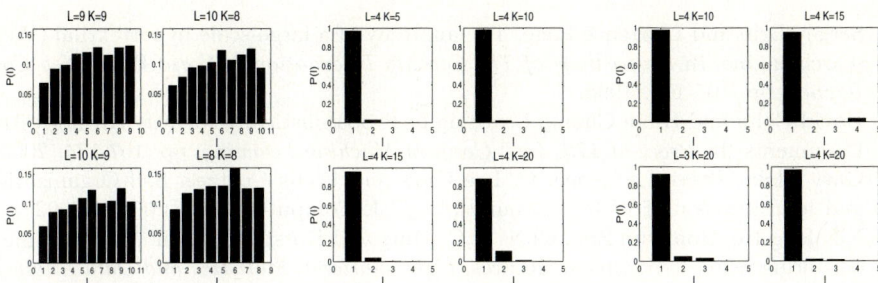

Fig. 4. The distribution of the memory depths, as estimated by the four best s_MAMC from IRC (leftmost plot), EPA (middle plot) and NASA (rightmost plot)

3.3 Chat Versus Browsing Traces

We also analysed two collections of web browsing traces, the EPA and the NASA data set (see http://ita.ee.lbl.gov/html/contrib for details). Interestingly, and contrarily to the clustered structure of static web link graphs [4], the dynamic browsing activity viewed globally (unconditional on particular users) has not displayed clusters of site locations. Instead, we noticed consistent structural differences between synchronous and one-along type online interactions: It is particularly illustrative to inspect the distribution of memory depths, as estimated by our model in the case of the two different online interaction scenarios. These are shown on Fig. 4, for four typical results for each of the data sets analysed. It can be observed that while in direct online communications through a single IRC channel, more distant past contributions consistently have a significant non-zero contribution due to concurrency, in the case of web browsing in turn, the distribution of memory depths tends to peak at the immediate past, i.e. $P(l=1)$ is the highest peak of $P(l)$. We believe these are rather insightful findings, which have not been noticed and studied before. A more detailed study may be conducted by employing of a mixture of MAMC models.

4 Conclusions

We developed and investigated probabilistic approaches of state clustering in higher-order Markov chains. A direct extension of the Aggregate Markov model to higher orders has proved to be impractical, and we created models that are able to infer the class-predictive saliency of past events and reduce the number of parameters. Our approach was able to unearth novel and insightful structural aspects from online interaction log sequences.

References

1. Sergey Brin and Lawrence Page. The anatomy of a large-scale hypertextual (Web) search engine. In *Proceedings of The Seventh International World Wide Web Conference*, pp. 107-117, 1998.
2. David Cohn and Huan Chang. Learning to Probabilistically Identify Authoritative Documents, In *Proc. of 17th Int'l Conf on Machine Learning*, pp. 167-174, 2000.
3. Gary Flake, Steve Lawrence, C. Lee Giles and Frans Coetzee. Self-Organization and Identification of Web Communities. IEEE Computer, **35** (3):66-71, 2002.
4. Xiaofeng He, Hongyun Zha, Chris H.Q. Ding and Horst D. Simon. Web document clustering using hyperlink structures. *Computational Statistics and Data Analysis*, **41**(1): 19–45, 2002.
5. Ata Kabán and Xin Wang. Deconvolutive Clustering of Markov States. Proc. 17-th European Conference on Machine Learning (ECML06), to appear.
6. Jon Kleinberg. Bursty and Hierarchical Structure in Streams. *Data Mining and Knowledge Discovery*, Vol. 7, Issue 4, 2003, pp. 373 - 397.
7. Jon Kleinberg. Authoritative sources in hyperlinked environment. *Journal of the ACM*, **46**(5): 604–632, 1999.
8. Mike E. J. Newman. Detecting community structure in networks. *Euro. Phys. J. B*, **38**: 321–330, 2004.
9. Adrian E. Raftery. A model for high-order Markov chains. *Journal of the Royal Statistical Society*, series B, **47**:528-539, 1985.
10. Lawrence K. Saul and Michael I. Jordan. Mixed Memory Markov Models: Decomposing Complex Stochastic Processes as Mixtures of Simpler Ones. *Machine Learning*, **37** (1):75-87, 1999.
11. Lawrence K. Saul and Fernando Pereira. Aggregate and Mixed-Order Markov Models for Statistical Language Processing. In *Proceedings of the Second Conference on Empirical Methods in Natural Language Processing*, pp. 81-89, 1997.
12. Xin Wang and Ata Kabán. Model-based Estimation of Word Saliency in Text. Proc. of the 9-th International Conference on Discovery Science (DS06), October 2006, Barcelona, Spain. To appear.

Functional Networks and Analysis of Variance for Feature Selection*

Noelia Sánchez-Maroño[1], María Caamaño-Fernández[1],
Enrique Castillo[2], and Amparo Alonso-Betanzos[1]

[1] University of A Coruña, Department of Computer Science, 15071 A Coruña, Spain
nsanchez@udc.es, infmcf00@ucv.udc.es, ciamparo@udc.es
[2] University of Cantabria, Department of Applied Mathematics and Computer Science, 39005 Santander, Spain
castie@unican.es

Abstract. In this paper a method for feature selection based on analysis of variance and using functional networks as induction algorithm is presented. It follows a backward selection search, but several features are discarded in the same step. The method proposed is compared with two SVM based methods, obtaining a smaller set of features with a similar accuracy.

1 Introduction

Reduction of feature dimensionality is of considerable importance in machine learning because it can reduce the computational complexity and it may improve the performance of the induction algorithm [1]. Moreover, reducing the number of features results in better understanding and interpretation of the data. Feature selection reduces the number of original features by selecting a subset of them that still retains sufficient information for obtaining a good performance result. In general, feature selection approaches can be grouped into two categories[2]:

- Filter algorithms, in which case the selection method is used as a preprocessing that does not attempt to optimize directly the predictor (machine learning method) performance. For example, in a classification problem, distance measures which reflect how well the classes separate from each other.
- Wrapper algorithms, in which the selection method optimizes directly the predictor performance. Based on the predictor performance, these methods evaluate the "goodness" of the selected subset of features.

In this paper, we present a wrapper algorithm based on a functional components decomposition of the function to be estimated and analysis of variance over this decomposition. Functional networks are employed as the induction algorithm. The method can be applied to regression and classification problems. However, most of the previous studies in feature selection are only devoted to classification

---
* This work has been partially funded by the Spanish Ministry of Science and Technology under project TIC-2003-00600 with FEDER funds.

problems. Then, the method presented is applied to real-world classification data sets and its performance results are compared to those obtained by other feature selection methods.

2 Previous Concepts

2.1 A Brief Introduction to Functional Networks

Functional networks are a generalization of neural networks that combine both knowledge about the structure of the problem, to determine the architecture of the network, and data, to estimate the unknown functional neurons [3]. Functional networks have been successfully applied to different problems [4]. Although functional networks are a generalization of neural networks, there are important differences between them, some of which are shown in Fig.1. It can be noticed that, in functional networks, there are no weights, i.e., they are incorporated into the neural functions $f_i; i = 1, 2, 3$. These neural functions are unknown functions from a given family, i.e., the polynomial or Fourier families, to be estimated during the learning process. For example, the neural function f_1 in figure 1(b) could be approximated by:

$$f_1(x_1, x_2) = \sum_{i=0}^{m_i} c_{1i} x_1^i + \sum_{j=0}^{m_j} c_{2j} x_2^j$$

and the parameters to be learned will be the coefficients c_{1i} and c_{2j}. As each function f_i is learnt, a different function is obtained for each neuron.

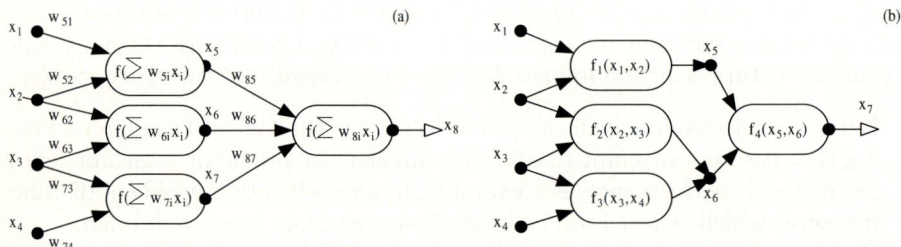

Fig. 1. (a)A neural network. (b)A functional network.

2.2 Functional Components Decomposition

According to Sobol[5], any square integrable function $f(x_1, \ldots, x_n)$ defined on the unit hypercube $[0, 1]^n$ can be written as

$$y = f(x_1, \ldots, x_n) = f_0 + \sum_{\nu=1}^{2^n - 1} f_\nu(\mathbf{x}_\nu), \qquad (1)$$

where $\{\mathbf{x}_\nu | \nu = 1, 2, \ldots, 2^n - 1\}$ is the set of all possible subsets of the set $\{x_1, x_2, \ldots, x_n\}$. In the case $\nu = 0$, corresponding to the empty set, the function $f_\nu(\mathbf{x}_\nu)$ has no arguments, and it is assumed to be the constant f_0. The decomposition (1) is called ANOVA iff

$$\int_0^1 f_\nu(\mathbf{x}_\nu) dx_i = 0; \quad \forall x_j \in \mathbf{x}_\nu \ i \neq j \ \forall \nu.$$

Then, the functions corresponding to the different summands are unique and orthogonal [5], i.e.:

$$\int_0^1 \int_0^1 \cdots \int_0^1 f_{\nu_1}(\mathbf{x}_{\nu_1}) f_{\nu_2}(\mathbf{x}_{\nu_2}) d\mathbf{x}_{\nu_1} d\mathbf{x}_{\nu_2} = 0; \quad \forall \nu_1 \neq \nu_2.$$

Note that, since the above decomposition includes terms with all possible kinds of interactions among the variables $x_1, x_2, \ldots, x_n$, it allows determining those interactions.

The main advantage of this decomposition is that there are closed or explicit formulas to obtain the different summands or components of $f(x_1, \ldots, x_n)$. These expressions were given by Sobol in [5], allowing that the $f(x_1, \ldots, x_n)$ function can always be written as the sum of the 2^n orthogonal summands:

$$f(x_1, \ldots, x_n) = f_0 + \sum_{i=1}^{n} f_i(x_i) + \sum_{i=1}^{n-1} \sum_{i<j}^{n} f_{ij}(x_i, x_j) + \cdots + f_{12\ldots n}(x_1, x_2, \ldots, x_n).$$

Since if $f(x_1, \ldots, x_n)$ is square integrable, then all $f_\nu(\mathbf{x}_\nu); \nu = 1, 2, \ldots, 2^n - 1$ also are square integrable, squaring $f(x_1, \ldots, x_n)$ and integrating over $(0, 1)^n$ one gets

$$\int_0^1 \int_0^1 \cdots \int_0^1 f^2(x_1, \ldots, x_n) dx_1 dx_2 \ldots dx_n - f_0^2 = \sum_{\nu=1}^{2^n-1} \int_0^1 f_\nu^2(\mathbf{x}_\nu) d\mathbf{x}_\nu,$$

and calling D to the left part of this equation and D_ν to each summand in the right part, it results

$$D = \sum_{\nu=1}^{2^n-1} D_\nu.$$

If $(x_1, x_2, \ldots, x_n)$ is a uniform random variable in the unit hypercube, then the constant D is its variance. With this, the following set of global sensitivity indices, adding up to one, can be defined

$$S_\nu = \frac{D_\nu}{D}; \quad \nu = 1, 2, 3, \ldots, 2^n - 1.$$

Therefore, the variance of the initial function can be obtained by summing up the variance of the components, and this allows assigning global sensitivity indices, adding to one, to the different functional components.

3 The AFN Method: Anova and Functional Networks for Feature Selection

The idea consists of approximating each functional component $f_\nu(\mathbf{x}_\nu)$ in (1), using some set $\{h^*_{\nu 1}(\mathbf{x}_\nu), h^*_{\nu 2}(\mathbf{x}_\nu), \ldots, h^*_{\nu k^*_\nu}(\mathbf{x}_\nu)\}$ of simple basic functions (polynomial, Fourier series, etc.). Then, those functions are orthonormalized, so each functional component in (1) is estimated by:

$$f_\nu(\mathbf{x}_\nu) \approx \sum_{j=1}^{k_\nu} c_{\nu j} p_{\nu j}(\mathbf{x}_\nu).$$

The parameters $c_{\nu j}$ will be estimated by solving an optimization problem and will be interpreted as global sensitivity indices that will suggest the variables to discard.

It is important to notice that the feature selection process depends on the function learnt. In order to get a good approximation, the following issues must be considered:

– The cost function. MSE was our first consideration [6] because it exhibits a good performance for classification and regression problems and the method proposed can be applied to both types of problems. However, as this work is devoted to classification problems and it is well-known that there are more adequate functions than MSE [7], several optimization problems were solved considering different functions (accuracy, cross-entropy and mean squared error(MSE)) in order to improve the function estimated. Cross-entropy obtained the best performance results, then the optimization problem to solve was:

$$\text{Minimize } J = -\sum_{i=1}^{M} y_i ln(\hat{y}_i) + (1 - y_i) ln(1 - \hat{y}_i), \qquad (2)$$

where M is the number of samples, y_i is the desired output for the sample i and $\hat{y}_i$ is the estimated output.
– The evaluation function. The evaluation function used is the mean accuracy from a five-fold cross-validation as done in [2]. The five-fold cross-validation is repeated several times in order to get a low standard deviation for the accuracy, i.e., we look for a training set as homogeneous as possible. The maximum number of repetitions was set to five in order to avoid a high-time consuming process.
– The set of basic functions. Several functions have to be tested for each problem in order to get a good approximation. Then, the elected functions are orthonormalized.

Once the proper functions were selected, the feature selection process may start. The method that allows to select the most relevant from the whole set of features is a backward selection method. It is divided into several steps that are briefly described in the next page. Figure 2 shows an overview of the selection process.

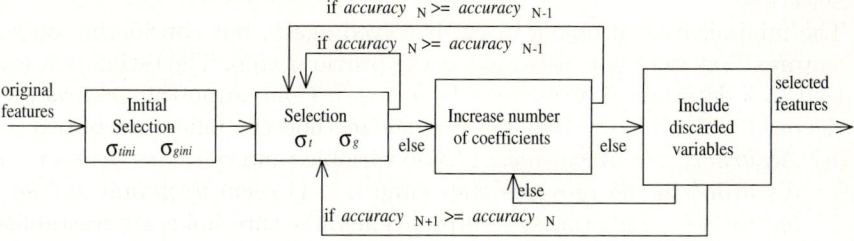

Fig. 2. The proposed method for feature selection. $\sigma_{gini}, \sigma_{tini}, \sigma_t$ and σ_g are thresholds. Stop condition: any smaller subset of features leads to worse accuracy results.

1. Initial selection

   As it was previously described, the coefficients are estimated by solving the optimization problem in (2) where the functional decomposition in (1) is used to estimate the desired output. All the original features of the problem are initially considered. After solving the problem, a mean accuracy is obtained for the test data ($accuracy_{n-1}$).

   Since the resulting basis functions have already been orthonormalized, the global sensitivity indices (importance factors) are the sums of the squares of those coefficients, i.e.:

$$S_\nu = \sum_{j=1}^{k_\nu} c_{\nu j}^2; \quad \nu = 1, 2, \ldots, 2^n - 1. \tag{3}$$

The total sensitivity index (TSI) for each variable is calculated by adding the global sensitivity index for that variable, x_i, and the global sensitivity index of each combination of variables where x_i is included, i.e., it is calculated by:

$$TSI_i = \sum_{j=1}^{2^{n-1}} S_{\nu_j} \text{ such that } x_i \in \nu_j. \tag{4}$$

The most relevant features are selected according to the total sensitivity indices; those features under an established threshold (σ_{tini}) are discarded. This threshold is calculated for each dataset considering the different values obtained for each variable trying to retain around a 90% of the variance. Also, it is necessary to determine if the feature is important by its own or by its combination with other variables. As global sensitivity indices provide this information, another threshold needs to be established for them (σ_{gini}). Those variables or combinations between variables under this threshold are eliminated.

As a wrong initial selection may lead to poor performance results, both thresholds were initially established to small values, so the number of features discarded in this step is reduced, being of one or two features at most.

2. Selection

   The minimization problem in (2) is solved again, but considering only the features that were not discarded in the previous step. The estimation learnt lead to a determined accuracy ($Accuracy_n$). Comparing this accuracy with the one obtained in the previous run, the method can follow one of two ways:

   (a) $Accuracy_n >= Accuracy_{n-1}$. The variables and relations between them discarded in the previous step (step $n-1$) seem irrelevant and so the feature selection process is correct. Then, the thresholds are reestablished (σ_t and σ_g) in order to get a new set of variables to discard and the feature selection process continues (go to step 2).

   (b) $Accuracy_n < Accuracy_{n-1}$. As several features are discarded in just one step, the number of coefficients can be considerably reduced. Even if the features are correctly selected, such a small number of coefficients may not lead to a good approximation of the problem, therefore, go to the next step where the number of coefficients is increased.

3. The number of coefficients of the basis functions are increased. If the polynomial family is being used, this can be done by increasing the degrees of the function. The goal is to use the same number of coefficients than those used when the classifier obtained the previous accuracy result. Once the number of coefficients has been increased, if the accuracy obtained with this subset of features is equal or higher than $accuracy_{n-1}$, the selection continues (go to step 2), otherwise some discarded variables may be reconsidered in the next step.

4. Discarded variables are included. If a highest accuracy was not reached by increasing the number of coefficients, variables that have already been discarded will be taken into account again. This can be done by changing the values of the thresholds (σ_t and σ_g).

   Notice that this point was included because several variables are discarded in just one step. This step allows to consider again variables eliminated by a too aggressive selection.

The process finishes when the accuracy obtained with a smaller subset of features cannot be improved by increasing the number of coefficients or including variables that had been discarded previously.

4 Experimental Results

The proposed method has been applied to some data sets used in previous studies [1,2], and that can be obtained in the Irvine repository [8]. A brief description for them is given in Table 1. Before applying the algorithm to each dataset, the values for each variable were normalized between 0.05 and 0.95. The exponential complexity to the number of features of the method proposed does not allow to consider data sets with a large number of features. The proposed method (AFN) is compared with two methods based on SVM (Support Vector Machines)[9]: (a) the novel work presented in [1] called FS-SFS (Filtered and Supported Sequential Forward Search) and (b) SFS (Sequential Forward Search).

Table 1. Dataset description. Baseline accuracy: accuracy when the main class is selected.

Dataset	Features	Classes	Number of Samples	Baseline Accuracy
Bupa liver	6	2	345	57.97
Breast cancer	9	2	683	65.01
Pima	8	2	768	65.10
Cleve	13	2	303	54.46

Table 2. Comparative results between the proposed method (AFN) and two methods based on SVM. Features indicates the mean number of features for the 20 simulations, with the maximum and minimum features selected in parenthesis. The accuracy for testing data sets is also presented.

Dataset	Features (min,max)			Test Accuracy		
	FS-SFS	SFS	AFN	FS-SFS	SFS	AFN
Bupa liver	4.6 (4,5)	4.6 (4,5)	3.5 (2,5)	70.2	71.7	70.4
Breast cancer	5.4 (5,6)	5.4 (5,6)	4.5 (2,7)	96.3	95.4	96.5
Pima	4.2 (4,5)	4.2 (4,5)	3.6 (2,6)	74.9	74.9	75.3
Cleve	6.6 (5,7)	6.6 (5,7)	6.3 (4,9)	84.8	84.8	82.1

For a fair comparison, the same technique to obtain the experimental results was used. The same solution for the missing values was chosen and so those samples containing missing values were discarded. Also, 20 simulations for each dataset were carried out as in [1], and for each simulation a 20% of the samples were randomly selected to construct the test set. The rest of the samples form the training set that will be used for the feature selection process. The performance results are shown in Table 2. The accuracy results are similar to those reached by the other methods. Besides, the mean number of features is smaller, although it exhibits more variability. This variability is obtained by two or three variables that are considered in some simulations, while the relevant variables remain in most of the cases. Figure 3 illustrates this problem for the Bupa set. As it can be seen, four variables are selected in most of the cases, while the rest only appears in very few simulations. Regarding the computational time, it takes around 30

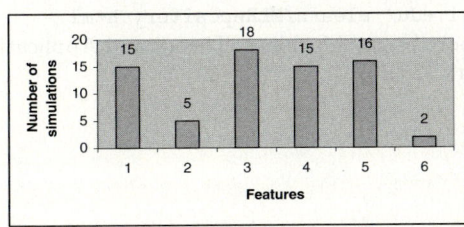

Fig. 3. Relation between each feature and the number of times selected for the Bupa set

seconds to compute the 20 simulations of the Bupa data set. Besides, only 6.5 different subsets were explored for this dataset, while 11 subsets will be explored with a sequential backward search from a set of 6 features to a subset compound by 4 features as the Bupa dataset.

5 Conclusions

This paper presents a new wrapper method based on functional networks and analysis of variance decomposition. The experimental results shown the adequacy of the method proposed, that exhibits a good accuracy results while maintaining a reduced set of variables. Besides, it allows to discard several variables in just one step and there is no need to check all the possible subsets as in a sequential backward search. Finally, the importance of each feature is given in terms of variance, allowing for interpretation of the results. Future work would address the main disadvantage of this method, that is, the exponential complexity of the functional decomposition.

References

1. Liu, Y., Zheng, Y.F.: A novel feature selection method for support vector machines. Pattern Recognition **39** (2006) 1333–1345
2. Kohavi, R., John, G.: Wrappers for feature subset selection. Artificial Intelligence journal, special issue on relevance **97**(1-2) (1997) 273–324
3. Castillo, E., Cobo, A., J.M. Gutiérrez, Pruneda, E.: Functional Networks with Applications. Kluwer Academic Publishers, Boston, Dordrecht, London (1998)
4. Castillo, E., Gutiérrez, J.M., Hadi, A.S., Lacruz, B.: Some applications of functional networks in statistics and engineering. Technometrics **43(1)** (2001) 10–24
5. Sobol, I.M.: Global sensitivity indices for nonlinear mathematical models and their Monte Carlo estimates. Mathematics and Computers in Simulation **55** (2001) 271–280
6. Sánchez-Maroño, N., Alonso-Betanzos, A., Castillo, E.: A new wrapper method for feature subset selection. In: Proc. European Symp. on Artificial Neural Networks. (2005) 515–520
7. Bishop, C.: Neural Networks for Patter Recognition. Oxford University Press, New York (1995)
8. Blake, C., Merz, C.: UCI repository of machine learning databases (1998) http://www.ics.uci.edu/~mlearn/MLRepository.html.
9. Wang, L., ed.: Support Vector Machines: Theory and Applications. Springer, Berlin Heidelberg New York (2005)

Automatic Categorization of Patent Applications Using Classifier Combinations

Henrik Mathiassen[1] and Daniel Ortiz-Arroyo[2]

Computer Science and Engineering Department
Aalborg University, Esbjerg
Niels Bohrs Vej 8, 6700 Esbjerg Denmark
[1] hm1464@student.cs.aaue.dk
[2] do@cs.aaue.dk

Abstract. In this paper we explore the effectiveness of combining diverse machine learning based methods to categorize patent applications. Classifiers are constructed from each categorization method in the combination, based on the document representations where the best performance was obtained. Therefore, the ensemble of methods makes categorization predictions with knowledge observed from different perspectives. In addition, we explore the application of a variety of combination techniques to improve the overall performance of the ensemble of classifiers. In our experiments a refined version of the WIPO-alpha[1] document collection was used to train and evaluate the classifiers. The combination ensemble that achieved the best performance obtained an improvement of 6.51% compared to the best performing classifier participating in the combination.

Keywords: Categorization, Machine Learning, Knowledge Management.

1 Introduction

A patent is a contract between the state and the applicant by which a temporary monopoly is granted in return for disclosing all details of an invention. Patent rights must be applied for at a patent office to gain rights in a country. Patent *classification schemes* are a hierarchical system of categories used to organize and index the technical content of patents so that a specific topic or area of technology can be identified easily and accurately. Different classification schemes are used in the different patent organizations. The most widely used classification scheme is the *International Patent Classification (IPC)*. The IPC is a hierarchical categorization system comprising sections, classes, subclasses and groups (main groups and subgroups). The eighth edition of the IPC contains approximately 70,000 groups. Every subdivision of the IPC is indicated by a symbol and has a title. The IPC divides all technological fields into eight sections designated by one of the capital letters A through H. The sections include from *Human Necessities* and *Physics* to *Electricity, Textiles* and *Mechanics* among others. Each section, in turn, is subdivided into classes labeled with a section symbol followed by a two-digit number. Each class then

---

[1] WIPO-alpha document collection available at http://www.wipo.int/ibis/datasets/index.html

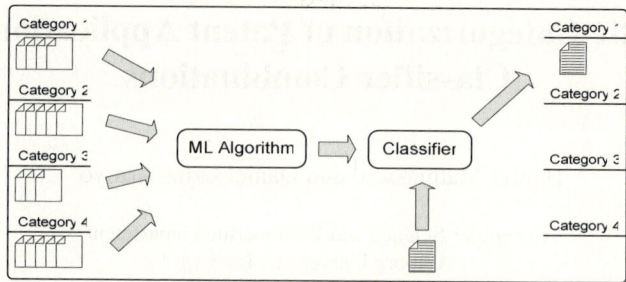

Fig. 1. Automated patent categorization based on machine learning

contains one or several subclasses labeled with a class id followed by a capital letter, e.g. A01B. Finally, each subclass is broken down into subdivisions referred to as groups and known as either main groups or subgroups. The IPC is developed and administered by *World Intellectual Property Organization (WIPO)*. The WIPO-alpha collection, a publicly available dataset aimed at encouraging research in automated categorization of patent documents, contains 75,000 patent documents in English divided into a training set of 46,324 documents and a test set with 28,926 documents.

An intellectually built (i.e. human made) taxonomy is the only solution when patent categories are new and empty. However, since normally a great amount of manually categorized patent examples exist, it is feasible to apply *machine learning* techniques. The machine learning techniques employed in patent categorization are normally based on *supervised* learning. In *supervised* learning some examples called training documents are assigned to the correct category first. Then, based on the learned information from these examples, new unseen documents are categorized. Fig. 1 shows the general scheme of an automated patent categorization method. The module used to categorize documents is called the *classifier*. The classifier is trained using machine learning algorithms from an inductive process called the training/learning phase.

Patents are normally processed within organizations in two main stages: *pre-categorization* where it is determined the technical unit that will handle a patent and the *categorization* stage where the final category is assigned.

In this paper we explore the effectiveness of applying diverse techniques for combining supervised machine learning methods to automatically categorize patents. The techniques presented in this paper are aimed to automate the pre-categorization stage of patents. The rest of the paper is organized as follows. Section 2 discusses related research on patent categorization. Section 3 describes our proposed model for a patent categorization system. Experimental results of our model are presented in Section 4. Finally, Section 5 describes future work and presents some conclusions.

2 Related Work

The first reported research on patent categorization is the work by Chakrabarti et al. In [2] they propose a statistical model that attempts to categorize patents into a hierarchical model containing 3 categories subdivided into 12 subcategories. The classifier obtained a precision of 64% when was applied to patents. The authors argue that this relatively poor performance is caused by the diversities in authorship performed across time and assignees. To improve performance they attempted to use information contained in links between referencing patents. Naively indexing features from referenced patents is reported to have a negative effect on the performance. Better results are obtained by including the labels from categorized referenced document in the indexing. This approach is reported to obtain a precision of 79%.

Larkey presents a system in [10] for searching and categorizing U.S. patent documents. The system uses a *kNN (K-Nearest Neighbor)* approach to categorize patents into a scheme containing around 400 classes and 135,000 subclasses. Larkey concludes that the best performance is obtained by using a vector, made up of the most frequent terms from the title, the abstract, the first twenty lines of the background summary, and the claims, with the title receiving three times as much weight as the rest of the text.

Koster et al. present in [8,9] some of the best published results on patent categorization using the *Winnow* algorithm. *Winnow* is a *mistake driven* learning algorithm that iterates over the training documents and computes for each category a vector of weights for approximating an optimal linear separator between relevant and non-relevant patents. Winnow is trained and tested with patent databases obtained from the *European Patent Office (EPO)*. In the experiments with Winnow, documents are represented as a bag of words and in contrast to [10] the internal structure of the documents is completely ignored. When Winnow is tested assigning only one category per document (*mono-categorization*), it achieves a precision exceeding 98%. To achieve such high precision as much as 1000 training examples for each of the 16 categories are utilized. When the amount of training examples is reduced to 280 documents per category the precision decreases to 85%. The F_1-measure was employed for evaluating Winnow's performance when set to categorize documents that belong to more than one category (*multi-categorization*). The F_1-measure is a standard measure used in information retrieval that combines precision and recall into a single value. The optimal performance obtained on multi-categorization is an F_1-measure of 68%. This result was obtained using 88,000 training examples distributed so that each of the 44 directorates[2] has 2000 examples. It is argued that this considerable decrease in performance (larger for multi than mono-categorization) is caused by noise, since training documents are labeled arbitrarily in the border cases.

In [6] different text categorization methods included in the *Rainbow* and *SNoW* package are tested on the WIPO-alpha document collection. The Rainbow package implements *Naïve Bayes*, *kNN*, and *Support Vector Machines (SVM)* algorithms. The SNoW package implements a network of linear functions where a variation of the Winnow algorithm is used for learning. In the Rainbow package indexing is performed at word level, accounting for term frequencies in each document. The output from all classifiers consists of a ranked list of categories for each test document. In the evaluation presented in [6] three different evaluation measures are used to asses the performance of the categorization process at class-level and at subclass-level. At class level the best performance is achieved when the first 300 words of each document are indexed. The best scoring text classification methods

---

[2] A directorate is an administrative defined cluster.

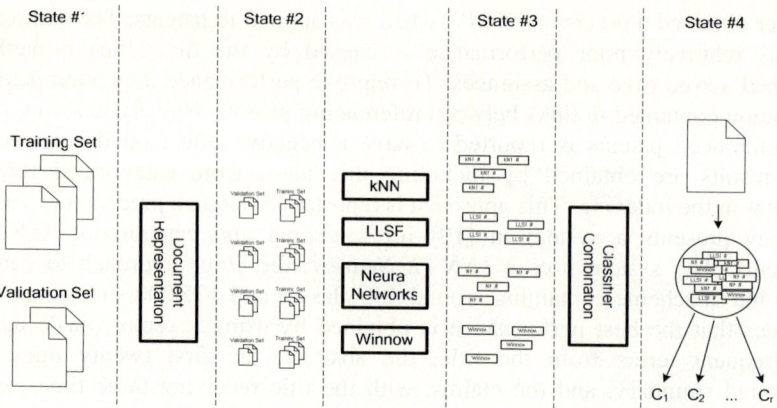

Fig. 2. The model used for constructing a combined classifier

were Naïve Bayes and SVM with a precision of 55%, whereas Winnow and kNN only achieved a precision of 51%. The research in [6] revealed that the distribution of errors of Naïve Bayes is strictly different from the error distribution in SVM. Using three-guesses the best scoring method is Naïve Bayes with a precision of 79%. The precision for the other algorithms is 77% (kNN), 73% (SVM) and 73% (SNoW). When measuring with all-categories Naïve Bayes still achieves the best precision at 63%. At subclass level the best performance is also achieved when the first 300 words are indexed. Here Naïve Bayes achieves the lowest precision of all TC methods tested with a top-prediction of 33% compared to 41% best achieved precision by SVM. In first three guesses kNN achieves the best precision of 62% and tested with all-categories SVM achieves the best precision of 48%. In a second article by Fall et al. [5], a customized language independent text classification system for categorization in the IPC is presented. The system is based on state-of-the-art Neural Network techniques, and applies in particular a variant of the Winnow algorithm.

To our knowledge, no previous work has investigated automatic patent categorization methods that rely on classifier combinations. The contribution presented in this paper is to explore the effectiveness of applying diverse combination techniques trained with different document representations to categorize patents.

3 Patent Categorization Model

The combined classifier proposed in this paper is constructed in several steps. The output of each step is shown in the states depicted in Fig. 2, where the rectangular boxes represent the software components responsible for the transformation between two states. The combined classifier is able to categorize patent documents in the categories represented in the document collection (State #4 in Fig. 2). The document collection is divided into a training set, a validation set, and a test set. The training set and the validation set are used to build the classifiers (State #1 in Fig. 2) and the test set is used to evaluate classifiers' performance. The *Document Representation* component is responsible for constructing different representations of the document collections (State #2). In our experiments the document representations used vary according to three characteristics a) how features are indexed, b) how features are represented, and c) how the process of feature reduction is performed. From each representation of the document collection, four classifiers are constructed (State #3). The classifiers are trained with one of the following machine learning methods: *kNN*, *LLSF (Linear Least Square Fit)*, *Neural Networks* and *Winnow*. The details of these algorithms can be found in [9,15,16].

The *Document Representation* stage consists of three separated processes: *Feature Indexing*, *Feature Weighting*, and *Feature Dimensionality Reduction*. The *Feature Indexing* process includes methods for stop-word removal and stemming and basically selects different document features to index documents. In the *Feature Weighting* process term frequencies can be used as feature weights but also other weighting schemes such as different versions of the *term frequency – inverse document frequency (tf-idf)* were included in our model. Methods for reducing the dimension of the feature collection were included in the *Feature Dimensionality Reduction* process. Our model employs two methods of *Feature Reduction*: by *Document Frequency* and by *Relevance Score*. In *Feature Reduction by Document Frequency* an upper and a lower bound obtained experimentally determines which features are included. *Feature Reduction by Relevance Score*, described in detail in [18], calculates for each feature a relevance score in each category. This score reveals how discriminative a feature is for one category in relation to all the other categories.

Our flexible patent categorization model includes also different methods to combine the machine learning based classifiers. Following sections briefly describe the methods employed to combine these classifiers; more details can be found in [16].

3.1 Combination Methods

In *Binary Voting*, voting is used to decide whether a document belongs or not to a category. Using this method it is possible to assign a document to several categories, since a voting round is conducted per category.

Weighted Classifier Combination uses the *Importance Weighted OWA* operator [14] to combine the prediction of several classifiers. The OWA operator is an averaging operator and its properties are defined by the quantifier *andness* ρ_Q applied to the algorithm using the OWA weights $\vec{w}$. Each classifier generates a value $y_i \in [0, 1]$ signifying a document's relationship to a category c_i and for each category it also contains a value $p \in [0, 1]$ representing the precision of the classifier on the validation set. In the combination method only classifiers producing a value exceeding some threshold are averaged for each main class. Thus, the input $\vec{a}$ to the *OWA* operator is the precision obtained by the classifiers exceeding the threshold in the specific main class. Additionally, a value v_i associated with y_i is used as importance weight for the respective value a_i. The computed average is multiplied with a value b representing the number of votes k_i. The values v_i and b have associated significance scores s_y and $s_v \in [0, 1]$, which can be used to grade the impact of y_i and k_i respectively.

Dynamic Classifier Selection is based on an approach for hand-printed digit recognition proposed by Sabourin et al. [13], which selects the classifier that correctly categorizes the most consecutive neighboring training examples to perform the final prediction. In case of a tie, the algorithm implemented in our model, performs a voting round between the classifiers holding the tie, predicting the category with the highest number of votes.

Adaptive Classifier Selection was introduced by Giacinto and Roli in [7]. This method predicts also according to the best performing classifier on the validation examples in the neighborhood of the document that will be categorized. The performance of the classifier is measured according to a *soft* probability, used to identify the classifier that obtains the highest probability in categorizing a document correctly. A *confidence score*, defined as the difference in probabilities obtained by a classifier and the others, is calculated. If the confidence score exceeds a threshold, the classifier with the highest probability is used to categorize the document. If any of the computed confidence scores does not exceed the threshold, the algorithm identifies all classifiers with differences in a range of the best classifier and performs a voting round between these classifiers.

3.2 Expert Advice Algorithms

Five different *Expert Advise* algorithms were implemented in our model: *WM* [12], *WMG* [12], *P* [4], *BW* [3] *and BW'* [3]. Additionally a *mistake driven* variation of P, denoted P', was also implemented. These algorithms aim at finding the optimal combination of *experts* by minimizing the number of mistakes over a worst case sequence of observations. The idea behind the expert advice algorithms is to optimize, in a series of trials, a set of weights used to properly combine the prediction of each expert. Based on the weighted linear combination of the prediction of each expert, the algorithm is able to predict if an unseen document belongs to a category or not.

4 Experimental Results

A comprehensive collection of classifier combinations was evaluated in our experiments using different document representations. As is described in [16], 23 different document representations were tested. The 4 document representations, where the classifiers obtained the best performance, were selected for training. Fig. 3 shows the performance obtained by the classifiers on six of these document representations. The document representation that obtained the best performance (DR23), from all the categorization methods within each of the 10 main classes comprised in the refined version of the WIPO-alpha document collection, used the following features: a) *indexed sections*: title, 200 first words from abstract, 200 first words from claims and 400 first words from description, b) *feature reduction*: using 500 features per main class, c) *section weight:* the title was weighted five times as much as the other sections, and d) *feature weigh*t: normalized term frequency weight was employed. It was also determined experimentally that the best performing of the classifiers participating in the combination was *LLSF*, which achieved an F_1 measure of 0.8137. The performance measures obtained by the different combination methods that were evaluated are depicted in Fig. 4. The combination method that achieved the best performance in the evaluations was *Weighted Classifier Combination* with an F_1 measure of 0.8667, which is an improvement of 6.51% compared to the best classifier

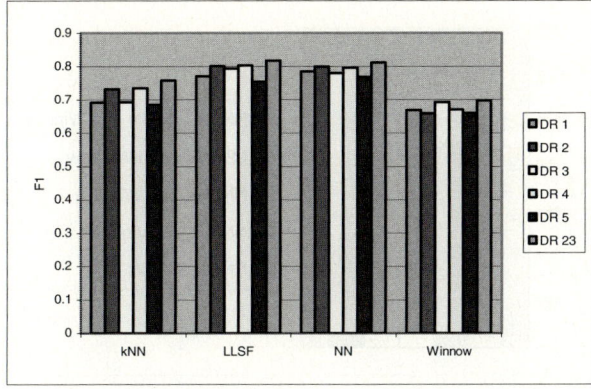

Fig. 3. Performance of four classifiers on six document representations

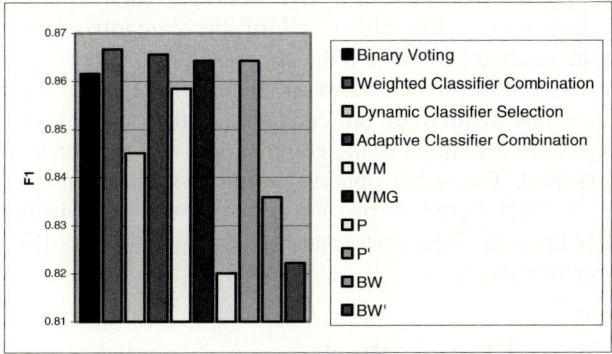

Fig. 4. F_1 measures obtained using the evaluated combination methods

participating in the combination. *Weighted Classifier Combination* achieves the best performance when the significance of voting is maximized, i.e. the voting phase of the algorithm is favored. Similar properties were observed with other combination methods. The great impact of voting in performance might be caused by the relatively large number of classifiers participating in the combinations.

Our results also show that the performance obtained by classifiers based on Winnow and kNN is inferior to the performance obtained by classifiers based on LLSF and Neural Networks. To determine the impact on performance of these classifiers, two of the combination methods were evaluated with and without classifiers based on Winnow and kNN participating in the combination. The evaluated combinations showed more effectiveness without a classifier based on kNN but including classifiers based on Winnow. To evaluate the contribution of the four categorization methods the *BestSelect* algorithm described in [1] was applied on five collections of classifiers. *BestSelect* predicts correctly whenever any of the classifiers in the combination predicts also correctly; otherwise the prediction remains

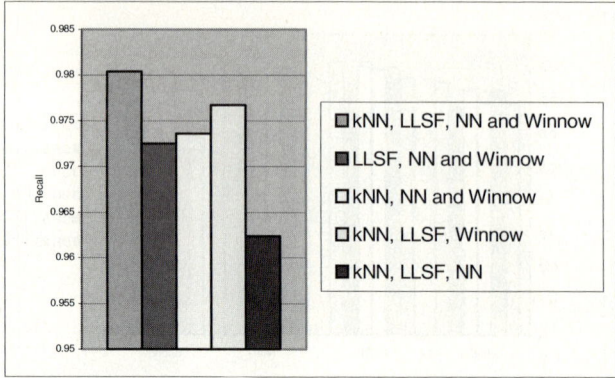

Fig. 5. Recall obtained using *BestSelect* with different combinations of categorization methods

undefined. We applied *BestSelect* on five settings, each comprising the same document representations where either, all of the categorization methods or all methods except the method from which the contribution should be tested, participated in the combination. The difference between the recall measured on a setting where classifiers based on one method are not contained in the combination and the setting where all classifiers are contained in the combination, can be seen as the contribution of a particular method. The recall obtained using *BestSelect* on the five settings is depicted in Fig. 5. This figure surprisingly reveals that combinations including a *Winnow* classifier have the best performance, although this classifier alone showed relatively poor performance.

5 Conclusions and Future Work

In this paper we have described a new model of an automatic patent categorization system based on an ensemble of classifiers. Our model was evaluated on a refined version of the WIPO-alpha document collection. However, since no previous research has been evaluated on this same collection no direct comparison with other methods can be done at this time. Instead, the performance results obtained by the ensemble were compared to the best performing categorization method used in the combination. As is described in Section 3, we evaluated 10 different techniques for combining the classifiers. Our experiments show that all of the combination methods achieved improved performance when compared to the best classifier participating in the combination. The best combination technique *Weighted Classifier Combination* achieves an F_1 score of 0.8667, which is an improvement of 6.51% to the best classifier participating in the ensemble. Among the four machine learning based categorization methods, the best performing were *Neural Networks* and *LLSF*, but they also have the worst training efficiency. However, their training can be improved reducing the feature collection. Interestingly, our experiments also show that reducing the feature collection improves the performance of some classifiers. The categorization methods employed in our model are representative of a variety of the available methods. As future research we plan to explore combining a broader class of classifiers and optimize the overall performance of the ensemble using genetic algorithms.

References

1. Bennett P.N., Dumais S. T., and Horvitz E.: Probabilistic Combination of Text Classifiers Using Reliability Indicators: Models and Result. Proceedings of the *25th Annual International ACM SIGIR Conference on Research and Development in Information Retrieval (SIGIR'02)*, Tampere, Finland, 2002.
2. Chakrabarti S., Dom B., and Indyk P.: Enhanced hypertext categorization using hyperlinks, Proceedings of SIGMOD98, *ACM International conference on Management of Data*, ACM Press, New York, 307-318, 1998.
3. Cesa-Bianchi N., Freund Y., Helmbold D. P., and Warmuth M. K.: On-line Prediction and Conversion Strategies, *Machine Learning* 25, pp. 71-110, 1996.
4. Cesa-Bianchi N., Freund Y., Hausler D., Helmbold D. P., Schapire R E. , and Warmuth M. K.: How to Use Expert Advice, *Journal of the ACM*, Vol. 44, No. 3, May 1997, pp. 427-485.
5. Fall C. J., Benzineb K., Goyot J., Törcsvári A., and Fiévet P.: Computer-Assisted Categorization of Patent Documents in the International Patent Categorization, *Proceedings of the International Chemical Information Conference*, Nîmes, October 2003.
6. Fall C. J., Törcsvári A., Benzineb K., and Karetka G.: Automated Categorization in the International Patent Classification, *ACM SIGIR Forum*, Vol 37(1), 10-25, 2003.
7. Giacinto G. and Roli F.: Adaptive Selection of Image Classifiers, *In Proceedings of ICIAP*, Springer Verlag LNCS, Vol. 1310, pp 38-45, 1997.
8. Koster C.H.A., Seutter M., and Beney J.: Classifying Patent Applications with Winnow, Proceedings Annual Machine Learning Conference Benelearn, Univ. Antwerp 2001.
9. Koster C.H.A., Seutter M. and Beney J.:Multi-categorization of Patent Applications with Winnow, *Ershov Memorial Conference 2003*, Novosibirsk, Russia, 546-555, 2003.
10. Larkey L. S.: A Patent Search and Categorization System, *Proceedings of the 4th ACM Conference on Digital Libraries*, 179-187, 1999.
11. Larkey L. S. and Croft W. B.: Combining Classifiers in Text Categorization, *In Proceedings of SIGIR-96, 19th ACM conference on Research and Development in Information Retrieval*, Zürich, Switzerland, 1996, p. 289-297.
12. Litlestone N. and Warmuth M. K.: The Weighted Majority Algorithm, *Information and Computation*, Vol. 108, 211-261, 1994.
13. Sabourin M., Mitiche A., Thomas D., and Nagy G.: Classifier Combination for Hand-printed Digit Recognition, *Proc. Second Int. Conf. Document Analysis and Recognition*, pp. 163–166, Tsukuba Saenie City, Japan, 20–22 Oct. 1993.
14. Yager R.R.: On ordered weighted averaging aggregation operators in multi-criteria decision making, *IEEE Transactions on Systems, Man and Cybernetics* 18(1988) 183-190.
15. Yang Y.: An Evaluation of Statistical Approaches to Text Categorization, *Information Retrieval*, Vol. 1, 69-90, 1999.
16. Mattiason H.: Automated categorization of Patent Applications, MSc Thesis. Computer Science and Engineering Department, Aalborg University Esbjerg, June 2006.

Best Subset Feature Selection for Massive Mixed-Type Problems

Eugene Tuv[1], Alexander Borisov[2], and Kari Torkkola[3]

[1] Intel, Analysis and Control Technology, Chandler, AZ, USA
eugene.tuv@intel.com
[2] Intel, Analysis and Control Technology, N.Novgorod, Russia
alexander.borisov@intel.com
[3] Motorola, Intelligent Systems Lab, Tempe, AZ, USA
Kari.Torkkola@motorola.com

Abstract. We address the problem of identifying a non-redundant subset of important variables. All modern feature selection approaches including filters, wrappers, and embedded methods experience problems in very general settings with massive mixed-type data, and with complex relationships between the inputs and the target. We propose an efficient ensemble-based approach measuring statistical independence between a target and a potentially very large number of inputs including any meaningful order of interactions between them, removing redundancies from the relevant ones, and finally ranking variables in the identified minimum feature set. Experiments with synthetic data illustrate the sensitivity and the selectivity of the method, whereas the scalability of the method is demonstrated with a real car sensor data base.

1 Introduction

Ensembles of decision trees have proven to be very efficient and versatile tools in classification and regression problems [2,4]. In addition, the structure of the trees can be used as a basis for variable selection methods. We have presented such a variable selection method that amends the ensemble with the concept of artificial contrast variables (ACE) [10].

The contribution of this paper is to extend ACE into the removal of redundant variables. This is an important problem in several domains. It may be expensive to observe all features at once. In medical diagnostics the smallest subset of tests for a reliable diagnosis is usually desirable. Similarly, in engineering problems concerned with a set of sensors, it is often necessary to design the lowest cost (the smallest) set of sensors to accomplish a particular task.

The generalization capability of a learner typically improves with a smaller set of parameters. Even with regularizing learners, removal of redundant features has shown improvement in domains such as cancer diagnosis from mass spectra or text classification [5].

Smaller model, in this case a smaller subset of relevant features, makes it easier to interpret the structure and the characteristics of the underlying domain. DNA microarray gene expression analysis is an example. As a reduced set of genes is chosen, it makes their biological relationship with the target diseases more explicit. New scientific knowledge of the disease domain is then provided by these important genes.

We describe first how ensembles of trees can produce a variable masking measure that forms the basis of the elimination of the redundant variables. Next we introduce the idea of artificial contrasts that is in the core of the proposed algorithm for the best subset feature selection. Experimentation with artificial as well as real data sets demonstrates the performance of the method.

2 Tree Ensemble Methods in Feature Ranking

In this paper we address the problem of feature filtering, or removal of irrelevant and redundant inputs in very general supervised settings. The target variable could be numeric or categorical, the input space could have variables of mixed type with non-randomly missing values, the underlying $X - Y$ relationship could be very complex and multivariate, and the data could be massive in both dimensions (tens of thousands of variables, and millions of observations). Ensembles of unstable but very fast and flexible base learners such as trees can address most of the listed challenges when equipped with embedded feature weighting [1]. They have proved to be very effective in variable ranking in problems with up to a hundred thousand predictors [1,7]. More comprehensive overview of feature selection with ensembles is given in [9].

Random Forest (RF) and *MART* are two distinguished representatives of tree ensembles. Random Forest extends the "random subspace" method [6]. It grows a forest of random trees on bagged samples showing excellent results comparable with the best known classifiers [2]. MART is a sequential ensemble of trees that fits a sequence of the shallow trees using gradient boosting approach [4].

2.1 Feature Masking

Decision trees can handle missing values gracefully using so-called *surrogate* splits. The surrogate splits, however, could also be used to detect *feature masking*. We describe now a novel masking measure assuming that the reader has an understanding of basic decision trees such as CART [3].

The predictive association of a surrogate variable x_s for the best splitter x^* at a tree node t is defined through the probability that x_s predicts the action of x^* correctly and this is estimated as:

$$p(x_s, x^*) = p_L(x_s, x^*) + p_R(x_s, x^*)$$

where $p_L(x_s, x^*)$ and $p_R(x_s, x^*)$ define the estimated probabilities that both x_s and x^* send a case in t left (right). The predictive measure of association $d(x^*|x_s)$ between x_s and x^* is defined as

$$d(x^*|x_s) = \frac{\min(p_L, p_R) - (1 - p(x_s, x^*))}{\min(p_L, p_R)} \qquad (1)$$

where p_L, p_R are the proportions of cases sent to the left(or right) by x^*. It measures the relative reduction in error due to using x_s to predict x^* $(1-p(x_s, x^*))$ as compared with the "naive" rule that matches the action with $\max(p_L, p_R)$ (with error $\min(p_L, p_R)$). $d(x^*|x_s)$ can take values in the range $(-\infty, 1]$. If $d(x^*|x_s) < 0$ then x_s is disregarded as a surrogate for x^*, otherwise we say that x^* masks x_s.

To comprehend the masking in terms of model impact, we define the masking metric for a pair of variables i, j as

$$M_{ij} = \sum_{t \in T, s=s_i} w(s_i, t) d(s|s_j) \tag{2}$$

where $w(s_i, t)$ is the decrease in impurity [3] due to the actual split on the variable s_i, and the summation is done over those tree ensemble nodes where the primary split s was made on the variable s_i. Here we take into account how well variable j "mimics" predictive action of the primary splitter i, and the contribution of the actual split on the variable i to the model.

2.2 Ranking Features

The main idea in this work relies on the following reasonable assumption: a stable feature ranking method, such as an ensemble of trees, that measures relative relevance of an input to a target variable Y would assign a significantly higher score to a relevant variable X_i than to an artificial variable created independently of Y from the same distribution as X_i. The same also applies to the masking measure. We compare the masking of all variables by a list of selected relevant variables, and consider only those masking values as real masking that are statistically higher than masking values of noise variables by selected variables. To select the minimal subset, the algorithm drops all masked (in a statistical sense) variables from the relevant variable list at every residual iteration.

We present now an algorithm for the best subset feature selection (BSFS) based on this idea. It is similar to the iterative procedure described in [10], but extends it in order to eliminate redundant features. The proposed approach encapsulates a new masking metric estimation scheme.

3 The Algorithm: The Best Subset Feature Selection

Our best subset selection method is a combination of the following steps: **A)** Estimating variable importance using a random forest of a fixed depth, such as 3-6 levels (we do split weight re-estimation usiing out-of-bag (OOB) samples because it gives more accurate and unbiased estimate of variable importance in each tree and filters out noise variables), **B)** Comparing variable importance against artificially constructed noise variables using a formal statistical test, **C)** Building a masking matrix for selected important variables, and selection of statistically important masking values using a formal test (here a series of short MART ensembles is used [4]), **D)** The masked variables are removed from the important variable list, and **E)** The effect of the identified important variables is iteratively removed to allow the detection of less important variables (because trees and a parallel ensemble of trees are not well suited for additive models). Steps **C)** and **D)** are novel and different from ACE [10].

A. Split Weight Re-estimation. We propose a modified scheme for calculating the split weight and for selecting the best split in each node of a tree. The idea is to use the training samples to find *the best split point* for each variable, and then to use the OOB samples that were not used in building the tree in order to select *the best split variable* in a node. The split weight used for variable importance estimation is also calculated using the OOB samples.

B. Selecting Important Features. In order to determine the cut-off point for the importance scores, there needs to be a *contrast* variable that is known to be truly independent of the target. By comparing variable importance to this contrast (or to several ones), one can then use a statistical test to determine which variables are truly important. These artificial contrast variables are obtained by randomly permuting the values of the original M variables across the N examples. Generating contrasts using unrelated distributions, such as Gaussian or uniform, is not sufficient, because the values of original variables may exhibit some special structure.

Trees in an ensemble are then broken into R short independent series of equal size $L = 10-50$, where each series is trained on a different but fixed permutation of the contrast variables. For each series, the importances are then computed for all variables including the artificial contrasts. Using these series is important when the number of variables is large or when the trees are shallow, because some (even important) features can be absent from a single tree. To gain statistical significance, importance score of all variables is compared to a percentile of importance scores of the M contrasts (we used 75th percentile). A statistical test (Student's t-test) is evaluated to compare the scores over all R series. Variables scoring significantly higher than the contrasts are selected as relevant.

C. Estimation of Masking Between Features. Next we calculate the masking matrix for the selected important features. Let their number be m. We build a set of R independent short MART models [4], with L=10-50 trees, and calculate all surrogates for all variables (including the contrasts) in all nodes of every tree. Note that the surrogate scores and the split weights are calculated using the OOB sample as in step A. For each pair of variables $i, j \in 1 \ldots, 2m$ and for each ensemble $r = 1 \ldots, R$ we compute the masking measure M_{ij}^r as a sum of the masking measure $M_{ij}(t)$ over all trees t in the ensemble. Let $M_{i,\alpha}^t$ be α - quantile of $M_{ij}^t, j = m+1, \ldots, 2m$. Then a square masking matrix M_{ij}^* is filled as follows. We set an element $M_{ij}^* = 1$ if the hypothesis $M_{ij}^r - M_{i,\alpha}^r > 0, r = 1, \ldots, R$ is accepted with a given significance level p (we used p=0.05). Otherwise we set $M_{ij}^* = 0$. We say variable j is masked by variable i if $M_{ij}^* = 1$.

D. Removal of Masked Features. After building the masking matrix, the masked variables are removed from the important variable list L as follows. Let L^* be initially an empty list of non-masked important features. We sort the items in L by the importance measure that is calculated as sum of the importances over the ensemble built on step E (or on step B for the initial pass). First, we move variable in L that has maximum importance from L to L^*. Next, all variables masked by this variable (in terms of matrix M_{ij}^*) are removed from L. Then this procedure is repeated for the remaining variables in L, until it is empty.

E. Removing Effects of Identified Important Variables. After a subset of relevant variables has been discovered in step B, we remove their effects on the target variable. To accomplish this, the target is predicted using only the identified important variables. The prediction residuals become then a new target. We return to step A, and continue iterating until no variables remain with scores significantly higher than those of the contrasts. It is important that step A uses all variables to build the ensemble not excluding identified important ones. This step is even more important here than in the ACE algorithm since it ensures that the algorithm will recover partially masked variables that still have their unique effect on the target.

To accommodate the step E in classification problems we adopted the multi-class logistic regression approach described in [4].

Note that the computational complexity of our method is of the same order as the maximal complexity of RF and MART models (usually MART is more complex, as it requires computing all surrogate splits at every tree node), but it could be significantly faster for datasets with large number of cases since the trees in RF are only built to a limited depth.

4 Experiments

We describe first experiments with the proposed method using synthetic data sets followed by a real example. Synthetic data sets allow one to vary systematically domain characteristics of interest, such as the number of relevant and irrelevant attributes, the amount of noise, and the complexity of the target concept. The relevance of the method is demonstrated using a real-life car sensor dataset.

4.1 Synthetic Data

To illustrate the sensitivity and the selectivity of the method, we simulated a dataset that conceptually should be challenging for our method, but optimal for the standard stepwise selection methods.

The data generated had 203 input variables and one numeric response. $x_1, ..., x_{100}$ are highly correlated with one another, and they are all reasonably predictive of the response ($R^2 \sim 0.5$). a, b, and c are independent variables that are much weaker predictors ($R^2 \sim 0.1$). $y_1, ..., y_{100}$ are i.i.d. $N(0, 1)$ noise variables. The actual response variable was generated using $z = x_1 + a + b + c + \epsilon$, where $\epsilon \sim N(0, 1)$.

Tables 1 and 2 compare stepwise best subset forward-backward selection with the significance level to enter/leave 0.05 to the proposed method.

Table 1. Ranked list of important variables (synthetic case) found by standard stepwise best subset forward-backward selection. Five of the important (but correlated) variables are at the head of the list. These are followed by eight noise variables before the weak (but important) predictors are discovered.

x1	x5	x37	x77	x93	y11	y13	y19	y25	y27	y67	y68	y74	a	b	c

Table 2. Ranked list of important variables (synthetic case) found by the proposed method together with their importances. Only one of the correlated variables appears in the list; the rest have been pruned as redundant variables. This is followed by the weak predictors. None of the noise variables have been picked.

variable	x13	a	b	c
importance	100%	10.6%	9.3%	5.9%

Note that even though this case is ideal for standard stepwise best subset selection, noise may be picked before weak but relevant predictors, whereas the proposed method is immune to independent noise. Naturally, the point of the paper, elimination of redundant variables is demonstrated.

4.2 Realistic Data

classification. Sensor data is collected in a driving simulator. This is a commercial product with a set of sensors that, at the behavioral level, simulate a rich set of current and future onboard sensors. This set consists of a radar for locating other traffic, a GPS system for position information, a camera system for lane positioning and lane marking, and a mapping data base for road names, directions, locations of points of interest etc. Thus, sensors are available that would be hard or expensive to arrange to a real vehicle. There is also a complete car status system for determining the state of engine parameters and driving controls (transmission gear selection, steering angle, brake and accelerator pedals, turn signal, window and seat belt status etc.). The simulator setup also has several video cameras, microphones and infrared eye tracking sensors to record all driver actions during the drive that is synchronized with all the sensor output and simulator tracking variables. Altogether there are 425 separate variables describing an extensive scope of driving data — information about the auto, the driver, the environment, and associated conditions.

The 29 driver activity classes in this study are related to maneuvering the vehicle with varying degrees of required attention [8]. The classes are not mutually exclusive. An instant in time can be labeled simultaneously as "TurningRight" and "Starting", for example. Thus, we performed variable selection separately for each of the 29 classes. We compare variable selection without redundancy elimination (ACE) to variable selection with redundancy elimination (BSFS).

Current database consists of 629375 data records (7.5 hours of driving) with 109 variables (this study excluded driver activity tracking variables). Of these variables, 82 were continuous, and 27 were catecorigal.

1054 E. Tuv, A. Borisov, and K. Torkkola

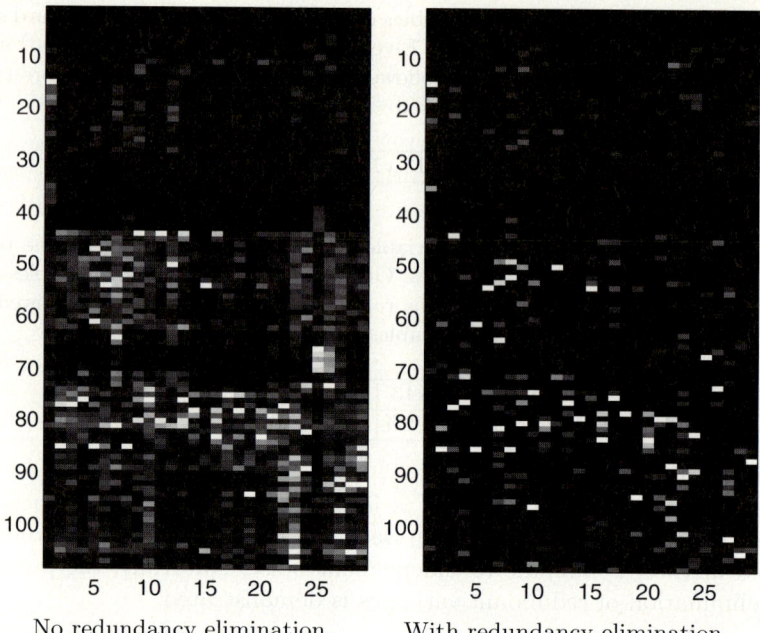

No redundancy elimination. With redundancy elimination.

Fig. 1. Variable importances for each driver activity class. 109 variables on the y-axis, 29 classes on the x-axis. The lightness of the square is proportional to the variable importance for the detection of the class. Thus the set of light squares in a column indicate the set of variables necessary for the detection of that particular class.

A visual overview of the results is presented in Fig. 1 (see caption for legend). Elimination of redundancies between important variables is clearly visible as the drastic reduction of the number of "light" squares in each column corresponding to each class.

We present a detailed view of one of the columns, class "TurningLeft" in Table 3. The three most important variables chosen by ACE have been retained as such even after the redundancy elimination ("steeringWheel", "LongAccel", "lateralAcceleration"). Of the following three variables on the list, "steeringWheel_abs" and "lateralAcceleration_abs" are absolute values of one of the three

Table 3. Variable importances for class "TurningLeft" without (ACE) and with (BSFS) redundancy elimination. See text for discusion

BSFS	ACE	Variables for "TurningLeft"
100.0	100.0	steeringWheel
74.2	75.9	LongAccel
72.2	72.2	lateralAcceleration
	69.8	acceleration
	49.3	steeringWheel_abs
	39.0	lateralAcceleration_abs
	36.7	aheadLaneBearing
2.2	32.8	steeringManeuver
40.5	23.0	speed
1.3	22.2	steeringWheel_rd3
2.8	20.5	laneBearingIfRightTurn
0.7	16.2	turnSignal
21.0	13.4	accelerator
	11.3	CultureType
0.3	9.5	steeringError
	9.0	laneOfLRtire
	8.8	LanePos
	8.7	laneNumber
	8.5	crossLaneVelocity_abs
	8.2	SubjectEngineRPM
0.4	8.0	laneBearingIfLeftTurn
	8.0	crossLaneAcceleration
	7.7	LaneIndex
1.9	7.4	inIntersection
	6.6	laneOffset
1.5	5.9	laneHeadingIfRightTurn
	5.8	crossLaneVelocity
11.9	5.6	laneOfLRtire
	5.3	distToRightLaneEdge
0.4	5.2	distToLeftLaneEdge
3.1	4.9	timeToCrossLeftEdge
	4.5	distanceToLaneChange
	4.5	minimumStoppingDistance
0.3	3.7	currentLaneHeading
0.2	3.7	laneOffsetVarShort
	3.6	LaneCount
	3.5	laneHeadingIfLeftTurn
	3.4	acceleratorManeuver
7.3	3.4	distToLeftLaneEdge_rd3

most important variables, and "acceleration" is a discretized version of the "LongAccel". All three have been completely (and correctly) eliminated as redundant variables. Variable "steeringManeuver" is a "virtual" sensor that has been calculated as a discretized nonlinear function of "steeringWheel", "speed", and "accelerator". We can see that "steeringManeuver" has been almost completely eliminated as a redundant variable and that its source variables have all been retained as important variables. These redundancy eliminations verify that the method is working as designed. The rest of the dependencies and their eliminations are subject to further analysis.

5 Discussion

We have presented an extension to feature selection with artificial contrasts, which also removes redundant variables from the result. Although some classifiers, such as Random Forest, for example, thrive with redundant information, there are application domains in which the minimum, most economical set of variables is needed. As an example, we presented a sensor selection example in the automotive domain.

Because in real engineering applications inclusion of a sensor incurs a cost, and the costs vary from one sensor to another, an interesting thread of future work would be to optimize the cost of a sensor set for a given fixed and required performance level. Medical diagnostics would also fall under the same scheme.

References

1. A. Borisov, V. Eruhimov, and E. Tuv. Dynamic soft feature selection for tree-based ensembles. In I. Guyon, S. Gunn, M. Nikravesh, and L. Zadeh, editors, *Feature Extraction, Foundations and Applications*. Springer, New York, 2005.
2. L. Breiman. Random forests. *Machine Learning*, 45(1):5–32, 2001.
3. L. Breiman, J.H. Friedman, R.A. Olshen, and C.J. Stone. *Classification and Regression Trees*. CRC Press, 1984.
4. J.H. Friedman. Greedy function approximation: a gradient boosting machine. Technical report, Dept. of Statistics, Stanford University, 1999.
5. E. Gabrilovich and S. Markovitch. Text categorization with many redundant features: Using aggressive feature selection to make svms competitive with c4.5. In *Proc. ICML'04*, 2004.
6. T. K. Ho. The random subspace method for constructing decision forests. *IEEE Transactions on Pattern Analysis and Machine Intelligence*, 20(8):832–844, 1998.
7. K. Torkkola and E. Tuv. Ensembles of regularized least squares classifiers for high-dimensional problems. In Isabelle Guyon, Steve Gunn, Masoud Nikravesh, and Lofti Zadeh, editors, *Feature Extraction, Foundations and Applications*. Springer, 2005.
8. Kari Torkkola, Mike Gardner, Chip Wood, Chris Schreiner, Noel Massey, Bob Leivian, John Summers, and Srihari Venkatesan. Toward modeling and classification of naturalistic driving. In *Proceedings of the 2005 IEEE Intelligent Vehicles Symposium*, pages 638–643, Las Vegas, NV, USA, June 6 - 8 2005.

9. E. Tuv. Feature selection and ensemble learning. In I. Guyon, S. Gunn, M. Nikravesh, and L. Zadeh, editors, *Feature Extraction, Foundations and Applications*. Springer, New York, 2005.
10. Eugene Tuv, Alexander Borisov, and Kari Torkkola. Feature selection using ensemble based ranking against artificial contrasts. In *Proceedings of the International Joint Conference on Neural Networks (IJCNN 2006)*, Vancouver, Canada, July 16-22 2006.

Planning Under Uncertainty with Abstraction Hierarchies

Letícia Maria Friske[1,2] and Carlos Henrique Costa Ribeiro[2]

[1] Dept. de Tecnologia – Universidade Regional do Noroeste do Estado do Rio Grande do Sul
– UNIJUÍ
98900-000 Santa Rosa – Brasil
leticia.friske@unijui.tche.br
[2] Div. de Ciência da Computação - Instituto Tecnológico de Aeronáutica
12228-900 São José dos Campos – Brasil
carlos@ita.br

Abstract. This article presents a hierarchical planner to actuate in uncertain domains named HIPU - Hierarchical Planner under Uncertainty. The uncertainties treated by HIPU include the probabilistic distribution of the operators effects and a distribution of probabilities on the possible initial states of the domain. HIPU automatically creates the abstraction hierarchy that will be used during planning, and for this it uses an extension of the Alpine method, adapted to act under uncertainty conditions. The planning process in HIPU happens initially in the highest level of abstraction, and the solution found in this level is refined by lower levels, until reaching the lowest level. During the search the plan evaluation is carried out, indicating if the plan achieves the goal with a success probability larger or equal to a previously defined value. To evaluate this probability, the planner uses the forward projection method.

Keywords: planning, reasoning under uncertainty, machine learning.

1 Introduction

In situations that involve choice of actions to reach an objective, it is natural that rational beings use a planning strategy to determine the sequence of actions to be taken. The approach for planning problems that is more challenging is Planning under Uncertainty or Decision Theoretical Planning [1], that involves partially observable environments, actions with non-deterministic effects, unknown initial state, and possibly other uncertainties.

There are many ways of tackling a planning problem under uncertainty. The most common approach considers adapting and generalizing classical planning through the use of techniques such as those based on Markov Decision Processes (MDPs), like Reinforcement Learning and Dynamic Programming [2]. These approaches cause modifications in several aspects in the structure of planning, both in action representation and plan evaluation. Many planners and theories in this area have been published, such as Buridan [3], CL-Buridan [4], Weaver [1], RTDP [5, 6], C-SHOP [7] and Drips [8].

The Buridan planner [3] uses classical planning techniques to build plans that probably achieve a goal, the C-Buridan [9] planner extends the representation and algorithm to handle sensing actions and conditional plans and the CL-Buridan planner adds the concept of a looping construct and introduces the idea of "plan blocks" which facilitate generating conditional and iterative plans. RTDP is a greedy search algorithm that learns to solve MDPs by repeatedly updating the heuristic values of the states that are visited, such updates eventually deliver an optimal behavior provided that the state space is finite and initial heuristic values are admissible [5]. Weaver is a planner that can handle uncertainty about actions taken by external agents, more than one possible initial state and non-deterministic outcomes of actions. It produces conditional plans and compute the plan's probability of success automatically, through a Bayesian belief net [1]. C-SHOP extends the classical hierarchical planner SHOP [10] to act in situations with incomplete and uncertain information about the environment and actions. Drips combines conditional planning with probabilistic distribution of effects, and accomplish abstraction of probabilistic operators with common pre-conditions and effects. This mechanism makes it possible that planning happens in different hierarchical abstraction levels. The association of the concepts of hierarchical structures and abstractions allow the reduction of the search space for solutions, converting the space complexity from exponential to linear [11],[12].

HIPU – Hierarchical Planner under Uncertainty – is inserted in the context of hierarchical planning and planning under uncertainties. Regarding uncertainties, it allows a probabilistic distribution of possible operators effects and a probabilistic choice under possible initial states of the domain. It is proposed as an extension of the Alpine method [12], adapted to act under uncertainty conditions, automatically generating an abstraction hierarchy and planning from this hierarchy. Many Alpine properties are modified due to the probabilistic operators. Planning in HIPU begins at the highest level of abstraction, and the solution found in this level is refined by lower levels. During refinement, the plan found so far is evaluated, verifying if the solution succeeds with probability equal or higher than a predefined value. Evaluation of the success probability is by forward assessment, as in [3]. This paper formalizes aspects of HIPU and presents a case study to a version of the Blocks World problem.

2 Definitions and Language

Classical Planning considers simplifying properties regarding the agent and the environment, for example: static, totally observable and deterministic, meaning respectively that the changes in the environment depend solely on actions executed by the agent, the agent completely knows the environment and its actions have pre-defined effects in the environmental states. In this context, planning means finding a sequence of operators (actions) that solve a problem in a problem space. The problem space is defined by a group of legal operators, where each operator consists of pre-conditions and effects. The pre-conditions should be satisfied before an operator can be applied, and the effects describe the state modifications generated by application of the operator [13]. A problem of classical planning can thus be formalized as a triple (L, S, O), where L is a logical language of first order; S is the set of states and O is a set of operators. Each operator $\alpha \in O$ is defined by a triple (P_α, D_α, A_α), where P_α is the set of literals that indicate the pre-conditions, and D_α e A_α are the operators effects, so that A_α encompasses the list of positive literals[1] and D_α the group of negative literals. A problem ρ consists of an initial state S_0 and a set of conditions that determines the objective state Sg. The solution (or plan) Π for a problem is a sequence of operators that, when executed, transform an initial state in a state that satisfies all the conditions of the objective state.

2.1 Planning in Uncertain Environments and Language

One of the uncertainties that an agent can find regards the actions, which can have stochastic effects, in other words, the next environmental state is expressed as a probability distribution over states. Problems that involve this type of uncertainty can be modeled as probabilistic processes, where the goal is find a plan or policy Π that maximizes the probability of achieving the goal state. Formally, this probabilistic process is a 3-uple (A, S, T), where S is a set of states, A is a set of possible actions, and T is the transition model for the system, that corresponds to a mapping $SxAxS$ with probabilities between [0, 1].Problems with probabilistic actions have been approached in IA through adaptations of classical planning and high-level languages, such as STRIPS [14], to actuate in uncertainty domains (for instance, RTDP [5] and Weaver [1]).

The adaptations proposed here modify the definition of the classical planning problem, specifically regarding operators. The space problem is defined by a set of legal operators, where each operator consists of preconditions and one or more subsets of effects. Each subset describes state modifications generated by the application of the operator. The set of effects is chosen non-deterministically. A planning problem under uncertainties can thus be formalized as a triple (L, S, O), where L is a first-order logic language; S is the set of states; and O is a set of probabilistic operators, where each operator $\alpha \in O$ is a probabilistic operator. Each subset of effects can be composed by a list of positive and negative literals, and all subsets are different from each other.

Definition 1. Subset of effects

$E_\alpha = \{e_{\alpha 0}, e_{\alpha 1}, ..., e_{\alpha k}\}$ is the set of effects of the operator α.

E_α^i is a subset i of effects such that:

1. n represents the number of possible subsets of effects to an operator α;
2. $E_\alpha^i \in$ Power Set(E_α), $1 \leq i \leq n$;
3. $\forall\ E_\alpha^i, E_\alpha^j \in$ Power Set(E_α), $i \neq j$, $E_\alpha^i - E_\alpha^j \neq \varnothing$

Definition 2. Probabilistic Operator

Let α be an operator belonging to O, α is probabilistic when for each subset of effects there is an occurrence probability $\wp_i(E_\alpha^i)$, such that $0 < \wp_i(E_\alpha^i) \leq 1$ and $\sum_i^n \wp_i = 1$.

---

[1] A literal is an atomic sentence (a positive literal) or a denied atomic sentence (a negative literal). Atomic sentences are indivisible syntactic elements, a proposition that can be true or false.

Figure 1 presents an example of a probabilistic operator. The probability distribution is given by $PD_\alpha = \{0,5(E_\alpha^0), 0,25(E_\alpha^1), 0,25(E_\alpha^2)\}$ and each subset contain the respective literals, $E_\alpha^0 = \{e_1, e_2, e_3\}$, $E_\alpha^1 = \{e_1, e_2, e_4\}$ and $E_\alpha^2 = \{e_1, e_2, e_3, e_5\}$. When there is more than a single possible subset of effects, only a subset will be considered in the moment of the execution. The choice of this subset is non-deterministic. An operator and its respective subset of effects will be called a realization α^i. The operator has three possible realizations, α^0, α^1, α^2, determined by the choice of one of each possible subset, E_α^0, E_α^1 and E_α^2.

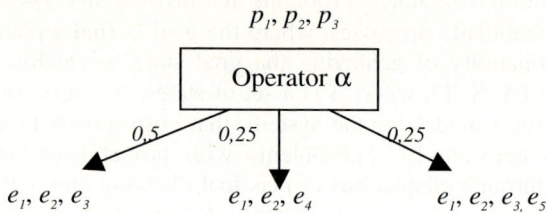

Fig. 1. Generic probabilistic operator

3 Automatically Generating Hierarchies in HIPU

The method used by HIPU for automatic generation of abstracting hierarchies is an extension of the Alpine method [12, 13], adapted to act in domains with probabilistic operators. The starting point is the algorithm for determining constraints (Algorithm 1). It establishes interactions among literals, creating constraints for the hierarchy. The definition of a relevant effect is very important. The relevant effects of an operator α relative to a goal S_g (Relevant(α, S_g)) are the effects of α that are either in S_g, or are preconditions of operators that have relevant effects with respect to S_g [12]. If α is probabilistic, its effects are distributed among the different subsets, then an operator α is relevant if one or more subsets contain relevant effects. The relevance of a probabilistic operator is associated with its realization that contain relevant effects, denoted Relevant(α^i, S_g) and $1 \leq i \leq n$, where n is the number of possible realizations.

After creating the graph of constraints, we find the strongly connected components using depth-first search [15]. The next step constructs a reduced graph where the nodes that comprise connected components in the original graph correspond to a single node. Literals within a node in the reduced graph must be placed in the same abstraction space, and connections between nodes define a partial order, transformed into a total order using topological sort or heuristics [12, 13]. The total order graph originates the hierarchy, each level of the graph corresponding to a hierarchical level.

Function Find-Constraints (graph, operators, goals):
Input: The operators of the apace problem and the goals of a problem.
Output: constraints to guarantee ordered monotonicity for the problem.
    For each *literal* in the goals **do**
        If not(Constraint-Determinated-*literal*)
                Constraint-Determinated-*literal*←TRUE;
        For each *operator* in Operators **do**
            Subset_relevant ←FALSE;
            For each Subset_Effects(*operator*) **do**
                For each *literal2* in Subset_Effects(*operator*) **do**
                      If (*literal* match *literal2*) Subset_Relevant←TRUE;
                      For each Effect in Subset_Effects(*operator*) **do**
                          Add_Directed_Edge(*literal*, Effect, graph);
                      Preconditions ← Preconditions(*operator*);
                      For each *precondition* in Preconditions **do**
                          Add-Directed-Edge(*literal*, *precondition*, graph);
            If (Subset_Relevant)
                Find_constraints(graph, operators, Preconditions);
  return(graph);

                    Algorithm 1. Algorithm for determining Constraints

4   Hierarchical Problem Solver

Given a hierarchy of abstractions, HIPU proceeds as follows. First the problem solver maps the original problem to the highest level of the hierarchy (level *i*) by deleting literals from the initial and goal states that are not relevant to the abstraction level. The planner then finds a pilot solution for that level. The pilot solution found in the level *i* will be used in the next abstraction level (level *i*-1), where the literals of the intermediate states of the pilot plan serve as sub goals at level *i*-1. The problem solver then solves each of the intermediate subproblems, using the final state of one subproblem as initial state for the next subproblem. The process is repeated until the pilot plan has been refined in all hierarchical levels.

The main purpose of HIPU is to find a plan such that the probability that it achieves the goal is no less than a user-supplied threshold. Searching for plans, HIPU performs depth-first search with modifications imposed by the probabilistic effects of operators. The search is initiated through expansion of the initial state in the highest level of abstraction. All applicable operators in the initial state (root node) are inserted in the search tree, and each subset of effects generates a new state (or node) at the tree. The child nodes are inserted in the tree in agreement with the occurrence probability associated with the subset of effects. The expansion continues on the nodes from the left, according to the depth search. When a plan that satisfies the goal state is found, the probability that the current plan will achieve the goal is computed. If the probability is high enough, then the plan is a solution, and planning terminates successfully, otherwise, the planner continues, choosing a new state for the expansion or returning fault.

Once HIPU has found a plan at an abstraction level, *forward assessment* [3] is executed to verify if the success probability exceeds the threshold δ. Execution of a probabilistic operator induces a transition from a probability distribution over states to another. The algorithm takes an operator sequence, executes each operator, and computes the probability of the goal literals in the final distribution [3]. To illustrate *forward assessment* see Figure 2, which contains two operators α and β. To calculate the final probability, it is necessary to evaluate all possible executions of the plan, which comprise all the possible realizations of probabilistic operators. Consider for example that *a* represents the initial state, and that *a, b* and *e* are goal literals. There are four possible combinations of *realizations*: (α^0, β^0), (α^0, β^1), (α^1, β^0), (α^1, β^1).

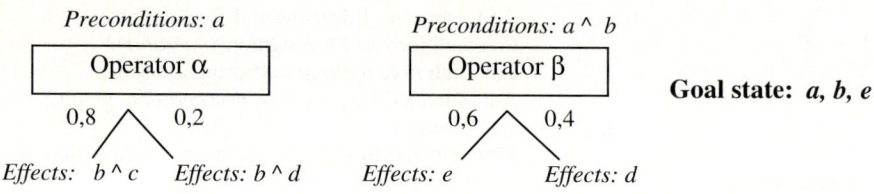

Fig. 2. Example of plan with probabilistic operator

Projecting effects of α at the initial state results in a state distribution with two states. The probability of these new states is the probability of the initial state (equal one) times the probability associated to realizations of α (0.8 to α^0 and 0,2 to α^1).

$S_0 = \text{Exec}(\alpha, \text{initial state})$ $\text{Exec}(\alpha^0, \text{initial state}) = \{(a, b, c), 1 \times 0,8 = 0,8\}$
$\text{Exec}(\alpha^1, \text{initial state}) = \{(a, b, d), 1 \times 0,2 = 0,2\}$

The next projection corresponds to the execution of operator β in states resulting from execution of α.

$S_1 = \text{Exec}(\beta, S_0)$
$\begin{cases} \text{Exec}(\beta^0, (a, b, c)) = \{(a, b, c, e)\ 0,8 \times 0,6 = 0,48\} \\ \text{Exec}(\beta 1, (a, b, c)) = \{(a, b, c, d)\ 0,8 \times 0,4 = 0,32\} \\ \text{Exec}(\beta^0, (a, b, d)) = \{(a, b, d, e)\ 0,2 \times 0,6 = 0,12\} \\ \text{Exec}(\beta 1, (a, b, d)) = \{(a, b, d)\ 0,2 \times 0,4 = 0,08\} \end{cases}$

After projecting all executions, the final probability of the plan is computed by adding the probabilities of states that accomplish the goal. In the example, the probability of reaching the goal in S_1 is $0,48 + 0,12 = 0,6$.

5 Hierarchical Planning and Assessment Probabilities in HIPU

This section presents the planning process and probability evaluation for the hierarchical planner's HIPU. The search begins in the highest level of abstraction that just possesses the initial state, the goal state and the group of relevant operators at the level. The initial state can be a distribution of probabilities under initial states or a single possible initial state. In the first case, the state with largest probability is expanded. Once defined the initial state, the search at level *i* is initiated.

HIPU is composed by six routines, with the functionalities: generate the hierarchy of abstractions (Section 3), manage the global planning, manage the flow among the hierarchical levels (planning inter-level), manage the planning inside an abstraction level (inter-level management), search for sub-objectives (intra-planning), and evaluate the generated plans. Figure 3 shows a process of hierarchical planning emphasizing where the planning routines act.

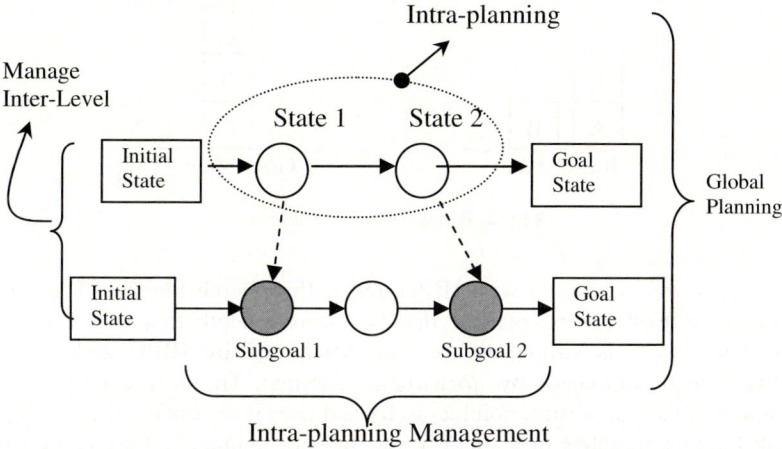

Fig. 3. Planning routines in a hierarchy of abstractions

Global planning controls the execution of planning in HIPU. It calls the routine that creates the abstraction hierarchy, define the abstraction spaces for each of the hierarchical levels and performs planning management among the hierarchical levels (inter-level management). When a pilot plan is found, the inter-level manager recovers each one of the intermediate states of the plan, designating them as sub-objectives for the immediately lower level. When search cannot be solved in the active abstraction level, the manager returns control for the immediately superior level, so that a new pilot plan is found and refined. The intra-planning manager is responsible for controlling execution of searches for sub-objectives in a same abstraction level. When a solution is found, the manager attributes the final state of the sub-plan for the initial state of the following sub-objective, and executes the intra-planning procedure, so that the next sub-plan is found. Sub-plans found in the same abstraction level are concatenated to compose the pilot plan of the respective level. If faults happen during the search by sub-plans, the manager controls backtracking among the sub-problems. In the search for objectives or intra-planning (depth-first search), the planner can detect a fault, when it is not possible to reach the goal state, or find a solution (sequence of operators that takes from the initial state to the goal state). In case of fault, the treatment will depend on the execution point in which the planner was, and in the case of success, the plan will be probabilistically evaluated by *forward assessment*. If the probability of the plan achieving the goal is less than a user-supplied probability δ, planning continues. The evaluation of the success probability defines a lower bound for the complete plan, and avoids that search continues in case the defined probability has already been reached.

6 Empirical Results

The Blocks World Problem [15] (Figure 4) was used to evaluate HIPU. We included two additional actions in the original problem: Paint Block (probabilistic operator) and Charge Paint. The Appendix shows the modified version of this domain, adapted to probabilistic operators.

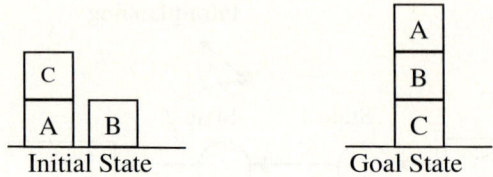

Fig. 4. Blocks World Problem

Experiments were executed with HIPU and with a Depth Planner. The latter is a non-hierarchical probabilistic planner that performs a depth first search to find the solution. The search is similar to the one performed by HIPU and the success probability is also computed by *forward assessment*. The difference is that HIPU automatically creates an abstraction hierarchy and uses it to conduct the search, whilst the Depth Planner searches in a single level. In both planners all plans are searched and evaluated, and the highest success probability plan chosen as solution.

The abstraction hierarchy created by HIPU to the Block's World Problem contains two levels. Literals and respective abstraction spaces are in Table 1. The problem in HIPU was indirectly divided in two stages, first to paint blocks (level 1) and then to stack the painted blocks as described in the goal state (level 0).

Table 1. Abstraction Spaces in the Blocks World

Level	*Literals*	*Abstraction Spaces*
Level 1	Paint, color(x)	Operator Paint Block(x) Preconditions: ~color(x),paint Effects: 0,80:color(x),paint 0,20:color(x),~paint Operator Charge Paint Preconditions: ~color(x), ~paint Effects: paint
Level 0	on(x,y), onTable(x), clear(x), clear(y)	Complete Domain (Appendix A)

The performance of the planners was evaluated as the number of nodes generated in the complete search tree. As HIPU divides the search in subproblems (subgoals), it created several tree searches. The number of nodes for each subproblem is showed in Table 2. The total number of nodes in HIPU is the sum of nodes generated at each abstraction level. The Depth planner creates a single search tree, however the number of nodes was nearly ten times larger. Concerning the plan solution, the number of operators and success probability were the same for both planners,.

Table 2. Experimental Results

	Nodes number in the complete tree.	Success Probability	Plan solution
HIPU	Level 1............: 52	0,512	PaintBlock(A), PaintBlock(B), PaintBlock(C)
	Level 0 subgoal 1: 938.403 Level 0 subgoal 2: 2.027 Level 0 subgoal 3: 154 Level 0 goal.......: 24	0,512	UnstackBlock(C,A), PaintBlock(A), PaintBlock(B), PaintBlock(C), Putton(B,C), Putton(A,B).
	Total nodes in HIPU: 940.661		
Depth Planner (single level)	9.441.837 nodes	0,512	PaintBlock(B), UnstackBlock(C,A), PaintBlock(A), PaintBlock(C), Putton(B,C), Putton(A,B).

7 Conclusions and Future Work

This paper presented HIPU, a framework for hierarchical planning under uncertainties. In HIPU, the classical planning representation was extended to handle uncertainty in the initial world state (via probability distributions over domain states) and in the effects of operators (via probability distributions over subsets of effects). The abstraction hierarchy is automatically generated through an adaptation of the Alpine algorithm to handle uncertainties. Results demonstrate that the hierarchical planner can reduce the plan search in probabilistic planning. A proposal for future work is to test and use different search strategies and heuristics to increase the planner's efficiency. The forward assessment strategy, although simple, can be inefficient. For example, there are domains in which the number of states with non-zero probability grows exponentially with the length of the plan. Assessing the probability of all possible plans and executions can thus be expensive. This motivates an investigation of alternative assessment algorithms. Some planners use Belief Networks [1] to calculate the probability of success of a plan. Another approaches evaluate the utility of a plan, and not its probability of success [8]. Comparing performance of HIPU with other planners is also a topic for further research.

References

1. Blyte, Jim. "Planning Under Uncertainty in Dynamic Domains". Doctor Thesis. Carnegie Mellon University. Pittsburgh, PA, May, 1998.
2. Tadepalli, Prasad; Givan, Robert; Driessens, Kurt. "Relational Reinforcement Learning: An Overview". In Procs. ICML 2004, Workshop on RRL, Canada, 2004.

3. Kushmerick, Nicholas; Hanks, Steve; Weld, Daniel. "An Algorithm for Probabilistic Planning". Artificial Intelligence, 1994.
4. Hanks, Steve. "Classical Planning under Uncertainty". In proceedings ARPI, 1996.
5. Geffner, Héctor; Bonet, Blai. "Solving Large POMDPs Using Real Time Dynamic Programming". Working Notes Fall AAAI Symposium on POMDPS. 1998.
6. Bonet, Blai; Geffner, Héctor. "Planning and Control in Artificial Intelligence: A Unifying Perspective". Appl. Intell. 14(3): 237-252, 2001.
7. Bougerra, Abdelhaki; Karlsson, Lars. "Hierarchical Task Planning under Uncertainty. In 3rd Italian Workshop on Planning and Scheduling. Perugia, Italy, 2004.
8. Doan, A., Haddawy, P. Decision-Theoretic Refinement Planning: Principles and Application. Technical Report TR 95-01-01, February, 1995.
9. Draper, D.; Hanks, S. and Weld, D. Probabilistic planning with information gathering and contingent execution. Proc. 2nd International Conference on Artificial Intelligence Planning Systems, 31-37. AAAI Press, 1994.
10. D. Nau, Y. Cao, A. Lotem, and H. Munoz-Avila. Shop: Simple hierarchical ordered planner. In Procs of the Int. Joint Conference on AI, pages 968-973, August 1999.
11. Korf, R. Planning as search: A quantitative approach. Artificial Intelligence, 33, 65-88, 1987.
12. Knoblock, Craig. "Automatically Generating Abstractions for Problem Solving". Doctoral Thesis, Carnegie Mellon University, May 1991.
13. Knoblock, Craig. "Automatically generating abstractions for planning". Artificial Intelligence, v. 68(2), p. 243-302, 1994.
14. Fikes, Richard E.; Nilsson, Nils J. "STRIPS: A new approach to the application of theorem proving to problem solving". Atificial Intelligence, 2:189-208, 1971.
15. Russel, Stuart J.; Norvig, Peter. *Artificial Intelligence: A Modern Approach.* New Jersey: Prentice Hall, 1995. 932 p.

Appendix

Modified Blocks World Domain

Operator Putton Block (x, y)
Preconditions: clear(x),clear(y),onTable(x)   Effects: on(x, y),~clear(y),~onTable (x)

Operator Unstack Block (x, y)
Preconditions: on(x, y),clear(x)   Effects: ~on(x, y),clear(y),onTable (x)

Operator Paint Block(x)
Preconditions: clear(x),onTable(x),~color(x),paint
Effects:0,80:color(x),paint 0,20:color(x),~paint

Operator Charge Paint
Preconditions: ~color(x), ~paint   Effects: paint

Fusion of Domain Knowledge for Dynamic Learning in Transcriptional Networks

Oscar Harari[1], R. Romero-Zaliz[1], C. Rubio-Escudero[1], and I. Zwir[1,2]

[1] Dept. Computer Science and Artificial Intelligence, University of Granada, E-18071, Spain
[2] Howard Hughes Medical Institute, Department of Molecular Microbiology,
Washington University School of Medicine, St. Louis, MO 63110-1093, USA
oharari@correo.ugr.es, rocio@decsai.ugr.es,
crubio@decsai.ugr.es, zwir@borcim.wustl.edu

Abstract. A critical challenge of the postgenomic era is to understand how genes are differentially regulated even when they belong to a given network. Because the fundamental mechanism controlling gene expression operates at the level of transcription initiation, computational techniques have been developed that identify *cis*-regulatory features and map such features into differential expression patterns. The fact that such co-regulated genes may be differentially regulated suggests that subtle differences in the shared *cis*-acting regulatory elements are likely significant. Thus, we carry out an exhaustive description of *cis*-acting regulatory features including the orientation, location and number of binding sites for a regulatory protein, the presence of binding site submotifs, the class and number of RNA polymerase sites, as well as gene expression data, which is treated as one feature among many. These features, derived from different domain sources, are analyzed concurrently, and dynamic relations are recognized to generate profiles, which are groups of promoters sharing common features. We apply this method to probe the regulatory networks governed by the PhoP/PhoQ two-component system in the enteric bacteria *Escherichia coli* and *Salmonella enterica*. Our analysis uncovered novel members of the PhoP regulon as and the resulting profiles group genes that share underlying biological that characterize the system kinetics. The predictions were experimentally validated to establish that the PhoP protein uses multiple mechanisms to control gene transcription and is a central element in a highly connected network.

1 Introduction

One of the biggest challenges in genomics is the elucidation of the design principles controlling gene networks. However, knowing the connectivity of a given network is not sufficient to define the expression dynamics of a group of genes; one also needs to specify the strength of the connections in a network, which are determined by the *cis*-promoter features participating in the regulation (Fig. 1a-b).

This work describes a machine learning method [1, 2] that integrates heterogeneous domains of knowledge to identify, differentiate and group genes by their expression patterns within a regulatory network. We encapsulate each source of information into model-based features, including fix-length DNA sequence motifs from transcription factor binding sites encoded as position weight matrices; variable-length motifs from RNA polymerase encoded as neural network edges; locations of these regulatory elements in the chromosome as data distributions encoded into fuzzy sets; and gene expression patterns from multiple experiments encoded as temporal vectors. Furthermore, we account for the variability of the data by treating these features as fuzzy (i.e., not precisely defined) instead of categorical entities [3-5].

We use conceptual clustering techniques [1] to integrate the regulatory features by combining features and promoters[1] into dynamic profiles, which are sets of promoters sharing a common set of features. The features are treated with equal weight, because it is not known beforehand which features are important for a profile to explain a differential gene behavior. The formulation of this clustering problem would result in the generation of many profiles with small extent, as it is easier to explain or profile-match smaller data subsets than those that constitute a significant portion of the dataset. For this reason, our approach also considers additional criteria to extract broader profiles based on their size, the number of retrieved profiles, and their diversity and extent of overlap [3, 5]. These are conflicting criteria that are formulated as a multi-objective and multimodal optimization problem [6].

We applied our method to characterize a network controlled by the PhoP/PhoQ regulatory system of *Escherichia coli* and *Salmonella enterica* serovar Typhimurium. We could identify key features that enable the PhoP protein to produce distinct kinetic patterns in target genes and uncover novel members of the PhoP regulatory network [7]. Our approach provides resources for the annotation of genome regulatory regions and their compilation in predictive databases.

2 Methods

Regulatory networks constitute a typical case of structural data, where genes can be viewed as objects described by several features including expression patterns and particular *cis*-acting promoter elements. Promoters are inherently complex combinations of objects that, in turn, are described by a number of features. For example, binding sites for one or more transcriptional regulators are characterized by their match to the binding motif of the regulators, and their locations relative to each other and to that of the RNA polymerase binding site(s).

The purpose of our proposed method is to identify interesting substructures, here termed profiles (i.e., groups of promoters sharing a common set of features), within a regulatory network, thus to suggest possible mechanisms by which the respective genes are controlled, which can further be used to classify additional (e.g., newly identified) promoters. Our method represents, learns and infers from structural data by following three main phases: (1) *Database representation by modeling the features of promoters*[8] ; (2) *Fusing distinct domain knowledge by dynamic learning profiles*; and (3) *Using the profiles to predict new members* [3].

---

[1] One gene can be regulated by the same transcription factor using more than one binding site. We consider each one of them and their corresponding relations with other regulatory elements as a promoter.

2.1 Dataset: Genes from *Escherichia Coli* and *Salmonella* Enterica Genomes

We built models based on microarray expression differed statistically between wild-type and *phoP E. coli* strains experiencing inducing conditions for the PhoP/PhoQ regulatory system and additional *S. enterica* promoters known to be regulated by the PhoP protein. This set of promoters constitutes the 70/30% training and test partitions (see [8] for a complete list of promoters as well as the codification for multiples promoters for a single gene). Expression values for *Salmonella* were inherited from its known orthologous genes in *E. coli*. Additional data for RNA polymerase and operons were obtained from RegulonDB database.

Representing Different Domain Knowledge: Modeling Promoter Features. We focused on four types of features [9] for describing our training set of promoters:

DNA Binding Site Motifs: (a) Fix-length Hierarchical Motifs: we modeled the PhoP box motifs by using position weight matrices[2] [10] (Fig. 1c) (see Consensus matrices in gps-tools.wustl.edu). Then, we used these preliminary models to describe promoters by using low thresholds corresponding to two standard deviations below the mean score obtained with the initial model [11]. We grouped the retrieved observations into subsets by using the possibilistic implementation of fuzzy C-means (PCM) [3] and rebuilt matrix models for each one (E-value < 10E-22), thus obtaining several more refined models, and increasing the sensitivity to departures from the consensus. These multiple matrices constitute the prototypes of the feature:

$$M_i(x_1,...,x_K) = \prod_{k=1}^{K} M(x_k) \qquad (1)$$

where $M(x_k)$ is the marginal probability of each nucleotide x_k in the k'th position on motifs of length K, and i indexes a family of prototypes M_i [12]. The degree of matching between an observation and a feature is measured by its similarity with the prototype by using the informational content scores normalized as fuzzy values in the unit interval. The prototypes can be combined and arranged as a multiclassifier (see Bagging consensus in gps-tools.wustl.edu).

(b) Variable-length Motifs: we gathered sigma 70 promoters [13] from the RegulonDB database and built models of the RNA polymerase site using a neuro-fuzzy method (see Promoter search (CPR-MOSS) in gps-tools.wustl.edu), and used the resulting models to perform genome-wide descriptions of the intergenic regions of the E. coli and Salmonella genomes with a false discovery rate <0.001. The time delay neural network constitutes the feature prototype [5] and the scores were also normalized.

Transcription Factor Binding Site Orientation: categorical data. We classified PhoP boxes as either in direct or opposite orientation relative to the open reading frame (Fig. 1d), and the prototype is a simple Boolean function.

---

[2] A matrix of log-odd score $\log \frac{P(x_k)}{P_0(x_k)}$ where $P_0(x_k)$ is a background distribution.

RNA Polymerase Distances: data distributions modeled as fuzzy sets. We built histograms with the distance between RNA polymerase and transcription factor from information available in RegulonDB database [13]. We encoded these distributions by using fuzzy set representations [5] into close, medium, and remote sets (Fig. 1e). These fuzzy sets constitute the prototypes of the feature, and can be viewed as approximation of data distributions:

$$D_i(x) = \begin{cases} 0 & \text{if } x < a_0 \text{ or } x > x_2 \\ (x - a_0)/(a_1 - a_0) & \text{if } x < a_1 \\ (a_2 - x)/(a_2 - a_1) & \text{if } x > a_2 \\ 1 & \text{otherwise} \end{cases} \qquad (2)$$

where x is any distance between the transcription start site of an RNA polymerase binding site and the center of a transcription factor binding site, and i indexes a family of distances D_{close}, D_{medium} and D_{remote}. Initial partitions are learned from the projection of the histograms onto the variable domains by simple regression and minimum squared methods [14]. The degree of matching between an observation and a prototype is calculated by specializing a value in a triangular fuzzy membership functions [15].

Microarray Expression Data: collection of fuzzy sets encoded as a fuzzy centroid. We clustered PhoP-regulated gene expression levels (Fig. 1f) by using PCM and built models for each cluster by calculating its centroid. These models represent the prototypes, where the values of the expression feature for each promoter in E. coli is calculated by its similarity to the centroids $\overline{V_i}$ as a vector of fuzzy sets:

$$E_i(x) = \left[1 + \left(\left\|x - \overline{V_i}\right\|_A^2 / w_i\right)^{1/m-1}\right]^{-1} \qquad (3)$$

where $x = \{x_1, ..., x_k\}$ corresponds to the expression of a gene in k microarray experiments; w_i is the "bandwidth" of the fuzzy set E_i; m is the degree of fuzzification which is initialized as 2; the type of norm, determinated by A, is Pearson correlation coefficient; and i indexes a family of prototypes E_i.

Composite Features. We combine several features with dependencies between each other into more informative models by using AND-connected fuzzy predicates:

$$C(F_i, F_j) = F_i{}^i \text{ AND } F_j = F_i \cap F_j \qquad (4)$$

where F_i and F_j are previously defined features. Fuzzy logic-based operations, such as *T-norm/T-conorm*, include operators like MINIMUM, PRODUCT, or MAXIMUM, which are used as basic logic operators, such as AND or OR, or their set equivalents INTERSECTION or UNION [3, 15]. In this work we used the MINIMUN and MAXIMUM as *T-norm* and *T-conorm*, respectively. For example, the RNA polymerase motif, learned by using a neural network method, it *sigma class*, identified by using an intelligent parser that differentiates *class* I from *class* II promoters, and the distance distributions ($D_{close}, D_{medium}, D_{remote}$) between RNA polymerase and transcription factor binding sites, learned by using fuzzy set representations [5], are normalized and combined into a single fuzzy vector (e.g., $P_i(x) = R_j \text{ AND } D_k \text{ AND } T_l$).

2.2 Fusing Distinct Domain Knowledge: Dynamic Learning Profiles

Initializing Profiles. Our method independently clusters each type of feature to build initial level-1 profiles (Fig. 1g) based on the PCM clustering method and a validity index [3] to estimate the number of clusters, as an unsupervised discretization of the features [5, 16]. For example, we obtained five level-1 profiles for the "submotifs" feature ($M_0^1,...,M_4^1$) (The superscript denotes the level, 1 in this case. The subscript denotes the specific profile, with subscript 0 corresponding to profiles containing promoters that do not have the corresponding type of feature).

Grouping Profiles. We group profiles by navigating in a lattice corresponding to the feature searching space [1, 2] and systematically creating compound higher level profiles (i.e., offspring profiles) based on combining parental profiles, by taking the fuzzy intersection (Fig. 1h). For example: level-1: (E_1^1, M_2^1 and P_3^1) $\mapsto$ level-2: ($E_1^2 M_2^2$, $M_2^2 P_3^2$ and $E_1^2 P_3^2$) $\mapsto$ level-3: ($E_1^3 M_2^3 P_3^3$), where level-3-profiles are obtained from intersection of the promoter members of level-2- profiles (e.g., $E_1^2 M_2^2$, $M_2^2 P_3^2$ and $E_1^2 P_3^2$) and not between those belonging to the initial profiles (E_1^1, M_2^1 and P_3^1). This is because our approach dynamically re-discretizes the original features at each level and allows re-assignments of observations between sibling profiles. In this hierarchical process, each level of the lattice increases the number of features shared by a profile. After searching through the whole lattice space, the most specific profiles (i.e., the most specific hypothesis [17]) are found. As a result of this strategy, one promoter observation can contribute to more than one profile in the same or a different level of the lattice, with different degrees of membership. This differentiates our approach from a hierarchical clustering process where, once an observation is placed in a cluster, it can only be re-assigned into offspring clusters. In contrast, our approach is similar to optimization clustering methods [18] in that it allows transfers among sibling clusters in the same level.

Prototyping Profiles. We learn profiles by using the PCM clustering method [3, 4], where promoters can belong to more than one cluster with different degrees of membership, and are not forced to belong to any particular cluster. This consists of individually evaluating the membership of the promoters to each feature, at each level in the lattice, and combining the results (equation (4)).

Selecting Profiles. Profile search and evaluation is carried out as a multi-objective optimization problem [5, 6], between the extent of the profile and the quality of matching among its members and the corresponding features. The extent of a profile is calculated by using the hypergeometric distribution that gives the chance probability (i.e., probability of intersection (PI)) of observing at least p candidates from a set V_i of size h within another set V_j of size n, in a universe of g candidates:

$$PI(V_{i,j}) = 1 - \sum_{q=0}^{p} \binom{h}{q}\binom{q-h}{n-q} \bigg/ \binom{g}{h} \quad (5)$$

where V_i is an alpha-cut of the offspring profile and V_j is an alpha-cut of the union of its parents. The PI [19] is a more informative measure than the number of promoters belonging to the profile, such as the Jaccard coefficient, in being an adaptive measure that is sensitive to small sets of examples, while retaining specificity with large datasets.

The quality of matching between promoters and features of a profile (i.e., similarity of intersection (SI)) is calculated using the following equation:

$$SI(V_i) = \frac{1}{f}\left(1 - \frac{\sum_{k \in U_\alpha} \mu_{ik}}{n_\alpha}\right) \quad U_\alpha = \{\mu_{ik} : \mu_{ik} > \alpha\} \quad (6)$$

where n_α is the number of elements in an arbitrary *alpha*-cut U_α.

The tradeoff between the opposing objectives (i.e., PI and SI) is estimated by selecting a set of solutions that are non-dominated, in the sense that there is no other solution that is superior to them in all objectives (i.e., Pareto optimal frontier) [5, 6]. The dominance relationship in a minimization problem is defined by:

$$a \prec b \text{ iif } \forall i\; O_i(a) \leq O_i(b)\; \exists j\, O_j(a) < O_j(b) \quad (7)$$

where the O_i and O_j are either PI or SI. The method applies the non-dominance relationship only to profiles in the local neighborhood or niche [6] by using the hypergeometric metric (equation (**5**)) between profiles and selecting an arbitrary threshold; in this way combining both multi-objective and multimodal optimization concepts [6].

2.3 Using the Profiles to Predict New Members

The method uses a fuzzy k-nearest prototype classifier (FKN) to predict new profile members using an unsupervised classification method [3] applied to regulatory regions of genomes described by regulatory features. First, we determine the lower-boundary similarity threshold for each non-dominated profile. This threshold is calculated based on the ability of each profile to retrieve its own promoters and to discard promoters from other profiles [20]. Second, we calculate the membership of a query observation x_q to a set of k profiles previously identified and apply a fuzzy OR logic operation:

$$FKN(x_q, V_1, ..., V_k) = i,\; i \in \{1,...,k\} \quad (8)$$

where $\mu_{i,q} = OP_{OR}\{\mu_{1,q},...,\mu_{k,q}\}$, μ is calculated based on (equation (**4**)) in which w_i (equation (**3**)) is initialized as:

$$w_i = \frac{r_1 PI(V_i) + r_2 (f/t')SI(V_i)}{r_1 + r_2} \qquad (9)$$

with t' being the number of distinct features observed in x_q and V_i, and f is the number of features in common between x_q and V_i, which are combined to obtain a measure of belief or rule weight [2]; r_1 and r_2 are user-dependent parameters, initialized as 1 if no preference exists between both objectives; and OP_{OR} is the Maximum fuzzy operator [3, 4].

Possibilistic Fuzzy C-means Clustering Method [3, 4]: (i) Initialize $L_0 = \{\overline{V_1},..,\overline{V_c}\}$; (ii) while ($s<S$ and $\|L_s - L_{s-1}\| > \varepsilon$), where S is the maximum number of iterations; (iii) calculate the membership of U_s in L_{s-1} as in (equation (3)); (iv) update L_{s-1} to L_s with U_s and $\overline{V_i} = \sum_{k=1}^{n} \mu_{ik} x_k / \sum_{k=1}^{n} \mu_{ik}$; (v) iterate.

3 Results

We investigated the utility of our approach by exploring the regulatory targets of the PhoP protein in *E. coli* and *S. enterica*, which is at the top of a highly connected network that controls transcription of dozens of genes mediating virulence and the adaptation to low Mg^{2+} environments [7]. We demonstrated that our method makes predictions at three levels [8]: (i) it makes an appropriate use of the regulatory features to perform genome-wide predictions; (ii) it detects new candidate promoters for a regulatory protein; and (iii) it indicates possible mechanisms by which genes previously known to be controlled by a regulator are expressed.

Performance of the Features. We illustrated the performance of the encoded features by analyzing three of them.. We evaluated the ability of the resulting models to describe PhoP-regulated promoters, we extended the dataset by including 772 promoters (RegulonDB V3.1 database [13]) that are regulated by transcription factors other than PhoP (see Search known transcription factor motifs in gps-tools.wustl.edu), by selecting the promoter region corresponding to the respective transcription factor binding site. We considered the compiled list of PhoP regulated genes as true positive examples and the binding sites of other transcriptional regulators as true negative examples to evaluate the performance of the submotif feature. Each matrix threshold has been optimized for classification purposes by using the overall performance measurement [20] based on the extended dataset. We found that the PhoP-binding site model increases its sensitivity from 66% to 90% when submotifs are used instead of a single consensus, while its specificity went from 98% to 97%. This allowed the recovery of promoters, such as that corresponding to the *E. coli* hdeD gene or the

Salmonella pmrD, that had not been detected by the single consensus position weight matrix model [10] despite being footprinted by the PhoP protein [7, 8].

The RNA polymerase site feature was evaluated using 721 RNA polymerase sites from RegulonDB as positive examples and 7210 random sequences as negative examples. We obtained an 82% sensitivity and 95% specificity for detecting RNA polymerase sites. These values provides an overall performance measurement [20] of 92% corresponding to a false discovery rate <0.001. In addition, we selected 34 examples of RNA polymerase sites reported to be of class II, which all differ from the typical class I promoter by exhibiting a degenerate -35 sequence motif [21], and obtained 74% sensitivity and 95% specificity.

Regarding the expression feature, results suggest that the sensitivity of the "expression" feature can be increased from 45% to the 76% by using the model-based approach in a complementary fashion to the original statistical approach, by just admitting a limited decrease in specificity. This approach allowed us to recover additional genes (e.g., the *hemL* and the *proP* promoters of *E. coli*) that have expression levels too weak to be initially detected using strict statistical filters (35). (see gps-tools.wustl.edu for predicted features in *E. coli* and *Salmonella*).

Performance of the Profiles. We recovered several profiles, some of which were experimentally validated [8]. In addition, here we measured the promoter activity and growth kinetics for GFP reporter strains with high-temporal resolution to evaluate the behavior of the profiles. For example, one of the profiles corresponds to the canonical PhoP-regulated promoters (PI=$1.57E^{-4}$, SI=0.002), and encompasses promoters (e.g., those of the *phoP, mgtA, rstA, slyB, yobG and yrbL* genes) that share the class II RNA polymerase sites situated close to the PhoP boxes, high expression patterns, and typically PhoP box submotif. This profile includes not only the prototypical *phoP* and *mgtA* promoters [22], but also other promoters, which was not known to be under PhoP control. The promoters sharing this profile produced the earlier rise times and the higher levels of transcription (Fig. 1i). Particularly, *phoP* itself, perhaps affected by its autoregulation, generates the top levels of expression during time. Another profile (PI=$3.53E^{-4}$, SI=0.032) includes promoters (e.g., those of the *mgtC, mig-14, pagC, pagK,* and *virK* genes of *Salmonella*) that share a PhoP boxes in the opposite orientation of the canonical PhoP-regulated promoters, as well as class I RNA polymerase sites situated at medium distances from the PhoP boxes, all of the features dynamically adapted for the current set of genes. This profile, exhibit the latest genes with the lowest levels of expression (Fig. 1i). Finally, another profile (PI=0.033, SI=0.044), which is slightly different from the former includes promoters (e.g., those of the *ompT* gene of *E. coli* and the *pipD, ugtL* and *ybjX* genes of *Salmonella*) that although exhibit a PhoP binding site in the opposite orientation, preserves the RNA polymerase of the canonical PhoP regulated promoters and present an intermediate kinetic behavior. The detailed analysis of the gene behavior would not be possible to be obtained by just inspecting each features independently, or by considering simple consensus of these features.

Predictions. To evaluate the ability of the method to retrieve PhoP-regulated promoters, we extended the test set by including 487 promoters from the RegulonDB database [13] that are regulated by transcription factors other than PhoP, by selecting the promoter region corresponding to the respective transcription factor binding site ±10 bp, its corresponding RNA polymerase site ±10 bp and expression levels from our own experiments. The method had a false positive rate of 5.3% and a 93.92% of overall performance measurement [20] as a particular correlation coefficient implementation, with a 94 and 92% specificity = TN/(TN + FP) and sensitivity = TP/(TP + FN) respectively, where P is positive examples, N is negative examples, T is true and F is false.

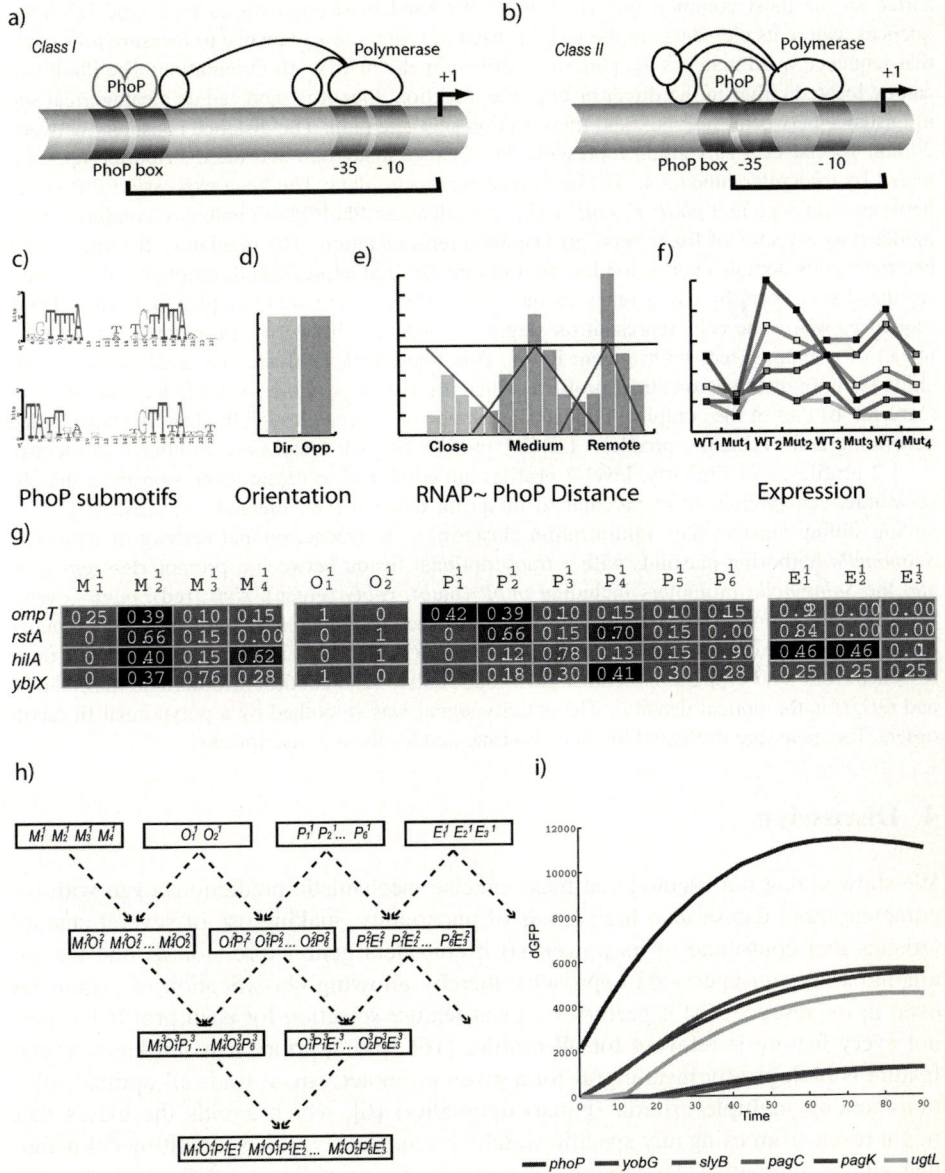

Fig. 1. Different *cis*-features participating in the regulation scheme. **a-b)** Two PhoP proteins had binded to a DNA strain and recruited RNA polymerase. Class I activators bind to upstream locations. By contrast Class II activators bind to sites that overlap the target promoter -35 region. A PhoP box might be located in the same strain as the polymerase (a) or in the opposite direction (b). **c)** PhoP binding box modeled as position weight matrices shown as logos: The characters representing the sequence are stacked on top of each other for each position in the aligned sequences. The height of each letter is made proportional to its frequency, and the letters are sorted so the most common one is on top. We used these matrices to prototype DNA sequences, where its elements are the weights used to score a test sequence to measure how close that sequence word matches the pattern described by the matrix. **d)** Orientation: The PhoP box can be located either in the direct or opposite direction, thus it is modeled as a categorical set. **e)** Distance between PhoP box and transcription start site (+1): The distance is usually between 20 and 100 bases. This graph represents the distance histogram and the distribution approximated by triangular functions. **f)** Microarray expression data: The gene expression difference between wild-type and *phoP E. coli* strains experiencing PhoP/PhoQ inducing condition were modeled as a vector of fuzzy sets. **g)** Database representation: The regulatory features model heterogeneous domains corresponding to different *cis*- and expression descriptions of the PhoP regulated promoters by using fuzzy membership values. Here we exemplify data from DNA sequences where the cells represent the degree of matching between a promoter value and the model of a feature (red: high; green: low). This framework facilitates the application of machine learning methods to extract profiles, which are sets of promoters sharing a common set of features. **h)** Part of the complete lattice: The method navigates through the feature-space lattice generating and evaluating profiles. Level-1 profiles of each feature are combined to identify level-2 profiles, and similarly, level-2 profiles are combined to create level-3 profiles; the observations can migrate from parental to offspring clusters (i.e., hierarchical clustering), and among sibling clusters (i.e., optimization clustering). **i)** Transcriptional activity of wild-type *Salmonella* harboring plasmids with a transcriptional fusion between a promoterless *gfp* gene and the *Salmonella* promoters including *phoP* (blue), *yobG* (green), *slyB* (red), *pagC* (cyan), *pagK* (magenta) and *ugtL* (yellow). The activity of each promoter is proportional to the number of GFP molecules produced per unit time per cell $[dG_i(t)/dt]/OD_i(t)]$, where $G_i(t)$ is GFP fluorescence from wild-type *Salmonella* strain 14028s culture and conditions described in Methods, and $OD_i(t)$ is the optical density. The activity signal was smoothed by a polynomial fit (sixth order). The genes are evaluated by their rise time and levels of transcriptions.

4 Discussion

We showed that our method can make precise mechanistic predictions even with incomplete input dataset and high levels of uncertainty; making use of several characteristics that contribute to its power: (i) it considers gene expression as one feature among many (unsupervised approach), thereby allowing classification of promoters even in its absence; (ii) it performs a local feature selection for each profile because not every feature is relevant for all profiles [16], and, a priori, it is not know which feature is biologically meaningful for a given promoter; (iii) it finds all optimal solutions among multiple criteria (Pareto optimality) [6], which avoids the biases that might result from using any specific weighing scheme; (iv) it has a multimodal nature that allows alternative descriptions of a system by providing several adequate solutions [5]; (v) it allows promoters to be members of more than one profile by using fuzzy clustering thus explicitly treating the profiles as hypotheses, which are tested and refined during the analysis; and (vi) it is particularly useful for knowledge discovery in environments with reduced datasets and high levels of uncertainty. The predictions made by our method were experimentally validated [8] to establish that the PhoP protein uses multiple mechanisms to control gene transcription, and is a central element in a highly connected network. These profiles can be used to effectively explain the different kinetic behavior of co-regulated genes.

Acknowledgments

This work was partly supported by the Spanish Ministry of Science and Technology under Project BIO2004-0270-E, and I.Z. is also supported by and by Howard Hughes Medical Institute.

References

1. Cook, D.J., et al., Structural mining of molecular biology data. IEEE Eng Med Biol Mag, 2001. 20(4): p. 67-74.
2. Cooper, G.F. and E. Herskovits, A Bayesian Method for the Induction of Probabilistic Networks from Data. Machine Learning, 1992. 9(4): p. 309-347.
3. Bezdek, J.C., Pattern Analysis, in Handbook of Fuzzy Computation, W. Pedrycz, P.P. Bonissone, and E.H. Ruspini, Editors. 1998, Institute of Physics: Bristol. p. F6.1.1-F6.6.20.
4. Gasch, A.P. and M.B. Eisen, Exploring the conditional coregulation of yeast gene expression through fuzzy k-means clustering. Genome Biol, 2002. 3(11): p. RESEARCH0059.
5. Ruspini, E.H. and I. Zwir, Automated generation of qualitative representations of complex objects by hybrid soft-computing methods, in Pattern recognition : from classical to modern approaches, S.K. Pal and A. Pal, Editors. 2002, World Scientific: New Jersey. p. 454-474.
6. Deb, K., Multi-objective optimization using evolutionary algorithms. 1st ed. Wiley-Interscience series in systems and optimization. 2001, Chichester ; New York: John Wiley & Sons. xix, 497.
7. Groisman, E.A., The pleiotropic two-component regulatory system PhoP-PhoQ. J Bacteriol, 2001. 183(6): p. 1835-42.
8. Zwir, I., et al., Dissecting the PhoP regulatory network of Escherichia coli and Salmonella enterica. Proc Natl Acad Sci U S A, 2005. 102(8): p. 2862-7.
9. Beer, M.A. and S. Tavazoie, Predicting gene expression from sequence. Cell, 2004. 117(2): p. 185-98.
10. Stormo, G.D., DNA binding sites: representation and discovery. Bioinformatics, 2000. 16(1): p. 16-23.
11. Robison, K., A.M. McGuire, and G.M. Church, A comprehensive library of DNA-binding site matrices for 55 proteins applied to the complete Escherichia coli K-12 genome. J Mol Biol, 1998. 284(2): p. 241-54.
12. Barash, Y., Elidan, G., Friedman, N., Kaplan, T. Modeling Dependencies in Protein-DNA Binding Sites. in RECOMB'03. 2003.
13. Salgado, H., et al., RegulonDB (version 4.0): transcriptional regulation, operon organization and growth conditions in Escherichia coli K-12. Nucleic Acids Res, 2004. 32(Database issue): p. D303-6.

14. Sugeno, M. and T. Yasukama, A Fuzzy-logic-based Approach to Qualitative Modeling. IEEE Transactions on Fuzzy Systems, 1993. 1(1): p. 7-31.
15. Klir, G.J. and T.A. Folger, Fuzzy sets, uncertainty, and information. 1988, London: Prentice Hall International. xi,355.
16. Kohavi, R. and G.H. John, Wrappers for feature subset selection. Artificial Intelligence, 1997. 97(1-2): p. 273-324.
17. Mitchell, T.M., Machine learning. 1997, New York: McGraw-Hill. xvii, 414.
18. Falkenauer, E., Genetic Algorithms and Grouping Problems. 1998, New York: John Wiley & Sons.
19. Tavazoie, S., et al., Systematic determination of genetic network architecture. Nat Genet, 1999. 22(3): p. 281-5.
20. Benitez-Bellon, E., G. Moreno-Hagelsieb, and J. Collado-Vides, Evaluation of thresholds for the detection of binding sites for regulatory proteins in Escherichia coli K12 DNA. Genome Biol, 2002. 3(3): p. RESEARCH0013.
21. Barnard, A., A. Wolfe, and S. Busby, Regulation at complex bacterial promoters: how bacteria use different promoter organizations to produce different regulatory outcomes. Curr Opin Microbiol, 2004. 7(2): p. 102-8.
22. Minagawa, S., et al., Identification and molecular characterization of the Mg2+ stimulon of Escherichia coli. J Bacteriol, 2003. 185(13): p. 3696-702.

An Improved Discrete Immune Network for Multimodal Optimization

Jing-Xin Xie[1,2], Chun-Tian Cheng[1], and Zhen-Hui Ren[2]

[1] Institute of Hydropower System & Hydroinformatics, Department of Civil Engineering,
Dalian University of Technology, Dalian, 116024, P.R. China
`xjxie@student.dlut.edu.cn`
[2] College of Mechanical and Electronic Engineering, Hebei Agricultural University,
Baoding 071001, P.R. China

Abstract. Aimed at multimodal optimization, the paper proposes an improved discrete immune network model (IDIN). In order to mention dynamic population and appropriate diversity, we introduce a bi-shape-space coding mechanism into a discrete immune network. To evaluate the efficiency of IDIN, we implemented three benchmark functions with various dimensions, and compared our results with other algorithms based on immune algorithm or the developed version of Genetic Algorithms. We have obtained similar or better results than those of others.

Keywords: Bi-shape-space coding; Discrete immune network; Benchmark functions.

1 Introduction

Multimodal optimization problems often have a global optimum and many local optima and are difficult to be solved by traditional search methods. Due to the inherent distinguished characteristics, Artificial Immune System (AIS), a developing biologically inspired intelligent method, has already attracted considerable attention from different areas [1-3]. Artificial Immune Optimization (AIO) methods provide us with superior performances when dealing with multi-modal, combinational and time dependent optimization problems. According to the underlying principles of the existing AIO methods, they can be classified into three main categories: GA-aided, clonal selection principle-based and immune networks-based approaches. Two classes of models: continuous network models and discrete network models and both have been successfully applied to complex problems such as autonomous navigation, optimization, and automatic control. Among those models, aiNet[4] employs a real-value vector in the Euclidean shape space for data analysis, and the adaptation of aiNet[5] is used to solve multimodal function optimization problems.

A great number of researches have focused on finding efficient methods for presentation of cells or population in immune network and they are all based on Euclidean distance measure in real-value shape-space. With regard to the shape-space of discrete immune network, just like de Castro said in his literature[5], those algorithms are not necessarily restricted to this shape-space and others could be used. Moreover, Empirical test of this paper over diversity maintenance shows that information-entropy-based bit-string coding in binary shape-space performs superior in measuring the distance between individuals. Based on Euclidean distance in real-value shape-space and information entropy coding in binary shape-space, we developed an improved discrete immune network model for multimodal function optimization. To improve performance, above processes are performed in parallel as much as possible.

2 IDIN

2.1 Bi-shape-space Encoding

According to biological immune theory, the B-cell is an integral part of the immune system, which will clone and mutate to produce a diverse set of antibodies via a process of recognition and stimulation. And Binding between antigens and antibodies is governed by how well the paratopes on the antibody matches the epitope of the antigen [6]. Bi-shape-space coding based Discrete Immune Network (IDIN) achieves the goal of seeking complex feasible solutions while maintaining diversity with the same concept of antibodies and B-cells which assumes defending responsibility within the immune network. Meanwhile, affinity and fitness are utilized in a way that the former corresponds to degrees of interaction between antibodies and between B-cells respectively, and the latter to the value of any defending individual when evaluated for a given multimodal function. Fig. 1 illustrates the bi-shape-space scheme for antibodies and B-cells defined in the IDIN.

Following operations are carried out. Firstly, real-value coding is implemented for initial antibodies in real-value shape-space. The model then uses (an adaptive version) fuzzy c-mean algorithm to cluster initial antibodies and yields a number of cluster centroids, namely B-cells. Bit-string coding of antibodies are work out based on which interaction level between antibodies inside each cluster are calculated in binary shape-space. The same process is then performed for all B-cells, but with real value coding in real-value shape-space. After mutation, clone and recombination over antibodies and B-cells respectively, selection is used to yield a new generation. The antibodies and B-cells corresponding to the objective functions and associated solution candidates in a computational model are expressed as Eq.1. Assume that one has a current generation G_t in iteration t. Then next generation G_{t+1} is transformed from G_t as follows:

$$\begin{aligned} G_t &\xrightarrow{I(\cdot)} \{Ab_i^r \mid i=1,2,...,N\} \\ &\xrightarrow{F(\cdot)} \{Ab_{jp}^b, Bc_j^r \mid p\in 1,2,...,NC_j; j=1,2,...Nc\} \\ &\xrightarrow{S(\cdot)} \{Ab_{jp}^{\prime b}, Bc_j^{\prime r} \mid p\in 1,2,...,NC_j'; j=1,2,...Nc'; \sum NC_j' + Nc' = N\} \\ &\xrightarrow{T(\cdot)} \{Ab_i^{\prime r} \mid i=1,2,...,N\} \to G_{t+1} \end{aligned} \qquad (1)$$

where $\{Ab_i^r \mid i=1,2,...,N\}$, $\{Ab_{jp}^b, Bc_j^r \mid p\in 1,2,...,NC_j; j=1,2,...Nc\}$, $\{Ab_{jp}^{\prime b}, Bc_j^{\prime r} \mid p\in 1,2,...,NC_j'; j=1,2,...Nc'; \sum NC_j' + Nc' = N\}$ and $\{Ab_i^{\prime r} \mid i=1,2,...,N\}$ denote

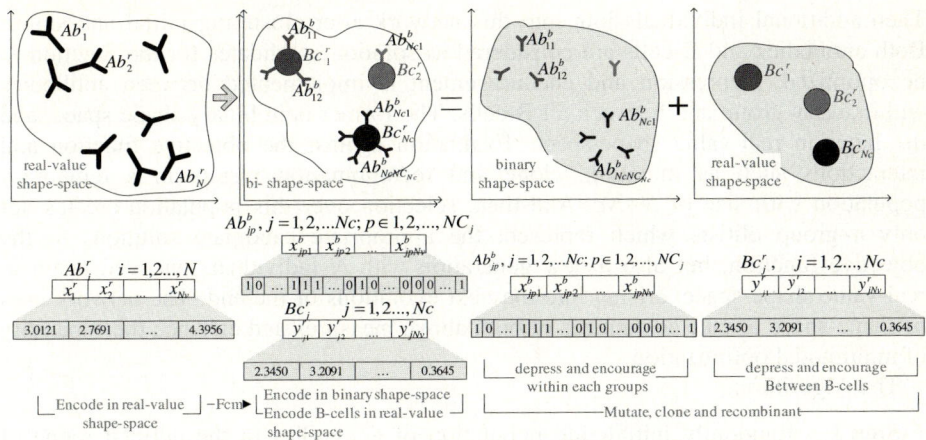

Fig. 1. Encoding in bi-shape-space for antibodies and B-cell

various sets with different coding individuals; N is the number of individuals within tth generation, Nc and NC_j (including Nc' and Nc'_j) represent the number of clusters and the size of jth cluster, respectively. In addition to, $I(.)$, $F(.)$, $S(.)$ and $T(.)$ are operator functions performing transformation on individuals. $I(.)$ initializes antibodies for G_t, $F(.)$ yields the B-cells with FCM cluster analysis, $S(.)$ implements selection between each clusters, B-cells and the ones from memory pool and $T(.)$ transforms the N individuals resulted from $S(.)$ into real-value coding. With regard to the bi-shape-space used in our model, we employ Ab^* and Bc^* to act as antibodies and B-cells of G_t where superscript $*$ including r and b represent coding in real-value shape-space and in binary shape-space respectively. In detail, the individuals can be encoded as Fig. 2.

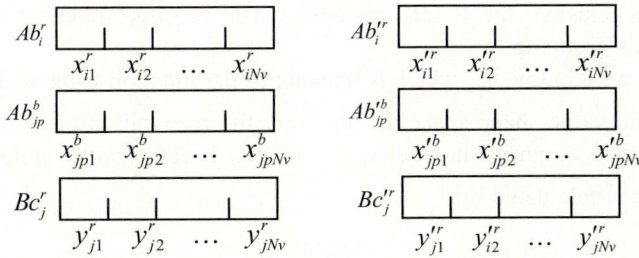

Fig. 2. All encodings within a certain iteration of evolution where Nv is the dimension of multimodal function

2.2 Implementing IDIN

IDIN evolves a dynamic population within each generation. In the beginning, only antibodies exist in real-value shape-space as defending individuals against antigens.

Then additional individuals join into this network after clustering initial antibodies. Both antibodies and B-cells are considered as solution candidates for the function to be optimized. Depression and encouragement is implemented between antibodies within every group and between all B-cells. The former is in binary shape-space, and the latter in real-value shape-space. Evaluation against the objective function and interactions such as mutation, clone and recombination results in a temporary population with size of $N+Nc$. And then, selection over this population creates not only a group elitists which represent the appropriate candidate solutions to the objective function, but also a new generation with N individuals encoded again in real-value shape-space, arising into the next evolutions or the end. The network uses bi-shape-space to take advantages of both above measures and enhance the capability of multimodal optimization.

The Algorithm:

Step 1. Randomly initializing population of antibodies in the defined scope of multimodal function;

Step 2. While (stopping criteria is not met) do

  step 2.1. Clustering antibody–antigen recognition to generate B-cells with maximum number of clustering Nc_{max};

  step 2.2. Calculating antibody–antigen recognition in real-value shape-space;

  step 2.3. Calculating Affinities of antibodies within each B-cell cluster and of whole B-cells respectively;

  step 2.4. Defining stimulation level of each individual including antibodies and B-cells;

  step 2.5. Implementing clone, mutation and recombination of individuals under the environment of step2.3;

  step 2.6. Randomly selecting N individuals into the next population and members of the memory pool;

Step 3. Determine highest affinity network cells and generated network cells.

In step 2.1, we use the fuzzy clustering validity function to measure the valid number of the clusters for B-cells grouping. The process above is undertaken to perform B-cells grouping.

In step 2.2, we employ R_j^r, which is relevant to the function value under jth B-cells encoded in real-value shape-space, to represent the recognition of jth B-cell against antigens and also of antibodies belonging to this B-cell against antigens(R_{ji}^r). The function value is calculated by:

$$R_j^r = R_{ji}^r = \frac{f(Bc_j^r) - f_{min}}{f_{max} - f_{min}}, \qquad (2)$$

Where $f(Bc_j^r)$ is the function value when with $Bc_j^r = \{y_{j1}^r, y_{j2}^r, ... y_{jNv}^r\}$ as variables; f_{min} and f_{max} represent the minimum and maximum function values of all variables respectively.

In step2.3 *for antibodies*, because of the remarkable efficiency of information entropy method in diversity maintenance, we attempt to exploit which latency-capacity in our model is. Here, unlike other conventional usage of information entropy in artificial immune system which is a usual measure to deal with concentrations, our paper utilizes information entropy to express the differences between any two antibodies surrounding the same B-cell. Note that from the type of coding for antibodies repertoire $Ab_{jp}^b = \{x_{jp1}^b, x_{jp2}^b, ..., x_{jpNv}^b\}$, we assumes that all individuals in our system are in an L-dimensional shape-space(S^L), in which the antibodies are represented by attribute strings defined over a alphabet of length 2. The function $H_l(N)$ is a measure of the information entropy of locus l in antibody repertoire. Then mean of the informative entropy between two antibodies p and q in the repertoires is displayed as:

$$H_{pq} = \frac{1}{L}\sum_{l}^{L} H_{pq}, \qquad (3)$$

Here we let matrix D^I to be the distance matrix among all antibodies within jth group, where I denotes information entropy. Affinity AA_{jp} of each antibody is performed according the following expression:

$$AA_{jp} = \frac{1}{1+da_{jp}}; da_{jp} = \frac{\frac{1}{NC_j}\sum_q d_{jpq}^I}{\sum_p \left(\frac{1}{NC_j}\sum_q d_{jpq}^I\right)}, \qquad (4)$$

Where da_{jp} denotes the distance between pth antibody and others in jth group, and it is calculated as the average over the results of information entropy distance.

For B-cells in our paper, Euclidean distance in real-value shape-space is used to measure affinities within whole B-cell population. The result for B-cell affinities is denoted as $DB = \{db_j \mid j = 1, 2, ..., Nc\}$.

In step 2.4, IDIN is composed of antibodies and B-cells as individuals of network. Antigens are presented as patterns of antibody–antigen recognition. The concept of stimulation is used to express the binding effects on a certain antibody from antigens and other antibodies. sa_{jp} denotes stimulation on pth antibody in jth cluster within the system.

$$\begin{cases} sa_{jp} = k_1 \times fs(f(Ab_{jp}^r)) + k_2 \times (1-da_{jp}) - k_3 \times da_{jp} \\ fs\left(f(Ab_{jp}^r)\right) = \dfrac{1}{1+\exp\left(-f(Ab_{jp}^r)\right)} \end{cases}, \qquad (5)$$

where $fs(\cdot)$, usually used as the threshold activation function in Networks, can limit the result in the scope of [0,1] by which the fitness of this antibody is inversely proportional to distance in the equation; k_1, k_2 and k_3 are arbitrary constants. The first term represents the stimulation of pth antibody-antigen recognition in jth cluster. The second and the last term represent the encouragement and depression between this antibody with others corresponding to its idiotope is recognized by the paratope of others. k_2 and k_3 represents a possible inequality between encouragement and depression. The concept stimulation denoted as sb_j is employed to express the synthesized effects on a certain B-cell from antigens and other B-cells.

$$\begin{cases} sb_j = k_4 \times fs(f(Ab_j^r)) + k_5 \times (1-db_j) - k_6 \times db_j \\ fs(f(Ab_j^r)) = \dfrac{1}{1+\exp(-f(Ab_j^r))} \end{cases}, \qquad (6)$$

where parameters are similar to Eq.10 except the fact that they are relevant to B-cells in real-value shape-space.

Because the calculations of stimulation level of antibodies within each group and overall B-cells can be carried out independently from each other, parallel computing techniques are used to reduce the cost of this step.

3 Experimental Results

The efficiency of IDIN was tested by a set of benchmark functions (with various variables), which are listed in Table 1.

Table 1. Mutimodal functions

Function name	Expression	Range
Rastrigin	$Ra_n(x) = 20 + \sum_{i=1}^{n}(x_i - 2\cos(2\pi x_i))^2$	[-5.12, 5.12]
Rosenbrock	$Ro_n = \sum_{i=1}^{n-1}\left(100(x_{i+1}-x_i^2)^2 + (x_i-1)^2\right)$	[-10, 10]
Zakharov	$Za_n = \left(\sum_{i=1}^{n}x_i^2\right) + \left(\sum_{i=1}^{n}0.5x_i^2\right)^2 + \left(\sum_{i=1}^{n}0.5x_i^2\right)^4$	[-5, 10]

Population diversity of IDIN was benchmarked with two other algorithms usually considered suitable for multimodal function optimization: Standard Genetic Algorithm (SGA), Information-entropy-based Immune Algorithm (IIA) with natural binary coding and Euclid-distance-based Immune Algorithm (EIA) with real value coding. The reciprocal of affinity is used to measure the diversity of a certain whole individuals population, and affinity is measured by information entropy and individuals encoded in bit-string. SGA, IIA, EIA and IDIN all start from the same set of initial individuals. Fig. 3 shows comparison of the three algorithms on average diversity for three functions. Although the diversity tendencies of all functions are similar, the three immune network based algorithms provide better diversities than SGA. The proposed IDIN achieves same or better performance as IIA and better performance than EIA, which implies better searching capability for multimodal optimization.

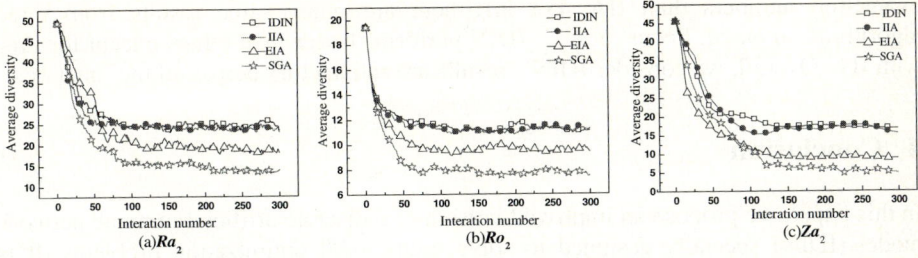

Fig. 3. Comparison of three alrorithms on average diversity of three functions: (a) Rastrigin, (b)Rosenbrock and (c) Zakharov

To evaluate IDIN's computational efficiency, we select four algorithms published in literatures. NHGA[8], an improved version of GA, provides a new architecture of hybrid algorithms, which organically merges the niche techniques and Nelder-Meads simplex method into GAs. Published results in the literature are used as is. The second benchmarking algorithm is IIA mentioned in diversity benchmarking section.

We choose three evaluation criterions used in works of Chelouah [8, 9]: the rate of successful minimizations R_s, the average of the objective function evaluation numbers C_{avg} and the mean errors *Mean*. When at least one of the stopping criterions is met, IDIN algorithm stops and outputs the coordinates of a located point, as well as the objective function value at this point. If the difference between the global optimum and the best solution in the current generation is less than 0.001, we consider that the first convergence happens. The average of the objective function evaluation numbers C_{avg} is evaluated in relation to the successful minimizations only, and *Mean* is the average of gaps between the best successful point found and the known global optimum.

Table 2. Optimization results comparison with different algorithms

	NHGA[9]			IIA			IDIN		
	R_s	C_{avg}	*Mean*	R_s	C_{avg}	*Mean*	R_s	C_{avg}	*Mean*
Ro_2	100	239	0.0007	100	289	0.00045	100	182	0.00023
Ro_5	100	1660	0.002	100	1846	0.0036	100	1264	0.0033
Ro_{10}	100	6257	0.003	100	8735	0.0031	100	6490	0.0029
Ro_{50}	100	46704	0.004	100	43562	0.0038	100	32617	0.004
Za_2	100	390	3.00E-06	100	255	3.00E-06	100	196	3.00E-06
Za_5	100	1310	4.00E-04	100	1032	3.50E-04	100	806	3.10E-04
Za_{10}	100	10734	1.00E-06	100	11368	1.00E-06	100	9876	1.00E-06
Za_{50}	100	84327	1.00E-05	100	54309	1.00E-05	100	58354	1.00E-05

Note: for IIA, concentration threshold $\delta c=0.85$;

Table 2 shows the results of two algorithms above and IDIN on 100 minimizations IDIN performs better than GA-based algorithm with respect to R_s, C_{avg} and *Mean*. Among the three IA-based algorithms, IDIN generally achieves better performance except for Ro_{50}, where IDIN gets slightly more error but less objective function evaluation numbers than IIA. For Za_n there are many same results from three algorithms on *mean*. Focus on C_{avg}, IDIN performs better than others except for Za_{50} with IIA. Overall, we consider IDIN's results are satisfactory across all the functions.

4 Conclusion

In this paper, we propose an improved version of a discrete artificial immune network model (IDIN) specially designed to solve multimodal optimization problems. It is shown that IDIN can be efficiently applied to the optimization of continuous multi-minima functions. The results are satisfactory, and for functions having various variables, we have obtained similar or better results than the ones provided by other methods based on immune algorithm or other versions of Genetic Algorithms.

Acknowledgments. This research was supported by the National Natural Science Foundation of China (No. 50479055).

References

1. de Castro, A.: A network model for clonal differentiation and immune memory Physica A: Statistical Mechanics and its Application 355 (2005) 408-426
2. Timmis, J., Neal, M., Hunt, J.: Data Analysis with Artificial Immune Systems and Cluster Analysis and Kohonen Networks : Some Comparisons Proceedings of IEEE international conference of systems, man and cybernetics, Tokyo, Japan (1999) 922-917
3. Dasgupta, D.: Artificial Immune systems and their applications. Springer (1998)
4. de Castro, L.N., Von Zuben, F.J.: aiNet: An Artificial Immune Network for Data Analysis, Vol. Chapter XII. Idea Group Publishing, USA (2001)
5. de Castro, L.N., Timmis, J.: An artificial immune network for multimodal function optimization. Proceedings of the IEEE Congress on Evolutionary Computation (2002) 699-704
6. Timmis, J., Neal, M., Hunt, J.: An artificial immune system for data analysis Biosystems 55 (2000) 143 - 150
7. Zheng, R.R., Mao, Z.Y.: A modified artificial immune algorithm. Computer Engineering and Application(Chinese) 33 (2003) 55-57
8. Chelouah, R., Siarry, P.: Genetic and Nelder-Mead algorithms hybridized for a more accurate global optimization of continuous multiminima functions. European Journal of Operational Research 148 (2003) 335-348
9. Chelouah, R., Siarry, P.: A continuous genetic algorithm designed for the global optimization of multimodal functions. Journal of Heuristics 6 (2000) 191-213

Using Fuzzy Patterns for Gene Selection and Data Reduction on Microarray Data

Fernando Díaz[1], Florentino Fdez-Riverola[2], Daniel Glez-Peña[2], and Juan M. Corchado[3]

[1] University of Valladolid, Plaza Santa Eulalia, 9-11, 40005, Segovia, Spain
fdiaz@infor.uva.es
[2] University of Vigo, Campus Universitario As Lagoas s/n, 32004, Ourense, Spain
{riverola, dgpena}@uvigo.es
[3] University of Salamanca, Plaza de la Merced s/n, 37008, Salamanca, Spain
corchado@usal.es

Abstract. The advent of DNA microarray technology has supplied a large volume of data to many fields like machine learning and data mining. Intelligent support is essential for managing and interpreting this great amount of information. One of the well-known constraints specifically related to microarray data is the large number of genes in comparison with the small number of available experiments. In this context, the ability of design methods capable of overcoming current limitations of state-of-the-art algorithms is crucial to the development of successful applications. In this paper we demonstrate how a supervised fuzzy pattern algorithm can be used to perform DNA microarray data reduction over real data. The benefits of our method can be employed to find biologically significant insights relating to meaningful genes in order to improve previous successful techniques. Experimental results on acute myeloid leukemia diagnosis show the effectiveness of the proposed approach.

1 Introduction

Microarrays are one of the latest high-throughput technologies in experimental molecular biology, which allow monitoring of gene expression for tens of thousands of genes in parallel and are already producing huge amounts of valuable data. Analysis and handling of such data is becoming one of the major bottlenecks in the utilization of this technology.

One of the major uses of DNA microarray experiments is to attempt to infer meaningful relationships among genes. Up to now, the analysis of DNA microarray data has been divided into four main interdependent branches: (*i*) gene identification, gene selection or gene reduction, (*ii*) clustering or class discovery, (*iii*) classification or class prediction and (*iv*) biological discovery. Nevertheless, there are two other parallel research areas in DNA microarray analysis: (*v*) graphical modeling, that allows the rapid interactive exploration of gene relationships and (*vi*) low-level analysis focused on providing better readouts and solving the expression level summarization problem. In addition, the characteristics of the data gathered from DNA microarray experiments determine which machine learning methods will apply, and can drive the extension of existing algorithms.

The systematic classification of types of tumors is crucial to achieve advances in cancer treatment and research. Although clustering is a popular way of analyzing data, input space reduction is often the key phase in the building of an accurate classifier [1]. We propose the use of a fuzzy prototype-based method able to perform gene selection. In this case, the goal is the identification of a simplified expression profile that can be used to identity relevant genes representing each class of cancer.

This paper describes our initial research in developing a sound method to perform gene selection over real data. Section 2 gives an overview of related work, section 3 explains the proposed algorithm, section 4 introduces the experimental test bed carried out, finally section 5 gives out the results and concluding remarks.

2 Previous Related Work

Classical gene selection methods tend to identify differentially expressed genes from a set of microarray experiments [2]. These genes are expected to be up- or down-regulated between healthy and diseased tissues or between different classes. A differentially expressed gene is a gene which has the same expression pattern for all samples of the same class, but different for samples belonging to different classes. The relevance value of a gene depends on its ability to be differentially expressed. However, a non-differentially expressed gene will be considered irrelevant and will be removed from a classification process even though it might well contain information that would improve classification accuracy. One way or another, the selected method has to pursue two main goals: (*i*) reduce the cost and complexity of the classifier and (*ii*) improve the accuracy of the model.

These methods rank genes depending on their relevance for discrimination. Then by setting a threshold, one can filter the less relevant genes among those considered. As such, these filtering methods may be seen as particular gene selection methods. An important task in microarray data analysis is therefore to identify genes, which are differentially expressed in this way. Statistical analysis of gene expression data relating to complex diseases is of course not really expected to yield accurate results. A realistic goal is to narrow the field for further analysis, to give geneticists a short-list of genes for analysis into which hard-won funds are worth investing.

The area of gene identification has been addressed by [3] through the utilization of information theory. Several methods have been proposed to reduce dimensions in the microarray data domain. These works include the application of genetic algorithms [4], wrapper approaches [5], support vector machines [6, 7], spectral biclustering [8] etc. Other approaches focus their attention on redundancy reduction and feature extraction [9, 10], as well as the identification of similar gene classes making prototypes-genes [11].

3 Gene Selection Using Fuzzy Patterns

This work proposes a method for selecting genes which is based on the notion of fuzzy pattern (see [12, 13] for more details). Briefly, given a set of microarrays which are well classified, for each class it can be constructed a fuzzy pattern (FP) from the fuzzy microarray descriptor (FMD) associated to each one of the microarrays. The FMD is a comprehensible description for each gene in terms of one from the following linguistic labels: LOW, MEDIUM and HIGH. Therefore, the fuzzy pattern is a prototype of the FMDs belonging to the same class where the membership criterion of each gene to the fuzzy pattern of the class is frequency-based. Obviously, this fact can be of interest, if the set of initial observations are labeled with the same kind of cancer. The pattern's quality of fuzziness is given by the fact that the selected labels come from the linguistic labels defined during the transformation into FMD of an initial observation. Moreover, if a specific label of one feature is very common in all the examples belonging to the same class, this feature is selected to be included in the pattern .

```
procedure DiscriminantFuzzyPatterns (input: ListFP; output: ListDFP)
{
00   begin
01      initialize_DFP: FP ← ∅
02      for each fuzzy pattern FPi ∈ ListFP do
03         Initialize_DFP: DFPi ← ∅
04         for each fuzzy pattern FPj ∈ ListFP and FPi <>FPj do
05            for each gen g ∈GetGenes(FPi) do
06               if (g ∈ GetGenes(FPj)) AND
                     (GetLabel(FPi, g) <> GetLabel(FPj, g)) then
07                  AddMember(DFPi, Member(FPi, g))
08         Add_to_List_of_DFP: Add(ListDFP, DFPi)
09   end.
}
```

Fig. 1. Proposed algorithm for selecting genes

3.1 Gene Selection Strategy

The goal of gene selection in this work is to determine a reduced set of genes, which are useful to classify new cases within one of the known classes. For each class it is possible to compute a fuzzy pattern from the available data. Since each pattern is representative of a collection of microarrays belonging to the same class, we can assume that the genes included in a pattern, are significant to the classification of any novel case within the class associated with that pattern. Now we are interested in those genes that allow us to discriminate the new case from one class with regard to the others. Here we introduce the notion of discriminant fuzzy pattern (DFP) with regard to a collection of fuzzy patterns. A DFP version of a FP only includes those genes that can serve to differentiate it from the rest of the patterns. The algorithm used to compute the DFP version of each FP in a collection of fuzzy patterns is shown in Figure 1.

As can be observed from the algorithm, the computed DFP for a specific FP is different depending on what other FPs are compared with it. It's not surprising that the genes used to discern a specific class from others (by mean of its DFP) will be different if the set of rival classes also changes.

4 Case Study: Acute Myeloid Leukemia

Acute myeloid leukemia (AML) is a heterogeneous group of hematological cancers with marked differences in their response to chemotherapy. As in many other human cancers, the diagnosis and classification of AML have been based on morphological, cytochemical and immunophenotipic features. More recently, genetic features have helped to define biologically homogeneous entities within AML as the Acute Promyelocytic Leukemia (APL). The correlation between morphologic characteristics, genetic abnormalities and prognostic features is very consistent within the APL group, whereas is more inconsistent in the remaining AML.

Bone marrow (BM) samples from 62 adult patients with newly de novo diagnosed AML were analyzed. All samples contained more than 80% blast cells. The median age was 36 years (range 14-70 years). Patients were classified according to the WHO classification into 4 subgroups: a) 10 APL with t(15;17), b) 4 AML with inv(16), c) 7 acute monocytic leukemias and d) 41 non-monocytic AML without recurrent cytogenetic translocations. Each case (microarray experiment) stores 22,283 ESTs corresponding to the expression level of thousands of genes. The data consisted of 1,381,546 scanned intensities.

The goal of this study is to characterize the Acute Promyelocytic Leukemia (APL) from the non-APL leukemias in terms of the genetic expression profile. As an additional requirement of this study, the number of selected genes must be the minimum (preserving the accuracy of a binary classifier).

4.1 Methodology

We are interested in determining a list of significant genes following the method described in section 3.1. Firstly, the selected genes can vary widely with the values of the parameters Θ and Π, which must be set up in order to compute the fuzzy patterns. Several configurations of these parameters have been tested. After some initial experiments, the tested values of parameters Θ and Π are the nine configurations of the Cartesian product $\{0.7, 0.8, 0.9\} \times \{0.55, 0.60, 0.65\}$. Each configuration has been used to select significant genes from the whole data set of microarrays. This is the first experiment carried out, herein referred to as EXP#1.

From a different point of view, the selected genes can be sensible to the specific microarrays from they are selected, namely the data sets used to select genes. Therefore, a second experiment is considered, herein referred to as EXP#2. It has been split the original data set in four chunks, following a stratified 4-fold cross validation strategy and then, the nine configurations have been tested.

In order to summarize the results of the tests, for each experiment (EXP#1 and EXP#2), a collection of three lists have been constructed (one list by each one value of parameter Π). Inside each list, the selected genes are ordered by the frequency of appearance of this gene in the tests carried out with the same Π parameter, but different Θ parameter. Namely, fixed the value of Π, a gene, which appears in the three tests (corresponding to the three possible values of Θ), appears before in the list that other gene which only appears in one test (of the three possible values).

Finally, in order to validate the obtained results we perform two different comparisons. Firstly, the selected genes by the proposed method are compared with the genes selected with the PAM software [14]. Secondly, a classifier is constructed from the data resulting of the projection of the original data within the selected features, and its accuracy is evaluated over the 4 test sets of the 4-fold cross validation. The selected classifier is growing cell structure (GCS) network [15]. Although this ANN is especially suitable for unsupervised learning, its choice is motivated by its use in current work about the same problem in other research tasks. To perform a classification task, the GCS simply responds with the majority class of the node that fires the new case. More detailed information about this network can be found in [12, 13].

Table 1. Selected genes in experiment EXP#1

μA Probeset	Π = 0.55 (filter1.1) Gene	tests	μA Probeset	Π = 0.60 (filter1.2) Gene	tests
209960_at	--	XOH	209960_at	--	XOH
210755_at	--	XOH	210755_at	--	XOH
210997_at	HGF	XOH	210997_at	HGF	XOH
220010_at	KCNE1L	XOH	220010_at	KCNE1L	XOH
209560_s_at	DLK1	XOH	209560_s_at	DLK1	XOH
203074_at	ANXA8	XOH	203074_at	ANXA8	-OH
207781_s_at	ZNF6	XOH	205110_s_at	FGF13	-OH
208894_at	HLA-DRA	XOH			
212187_x_at	PTGDS	XOH		Π = 0.65 (filter1.3)	
222317_at	PDE3B	XOH	μA Probeset	Gene	tests
209686_at	S100B	XOH	209960_at	--	XOH
211748_x_at	PTGDS	XOH	210755_at	--	XOH
212013_at	Q92626_HUMAN	XOH	210997_at	HGF	XOH
213385_at	CHN2	XOH	220010_at	KCNE1L	XOH
207996_s_at	CS001_HUMAN	XOH			
209815_at	PTCH	XOH			
213355_at	SIA10_HUMAN	XOH			
212012_at	Q92626_HUMAN	XOH			
219090_at	SLC24A3	XOH			
210998_s_at	HGF	XOH			
211474_s_at	SERPINB6	XOH			
212590_at	RRAS2	XOH			
212590_at	FGF13	-OH			

Table 2. Accuracy of the GCS network trained with selected genes in EXP#1

Filter	Set	Mean	Std. Err.
filter1.1	training	0.00%	0.00%
	test	0.00%	0.00%
filter1.2	training	0.53%	0.46%
	test	0.00%	0.00%
filter1.3	training	1.62%	0.89%
	test	1.47%	1.27%

Table 3. Selected genes in experiment EXP#2

μA Probeset	Π = 0.55 (filter2.1) Gene	tests		μA Probeset	Π = 0.60 (filter2.2) Gene	tests
220010_at	KCNE1L	12/12		220010_at	KCNE1L	12/12
210997_at	HGF	12/12		210997_at	HGF	12/12
210755_at	--	12/12		210755_at	--	12/12
209960_at	--	12/12		209960_at	--	12/12
207996_s_at	CS001_HUMAN	11/12		203074_at	ANXA8	11/12
203074_at	ANXA8	11/12		205110_s_at	FGF13	8/12
209560_s_at	DLK1	11/12		212187_x_at	PTGDS	10/12
211748_x_at	PTGDS	11/12				
213355_at	SIA10_HUMAN	10/12			Π = 0.65 (filter2.3)	
207781_s_at	ZNF6	11/12		μA Probeset	Gene	tests
212912_at	RPS6KA2	9/12		220010_at	KCNE1L	11/12
209686_at	S100B	10/12		210997_at	HGF	10/12
220570_at	RETN	9/12		210755_at	--	9/12
211474_s_at	SERPINB6	11/12		209960_at	--	9/12
209815_at	PTCH	10/12				
205110_s_at	FGF13	8/12				
212187_x_at	PTGDS	10/12				
208894_at	HLA-DRA	10/12				
222317_at	PDE3B	8/12				
219090_at	SLC24A3	10/12				
213385_at	CHN2	10/12				
214617_at	PRF1	7/12				

Table 4. Accuracy of the GCS network trained with selected genes in EXP#2

Filter	Set	Mean	Std. Err.
Filter2.1	training	0.00%	0.00%
	test	0.00%	0.00%
Filter2.2	training	0.00%	0.00%
	test	0.00%	0.00%
Filter2.3	training	1.62%	0.89%
	test	1.47%	1.27%

5 Results and Conclusions

Table 1 shows the selected genes in the experiment EXP#1. In this table, the column 'tests' indicates if the gene appears in tests with the same Π value, but different Θ value ('X' stands for Θ=0.7, 'O' for Θ=0.8 and 'H' for Θ=0.9). Analyzing these results, for the value Π=0.55, it has been selected a list with 23 probesets (21 of them corresponding to known genes). The list is reduced to 7 probesets when the parameter Π is 0.60 and only 4 probesets when Π=0.65. The HGF (Hepatocyte growth factor precursor) and KCNE1L (Potassium voltage-gated channel, AMMECR2 protein) genes appear in the first positions of the three lists. The HGF gene has been selected by PAM software, and its significance has been validated by the biological technique qr-PCR, whereas PAM has also detected the KCNE1L gene. The FGF13 gene (Fibroblast growth factor 13) also appears as a significant gene when Π=0.55 and Π=0.60. The relative relevance of the FGF13 increases when the Θ parameter increases (this gene appears as significant when Π=0.60 for the two higher values of parameter Θ). Moreover, this gene has been detected by PAM software and validated by a qr-PCR analysis. The S100B, ANXA8 and SLCS24A3 genes have been also selected by PAM software, whereas the rest of genes are different. Finally, the three lists of genes (respectively referred to as filter1.1, filter1.2 and filter1.3) have been used to train a GCS network. It has been considered the training and test sets of the 4-fold cross validation used in EXP#2. The accuracy of the different classifiers is shown in Table 2.

Table 3 shows the genes selected in the experiment EXP#2. Now, the column 'tests' of the table indicates the number of appearances of a gene in all the possible test for the same value of Π. Additionally, the appearances of the same gene in tests with a great specificity (a higher value of parameter Θ) weigh more than appearances with a lower specificity, when the genes are ranked. As shown in Table 3, the number of selected genes is quite similar in the two experiments (there is only a difference of one gene among filter1.1 and filter2.1). With regard to the degree of overlapping of selected genes in the two experiments, it is also quite similar. The similarity of filter2.1 with regard to filter1.1 is 19/23=82.6%, the similarity of filter 1.1 with regard to filter2.1 is 19/22=86.4%. The degree of overlapping of filter1.2 and filter2.2 is 6/7=85.7% and, it is a 100% in the case of filter1.3 and filter2.3. Finally, Table 4 shows the accuracy of the GCS network when it is trained with the selected genes (filter2.1, filter2.2 and filter3.3). It is remarkable that filter2.2 has an error of 0% predicting novel cases (both within the training set and the test set).

The experiments carried out, show that the number of genes, which are sufficient to correctly classify novel cases, are 7 genes. The genes selected in filter2.2 are especially remarkable, since with a minimal number of genes (7) it is reached a 100% accuracy of the classifier on both training and test sets. The minimal number of genes selected by PAM software, which reaches also an accuracy of 100%, was 23 genes. Therefore, the proposed method has achieved a reduction of the number of genes about the 70% with regard to the PAM software (preserving the classifier accuracy).

From Tables 2 and 4, it can be observed that errors on tests sets are always lesser than errors on training sets. This can also be interpreted as the selected genes are meaningful genes, since they provide an excellent ability of generalization to the constructed classifier.

Finally, from the comparison of similarity among genes selected in the two experiments, we can claim that the proposed method is robust against slight variations of the data set from where genes are selected. It is a desirable feature of the algorithm in order to select truly meaningful genes.

Summarizing our work, in this article we have presented and tested a successful approach of applying fuzzy logic to the process of gene selection and data reduction in the microarray data domain. Our proposed method of fuzzy pattern construction takes advantage of the ability inherent to fuzzy logic to process uncertain, imprecise and incomplete information. In this sense, we have applied fuzzy logic to discretize the original data within the three linguistic labels. This fact leads to the possibility of clearly identifying those genes with a great capacity of discriminate patients based on the selected genes that compose the discriminant fuzzy patterns.

References

1. Cakmakov, D., Bennani, Y.: Feature selection for pattern recognition, Informa Press (2002)
2. Zheng, G., Olusegun, E. Narasimhan, G.: Neural network classifiers and gene selection methods for microarray data on human lung adenocarcinoma. Proc. of the CAMDA 2003 Conference, (2003) 63-67
3. Fuhrman, S. Cunningham, M.J., Wen, X., Zweiger, G., Seilhamer, J.J., Somogyi, R.: The application of Shannon entropy in the identification of putative drug targets. Biosystems 55 (2000) 5-14
4. Li, L., Darden, T.A., Weinberg, C.R., Levine, A.J., Pedersen, L.G.: Gene assessment and sample classification for gene expression data using a genetic algorithm/k-nearest neighbor method. Combinatorial Chemistry and High Throughput Screening, 4(8) (2001) 727-739
5. Blanco, R., Larrañaga, P., Inza, I., Sierra. B.: Gene selection for cancer classification using wrapper approaches. International Journal of Pattern Recognition and Artificial Intelligence 18(8) (2004) 1373-1390
6. Guyon, I., Weston, J., Barnhill, S., Vapnik, V.: Gene selection for cancer classification using support vector machines. Machine Learning 46(1-3) (2002) 389-422
7. Chu, F., Wang, L.: Gene Expression Data Analysis Using Support Vector Machines. Bioinformatics using Computational Intelligence Paradigms. Udo Seiffert and Lakhmi C. Jain (Editors). Springer, Berlin (2005) 167-189
8. Liu, L., Wan, C.R., Wang, L.P.: Unsupervised gene selection via spectral biclustering. Proc. of the International Joint Conference on Neural Networks, (2005) 1681-1686
9. Jaeger, J., Sengupta, R., Ruzzo, W.L.: Improved gene selection for classification of microarrays. Proc. of the PSB 2003 Conference, (2003) 53-64
10. Qi, H.: Feature selection and kNN fusion in molecular classification of multiple tumor types. Proc. of the METMBS 2002 Conference, (2002)
11. Hanczar, B., Courtine, M., Benis, A., Hennegar, C., Clément, K., Zucker, J.D.: Improving classification of microarray data using prototype-based feature selection. ACM SIGKDD Explorations Newsletter 5(2) (2003) 23-30
12. Fdez-Riverola, F., Díaz, F., Corchado, J.M., Hernández, J.M., San Miguel, J.: Improving Gene Selection in Microarray Data Analysis using Fuzzy Patterns inside a CBR System. Proc. of the ICCBR 2005 Conference, (2005) 23-26
13. Díaz, F., Fdez-Riverola, F., Corchado, J. M.: GENE-CBR: a Case-Based Reasoning Tool for Cancer Diagnosis using Microarray Datasets. Computational Intelligence. ISSN 0824-7935. In Press.
14. Tibshirani, R., Hastie, T., Narasimhan, B., Chu, G.: Diagnosis of multiple cancer types by shrunken centroids of gene expression. Proc. of the National Academy of Sciences, Vol. 99:(10) (2002) 6567-6572
15. Fritzke, B.: Growing Cell Structures – A Self-Organizing Network for Unsupervised and Supervised Learning. Neural Networks 7 (1994) 1441-1460

Applying GCS Networks to Fuzzy Discretized Microarray Data for Tumour Diagnosis

Fernando Díaz[1], Florentino Fdez-Riverola[2], Daniel Glez-Peña[2], and J.M. Corchado[3]

[1] Dept. Informática, University of Valladolid, Escuela Universitaria de Informática,
Plaza Santa Eulalia, 9-11, 40005, Segovia, Spain
fdiaz@infor.uva.es

[2] Dept. Informática, University of Vigo, Escuela Superior de Ingeniería Informática,
Edificio Politécnico, Campus Universitario As Lagoas s/n, 32004, Ourense, Spain
{riverola, dgpena}@uvigo.es

[3] Dept. Informática y Automática, University of Salamanca,
Plaza de la Merced s/n, 37008, Salamanca, Spain
corchado@usal.es

Abstract. Gene expression profiles belonging to DNA microarrays are composed of thousands of genes at the same time, representing the complex relationships between them. In this context, the ability of designing methods capable of overcoming current limitations is crucial to reduce the generalization error of state-of-the-art algorithms. This paper presents the application of a self-organised *growing cell structures* network in an attempt to cluster biological homogeneous patients. This technique makes use of a previous successful supervised fuzzy pattern algorithm capable of performing DNA microarray data reduction. The proposed model has been tested with microarray data belonging to bone marrow samples from 43 adult patients with cancer plus a group of six cases corresponding to healthy persons. The results of this work demonstrate that classical artificial intelligence techniques can be effectively used for tumour diagnosis working with high-dimensional microarray data.

1 Introduction and Motivation

In recent years, machine learning and data mining fields have found a successful application area in the field of DNA microarray technology. Microarrays are one of the latest high-throughput technologies in experimental molecular biology, which allow monitoring of gene expression for tens of thousands of genes in parallel and are already producing high amounts of valuable data. One of the major uses of DNA microarray experiments is to attempt to infer meaningful relationships among genes, but the analysis and handling of such data is becoming one of the major bottlenecks in the utilization of this technology [1]. Since the number of examined genes in an experiment is measured in terms of thousands, different data mining techniques have been intensively used to analyse and discover knowledge from gene expression data [2]. However, having so many fields relative to so few samples creates a high likelihood of finding false positives.

Recent studies in human cancer have demonstrated that microarrays can be used to develop a new taxonomy of cancer, including major insights into the genesis, progression, prognosis, and response to therapy on the basis of gene expression profiles [3].

However, there continues to be a need to develop new approaches to (*i*) diagnose cancer early in its clinical course, (*ii*) more effectively treat advanced stage disease, (*iii*) better predict a tumour's response to therapy prior to the actual treatment, and (*iv*) ultimately prevent disease from arising through chemopreventive strategies. Given the fact that systematic classification of types of tumours is crucial to achieve advances in cancer treatment, several research works have been developed in this direction [4, 5].

Following a novel approach, in this paper we explore the capabilities of a growing cell structures (GCS) neural network to discover relevant knowledge for clustering patients suffering for acute myeloid leukemia (AML). This knowledge can be easily conveyed to and understood by humans via available visualization techniques. A key advantage of the proposed method is that it allows incorporating biological meaningful information to the network operation in the form of a gene-based distance metric. Our GCS network makes use of a previous successful fuzzy discretization method for data reduction on microarray data domain.

The rest of the paper is organized as follows: Section 2 summarizes our previous successful fuzzy discretization algorithm for data dimensionality reduction, Section 3 presents the main issues about the proposed model based on a modified GCS network, Section 4 presents the experiments carried out and discusses the obtained results, finally, Section 5 gives out the concluding remarks.

2 Discovering Relevant Genes Using a Discriminant Fuzzy Microarray Descriptor

Input space reduction is often the key phase in the building of an accurate classifier [6]. Based on a novel fuzzy discretization method working as the retrieval stage in the GENECBR system [7], it is possible to represent any microarray by means of its generalized fuzzy microarray descriptor (FMD). This descriptor is a comprehensible representation for each gene expression level in terms of one from the following linguistic labels: LOW, MEDIUM and HIGH. Moreover, from a set of FMDs the method is also able to construct a prototype, known as a fuzzy pattern (FP), which characterizes and summarizes the most relevant values of gene expression levels within a given set of microarrays. A FP is a higher concept constructed from a set of FMDs. A fuzzy pattern can be viewed as a prototype of the set of FMDs from which it is constructed. Therefore, the fuzzy pattern can capture relevant and common information about the gene expression levels of these FMDs. The final goal of the proposed method is to select a reduced number of relevant and representative genes allowing other artificial intelligence techniques being able to tackle with this high-dimensional domain.

As aforementioned, the proposed method employs a fuzzy codification for the gene expression levels of each microarray, based on the discretization of real gene expression data into a small number of fuzzy membership functions. The whole algorithm comprises of three main steps: (*i*) first, we discretize the gene expression levels into binary variables according to a supervised learning process generating several FMDs; then, (*ii*) a unique FP is generated from the patients belonging to each specific pathology; finally, (*iii*) we discriminate between those genes belonging to the existing FPs and we select a subset of relevant genes in order to construct the final discriminant fuzzy pattern (DFP). When the algorithm finishes each microarray can be represented by a simplified fuzzy vector of common genes that we call FMD_{DFP}. The details of the whole process can be found in [8].

In this work we plan to employ this new representation of the available samples (FMD_{DFP}) as input data for a GCS network. The target goal of the GCS network is to group those patients that are most similar to a new one but only taking into account the genetic information provided by the previously selected genes (DFP vector descriptor).

3 GCS Networks for Clustering Biologically Homogeneous Patients

GCS neural networks [9] constitute an extension to Kohonen's self-organising maps [10], and are only one member in the family of self-organising incremental models. GCS networks have the advantage of being able to automatically construct the network topology, and to support easy visualisation of semantic similarity in high-dimensional data. More importantly, the extracted knowledge that is relevant to clustering can provide meaningful explanations for the clustering process and useful insight into the underlying domain.

To illustrate the working model of the GCS network used in our experimentation, a two-dimensional space is used, where the cells (neurons) are connected and organized into triangles [11]. Each cell in the network is associated with a weight vector, w, of the same dimension as the number of relevant genes selected in the previous step (size of the DFP vector). At the beginning of the learning process, the weight vector of each cell is initialized with random values [11]. The basic learning process in a GCS network consists of topology modification and weight vector adaptations carried out in three steps.

In the first step of each learning cycle, the cell c, with the smallest distance between its weight vector, w_c, and the actual FMD_{DFP} is chosen as the *winner cell* or best-match cell. The selection process is succinctly defined by using the Euclidean distance measure as indicated in Expression (1) where O denotes the set of cells within the structure at a given point in time.

$$c : \|FMD_{DFP} - w_c\| \leq \|FMD_{DFP} - w_i\|; \forall i \in O \qquad (1)$$

The second step of the learning process consists of the adaptation of the weight vector, w_c, of the winning cell, and the weight vectors, w_n, of its directly connected neighbouring cells, N_c, by means of Equations (2) and (3).

$$w_c(t+1) = w_c(t) + \varepsilon_c(FMD_{DFP} - w_c) \qquad (2)$$

$$w_n(t+1) = w_n(t) + \varepsilon_n(FMD_{DFP} - w_n); \forall n \in N_c \qquad (3)$$

where ε_c and ε_n represent the learning rates for the winner and its neighbours respectively, belonging to the [0, 1] interval, and N_c stands for the set of direct neighbour cells of the winning cell, c.

In the third step, a *signal counter*, τ, is assigned to each cell, which reflects how often a cell has been chosen as winner. Equations (4) and (5) define how the signal counter is updated with parameter α acting as a constant rate of counter reduction for the rest of the cells at the current learning cycle, t.

$$\tau_c(t+1) = \tau_c(t) + 1 \qquad (4)$$

$$\tau_i(t+1) = \tau_i(t) - \alpha \tau_i(t); i \neq c \qquad (5)$$

Growing cell structures also modify the overall network structure by inserting new cells into those regions that represent large portions of the input data (genetically similar patients), or removing cells that do not contribute to the input data representation. The cell deletion policy has not been used in our work due to the lack of great amounts of data. The adaptation process is then performed after a fixed number of learning cycles of input presentations (epochs). Therefore, the overall structure of a GCS network is modified through the learning process by performing only cell insertion. Equations (6), (7) and (8) define the rules that govern the insertion behaviour of the network.

$$h_i = \tau_i / \sum_j \tau_j; \forall i, j \in O \qquad (6)$$

$$q : h_q \geq h_i; \forall i \in O \qquad (7)$$

$$r : \|w_r - w_q\| \geq \|w_p - w_q\|; \forall p \in N_q \qquad (8)$$

Insertion starts with selecting the cell, which served the most often as the winner, on the basis of the signal counter, τ. The cell, q, with the highest relative counter value, h, is selected. The neighbouring cell, r, of q with the most dissimilar weight vector is determined using Expression (8). In this expression, N_q denotes the set of neighbouring cells of q. A new cell, s, is inserted between the cells q and r, and the initial weight vector, w_s, of this new cell is set to the mean of the two existing weight vectors, w_q and w_r. Finally, the signal counters, τ, in the neighbourhood, N_s, of the newly inserted cell, s, are adjusted. The new signal counter values represent an approximation to a hypothetical situation where s would have been existing since the beginning of the process.

An important issue in the network operation is the distance calculation between two cells or one cell and the actual FMD_{DFP}. Every time the network needs to compute a distance between two nodes, Expression (1) is used. In this work, we propose to hybridise our GCS network by using biological knowledge for the distance computation. Given that each cell in the network have a weight vector, w_c, representing their location in the input space (FMD_{DFP} space) and that each position in w_c stands for a gene expression value, we can use the similarity between linguistic labels (represented by fuzzy sets) as a measure of the relation between each point belonging to w_c and the corresponding value in the FMD_{DFP} vector.

In order to explain how we calculate this correspondence we need to previously define the similarity between linguistic labels (represented by fuzzy sets). In this case, it has been considered that the fuzzy intersection of two fuzzy sets A and B (represented by its membership functions, μ_A and μ_B, respectively) is given by the application of the min operator to the two membership functions, namely, $\mu_{A \cap B} = \min\{\mu_A, \mu_B,\}$. On the other hand, the cardinality operator can be replaced by the integral operator (see

[8] for details). In this way, the metric *Sim(A, B)* varies between the values 0 (total dissimilarity) and 1 (total similarity).

It is important to highlight that the final goal of our GCS network is to cluster all patients that are genetically similar given a selected group of genes (DFP vector descriptor) and without taking into account their previous assigned classes. Our proposed method aims to find new relations between the patients even now unknown. Therefore, it is possible and not contradictory to group together patients suffering different (but genetically related) diseases. Such a topology has the added advantage that inter-cluster distances can be precisely quantified. Since such networks contain explicit distance information, they can be used effectively to (*i*) represent an *indexing structure* which indexes sets of related patients and to (*ii*) serve as a similarity measurement between individual patients.

Every time a new microarray needs to be classified a new FMD_{DFP} is constructed and presented to the trained CGS network. A sorted vector of pairs, *S*, holding the similarity of each selected patient with the new microarray is generated. In order to produce a new classification, a proportional weighted voting schema is proposed. For this purpose, we need to ponder the vote of each patient contained in vector *S*. In this case, a weight α_j for each retrieved patient, k_j, is calculated based on the position (*pos*) that it occupies in the vector *S* and the level of similarity with the target case, Sim_j. For this task, Expression (9) is used.

$$\alpha_j = Sim_j \frac{2^{|S|-1}}{(2^{|S|}-1)2^{pos-1}} \quad (9)$$

Therefore, the classification made by the GCS network when a target patient is presented to the system depends on both the number of selected patients (those genetically similar taking into account the genes belonging to the DPF vector descriptor) and the level of similarity with the target patient. The solution proposed by the system is the class corresponding to the disease with the highest score.

As we can surmise, it is easy to introduce a rejection mechanism in the voting model. We simply use a threshold *T* to indicate whether the score received by the best matching class is sufficiently strong (passing quota). In the event that the score received by the matching class is less than *T*, the target patient remains unclassified.

4 Evaluation

The goal of this section is to evaluate the performance of the GCS network in conjunction with the dimensionality reduction technique based on the notion of FMDs. The GCS is trained and tested over an available set of 49 microarrays from the Haematology Service of the University Hospital of Salamanca (Spain).

Acute myeloid leukemia is a heterogeneous group of hematological cancers with marked differences in their response to chemotherapy. As in many other human cancers, the diagnosis and classification of AML have been based on morphological, cytochemical and immunophenotipic features. More recently, genetic features have helped to define biologically homogeneous entities within AML [12]. Karyotype is the most important independent prognostic factor and therefore the most useful parameter for stratifying patients into risk groups. Thus, the favorable outcome group is composed of well-defined subtypes in terms of cytogenetics: t(15;17), inv(16) and t(8;21) [13, 14]. In contrast, the correlation between morphologic characteristics, genetic abnormalities and prognostic features is more inconsistent in the remaining AML. Analysis of gene expression profiles of tumors using microarray technology has become a powerful tool for classifying hematopoietic neoplasms [15].

Bone marrow samples from 43 adult patients with newly de novo diagnosed AML were analyzed. All samples contained more than 80% blast cells. The median age was 36 years (range 14-70 years). Patients were classified according to the WHO classification into 4 subgroups: (*i*) 10 APL with t(15;17) confirmed by FISH studies with LSI PML/RARA probe (Vysis, Stuttgart, Germany), (*ii*) 4 AML with inv(16) confirmed by FISH analysis with LSI CBFB probe (Vysis); (*iii*) 7 acute monocytic leukemias and (*iv*) 22 non-monocytic AML without recurrent cytogenetic translocations. In addition to this data, a set of 6 samples from healthy persons are also available and they constitute the group of control. Each case (microarray experiment) stores 22,283 expressed sequence tags (ESTs) corresponding to the expression level of thousands of genes. The data consisted of 1,091,867 scanned intensities.

The employed methodology splits the available data within a test set and a training set with 1/3 and 2/3 of the whole observations, respectively. In order to asses the maximum number of nodes of the GCS network an strategy of cross-validation is used, concretely a three fold stratified cross validation. In each round, each fold of the original training set is used to estimate the predictive accuracy of the GCS network which has been trained from the rest of folds. The mean error (and its standard error) for each number of nodes of the GCS are depicted in Figure 1, which shows the training and evaluation errors. As it can be seen, the configuration of 6 nodes as maximum number of cells of the GCS networks involves the minimal value of the error in the evaluation sets, so this value was used to train a GCS network from the training set.

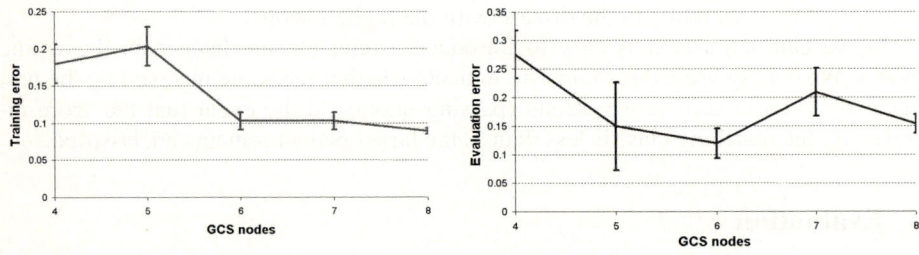

Fig. 1. CV#3 error of GCS network v.s. maximum number of cells at the parameter estimation

Before the training of the GCS network, a reduced number of features (genes) are selected using the FMD representation of the available microarrays. Specifically, the original number of 22,283 ESTs per microarray was reduced to only 165 meaningful ESTs. After the training of the GCS network (with a maximum number of cells equal to 6) over the training set (with 34 observations) the classification error of the GCS network over training was a 8.82 % and a 6.67% over the test set (with 15 observations).

Finally, the following considerations can be made from the clustering performed by the GCS network. The control group (samples from healthy persons) can be adequately differentiated from patients with any kind of AML (see Figure 2). The APL and AML-mono groups are also well differentiated from the rest of AML groups, and there is some kind of overlapping among the AML-inv and the AML-other groups. It must be remembered that the AML-other group is the uncertain area at the current knowledge in the field of AML. The APL group is a kind of AML well characterized (morphologically, cytogenetically and genetically), whereas the AML-mono or AML-inv are possible kinds of AML which are partially characterized. Finally, the AML-other is no characterized in any way. Therefore, at the present state-of-the-art, the given classification can present mistakes and it is possible that some samples from the AML-other group belongs to the AML-mono, AML-inv or new subtypes of AML.

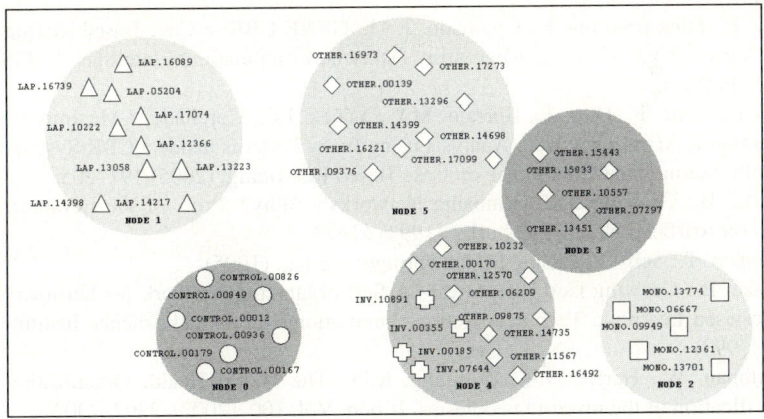

Fig. 2. Final mapping between patients and cells in the GCS network space

5 Conclusions

This work explores the capabilities of a growing cell structure neural network to discover relevant knowledge for clustering patients suffering for acute myeloid leukemia. A key advantage of the proposed method is that it allows incorporating biological meaningful information to the network operation in the form of a gene-based distance metric. Moreover, the GCS network makes use of a previous successful fuzzy discretization method for data reduction on microarray data domain.

Using self-organising GCS networks to meaningfully cluster filtered microarray data has a number of appealing features over other approaches. For example, incremental self-construction, and easy visualisation of biological relationships among the input data. The explanations of the clustering process carried out by the network can be addressed by means of our DFP vector. The most relevant knowledge for each cluster can be highlighted, and provide meaningful explanations about the clustering process and useful insight into the underlying problem and data. The experimental results show that with only a small subset of the genes belonging to a microarray, the performance of the network in terms of the clustering accuracy rate raises to 100%.

References

1. Piatetsky-Shapiro, G., Tamayo, P.: Microarray data mining: facing the challenges. ACM SIGKDD Explorations Newsletter, Vol. 5 (2). (2003) 1–5
2. Cho, S.B., Won, H.H.: Machine learning in DNA microarray analysis for cancer classification. Proc. of the First Asia-Pacific Bioinformatics Conference, (2003) 189–198
3. Ochs, M.F., Godwin A.K.: Microarrays in Cancer: Research and Applications. BioTechniques, Vol. 34. (2003) s4–s15
4. Xiang, Z.Y., Yang, Y., Ma, X., Ding, W.: Microarray expression profiling: Analysis and applications. Current Opinion in Drug Discovery & Development, Vol. 6 (3). (2003) 384–395
5. Golub, T.: Genome-Wide Views of Cancer. The New England Journal of Medicine, Vol. 344. (2001) 601–602
6. Cakmakov, D., Bennani, Y.: Feature selection for pattern recognition. Informa Press, (2003)
7. Díaz, F., Fdez-Riverola, F., Corchado, J. M.: GENE-CBR: a Case-Based Reasoning Tool for Cancer Diagnosis using Microarray Datasets. Computational Intelligence. ISSN 0824-7935. In Press.
8. Fdez-Riverola, F., Díaz, F., Borrajo, M.L., Yáñez, J.C., Corchado, J.M.: Improving Gene Selection in Microarray Data Analysis using fuzzy Patterns inside a CBR System. Proc. of the 6th International Conference on Case-Based Reasoning, (2005) 191–205
9. Fritzke, B.: Growing Self-organising Networks – Why?. Proc. of the European Symposium on Artificial Neural Networks, (1993) 61–72
10. Kohonen, T.: Self-Organising Maps. Springer-Verlag, (1995)
11. Fritzke, B.: Growing Cell Structures - A Self-organizing Network for Unsupervised and Supervised Learning. Technical Report, International Computer Science Institute, Berkeley, (1993)
12. Vardiman, W., Harris, N.L., Brunning, R.D.: The World Health Organization (WHO) classification of the myeloid neoplasms. Blood, Vol. 100. (2002). 2292–2302
13. Grimwade, D., Walker, H., Oliver, F., Wheatley, K., Harrison, C., Harrison, G., Rees, J., Hann, I., Stevens, R., Burnett, A., Goldstone, A.: The importance of diagnostic cytogenetics on outcome in AML: analysis of 1,612 patients entered into the MRC AML 10 trial. Blood, Vol. 92. (1998) 2322–2333
14. Slovak, M.L., Kopecky, K.J., Cassileth, P.A., Harrington, D.H., Theil, K.S., Mohamed, A., Paietta, E., Willman, C.L., Head, D.R., Rowe, J.M., Forman, S.J., Appelbaum, F.R.: Karyotypic analysis predicts outcome of preremission and postremission therapy in adult acute myeloid leukemia: a Southwest Oncology Group/Eastern Cooperative Oncology Group Study. Blood, Vol. 96. (2000). 4075–4083
15. Golub, T.R., Slonim, D.K., Tamayo, P., Huard, C., Gaasenbeek, M., Mesirov, J.P., Coller, H., Loh, M.L., Downing, J.R., Caligiuri, M.A., Bloomfield, C.D., Lander, E.S.: Molecular classification of cancer: class discovery and class prediction by gene expression monitoring. Science, Vol. 286. (1999) 531–537

Refractory Effects of Chaotic Neurodynamics for Finding Motifs from DNA Sequences

Takafumi Matsuura* and Tohru Ikeguchi

Graduate School of Science and Engineering, Saitama University,
225 Shimo-Ohkubo, Sakura-ku, Saitama-city 338-8570, Japan
*takafumi@nls.ics.saitama-u.ac.jp

Abstract. To discover a common and conserved pattern, or motif, from DNA sequences is an important step to analyze DNA sequences because the patterns are acknowledged to reflect biological important information. However, it is difficult to discover unknown motifs from DNA sequences because of its huge number of combination. We have already proposed a new effective method to extract the motifs using a chaotic search, which combines a heuristic algorithm and a chaotic dynamics. To realize the chaotic search, we used a chaotic neural network. The chaotic search exhibits higher performance than conventional methods. Although we have indicated that the refractory effects realized by the chaotic neural network have an essential role, we did not clarify why the refractory effects are important to search optimal solutions. In this paper, we further investigate this issue and reveal the validity of the refractory effects of the chaotic dynamics using surrogate refractory effects. As a result, we discovered that it is important for searching optimal solutions to increase strength of the refractory effects after a firing of neurons.

1 Introduction

In April 2003, the Human Genome Project had completed. This project generated large data sets of genomic sequence data. The human genomes consist of about 3 billions base pairs and approximately 25,000 genes. A deoxyribo nucleic acid (DNA) sequence is composed of four bases: Adenine, Cytosine, Guanine, and Thymine. Then, the most important present issue is to identify important parts in which biological information is embedded. In general, the biologically essential alignment is thought to appear repeatedly in the DNA sequences. Therefore, one of the popular analyses is to find a common and conserved pattern, which is often called a motif.

Such a problem, how to discover motifs, is mathematically described as follows [1]: we have a DNA data set $S = \{s_1, s_2, ..., s_N\}$, where s_i is the i-th DNA sequence (Fig.1). Each sequence consists of m_i ($i = 1, 2, ..., N$) bases, and length of the motif is L. This problem has several varieties: the number of embedded motifs in each sequence is exactly one, plural, or random (contains zero). An enumeration method is an exact method to discover the motifs. However, there are 4^L motif patterns to be considered for DNA sequence in case of using the enumeration method. If L is large, it is almost impossible to explore all motif patterns in real time, because the number of the motif patterns exponentially diverges. It is also proved that this problem is $\mathcal{NP}$-complete[3]. Thus, it is inevitable to develop an effective approximation method to detect the motifs. Several approximation methods have been developed for the motif detection. One of the popular methods is the Gibbs sampling [11]. Its strategy is based on a stochastic search for exploring possible states and it is shown that the Gibbs sampling method works very well.

As for combinational optimization, many effective algorithms have been proposed, for example, a tabu search [4,5], an exponential tabu search [7], and a chaotic search [8,9]. It has been shown that the chaotic search [8,9] exhibits higher performance than stochastic approaches for solving Traveling Salesman Problem (TSP) [6,9] and Quadratic Assignment Problem (QAP) [8]. To solve the motif extraction problem, we have already proposed a chaotic search, called *Chaotic Motif Sampler* (CMS) [13], which combines a heuristic algorithm and a chaotic dynamics. This method exhibits higher performance than conventional methods [11,12,13]. In CMS, we used the chaotic neural network model [2] which has a refractory effect. This effect emulates real biological neurons: neuron cannot fire just after a firing. Because motif selection is defined by a firing of a chaotic neuron in CMS [13], the refractory effect has a similar effect as tabu search [7] on memorizing previous searching status. Then, the same selection of a motif can be avoided after the firing of the corresponding neuron due to the refractory effect.

We have already indicated that the refractory effects have a significant role in finding motifs in the chaotic search [6,8,9,13]. However, we do not have clarified yet why the refractory effect are so effective to find optimal solutions and which aspects of the refractory effect contribute to the good performance. Therefore, in this paper, we further investigate the validity of the refractory effect for finding optimal solutions through CMS [13]. Although the issue raised in this paper is directly discussed with to the motif extraction problem, the concepts of the analyses can be easily extended and applicable to a more general class of solving combinatorial optimization problems, such as TSP or QAP, by the chaotic search [6,8,9].

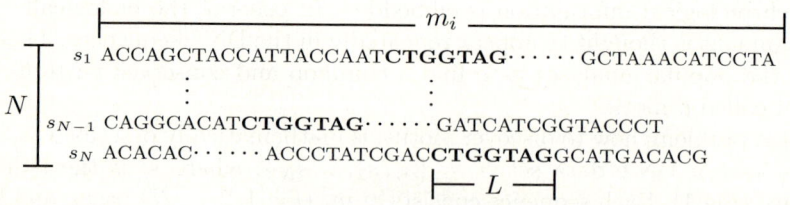

Fig. 1. An example of a data set for DNA sequences. Bold face alignments indicate a motif. A, C, G, and T stand for Adenine, Cytosine, Guanine, and Thymine.

2 Chaotic Motif Sampler

We use a chaotic dynamics to decide a new motif position. To realize the chaotic search, we used a chaotic neural network [2] composed of $\sum_{i=1}^{N}(m_i-L+1)$ neurons (Fig.2). A firing of a neuron encodes the head position of a motif candidate (Fig.2). The firing of the (i,j)-th neuron is defined by $x_{ij}(t) = f(y_{ij}(t)) > \frac{1}{2}$, where $f(y) = 1/(1 + \exp(-y/\epsilon))$, and $y_{ij}(t)$ is an internal state of the (i,j)-th neuron at time t. The internal state of the chaotic neural network [2] is decomposed into three parts, $\xi_{ij}(t)$, $\zeta_{ij}(t)$, and $\eta_{ij}(t)$, which represent different influence to the firing of the neuron in the algorithm; a gain effect, a refractory effect, and mutual inhibition, respectively. The first part, $\xi_{ij}(t)$, which expresses the gain effect, is defined by,

$$\xi_{ij}(t+1) = \beta(\frac{E_{ij}(t) - \hat{E}}{\hat{E}}), \tag{1}$$

where β is a scaling parameter; $E_{ij}(t) = \frac{1}{L}\sum_{k=1}^{L}\sum_{a\in\Omega} f_k(\omega) \log_2 \frac{f_k(\omega)}{p(\omega)}$ is a relative entropy score when a subsequence is at the j-th position of the sequence s_i; $\hat{E}$ is the entropy score of a current state; $f_k(\omega)$ is the number of appearances of a base $\omega \in \Omega$ at the k-th position of subsequences, $p(\omega)$ is the probability of appearance of the base ω and Ω is a set of bases (Ω={A, C, G ,T}). The second part, $\zeta_{ij}(t)$, is related to the refractoriness of the neuron. The refractoriness is one of the important properties of real neurons; once a neuron fires, the neuron becomes hard to fire for a while. Then the second part is expressed as:

$$\zeta_{ij}(t+1) = -\alpha\sum_{d=0}^{t} k_r^d x_{ij}(t-d) + \theta = -\alpha x_{ij}(t) + k_r \zeta_{ij}(t) + \theta(1-k_r) \tag{2}$$

where α is a scaling factor, θ is a threshold; $\zeta_{ij}(t+1)$ expresses a refractory effect with a factor k_r. To obtain a reasonable firing rate of neurons, the third part, $\eta_{ij}(t)$, related to mutual inhibitory connections is introduced,

$$\eta_{ij}(t+1) = W - \frac{W}{m_i - L}\sum_{\substack{l=1\\l\neq j}}^{(m_i-L+1)} x_{il}(t), \tag{3}$$

where W corresponds to a control parameter of the firing rate. This function is not always necessary for solving the problem: If we want to adjust the firing rate of the neuron, we use this function.

Being guided by the above searching machine, we construct an algorithm for extracting motifs described as follows:

1. Let us have a set of sequences, and denote the number of the sequences as N, the length of each sequence as m_i ($i = 1, 2, ..., N$), and the length of a subsequence (motif) as L (Fig.2).
2. A position of an initial subsequence t_{ij} ($i=1, 2, ..., N$; $j=1, 2, ..., m_i - L + 1$) is selected from the i-th sequence at uniformly random.
3. The i-th sequence s_i is selected cyclically.
4. For a selected sequence s_i at the third step, a position of a motif candidate is changed to a new position. $x_{ij}(t + 1)$ is calculated from the first neuron ($j = 1$) to the last neuron ($j = m_i - L + 1$) in the sequence s_i. The new motif position is determined by which the internal state is maximum. If $x_{ij}(t+1) > \frac{1}{2}$, a new motif position is set to t_{ij}, and $\hat{E}$ is updated.
5. Repeat the steps 3-4 for sufficiently many times.

In this report, the parameters are k_r=0.8, θ=0.9, α=0.45, β=12.0, W=0.001, and ϵ=0.01.

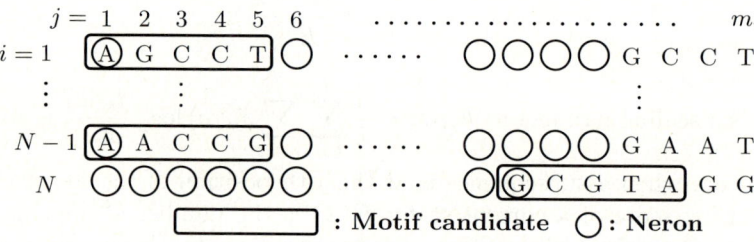

Fig. 2. A coding scheme by the chaotic neural network

3 Results

We used Sun Blade 2000 with 1GB memory and gcc compiler on Solaris 8. To investigate a refractory effect for chaotic search, we prepared an artificial data set, because it might be better to clarify the effectivity of the refractory effect with a simpler data set. The data set has 20 sequence (N=20), and each sequences is composed of 600 bases (m_i=600, $i = 1, 2, ..., 20$). We introduced the same background probability as real DNA sequences [1]. In the data set, only one

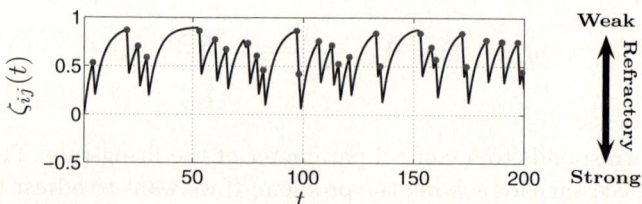

Fig. 3. An example of a time-series of $\zeta_{ij}(t)$ in a chaotic neuron. Dots show time at which the (i, j)-th neuron fires.

motif is embedded in each sequence. The length of the motif is 16 ($L = 16$). If the motif is extracted exactly, the relative entropy score takes 1.9632 in this case.

We extracted motifs from the data set using CMS. When the motif position is changed for 500 times for each sequence in one trial, CMS can find the motif in a high rate, 96.0% (Table 1). One of the possible reasons for finding the motif with such a high rate is that the refractory effect efficiently controls firings of the neurons. Figure 3 shows an example time-series data of refractory effects of the CMS. The refractory effect suddenly increases after firing a neuron, then it gradually decreases with exponential decay.

To investigate the refractory effects of the chaotic neurons, we replaced the original refractory effect $\zeta_{ij}(t)$ by its possible surrogates [10] with which we tried to extract the motifs. The four surrogates are described as follows:

Case 1: Random time-series whose dynamic range is [0,1] (Fig.4(a)).
Case 2: Random time-series whose dynamic range is same as the original $\zeta_{ij}(t)$ (Fig.4(b)).
Case 3: Random shuffled time-series of $\zeta_{ij}(t)$ (Fig.4(d)).
Case 4: Random shuffling of exponentially decaying short segments between two successive firing timings in $\zeta_{ij}(t)$ (Fig.4(e)).

Results of computer simulations are summarized in Table 1. From Table 1, Case 1 and Case 2 cannot extract the motif. The low performance of Case 1 may come from a different dynamic range from $\zeta_{ij}(t)$. However, we cannot extract motif with Case 2, whose dynamic range is same as that of the original refractory effects of CMS. Another possible hypothesis is that frequency histograms of Case 1 and Case 2 described above is different from that of the original $\zeta_{ij}(t)$, because the surrogate series are produced randomly. Then, we try to extract motifs by introducing a constraint: the surrogate time-series has the same frequency histogram as $\zeta_{ij}(t)$. Then, we randomly shuffled temporal indices of the original $\zeta_{ij}(t)$ (Case 3). This approach, however, cannot extract the motif again.

The most different point between the surrogate refractory effects of Cases 1, 2 and 3 and the original $\zeta_{ij}(t)$ is now clear: The original $\zeta_{ij}(t)$ has exponential decay parts between successive firing timings. The values of the original $\zeta_{ij}(t)$ recover exponentially with time. On the other hand, the surrogate refractory effects described above do not show such behavior. It may be important to weaken the value of the refractoriness gradually. To investigate this effect, we made the fourth surrogate. In the fourth surrogate (Case 4), exponential decay segments in the original $\zeta_{ij}(t)$ are identified and are randomly shuffled (Fig.1(e))). However, the motif cannot be found even by this method (Table 1).

The firing rates of Cases 1, 2, 3, and 4 ($\beta = 12.0$) and the original are different. In order to increase the firing rate, we change the value of β. As a result, although the firing rates of the neurons increase ($\beta = 8.0$), these cases cannot extract the motifs. Thus, the low performance does not originate from the low firing rates. The results indicate that the refractory series of the above methods cannot effectively control the neurons. This is attributed to the fact that the strength of these surrogate refractory effects do not increase after firings of neurons, because

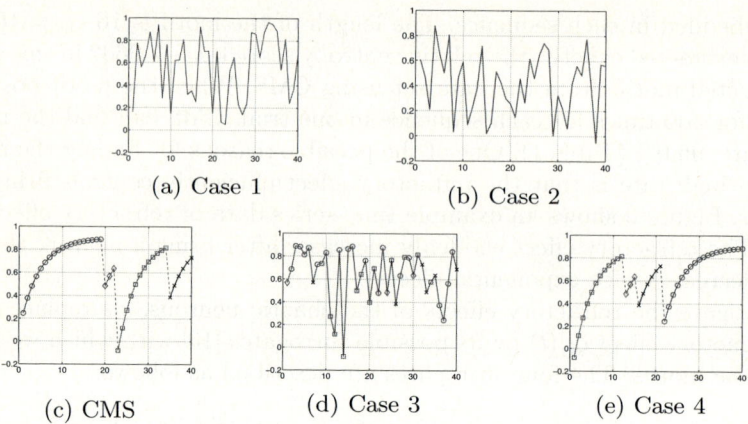

Fig. 4. Examples of time-series of $\zeta_{ij}(t)$

they are decided without relation to states of the neurons. It may be important to strengthen the refractory effects after firings of neurons.

In the CMS, parameter α controls strength of the refractory effects after the firing. Then, to investigate the refractory effects of post firings of the neurons, we tried to extract the motifs by replacing Eq.(2) by the following three cases:

Case 5: $\zeta_{ij}(t+1) = -U(t)x_{ij}(t) + k_r\zeta_{ij}(t) + \theta(1-k_r)$, where $U(t)$ is a uniform random number whose dynamic range is $[0,1]$.

Case 6: $\zeta_{ij}(t+1) = -U'_{ij}(t)x_{ij}(t) + k_r\zeta_{ij}(t) + \theta(1-k_r)$, where $U'_{ij}(t)$ is a uniform random number whose dynamic range is same as $R_{ij}(n)$. Here, $R_{ij}(n)$ is the n-th value of the strength of refractory effects after the n-th firing of the (i,j)-th neuron in the CMS (Fig. 5).

Case 7: $\zeta_{ij}(t+1) = -R'_{ij}(n)x_{ij}(t) + k_r\zeta_{ij}(t) + \theta(1-k_r)$, where $R'_{ij}(n)$ is a random shuffled time-series of $R_{ij}(n)$ (Fig. 5).

At first, we extracted the motif in Case 5. Although the firing rate of the neurons is the same as the CMS, Case 5 cannot extract the motifs. This low performance may come from a difference in the strength of refractoriness. Thus, we extracted the motif with refractoriness whose dynamic range is same as the range of the CMS (Case 6). As a result, we can find the motifs with very high performance 94.0% (Table 1). The result of Case 6 indicates that if we use the same frequency histogram of $R_{ij}(n)$ as the original CMS, the success rate becomes closer to the CMS. In addition, we also introduce the random shuffled time-series of $R_{ij}(n)$, denoted by $R'_{ij}(n)$ (Case 7). As a result, we can get almost the same performance with Case 6. The results of Cases 6 and 7 indicate that it is important to increase the refractory effect after firing of the neuron with a proper strength.

4 Conclusions

In this paper, we examined the refractory effect, probably a simple mechanism of memorizing the past searching history, to the motif extraction problems by

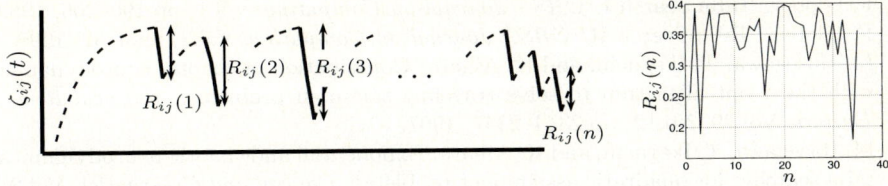

Fig. 5. Schematic representation of refractory effect time-series of $R_{ij}(n)$ in the CMS

Table 1. Solving performance of CMS, and the surrogate refractory effects. Numerals are average probabilities for finding motifs, and firing rates of the neurons in 100 trials(%).

Refractory effect	Success rate (%) / Firing rate of neurons (%)	
CMS	96.0 / 13.4117	
	$\beta = 12.0$	$\beta = 8.0$
Case 1	4.0 / 8.3438	10.0 / 13.6525
Case 2	6.0 / 7.2327	6.0 / 12.4478
Case 3	8.0 / 4.8701	4.0 / 11.5785
Case 4	6.0 / 4.7689	8.0 / 11.3286
Case 5	17.0 / 13.5295	
Case 6	94.0 / 12.7001	
Case 7	94.0 / 13.4910	

CMS. As a result, the motifs can be found in case that dynamic range of strength of refractory effects after the corresponding neuron fires is same as the CMS. The results indicate that the refractory effect after firing of a neuron is an important factor. However we cannot find the motif if we set the strength too strong. It is important to set appropriate amount of the strength.

The authors thank K.Aihara, Y.Horio, M. Adachi, N. Ichinose, M. Hasegawa and R.Hosaka, for their valuable comments and discussions. This research was partially supported by Grant-in-Aids for Scientific Research on Priority Areas (Genome Information Science, No.15014101) from the Ministry of Education, Culture, Sports, Science and Technology and for Scientific Research (B) (No.16300072) from the Japan Society for the Promoion of Science.

References

1. "http://contest.genome.ad.jp/2003/".
2. K. Aihara, T. Takebe, and M. Toyoda. Chaotic neural networks. *Physics Letters A*, Vol.144, 1990.
3. T. Akutsu, H. Arimura, and S. Shimozono. On approximation algorithms for local multiple alignment. *Proceedings of the Fourth International Conference on Computational Molecular Biology*, pp.1–7, 2000.

4. F. Glober. Tabu Search I. *ORSA Journal on Computing*, Vol.1, pp.190–206, 1989.
5. F. Glober. Tabu Search II. *ORSA Journal on Computing*, Vol.2, pp.4–32, 1990.
6. M. Hasegawa, T. Ikeguchi, and K. Aihara. Combination of chaotic neurodynamics with the 2-opt algorithm to solve traveling salesman problems. *Physical Review Lettters*, Vol.79, No.12, pp.2344–2347, 1997.
7. M. Hasegawa, T. Ikeguchi, and K. Aihara. Exponential and chaotic neurodynamical tabu searches for quadratic assignment problems. *Control and Cybernetics*, Vol.29, No.3, pp.773–788, 2000.
8. M. Hasegawa, T. Ikeguchi, and K. Aihara. A novel chaotic search for quadratic assignment problems. *European Journal of Operational Research*, Vol.139, No.3, pp.543–556, 2002.
9. M. Hasegawa, T. Ikeguchi, and K. Aihara. Solving large scale traveling salesman problems by chaotic neurondynamics. *Neural Networks*, Vol.15, No.2, pp.271–283, 2002.
10. H.Kantz and T.Schrieber. Nonlinear time series analysis. *Cambridge university press*, 2003.
11. C. E. Lawrence, S. F. Altschul, M. S. Boguski, J. S. Liu, A. F. Neuwald, and J. C. Wootton. Detecting subtle sequence signals: A gibbs sampling strategy for multiple alignment. *Science*, Vol.262, pp.208–214, October 1993.
12. T. Matsuura, T. Anzai, T. Ikeguchi, Y. Horio, M. Hasegawa, and N. Ichinose. A tabu search for extracting motifs from dna sequences. *Proceedings of 2004 RISP international Workshop on Nonlinear Civcuits and Signal Processing*, pp.347–350, 2004.
13. T. Matsuura and T. Ikeguchi. A tabu search and chaotic search for extracting motifs from dna sequences. *Procceedings of the Sixth Metaheuristics International Conference 2005*, pp.677–682, 2005.

Neighborhood-Based Clustering of Gene-Gene Interactions

Norberto Díaz–Díaz, Domingo S. Rodríguez–Baena,
Isabel Nepomuceno, and Jesús S. Aguilar–Ruiz

BioInformatics Group Seville; Seville and Pablo de Olavide University. Spain
{ndiaz, dsavio, isabel}@lsi.us.es, jsagurui@upo.es

Abstract. In this work, we propose a new greedy clustering algorithm to identify groups of related genes. Clustering algorithms analyze genes in order to group those with similar behavior. Instead, our approach groups pairs of genes that present similar positive and/or negative interactions. Our approach presents some interesting properties. For instance, the user can specify how the range of each gene is going to be segmented (labels). Some of these will mean expressed or inhibited (depending on the gradation). From all the label combinations a function transforms each pair of labels into another one, that identifies the type of interaction. From these pairs of genes and their interactions we build clusters in a greedy, iterative fashion, as two pairs of genes will be similar if they have the same amount of relevant interactions. Initial two–genes clusters grow iteratively based on their neighborhood until the set of clusters does not change. The algorithm allows the researcher to modify all the criteria: discretization mapping function, gene–gene mapping function and filtering function, and provides much flexibility to obtain clusters based on the level of precision needed.

The performance of our approach is experimentally tested on the yeast dataset. The final number of clusters is low and genes within show a significant level of cohesion, as it is shown graphically in the experiments.

1 Introduction

In any biologic process, cells and genes in particular play an important role which can be measured by their different levels of expression. These levels depend on the type of process, on the stage, and on the experimental condition that is analyzed. The knowledge about these, under a specific situation, helps to understand the function that genes play in a particular biological process.

Current works accomplished by researchers in the Bioinformatic field, like SAGE [1] for measuring gene expression, or like [2, 3] to store this gene expression in structure denominated microarray, make possible the simultaneous study of numerous genes under different conditions. Many different approaches have been applied to analyze this structure, including principal component analysis [4] as well as supervised [5] and unsupervised [6–10] learning. In unsupervised learning, clustering techniques are used to identify groups of genes that show the same expression pattern under different conditions.

[6] applied the k–means algorithm to find clusters in yeast data. In [7] graph–theoretic and statistical techniques were used to identify tight groups of highly similar elements. In [8] a memetic algorithm is presented, i.e., a genetic algorithm combined with local search -based on a tree representation of the data - for clustering gene expression data. With this aim, in [9] is explored a novel type of gene–sample–time microarray data sets, which records the expression levels of various genes under a set of samples during a series of time points. Even evolutionary algorithm [10] have been used to discover clusters in gene expression data.

All of these methods are based on the idea of grouping those genes that show the same behavior. In this work, we propose a novel clustering algorithm to identify groups of related genes based on the idea of clustering pair of genes which present the same type of interaction.

In broad outlines, the remainder of the paper is organized as follows. In section 2, the characteristics of our approach are detailed. Later in Section 3, we describe the results of our experiments. Finally, the most interesting conclusions are summarized in Section 4.

2 Description

The algorithm presented in this paper can be divided into four steps: encoding of each gene expression (*segmentation*), representation of the interaction of every two genes (*gene–gene interaction*), filtering of most representative interactions (*filtering*), and clustering interactions (*neighborhood–based clustering*). The overall approach, named INTERCLUS, is illustrated in Algorithm 1. Each step represents a line of code in the algorithm.

Algorithm 1. INTERCLUS

INPUT M: microarray (*Conditions,Genes*)
Ω: alphabet of discretization
α: discretization mapping
Π: alphabet of interactions
β: interactions mapping
F: Filter
OUTPUT S: Set of Clusters
begin
  M'=Segmentation(M,Ω,α)
  M''=Encoding_Gene–Gene_Interactions(M',Π,β)
  L=Filtering(M'',F,Π)
  S=Build_Set_of_Clusters(L)
end

The first three steps of the process are depicted in Figure 1. Each of these steps is described in detail in the next subsections. In addition, the last step, neighborhood–based clustering is also explained.

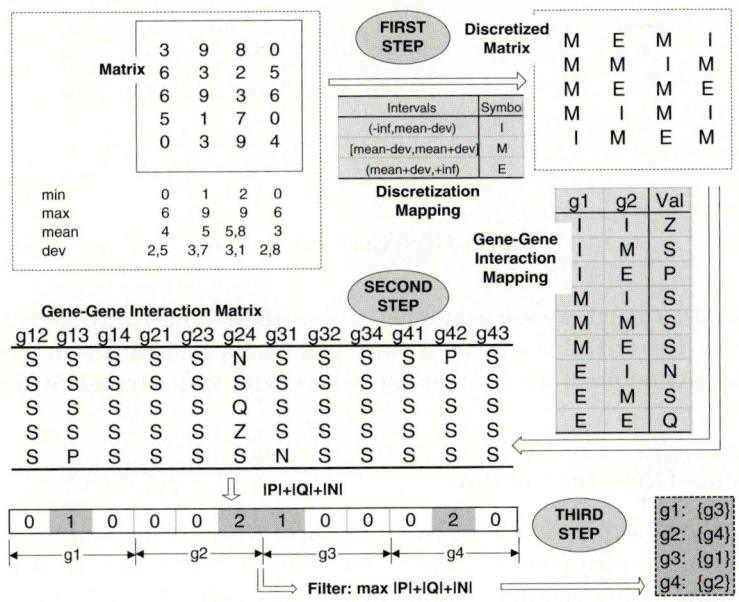

Fig. 1. First three steps of Algorithm 1. First step: definition of the discretization mapping function to obtain a discretized matrix. Second step: definition of the gene–gene interaction mapping function to obtain the gene–gene interaction matrix. Third step: selection of gene–gene interactions that satisfy the filtering criterion.

2.1 Segmentation

The first step addresses the segmentation of each gene expression level. Due to the fact these levels are represented by numerical values, the segmentation is done by discretizing the range of values. In this way, different labels are obtained according to the gene expression level under particular stimulus (experimental condition). However, the discretization is local, i.e., the same expression level for two different genes might transform into different labels.

To carry out the discretization, we need to define an alphabet Ω, which is used to provide labels for the mapping, and a mapping function α, which is used to assign labels from Ω to the numerical values. The definition of Ω and α is provided by the user: characters for Ω and a discretization mapping table for α, in which the user can also make use of symbols ∞, μ and σ, standing for *infinite*, *mean* and *standard deviation*. Any expression that uses these special symbols is valid, together with arithmetical operators and numbers. For instance, in Figure 1, the first step transforms the gene expression level matrix into a discretized matrix by using the discretization mapping α, defined over a three–symbol alphabet $\Omega = \{I, M, E\}$. If the gene expression level is in $(-\infty, \mu - \sigma)$ then the label "I" is assigned (inhibited); if it is in $[\mu - \sigma, \mu + \sigma]$, then the label is "M" (medium); and finally, if it is in $(\mu + \sigma, +\infty)$, then "E" (expressed). An expression like $\mu + 2\sigma$ is also feasible, and any number of labels as well.

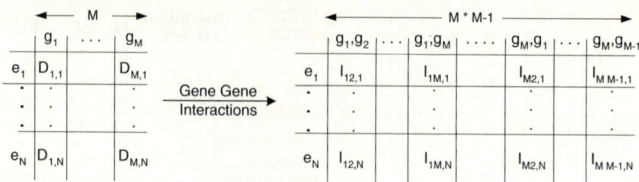

Fig. 2. Gene-Gene Interactions

Note that although we use values like μ or σ, these values are different for each gene, so the discretization is local. A value of 0.6 for a gene can mean "expressed", and perhaps "inhibited" for another one, where both states translate further into labels.

2.2 Gene–Gene Interaction

Once each gene expression level has been labelled, we will focus on the interaction between every pair of genes. Firstly, another alphabet Π is needed to assign a label to any possible combination of gene pairs. For example, we might be interested in differentiating the interaction *inhibited–expressed* from the interaction *expressed–expressed*. In general, the size of the set Π is, at maximum, the square of the size of the set Ω, although usually should be lower. In Figure 1, it is shown in the first step that $|\Omega| = 3$, and in the second step, the gene–gene interaction mapping has exactly 9 combinations, but the size of the alphabet Π is 5, corresponding to {Z,S,P,N,Q}. In this example, Z stands for *null*, S for *similar*, P for *positive*, N for *negative*, and Q for *both expressed*. The interaction mapping function β is also defined by the user, as a mapping table, $\beta : \Omega \times \Omega \to \Pi$.

As the microarray has M genes and N experiments, for each gene, $M - 1$ interactions with the remaining genes are needed. In short, there will be $M \times (M - 1)$ interactions, as it is illustrated in Figure 2. The left–hand side of Figure 2 represents the discretized matrix obtained after the first step, in which rows mean experiments and columns mean genes. The values D_{ij} of a specific row and column are discrete, belonging to the alphabet Ω. To the right, any possible pair of different genes is enumerated in columns. In general, gene i can interact with other $M - 1$ genes. The value $I_{ij,k}$ of a row k and a column represents the symbol from the alphabet Π obtained after analyzing the two genes i and j involved in the interaction under the experiment k.

The new matrix M'' encodes the information of all possible interactions, although not every one might be interesting. For example, in Figure 1, we see in the table generated by the second step that many columns have only the symbol "S", which means similar, i.e., there is no significant up– or down–regulation in this case. The first column shows that genes 1 and 2 have similar behavior, so its interaction is not relevant. In this way, we might withdraw much irrelevant information if we were able to select the most interesting patterns in columns. That is the aim of the third step, described in the next subsection.

Algorithm 2. STEP–3 Filtering

INPUT M'': Interaction Matrix
F: Filter
Π: alphabet of interactions
OUTPUT L_F: List of gene subsets
begin
  $L_F := \{\}$
  for all pair of gene (g_i, g_j) with $i \neq j$ **do**
    $S_e := \{\}$
    for all experiment e_k **do**
      $S_e := S_e + I_{ij,k}$
    end for
    $S'_e := Filter(S_e, F)$
    $L_F := L_F + S'_e$
  end for
end

2.3 Filtering

The fact that two genes are inhibited under most or all of the experimental conditions, has no biological importance. Therefore, this situation can be easily ignored. When two genes are both expressed under most or all of the experimental conditions, that might have biological meaning. In fact, many studies only focus on this aspect: the interaction expressed–expressed. In this work, we are also interested in other cases: for example, when most of the time an inhibited gene is related to an expressed gene, and vice verse. And this situation is especially interesting when the complementary is true as well, i.e., if gene 1 is expressed then gene 2 is inhibited and if gene 1 is inhibited then gene 2 is expressed. The last situation is more difficult to detect and is one of the main goals in this work.

Another interesting issue is that what means "most of the time" for a pair of genes may not have the same meaning for another pair. For example, in Figure 1 the gene 1 is related to genes 2, 3 and 4, in the first three columns. The most significant behavior is shown by the interaction 1–3, because for the last experiment the label is "P". However, if we analyze the gene 2 against genes 1, 3 and 4, the most significant behavior is shown by the interaction 2–4, because for the experiments 1 and 3 the labels are "N" and "Q", respectively. This gives some clues about the strength of interactions, and provides us a specific criterion for each gene regarding the remainder. Therefore, although the filtering function is global, the value provided by the filtering function might be different for each gene. That happens in Figure 1, in the third step, as gene 1 is related to gene 3 (the filter function value is 1), gene 2 is related to gene 4 (the filter function value is 2), etc. Note that if gene 2 were also related to gene 3 with filter function value equal to 1, this interaction will not be chosen as the maximum value for the filter function was 2.

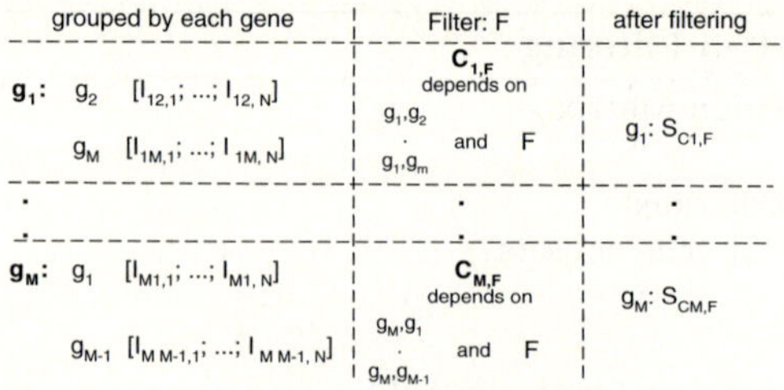

grouped by each gene	Filter: F	after filtering
g_1: g_2 $[I_{12,1}; ...; I_{12,N}]$ g_M $[I_{1M,1}; ...; I_{1M,N}]$	$C_{1,F}$ depends on g_1,g_2 . . . g_1,g_m and F	g_1: $S_{C1,F}$
. . .	. . .	. . .
g_M: g_1 $[I_{M1,1}; ...; I_{M1,N}]$ g_{M-1} $[I_{M M-1,1}; ...; I_{M M-1,N}]$	$C_{M,F}$ depends on g_M,g_1 . . . g_M,g_{M-1} and F	g_M: $S_{CM,F}$

Fig. 3. Filtering process

In Figure 3 is depicted the use of filtering, where $C_{i,F}$ denotes the conditions established for the g_i–interactions using the filter F, and $S_{C_{i,F}}$ represents the subset of genes whose interactions satisfy the condition $C_{i,F}$. As explained earlier, for the example in Figure 1, the condition $C_{1,F}$ would be $max(|P|+|Q|+|N|) = 1$, but $C_{2,F}$ would be $max(|P|+|Q|+|N|) = 2$.

The filtering algorithm is illustrated in Algorithm 2, where L_F denotes the list of all the subsets $S_{C_{i,F}}$. That is, $L_F = \{S_{C_{1,F}}, S_{C_{2,F}}, ..., S_{C_{M,F}}\}$. After this process, the filtering algorithm will generate the list of subsets of genes related to each one, if exists. In Figure 1 is provided, in the third step, the list of four subsets of genes, each of them with only one gene, by using the filter $max(|P|+|Q|+|N|)$.

Also, in this filtering process is possible to establish a minimum threshold. This value will have been satisfied for each $C_{i,F}$, so that if the condition established for g_i-interactions do not satisfy it, $S_{C_{i,F}}$ will be empty and, therefore, it will not be part of L_F. In this way, we manage to give greater power to the filter function, since it is possible to select those gene interactions that fulfil the filtering criterion a minimum number of times.

Note that it does not make sense to establish this threshold in a value greater than the number of experiments of the original dataset, because all of the $S_{C_{i,F}}$ subsets will be empty, and so, the L_F list as well.

2.4 Neighborhood–Based Clustering

Once the relevant interactions between each pair of genes have been obtained, it is time to cluster them. The clustering algorithm, named SNN (Similar Nearest Neighbor), is based on the similarity of groups, instead of analyzing pairs of elements. It builds clusters by grouping genes whose neighbors are similar. SNN stars considering each gene as a separate cluster and at each step merges clusters which have exactly the same neighbors. Thus, the concept of neighborhood is redefined to handle correctly with clusters of neighbors.

Definition 1 (Neighborhood of a gene). *The neighborhood $N_g(i, F)$ of a gene g_i using the Filter F, is the set of genes whose amount of relevant interactions with regards to the gene i fulfils the condition $C_{i,F}$.*

$$N_g(g_i) = S_{C_i} \qquad (1)$$

Algorithm 3. STEP–4 SNN

INPUT L_F: List of gene subsets
OUTPUT RSC: Set of Clusters
begin
  $SC := \theta$
  for all gene g_i **do**
    $RSC[i] := \{g_i\}$
  end for
  repeat
    for all cluster $C_h \in RSC, 1 \leq h \leq |RSC|$ **do**
      $NSC[h] := N_c(C_h)$
    end for
    $SC := RSC$
    $RSC := Reduction(SC, NSC)$
  until $SC = RSC$
end

Algorithm 4. Reduction

INPUT C: Set of Cluster
  NSC: Neighbor Set of Cluster
OUTPUT R: Reduced set of clusters
begin
  $R := C$
  for all pair (i, j), with $1 \leq i \leq j \leq |C|$ **do**
    if $S[i] = S[j]$ **then**
      $R[i] := R[i] \bigcup C[j]$
      remove $R[j]$
    end if
  end for
end

Definition 2 (Neighborhood of a cluster). *The neighborhood $N_c(C, F)$ of a cluster c (cluster neighborhood) using the Filter F, is the set formed by all the neighborhoods of each gene belonging to the cluster C.*

$$N_c(C) = \bigcup_{g \in C} N_g(g) \qquad (2)$$

Once every necessary definition to support the algorithm at this step have been presented, we will describe the code depicted in Algorithm 3. The input parameter is L_F, containing in each position i the neighbors of g_i. And the output parameter is RSC, the reduced set of clusters, where each one comprises a group of genes. SC is an auxiliary set of clusters and RSC is initially set with clusters containing only one gene. The process is repeated until RSC has no change at an iteration. The neighborhood of every cluster is calculated in order to analyze the possible reduction of the set of cluster, task done by the Reduction function

(Algorithm 4). The reduction of a set of cluster follows the next criterion: two clusters are joined if both have exactly the same neighborhood. We are aware of the restrictive character of this criterion and a relaxation of it is considered among our future research directions.

3 Experiments

In this section, we address the evaluation of the performance of our approach, which is experimentally tested on the yeast dataset [6]. This dataset has information on 2884 genes under 17 different experimental conditions.

In Table 1 it is shown the discretization mapping. The symbols μ_i and σ_i denote the mean and the standard deviation, respectively, of the expression levels of g_i under the whole set of experiments. Thus, the g_i expression level under e_k will be labelled as **I** (inhibited) if it belongs to $(-\infty, \mu_i + \sigma_i)$, or as **E** (expressed) if it belongs to $[\mu_i + \sigma_i, +\infty)$.

The alphabet Π, used to encode each pair of gene–gene interaction, and the interaction mapping function β are shown in Table 2. Highly relevant interactions are those where genes change their state from inhibited to expressed (P) or from expressed to inhibited (N).

The interaction encoded as Z means that the gene does not take part in the experiment, and the interaction encoded as S means that there is no visible influence on each other. Thus, the used filter aims to select those interactions in which the highest number of P and N is reached. For this dataset we will establish a threshold value equal to 14 (note that 17 is the maximum). In this way, we will manage to select those gene–gene interactions which change their state from inhibited to expressed or from expressed to inhibited in at least 14 of the 17 experiments. With this filter, those genes whose interaction with others are P or N are selected, and those whose interaction is S or N are not. These two last interactions might be chosen as well, although not because of their biological relevance, but to make possible the comparison of the clusters obtained by using the filter *highest(P,N)*. Thus, the INTERCLUS process will be repeated three times with the same configuration but with different filter functions. These filters will be *highest(P,N)*, *highest(Z)* and *highest(S)*, respectively. However, we do not show the cluster obtained with *highest(Z)* because of its lack of biological interest.

The results obtained using our approach over the yeast dataset has been shown in Table 3, in which it is shown the five clusters with the highest size for each filter function. These clusters are ordered decreasingly according to their sizes. The dimension of each cluster will be shown at column "Size". The other column, "Number", represents the number of clusters which have been obtained

Table 1. Disretization mapping α

Intervals	Ω
$(-\infty, \mu_i + \sigma_i)$	I
$[\mu_i + \sigma_i, +\infty)$	E

Table 2. Gene–Gene Interaction Mapping Function β

$\Omega \times \Omega$		Π
I	I	Z
I	E	P
E	I	N
E	E	S

Table 3. Results obtained using the yeast dataset

	F_1 =Highest(Z)		F_2 =Highest(P,N)		F_3 =Highest(S)	
	Number	Size	Number	Size	Number	Cluster
1°	1	164	1	89	1	5
2°	1	116	1	2	-	-
3°	1	84	-	-	-	-
4°	1	54	-	-	-	-
5°	1	45	-	-	-	-

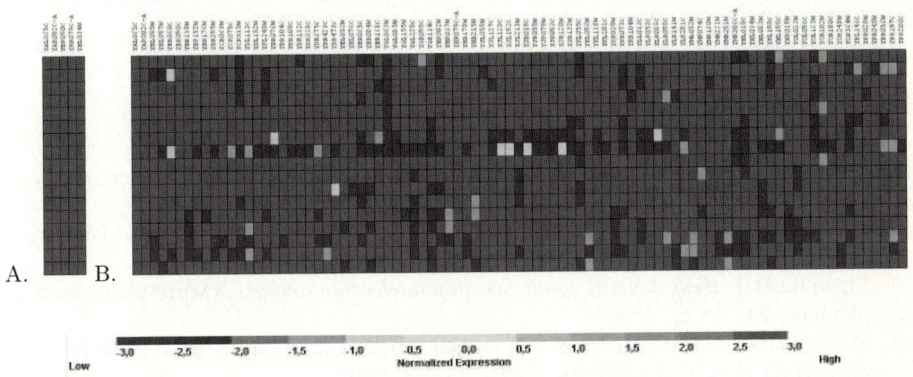

Fig. 4. A. Cluster (5 genes) using F_3 =Highest(S); **B.** Cluster (89 genes) using F_2 =Highest(P,N).

with that size. The symbol "-" means that no cluster has been found with at least two genes. For example, the size of the bigger cluster obtained using F_1 is 164 genes, using F_2 is 89 genes and 5 using the filter F_3. The next clusters found with these filters (second row) have been one with 116 genes, one with 2 genes and none, respectively.

We will show two examples of clusters. Figure 4.A shows the first cluster (5 genes) obtained with F_3 =Highest(S). Obviously all of the genes are highly expressed. Figure 4.B shows the first cluster (89 genes) obtained with F_2 =Highest(P,N). In this case, we are mainly interested in the interactions that lead to changes in the regulation, from inhibited to expressed and vice versa. These expression levels are encoded using the *GenePattern* tools [11]. For each gene under one experimental condition is generated a color which represents the expression level for this pair gene–experiment. The meaning of this colors is depicted at the bottom in Figure 4. A preprocessing of the expression level (standardization and normalization by column) was carried out in order to draw the clusters using using regular levels of blue (inhibited) and red (expressed).

Figure 4 shows that each cluster groups genes with very similar behavior pattern, as the colors are almost alike.

4 Conclusions

In this work, we propose a new greedy clustering algorithm to identify groups of related genes. The approach is based on neighborhood of gene–gene interactions instead of on expression levels. One of the main features is that the algorithm allows the researcher to modify all the criteria: discretization mapping function, gene–gene mapping function and filtering function, and provides much flexibility to obtain clusters based on the level of precision needed. The performance of our approach is experimentally tested on the yeast dataset. The final number of clusters is low and genes within show a significant level of cohesion, as it is shown graphically in the experiments.

References

1. Velculescu, V.E. *Characterization of the yeast transcriptome.* Cell, **88**, 243-251,1997
2. Schena, M. (1996) *Genome analysis with gene expression microarray.* Bioessaya, **18**, 427-431, 1996
3. Lipshutz,R.J *High density synthesis oligonucleotide arrays,* Nature Genetics Supplement, **21**, 20-24, 2000
4. K.Y. Yeung and W.L. Ruzzo *Principal component analysis for clustering gene expression data* Bioinformatics, **17**, 763-774, 2001
5. T.R. Golub, D.K. Slonim, P. Tamayo, C. Huard, M. Gaasenbeed, J.P. Mesirov, H. Coller, M.L. Loh, F.R. Downing, M.A. Caliguri, C.d. *Molecular classification of cancer: Class discovery by gene expression monitoring* Science, **286**, 531-537,1999
6. S. Tavazoie, J.D. Hughes, M.J. Campbell, R.J. Cho, and G.M. Church *Systematic determination of genetic network architecture* Nature Genetics, **22**, 281-285, 1999
7. R Sharan and R Shamir *CLICK: A clustering Algorithm for Gene Expression Analysis* Proc Int Conf Intell Syst Mol Biol, **8**, 307-316, 2000
8. N. Speer and P. Merz and C. Spieth and A. Zell *Clustering Gene Expression Data with Memetic Algorithms based on Minimum Spanning Trees* IEEE Press, **3**, 1848-1855, 2003
9. Daxin Jiang, Jian Pei, Murali Ramanathan, Chung Tang, and Aidong Zhang *Mingin Coherent Gene Clusters from Gene-Sample-Time Microarray Data* KDD, 430-439, 2004
10. Patrick C.H. Ma, and Keith C.C. Chan *Discovering Clusters in Gene Expression Data using Evolutionary Approach* ICTAI, 459-466, 2003
11. http://www.broad.mit.edu/cancer/software /genepattern/

Gene Expression Profiling Using Flexible Neural Trees

Yuehui Chen[1], Lizhi Peng[1], and Ajith Abraham[1,2]

[1] School of Information Science and Engineering
Jinan University, Jinan 250022, P.R. China
yhchen@ujn.edu.cn
[2] IITA Professorship Program, School of Computer Science and Engg.
Chung-Ang University, Seoul, Republic of Korea
ajith.abraham@ieee.org

Abstract. This paper proposes a Flexible Neural Tree (FNT) model for informative gene selection and gene expression profiles classification. Based on the pre-defined instruction/operator sets, a flexible neural tree model can be created and evolved. This framework allows input variables selection, over-layer connections and different activation functions for the various nodes involved. The FNT structure is developed using the Extended Compact Genetic Programming and the free parameters embedded in the neural tree are optimized by particle swarm optimization algorithm. Empirical results on two well-known cancer datasets shows competitive results with existing methods.

1 Introduction

The classification of cancers from gene expression profiles is actively investigated in bioinformatics. It commonly consists of feature selection and pattern classification. In advance, feature selection selects informative features useful to categorize a sample into predefined classes from lots of gene expression profiles. Pattern classification is composed of learning a classifier with those features and categorizing samples with the classifier.

Much research effort has been devoted to exploring the informative gene selection from microarray data. Typical effective feature reduction methods include principal components analysis (PCA), class-separability measure, Fisher ratio and t-test. Evolutionary based feature selection methods are alternatives of the gene selection approaches. A probabilistic model building genetic algorithm based informative selection method was proposed in [1]. Genetic programming can be also used to select informative gene and classification of gene expression profiles [2]. After the gene selection was performed, many candidate classifiers can be employed for classification of microarray data, including Bayesian network, KNN, neural networks, support vector machine [12], random forest [4] etc.. For a recent review, the reader is refer to ref. [3]. Classification algorithms that directly provide measures of variable importance are of great interest for gene selection, specially if the classification algorithm itself presents features that make it well suited for the types of problems frequently faced with microarray data. Random forest is one such algorithm [4]. The proposed FNT method is another alternative.

This papers proposes a Flexible Neural Tree (FNT) [5][6] for selecting the input variables and forecasting exchange rates. Based on the pre-defined instruction/operator sets, a flexible neural tree model can be created and evolved. FNT allows input variables selection, over-layer connections and different activation functions for different nodes. In our previous work, the hierarchical structure was evolved using Probabilistic Incremental Program Evolution algorithm (PIPE) with specific instructions. In this research, the hierarchical structure is evolved using the Extended Compact Genetic Programming (ECGP), a tree-structure based evolutionary algorithm. The fine tuning of the parameters encoded in the structure is accomplished using particle swarm optimization (PSO). The proposed method interleaves both optimizations. Starting with random structures and corresponding parameters, it first tries to improve the structure and then as soon as an improved structure is found, it fine tunes its parameters. It then goes back to improving the structure again and, fine tunes the structure and rules' parameters. This loop continues until a satisfactory solution is found or a time limit is reached. The novelty of this paper is in the usage of flexible neural tree model for selecting the informative genes and for classification of microarray data.

2   The Flexible Neural Tree Model

The function set F and terminal instruction set T used for generating a FNT model are described as $S = F \bigcup T = \{+_2, +_3, \ldots, +_N\} \bigcup \{x_1, \ldots, x_n\}$, where $+_i(i = 2, 3, \ldots, N)$ denote non-leaf nodes' instructions and taking i arguments. $x_1, x_2, \ldots, x_n$ are leaf nodes' instructions and taking no other arguments. The output of a non-leaf node is calculated as a flexible neuron model (see Fig.1). From this point of view, the instruction $+_i$ is also called a flexible neuron operator with i inputs.

In the creation process of neural tree, if a nonterminal instruction, i.e., $+_i(i = 2, 3, 4, \ldots, N)$ is selected, i real values are randomly generated and used for representing the connection strength between the node $+_i$ and its children. In addition, two adjustable parameters a_i and b_i are randomly created as flexible activation function parameters. For developing the forecasting model, the flexible activation function $f(a_i, b_i, x) = e^{-(\frac{x - a_i}{b_i})^2}$ is used. The total excitation of $+_n$ is $net_n = \sum_{j=1}^{n} w_j * x_j$, where $x_j(j = 1, 2, \ldots, n)$ are the inputs to node $+_n$. The output of the node $+_n$ is then calculated by $out_n = f(a_n, b_n, net_n) = e^{-(\frac{net_n - a_n}{b_n})^2}$. The overall output of flexible neural tree can be computed from left to right by depth-first method, recursively.

2.1   Tree Structure Optimization

Finding an optimal or near-optimal neural tree is formulated as a product of evolution. In our previous studies, the Genetic Programming (GP) and Probabilistic

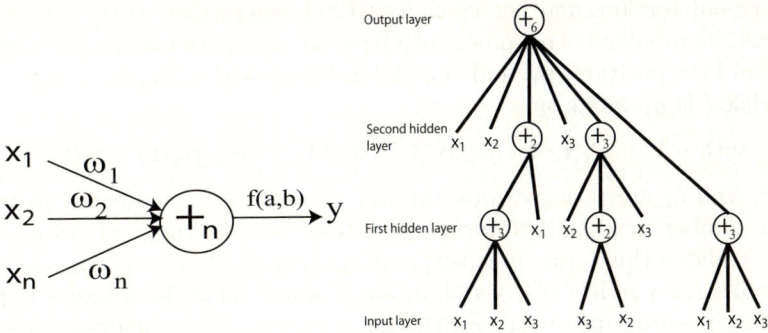

Fig. 1. A flexible neuron operator (left), and a typical representation of the FNT with function instruction set $F = \{+_2, +_3, +_4, +_5, +_6\}$, and terminal instruction set $T = \{x_1, x_2, x_3\}$ (right)

Incremental Program Evolution (PIPE) have been explored for structure optimization of the FNT [5][6]. In this paper, the Extended Compact Genetic Programming (ECGP) [7] is employed to find an optimal or near-optimal FNT structure.

ECGP is a direct extension of ECGA to the tree representation which is based on the PIPE prototype tree. In ECGA, Marginal Product Models (MPMs) are used to model the interaction among genes, represented as random variables, given a population of Genetic Algorithm individuals. MPMs are represented as measures of marginal distributions on partitions of random variables. ECGP is based on the PIPE prototype tree, and thus each node in the prototype tree is a random variable. ECGP decomposes or partitions the prototype tree into sub-trees, and the MPM factorises the joint probability of all nodes of the prototype tree, to a product of marginal distributions on a partition of its sub-trees. A greedy search heuristic is used to find an optimal MPM mode under the framework of minimum encoding inference. ECGP can represent the probability distribution for more than one node at a time. Thus, it extends PIPE in that the interactions among multiple nodes are considered.

2.2 Parameter Optimization with PSO

The Particle Swarm Optimization (PSO) conducts searches using a population of particles which correspond to individuals in evolutionary algorithm (EA) [9]. A population of particles is randomly generated initially. Each particle represents a potential solution and has a position represented by a position vector $\mathbf{x_i}$. A swarm of particles moves through the problem space, with the moving velocity of each particle represented by a velocity vector $\mathbf{v_i}$. At each time step, a function f_i representing a quality measure is calculated by using $\mathbf{x_i}$ as input. Each particle keeps track of its own best position, which is associated with the best fitness it has achieved so far in a vector $\mathbf{p_i}$. Furthermore, the best position among all the particles obtained so far in the population is kept track of as $\mathbf{p_g}$. In addition to this global version, another version of PSO keeps track of the best position among all the topological neighbors of a particle. At each time step t, by using the individual best position, $\mathbf{p_i}$, and the global best position, $\mathbf{p_g(t)}$, a new velocity for particle i is updated by

$$\mathbf{v_i(t+1)} = \mathbf{v_i(t)} + c_1\phi_1(\mathbf{p_i(t)} - \mathbf{x_i(t)}) + c_2\phi_2(\mathbf{p_g(t)} - \mathbf{x_i(t)}) \qquad (1)$$

where c_1 and c_2 are positive constant and ϕ_1 and ϕ_2 are uniformly distributed random number in [0,1]. The term $\mathbf{v_i}$ is limited to the range of $\pm\mathbf{v_{max}}$. If the velocity violates this limit, it is set to its proper limit. Changing velocity this way enables the particle i to search around its individual best position, $\mathbf{p_i}$, and global best position, $\mathbf{p_g}$. Based on the updated velocities, each particle changes its position according to the following equation:

$$\mathbf{x_i(t+1)} = \mathbf{x_i(t)} + \mathbf{v_i(t+1)}. \qquad (2)$$

2.3 Procedure of the General Learning Algorithm

The general learning procedure for constructing the FNT model can be described as follows.

1) Create an initial population randomly (FNT trees and its corresponding parameters);
2) Structure optimization is achieved by using the ECGP algorithm;
3) If a better structure is found, then go to step 4), otherwise go to step 2);
4) Parameter optimization is achieved by the PSO algorithm as described in subsection 2. In this stage, the architecture of FNT model is fixed, and it is the best tree developed during the end of run of the structure search. The parameters (weights and flexible activation function parameters) encoded in the best tree formulate a particle.
5) If the maximum number of local search is reached, or no better parameter vector is found for a significantly long time then go to step 6); otherwise go to step 4);
6) If satisfactory solution is found, then the algorithm is stopped; otherwise go to step 2).

2.4 Feature/Input Selection Using FNT

It is often a difficult task to select important variables for a forecasting or classification problem, especially when the feature space is large. A fully connected NN classifier usually cannot do this. In the perspective of FNT framework, the nature of model construction procedure allows the FNT to identify important input features in building a forecasting model that is computationally efficient and effective. The mechanisms of input selection in the FNT constructing procedure are as follows. (1) Initially the input variables are selected to formulate the FNT model with same probabilities; (2) The variables which have more contribution to the objective function will be enhanced and have high opportunity to survive in the next generation by a evolutionary procedure; (3) The evolutionary operators i.e., crossover and mutation, provide a input selection method by which the FNT should select appropriate variables automatically.

3 Cancer Classification Using FNT Paradigms

3.1 Data Sets

The colon cancer dataset contains gene expression information extracted from DNA microarrays [1]. The dataset consists of 62 samples in which 22 are normal samples and 40 are cancer tissue samples, each having 2000 features. We randomly choose 31 samples for training set and the remaining 31 samples were used as testing set. (http://sdmc.lit.org.sg/GEDatasets/Data/ColonTumor.zip). The leukemia dataset consists of 72 samples divided into two classes ALL and AML [14]. There are 47 ALL and 25 AML samples and each contains 7129 features. This dataset was divided into a training set with 38 samples (27 ALL and 11 AML) and a testing set with 34 samples (20 ALL and 14 AML) (Availble at: http://sdmc.lit.org.sgGEDatasets DataALL-AML_Leukemia.zip).

3.2 Colon Cancer

The data was randomly divided into a training set of 30 samples and testing set of 12 for 50 times, and our final results were averaged over these 30 independent trials (Fig. 2). A FNT model was constructed using the training data and then the model was used on the test data set. The instruction sets used to create an optimal FNT forecaster is $S = F \bigcup T = \{+_5, +_6, \ldots, +_9\} \bigcup \{x_0, x_1, \ldots, x_{1999}\}$. Where $x_i (i = 0, 1, \ldots, 1999)$ denotes the 2000 input variables (genes) of the classification model.

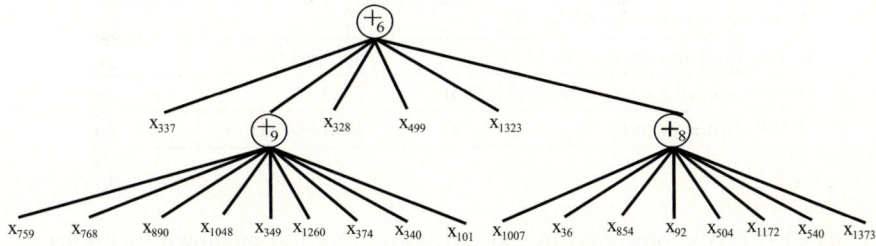

Fig. 2. An evolved best FNT for colon data classification

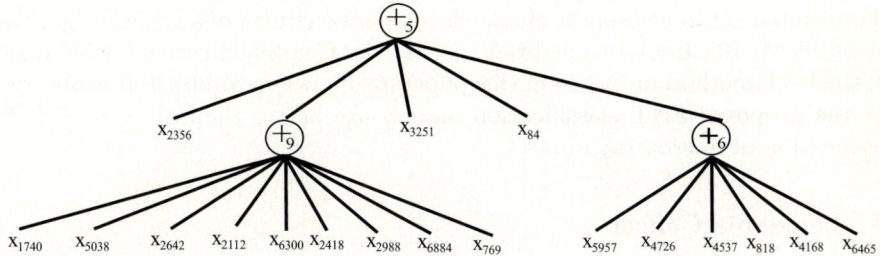

Fig. 3. An evolved best FNT for leukemia data classification

Table 1. The extracted informative genes in case of Colon dataset

$x_{337}, x_{328}, x_{759}, x_{768}, x_{890}, x_{1048}, x_{349}, x_{1260}, x_{374}, x_{340}, x_{101}, x_{499}, x_{1007}, x_{36}, x_{854}, x_{92}, x_{504}, x_{1172}, x_{540}, x_{1373}, x_{1323}$

Table 2. The extracted informative genes in case of leukemia dataset

$x_{2356}, x_{3251}, x_{1740}, x_{5038}, x_{2642}, x_{2112}, x_{6300}, x_{2418}, x_{2988}, x_{6884}, x_{769}, x_{5957}, x_{4726}, x_{4537}, x_{818}, x_{4168}, x_{6465}, x_{84}$

Table 3. The best prediction rate of some studies in case of Colon dataset

Classifier	Classification rate (%)
GA+SVM [10]	84.7± 9.1
Bootstrapped GA+SVM [11]	80.0
Combined kernel for SVM [12]	75.33±7.0
FNT (This paper)	97.09±0.018

Table 4. The best prediction rate of some studies in case of Colon dataset

Classifier	Classification rate (%)
Weighted voting [8]	94.1
Bootstrapped GA+SVM [11]	97.0
Combined kernel for SVM [12]	85.3±3.0
Multi-domain gating network [13]	75.0
FNT (This paper)	99.6±0.021

A best FNT tree obtained by the proposed method is shown in Figure 2. It should be noted that the important features for constructing the FNT model were formulated in accordance with the procedure mentioned in the previous section. These informative genes selected by FNT algorithm is shown in Table 1.

For comparison purpose, the classification performances of a genetic algorithm trained SVM [10], Bootstrapped GA+SVM [11], Combined kernel for SVM [12] and the FNT method proposed in this paper are shown in Tables 3. It is observed that the proposed FNT classification models are better than other models for classification of microarray dataset.

3.3 Leukemia Cancer

As mentioned in Sec. 3.1, the Leukemia dataset is already divided into training and testing set. To setup the 30 independent trials, A FNT model was constructed using the training data and then the model was used on the test data set. The instruction sets used to create an optimal FNT forecaster is $S = F \bigcup T = \{+_5, +_6, \ldots, +_9\} \bigcup \{x_0, x_1, \ldots, x_{7128}\}$. Where $x_i (i = 0, 1, \ldots, 7128)$ denotes the 7129 input variables (genes) of the classification model.

A best FNT tree obtained by the proposed method for leukemia cancer classification is shown in Figure 3. It should be noted that the important features for constructing the FNT model were formulated in accordance with the procedure mentioned in the previous section. These informative genes selected by FNT algorithm is shown in Table 2.

For comparison purposes, the classification performances of Weighted voting method [8], Bootstrapped GA+SVM [11], Combined kernel for SVM [12], Multi-domain gating network [13] and the FNT method proposed in this paper are shown in Table 4. It is observed that the proposed FNT classification models are better than other models for classification of microarray dataset.

4 Conclusions

In this paper, we presented a Flexible Neural Tree (FNT) model for informative gene selection and classification of microarray data simultaneously. We have demonstrated that the FNT classification model may provide better classifier than the other classification models. The experimental results also shown a significantly improvement in classification accuracy compare to other classifiers especially in case of Leukemia cancer dataset. This implies that the proposed FNT model can be used as a feasible solution for classification of microarray data.

Acknowledgment

This research was partially supported the Natural Science Foundation of China under contract number 60573065, and The Provincial Science and Technology Development Program of Shandong under contract number SDSP2004-0720-03.

References

1. Topon, K. P. and Hitoshi, I.: Gene Selection for Classification of Cancers using Probabilistic Model Building Genetic Algorithm. BioSystems 82(3)(2005) 208-225.
2. Hong, J.-H. and Cho, S.-B.: The classification of cancer based on DNA microarray data that uses diverse ensemble genetic programming. Artificial Intelligence in Medicine, 36 (2006) 43-58
3. Asyali, M.H., Colak, D., Demirkaya, O., Inan, M. S.: Gene Expression Profile Classification: A Review. Current Bioinformatics. 1 (2006) 55-73.
4. Ramn Daz-Uriarte and Sara Alvarez de Andrs: Gene selection and classification of microarray data using random forest. BMC Bioinformatics. 7 (2006) 3.
5. Chen, Y., Yang, B. and Dong, J.: Nonlinear System Modeling via Optimal Design of Neural Trees. International Journal of Neural Systems. 14 (2004) 125-137

6. Chen, Y., Yang, B., Dong, J. and Abraham, A.: Time-series Forecasting using Flexible Neural Tree Model. Information Science. 174 (2005) 219-235
7. Sastry, K. and Goldberg, D. E.: Probabilistic model building and competent genetic programming. In: R. L. Riolo and B. Worzel, editors, Genetic Programming Theory and Practise. (2003) 205-220
8. Golub, T. R., Slonim, D. K., Tamayo, P., Huard, C., Gaasenbeek, J. P., Mesirov, J., Coller, H., Loh, M. L., Downing, J.R., Caligiuri, M. A., Bloomfield, C. D., and Lander, E.: Mo-lecular Classification of Cancer: Class Discovery and Class Prediction by Gene Expression Monitoring, Science, vol. 286 (1999): 531-537.
9. Kennedy, J., Eberhart, R.: Particle Swarm Optimization. Proc. IEEE Int. Conf. on Neural Networks, Perth, (1995) 1492-1948.
10. Frohlich, H., Chapelle, O., and Scholkopf, B.: Feature Selection for Support Vector Ma-chines by Means of Genetic Algorithms, 15th IEEE International Conference on Tools with Artificial Intelligence (2003): 142
11. Chen, Xue-wen: Gene Selection for Cancer Classification Using Bootstrapped Genetic Algorithms and Support Vector Machines, IEEE Computer Society Bioinformatics Confer-ence (2003): 504
12. Nguyen, H.-N, Ohn, S.-Y, Park, J., and Park, K.-S.: Combined Kernel Function Approach in SVM for Diagnosis of Cancer, Proceedings of the First International Conference on Natural Computation (2005)
13. Su, T., Basu, M., Toure, A.: Multi-Domain Gating Network for Classification of Cancer Cells using Gene Expression Data, Proceedings of the International Joint Conference on Neural Networks (2002): 286-289
14. Alon, U., Barkai, N., Notterman, D., Gish, K., Ybarra, S., Mack, D., and Levine, A.: Broad Patterns of Gene Expression Revealed by Clustering Analysis of Tumor and Normal Colon Tissues Probed by Oligonucleotide Arrays, Proceedings of National Academy of Sciences of the United States of American, 96 (1999) : 6745-6750.

Multivariate Crosstalk Models

Natasha Young and Zheng Rong Yang

School of Engineering, Computer Science and Mathematics
University of Exeter, UK
N.Young@ex.ac.uk

Abstract. Since 1960s unexpected communication activity between signaling pathways and signaling molecules in cells has been very often observed. As there is no biological theory to interpret it, this activity has been termed as crosstalk, unwanted communication. So far, no computer or statistical models have been developed for modeling crosstalk between signaling proteins although studying crosstalk between signaling pathways in wet laboratory has been one of the main stream. As the first attempt in the world, we have investigated multivariate crosstalk models. The simulation shows that such statistical crosstalk models work very well although more investigations are needed.

Keywords: Multivariate models, crosstalk, systems biology.

1 Introduction

Over the past decades, many signaling molecules (proteins, lipids and ions) have been identified and the way through which they communicate via signaling pathways have been elucidated. Extracellular cues trigger multiple sequential events in which signaling proteins are physically and chemically modified; e.g. covalent modifications (phosphorylation), recruitment, allosteric activation or inhibition and binding of proteins; affect subsequent proteins and culminate in a specific phenotypic cellular response [1]. As more and more interactions between signaling pathways are identified, it has become apparent that signaling does not necessarily occur only in parallel linear pathways, but rather through a large and complex network of interacting signaling networks [2]. With signaling proteins from different pathways interacting directly (e.g. phosphorylation) or indirectly (e.g. via regulation of gene expression), it is now understood that interpathway *cross-talk* can reflect underlying complexities within a cellular signaling network causing the output of a signaling pathway to depend non-linearly on the input [3], [4].

Crosstalk is generally described in biochemistry and molecular biology as indirect influences between signaling pathways. The term encompasses positive and negative signaling, layered changes in gene expression and feedback between signaling proteins [5]. Crosstalk can also be described as specific interactions between proteins of more than one signaling pathway. Crosstalk events can be observed when there is a shared component between two or more different pathways or in protein-protein interactions. This general and specific description implies that crosstalk acts to balance signal specificity (e.g. one output for one specific input) and signal integration (e.g. one output for many inputs).

While to some researchers crosstalk is unwanted or insignificant exchange of information and specific crosstalk between signaling components are exciting but apparently rare, many biological experiments have documented and confirmed that inhibiting one signaling pathway may have a positive or negative influence on other signaling proteins in other pathways. Since 1960, biological studies of crosstalk have increased exponentially suggesting that crosstalk is an important phenomenon in cell signaling; which begs the question: to what extent does the consequence of crosstalk affect the robustness of a signaling cell. Fig 1 shows the number of published articles in PubMed since 1960.

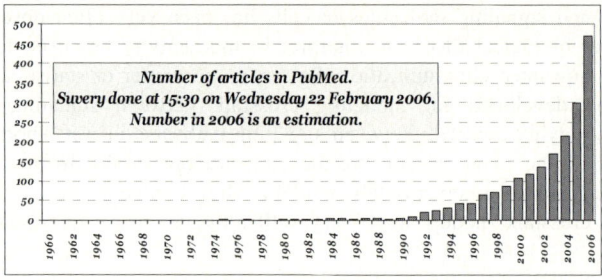

Fig. 1. Experimental studies on crosstalk since 1960 till date

Machine learning techniques have a rich history in bioinformatics studies. In recent research, machine learning methods have been applied to protein data to understand signal-response cascade relationships [6] and find casual relationships among biological pathways with success. They can represent complex non-linear relationships among multiple interacting molecules; they can accommodate noise which is inherent in biological data and describe statistically meaningful direct as well as indirect influences that proceed through addition unobserved components. As a motivating study, we test the use of linear systems to study potential crosstalk between proteins with a view of developing a sophisticated multivariate method for further in-depth study of crosstalk in cell signaling.

2 Methodology

2.1 Data

Quantitative experimental measurements of proteins – their levels, states, location and activity – is more challenging when relative to gene level measurements. The dataset employed in this study are intracellular multicolor flow cytometry measurements of phosphorylated proteins and phospholipids [6]. Flow cytometry data $is correlated and allows for the simultaneous quantitative measurement of the protein's expression level as well as measures of protein modification states such as phosphorylation. The datasets were created to analyse the crosstalk between proteins from one pathway (source proteins) with a protein from another pathway (target proteins). The proteins were studied under initial and inhibited conditions.

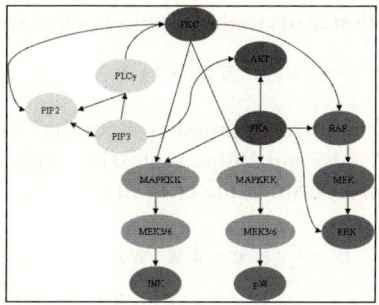

Fig. 2. A graphical illustration of conventionally accepted signalling molecule interactions

For the first study, we use as source proteins PKC (protein kinase C), PKA (protein kinase A), Raf-1, MEK and ERK and as the target protein p38. Stimulations are done on two datasets: (a) uninhibited data (853 data points) (b) inhibited data using MEK inhibitor U0126 (799 data points). For the second study, we use as source proteins: PKC (protein kinase C), Raf-1, MEK, PIP3 and Akt, and as the target protein we use ERK. Stimulations are done on two datasets: (a) uninhibited data (853 data points) (b) inhibited data with PI3K inhibitor LY294002 (848 data points).

2.2 Algorithms

In this study, we have employed three simple multivariate regression algorithms. They are least squares error regression [7], Lasso regression [8] and Ridge regression [9]. Denote the data set as $\mathcal{D} = \{\mathbf{x}_n, t_n\}_{1 \leq n \leq \ell}$, where $\mathbf{x}_n \in \mathrm{R}^d$ is the nth input vector (d is the dimensionality indicator) and $t_n \in \mathrm{R}$ is the nth target. Note that $\mathbf{x}_n$ is a collection of flow cytometry measurements for d phosphorylated source proteins in the nth cells and t_n is the flow cytometry measurements for the target protein in the nth cell. Because of many uncertainty factors, both $\mathbf{x}_n$ and t_n vary with cells. It is believed that there must be some quantitative relationship between $\mathbf{x}_n$ and t_n. A regression model is therefore defined as

$$\mathbf{y} = \mathbf{X}\mathbf{w} \qquad (1)$$

where $\mathbf{y} = (y_1, y_2, \cdots, y_\ell)^\mathrm{T}$ is the model output vector, $\mathbf{w} = (w_1, w_2, \cdots, w_d)^\mathrm{T}$ is the model weight vector and $\mathbf{X} = \{x_{nm}\}_{1 \leq n \leq \ell, 1 \leq m \leq d}$ is the input matrix. The error model can be defined as

$$\mathbf{e} = \mathbf{t} - \mathbf{y} \qquad (2)$$

where $\mathbf{e} = (e_1, e_2, \cdots, e_\ell)^\mathrm{T}$ is the error vector and $\mathbf{t} = (t_1, t_2, \cdots, t_\ell)^\mathrm{T}$ is the target vector. Using the least squares error regression algorithm, the error function is defined as

$$\mathcal{O} = \frac{1}{2}\mathbf{e}^\mathrm{T}\mathbf{e} \qquad (3)$$

Minimizing the error function leads to the pseudo-inverse solution as

$$\mathbf{w} = (\mathbf{X}^T\mathbf{X})^{-1}\mathbf{X}^T\mathbf{t} \qquad (4)$$

The use of the least squares error regression algorithm may make the built model over-fitting to data. The Lasso and Ridge regression algorithms are the alternatives. Using the Ridge regression algorithm, the error function is

$$\mathcal{O} = \frac{1}{2}(\mathbf{e}^T\mathbf{e} + \lambda\,\mathbf{w}^T\mathbf{w}) \qquad (5)$$

Minimizing the error function leads to the solution as

$$\mathbf{w} = (\mathbf{X}^T\mathbf{X} + \lambda\,\mathbf{I})^{-1}\mathbf{X}^T\mathbf{t} \qquad (6)$$

Using the Lasso regression algorithm, the error function is

$$\mathcal{O} = \frac{1}{2}(\mathbf{e}^T\mathbf{e} + \lambda\,|\,\mathbf{w}\,|) \qquad (7)$$

As the derivative function is not continuous, the solution to the equation is a little complicated. Limited by the space, we don't expand to this subject. Readers are referred to the article [8].

2.3 Experimental Design

In simulation, each model is built on randomly selected 90% of data points and validated on the rest. This is repeated for 10,000 times. Based on 10,000 models, mean and standard deviation values are calculated for each weight. We then review literatures to see if the multivariate crosstalk models are able to identify

1) Enhanced or inhibited crosstalk
2) Direct or indirect crosstalk

We use the following hypothesis in interpreting the results biologically. We propose that the signs of the derived weights suggest that the relationship between the source protein and target protein is enhanced in case of a positive sign (+) or inhibition in the case of a negative sign (-). We also propose that the magnitude of each weight could determine how much influence the source protein exerts on the target protein. In the case of a low magnitude, we propose a reduced influence while a strong magnitude suggests a direct influence. Otherwise it is regarded as indirect.

3 Results and Discussions

A. Case study 1

Mitogen-activated protein kinases (MAPKs) are serine/theorine kinases that transmit signals from extracellular stimuli to multiple substrates controlling such fundamental cellular processes as proliferation, differentiation, cell growth, survival and apoptosis [10]. There are three major subfamilies of the MAPKs: extra-cellular signal-regulated kinases (ERKs), JNKs and p38 kinases. While the ERK family MAPKs generally regulate cell growth and differentiation, the JNK and p38 family MAPKs mediate stress and inflammatory responses [10]. It has been proposed that the balance between the stress kinases activity (JNK and p38) and that of ERK decides the fate of the cell [11].

In the case study, we studied possible crosstalk between the Raf-MEK-ERK pathway and the p38 pathway in the presence of a MEK inhibitor. Figure 3 shows only the derived weights for Lasso regression due to lack of space. For the dataset with inhibition, the Mek inhibitor U0126 prevents phosphorylation of Erk 1/2 in the MAPK cascade. The results obtained from our stimulations suggested that crosstalk takes place upstream of MEK when considering the assigned weights to both proteins Raf and MEK.MEKK1, an upstream mediator of the MEK pathway, has reported to act as an E3 ligase and mediate ubiquitination and degradation of ERK [12], which suggests that a signal transduction molecule can directly suppress other signaling molecules as well as implies that the crosstalk with p38 might have occurred upstream from MEK. Phosphatases or scaffold proteins for the MAPK kinase could also have been involved in the crosstalk events [11].

The weights assigned to PKC and PKA also suggests relationships between the proteins and p38 for both datasets. While the influence of PKA and PKC on p38 could be via their respective MAPK kinases, PKA is also known to crosstalk with the MAP kinase cascade. There is evidence of crosstalk between MAP-kinase p38 and PKA in the form of a negative feedback when p38 activity is inhibited as seen in adult mouse cardiomyocytes [13]. Figure 4 denotes the correlation of targets to prediction for the Lasso regression algorithm.

B. Case study 2

Phosphatidylinositol 3 kinase (PI3K) kinases and mitogen-activated protein kinases (MAPKs) have been implicated in diverse cellular functions, including proliferation, migration and survival. A crucial downstream target of the PI3K is the serine/threonine kinase Akt. Akt activation promotes various cell responses that are associated with cell division, including increased cell size, suppression of apoptosis, inactivation of cell cycle inhibitors, and induction of cyclin and cytokine gene expression [14].

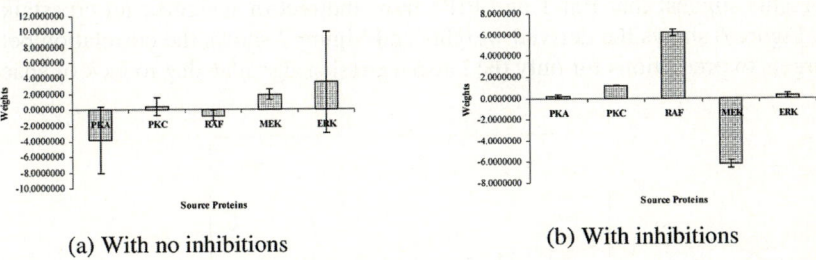

(a) With no inhibitions   (b) With inhibitions

Fig. 3. Lasso results for ERK pathway – p38 pathway with and without inhibitions

In this case study, we investigate the crosstalk phenomenon between the Raf-MEK-ERK and PI3K-AKT pathways. We use ERK as the target protein since ERK activity mirrors the activity of Raf-1, although with slightly delayed kinetics due to the downstream position of ERK. Our results shows a relationship between Akt and ERK, with the weight assigned to Akt reflecting the crosstalk influence of Akt on the ERK pathway. On analysing results of the inhibited dataset, inhibition of PI3K with LY294002 should reduce the phosphorylation of Akt; however a positive weight is assigned to Akt in relation with ERK. Figure 5 shows that the partial correlation graph for the ERK and Akt data used depict a linear relationship between the two proteins suggesting the results have been true to the data provided.

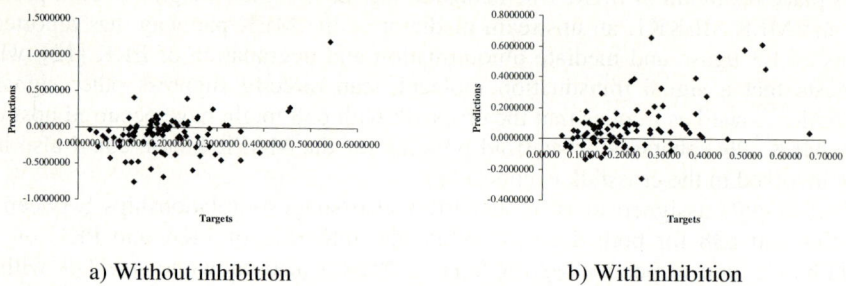

a) Without inhibition   b) With inhibition

Fig. 4. Correlation between targets and prediction for Lasso regression algorithm for ERK – p38 dataset

MEK is upstream of ERK in the MAPK cascade and the weight assigned to the protein kinase MEK reflects an inhibited influence on ERK which is seen in the Ras-Raf-MEK-ERK pathway when Raf-1 is phosphorylated by Akt. Various PKC family members have been shown to activate the ERK pathway in vitro and in intact cells. In some cells, it is possible that crosstalk between PI3K/Akt and Raf-1 pathways is mediated in part by PKC [15]. There is also a positive feedback loop between ERK and PKC in the MAPK cascade. Our results suggest a relationship between PKC and ERK either as part of the crosstalk with PI3K/Akt or via direct interactions with MEK downstream of Ras. On considering the weights of Raf-1 and PIP3, the magnitudes of the weights suggest that Raf-1 and PIP3 have indirect or insignificant crosstalk with ERK. Figure 6 shows the derived weights and Figure 7 shows the correlation between the targets to predictions for only the Lasso regression algorithm due to lack of space.

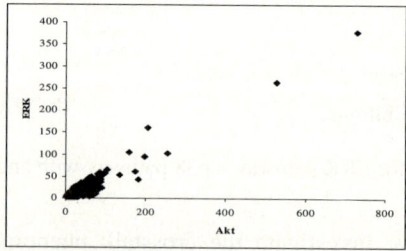

Fig. 5. Correlation graph of ERK and AKT with inhibition

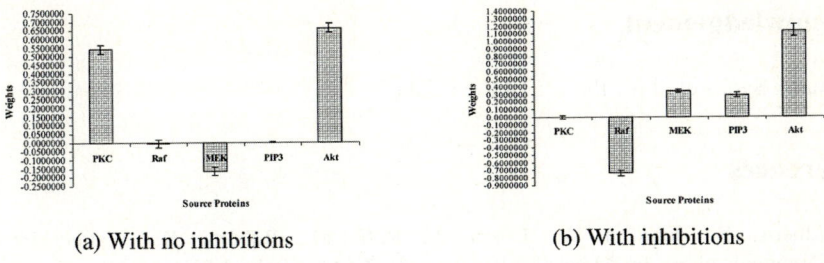

(a) With no inhibitions (b) With inhibitions

Fig. 6. Lasso results for PI3K pathway – ERK pathway with and without inhibitions

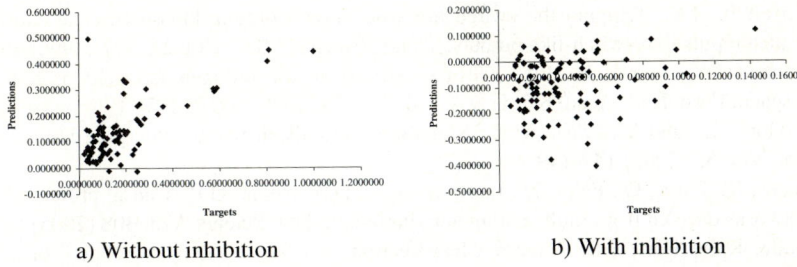

a) Without inhibition b) With inhibition

Fig. 7. Correlation between targets and prediction for Lasso regression algorithm for PI3K pathway – ERK pathway

Crosstalk between proteins can be quite complex depending on type of ligand, ligand concentration and intensity of signaling. Given time series data, the algorithms could have potentially captured precise results at different time points. In our stimulations we have only captured crosstalk between proteins of only two pathways. However, considering the overall signaling in a cell, crosstalk between proteins of two specific pathways might actually be influenced by crosstalk with a third pathway, which we have not measured. Improvement in the quality of data points and the implementation of time series data could provide more in-depth and precise insight into crosstalk, thereby analysing the robustness of cell signaling as a consequence of crosstalk.

4 Conclusion

It is now a well-established fact that cell signaling pathways are not independent and the increasing evidence for the complex signaling topology suggest non-linear inter-pathway crosstalk. As the first attempt, we have studied the potential crosstalk between signaling proteins from one pathway with another in both initial and inhibited conditions. While linear statistical models have proven to work well with analyzing crosstalk between proteins as initial research, correlation graphs between proteins in the dataset depict a more non-linear relationship. Further work would focus on developing more sophisticated multivariate models to capture the non-linearity of crosstalk activity between pathways.

Acknowledgement

We thank Sachs et al for the use of their data.

References

1. Alberts, B., Johnson, A., Lewis, J., Raff, M., Roberts, K., Walter, P.: Cell Communications. In: Molecular Biology of the Cell. Garland Science, New York (2002) 831-90
2. Weng, G., Bhalla, U.S., Iyengar, R.: Complexity in Biological Signaling Systems. Science Vol. 284 (5411) (1999) 92-96
3. Ferrell Jr., J.E.: Tripping the switch fantastic: how a protein kinase cascade can convert graded inputs into switch-like outputs. Trends Biochem. Sci., Vol. 21 (12) (1996) 460-466
4. Huang, C.Y., Ferrell Jr., J.E..: Ultra sensitivity in the mitogen-activated protein kinase cascade. Proc. Natl. Acad. Sci. U.S.A Vol. 93 (19) (1996) 10078-10783
5. Taylor, J.E., and McAnish, M.R.: Signaling crosstalk in plants: emerging issues. J. Exp. Bot. Vol. 55 (2003) 147-149
6. Sachs, K., Perez, O., Pe'er, D., Lauffenburger, D.A.,Nolan, G.P.: Causal protein-signaling networks derived from multi-parameter single-cell data. Science Vol. 308 (2005) 523-529
7. Duda, R.O., Hart, P.E.: Pattern Classification and Scene Analysis. New York, Wiley, (2002)
8. Tibshirani, R.: Regression shrinkage and selection via the Lasso. J. Royal Statistical Sco. (B), Vol. 58, (1996) 267-288
9. Lay, D.C.: Linear Algebra and Its Applications, 3rd Edition, Boston San Francisco New York, Pearson Education Inc, (2003)
10. Kolch, W.: Meaningful relationships: the regulation of the Ras/Raf/MEK/ERK pathway by protein interactions. Biochem. J. Vol. 351 (2000) 289-305
11. Hotokezaka, H., Sakai,E., Kanaoka, K., Saito, K., Matsuoi, K., Kitaura, H., Yoshida, N., Nukayama, K.: U0126 and PD98059,Specific inhibitors of MEK,accelerate differentiation of RAW264.7 cells into osteoclast-like cells. J. Biol. Chem. Vol.277 (49) (2002)
12. Lu, Z.,Xu, S., Joazeiro, C., Cobb, M.H., and Hunter, T.: The PHD Domain of MEKK1 Acts as an E3 Ubiquitin Ligase and Mediates Ubiquitination and Degradation of ERK1/2. Mol. Cell Vol. 9 (2002) 945-956
13. Zheng M., Zhang, S-J., Zhu, W-Z., Ziman,B., Kobilka, B. K.,Xiao, R-P.: Beta$_2$-Adrenergic Receptor-induced p38 MAPK Activation Is Mediated by Protein Kinase A Rather than by G$_i$ or G-beta-gamma in Adult Mouse Cardiomyocytes J. Biol. Chem., Vol. 275 (2000) 51, 40635-40640
14. Fruman, D.A.: Phosphoinositide 3-kinase and its targets in B-cell and T-cell signaling. Current Opinion in Immunology Vol. 16 (2004)
15. Langford, D.,Hurford, R.,Hashimoto, M., Digicaylioglu, M.,Masliah, E.: Signalling crosstalk in FGF2-mediated protection of endothelial cells from HIV-gp120.BMC Neuroscience.Vol. 6 (2005)

Decision Making Association Rules for Recognition of Differential Gene Expression Profiles

C. Rubio-Escudero[1], Coral del Val[1], O. Cordón[1,2], and I. Zwir[1,3]

[1] Department of Computer Science and Artificial Intelligence, University of Granada, Spain
[2] European Center for Soft Computing, Mieres, Spain
[3] Howard Hughes Medical Institute, Washington University School of Medicine, St. Louis, MO
{crubio, delval, ocordon, zwir}@decsai.ugr.es

Abstract. The rapid development of methods that select over/under expressed genes from RNA microarray experiments have not yet satisfied the need for tools that identify differential profiles that distinguish between experimental conditions such as time, treatment and phenotype. We evaluate several microarray analysis methods and study their performance, finding that none of the methods alone identifies all observable differential profiles, nor subsumes the results obtained by the other methods. Therefore, we propose a machine learning based methodology that identifies and combines the abilities of microarray analysis methods to recognize differential profiles. We encode the results of this methodology in decision making association rules able to decide which method or method-aggregation is optimal to retrieve a set of genes exhibiting a common profile. These solutions are optimal in the sense that they constitute partial ordered subsets of all method-aggregations bounded by the most specific and the most sensitive available solution. This methodology was successfully applied to a study of inflammation and host response to injury data set derived from the analysis of longitudinal blood microarray profiles of human volunteers treated with intravenous endotoxin compared to placebo. Our approach was able to uncover a cohesive set of differentially expressed genes and novel members exhibiting previously studied differential profiles. This guideline serves as a means to support decisions on new microarray problems.

1 Background

Advances in molecular biology and computational techniques permit the systematical study of molecular processes that underlie biological systems [1]. Particularly, microarray technology has revolutionized modern biomedical research by its capacity to monitor changes in RNA abundance for thousands of genes simultaneously [2].

To address the statistical challenge of analyzing these large data sets, new methods have emerged ([3], [4], [5], [6], [7]). However, there is a dearth of computational methods to facilitate understanding of differential gene expression profiles (e.g., profiles that change over time and/or over treatments and/or over patients) and to decide which is the most reliable method to identify differences across profiles.

We develop a detailed evaluation of the performance of several commonly used statistical methods to identify differential expression profiles. We found that the application of these methods return different results applied over the same set of data: the methods do not identify all observable differential profiles (genes exhibiting a common behavior throughout experimental conditions). Moreover, none of the methods subsume the results obtained by the other methods.

Our study reveals how some methods are able to recognize some differential profiles and not others and that some of the not retrieved profiles might contain significant genes for the experiment under study. Therefore, we propose a methodology that combines the properties of each method into a set of decision making association rules ([8], [9], [10]) devoted to discover optimal aggregations of microarray analysis methods in an effort to identify differential gene expression profiles. The association rules allow users to query for the most appropriate method or aggregation of them to retrieve significant genes based on the differential profiles they exhibit.

To create such set of decision association rules we perform the following steps over a set of microarray gene expression data (Fig. 1). First, we extract from the data set all genes which behave in a different way from one experimental condition to the others (i.e., genes that change over time, treatments and phenotype). We apply several classical microarray analysis methods (T-Tests [11], Permutation Tests [6], Analysis of Variance [5] and Repeated Measures ANOVA [12]). Second, we create a database containing distinct types of differential profiles over time, experiment and subjects from previously recovered genes.

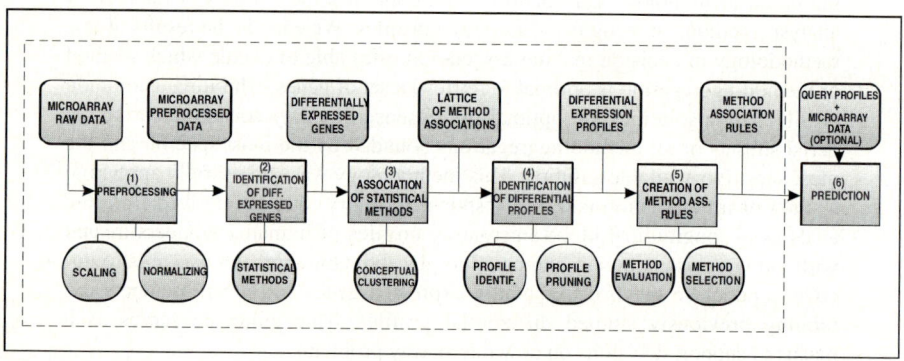

Fig. 1. Graphical representation of the methodology. The squared boxes represent the phases of the methodology, the round cornered boxes correspond to the input/output data at each step, and the ellipses the operations performed at each phase.

Third, we create decision making association rules, where the antecedents are differential profiles and the consequents are methods or aggregations of them capable to identify the profiles. Fourth, we arrange the association rules into a lattice, where the rules are ordered from the most general (top) to the most specific solution (bottom). We use this structure to evaluate the performance of the rules by analyzing their specificity, sensitivity and cost, applying multiobjective optimization techniques. Fifth, we use a selected set of optimal rules as a framework to support new decisions about the applicability of microarray analysis methods to retrieve differential gene expression profiles.

2 Results

The results are obtained from the application of our procedure to a data set derived from longitudinal blood expression profiles of human volunteers treated with intravenous endotoxin compared to placebo. The motivation of these experiments is to provide insight to the host response to injury as part of a Large-scale Collaborative Research Project sponsored by the National Institute of General Medical Sciences (www.gluegrant.org) [13]. Analysis of the set of gene expression profiles obtained from this experiment is complex, given the number of samples taken and variance due to treatment, time, and subject phenotype. Therefore, we believe this problem is typical and informative as a microarray case study. The data were acquired from blood samples collected from eight normal human volunteers, four treated with intravenous endotoxin (i.e., patients 1 to 4) and four with placebo (i.e., patients 5 to 8). Complementary RNA was generated from circulating leukocytes at 0, 2, 4, 6, 9 and 24 hours after the i.v. infusion and hybridized with GeneChips® HG-U133A v2.0 from Affymetrix Inc., which contains 22216 probe sets, analyzing the expression level of 18400 transcripts and variants, including 14500 well-characterized human genes.

2.1 Accuracy of the Statistical Methods

We investigate the performance of several commonly used statistical methods in identifying differential expression profiles that change over time, treatments and phenotype. We name T-Test as M^1, T-Test considering time as M^2, Permutation Test as M^3, Permutation Test considering time as M^4, ANOVA over treatment as M^5, ANOVA over time as M^6, ANOVA over treatment and time as M^7, RMANOVA over treatment as M^8, RMANOVA over time as M^9 and RMANOVA over treatment and time as M^{10}, where considering time refers to the fact that the tests have been specifically applied to find differences between time points. For our set of data, we found that these methods do not identify all observable distinct profiles. Moreover, none of them subsumes the results obtained by other methods (Table 1). Different methods retrieve different amounts of probe sets (e.g., the application of M^1 over the microarray dataset retrieves 962 genes as differentially expressed, whereas M^5 retrieves 1734 genes, and M^3 retrieves 612 genes). The concordance rates between the sets of genes retrieved also varies widely, indicating that none of the methods subsumes the others (Table 1)(e.g., from the genes retrieved by M^3, only 31.11% are also retrieved by M^5, and 52.29% by M^1.

2.2 Statistical Methods and Differential Profiles

We found that there is a relationship between the statistical methods and the differential profiles they are able to identify, having differential profiles identified by some methods and not by others. This type of relation is what we encode in the set of decision making association rules that we obtain from the application of our methodology. In our particular problem, there are genes highly related with the inflammation problem which exhibit profiles that would not be retrieved applying some of the classic microarray analysis methods individually. That is the case of probe set 206011_at, which is related in behavior and in function (apoptosis-related cysteine peptidase) to probe sets 211367_s_at and 211368_s_at (Fig. 2(a)), stated as relevant for the inflammation problem in [13]. For these particular probe set, the isolated application of classical methods such as M^1 or M^3 with either default *p-value or* false discovery, rate, depending on what each method uses, would not retrieve such probe set as differentially expressed. The same situation applies to probe sets 202076_at and 210538_s_at, related both in behavior and in function (inhibitor of apoptosis protein 2 and 1 respectively) (Fig. 2(b)).

Table 1. Intersection of the results between methods recognizing differentially expressed genes. The number in each cell represents the ratio of coincidence between genes retrieved by the statistical method in the column and in the row relative to the total number of genes recovered by the method in the row $((Row \cap Column)/Row)$.

%	M^1	M^2	M^3	M^4	M^5	M^6	M^7	M^8	M^9	M^{10}
M^1	--	92.20	52.29	75.05	96.48	69.23	85.55	70.06	61.33	50.52
M^2	56.06	--	34.07	57.84	85.27	59.54	71.11	62.64	50.57	42.98
M^3	82.19	88.07	--	96.24	94.77	57.35	78.75	72.87	56.86	46.73
M^4	67.22	85.19	54.84	--	95.16	55.49	73.65	70.20	51.49	42.83
M^5	55.20	77.80	33.45	58.94	--	50.28	66.72	66.38	46.42	38.93
M^6	59.04	83.51	31.11	52.84	77.30	--	89.63	56.56	60.64	49.38
M^7	58.36	79.79	34.18	56.10	82.05	71.70	--	62.34	57.23	49.07
M^8	57.36	84.34	37.96	64.17	95.96	54.30	74.80	--	49.62	40.51
M^9	62.10	84.21	36.63	58.21	84.74	72.00	84.95	61.36	--	72.31
M^{10}	59.56	83.34	35.05	56.37	82.72	68.26	84.80	58.34	84.19	--

In contrast, some other available methods retrieve profiles that do not differ between the considered experimental conditions. For example, ANOVA, perhaps based on the violation of statistical constraints ([14]), retrieves a 43% of genes lacking an observable change with the default parameter values. The increase of the specificity of these parameters generates severe effects on the sensitivity of other true changes.

These findings reveal that there are desired and undesired differential profiles termed positive and negatively, respectively. For example, some profiles exhibiting similarly arranged patterns but shifted over time may be relevant for a specific experiment but not for other. In addition, we also found that methods applied to microarray profiles are focused on identifying differences among expression patterns over treatment and/or time since biological replicates are averaged in the same experimental group. However, we might also need to detect differences among subjects.

We create a database with all possible differential profiles derived from genes retrieved in our inflammation problem by all available methods (i.e., 28 differential profiles). This database contains differential profiles that can be labeled as positive or negative according to their interest to be retrieved for a particular study. To validate biologically these profiles we calculate the coincidence the coincidence between our retrieved differential profiles and external information provided by the Gene Ontology database ([15]) showing that genes sharing behaviour are related in function ([16]).

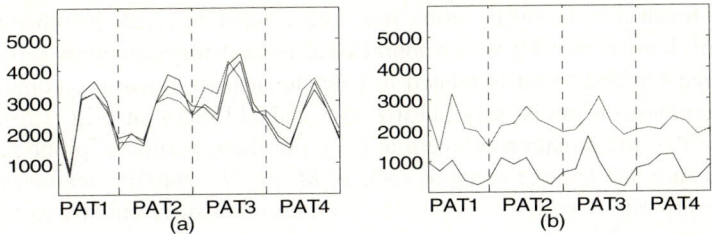

Fig. 2. Probe sets in blue are stated as relevant for the inflammation problem in ([13]). Probe sets in red are detected by application of our methodology but not by applying some classical microarray analysis methods individually. In (a) the probe set in red, 206011_at, is related to probe sets 211367_s_at and 211368_s_at (blue) both in expression throughout time and in function (apoptosis-related cysteine peptidase). In (b) we see the same situation between 202076_at in red and 210538_s_at in blue, which have correlated level of expression throughout time and share their function (inhibitor of apoptosis protein 2 and 1 respectively).

The temporal expression data in our database can be averaged or sequentially represented for each biological replicate. Originally, the database was built based on the inflammatory response patterns, which is based on a very robust microarray experiment ([13]). Now, it is being updated with experiments provided from different sources such as the Ventilator Associated Pneumonia (unpublished results).

The application of our methodology to the database of differential profiles allowed the optimal retrieval of the desired differential profiles. For example, if we were interested in probe exhibiting any of 27 of the profiles in the database and not exhibiting one of the profiles, we are able to do applying $M^5 \cup M^6$ with specificity and sensitivity levels of 94% and 92% respectively. In Fig. 3 we show the method-aggregations from the optimal rules to retrieve individually each of the 28 profiles in our database.

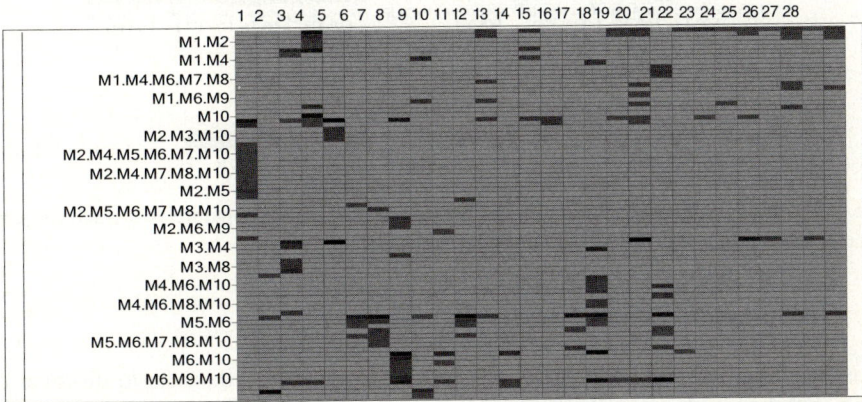

Fig. 3. Microarray analysis methods are able to retrieve some differential profiles and not others. Rows correspond to method-aggregations using the union operator and columns to each of the 28 individual differential profiles from our example. The coloring scheme corresponds to the sensitivity in retrieving the differential profile: from green, the lowest, to black, the highest.

Our approach also recovers probe sets with related behavior to other probe sets with already known profiles which might have related functionalities ([16]). For instance, probe set 206011_at is related in behavior and in function (apoptosis-related cysteine peptidase) to probe sets 211367_s_at and 211368_s_at (Fig. 2(a)), stated as relevant for the inflammation problem in [13]. For these particular probe set, the isolated application of classical methods such as M^1 or M^3 with the default *p-value* and false discovery rate would not retrieve such probe set as differentially expressed. We retrieve such probe set applying the rule that implies the method aggregation $M^7 \cup M^{10}$ with values (1, 0.25, *0.8*) for sensitivity, specificity and cost respectively. The same situation applies to probe sets 202076_at and 210538_s_at, related both in behavior and in function (inhibitor of apoptosis protein 2 and 1 respectively) (Fig. 2(b)). It is retrieved applying the rule of methods $M^3 \cup M^6$ with values *(0.93, 0.35, 0.8)*.

In addition, the representation used in the inflammation problem (Fig. 4) allows us to independently examine the gene behavior in each subject, helping to uncover individual tendencies among biological replicates that could represent conditions not previously considered such as gender or age (e.g., differential profile #15 (Fig. 5), where some of the probe sets from patient 1 exhibit a very different behavior than the rest of the patients).

We illustrate the obtained association rules for Profile #19 from our database (Table 2) and the Pareto-optimal front for the three objectives corresponding to the selected rules (Fig. 6).

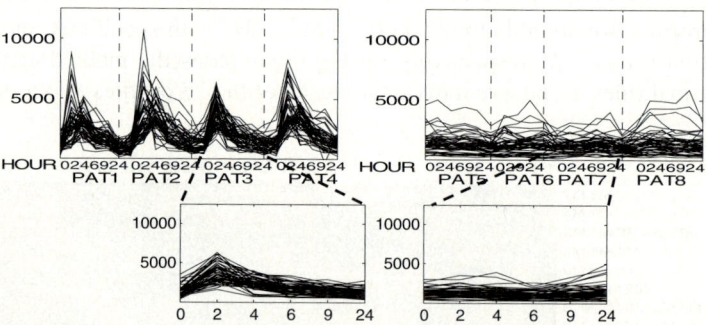

Fig. 4. Profile #19: the expression profiles have been represented separately for each subject the experimental group and patients are arranged individually

3 Methods

Most machine learning techniques are applied to mine into datasets to discover concepts involving objects which share a common methodological framework, even though they employ distinct metrics, heuristics or probability interpretations ([17], [18]): (1) *identification of a database*, different data types can be efficiently organized by taking advantage of a naturally occurring structure over feature space. (2) *learning rules from the database*, searching through the feature space for potential relationships among data, and either returning the best one found or an optimal sample of them. This learning process would result in the generation of many rules with small extent, as it is easier to explain or match small data subsets than those that constitute a significant portion of the dataset. For this reason, any successful methodology should also consider additional criteria ([19]) to extract broader or more comprehensive rules as a multiobjective optimization problem, based on their specificity, sensitivity and cost as a measures of the rule quality. (3) *Inference*, where new observations can be predicted from previously learned rules by using classifiers that optimize their matching to the rules based on distance ([18]) or probabilistic metrics ([20], [21]).

We propose a method, inspired on conceptual clustering and optimization techniques ([9], [10], [17]), that identifies a database of gene profiles that change their expression over time and/or over treatments and/or over subjects, learns associations rules and make decisions about the microarray analysis method or the best aggregation of methods capable of detecting a desired set of differential profiles, and finally uses these rules to make decisions based on new situations (Fig.1).

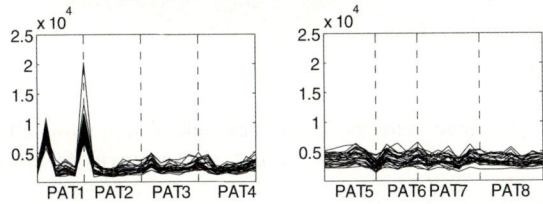

Fig. 5. Profile #15: patient 1 behaves different than patients 2, 3 and 4 for the treatment group

Table 2. Set of decision making association rules generated to retrieve Profile #19. The axes (X,Y,Z) represent the number of methods, specificity and sensitivity for each of the 35 solutions generated.

RULES	Sensitivity	Specificity	Cost
R^1:IF x_1 IS $(P_TP_C)_{19}$ THEN Z^1 IS M^1	0.878378	0.0675676	0.9
$R2$:IF x_1 IS $(P_TP_C)_{19}$ THEN Z^2 IS M^2	0.972973	0.045512	0.9
R^3:IF x_1 IS $(P_TP_C)_{19}$ THEN Z^3 IS M^7	0.905405	0.0475177	0.9
R^4:IF x_1 IS $(P_TP_C)_{19}$ THEN Z^4 IS $M^1 \cap M^2$	0.864865	0.0721533	0.8
R^5:IF x_1 IS $(P_TP_C)_{19}$ THEN Z^5 IS $M^2 \cup M^{10}$	1	0.0430733	0.8
R^7:IF x_1 IS $(P_TP_C)_{19}$ THEN Z^7 IS $M^1 \cap M^{10}$	0.594595	0.090535	0.8
R^8:IF x_1 IS $(P_TP_C)_{19}$ THEN Z^8 IS $M^2 \cap M^7$	0.891892	0.0538776	0.8
R^9:IF x_1 IS $(P_TP_C)_{19}$ THEN Z^9 IS $M^3 \cap M^9$	0.472973	0.100575	0.8
R^{10}:IF x_1 IS $(P_TP_C)_{19}$ THEN Z^{10} IS $M^3 \cap M^{10}$	0.405405	0.104895	0.8
R^{11}:IF x_1 IS $(P_TP_C)_{19}$ THEN Z^{11} IS $M^1 \cap M^2 \cap M^7$	0.797297	0.0732919	0.7
R^{12}:IF x_1 IS $(P_TP_C)_{19}$ THEN Z^{12} IS $M^1 \cap M^2 \cap M^9$	0.662162	0.0853659	0.7
R^{13}:IF x_1 IS $(P_TP_C)_{19}$ THEN Z^{13} IS $M^1 \cap M^3 \cap M^7 \cap M^{10}$	0.459459	0.112211	0.6
R^{14}:IF x_1 IS $(P_TP_C)_{19}$ THEN Z^{14} IS $M^3 \cap M^6 \cap M^9 \cap M^{10}$	0.364865	0.135	0.6
R^{15}:IF x_1 IS $(P_TP_C)_{19}$ THEN Z^{15} IS $M^1 \cap M^3 \cap M^6 \cap M^9 \cap M^{10}$	0.364865	0.140625	0.6
R^{16}:IF x_1 IS $(P_TP_C)_{19}$ THEN Z^{16} IS $M^1 \cap M^3 \cap M^4 \cap M^6 \cap M^9 \cap M^{10}$	0.364865	0.141361	0.4

3.1 Identification of the Database

Our database is composed of differential profiles obtained from the probe sets differentially expressed retrieved from the expression datasets. The probe sets are obtained using several classical microarray analysis methods. These methods include Student's T-Test proposed in [11], with variants that distinguish changes in the abundance of RNA occurring not only over treatment but also over time; Permutation Test described in ([6]), also including a time approach; Analysis of Variance described in ([5]); and Longitudinal Data approach using Repeated Measures Analysis of Variance described in ([12]).

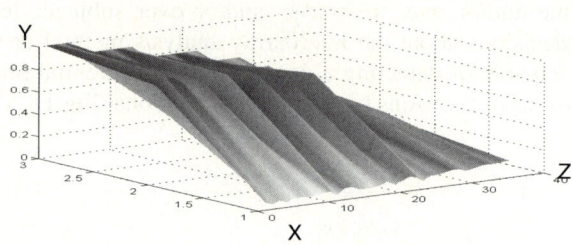

Fig. 6. Pareto-front representation for the set of rules generated to retrieve Profile #19. The axes (X,Y,Z) represent the number of methods, specificity and sensitivity for each of the 35 solutions generated.

The probe sets identified by the statistical methods serve as a means to create differential expression profiles (i.e., sets of genes with coordinate changes in RNA abundance) expressed from one experimental condition to the others (i.e., probe sets that change over time, treatments and phenotype). We group separately probe sets for different experimental conditions, treatment and P_T control P_C by applying the K-means clustering algorithm ([22]), which takes three input parameters: first, number of resulting clusters K, which is estimated by application of the Davies-Bouldin validity index ([23]); second, the similarity measure applied, Euclidean distance, which yields the best results in the clustering of this problem and third, the initialization strategy, random generation of the cluster centroids.

Particularly, in our inflammation problem, we consider the temporal expression data sequentially represented for each biological replicate (i.e., patients in the same experimental group) instead of averaging them to uncover phenotype differences.

We identify differential profiles by applying a coincidence index (CI) based on the hypergeometric distribution (p-value <0.05), which determines the statistical significance of overlap between pairwise profile association in treatment and control conditions ([16]):

$$CI(P_T, P_C) = 1 - (\sum_{q=0}^{p} \binom{h}{q}\binom{q-h}{n-q} / \binom{g}{h}) \tag{1}$$

that gives the chance probability of observing at least p candidates from a set P_T of size h within another set P_C of size n, in a universe of g candidates. Therefore, probe sets belonging to a cluster in treatment, P_T, can fit in more than one cluster in control,

P_C, and vice versa. We define a differential profile by a triplet ($P_T P_C G$), which represents a set of genes G with similar behavior in treatment P_T and control P_C experiments. The available profiles can be labeled as positive or negative examples for the decision process according to their relevance for a desired analysis.

3.2 Learning Association Rules

We create a set of decision making association rules from the database that, given a desired differential profile or set of profiles, suggests the most appropriate method-aggregations to recognize it. The rules are created to retrieve all possible combinations of differential profiles $P = \{(P_T P_C G)_1, ..., (P_T P_C G)_l\}$ present in our database.

We say that a method M^i is able to retrieve a differential profile $(P_T P_C G)_j$ if it identifies a sufficient number of the genes exhibiting that profile in the data set. That is, $M^i(G) > t$, where t satisfies a statistical power of 80%. Then, an association rule is defined as:

$$R : \text{IF } X \text{ IS } (P_T P_C G)_j \text{ THEN } Z \text{ IS } M^i, \tag{2}$$

where X is the profile queried by the user and Z is a latent class returned from M^i, which represents a method or a method-aggregation. The antecedent of the rule is activated by considering the degree of matching between a query and a profile, both of which are represented by their centroids as a fuzzy set prototype ([19]). We use the Euclidean distance normalized in the unit interval to account for this matching. We extend the antecedent to encode several profiles linked by using typical AND-operations in fuzzy rules (e.g., *T-norms* including the MINIMUM or the PRODUCT ([24]). The consequent of the rules is composed of a single or a method-aggregation (e.g., $M^i \& M^h (G) > t$). The potential method-aggregations are defined as:

$$M = \{M^1, M^2, M^n, M^1 \oplus M^2, M^1 \oplus M^3, \ldots, M^1 \oplus M^2 \oplus \ldots \oplus M^n\} \tag{3}$$

where $\oplus$ is a classical set operator (e.g., the union ($\cup$) or the intersection ($\cap$)). The association rules are arranged into a lattice (Fig. 7) for one or a set of desired profiles, and structured from top (i.e., intersection of all methods, increasing Type I error) to bottom (i.e., union of all methods increasing error of Type II) [21].

3.3 Selecting Association Rules

We evaluate a rule by the ability of a method-aggregation to recognize a desired positive and not to detect an undesired negative differential profile, as well as the number of methods being considered in the consequent. We explicitly perform a multiobjective evaluation of the performance of the rules by considering three objectives: *specificity, sensitivity* and *cost*:

$$\begin{aligned} Specificity &= TN/(TP+FN) \quad Sensitivity = TP/(TP+FN) \\ Cost &= 1-(\#\,Methods\,/\,Max(Methods)), \end{aligned} \tag{4}$$

where *TP* stands for *True Positive*, *TN* stands for *True Negative*, *FP* stands for *False Positive*, *FN* stands for *False Negative*, *#Methods* is the number of methods included in the consequent and *Max(Methods)* is the total number of methods available.

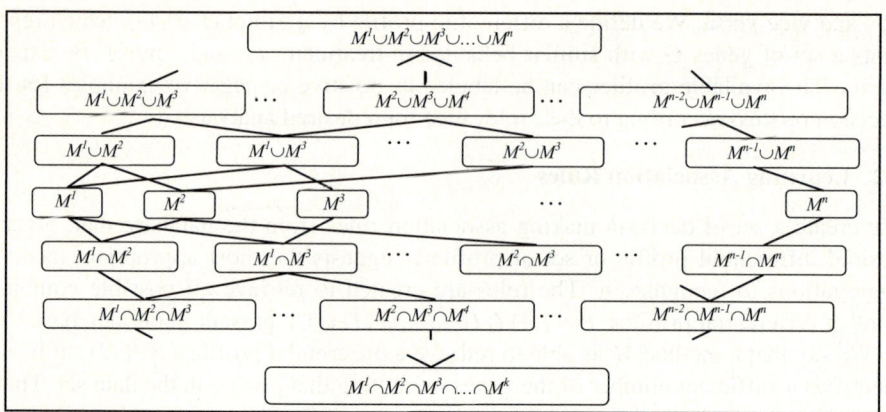

Fig. 7. Lattice structure containing possible association rules

We obtain a set of optimal rules by calculating a trade-off between the opposing objectives that is estimated by selecting a set of solutions that are non-dominated, in the sense that there is no solution that is superior to them in all objectives (i.e., Pareto optimal frontier ([25])). The dominance relationship in a maximization problem of at least two objectives is defined as:

$$a > b \text{ iff } \forall i O_i(a) \geq O_i(b) \exists j O_j(a) > O_j(b) \qquad (5)$$

where the O_i and O_j are either one or another defined objective.

3.4 Inferring from Association Rules

We use the set of non-dominated rules and the corresponding metrics derived from the multiobjective optimization process to update the rule defined in equation (2):

$$R: \text{IF } X \text{ IS } (P_T P_C G)_j \text{ THEN } Z \text{ IS } M^i \text{ WITH } C \qquad (6)$$

where C is the confidence of the rule, defined as a weighted sum of the sensitivity, specificity and cost. The rules are fired as typical fuzzy classification rules ([26]):

$$\text{INFERENCE}(R_1(X),...,R_n(X)) = i, i \in \{1,...,n\} \qquad (7)$$

where:

$$R_i(X) = T - conorm\{R_1(X),...,R_n(X)\}, \qquad (8)$$

and,

$$R_k(X) = \alpha_k \times C_k, \forall k \in \{1,...,n\} \qquad (9)$$

with α_k and C_k being the degree of matching of the antecedent and the confidence value of the rule k when the profile $(P_T P_C G)_j$ is evaluated, and the *T-conorm* is the fuzzy operation defined as the MAXIMUM.

4 Discussion

The emergence of microarray technology as a standard tool for biomedical research has necessarily led to the rapid development of specific analytical methods to handle these large data sets. Based on what we learnt from studying the performance of classical microarray analysis methods, different methods yield different results for the same set of input data, and some methods are more capable to retrieve certain differential profiles than others, we create a set of decision making association rules between methods or aggregation of them, and differential profiles, that will help us in the decision of which microarray analysis methods to apply on new data sets in order to retrieve the genes exhibiting the desired differential profile.

Our method addressed the need for computational methods to facilitate understanding of differential gene expression profiles, to establish comparisons among them, and to decide which is the most reliable method to identify informational profiles. The proposed methodology is valid for either providing the optimal method-aggregations for a query profiles, or identifying all differential profiles in a given set of microarray data, suggesting the optimal method-aggregations for them and updating the set of possible profiles used for prediction. Although we have applied our procedure to time-course structured experiments, they constitute more general cases of simpler microarray problems where microarray samples are taken as single data points. Therefore, the methodology presented is also useful for simpler microarray experiments with single data points.

Our approach presents various advantages over the standard analytical methods for microarray experiments. First, our proposal consists of machine learning techniques that combine the properties of the methods applied. Second, it permits interaction with the user: given the differential profile queried from the set of data obtains the optimal combination of statistical methods to retrieve the genes exhibiting such profile. Third, the representation used for the profiles, allowing us to examine the behavior of the genes independently in each subject, facilitates the identification of different behaviors of genes across the subjects in the same experimental group. Finally, the system provides solutions based on a trade-off of specificity, sensitivity and cost and the number of methods applied, whereas other methods evaluate their solutions only over one measure, usually a ratio between False Positives and the total number of genes retrieved ([6], [11]).

The computational procedure we propose solves many of the problems actually present in the process of analyzing a microarray experiment, such as the decision of analytical methodology to follow, extraction of biologically significant results, proper management of complex experiments harboring experimental conditions, time-series and intersubject variation. Therefore, it provides a robust platform for the analysis of many types of microarray experiments, from the simplest experimental design to the most complex, providing accurate and reliable results.

References

1. Durbin,R., Eddy,S., Krogh,A. and Mitchison,G. (1998) Biological Sequence Analysis: Probabilistic Models of Proteins and Nucleic Acids. Cambridge University Press.
2. Brown,P. and Botstein,D. (1999) Exploring the new world of the genome with DNA microarrays. Nature Genet., 21 (Suppl.), 33-37.

3. Inza, I., Larranaga, P., Blanco, R., Cerrolaza, A.J. (2004) Filter versus wrapper gene selection approaches in DNA microarray domains. Artif Intell Med. 31(2):91-103.
4. Pan,W., Lin.J. and Le.C. (2001) A mixture model approach to detecting differentially expressed genes with microarray data. Funct. Integr. Genomics, 3(3), 117-124.
5. Park,T., Yi,S.G., Lee,S., Lee,S.Y., Yoo,D.H., Ahn, J.I. and Lee, Y.S. (2003) Statistical tests for identifying differentially expressed genes in time-course microarray experiments. Bioinformatics, 19(6), 694-703.
6. Tusher,V.G., Tibshirani,R. and Chu,G. (2001) Significance analysis of microarrays applied to the ionizing radiation response. Proc. Natl. Acad. Sci. USA. 98, 5116-5121.
7. Vaquerizas, J.M., Conde, L., Yankilevich, P., Cabezon, A., Minguez, P., Diaz-Uriarte, R., Al-Shahrour, F., Herrero, J., Dopazo, J. (2005) GEPAS, an experiment-oriented pipeline for the analysis of microarray gene expression data. Nucleic Acids Res. 1;33(Web Server issue):W616-20.
8. Agrawal,R., Imielinski,T., Swami,A.N. (1993) Mining association rules between sets of items in large databases. In Buneman, P., Jajodia, S., eds.: Proceedings of the ACM SIGMOD. International Conference on Management of Data, Washington, D.C., 207—216.
9. Zwir,I., Shin,D., Kato,A., Nishino,K., Latifi,K., Solomon,F., Hare,J.M., Huang,H. and Groisman,E.A. (2005a) Dissecting the PhoP regulatory network of Escherichia coli and Salmonella enterica. Proc Natl Acad Sci, 102, 2862-2867.
10. Zwir,I., Huang,H. and Groisman,E.A. (2005b) Analysis of Differentially-Regulated Genes within a Regulatory Network by GPS Genome Navigation, Bioinformatics 21(22):4073-83.
11. Li,C. and Wong,W.H. (2003) DNA-Chip Analyzer (dChip). In Parmigiani,G., Garrett,E.S., Irizarry,R. and Zeger,S.L. (eds), The analysis of gene expression data: methods and software. Springer.
12. Der,G. and Everitt,B.S. (2001) Handbook of Statistical Analyses using SAS. Chapman and Hall/CRC.
13. Calvano,S.E., Xiao,W., Richards,D.R., Feliciano,R.M., Baker, H.V., Cho, R.J., Chen, R.O., Brownstein,B.H., Cobb,J.P., Tschoeke,S.K., Miller-Graziano,C., Moldawer,L.L., Mindrinos, M.N., Davis, R.W., Tompkins,R.G. and Lowry,S.F. (2005) The Inflammation and Host Response to Injury Large Scale Collaborative Research Program. A Network-Based Analysis of Systemic Inflammation in Humans. Nature, 13,437(7061):1032-7.
14. Gao, X., Song, PX. (2005) Nonparametric tests for differential gene expression and interaction effects in multi-factorial microarray experiments. BMC Bioinformatics, 21,6:186
15. Romero-Zaliz, R., Rubio-Escudero, C., Cordón, O., Harari, O., del Val, C., Zwir, I. Mining Structural Databases : An Evolutionary Multi-Objective Conceptual Clustering Methodology. Applications of Evolutionary Computing, LNCS 3907, 2006.
16. Tavazoie,S., Hughes,J.D., Campbell,M.J., Cho,R.J. and Church,G.M. (1999) Systematic determination of genetic network architecture, Nat Genet, 22, 281-285.
17. Cheeseman,P. and Oldford,R.W. (1994) Selecting models from data : artificial intelligence and statistics IV. Springer-Verlag, New York.
18. Cooper, G. and Herskovits, E. (1992) Bayesian method for the induction of probabilistic networks from data. Machine Learning, 9:309--347.
19. Ruspini, E. (2002) Introduction to Longitudinal Research. Edited by M. Bulmer, Social Research Today. London: Routledge.
20. Bezdek, J.C. (1998) Pattern Analysis. In Pedrycz, W., Bonissone, P.P. and Ruspini, F. H. (eds), Handbook of Fuzzy Computation. Institute of Physics, Bristol, F6.1.1-F6.6.20.
21. Mitchell, T. (1997) Machine Learning. McGraw Hill.

22. Duda, R. O., and Hart, P. E. (1973) Pattern Classification and Scene Analysis. John Wiley & Sons, New York, USA.
23. Davies D.L. and Bouldin D.W. (1979) A cluster separation measure. IEEE Trans. On Pattern Analysis and Machine Intelligence, (1)2: 224-227.
24. Klir, G.J. and Yuan, B. (2005) Fuzzy Sets and Fuzzy Logic: Theroy and Applications. Prentice-Hall.
25. Deb, K. (2001) Multi-objective optimization using evolutionary algorithms. John Wiley & Sons, Chichester, New York.
26. Cordón O., del Jesus, M.J., Herrera, F. (1999) A Proposal on Reasoning Methods in Fuzzy Rule-Based Classification Systems. International Journal of Approximate Reasoning, 20: 21-45.

Application of Chemoinformatics to the Structural Elucidation of Natural Compounds

José Luis López-Pérez[1], Roberto Theron[2], Esther del Olmo[1], David Díez[2], Miguel Vaquero[2], and José Francisco Adserias[3]

[1] Departamento de Química Farmacéutica-Facultad de Farmacia,
[2] Departamento de Informática y Automática-Facultad de Ciencias
[3] Fundación General. Universidad de Salamanca, Spain
lopez@usal.es, theron@usal.es

Abstract. This paper describes the characteristics of a free web-based spectral database for the chemical research community, containing ^{13}C NMR spectra data from more than 4.000 natural compounds. The number of entries is constantly growing. This database allows for searches by chemical structure, substructure, name, family compounds, and by spectral features i.e. chemical shifts and multiplicities, which enable the structural elucidation of known and unknown compounds by comparison of their ^{13}C NMR data.

Keywords: structural elucidation, ^{13}C NMR spectral database, natural compounds.

1 Introduction

Chemoinformatics is the application of informatics methods to chemical problems [1]. All areas of chemistry can profit from the use of information technology and management, since both a deep chemical knowledge and the processing of a huge amount of information are needed. Natural products structure elucidation requires spectroscopic experiments. The results of these spectroscopic experiments need to be compared with those of the previously described compounds. This methodology provides highly interesting challenges for chemoinformatics practitioners.

Natural products from microbial, plant, marine, or even mammalian sources have traditionally been a major drug source and continue to play a significant role in today's drug discovery environments [2][3]. In fact, in some therapeutic areas, for example, oncology, the majority of currently available drugs are derived from natural products. However, natural products have not always been as popular in drug discovery research as one might expect, since in the natural products research, tedious purifications are needed in order to isolate the constituents. These procedures are often performed with the main purpose of structure identification or elucidation. Because of that, ultra-highthroughput screening and large-scale combinatorial synthetic methods have been the major methods employed in drug discovery [4]. Yet if the structures of natural extract constituents could be known in advance, the isolation efforts could be focused on truly novel and interesting components, avoiding re-isolation of known or trivial constituents and their increasing productivity [5]. Furthermore, it is generally known that the intrinsic diversity of natural products exceeds the degree of molecular diversity that can be created by synthetic means, and the vast majority of biodiversity is yet to be explored [3][6]. At present, it is unanimously assumed that the size of a chemical library is not a key issue for successful developmental leads and that molecular diversity, biological functionality and "drug likeness" are decisive factors for drug discovery processes [3]. For this reason the natural products-based drug discovery is on the rise again.

Some chemoinformatics methods include predictive classification, regression and clustering of molecules and their properties. In order to develop these statistical machine learning methods the need for large and well-annotated datasets has been already pointed out. These datasets need to be organized in rapidly searchable databases to facilitate the development of computational methods that rapidly extract or predict useful information for each molecule [7].

In this paper we present a web-based spectral database that tries to facilitate the structural identification of the natural compounds even previously to their purification.

For the identification and elucidation of natural compounds, ^{13}C NMR spectroscopy is the more powerful tool. This is largely due to the well-known and exquisite dependence of the ^{13}C chemical shift of each carbon atom on its local chemical environment and its number of attached protons. Furthermore, the highly resolved spectra, provided by a large chemical shift range and narrow peak width, could by easily converted into a highly reduced numerical lists of chemical shift positions with minimal loss of peak intensity and width information. These features are not generally used in dereplication. ^{13}C NMR spectroscopy can also provide the molecular formula. The analysis of spectral data for the determination of unknown compound structure remains a usual and laborious task in chemical practice.

Since the advent of computers many efforts have been directed toward facilitating the solution to this problem [1]. Libraries of such spectral lists of data are common for synthetic organic compounds and are an invaluable tool for confirming the identity of known compounds [8]. However, the methods for structure elucidation of compounds outside a database have not been exhaustively studied. In the field of natural products, where hundreds of thousands compounds have been reported in the literature, most compounds are absent from commercially available spectral libraries.

When a researcher in natural products isolates and purifies a compound he needs to know, as soon as possible, what skeleton this compound has, its structure, and if it has been previously described. If a database of natural products and their NMR spectral data were available, searching databases would allow for quick identifications by comparison with previously registered compounds. They would also provide insight into the structural elucidation of unknown compounds.

2 Structural Elucidation Trough the Web

The structural elucidation of natural compounds poses a great challenge because of its great structural diversity and complexity. For this reason, we are developing a database accessible through a standard browser (http://c13.usal.es). It provides retrieval of natural compounds structures with ^{13}C NMR spectral data related to the query. At present it contains the structures of several thousands compounds with their ^{13}C NMR information. This database is constantly increasing and it has capacity to store hundreds of thousands of compounds. The utility of the database will be conditioned by the number of entries created and, certainly, by the quality of the spectral information of the entered compounds.

This database has many search facilities and a set-up that allows comparative studies of related compounds. At present, new search tools are being developed and the data input methods are being improved so as to allow researchers from different institutions to enter the information over the Net. The aim of this database is to help identify and elucidate the structure of hypothetical new compounds, by comparing their ^{13}C NMR data with those of already published related compounds. We have developed several tools that facilitate this task:

- search by substructure in graphics environment
- search by chemical shift and number of carbons and hydrogens
- a combination of substructure and chemical shift searches
- search refinements
- results are displayed in different layouts so as to enable comparative studies
- deviation calculus in fixed positions, etc.

This tool is designed for researchers willing to enter the information of their own compounds and share information over the Net. We have also developed scripts to automatically parse input data, run different tests and populate the database.

2.1 Implementation

To build this database we have used MySQL (http://www.mysql.com), one of the leading open-source relational database managers, based on SQL (Structured Query Language). This manager is fast, multi-thread, multi-user and robust. MySQL server controls the access to the information and ensures that several users can work at the same time. We use the open-source Apache Tomcat Web server and JSP to create Web pages that show contents dynamically generated. By means of proper JSP programming we bring about the communication between applets and database. These tools are convenient for systems in which security is not important and in which the speed and the simultaneous number of accesses to the database is important.

The database contains natural compounds. The largest number of heavy atoms of a compound in the database is 99, and its molecular formula is $C_{66}H_{106}O_{33}$. The database contains mainly compounds from more than 30 Carbons. Structures and spectral data collected in the database proceeds from books, journals and our measurements.

2.2 Database Schema and Data Format

The basic database schema is relationally organized and the molecular structures are defined and stored in the database with SMILES (Simplified Molecular Input Line Entry Specification) [9][10] code. This format of structural specification, that uses one line notation, is designed to share chemical structure information over the Internet [1]. The substructural searches are performed by SMARTS code (SMILES ARbitrary Target Specification), a variation of the SMILES code. While SMILES defines the molecules in the form of alphanumeric chains, that enable an easy manipulation, SMARTS is a more complex code. It uses a Boolean operator that allows choosing all-purpose atoms, groups of alternative atoms, donor and acceptor groups of hydrogen bonds or lipophilic atoms. The spectral ^{13}C NMR data in form of a numerical list of chemical shift and their multiplicity is always associated with the structure.

Evidently, the type of patterns and notations that are used, both SMARTS and SMILES, are too complex to be interpreted by organic chemists without specific training in this area. For this reason we use a tool able to convert these notations into a graph that represents a substructure that will act as question. The applet used in this database realizes this task.

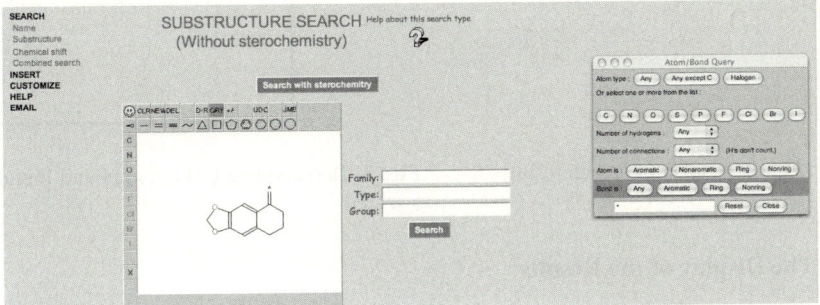

Fig. 1. Substructure searching using the JME editor

Inevitably, as the database of this nature grows, errors from the manual transcription process and even from the data spread in the literature, are present. Scripts were used to detect obvious chemical shift errors, such as shifts >240.0 ppm, as well as errors based on a few simple rules regarding proper ranges of chemical shift ranges for several easily identifiable functional groups. In this way many errors published in the literature could be corrected.

2.3 Web Interface

The high search speed facilitates the entry of query molecules through a Web interface. Users can address questions in a graphic form to the database. These are answered by JME[1], a structure editor that enables the user to draw several fragments that may not be related to each other (see Figure 1). This permits selective searches. This editor is an embedded Java applet that allows the match between a 2D query and the structures available in the database and then displays the structures found over the Net.

The JME molecular editor has a palette that speeds up the creation of structures and uses IUPAC recommendations to depict the stereochemistry. By using this palette it is possible to add preformed substructures, i.e., different size cycles, aromatic rings, simple and multiple bonds, frequently used atoms. The control panel allows to enter directly functional groups, i.e., carboxyl acids, nitro groups and other groups, for example *terc*-butyl, etc. The facilities of this applet rapidly generate a new structure and to speed up the search process.

---

[1] JME, version 1.2. The authors wish to thank the courtesy of Dr. Peter Ertl for consenting to the use in this non-profit database.

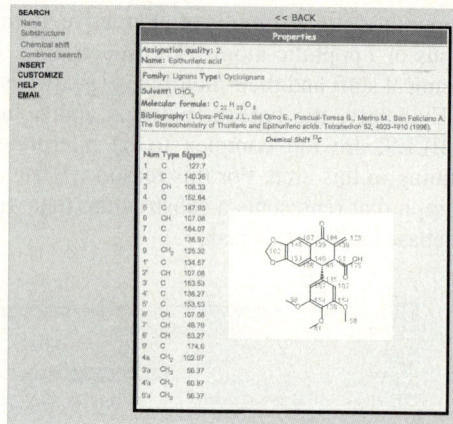

Fig. 2. Display of search results

Fig. 3. Detailed chart of a compound found by a search

2.4 The Display of the Results

As can be seen in Figure 2, search results are displayed graphically. The example in Figure 2 shows the results for the query substructure drawn in Figure 1. Each of the structures found by the search can be visualized individually in more detail, showing the chemical shift of every carbon, the molecular formula, the family and type to which they belong, the deuterated solvent used in the NMR experiment, etc., as well as the literature references (the details for the upper-left result of Figure 2 are shown in Figure 3).

One script calculates and represents the ^{13}C NMR spectra of the selected compound in a very similar way to the experimentally obtained data, that it shows the decoupled proton (broad band) and the DEPTs (Distortionless Enhancement by Polarization Transfer) (Figure 4 shows the ^{13}C NMR spectrum calculated for the substance of Figure 3). Another script calculates and represents the signals corresponding to the deuterated solvent used in the experiment.

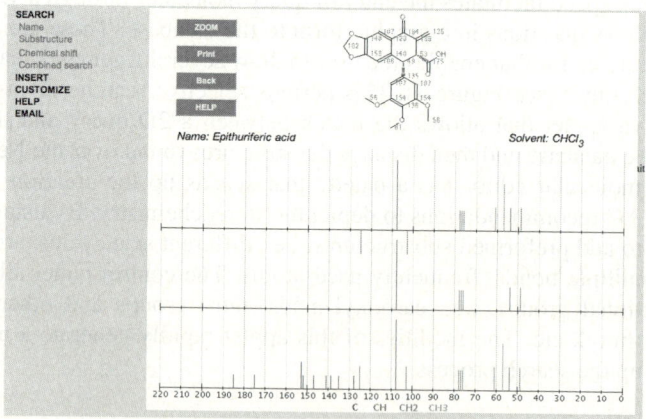

Fig. 4. Chart of the ^{13}C NMR spectra of a substance

3 Searches

This database allows for flexible searches by chemical structure, substructure of structures as well as spectral features, chemical shifts and multiplicities. Searches for names, formulas, molecular weights, family, type and group of compound according to the IUPAC classification and other parameters are also included.

3.1 Substructure Search

The best method to locate structures with a particular fragment is by means of substructure searches. Loosely defined, substructure is a particular combination of atoms or of functional groups that makes up part of a larger structure. Substructure searching is very useful in locating related compounds reported in the literature that contains the substructures we want [11]. Substructure searches can be made more or less specific with the addition of the Boolean operators AND, OR, and NOT. In addition, the degree of search can be specified. A substructure search can be so specific as to define a substructure of a single atom or general enough so as to specify a substructure consisting of several functional groups. The smaller the restricted fragment, the bigger the number of compounds found in the database.

Frequently, from the spectroscopic analysis of several two-dimensional experiments of NMR, like COSY (Correlated Spectroscopy), HMQC (Heteronuclear Multiple Quantum Coherence), HMBC (Heteronuclear Multiple Bond Coherence), we can infer the presence of different structural fragments. These fragments can be drawn with the editor in order to find all of the compounds that simultaneously fulfill these requirements. We can also specify the stereochemistry according to the IUPAC notations.

3.2 Search by Chemical Shift

The database offers several alternatives of the chemical shift search process. The user can submit a query introducing the experimentally obtained chemical shift. The multiplicity for each chemical shift is always required and this constitutes a useful search restriction (see Figure 5). The search can be undertaken for one specific position in the molecule. Furthermore, the user can carry out a combined search that implies a simultaneous search by substructure and chemical shift.

The system permits to formulate the enquiry with the required number of carbons, by one carbon or more, up to the totality of the carbons of the compound.

There is a default established deviation (+/-1 ppm) for all chemical shifts, but the user can specify a particular deviation for every carbon. It is convenient to repeat the search with different deviations and to select the search that provides the best results. If the deviation is too small, it may occur that an interesting compound will not be selected. In this way the researcher will obtain a reasonable and manageable number of compounds.

Even a search based only on the most significant carbons of the studied compound ^{13}C NMR spectrum will lead to the identification of the family they belong to.

If the skeleton of the studied substance is already known, and if some distinctive chemical shifts of the most important signals are also available, a search by shifts in each particular position of the molecule can be carried out. Therefore the researcher will only obtain the compounds of the family whose shifts, in those positions, match those of the problem compound.

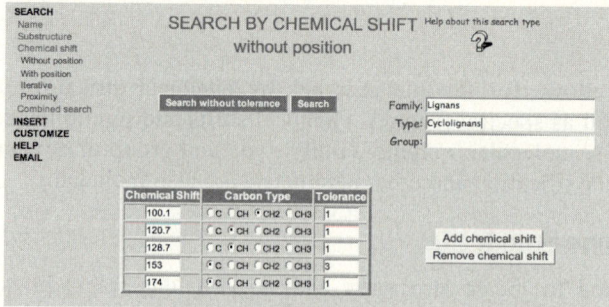

Fig. 5. Chemical shift search without carbon position

It is also possible to undertake a combined and simultaneous search by substructure and by chemical shifts, a feature that undoubtedly enhances the search capacity and increases the possibilities of finding compounds related with the problem substance.

The iterative search is probably the most characteristic and idiosyncratic search of this application. The user can include in his/her search from one only chemical shift, to the totality of the signals of the problem compound ^{13}C NMR spectrum. This tool will initially carry out a search of all the entered chemical shifts. If it does not find any compound that does not fulfill the full requirements, it will undertake a new iterative search by all the shifts except one. It will perform all the possible combinations until it finds a compound that fulfills some of the requirements.

3.3 Search by Proximity

By HMBC and HMQC NMR 2D experiments the researcher can find long-range correlations between carbons that are one or two bonds away. In this application a query into the chemical shift of these related carbons can by submitted and the maximum number of bonds between the carbons for which the chemical shift are introduced have to be specified. In this way, we can find compounds which possess a determinate substructure and whose chemical shifts are in agreement with our substance problem (see Figure 6).

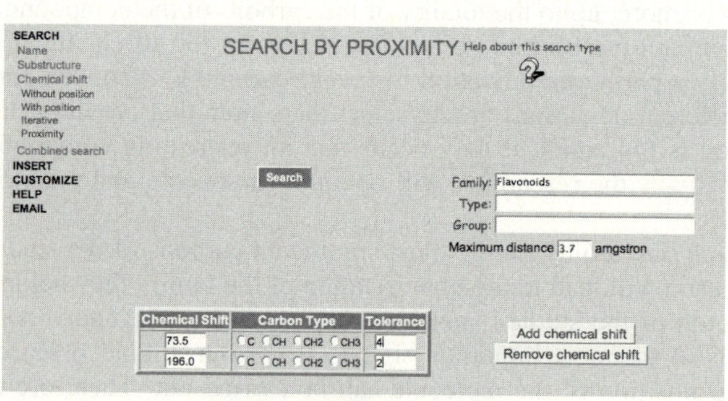

Fig. 6. Proximity search

Finally if the number of found compounds is too large and difficult to manage, the user can refine the search of the compounds obtained in the previous search. In this way the results are limited to a reasonable number that will enable him/her to find the target compound or at least a series of molecules closely related to it. By means of them, we will then be able to deduce a structure for the problem compound.

4 Conclusions and Further Work

The development of this database, provides an excellent tool to deal with complex chemical problems such as structure elucidation, which necessitates the joint efforts of information science and chemistry experts.

Currently we are working in order to increase the number of stored compounds and to add new search methods, such as the *hot spot* search, a powerful search for chemical shifts of carbons of one area of the molecule. We also want to improve information visualization techniques that will give more insight into analysis processes and to include supervised and unsupervised machine learning methods conducive to interesting predictions for assignment of the NMR spectral data of new compounds.

Acknowledgements

We would like to acknowledge Carolina Smith de la Fuente help with the translation.

References

1. Gasteiger, J.: Chemoinformatics: a new field with a long tradition. Anal. Bioanal. Chem. **384** (2006) 57–64.
2. Grabley, S. and Thiericke, R.: Bioactive agents from natural sources: trends in discovery and application. Adv. Biochem. Eng. Biotechnol. **64** (1999) 101-54.
3. Harvey, A.: Strategies for discovering drugs from previously unexplored natural products. Drug. Discov. Today **5**, (2000) 294-300.
4. Shoichet, B. K.: Virtual screening of chemical libraries. Nature **432** (2004) 862-5.
5. Clarkson, C., Stærk, D., Hansen, S.H., Smith, P.J., Jaroszewski, J.W.: Discovering new natural products directly from crude extracts by hplc-spe-nmr: Chinane diterpenes in harpagophytum procumbens. J. Nat. Prod. **69** (2006) 527–30
6. Strohl, W.R.: The role of natural products in a modern drug discovery program. Drug Discov. Today, **5** (2000) 39–41
7. Chen, J., Swamidass, S.J., Dou, Y., Bruand, J., Baldi, P.: Chemdb: a public database of small molecules and related chemoinformatics resources. Bioinformatics **21** (2005) 4122-39
8. Robien, W.: NMR data correlation with chemical structure. In v. R. Schleyer, P., Allinger, N.L., Clark, T., Gasteiger, J., Kollman, P.A., III, H.F.S., Schreiner, P.R., eds.: Encyclopedia of Computational Chemistry. Volume 3. John Wiley & Sons, Limited, Chichester, England (1998) 1845–57
9. Weininger, D.: Smiles, a chemical language and information system. 1. introduction to methodology and encoding rules. J. Chem. Inf. Comput. Sci. **28** (1988) 31–6
10. Weininger, D., Weininger, A., Weininger, J.L.: Smiles. 2. algorithm for generation of unique smiles notation. J. Chem. Inf. Comput. Sci. **29** (1989) 97–101
11. Kochev, N., Monev, V., Bangov, I.: Searching Chemical Structures. In: Chemoinformatics: A textbook. Wiley-VCH (2003) 291–318

Intelligent Coordinated Control of Multiple Teleoperated Robots

Wusheng Chou and Tianmiao Wang

Robotics Institute
Beijing University of Aeronautics and Astronautics,
Beijing, 100083, P.R. China
wschou@buaa.edu.cn

Abstract. Multiple teleoperated robots are more powerful to accomplish complex tasks than single robot does, and coordinated control of multiple robots play an important role in improving their performances. A knowledge based intelligent control method is proposed to coordinate the autonomous actions of the two teleoperated robots. In this method, each intelligent agent of the teleoperated robots has a model of other robots and a knowledge base of the task in a virtual distributed graphic predictive display system. Based on minimum distance query and collision detection, the autonomous motion of each robot is then planned via knowledge based reasoning to accomplish the given task. Experimental simulation results show that the method is effective for multiple robots to work coordinately.

Keywords: Multiple robots, Virtual reality, Intelligent control.

1 Introduction

Besides of the simple tasks which can be done by a robot via teaching and replication, many tasks have to be done by the teleoperated robot, because of the limitation of current robot intelligence [1]. In a teleoperated robotic system, the robot is fully controlled by human in coarse phases (for instance, when the robot can be moved freely) and work autonomously in fine phase (for instance, when the robot begin to perform contact task). Thus the telerobot can extend human operator's action abilities and can accomplish some complex tasks which cannot be done only by the robot itself in fully autonomous way.

Virtual reality has been used to deal with the control problems [2] of teleoperated robotic system. Virtual predictive/preview display which models the environment of robot graphically can provide a pseudo real-time response to teleoperator commands and an enhanced telepresence of remote environment. Through the predictive display, teleoperator can control the robot consecutively and obtain needed information which can not be gained from physical sensors, and the real remote robot replicates the actions of commands [3],[4]. On the other hand, it is ineluctable that there are discrepancies between the predictive display and real remote environment. High fidelity fusion of predictive display and real live images is developed to modify the predictive display [5],[6],[7].

Most of above researches are concentrated on single teleoperated robot. In fact, multiple telerobotic system has more functions than single telerobotic system, and they can accomplish some tasks which are not suitable for single robot to do, such as transfer heavy object, assembly and space operations. For instance, in the total 195 kinds of EVA space operations, there are more than 166 kinds of EVA space operation needing dual arm to work coordinately [8].

In multiple telerobotic system, each robot is controlled separately. Cooperation is a main theme in multiple telerobotic system. "Hidden robot" [9] and "projective virtual reality" [10] (which is a virtual hand to present a robot) was used to simplify the teleoperation of multiple robots with little coordination. Event based cooperation methods have been proposed to coordinated robots via internet [11]. These methods did not concern with the coordination under constrains.

In this paper, we propose an intelligent coordinated control method for multiple teleoperated robots. A distributed virtual predictive environment is implemented, and robot is modeled as an agent which has a model of other robots and a knowledge base of the task. In the coarse phase, the robots are controlled by the human operator respectively. When the robots reach each other in a certain area, they are fully autonomous. According to minimum distance calculation, collision detection and updated status information of other robots, the intelligent agent can conduct knowledge based reasoning to give motion plan for the robot to work coordinately with other robots.

The rest of this paper is organized as follows. Section II describes the distributed virtual predictive environment. Section III gives the method of minimum distance calculation and collision detection. Section IV presents the knowledge based coordination method. Section V describes our primary experimental results, and Section VI concludes the paper.

2 The Distributed Virtual Predictive Environment

There are two redundant robots in the virtual environment, a PA-10 made in Japan and a modular 7 DOF redundant robot made in German. Each robot has a 3-figer dexterous hand mounted at its wrist. At the on spot site, the PA-10 robot and the modular redundant robot are located on two pair of guide rail respectively, and they can move along these guide rails.

The Distributed Virtual Environment (DVE) for multiple teleoperated robots is modularized to enhance whole system's reliability, expansibility and maitainability. There are three main modules designed and implemented in DVE: Control center and two predictive display modules that can be used by two human operators respectively. These three logic modules are connected by networks. The module of Control Center is a multi-thread applied program adopting client-server structure. It is responsible for administrating the whole system, the ownership of nodes, and synchronizing whole system.

Each module of predictive display has the similar structure and consists of several sub-modules. Fig.1 illustrates the components of the module of predictive display.

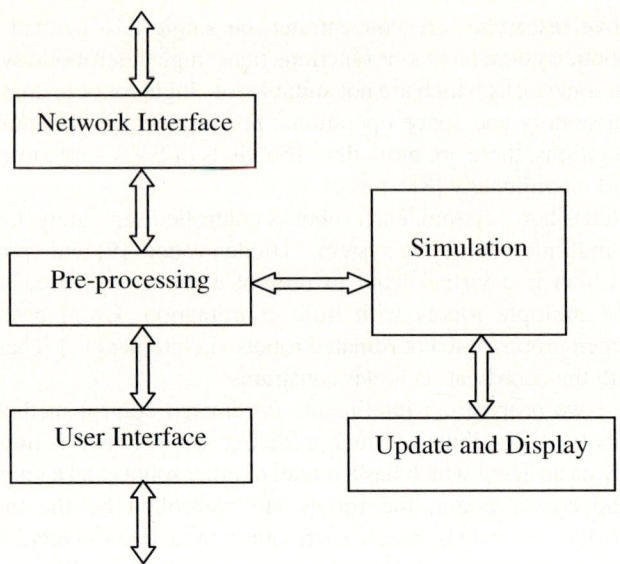

Fig. 1. Predictive display module

In Fig.1, the user interface module receives human operator's control command, and reflects the simulated results to human operator. The network interface module is responsible for communication via the networks (LAN /Internet). Three pairs of communication Socket connect the control center and the two predictive display modules. Pre-processing module can be used to construct and modify the knowledge base of the agents which represent the robots.The simulation module is a kernel module. It contains geometric models and two agents. Each agent has a knowledge base and a data base and can conduct knowledge based reasoning.

The control center can be seen as a server, and the predictive display units can be seen as clients. The objects in each predictive display unit can be categorized into three classes. First one is controllable object whose displacement can be controlled directly by the human teleoperator using haptic interactive device at the same unit, such as redundant robot, dexterous hand and the object that can be moved by the teleoperator. The second is uncontrollable object that cannot be controlled directly by the human teleoperator at the same unit, such as the robot and dexterous hand directly controlled by other human teleoperator. The third is unmovable object, such as guide rails and platform.

In each period of simulation, if the states of some objects in some predictive display unit are changed, the unit sends request to the server. After client's requests are acknowledged, client sends the information of its current states accompanied with time stamp to the server. Then the server sends the information to other units. Each unit listen the commands that come from the server through network interface module.

When it receives the server's command including object's state information, it interprets the command, and according to the current time and the stamped time it calculates the current state of the object which is identified in the command. Then it refreshes its own local models. All the uncontrollable objects in each predictive display unit can be refreshed under the control of the synchronous center.

3 Minimum Distance Query and Collision Detection

Starting autonomous control and planning the coordinated motion need the information of collision and the minimum distance and the closest features between the two robots.

We establish geometric representations of objects in terms of polygonal meshes. We use these vertices of triangles to bridge the closest points and the geometric features of objects. A special data structure is developed for these vertices, where the correspondences between each vertex and the triangles as well as the feature to which it belongs are stored as the result of the preprocessing. The 3-dimentional coordinates of a vertex is defined in the object's coordinate frame. We developed an extended algorithm based on the GJK method [12] to track the minimum distance between the polygonal models of two objects in real-time.

At runtime, the pair of point s1 and s2 for finding the minimum distance and the closest pair of points on two features f and h of two objects O1 and O2 can be obtained dynamically from the closest points between the polygonal approximations of the two objects. The closest feature h of O2 corresponds to p1 can be decided similarly. The above rules are stored in the knowledge base of the robot agent.

We also developed an octagonal bounding box method to detect the collision between polygonal models [13]. The collision checking between bounding boxes is based on the theory of separating axis. There are total 15 separating axes between rectangular bounding boxes. The number of separating axis between rectangular and octagonal bounding box is 20.

4 Intelligent Control Strategies for Multiple Teleoperated Robot Cooperation

Generally speaking, the motion of muti-telerobot can be classed as coarse motion and fine motion. For instance, when robot's end effector is far away from its destination, its motion belongs to coarse motion. When robot's end effector is close to its destination or when multi-robot begin to work coordinately, their motion belongs to fine motion. When robot does gross motion, the master/slave control mode is adopted. Under this condition, multiple robot cooperation is mainly conducted by teleoperators who communicated each other via interaction device, and what the DVE does is to calculate minimum distance and detects potential collisions and show results to human operator. In the condition that robot is close to its destination, the robots are fully autonomous.

The autonomous motion planning is conducted by the intelligent agent of robot. The structure of each agent is shown as Fig.2.

The meta-system is the core of this system. It has the knowledge base, real-time inference engine and data base. The real-time inference mechanism guarantees the real-time performance of system. The knowledge base is a key model, and it affects the performance of motion planning greatly. It is composed of meta-knowledge, task knowledge, maintaining method base, status base (minimum distance and contact status) and simulation models. Meta-knowledge is in charge of the control and management of the whole system, task coordination knowledge comprises case based coordination; maintaining method base saves the disposal methods of motion planning, and simulation models runs synchronously with the practical system to provide quantitative information for the data and knowledge base.

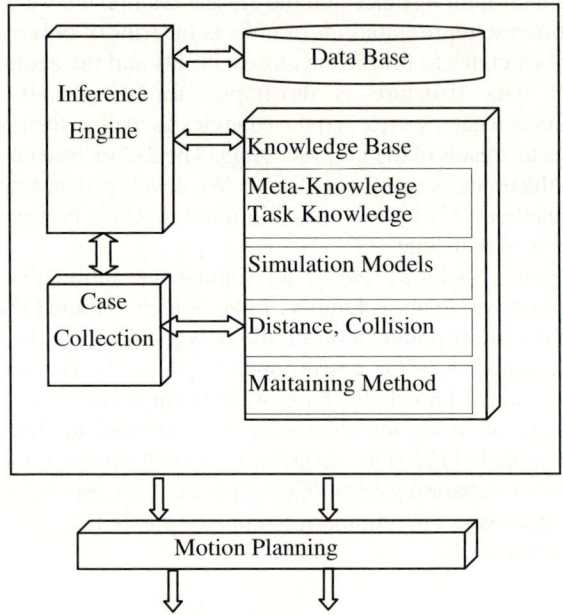

Fig. 2. Structure of Agent

The model of other robot is pre-built. Data base saves the data produced or needed during the period of system's running. The agent updated its data base and other robot models in each cycle. Case collection model saves all important events and experience about task for knowledge acquirement.

If-then rules (closest feature determination, actions according to minimum distance, contact status, virtual contact force, task decomposition, etc.) are built in knowledge base. For example, we can obtain the contact status of the end effectors of the two robots through the contact force and moment [14].The motion planning for coordination is given by real time reasoning.

We use object oriented programming method to implement the knowledge base motion planning. We define a new class containing both numeric attributions and symbolic attributions, and each attribution corresponding to motion planning output is attached a variable of valid period. The knowledge base is embedded in the process of reasoning. The rules in knowledge base describe the relationships among numeric data and symbolic data and the relationships among system data. Because the knowledge base of each agent is small, the matching process during reasoning is fast. The variable of valid period attached to the attribution of output data can be used to maintain information coincidence and real time reasoning. When some attribution about output data is needed, its valid period is checked first. If it is still valid, then there is not necessary to initiate reasoning. If its valid period is expired, then backward chain reasoning is initiated.

5 Preliminary Experimental Results

As the stage of collision detection, the running time for collision detection is presented in Tables 1. Table 1 illustrates the time of collision detection between a pair of bounding volumes. The data show that the entire intersecting checking is very fast in the order of hundreds of microseconds (μs) compared to traditional Orientation Bounding Box (OBB) method.

Table 1. Average time (in millisecond) for intersection checking of one pair of bounding volume nodes

	disjoint	intersected
OBBs	0.005	0.008
Octagonal	0.006	0.017

Fig. 3 shows that the average running time of the minimum distance algorithm ranges from 1.0 to 1.8 millisecond.

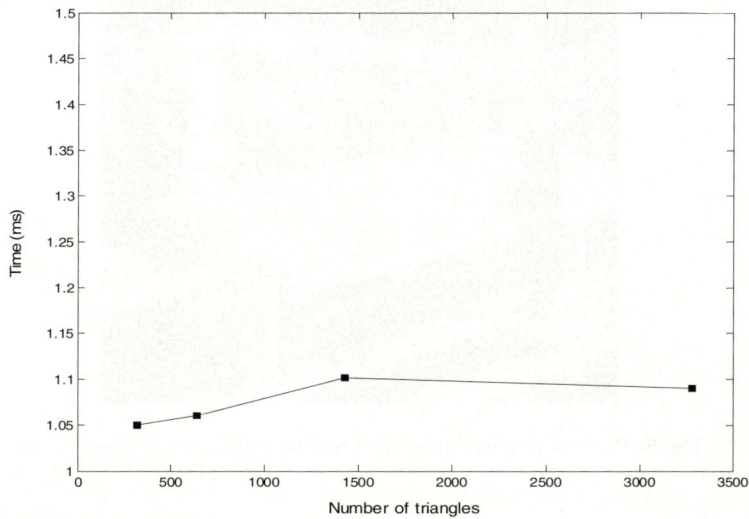

Fig. 3. Time cost with respect to different number of triangles of geometric model

We use the peg in hole task to test the proposed coordination method. There are a peg and a cylindrical part with a hole on the experimental table. The task is that each arm/hand integrated robotic system grasps the two parts respectively, then inserts the peg into the hole on the cylindrical part and move them coordinately.

Fig.4 illustrates the fine motion phase that the two robots need cooperation. In Fig.5, the two arm/hand integrated robotic systems can work coordinately to accomplish the task and can rotate and move the cylindrical part with the peg in hole.

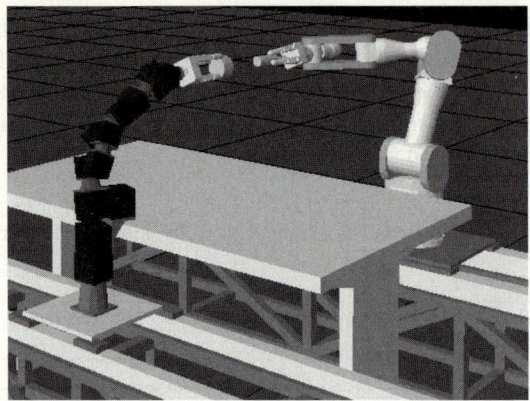

Fig. 4. The predictive display in fine motion phase

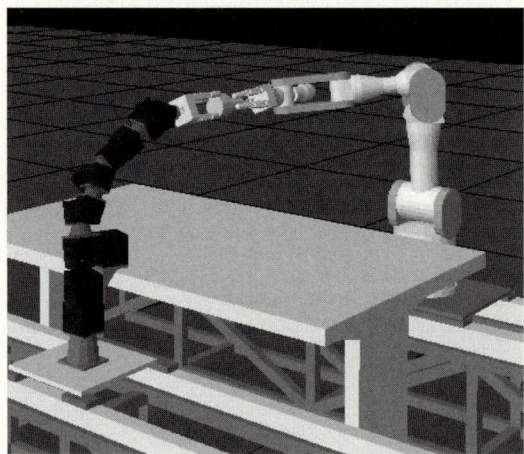

Fig. 5. The two arm/hand integrated robotic systems work coordinately

6 Conclusions

This paper proposes an intelligent control method for the coordination of multiple teleoperated robots. By developing intelligent agent of each robot, the coordinated motion can be planned by knowledge based reasoning, which embedded the heuristic intelligence of human operator when he conducts the same task. The knowledge based reasoning of each agent is conducted based on the knowledges about the task and system status in a virtual distributed environment, and the coordinated motion planning results can be outputted for the real robotic system to carry on.

Experimental shows this system can run in real time and can fulfill the requirement of intelligent coordination of multiple teleoperated robots.

Acknowledgments. This work was supported by the National Key Basic Research Program (973 program) under grant No. 2002CB312204.

References

1. Hirzinger G.., Brunner B., Dietrich J. and Heindl J.: Sensor-Based Space Robotics-ROTEX and Its Telerobotic Features. IEEE Trans. onRobotics and Automation, Vol. 9, No. 5 (1993) 649–663
2. Funds J., Lindsay T., Paul R.: Teleprogramming : Toward Delay-Invariant Remote Manipulation. Presence, Vol. 1, No. 1(1992):29-44
3. Sheridan T.B.: Space Teleoperation through Time Delay:Review and Prognosis. IEEE Transactions on Robotics and Automation, Vol. 9, No. 5 (1993)592-606
4. Li L.: Development of a Telepresence Controlled Ambidextrous Robot for Space Application. Proceedings of IEEE International Conference on R&A (1996)58-63,
5. Kim W.S.: Computer Vision Assisted Virtual Reality Calibration. IEEE Transactions on Robotics and Automation, Vol. 15, No. 3 (1999)450-464
6. Bejczy A.K., Fiorini P., et al..: Toward Integrated Operator Interface for Advanced Teleoperation under Time Delay. Intelligent Robots and Systems, Vol. 28, No. 6 (1995)327-349
7. Yoon W.K., Goshozono T., Kawabe H., et al..: Model-Based Teleoperation of a Space Robot on ETS-VII Using a Haptic Interface. IEEE International Conference on Robotics & Automation (2001)407-412
8. Jau B.M.: Dexterous Telemanipulation with Four Fingered Hand System. IEEE International Conference on Robotics and Automation (1995)338-343
9. Kheddar A., Tzafestas C. Coiffet P., et al..: Parallel Multi-Robots Long Distance Teleoperation. Proc. Int. Conf. on Advanced Robotics (1997)1007-1012,
10. Freund E., Rosmann J.: Projective Virtual Reality: Bridging the Gap between Virtual Reality and Robotics. IEEE Transactions on Robotics and Automation, Vol. 15, No. 3 (1999)411-424
11. Xi N., Tarn T.J., and Bejczy A.K..: IntelligentPlanning and Controlfor Multi-Robot Coordination-An Event-Based Approach. IEEE Trans. On Robotics and Automation, Vol.1 (1999)219-224
12. Gilbert E. G., Johnson D.W., and Keerthi S. S.: A Fast Procedure for Computing the Distance between Complex Objects in Three- Dimensional Space. IEEE J. Robot. Automat.,Vol. 4 (1988) 193-203
13. Chou W.S., Xiao J.: A Collision Detection Method for Virtual Manufacturing. Transactions of the North American Manufacturing Research Institute of SME, Vol. 32 (2004)319-326
14. Chou W.S., Wang T.M.: The Arm/Hand Integrated Telerobotic System Based on Sensory Information. IEEE International Conference on Robotics, Intelligent Systems and Signal Processing, Vol.2 (2003)809–814

SMas: A Shopping Mall Multiagent Systems

Javier Bajo[1], Yanira de Paz[2], Juan Francisco de Paz[2], Quintín Martin[3], and Juan M. Corchado[2]

[1] Universidad Pontificia de Salamanca, Compañía 5 37002, Salamanca, Spain
jbajope@upsa.es
[2] Departamento Informática y Automática, Universidad de Salamanca,
Plaza de la Merced s/n 37008, Salamanca, Spain
yanira@usal.es, fcofds@gmail.com, corchado@usal.es
[3] Departamento Estadística, Universidad de Salamanca,
Plaza de la Merced s/n 37008, Salamanca, Spain
qmm@usal.es

Abstract. This paper presents a multiagent model that facilitates aspects of shopping mall management, as well as increasing the quality of leisure facilities and shopping on offer. The work presented focuses on the use of a multi agent architecture, based on the use of deliberative agents that incorporates case-based planning. The architecture considers a dynamic framework, and the need to use autonomous models that are able to evolve over time. The architecture incorporates agents whose aim is to acquire knowledge and adapt themselves to the environmental changes. The system has been tested successfully, and the results obtained are presented in this paper.

Keywords: CBR, CBP-BDI, wireless multiagent system, shopping mall, SMAS.

1 Introduction

Agents and multiagent systems are adequate for developing applications in dynamic, flexible environments. Agents can be characterized through their capacities in areas such as autonomy, reactivity, pro-activity, social abilities, reasoning, learning and mobility. These capacities can be modelled in various ways, using different methodologies [1]. One of the possibilities is to use Case Based Reasoning (CBR). This paper presents a distributed architecture whose principal characteristic is the use of CBP agents [2, 3, 4]. These deliberative agents incorporate a reasoning CBP (Case Based Planning) engine, a variant of the CBR (Case Based Reasoning) system [5, 6]. The CBP system makes it possible for the agents to learn from initial knowledge, interact autonomously with the environment and system users, and allows it to adapt itself to environmental changes.

The aim of this work is to obtain an architecture that allows the development of multi-objective agents, which incorporate CBP reasoning mechanisms, for dynamic environments. To achieve this aim we have concentrated in a specific problem, the management of some aspects of a shopping mall, and we use an architecture that makes it possible to construct agents capable of adapting its knowledge to environmental changes. There are many different architectures for constructing deliberative agents and many of them are based on the BDI model. In the BDI model, the internal structure of an agent and its capacity to choose, is based on mental aptitudes. The BDI model uses the agent's beliefs as informational aptitudes, its desires as motivational aptitudes and its intentions as deliberative aptitudes. The method proposed in [7] facilitates the incorporation of CBR systems as a deliberative mechanism within BDI agents, allowing them to learn and adapt themselves, lending them a greater level of autonomy than pure BDI architecture [4]. The management of a shopping mall is a problem in a dynamic environment. Moreover several goals must be controlled, such as offers, product or service promotions, plans generation for a user profile and preferences, etc.

SMas incorporates "lightweight" agents that can live in mobile devices, such as phones, PDAs, etc. These agents make it possible for a client to interact with the SMas in a very simple way, downloading and installing a personal agent in his mobile phone or PDA. The system also incorporates one agent for each shop in the shopping mall. These agents can calculate the optimal promotions and services at a given moment. The core of the SMas is a Coordinator agent in change of the plans (routes) generation in response to a client's request, looking for the best shopping or leisure time alternatives. The agent has to take into account the client profile, the maximum amount of money that the client wants to spend, the time available and the client profile. The generation of routes must be independent of the shopping mall management, in the sense that it is not appropriate to use the same knowledge base (or all the knowledge) that the directorship controls. Only the knowledge corresponding to the offers and promotions at the moment of the client request should be used. Otherwise the client will be directed to the objectives of the shopping mall management. The agents are adapted to work in mobile devices, so they support wireless communication (Wi-Fi, Bluetooth) which facilitates the portability to a wide range of mobile devices [4]. The multiagent system can be designed using a number of methodologies: Gaia [8], AUML [9], MAS-CommonKADS, MaSE, ZEUS and MESSAGE. We have decided to opt for a combination of elements from Gaia and Agent Unified Modeling Language (AUML) for our MAS.

In the next section, we will explain the shopping mall problem that has led to most of this research. In the third section we will describe the wireless multiagent system developed, paying special attention to the Planner agent. Finally, some preliminary results and the conclusions will be presented.

2 Shopping Mall Problem

The Mall has become one of the most prevalent alternatives to traditional shopping [10]. A shopping mall is a cluster of independent shops, planned and developed by one or several entities, with a common objective. The size, commercial mixture, common services and complementary activities developed are all in keeping with their surroundings [10]. Our aim is to develop an open system, capable of incorporating as many agents as necessary, agents that can provide useful services to the clients not only in this shopping centre, but also in any other environment such as the labor market, educational system, medical care, etc. The system provides mechanisms for free easy data consulting. A user will be able to gain access to commercial (shopping and sales) and leasing time information (entertainment, events, attractions, etc.) by using their mobile phone or PDA. Mechanisms for route planning when a user wants to spend their time in the mall will also be available. Moreover, it provides a tool for advertising offers (a commercial manager will be able to make his offers available to the shopping mall clients), or provides a tool to the shopping mall management team in order to contact commercial managers or shopping mall clients, providing an interaction between users interested in the same topics.

The SMas incorporate agents based on a multi objective architecture, such as BDI, which incorporates Case Based Planning mechanisms as a reasoning engine and includes dynamic replanning algorithms. The CBP uses the CBR concepts to reason and create plans. Moreover, the incorporation of a dynamic replanning technique (Most-Re-plan-able Intention) offers the possibility of replanning at time of execution [5, 2] thereby ensuring that every client will use optimal plans at execution time. The use of artificial intelligence models makes it possible to take decisions about the optimal route for a user with a given profile and his preferences at the moment when the suggestion is requested.

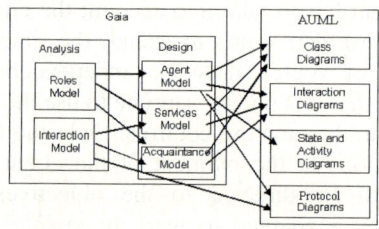

Fig. 1. Methodology used in the development process

3 SMas System Architecture

The option chosen to define an appropriate analysis and design methodology for the problem to be resolved is one that combines Gaia [8] and AUML [9], in an attempt to take advantage of both. Through Gaia it is possible to make an analysis of the problem using organizational criteria and a later design. After applying Gaia, the result consists of a design at the elevated abstraction level. At this point the Gaia design is transformed so that AUML techniques can be applied. Figure 1 illustrates the paths followed in order to obtain the different models used. It shows how Gaia is used initially in order to obtain an analysis and high level design and then AUML is used in order to obtain a detailed, low level design.

Studying the requirements of the problem we have come to the conclusion that we need nine roles: The Communicator role manages all the communications of a client. The Finder role looks for near devices. The Profile Manager role obtains a client profile. The Store operator is in charge of manage the store: data base operations on stored products. Moreover monitors the products shortage, in order to prevent desupply. The Promotions manager role controls the shells in each shop, as well as the promotions that every shop offers to its clients. The Clients Manager role deals with the client profiles management and controls the connected clients at a given moment. The Analist role carries out periodic evaluations on shells, promotions and surveys data trying to provide a good quality service. The Incidents Manager role manages incidents, such as sending advices, or solving a wide range of problems. The Planner role is the most important role in our system. The Planner creates a route printing the most suitable shops, promotions or events to the client profile and available resources at one particular moment. As can be seen in Figure 2, the Incidents Manager role is composed of responsibilities, permissions, activities and protocols. The Incidents Manager is authorized to read and change the Incidents DB, and it is responsible for the incidents management, product orders and sending advices. Besides it must maintain a successful connection with the Incidents DB.

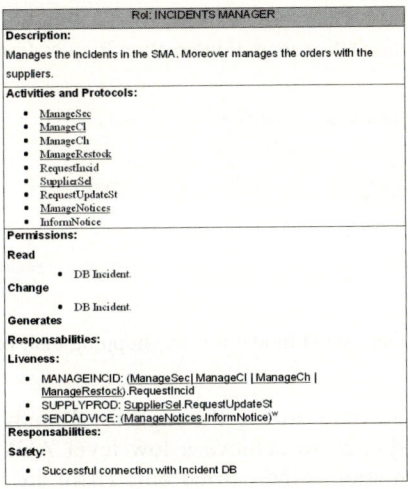

Fig. 2. Gaia roles model: Incidents Manager role

As far as interaction model is concerned, the dependences and relations between roles are described. Each interaction in which two roles are involved requires protocols (described in the roles model). In the SMA presented in this work the next protocols have been considered: RequestPromotionsData, SolveConsult, StoreProducts, AlertShortage, OrderSupplier, InformProductsState, InformPromotionsState, SolveIncident, SolveSuggestion, Notify. Figure 3 shows the interaction diagram that represents the interaction between the Analist and the Store Manager roles when the Analist requests a promotion inform.

Traditional techniques of software engineering are not followed in terms of detailing the analysis to the extent that a direct implementation can be made. Instead, the level of abstraction is reduced so that traditional techniques can be applied. In the design process three models are considered: agent model, services model and acquaintance model [8]. As we can see in Figure 4, the agent model shows the types of agents that are going to appear in the system, as well as the number of instances for each agent type that can be executed within the execution time. For example agent Store plays the Promotions Manager and Store Operator roles.

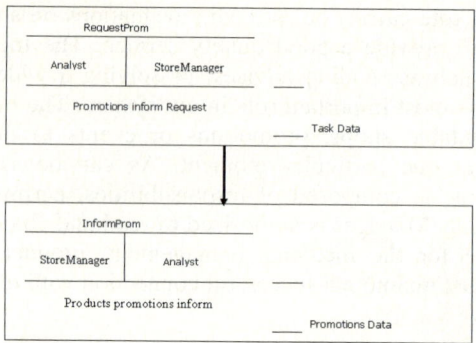

Fig. 3. Gaia interaction model: interaction RequestPromotionsData

Fig. 4. Gaia agent model for the shopping mall problem

Our proposal deals with how to use the high level analysis and design obtained through the Gaia methodology to achieve a low level AUML design, with enough detailed for an implementation to be carried out. There are three concepts that vary slightly with respect to their meaning in Gaia and AUML: role, service and capability [9]. The AUML design provides class diagrams for each agent, collaboration or sequence diagrams for each interaction, state and activity diagrams to represent internal states and protocol diagrams to model communicative acts [9].

In our system a CBP agent is used, the Coordinator agent. It is an agent that deals with multiple objectives derived from the tasks of coordinating all the shops in the shopping mall, client management and its main task, planning and optimization of routes. The routes and promotions proposed to a client consider the client profile and his resources (money and time) at the moment of the route request. In the Figure 5 it is possible to observe that the Coordinator agent is able to generate routes, analyze shell and promotion data, manage incidents and manage clients at the same time. To solve the problem of routes generation the Coordinator uses an innovative planning mechanism: the case based planning. CBP provides the agent with the capabilities of learning and adaptation to the dynamic environment. Moreover, the Coordinator will be able to apply a dynamic replanning technique, the MRPI (Most RePlan-able Intention), which allows the agent to change a plan at execution time when an incident happens [3]. The Coordinator agent has seven capabilities and offers three services that are available to the rest of the agents of the SMA. It is necessary play especial attention to the Update, KBase y VCBP capabilities. The reason is that these capabilities implement the reasoning cycle of the CBP system. The Update capability implements the retrieve and retain stages, while the KBase capability implements the reuse stage and the capability VCBP the revise stage. The VCBP capability is also in charge of dynamic replanning task. The AUML roles are obtained through the liveness properties described in the Gaia role model role.

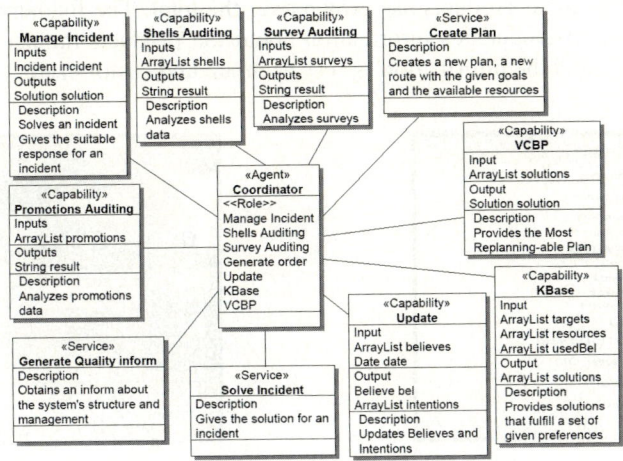

Fig. 5. Coordinator agent class diagram

Finally, to complete the AUML design, the collaboration and sequence diagrams are obtained. The protocol diagrams represent the communicative acts in the system. Once the design is finished, the implementation is carried out. The platform chosen is Jadex, a Jade [11] add-on that incorporates the BDI model to the Jade agents.

4 Results and Conclusions

The previously described system was tested at the Tormes Shopping Mall in the city of Salamanca during 2005. During this period of time, the multiagent system has been tuned and updated, and the first autonomous prototype started to work in October 2005. Although the system is not fully operational and the aim of the project is to construct a research prototype and not a commercial tool, the initial results have been very successful from the technical and scientific point of view. Figure 6 presents two screen shots of the User agent. Figure 6 shows the form for introducing personal data. It also shows the route generated for a client that wants buy clothes and take coffee. The fundamental concept when we work with a CBR system is the concept of case, and it is necessary to establish a case definition. A case in our problem, managed by the Coordinator agent, is composed of the attributes described in Table 1. Cases can be viewed, modified and deleted manually or automatically by the agent (during its revision stage). The agent plans (intentions) can be generated using different strategies since the agent integrates different algorithms.

SMas has been tested during the last three months of 2005 and the results have been very accurate. The system implementation has involved an increase in benefits due to the generation of automatic promotions. The e-commerce techniques [10] have facilitated custom-designed services for the clients. A user can easily find the products he is interested in, spend his leisure time in a more efficient way and make contact with other clients with whom he can share hobbies or opinions. So the degree of client satisfaction has been improved as observed in the surveys. The percentage of the sale of promotional products has grown over the total. The fundamental reason is that clients have instantaneous information about the products the agent thinks they are interested in, and the information is very accurate and customized.

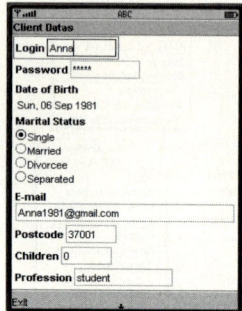 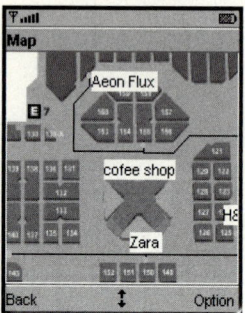

Fig. 6. Screen shots for user profile and inform route

Table 1. Case fields

Case Field	Measurement
CLIENT	Client personal profile (ClientProfile)
MONEY	Money to spend (Money)
TIME	Available Time (Time)
INIT	User initial location (Location)
PREF	User preferences (Preference)

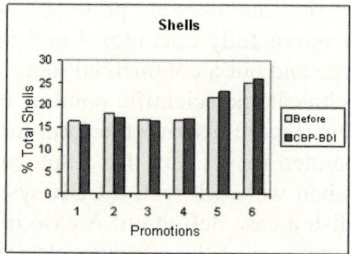

Fig. 7. Shell promotional products and shell total products

The increase in promotional products sold can be seen in Figure 7. Figure 7 shows how new promotions are launched, and the increased percentage in promotional products sold in comparison with the promotional products sold using traditional commercial techniques carried out the year before. We can observe that at the beginning, the results obtained with the multiagent system were worse than traditional techniques. However, as the system obtained more information about client profiles, products and habits, so the knowledge it obtained became more suitable and it was able to create optimal plans. Moreover the clients also needed some time to get used to the new system.

Acknowledgements. This work has been partially supported by the MCYT TIC2003-07369-C02-02 and the JCYL-2002-05 project SA104A05.

References

1. Wooldridge, M. and Jennings, N. R. (1995) Agent Theories, Architectures, and Languages: a Survey. In: Wooldridge and Jennings, editors, Intelligent Agents, Springer-Verlag, pp. 1-22.
2. Corchado J. M., Pavón J., Corchado E. and Castillo L. F. (2005) Development of CBR-BDI Agents: A Tourist Guide Application. 7th European Conference on Case-based Reasoning 2004. Lecture Notes in Artificial Intelligence 3155, Springer Verlag. pp. 547-559.
3. Glez-Bedia M. and Corchado J. M. (2002) A planning strategy based on variational calculus for deliberative agents. Computing and Information Systems Journal. Vol 10, No 1, 2002. ISBN: 1352-9404, pp. 2-14.
4. Glez-Bedia M., Corchado J. M., Corchado E. S. and Fyfe C. (2002) Analytical Model for Constructing Deliberative Agents, Engineering Intelligent Systems, Vol 3: pp. 173-185.
5. Bajo J. and Corchado J.M. Evaluation and monitoring of the air-sea interaction using a CBR-Agents approach Proccedings of the 6th Internacional Conference on Case-based Reasoning, ICCBR'05 pp. 50-62. Springer Verlag. (2005)
6. Corchado J. M. and Laza R. (2003). Constructing Deliberative Agents with Case-based Reasoning Technology, International Journal of Intelligent Systems. Vol 18, No. 12, December. pp.: 1227-1241
7. Bratman, M.E. (1987). Intentions, Plans and Practical Reason. Harvard University Press, Cambridge, M.A.
8. Wooldridge, M. and Jennings, N. R. and Kinny, D. (2000) The Gaia Methodology for Agent-Oriented Analysis and Design. Journal of Autonomous Agents and Multi-Agent Systems, 3 (3). pp. 285-312.
9. Bauer, B. and Huget, M. P. (2003) FIPA Modeling: Agent Class Diagrams.
10. Adams, F.G. (2003): The E-Business Revolution & the New Economy: E-conomics after the Dot-Com Crash. South-Western Educational Pub.
11. Bellifime, F. Poggi, A. and Rimasa, G. (2001) JADE: a FIPA2000 compliant agent development environement. Proceedings of the 5th international conference on autonomous agents (ACM).

Protecting Agent from Attack in Grid Computing[II]

Byungryong Kim

DongBang Data Technology Co., Ltd. No.417, Hanshin IT Tower #235, Kuro-Dong,
Kuro-Ku, Seoul, Korea, 152-050
doolyn@gmail.com

Abstract. Peer-to-peer computing has been emerged as very popular application due to the strong retrieval performance and the easiness of sharing resource and information. Nonetheless in reality p2p users are demanding more privacy rather than share of information. In this study we propose mutual anonymity technique based on length-restricted multi-path for identity of initiator and responder and the anonymous communication between initiator and responder. In this technique is not easily revealed to denial of service attack by ensuring the anonymity of initiator and responder and anonymous communication is possible by means of grouping technique of intermediate nodes. Compared with the previous studies privacy can easily be ensured without causing cryptography processing overhead by using former protocol only. Overhead, expected in the proposed technique of intermediate node grouping, is evaluated through test.

1 Introduction

Privacy is critical for many networked applications. Yet current Internet protocols provide no support for masking the identity of communication endpoints. In fact the most important protocol, TCP/IP protocol puts more emphasis on the improvement of performance such as scalability or efficiency rather than privacy of users. Therefore under open internet environment when sending information, private information which should be secured may be attacked or detected. Anonymity can largely be classified into three types: resistant-censorship; anonymity of initiator or responder; mutual anonymity. Mutual anonymity is composed of the following three parts: initiator having anonymity; responder having anonymity; and communication having anonymity between the initiator and the responder. In the most recent studies on mutual anonymity, trusted agent, random agent and random or static proxy techniques are included.

Peer-to-Peer(P2P) systems can largely be classified into centralized system and decentralized system. Centralized system such as Napster[2] can be attacked by denial of service. Decentralized system is strong in terms of high fault-tolerance, high autonomy and flexible scalability. This study puts focus on decentralized and unstructured P2P systems. Nodes participating in P2P systems communicate only with neighbor nodes and finally any node is unable to know the information of node which is more than 2 hops away. Hence Query message requesting for retrieval does not include IP address of node to process the Query[1]. identity of peer is exposed to all the neighbors and some of malicious peers collect and analyze information with no difficulty by monitoring packet flow. For example type of packet or TTL value, Hops value, retrieval character and so forth can be obtained. Therefore through this method initiator and responder lose the anonymity among their neighbors and at last P2P system as well loses the anonymity.

This study proposes length-restricted multi-path technique through grouping nodes that can avoid denial of service. Identity is exposed on responder side by initiator receiving QueryHit[1] packet and initiator's identity comes to get exposed to responder by initiator's download request made to responder. Therefore through packet monitoring malicious peer knows who the initiator and responder are. In addition using the information obtained from the information, it can fail initiator and responder with denial of service attack. The proposed technique not only protects identity of initiator and responder through grouping but also enables anonymous communication by performing packet relay for nodes belonging to group in random order. Since cryptography processing implemented in previous papers is not used, it is advantageous in that mutual anonymity can easily be provided using previous protocol as it is without additional overhead.

2 Related Researches

Gnutella[3] is a decentralized P2P file-sharing model developed in the early 2000. To the share files on the Gnutella network, a user starts with a networked computer that runs one of the Gnutella clients. Since the node will work both as a server and a client, it is generally referred to as a servent. Node A connect to another Gnutella-enabled networked computer node B and then node A will announce existence to B. Node B will in turn announce to all its neighboring nodes that A is live. This pattern will continue recursively with each new level of nodes announcing to its neighbors that node A is alive. Once the node A has announced its existence to the rest of the network, the user at this node can now query the contents of the data shared across the network. This announcement broadcasting will end when the TTL packet information expires; that is, at each level the TTL counter will be decreased by one from some initial value until it reaches zero at which point its broadcasting will stop. To prevent users from setting this initial TTL value too high, the majority of the Gnutella servents will refuse packets with excessively high TTL value. However, from the users perspective, maximizing the chances of finding the required file means using as high as possible TTL value therefore creating a trade-off point for this network.

After a connection is established, two servents communicate with each other by exchanging Gnutella protocol descriptors(Ping, Pong, Query, QueryHit, Push)[1]. The Gnutella protocol rules also indicate for all descriptors that a particular response message can only be sent along the same path that carried the matching request-for-response descriptor. For example, Pong descriptor can only be sent along the same path that carried the incoming Ping descriptor, and the analog holds for QueryHit and Query, and Push and Query descriptors respectively. Ping and Query descriptors are broadcasted to all neighbors, and the servent that is recognized as the target of a particular descriptor will not forward that descriptor further. The downloading process is done using the HTTP protocol scheme based on the information extracted from the Result-Set field from the QueryHit descriptor.

The 0.4 version of Gnutella protocol provides an almost ideal environment for the self-replicating malicious agents primarily due to two main features of P2P's design:

the anonymity in the peer-to-peer communication and the variety of the shared files. The anonymity feature involves weakness because each individual servent for the combination of low accountability and over-trust. In a traditional Internet-based transaction, the administrator would be notified when discovering malicious content, so Napster with a centralized index server can disable a user's account if he or she was caught distributing malicious content. However in Gnutella 0.4, every servent with equal right can continuously provide spoofed content to any search request, which is difficult to prevent even by blacklisting the hostile IPs because of many servents using dynamic IP. Moreover, without trusted central supervisor in pure P2P networks, there is no mechanism to propagate the deceiving information to other servents. Various attacks relying on the anonymity have been observed. For instance, the well-known VBS.Gnutella worm[4] (often wrongly referred the Gnutella virus) spreads by making a copy of itself in the Gnutella program directory; then it modifies the Gnutella.ini file to allow sharing the .vbs format files in the Gnutella program folder. Another Gnutella worm called Mandragore[5] establishes a connection with local Gnutella client and pretends an active neighboring peer with local IP address. Then Mandragore will respond affirmatively to any intercepted request with a renamed copy of itself for the requesting peer to download.

The primary goal for Freenet[6] security is protecting the anonymity of requestors and inserters of files. As Freenet communication is not directed towards specific receivers, receiver anonymity is more accurately viewed as key anonymity, that is, hiding the key which is being requested or inserted. Anonymous point-to-point channels based on Chaum's mix-net scheme[7] have been implemented for email by the Mixmaster remailer[8] and for general TCP/IP traffic by onion routing[9,10] and freedom[11]. Such channels are not in themselves easily suited to one-to-many publication, however, and are best viewed as a complement to Freenet since they do not provide file access and storage. Anonymity for consumers of information in the web context is provided by browser proxy services such as the Anonymizer[12], although they provide no protection for producers of information and do not protect consumers against logs kept by the services themselves. Private information retrieval schemes[13] provide much stronger guarantees for information consumers, but only to the extent of hiding which piece of information was retrieved from a particular server. In many cases, the fact of contacting a particular server in itself can reveal much about the information retrieved, which can only be counteracted by having every server hold all information. Reiter and Rubin's Crowds system[14] uses a similar method of proxying requests for consumers, although Crowds does not itself store information and does not protect information producers. Berthold *et al.* propose Web MIXes[15], a stronger system that uses message padding and reordering and dummy messages to increase security, but again does not protect information producers.

Free Haven[16] is an interesting anonymous publication system that uses a trust network and file trading mechanism to provide greater server accountability while maintaining anonymity. MUTE[17] forces all intermediate nodes along the path between the client and the server node to work as proxies to protect the identities of the client and the server. Every node in the path including the client and the server thinks its previous node is the client and its next one the server. Therefore the data from the true server will be relayed node by node along the path causing a heavy traffic, especially for large multimedia files. Tarzan[18] is a peer-to-peer anonymous IP network overly. so it works with any internet application. Its peer-to-peer design makes it decentralized, scalable, and easy to manage. But Tarzan provides anonymity to either clients or servers. Mantis[19] is similar to Crowds in that there are helping nodes to propagate the request to the candidate servers anonymously. Since Mantis preserves the anonymity of the server only, the server knows where is the client. The server sends the requested data to the client directly but in UDP hiding its IP. UDP is convenient to hide the server's identity but due to the packet loss inevitable in UDP Mantis needs additional packet retransmission mechanism.

3 Length-Restricted Multi-path Technique by Means of Intermediate Node Grouping

With the technique proposed in this paper neighbor nodes are tied into a group and the group becomes a fixed proxy. Each node belonging to the group processes the request of client in part. Fig. 1 shows the p2p retrieval system (ie. Gnutella) of general flooding basis. Whenever client sends Query it has GUID value of its own. Therefore when client receives QueryHit packet, in case that the current GUID value and the GUID value of received QueryHit packet are different it is ignored since it is the answer to the former request.

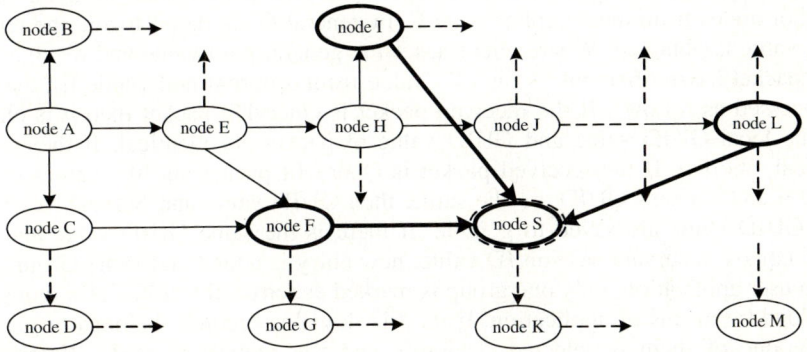

Fig. 1. Packet flow at gnutella system

In Fig. 1 client broadcasts Query packet to neighbor node and the node receiving the packet broadcasts it to the neighbor node again. If retrieval matches to among these nodes, it responds as QueryHit packet. In general Gnutella system, if receiving Query packet having the same quid value again, it is aborted. If not, numerous query packets are generated and substantial network traffic may be found. In the proposed technique these rules are ignored according to certain standard. In Fig. 1 Nodes B, C, and E initially received the packet having the same GUID value. Then they broadcasts it again to server, the neighbor node. According to general rule, server(node S) will respond to one of Queries sent by node I, F, or L if it matches to retrieval. However with technique proposed in Fig. 2, if it matches to retrieval, it will respond to all Queries having the same GUID value.

Nodes I, F, L receiving QueryHit packet from server are grouped as one through the exchange of SetGroup packet. Through the exchange of SetGroup packet, it is known that nodes I, F, L belong to the same group and finally client communicates with server through the group in the end.

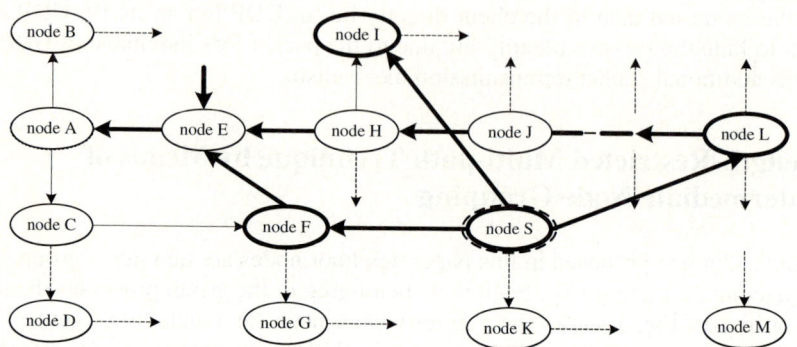

Fig. 2. Grouping intermediate nodes through overlapping receipt of Query message

When downloading a file, client can download file from all the nodes, I, F, L belonging to group. In Fig. 2, client receives QueryHit packet sent by I,F,L server's neighbor nodes from the neighbor node E. In general Gnutella protocol, one retrieval result value is obtained. Where client has same general guid value and receives QueryHit packet having Servant Session ID value from different node(node E), the client is processed as follows. If the received packet is QueryHit packet then it is checked that the local GUID value and GUID value of packet are identical. If they are not identical, abort it. If the received packet is QueryHit packet and the values of local GUID d and packet's GUID are the same, then GUID value and Servant Session ID local GUID value are saved to g_table. If there is the same GUID value and entry which equals to servant session ID value, new entry is added and same Group is set. and In user application, only one group is marked as retrieval result. Users request file download by means of application. If the file download request belongs to g_table a Group, one of them is selected randomly and file request is made. Namely, file download request can be sent to node other than node requested by user.

Fig 3 shows client's downloading flow. In Fig. 2, client tries to download among retrieval list obtained by received QueryHit. If it belongs to a group at g_table, one of them is randomly selected. In Fig. 3 node I was selected. For node I it conforms to the following process. In node I value obtained from SetGroup packet exchange performed at Fig. 2 process is stored at g_table. So it is known that nodes L and F belong to the same group. Node I randomly fixes order within the Group. In Fig. 3, number one is I, number two, L, and number three, F. Node I sends these order information, SetOrderGroup packet to nodes, L and F. Node I sends the IP address and Port value of PUSH packet after setting them as IP address and Port of the last node in order, node F. Because Server received PUSH packet it tries to connect to node F and sends filed requested by client. Node F knows node L with order number 2 and sends the file sent by Sever to node L. Node L sends it to node I with order number 1 again. Finally, Node I sends the file to Node A(client).

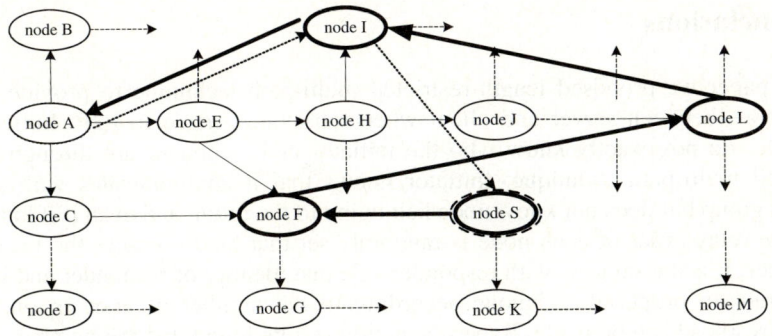

Fig. 3. Anonymous communication flow between server and client

4 Experimentation

In chapter 3 algorithm proposed in this paper was explained. As shown on Fig. 3 several nodes are grouped and nodes in the group relay file between server and client in turn. However there is problem here. If all the nodes between server and client are grouped in one, relay nodes are so many as MUTE so it leads to cause lots of packet and the sending speed is fixed to the lowest bandwidth of nodes within group as well. Accordingly the number of nodes in the same group is needed to be properly fixed.

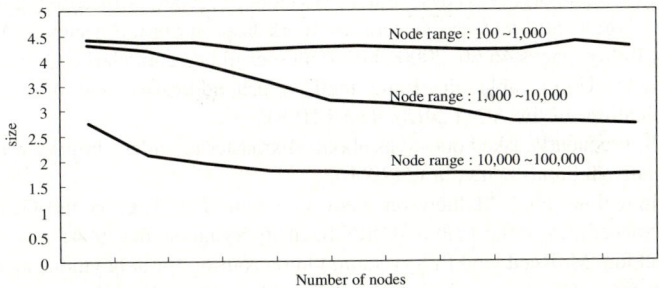

Fig. 4. The number of relay nodes included in Group simulated with Minism

Fig. 4 shows the number of relay nodes included in Group simulated with Minism [20,21]. Maximum neighbor nodes per node is 5, the TTL value is 7, and the probability to be retrieved is 30%. Probability to be retrieved here means that approximately 30 % of all the nodes have matching file. The number of nodes in a group when the size of P2P network is classified as small, medium, and large unit each. As shown on the figures although the number of nodes participating in network is diminished or increased, the number of node in Group is not so variable. Therefore packet overload is not caused as MUTE.

5 Conclusions

In this paper we proposed length-restricted multi-path technique to provide mutual anonymous between server and client when retrieval is made in P2P. Initiator and responder do not exactly know who the initiator and responder are through length-restricted multi-path technique. Initiator knows that it communicates with specific node of group but does not know node belonging to the group and even if it knows the node the relay order of each node is randomly set that hardly knows the location of responder. It is the same as with responder side that identity of responder and initiator is secured. In proposed technique according to the number of node in one group packet overhead can be made. Experimentation results found that the number of relay nodes included in Group is constantly maintained to a certain level regardless of the number of node. Therefore with length-restricted multi-path technique, since overhead such as cryptography processing is not aroused the mutual anonymity can be provided with relatively little overhead.

References

1. The Gnutella Protocol Specification v0.41 Document Revision 1.2., http://rfc-gnutella.sourceforge.net/developer/stable/index.html/
2. Napster, http://www.napster.com/ 2000
3. Gnutella, http://gnutella.wego.com/ 2000
4. VBS.Gnutella worm, http://vil.nai.com/vil/content/Print98666.htm/
5. Mandragore. http://www.openp2p.com/pub/a/p2p/2001/03/22/truelove.html?page=4
6. I. Clarke, O. Sandberg, B. Wiley, and T. W. Hong, Freenet: A distributed anonymous information storage and retrieval system, In Workshop on Design Issues in Anonymity and Unobservability, pages 46.66, 2000., http://citeseer.nj.nec.com/clarke00freenet.html.
7. D.L. Chaum, Untraceable electronic mail, return addresses, and digital pseudonyms, Communications of the ACM 24(2), 84-88 (1981)
8. L. Cottrell, Frequently asked questions about Mixmaster remailers, http://www.obscura.com/~loki/remailer/mixmaster-faq.html (2000).
9. Roger Dingledine, Nick Mathewson, Paul Syverson, Tor: The Second-Generation Onion Router, Proceedings of the 13th USENIX Security Symposium (2004)
10. D. Goldschlag, M. Reed, and P. Syverson, Onion routing for anonymous and private Internet connections, Communications of the ACM 42(2), 39-41 (1999)
11. Zero-Knowledge Systems, http://www.zks.net/ (2000)
12. Anonymizer, http://www.anonymizer.com/ (2000)
13. B. Chor, O. Goldreich, E. Kushilevitz, and M. Sudan, Private information retrieval, Journal of the ACM 45(6), 965-982 (1998)
14. M.K. Reiter and A.D. Rubin, Anonymous web transactions with Crowds, Communications of the ACM 42(2), 32-38 (1999)
15. O. Berthold, H. Federrath, and S. Kopsell, Web MIXes: a system for anonymous and unobservable Internet access, in Proceedings of the Workshop on Design Issues in Anonymity and Unobservability, Berkeley, CA, USA. Springer: New York (2001)
16. R. Dingledine, M.J. Freedman, and D. Molnar, The Free Haven project: distributed anonymous storage service, in Proceedings of the Workshop on Design Issues in Anonymity and Unobservability, Berkeley, CA, USA. Springer: New York (2001)

17. MUTE: Simple, Anonymous File Sharing., http://mute-net.sourceforge.net/
18. Michael J. Freedman, Robert Morris, Tarzan: A Peer-to-Peer Anonymizing Network Layer, in Proceedings of the 1st International Workshop on Peer-to-Peer Systems (IPTPS '02), Cambridge, MA, USA (2002)
19. Stephen C. Bono, Christopher A. Soghoian, Fabian Monrose, Mantis: A Lightweight, Server-Anonymity Preserving, Searchable P2P, Information Security Institute of The Johns Hopkins University, Technical Report TR-2004-01-B-ISI-JHU (2004)
20. Byung-Ryong Kim, Ki-Chang Kim, Anonymous Communication System in P2P Network with Random Agent Nodes, Lecture Notes in Computer Science, Vol.3795 (2005)
21. Gnutella Developer Forum., http://groups.yahoo.com/group/the_gdf/

A Graph Transformation System Model of Dynamic Reorganization in Multi-agent Systems

Zheng-guang Wang, Xiao-hui Liang, and Qin-ping Zhao

Department of Computer Science and Engineering, Beihang University, Beijing,
P.R. China, 100083
{wangzg, lxh, zhaoqp}@vrlab.buaa.edu.cn

Abstract. In an open and dynamic environment, an organization has to cope with various changes from both the external environment and the internal elements in multi-agent systems. Reorganization is the essential capability for an organization to achieve organizational objectives flexibly and becomes one of the key issues of organization theories. To represent formally the dynamic process of reorganization in multi-agent systems, in this paper, we formulate a graph transformation based model of reorganization process in the context of organizational structures. In this model, a multi-level graph is proposed to capture main elements and their inter-relations of the organization and the specific operational semantics of organizational changes are defined with the graph manipulation of this graph based on graph transformation rules. Finally, for methodologies, we specify the examples of applying this graph transformation approach to the transition of organizational structures during the reorganization process.

Keywords: Dynamic reorganization; multi-level graph; graph transformation, multi-agent system.

1 Introduction

Organizations are well recognized as an effective approach to enhance the efficiency of problem solving based on agent computing and decrease conflicts between agents performing the shared tasks cooperatively. However, agent organizations have to cope with various changes from both the external environments, i.e. changing the organizational objectives, and the internal elements in multi-agent systems, i.e. agents leaving from the organizations, which lead to the structural changes of organizations or emergent changes of agent behaviors. Therefore, reorganization is an essential capability provided by agent organizations to achieve organizational objectives flexibly.

In the literature of reorganization and organizational evolution, the existing methodologies can be distinguished by agent-centered and organization-centered approaches. The former emphasizes combining social concepts into agent architectures, i.e. G. Boella et al [5] propose social laws as the set of restrictions on the agents' activities, by which artificial social systems can reason about the evolution of them. Glaser N. et al [6] introduce an agent model with social competences, with which an agent can agree with other agents on the assignment of roles. The latter concentrates on main concepts, namely agents, roles and groups, by which organizational evolution can originate from both the structural changes and behavioral changes of organizations [13]. From the organization-centered view, the existing typical researches relate to organizational self-design [2], [11], formal transition of organizational states [10], dynamic reorganization [8], [13]. In addition, reorganization-oriented simulation is also concerned [12], but it is still at the exploring stage.

In this paper, we aim at formulating the formal process of reorganization in multi-agent systems in the context of organizational structures. Especially, organizational structures describe how agents in the organizations should coordinate their activities to achieve organizational objectives, and also influence the reorganization process in multi-agent systems in some extent. Comparing with the above existing work, our contributions involve giving a formal representation of organizational structures and a graph transformation based formal model of reorganization process in multi-agent systems. To understand the concrete process of reorganization, we introduce the examples of applying this graph transformation approach to analyzing organizational changes.

The remainder of this paper is structured as follows. In section 2, the characteristics of organizational structures are specified. The graph based approach of representing the organizational structure and the analysis of dynamic reorganization with graph transformation are presented in section 3 and 4, respectively. Finally, section 5 draws the conclusions and points the directions of future work.

2 Characteristics of Organizational Structures

Previous work on organizational structures focuses on many central concepts, i.e. agents, roles and social structures (e.g. AGR, MOISE+, OMNI and etc. in [9]). Generally, organizational structures can appear either from the emergent cooperation among agents performing shared task together according to the certain dependence relations [7] or by instantiating the above organizational concepts. In order to capture main elements and their inter-relations of organizational structures, we consider them from three aspects of the social structure, the coordination relations between agents and the role enactment for agents. A diagram of these aspects is shown in Fig.1. The social structure shapes the abstraction of an organizational structure and consists of roles and their inter-relations in the organizational structure. Agent coordination builds the solid organization according to the social structure, in which agents act as the components or entities in multi-agent systems and relate to the given roles by the certain role enactment relations that can be assigned either at the design stage or at the stage of system runtime.

As shown in Fig. 1, a social structure is defined, i.e. there exist three roles supervisor, product manager and engineer labeled by SP, PM and PE associating to the nodes respectively and five agents. In the social structure of this graph, directed arrows linking two roles indicate the relations of dependences between roles. The directed arrows between agents express the relations of coordination that can be considered as the instantiation of dependences between roles after agents enact the corresponding roles.

Fig. 1. An exemplar diagram containing the social structure, agent coordination and role enactment in a manufacturing organization

In multi-agent systems, organizational changes can be considered from the above three aspects. A full formal specification of these aspects is discussed in the next section.

3 The Graph Based Representation of Organizations

In order to model the above three aspects of the organizational structure, we propose a multi-level graph model consisting of the rolegraph, agentgraph and connection graph as follows:

- The top level: namely rolegraph level, which is composed of roles and their inter-relations, i.e. dependences between roles. Roles can be considered as the constructed notion according to their objectives. If an objective of the role is the set of sub-objectives accomplished by other roles, then the role is viewed as the notion of the group. In addition, we only consider the dependences between roles marked by the directed edges in the rolegraph. Dependences describe the constraints on roles and imply other relations between roles, i.e. power and authorization [3].
- The bottom level: namely agentgraph level, which consists of agents and their inter-relations, i.e. coordination between agents.
- The middle level: namely connection graph level having roles and agents in rolegraph and agentgraph respectively as nodes, and the role enactment for agents as its directed edges. Connection graph links the top and bottom level with its directed edges.

The formal specification of the multi-level graph is presented here.

Definition 1 (Rolegraphs)
Let Σr and Δr are two fixed sets of alphabets marking the nodes and edges respectively. A rolegraph is a labeled, directed acyclic graph:

$$G_r = (N_r, E_r, s_r, t_r, l_r, m_r) \quad (1)$$

Where N_r and E_r are two finite sets of nodes and edges with $N_r \cap E_r = \Phi$. $s_r, t_r : E_r \mapsto N_r$ are two functions mapping each edge to its source and target node respectively, and $l_r : N_r \mapsto \Sigma r$, $m_r : E_r \mapsto \Delta r$ are the node and edge labeling functions respectively.

Definition 2 (Agentgraphs)
Let Σa and Δa are two fixed sets of the node and edge alphabets respectively. An agentgraph is a labeled, directed acyclic graph:

$$G_a = (N_a, E_a, s_a, t_a, l_a, m_a) \tag{2}$$

Where N_a and E_a are the finite sets of nodes and edges with $N_a \cap E_a = \Phi$. s_a, t_a, l_a, m_a are the functions of the source, target, node and edge labeling mapping, respectively.

As above, for $< a1, a2 > \in E_a$, there exists a coordination relation between the agent $a1$ and $a2$, that is, the agent $a1$ can manage the activities of the agent $a2$ for their shared tasks, and then, $a1$ will form the coordination relation with $a2$ after they enact the corresponding roles as expressed by the equation (3).

$$R_{dep}(r1, r2) \wedge R_{act}(a1, r1) \wedge R_{act}(a2, r2) \rightarrow R_{cor}(a1, a2) \tag{3}$$

Where $r1$ and $r2$ are two nodes of roles in the rolegraph, $a1$ and $a2$ are two nodes of agents in the agentgraph. R_{dep}, R_{cor} and R_{act} are the binary relations of dependences, coordination and role enactment, respectively. The role enactment is implied by the corresponding edges of the connection graph.

Definition 3 (Connection Graphs)
Let Σc and Δc are two fixed sets expressing the node and edge alphabets with $\Sigma c = \Sigma r \cup \Sigma a$, a connection graph is a bipartite graph G_c:

$$G_c = (N_c, E_c, s_c, t_c, l_c, m_c) \tag{4}$$

Where $N_c = N_r \cup N_a$ is a finite set of nodes including the nodes in the rolegraph and agentgraph, E_c is a finite set of edges partitioning the nodes into two sets N_r and N_a. For each $e \in E_c$, s.t. $s_c(e) \in N_a$ and $t_c(e) \in N_r$. s_a, t_a, l_a, m_a are the source, target, node and edge labeling mappings, respectively.

In the connection graph, each edge indicates the relation of role enactment mapping an agent into a role. We can define a role enactment relation R_{act}:

$$R_{act} = \{(a, r) \mid a \in N_a, r \in N_r, \exists e \in E_c \text{ s.t. } a = s_c(e) \wedge r = t_c(e)\} \tag{5}$$

The multi-level graph model is constructed with rolegraph, agentgraph and connection graph as the Definition 4.

Definition 4 (Multi-level Graph of Organization)
A multi-level graph of organization is a tuple G_m:

$$G_m = (G_r, G_a, G_c) \qquad (6)$$

Where G_r is a rolegraph, G_a is an agentgraph and G_c is a connection graph with $N_c = N_r \cup N_a$.

Based on the multi-level graph, the dynamic process of reorganization can be characterized as the transformation between different graphs by applying certain graph rules in the specific scenarios. We specify a graph transformation system formalizing this dynamic process and the operational semantics of organizational changes in section 4.

4 The Analysis of Dynamic Reorganization Based on Graph Transformation System

The focus here is to provide a formal specification of the reorganization process. For simplicity, we consider that reorganization is enforced based on certain rules, that is, the transition between organizational states can be expressed by the transformation between different instances of the multi-level graph model of organizations. Graph transformation provides a formal basis of graph manipulation [1], [4]. In this section, this process here will be detailed by the notions of the algebraic graph transformation approach.

4.1 Multi-level Graph Transformation System

As above, a multi-level graph transformation system can be constructed by the rolegraph, agentgraph and connection graph shown in the Definition 5.

Definition 5 (Multi-level Graph Transformation System)
A multi-level graph transformation system is a tuple:

$$A_m = (\Gamma_m, \Re_m, \Rightarrow_m, C_m, \varepsilon_m) \qquad (7)$$

Where:

- $\Gamma_m = (\Gamma_r, \Gamma_a, \Gamma_c)$ is a class of multi-level graphs of an organization. Γ_r, Γ_a and Γ_c are the classes of rolegraphs, agentgraphs and connection graphs of the organization.

- $\Re_m$ is a class of graph transformation rules denoted by $\Re_m = \Re_r \times \Re_a \times \Re_c$. $\Re_r$, $\Re_a$ and $\Re_c$ are the classes of the graph rules of rolegraphs, agentgraphs and connection graphs.

- $\Rightarrow_m$ is a rule application operator, its semantics can be defined here. For a rule $p = (\alpha, \beta, \gamma)$, $G_m = (G_r, G_a, G_c) \in \Gamma_m$ and $G_m' = (G_r', G_a', G_c') \in \Gamma_m$, $G_m \stackrel{p}{\Rightarrow}_m G_m'$ iff $G_r \stackrel{\alpha}{\Rightarrow}_r G_r'$, $G_a \stackrel{\beta}{\Rightarrow}_a G_a'$ and $G_c \stackrel{\gamma}{\Rightarrow}_c G_c'$.

- C_m is a class of controlling conditions that specify the destination graph from a given scenario and an initial graph denoted by $C_m = C_r \times C_a \times C_c$, and its semantics can be defined as follows. For $\forall c_m = (c_r, c_a, c_c) \in C_m$, the semantics $SEM(c_m)$ of c_m is presented in the equation (8).

$$SEM(c_m) = \{((G_r, G_a, G_c), (G_r', G_a', G_c')) \in \Gamma_m \times \Gamma_m \mid \\ (G_r, G_r') \in SEM(c_r) \wedge (G_a, G_a') \in SEM(c_a) \wedge (G_c, G_c') \in SEM(c_c)\} \quad (8)$$

- ε_m is a class of graph class expressions denoted by $\varepsilon_m = \varepsilon_r \times \varepsilon_a \times \varepsilon_c$ and its semantics can be specified here, $\forall \chi_m = (\chi_r, \chi_a, \chi_c) \in \varepsilon_m$, the semantics $SEM(\chi_m)$ of χ_m is given in the equation(9).

$$SEM(\chi_m) = SEM(\chi_r) \times SEM(\chi_a) \times SEM(\chi_c) \cap \Gamma_m \quad (9)$$

With graph transformation, we can associate various organizational changes to specific graph manipulation, i.e. the addition or deletion of the nodes or edges in rolegraph, agentgraph and connection graph. The analysis of this reorganization process is discussed as follows.

4.2 The Analysis Process of Reorganization

The graph transformation based approach characterizes the formal process of reorganization that can reflect adaptive mechanisms of organizational structures in multi-agent systems [14]. To specify various changes of organizational structures in multi-agent systems, we present the example indicating the three aspects of the organizational structure in a manufacturing organization as shown in Fig. 1. In this example, for simplicity, we assume that an objective is assigned to a role and each agent plays one role. Formally, graph transformation rules can be constructed by the double pushout approach [1], which specifies the application conditions of these rules, i.e. dangling and identification conditions to ensure that these rules can control exactly in their context some node or edge of the multi-level graph should be deleted or preserved.

As above, a rule of multi-level graph m can be constructed by the product of graph rules of rolegraph, agentgraph and connection graph according to the Definition 5. Fig.2 shows the examples of two graph transformation rules.

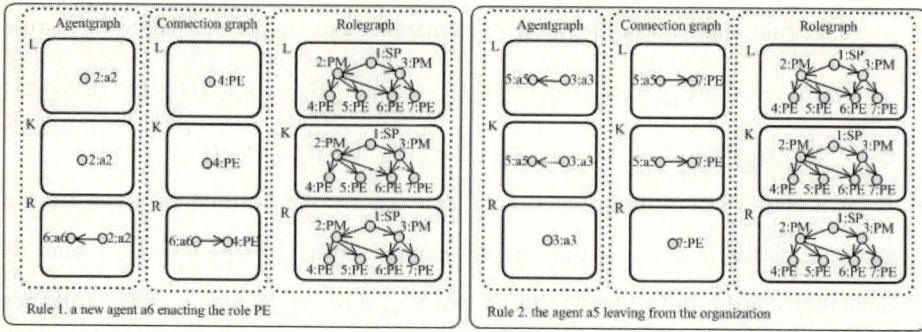

Fig. 2. A diagram indicating two graph transformation rules of a new agent *a6* enacting the role *PE* and the agent *a5* leaving from the organization

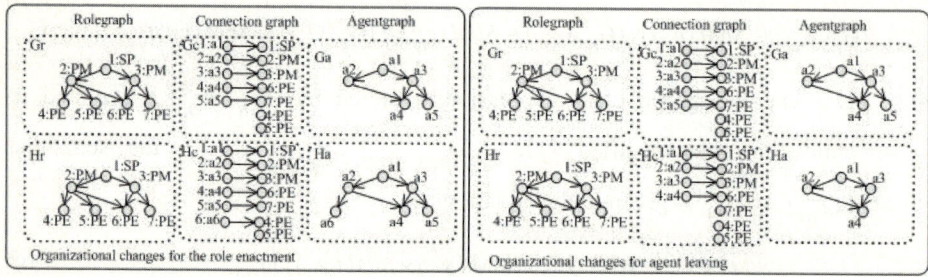

Fig. 3. The two scenarios indicating organizational changes for the role enactment and agent leaving

As shown in Fig.2, there are two graph transformation rules involving a new agent *a6* enacting the role *PE* and the agent *a5* leaving from the organization denoted by *ENACT* and *LEAVING*, respectively. We assume two scenarios of organizational changes, that is, an agent enacting a role in the organization and an agent leaving from the organization, in which the initial scenario is shown in Fig.1 and the destination scenarios are depicted in the left-side and right-side graphs of Fig.3, respectively. The analysis of the scenarios is discussed as follows.

Example 1 (A new agent a6 enacting the role PE).

In the left-side graph of Fig.3, $G_m = (G_r, G_a, G_c)$ is the initial graph. When the agent *a6* enacts the role *PE*, the instance G_m of the multi-level graph of the organization is transformed into $H_m = (H_r, H_a, H_c)$ by applying the rule *ENACT* to G_m. After enacting the role *PE*, the agent *a2* will form the coordination relation with *a6* in the agentgraph of H_m according to the dependence between *PM* and *PE*, and an edge from *a6* to the role *PE* is also added in the connection graph of H_m as shown in the left-side graph of Fig.3.

Example 2 (The agent a5 leaving from the organization).
The right-side graph of Fig.3 shows the scenario that the agent $a5$ leaves from the organization. In this scenario, the destination graph H_m originates from the initial graph G_m by applying the rule *LEAVING* . After the agent $a5$ leaves from the organization, the node $a5$ is deleted and the edge from $a3$ to $a5$ is removed from the agentgraph of G_m. Similarly, the node $a5$ and an edge indicating the role enactment from $a5$ to the role *PE* are also removed from the connection graph of G_m.

In the above examples, there are no changes in the rolegraphs of the initial graphs and destination graphs since the graph rules only specify the behavioral changes in the organization. To enforce the transformation of organizational structures in multi-agent systems, the particular components should be provided by these systems to monitor and control this reorganization process.

5 Conclusions

We have presented a graph transformation system based approach to formulate the process of dynamic reorganization in multi-agent systems. In this approach, we introduced a multi-level graph model involving the rolegraph, agentgraph and connection graph to characterize main elements and their inter-relations of organizational structures and specified a graph transformation system based on this multi-level graph. Based on this graph transformation based approach, various organizational changes can be integrated into the graph transformation system. Finally, we discussed the examples of reorganization process with this graph transformation approach.

In our further work, we will refine the graph transformation model, and elaborate the graph transformation rules and controlling conditions in order to represent the mechanisms of reorganization and combine this graph transformation approach with quantitative simulation analysis as well.

References

1. Andrea Corradini, Hartmut Ehrig, Reiko Heckel, Michael Lowe, Ugo Montanari, and Francesca Rossi.: Algebraic approaches to graph transformation part I: Basic concepts and double pushout approach. In Grzegorz Rozenberg, editor, Handbook of Graph Rewriting. Vol. I: Foundations. World Scientific (1996)
2. B. Horling, B. Benyo, and V. Lesser: Using Self-Diagnosis to Adapt Organizational Structures. Computer Science Technical Report TR-99-64, University of Massachusetts at Amherst (1999)
3. D. Grossi, F. Dignum, L. Royakkers, M. Dastani: Foundations of Organizational Structures in Multi-Agent Systems. Fourth International Conference on Autonomous Agents and Multiagent Systems, Utrecht, ACM Press (2005) 690-697
4. Ehrig, H., Pfender, M., Schneider, H.: Graph Grammars: an Algebraic Approach. In 14th Annual IEEE Symposium on Switching and Automata Theory, IEEE (1973)167– 180

5. G. Boella and L. van der Torre: Organizations in Artificial Social Systems. Postproceedings of AAMAS-05 workshop on From Organizations to Organization Oriented Programming (OOOP@AAMAS05), Springer, LNCS (2006)
6. Glaser, N. and Morignot, P.: The Reorganization of Societies of Autonomous Agents. In Modelling Autonomous Agents in Multi-Agent Worlds (MAAMAW). (Ronneby, Sweden), LNAI, Vol. 1237, Springer Verlag (1997)98-111
7. Jaime Simão Sichman and Rosaria Conte: Multi-Agent Dependence by Dependence Graphs. In Proc. 1st International Joint Conference on Autonomous Agents and Multi-Agent Systems (AAMAS'02), Bologna, Italy (2002) 483-492
8. Jomi Fred Hübner, Jaime Simão Sichman, and Olivier Boissier: Using the MOISE+ for a cooperative framework of MAS reorganisation. In Ana L. C. Bazzan and Sofiane Labidi, editors, Proceedings of the 17th Brazilian Symposium on Artificial Intelligence (SBIA'04), volume 3171 of LNAI, Berlin, Springer (2004) 506-515
9. Luciano R. Coutinho, Jaime S. Sichman, Olivier Boissier: Modeling Organization in MAS: A Comparison of Models. First Workshop on Software Engineering for Agent-oriented Systems (2005)
10. Matson, E., DeLoach, S.: Formal transition in agent organizations. International Conference on Integration of Knowledge Intensive Multi-Agent Systems (2005)235 – 240
11. So, Y. and Durfee, E. H.: An organizational self-design model for organizational change. In AAAI-93 Workshop on AI and Theories of Groups and Organizations: Conceptual and Empirical Research, Washington, D.C. (1993)8-15
12. Vasco Furtado, Adriano Melo, Virginia Dignum, Frank Dignum, Liz Sonenberg: Exploring congruence between organizational structure and task performance: a simulation approach. OOOP@AAMAS'05 (2005)
13. Virginia Dignum, Liz Sonenberg, Frank Dignum: Towards Dynamic Reorganization of Agent Societies, Proceedings of Workshop on Coordination in Emergent Agent Societies at ECAI 2004, Valencia, Spain (2004)
14. Wang Zheng-guang, Liang Xiao-hui, and Zhao Qin-ping: Adaptive Mechanisms of Organizational Structures in Multi-agent Systems. Proceedings of Ninth Pacific Rim International Workshop on Multi-Agents, Guilin, Z. Shi and R. Sadananda (Eds.): PRIMA 2006, LNAI 4088, Springer Verlag (2006)471 – 477

Efficient Search of Winning Strategies in Multi-agent Systems on Random Network: Importance of Local Solidarity

Tin Yau Pang and K.Y. Szeto

Department of Physics,
Hong Kong University of Science and Technology,
Hong Kong
phszeto@ust.hk

Abstract. Multi-agent systems defined on a network can be used for modelling the competition between companies in terms of market dominance. In view of the enormous size of the search space for winning strategies of initial configuration of resource allocation on network, we focus our search on the subspace defined by special local clustering effects, using the recently developed evolutionary computational algorithm. Strategies that emphasize local solidarity, measured by the formation of clusters in the form of triangles linkage between members of the same company, prove to be effective in winning both the market share with high probability and high speed. The result provides a good guideline to improve the collective competitiveness in a network of agents. The formulation is based on the Ising model in statistical physics and the evolutionary game is based on Monte Carlo simulation. Significance and the application of the algorithm in the context of econophysics and damage spreading in network are discussed.

1 Introduction

The resource allocation problem is an interesting problem in econophysics where it considers different competitors on the market trying to achieve market dominance in the shortest time [1]. A good example can be found in the competition between telecommunication service providers on a social network. The telecommunication service providers are interested in expanding their business in terms of subscribing clients by good allocation of their resource. It is a common promotional practice that the service providers offer a lower price or other bonus to reward the clients to make intra-network phone calls, that is, phone call made between users subscribing the same company. In this way, clustering in social networks becoming clustering of the clients for the company. Users will find the promotional offer of intra-network call attractive, as most calls will be made between friends. We therefore anticipate that clustering effects will be a useful guideline in the design of winning strategy in resource allocation.

If one maps the clustering effect of social networks to the problem of local interactions in econophysics, one natural description will be the localized magnetic moment models commonly studied in statistical physics. A simplest model for two competing companies is the Ising model on the network. The model consists of a set of Ising spins with two possible values, up or down, (representing two companies, say, black or white). The local interaction with neighbouring spins will determine the spin orientation probabilistically, according to the Boltzmann factor. In the ferromagnetic version of the Ising model, if most of the spin in the neighbouring sites are pointing up (down), then it is likely to point up (down). In order to relate this model to the problem of the resource allocation for the telecommunication service provider, we assume that the clients are living in an artificial society defined by a social network [2] where every node of the network represents a client and a pair of connected nodes means that the pair of clients communicates frequently on the phone. (Here we consider a bi-directional network). We approach the problem with the Ising model of statistical mechanics in physics [3] and model the social network with a random network [4]. Every node of the network has an Ising spin [5], with a freedom to choose its state (up or down), corresponding to the service provider subscribed. The approach to the resource allocation problem is: (1) generate a set of initial spin configuration on the network, (2) simulate the initial configurations using Monte Carlo simulation [6] to find the probability and speed for the different telecommunication service provider to achieve dominance on the network and (3) evolve the initial spin configuration with Mutation Only Genetic Algorithm (MOGA) [7,8,9] to improve the winning probability and speed of dominance of the spin configuration. Here speed is the inverse of time required for a service provider to achieve dominance, which is a good parameter to assess the competence of a strategy.

2 Modelling of the Resource Allocation Problem

The resource allocation problem of the telecommunication service providers can be modelled by multi-agent system defined on a random network simulated by Monte Carlo simulation [1]. A random network with L nodes with connection probability p is formed by linking every pair of nodes with probability p. Every node on the network represents a client in the model, and a link between two nodes represents their established communication. Here we assume that only two telecommunication service providers are competing in order to simplify the model. For a node i there is a spin s_i residing on it. The state of spin (up: $s_i = +1$ or down: $s_i = -1$) represents the subscribed telecommunication service provider. The interaction energy E between two spins is defined as

$$E = -\sum_{i>j}^{L} J_{ij} s_i s_j \qquad (1)$$

Here J_{ij} is 1 if node i and j are connected in the network and 0 otherwise. The energy E is raised by a pair of nodes with opposite spin type and lowered otherwise. If we interpret E as some monotonic increasing function of the total spending of the client on the telecommunication service, then we expect that E tends to drop throughout the simulation since people are eager to minimize their cost. To make a fair game, we assume that none of the service providers has enough resource to supersede its competitors so that we constrain the initial configuration of the model to be any spin configuration with equal dominance of different spin types: the two service providers have 50% market share at the beginning. In our simulation we studied two random network both having $L=60$, one with $p = 0.05$ and the other with $p = 0.1$.

3 Monte Carlo Simulation to Evolve the Initial Spin Configuration on the Random Network

The initial spin configurations in the model are evolved by Monte Carlo simulation. In every step of the Monte Carlo simulation a spin s_i is chosen from the network. Let ΔE be the energy change associated with the switching of s_i, the probability to switch s_i in the Monte Carlo step is 1 if $\Delta E \leq 0$. If $\Delta E > 0$ then it is switched with probability P:

$$P = \exp\left(-\frac{\Delta E}{kT}\right) \qquad (2)$$

where k is the Boltzmann constant and T is the temperature of the network. The presence of a temperature in the equation is related to the noise in the competition that affects the decision of a client. Government policies and various advertisements or promotions are examples of the noise [1]. We set $kT=1$ in our simulation. This is a temperature sufficiently low to guarantee that one of the two spin type will be able to dominate the network. If kT is too high then none of the spin types will be able to dominate the network. (In the language of the physics of magnetism, the high temperature phase is paramagnetic, without ferromagnetic order [5].) This is an undesirable condition since we are not able tell which one has achieved dominance and we cannot make any conclusion.

In the Monte Carlo simulation the steps are carried on until one of the spin types has achieved dominance. To save computational resource we do not wait for a spin type to dominate the whole network. Instead we declare dominance of one spin type once it has occupied 87.5% of the network. Furthermore it is possible but rarely occurs that the simulation will enter a deadlock where none of the spin type is able to defeat the other and achieve dominance. When such cases occur we declare a draw. In our simulation, we define a draw if no winner appears after 100,000 Monte Carlo steps. This is a rare situation and we do not count such cases in our analysis.

4 Search of Winning Configurations by Genetic Algorithm

On an $L = 60$ random network, there are $_{60}C_{30}$ (1.2×10^{17}) valid initial spin configurations. To handle the search for winning initial configuration in such an enormous search space, we applied the recently developed Mutation Only Genetic Algorithm (MOGA) [7,8,9] which we found to be very efficient in solving the Knapsack problem. We first map the spin configuration bijectively on a chromosome containing 60 elements, where each element could be 0 or 1. Let the entire population of N chromosome each having a length $L(=60)$ expressed as a matrix $A_{ij}(t)$, $i=1,...,N$; $j=1,...,L$, where A has been sorted according to the fitness of chromosome such that the ith chromosome has a fitness equal or higher than the $i+1^{th}$ chromosome. We consider the mutation matrix $M(t)$ such that $M_{ij}(t) = a_i(t)b_j(t)$, $i = 1,...,N$; $j = 1,...,L$, where $0 \leq a_i(t)$, $b_j(t) \leq 1$ are respectively called the row (column) mutation probability. We should mutate loci on an unfit chromosome and we set

$$a_i(t) = 1 - \left(\frac{\sum_{n=i}^{N} f(n)}{\sum_{n=1}^{N} f(n)} \right) \qquad (3)$$

where $f(n)$ is the fitness of the chromosome n and $a_i(t)$ is zero for the fittest chromosome in the population and largest for the weakest chromosome. We then consider the column mutation probability $b_j(t)$. Let's define the locus mutation probability of changing to X ($X=0$ or 1) at locus j as p_{jX}:

$$p_{jX} = \frac{1}{\sum_{m=1}^{N} m} \left(\sum_{k=1}^{N} (N+1-k) \delta_{kj}(X) \right) \qquad (4)$$

where $\delta_{kj}(X)$ is 1 if the jth element of the ith chromosome has locus X, and 0 otherwise. Note that p_{jX} contains information of both locus and row, and the locus statistics is biased so that heavier weight for chromosomes with high fitness is assumed. After defining p_{jX} we define the $b_j(t)$ as:

$$b_j = \frac{1}{\sum_{j=1}^{L} b_j} \left(1 - |p_{j0} - 0.5| - |p_{j1} - 0.5| \right) \qquad (5)$$

Let's consider an example. If 0 and 1 are randomly distributed then $p_{j0} = p_{j1} = 0.5$, we have no useful information about the locus and we set $b_j = 1$. When there is definitive information, such as when $p_{j0} = 1-p_{j1} = 0$ or 1, we should not mutate and $b_j(t)=0$. As there are sixty nodes in the network and the spins in every node can take two values, we can represent all configurations by a chromosome which is a sequence having thirty 1s and thirty 0s. To compare different strategies for the initial allocation of resource, we define a fitness for the spin configuration. The evolution of initial spin configurations affects both spin types. If the evolution favours one spin type and make it more competent then at the same time it will reduce the competitiveness of the other spin types. Here we set the evolution process to favour the spin up type and so the fitness of a chromosome solely reflects the competitiveness of the spin up type. Given a chromosome representing a particular initial spin configuration, we perform U trials of Monte Carlo simulation. If there are u out of the U trials of Monte Carlo simulations spin up achieve 87.5% dominance, then $U-u$ times spin down will win. We now define for a given trial the number s as the metropolis steps required to evolve the initial configuration to one that has 87.5% dominance by one spin type, say the spin up type. Therefore, among the U trials, we see that the average speed to dominance by spin up is given by $<1/s>_u$, while the average speed to dominance by spin down is given by $<1/s>_{U-u}$. Other than the speed and probability for spin up type to achieve dominate, we are interested in the number of triangles formed by the two spin types. Here a triangle is defined as a group of three interconnected nodes that share the same spin type, and we denote T^U and T^D the number of triangles of spin up type and spin down type. We expect that the number of triangle is a good indicator for solidarity of the two spin types: the larger the different of number of triangle between the two spin the larger the disparity in terms of solidarity. Thus the term $T^U - T^D$ should be included in our consideration of fitness of the chromosome. Furthermore, we normalize this factor by dividing $(T^U - T^D)$ by $(T^U + T^D)$, and add a constant factor 1 so that the fitness is non-negative. This inclusion of the effect of local solidarity, represented by the factor $\{1+(T^U-T^D)/(T^U+T^D)\}$ into the fitness definition allows us to direct our search to the subspace with concentrated clustering effects. We now define the fitness f_c of chromosome c by the average speed to dominance by spin up, multiplied by the probability that spin up dominates among U (=1000) trials,

$$f_c = \left\langle \frac{1}{s} \right\rangle_u \times \left(\frac{u}{U} \right) \times \left[1 + \frac{T^U - T^D}{T^U + T^D} \right] \quad (6)$$

Since we want to compare the strategies of two companies with initially equal market share, we must make sure that in the construction of initial spin configurations there are equal number of spin up and spin down. However, the mutation operation in genetic algorithm will not conserve the number of spin up and down (represented by 1 and 0). We thus need to modify MOGA. Let's assume that the mutation probability for the locus in the chromosome has been calculated in the usual way [8], and that the chromosome c has k loci to be mutated. Out of these k loci k_0 of them are 0s and k_1 of them are 1s. We only mutate $2 \times min(k_0, k_1)$, and reject those 0s or 1s in excess which have the least mutation probability in order to conserve the number of 0s and 1s. For example, MOGA has designated the first six loci of the chromosome 1111000010 to mutate, and the corresponding mutation probabilities are: 0.9 0.7 0.5 0.3 0.8 0.6 0.2 0.1 0.05 0.04 respectively. To conserve the number of 0s and 1s, two 1s should not mutate. Since the third and the fourth 1 are the least probable to mutate among all chosen 1s, they won't mutate. So far the final outcome is 0011110010. In our evolutionary computation using MOGA, we set the population size of chromosome to be 100 (=N) and the number of generation for the chromosomes to evolve to be 100.

5 Result of the Simulation

We performed simulations on two random networks which have $N=60$ nodes, one with $p=0.05$ and the other $p=0.1$. For each random network we performed evolution with genetic algorithm described in Section 4, with the fitness evaluation defined by the Monte Carlo process in Section 3, and output the chromosome with the highest fitness. We repeat this 10 times with different initial population and random number seed, so as to obtain 10 best chromosomes for the random network, corresponding to 10 best initial spin configurations. We measured $<u/U>$, $<1/s>_u$ and $\{1+(T^U-T^D)/(T^U+T^D)\}$ on these 10 initial spin configurations, as well as their distributions of connectivity of nodes and the clustering coefficient. Here the connectivity of node i, denoted as $k_i \equiv C_i^S + C_i^D$, stands for the number (C_i^S) of the neighbours having the **same** spin type as i's plus the number of the neighbors (C_i^D) having **opposite** spin types as node i. Let's denote **U** and **D** to be the set that contains nodes with spin up type and spin down type respectively, the distribution of spin up type (the favoured spin type) and spin down type (the hampered spin type) are defined as the distribution of elements in the set $\{k_i, i \in U\}$ and $\{k_i, i \in D\}$. Next denote T_i as the number of triangles having a node being i, and let's introduce a local measure d_i on node i

$$d_i = \begin{cases} 0 & if \quad k_i < 2 \\ \dfrac{T_i}{k_i(k_i-1)/2} & if \quad k_i \geq 2 \end{cases} \quad (7)$$

The clustering coefficient of the spin up type and spin down type is defined as the average $\langle d_i \rangle \{i \in U, D\}$. Statistics shows (i) the enhanced strategies have a higher probability to achieve dominance on the network, (ii) the favoured spin have more triangles than its counterpart (Table 1). This is very natural if we interpret the number of triangle as the indicator of solidarity: the more united it is the harder to break it.

Table 1. Averaged $<1/s>_u$, u/U and $1+(T^U-T^D)/(T^U+T^D)$ for 10 random spin configurations and 10 good spin configurations on the two networks

P = 0.05						
Random Spin Configuration			**Good Spin Configuration**		
$<1/s>_u$	u/U	$1+\dfrac{T^U-T^D}{T^U+T^D}$	$<1/s>_u$	u/U	$1+\dfrac{T^U-T^D}{T^U+T^D}$
0.0023±0.0002	0.47±0.22	1.0±1.0	0.0036±0.0003	0.93±0.05	1.8±0.6
p = 0.1						
Random Spin Configuration			**Good Spin Configuration**		
$<1/s>_u$	u/U	$1+\dfrac{T^U-T^D}{T^U+T^D}$	$<1/s>_u$	u/U	$1+\dfrac{T^U-T^D}{T^U+T^D}$
0.0049±0.0003	0.53±0.13	0.8±1.0	0.0068±0.0005	0.93±0.05	1.8±0.6

We observe that the distribution of connectivity of the favoured spin type has shift to the left of the hampered spin's (Fig.1). This implies that the enhanced spin type should have more nodes with the same spin type in contact compared with the hampered one, a sign of the importance of local solidarity.

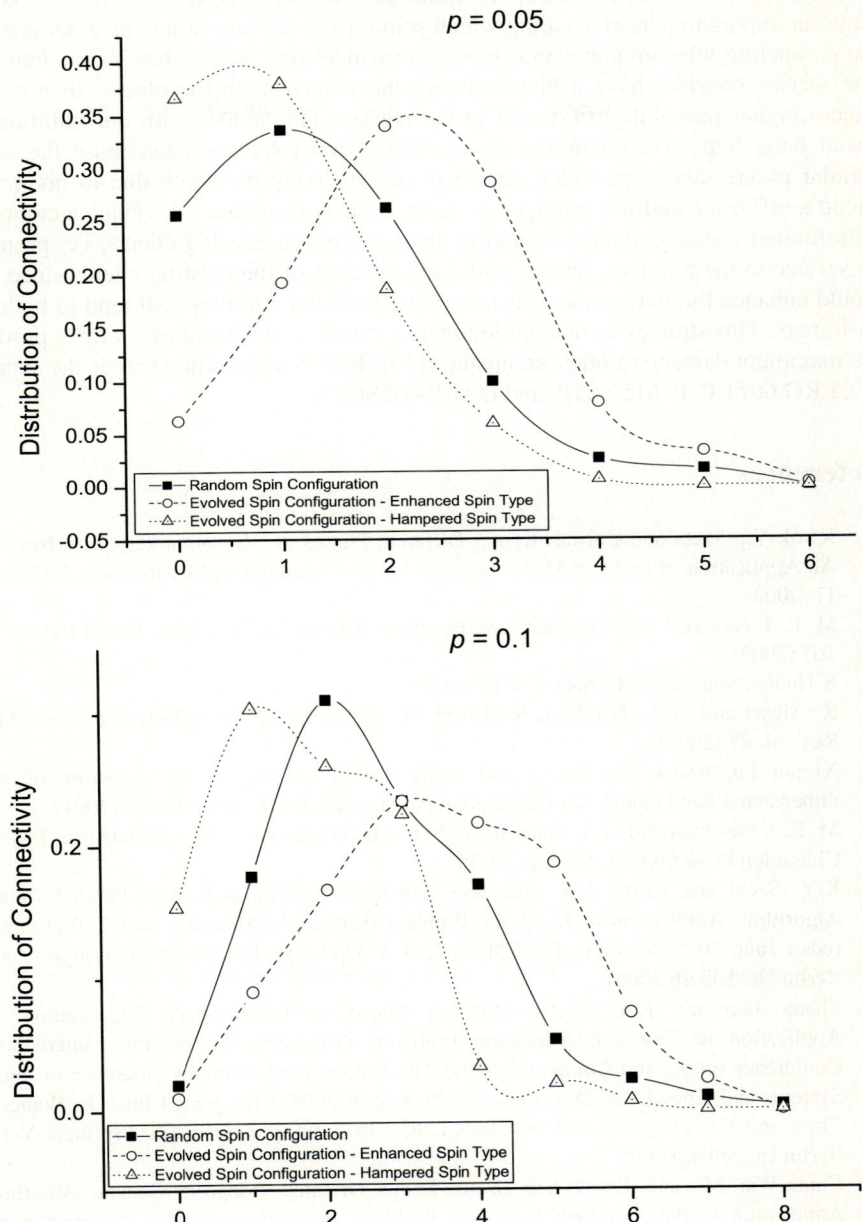

Fig. 1. Averaged Distribution of Connectivity k_i for (1) spin up type in random configurations (Filled Square), (2) enhanced spin in evolved configurations (empty circle) and (3) hampered spin in evolved configurations (triangle)

Based on numerical evidence, we conclude that the interconnectedness of nodes plays an important part in deciding which spin type to achieve dominance. In terms of the competing telecommunication service providers this means that if the clients of one service provider have a higher interconnectedness than the others' then it will have a higher probability to dominate the market. This agrees with our intuition on social behaviour: if a client has many friends and relatives subscribing the same cellular phone service provider, he/she is very unlikely to switch due to his or her friend's influence and the lower price on intra-network phone call. Thus, a company with limited resource should expand its market through existing clients, i.e. promote its service to the relatives, friends and acquaintances of the existing clients since this would enhance the interconnectedness among its client and they will tend to be loyal customers. This strategy to market dominance can also be viewed as a way to produce the maximum damage to other companies [10]. K.Y. Szeto acknowledges the support of CERG 6071-02P, 6157-01P, and DAG04/05SC23.

References

1. Kwok Yip Szeto and Chiwah Kong, Different Phases in a Supermarket Chain Network: An Application of an Ising Model on Soap Froth, Computational Economics, 22(2): 163-17, 2003.
2. M. E. J. Newman, The Structure and Function of Complex Networks, SIAM Review 45, 167 (2003).
3. K.Huang, Statistical Mechanics, Wiley, 1987.
4. R. Albert and A.-L. Barabási, Statistical Mechanics of Complex Networks, Rev. Mod. Rev. 74, 47 (2002).
5. Xiujun Fu, Kwok Yip Szeto, and Wing Keung Cheung, Phase transition of two-dimensional Ising model on random point patterns, Phys. Rev.E70, 056123(2004).
6. M. E. J. Newman and G. T. Barkema (1999), Monte Carlo Methods in Statistical Physics, Clarendon Press Oxford, 1999, p. 45-59
7. K.Y. Szeto and Zhang Jian, Adaptive Genetic Algorithm and Quasi-Parallel Genetic Algorithm: Application to Knapsack Problem (Lirkov, S. Marenov, and J. Wasniewski (eds.) June 2005, Sozopol, LSSC2005, LNCS 3743, pp.189-96, 2006,Springer-Verlag Berlin Heidelberg 2006).
8. Zhang Jian and K.Y. Szeto, Mutation Matrix in Evolutionary Computation: An Application to Resource Allocation Problem; Proceeding of the First International Conference on Natural Computation and The Second International Conference on Fuzzy Systems and Knowledge Discovery, 27-29 August 2005, Changsha, China, L. Wang, K. Chen, and Y.S. Ong (Eds.): ICNC 2005, LNCS 3612, pp. 112–119, 2005, Springer-Verlag Berlin Heidelberg 2005.
9. Chun Wai Ma and Kwok Yip Szeto, Locus Oriented Adaptive Genetic Algorithm: Application to the Zero/One Knapsack Problem, Proceeding of The 5th International Conference on Recent Advances in Soft Computing, RASC2004 Nottingham, UK. p.410-415, 2004.
10. Z. Z. Guo, K.Y. Szeto, and Xiujun Fu, Damage spreading on two-dimensional trivalent structures with Glauber dynamics: Hierarchical and random lattices,Phys. Rev. E70, 016105(2004).

Heterogeneous Domain Ontology for Location Based Information System in a Multi-agent Framework*

Virginia Fuentes, Javier Carbó, and José Manuel Molina

Computer Science Department-GIAA
Universidad Carlos III de Madrid
Colmenarejo, Spain
{vfuentes, jcarbo}@inf.uc3m.es, molina@ia.uc3m.es

Abstract. The growing interest in mobile devices in new different scenarios increases the need to create context-aware multi-agent systems. Interaction between users is produced in many environments and new mobility technologies allow access information anytime and anywhere. Many researches and location systems have focused in specific domains to share knowledge between agents. This article proposes a global ontology to let agents work with heterogeneous domains using a wireless network. The intention of the proposed ontology is to provide customization about different environment services based on user location and profile.

Keywords: ontology, heterogeneous domain, multi-agent system, wireless network.

1 Introduction

Nowadays, mobile devices have a series of powerful computation capacities, which opens us towards new environments where the users interact between them and access to the information anywhere and anytime [9]. User mobility, new wireless technologies and the need to receive context-dependent information, promote new user location systems that adapt and customize information according to user position, rather than classic systems which do not support automatic detection of user location. [10]. Mobility allows users to access information anytime and anywhere, so due to user position, these location based systems provide context-aware information in the environment where the user is located. In the same way scenarios change, the system has to adapt itself to new domain information. This article proposes a high level conceptualization ontology allowing systems to adapt to heterogeneous domains in commercial area.

Museum domain is one of most used domains, and several applications based on user location have been implemented, addressed mainly for Semantic Web. One of them is KORE [8] that uses agents to obtain visitor position in the museum, and to customize information according to the visitor profile. In KORE, information

---

* Funded by projects CICYT TSI2005-07344, CICYT TEC2005-07 186 and CAM MADRINET S-0505/TIC/0255.

exchanged between agents is defined by an ontology, which only covers a specific domain. Other research projects propose the introduction of a mediator agent, which contains user location knowledge, defined by a location ontology, and determines the best service for the user [11] [12]. The main point of ontologies is the connection between physical information in real world and conceptual information in digital world. Several researches have later identified three basic features for this kind of systems: previous knowledge of agents, cooperation between context and devices, and independence of application [6].

The intention in this contribution is to apply user location and information personalization to large and dynamic domains, using a more versatile ontology to allow very different information exchanges between agents. The proposal here is to design and implement such ontology that should cover a wide application domain. The ontology aim is to be shared and re-used by agents. Ontology universe allows using agents in several business area contexts (conferences, department stores, fairgrounds etc.) agents obtain user position and profile user information, and according to these, they provide personalized and recommended information about the context. The proposed multi-agent system runs on a wireless network, where visitor information, as well as supplier information, will be managed by visitor/supplier agents while one special agent handles all position information.

The chosen internal architecture of agents is based on the BDI model (Belief-Desire-Intention) [3], who is one of the most used deliberative paradigms to model and implement internal reasoning of agents. The BDI model allows viewing an agent as a goal-directed entity that acts in a rational way [2]. The framework Jadex has been selected as development platform to support the use of the reasoning capacities by BDI model deployment with software engineering technologies as XML and Java [1].

For accomplishing objectives, agents need to communicate between them. Since there are a large variety of communication environments, we focus in ontology development to allow sharing knowledge in a global domain which may cover several contexts [7]. Communicative acts between agents are expressed through FIPA-ACL messages (Foundation for Intelligent Physical Agent ACL), which allows selecting content language and ontology inside messages. We adopt as content language RDF (Resource Description Framework) and RDFS (RDF Schema) [6] for information description. As ontology development tool Protégé-2000 is selected, because it allows performing in different platforms and interacting with standard storage formats as XML and RDF [5].

This article describes a generic ontology for a multi-agent system to be applied to in any context of commercial or business nature. Section 2 presents different research related to the objective of this contribution. Section 3 explains the problem of using a single ontology for different contexts, and its motivation. It describes the proposed ontology, including abstract concepts and relations between them, which constitute the communication language domain between agents. Section 4 illustrates the problem with some example cases. Finally, Section 5 reports some conclusions.

2 Previous Works

At present, mobile devices establish new scenarios where users can interact in many environments and access to information anywhere and anytime [9]. Numerous researches have focused on ubiquitous computing problems as well as Semantic Web, in order to provide context-aware information from real world, emphasizing the combination of physical sensors and ontologies, to establish a connection between real world and digital world [6]. One limitation of these works is the use of specific domain ontologies. Museum domain is one of most used domains, because users walk freely in a building without a fixed way, and they need information relative to the environment. Therefore, museums are an ideal area for testing the human-computer interaction with mobile devices [9].

There are many approaches which use museum domain to show and implement their solutions. PGAA architecture [6] is one of them. Its intelligent navigation and guide's services recognize the context by environment sensor-based information, and presents customized contents dependent on user location. To standardize communication between agents and knowledge representation, PGAA uses an ontology that represents context information and it allows a flexible cooperation between several agents. Although in this research, it is not expressly defined what type of ontological information is gathered, at least it contemplates user location information, as well as services in museum domain.

CONSORTS system [12] offers a solution implemented for a museum and for a Wireless-LAN network, respectively, to determine which service is better adjusted to user location, translating real location sensor-based representation, to a contextual ones. CONSORTS ontology defines ubiquitous computing locations, and describes spatial region (buildings, floors, rooms, objects in space) and temporary region.

KORE architecture [8] allows recognizing user position by PDA or cellular phone in museum environment too. KORE does not focus on information representation with ontology, but focuses on architecture to provide the services that user needs inside the museum specific domain, according to user location and profile. The restriction of a concrete domain constitutes a limitation and moves away from the principal intention of this article. PDA applications designed for conscious and indoor location supposes an advantage in user position location and in adaptation information to context [9]. It is similar to our research as for PDA devices to receive personalized information, but not as for ontology creation which includes multiple heterogeneous scenarios in commercial scope.

Museum domain is not the only application domain. The wireless communication offers new opportunities such as mobile learning [15] where the most important challenge is information security. This work proposes a model based on ontologies and agents for information security. Although other studies do not reach the ontology definition for a global and heterogeneous domain, they bring near enough. Conference Center project ontology for conference domain [13], describes conference social activities, and focuses on different people roles, locations and activities, conference areas and event scheme. Users try to obtain great variety of services information in different situations. Conconf prototype is designed to analyze and evaluate the viability of the framework for essential services [14]. It consists of a content-based conference environment. Conconf needs one or more ontologies to complete the task of reasoning satisfactorily.

In general, all these approaches with specific domains constitute precedents of this article. Although some researches are close to our proposal, they do not focus on the principal aim: create and handle a global domain for heterogeneous and different environments of commercial nature.

3 The Proposed Ontology

The main motivation to define ontologies relies on the need of communication between persons, organizations and software, and on integrating different domains in a coherent framework. Due to the different needs and contexts, there is a great variety of points of view and assumptions relating to the same question [4]. The ontology aim relies on a common vocabulary definition to share information in an interest domain, and provide interoperability between heterogeneous systems [16].

To define the ontology we have used a generic methodology which combines Top-Down and Bottom-Up strategies for concepts extraction. First, it is important to have clearly requirements, and the use intentions. Identifying the scope of the ontology provides a reasonable and good defined aim [4]. The intention of this article is to define an ontology that provides context-aware information in a heterogeneous domain, which covers different and specific contexts in commercial area. Different multi-agents solutions and architectures have been proposed to solve problems in specific environments and have supported on restricted ontology definition to a specific domain, which constitutes a limitation [6], [11], [12], [13], [14]. With a generic ontology design we try to solve the problem of applying agents to user location and personalized information in restricted domains. The ontology role in communication is a main point, because it provides not ambiguous terms definitions that agents share and communicate between them inside a domain.

Once the goal is fixed, it is considered integration of existing ontologies, or part of them, in case they have concepts in common [16]. Examining the ontologies used by the most researches related with this article, they agree with our study in the need of user location system providing customized information according to the location. Furthermore, the design of location ontology to describe user position is equivalent to a part of the proposed meta-ontology. They not only have described user position, but also the geographical space in which users move, the position of elements and objects in it [6], [11], [12]. In our study location concept is similar to these researches, for people and places, with the difference that this environment can be re-used in different commercial area contexts.

Defining the ontology implies a process of ontological acquisition, which consists on the identification of the key concepts and relationships of interest domain [4]. For this acquisition we have combined a Top-Down strategy with Bottom-Up strategy. Top-Down starts with a general vision of the problem, and go down to instantiate the specific concepts of the domain. Bottom-Up strategy obtains a high level abstract conceptualization from different specific domain applications. Thanks to this combination, the aim of meta-ontology definition is accomplished with a high level abstraction by distinguishing the details according to different contexts include in global domain. The created ontology focuses mainly on all concepts definition in order to be valid for a set of heterogeneous domains. These ontological high level concepts are considered to be meta-concept or meta-object and can be described as follows:

- *Framework:* general application which includes high level system concepts. It has two properties or slots: system sector (technology, entertainment, market etc.) and event (fairground, conference, congress, exhibition etc.). These slots are properties of whole subclasses of Framework.
- *Location*: includes (x, y) coordinates. System requires knowing coordinates about any place, participant or object.

- *Spatial Region or environment*: defines principal area or map and is composed by segments according to a range of coordinates
- *Place or interest points:* defined in one segment or a group of segments, or in a specific localization. It contains different kind of places: stands, departments, conference room, exhibition area etc.
- *Temporal Region*: gathers temporal system information, hour and date when user is in any localization in spatial region.
- *Participants*: persons, companies and their roles in the environment: user or visitant, supplier, seller, buyer etc. It contains a slot about preferences participants' information.
- *Services:* different kind of system provision offered to users referred to places or interest points: notice or notifications about publicity information, product information etc.
- *Products:* offers, solutions, applications, objects.
- *Devices*: information about different devices profiles and hardware to present information to user anywhere and anytime [14].

System super class Framework includes generic meta-concepts or meta-classes. Location, spatial region, temporary region, places, participants and devices, constitute a generic valid part for any location system that appears in other similar works and all these concepts are related between them. Particular development in this article consists on an abstract conceptualization of services and products. There is a bidirectional interchange of services and products information between system and users, and it is valid in whatever commercial area. Sector and event are common properties to all concepts included in the framework and they determine which domain is currently used.

Once ontology concepts are obtained, codification process is the next step and consists on specific and formal representation of the conceptualization gathered in the capture phase and it allows selecting representation language. In this step the meta-ontology is created. This ontology describes representative terms used to express the principal ontology, as shown in Figure1.

Developing on appropriated semantic for a concrete expression inside context requires the classification of all the possible elements of discourse domain. High level conceptualization is common to any context in commercial and business area and covers the heterogeneous application domains of this nature. Ontology application to a multi-agent system describes handled agents knowledge in communication process. Communication is achieved by FIPA-ACL and uses ontological concepts for messages. This means that it is necessary to add other important aspects to gather the appropriate semantic in agreement to ACL messages agents exchange, besides common concepts on heterogeneous system domain. According to this, multi-agent system ontology must include [17]:

- *Predicate*: represents a base of facts or expressions that says something about world state, and can be true or false.
- *Agent action*: represents special concepts that indicates some action developed by several agents, like communicative acts or ACL messages;
- *Agent identification*: represents expressions which identify entities or agents.

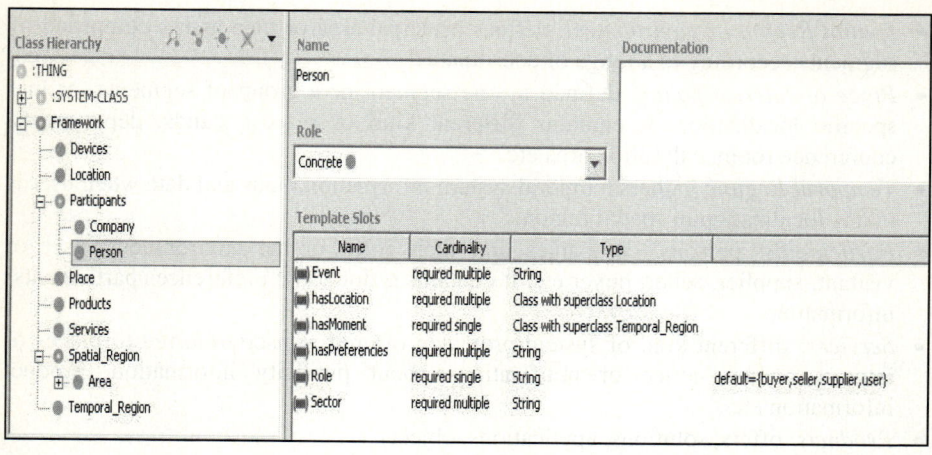

Fig. 1. Ontology high level concepts

4 Evaluation

To analyze and evaluate the viability of ontology framework, this paper proposes two particular application contexts to show that are covered by ontology, although they belong to different domains. Several possible application domains of built ontology in proposed multi-agent architecture for a wireless network are a mobile fair and a shopping centre. Meta-concepts in the ontology have specific terms in this concrete domain as instances, and these terms match perfectly with generic concept pattern defined (Figure 2 shows an example). In this conceptual framework some example meta-class instances are included, as follows:

- *Sector*: Framework slot. It takes "mobile" value in mobile fair domain and "commercial" value in shopping centre domain.
- *Event*: Framework slot. It takes "fair" value in mobile fair domain and "shopping centre" value in correspondent domain.
- *Location*: user is in (x, y) position in any domain.
- *Spatial Region*: map or NxM area, composed by segments with a range of positions each one. For example, segment1 is a segment with the range of positions: (1,1) (1,2). This is shared for all domains.
- *Place or interest point*: in fair domain, places are participant companies expositors like Nokia, Siemens etc.; and in shopping centre domain places are departments or counters close to users and composed by one or some segments.
- *Temporal region*: user date (dd/mm/yyyy) and hour (hh:mm) when is in a concrete position inside map. This is shared for all domains.
- *Participants*: in mobile fair domain, participants are users (registered with an identifier each one), and companies like Nokia, Siemens, Motorola. Preferences are one Participants' slot, and they can be preferential-product, firm, price, model etc. in fair domain; slots in shopping centre could be firm, price and size.

- *Product*: in fair domain a product is a mobile, for example. In the other domain a product is footwear.
- *Service*: for fair domain a service could be a notification in user device about preferential user product. In shopping centre, services could be different offers in footwear product.
- *Device*: PDA in both domains.

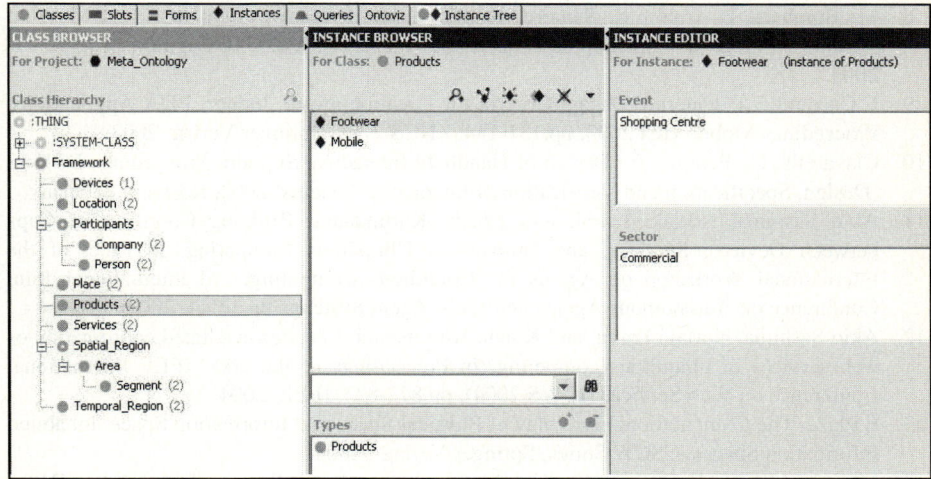

Fig. 2. Particular domain application ontology

5 Conclusions

This paper presents a framework for generic and heterogeneous ontology to cover several commercial domains, and describes knowledge for multi-agent communication process in wireless networks. User mobility in a great variety of environments increases the need of developing context-aware information systems based on user location and profile for providing different services to users. In this work a global ontology is designed in a high level of conceptualization and its viability is analyze and evaluated with two specific cases, which show that first level defined concepts match perfectly with specific concepts taken out from examples.

References

1. L. Braubach, A. Pokahr, and W. Lamersdorf, "Jadex: A short overview," in Main Conference Net.ObjectDays 2004, 9 2004, pp. 195–207.
2. A. Pokahr, L. Braubach, and W. Lamersdorf. Jadex: Implementing a BDI Infrastructure for JADE Agents. EXP – in search of innovation, 3(3):76–85, 2003.
3. A. Rao and M. Georgeff. BDI Agents: from theory to practice. In V. Lesser, editor, Proceedings of the First International Conference on Multi-Agent Systems (ICMAS'95), pages 312–319. The MIT Press: Cambridge, MA, USA, 1995.

4. Uschold, M.; Gruninger, M. Ontologies: principles, methods and applications. Knowledge Engineering Review, 1996, vol. 11, nº 2, p. 320-321.
5. J. Gennari, M. A. Musen, R. W. Fergerson, W. E. Grosso, M. Crubezy, H. Eriksson, N. F. Noy, S. W. Tu. The Evolution of Protégé: An Environment for Knowledge-Based Systems Development. 2002 Academic Press, Inc. USA
6. Sashima, A., Kurumatani, K and Izumi, N (2002) Physically Grounding Agents in Ubiquitous Computing, Proc.Joint Agent Workshop (JAWS2002) pp. 196-203, 2002.
7. The Foundation for Intelligent Physical Agents. http://www.fipa.org. 2002
8. M. Bombara, D. Cali' , C. Santoro. KORE: a Multi-Agent System to Assist Museum Visitors. In Proc. of Workshop on Objects and Agents (WOA2003), Cagliari, Sept. 10-11, 2003.
9. C.Ciavarella, F. Paternò. Design Criteria for Location-aware, Indoor, PDA Applications. Proceedings Mobile HCI 2003, pp.131-144, LNCS 2795, Springer Verlag, 2003.
10. Ciavarella, C., Paternò, F.: Design of Handheld Interactive Support, Proceedings DSV-IS (Design, Specification and Verification of Interactive Systems) 2002, Rostock, Germany.
11. Akio Sashima, Noriaki Izumi, and Koichi Kurumatani. Bridging Coordination Gaps between Devices, Services, and Humans in Ubiquitous Computing. In Proc. of the International Workshop on Agents for Ubiquitous Computing, 3rd International Joint Conference on Autonomous Agents and Multi Agent Systems, pp.37-44, 2004.
12. Akio Sashima, Noriaki Izumi, and Koichi Kurumatani. Location-mediated coordination of web services in ubiquitous computing. In Proceedings of the 2004 IEEE International Conference on Web Services (ICWS 2004), pp.822-823. IEEE, 2004.
13. E.Plaza, The Computational Interplay of Physical Space and Information Space. Inhabited Information Spaces. CSCW Series, Springer Verlag. (2004)
14. Mohamed Khedr. Enhancing Applicability of Context-Aware Systems Using Agent-Based Hybrid Inference Approach. Arab Academy for Science and Technology
15. Hentea M, "Multi-Agent Security Service Architecture for Mobile Learning", Proceedings, 2nd International Conference Information Technology: Research and Education, June 2004, London Metropolitan University, UK
16. Natalya F. Noy and Deborah L. McGuinness. ``Ontology Development 101: A Guide to Creating Your First Ontology''. Stanford Knowledge Systems Laboratory Technical Report KSL-01-05 and Stanford Medical Informatics Technical Report SMI-2001-0880, March 2001.
17. Giovanni Caire. JADE Tutorial. Application-Defined Content Languages and Ontologies. 2002

Intelligent Data Analysis for the Verification of Multi-Agent Systems Interactions

Juan A. Botía, Jorge J. Gómez-Sanz, and Juan Pavón

[1] Universidad de Murcia, Murcia, Facultad de Informática,
Campus Espinardo, s/n, 30071 Murcia, Spain
juanbot@um.es
[2] Universidad Complutense Madrid, Facultad de Informática
Ciudad Universitaria s/n, 28040 Madrid, Spain
{jjgomez, jpavon}@sip.ucm.es

Abstract. Testing interactions in multi-agent systems is a complex task because of several reasons. Agents are distributed and can move through different nodes in a network, so their interactions can occur concurrently and from many different sites. Also, agents are autonomous entities with a variety of possible behaviours, which can evolve during their lives by adapting to changes in the environment and new interaction patterns. Furthermore, the number of agents can vary during system execution, from a few dozens to thousands or more. Therefore, the number of interactions can be huge and it is difficult to follow up their occurrence and relationships. In order to solve these issues we propose the use of a set of data mining tools, the ACLAnalyser, which processes the results of the execution of large scale multi-agent systems in a monitored environment. This has been integrated with an agent development toolset, the INGENIAS Development Kit, in order to facilitate the verification of multi-agent system models at the design level rather than at the programming level.

1 Introduction

Agent execution platforms usually provide some tools for debugging interactions of multi-agent systems (MAS). However, these tools are currently very limited in functionality and just provide the visualization of a small number of interactions and agents in the system. Therefore they can be applied just for simple debugging of agent code and are not integrated with other activities of the software development lifecycle, such as analysis and design. They are impractical to test MAS with hundreds or thousands of agents. In such cases, strong and flexible tools are needed to log and recover all necessary data and to analyze these and extract some results and views of the system behaviour. These views should maintain the appropriate abstraction level because, in scenarios that involve the execution of large-scale MAS, there is a clear need to summarize in order to gain insight about what is actually happening in the MAS.

In this paper we address these issues by integrating the ACLAnalyser tool [2] with the INGENIAS Development Kit (IDK) framework [6]. On the one hand, the ACLAnalyser facilitates the analysis of the interactions of large scale MAS, by applying clustering techniques to the logs of interactions resulting from the execution of a MAS on the JADE platform [1]. This solves part of the problem, managing thousands of agent interactions. On the other hand, the IDK provides a development environment for modelling MAS and tools for automatic code generation. The integration of ACLAnalyser with the IDK consists basically on the generation of a JADE implementation of the MAS under development to perform extensive executions, analysing the resulting logs with ACLAnalyser, and interpreting back the results in terms of the INGENIAS models. In this way, the developer gets feedback in terms of the model (rather than the programming language level) and, besides, the ACLAnalyser is integrated with the MAS design activity. This improves considerably the productivity of the developers as they are able to validate their MAS models without concerns about the actual program code for the target platform.

The rest of the paper is structured as follows. Section 2 presents the ACLAnalyser tool, and section 3 the INGENIAS framework. Their integration is explained in section 4, where it is illustrated with one example. Conclusions in section 5 discuss the results and points out issues to be considered in the coming future.

2   The ACLAnalyser Tool

A MAS can be analysed at the intra-agent level or at the inter-agent level. At the intra-agent level, the purpose is to check the right evolution of goals with respect to intentions, the correct accomplishment of tasks semantics, and possibly belief revisions. In this case, the nature of the analysed information influences the kind of properties that can be verified because they will depend on the concrete agent model under consideration (e.g., BDI agents, mobile agents, etc.) Examples of this approach for MAS verification and validation can be found in [3][8]. At the inter-agent level, information comes only from interactions occurred during the execution of the MAS. This information consist of messages in an Agent Communication Language (ACL). This level considers the social perspective of agents and their communication activity. Examples of such analysis are [7][8] (this last works at both levels) and also concrete tools integrated in the JADE and Zeus agent platforms. In their current state, however, these tools work at the micro social layer (i.e. they study only the correct accomplishment of single dialogues among a few number of agents). The ACLAnalyser works at the inter-agent level but it also works at the macro social layer.

The ACLAnalyser tool has been designed to analyze executions on any FIPA compliant platform. It has been implemented, as a proof of concept, for the JADE platform. The tool consists of the following elements:

- A special *sniffer* agent: it is in charge of receiving a copy of all messages exchanged in the MAS under test. Messages are stored in a relational database for further processing. This sniffer agent subscribes to the Agent Management System (AMS, the central element of management in a FIPA platform) to indicate that it is interested in receiving messages of each new agent. The sniffer is notified when a new agent is started. After that, it asks the AMS to receive a copy of all messages which come out from it.

- A relational database: this is actually a log of all messages. The main entity of the database is a session. A session is a logical entity that groups all messages exchanged in a run of the MAS under test. A session consists of a number of conversations (different conversations are detected by using the *conversation-id* parameter value, generated by the FIPA platform in the case of JADE). Finally, conversations contain messages. Messages come with a number of receivers (interaction protocols may be multi-party) and the message content.
- A monitor: the monitor is actually a GUI for the sniffer agent. It can be activated or not, depending on whether we are interested to follow the evolution of the run in terms of what new agents start executing and what messages are exchanged on the fly.
- The analyzer: this is a stand-alone Java program that interacts with the database and carries out all tasks related to the analysis of the logs that have been produced in the different runs.

Among the components of the tool, the analyzer is the most important. Its functionality can be divided in two different groups depending on the abstraction level from which we look at the agent society:

- At the group level, the analyser allows verification of formally specified protocols. This definitely supports the ability of detecting unfinished or wrong dialogues between agents and, in consequence, locating bugs in interaction protocol implementations. In the first version and implementation of the tool (see details in [2]) the protocol specification was based on the definition of a deterministic finite automaton by specifying states and transitions between them. However, this approach has some limitations, which are addressed by the improvements exposed in this paper.
- At the society level, it supports testing of large scale multi-agent societies (i.e. compound by more than one thousand agents). At this level of abstraction, we are not interested in single conversations between a few agents but in macro-parameters which, in some sense, reflect the global behaviour of the society. For example, we might be interested in discovering hierarchical arrangements in the society that were not directly specified in the design. For that, the ACLAnalyser performs data mining over the ACL messages. One typical data mining task is *complex data visualization* [9]. In this task, data is analysed to find adequate graphical representations that, at a first sight, are capable of representing information in a manner that may allow to obtain quick answers to questions made on source data. This is particularly useful in the development of complex MAS in order to highlight the specific properties of the system under study.

3 The INGENIAS Development Kit (IDK) and the Interaction Analysis Module

The basic assumption of the INGENIAS approach is that agent related concepts facilitate the modelling of complex systems, and consequently their analysis and design. These concepts are organized in five viewpoints: organization, interactions, agents, goals/tasks, and environment [6].

The system architecture is defined as a MAS organization. The concept of organization supports the definition of structural relationships (i.e., groups) and dynamics (i.e., workflows). Organization rules determine how agents can participate in organizations and constraint agent relationships. The organization view is complemented by the interaction view, which provides the description of the interactions among agents. Precisely, the need for analysis of such interactions is the motivation for using the ACLAnalyser tool in this work. The behaviour of the active entities in the system, i.e. the agents, is defined in the agent and the goals/tasks viewpoints. As agent agents are considered as intentional entities, their interactions are the result of their decisions. These decisions are determined by the evolution of the agent mental state, which is described in the agent viewpoint. The agent mental state consists of goals, knowledge about the world, and agent capabilities. The decomposition of goals and their relationship with tasks are expressed in the goals/tasks viewpoint. Finally, the environment viewpoint specifies what agents can perceive and how they can act on the surrounding world.

With these elements it is possible to model a MAS. The IDK provides a customizable editor for the creation and modification of MAS models, which consist of several diagrams for each viewpoint. While defining the models, the developer needs to check their validity, i.e. whether models represent what they intend to, and to verify that the system satisfies certain properties. The IDK offers for this purpose a framework for the implementation of modules that can perform different types of functions with the MAS models. This framework includes APIs that allow to navigate through the MAS models and basic classes to plugin new modules into the editor. It was initially conceived to support automatic code generation but soon its suitability to build verification and validation tools has shown up, as it is demonstrated in this paper.

The purpose of the integration of the ACLAnalyser into the IDK, as it has been mentioned in the introduction, is to support the analysis of the interactions during design, which means working with models instead of program code. This is done by wrapping the ACLAnalyser into the new *Interaction Analysis* module in the IDK. This new module works as follows:

1. It browses the MAS models to identify which agent types have been specified and in which interactions do they participate. In this step, the module checks whether all necessary information for describing interactions has been provided. If some information is missing, code generation could not be performed, so the module reports an error to the developer with the required information.
2. With the information from the model, the module instantiates templates for agents in the JADE platform according to the agent types in the MAS and the requirements of the ACLAnalyser tool (basically, to facilitate the log of their activity). There is also a default sniffer agent typefor the ACLAnalyser. This process reuses the JADE code generator modules already existing in the IDK. The result is a set of Java classes ready for compilation.
3. The module generates also one ant script (information about the ant tool is available at http://ant.apache.org). The script incorporates tasks for compilation of all Java classes and for the deployment and execution of the

agents in JADE agencies or platforms. In order to get deployment information, an extension to the INGENIAS MAS modelling language has been required. The extension specifies how many agents of each type are created at each agency (node of the agent platform).
4. The module executes the scripts and while running the MAS on the JADE platform, ACLAnalyser sniffer agents prepare logs with information concerning the interactions.
5. Information from the logs is used by the Analyzer component. This information is then visualized in a new window in the IDK with the results of the ACLAnalyser in terms of agents as identified in the IDK model diagrams. This is made by integrating ACLAnalyser GUI with IDK windows management hierarchy and maintaining hooks between agent entities in IDK models and the corresponding JADE agents (which where automatically generated).

Note that most of the work for integrating ACLAnalyser in the IDK as the Interactions Analysis Module reuses the JADE automatic code generation module of IDK and the ACLAnalyser itself.

4 Example of Analysis of MAS Interactions

The use of this module is illustrated with an example of a MAS where agents have to choose a leader. This is useful in situations where a set of agents has to choose one to perform a certain task, for instance, to act as a coordinator. We start from a community of agents of type *group member agent*, which are agents that know how to choose a leader, as it is shown in Fig. 1. This shows that an agent can play several roles, in this case, a *leader* or a *follower*.

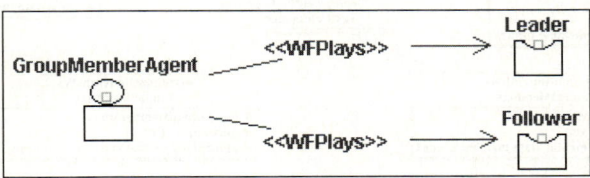

Fig. 1. Roles associated to a GroupMemberAgent

Agents interact to select who plays the *leader* role in a group. This interaction is declared in Fig. 2. In INGENIAS, the interaction is described by the goal why agents get engaged in the interaction (*Choose a leader* in this case), the participants, and a protocol (the possible sequences of messages that agents exchange in the interaction). The protocol is specified in another diagram (referenced as Leader Selection Protocol) as INGENIAS allows the use of several ways to specify it (collaboration diagrams and AUML sequence diagrams, for instance). [This is not shown here because of space limitations.]

The interaction protocol *Leader Selection* describes the algorithm by which all agents decide who will be the leader. For this example we have considered the

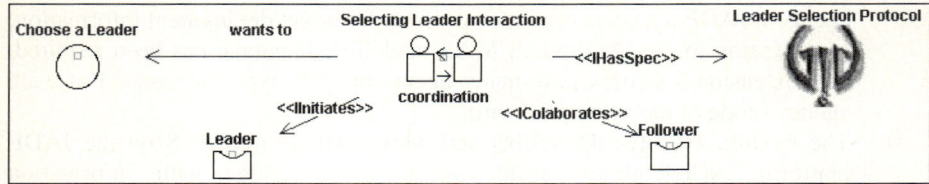

Fig. 2. High level representation of the interaction to select a leader

algorithm proposed by Muller in [5], page 101, where the leader will be the agent with the greatest identifier (considered this as a number). The algorithm consists on sending to all the acquaintances the own identifier and if no received message comes from an agent with a greater identifier than the own, the agent will claim to be a *leader*, and a *follower* elsewhere.

For this particular example, 500 agents have been arranged in five different groups with the same size. Each group will have to choose a coordinator (i.e. all agents in a group only communicate with the leader agent within the group) and coordinators communicate between them. This deployment is described in the diagram of Fig. 3. There are five *deployment units,* to describe the deployment configuration of each group. Each deployment unit indicates the type of agent to instantiate, i.e. *GroupMemberAgent*, the number of times, i.e., 100, and initial mental state for each agent (this is a reference to a particular configuration of an agent mental state).

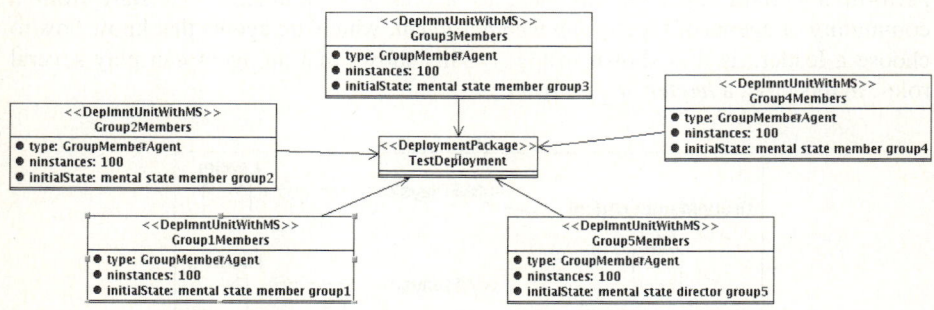

Fig. 3. Description of the deployment configuration

It is not possible to know in advance who will be the leader. In runtime, all agents could be asked whether they are the leader or they could be programmed to notify when they are playing the leader role. The problem is that, during the execution of the algorithm, there can be several leaders at some moment (there can be local maximals agent ID, but we look for a maximal ID within the group). Also, agents can get in and out of the system, so a chosen leader may vanish, leading again to a leader selection process. Instead of asking or being informed, the ACLAnalyser can help to guess who is finally the leader. A graphical representation of the MAS through a communication graph may be useful in order to discover which hierarchy is hidden in the distributed system, in terms of the interactions which took place when simulating the society.

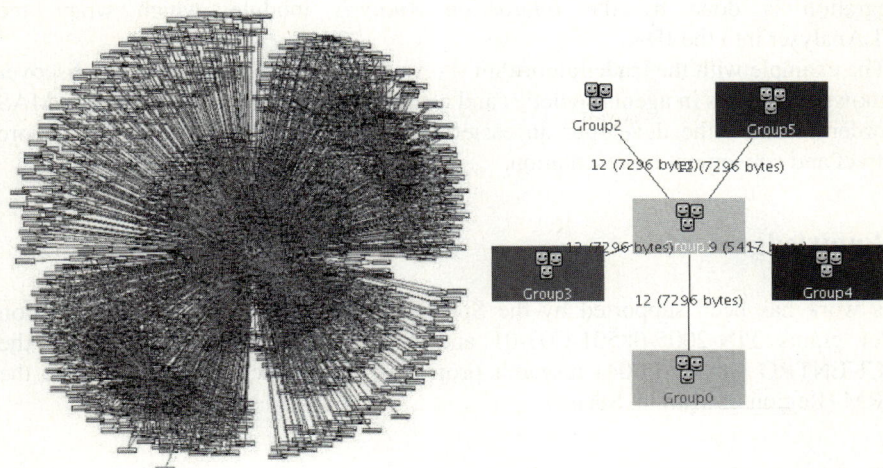

Fig. 4. A communication graph in a five hundred agents deployment. It is compound by a set of nodes that represent the agents in the system and arcs between nodes when the corresponding agents exchange messages. Arcs may be labelled with the number of bytes exchanged through the link.

The communication graph generated by the ACLAnalyser for this example appears on the left of Fig. 4. Clearly, this graph is so complex that it results useless. But a more abstract representation is still useful. In this example, the use of a k-means clustering approach [4] finally arranges agents as they appear on the right of Fig. 4. This representation is also a graph whose nodes represent subsets of agents that are grouped together because they interact with the same agents. Cluster 5 contains the directory facilitator agent and the agent that creates the 500 agents in the example, and, for this reason, it appears in the center. In the rest of clusters, agents within the node are grouped because they interact with the coordinator within their group. Coordinators appear as dense communication points within each group.

5 Conclusions

The integration of the ACLAnalyser into the IDK facilitates the development of large scale MAS as it allows the verification of some MAS properties at the design level, which is more convenient than working at program code level for several reasons. Firstly, as the developer works at a higher abstraction level, details of the target platform do not need to be taken into consideration. Secondly, as interactions are specified at model level, they are independent of a concrete target platform, and once the design has been validated, they can be implemented in any target platform without effort, given that there is a module for automatic code generation for such platform. Third, the automation that is provided by the tool eases the work of the developer, who does not need to generate specific code, compile, configure the deployment on the target platform, monitor the execution, capture and interpret the results. This integration is done by the *Interaction Analysis* module, which wraps the ACLAnalyser into the IDK.

The example with the leader algorithm shows how the tool may be used to discover unknown groupings in agents societies and also to visually arrange a large scale MAS in order to allow the developer an easier inspection of the MAS through a more abstract and convenient representation.

Acknowledgements

This work has been supported by the Spanish Council for Science and Education under grants TIN-2005-08501-C03-01 and TIN-2005-08501-C03-02, and by the ENCUENTRO (00511/PI/04) research project of the Seneca Foundation with the CARM (Region of Murcia, Spain).

References

[1] Bellifemine F., Poggi A., Rimassa, G.: Developing multi-agent systems with a FIPA-compliant agent framework. Software Practice and Experience 31, 2 (2001) 103—128
[2] Botía, J., Hernández, J.M., Gómez-Skarmeta, A.: Towards an approach for debugging MAS through the analysis of ACL messages. Computer Systems Science and Engineering, 20 (2005)
[3] Lam, D. N., Barber, K. S.: Comprehending agent software. In: Proc. of the Fourth Int. Joint Conference on Autonomous Agents and Multiagent Systems. ACM Press (2005) 586–593
[4] MacQueen, J. B.: Some methods for classification and analysis of multivariate observations. In: 5-th Berkeley Symposium on Mathematical Statistics and Probability, Berkeley. University of California Press (1967).
[5] Müller, J.P. The Design of Intelligent Agents. A Layered Approach. Springer-Verlag (1996)
[6] Pavón J., Gómez-Sanz J., Fuentes, R.: The INGENIAS Methodology and Tools. In: Agent-Oriented Methodologies. Idea Group Publishing (2005) 236—276
[7] Poutakidis, D., Padgham, L.,Winikoff, M.: Debugging multi-agent systems using design artifacts: The case of interaction protocols. In AAMAS'02.
[8] Sudeikat, J. et al.: Validation of BDI Agents. In: Workshop on Programming Multi-Agent Systems (ProMAS 2006)
[9] Wills, G. and Keim, D.: Data Visualization for Domain Exploration. In: Handbook of Data Mining and Knowledge Discovery. Oxford University Press (2002) 226–232

Multi-agent Based Hybrid System for Dynamic Web-Content Adaptation*

Jaewoo Cho, Seunghwa Lee, and Eunseok Lee[**]

School of Information and Communication Engineering, Sungkyunkwan University
300 Chunchun Jangahn Suwon 440-746, Korea
{jwcho, shlee, eslee}@ece.skku.ac.kr

Abstract. Context-aware adaptation service is rapidly becoming an important issue. This service overcomes the limitations of wireless devices and maintains adequate service levels in changing environments. The majority of existing studies concentrate on adaptation modules on the client, proxy, or server. These existing studies thus suffer from the problem of having the workload concentrated on a single system. This means that increasing the number of users increases the response time of a user's request. In this paper, the adaptation module is dispersed and arranged over the client, proxy, and server. The module monitors the context of each system and creates a dispersed adaptation system, optimized for efficient operation. Through this method, faster adaptation work is made possible, even when the number of users increases, and the dividing workload makes more stable system operation possible. In order to evaluate the proposed system, a prototype is constructed and dispersed operations are tested using multimedia content, simulating server overload and comparing the response times and system stability with existing server based adaptation systems. The effectiveness of the system is confirmed through the results.

1 Introduction

The developments made in computing technologies have accentuated the supply of wireless devices of various forms, enabling the internet to be accessed anywhere, at anytime. In addition, many tasks that must be achieved at fixed locations using wired internet and desktop PC's are being transformed into tasks that can be completed at any location. However, wireless devices still suffer from limited performance, due to small screens, slower CPU's, and reduced memory sizes. In addition, unlike fixed wired network environments, the wireless network environment often experiences fluctuations in performance as users move from one point to another. In an effort to overcome such limitations and maintain adequate service level, various institutions worldwide are carrying out studies relating to adaptive systems. In the majority of cases, when the number of users increases, these systems suffer from the problem of the workload being concentrated in one place.

---

[*] This work was supported in parts by *Ubiquitous Autonomic Computing and Network Project*, 21th Century Frontier R&D Program, MIC, Korea, ITRC IITA-2005-(C1090-0501-0019), Grant No. R01-2006-000-10954-0, *Basic Research Program* of the Science & Engineering Foundation, and the *Post-BK21 Project*.
[**] Corresponding author.

Therefore, in an effort to solve this problem, this paper proposes a system for dispersing the adaptation module over the client, proxy, and server, dividing adaptation work adequately according to the situation of each system. With such a system, as the number of users increase and the response speed of a request increases, faster adaptation is made possible. In addition, this results in more stable operation of the server.

In order to evaluate the proposed system a prototype is constructed, and dispersed operations are tested by applying the system to multimedia based learning content. In comparing the response time and stability of the system with existing systems, and the adaptation module concentrated at a single location, the overload of the server is simulated and the effectiveness of the proposed system is demonstrated.

The paper is organized as follows. Chapter 2 divides the well known existing studies into three types and discusses their characteristics. Chapter 3 explains the proposed system, designed after considering the problems of other studies. Chapter 4 discusses construction of a prototype of the proposed system and evaluates the system by conducting tests. The conclusion and future tasks are presented in chapter 5.

2 Related Work

Depending on the location adaptation occurs, existing adaptation systems can be divided into client, server, or proxy side. The first system, the client side adaptation system, refers to the type of system where the adaptation module is installed in the user's device, monitoring the changing environment, and converting and displaying downloaded content accordingly[1]. However, as a client in the mobile environment is a portable machine that possesses peer computing power, this system suffers from the problem of making it difficult to perform work that consumes substantial resources, such as converting the format of multimedia content.

The second, the server side adaptation system, is a type of system that supplies content, and connects to the client with the appropriate pre-constructed content, according to the context of the client requesting the content, or dynamically creating the content[2][3][4]. This type of system offers the advantage of being able to create more accurate content, as adaptation can be carried out according to the requirements of the author. However, the server is burdened by the workload required for adaptation, in addition to supplying the content, resulting in a serious disadvantage.

The third type of system, the proxy side adaptation system, refers to a system that removes the function of conducting content adaptation at the server, to decrease the workload of the server, and conducts adaptation work at the proxy[5][6]. This system is being used in many studies and has advantages of decreasing the workload concentrated on the server, and making adaptation possible simply by adding the adaptation module to the proxy. However, tasks such as converting media content consume considerable resources, as the requests of user increases with the workload of the proxy.

As presented above, existing systems suffer from the problem of the adaptation module being concentrated in one place, either in the client, proxy, or server. This means the workload will be concentrated at a single location, resulting in increased response time to a user's request when the number of users increases. The subsequent section considers the problems of existing systems and explains the proposed system.

3 Proposed System

3.1 The Proposed System Architecture

- *Monitoring Agent (MA)*: The MA is inserted into each adaptation module located at the client, proxy, and server, gathering dynamically changing context information such as resource state and workload.
- *Analysis Agent (AA)*: The AA analyzes the current situation based on information gathered by the MA. In addition, the AA of the client decides the adaptation services to be performed by the client in each situation. This decision has priority over others when a server finally decides on the type of adaptation services and location for performing adaptation work.
- *Context Synthesis Agent (CSA)*: The CSA combines the information collected by the MA and the information analyzed by the AA.
- *Decision Agent (DA)*: The DA selects the type and intensity of the adaptation service, decides the location to perform is based on the integrated context information and the rules in the Rule DB.
- *Rule DB*: The Rule DB is composed of the response plans for each context.
- *Repository*: The Repository saves the service components required for adaptation.
- *Content DB*: The Content DB saves the original copies of web content.
- *Executor*: The Executor executes the adaptation service components
- *Communicator*: The Communicator performs the interaction between modules.

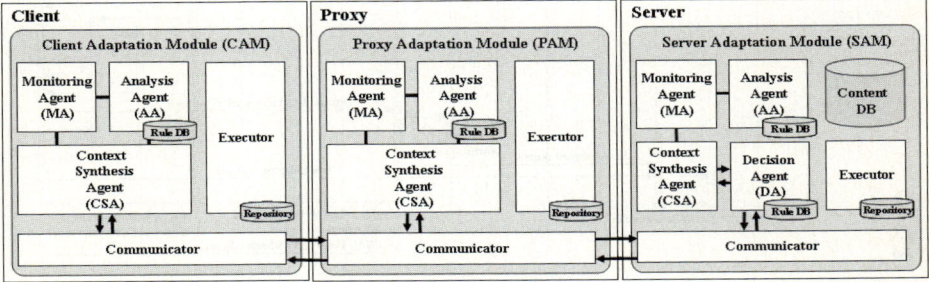

Fig. 1. Proposed system architecture

3.2 Overall System Behavior

The overall behavior of proposed system is as follows. First, the Monitoring Agent (MA), gather the context information of itself, accessible by being embedded in each system. The collected information is presented in Table 1. The component representing the static capacity of the client can use HTTP 1.1 to represent the server. However, the proposed system used the MA in order to collect dynamic context and to extend the new context type in response to the addition of adaptation services.

Table 1. The context information collected at each location

Location	Context type	Application
Client	CPU-RAM usage, current usage	Decides the type and intensity of the adaptation service
	Display size, Acceptable color depth of device	
	Acceptable media format of device	
	Adaptation service to be performed	Decides the distribution of adaptation jobs such as web page reconfiguration.
Proxy	CPU-RAM usage, current usage, Size of work queue	Decides the distribution of adaptation jobs such as media format conversion which is consuming the resource
	List of adaptation service	
Server	CPU-RAM usage, current usage, Size of work queue	Decides the distribution of adaptation jobs such as media format conversion which is consuming the resource

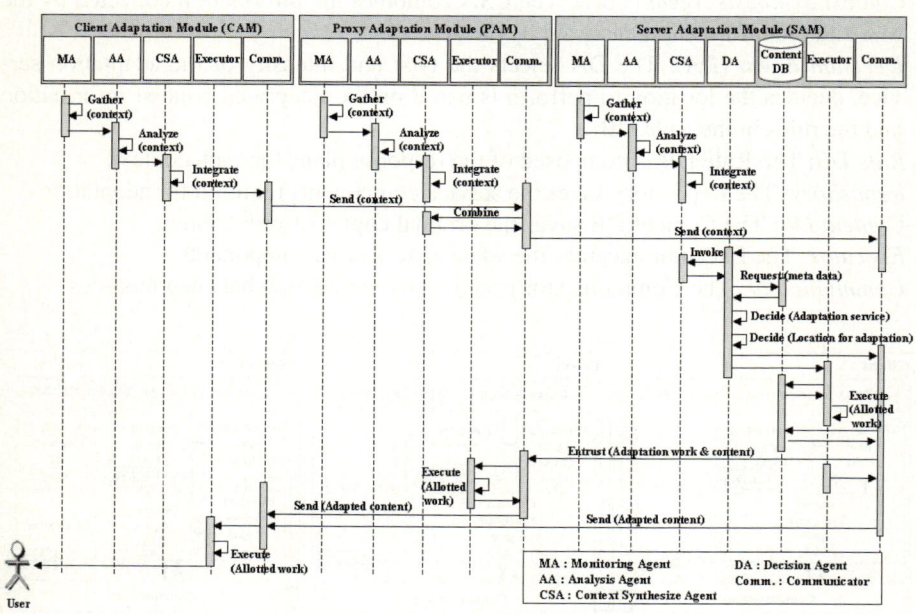

Fig. 2. Sequence diagram for the interaction between agents

The AA calculates and analyzes the collected information. The AA of client decides the adaptation services to be performed, in the analyzing phase. Section 3.3 presents more detailed explanation of this decision. Then, the CSA combines collected static information using the MA and calculated information from the AA.

The client content request makes the *Client Adaptation Module(CAM)* transmit collected context information to the *Proxy Adaptation Module(PAM)*. Then, the CSA of the proxy attaches the context information of the proxy to the request information of the client. This information is transmitted to the *Server Adaptation Module(SAM)*.

The Decision Agent(DA) of the server analyzes metadata for the requested information, then decides the type of adaptation service and its intensity, based on context information of the client, proxy, and server attached to the request message. This decision uses rules described in advance by an expert, however research relating to self-extension of rules[7] will be integrated in future research.

Then, the proposed system performs a decision for the location which adaptation service to be performed. At this time, the requested first decision by CAM has priority over others, then, by calculating the workload of the each system, adaptation work is distributed and processed. Hence, the original web content of the Content DB is distributed to each system. A sequence diagram corresponding to the interaction between agents is presented in Figure 2.

3.3 Behavior of Decision Agent

In the proposed system, the resource consumption of the system and the length of the queue, which refers to the amount of work being carried out, are incorporated into the decision for the location adaptation work is to be conducted.

$$Current_{resource} = \frac{Current_{CPU} + Current_{RAM}}{W_{CPU} + W_{RAM}} \tag{1}$$

$$Current_{CPU} = W_{CPU}(1 - CPU_{load})\frac{CPU_{speed}}{CPU_{min}} \tag{2}$$

$$Current_{RAM} = W_{RAM}(1 - RAM_{usage})\frac{RAM_{size}}{RAM_{min}} \tag{3}$$

The formulae used in previous *grid computing* studies[8] can be used to determine the first necessary factor, the resource consumption of the client, proxy, and server.

In these formulas, W is the weight assigned to the CPU and RAM. For example, when it is assumed that the resources consumed by the image_convertor carrying out the decided adaptation work is 10, the weight consumed by the CPU and RAM can be defined as 4 and 6, respectively. W_{cpu} is the work assigned to the CPU, CPU_{load} is the current usage of the CPU, CPU_{speed} is the operational speed of the CPU, and CPU_{min} is the minimum level required for the CPU to carry out the requested task. In addition W_{RAM} is the work assigned to the RAM, RAM_{usage} is the current usage of the RAM, RAM_{size} is the size of the RAM, and RAM_{min} is the minimum amount of RAM required to carry out the requested task.

The second factor is to determine the amount of work presently being conducted. The current length of the queue can determine this factor. The queue length calculation formula defined as Little's law[9] can be used to calculate the length of the queue on the model.

$$r = \lambda \text{Tr} \tag{4}$$

r refers to the length of the queue, λ refers to the rate of the arrival time of the packet arriving at the system, and Tr refers to the average standby time.

The resource usage and length of the queue can be used to calculate the current workload handled by the system. Based on this information, distributed processing can be determined. The equation to express the current state of the system ($System_{Context}$) used in the proposed system, is as follows.

$$System_{Context} = Current_{resource} + r \tag{5}$$

In the case where the number of users rapidly increases and the server processes all workload, increasing the resource usage of the server to a near critical value occurs, distributing processing among the client, proxy, and server. The real time determination of the resource usage of the client and proxy is necessary, because the condition for distributed processing is such that the resource usage of the client and proxy must be lower than that of the server.

4 System Evaluation

In this paper, a prototype is presented, and multimedia based learning content was applied to the proposed system to evaluate the proposed system. The evaluations were conducted for response time and stability. The evaluations were conducted using the materialized system to simulate server overload and checking the system workload of the standard adaptation system in which the adaptation module was processed at a single location. The change in response time was tested.

The device used for the prototypes are as follows. The client's device consists of general portable wireless devices, and an HP 5500 PDA with 240 * 320 resolution, a 400MHz CPU, and 128 MB RAM. The proxy refers to the server located at or around the AP, and its role executes adaptation services of the proposed system and acts as a general gateway. A general desktop PC with a 2.8 GHz CPU and 512 MB RAM was used in the test. For the content server, a HP 4300 workstation with a 3.4 GHz CPU and 2 GB RAM was used, and the provided content was multimedia content, which included movie clips, images, and documents. For tests on the adaptation services used in the prototype, *Image_size_convert*, *Image_colordepth_convert*, and *Image_format_convert* were used.

4.1 Evaluation for Response Time

The first test was to test the system's response time. This was achieved by checking the time required to complete the output on the client screen and changing conditions by increasing the number of users through simulation. Through this test, the goal is to demonstrate that as the number of clients increases, the overall workload is distributed, making the proposed system's response time the fastest. In a standard system, when a web page is requested, the work is conducted at one point of the server, increasing the workload of the system server and decreasing processing speed. However, in the proposed system, the workload for adaptation is distributed among the client, proxy, and server, according to the context, resulting in the processing speed of adaptation pages being faster than the standard system. The test graphs are presented in Figure 3. Through this process, by distributing adaptation work, the proposed system maintains system stability better than that of the standard adaptation system, and the system's response time improved.

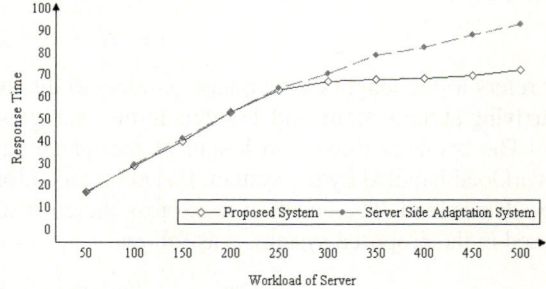

Fig. 3. Response time comparison graph

4.2 Evaluation for System Stability

The second test was to test the stability of the system when adaptation modules were distributed among the client, proxy, and server. The test conditions were normal (CASE1), increasing the number of users, but most adaptation service work was achieved by the server (CASE2), and increasing users on the proposed system (CASE3). For the normal state, it is assumed that the server completed all adaptation work and that there were few users. In the event of increasing users, it is assumed that the server completed all adaptation work, rapidly increasing the resource workload of the server. In the proposed system, it is assumed that the number of users constantly increased and adaptation work is being distributed among the client, proxy, and server. Equation (5) was used to calculate and compare the resource value and usage, respectively, in order to test the resource distribution effects of this situation.

For the values used in the test, it is assumed that there was a certain process requiring adaptation work with weight 10 and adaptation work was distributed among the client, proxy, and server, with the weight for each being decided according to whether there was adaptation work to be completed in the system. The result for this experiment is presented in Table 2.

Table 2. Resource factor for the each case

	CASE	CPU_{load} (%)	RAM_{usage} (%)	W_{cpu}	W_{RAM}	CPU_{min} (GHz)	RAM_{min} (MB)	$Current_{resource}$	Usage (%)
Client	1	8	16	0	0	0	0	-	-
	2	12	20	0	0	0	0	-	-
	3	22	24	1	1	0.1	64	2.26 / 3	25
Proxy	1	21	17	0	0	0	0	-	-
	2	19	24	0	0	0	0	-	-
	3	42	29	2	1	0.2	128	1.07 / 1.66	36
Server	1	51	43	6	4	0.3	128	7.37 / 13.2	45
	2	77	72	6	4	0.3	128	3.68 / 13.2	73
	3	48	56	3	2	0.3	128	6.6 / 15.2	57

In CASE 1, few users request content and all adaptation work is completed on the server. The server does not contain large workload even though all work is conducted on the server. In CASE 2, the number of users rapidly increased, increasing the work for the server and decreasing system stability. Through this result, it is confirmed that system stability is improved by distributing work among the server and proxy.

5 Conclusion

In this paper, a multi-agent based hybrid system is proposed. This system complements the weaknesses of adaptation systems currently being researched, by distributing the adaptation modules among client, proxy, and server and distributing adaptation work adequately, depending on each system's resource usage.

The proposed system makes adaptation faster, improving response time for requests. Therefore, stability of the system is improved. In addition, it is expected to alleviate many restrictions in limited mobile computing environments and create a more convenient mobile computing environment. Future work includes the following topics.

- Usage of various context found in the ubiquitous computing environment
- A more effective algorithm for monitoring, analysis, and management of context
- Security of messages transmitted and received between modules
- Prediction of context changes through the pattern analyzing

References

1. Daniel Billsus, Clifford A. Brunk, Craig Evans, Brian Gladish, and Michael Pazzani, "Adaptive Interfaces for Ubiquitous Web Access", Communication of the ACM, Vol.45, No.5, pp.34-38, May.2002
2. Ariel Pashtan, Shriram Kollipara, and Michael Pearce, "Adapting Content for Wireless Web Services", IEEE Internet Computing, Vol.7, No.5, pp.79-85, Sep.2003
3. Rakesh Mohan, John R. Smith, and Chung-Sheng Li, "Adapting Multimedia Internet Content for Universal Access", IEEE Trans. on Multimedia, Vol.1, No.1, Mar.1999
4. Chulho Jung, Sanghee Lee and Eunseok Lee, "Dynamic Adaptive Architecture for Self-adaptation in VideoConferencing System", LNCS 3768, pp.36-47, Nov.2005
5. IBM WebSphere® Transcoding Publisher, http://www-306.ibm.com/software/pervasive/transcoding_publisher
6. Timo Laakko and Tapio Hiltunen, "Adapting Web Content to Mobile User Agents", IEEE Internet Computing, Vol.9, No.2, pp.46-53, Mar.2005
7. Seunghwa Lee, Jehwan Oh, and Eunseok Lee, "An Architecture for Multi-agent based Self-adaptive System in Mobile Environment", LNCS 3578, pp.494-500, Jul.2005
8. Maozhen Li, Mark A. Baker, "The Grid: Core Technologies", Wiley, pp.243–300, Chapter 6 Grid Scheduling and Resource Management, 2005
9. Little, J. D., "A proof of the queueing formula L = Lambda * W," Operations Research, vol.9, pp.383-387, 1961

Strategic Software Agents in Continuous Double Auction Under Dynamic Environments

Marta Posada

INSISOC, Universidad de Valladolid,
E.T.S. de Ingenieros Industriales, Paseo del Cauce s/n, 47011 Valladolid, Spain
posada@eis.uva.es

Abstract. Internet auctions in open dynamic environments have been attracting increasing attention. We analyze with a bottom-up approach the competition between artificial intelligent agents in Continuous Double Auction markets. In almost all previous works agents have a fixed bidding strategy during the auction, usually under static symmetric environments. In our simulations we allow the soft-agents to learn not only about how much they should bid or ask, but also about possible switching between the alternative strategies. We examine the behaviour of strategic traders under dynamic asymmetric environments thus extending previous results. This analysis is important in the design and performance of auctions in the real world (stock exchanges, commodity markets, emission permits, and B2B exchanges) and in the applications of auction theory to many problems in management and production, far beyond market design (market oriented programming).

1 Electronic Commerce and Software Agents in Continuous Double Auction Markets

The advent of Internet has significantly contributed to the development of electronic commerce. Internet is not only an integral part of electronic commerce but it is also becoming a promising field for applying autonomous agents and multi-agent system technologies (Chen and Hu [3]). Autonomous agents that participate in online trading environments with the goal to increase revenue for humans, represent such an advanced paradigm of process automation (Kehagias et al. [9]). Software agents execute their transactions on electronic marketplaces. Some good references are Kasbah (Chavez and Maes [1]), the Fishmarket project (Rodríguez et al. [15]) and AuctionBot (Wurman [21]).

The challenge now is to see how agents bargain and learn in a more complex environment. We focus on continuous double auction (CDA). It is one of the most common exchange institutions and is extensively used in the stock and commodity markets, emission permits, and B2B exchanges. The prevalence of this institution comes from its operational simplicity (any trader may submit or accept an offer or a bid at any time) and its high efficiency.

Never mind these properties, the CDA remains as a persistent puzzle in economic theory. The research on CDA has its root in early experimental economics work (Smith [17]). When Gode and Sunder [7] replaced the human traders with *zero-intelligence* (ZI) software agents, a new area research began (*beyond experimental economics*, López et al. [11]).

Since Gode and Sunder [7] several studies have examined CDA with various computerized bidding agents. Cliff and Bruten [4] designed the *zero intelligence plus* (ZIP) agents to demonstrate that institutions matters and so does intelligence. They employed an elementary form of machine learning to explore the minimum degree of agent intelligence required to reach market equilibrium in a simple version of the CDA. Preist and van Tol [14] used different heuristics for determining target profit margins in ZIP agents to faster achieve market equilibrium. Gjerstad and Dickhaut [6] proposed an agent (GD) who places the bid or offer that maximizes the expected surplus (calculated as the product of the gain and the probability for the bid or offer to be accepted). Das et al. [5] made improvements on the GD agents and described a series of laboratory experiments that, for the first time, allow human subjects to interact with two types of software bidding agents (ZIP and GD). He et al. [8] introduced fuzzy sets and fuzzy reasoning into the heuristic rules for traders. They proposed an agent (A-FL) who has an Adaptive Fuzzy Logic strategy. An A-FL becomes more risk-averse in the next round, if he waits too long to trade. On the contrary, he becomes risk-seeking if he transacts too often. This adaptability helps the agent to achieve more profit when supply is less (greater) than demand. Although these strategies achieve good performance in the CDA market, there is still room for improvement. Ma and Leung [12] proposed an adaptive attitude (AA) agent who employs a $\theta - \omega$ method and two levels of adaptability, long term and short term. The result demonstrates that its performance is better than ZI, ZIP, GD and A-FL.

We focus on the interactions between software bidding strategies. In this sense, Tesauro and Das [18] tested agent performance in homogeneous populations and in two heterogeneous settings:

1. A single agent of one type competes against an otherwise homogeneous populations of a different type.
2. Two types of agents compete in a market where one has a counterpart of the other type.

These are important contributions, but they are restricted to fixed strategies and static environments. Li and Smith [10], developed a speculation agent for a B2B a dynamic environment where both demand and supply change from period to period. But their agents are not strategic. We extend their experiment to agents that learn to change their strategies when the environment is dynamic and the strategies of other agents change.

A typical approach to evaluate bidding strategies in heterogeneous populations has been to establish a tournament, like the Santa Fe Double Auction (Rust et al. [16]) or the Trading Agent Competition (TAC) (Wellman et al. [20]). We agree with Walsh et al. [19] in that the tournament-play is one trajectory through the space of possible interactions and the question of which strategy is the best is often not the most appropriate given that a mix of strategies may constitute an equilibrium. Accordingly we allow for interactions among heterogeneous agents strategies in all the strategy space.

2 The Model

We describe our model in terms of the essential dimensions of any market experiment (IxExA): institution (I), environment (E) and agent behaviour (A) proposed by Smith [17].

2.1 The Environment (E)

Our model have not restrictions and it allows us to simulate any environment in terms of the number of traders, their number of units and both static or dynamic valuations of each trader. Each trader is either a seller or a buyer. The assumption of fixed roles conforms to extensive prior studies of the CDA, including experiments involving human subjects and automated bidding agents. Each agent is endowed with a finite number of units. Seller i has n_i units to trade and he has a vector of marginal costs $(MaC_{i1t}, MaC_{i2t}, \ldots, MaC_{in_it})$ for the corresponding units. Here MaC_{i1t} is the marginal cost to seller i of the first unit in the period t, MaC_{i2t} is the cost of the second unit in the period t, and so on. Similarly, buyer j has n_j units to trade and he has a vector of reserve prices $(RP_{j1}, RP_{j2}, \ldots, RP_{jn_j})$ for the corresponding units. Here RP_{j1} is the reserve price to seller j of the first unit, RP_{j2} is the reserve price of the second unit, and so on.

2.2 The Institution (I)

We consider a Continuous Double Auction (CDA) with a bid-ask spread reduction (a new bid/ask has to provide better terms than previous outstanding bid/out-standing asks). There are not restrictions on the sequencing of messages. Any trader can send a message at any time during the trading period. A period has several rounds. The CDA protocol is detailed in He *et al.* [8].

2.3 Agents' Behaviour (A)

In CDA markets traders face three non-trivial decisions (Chen [2]):

- How much should they bid or ask?
- When should they place a bid or an ask?
- When should they accept an outstanding order?

Each agent type: ZIP, GD and K (defined below) corresponds to particular values for these decisions.

Each ZI-Plus agent (Cliff and Bruten [4]) has a mark up μ that determines the price at which he is willing to buy or sell in adaptative way. The agents learn to modify the profit margin over the auction using the information about the last market activity. For example, the profit margin of a buyer is:

$$\mu = 1 - \frac{\text{howMuchBid}_{t-1} + \Delta_t}{\text{ReservePrice}}, \qquad (1)$$

where Δ_t is calculated using the individual trader's learning rate (β), the momentum learning coefficient (γ) and the difference between the target bid and the bid in the last round.

The GD agent is a more sophisticated one (Gjerstad and Dickhaut [6]) and it has belief-learning skills. Each seller chooses the bid that maximizes his expected surplus, defined as the product of the gain from trade and the probability for an ask to be accepted. GD agents modify this probability using the history HM of the recent market activity (the bids and asks leading to the last M traders: ABL accepted bid less than b, AL accepted bid and ask less than b, RBG rejected bid greater than b, etc.) to calculate a belief function. Interpolation is used for prices at which no orders or traders are registered in HM. For example, the belief function of a buyer is:

$$\hat{q}(b) = \frac{ABL(b) + AL(b)}{ABL(b) + AL(b) + RBG(b)}. \qquad (2)$$

The Kaplan (K) agent is the third type agent we consider. It was the winner in the tournament of Santa Fe Institute in 1993 (Rust *et al.* [16]). The basic idea behind the Kaplan strategy is: "wait in the background and let others negotiate. When an order is interesting, accept it". K agents must be parasitic on the intelligent agents to trade and to obtain profit. If all traders in the market are K agents no trade will take place.

In our model, we consider one more decision: Which strategy should they choose to obtain higher profit? Each agent chooses a strategy from a set of three alternatives (GD, K and ZIP). To take this decision each trader only knows their own reservation prices and the information generated in the market, but he doesn't know the bidding strategy of the other agents or the profit achieved by them.

Each agent learns to change his strategy looking for the best bidding strategy in the following way: *An agent will consider to change his strategy if the profit is less than the profit from the previous period. The agent will actually change his strategy if he believes that he could have reached higher profit following an alternative strategy* (see table 1).

Table 1. Strategic behaviour

If profit $\geq$ profit of previous period
Then No change the strategy
Else If profit $\neq 0$
    Then If profit $>$ profit belief
        Then No change the strategy
        Else Choice the strategy with the highest profit belief
    Else Random Choice

Table 2 details how a buyer forms his beliefs. The buyer compares if the bid of an alternative strategy (BA) could have been lower or greater than the realized bids or accepted offers under the current strategy.

Table 2. Buyer's beliefs

If BA< realized bid
Then If BA> minimum transaction price for that period
      Then greater profits
      Else profits= 0
Else lower profits

If BA< accepted ask
Then profits= 0
Else same profits

---

3 The Experiments

Twenty agents were used to isolate the effects of their behaviour under dynamic symmetric and asymmetric environments. We have simulated six scenarios that accommodate three static environments (E) and two kinds of agent strategic behaviours (A) for each of them: fixed strategies and adaptive change of strategies from the three pure agent's strategies (See table 3). To prevent some agents having relative initial advantage, each trader has the same number (ten) of trading units and the valuations of the agents on the same side of the market are the same.

Table 3. Experiments: static environments (E) and different agent behaviour (A)

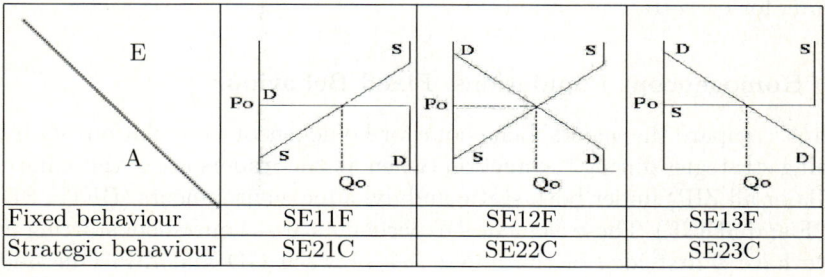

We also check two scenarios where the environment is dynamic (see table 4). The valuations change from step to step in the following way. A step can be one period or more.

$$MaC_t = \frac{10q(t_0 - t)}{t_0 - 1} + \frac{100t}{t_0 - 1} + \frac{150(t_0 - 1) - 100}{t_0 - 1}, \qquad (3)$$

where $q(\text{units}) = 1, 2, \ldots, n_i$, $t(\text{step}) = 1, 2, \ldots, t_0$.

$$RP_t = \frac{10q(1-t)}{t_0 - 1} + \frac{100t}{t_0 - 1} + \frac{210(t_0 - 1) - 100}{t_0 - 1}, \quad (4)$$

where $q(\text{units}) = 1, 2, \ldots, n_i$, $t(\text{step}) = 1, 2, \ldots, t_0$.

Table 4. Experiments: dynamic environment (E) and different agent behaviour (A)

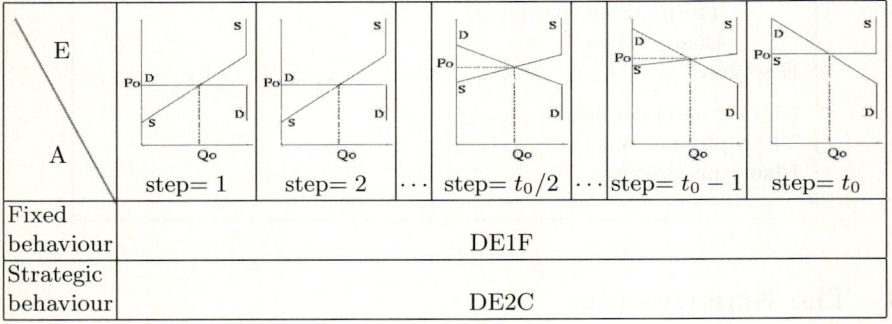

4 Main Findings

Results will be reported for the eight scenarios (SE11F to DE2C) above. Following we will comment on the qualitative results of the simulations for a representative sample of the emerging prices dynamics in terms of allocative efficiency, rate of convergence, volatility and agents' surplus. We also report about attractor points in the simplex space of proportions of the three kinds of strategies for the static environments scenarios (SSE21S to SE23S) in which the agents can choose their strategies in an evolutionary way according to individual and social learning for each trading period.

4.1 Homogeneous Populations. Fixed Behaviour

We first compare the agents' behaviour for homogeneous populations with fixed learning strategies during the auction (when all the traders are of the same class: all GD or all ZIP) under both static and dynamic environments (DE1F, SE11F, SE12F and SE13F). These elemental experiments are a convenient starting point. So we have a first idea of the differences between GD and ZIP. Our findings are:

– Efficiency: Efficiency near 1 is always achieved under static environments, even if the agents are zero intelligence. The highest efficiency is achieved in GD homogeneous populations. Under dynamic environments the efficiency decreases in both GD homogeneous population and ZIP homogeneous population.

- Prices: Price convergence needs at least ZIP agents (some learning). GD agents take less time than ZIP agents both to exchange and to learn in any environment (compare the first and the second rows of table 5). GD agents make transactions in the first rounds of each period. They learn very soon to trade at a price very close to the competitive under every environment. The prices converge from above (below) when the supply (demand) is perfectly or more elastic than demand (supply) (compare the first and the third column of table 5). We observe that agents have the same behaviour under dynamic environments (fourth column).

Table 5. Transaction price time series for homogeneous populations (3 periods, 100 rounds per session, $t_0 = 3$, step=1 period)

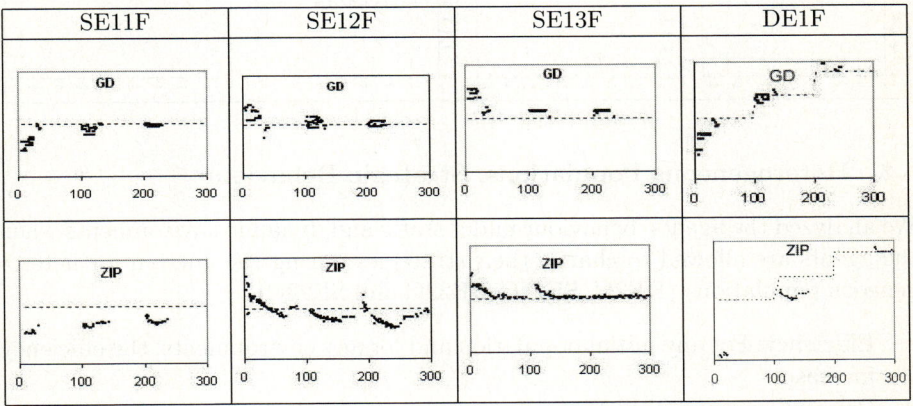

4.2 Heterogeneous Populations. Fixed Behaviour

We analyzed the agents' behaviour for heterogeneous populations with fixed learning strategies during the auction under static and dynamic environments (DE1F, SE11F, SE12F and SE13F). Each scenario is a game with 20 agents, each one with 3 strategies (ZIP, GD and K). It will require the computation of 231 populations.

- Efficiency: In heterogeneous populations where more than 50% of the agents are Kaplan, the efficiency goes down static asymmetric environment as it happened under static symmetric environment (SE12F, Posada et al. 2006). The reason is when one side of the market are all K agents, Kaplan can change the institution rules through their strategy. The volatility under static asymmetric environments is higher than it was in static symmetric environments. Under dynamic environments, the efficiency goes down for any initial population.
- Prices: In heterogeneous populations where more than 50% of the agents are Kaplan, competitive equilibrium convergence is not achieved in almost all the environments analyzed, except when the less elastic side of the market

is populated only by the Kaplan agents. For example, for a population where the buyers are K and the sellers are GD, there is only convergence to the competitive equilibrium price when the supply is perfectly elastic (third column of table 6, SE13F). So, the price convergence may depend, not only on the intersection and the shapes of the supply and demand schedules, but also upon the agent behaviour.

Table 6. Price dynamics for heterogeneous populations with fixed strategies

SE11F	SE12F	SE13F	DE1F

4.3 Heterogeneous Populations. Strategic Behaviour

We analyzed the agents' behaviour under static and dynamic environments when the agents are allowed to change their strategies during the auction for heterogeneous populations (DE2C, SE21C, SE22C and SE23C).

- Efficiency: For any initial population and for any environments, the efficiency increases.
- Prices: Convergence to the competitive price is achieved after some previous learning periods (compare the price convergence in the scenarios of table 6 with the scenarios of table 7).
- Nash equilibrium: To have a graphical idea of the dynamics of populations, we represent the strategy space by a two dimensional simplex grid with vertices corresponding to the pure strategies (all ZIP, all GD or all K). We draw three regions to represent the populations that have a dominant strategy when more than 33% of the agents use the strategy. As it happens, the ZIP agents are a majority in the region (abSc), the GD agents settle in the region (bdeS) and the K agents choice is the region (cSef). Under

Table 7. Price dynamics for the initial population: all buyers are K and sellers are GD

SE21C	SE22C	SE23C	DE2C

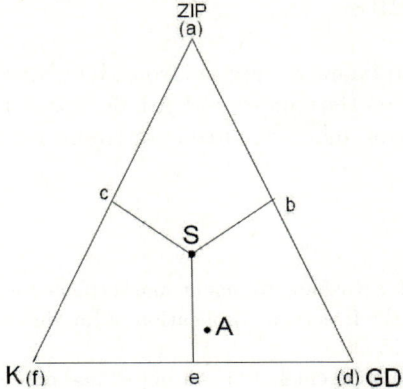

Fig. 1. Nash equilibrium

symmetric environments, there is an attractor zone where no strategy seems to dominate but there are no Nash equilibriums (see figure 1, point S). When the environment is asymmetric there is an attractor point but it is not Nash, with the GD becoming dominant (see figure 1, point A).

5 Conclusions

We have extended in several ways related works following Gode and Sunder [7] seminal contribution in experimental economics with programmed agents: beyond experimental economics. We allow the agents to change their strategies autonomously so that we can trace the patterns of the emerging proportion of agents' behaviour not only with static symmetric environment as in Posada *et al.* [13] but also with dynamics asymmetric environments. The results confirm that:

- The quality of price convergence and allocative efficiency, depend on alternative degrees of agents intelligence.
- Price dynamics and agents surplus depend on the proportion of the types of intelligent agents (K, ZIP, GD).
- It also matters whether the environment is symmetric or not. Nevertheless convergence is achieved if we allow the agents to change their strategy. There is not Nash equilibriums in the strategy proportions, but under asymmetric environments the GD strategy becomes dominant.

These results are of importance in the design and functioning of auctions in the real world: stock exchanges, commodity markets, B2B exchanges and trading permits, a prominent recent approach in economics for coping with the problem of rationing access to the commons and natural resources regulations. Last but no least, since auctions is/are a matter of scarcity and choice, our results can be ex-ported to management and production as pointed out by Wellman [20] (market oriented programming).

Acknowledgements

This work has received financial support from the Spanish MEC, n⁰ 2005-05676. I want to thank Cesáreo Hernández and Adolfo López for many helpful suggestions and encouragement and to the two anonymous referees for their comments.

References

1. Chavez, A., Maes, P.: Kasbah: An agent marketplace for buying and selling goods. In 1st Int. Conf. on the Practical Application of Intelligent Agents and Multi-Agent Technology (1996) 75–90.
2. Chen, S.-H.: Toward an agent-based computational modelling of bargaining strategies in double auction markets with genetic programming. Lecture Notes in Computer Science **1983** (2000) 517–531.
3. Chen, X. Hu, S-l.: A Vickrey-type multiattribute auction model. Lecture Notes in Computer Science **3955** (2006) 21–29.
4. Cliff, D., Bruten, J.: Zero is not enough: On the lower limit of agent intelligence for continuous double auction markets. HP Laboratories, Tech. Rep. HPL-97-141 (1997).
5. Das, R., Hanson, J., Kephart, J., Tesauro, G.: Agent-human interactions in the continuous double auction. Proceedings of the International Joint Conferences on Artificial Intelligence (2001) 1169–1187.
6. Gjerstad, S., Dickhaut, J.: Price formation in double auctions. Games and Economic Behaviour **22** (1998) 1–29.
7. Gode, D., Sunder, S.: Allocative efficiency of market with zero-intelligent traders: Market as a partial substitute for individual rationality. J. of Political Economy **101** (1993) 119–137.
8. He, M., Leung, H., Jennings, N. R.: A Fuzzy-Logic Based Bidding Strategy for Autonomous Agents in Continuous Double Auctions. IEEE Transactions on Knowledge and Data Engineering **15** (6) (2003) 1345–1363.
9. Kehagias, D., Toulis, P., Mitkas, P.: A long term profit seeking strategy for continuous double auction in a trading agent competition. Lecture Notes in Computer Science **3955** (2006) 116–126.
10. Li, L., Smith, S.: Speculation agents for dynamic, multiperiod continuous double auctions in B2B exchanges. Proceedings 37th Hawaii International Conference on System Sciences (2004).
11. López, A., Hernández, C., Pajares, J.: Towards a new experimental socio-economics. Complex behaviour in bargaining. Journal of Socio-Economics **31** (2002) 423–429.
12. Ma, H., Leung, H.: An Adaptive Attitude Bidding strategy for Agents in Continuous Double Auctions. IEEE International Conference on e-Technology, e-Commerce and e-Service (2005) 38–43.
13. Posada, M., Hernández, C., López, A.: Learning in a continuous double auction market. Artificial Economics - Lecture Notes in Economics and Mathematical Systems **564** (2006) 41–51.
14. Preist, C., van Tol, M.: Adaptive agents in a persistent shout double auction. Proceedings of the First International Conference on Information and Computation Economics (1998) 11–18.

15. Rodríguez, J.A., Noriega, P., Sierra, C. Padget, J.A.: FM96.5 A Java-based Electronic Auction House. In 2nd International Conference on the practical application of intelligent agents and multi-agent technology (1997) 207–226.
16. Rust, J., Miller, J., Palmer, R.: Behaviour of trading automata in computerized double auctions. In: Friedman and Rust (eds.), The double auction markets: Institutions, theories and evidence (1993) 155–198, Addison-Wesley.
17. Smith, V.L.: An experimental study of competitive market behavior. Journal of Political Economy **70** (1962) 111–137.
18. Tesauro, G., Das, R.: High performance bidding agents for the continuous double auction. In Proceedings of the Third ACM Conference on Electronic Commerce (2001) 206–209.
19. Walsh, W., Das, G., Tesauro, G., Kephart, J.: Analyzing complex strategic interactions in multi-agent games. AAAI-02 Workshop on Game Theoretic and Decision Theoretic Agents (2002) 109–118.
20. Wellman, M., Wurman, P., O'Malley, K., Bangera, R., Lin, S., Reeves, D., Walsh, W.: Designing the market game for a trading agent competition. IEEE Internet Computing **5**(2) (2001) 43–51.
21. Wurman, P., Wellman, M., Walsh, W.: The Michigan Internet AuctionBot: a configurable auction server for human and software agents. Proceedings of the 2nd International Conference on Autonomous Agents (1998) 301–308, ACM Press, New York.

Student Modeling for Adaptive Teachable Agent to Enhance Interest and Comprehension

Sung-il Kim[1], Myung-Jin Lee[1], Woogul Lee[1], Yeonhee So[1],
Cheon-woo Han[1], Karam Lim[1], Su-Young Hwang[1], Sung-Hyun Yun[2],
Dong-Seong Choi[3], and Misun Yoon[4]

[1] Department of Education, Korea University, Seoul, Korea
sungkim@korea.ac.kr
[2] Division of Information and Communication Engineering, Baekseok University,
Cheonan, Korea
[3] Division of Design and Image, Baekseok University, Cheonan, Korea
[4] Department of Teacher Education, Jeonju University, Jeonju, Korea

Abstract. Recent development of teachable agent focuses on individualization and provides learners with active roles of knowledge constructors. The adaptive agent aims to maximize the learner's cognitive functions as well as to enhance the learner's interests in and motivation for learning. To establish the relationships between user characteristics and response patterns and to develop an algorithm based on the relationship, the individual characteristics of the learner were measured and the log data during interaction with the teachable agent named KORI were collected. A correlation analysis was conducted to identify the relationships among individual characteristics, user responses, and learning. Of the hundreds of possible relationships among numerous variables in three dimensions, nine key user responses were extracted, which were highly correlated with either the individual characteristics or learning outcomes. The results suggested that the construction of an individualized student model based on the ongoing response pattern of the user would be useful indices for predicting the learners' individual characteristics and ongoing learning outcome. This study proposes a new type of method for assessing individual differences and dynamic cognitive/motivational changes rather than measuring them directly before or after learning.

Keywords: Adaptive agent, Teachable agent, Student modeling, Motivation, Interest, Comprehension, Individualization.

1 Introduction

One-on-one instruction has long been considered the ideal method for learning because this kind of learning environment has been expected to provide individual learners with adaptive instruction. In this respect, Intelligent Tutoring System (ITS) aroused research interest in the educational field because it offered solutions to problems of one-on-one instruction in the school environment such as limitations of time, space, and money. Researchers expected that individual learners would receive expert-tutor-like assistance by ITS as it became popular. However, frequently, the effectiveness of ITS was below expectations, mainly because learners tended to be involved in shallow learning such as practice and drills or solving test questions through ITS rather than deep learning. As learners became more passive with ITS, their motivation to learn decreased and their cognitive processes became less active.

One way to solve these kinds of problems is to provide the learner with of role of a tutor. The researchers in the field of cognitive science and learning science suggested that activity of teaching enhances a learner's motivation. For example, Kim et al. (2003) suggested that a learner's motivation can be enhanced by assigning the learner to tutor roles, which give the learner a sense of responsibility, feeling of engagement, and situational interest to persist in learning [1]. These motivated learners can become more deeply involved in the sub-activities of teaching such as memory and comprehension, knowledge reorganization, explanation, demonstration, questioning, answering, evaluation. Biswas et al. (2001) developed the new concept of intelligent agent called Teachable Agent (TA) based on this learning-by-teaching paradigm [2]. A TA provides students with tutor roles by using ITS so that the students can have an active attitude toward subject matters like peer tutoring.

The adaptive response of an agent is one of the key factors in the enhancement of TA effectiveness. To improve this individualized adaptivity, the system developers need to use a new methodology to obtain the learner's responses and infer the individual characteristics and the current motivational and cognitive state of each learner based on the analysis of indirect measurement like the user's behavior log data through student modeling. As the first step of developing an adaptive teachable agent, a student model is proposed based on the correlation among three dimensions: individual differences, learner responses, and learning outcome. Four variables of individual difference in metacognition and motivation were selected because differences in the level or type of motivation result in huge differences in persistence and effort in learning [3]. Among the various motivational factors, self-efficacy, learning and performance goal orientations were used in this study. Metacognitive awareness including planning, monitoring, and evaluation was measured since elementary school students may lack of this skill though it is a critical factor in their future learning.

2 Method

2.1 Teachable Agent (KORI)

KORI (KORea university Intelligent agent) is a new type of teachable agent developed to enhance learners' motivation to learn and to facilitate their learning [1]. It was made by JAVA Swing and Jgraph components and implemented based on the JAVA platform. The domain of KORI was science and the topic was 'rock and rock cycle' which includes kinds of rocks, transformation of rocks, and characteristic and usage of each rock and so on. KORI consists of four independent modules: planning module, teaching module, learning resource module, and quiz module. In the planning module, users make a specific plan for teaching KORI and collect and sort the learning materials from learning resources. With this module, the user realizes the role of a tutor, gets deeply involved in the teaching situation, and has more responsibility. This module is expected to assess the metacognitive ability of users by examining the quality of the lesson plan and planning duration.

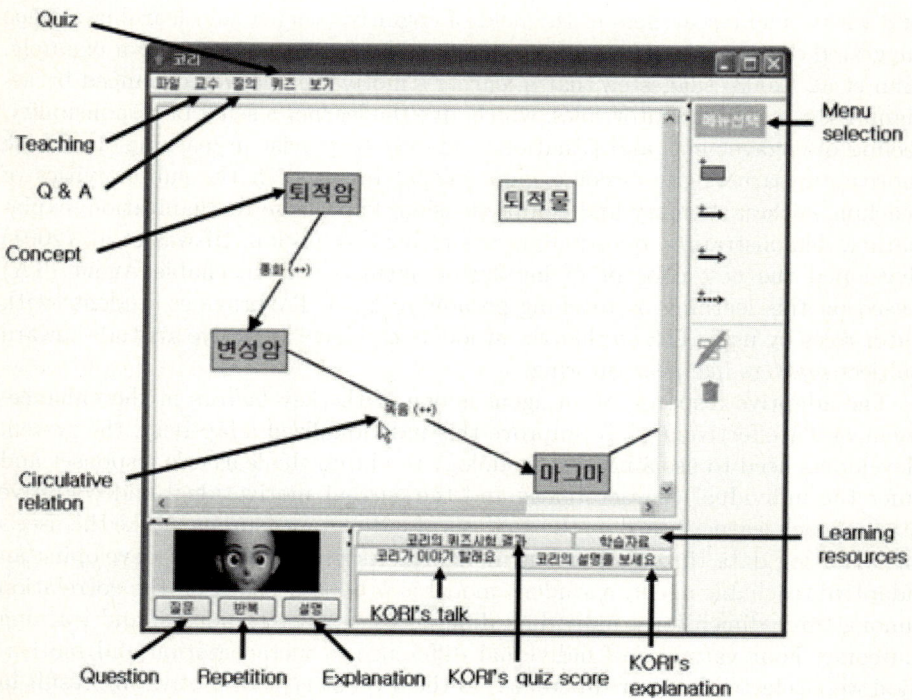

Fig. 1. Relation teaching interface of KORI

In the teaching module, users teach KORI by providing the basic characteristics of various rocks and constructing a concept map on the transformation of the rocks. The basic concepts were described in the form of simple propositions. The concept map is a kind of relational diagram that represents the relationships among the concepts in the learning materials [4]. The teaching module consists of two activities: concept teaching and transformation teaching. In the concept teaching activity, users teach the basic concepts of three kinds of rocks: igneous rock, sedimentary rock, and metamorphic rock. They teach KORI by inputting five correct propositions and taking out five incorrect propositions among the 15 given propositions. After teaching the basic concepts, users rock transformation by drawing a concept map. To teach KORI, users should understand and remember the basic concept of rock and recognize the relationships and transformation among rocks.

Figure 1 shows relation teaching interface of KORI. Users can put whatever concepts he/she wants and draw arrows between concepts to indicate their relations. In the main window of the screen, users put the name of the rock in the box and make a transformation relation between rocks with an arrow. The transformation process is represented by a mathematical symbol. The plus symbol (+) means the increase of the weathering factors, while the minus symbol (-) means the decrease. Below the concept-mapping window, there is a dialogue box that users can use to interact with KORI.

The learning resource module provides basic and expanded knowledge about rocks and their transformation. Users can access to this module by clicking the icon whenever they want to know more about rocks while teaching KORI. The resource is made of hypertext that is linked basic concepts as well as concrete images and examples. There are two different levels of learning resource: basic learning resource and additional learning resource. The basic learning resource is comprised of the minimum amount of knowledge essential to teach KORI. Additional learning resource is comprised of the expanded knowledge not directly related to teach KORI. It is expected that the durations and frequencies of exploring both types of learning resource would be correlated with the individual's characteristics or motivation. In the quiz module, KORI takes a quiz at the end of teaching. The quiz consists of 6 questions related to rocks. Since KORI's answers for the quiz are based on the information taught by the users, KORI's achievement level is equivalent to the cognitive learning outcome of the users.

When exploring the four modules of KORI, the user is given diverse choices to increase learner control and to promote learning motivation. For example, before the concept teaching, the user is asked to estimate the KORI's quiz score at the end of teaching and the difficulty level of teaching. In addition, while teaching KORI, the user can give his/her own feedback for unexpected KORI behavior through a dialogue box, which is predetermined, such as dozing off during learning. The increase in the user's self-determination in using KORI would enhance the feeling of autonomy and self-relevance to the learning material, which would result in more active engagement in teaching KORI with enthusiasm.

2.2 Procedure

Twelve fifth graders (8 males and 4 females) participated in student modeling. Participants took a 30-minute lesson on 'rock cycle' to acquire the base knowledge in the domain. Since 'rock cycle' is the content for seventh graders, it was revised to be suitable for fifth graders. After the lesson, participants filled out questionnaires on self-efficacy, goal- orientation, and metacognition. Then, each participant's behaviors based on the structured checklist were videotaped as a teaching scene of KORI. The log data of each participant's responses (e.g., mouse-click pattern, duration & frequency at particular task, individual choice etc) were recorded automatically by a computer during the participant's interaction with KORI. It took approximately 30 - 40 minutes to complete teaching KORI. After teaching KORI, participants completed the interest and comprehension questionnaires. And while watching the video of their own behaviors, they were given a structured interview on the reason for each response and their emotional and motivational reaction at a particular point of time.

3   Node and Structure in Student Model

A correlation analysis among the log data, questionnaire scores, and learning measurements was conducted. Out of hundreds of possible relationships among numerous variables in the three dimensions, the relationships of which the correlation coefficient was higher than 0.3 were included in the student model (see Figure 2). The nodes and structure of the student model showed (a) the overall relationship between individual characteristics and participants' responses, (b) the specific relationships between participants' responses and learning outcomes. Each dimension in the student model is described in detail in the following section.

3.1   Learner Responses

The log data included about 150 learner responses. Among these, eleven key learner responses were extracted based on the correlation coefficient between individual characteristics and learner responses, and between learning outcomes and learner responses. Eleven key learner responses were as follows.
Learning resource (d) represents the durations of exploring the resources.
Learning resource (f) represents the frequency of exploring the resources.
Prediction (d) represents the durations of predicting the level of performance that KORI would achieve.
Prediction (s) represents the predicted score of the KORI's performance.
Difference between predicted and actual performance represents the differences between the predicted score of KORI and the actual test score of each learner.
Planning (d) represents the planning time for teaching KORI at the beginning.
Concept teaching (d) represents the duration of inputting the correct propositions and taking out the incorrect propositions among 15 propositions.
Concept map teaching (d) represents the duration of drawing the concept map.
Response to interruption (d) represents the response time to interruptive stimulus.
Correct concepts included (n) represents the number of correct propositions that were input.
Wrong concepts excluded (n) represents the number of wrong propositions taken out.

3.2   Individual Characteristics

The results indicated that the pattern of the learner responses in teaching KORI varied depending on each of the four measures of individual characteristics.
Self-efficacy: It was found that participants who were highly self-efficacious were likely (a) to spend more time in exploring learning resources; (b) to teach more correct concepts; (c) to show less difference between learner's actual test

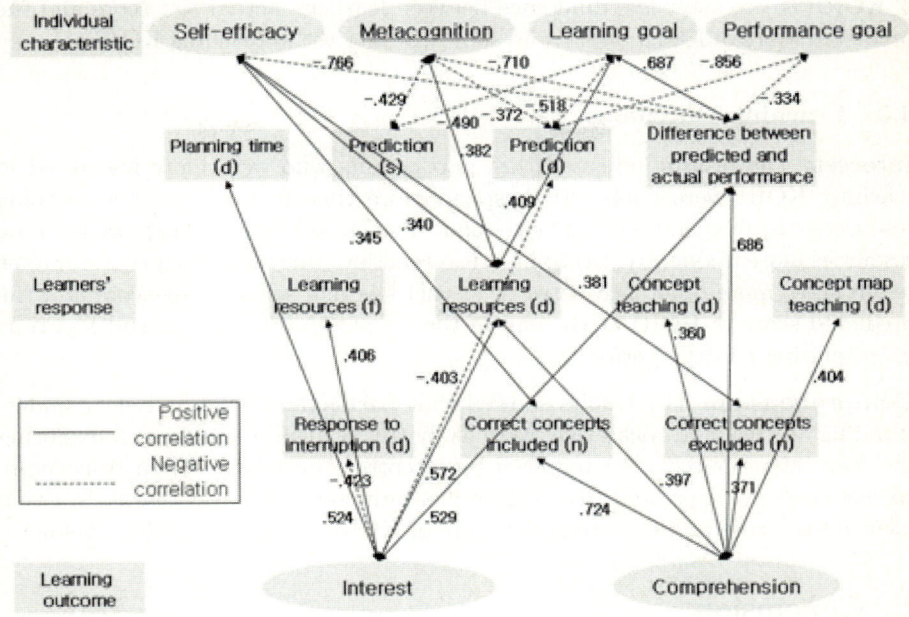

Fig. 2. Structure of nodes (d: duration, f: frequency, n: number, s: score)

score and the predicted score of KORI at the end of the teaching, indicating that those who had high self-efficacy tended to predict the score of KORI based on their actual test score.

Metacognition: Metacognition was found to be the most significant individual characteristic to influence participants' responses during their interaction with the KORI. The result indicated that participants who had higher metacognitive awareness have a tendency (a) to spend less time in exploring the learning resources, indicating they knew what they needed to know to teach KORI and where the necessary information was; (b) to spend less time in predicting the performance of KORI; (c) to show low estimation score; (d) to show less difference between learner's actual test score and the predicted score of KORI, indicating that those who had high metacognitive awareness tended to predict the KORI's test score based on the cognition of their own ability.

Learning goal: The student model showed that the level of learning goal orientation affected participants' response pattern. Participants who had high goal orientation were likely (a) to spend more time in exploring the learning resources; (b) to spend less time predicting the performance of KORI; (c) to show more difference between learner's actual test score and the predicted score of KORI, indicating quick but incorrect prediction of performance.

Performance goal: The correlational analysis showed that high performance goal oriented participants tended (a) to spend less time in predicting the performance of KORI; (b) to show less difference between learner's actual test score and the predicted score of KORI; and (c) to show less interest in teaching KORI.

3.3 Learning Outcomes

Interest: The results indicated that participants who were more interested in teaching KORI were likely (a) to spend more time in exploring the learning resources; (b) to spend more time to plan to teach KORI; (c) to explore learning resources more frequently; (d) to have less reaction time to interruptive stimulus; (e) to show more difference between learner's actual science test score and the predicted score of KORI at the end of the teaching; and (f) to spend less time in estimating KORI's performance.

Comprehension: The results showed that participants who had clear understanding of 'rock and rock cycle' were likely (a) to spend more time in exploring the learning resources; (b) to teach more correct concepts; (c) to draw more correct concept maps; and (d) to show more difference between learner's actual science test score and the predicted score of KORI at the end of the teaching.

4 Conclusion

The results of student modeling indicated that the participants' individual differences in metacognition, self-efficacy, goal-orientation and ongoing status of learning can be predicted by a combination of a variety of learner responses during the learning process. In the student model, all data were classified into three dimensions and described in terms of these three dimensions: individual differences, participants' responses, and learning outcomes. The duration of exploring the learning resources and the difference between predicted and actual performance might be useful indices to estimate the ongoing level of comprehension and interests of each learner. In particular, the difference between predicted and actual performance is the only response that is related to all four individual characteristics and two learning outcomes.

Individualization is the significant issue in developing a computer assisted learning system including an intelligent tutoring agent. The ultimate goal of developing an adaptive learning agent is to make the agent respond intelligently to the individual learner. Therefore, it should reflect the individual differences and ongoing changes in terms of cognition and motivation. Traditional measurements for individual characteristics include assessment by standardized tests or questionnaires at the beginning or at the end of the learning session. This study proposed a new type of assessment for individual differences and ongoing cognitive/motivational changes. In this new assessment process, the response patterns are computed without direct measurement before or after the learning. In the near future, various physiological indices such as temperature of fingers, eye-movement, facial expression, and brainwaves combined with the response pattern are likely to be used to measure individual differences or learning outcomes. However, for now, it is essential to develop an algorithm of learner response pattern during learning. The construction of the student model consisted of a structure of nodes which were formed by collecting and classifying the log data of the learner that were correlated with the individual characteristics and learning outcomes. This model can be used to understand the learner's dynamic changes during a specific learning situation.

The limitation of this study is that the log data were collected from a very small sample. If the sample size were large enough, it would be possible to conduct a regression analysis to give different weights to the responses. Then the algorithm for the adaptive teachable agent would be computed from the regression equation. Once the algorithm is extracted, the teachable agent would collect the information of the learner's learning states from the responses and can automatically predict the learner's cognitive and motivational states, and then respond to the learner according to the learners' individual data.

Acknowledgements

This research was supported as a Brain Neuroinformatics Research Program sponsored by Korean Minister of Commerce, Industry and Energy.

References

1. Kim. S., Kim, W.S., Yun, M.S., So, Y.H., Kwon, E.J., Choi, J.S., Kim, M.S. Lee, M.J., & Park, T.J. (2003). Conceptual understanding and Designing of Teachable Agent. Journal of Korean Cognitive Science, 14(3), 13-21.
2. Biswas, G., Schwartz, D., Bransford, J. & TAG-V. (2001). Technology support for complex problem solving: From SAD environment to AI. In Forbus and Feltovich, (Eds.), Smart machines in education, Menlo Park, CA: AAAI Press.
3. Pintrich, P.R. & Schunk, D.H. (1996). Motivation in Education; Theory, Research, and Application. Englewood Cliffs, NJ: Prentice-Hall.
4. Stoyanov, S., & Kommers, P. (1999). Agent-support for problem solving through concept-mapping. Journal of Interactive Learning Research, 10(3), 401-442.

An Agent-Based Model of Personal Web Communities

José I. Santos, José M. Galán, and Ricardo del Olmo

University of Burgos, Avda. Cantabria s/n, 09006, Burgos, Spain
{jisantos, jmgalan, rdelolmo}@ubu.es

Abstract. The idea that people use the Web and make the Web at the same time is an interesting starting point to study it. Personal homepages, blogs and similar websites can be studied as a social network phenomenon because social characteristics can explain their nature and dynamic. We present a computational Agent-Based model of personal web communities. Agents maintain their homepages and the web network emerges as they make links to colleagues' homepages, with whom they share common interests. Three simple rules we have summarized in the "similarity", "bookmarks" and "activity" concepts allow to explain most of the network properties presented in real web communities. The similarity in personal interests conditions the network structure, mainly the average social distance between individuals. The way in which agents search information in the Web influences the probability of meeting new people and has a big effect on the transitivity of the web network.

Keywords: blogs, personal homepages, Social Networks, Agent-Based Modeling.

1 Introduction

The Internet and his big brother the WWW are in the centre of many scientific research projects. The different study dimensions of this topic, technological, economic or social, have found a common knowledge reference in the Network Theory, a branch of applied mathematics that is arousing new interest in scientific community thanks to the major advances in computing algorithms and statistical methods for large networks [1].

The Network Theory provides a basis not only for developing advanced Web search engines, or improving the electronic traffic over the Net, but also a set of theoretical concepts and applied tools for understanding the nature and the dynamic of these systems. That is how some research lines focus their activities on explaining how the WWW comes to have their scale free characteristic [2], while others try to exploit the information collected in the WWW to show the social characteristics presented in many online communities [3].

In our opinion, the last two examples of research lines are very interesting and complementary. In order to develop models of some sort of web networks we should take account of the social nature of the main actors, people. Many online phenomena show a small world effect or a clustering property like real social networks [4]. We can see the Net as a new virtual social space where people behave in a similar way as they do in the real world. Agent-Based modeling (ABM) allows us to design more realistic models applying a bottom-up methodology that can offer new insights to this kind of technological and social phenomenon.

The structure of the rest of the paper is as follows: in the next section we summarize the knowledge background about online communities' phenomena and some approaches from the Network Theory; the model section describes the main features of our agent-based model; simulations section summarizes important results of the model; and conclusions are discussing in the last section.

2 Online Websites Communities and Social Networks

We are interested in online websites communities where personal interests are determinant to understand the contents and the structure of relationships. Two important examples of these web communities are personal homepages and weblogs.

Personal homepages are like windows on the world where people put diverse objects, such as personal information, opinions, hobbies and many other interests. Blogs are a more recent event, whose successful is due to blog service providers that facilitate publishing contents in the WWW [5]. They are much more dynamic and personal content-oriented where someone periodically adds new contents like personal notes, called posts, that everybody in the Net can read and comment.

Homepages and blogs can be a social research source, because they not only show individual portraits of their users but also draw the big picture of social relationships through the links between websites. Although the WWW depicts a virtual space without physical references, the absence of geographic proximity does not reduce the social nature of these phenomena. Unlike other social network information resources, they are more affordable and provide much more rigorous data due to the electronic nature of the Internet [6].

There is no doubt that the relationships between websites such as homepages and blogs are an interesting object of study for Social Network researchers. Adamic and Aldar [3] analyze the social structure of two personal homepage communities form the MIT and Stanford University. These personal webs and their links between them are studied using social network techniques. The small world characteristic, common in real social networks, is presented in these web networks too. The existence of a giant component shows that an important fraction of homepages are connected and therefore different types of electronic communications between them are possible. The link distribution follows a typical power law function with a fat tail, very different from a Binomial distribution we would expect if the linking process was driven by a pure random mechanism. And the clustering coefficient manifests a transitivity property that it is always present in social networks.

An interest of the authors [3] is to identify proximity measures that allow explaining the social proximity in the network. They define some indicators and develop some computing techniques to measure the grade of similarity between agents, which allow characterizing communities. This study evidences how the social similarity between agents falls as the corresponding social distance goes up, measured by the geodesic distance in the graph.

The works cited before look at real web networks focusing on the graph properties that characterize them. Other researchers exploit other work line proposing dynamic network models that explain these properties. Most of these models are based on the "preferential attachment" principle [1], [7]. The idea is simple, but not less powerful, as the network grows the new edges appear preferentially between vertices with a high number of links. These models are elegant and fit well many real networks, not only web networks.

The idea that "famous" agents, in terms of the number of relationships, become "more famous" has an interesting meaning in many physical and social phenomena, but it does not give much more understanding about the micro-foundation of the social system and the agents' behaviors. This is the main reason why we propose an agent-based model of web communities set up on a bottom-up analysis.

3 The Model

The simulation model is composed of *Na* agents who maintain personal homepages. The type of website is not important for our purpose, because we are more interested in the agents' routines and the corresponding network dynamic. The web community emerges as an agent makes a link to a colleague's homepage, with whom he shares common interests. The equivalent graph is a directed network where vertices represent agents' homepages, and directed edges the links between them.

Unlike preferential attachment models family, our agent-based model is characterized by:

1. It is not a dynamic network, a non-equilibrium network where new vertices and edges come along at each time step. We start from a stable set of non-connected vertices, let agents interact and make new links and stop the simulation when the system reaches a saturation point where agents can not make new links.
2. The agents' behaviors in the model reproduce behaviors in the real world. The actual process by which an agent participates in a web community can be very complex, but we are interested in identifying those individual routines that drive the social network dynamic.

3.1 Principles of the Model

The basic principles of the model coming from the observations we have made from our own experience and different works about personal homepages, web communities and blogs [3], [4], [8]. They can be summarized as follows:

Similarity. The more interest proximity between two agents the more likely they make a link with each other [3]. Similarity is measure in terms of sharing common interests.

Each agent is endowed with a vector of personal interests. You can see an element in this vector as an interest category or topic, and the corresponding value as the personal expression of the agent's interest in the topic. The probability that agent i makes an out link to agent j is a function of the number of topics with a common value he shares and a similarity parameter (1). Note that *SimilaritySigma* parameter governs this probability, the higher it is the less common interests agents need share to have enough likely to make a link.

$$P(iLinkToj) = \exp((nCommonTopic(i,j) - nTopic)/SimilaritySigma) . \qquad (1)$$

Bookmarks. An agent uses preferentially his bookmarks (list of out links) as source for his searches. This rule feeds a transitivity effect in the networks because the links of my link have more likely to have a link from me.

At each time step (tick), an agent updates a vector of preference weights that take into account the social distance (length of the corresponding directed path between two agents) with the rest of agents (2). Note that *PreferenceSigma* parameter governs the weight distribution that drives the agents' choice. The higher it is the more sensitive the weights are to distance. Agents who receive a link from me have a distance of 1 and they are out of future searches, so the corresponding weight will be cero. Agents who are in the bookmarks of my links have a distance of 2 and therefore will have a high weight. And so on.

$$W(i,j) = \min(1, \text{WeightBase}*\exp(-(\text{Distance}(i,j)-2)/\text{PreferenceSigma}) \,. \tag{2}$$

Activity. Surfing the web and updating a homepage is a time consuming activity. Not everybody dedicates the same time and energy to do it [8]. Each agent is endowed with an activity parameter that conditions the probability of starting new searches (3). Note that the agent's energy to look for new colleagues decays with the number of out links. The *ActivitySigma(i)* parameter determines the function increasing the probability as it has high values.

$$P(i\text{NewSearch}) = \exp(-n\text{OutLink}/\text{ActivitySigma}(i)) \,. \tag{3}$$

3.2 Network Dynamic

The model describes a directed network where agents are the vertices and each link from one to another is a directed edge between the corresponding vertices. The network evolves as follows. At each tick an agent has an opportunity to surf the web looking for new colleagues:

1. If he shows enough interest (depending on his individual activity parameter and his current number of out links) he will look for a new colleague in the Web.
2. He chooses a new guy at random (taking account the preferential function (2) commented before).
3. The probability of making an out link to the new colleague depends on the similarity (1). If there is enough interest proximity, the corresponding directed edge will be added to the graph.

We are particularly interested in the similarity distance effects on the social network dynamic and their graph properties.

4 The Simulation

This section describes the design and results of the computational simulation of the model. The model[1] is composed of $Na=500$ agents endowed with a vector of personal interests with $k=5$ topics. The corresponding value an agent has in each topic is an

---

[1] The model has been developed using REPAST (http://repast.sourceforge.net/) and JUNG (http://jung.sourceforge.net/) java libraries.

integer value generated from a Normal distribution *N(5, 1)*. The distribution of agents' interests is not important for the purpose of this paper because our curiosity focuses on how interest distance between agents conditions the network structure.

The agents' *ActivitySigma* parameter follows a Normal distribution *N(2,1)*. Note that this value is directly related with the number of out links an agent maintains (3). The chosen distribution has a mean close to the average out links of a particular web community studied by Adamic and Aldar [3].

We vary the main parameters of the model, *PreferenceSigma* and *SimilaritySigma*. A simulation run is composed of 200 ticks, and ten replications or samples are recorded for each run. Some network properties have been computing using the network analysis tool Pajek [9].

The network evolves following the rules described in the previous section until agents can not make new links. The network properties are computing at this steady state, which is reached at about 180 ticks for all simulations.

The figure 1 shows a sensitivity analysis to changes in the main parameters. We use contour plots to display the average path length and the clustering coefficient in the *PreferenceSigma-SimilaritySigma* space. The small world effect comes along when every agent can reach others in a small number of steps, and is measured by the average path length between agents. The simulation results show that this property is not sensitive to changes in the *PreferenceSigma* parameter, but *SimilaritySigma* has a significant influence. It is easily understandable, the facility to make friends because agents do not mind their interest distance (that corresponds with high *SimilaritySigma* values) reduces the social distance between individuals.

The transitivity property of a social network describes the nature of the triple relationships. The clustering coefficient can be described in the model as the probability that the links of my links are my links too. When *PreferenceSigma* is high enough (2) the model follows a sort of random process, because all agents can be chosen with the same probability by anyone. As a result of this random selection

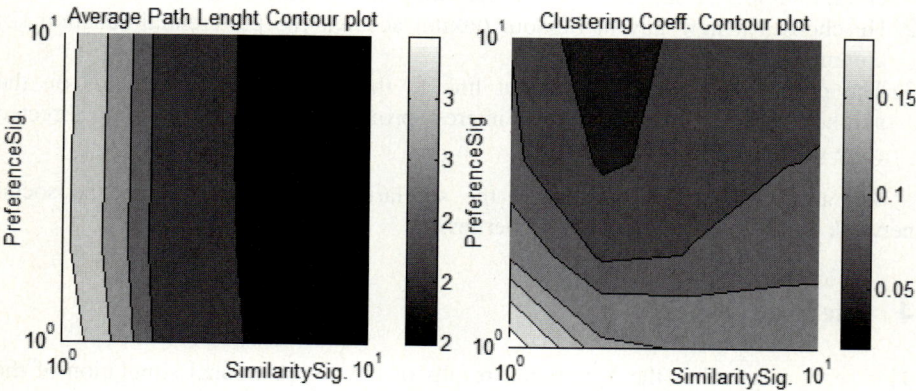

Fig. 1. Contour plots of the average path length and the clustering coefficient for the *PreferenceSigma* and *SimilaritySigma* parameters

process the corresponding clustering coefficient is low whatever *SimilaritySigma* value is. On the other hand, when *PreferenceSigma* is close to 1 the network gets a high clustering coefficient, much higher when the *SimilaritySigma* value is lower. For high *SimilaritySigma* values the *PreferenceSigma* effect on the clustering coefficient is a bit lower because any pick causes a link and therefore the network dynamic evolves much more randomly.

We chose a particular combination of the main parameters to comment the rest of network properties, a model where similarity is important to make links (*SimilaritySigma*=1) and agents search new colleagues preferentially over the links of their current links (*PreferenceSigma*=1). This model gets a clustering coefficient similar to the web communities of MIT and Stanford University studied by Adamic and Aldar [3].

The degree of a vertex in a graph is the number of edges connected to it. In the model, the emergent structure is a directed network where an agent maintains links to his colleagues (that is called out-degree) and is pointed by the links of other agents (in-degree). Random networks follow a binomial degree distribution but social networks show a different distribution, usually a power-law distribution [7].

The figure 2 shows the cumulative degree (in and out) distribution for a network sample with *SimilaritySigma*=1 and *PreferenceSigma*=1. A power law function can be easily observed in the log-log plot. Note the difference between the two degree distributions. The maximum in-degree is 9 but the maximum out-degree is 28, which reveals the presence of a few popular agents in the community. All these network characteristics are common in real web communities [3].

Finally, we are going to pay special attention to the similarity distribution between agents. Remember that the *SimilaritySigma* parameter governs the probability an agent makes a link to other taking into account the common interests they share. For two agents, we can compare the number of common interests and the path length that separates them in the network. If similarity was important in the link making process, one could expect that the interest distance goes up with the social distance.

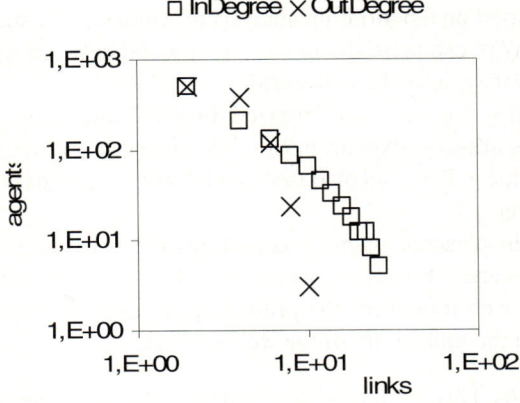

Fig. 2. Cumulative in-degree and out-degree distribution of a sample network where *PreferenceSigma*=1 and *SimilaritySigma*=1

The figure 3 shows the average number of common interests and the path length between agents when we vary the *SimilaritySigma* parameter. We observe that when the parameter is low enough, the proximity in interests between agents grows with the social proximity in the network. On the other hand when the value is high the network presents a much more heterogeneous map of relationships.

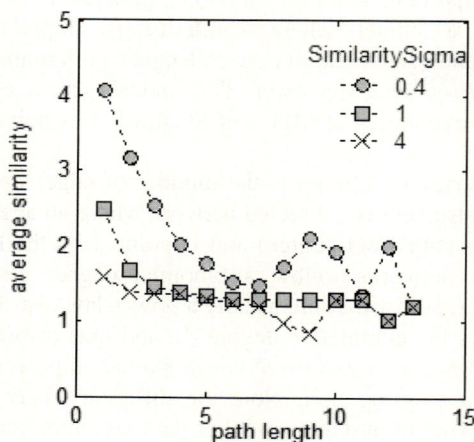

Fig. 3. The average similarity (measured as the average number of common interests) and the path length between agents of tree sample networks where *PreferenceSigma*=1 and *SimilaritySigma*={0.4, 1, 4}

5 Conclusions

We have presented a computational Agent-Based model of personal web communities. Unlike other models based on the preferential attachment principle, we have design one based on a bottom-up analysis that looks at the social actors and their behaviors. The WWW can be studied as a virtual social network where people behave in a similar way as they do in the real world.

Tree simple rules we have summarized in the "similarity", "bookmarks" and "activity" concepts allow to explain most of the network properties that we found in real web communities. This Agent-Based model gives new ideas to understand this type of phenomenon.

The similarity in personal interests conditions the network structure, mainly the average social distance between individuals. The way in which agents search information in the web influences the probability of meeting new people and has an important effect on the transitivity of the web network.

Acknowledgements. This work has been supported by the Spanish MICYT, research project DPI2004-06590.

References

1. Newman, M.E.J.: The structure and function of complex networks. SIAM Review, Vol. 45 (2003) 167-256
2. Barabási, A.-L., Albert, R., Jeong, H.: Scale-free characteristics of random networks: The topology of the World Wide Web. Physica A, Vol. 281 (2000) 69–77
3. Adamic, L.A., Adar, E.: Friends and neighbors on the Web. Social Networks, Vol. 25 (2003) 211-230
4. Bachnik, W., Szymczyk, S., Leszczynski, P., Podsiadlo, R., Rymszewicz, E., Kurylo, L., Makowiec, D., Bykowska, B.: Quantitive and sociological analysis of blog networks. Acta Physica Polonica B, Vol. 36 (2005) 3179-3191
5. Lindahl, C., Blount, E.: Weblogs: simplifying web publishing. Computer, Vol. 36 (2003) 114-116
6. Adamic, L.A., Buyukkokten, O., Adar, E.: A social network caught in the Web. First Monday, Vol. 8, No. 6 (2003)
7. Dorogovtsev, S.N., Mendes, J.F.F.: Evolution of Networks. From Biological Nets to the Internet and WWW. Oxfrod University Press (2003) 112-131
8. Lenhart, A., Fallows, D., Horrigan, J.: Content Creation Online: 44% of U.S. Internet users have contributed their thoughts and their files to the online world. Report: Online Activities&Pursuits. Pew Internet & American Life Project (2004)
9. Batagelj, V., Mrvar, A.: Pajek – Program for Large Network Analysis [http://vlado.fmf.uni-lj.si/pub/networks/pajek/]

A Conceptual Framework for Automated Negotiation Systems

Manuel Resinas, Pablo Fernandez, and Rafael Corchuelo

ETS Ingenieria Informatica
Universidad de Sevilla, Spain
http://www.tdg-seville.info

Abstract. In the last years, much work have been done in the development of techniques for automated negotiation, and, particularly, in the automated negotiation of SLAs. However, there is no work that describes how to develop advanced software systems that are able to negotiate automatically in an open environment such as the Internet. In this work, we develop a conceptual framework for automated negotiations of SLAs that serves as a starting point by identifying the elements that must be supported in those software systems. In addition, based on that conceptual framework, we report on a set of properties for automated negotiation systems that may be used to compare different proposals.

1 Introduction

In this work, we focus on SLA negotiations[1]. The goal of this kind of negotiations is to reach an agreement between a service provider and a service consumer about the terms and guarantees of the service consumption. We are interested in developing software systems that are able to negotiate in open environments, such as the Internet, with temporal restrictions. That is, the agreement has to be reached in a limited amount of time. This scenario defines the characteristics of the negotiation that shall be carried out: it is a non-cooperative negotiation between two or more parties with partial information of the world and hard computational constraints.

In the last years, much work have been done on automated negotiations. These works are focused on the development of new decision-making algorithms or the construction of new protocols that presents certain desirable characteristics for automated negotiations. However, much less attention has been paid to the software artefacts that are necessary to carry out this automated negotiation. In this work, we analyse the problem of automated negotiation of service level agreements from a software engineering perspective. Specifically, we want to identify the elements that are required to build a system that develops an automated negotiation of SLAs.

To reach this goal, we present a novel conceptual framework of SLA automated negotiations. Unlike other works, we take a software engineering perspective and

---
[1] SLA negotiations are equivalent to the so-called service-oriented negotiations [1].

centre on the elements that are required to build an automated negotiation system. This conceptual framework settles the bases for a later analysis of the different negotiation proposals and defines a common vocabulary for automated negotiation systems. In addition, we obtain a set of properties of automated negotiation systems as a consequence of the conceptual framework. These properties may be used to evaluate and compare different proposals on automated negotiation of SLAs.

This paper is structured as follows: first, we describe the conceptual framework in Section 2, then, in Section 3, we use the conceptual framework to obtain a set of properties of automated negotiation systems. Finally, we present our conclusions and future work in Section 4.

2 A Conceptual Framework for Automated Negotiations

Traditionally, an automated negotiation system has been characterised by three elements [2]: protocol, negotiation object and decision-making model. In our conceptual framework we propose to extend this characterisation with two additional elements: information and preferences. Additionally, we detail more precisely the decision-making and protocol elements, and we also provide a concrete description of the negotiation object.

2.1 Negotiation Object

In a SLA negotiation, the object that is being negotiated is an agreement between parties. An agreement defines a dynamically-established and dynamically-managed relationship between parties [3]. The goal of the agreement is to establish the guarantees that must be observed during the execution of a service. An agreement is composed at least by the following:

- A specification of the *parties* involved in it. In principle, the number of parties involved in an agreement is not constrained. However, the most common case is two-party agreements.
- A collection of *terms* that describes both functional descriptions and non-functional guarantees of the service. Additionally a term can also express other aspects of an agreement such as termination clauses. A term is composed of three parts:
    - The *counterparty* whom the term is applied to. Each term is to be applied to one of the parties involved in the agreement and the party is obligated to fulfil what it is specified in it. Obviously, the *counterparty* must be one of those that have been designated in the agreement as one of the parties that are involved in it.
    - A set of *constraints* to specify functional or non-functional descriptions or guarantees of the service. It is expected that the content of these constraints will be very broad and domain-specific.
    - A set of *compensations* that will be applied in case the party does not fulfil the constraints specified in the term. This element is optional and it is not supported by the majority of the negotiation strategies.

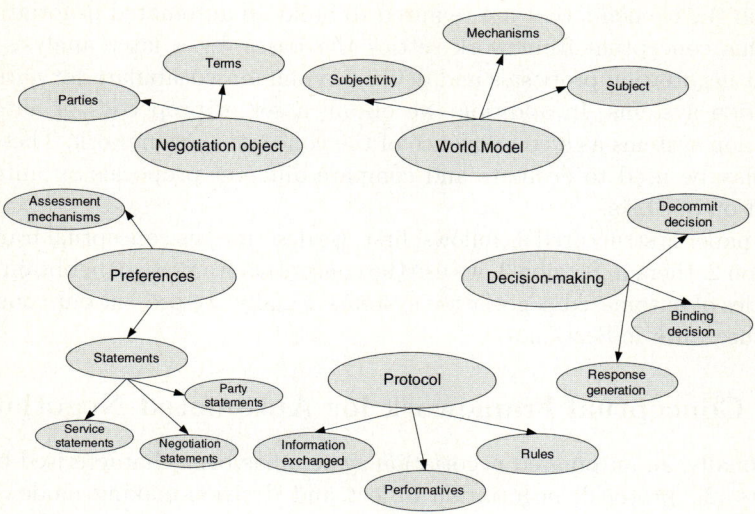

Fig. 1. Conceptual framework

2.2 Preferences

The agreement preferences express the data that is used to assure that the user needs are correctly dealt among the negotiation process. These preferences comprise: a set of *statements* expressing the *features* and *requirements* of the user, and an *assessment mechanism* to evaluate and compare agreement proposals. The most common way of evaluating proposals is through the definition of utility functions [4]. Statements can be classified depending on the domain in which they are applied:

- **Service statements**. These statements are applied to the service offered (or demanded). They can refer to either functional or non-functional characteristics of the service such as the *service interface* or the *service price*.
- **Party statements**. In this case, an expression about the party is stated. These statements can express either features or requirement over a given party. Examples of this can be: *Party Z is located in Iran* or *Party X must have a high reputation on service Y*.
- **Negotiation statements**. They specify features about the negotiation process itself, such as the negotiation deadline.

Each statement is linked to a set of *languages* that give semantics to the vocabulary used within the statement. Ontologies can be seen as an example of languages describing the relationship amongst concepts of a given semantic domain. Usually, the statements are expressed using two different formalisms: rules and constraints. However, other formalisms could be used.

2.3 World Model

While negotiating, the more information we have about other parties, the better our performance is [5]. Furthermore, it has been shown that taking the conditions of the market into account does improve the outcome of negotiations with several simultaneous opponents [6]. Therefore, it is essential for an automated negotiation system to build a model of the counterparties and the market. We call this model, the world model of an automated negotiation system and it may cover three different domains:

- Counterparties: including the characteristics of the service demanded or offered, the negotiation process followed by the counterparty and the counterparty itself (e.g. reputation or geographical location).
- Market: for instance, the market reservation price, or the probability of appearing outside options during the negotiation [7].
- Service-domain: such as knowledge about the vocabulary used in the terms of the agreement.

The information used to build the world model may be either objective or subjective: objective information typically includes the public features about the service demanded/supplied, but it may also include information about the counterparties themselves (e.g. their geographical location) and the market. Subjective information comprises elements such as the reputation of a counterparty or the market price of a certain service.

Finally, there are three different mechanisms to obtain the information that is used to build the world model: (i) Directly polling the potential counterparty. In this case, the system must implement a compatible specification of a format to express functional and non-functional features of services and a procedure to query and to inspect services. (ii) Querying a third party entity to obtain information related to a specific counterparty. For instance, to obtain information about its reputation or its geographical location. (iii) Analysing previous interactions with a potential counterparty. The results of the analysis may be stored in order to be used later while making decision about proposals related to the potential counterparty.

We envision that the first procedure shall be commonly used in gathering objective information about the counterparties, while the second and third procedures shall be more common in obtaining subjective information about the market and the potential counterparty itself.

2.4 Protocol

The negotiation protocol establishes the rules that govern the negotiation and the way the communication between the different parties involved in the negotiation is carried out as well as the information exchanged between the parties. We distinguish three different, although strongly related, aspects in a negotiation protocol: rules, performatives and information exchanged.

Performatives. A performative is the expression of the intention of the sender of a message. The set of performatives used in a negotiation protocol may differ significantly. However, there are a minimum subset of performatives that are common to the majority of negotiation protocols. Namely, *accept* (accept a proposal), *reject proposal* (withdraws the proposal), *reject negotiation* (cancel the whole negotiation process), and *commit*[2] (commit to a given proposal). Depending on the specific protocol that is being used, other performatives may be necessary. For instance, in auctions, it is common to use the *inform* performative to notify events occurred during the negotiation such as that a new bid has been done. In protocols that differentiates between binding and non-binding proposals, the *propose* (make a non-binding proposal) performative may be introduced. Other protocols use a vote system to decide which is the preferred offer [8]. In such protocols, a *vote* performative may be used. Finally, in negotiation protocols that use argumentation [9], other performatives to introduce arguments supporting our proposal are used such as *argue* and *challenge* [9].

Rules. In a negotiation protocol, there are usually some restrictions regarding a variety of aspects of the negotiation such as how the proposals must be built, when a participant can post a proposal, which performative can be used in each moment, when a participant may join to the negotiation, or when the negotiation can finish. In [10], a taxonomy of rules for negotiation protocols is presented. However, although it is a thorough taxonomy and the majority of the aspects of automated negotiation are covered, we believe that it should be extended with rules for decommitting from previously created agreements. We argue that there must be rules that explicitly specify whether a decommitment may take place, and, if so, when it may occur and which are the penalties to be paid as a compensation.

Information Exchanged. The third aspect in a negotiation protocol is the type of information exchanged amongst the participants in the negotiation. A variety of approaches has been presented in the literature. Those approaches may be classified into three broad groups:

- The information exchanged explicitly states the parts of the agreement that are disliked by the party as well as the proposed changes.
- The information exchanged consists only of proposals. In other words, the negotiation protocol is proposal-based. The advantage of this approach is that it unveils less information to the other parties. The disadvantage is that the lack of explicit information implies a blind search of a mutually acceptable agreement that may lead to longer negotiations and even to not to find any agreement at all.
- The information exchanged includes proposals, as in proposal-based protocols, and statements that are used to persuade or convince the opponent to

---

[2] In the literature, this performative is usually called *propose* meaning making a binding proposal. However, we prefer to leave the term *propose* to non-binding proposals and to use *commit* for binding proposals.

accept our proposal [11]. This approach is called argumentation and it is a promising field that may eventually overcome the drawbacks of the proposal-based negotiation [9]. However, the negotiators that support argumentation tend to be very complex and no argumentation approach has been applied to a real scenario yet.

2.5 Decision-Making

The decision-making model determines the way a party behaves while involved in a negotiation process. Three elements form part of the decision-making model of an automated negotiation system: the decision of what is considered an acceptable agreement and whether to commit to it, the construction of responses to this information, and the decision to decommit from a previously established agreement if possible.

Binding Decision. This decision includes determining when a binding proposal must be submitted and whether a binding proposal that has been received should be accepted. The binding decision depends on several factors that may vary depending on whether it is a service consumer who is making the decision or it is a service provider. Nevertheless, we can divide these factors into three broad groups:

- Preferences of the user. These preferences may be related to the contents of the agreement, the party we are negotiating the agreement and the negotiation process.
- The information the system have about the status of the market and other possible concurrent negotiations. For instance, we may be more reluctant to accept a proposal if we know it is very likely that in a short amount of time we will receive a proposal better than the current one [7].
- External factors that may prevent a party to commit to an agreement. For instance, the provider's capability to accept new agreements or the existence of dependencies amongst the agreements a service consumer wants to reach.

Together with the decision of making or accepting a binding proposal, it has to be decided when this decision take place. Usually, the decision is made as the proposals are received like in [12]. However, other approaches may be followed such as making the decision in some certain points in time previously defined.

Response Generation. Other important task in an automated negotiator is to decide which response must be sent to the other participants in the negotiation. On the one hand, this response is subordinated to the binding decision. On the other hand, the response generated must obey the rules imposed by the negotiation protocol. The process followed to generate the responses varies significantly. However, in general, it depends on the performatives of the negotiation protocol and the expressivity of the information exchanged during the negotiation:

- In auctions, the unique possible response is a bid together with the bidding price. Therefore, in this case the problem is centred on deciding in which auction must be placed the bid [13].
- In bilateral proposal-based protocols, a counterproposal must be generated. A wide variety of techniques have been developed to generate them. The most significant are: those that use time-dependant functions, resource-dependant functions, etcetera to obtain the counterproposal by modifying the values of the terms of the offer [4]; those that try to make the counterproposal more appealing to the opponent by sending the counteroffer with the highest similarity to the received offer [14]; those that use fuzzy constraint techniques [15], and those that interpret the negotiation as if it were a game and use techniques similar to those used in chess games [16]. Genetic algorithms have also been used to calculate offline which is the best strategy to use depending on the conditions of the negotiation in a certain instant [17].
- In negotiation protocols that supports argumentation, the response generation includes two problems [9]. First, the different arguments must be generated and then, the best argument from the point of view of the speaker must be selected. However, both the generation of arguments and the selection of the best one may occur at the same time. Nevertheless, whether or not this is possible depends on the specific argumentation framework.

Decommit Decision. It has been proved [18,12] that decommitment is a valuable resource when dealing with multiple simultaneous negotiations and, hence, it is another decision element that must be included in an automated negotiation system. The decommit decision is highly related to the binding decision and depends on the same factors. Therefore, in many cases, both the binding and decommit decisions are made by the same element [12].

3 Properties of Automated Negotiation Systems

The following properties for automated negotiation systems (ANS) have been obtained based on the conceptual framework (Section 2). We must remark that these properties are just centred on high-level details of automated negotiation systems and do not cover lower-level elements such as concrete technologies, protocols or algorithms.

1. *Information query*: An information query is an inquiry made by one party to another to obtain more detailed information about it or about the service it provides or demands.
2. *World model*: An ANS builds a world model if it analyses previous interactions with the elements external to the architecture and uses the results to make better decisions [2] during the negotiation.
3. *Third party information*: An ANS uses third party information if it explicitly queries a third party entity to obtain information related to another party.

4. *Information managed about the parties*: There are three types of information that can be managed: about the parties, the service and the negotiation process itself.
5. *Multiple negotiation protocols supported*: An ANS supports multiple negotiation protocols if it is able to use a number of negotiation protocols such as different bilateral negotiation protocols or several auction protocols [2].
6. *Decommitment from previously established agreements*: An ANS supports the decommitment [18] from previously established agreements if it can revoke previous agreements before the execution of the service.
7. *External factors in binding decisions*: An ANS may make use of a capacity estimator to determine whether the provider can provision a certain agreement before committing to an agreement [19].
8. *Cooperative or non-cooperative agreement creation*: An ANS supports non-cooperative agreement creation when it acts as a self-interested party reaching agreements with other self-interested parties. Alternatively, an ANS supports cooperative agreement creation when it can reach agreements with other parties trying to maximise the social welfare.
9. *Assessment mechanisms used*: The assessment mechanisms of an ANS is the kind of information used to evaluate the goodness of a proposal or agreement in relation to some criteria provided by the user.
10. *Forms of expressing preferences*: The preferences about the service and the parties can be expressed in different ways such as rules or constraints (see Section 2).

4 Conclusions

In this work, we analyse the problem of automated negotiation of service level agreements from a software engineering perspective. To develop advanced automated negotiation systems, it is necessary to identify the elements that are required in them. We present a conceptual framework for automated negotiation of SLAs that identifies the elements that must be supported by an advanced automated negotiation system. We extend the classical elements of automated negotiation with two new ones: world model and preferences. Furthermore, we detail more precisely the parts that compose the other three: negotiation object, protocol and decision-making. In addition, taking the conceptual framework as a basis, we also present a set of properties of automated negotiation systems that can be used to compare them.

Moreover, we believe that this work is a necessary step to develop a software framework for automated negotiation system that gives support to the most significant proposals of negotiation protocols and strategies that have been done in the last years.

Further work includes refining the categorisation of automated negotiation proposals in order to identify which alternative is better in each case. In this way, an automated selection of the algorithms used to carry out the negotiation can be made depending on the context of the negotiation.

References

1. Sierra, C., Faratin, P., Jennings, N.R.: A Service-Oriented Negotiation Model Between Autonomous Agents. In: Proc. of the 8th European Workshop On Modelling Auton. Agents in a Multi-Agent World, Springer-Verlag (1997) 17–35
2. Jennings, N.R., Faratin, P., Lomuscio, A.R., Parsons, S., Wooldridge, M., Sierra, C.: Automated Negotiation: Prospects, Methods and Challenges. Group Decision and Negotiation **10** (2001) 199–215
3. Andrieux, A., Czajkowski, K., Dan, A., Keahey, K., Ludwig, H., Pruyne, J., Rofrano, J., Tuecke, S., Xu, M.: WS-Agreement Specification (2004)
4. Faratin, P., Sierra, C., Jennings, N.R.: Negotiation Decision Functions For Autonomous Agents. Int. Journal of Robotics and Autonomous Systems **24** (1998) 159–182
5. Zeng, D., Sycara, K.: Bayesian Learning in Negotiation. Int. J. Hum.-Comput. Stud. **48** (1998) 125–141
6. Sim, K.M., Wong, E.: Toward market-driven agents for electronic auction. Systems, Man and Cybernetics, Part A, IEEE Transactions on **31** (2001) 474–484
7. Li, C., Giampapa, J., Sycara, K.: Bilateral negotiation decisions with uncertain dynamic outside options. In: Electronic Contracting, 2004. Proceedings. First IEEE International Workshop on. (2004) 54–61
8. Klein, M., Faratin, P., Sayama, H., Bar-Yam, Y.: Protocols For Negotiating Complex Contracts. IEEE Intelligent Systems **18** (2003) 32–38
9. Rahwan, I., Ramchurn, S.D., Jennings, N.R., McBurney, P., Parsons, S., Sonenberg, L.: Argumentation-Based Negotiation. The Knowledge Engineering Review **18** (2003) 343–375
10. Bartolini, C., Preist, C., Jennings, N.R.: Architecting For Reuse: A Software Framework For Automated Negotiation. In: Agent-Oriented Software Engineering III: AOSE 2002. Volume 2585 of Lecture Notes in Computer Science., Springer-Verlag (2003) 88–100
11. Ramchurn, S.D., Jennings, N.R., Sierra, C.: Persuasive Negotiation For Autonomous Agents: A Rhetorical Approach. In: Proc. IJCAI Workshop On Computational Models of Natural Argument. (2003) 9–17
12. Nguyen, T., Jennings, N.: Managing commitments in multiple concurrent negotiations. Electronic Commerce Research and Applications **4** (2005) 362–376
13. Anthony, P., Jennings, N.R.: Developing a Bidding Agent For Multiple Heterogeneous Auctions. ACM Trans. Internet Technology **3** (2003) 185–217
14. Faratin, P., Sierra, C., Jennings, N.R.: Using Similarity Criteria to Make Trade-Offs in Automated Negotiations. Artificial Intelligence **142** (2002) 205–237
15. Kowalczyk, R.: Fuzzy e-negotiation agents. Soft Computing **6** (2002) 337–347
16. Karp, A.H., Wu, R., Chen, K.Y., Zhang, A.: A Game Tree Strategy For Automated Negotiation. In: ACM Conference On Electronic Commerce. (2004) 228–229
17. Fatima, S.S., Wooldridge, M., Jennings, N.R.: A Comparative Study of Game Theoretic and Evolutionary Models of Bargaining For Software Agents. Artificial Intelligence Review **23** (2005) 187–205
18. Sandholm, T., Lesser, V.: Leveled commitment contracts and strategic breach. Games and Economic Behavior **35** (2001) 212–270
19. Ludwig, H., Gimpel, H., Dan, A., Kearney, R.: Template-Based Automated Service Provisioning - Supporting the Agreement-Driven Service Life-Cycle. In: ICSOC. (2005) 283–295

Development of New IFC-BRIDGE Data Model and a Concrete Bridge Design System Using Multi-agents

Nobuyoshi Yabuki and Zhantao Li

Department of Civil Engineering and Architecture, Muroran Institute of Technology,
27-1 Mizumoto-cho, Muroran-shi, Hokkaido, 050-8585, Japan
yabuki@news3.ce.muroran-it.ac.jp

Abstract. In this paper, first, our J-IFC-BRIDGE product model, which is a combination of YLPC-BRIDGE and YLSG-BRIDGE, and French IFC-BRIDGE product models were described. Then, the process of merging these models into the New IFC-BRIDGE was presented, and New IFC-BRIDGE was introduced. Further, the concrete bridge design system using multi-agents that had been developed before was modified to follow the changes of the product model, and the new system and the product model were verified by applying the design scenario of a prestressed concrete girder. Both the New IFC-BRIDGE and the concrete bridge design system showed the feasibility and practicality.

Keywords: product data model, IFC, bridge, design checking, multi-agents.

1 Introduction

Much effort has been seen in developing product models for building design and construction in order to enable the interoperability among heterogeneous application systems and software packages such as CAD, analysis, conformance checking, cost estimation, construction scheduling, for more than two decades. Recently, Industry Foundation Classes (IFC) of International Alliance for Interoperability (IAI) [1] seems to be considered as a de facto standard for building product models. However, as for bridges, each CAD and design software company, nation, or organization has been developing its own product model such as Japan Highway Product Model (JHDM) [2], TransXML [3], and there is little interoperability among those models and application systems.

The importance of product models resides not only in the interoperability but also in representing knowledge related to engineering structures such as bridges. In knowledge engineering, many expert systems were developed to design, inspect, diagnose, or manage civil engineering structures. However, most knowledge systems developed then were not used because rather than generalized textbook knowledge, more specific knowledge related to concrete cases and experiences is usually useful and effective for high-level engineering judgment. To represent such knowledge, product data must be represented exactly and precisely. Thus, such representation methodologies have been explored and discussed by many researchers in terms of knowledge and data engineering for more than two decades.

In our research group, a bridge product model named Yabuki Laboratory (YL) Prestressed Concrete (PC) Bridge (YLPC-BRIDGE) product model was developed by expanding IFC in collaboration with Japan Prestressed Concrete Contractors Association [4] [5]. Then, programs for data converting among CAD systems, structural design analysis systems, design a checking systems, etc., were developed to verify the interoperability among the systems based on the developed product model. Among the integrated systems, three design checking programs, i.e., interference checking, reinforcing bar cover checking, and reinforcing bar space checking programs, were developed as multi-agents, which can act behind the CAD system to support the user by checking the design while the engineer is designing and by giving alert if the design violates a provision of design codes [6]. A concrete bridge design system was developed by integrating YLPC-BRIDGE, application systems and the multi-agents. In parallel, a steel girder bridge product model called YL Steel Girder (SG) Bridge (YLSG-BRIDGE) was developed by the similar method [7]. These two bridge product models were merged and the merged one was called J-IFC-BRIDGE, where J stands for Japan.

Around the same time as our group developed the YLPC-BRIDGE, IAI French Speaking Chapter developed a bridge product model called IFC-BRIDGE based on the IFC and OA-EXPRESS, which is a bridge product model developed by SETRA, French governmental technical center for roads and highways, and it has been open to public since 2002 via the Internet web site [8].

Both Japanese and French groups did not know their efforts in developing bridge product models each other by 2002, although their approaches were quite similar. To make the product model internationally accepted de facto standard in the future, both groups agreed that international collaboration would be necessary and both of the models should be merged into one and that the integrated product model should be verified internationally. Recently both Japanese and French groups have proposed New IFC-BRIDGE by merging their product models by the support of IAI. At our laboratory, the concrete bridge design system including various data converters, multi-agents was modified following the changes from the YLPC-BRIDGE to New IFC-BRIDGE.

In this paper, first, the J-IFC-BRIDGE and the previous French IFC-BRIDGE product models are described. Then, the merging process of these models and the New IFC-BRIDGE are presented. Finally, the modification of the concrete bridge design system using the multi-agents is described.

2 J-IFC-BRIDGE Product Model

As described earlier, our research group developed a PC bridge product model named YLPC-BRIDGE based on IFC2x as shown in Fig. 1. In this product model, new classes representing slabs, prestressing strands, sheaths, voids, reinforcing bars (rebars), and anchoring devices were added to IFC. A feature of this model is that it clearly represents the relationship that the concrete contains elements such as reinforcing bars, prestressing strands, and voids by representing the concrete as a spatial structure element by B-rep (Boundary representation). Then, they implemented the schema of the product model and instances of PC bridges by using ifcXML.

Development of New IFC-BRIDGE Data Model and a Concrete Bridge Design System

The characteristics of the YLPC-BRIDGE are as follows. 1) The basic structure of IFC2x has been retained, and new classes of members for PC bridges have been defined as 3D models based on the object-oriented technology. 2) New classes of property sets for a slab and contained members such as rebars, prestressing strands, voids, etc., have been defined. 3) A modern model developing technique, i.e., separating property sets from object classes rather than representing all attributes in product classes, was employed, which makes the model more flexible. 4) ifcXML has been selected for implementing the product model. ifcXML is compatible with the standardized modeling language, EXPRESS of International Organization for Standardization (ISO) – Standards for The Exchange of Product Model data (STEP).

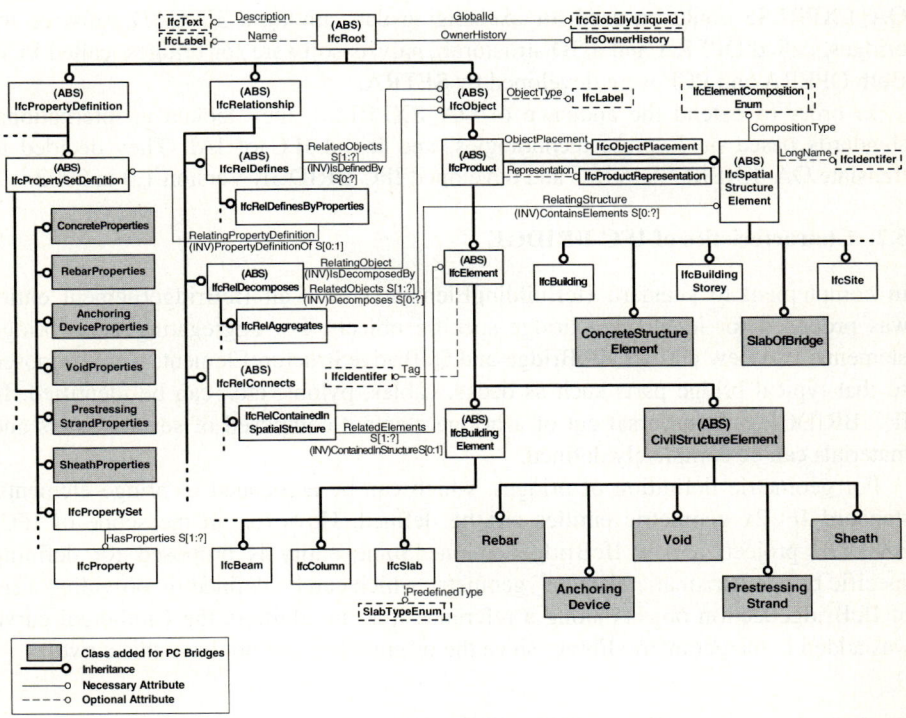

Fig. 1. A part of YLPC-BRIDGE product model for representing prestressed concrete bridges

A product model for steel girder bridges, YLSG-BRIDGE, was developed by adding three classes, Bridge, PlateGirder, and OtherSteelBuiltupElement, as subclasses of IfcSpatialStruc-tureElement to IFC2x2 of IAI. The Bridge class represents the whole bridge superstructure. PlateGirder and OtherSteelBuiltup-Element classes represent objects which are contained in the Bridge class. Those classes are linked with the Bridge class by using IfcRelContainedInSpatial-Structure. In addition, CivilStructureElement, which has subclasses of SteelStructureElement and SteelShapeElement, was added as a subclass of IfcElement. SteelStructure-Element class can represent elements such as webs and flanges. SteelShapeElement class represents general steel shapes such as I, H, box, angle, pipe types.

Both YLPC-BRIDGE and YLSG-BRIDGE product models were merged into one and is called J-IFC-BRIDGE in this research.

3 French IFC-BRIDGE

3.1 Development of IFC-BRIDGE

In 1998, a French bridge data model named OA_EXPRESS was developed by SETRA with building firms, design offices, etc. In 2000, they demonstrated that OA_EXPRESS could be used for exchanging data among a 3D-CAD software for bridges, called OPERA and a 3D structural analysis software for bridges, called PCP. Both OPERA and PCP were developed by SETRA.

In order to extend the audience of OA_EXPRESS, they looked at international standards based on Express technologies, and found IFC of IAI. They decided to translate OA_EXPRESS to IFC and developed IFC-BRIDGE Version 1.0 in 2002.

3.2 Characteristics of IFC-BRIDGE

In complement to standard IfcBuildingElement entity, an IfcBridgeElement entity was proposed for identifying bridge specific objects. For aggregating these bridge elements, two new entities, IfcBridge and IfcBridgeStructureElement, were proposed so that typical bridge parts such as decks, cables, pylons, etc., can be identified. In IFC-BRIDGE, a transversal cut of a bridge element composed of several fibers and materials can be completely defined.

For geometric definition of bridges, which can be associated to bridge elements, standard IFC2x geometric entities can be defined. However, in the scope of IFC-BRIDGE project, a new IfcBridgeSectionedSpine entity is proposed for defining specific bridge "prismatic element" geometry which can be defined by providing a set of IfcBridgeSection objects along a reference line. In addition, the Clothoidal curve was added to the geometric library since the original IFC did not have this curve.

4 Development of New IFC-BRIDGE

The first meeting was held by the Japanese and French groups at SETRA in April 2004 for searching ways for international collaboration and agreed to merge the two models into one, developing a new IFC-BRIDGE. After the meeting, the Civil Engineering Group was newly established in IAI Japan Chapter in November 2004 as a counterpart of the IFC-BRIDGE group of IAI French Speaking Chapter.

In August 2005, the French group revised IFC-BRIDGE and proposed the Version 2.0. The Japanese group had reviewed the Version 1.0 and quickly reviewed the Version 2.0, and wrote up a proposal for modifying the IFC-BRIDGE Version 2.0 by merging the YLPC-BRIDGE. Three researchers of the Japanese group visited the Center for Science and Technique of Buildings (CSTB) at Sophia-Antipolis in France in September 2005 and discussed the integration of the two data models. They agreed the modification proposal of the Japanese group there. In November 2005, four researchers of the French group visited Japan and discussed with many of Japanese researchers and engineers. Fig. 2 shows a part of the New IFC-BRIDGE product model. The New IFC-BRIDGE is being implemented into the next version of IFC by IFC experts and will be released in the near future.

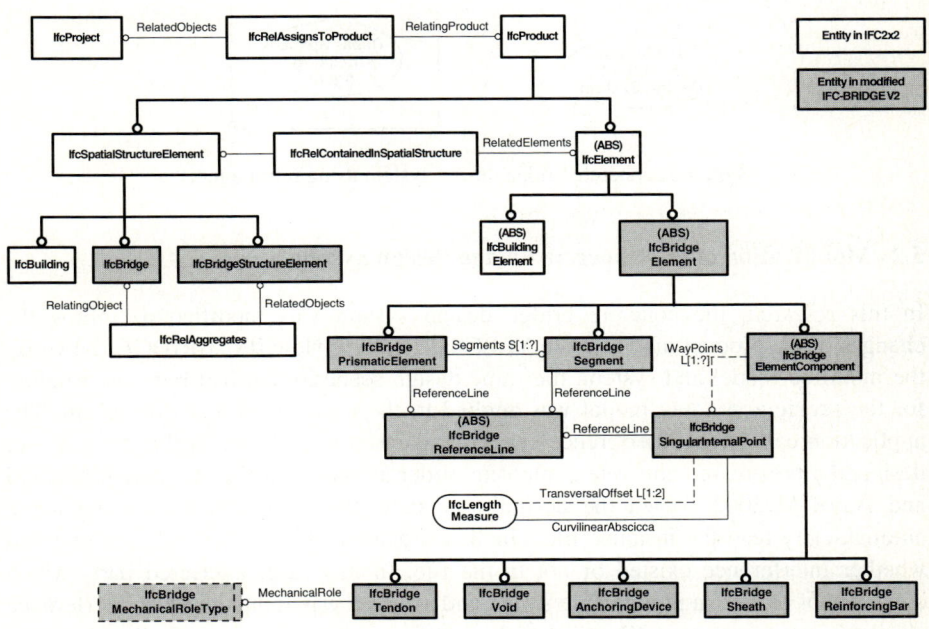

Fig. 2. A part of NEW IFC-BRIDGE product model

5 Concrete Bridge Design System Using Multi-agents

5.1 Development of the Concrete Bridge Design System

Previously, our research group integrated the product model with three application systems, namely, 3D-CAD, a PC bridge structural design system, and Multi-Agent system by developing converter programs as shown in Fig. 3. The converter program named CAD2PM (CAD to Product Model) can generate product model data of PC bridge objects as an ifcXML, and PM2CAD (Product Model to CAD) retrieves data from the instance file and renders the 3D model in AutoCAD automatically. The Multi-Agent consists of interference checking agent, reinforcing bar (rebar) cover checking agent and rebar space checking agent.

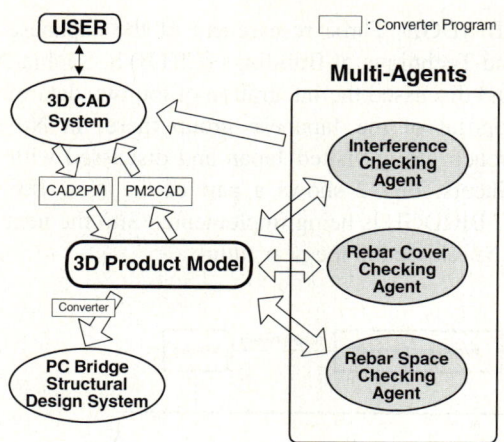

Fig. 3. A concrete bridge design system using multi-agents

5.2 Modification of the Concrete Bridge Design System

In this research, the concrete bridge design system was modified to follow the changes of the product models from YLPC-BRIDGE to New IFC-BRIDGE. To verify the modified model and system, the same design scenario that had been used before for the previous product model was applied to the new model and the system. The application case of an interference checking agent is as follows. In this case, a user designed a prestressed concrete composite girder as shown in Fig. 4, using CAD2PM and AutoCAD2002. When the design was done, the interference checking agent automatically read the instance file which was generated by CAD2PM, and checked whether interference existed or not in the file. In this case, interfered parts which consisted of re-bars, a prestressing strand and a sheath was found, and the interference checking agent generated 3D solids of the interfered objects as shown in Fig. 4.

The application case of the rebar cover checking agent and the rebar space checking agent is the following. A user designed a 3D CAD model of a precast segment, using CAD2PM and AutoCAD2002. Since the instance file was generated by executing CAD2PM, the rebar cover checking agent and the rebar space checking agent worked autonomously and checked rebar cover and space, retrieving data from the instance file. In this case, the rebar space checking agent sent no message, but the rebar cover checking agent sent a message saying, "Some rebars violate the cover provision." And then, the rebar cover checking agent displayed the result of checking (Fig. 5). At the same time, this system output this result into the instance file as a new property value. Then, the user executed PM2CAD, which constructed a 3D CAD model form the new instance file. Fig. 5 shows that rebars which have yellow color, need to be modified. Then, the user modified the rebars and updated the product model data.

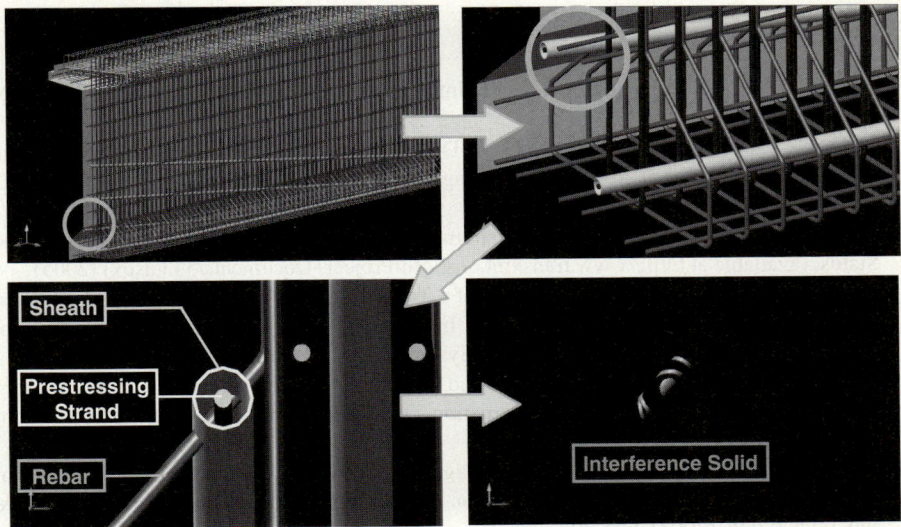

Fig. 4. An interfering reinforcing bar and interference solid in a prestressed concrete girder

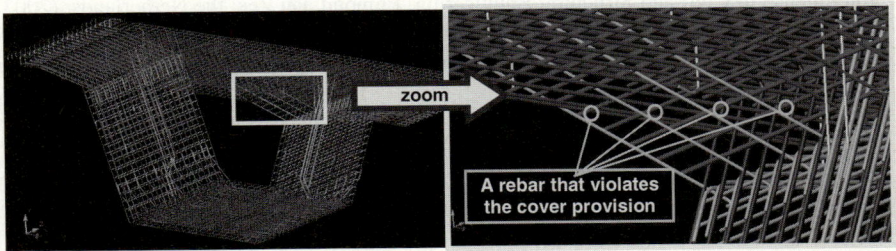

Fig. 5. Detection of reinforcing bars violating the provision concerning the cover

6 Conclusion

In this paper, first, our J-IFC-BRIDGE product model, which is a combination of YLPC-BRIDGE and YLSG-BRIDGE, and French IFC-BRIDGE product models were described. Then, the process of merging these models into the New IFC-BRIDGE was presented, and New IFC-BRIDGE was introduced. Further, the concrete bridge design system using multi-agents that had been developed before was modified to follow the changes of the product model, and the new system and the product model were verified by applying the design scenario of a prestressed concrete girder. Both the New IFC-BRIDGE and the concrete bridge design system showed the feasibility and practicality.

Acknowledgments. This research has been partially supported by Japan Society for the Promotion of Science (JSPS) and the Foreign Affairs of France as joint research project of Japan-France Integrated Action Program (SAKURA). The authors would like to express their gratitude to Dr. Tomoaki Shitani of Taisei Corporation.

References

1. Liebich, T. (ed.): IFC 2x Edition 2 Model Implementation Guide. International Alliance for Interoperability (2004)
2. Hongo, T. and Ishimura H.: A Study on Development JHDM for the Superstructures in Metal Bridge. Journal of Applied Computing in Civil Engineering, JSCE, 12, (2003) 11-20, in Japanese.
3. Harrison, F.: XML Schema for Transportation Data Exchange: Project Overview and Status. (available at http://www.transxml.org/Info/Project+Documents/543.aspx) (2005)
4. Yabuki, N. and Shitani, T.: Development of a 3 Dimensional Product Model for Prestressed Concrete Hollow Slab Bridges Based on Industry Foundation Classes (IFC). Journal of Civil Engineering Information Processing System, JSCE, 11, (2002) 35-44, in Japanese.
5. Yabuki, N. and Shitani, T.: An IFC-Based Product Model for RC or PC Slab Bridges, Proceedings of the CIB W78's 20th International Conference on Information Technology for Construction, (2003), 463-470.
6. Shitani, T. and Yabuki, N.: A Concrete Bridge Design System Using Multi-Agents, Proc. of the fourth IEEE International Workshop on Soft Computing as Transdisciplinary Science and Technology, (2005), 695-704.
7. Yabuki, N., Kotani, J.: A Steel Member Design System Using Distributed Multi-Agent and SOAP, Proceedings of the Seventh International Conference on the Application of Artificial Intelligence to Civil and Structural Engineering, Egmond aan Zee, the Netherlands, (2003), Paper No.5, 1-11.
8. Lebegue, E.: IFC-BRIDGE Introduction. (PowerPoint file available at http://www.iai-france.org/bridge/) (2002)

Multi-Agent Systems over RT-Java for a Mobile Robot Control

Marti Navarroa, Vicente Julian, Stella Heras, Jose Soler, and Vicent Botti

Departamento de sistemas informáticos y computación
Universidad Politécnica de Valencia
Camino de Vera S/N 46022 Valencia, Spain
{mnavarro, vinglada, sheras, jsoler, vbotti}@dsic.upv.es

Abstract. There are a great number of programming languages and frameworks for multi-agent system development, but most of them do not allows us create and later manage real-time multi-agent systems. In this paper, we propose the use of the RT-Java language for real-time multi-agent development. We also present the jART platform as an appropriate framework for the execution of agents of this kind. A mobile robot control is implemented and analyzed using this framework.

1 Introduction

Nowadays, there are specific programming languages (Aglets [2] or Javalog [3]) and frameworks (Madkit [5] or Jade [4]) that facilitate agent development. These languages and frameworks have been fundamentally characterized by providing the multi-agent system developer with mechanisms to facilitate the creation of agents, their control, and the easy definition of the communication processes among them. Moreover, these languages and frameworks allow representation of agent knowledge (their beliefs, desires and intentions, or their ontology).

Nevertheless, the current approaches have certain deficiencies in some environments. Specifically, the applicability of multi-agent systems to real-time environments requires specific functionalities that are not available in current agent languages or frameworks. Agents that work in these environments must fulfill specific temporal restrictions, which implies the use of real-time programming languages and real-time agent architectures.

A Real-Time Multi-Agent System (RTMAS) is a multi-agent system with at least one agent with temporal constraints in any of its responsibilities [1]. In order to implement RTMAS, the developer must be able to declare the temporal features that will define the temporal behaviour of the different agent actions. Typically these features are: cost, deadline, priority, and period for each agent task. In addition, RTMAS must be executed over a Real-Time Operating System (RTOS) which can to manage the temporal features appropriately.

This article presents a solution for the development of RTMAS using a new extension of the Java language, called RT-Java [7]. This extension covers all the aspects regarding real-time systems. However, it is necessary to add more functionalities in order to employ it as an agent development language. To solve this problem, we have developed a middleware platform for the creation and management of RTMAS that is implemented using RT-Java. The platform, called jART[11], has been used to develop a mobile robot control example, which has been analyzed in order to validate the use of RT-Java.

2 Java and Real-Time Multi-Agent Systems

Java is the language that is most widely used to develop both agent programming languages and multi-agent frameworks. Currently, the use of Java for developing Real-Time Systems (RTS) is inadequate because is not a specific programming language for RTS.

There are a proposal that extend Java for developing real-time systems called *The Real-Time Specification for Java* (RTSJ), was developed by *The Real-Time for Java Expert Group* (RTJ) [7]. This specification proposes an extension of the Java language without modifying the standard. The use of RT-Java instead of other programming languages such as C or Ada comes from the desire to obtain a platform for real-time multi-agent systems that is easy to use by a great number of expert Java programmers.

The RTSJ specification provides a series of improvements with respect to the Java language and allows us to create RTAs. The following points describe some of these improvements and how to use them to develop RTA and RTMAS:

Memory management: The extension RTSJ offers a new memory area called *NoHeapMemory*. This new memory area is not released by the *garbage collector* (GC). Thus, if the execution of the tasks associated to the RTAs are not to be interrupted, the developer should use *NoHeapMemory* to store the agent knowledge, their associated tasks and shared resources.
High precision clocks: The use of these high precision clocks allows us to associate precise values to the temporal features of the task.
Scheduler and schedulable objects: The RTSJ extension allows us to define the scheduling algorithm used by the Scheduler of the operative system. In addition, the schedulable objects will be scheduled by the RTOS as tasks with temporal features.
Real-Time threads: These new threads are schedulable objects, and they have temporal features. These threads have a higher priority than the GC and will never be interrupted by GC. We can define the agent task behaviours using the real-time threads. These behaviours can be executed periodically or sporadically.
Asynchronous event handlers: This allows the agents to capture events that are produced randomly in the environment in a controlled way and treat them in an asynchronous way.
Asynchronous transfer of control: An agent, *agent management system*, for example, will be able to take the control of the execution of another agent by using this mechanism in a controlled way.
Resource sharing: RTSJ provides the necessary mechanisms for the control of the shared resources by the agent developer. The Scheduler deals with this by assigning the resources according to the developed plan.

Direct access to physical memory: RTSJ allows direct access to the physical memory. This provides better control of access to the memory area used for communication with the different physical devices, such as ports and registers.

3 The jART Platform

RT-Java allows Java programming language to be used in real-time environments. However, to create RTMAS must be provided to the programmer components for agent management and communication control. A platform for RT-MAS, called jART (Java for Agents in Real-Time) has been developed and is presented in [11]. The jART platform must be executed on a Java virtual machine (JVM) that must comply with the RTSJ as, for example, the reference implementation [10]. In order to ensure the correct execution, it is mandatory to execute the JVM on a RTOS.

For brevity reasons, only main jART platform properties are presented:

- jART complies with FIPA specifications. This platform uses FIPA-ACL [8] as the communication language and FIPA-SL [9] as the content language.
- In a jART platform, two types of agents can co-exist: (1) The **NonRT-Agents** are agents without temporal restrictions in their responsibilities.(2) The **RT-Agents** are agents with at least one responsibility with temporal characteristics.
- Each agent is formed by a set of behaviours. There are mainly two types of behaviours in jART: (1) **NonRT-Behaviour:** without temporal characteristics. NonRT-Agents can only include NonRT-Behaviours. (2) **RT-Behaviour:** with temporal characteristics. RT-Behaviours can only be employed in RT-Agents and it is discomposed in: (i) Periodic-Behaviour: this behaviour will be executed periodically. (ii) NonPeriodic-Behaviour: it may become active at any time.
- This platform includes an agent management system for the control of the agents inside the platform. Moreover, it has a message transport service for the communication management among the agents.

4 Robot Control Problem

In an environment with obstacles, we placed a series of objects on the ground randomly. These objects had to be gathered and deposited in specific places. To do this, we need a Khepera mobile robot that could gather these objects. This robot knew a priori where the objects were placed, and hence, it was able to schedule the optimum order for all the objects to be gathered efficiently. Efficiency was considered to be the shortest distance traveled by the robot.

The use of real-time agents was determined by the need to guarantee the physical integrity of the robot. To do this, the robot had to detect the obstacle and avoid it before the crash took place.

4.1 Implementation Details

In this example the main goal is to pick up objects that are located in a given environment. This goal is complex due to the fact that the robot must navigate towards the different objects, dodge obstacles, and pick up the object. Thus, this goal can be split into four sub-goals: to **maintain robot integrity**, to **navigate** to the objects, to **plan** the shortest route, and finally, to **pick up an object** and deposit it in a specified location. Four different types of agents have been identified:

Collect Agent: This agent is in charge of controlling the collection process when the mobile robot is close to one of the objects.
Planning agent: This agent planned a route among the objects to pick up. The route has to travel across all the points where the objects are located. Once the object collection is finished, the route should provide the road towards the final position where the robot should place the objects. In turn, this agent will take charge of the robot navigation along the planned route.
Sensor agent: This agent is in charge of maintaining for the robots physical integrity. It prevents the robot from crashing into obstacles.
Manager Agent: This agent is the only one that communicates directly with the robot's hardware. It extracts environment information using the robot sensor. This agent also decides which action proposed by the other agents should be executed. This decision process is done using an auction mechanism. The first-price sealed-bid auction [6] is the auction mechanism used.

The Collect agent, the Sensor agent, and the Planning agent take the role of bidders, competing for the right to propose the next action to be executed by the robot. The Manager agent takes the role of auctioneer, choosing the bid with the highest value. This value will be determined by the need of each bidder agent yo perform the next robot movement (For instance, the Sensor agent increased its bid as the robot approaches an obstacle). These bids are performed by means of FIPA-ACL [8] messages between the bidder agents and the controller agent, according to the auction protocol. Figure 1 shows a graphical view of the proposed system.

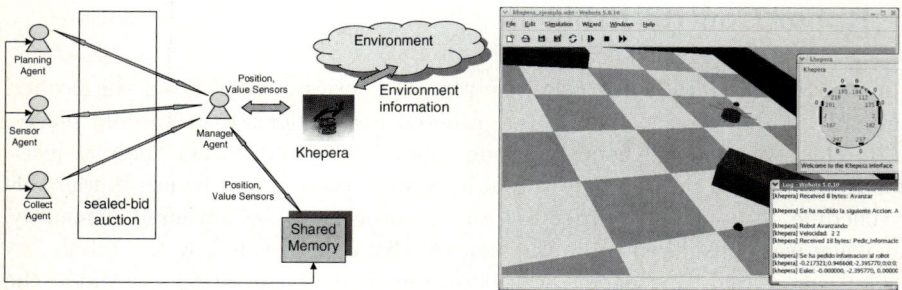

Fig. 1. Example system architecture graph **Fig. 2.** Webots simulation environment

The auction management behaviour of the Manager agent must also guarantee a periodic answer with the most appropriate movement to be performed by the Khepera robot. If the period fulfillment is not guaranteed, the robot control would be unstable. This is because many necessary actions will not be performed at the right moment, or they may never be performed.

A special case is the management of the blackboard performed by the Manager agent. This behaviour is in charge of gathering the information provided by the robot through its sensors. This information is stored to be used by the other agents in the system. Therefore, the periodic update of this information is essential so that the most recent data is available.

We used the mobile robot simulator *webots* [12] (Figure 2) created by *Ciberbotics* company to realize the test. This multi-agent system runs on a jART platform, which must be executed inside a RTOS (we used the RTOS developed by Timesys [10]) and The reference implementation of RTSJ has been used as virtual machine. The multi-agent system was connected to the simulator, which was run on another computer through an intranet using the TCP/IP protocol.

4.2 Results

In order to analyze the viability of using RT-Java as an agent programming language with temporal constraints, a set of performance and reliability tests has been carried out. First, a temporal analysis of the different system tasks was performed to fit their computation times. Next, a battery of tests was developed in order to verify whether the system works as a RTS.

Temporal Analysis

Before, performing a study of the behaviour that the multi-agent system would have we made an estimation of the temporal cost that the different agent behaviours would have in order to determine the Worst Case Execution Time (WCET) associated to each behaviour. This WCET is used by the RTOS to determine whether the task is schedulable. Therefore, it is necessary to adjust the WCET so that the tasks do not exceed the estimated cost, since this might affect the possibility of their being scheduled. To estimate the WCET, each task was carried out 100.000 times. The WCET for the sensor task is 20 ms.; for the navigation task is 40 ms.; for pick up task is 20 ms.; for auction task is 20 ms.; and finally, for blackboard management task is 290 ms.

The blackboard management task needs more processor time to complete its assignment. This task, which is executed by the Manager agent, is in charge of requesting the Webots simulator (via TCP/IP) for the information about the state of the robot, its current position, the readings of the eight infrared sensors, and the robot's orientation. Once the controller agent receives this information, it stores it in a memory area that is shared by the multi-agent system. This process is very expensive mainly due to the TCP/IP messages required for the information gathering.

The rest of the tasks are dependent on the shared information. This dependence allows us to deduce that, if we modify the period of the task associated to the blackboard management, we are indirectly affecting the rest of the system tasks. If the time interval in which the robot's information is gathered is too large, the available information will not be correct. This will make the tasks take incorrect actions due to the incorrect information. Thus, the other tasks should adapt their periods to the blackboard management task period.

Analysis of the System Behaviour

A total of 500 complete simulations were performed, modifying the period of the tasks associated to the blackboard management task by 50 ms every 100 simulations. The first period assigned to the task was 300 ms, which is, a period that is equal to the WCET of the task that was managing the blackboard. This is because a lower value didn't make sense. The last simulations were performed with a period of 500 ms, because it was observed that a higher period would result in lost of control over the robot. Figure 3 shows a chronogram of the system obtained by means of a modification in the Java virtual machine to be able to generate temporal information that can be visualized by the *Kiwi* tracing tool [13]. This figure presents the different executions for each period, showing only the considered task set. The blackboard management task is the one that consumes the most resources as pointed out above. The black vertical lines mark the deadline of each task. The dot indicates the beginning of a task execution, and the rectangle represents the execution time of a task. Note that the tasks are executed periodically and that each task has an execution time that is smaller than its deadline.

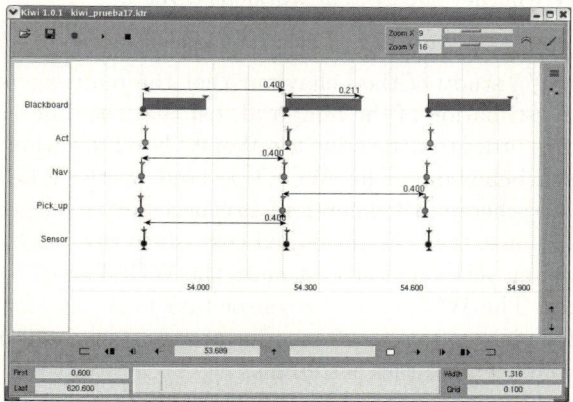

Fig. 3. Kiwi trace of the different executed tasks

The first test analyzed was the average of crashes and the standard deviation as the period was increased. Figure 4 indicates that if the period of the tasks was increased a belated answer by the robot causing an increase in crashes. This is logical if the system is a real-time system. Figure 5 shows the relation between the increase in the period and the time required to complete a simulation. If the task periods are increased, the actions on the robot are executed later. This could cause an action which might not be the most correct to be performed.

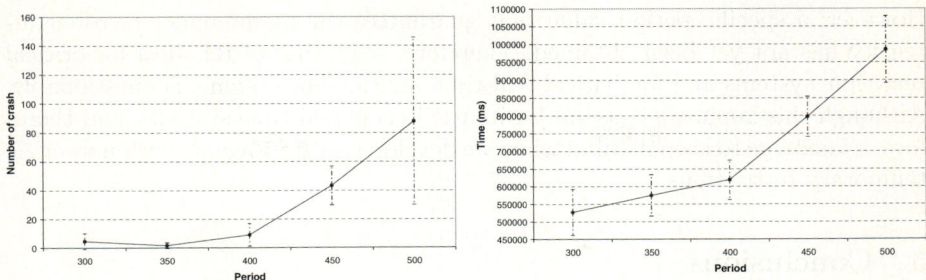

Fig. 4. Average number of crashes per period and the standard deviation

Fig. 5. Average time to complete a simulation per period and the standard deviation

Therefore, more time is needed to complete the simulation, since the way the robot pursues the different objectives must be connected more aften. This behaviour is completely logical and expected in real-time conditions.

The number of missed deadlines for the different tasks were analyzed (see Figure 6). This figure shows how the number of missed deadlines is very high for a small period, as can be expected. It also shows how the deadlines approach zero as the period is increased. This is a logical behaviour from a real-time point of view. Even so, Figure 7 which shows the percentage of missed deadlines per total number of tasks executed, indicates that the percentage in every period is low. It is about one percent in the worst still case. Even though the scheduler loses a deadline, it still attempts to the best schedule.

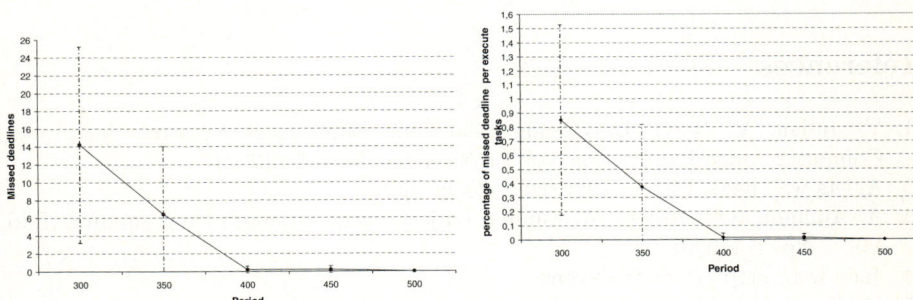

Fig. 6. Average of missed deadlines and the standard deviation

Fig. 7. Percentage of missed deadlines per number of task execution and the standard deviation

Finally, if the different graphics are analyzed, they show that as the period increases, the blackboard information is deactivated longer. However, this fact produces an increase in the probability of the robot crashing. If the graphics are overlapped, it can be observed that the best period is 400 ms. At this period, the number of crashes and missed deadlines is minimal. Thus, in a global way, the multi-agent system performs as expected from a real-time point of view.

However, a specific period value that guarantees the maintenance of robot integrity has not yet been obtained. Therefore, it the use of RT-Java for critical real-time systems and for critical real-time multi-agent systems is questionable. Although this language is useful for its use in soft real-time systems, and therefore, a language to keep in mind when we develop real-time agents with non-critic temporary restrictions.

5 Conclusions

The appearance of RT-Java constitutes an important advance in the development of distributed real-time applications, since, it encapsulates a lange part of the complexity and specific details of such applications. Moreover, it guarantees the predictability of the developed system to some extent. However, in applications of this type, the level of complexity is high, especially if we want to develop systems that integrate high-level planning processes or coordination within temporal bounded processes. Here is where the use of the agents in the development of distributed real-time applications becomes a great interest.

This paper presents an example of an application of RT-Java as a development language for a real-time multi-agent system using the jART platform. An analysis of the expected behaviour indicates that its use is valid for the development of non-critical real-time multi-agent systems. Real-time tasks have been integrated with scheduling processes of routes and auction-based negotiation. However, the results show that strictly guaranteeing the fulfilment of the estimated terms. The reference implementation of RT-Java and the operative system used in the tests must be analyzed in more detail.

References

1. V. Julian, V. Botti: Developing Real-Time Multi-agent Systems. Integrated Computer-Aided Engineering Vol. 11 No. 2 pp. 135-149. (2004)
2. Aglets web page: http://www.trl.ibm.com/aglets/
3. A. Amandi, R. Iturregui, A. Zunino: Object-Agent Oriented Programming. EJS Vol. 2 No. 1. (1999)
4. Jade web. http://jade.tilab.com.
5. Madkit web. http://www.madkit.org.
6. P. McAfee, J. McMillan: Auctions and Bidding. JEL, Vol. 25 (1987)
7. RTJ web. http://www.rtj.org
8. FIPA Technical Report SC00061G. http://www.fipa.org/specs/fipa00061/
9. FIPA Technical Report SC00008G. http://www.fipa.org/specs/fipa00008/
10. http://www.timesys.com
11. M. Navarro, V. Julián, Jose Soler, V Botti: jART: A Real-Time Multi-Agent Platform with RT-Java. In Proc. 3rd IWPAAMS'04, pp. 73-82, 2004.
12. Webots: http://www.cyberbotics.com/
13. Kiwi: http://rtportal.upv.es/apps/kiwi/

Financial Risk Modeling with Markov Chains

Arturo Leccadito[1], Sergio Ortobelli Lozza[2],
Emilio Russo[3], and Gaetano Iaquinta[2]

[1] Cass Business School, 106 Bunhill Row, EC1Y 8TZ, London (U.K.)
abbg233@city.ac.uk
[2] University of Bergamo,
Via dei Caniana 2, 24127 Bergamo, Italy
sol@unibg.it,
gaetano.iaquinta@unibg.it
[3] CARISMA, Brunel University, West London (U.K.)
russo_emilio@yahoo.it

Abstract. This paper proposes markovian models in portfolio theory and risk management. In a first analysis, we describe discrete time optimal allocation models. Then, we examine the investor's optimal choices either when returns are uniquely determined by their mean and variance or when they are modeled by a Markov chain. Moreover we propose different models to compute VaR and CVaR when returns are modeled by a Markov chain.

1 Introduction

In this paper we pursue two objectives. We first propose different markovian models that may be used to determine optimal portfolio strategies and to value opportunely the risk of a given portfolio. Then we compare portfolio selection strategies obtained either by modeling the return distributions with a Markov chain or by using a mean–variance analysis.

Following the methodology proposed by Christoffersen [3], it is possible to test the null hypothesis that the intervals of the distributional support of a given portfolio are independent against the hypothesis that the intervals follow a Markov chain. Several empirical analyses, carried out by considering both different distributional hypotheses for many return portfolios (Gaussian, Stable Paretian, Student's t, and semi-parametric), and different percentiles θ, have shown that we cannot reject the markovian hypothesis. Therefore, the sequence of intervals of the distributional support are significantly dependent along time (see [8,7]).

Accordingly, in this paper we assume that interval dependence of portfolios can be characterized by a Markov chain so that we can describe different portfolio selections, VaR and CVaR models. As a matter of fact, given a portfolio of gross returns, we share the support of the portfolio in N intervals and each interval is assumed to be a state of a Markov chain. Then, we build up the transition matrix and maximize the expected logarithmic utility function by assuming that in each interval the return is given by the middle point.

When we have large portfolios the problem is computationally too complex and the algorithm used may give only a local optimum. In order to solve portfolio choice problems therefore we use a Simulated Annealing type algorithm (see [1]).

The main contribution of this paper is the presentation of a general theory and a unifying framework with the following aims: 1) examining the portfolio selection problem when the portfolio of returns evolves along time following a Markov chain; 2) assessing the presented portfolio selection model and the mean–variance one; 3) studying and understanding VaR and CVaR markovian models.

The paper is organized as follows: in Section 2 we formalize portfolio selection with Markov chains. Section 3 presents the approaches to compute VaR and CVaR when the portfolio follows a Markov chain. Finally, we briefly summarize the paper.

2 Portfolio Selection with Homogeneous Markov Chains

In this section we propose a non-parametric distributional analysis of the optimal portfolio choice problem by describing the behavior of portfolios through a homogeneous Markov chain.

Let us consider $n+1$ assets: n of these assets are risky with gross returns[1] $z_{t+1} = [z_{1,t+1}, \ldots, z_{n,t+1}]'$ and the $(n+1)$-th asset is characterized by a risk-free gross return $z_{0,t+1}$. If we denote with x_0 the weight of the riskless asset and with $x = [x_1, \ldots, x_n]'$ the vector of the positions taken in the n assets forming the risky portfolio, then the return portfolio during the period $[t, t+1]$ is given by

$$z_{(x),t+1} = \sum_{i=1}^{n} x_i z_{i,t+1} + x_0 z_{0,t+1} . \tag{1}$$

Let us assume that the portfolio of gross returns has support on the interval $(\min_k z_{(x),k}; \max_k z_{(x),k})$, where $z_{(x),k}$ is the k-th past observation of the portfolio $z_{(x)}$. We first share the portfolio support $(\min_k z_{(x),k}; \max_k z_{(x),k})$ in N intervals $(a_{(x),i}; a_{(x),i+1})$ where $a_{(x),i} = \left(\frac{\max_k z_{(x),k}}{\min_k z_{(x),k}}\right)^{i/N} \min_k z_{(x),k}$, $i = 0, 1, \ldots, N$. For simplicity, we assume that on the interval $(a_{(x),i}; a_{(x),i+1})$ the state of the return is given by the geometric mean of the extremes $z_{(x)}^{(i)} := \sqrt{a_{(x),i} a_{(x),i+1}}$. Moreover, we add an additional state, $z_{(x)}^{(N+1)} := z_0$, in the case we assume a fixed riskless return. Secondly, we build the transition matrix $\boldsymbol{P}_t = [p_{i,j;t}]_{1 \leq i,j \leq N}$ valued at time t where the probability $p_{i,j;t}$ points out the probability (valued at time t) of a transition of the process between the state $z_{(x)}^{(i)}$ and the state $z_{(x)}^{(j)}$. On the other hand, if we consider an homogeneous Markov chain, the transition matrix

---

[1] Generally, we assume the standard definition of i-th gross return between time t and time $t + 1$, $z_{i,t} = \frac{P_{i,t+1} + d_{i,[t,t+1]}}{P_{i,t}}$, where $P_{i,t}$ is the price of the i-th asset at time t and $d_{i,[t,t+1]}$ is the total amount of cash dividends generated by the instrument between t and $t + 1$.

is independent of time and it can be denoted simply by $\boldsymbol{P}$. We observe that the transition probability matrix associated with the Markov chain is usually sparse and this deeply reduces the computational costs. In constructing the approximating Markov chain, we need to choose the length of a time step and the number of states of the process. In portfolio selection problems we assume daily step with the convention that the Markov chain is computed on returns valued with respect to investor's temporal horizon T. For instance, if the investor recalibrates the portfolio every month ($T = 20$ working days), we consider monthly returns with daily frequency and compute on the portfolio series the relative transition matrix. Moreover, for portfolio selection problems, it is better to use a limited number of states since the transition matrix is strictly dependent on the portfolio composition. As the portfolio composition is the variable of the optimization problem, the complexity of the problems becomes relevant when the number of states increases. However this does not excessively compromise the goodness of the investor's choices.

Under these assumptions, the final wealth (after T periods (days)) obtained investing W_0 in the portfolio with composition (x_0, x) is simply given by:

$$S_{(x),t+T} = \prod_{h=1}^{N+1} \left(z_{(x)}^{(h)}\right)^{\sum_{i=1}^{T} \nu_{(t+i)}^{(h)}} \tag{2}$$

where $\nu_{(t+i)}^{(h)} = \begin{cases} 1 & \text{if at } (t+i)\text{-th period the portfolio return is in the } s\text{-th state} \\ 0 & \text{otherwise} \end{cases}$.

As a consequence of the Chapman-Kolmogorov equations, when at t-th time the portfolio is in the m-th state, the expected value of the logarithm of the final wealth is given by:

$$E_m\left(\log\left(S_{(x),t+T}\right)\right) = \log(W_0) + \sum_{s=1}^{N+1} \left(\sum_{i=1}^{T} p_{m,s}^{(i)}\right) \log\left(z_{(x)}^{(s)}\right) \tag{3}$$

where $p_{m,s}^{(i)}$ is the element in position (m, s) of the i-th power of the transition matrix $\boldsymbol{P}^i$. The expected value of the log final wealth is

$$E\left(\log\left(S_{(x),t+T}\right)\right) = \log(W_0) + \sum_{m=1}^{N+1} p_m \sum_{s=1}^{N+1} \left(\sum_{i=1}^{T} p_{m,s}^{(i)}\right) \log\left(z_{(x)}^{(s)}\right) \tag{4}$$

where p_m is the probability of being in the state m. When no short sales are allowed, an investor with logarithmic utility function and temporal horizon T tries to solve the following optimization problem:

$$\begin{aligned} &\max_x E\left(\log\left(S_{(x),t+T}\right)\right) \\ &\text{subject to} \\ &x_0 + \sum_{i=1}^{n} x_i = 1; \quad x_i \geq 0; \quad i = 0, 1, \ldots, n \end{aligned} \tag{5}$$

in order to maximize his expected utility. The above problem generally admits many local maximum and the optimization problem appears computationally complex. This fact is a consequence of the discretization process we adopt in building the approximating transiction matrix that depends on the portfolio composition. Thus, the sensitivity of the maximum expected utility respect to the portfolio composition implies that we have many local maximum in the above optimization problem. In order to approximate the optimal solution of portfolio problem (5), we consider two procedures.

Procedure 1

First we look for a local optimum near a potential optimal point. To verify our model, we consider the optimal allocation amongst 24 assets: 23 of these assets are risky and the 24-th is risk-free with annual rate 6%. Our dataset consists of monthly gross returns (20 working days) with daily frequency taken from 23 international risky indexes valued in USD and quoted from January 1993 to January 1998 (for a complete description of the data see [9]). We assume that short selling is not allowed and that there are no transaction costs. Figure 1 reports a comparison between the markovian approach and the mean–variance one. In both cases the initial wealth is one and the portfolio is calibrated 27 times according to the procedure proposed in Leccadito et al., [9].

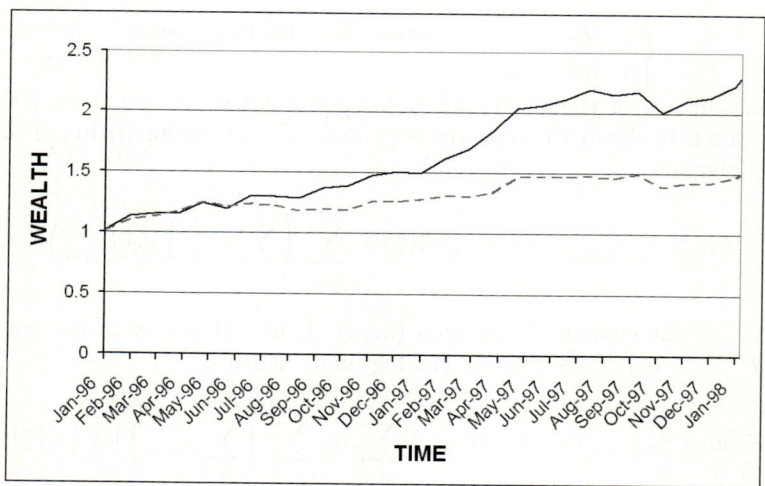

Fig. 1. (Adapted from Leccadito et al., [9]). This figure summarizes the ex-post sample paths of final wealth (with procedure 1 and without transaction costs) when we assume a markovian behaviour of returns (continuous line), or when we use a mean–variance analysis (dashed line).

It is clear that the markovian approach presents a final wealth that is greater (75% of the initial one) than the classic mean–variance one even during the crisis of the Asian market (September 1997–January 1998).

Procedure 2

We use a simulated annealing-type procedure in order to obtain the global maximum. Now the data consists of six-month returns (123 working days) with daily frequency taken from 9 risky assets contained in the Dow Jones Industrial index quoted from January 1995 to April 2005. We assume that short selling is not allowed and that there are no transaction costs. We examine optimal allocation amongst the Treasury Bill three months return and 9 asset returns: Altria, Boeing, Citigroup, Coca Cola, Intel, Johnson, Microsoft, Procter & Gamble, Pfizer. Figure 2 reports a comparison between the markovian approach and the mean–variance one.

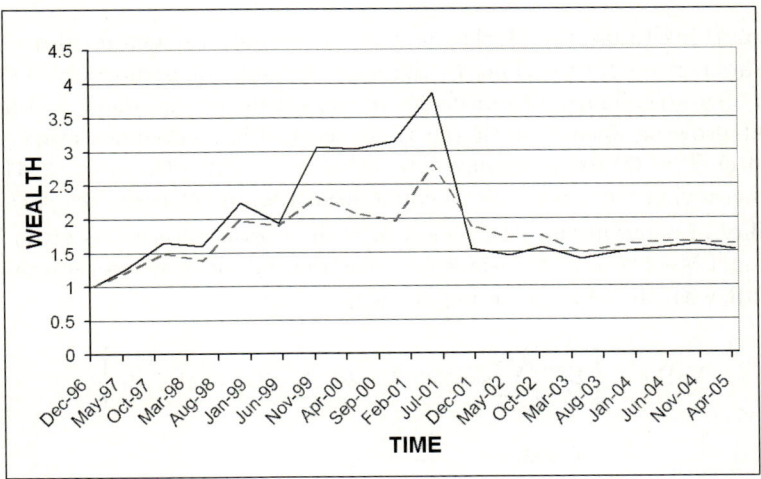

Fig. 2. (Adapted from Leccadito et al., [9]). This figure summarizes the ex-post sample paths of final wealth (with procedure 2 without transaction costs) when we assume a markovian behavior of returns (continuous line), or when we use a mean–variance analysis (dashed line).

This comparison shows that the markovian approach significantly increases the final wealth on these 10 assets until September 11th 2001. The markovian approach performs better that the mean–variance one during the high volatility period of the late 1990's (Asian and Russian crises) as well. Before September 11th the markovian approach presented a greater wealth (115% of the initial wealth) than the mean–variance one, whilst in December 2001 there is a dramatic loss of value of both portfolios. From December 2001 we find that the two strategies give almost the same final wealth.

3 VaR and CVaR Models with Markov Chains

In this section we propose some alternative models to compute Value at Risk (VaR) and Conditional Value at Risk (CVaR) with an homogeneous Markov chain. If we denote with τ the investor's temporal horizon, with $W_{t+\tau} - W_t$ the profit/loss realized in the interval $[t, t+\tau]$ and with θ the level of confidence, then the VaR is the percentile at the $(1-\theta)$ of the profit/loss distribution in the interval $[t, t+\tau]$:

$$\text{VaR}_{\theta, t+\tau}(W_{t+\tau} - W_t) = \inf \{q | Pr(W_{t+\tau} - W_t \leq q) > 1 - \theta\} \ .$$

On the other hand the CVaR measures the expected value of profit/loss given that the VaR has not been exceeded:

$$\text{CVaR}_{\theta, t+\tau}(W_{t+\tau} - W_t) = \frac{1}{1-\theta} \int_0^{1-\theta} \text{VaR}_{q, t+\tau}(W_{t+\tau} - W_t) dq \ .$$

We can think to use the Markovian tree to compute the possible losses (VaR, CVaR) at a given future time T. Suppose we build a homogeneous Markov chain of 50 states. Thus, for our choice of the states, we can make a Markovian tree that growths linearly with the time because it recombines every period. Then, after $T = 60$ days, we have $(N-1)T + 1 = 49 * 60 + 1 = 2941$ nodes in the markovian tree. Starting to count from the lowest node, let $p(j)$ be the probability of being at the j-th node where the portfolio return is given by $z_T^{(j)}$ ($j = 1, \ldots, (N-1)T+1$). Considering a confidence level θ, we can compute VaR and CVaR with the Markovian hypothesis:

$$\text{VaR}_\theta = \left\{ z_T^{(s)} \middle| \sum_{i=1}^{s-1} p(i) < (1-\theta); \sum_{i=1}^{s} p(i) \geq (1-\theta) \right\} \ ; \qquad (6)$$

$$\text{CVaR}_\theta = \frac{1}{1-\theta} \sum_{i : z_T^{(i)} \leq \text{VaR}_\theta} p(i) z_T^{(i)} \ . \qquad (7)$$

An ex-post analysis on 60 days portfolio return distributions shows that the markovian tree better approximates the heavy tails than the Riskmetrics Gaussian model (B&S).

Figure 3 compares the ex post empirical return distribution (of an arbitrary portfolio) with the forecasted 60 days Markovian (mkv) and Riskmetrics (B&S) ones. This graphical comparison is confirmed by some simple statistical tests (Kolmogorv Smirnov and Anderson Darling) valuated on some US indexes (see S&P 500, Nasdaq and Dow Jones Industrial) quoted from January 1996 to January 2006. Table 1 is obtained by considering Kolmogorov-Smirnoff test

$$\text{KS} = \sup_x |F_{\text{emp}}(x) - F_{\text{theo}}(x)|$$

and Anderson-Darling test

$$\text{AD} = \sup_x \frac{|F_{\text{emp}}(x) - F_{\text{theo}}(x)|}{\sqrt{F_{\text{theo}}(x)(1 - F_{\text{theo}}(x))}}$$

on the ex-post return distributions forecasted after 60 days.

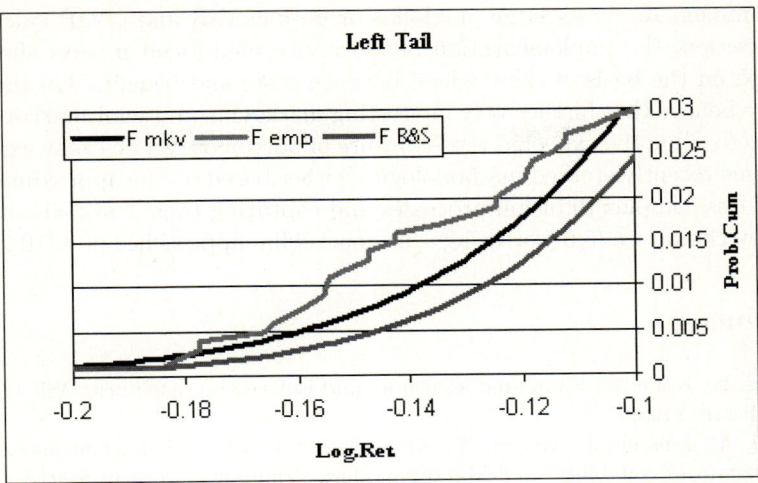

Fig. 3. Ex post comparison among empirical, Markovian and Gaussian c.d.f. left tails of 60 days returns

As we can see from Table 1 the Markovian approach presents the best performance in approximating the 60 days return distributions. These results are confirms that the proposed Markovian approach takes into account much better the aggregated 60 days risk as compared to classical Riskmetrics model.

Table 1. Kolmogorov-Smirnoff and Anderson-Darling tests for the indexes: Nasdaq, S&P500, and Dow Jones Industrials

		RiskMetrics	Markovian
S&P500	KS	0.0555	0.0692
	AD	37.024	32.021
Nasdaq	KS	0.0424	0.0401
	AD	41.027	36.012
DJ ind	KS	0.0509	0.0463
	AD	42.057	28.018

4 Concluding Remarks

This paper proposes alternative models for the portfolio selection and the VaR and CVaR calculation. In the first part we describe a portfolio selection model that uses a Markov chain to capture the behavior and the evolution of portfolio returns. In the second part we present some alternative markovian VaR and CVaR models. It is important to underline that the numerical procedure to compute the percentiles and the expected loss with the markovian approach is quite complex. As far as large portfolios or on-line VaR and CVaR calculation are concerned, the implementation of the above mentioned models should be evaluated on the basis of the tradeoff between costs and benefits. On the other hand, we believe that further very interesting markovian and semi-markovian approaches to value the expected risk exposure of portfolios can be easily expressed using some recently studied methodologies: either based on the approximation of more or less complex diffusion processes and capturing their markovianity with a Markov chain (see [5,6]) or using semi-markovian approaches (see [10,2,4]).

References

1. Aarts, E., Korst, J.: Simulated annealing and Boltzmann machines. Wiley & Sons, Chichester (1989)
2. Blasi, A., Janssen, J., Manca, R.: Numerical treatment of homogeneous and non-homogeneous reliability semi-Markov models. Communications in Statistics, Theory and Models (2003)
3. Christoffersen, P.: Evaluating interval forecasts. International Economic Review **39** (1998) 841–862
4. D'Amico, G., Janssen, J., Manca, R.: Non-homogeneous backward semi-markov reliability approach to downward migration credit risk problem. Proceedings of the 8th Italian Spanish Meeting on Financial Mathematics, Verbania (2005)
5. Duan, J., Dudley, E., Gauthier, G., Simonato, J.: Pricing discretely monitored barrier options by a Markov chain. Journal of Derivatives (2003) **10** 9–23
6. Duan, J., Simonato, J.: American option pricing under GARCH by a Markov chain approximation. Journal of Economic Dynamics and Control **25** (2001) 1689–1718
7. Iaquinta, G., A. Leccadito, and S. Ortobelli. Markovian trees and markovian choices. Proceedings of the 8th Italian Spanish Meeting on Financial Mathematics, Verbania (2005)
8. Lamantia, F., S. Ortobelli and S. T. Rachev: An empirical comparison among VaR models and time rules with elliptical and stable distributed returns. To appear in Investment Management and Financial Innovations (2006)
9. Leccadito, A., Ortobelli, S., Russo, E.: Portfolio selection and risk management with Markov chains. Technical report, M.S.I.A. Department, Bergamo University. Submitted to Journal of Multinational Financial Management (2006)
10. Limnios, N., Oprisan, G.: Semi-Markov processes and reliability modeling. World Scientific, Singapore (2001)

CNY Realignment and USD Expectation: Empirical Study Based on RND Function of Currency Option

Zhongzhong Ning

Ph.D candidate, Financial Engineering Research Center, South China University of Technology,
510641, Guangzhou, P.R. China
ningzhongzhong@sina.com

Abstract. This paper analysis dynamics of JPY/USD and USD/EUR currency option RND (Risk-Neutral Density) function and moments during CNY realignment. Empirical study shows CNY realignment only has limited impact on USD expectation. The influence of CNY on FX market should not be exaggerated.

Keywords: CNY realignment, USD expectation, Currency option, RND function.

1 Introduction

On 21 July 2005, CNY (Chinese currency, Renminbi) appreciated 2% against U.S. Dollar, caused turbulence in international foreign exchange (FX) market. In New York market, U.S. Dollar against Japanese Yen (JPY/USD) dropped 2.2% to 110.34, the largest one-day drop from March 2002. Euro against Japanese Yen (JPY/EUR) dropped 2% to 134.28, also the largest one-day drop from May 2001. As we review the FX market since 2005, market sentiment changed as the expectation of CNY appreciation fluctuated. When CNY realigned with market unconscious on 21 July, we need to focus on this question: to what extend the CNY realignment will impact the FX market, especially on the expectation of USD.

In general, asset prices reflect market expectations about the future. Derivative prices have been used to analyze FX market expectations concerning future asset prices. We can use currency option price information to observe implied volatility estimated by the Garman-Kohlhagen Model, and to evaluate dispersion of expectations concerning future asset prices. By estimating the entire expectation distribution, we can examine FX market expectations concerning future outcomes in detail. We can obtain information about the dispersion of market expectations concerning currency fluctuations, as well as about market participants' beliefs about direction of market price changes and probability of an extreme outcome. This method is deemed useful for close monitoring of the impact of currency realignment on market expectations. By using the RND function of currency option to analysis FX market expectation, this work contributes to a new and growing literature on options-based approaches to model expected asset returns and focus on CNY realignment and USD expectation.

The rest of this paper is organized as follows. Section 2 describes the theoretical background of extracting expectations through RND function from currency option. Section 3 discusses some particular features of OTC currency option data that used in our empirical work. Section 4 presents the results of estimating implied RND and discusses how several measures calculated from these distributions behaved. Section 5 concludes this paper.

2 Framework of RND Function from Currency Option

RND (Risk-Neutral Distribution) function from currency option is the option implied density function of currency's future volatility. Campa et.al. (1998), Malz (1996) showed RND function is an appropriate indicator for FX risk in ERM. Bhar (1996) reckon RND function will change significantly before some major fundamental change, such as monetary policy change. Campa,et.al. (2002) studied RND function of currency option in emerging market, this function can be used to analysis the credibility of currency target zone and realignment.

RND function is risk-neutral, they can be considered as distributions that are consistent with observed market prices under the assumption that market agents are risk neutral. However, as investors are generally considered to be risk-averse – and as a consequence options prices contain information about both expectations and preferences for risk-taking – the option-implied PDFs may deviate from 'true' probability distribution that market participants attach to different outcomes of the underlying asset's price. We will be working exclusively with European call options. Reflecting this interest, nearly all analysis are based on one of three basic approaches: Estimating parameters of a particular stochastic process for the underlying asset price from options prices and constructing the implied RND from the estimated process, see Malz (1996), Bates (1996); Fitting a particular parametric functional form for terminal asset price, see Bahra (1996); Interpolating across call pricing function or the volatility smile, employing the Breeden and Litzenberger (1978) result that implied distribution may be extracted by calculating the second partial derivative of that function with respect to the strike price. Caused we cannot observe whether the assumed process can capture the density functions that are implicit within options' prices, we focus on the second and third approaches, which are more flexible. It was first shown in Breeden and Litzenberger (1978) that decline in value of European call option for an infinitesimal increase in its strike price equals the (discounted) risk-neutral probability the option will, at expiration, finish in-the-money, i.e. with positive value. The option expires in-the-money whenever the exchange rate at expiration is above the strike price, at all points right of the strike price (assuming the exchange rate is on a graph's horizontal axis). We denote spot rate on maturity as S_T, pricing model for European-style call option C :

$$S_T = S_t + S_t \left(\frac{1+r'\tau}{1+r\tau} - 1 \right) \tag{1}$$

$$C = e^{[-r(T-t)]} E[\max(0, S_T - K)] = e^{[-r(T-t)]} \int_K^{+\infty} f(S_T)(S_T - K) dS_T \tag{2}$$

Where S_t is spot rate, K is strike price, r and r' is risk free risk of home and foreign currency respectively, $T - t = \tau$ is maturity of option, $f(S_T)$ is the density function of S_T. Exploits the result derived by Breeden and Litzenberger (1978) that the RND can be recovered by calculating the second partial derivative of the call-pricing function with respect to strike price. This result can be derived simply by taking the second partial derivative of equation (1) with respect to the strike price to get:

$$\frac{\partial^2 C}{\partial K^2} = e^{[-r(T-t)]} f(S_T) \qquad (3)$$

So we just have to adjust up the second partial derivative by $e^{-r\tau}$ to get the RND $f(S_T)$. Therefore four types of statistics can be shown as mean, standard deviation (SD), skewness (Skew) and kurtosis (Kurt). Following Malz (1996), we use delta of the option to measure the moneyness of options. We calculate the second partial derivative with respect to strike price numerically and adjust for the effect of the discount factor. The rate of change of the Garman-Kohlhagen price with respect to the spot exchange rate, the first order derivative of C_{GK} against S_t is called delta, δ_{GK}, and is often used as a measure of options' moneyness. The δ_{GK} of a call option is always between 0 and 1. The quoted prices of at-the-money vanilla call σ_{atm}, risk reversals rr_t, and strangles str_t are quoted directly in terms of volatility and delta. Using $\sigma(\delta_{GK})$ as notation for volatility smile function, the quoting conventions can be written in the Malz's method. This method assumes implied volatility function, $\sigma(\delta_{GK})$ can be expressed as second-order Taylor approximation around $\delta = 0.5$. Substituting the values of $\hat{\sigma}(\delta_{GK})$ into Garman-Kohlhagen model, we can transform it to corresponding strike price K, and form a smooth volatility smile curve with only few option data from market. Finally, the implied risk-neutral probability distribution is derived using the Breeden-Litzenberger method.

3 Data Description

Our data comes form BBA-Reuters FX option volatilities database. The database is almost a universally-accepted pricing standard on which market participants could rely particularly for market to market purposes. The database provides a panel of 12 contributors, providing rates on a daily basis. Among currency contributors are strong market participants, such as BNP Paribas, Barclays Capital etc. Our data consist of market quotes of OTC options on two actively traded currency pairs: JPY/USD and USD/EUR. Observations are daily quotes. While exact quotes may differ slightly from OTC to ETO, the OTC options market is relatively liquid and competitive. The risk free rates for both home and foreign country come form LIBOR. We wrote Matlab code for all calculation.

4 Empirical Findings

We focus on date 21st July 2005, when CNY realigned to 2% higher against USD. The realignment caused relatively large fluctuation in FX market. We used the London close (GMT) data on the realignment day, one week before and after the realignment, and one month after the realignment, that is 14th July, 21st July, 29th July and 22nd August.

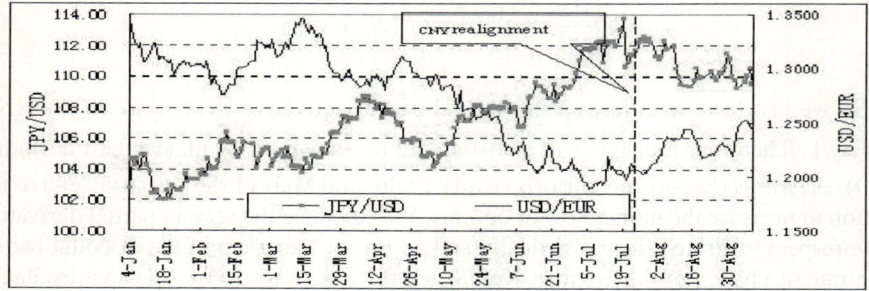

Fig. 1. USD/EUR、JPY/USD spot rate (Jan.2005-Sept.2005)

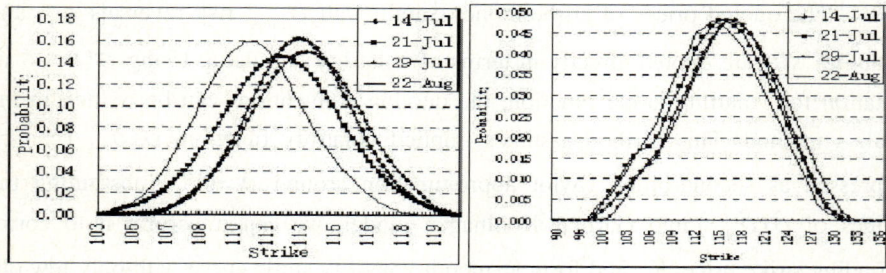

Fig. 2. JPY/USD 1-Month RND **Fig. 3.** JPY/USD 1-Year RND

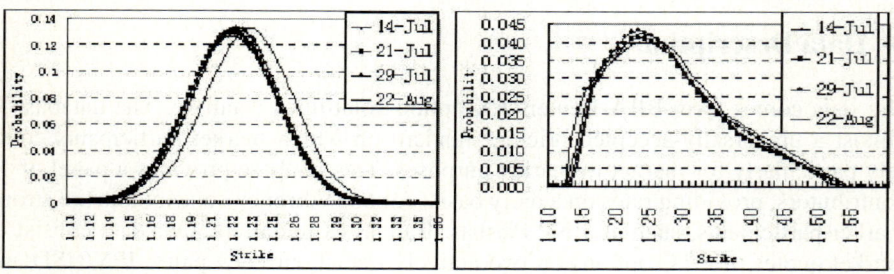

Fig. 4. USD/EUR 1-Month RND **Fig. 5.** USD/EUR 1-Year RND

Table 1. Moment of JPY/USD RND

	1-month				1-year			
	Mean	S.D.	Skew	Kurt	Mean	S.D.	Skew	Kurt
14th Jul	112.93	2.44	-0.01	2.87	115.97	6.12	-0.22	2.61
21st Jul	112.04	2.79	-0.01	2.75	115.12	6.41	-0.14	2.49
29th Jul	113.23	2.52	-0.03	2.58	116.78	6.19	-0.09	2.47
22nd Aug	110.70	2.50	0.09	2.74	114.43	6.22	-0.07	2.48

Table 2. Moment of USD/EUR RND

	1-month				1-year			
	Mean	S.D.	Skew	Kurt	Mean	S.D.	Skew	Kurt
14th Jul.	1.21	0.03	-0.01	3.02	1.25	0.08	0.65	2.79
21st Jul	1.21	0.03	-0.01	3.08	1.25	0.08	0.66	2.81
29th Jul	1.22	0.02	-0.01	3.12	1.25	0.08	0.55	2.62
22nd Aug	1.23	0.03	0.00	3.15	1.26	0.08	0.57	2.63

Sine then, market volatility soared, indicated realignment's negative shock on dollar-dominated asset. Investors in FX market sold dollar against EURO and Japanese Yen. As in figure 1, USD goes up against EUR and JPY sine May 2005, and consolidated until 21st July, when CNY realigned. Till the end of September, dollar's weak trend prevailed. It seems CNY realignment is also a negative shock on USD expectation, but when we looked at the RND function from currency option, it is not exactly that case. Figure 2 –figure 5 denoted these currency pares' 1-month and 1-year RND function. We also get four moments for these RND function (Table1 -Table2). The dynamic of these RND function and moment, especially skewness and kurtosis indicated some significant characteristic.

Compare to the day before 21st July 2005, RND function of JPY/USD move dramatically. Both long and short-term RND moved to the left, first moment (mean) dropped 90 bps with enlarged standard deviation. The movement implicated market expectation for USD is negative, and increasing volatility. No significant change for USD/EUR RND function. One week after the realignment, the first and second moment of JPY/USD RND function almost goes back to the original level. The negative trend of market expectation for USD caused by CNY realignment did not prevailed. Another notable change came one month later, by that time the market sentiment had change, CNY realignment is no longer the pivot of market. The third moment (skewness) of Short term JPY/USD and USD/EUR RND function on 21st July is relatively small, indicated market had no clear future direction. The long-term skewness of JPY/USD RND function of skewed to left, and indicated a clear trend to zero. Skewness of USD/EUR RND function skewed to right also had an increasing trend. Both evidences showed the market expect dollar will devaluate in the long term, but this sentiment faded out during the period of CNY realignment, it is very different from what we discover in the spot market. Kurtosis of Both currency pairs showed no clear direction. On the initial stages of the realignment, both long term and short term kurtosis declined, standard deviation raised, investors expect higher volatility for USD. When this sentiment faded out, Kurtosis stands still, while standard deviation declined remarkably.

Theoretically, the formation of expectation in FX market is still unknown, as well as other equity market. The chance of using only one factor to satisfactorily explain the movement of this expectation is very slim. So we must note the pitfall of the RND function of currency option. We can't separate the exact affection that came form CNY realignment. But we also noted that almost one week before and after the realignment, the news about CNY is the most significant shock for the FX market among others. Under this consideration, RND function still had no remarkable change, so we conclude that CNY realignment had no substantial affect on USD expectation.

5 Conclusion

RND function shows USD expectation fluctuated during CNY realignment, but indicated no clear direction, and CNY realignment had no substantial affect on USD expectation. This conclusion will make sense when we manage foreign exchange risk concerned about CNY. The most distinctive factor of our conclusion is that, because of the steady RND function, investors in FX market consider the timing and intensity of CNY realignment is appropriate. In the other hand, we noted that CNY is still not a strong currency that can affect FX market significantly, and one can not counted on this currency's realignment to adjust the trading balance. The influence of CNY on international FX market should not be exaggerated.

References

1. Bahra, B. Probability Distributions of Future Asset Prices Implied By Option Prices. Bank of England Quarterly Bulletin, August (1996) 299-311.
2. Bates, D. Jumps and Stochastic Volatility: Exchange Rate Processes Implicit in Deutsche Mark Options [J]. Review of Financial Studies, (1996).9(1) 69-107.
3. Breeden, D. and Litzenberger, R. Prices of state-contingent claims implicit in option price [J]. Journal of Business, (1978) 51:621-651.
4. Campa, J.M. Chang, P.H.K and Reiderc, R.L. Implied exchange rate distributions: evidence from OTC option markets [J]. Journal of International Money and Finance, (1998).17: 117-160
5. Campa, J.M. Chang, P.H.K Refalo, J.F. An options-based analysis of emerging market exchange rate expectations: Brazil's Real Plan, 1994–1999. [J]. Journal of Development Economics, (2002).69: 227– 253.
6. Malz, Allan M. Using Option Prices to Estimate Realignment Probabilities in the European Monetary System: The Case of Sterling-Mark [J]. Journal of International Money and Finance, (1996). 15: 717-748.

Investment Selection and Risk Management for Insurance Corporation

Yan-Ling Wang[1,2] and De-Li Yang[2]

[1] School of Law, Dalian Maritime University, 116026 Dalian, P.R. China
yanling_wang1@yahoo.com.cn
[2] School of Management, Dalian University of Technology,
116024 Dalian, P.R. China

Abstract. The problems related to the investment selection and risk management are very important for the insurance corporation and are considered in this paper. When performing the investment selection and risk management, the insurance corporation should suitably choose the policy among a variety of production/business policies with different risk and profit potential. In this paper, the optimal investment selection and risk management policy for the insurance corporation is defined as the objective to find the policy which maximizes the expected total discounted dividend pay-out until the time of bankruptcy.

Keywords: Investment selection, Risk Management, Insurance Corporation.

1 Introduction

Since the existence of the unprecedented scale of the losses (claims) caused by catastrophic events such as ship collision, oil pollution, hurricanes and earthquakes, it is very important for the insurance corporations to suitably perform the investment selection and risk management in order to avoid the bankruptcy.

The risk the insurance corporation takes effects the potential profit it can receive [1], [2], [3]. The insurance corporation we considered here is the one who has the possibility to choose among a variety of production/business policies with different expected risk and profit potential. A typical example of such an insurance corporation is the one whose different business activities correspond to choosing different levels of long-term investment. For an insurance corporation, there is usually a constant payment of a corporation debt, such as bond liability or loan amortization, to be paid-out, for example the dividends paid-out to other shareholders [4], [5], [6]. In such cases, the investment selection and risk management of the insurance corporation has to decide about the amount of dividends paid-out to other shareholders [6]. When the cash reserve of a corporation vanishes, the corporation will be bankrupt and its operation will seize [7]. Therefore, the policies of the investment selection and risk management are very important for the insurance corporation.

2 Investment Selection and Risk Management Policy

As an insurance corporation, it has an obligation to pay "coupon" bond or amortize its debt at a constant rate. When the cash reserve of the corporation vanishes, the corporation will be bankrupt and its operation will seize. Therefore, the objective of the investment selection and risk management for an insurance corporation is to choose the revenue policy and the dividends distribution in such a way to maximize the total expected discounted dividends pay-outs until the time of bankruptcy [4], [5], [7].

Consider an economy in which risk-sharing takes place over several (and possibly an infinity of) discrete time periods. At the beginning of period t (dated $(t-1)$), the insurance corporation collects revenue p_{t-1} for the coverage that it provides its clients. Total losses (claims) for each period are realized at the end of the period and can be thought of as independent draws from the distribution of the random variable

$$\tilde{U} = \mu + \tilde{\varepsilon},$$
$$\tilde{\varepsilon} \equiv N(0, \sigma^2) \tag{1}$$

In other words, losses (claims) at date t (noted U_t) are independent realizations of $\tilde{U}$ and can be thought of as random variables $\tilde{U}_t$ such that

$$\tilde{U}_t = \mu + \tilde{\varepsilon}_t,$$
$$\tilde{\varepsilon}_t \equiv N(0, \sigma^2) \tag{2}$$

where $\tilde{\varepsilon}_t$ are independently and identically distributed, i.i.d., random variables. In this expression, $\tilde{\varepsilon}$ is a random variable that is beyond the insurance corporation's control; noise variables $\tilde{\varepsilon}_t$ in different periods are independent of each other. The parameter μ is characteristic of the insurance corporation's exposure to catastrophic losses (claims). μ can be interpreted as the result of the insurance corporation's previous decisions relating to selecting the risks that it wants to insure [8].

In any period, in addition to the losses (claims) themselves, the insurance corporation incurs an additional cost that can be interpreted as the cost of a higher likelihood of insolvency. In this case, the volatility of losses (claims) is a variable that the insurance corporation can choose by adjusting the level of investment selection and risk management [9].

From above discussion, we can see that the dynamics of the insurance corporate assets (cash reserve) can be modelled as a diffusion process with controlled drift (determined by the parameter μ) and with another additive type control (determined by the parameter $\tilde{\varepsilon}$), modelled by a general increasing process. This leads to a mixed regular-singular control problem for diffusion processes.

The optimal investment selection and risk management policy can be modelled as a function of the current reserve (wealth) [10]. Using the current reserve indexes, the optimal investment selection and risk management policy can be determined for the insurance corporation.

In the classical Cramer–Lundberg model of an insurance corporation [8], claims arrive according to a Poisson process $A(t)$ with rate λ and the size of ith claim is U_i, where $\{U_i\}$ are independent and identical distribution (i.i.d.) with mean $\hat{\mu}$ and variance σ^2. The risk process representing the liquid assets of the corporation, also called reserve or surplus [10], is governed by the following equation

$$r_t = r_0 + pt - \sum_{i=1}^{A(t)} U_i \tag{3}$$

Where r_t and r_0, respectively, denotes the reserve up to time t and at the beginning.

This process can be approximated by a diffusion process [11] with a constant drift $\mu = p - \lambda\hat{\mu}$ and diffusion coefficient $\delta = \sqrt{\sigma^2 + \hat{\mu}^2}$. It should be noted that to make this approximation rigorous, one needs to consider a sequence of processes governed by (3) with $\hat{\mu} = \hat{\mu}_n$ and $p = p_n$ converging to zero at the rate of $\sqrt{n}$ and then make a standard diffusion approximation transformation. Thus, in the absence of control, the reserve process $R(t)$ can be modelled as

$$dR(t) = \mu\, dt + \delta\, dw(t) \tag{4}$$
$$R(0) = x \tag{5}$$

where $w(t)$ is a standard Brownian motion, representing the uncertainty in the system.

Assume that the insurance corporation can control its current reserve through the long-term investment selections. One case of the long-term investments for the insurance corporate can be simply modelled as that the insurance corporation pays a certain fraction of the premiums to other corporations in exchange for an obligation from the latter to pick up the same fraction of each claim.

In such a long-term investment case, at each moment t, it is assumed that there is an option for the insurance corporation to choose and disperse part of the insurance corporation's losses (claims). If $1-a$ is the fraction of each claim picked up by the long-term investment, then we call a the risk exposure of the insurance corporation. When the risk exposure a is fixed, the reserve of the insurance corporation is governed by

$$r_t = r_0 + apt - \sum_{i=1}^{A(t)} aU_i \tag{6}$$

If the diffusion approximation [11], [12] is used for (6), the above long-term investment process yields a Brownian motion with drift $a\mu$ and diffusion coefficient $a\delta$, where μ and δ are the same as before.

Considering $a = a(t)$, $0 \leq a(t) \leq 1$, to be a decision variable at time t, and introducing in addition $C(t)$, the cumulative amount of dividends paid-out up to time t, we get a controlled diffusion model for the reserve of the insurance corporation. In this model, the dynamics of the controlled process R is governed by

$$dR(t) = a(t)\mu\, dt + a(t)\delta\, dw(t) - dC(t) \tag{7}$$

Since the long-term investment objective of the insurance corporation is to maximize the dividends, and the insurance corporation has an option of choosing among a variety of business activities with associated risk proportional to potential profit, we can see that the optimal long-term investment objective of the insurance corporation is to find a policy which maximizes the expected present value of the total dividend pay out plus the terminal value of the insurance corporation. This is a mixed regular-singular stochastic control problem with the $a(t)$ representing the regular part of the control, and with the functional $C(t)$ representing the singular part.

Mathematically expressing the problem of optimal long-term investment of the insurance corporation can be formulated as follows. We start with a filtered probability space (Ω, F, F_t, P) and a standard Brownian motion $w(t)$ adapted to the filtration F_t. The latter plays the role of the information available at time t. A policy is a pair of F_t-adapted processes $(a(t), C(t))$, such that

(i) $0 \leq a(t) \leq 1$;

(ii) $C(t)$ is a nonnegative increasing right continuous process.

Given any policy $\pi = (a(t), C(t))$, we define the bankruptcy time for the insurance corporation as $\tau = \inf\{t : R(t) = 0\}$, where $R(t)$ is given by (6), (7). With each π we associate its performance index as

$$J_x(\pi) = E_x\left[\int_0^\tau e^{-ct} dC(t) + e^{-c\tau} P\right] \tag{8}$$

where x is the initial position of the reserve, c is the discount factor, and P is the terminal value of the insurance corporation non liquid assets (such as real estate or the rights to conduct business or the trade name), which are subject to sale with proceeds distributed among shareholders at the time of bankruptcy.

Then, the long-term investment objective is to find the optimal function [13]

$$V(x) = \sup_\pi J_x(\pi) \tag{9}$$

and the optimal long-term investment policy $\pi^* = (a^*(t), C^*(t))$ must be

$$V(x) = J_x(\pi^*) \tag{10}$$

The constrained condition of the optimal long-term investment policy is $V(0) = P$. It is easy to proof that functions (8) and (9) both are nonnegative concave functions, so, the optimal long-term investment policy can be determined by the solution of the Hamilton-Jacobi-Bellman equation for the function V of (9) [11], [13], [14].

The Hamilton-Jacobi-Bellman equation for the function V of (9) is [14]

$$\max\left\{\max_{0 \leq a \leq 1}\left\{\left[\frac{1}{2}\delta^2 a^2 \frac{d^2 V(x)}{dx^2} + \mu a \frac{dV(x)}{dx} - cV(x)\right], \left[1 - \frac{dV(x)}{dx}\right]\right\}\right\} = 0 \tag{11}$$

Most of the researching works on the optimal economy decision problems for a corporation are assumed that the terminal value of the corporation P is equal to 0 [15], [16].

From [17], [18], if $V(0) = P = 0$, the solution $v_{zero}(x)$ of (11) can be calculated and given by

$$v_{zero}(x) = \begin{cases} (2\alpha\mu/\delta^2)(x/d_0)^\beta, & x < d_0, \\ -\alpha(\theta_1 e^{-\theta_2(x-d_0)} - \theta_2 e^{\theta_1(x-d_0)}), & d_0 \leq x < d, \\ x - d + \gamma, & x \geq d, \end{cases} \quad (12)$$

where

$$\theta_1, \theta_2 = \left(\sqrt{\mu^2 + 2\delta^2 c} \pm \mu\right)/(\delta^2) \quad (13)$$

$$\beta = c/[c + \mu^2/(2\delta^2)] \quad (14)$$

$$d_0 = [(1-\beta)\delta^2]/\mu \quad (15)$$

$$d = d_0 + 2/(\theta_1 + \theta_2)\log|\theta_2/\theta_1| \quad (16)$$

$$\alpha = 1/[\theta_1\theta_2(\theta_1 e^{\theta_1(d-d_0)} + \theta_2 e^{-\theta_2(d-d_0)})] \quad (17)$$

$$\gamma = -\alpha(\theta_1 e^{-\theta_2(d-d_0)} - \theta_2 e^{\theta_1(d-d_0)}) \quad (18)$$

However, practically, when an insurance corporation is put in for bankruptcy, the terminal value of the insurance corporation $V(0) = P$ may be not equal to 0, but $V(0) = P < 0$ or $V(0) = P > 0$.

For the case of negative bankruptcy value $V(0) = P < 0$, we have

$$v_{zero}(x) \geq V(x) \quad (19)$$

Meanwhile, if we select the optimal long-term investment policy $\pi^* = (a^*(t), C^*(t))$ corresponding to the zero bankruptcy value $V(0) = P = 0$ as the optimal long-term investment policy corresponding to the negative bankruptcy value $V(0) = P < 0$, we have

$$\tau = \infty \quad (20)$$

Thus,

$$V(x) \geq v_{zero}(x) \quad (21)$$

From (19) and (21), we can see that for the case of negative bankruptcy value $V(0) = P < 0$, the solution $v_{negative}(x)$ of (11) can also be calculated and given by (12).

From (11) and (12), we can see that the Hamilton-Jacob-Bellman equation does not explicitly depend on x. So, if $v(x)$ is the solution of (12), then [17], [18]

$$V(x) = v(x + \rho) > 0, \quad \rho > 0 \quad (22)$$

is also a solution to the same equation (12) with the condition

$$V(x) = v(\rho) \quad (23)$$

From (12), (22), and (23), for the case of positive bankruptcy value $V(0) = P > 0$, the solution $v_{positive}(x)$ of (11) can be calculated and given by

$$v_{\text{positive}}(x) = \begin{cases} (2\alpha\mu/\delta^2)(x+\rho/d_0)^\beta, & 0 \leq x < d_0 - \rho, \\ -\alpha\left(\theta_1 e^{-\theta_2(x-d_0+\rho)} - \theta_2 e^{\theta_1(x-d_0+\rho)}\right), & d_0 - \rho \leq x < d - \rho, \\ x - d + \gamma + \rho, & x \geq d - \rho, \end{cases} \quad (24)$$

where ρ is the root of

$$(2\alpha\mu/\delta^2)\left[(\rho/d_0)^\beta\right] = P \tag{25}$$

Therefore, the optimal long-term investment must satisfy the condition that the maximal level of reserve which the insurance corporation must be kept is $D = d - \rho$. The insurance corporation does not distribute dividends until the reserve reaches the level D, and it pays-out everything whenever the reserve exceeds D.

From above discussion, we can see that the major optimal investment policy control parameters depend on the terminal value P. From (12) and (24), it can be seen that the optimal risk exposure is a linear function of the current reserve x when $P \leq 0$ and is an affine function when $P > 0$. The need for reducing risk, simultaneously reducing potential profit stems from the necessity to extend the time before bankruptcy occurs. However, with increasing terminal value, the insurance corporation can be less sensitive to the bankruptcy, since the distribution of the terminal wealth hedges against potential losses (claims) of the future profits.

3 Conclusions

In this paper, the problems of the investment selection and risk management for an insurance corporation are considered. The policies of the investment selection and risk management should be carefully designed for the insurance corporation in order both to gain the most of future profits and to avoid the bankruptcy.

Acknowledgments. This work was supported in part by the fund of Educational Department of Liaoning Province (No.05W021) and the fund of Personnel Department of Liaoning Province.

References

1. Carter R. L.: Reinsurance. Kluwer Academic Publishers, Dordrecht, in association with the Mercantile and General Reinsurance Co., London (1979)
2. Bennett P.: Mutual risk: P&I insurance clubs and maritime safety and environmental performance. Policy, 25 (2001) 13–21
3. Panjer H. H.: Financial Economics: With Applications to Investments, Insurance and Pensions. The Society of Actuaries, Schaumburg IL (1998)
4. Baton B., Lemaire J.: The core of a reinsurance market. Astin Bulletin, 12 (1981) 57–71
5. Baton B., Lemaire J.: The bargaining set of a reinsurance market. Astin Bulletin, 12 (1981) 101–114
6. Radner R., Shepp L.: Risk vs. profit potential: A model for corporate strategy. J. Optimization Theory and Applications, 20 (1996) 1373–1393

7. Embrechts P., Klüppelberg C., Mikosch T.: Modelling Extremal Events for Insurance and Finance. Springer, Berlin (1997)
8. Panjer H. H., Willmot G. E.: Insurance risk models. Society of Actuaries, Schaumburg IL (1992)
9. Klugman S. A., Panjer H. H., Willmot G. E.: Loss Models: From Data to Decisions. Wiley, New York (1998)
10. Grandell J.: Aspects of Risk Theory. Springer, New York (1991)
11. Guillermo L., Gomez M.: Stopping times in economic development planning. Some modelling issues, International J. Systems Science, 22 (1991) 415–432
12. Markowitz D. M., Reiman M. I., Wein L. M.: Stochastic economic lot scheduling problem: heavy traffic analysis of dynamic cyclic policies. Operations Research, 48 (2000) 136–154
13. Browne S.: Survival and growth with a liability: Optimal portfolio strategies in continuous time. Mathematics of Operations Research, 22 (1997) 468–493
14. Munk C.: Optimal consumption/investment policies with undiversifiable income risk and liquidity constraints. J. Economic Dynamics & Control, 24 (2000) 1315–1343
15. Huang C., Litzenberger R.: Foundations for Financial Economics. Elsevier Science, London (1988)
16. BORCH K. H.: Economics of Insurance. In K. K. Aase and A. Sandmo (Eds.), Amsterdam: North-Holland (1990)
17. Evans L.C.: Classical solutions of the Hamilton-Jacobi-Bellman equation for uniformly elliptic operators. Transactions of the American Mathematical Society, 275 (1983) 245–255
18. Soner H. M., Touzi N.: Superreplication under gamma constraints. SIAM J. Control and Optimization, 39 (2000) 73–96

Knowledge-Based Risk Assessment Under Uncertainty in Engineering Projects

Rashid Hafeez Khokhar, David A. Bell, Jiwen Guan, and QingXiang Wu

The School of Electronics, Electrical Engineering and Computer Science
Queen's University Belfast, Belfast, BT7 1NN, N.I. UK
{r.khokhar, da.bell, j.guan, q.wu}@qub.ac.uk

Abstract. In this paper we describe how an evidential-reasoner can be used as a component of risk assessment of engineering projects using a direct way of reasoning. Guan & Bell (1991) introduced this method by using the mass functions to express rule strengths. Mass functions are also used to express data strengths. The data and rule strengths are combined to get a mass distribution for each rule; i.e., the first half of our reasoning process. Then we combine the prior mass and the evidence from the different rules; i.e., the second half of the reasoning process. Finally, belief intervals are calculated to help in identifying the risks. We apply our evidential-reasoner on an engineering project and the results demonstrate the feasibility and applicability of this system in this environment.

Keywords: Evidential reasoning, Risk assessment, Dempster-Shafer theory, Knowledge-based, Uncertainty.

1 Introduction

Due to the high costs of failure of projects the demand for efficient risk assessment approaches have dramatically increased for the last few years. Different types of risks are being faced in daily life such as health risks, communication risks, management risks, e-commerce development risks and engineering risks. Risk assessment involves finding some allocation of belief by using an *uncertainty value* (usually probabilities) to risk factors before multiplying this by a *loss factor* (which shows how much a definite failure would cost). In the present study we are not considering the loss factor and are simply trying to estimate the chance of failure. We focus on using a generalization of probability (evidence theory) to capture the uncertainty value of risk calculation. The risk assessment of engineering projects is discussed in this study.

Previously, we showed how e-commerce developments are usually complex and unpredictable [8]. The Standish Group CHAOS Report in 2004 indicated that 53% of software projects were unable to deliver on schedule, within budget, and with the required functions, while 18% of the software projects were cancelled [9]. This stresses the fact that software projects pose various risks and daunting tasks for many organizations [4]. Addison [1] used a Delphi technique to gather the data from 32 experts and to rank the 28 risks for EC projects. In another attempt a risk analysis model for the assessment of risk in EC development using a fuzzy set approach is proposed and incorporated into the fuzzy decision support system (FDSS) [7].

However, FDSS is not be able to test it with real life EC projects, and variables membership functions need to be as realistic as possible.

Similarly, the engineering industry is also plagued by various risks, and poor performance has often been the result. Although risk management techniques have been applied, the lack of a formalized approach has produced inconsistent results. Car and Tah [3] present a hierarchical risk breakdown structure to represent a formal model for qualitative risk assessment. They present the relationships between risk factors, risks and their consequences on case and effect diagrams. Zed and Martin [12] use the PERT approach to develop a linear model for the assessment of contractor data. The model incorporates multiple ratings permitting the uncertainty in contractor data to be evaluated. Baloi and Price [2] develop a fuzzy decision framework for contractors to handle global risk factors affecting construction cost performance at a project level. All these attempts are reasonable but not enough to handle vague, incomplete, uncertainty or inexact information. Also construction projects are becoming increasingly complex and dynamic in their nature, and the introduction of new procurement methods means that contractors have to rethink their approach to the way risks are treated within their projects and organizations.

In the above mentioned literature for engineering environments the basic problem is to handle uncertainty. In such situation where analysis is highly subjective, the Dempster-Shafer theory of evidence has an advantage. In this paper, an evidential reasoning based system is used to assess the risk in engineering projects using a direct way of reasoning in a single step [5, 6]. This is actually an extension of the Dempster-Shafer theory of evidence.

Section 2 presents a direct way of reasoning in single step and the risk assessment results using a case study is presented in section 3. Finally, conclusions are in section 4.

2 Reasoning in a Single Step

In an expert systems evidence is some times associated with a group of mutually exclusive hypotheses but details are not provided about the individual members of the group. So an appropriate formalism for representing evidence should have the ability to assign beliefs to (not necessarily disjoint) sets of hypotheses and to combine these beliefs in a consistent way, when they represent evidence from different sources. The Dempster-Shafer theory of evidence is one such formalism. In this theory, beliefs are assigned to subsets of a set of mutually exclusive and exhaustive hypotheses, and Dempster rule is used to combine beliefs coming from different sources of evidence [5, 6]. The subsections below describe the procedure for direct reasoning about situations where we have a knowledge base of (uncertain) rules, and (uncertain) data which triggers them becomes available. We use mass functions in the Dempster-Shafer theory to express uncertain relationships.

2.1 Knowledge Base and Rule Strengths

Consider a frame of discernment with 5 exhaustive and mutually exclusive hypotheses $\Theta = \{h_1, h_2, h_3, h_4, h_5\}$:

$h_1 =$ "VeryLow", $h_2 =$ "Low", $h_3 =$ "Medium", $h_4 =$ "High", $h_5 =$ "VeryHigh" roughly representing the degrees of likelihood of a negative effect on the project completion.

Consider a particular source of evidence e_1 e.g., *"inadequate cash flow"*, which comes from an interview with the engineering project manager for the *"New Library"* project. We can obtain a general rule which uses this evidence, when present indicated by $\{e_1\}$, strongly supports $h = \{h_1, h_2, h_3\}$ of Θ and refutes $\bar{h} = \{h_4, h_5\}$. That is, it basically supports the hypothesis that "there is tolerable risk". When the evidence is not present, indicated by $\{\bar{e}_1\}$, the support strengths are divided between $\bar{h}$ and Θ. More specifically, we say here that there is an evidence space $\Xi_1 = \{e_1, \bar{e}_1\}$ and mass functions $s_{11}, s_{12}, s_{13} : 2^\Theta \rightarrow [0,1]$ such that

$s_{11}(\{h_1,h_2,h_3\}|\{e_1\}) = 0.85, s_{11}(\{h_4,h_5\}|\{e_1\}) = 0.05, s_{11} = (\{\Theta\}|\{e_1\}) = 0.10;$
$s_{12}(\{h_1,h_2,h_3\}|\{\bar{e}_1\}) = 0.00, s_{12}(\{h_4,h_5\}|\{\bar{e}_1\}) = 0.50, s_{12} = (\{\Theta\}|\{\bar{e}_1\}) = 0.50;$
$s_{13}(\{h_1,h_2,h_3\}|\{\Xi_1\}) = 0.20, s_{13}(\{h_4,h_5\}|\{\Xi_1\}) = 0.40, s_{13} = (\{\Theta\}|\{\Xi_1\}) = 0.40.$

Guan and Bell [5, 6] used mass function $m(X) = s(X | E)$ on the power set of hypothesis space Θ to express the rule strength for each subset E of the evidence space Ξ. Yen [10, 11] used $m(X) = s(X | e)$ for each element e of the evidence space to express the rule strength. This means that Guan and Bell [5, 6] have generalized Yen's *subset-probability-pair-collection-valued (s-p-p-c-v)* mapping to a *subset-mass-pair-collection-valued (s-m-p-c-v)* mapping. The s-m-p-c-v mapping Γ from the power set 2^Ξ of evidence space Ξ to $2^{2^\Theta \times [0,1]}$ is

$$\Gamma : (2^\Xi - \{\phi\}) \rightarrow 2^{2^\Theta \times [0,1]} \qquad (1)$$

such that for every non-empty $E \subseteq \Xi$

$$\Gamma(E) = \{(A_{E1}, s_E(A_{E1}|E)), (A_{E2}, s_E(A_{E2}|E)), \ldots, (A_{En_E}, s_E(A_{En_E}|E))\} \qquad (2)$$

Where $A_{E1}, A_{E2}, \ldots, A_{En_E} \in 2^\Theta; i.e., A_{E1}, A_{E2}, \ldots, A_{En_E} \subseteq \Theta$ are the focal elements of mass function $m_E(X) = s_E(X | E)$ on 2^Θ:

$$0 < s_E(A_{E1}|E), s_E(A_{E2}|E), \ldots, s_E(A_{En_e}|E) \leq 1 \qquad (3)$$

and

(1) $A_{Ei} \neq \phi$ for $i = 1, \ldots, n_E$;
(2) $s_E(A_{Ei}|E) > 0$ for $i = 1, \ldots, n_E$;
(3) $\sum_{i=1}^{nE} s_E(A_{Ei}|E) = 1$

Then a rule is a collection $RULE =< \Xi, \Theta, \Gamma >$, where Ξ is an evidence space, Θ is a hypothesis space, and Γ is a s-m-p-c-v mapping from the power set 2^Ξ of evidence space Ξ to hypothesis space Θ (more precisely, to $2^{2^\Theta \times [0,1]}$).

Also, a rule can be expressed by a collection of $|2^\Xi|-1$ "strength" mass functions $m_E(A) = s_E(A|E)$ for $A \subseteq \Theta$,
$RULE = \{s_E(A|E) | E \in (2^\Xi - \{\phi\})\} = \{s_1(A|E_1), s_2(A|E_2),...,s_{|2^\Xi|-1}(A|E_{|2^\Xi|-1})\}$,

$$2^\Xi - \{\phi\} = \{E_1, E_2,...,E_{|2^\Xi|-1}\}; \ s_i = s_{Ei}, E_i \neq \phi \text{ for } i = 1,........|2^\Xi|-1 \quad (4)$$

Consider a second source of evidence e_2 e.g., *"shortage of machinery"* for the *"New Library"* project. This evidence when present indicated by $\{e_2\}$, strongly support subset $h = \{h_3, h_4, h_5\}$ of Θ, and refutes $\overline{h} = \{h_1, h_2\}$. When the evidence is not present, indicated by $\{\overline{e}_2\}$, the support strengths are divided between $\overline{h}$ and Θ. More specifically, we say here that there is an evidence space $\Xi_2 = \{e_2, \overline{e}_2\}$ and mass functions $s_{21}, s_{22}, s_{23} : 2^\Theta \to [0,1]$ such that

$s_{21}(\{h_3,h_4,h_5\}|\{e_2\}) = 0.90, s_{21}(\{h_1,h_2\}|\{e_2\}) = 0.02, s_{21} = (\{\Theta\}|\{e_2\}) = 0.08;$
$s_{22}(\{h_3,h_4,h_5\}|\{\overline{e}_2\}) = 0.00, s_{22}(\{h_1,h_2\}|\{\overline{e}_2\}) = 0.50, s_{22} = (\{\Theta\}|\{\overline{e}_2\}) = 0.50;$
$s_{23}(\{h_3,h_4,h_5\}|\{\Xi_2\}) = 0.15, s_{23}(\{h_1,h_2\}|\{\Xi_2\}) = 0.45, s_{23} = (\{\Theta\}|\{\Xi_2\}) = 0.40.$

Summarizing, following the method in [5], the knowledge base includes the following rules:

RULE-1
IF EVIDENCE $\{e_1\}$ THEN
HYPOTHESIS $\{h_1, h_2, h_3\}$ WITH STRENGTH $s_{11}(\{h_1,h_2,h_3\}|\{e_1\}) = 0.85$
HYPOTHESIS $\{h_4, h_5\}$ WITH STRENGTH $s_{11}(\{h_4,h_5\}|e_1) = 0.05$
HYPOTHESIS $\{\Theta\}$ WITH STRENGTH $s_{11}(\{\Theta\}|\{e_1\}) = 0.10$
ELSE IF EVIDENCE $\{\overline{e}_1\}$ THEN
HYPOTHESIS $\{h_1, h_2, h_3\}$ WITH STRENGTH $s_{12}(\{h_1,h_2,h_3\}|\{\overline{e}_1\}) = 0.00$
HYPOTHESIS $\{h_4, h_5\}$ WITH STRENGTH $s_{12}(\{h_4,h_5\}|\{\overline{e}_1\} = 0.50$
HYPOTHESIS $\{\Theta\}$ WITH STRENGTH $s_{12}(\{\Theta\}|\{\overline{e}_1\} = 0.50$
ELSE IF EVIDENCE $\{\Xi_1\}$ THEN
HYPOTHESIS $\{h_1, h_2, h_3\}$ WITH STRENGTH $s_{13}(\{h_1,h_2,h_3\}|\Xi_1) = 0.20$
HYPOTHESIS $\{h_4, h_5\}$ WITH STRENGTH $s_{13}(\{h_4,h_5\}|\Xi_1) = 0.40$
HYPOTHESIS $\{\Theta\}$ WITH STRENGTH $s_{13}(\{\Theta\}|\{\Xi_1\}) = 0.40$
Here $\Xi_1 = \{e_1, \overline{e}_1\}$ is an evidence space and

$$m_{11}(X) = s_{11}(X | e_1) \tag{5}$$

$$m_{12}(X) = s_{12}(X | \bar{e}_1) \tag{6}$$

$$m_{13}(X) = s_{13}(X | \Xi_1) \tag{7}$$

are mass functions $2^\Theta \to [0,1]$; i.e., they are the functions $m: 2^\Theta \to [0,1]$ such that

$$m(\phi) = 0, \sum_{X \subseteq \Theta} m(\Theta) = 1. \tag{8}$$

RULE-2
IF EVIDENCE $\{e_2\}$ THEN
HYPOTHESIS $\{h_3, h_4, h_5\}$ WITH STRENGTH $s_{21}(\{h_3, h_4, h_5\} | \{e_2\}) = 0.90$
HYPOTHESIS $\{h_1, h_2\}$ WITH STRENGTH $s_{21}(\{h_1, h_2\} | \{e_2\} = 0.02$
HYPOTHESIS $\{\Theta\}$ WITH STRENGTH $s_{21}(\{\Theta\} | e_2) = 0.08$
ELSE IF EVIDENCE $\{\bar{e}_2\}$ THEN
HYPOTHESIS $\{h_3, h_4, h_5\}$ WITH STRENGTH $s_{22}(\{h_3, h_4, h_5\} | \{\bar{e}_2\} = 0.00$
HYPOTHESIS $\{h_1, h_2\}$ WITH STRENGTH $s_{22}(\{h_1, h_2\} | \{\bar{e}_2\} = 0.50$
HYPOTHESIS $\{\Theta\}$ WITH STRENGTH $s_{22}(\{\Theta\} | \{\bar{e}_2\} = 0.50$
ELSE IF EVIDENCE $\{\Theta\}$ THEN
HYPOTHESIS $\{h_3, h_4, h_5\}$ WITH STRENGTH $s_{23}(\{h_3, h_4, h_5\} | \{\Xi_2\} = 0.15$
HYPOTHESIS $\{h_1, h_2\}$ WITH STRENGTH $s_{23}(\{h_1, h_2\} | \{\Xi_2\}) = 0.45$
HYPOTHESIS $\{\Theta\}$ WITH STRENGTH $s_{23}(\{\Theta\} | \{\Xi_2\} = 0.40$
Here $\Xi_2 = \{e_2, \bar{e}_{12}\}$ is an evidence space and

$$m_{21}(X) = s_{21}(X | e_2) \tag{9}$$

$$m_{22}(X) = s_{22}(X | \bar{e}_2) \tag{10}$$

$$m_{23}(X) = s_{23}(X | \Xi_2) \tag{11}$$

are mass functions $2^\Theta \to [0,1]$

Now the data items e_1 and e_2 are not certain for example in the case above

$$c_1(\{e_1\}) = 0.80, c_1(\{\bar{e}_1\}) = 0.10, c_1(\Xi_1) = 0.10$$

$$c_2(\{e_2\}) = 0.65, c_2(\{\bar{e}_2\}) = 0.25, c_2(\Xi_2) = 0.10$$

For example informally the confidence we have that adequate cash will be available is about 8 in 10. So we refer to these inputs e_1 and e_2 as 'data' to be used with the rules and the data has strength associated with it.

2.2 Evidence Combination Rules

Now, if μ_1 and μ_2 are two mass functions corresponding to two independent evidential sources, then the combined mass function $\mu_1 \otimes \mu_2$ is calculated according to Dempster rule of combination:

1. $(\mu_1 \otimes \mu_2)(\phi) = 0$;
2. For every $A \subseteq \Theta, A \neq \phi$,

$$(\mu_1 \otimes \mu_2)(A) = \frac{\sum_{X \cap Y = A} [P(A) \frac{\mu_1(X)}{P(X)} \frac{\mu_2(Y)}{P(Y)}]}{\sum_{\theta \subseteq \Theta, \theta \neq \phi} (\sum_{X \cap Y = \theta} [P(\theta) \frac{\mu_1(X)}{P(X)} \frac{\mu_2(Y)}{P(Y)}])}. \tag{12}$$

Finally, belief intervals are determined using the two pieces of evidence, "*inadequate cash flow*" and "*shortage of machinery*" for "*New Library*" project, the overall project risk is "$\{h_3\} = medium$" with belief intervals: $[bel_\mu(A), pls_\mu(A)] = [0.2399, 0.5234]$ and *ignorance* $(A) = 0.2834$.

3 Risk Assessment

We have developed an evidential reasoning based system and we test it using the potential risk factors associated with engineering projects. These risk factors are based on interview with engineering personnel. The second and third columns in table 1 present the names of 8 engineering projects and pieces of evidence (risk factors) respectively. In the evidential-reasoner, all possible hypothesis (e.g., *VeryLow*, *Low*,

Table 1. Belief intervals and ignorance for EC and engineering projects

No	Projects	Pieces of Evidence	Conclusions	$[bel_\mu(A), pls_\mu(A)]$	$ign(A)$
1	New Library	$E_1, E_2,...,E_{10}$	VeryLow	[0.7215, 0.7834]	0.0619
2	Students Union	$E_1, E_2,...,E_{10}$	Medium	[0.6456, 0.6701]	0.0245
3	Elms Centre	$E_1, E_2,...,E_{10}$	VeryLow	[0.7524, 0.8413]	0.0889
4	ILL	$E_1, E_2,...,E_{10}$	Medium	[0.6074, 0.7819]	0.1745
5	New GRC	$E_1, E_2,...,E_{10}$	Low	[0.6328, 0.6466]	0.0138
6	CCRCB	$E_1, E_2,...,E_{10}$	Low	[0.0214, 0.0634]	0.0400
7	CHRONO	$E_1, E_2,...,E_{10}$	VeryLow	[0.3788, 0.5487]	0.1699
8	PEC extension	$E_1, E_2,...,E_{10}$	Low	[0.9220, 0.9747]	0.0527

Medium, High, VeryHigh) and pieces of evidence (risk factors) are provided by the user as input method. For example the *"New Library"* project in the first row of table 1 has 10 pieces of evidence. In the evidential-reasoner the user can select two types of evidence: data (i.e. direct evidence) or data + rule. We have developed a rule database and assign rule strength to each rule. However, the user can also edit the rules strengths dynamically. After collecting all pieces of evidence related to a particular engineering project, we combine prior masses and different rules using our direct way of reasoning (i.e. extended Dempster-Shafer theory) for the best supported decision. The last three columns in table 1 present the summary of the results for the engineering projects.

For example, the result for *"New Graduate Research Centre"* project using 10 pieces of evidence is demonstrated in figure 1 with the help of pie chart. The conclusion is for this particular project is: the overall project risk is *"Low"* with the belief intervals [*bel, pls*] = [0.6328, 0.6466] and *ignorance* = 0.0138.

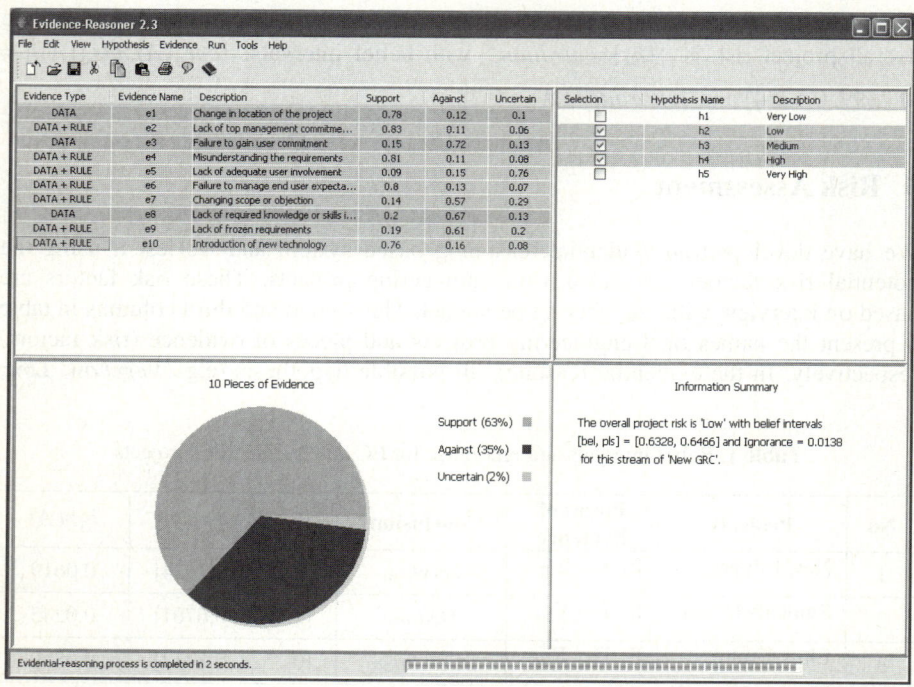

Fig. 1. Risk assessment results of New Graduate Research Centre project

4 Conclusions

Evidence shows that both clients and developers suffer significant financial losses due to poor risk management in engineering projects. In this paper, we have used an evidential reasoning based system using a direct way of evidence reasoning with an extended Dempster-Shafer theory for the risk assessment of engineering projects. In this method, mass function is used to express rule strengths for subsets of the evidence space. The system is tested using 10 risk factors from interviews with project staff on engineering projects. The results of the evaluation show the viability of the approach to the uncertainty handling aspects of risk assessment using evidential reasoning.

References

1. Addison. T.: E-commerce project development risks: evidence from a Delphi survey, International Journal of Information Management. 1 (2003) 25–40.
2. Baloi, D., Price, A. D. F.: Modelling global risk factors affecting construction cost performance. International Journal of Project Management, Volume 21, Number 4, May 2003, 261-269(9)
3. Carr, V., Tah, J.H.M.: A fuzzy approach to construction project risk assessment and analysis: construction project risk management system. Advances in Engineering Software, Volume 32, Number 10, October 2001, 847-857(11)
4. 4 Charette, R.N.: Why software fails [software failure]. Spectrum, IEEE, Volume 42, Issue 9, Sept. 2005 42 – 49
5. Guan, J. W., Bell, D. A.: Evidence theory and its applications. Vol.1, Studies in Computer Science and Artificial Intelligence 7, Elsevier, The Netherlands, (1991).
6. Guan, J. W., Bell, D. A.: Evidence theory and its applications. Vol.2, Studies in Computer Science and Artificial Intelligence 8, Elsevier, The Netherlands, (1992).
7. Ngai, E.W.T., Wat, F.K.T.: Fuzzy decision support system for risk analysis in e-commerce development. Journal of Decision Support Systems. Volume 40, Issue 2, August (2005), 235-255
8. Rashid. H. K., David A. Bell., Guan. J. W., QingXiang Wu.: Risk Assessment of E-Commerce Projects using Evidential Reasoning. The 2nd International Conference on Natural Computation (ICNC'06) and the 3rd International Conference on Fuzzy Systems and Knowledge Discovery (FSKD'06), China, September (2006), 621-630
9. Standish Group International, 2004 Standish Group International, Inc., 2004. 2004 Third Quarter Research Report.
10. Yen, J. A.: reasoning model based on an extended Dempster-Shafer theory. Proceedings aaai-(1986) 125-131.
11. Yen, J.: GERTIS: A Dempster-Shafer Approach to Diagnosing Hierarchical Hypotheses", Communications of the ACM 5 vol. 32, (1989), 573-585.
12. Zed, H., Martin, S.: Assessment and evaluation of contractor data against client goals using PERT approach. Construction Management & Economics, Volume 15, Number 4 / July 1, 1997 327-340

Fuzzy Regression with Quadratic Programming: An Application to Financial Data

Sergio Donoso[1], Nicolás Marín[2], and M. Amparo Vila[2]

[1] UTEM - Santiago de Chile - Chile
sdonosos@vtr.net
[2] Dept. of Computer Science and A. I.,
University of Granada, 18071, Granada, Spain
{nicm, vila}@decsai.ugr.es

Abstract. The fuzzy approach to regression has been traditionally considered as a problem of linear programming. In this work, we introduce a variety of models founded on quadratic programming together with a set of indices useful to check the quality of the obtained results. In order to test the validness of our proposal, we have done an empirical study and we have applied the models in a case with financial data: the Chilean COPEC Company stock price.

1 Introduction

Probabilistic regression assumes the existence of a crisp aleatory term in order to compute the uncertainty of a regression model. In contrast, fuzzy regression (first proposed by Tanaka et al. [12]) considers the use of fuzzy numbers and possibilisic restrictions.

Fuzzy regression analysis (with crisp input variables and fuzzy output) can be categorized in two alternative groups: proposals based on the use of *possibility* concepts [7,8,10,6]; and proposals based on the minimization of central values, mainly through the use of the least squares method[3,5,9].

In this work we introduce a new proposal where both approaches of fuzzy regression analysis are integrated. As we will see in Section 2, the use of *quadratic programming* makes possible to reconcile the minimization of estimated deviations of the central tendency with the minimization of estimated deviations in the membership functions' spreads.

This work also analyzes several *goodness of fit indices* beyond the conventional ones, which can be used to measure the quality of the fitness of a given regression model. Section 3 and 4 are devoted to this point.

We also apply these *goodness of fit indices indexes* to COPEC stock price with our possibilistic regression models. Section 5 describes this case study.

2 The Regression Models

Let X be a data matrix of m variables $X_1, ..., X_m$, with n observations each one (all of them real numbers), and Y_i ($i = 1, .., n$) be a fuzzy set characterized by a

LR membership function $\mu_{Y_i}(x)$, with center y_i, left spread p_i, and right spread q_i ($Y_i = (y_i, p_i, q_i)$).

The problem of fuzzy regression is to find fuzzy coefficients $A_j = (a_j, c_{Lj}, c_{Rj})$ such that the following model holds:

$$Y_i = \sum_{j=1}^{m} A_j X_{ij} \qquad (1)$$

The first model formulated by Tanaka et al. [12] considers that the fuzzy coefficients to estimate are affected by imprecision. That model was replaced by the following optimization criterion [11]:

$$Min \sum_{i=1}^{n} \sum_{j=1}^{m} (c_{Li} + c_{Ri})|X_{ij}| \qquad (2)$$

subject to the usual condition that, at a given level of possibility (h), the h-cut of the estimated value $\widetilde{Y}_i$ contains the h-cut of the empiric value Y_i. This restriction can be expressed by means of the following formulation[1]:

$$\sum_{j}^{m} a_j X_{ij} + (1-h) \sum_{j}^{m} c_{Rj} |X_{ij}| \geq y_i + (1-h)q_i \quad for\ i = 1, ..., n \qquad (3)$$

$$\sum_{j}^{m} a_j X_{ij} - (1-h) \sum_{j}^{m} c_{Lj} |X_{ij}| \leq y_i - (1-h)p_i \quad for\ i = 1, ..., n \qquad (4)$$

$$c_{Rj}, c_{Lj} \geq 0 \quad for\ j = 1, ..., m \qquad (5)$$

where h is a possibility degree for the estimate ($\mu(Y_i) \geq h$).

The model made up of objective function (2) and restrictions (3)-(5) will be called Linear Model (LIN) in this work. This model has been the most used in fuzzy regression analysis and it is stable with respect to changes in the measurement unit of variables X.

Fuzzy Regression with linear programming (based on the above mentioned Tanaka's studies) has the inconvenience that the optimal solution is located in one of the vertex of the polyhedron of feasible solutions. This fact increases the possibility that coefficients c_i are equal to zero in the estimation. In order to deal with this problem, the idea that guide this paper is to substitute the usual objective function (equation (2)) by an extended formulation with quadratic functions.

If we want to minimize the extensions, taking into account the criterion of least squares and that we use non symmetrical triangular membership functions, we have the objective function

$$J = k_1 \sum_{i=1}^{n} (y_i - a' X_i)^2 + k_2(c_L X' X c_L' + c_R X' X c_R') \qquad (6)$$

where k_1 and k_2 are weights that perform a very important role: they allow to give more importance to the central tendency ($k_1 > k_2$) or to the reduction of estimate's uncertainty ($k_1 < k_2$) in the process.

The model with objective function (6) and restrictions (3)-(5) will be called Extended Tanaka Model (ETM).

In order to reach a more precise adjustment of the extensions, let us now focus not in the minimization of the uncertainty of the estimated results but on the quadratic deviation with respect to the empiric data. According to this new criterion, the objective function represents the quadratic error for both the central tendency and each one of the spreads:

$$J = k_1 \sum_{i=1}^{n}(y_i - a' X_i)^2 +$$

$$+ k_2 (\sum_{i=1}^{n}(y_i - p_i - (a' - c'_L)X_i)^2 + \sum_{i=1}^{n}(y_i + q_i - (a' + c'_R)X_i)^2) \qquad (7)$$

The model with objective function (7) and restrictions (3)-(5) will be called Quadratic Possibilistic Model (QPM). This model does not depend on the data unit.

In the non-possibilistic side, we propose a new model, called Quadratic Non-Possibilistic (QNP), which considers the objective function (7) and which incorporates the only restriction (5).

3 Quality Measures

We complete our proposal with a set of indexes useful to measure the similarity between the original output data $Y_i = (y_i, p_i, q_i)$ and the estimated data $\widetilde{Y}_i$.

The first similarity index we are going to consider computes the quotient between the cardinal of the intersection of Y_i and $\widetilde{Y}_i$ and the cardinal of their union:

$$S_i = \frac{|Y_i \cap \widetilde{Y}_i|}{|Y_i \cup \widetilde{Y}_i|} \qquad (8)$$

where the cardinal of a fuzzy set can be defined as $|A| = \int \mu_A(x)dx$. For the whole data set, we have

$$SIM_1 = \frac{\sum_{i=1}^{n} S_i}{n} \qquad (9)$$

which varies from 0 to 1. A measure of the same family is used in the work of Kim and Bishu [4]:

$$D = \int_{S_Y \cup S_{\widetilde{Y}}} |\mu_Y(x) - \mu_{\widetilde{Y}}(x)|dx \qquad (10)$$

Kim et al. proposes a measure of relative divergence, where the measure is 0 when both fuzzy numbers are identical, but can reach values over 1.

Alternative measures can be computed with the fuzzy numbers of $Y_i = [y_i - p_i, y_i + q_i]$ and $\widetilde{Y}_i = [\widetilde{y}_i - \widetilde{p}_i, \widetilde{y}_i + \widetilde{q}_i]$. The similarity between these intervals, considered as membership functions, can be measured as follows:

$$\nabla(Y_i, \widetilde{Y}_i) = \frac{|\widetilde{y}_i - \widetilde{p}_i - (y_i - p_i)| + |\widetilde{y}_i + \widetilde{q}_i - (y_i + q_i)|}{2(\beta_2 - \beta_1)} \quad (11)$$

where $\beta_1 = min(\widetilde{y}_i - \widetilde{p}_i, y_i - p_i)$ and $\beta_2 = max(\widetilde{y}_i + \widetilde{q}_i, y_i + q_i)$.

Taking this formulation into account, we can define the index for the i datum in the test as

$$T_i = \frac{|\widetilde{y}_i - \widetilde{p}_i - (y_i - p_i)| + |\widetilde{y}_i + \widetilde{q}_i - (y_i + q_i)| + (|\widetilde{p}_i - p_i| + |\widetilde{q}_i - q_i|)}{2(\beta_2 - \beta_1)} \quad (12)$$

and, for the whole dataset, a index varies from 0 to approximately 1:

$$SIM_2 = \frac{\sum_i^n T_i}{n} \quad (13)$$

The same idea can be used to add the deviation of the central tendency to this measure:

$$R_i = \frac{|\widetilde{y}_i - \widetilde{p}_i - (y_i - p_i)| + |\widetilde{y}_i + \widetilde{q}_i - (y_i + q_i)| + (|\widetilde{y}_i - y_i|)}{3(\beta_2 - \beta_1)} \quad (14)$$

With this modification, we build a third index which also varies from 0 to 1:

$$SIM_3 = \frac{\sum_i^n R_i}{n} \quad (15)$$

A similarity measure based on the Hausdorff metric [13], is given by the relation

$$U_i = \frac{max(|\widetilde{y}_i - \widetilde{p}_i - (y_i - p_i)|, |\widetilde{y}_i + \widetilde{q}_i - (y_i + q_i)|)}{(\beta_2 - \beta_1)} \quad (16)$$

where the index for the set of observations, which fluctuates from 0 to 1, is

$$SIM_4 = \frac{\sum_i^n (1 - U_i)}{n}. \quad (17)$$

Finally, a measure based on only one point of the membership function is $V_i = sup(\mu_{Y_i \cap \widetilde{Y}_i}(x))$ and can be extended for the whole dataset:

$$SIM_5 = \frac{\sum_i^n (V_i)}{n} \quad (18)$$

The R^2 index (which varies from 0 to 1) is commonly used in order to measure the quality of the fitness of the central tendency. We propose to use the following index for the central tendency, where, as the error between the observed value and the estimated central value tends to 0, the index value tends to 1:

$$R^2_{fuzzy} = max\left(0, \ 1 - \frac{\sum_i^n (y_i - \widetilde{y}_i)^2}{\sum_i^n (y_i - y_{mean})^2}\right) \quad (19)$$

Table 1. Summary of the proposed quality measures

Index	Formulation
SIM_1	$SIM_1 = \frac{\sum_i^n \frac{|Y_i \cap \widetilde{Y_i}|}{|Y_i \cup \widetilde{Y_i}|}}{n}$
SIM_2	$SIM_2 = \frac{\sum_i^n \frac{|\widetilde{y_i} - \widetilde{p_i} - (y_i - p_i)| + |\widetilde{y_i} + \widetilde{q_i} - (y_i + q_i)| + (|\widetilde{p_i} - p_i| + |\widetilde{q_i} - q_i|)}{2(\beta_2 - \beta_1)}}{n}$
SIM_4	$SIM_4 = \frac{\sum_i^n (1 - \frac{max(|\widetilde{y_i} - \widetilde{p_i} - (y_i - p_i)|,\ |\widetilde{y_i} + \widetilde{q_i} - (y_i + q_i)|)}{(\beta_2 - \beta_1)})}{n}$
R^2_{fuzzy}	$R^2_{fuzzy} = max\left(0,\ 1 - \frac{\sum_i^n (y_i - \widetilde{y_i})^2}{\sum_i^n (y_i - y_{mean})^2}\right)$

4 Empirical Analysis

In order to make an empirical study of the proposed regression models we have carried out an experimentation process with different problems:

- Three well known examples from the literature: Tanaka and Lee[11], Chang[2], and Kao [3].
- A variation of a given Chilean company weekly stock price with 46 observations.
- A given accident data base with 9 observations.

The output variable has symmetrical membership function in three of the examples while this membership function is non-symmetrical in the other three. In the experimentation, we have computed a variance analysis for each index, where the factors are the methods and the cases.

From the above described empirical study we have obtained the following conclusions:

- With respect to the methods:
  - In general, the LIN method does not produce good results.
  - QNP and QPM seem to be the most accurate methods. The QNP method yields the highest value for indexes SIM_2, SIM_4, and R^2_{fuzzy}, while QPM produces the best results for the other three goodness of fit indices.
  - QPM gets better values of similarity than ETM in almost all the indexes.
- With respect to the goodness of fit indices
  - Within the family of indexes based on geometric distances, we had chosen SIM_3 because it considers not only the fitness of the extremes but also the fitness of the center. However, in spite of its good results for index R^2_{fuzzy}, method QNP presents the lowest value for SIM_3. Thus, we conclude that SIM_3 is not a good index to evaluate the central similarity.
  - Index SIM_5 is the most unstable of the six indexes.

5 Application to Financial Data: A Case Study

The Chilean COPEC company is a holding whose main goal is the production of cellulose and the distribution of fuel. It is owned by the main enterprise group of the country, the Angelini group.

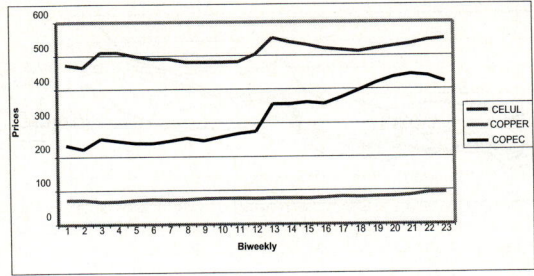

Fig. 1. *COPECT Data: Internacional CELLULOSE and COOPER prices*

In this section, we apply our regression models in order to explain its stock price. We take data related to 23 periods of two weeks described by means of six input variables. After a variable selection process, we have reduced the model to two input variables: the international cellulose price (important from the company point of view) and the copper price (important from the Chilean economy point of view). Data can be seen in Figure 1.

Every period's minimum stock price is the left end of the membership function, while the maximum is the right end. The average of the closing COPEC prices is the center.

We give the results of the three fuzzy regression models in table 2. The central estimated coefficients are *const*, *cell*, and *copper*. First line of c_i refers to the left spreads and the second line refers to the right spread. As can be observed, index SIM_1 is the strictest one among the indicators. The LIN estimation is the usual fuzzy regression. As can be seen, both our possibilistic and non-possibilistic models maintain or improve the results for every considered index.

Table 2. Estimated factors: cellulose and copper prices

	Const	Cell.	Copper	Const	Cell.	Copper				
Model	a_1	a_2	a_3	c_1	c_2	c_3	$R2$	SIM_1	SIM_2	SIM_4
LIN	5.18	.003	.018	.006	0	.002	0.77	0.09	0.36	0.31
				.005	0	.002				
QNP	4.05	.005	.018	0	0	.004	0.85	0.10	0.46	0.96
				0	0	.004				
QPM	4.73	.004	.014	0	0	.002	0.82	0.09	0.36	0.70
				0	0	.003				

As an example, Figure 2 plots the observed price and the estimated price with the QPM model. As can be appreciated, this possibilictic estimation incorporates all the observed data.

Figure 3 depicts the observed and the estimated price, with the QNP model. In this case, due to the non-possibilistic approach, the estimated spreads have an amplitude similar to the observed data.

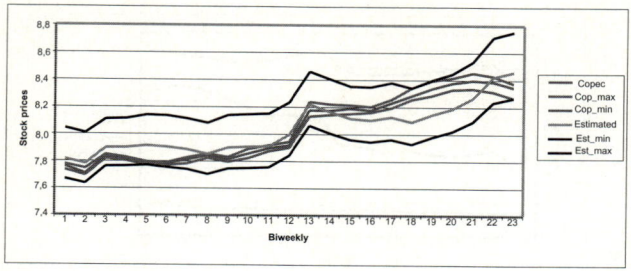

Fig. 2. *COPEC stock price, and QPM possibilistic estimated price*

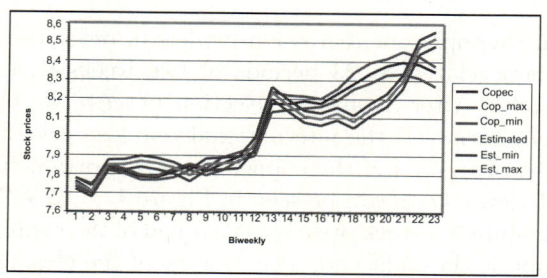

Fig. 3. *COPEC stock price, and QNP no possibilistic estimated prices*

6 Conclusions

In this paper we have used quadratic programming in order to obtain a good fitness in fuzzy linear regression. To accomplish this task, we have adapted the conventional model of Tanaka (ETM) and we have proposed two new models (QPM and QNP). We have also proposed a new set of goodness of fit indices useful to analyze the goodness of each regression method.

According to the results of our experimentation, the quadratic methods introduced in this work improve the results obtained with the linear programming approach:

- Method QPM is a good choice when possibilistic restrictions are important in the problem.
- If we do not want to pay special attention to the possibilistic restriccions, QNP is an appropriate alternative.

Further work in this line will be directed to extend the set of restrictions of methods QPM and QNP to other possibilistic measures. Additionally, we are involved in the study of new indexes which merge several of the proposed goodness criteria and which use an aggregator operator (like OWA, for example).

Finally, also in this work, we have applied our models to a problem of financial data, analyzing the COPEC stock price. As a conclusion of our analysis, we have observed that both selected variables are very informative of the behaviour of the COPEC stock price taking into account that $R2fuzzy > 0.8$. Copper price is the only factor that produces uncertainty in the system (its spread is greater than zero). Further work in this case will be focused on the explanation of the difference in terms of spread between the possibilistic and non-possibilistic models.

References

1. A. Bárdossy. Note on fuzzy regression. *Fuzzy Sets and Systems*, 37:65–75, 1990.
2. Yun-His O. Chang. Hybrid fuzzy lest-squares regression analysis and its reliability measures. *Fuzzy Sets and Systems*, 119:225–246, 2001.
3. C. Kao and C.L. Chyu. Least-squares estimates in fuzzy regression analysis. *European Journal of Operational Research*, 148:426–435, 2003.
4. B. Kim and R.R. Bishu. Evaluation of fuzzy linear regression models by comparing membership functions. *Fuzzy Sets and Systems*, 100:342–353, 1998.
5. K. J. Kim, H. Moskowitz, and M. Koksalan. Fuzzy versus statistical linear regression. *European Journal of operational Research*, 92:417–434, 1996.
6. E. C. Ozelkan and L. Duckstein. Multi-objective fuzzy regression: a general framework. *Computers and Operations Research*, 27:635–652, 2000.
7. G. Peters. Fuzzy linear regression with fuzzy intervals. *Fuzzy Sets and Systems*, 63:45–53, 1994.
8. D. T. Redden and W. H. Woodall. Properties of certain fuzzy linear regression methods. *Fuzzy Sets and Systems*, 64:361–375, 1994.
9. D. A. Savic and W. Pedrycz. Evaluation of fuzzy linear regression models. *Fuzzy Sets and Systems*, 39:51–63, 1991.
10. H. Tanaka and J. Wataka. Possibilistic linear systems and their applications to the linear regresion model. *Fuzzy Sets and Systems*, 27:275–289, 1988.
11. Hideo Tanaka and Haekwan Lee. Interval regression analysis by quadratic programming approach. *IEEE Trans. on Fuzzy Systems*, 6(4), 1998.
12. Hideo Tanaka, S. Uejima, and K. Asai. Linear regression analysis with fuzzy model. *IEEE Trans. on Systems, Man, and Cybernetics*, 12(6):903–907, 1982.
13. R. Zwick, E. Carlstein, and D. V. Budescu. Measures of similarity among fuzzy concepts: A comparative analysis. *International Journal of Aproximate Reasoning*, 1:221–242, 1987.

Improving Search in Unstructured P2P Systems: Intelligent Walks (I-Walks)

Francis Otto[1] and Song Ouyang[2]

School of Information Science and Engineering, Central South University, Changsha, Hunan, P.R. China 410083
[1] ottofrancis@yahoo.com, [2] ouyangsong@yahoo.com

Abstract. Random Walks (RW) search technique can greatly reduce bandwidth production but generally fails to adapt to different workloads and environments. A Random Walker can't learn anything from its previous successes or failures, displaying low success rates and high latency. In this paper, we propose Intelligent Walks (IW) search mechanism - a modification of RW, exploiting the learning ability and the shortest path distance of node neighbors. A node probes its neighbors before forwarding the query. The probe is to find a candidate that has the shortest distance from the query source and/or has ever seen before the object that is going to be sent. If there isn't such candidate, then a node is chosen as usual (at random). The experimental results demonstrate that new method achieves better performance than RW in terms of success rate.

Keywords: Unstructured P2P, Search, Random Walks and Intelligent Walks.

1 Introduction

Peer-to-Peer (P2P) computing has emerged as a popular fully-distributed and cooperative model, attracting a lot of attention by the Internet community. Its advantages (although application-dependent in many cases) include robustness in failures, extensive resource-sharing, self-organization, load balancing, data persistence, anonymity, etc. One significant challenging aspect in P2P resource sharing environments is efficient searching mechanism. The usability of P2P systems depends on effective techniques to locate and retrieve data. However, existing search techniques in pure P2P networks are inefficient due to the decentralized nature of such networks.

Today, the most popular P2P applications operate on unstructured networks as they are simple, robust and dynamic. Unstructured systems are designed more specifically for the heterogeneous Internet environment, where the nodes' persistence and availability are not guaranteed. Under these conditions, it is impossible to control data placement and to maintain strict constraints on overlay network topology, as structured applications require. Currently, these systems (such as Napster [1], Gnutella [2], and Freenet [3], etc) are widely deployed in real life – hence their paramount importance and applicability. Efficient resource discovery is the first step towards the realization of distributed resource-sharing.

Random walks algorithm can greatly improve the scalability problem [4]. However, random walks search algorithm suffers from poor search efficiency in the short term [5]. A Random Walker can't learn anything from its previous successes or failures, hence displaying low success rate and high latency.

In this paper, we propose a new search method, Intelligent Walks that uses node's distance and its knowledge from previous searches to guide random walkers. In our case, in order to intelligently select a neighbor to forward the query to, a node will use the *Dijkstra's* algorithm to determine the length between the candidate node and the originating node. Also a simple matching of the node's content is performed to determine whether or not the neighbor has ever seen before the message that is going to be sent. If there isn't such a neighbor, then a node is chosen as usual (at random).

2 Related Work

Search methods for unstructured P2P networks have been studied a lot in the last few years. Studies on Random Walks algorithm show how it can be modified to achieve greater level of efficiency. E.g. a study in [6] led to a proposal of equation based adaptive search mechanism that uses estimate of popularity of a resource in order to choose the parameters of random walk such that a targeted performance level is achieved by the search. In [7] each object is probed with probability proportional to the square root of its query popularity. It was shown that with the guidance of the Metropolis algorithm, each step of the random walks is determined based on the content popularity of current neighbors. Another modification includes APS [8], which utilizes feedback from previous searches to probabilistically guide future ones. It performs efficient object discovery while inducing zero overhead over dynamic network.

Although the above approaches to modify Random Walk have yielded good results, our approach is different and applies the concept of distance, which previous researches have not emphasized. In *I-Walks* we exploit the neighbor node distance from the querying node and, at the same time, the learning ability so that the walkers are guided to nearby neighbors, having ever before transferred the object being queried.

3 Background

3.1 Random Walks

Random walk search mechanism does not generate as much message traffic as other flood-based algorithms. In Random Walks, the requesting node sends out k query messages to an equal number of randomly chosen neighbors. Each of these messages follows its own path, having intermediate nodes forward it to a randomly chosen neighbor at each step. These queries are also known as walkers. A walker terminates either with a success or a failure. Termination can be determined by two different methods: The TTL-based method, whereby search is terminated when TTL value is zero, and the checking method, where walkers periodically contact the query source asking whether the termination conditions have been satisfied [8].

Random Walks Search Algorithm, GSCP (Generic Semantic Constraint Parsing):

```
define kRandomWalk(Graph g, int numWalkers, Node
startNode, Node    destinationNode)
     Node n := startNode;
     while( n not equals destinationNode)
          for walker (1...numWalkers)
               int count := numNeighbors(g, n);
               if (count > 1)
                    int randomNumber := rand(count);
                    Node prev = n;
                    n := getNeighbor(g,n,randomNumber);
               else
                    n = prev;
               end if;
          end for;
     end while;
end;
```

Simulation results in [9, 10] show that messages are reduced by more than an order of magnitude compared to the standard flooding schemes.

3.2 Dijkstra's Shortest Path Algorithm

Dijkstra's algorithm (fig.1), when applied to a graph, quickly finds the shortest path from a chosen source to a given destination. In fact, the algorithm is so powerful that it finds all shortest paths from the source to all destinations! This is known as the single-source shortest paths problem.

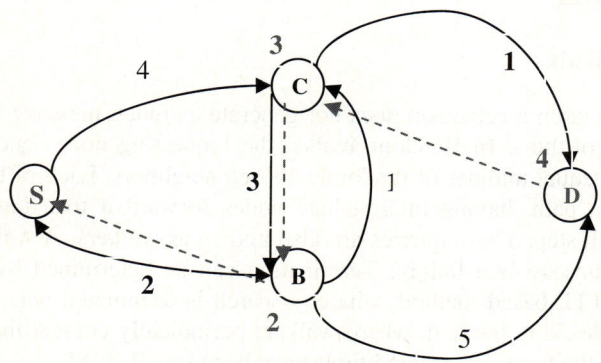

Fig. 1. Dijkstra's Shortest Path of D from S

The graph is made of nodes and edges which link vertices together. Edges are directed and have an associated distance, sometimes called the weight or the cost. The distance between the vertex u and the vertex v is noted [u, v] and is always positive.

$$d(C) = d(S) + [S,C] = 0 + 4 = 4 \tag{1}$$

$$d(C) = 4 > d(B) + [B,C] = 2 + 1 = 3 \tag{2}$$

$$d(D) = 7 > d(C) + [C,D] = 3 + 1 = 4 \tag{3}$$

We believe that if an object is stored in a nearby node then the cost of locating and transferring it is much less compared to distant nodes. Our algorithm uses this concept to determine which neighbor to be chosen for forwarding the query since the physical path delay strongly influences the performance of searches. Thus a random walker, conscious of the distance, is passed through the network. We use Dijkstra's algorithm to determine which node neighbor is closest to the source node.

4 Intelligent Walks (I-Walks)

I- Walks can reduce the routing cost in terms of the number of routing messages. By making informed choice of 'good' neighbors, this technique can maintain the quality of query results and decrease the query response time. We can develop two heuristics to help node select the best neighbor to send the query. These heuristics are:

- Select a neighbor that is closer to the query originating node and containing useful data (or has ever seen the message to be sent).
- Select a neighbor that has ever answered same query before.

The latter heuristic will ensure the successes of the search while the former ensures the success at the same time reducing the retrieval cost.

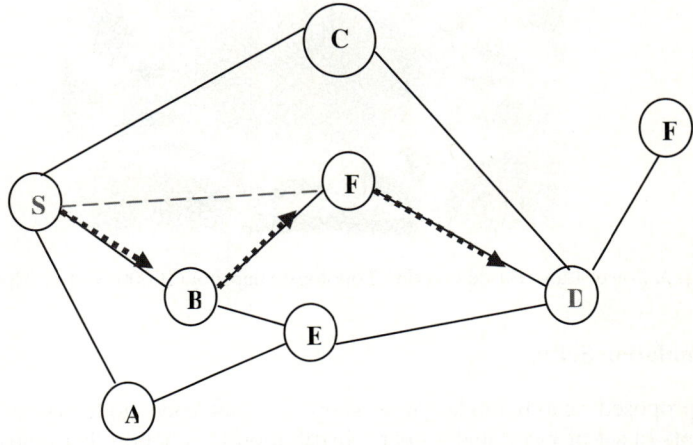

Fig. 2. Intelligent Walk (I-Walk) Search

Observation 1. In fig.2, node B is chosen as the next hope basing the length from the query originator N. If all neighbors A, B, and C have ever seen the object to be sent, the choice of B is made after considering the distances of SA, SB and SC.

Observation 2. Assuming both E and F have seen the object to be transferred, F is considered because of its distance from N. I.e. dist [S,F] < dist [S,E].

$$[S,D] = [S,B] + [B,F] + [F,D] \qquad (4)$$

5 Simulations

5.1 General Topology Scenario

Our environment, using peersim simulator [11], consists of an Internet-like tree topology, based on power Law principle [12] because of its specific, location dependent preferential attachment. It takes into account geometric and network constraints to better mimic real world networks. Preferential attachment is tuned by the parameter α that amplifies or reduces the influence of the geometric location.

The rule strategy is the following: we consider a unit square, and we place χ_0 in the middle, that is, $\chi_0 = (0.5, 0.5)$. This node is called the root. Let $W()$ denote the number of hops to the root. For each, i = 1, ..., i = n-1; we select a point χ_i in the unit square at random, and we connect it to an already existing node χ_j that minimizes the following formula: $W(\chi_j) + \alpha \cdot dist(\chi_i, \chi_j)$ where $dist()$ is the Euclidean distance and α is a weight parameter.

Certainly, $W(\chi_i) = W(\chi_j) + 1$. This way we obtain a tree rooted in χ_0. This topology implies that every node (except the root) has an out-degree of exactly one link (fig.3).

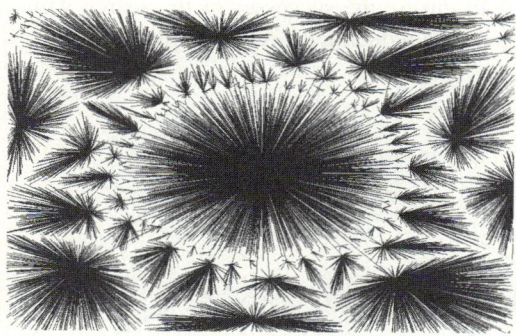

Fig. 3. Power Law- Based Overlay Topology Snapshot (10000 Nodes, Alpha $\alpha = 4$)

5.2 Simulation Setup

In our proposed search model, it is supposed that each node has a repository of documents (a set of keys) and a query distribution (a function that maps which query to perform at each simulation cycle for each node). Each query may contain one or more keys to search for each node to initiate at most a query at each cycle and/or to forward all the messages received (stored in a buffer); each message packet can only perform one hop per cycle. Each node is allowed to initiate at most a query at each cycle and/or to forward all the messages received (stored in a buffer); each message packet can only perform one hop per cycle.

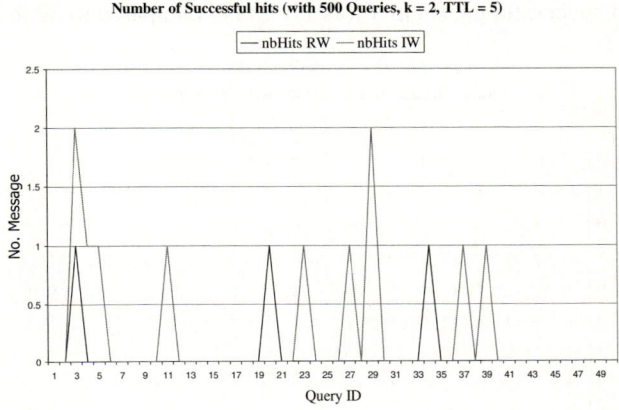

Fig. 4. Number of successful packet hits per query

The experiment was performed to compare two search techniques i.e. Random Walk (RW) and Intelligent Walk (IW). The parameters were varied as follows: First, a maximum of 50 queries were deployed on the network. Second, the maximum number of queries was increased to 500. The number of walkers was 2, TTL was 5.That means the total number of messages sent for this query was 10 in each case.

The idea was thus to compare the number of successful packet hits per query for the two methods and to compare the learning ability by comparing the number of times the packets has been seen.

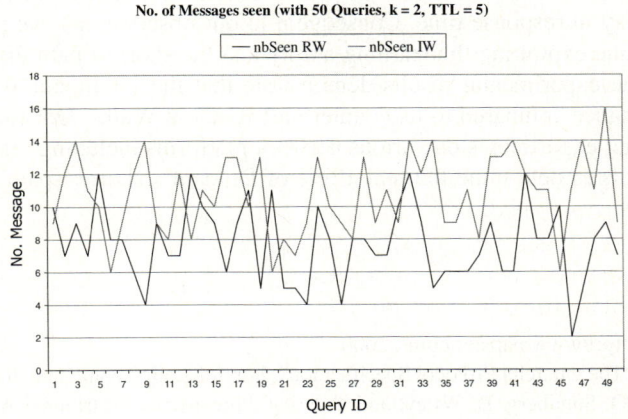

Fig. 5a. Number of times the packets has been seen for 50 queries

5.3 Simulation Results

Fig.4 and Fig.5 present the number of successful packet hits per query and number of times packets has been seen respectively. It was observed that IW performs better especially with increased number of queries deployed. With 500 queries deployed, the number of times the packets has been seen was 4920 in IW compared to 3720 in RW. The number of successful packet hits was 110 in IW compared to 50 in RW.

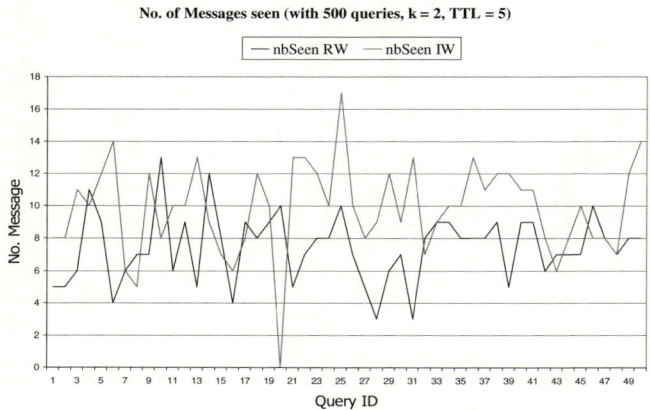

Fig. 5b. Number of times the packets has been seen for 500 queries

6 Conclusion and Future Work

The existing search techniques in unstructured P2P networks are inefficient due to the decentralized nature of such networks. In this paper we investigate Random Walk search algorithm primarily in decentralized, unstructured P2P network environment. Two major deficiencies of Random Walks search technique are addressed: Learning ability and distance, which affect its efficiency in terms number of successful hits per query and delay in response time. Consequent to our observations, we propose a new search technique exploiting the learning ability and the shortest path distance of node neighbors. The experimental results demonstrate that the Intelligent Walks achieves better performance compared to its counter part Random Walks. Our future work will focus on further experiments on various network platforms including real network and simulation tools to determine the real effect of Dijkstra's shortest path in the overall search process.

References

1. Napster, http://www.napster.com/, 2000
2. Gnutella, "The Gnutella Protocol Specification", http://dss.clip2.com/GnutellaProtocol04.pdf
3. I. Clarke, O. Sandberg, B. Wiley, and T. Hong, "Freenet: A Distributed Anonymous File Storage and Retrieval System", Workshop on Design Issues in Anonymity and Unobservability, 2000.

4. Dimitrios Tsoumakos and Nick Roussopoulos Analysis and Comparison of P2P Search Methods, University of Maryland, USA, 2003
5. Tsungnan Lin, Hsinping Wang. Search Performance Analysis in Peer-to-Peer Networks, Taiwan.
6. Nabhendra Bisnik and Alhussein Abouzeid. Modeling and Analysis of Random Walk Search Algorithms in P2P Networks, Rensselaer Polytechnic Institute, Troy, New York, 2005
7. M. Zhong, and K. Shen Popularity- Biased Random Walks for Peer-to-Peer Search under the Square-Root Principle, University of Rochester, 2006
8. 8. D. Tsoumakos and N. Roussopoulos. Adaptive Probabilistic Search (APS) for Peer-to-Peer Networks.   Technical Report CS-TR-4451, Univerisity of Maryland, 2003.
9. N. Metropolis, A.W. Rosenbluth, M.N. Rosenbluth, A.H. Teller, and E. Teller. Equation of State Calculations by Fast Computing Machines. J. Chem. Phys., 21:1087.1092, 1953.
10. S. Daswani and A. Fisk. Gnutella UDP Extension for Scalable Searches (GUESS) v0.1.
11. Peersim simulator. http://sourceforge.net/projects/peersim
12. Alex Fabrikant, et al; Heuristically Optimized Trade-offs: A New Paradigm for Power Laws in the Internet" (http://cgi.di.uoa.gr/~elias/publications/paper-fkp02.pdf)e

Evolutionary Product-Unit Neural Networks for Classification*

F.J. Martínez-Estudillo[1,**], C. Hervás-Martínez[2], P.A. Gutiérrez Peña[2]
A.C. Martínez-Estudillo[1], and S. Ventura-Soto[2]

[1] Department of Management and Quantitative Methods, ETEA,
Escritor Castilla Aguayo 4, 14005, Córdoba, Spain
Tel.: +34957222120; Fax: +34957222107
fjmestud@etea.com, acme@etea.com
[2] Department of Computing and Numerical Analysis of the
University of Córdoba, Campus de Rabanales, 14071, Córdoba, Spain
chervas@uco.es, zamarck@yahoo.es, sventura@uco.es

Abstract. We propose a classification method based on a special class of feed-forward neural network, namely product-unit neural networks. They are based on multiplicative nodes instead of additive ones, where the nonlinear basis functions express the possible strong interactions between variables. We apply an evolutionary algorithm to determine the basic structure of the product-unit model and to estimate the coefficients of the model. We use softmax transformation as the decision rule and the cross-entropy error function because of its probabilistic interpretation. The empirical results over four benchmark data sets show that the proposed model is very promising in terms of classification accuracy and the complexity of the classifier, yielding a state-of-the-art performance.

Keywords: Classification; Product-Unit; Evolutionary Neural Networks.

1 Introduction

The simplest method for classification provides the class level given its observation via linear functions in the predictor variables. Frequently, in a real-problem of classification, we cannot make the stringent assumption of additive and purely linear effects of the variables. A traditional technique to overcome these difficulties is augmenting/replacing the input vector with new variables, the basis functions, which are transformations of the input variables, and then to using linear models in this new space of derived input features. Once the number and the structure of the basis functions have been determined, the models are linear in these new variables and the fitting is a well known standard procedure. Methods like sigmoidal feed-forward neural networks, projection pursuit learning, generalized additive models [1], and PolyMARS [2], a hybrid of multivariate adaptive splines (MARS) specifically

---

* This work has been financed in part by TIN 2005-08386-C05-02 projects of the Spanish Inter-Ministerial Commission of Science and Technology (MICYT) and FEDER funds.
** Corresponding author.

designed for classification problems, can be seen as different basis function models. The major drawback of these approaches is to state the optimal number and the typology of corresponding basis functions. We tackle this problem proposing a nonlinear model along with an evolutionary algorithm that finds the optimal structure of the model and estimates the corresponding parameters. Concretely, our approach tries to overcome the nonlinear effects of variables by means of a model based on nonlinear basis functions constructed with the product of the inputs raised to arbitrary powers. These basis functions express the possible strong interactions between the variables, where the exponents may even take on real values and are suitable for automatic adjustment. The proposed model corresponds to a special class of feed-forward neural network, namely product-unit neural networks, PUNN, introduced by Durbin and Rumelhart [3]. They are an alternative to sigmoidal neural networks and are based on multiplicative nodes instead of additive ones. Up to now, PUNN have been used mainly to solve regression problems [4], [5].

Evolutionary artificial neural networks (EANNs) have been a key research area in the past decade providing a better platform for optimizing both the weights and the architecture of the network simultaneously. The problem of finding a suitable architecture and the corresponding weights of the network is a very complex task (for a very interesting review on this subject the reader can consult [6]). This problem, together with the complexity of the error surface associated with a product-unit neural network, justifies the use of an evolutionary algorithm to design the structure and training of the weights. The evolutionary process determines the number of basis functions of the model, associated coefficients and corresponding exponents. In our evolutionary algorithm we encourage parsimony in evolved networks by attempting different mutations sequentially. Our experimental results show that evolving parsimonious networks by sequentially applying different mutations is an alternative to the use of a regularization term in the fitness function to penalize large networks. We use the softmax activation function and the cross-entropy error function. From a statistical point of view, the approach can be seen as a nonlinear multinomial logistic regression, where we optimize the log-likelihood using evolutionary computation. Really, we attempt to estimate conditional class probabilities using a multilogistic model, where the nonlinear model is given by a product-unit neural network.

We evaluate the performance of our methodology on four data sets taken from the UCI repository [7]. Empirical results show that the proposed method performs well compared to several learning classification techniques. This paper is organized as follows: Section 2 is dedicated to a description of product-unit based neural networks; Section 3 describes the evolution of product-unit neural networks; Section 4 explains the experiments carried out; and finally, Section 5 shows the conclusions of our work.

2 Product-Unit Neural Networks

In this section we present the family of product-unit basis functions used in the classification process and its representation by means of a neural network structure. This class of multiplicative neural networks comprises such types as sigma-pi networks and product unit networks. A multiplicative node is given by $y_j = \prod_{i=1}^{k} x_i^{w_{ji}}$, where k is the number of the inputs. If the exponents are $\{0,1\}$ we obtain a higher-order unit, also known by the name of sigma-pi unit. In contrast to the sigma-pi unit, in the product-unit the exponents are not fixed and may even take real values.

Some advantages of product-unit based neural networks are increased information capacity and the ability to form higher-order combinations of the inputs. Besides that, it is possible to obtain upper bounds of the VC dimension of product-unit neural networks similar to those obtained for sigmoidal neural networks [8]. Moreover, it is a straightforward consequence of the Stone-Weierstrass Theorem to prove that product-unit neural networks are universal approximators, (observe that polynomial functions in several variables are a subset of product-unit models).

Despite these advantages, product-unit based networks have a major drawback: they have more local minima and more probability of becoming trapped in them [9]. The main reason for this difficulty is that small changes in the exponents can cause large changes in the total error surface and therefore their training is more difficult than the training of standard sigmoidal based networks. Several efforts have been made to carry out learning methods for product units [9],[10]. Studies carried out on PUNNs have not tackled the problem of the simultaneously design of the structure and weights in this kind of neural network, either using classic or evolutionary based methods. Moreover, so far, product units have been applied mainly to solve regression problems. We consider a product-unit neural network with the following structure (Fig. 1): an input layer with k nodes, a node for every input variable, a hidden layer with m nodes and an output layer with J nodes, one for each class level. There are no connections between the nodes of a layer and none between the input and output layers either. The activation function of the j-th node in the hidden layer is given by $B_j(\mathbf{x}, \mathbf{w}_j) = \prod_{i=1}^{k} x_i^{w_{ji}}$, where w_{ji} is the weight of the connection between input node i and hidden node j and $\mathbf{w}_j = (w_{j1},...,w_{jk})$ the weights vector. The activation function of each output node is given by $f_l(\mathbf{x}, \boldsymbol{\theta}) = \beta_0^l + \sum_{j=1}^{m} \beta_j^l B_j(\mathbf{x}, \mathbf{w}_j)$, $l = 1, 2,..., J$, where β_j^l is the weight of the connection between the hidden node j and the output node l. The transfer function of all hidden and output nodes is the identity function. We consider the softmax activation function given by:

$$g_l(\mathbf{x}, \boldsymbol{\theta}_l) = \frac{\exp f_l(\mathbf{x}, \boldsymbol{\theta}_l)}{\sum_{l=1}^{J} \exp f_l(\mathbf{x}, \boldsymbol{\theta}_l)}, l = 1, 2,..., J. \quad (1)$$

where $\boldsymbol{\theta}_l = (\boldsymbol{\beta}^l, \mathbf{w}_1,..., \mathbf{w}_m)$, $\boldsymbol{\theta} = (\boldsymbol{\theta}_1,..., \boldsymbol{\theta}_J)$ and $\boldsymbol{\beta}^l = (\beta_0^l, \beta_1^l,..., \beta_m^l)$. It interesting to note that the model can be regarded as the feed-forward computation of a three-layer neural network where the activation function of each hidden units is $\exp(t) = e^t$ and where we have to do a logarithmic transformation of the input variables x_i, [11].

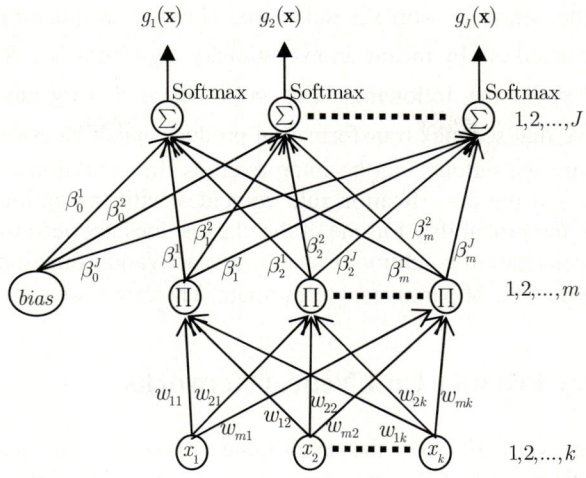

Fig. 1. Model of a product-unit based neural network

3 Classification Problem

In a classification problem, measurements x_i, $i = 1, 2, ..., k$, are taken on a single individual (or object), and the individuals have to be classified into one of the J classes based on these measurements. A training sample $D = \{(\mathbf{x}_n, \mathbf{y}_n); n = 1, 2, ..., N\}$ is available, where $\mathbf{x}_n = (x_{1n}, ..., x_{kn})$ is the random vector of measurements taking values in $\Omega \subset \mathbb{R}^k$, and $\mathbf{y}_n$ is the class level of the n-th individual. We adopt the common technique of representing the class levels using a "1-of-J" encoding vector $\mathbf{y} = \left(y^{(1)}, y^{(2)}..., y^{(J)}\right)$, such as $y^{(l)} = 1$ if $\mathbf{x}$ corresponds to an example belonging to class l; otherwise, $y^{(l)} = 0$. Based on the training sample we try to find a decision function $C : \Omega \to \{1, 2, ..., J\}$ for classifying the individuals. A misclassification occurs when the decision rule C assigns an individual to a class j, when it actually comes from a class $l \neq j$. We define the corrected classified rate by $CCR = \frac{1}{N} \sum_{n=1}^{N} I(C(\mathbf{x}_n) = \mathbf{y}_n)$, where $I(\bullet)$ is the zero-one loss function. A good classifier tries to achieve the highest possible CCR in a given problem. We define the cross-entropy error function for the training observations as:

$$l(\mathbf{\theta}) = -\frac{1}{N} \sum_{n=1}^{N} \sum_{l=1}^{J} y_n^{(l)} \log g_l(\mathbf{x}_n, \mathbf{\theta}_l) = \frac{1}{N} \sum_{n=1}^{N} \left[-\sum_{l=1}^{J} y_n^{(l)} f_l(\mathbf{x}_n, \mathbf{\theta}_l) + \log \sum_{l=1}^{J} \exp f_l(\mathbf{x}_n, \mathbf{\theta}_l) \right] \quad (2)$$

The Hessian matrix of the error function $l(\mathbf{\theta})$ is, in general, indefinite and the error surface associated with the model is very convoluted with numerous local optimums. Moreover, the optimal number of basis functions of the model (i.e. the number of hidden nodes in the neural network) is unknown. Thus, the estimation of the vector parameters $\hat{\boldsymbol{\theta}}$ is carried out by means an evolutionary algorithm (see Section 4). The optimum rule $C(\mathbf{x})$ is the following: $C(\mathbf{x}) = \hat{l}$, where $\hat{l} = \arg\max_l g_l(\mathbf{x},\hat{\boldsymbol{\theta}})$, for $l = 1,...,J$. Observe that softmax transformation produces positive estimates that sum to one and therefore the outputs can be interpreted as the conditional probability of class membership and the classification rule coincides with the optimal Bayes rule. On the other hand, the probability for one of the classes does not need to be estimated, because of the normalization condition. Usually, one activation function is set to zero and we reduce the number of parameters to estimate. Therefore, we set $f_J(\mathbf{x},\boldsymbol{\theta}_J) = 0$.

4 Evolutionary Product-Unit Neural Networks

In this paragraph we carry out the evolutionary product-unit neural networks algorithm (EPUNN) to estimate the parameter that minimizes the cross-entropy error function. We build an evolutionary algorithm to design the structure and learn the weights of the networks. The search begins with an initial population of product-unit neural networks, and, in each iteration, the population is updated using a population-update algorithm. The population is subjected to the operations of replication and mutation. Crossover is not used due to its potential disadvantages in evolving artificial networks. With these features the algorithm falls into the class of evolutionary programming .The general structure of the EA is the following:

(1) Generate a random population of size N_p.
(2) Repeat until the stopping criterion is fulfilled
    (a) Calculate the fitness of every individual in the population.
    (b) Rank the individuals with respect to their fitness.
    (c) The best individual is copied into the new population.
    (d) The best 10% of population individuals are replicated and substitute the worst 10% of individuals.
    Over that intermediate population we:
    (e) Apply parametric mutation to the best 10% of individuals.
    (f) Apply structural mutation to the remaining 90% of individuals.

We consider $l(\boldsymbol{\theta})$ being the error function of an individual g of the population. Observe that g can be seen as the multivaluated function $g(\mathbf{x},\boldsymbol{\theta}) = (g_1(\mathbf{x},\boldsymbol{\theta}_1),...,g_l(\mathbf{x},\boldsymbol{\theta}_l))$. The fitness measure is a strictly decreasing transformation of the error function $l(\boldsymbol{\theta})$ given by $A(g) = (1+l(\boldsymbol{\theta}))^{-1}$. Parametric mutation is accomplished for each coefficient w_{ji}, β_j^l of the model with Gaussian noise: $w_{ji}(t+1) = w_{ji}(t) + \xi_1(t)$, $\beta_j^l(t+1) = \beta_j^l(t) + \xi_2(t)$, where $\xi_k(t) \in N(0,\alpha_k(t))$, $k = 1,2$, represents a one-dimensional normally-distributed random variable with mean 0 and variance $\alpha_k(t)$, where $\alpha_1(t) < \alpha_2(t)$, and t is the t-th generation. Once the mutation is performed, the fitness of the individual is recalculated and the usual simulated annealing is applied. Thus, if ΔA is the difference in the fitness function after and preceding the random step, the criterion is: if $\Delta A \geq 0$ the step is accepted, if $\Delta A < 0$, the step is accepted with a probability $\exp(\Delta A / T(g))$, where the temperature $T(g)$ of an individual g is given by $T(g) = 1 - A(g)$, $0 \leq T(g) < 1$.

The variance $\alpha_k(t)$ is updated throughout the evolution of the algorithm. There are different methods to update the variance. We use the 1/5 success rule of Rechenberg, one of the simplest methods. This rule states that the ratio of successful mutations should be 1/5. Therefore, if the ratio of successful mutations is larger than 1/5, the mutation deviation should increase; otherwise, the deviation should decrease. Thus:

$$\alpha_k(t+s) = \begin{cases} (1+\lambda)\alpha_k(t) & \text{if } s_g > 1/5 \\ (1-\lambda)\alpha_k(t), & \text{if } s_g < 1/5 \\ \alpha_k(t) & \text{if } s_g = 1/5 \end{cases} \qquad (3)$$

where $k = 1, 2$, s_g is the frequency of successful mutations over s generations and $\lambda = 0.1$. The adaptation tries to avoid being trapped in local minima and also to speed up the evolutionary process when searching conditions are suitable.

Structural mutation implies a modification in the neural network structure and allows explorations of different regions in the search space while helping to keep up the diversity of the population. There are five different structural mutations: node deletion, connection deletion, node addition, connection addition and node fusion. These five mutations are applied sequentially to each network. In the node fusion, two randomly selected hidden nodes, a and b, are replaced by a new node, c, which is a combination of both. The connections that are common to both nodes are kept, with weights given by: $\beta_c^l = \beta_a^l + \beta_b^l$, $w_{jc} = \dfrac{1}{2}(w_{ja} + w_{jb})$. The connections that are not shared by the nodes are inherited by c with a probability of 0.5 and its weight is unchanged. In our algorithm, node or connection deletion and node fusion is always attempted before addition. If a deletion or fusion mutation is successful, no other mutation will be made. If the probability does not select any mutation, one of the mutations is chosen at random and applied to the network.

5 Experiments

The parameters used in the evolutionary algorithm are common for the four problems. We have considered $\alpha_1(0) = 0.5$, $\alpha_2(0) = 1$, $\lambda = 0.1$ and $s = 5$. The exponents w_{ji} are initialized in the $[-5,5]$ interval, the coefficients β_j^l are initialized in $[-5,5]$. The maximum number of hidden nodes is $m = 6$. The size of the population is $N_P = 1000$. The number of nodes that can be added or removed in a structural mutation is within the $[1,2]$ interval. The number of connections that can be added or removed in a structural mutation is within the $[1,6]$ interval. The stop criterion is reached if the following condition is fulfilled: for 20 generations there is no improvement either in the average performance of the best 20% of the population or in the fitness of the best individual. We have done a simple linear rescaling of the input variables in the interval $[1,2]$, being X_i^* the transformed variables.

We evaluate the performance of our method on four data sets taken from the UCI repository [7]. For every dataset we performed ten runs of ten-fold stratified cross-validation. This gives a hundred data points for each dataset, from which the average classification accuracy and standard deviation is calculated. Table 1 shows the statistical results over 10 runs for each fold of the evolutionary algorithm for the four data sets. With the objective of presenting an empirical evaluation of the performance of the EPUNN method, we compare our approach to the most recent results [12] obtained using different methodologies (see Table 2). Logistic model tree, LMT, to logistic regression (with attribute selection, SLogistic, and for a full logistic model, MLogistic); induction trees (C4.5 and CART); two logistic tree algorithms: LTreeLog and finally, multiple-tree models M5´ for classification, and boosted C4.5 trees using AdaBoost.M1 with 10 and 100 boosting interactions. We can see that the results obtained by EPUNN, with architectures (13:2:2), (34:3:2), (4:5:3) and (51:3:2) for each data set, are competitive with the learning schemes mentioned previously.

Table 1. Statistical results of training and testing for 30 executions of EPUNN model

Data set	CCR_T				CCR_G				#connect		#node
	Mean	SD	Best	Worst	Mean	SD	Best	Worst	Mean	SD	
Heart-stat	84.65	1.63	88.48	80.25	**81.89**	6.90	**96.30**	62.96	14.78	3.83	2
Ionosphere	93.79	1.46	97.15	90.19	**89.63**	5.52	**100**	74.29	43.97	13.87	3
Balance	97.26	0.98	99.47	94.32	**95.69**	2.36	**100**	90.32	25.62	2.18	5
Australian	87.01	0.82	88.57	85.02	**85.74**	3.90	**95.65**	78.26	44.13	16.26	3

Table 2. Mean classification accuracy and standard deviation for: LMT, SLogistic, MLogistic, C4.5, CART, NBTree, LTreeLin, LTreeLog, M5', ABOOST and EPUNN method

Data set	LMT	SLogistic	MLogistic	C4.5	CART	NBTree
Heart-stat	83.22±6.50	83.30±6.48	**83.67±6.43**	78.15±7.42	78.00±8.25	80.59±7.12
Ionosphere	92.99±4.13	87.78±4.99	87.72±5.57	89.74±4.38	89.80±4.78	89.49±5.12
Balance	89.71±2.68	88.74±2.91	89.44±3.29	77.82±3.42	78.09±3.97	75.83±5.32
Australian	85.04±3.84	85.04±3.97	85.33±3.85	85.57±3.96	84.55±4.20	85.07±4.03
Data set	LTreeLin	LTreeLog	M5'	ABoost(10)	ABoost(100)	EPUNN	W/L
Heart-stat	83.52±6.28	83.00±6.83	82.15±6.77	78.59±7.15	80.44±7.08	81.89±6.90	5/6
Ionosphere	88.95±5.10	88.18±5.06	89.92±4.18	93.05±3.92	**94.02±3.83**	89.63±5.52	7/4
Balance	**92.86±3.22**	92.78±3.49	87.76±2.23	78.35±3.78	76.11±4.09	95.69±2.36	11/0
Australian	84.99±3.91	84.64±4.09	85.39±3.87	84.01±4.36	**86.43±3.98**	85.74±3.90	10/1

6 Conclusions

We propose a classification method that combines a nonlinear model, based on a special class of feed-forward neural network, namely product-unit neural networks, and an evolutionary algorithm that finds the optimal structure of the model and estimates the corresponding parameters. Up to now, the studies on product units have been applied mainly to solve regression problems and have not addressed the problem of the design of both structure and weights simultaneously in this kind of neural network, either using classic or evolutionary based methods. Our approach uses softmax transformation and the cross-entropy error function. From a statistical point of view, the approach can be seen as nonlinear multinomial logistic regression, where optimization of the log-likelihood is made by using evolutionary computation. The empirical results show that the evolutionary product-unit model performs well compared to other learning classification techniques. We obtain very promising results in terms of classification accuracy and the complexity of the classifier.

References

[1] T. J. Hastie and R. J. Tibshirani, Generalized Additive Models. London: Chapman & Hall, 1990.
[2] C. Kooperberg, S. Bose, and C. J. Stone, "Polychotomous Regression," Journal of the American Statistical Association, vol. 92, pp. 117-127, 1997.
[3] R. Durbin and D. Rumelhart, "Products Units: A computationally powerful and biologically plausible extension to backpropagation networks," Neural Computation, vol. 1, pp. 133-142, 1989.
[4] A. C. Martínez-Estudillo, F. J. Martínez-Estudillo, C. Hervás-Martínez, et al., "Evolutionary Product Unit based Neural Networks for Regression," Neural Networks, pp. 477-486, 2006.
[5] A. C. Martínez-Estudillo, C. Hervás-Martínez, A. C. Martínez-Estudillo, et al., "Hybridation of evolutionary algorithms and local search by means of a clustering method," IEEE Transactions on Systems, Man and Cybernetics, Part. B: Cybernetics, vol. 36, pp. 534-546, 2006.
[6] X. Yao, "Evolving artificial neural network," Proceedings of the IEEE, vol. 9 (87), pp. 1423-1447, 1999.
[7] C. Blake and C. J. Merz, " UCI repository of machine learning data bases," www.ics.uci.edu/ mlearn/MLRepository.thml, 1998.
[8] M. Schmitt, "On the Complexity of Computing and Learning with Multiplicative Neural Networks," Neural Computation, vol. 14, pp. 241-301, 2001.
[9] A. Ismail and A. P. Engelbrecht, "Global optimization algorithms for training product units neural networks," presented at International Joint Conference on Neural Networks IJCNN`2000, Como, Italy, 2000.
[10] A. P. Engelbrecht and A. Ismail, "Training product unit neural networks," Stability and Control: Theory and Applications, vol. 2, pp. 59-74, 1999.
[11] K. Saito and R. Nakano, "Extracting Regression Rules From Neural Networks," Neural Networks, vol. 15, pp. 1279-1288, 2002.
[12] N. Landwehr, M. Hall, and F. Eibe, "Logistic Model Trees," Machine Learning, vol. 59, pp. 161-205, 2005.

Answers to the Referees

Referee 1

The functional model defined by the product-unit neural network is given by

$$(1) \quad f_l(\mathbf{x},\boldsymbol{\theta}) = \beta_0^l + \sum_{j=1}^{m} \beta_j^l B_j(\mathbf{x},\mathbf{w}_j), \quad l=1,2,\ldots,J$$

where $B_j(\mathbf{x},\mathbf{w}_j) = \prod_{i=1}^{k} x_i^{w_{ji}}$. We are agreeing with the referee 1 that this expression is analytically equivalent to the expression:

$$(2) \quad f_l(\mathbf{x},\boldsymbol{\theta}) = \beta_0^l + \sum_{j=1}^{m} \beta_j^l \exp\left(\sum_{j=1}^{n} w_{ji} \ln(x_i)\right), \quad l=1,2,\ldots,J$$

This equation can be regarded as the feed-forward computation of a three-layer neural network where the activation function of each hidden units is $\exp(t) = e^t$ and where we have done a logarithmic transformation inputs variables x_i. Therefore we can have different architectures of the same functional model. We have chosen the architecture associated to the first equation because it is easier.

However, the functional model given by (1), or equivalent by (2), is different from the functional model of MLP. The function that a classic multilayer feed-forward network computes is

$$(3) \quad f_l(\mathbf{x},\boldsymbol{\theta}) = \beta_0^l + \sum_{j=1}^{m} \beta_j^l \sigma\left(\sum_{j=1}^{n} w_{ji} x_i - \theta_j\right), \quad l=1,2,\ldots,J$$

where σ is a sigmoidal function.

From an analytical point of view, the model defined by (3) is different to the (1) and (2) ones.

We have included in the page 3 of the paper a brief comment about this question.

Referee 2

There are a reduced number of papers dealing with product-unit neural networks. For this, the references could seem a bit outdated. We have included in the paper more recent references ([4], [5], [11]) to solve this question. On the other hand, a deeper analysis about the "why" of the motivation on the problem and the theoretical justification of the product-unit approach would need a long and extensive paper to explain the VC dimension of the PU and the upper bounds of the VC dimension obtained in Schmitt [10].

Uncentered (Absolute) Correlation Clustering Method Fit for Establishing Theoretical SAPK/JNK Signaling Pathway in Human Soft Tissue Sarcoma Samples

Jinling Zhang[1], Yinghua Lu[1], Lin Wang[1,2], Hongxin Zhang[1], Bo Zhang[1], Yeqiu Wang[1], Kai Wu[1], and Stefan Wolfl[2]

[1] Biomedical center, School of Electronic Eng.,
Beijing University of Posts and Telecommunication, Beijing 100876, China
[2] Institute of Pharmacia & Molecular Biotech., Dept. Biology - Bioanalytic,
University Heidelberg, 69120 Heidelberg, Germany
yangjsh218@sohu.com, wanglin98@tsinghua.org.cn

Abstract. The aim of this research is to use and compare clustering technologies and find the best method for establishing theoretical SAPK/JNK signaling pathway in human soft tissue sarcoma samples. Centroid linkage, Single linkage, complete linkage and average linkage hierarchical clustering are used to arrange genes for setup signaling pathways according to similarity in pattern of gene. The results show that centriod linkage, complete linkage, and average linking clustering architecture is consistent with the core unit of the cascade composed of a CDC42, a MEKK1 (map3k1), a MKK4 (map2k4), a JNK1(mapk8) to a ATF2 in hierarchical clustering. An activated Jnk phosphorylates a variety of transcription factors regulating gene expression, such as ATF2. This study implies that centroid linkage, complete linkage and average linkage clustering method in uncentered (absolute) correlation similarity measures fits for establishing theoretical SAPK/Jnk signaling pathway in human soft tissue sarcoma samples which is consistent with biological experimental SAPK/Jnk signaling pathway

1 Introduction

Molecular biologists and geneticists are working energetically to understand the function of genes and signaling pathways by bioinformatics. There is a great demand to develop an analytical methodology to analyze and to exploit the information contained in gene expression data. Because of the large number of genes and the complexity of biological networks, clustering is a useful exploratory technique for analysis of gene expression data. Many clustering algorithms have been proposed for gene expression data. For example, Eisen et al [1] applied a variant of the hierarchical average link clustering algorithm to identify groups of co-regulated yeast genes. Ben-Dor and Yakhini reported success with their CAST algorithm [2]. Other classical techniques, such as principal component analysis, have also been applied to analyze gene expression data [3]. Using different data analysis techniques and different cluster algorithms to analyze the same datasets can lead to very different conclusions.

Signaling pathway study has driven the development of methods to exploit this information by characterizing biological processes in new ways, and already provided a wealth of biological insight. Hierarchical clustering is widely used to find patterns in multi-dimensional datasets, especially for genomic microarray data [4, 5]. We use hierarchical clustering to studied SAPK/JNK signaling pathway.

Stress-activated protein kinases (SAPK) /Jun N-terminal kinase (JNK) are members of the MAPK family and are activated by variety of environmental stresses, inflammatory cytokines, growth factors and GPCR agonists. Stress signals are delivered to this cascade by members of small GTPases of the Rho family (Rac, Rho, cdc42). As with the other MAPKs, the membrane proximal kinase is a MAPKKK, typically MEKK1-4, or a member of the mixed lineage kinases (MLK) that phosphorylates and activates MKK4 (SEK) or MKK7, the SAPK/JNK kinase Alternatively, MKK4/7be can activated by a member of the germinal center kinase (GCK) family in a GTPase-independent manner. SAPK/JNK translocates to the nucleus where it regulates the activity of several transcription factors such as c-Jun, ATF-2 AND p53 [6-10].

Cdc is named as Cell division cycle 42 (GTP binding protein, 25kDa). MEKK1 also called map3k1, which is named as MAP/ERK kinase kinase 1. MKK1 is also called MAP2K4, which is named Mitogen-activated protein kinase kinase 4. JNK1 is also called mapk8, which is named Mitogen-activated protein kinase 8. ATF2 is named as cAMP responsive element binding protein 2, and is also called creb-2.

2 Materials and Methods

2.1 Data Sources

Our gene expression data are downloaded from http://www.ncbi.nlm.nih.gov/geo in 3/12/2006. Database Name is Gene Expression Omnibus (GEO), Database ref is Nucleic Acids Res. 2005 Jan 1; 33 Database Issue: D562-6. Dataset title is Sarcoma and hypoxia. Dataset type is gene expression array-based, dataset platform organism is Homo sapiens by situ oligonucleotide of cDNA, dataset feature count is 22283, dataset channel count is 1, dataset sample count is 54.

2.2 Clustering Techniques

A variety of clustering methods have been used in many areas to discover interesting patterns in large datasets. Among the methods, hierarchical clustering has been shown to be effective in microarray data analysis. This approach finds the pair of genes with the most similar expression profiles, and iteratively builds a hierarchy by pairing genes (or existing clusters) that are most similar. The resulting hierarchy is shown using dendrograms.

There are a variety of ways to compute distances when we are dealing with pseudo-items, and Cluster currently provides four choices, which are called centroid linkage, single linkage, complete linkage and average linkage. Centroid Linkage Clustering is that a vector is assigned to each pseudo-item, and this vector is used to compute the distances between this pseudo-item and all remaining items or pseudo-items using the same similarity metric as were used to calculate the initial similarity matrix. The vector is the average of the vectors of all actual items (e.g. genes) contained within the pseudo-item. In Complete Linkage Clustering the distance between two items x and y is the maximum of all pairwise distances between items contained in x and y. In average linkage clustering, the distance between two items x and y is the mean of all pairwise distances between items contained in x and y. In Single Linkage Clustering the distance between two items x and y is the minimum of all pairwise distances between items contained in x and y.

2.2.1 Distance / Similarity Measurement

Distance measurement based on the Pearson correlation. The most commonly used similarity metrics are based on Pearson correlation. The Pearson correlation coefficient between any two series of numbers $x = \{x_1, x_2, \cdots, x_n\}$ and $y = \{y_1, y_2, \cdots, y_n\}$ is defined as:

$$r = \frac{1}{n}\sum_{i=1}^{n}\left(\frac{x_i - \bar{x}}{\sigma_x}\right)\left(\frac{y_i - \bar{y}}{\sigma_y}\right) \tag{1}$$

$$\sigma_x = \sqrt{\sum_{i=1}^{n}\frac{(x-\bar{x})^2}{n}} \tag{2}$$

Where $\bar{x}$ is the average of values in x, and σ_x is the standard deviation of these values. The Pearson correlation coefficient is always between -1 and 1, with 1 meaning that the two series are identical, 0 meaning they are completely uncorrelated, and -1 meaning they are perfectly opposites. The correlation coefficient is invariant under linear transformation of the data.

Cluster actually uses four different flavors of the Pearson correlation. Pearson correlation coefficient, given by the formula above, is used if you select Correlation (centered) in the Similarity Metric dialog box. Correlation (uncentered) uses the following modified equation:

$$r = \frac{1}{n}\sum_{i=1}^{n}\left(\frac{x_i}{\sigma_x^{(0)}}\right)\left(\frac{y_i}{\sigma_y^{(0)}}\right) \tag{3}$$

where

$$\sigma_x^{(0)} = \sqrt{\frac{1}{n}\sum_{i=1}^{n}(x_i)^2}, \quad \sigma_y^{(0)} = \sqrt{\frac{1}{n}\sum_{i=1}^{n}(y_i)^2} \tag{4}$$

This is basically the same function, except that it assumes the mean is 0, even when it is not. The difference is that, if you have two vectors x and y with identical shape, but which are offset relative to each other by a fixed value, they will have a standard Pearson correlation (centered correlation) of 1 but will not have an uncentered correlation of 1. The uncentered correlation is equal to the cosine of the angle of two n-dimensional vectors x and y, each representing a vector in n- dimensional space that passes through the origin. Cluster provides two similarity metrics that are the absolute value of these two correlation functions, which consider two items to be similar if they have opposite expression patterns; the standard correlation coefficients considering opposite genes are being very unrelated.

Distance measurement related to the Euclidean distance. A newly added distance function is the Euclidean distance, which is defined as:

$$d(\underline{x},\underline{y}) = \sum_{i=1}^{n}(x_i - y_i)^2 \qquad (5)$$

The Euclidean distance takes the difference between two gene expression levels directly. It should therefore only be used for expression data that are suitably normalized. An example of the Euclidean distance applied to k-means clustering can be found in De Hoon, Imoto, and Miyano [11].

Harmonically summed Euclidean distance. The harmonically summed Euclidean distance is a variation of the Euclidean distance, where the terms for the different dimensions are summed inversely (similar to the harmonic mean):

$$d(\underline{x},\underline{y}) = \left[\frac{1}{n}\sum_{i=1}^{n}\left(\frac{1}{x_i - y_i}\right)^2\right]^{-1} \qquad (6)$$

The harmonically summed Euclidean distance is more robust against outliers compared with the Euclidean distance. Note that the harmonically summed Euclidean distance is not a metric.

Hierarchical clustering using spearman rank correlation. Spearman's rank coefficient requires data that are at least ordinal and the calculation, which is the same as for Pearson correlation, is carried out on the ranks of the data. Each variable is ranked separately by putting the values of the variable in order and numbering them: the lowest value is given rank 1, the next lowest is given rank 2 and so on. If two data values for the variable are the same they are given averaged ranks. Spearman's rank correlation coefficient is used as a measure of linear relationship between two sets of ranked data, that is, it measures how tightly the ranked data clusters around a straight line.

Hierarchical clustering using kendall's tau. Kendall's tau is a measure of correlation, and so measures the strength of the relationship between two variables. We require that the two variables, X and Y, are paired observations. for example, degree of deviation from diet guidelines and degree of deviation from fluid guidelines, for each patient in the sample. Then, provided both variables are at least ordinal, it would be possible to calculate the correlation between them.

Hierarchical clustering using City-block distance. The city-block distance, alternatively known as the Manhattan distance, is related to the Euclidean distance. Whereas the Euclidean distance corresponds to the length of the shortest path between two points, the city-block distance is the sum of distances along each dimension:

$$d = \sum_{i=1}^{n} |x_i - y_i| \qquad (7)$$

The city-block distance is a metric, as it satisfies the triangle inequality. As for the Euclidean distance, the expression data are subtracted directly from each other, and we should therefore make sure that they are properly normalized.

2.2.2 Clustering Method

Sample data which from http://www.ncbi.nlm.nih.gov/geo, we use correlation uncentered, correlation centered, absolute correlation uncentered, absolute correlation centered, spearman rank correlation, kendall's tau, Edclidean distance, city-block distance, Edclidean distance harmonic in single linkage, centroid linkage, complete linkage and average linkage of Hierarchical clustering respectively, and the steps are as follows :

Step 1 Loading and filtering data;
Step 2 Normalizing for adjusting data;
Step 3 Choosing similarity methods, measuring the distance/similarity;
Step 4 Choosing Hierarchical Cluster;
Step 5 Doing TreeView.

3 Results and Discussion

Sample data as shown in table.1 (7 sample data of 54 sample data), we use Pearson correlation, absolute correlation, Euclidean distance, spearman rank correlation, kendall's tau, and City-block distance, etc. in single linkage, centroid linkage, complete linkage and average linkage of Hierarchical clustering respectively, and the steps repeat the above steps from 1 to 6. The complete source code of Cluster is now open. If you are interested, it can be easily found and downloaded from http://bonsai.ims.tokyo.ac.jp/~mdehoon/software/cluster. The process is summarized by the following hierarchical tree as shown in Fig.1, Fig.2 and Fig.3.

Table 1. The genes expression data human soft tissue sarcoma samples

Genes	GSM 52556	GSM 52557	GSM 52558	GSM 52559	GSM 52560	GSM 52561	...	GSM 52609
Cdc42	2525.9	268.5	2343.1	435.8	999.7	266.9	...	527.5
mekk1	19.8	242.1	174.8	16.4	178.3	190.7	...	193
Mkk4	403.6	299.8	183.7	286.9	229.6	267.1	...	541.9
Jnk1	202.2	28.6	57.7	274.4	175.3	89	...	156.3
Atf2	336.9	288.9	153.4	164.1	223.4	240.6	...	383.4

Centroid linkage, complete linkage and average linkage clustering methods are used in uncentered (absolute) correlation similarity, the dendrograms as shown in Fig.1. The pattern is ATF2 and JNK1 clustering then and MKK4, MEKK1, CDC42 clustering which form their relative signaling pathway take turns, this clustering results is in accorded with main pathways of SAP kinase(Jnk) signaling pathways by experiment (show in Fig.4) from http://www.cellsignal.com. Because of data is quite approximate and all plus, we used uncentered similarity clustering method. It is shown that our method is suitable for establishing theoretical SAPK/Jnk signaling pathway of human soft tissue sarcoma samples.

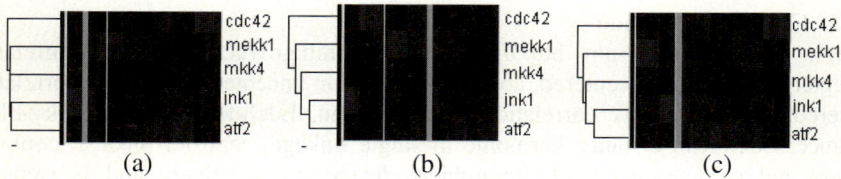

Fig. 1. Uncentered (absolute) correlation (a) in centroid linkage, (b) in complete linkage, (c) in everage linkage. ATF2 and JNK1 clustering then and MKK4, MEKK1, CDC42 clustering take turns

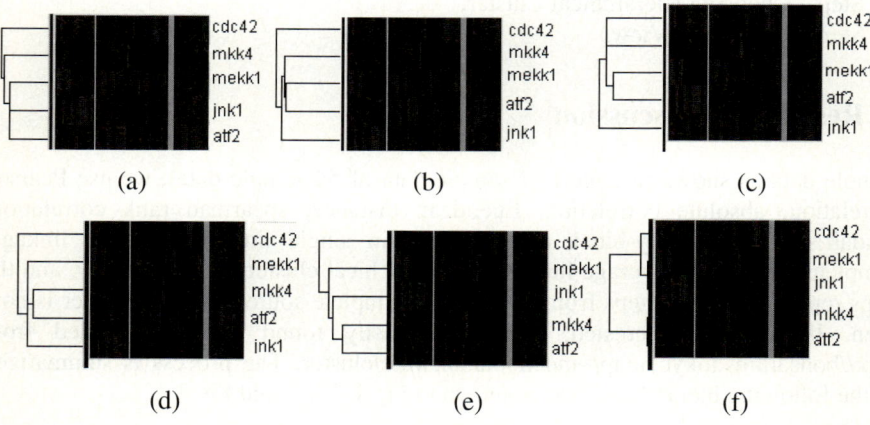

Fig. 2. In single linkage (a) correlation uncentered and absolute correlation (uncentered), (b) correlation centered, (c) absolute correlation (centered), (d) spearman rank correlation and kendall's tau, (e) Edclidean distance and city-block distance, (f) Edclidean distance harmonic

The single linkage cluster result about CDC42, MEKK1, MKK4, JNK1 and ATF2, as shown in Fig.2 is not consistent with biological experimental SAPK/Jnk signaling pathway. Because in Single Linkage Clustering the distance between two items x and y is the minimum of all pairwise distances between items contained in x and y, however, in our dataset two items similarity can be lower. It is obvious that These data is not fit to the clustering analysis using single linkage, but Single Linkage Clustering is fit for establish MAPK/Erk signaling pathway of human soft tissue sarcoma samples. It is also shown that methods are different for different signaling pathways in the same gene dataset.

The agreement is not generally good among our results in centroid linkage, single linkage, complete linkage and average linkage clustering methods and experiments results in genes signaling pathway as shown in Fig.3, which only showed average linkage clustering method's dendrograms. It is shown that these clustering methods are not fit for establishing theoretical SAPK/Jnk signaling pathway of human soft tissue sarcoma samples.

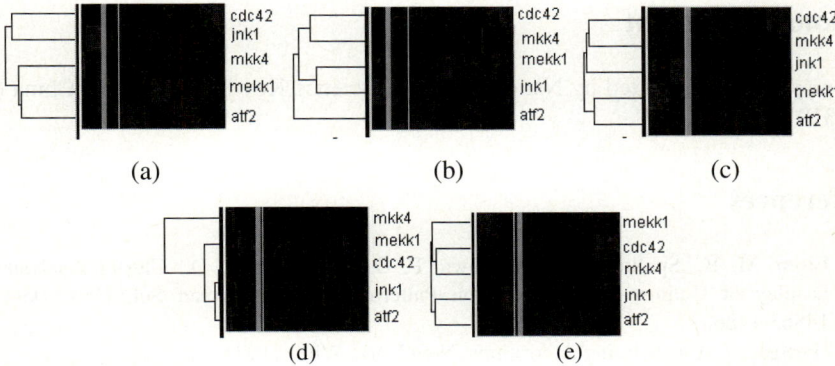

Fig. 3. In average linkage (a) centered and pearman rank correlation and kendall's tau, (b) absolute correlation (centered), (c) Edclidean distance and spearman rank correlation, (d) Edclidean distance harmonic, (e) city-block distance

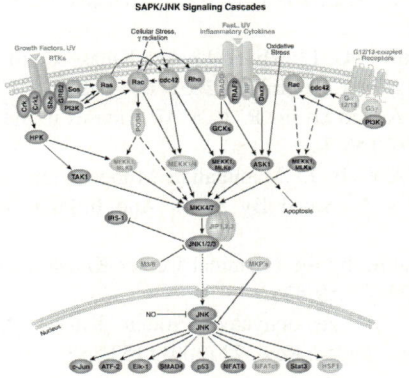

Fig. 4. SAP kinase (Jnk) signaling pathway

4 Conclusion

This study implies that uncentered (absolute) correlation in centroid linkage, complete linkage and average linkage clustering from a CDC42, a MEKK1, a MKK4, a JNK1 to a ATF2.fist for establishing theoretical SAPK/Jnk signaling pathway in human soft tissue sarcoma samples which is consistent with biological experimental SAPK/Jnk signaling pathway Fig.4 from http://www.cellsignal.com. We are able to determine that how many genes are needed in order to estimate the unknown signaling pathway of human soft tissue sarcoma samples. Our clustering method may be one of the methods that establish unknown signaling pathway of human soft tissue sarcoma samples, which can also give a new method in drug making for anti cancer, because when the signaling pathway is broken, the soft tissue sarcoma can be suppressed.

Acknowledgement

The project was supported by National Natural Science Key Foundation of China (No. 60331010).

References

1. Eisen, M. B., Spellman, P. T., Brown, P. O., and Botstein, D.: Cluster Analysis and Display of Genome-wide Expression Patterns. Proc Natl Acad Sci, USA, 95(1998) 14863-14868
2. Hartigan, J. A. Clustering Algorithms, New York: Wiley (1975)
3. Yeung, K. Y., and Ruzzo, W. L.: Principal Component Analysis for Clustering Gene Expression Data. Bioinformatics, 17(2001) 763-774
4. Johnson, S.C.: Hierarchical Clustering Schemes. Psychometrika, 32 (1967) 241-254
5. Karypis, G., Eui-Hong H., Kumar, V.: Chameleon: A Hierarchical Clustering Algorithm Using Dynamic Modeling. IEEE Computer, 32(8), (1999) 68 -75
6. Weston, C R. and Davis, R. J.: The JNK Signal Transduction Pathway. Curr Opin. Genet . Dev., 12 (2002) 14-21
7. Gallo, K. A. and Johnson, G. L.: Mixed-lineage Kinase Control of JNK and p38 MAPK Pathway. Nature Rev. Mol. Cell Biol., 3 (2002) 663-672
8. Dong, C., Flavell, R. A. and Dvais, R. J.: MAP Kinases in the Immune Response. Annu. Rev. Immunol, 20 (2002) 55-72
9. Kyriakis, J. M. and Avruch, J.: Mammalian Mitogen-Activated Protein Kinase Signal Transduction Pathways Activated By Stress And Inflammation. Physiol Reviews, 81 (2001) 807-886
10. Kyriakis, J. M.: Signaling by the Germinal Center Kinase Family of Protein Kinases. J. BIOL. Chem., 274 (1999) 5259-5262
11. Pearson, G., et al.: Mitogen-activated Protein Kinase Pathways: Regulation and Physiological Functions. Endoc. Rev., 22 (2001) 153-183

Guiding Genetic Program Based Data Mining Using Fuzzy Rules

James F. Smith III and ThanhVu H. Nguyen

Code 5741
Naval Research Laboratory
Washington, DC, 20375-5320
jfsmith@drsews.nrl.navy.mil

Abstract. A data mining procedure for automatic determination of fuzzy decision tree structure using a genetic program is discussed. A genetic program (GP) is an algorithm that evolves other algorithms or mathematical expressions. Methods for accelerating convergence of the data mining procedure are examined. The methods include introducing fuzzy rules into the GP and a new innovation based on computer algebra. Experimental results related to using computer algebra are given. Comparisons between trees created using a genetic program and those constructed solely by interviewing experts are made. Connections to past GP based data mining procedures for evolving fuzzy decision trees are established. Finally, experimental methods that have been used to validate the data mining algorithm are discussed.

Keywords: Genetic Programs, Fuzzy Logic, Data Mining, Control Algorithms, Planning Algorithms.

1 Introduction

Two fuzzy logic based resource managers (RMs) have been developed that automatically allocate resources in real-time [1-3]. Both RMs were evolved by genetic programs (GPs). The GPs were used as data mining functions. Both RMs have been subjected to a significant number of verification experiments.

The most recently developed RM is the main subject of this paper. This RM automatically allocates unmanned aerial vehicles (UAVs) that will ultimately measure atmospheric properties in a cooperative fashion without human intervention [2,3]. This RM will be referred to as the UAVRM. It consists of a pre-mission planning algorithm and a real-time control algorithm that runs on each UAV during the mission allowing the UAVs to automatically cooperate.

The previous RM was evolved to control electronic attack functions distributed over many platforms [1]. It will be referred to as the electronic attack RM (EARM).

This paper introduces many novel features not found in the literature. These include several new approaches for improving the convergence of the genetic program that evolves control and planning logic. Such procedures involve the use of symbolic algebra techniques not previously explored, a terminal set that includes both fuzzy concepts and their complements, the use of fuzzy rules, etc. The control algorithm evolved by a GP is compared to one created through expertise. Experiments to validate the evolved algorithm are discussed.

Section 2 gives a brief discussion of fuzzy decision trees (FDTs), how FDTs are used in the UAVRM, genetic programs and GP based data mining (DM). Section 3 describes the UAVRM's FDT that assign UAVs to paths. Section 4 examines how a fuzzy decision tree for the UAVRM was created through GP based data mining. Section 5 discusses experiments that have been conducted to validate the FDT that assigns UAVs to paths (AUP). Finally, section 6 provides a summary.

2 Fuzzy Decision Trees and Genetic Program Based Data Mining

The particular approach to fuzzy logic used by the UAVRM is the fuzzy decision tree [1-5]. The fuzzy decision tree is an extension of the classical artificial intelligence concept of decision trees. The nodes of the tree of degree one, the leaf nodes are labeled with what are referred to as root concepts. Nodes of degree greater than unity are labeled with composite concepts, i.e., concepts constructed from the root concepts [6,7] using logical connectives and modifiers. Each root concept has a fuzzy membership function assigned to it. Each root concept membership function has parameters to be determined. For the UAVRM, the parameters were set based on expertise.

The UAVRM consists of three fuzzy decision trees. Only the creation of the FDT by GP based data mining for assigning UAVs to paths will be considered in this paper. This FDT is referred to as the AUP tree; and the associated fuzzy concept, as AUP. The AUP tree makes use of the risk tree which is discussed in the literature [2, 3].

Data mining is the efficient extraction of valuable non-obvious information embedded in a large quantity of data [8]. Data mining consists of three steps: the construction of a database that represents truth; the calling of the data mining function to extract the valuable information, e.g., a clustering algorithm, neural net, genetic algorithm, genetic program, etc; and finally determining the value of the information extracted in the second step, this generally involves visualization.

In a previous paper a genetic algorithm (GA) was used as a data mining function to determine parameters for fuzzy membership functions [7]. Here, a different data mining function, a genetic program [9] is used. A genetic program is a problem independent method for automatically evolving computer programs or mathematical expressions.

The GP data mines fuzzy decision tree structure, i.e., how vertices and edges are connected and labeled in a fuzzy decision tree. The GP mines the information from a database consisting of scenarios.

3 UAV Path Assignment Algorithm, the AUP Tree

Knowledge of meteorological properties is fundamental to many decision processes. The UAVRM enables a team of UAVs to cooperate and support each other as they measure atmospheric meteorological properties in real-time. Each UAV has onboard its own fuzzy logic based real-time control algorithm. The control algorithm renders each UAV fully autonomous; no human intervention is necessary. The control algorithm aboard each UAV will allow it to determine its own course, change course to avoid danger, sample phenomena of interest that were not preplanned, and cooperate with other UAVs.

The UAVRM determines the minimum number of UAVs required for the sampling mission. It also determines which points are to be sampled and which UAVs will do the sampling. To do this, both in the planning and control stages it must solve an optimization problem to determine the various paths that must be flown. Once these paths are determined the UAVRM uses the AUP fuzzy decision tree to assign UAVs to the paths.

The AUP fuzzy decision tree is displayed in Figure 1. The various fuzzy root concepts make up the leaves of the tree, i.e., those vertices of degree one. The vertices of degree higher than one are composite concepts.

Starting from the bottom left of Figure 1 and moving to the right, the fuzzy concepts "risk-tol," "value", "fast," and "low risk," are encountered. These concepts are developed in greater mathematical detail in the literature [2,3]. The fuzzy concept "risk-tol" refers to an individual UAV's risk tolerance. This is a number assigned by an expert indicating the degree of risk the UAV may tolerate. A low value near zero implies little risk tolerance, whereas, a high value near one implies the UAV can be subjected to significant risk.

The concept "value" is a number between zero and one indicating the relative value of a UAV as measured against the other UAVs flying the mission. The concept "value" changes from mission to mission depending on which UAVs are flying.

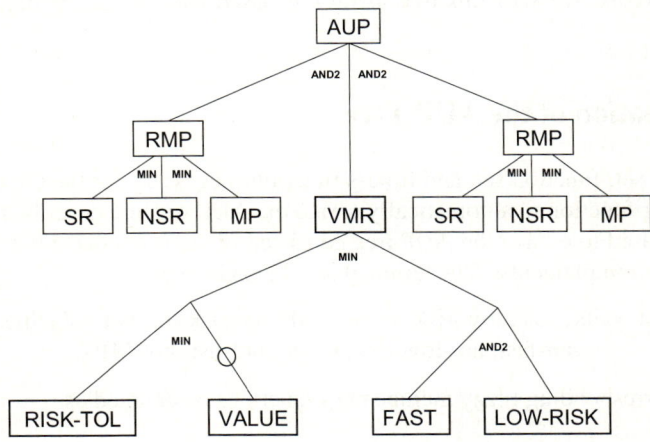

Fig. 1. The AUP subtree for the UAVRM

The concept "fast" relates to how fast the UAV is and builds in measures of the UAV's reliability estimates as well as its risk tolerance and the mission's priority.

The rightmost concept is "low risk." It quantifies experts' opinions about how risky the mission is. It takes a value of one for low risk missions and a value near zero for high risk missions.

These four fuzzy root concepts are combined through logical connectives to give the composite concept "VMR." Although four concepts are now used to construct

VMR it originally only used the concepts related to value and mission risk, and was called the Value-Mission-Risk (VMR) subtree.

Each vertex of the "VMR" tree uses a form of "AND" as a logical connective. In fuzzy logic, logical connectives can have more than one mathematical form. Based on expertise it was useful to allow two types of ANDs to be used. The two mathematical forms of AND used are the "min" operator and the algebraic product denoted in Figure 1 as "AND2." When a "min" appears on a vertex then the resulting composite concept arises from taking the minimum between the two root concepts connected by the "min." When an "AND2" appears it means that the resulting composite concept is the product of the fuzzy membership functions for the two concepts connected by the AND2.

The final subtree of AUP that needs to be described is the reliability-mission priority (RMP) subtree. The RMP tree appears twice on the AUP tree. RMP consists of a "min" operation between three fuzzy concepts. These concepts are "sr" which refers to an expert's estimate of the sensor reliability, "nsr" which refers to an expert's estimate of the non-sensor system reliability and "MP" a fuzzy concept expressing the mission's priority.

The AUP tree is observed to consist of the VMR subtree and two copies of the RMP subtree with AND2 logical connectives at each vertex. These fuzzy concepts and their related fuzzy membership functions, as well as additional details are given in much greater detail in [2, 3].

The AUP tree given in Figure 1 was originally created using human expertise alone. The rediscovery of this tree using GP based data mining is described in the next section.

4 GP Creation of the AUP Tree

The terminal set, function set, and fitness functions necessary for the GP to be used as a data mining function to automatically create the AUP tree are described below. The terminal set used to evolve the AUP tree consisted of the root concepts from the AUP tree and their complements. The terminal set, T, is given by

$$T=\{\text{risk-tol, value, fast, low-risk, sr, nsr, MP, not-risk-tol, not-valuable,} \\ \text{not-fast, not-low-risk, not-sr, not-nsr, not-MP}\}. \quad (1)$$

Let the corresponding fuzzy membership functions be denoted as

$$\{\mu_{risk-tol}, \mu_{value}, \mu_{fast}, \mu_{low-risk}, \mu_{sr}, \mu_{nsr}, \ldots \\ \mu_{MP}, \mu_{not-risk-tol}, \mu_{not-valuable}, \mu_{not-fast}, \ldots \\ \mu_{not-low-risk}, \mu_{not-sr}, \mu_{not-nsr}, \mu_{not-MP}\}. \quad (2)$$

When mathematical expressions are constructed by a GP that reproduce the entries in a database within some tolerance, the process is referred to as symbolic regression [10]. It is found in symbolic regression that candidate solutions are frequently not in algebraic simplest form and this is the major source of their excess length. When candidate solutions are too long this is referred to as bloat [10].

By including in the terminal set a terminal and its complement, e.g., "risk-tol," and "not-risk-tol"; "value" and "not-valuable"; etc., it is found that bloat is less and convergence of the GP is accelerated. This is a recent innovation which was not used when the EARM was evolved using GP based data mining (DM) [1]. Additional bloat control procedures are described below.

The mathematical form of the complement whether it appears in the terminal set or is prefixed with a "NOT" logical modifier from the function set is one minus the membership function. To make this more explicit

$$\mu_{NOT(A)} = \mu_{not-A} = 1 - \mu_A, \tag{3}$$

where *NOT(A)* refers to the application of the logical modifier *NOT* from the function set to the fuzzy concept *A* from the terminal set. The notation, *not-A* refers to the terminal which is the complement of the terminal *A*.

The function set, denoted as F, consists of

$$F = \{AND1, OR1, AND2, OR2, NOT\}, \tag{4}$$

where the elements of (4) are defined in (5-9). Let A and B represent fuzzy membership functions then elements of the function set are defined as

$$AND1(A,B) = min(A,B); \tag{5}$$
$$OR1(A,B) = max(A,B); \tag{6}$$
$$AND2(A,B) = A \cdot B; \tag{7}$$
$$OR2(A,B) = A + B - A \cdot B; \tag{8}$$

and

$$NOT(A) = 1 - A. \tag{9}$$

The database to be data mined is a scenario database kindred to the scenario database used for evolving the EARM [1]. In this instance scenarios are characterized by values of the fuzzy membership functions for the elements of the terminal set plus a number from zero to one indicating the experts' opinion about the value of the fuzzy membership function for AUP for that scenario.

GPs require a fitness function [9]. As its name implies the fitness function measures the merit or fitness of each candidate solution represented as a chromosome. The fitness used for data mining is referred to as the input-output fitness.

The input-output fitness for mining the scenario database takes the form

$$f_{IO}(i, n_{db}) \equiv \frac{1}{1 + 2 \cdot \sum_{j=1}^{n_{db}} \left| \mu_{gp}(i, e_j) - \mu_{expert}(e_j) \right|}. \tag{10}$$

where e_j is the jth element of the database; n_{db} is the number of elements in the database; $\mu_{gp}(e_j)$ is the output of the fuzzy decision tree created by the GP for the ith element of the population for database element e_j; and $\mu_{expert}(e_j)$ is an expert's estimate as to what the fuzzy decision tree should yield as output for database element e_j.

The AUP tree is evolved in three steps. The first step involves evolving the VMR subtree; the second step, the RMP subtree and the final step, the full AUP tree. In the second and third steps, i.e., evolving the RMP subtree and full AUP tree from the RMP and VMR subtrees, only the input-output (IO) fitness in (10) is calculated, i.e., the rule-fitness described below is not used.

When evolving the VMR subtree a rule-fitness is calculated for each candidate solution. Only when the candidate's rule fitness is sufficiently high is its input-output fitness calculated. The use of the rule-fitness helps guide the GP toward a solution that will be consistent with expert rules. Also the use of the rule fitness reduces the number of times the IO fitness is calculated reducing the run time of the GP. After some preliminary definitions of crisp and fuzzy relations, a set of crisp and fuzzy rules that were used to help accelerate the GP's creation of the VMR subtree are given. The rules are combined to formulate the rule fitness. The mathematical form of the rule fitness has not been included due to space limitations.

Let T be a fuzzy decision tree that represents a version of the VMR subtree, that is to be evolved by a genetic program. Let A and B be fuzzy concepts. Then let $\gamma_{share}(T,A,B) = 1$ if A and B share a logical connective denoted as C and $\gamma_{share}(T,A,B) = 0$, otherwise.

Furthermore, define the fuzzy relation

$$\mu_{com}(T,A,B,C) = \begin{cases} 0.4 & if \quad C = AND1 \quad or \quad AND2 \\ 0.1 & if \quad C = OR1 \quad or \quad OR2 \\ 0, & otherwise \end{cases} \quad . \quad (11)$$

The following is a subset of the rules used to accelerate the GP's convergence and to help produce a result consistent with human expertise.

R1. "not-valuable" and "risk-tol" must share a logical connective, denoted as C_1, i.e., it is desired that $\gamma_{share}(T, not-valuable, risk-tol) = 1$

R2. "not-valuable" and "risk-tol" strongly influence each other, so they should be connected by AND1 or AND2. So it is desired that $\mu_{com}(T, not-valuable, risk-tol, C_1) = .4$

R3. "fast" and "low-risk" have an affinity for each other. They should share a logical connective, denoted as C_2, i.e., it is desired that $\gamma_{share}(T, fast, low-risk) = 1$

R4. The fuzzy root concepts "fast" and "low-risk" strongly influence each other, so they should be connected by AND1 or AND2. So it is desired that $\mu_{com}(T, fast, low-risk, C_2) = .4$.

R5. There is an affinity between the fuzzy root concepts $C_1(not-valuable, risk-tol)$ and $C_2(fast, low-risk)$, they are connected by a logical connective denoted as C_3, i.e., it is desired that,

$$\gamma_{share}(T, C_1(not-valuable, risk-tol), C_2(fast, low-risk)) = 1. \quad (12)$$

When the EARM was evolved by GP based data mining [1] bloat was controlled using adhoc procedures based on tree depth and parsimony pressure. Most of the bloat in evolving mathematical expressions with a GP arises from the expressions not being in algebraic simplest form [10]. With that observation in mind, computer algebra routines have been introduced that allow the GP to simplify expressions. The following is a partial list of algebraic simplification techniques used during the evolution of the EARM and the AUP tree. The simplification routines used when evolving AUP are more sophisticated than those applied to the creation of EARM [1].

One routine simplifies expressions of the form *NOT(NOT(A)) = A*. This can be more complicated than it initially appears, since the NOT logical modifiers can be separated on the fuzzy decision tree.

Another simplification procedure consists of eliminating redundant terminals connected by an AND1 logical connective. An example of this is *AND1(A,A) =A*. Like the case with the logical modifier NOT there can be a separation between the AND1s and the terminals that add complexity to the simplification operation.

The third algebraic simplification example is like the second. It involves simplifying terminals connected by OR1s. Like AND1, separation between terminals and OR1 can increase the complexity of the operation.

Other types of algebraic simplification use DeMorgan's theorems in combination with the above procedures. This can significantly reduce the length of an expression.

Another algebraic procedure that reduces the length of expressions includes replacement of forms like AND2(A,A) by the square of "A," i.e., A^2. Still another length reducing simplification includes replacing NOT(A) with not-A, its complement from the terminal set listed in (1).

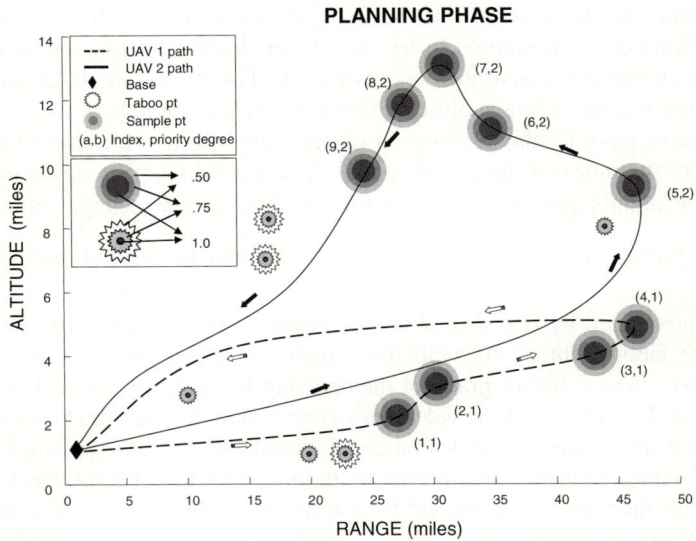

Fig. 2. Trajectory of two UAVs as determined by the planning algorithm and their paths assigned by AUP

There is always a question of how much algebraic simplification should be conducted from generation to generation as such the simplification algorithm allows levels of simplification. If a low level of simplification is selected then some parts of an expression remain that might be eliminated during full simplification. This has two advantages: it leaves chromosome subcomponents that may prove useful during mutation or crossover and it takes less CPU time.

Algebraic simplification produces candidate solutions in simpler form making it easier for human observers to understand what is being evolved. Having candidate solutions that are easier to understand can be an important feature for improving the evolution of GPs.

5 Computational Experiments

The AUP tree described above has been the subject of a large number of experiments. This section provides a description of an experiment that is representative of the type of scenarios designed to test the AUP tree. Due to space limitations only an experiment involving two UAVs is discussed.

In Figure 2 a scenario using two UAVs illustrates how AUP properly assigns the UAVs to the best path. The two paths were created by the planning algorithm so that the UAV could most efficiently sample the atmosphere's electromagnetic index of refraction [2, 3].

Sample points are labeled by concentric circular regions colored in different shades of gray. The lighter the shade of gray used to color a point, the lower the point's grade of membership in the fuzzy concept "desirable neighborhood." [2, 3] The legend provides numerical values for the fuzzy grade of membership in the fuzzy concept "desirable neighborhoods." If the fuzzy degree of desirability is high then the index of refraction is considered to be close to the index of refraction of the sample point at the center of the desirable neighborhood. This allows the UAV to make significant measurements while avoiding undesirable neighborhoods.

Each sample point is labeled with an ordered pair. The first member of the ordered pair provides the index of the sample point. The second member of the ordered pair provides the point's priority. For example, if there are n_{sp} sample points and the qth sample point is of priority p, then that point will be labeled with the ordered pair (q,p).

Points surrounded by star-shaped neighborhoods varying from dark grey to white in color are taboo points. As with the sample points, neighborhoods with darker shades of gray have a higher grade of membership in the fuzzy concept "undesirable neighborhood." The legend provides numerical values for the fuzzy grade of membership in the fuzzy concept "undesirable neighborhood." UAVs with high risk tolerance may fly through darker grey regions than those with low risk tolerance.

UAVs start their mission at the UAV base which is labeled with a diamond-shaped marker. They fly in the direction of the arrows labeling the various curves in Figure 2.

Figure 2 depicts the sampling path determined by the planning algorithm for an experiment involving two UAVs. The first, UAV(1) follows the dashed curve; the second, UAV(2), the solid curve. The UAVs were assigned to the different paths by the

AUP fuzzy decision tree described in section 2. UAV(1) is assigned to sample all the highest priority points, i.e., the priority one points. UAV(2) samples the lower priority points, i.e.; those with priority two. Due to the greedy nature of the point-path assignment algorithm, the highest priority points are assigned for sampling first.

6 Summary

A genetic program (GP) has been used as a data mining (DM) function to automatically create decision logic for two different resource managers (RMs). The most recent of the RMs, referred to as the UAVRM is the topic of this paper. It automatically controls a group of unmanned aerial vehicles (UAVs) that are cooperatively making atmospheric measurements.

The DM procedure that uses a GP as a data mining function to create a subtree of UAVRM is discussed. The resulting decision logic for the RMs is rendered in the form of fuzzy decision trees. The fitness function, bloat control methods, data base, etc., for the tree to be evolved are described. Innovative bloat control methods using computer algebra based simplification are given. A subset of the fuzzy rules used by the GP to help accelerate convergence of the GP and improve the quality of the results is provided. Experimental methods of validating the evolved decision logic are discussed to support the effectiveness of the data mined results.

References

1. Smith, III, J. F.: Fuzzy logic resource manager: decision tree topology, combined admissible regions and the self-morphing property, In: Kadar, I. (ed.): Signal Processing, Sensor Fusion, and Target Recognition XII: Vol. 5096, SPIE Proceedings, Orlando (2003) 104-114.
2. Smith, III, J. F., Nguyen, T., H.: Distributed autonomous systems: resource management, planning, and control algorithms, In: Kadar, I. (ed.): Signal Processing, Sensor Fusion, and Target Recognition XIV: Vol. 5096, SPIE Proceedings, Orlando (2005) 65-76.
3. Smith, III, J. F., Nguyen, T., H.: Resource manager for an autonomous coordinated team of UAVs, In: Kadar, I. (ed.): Signal Processing, Sensor Fusion, and Target Recognition XV: 62350C, SPIE Proceedings, Orlando (2006) 104-114.
4. Blackman, S., Popoli, R.: Design and Analysis of Modern Tracking Systems. Artech House, Boston (1999)
5. Tsoukalas, L.H., Uhrig, R.E.: Fuzzy and Neural Approaches in Engineering: John Wiley and Sons, New York (1997)
6. Zimmerman, H. J.: Fuzzy Set Theory and its Applications. Kluwer Academic Publishers Group, Boston (1991)
7. Smith, III, J.F., Rhyne, II, R.: A Resource Manager for Distributed Resources: Fuzzy Decision Trees and Genetic Optimization. In: Arabnia, H. (ed.): Proceeding of the International Conference on Artificial Intelligence, IC-AI'99, Vol. II. CSREA Press, Las Vegas (1999) 669-675.
8. Bigus, J.P.: Data Mining with Neural Nets. McGraw-Hill, New York, (1996).
9. Koza, J.R., Bennett III, F.H.: Andre, D., Keane, M.A.: Genetic Programming III: Darwinian Invention and Problem Solving. Morgan Kaufmann Publishers, San Francisco (1999).
10. Luke, S., Panait, L.: Fighting Bloat with Nonparametric Parsimony Pressure. In: Guervos, J.J.M (ed.): Parallel Problem Solving from Nature - PPSN VII, 7th International Conference. Proceedings. LNCS Vol. 2439, Springer-Verlag, Berlin, (2002) 411-421.

Neural Network Models for Language Acquisition: A Brief Survey

Jordi Poveda[1] and Alfredo Vellido[2]

[1] TALP Research Center
[2] Soft Computing Research Group
Technical University of Catalonia (UPC), Barcelona, Spain
{jpoveda, avellido}@lsi.upc.edu

Abstract. Since the outbreak of connectionist modelling in the mid eighties, several problems in natural language processing have been tackled by employing neural network-based techniques. Neural network's "biological plausibility" offers a promising framework in which the computational treatment of language may be linked to other disciplines such as cognitive science and psychology. With this brief survey, we set out to explore the landscape of artificial neural models for the acquisition of language that have been proposed in the research literature.

1 Introduction

Human language, as a canonical representative of human cognitive faculties, has gathered wide attention in such diverse fields as cognitive science, psychology, artificial intelligence and, of course, linguistics. There are strong intuitive reasons to believe that human cognition, at least at its higher levels, revolves around mental representations that have language at the base. This is why a better understanding of the mechanisms behind language acquisition and its representation in the brain could shed some light in unresolved questions about the working of the human mind. In this respect, the ability to have computational models run and interact with linguistic input data, and to analyze quantitave and qualitative results, plays a very important role. Whether artificial neural networks (ANNs) provide meaningful models of the brain and to what degree, and whether they constitute a useful approach to natural language processing (NLP) is subject to debate [1]. Throughout this survey, we will examine some of the main arguments raised for and against the explanatory potential of ANNs as models for language acquisition, while supporting the position that they do indeed possess at least potential as useful tools and models.

First language acquisition concerns itself with the processes involved in the development of language in children. There have been traditionally two schools of thought: nativists and non-nativists or "emergencionists". Nativists assume that the ability for language is for the most part innate, and thus the underlying principles of language are universal and inborn to all humans. Proponents of nativism are Chomsky, Fodor and Pinker, among others. A central idea to nativism is the well-known Chomskian postulate of the existence of a Universal Grammar [2], which is innate to all individuals and which underlies all specific instances of human languages. Non nativists (among them, Mac Whinney, Bates and Snow), despite admitting that some of the ability for developing language may be innate, see language acquisition as a rather emergent process and a result of children's social interaction and exposure to linguistic stimuli. As we will see later, connectionist models of the brain in general, and self-organizing models in particular, due to their design characteristics, have a lot to say as advocates of the view of language acquisition as an emergent process.

The acquisition of a second language and bilingual development in children present their own of set of issues: the interference and coupling effects between the two languages, how the two languages and their respective lexicons are represented in the brain, the effects of age of acquisition, etc. We will also see a neural-network based model of bilingualism that particially addresses these issues.

The goal of this survey is to explore ANN-based approaches for an specific NLP problem: that of language acquisition; what research efforts have historically been made, where this area of research currently stands, and to what degree ANNs are viable and biologically plausible models of language acquisition. It was conceived in the light of a perceived prevalence of statistical (e.g. HMMs, linear classifiers, Gaussian models, SVMs, ...) and relational (rule induction) methods for NLP problems in general in current AI research, in detriment of more generalized use of ANN (connectionist) methods, although connectionist models of language cognitive development are being reappraised [3]. Nonetheless, it can also be argued that statistical and connectionist methods are not necessarily mutually exclusive fields. Much work has been done both to provide a probabilistic interpretation of neural networks and to insert neural networks within a probabilistic framework [4,5,6]. Some of the most recent theories of cortical activity draw heavily both from connectionist models and from probability theory [7].

The rest of this work is structured as follows. In Sect. 2, we provide some historical perspective on connectionist modelling of natural language. Section 3 deals with the strengths of two specific neural architectures that have been proposed to model aspects of language acquisition, namely Self-Organizing Maps (SOM) and the Simple Recurrent Network (SRN). In Sect. 4, we describe four particular proposed architectures commented in a greater level of detail: the ANN for learning english verbs past tenses by Rummelhart and McClelland [8], TRACE [9], SOMBIP [10] and DevLex [11]. We will examine in turn the rationale behind these models, their architectures, training methods and their main results and implications. Section 5 briefly compares connectionist modelling of lexical acquisition with statistical and other approaches. Finally, Sect. 6 presents the conclusions.

2 The Connectionism vs. Symbolism Controversy: An Historical Perspective

Connectionism attempts to construct biologically-inspired computacional models of cognitive processes as a network of connections between processing units or nodes, known as neurons [12]. According to this view of computation, information is stored in the form of weights between the nodes' connections, or synapses, in imitation of biological synapses. Connectionist models of NLP took off in the late eighties thanks to the pioneering work of Rummelhart & McClelland [8], with their famous ANN model of the acquisition of past tenses of English verbs. Rummelhart and McClelland's model was intended as a proof-of-concept against symbolism (and simultaneously against the prevailing nativist view of the time that language ability was hardwired into the brain from birth): they argued, information could be better captured in the form of connections among processing units, thus eliminating the need for formulating explicit rules that try to explain the details of acquisition phenomena. This claim was widely contested from symbolist circles (e.g. [13]).

The proponents of symbolism picture the human brain as a digital processor of symbolic information, and argue that computational models of the brain should be based on algorithmic programs manipulating symbols. This is the traditional school of thought, antagonist to connectionism, which denies the validity of connectionist models altogether and doesn't credit them with any explanatory potential. A halfway position between these two opposite views is that of implementational connectionists (e.g. Fodor, Pinker and Pylyshyn), who admit the utility of ANNs in modelling cognitive processes, but hold that they should be employed ultimately to implement symbolic processing (*"the mind is a neural net; but it is also a symbolic processor at a higher and more abstract level of description"* [14]). According to them, research of models should be made at the symbolic (psychological) level, whereas ANNs are the tools through which these models are implemented in practice.

Fodor raised in [15] a well-known argument against the adequacy of connectionism as a model of the mind, based on a characteristic of human intelligence which he called systematicity. Neural networks, he said, are good at capturing associations, but they alone cannot account for higher cognitive abilities required, for instance, for human language. Still another main criticism against connectionist models of language is based on the *compositionality* of language (the meaning of a complex statement can be decomposed in terms of the individual meanings of its simpler constituents). As if to contest this challenge launched against connectionism about the recursive nature of language, Pollack devised a neural network architecture that was well-suited to represent recursive data structures, such as trees and lists: the recursive auto-associative memory (RAAM) [16]. Due to their ability to represent recursive data structures, RAAM networks are useful for working with syntactic and semantic representations in NLP applications. In the field of speech processing, the TRACE architecture by McClelland and Elman [9] set another milestone in early connectionist modelling of language.

More recent systems have used SOM as neural-network models of language acquisition. One such model is Miikkulainen's DISLEX [17], which is composed of multiple self-organizing feature maps. DISLEX is a neural network model of the mental lexicon, intented to explain the phenomena involved in lexical aphasia. We will conclude this historical revision by making a reference to the CHILDES database project [18]. The CHILDES database is a corpus of child-directed speech, that is, recordings and transcripts of conversations between parents and young children. It has been subsequently used by other experiments on neural network modelling of lexical acquisition, in order to gather training data for the model, and to build a restricted lexicon, representative of the first stages of language learning.

3 Artificial Neural Network Architectures for Language Acquisition

In this section we will discuss how two specific neural network architectures, Kohonen's SOM [19] and Elman's SRN [20], have been applied for modelling aspects of language acquisition and have served as building blocks for larger ANN models.

3.1 Kohonen Self-Organizing Maps

A SOM network defines a topology-preserving mapping between a often highly dimensional input space and a low dimensional, most typically 2-D, space. Self-organization is introduced by having the notion of neighbouring units, whose weights are adjusted in proportion to their distance from the winning unit. Several characteristics of SOM make this architecture especially suitable for modelling language acquisition [10]:

1. *Unsupervised learning*: SOM is trained by presenting inputs to the network (without correcting feedback). This is coherent with the way in which children are for the most part exposed to language.
2. *Self-organization*: Activation of the best-matching unit and propagation of activation yield network units that specialize in specific groups of related words, and resonance between the input and the matching neuron(s) is increased. This presents a coherent picture of memory and the process of remembering.
3. *Representation*: Inputs that are close in the high dimensional space will activate nearby units in the 2-D space. Also, semantic categories emerge in SOM in the form of clusters of related words.
4. *Neighbourhood function*: Acting on the neighbourhood ratio allows the modelling of different levels of brain plasticity. Early plasticity and formation of gross categories, and posterior establishment and fine-grained specialization of the learned structures can be modelled by decreasing the neighbourhood ratio through the learning process.

5. *Hebbian learning*: SOM maps interconnected through hebbian associative links can be used to model the interactions among different levels of language, as is done in DISLEX architecture [17].

Anderson reports in [21] the results of several experiments he conducted with SOM simulations in order to model a number of aspects of language acquisition, including: the modelization of the process of learning to distinguish word boundaries in a continuous stream of speech; the modelization of the disappearance with age of the ability to recognize phonemes other than those of one's own language; and the modelization of the clinical occurrences of semantically bounded anomia (i.e. inability to distinguish correctly among words belonging to some semantic category).

3.2 SRN for Building Word Meaning Representations

A simple recurrent network (SRN) architecture, as introduced by Elman in [20], can be employed to construct distributed representations (i.e. as a vector of weights) for the meaning of a word. The word meaning representations are built from contextual features, by putting the word in relation to its context, as it occurs in a stream of input sentences. This is indeed what Li and Farkas do in the WCD (Word Co-ocurrence Detector) subsystem of their DevLex [11] and SOMBIP [10] models, both of which are described in Sect. 4.

The SRN network has two layers, an input layer and a hidden layer (which we will call copy layer). This model assigns to each word w_i of a lexicon of size N a unary encoding as a vector of N dimensions, where the i-th component is 1 and the rest of components are 0. The input layer has N input units (as many units as the number of components in a word's encoding). At each time instant t, the hidden or copy layer contains a one-to-one copy of the previous vector on the input layer (the input word at time $t-1$). L and R are two arrays of associative vectors, fully connecting the units of the copy layer to input layer and viceversa. Training consists in presenting the network with words from a stream of input sentences, one word at a time. The weight l_{ij}, connecting unit j in the copy layer to unit i in the input layer, expresses the probability $P(j^{t-1}|i^t)$ that word w_i is preceded by word w_j. Similarly, the weight r_{ij} expresses the probability $P(i^t|j^{t-1})$ that word w_i follows word w_j. These weights are updated by hebbian learning after each input word is presented. By the end of the training, $l_i = [l_{i1} \ldots l_{iN}]$ contains a representation of the left context of word w_i (the probability distribution of the words preceding i), and $r_i = [r_{1i} \ldots r_{Ni}]$ contains a representation of the right context of w_i (the probability distribution of the words following i). The concatenation of these two vectors forms the distributed representation of the meaning of a word.

4 Case Studies

In the previous sections, we have examined general questions about the subject of language acquisition, trying to relate the viewpoints of different disciplines.

In this section we examine four complete ANN models that have been proposed in the literature to tackle different problems in language acquisition. These four models are presented here in chronological order of appearance in the research literature, so that the reader will realize how each one draws on the experience and foundations laid out by the previous ones.

A first attempt to establish a typology of neural lexical models may be established with regard to the type of representation they use, and to the behaviour of the network over time: in *localist* representations, each word or the meaning of the concept that it conveys is represented by a single neuron or processing unit (i.e. localized), whereas in *distributed* representations, the representation of each word or its corresponding concept is spread through multiple units of the network; likewise, regarding evolution with time, *stationary* or permanent models are those in which the connection weights (and the network architecture) are prespecified, whereas in *dynamic* or learning models the connection weights (and/or the network architecture) evolve through time. The TRACE architecture, for instance, is a localist and stationary model. In constrast, systems based on the SRN architecture introduced by Elman [20] are usually distributed and dynamic. Dynamic models afford a better interpretability of the observed results than stationary ones, by putting the model dynamics in relation with the dynamics of human lexical learning evidenced by psychology and cognitive science experimentation. Localist and distributed representations serve different purposes and are not mutually exclusive: some complex multi-level ANN models such as DevLex and others based on SOM maps exhibit both types of unit-word correspondence simultaneously at different levels of representation.

A second attempt at establishing a taxonomy of these models refers to the type of basic ANN architecture underlying the model. Table 1 summarizes this distinction and presents some highlights of each type of model.

4.1 Rummelhart and McClelland: Acquisition of Past Tenses of English Verbs

Rummelhart and McClelland [8] used a one-layer feedforward network based on the perceptron learning algorithm in order to map verb roots to their past tense forms. The representation of verbs was based on a system of phonological features (Wickelphones), into which verb roots were encoded prior to being inputs to the network, and which were decoded at the output. Rummelhart and McClelland wanted to model the U-shaped learning curve typically found in children: early correct production of a few irregular verbs, middle confusion due to mixing of regular and irregular verbs' patterns, and late correct production of the majority of verbs. To this end, they split a training of 200 epochs in two stages: in the first 10 epochs, they presented the network with 10 highly-ocurring verbs; later, during the remaining 190 epochs, they introduced 410 medium-frequency verbs. The testing set consisted of 86 low-frequency verbs (14 irregular and 72 regular). They report having observed the U-shaped pattern of learning, as many irregulars were incorrectly produced during the middle stages of training due to overregularization.

Table 1. A comparison of ANN models of lexical acquisiton by underlying architecture

Type	Examples	Training	Highlights
Feed-forward	Rummelhart & McClelland [8]	Back-propagation	– Supervised learning: poor reflection of human lexical acquisition – The earliest architecture defined – Able to capture only a highly limited range of phenomena – Inadequate to capture temporal dimension of language
Interactive activation	TRACE [9]	Preset weights	– Multi-level architecture – Interactions among different abstraction levels – Competition and cooperation among candidate hypotheses through inhibitory synapses – Temporal context captured by interconnecting multiple copies of the network
SOM-based	DISLEX [17] SOMBIP [10] DevLex [11]	SOM learning + Hebbian learning	– Unsupervised learning: reflects main mode of human language learning – Self-organization allows for emergence of lexical categories – Interaction among different levels of language – Distributed encoding for word semantics based on contextual features – Capture a wide range of phenomena

This model has received a number of critiques, among them:

- that it is not a valid model of language acquisition, because the direct mapping from phonological forms of verb roots to past tenses is considered in isolation from the rest of the language;
- criticisms about the features chosen for representation (that Wickelphones tend to favour positively the aspects of data that convey most information);
- that the results obtained fall short of being generalizable (due to relatively low performance);
- and that the training and testing procedures were unrealistic, as a result of an excessive zeal in modeling the U-shaped learning curve.

4.2 TRACE: A Model of Speech Processing

TRACE by McClelland and Elman [9] is a neural model of human speech perception, which implements activation of words in a lexicon through a combination of phonological and phonotactical features. It set a hallmark in connectionist treatment of language by introducing the notion of interconnection among different abstraction levels of language. A particularly interesting characteristic of TRACE is found in its ability to perform word segmentation without an explicit marker, based only on phonetic interactions.

The TRACE model was based on the principle of *interactive activation* (IA), where units are related by connections that exercise either an inhibitory or excitatory action on their neighbours. TRACE has three layers of neurons, each one representing a higher level of abstraction in language: first, phonetic features; second, individual phonemes; and third, words. Connections exist within and across layers. Inhibitory synapses model situations where the items represented by the co-activating units can not co-exist (competition), whereas excitatory ones model items that are somehow related (cooperation). In addition, the temporal dimension is captured by having multiples copies of the whole network, among which neurons are also interconnected.

There is one particular novelty about TRACE that challenged the traditional perception of the scientific community regarding how the brain network is organized. It is that activation between layers in TRACE works top-down (words to phonemes) as well as bottom-up (phonemes to words). It is a matter of debate whether layers of higher abstraction feed information back to lower layers. Another particular characteristic of TRACE is that the connection weights are all preset to account for the desired model of language: the network does not learn.

4.3 SOMBIP: A Model of Bilingual Lexicon Acquisition

SOMBIP is an ANN model by Li and Farkas [10] of how a bilingual lexicon (i.e. a lexicon where words of two languages appear mixed) is acquired by bilingual learners. The network architecture consists of two Kohonen SOM maps, one phonological (SOM1) and one semantical (SOM2), interconnected via associative hebbian links. The network was trained to learn a bilingual English-Chinese lexicon of 400 words (184 Chinese, 216 English), extracted from the CHILDES database [18].

In order to allow the network to create associations between translation equivalents in the two languages that occur in the bilingual lexicon, if the phonological representation of an English (or Chinese) word is presented to SOM1 and it has a translation equivalent in the lexicon, not only the semantic representation of the same English (or Chinese) word is presented to SOM2 coupled with the word form, but also the semantic representation of the translation equivalent in Chinese (or English) is presented.

Emergence of grammatical and lexical categories in the form of visible clusters appears in SOMBIP, with the particularity that the network is able as well to effectively separate words from the two languages. Interference effects between words, both intra-language and inter-language, were verified by presenting the network with a phonological representation and observing the response it triggers in the semantic map, and vice versa. Different levels of the learner's proficiency in one of the languages were modelled by building the word meaning representations for one of the languages from a smaller portion of the corpus. Words from the dominant language tended to occupy a larger area of the semantic map than before, which caused lexical confusion in the disadvantaged language.

4.4 DevLex: A Model of Early Lexical Acquisition

DevLex [11], by Li, Farkas & MacWhinney, is a neural network model of the development of the lexicon in young children, based mainly in the SOM architecture and inspired by Miikkulainen's DISLEX model [17]. The authors observe that most previous ANN models of lexical acquisition have been based on the supervised back-propagation algorithm for training, thus misrepresenting the mainly unsupervised nature of lexical acquisition in children, and most have also failed at modelling the incremental nature of vocabulary acquisition. To address this issues, DevLex introduces through a combination of SOM and ART (Adaptive Resonance Theory, [22]) modes of operation.

The DevLex architecture is composed of two GMAPs (Growing Maps), one phonological map for dealing with phonological information of words (P-MAP) and one semantic map (S-MAP) for dealing with word's meanings. A GMAP is an arrangement that combines both the self-organization properties of SOM, and the ability of ART networks to create new nodes that become representatives of a new class of inputs. The learning process is modelled like a gradual transition between the SOM and ART modes of learning. During SOM mode, the network undergoes reorganization as a result of exposure to the input patterns. In ART mode, the network is allowed to create new units when the input pattern (word forms or meanings) is sufficiently different from all the patterns stored in existing nodes. At any time, showing the network a word form causes a response in the S-MAP, which models *language comprehension*; while showing the network a word meaning causes a response in the P-MAP, which models *language production*.

The results observed concerted three types of phenomena: category emergence, lexical confusion and effects of age of acquisition. The target 500-word vocabulary from the CHILDES database is structured in 4 major lexical categories (nouns, verbs, adjectives and closed-class words). By comparing each S-MAP unit against its 5-nearest neighbours, category compaction was observed in nouns (more than 90%), then in verbs, in adjectives (circa 80%), and last closed-class words. Lexical confusion in the network was evaluated by looking inside individual units, in order to observe how many words of the lexicon were cluttered into the same unit, and over the associative links that relate phonology and meaning. Largely in agreement with the way how this phenomenon manifests in children, it was found that lexical confusion is very high during early stages of high reorganization (in SOM mode), and then decreases steeply just to reach a minimum in ART mode. Regarding age of acquisition, it was observed that, after the network starts operating in ART mode, the earlier a word was entered for learnig, the less it took the network to construct an unique representation for it and with a correct association between form and meaning.

5 Comparison to Statistical Approaches

Statistical NLP has typically concerned itself with problems that depart from the interpretation of language acquisition (or lexical acquisition) addressed in this survey. Rather than modelling the identification and learning of words of a lexicon from phonological and/or semantic contextual information, as the ANN models we have reviewed in the previous sections do, the methods employed in statistical NLP extract a series of lexical, morphological, syntactic and semantic features from text documents, in order to apply them to higher-level tasks where the focus is on performance on the task at hand, as opposed to interpretability of the results, or imitation of biological or cognitive processes. Examples of such tasks are text categorization, information extraction, machine translation or word sense disambiguation, among others.

An outstanding difference regarding the way features extracted from words and text are employed in statistical NLP with respect with the connectionist models we have seen here, is that in statistical NLP information flows only from lower-level features (i.e. levels of language) to higher-level problems. Lower levels of language (e.g. morphological) are used to solve the NLP problems in the higher levels (e.g. syntactic or semantic). There is no notion of information flowing forward and backwards across language levels (as in the TRACE model in [9]) or interaction (in a hebbian sense) among different levels.

Although some research literature on the application of ANNs to NLP tasks in general has been published in recent years, the overwhelming majority of instances have employed either statistical or symbolic approaches. This scarcity of ANN-related publications might be due, at least in part, to two of the limitations that are usually associated to ANN models: that of the difficult interpretability of results, and the excessive tuning of the network architecture and learning parameters that is required. Moreover, it is hard to integrate existing background linguistic knowledge for use by an ANN, if so desired. Nevertheless, and as mentioned in the introduction, some connectionist models have been reinterpreted within the framework of probability theory. Among the frequently quoted advantages of this reformulation, we find: the possibility of defining principled model extensions, and the explicit addressing of the model complexity problem. Among the disadvantages: the likely increase of computational effort, and the requirement of data distributional assumptions that might hamper biological plausibility.

With respect to the effect of lexical category emergence of which we have seen occurrences in SOM-based models, and which has an intrinsic interest from the standpoint of modelling cognitive processes, a similar category separation could have been attained by resorting to traditional statistical clustering techniques. Nevertheless, models based on SOM offer an additional value concerning analysis and visualization of the resulting clusters, which is afforded by the reduction-of-dimensionality characteristic of SOM.

6 Conclusions

Throughout this brief survey, we have seen a variety of neural network connectionist architectures that can be used to capture phenomena that arise in language acquisition. Arguments that have been raised for and against ANNs as valid models of language acquisition have been presented. This has lead to the explanation of two particular instances of ANN-based models for lexical acquisition, and has enabled us to prove the point that such full-scale neural models as DevLex (for early lexical acquisition) and SOMBIP (for modelling the acquisition of a bilingual lexicon) can reproduce a variety of phenomena that have a parallel in empirical evidence: lexical confusion, interference between languages, effects of proficiency and learning capacity, etc. In fact, ANNs such as these, as well as other machine learning methods (as in [23]), provide a computational basis for certain biological and psychological explanations of empirically observed phenomena.

References

1. Quartz, S. R., Sejnowski, T. J.: The Neural Basis of Cognitive Development: A Constructivist Manifesto. Behavioural and Brain Sciences **20** (1997) 537–596
2. Chomsky, N.: Aspects of the Theory of Syntax (1965). MIT Press, Cambridge
3. Quinlan, P. T., van der Maas, H. L. J., Jansen, B. R. J., Booij, O., Rendell, M.: Re-Thinking Stages of Cognitive Development: An Appraisal of Connectionist Models of the Balance Scale Task. Cognition, in press (2006)
4. MacKay, D. J. C.: Bayesian Methods for Back-propagation Networks. In Domany, E., van Hemmen, J. L., and Schulten, K. (eds.), Models of Neural Networks III, Ch. 6 (1994). Springer, New York.
5. Neal, R.: Bayesian Learning for Neural Networks, PhD thesis (1994). University of Toronto, Canada
6. Bishop, C.: Neural Networks for Pattern Recognition (1995). Oxford University Press, New York
7. Friston, K.: A Theory of Cortical Responses. Philosophical Transactions of the Royal Society, B, **360** (2005) 815–836
8. Rumelhart, D., McClelland, J.: On the Learning of the Past Tenses of English Verbs. Parallel distributed processing: Explorations in the microstructure of cognition **2** (1986) 216–271
9. McClelland, J. L., Elman, J. L.: Interactive Processes in Speech Perception: The TRACE Model. Parallel distributed processing **2** (1986) 58–121
10. Li, P., Farkas, I.: A Self-Organizing Connectionist Model of Bilingual Processing. Bilingual Sentence Processing (2002) 59–85
11. Li, P., Farkas, I., MacWhinney, B.: Early Lexical Development in a Self-Organizing Neural Network. Neural Networks **17** (2004) 1345–1362
12. Christiansen, M. H., Chater, N.: Connectionist Natural Language Processing: The State of the Art. Cognitive Science **23** (1999) 417–437
13. Pinker, S., Prince, A.: On Language and Connectionism: Analysis of A Parallel Distributed Processing Model of Language Acquisition. Cognition **28** (1988) 73–193
14. Garson, J.: Connectionism. The Stanford Encyclopedia of Philosophy (2002). Edward N. Zalta (ed.)

15. Fodor, J. A., Pylyshyn, Z.: Connectionism and Cognitive Architecture: A Critical Analysis. Cognition **28** (1988) 3–71
16. Pollack, J. B.: Recursive Distributed Representations. Artificial Intelligence **46** (1990) 77–105
17. Miikkulainen, R.: Dyslexic and Category-Specific Impairments in a Self-Organizing Feature Map Model of the Lexicon. Brain and Language **59** (1997) 334–366
18. MacWhinney, B.: The CHILDES Project: Tools for Analyzing Talk (2000). Mahwah, NJ: Lawrence Erlbaum Associates
19. Kohonen, T.: Self-Organizing Maps. Springer Series in Information Sciences **30** (1995)
20. Elman, J. L.: Finding Structure in Time. Cognitive Science **14** (1990) 179–211
21. Anderson, B.: Kohonen Neural Networks and Language. Brain and Language **70** (1999) 86–94
22. Carpenter, G. A., Grossberg, S.: The ART of Adaptive Pattern Recognition by a Self-Organizing Neural Network. Computer **21(3)** (1988) 77–88
23. Yu, C., Ballard, D. H., Aslin, R. N.: The Role of Embodied Intention in Early Lexical Acquisition. Cognitive Science **29** (2005) 961–1005

Incorporating Knowledge in Evolutionary Prototype Selection

Salvador García[1], José Ramón Cano[2], and Francisco Herrera[1]

[1] University of Granada, Department of Computer Science and Artificial Intelligence,
E.T.S.I. Informática, 18071 Granada, Spain
{salvagl, herrera}@decsai.ugr.es
[2] University of Jaén, Department of Computer Science, 23700 Linares, Jaén, Spain
jrcano@ujaen.es

Abstract. Evolutionary algorithms has been recently used for prototype selection showing good results. An important problem in prototype selection consist in increasing the size of data sets. This problem can be harmful in evolutionary algorithms by deteriorating the convergence and increasing the time complexity. In this paper, we offer a preliminary proposal to solve these drawbacks. We propose an evolutionary algorithm that incorporates knowledge about the prototype selection problem. This study includes a comparison between our proposal and other evolutionary and non-evolutionary prototype selection algorithms. The results show that incorporating knowledge improves the performance of evolutionary algorithms and considerably reduces time execution.

1 Introduction

Most machine learning methods use all examples from the training data set. However, data sets may contain noisy examples, that make the performance worse of these methods, or they may contain great amount of examples, increasing the complexity of computation. This fact is important especially for algorithms such as the k-nearest neighbors (k-NN) [1]. Nearest neighbor classification is one of the most well known classification methods in the literature. In its standard formulation, all training patterns are used as reference patterns for classifying new patterns.

Instance selection (IS) is a data reduction process applied as preprocessing in data sets which are used as inputs for learning algorithms [2]. We consider data as stored in a flat file and described by terms called attributes or features. Each line in the file consists of attribute-values and forms an instance. By selecting instances, we reduce the number of rows in the data set. When we use the selected instances for direct classification with k-NN, then the IS process is called Prototype Selection (PS).

Various approaches were proposed in order to carry out PS process in the literature, see [3] and [4] for review. Evolutionary Algorithms (EAs) have been used to solve the PS problem with promising results [5,6]. These papers show that EAs outperform the non-evolutionary ones obtaining better instance reduction rates and higher classification accuracy. However, the increasing of the size of data is always present in PS. The Scaling Up problem produces excessive storage requirement, increases times complexity and affects to generalization accuracy.

When we use EAs for selecting prototypes (we call it as Evolutionary Prototype Selection (EPS)), we have to add to these drawbacks the ones produced by the chromosomes size associated to the representation of the PS solution. Large chromosomes size increases the storage requirement and time execution and reduces significantly the convergence capabilities of the algorithm. A way of avoid the drawbacks of this problem can be seen in [7], where data sets stratification is used.

In order to improve the capacity of convergence and reduce time execution on EPS, we propose an evolutionary model that incorporates knowledge through the local improvement of chromosomes based on removing prototypes and adapting chromosome evolution. The aim of this paper is to present our proposal model and compare it with others PS algorithms studied in the literature. To address this, we have carried out experiments with increasing complexity and size of data sets.

To achieve this objective, this contribution is set out as follows. Section 2 summarizes the main features of EPS. In Section 3, we explain how to incorporate knowledge in EPS. Section 4, describes the methodology used in the experiments and analyzes the results obtained. Finally, in Section 5, we point out our conclusion.

2 Evolutionary Prototype Selection

EAs [8] are stochastic search methods that mimic the metaphor of natural biological evolution. All EAs rely on the concept of *population* of individuals (representing search points in the space of potential solutions to a given problem), which undergo probabilistic operators such as *mutation*, *selection* and *recombination*. The *fitness* of an individual reflects its objective function value with respect to particular objective function to be optimized. The mutation operator introduces innovation into the population, the recombination operator performs an information exchange between individuals from a population and the selection operator imposes a driving force on the evolution process by preferring better individuals to survive and reproduce.

PS problem can be considered as a search problem in which EAs can be applied. To accomplish this, we take into account two important issues: the specification of the representation of the solutions and the definition of the fitness function.

  – *Representation:* Let us assume a data set denoted TR with n instances. The search space associated is constituted by all the subsets of TR. This is accomplished by using a binary representation. A chromosome consists of n genes (one for each instance in TR) with two possible states: 0 and 1. If the gene is 1, its associated instance is included in the subset of TR represented by the chromosome. If it is 0, this does not occur.

- *Fitness Function:* Let S be a subset of instances of TR to evaluate and be coded by a chromosome. We define a fitness function that combines two values: the classification rate ($clas\_rat$) associated with S and the percentage of reduction ($perc\_red$) of instances of S with regards to TR.

$$Fitness(S) = \alpha \cdot clas\_rat + (1-\alpha) \cdot perc\_red. \quad (1)$$

The 1-NN classifier is used for measuring the classification rate, $clas\_rat$, associated with S. It denotes the percentage of correctly classified objects from TR using only S to find the nearest neighbor. For each object y in S, the nearest neighbor is searched for amongst those in the set $S \setminus \{y\}$. Whereas, $perc\_red$ is defined as

$$perc\_red = 100 \cdot \frac{|TR| - |S|}{|TR|}. \quad (2)$$

The objective of the EAs is to maximize the fitness function defined, i.e., maximize the classification rate and minimize the number of instances obtained.

Considering this issues, four models of EAs have been studied as EPS [6]. The first two are the classical Genetic Algorithm (GA) models [9]; the generational one and the steady-state one. The third one, heterogeneous recombinations and cataclysmic mutation (CHC), is a classical model that introduces different features to obtain a tradeoff between exploration and exploitation [10], and the fourth one, PBIL [11], is a specific EA approach designed for binary spaces.

Our proposal of EA is a steady-state model with the following characteristics:

- The *fitness function* is calculated by the number of instances correctly classified, without obtain the reduction rate.
- Selection mechanism used is binary tournament.
- As genetic operators we use a crossover operator that randomly replace 20% of first parent's bits with second parent's bits and vice versa, and standard mutation of bit representation of chromosomes.
- Our proposal will use a replacement of the worst individuals of the population in all cases.

3 Incorporating Knowledge in Prototype Selection

Incorporation of knowledge can help to improve the behavior of an algorithm for a determined problem. We have designed a Local Search (LS) procedure based on knowledge on the PS problem that will be applied to improve individuals of a population of an EA. LS that incorporates knowledge procedure is an iterative process that tries to enhance the accuracy classification of a chromosome representation by using 1-NN method and to reduce the number of instances selected in a solution.

To achieve this double objective, it considers neighborhood solutions with $m-1$ instances selected, being m equal to the number of instances selected in a current solution (all positions with value 1 in the chromosome). In other words, a neighbor is obtained by changing 1 to 0 in a gene. In this way, the number of instances represented in a chromosome after the optimization always will be less than or equal to the number of instances of the original chromosome.

Now we describe the local search. It has a standard behavior when we improve the fitness, and a strategy for dealing with the problem against premature convergence in the second half of the run. In the following, we describe them:

- *Standard behavior*: It starts from an initial assignment (a recently generated offspring) and iteratively try to improve the current assignment by local changes. If in the neighborhood of the current assignment, a better assignment is found, it replaces the current assignment and it continues from the new one. The selection of a neighbor is made randomly without repetition among all solutions that belongs to the neighborhood. In order to consider an assignment better than the current one, the accuracy of classification must be better than or equal to the previous one, but in this last case, the number of instances selected must be less than current assignment. The procedure stops when there are not solutions considered better than the current one in its neighborhood.
- *Avoiding premature convergence*: When the search process advances, a tendency of the population to premature convergence toward a certain area of the search space takes place. A local optimization promotes this behavior when it considers solutions with better classification accuracy. In order to prevent this conduct, LS proposed will accept worse solutions in the neighborhood provided two conditions are carried out: the difference of fitness between current and neighbor solution will be not greater than one unit and a certain number of evaluations of EA in the execution have been reached (we consider overcome the half of total number of them).

By using this strategy of local optimization of a chromosome, we can distinguish between *Total evaluation* and *Partial evaluation*.

- *Total Evaluation*: It consists in a standard evaluation of performance of a chromosome in EPS, that bears to compute the nearest neighbor of each instance belongs to subset selected and take the account of the instances classified correctly.
- *Partial Evaluation*: It can take place when it accomplish on a neighbor solution of a current already evaluated and differs only in a bit position, which have changed from value 1 to 0. If a total evaluation counts as one evaluation in terms of taking account of number of evaluations for the stop condition, a partial evaluation counts as:

$$\frac{N_{nu}}{|TR|} \quad (3)$$

where N_{nu} is the number of neighbors updated when a determined instance is removed by LS procedure and $|TR|$ is the size of the original set of instances (also is the size of the chromosome).

If a structure $U = \{u_1, u_2, ..., u_n\}$ is defined, where $u_i/i = 1, ..., n$ represents the identifier of the nearest instance to the instance i, considering only instance subset selected by the chromosome, a reduction of time complexity can be achieved. A partial evaluation can take advantage of U and of the divisible nature of the PS problem when instances are removed. Note that if instances are added (changes from 0 to 1 are allowed), the update of U is neither partial nor an efficient process because all neighbors have to been computed again. In this sense, the PS problem have characteristics of divisible nature.

An example is illustrated in figure 1, where a chromosome of 13 instances is considered. LS procedure removes the instance number 3. Once removed, the instance number 3 can not appears into U structure as nearest neighbor of another instance. U must be updated at this moment obtaining the new nearest neighbors for the instances that had instance number 3 as nearest neighbor. Then, a relative fitness with respect original chromosome fitness is calculated (instances 1, 5, 11 and 13).

Class	Instances
A	{1,2,3,4,5,6,7}
B	{8,9,10,11,12,13}

	Current Solution	→	Neighbor Solution
Representation	0110110100010	→	0100110100010
U structure	{3, 5, 8, 8, 3, 2, 6, 2, 8, 8, 3, 2, 3}	→	{**12**, 5, 8, 8, **2**, 2, 6, 2, 8, 8, **8**, 2, **8**}
Fitness	{1,1,0,0,1,1,1,0,1,1,0,0,0}	→	{-1,*,*,*,0,*,*,*,*,*,+1,*,+1}
	7	→	7 − 1 + 1 + 1
	Partial evaluation account: $\frac{N_{nu}}{|T|} = \frac{4}{13}$		
	Neighbor Fitness: 8		

Fig. 1. Example of a move in LS procedure and a partial evaluation

4 Experiments and Results

In this section, the behavior of the EPS proposed is analyzed using 13 data sets taken from the UCI Machine Learning Database Repository [12] and compared with others non-evolutionary PS algorithms, such as ENN [13], CNN [14], RNN [15], IB3 [16], DROP3 [3] and RMHC [17] (brief descriptions can be found in [3]). The main characteristics of these data sets are summarized in Table 1.

The data sets considered are partitioned using the *ten fold cross-validation (10-fcv)* procedure. Whether either small or medium data sets are evaluated, the parameters used are the same, see Table 2. The scale of size of data sets and parameters for the algorithms follow the instructions given in [6].

Tables 3 and 4 show us the average of the results offered by each algorithm for small data sets and medium data sets, respectively. Each column shows:

- The first column shows the name of the algorithm. Our proposal of Incorporating Knowledge in a Genetic Algorithm for PS problem will be labeled by *IKGA* and will be followed by the number of evaluations executed to reach the stop condition. It has been executed considering 5000 and 10000 evaluations in order to check its behavior.

Table 1. A brief summary of the experimental data sets

Name	N. Instances	N. Features.	N. Classes.	Size
Bupa	345	7	2	small
Cleveland	297	13	5	small
Glass	294	9	7	small
Iris	150	4	3	small
Led7Digit	500	7	10	small
Lymphography	148	18	4	small
Monks	432	6	2	small
Pima	768	8	2	small
Wine	178	13	3	small
Wisconsin	683	9	2	small
Pen-Based	10992	16	10	medium
Satimage	6435	36	7	medium
Thyroid	7200	21	3	medium

Table 2. Parameters considered for the algorithms

Algorithm	Parameters
CHC	$Pop = 50, Eval = 10000, \alpha = 0.5$
IB3	$Acept.Level = 0.9, DropLevel = 0.7$
IKGA	$Pop = 10, Eval = [5000|10000], p_m = 0.01, p_c = 1$
PBIL	$LR = 0.1, Mut_{shift} = 0.05, p_m = 0.02, Pop = 50$
	$Negative_{LR} = 0.075, Eval = 10000$
RMHC	$S = 90\%, Eval = 10000$

– The second column contains the average execution time associated to each algorithm. The algorithms have been run in a Pentium 4, 3 GHz, 1 Gb RAM.
– The third column shows the average reduction percentage from the initial training sets.
– Fourth and Fifth columns contains the training accuracy when using the training set selected S_i from the initial set TR_i and the test accuracy of S_i over the test data set TS_i, respectively.

In the third, fourth and fifth columns, the best result per column are shown in bold.

By studying the tables 3 and 4, two drawbacks can be appreciated:

– The evaluation of just the mean classification accuracy over all the data sets hides important information due to a better/worse behavior of an algorithm associated to a determined data set.
– Each data set represents a different classification problem and different data sets have many different degrees of difficulty.

To avoid these drawbacks, we have included a second type of table accomplishing a statistical comparison of methods over multiple data sets. Demšar [18] recommends a set of simple, safe and robust non-parametric tests for statistical comparisons of classifiers. One of them is Wilcoxon Signed-Ranks Test [19,20]. Table 5 collects results of applying Wilcoxon test between our proposed methods and rest of PS algorithm studied in this paper over the 13 data sets considered. This table is divided in three parts: In the first part, we accomplish Wilcoxon test by using as performance measure only the reduction of the training set; in the second part, the measure of performance used is the accuracy

Table 3. Average results for small data sets

Algorithm	Time(s)	Reduction	Ac. Train	Ac. Test
1NN	0.02	-	73.52	72.52
CHC	8.67	97.45	79.91	74.14
CNN	0.03	65.70	64.76	68.35
DROP3	0.17	83.53	73.50	67.90
ENN	0.02	25.21	77.68	73.44
IB3	0.02	69.17	64.17	69.90
PBIL	31.05	93.99	81.55	73.96
IKGA 5000 Ev.	6.20	98.43	74.77	**76.37**
IKGA 10000 Ev.	13.49	**98.46**	74.71	75.97
RMHC	17.50	90.18	**83.80**	74.98
RNN	4.63	92.43	74.59	73.37

Table 4. Average results for medium data sets

Algorithm	Time(s)	Reduction	Ac. Train	Ac. Test
1NN	31.56	-	94.19	94.18
CHC	8945.91	**99.55**	93.02	92.45
CNN	2.31	88.80	88.86	90.58
DROP3	186.82	94.62	89.17	87.71
ENN	10.78	5.88	95.11	**94.41**
IB3	5.48	73.02	91.87	92.80
PBIL	51165.29	83.82	94.79	93.80
IKGA 5000 Ev.	2394.07	99.29	94.84	93.81
IKGA 10000 Ev.	4996.26	99.34	94.95	93.74
RMHC	8098.15	90.00	**96.35**	94.06
RNN	23822.91	96.57	94.22	92.81

Table 5. Wilcoxon test

	IKGA 5000 Ev.	IKGA 10000 Ev.	CHC	CNN	DROP3	ENN	IB3	PBIL	RMHC	RNN
Reduction Performance										
IKGA 5000 Ev.	=	=	+	+	+	+	+	+	+	+
IKGA 10000 Ev.	=	=	+	+	+	+	+	+	+	+
Accuracy in Test Performance										
IKGA 5000 Ev.	=	=	+	+	+	=	+	=	=	=
IKGA 10000 Ev.	=	=	+	+	+	=	+	=	=	=
Accuracy in Test ∗ 0.5 + Reduction ∗ 0.5										
IKGA 5000 Ev.	=	=	+	+	+	+	+	+	+	+
IKGA 10000 Ev.	=	=	+	+	+	+	+	+	+	+

classification in test set; in third part, a combination of reduction an classification accuracy is used for performance measure. This combination corresponds to $0.5 \cdot clas\_rat + 0.5 \cdot perc\_red$. Each part of this table contains two rows, representing our proposed methods, and N columns where N is the number of algorithms considered in this study. In each one of the cells can appear two symbols: + or =. They represent that the algorithm situated in that row outperforms (+) or is similar (=) in performance that the algorithm which appear in the column (Table 5).

The following analysis seeing this results can be made:

- IKGA presents the best reduction and test accuracy rates in Table 3.
- In Table 4, IKGA offers a good test accuracy rate and maintains a high reduction rate.

- When the problem scales up to medium data sets, IKGA avoids premature convergence observed in CHC and reach similar test accuracy than PBIL, but provides more reduction rate.
- Time execution over small and medium data sets decreases considerably by using IKGA with respect the remaining EAs.
- IKGA executed with 5000 evaluations and 10000 evaluations have similar behavior. This indicates that this algorithm carries out a good trade-off between exploitation and exploration over the search space.
- In Table 5, IKGA outperforms all methods considering that both objectives (reduction and test accuracy) have the same importance. Furthermore, Wilcoxon accuracy test considers it equal to classical algorithms such as ENN, RNN or RMHC, but these algorithms don't reach its reduction rate.

5 Concluding Remarks

In this paper, we have presented an Evolutionary Algorithm that incorporates knowledge on the Prototype Selection problem. The results shows that incorporating knowledge can obtain an improvement on accuracy and a better reduction of data. Furthermore, a decrement of time complexity is got with respect others Evolutionary Prototype Selection algorithms studied in the literature.

Acknowledgement. This work was supported by TIN2005-08386-C05-01 and TIN2005-08386-C05-03.

References

1. Cover, T.M., Hart, P.E.: Nearest neighbor pattern classification. IEEE Transactions on Information Theory **13** (1967) 21–27
2. Liu, H., Motoda, H.: On issues of instance selection. Data Min. Knowl. Discov. **6** (2002) 115–130
3. Wilson, D.R., Martinez, T.R.: Reduction techniques for instance-based learning algorithms. Machine Learning **38** (2000) 257–286
4. Grochowski, M., Jankowski, N.: Comparison of instance selection algorithms II. Results and comments. In: ICAISC. (2004) 580–585
5. Ishibuchi, H., Nakashima, T.: Evolution of reference sets in nearest neighbor classification. In: SEAL'98: Selected papers from the Second Asia-Pacific Conference on Simulated Evolution and Learning on Simulated Evolution and Learning, London, UK, Springer-Verlag (1999) 82–89
6. Cano, J.R., Herrera, F., Lozano, M.: Using evolutionary algorithms as instance selection for data reduction in KDD: An experimental study. IEEE Transactions on Evolutionary Computation **7** (2003) 561–575
7. Cano, J.R., Herrera, F., Lozano, M.: Stratification for scaling up evolutionary prototype selection. Pattern Recogn. Lett. **26** (2005) 953–963
8. Eiben, A.E., Smith J.E.: Introduction to Evolutionary Computing. SpringerVerlag (2003)
9. Goldberg, D.E.: Genetic Algorithms in Search, Optimization, and Machine Learning. Addison Wesley (1989)

10. Eshelman, L.J.: The CHC adaptative search algorithm: How to safe search when engaging in nontraditional genetic recombination. In: FOGA. (1990) 265–283
11. Baluja, S.: Population-based incremental learning: A method for integrating genetic search based function optimization and competitive learning. Technical report, Pittsburgh, PA, USA (1994)
12. Newman, D.J., Hettich, S., Merz, C.B.: UCI repository of machine learning databases (1998)
13. Wilson, D.L.: Asymptotic properties of nearest neighbor rules using edited data. IEEE Transactions on Systems, Man and Cybernetics **2** (1972) 408–421
14. Hart, P.E.: The condensed nearest neighbour rule. IEEE Transactions on Information Theory **18** (1968) 515–516
15. Gates, G.W.: The reduced nearest neighbour rule. IEEE Transactions on Information Theory **18** (1972) 431–433
16. Aha, D.W., Kibler, D., Albert, M.K.: Instance-based learning algorithms. Machine Learning **7** (1991) 37–66
17. Skalak, D.B.: Prototype and feature selection by sampling and random mutation hill climbing algorithms. In: ICML. (1994) 293–301
18. Demšar, J: Statistical comparisons of classifiers over multiple data sets. Journal of Machine Learning Research **7** (2006) 1–30
19. Wilcoxon, F.: Individual comparisons by rankings methods. Biometrics **1** (1945) 80–83
20. Sheskin, D.J.: Handbook of Parametric and Nonparametric Statistical Procedures. CRC Press (1997)

Evidence Relationship Matrix and Its Application to D-S Evidence Theory for Information Fusion

Xianfeng Fan, Hong-Zhong Huang, and Qiang Miao

School of Mechatronics Engineering,
University of Electronic Science and Technology of China,
Chengdu, Sichuan, 610054, China
fanxf@yahoo.com, hzhuang@uestc.edu.cn, mqiang@uestc.edu.cn

Abstract. D-S evidence theory has been studied and used for information fusion for a while. Though D-S evidence theory can deal with uncertainty reasoning from imprecise and uncertain information by combining cumulative evidences for changing prior opinions using new evidences. False evidence generated by any fault sensor will result in evidence conflict increasing and inaccurate fused results. Evidence relationship matrix proposed in this paper depicts the relationship among evidences. False evidences can be identified through the analysis of relationships among evidences. Basic probability assignments related to the false evidences may be decreased accordingly. The accuracy of information fusion may be improved. Case studies show the effectiveness of the proposed method.

Keywords: evidence relationship matrix, D-S evidence theory, and information fusion.

1 Introduction

The Dempster-Shafer (D-S) evidence theory was proposed by Shafer, who built upon Dempster's research [1]. It is able to calculate probabilities that evidence supports the propositions and offers an alternative approach to dealing with uncertainty reasoning from imprecise and uncertain information. The theory is suitable to taking into account the disparity of knowledge types due to the fact that it is able to provide a federative framework, and combine cumulative evidences for changing prior opinions in the light of new evidences [1, 2]. Therefore, the study and application of D-S evidence theory for information fusion attract researchers interests [3, 4, 5].

We still face some challenges during using the theory in practice. For example, evidence may not be sufficient to support the basic probability assignment because of the measurement errors incurred by sensors. Recently, fuzzy theory was introduced to modify the basic probability assignment (BPA) with the consideration of evidence sufficiency [6, 7]. But, false evidences are not considered. If any sensor has fault, the acquired data is not correct any more. False evidences will occur. The conflicts among evidences may be bigger than before. Wrong fusion results may arise. In this paper, evidence relationship matrix that can reflect the relationships among evidences is proposed. Through studying the evidence relationship, we can identify false evidences. The BPAs related to the false evidences can be decreased greatly. Therefore, the accuracy of information fusion through D-S evidence theory can be improved accordingly.

The rest of the paper is organized as follows. D-S evidence theory is illustrated briefly in Section 2. Evidence relationship matrix is proposed in Section 3. The modification of BPAs based on evidence relationship matrix is investigated. An example is given out to validate the proposed method in Section 4. Conclusions and discussion are presented in the last section.

2 D-S Evidence Theory

Let Θ be a finite nonempty set of mutually exclusive alternatives, and be called discernment frame containing every possible hypothesis.

Basic probability assignment is a function, $m: 2^{\Theta} \to [0,1]$, such that $m(\emptyset)=0$ where $\emptyset$ denotes an empty set, and $\sum m(X) = 1$ for any $X \subseteq \Theta$. The power set 2^{Θ} is the set of all the subsets of Θ including itself [1]. Given a piece of evidence, a belief level between [0, 1], denoted by $m(\cdot)$, is assigned to each subset of Θ. Each subset contains one or more hypothesis. If a feature for a hypothesis exists, the corresponding BPA is said to be fired by the feature and the feature is called evidence. This BPA will be involved in information fusion. Otherwise, the BPA for the hypothesis will not be fired and considered for information fusion.

The total belief level committed to X, $Bel: 2^{\Theta} \to [0,1]$, is obtained by calculating the belief function for X as Eq. (1). $Bel(X)$ represents the belief level that a proposition lies in X or any subset of X.

$$Bel(X) = \sum_{Y \subseteq X, X \subseteq \Theta} m(Y). \tag{1}$$

The plausibility function defined below measures the extent, to which we fail to disbelieve the hypothesis of X, $Pl: 2^{\Theta} \to [0,1]$.

$$Pl(X) = \sum_{Y \cap X \neq \emptyset, X, Y \subseteq \Theta} m(Y). \tag{2}$$

Both imprecision and uncertainty can be represented by Bel and Pl. The relationship between them is

$$\begin{cases} Pl(A) = 1 - Bel(\bar{A}) \\ Pl(A) \geq Bel(A) \end{cases}. \tag{3}$$

Where, $\bar{A}$ is the negation of hypothesis A. $Bel(A)$ and $Pl(A)$ are the lower limit and the upper limit of belief level of A, respectively. $Pl(A)$-$Bel(A)$ for $A \subseteq \Theta$ represents the ignorance level in hypothesis A.

Multiple evidences can be fused using Dempster's combination rule, shown as Eq. (4) [1]. Evidences of any subsets X and Y of Θ can be used to calculate the belief level in a new hypothesis C. $C = X \cap Y$. If $C = \emptyset$, it means evidences conflict with each other totally and the belief level in hypothesis C is then null.

$$m(C) = m_i(X) \oplus m_{i'}(Y) = \begin{cases} 0, & \text{If } X \cap Y = \emptyset \\ \dfrac{\sum_{X \cap Y = C, \forall X, Y \subseteq \Theta} m_i(X) \times m_{i'}(Y)}{1 - \sum_{X \cap Y = \emptyset, \forall X, Y \subseteq \Theta} m_i(X) \times m_{i'}(Y)}, & \text{If } X \cap Y \neq \emptyset \end{cases} \quad (4)$$

where i (i') denotes the ith (i'^{th}) evidence. $m_i(X)$ and $m_{i'}(Y)$ are the BPA of X supported by evidence i and the BPA of Y supported by evidence i', respectively. Let

$$k_{i,i'} = \sum_{X \cap Y = \emptyset} m_i(X) \times m_{i'}(Y), \quad (5)$$

$k_{i,i'}$ is called the conflict factor between the two evidences i and i', where $k_{i,i'} \neq 1$.

Dempster's combination rule can be generalized to more than two hypotheses, as Eq. (6). The final result represents the synthetic effects of all evidences.

$$m = m_1 \oplus m_2 \oplus \cdots \oplus \cdots = (((m_1 \oplus m_2) \oplus \cdots) \oplus \cdots). \quad (6)$$

In practice, because the collected data from sensors have errors and the features extracted may not be sufficient, we may have no adequate evidence to support a certain hypothesis. Fan and Zuo solve the issue through the introduction of fuzzy theory [6]. For evidence e_i, the evidence sufficiency can be realized by the attenuation of BPA using sufficiency index μ_i, as Eq. (7). The new BPA is denoted by $m_{i,*}(\cdot)$.

$$m_{i,*}(A) = \begin{cases} \mu_i \cdot m_i(A), & A \subset \Theta \\ 1 - \sum_{B \subset \Theta} \mu_i \cdot m_i(B), & B \subset \Theta, A = \Theta \end{cases} \quad (7)$$

where $i = 1, 2, \cdots, n$, n is the number of evidences, and $*$ denotes that the BPA has incorporated evidence sufficiency. All the above analysis is based on the assumption that all sensors are normal. In practice, we may collect false data and obtain false evidence if any unknown fault sensor exists. For this case, information fusion results are suspect and may be wrong.

3 The Evidence Relationship Matrix and the Modification of BPAs

Because all the information comes from a same system usually, there may be a relationship between any two evidences. E is used to represent evidence set in this paper. $E = \{e_i \mid i = 1, 2, \cdots, n\}$. n is the number of all the evidences that may be obtained for information fusion. $r_{i,j}$ represents the relationship between evidences e_i and e_j. $j = 1, 2, \cdots, n$. It means that if evidences e_i appear, the appearance probability of evidence e_j should be $r_{i,j}$. $r_{i,j} \in [0,1]$. If there is no relationship between evidences e_i and e_j, $r_{i,j} = 0.5$. It means that if e_i appears, the appearance possibility of e_j is 50%. The meaning of $r_{i,j} < 0.5$ is that if e_i appears, the appearance possibility of e_j is less than 50%. For evidence self, $r_{i,i} = 1$. In this paper, $r_{i,j}$ are determined through system analysis. For example, machine faults are usually reflected through vibration, acoustic, wear debris, oil temperature, electrical current, and function performance. The pattern identification accuracy of machine faults is greatly depended on the above multi signatures. The determination of $r_{i,j}$ is based on the following relationships. Such as: if the vibration increases, acoustic level will increase with the possibility of 80%. If there are lots of metal particles in oil debris, vibration will increase with the possibility of 90%. These possibilities $r_{i,j}$ can be obtained by experts experience and statistic based on past fault modes. Then, we may have the following matrix, called evidence relationship matrix.

$$R = \begin{bmatrix} r_{1,1} & r_{1,2} & \cdots & r_{1,n} \\ r_{2,1} & r_{2,2} & \cdots & r_{2,n} \\ \vdots & \vdots & \ddots & \vdots \\ r_{n,1} & r_{n,2} & \cdots & r_{n,n} \end{bmatrix} = \begin{bmatrix} 1 & r_{1,2} & \cdots & r_{1,n} \\ r_{2,1} & 1 & \cdots & r_{2,n} \\ \vdots & \vdots & \ddots & \vdots \\ r_{n,1} & r_{n,2} & \cdots & 1 \end{bmatrix}. \tag{8}$$

In this matrix, for evidence e_i, when the number of j that satisfies $r_{j,i} > 0.5$ is more than one, it means that more than one evidences support the appearance of e_i. In other words, the appearance possibility of e_i becomes bigger. For each row in Eq. (8), we can obtain the appearance possibility of e_i, P_i^R, from total other evidences by

$$P_i^R = \sum_j r_{i,j}. \tag{9}$$

Accordingly, for each column in Eq. (8), we can obtain the appearance possibility of e_i, P_i^C, from total other evidences by

$$P_j^C = \sum_i r_{i,j}. \tag{10}$$

Because $i, j = 1, 2, \cdots, n$, we may write P_j^R as P_i^R. At last, we can reach the general appearance possibility of an evidence i by

$$P_i = (P_i^R + P_i^C)/2. \tag{11}$$

The modification of BPAs can be performed. Firstly, construct the matrix in Eq. (8). Secondly, calculate P_i using Eqs. (8)-(11). Thirdly, define an appearance possibility index $\hat{P}_i$. $\hat{P}_i = P_i / \max(P_i)$. At last, we obtain the modified BPAs $m_i^*(X) = \hat{P}_i m_i(X)$. $X \subset \Theta$. In addition, considering sensor error, we introduce synthetical index ξ_i. $\xi_i = \hat{P}_i \cdot \mu_i$. μ_i is evidence sufficiency index. The details can be referred to [6]. Therefore, the modified BPAs can be obtained by

$$\begin{cases} m_i^*(X) = \xi_i m_i(X) \\ m_i^*(\Theta) = 1 - \sum m_i^*(X) \end{cases} \text{for } X \subset \Theta. \tag{12}$$

In Eq. (12), we assume that all the evidences have same importance in order to focus on the issue mentioned in this paper.

In practice, it is impossible that all evidences appear at a same time. Only the evidences related to a hypothesis, which is true, appear. Therefore, we have the practical relationship matrix $\hat{R}$. The dimension of $\hat{R}$ is less than that of R.

At last, we substitute the $m_i(X)$ and $m_i(Y)$ by $m_i^*(X)$ and $m_i^*(Y)$, respectively. Using Eq. (4), we can fuse information and greatly avoid the affect of false evidences.

4 Case Studies

In order to verify the proposed method, an example is studied. Suppose $\Theta = \{F_1, F_2, F_3\}$, $E = \{e_i \mid i=1,2,3\}$. The BPAs are shown in Table 1.

Table 1. The basic possibility assignments

	$m(\{F_1\})$	$m(\{F_2\})$	$m(\{F_3\})$	$m(\Theta)$
e_1	0.1	0.2	0.7	0
e_2	0.4	0.5	0	0.1
e_3	0.8	0.1	0.1	0

In this example, we assume that all the evidences are sufficient and have the same importance for information fusion. Therefore, $\mu_i = 1$. In Table 1, we find that evidences e_1 support $\{F_3\}$ greatly. While, evidences e_2 and e_3 do not support $\{F_3\}$ very well. Obviously, both of evidences e_2 and e_3 conflict with evidence e_1. Therefore, e_1 may be false evidence.

If we do not consider the phenomena discussed above, according to Eq. (4), we fuse the evidence $\{e_i \mid i=1,2,3\}$ and obtain the following results. $m(\{F_1\}) = 0.6778$, $m(\{F_2\}) = 0.2035$, $m(\{F_3\}) = 0.1187$. Correspondingly, belief level and plausibility can be obtained using Eqs. (1) and (2), respectively. Such as, $Bel(\{F_1\}) = 0.6778$, $Pl(\{F_1\}) = 0.6778$.

We then consider the relationship among evidences in order to embody the conflict issue mentioned above. The evidence relationship matrix is shown in Eq. (13). Based on Eqs. (8)-(11), we are able to calculate $\hat{p}_i$. $\hat{p}_i$ are equal to 0.6667, 0.911, and 1, respectively, when i is equal to 1, 2 and 3. Based on Eq. (12), Table 1 is modified to Table 2.

$$R = \begin{array}{c} e_1 \\ e_2 \\ e_3 \end{array} \begin{array}{ccc} e_1 & e_2 & e_3 \end{array} \\ \begin{bmatrix} 1 & 0.1 & 0.6 \\ 0.2 & 1 & 0.9 \\ 0.1 & 0.9 & 1 \end{bmatrix}. \tag{13}$$

Table 2. The modified basic possibility assignments

	$m^*(\{F_1\})$	$m^*(\{F_2\})$	$m^*(\{F_3\})$	$m^*(\Theta)$
e_1	0.0667	0.1333	0.4667	0.333
e_2	0.3644	0.4544	0	0.1801
e_3	0.8	0.1	0.1	0

According to Eq. (4) and Table 2, we fuse the evidence $\{e_i \mid i=1,2,3\}$ again and obtain the following results. $m(\{F_1\}) = 0.7960 \cdot m(\{F_2\}) = 0.1368 \cdot m(\{F_3\}) = 0.0672$. Correspondingly, belief level and plausibility can be obtained using Eqs. (1) and (2), respectively. Such as, $Bel(\{F_1\}) = 0.7960 \cdot Pl(\{F_1\}) = 0.7960$.

Compared with the fusion results without introduction of evidence relationship matrix, the BPA of $\{F_1\}$ increases using the proposed method. The comparisons are shown in Fig. 1. According to Eqs. (1) and (2), the *Bel* and *Pl* of $\{F_1\}$ will increase using the proposed method, correspondingly. The BPA, *Bel* and *Pl* of $\{F_3\}$ decrease greatly. These results show that the role of evidence e_1 for fusion is decreased greatly.

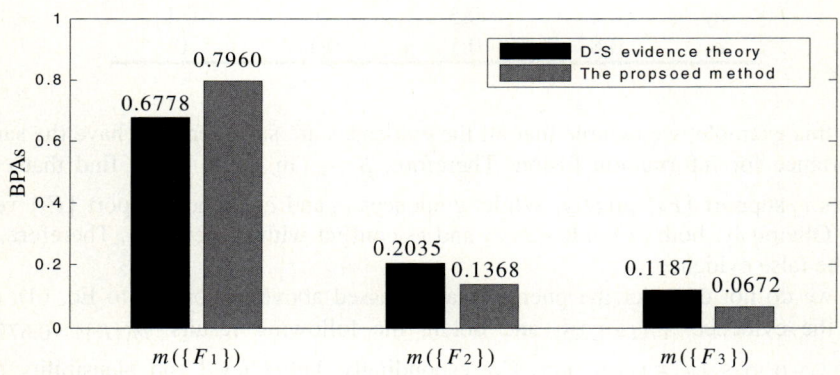

Fig. 1. The comparison between D-S evidence theory and the proposed method

5 Conclusions and Discussions

In this study, relationships among evidences are considered in D-S evidence theory for information fusion. Evidence relationship matrix is proposed to depict these relationships. Appearance possibility index obtained using the evidence relationship matrix is proposed as well. Case studies show that the proposal of evidence relationship matrix and appearance possibility index can help to decrease the role of false evidences for information fusion. The credibility of information fusion is improved compared with the information fusion using traditional D-S evidence theory. The evaluation of relationships between any two evidences needs study further.

Acknowledgments

The work reported in this paper was partially supported by the Open Fund of the State Key Laboratory of Vibration, Shock and Noise of Shanghai Jiaotong University under grant VSN-2006-03.

References

[1] Shafer, G.: A Mathematical Theory of Evidence, Princeton, NJ: Princeton University Press, (1976).
[2] Fabre, S., Appriou A., Briottet X.: Presentation and Description of Two Classification Methods using Data Fusion based on Sensor Management. Information Fusion. 2 (2001) 49-71
[3] Rottensteiner F., Trinder J., Clode S., Kubik K.: Using the Dempster - Shafer Method for the Fusion of LIDAR Data and Multi - Spectral Images for Building Detection. Information Fusion 6 (2005) 283-300
[4] Basir O., Karray F., Zhu H.: Connectionist-Based Dempster–Shafer Evidential Reasoning for Data Fusion. IEEE Transactions on Neural Networks. 6(2005) 1513-1530
[5] Fan X., Huang H., Miao Q.: Agent-based Diagnosis of Slurry Pumps Using Information Fusion. Proceedings of the International Conference on Sensing, Computing and Automation. ICSCA 2006. Chongqing, China. May 8-11 (2006) 1687-1691
[6] Fan X., Zuo, M. J.: Fault Diagnosis of Machines based on D-S Evidence Theory. Part 1: D-S Evidence Theory and Its Improvement. Pattern Recognition Letters. 5(2006) 366-376
[7] Huang H. Z.: Fuzzy Multi-Objective Optimization Decision-Making of Reliability of Series System. Microelectronics and Reliability. 3 (1997) 447- 449

Soft Computing in Context-Sensitive Multidimensional Ranking

Weber Martins[1,2], Lauro Eugênio Guimarães Nalini[2],
Marco Antonio Assfalk de Oliveira[1], and Leonardo Guerra de Rezende Guedes[1]

[1] Federal University of Goias, School of Computer and Electrical Engineering,
PIRENEUS Research Group, Bloco D, Goiania, Goias, 74605-220, Brazil
{weber, assfalk, lguedes}@eee.ufg.br
http://www.pireneus.eee.ufg.br/~weber

[2] Catholic University of Goias, Department of Psychology,
LAEC Research Group, Bloco H, Goiania, Goias, 74605-010, Brazil
{weber, nalini}@ucg.br

Abstract. Many applications require ordering of instances represented by high dimensional vectors. Despite the reasonable quantity of papers on classification and clustering, papers on multidimensional ranking are rare. This paper expands a generic ranking procedure based on one-dimensional self-organizing maps (SOMs). The typical similarity metric is modified to a weighted Euclidean metric and automatically adjusted by a genetic search. The search goal is the best ranking that matches the desired probability distribution (provided by experts) leading to a context-sensitive metric. To ease expert agreement the technique relies on consensus about the best and worst instances. Besides the ranking task, the derived metric is also useful on reducing the number of dimensions (questionnaire items in some situations) and on modeling the data source. Promising results were achieved on the ranking of data from blood bank inspections and client segmentation in agribusiness.

1 Introduction

Despite the existence of few reported works, the area of context-sensitive multi-dimensional ranking is interesting to many areas [2,3,4]. Some studies are undertaken regarding the problem faced in web search engines, where pages must be ranked, but this problem has a different nature since dimensions are not clearly available in the text and query-time is very important. This paper presents a general technique introduced in [1] by one of the authors and exemplifies its use with two practical examples based on questionnaires: quality evaluation of Brazilian blood banks and client segmentation in agribusiness.

Generally, multidimensional data represents any phenomenon or entity of the real world, assuming an attribute vector format. Which attributes of the phenomenon will be selected depend on the application. Many times, the available attributes are not of direct interest. They are only paths to discover the attributes that we are really interested. An example would be the multidimensional data that reports a blood bank sanitary inspection or a client interview.

By using the first example in order to clarify, the interest of the application is to rank Brazilian blood banks according to the quality of available services. The attribute 'quality', however, is not directly measurable. It is obtained through observation and analysis of other attributes (component variables), more precisely 77 recorded attributes for each blood bank. Therefore, the attribute we are really interested at is a latent attribute.

When 'ranking' (ordinal number) is mentioned, a meaningful sequence (e.g., positions in a race car) is thought of. Therefore, when it is mentioned the Goiania city blood bank position in the Brazilian blood bank quality ranking, there is always a criteria to discover (or set) that position. In fact, ranking leads to the idea of one-dimensional criteria. To rank instances represented by multidimensional data, there must be a dimensionality reduction and the performing of some type of regression that, when they are combined, will reveal the criteria employed to build the ranking. The SOM neural network [5,6] has these two characteristics needed to build a ranking of multidimensional data.

The use of SOM artificial neural networks (ANNs) to solve ordering problems of high dimensional vectors is not common. Problems of this kind are generally approached by using probabilistic classifiers and other strategies [7]. Kohonen, SOM creator, lists only one reference about this issue among other 1700 references. Some works have been published since then [8].

Besides SOM's ability to visualize nonlinear relationships in multidimensional data, the development of a topological order is an effect already empirically confirmed. However, the analytical proof of the ordering property does not prove they can be used to order instances represented by high dimensional vectors (the proof was undertaken to the case of one-dimensional networks and one dimensional input vectors, scalar values) [9]. Kohonen himself [6] states that it is not likely the existence of ordered convergent states in high dimensions. In [10], by observing geometric aspects of the ordering phenomenon described by the Kohonen ordering theorem [6], authors have shown that an unique convergent ordered state in dimensions greater than one has zero probability of existence, that is, it is an impossible event. The fact that SOM maps do not converge voluntarily to an (unique) ordered state in high dimensional input spaces requires the imposition of external constraints in order to use their properties of dimension reduction and topological ordering. These constraints should force the convergence to the desired state and conduct the learning process properly.

Another important aspect to be analyzed is the similarity metric used by the SOM algorithm to choose the winner unit. In the standard algorithm, the Euclidean distance is employed. The unit with the lowest distance between its weight and the current input (in terms of Euclidean distance) is the winner neuron and has its weight vector updated (together with its neighboring). In real-world ordering of instances, however, the 'pure' Euclidean distance does not always points to the desired ordering. In a vector of attributes, each one can provide a different weight to the ordering. The 'pure' Euclidean distance does not take into account this attribute weighting. Therefore, a generic technique of ordering should consider the weighting of components of an attribute vector. In this work, it is suggested the weighting of attributes by using a genetic algorithm to automatically find the values used by the weighting process.

The expected distribution function of samples in the ranking (provided by domain experts) combined with the references for the first (best) and last (worst) instances in the desired ordering (also provided by the domain expert) are the external constraints employed to force the convergence of the network. The confirmed hypothesis of this work is that the distribution function and references provided by domain experts are enough to cause the convergence of the ordering at the desired context. Such strategy is justified since looking at the direct evaluation of the relative importance of each attribute is a controversial process even among experts. In this work, we have used a distribution based on a histogram obtained from a normal (Gaussian) distribution due to its ability to represent the reality in different situations. To the expert, it is left only the definition of the best and the worst cases.

2 Proposed System

This work proposes the use of one-dimensional SOM maps to order multidimensional data. It consists on searching and adjusting a population of distance metrics to find the one that conducts the one-dimensional map to generate a ranking where the difference of importance among the attributes is considered. This is carried on by presetting the neuron weights that occupy ending positions (with the best and worst instances provided by the domain expert) and adjusting the sample distribution to make it as near as possible to the one desired by the expert.

The search in the distance domain is performed by a Genetic Algorithm [11]. It looks for the recombination of the best chromosomes (best distances) by using the fitness criteria. In this paper, on the case of quality evaluation of Brazilian blood banks, this criteria is the similarity of the ranking distribution generated by the network with the reference distribution defined by the expert (usually, a histogram obtained from the normal distribution). On the second case, client segmentation in agribusiness, the criteria is the correlation between subjective (human, expert) classification and objective classification (derived from the resulting mathematical model).

The algorithm of the proposed procedure is shown below.

1. Set up the network in order to cope with the desired ranking (e.g., 10 neurons in the example of Brazilian blood banks)
2. Generate the initial population of distances (chromosomes) with random scalar numbers in the range from zero to one.
3. While the quality of the distribution is not adequate, do:
   – Fix weights of the first and last neuron by using the samples provided by domain experts as the best and the worst of the whole sample. All the rest of them receive random values chosen in the same range of the examples as suggested in [5]
   – Recombine the distance population (chromosomes)

- Train the network with the available samples by using the distance (chromosome), generated by the recombination.
- Calculate the quality (fitness) of the 'ranking' generated by the network with respect to the expected distribution.
4. Train a significant number of networks with the chosen distance and generates a final ranking by using the average of the ranking position in all trained networks.

The distance (or similarity measure) used in the standard SOM is the square of the Euclidean distance between the input and the vector of neuron weights. Let **X** be the input vector, **W** be the weight vector and n be the dimensionality of the input vector, the standard Euclidean distance is given by:

$$d^2 = \sum (X_i - w_i)^2 \tag{1}$$

where: X_i is the value of the i-th input; and w_i is the weight value of the i-th connection. In this work, the distance has been modified to the following expression:

$$d^2 = \sum p_i . (X_i - w_i)^2 \tag{2}$$

where: p_i is a weighting factor that indicates the importance of the i-th attribute.

The genetic algorithm will look for the **p** vector that imposes the best ranking, in accordance with the criteria of the best example distribution (the highest similarity with the chosen distribution). The fixation of weights for the first and last neurons forces the map to have only one ordering direction, not allowing inversions that are common at trained one-dimensional SOMs. This procedure also forces that the ranking position difference between the two references (the best and the worst ones) indicated by the expert to be naturally the highest of the ranking.

3 Experiments

3.1 Quality Evaluation of Brazilian Blood Banks

Data were obtained by sanitary inspections in Brazilian blood banks. In total, it was analyzed data from 85 inspections. Each inspection was recorded by 77 items. Each item has received the values '1', '-1' and '0', corresponding, respectively, to 'yes', 'no' and 'not applicable' or 'not informed'. Data were ordered in three situations, each one generates a ranking. The first ranking is generated by using a statistical method (PCA - Principal Component Analysis and regression) [12,13]. The second ranking was generated by a SOM network without the use of weighting and the third one uses the SOM network with adjust of similarity metric by the genetic algorithm.

Statistical (PCA) Approach. The use of the technique of PCA to reach the ordering criteria has resulted in 23 components (greater than one), that explained, together, 78,43% of the data variability. The first principal component, chosen for the ordering criteria, has represented only 13,68% of the data variability. Figure 1 shows the resulting ranking distribution.

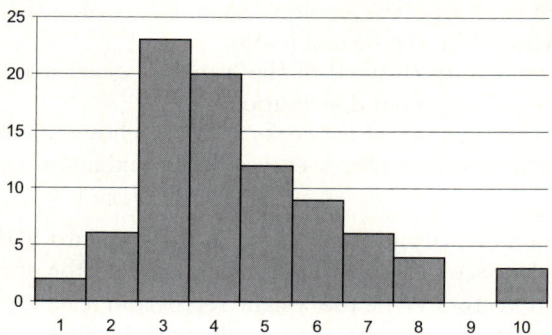

Fig. 1. Histogram of instances distribution using Principal Component Analysis

Standard SOM. The second approach was a SOM network modified by fixing the weights of the ending neurons with the references pointed out by experts. The weighting and the subsequent genetic search of the best distribution were not employed. The parameters to the training of the network at the first phase were learning rate equals to 0.9, neighboring radius of 6 and number of epochs equals to 1044. At the second phase, it was used learning rate equals to 0.02, neighboring radius of 3 and number of epochs equals to 10440. The presentation order was random and the values of the parameters were obtained empirically taking into account suggestions in [6]. The obtained shape of sample distribution is shown in Figure 2.

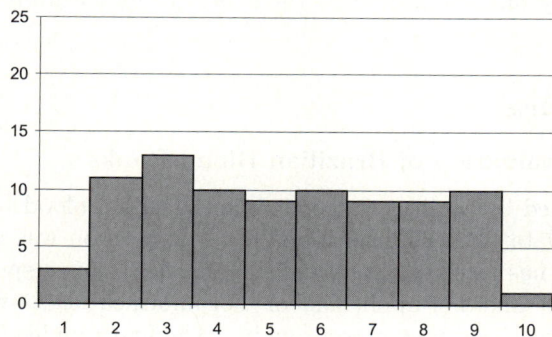

Fig. 2. Histogram of instances distribution using standard Self-Organizing Maps

It was verified by the experiments, in accordance with what has been expected in theoretical studies that, in each training, the one-dimensional SOM network generates a different ranking (by using the same parameters). Nevertheless, it was also perceived that the network presents 'statistical convergence'. In other words, as the number of trained networks is increased, a specific ranking has a higher probability to occur. Therefore, to obtain the final ranking there is a need to train a significant number of networks and, from them, adopt the average positions to each example. In this work, the number of trained networks was 1000.

Proposed System. The parameters employed to test the proposed system concerning SOM networks were the same as the standard SOM. The parameters of the genetic algorithm were: size of initial population equals to 100, mutation rate equals to 1%, uniform crossover, and random initialization of genes in the range of 0 to 5. After the weighting values have been obtained by the genetic algorithm, 1000 networks have been trained and average values of the ranking positions have been adopted as final values, as before. The ranking distribution can be seen in Figure 3.

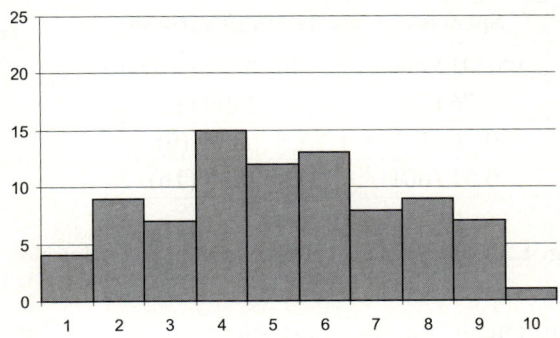

Fig. 3. Histogram of instances distribution using the Proposed System

Results. Besides visual inspection, the use of skewness and curtosis shows that the proposed system has lead to the best solution, that is, the best resemblance of a Gaussian histogram. For instance, the skewness of the proposed system soluction is only 0.05 compared to PCA solution's 0.91. To compare among solutions, it was employed the Spearman coefficient (r_S), non-parametric measure of ordinal data correlation, to assess the similarity between two rankings. The statistical technique, PCA is the most uncorrelated with the proposed system (r_S=0.860). The traditional SOM technique is more correlated with the proposed system (r_S=0.916) but not as much as it is with PCA ($r_S = 0.937$).

3.2 Client Segmentation in Agribusiness

The dataset for the study of client segmentation in agribusiness is composed of 98 client interviews and derived from commercial consulting. Experts have analyzed the agriculture context in three subdomains (production, administration and commercial) and each subdomain in three subjective classes (elementary, intermediary and advanced). Each client has received a subjective classification. The main goal was to obtain a model to turn classification into an objective procedure and, after that, use the derived mathematical model to classify other clients.

Most of variables were binary, but a 'statistical normalization' (based on the histogram of the variable) was necessary to make all of them cover a range between zero and one. Many constraints were imposed by the experts to the weighted Euclidean distance. For example, the weight of X_1 should be greater than the one associated with X_2 and so on.

The main criterion has maintained the number of clients per class as stated by experts and the Spearman correlation between subjective and objective (optimized) ordering has been calculated and optimized, that is, the Spearman correlation was the fitness function of the problem. Notice that only three neurons are used to build the one-dimensional SOM in this case. Figure 4 summarizes the results.

subdomain	Spearman Correlation (# variables)		reduction of # variables
	expert values	proposed system	
production	0.76 (78)	0.90 (12)	15.38%
commercial	0.76 (17)	0.89 (9)	52.94%
administration	0.51 (60)	0.88 (16)	26.67%

Fig. 4. Results of Client Segmentation in Agribusiness

The production domain was the most successful in terms of Spearman correlation and reduction of variables. At first, it seems that no great success has happened in the commercial domain, but it should be noted that it has few variables originally and, therefore, less space for improvement. In terms of relative correlation improvement, the administration domain was the most successful. Finally, it should be highlighted the significant gain in terms of questionnaire reduction, from 155 to 37 items. In practical terms, the interview has been reduced from 3 hours to 30 minutes (a much better session according to interview guidelines).

4 Conclusions

This article has presented a system dedicated to the discovery of rankings in situations where the techniques from traditional statistics are not adequate. By combining Kohonen self-organizing maps, genetic algorithms and expert previous knowledge, it was developed an interesting technique to attend to expert expectations and to find the relative importance (weight) of each attribute of the vector of features that describes the phenomenon. Additional constraints can be imposed on the definition of genetic populations as well.

The proposed technique has behaved quite well for the academic problem of Brazilian blood banks ranking by using the criteria of quality and has shown the importance of each attribute present in the questionnaire of the sanitary inspection. A brief exposition was given to a consulting problem of client segmentation in agribusiness. The reduction of questionnaire items and the improvement of Spearman correlation, fitness function for genetic algorithm optimization, between subjective and objective classification were achieved simultaneously. Future works will be directed to the exploration of logical combinations of the questionnaire variables to reduce even more the number of questionnaire items that have strong influence on the success of a marketing research.

References

1. Martins, W., Meira e Silva, J. C.: Multidimensional Data Ranking Using Self-Organising Maps and Genetic Algorithms. Proceedings of IEEE INNS International Joint Conference on Neural Networks (IJCNN '01). **4** Washington, DC, USA. (2001) 2382–2387
2. Page, L., Brin, S., Motwani, R., Winograd, T.: The PageRank Citation Ranking: bringing order to the web. Technical report, Stanford University, USA. (1998)
3. Kamishima, T., Akaho, S.: Learning From Order Examples. Proceedings of The IEEE Intl Conf. on Data Mining. (2002) 645-648
4. Richardson, M., Domingos, P.: The Intelligent Surfer: Probabilistic combination of link and content information in pagerank. Advances in Neural Information Processing Systems. **14** Proc. of NIPS'01. MIT Press. (2002) 1441–1448
5. Kohonen, T.: Self-Organized Formation of Topologically Correct Feature Maps. Biological Cybernetics. **43** (1982) 59–69
6. Kohonen, T.: Self-Organizing Maps. 3rd extended edition. Springer Series in Information Sciences. **30** Springer-Verlag - Berlin, Heidelberg, New York. (2001)
7. Cohen, W. W., Schapire, R. E., Singer, Y.: Learning to Order Things. Advances in Neural Information Processing Systems. **11** Proc. of NIPS'97. MIT Press. (1998) 451–457
8. Azcarraga, A. P.: Assessing Self-Organization Using Order Metrics. Proceedings of IEEE INNS International Joint Conference on Neural Networks (IJCNN '00). **6** Piscataway, NJ, USA. (2000) 159–164
9. Erwin, E., Obermayer, K., Schulten, K.: Self-Organizing Maps: ordering, convergence properties, and energy funcions. Biological Cybernetics. **67** (1992) 47–55
10. Budinich, M., Taylor, J. G.: On the Ordering Conditions for Self-Organizing Maps. Centre for Neural Networks - Kings College. London, UK. (1995)
11. Michalewicz, Z.: Genetic Algorithms + Data Structures = Evolution Programs. Springer-Verlag. Heidelberg, Germany. (1992)
12. Jolliffe, I.T.: Principal Component Analysis. Springer-Verlag, New York, USA. (1986)
13. Carreira-Perpinan, M. A.: A Review of Dimension Reduction Techniques. Technical Report CS-96-09. University of Shefield, UK. (1999)

Ontology-Based Classifier for Audio Scenes in Telemedicine

Cong Phuong Nguyen, Ngoc Yen Pham, and Eric Castelli

International Research Center MICA
HUT - CNRS/UMI2954 – INPGrenoble
1, Dai Co Viet, Hanoi, Vietnam
{Cong-Phuong.Nguyen, Ngoc-Yen.Pham,
Eric.Castelli}@mica.edu.vn

Abstract. Our work is within the framework of studying and implementing a sound analysis system in a telemedicine project. The task of this system is to detect situations of distress in a patient's room based sound analysis. In this paper we present our works on building domain ontologies of such situations. They gather abstract concepts of sounds and these concepts, along with their properties and instances, are represented by a neural network. The ontology-based classifer uses outputs of networks to identify classes of audio scenes. The system is tested with a database extracted from films.

1 Introduction

The system that we present is developed for the surveillance of elderly, convalescent persons or pregnant women. Its main goal is to detect serious accidents such as falls or faintness at any place in the apartment. Firstly most people do not like to be supervised by cameras all day long while the presence of microphone can be acceptable. Secondly the supervision field of a microphone is larger than that of a camera. Thirdly, sound processing is much less time consuming than image processing, hence a real time processing solution can be easier to develop. Thus, the originality of our approach consists in replacing the video camera by a system of multichannel sound acquisition. The system analyzes in real time the sound environment of the apartment and detects abnormal sounds (falls of objects or patient, scream, groan), that could indicate a distress situation in the habitat.

This system is divided into different small modules. In the process of developing it, a sound acquisition module, a sound classifier, a speech/nonspeech discriminator and a speech/scream-groan discriminator are constructed [1], [2]. They are now being implemented in a room of Mica Centre. Audio signals are acquired by five microphones installed in different positions and fed to a multichannel data acquisition card, at the moment it is of National Instruments. The four modules mentioned above, developed in LabWindows/CVI, process acquired signals to detect situations of distress.

In order to complete the system, we propose sound ontologies which can be used in an ontology-based classifier. Each ontology is an abstract concept of an audio scene representing a situation of distress in the house. It can be used to detect situations of distress, classify audio scenes, to share informations of audio scenes among people and software, to analyze domain knowledge, or to save (as metadata) audio scenes in a database for further usages.

This article is structured as follows. Section 2 discusses works related to ontology-based audio applications. Section 3 describes the proposed ontology of audio scenes, the neural network used to represent ontologies and the ontology-based classifier. Section 4 presents the database of audio scene and the evaluation of ontologies. Section 5 outlines our conclusion and next steps in future to complete this ontology-based system.

2 Related Work

Ontology has been researched and developed for years. In audio applications, it is applied probably for the first time by Nakatani and Okuno [3]. They propose a sound ontology and its three usages: ontology-based integration (for sound stream segregation), interfacing between speech processing systems, and integration of bottom-up and top-down processing. Their sound stream segregation means generating an instance of a sound class and extracting its attributes from an input sound mixture. Khan and McLeod [4] utilizes a domain-specific ontology for the generation of metadata for audio and the selection of audio information in a query system. In this work, an audio ontology is defined by its identifier, start time, end time, description (a set of tags or labels) and the audio data. MPEG-7 Description Definition Language and a taxonomy of sound categories are employed by Casey [5] for sound recognitions. The audio content is described by qualitative descriptors (taxonomy of sound categories) and quantitative descriptors (set of features). Amatriain and Herrera [6] use semantic descriptors for sound ontology to transmit audio contents. Their description includes both low-level descriptors (e.g. fundamental frequency) and high-level descriptors (e.g. 'loud'). WordNet, an existing lexical network, is used by Cano et al. in [7] as a ontology-backbone of a sound effects management system. Ontology is applied to the disambiguation of the terms used to label a database in order to define concepts of sound effects, for example, the sound of a jaguar and the sound of a Jaguar car. A system of ontology-based sound retrieval is proposed by Hatala et al. in [8] to serve museum visitors. Ontology is used to describe concepts and characteristics of sound objects as an interface between users and audio database. In most cases, ontology is used to describe an audio file (e.g. a sound effect) and to manage the database.

Our work is to build a sound ontology applied to classifying an unknown audio sample detected in habitat. We will present in the next section ontologies for abstract concepts of audio scenes and for detecting situations of distress.

3 Ontology-Based Sound Classification

An ontology-based sound classification includes three problems: defining ontologies, representing them, and applying them to classification. These problems will be presented in this section.

3.1 Sound Ontology

From the classified sounds, we intend to extract the true meaning of the scene. For example, when a sound of a fallen chair and a sound of scream are detected, it should be interpreted as "the patient has tumbled down" (making the chair fall). Or when we detect a sound of groan, we can say that the patient is ill or hurt. This is a mapping between concrete sounds and abstract concepts. In other words, an abstract concept is defined by sounds.

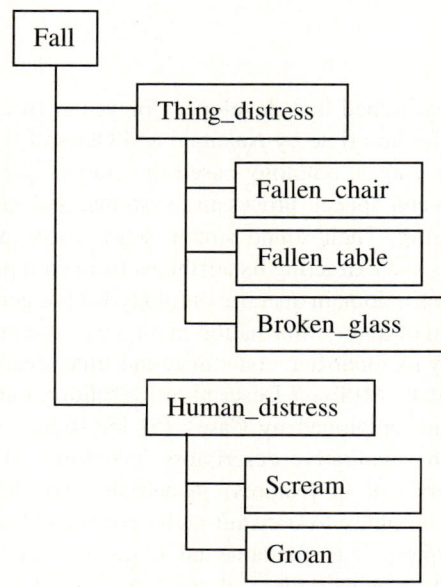

Fig. 1. An example of the ontology representing the "fall" concept. It has two properties and five facets.

An ontology is a definition of a set of representational terms as defined by Gruber in [9]. In this paper, some situations are defined as ontologies. An ontology consists of concept, concept properties, relations and instances. The hierarchical relations between concepts in text or image applications can be established. But in our applications, such relations between situation are not obvious. So we simply define concepts of situations based on concept properties and their facets. The ontology of the situation of patient falling in house is depicted in Fig. 1 as an example. When the patient falls, he can make a chair or a table fall over, or can break something such as a glass. After the fall, the patient probably screams or groans. Sound of fallen chair, fallen table and broken glass are categorized in the "thing_distress" class, sound of scream and groan are of "human_distress". So if a sound of "thing_distress" and/or a sound of "human_distress" are successively detected, we can probably say that the patient has fallen. Of course it can also be said that those sounds come from a chair tumbled down by a man and from another man being hurt. But if we suppose that normally the patient lives alone in the house then the "fall" interpretation is the most appropriate.

Table 1. Properties and facets of three ontologies. "Hurt" concept has no thing_distress property. "Water_in_toilet" facet taken into account is due to the fact that when the patient is sick/ill in the toilet, sound of water is often detected.

	Fall	Hurt	Sick/ill
Thing_distress	Fallen_chair, Fallen_table, Broken_glass		Water_in_toilet
Human_distress	Scream, Groan	Scream, Groan	Cough, Pant, Vomit

Two other concepts of hurt and sick/ill are listed in Table 1. In short, the concept of sound can be identified based on its attached concept properties and their respective facets.

3.2 Ontology-Based Sound Classification

Ontology-based classifications are mostly applied in text and image applications. The image classification system presented by Breen et al. in [10] uses a neural network to identify objects in a sports image. Category of the image is determined by a combination of detected image objects, each objects being assigned an experimental weight. Image ontology in this case is used to prune the selection of concepts: if the parent and the children are selected, the later will be discarded. In order to automatically classify web page, Prabowo et al in [11] apply a feed-forward neural network represent relationships in an ontology. The output of this network is used to estimate similarity between web pages. Mezaris et al. in [12] propose an object ontology for an object-based image retrieval system. In this ontology, each immediate-level descriptors is mapped to an appropriate range of values of the corresponding low-level arithmetic feature. Based on low-level features and query keywords, a support vector machine will result the final query output. In [13], Noh et al. classify web pages using an ontology. In this ontology, each class is predefined by a certain keyword and their relations. Classes of web pages are classified by extracting term frequency, document frequency and information gain, and by using several machine learning algorithms. Taghva et al. in [14] construct an email classification system in which an ontology is applied to extract useful feature, these feature are inputs of a Bayesian classifier. The text categorization system of Wu et al. in [15] also employ an ontology predefined by keywords and semantic relationship of word pair. These keywords are chosen by a term frequency / inverse document frequency classifier. The domain of a text is categorized by a "score". Maillot et al. in [16] introduce their ontology-based application for image retrieval. Each image object in an image is detected by a trained detectors. The relations of detected image object, established in ontology, will determine the category.

In ontology-based image applications, an image object is often defined by lower properties, such as form, color, viewing angle, background, etc. The method of defining related lower properties in image applications is hard to apply to audio domain, because an audio object, such as a laugh, is hard to be defined.

Text applications use relationships between text objects to classify. They are often known or predefined. For example, in a text application "net" can be interpreted as "a fishing tool" if words such as "fish", "boat", "river" are found in the same sentence of paragraph because they have obvious relation; or it can be a "group of connected computers" if there are "port", "cable", "TCP/IP", "wi-fi" nearby.

In our work methods used in text applications are considered because we hope to find the meaning of an audio scene by a group of sounds. The predefined classifying rules of Noh et al. is hard to apply to audio domain because so far we do not know a predefined rule for sounds. The keyword-based ontology of Wu et al. is also difficult to be used in our work because it needs relationship between sounds. The method of using neural netwok to represent ontology of Prabowo et al. [11] seems to be the most appropriate for us since it demands only two levels of concept and properties. Therefore in our work the relationship among concept, concept properties and facets is represented by a feed forward neural network described in [11]. The task of this network is to produce an output value that is used to estimate the similarity between the ontology and a new sound situation.

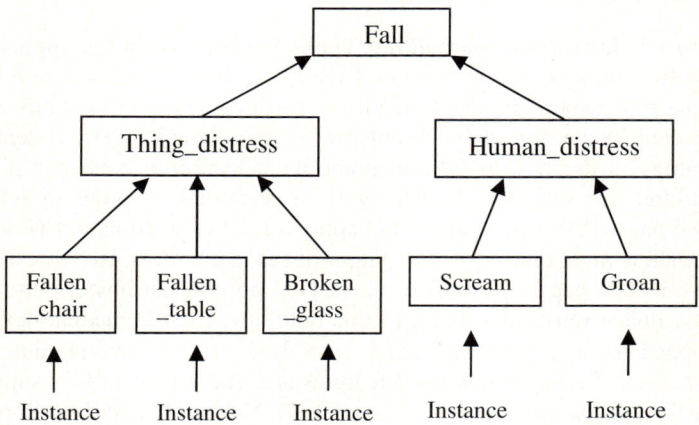

Fig. 2. The feed-forward neural network representing the "fall" ontology. Weights of links between layers depend on number of properties, number of facets and number of detected instances.

This model has three layers: input, hidden and output. The input layer of the network represents a set of instances. The hidden layer represents a set of concept properties. The number of neurons in the hidden layer equals the number of concept properties. The neuron output layer is the concept representatives. The two reasons to choose sigmoid transfer function, $f(x) = 1/(1 + e^{-x})$, for neurons, are as follows. Different concepts have different numbers of properties, so their outputs are normalised form 0 to 1. And they vary continously. The neural network representing the "fall" concept is depicted in Fig. 2. In this example there are two hidden neurons and five input neurons.

The weights of links between the output and hidden layer depend on the number of hidden neurons. The weights of links between a hidden neuron also depend on the number of its attached input neurons. Details of calculation of those weights can be found in [11]. If n instances are matched, the weight of each instance is the square root of n.

During the classification phase, similarities between an input sample and each concepts are calculated in order to assign a concept to the sample. Classes of sounds are extracted. If an instance is found, its respective concept properties input is set to 1, otherwise it is zero. According to detected instances and their classes, weights of links of layers are determined. The output of each neural network therefore is a function of weighted properties of the respective concept and is the similarity between the sample and the concept. The input sample will be assigned to the concept with which it has the highest similarity.

4 Experimental Evaluation

An audio scene database of situations of distress is difficult to build. Firstly, recording this type of audio scenes in hospital is nearly impossible due to the concerns of privacy. Secondly, recording them in a studio is feasible, but situations of distress are hard to be simulated by speakers, making a not true corpus. And finally in fact audio scenes are so numerous that it is hard to build a database (from a sound effect database) that can cover many situations. Therefore we collect manually audio scenes from films. The scenes we target are the ones in which the character is in house and in a situation of distress: falling down, being hurt, sick or ill. From 150 films, 44 scenes of situations of distress with total duration of 680 seconds are collected.

This classifier should function automatically: detects sounds, estimates similarities between the sample and ontologies, and outputs the concept of the scene. But in this first stage of building an ontology-based classification system, the first steps are manually carried out. 44 audio scenes of situations of distress and 50 of normal (non distress) situations are tested. Results are presented in Table 2.

The misidentified scene of "fall" is the one in which the character falls down unconsciously making the door shut, and the unique sound we get is a shutting door. But if we add this type of sound into the ontology, the system will identify actions of shutting doors as "fall", and that will be wrong. Therefore the fall ontology does not need to be redefined. There is one normal situation that is wrongly identified as a "hurt" one. In this situation the character cries when she is too happy. Based on results of classification, it can be said that the ontologies are appropriate for audio scenes of situations of distress.

Table 2. Results of classification. Number of correctly identified is the number of audio scenes of situations of distress which are correctly identified as its assigned concept in the database. Number of wrongly identified is the number of audio scenes of normal situations which are identified as a situation of distress.

	Fall	Hurt	Sick/ill
Number of scene	20	19	5
Number of correctly identified	19	19	5
Number of wrongly identified	0	1	0

5 Conclusion and Future Works

We present in this article an ontology-based audio scene classifier which can be used to detect audio scenes of situations of distress. The construction of the ontology is within the framework of a telemedicine project. Three ontologies of sounds are defined. Concept, properties and instances of an ontology are modeled by a feed forward neural network. The output of a neural network presenting a concept is the similarity between it and the input sample. At first stages, we defined three domain ontologies and tested them manually. These ontologies work well with our first audio database of situations of distress.

In the future a fully automatic ontology-based system needs to be built. In order to archieve this, the following tasks must be undertaken. First, more sound classes should be classified to cover a larger range of different types of sound. Second, sounds need to be separated from music because audio scenes collected from film are often mixed with music, making sound classifiers work inexactly. Third a combination of ontologies and sound classifier should be built. Fourth more situations of distress need to be defined. And finally, a bigger database should be acquired to obtain more complete domain ontologies. Besides the extension of this audio database, we also think of acquiring a text database from the Internet. This text database will consist of paragraphs that use types of sound in order to describe audio scenes in house. In short it is a text database of audio scenes. Audio object classes, context of the scene, or distribution of audio object can probably be extracted from this database.

References

1. Istrate, D., Vacher, M., Castelli, E., Sérignat, J.F.: Distress situation identifcation though sound processing. An application to medical telemonitoring. European Conference on Computational Biology, Paris (2003)
2. Nguyen, C.P., Pham, N.Y., Castelli, E.: Toward a sound analysis system for telemedicine. 2nd International Conference on Fuzzy Systems and Knowledge Discovery, Chansha China (2005)
3. Nakatani, T., Okuno, H.G.: Sound ontology for computational auditory scene analysis. Proc. AAAI-98, Vol.~1 (1998) 30-35
4. Khan, L., McLeod, D.: Audio Structuring and Personalized Retrieval Using Ontologies. Proc. of IEEE Advances in Digital Libraries, Library of Congress, Washington, DC (2000) 116-126
5. Casey, M.: MPEG-7 sound-recognition tools. IEEE Transaction on Circuits and Systems for Video Technology, Vol. 11, No. 6 (2001)
6. Amatriain, X., Herrera, P.: Transmitting audio contents as sound objects. Proceedings of AES22 International Conference on Virtual, Synthetic and Entertainment Audio, Espoo, Finland (2002)
7. Cano, P., Koppenberger, M., Celma, O., Herrera, P., Tarasov, V.: Sound effects taxonomy management in production environments. AES 25th International Conference, UK (2004)
8. Hatala, M., Kalantari, L., Wakkary, R., Newby, K, : Ontology and rule based retrieval of sound objects in augmented audio reality system for museum visitors. Proceedings of the 2004 ACM symposium on Applied computing, Nicosia, Cyprus (2004) 1045 – 1050

9. Gruber, T.R.: A Translation Approach to Portable Ontology Specifications. Knowledge Acquisition 5(2) (1993) 199-220
10. Breen, C., Khan, L., Kumar, A., Wang, L.: Ontology-based image classification using neural networks. Proc. SPIE Vol. 4862 (2002) 198-208
11. Prabowo, R., Jackson, M., Burden, P., Knoell, H.D.: Ontology-based automatic classification for the web pages: design, implimentation and evaluation. The 3rd International Conference on Web Information Systems Engineering, Singapore (2002)
12. Mezaris, V., Kompatsiaris, I., Strintzis, M.G.: An Ontology Approach to Object-Based Image Retrieval. IEEE Intl. Conf. on Image Processing (2003)
13. Noh, S., Seo, H., Choi, J., Choi, K., Jung, G.: Classifying Web Pages Using Adaptive Ontology. In Proceedings of the IEEE International Conference on Systems, Man and Cybernetics, Washington, D.C. (2003) 2144-2149
14. 14 Taghva, K., Borsack, J., Coombs, J., Condit, A., Lumos, S., Nartker, T: Ontology-based classification of email. International Conference on Information Technology: Computers and Communications, Las Vegas, Nevada (2003)
15. Wu, S.H., Tsai, T.H., Hsu, W.L.: Text Categorization Using Automatically Acquired Domain Ontology. The Sixth International Workshop on Information Retrieval with Asian Languages (IRAL-03), Sapporo, Japan (2003) 138-145
16. Maillot, N., Thonnat, M., Hudelot, C.: Ontology based object learning and recognition: application to image retrieval. ICTAI 2004

PSO and ACO in Optimization Problems

Lenka Lhotská, Martin Macaš, and Miroslav Burša

Gerstner Laboratory, Czech Technical University in Prague
Technicka 2, 166 27 Prague 6, Czech Republic
lhotska@fel.cvut.cz
http://cyber.felk.cvut.cz

Abstract. Biological processes and methods have been influencing science and technology for many decades. The ideas of feedback and control processes Norbert Wiener used in his cybernetics were based on observation of these phenomena in biological systems. Artificial intelligence and intelligent systems have been fundamentally interested in the phenomenology of living systems, namely perception, decision-making, action, and learning. Natural systems exhibit many properties that form fundamentals for a number of nature inspired applications – dynamics, flexibility, robustness, self-organisation, simplicity of basic elements, and decentralization. This paper reviews examples of nature inspired software applications focused on optimization problems, mostly drawing inspiration from collective behaviour of social colonies.

1 Introduction

Nature has served as inspiration in a number of different areas of human activity for centuries. In recent decades it has attracted the attention of researchers in computer science, artificial intelligence and related disciplines because most of the modern technological systems that have been and are being developed have become very complex, often distributed, and interconnected to a very high degree. Thus they depend on effective communication; they require high flexibility, adaptability, and ability to cope with changing demands. However, these systems are often designed and constructed as inflexible and centralized. There are several reasons for this approach: need for clear control of the operation of the system (easier in a centralised system than in a distributed one); requirement for an exact specification of what needs to be built on the first place; traditional routinely used way of design. It is obvious that such approach results in a number of technical problems, often due to the failure to adapt to changing circumstances.

When we inspect natural systems more closely, we can find that they are typically characterized by a great degree of complexity, at various levels of description. This complexity means that the behaviour of natural systems may appear unpredictable and imprecise, but at the same time living organisms, and the ecosystems in which they are found, show a substantial degree of resilience. Examples of such resilient systems include social insect colonies, mammalian nervous systems, and temperate woodland communities [1]. This resilience arises from several sources: large number of elements in each system, each of which may be interchangeable for another; loose but flexible interconnections between elements; differences between elements in the system, allowing a diversity of responses to a changing environment; resulting complex environment that all the interacting parts produce, which stimulates diverse responses from living organisms. Natural organisms have proved by their existence that they have the ability to deal with complex and dynamic situations in the world. They adapt to the changing environment by learning during their lifetime (development of an individual) and by evolving over the course of many generations (development of the species).

The sources of inspiration for design of both hardware and software systems come from many aspects of natural systems – evolution [2], ecology [3], development [4], cell and molecular phenomena [5], behaviour [6], cognition and neurosystems [7], and other areas. The developed techniques have led to applications in many different areas including networks [8], [9], data mining [10], [11], optimization [12], robotics [13], automatic control [14], [15], and many others.

2 Optimization

When looking at many practical problems we find out that the core of the problems is the optimization task. Optimization means that we are looking for input values that minimize or maximize the result of some function. In other words the aim is to get the best possible outcome. However, in some cases the search for the very best outcome is hopeless or unnecessary (too expensive or time demanding). Therefore a "good" outcome (being relatively close to the best solution) might be satisfactory.

Let us identify the most frequent areas where optimization is necessary. One example is parameter setting in different systems. For example, in training a feedforward neural network we want to minimize error at the output, which means that we want to find optimal combination of weights. Similar problem is feature weighting and model parameter setup in instance-based reasoning or optimization of parameters of kernel functions in support vector machines. In data mining algorithms we frequently face the problem of feature extraction and selection. Mostly we do not use all the attributes we can collect or extract. We try to identify the smallest possible subset that provides maximum class separation or consistent, one-to-one mapping (in regression). Feature optimization can be done in two ways: feature ranking via combinatorial optimization or dimension reduction via feature transformation.

In networks (communications, transport), the most frequent problems are connected with optimization of load balance, optimization of distance (travelling salesman problem), optimization of (re-)routing. Planning and scheduling inherently represent optimization problems.

3 Nature Inspired Systems

Biologically or nature inspired systems, methods and technologies represent a very broad area covering many interesting topics. Recently this area has attracted more attention and many interesting methods and their applications have been developed. We have decided to focus only on two methods and their application to various optimization tasks, namely ant colony optimization, and particle swarm optimization.

3.1 Swarm Intelligence

Swarm intelligence [16] can be defined as the collective intelligence that emerges from a group (usually a large one) of simple entities, mostly called agents. These entities enter into interactions, sense and change their environment locally. Furthermore, they exhibit complex, emergent behaviour that is robust with respect to the failure of individual entities. Most frequently used agent-based models are ant colonies, flocks of birds, termites, swarms of bees, or fish schools. Some of the developed algorithms are inspired by the biological swarm social behaviour, e.g. the ant colony foraging.

There are two popular swarm inspired methods in computational intelligence areas: Ant colony optimization (ACO) and particle swarm optimization (PSO). ACO was inspired by the behaviours of ants and has many successful applications in discrete optimization problems [17]. The particle swarm concept originated as a simulation of simplified social system. It was found that particle swarm model could be used as an optimizer [18]. These algorithms have been already applied to solving problems of clustering, data mining, dynamic task allocation, and optimization.

3.1.1 Ant Colony Optimization

ACO was introduced by Marco Dorigo [19] and his colleagues in the early 1990s. The first computational paradigm appeared under the name Ant System. It is another approach to stochastic combinatorial optimization. The search activities are distributed over "ants" – agents with very simple basic capabilities that mimic the behaviour of real ants. There emerges collective behaviour that has a form of autocatalytic behaviour (positive feedback loop). The more the ants follow a trail, the more attractive that trail becomes for being followed. The main aim was not to simulate ant colonies, but to use artificial ant colonies as an optimization tool. Therefore the system exhibits several differences in comparison to the real (natural) ant colony: artificial ants have some memory; they are not completely blind; they live in an environment with discrete time. In ACO algorithms, artificial ants construct solutions from scratch by probabilistically making a sequence of local decisions. At each construction step an ant chooses exactly one of possibly several ways of extending the current partial solution. The rules that define the solution construction mechanism in ACO implicitly map the search space of the considered problem (including the partial solutions) onto a search tree.

ACO was applied to many optimization problems and nowadays it belongs to the class of metaheuristic algorithms. ACO algorithms are state-of-the-art for combinatorial optimization problems such as open shop scheduling (OSS) [20], quadratic assignment [21], and sequential ordering [22]. They can be found in other types of applications as well. Dorigo and Gambardella have proposed Ant Colony System (ACS) [22], while Stützle and Hoos have proposed MAX-MIN Ant System (MMAS) [21]. They have both have been applied to the symmetric and asymmetric travelling salesman problem with excellent results. Dorigo, Gambardella and Stützle have also proposed new hybrid versions of ant colony optimization with local search. In problems like the quadratic assignment problem and the sequential ordering problem these ACO algorithms outperform all known algorithms on vast classes of benchmark problems. The recent book "Ant Colony Optimization" [23] gives a full overview of the many successful applications of Ant Colony Optimization.

3.1.2 Particle Swarm Optimization

Particle swarm optimization (PSO) is a population based stochastic optimization technique developed by Dr. Eberhart and Dr. Kennedy in 1995 [24], [25], inspired by social behaviour of bird flocking or fish schooling.

PSO shares many similarities with evolutionary computation techniques such as Genetic Algorithms (GA). The system is initialized with a population of random solutions, has fitness values, updates the population, and searches for optima by updating generations. However, unlike GA, PSO has no evolution operators such as crossover and mutation. In PSO, the potential solutions, called particles, fly through the problem space by following the current optimum particles. Particles update themselves with the internal velocity. They also have memory, which is important to the algorithm. Compared with genetic algorithms (GAs), the information sharing mechanism in PSO is significantly different. In GAs, chromosomes share information with each other. In PSO, only gBest (or lBest) gives out the information to others. It is a one-way information sharing mechanism. The evolution only looks for the best solution. Compared with GA, all the particles tend to converge to the best solution quickly even in the local version in most cases.

3.2 Applications

As we have already mentioned there have appeared many interesting applications in different areas. In principle all tasks can be viewed as optimization tasks. However, we can divide them into several groups according to the main solved problems, namely optimization (of parameters, topology), state space search (travelling salesman problem, routing in telecommunication networks), data mining and classification (clustering, feature extraction), and data visualization. Let us briefly describe several examples of applications representing the areas of telecommunication networks, data mining, design of digital circuits, optimization, and detection of objects in images.

Emission sources localization [31]. In this application, a biasing expansion swarm approach is used. It is based on swarm behaviour and utilizes its three properties: separation, cohesion and alignment. This approach is applied to multiple simple mobile agents, with limited sensing and communication capabilities. The agents search collaboratively and locate an indeterminate number of emission sources in an unknown large-scale area. Each agent considers all concentration values collected by other swarm members and determines the positive gradient direction of the whole coverage area of the swarm.

Open shop scheduling. ACO can be combined with tree search methods with the aim to improve methods for solving combinatorial optimization problems. In [20] a combination of ACO and beam search is described. It has been applied to open shop scheduling, which is a NP-hard scheduling problem. The obtained results compared with two best approaches currently available (GA by Prins [32] and Standard-ACO-OSS) show that the Beam-ACO performs better.

Communications. A number of applications have appeared quite naturally in the area of communications. There can be identified many optimization tasks. One of them is *routing in mobile ad hoc networks* [33]. Mobile ad hoc networks are wireless mobile networks formed spontaneously. Communication in such a decentralized network typically involves temporary multi-hop relays, with the nodes using each other as the relay routers without any fixed infrastructure. This kind of network is very flexible and suitable for applications such as temporary information sharing in conferences, military actions and disaster rescues. However, multi-hop routing, random movement of mobile nodes and other features lead to enormous overhead for route discovery and maintenance. Furthermore, this problem is worsened by the resource constraints in energy, computational capacities and bandwidth. The developed algorithm is an on-demand multi-path routing algorithm, inspired by the foraging intelligence. It incorporates positive feedback, negative feedback and randomness into the routing computation. Positive feedback originates from destination nodes to reinforce the existing pheromone on good paths. The negative feedback is represented by exponential pheromone decay that prevents old routing solutions from remaining in the current network status. Each node maintains a probabilistic routing table.

Ant Based Control in Telecommunication Networks. In [34] the authors propose a new migration scheme for the ant-like mobile agents and a new routing table management scheme. The main objective is to achieve better load balancing. Load balancing in a telecommunication network can provide better utilization of the available resources, which results in better services for the end users. The agents update the routing tables of nodes based on their acquired knowledge (Ant Based Control is a reinforcement learning technique.) In addition to the parameter of the shortest delay, the call capacity of the path is considered. That means if the shortest-delay path becomes congested a new path with less congestion, if it exists, will be chosen.

PSO algorithm in signal detection and blind extraction. In signal processing there are among others two important problems, namely multi-user detection and blind extraction of sources. The optimal multi-user detection is a NP-complete problem. Therefore the research effort has been focused on the development of suboptimum techniques with the aim to achieve a trade-off between complexity and performance. Binary PSO algorithm was used [35] and reached better results than genetic algorithm. Similar results were achieved in blind source separation, which is an important issue in many science and engineering scenarios as well.

Optimization of FPGA placement and routing [36]. FPGAs are becoming increasingly important implementation platforms for digital circuits. One of the necessary requirements to effectively utilize the FPGA's resources is an efficient placement and routing mechanism. Initial FPGA placement and routings generated in a standard way are then optimized by PSO. According to [36] the interconnection lengths between the configurable logic blocks and input/output blocks for a counter and an arithmetic logic unit were minimized.

PSO for Solving Travelling Salesman Problem (TSP) [37]. TSP is a well-known NP-hard problem. Modification of PSO using fuzzy matrices to represent the position and velocity of the particles in PSO was developed. The algorithm can be used for resolving common routing problems and other combinatorial optimization problems.

Discovering clusters in spatial data [38]. In this application, each agent represents a simple task and the success of the method depends on the cooperative work of the agents. The algorithm combines a smart exploratory strategy based on the movements of a flock of birds with a shared nearest-neighbour clustering algorithm to discover clusters in parallel. Birds are used as agents with an exploring behaviour foraging for clusters. This strategy can be used as a data reduction technique to perform approximate clustering efficiently.

Discovering clusters in biomedical signals (ongoing research of paper authors). In this application, individual parts of the signal are characterized by real valued features and the resulting set of samples is partitioned into groups using a clustering method based on Particle Swarm Optimization (PSO) algorithm. The signal is segmented according to the resulting division into the corresponding groups, where each group represents certain type of segments, thus a certain cluster. The clustering method is applied on real data extracted from electrooculographic signals.

Combination of ants and cellular automata – application to clustering problem in data mining [39]. Ant Sleeping Model combines advantages of the classical cellular automata model and the swarm intelligence. The ants have two states: sleeping state and active state. The ant's state is controlled by a function of the ant's fitness to the environment it locates and a probability for the ants becoming active. The state of an ant is determined only by its local information. By moving dynamically, the ants form different subgroups adaptively. The algorithm was applied to clustering problem in data mining. Results show that the algorithm is significantly better than other clustering methods in terms of both speed and quality. It is adaptive, robust and efficient, achieving high autonomy, simplicity and efficiency.

PSO for buoys-arrangement design. In [40] PSO deals with constrained multiobjective optimization problems. In this case PSO is modified by using the bidirectional searching strategy to guide each particle to search simultaneously in its neighbourhood and the region where particles are distributed sparsely. Constrained multiobjective optimization problems are very common in engineering applications, such as structural optimization, design of complex hardware/software systems, production scheduling, etc. Buoys-arrangement problem mainly researches on how to design the longitudinal position and buoyancy value of each pair of buoys. It is the main component of submarine salvage engineering.

4 Conclusion

This paper has tried to show using few examples that nature inspired techniques represent promising approaches to solving complex problems, frequently having optimization component. We can see that especially computing and telecommunication systems tend to become more complicated. They will require adequate solutions for which the use of nature inspired techniques promises substantial benefits. One of the important features of PSO and ACO is their convergence to the optimal solution. Another one is relatively easy representation of the real-world problem.

However, many areas still require further investigation before they will be used in real-world applications. Therefore nature inspired systems remain an active area of research.

Acknowledgement

The research has been supported by the research program No. MSM 6840770012 "Transdisciplinary Research in the Area of Biomedical Engineering II" of the CTU in Prague, sponsored by the Ministry of Education, Youth and Sports of the Czech Republic and by the FP6-IST project No. 13569 NiSIS (Nature-inspired Smart Information Systems).

References

1. Begon, M.; Harper, J.L.; Townsend C.R., 1990, "Ecology: individuals, populations and communities". Blackwell Scientific, Oxford.
2. Banzhaf, W.; Daida, J.; Eiben, A. E.; Garzon, M. H.; Honavar, V.; Jakiela, M.; Smith, R. E. (Eds), 1999, "GECCO-99: Proceedings of the Genetic and Evolutionary Computation Conference", Morgan Kauffman, San Francisco.
3. Huberman, B. (Ed), 1988 "The Ecology of Computation", North-Holland, Amsterdam.
4. Tateson, R., 1998, "Self-organising pattern formation: fruit flies and cell phones'", Eiben, A. E.; Bäck, T.; Schoenauer, M.; Schwefel, H.-P. (Eds), Parallel problem solving from nature — PPSN V, Springer, Berlin, pp 732—741.
5. Conrad, M., 1990, "Molecular computing", Advances in Computers, 30, pp 235—324.
6. Proctor, G.; Winter, C., 1998, "Information flocking: data visualisation in virtual worlds using emergent behaviours", Proceedings of Virtual Worlds 1998.
7. Smith, T.; Philippides, A., 2000, "Nitric oxide signalling in real and artificial neural networks", BT Technol J, 18, No 4, pp 140—149.
8. Zhang, Y.; Ji, C.; Yuan, P.; Li, M.; Wang, C.; Wang, G., 2004, "Particle swarm optimization for base station placement in mobile communication", Proceedings of 2004 IEEE International Conference on Networking, Sensing and Control 2004, pp. 428-432.
9. Ji, C.; Zhang, Y.; Gao, S.; Yuan, P.; Li, Z., 2004, "Particle swarm optimization for mobile ad hoc networks clustering", Proceedings of IEEE International Conference on Networking, Sensing and Control 2004, p. 375.
10. Van der Merwe, D. W.; Engelbrecht, A. P., 2003, "Data clustering using particle swarm optimization", Proceedings of IEEE Congress on Evolutionary Computation 2003 (CEC 2003), pp. 215-220.
11. Sousa, T.; Silva, A.; Neves, A., 2003, "A particle swarm data miner", Lecture Notes in Computer Science(LNCS) No. 2902: Progress in Artificial Intelligence, Proceedings of 11th Portuguese Conference on Artificial Intelligence (EPIA 2003), pp. 43-53.
12. Fourie, P. C.; Groenwold, A. A., 2001, "Particle swarms in topology optimization", Extended Abstracts of the Fourth World Congress of Structural and Multidisciplinary Optimization, pp. 52-53.
13. Floreano, D., 1997, "Evolutionary mobile robotics", Quagliarelli, D.; Periaux, J.; Poloni, C.; Winter, G. (eds.) Genetic Algorithms in Engineering and Computer Science. John Wiley, Chichester.
14. Oliveira, P. M.; Cunha, J. B.; Coelho, J. o. P., 2002, "Design of PID controllers using the particle swarm algorithm", Twenty-First IASTED International Conference: Modelling, Identification, and Control (MIC 2002)
15. Conradie, A.; Miikkulainen, R.; Aldrich, C., 2002, "Adaptive control utilizing neural swarming", Proceedings of the Genetic and Evolutionary Computation Conference 2002 (GECCO 2002).

16. Bonabeau, E.; Dorigo, M.; Theraulaz, G., 1999, "Swarm Intelligence: From Natural to Artificial Systems", Oxford University Press, New York, NY.
17. http://iridia.ulb.ac.be/~mdorigo/ACO/ACO.html
18. http://www.engr.iupui.edu/~shi/Conference/psopap4.html
19. Dorigo, M., 1992, "Optimization, learning and natural algorithms", PhD thesis, Dipartimento di Elettronica, Politecnico di Milano, Italy.
20. Blum, C., 2005, "Beam-ACO – Hybridizing ant colony optimization with beam search: An application to open shop scheduling", Comput. Oper. Res. 32 (6) (2005), pp. 1565-1591.
21. Stützle, T.; Hoos, H.H., 2000, „MAX-MIN Ant system". Future Gen. Comput. Syst. 16 (8) (2000), pp. 889-914.
22. Gambardella, L.M.; Dorigo, M., 2000, "Ant Colony System hybridized with a new local search for the sequential ordering problem", INFORMS J. Comput. 12 (3) (2000), pp. 237-255.
23. Dorigo, M.; Stützle, T., 2004, "Ant Colony Optimization", MIT Press, Cambridge, MA.
24. Kennedy, J.; Eberhart, R. C., 1995, "Particle swarm optimization", Proceedings IEEE International Conference on Neural Networks Vol. IV, pp. 1942-1948.
25. Eberhart, R. C.; Kennedy, J., 1995, "A new optimizer using particle swarm theory", Proceedings of the Sixth International Symposium on Micro Machine and Human Science, pp. 39-43.
26. Parker, L.E., 2000, "Current State of the Art in Distributed Autonomous Mobile Robotics", Parker, L.E.; Bekey, G.A.; Barhen, J. (eds.) Proceedings of the 5th International Symposium on Distributed Autonomous Robotic Systems, pp 3-12, Springer Verlag, Berlin.
27. Dasgupta D., Balachandran S.: Artificial Immune Systems: A Bibliography, Computer Science Devision, University of Memphis, Technical Report No. CS-04-003, June 2005.
28. Dasgupta D. An Overview of Artificial Immune Systems and Their Applications. In: Artificial Immune Systems and Their Applications, Publisher: Springer-Verlag, Inc., Page(s): 3-23, 1999.
29. Ji Z. and Dasgupta D. Artificial Immune System (AIS) Research in the Last Five Years. Published in the proceedings of the Congress on Evolutionary Computation Conference (CEC) Canberra, Australia December 8-12, 2003.
30. Branco C. P.J., Dente J.A. und Mendes R.V.: Using Immunology Principles for Fault Detection, IEEE Transactions on Industrial Electronics, Vol. 50 No. 2, April 2003
31. Cui, X.; Hardin, C.T.; Ragade, R.K.; Elmaghraby, A.S., 2004, "A Swarm Approach for Emission Sources Localization", Proceedings of the 16th IEEE International Conference on Tools with Artificial Intelligence (ICTAI 2004), IEEE Computer Society.
32. Prins, C., 2000, "Competitive genetic algorithms for the open-shop scheduling problem", Mathematical Methods of Operations Research 2000, 52(3), pp. 389-411.
33. Liu, Z.; Kwiatkowska, M.Z.; Constantinou, C., 2005, "A Biologically Inspired QoS Routing Algorithm for Mobile Ad Hoc Networks", Proceedings of the 19th International Conference on Advanced Information Networking and Applications (AINA'05), IEEE.
34. Akon, M.M.; Goswani, D.; Jyoti, S.A., 2004, "A New Routing Table Update and Ant Migration Scheme for Ant Based Control in Telecommunication Networks", Proceedings of the 7th International Symposium on Parallel Architectures, Algorithms and Networks (ISPAN'04), IEEE Computer Society.
35. Zhao, Y.; Zheng, J., 2004, "Particle Swarm Optimization Algorithm in Signal Detection and Blind Extraction", Proceedings of the 7th International Symposium on Parallel Architectures, Algorithms and Networks (ISPAN'04), IEEE Computer Society.

36. Venayagamoorthy, G.K.; Gudise, V.G., 2004, "Swarm Intelligence for Digital Circuits Implementation on Field Programmable Gate Arrays Platforms", Proceedings of the 2004 NASA/DoD Conference on Evolution Hardware (EH'04), IEEE Computer Society.
37. Pang, W.; Wang, K.; Zhou, C.; Dong, L., 2004, "Fuzzy Discrete Particle Swarm Optimization for Solving Traveling Salesman Problem", Proceedings of the 4th International Conference on Computer and Information Technology (CIT'04), IEEE Computer Society.
38. Folino, G.; Forestiero, A.; Spezzano, G., 2003, "Swarming Agents for Discovering Clusters in Spatial Data", Proceedings of the 2nd International Symposium on Parallel and Distributed Computing (ISPDC'03), IEEE Computer Society.
39. Chen, L.; Xu, X.; Chen, Y.; He, P., 2004, "A Novel Ant Clustering Algorithm Based on Cellular Automata", Proceedings of the IEEE/WIC/ACM International Conference on Intelligent Agent Technology (IAT'04), IEEE Computer Society.
40. Zhang, Y.; Huang, S., 2004, "A Novel Multiobjective Particle Swarm Optimization for Buoys-Arrangement Design", Proceedings of the IEEE/WIC/ACM International Conference on Intelligent Agent Technology (IAT'04), IEEE Computer Society.

Constraints in Particle Swarm Optimization of Hidden Markov Models

Martin Macaš, Daniel Novák, and Lenka Lhotská

Czech Technical University, Faculty of Electrical Engineering, Dep. of Cybernetics,
Prague, Czech Republic
mmacas@seznam.cz
http://gerstner.felk.cvut.cz/nit

Abstract. This paper presents new application of Particle Swarm Optimization (PSO) algorithm for training Hidden Markov Models (HMMs). The problem of finding an optimal set of model parameters is numerical optimization problem constrained by stochastic character of HMM parameters. Constraint handling is carried out using three different ways and the results are compared to Baum-Welch algorithm (BW), commonly used for HMM training. The global searching PSO method is much less sensitive to local extremes and finds better solutions than the local BW algorithm, which often converges to local optima. The advantage of PSO approach was markedly evident, when longer training sequence was used.

1 Introduction

Hidden Markov Model (HMM) is statistical modelling technique which enables to characterize real-world stochastic signals in terms of signal models. There are many real world problems which have been solved by HMMs. The examples are speech recognition [1], biomedical signal processing, bioinformatics, robotics, handwriting recognition or economy.

There are two main problems connected with HMMs - the choice of model topology (e.g. number of hidden states and type of connections) and search for the model parameters. This problem is mostly solved using Baum-Welch algorithm (BW). The main drawback of the method is frequent convergence to local optima resulting from local character of searching. One solution of this problem is to use some global searching methods [2].

In this paper, the model parameters are searched while the topology is given in advance for all experiments. The model parameters are searched in terms of likelihood maximization. The problem of reaching the global maxima is solved using nature inspired Particle Swarm Optimization (PSO) method, which is described below. However, the problem of searching some parameters of HMM is made difficult by constraints arising from the probabilistic character of this type of parameters. Furthermore, some other parameters representing covariance are searched and therefore a positivity constraint arises from this fact. This implies a need for some constraint handling mechanism to be used in PSO.

2 Methods

2.1 Hidden Markov Models

An HMM is a stochastic finite state automata defined by the following parameters: $\lambda = (A, p, B)$, where $A = \{a_{ij}\}$ is a matrix of state transition probabilities a_{ij} representing probability of transition from state i to state j, p is the initial state probability and B is the emission probability density function of each state. This paper considers continuous HMMs with B represented by a finite mixture of Gaussian distributions. For simplicity, only one Gaussian distribution was used for all experiments and therefore the B is set of N Gaussian distributions $G_i(m_i, U_i)$, where the m_i and U_i are mean and variance of the distribution for ith state respectively.

Consider an observation sequence $\mathbf{O} = O_1, \ldots, O_T$. There are three problems connected with HMM. The first one is to compute $P(\mathbf{O}|\lambda)$, the probability of observing the sequence, given the model (model evaluation). The second problem is to find a corresponding state sequence $\mathbf{Q} = Q_1, \ldots, Q_T$, given the observation sequence $\mathbf{O}$ and model parameters λ. The third problem is crucial and by far the most difficult one. How to find the model parameters λ maximizing $P(\mathbf{O}|\lambda)$ (fitting the training sequence). This problem of model training consists of adjusting the model parameters λ to maximize likelihood - the probability of the observation sequence given the model. There is no known way to analytically solve this problem. Usually the alternative solutions are iterative procedures like Baum-Welch algorithm [3].

Baum-Welch algorithm [1] is a standard solution for solving the training problem based on maximization of data likelihood. However, this hill-climbing algorithm leads to local maxima only, and in most problems of interest, the optimization surface is very complex and has many local optima. The BW algorithm uses a set of re-estimation formulas and guarantees that the likelihood of re-estimated model will be equal to or greater than the likelihood of model in previous iteration.

2.2 Particle Swarm Optimization

The PSO method is one of optimization method developed for finding a global optima of some nonlinear function [4]. It has been inspired by social behavior of birds and fish. The method applies the approach of problem solving in groups. Each solution consists of set of parameters and represents a point in multidimensional space. The solution is called "particle" and the group of particles (population) is called "swarm".

Each particle i is represented as a D-dimensional position vector $\vec{x}_i(t)$ and has a corresponding instantaneous velocity vector $\vec{v}_i(t)$. Furthermore, it remembers its individual best value of fitness function and position $\vec{p}_i$ which has resulted in that value. During each iteration t, the velocity update rule (1) is applied on each particle in the swarm. The $\vec{p}_g$ is the best position of the entire swarm and represents the social knowledge.

$$\vec{v}_i(t) = w\vec{v}_i(t-1) + \varphi_1 R_1(\vec{p}_i - \vec{x}_i(t-1)) + \varphi_2 R_2(\vec{p}_g - \vec{x}_i(t-1)) \quad (1)$$

The parameter w is called inertia weight and during all iterations decreases linearly from w_{start} to w_{end}. The symbols R_1 and R_2 represent the diagonal matrices with random diagonal elements drawn from a uniform distribution between 0 and 1. The parameters φ_1 and φ_2 are scalar constants that weight influence of particles' own experience and the social knowledge.

Next, the position update rule (2) is applied:

$$\vec{x}_i(t) = \vec{x}_i(t-1) + \vec{v}_i(t) . \qquad (2)$$

If any component of $\vec{v}_i$ is less than $-V_{max}$ or greater than $+V_{max}$, the corresponding value is replaced by $-V_{max}$ or $+V_{max}$, respectively. The V_{max} is maximum velocity parameter.

The update formulas (1) and (2) are applied during each iteration and the $\vec{p_i}$ and $\vec{p_g}$ values are updated simultaneously. The algorithm stops if maximum number of iterations is achieved.

2.3 Particle Structure and Evaluation

The quality of particle (candidate solution) is evaluated using a fitness function. Each particle is built of A, p, m, U parameters reconfigured to one dimensional vector. Two sorts of structure of particles (encoding) were used here (see the Table 1) - the *Type A* encoding is used when the particle corresponds to all parameters λ, the type B encoding does not include last component of probabilistic parameters, because it can be computed from stochastic constraints described in the next section. Particles of both types are equivalent to parameters λ of HMM. The *Type A* representation was used for repair based method and the *Type B* encoding was used for penalty based method.

Table 1. Two types of representation of a particle

Type A

$A\{N \times N\}$						$p\{N\}$			$m\{N\}$			$U\{N\}$		
a_{11}	...	a_{1N}	...	a_{N1}	...	a_{NN}	p_1	...	p_N	m_1	...	m_N	U_1	...	U_N

Type B

$A\{N \times (N-1)\}$						$p\{N-1\}$			$m\{N\}$			$U\{N\}$		
a_{11}	...	a_{1N-1}	...	a_{N1}	...	a_{NN-1}	p_1	...	p_{N-1}	m_1	...	m_N	U_1	...	U_N

In this paper, the maximization of likelihood is performed as minimization of the value of function described by Equation 3.

$$eval_F(\lambda) = -\ln P(\mathbf{O}|\lambda) \qquad (3)$$

2.4 Constraint Handling

An important aspect of the Baum-Welch algorithm is that the stochastic constraints of the HMM parameters are automatically satisfied at each iteration.

Generally, this is not true for all training algorithms. The problem of training must be therefore understood as constraint optimization task and could be described as following:

Find $\lambda = \{A, p, B\}$, which maximizes $P(\mathbf{O}|\lambda)$, subject to

$$a_{ik} \geq 0 \qquad (4)$$

$$\sum_{j=1}^{N} a_{ij} = 1 \qquad (5)$$

$$p_j \geq 0 \qquad (6)$$

$$\sum_{j=1}^{N} p_j = 1 \qquad (7)$$

$$U_i > 0, \qquad (8)$$

where $i = 1 \ldots N$, $k = 1 \ldots N$ and N is number of hidden states.

However, the PSO was originally developed for unconstrained optimization and hence the algorithm described in previous section must be modified to be able to handle with constraints [5]. In this paper, the following constraint handling methods are compared:

Methods based on repair algorithm (PSOr, PSOrf). The unfeasible solutions are "repaired" by moving them into feasible space. The unfeasible solutions can be replaced by its repaired version or the repair procedure can be used for fitness evaluation only.

The two following repair methods are used in this paper. First approach, reffered to as *PSOr*, replaces unfeasible particles by their repaired version. The second one, referred to as *PSOrf*, uses modification of fitness function, which evaluates the repaired version of unfeasible particle, however, the unfeasible particles are not replaced. The repair procedure consists of normalization operations. First, all negative elements of state transition matrix A are assigned to be zero. Next, each element a_{ij} of the matrix is transformed to $a_{ij}/\sum_{j=1}^{N} a_{ij}$ which ensures that the constraint (5) is not violated.

The same procedure is applied on initial probabilities p. Finally, a violation of positivity constraint (8) (for multivariate observations, it is constraint of positive-definity) is repaired by setting all C_i which are smaller than a constant c (e.g. $c = 10^{-5}$) to c.

Method based on penalty function (PSOp). The unfeasible solutions are penalized using $eval_U(\lambda) = eval_F(\lambda) + penalty(\lambda)$. However, the likelihood can not be computed for model parameters violating the stochastic constraints. Therefore, a constant K could be used in place of $eval_F(\lambda)$. For instance, the suitable value for K could be the fitness function of the worst particle in the initial swarm. The following form of fitness evaluation was used:

$$eval_U(\lambda) = K + \xi[(\sum_{a_{ij}<0} a_{ij}^2 + \sum_{p_i<0} p_i^2)] + \sum_{U_i<c}(c - U_i)^2 . \qquad (9)$$

The constant c in Equation 9 has similar meaning as in the previous section and was set to $c = 10^{-5}$. The penalty term computes the degree of constraint violation. The constant ξ is weight which scales an influences of stochastic constraints (4, 6) and the positivity constraint (8). The suitable value of ξ is determined by the observation sequence and was set to $\xi = 10$ for all experiments.

The implementation of penalty function uses different conception of feasibility. The parameters of HMM are encoded into particle using the *Type B* encoding. Thus, the last column of transition matrix A and last component of vector of initial state probabilities are removed from particle. In the beginning of each evaluation, these parameters must be computed using Equations 5 and 7. For instance, the p_N parameter is $p_N = 1 - \sum_{i=1}^{N-1} p_i$.

Thus, the feasibility is equivalent to satisfaction of the Equations 4, 6 and 8. In the case of violating these three inequality constraints, the particle is evaluated using Equation 9. In the case, that the particle represents feasible solution, it is evaluated using log-likelihood function (3). In experimental results, the penalty method is referred to as *PSOp*.

3 Results

The approaches described above were tested using three observation sequences generated by three predefined artificial HMMs (*Model 1-3*). The number of hidden states was $N = 4$ because of two reasons. First, authors of this work will utilize the results in application of HMM to classification of 4 substages of non-REM sleep from sleep EEG record. Secondly, the PSO method fits to optimize smaller HMMs as it will be discussed at the end of this section. The initial state probabilities were set uniform (to 0.25) for all three models ($p_1 = p_2 = p_3 = (0.25, 0.25, 0.25, 0.25)$). For the models 1 and 2, the transition probabilities were set also uniformly to 0.25. On the other hand, the diagonal elements of matrix A_3 (probabilities of staying in the previous state) were 0.85 and the others (probabilities of transition to different state) were set to 0.05. The Gaussian distributions representing the emission probabilities are described in Equation 10.

$$B_1 = \begin{pmatrix} G(-2, 0.5) \\ G(0, 0.5) \\ G(2, 0.5) \\ G(4, 0.5) \end{pmatrix}, B_2 = \begin{pmatrix} G(0, 0.2) \\ G(0, 2.0) \\ G(-4, 0.5) \\ G(4, 0.5) \end{pmatrix}, B_3 = \begin{pmatrix} G(0, 0.2) \\ G(0, 2.0) \\ G(-4, 0.5) \\ G(4, 0.5) \end{pmatrix} \quad (10)$$

The BW algorithm and the three constraint handling PSO methods were compared. The comparison criterion was the final log-likelihood function described by Equation 3 averaged over 30 runs of experiment. First, a training observation sequence of length T was generated by the model (T was 100 and 200). Further, the optimization algorithm was launched 30 times searching for the model which best fits the training sequence.

For all PSO experiments, the algorithm parameters were set as following: the weight parameters were $\varphi_1 = \varphi_2 = 2$, number of iterations was 500, swarm size was 100. The inertia weight w has decreased linearly from $w = 1$ to $w = 0.2$

during 350 iterations and then it remained constant for the rest of optimization process. The maximum velocity parameter was set variously for different dimensions. Concretely, the change of probabilistic parameters representing the transition matrix and initial state probability was limited by $V_{max} = 0.2$, the rest of velocity dimensions was limited by $V_{max} = 2$. The value of V_{max} is problem dependent and was selected experimentally.

Table 2. Experimental results: means, standard deviations of $-\ln P(\mathbf{O}|\lambda)$ obtained from 30 runs of experiments and the results of t-test ($\alpha = 0.05$) of difference between BW results and results for particular PSO modifications. The 1 behind the slash means that the PSO method found significantly better solutions than the BW algorithm.

Method	$T = 100$ Model 1	Model 2	Model 3
BW	209.55(4.71)/-	229.46(5.66)/-	158.41(27.13)/-
PSOr	207.19(2.67)/0	229.35(5.46)/0	143.25(1.54)/1
PSOrf	207.34(3.50)/0	225.81(4.69)/1	144.91(2.03)/1
PSOp	204.66(2.04)/1	223.25(4.87)/1	142.74(2.46)/1

Method	T=200 Model 1	Model 2	Model 3
BW	435.18(3.46)/-	449.12(22.52)/-	374.13(30.54)/-
PSOr	428.76(3.44)/1	427.33(3.02)/0	316.92(2.64)/1
PSOrf	428.01(5.22)/1	429.92(6.40)/0	317.66(1.66)/1
PSOp	425.38(1.26)/1	422.68(0.72)/1	315.61(1.65)/1

The final values of $-\ln P(\mathbf{O}|\lambda)$ obtained for the three models fitting the sequences of two different lengths ($T = 100$ and $T = 200$) are depicted in Table 2. The Figure 1 shows the training curves averaged over 30runs. The three PSO variants can be compared from this figure. The difference between BW and PSO algorithms can be seen from the Table 2. The standard deviation of final fitness value represents the ability of method to reach the minimum independently on initialization. In addition, the test of significance was performed using paired t-test ($\alpha = 0.05$) of the hypothesis that two matched samples X, Y come from distributions with equal means. However, the test makes an assumption that the distribution of $X - Y$ comes from a normal distribution. This assumption was not satisfied for some samples (e.g. comparison for Model 3) and hence the testing was just additional comparison tool. For all experiments, the means of final fitness obtained for PSO methods are smaller. For the short training sequence ($T = 100$), only the Model 3 was identified significantly better by all PSO approach. On the other hand, if the longer training sequence is used for training, the PSO algorithms reached much smaller values of the function $eval_F$ than the BW algorithm.

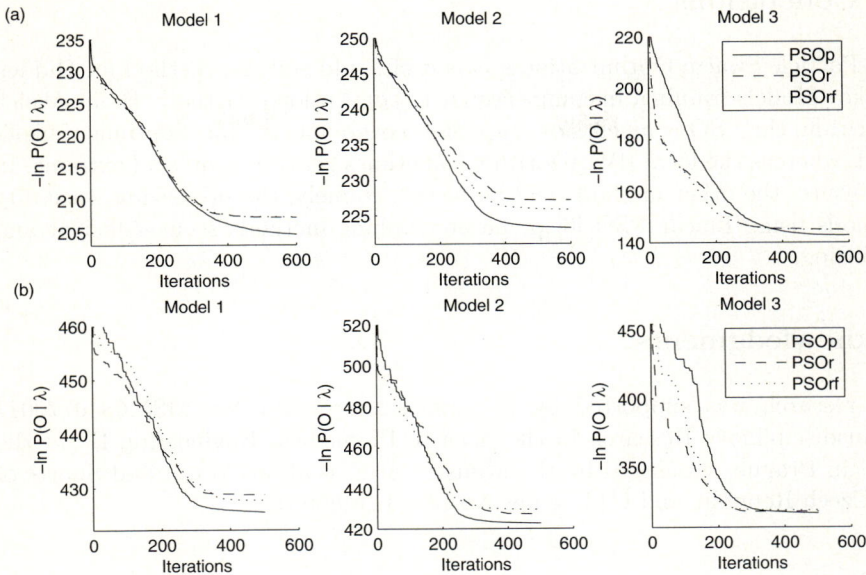

Fig. 1. The training curves averaged over 30 runs of experiment. An observation sequence with length (a) $T = 100$ and (b) $T = 200$ samples was used for training the HMM.

Further, the different PSO constraint handling methods may be compared using the Table 2 and the Figure 1. The figure depicts the optimization process using the dependence of the best fitness in the swarm on time. The curves are averaged over 30 runs of experiment. The figures show strong similarity between the two repair methods (PSOr, PSOrf). At the beginning of optimization, the curve decreases faster for the PSOr and PSOrf methods, however, for PSOp, the rapidity of fall increases during first 200-300 iterations. Furthermore, it even outruns the repair methods and reaches better value. Apparently, the concave-like shape of first part of training is caused by increasing number of feasible particles in the swarm. Finally, the penalty method PSOp seems least sensitive to initialization, because the minimum is reached with the smallest standard deviation and the difference of mean of results from the BW results was statistically significant.

Finally, some temporal aspects of the methods must be mentioned. The main disadvantage of all population based techniques are time requirements. During each iteration of PSO using a swarm of 100 particles, the calculation of fitness function must be repeated 100 time. During the whole optimization process with 500 iterations, there are 50000 fitness evaluations. The fitness evaluation depends on the order of HMM and on length of the observation sequence. Therefore, it can be concluded, that PSO should be used for HMM training in the case of reasonable model order and not very long training sequence. The detailed experiments with time requirements were not performed for this paper.

4 Conclusions

The Particle Swarm Optimization seems useful and suitable method for Hidden Markov Models training. In comparison with conventional method - Baum-Welch algorithm, the PSO is much more capable to overcome the local optima of likelihood, whereas the local BW algorithm sometimes gets stuck in local extreme. In the future, the other methods will be tested. Namely, the preserving feasibility methods using Linear PSO [6] or pareto-ranking methods seem sufficient and promising.

Acknowledgments

The research was supported by the research program No. MSM6840770012 "Transdisciplinary Research in the Area of Biomedical Engineering II" of the CTU in Prague, sponsored by the Ministry of Education, Youth and Sports of the Czech Republic and CTU grant No.13133 10-86084.

References

1. Rabiner, R.: A tutorial on hidden markov models and selected applications in speech recognition. Proceedings of the IEEE **77**(2) (1989) 257–285
2. Kwong, S., Chau, C.: Analysis of paralell genetic algortihms on hmm based speech recognition system. In: ICASSP. (1997) 1229–1233
3. Dempster, A., Laird, N., Rubin, D.: Maximum-likelihood from incomplete data via the em algorithm. Journal of Royal Statistics **39** (1977) 1–38
4. Kennedy, J., Eberhart, R.: Particle swarm optimization. In: Proceedings International Conference on Neural Networks IEEE. Volume 4. (1995) 1942–1948
5. X.Hu, R.C.Eberhart: Solving constrained nonlinear optimization problems with particle swarm optimization. In: Proceedings of the Sixth World Multiconference on Systems, Cybernetics and Informatics. (2002)
6. Paquet, U., p Engelbrecht, A.: A New Particle Swarm Optimiser for Linearly Constrained Optimization. In: Proceedings of the Congress on Evolutionary Computation 2003 (CEC'2003). Volume 1., Piscataway, New Jersey, Canberra, Australia, IEEE Service Center (2003) 227–233

Nature-Inspired Approaches to Mining Trend Patterns in Spatial Databases*

Ashkan Zarnani[1], Masoud Rahgozar[2], and Caro Lucas[3]

[1,2,3] Database Research Group, Faculty of ECE, School of Engineering, University of Tehran
[2,3] Control and Intelligent Processing Center of Excellence
no. 9 Alley, Amir Abad St., Tehran, Iran
[1]`a.zarnani@ece.ut.ac.ir`, [2]`rahgozar@ut.ac.ir`, [3]`lucas@ipm.ir`

Abstract. Large repositories of spatial data have been formed in various applications such as Geographic Information Systems (GIS), environmental studies, banking, etc. The increasing demand for knowledge residing inside these databases has attracted much attention to the field of Spatial Data Mining. Due to the common complexity and huge size of spatial databases the aspect of efficiency is of the main concerns in spatial knowledge discovery algorithms. In this paper, we introduce two novel nature-inspired algorithms for efficient discovery of *spatial trends*, as one of the most valuable patterns in spatial databases. The algorithms are developed using ant colony optimization and evolutionary search. We empirically study and compare the efficiency of the proposed algorithms on a real banking spatial database. The experimental results clearly confirm the improvement in performance and effectiveness of the discovery process compared to the previously proposed methods.

1 Introduction

The major improvements in geo-referenced data collection technologies such as remote sensing, Geographic Positioning System (GPS) and Geo-coding has formed huge repositories of spatial data. Such geo-spatial databases are now available in many application domains e.g. environmental studies, banking, retailing, etc. Implicit patterns and rules inside these databases are invaluable spatial knowledge that is so useful in many strategic decision making processes. This is the reason why the field of spatial data mining (i.e., the discovery of interesting, implicit knowledge from large amounts of spatial data [10]) has attracted so much attention in the research community as well as the industrial community.

The common huge size and complexity of geo-spatial databases has turned the aspect of efficiency into one of the most important challenges in the development of spatial data mining algorithms. So far many algorithms have been designed for efficient discovery of various types of knowledge from spatial databases. Spatial association rules were first introduced by Koperski et. al [10]. Many improved spatial association rule mining algorithms are also recently proposed including [15]. Spatial classification models that predict some spatial phenomena are also studied in many research works [11, 14]. One of the most valuable and interesting patterns potentially found in spatial databases are spatial

---
* This work is supported in part by the TAKFA Grant Program and Mellat Bank R&D Center.

trends [5, 6, 8]. In spatial trend analysis, patterns of change of some non-spatial attributes in the neighborhood of an object are explored [5, 6]; e.g. moving towards north-west from the city center, the average income of the population decreases (confidence 81%).

Ester *et al.* studied the task of spatial trend discovery in [8]. This algorithm was further improved in [6] by exploiting the database primitives for spatial data mining introduced in [7]. In this approach the search space becomes exponentially huge by increasing the size of neighborhood graph and makes it impossible to perform an exhaustive search. In order to prune the search space it applies a heuristic rule based on a user-given threshold [6]. Here it will be shown that this rule is restrictive and makes some valid trends to be missed and never found.

Many efficient solutions for NP-Hard search and optimization problems have been developed inspired by the mechanisms observed in the nature [4]. However, less attention has been given to this powerful source in the tasks of spatial data mining. In this research, we introduce two novel algorithms for efficient mining of spatial trends in large geo-spatial databases, by applying two of the most successful nature-inspired meta-heuristics. In the first algorithm we exploit the phenomenon of *stigmergy* observed in the ant colonies [2, 3] to handle the huge search space encountered in the discovery of spatial trends [16]. In the second approach we have developed a genetic algorithm for evolutionary mining of the trend patterns [17]. Some customized genetic operators are defined so that the genetic search can conform to the nature of the problem [17]. In contrast to the algorithm proposed in [5, 6], our nature-inspired algorithms, are not dependent on the user's initial inputs. We have conducted many experiments on a real-life banking spatial database to study the performance and properties of the proposed algorithms. In both of the algorithms we succeeded to handle the non-polynomial growth of the search space. The results clearly show noticeable improvement in the performance of the pattern mining process compared to the previously proposed method.

2 Mining Spatial Trends: Problem Definition and Applications

In order to model the mutual influence between the spatial objects some spatial relations between objects (called neighborhood relations) are formally defined [5]. These include direction, metric and topological relations. Based on these spatial relations the notions of neighborhood graph and neighborhood path are defined as follows [5, 7]:

Definition 1. let neighbor be a neighborhood relation and DB be a database of spatial objects. A *neighborhood graph* G = (N, E) is a graph with nodes $N = DB$ and edges $E \subseteq N \times N$ where an edge $e = (n_1, n_2)$ exists iff $neighbor(n_1, n_2)$ holds.

Definition 2. A *neighborhood path* of length k is defined as a sequence of nodes $[n_1, n_2, ..., n_k]$, where $neighbor(n_i, n_{i+1})$ holds for all $n_i \in N$, $1 \leq i < k$.

Having available the desired neighborhood graph, a spatial trend pattern can be defined as follows [6]:

Definition 3. A *spatial trend* is a path on the neighborhood graph with a length k that the confidence of regression on its nodes data values based on their distance from the start node is above a user-given threshold (Figure 1.a).

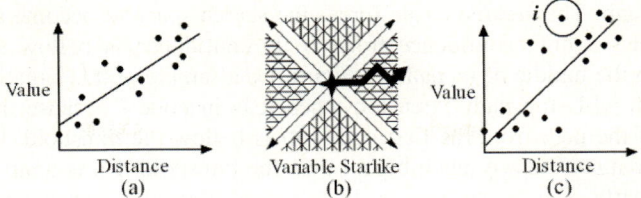

Fig. 1. (a) Regression line for a trend (b) A direction filter (c) Missing a trend in node i

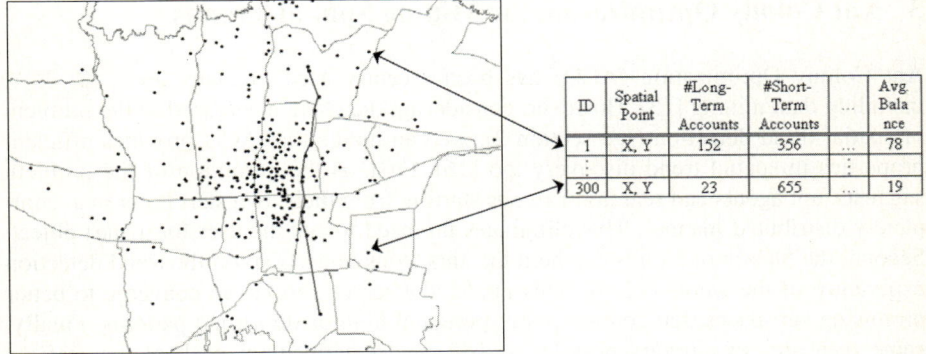

Fig. 2. The City Regions with Bank Points

Our example spatial database contains the agency locations of a national bank and their various (non-spatial) financial data like the count and balance of different kinds of accounts. A map of these points and a sample trend are provided in Figure 2. As an example we may need to find trends of "the number of long term accounts" in the bank agencies starting from any arbitrary agency points. Having discovered such trends, we can try to explain their existence by some spatial attributes [6, 7]. As an example a trend may approximately match with a road or a highway. We can also check if there are any matching trends on the same path but in other thematic layers such as demographic or land use layers. A trend can predict the non-spatial attribute value of a new point on its path using the regression equation. The reliability of this prediction is equal to the regression confidence. A desired informative spatial trend pattern would not be crossing the space in an arbitrary manner [5, 6]. So a direction filter is applied when forming the path of a candidate trend [5] like the variable star-like filter depicted in Figure 1.b.

To discover the trends in a neighborhood graph by the algorithm proposed in [6] the user first specifies the starting object o. Having an average of 'a' eligible nodes to extend a path, we will then have to check a^{n-1} paths starting from o to examine their regression confidence, where n is the user-given maximum trend length. It is impractical to examine this amount of paths even for small values of n. This condition gets worse when the user has not any specific start object in mind, and expects the algorithm to check different start objects. So for higher efficiency, the algorithm allows a path to be extended further by the next set of feasible nodes only if its current confidence is not bellow the given threshold [6]. This is continued until we reach the maximum length. This heuristic rule forces the search space to become smaller but it can easily miss a high confidence trend if its confidence is bellow the threshold somewhere in the middle of its path. In Figure 1.c a sample of this situation is shown. The algorithm will stop path extension when it is in node i because the regression confidence of the path from the first node to i is bellow the threshold. However this path will have a confidence much higher than the threshold if it is continued and not stopped too early. Hence the previously proposed algorithm can not ever discover such valid trends.

3 Ant Colony Optimization for Mining Spatial Trends

Ant Colony Optimization (ACO) has been recently used in many areas [2, 3, 4] including data mining [13]. However, considering the challenges faced in the problem of spatial trend detection (see section 2), we can notice that ACO provides efficient properties in spatial trend discovery too [16]. First, as the definition of the problem suggests, ant agents can search for trends starting from their own start point in a completely distributed manner. This eliminates the need to ask the user for a start object. Second, the pheromone trails can help the ants to share and exploit the trend detection experience of the whole colony. This guides the search process to converge to better promising subspaces that contains more potential high quality trend patterns. Finally, some measures of attractiveness [3, 4, 16] can be defined for each of the feasible spatial nodes to extend a path. This can effectively guide the trend discovery process of each ant.

We assign a pheromone trail value $\tau_{i,j}$ to each directed edge $E_{i,j}$ of the neighborhood graph. When an ant is in node P_i and selects P_j as the next node, its pheromone will be laid on $E_{i,j}$. Thus $\tau_{i,j}$ encodes the favorability of selecting P_j when in P_i to form a high quality spatial trend. We applied two heuristics to guide the discovery of spatial trends [16]. Closer nodes are preferable to the ones far from the current node (equation 1). Also, we would like the value of the next node to match better with an increasing linear regression model (equation 2). Thus $\eta_{i,j}$ which is the attractiveness of P_j for selection when in P_i will be calculated by the following formulas:

$$D_{i,j} = 1/Distance(i,j) \tag{1}$$

$$S_{i,j} = 1 - \left| \frac{Slope(i,j) - 45}{135} \right| \tag{2}$$

$$\eta_{i,j} = S_{i,j}^{\beta} \cdot D_{i,j}^{\gamma} \tag{3}$$

For details of the parameters and their explanation please refer to [16]. Now each ant agent starts from a node and forms a candidate trend by iteratively selecting a new node [3]. Ant k stochastically selects the next node by assigning a probability $P^k_{i,j}$ to select P_j when in P_i by the following formula:

$$P^k_{i,j} = \begin{cases} \dfrac{[\tau_{i,j}]^{\alpha} \cdot [\eta_{i,j}]}{\sum_{l \in allowed_k} [\tau_{i,l}]^{\alpha} \cdot [\eta_{i,l}]} & \text{if } j \in allowed_k \\ 0 & \text{otherwise} \end{cases} \tag{4}$$

This process is repeated until the number of nodes in the candidate trends reach to *TrendLength* which is an input of the ACO and genetic algorithm proposed. To update the pheromone trail information [3, 4], we will consider the quality of the trends (i.e. their regression confidence) [16].

$$\tau_{i,j}(t+1) = \rho.\tau_{i,j}(t) + \Delta\tau_{i,j} \quad (5)$$

$$\Delta\tau_{i,j} = \sum_{k=1}^{m} \Delta\tau_{i,j}^{k} \quad (6)$$

$$\Delta\tau_{i,j}^{k} = \begin{cases} Q \times confidence(k) & \text{if ant k uses edge(i,j) in its trend} \\ 0 & \text{otherwise} \end{cases} \quad (7)$$

In each cycle of the algorithm m ants form their candidate trends with *TrendLength* nodes. At the end of a cycle the pheromone matrix is updated by the above formulas.

4 Genetic Algorithm for Mining Spatial Trends

Genetic algorithms have become a popular search strategy that uses simulated evolution for search and optimization problems in many fields [1, 12] including data mining [1, 9]. Genetic algorithms have been applied in many KDD tasks such as feature selection, clustering, and decision rule discovery [9].

In the problem of discovering spatial trends there are many motivations to apply the evolutionary search strategy used in a genetic algorithm [17]. First, the problem of mining spatial trends is NP-Hard and the full exploration of the search space is impossible in the large geo-spatial databases available today. Second, the graph representation of the problem suggests easy coding and assessment of the chromosomes. Third, the search for trends with different start nodes can be easily integrated. Finally, the nature of the problem matches well with the search mechanism used in genetic algorithms. To explain this final aspect, one must notice that a good spatial trend search strategy can be obtained if we use the previously found high quality trends to effectively guide the search. The mutation genetic operator can perform this utilization by modifying a high confidence spatial trend in few edges. Also the crossover genetic operator can combine two good spatial trends to generate another two paths in the spatial graph that are likely to have high confidence.

The sequence of nodes on a candidate trend is encoded on a chromosome [1, 12]. The interested reader can refer to [17] for detailed explanations. A key aspect is the fitness function that is defined to assess the individuals in order to guide the evolution process towards the promising areas [1, 12]. For the fitness evaluation of candidate trend individuals, we consider the same criteria used to update the pheromone trail in the ACO algorithm (i.e. regression confidence). Then the selection operator is applied to improve the expected average quality of the next generation. Here we use a roulette-wheel selection method.

We use a neighborhood local selection method [12] to perform the crossover combination. The local neighborhood of an individual used in the algorithm is defined in [17]. The two offspring are gained by exchanging the subsequence after the crossover point (the common node) in the two path sequences [17]. We argue that the mutation operation is of high importance in our genetic algorithm for spatial trend discovery [17]. Therefore, a proportion of the next generation (mutation percentage) will be populated by merely mutating selected individuals. The mutation operator changes a node in the path sequence with a probability equal to the mutation rate. Please refer to [17] for details of the crossover and mutation procedures. The initial generation will be populated with randomly generated valid paths with *TrendLength* nodes. In the spatial trend mining problem we prefer to have a high exploration. Therefore, a small proportion of the next generation (insertion percentage) will be populated with randomly generated individuals.

5 Performance Study on a Real-Life Spatial Database

In our experimental study spatial trends of banking attributes among the agencies beginning from arbitrary points were targeted at search. Here we used the "number of long-term accounts" as the non-spatial attribute. To get an insight to the values of this attribute some statistics are provided in Table 1. Also some properties of our spatial neighborhood graph subject to search are given in Table 2.

Table 1. Non-spatial values

Min.	Max.	Avg.	Std. Deviation
1	39025	4623	15631

Table 2. Neighborhood graph

Nodes	Edges	Max.Degree	Min.Degree	Avg.Degree
300	9220	51	2	30.73

To compare the performance of the algorithms they were run with their best known setup to discover the spatial trends in the same neighborhood graph. All of the algorithms were run to discover trends with *TrendLength* equal to 10 and Minimum Confidence equal to %80. In the ACO algorithm one ant was put in each of the possible start nodes. The best result was gained by the values of α, β, γ, ρ being respectively equal to 1, 2, 0.2, and 0.9. In the Genetic Algorithm an individual was initially created for each possible start node. Mutation rate was set to 0.2. Mutation percentage and insertion percentage were %40 and %5. Finally, for the execution of the algorithm proposed by Ester et. al [5, 6] an equal number of paths starting from each possible node were checked in each cycle. In Figure 3 the performance of the three algorithms are compared (averaged over 3 independent runs). This comparison is based on the number of trends that each algorithm was able to discover when a certain number of paths in the graph have been checked. As can be seen both of the nature-inspired algorithms improve their efficiency as the search continues and its experience is saved and exploited. However, this is not seen in the algorithm proposed in [5, 6]. Also in Figure 4 the average confidence of the paths that were examined in each cycle are shown. The fast increase in this metric approves the effective use of the search experience too. This utilization is done by means of stigmergy in the ACO algorithm and evolution in the Genetic Algorithm. The higher number of discovered trends in the ACO algorithm compared to the genetic algorithm seems to be because of the attractiveness heuristic defined for the nodes and its effective guidance [16].

As the candidate trends in the genetic algorithm are formed purely based on the previous generation, the number of trends found in near cycles do not differ much. In contrast, in the ACO algorithm the candidate trend generation is independent from the previous cycle and is indirectly guided by all of the previous cycles. This seems to be the reason why there are major changes in the number of discovered trends in some near cycles of this algorithm.

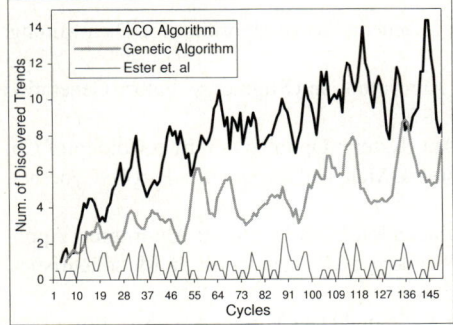 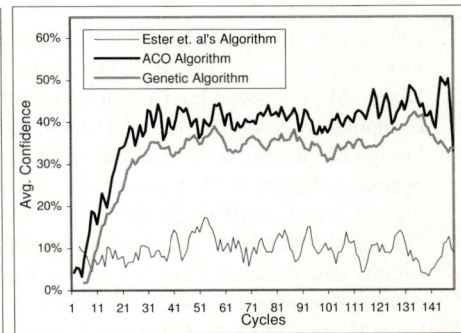

Fig. 3. Performance comparison   **Fig. 4.** Improvement in average confidence

The experiments also revealed an important and interesting distinction between the two algorithms. When we aim to initially form a valid candidate trend of a certain length, we have to iteratively add an eligible node to the last node in the path. If there are no feasible nodes to be added we have to restart this process from the start node and repeat this procedure until a valid candidate trend is formed. In the ACO algorithm the construction of the candidate trends has to be done from scratch in every cycle. However, in the genetic algorithm we construct the valid candidate trends by merely modifying and recombining the current valid paths [17]. Due to this fact the ACO algorithm needs a higher amount of CPU time compared to the genetic algorithm to discover a certain number of trends. The ACO algorithm took 370 minutes of CPU time to discover 100 trends. However, this time was about 183 minutes in the genetic algorithm (experiments run on PC with CPU Intel(R) Xeon 2.4GHz, 2GB RAM).

6 Conclusions

In this paper we introduced and compared two novel spatial trend mining algorithms inspired by two successful nature-inspired search strategies. To handle the huge search space encountered in the discovery of trend patterns in today's large spatial databases, an Ant Colony Optimization algorithm and a Genetic Algorithm were designed. In the ACO algorithms the colony's experience of trend discovery was shared between its agents by means of stigmergy. In the genetic algorithm customized operators were designed to effectively guide the search by an evolutionary process. The experimental studies on a real-life spatial database confirmed noticeable improvement in the performance of the mining process. Consequently, we succeeded to remove the restriction with the previously used pruning rule. Also the search for the trends with different start nodes are integrated, so that there will be no need to ask the start node from the user. For future work, we plan to study the behavior of the proposed algorithms and the effects of their parameters in more details. We also plan to integrate the search for trends with different lengths.

References

1. Choenni A.: Design and Implementation of a Genetic-based Algorithm for Data Mining. Proc. 26th Int. Conf. VLDB (2000) 33-42
2. Dorigo M., Bonabeau E., Theraulaz G.: Ant Algorithms and Stigmergy. Future Generation Computer Systems. vol. 17, no.8 (2000) 851–871
3. Dorigo M., Maniezzo V., Colorni A.: The Ant System: Optimization by a Colony of Co-operating Agents. IEEE Transactions on Systems, Man, and Cybernetics Part B: Cybernetics, vol. 26, no.1 (1996) 29–41
4. Dorigo M., Stützle T.: The Ant Colony Optimization Meta-Heuristic: Algorithms, Applications and Advances. In: Glover F., Kochenberger G.: Handbook of Meta-heuristics. Kluwer Academic Publishers (2002)
5. Ester M., Frommelt A., Kriegel H.P., Sander J.: Spatial Data Mining: Database Primitives, Algorithms and Efficient DBMS Support. Int. Journal of Data Mining and Knowledge Discovery, vol. 4, no.2/3 (2000) 193-217
6. Ester M., Frommelt A., Kriegel H.P., Sander J.: Algorithms for Characterization and Trend Detection in Spatial Databases. Proc. 4th Int. Conf. on Knowledge Discovery and Data Mining, (1998) 44-50
7. Ester M., Kriegel H.P., Sander J.: Spatial Data Mining: A Database Approach. Proc. 5th Int. Symp. On Large Spatial Databases. (1997) 320-328
8. Ester M., Kriegel H.P., Sander J., Xu X.: Density-Connected Sets and Their Application for Trend Detection in Spatial Databases. Proc. 3rd Int. Conf. on Knowledge Discovery and Data Mining. (1997) 44-50
9. Freitas A.A.: A Survey of Evolutionary Algorithms for Data Mining and Knowledge Discovery. In: Ghosh A., Tsutsui S.: Advances in Evolutionary Computation. Springer-Verlag (2002) 819-846
10. Koperski K., Han J.: Discovery of Spatial Association Rules in Geographic Information Databases. Proc. 4th Int. Symp. on Large Spatial Databases (1995) 47-66
11. Koperski K., Han J., Stefanovic N.: An Efficient Two-step Method for Classification of Spatial Data. Proc. International Symp. On Spatial Data Handling (1998) 320-328
12. Michalewicz, Z.: Genetic Algorithms + Data Structures = Evolution Programs. 3rd edn. Springer-Verlag, Berlin Heidelberg New York (1996)
13. Parpinelli R.S., Lopes H.S., Freitas A.A.: Data Mining with an Ant Colony Optimization Algorithm. IEEE Transactions on Evolutionary Computation, vol. 6, no.4 (2002) 321-332
14. Shekhar S., Schrater P., Vatsavai W. R., Wu W., S. Chawla: Spatial Contextual Classification and Prediction Models for Mining Geospatial Data. IEEE Transactions on Multmedia, vol. 2, no.4 (2002) 174-188
15. Wang L., Xie K., Chen T., Ma X.: Efficient Discovery of Multilevel Spatial Association Rules Using Partitions. Information and Software Technology, Vol. 47, no. 13 (2005) 1829-840
16. Zarnani A., Rahgozar M., Lucas C., Memariani A.: AntTrend: Stigmergetic Discovery of Spatial Trends. To Appear in Proc. 16th Int. Symp. On Methodologies for Intelligent Systems (2006)
17. Zarnani A., Rahgozar M., Lucas C.: Efficient Discovery of Knowledge form Large Geo-Spatial Databases: An Evolutionary Approach. To Appear in Proc. Int. Conf. on Data Mining(DMIN'06) Part of the WORDCOMP'06 (2006)

A Proposal of Evolutionary Prototype Selection for Class Imbalance Problems

Salvador García[1], José Ramón Cano[2],
Alberto Fernández[1], and Francisco Herrera[1]

[1] University of Granada, Department of Computer Science and Artificial Intelligence,
E.T.S.I. Informática, 18071 Granada, Spain
salvagl@decsai.ugr.es, alfh@ugr.es, herrera@decsai.ugr.es
[2] University of Jaén, Department of Computer Science, 23700 Linares, Jaén, Spain
jrcano@ujaen.es

Abstract. Unbalanced data in a classification problem appears when there are many more instances of some classes than others. Several solutions were proposed to solve this problem at data level by under-sampling. The aim of this work is to propose evolutionary prototype selection algorithms that tackle the problem of unbalanced data by using a new fitness function. The results obtained show that a balancing of data performed by evolutionary under-sampling outperforms previously proposed under-sampling methods in classification accuracy, obtaining reduced subsets and getting a good balance on data.

1 Introduction

The class unbalance problem emerged when machine learning started being applied to the technology, industry and scientific research. A set of examples that will be used as input of classification algorithms is said to be unbalanced when one of the classes is represented by a very small number of cases compared to the other classes. In such cases, standard classifiers tend to be flooded by the large classes and ignore the small ones.

A number of solutions have been proposed at the data and algorithmic levels [1]. At the data level, we found forms of re-sampling such as over-sampling, where replication of examples or generation of new instances is performed [2]; or under-sampling, where elimination of examples is performed. At the algorithmic level, an adjust of the operation of the algorithm is carried out to treat with unbalanced data, see [3] for an example.

Various approaches of under-sampling methods were proposed in the literature considering two-classes problems, see [4] for review. Most of them are modifications of Prototype Selection (PS) algorithms [5].

Evolutionary Algorithms (EAs) [6] are stochastic search methods that mimic the metaphor of natural biological evolution. All EAs rely on the concept of *population* of individuals (representing search points in the space of potential solutions to a given problem), which undergo probabilistic operators such as *mutation*, *selection* and *recombination*. EAs have been used to solve the PS problem with promising results [7]. Its application is denoted by Evolutionary Prototype Selection (EPS).

In this work, we propose the use of EAs for under-sampling unbalanced data sets, we call it Evolutionary Under-Sampling (EUS), in order to improve balanced classification accuracy and distribution of classes. The aim of this paper is to present our proposal model and compare it with others under-sampling methods studied in the literature. To address this, we have carried out experiments with unbalanced data sets with distinct degrees of distribution of classes.

The remainder of the paper is divided into four sections. Section 2 summarizes the main characteristics of EUS. Section 3 briefly describes the previous under-sampling methods. Section 4 presents the way to evaluate classification systems in domains with unbalanced data sets. Section 5 discusses the methodology used in the experiments, as well as the results achieved. Finally, Section 6 concludes the paper.

2 Evolutionary Under-Sampling

Let's assume that there is a training set TR which consists of pairs $(x_i, y_i), i = 1, ..., n$, where x_i defines input vector of attributes and y_i defines the corresponding class label. TR contains n instances, which have m input attributes each one and they should belong to positive or negative class. Let $S \subseteq TR$ be the subset of selected instances resulted for the execution of an algorithm.

PS problem can be considered as a search problem in which EAs can be applied. To accomplish this, we take into account two important issues: the specification of the representation of the solutions and the definition of the fitness function.

- *Representation:* Let us assume a data set TR with n instances. The search space associated is constituted by all the subsets of TR. This is accomplished by using a binary representation. A chromosome consists of n genes (one for each instance in TR) with two possible states: 0 and 1. If the gene is 1, its associated instance is included in the subset of TR represented by the chromosome. If it is 0, this does not occur.
- *Fitness Function:* Let S be a subset of instances of TR to evaluate and be coded by a chromosome. Classically, we define a fitness function that combines two values: the classification rate (*clas_rat*) associated with S and the percentage of reduction (*perc_red*) of instances of S with regards to TR [7].

$$Fitness(S) = \alpha \cdot clas\_rat + (1 - \alpha) \cdot perc\_red. \qquad (1)$$

The 1-NN classifier is used for measuring the classification rate, *clas_rat*, associated with S. It denotes the percentage of correctly classified objects from TR using only S to find the nearest neighbor. For each object y in S, the nearest neighbor is searched for amongst those in the set $S \setminus \{y\}$. Whereas, *perc_red* is defined as

$$perc\_red = 100 \cdot \frac{|TR| - |S|}{|TR|}. \qquad (2)$$

The objective of the EAs is to maximize the fitness function defined, i.e., maximize the classification rate and minimize the number of instances obtained. The EAs with this fitness function will be denoted with the extension PS in the name.

In order to approach the unbalance data problem, EPS algorithms can be adjusted making use of a new fitness function defined as follows:

$$Fitness_{Bal}(S) = g - |1 - \frac{n_+}{n_-}| \cdot P, \qquad (3)$$

where g is geometric mean of balanced accuracy defined in Section 4, n_+ is the number of positive instances selected (minority class), n_- is the number of negative instances selected (majority class), and P is a penalization factor.

This fitness function try to find subsets of instances making a trade-off between the classification balanced accuracy and an equal number of examples selected of each class. This second objective is obtained through the penalization applied to g in fitness value.

In this paper, we have applied this fitness function in two models of EAs. The first one, heterogeneous recombinations and cataclysmic mutation (CHC), is a classical model that introduces different features to obtain a tradeoff between exploration and exploitation [8], and the second one, PBIL [9], is a specific EA approach designed for binary spaces. We denote them as CHC-US and PBIL-US respectively.

3 Under-Sampling and Prototype Selection Methods

In this section, we describe the under-sampling methods and PS algorithms used in this study.

3.1 Under-Sampling Methods for Balance of Class Distribution

In this work, we evaluate six different methods of under-sampling to balance the class distribution on training data:

Random under-sampling: It is a non-heuristic method that aims to balance class distribution through the random elimination of majority class examples to get a balanced instance set.

Tomek Links [10]: It can be defined as follows: given two examples $E_i = (x_i, y_i)$ and $E_j = (x_j, y_j)$ where $y_i \neq y_j$ and $d(E_i, E_j)$ being the distance between E_i and E_j. A pair (E_i, E_j) is called Tomek link if there is not an example E_l, such that $d(E_i, E_l) < d(E_i, E_j)$ or $d(E_j, E_l) < d(E_i, E_j)$. Tomek links can be used as an under-sampling method eliminating only examples belonging to the majority class in each Tomek link found.

Condensed Nearest Neighbor Rule (CNN-US) [11]: First, randomly draw one majority class example and all examples from the minority class and put these examples in S. Afterwards, use a 1-NN over the examples in S to classify the examples in TR. Every misclassified example from TR is moved to S.

One-sided Selection (OSS) [12]: It is an under-sampling method resulting from the application of Tomek links followed by the application of CNN-US.

CNN-US + Tomek Links [4]: It is similar to OSS, but the method CNN-US is applied before the Tomek links.

Neighborhood Cleaning Rule (NCL) [13]: Uses the *Wilsons Edited Nearest Neighbor Rule (ENN)* [14] to remove majority class examples. For each example $E_i = (x_i, y_i)$ in the training set, its three nearest neighbors are found. If E_i belongs to the majority class and the classification given by its three nearest neighbors contradicts the original class of E_i, then E_i is removed. If E_i belongs to the minority class and its three nearest neighbors misclassify E_i, the the nearest neighbors that belongs to the majority class are removed.

3.2 Prototype Selection Methods

Two classical models for PS are used in this study: DROP3 [5] and IB3 [15]. Furthermore, same two EAs used as EUS are employed as EPS with classical objective and we denote them as CHC-PS and PBIL-PS [7].

4 Evaluation on Unbalanced Data Classification

The most correct way of evaluating the performance of classifiers is based on the analysis of the confusion matrix. In Table 1, a confusion matrix is illustrated for a problem of two classes, with the values for the positive and negative classes. From this matrix it is possible to extract a number of widely used metric to measure the performance of learning systems, such as *Error Rate*, defined as $Err = \frac{FP+FN}{TP+FN+FP+TN}$ and *Accuracy*, defined as $Acc = \frac{TP+TN}{TP+FN+FP+TN} = 1 - Err$.

Table 1. Confusion matrix for a two-class problem

	Positive Prediction	Negative Prediction
Positive Class	True Positive (TP)	False Negative (FN)
Negative Class	False Positive (FP)	True Negative (TN)

Face to the use of error (or accuracy) rate, another type of metric in the domain of the unbalanced problems is considered more correct. Concretely, from Table 1 it is possible to obtain four metrics of performance that measure the classification performance for the positive and negative classes independently:

- **False negative rate** $FN_{rate} = \frac{FN}{TP+FN}$ is the percentage of positive cases misclassified.
- **False positive rate** $FP_{rate} = \frac{FN}{FP+TN}$ is the percentage of negative cases misclassified.
- **True negative rate** $TN_{rate} = \frac{TN}{FP+TN}$ is the percentage of negative cases correctly classified.

- **True positive rate** $TP_{rate} = \frac{TP}{TP+FN}$ is the percentage of positive cases correctly classified.

These four performance measures have the advantage of being independent of the costs for class and prior probabilities. The goal of a classifier is to minimize the false positive and false negative rates or, in a similar way, to maximize the true positive and true negative rates.

In [16] it was proposed another metric called *Geometric Mean (GM)*, defined as $g = \sqrt{a^+ \cdot a^-}$, where a^+ denotes accuracy on positive examples (TP_{rate}), and a^- is accuracy on negative examples (TN_{rate}). This measure try to maximize accuracy in order to balance both classes at the same time. It is an evaluation measure that joins two objectives.

5 Experiments and Results

Performance of the under-sampling and PS methods, described in Sections 2 and 3, is analyzed using 7 data sets taken from the UCI Machine Learning Database Repository [17]. These data sets are transformed to obtain two-class non-balanced problems. The main characteristics of these data sets are summarized in Table 2. For each data set, it shows the number of examples (#Examples), number of attributes (#Attributes), name of the class (minority and majority) together with class distribution.

The data sets considered are partitioned using the *ten fold cross-validation (10-fcv)* procedure. The parameters of algorithms used are presented in Table 3.

Table 4 shows class distribution after balancing with each method. Table 5 shows us the average of the results offered by each algorithm. Each column shows:

Table 2. Relevant information about each data set used in this study

Data Set	#Examples	#Attributes	%Class (min., maj.)	%Class (min., maj.)
Ecoli	336	7	(iMU, Remainder)	(10.42,89.58)
German	1000	20	(Bad, Good)	(30.00,70.00)
Glass	214	9	(Ve-win-float-proc, Remainder)	(7.94,92.06)
Haberman	306	3	(Die, Survive)	(26.47,73.53)
New-thyroid	215	5	(hypo, Remainder)	(16.28,83.72)
Pima	768	8	(1,0)	(34.77,66.23)
Vehicle	846	18	(van, Remainder)	(23.52,76.48)

Table 3. Parameters considered for the algorithms

Algorithm	Parameters
CHC-PS	$Pop = 50, Eval = 10000, \alpha = 0.5$
IB3	$Acept.Level = 0.9, DropLevel = 0.7$
PBIL-PS	$LR = 0.1, Mut_{shift} = 0.05, p_m = 0.02, Pop = 50$
	$Negative_{LR} = 0.075, Eval = 10000$
CHC-US	$Pop = 50, Eval = 10000, P = 20$
PBIL-US	$LR = 0.1, Mut_{shift} = 0.05, p_m = 0.02, Pop = 50$
	$Negative_{LR} = 0.075, Eval = 10000, P = 20$

Table 4. Class distribution after balancing

Balancing Method	% Minority Class (Positive)	% Majority Class (Negative)
CHC-PS	34.74	65.26
PBIL-PS	33.94	66.06
DROP3	45.10	54.90
IB3	33.95	66.05
CNN-US + TomekLinks	87.14	12.86
CNN-US	58.25	41.75
NCL	31.52	68.48
OSS	38.76	61.24
RandomUnderSampling	50.00	50.00
TomekLinks	29.29	70.71
CHC-US	50.00	50.00
PBIL-US	49.99	50.01

- The balancing method employed. *None* indicates that no balancing method is employed (original data set is used to classification with 1-NN).
- Percentage of reduction with respect to the original data set size.
- Accuracy percentage for each class by using a 1-NN classifier (a^+ and a^-), where subindex *tra* refers to training data and subindex *tst* refers to test data. GM value also is showed to training and test data.

Tables 4 and 5 are divided in three parts by separator lines: PS methods, Under-Sampling methods and proposed methods.

The following analysis of results can be made for these tables:

- CHC-US and PBIL-US present the best trade-off accuracy between both classes, they have the higher value of average GM in training and test (Table 5).
- The new fitness function used in EUS allows us to obtain a well-balanced class distribution (Table 4).
- There are algorithms that discriminate the negative class to a great extent, such as CNN-US+Tomek Links. PS algorithms discriminate positive class because they only take into account the global performance of classification, which is highly conditioned for negative (majority) class examples.

We have included a second type of table accomplishing a statistical comparison of methods over multiple data sets. Demšar [18] recommends a set of simple, safe and robust non-parametric tests for statistical comparisons of classifiers. One of them is Wilcoxon Signed-Ranks Test [19,?]. Table 7 collects results of applying Wilcoxon test between our proposed methods and the rest of Under-Sampling algorithm studied in this paper over the 7 data sets considered. This table is divided in two parts: In the first part, the measure of performance used is the accuracy classification in test set through geometric mean. In the second part, we accomplish Wilcoxon test by using as performance measure only the reduction of the training set. Each part of this table contains two rows, representing our proposed methods, and N columns where N is the number of algorithms considered in this study. Algorithms order is given at Table 6. In each one of the cells can appear three symbols: +, = or −. They represent that the

Table 5. Average results

Balancing Method	% Red	$\%a_{tra}^-$	$\%a_{tra}^+$	GM_{tra}	$\%a_{tst}^-$	$\%a_{tst}^+$	GM_{tst}
None (1-NN)	-	89.34	57.69	70.46	88.71	56.19	69.38
DROP3	87.75	84.51	67.31	74.90	81.42	56.88	67.08
IB3	71.61	84.96	48.84	62.47	85.35	51.88	65.18
CHC-PS	**98.67**	94.88	57.07	67.04	**93.16**	50.11	61.73
PBIL-PS	95.48	**95.58**	61.19	69.78	91.59	53.81	63.49
CNN-US	61.70	79.08	63.00	69.41	81.26	63.53	70.76
CNN-US + TomekLinks	74.77	54.05	**91.66**	68.28	54.29	**89.16**	67.43
NCL	17.70	81.72	82.30	81.38	80.17	73.47	75.96
OSS	75.39	81.23	69.01	74.23	81.72	67.33	73.43
RandomUnderSampling	57.32	75.25	76.85	75.99	74.70	75.88	75.21
TomekLinks	11.88	85.64	76.50	80.15	83.77	68.58	75.19
CHC-US	95.45	82.46	88.78	85.54	79.17	75.91	77.48
PBIL-US	77.66	86.98	90.82	**88.87**	81.08	74.32	**77.56**

Table 6. Algorithms order

Algorithm	Number	Algorithm	Number
DROP3	1	NCL	7
IB3	2	OSS	8
CHC-PS	3	RandomUnderSampling	9
PBIL-PS	4	Tomek Links	10
CNN-US	5	CHC-US	11
CNN-US+Tomek Links	6	PBIL-US	12

Table 7. Wilcoxon test

	GM_{tst} Accuracy Performance											
	1	2	3	4	5	6	7	8	9	10	11	12
CHC-US (11)	+	+	+	+	=	+	=	=	=	=		=
PBIL-US (12)	+	+	=	=	=	+	=	=	=	=	=	

	Reduction Performance											
	1	2	3	4	5	6	7	8	9	10	11	12
CHC-US (11)	+	+	-	=	+	+	+	+	+	+		+
PBIL-US (12)	-	=	-	-	+	=	+	=	+	+	-	

algorithm situated in that row outperforms (+), is similar (=) or is worse (−) in performance than the algorithm which appear in the column (Table 7).

We make a brief analysis of results summarized in Table 7:

– Wilcoxon test shows us that our proposed algorithms are statistically equal to other Under-Sampling methods and outperforms PS methods, in terms of accuracy in test.
– However, in reduction performance, EUS obtain better reduction than non-evolutionary under-sampling methods. It points out that EUS provides reduced subsets without loss of balanced accuracy classification performance with respect to the rest of algorithms.
– Note that Wilcoxon test is performed using a low number of data sets (the minimum possible number of them to carry out the test). This implies that the results obtained may need a more depth study (see for example the difference between CHC-PS and PBIL-US in GM test with similar statistical behavior). It is necessary to use more data sets in a future study.

6 Conclusions

The purpose of this paper is to present a proposal of Evolutionary Prototype Selection Algorithm with balance of data through under-sampling for imbalanced data sets. The results shows that our proposal is better analyzing the mean, equal statistically and better in reduction versus the remainder of under-sampling methods. Furthermore, a good balance of distribution of classes is achieved.

The paper also points out that standard Prototype Selection must not be employed to manage non-balanced problems.

Acknowledgement. This work was supported by TIN2005-08386-C05-01 and TIN2005-08386-C05-03.

References

1. Chawla, N.V., Japkowicz, N., Kotcz, A.: Editorial: special issue on learning from imbalanced data sets. SIGKDD Explorations **6** (2004) 1–6
2. Chawla, N.V., Bowyer, K.W., Hall, L.O., Kegelmeyer, W.P.: Smote: Synthetic minority over-sampling technique. Journal of Artificial Intelligence and Research **16** (2002) 321–357
3. Tan, S.: Neighbor-weighted k-nearest neighbor for unbalanced text corpus. Expert Systems with Applications **28** (2005) 667–671
4. Batista, G.E.A.P.A., Prati, R.C., Monard, M.C.: A study of the behavior of several methods for balancing machine learning training data. SIGKDD Explor. Newsl. **6** (2004) 20–29
5. Wilson, D.R., Martinez, T.R.: Reduction techniques for instance-based learning algorithms. Machine Learning **38** (2000) 257–286
6. Eiben, A.E., Smith J.E.: Introduction to Evolutionary Computing. SpringerVerlag (2003)
7. Cano, J.R., Herrera, F., Lozano, M.: Using evolutionary algorithms as instance selection for data reduction in KDD: An experimental study. IEEE Transactions on Evolutionary Computation **7** (2003) 561–575
8. Eshelman, L.J.: The CHC adaptative search algorithm: How to safe search when engaging in nontraditional genetic recombination. In: FOGA. (1990) 265–283
9. Baluja, S.: Population-based incremental learning: A method for integrating genetic search based function optimization and competitive learning. Technical report, Pittsburgh, PA, USA (1994)
10. Tomek, I.: Two modifications of CNN. IEEE Transactions on Systems, Man, and Communications **6** (1976) 769–772
11. Hart, P.E.: The condensed nearest neighbour rule. IEEE Transactions on Information Theory **18** (1968) 515–516
12. Kubat, M., Matwin, S.: Addressing the course of imbalanced training sets: One-sided selection. In: ICML. (1997) 179–186
13. Laurikkala, J.: Improving identification of difficult small classes by balancing class distribution, In: AIME '01: Proceedings of the 8th Conference on AI in Medicine in Europe, London, UK, Springer-Verlag (2001) 63–66
14. Wilson, D.L.: Asymptotic properties of nearest neighbor rules using edited data. IEEE Transactions on Systems, Man and Cybernetics **2** (1972) 408–421

15. Aha, D.W., Kibler, D., Albert, M.K.: Instance-based learning algorithms. Machine Learning **7** (1991) 37–66
16. Barandela, R., Sánchez, J.S., García, V., Rangel, E.: Strategies for learning in class imbalance problems. Pattern Recognition **36** (2003) 849–851
17. Newman, D.J., Hettich, S., Merz, C.B.: UCI repository of machine learning databases (1998)
18. Demšar, J: Statistical comparisons of classifiers over multiple data sets. Journal of Machine Learning Research **7** (2006) 1–30
19. Wilcoxon, F.: Individual comparisons by rankings methods. Biometrics **1** (1945) 80–83
20. Sheskin, D.J.: Handbook of Parametric and Nonparametric Statistical Procedures. CRC Press (1997)

MOVICAB-IDS: Visual Analysis of Network Traffic Data Streams for Intrusion Detection

Álvaro Herrero, Emilio Corchado, and José Manuel Sáiz

Department of Civil Engineering, University of Burgos, Spain
`{ahcosio, escorchado, jmsaiz}@ubu.es`

Abstract. MOVICAB-IDS enables the more interesting projections of a massive traffic data set to be analysed, thereby providing an overview of any possible anomalous situations taking place on a computer network. This IDS responds to the challenges presented by traffic volume and diversity. It is a connectionist agent-based model extended by means of a functional and mobile visualization interface. The IDS is designed to be more flexible, accessible and portable by running on a great variety of applications, including small mobile ones such as PDA's, mobile phones or embedded devices. Furthermore, its effectiveness has been demonstrated in different tests.

Keywords: Unsupervised Learning, Neural Networks, Exploratory Projection Pursuit, Multiagent Systems, Computer Network Security, Intrusion Detection.

1 Introduction and Previous Work

In the context of a computer network, an IDS (Intrusion Detection System) can roughly be defined as a tool that is designed to detect suspicious patterns that may be related to a network or system attack. To do so, a Network IDS (NIDS) analyses the events occurring along the computer network. Such tools have now become very necessary additions to reinforce security infrastructure.

Many different forms of Artificial Intelligence (such as Genetic Programming [1], Data Mining [2], [3] or Neural Networks [4], [5], [6] among others), and statistical [7] and signature verification [8] techniques have been applied in the field of IDSs. There are several IDSs that can generate different alarms when an anomalous situation occurs, but they can not provide a general overview of what is happening inside a network. Various visualization techniques have been applied in the field of IDSs [4], [5], [9], [10], [11], [12] to tackle this issue. Some of them (The Multi Router Traffic Grapher [12] for example) offer visual measurements of network traffic. MOVICAB-IDS goes further and offers a complete and more intuitive visualization of network traffic by depicting each simple packet and providing the network administrator with a snapshot of network traffic, protocol interactions, and traffic volume, generally in order to identify anomalous situations.

Knowledge discovery, pattern recognition, data mining and other such techniques, deal with the problem of extracting interesting classifications, clusters, associations and other patterns from data. Furthermore, the existence of laptops, palmtops, handhelds, embedded systems, and wearable computers is making ubiquitous access to a large quantity of distributed data a reality. Advanced analysis of distributed data for extracting useful knowledge is the next natural step in the increasingly interconnected world of ubiquitous and distributed computing.

We have therefore extended our agent-based IDS model [4], [5] to make it accessible from any wireless device, such as a palmtop, laptop or mobile phone to give more accessibility to network administrators, enabling permanent mobile visualization, monitoring and supervision of their networks.

The remaining five sections of this paper are structured as follows: section 2 contains an overview of MOVICAB-IDS; data management is then explained in depth in section 3; some experimental results are described in section 4; the model is evaluated in section 5; finally, section 6 puts forward a number of conclusions and pointers for future work.

2 MOVICAB-IDS

Our model is designed to split massive traffic data sets into segments and analyse them, thereby providing administrators with a visual tool to analyse the kinds of events taking place on the computer network. This tool also provides an analysis of several subsequent segments as unique ones (simple segments) and also as an accumulated data set.

Thus, MOVICAB-IDS (MObile VIsualization Connectionist Agent-Based Intrusion Detection System) may be defined as an IDS formed of different software agents [13] that work in unison in order to detect anomalous situations by taking full advantage of an unsupervised connectionist model [4], [5], [14], [15], [16].

To detect anomalous situations, MOVICAB-IDS performs the following functions:

- 1st step.- Network Traffic Capture: captures packets travelling over the different network segments.
- 2nd step.- Data Pre-processing: the captured data is selected and pre-processed. A set of packets and features contained in the headers of the captured data is selected from the raw network traffic. (See Sect. 3)
- 3rd step.- Segmentation: the data stream is divided into simple segments and accumulated ones (consisting of the addition of several consecutive simple segments). (See Sect. 3.1)
- 4th step.- Data Analysis: a connectionist model is applied to analyse the data. (See Sect. 2.1)
- 5th step.- Visualization: the projections of both, simple and accumulated segments, are presented to the network administrator for the analysis and monitoring.

The visualization step may be displayed on a different device than the one used for the first four steps. To improve the accessibility of the system, the administrator may visualize the results on a mobile device, enabling informed decisions to be taken anywhere and at any time.

2.1 The Unsupervised Connectionist Model

The data analysis task is based on the use of a neural Exploratory Projection Pursuit (EPP) [17], [18] model called Cooperative Maximum Likelihood Hebbian Learning

(CMLHL) [14], [15], [16]. It was initially applied in the field of Artificial Vision [14], [15] to identify local filters in space and time. In MOVICAB-IDS it is applied in the field of Computer Network Security. CMLHL is based on Maximum Likelihood Hebbian Learning (MLHL) [19], [20] adding lateral connections [14], [15] which have been derived from the Rectified Gaussian Distribution [21]. The resultant net can find the independent factors of a data set but does so in a way that captures some type of global ordering in the data set.

Considering an N-dimensional input vector (x), an M-dimensional output vector (y) and with W_{ij} being the weight (linking input j to output i), CMLHL can be expressed [14], [15], [16] as:

1. Feed-forward step:

$$y_i = \sum_{j=1}^{N} W_{ij} x_j, \forall i \ . \tag{1}$$

2. Lateral activation passing:

$$y_i(t+1) = [y_i(t) + \tau(b - Ay)]^+ \ . \tag{2}$$

3. Feedback step:

$$e_j = x_j - \sum_{i=1}^{M} W_{ij} y_i, \forall j \ . \tag{3}$$

4. Weight change:

$$\Delta W_{ij} = \eta . y_i . sign(e_j) | e_j |^{p-1} \ . \tag{4}$$

Where: η is the learning rate, τ is the "strength" of the lateral connections, b the bias parameter, p a parameter related to the energy function [15], [19], [20] and A a symmetric matrix used to modify the response to the data. The effect of this matrix is based on the relation between the distances among the output neurons.

3 Data Stream and Data Sets

As previously mentioned, NIDSs have to deal with the practical problem of high volumes of quite diverse data [22]. To deal with the problem of high diversity, MOVICAB-IDS splits the traffic into different groups, taking into account the protocol (either UDP, TCP, ICMP…) over IP. For the sake of simplicity, only UDP traffic is considered in this work due to its potential dangers.

Once the data set is classified by the protocol over IP, our model is based on the analysis of five main numerical variables (timestamp, source and destination port, packet size and protocol) existing on the packets headers. The capability of these variables to identify different anomalous situations has already been demonstrated [4], [5].

Then, MOVICAB-IDS divides the pre-processed data sets as follows:

- Equal simple segments. Each simple segment contains all the packets whose timestamps are between its initial and final limits. As can be seen in Fig. 1, there is a time overlap between each consecutive simple segments. This is done because anomalous situations could conceivably take place between simple segment S_x and S_{x+1} (the next segment following S_x). In this case, it would be necessary to consider some packets twice in order to visualize the end of the anomalous situation and the evolution between simple segments. Both the length (time duration) of the simple segments and the overlap time can be set up by the administrator.
- Accumulated segments. Each one of these segments contains several consecutive simple ones (Fig. 1). The main considerations are, firstly, to present a long-term picture of the evolution of network traffic to the network administrator and, secondly, to allow the visualization of attacks lasting longer than the length of a simple segment. The number of simple segments making up the accumulated segments is configurable.

3.1 Fragmentation

Fig. 1 shows the fragmentation system used by MOVICAB-IDS. In this study we have fixed a length of 10 minutes for each simple segment, and 2 minutes of overlap between consecutive segments. All these values can be fixed to make the system more suitable for the administrator by taking into account issues such as the traffic volume (packets), the available calculus power, and so on.

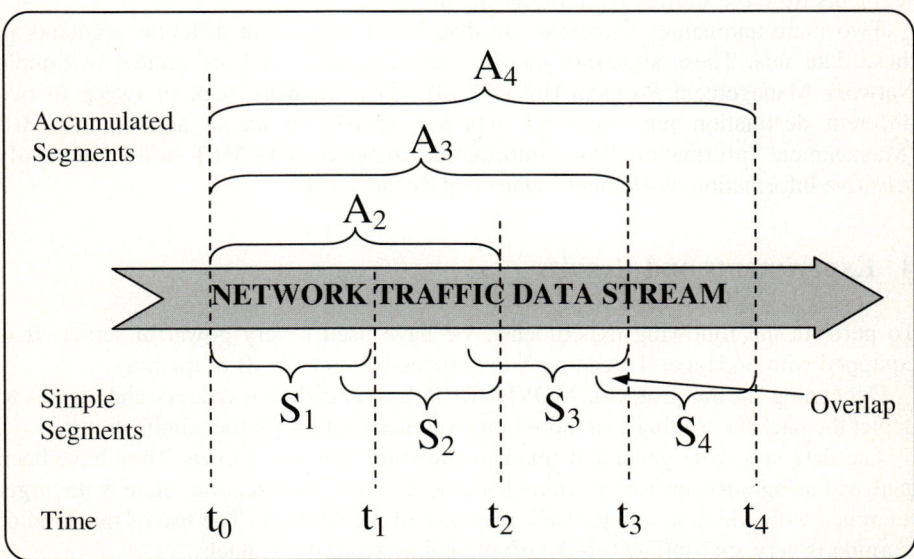

Fig. 1. Data stream fragmentation. Each data set is divided into several simple segments (e.g. S_1, S_2 and so on) and accumulated ones (e.g. A_2, A_3 ...)

Table 1. Data sets description

Data set	# packets	Initial timestamp (ms)	Final timestamp (ms)
S_1	3122	1	600000
S_2	3026	480000	1080000
S_3	3052	960000	1560000
S_4	9673	1440000	2040000
S_5	10249	1920000	2520000
S_6	3584	2400000	3000000
S_7	3051	2880000	3480000
S_8	2818	3360000	3960000
...			
A_2	5553	1	1080000
A_3	8036	1	1560000
A_4	17079	1	2040000
A_5	20227	1	2520000
A_6	23169	1	3000000
A_7	25450	1	3480000
A_8	27787	1	3960000
...			
A_{13}	49464	1	6360000

Table 1 describes the data sets used in this work.

Datasets from A_2 to A_{13} have been developed to show the evolution of accumulated segments from the starting point of the capture.

Two main anomalous situations are distributed throughout different segments in these data sets. These situations can be very dangerous and are related to Simple Network Management Protocol (SNMP) [4], [5]: a network scan (a sweep to two different destination port to check whether SNMP service is active) and MIB (Management Information Base) information transfers. The MIB stores potentially sensitive information on elements controlled by the SNMP.

4 Experiments and Results

To perform the following experiments, we have used a very powerful server. It is equipped with 64 Hyper-Threading Xeon processors and 12 GB of memory.

Depending on the protocol, MOVICAB-IDS uses different colours and shapes to depict the packets, leading to a more intuitive visualization for the administrator.

The data sets were generated 'made-to-measure' and are known. They have been analysed using unsupervised learning because in a real-life situation, there is no target reference with which to compare the response of the network. The use of this kind of learning is very appropriate for identifying unknown (0-day) attacks.

In the following figures (Fig. 2 and Fig. 3), we show some examples of how our system performs when applied to simple segments of 10 minutes. Fig. 2 (for data set S_1) is an example of normal traffic with no anomalous situations as all the packets evolve in "normal" parallel directions over time [4], [5]. On the other hand, Fig. 3 (for data set S_4) shows how the system identifies an anomalous situation related to a MIB information transfer [4], [5]. This situation (Groups 1 and 2 in Fig. 2) is identified as anomalous due to its high temporal concentration of packets in comparison to a "normal" one [4], [5], that is visualized as smooth, straight lines running in parallel to each other as can be seen in Fig. 2.

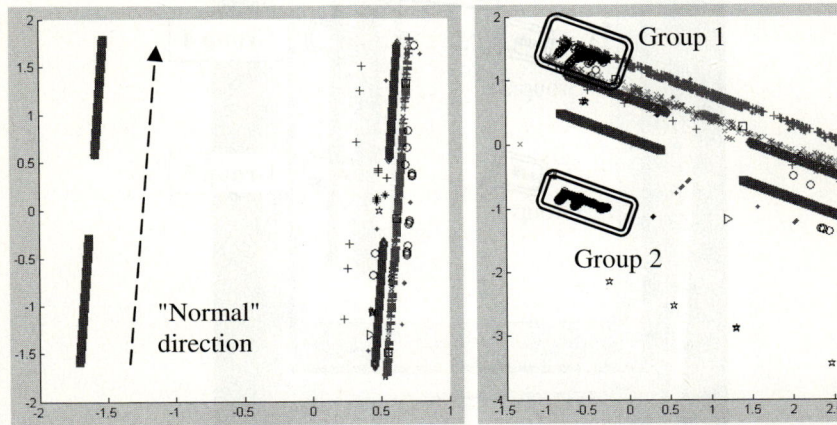

Fig. 2. Visualization of S_1.

Fig. 3. Visualization of S_4.

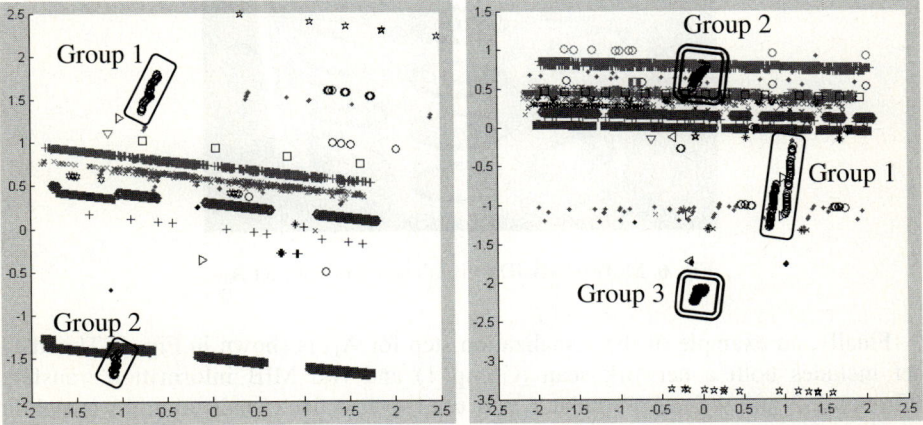

Fig. 4. Visualization of A_2.

Fig. 5. Visualization of A_8.

The following two figures show the evolution of a 20 minute-long accumulated segment (A_2 - Fig. 4) and then an 80 minute-long one (A_8 - Fig. 5). As can be seen, the same network scan can be identified in both data sets in which it is contained (Groups 1 and 2 in Fig. 4, and Group 1 in Fig. 5). Additionally, A_8 includes a MIB information transfer (Groups 2 and 3 in Fig. 5).

1430 Á. Herrero, E. Corchado, and J.M. Sáiz

Fig. 6. MOVICAB-IDS visualization of data set A_{13}.

Finally, an example of the visualization step for A_{13} is shown in Fig. 6. This data set includes both a network scan (Group 1) and two MIB information transfers (Groups 2-3 and 4-5). An emulator was used to test the visualization on a mobile platform.

In these examples, the administrator can easily identify a network scan represented by its evolution along a non-parallel direction to the normal one while an MIB transfer is characterized by its high packet density.

5 Evaluation

Up until the present, there has been no specific evaluation technique for numerical IDSs. We have therefore used a novel mutation-based method to evaluate the performance of MOVICAB-IDS. In general, a mutation can be defined as a random change. In keeping with this idea, this evaluation modifies different features of the numerical information. Thus, both the destination ports and the number of packets (included in the scan) in data set A_2 have been mutated. As can be seen in Fig. 7, MOVICAB-IDS detects the mutated scans (Groups 1 and 2). Once again, these anomalous situations are identified by their evolution along a non-parallel direction that intersects with the normal one that represents the rest of the traffic. The goal is to test the system in real-life situations that differ from those used to train the model and which might be generated by a hacker.

Moreover, the statistical technique known as Principal Component Analysis (PCA) [23] was applied to data set S_4 (as can be seen in Fig. 8) for comparison purposes. This technique, already used in the field of IDSs [9], failed to detect the MIB information transfer contained in the data set.

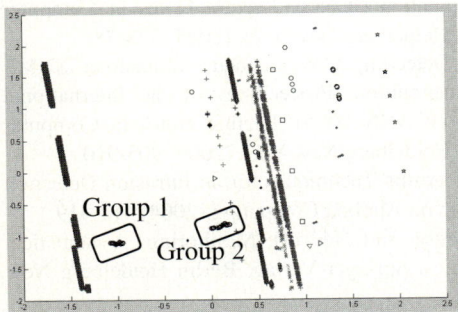

Fig. 7. Visualization of mutated A_2.   Fig. 8. PCA visualization of S_4.

6 Conclusions and Future Work

We have presented an IDS which offers network administrators greater accessibility using any mobile devices to its visualization features. The system can deal with a high-volume network traffic data stream by pre-processing and splitting it into simple and accumulated segments. Simple segments are characterized by a time overlap with the preceding and the following simple segment in order to prevent any short anomalous situation passing by unnoticed at the very end or at the beginning of a simple segment. To provide a continual analysis of the network traffic, this IDS also studies accumulated segments for more general purposes to monitor and analyse traffic. To achieve this, we have performed the experiments using a supercomputer, which allow us the possibility of increasing the segment length.

This system can be used in combination with other IDS to overcome their limitations (e.g: identification of 0-day attacks).

Further work will focus on the study of different anomalous situations to extend the model to cover several protocols, and the application of different learning rules in the Analysis Step.

Acknowledgments. This research has been supported by the MCyT project TIN2004-07033 and the project BU008B05 of the JCyL.

References

1. Abraham, A., Grosan, C., Martin-Vide, C.: Evolutionary Design of Intrusion Detection Programs. International Journal of Network Security (2006)
2. Julisch, K.: Data Mining for Intrusion Detection: A Critical Review. Research Report RZ 3398, IBM Zurich Research Laboratory. Switzerland (2002)
3. Lee, W., Stolfo, S.J.: A Framework for Constructing Features and Models for Intrusion Detection Systems. ACM Transactions on Information and System Security (TISSEC), Vol. 3(4). ACM Press, New York (2000) 227 – 261
4. Herrero, Á., Corchado, E., Sáiz, J.M.: A Cooperative Unsupervised Connectionist Model Applied to Identify Anomalous Massive SNMP Data Sending. Proceedings of the International Conference on Natural Computation (ICNC). Lecture Notes in Computer Science, Vol. 3610. Springer-Verlag, Berlin Heidelberg New York (2005) 778-782
5. Corchado, E., Herrero, Á., Sáiz J.M.: Detecting Compounded Anomalous SNMP Situations Using Unsupervised Pattern Recognition. Proceedings of the International Conference on Artificial Neural Networks (ICANN 2005). Lecture Notes in Computer Science, Vol. 3697. Springer-Verlag, Berlin Heidelberg New York (2005) 905-910
6. Zanero, S., Savaresi, S.M.: Unsupervised Learning Techniques for an Intrusion Detection System. Proceedings of the ACM Symposium on Applied Computing (2004) 412-419
7. Marchette, D.J.: Computer Intrusion Detection and Network Monitoring: A Statistical Viewpoint. Information Science and Statistics. Springer-Verlag, Berlin Heidelberg New York (2001)
8. Roesch, M.: Snort - Lightweight Intrusion Detection for Networks. Proceedings of the 13th Systems Administration Conference (LISA '99) (1999)
9. Goldring, T.: Scatter (and Other) Plots for Visualizing User Profiling Data and Network Traffic. Proceedings of the ACM Workshop on Visualization and Data Mining for Computer Security (2004)
10. Muelder, Ch., Ma, K-L., Bartoletti, T.: Interactive Visualization for Network and Port Scan Detection. Proceedings of the 8th International Symposium on Recent Advances in Intrusion Detection (RAID). Lecture Notes in Computer Science, Vol. 3858. Springer-Verlag, Berlin Heidelberg New York (2005)
11. Abdullah, K., Lee, Ch., Conti, G., Copeland, J.A.: Visualizing Network Data for Intrusion Detection. Proceedings of the IEEE Workshop on Information Assurance and Security (2002) 100-108
12. MRTG: The Multi Router Traffic Grapher, http://people.ee.ethz.ch/~oetiker/webtools/mrtg/
13. Wooldridge, M.: Multiagent Systems: A Modern Approach to Distributed Artificial Intelligence. Gerhard Weiss (1999)
14. Corchado, E., Han, Y., Fyfe, C.: Structuring Global Responses of Local Filters Using Lateral Connections. Journal of Experimental and Theoretical Artificial Intelligence, Vol. 15(4) (2003) 473-487
15. Corchado, E., Fyfe, C.: Connectionist Techniques for the Identification and Suppression of Interfering Underlying Factors. International Journal of Pattern Recognition and Artificial Intelligence, Vol. 17(8) (2003) 1447-1466

16. Corchado, E., Corchado, J.M., Sáiz, L., Lara, A.: Constructing a Global and Integral Model of Business Management Using a CBR System. Proceedings of the 1st International Conference on Cooperative Design, Visualization and Engineering (CDVE). Lecture Notes in Computer Science, Vol. 3190. Springer-Verlag, Berlin Heidelberg New York (2004) 141-147
17. Friedman J., Tukey. J.: A Projection Pursuit Algorithm for Exploratory Data Analysis. IEEE Transaction on Computers, Vol. 23 (1974) 881-890
18. Hyvärinen A.: Complexity Pursuit: Separating Interesting Components from Time Series. Neural Computation, Vol. 13(4) (2001) 883-898
19. Corchado, E., MacDonald, D., Fyfe, C.: Maximum and Minimum Likelihood Hebbian Learning for Exploratory Projection Pursuit. Data Mining and Knowledge Discovery, Vol. 8(3), Kluwer Academic Publishing (2004) 203-225
20. Fyfe, C., Corchado, E.: Maximum Likelihood Hebbian Rules. Proceedings of the European Symposium on Artificial Neural Networks (2002) 143-148
21. Seung, H.S., Socci, N.D., Lee, D.: The Rectified Gaussian Distribution. Advances in Neural Information Processing Systems, Vol. 10 (1998) 350-356
22. Dreger, H., Feldmann, A., Paxson, V., Sommer, R.: Operational Experiences with High-Volume Network Intrusion Detection. Proceedings of the ACM Conference on Computer and Communications Security. ACM Press, New York, USA. (2004) 2-11
23. Oja, E.: Neural Networks, Principal Components and Subspaces. International Journal of Neural Systems, Vol. 1 (1989) 61-68

Maximum Likelihood Topology Preserving Ensembles

Emilio Corchado[1], Bruno Baruque[1] and Bogdan Gabrys[2]

[1] Department of Civil Engineering. University of Burgos. Spain
`escorchado@ubu.es, bbaruque@ubu.es`
[2] Computational Intelligence Research Group. Bournemouth University. United Kingdom
`bgabrys@bournemouth.ac.uk`

Abstract. Statistical re-sampling techniques have been used extensively and successfully in the machine learning approaches for generations of classifier and predictor ensembles. It has been frequently shown that combining so called unstable predictors has a stabilizing effect on and improves the performance of the prediction system generated in this way. In this paper we use the re-sampling techniques in the context of a topology preserving map which can be used for scale invariant classification, taking into account the fact that it models the residual after feedback with a family of distributions and finds filters which make the residuals most likely under this model. This model is applied to artificial data sets and compared with a similar version based on the Self Organising Map (SOM).

1 Introduction

Topographic map formation is an organizing principle in the mammalian cerebral cortex. It consists of an orderly topographical arrangement of motor and sensory neurons with similar response properties across the cortical surface. There is an experimental evidence of the existence of cortical maps in the brain, and some examples have been identified in the visual cortex, somatosensory cortex and the auditory cortex.

The most typical example of an artificial topographic map formation is the Self-Organising Map (SOM) [1], [2], [3]. SOM is composed of a discrete array of L nodes arranged on an N-dimensional lattice and it maps these nodes into D-dimensional data space while maintaining their ordering. The dimensionality, N, of the lattice is normally less than that of the data. With the SOM, all data in a partition is quantised to a single point, and the combined effect of all of the vector-quantising nodes is to give a globally non-linear representation of the data set. Typically, the array of nodes is one or two-dimensional, with all nodes connected to the N inputs by an N-dimensional weight vector.

Another example of a topographic mapping algorithm is the Maximum Likelihood Scale Invariant Map (MLSIM) [4], [5], [6]. It is similar model to a Self-Organising Map (SOM) [3] but in this case training is based on the use of a particular Exploratory Projection Pursuit (EPP) model [7], [8] called Maximum Likelihood Hebbian Learning (MLHL) Network [6], [9]. The competitive learning and a neighbourhood function are then used in a similar way as with the SOM.

Competitive learning based networks are inherently instable, due to the nature of their learning algorithm. That means that even running the same algorithm, under the same learning conditions several times can give quite different results. To try to minimize the effect of this instability several methods are being studied. One of the most popular is the bagging technique [10]. This technique consists of constructing several different classifiers of the same type and combining their outputs. To train each one of the classifiers, a different subset of the training data is used, so a bit of diversity is included in the ensemble.

Tests on real and simulated datasets using classification and regression trees and subset selection in linear regression show that bagging can give substantial gains in accuracy. The vital element is the instability of the classifying method. It has been observed that if perturbing the learning set can cause significant changes in the classifier decisions, the bagging can improve accuracy [11], [12], [13].

In this paper the instability of individual MLSIMs and potential for improvement of the performance using ensembles of classifiers are exploited by utilising bagging like combination approaches and MLSIM weight initialisation procedures described in the following sections.

2 Bagging

The term "bagging" refers to the union of two other words: "bootstrapping" and "aggregating" [10]. The first one refers to the way the inputs are extracted from the dataset used for training the predictor(s). The second refers to the fact that, instead of a unique one, a set or aggregation of predictors should be constructed. The aggregated predictor is potentially much more powerful than any individual predictor trained on the same data.

This technique, utilized in this study to improve the classifying capacity of certain topography preserving maps, is based on statistical re-sampling theory. The description of this "bootstrap aggregating" or "bagging" technique can be found in [10] and a version of bagging will be exploited in this paper in the context of topology preserving maps.

When dealing with classification trees for instance, this technique has been employed to generate n subsets of the main dataset under analysis through re-sampling with replacement and training individual decision trees on such re-sampled subsets. This permits to generate n classifiers which are most often combined by simple majority voting of their decisions [11], [12].

In our case, the idea is to employ the bagging like technique in combination with the MLSIM training carried out on several re-sampled subsets of the original training set. Once the multiple versions of MLSIM are generated the ensemble output is computed by simple voting procedure [14], [15].

3 Maximum Likelihood Scale Invariant Maps

Maximum Likelihood Scale Invariant Map (MLSIM) [4], [5] is an extension of the Scale Invariant Map (SIM) [16] based on the application of the Maximum Likelihood Hebbian Learning (MLHL) [6], [9].

As mentioned earlier an MLSIM is a regular array of nodes arranged on a lattice. Competitive learning and a neighbourhood function are used in a similar way as with the SOM. The input data (x) is fed forward to the outputs y_i in the usual way. After selection of a winner, the winner, c, is deemed to be firing ($y_c=1$) and all other outputs are suppressed ($y_i = 0, \forall i \neq c$).

The winner's activation is then fed back through its weights and this is subtracted from the inputs to calculate the error or residual **e** as shown in Eq. 1.

$$\mathbf{e} = x - W_c \cdot y_c, (y_c = 1) \tag{1}$$

Following this, the Maximum Likelihood Hebbian Learning is used to update the weights of all nodes in the neighbourhood of the winner which can be expressed as in Eq. 2.

$$\Delta W_i = h_{ci} \cdot \eta \cdot sign(\mathbf{e} - W_c) \mid \mathbf{e} - W_c \mid^{p-1}, \forall i \in N_c \text{ with different values of } p \tag{2}$$

By giving different values to p [6], [9], the learning rule is optimal for different probability density functions of the residuals. h_{ci} is the neighbourhood function as in the case of the SOM and N_c is the number of output neurons. Finally, η represents the learning rate.

While training of a SOM relies on iteratively selecting a winner stimulated by the inputs, and updating the weights, in the case of the MLSIM, the weights of the winning node are fed back as inhibition at the inputs, and then, MLH learning is used to update the weights of all nodes in the neighbourhood of the winner as explained above.

4 MLSIM Ensembles

As explained before we intend to apply bagging in combination with MLSIM with the main objective of improving the classification performance of the ensemble of MLSIMs in comparison to individual MLSIM and some other topology preserving maps i.e. SOM.

4.1 Training the MLSIM Ensemble

When constructing MLSIM ensemble, first a subset of data is randomly drawn from the training dataset and used to train only one of the networks. For the next trained network the process is repeated. Thus, the networks of the ensemble are trained using slightly different datasets, giving as a result the desired diversity.

In our investigations we have conducted three distinctive procedures for constructing the ensemble of MLSIMs related to the initialisation of weights in the trained individual MLSIMs which have had a significant effect on the performance.

In the first approach we have trained several MLSIMs separately with completely random initialisation of the weights. However due to the random initialisation of the weights it was very difficult to compare the results of individual output neurons from different networks. In order to remedy this problem a more controlled way of setting the initial weights was required.

Our next step was to initialize the weights of several neurons of each network according to the first and second Principal Components of the training dataset in order to initiate all the networks within the constructed ensemble in a similar manner, but still maintaining a certain degree of independence (in a similar way it is done in [17]). To obtain these two first Principal Components (PCs), we have applied a PCA ensemble described in one of our previous papers [18]. Specifically, the weights of the first *(1)* and the middle *(n/2)* neurons were initiated to the values representing the first principal component, while the weights of the neurons situated in positions *(n/4)* and *((3*n)/4)* (with *n* being the number of neurons in the network) were initiated with the values representing the second principal component. This procedure has been applied to all the networks in the ensemble.

The first and second PCs are orthogonal, so the mentioned neurons (labelled as *1, n/2, n/4 and (3*n)/4*) are going to be initially located forming a kind of cross, along the two PCs as it can be seen in Fig. 1. This initialization has been performed deliberately in this way as it is known that MLSIM weights are commonly distributed forming a circular shape [4], [5], [16].

Additional benefit of such coordinated initialisation of the weights is the fact that the results of all individual networks are much easier to compare by visual inspection, as the networks tend to update their weights in a similar way.

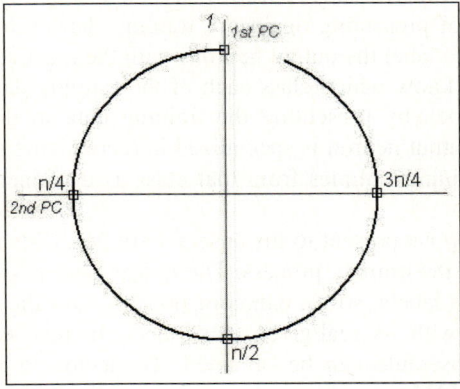

Fig. 1. Initialization of the MLSIM weights along the first two PCs

Although it is not critical in the examined context, in the third approach to weights initialisation we have tried to force even more of a commonality to the ensemble. This has been carried out mainly having in mind a possible future study of combination at the model rather than a decision level [13], [19] and also to make the networks even more easily comparable by visual inspection. In order to do so, we use the final weights obtained after training one network to initiate the next. The first trained network of the ensemble was initialized with the Principal Components as explained before, while the following ones were initiated with the final weights of their corresponding predecessors. In this way, the set of networks is quite more "compact", although it keeps its diversity element by using different bootstrap samples of the dataset used to train them.

The results showed below have been obtained by using this last initialisation and training procedure.

4.2 Testing the Classification

We have tested the effectiveness of the classification made by our proposed model using a similar semi-supervised technique as the one described in [17] and in combination with a classical ten-fold cross validation.

We randomly divide the input dataset into ten subsets and perform training and testing process ten times. Each time we iterate over this main algorithm we select a different part of the input dataset as a testing dataset, while the other nine parts are used for training. In this way all data were used to train and test the ensemble. At the end, we average the testing results obtained in the ten tests to achieve a final classification accuracy result.

Each of the ten times we perform the previously explained "outer loop", we take three steps.

1. **Training.** In this case the ensemble of MLSIMs is trained using the novel technique explained in section 4.1. We use the 9/10 of data considered as training data in the current iteration.
2. **Labelling of output neurons.** As MLSIMs use an unsupervised learning technique this step consists of presenting again the training dataset to the recently trained ensemble in order to label the output neurons with the most consistently recognised class label. As we know which class each of the training data belongs to through the given class label, by presenting the training data to the ensemble, we will consider that the output neuron is specialized in recognizing data from that class if it responded to training samples from that class as a winner in a majority of the cases.
3. **Testing.** In this step we present to the ensemble of MLSIMs the other 1/10 of data that was left out of the training process. The testing dataset is also labelled with its corresponding class labels, so we can compare the class the ensemble classifies a testing sample as with its real/given class label. In this way a measure of the accuracy of the ensemble can be obtained. To decide to which class an input belongs to, the MLSIM ensemble performs a majority voting among its composing MLSIMs [15]. The input is presented to each network individually, each one finds the winner neuron for that input and gives as an answer the class that winner neuron is supposed to recognize better (as determined in step 2). The ensemble collects the answers from all its composing networks and returns the answer that was repeated the largest number of times (i.e. in the majority of the cases).

5 Data Set and Results

In order to test the performance of our model in a dataset where it is supposed to do best [16] we have generated a radial dataset. It is composed of six normal distributions of 2 dimensions disposed in a radial way. Their centres are situated in points (3,2), (1,4), (-2,4), (-3,1), (-2,-4) and (1,-2) respectively. The number of samples corresponding to each distribution is as follows: 50, 100, 70, 50, 20 and 100.

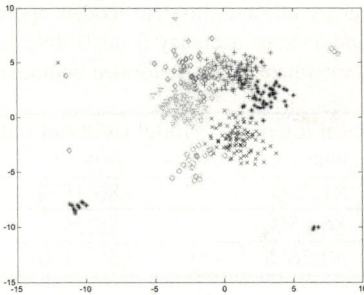

Fig. 2. Samples of the radial artificial data used in this study.

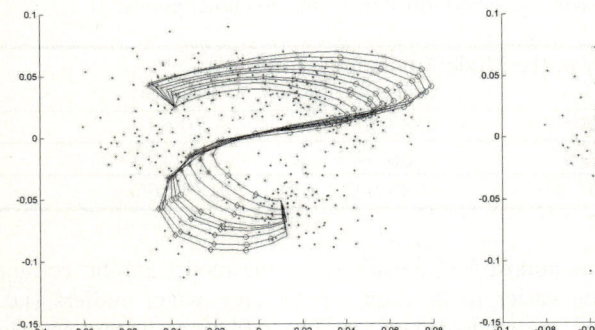

Fig. 3. Ten SOMs trained on the bagged data. The weights of the first one were initialized to the Principal Components of the dataset. The following ones were initialized to the final weights of its predecessor.

Fig. 4. Ten MLSIMs trained on the bagged data. The weights of the first one were initialized to the Principal Components of the dataset. The following ones were initialized to the final weights of its predecessor.

We have also included several outlier points to compare the results of different classification models when they are or are not present.

Fig. 3 and Fig. 4 show the results of training the ensembles of ten SOMs [17] and ten MLSIMs, respectively. As it can be seen the SOM ensemble tries to expand and cover the whole dataset range by forming a kind of inverted 'S', while the MLSIM ensemble does the same thing by using a circular form. In this particular case of a radial form dataset, the second approach should give better results, as the second form fits better the form of the considered dataset.

This difference in the form the two ensembles try to approximate to the data is mainly due to the training algorithm used (particularly the weights update) [3], [4], [5], [16] but also because of the initialization of the weights of the trained networks, as explained in section 4.1.

We have applied three classification models to the above described data set (including and without outliers). As expected the MLSIM ensemble model obtains better results than the single MLSIM and the SOM ensemble models, without and with outliers in the data set, as can be seen in Table 1 and Table 2. In the case of a single MLSIM, the variation between the best and worse accuracy results

Table 1. Classification accuracy of three different models applied to the data set from Fig. 2. The minimum, maximum and average accuracy from 10-fold cross validation testing runs are shown in the table. All the experiments were performed without the 20 outlier points.

	Accuracy of the Model (without outliers)		
	min	max	average
Single MLSIM	81.28%	86.15 %	83.58%
Ensemble (10 MLSIMs)	86.15%	88.2%	87.02%
Ensemble (10 SOM)	80.76 %	86.41 %	83.11%

Table 2. Classification accuracy of three different models applied to the data set from Fig. 2. The minimum, maximum and average accuracy from 10-fold cross validation testing runs are shown in the table. All the experiments were performed including 20 outlier points.

	Accuracy of the Model (including outliers)		
	min	max	average
Single MLSIM	75.36%	83.17 %	79.6 %
Ensemble (10 MLSIMs)	82.19%	86.34%	84.15%
Ensemble (10 SOM)	79.20 %	85.6 %	82.86%

(for dataset without outliers), is almost 5%, meaning that the model exhibit certain instability. This issue is even easier to be seen, in the case when outliers (i.e. mislabelled data) are present in the studied data set. The difference in this case is close to 8%. In the case of the model presented in this study, the MLSIM ensemble, we can see that the difference in both cases is smaller than in the case of a single one. It is around 2% for the case without outliers present, and around 4% when outliers are present.

For comparison purposes, we have applied an ensemble version of a SOM [17]. In the first case, when no outliers are present, the difference is less than 6%, and above 6% with outliers in the data set.

All these experiments have demonstrated how the MLSIM ensemble performs better than a single MLSIM model and an SOM ensemble version, in the case of radial data sets.

6 Conclusions

In this study we have applied a statistical re-sampling method for creating ensembles of classifiers based on a topology preserving model, MLSIM, trained in an unsupervised manner. We have studied and compared different ways to initialise the centres of individual MLSIMs and proposed an approach based on utilising Principal Components Analysis and sequential initialisation of subsequent MLSIMs within created ensemble.

We have compared the novel ensemble model with a SOM ensemble version and showed how our model improved the results obtained by the SOM when using radial data sets.

This study shows how the use of an ensemble version of an MLSIM improves the single model providing it with more stability and accuracy.

Future work will also investigate these ensemble methods on a range of artificial and real data sets, and the application of other viable classifier combining techniques such as the one known as bumping.

Acknowledgments

This research has been supported by the MCyT project TIN2004-07033 and the project BU008B05 of the JCyL.

References

1. Kohonen, T. Self-Organization and Associative Memory. Springer-Verlag, Heidelberg, Germany, 1984.
2. Kohonen, T. Barna, G and Chrisley R. Statistical Pattern Recognition with Neural Networks. In Proceeding of International Joint Conference of Neural Networks (pp. 61-88), IEEE Press, 1988.
3. Kohonen, T. The Self-Organizing Map. In Proceedings of the IEEE 78 (pp. 1464-1480), 1990.
4. Corchado, E. and Fyfe, C. Maximum Likelihood Topology Preserving Algorithms. In Proceedings of the U.K. Workshop on Computational Intelligence, Birmingham, UK, 2002.
5. Corchado, E. and Fyfe C. The Scale Invariant Map and Maximum Likelihood Hebbian Learning. International Conference on Knowledge-Based & Intelligent Information & Engineering System, IOS Press, 2002.
6. Corchado, E., MacDonald, D., Fyfe C., Maximum and Minimum Likelihood Hebbian Learning for Exploratory Projection Pursuit. Data Mining Knowledge Discovery 8(3): 203-225 (2004).
7. Friedman J., Tukey. J.: A Projection Pursuit Algorithm for Exploratory Data Analysis. IEEE Transaction on Computers, Vol. 23 (1974) 881-890.
8. Hyvärinen A.: Complexity Pursuit: Separating Interesting Components from Time Series. Neural Computation, Vol. 13(4) (2001) 883-898.
9. Fyfe, C. and Corchado, E. Maximum likelihood Hebbian rules. ESANN (European Symposium on Artificial Neural Networks), ISBN 2-930307-02-1, 2002.
10. Breiman, L. Bagging Predictors. Machine Learning, 24 (pp. 123–140), 1996.
11. Ruta, D. and Gabrys, B. A Theoretical Analysis of the Limits of Majority Voting Errors for Multiple Classifier Systems, Pattern Analysis and Applications, vol. 5, pp. 333-350, 2002.
12. Schapire, R.E; Freud, Y; Bartlett, P. and Lee, W.S. Boosting the margin: a new explanation for the effectiveness of voting methods. The Annals of Statistics, 26(5):1651–1686, 1998.
13. Gabrys, B. Learning Hybrid Neuro-Fuzzy Classifier Models From Data: To Combine or not to Combine? *Fuzzy Sets and Systems*, vol. 147, pp. 39-56, 2004.
14. Kuncheva, L. Combining Pattern Classifiers: Methods and Algorithms. Wiley-Interscience, 2004.

15. Ruta, D. and Gabrys, B. Classifier Selection for Majority Voting, Special issue of the journal of information fusion on Diversity in Multiple Classifier Systems, vol. 6, issue 1, pp. 63-81, 1 March 2005.
16. Fyfe, C. A Scale Invariant Map. Network: Computation in Neural Systems, 7 (pp 269-275), 1996.
17. Petrakieva, L. and Fyfe, C. Bagging and Bumping Self-organising Maps. Computing and Information Systems, 2003.
18. Gabrys, B., Baruque, B. and Corchado, E. Outlier Resistant PCA Ensembles. To appear in the proceedings of the International Conference on Knowledge-Based & Intelligent Information & Engineering System, KES'2006, 2006.
19. Gabrys, B., Combining Neuro-Fuzzy Classifiers for Improved Generalisation and Reliability, Proceedings of the Int. Joint Conference on Neural Networks, (IJCNN'2002) a part of the WCCI'2002 Congress, ISBN: 0-7803-7278-6, pp. 2410-2415, Honolulu, USA, May 2002.

Author Index

Abella, Jaume   488
Abraham, Ajith   707, 1121
Adachi, Jun   904
Adserias, José Francisco   1150
Aguilar–Ruiz, Jesús S.   1111
Ahmad, Khurshid   1003
Ahn, Seongjin   444
Ahn, Tae-Chon   133
Alatas, Bilal   386
Alejo, R.   371, 464
Alexandre, Enrique   306
Alhajj, Reda   163, 454, 920
Allende, Héctor   570
Allinson, Nigel M.   721
Alonso-Betanzos, Amparo   249, 1031
Álvarez, Lorena   306
Annunziato M.   554
Aoki, Terumasa   869
Araujo, Lourdes   771
Assfalk de Oliveira, Marco Antonio   1374
Aznar, F.   472
Azvine, Ben   207

Bäck, Thomas   410
Bajo, Javier   1166
Banchs, Rafael E.   147
Bao, Yongguang   57
Bao, Yukun   504
Barbakh, Wesam   283
Barker, Ken   454
Baruque, Bruno   1434
Bell, David A.   1296
Bellotti, Tony   978
Bertini, I.   554
Borisov, Alexander   1048
Botía, Juan A.   1207
Botti, Vicent   663, 1267
Burša, Miroslav   1390

Caamaño-Fernández, María   1031
Cabello, Enrique   645
Cano, José Ramón   1358, 1415
Carbó, Javier   1199

Cardot, H.   99, 108
Carrasco-Ochoa, J.A.   512
Castanedo, F.   216
Castelli, Eric   1382
Castillo, Enrique   1031
Chan, Lai-Wan   530
Charrier, C.   99, 108
Charro, M.   849
Chen, Ping   25
Chen, Yuehui   355, 1121
Cheng, Chun-Tian   1079
Cho, Jaewoo   1215
Cho, Sung-Bae   538
Choi, Dong-Seong   1234
Choi, In-Chan   807
Choi, Yun Jeong   688
Chou, Wusheng   1158
Chung, Jinwook   444
Chung, Ji-Won   807
Conde, Cristina   645
Corbacho, Fernando J.   944
Corchado, Emilio   1424, 1434
Corchado, Juan M.   1087, 1095, 1166
Corchuelo, Rafael   1250
Cordón, O.   1137
Corral, Guiomar   488
Cortizo, José Carlos   419
Crowe, Malcolm   283
Cuadra, Lucas   306
Cuadrado, J.J.   849

Díaz, Fernando   1087, 1095
Díaz–Díaz, Norberto   1111
Díez, David   1150
de Castro, Antonio J.   754
de Castro, Carlos   887
de Diego, Isaac Martín   330
de la Mata-Moya, D.   298
De Paz, Juan Francisco   191, 1166
de Paz, Yanira   1166
del Castillo, M. Dolores   779
del Olmo, Esther   1150
del Olmo, Ricardo   1242
del Val, Coral   1137

del Valle, Manuel   944
Dong, Xingye   25
Donoso, Sergio   1304
Dorronsoro, José R.   578
Du, Shihong   729

Eruhimov, Victor   480
Etchells, Terence A.   970

Fan, Xianfeng   1367
Fdez-Riverola, Florentino   1087, 1095
Feng, Honghai   713
Feng, Shuijuan   428
Feng, Yucai   798
Fernández, Alberto   1415
Fernandez, Pablo   1250
Flores, Victor   896
Fontenla-Romero, Oscar   249
Fornells, Albert   116, 488
Freeman, Richard T.   789
Friske, Letícia Maria   1057
Fuentes, Virginia   1199
Fyfe, Colin   241, 283

Gabrys, Bogdan   1434
Galán, José M.   1242
Galván, Inés M.   754
Gammerman, Alex   978
Gao, Zhuye   713
García, Daniel   578
García, David L.   970
García, Enrique   887
García, Salvador   1358, 1415
García, V.   371, 464
García-Cuesta, Esteban   754
García-Moratilla, Sergio   995
García-Pardo, Juan Ángel   663
Garre, M.   849
Gil-Pita, R.   496, 522
Giraldez, Ignacio   419
Girgin, Sertan   163
Glez-Peña, Daniel   1087, 1095
Golobardes, Elisabet   116, 488
Gómez-Sanz, Jorge J.   1207
González, Ana   578
Gopych, Petro   199
Gu, Jie   637, 841
Guan, Jiwen   1296
Guerra de Rezende Guedes, Leonardo   1374

Guimarães Nalini, Lauro Eugênio   1374
Gutiérrez Peña, P.A.   1320

Hakala, Risto   73
Han, Cheon-woo   1234
Hao, Zhifeng   48
Haraki, Daisuke   155
Harari, Oscar   1067
He, Yong   428
He, Yuguo   859
Heikkinen, Mikko   224
Heras, Stella   1267
Heras Barberá, Stella   663
Hernández-Lobato, Daniel   322
Hernández-Lobato, José Miguel   322
Herrera, Francisco   1358, 1415
Herrero, Álvaro   1424
Hervás-Martínez, C.   1320
Hong, Jin-Hyuk   538
Hong, Kwang-Seok   338
Hong, Xin   961
Huang, Fenggang   275
Huang, Hong-Zhong   1367
Huang, Houkuan   25
Hussain, Israr   595
Hwang, Su-Young   1234
Hwang, Yi-Gyu   346

Iannone, R.   554
Iaquinta, Gaetano   1275
Ikeguchi, Tohru   155, 363, 1103
Ishii, Naohiro   57
Izquierdo, Luis R.   172
Izquierdo, Segismundo S.   172

Jang, Myung-Gil   346
Jarabo-Amores, P.   298
Jin, Xiaoming   841, 986
Julián, Vicente   663, 1267

Kabán, Ata   1023
Karci, Ali   386
Khan, M. Sulaiman   1014
Khokhar, Rashid Hafeez   1296
Kianmehr, Keivan   920
Kim, Byungryong   1174
Kim, Eun Hee   928
Kim, Eun Yi   562
Kim, Hyeon-Jin   346
Kim, Jung-Hyun   338
Kim, Sung-il   1234

Kimura, Takayuki 363
King, Irwin 953
Klami, Mikaela 912
Klie, Hector 147
Kok, Joost N. 410
Kolehmainen, Mikko 224

Lago-Fernández, Luis F. 944
Lagus, Krista 912
Lau, Po Chi 265
Lebrun, G. 99, 108
Leccadito, Arturo 1275
Lee, Changki 346
Lee, Chung-Hee 346
Lee, Eric Wai Ming 265
Lee, Eunseok 1215
Lee, Myung-Jin 928, 1234
Lee, Seunghwa 1215
Lee, Woogul 1234
Lei, Qin 738
León, Carlos 402
Lezoray, O. 99, 108
Lhotská, Lenka 1390, 1399
Li, Hui 637
Li, Wenhai 798
Li, Xiang-Yang 637
Li, Xiaohe 183
Li, Yueli 713
Li, Zhantao 1259
Li, Zhihui 275
Liang, Xiao-hui 1182
Lim, Donghyun 444
Lim, Karam 1234
Lin, Charles 832
Linckels, Serge 612
Liu, Baoyan 713
Liu, Dexi 763
Liu, Jing 936
Liu, Xinggao 379
Liu, Yongmei 275
Liu, Zhitao 504
Lopes, José 291, 823, 832
López-Escobar, Saúl 512
López-Ferreras, Francisco 298, 306
López-Pérez, José Luis 1150
Lu, Jie 48
Lu, Yinghua 1329
Lucas, Caro 1407
Luo, Zhiyuan 978
Lv, Zehua 798

Ma, Haijian 729
Ma, Xiaoming 798
Macaš, Martin 1390, 1399
Majewski, Pawel 314
Malik, Zarrar 1014
Manomaisupat, Pensiri 1003
Manuel, Martín-Merino 654
Marín, Nicolás 1304
Martí, J. 116
Martín, Antonio 402
Martin, Quintín 1166
Martínez-Estudillo, A.C. 1320
Martínez-Estudillo, F.J. 1320
Martínez-Muñoz, Gonzalo 995
Martínez-Trinidad J., Fco 512
Martins, Weber 1374
Martyanov, Vladimir 480
Marzal, Andrés 436
Masada, Tomonari 904
Mathiassen, Henrik 1039
Matsuura, Takafumi 1103
McClean, Sally 961
Meinel, Christoph 612
Miao, Qiang 1367
Mínguez, Roberto 394
Mira Mira, José 1
Miura, Takao 697
Moguerza, Javier M. 330
Molina, José Manuel 216, 1199
Molina, Martin 896
Mollineda, R.A. 371, 464
Monedero, Iñigo 402
Moraga, Claudio 570
Moreno, Antonio 629
Morrow, Philip 961
M.P., Jarabo-Amores 522
Muñ, Alberto 330
Murai, Tsuyoshi 57
Muyeba, Maybin 1014

Nagata, Kenji 125
Ñanculef, Ricardo 570
Nauck, Detlef 207
Navarroa, Marti 1267
Nebot, Ángela 970
Nepomuceno, Isabel 1111
Nguyen, Cong Phuong 1382
Nguyen, ThanhVu H. 1337
Nguyen, Trung Thanh 586
Ning, Zhongzhong 1283

Niska, Harri   224
Novák, Daniel   1399

Oh, Hyo-Jung   346
Olier, Iván   40
Ortiz-Arroyo, Daniel   1039
Ortobelli, Lozza Sergio   1275
Otero, Adolfo   232
Otero, José   232
Otto, Francis   1312
Ouyang, Song   1312
Oyanagi, Shigeru   620
Özyer, Tansel   454

Pacheco, Joaquín   815
Palaniappan, Ramaswamy   604
Palazón, Vicente   436
Palma, Ana Maria Lara   815
Palomares, Alberto   663
Pang, Tin Yau   1191
Park, Ho-Sung   133
Park, Moon-Hee   538
Park, Se Hyun   562
Park, Seung Soo   688
Parviainen, Jukka   73
Pascual, Damaris   671
Patricio, M.A.   216
Pavlou, Maria   721
Pavón, Juan   1207
Peña, Marian   241
Peng, Lizhi   1121
Peng, Xiang   953
Pérez-Agüera, José R.   771
Pham, Ngoc Yen   1382
Pizzuti, S.   554
Pla, Filiberto   671
Platero-Santos, Sabela   249
Polat, Faruk   163
Posada, Marta   1223
Poveda, Jordi   1346
Pujol, M.   472

Qin, Qimin   729
Quang, Tran Minh   620

Rahgozar, Masoud   1407
Ramos-Garijo, Rafael   663
Raulefs, Peter   480
Rebollo, Miguel   663
Ren, Zhen-Hui   1079

Resinas, Manuel   1250
Ribeiro, Bernardete   878
Ribeiro, Carlos Henrique Costa   1057
Ríos, Sebastián A.   869
Rizo, R.   472
Rodriguez, Adolfo   147
Rodríguez-Aragón, Licesio J.   645
Rodríguez–Baena, Domingo S.   1111
Román, Jesus   654
Romero, Cristóbal   887
Romero, Enrique   90
Romero-Zaliz, R.   1067
Rosa-Zurera, Manuel   298, 306, 522
Rubio-Escudero, C.   1067, 1137
Ruiz-Torrubiano, Rubén   322
Russo, Emilio   1275
Ruta, Dymitr   207
Ryu, Keun Ho   928

Sáiz, José Manuel   1424
Sáiz Bárcena, Lourdes   815
Sala-Burgos, N.   496
Sánchez, David   629
Sánchez, J. Salvador   371, 464, 671
Sánchez, Luciano   232
Sánchez-Maroño, Noelia   1031
Sanchís, F.A.   472
Santos, José I.   1242
Sas, Jerzy   679
Scotney, Bryan   961
Sempere, M.   472
Serrano, Ángel   645
Serrano, J. Ignacio   779
Shang, Haichuan   986
Shao, Yongni   428
Shi, Chaojian   746
Shiga, Motoki   139
Shin, Hyoseop   546
Shin, Kwangcheol   707
Shir, Ofer M.   410
Sicilia, M.A.   849
Silva, Catarina   878
Similä, Timo   73
Singh, Sameer   257, 291, 823, 832
Sirola, Miki   73
Smith III, James F.   1337
So, Yeonhee   1234
Solares, Cristina   394
Soler, Jose   1267
Sotoca, J.M.   371, 464

Suárez, Alberto   995
Sun, Jun   936
Suzuki, Tomoya   155
Szeto, K.Y.   1191

Takasu, Atsuhiro   904
Therón, Roberto   191, 1150
Thomas, Sunil G.   147
Tjortjis, Christos   1014
Toppo, Daniel   90
Torkkola, Kari   1048
Trunfio, Giuseppe A.   81
Tuv, Eugene   480, 1048

Valle, Ángel   322
Valle, Carlos   570
Vaquero, Miguel   1150
Velásquez, Juan D.   869
Vellido, Alfredo   40, 970, 1346
Ventura, Sebastián   887
Ventura-Soto, S.   1320
Vicen-Bueno, R.   298, 522
Vieira, Eduardo W.   394
Vila M., Amparo   1304
Vilasís, X.   116
Villar, José   232
Vrakking, Marc J.J.   410
Vrusias, Bogdan   1003

Wakaki, Hiromi   904
Wang, Bin   746
Wang, Jessica   257
Wang, Ji-Hyun   346
Wang, Lin   1329
Wang, Qiao   729
Wang, Tianmiao   1158
Wang, Xin   1023
Wang, Yan-Ling   1289
Wang, Yeqiu   1329
Wang, Zheng-guang   1182
Watanabe, Kazuho   139
Watanabe, Sumio   125, 139
Wen, Wen   48

Wheeler, Mary F.   147
Wolfl, Stefan   1329
Wu, Di   428
Wu, Kai   1329
Wu, QingXiang   1296

Xie, Jing-Xin   1079
Xu, Cunlu   738
Xu, Hao   713
Xu, Wenbo   936
Xu, Zeshui   16

Yabuki, Nobuyoshi   1259
Yamada, Takahiro   57
Yamazaki, Katsuhiro   620
Yan, Zhengbing   379
Yang, Bingru   713
Yang, De-Li   1289
Yang, Shulin   738
Yang, Xiaowei   48
Yang, Yong   65
Yang, Zheng Rong   33, 1129
Yao, Xin   586
Yasuda, Hiroshi   869
Yin, Hujun   595
Yoon, Misun   1234
Yoshihara, Yukiteru   697
Young, Natasha   1129
Yuen, Kitty Kit Yan   265
Yun, Sung-Hyun   1234

Zarnani, Ashkan   1407
Zhang, Bo   1329
Zhang, Guangquan   48
Zhang, Hongxin   1329
Zhang, Jinling   1329
Zhang, Kun   530
Zhang, Taiyi   183
Zhang, Zengchang   763
Zhao, Qin-ping   1182
Zhao, Yaou   355
Zhou, Yatong   183
Zwir, I.   1067, 1137

Lecture Notes in Computer Science

For information about Vols. 1–4105

please contact your bookseller or Springer

Vol. 4228: D.E. Lightfoot, C.A. Szyperski (Eds.), Modular Programming Languages. X, 415 pages. 2006.

Vol. 4224: E. Corchado, H. Yin, V. Botti, C. Fyfe (Eds.), Intelligent Data Engineering and Automated Learning – IDEAL 2006. XXVII, 1447 pages. 2006.

Vol. 4219: D. Zamboni, C. Kruegel (Eds.), Recent Advances in Intrusion Detection. XII, 323 pages. 2006.

Vol. 4213: J. Fürnkranz, T. Scheffer, M. Spiliopoulou (Eds.), Knowledge Discovery in Databases: PKDD 2006. XXII, 660 pages. 2006. (Sublibrary LNAI).

Vol. 4212: J. Fürnkranz, T. Scheffer, M. Spiliopoulou (Eds.), Machine Learning: ECML 2006. XXIII, 851 pages. 2006. (Sublibrary LNAI).

Vol. 4208: M. Gerndt, D. Kranzlmüller (Eds.), High Performance Computing and Communications. XXII, 938 pages. 2006.

Vol. 4206: P. Dourish, A. Friday (Eds.), UbiComp 2006: Ubiquitous Computing. XIX, 526 pages. 2006.

Vol. 4205: G. Bourque, N. El-Mabrouk (Eds.), Comparative Genomics. X, 231 pages. 2006. (Sublibrary LNBI).

Vol. 4202: E. Asarin, P. Bouyer (Eds.), Formal Modeling and Analysis of Timed Systems. XI, 369 pages. 2006.

Vol. 4197: M. Raubal, H.J. Miller, A.U. Frank, M.F. Goodchild (Eds.), Geographic, Information Science. XIII, 419 pages. 2006.

Vol. 4196: K. Fischer, E. André, I.J. Timm, N. Zhong (Eds.), Multiagent System Technologies. X, 185 pages. 2006. (Sublibrary LNAI).

Vol. 4194: V.G. Ganzha, E.W. Mayr, E.V. Vorozhtsov (Eds.), Computer Algebra in Scientific Computing. XI, 343 pages. 2006.

Vol. 4193: T.P. Runarsson, H.-G. Beyer, E. Burke, J.J. Merelo-Guervós, L. D. Whitley, X. Yao (Eds.), Parallel Problem Solving from Nature - PPSN IX. XIX, 1061 pages. 2006.

Vol. 4192: B. Mohr, J.L. Träff, J. Worringen, J. Dongarra (Eds.), Recent Advances in Parallel Virtual Machine and Message Passing Interface. XVI, 414 pages. 2006.

Vol. 4189: D. Gollmann, J. Meier, A. Sabelfeld (Eds.), Computer Security – ESORICS 2006. XI, 548 pages. 2006.

Vol. 4188: P. Sojka, I. Kopeček, K. Pala (Eds.), Text, Speech and Dialogue. XIV, 721 pages. 2006. (Sublibrary LNAI).

Vol. 4187: J.J. Alferes, J. Bailey, W. May, U. Schwertel (Eds.), Principles and Practice of Semantic Web Reasoning. XI, 277 pages. 2006.

Vol. 4186: C. Jesshope, C. Egan (Eds.), Advances in Computer Systems Architecture. XIV, 605 pages. 2006.

Vol. 4185: R. Mizoguchi, Z. Shi, F. Giunchiglia (Eds.), The Semantic Web – ASWC 2006. XX, 778 pages. 2006.

Vol. 4184: M. Bravetti, M. Núñez, G. Zavattaro (Eds.), Web Services and Formal Methods. X, 289 pages. 2006.

Vol. 4183: J. Euzenat, J. Domingue (Eds.), Artificial Intelligence: Methodology, Systems, and Applications. XIII, 291 pages. 2006. (Sublibrary LNAI).

Vol. 4180: M. Kohlhase, OMDoc – An Open Markup Format for Mathematical Documents [version 1.2]. XIX, 428 pages. 2006. (Sublibrary LNAI).

Vol. 4179: J. Blanc-Talon, W. Philips, D. Popescu, P. Scheunders (Eds.), Advanced Concepts for Intelligent Vision Systems. XXIV, 1224 pages. 2006.

Vol. 4178: A. Corradini, H. Ehrig, U. Montanari, L. Ribeiro, G. Rozenberg (Eds.), Graph Transformations. XII, 473 pages. 2006.

Vol. 4176: S.K. Katsikas, J. Lopez, M. Backes, S. Gritzalis, B. Preneel (Eds.), Information Security. XIV, 548 pages. 2006.

Vol. 4175: P. Bücher, B.M.E. Moret (Eds.), Algorithms in Bioinformatics. XII, 402 pages. 2006. (Sublibrary LNBI).

Vol. 4174: K. Franke, K.-R. Müller, B. Nickolay, R. Schäfer (Eds.), Pattern Recognition. XX, 773 pages. 2006.

Vol. 4173: S. El Yacoubi, B. Chopard, S. Bandini (Eds.), Cellular Automata. XV, 734 pages. 2006.

Vol. 4172: J. Gonzalo, C. Thanos, M. F. Verdejo, R.C. Carrasco (Eds.), Research and Advanced Technology for Digital Libraries. XVII, 569 pages. 2006.

Vol. 4169: H.L. Bodlaender, M.A. Langston (Eds.), Parameterized and Exact Computation. XI, 279 pages. 2006.

Vol. 4168: Y. Azar, T. Erlebach (Eds.), Algorithms – ESA 2006. XVIII, 843 pages. 2006.

Vol. 4167: S. Dolev (Ed.), Distributed Computing. XV, 576 pages. 2006.

Vol. 4165: W. Jonker, M. Petković (Eds.), Secure, Data Management. X, 185 pages. 2006.

Vol. 4163: H. Bersini, J. Carneiro (Eds.), Artificial Immune Systems. XII, 460 pages. 2006.

Vol. 4162: R. Královič, P. Urzyczyn (Eds.), Mathematical Foundations of Computer Science 2006. XV, 814 pages. 2006.

Vol. 4160: M. Fisher, W.v.d. Hoek, B. Konev, A. Lisitsa (Eds.), Logics in Artificial Intelligence. XII, 516 pages. 2006. (Sublibrary LNAI).

Vol. 4159: J. Ma, H. Jin, L.T. Yang, J.J.-P. Tsai (Eds.), Ubiquitous Intelligence and Computing. XXII, 1190 pages. 2006.

Vol. 4158: L.T. Yang, H. Jin, J. Ma, T. Ungerer (Eds.), Autonomic and Trusted Computing. XIV, 613 pages. 2006.

Vol. 4156: S. Amer-Yahia, Z. Bellahsène, E. Hunt, R. Unland, J.X. Yu (Eds.), Database and XML Technologies. IX, 123 pages. 2006.

Vol. 4155: O. Stock, M. Schaerf (Eds.), Reasoning, Action and Interaction in AI Theories and Systems. XVIII, 343 pages. 2006. (Sublibrary LNAI).

Vol. 4154: Y.A. Dimitriadis, I. Zigurs, E. Gómez-Sánchez (Eds.), Groupware: Design, Implementation, and Use. XIV, 438 pages. 2006.

Vol. 4153: N. Zheng, X. Jiang, X. Lan (Eds.), Advances in Machine Vision, Image Processing, and Pattern Analysis. XIII, 506 pages. 2006.

Vol. 4152: Y. Manolopoulos, J. Pokorný, T. Sellis (Eds.), Advances in Databases and Information Systems. XV, 448 pages. 2006.

Vol. 4151: A. Iglesias, N. Takayama (Eds.), Mathematical Software - ICMS 2006. XVII, 452 pages. 2006.

Vol. 4150: M. Dorigo, L.M. Gambardella, M. Birattari, A. Martinoli, R. Poli, T. Stützle (Eds.), Ant Colony Optimization and Swarm Intelligence. XVI, 526 pages. 2006.

Vol. 4149: M. Klusch, M. Rovatsos, T.R. Payne (Eds.), Cooperative Information Agents X. XII, 477 pages. 2006. (Sublibrary LNAI).

Vol. 4148: J. Vounckx, N. Azemard, P. Maurine (Eds.), Integrated Circuit and System Design. XVI, 677 pages. 2006.

Vol. 4146: J.C. Rajapakse, L. Wong, R. Acharya (Eds.), Pattern Recognition in Bioinformatics. XIV, 186 pages. 2006. (Sublibrary LNBI).

Vol. 4144: T. Ball, R.B. Jones (Eds.), Computer Aided Verification. XV, 564 pages. 2006.

Vol. 4142: A. Campilho, M. Kamel (Eds.), Image Analysis and Recognition, Part II. XXVII, 923 pages. 2006.

Vol. 4141: A. Campilho, M. Kamel (Eds.), Image Analysis and Recognition, Part I. XXVIII, 939 pages. 2006.

Vol. 4139: T. Salakoski, F. Ginter, S. Pyysalo, T. Pahikkala, Advances in Natural Language Processing. XVI, 771 pages. 2006. (Sublibrary LNAI).

Vol. 4138: X. Cheng, W. Li, T. Znati (Eds.), Wireless Algorithms, Systems, and Applications. XVI, 709 pages. 2006.

Vol. 4137: C. Baier, H. Hermanns (Eds.), CONCUR 2006 – Concurrency Theory. XIII, 525 pages. 2006.

Vol. 4136: R.A. Schmidt (Ed.), Relations and Kleene Algebra in Computer Science. XI, 433 pages. 2006.

Vol. 4135: C.S. Calude, M.J. Dinneen, G. Păun, G. Rozenberg, S. Stepney (Eds.), Unconventional Computation. X, 267 pages. 2006.

Vol. 4134: K. Yi (Ed.), Static Analysis. XIII, 443 pages. 2006.

Vol. 4133: J. Gratch, M. Young, R. Aylett, D. Ballin, P. Olivier (Eds.), Intelligent Virtual Agents. XIV, 472 pages. 2006. (Sublibrary LNAI).

Vol. 4132: S. Kollias, A. Stafylopatis, W. Duch, E. Oja (Eds.), Artificial Neural Networks – ICANN 2006, Part II. XXXIV, 1028 pages. 2006.

Vol. 4131: S. Kollias, A. Stafylopatis, W. Duch, E. Oja (Eds.), Artificial Neural Networks – ICANN 2006, Part I. XXXIV, 1008 pages. 2006.

Vol. 4130: U. Furbach, N. Shankar (Eds.), Automated Reasoning. XV, 680 pages. 2006. (Sublibrary LNAI).

Vol. 4129: D. McGookin, S. Brewster (Eds.), Haptic and Audio Interaction Design. XII, 167 pages. 2006.

Vol. 4128: W.E. Nagel, W.V. Walter, W. Lehner (Eds.), Euro-Par 2006 Parallel Processing. XXXIII, 1221 pages. 2006.

Vol. 4127: E. Damiani, P. Liu (Eds.), Data and Applications Security XX. X, 319 pages. 2006.

Vol. 4126: P. Barahona, F. Bry, E. Franconi, N. Henze, U. Sattler, Reasoning Web. XII, 269 pages. 2006.

Vol. 4124: H. de Meer, J.P. G. Sterbenz (Eds.), Self-Organizing Systems. XIV, 261 pages. 2006.

Vol. 4121: A. Biere, C.P. Gomes (Eds.), Theory and Applications of Satisfiability Testing - SAT 2006. XII, 438 pages. 2006.

Vol. 4120: J. Calmet, T. Ida, D. Wang (Eds.), Artificial Intelligence and Symbolic Computation. XIII, 269 pages. 2006. (Sublibrary LNAI).

Vol. 4119: C. Dony, J.L. Knudsen, A. Romanovsky, A. Tripathi (Eds.), Advanced Topics in Exception Handling Components. X, 302 pages. 2006.

Vol. 4117: C. Dwork (Ed.), Advances in Cryptology - CRYPTO 2006. XIII, 621 pages. 2006.

Vol. 4116: R. De Prisco, M. Yung (Eds.), Security and Cryptography for Networks. XI, 366 pages. 2006.

Vol. 4115: D.-S. Huang, K. Li, G.W. Irwin (Eds.), Computational Intelligence and Bioinformatics, Part III. XXI, 803 pages. 2006. (Sublibrary LNBI).

Vol. 4114: D.-S. Huang, K. Li, G.W. Irwin (Eds.), Computational Intelligence, Part II. XXVII, 1337 pages. 2006. (Sublibrary LNAI).

Vol. 4113: D.-S. Huang, K. Li, G.W. Irwin (Eds.), Intelligent Computing, Part I. XXVII, 1331 pages. 2006.

Vol. 4112: D.Z. Chen, D. T. Lee (Eds.), Computing and Combinatorics. XIV, 528 pages. 2006.

Vol. 4111: F.S. de Boer, M.M. Bonsangue, S. Graf, W.-P. de Roever (Eds.), Formal Methods for Components and Objects. VIII, 447 pages. 2006.

Vol. 4110: J. Díaz, K. Jansen, J.D.P. Rolim, U. Zwick (Eds.), Approximation, Randomization, and Combinatorial Optimization. XII, 522 pages. 2006.

Vol. 4109: D.-Y. Yeung, J.T. Kwok, A. Fred, F. Roli, D. de Ridder (Eds.), Structural, Syntactic, and Statistical Pattern Recognition. XXI, 939 pages. 2006.

Vol. 4108: J.M. Borwein, W.M. Farmer (Eds.), Mathematical Knowledge Management. VIII, 295 pages. 2006. (Sublibrary LNAI).

Vol. 4106: T.R. Roth-Berghofer, M.H. Göker, H. A. Güvenir (Eds.), Advances in Case-Based Reasoning. XIV, 566 pages. 2006. (Sublibrary LNAI).